20

Estate & Gift Tax Handbook

Susan Flax Posner J.D., LL.M. in Taxation

Wolters Kluwer

CCH

Editorial Staff

Editor. . . . . Barbara L. Post, Esq.

Production . . . . Linda Kalteux

ISBN 978-0-8080-3876-4

©2014 CCH Incorporated. All Rights Reserved.
4025 W. Peterson Ave.
Chicago, IL 60646-6085
800 248 3248
CCHGroup.com

Certified Chain of Custody
Product Line Contains At Least
20% Certified Forest Content
www.sfiprogram.org
SFI-00756

- *Estate of Costanza, Estate of Moss* and GCM 39503;

- Chief Counsel Advice 201330033 where the IRS addressed (1) whether transfers of stock from the seller to grantor trusts in exchange for self-cancelling installment notes constituted a taxable gift: (2) how to determine the amount of the gift for gift tax purposes when property is exchanged for a SCIN; and (3) whether the SCIN should be included in the decedent/seller's gross estate and therefore subject to federal estate tax;

- *Estate of Robert Frane,* where the Court of Appeals for the Eighth Circuit concluded that the automatic cancellation of an installment obligation when the seller died required the seller's estate to recognize gain from the original transaction as income in respect of decedent;

- Discussion of IRC Sec. 2512(b) which addresses the tax treatment of property transferred for less than adequate and full consideration in money or money's worth;

- Discussion of the IRC Sec. 7520 tables that apply in valuing private annuities;

- Reg. Sec. 1.7520-3(b)(3) which addresses using the IRC Sec. 7520 tables when the creator of the private annuity has a greater than 50 percent likelihood of living at least one year after the transfer and will likely live at least 18 months afterward;

- *Frank Aragona Trust,* where the Tax Court concluded that a trust that owned rental real estate property qualified under IRC Sec. 469(c)(7) as a real estate professional;

- *Estate of Woodbury,* where the Tax Court held that an estate was not entitled to pay its estate tax in installments because it did not make a timely IRC Sec. 6166 election;

- Discussion of the final regulations released under Reg. Sec. 1.67-4 that provide guidance on which costs incurred by estates or nongrantor trusts are subject to the 2-percent floor for miscellaneous itemized deductions under IRC Sec. 67(a);

- *Estate of Hurford,* where the Tax Court held that the transfer of a surviving spouse's interests in a family limited partnership to her children for private annuity agreements, while the surviving spouse was being treated for stage 3 liver cancer, was not bona fide;

- *Estate of Kite,* where the court addressed whether an annuity transaction was a bona fide sale for adequate and full consideration;

- The meaning of the term "incidents of ownership";

- Letter Ruling 201327010, where the IRS concluded that proceeds of life insurance policies purchased by the insured's predeceased spouse, naming the purchasing spouse's estate as beneficiary, and held in a trust of which the insured is the trustee, will not be included in the insured's gross estate if he relinquishes his role as a trustee and survives the three-year period of IRC Sec. 2035(a);

- The right to receive life insurance policy dividends;

- *Estate of Bowers,* where the court addressed whether "dividends paid on an insurance policy" is an economic benefit that would cause the value of the insurance proceeds to be includible in a decedent's gross estate;

- Chief Counsel Advice 201328030, where the IRS addressed whether the decedent was required to insure his life for a certain amount in conjunction with his property settlement agreement;
- IRC Sec. 2701, which provides rules to determine the amount of the gift that occurs when an equity interest in a corporation or partnership is transferred from an individual to a member of that individual's family;
- How to measure the amount of a gift under Reg. Sec. 25.2701-3;
- How to determine the value of a retained interest held by the transferor or an applicable family member including any put, call, or conversion right, right to compel liquidation, or right to receive dividends which is valued at zero if the right is an "extraordinary payment right" under Reg. Sec. 25.2701-1(a)(2);
- The definition of the term "transfer" for purposes of IRC Sec. 2701;
- Updated discussion of GRATs under IRC Sec. 2702;
- The estate and gift tax consequences of the creation of a GRAT;
- The income tax consequences of the creation of a GRAT;
- How to "zero out" a GRAT;
- President Obama's proposal to impose a requirement that a GRAT have a minimum term of ten years and a maximum term of the life expectancy of the annuitant plus ten years;
- The good faith/reasonable cause defense to the imposition of tax penalties;
- Reliance on professional advice as a defense under Reg. Sec. 1.6664-4(b)(1) to the imposition of tax penalties;
- The gift tax annual exclusion amounts in effect for transfers made from 1939 through 2014;
- The required contents of a *Crummey* letter;
- How the IRS will challenge a *Crummey* letter;
- The sale by a grantor of a retained interest;
- Proposed regulations providing rules for determining a taxable beneficiary's basis in a term interest in a CRT upon a sale or other disposition of all interests in the trust to the extent that basis consists of a share of adjusted uniform basis;
- "Abusive" transactions as listed in Notice 2008-99;
- The uniform basis rule for property acquired by a trust from a decedent or as a gift under Reg. Secs. 1.1014-4(a)(1) and 1.1015-1(b);
- Basis of term and remainder interests in a CRT;
- Proposed regulations that attempt to prevent the taxable beneficiary of a CRT from benefiting from a basis step-up attributable to tax-exempt gains under Prop. Reg. Sec. 1.1014-5(c)(1);
- Reg. Sec. 25.2519-1(f) which provides that the sale of a QTIP, followed by the payment to the surviving spouse of a portion of the proceeds equal to the value of the surviving spouse's income interest, is considered a disposition of a qualifying income interest;

- *Estate of Kite*, where the Tax Court concluded that the sale of a decedent's interest in two qualified terminable interest property (QTIP) trusts was subject to gift tax;
- The importance of the date of expatriation;
- Gifts by expatriates of stock/debt of foreign corporation;
- The computation of gift tax under IRC Sec. 2501(a)(5)(C);
- Rules for expatriation on or after June 17, 2008;
- The impact of the IRS report that the number of filed gift tax returns has increased;
- How to extend the time for filing the Form 709;
- What's new on Form 709 in 2014;
- How to elect out of QTIP treatment of annuities for joint and survivor annuities;
- The notice of allocation of GST exemption to an indirect skip;
- The election not to have automatic GST tax exemption allocation rules apply to a current-year transfer reported on Form 709;
- The impact of special use valuation on the basis of property;
- *Van Alen*, where the Tax Court concluded that the alternate use valuation determined the basis of the property that carried over to the trust that inherited the property, and then to the taxpayers who were the beneficiaries of the trust;
- *Estate of Koons*, where the court allowed a 7.5 percent discount for lack of marketability for the transfer to an LLC of proceeds of the sale of the family's Pepsi distributorship business;
- *Estate of Tanenblatt*, where the court allowed a 26 percent discount for lack of marketability for the transfer to an LLC of a commercial building;
- *Estate of Elkins*, where the decedent and his wife created a grantor retained income trust (GRIT) to hold 64 famous works of art and the court held that IRC Sec. 2703(a)(2) required that the artwork be valued without regard to the restrictions on transferability in the co-tenancy agreement;
- Deduction of an administration expense against the gross estate under Reg. Sec. 20.2053-3(a);
- *Estate of Koons*, where the Tax Court concluded that an estate was not entitled to deduct the projected interest expense on a loan from a limited liability company (LLC) to the decedent's revocable trust;
- *Estate of Saunders*, where the Tax Court concluded that a decedent's estate was only able to take an estate tax deduction for the amount of a claim against the estate that was actually paid, not the value claimed upon the date of death;
- Limitations on the type of claim that can be deducted on an estate tax return are provided in Reg. Sec. 20.2053-1(b)(3);
- *Marshall Naify Revocable Trust*, where the Ninth Circuit concluded that a decedent's estate was limited to a deduction for the amount of state income tax actually paid in settlement with the state taxing authority and not a deduction for potential state income tax liability;
- Special rules for computing the value of the decedent's estate;

- Exclusions, deductions, and credits available on Form 706-NA;
- Foreign countries where the United States has entered into death tax conventions;
- Table of estimated values as required by Temp. Reg. Sec. 20.2010-2T(a)(7)(ii);
- When simplified reporting is unavailable under Temp. Reg. Sec. 20.2010-2T(a)(7)(ii);
- What's new on Form 706 in 2014;
- New Schedule PC added to Form 706 in 2013;
- Simplified reporting on Form 706 for estates making a portability election if under the filing threshold as provided in Temp. Reg. Sec. 20.2010-2T(a)(7)(ii);
- What expenses are claimed on Form 706, Schedule J;
- When to complete Form 706, Schedule K;
- Deductibility of claims against the estate;
- Validity of claims between related parties under Reg. Sec. 20.2053-1(b)(2)(ii);
- An update on QTIP requirements;
- Limitations on the amount of the foreign death tax credit;
- Filing requirements for generation-skipping transfers;
- How to opt-out of the portability election;
- DSUE of first spouse to die is subject to review when the surviving spouse dies;
- Special rules where the value of certain property need not be reported on Form 706;
- The DSUE amount portable to the surviving spouse;
- Application of GST tax provisions to nonresidents, noncitizens;
- GST tax exemption amounts in effect from 1999-2014;
- Extension of time to make an election out of the automatic allocation of GST exemption under IRC Sec. 2642(g) and Reg. Sec. 310.9100-3;
- When to file Form 1040, Form 1040A and Form 1040EZ;
- What's new on Form 1040;
- Earned income tax credit inflation adjustments;
- Net investment income tax imposed on unearned income of individuals;
- Line-by-line explanation of how to complete Form 8960, "Net Investment Income Tax Individuals, Estates, and Trusts," which is attached to Form 1040 (individuals);
- Definition of net investment income (NII);
- Increased 0.9% Additional Medicare Tax (hospital insurance tax) payroll tax imposed on employees and self-employed taxpayers above certain filing thresholds;
- Long-term capital gain and dividend tax rate increases in 2013;
- Impact of increased long-term capital gains and dividend tax rate and 3.8 percent NII tax;

- Reinstatement of limitation on individuals' itemized deductions;
- Increase in floor for deducting medical and dental expenses;
- Changes to health flexible spending arrangements starting in 2013;
- Reinstatement of personal exemption phaseout;
- IRS Simplification changes how taxpayers claim home office deduction;
- Changes to how taxpayers can claim a theft loss deduction for Ponzi-type investment schemes;
- How and when trusts and estates must complete Form 8949 to report capital transactions in 2013;
- New direct payment option for Form 1040 filers;
- Standard mileage rate changes;
- Credit for prior year minimum tax;
- IRS attempts to thwart identity theft;
- Imposition of net investment income tax in estates and trusts beginning in 2013;
- Line-by-line explanation of how to complete Form 8959, "Additional Medicare Tax" used to compute 0.9 percent additional Medicare tax on earned income;
- Discussion of abusive trust arrangements;
- Discussion of trust terms authorizing decanting;
- What trusts and estates are subject to the 3.8 percent NII tax;
- How to compute AGI of estate or trust for NII tax purposes;
- Trusts not subject to NII tax;
- Net investment income defined with regard to trusts and estates subject to NII tax;
- What income/gain is excluded from definition of NII;
- How estates and trust can minimize exposure to the 3.8 percent NII tax;
- How trusts can establish material participation under IRC Sec. 469 passive loss rules under IRC Sec. 1411(c)(2)(A) and IRC Sec. 469(h)(1) to minimize exposure to the 3.8 percent NII tax;
- How trusts can use installment sales method to spread out taxable gain and avoid imposition of NII tax;
- Trust reformation when trust documents no longer accomplish their intended goal;
- New rule requiring trusts to use Form 8949, "Sales and Other Dispositions of Capital Assets" to report most capital gains and losses in 2013;
- Higher tax rates imposed on trusts and estates beginning in 2013;
- Increase in long-term capital gain and dividend tax rates in 2013 and impact on trust and estate tax planning;
- IRC Sec. 645 election;
- Changes in 2013 in reporting net operating loss deduction (NOLD) on Form 1041;

- Changes in how miscellaneous itemized deductions subject to the 2 percent floor are reported;

- New Form 1041 e-filing for tax year 2013;

- The Legacy Electronic Management System (EMS) and the Modernized e-File (MeF) System;

- Form 8453-F, "U.S. Estate or Trust Income Tax Declaration and Signature for Electronic Filing";

- New Form 8453-FE, "U.S. Estate or Trust Declaration for an IRS e-file Return";

- Increase in bankruptcy estate filing threshold in 2013;

- Changes to qualified disability trusts in 2013;

- AMT tax bracket increases in 2013;

- AMT exemption amount and phaseout in 2013;

- The IRC Sec. 645 election to treat a revocable trust as part of the decedent's estate;

- How trusts and estates report capital gains in 2013;

- Line-by-lines explanation of how estates and trusts complete Form 8949, "Sales and Other Dispositions of Capital Assets" to report sales and exchanges of capital assets not reported on another form or schedule;

- Special rule on how to report basis of trust property;

- Detailed background discussion on the additional 3.8 percent net investment income tax;

- What trusts are subject to the NII tax;

- Computing the amount of the NII tax;

- Income/gains excluded from computation of NII;

- How to calculate the NII tax;

- How to report and pay NII tax;

- Special Rules for Electing Small Business Trusts (ESBTs);

- Line-by-line discussion of how to complete Form 8969 for Trent Trust;

- Special rule on how to report basis of the decedent's estate property.

7/14

To Jeffrey, Joel and Andrew who are an endless source of laughter, joy and inspiration.

Susan Flax Posner

PREFACE

Estate & Gift Tax Handbook is a practical exploration of federal estate and gift taxation. Providing timely and effective advice on estate and gift tax practice and procedure, this text will be a useful resource for estate-planning practitioners, fiduciaries, attorneys, and others dealing with the complexities of the estate and gift tax system, especially at a time when the American Taxpayer Relief Act of 2012 changed estate planning in a fundamental way. In one place, the reader will find all the information, explanations, completed IRS forms, and checklists necessary to arrange a person's affairs, both before and after death, to minimize the estate and gift tax burden and to maximize wealth transfers through lifetime and testamentary giving.

The book is organized in an outline format that provides the reader several ways to locate any covered topic instantly. Key concepts are explained and illustrated, with numerous examples and sample completed Internal Revenue Service forms, schedules, and worksheets. Included in each chapter are useful cross references to related matters dealt with elsewhere in the book. In addition, citations to statutes, regulations, and cases are provided within the text and in footnotes. A comprehensive index is located at the back of the book to direct the reader to the precise location of each topic discussed. Also included at the back is a complete glossary of important terms related to the federal estate and gift tax system.

Written in concise, jargon-free language to elucidate and demystify this complicated area of the law, the book will be a valuable resource to readers approaching the subject from varied backgrounds and disciplines. All relevant terms and key concepts are thoroughly defined and illustrated. Topics addressed include:

- The wealth transfer taxes defined, and who is affected;
- What had to be done for decedents who died in 2010 and beyond;
- Estate tax planning for 2012 and beyond;
- Necessary federal income, estate tax, and gift tax forms, how they are completed, and when they are due with line-by-line explanations;
- Planning strategies available to reduce the burden of these taxes including discussion of family limited partnerships, intentionally defective grantor trusts, and valuation discounts for lack of control and lack of marketability;
- The generation-skipping transfer tax and application of the generation skipping transfer tax exemption;
- Federal estate taxes, determination of the gross estate, computation of the taxable estate, exemptions, and exceptions;
- The decedent's final income tax return and tax treatment of income in respect of a decedent; and
- Federal income taxation of trusts and estates including discussion of the throwback rules.

ABOUT THE AUTHOR

Susan Flax Posner received her LL.M. in taxation from The George Washington University National Law Center and served as a law clerk to Judge Irene F. Scott, U.S. Tax Court for two years. Ms. Posner co-authored *Tax Planning Strategies* and *Taxation of Investments*. Ms. Posner currently writes a monthly newsletter for CCH entitled *The Federal Tax Course Letter* as well as a publication entitled *Federal Tax Course—A Guide for the Tax Practitioner* also for CCH. She also wrote *Taxation of Investments Handbook*. She is a graduate of McGill University and University of Baltimore Law School. She has practiced law in Washington, D.C., and in Baltimore, Maryland.

ACKNOWLEDGMENTS

The author would like to express her sincere appreciation to the dedicated and talented staff at CCH whose talents and expertise were invaluable in updating this book. Special thanks go to Barbara Post, Esq., Senior Developmental Editor, and Kurt Diefenbach, J.D., Managing Editor, for their hard work, high standards, dedication, patience, and valuable advice and suggestions.

Table of Contents

Chapter 28—Income Taxation of Trusts and Estates

ESTATE AND GIFT TAX PLANNING IN LIGHT OF AMERICAN TAXPAYER RELIEF ACT OF 2012

TABLE OF CONTENTS

This book provides a working knowledge of estate and gift taxation. Estate and gift taxes are imposed by the federal government on transfers of wealth that occur when gifts are made during a person's life or when someone dies and wealth is inherited. The federal government considers it a privilege to freely transfer property to loved ones. For this privilege, taxpayers are subject to a gift tax on any lifetime transfers, an estate tax on transfers at death, and a generation-skipping transfer (GST) tax on transfers that bypass a generation. The book details the operation of wealth transfer taxes and discusses the many tools available to reduce the taxes. The book also provides filed-in examples and explanations of the various federal estate, gift and income tax returns that executors must file on behalf of decedents.

When estate planning and wealth transfers are mentioned, people often think they apply only to the super-rich. Nothing could be further from the truth. Estate planning should be considered by anyone who, for example, has built a business, owns a home or two, has a retirement plan or savings, owns stock, or has life insurance, so that all the wealth that he or she has created will be transferred intact to loved ones, rather than going to Uncle Sam.

¶100 ESTATE AND GIFT TAX PLANNING IN 2010-2012

(a) Impact of EGTRRA. The Economic Growth and Tax Relief Reconciliation Act of 2001 (EGTRRA) made sweeping changes to our estate, gift and generation skipping transfer tax laws. The changes were gradually phased in over nine years rather than becoming effective immediately.

The most notable change made by EGTRRA was the elimination of the estate and generation-skipping transfer (GST) tax for decedents dying in 2010. But nobody actually expected January 1, 2010 to dawn without Congress changing the law. But January 1, 2010 did arrive and we found ourselves in the predicament no one expected to occur when EGTRRA was enacted. As a result of Congress's preoccupation with other matters and their failure to change the law in time, both the estate and generation-skipping transfer (GST) taxes did not exist in 2010 and the stepped-up basis at death rules were replaced with modified carryover basis at death rules in order to deny taxpayers a step-up in the basis of appreciated assets received at death. However, in 2010, the gift tax remained in place with a $1 million exemption and a 35 percent maximum tax rate. What a mess we faced in 2010. To make matters worse, many lawyers who drafted estate planning documents from 2002 through 2009 failed to consider the possibility that there would be a year when there would be zero estate tax. This left many drafting glitches which lead to unforeseen consequences for surviving spouses and other beneficiaries, including charitable remainder beneficiaries.

The practical ramifications of zero estate tax in 2010 were almost ludicrous. Only people dying in 2010 were able to escape estate tax. If people did not die in that 365-day window their estates would be subject to tax. As one estate planning expert so aptly put it, "[w]ealthy persons with families that are less than totally harmonious may wish to employ bodyguards and tasters during calendar year 2010, if Congress does not eliminate the sunset rules or make the estate tax permanent before that date" [Zaritsky, Practical Estate Planning and Drafting After the Economic Growth and Tax Relief Reconciliation Act of 2001, page 1–30 fn 71].

Example 1: Mom's estate is worth $10 million. She has terminal cancer. She is near death on December 1, 2009. Because there is only a $3.5 million exemption equivalent in 2009, she is put on a respirator on December 1, 2009. Mom is taken off the respirator on January 2, 2010 when the estate tax is repealed. Her estate will owe no estate or generation-skipping tax. If they wait until January 2, 2011, to take her off the respirator her estate will owe estate tax on a $5 million estate because the exemption equivalent is reduced to $5 million in 2011.

¶100

(b) Gift Tax Not Repealed. EGTRRA created confusion regarding the gift tax because the gift tax was not repealed. The gift tax was retained following the repeal by EGTRRA of the estate and GST taxes in 2010. For gifts made after December 31, 2009, the gift tax was computed using a rate schedule with a top marginal rate of 35 percent [IRC Sec. 2502(a)]. Taxpayers were advised to continue to make annual exclusion gifts to reduce the amount of their eventual estate and/or gift tax liability. Lifetime annual exclusion gifts always make sense because they shift future appreciation and income to loved ones without the donor paying any added gift or estate tax.

¶101 CHANGES MADE BY TAX RELIEF ACT OF 2010 AND AMERICAN TAXPAYER RELIEF ACT OF 2012

(a) Estate and GST Taxes Made Permanent. The Tax Relief Act of 2010 provided that the federal estate and generation-skipping transfer (GST) taxes will again apply to the estates of decedents dying and GSTs made in 2010, 2011, and 2012. The estate tax applicable exclusion amount was $5 million in 2010 and 2011. In 2012, the amount increased to $5,120,000. The federal estate, gift, and GST tax changes enacted by EGTRRA and the Tax Relief Act of 2010 that were set to expire with respect to the estates of decedents dying and gifts and GSTs made after December 31, 2012, by operation of the sunset provision of EGTRRA, were made permanent for estates of decedents dying, gifts made, or GSTs after December 31, 2012. However, the maximum transfer tax rate will now be 40 percent, rather than 35 percent as it had been under the Tax Relief Act of 2010. The estates of decedents who die before December 31, 2014 have an applicable exclusion amount of $5,340,000 in 2014 (up from $5,250,000 in 2013).

The increase of the estate tax exclusion amount in 2014 to $5,340,000 (which also serves as the estate tax return filing threshold) will presumably serve to continue the decline in the number of federal estate tax returns filed and the corresponding revenue collected. According to the IRS (http://www.irs.gov/pub/irs-soi/12estateonesheet.pdf), the number of estate tax returns declined 87 percent from about 73,100 in 2003 to about 9,400 in 2012. It is expected that they will drop even more in 2013 and 2014 as the exclusion amount increases and the estate tax affects fewer and fewer decedents.

(b) Gifts. For gifts made in 2010, the applicable exclusion amount for gift tax purposes was $1 million and the gift tax rate was 35 percent [IRC Sec. 2010]. For gifts made in 2011 and 2012, the gift tax was reunified with the estate tax. In 2011, the applicable exclusion amount was $5 million with a top unified estate and gift tax rate of 35 percent. In 2012, the amount of the gift tax applicable exclusion amount was $5,120,000 with a top unified estate and gift tax rate of 35 percent. The lifetime exclusion from gift tax under IRC Sec. 2505 was $5,250,000 for gifts made in 2013. In 2014, the exclusion amount for gifts is $5,340,000. [See ¶ 101(i) for applicable credit and exclusion amount chart].

(c) GST Tax Rate and Exemption Amount. Every individual is allowed a lifetime GST tax exemption equal to the "basic exclusion amount" in the calendar year of the allocation ($5,340,000 in 2014) [IRC Sec. 2631(a)]. The GST exemption may be allocated by the individual or his or her executor to the transfer of any property if the individual is the transferor [IRC Sec. 2631(a)]. Once made, the allocation of GST exemption is irrevocable [IRC Sec. 2631(b)]. The GST tax is assessed at the highest transfer tax rate in effect in the year of the event that triggered the GST tax. The tax rate is 40 percent in 2014. The tax is assessed in addition to any estate or gift tax that applies to the transfer. For further discussion, see ¶ 2509.

The following chart illustrates the GST tax exemption amounts in effect from 1999–2014.

GST Tax Exemption Amounts

For Transfers Made in:	Exemption
1999	1,010,000
2000	1,030,000
2001	1,060,000
2002	1,100,000
2003	1,120,000
2004–2005	1,500,000
2006–2008	2,000,000
2009	3,500,000
2010–2011	5,000,000
2012	5,120,000
2013	5,250,000
2014	5,340,000

(d) Stepped-Up Basis Rules. The stepped-up basis at death rules of IRC Sec. 1014 continue to generally apply to the property acquired from the estates of decedents dying before and after 2012. Under the stepped-up basis rules, the income tax basis of property acquired from a decedent at death generally is stepped-up (or stepped-down) to equal its value as of the date of the decedent's death (or on the date six months after the date of death, if alternate valuation under IRC Sec. 2032 is elected on the decedent's estate tax return). An estate's ability to elect the carryover basis rules of IRC Sec. 1022 applied only with respect to the estates of decedents dying in 2010 [see ¶ 103].

The Tax Relief Act of 2010 generally repealed the modified carryover basis rules that, under EGTRRA, applied for purposes of determining basis in property acquired from a 2010 decedent. Under the Tax Relief Act of 2010, the recipient of property acquired from a decedent who dies after December 31, 2009, generally received a step up in basis under IRC Sec. 1014.

(e) Portability. The Tax Relief Act of 2010 dramatically changed the estate tax laws by amending IRC Sec. 2010(c), to add the portability feature which generally allows the surviving spouse to use the decedent's unused exclusion amount in addition to the surviving spouse's own basic exclusion amount if an election is made on a timely-filed and complete estate tax return. Portability was designed to simplify estate planning by eliminating the need for spouses to retitle property and create credit shelter trusts solely to take full advantage of each spouse's applicable exclusion amount.

¶101

Example 1: Wife died in 2014 when the applicable exclusion amount is $5,340,000. During her life she made no taxable gifts. Her timely filed estate tax return includes a portability election. Husband also dies in 2014 and assuming he has made no taxable gifts, his applicable exclusion amount is $10,680,000 (his applicable exclusion amount of $5,340,000 plus her unused applicable exclusion amount of $5,340,000).

Portability now permanent. The concept of "portability" of a deceased spouse's unused exclusion (DSUE) amount was made permanent for the estates of decedents dying after December 31, 2012 by the American Taxpayer Relief Act of 2012. Portability applies to the gift tax exemption as well as the estate tax exemption. Portability does not, however, apply to the generation skipping transfer tax exemption. For a detailed discussion of portability, see Chapter 15.

(f) State Death Tax Deduction. The Tax Relief Act of 2010 allowed a deduction for certain death taxes paid to any state or the District of Columbia for decedents dying in 2010, 2011 and 2012. The state death tax deduction in IRC Sec. 2058 was scheduled to expire for the estates of decedents dying after December 31, 2012, under the sunset provision of EGTRRA, as extended by the Tax Relief Act of 2010. The state death tax deduction is now permanent for the estates of decedents dying after December 31, 2012. Accordingly, the estates of decedents dying after December 31, 2012, will be able to deduct state death taxes paid to a state or the District of Columbia from a decedent's gross estate [IRC Sec. 2058]. The state death tax credit has been permanently repealed.

(g) Summary of Major Changes to Transfer Taxes. The reduction and ultimate repeal of the federal estate and GST taxes were accompanied by a number of changes to the transfer tax system generally, as depicted in the following timeline.

2001

- Distance requirement for conservation easement exclusion lifted [IRC Sec. 2031(c)(2)];

- Deemed and retroactive allocations of GST tax exemption allowed [IRC Sec. 2632];

- Qualified severance of GST trusts available [IRC Sec. 2642(a)];

- Valuation rules concerning date when allocation of GST tax exemption becomes final modified [IRC Sec. 2642(b)];

- Relief provided for late elections to allocate GST tax exemption and for substantial compliance with regulations [IRC Sec. 2642(g)].

2002

- Maximum estate, gift, and GST tax rate: 50 percent [IRC Secs. 2001, 2502, and 2602];

- Five-percent surtax on large estates and gifts in excess of $10 million up to $17,184,000 repealed [IRC Sec. 2001(c)(2)];

- Applicable exclusion amount for estate and gift taxes: $1 million [IRC Secs. 2010 and 2505];

- GST tax exemption: $1,100,000 (as adjusted for inflation) [IRC Sec. 2631];

- State death tax credit reduced to 75 percent of prior law amount [IRC Sec. 2011(b)(2)];
- Rules on installment payment of estate taxes liberalized [IRC Sec. 6166(b)(1), (9), and (10)].

2003

- Maximum estate, gift, and GST tax rate: 49 percent;
- Applicable exclusion amount for estate, gift, and GST tax: $1 million;
- GST tax exemption: $1,120,000 (as adjusted for inflation);
- State death tax credit reduced to 50 percent of prior law amount.

2004

- Maximum estate, gift, and GST tax rate: 48 percent;
- Applicable exclusion amount for estate and GST tax: $1.5 million;
- Inflation adjustment for GST tax exemption ends;
- Applicable exclusion amount for gift tax: $1 million;
- State death tax credit reduced to 25 percent of prior law amount;
- Deduction for qualified family-owned business interests repealed [IRC Sec. 2057].

2005

- Maximum estate, gift, and GST tax rate: 47 percent;
- Applicable exclusion amount for estate and GST tax: $1.5 million;
- Applicable exclusion for gift tax: $1 million;
- State death tax credit becomes a deduction [IRC Sec. 2058].

2006

- Maximum estate, gift, and GST tax rate: 46 percent;
- Applicable exclusion amount for estate and GST tax: $2 million;
- Applicable exclusion for gift tax: $1 million.

2007-2008

- Maximum estate, gift, and GST tax rate: 45 percent;
- Applicable exclusion amount for estate and GST tax: $2 million;
- Applicable exclusion for gift tax: $1 million.

2009

- Maximum estate, gift, and GST tax rate: 45 percent;.
- Applicable exclusion amount for estate and GST tax: $3.5 million;
- Applicable exclusion for gift tax: $1 million.

2010

- Decedents dying in 2010 have the option of paying zero estate tax and having a carryover basis apply to assets inherited by their heirs or choosing to pay estate tax as described below and having stepped-up basis apply to assets inherited by their heirs;

¶101

- Estate tax reinstated by the Tax Relief Act of 2010 with a $5 million exclusion and maximum 35-percent rate [IRC Secs. 2001 and 2010(c)];
- GST tax reinstated by the Tax Relief Act of 2010 with a $5 million exemption amount and zero-percent tax rate (2010 GSTs only) [IRC Secs. 2010(c) and 2631(c)];
- Gift tax exclusion amount remains at $1 million with a maximum rate of 35 percent [IRC Secs. 2502(a)and 2505(a)];
- Stepped-up basis restored by the Tax Relief Act of 2010 for assets inherited by the decedent's heirs, but election available for 2010 decedents only to pay zero estate tax and have carryover basis apply to assets inherited by the decedent's heirs [IRC Sec. 1022].

2011

- Maximum estate, gift, and GST tax rate is 35 percent [IRC Secs. 2001, 2502(a), and 2602];
- Applicable exclusion amount for estate and gift taxes is $5 million [IRC Secs. 2010 and 2505];
- "Portability" of unused applicable exclusion amount allowed for estate and gift (not GST) tax purposes [IRC Sec. 2010(c)(4)];
- GST exemption amount is $5 million [IRC Sec. 2631(c)];
- Stepped-up basis applies for assets inherited by the decedent's heirs [IRC Sec. 1014].

2012

- Maximum estate, gift, and GST tax rate is 35 percent [IRC Secs. 2001, 2502(a), and 2602];
- Applicable exclusion amount for estate and gift taxes is $5,120,000 (as adjusted for inflation) [IRC Secs. 2010 and 2505];
- "Portability" of unused applicable exclusion amount allowed for estate and gift (not GST) tax purposes [IRC Sec. 2010(c)(4)];
- GST exemption amount is $5,120,000 (as adjusted for inflation) (IRC Sec. 2631(c));
- Stepped-up basis applies for assets inherited by the decedent's heirs [IRC Sec. 1014].

2013 and 2014

- Maximum estate, gift, and GST tax rate: generally 40 percent [IRC Sec. 2001(c)(1)];
- Applicable exclusion amount for estate and gift taxes: $5,250,000 in 2013, increasing to $5,340,000 in 2014 [IRC Sec. 2010];
- Exemption amount for GST tax: $5,250,000 in 2013, increasing to $5,340,000 in 2014 [IRC Sec. 2631(c)];
- Portability of the deceased spousal unused exclusion (DSUE) amount for estate and gift tax purposes continues to be available [IRC Sec. 2010(c)].

Maximum Estate and Gift Tax Rates—2002 through 2014

- 2002: 50 percent
- 2003: 49 percent
- 2004: 48 percent

¶101

- 2005: 47 percent

- 2006: 46 percent

- 2007 through 2009: 45 percent

- 2010* through 2012: 35 percent

- 2013 and thereafter: 40 percent

  * The estates of decedents dying in 2010 were allowed to elect out of the estate tax regime, effectively reducing their estate tax rate to zero.

(h) Unified Estate and Gift Tax Rate Schedule (After 2012).

(A) Amount subject to tax equal to or more than—	(B) Amount subject to tax less than—	(C) Tax on amount in column (A)	(D) Rate of tax on excess over amount in column (A) Percent
	$10,000		18
$10,000	20,000	$1,800	20
20,000	40,000	3,800	22
40,000	60,000	8,200	24
60,000	80,000	13,000	26
80,000	100,000	18,200	28
100,000	150,000	23,800	30
150,000	250,000	38,800	32
250,000	500,000	70,800	34
500,000	750,000	155,800	37
750,000	1,000,000	248,300	39
1,000,000		345,800	40

(i) Applicable Credit and Exclusion Amounts.

Applicable Credit and Exclusion Amounts

For Transfers Made in:	Estates		Gifts	
	Maximum Credit	Exclusion Amount	Maximum Credit	Exclusion Amount
2006-2008	$ 780,800	$ 2,000,000	$ 345,800	$ 1,000,000
2009	1,455,800	3,500,000	345,800	1,000,000
2010	1,730,800*	5,000,000*	330,800	1,000,000
2011	1,730,800**	5,000,000**	1,730,800**	5,000,000**
2012	1,772,800**	5,120,000**	1,772,800**	5,120,000**
2013	2,045,800**	5,250,000**	2,045,800**	5,250,000**
2014	2,081,800**	5,340,000**	2,081,800**	5,340,000**

* Unless executor elected modified carryover basis rules.
** Increased by amount unused by first spouse that is transferred to a surviving spouse, if elected.

¶101

¶102 IMPORTANCE OF ESTATE PLAN REVIEW

Estate plans should be reviewed at least every five years to take into account life changes and shifts in one's financial situation. Changes that would mandate a review would include health changes, marriage, divorce, and a birth or a death in the family.

Formula clauses are clauses inserted in estate planning documents such as wills and trusts to express the beneficiary's interest in terms of a pecuniary or fractional formula. The use of formula clauses is frequently used by estate planners to ensure the proper division of property but it is extremely important that formula clauses be reviewed or eliminated entirely especially in light of recent legislative changes to make certain that they continue to implement the testator's long-term intent for his or her loved ones. A common problem is transferring too little or too much to the surviving spouse because of overfunding of the credit shelter trust in the typical split estate plan.

All estate planning documents that contain formula dispositions should be reviewed and revised to make it absolutely clear what happens when death occurs. It may be possible to simply add a short codicil or trust amendment, but the most important goal is to make sure that the documents implement the owner's intent and understanding. The problem areas that deserve special attention are the documents employing the split estate plan that relied on formula bypass language to fund the bypass or credit shelter trust with the remainder to the marital trust in order to qualify for the marital deduction. Here's how they work. Typically, estate planners divide the estate of a married couple into two shares. This so-called split-estate plan operates so that one share (called the bypass or credit shelter trust) is funded with the amount of the federal estate tax exemption equivalent ($5,250,000 in 2013) and the other share is in a form qualifying for the estate tax marital deduction (called the marital deduction trust).

Unexpected problems can arise for taxpayers with formula bypass provisions now that the federal estate tax exemption amount is $5,340,000. If someone dies with a provision in his or her will stating that the bypass trust be funded with the amount needed to make maximum use of the exemption equivalent or something to that effect, $5,340,000 may be used to fund the bypass trust leaving little to fund the marital trust in an estate of between $5 million and $7.5 million.

Now that portability is permanent and the exemption equivalent of the first spouse to die can be used by the surviving spouse, the need for estate planners to create the bypass trust is called into question. The whole purpose of portability was to simplify estate planning and, by eliminating the need for the split estate plan, it does just that. Portability does not require estate planners to create a special trust in order for the surviving spouse to take advantage of the first spouse to die's exemption equivalent. The only requirement is that the executor of the first spouse to die must file a timely, complete estate tax return. There may be other reasons for estate planners to still create bypass trusts, including: (1) there may be no portability of state estate tax exemption amounts; (2) the unused exclusion from one predeceased spouse will be lost if the surviving spouse remarries and survives his or her next spouse; (3) there is no portability of the GST exemption; (4) beneficiaries other than just the surviving spouse can use the assets that are left to a bypass trust; (5) there is no statute of limitations on values for purposes of determining the unused exclusion amount that begins to run from the time the first deceased spouse's estate tax return is filed whereas the statute of limitations does run on values if a bypass trust is funded at the first spouse's death; (6) the estate of the first spouse to die may not need to file an estate tax return just to elect portability if the assets passing to the credit shelter and marital deduction trust are small enough; and (7) the bypass trust offers asset protection, centralized management and protection of the assets by restricting transfers by the surviving spouse.

As soon as possible, wills need to be revised to use fixed amounts or sliding scales.

An overriding theme is to add maximum flexibility for the surviving spouse and other beneficiaries after the decedent's death. For example, a new provision could be inserted in the documents providing, for example, that a surviving spouse's interest in the marital trust is contingent on a QTIP election by the executor of the decedent's estate. Assets which are not encompassed by the QTIP election would pass outright to the surviving spouse or to the decedent's other beneficiaries outright or in trust. The *"Clayton* QTIP" format as allowed under Reg. Sec. 20.2056(b)-7(d)(3) and Reg. Sec. 20.2056(b)-7(h), Example 6, allows a fiduciary to wait and see how the tax law, beneficiary needs, and other factors fall into place before determining what the surviving spouse receives.

¶103 STEPPED-UP BASIS FOR PROPERTY ACQUIRED FROM DECEDENT

(a) Stepped-Up Basis. The stepped-up basis at death rules in IRC Sec. 1014 applied to estates of decedents dying after 2012. The carryover basis at death rules of IRC Sec. 1022 only applied to the estates of decedents dying in 2010 for which a carryover basis election had been made. Under the stepped-up basis rules, the income tax basis of property acquired from a decedent at death generally is stepped up (or stepped down) to equal its value as of the date of the decedent's death (or on the date six months after the date of death, if alternate valuation under IRC Sec. 2032 is elected on the decedent's estate tax return).

(b) Mechanics of COB Rule. In conjunction with the repeal of the estate tax with respect to the estates of decedents dying after December 31, 2009 [IRC Sec. 2210], EGTRRA replaced the long-standing "stepped-up" basis at death rules with a modified carryover basis regime [IRC Secs. 1014(f), 1022(a)]. Effective for property acquired from a decedent dying in 2010, to make up for the revenue lost as a result of the estate tax repeal, the law provided that the income tax basis of property acquired from a decedent would generally be carried over from the decedent. More specifically, the recipient of the property was to receive a basis equal to the lesser of (1) the adjusted basis of the property in the hands of the decedent, or (2) the fair market value of the property on the date of the decedent's death. The COB rule replaced the stepped-up basis rules that have long applied to property received from a decedent.

The carryover basis rule only applied to "property acquired from a decedent," which is defined in IRC Sec. 1022(e) as follows:

- Property acquired by bequest, devise, or inheritance, or by the decedent's estate from the decedent;
- Property transferred by the decedent during his lifetime to a qualified revocable trust or to any other trust with respect to which the decedent reserved the right to make any change in the enjoyment thereof through the exercise of a power to alter, amend, or terminate the trust; and
- Any other property passing from the decedent by reason of death to the extent that such property passed without consideration.

The results produced when the stepped-up basis rules are applied to property acquired from a decedent contrast sharply with the results produced when the basis of property is computed under the COB rules. Under the COB rule, the basis of property transferred by a decedent to another person becomes the basis in the hands of the recipient; the decedent's basis is "carried over" to the recipient. If the property transferred at death appreciated greatly in the decedent's lifetime, the recipient would face a significant capital gain on a later sale of the property.

Example 1: When her mother died, Sally received 2,500 shares of ABCo stock from her mother testamentary trust. At her death on January 1, 2011, Mother had a basis of $100 per share in the stock, and each share had a fair market value of $1,000. In each of the 2,500 shares received Sally will have a basis stepped up to its date of death value, that is, $1,000. If, upon receipt of her shares, Sally chooses to immediately sell them (assuming the value of each share is still $1,000), she will incur no taxable gain because her basis is equal to the stock's fair market value. Thus, the taxation of the $900 gain per share that had occurred during her mother's lifetime is permanently excused: none of Sally's $2.25 million gain (2,500 shares × $900) will be taxed.

Example 2: Assume the same facts as in the Example above, except that Mother died on December 31, 2010. The 2,500 shares transferred to Sally will have a carryover basis of $100, assuming that the executor elects to have the EGTRRA rules apply. If Sally were to immediately sell her stock at $1,000 per share, she would incur a taxable gain of $900 per share. If the executor of Sally's estate allocates the full $1.3 million general basis increase to the ABCo stock, Sally will still have a taxable gain of $950,000 ($2.25 million – $1.3 million).

For the estates of decedents dying after December 31, 2009 and before January 1, 2011, the executor could elect out of the estate tax system and use the carryover basis rules established under EGTRRA. Under EGTRRA, a recipient's basis in assets acquired from the decedent who died in 2010 is the lesser of the decedent's adjusted basis (carryover basis) or the fair market value of the property on the date of the decedent's death.

However, there are two exceptions to this general rule:

- The executor can allocate up to $1.3 million, increased by unused losses and loss carryovers ($60,000 in the case of a decedent nonresident not a citizen of the United States, but with no loss or loss carryover increase) to increase the basis of assets owned by the decedent at death; and

- The executor can also allocate an additional amount, up to $3 million, to increase the basis of assets passing to a surviving spouse, either outright or in a Qualified Terminable Interest Property trust.

Form 8939. The executor of the estate of a decedent who died in 2010 was required to make the irrevocable IRC Sec. 1022 Election by filing a Form 8939, "Allocation of Increase in Basis for Property Acquired From a Decedent," on or before January 17, 2012. The IRS did not grant extensions of time to file Form 8939.

On Form 8939, the executor must report and value property (excluding cash and property that constitutes the right to receive an item of income in respect of a decedent) acquired from the decedent [IRC Sec. 6018(b)(1)]. In addition, the executor must report all appreciated property acquired from the decedent, valued as of the decedent's date of death, that was required to be included on the donor's Form 709, "United States Gift (and Generation-Skipping Transfer) Tax Return," if such property was acquired by the decedent by gift or by inter vivos transfer for less than adequate and full consideration during the 3-year period ending on the date of the decedent's death [IRC Sec. 6018(b)(2)]. An exception is available for property transferred to the decedent by the decedent's spouse, who had not acquired the property by gift or by inter vivos transfer for less than adequate and full consideration during that same 3-year period.

Ineligible property. The following types of property transfers were ineligible for the basis increase [IRC Sec. 1022(d)(1)(D)]:

- Property acquired by a decedent by gift from a non-spouse less than three years before death;

- Property that constituted a right to receive income in respect of a decedent;

- Stock in foreign investment and personal holding companies;

- Stock or securities of a foreign personal holding company;

- Stock of a domestic international sales corporation (or former domestic international sales corporation);

- Stock of a foreign investment company; and

- Stock of a passive foreign investment company (except for which a decedent share-holder had made a qualified electing fund election).

Rules applicable to basis increase. Basis increase was allocable on an asset-by-asset basis (e.g., basis increase could be allocated to a share of stock or a block of stock). However, in no case could the basis of an asset be adjusted above its fair market value. If the amount of basis increase was less than the fair market value of assets whose bases could increase under these rules, the executor had the discretion to determine which assets and to what extent each asset received a basis increase.

▶ **PLANNING POINTER:** *Carryover Basis Rules Require Beefed-up Record Retention.* The carryover basis rules make it mandatory for taxpayers to maintain records of their original cost basis as well as the adjusted basis for some if not all of their property. This adds a whole new level of complexity to the recordkeeping and retention rules imposed on taxpayers. To comply with the rules, taxpayers must retain records detailing the tax basis of all assets of significant value. From a planning perspective, it is easier to collect and retain this information now while the purchaser is still alive rather than trying to recreate the basis history many years from now after the original purchaser has died. Proving basis can be particularly nettlesome for assets, such as mutual fund shares that may have been purchased over a number of years.

Under a carryover basis regime, record retention becomes very important for collectibles purchased over a lifetime, such as rare books, artwork, coins, and antiques. It will be difficult, if not impossible, to recreate the basis history for these assets years from now after the original purchaser is dead and has given the property away. Moreover, in the absence of clear and complete records establishing the basis of the assets, the IRS will be forced to reconstruct the basis for the asset. You can be sure that they most likely will approximate a basis that will not be favorable to the taxpayer.

¶104 2014 ESTATE AND GIFT TAX INFLATION ADJUSTMENTS

- **Estate and GST exemption amount.** In 2014, the estate and GST exemption amount is $5,340,000 (increasing from $5,250,000 in 2013).

- **Gift tax applicable credit amount.** In 2014, the gift tax applicable credit amount or gift tax exemption amount is $5,340,000 (increasing from $5,250,000).

- **Top estate tax rate.** In 2014, the top estate tax rate is 40 percent (no change).

- **Gift tax exclusion.** In 2014, the annual gift tax exclusion is $14,000 (no change) or $28,000 if a couple elects to gift split. (This does not apply to gifts of future interests in property.)

- **Gifts to noncitizen spouses.** For gifts made in 2014 to noncitizen spouses, the annual gift tax exclusion increases to $145,000 (increasing from $143,000 in 2013).

- **Special use valuation.** The special use valuation under IRC Sec. 2032A increases to $1,090,000 for the estates of decedents dying in 2014 (increasing from $1,070,000 in 2013).

- **Determining 2 percent portion for interest on deferred estate tax.** When you are determining the part of the estate tax that is deferred on a farm or closely-held business that is subject to interest at a rate of 2 percent per year, for decedents dying in 2014, the tentative tax will be computed on $1,450,000 (up from $1,430,000).

- **Generation-skipping transfer tax exemption amount.** The generation-skipping transfer tax exemption is $5,340,000 in 2014. That amount was $5,250,000 in 2013.

- **Notice of large gifts received from foreign persons.** In 2014, IRC Sec. 6039F authorizes the IRS to require recipients of gifts from certain foreign persons to report these gifts if the aggregate value of gifts received in the tax year exceeds $15,358.

- **Expatriation rules.** For 2014, a tax avoidance motive is presumed for an expatriate (except certain former citizens) whose average annual net income tax liability for the five tax years ending before the date of loss of citizenship or residence exceeds $157,000 (increased from $155,000 in 2013).

¶104

- **Tax responsibilities of expatriation.** In 2014, the amount that would be includible in the gross income of a covered expatriate by reason of IRC Sec. 877 is reduced (but not below zero) by $680,000 (increased from $668,000 in 2013).

¶105 IRS PUBLICATION 559: SURVIVORS, EXECUTORS, AND ADMINISTRATORS

Department
of the
Treasury

**Internal
Revenue
Service**

Publication 559
Cat. No. 15107U

Survivors, Executors, and Administrators

For use in preparing

2013 Returns

**Get forms and other information faster and easier by
Internet at IRS.gov**

Jan 31, 2014

Contents

Future Developments

For the latest information about developments affecting Publication 559, such as legislation enacted after we release it, go to *www.irs.gov/pub559*.

Reminders

Throughout this publication, section references are to the Internal Revenue Code unless otherwise noted.

Consistent treatment of estate and trust items. Beneficiaries must generally treat estate items the same way on their individual returns as they are treated on the estate's return.

Photographs of missing children. The Internal Revenue Service is a proud partner with the National Center for Missing and Exploited Children. Photographs of missing children selected by the Center may appear in this publication on pages that would otherwise be blank. You can help bring these children home by looking at the photographs and calling 1-800-THE-LOST (1-800-843-5678) if you recognize a child.

Introduction

This publication is designed to help those in charge (personal representatives) of the property (estate) of an individual who has died (decedent). It shows them how to complete and file federal income tax returns and explains their responsibility to pay any taxes due on behalf of the decedent. A comprehensive example of the decedent's final tax return, Form 1040, and estate's income tax return, Form 1041, are included in this publication.

The publication also explains how much money or property a taxpayer can give away during their lifetime or leave to their heirs at their death before any tax will be owed. A discussion of Form 709, United States Gift (and Generation-Skipping Transfer) Tax Return, and Form 706, United States Estate (and Generation-Skipping Transfer) Tax Return, is included.

Also included in this publication are the following items:

- A checklist of the forms you may need and their due dates.
- A worksheet to reconcile amounts reported in the decedent's name on information returns including Forms W-2, 1099-INT, 1099-DIV, etc. The worksheet will help you correctly determine the income to report on the decedent's final return and on the return for either the estate or a beneficiary.

Comments and suggestions. We welcome your comments about this publication and your suggestions for future editions.

You can send us comments from *http://www.irs.gov/formspubs*. Click on "More Information" and then on "Give us Feedback." Or you can also send your comments to the Internal Revenue Service, Tax Forms and Publications Division, 1111 Constitution Ave. NW, IR-6526, Washington, DC 20224.

Useful Items

You may want to see:

Publication

- ❑ 3   Armed Forces' Tax Guide

Form (and Instructions)

- ❑ SS-4   Application for Employer Identification Number
- ❑ 56   Notice Concerning Fiduciary Relationship
- ❑ 1040   U.S. Individual Income Tax Return
- ❑ 1041   U.S. Income Tax Return for Estates and Trusts
- ❑ 706   United States Estate (and Generation-Skipping Transfer) Tax Return
- ❑ 709   United States Gift (and Generation-Skipping Transfer) Tax Return
- ❑ 1310   Statement of Person Claiming Refund Due a Deceased Taxpayer

See *How To Get Tax Help* near the end of this publication for information about getting publications and forms. Also near the end of this publication is *Table A*, a checklist of forms and their due dates for the executor, administrator, or personal representative.

Personal Representative

A *personal representative* of an estate is an executor, administrator, or anyone who is in charge of the decedent's property. Generally, an *executor* (or *executrix*) is named in a decedent's will to administer the estate and distribute properties as the decedent has directed. An *administrator* (or *administratrix*) is usually appointed by the court if no will exists, if no executor was named in the will, or if the named executor cannot or will not serve.

In general, an executor and an administrator perform the same duties and have the same responsibilities.

For estate tax purposes, if there is no executor or administrator appointed, qualified, and acting within the United States, the term "executor" includes anyone in actual or constructive possession of any property of the decedent. It includes, among others, the decedent's agents and representatives; safe-deposit companies, warehouse companies, and other custodians of property in this country; brokers holding securities of the decedent as collateral; and the debtors of the decedent who are in this country.

Duties

The primary duties of a personal representative are to collect all the decedent's assets, pay his or her creditors, and distribute the remaining assets to the heirs or other beneficiaries.

The personal representative also must perform the following duties.

- Apply for an employer identification number (EIN) for the estate.

- File all tax returns, including income, estate and gift tax returns, when due.
- Pay the tax determined up to the date of discharge from duties.

Other duties of the personal representative in federal tax matters are discussed in other sections of this publication. If any beneficiary is a nonresident alien, see Publication 515, Withholding of Tax on Nonresident Aliens and Foreign Entities, for information on the personal representative's duties as a withholding agent.

Penalty. There is a penalty for failure to file a tax return when due unless the failure is due to reasonable cause. Reliance on an agent (attorney, accountant, etc.) is not reasonable cause for late filing. It is the personal representative's duty to file the returns for the decedent and the estate when due.

Identification number. The first action you should take if you are the personal representative for the decedent is to apply for an EIN for the estate. You should apply for this number as soon as possible because you need to enter it on returns, statements, and other documents you file concerning the estate. You also must give the number to payers of interest and dividends and other payers who must file a return concerning the estate.

You can get an EIN by applying online at *www.irs.gov* (click on "Apply for an EIN Online" under the Tools heading). Generally, if you apply online, you will receive your EIN immediately upon completing the application. You can also apply using Form SS-4, Application for Employer Identification Number. Generally, if you apply by mail, it takes about 4 weeks to get your EIN. See the form instructions for other ways to apply.

Payers of interest and dividends report amounts on Forms 1099 using the identification number of the person to whom the account is payable. After a decedent's death, Forms 1099 must reflect the identification number of the estate or beneficiary to whom the amounts are payable. As the personal representative handling the estate, you must furnish this identification number to the payer. For example, if interest is payable to the estate, the estate's EIN must be provided to the payer and used to report the interest on Form 1099-INT, Interest Income. If the interest is payable to a surviving joint owner, the survivor's identification number, such as an SSN or ITIN, must be provided to the payer and used to report the interest.

If the estate or a survivor may receive interest or dividends after you inform the payer of the decedent's death, the payer should give you (or the survivor) a Form W-9, Request for Taxpayer Identification Number and Certification (or a similar substitute form). Complete this form to inform the payer of the estate's (or if completed by the survivor, the survivor's) identification number and return it to the payer.

 Do not use the deceased individual's identifying number to file an individual income tax return after the decedent's final tax return. Also do not use it to make estimated tax payments for a tax year after the year of death.

¶105

Penalty. If you do not include the EIN or the taxpayer identification number of another person where it is required on a return, statement, or other document, you are liable for a penalty for each failure, unless you can show reasonable cause. You also are liable for a penalty if you do not give the taxpayer identification number of another person when required on a return, statement, or other document.

Notice of fiduciary relationship. The term *fiduciary* means any person acting for another person. It applies to persons who have positions of trust on behalf of others. A personal representative for a decedent's estate is a fiduciary.

Form 56. If you are appointed to act in a fiduciary capacity for another, you must file a written notice with the IRS stating this. Form 56, Notice Concerning Fiduciary Relationship, is used for this purpose. See the Instructions for Form 56 for filing requirements and other information.

File Form 56 as soon as all the necessary information (including the EIN) is available. It notifies the IRS that you, as the fiduciary, are assuming the powers, rights, duties, and privileges of the decedent. The notice remains in effect until you notify the IRS (by filing another Form 56) that your fiduciary relationship with the estate has terminated.

Termination of fiduciary relationship. Form 56 should also be filed to notify the IRS if your fiduciary relationship is terminated or when a successor fiduciary is appointed if the estate has not been terminated. See Form 56 and its instructions for more information.

At the time of termination of the fiduciary relationship, you may want to file Form 4810, Request for Prompt Assessment Under Internal Revenue Code Section 6501(d), and Form 5495, Request for Discharge From Personal Liability Under Internal Revenue Code Section 2204 or 6905, to wind up your duties as fiduciary. See below for a discussion of these forms.

Request for prompt assessment (charge) of tax. The IRS ordinarily has 3 years from the date an income tax return is filed, or its due date, whichever is later, to charge any additional tax due. However, as a personal representative, you may request a prompt assessment of tax after the return has been filed. This reduces the time for making the assessment to 18 months from the date the written request for prompt assessment was received. This request can be made for any tax return (except the estate tax return) of the decedent or the decedent's estate. This may permit a quicker settlement of the tax liability of the estate and an earlier final distribution of the assets to the beneficiaries.

Form 4810. Form 4810 can be used for making this request. It must be filed separately from any other document.

As the personal representative for the decedent's estate, you are responsible for any additional taxes that may be due. You can request prompt assessment of any of the decedent's taxes (other than federal estate taxes) for any years for which the statutory period for

assessment is open. This applies even though the returns were filed before the decedent's death.

Failure to report income. If you or the decedent failed to report substantial amounts of gross income (more than 25% of the gross income reported on the return) or filed a false or fraudulent return, your request for prompt assessment will not shorten the period during which the IRS may assess the additional tax. However, such a request may relieve you of personal liability for the tax if you did not have knowledge of the unpaid tax.

Request for discharge from personal liability for tax. An executor can make a request for discharge from personal liability for a decedent's income, gift, and estate taxes. The request must be made after the returns for those taxes are filed. To make the request, file Form 5495. For this purpose, an executor is an executor or administrator that is appointed, qualified, and acting within the United States.

Within 9 months after receipt of the request, the IRS will notify the executor of the amount of taxes due. If this amount is paid, the executor will be discharged from personal liability for any future deficiencies. If the IRS has not notified the executor, he or she will be discharged from personal liability at the end of the 9-month period.

 Even if the executor is discharged from personal liability, the IRS will still be able to assess tax deficiencies against the executor to the extent he or she still has any of the decedent's property.

Insolvent estate. Generally, if a decedent's estate is insufficient to pay all the decedent's debts, the debts due to the United States must be paid first. Both the decedent's federal income tax liabilities at the time of death and the estate's income tax liability are debts due to the United States. The personal representative of an insolvent estate is personally responsible for any tax liability of the decedent or of the estate if he or she had notice of such tax obligations or failed to exercise due care in determining if such obligations existed before distribution of the estate's assets and before being discharged from duties. The extent of such personal responsibility is the amount of any other payments made before paying the debts due to the United States, except where such other debt paid has priority over the debts due to the United States. Income tax liabilities need not be formally assessed for the personal representative to be liable if he or she was aware or should have been aware of their existence.

Fees Received by Personal Representatives

All personal representatives must include fees paid to them from an estate in their gross income. If you are not in the trade or business of being an executor (for instance, you are the executor of a friend's or relative's estate), report these fees on your Form 1040, line 21. If you are in the trade or business of being an executor, report fees received from the estate as

self-employment income on Schedule C or Schedule C-EZ of your Form 1040.

If the estate operates a trade or business and you, as executor, actively participate in the trade or business while fulfilling your duties, any fees you receive related to the operation of the trade or business must be reported as self-employment income on Schedule C (or Schedule C-EZ) of your Form 1040.

Final Income Tax Return for Decedent—Form 1040

The personal representative (defined earlier) must file the final income tax return (Form 1040) of the decedent for the year of death and any returns not filed for preceding years. A surviving spouse, under certain circumstances, may have to file the returns for the decedent. See *Joint Return*, later.

Return for preceding year. If an individual died after the close of the tax year, but before the return for that year was filed, the return for the year just closed will not be the final return. The return for that year will be a regular return and the personal representative must file it.

Example. Samantha Smith died on March 21, 2013, before filing her 2012 tax return. Her personal representative must file her 2012 return by April 15, 2013. Her final tax return covering the period from January 1, 2013, to March 20, 2013, is due April 15, 2014.

Name, Address, and Signature

Write the word "DECEASED," the decedent's name, and the date of death across the top of the tax return. If filing a joint return, write the name and address of the decedent and the surviving spouse in the name and address fields. If a joint return is not being filed, write the decedent's name in the name field and the personal representative's name and address in the address field.

Third party designee. You can check the "Yes" box in the Third Party Designee area on page 2 of the return to authorize the IRS to discuss the return with a friend, family member, or any other person you choose. This allows the IRS to call the person you identified as the designee to answer any questions that may arise during the processing of the return. It also allows the designee to perform certain actions. See the Instructions for Form 1040 for details.

Signature. If a personal representative has been appointed, that person must sign the return. If it is a joint return, the surviving spouse must also sign it. If no personal representative has been appointed, the surviving spouse (on a joint return) signs the return and writes in the signature area "Filing as surviving spouse." If no personal representative has been appointed and if there is no surviving spouse, the person in charge of the decedent's property must file and sign the return as "personal representative."

Paid preparer. If you pay someone to prepare, assist in preparing, or review the tax return, that person must sign the return and fill in the other blanks in the *Paid Preparer Use Only* area of the return. See the Form 1040 instructions for details.

When and Where To File

The final income tax return is due at the same time the decedent's return would have been due had death not occurred. A final return for a decedent who was a calendar year taxpayer is generally due on April 15 following the year of death, regardless of when during that year death occurred. However, when the due date falls on a Saturday, Sunday, or legal holiday, the return is filed timely if filed by the next business day.

The tax return must be prepared for the year of death regardless of when during the year death occurred.

Generally, you must file the final income tax return of the decedent with the Internal Revenue Service Center for the place where you live. A tax return for a decedent can be electronically filed. A personal representative may also obtain an income tax filing extension on behalf of a decedent.

Filing Requirements

The gross income, age, and filing status of a decedent generally determine whether a return must be filed. Gross income is all income received by an individual from any source in the form of money, goods, property, and services that is not tax-exempt. It includes gross receipts from self-employment, but if the business involves manufacturing, merchandising, or mining, subtract any cost of goods sold. In general, filing status depends on whether the decedent was considered single or married at the time of death. See the income tax return instructions or Publication 501, Exemptions, Standard Deduction, and Filing Information.

Refund

A return must be filed to obtain a refund if tax was withheld from salaries, wages, pensions, or annuities, or if estimated tax was paid, even if a return is not otherwise required to be filed. Also, the decedent may be entitled to other credits that result in a refund. These advance payments of tax and credits are discussed later under *Credits, Other Taxes, and Payments.*

Form 1310, Statement of Person Claiming Refund Due a Deceased Taxpayer. Form 1310 does not have to be filed if you are claiming a refund and you are:
- A surviving spouse filing an original or amended joint return with the decedent, or
- A court-appointed or certified personal representative filing the decedent's original return and a copy of the court certificate showing your appointment is attached to the return.

If the personal representative is filing a claim for refund on Form 1040X, Amended U.S. Individual Income Tax Return, or Form 843, Claim for Refund and Request for Abatement, and the court certificate has already been filed with the IRS, attach Form 1310 and write "Certificate Previously Filed" at the bottom of the form.

Example. Edward Green died before filing his tax return. You were appointed the personal representative for Edward's estate, and you file his Form 1040 showing a refund due. You do not need Form 1310 to claim the refund if you attach a copy of the court certificate showing you were appointed the personal representative.

TIP *If you are a surviving spouse and you receive a tax refund check in both your name and your deceased spouse's name, you can have the check reissued in your name alone. Return the joint-name check marked "VOID" to your local IRS office or the service center where you mailed your return, along with a written request for reissuance of the refund check. A new check will be issued in your name and mailed to you.*

Death certificate. When filing the decedent's final income tax return, do not attach the death certificate or other proof of death to the final return. Instead, keep it for your records and provide it if requested.

Nonresident Alien

If the decedent was a nonresident alien who would have had to file Form 1040NR, U.S. Nonresident Alien Income Tax Return, you must file that form for the decedent's final tax year. See the Instructions for Form 1040NR for the filing requirements, due date, and where to file.

Joint Return

Generally, the personal representative and the surviving spouse can file a joint return for the decedent and the surviving spouse. However, the surviving spouse alone can file the joint return if no personal representative has been appointed before the due date for filing the final joint return for the year of death. This also applies to the return for the preceding year if the decedent died after the close of the preceding tax year and before filing the return for that year. The income of the decedent that was includible on his or her return for the year up to the date of death (see *Income To Include,* later) and the income of the surviving spouse for the entire year must be included in the final joint return.

A final joint return with the decedent cannot be filed if the surviving spouse remarried before the end of the year of the decedent's death. The filing status of the decedent in this instance is married filing a separate return.

For information about tax benefits to which a surviving spouse may be entitled, see *Tax Benefits for Survivors,* later, under *Other Tax Information.*

Personal representative may revoke joint return election. A court-appointed personal representative may revoke an election to file a joint return previously made by the surviving spouse alone. This is done by filing a separate return for the decedent within one year from the due date of the return (including any extensions). The joint return made by the surviving spouse will then be regarded as the separate return of that spouse by excluding the decedent's items and refiguring the tax liability.

Relief from joint liability. In some cases, one spouse may be relieved of joint liability for tax, interest, and penalties on a joint return for items of the other spouse that were incorrectly reported on the joint return. If the decedent qualified for this relief while alive, the personal representative can pursue an existing request, or file a request, for relief from joint liability. For information on requesting this relief, see Publication 971, Innocent Spouse Relief.

Income To Include

The decedent's income includible on the final return is generally determined as if the person were still alive except that the taxable period is usually shorter because it ends on the date of death. The method of accounting regularly used by the decedent before death also determines the income includible on the final return. This section explains how some types of income are reported on the final return.

For more information about accounting methods, see Publication 538, Accounting Periods and Methods.

Cash Method

If the decedent accounted for income under the cash method, only those items actually or constructively received before death are included on the final return.

Constructive receipt of income. Interest from coupons on the decedent's bonds is constructively received by the decedent if the coupons matured in the decedent's final tax year, but had not been cashed. Include the interest income on the final return.

Generally, a dividend is considered constructively received if it was available for use by the decedent without restriction. If the corporation customarily mailed its dividend checks, the dividend was includible when received. If the individual died between the time the dividend was declared and the time it was received in the mail, the decedent did not constructively receive it before death. Do not include the dividend in the final return.

Accrual Method

Generally, under an accrual method of accounting, income is reported when earned.

If the decedent used an accrual method, only the income items normally accrued before death are included on the final return.

Publication 559 (2013)

¶105

Interest and Dividend Income (Forms 1099)

Form(s) 1099 reporting interest and dividends earned by the decedent before death should be received and the amounts included on the decedent's final return. A separate Form 1099 should show the interest and dividends earned after the date of the decedent's death and paid to the estate or other recipient that must include those amounts on its return. You can request corrected Forms 1099 if these forms do not properly reflect the right recipient or amounts.

For example, a Form 1099-INT, reporting interest payable to the decedent, may include income that should be reported on the final income tax return of the decedent, as well as income that the estate or other recipient should report, either as income earned after death or as income in respect of the decedent (discussed later). For income earned after death, you should ask the payer for a Form 1099 that properly identifies the recipient (by name and identification number) and the proper amount. If that is not possible, or if the form includes an amount that represents income in respect of the decedent, report the interest as shown next under *How to report.*

See *U.S. savings bonds acquired from decedent* under *Income in Respect of a Decedent,* later, for information on savings bond interest that may have to be reported on the final return.

How to report. If you are preparing the decedent's final return and you have received a Form 1099-INT for the decedent that includes amounts belonging to the decedent and to another recipient (the decedent's estate or another beneficiary), report the total interest shown on Form 1099-INT on Schedule B (Form 1040A or 1040), Interest and Ordinary Dividends. Next, enter a subtotal of the interest shown on Forms 1099, and the interest reportable from other sources for which you did not receive Forms 1099. Then, show any interest (including any interest you receive as a nominee) belonging to another recipient separately and subtract it from the subtotal. Identify the amount of this adjustment as "Nominee Distribution" or other appropriate designation.

Report dividend income for which you received a Form 1099-DIV, Dividends and Distributions, on the appropriate schedule using the same procedure.

Note. If the decedent received amounts as a nominee, you must give the actual owner a Form 1099, unless the owner is the decedent's spouse. See General Instructions for Certain Information Returns (Forms 1097, 1098, 1099, 3921, 3922, 5498, and W-2G) for more information on filing Forms 1099.

Partnership Income

The death of a partner closes the partnership's tax year for that partner. Generally, it does not close the partnership's tax year for the remaining partners. The decedent's distributive share of partnership items must be figured as if the partnership's tax year ended on the date the partner died. To avoid an interim closing of the

partnership books, the partners can agree to estimate the decedent's distributive share by prorating the amounts the partner would have included for the entire partnership tax year.

On the decedent's final return, include the decedent's distributive share of partnership items for the following periods.

1. The partnership's tax year that ended within or with the decedent's final tax year (the year ending on the date of death).

2. The period, if any, from the end of the partnership's tax year in (1) to the decedent's date of death.

Example. Mary Smith was a partner in XYZ partnership and reported her income on a tax year ending December 31. The partnership uses a tax year ending June 30. Mary died August 31, 2013, and her estate established its tax year through August 31.

The distributive share of partnership items based on the decedent's partnership interest is reported as follows.

- Final Return for the Decedent—January 1 through August 31, 2013, includes XYZ partnership items from (a) the partnership tax year ending June 30, 2013, and (b) the partnership tax year beginning July 1, 2013, and ending August 31, 2013 (the date of death).
- Income Tax Return of the Estate—September 1, 2013, through August 31, 2014, includes XYZ partnership items for the period September 1, 2013, through June 30, 2014.

S Corporation Income

If the decedent was a shareholder in an S corporation, include on the final return the decedent's share of the S corporation's items of income, loss, deduction, and credit for the following periods.

1. The corporation's tax year that ended within or with the decedent's final tax year (the year ending on the date of death).

2. The period, if any, from the end of the corporation's tax year in (1) to the decedent's date of death.

Self-Employment Income

Include self-employment income actually or constructively received or accrued, depending on the decedent's accounting method. For self-employment tax purposes only, the decedent's self-employment income will include the decedent's distributive share of a partnership's income or loss through the end of the month in which death occurred. For this purpose, the partnership's income or loss is considered to be earned ratably over the partnership's tax year.

Community Income

If the decedent was married and domiciled in a community property state, half of the income received and half of the expenses paid during the decedent's tax year by either the decedent or spouse may be considered to be the income

and expenses of the other. For more information, see Publication 555, Community Property.

HSA, Archer MSA, or Medicare Advantage MSA

The treatment of an HSA (health savings account), an Archer MSA (medical savings account), or a Medicare Advantage MSA at the death of the account holder, depends on who acquires the interest in the account. If the decedent's estate acquires the interest, the fair market value (FMV) of the assets in the account on the date of death is included in income on the decedent's final return. The estate tax deduction, discussed later, does not apply to this amount.

If a beneficiary acquires the interest, see the discussion under *Income in Respect of a Decedent,* later. For other information on HSAs, Archer MSAs, or Medicare Advantage MSAs, see Publication 969, Health Savings Accounts and Other Tax-Favored Health Plans.

Coverdell Education Savings Account (ESA)

Generally, the balance in a Coverdell ESA must be distributed within 30 days after the individual for whom the account was established reaches age 30, or dies, whichever is earlier. The treatment of the Coverdell ESA at the death of an individual under age 30 depends on who acquires the interest in the account. If the decedent's estate acquires the interest, the earnings on the account must be included on the final income tax return of the decedent. The estate tax deduction, discussed later, does not apply to this amount. If a beneficiary acquires the interest, see the discussion under *Income in Respect of a Decedent,* later.

The age 30 limitation does not apply if the individual for whom the account was established or the beneficiary that acquires the account is an individual with special needs. This includes an individual who, because of a physical, mental, or emotional condition (including a learning disability), requires additional time to complete his or her education.

For more information on Coverdell ESAs, see Publication 970, Tax Benefits for Education.

Accelerated Death Benefits

Accelerated death benefits are amounts received under a life insurance contract before the death of the insured individual. These benefits also include amounts received on the sale or assignment of the contract to a viatical settlement provider.

Generally, if the decedent received accelerated death benefits on the life of a terminally or chronically ill individual, whether on his or her own life or on the life of another person, those benefits are not included in the decedent's income. For more information, see the discussion under *Gifts, Insurance, and Inheritances* under *Other Tax Information,* later.

Exemptions and Deductions

Generally, the rules for exemptions and deductions allowed to an individual also apply to the decedent's final income tax return. Show on the final return deductible items the decedent paid (or accrued, if the decedent reported deductions on an accrual method) before death. This section contains a detailed discussion of medical expenses because the tax treatment of the decedent's medical expenses can be different. See *Medical Expenses*, later.

Exemptions

You can claim the decedent's personal exemption on the final income tax return. If the decedent was another person's dependent (for example, a parent's), you cannot claim the personal exemption on the decedent's final return.

Standard Deduction

If you do not itemize deductions on the final return, the full amount of the appropriate standard deduction is allowed regardless of the date of death. For information on the appropriate standard deduction, see the Form 1040 income tax return instructions or Publication 501.

Medical Expenses

Medical expenses paid before death by the decedent are deductible, subject to limits, on the final income tax return if deductions are itemized. This includes expenses for the decedent, as well as for the decedent's spouse and dependents.

 Beginning in 2013, medical expenses exceeding 10% of adjusted gross income (AGI) may be deducted, unless the decedent or their spouse is age 65 or older. In that case medical expenses exceeding 7.5% of AGI may be deducted.

 Qualified medical expenses are not deductible if paid with a tax-free distribution from an HSA or an Archer MSA.

Election for decedent's expenses. Medical expenses not paid before death are liabilities of the estate and are shown on the federal estate tax return (Form 706). However, if medical expenses for the decedent are paid out of the estate during the 1-year period beginning with the day after death, you can elect to treat all or part of the expenses as paid by the decedent at the time they were incurred.

If you make the election, you can claim all or part of the expenses on the decedent's income tax return (if deductions are itemized) rather than on the federal estate tax return (Form 706). You can deduct expenses incurred in the year of death on the final income tax return. You should file an amended return (Form 1040X) for medical expenses incurred in an earlier year, unless the statutory period for filing a claim for that year has expired.

The amount you can deduct on the income tax return is the amount above 10% of adjusted gross income (or 7.5% of adjusted gross income if the decedent or the decedent's spouse was born before January 2, 1949). Amounts not deductible because of this percentage cannot be claimed on the federal estate tax return.

Making the election. You make the election by attaching a statement, in duplicate, to the decedent's income tax return or amended return. The statement must state that you have not claimed the amount as an estate tax deduction, and that the estate waives the right to claim the amount as a deduction. This election applies only to expenses incurred for the decedent, not to expenses incurred to provide medical care for dependents.

Example. Richard Brown used the cash method of accounting and filed his income tax return on a calendar year basis. Richard died on June 1, 2013, at the age of 78, after incurring $800 in medical expenses. Of that amount, $500 was incurred in 2012 and $300 was incurred in 2013. Richard itemized his deductions when he filed his 2012 income tax return. The personal representative of the estate paid the entire $800 liability in August 2013.

The personal representative may file an amended return (Form 1040X) for 2012 claiming the $500 medical expense as a deduction, subject to the 7.5% limit. The $300 of expenses incurred in 2013 can be deducted on the final income tax return if deductions are itemized, subject to the 7.5% limit. The personal representative must file a statement in duplicate with each return stating that these amounts have **not** been claimed on the federal estate tax return (Form 706), and waiving the right to claim such a deduction on Form 706 in the future.

Medical expenses not paid by estate. If you paid medical expenses for your deceased spouse or dependent, claim the expenses on your tax return for the year in which you paid them, whether they are paid before or after the decedent's death. If the decedent was a child of divorced or separated parents, the medical expenses can usually be claimed by both the custodial and noncustodial parent to the extent paid by that parent during the year.

Insurance reimbursements. Insurance reimbursements of previously deducted medical expenses due a decedent at the time of death and later received by the decedent's estate are includible in the income tax return of the estate (Form 1041) for the year the reimbursements are received. The reimbursements are also includible in the decedent's gross estate.

 No deduction for funeral expenses can be taken on the final Form 1040 of a decedent. These expenses may be deductible for estate tax purposes on Form 706.

Deduction for Losses

A decedent's net operating loss deduction from a prior year and any capital losses (including capital loss carryovers) can be deducted only on the decedent's final income tax return. A net operating loss on the decedent's final income tax return can be carried back to prior years. (See Publication 536, Net Operating Losses (NOLs) for Individuals, Estates, and Trusts.) You cannot deduct any unused net operating loss or capital loss on the estate's income tax return.

At-risk loss limits. Special at-risk rules apply to most activities that are engaged in as a trade or business or for the production of income.

These rules limit the deductible loss to the amount which the individual was considered at-risk in the activity. An individual generally will be considered at-risk to the extent of the money and the adjusted basis of property that he or she contributed to the activity and certain amounts the individual borrowed for use in the activity. An individual will be considered at-risk for amounts borrowed only if he or she was personally liable for the repayment or if the amounts borrowed were secured by property other than that used in the activity. The individual is not considered at-risk for borrowed amounts if the lender has an interest in the activity or if the lender is related to a person who has an interest in the activity. For more information, see Publication 925, Passive Activity and At-Risk Rules.

Passive activity rules. A *passive activity* is any trade or business activity in which the taxpayer does not materially participate. To determine material participation, see Publication 925. Rental activities are passive activities regardless of the taxpayer's participation, unless the taxpayer meets certain eligibility requirements.

Individuals, estates, and trusts can offset passive activity losses only against passive activity income. Passive activity losses or credits not allowed in one tax year can be carried forward to the next year.

If a passive activity interest is transferred because a taxpayer dies, the accumulated unused passive activity losses are allowed as a deduction against the decedent's income in the year of death. Losses are allowed only to the extent they are greater than the excess of the transferee's (recipient of the interest transferred) basis in the property over the decedent's adjusted basis in the property immediately before death. The part of the accumulated losses equal to the excess is not allowed as a deduction for any tax year.

Use Form 8582, Passive Activity Loss Limitations, to summarize losses and income from passive activities and to figure the amounts allowed. For more information, see Publication 925.

Credits, Other Taxes, and Payments

Discussed below are some of the tax credits, types of taxes that may be owed, income tax withheld, and estimated tax payments reported on the final return of a decedent.

Publication 559 (2013)

Credits

On the final income tax return, you can claim any tax credits that applied to the decedent before death. Some of these credits are discussed next.

Earned income credit. If the decedent was an eligible individual, you can claim the earned income credit on the decedent's final return even though the return covers less than 12 months. If the allowable credit is more than the tax liability for the year, the excess is refunded.

For more information, see Publication 596, Earned Income Credit (EIC).

Credit for the elderly or the disabled. This credit is allowable on a decedent's final income tax return if the decedent met both of the following requirements in the year of death. The decedent:

- Was a "qualified individual," and
- Had income (adjusted gross income (AGI) and nontaxable social security and pensions) less than certain limits.

For details on qualifying for or figuring the credit, see Publication 524, Credit for the Elderly or the Disabled.

Child tax credit. If the decedent had a qualifying child, you may be able to claim the child tax credit on the decedent's final return even though the return covers less than 12 months. You may be able to claim the additional child tax credit and get a refund if the credit is more than the decedent's liability. For more information, see the Instructions for Form 1040.

Adoption credit. Depending upon when the adoption was finalized, this credit may be taken on a decedent's final income tax return if the decedent:

- Adopted an eligible child and paid qualified adoption expenses, or
- Has a carryforward of an adoption credit from a prior year.

Also, if the decedent is survived by a spouse who meets the filing status of qualifying widow(er), unused adoption credit may be carried forward and used following the death of the decedent. See Form 8839, Qualified Adoption Expenses, and its instructions for more details.

General business tax credit. The general business credit available to a taxpayer is limited. Any credit arising in a tax year beginning before 1998 that has not been used up can be carried forward for up to 15 years. Any unused credit arising in a tax year beginning after 1997 has a 1-year carryback and a 20-year carryforward period.

After the carryforward period, a deduction may be allowed for any unused business credit. If the taxpayer dies before the end of the carryforward period, the deduction generally is allowed in the year of death.

For more information on the general business credit, see Publication 334, Tax Guide for Small Business.

Other Taxes

Taxes other than income tax that may be owed on the final return of a decedent include self-employment tax and alternative minimum tax, which are reported on Form 1040.

Self-employment tax. Self-employment tax may be owed on the final return if either of the following applied to the decedent in the year of death:

1. Net earnings from self-employment (excluding income described in (2)) were $400 or more; or

2. Wages from services performed as a church employee were $108.28 or more.

Alternative minimum tax (AMT). The tax laws give special treatment to certain types of income and allow special deductions and credits for certain types of expenses. The alternative minimum tax (AMT) was enacted so taxpayers who benefit from these laws still pay at least a minimum amount of tax. In general, the AMT is the excess of the tentative minimum tax over the regular tax shown on the return.

Form 6251. Use Form 6251, Alternative Minimum Tax—Individuals, to determine if this tax applies to the decedent. See the form instructions for information on when you must attach Form 6251 to Form 1040.

Form 8801. If the decedent paid AMT in a previous year or had a credit carryforward, the decedent may be eligible for a minimum tax credit. See Form 8801, Credit for Prior Year Minimum Tax—Individuals, Estates, and Trusts.

Payments of Tax

The income tax withheld from the decedent's salary, wages, pensions, or annuities, and the amount paid as estimated tax are credits (advance payments of tax) that must be claimed on the final return.

Tax Forgiveness for Armed Forces Members, Victims of Terrorism, and Astronauts

Income tax liability may be forgiven for a decedent who dies due to service in a combat zone, due to military or terrorist actions, as a result of a terrorist attack, or while serving in the line of duty as an astronaut.

Combat Zone

If a member of the Armed Forces of the United States dies while in active service in a combat zone or from wounds, disease, or injury incurred in a combat zone, the decedent's income tax liability is abated (forgiven) for the entire year in which death occurred and for any prior tax year ending on or after the first day the person served in a combat zone in active service. For this purpose, a qualified hazardous duty area is treated as a combat zone.

If the tax (including interest, additions to the tax, and additional amounts) for these years has been assessed, the assessment will be forgiven. If the tax has been collected (regardless of the date of collection), that tax will be credited or refunded.

Any of the decedent's income tax for tax years before those mentioned above that remains unpaid as of the actual (or presumptive) date of death will not be assessed. If any unpaid tax (including interest, additions to the tax, and additional amounts) has been assessed, this assessment will be forgiven. Also, if any tax was collected after the date of death, that amount will be credited or refunded.

The date of death of a member of the Armed Forces reported as missing in action or as a prisoner of war is the date his or her name is removed from missing status for military pay purposes. This is true even if death actually occurred earlier.

For other tax information for members of the Armed Forces, see Publication 3, Armed Forces' Tax Guide.

Military or Terrorist Actions

The decedent's income tax liability is forgiven if, at death, he or she was a military or civilian employee of the United States who died because of wounds or injury incurred:

- While a U.S. employee, and
- In a military or terrorist action.

The forgiveness applies to the tax year in which death occurred and for any earlier tax year, beginning with the year before the year in which the wounds or injury occurred.

Example. The income tax liability of a civilian employee of the United States who died in 2013 because of wounds incurred while a U.S. employee in a terrorist attack that occurred in 2008 will be forgiven for 2013 and for all tax years in the period 2007 through 2012. Refunds are allowed for the tax years for which the period for filing a claim for refund has not ended, as discussed later.

Military or terrorist action defined. A *military or terrorist action* means the following.

- Any terrorist activity that most of the evidence indicates was directed against the United States or any of its allies.
- Any military action involving the U.S. Armed Forces and resulting from violence or aggression against the United States or any of its allies, or the threat of such violence or aggression.

Terrorist activity includes criminal offenses intended to coerce, intimidate, or retaliate against the government or civilian population. Military action does not include training exercises. Any multinational force in which the United States is participating is treated as an ally of the United States.

Determining if a terrorist activity or military action has occurred. You may rely on published guidance from the IRS to determine if a particular event is considered a terrorist activity or military action.

Specified Terrorist Victim

The Victims of Terrorism Tax Relief Act of 2001 (the Act) provides tax relief for those injured or killed as a result of terrorist attacks, certain survivors of those killed as a result of terrorist attacks, and others who were affected by terrorist attacks. Under the Act, the federal income tax liability of those killed in the following attacks (specified terrorist victim) is forgiven for certain tax years.

- The April 19, 1995, terrorist attack on the Alfred P. Murrah Federal Building (Oklahoma City).
- The September 11, 2001, terrorist attacks.
- The terrorist attacks involving anthrax occurring after September 10, 2001, and before January 1, 2002.

The Act also exempts from federal income tax the following types of income.

- Qualified disaster relief payments made after September 10, 2001, to cover personal, family, living, or funeral expenses incurred because of a terrorist attack.
- Certain disability payments received in tax years ending after September 10, 2001, for injuries sustained in a terrorist attack.
- Certain death benefits paid by an employer to the survivor of an employee because the employee died as a result of a terrorist attack.
- Payments from the September 11th Victim Compensation Fund 2001.

The Act also reduces the estate tax of individuals who die as a result of a terrorist attack. See Publication 3920, Tax Relief for Victims of Terrorist Attacks, for more information.

Astronauts

Legislation extended the tax relief available under the Victims of Terrorism Tax Relief Act of 2001 (the Act) to astronauts who died in the line of duty after December 31, 2002. The decedent's income tax liability is forgiven for the tax year in which death occurs, and for the tax year prior to death. For information on death benefit payments and the reduction of federal estate taxes, see Publication 3920. However, the discussions in that publication under *Death Benefits* and *Estate Tax Reduction* should be modified for astronauts (for example, by using the date of death of the astronaut instead of September 11, 2001).

For more information on the Act, see Publication 3920.

Claim for Credit or Refund

If any of these tax-forgiveness situations applies to a prior year tax, any tax paid for which the period for filing a claim has not ended will be credited or refunded. If any tax is still due, it will be canceled. The normal period for filing a claim for credit or refund is 3 years after the return was filed or 2 years after the tax was paid, whichever is later.

If death occurred in a combat zone or from wounds, disease, or injury incurred in a combat zone, the period for filing the claim is extended by:

1. The amount of time served in the combat zone (including any period in which the individual was in missing status), plus

2. The period of continuous qualified hospitalization for injury from service in the combat zone, if any, plus

3. The next 180 days.

Qualified hospitalization means any hospitalization outside the United States and any hospitalization in the United States of not more than 5 years.

This extended period for filing the claim also applies to a member of the Armed Forces who was deployed outside the United States in a designated contingency operation.

Filing a claim. Use the following procedures to file a claim.

- If a U.S. individual income tax return (Form 1040, 1040A, or 1040EZ) has not been filed, you should make a claim for refund of any withheld income tax or estimated tax payments by filing Form 1040. Form W-2, Wage and Tax Statement, must accompany all returns.
- If a U.S. individual income tax return has been filed, you should make a claim for refund by filing Form 1040X. You must file a separate Form 1040X for each year in question.

You must file these returns and claims at the following address for regular mail (U.S. Postal Service).

  Internal Revenue Service
333 W. Pershing, P5–6503
Kansas City, MO 64108

Identify all returns and claims for refund by writing "Iraq—KIA," "Enduring Freedom—KIA," "Kosovo Operation—KIA," "Desert Storm—KIA," or "Former Yugoslavia—KIA" in bold letters on the top of page 1 of the return or claim. On the applicable return, write the same phrase on the line for total tax. If the individual was killed in a terrorist or military action, put "KITA" on the front of the return and on the line for total tax.

Include an attachment showing the computation of the decedent's tax liability and a computation of the amount to be forgiven. On joint returns, make an allocation of the tax as described below under *Joint returns*. If you cannot make a proper allocation, attach a statement of all income and deductions allocable to each spouse and the IRS will make the proper allocation.

You must attach Form 1310 to all returns and claims for refund. However, for exceptions to filing Form 1310, see *Form 1310. Statement of Person Claiming Refund Due a Deceased Taxpayer,* under *Refund*, earlier.

You must also attach proof of death that includes a statement that the individual was a U.S. employee on the date of injury and on the date of death and died as the result of a military

or terrorist action. For military and civilian employees of the Department of Defense, attach DD Form 1300, Report of Casualty. For other U.S. civilian employees killed in the United States, attach a death certificate and a certification (letter) from the federal employer. For other U.S. civilian employees killed overseas, attach a certification from the Department of State.

If you do not have enough tax information to file a timely claim for refund, you can suspend the period for filing a claim by filing Form 1040X. Attach Form 1310, any required documentation currently available, and a statement that you will file an amended claim as soon as you have the required tax information.

Joint returns. If a joint return was filed, only the decedent's part of the income tax liability is eligible for forgiveness. Determine the decedent's tax liability as follows.

1. Figure the income tax for which the decedent would have been liable if a separate return had been filed.

2. Figure the income tax for which the spouse would have been liable if a separate return had been filed.

3. Multiply the joint tax liability by a fraction. The numerator of the fraction is the amount in (1), above. The denominator of the fraction is the total of (1) and (2).

The resulting amount from (3) above is the decedent's tax liability eligible for forgiveness.

Filing Reminders

To minimize the time needed to process the decedent's final return and issue any refund, be sure to follow these procedures.

1. Write "DECEASED," the decedent's name, and the date of death across the top of the tax return.

2. If a personal representative has been appointed, the personal representative must sign the return. If it is a joint return, the surviving spouse must also sign it.

3. If you are the decedent's spouse filing a joint return with the decedent and no personal representative has been appointed, write "Filing as surviving spouse" in the area where you sign the return.

4. If no personal representative has been appointed and if there is no surviving spouse, the person in charge of the decedent's property must file and sign the return as "personal representative."

5. To claim a refund for the decedent, do the following.

   a. If you are the decedent's spouse filing a joint return with the decedent, file only the tax return to claim the refund.

   b. If you are the personal representative and the return is not a joint return filed with the decedent's surviving spouse, file the return and attach a copy of the certificate that shows your appointment by the court. (A power of attorney or a copy of the decedent's will is not acceptable evidence of your appointment as the personal representative.) If you are filing an amended return, attach Form 1310 and a copy of the certificate of appointment (or, if you have already sent the certificate of appointment to IRS, write "Certificate Previously Filed" at the bottom of Form 1310).

c. If you are not filing a joint return as the surviving spouse and a personal representative has not been appointed, file the return and attach Form 1310.

Other Tax Information

Discussed below is information about the effect of an individual's death on the income tax liability of the survivors (including widows and widowers), the beneficiaries, and the estate.

Tax Benefits for Survivors

Survivors can qualify for certain benefits when filing their own income tax returns.

Joint return by surviving spouse. A surviving spouse can file a joint return for the year of death and may qualify for special tax rates for the following 2 years, as explained under *Qualifying widows and widowers*, later.

Decedent as your dependent. If the decedent qualified as your dependent for a part of the year before death, you can claim the exemption for the dependent on your tax return, regardless of when death occurred during the year.

If the decedent was your qualifying child, you may be able to claim the child tax credit or the earned income credit. To determine if you qualify for the child tax credit, see the instructions for Form 1040, line 51; Form 1040A, line 33; or Form 1040NR, line 48. To determine if you qualify for the earned income credit, see the instructions for Form 1040, lines 64a and 64b or Form 1040A, lines 38a and 38b.

Qualifying widows and widowers. If your spouse died within the 2 tax years preceding the year for which your return is being filed, you may be eligible to claim the filing status of qualifying widow(er) with dependent child and qualify to use the married-filing-jointly tax rates.

Requirements. Generally, you qualify for this special benefit if you meet all of the following requirements.

- You were entitled to file a joint return with your spouse for the year of death—whether or not you actually filed jointly.
- You did not remarry before the end of the current tax year.
- You have a child, stepchild, or foster child who qualifies as your dependent for the tax year.
- You provide more than half the cost of maintaining your home, which is the principal residence of that child for the entire year except for temporary absences.

Example. William Burns' wife died in 2010. William has not remarried and continued throughout 2011 and 2012 to maintain a home for himself and his dependent child. For 2010, he was entitled to file a joint return for himself and his deceased wife. For 2011 and 2012, he qualifies to file as a qualifying widower with dependent child. For later years, he may qualify to file as a head of household.

Figuring your tax. Check the box on line 5 (Form 1040 or 1040A) under Filing Status on your tax return. Use the Tax Rate Schedule or the column in the Tax Table for Married filing jointly, which gives you the split-income benefits.

The last year you can file jointly with, or claim an exemption for, your deceased spouse is the year of death.

Joint return filing rules. If you are the surviving spouse and a personal representative is handling the estate for the decedent, you should coordinate filing your return for the year of death with this personal representative. See *Joint Return* under *Final Income Tax Return for Decedent—Form 1040*, earlier.

Income in Respect of a Decedent

All income the decedent would have received had death not occurred that was not properly includible on the final return, discussed earlier, is income in respect of a decedent.

 If the decedent is a specified terrorist victim (see Specified Terrorist Victim, *earlier), income received after the date of death and before the end of the decedent's tax year (determined without regard to death) is excluded from the recipient's gross income. This exclusion does not apply to certain income. For more information, see Publication 3920.*

How To Report

Income in respect of a decedent must be included in the income of one of the following.

- The decedent's estate, if the estate receives it.
- The beneficiary, if the right to income is passed directly to the beneficiary and the beneficiary receives it.
- Any person to whom the estate properly distributes the right to receive it.

TIP *If you have to include income in respect of a decedent in your gross income and an estate tax return (Form 706) was filed for the decedent, you may be able to claim a deduction for the estate tax paid on that income. See* Estate Tax Deduction, *later.*

Example 1. Frank Johnson owned and operated an apple orchard. He used the cash method of accounting. He sold and delivered 1,000 bushels of apples to a canning factory for $2,000, but did not receive payment before his death. The proceeds from the sale are income in respect of a decedent. When the estate was

settled, payment had not been made and the estate transferred the right to the payment to his widow. When Frank's widow collects the $2,000, she must include that amount in her return. It is not reported on the final return of the decedent or on the return of the estate.

Example 2. Assume the same facts as in Example 1, except that Frank used the accrual method of accounting. The amount accrued from the sale of the apples would be included on his final return. Neither the estate nor the widow would realize income in respect of a decedent when the money is later paid.

Example 3. On February 1, George High, a cash method taxpayer, sold his tractor for $3,000, payable March 1 of the same year. His adjusted basis in the tractor was $2,000. George died on February 15, before receiving payment. The gain to be reported as income in respect of a decedent is the $1,000 difference between the decedent's basis in the property and the sale proceeds. In other words, the income in respect of a decedent is the gain the decedent would have realized had he lived.

Example 4. Cathy O'Neil was entitled to a large salary payment at the date of her death. The amount was to be paid in five annual installments. The estate, after collecting two installments, distributed the right to the remaining installments to you, the beneficiary. The payments are income in respect of a decedent. None of the payments were includible on Cathy's final return. The estate must include in its income the two installments it received, and you must include in your income each of the three installments as you receive them.

Example 5. You inherited the right to receive renewal commissions on life insurance sold by your father before his death. You inherited the right from your mother, who acquired it by bequest from your father. Your mother died before she received all the commissions she had the right to receive, so you received the rest. The commissions are income in respect of a decedent. None of these commissions were includible in your father's final return. The commissions received by your mother were included in her income. The commissions you received are not includible in your mother's income, even on her final return. You must include them in your income.

Character of income. The character of the income you receive in respect of a decedent remains the same as it would have been to the decedent if he or she were alive. If the income would have been a capital gain to the decedent, it will be a capital gain to you.

Transfer of right to income. If you transfer your right to income in respect of a decedent, you must include in your income the greater of:

- The amount you receive for the right, or
- The fair market value of the right you transfer.

If you make a gift of such a right, you must include in your income the fair market value of the right at the time of the gift.

If the right to income from an installment obligation is transferred, the amount you must include in income is reduced by the basis of the obligation. See *Installment obligations,* later.

Transfer defined. A transfer for this purpose includes a sale, exchange, or other disposition, the satisfaction of an installment obligation at other than face value, or the cancellation of an installment obligation.

Installment obligations. If the decedent sold property using the installment method and you are collecting payments on an installment obligation acquired from the decedent, use the same gross profit percentage the decedent used to figure the part of each payment that represents profit. Include in your income the same profit the decedent would have included had death not occurred. For more information, see Publication 537, Installment Sales.

If you dispose of an installment obligation acquired from a decedent (other than by transfer to the obligor), the rules explained in Publication 537 for figuring gain or loss on the disposition apply to you.

Transfer to obligor. A transfer of a right to income, discussed earlier, has occurred if the decedent (seller) sold property using the installment method and the installment obligation was transferred to the obligor (buyer or person legally obligated to pay the installments). A transfer also occurs if the obligation was canceled either at death or by the estate or person receiving the obligation from the decedent. An obligation that becomes unenforceable is treated as having been canceled.

If such a transfer occurs, the amount included in the income of the transferor (the estate or beneficiary) is the greater of the amount received or the fair market value of the installment obligation at the time of transfer, reduced by the basis of the obligation. The basis of the obligation is the decedent's basis, adjusted for all installment payments received after the decedent's death and before the transfer.

If the decedent and obligor were related persons, the fair market value of the obligation cannot be less than its face value.

Specific Types of Income in Respect of a Decedent

This section explains and provides examples of some specific types of income in respect of a decedent.

Wages. The entire amount of wages or other employee compensation earned by the decedent but unpaid at the time of death is income in respect of a decedent. The income is not reduced by any amounts withheld by the employer. If the income is $600 or more, the employer should report it in box 3 of Form 1099-MISC, Miscellaneous Income, and give the recipient a copy of the form or a similar statement.

Wages paid as income in respect of a decedent are not subject to federal income tax withholding. However, if paid during the calendar year of death, they are subject to withholding for social security and Medicare taxes. These taxes should be included on the decedent's

Form W-2 along with the taxes withheld before death. These wages are not included in box 1 of Form W-2.

Wages paid as income in respect of a decedent after the year of death generally are not subject to withholding for any federal taxes.

Farm income from crops, crop shares, and livestock. A farmer's growing crops and livestock at the date of death normally would not give rise to income in respect of a decedent or income to be included in the final return. However, when a cash method farmer receives rent in the form of crop shares or livestock and owns the crop shares or livestock at the time of death, the rent is income in respect of a decedent and is reported in the year in which the crop shares or livestock are sold or otherwise disposed of. The same treatment applies to crop shares or livestock that the decedent had a right to receive as rent at the time of death for economic activities that occurred before death.

If the individual died during a rental period, only the proceeds from the part of the rental period ending on the date of death are income in respect of a decedent. The proceeds from the rental period from the day after death to the end of the rental period are income to the estate. Cash rent or crop shares and livestock received as rent and reduced to cash by the decedent are includible on the final return even though the rental period did not end until after death.

Example. Alonzo Roberts, who used the cash method of accounting, leased part of his farm for a 1-year period beginning March 1. The rental was one-third of the crop, payable in cash when the crop share is sold at the direction of Alonzo. He died on June 30 and was alive during 122 days of the rental period. Seven months later, Alonzo's personal representative ordered the crop to be sold and was paid $1,500. Of the $1,500, 122/365, or $501, is income in respect of a decedent. The balance of the $1,500 received by the estate, $999, is income to the estate.

Partnership income. If the decedent had been receiving payments representing a distributive share or guaranteed payment in liquidation of his or her interest in a partnership, the remaining payments made to the estate or other successor in interest are income in respect of a decedent. The estate or the successor receiving the payments must include them in income when received. Similarly, the estate or other successor in interest receives income in respect of a decedent if amounts are paid by a third person in exchange for the successor's right to the future payments.

For a discussion of partnership rules, see Publication 541, Partnerships.

U.S. savings bonds acquired from decedent. If series EE or series I U.S. savings bonds, owned by a cash method taxpayer who reported the interest each year, or by an accrual method taxpayer are transferred because of death, the increase in value of the bonds (interest earned) in the year of death up to the date of death must be reported on the decedent's final return. The transferee (estate or beneficiary) reports on its return only the interest earned after the date of death.

The redemption values of U.S. savings bonds generally are available from local banks, credit unions, savings and loan institutions, or your nearest Federal Reserve Bank.

You also can get information by writing to the following address.

Series EE and I
Bureau of the Fiscal Service
Division of Customer Assistance
P.O. Box 7015
Parkersburg, WV 26106-7015

Or, on the Internet, visit:
www.treasurydirect.gov.

If the bonds transferred because of death were owned by a cash method taxpayer who chose not to report the interest each year and had purchased the bonds entirely with personal funds, interest earned before death must be reported in one of the following ways.

1. The person (executor, administrator, etc.) who is required to file the decedent's final income tax return can elect to include all of the interest earned on the bonds before the decedent's death on the return. The transferee (estate or beneficiary) then includes only the interest earned after the date of death on its return.

2. If the election in (1), above, was not made, the interest earned to the date of death is income in respect of the decedent and is not included on the decedent's final return. In this case, all of the interest earned before and after the decedent's death is income to the transferee (estate or beneficiary). A transferee who uses the cash method of accounting and who has chosen not to report the interest annually may defer reporting any of it as income until the bonds are either cashed or reach the date of maturity, whichever is earlier. In the year the interest is reported, the transferee may claim a deduction for any federal estate tax paid that arose because of the part of interest (if any) included in the decedent's estate.

Example 1. Your uncle, a cash method taxpayer, died and left you a $1,000 series EE bond. He bought the bond for $500 and had not chosen to report the increase in value each year. At the date of death, interest of $94 had accrued on the bond, and its value of $594 at date of death was included in your uncle's estate. Your uncle's personal representative did not choose to include the $94 accrued interest on the decedent's final income tax return. You are a cash method taxpayer and do not choose to report the increase in value each year as it is earned. Assuming you cash it when it reaches maturity value of $1,000, you would report $500 interest income (the difference between maturity value of $1,000 and the original cost of $500) in that year. You also are entitled to claim, in that year, a deduction for any federal estate tax resulting from the inclusion in your uncle's estate of the $94 increase in value.

Example 2. If, in Example 1, the personal representative had chosen to include the $94 interest earned on the bond before death in the final income tax return of your uncle, you would report $406 ($500 – $94) as interest when you cashed the bond at maturity. This $406 represents the interest earned after your uncle's death and was not included in his estate, so no deduction for federal estate tax is allowable for this amount.

Example 3. Your uncle died owning series HH bonds he acquired in exchange for series EE bonds. You were the beneficiary on these bonds. Your uncle used the cash method of accounting and had not chosen to report the increase in redemption price of the series EE bonds each year as it accrued. Your uncle's personal representative made no election to include any interest earned before death on the decedent's final return. Your income in respect of the decedent is the sum of the unreported increase in value of the series EE bonds, which constituted part of the amount paid for series HH bonds, and the interest, if any, payable on the series HH bonds but not received as of the date of the decedent's death.

Specific dollar amount legacy satisfied by transfer of bonds. If a beneficiary receives series EE or series I bonds from an estate in satisfaction of a specific dollar amount legacy and the decedent was a cash method taxpayer who did not elect to report interest each year, only the interest earned after receipt of the bonds is income to the beneficiary. The interest earned to the date of death plus any further interest earned to the date of distribution is income to (and reportable by) the estate.

Cashing U.S. savings bonds. When you cash a U.S. savings bond that you acquired from a decedent, the bank or other payer that redeems it must give you a Form 1099-INT if the interest part of the payment you receive is $10 or more. Your Form 1099-INT should show the difference between the amount received and the cost of the bond. The interest shown on your Form 1099-INT will not be reduced by any interest reported by the decedent before death, or, if elected, by the personal representative on the final income tax return of the decedent, or by the estate on the estate's income tax return. Your Form 1099-INT may show more interest than you must include in your income.

You must make an adjustment on your tax return to report the correct amount of interest. Report the total interest shown on Form 1099-INT on your Schedule B (Form 1040A or 1040). Enter a subtotal of the interest shown on Forms 1099, and the interest reportable from other sources for which you did not receive Forms 1099. Show the total interest that was previously reported and subtract it from the subtotal. Identify this adjustment as "U.S. Savings Bond Interest Previously Reported."

Interest accrued on U.S. Treasury bonds. The interest accrued on U.S. Treasury bonds owned by a cash method taxpayer and redeemable for the payment of federal estate taxes that was not received as of the date of the individual's death is income in respect of a decedent. This interest is not included in the decedent's final income tax return. The estate will treat such interest as taxable income in the tax year received if it chooses to redeem the U.S. Treasury bonds to pay federal estate taxes. If the person entitled to the bonds (by bequest, devise, or inheritance, or because of the death of the individual) receives them, that person will treat the accrued interest as taxable income in the year the interest is received. Interest that accrues on the U.S. Treasury bonds after the owner's death does not represent income in respect of a decedent. The interest, however, is taxable income and must be included in the income of the respective recipients.

Interest accrued on savings certificates. The interest accrued on savings certificates (redeemable after death without forfeiture of interest) for the period from the date of the last interest payment and ending with the date of the decedent's death, but not received as of that date, is income in respect of a decedent. Interest accrued after the decedent's death that becomes payable on the certificates after death is not income in respect of a decedent, but is taxable income includible in the income of the respective recipients.

Inherited IRAs. If a beneficiary receives a lump-sum distribution from a traditional IRA he or she inherited, all or some of it may be taxable. The distribution is taxable in the year received as income in respect of a decedent up to the decedent's taxable balance. This is the decedent's balance at the time of death, including unrealized appreciation and income accrued to date of death, minus any basis (nondeductible contributions). Amounts distributed that are more than the decedent's entire IRA balance (includes taxable and nontaxable amounts) at the time of death are the income of the beneficiary.

If the beneficiary of a traditional IRA is the decedent's surviving spouse who properly rolls over the distribution into another traditional IRA, the distribution is not currently taxed. A surviving spouse can also roll over tax free the taxable part of the distribution into a qualified plan, section 403 annuity, or section 457 plan.

For more information on inherited IRAs, see Publication 590, Individual Retirement Arrangements (IRAs).

Roth IRAs. Qualified distributions from a Roth IRA are not subject to tax. A distribution made to a beneficiary or to the Roth IRA owner's estate on or after the date of death is a qualified distribution if it is made after the 5-tax-year period beginning with the first tax year in which a contribution was made to any Roth IRA of the owner.

Generally, the entire interest in the Roth IRA must be distributed by the end of the fifth calendar year after the year of the owner's death unless the interest is payable to a designated beneficiary over his or her life or life expectancy. If paid as an annuity, the distributions must begin before the end of the calendar year following the year of death. If the sole beneficiary is the decedent's spouse, the spouse can delay the distributions until the decedent would have reached age 70½ or can treat the Roth IRA as his or her own Roth IRA.

The part of any distribution made to a beneficiary that is not a qualified distribution may be includible in the beneficiary's income. Generally, the part includible is the earnings in the Roth IRA. Earnings attributable to the period ending with the decedent's date of death are income in respect of a decedent. Additional earnings are the income of the beneficiary.

For more information on Roth IRAs, see Publication 590.

Coverdell education savings account (ESA). Generally, the balance in a Coverdell ESA must be distributed within 30 days after the individual for whom the account was established reaches age 30 or dies, whichever is earlier. The treatment of the Coverdell ESA at the death of an individual under age 30 depends on who acquires the interest in the account. If the decedent's estate acquires the interest, see the discussion under *Final Income Tax Return for Decedent—Form 1040,* earlier.

⚠ *The age 30 limitation does not apply if the individual for whom the account was established or the beneficiary that acquires the account is an individual with special needs. This includes an individual who, because of a physical, mental, or emotional condition (including a learning disability), requires additional time to complete his or her education.*

If the decedent's spouse or other family member is the designated beneficiary of the decedent's account, the Coverdell ESA becomes that person's Coverdell ESA. It is subject to the rules discussed in Publication 970.

Any other beneficiary (including a spouse or family member who is not the designated beneficiary) must include in income the earnings portion of the distribution. Any balance remaining at the close of the 30-day period is deemed to be distributed at that time. The amount included in income is reduced by any qualified education expenses of the decedent that are paid by the beneficiary within one year after the decedent's date of death. An estate tax deduction, discussed later, applies to the amount included in income by a beneficiary other than the decedent's spouse or family member.

HSA, Archer MSA, or a Medicare Advantage MSA. The treatment of an HSA, Archer MSA, or a Medicare Advantage MSA at the death of the account holder depends on who acquires the interest in the account. If the decedent's estate acquired the interest, see the discussion under *Final Income Tax Return for Decedent—Form 1040,* earlier.

If the decedent's spouse is the designated beneficiary of the account, the account becomes that spouse's Archer MSA. It is subject to the rules discussed in Publication 969.

Any other beneficiary (including a spouse that is not the designated beneficiary) must include in income the fair market value of the assets in the account on the decedent's date of death. This amount must be reported for the beneficiary's tax year that includes the decedent's date of death. The amount included in income is reduced by any qualified medical expenses for the decedent paid by the beneficiary within one year after the decedent's date of death. An estate tax deduction, discussed later, applies to the amount included in income by a beneficiary other than the decedent's spouse.

Deductions in Respect of a Decedent

Items such as business expenses, income-producing expenses, interest, and taxes, for which the decedent was liable but that are not properly allowable as deductions on the decedent's final income tax return will be allowed as a deduction to one of the following when paid:

- The estate, or
- The person who acquired an interest in the decedent's property (subject to such obligations) because of the decedent's death, if the estate was not liable for the obligation.

Note. Similar treatment is given to the foreign tax credit. A beneficiary who must pay a foreign tax on income in respect of a decedent will be entitled to claim the foreign tax credit.

Depletion. The deduction for percentage depletion is allowable only to the person (estate or beneficiary) who receives income in respect of a decedent to which the deduction relates, whether or not that person receives the property from which the income is derived. An heir who (because of the decedent's death) receives income as a result of the sale of units of mineral by the decedent (who used the cash method) will be entitled to the depletion allowance for that income. If the decedent had not figured the deduction on the basis of percentage depletion, any depletion deduction to which the decedent was entitled at the time of death is allowable on the decedent's final return, and no depletion deduction in respect of a decedent is allowed to anyone else.

For more information about depletion, see chapter 9 in Publication 535, Business Expenses.

Estate Tax Deduction

Income that the decedent had a right to receive is included in the decedent's gross estate and is subject to estate tax. This income in respect of a decedent is also taxed when received by the recipient (estate or beneficiary). However, an income tax deduction is allowed to the recipient for the estate tax paid on the income.

The deduction for estate tax paid can only be claimed for the same tax year in which the income in respect of a decedent must be included in the recipient's income. (This also is true for income in respect of a prior decedent.)

Individuals can claim this deduction only as an itemized deduction on line 28 of Schedule A (Form 1040). This deduction is not subject to the 2% limit on miscellaneous itemized deductions. Estates can claim the deduction on line 19 of Form 1041. For the alternative minimum tax computation, the deduction is not included as an itemized deduction that is an adjustment to taxable income.

If income in respect of a decedent is capital gain income, you must reduce the gain, but not below zero, by any deduction for estate tax paid

on such gain. This applies in figuring the following.

- The maximum tax on net capital gain (including qualified dividends).
- The 50% exclusion for gain on small business stock.
- The limitation on capital losses.

Computation

To figure a recipient's estate tax deduction, determine:

- The estate tax that qualifies for the deduction, and
- The recipient's part of the deductible tax.

Deductible estate tax. The estate tax is the tax on the taxable estate, reduced by any credits allowed. The estate tax qualifying for the deduction is the part of the net value of all the items in the estate that represents income in respect of a decedent. Net value is the excess of the items of income in respect of a decedent over the items of expenses in respect of a decedent. The deductible estate tax is the difference between the actual estate tax and the estate tax determined without including net value.

Example 1. Jack Sage used the cash method of accounting. At the time of his death, he was entitled to receive $12,000 from clients for his services and he had accrued bond interest of $8,000, for a total income in respect of a decedent of $20,000. He also owed $5,000 for business expenses for which his estate is liable. The income and expenses are reported on Jack's estate tax return.

The tax on Jack's estate is $9,460, after credits. The net value of the items included as income in respect of the decedent is $15,000 ($20,000 − $5,000). The estate tax determined without including the $15,000 in the taxable estate is $4,840, after credits. The estate tax that qualifies for the deduction is $4,620 ($9,460 − $4,840).

Recipient's deductible part. Figure the recipient's part of the deductible estate tax by dividing the estate tax value of the items of income in respect of a decedent included in the recipient's income (the numerator) by the total value of all items included in the estate that represents income in respect of a decedent (the denominator). If the amount included in the recipient's income is less than the estate tax value of the item, use the lesser amount in the numerator.

Example 2. As the beneficiary of Jack's estate (Example 1), you collect the $12,000 accounts receivable from his clients. You will include the $12,000 in your income in the tax year you receive it. If you itemize your deductions in that tax year, you can claim an estate tax deduction of $2,772 figured as follows:

$$\frac{\text{Value included in your income}}{\text{Total value of income in respect of decedent}} \times \text{Estate tax qualifying for deduction}$$

$$\frac{\$12,000}{\$20,000} \times \$4,620 = \$2,772$$

If the amount you collected for the accounts receivable was more than $12,000, you would still claim $2,772 as an estate tax deduction because only the $12,000 actually reported on the estate tax return can be used in the above computation. However, if you collected less than the $12,000 reported on the estate tax return, use the smaller amount to figure the estate tax deduction.

Estates. The estate tax deduction allowed to an estate is figured in the same manner discussed earlier. However, any income in respect of a decedent received by the estate during the tax year is reduced by any such income properly paid, credited, or required to be distributed by the estate to a beneficiary. The beneficiary would include such distributed income in respect of a decedent for figuring the beneficiary's estate tax deduction.

Surviving annuitants. For the estate tax deduction, an annuity received by a surviving annuitant under a joint and survivor annuity contract is considered income in respect of a decedent. The deceased annuitant must have died after the annuity starting date. You must make a special computation to figure the estate tax deduction for the surviving annuitant. See Regulations section 1.691(d)-1.

Gifts, Insurance, and Inheritances

Property received as a gift, bequest, or inheritance is not included in your income. However, if property you receive in this manner later produces income, such as interest, dividends, or rents, that income is taxable to you. The income from property donated to a trust that is paid, credited, or distributed to you is taxable income to you. If the gift, bequest, or inheritance is the income from property, that income is taxable to you.

If you receive property from a decedent's estate in satisfaction of your right to the income of the estate, it is treated as a bequest or inheritance of income from property. See *Distributions to Beneficiaries*, later.

Insurance

The proceeds from a decedent's life insurance policy paid by reason of his or her death generally are excluded from income. The exclusion applies to any beneficiary, whether a family member or other individual, a corporation, or a partnership.

Veterans' insurance proceeds. Veterans' insurance proceeds and dividends are not taxable either to the veteran or to the beneficiaries.

Interest on dividends left on deposit with the Department of Veterans Affairs is not taxable.

Life insurance proceeds. Life insurance proceeds paid to a beneficiary because of the death of the insured (or because the insured is a member of the U.S. uniformed services who is missing in action) are not taxable unless the policy was turned over to the recipient for a price. This is true even if the proceeds are paid

¶105

under an accident or health insurance policy or an endowment contract. If the proceeds are received in installments, see the discussion under *Insurance received in installments,* later.

Accelerated death benefits. A beneficiary can exclude from income accelerated death benefits received on the life of an insured individual if certain requirements are met. Accelerated death benefits are amounts received under a life insurance contract before the death of the insured. These benefits also include amounts received on the sale or assignment of the contract to a viatical settlement provider. This exclusion applies only if the insured was a terminally ill individual or a chronically ill individual. This exclusion does not apply if the insured is a director, officer, employee, or has a financial interest, in any trade or business carried on by the beneficiary.

Terminally ill individual. A *terminally ill individual* is one who has been certified by a physician as having an illness or physical condition that reasonably can be expected to result in death in 24 months or less from the date of certification.

Chronically ill individual. A *chronically ill individual* is one who has been certified as one of the following.

- An individual who, for at least 90 days, is unable to perform at least two activities of daily living without substantial assistance due to a loss of functional capacity.
- An individual who requires substantial supervision to be protected from threats to health and safety due to severe cognitive impairment.

A certification must have been made by a licensed health care practitioner within the previous 12 months.

Exclusion limited. If the insured was a chronically ill individual, exclusion of accelerated death benefits is limited to the cost incurred in providing qualified long-term care services for the insured. In determining the cost incurred, do not include amounts paid or reimbursed by insurance or otherwise. Subject to certain limits, exclude payments received on a periodic basis without regard to costs.

Interest option on insurance. If an insurance company pays interest only on proceeds from life insurance left on deposit, the interest is taxable.

Insurance received in installments. If a beneficiary receives life insurance proceeds in installments, he or she can exclude part of each installment from income.

To determine the part excluded, divide the amount held by the insurance company (generally the total lump sum payable at the death of the insured person) by the number of installments to be paid. Include anything over this excluded part in income as interest.

Specified number of installments. If a beneficiary will receive a specified number of installments under the insurance contract, figure the part of each installment he or she can exclude by dividing the amount held by the insurance company by the number of installments to

which he or she is entitled. In case he or she dies before receiving all the installments, a secondary beneficiary is entitled to the same exclusion.

Example. As beneficiary, you choose to receive $100,000 of life insurance proceeds in 10 annual installments of $11,000. Each year, you can exclude from your income $10,000 ($100,000 ÷ 10) as a return of principal. The balance of the installment, $1,000, is taxable as interest income.

Specified amount payable. If each installment received under the insurance contract is a specific amount based on a guaranteed rate of interest, but the number of installments that will be received is uncertain, the part of each installment excluded from income is the amount held by the insurance company divided by the number of installments necessary to use up the principal and guaranteed interest in the contract.

Example. The face amount of the policy is $200,000, and as beneficiary you choose to receive annual installments of $12,000. The insurer's settlement option guarantees you this amount for 20 years based on a guaranteed rate of interest. It also provides that extra interest may be credited to the principal balance according to the insurer's earnings. The excludable part of each guaranteed installment is $10,000 ($200,000 ÷ 20 years). The balance of each guaranteed installment, $2,000, is interest income to you. The full amount of any additional payment for interest is income to you.

Installments for life. If the beneficiary under an insurance contract is entitled to receive the proceeds in installments for the rest of his or her life without a refund or period-certain guarantee, the excluded part of each installment can be determined by dividing the amount held by the insurance company by his or her life expectancy. If there is a refund or period-certain guarantee, the amount held by the insurance company for this purpose is reduced by the actuarial value of the guarantee.

Example. As beneficiary, you choose to receive the $50,000 proceeds from a life insurance contract under a life-income-with-cash-refund option. You are guaranteed $2,700 a year for the rest of your life (which is estimated by use of mortality tables to be 25 years from the insured's death). The actuarial value of the refund feature is $9,000. The amount held by the insurance company, reduced by the value of the guarantee, is $41,000 ($50,000 − $9,000) and the excludable part of each installment representing a return of principal is $1,640 ($41,000 ÷ 25). The remaining $1,060 ($2,700 − $1,640) is interest income to you. If you should die before receiving the entire $50,000, the refund payable to the refund beneficiary is not taxable.

Flexible premium contracts. A life insurance contract (including any qualified additional benefits) qualifies as a flexible premium life insurance contract if it provides for the payment of one or more premiums that are not fixed by the insurer as to both timing and amount. For a flexible premium contract issued before January 1, 1985, the proceeds paid under the contract be-

cause of the death of the insured will be excluded from the recipient's income only if the contract meets the requirements explained under section 101(f).

Basis of Inherited Property

The basis of property inherited from a decedent is generally one of the following.

- The FMV of the property on the date of the individual's death.
- The FMV on the alternate valuation date (discussed in the instructions for Form 706), if elected by the personal representative.
- The value under the special-use valuation method for real property used in farming or other closely held business (see *Special-use valuation,* later), if elected by the personal representative.
- The decedent's adjusted basis in land to the extent of the value excluded from the decedent's taxable estate as a qualified conservation easement (discussed in the Instructions for Form 706).

Exception for appreciated property. If you or your spouse gave appreciated property to an individual during the 1-year period ending on the date of that individual's death and you (or your spouse) later acquired the same property from the decedent, your basis in the property is the same as the decedent's adjusted basis immediately before death.

Appreciated property. Appreciated property is property that had an FMV greater than its adjusted basis on the day it was transferred to the decedent.

Special-use valuation. If you are a qualified heir and you receive a farm or other closely held business real property for which the personal representative elected special-use valuation, the property is valued on the basis of its actual use rather than its FMV.

If you are a qualified heir and you buy special-use valuation property from the estate, your basis is equal to the estate's basis (determined under the special-use valuation method) immediately before your purchase plus any gain recognized by the estate.

You are a qualified heir if you are an ancestor (parent, grandparent, etc.), the spouse, or a lineal descendant (child, grandchild, etc.) of the decedent, a lineal descendant of the decedent's parent or spouse, or the spouse of any of these lineal descendants.

For more information on special-use valuation, see the instructions for Form 706.

Increased basis for special-use valuation property. Under certain conditions, some or all of the estate tax benefits obtained by using the special-use valuation will be subject to recapture. Generally, an additional estate tax must be paid by the qualified heir if the property is disposed of, or is no longer used for a qualifying purpose within 10 years of the decedent's death.

If you must pay any additional estate (recapture) tax, you can elect to increase your basis in the special-use valuation property to its FMV on the date of the decedent's death (or on the alternate valuation date, if it was elected by the personal representative). If you elect to increase your basis, you must pay interest on the recapture tax for the period beginning 9 months after the decedent's death until the date you pay the recapture tax.

For more information on the recapture tax, see the Instructions for Form 706-A, United States Additional Estate Tax Return.

S corporation stock. The basis of inherited S corporation stock must be reduced if there is income in respect of a decedent attributable to that stock.

Joint interest. Figure the surviving tenant's new basis of jointly owned property (joint tenancy or tenancy by the entirety) by adding the surviving tenant's original basis in the property to the value of the part of the property included in the decedent's estate, discussed earlier. Subtract from the sum any deductions for wear and tear, such as depreciation or depletion, allowed to the surviving tenant on that property.

Example. Fred Maple and his sister Anne owned, as joint tenants with right of survivorship, rental property they purchased for $60,000. Anne paid $15,000 of the purchase price and Fred paid $45,000. Under local law, each had a half interest in the income from the property. When Fred died, the FMV of the property was $100,000. Depreciation deductions allowed before Fred's death were $20,000. Anne's basis in the property is $80,000 figured as follows:

Anne's original basis	$15,000	
Interest acquired from Fred (³⁄₄ of $100,000)	75,000	$90,000
Minus: ¹⁄₂ of $20,000 depreciation		10,000
Anne's basis		**$80,000**

Qualified joint interest. One-half of the value of property owned by a decedent and spouse as tenants by the entirety, or as joint tenants with right of survivorship if the decedent and spouse are the only joint tenants, is included in the decedent's gross estate. This is true regardless of how much each contributed toward the purchase price.

Figure the basis for a surviving spouse by adding one-half of the property's cost basis to the value included in the gross estate. Subtract from this sum any deductions for wear and tear, such as depreciation or depletion, allowed on that property to the surviving spouse.

Example. Dan and Diane Gilbert owned, as tenants by the entirety, rental property they purchased for $60,000. Dan paid $15,000 of the purchase price and Diane paid $45,000. Under local law, each had a half interest in the income from the property. When Diane died, the FMV of the property was $100,000. Depreciation deductions allowed before Diane's death were $20,000. Dan's basis in the property is $70,000 figured as follows:

One-half of cost basis (¹⁄₂ of $60,000)	$30,000	
Interest acquired from Diane (¹⁄₂ of $100,000)	50,000	$80,000
Minus: ¹⁄₂ of $20,000 depreciation		10,000
Dan's basis		**$70,000**

See Publication 551, Basis of Assets, for more information on basis. If the decedent and his or her spouse lived in a community property state, see the discussion in that publication about figuring the basis of community property after a spouse's death.

Depreciation. If a beneficiary can depreciate inherited property, the modified accelerated cost recovery system (MACRS) must be used to determine depreciation.

For joint interests and qualified joint interests, use the following computations to figure depreciation.

- The first computation is for the original basis in the property.
- The second computation is for the inherited part of the property.

Continue depreciating the original basis under the same method used in previous years. Depreciate the inherited part using MACRS.

MACRS consists of two depreciation systems, the General Depreciation System (GDS) and the Alternative Depreciation System (ADS). For more information on MACRS, see Publication 946, How To Depreciate Property.

Valuation misstatements. If the value or adjusted basis of any property claimed on an income tax return is 150% or more of the amount determined to be the correct amount, there is a substantial valuation misstatement. If the value or adjusted basis is 200% or more of the amount determined to be the correct amount, there is a gross valuation misstatement.

Understatements. A substantial estate or gift tax valuation misstatement occurs when the value of property reported is 65% or less of the actual value of the property. A gross valuation misstatement occurs if any property on a return is valued at 40% or less of the value determined to be correct.

Penalty. If a misstatement results in an underpayment of tax of more than $5,000, an addition to tax of 20% of the underpayment can apply. The penalty increases to 40% if the value or adjusted basis reported is a gross valuation misstatement.

The IRS may waive all or part of the 20% addition to tax (for substantial valuation overstatement) if the following apply.

- The claimed value of the property was based on a qualified appraisal made by a qualified appraiser.
- In addition to obtaining such appraisal, the taxpayer made a good faith investigation of the value of the contributed property.

No waiver is available for the 40% addition to tax (for gross valuation overstatement).

For transitional guidance on the definitions of "qualified appraisal" and "qualified appraiser," see Notice 2006-96, 2006-46 I.R.B. 902, available at *www.irs.gov/pub/irs-irbs/irb06-46.pdf*.

The definitions apply to appraisals prepared for the following.

- Donated property for which a deduction of more than $5,000 is claimed.
- Returns filed after August 17, 2006.

Holding period. If you sell or dispose of inherited property that is a capital asset, the gain or loss is considered long-term, regardless of how long you held the property.

Property distributed in kind. Your basis in property distributed in kind by a decedent's estate is the same as the estate's basis immediately before the distribution plus any gain, or minus any loss, recognized by the estate. Property is distributed in kind if it satisfies your right to receive another property or amount, such as the income of the estate or a specific dollar amount. Property distributed in kind generally includes any noncash property you receive from the estate other than the following:

- A specific bequest (unless it must be distributed in more than three installments), or
- Real property, the title to which passes directly to you under local law.

For information on an estate's recognized gain or loss on distributions in kind, see *Income To Include* under *Income Tax Return of an Estate—Form 1041,* later.

Other Items of Income

Some other items of income that a survivor or beneficiary may receive are discussed below. Lump-sum payments received by the surviving spouse or beneficiary of a deceased employee may represent the following.

- Accrued salary payments.
- Distributions from employee profit-sharing, pension, annuity, and stock bonus plans.
- Other items that should be treated separately for tax purposes.

The treatment of these lump-sum payments depends on what the payments represent.

Public safety officers. Special rules apply to certain amounts received due to the death of a public safety officer (a law enforcement officer, fire fighter, chaplain, or member of an ambulance crew or rescue squad).

⚠️ *The provisions for public safety officers apply to a chaplain killed in the line of duty after September 10, 2001, if the chaplain was responding to a fire, rescue, or police emergency as a member or employee of a fire or police department.*

Death benefits. The death benefit payable to eligible survivors of public safety officers who die as a result of traumatic injuries sustained in the line of duty is not included in either the beneficiaries' income or the decedent's gross estate. This benefit is administered through the Bureau of Justice Assistance (BJA).

The BJA can pay the eligible survivors an emergency interim benefit up to $3,000 if it determines that a public safety officer's death is one for which a death benefit will probably be paid. If there is no final payment, the recipient of the interim benefit is liable for repayment.

¶105

However, the BJA may waive all or part of the repayment if it will cause a hardship. Any repayment waived is not included in income.

Survivor benefits. Generally, a survivor annuity received by the spouse, former spouse, or child of a public safety officer killed in the line of duty is excluded from the recipient's income. The annuity must be provided under a government plan and is excludable to the extent that it is attributable to the officer's service as a public safety officer.

The exclusion does not apply if the recipient's actions were responsible for the officer's death. It also does not apply in the following circumstances.

- The death was caused by the intentional misconduct of the officer or by the officer's intention to cause such death.
- The officer was voluntarily intoxicated at the time of death.
- The officer was performing his or her duties in a grossly negligent manner at the time of death.

Salary or wages. Salary or wages paid after the employee's death are usually taxable income to the beneficiary. See *Wages,* earlier, under *Specific Types of Income in Respect of a Decedent.*

 If the decedent is a specified terrorist victim (see Specified Terrorist Victim, earlier), certain income received by the beneficiary or the estate is not taxable. For more information, see Publication 3920.

Rollover distributions. An employee's surviving spouse who receives an eligible rollover distribution may roll it over tax free into an IRA, a qualified plan, a section 403 annuity, or a section 457 plan. For more information, see Publication 575, Pension and Annuity Income, and Form 4972, Tax on Lump-Sum Distributions.

Rollovers by nonspouse beneficiary. A beneficiary other than the employee's surviving spouse may be able to roll over all or part of a distribution from an eligible retirement plan of a deceased employee. The nonspouse beneficiary must be the designated beneficiary of the employee. The distribution must be a direct trustee-to-trustee transfer to his or her IRA set up to receive the distribution. The transfer will be treated as an eligible rollover distribution and the receiving plan will be treated as an inherited IRA. For more information on inherited IRAs, see Publication 590.

Pensions and annuities. For beneficiaries who receive pensions and annuities, see Publication 575. For beneficiaries of federal civil service employees or retirees, see Publication 721, Tax Guide to U.S. Civil Service Retirement Benefits.

Inherited IRAs. If a person other than the decedent's spouse inherits the decedent's traditional IRA or Roth IRA, that person cannot treat the IRA as one established on his or her behalf. If a distribution from a traditional IRA is from contributions that were deducted or from earnings and gains in the IRA, it is fully taxable income. If there were nondeductible contributions, an allocation between taxable and

nontaxable income must be made. For information on distributions from a Roth IRA, see the discussion earlier under *Income in Respect of a Decedent.* The inherited IRA cannot be rolled over into, or receive a rollover from, another IRA. No deduction is allowed for amounts paid into that inherited IRA. For more information about IRAs, see Publication 590.

Estate income. Estates may have to pay federal income tax. Beneficiaries may have to pay tax on their share of estate income. However, there is never a double tax. See *Distributions to Beneficiaries,* later.

Income Tax Return of an Estate— Form 1041

An estate is a taxable entity separate from the decedent and comes into being with the death of the individual. It exists until the final distribution of its assets to the heirs and other beneficiaries. The income earned by the assets during this period must be reported by the estate under the conditions described in this publication. The tax generally is figured in the same manner and on the same basis as for individuals, with certain differences in the computation of deductions and credits, as explained later.

The estate's income, like an individual's income, must be reported annually on either a calendar or fiscal year basis. The personal representative chooses the estate's accounting period upon filing the first Form 1041. The estate's first tax year can be any period that ends on the last day of a month and does not exceed 12 months.

Generally, once chosen the tax year cannot be changed without IRS approval. Also, on the first income tax return, the personal representative must choose the accounting method (cash, accrual, or other) to report the estate's income. Once a method is used, it ordinarily cannot be changed without IRS approval. For a more complete discussion of accounting periods and methods, see Publication 538.

Filing Requirements

Every domestic estate with gross income of $600 or more during a tax year must file a Form 1041. If one or more of the beneficiaries of the domestic estate are nonresident aliens, the personal representative must file Form 1041, even if the gross income of the estate is less than $600.

A fiduciary for a nonresident alien estate with U.S. source income, including any income that is effectively connected with the conduct of a trade or business in the United States, must file Form 1040NR, U.S. Nonresident Alien Income Tax Return, as the income tax return of the estate.

A nonresident alien who was a resident of Puerto Rico, Guam, American Samoa, or the Commonwealth of the Northern Mariana Islands for the entire tax year will, for this purpose, be treated as a resident alien of the United States.

Schedule K-1 (Form 1041)

The personal representative must file a separate Schedule K-1 (Form 1041), or a substitute (described below), for each beneficiary. File these schedules with Form 1041.

The personal representative must ask each beneficiary to provide a taxpayer identification number (TIN), which must be reported on the Schedule K-1 (Form 1041). A $50 penalty is charged for each failure to provide the identifying number of each beneficiary unless reasonable cause is established. A nonresident alien beneficiary with a withholding certificate generally must provide a TIN (see Publication 515). A TIN is not required for an executor or administrator of the estate unless that person is also a beneficiary.

The personal representative must also give a Schedule K-1 (Form 1041), or a substitute, to each beneficiary by the date on which the Form 1041 is filed. Failure to provide this payee statement can result in a penalty of $50 for each failure. This penalty also applies if information is omitted or incorrect information is included on the payee statement.

No prior approval is needed for a substitute Schedule K-1 (Form 1041) that is an exact copy of the official schedule or that follows the specifications in Publication 1167, General Rules and Specifications for Substitute Forms and Schedules. Prior approval is required for any other substitute Schedule K-1 (Form 1041).

Beneficiaries. The personal representative has a fiduciary responsibility to the ultimate recipients of the income and the property of the estate. While the courts use a number of names to designate specific types of beneficiaries or the recipients of various types of property, this publication refers to all of them as beneficiaries.

Liability of the beneficiary. The income tax liability of an estate attaches to the assets of the estate. If the income is distributed or must be distributed during the current tax year, the income is reportable by each beneficiary on his or her individual income tax return. If the income does not have to be distributed, and is not distributed but is retained by the estate, the income tax on the income is payable by the estate. If the income is distributed later without the payment of the taxes due, the beneficiary can be liable for tax due and unpaid to the extent of the value of the estate assets received.

Income of the estate is taxed to either the estate or the beneficiary, but not to both.

Nonresident alien beneficiary. In addition to filing Form 1041, the personal representative may need to file Form 1040NR and pay the tax due, if any, if there is a nonresident alien beneficiary. There are a number of factors which determine whether a Form 1040NR is required. For information on who must file Form 1040NR, see Publication 519, U.S. Tax Guide for Aliens.

If a nonresident alien has an appointed agent in the United States, the personal representative is not responsible for filing Form 1040NR and paying any tax due. However, a copy of the document appointing the agent must be attached to the estate's Form 1041.

The personal representative also must file Form 1042, Annual Withholding Tax Return for U.S. Source Income of Foreign Persons, and Form 1042-S, Foreign Person's U.S. Source Income Subject to Withholding, to report and transmit withheld tax on distributable net income (discussed later) actually distributed. This applies to the extent the distribution consists of an amount subject to withholding. For more information, see Publication 515.

Amended Return

If an amended Form 1041 must be filed, use a copy of the form for the appropriate year and check the "Amended return" box. Complete the entire return, correct the appropriate lines with the new information, and refigure the tax liability. On an attached sheet, explain the reason for the changes and identify the lines and amounts changed.

Note. If the amended return results from a net operating loss carryback, check the "Net operating loss carryback" box. For more information, see the Instructions for Form 1041.

If the amended return results in a change to income, or a change in distribution of any income or other information provided to a beneficiary, an amended Schedule K-1 (Form 1041) must be filed with Form 1041 and a copy given to each beneficiary. Check the "Amended K-1" box at the top of Schedule K-1 (Form 1041).

Information Returns

Even though the personal representative may not have to file an income tax return for the estate, Form 1099-DIV, Form 1099-INT, or Form 1099-MISC may need to be filed if the estate received income as a nominee or middleman for another person. For more information on filing information returns, see the General Instructions for Certain Information Returns.

The personal representative will **not** have to file information returns for the estate if the estate is the owner of record, Form 1041 is filed for the estate (reporting the name, address, and identifying number of each actual owner), and a completed Schedule K-1 (Form 1041) is provided to each actual owner.

Penalty. A penalty of up to $50 can be charged for each failure to file or failure to include correct information on an information return. (Failure to include correct information includes failure to include all the information required.) If it is shown that such failure is due to intentional disregard of the filing requirement, the penalty amount increases.

See the General Instructions for Certain Information Returns, for more information.

Copy of the Will

The personal representative does **not** have to include a copy of the decedent's will with Form 1041. If the will is later requested, attach a statement to it indicating the provisions that determine how much of the estate's income is taxable to the estate or to the beneficiaries. A

statement signed by the personal representative under penalties of perjury that the will is a true and complete copy should also be attached.

Income To Include

The estate's taxable income generally is figured the same way as an individual's income, except as explained in the following discussions.

 If the decedent is a specified terrorist victim (see Specified Terrorist Victim, earlier), certain income received by the estate is not taxable. See Publication 3920.

Gross income of an estate consists of all items of income received or accrued during the tax year. It includes dividends, interest, rents, royalties, gain from the sale of property, and income from business, partnerships, trusts, and any other sources. For a discussion of income from dividends, interest, and other investment income, as well as gains and losses from the sale of investment property, see Publication 550, Investment Income and Expenses. For a discussion of gains and losses from the sale of other property, including business property, see Publication 544, Sales and Other Dispositions of Assets.

If the personal representative's duties include the operation of the decedent's business, see Publication 334. That publication provides general information about the tax laws that apply to a sole proprietorship.

Income in respect of a decedent. The personal representative of the estate may receive income the decedent would have reported had death not occurred. For an explanation of this income, see *Income in Respect of a Decedent* under *Other Tax Information*, earlier. An estate may qualify to claim a deduction for estate taxes if the estate must include in gross income for any tax year an amount of income in respect of a decedent. See *Estate Tax Deduction*, under *Other Tax Information*, earlier.

Gain (or loss) from sale of property. During the administration of the estate, the personal representative may find it necessary or desirable to sell all or part of the estate's assets to pay debts and expenses of administration, or to make proper distributions of the assets to the beneficiaries. While the personal representative may have the legal authority to dispose of the property, title to it may be vested (given a legal interest in the property) in one or more of the beneficiaries. This is usually true of real property. To determine whether any gain or loss must be reported by the estate or by the beneficiaries, consult local law to determine the legal owner.

Redemption of stock to pay death taxes. Under certain conditions, a distribution to a shareholder (including the estate) in redemption of stock included in the decedent's gross estate may be allowed capital gain (or loss) treatment.

Character of asset. The character of an asset in the hands of an estate determines whether gain or loss on its sale or other disposition is capital or ordinary. The asset's character

depends on how the estate holds or uses it. If it was a capital asset to the decedent, it generally will be a capital asset to the estate. If it was land or depreciable property used in the decedent's business and the estate continues the business, it generally will have the same character to the estate that it had in the decedent's hands. If it was held by the decedent for sale to customers, it generally will be considered to be held for sale to customers by the estate if the decedent's business continues to operate during the administration of the estate.

 The gain from a sale of depreciable property between an estate and a beneficiary of that estate will be treated as ordinary income, unless the sale or exchange was made to satisfy a pecuniary (cash) bequest.

Sale of decedent's residence. If the estate is the legal owner of a decedent's residence and the personal representative sells it in the course of administration, the tax treatment of gain or loss depends on how the estate holds or uses the former residence. For example, if, as the personal representative, you intend to realize the value of the house through sale, the residence is a capital asset held for investment and gain or loss is capital gain or loss (which may be deductible). This is the case even though it was the decedent's personal residence and even if you did not rent it out. If, however, the house is not held for business or investment use (for example, if you intend to permit a beneficiary to live in the residence rent-free and then distribute it to the beneficiary to live in), and you later decide to sell the residence without first converting it to business or investment use, any gain is capital gain, but a loss is not deductible.

Holding period. An estate (or other recipient) that acquires property from a decedent and sells or otherwise disposes of it is considered to have held that property for more than 1 year, no matter how long the estate and the decedent actually held the property.

Basis of property. The basis used to figure gain or loss for property the estate receives from the decedent usually is its fair market value at the date of death. See *Basis of Inherited Property* under *Other Tax Information*, earlier, for other basis in inherited property.

If the estate purchases property after the decedent's death, the basis usually will be its cost.

The basis of certain appreciated property the estate receives from the decedent will be the decedent's adjusted basis in the property immediately before death. This applies if the property was acquired by the decedent as a gift during the 1-year period before death, the property's fair market value on the date of the gift was greater than the donor's adjusted basis, and the proceeds of the sale of the property are distributed to the donor (or the donor's spouse).

Schedule D (Form 1041) and Form 8949. Use Form 8949, Sales and Other Dispositions of Capital Assets, to report most sales and exchanges of capital assets. Use Schedule D (Form 1041), to report the overall capital gains and losses from transactions reported on Form

8949, certain transactions that do not have to be reported on Form 8949, and certain other capital gains and losses. For additional information, see the Instructions for Form 8949 and the Instructions for Schedule D (Form 1041).

Installment obligations. If an installment obligation owned by the decedent is transferred by the estate to the obligor (buyer or person obligated to pay) or is canceled at death, include the income from that event in the gross income of the estate. See *Installment obligations* under *Income in Respect of a Decedent,* earlier. See Publication 537 for information about installment sales.

Gain from sale of special-use valuation property. If the personal representative elected special-use valuation for farm or other closely held business real property and that property is sold to a qualified heir, the estate will recognize gain on the sale if the fair market value on the date of the sale exceeds the fair market value on the date of the decedent's death (or on the alternate valuation date if it was elected).

Qualified heirs. Qualified heirs include the decedent's ancestors (parents, grandparents, etc.) and spouse, the decedent's lineal descendants (children, grandchildren, etc.) and their spouses, and lineal descendants (and their spouses) of the decedent's parents or spouse.

For more information about special-use valuation, see Form 706 and its instructions.

Gain from transfer of property to a political organization. Appreciated property transferred to a political organization is treated as sold by the estate. Appreciated property is property that has a fair market value (on the date of the transfer) greater than the estate's basis. The gain recognized is the difference between the estate's basis and the fair market value on the date transferred.

A political organization is any party, committee, association, fund, or other organization formed and operated to accept contributions or make expenditures for influencing the nomination, election, or appointment of an individual to any federal, state, or local public office.

Gain or loss on distributions in kind. An estate recognizes gain or loss on a distribution of property in kind to a beneficiary only in the following situations:

1. The distribution satisfies the beneficiary's right to receive either:

    a. A specific dollar amount (whether payable in cash, in unspecified property, or in both); or

    b. A specific property other than the property distributed.

2. An election is made to recognize the gain or loss on the estate's income tax return (section 643(e)(3) election).

The gain or loss is usually the difference between the fair market value of the property when distributed and the estate's basis in the property. However, see *Gain from sale of special-use valuation property,* earlier, for a limit on

the gain recognized on a transfer of such property to a qualified heir.

If you elect to recognize gain or loss, the election applies to all noncash distributions during the tax year except charitable distributions and specific bequests. To make the election, report the transaction on Form 8949 and/or Schedule D (Form 1041) as applicable, and check the box on line 7 in the "Other Information" section of Form 1041. The election must be made by the due date (including extensions) of the estate's income tax return for the year of distribution. However, if the return is timely filed without making the election, the election can be made by filing an amended return within 6 months of the due date of the return (excluding extensions). Attach Form 8949 and/or Schedule D (Form 1041) as applicable, to the amended return and write "Filed pursuant to section 301.9100-2" on the form. File the amended return at the same address you filed the original return. IRS consent is required to revoke the election.

For more information, see *Property distributed in kind* under *Income Distribution Deduction,* later.

⚠ **CAUTION** *Under the related persons rules, a loss cannot be claimed for property distributed to a beneficiary unless the distribution is in discharge of a pecuniary bequest. Also, any gain on the distribution of depreciable property is ordinary income.*

Exemption and Deductions

In figuring taxable income, an estate is generally allowed the same deductions as an individual. Special rules, however, apply to some deductions for an estate. This section includes discussions of those deductions affected by the special rules.

Exemption Deduction

An estate is allowed an exemption deduction of $600 in figuring its taxable income. No exemption for dependents is allowed to an estate. Even though the first return of an estate may be for a period of less than 12 months, the exemption is $600. If, however, the estate was given permission to change its accounting period, the exemption is $50 for each month of the short year.

Charitable Contributions

An estate qualifies for a deduction for gross income paid or permanently set aside for qualified charitable organizations. The adjusted gross income limits for individuals do not apply. However, to be deductible by an estate, the contribution must be specifically provided for in the decedent's will. If there is no will, or if the will makes no provision for the payment to a charitable organization, then a deduction will not be allowed even though all beneficiaries may agree to the gift.

You cannot deduct any contribution from income not included in the estate's gross income.

If the will specifically provides that the contributions are to be paid out of the estate's gross income, the contributions are fully deductible. However, if the will contains no specific provisions, the contributions are considered to have been paid and are deductible in the same proportion as the gross income bears to the total of all classes (taxable and nontaxable) of income.

You cannot deduct a qualified conservation easement granted after the date of death and before the due date of the estate tax return. A contribution deduction is allowed to the estate for estate tax purposes.

For more information about contributions, see Publication 526, Charitable Contributions, and Publication 561, Determining the Value of Donated Property.

Losses

Generally, an estate can claim a deduction for a loss it sustains on the sale of property. This includes a loss from the sale of property (other than stock) to a personal representative of the estate, unless that person is a beneficiary of the estate.

For a discussion of an estate's recognized loss on a distribution of property in kind to a beneficiary, see *Income To Include,* earlier.

⚠ **CAUTION** *An estate and a beneficiary of that estate are generally treated as related persons for purposes of the disallowance of a loss on the sale of an asset between related persons. The disallowance does not apply to a sale or exchange made to satisfy a pecuniary bequest.*

Net operating loss deduction. An estate can claim a net operating loss deduction, figured in the same way as an individual's, except that it cannot take the income distribution deduction (discussed later) or the deduction for charitable contributions in figuring the loss or the loss carryover. For a discussion of the carryover of an unused net operating loss to a beneficiary upon termination of the estate, see *Termination of Estate,* later.

For information on net operating losses, see Publication 536.

Casualty and theft losses. Losses incurred from casualties and thefts during the administration of the estate can be deducted only if they have not been claimed on the federal estate tax return (Form 706). The personal representative must file a statement with the estate's income tax return waiving the deduction for estate tax purposes. See *Administration Expenses,* later.

The same rules that apply to individuals apply to the estate, except that in figuring the adjusted gross income of the estate used to figure the deductible loss, you deduct any administration expenses claimed. Use Form 4684, Casualties and Thefts, and its instructions to figure any loss deduction.

Carryover losses. Carryover losses resulting from net operating losses or capital losses sustained by the decedent before death cannot be deducted on the estate's income tax return.

Administration Expenses

Expenses of administering an estate can be deducted either from the gross estate in figuring the federal estate tax on Form 706 or from the estate's gross income in figuring the estate's income tax on Form 1041. However, these expenses cannot be claimed for both estate tax and income tax purposes. In most cases, this rule also applies to expenses incurred in the sale of property by an estate (not as a dealer).

To prevent a double deduction, amounts otherwise allowable in figuring the decedent's taxable estate for federal estate tax on Form 706 will not be allowed as a deduction in figuring the income tax of the estate or of any other person unless the personal representative files a statement, in duplicate, that the items of expense, as listed in the statement, have not been claimed as deductions for federal estate tax purposes and that all rights to claim such deductions are waived. One deduction or part of a deduction can be claimed for income tax purposes if the appropriate statement is filed, while another deduction or part is claimed for estate tax purposes. Claiming a deduction in figuring the estate income tax is not prevented when the same deduction is claimed on the estate tax return so long as the estate tax deduction is not finally allowed and the preceding statement is filed. The statement can be filed with the income tax return or at any time before the expiration of the statute of limitations that applies to the tax year for which the deduction is sought. This waiver procedure also applies to casualty losses incurred during administration of the estate.

Accrued expenses. The rules preventing double deductions do not apply to deductions for taxes, interest, business expenses, and other items accrued at the date of death. These expenses are allowable as a deduction for estate tax purposes as claims against the estate and also are allowable as deductions in respect of a decedent for income tax purposes. Deductions for interest, business expenses, and other items not accrued at the date of the decedent's death are allowable only as a deduction for administration expenses for both estate and income tax purposes and do not qualify for a double deduction.

Expenses allocable to tax-exempt income. When figuring the estate's taxable income on Form 1041, you cannot deduct administration expenses allocable to any of the estate's tax-exempt income. However, you can deduct these administration expenses when figuring the taxable estate for federal estate tax purposes on Form 706.

Interest on estate tax. Interest paid on installment payments of estate tax is not deductible for income or estate tax purposes.

Depreciation and Depletion

The allowable deductions for depreciation and depletion that accrue after the decedent's death must be apportioned between the estate and the beneficiaries, depending on the income of the estate allocable to each.

 An estate cannot elect to treat the cost of certain depreciable business assets as an expense under section 179.

Example. In 2013, the decedent's estate realized $3,000 of business income during the administration of the estate. The personal representative distributed $1,000 of the income to the decedent's son, Ned, and $2,000 to another son, Bill. The allowable depreciation on the business property is $300. Ned can take a deduction of $100 [($1,000 ÷ $3,000) × $300], and Bill can take a deduction of $200 [($2,000 ÷ $3,000) × $300].

Income Distribution Deduction

An estate is allowed a deduction for the tax year for any income that must be distributed currently and for other amounts that are properly paid, credited, or required to be distributed to beneficiaries. This deduction is limited to the distributable net income of the estate.

For special rules about distributions that apply in figuring the estate's income distribution deduction, see *Bequest* under *Distributions to Beneficiaries,* later.

Distributable net income. Distributable net income (figured on Form 1041, Schedule B) is the estate's taxable income, excluding the income distribution deduction, with the following additional modifications.

Tax-exempt interest. Tax-exempt interest, including exempt-interest dividends, is included in the distributable net income but is reduced by the following items.

- Expenses not allowed in computing the estate's taxable income because they were attributable to tax-exempt interest (see *Expenses allocable to tax-exempt income* under *Administration Expenses,* earlier).
- The portion of tax-exempt interest deemed to have been used to make a charitable contribution. See *Charitable Contributions,* earlier.

The total tax-exempt interest earned by an estate must be shown in the "Other Information" section of Form 1041. The beneficiary's portion of the tax-exempt interest is shown on Schedule K-1 (Form 1041).

Exemption deduction. The exemption deduction is not allowed.

Capital gains. Capital gains are not automatically included in distributable net income. However, they can be included in distributable net income if any of the following apply.

- The gain is allocated to income in the accounts of the estate or by notice to the beneficiaries under the terms of the will or by local law.

- The gain is allocated to the corpus or principal of the estate and is actually distributed to the beneficiaries during the tax year.
- The gain is used, under either the terms of the will or the practice of the personal representative, to determine the amount that is distributed or must be distributed.
- Charitable contributions are made out of capital gains.

Generally, when you determine capital gains to be included in distributable net income, the exclusion for gain from the sale or exchange of qualified small business stock is not taken into account.

Capital losses. Capital losses are excluded in figuring distributable net income unless they enter into the computation of any capital gain that is distributed or must be distributed during the year.

Separate shares rule. The separate shares rule must be used if both of the following are true.

- The estate has more than one beneficiary.
- The economic interest of a beneficiary does not affect and is not affected by the economic interest of another beneficiary.

A bequest of a specific sum of money or of property is not a separate share (see *Bequest,* later).

If the separate shares rule applies, the separate shares are treated as separate estates for the sole purpose of determining the distributable net income allocable to a share. Each share's distributable net income is based on that share's portion of gross income and any applicable deductions or losses. The personal representative must use a reasonable and equitable method to make the allocations.

Generally, gross income is allocated among the separate shares based on the income each share is entitled to under the will or applicable local law. This includes gross income not received in cash, such as a distributive share of partnership tax items.

If a beneficiary is not entitled to any of the estate's income, the distributable net income for that beneficiary is zero. The estate cannot deduct any distribution made to that beneficiary and the beneficiary does not have to include the distribution in its gross income. However, see *Income in respect of a decedent,* later in this discussion.

Example. Patrick's will directs you, the executor, to distribute ABC Corporation stock and all dividends from that stock to his son, Edward, and the residue of the estate to his son, Michael. The estate has two separate shares consisting of the dividends on the stock left to Edward and the residue of the estate left to Michael. The distribution of the ABC Corporation stock qualifies as a bequest, so it is not a separate share.

If any distributions, other than the ABC Corporation stock, are made during the year to either Edward or Michael, you must determine the distributable net income for each separate share. The distributable net income for Edward's separate share includes only the dividends attributable to the ABC Corporation stock. The distributable net income for Michael's separate share includes all other income.

Income in respect of a decedent. This income is allocated among the separate shares that could potentially be funded with these amounts, even if the share is not entitled to receive any income under the will or applicable local law. This allocation is based on the relative value of each share that could potentially be funded with these amounts.

Example 1. Frank's will directs you, the executor, to divide the residue of his estate (valued at $900,000) equally between his two children, Judy and Ann. Under the will, you must fund Judy's share first with the proceeds of Frank's traditional IRA. The $90,000 balance in the IRA was distributed to the estate during the year. This amount is included in the estate's gross income as income in respect of a decedent and is allocated to the corpus of the estate. The estate has two separate shares, one for the benefit of Judy and one for the benefit of Ann. If any distributions are made to either Judy or Ann during the year, then, for purposes of determining the distributable net income for each separate share, the $90,000 of income in respect of a decedent must be allocated only to Judy's share.

Example 2. Assume the same facts as in Example 1, except that you must fund Judy's share first with DEF Corporation stock valued at $300,000, instead of the IRA proceeds. To determine the distributable net income for each separate share, the $90,000 of income in respect of a decedent must be allocated between the two shares to the extent they could potentially be funded with that income. The maximum amount of Judy's share that could be funded with that income is $150,000 ($450,000 value of share less $300,000 funded with stock). The maximum amount of Ann's share that could be funded is $450,000. Based on the relative values, Judy's distributable net income includes $22,500 ($150,000/$600,000 X $90,000) of the income in respect of a decedent and Ann's distributable net income includes $67,500 ($450,000/$600,000 X $90,000).

Income required to be distributed currently. The income distribution deduction includes any income that, under the terms of the decedent's will or by reason of local law, must be distributed currently. This includes an amount that may be paid out of income or corpus (such as an annuity) to the extent it is paid out of income for the tax year. The deduction is allowed to the estate even if the personal representative does not make the distribution until a later year or makes no distribution until the final settlement and termination of the estate.

Any other amount paid, credited, or required to be distributed. Any other amount paid, credited, or required to be distributed is included in the income distribution deduction of the estate only in the year actually paid, credited, or distributed. If there is no specific requirement by local law or by the terms of the will that income earned by the estate during administration be distributed currently, a deduction for dis-

tributions to the beneficiaries will be allowed to the estate, but only for the actual distributions during the tax year.

If the personal representative has discretion as to when the income is distributed, the deduction is allowed only in the year of distribution.

The personal representative can elect to treat distributions paid or credited within 65 days after the close of the estate's tax year as having been paid or credited on the last day of that tax year. The election is made by completing line 6 in the "Other Information" section of Form 1041. If a tax return is not required, the election is made on a statement filed with the IRS office where the return would have been filed. The election is irrevocable for the tax year and is only effective for the year of the election.

Interest in real estate. The value of an interest in real estate owned by a decedent, title to which passes directly to the beneficiaries under local law, is not included as any other amount paid, credited, or required to be distributed.

Property distributed in kind. If an estate distributes property in kind, the estate's deduction ordinarily is the lesser of its basis in the property or the property's fair market value when distributed. However, the deduction is the property's fair market value if the estate recognizes gain on the distribution. See *Gain or loss on distributions in kind* under *Income To Include*, earlier.

Property is distributed in kind if it satisfies the beneficiary's right to receive another property or amount, such as the income of the estate or a specific dollar amount. It generally includes any noncash distribution other than the following.

- A specific bequest (unless it must be distributed in more than three installments).
- Real property, the title to which passes directly to the beneficiary under local law.

Tax-exempt income not deductible. The estate cannot take an income distribution deduction for any item of distributable net income not included in the estate's gross income.

Example. An estate has distributable net income of $2,000, consisting of $1,000 of dividends and $1,000 of tax-exempt interest. Distributions to the beneficiary total $1,500. Except for this rule, the income distribution deduction would be $1,500 ($750 of dividends and $750 of tax-exempt interest). However, as the result of this rule, the income distribution deduction is limited to $750, because no deduction is allowed for the tax-exempt interest distributed.

Denial of double deduction. A deduction cannot be claimed twice. If an amount is considered to have been distributed to a beneficiary of an estate in a preceding tax year, it cannot again be included in figuring the deduction for the year of the actual distribution.

Example. The decedent's will provides that the estate must distribute currently all of its income to a beneficiary. For administrative convenience, the personal representative did not make a distribution of part of the income for the

tax year until the first month of the next tax year. The amount must be deducted by the estate in the first tax year, and must be included in the income of the beneficiary in that year. This amount cannot be deducted again by the estate in the following year when it is paid to the beneficiary, nor must the beneficiary again include the amount in income in that year.

Charitable contribution. Any amount allowed as a charitable deduction by the estate in figuring the estate's taxable income cannot be claimed again as a deduction for a distribution to a beneficiary.

Funeral and Medical Expenses

No deduction can be taken for funeral expenses or medical and dental expenses on the estate's Form 1041.

Funeral expenses. Funeral expenses paid by the estate are not deductible in figuring the estate's taxable income on Form 1041. They are deductible only for determining the taxable estate for federal estate tax purposes on Form 706.

Medical and dental expenses of a decedent. The medical and dental expenses of a decedent paid by the estate are not deductible in figuring the estate's taxable income on Form 1041. You can deduct them in figuring the taxable estate for federal estate tax purposes on Form 706. If these expenses are paid within the 1-year period beginning with the day after the decedent's death, you can elect to deduct them on the decedent's income tax return (Form 1040) for the year in which they were incurred. See *Medical Expenses* under *Final Income Tax Return for Decedent—Form 1040,* earlier.

Credits, Tax, and Payments

This section includes brief discussions of some of the tax credits, types of taxes that may be owed, and estimated tax payments reported on the estate's Form 1041.

Credits

Estates generally are allowed some of the same tax credits that are allowed to individuals. The credits generally are allocated between the estate and the beneficiaries. However, estates are not allowed the credit for the elderly or the disabled, the child tax credit, or the earned income credit discussed earlier under *Final Income Tax Return for Decedent—Form 1040.*

Foreign tax credit. The foreign tax credit is discussed in Publication 514, Foreign Tax Credit for Individuals.

General business credit. The general business credit is available to an estate involved in a business. For more information, see Publication 334.

Tax

You cannot use the Tax Table for individuals to figure the estate tax. You must use the tax rate schedule in the Instructions for Form 1041 to figure the estate tax.

Alternative minimum tax (AMT). An estate may be liable for the alternative minimum tax. To figure the alternative minimum tax, use Schedule I (Form 1041), Alternative Minimum Tax. Certain credits may be limited by any tentative minimum tax figured on Schedule I (Form 1041), Part III, line 54, even if there is no alternative minimum tax liability.

If the estate takes a deduction for distributions to beneficiaries, complete Parts I and II of Schedule I (Form 1041) even if the estate does not owe alternative minimum tax. Allocate the income distribution deduction figured on a minimum tax basis among the beneficiaries and report each beneficiary's share on Schedule K-1 (Form 1041). Also, show each beneficiary's share of any adjustments or tax preference items for depreciation, depletion, and amortization.

For more information, see the Instructions for Schedule I (Form 1041).

Payments

The estate's income tax liability must be paid in full when the return is filed. You may have to pay estimated tax, however, as explained below.

Estimated tax. Estates with tax years ending 2 or more years after the date of the decedent's death must pay estimated tax in the same manner as individuals.

If you must make estimated tax payments for 2014, use Form 1041-ES, Estimated Income Tax for Estates and Trusts, to determine the estimated tax to be paid.

Generally, you must pay estimated tax if the estate is expected to owe, after subtracting any withholding and credits, at least $1,000 in tax for 2014. You will not, however, have to pay estimated tax if you expect the withholding and credits to be at least:

1. 90% of the tax to be shown on the 2014 return, or

2. 100% of the tax shown on the 2013 return (assuming the return covered all 12 months).

The percentage in (2) above is 110% if the estate's 2013 adjusted gross income (AGI) was more than $150,000 (and less than ⅔ of gross income for 2013 or 2014 is from farming or fishing). To figure the estate's AGI, see the instructions for Form 1041, line 15c.

The general rule is that the first estimated tax payment must be made by the 15th day of the 4th month of the tax year (whether calendar or fiscal). The estimated tax may be paid in full at that time or paid in four equal installments on the 15th day of the 4th, 6th, and 9th months of the tax year, and the 1st month of the following tax year. If any of these dates fall on a Saturday, Sunday, or legal holiday, the payment must be made by the next business day. For

2014, calendar year taxpayers estimated tax payments are due on April 15, 2014; June 16, 2014; September 15, 2014; and January 15, 2015.

For exceptions to the general rule, see the instructions for Form 1041-ES and Publication 505, Tax Withholding and Estimated Tax.

A penalty may be charged for not paying enough estimated tax or for not making the payment on time in the required amount (even if there is an overpayment on the tax return). Use Form 2210, Underpayment of Estimated Tax by Individuals, Estates, and Trusts, to figure any penalty, or let the IRS figure the penalty.

For more information, see the instructions for Form 1041-ES and Publication 505. Also, see *Transfer of Credit for Estimated Tax Payments,* later, for information regarding the transfer of the estate's estimated tax payments to the beneficiary(ies).

Name, Address, and Signature

In the top space of the name and address area of Form 1041, enter the exact name of the estate used to apply for the estate's employer identification number. In the remaining spaces, enter the name and address of the personal representative of the estate.

Signature. The personal representative (or its authorized officer if the personal representative is not an individual) must sign the return. An individual who prepares the return for pay must sign the return as preparer. You can check a box in the signature area that authorizes the IRS to contact that paid preparer for certain information. See the instructions for Form 1041 for more information.

When and Where To File

When Form 1041 (or Form 1040NR if it applies) is filed depends on whether the personal representative chooses a calendar year or a fiscal year as the estate's accounting period. Where Form 1041 is filed depends on where the personal representative lives or has their principal business office.

When to file. If the calendar year is the estate's accounting period, the 2013 Form 1041 is due by April 15, 2014 (June 16, 2014, in the case of Form 1040NR for a nonresident alien estate that does not have an office in the United States). If the personal representative chooses a fiscal year, Form 1041 is due by the 15th day of the 4th month (6th month for aForm 1040NR) after the end of the tax year. If the due date is a Saturday, Sunday, or legal holiday, the form must be filed by the next business day.

Extension of time to file. An automatic 5-month extension of time to file Form 1041 can be requested by filing Form 7004, Application for Automatic Extension of Time To File Certain Business Income Tax, Information, and Other Returns. The extension is automatic, so no signature or reason for the request is required. File Form 7004 on or before the regular due date of Form 1041. Form 7004 can be electronically

filed. For additional information, see the Instructions for Form 7004.

An extension of time to file a return does not extend the time for payment of tax due. The total income tax estimated to be due on Form 1041 must be paid in full by the regular due date of the return. For additional information, see the Instructions for Form 7004.

Where to file. The personal representative of an estate files the estate's income tax return (Form 1041) with the Internal Revenue Service Center assigned to the state where the personal representative lives or has its principal place of business. A list of the states and assigned Service Centers is in the instructions for Form 1041.

Form 1040NR must be filed at the following address:

> Department of the Treasury
> Internal Revenue Service Center
> Cincinnati, OH 45999-0048, U.S.A.

If enclosing a payment, mail Form 1040NR to:

> Internal Revenue Service
> P.O. Box 1303
> Charlotte, NC 28201-1303 USA

Electronic filing. Form 1041 can be filed electronically. See the instructions for more information.

Distributions to Beneficiaries

If you are the beneficiary of an estate that is required to distribute all its income currently, you must report your share of the distributable net income, whether or not you have actually received the distribution.

If you are a beneficiary of an estate that is not required to distribute all its income currently, you must report all income that is required to be distributed to you currently (whether or not actually distributed), plus all other amounts paid, credited, or required to be distributed to you, up to your share of distributable net income. As explained earlier in *Income Distribution Deduction,* for an amount to be income required to be distributed currently, there must be a specific requirement for current distribution either under local law or the terms of the decedent's will. If there is no such requirement, the income is reportable only when distributed.

If the estate has more than one beneficiary, the separate shares rule discussed earlier under *Income Distribution Deduction* may have to be used to determine the distributable net income allocable to each beneficiary. The beneficiaries in the examples shown next do not meet the requirements of the separate shares rule.

Income That Must Be Distributed Currently

Beneficiaries entitled to receive currently distributable income generally must include in gross income the entire amount due them. However, if the income required to be distributed currently is more than the estate's distributable net income figured without deducting charitable contributions, each beneficiary must include in gross income a ratable part of the distributable net income.

Example. Under the terms of the will of Gerald Peters, $5,000 a year is to be paid to his widow and $2,500 a year is to be paid to his daughter out of the estate's income during the period of administration. There are no charitable contributions. For the year, the estate's distributable net income is only $6,000. The distributable net income is less than the currently distributable income, so the widow must include in her gross income only $4,000 [($5,000 ÷ $7,500) × $6,000], and the daughter must include in her gross income only $2,000 [($2,500 ÷ $7,500) × $6,000].

Annuity payable out of income or corpus. Income that is required to be distributed currently includes any amount that must be paid out of income or corpus (principal of the estate) to the extent the amount is satisfied out of income for the tax year. An annuity that must be paid in all events (either out of income or corpus) would qualify as income that is required to be distributed currently to the extent there is income of the estate not paid, credited, or required to be distributed to other beneficiaries for the tax year.

Example 1. Henry Frank's will provides that $500 be paid to the local Community Chest out of income each year. It also provides that $2,000 a year is currently distributable out of income to his brother, Fred, and an annuity of $3,000 is to be paid to his sister, Sharon, out of income or corpus. Capital gains are allocable to corpus, but all expenses are to be charged against income. Last year, the estate had income of $6,000 and expenses of $3,000. The personal representative paid $500 to the Community Chest and made the distributions to Fred and Sharon as required by the will.

The estate's distributable net income (figured before the charitable contribution) is $3,000. The currently distributable income totals $2,500 ($2,000 to Fred and $500 to Sharon). The income available for Sharon's annuity is only $500 because the will requires that the charitable contribution be paid out of current income. The $2,500 treated as distributed currently is less than the $3,000 distributable net income (before the contribution), so Fred must include $2,000 in his gross income and Sharon must include $500 in her gross income.

Example 2. Assume the same facts as in *Example 1* except the estate has an additional $1,000 of administration expenses, commissions, etc., chargeable to corpus. The estate's distributable net income (figured before the charitable contribution) is now $2,000 ($3,000 – $1,000 additional expense). The amount treated as currently distributable income is still $2,500 ($2,000 to Fred and $500 to Sharon). The $2,500 treated as distributed currently is more than the $2,000 distributable net income, so Fred has to include only $1,600 [($2,000 ÷ $2,500) × $2,000] in his gross income and

Sharon has to include only $400 [($500 ÷ $2,500) × $2,000] in her gross income. Fred and Sharon are beneficiaries of amounts that must be distributed currently, so they do not benefit from the reduction of distributable net income by the charitable contribution deduction.

Other Amounts Distributed

Any other amount paid, credited, or required to be distributed to the beneficiary for the tax year also must be included in the beneficiary's gross income. Such an amount is in addition to those amounts that are required to be distributed currently, as discussed earlier. It does not include gifts or bequests of specific sums of money or specific property if such sums are paid in three or fewer installments. However, amounts that can be paid only out of income are not excluded under this rule. If the sum of the income that must be distributed currently and other amounts paid, credited, or required to be distributed exceeds distributable net income, these other amounts are included in the beneficiary's gross income only to the extent distributable net income exceeds the income that must be distributed currently. If there is more than one beneficiary, each will include in gross income only a *pro rata* share of such amounts.

The personal representative can elect to treat distributions paid or credited by the estate within 65 days after the close of the estate's tax year as having been paid or credited on the last day of that tax year.

The following are examples of other amounts distributed.

- Distributions made at the discretion of the personal representative.
- Distributions required by the terms of the will when a specific event occurs.
- Annuities that must be paid in any event, but only out of corpus (principal).
- Distributions of property in kind as defined earlier in *Income Distribution Deduction* under *Income Tax Return of an Estate—Form 1041*.
- Distributions required for the support of the decedent's surviving spouse or other dependent for a limited period, but only out of corpus (principal).

If an estate distributes property in kind, the amount of the distribution ordinarily is the lesser of the estate's basis in the property or the property's fair market value when distributed. However, the amount of the distribution is the property's fair market value if the estate recognizes gain on the distribution. See *Gain or loss on distributions in kind* in the discussion *Income To Include*, earlier.

Example. The terms of Michael Scott's will require the distribution of $2,500 of income annually to his wife, Susan. If any income remains, it may be accumulated or distributed to his two children, Joe and Alice, in amounts at the discretion of the personal representative. The personal representative also may invade the corpus (principal) for the benefit of Michael's wife and children.

Last year, the estate had income of $6,000 after deduction of all expenses. Its distributable

net income is also $6,000. The personal representative distributed the required $2,500 of income to Susan. In addition, the personal representative distributed $1,500 each to Joe and Alice and an additional $2,000 to Susan.

Susan includes in her gross income the $2,500 of currently distributable income. The other amounts distributed totaled $5,000 ($1,500 + $1,500 + $2,000) and are includible in the income of Susan, Joe, and Alice to the extent of $3,500 (distributable net income of $6,000 minus currently distributable income to Susan of $2,500). Susan will include an additional $1,400 [($2,000 ÷ $5,000) × $3,500] in her gross income. Joe and Alice each will include $1,050 [($1,500 ÷ $5,000) × $3,500] in their gross incomes.

Discharge of a Legal Obligation

If an estate, under the terms of a will, discharges a legal obligation of a beneficiary, the discharge is included in that beneficiary's income as either currently distributable income or other amount paid. This does not apply to the discharge of a beneficiary's obligation to pay alimony or separate maintenance.

The beneficiary's legal obligations include a legal obligation of support, for example, of a minor child. Local law determines a legal obligation of support.

Character of Distributions

An amount distributed to a beneficiary for inclusion in gross income retains the same character for the beneficiary that it had for the estate.

No charitable contribution made. If no charitable contribution is made during the tax year, treat the distributions as consisting of the same proportion of each class of items entering into the computation of distributable net income as the total of each class bears to the total distributable net income. Distributable net income was defined earlier in *Income Distribution Deduction* under *Income Tax Return of an Estate—Form 1041*. However, if the will or local law specifically provides or requires a different allocation, use that allocation.

Example 1. An estate has distributable net income of $3,000, consisting of $1,800 in rents and $1,200 in taxable interest. There is no provision in the will or local law for the allocation of income. The personal representative distributes $1,500 each to Jim and Ted, beneficiaries under their father's will. Each will be treated as having received $900 in rents and $600 of taxable interest.

Example 2. Assume in *Example 1* that the will provides for the payment of the taxable interest to Jim and the rental income to Ted and that the personal representative distributed the income under those provisions. Jim is treated as having received $1,200 in taxable interest and Ted is treated as having received $1,800 of rental income.

Charitable contribution made. If a charitable contribution is made by an estate and the terms of the will or local law provide for the contribution to be paid from specified sources, that provision governs. If no provision or requirement exists, the charitable contribution deduction must be allocated among the classes of income entering into the computation of the income of the estate before allocation of other deductions among the items of distributable net income. In allocating items of income and deductions to beneficiaries to whom income must be distributed currently, the charitable contribution deduction is not taken into account to the extent that it exceeds income for the year reduced by currently distributable income.

Example. The will of Harry Thomas requires a current distribution from income of $3,000 a year to his wife, Betty, during the administration of the estate. The will also provides that the personal representative, using discretion, may distribute the balance of the current earnings either to Harry's son, Tim, or to one or more designated charities. Last year, the estate's income consisted of $4,000 of taxable interest and $1,000 of tax-exempt interest. There were no deductible expenses. The personal representative distributed the $3,000 to Betty, made a contribution of $2,500 to the local heart association, and paid $1,500 to Tim.

The distributable net income for determining the character of the distribution to Betty is $3,000. The charitable contribution deduction to be taken into account for this computation is $2,000 (the estate's income ($5,000) minus the currently distributable income ($3,000)). The $2,000 charitable contribution deduction must be allocated: $1,600 [($4,000 ÷ $5,000) × $2,000] to taxable interest and $400 [($1,000 ÷ $5,000) × $2,000] to tax-exempt interest. Betty is considered to have received $2,400 ($4,000 − $1,600) of taxable interest and $600 ($1,000 − $400) of tax-exempt interest. She must include the $2,400 in her gross income. She must report the $600 of tax-exempt interest, but it is not taxable.

To determine the amount to be included in Tim's gross income, however, take into account the entire charitable contribution deduction. The currently distributable income is greater than the estate's income after taking into account the charitable contribution deduction, so none of the amount paid to Tim must be included in his gross income for the year.

How and When To Report

How income from the estate is reported depends on the character of the income in the hands of the estate. When the income is reported depends on whether it represents amounts credited or required to be distributed to beneficiaries or other amounts.

How to report estate income. Each item of income keeps the same character in the hands of a beneficiary as it had in the hands of the estate. If the items of income distributed or considered to be distributed include dividends, tax-exempt interest, or capital gains, they will keep the same character in the beneficiary's hands for purposes of the tax treatment given

those items. Generally, a beneficiary reports dividends on Form 1040, line 9a, and capital gains on Schedule D (Form 1040). The tax-exempt interest, while not included in taxable income, must be shown on Form 1040, line 8b. Report business and other nonpassive income in Part III of Schedule E (Form 1040).

The estate's personal representative must provide the beneficiary with the classification of the various items that make up his or her share of the estate income and the credits he or she takes into consideration to properly prepare his or her individual income tax return. See *Schedule K-1 (Form 1041),* later.

When to report estate income. If income from the estate is credited or must be distributed to a beneficiary for a tax year, he or she reports that income (even if not distributed) on his or her return for that year. The personal representative can elect to treat distributions paid or credited within 65 days after the close of the estate's tax year as having been paid or credited on the last day of that tax year. If this election is made, the beneficiary must report that distribution on his or her return for that year.

Other income from the estate is reported on his or her return for the year in which it was received. If the beneficiary's tax year is different from the estate's tax year, see *Different tax years,* next.

Different tax years. Each beneficiary must include his or her share of the estate income in his or her return for the tax year in which the last day of the estate's tax year falls. If the tax year of the estate is a fiscal year ending on June 30, 2013, and the beneficiary's tax year is the calendar year, the beneficiary will include in gross income for the tax year ending December 31, 2013, his or her share of the estate's distributable net income distributed or required to be distributed during the fiscal year ending the previous June 30.

Death of individual beneficiary. If an individual beneficiary dies, the beneficiary's share of the estate's distributable net income may be distributed or be considered distributed by the estate for its tax year that does not end with or within the last tax year of the beneficiary. In this case, the estate income that must be included in the gross income on the beneficiary's final return is based on the amounts distributed or considered distributed during the tax year of the estate in which his or her last tax year ended. However, for a cash basis beneficiary, the gross income of the last tax year includes only the amounts actually distributed before death. Income that must be distributed to the beneficiary but, in fact, is distributed to the beneficiary's estate after death is included in the gross income of the beneficiary's estate as income in respect of a decedent.

Termination of nonindividual beneficiary. If a beneficiary that is not an individual, for example a trust or a corporation, ceases to exist, the amount included in its gross income for its last tax year is determined as if the beneficiary were a deceased individual. However, income that must be distributed before termination, but which is actually distributed to the beneficiary's successor in interest, is included

in the gross income of the nonindividual beneficiary for its last tax year.

Schedule K-1 (Form 1041). The personal representative of the estate must provide the beneficiary with a copy of Schedule K-1 (Form 1041) or a substitute Schedule K-1. The beneficiary should not file Schedule K-1 (Form 1041) with his or her Form 1040, but should keep it for their personal records.

Each beneficiary (or nominee of a beneficiary) who receives a distribution from the estate for the tax year or to whom any item is allocated must receive a Schedule K-1 or substitute. The personal representative must furnish the form to each beneficiary or nominee by the date on which the Form 1041 is filed.

Nominees. A person who holds an interest in an estate as a nominee for a beneficiary must provide the estate with the name and address of the beneficiary, and any other required information. The nominee must provide the beneficiary with the information received from the estate.

Penalty. A personal representative (or nominee) who fails to provide the correct information may be subject to a $50 penalty for each failure.

Consistent treatment of items. Beneficiaries must treat estate items the same way on their individual returns as those items are treated on the estate's income tax return. If their treatment is different from the estate's treatment, the beneficiary must file Form 8082, Notice of Inconsistent Treatment or Administrative Adjustment Request (AAR), with his or her return to identify the difference. If he or she does not file Form 8082 and the estate has filed a return, the IRS can immediately assess and collect any tax and penalties that result from adjusting the item to make it consistent with the estate's treatment.

Bequest

A bequest is the act of giving or leaving property to another through the last will and testament. Generally, any distribution of income (or property in kind) to a beneficiary is an allowable deduction to the estate and is includible in the beneficiary's gross income to the extent of the estate's distributable net income. However, a distribution will not be an allowable deduction to the estate and will not be includible in the beneficiary's gross income if the distribution meets all the following requirements.

- It is required by the terms of the will.
- It is a gift or bequest of a specific sum of money or property.
- It is paid out in three or fewer installments under the terms of the will.

Specific sum of money or property. To meet this test, the amount of money or the identity of the specific property must be determinable under the decedent's will as of the date of death. To qualify as specific property, the property must be identifiable both as to its kind and its amount.

Example 1. Dave Rogers' will provided that his son, Ed, receive Dave's interest in the Rogers-Jones partnership. Dave's daughter, Marie, would receive a sum of money equal to the value of the partnership interest given to Ed. The bequest to Ed is a gift of a specific property ascertainable at the date of Dave Rogers' death. The bequest of a specific sum of money to Marie is determinable on the same date.

Example 2. Mike Jenkins' will provided that his widow, Helen, would receive money or property to be selected by the personal representative equal in value to half of his adjusted gross estate. The identity of the property and the money in the bequest are dependent on the personal representative's discretion and the payment of administration expenses and other charges, which are not determinable at the date of Mike's death. As a result, the provision is not a bequest of a specific sum of money or of specific property, and any distribution under that provision is a deduction for the estate and income to the beneficiary (to the extent of the estate's distributable net income). The fact that the bequest will be specific sometime before distribution is immaterial. It is not ascertainable by the terms of the will as of the date of death.

Distributions not treated as bequests. The following distributions are not bequests that meet all the requirements listed earlier that allow a distribution to be excluded from the beneficiary's income and do not allow it as a deduction to the estate.

Paid only from income. An amount that can be paid only from current or prior income of the estate does not qualify even if it is specific in amount and there is no provision for installment payments.

Annuity. An annuity or a payment of money or of specific property in lieu of, or having the effect of, an annuity is not the payment of specific property or a sum of money.

Residuary estate. If the will provides for the payment of the balance or residue of the estate to a beneficiary after all expenses and other specific legacies or bequests, that residuary bequest is not a payment of specific property or a sum of money.

Gifts made in installments. Even if the gift or bequest is made in a lump sum or in three or fewer installments, it will not qualify as specific property or a sum of money if the will provides that the amount must be paid in more than three installments.

Conditional bequests. A bequest of specific property or a sum of money that may otherwise be excluded from the beneficiary's gross income will not lose the exclusion solely because the payment is subject to a condition.

Installment payments. Certain rules apply in determining whether a bequest of specific property or a sum of money has to be paid or credited to a beneficiary in more than three installments.

Personal items. Do not take into account bequests of articles for personal use, such as personal and household effects and automobiles.

Real property. Do not take into account specifically designated real property, the title to which passes under local law directly to the beneficiary.

Other property. All other bequests under the decedent's will for which no time of payment or crediting is specified and that are to be paid or credited in the ordinary course of administration of the estate are considered as required to be paid or credited in a single installment. Also, all bequests payable at any one specified time under the terms of the will are treated as a single installment.

Testamentary trust. In determining the number of installments that must be paid or credited to a beneficiary, the decedent's estate and a testamentary trust created by the decedent's will are treated as separate entities. Amounts paid or credited by the estate and by the trust are counted separately.

Termination of Estate

The termination of an estate generally is marked by the end of the period of administration and by the distribution of the assets to the beneficiaries under the terms of the will or under the laws of succession of the state if there is no will. These beneficiaries may or may not be the same persons as the beneficiaries of the estate's income.

Period of Administration

The period of administration is the time actually required by the personal representative to assemble all the decedent's assets, pay all the expenses and obligations, and distribute the assets to the beneficiaries. This may be longer or shorter than the time provided by local law for the administration of estates.

Ends if all assets distributed. If all assets are distributed except a reasonable amount set aside, in good faith, for the payment of unascertained or contingent liabilities and expenses (but not including a claim by a beneficiary, as a beneficiary), the estate will be considered terminated.

Ends if period unreasonably long. If settlement is prolonged unreasonably, the estate will be treated as terminated for federal income tax purposes. From that point on, the income, deductions, and credits of the estate are considered those of the person or persons succeeding to the property of the estate.

Transfer of Unused Deductions to Beneficiaries

If the estate has unused loss carryovers or excess deductions for its last tax year, they are allowed to those beneficiaries who succeed to the estate's property. See *Successor beneficiary,* later.

Unused loss carryovers. An unused net operating loss carryover or capital loss carryover existing upon termination of the estate is allowed to the beneficiaries succeeding to the property of the estate. That is, these deductions will be claimed on the beneficiary's tax return. This treatment occurs only if a carryover would have been allowed to the estate in a later tax year if the estate had not been terminated.

Both types of carryovers generally keep their same character for the beneficiary as they had for the estate. However, if the beneficiary of a capital loss carryover is a corporation, the corporation will treat the carryover as a short-term capital loss regardless of its status in the estate. The net operating loss carryover and the capital loss carryover are used in figuring the beneficiary's adjusted gross income and taxable income. The beneficiary may have to adjust any net operating loss carryover in figuring the alternative minimum tax.

The first tax year to which the loss is carried is the beneficiary's tax year in which the estate terminates. If the loss can be carried to more than one tax year, the estate's last tax year (whether or not a short tax year) and the beneficiary's first tax year to which the loss is carried each constitute a tax year for figuring the number of years to which a loss may be carried. A capital loss carryover from an estate to a corporate beneficiary will be treated as though it resulted from a loss incurred in the estate's last tax year (whether or not a short tax year), regardless of when the estate actually incurred the loss.

If the last tax year of the estate is the last tax year to which a net operating loss may be carried, see *No double deductions,* later. For a general discussion of net operating losses, see Publication 536. For a discussion of capital losses and capital loss carryovers, see Publication 550.

Excess deductions. If the deductions in the estate's last tax year (other than the exemption deduction or the charitable contributions deduction) are more than gross income for that year, the beneficiaries succeeding to the estate's property can claim the excess as a deduction in figuring taxable income. To establish these deductions for the beneficiaries, a return must be filed for the estate along with a schedule showing the computation of each kind of deduction and the allocation of each to the beneficiaries.

An individual beneficiary must itemize deductions to claim these excess deductions. The deduction is claimed on Schedule A (Form 1040), subject to the 2% limit on miscellaneous itemized deductions. The beneficiaries can claim the deduction only for the tax year in which or with which the estate terminates, whether the year of termination is a normal year or a short tax year.

No double deductions. A net operating loss deduction allowable to a successor beneficiary cannot be considered in figuring the excess deductions on termination. However, if the estate's last tax year is the last year in which a deduction for a net operating loss can be taken, the deduction, to the extent not absorbed in the last return of the estate, is treated as an excess deduction on termination. Any item of income or deduction, or any part thereof, taken into account in figuring a net operating loss or a capital loss carryover of the estate for its last tax year cannot be used again to figure the excess deduction on termination.

Successor beneficiary. A beneficiary entitled to an unused loss carryover or an excess deduction is the beneficiary who, upon the estate's termination, bears the burden of any loss for which a carryover is allowed or of any deductions more than gross income.

If decedent had no will. If the decedent had no will, the beneficiaries are those heirs or next of kin to whom the estate is distributed. If the estate is insolvent, the beneficiaries are those to whom the estate would have been distributed had it not been insolvent. If the decedent's spouse is entitled to a specified dollar amount of property before any distributions to other heirs and the estate is less than that amount, the spouse is the beneficiary to the extent of the deficiency.

If decedent had a will. If the decedent had a will, a beneficiary normally means the residuary beneficiaries (including residuary trusts). Those beneficiaries who receive specific property or a specific amount of money ordinarily are not considered residuary beneficiaries, except to the extent the specific amount is not paid in full.

Also, a beneficiary who is not strictly a residuary beneficiary, but whose devise or bequest is determined by the value of the estate as reduced by the loss or deduction, is entitled to the carryover or the deduction. This includes the following beneficiaries:

- A beneficiary of a fraction of the decedent's net estate after payment of debts, expenses, and specific bequests.
- A nonresiduary beneficiary, when the estate is unable to satisfy the bequest in full.
- A surviving spouse receiving a fractional share of the estate in fee under a statutory right of election when the losses or deductions are taken into account in determining the share. However, such a beneficiary does not include a recipient of a dower or curtesy, or a beneficiary who receives any income from the estate from which the loss or excess deduction is carried over.

Allocation among beneficiaries. The total of the unused loss carryovers or the excess deductions on termination that may be deducted by the successor beneficiaries is to be divided according to the share of each in the burden of the loss or deduction.

Example. Under his father's will, Arthur is to receive $20,000. The remainder of the estate is to be divided equally between his brothers, Mark and Tom. After all expenses are paid, the estate has sufficient funds to pay Arthur only $15,000, with nothing to Mark and Tom. In the estate's last tax year, there are excess deductions of $5,000 and $10,000 of unused loss carryovers. The total of the excess deductions and unused loss carryovers is $15,000 and Arthur is considered a successor beneficiary to the extent of $5,000, so he is entitled to one-third of the unused loss carryover and one-third of the excess deductions. His brothers may divide the other two-thirds of the excess deductions and the unused loss carryovers between them.

Transfer of Credit for Estimated Tax Payments

When an estate terminates, the personal representative can elect to transfer to the beneficiaries the credit for all or part of the estate's estimated tax payments for the last tax year. To make this election, the personal representative must complete Form 1041-T, Allocation of Estimated Tax Payments to Beneficiaries, and file it either separately or with the estate's final Form 1041. The Form 1041-T must be filed by the 65th day after the close of the estate's tax year.

 Filing Form 1041-T with Form 1041 does not change the due date for filing Form 1041-T. The IRS will reject a late filed election. If Form 1041-T is rejected and Form 1041 was filed based on a successful election, then the personal representative must file an amended Form 1041, including amended Schedule K-1(s).

The estimated tax allocated to each beneficiary is treated as paid or credited to the beneficiary on the last day of the estate's final tax year and must be reported in box 13, Schedule K-1 (Form 1041) using code A. If the estate terminated in 2013, this amount is treated as a payment of 2013 estimated tax made by the beneficiary on January 15, 2014.

Estate and Gift Taxes

 This publication does not contain all the rules and exceptions for federal estate, gift or GST taxes. Nor does it contain all the rules that apply to nonresident aliens. If you need more information, see Form 709, United States Gift (and Generation-Skipping Transfer) Tax Return; Form 706, United States Estate (and Generation-Skipping Transfer) Tax Return; Form 706-NA, United States Estate (and Generation-Skipping Transfer) Tax Return, Estate of nonresident not a citizen of the United States, and the related instructions. This publication also does not contain any information about state or local taxes. That information should be available from your state or local taxing authority.

If you give someone money or property during your life, you may be subject to federal gift tax. The money and property you own when you die (your estate) may be subject to federal estate tax. This is in addition to any federal income tax that you may owe on the gross income of your estate. The discussion below is to give you a general understanding of when these taxes apply and when they do not. It explains how much money or property you can give away during your lifetime or leave to your heirs at your death before any tax will be owed.

Most gifts are not subject to the gift tax and most estates are not subject to the estate tax. For example, there is usually no tax if you make a gift to your spouse or to a charity or if your estate goes to your spouse or to a charity at your death. If you make a gift to someone else, the gift tax usually does not apply until the value of the gifts you give that person exceeds the annual exclusion for the year. See *Annual*

exclusion under *Gift Tax*, below. Even if tax applies to your gifts or your estate, it may be eliminated by the *Applicable Credit Amount*, discussed later.

Person receiving your gift or bequest. Generally, the person who receives your gift or bequest of property from your estate will not have to pay any federal gift tax or estate tax. Also, that person will not have to pay income tax on the value of the gift or inheritance received.

Note. Gifts or bequests received from expatriates after June 16, 2008, may be subject to tax which must be paid by the recipient. Consult a qualified tax professional for more information.

No income tax deduction. Making a gift or leaving your estate to your heirs does not ordinarily affect your federal income tax. You cannot deduct the value of gifts you make (other than gifts that are deductible as charitable contributions) or any federal gift tax resulting from making those gifts. You also cannot deduct the value of any bequests made or estate tax resulting from making bequests.

Filing requirements. For estate tax purposes, the personal representative may be required to file Form 706. If death occurred in 2013, Form 706 must be filed if the gross estate of the decedent is valued at more than $5,250,000 or if the estate elects to transfer any deceased spousal unused exemption (DSUE) to a surviving spouse (this is also known as the portability election), regardless of the size of the gross estate.

If Form 706 is required, the return and payment of any tax is due within 9 months after the date of the decedent's death. To apply for an extension of time to file the return and/or pay the tax due, use Form 4768, Application for Extension of Time To File a Return and/or Pay U.S. Estate (and Generation-Skipping Transfer) Taxes.

Note. For the estate of decedents, who died after December 31, 2010 and on or before December 31, 2013, that were not required to file a Form 706 and did not timely file a Form 706 to make the portability election, see Rev. Proc. 2014-18, 2014-7 I.R.B. to see if the estate qualifies to be granted an extension to make the portability election on or before December 31, 2014.

The federal gift tax return, Form 709, United States Gift (and Generation-Skipping Transfer) Tax Return, is filed for every year in which a gift is made. However, you generally do not need to file a gift tax return unless you give someone, other than your spouse, money or property worth more than the annual exclusion for that year, or a gift not subject to the annual exclusion. The annual gift exclusion is $14,000 for 2013. See *Annual exclusion*, later, for more information.

Generally, you must file Form 709 by April 15, of the year after the gift was made. An extension of time to file the return is available by filing Form 8892, Application for Automatic Extension of Time To File Form 709 and/or Payment of Gift/Generation-Skipping Transfer Tax.

Note. Any extension of time granted for filing an individual tax return will also automatically extend the time to file your gift tax return. An income tax return extension is made on Form 4868, Application for Automatic Extension of Time To File U.S. Individual Income Tax Return.

Basic exclusion amount. The basic exclusion amount for gifts made during your lifetime and estates of decedents is $5,000,000. This amount is indexed for inflation. The basic exclusion amount for decedents who died in 2013 is $5,250,000.

Beginning in 2011, a predeceased spouse's unused exclusion, the Deceased Spousal Unused Exclusion (DSUE) amount, may be added to the basic exclusion amount to determine the applicable exclusion amount. The DSUE amount is only available if an election is made on the Form 706 filed by the predeceased spouse's estate.

The total of the basic exclusion amount and any DSUE amount received from the estate of a predeceased spouse is the applicable exclusion amount. This amount may be applied against tax due on lifetime gifts and/or transfers at death.

Note. Section 303 of the Tax Relief, Unemployment Insurance Reauthorization, and Job Creation Act of 2010, which increased the basic exclusion amount and authorized portability of the DSUE amount, was scheduled to expire on December 31, 2012. The provision was made permanent by section 101(a)(2) of the American Taxpayer Relief Act (ATRA), P.L. 112-240, effective January 1, 2013.

Applicable Credit Amount

A credit is an amount that reduces or eliminates tax. The applicable credit applies to both the gift tax and the estate tax and it equals the tax on the applicable exclusion amount. You must subtract the applicable credit from any gift or estate tax that you owe. Any applicable credit you use against gift tax in one year reduces the amount of credit that you can use against gift or estate taxes in a later year.

In 2013, the credit on the basic exclusion amount is $2,045,800 (exempting $5,250,000 from tax). The total amount of applicable credit available to a person will equal the tax on the basic exclusion amount plus the tax on any deceased spousal unused exclusion (DSUE) amount.

For examples of how the credit works, see *Applying the applicable credit to gift tax* and *Applying the applicable credit to estate tax*, later.

Gift Tax

The gift tax applies to lifetime transfers of property from one person (the donor) to another person (the donee). You make a gift if you give tangible or intangible property (including money), the use of property, or the right to receive income from property without expecting to receive something of at least equal value in return. If you sell something for less than its full

value or if you make an interest-free or reduced-interest loan, you may be making a gift.

The general rule is that any gift is a taxable gift. However, there are many exceptions to this rule.

Generally, the following gifts are not taxable gifts:
- Gifts, excluding gifts of future interests, that are not more than the annual exclusion for the calendar year,
- Tuition or medical expenses paid directly to an educational or medical institution for someone else,
- Gifts to your spouse,
- Gifts to a political organization for its use, and
- Gifts to charities.

Annual exclusion. A separate annual exclusion applies to each person to whom you make a gift. The gift tax annual exclusion is subject to cost-of-living increases.

Gift Tax Annual Exclusion

Year(s)	Annual Exclusion
1998 — 2001	$10,000
2002 — 2005	$11,000
2006 — 2008	$12,000
2009 — 2012	$13,000
2013	$14,000

In 2013, you generally could have given gifts valued up to $14,000 per person to any number of people, and none of the gifts will be taxable. However, gifts of future interests cannot be excluded under the annual exclusion. A gift of a future interest is a gift that is limited so that its use, possession, or enjoyment will begin at some point in the future. If you are married, both you and your spouse could have separately given gifts valued up to $14,000 to the same person without making a taxable gift. If one of you gave more than the $14,000 exclusion, see *Gift splitting*, later.

Example 1. You gave your niece a cash gift of $8,000. It is your only gift to her in 2013. The gift is not a taxable gift because it is not more than the $14,000 annual exclusion.

Example 2. You paid the $15,000 college tuition of your friend directly to his college. Because the payment qualifies for the educational exclusion, the gift is not a taxable gift.

Example 3. You gave $25,000 to your 25 year-old daughter. The first $14,000 of your gift is not subject to the gift tax because of the annual exclusion. The remaining $11,000 is a taxable gift. As explained later under *Applying the applicable credit to gift tax*, you may not have to pay the gift tax on the remaining $11,000. However, you do have to file a gift tax return.

More information. See Form 709 and its instructions for more information about taxable gifts.

Gift splitting If you or your spouse made a gift to a third party, the gift can be considered as made one-half by you and one-half by your

spouse. This is known as gift splitting. Both of you must agree to split the gift. If you do, you each can take the annual exclusion for your part of the gift. For gifts made in 2013, gift splitting allows married couples to give up to $28,000 to a person without making a taxable gift. If you split a gift you made, both of you must file a gift tax return to show that you and your spouse agree to use gift splitting. Form 709 must be filed even if half of the split gift is less than the annual exclusion.

Example. Harold and his wife, Helen, agreed to split the gifts that they made during 2013. Harold gave his nephew, George, $21,000, and Helen gave her niece, Gina, $18,000. Although each gift is more than the annual exclusion ($14,000), by gift splitting they made these gifts without making a taxable gift. Harold's gift to George is treated as one-half ($10,500) from Harold and one-half ($10,500) from Helen. Helen's gift to Gina is also treated as one-half ($9,000) from Helen and one-half ($9,000) from Harold. In each case, because one-half of the split gift is not more than the annual exclusion, it is not a taxable gift. However, each of them must file a gift tax return.

Applying the applicable credit to gift tax. After you determine which of your gifts are taxable, figure the amount of gift tax on the total taxable gifts and apply your applicable credit for the year.

Example. In 2013, you gave your niece, Mary, a cash gift of $8,000. It is your only gift to her this year. You paid the $15,000 college tuition of your friend, David. You gave your 25 year-old daughter, Lisa, $25,000. You also gave your 27 year-old son, Ken, $25,000. You have never given a taxable gift before. Apply the exceptions to the gift tax and the applicable credit as follows:

1. Apply the educational exclusion. Payment of tuition expenses is not subject to the gift tax. Therefore, the gift to David is not a taxable gift.

2. Apply the annual exclusion. The first $14,000 you give someone is not a taxable gift. Therefore, your $8,000 gift to Mary, the first $14,000 of your gift to Lisa, and the first $14,000 of your gift to Ken are not taxable gifts.

3. Apply the applicable credit. The gift tax on $22,000 ($11,000 remaining from your gift to Lisa plus $11,000 remaining from your gift to Ken) is $4,240. Subtract the $4,240 from your applicable credit of $2,045,800 for 2013. The applicable credit that you can use against the gift or estate tax in a later year is $2,041,560.

You do not have to pay any gift tax for 2013. However, you do have to file Form 709.

For more information, see the *Table for Computing Gift Tax* in the Instructions for Form 709.

Filing a gift tax return. Generally, you must file a gift tax return if any of the following apply:
- You gave gifts to at least one person (other than your spouse) that are more than the annual exclusion for the year.

- You and your spouse are splitting a gift.
- You gave someone (other than your spouse) a gift of a future interest that he or she cannot actually possess, enjoy, or receive income from until some time in the future.
- You gave your spouse an interest in property that will be ended by some future event.

You do not have to file a gift tax return to report gifts to (or for the use of) political organizations and gifts made by paying someone's tuition or medical expenses.

You also do not need to report the following deductible gifts made to charities:

- Your entire interest in property, if no other interest has been transferred for less than adequate consideration or for other than a charitable use, or
- A qualified conservation contribution that is a perpetual restriction on the use of real property.

More information. If you think you need to file a gift tax return, see Form 709 and its instructions for more information. You can get publications and forms from the IRS website, *IRS.gov*. You may want to speak with a qualified tax professional to receive help with gift tax questions.

Estate Tax

Estate tax may apply to your taxable estate at your death. Your taxable estate is your gross estate less allowable deductions.

Gross estate. Your gross estate includes the value of all property you own partially or outright at the time of death. Your gross estate also includes the following:

- Life insurance proceeds payable to your estate or, if you owned the policy, to your heirs,
- The value of certain annuities payable to your estate or your heirs, and
- The value of certain property you transferred within 3 years before your death.

Taxable estate. The allowable deductions used in determining your taxable estate include:

- Funeral expenses paid out of your estate,
- Debts you owed at the time of death,
- The marital deduction (generally, the value of the property that passes from your estate to your surviving spouse),
- The charitable deduction (generally, the value of the property that passes from your estate to the United States, any state, a political subdivision of a state, the District of Columbia, or to a qualifying charity for exclusively charitable purposes), and
- The state death tax deduction (generally any estate, inheritance, legacy, or succession taxes paid as the result of the decedent's death to any state or the District of Columbia.

More information. For more information on what is included in your gross estate and the allowable deductions, see Form 706 and Form 706-NA and their instructions.

Applying the applicable credit to estate tax. Basically, any applicable credit not used to eliminate gift tax can be used to eliminate or reduce estate tax. However, to determine the applicable credit available for use against the estate tax, you must complete Form 706.

Filing an estate tax return. An estate tax return must be filed if the gross estate, plus any adjusted taxable gifts and specific gift tax exemption, is more than the basic exclusion amount. The basic exclusion amount is generally equal to the filing requirement. The basic exclusion amount is $5,000,000, indexed for inflation. For 2013, the basic exclusion amount is $5,250,000.

Note. The federal estate tax return generally does not need to be filed unless the total value of lifetime transfers and the estate is worth more than the basic exclusion amount for the year of death. However, a complete and timely filed return is required if a deceased spouse's estate elects portability of any unused exclusion amount for use by the surviving spouse.

Adjusted taxable gifts is the total of the taxable gifts you made after 1976 that are not included in your gross estate.

Note. The *specific gift tax exemption* applies only to gifts made after September 8, 1976, and before January 1, 1977.

The *applicable exclusion amount* is the total amount exempted from gift and/or estate tax. For estates of decedents dying after December 31, 2010, the applicable exclusion amount equals the basic exclusion amount plus any deceased spousal unused exclusion (DSUE) amount. The DSUE amount is the remaining applicable exclusion amount from the estate of a predeceased spouse who died after December 31, 2010. The DSUE amount is only available where an election was made on the Form 706 filed by the deceased spouse's estate.

Note. For the estate of decedents, who died after December 31, 2010 and on or before December 31, 2013, that were not required to file a Form 706 and did not timely file a Form 706 to make the portability election, see Rev. Proc. 2014-18, 2014-7 I.R.B., to make the portability election on or before December 31, 2014.

Filing requirement. The following table lists the filing requirements for estates of decedents dying after 2001.

Basic Exclusion Amount

Year of Death:	File return if estate's value is more than:
2002 and 2003	$1,000,000
2004 and 2005	$1,500,000
2006, 2007, and 2008	$2,000,000
2009	$3,500,000
2010 and 2011	$5,000,000
2012	$5,120,000
2013	$5,250,000

More information. If you think you will have an estate on which tax must be paid, or if your estate will have to file an estate tax return even if no tax will be due, see Form 706, Form 706-NA, and the forms' instructions for more information. You (or your estate's representative) may want to speak with a qualified tax professional to receive help with estate tax questions.

Generation-Skipping Transfer Tax

The *generation-skipping tax* (GST) may apply to gifts during your life or transfers occurring at your death, called *bequests*, made to skip persons. A *skip person* is a person who belongs to a generation that is two or more generations below the generation of the donor. For instance, your grandchild will generally be a skip person to you or your spouse. The GST tax is figured on the amount of the gift or bequest transferred to a skip person, after subtracting any GST exemption allocated to the gift or bequest at the maximum gift and estate tax rates. Each individual has a GST exemption equal to the basic exclusion amount, as indexed for inflation, for the year the gift or bequest was made. GSTs have three forms: direct skip, taxable distribution, and taxable termination.

- A *direct skip* is a transfer made during your life or occurring at your death that is:
  1. Subject to the gift or estate tax,
  2. Of an interest in property, and
  3. Made to a skip person.
- A *taxable distribution* is any distribution from a trust to a skip person which is not a direct skip or a taxable termination.
- A *taxable termination* is the end of a trust's interest in property where the property interest will be transferred to a skip person.

More information. If you think you will have a gift or bequest on which GST tax must be paid, see Form 709, Form 706, Form 706-NA, and the forms' instructions for more information. You (or your estate's representative) may want to speak with a qualified tax professional to receive help with GST questions.

Comprehensive Example

The following is an example of a typical situation. All figures on the filled-in forms have been rounded to the nearest whole dollar.

On April 9, 2013, your father, John R. Smith, died at the age of 72. He had not resided in a community property state. His will named you to serve as his executor (personal representative). Except for specific bequests to your mother, Mary, of your parents' home and your father's automobile and a bequest of $5,000 to his church, your father's will named your mother and his brother as beneficiaries.

After the court has approved your appointment as the executor, you should obtain an employer identification number for the estate. (See *Duties* under *Personal Representatives,* earlier.) Next, you use Form 56 to notify the Internal

¶105

Revenue Service that you have been appointed executor of your father's estate.

Assets of the estate. Your father had the following assets when he died.

- His checking account balance was $2,550 and his savings account balance was $53,650.
- Your father inherited his home from his parents on March 5, 1980. At that time it was worth $42,000, but was appraised at the time of your father's death at $150,000. The home was free of existing debts (or mortgages) at the time of his death.
- Your father owned 500 shares of ABC Company stock that cost $10.20 a share in 1984. The stock had a mean selling price (midpoint between highest and lowest selling price) of $25 a share on the day he died. He also owned 500 shares of XYZ Company stock that cost $30 a share in 1989. The stock had a mean selling price on the date of death of $22.
- The appraiser valued your father's automobile at $6,300 and the household effects at $18,500.
- Your father's employer sent a check to your mother for $11,082 ($12,000 – $918 for social security and Medicare taxes), representing unpaid salary and payment for accrued vacation time. The statement that came with the check indicated that no amount was withheld for income tax. The check was made out to the estate, so your mother gave you the check.
- The Easy Life Insurance Company gave your mother a check for $275,000 because she was the beneficiary of his life insurance policy.
- Your father was the owner of several series EE U.S. savings bonds on which he named your mother as co-owner. Your father purchased the bonds during the past several years. The cost of these bonds totaled $2,500. After referring to the appropriate table of redemption values (see *U.S. savings bonds acquired from decedent*, earlier), you determine that interest of $840 had accrued on the bonds at the date of your father's death. You must include the redemption value of these bonds at date of death, $3,340, in your father's gross estate.
- On July 1, 1996, your parents purchased a house for $90,000. They have held the property for rental purposes continuously since its purchase. Your mother paid one-third of the purchase price, or $30,000, and your father paid $60,000. They owned the property, however, as joint tenants with right of survivorship. An appraiser valued the property at $120,000. You include $60,000, one-half the value, in your father's gross estate because your parents owned the property as joint tenants with right of survivorship and they were the only joint tenants.

Your mother also gave you a Form W-2, Wage and Tax Statement, that your father's employer had sent. In examining it, you discover that your father had been paid $11,000 in salary between January 1, 2013, and April 9, 2013 (the date he died). The Form W-2 showed

$11,000 in box 1 and $23,000 ($11,000 + $12,000) in boxes 3 and 5. The Form W-2 indicated $845 as federal income tax withheld in box 2. The estate received a Form 1099-MISC from the employer showing $12,000 in box 3. The estate received a Form 1099-INT for your father showing he was paid $1,900 interest on his savings account at the First S&L of Juneville in 2013, before he died.

Final Return for Decedent—Form 1040

From the papers in your father's files, you determine that the $11,000 paid to him by his employer (as shown on the Form W-2), rental income, and interest are the only items of income he received between January 1 and the date of his death. You will have to file an income tax return for him for the period during which he lived. (You determine that he timely filed his 2012 income tax return before he died.) The final return is not due until April 15, 2014, the same date it would have been due had your father lived during all of 2013.

The check representing unpaid salary and earned but unused vacation time was not paid to your father before he died, so the $12,000 is not reported as income on his final return. It is reported on the income tax return for the estate (Form 1041) for 2013. The only taxable income to be reported for your father will be the $11,000 salary (as shown on the Form W-2), the $1,900 interest, and his portion of the rental income that he received in 2013.

Your father was a cash basis taxpayer and did not report the interest accrued on the series EE U.S. savings bonds on prior tax returns that he filed jointly with your mother. As the personal representative of your father's estate, you choose to report the interest earned on these bonds before your father's death ($840) on the final income tax return.

The rental property was leased the entire year of 2013 for $1,000 per month. Under local law, your parents (as joint tenants) each had a half interest in the income from the property. Your father's will, however, stipulates that the entire rental income is to be paid directly to your mother. None of the rental income will be reported on the income tax return for the estate. Instead, your mother will report all the rental income and expenses on Form 1040.

Checking the records and prior tax returns of your parents, you find that they previously elected to use the alternative depreciation system (ADS) with the mid-month convention. Under ADS, the rental house is depreciated using the straight-line method over a 40-year recovery period. They allocated $15,000 of the cost to the land (which is never depreciable) and $75,000 to the rental house. Salvage value was disregarded for the depreciation computation. Before 2013, $23,359 had been allowed as depreciation. (For information on ADS, see Publication 946.)

Deductions. During the year, you received a bill from the hospital for $945 and bills from your father's doctors totaling $685. You paid these bills as they were presented. In addition, you

find other bills from his doctors totaling $302 that your father paid in 2013 and receipts for prescribed drugs he purchased totaling $724. The funeral home presented you a bill for $6,890 for the expenses of your father's funeral, which you paid.

The medical expenses you paid from the estate's funds ($945 and $685) were for your father's care and were paid within 1 year after his death. They will not be used to figure the taxable estate so you can treat them as having been paid by your father when he received the medical services. See *Medical Expenses* under *Final Income Tax Return for Decedent—Form 1041*, earlier. However, you cannot deduct the funeral expenses either on your father's final return or on the estate's income tax return. They are deductible only on the federal estate tax return (Form 706).

In addition, after going over other receipts and canceled checks for the tax year with your mother, you determine that the following items are deductible on your parents' 2013 income tax return.

Health insurance	$4,250
State income tax paid	1,391
Real estate tax on home	3,100
Contributions to church	3,830

Rental expenses included real estate taxes of $700 and mortgage interest of $410. In addition, insurance premiums of $260 and painting and repair expenses for $350 were paid. These rental expenses totaled $1,720 and are reflected on Schedule E (Form 1040).

Your mother and father owned the property as joint tenants with right of survivorship and they were the only joint tenants, so her basis in this property upon your father's death is $93,047. This is figured by adding the $60,000 value of the half interest included in your father's gross estate to your mother's $45,000 share of the cost basis and subtracting your mother's $11,953 share of depreciation (including 2013 depreciation for the period before your father's death), as explained next.

For 2013, you must make the following computations to figure the depreciation deduction.

1. For the period before your father's death, depreciate the property using the same method, basis, and life used by your parents in previous years. They used the mid-month convention, so the amount deductible for three and a half months is $547. (This brings the total depreciation to $23,906 ($23,359 + $547) at the time of your father's death.)

2. For the period after your father's death, you must make two computations.

    a. Your mother's cost basis ($45,000) minus one-half of the amount allocated to the land ($7,500) is her depreciable basis ($37,500) for half of the property. She continues to use the same life and depreciation method as was originally used for the property. The amount deductible for the remaining eight and a half months is $664.

    b. The other half of the property must be depreciated using a depreciation method that is acceptable for property placed in service in 2013. You chose to use ADS with the mid-month convention. The value included in the estate ($60,000) less the value allocable to the land ($10,000) is the depreciable basis ($50,000) for this half of the property. The amount deductible for this half of the property is $886 ($50,000 × .01771). See chapter 4 and *Table A-13* in Publication 946.

Show the total of the amounts in (1) and (2) (a), above, on line 17 of Form 4562, Depreciation and Amortization. Show the amount in (2) (b) on line 20c. The total depreciation deduction allowed for the year is $2,097.

Filing status. After December 31, 2013, when your mother determines the amount of her income, you and your mother must decide whether you will file a joint return or separate returns for your parents for 2013. Your mother has rental income and $400 of interest income from her savings account at the Mayflower Bank of Juneville, so it appears to be to her advantage to file a joint return.

Tax computation. The illustrations of Form 1040 and related schedules appear near the end of this publication. These illustrations are based on information in this example. The tax refund is $748. The computation is as follows:

Income:		
Salary (per Form W-2)	$11,000	
Interest income	3,140	
Net rental income	8,183	
Adjusted gross income		$22,323
Minus: Itemized deductions		13,553
Balance		$8,770
Minus: Exemptions (2)		7,800
Taxable income		$970
Income tax from tax table		$96
Minus: Tax withheld		$845
Refund of taxes		**$749**

Income Tax Return of an Estate—Form 1041

The illustrations of Form 1041 and the related schedules for 2013 appear near the end of this publication. These illustrations are based on the information that follows.

2013 income tax return. Having determined the tax liability for your father's final return, you now figure the estate's taxable income. You decide to use the calendar year and the cash method of accounting to report the estate's income. This return also is due by April 15, 2014.

In addition to the amount you received from your father's employer for unpaid salary and for vacation pay ($12,000) entered on line 8 (Form 1041), you received a dividend check from the XYZ Company on June 16, 2013. The check was for $750 and you enter it on line 2a (Form 1041). The amount is a qualified dividend and you show the allocation to the beneficiaries and the estate on line 2b. The amount allocated to the beneficiary ($179) is based on the distributable dividend income before any deductions.

Page 28

The estate received a Form 1099-INT showing $2,250 interest paid by the bank on the savings account in 2013 after your father died. Show this amount on line 1 (Form 1041).

Deductions. In November 2013, you received a bill for the real estate taxes on your parents' home. The bill was for $2,250, which you paid. Include real estate taxes on line 11 (Form 1041).

You paid $1,325 for attorney's fees in connection with administration of the estate. This is an expense of administration and is deducted on line 14 (Form 1041). You must, however, file with the return a statement in duplicate that such expense has not been claimed as a deduction from the gross estate for figuring the federal estate tax on Form 706, and that all rights to claim that deduction on Form 706 are waived.

Distributions. You made a distribution of $2,000 to your father's brother, James. The distribution was made from current income of the estate under the terms of the will.

The income distribution deduction ($2,000) is figured on Schedule B of Form 1041 and deducted on line 18 (Form 1041).

You characterized the $2,000 that is included in income and reported it on Schedule K-1 (Form 1041) as follows:

Step 1
Allocation of Income & Deductions

Type of Income	Amount	Deductions	Distributable Net Income
Interest (15%)	$2,250	(536)	$1,714
Dividends (5%)	750	(179)	571
Other Income (80%)	12,000	(2,860)	9,140
Total	**$15,000**	**(3,575)**	**$11,425**

Step 2
Allocation of Distribution
(Report on the Schedule K-1 for James)

Line 1 – Interest	
$2,000 × (1,714 ÷ 11,425)	$300
Line 2b – Total dividends	
$2,000 × (571 ÷ 11,425)	100
Line 5 – Other income	
$2,000 × (9,140 ÷11,425)	1,600
Total Distribution	**$2,000**

The estate took an income distribution deduction, so you must prepare Schedule I (Form 1041), Alternative Minimum Tax—Estates and Trusts, regardless of whether the estate is liable for the alternative minimum tax.

The other distribution you made out of the assets of the estate in 2013 was the transfer of the automobile to your mother on July 1. This is included in the bequest of property, so it is not taken into account in computing the distribution of income to the beneficiary. The life insurance proceeds of $275,000 paid directly to your mother by the insurance company are not an asset of the estate.

Tax computation. The taxable income of the estate for 2013 is $8,825, figured as follows:

Gross income:		
Income in respect of a decedent		$12,000
Dividends		750
Interest		2,250
		$15,000
Minus: Deductions and income distribution		
Real estate taxes	$2,250	
Attorney's fee	1,325	
Exemption	600	
Distribution	2,000	6,175
Taxable income		**$8,825**

The estate had taxable income of $8,825 which included $571 of qualified dividends for the year, which leaves the estate with a tax due of $1,981 for 2013.

2014 income tax return for estate. On January 7, 2014, you receive a dividend check from the XYZ Company for $500. You also have interest posted to the savings account in January totaling $350. On January 28, 2014, you make a final accounting to the court and obtain permission to close the estate. In the accounting, you list $1,650 as the balance of the expense of administering the estate.

You advise the court that you plan to pay $5,000 to Hometown Church under the provisions of the will, and that you will distribute the balance of the property to your mother, the remaining beneficiary.

Gross income. After making the distributions already described, you can wind up the affairs of the estate. The gross income of the estate for 2014 is more than $600, so you must file a final income tax return, Form 1041, for 2014 (not shown). The estate's gross income for 2014 is $850 (dividends $500 and interest $350).

Deductions. After making the following computations, you determine that none of the distributions made to your mother must be included in her taxable income for 2014.

Gross income for 2014:		
Dividends		$500
Interest		350
		$850
Less deductions:		
Administration expense		$1,650
Loss		**($800)**

Note that because the contribution of $5,000 to Hometown Church was not required under the terms of the will to be paid out of the gross income of the estate, it is not deductible and was not included in the computation.

The estate had no distributable net income in 2014, so none of the distributions made to your mother have to be included in her gross income. Furthermore, because the estate in the year of termination had deductions in excess of its gross income, the excess of $800 will be allowed as a miscellaneous itemized deduction subject to the 2%-of-adjusted-gross-income limit to your mother on her individual return for the year 2014, if she itemizes deductions.

Deceased: John R. Smith -- April 9, 2013

Form **1040** Department of the Treasury – Internal Revenue Service (99)	20**13**	U.S. Individual Income Tax Return	OMB No. 1545-0074	IRS Use Only—Do not write or staple in this space.

U.S. Individual Income Tax Return

For the year Jan. 1–Dec. 31, 2013, or other tax year beginning _____, 2013, ending _____, 20__   See separate instructions.

Your first name and initial	Last name		Your social security number
John R.	Smith		234 | 00 | 7890
If a joint return, spouse's first name and initial	Last name		Spouse's social security number
Mary L.	Smith		567 | 00 | 0123

Home address (number and street). If you have a P.O. box, see instructions.   Apt. no.   ▲ Make sure the SSN(s) above and on line 6c are correct.

6406 Mayflower St.

City, town or post office, state, and ZIP code. If you have a foreign address, also complete spaces below (see instructions).

Juneville, ME 00000

Presidential Election Campaign
Check here if you, or your spouse if filing jointly, want $3 to go to this fund. Checking a box below will not change your tax or refund.   ☐ You   ☐ Spouse

Foreign country name	Foreign province/state/county	Foreign postal code

Filing Status

Check only one box.

1. ☐ Single
2. ☑ Married filing jointly (even if only one had income)
3. ☐ Married filing separately. Enter spouse's SSN above and full name here. ▶
4. ☐ Head of household (with qualifying person). (See instructions.) If the qualifying person is a child but not your dependent, enter this child's name here. ▶
5. ☐ Qualifying widow(er) with dependent child

Exemptions

6a ☑ **Yourself.** If someone can claim you as a dependent, **do not** check box 6a . . . . . .
b ☑ **Spouse** . . . .

Boxes checked on 6a and 6b   **2**

c **Dependents:**

(1) First name Last name	(2) Dependent's social security number	(3) Dependent's relationship to you	(4) ✓ if child under age 17 qualifying for child tax credit (see instructions)
			☐
			☐
			☐
			☐

If more than four dependents, see instructions and check here ▶ ☐

No. of children on 6c who:
• lived with you
• did not live with you due to divorce or separation (see instructions)

Dependents on 6c not entered above

Add numbers on lines above ▶   **2**

d Total number of exemptions claimed . . . .

Income

Attach Form(s) W-2 here. Also attach Forms W-2G and 1099-R if tax was withheld.

If you did not get a W-2, see instructions.

7	Wages, salaries, tips, etc. Attach Form(s) W-2	7	11,000
8a	Taxable interest. Attach Schedule B if required	8a	3,140
b	Tax-exempt interest. **Do not** include on line 8a . . .	8b	
9a	Ordinary dividends. Attach Schedule B if required	9a	
b	Qualified dividends	9b	
10	Taxable refunds, credits, or offsets of state and local income taxes	10	
11	Alimony received	11	
12	Business income or (loss). Attach Schedule C or C-EZ	12	
13	Capital gain or (loss). Attach Schedule D if required. If not required, check here ▶ ☐	13	
14	Other gains or (losses). Attach Form 4797	14	
15a	IRA distributions .	15a	b Taxable amount . . .	15b	
16a	Pensions and annuities	16a	b Taxable amount . . .	16b	
17	Rental real estate, royalties, partnerships, S corporations, trusts, etc. Attach Schedule E	17	8,183
18	Farm income or (loss). Attach Schedule F	18	
19	Unemployment compensation	19	
20a	Social security benefits	20a	b Taxable amount . . .	20b	
21	Other income. List type and amount	21	
22	Combine the amounts in the far right column for lines 7 through 21. This is your **total income** ▶	22	22,323

Adjusted Gross Income

23	Educator expenses	23	
24	Certain business expenses of reservists, performing artists, and fee-basis government officials. Attach Form 2106 or 2106-EZ	24	
25	Health savings account deduction. Attach Form 8889 .	25	
26	Moving expenses. Attach Form 3903	26	
27	Deductible part of self-employment tax. Attach Schedule SE .	27	
28	Self-employed SEP, SIMPLE, and qualified plans . .	28	
29	Self-employed health insurance deduction . . .	29	
30	Penalty on early withdrawal of savings	30	
31a	Alimony paid b Recipient's SSN ▶	31a	
32	IRA deduction	32	
33	Student loan interest deduction	33	
34	Tuition and fees. Attach Form 8917	34	
35	Domestic production activities deduction. Attach Form 8903	35	
36	Add lines 23 through 35	36	
37	Subtract line 36 from line 22. This is your **adjusted gross income** . . . . ▶	37	22,323

For Disclosure, Privacy Act, and Paperwork Reduction Act Notice, see separate instructions.   Cat. No. 11320B   Form **1040** (2013)

Form 1040 (2013)   Page **2**

Tax and Credits	38	Amount from line 37 (adjusted gross income)	38	22,323

39a Check if: ☑ You were born before January 2, 1949, ☐ Blind. ☐ Spouse was born before January 2, 1949, ☐ Blind. Total boxes checked ▶ 39a **1**

b If your spouse itemizes on a separate return or you were a dual-status alien, check here ▶ 39b ☐

Standard Deduction for—

- People who check any box on line 39a or 39b or who can be claimed as a dependent, see instructions.
- All others:

Single or Married filing separately, $6,100

Married filing jointly or Qualifying widow(er), $12,200

Head of household, $8,950

Line	Description		Amt	Value
40	Itemized deductions (from Schedule A) **or** your **standard deduction** (see left margin)		40	13,553
41	Subtract line 40 from line 38		41	8,770
42	**Exemptions.** If line 38 is $150,000 or less, multiply $3,900 by the number on line 6d. Otherwise, see instructions		42	7,800
43	**Taxable income.** Subtract line 42 from line 41. If line 42 is more than line 41, enter -0-		43	970
44	**Tax** (see instructions). Check if any from: **a** ☐ Form(s) 8814 **b** ☐ Form 4972 **c** ☐		44	96
45	**Alternative minimum tax** (see instructions). Attach Form 6251		45	0
46	Add lines 44 and 45 ▶		46	96
47	Foreign tax credit. Attach Form 1116 if required	47		
48	Credit for child and dependent care expenses. Attach Form 2441	48		
49	Education credits from Form 8863, line 19	49		
50	Retirement savings contributions credit. Attach Form 8880	50		
51	Child tax credit. Attach Schedule 8812, if required	51		
52	Residential energy credits. Attach Form 5695	52		
53	Other credits from Form: **a** ☐ 3800 **b** ☐ 8801 **c** ☐	53		
54	Add lines 47 through 53. These are your **total credits**		54	
55	Subtract line 54 from line 46. If line 54 is more than line 46, enter -0-		55	96

Other Taxes

Line	Description		Amt	Value
56	Self-employment tax. Attach Schedule SE		56	
57	Unreported social security and Medicare tax from Form: **a** ☐ 4137 **b** ☐ 8919		57	
58	Additional tax on IRAs, other qualified retirement plans, etc. Attach Form 5329 if required		58	
59a	Household employment taxes from Schedule H		59a	
b	First-time homebuyer credit repayment. Attach Form 5405 if required		59b	
60	Taxes from: **a** ☐ Form 8959 **b** ☐ Form 8960 **c** ☐ Instructions; enter code(s)		60	
61	Add lines 55 through 60. This is your **total tax** ▶		61	

Payments

If you have a qualifying child, attach Schedule EIC.

Line	Description		Amt	Value
62	Federal income tax withheld from Forms W-2 and 1099	62	845	
63	2013 estimated tax payments and amount applied from 2012 return	63		
64a	**Earned income credit (EIC)**	64a		
b	Nontaxable combat pay election	64b		
65	Additional child tax credit. Attach Schedule 8812	65		
66	American opportunity credit from Form 8863, line 8	66		
67	Reserved	67		
68	Amount paid with request for extension to file	68		
69	Excess social security and tier 1 RRTA tax withheld	69		
70	Credit for federal tax on fuels. Attach Form 4136	70		
71	Credits from Form: **a** ☐ 2439 **b** ☐ Reserved **c** ☐ 8885 **d** ☐	71		
72	Add lines 62, 63, 64a, and 65 through 71. These are your **total payments** ▶		72	845

Refund

73	If line 72 is more than line 61, subtract line 61 from line 72. This is the amount you **overpaid**		73	749
74a	Amount of line 73 you want **refunded to you.** If Form 8888 is attached, check here ▶ ☐		74a	749

Direct deposit? See instructions.
b Routing number ▶   **c** Type: ☐ Checking ☐ Savings
d Account number ▶

75	Amount of line 73 you want **applied to your 2014 estimated tax** ▶	75		

Amount You Owe

76	**Amount you owe.** Subtract line 72 from line 61. For details on how to pay, see instructions ▶		76	
77	Estimated tax penalty (see instructions)	77		

Third Party Designee

Do you want to allow another person to discuss this return with the IRS (see instructions)? ☐ **Yes.** Complete below. ☐ **No**

Designee's name ▶   Phone no. ▶   Personal identification number (PIN) ▶

Sign Here

Under penalties of perjury, I declare that I have examined this return and accompanying schedules and statements, and to the best of my knowledge and belief, they are true, correct, and complete. Declaration of preparer (other than taxpayer) is based on all information of which preparer has any knowledge.

Joint return? See instructions. Keep a copy for your records.

Your signature: *Charles R. Smith, Executor*   Date: 3-25-14   Your occupation   Daytime phone number

Spouse's signature. If a joint return, **both** must sign. *Mary L. Smith*   Date: 3-25-14   Spouse's occupation   If the IRS sent you an Identity Protection PIN, enter it here (see inst.)

Paid Preparer Use Only

Print/Type preparer's name   Preparer's signature   Date   Check ☐ if self-employed   PTIN

Firm's name ▶   Firm's EIN ▶

Firm's address ▶   Phone no.

Form **1040** (2013)

¶105

SCHEDULE A (Form 1040) Department of the Treasury Internal Revenue Service (99)	**Itemized Deductions** ▶ Information about Schedule A and its separate instructions is at *www.irs.gov/schedulea*. ▶ Attach to Form 1040.	OMB No. 1545-0074 20**13** Attachment Sequence No. **07**

Name(s) shown on Form 1040

John R. (Deceased) & Mary L. Smith

Your social security number

234-00-7890

Medical and Dental Expenses		**Caution.** Do not include expenses reimbursed or paid by others.			
	1	Medical and dental expenses (see instructions)	**1**	6,906	
	2	Enter amount from Form 1040, line 38 | **2** | 22,323			
	3	Multiply line 2 by 10% (.10). But if either you or your spouse was born before January 2, 1949, multiply line 2 by 7.5% (.075) instead	**3**	1,674	
	4	Subtract line 3 from line 1. If line 3 is more than line 1, enter -0-		**4**	5,232
Taxes You Paid	5	State and local (**check only one box**): a ☑ Income taxes, **or** b ☐ General sales taxes }	**5**	1,391	
	6	Real estate taxes (see instructions)	**6**	3,100	
	7	Personal property taxes	**7**		
	8	Other taxes. List type and amount ▶ _____	**8**		
	9	Add lines 5 through 8		**9**	4,491
Interest You Paid **Note.** Your mortgage interest deduction may be limited (see instructions).	10	Home mortgage interest and points reported to you on Form 1098	**10**		
	11	Home mortgage interest not reported to you on Form 1098. If paid to the person from whom you bought the home, see instructions and show that person's name, identifying no., and address ▶ _____	**11**		
	12	Points not reported to you on Form 1098. See instructions for special rules	**12**		
	13	Mortgage insurance premiums (see instructions)	**13**		
	14	Investment interest. Attach Form 4952 if required. (See instructions.)	**14**		
	15	Add lines 10 through 14		**15**	
Gifts to Charity If you made a gift and got a benefit for it, see instructions.	16	Gifts by cash or check. If you made any gift of $250 or more, see instructions	**16**	3,830	
	17	Other than by cash or check. If any gift of $250 or more, see instructions. You **must** attach Form 8283 if over $500 . . .	**17**		
	18	Carryover from prior year	**18**		
	19	Add lines 16 through 18		**19**	3,830
Casualty and Theft Losses	20	Casualty or theft loss(es). Attach Form 4684. (See instructions.)		**20**	
Job Expenses and Certain Miscellaneous Deductions	21	Unreimbursed employee expenses—job travel, union dues, job education, etc. Attach Form 2106 or 2106-EZ if required. (See instructions.) ▶ _____	**21**		
	22	Tax preparation fees	**22**		
	23	Other expenses—investment, safe deposit box, etc. List type and amount ▶ _____	**23**		
	24	Add lines 21 through 23	**24**		
	25	Enter amount from Form 1040, line 38 | **25**			
	26	Multiply line 25 by 2% (.02)	**26**		
	27	Subtract line 26 from line 24. If line 26 is more than line 24, enter -0-		**27**	
Other Miscellaneous Deductions	28	Other—from list in instructions. List type and amount ▶ _____		**28**	
Total Itemized Deductions	29	Is Form 1040, line 38, over $150,000? ☑ **No.** Your deduction is not limited. Add the amounts in the far right column for lines 4 through 28. Also, enter this amount on Form 1040, line 40. ☐ **Yes.** Your deduction may be limited. See the Itemized Deductions Worksheet in the instructions to figure the amount to enter. }		**29**	13,553
	30	If you elect to itemize deductions even though they are less than your standard deduction, check here . . . . ▶ ☐			

For Paperwork Reduction Act Notice, see Form 1040 instructions.   Cat. No. 17145C   Schedule A (Form 1040) 2013

SCHEDULE B (Form 1040A or 1040)	**Interest and Ordinary Dividends**	OMB No. 1545-0074
Department of the Treasury Internal Revenue Service (99)	▶ **Attach to Form 1040A or 1040.** ▶ Information about Schedule B (Form 1040A or 1040) and its instructions is at *www.irs.gov/scheduleb*.	20**13** Attachment Sequence No. **08**

Name(s) shown on return

John R. (Deceased) & Mary L. Smith

Your social security number

234-00-7890

Part I

Interest

(See instructions on back and the instructions for Form 1040A, or Form 1040, line 8a.)

Note. If you received a Form 1099-INT, Form 1099-OID, or substitute statement from a brokerage firm, list the firm's name as the payer and enter the total interest shown on that form.

1 List name of payer. If any interest is from a seller-financed mortgage and the buyer used the property as a personal residence, see instructions on back and list this interest first. Also, show that buyer's social security number and address ▶

	Amount
First S&L of Juneville	1,900
Mayflower Bank of Juneville	400
Series EE U.S. Saving Bonds -- Interest includible before decedent's death	840

2 Add the amounts on line 1 . . . . | **2** | 3,140 |

3 Excludable interest on series EE and I U.S. savings bonds issued after 1989. Attach Form 8815 . . . . | **3** | -0- |

4 Subtract line 3 from line 2. Enter the result here and on Form 1040A, or Form 1040, line 8a . . . . ▶ | **4** | 3,140 |

Note. If line 4 is over $1,500, you must complete Part III.

Part II

Ordinary Dividends

(See instructions on back and the instructions for Form 1040A, or Form 1040, line 9a.)

Note. If you received a Form 1099-DIV or substitute statement from a brokerage firm, list the firm's name as the payer and enter the ordinary dividends shown on that form.

5 List name of payer ▶

	Amount

6 Add the amounts on line 5. Enter the total here and on Form 1040A, or Form 1040, line 9a . . . . ▶ | **6** | |

Note. If line 6 is over $1,500, you must complete Part III.

Part III

Foreign Accounts and Trusts

(See instructions on back.)

You must complete this part if you **(a)** had over $1,500 of taxable interest or ordinary dividends; **(b)** had a foreign account; or **(c)** received a distribution from, or were a grantor of, or a transferor to, a foreign trust.

		Yes	No
7a	At any time during 2013, did you have a financial interest in or signature authority over a financial account (such as a bank account, securities account, or brokerage account) located in a foreign country? See instructions		✓
	If "Yes," are you required to file FinCEN Form 114, Report of Foreign Bank and Financial Accounts (FBAR), formerly TD F 90-22.1, to report that financial interest or signature authority? See FinCEN Form 114 and its instructions for filing requirements and exceptions to those requirements		
b	If you are required to file FinCEN Form 114, enter the name of the foreign country where the financial account is located ▶		
8	During 2013, did you receive a distribution from, or were you the grantor of, or transferor to, a foreign trust? If "Yes," you may have to file Form 3520. See instructions on back		✓

For Paperwork Reduction Act Notice, see your tax return instructions.   Cat. No. 17146N   Schedule B (Form 1040A or 1040) 2013

¶105

SCHEDULE E (Form 1040) Department of the Treasury Internal Revenue Service (99)	**Supplemental Income and Loss** (From rental real estate, royalties, partnerships, S corporations, estates, trusts, REMICs, etc.) ▶ Attach to Form 1040, 1040NR, or Form 1041. ▶ Information about Schedule E and its separate instructions is at *www.irs.gov/schedulee.*	OMB No. 1545-0074 20**13** Attachment Sequence No. **13**

Name(s) shown on return	Your social security number
John R. (Deceased) & Mary L. Smith	234-00-7890

Part I Income or Loss From Rental Real Estate and Royalties **Note.** If you are in the business of renting personal property, use **Schedule C or C-EZ** (see instructions). If you are an individual, report farm rental income or loss from **Form 4835** on page 2, line 40.

A Did you make any payments in 2013 that would require you to file Form(s) 1099? (see instructions) ☐ Yes ☑ No

B If "Yes," did you or will you file required Forms 1099? ☐ Yes ☐ No

1a Physical address of each property (street, city, state, ZIP code)

A 137 Main Street, Juneville, ME 00000

B

C

1b	Type of Property (from list below)	2 For each rental real estate property listed above, report the number of fair rental and personal use days. Check the **QJV** box only if you meet the requirements to file as a qualified joint venture. See instructions.		Fair Rental Days	Personal Use Days	QJV
A	1		**A**	365		☑
B			**B**			☐
C			**C**			☐

Type of Property:

1 Single Family Residence 3 Vacation/Short-Term Rental 5 Land 7 Self-Rental
2 Multi-Family Residence 4 Commercial 6 Royalties 8 Other (describe)

Income:		Properties:		A	B	C
3	Rents received		3	12,000		
4	Royalties received		4			
Expenses:						
5	Advertising		5			
6	Auto and travel (see instructions)		6			
7	Cleaning and maintenance		7			
8	Commissions.		8			
9	Insurance		9	260		
10	Legal and other professional fees		10			
11	Management fees		11			
12	Mortgage interest paid to banks, etc. (see instructions)		12	410		
13	Other interest.		13			
14	Repairs.		14	350		
15	Supplies		15			
16	Taxes		16	700		
17	Utilities.		17			
18	Depreciation expense or depletion		18	2,097		
19	Other (list) ▶		19			
20	Total expenses. Add lines 5 through 19		20	3,817		
21	Subtract line 20 from line 3 (rents) and/or 4 (royalties). If result is a (loss), see instructions to find out if you must file **Form 6198**		21	8,183		
22	Deductible rental real estate loss after limitation, if any, on **Form 8582** (see instructions)		22	( )	( )	( )

23a	Total of all amounts reported on line 3 for all rental properties	**23a**	12,000
b	Total of all amounts reported on line 4 for all royalty properties	**23b**	
c	Total of all amounts reported on line 12 for all properties	**23c**	410
d	Total of all amounts reported on line 18 for all properties	**23d**	2,097
e	Total of all amounts reported on line 20 for all properties	**23e**	3,817

24	**Income.** Add positive amounts shown on line 21. **Do not** include any losses	**24**	8,183
25	**Losses.** Add royalty losses from line 21 and rental real estate losses from line 22. Enter total losses here	**25**	( )
26	**Total rental real estate and royalty income or (loss).** Combine lines 24 and 25. Enter the result here. If Parts II, III, IV, and line 40 on page 2 do not apply to you, also enter this amount on Form 1040, line 17, or Form 1040NR, line 18. Otherwise, include this amount in the total on line 41 on page 2	**26**	8,183

For Paperwork Reduction Act Notice, see the separate instructions.   Cat. No. 11344L   Schedule E (Form 1040) 2013

Form **4562**	**Depreciation and Amortization**	OMB No. 1545-0172
Department of the Treasury Internal Revenue Service (99)	**(Including Information on Listed Property)** ▶ See separate instructions. ▶ Attach to your tax return.	20**13** Attachment Sequence No. **179**

Name(s) shown on return	Business or activity to which this form relates	Identifying number
John R. (Deceased) & Mary L. Smith		234-00-7890

Part I   **Election To Expense Certain Property Under Section 179**
Note: *If you have any listed property, complete Part V before you complete Part I.*

1	Maximum amount (see instructions)	**1**	
2	Total cost of section 179 property placed in service (see instructions)	**2**	
3	Threshold cost of section 179 property before reduction in limitation (see instructions)	**3**	
4	Reduction in limitation. Subtract line 3 from line 2. If zero or less, enter -0-	**4**	
5	Dollar limitation for tax year. Subtract line 4 from line 1. If zero or less, enter -0-. If married filing separately, see instructions	**5**	

6	(a) Description of property	(b) Cost (business use only)	(c) Elected cost

7	Listed property. Enter the amount from line 29	**7**		
8	Total elected cost of section 179 property. Add amounts in column (c), lines 6 and 7		**8**	
9	Tentative deduction. Enter the **smaller** of line 5 or line 8		**9**	
10	Carryover of disallowed deduction from line 13 of your 2012 Form 4562		**10**	
11	Business income limitation. Enter the smaller of business income (not less than zero) or line 5 (see instructions)		**11**	
12	Section 179 expense deduction. Add lines 9 and 10, but do not enter more than line 11		**12**	
13	Carryover of disallowed deduction to 2014. Add lines 9 and 10, less line 12 ▶	**13**		

Note: *Do not use Part II or Part III below for listed property. Instead, use Part V.*

Part II   **Special Depreciation Allowance and Other Depreciation (Do not** include listed property.) (See instructions.)

14	Special depreciation allowance for qualified property (other than listed property) placed in service during the tax year (see instructions)	**14**	
15	Property subject to section 168(f)(1) election	**15**	
16	Other depreciation (including ACRS)	**16**	

Part III   **MACRS Depreciation (Do not** include listed property.) (See instructions.)

Section A

17	MACRS deductions for assets placed in service in tax years beginning before 2013	**17**	1,211
18	If you are electing to group any assets placed in service during the tax year into one or more general asset accounts, check here . . . . ▶ ☐		

Section B—Assets Placed in Service During 2013 Tax Year Using the General Depreciation System

(a) Classification of property	(b) Month and year placed in service	(c) Basis for depreciation (business/investment use only—see instructions)	(d) Recovery period	(e) Convention	(f) Method	(g) Depreciation deduction
19a 3-year property						
b 5-year property						
c 7-year property						
d 10-year property						
e 15-year property						
f 20-year property						
g 25-year property			25 yrs.		S/L	
h Residential rental property			27.5 yrs.	MM	S/L	
			27.5 yrs.	MM	S/L	
i Nonresidential real property			39 yrs.	MM	S/L	
				MM	S/L	

Section C—Assets Placed in Service During 2013 Tax Year Using the Alternative Depreciation System

20a Class life					S/L	
b 12-year			12 yrs.		S/L	
c 40-year	4-13	50,000	40 yrs.	MM	S/L	886

Part IV   **Summary** (See instructions.)

21	Listed property. Enter amount from line 28	**21**	
22	**Total.** Add amounts from line 12, lines 14 through 17, lines 19 and 20 in column (g), and line 21. Enter here and on the appropriate lines of your return. Partnerships and S corporations—see instructions .	**22**	2,097
23	For assets shown above and placed in service during the current year, enter the portion of the basis attributable to section 263A costs	**23**		

For Paperwork Reduction Act Notice, see separate instructions.   Cat. No. 12906N   Form **4562** (2013)

Form **1041**	Department of the Treasury—Internal Revenue Service **U.S. Income Tax Return for Estates and Trusts**	20**13**	OMB No. 1545-0092

▶ Information about Form 1041 and its separate instructions is at *www.irs.gov/form1041.*

| For calendar year 2013 or fiscal year beginning | April 9 , 2013, and ending | December 31, 2013 |

A Check all that apply:

☑ Decedent's estate
☐ Simple trust
☐ Complex trust
☐ Qualified disability trust
☐ ESBT (S portion only)
☐ Grantor type trust
☐ Bankruptcy estate-Ch. 7
☐ Bankruptcy estate-Ch. 11
☐ Pooled income fund

Name of estate or trust (if a grantor type trust, see the instructions.)
Estate of John R. Smith

Name and title of fiduciary
Charles R. Smith, Executor

Number, street, and room or suite no. (If a P.O. box, see the instructions.)
6406 Mayflower St.

City or town, state or province, country, and ZIP or foreign postal code
Juneville, ME 00000

C Employer identification number
10-0123456

D Date entity created
04/09/2013

E Nonexempt charitable and split-interest trusts, check applicable box(es). see instructions.
☐ Described in sec. 4947(a)(1). Check here if not a private foundation . . ▶ ☐
☐ Described in sec. 4947(a)(2)

B Number of Schedules K-1 attached (see instructions) ▶

F Check applicable boxes:
☑ Initial return ☐ Final return ☐ Amended return
☐ Change in trust's name ☐ Change in fiduciary ☐ Change in fiduciary's name
☐ Net operating loss carryback
☐ Change in fiduciary's address

G Check here if the estate or filing trust made a section 645 election . . . . . . ▶ ☐   Trust EIN ▶

Income	1	Interest income	1	2,250
	2a	Total ordinary dividends	2a	750
	b	Qualified dividends allocable to: (1) Beneficiaries ___179___ (2) Estate or trust ___571___		
	3	Business income or (loss). Attach Schedule C or C-EZ (Form 1040) . . .	3	
	4	Capital gain or (loss). Attach Schedule D (Form 1041)	4	
	5	Rents, royalties, partnerships, other estates and trusts, etc. Attach Schedule E (Form 1040)	5	
	6	Farm income or (loss). Attach Schedule F (Form 1040)	6	
	7	Ordinary gain or (loss). Attach Form 4797	7	
	8	Other income. List type and amount ___IRD Salary and Vacation Pay___	8	12,000
	9	**Total income. Combine lines 1, 2a, and 3 through 8** . . . . . ▶	9	15,000
Deductions	10	Interest. Check if Form 4952 is attached ▶ ☐	10	
	11	Taxes	11	2,250
	12	Fiduciary fees	12	
	13	Charitable deduction (from Schedule A, line 7)	13	
	14	Attorney, accountant, and return preparer fees	14	1,325
	15a	Other deductions **not** subject to the 2% floor (attach schedule) . . .	15a	
	b	Net operating loss deduction (see instructions)	15b	
	c	Allowable miscellaneous itemized deductions subject to the 2% floor .	15c	
	16	Add lines 10 through 15c . . . . ▶	16	3,575
	17	Adjusted total income or (loss). Subtract line 16 from line 9 . .	17	11,425
	18	Income distribution deduction (from Schedule B, line 15). Attach Schedules K-1 (Form 1041)	18	2,000
	19	Estate tax deduction including certain generation-skipping taxes (attach computation) . . .	19	
	20	Exemption	20	600
	21	Add lines 18 through 20 . . . . ▶	21	2,600
	22	Taxable income. Subtract line 21 from line 17. If a loss, see instructions	22	8,825
	23	**Total tax** (from Schedule G, line 7)	23	1,981
Tax and Payments	24	**Payments: a** 2013 estimated tax payments and amount applied from 2012 return . . .	24a	
	b	Estimated tax payments allocated to beneficiaries (from Form 1041-T) . . .	24b	
	c	Subtract line 24b from line 24a	24c	
	d	Tax paid with Form 7004 (see instructions)	24d	
	e	Federal income tax withheld. If any is from Form(s) 1099, check ▶ ☐ . . .	24e	
		Other payments: **f** Form 2439 _____ ; **g** Form 4136 _____ ; Total ▶	24h	
	25	**Total payments. Add lines 24c through 24e, and 24h** . . . . . ▶	25	
	26	Estimated tax penalty (see instructions)	26	
	27	**Tax due.** If line 25 is smaller than the total of lines 23 and 26, enter amount owed . . .	27	1,981
	28	**Overpayment.** If line 25 is larger than the total of lines 23 and 26, enter amount overpaid	28	
	29	Amount of line 28 to be: **a** Credited to 2014 estimated tax ▶ _____ ; **b** Refunded ▶	29	

Sign Here

Under penalties of perjury, I declare that I have examined this return, including accompanying schedules and statements, and to the best of my knowledge and belief, it is true, correct, and complete. Declaration of preparer (other than taxpayer) is based on all information of which preparer has any knowledge.

▶ _Charles R. Smith_   03/24/2014 ▶
Signature of fiduciary or officer representing fiduciary   Date   EIN of fiduciary if a financial institution

May the IRS discuss this return with the preparer shown below (see instr.)? ☐ Yes ☐ No

Paid Preparer Use Only

Print/Type preparer's name	Preparer's signature	Date	Check ☐ if self-employed	PTIN
Firm's name ▶			Firm's EIN ▶	
Firm's address ▶			Phone no.	

For Paperwork Reduction Act Notice, see the separate instructions.   Cat. No. 11370H   Form **1041** (2013)

Form 1041 (2013)   Page **2**

Schedule A	**Charitable Deduction.** Do not complete for a simple trust or a pooled income fund.		
1	Amounts paid or permanently set aside for charitable purposes from gross income (see instructions)	**1**	
2	Tax-exempt income allocable to charitable contributions (see instructions)	**2**	
3	Subtract line 2 from line 1	**3**	
4	Capital gains for the tax year allocated to corpus and paid or permanently set aside for charitable purposes	**4**	
5	Add lines 3 and 4	**5**	
6	Section 1202 exclusion allocable to capital gains paid or permanently set aside for charitable purposes (see instructions)	**6**	
7	**Charitable deduction.** Subtract line 6 from line 5. Enter here and on page 1, line 13	**7**	

Schedule B	**Income Distribution Deduction**		
1	Adjusted total income (see instructions)	**1**	11,425
2	Adjusted tax-exempt interest	**2**	
3	Total net gain from Schedule D (Form 1041), line 19, column (1) (see instructions)	**3**	
4	Enter amount from Schedule A, line 4 (minus any allocable section 1202 exclusion)	**4**	
5	Capital gains for the tax year included on Schedule A, line 1 (see instructions)	**5**	
6	Enter any gain from page 1, line 4, as a negative number. If page 1, line 4, is a loss, enter the loss as a positive number	**6**	
7	**Distributable net income.** Combine lines 1 through 6. If zero or less, enter -0-	**7**	11,425
8	If a complex trust, enter accounting income for the tax year as determined under the governing instrument and applicable local law **8**		
9	Income required to be distributed currently	**9**	
10	Other amounts paid, credited, or otherwise required to be distributed	**10**	2,000
11	Total distributions. Add lines 9 and 10. If greater than line 8, see instructions	**11**	2,000
12	Enter the amount of tax-exempt income included on line 11	**12**	
13	Tentative income distribution deduction. Subtract line 12 from line 11	**13**	2,000
14	Tentative income distribution deduction. Subtract line 2 from line 7. If zero or less, enter -0-	**14**	11,425
15	**Income distribution deduction.** Enter the smaller of line 13 or line 14 here and on page 1, line 18	**15**	2,000

Schedule G	**Tax Computation** (see instructions)			
1	**Tax: a** Tax on taxable income (see instructions)	**1a**	1,981	
	b Tax on lump-sum distributions. Attach Form 4972	**1b**		
	c Alternative minimum tax (from Schedule I (Form 1041), line 56)	**1c**		
	d **Total.** Add lines 1a through 1c	▶ **1d**		1,981
2a	Foreign tax credit. Attach Form 1116	**2a**		
b	General business credit. Attach Form 3800	**2b**		
c	Credit for prior year minimum tax. Attach Form 8801	**2c**		
d	Bond credits. Attach Form 8912	**2d**		
e	**Total credits.** Add lines 2a through 2d	▶ **2e**		
3	Subtract line 2e from line 1d. If zero or less, enter -0-	**3**		1,981
4	Net investment income tax from Form 8960, line 21	**4**		
5	Recapture taxes. Check if from: ☐ Form 4255 ☐ Form 8611	**5**		
6	Household employment taxes. Attach Schedule H (Form 1040)	**6**		
7	**Total tax.** Add lines 3 through 6. Enter here and on page 1, line 23	▶ **7**		1,981

	Other Information	Yes	No
1	Did the estate or trust receive tax-exempt income? If "Yes," attach a computation of the allocation of expenses. Enter the amount of tax-exempt interest income and exempt-interest dividends ▶ $ _____		✓
2	Did the estate or trust receive all or any part of the earnings (salary, wages, and other compensation) of any individual by reason of a contract assignment or similar arrangement?		✓
3	At any time during calendar year 2013, did the estate or trust have an interest in or a signature or other authority over a bank, securities, or other financial account in a foreign country?		✓
	See the instructions for exceptions and filing requirements for FinCEN Form 114. If "Yes," enter the name of the foreign country ▶		
4	During the tax year, did the estate or trust receive a distribution from, or was it the grantor of, or transferor to, a foreign trust? If "Yes," the estate or trust may have to file Form 3520. See instructions		✓
5	Did the estate or trust receive, or pay, any qualified residence interest on seller-provided financing? If "Yes," see the instructions for required attachment		✓
6	If this is an estate or a complex trust making the section 663(b) election, check here (see instructions) ▶ ☐		
7	To make a section 643(e)(3) election, attach Schedule D (Form 1041), and check here (see instructions) ▶ ☐		
8	If the decedent's estate has been open for more than 2 years, attach an explanation for the delay in closing the estate, and check here ▶ ☐		
9	Are any present or future trust beneficiaries skip persons? See instructions		✓

Form **1041** (2013)

¶105

SCHEDULE I (Form 1041) Department of the Treasury Internal Revenue Service	**Alternative Minimum Tax—Estates and Trusts** ► Attach to Form 1041. ► Information about Schedule I (Form 1041) and its separate instructions is at *www.irs.gov/form1041.*	OMB No. 1545-0092 20**13**

Name of estate or trust	Employer identification number
Estate of John R. Smith	10-0123456

Part I Estate's or Trust's Share of Alternative Minimum Taxable Income

1	Adjusted total income or (loss) (from Form 1041, line 17)	**1**	11,425
2	Interest	**2**	
3	Taxes	**3**	1,981
4	Miscellaneous itemized deductions (from Form 1041, line 15c)	**4**	
5	Refund of taxes	**5**	( )
6	Depletion (difference between regular tax and AMT)	**6**	
7	Net operating loss deduction. Enter as a positive amount	**7**	
8	Interest from specified private activity bonds exempt from the regular tax	**8**	
9	Qualified small business stock (see instructions)	**9**	
10	Exercise of incentive stock options (excess of AMT income over regular tax income)	**10**	
11	Other estates and trusts (amount from Schedule K-1 (Form 1041), box 12, code A)	**11**	
12	Electing large partnerships (amount from Schedule K-1 (Form 1065-B), box 6)	**12**	
13	Disposition of property (difference between AMT and regular tax gain or loss)	**13**	
14	Depreciation on assets placed in service after 1986 (difference between regular tax and AMT)	**14**	
15	Passive activities (difference between AMT and regular tax income or loss)	**15**	
16	Loss limitations (difference between AMT and regular tax income or loss)	**16**	
17	Circulation costs (difference between regular tax and AMT)	**17**	
18	Long-term contracts (difference between AMT and regular tax income)	**18**	
19	Mining costs (difference between regular tax and AMT)	**19**	
20	Research and experimental costs (difference between regular tax and AMT)	**20**	
21	Income from certain installment sales before January 1, 1987	**21**	( )
22	Intangible drilling costs preference	**22**	
23	Other adjustments, including income-based related adjustments	**23**	
24	Alternative tax net operating loss deduction (See the instructions for the limitation that applies.)	**24**	( )
25	Adjusted alternative minimum taxable income. Combine lines 1 through 24	**25**	13,406
	Note: *Complete Part II below before going to line 26.*		
26	Income distribution deduction from Part II, line 44	**26** 2,000	
27	Estate tax deduction (from Form 1041, line 19)	**27**	
28	Add lines 26 and 27	**28**	2,000
29	Estate's or trust's share of alternative minimum taxable income. Subtract line 28 from line 25	**29**	11,406
	If line 29 is: • $23,100 or less, stop here and enter -0- on Form 1041, Schedule G, line 1c. The estate or trust is not liable for the alternative minimum tax. • Over $23,100, but less than $169,350, go to line 45. • $169,350 or more, enter the amount from line 29 on line 51 and go to line 52.		

Part II Income Distribution Deduction on a Minimum Tax Basis

30	Adjusted alternative minimum taxable income (see instructions)	**30**	13,406
31	Adjusted tax-exempt interest (other than amounts included on line 8)	**31**	
32	Total net gain from Schedule D (Form 1041), line 19, column (1). If a loss, enter -0-	**32**	
33	Capital gains for the tax year allocated to corpus and paid or permanently set aside for charitable purposes (from Form 1041, Schedule A, line 4)	**33**	
34	Capital gains paid or permanently set aside for charitable purposes from gross income (see instructions)	**34**	
35	Capital gains computed on a minimum tax basis included on line 25	**35**	( )
36	Capital losses computed on a minimum tax basis included on line 25. Enter as a positive amount	**36**	
37	Distributable net alternative minimum taxable income (DNAMTI). Combine lines 30 through 36. If zero or less, enter -0-	**37**	13,406
38	Income required to be distributed currently (from Form 1041, Schedule B, line 9)	**38**	
39	Other amounts paid, credited, or otherwise required to be distributed (from Form 1041, Schedule B, line 10)	**39**	2,000
40	Total distributions. Add lines 38 and 39	**40**	2,000
41	Tax-exempt income included on line 40 (other than amounts included on line 8)	**41**	
42	Tentative income distribution deduction on a minimum tax basis. Subtract line 41 from line 40	**42**	2,000

For Paperwork Reduction Act Notice, see the Instructions for Form 1041.   Cat. No. 51517Q   Schedule I (Form 1041) (2013)

Schedule I (Form 1041) (2013)   Page **2**

Part II	Income Distribution Deduction on a Minimum Tax Basis *(continued)*			
43	Tentative income distribution deduction on a minimum tax basis. Subtract line 31 from line 37. If zero or less, enter -0-		**43**	13,406
44	**Income distribution deduction on a minimum tax basis.** Enter the smaller of line 42 or line 43. Enter here and on line 26		**44**	2,000

Part III	Alternative Minimum Tax					
45	Exemption amount			**45**	$23,100	00
46	Enter the amount from line 29	**46**	11,406			
47	Phase-out of exemption amount	**47**	$76,950	00		
48	Subtract line 47 from line 46. If zero or less, enter -0-	**48**	0			
49	Multiply line 48 by 25% (.25)			**49**	0	
50	Subtract line 49 from line 45. If zero or less, enter -0-			**50**	23,100	
51	Subtract line 50 from line 46			**51**	0	
52	Go to Part IV of Schedule I to figure line 52 if the estate or trust has qualified dividends or has a gain on lines 18a and 19 of column (2) of Schedule D (Form 1041) (as refigured for the AMT, if necessary). Otherwise, if line 51 is—					
	• $179,500 or less, multiply line 51 by 26% (.26).					
	• Over $179,500, multiply line 51 by 28% (.28) and subtract $3,590 from the result			**52**	0	
53	Alternative minimum foreign tax credit (see instructions)			**53**		
54	Tentative minimum tax. Subtract line 53 from line 52			**54**	0	
55	Enter the tax from Form 1041, Schedule G, line 1a (minus any foreign tax credit from Schedule G, line 2a)			**55**	1,981	
56	**Alternative minimum tax.** Subtract line 55 from line 54. If zero or less, enter -0-. Enter here and on Form 1041, Schedule G, line 1c			**56**	0	

Part IV	Line 52 Computation Using Maximum Capital Gains Rates			
	Caution: *If you did not complete Part V of Schedule D (Form 1041), the Schedule D Tax Worksheet, or the Qualified Dividends Tax Worksheet in the Instructions for Form 1041, see the instructions before completing this part.*			
57	Enter the amount from line 51		**57**	
58	Enter the amount from Schedule D (Form 1041), line 26, line 13 of the Schedule D Tax Worksheet, or line 4 of the Qualified Dividends Tax Worksheet in the Instructions for Form 1041, whichever applies (as refigured for the AMT, if necessary)	**58**		
59	Enter the amount from Schedule D (Form 1041), line 18b, column (2) (as refigured for the AMT, if necessary). If you did not complete Schedule D for the regular tax or the AMT, enter -0-	**59**		
60	If you did not complete a Schedule D Tax Worksheet for the regular tax or the AMT, enter the amount from line 58. Otherwise, add lines 58 and 59 and enter the **smaller** of that result or the amount from line 10 of the Schedule D Tax Worksheet (as refigured for the AMT, if necessary) . .	**60**		
61	Enter the **smaller** of line 57 or line 60		**61**	
62	Subtract line 61 from line 57		**62**	
63	If line 62 is $179,500 or less, multiply line 62 by 26% (.26). Otherwise, multiply line 62 by 28% (.28) and subtract $3,590 from the result . . . . ▶		**63**	
64	Maximum amount subject to the 0% rate	**64**	$2,450	00
65	Enter the amount from line 27 of Schedule D (Form 1041), line 14 of the Schedule D Tax Worksheet, or line 5 of the Qualified Dividends Tax Worksheet in the Instructions for Form 1041, whichever applies (as figured for the regular tax). If you did not complete Schedule D or either worksheet for the regular tax, enter the amount from Form 1041, line 22; but do not enter less than -0-	**65**		
66	Subtract line 65 from line 64. If zero or less, enter -0-	**66**		
67	Enter the **smaller** of line 57 or line 58	**67**		
68	Enter the **smaller** of line 66 or line 67. This amount is taxed at 0% . .	**68**		
69	Subtract line 68 from line 67	**69**		

Schedule I (Form 1041) (2013)

¶105

661113

| | Final K-1 | | Amended K-1 | OMB No. 1545-0092 |

Schedule K-1
(Form 1041)
Department of the Treasury
Internal Revenue Service

2013

For calendar year 2013,
or tax year beginning ___April 9___ , 2013,
and ending ___December 31___, 20 __13__

Beneficiary's Share of Income, Deductions, Credits, etc.

▶ See back of form and instructions.

| Part I | Information About the Estate or Trust |

A Estate's or trust's employer identification number

10-0123456

B Estate's or trust's name

Estate of John R. Smith

C Fiduciary's name, address, city, state, and ZIP code

Charles R. Smith, Executor
6406 Mayflower Street
Juneville, ME 00000

D ☐ Check if Form 1041-T was filed and enter the date it was filed
_____

E ☐ Check if this is the final Form 1041 for the estate or trust

| Part II | Information About the Beneficiary |

F Beneficiary's identifying number
123-00-6789

G Beneficiary's name, address, city, state, and ZIP code

James Smith
6407 Mayflower Street
Juneville, ME 00000

H ☒ Domestic beneficiary   ☐ Foreign beneficiary

Part III	Beneficiary's Share of Current Year Income, Deductions, Credits, and Other Items
1 Interest income	**11** Final year deductions
300	
2a Ordinary dividends	
100	
2b Qualified dividends	
100	
3 Net short-term capital gain	
4a Net long-term capital gain	
4b 28% rate gain	**12** Alternative minimum tax adjustment
4c Unrecaptured section 1250 gain	
5 Other portfolio and nonbusiness income	
1,600	
6 Ordinary business income	
7 Net rental real estate income	
	13 Credits and credit recapture
8 Other rental income	
9 Directly apportioned deductions	
	14 Other information
10 Estate tax deduction	

*See attached statement for additional information.

Note. A statement must be attached showing the beneficiary's share of income and directly apportioned deductions from each business, rental real estate, and other rental activity.

For IRS Use Only

For Paperwork Reduction Act Notice, see the Instructions for Form 1041.   IRS.gov/form1041   Cat. No. 11380D   **Schedule K-1 (Form 1041) 2013**

¶105

Table A. Checklist of Forms and Due Dates For Executor, Administrator, or Personal Representative

Form No.	Title	Due Date**
SS-4	Application for Employer Identification Number	As soon as possible. The identification number must be included in returns, statements, and other documents.
56	Notice Concerning Fiduciary Relationship	As soon as all necessary information is available.*
706	United States Estate (and Generation-Skipping Transfer) Tax Return	9 months after date of decedent's death.
706-A	United States Additional Estate Tax Return	6 months after cessation or disposition of special-use valuation property.
706-GS(D)	Generation-Skipping Transfer Tax Return for Distributions	Generally, April 15th of the year after the distribution.
706-GS(D-1)	Notification of Distribution From a Generation-Skipping Trust	Generally, April 15th of the year after the distribution.
706-GS(T)	Generation-Skipping Transfer Tax Return for Terminations	Generally, April 15th of the year after the taxable termination.
706-NA	United States Estate (and Generation-Skipping Transfer) Tax Return, Estate of nonresident not a citizen of the United States	9 months after date of decedent's death.
709	United State Gift (and Generation-Skipping Transfer) Tax Return	April 15th of the year after the gift was made.
712	Life Insurance Statement	Part I to be filed with estate tax return.
1040	U.S. Individual Income Tax Return	Generally, April 15th of the year after death.**
1040NR	U.S. Nonresident Alien Income Tax Return	See form instructions.
1041	U.S. Income Tax Return for Estates and Trusts	15th day of 4th month after end of estate's tax year.**
1041-T	Allocation of Estimated Tax Payments to Beneficiaries	65th day after end of estate's tax year.
1041-ES	Estimated Income Tax for Estates and Trusts	Generally, April 15th, June 15th, Sept. 15th, and Jan. 15th for calendar-year filers.**
1042	Annual Withholding Tax Return for U.S. Source Income of Foreign Persons	March 15th.**
1042-S	Foreign Person's U.S. Source Income Subject to Withholding	March 15th.**
4768	Application for Extension of Time To File a Return and/or Pay U.S. Estate (and Generation-Skipping Transfer) Taxes	See form instructions.
4810	Request for Prompt Assessment Under Internal Revenue Code Section 6501(d)	As soon as possible after filing Form 1040 or Form 1041.
4868	Application for Automatic Extension of Time To File U.S. Individual Income Tax Return	April 15th.**
5495	Request for Discharge From Personal Liability Under Internal Revenue Code Section 2204 or 6905	See form instructions.
7004	Application for Automatic Extension of Time to File Certain Business Income Tax, Information, and Other Returns	15th day of 4th month after end of estate's tax year.**
8300	Report of Cash Payments Over $10,000 Received in a Trade or Business	15th day after the date of the transaction.
8822	Change of Address	As soon as the address is changed.

* A personal representative must report the termination of the estate, in writing, to the Internal Revenue Service. Form 56 can be used for this purpose.
** If the due date falls on a Saturday, Sunday, or legal holiday, file on the next business day.

¶105

Table B. Worksheet To Reconcile Amounts Reported in Name of Decedent on Information Returns (Forms W-2, 1099-INT, 1099-DIV, etc.)

Keep for Your Records

Name of Decedent	Date of Death	Decedent's Social Security Number		
Name of Personal Representative, Executor, or Administrator		Estate's Employer Identification Number (If Any)		

Source (list each payer)	A Enter total amount shown on information return	B Enter part of amount in column A reportable on decedent's final return	C Amount reportable on estate's or beneficiary's income tax return (column A minus column B)	D Part of column C that is *income in respect of a decedent*
1. Wages				
2. Interest income				
3. Dividends				
4. State income tax refund				
5. Capital gains				
6. Pension income				
7. Rents, royalties				
8. Taxes withheld*				
9. Other items, such as social security, business and farm income or loss, unemployment compensation, etc.				

* List each withholding agent (employer, etc.)

¶105

How To Get Tax Help

Whether it's help with a tax issue, preparing your tax return or a need for a free publication or form, get the help you need the way you want it: online, use a smart phone, call or walk in to an IRS office or volunteer site near you.

Free help with your tax return. You can get free help preparing your return nationwide from IRS-certified volunteers. The Volunteer Income Tax Assistance (VITA) program helps low-to-moderate income, elderly, people with disabilities, and limited English proficient taxpayers. The Tax Counseling for the Elderly (TCE) program helps taxpayers age 60 and older with their tax returns. Most VITA and TCE sites offer free electronic filing and all volunteers will let you know about credits and deductions you may be entitled to claim. In addition, some VITA and TCE sites provide taxpayers the opportunity to prepare their own return with help from an IRS-certified volunteer. To find the nearest VITA or TCE site, you can use the VITA Locator Tool on IRS.gov, download the IRS2Go app, or call 1-800-906-9887.

As part of the TCE program, AARP offers the Tax-Aide counseling program. To find the nearest AARP Tax-Aide site, visit AARP's website at *www.aarp.org/money/taxaide* or call 1-888-227-7669. For more information on these programs, go to IRS.gov and enter "VITA" in the search box.

Internet. IRS.gov and **IRS2Go** are ready when you are —24 hours a day, 7 days a week.

- Download the free IRS2Go app from the iTunes app store or from Google Play. Use it to check your refund status, order transcripts of your tax returns or tax account, watch the IRS YouTube channel, get IRS news as soon as it's released to the public, subscribe to filing season updates or daily tax tips, and follow the IRS Twitter news feed, @IRSnews, to get the latest federal tax news, including information about tax law changes and important IRS programs.
- Check the status of your 2013 refund with the *Where's My Refund?* application on IRS.gov or download the IRS2Go app and select the *Refund Status* option. The IRS issues more than 9 out of 10 refunds in less than 21 days. Using these applications, you can start checking on the status of your return within 24 hours after we receive your e-filed return or 4 weeks after you mail a paper return. You will also be given a personalized refund date as soon as the IRS processes your tax return and approves your refund. The IRS updates *Where's My Refund?* every 24 hours, usually overnight, so you only need to check once a day.
- Use the *Interactive Tax Assistant* (ITA) to research your tax questions. No need to wait on the phone or stand in line. The ITA is available 24 hours a day, 7 days a week, and provides you with a variety of tax information related to general filing topics, deductions, credits, and income. When you reach the response screen, you can print the entire interview and the final response

for your records. New subject areas are added on a regular basis.

Answers not provided through ITA may be found in *Tax Trails*, one of the Tax Topics on IRS.gov which contain general individual and business tax information or by searching the *IRS Tax Map*, which includes an **international subject index.** You can use the **IRS Tax Map,** to search publications and instructions by topic or keyword. The IRS Tax Map integrates forms and publications into one research tool and provides single-point access to tax law information by subject. When the user searches the IRS Tax Map, they will be provided with links to related content in existing IRS publications, forms and instructions, questions and answers, and Tax Topics.

- Coming this filing season, you can immediately view and print for free all 5 types of individual federal tax transcripts (tax returns, tax account, record of account, wage and income statement, and certification of non-filing) using **Get Transcript.** You can also ask the IRS to mail a return or an account transcript to you. Only the mail option is available by choosing the *Tax Records* option on the IRS2Go app by selecting *Mail Transcript* on IRS.gov or by calling 1-800-908-9946. Tax return and tax account transcripts are generally available for the current year and the past three years.
- Determine if you are eligible for the EITC and estimate the amount of the credit with the *Earned Income Tax Credit (EITC) Assistant.*
- Visit *Understanding Your IRS Notice or Letter* to get answers to questions about a notice or letter you received from the IRS.
- If you received the First Time Homebuyer Credit, you can use the *First Time Homebuyer Credit Account Look-up* tool for information on your repayments and account balance.
- Check the status of your amended return using *Where's My Amended Return?* Go to IRS.gov and enter *Where's My Amended Return?* in the search box. You can generally expect your amended return to be processed up to 12 weeks from the date we receive it. It can take up to 3 weeks from the date you mailed it to show up in our system.
- Make a payment using one of several safe and convenient electronic payment options available on IRS.gov. Select the Payment tab on the front page of IRS.gov for more information.
- Determine if you are eligible and apply for an *online payment agreement,* if you owe more tax than you can pay today.
- Figure your income tax withholding with the *IRS Withholding Calculator* on IRS.gov. Use it if you've had too much or too little withheld, your personal situation has changed, you're starting a new job or you just want to see if you're having the right amount withheld.
- Determine if you might be subject to the Alternative Minimum Tax by using the *Alternative Minimum Tax Assistant* on IRS.gov.

- Request an **Electronic Filing PIN** by going to IRS.gov and entering *Electronic Filing PIN* in the search box.
- Download forms, instructions and publications, including accessible versions for people with disabilities.
- Locate the nearest **Taxpayer Assistance Center (TAC)** using the *Office Locator* tool on IRS.gov, or choose the *Contact Us* option on the IRS2Go app and search *Local Offices.* An employee can answer questions about your tax account or help you set up a payment plan. Before you visit, check the *Office Locator* on IRS.gov, or *Local Offices* under Contact Us on IRS2Go to confirm the address, phone number, days and hours of operation, and the services provided. If you have a special need, such as a disability, you can request an appointment. Call the local number listed in the Office Locator, or look in the phone book under United States Government, Internal Revenue Service.
- Apply for an **Employer Identification Number (EIN).** Go to IRS.gov and enter *Apply for an EIN* in the search box.
- Read the Internal Revenue Code, regulations, or other official guidance.
- Read Internal Revenue Bulletins.
- Sign up to receive local and national tax news and more by email. Just click on "subscriptions" above the search box on IRS.gov and choose from a variety of options.

Phone. You can call the IRS, or you can carry it in your pocket with the IRS2Go app on your smart phone or tablet. Download the free IRS2Go app from the iTunes app store or from Google Play.

- Call to locate the nearest volunteer help site, 1-800-906-9887 or you can use the VITA Locator Tool on IRS.gov, or download the IRS2Go app. Low-to-moderate income, elderly, people with disabilities, and limited English proficient taxpayers can get free help with their tax return from the nationwide Volunteer Income Tax Assistance (VITA) program. The Tax Counseling for the Elderly (TCE) program helps taxpayers age 60 and older with their tax returns. Most VITA and TCE sites offer free electronic filing. Some VITA and TCE sites provide IRS-certified volunteers who can help prepare your tax return. Through the TCE program, AARP offers the Tax-Aide counseling program; call 1-888-227-7669 to find the nearest Tax-Aide location.
- Call the automated *Where's My Refund?* information hotline to check the status of your 2013 refund 24 hours a day, 7 days a week at 1-800-829-1954. If you e-file, you can start checking on the status of your return within 24 hours after the IRS receives your tax return or 4 weeks after you've mailed a paper return. The IRS issues more than 9 out of 10 refunds in less than 21 days. *Where's My Refund?* will give you a personalized refund date as soon as the IRS processes your tax return and approves your refund. Before you call this automated hotline, have your 2013 tax return handy so you can enter your social

¶105

security number, your filing status, and the exact whole dollar amount of your refund. The IRS updates *Where's My Refund?* every 24 hours, usually overnight, so you only need to check once a day. Note, the above information is for our automated hotline. Our live phone and walk-in assistors can research the status of your refund only if it's been 21 days or more since you filed electronically or more than 6 weeks since you mailed your paper return.

- Call the *Amended Return Hotline*, 1-866-464-2050, to check the status of your amended return. You can generally expect your amended return to be processed up to 12 weeks from the date we receive it. It can take up to 3 weeks from the date you mailed it to show up in our system.
- Call 1-800-TAX-FORM (1-800-829-3676) to order current-year forms, instructions, publications, and prior-year forms and instructions (limited to 5 years). You should receive your order within 10 business days.
- Call **TeleTax**, 1-800-829-4477, to listen to pre-recorded messages covering general and business tax information. If, between January and April 15, you still have questions about the Form 1040, 1040A, or 1040EZ (like filing requirements, dependents, credits, Schedule D, pensions and IRAs or self-employment taxes), call 1-800-829-1040.
- Call using TTY/TDD equipment, 1-800-829-4059 to ask tax questions or order forms and publications. The TTY/TDD telephone number is for people who are deaf, hard of hearing, or have a speech disability. These individuals can also contact the IRS through relay services such as the *Federal Relay Service*.

Walk-in. You can find a selection of forms, publications and services — in-person.

- Products. You can walk in to some post offices, libraries, and IRS offices to pick up

certain forms, instructions, and publications. Some IRS offices, libraries, and city and county government offices have a collection of products available to photocopy from reproducible proofs.

- Services. You can walk in to your local TAC for face-to-face tax help. An employee can answer questions about your tax account or help you set up a payment plan. Before visiting, use the *Office Locator* tool on IRS.gov, or choose the *Contact Us* option on the IRS2Go app and search *Local Offices* for days and hours of operation, and services provided.

Mail. You can send your order for forms, instructions, and publications to the address below. You should receive a response within 10 business days after your request is received.

Internal Revenue Service
1201 N. Mitsubishi Motorway
Bloomington, IL 61705-6613

The Taxpayer Advocate Service Is Here to Help You. **The Taxpayer Advocate Service (TAS)** is your voice at the IRS. Our job is to ensure that every taxpayer is treated fairly and that you know and understand your rights.

What can TAS do for you? We can offer you free help with IRS problems that you can't resolve on your own. We know this process can be confusing, but the worst thing you can do is nothing at all! TAS can help if you can't resolve your tax problem and:

- Your problem is causing financial difficulties for you, your family, or your business.
- You face (or your business is facing) an immediate threat of adverse action.
- You've tried repeatedly to contact the IRS but no one has responded, or the IRS hasn't responded by the date promised.

If you qualify for our help, you'll be assigned to one advocate who'll be with you at every turn and will do everything possible to resolve your problem. Here's why we can help:

- TAS is an independent organization within the IRS.
- Our advocates know how to work with the IRS.
- Our services are free and tailored to meet your needs.
- We have offices in every state, the District of Columbia, and Puerto Rico.

How can you reach us? If you think TAS can help you, call your local advocate, whose number is in your local directory and at *Taxpayer Advocate*, or call us toll-free at 1-877-777-4778.

How else does TAS help taxpayers?

TAS also works to resolve large-scale, systemic problems that affect many taxpayers. If you know of one of these broad issues, please report it to us through our *Systemic Advocacy Management System*.

Low Income Taxpayer Clinics

Low Income Taxpayer Clinics (LITCs) serve individuals whose income is below a certain level and need to resolve tax problems such as audits, appeals and tax collection disputes. Some clinics can provide information about taxpayer rights and responsibilities in different languages for individuals who speak English as a second language. Visit *Taxpayer Advocate* or see IRS Publication 4134, Low Income Taxpayer Clinic List.

THE FEDERAL GIFT TAX

TABLE OF CONTENTS

LIFETIME GIFTS

The federal gift tax is an excise tax on the privilege of making a gift during your lifetime [IRC Sec. 2502(c)]. The starting point for federal gift taxation is determining whether you have made a "taxable gift" [IRC Sec. 2501(a); see ¶201]. Deciding if a taxable gift has been made is not always as straightforward as it sounds.

¶200 GIFT TAX BASICS

(a) Gift Tax Rules. The American Taxpayer Relief Act of 2012 provides that gifts made after December 31, 2012, will be subject to an exclusion amount of $5,340,000 in 2014. This is an increase from the exclusion amount of $5,250,000 available in 2013. A maximum transfer tax rate of 40 percent will be imposed on gifts in excess of the exclusion amount. The following table summarizes the federal estate tax applicable exclusion amount, gift tax exemption equivalent, and highest marginal tax rate for the years 2010 through 2014.

	2010	2011	2012	2013	2014
Applicable Exclusion Amount	No estate tax	$5,000,000	$5,120,000	$5,250,000	$5,340,000
Gift Tax Exemption Equivalent	$1,000,000	$5,000,000	$5,120,000	$5,250,000	$5,340,000
Highest Marginal Tax Rate	No estate tax, 35% gift tax	35%	35%	40%	40%

Previously made gifts will "consume" part of donor's applicable exclusion amount, but at gift tax rates imposed at the time of the currently made gift. Thus, if a donor made a gift of $1 million in 2010, the person should still be able to make $4,250,000 of additional gifts in 2014 and have such additional gifts "sheltered" from gift tax by the donor's remaining applicable exclusion amount.[1]

(b) Gift Tax Basics. The law provides that the gift tax is imposed on the "transfer of property by gift" by an individual, resident, or nonresident [IRC Sec. 2501(a)(1)]. A gift generally includes any property transferred during someone's lifetime for less than adequate consideration [IRC Sec. 2511(a)]. "Gifts" are defined in Reg. Sec. 25.2511-1(c) as "all transactions whereby property, or property rights or interests are gratuitously passed or conferred upon another, regardless of the means or device employed." IRC Sec. 2511(a) provides further that the gift tax applies to all

---

[1] **¶200** See ¶2202, *infra*, for the Applicable Credit and Exclusion Amount Chart for transfers made in 2006-2014.

gratuitous transfers, whether direct or indirect, whether outright or in trust, and whether the property transferred is real or personal, tangible or intangible [Reg. Sec. 25.2511-1(a)]. The gift tax does not apply, however, to transfers of property that does not have a United States situs, made by a nonresident alien.

The gift tax is levied on an annual basis during the donor's lifetime and is cumulative in nature. The gift tax is computed and reported on Form 709, "United States Gift (and Generation-Skipping Transfer) Tax Return."[2] This form is generally due on the April 15th following the year the gift(s) were made, unless the donor dies during the year in which the gift(s) were made. If you give any one person gifts in 2014 that are valued at more than $14,000, you must report the total gifts to the IRS and may have to pay tax on the gifts. See ¶901 for further discussion of the annual gift tax exclusion. Note that the person who received the gift (the donee) does not have to report the gift to the IRS or pay gift or income tax on its value. Gifts can be in the form of money or property, and include the use of property and are made without expecting to receive something of equal value in return. If you sell something at less than its value or make an interest-free or reduced-interest loan, you may be making a gift.

(c) Fair-Market Value. Adequate consideration is generally the fair-market value of the property that has been transferred. The Treasury Regulations (the Regulations) define fair-market value of property as the price at which the property would change hands between a willing buyer and a willing seller, neither being under any compulsion to buy or to sell, and both having knowledge of relevant facts [Reg. Sec. 25.2512-1].

> **Example 1:** In 2014, Dad sells his car to Child for $5,000. The car is worth $19,000. Dad has made a taxable gift to Child of $14,000 [Reg. Sec. 25.2512-8]. Dad may not owe gift tax on this transfer if he can use his annual gift tax exclusion of $14,000 in 2014 to shelter this below-market transfer from gift tax [See discussion at ¶901].

The gift tax must be paid on all below-fair-market or gratuitous transfers of property that are made during the donor's lifetime unless the Internal Revenue Code (the IRC) specifically excludes that particular transfer. Exceptions exist for certain types of transfers deemed to promote public policy, such as gifts to charity [IRC Sec. 2522] and gifts to one's spouse provided the spouse is a citizen of the United States [IRC Secs. 2056, 2523].

(d) Exceptions to Gift Tax Rule. The following are exceptions to the gift tax rule and therefore are not subject to gift tax:

1. Charitable and marital deductions [IRC Secs. 2522, 2523; see ¶¶910–1107];

2. Annual per donee gift tax exclusion [IRC Sec. 2503(b); see ¶901];

3. Exclusion for a transfer for a benefit of a minor [IRC Sec. 2503(c); see ¶907];

---

[2] See Chapter 17 for a sample completed gift tax return.

4. Exclusion for certain transfers for educational or medical expenses [IRC Sec. 2503(e); see ¶ 908];

5. Exclusion for lending certain artworks to charitable organizations [IRC Sec. 2503(g); see ¶ 909];

6. Exclusion for qualified disclaimers [IRC Sec. 2518; see ¶ 1201]; and

7. Exclusion for transfers of money or other property to a qualified political organization [IRC Sec. 2501(a)(4)]. A qualified political organization is a party, committee, association, fund, or other organization (whether or not incorporated) that is organized and operated primarily for purposes of directly or indirectly accepting contributions or making expenditures, or both, for the purpose of electing, appointing, selecting or nominating public officials to positions in a political organization [IRC Sec. 527(e)(1)];

8. Exclusion for contributions to newsletter funds established and maintained by an individual who holds, has been elected to, or is a candidate for nomination or election to, any federal, state, or local elective public office for use by such individual exclusively for the preparation and circulation of such individual's newsletter [Reg. Sec. 25.2501-1(a)(5); IRC Sec. 527(g)].

It may be surprising to learn that some unexpected types of property transfers raise gift tax issues. These include joint ownership of property, community property, revocable trusts, irrevocable (unchangeable) trusts, disposition of a qualified terminable interest property (QTIP) life income interest, life insurance, and retirement funds. (These are discussed further at ¶ ¶ 207, 1105, 400. See ¶ 211 for a checklist of surprise transfers that may result in a taxable gift.)

(e) Who Must File Form 709. The person who gives the gift (called the "donor") is responsible for paying the gift tax [IRC Sec. 2502(d); Reg. Sec. 25.2502-2]. A donee may be liable for the gift tax if the donor fails to pay but typically the person who receives the gift does not have to report the gift to the IRS or pay gift or income tax on its value [IRC Sec. 6901]. The donor must file IRS Form 709, "United States Gift (and Generation-Skipping Transfer) Tax Return" for gifts to a donee of present interests that exceed the annual gift tax exclusion in the calendar year and for gifts of future interests, regardless of the amount. A $14,000 annual gift tax exclusion is available in 2014.

(f) Why Form 709 Should Be Filed. The gift tax return should be filed by a taxpayer to report a gift of real or personal property, whether tangible or intangible, that has been made either directly or indirectly, in trust, or by any other means. For example, a gift tax return should be filed in the following situations:

1. To report sales or exchanges, not made in the ordinary course of business, where value of the money (or property) received is less than the value of what is sold or exchanged. The gift tax is in addition to any other tax, such as federal income tax, paid or due on the transfer;

2. As part of the exercise or release of a general power of appointment by the individual possessing the power. The holder of a general power of appointment can appoint the property under the power to themselves, their creditors, their estates, or the creditors of their estates. To qualify as a power of appointment, it must be

created by someone other than the holder of the power [For further discussion, see ¶ 205];

3. To report debt forgiveness;

4. To report that the taxpayer has made an interest-free or below market interest rate loan [For further discussion, see ¶ 204];

5. To report transferring the benefits of an insurance policy;

6. To report certain property settlements in conjunction with a divorce [For further discussion, see ¶ 203];

7. To report the giving up of some amount of annuity in exchange for the creation of a survivor annuity [For further discussion, see ¶ 204];

8. To report bonds that are exempt from federal income tax but not exempt from federal gift tax;

9. To report certain transfers under IRC Secs. 2701 and 2702 to a family member of interests in corporations, partnerships, and trusts [For further discussion, see ¶ 500];

10. To report the lapse of any voting or liquidation right if such is a gift under IRC Sec. 2704 [For further discussion, see ¶ 512];

11. To report a gift to a spouse of a terminable interest that does not qualify as a life estate with power of appointment as discussed in ¶ 1107.

12. To make the Qualified Terminable Interest Property (QTIP) election described in Form 709, Line 12. Election Out of QTIP Treatment of Annuities. IRC Sec. 2523(f)(6) creates an automatic QTIP election for gifts of joint and survivor annuities where the spouses are the only possible recipients of the annuity prior to the death of the last surviving spouse. The donor spouse can elect out of QTIP treatment, however, by checking the box on Form 709, line 12 and entering the item number from Schedule A for the annuities for which the spouse is making the election [For further discussion, see ¶ 1708];

13. To report a gift that a taxpayer is splitting with a spouse;

14. To report gifts that are more than the annual exclusion for the year to someone other than a spouse unless the gift qualifies under one of the exceptions as discussed in ¶ 200(d);

15. To report gifts that a taxpayer gave to someone (other than a spouse) when the recipient cannot actually possess, enjoy, or receive income from the gift until some time in the future;

16. To report transfers subject either to the gift tax and/or the generation-skipping transfer (GST) tax [see ¶ 2500];

17. To compute the federal gift and/or GST tax due on any taxable transfers [see ¶ 2500];

18. To allocate GST exemption to property transferred during the transferor's lifetime [see ¶ 2509]. The instructions for Form 709 appear in Appendix A. Completed Form 709 with line-by-line explanations appears in Chapter 17,

19. To limit the ability of the IRS many years after a gift has been made to revalue the gift for purposes of determining the applicable estate tax bracket and the available unified credit at death, it is a good idea to file a protective gift tax return where you adequately disclose gifts made that year [see ¶ 1910];

20. A nonresident alien must file a gift tax return if the taxpayer's outright gifts to his or her spouse, who is not a U.S. citizen, total more than $145,000 in 2014.

(g) When Form 709 Not Required. In the following situations, taxpayers need not file Form 709:

1. The taxpayer did not give more than $14,000 to any one donee;

2. If the taxpayer only made tax-deductible gifts to charities, the taxpayer need not file Form 709 as long as the taxpayer transferred his or her entire interest in the property to qualifying charities. If, however, the taxpayer transferred only a partial interest, or transferred part of his or her interest to someone other than a charity, the taxpayer must still file Form 709 to report all of his or her gifts to charities. Note that if the taxpayer is required to file a Form 709 to report noncharitable gifts and the taxpayer also made gifts to charities, the taxpayer must include all gifts to charities on the return;

3. If the taxpayer made a transfer to a political organization (defined in IRC Sec. 527(e)(1)) for the use of the organization, the taxpayer need not file Form 709;

4. If the taxpayer paid an amount on behalf of an individual to a qualifying domestic or foreign educational organization as tuition for the education or training of the individual, the taxpayer need not file Form 709 to report that transfer. A qualifying educational organization is one that normally maintains a regular faculty and curriculum and normally has a regularly enrolled body of pupils or students in attendance at the place where its educational activities are regularly carried on. The payment must be made directly to the qualifying educational organization and it must be for tuition. No educational exclusion is allowed for amounts paid for books, supplies, room and board, or other similar expenses that are not direct tuition costs. To the extent that the payment to the educational organization was for something other than tuition, it is a gift to the individual for whose benefit it was made, and may be offset by the annual exclusion if it is otherwise available. Contributions to a qualified tuition program (QTP) on behalf of a designated beneficiary do not qualify for the educational exclusion [see ¶ 1708];

5. If the taxpayer paid an amount on behalf of an individual to a person or institution that provided medical care for the individual, the taxpayer need not file Form 709 to report the payment. However, the payment must be to the care provider and the payment must be for the diagnosis, cure, mitigation, treatment, or prevention of disease or for the purpose of affecting any structure or function of the body, or for transportation primarily for and essential to medical care. Medical care also in-cludes amounts paid for medical insurance on behalf of any individual. The medical exclusion does not apply to amounts paid for medical care that are reimbursed by the donee's insurance. If payment for a medical expense is reimbursed by the donee's insurance company, the payment for that expense, to the extent of the reimbursed amount, is not eligible for the medical exclusion and the taxpayer is

considered to have made a gift to the donee of the reimbursed amount. To the extent that the payment was for something other than medical care, it is a gift to the individual on whose behalf the payment was made and may be offset by the annual exclusion if it is otherwise available [For further discussion, see ¶ 908].

(h) When Form 709 Should Be Filed. Because the gift tax is determined on a calendar year basis, the gift tax return and gift tax are due when the taxpayer is required to file his or her federal income tax return, including extensions [IRC Sec. 2502(a)(1)]. This means that the taxpayer must file the gift tax return on or before April 15 following the close of the calendar year in which the taxpayer makes the gift.

If the taxpayer reports income on a calendar year basis and files for an extension to file his or her tax return, the taxpayer automatically receives an extension to file your income tax return, you automatically get an extension to file the gift tax return. If a donor dies during the calendar year the gift is made, the gift tax return is due when the estate tax return is due [IRC Sec. 6075]. [See Chapter 17 for a thorough discussion of how to complete the gift tax return; for discussion of extensions of time to file, see ¶ 1702].

¶201 WHAT IS A GIFT

Even though the term "gift" is not expressly defined in the Internal Revenue Code, some guidance is provided in IRC Sec. 2512(b) and in court decisions. IRC Sec. 2512(b) provides that "where property is transferred for less than an adequate and full consideration in money or money's worth, then the amount by which the value of the property exceeded the value of the consideration shall be deemed a gift." In other words, the value of the gift for gift tax purposes is the amount that the value of the property transferred by the donor exceeds the value in money or money's worth of the consideration given for the property. Accordingly, it is necessary to determine a value for the consideration received to determine whether it is adequate consideration for gift tax purposes [Reg. Sec. 25.2512-8].

The Supreme Court in *Duberstein*[1] provided that taxpayers seeking to determine whether a payment is a gift or compensation must consider the facts in each case. If the payee performs services at the same time for the payor, that is one factor to consider, but not the only one. If a payment is made out of affection, admiration, charity or a disinterested generosity, then it will be treated as a gift for tax purposes. The most important factor according to the Supreme Court is the donor's intent. For example, in *Lane*[2] the Court of Appeals for the Fourth Circuit concluded that substantial payments that a businessman made to his former secretary were gifts rather than compensation because the facts revealed that the payments were made to her out of his deep affection and concern for her welfare. There was no evidence that the payments were made to compensate her for secretarial services that she performed.

You have to be the owner of the property to give it away for gift tax purposes. A transfer by a trustee of trust property in breach of his or her fiduciary duty will not be a taxable

---

[1] ¶ **201** Duberstein, 363 U.S. 278 (1960).   [2] Lane, 286 F.3d 723 (4th Cir. 2002).

gift because the trustee did not retain any beneficial interest in the trust assets, and therefore had nothing to give away.[3] Reg. Sec. 25.2511-1(g)(1) supports this view. It provides that a transfer by a trustee of trust property in which he or she has no beneficial interest does not constitute a gift by the trustee. It could, however, be a gift by the creator of the trust if he or she had the power at the time of the transfer to amend or revoke the trust.

(a) Value Measurable in Money. Consideration not reducible to a value in money or measurable in money's worth, such as love, affection, or a promise of marriage, is not viewed as a taxable gift [Reg. Sec. 25.2512-8]. However, a transfer made in discharge of a legal obligation of support constitutes consideration measurable in money or money's worth.[4] But the relinquishment (or the promise to relinquish) of marital rights, such as dower or curtesy, in a spouse's property or estate, is not considered to be consideration "in money or money's worth" [Reg. Sec. 25.2512-8]. Note that special rules exempt marital dissolution property settlements in the event of a divorce from gift tax [see ¶ 203].

The concept of property is at the heart of the IRC's gift tax provisions. The federal gift tax applies whether the transfer is outright or in trust, whether the gift is direct or indirect, and whether the property is real or personal, tangible or intangible [Reg. Sec. 25.2511-1]. The following are key definitions of types of property:

- *Real property* is something that is permanent, fixed, and immovable. It includes land and anything that is attached to land or soil, including buildings and tracks. In addition, the term includes all things that are incidental to the land, such as gas, oil, minerals, crops, and trees that have not been severed from the ground.

- *Personal property* is anything that is not real property. It includes money and any real property that has been separated from the land with an intention to change it into personal property.

- *Intangible property* is property that has no intrinsic value, but represents something of value. It includes stocks, bonds, and promissory notes. The special statutory provisions that exempt bonds, notes, bills, and certificates of indebtedness of the federal government or its agencies and the resulting interest from income tax do not apply to the gift tax [Reg. Sec. 25.2511-1(a)]. Therefore, the transfer of these items can be subject to gift tax.

A taxable gift may result from the creation of a trust, the forgiving of a debt, the assignment of a judgment, the assignment of the benefits of an insurance policy, or the transfer of cash, certificates of deposit, or federal, state, or municipal bonds. A gift can be of an entire interest in property or of only a fraction or remainder interest in the property.

Examples of indirect transfers that are subject to gift tax are forgiveness of debts where the borrower is a related party who is financially able to repay the debt and interest-free loans (subject to certain exceptions as discussed at ¶ 205).

Some transactions that are not ordinarily considered transfers constitute gifts because they indirectly enrich someone else.

---

[3] Saltzman, 131 F.3d 87 (2d Cir. 1997).   [4] Rev. Rul. 77-314, 1977-2 CB 349.

> **Example 1:** A controlling shareholder fails to take action to protect his or her right to annual preferred noncumulative dividends, which were within the corporation's earnings to pay. This can result in indirect gifts to minority common shareholders.[5]

You need not be motivated by disinterested generosity or have "donative intent" in order for a transfer to be subject to gift tax. In other words, the intention of the transferor is not as important as whether the property was transferred for less than full and adequate consideration [Reg. Sec. 25.2511-(1)(g)(1)]. The tax applies based on the objective facts of the transfer and the circumstances under which it is made, rather than on the subjective motives of the person making the gift.

The gift tax applies only to voluntary transfers of property. Thus, a payment made under duress or fear of a lawsuit will not constitute a gift.

(b) Sale of Property Below Fair-Market Value. Also keep in mind that when you sell property to family members or friends at a price that is below market value, a taxable gift may result. For this reason, the Internal Revenue Service (the IRS) closely examines all of the facts and circumstances of these types of transactions to see if the price paid reflects fair market value for the asset or item of property that was sold.

Property that comes into existence when someone dies is outside the scope of the federal gift tax. For example, death benefits that an employer provides to a surviving spouse based on the deceased employee's compensation are not subject to gift tax [see ¶ 1814].[6]

No gift tax is imposed on the contribution of personal services without compensation because the gift tax applies only to transfers of property.[7] The performance of services without compensation does not constitute a gift. Once the personal services are performed for compensation, however, they are converted into property rights, which are subject to federal gift tax.[8]

> **Example 2:** Mary Bell is a very good cook who is not in the trade or business of being a chef. She prepares a gourmet dinner party for a friend's business colleagues. Mary informs her friend in advance that she wants no payment for her services. No gift tax results. If Mary Bell had sent a bill for the services performed and then returned the check uncashed once she received it, she would have made a gift to her friend.

---

[5] Ltr. Rul. 8723007; Estate of Hundley, 52 TC 495, *aff'd*, 435 F.2d 1311 (4th Cir. 1971), *acq.*, 1978-1 CB 2. In Daniels, TC Memo 1994-591, the IRS characterized the corporation's failure to declare dividends as a gift by the controlling shareholders. The Tax Court disagreed where the particular circumstances of the case supported the shareholders' argument that retention of funds at the corporate level had legitimate business justification.

[6] Estate of DiMarco, 87 TC 653 (1986), *acq. in result in part*, 1990-2 CB 1.

[7] Rev. Rul. 66-167, 1966-1 CB 20. Rev. Rul. 56-472, 1956-2 CB 21.

[8] Estate of Bogley, 514 F.2d 1027 (Ct. Cl. 1975), *later proceeding* 207 Ct. Cl. 1059 (1975).

Transfers made in the ordinary course of business are not subject to federal gift tax [Reg. Sec. 25.2512-8]. The Regulations define a business transaction as one that is "bona fide, at arm's length, and free from any donative intent."

> **Example 3:** *Situation 1*—You sell property for less than its fair-market value because business reasons motivate a bargain sale to customers. *Situation 2*—You transfer property to settle a claim against you. No gift tax results in either situation [Reg. Sec. 25.2512-8].

¶202 WHO MUST PAY THE GIFT TAX

The gift tax applies only to transfers made by individuals, whether or not they are residents of the United States [IRC Sec. 2501(a)(1)] (see ¶ 1500 for gifts by nonresidents). The gift tax does not apply to transfers that corporations and other business entities make [Reg. Sec. 25.0-1(b)].

Unfortunately, the rule exempting corporations from gift tax is not as simple as it sounds. Because the gift tax applies to direct and indirect transfers, as mentioned above, a transfer by or to a corporation is considered a transfer by or to its shareholder. Transfers of property that a corporation makes are attributed to the shareholders. In addition, a gift to a corporation generally is considered a gift to its individual shareholders [Reg. Sec. 25.2511-1(h)(1)]. However, a gift made to a charitable, public, political, or similar organization may be considered a gift to the organization.

> **Example 1:** ABC, Inc. transfers property to Paul, who owns no ABC stock. The transfer was not made for an adequate and full consideration in money or money's worth. This transfer will be a gift to Paul from the ABC stockholders.

> **Example 2:** Paul transfers property to ABC. The transfer was not made for an adequate and full consideration in money or money's worth. This will be a gift from Paul to the other ABC shareholders to the extent of their proportionate interests in ABC. See Example 3 for the exceptions to this rule.

> **Example 3:** If Paul makes a similar transfer to that in Example 2 (i.e., one that was not made for an adequate and full consideration in money or money's worth) to a charitable, public, political, or similar organization, it will constitute a gift to the organization as a single entity [Reg. Sec. 25.2511-1(h)(1)].

(a) Net Gifts. The obligation to pay the gift tax owed on a gift is primarily the financial responsibility of the donor (i.e., the gift giver) [IRC Sec. 2502(c); Reg. Sec. 25.2502-2]. The gift tax is imposed upon the donor's act of making the transfer, rather than upon receipt by the donee, and it is measured by the value of the property passing from the donor, rather than the value of enrichment resulting to the donee [Reg. Sec. 25.2511-2(a)]. The value of the property is the price at which it would change hands between a willing buyer and a willing seller, neither being under any compulsion to buy or to sell and both having reasonable knowledge of the relevant facts [Reg. Sec. 25.2512-1]. The amount of the gift is the amount by which the value of the property transferred exceeds the value of consideration received in money or money's worth [IRC Sec. 2512(b); Reg. Secs. 25.2511-1(g)(1), 25.2512-8]. Thus, if a donor makes a gift subject to the condition that the donee pay the resulting gift tax, the amount of the gift is reduced by the amount of the gift tax.[1] This type of gift is commonly referred to as a "net gift." When a net gift occurs, the donor calculates his or her gift tax liability by reducing the amount of the gift by the amount of the gift tax.[2] The rationale is that "because the donee incurred the obligation to pay the tax as a condition of the gift, 'the donor did not have the intent to make other than a net gift.'"[3] In other words, the donor reduces the value of the gift by the amount of the tax because the donor has received consideration for a part of the gift equal to the amount of the applicable gift tax. In a net gift, the donee can contractually assume the responsibility of paying the gift tax on the transfer.[4]

The net gift takes the form of a signed agreement which provides that the donee promises to pay any additional estate taxes due on the donor's estate as a result of the inclusion of the gift in the donor's estate tax calculation as an adjusted taxable gift. The net gift is the amount of the taxable gift reduced for gift tax purposes by the estate tax liability assumed by the donee. Typically, in a net gift situation, the donee agrees to be obligated to pay the gift tax resulting from the gift. The gift tax payable is often easily calculated and even where valuation uncertainty exists; it may be determined within a year or two of the filing of the gift tax return. Estate taxes attributable to the inclusion of a lifetime gift might not be calculable for many years, rendering valuation of the net gift difficult to ascertain.

In Rev. Rul. 75-72,[5] the IRS concluded that gift tax paid by a donee may be deducted from the value of the transferred property when it is expressly shown or is implied that payment of the tax by the donee or from the property itself is a condition of the transfer. The IRS provided a formula showing how to calculate the true tax to be deducted from the value of the transferred property. The formula is:

$$\frac{\text{Tentative tax}}{1 \text{ plus rate of tax}} = \text{True tax}$$

Rev. Rul. 75-72 provides that the payment of tax by the donee or from the property must be a condition of the transfer. It is not sufficient that the donee pay the tax voluntarily. In fact, if he or she does, not only do the parties lose the gift tax deduction, but the donee will also be in a position of having made a gift to his donor, which might or might not be taxable to him or her, depending on the available exclusions or deductions.

If the obligation to pay the gift tax is illusory or too "contingent and speculative" as it was in *Estate of Armstrong*,[6] the donees cannot apply the net gift doctrine to reduce the

---

[1] ¶202 Harrison, 17 TC 1350 (1952).

[2] Morgens, 133 TC 401 (2009), aff'd, 678 F.3d 769 (9th Cir. 2012).

[3] Turner, 49 TC 356 (1968), aff'd per curiam, 410 F.2d 752 (6th Cir. 1969).

[4] Diedrich, 457 U.S. 191 (1982); Rev. Rul. 80-111, 1980-1 CB 208.

[5] Rev. Rul. 75-72, 1975-1 CB 310.

[6] Armstrong Trust, 277 F.3d 490 (4th Cir. 2002).

value of the property. Although the decedent's children signed a transferee liability agreement indicating that they would pay any gift tax liability resulting from a higher valuation of the stock than that reported by the decedent, the potential liability was too speculative at the time of the transfer and created no lien or encumbrance that would reduce the gift tax value of the stock. In addition, the possibility that the donees would incur transferee liability for estate tax incurred because of the gross-up rule under IRC Sec. 2035(b) was too speculative at the time of the transfer to reduce the gift tax value of the stock.

In Steinberg,[7] a mother entered into a binding net gift agreement with her four daughters when she was 89 years old. The mother agreed to make gifts to the daughters of cash and securities in exchange for the daughters' agreement to assume and to pay any federal gift tax liability imposed as a result of the gifts. The daughters also agreed to pay any estate tax liability imposed under IRC Sec. 2035(b) as a result of the gifts in the event that their mother passed away within three years of the gifts. IRC Sec. 2035(b) provides that the value of a decedent's gross estate is increased by the amount of any gift taxes actually paid on a gift made by a decedent within the three-year period preceding the decedent's date of death.

The mother retained an appraiser to calculate the gross fair market value of the property transferred to the donees. The appraiser also calculated the aggregate fair market value of the "net gift." The appraiser determined the value of the net gift by reducing the fair market value of the cash and securities by both (1) the gift tax the donees paid and (2) the actuarial value of the donees' assumption of the potential IRC Sec. 2035(b) estate tax liability. The appraiser determined the actuarial value of the donees' assumption of the potential IRC Sec. 2035(b) estate tax by calculating the mother's annual mortality rate for the three years after the gift (i.e., the probability that she would pass away within one year, two years, or three years of the gift), among other things.

The Tax Court concluded that the fair market value of the mother's taxable gifts to her four daughters could be reduced by the daughters' assumption of the potential IRC Sec. 2035(b) estate tax liability. In reaching its decision, the court reconsidered its decision in McCord,[8] analyzing whether the daughters' assumption of the potential estate tax liability was too speculative to be reduced to a monetary value. The court reasoned that although tax rates and exclusion amounts are subject to change, methods exist to determine potential estate tax liability. The donees' assumption of the potential estate tax liability could be quantifiable and reducible to a monetary value and, therefore, would be consideration in money or money's worth. The court therefore stated that it would no longer follow McCord.

In McCord, the taxpayers (husband and wife) formed McCord Interests, Ltd., L.L.P. (MIL). The taxpayers were both class A limited partners and class B limited partners in MIL. The taxpayers' four adult sons were class B limited partners and general partners. On formation, MIL held stocks, bonds, real estate, oil and gas investments, and other closely held business interests.

---

[7] Steinberg, 141 TC No. 8 (2013).

[8] McCord, 120 TC 358 (2003), *rev'd and remanded sub. nom.* Succession of McCord, 461 F.3d 614 (5th Cir. 2006).

The taxpayers assigned their respective class A limited partnership interests in MIL to a charitable organization. On the valuation date, the taxpayers entered into an assignment agreement, in which the taxpayers relinquished all dominion and control over their class B limited partnership interests in MIL to (1) their four sons, (2) four trusts for the benefit of their sons, and (3) two charitable organizations.

Under the terms of the "formula clause" contained in the assignment agreement, the four sons and the four trusts were to receive the portion of the gift interest having an aggregate fair market value of $6,910,933. If the fair market value of the gift interest exceeded $6,910,933, the excess was to be allocated to the two charitable organizations. The four sons—individually and as trustees of the four trusts—agreed to be liable for all transfer taxes (federal gift, estate, and generation-skipping transfer taxes and any resulting state taxes) imposed on the taxpayers as a result of the gifts. On their gift tax return, both taxpayers reduced the gross value amounts of their respective shares of the gifts by the amount of federal and state gift tax generated by the transfer, which the four sons had agreed to pay as a condition of the gifts. Each taxpayer further reduced that gross value amount by the actuarially determined value of the four sons' contingent obligation to pay any estate tax that would result from the transaction if that taxpayer were to pass away within three years of the valuation date.

The Tax Court concluded that the McCord sons' assumption of the taxpayers' potential IRC Sec. 2035(b) estate tax liability was too speculative to be reduced to a monetary value. The court therefore found that the taxpayers had improperly reduced their gross value amounts by the actuarial value of the four sons' obligation to pay any potential estate taxes arising from the transactions. The court reasoned that "the dollar amount of a potential liability to pay the IRC Sec. 2035 tax is by no means fixed; rather, such amount depends on factors that are subject to change, including estate tax rates and exemption amounts (not to mention the continued existence of the estate tax itself)."

The taxpayers appealed *McCord* and the Court of Appeals for the Fifth Circuit reversed and remanded *McCord*, holding, among other things, that a willing buyer and a willing seller may take into account a donee's assumption of potential IRC Sec. 2035(b) estate tax liability in arriving at a sale price. The court reasoned that there was nothing too speculative about the McCord sons' legally binding assumption of the potential IRC Sec. 2035(b) estate tax at the time the gift was made. A willing buyer would insist at the time a gift is made that a willing seller take into account the effect of the three-year exposure to IRC Sec. 2035 estate taxes when calculating a purchase price and it was therefore appropriate to reduce the value of the gifts by the actuarial date-of-gift value of the IRC Sec. 2035(b) obligation.

▶ **CAUTION:** Care should be exercised in using a net gift because the donor could realize taxable income to the extent that the gift tax paid by the donee exceeds the donor's adjusted basis in the gifted property. In *Diedrich*,[9] the U.S. Supreme Court affirmed the Eighth Circuit which held that, to the extent the gift taxes paid by donees exceeded the donors' adjusted bases in the property transferred, the donors realized taxable income. The court reasoned that the donor received a benefit when a donee discharged the donor's legal obligation to pay gift taxes and that the discharge by a third party of an obligation is

---

[9] Diedrich, 457 U.S. 191 (1982).

equivalent to the receipt of income. The Supreme Court compared the net gift to a situation in which the donor is treated as having sold the property to the donee for less than full fair market value. The sale price is the amount of the discharge of the gift tax indebtedness, and the balance of the value of the transfer is treated as a gift. Therefore the court concluded that the donor realizes a gain on the sale portion of the transaction.

Net gift after disclaimer of QTIP trust. The IRS ruled in Technical Advice Memorandum 9736001 that a net gift occurred where a surviving spouse made a nonqualified disclaimer of her interest in a QTIP trust. Upon making the disclaimer, a taxable gift to the trust remaindermen occurred pursuant to IRC Sec. 2519. Moreover, because the trust was includible in the surviving spouse's estate under IRC Sec. 2044, IRC Sec. 2207A(b) statutorily shifted the burden for paying the gift tax to the remaindermen. Nonetheless, the surviving spouse remained liable for the gift tax. Thus, a net gift occurred upon payment of the gift tax by the remaindermen. (Similarly, see IRS Letter Ruling 200604006.)[10]

(b) Disability of the Gift Giver. If the donor is incompetent, any attempted gift is void and no federal gift tax is imposed. A gift by the legally appointed guardian or conservator of the incompetent donor will result in federal gift taxation if the guardian or conservator is authorized to make a gift.[11]

If the donor is under a temporary disability and can affirm or rescind the transfer when the disability has been removed, there is no gift at the time of the transfer. However, a gift will be deemed to have been made when the donor's disability is removed and no rescission of the transfer occurs within a reasonable time.[12]

If the donor dies before the gift tax is paid, the amount of the tax is a debt due the United States from the decedent's estate, and the decedent's executor or administrator is responsible for paying the tax out of the estate. If there is no executor or administrator, the heirs and distributees are liable for and must pay the gift tax to the extent of the value of their inheritances or distributive shares of the donor's estate [Reg. Sec. 25.2502-2].

GIFTS WITHIN THE FAMILY

¶203 GIFT TAX CONSEQUENCES OF DIVORCE

A party in a divorce can get relief from the gift tax if certain spousal rights are given up in the divorce or in a separation agreement. IRC Sec. 2516 provides that a transfer of property (or property interests) from one spouse to the other pursuant to a written agreement in settlement of their marital and property rights is deemed to be for "full and adequate consideration in money or money's worth." As a result, the transfer

---

[10] Ltr. Rul. 200604006; Ltr. Rul. 200116006 (involved renunciation by surviving spouse rather than disclaimer); Ltr. Rul. 200122036 (involved renunciation by surviving spouse rather than disclaimer).

[11] Rev. Rul. 67-280, 1967-2 CB 349.

[12] Allen, 108 F.2d 961 (3d Cir. 1969), *cert. denied*, 309 U.S. 680 (1940).

will be exempt from gift tax provided the spouses are divorced within the three-year period beginning one year before the agreement was entered into.

The tax-free transfer rule of IRC Sec. 2516 does not apply if the divorce precedes the agreement by more than one year or follows the agreement by more than two years. Divorce in this context means a final decree of divorce, although the decree need not incorporate or make reference to the marital property settlement agreement [Reg. Sec. 25.2516-1(a)]. As long as transfers of property are made pursuant to the written agreement, they can be made at any time.

(a) Gifts to Provide Child Support. Transfers to provide a reasonable allowance for the support of minor (not adult) children (including legally adopted children) of the marriage are not subject to the gift tax if these transfers are made under an agreement satisfying the requirements for marital property settlements [IRC Sec. 2516; Reg. Sec. 25.2516-2].

(b) Property Settlement Transfers. If divorcing spouses have entered into a written property settlement, but the final decree of divorce is not granted by the due date for filing the transferor's gift tax return for the calendar year in which the settlement agreement becomes effective, they must:

1. Show the transfer on their gift tax return for that calendar year; and

2. Attach a copy of the settlement agreement to the return.

A certified copy of the final divorce decree must be sent to the IRS office where the gift tax return was filed no later than 60 days after the divorce is granted. Until the IRS receives evidence that the final divorce decree has been granted (provided the decree is granted not more than two years from the effective date of the settlement agreement), it tentatively treats the transfer as made for adequate consideration [Reg. Sec. 25.2516-1(a)].

(c) Voluntary Increases in Support. Voluntary increases in support payments after a final divorce decree are subject to gift tax if, under state law, the court has no authority to modify the decree as it pertains to the payments. In this situation, the value of the gift equals the amount by which each payment exceeds the amount specified in the original written agreement between the spouses.

¶204 INTRAFAMILY TRANSACTIONS AS GIFT ALTERNATIVES

Several types of intrafamily transactions in lieu of gifts are available to reduce or "freeze" the value of an estate. The objective of these freeze techniques is to move appreciated assets out of the parents' estate into the hands of their children and grandchildren. Future appreciation of these assets is accordingly shifted to the younger generation, whose members typically are in lower tax brackets. Therefore, when you transfer wealth from one generation to the next, you must always keep in mind the impact of the different individual tax rates that apply to different family members as well as the possible impact of the kiddie tax rules.[1]

> **Example 1:** Dad sells stock worth $25 per share to Son. Five years later, the stock is worth $85 per share in the hands of Son. This transfer is an excellent example of an outright family sale that removed all stock appreciation from Dad's estate without his having to pay any income, gift, or estate tax on the appreciation. The downside to selling the stock is that Dad, who may already be in a high tax bracket, realized taxable capital gain when he sold the stock.

Intrafamily transactions, which are discussed below, include the following:

- Ordinary installment sales;
- Self-cancelling installment notes (SCINs);
- Private annuities;
- Interest-free loans; and
- Loan guarantees.

(a) Ordinary Installment Sales. An individual holding appreciated property such as shares of stock or an interest in real estate should consider selling the property to family members by means of an installment sale.

In such a sale, the parent transfers an asset to a child in exchange for either a promissory note or part cash and a promissory note for the remainder of the purchase price. The terms of the promissory note require the child to pay the parent the principal balance of the sales price plus interest.

IRC Sec. 453(b)(1) only requires that the parent receive one or more installment payments in a year other than the year in which the sale of the property occurred to qualify for use of the installment sale method. A single payment is therefore sufficient provided it occurs after the end of the year of sale.

To avoid a situation where parents are pushed into a higher tax bracket simply because of the proceeds from the installment sale, the gain from the sale of appreciated property can be spread over a number of years. Spreading the payments out may also be better for the buyer-child who has to make the actual installment payments [IRC Sec. 453].

Advantages. Four major benefits of the installment sale are that:

1. The buyer-child receives a basis stepped up to equal the purchase price of the asset rather than the carryover basis that would apply to a gift;

2. Any income generated by the asset that was sold to the child will be taxed to the child, who will typically be in a lower tax bracket than his or her parent;

3. Gain on the sale is deferred and taxed as payments are received or the notes are forgiven; and

---

[1] ¶204 For a further discussion of the kiddie tax rules, see ¶900 and ¶2751, *infra.*

4. If the property has been sold for full and adequate consideration, only the value of the outstanding installment obligation is includible in the seller's estate, rather than any subsequent asset appreciation.

Problem areas. One of the dangers of the intrafamily installment sale is the risk that the IRS will say that the parent has made a taxable gift to the child. The key to avoiding gift tax consequences is making sure that the consideration received under the installment promissory note is equal to the value of the property sold [Reg. Sec. 25.2511-1(g)(1)].

This simply means that parent and child must determine an arm's-length price to avoid gift tax consequences. In addition, the parties must agree to an appropriate interest rate to avoid the challenge that the interest rate stipulated in the promissory note is "below market."

▶ **PRACTICE POINTER:** It behooves you to get independent professional appraisals of all transferred assets. Two special rules apply to installment sales between related persons.

First, the installment method is unavailable for the sale of a depreciable asset to a related person. All the gain from the sale of depreciable assets must be reported in the year of sale.

Second, related taxpayers cannot use the installment sales rules to avoid current tax on an asset's appreciation. As a result, a resale by a related purchaser within two years of the initial sale will trigger recognition of gain by the initial seller (i.e., the parent). Gain is recognized, based on the parent's gross profit ratio, to the extent the amount realized on the resale exceeds actual payments made under the installment sale [IRC Sec. 453(e)]. The term "related persons" includes you and members of your immediate family.

If the parent dies before the installment payments are completed, the unpaid installment obligation will be considered income in respect of a decedent (IRD) [IRC Sec. 691(a)(2)]. See ¶ 2614 for a detailed discussion of IRD.

Interest rate guidelines. Generally, IRC Sec. 483 contains a safe harbor rate of interest for federal income tax purposes. Although the focus of Section 483 is on the federal income tax, its safe harbor protection has been recognized for federal gift tax purposes.[2] To play it safe and avoid unwanted income and gift tax consequences, the interest rate should be the higher of:

• The lowest applicable federal rate (AFR) during the three months ending in the month the binding sales contract is signed, and

• The AFR for the month in which the sale closes.

(b) Self-Cancelling Installment Notes. A self-cancelling installment note (SCIN) is a debt obligation which by its terms specifically provides that the debt and any outstanding balance owed on the note will be cancelled automatically if the seller dies before the note's maturity date. In order to compensate the seller for the risk of the note being cancelled, the amount due to the seller under the terms of the SCIN must include a risk premium which could be in the form of either an increased

[2] Ballard, TC Memo 1987-128, *rev'd*, 854 F.2d 185 (7th Cir 1988).

purchase price or an increased interest rate. The inclusion of this risk premium in the note will also reflect the fact that the SCIN was bargained for and help establish that the sale was bona fide and for full and adequate consideration.

Estate tax treatment. SCINs are frequently used to transfer property between family members because SCINs can eliminate estate taxes on the value of both the transferred property and the unpaid balance of the purchaser's obligation if the obligation terminates when the seller dies.

> **Example 2:** Mom sells property to Son for an installment note which is for a period of ten years or Mom's life, whichever is shorter. If Mom dies before Son pays off the note in full, the note is deemed to have been paid and is cancelled. There will be nothing to include in Mom's taxable estate for federal estate tax purposes. However, in order for Mom not to have made a gift to Son, the consideration for the property would have had to include a risk premium to reflect the fact that Son would not have to pay the note in full if Mom died during the term of the installment note. If, however, Mom's life expectancy was less than the term of the note, the transaction will be taxed for income tax purposes as a private annuity.

Because a SCIN will eliminate estate tax only if the note holder dies before the maturity date of the note, the ideal candidate for a SCIN is someone in poor health or with a poor family health history. However, since an exception exists to the use of the mortality tables in the event of a "terminal illness," SCINs should not be used if the note holder is terminally ill which is defined as someone who has a 50 percent chance of dying within one year.

The ideal property to be used in a SCIN transaction is property with a high basis and a potential for future appreciation because the property sold and any post-sale appreciation will be removed from the decedent's taxable estate.

Estate of Costanza. The first appellate court to validate the use of SCINs as an estate planning technique was the Sixth Circuit in *Estate of Costanza*.[3] In that case, the decedent sold real property to his son in exchange for a SCIN. The decedent died unexpectedly five months after the issuance of the note. Reversing the Tax Court, the Sixth Circuit stated that, at the time of the transaction, there was a real expectation of repayment and intent to enforce the collection of the indebtedness. Thus, the Sixth Circuit concluded that the transaction was bona fide. The appellate court stated that even though "a SCIN signed by family members is presumed to be a gift and not a bona fide transaction," the presumption may be rebutted by an affirmative showing that there existed at the time of the transaction a real expectation of repayment and intent to enforce the collection of the indebtedness. The court concluded that, on the facts before it, the presumption had been rebutted because the decedent would not have gifted the business properties to his son because he needed a steady stream of income in order to retire. Moreover, the taxpayer proved that, at the time of the transaction, a real

---

[3] Estate of Costanza, TC Memo 2001-128, *rev'd and rem'd*, 320 F.3d 595 (6th Cir. 2003).

¶204

expectation of repayment existed and that the decedent intended to enforce the collection of the indebtedness. Therefore, there was a bona fide transaction.

Estate of Moss. In *Estate of Moss*,[4] a 72-year-old minority shareholder sold stock and other property to a corporation in exchange for SCINs that included a cancellation clause providing that the principal and interest due on the notes would cancel on the decedent's death. At the time of the transaction, the decedent had a ten-year life expectancy under the actuarial tables. Nevertheless, the decedent died unexpectedly only 18 months after execution of the SCIN. The Tax Court held that the notes were not included in the decedent's estate because the parties had stipulated that the sales of shares of the notes were bona fide transactions for full and adequate consideration and that the cancellation provision was part of the bargained for consideration provided by the decedent for the purchase price of the stock. In addition, there was no reason to believe that the decedent's life expectancy would have been shorter than the ten years of life expectancy indicated by the mortality tables.

GCM 39503. After acquiescing in the result only in *Moss*, in GCM 39503, the IRS Chief Counsel's Office concluded that if a SCIN expressly contains a debt cancellation clause in the event of the seller's death, the SCIN will not be included in the transferor's gross estate for federal estate tax purposes. (GCMs are prepared by a Chief Counsel attorney for internal use, most often for evaluating proposed rulings. Like CCAs, they have no precedential value.) In addition, the IRS concluded that the SCIN would not be subject to gift tax if the sales price and length of payment are reasonable when compared with the value of the property transferred. The SCIN must contain a risk premium reflected as either an increase in the sales price or a higher interest rate in order to account for the possibility that the seller will die prior to the end of the installment term. If the fair market value of the property exceeds the SCIN's value, the seller has made a gift of the excess.

In GCM 39503 (1986) the IRS provided the following basic guidelines to help taxpayers determine whether a sale for deferred payments is a SCIN or a private annuity:

1. If the transferor of property receives a right to periodic payments for life, with no monetary limit provided, the payments represent an annuity and should be governed by IRC Sec. 72;

2. If the terms of the property sale are structured so that there is a stated maximum payout that will be achieved in a period less than the life expectancy of the transferor (as determined at the time of the transfer in accordance with the tables in Reg. Sec. 1.72-9), the transaction will be characterized as an installment sale with a contingent sales price, and will be treated in accordance with the installment rules;

3. If the terms of the property sale are such that the life expectancy of the transferor is less than or equal to the stated maximum payout period, the transaction will be an annuity.

---

[4] Estate of Moss, 74 TC 1239 (1980), *acq. in result in part*, 1981-2 CB 2; GCM 39503 (1986).

The IRS provided further in GCM 39503 (1986) that SCINs and private annuities should be treated in the same way for federal estate tax purposes:

> We conclude that in the case of an installment sale, when a death-extinguishing provision is expressly included in the sales agreement and any attendant installment notes, the notes will not be included in the transferor's gross estate for federal estate tax purposes.

> A private annuity also should not be included in the transferor's gross estate for federal estate tax purposes. Thus, the estate tax consequences of a private annuity and an installment obligation with a death terminating provision are identical in our opinion.

There is a risk, however, that the value of the property transferred into the SCIN will be included in the decedent/seller's estate under IRC Secs. 2035-2039 if the decedent/seller receives less than full and adequate consideration. Therefore the seller should not retain any interests or controls that could cause inclusion under these Code provisions.

Gift tax treatment. To avoid any adverse gift tax consequences on the transfer of property in exchange for a self-cancelling installment note, the SCIN must be a bona fide note, and the price paid must include a bargained-for risk premium designed to compensate the seller for the note's self-cancelling clause. If the property that is transferred in exchange for the self-cancelling installment note is of equal value to the value of the note, a gift will not result. However, the transaction could constitute a bargain sale if the property is exchanged for a note of lesser value. In this case, the gift could be made by the seller to the transferee of the property.

Chief Counsel Advice 201330033. In Chief Counsel Advice (CCA) 201330033,[5] the IRS addressed: (1) whether transfers of stock from the seller to grantor trusts in exchange for self-cancelling installment notes constituted a taxable gift: (2) how to determine the amount of the gift for gift tax purposes when property is exchanged for a SCIN; and (3) whether the SCIN should be included in the decedent/seller's gross estate and therefore subject to federal estate tax.

The IRS concluded that (1) the transfers resulted in taxable gifts because the value of the stock transferred by the decedent exceeded the value of the SCINs received by the decedent; (2) the SCINs should be valued based on a method that takes into account the willing-buyer willing-seller standard of Reg. Sec. 25.2512-8 and should also account for the decedent's medical history on the date of the gift; (3) no estate tax is associated with the cancellation of the notes with the self-cancelling feature when the decedent died.

Facts. In CCA 201330033, the decedent/seller transferred stock to a grantor trust in exchange for SCINs. The terms of the SCINs were based on the taxpayer's life expectancy as determined in the IRC Sec. 7520 tables. The IRC Sec. 7520 tables are a series of IRS tables that must be used to value noncommercial annuities, any interest for life or a term of years, any remainder interest and any reversionary interest [IRC Sec. 7520(a)]. Each note required only payments of interest during the note term and the payment of principal to the note holder on the last day of the term. Each of the notes

---

[5] Chief Counsel Advice 201330033 (July 26, 2013).

¶204

contained a self-cancelling feature. This feature relieved the issuer of the obligation to make any further payments on the note if the taxpayer died before all of the payments under the note came due. The total face value of one group of the notes was almost double the appraised value of the stock transferred for those notes. The higher value of the notes represented a risk premium that compensated the seller for the risk that he would die before the end of the note term and thus not receive the full amount of interest or any principal due under the note. The total face value of the rest of the notes equaled the appraised value of the stock transferred for those notes. To account for the possibility that the self-cancelling feature would take effect, these notes also contained an above-market interest rate.

The taxpayer was in very poor health at the time of the transfer and died less than six months after the transfer. He therefore received neither the interest payments nor any principal due on the notes. Although CCA 201330022 was redacted for personal information, a recent Tax Court petition indicates that the decedent was William M. Davidson, owner of the NBA Detroit Pistons and the deficiency at issue is in excess of $2 billion in gift, estate, and generation-skipping transfer tax, including penalties and interest.

Issue 1: The IRS explained that based on IRC Sec. 2512(b) a taxable gift will result if property is transferred for less than an adequate and full consideration in money or money's worth. The amount by which the value of the property exceeds the value of the consideration is deemed to be a gift. In order to determine if the decedent made a taxable gift, the IRS had to determine if the face value and length of payment of the notes that the decedent transferred to the grantor trusts shortly before his death was greater than the value of the notes taking into consideration the notes' self-cancelling feature. Since the IRS concluded that the FMV of the notes received by the decedent was less than the FMV of the property he transferred to the grantor trusts, the difference constituted a gift under IRC Sec. 2512(b) and Reg. Sec. 25.2512-8.

The decedent structured the SCIN so that the payments received during the term of the note consisted of only interest with a large payment on the last day of the term of the note (balloon payment). Therefore, it was apparent that a steady stream of income was not contemplated by the decedent/seller when the SCIN was drafted. Moreover, the decedent had substantial assets and did not require the income from the notes to cover his daily living expenses. The IRS characterized the SCIN as "nothing more than a device to transfer the stock to other family members at a substantially lower value than the fair market value of the stock." Moreover, the IRS reasoned that the decedent's poor health made it unlikely that the full amount of the note would ever be paid. Since, there was no reasonable expectation that the debt would be repaid the SCINS did not therefore constitute a bona fide debt and the transfers of stock from the seller to the grantor trusts in exchange for the SCINs constituted taxable gifts. Since the note was worth significantly less than its stated amount, the difference between the note's fair market value and its stated amount constituted a taxable gift.

Issue 2: In determining the FMV of the gift, the IRS concluded that the IRC Sec. 7520 tables should not apply to value the decedent's notes because IRC Sec. 7520 applies only to value an annuity, any interest for life or a term of years, or any remainder. The IRS reasoned that since the items to be valued were the notes that the decedent received in exchange for the stock sold to the grantor trust, the valuation method should take into account the willing-buyer willing-seller standard in Reg. Sec. 25.2512-8. In applying that standard, the IRS reasoned that the decedent's life expectancy, taking into consideration the decedent's medical history on the date of the gift, should also be taken into account. Reg. Sec. 25.2512-8 provides, in part, that a sale, exchange, or other transfer of property made in the ordinary course of business (a transaction that is bona fide, at arm's length, and free from any donative intent) will be considered as made for an adequate and full consideration in money or money's worth.

Reg. Sec. 25.7520-3(b)(3)(i) limits the use of the IRC Sec. 7520 valuation tables to determine the present value of an annuity, income interest, remainder interest, or reversionary interest if the seller suffers from a terminal illness at the time the gift is completed. For these purposes, "terminal illness" means an incurable illness or other deteriorating physical condition such that the transferor has at least a 50 percent probability of dying within one year from the date of the transaction. If the individual survives for 18 months or longer after the date the gift is completed, that individual will be presumed to have not been terminally ill at the date the gift was completed unless the contrary is *established by clear and convincing evidence* [emphasis added].

The IRS explained that the SCINs "lack the indicia of genuine debt because there must be a reasonable expectation that the debt will be repaid." The IRS found that the notes should be valued based on a method that takes into account the willing buyer/willing seller standard of Reg. Sec. 25.2512-8 and also should account for the seller's medical history on the date of the gift. The IRS relied on the following statement in Reg. Sec. 25.2512-8 to support the proposition that it should use the willing buyer/willing seller standard for determining the value of the SCINs "a sale, exchange, or other transfer of property made in the ordinary course of business (a transaction which is bona fide, at arm's length, and free from any donative intent), will be considered as made for an adequate and full consideration in money or money's worth." Any transaction that does not meet this standard will be considered a gift to the extent that the property transferred by the donor exceeds the value of consideration received.

Income tax treatment. For income tax purposes, a SCIN will be classified as either an installment sale or as a private annuity. If the transaction is treated as an installment sale, the income tax consequences will be determined according to the installment sale rules of IRC Sec. 453 [For a discussion of private annuities, see 204(c)]. In *Estate of Robert Frane*,[6] the Court of Appeals for the Eighth Circuit concluded that the automatic cancellation of an installment obligation when the seller died required the seller's estate to recognize the gain from the original transaction as income in respect of decedent.

(c) Private Annuity. A private annuity is an intrafamily sale of property (or money) for an unsecured promise to pay the seller a fixed dollar amount at least annually, for the lifetime of a named measuring life (usually the seller). Typically, the private annuity sale is an estate planning device that involves the transfer of appreciated property, such as undeveloped real estate or small business stock, from a parent or grandparent to a third party (an insurance company or a child) in exchange for the third party's promise to pay the senior family member a specified sum for the rest of his or her lifetime. The size of the payments is determined by the value of the property

---

[6] Estate of Frane, 98 TC 341, *aff'd and rev'd*, 998 F.2d 567 (8th Cir. 1993); Rev. Rul. 86-72, 1986-1 CB 253.

¶204

transferred, current interest rates and the life expectancy of the annuitant. A private annuity can be a very valuable estate-planning tool because it can accomplish two important goals. A properly structured private annuity can be used to shift appreciated assets out of a parent's taxable estate into the hands of the younger generation while providing the parent with a fixed income stream for life. The private annuity is popular because it allows a parent to pass appreciated property on to children, while guaranteeing income for the parent.

Private annuities typically work in this way. The parent transfers appreciated property (not cash) to his or her child in exchange for the child's promise to pay the parent a specified periodic sum for an agreed period, which is usually the duration of the parent's lifetime [See ¶ 1808 for a discussion of commercial annuities].

> **Example 3:** Mom sells her beach house worth $1 million to Son in exchange for Son's promise to pay her $50,000 per year for the rest of her life. This is a private annuity.

Gift tax consequences. There are no federal gift tax consequences when a private annuity is established provided the fair market value of the property sold in exchange for the private annuity does not exceed the present value of the payments expected to be made under the terms of the annuity. IRC Sec. 2512(b) provides that "[w]here property is transferred for less than an adequate and full consideration in money or money's worth, then the amount by which the value of the property exceeded the value of the consideration shall be deemed a gift." Thus, the gift tax does not apply to a transfer for full and adequate consideration in money or money's worth [Reg. Sec. 25.2511-1(g)(1)]. In the context of a private annuity, the issue becomes whether the transfer of the property interests to the children in exchange for the annuity agreements was made for adequate and full consideration and whether there was an expectation of payment. The IRS will closely examine the facts and circumstances of each private annuity to determine whether the transfer was a disguised gift subject to gift tax.

> **Example 4:** Dad sells the farm to Son for $500,000 in exchange for Son's promise to pay Dad $50,000 per year for the rest of Dad's life. If the present value of the payments that Dad will receive is also $500,000, no gift has occurred. If the present value of the payments is only $400,000, Dad has made a gift to Son in the amount of $100,000.

The IRS provides actuarial tables for taxpayers to use in determining the present value of annuities [IRC Sec. 7520]. These can be found in IRS Publications 1457 (Actuarial Values, Aleph Volume) and 1458 (Actuarial Values, Beth Volume). The value of life estates, term interests, remainders, and reversions for estate, gift, and income tax purposes is generally determined under tables promulgated under IRC Sec. 7520. The valuation depends on both an actuarial factor dependent on life expectancies and an interest factor. The IRC Sec. 7520 tables apply in valuing private annuities and if the creator of the private annuity has a greater than 50 percent likelihood of living at least one year after the transfer and will likely live at least 18 months afterward, the IRC Sec. 7520 tables may be used [Reg. Sec. 1.7520 3(b)(3)].

▶ **PRACTICE POINTER:** To be certain that no gift tax consequences result, the private annuity sale should satisfy the following requirements:

1. The annuity payments must accurately reflect the current value of the property;

2. The amount of each annuity payment must be computed using the IRC Sec. 7520 valuation tables set forth in IRS Publication 1457 unless death of the parent is clearly imminent. Death is not clearly imminent if there is a reasonable possibility of survival for more than a brief period. For example, death is not clearly imminent if the individual may be expected to survive for a year or more;[7]

3. There must be a real expectation of payment;

4. The obligor must actually hand over an annuity check to the parent each payment period. Avoid private annuities if the obligor is a child who is not in a financial position to make the annuity payments;

5. The parent may not retain any interest in the property that is exchanged for the child's promise to make the annuity payments.

Example 5: Dad sells farm to Daughter in exchange for Daughter's promise to pay him $50,000 per year for the rest of his life. Dad has not made a gift to Daughter if the present value of all payments expected to be made under the annuity contract equal the fair-market value of the farm. To make this determination, they consult the IRC Sec. 7520 actuarial tables found in IRS Publications 1457 which is used to determine the value of the annuity payments.

When determining whether adequate and full consideration has been exchanged, the courts generally consider whether the consideration received by the transferor is roughly equivalent to the value of the property given up. In *Estate of Hurford*,[8] for example, the Tax Court held that the transfer of a surviving spouse's interests in a family limited partnership (FLP) to her children for private annuity agreements, while the surviving spouse was being treated for stage 3 liver cancer was not bona fide. In reaching this holding, the court relied upon the following: (1) the parties to the private annuity agreements intended to ignore the agreements they signed; and (2) the children, who did not have assets of their own to make the annuity payments, used the assets underlying the FLP interests to transfer income back to their mother beginning with the first month after the agreements were executed and each month thereafter.

Unlike the private annuity agreements in *Estate of Hurford*, the private annuity agreements considered by the Tax Court in *Estate of Kite*,[9] between a mother and her children were found by the court to be bona fide and enforceable because the mother demonstrated an expectation that she would receive payments under the terms of the private annuity. It was clear to the court that the Kite children expected to make payments under the annuity agreements and were prepared to comply with the terms of

---

[7] McLendon, TC Memo 1993-459, *rev'd*, 135 F.3d 1017 (5th Cir. 1998).

[8] Estate of Hurford, TC Memo 2008-278.

[9] Estate of Kite, TC Memo 2013-43.

the annuity agreement. The court therefore found that the "the annuity transaction was a bona fide sale for adequate and full consideration."

The court considered the facts and circumstances in *Kite* before reaching its conclusion that the private annuity agreements constituted adequate and full consideration and consequently were not subject to gift tax. Taxpayers hoping to have their private annuity transactions successfully upheld should consider the following facts considered by the *Kite* court as a model:

> Before the annuity transaction, Mrs. Kite received a letter from her physician attesting to her health and longevity. He affirmed that Mrs. Kite did not have an incurable illness or other deteriorating physical condition that would cause her to die within one year. The physician further opined that Mrs. Kite had at least a 50 percent probability of surviving for 18 months or longer. This established that Mrs. Kite and her children reasonably expected that she would live through the life expectancy determined by the IRS actuarial tables, which was 12.5 years after the annuity transaction. Mrs. Kite was therefore not precluded from relying on the IRS actuarial tables to value the annuity transaction.

- Mrs. Kite demonstrated her intention to demand compliance with the terms of the annuity agreements.
- The Kite children established that they had sufficient assets independent of the assets already held by the annuities to make the annuity payments under the terms of the annuity agreements.
- The Kite children demonstrated that they expected to make payments under the annuity agreements and were prepared to do so.
- Mrs. Kite demonstrated an expectation that she would receive payments. She actively participated in her finances and over the course of her life demonstrated an immense business acumen. Therefore, the court concluded that it was unlikely that Mrs. Kite would have entered into the annuity agreements unless they were enforceable and profitable.

Income tax treatment of annuities. IRC Sec. 72 provides that each payment received by the annuitant reflects a partial return of the annuitant's basis in the transferred asset, and the balance represents a combination of ordinary (annuity) income and gain from the appreciation in the transferred assets. Each annuity payment is divided into two parts for tax purposes: a capital portion (return of basis and capital gain) and an annuity portion. The capital portion is taxed as a return of the annuitant's adjusted basis over the annuitant's life expectancy and the gain realized on the sale. The annuity portion is equal to the excess of the amounts the obligor promises to pay for the annuity property over the capital portion, and it is taxed to the annuitant as ordinary income.

The capital portion of each annuity payment is divided between the return of the annuitant's basis and the taxable gain based on an "exclusion ratio." The exclusion ratio is the result of dividing the annuitant's investment in the contract by the expected return on the annuity contract. The investment in the contract is the annuitant's income tax basis in the annuity property. The expected return from the contract is the product of the annuitant's life expectancy and the annuity payments [IRC Sec. 72(b); Reg. Sec.

¶204

1.72-4(a)(4)]. The capital gain portion of each annuity payment is the difference between the present value of the annuity promise on the date of the sale, and annuitant's adjusted basis in the property, divided by the annuitant's life expectancy. The entire capital portion of any payments that the annuitant received after his or her entire basis has been recovered is taxed as a gain.

IRS eliminates tax perks associated with private annuity arrangements. The IRS has released proposed regulations that change the income tax treatment of a popular tax-deferral transaction known as the private annuity arrangement in which the seller exchanges real estate or other appreciated property for an annuity contract and receives payments for the rest of his or her life. Taxpayers have entered into these arrangements in order to avoid paying the up-front capital gains that the seller would owe if the taxpayer sold appreciated property outright. By establishing the private annuity trust, the taxpayer only paid tax on the annuity payments when they were distributed from the trust, thus deferring the payment of tax over a longer period of time. The new rules are designed to combat the problem of taxpayers who have been inappropriately avoiding or deferring gain on the exchange of highly appreciated property for the issuance of annuity contracts. Under the proposed regulations, the seller's gain is recognized in the year the transaction is completed rather than as payments under the annuity contract are received. The transferor is thus taxed on any appreciation in the property as if that transferor had sold the property for cash and then used the proceeds to purchase the annuity. Under previous IRS guidance, the transferor had recognized the gain evenly over the life expectancy of the annuitant. As a result of this significant reversal in tax treatment, the proposed regulations are essentially the death knell of private annuity arrangements involving transfers of appreciated property.

IRS declares decades-old rule obsolete. In Rev. Rul. 69-74,[10] the IRS sanctioned the deferral of tax on the exchange of appreciated property for a private annuity over the life expectancy of the transferor. In conjunction with the release of the proposed regulations, the IRS declared Rev. Rul. 69-74 obsolete contemporaneous with the effective date of the regulations. Thus the obsolescence would be effective April 18, 2007, for exchanges described in Prop. Reg. Sec. 1.72-6(e)(2)(ii) and Prop. Reg. Sec. 1.1001-1(j)(2)(ii) and effective October 18, 2006 for all other exchanges of property for an annuity contract. The IRS noted that the result in Rev. Rul. 69-74 is inconsistent with the tax treatment of exchanges for commercial annuities or other kinds of property. This ruling was originally based in part on the assumption that the value of a private annuity contract could not be determined for federal income tax purposes. The IRS pointed out that this assumption is no longer correct. The ruling has its roots in authorities that applied the "open transaction doctrine," which has been eroded in recent years. Moreover, the IRS learned that the ruling has been relied upon inappropriately in a number of abusive transactions that were designed to avoid paying income tax on the exchange of appreciated property.

Tax treatment under proposed regulations. In response to the use of private annuities to shelter taxable gain on appreciated assets, which the IRS characterizes as "abusive" and "inappropriate," the IRS has completely reversed its prior tax treatment of

---

[10] Rev. Rul. 69-74, 1969-1 CB 43.

private annuity trusts. Under the proposed regulations, if an annuity contract is received in exchange for property other than money:

- The amount realized attributable to the annuity contract is the fair market value (as determined under the valuation tables issued under IRC Sec. 7520) of the annuity contract at the time of the exchange;

- The entire amount of the gain or loss, if any, is recognized at the time of the exchange, regardless of the taxpayer's method of accounting; and

- For purposes of determining the initial investment in the annuity contract, the aggregate amount of premiums or other consideration paid for the annuity contract equals the amount realized attributable to the annuity contract (the fair market value of the annuity contract) [Prop. Reg. Sec. 1.72-6(e)(1); Prop. Reg. Sec. 1.1001-1(j)(1)].

Application to charitable gift annuities. The proposed regulations do not apply to charitable gift annuities or in circumstances in which there is a legitimate use of the installment sales rules.

Advantages.

- The private annuity allows you to keep the transferred asset within the family and allows for the easy transfer of management responsibilities to the younger generation.

- The parent receives a predetermined payment during the annuity payout period, which is either the life of the parent or a fixed term of years.

- Any appreciation on the transferred property flows to the junior family member.

Disadvantages.

- The parent is exposed to the financial loss resulting from the nonpayment of the annuity by the child. To obtain the desired tax benefits, the risk of nonpayment cannot be lessened through the collateralization of the annuity with some form of security. The receipt of collateral or security will result in the parent's gain being realized and recognized for federal income tax purposes in the year the parties enter into the transaction.[11]

- The annuity payment may cause a financial strain on the child, particularly if the annuity runs for the parent's life expectancy and the parent outlives his or her life expectancy.

- When the parent dies, the child's basis in the property becomes the total of all of the annuity payments made by the child. When the child's basis is low, which is usually the case, the child's taxable gain will be higher when he or she sells the property.

Estate tax consequences. The property transferred to the child is excluded from the parent's gross estate. However, the annuity payments, to the extent that they are not consumed by the parents, constitute property within the parent's taxable gross estate [IRC Sec. 2033].

---

[11] Estate of Bell, 60 TC 469 (1973).

Example 6: Mom sells her beach house worth $1 million to Son in exchange for Son's promise to pay her $50,000 per year for the rest of her life. This is a private annuity and the beach house will be excluded from Mom's estate. If she lives for five years after she has sold the house to Son and has received $250,000 in annuity payments, these payments will be included in her taxable gross estate to the extent that she has not spent the money.

Additional estate tax problems arise if:

1. The value of the transferred property exceeds the value of the annuity. The failure to receive full and adequate consideration in exchange for the transferred property results in the difference being subject to estate tax under IRC Sec. 2043(a) as a transfer for insufficient consideration [see ¶ 1811].

Example 7: Mom sells the beach house worth $1 million to Son in exchange for Son's promise to pay her $50,000 per year for the rest of her life. If the present value of the payments that Mom will receive is also worth $1 million, the beach house is not included in her taxable gross estate. If the present value of the payments is only worth $400,000, after Mom's death, $600,000 must be included in her taxable gross estate because the annuity was a transfer for insufficient consideration [IRC Sec. 2043].

1. The annuity with a survivorship component that pays someone else when the parent dies triggers inclusion in the parent's estate under IRC Sec. 2039 [see ¶ 1808].

Example 8: Same example as above, except that after Mom dies, the annuity agreement provides that Sister will receive the annuity payments instead of Mom. The value of the remaining payments due to Sister must be included in Mom's taxable gross estate [IRC Sec. 2039].

1. If the annuity is issued by a trust, particularly a trust where the parent retains some control over the trust, the retained string may result in taxation under IRC Sec. 2036.
2. If the parent retains use of the property through an implied understanding or agreement with the child, the implied understanding triggers inclusion under IRC Sec. 2036 [see ¶ 1807].

If the child dies before the parent, the child's estate can take a deduction for the actuarial value of the payments the estate must make (or in fact makes) if the parent dies before the child's federal estate tax return is filed [see ¶ 2001].

(d) Intra-Family Interest-Free Loans. A popular technique for shifting income within a family used to be a low-interest or interest-free loan to children and grandchildren. Typically, the children could invest the loan proceeds and pay tax on the income at a lower tax rate than the parents. Unfortunately, the U.S. Supreme Court eliminated this technique in *Dickman*,[12] where the Court held that the economic value associated with money in an intrafamily interest-free or below-market loan, if uncol-

---

[12] 465 U.S. 330 (1984).

lected by the lender, is really a taxable gift.[13] The amount of the gift was not determined by the Court. The enactment of IRC Sec. 7872 and IRC Sec. 1274 soon thereafter filled this void. IRC Sec. 7872 governs the tax treatment of below market loans in several types of transactions, including loans between family members. IRC Sec. 7872 applies to any transaction that (1) is a bona fide loan, (2) is below market, (3) falls within one of four categories of below-market loans, and (4) does not qualify for one of several exceptions. The four categories are loans (1) from a donor to a donee, (2) from an employer to an employee, (3) from a corporation to a shareholder, and (4) with interest arrangements made for tax avoidance purposes [IRC Sec. 7872(c)]. IRC Sec. 7872 will not impute gift or income tax consequences to a loan providing sufficient stated interest which is defined as interest at a rate no lower than the appropriate AFR, based on the appropriate compounding period [Prop. Reg. Sec. 1.7872-3(c)(1)].

IRC Sec. 1274 provides monthly factors for short term (0-3 years), mid-term (over 3 up to 9 years), and long-term (over 9 years) notes. There are factors for annual, semiannual, or monthly compounding. If a loan bears interest at the applicable federal rate (AFR) using the appropriate factor based on the timing of compounding under the note, it will not be considered a below market loan under IRC Sec. 7872 and there will no imputed gift from the lender to the borrower or imputed interest income to the lender [Prop. Reg. Sec. 1.7872-3(c)(1)]. A below market loan is defined as a demand loan for which the amount loaned exceeds the present value of all payments due under the loan [IRC Sec. 7872(e)(1)(A)]. Because the present value of a term loan is determined using the AFR, a demand or term loan with an interest rate at least equal to the AFR is not a below market loan [Prop. Reg. Sec. 1.7872-3(c)(1)]. The AFR schedules are published by the IRS each month on about the 20th day of the month.

The taxpayer computes forgone interest by taking the present value of all payments due under the loan (discounted using the appropriate AFR) and comparing it to the actual loan amount. If the present value is less, there is forgone interest. This forgone interest is deemed to have been transferred from the lender to the borrower as a gift and then transferred from the borrower to the lender as interest income. The forgone interest is imputed as interest income on the last day of each taxable year.

For demand loans, the forgone interest each year is deemed to be given on December 31 (or when the loan is repaid). For term loans, 100 percent of the forgone interest is treated as a gift upfront when the loan is made. In order to avoid these deemed and imputed tax treatments, the parties in an intra-family loan transaction should use an interest rate at least equal to the AFR for all loans.

Exceptions. In the following two situations interest does not have to be charged on the loan at the AFR in order to avoid imputed income or gift tax:

1. **$10,000 *De Minimis* Exemption.** Under a *de minimis* exception, a loan is exempt from IRC Sec. 7872 if it is made between individuals (not trusts, estates or corporations) and the aggregate outstanding balance of the loans between such individuals does not exceed $10,000 and the loan is directly attributable to the purchase or carrying of income-producing assets [IRC Sec. 7872(c)(2)(B)];

---

[13] 465 U.S. 330 (1984).

2. **$100,000 Exemption (Income Exception Only).** If the aggregate outstanding amount of loans between individuals does not exceed $100,000, the imputed interest amount (the amount treated as retransferred from the borrower to the lender at the end of the year) for income tax purposes is limited to the borrower's net investment income for the year [IRC Sec. 7872(d)]. A *de minimis* rule allows the lender to report zero interest income if the borrower's net investment income does not exceed $1,000. The limitation on the amount of interest applies for income tax rather than gift tax purposes. The full amount of imputed interest must be included as a gift. The deduction that may be available to the borrower is limited to the amount of imputed interest reported by the lender.

There are two types of below-market-rate loans:

1. A demand loan, which is a loan payable in full at any time that the lender asks for the money back [IRC Sec. 7872(f)(5)]. If the interest is less than the AFR, it is a below-market-rate loan and special rules discussed below apply.

2. A term loan, which is any loan other than a demand loan. A term loan states a specific time period for repayment. If the amount loaned exceeds the present value (applying the appropriate AFR) of all payments due under the loan, it is a below-market-rate loan and special rules apply.

IRC Sec. 7872(a)(1) recharacterizes the below-market-rate demand loan as a two-step transaction:

1. The lender (parent) is treated as having transferred on the last day of the calendar year an amount equal to the forgone interest (the prevailing federal rate of interest less the loan's actual interest rate) to the borrower (child); and

2. The borrower (child) is then treated as retransferring that amount back to the lender (parent) as imputed interest.

If the parent has made a long-term loan to a child, the child is treated as having received cash (generally as of the date of the loan) equal to the excess of the amount loaned over the present value of all payments required under the loan's terms.

Forgone interest is the difference between the interest that would have been payable on the loan for the period the interest accrues at the AFR, assuming that such payment would be payable annually on the last day of the calendar year, over any interest actually payable on the loan properly allocable to such period. To help taxpayers determine the AFR, the IRS issues on a monthly basis the rate for the next month.

Bottom line. There is phantom income (the amount of the forgone interest) passing from the parent to the child and back again [IRC Sec. 7872]. This undercuts dramatically the value of making a low-interest or interest-free loan to family members as an income-shifting tool.

> **Example 9:** On January 1, Mom, a calendar year taxpayer, makes a $200,000 loan to Son, who is a calendar year taxpayer, for two years at 5 percent simple interest payable annually. If the AFR is 12 percent compounded semiannually, the amount treated as transferred by Mom to Son for gift tax purposes would be $24,760 (the excess of $200,000 over the present value of all payments due under the loan discounted at the AFR). The amount treated as retransferred by Son to

Mom on the last day of each of the two calendar years would be $14,720 (the excess of interest computed at the AFR compounded semiannually over interest actually payable on the loan). Mom would therefore have to include in income each year $14,720 plus the $10,000 interest stated in the loan agreement. The interest payment may or may not be deductible by Son, depending on the interest deduction rules.

Loan or Gift? In intra-family loan transactions, there is always a possibility that the IRS will treat the loan as a gift even if a note was given in return for the transfer if the loan is not bona fide or if there appears to be an intention that the loan will not be repaid by the borrower. The IRS may look askance at intra-family loans that result in estate freezing and the avoidance of estate tax on the lender's assets. Estate freezing can occur if the asset that the borrower acquires with the loan proceeds has combined income and appreciation above the interest rate that is paid on the note resulting in a transfer by the lender of wealth without gift or estate tax consequences.

The IRS has a presumption that a transfer of property in an intra-family situation will be presumed to be a gift unless the transferor can prove the receipt of "an adequate and full consideration in money or money's worth" [Reg. Sec. 25.2512-8; 25.2511-1(g)(1)].[14] This gift presumption can be overcome if the parties can show the existence of a bona fide loan with a "real expectation of repayment and an intention to enforce the debt."[15] The court in *Miller*,[16] applied the following factors to determine whether a bona fide loan existed: (1) existence of a note or other evidence of indebtedness; (2) payment of reasonable interest; (3) presence of security or collateral in the transaction; (4) whether there was a fixed maturity date; (5) whether a demand for repayment was made; (6) whether actual repayment was made; (7) whether the transferee had the ability to repay; (8) whether any records maintained by the transferor or the transferee reflected the transaction as a loan; and (9) if the manner in which the transaction was reported for federal tax purposes was consistent with a loan.

Gift loans or interest-free loans involve gratuitous transfers of the type subject to gift taxes. More specifically, the term "gift loan" connotes any below-market interest loan where the forgone interest is in the nature of a loan [IRC Sec. 7872(f)(3)].

The forgone interest means, for any period during which the loan is outstanding, the excess of:

1. The amount of interest that would have been payable for the period if interest accrued at the AFR and were payable annually on the last day of the calendar year, minus

2. Any interest payable on the loan allocable to that period [IRC Sec. 7872(e)(2)].

Gift loans. A gift loan is a below market loan if the lender does not charge interest at the rate of interest required under IRC Sec. 7872 [IRC Sec. 7872(f)(3); Prop. Reg. Sec. 1.7872-4(b)(1)]. The IRS will assume that a transfer of money from one family member to another is a gift.

---

[14] Harwood, 82 TC 239 (1984), *aff'd*, 786 F.2d 1174 (9th Cir. 1986), *cert. den.*, 479 U.S. 1007 (1987).

[15] Estate of Van Anda, 12 TC 1158 (1949).
[16] TC Memo 1996-3.

A loan between related (as well as unrelated) persons can qualify as a gift loan. For example, if a parent does not charge interest when money is loaned to children, the parent is deemed to make a gift to the children in the amount of the forgone interest for gift and income tax purposes and to receive an equivalent amount of interest income for income tax purposes. The child is treated as having received a gift and as having used it to pay the phantom interest income to the parent. The parent owes income tax on the phantom income received from the child. The child, on the other hand, owes no income tax on his or her phantom income. It is an income tax-free gift that is subject to gift tax. For federal income tax purposes, the child may be able to claim an interest deduction equal to the amount of the parent's phantom income.

If the gift loan is a below-market demand loan, the forgone interest is treated as a gift made by the lender to the borrower. Any forgone interest attributable to periods during any calendar year is treated as transferred on the last day of that calendar year [IRC Secs. 7872(a)(1), 7872(a)(2)].

If the gift loan is a below-market term loan, the lender is treated as having transferred as a gift on the date the loan was made an amount equal to:

1. The excess of the amount lent, less

2. The present value of all payments that are required to be made under the terms of the loan [IRC Sec. 7872(b)(1)].

Present value is determined on the date of the loan by using a discount rate equal to the AFR.

For demand loans, the AFR equals the federal short-term rate in effect for the period for which the amount of forgone interest is being determined, compounded semiannually [IRC Sec. 7872(f)(2)(B)].

For term loans, the AFR equals the federal short-term, mid-term, or long-term rate, based on the term of the loan (not longer than three years, over three years but not over nine years, or over nine years) in effect on the day the loan was made, compounded semiannually [IRC Sec. 7872(f)(2)(A)].

A below-market interest loan constitutes a completed gift for federal gift tax purposes when made and qualifies for the annual per donee exclusion [see ¶ 901] if made to:

1. An individual;

2. A present interest trust (see discussion at ¶ 905); or

3. A trust containing a "*Crummey* power" (see ¶ 906 for a more detailed discussion of this concept).

Exceptions. The below-market loan rules generally do not apply to any day the aggregate amount of outstanding loans (all loans whether or not involving forgone interest) between two individuals is $10,000 or less. However, this de minimis break does not apply to gift loans between individuals if the loans are directly attributable to the acquisition or carrying of income-producing assets [IRC Sec. 7872(c)(2)]. There is a special ceiling for any day the amount of a gift loan's outstanding balance does not exceed $100,000. The amount of interest that is deemed to have been transferred between the lender and the borrower is limited to the borrower's net investment income for the year. But if the net investment income is $1,000 or less, the net investment

¶204

income is deemed to be zero and there are no tax consequences to the gift loan [IRC Sec. 7872(d)].

(e) Loan Guarantees. An individual may even incur a gift tax liability by paying off a loan he or she guaranteed for a child or someone else. In addition, the IRS has said that a parent's promise to pay a child's debts can itself be taxable.[17] The guarantor transfers a valuable property interest, which is deemed a completed gift on the date the promise becomes binding and determinable in value.

¶205 POWERS OF APPOINTMENT

A power of appointment can be defined as the power or right that enables someone (the "donee" or "powerholder") to designate the recipients of property or interests in property.[1] Powers of appointment can be one of the most useful estate-planning tools because they afford you the opportunity to draft estate-planning documents with a measure of flexibility [see ¶ 1810]. With a power of appointment in place, long after a person has died, the heirs have the ability to make changes to the estate plan if circumstances have changed and mandate such action.

There are many terms of art in the power of appointment world. Understanding these terms is a prerequisite to understanding the tax consequences of these powers. Basically a power of appointment, which is also just called a power, is the power the donor of property grants to someone else, who is called the holder, enabling the holder to designate who will own the property down the road. A power of appointment must be created by someone other than the possessor (or holder) of the power.

> **Example 1:** Dad creates a trust. The trust owns a piece of land. After Dad dies, the trust provides that the land goes to Son and Daughter. Dad gives Mom an unlimited or general power of appointment over the property in the trust. Mom can give the land to whomever she pleases, including her boyfriend or her children from a prior marriage.

The power could be a general power of appointment or a special power of appointment. Why is this distinction important? The different types of powers have different tax ramifications. In general, property subject to a general power of appointment is subject to gift and estate taxation when the power is exercised or released. In addition, if a holder had a general power of appointment over property at the time of death, the property is included in his or her estate [IRC Sec. 2041(a)(2)].

(a) General Power of Appointment. A general power of appointment is a power exercisable in favor of the power holder, the power holder's estate, creditors, or creditors of the power holder's estate [IRC Sec. 2514(c); Reg. Sec. 25.2514-1(c)(1)]. An individual has a general power of appointment if he has the power to determine, who, including himself, may become the owner of the property. The mere possession of

---

[17] Ltr. Rul. 9113009.

[1] ¶ 205 Restatement (Second) Property, Section 11.1 (1986).

certain general powers can cause inclusion in the power holder's gross estate. A general power of appointment includes the unlimited power to consume or invade the trust principal or income, or both, for the benefit of the holder of the power. A power of appointment exercisable to meet the estate tax, or any other taxes, debts, or charges which is enforceable against the estate, is included within the meaning of a power of appointment exercisable in favor of the decedent's estate, his creditors, or the creditors of his estate. A power of appointment exercisable for the purpose of discharging a legal obligation of the decedent or for his pecuniary benefit is considered a power of appointment exercisable in favor of the decedent or his creditors. However, a power of appointment will not be considered a general power of appointment just because an appointee may be a creditor of the decedent or his estate. A power of appointment is not a general power if by its terms it is either exercisable only in favor of one or more designated persons or classes other than the decedent or his creditors, or the decedent's estate or the creditors of his estate, or expressly not exercisable in favor of the decedent or his creditors, or the decedent's estate or the creditors of his estate.

A decedent may have two powers under the same instrument, one of which is a general power of appointment and the other which is not. For example, a beneficiary may have a power to withdraw trust corpus during his life, and a testamentary power to appoint the corpus among his descendants. The testamentary power is not a general power of appointment [Reg. Sec. 25.2541-1(c)(1)].

If the holder of the general power of appointment exercises or releases (as discussed below) the power during his or her lifetime, the holder has made a gift [IRC Sec. 2514(b)].

> **Example 2:** Dad establishes a trust for Daughter. She is the trustee and has the power to invade the trust for any purpose. Daughter has a general power of appointment.

(b) Special or Limited Power of Appointment. A special or limited power of appointment is:

1. Any power of appointment that cannot be exercised in favor of the holder, the holder's estate, creditors, or creditors of the holder's estate [Reg. Sec. 25.2514-1(c)(1)]; or

2. A general power of appointment that is limited by an ascertainable standard relating to the holder's health, education, maintenance, or support (HEMS) [IRC Sec. 2514(c)(1); Reg. Sec. 25.2514-1(c)(2)].

> **Example 3:** Dad creates a trust for Son. Son is the trustee and can only withdraw funds to pay for medical bills. For transfer tax purposes, Son has a limited power of appointment.

> ▶ **PRACTICE POINTER:** Do not deviate from this exact HEMS language contained in the Regulations. The IRS and the courts are not flexible. Do not get too creative when drafting your ascertainable standards. According to the IRS and the courts, you cannot use just the words "comfort," "welfare," "benefit" or

"happiness."[2] These words will taint the ascertainable standard and cause the power to be taxed as a general power of appointment. Use the full HEMS language.

The Regulations permit the use of the following phrases: "support," "support in reasonable comfort," "maintenance in health and reasonable comfort," "support in his accustomed manner of living," "education, including college and professional education," "health," and "medical, dental, hospital, and nursing expenses and expenses of invalidism." In determining whether a power is limited by an ascertainable standard, it is immaterial whether the beneficiary is required to exhaust his other income before the power can be exercised [Reg. Sec. 25.2514-1(c)(2)].

Some powers are not powers of appointment. A power to manage or invest trust assets or to allocate trust receipts and disbursements, when exercisable only in a fiduciary capacity, is not a power of appointment. A power to amend the administrative provisions of a trust that do not substantially affect the beneficial enjoyment of the trust property or income is also not considered a power of appointment.

If a power of appointment can be exercised by the holder but only with the consent of (1) the creator of the power, or (2) a person having a substantial adverse interest in the property subject to the power, the holder does not have a general power of appointment [IRC Sec. 2514(c)(3); Reg. Sec. 25.2514-3(b)(2)]. A person is considered to have an interest adverse to the exercise of the power if there is a possibility, now or in the future, that the person may obtain a personal benefit from the property. A trustee administering a trust in a fiduciary capacity does not, by that fact alone, have an adverse interest in the trust.

> **Example 4:** *Adverse interest.* Tom and Larry are trustees of a trust under which the income is to be paid to Larry for life and then to Meg for life, and Tom is the remainderman. Tom and Larry have the power to distribute corpus to Tom during Larry's life. Because Larry's interest is adverse to an exercise of the power in favor of Tom, Tom does not have a general power of appointment. If Tom and Meg were trustees, Meg's interest would likewise be adverse [Reg. Sec. 25.2514-3(b)(2), Example (2)].

> **Example 5:** *Interest that is not adverse.* Tom and Larry are trustees of a trust under which the income is to be paid to Larry for life. Tom and Larry can designate whether corpus is to be distributed to Tom or to Alice after Larry's death. Larry's interest is not adverse to an exercise of the power in favor of Tom, and Tom therefore has a general power of appointment [Reg. Sec. 25.2514-3(b)(2), Example (3)].

(c) Consequences of Exercise, Release, or Lapse.
The lifetime exercise or release of a general power of appointment in favor of someone other than the holder of the power is a transfer for gift tax purposes unless the exercise or release was for

---

[2] Miller, 387 F.2d 866 (3d Cir. 1968); Lehman, 448 F.2d 1318 (5th Cir. 1971); Estate of Jones, 56 TC 35 (1971), *aff'd*, 73-1 USTC ¶12,924 (3d Cir 1973), *cert. denied*, 414 U.S. 820 (1974); Rev. Rul. 77-194, 1977-1 CB 283; Rev. Rul. 82-63, 1982-1 CB 135.

adequate consideration [IRC Sec. 2514(b)]. By *exercising* the power in favor of the other person rather than in favor of himself or herself, the power holder has diminished his or her wealth.

> **Example 6:** Grandfather transfers $100,000 to Son in an irrevocable trust, income to Grandson for life, remainder to Granddaughter. Son has the power to invade corpus for anyone, including himself. He invades $40,000 of corpus for Girlfriend. IRC Sec. 2514 treats Son as having made a gift to Girlfriend of $40,000, of which $28,000 is taxable and $13,000 is excludable under the annual exclusion rules found in IRC Sec. 2503(b) [see ¶ 901].

The exercise of a general power in favor of the holder of the power is not a gift for tax purposes because the gift tax applies only to transfers that diminish the wealth of the holder-donor. In this context, the donee and the donor (in the tax sense) are one and the same.

Sec. 2514 also applies if the power holder *releases* the power, so that he or she will not hold the power at his or her death. The release diminishes his or her estate by preventing operation of IRC Sec. 2041, which requires that the power be held at death to be estate taxable [see ¶ 1810]. Not surprisingly, the definition of general power of appointment is the same for both gift and estate tax purposes [IRC Secs. 2514(c), 2041(b)(1)].

A qualified disclaimer of a general power of appointment is not considered a release of the power and does not result in a gift [see ¶ 1201].

The failure to exercise a general power of appointment (created after October 21, 1942) within a specific time period so that the power *lapses* constitutes a lapse or a taxable release of the power [Reg. Sec. 25.2514-3(c)(4)]. The lapse is treated as a taxable release only to the extent that the value of the property subject to the power exceeds the greater of $5,000 or 5 percent of the total value of the property out of which the appointment could have been satisfied [IRC Sec. 2514(e)]. The gift tax consequences of the 5 and 5 limitation are discussed further at ¶ 906.

The exercise or release of a special power of appointment is generally not treated as a transfer for gift tax purposes. An exception exists for certain circumstances in which a special power of appointment is exercised to create another power [IRC Sec. 2514(d)].

> **Example 7:** Brother has transferred property in trust to Sister with the remainder payable to Nephew at Sister's death. The income is accumulated during Sister's life. Sister has the power to have the income distributed to herself. If Sister's power is limited by an ascertainable standard (relating to health, etc.), the lapse of such power will not constitute a transfer of property for gift tax purposes. If Sister's power is not limited by an ascertainable standard, its lapse or release during Sister's lifetime may constitute a transfer of property for gift tax purposes [Reg. Sec. 25.2514-3(c)(4)].

A gift results when a general power of appointment created before October 22, 1942, is exercised. However, the release or lapse of such a power does not result in a gift [IRC Sec. 2514(a)]. A power created before October 22, 1942, that is exercisable by the

¶205

holder together with another person, regardless of that person's adverse interest, is not treated as a general power of appointment [IRC Sec. 2514(c)(2)].

A testamentary power of appointment (i.e., one created by will) is generally considered as created on the date of the testator-creator's death. However, a power of appointment created by will executed before October 22, 1942, is considered created before that date if the creator died before July 1, 1949, without having republished his or her will after October 21, 1942 [Reg. Sec. 25.2514-1(e)].

A general power of appointment created by a lifetime (or inter vivos) instrument is considered created on the date the instrument takes effect. This type of power is not considered created at some future date just because it can be revoked, it cannot be exercised immediately, or its holders cannot be identified until after the date the document takes effect [Reg. Sec. 25.2514-1(e)].

¶206 WHEN IS A GIFT TRANSFER COMPLETE

A taxable gift is considered to have been made when the donor has made a completed, gratuitous transfer of property. The gift transfer is completed when the donor has relinquished sufficient dominion and control over the property so that it is no longer subject to the donor's will or the donor no longer has the power to change its disposition (whether for the donor's own benefit or the benefit of others) [Reg. Sec. 25.2511-2(b)]. In other words, a gift occurs when a person has completely parted with and retains no strings over the property transferred in the gift.

Consequences of retention of testamentary power of appointment. In Reg. Sec. 25.2511-2(b) the IRS addresses whether a gift is complete when the donor has retained a testamentary power of appointment:

> As to any property, or part thereof or interest therein, of which the donor has so parted with dominion and control as to leave in him no power to change its disposition, whether for his own benefit or for the benefit of another, the gift is complete. But if upon a transfer of property (whether in trust or otherwise) the donor reserves any power over its disposition, the gift may be wholly incomplete, or may be partially complete and partially incomplete... For example, if a donor transfers property to another in trust to pay the income to the donor or accumulate it in the discretion of the trustee, and the donor retains a testamentary power to appoint the remainder among his descendants, no portion of the transfer is a completed gift. On the other hand, if the donor had not retained the testamentary power of appointment, but instead provided that the remainder should go to X or his heirs, the entire transfer would be a completed gift. However, if the exercise of the trustee's power in favor of the grantor is limited by a fixed or ascertainable standard, enforceable by or on behalf of the grantor, then the gift is incomplete to the extent of the ascertainable value of any rights thus retained by the grantor.

In Chief Counsel Advice 201208026, the IRS concluded that under IRC Sec. 2511, donors made completed gifts of beneficial term interests when they transferred property to a trust, even though they retained limited testamentary powers of appointment over the remaining trust corpus. The donors each retained a limited testamentary power of appointment over only so much of the trust that would remain at their deaths. The trustee, who was one of the donors' children, had absolute discretion over the trust's administration. Pursuant to the trust instrument, the donors did not retain any power or right to affect the beneficial term interests of the beneficiaries during the trust term. The donors completely divested themselves of dominion and control over that portion of the trust property on the date of transfer. As a result, the donors' transfers to the trust constituted a completed gift of the beneficial term interests. Because the limited testamentary powers of appointment related only to the remainder, if the donors relinquished this power during the trust term, the relinquishment would only affect the disposition of the remainder of the trust property and would constitute a transfer of the remainder.

Consequences of retention of powers. In Reg. Sec. 25.2511-2(c), the IRS provides that a gift is incomplete if a donor reserves the power to revest the beneficial title to the property in himself. A gift is also incomplete if a reserved power gives the donor the power to name new beneficiaries or to change the interests of the beneficiaries unless the power is a fiduciary power limited by a fixed or ascertainable standard.

In Reg. Sec. 25.2511-2(d), the IRS provides that a gift is not considered incomplete merely because the donor reserves the power to change the manner or time of enjoyment.

In Reg. Sec. 25.2511-2(f), the IRS provides that the relinquishment or termination of a power to change the beneficiaries of transferred property is regarded as the event which completes the gift and causes the tax to apply. For example, if A transfers property in trust for the benefit of B and C but reserves the power as trustee to change the proportionate interests of B and C, and if A thereafter has another person appointed trustee in place of himself, such later relinquishment of the power by A to the new trustee completes the gift of the transferred property. The receipt of income or other enjoyment of the transferred property by the transferee or by the beneficiary (other than by the donor himself) during the interim between the making of the initial transfer and the relinquishment or termination of the power operates to free such income or other enjoyment from the power, and constitutes a gift of such income or of such other enjoyment.

(a) Deciding Whether Check Is Gift Upon Receipt or When Cashed.

Year-end is a good time for taxpayers to be sure that they have made their annual exclusion gifts. Taxpayers should not wait until December 31 to make the gift. The IRS could argue that the gift was made the following year when the check cleared the bank rather than in the year that the taxpayer wrote the check and delivered it to the donee. The gift giver would then lose the opportunity to take advantage of his or her annual gift tax exclusion in the year of the gift and any subsequent gifts made the following year would exceed that year's quota. When an individual makes late year-end gifts by check, it is thus important to figure out in which year the gift was made because the gift tax exclusion is determined on an annual basis [see ¶ 602]. Any portion of the annual gift tax exclusion that is not used up by year-end cannot be carried over to the next year. The law provides that a gift made by check is not complete until the check is cashed, certified, or negotiated for value to a third person. As a result, if you are giving a check and intend to claim an exclusion for the gift, allow enough time for the check to be cashed before the end of the year. Alternatively, consider giving a certified check, which is as good as cash because it is considered a completed gift when you hand over the check regardless when the donee cashes it.

Rev. Rul. 96-56[1] provides that if a check is delivered to a noncharitable donee, completion of the gift will relate back to the earlier of:

1. The date on which the donor parted with dominion and control under local law so the donor cannot change his or her mind; or

2. The date on which the donee deposited, cashed, or presented the check for payment if:

- The drawee bank paid the check when it was first presented;
- The donor was alive when the bank paid the check;
- The donor intended to make a gift;
- Delivery was unconditional; and
- The check was deposited, cashed or presented in the calendar year in which the favorable gift treatment was sought and within a reasonable time of issuance.

(b) Relation-Back Rule. This rule, which is known as the relation-back doctrine, also applies to noncharitable donees where the donor was alive when the checks were paid.[2] For example, a donor's gift by check that is drawn and presented for payment predeath to the donee's bank in December, but is not accepted until January of the following year will constitute a completed gift in December in the year the check was delivered and presented for payment. The relation-back doctrine will apply if the taxpayer establishes that:

- There was an intent to make a gift;
- The predeath delivery of the check was unconditional; and
- The check was presented for payment prior to the death of the decedent and within the year for which favorable tax treatment was sought and within a reasonable time of issuance.

Example 1: Mom gives Son a $14,000 check on December 31, 2014. Mom wants the check to qualify as a 2014 annual gift tax exclusion gift. Son cashes the check on January 3, 2015. The check is considered a 2014 gift, even though it is not cashed until 2015. All three of the following elements existed for the relation-back theory to apply: (1) Mom intended to make a 2014 gift; (2) Mom delivered the check unconditionally (e.g., there were enough funds in the account to cover the check and there was no understanding between Mom and Son not to cash the check); and (3) Son could have presented the check to the bank before the end of 2014, but waited until 2015 to cash it.

---

[1] ¶ 206 Rev. Rul. 96-56, 1996-2 CB 161.

[2] Estate of Metzger, 100 TC 204, *aff'd*, 38 F.3d 118 (4th Cir. 1994).

The relation-back doctrine will save the annual exclusion for a check that is not paid before the end of the calendar year, if:

- The donor is alive when the check is paid;
- Delivery of the check is unconditional;
- There are sufficient funds in the account on which the check is drawn; and
- The check is deposited in the calendar year for which completed gift treatment is sought and within a reasonable time of its issuance.

(c) Exception to Relation-Back Rule. The relation-back rule does not apply when gifts are made to noncharitable donees and when the donor dies before the checks are cashed.[3] This means that the value of checks drawn on a decedent's checking account prior to death will be included in the decedent's gross estate if they are cashed after the decedent has died because the decedent possessed, until death, the power to revoke the checks until accepted or paid by the drawee bank. Therefore, they were not completed gifts because the decedent maintained dominion and control over the amounts in the checking account against which the checks were written until death.

It therefore behooves taxpayers who are elderly or seriously ill to avoid procrastinating and to make annual exclusion gifts as soon as possible rather than wait until December 31. In addition, donees should deposit the checks immediately to avoid any IRS challenge of annual exclusion gifts.

¶207 JOINT OWNERSHIP

The creation or termination of a joint tenancy can have gift tax consequences. The joint ownership of property refers to the simultaneous ownership of property by at least two persons. While both joint owners are still alive, each co-owner has an equal, undivided interest in the entire property and the right to use and enjoy it. Joint ownership applies to all forms of property, real property, tangible personal property, and intangible personal property.

In a tenancy in common, two or more people each have a separate interest in the property but all of them have a common right of possession. Therefore, there is no survivorship right to property held as tenants in common and creditors can reach the entire property to satisfy a debt of only one tenant.

Joint ownership between spouses may, in states where it is recognized, take the form of a tenancy by the entirety. The tenancy by entirety is distinguished from the usual form of joint ownership because a tenancy by entirety can neither be conveyed, severed, or terminated by one spouse acting alone nor be reached by a creditor of only one spouse. Each spouse or joint tenant has the same interest and same rights in the property as his or her spouse. A tenancy by entirety is a form of property ownership available only to a husband and wife as a marital unit. The key feature of the tenancy by the entirety form

---

[3] Estate of Newman, 111 TC 81 (1998), *aff'd*, 203 F.3d 53 (D.C. Cir. 1999); see also Estate of Rosano, 67 F. Supp. 2d 113 (E.D.N.Y. 1999), *aff'd*, 245 F.3d 212 (2d Cir. 2001), *cert. denied*, 534 U.S. 1135 (2002).

of property ownership is the right of survivorship—the survivor becomes the fee simple owner of the property when the other spouse dies. The tenancy terminates when the property is transferred or sold or when the couple divorce.

Community property is property acquired during a couple's marriage (except by gift, devise, descent, or as compensation for personal injuries) in nine community property states (Arizona, California, Idaho, Louisiana, Nevada, New Mexico, Texas, Washington, and Wisconsin). When one spouse dies, the surviving spouse owns one-half of all community property and the other one-half is included in the decedent's probate estate. In addition, the entire community property may be liable for the debts of only one spouse.

(a) Nonspousal Joint Ownership. Federal gift tax principles generally govern gifts to nonspouses. No special or unique treatment is accorded this type of gift. In general, if each joint owner contributes a proportional share of the consideration for the property and when the property is severed would receive this proportional interest, no gift occurred on the creation of the joint property and there are no federal gift tax consequences. If, however, one of the joint owners contributes more than his or her proportional share of the consideration, a gift results. The amount of the gift equals the excess consideration.

> **Example 1:** If you buy land for $100,000 with your own funds and title is taken in your name and your brother's as tenants in common, you have made a gift of $50,000 to your brother because your brother received an interest in property worth $50,000. Because your brother can dispose of his share at will without your permission in the normal course, his interest is "severable" [Reg. Sec. 25.2511-1(h)(5)] and its creation is taxed.

> **Example 2:** You and your sister buy land for $100,000 and take title as joint tenants with a right of survivorship, respectively, providing $70,000 and $30,000 of the purchase price. You have made a gift to your sister of $20,000, the amount by which her half of the property exceeds her consideration.

The relative ages of the joint owners are immaterial if any owner could, in theory, sever the joint tenancy and thus obtain a pro rata share of the property. However, where severance of the property can be accomplished only by the joint action of all joint owners, then the ages of the joint owners are material and the value of the gift must be determined actuarially. In most states, one tenant acting alone can sever the traditional joint tenancy.

The value of the gift can be determined actuarially by consulting the actuarial tables published by the Treasury Department [Reg. Sec. 25.2512-5].

Also, in accordance with general gift tax principles, the termination of a nonspousal joint tendency represents a taxable gift to the extent the donor's share of the proceeds is less than the donor's interest in the property.

(b) Spousal Joint Ownership. Gifts between spouses are not taxed as a result of the unlimited federal gift tax marital deduction unless the donee spouse is a non-U.S. citizen [IRC Sec. 2523(i)(3); see ¶ 1107 for an in-depth analysis of the marital deduction]. For spouses who are not citizens of the United States, there is a special $145,000 annual exclusion in 2014 [see ¶ 1501]. If the amount of the gift exceeds this exclusion, then gift tax liability arises but no tax is owed if the donor has available unified credit. To the extent that gifts are made in excess of $145,000 in 2014, no marital deduction will apply to reduce the gift tax. However, the annual exclusion for transfers by gift to a noncitizen spouse is allowed only for transfers that would qualify for the marital deduction if the donee were a U.S. citizen. For example, a gift in trust will not qualify for the increased annual exclusion unless it qualified for one of the exceptions to the terminable interest rule.

> **Example 3:** Husband and Wife are both residents of the United States, but Wife is a Brazilian citizen. In 2003, Husband bought real property entirely out of his own funds for himself and Wife as tenants by the entirety. The creation of the joint tenancy did not result in a gift. In 2014, they sell the real property at a gain of $625,000, and Wife keeps all the proceeds. Result: in 2014, Husband is treated as making a gift of $625,000 to Wife, the first $145,000 of which is sheltered by the special annual exclusion available to spouses who are not U.S. citizens. The remaining $480,000 is subject to tax. Note that if Wife were a citizen of the United States, the entire gift on the termination of the joint tenancy would be sheltered by the gift tax marital deduction.

(c) Tenancy by the Entirety. A tenancy by the entirety is a form of joint property ownership available only to a husband and wife as a marital unit. A tenancy by the entirety can neither be conveyed, severed, or terminated by one spouse acting alone nor be reached by a creditor of only one spouse. Each spouse or joint tenant has the same interest and same rights in the property as his or her spouse. Entireties property is, however, subject to the claims of the creditors of both spouses. Most states that recognize tenancy by the entireties, so-called full bar jurisdictions, completely prohibit creditors from attaching entireties property to satisfy the debts of only one spouse. The other states that recognize tenancy by the entirety, so-called modified or partial bar jurisdictions, permit creditors to attach one spouse's interest in entireties property for that spouse's debts only, subject to the rights of the nonliable spouse.

The most important aspect of a joint tenancy is that it contains the rights of survivorship which means that the interest of a deceased joint tenant does not pass in accordance with the provisions in a will, but passes to the surviving joint tenant directly by operation of law without any additional legal action.

The right of survivorship and the protection from separate creditors makes tenancy by the entirety an attractive and simple estate planning device. As a result of this automatic survivorship feature, the joint tenancy form of property ownership functions as a means of probate avoidance because probate only applies to property that is titled in an individual's name alone. Thus probate is avoided for property titled as tenants by the entirety.

> ▶ **PRACTICE POINTER:** Many couples have the misconception that they can avoid all other estate planning by simply titling all of their assets as tenants by the entireties because when the first spouse dies, the property passes automatically, by operation of law to the surviving spouse. Jointly held property also

¶207

avoids the often time-consuming and expensive state probate process. In addition, the property is protected from the creditors of one of the spouses. But couples who use tenancies by the entireties as their sole means of estate planning, are failing to take advantage of estate tax savings techniques sanctioned by the IRS and will end up paying in taxes the very money they had intended to leave to their loved ones. Ownership of excessive amounts of jointly owned property between husband and wife can result in what is called "overfunding" the marital deduction. This occurs when too much property is transferred to the surviving spouse causing an unnecessarily large estate tax at the surviving spouse's death. If property is jointly owned with rights of survivorship, no estate tax will be due at the death of the first spouse because of the unlimited marital deduction that allows all property to pass tax-free to a surviving spouse. But when the second spouse dies, the beneficiaries will be hit with a big estate tax bill because the first spouse's unified credit was wasted.

A simple solution to this problem is to sever all the joint tenancies so that each spouse has separate ownership of an amount at least equal to the applicable exclusion amount. Then, take advantage of the bypass or credit shelter trust to shelter assets totaling up to twice the applicable exclusion amount from estate tax.

As a general rule, if one tenant furnishes more consideration than another, that first person is treated as having made a taxable gift to the other. If the donee is the donor's spouse and is a U.S. citizen, no gift tax has to be paid because of the unlimited gift tax marital deduction. The unlimited gift tax marital deduction is not available for donees who are not U.S. citizens [IRC Sec. 2523(i)(1)]. However, such gifts are eligible for a special gift tax annual exclusion of $145,000 in 2014 [IRC Sec. 2523(i)(2)]. If the joint tenancy or tenancy by the entirety is in real property and the spouse furnishing less than his or her share of the consideration is not a U.S. citizen, the creation of the joint tenancy or tenancy by the entirety will not be treated as a taxable gift; if the joint tenancy or tenancy by the entirety is in personal property, each spouse will be treated as having furnished one-half of the consideration [IRC Sec. 2523(i)(3)]. If, during the lifetime of the tenants, the property is sold or the tenancy is otherwise terminated, a gift tax is imposed unless the proceeds are divided in proportion to the amount paid (or deemed paid) by each party in acquiring the property. But the marital deduction shelters the tax, unless the donee spouse is a noncitizen [IRC Sec. 2523(i)(1)]. For gifts made in 2014, the first $145,000 of gifts per year to an alien spouse will not be taxed [IRC Sec. 2523(i)(2)]. To the extent that gifts are made in excess of this amount, no marital deduction will apply to reduce the gift tax. However, the annual exclusion for transfers by gift to a noncitizen spouse is allowed only for transfers that would qualify for the marital deduction if the donee were a U.S. citizen. For example, a gift in trust would not qualify for the increased annual exclusion unless it was within one of the exceptions to the terminable interest rule.

The creation of a nonspousal joint tenancy is a taxable gift to the extent that the funds furnished by one party exceed the value of that person's interest. If the joint tenancy is in a bank account, the depositor who opens a joint bank account with his or her own funds generally is not considered to make a completed gift until the other joint owner makes a withdrawal without any obligation to account for the withdrawal. The termination of a nonspousal joint tenancy is a taxable gift to the extent the donor's share of the proceeds is less than the donor's interest in the property.

If the property is sold, exchanged, or otherwise disposed of or the tenancy is otherwise terminated during the lifetime of spouses who hold title to property in a tenancy by entirety, a gift tax is imposed unless the proceeds are divided in proportion to the amount that each party paid for acquiring the property [Reg. Sec. 25.2523(i)-(2)].

(d) Joint Bank or Brokerage Accounts. The creation of a joint bank account or joint stock brokerage account generally constitutes an incomplete transfer. Because the creator may unilaterally withdraw any or all of the funds or investments on deposit, the depositor-donor has not parted with dominion or control.

When the nondepositor-donee withdraws funds from the account for his or her benefit without any obligation to account for the withdrawal, thereby removing those funds from the control of the creator, there is a completed gift of the withdrawn funds at the date of withdrawal [Reg. Sec. 25.2511-1(h)(4)].[1]

A similar result occurs when a purchase of a U.S. savings bond is registered as payable to "A or B." There is no gift to B until B cashes the bond for his or her own benefit [Reg. Sec. 25.2511-1(h)(4)].

However, if local law treats the creation of a joint bank account as an irrevocable (unchangeable) transfer of a proportionate interest in the account to the nondepositor-donee, the creation of the joint account constitutes a completed gift for gift tax purposes.[2]

(e) Impact of a Disclaimer. The use of a qualified disclaimer, specifically when you use a disclaimer to reorder the disposition of property, can also result in the creation or termination of joint property. Use of the disclaimer in this fashion will have federal gift tax consequences and is discussed further in ¶ 1201.

¶208 COMMUNITY PROPERTY

A special form of co-ownership between spouses arising from interests in property acquired during marriage (except property acquired by gift or inheritance by a particular spouse) exists in Arizona, California, Idaho, Louisiana, Nevada, New Mexico, Texas, Washington, and Wisconsin. This special form of spousal co-owned property is called community property. Community property encompasses any form of property, real property, tangible personal property, or intangible personal property.

An individual who at any time during his or her married life lives in one of the above jurisdictions may have any one or more of the following types of property:

1. *Separate property,* which exists prior to marriage from any source, including the labors of the owner-spouse, or is received during marriage by one spouse by gift or inheritance from any person (including a gift from a spouse of the donor-spouse's interest in community property). The owner-spouse has complete and unrestricted control and dominion over his or her separate property.

---

[1] ¶ **207** Rev. Rul. 69-148, 1969-1 CB 226.   [2] Estate of Buchholtz, TC Memo 1977-396.

2. *Community property*, which exists only between a married couple and pertains only to property acquired during marriage. Both the husband and wife have an equal, undivided interest in community property.

3. *Combined community property*, which is acquired from both community and separate property sources. Combined community and separate property exists during the marriage and pertains only to property whose origin is traceable to the combining, but not commingling, of community and separate property. Decisions regarding the use and disposition of this type of property are managed as in a partnership with one spouse acting like a general partner. Each spouse has an undivided ownership interest in the property, with each spouse's percentage dependent on his or her interests in the community property and the separate property that has gone into the combined property.

4. *Quasi-community property*, which creates property rights in a spouse as a result of dissolution of a marriage by divorce or when one spouse dies. In a divorce, quasi-community property is all real and personal property, located outside of the community property state, that would have been community property had the acquiring spouse been living in a community property state when the property was acquired. At death, quasi-community property is personal property wherever located and real estate located in a community property state acquired while the acquiring spouse-decedent was domiciled outside of a community property state.

The federal gift tax consequences of transferring community property by gift to a third party are identical to those applicable to a transfer of separate property by an individual owner. A transfer of community property by gift to a third party constitutes a gift by each spouse of his or her one-half of the community property.[1]

Most community property jurisdictions restrict the ability of one spouse to make unilateral transfers of community property to a nonspouse, particularly when the subject matter is the couple's residence. Such a unilateral transfer is likely to be viewed as an incomplete transfer of the nonconsenting spouse's interest, which the nonconsenting spouse is able to recall.

Completed interspousal transfers of community property constitute the transfer of the donor spouse's one-half of the community property to the donee-spouse. This transfer qualifies for the gift tax marital deduction [see ¶1107].

The conversion of community property into the separate property of one spouse or the conversion of separate property into community property without consideration also results in a gift for federal gift tax purposes. The conversion of community property into the separate property of one spouse generally qualifies for the gift tax marital deduction [see ¶1107]. However, the partition of community property into equal amounts of spousal separate property does not constitute a transfer subject to federal gift tax because each spouse receives the interest he or she previously held as community property. The division is unaffected by the separate property interest created, whether joint tenancy or tenancy in common.

---

[1] ¶208 Roeser, 2 TC 298 (1943), *acq.*, 1943 CB 19.

The migration of a couple from or into a community property jurisdiction may create a situation where the community property and separate property are commingled. This commingling process may result in one spouse's interest being voluntarily terminated or, conversely, voluntarily arising. In either situation, a gift from one spouse to the other will occur. However, the unlimited federal gift tax marital deduction as discussed further in ¶1107 generally eliminates any federal gift tax consequences.

Other interspousal transfers may take the form of:

* Transfers of separate property into community property;
* The conversion of an "expectant interest" in community property into conventional community property;
* The transfer of community property into joint ownership property with right of survivorship;
* The commingling of joint ownership property with community property as couples move in and out of community property states.

In each of these instances, the federal gift tax unlimited marital deduction [see ¶1107] shelters the transaction from federal gift taxation.

Even though a couple lives in a community property state, they may also own joint property. This will usually occur when couples move into a community property state from a noncommunity property state where they initially acquired the joint property. Joint property has the same characteristics regardless of whether it exists in a community or noncommunity property state. See ¶207 for an analysis of joint property.

¶209 RETAINED POWERS

Property has not been given away for gift tax purposes if it is transferred or given away, but the transferor retains the power to:

* Control who will benefit from and enjoy the trust property;
* Remove or appoint a trustee;
* Administer or manage the trust; or
* Have the trust property revert or go back to the transferor.

Under these circumstances, a complete gift has not occurred [Reg. Sec. 25.2511-2]. Complete control of the property has not been surrendered at the time of the transfer into the trust, resulting in an incomplete transfer. Remember that for a taxable gift to occur, there must be a completed transfer of the property where no strings whatsoever have been retained over the property in the trust.

This is important because by retaining certain powers over the gift, the gift is incomplete and will not be eligible for the annual gift tax exclusion. In addition, the value of the property in the trust will be included in the taxable gross estate when the settlor dies.

Why make an incomplete gift? This is a helpful device when the donor wants to make a transfer of property but postpone the gift tax until death. It also may be helpful in divorce planning when a divorcing spouse may wish to transfer property into a trust for the benefit of children but postpone paying tax on the transfer.

(a) Reservation of Power to Change Beneficial Enjoyment. Reservation of the right to determine who will benefit from the trust property will enable the settlor to take a "second look" at the class of beneficiaries. This power will allow the trust creator to adjust for events or circumstances that might unfold in the future, such as an unexpected change in the financial worth or maturity of a trust beneficiary. The existence of this power provides a settlor with the ability to fine-tune distributions during his or her lifetime and/or after death without having to revise the trust provisions.

The following examples illustrate reservation of a power to affect beneficial enjoyment of trust property. The reservation of this power renders the transfers into the trust incomplete gifts for gift tax purposes. In these examples, it does not matter whether the settlor reserves the right as settlor or appoints himself or herself trustee and exercises the right as trustee.

> **Example 1:** Mom established an irrevocable trust to pay income to Daughter for life and at her death to pay the principal to Son. Mom retains the right to direct that the income in any one year be accumulated and added to the principal. This is an incomplete gift for gift tax purposes.

> **Example 2:** Mom establishes an irrevocable trust to pay income to her three children for life in such amounts as Mom shall determine and at her death to pay the principal to the children in equal shares. This is an incomplete gift for gift tax purposes.

The power to change beneficial enjoyment may attach to either the trust income or principal or both interests. For federal gift tax purposes, where the settlor retains this power, that segment of the trust affected by the power is incomplete, and a taxable transfer therefore does not occur [Reg. Sec. 25.2511-2(c)].

However, the the settlor's relinquishment of the power to change the beneficial enjoyment of the transferred property is regarded as the event that completes the gift, resulting in gift tax liability [Reg. Sec. 25.2511-2(f)].

> **Example 3:** Mom established an irrevocable trust to pay income to Daughter for life and at Daughter's death to pay the principal to Son. Mom retains the right to direct that the income in any one year be accumulated and added to the principal. When the transfer into the trust is made, Mom has made a completed gift to Son because Mom's right does not apply to principal. Each year Mom makes a gift of the income to Daughter, if it is distributed to Daughter, or to Son, if it is accumulated. The power to alter the amount enjoyed by Daughter makes this part of the transfer an incomplete transfer for federal gift tax purposes. At the time the income passes out of your control, the transfer becomes complete.

¶209

However, a transfer in trust is considered complete if the settlor retains only the power to change a beneficiary's time or manner of enjoyment [Reg. Sec. 25.2511-2(d)].

> **Example 4:** Mom established an irrevocable trust for Daughter for 20 years, and at the end of 20 years to pay the principal to Daughter. Mom, as trustee, retains the power to distribute the income annually or to accumulate the trust income and distribute it to Daughter at the end of 20 years. The gift is complete at the creation of the trust because Mom has only retained the power to change a beneficiary's time of enjoyment.

A transfer involving a retained power in the donor-settlor to amend or modify the beneficial interests through control over trust income and/or principal represents a completed gift provided the power is a fiduciary power limited by an ascertainable standard [Reg. Secs. 25.2511-2(c), 25.2511-2(g)]. A standard that is articulated in terms of the beneficiary's health, education, maintenance, or support is an ascertainable standard.

When the power to change the beneficial enjoyment of the transferred property is held by an independent trustee, the gift is complete at the date of the transfer.

(b) Reservation of Power to Change Trustee. Selecting a trustee is an important decision that must be made when establishing a trust. The settlor may choose a professional to serve in the role of trustee, particularly where the settlor is inexperienced in financial matters and would benefit from the guidance of such a professional while the settlor gains experience. In such a situation, the settlor would likely reserve the power to remove the designated trustee and appoint a successor, including the settlor.

The reservation of the power to remove a trustee or appoint a new trustee is tax neutral for gift tax purposes. [For discussion of estate tax consequences, see ¶ 1807].

(c) Reservation of Administrative or Managerial Powers. The retention by the settlor of administrative or managerial powers over property transferred into a trust renders the gift incomplete for gift tax purposes [Reg. Sec. 25.2511-2(b)].

(d) Reservation of Reversionary Interest. Reversions to the settlor or the settlor's estate may come about intentionally, such as an express reservation, or unintentionally, as with the impact of a state statute that causes the property to revert to the settlor's estate if no beneficiaries exist.

> **Example 5:** Mom establishes a trust to pay Son income for 15 years, at which time the trust terminates and the trust property is returned to Mom, if living (an express reversion), or if not, to Son if Son survives Mom. If state law causes the trust property to revert to Mom's estate (in the event Son predeceases Mom), an implied reversion exists.

¶209

Transfers of property in which the donor retains a reversionary interest are subject to the gift tax.[1] The value of the gift is determined by subtracting the value of the settlor's reversionary interest (determined at the time of the transfer) from the value of the property transferred to the trust. As with all gifts, the donor has the burden of proof regarding valuation. If the reversion is so speculative as to have no ascertainable value under recognized actuarial methods, the amount of the gift equals the entire value of the property transferred [Reg. Sec. 25.2511-1(e)].

¶210 GIFT TAX CONSEQUENCES OF NONQUALIFIED STOCK OPTIONS

Stock options that do not satisfy the strict statutory requirements for incentive stock options (ISOs) are nonqualified stock options (NQSOs) and their income tax treatment is governed by IRC Sec. 83. NQSOs are often favored over ISOs because employees and employers are afforded greater flexibility in structuring an NQSO. The granting of nonqualified executive stock options is a popular way for corporations to compensate executives and key employees. These stock options are used frequently in lieu of cash compensation now that publicly traded companies cannot deduct more than $1 million annually in compensation paid to executives [IRC Sec. 162(m)]. Employers favor nonqualified stock options because the granting of stock options to key employees gives employees an added incentive to contribute to the growth and development of the company and encourages them to "stay on board." Employees like them because the stock options afford them an excellent risk-free opportunity to participate in the potential growth of the company.

Here's how nonqualified stock options work. The executive who receives the stock options as a form of compensation has the right for a fixed period of time (usually ten years) to buy shares in the company at a pre-set price ("exercise price"), no matter what the fair market value (FMV) of the stock is on the stock market at the time the stock options are exercised. Typically, the options will be granted or issued with an exercise price equal to the FMV of the stock at the date of the grant. When the price of the stock rises above the exercise price, the executive has the opportunity to purchase stock at the lower "exercise price." The difference between the FMV of the stock on the exercise date and the "exercise price" is called the stock option's "bargain element."

There are two types of stock options, which are subject to very different tax rules. This text focuses on nonstatutory stock options. The other type is called incentive stock options, or ISOs, which must meet the statutory requirements of IRC Sec. 422. ISOs are not discussed here because they are nontransferable and therefore cannot be gifted by executives to family members as a wealth transfer device [IRC Sec. 422(b)(5)].

Nonstatutory or nonqualified employee stock options are the most common type of stock options offered by employers today. They are very popular with start-up companies, typically in the technology field where tremendous growth is anticipated. The

---

[1] **¶209** Smith v. Shaughnessy, 318 U.S. 176 (1943).

executive typically does not recognize income when the stock options are granted, but, when the FMV of the stock increases and the stock options are exercised, the increase in value over the "exercise price" is taxed as ordinary income. The company gets a tax deduction equal to the increase in value at the time the employee exercises the stock options.

ISOs are subject to different tax rules. If you hold onto your ISOs for at least two years after receipt, the difference between "the exercise price" and the stock selling price is taxed as capital gain. The bad news, however, is that this amount, which is called the "bargain element," is considered an adjustment for alternative minimum tax purposes [IRC Sec. 56(b)(3)].

It is obvious that stock options offer the potential for tremendous appreciation because the executive is locked into purchasing the stock at a pre-set bargain price, which can become quite lucrative if the value of the stock skyrockets. The following example illustrates how the exercise of stock options that have appreciated in value can generate big profits for executives.

> **Example 1:** Executive receives nonstatutory stock options from his employer. The stock options entitle him to purchase 10,000 shares of the company's stock at $50 a share. Eighteen months later the stock is worth $150 a share. Executive could purchase 50 shares of the stock for $500,000. The street value for those shares is $1.5 million. Executive has increased his wealth by $1 million with none of his or her own money at risk.

    (a) Estate Planning with Stock Options. In 1996, the Securities and Exchange Commission (SEC) changed its rules to allow the transfer of nonqualified employee stock options. As a result of this liberalizing of the transfer rules and the surge in stock prices of publicly traded companies, executives began gifting their nonstatutory stock options to family members almost as soon as they were granted. They viewed it as a way to move substantial amounts of wealth out of their estate without paying a cent of wealth transfer tax. There were no tax implications at first, as wealthy taxpayers took advantage of the annual per-donee gift tax exclusion when they gifted nonstatutory stock options to loved ones. Stock options were ideally suited for gifting because of their low valuation when granted and their potential to greatly appreciate in value. The valuation of the stock options was low because at the time they were granted there was very little difference between the price when granted (the "exercise price") and the price for the stock on the stock exchange when the option was exercised. The IRS took a hard look at this picture, which resulted in a zero gift tax bill, and decided to put the kibosh on this popular estate-planning technique.

In Rev. Rul. 98-21,[1] the IRS found that the gifting of unvested nonstatutory stock options to family members does not qualify as a completed gift eligible for the annual gift tax exclusion because the gift is incomplete at the time of the transfer and will not be a completed gift until the stock option becomes vested. The stock option becomes vested only when the donee's right to exercise the option is no longer conditioned on the executive-transferor working for the company for a specified number of years. This

---

[1] ¶ **210** Rev. Rul. 98-21, 1998-1 CB 975.

¶**210**

means that the transfer to a family member of a nonstatutory stock option whose exercise is conditioned on the executive performing future services will only be a completed gift when the employee has satisfied the condition and the stock options can be exercised. Presumably, this usually occurs when the stock has already risen dramatically in value, thereby increasing the transfer tax cost of making the gift.

The following example illustrates how the IRS intended Rev. Rul. 98-21 to work in reducing the benefits of gifting nonstatutory stock options to family members.

> **Example 2:** Executive receives nonstatutory stock options from Employer. Executive cannot exercise the option until he has worked at the company for four years. The stock options entitle him to purchase 1,000 shares of the company's stock at $50 a share. Immediately upon receipt, Executive gifts the stock options to Child. At this time, the stock price and the exercise price (value when granted) are the same. Prior to the issuance of Rev. Rul. 98-21, this transfer would have resulted in zero gift tax liability because the options had no value when granted. Four years later the stock is worth $150 a share. Rev. Rul. 98-21 says that there was no completed gift of the options until four years later when the stock option had vested and the price of the stock had skyrocketed to $150 a share. The taxable gift (before application of the annual per-donee exclusion and the unified credit) at that time is $100,000 [$150,000 ($150 × 1,000) minus $50,000 (1,000 × $50)].

> ▶ **PRACTICE TIP:** Rev. Rul. 98-21 does not kill the gifting of all nonstatutory stock options. It only controls the gift tax consequences of nonvested stock options. You can therefore continue to gift vested stock options as a way to remove wealth and potential appreciation out of your estate because they will be considered present interests eligible for the annual gift tax exclusion. Another way around the problem presented in Rev. Rul. 98-21 is to continue to gift nonvested options but to include along with them an enforceable guarantee if vesting does not occur.

(b) How to Value Nonstatutory Stock Options. In Rev. Proc. 98-34,[2] the IRS outlined the method to use when valuing compensatory stock options for purposes of determining gift, estate, and generation-skipping transfer taxes. Specifically, Rev. Proc. 98-34 provides that you may use a generally recognized option pricing model, such as the Black-Scholes model or an accepted version of the binomial model, when valuing compensatory stock options for gift, estate, or GSTT purposes. The model that is selected must consider the following factors as of the valuation date:

1. The option's exercise price;
2. The option's expected life;
3. The current trading price of the underlying stock;
4. The expected volatility of the underlying stock;
5. The expected dividends on the underlying stock; and
6. Risk-free interest rate over the remaining option term.

---

[2] Rev. Rul. 98-34, 1998 2 CB 118.

In addition, you must satisfy the following requirements:

1. Compute the option's expected life in the manner outlined in Rev. Proc. 98-34;

2. Use the maximum remaining term as the option's expected life on the valuation date provided specified conditions are present;

3. Apply the option pricing model properly;

4. Use reasonable factors when applying the option pricing model;

5. Apply no discount to the valuation produced by the option pricing model;

6. Compute the expected volatility factor of the underlying stock in the manner outlined in Rev. Proc. 98-34; and

7. You must determine the factor for the risk-free interest rate in the manner outlined in Rev. Proc. 98-34.

The IRS also provides that you must write "FILED PURSUANT TO Rev. Proc. 98-34," if you use the methodology outlined in Rev. Proc. 98-34 to value your compensatory stock options.

¶211 CHECKLIST OF TRANSFERS THAT MAY RESULT IN A TAXABLE GIFT

☐ Transfer of tax-exempt bonds or property for less than adequate and full consideration.

☐ Below market loans are a gift from the lender to the borrower (certain exceptions and a de minimis rule exist).

☐ Forgiveness of a debt, including allowing a statute of limitation to run on the right to collect a debt.

☐ Parents' guarantee of loans to children's companies.

☐ General support of adult children.

☐ Monthly mortgage payments made on a child's or another person's property.

☐ Transfer of property to a child where the consideration received from the child is less than the value of the property.

☐ Assignment of future income.

☐ Transfer of jointly held property.

☐ Payment of another person's tax liability.

☐ Transfer in trust for benefit of other persons.

☐ Distributions of cash or property from a revocable trust to persons other than the grantor.

☐ Permitting a beneficiary to receive income from a trust over which the grantor has ownership.

☐ A transfer of a remainder interest to an adult child where an obligation for support does not exist.

¶211

- ☐ Transfer of a future interest.
- ☐ Payment of an adult's medical expenses where the funds are transferred directly to the adult, rather than the provider of medical services.
- ☐ Payment of tuition expenses for an adult child when not made directly to the educational institution.
- ☐ Exercise or release of a power of appointment.
- ☐ Transfer to a life insurance trust or the payment of premiums on a policy.
- ☐ Transfer of property by one spouse to another under a marital settlement except when (1) the transfer is in exchange for release of the other spouse's support rights; (2) the transfer is made under a written agreement and final divorce occurs within one year before or two years after the date of the agreement; or (3) the transfer is made under a divorce decree that includes a marital settlement agreement.
- ☐ Transfer to a trust for the benefit of adult children even though required under a divorce decree.
- ☐ Entering into a disclaimer for the receipt of property.
- ☐ Relinquishing of rights to a pension plan.
- ☐ Election of lesser annuity in exchange for survivor annuity under employee plan (certain exemptions do exist).
- ☐ Gift or transfer to a charity.
- ☐ Election to take property under a will instead of a spouse asserting community property rights.
- ☐ Life estate interest to a spouse unless the QTIP provisions apply.
- ☐ Certain transfers related to estate tax valuation freezes.
- ☐ Transfer of property to a corporation or partnership where there is an indirect shifting of value to other family members.
- ☐ Transfer of a family partnership interest.
- ☐ Transfer of property located in the United States by a nonresident alien.
- ☐ Transfer of lottery ticket to family corporation where there was no enforceable contract to share the lottery prize with the family.[1]

¶212 GIFTS BY NONRESIDENT NONCITIZENS

The gift tax also applies to nonresidents who are not citizens of the United States [IRC Sec. 2501(a)(1)]. However, for these donors the gift tax applies only to gifts of property situated in the United States [IRC Sec. 2511(a); Reg. Sec. 25.2511-3(a)]. The gift tax applies only to transfers of real and tangible personal property, such as clothing, jewelry, automobiles, furniture, or currency. It does not apply to intangible personal property, except in the case of a noncitizen who expatriated (voluntarily

---

[1] ¶211 Dickerson, TC Memo 2012-60.

surrendered his or her citizenship) in order to avoid U.S. taxation [IRC Secs. 2501(a)(2), 2501(a)(3); Reg. Sec. 25.2501-1(a)(3)].

Special situs rules exist for shares of stock and debt obligations [Reg. Sec. 25.2511-3(b)]. In brief, the following intangibles constitute property located in the United States:

1. Shares of stock that a domestic corporation issues [IRC Sec. 2104(a)];

2. Debt obligations of a U.S. citizen or resident, a domestic partnership, a domestic corporation (including moneys on deposit with a domestic corporation or its foreign branch), and of any estate or trust (other than a foreign estate or trust) [IRC Sec. 2104(c)];

3. Debt obligations of the United States, a state (or political subdivision of a state), or the District of Columbia;

4. Deposits with a domestic branch of a foreign bank that are effectively connected with a U.S. trade or business [IRC Secs. 2104(c), 2105(b), 871(i)(3)]; and

5. Currency situated in the United States at the date of transfer [Reg. Sec. 20.2104-1(a)(7)].

If a person is a resident of a U.S. possession and acquired U.S. citizenship only because of citizenship, birth, or residence in the U.S. possession, the person is considered a nonresident noncitizen for gift tax purposes [IRC Sec. 2501(c); Reg. Sec. 25.2501-1(d)].

In order to prevent two or more countries from imposing a tax on the same gift, the U.S. has gift tax treaties for the avoidance of the double taxation with a number of countries, including Australia, Austria, Denmark, France, Japan, Sweden, the United Kingdom, and Germany. Among other provisions, these treaties provide certain rules for determining the situs of property. These situs rules are used for determining the situs of property subject to gift tax by nonresident noncitizen donors who come within the scope of the treaties.

¶213 HOW GIFT TAX RULES APPLY TO NONRESIDENT ALIENS

Aliens application of rate schedule. The rate schedule [see ¶1403] applicable to citizens and residents of the United States also applies to nonresident noncitizens.

Unified credit. A nonresident noncitizen is not entitled to the unified credit against the gift tax [see ¶1404; IRC Sec. 2505(a)]. Note that the estates of nonresident noncitizens are allowed a unified credit of only $14,000 unless they are entitled to a greater amount under a treaty [IRC Sec. 2102(c)(1); Reg. Sec. 20.2102-1(c)]. This amounts to an exemption on the first $60,000 of the taxable estate of the nonresident alien.

Marital deduction. A gift tax marital deduction [see ¶1107] is not available for a gift to a spouse who is not a citizen of the United States [IRC Sec. 2523(i)(1)]. Note that a transfer to a noncitizen spouse can qualify for the estate tax marital deduction if a QDOT is established [see ¶1100].

Annual exclusion. For gifts made in 2014, the first $145,000 (up from $143,000 in 2013) of gifts per year to an alien spouse will not be taxed [IRC Sec. 2523(i)(2)]. To the extent that gifts are made in excess of this amount, no marital deduction will apply to reduce the gift tax. However, the annual exclusion for transfers by gift to a noncitizen spouse is allowed only for transfers that would qualify for the marital deduction if the donee were a U.S. citizen. For example, a gift in trust would not qualify for the increased annual exclusion unless it was within one of the exceptions to the terminable interest rule.

Gift splitting. A nonresident alien spouse is not entitled to the benefits of gift splitting with his or her spouse [IRC Sec. 2513(a)(1)].

Exclusion for payment of medical and education expenses. Nonresident aliens are able to take advantage of the unlimited exclusion for educational or medical purposes [IRC Sec. 2503(e); see ¶ 908].

Charitable deduction. The deduction for charitable gifts by nonresident noncitizens is governed by the same rules that apply to U.S. citizens and residents [see ¶ 910; IRC Sec. 2522(b)]. However, gifts to or for the use of a trust, community chest, fund, foundation, or fraternal order or society operating under the lodge system are deductible only if the gifts are to be used within the United States exclusively for tax exempt purposes [IRC Secs. 2522(b)(3), 2522(b)(4)]. If the gifts are made to or for the use of a corporation, the corporation must be one created or organized under the laws of the United States or of a state or territory thereof [IRC Sec. 2522(b)(2)].

In sum, a gift made by a nonresident noncitizen to a noncharitable donee of real or tangible personal property situated in the United States is subject to federal gift tax to the extent the value of the gift exceeds the annual per donee exclusion and the gift fails to qualify for the exclusion for educational expenses or medical expenses.

REVOCABLE LIVING TRUSTS

TABLE OF CONTENTS

¶300 REVOCABLE LIVING TRUST BASICS

A revocable living trust is a heavily promoted estate-planning device that can be valuable for some people but is totally inappropriate for others. Before you sign one, be sure the revocable living trust addresses your estate-planning needs. Living trusts are commonly referred to as the panacea for all estate-planning woes. You should know that they are not for everyone and they do *not* solve all estate-planning problems. See ¶2826 for more discussion of revocable living trusts.

A revocable living trust is used to manage assets including property, money, and investments in case you become mentally or physically disabled. The trust is established during your lifetime with you as trustee and another person or financial institution named as successor trustee. A revocable trust is appropriate for anyone who is expected to become incapacitated or experience decreased mental acuity as a result of illness or a disease. Persons diagnosed with Alzheimer's disease or with a terminal illness would be perfect candidates provided their gross estate is less than the applicable exclusion amount and saving estate taxes is not their prime concern. Just keep in mind that assets in your revocable living trust are fully includible in your taxable gross estate when you die because the assets remain under your control.

In this type of trust, the settlor or the creator of the trust reserves the power to revoke or cancel the trust at any time before death or disability. That is why it is called a revocable trust. For example, the settlor can change the beneficiaries or the trustee, or alter or amend the terms of the trust agreement while still alive. The living trust only becomes irrevocable (unchangeable) when the settlor dies or becomes disabled. At that time, the assets in it are disposed of as provided in the trust agreement, which essentially becomes a will substitute. This means that the living trust will provide for the disposition of your assets at death but the terms of the disposition will not be a matter of public record because assets transferred to the living trust will not be subject to probate. Probate is the state-supervised process for validating a will, appointing the decedent's named executor or representative, notifying creditors, and administering the estate. Assets that have been transferred to the living trust are not subject to probate because those assets are owned by the trust, which is treated as a separate legal entity at death.

A revocable trust gives the settlors the opportunity to:

- Plan for the orderly disposition of their wealth after death without the delay inherent in probate proceedings;
- Preselect who will handle their financial affairs if they become incapacitated;
- Avoid the expense of a state court supervised guardianship or conservatorship proceeding;
- Dispose of property in private without the public scrutiny associated with the probate process;
- Avoid ancillary estate proceedings in those non-domiciliary jurisdictions where the settlor owns property subject to estate administration;
- Have immediate access to trust assets without the two or three-year delay normally associated with the probate process.

The most important reason to use a living trust or revocable trust is to manage assets including property, money, and investments in case of mental or physical disability. The trust is established during your lifetime with you as trustee and another person or financial institution named as successor trustee.

> ▶ **PRACTICE POINTER:** *You still need a pour-over will.* Living trusts should always be accompanied by a pour-over will, which will dispose of all assets that were not transferred into the trust. In addition, the will can accomplish things that cannot be achieved with a trust. This includes appointing guardians for minor and/or disabled children and appointing an executor to handle any probate assets.

For the revocable trust to be able to manage your assets when you become disabled, you must transfer everything you own into the trust during your lifetime. The terms of the trust designate the trustee and govern the management and disposition of the assets in the trust by directing how they are to be invested and indicating who will receive income and principal distributions from the trust.

¶301 SELECTING GOOD CANDIDATE FOR LIVING TRUST

A revocable trust should be considered whenever you expect someone to become incapacitated or experience decreased mental acuity as a result of illness or a disease. Someone diagnosed with Alzheimer's disease would be a perfect candidate provided saving estate taxes is not their prime concern. Someone with a terminal illness would also be a good candidate for a living trust because they can expect to experience physical or mental incapacity before death.

¶302 REVOCABLE LIVING TRUSTS WILL NOT AVOID ESTATE TAXES

Living trusts do *not* save the settlor estate taxes. The assets in the settlor's living trust are fully includible in his or her taxable estate upon death because the assets remain under his or her control and are therefore includible in the settlor's estate under IRC Sec. 2038 [see ¶1806]. If the value of the settlor's taxable estate is less than the applicable exclusion amount, saving estate taxes is not his or her concern and revocable trusts may be appropriate.

¶303 GIFT TAX CONSEQUENCES OF CREATING REVOCABLE TRUST

In general, there are no gift tax consequences when the settlor transfers property into the revocable trust because the settlor retains dominion and control over the trust assets [see ¶210]. Therefore, no gift has been made [Reg. Sec. 25.2511-2(c)]. The flip side to this is that the property in the trust will be included in the settlor's taxable gross estate when he or she dies.

No taxable gift has occurred if the settlor holds the power to revoke provided the settlor exercises the power alone or in conjunction with any party (or parties) who does not have a substantial adverse interest [Reg. Sec. 25.2511-2(e)]. However, if the settlor's power to revoke is exercisable only with the consent of a party with a substantially adverse interest, the transfer is complete for gift tax purposes.[1] An adverse party is a person who may be substantially and adversely impacted economically by an action of the settlor [IRC Sec. 672(a)].[2]

> **Example 1:** Mom transfers property to State Bank as the trustee, in trust for herself for life, remainder to Son, when she dies. She reserves the power to revoke the trust. The transfer is not complete and there is no taxable gift. If, however, the trust provides that Mom can exercise the power to revoke only with the consent of Son, then on the funding of the revocable trust, there is a completed transfer. Mom will make a taxable gift to Son of the value of the remainder interest. Son has an adverse interest with respect to Mom's revocation of the remainder interest in the trust. Thus, Son's consent to such revocation renders the transfer a completed gift.

If during the trust term the trustee distributes income or principal to a beneficiary other than the settlor, or if the settlor subsequently relinquishes the power to revoke the trust, a taxable gift has been made [Reg. Sec. 25.2511-2(f)]. These rules apply regardless of whether the settlor or some other party is serving as trustee.

---

[1] ¶303 Camp, 195 F.2d 999 (1st Cir. 1952).   [2] Prouty, 115 F.2d 331 (1st Cir. 1940).

¶304 GIFTS FROM REVOCABLE TRUSTS

The value of property transferred to a donee from a decedent's revocable trust within three years of the decedent's death is not includible in the decedent's gross estate under IRC Sec. 2038 because it is treated as having been made directly by the decedent [IRC Sec. 2035(e)]. Nor is it includible in a decedent's gross estate as a proscribed transfer within three years of death.

Gifts made by a trustee from a revocable trust are treated as if they were made by the decedent and are eligible for the annual gift tax exclusion [IRC Sec. 2035(e)]. As a result, gifts from a revocable trust within three years of the settlor's death will *not* be included in the grantor's estate. This change codifies the conclusions reached by the courts that had previously addressed the issue.[1]

Thus, a settlor who has created a revocable trust can continue his or her lifetime program of making annual exclusion gifts to loved ones even after disability, thanks to IRC Sec. 2035(e), which provides that a gift made from a revocable trust is treated as direct gift made by the settlor.

▶ **DRAFTING TIP:** Be sure that the revocable trust includes language expressly authorizing the trustee to make annual exclusion gifts to designated beneficiaries. In the absence of the necessary language authorizing gift-giving from the revocable trust, the gifts will be included in the donor's gross estate.

¶305 FUNDING WITH COMMUNITY PROPERTY

Creating and funding a revocable trust by both spouses with community property does not constitute a completed gift for federal gift tax purposes.[1] Couples frequently use this technique to preserve the character of their respective interests in the community property, especially when the couple plans a move to a non-community property state.

¶306 ELECTION TO TREAT REVOCABLE TRUST AS PART OF ESTATE

Executors can now make an irrevocable election to treat revocable trusts as part of the deceased person's probate estate for income tax purposes [IRC Sec. 645(a)] [For further discussion, see ¶2826].

---

[1] **¶304** McNeely, 16 F.3d 303 (8th Cir. 1994); Estate of Kisling, 32 F.3d 1222 (8th Cir. 1994), *acq.* 1995-2 CB 1.

[1] **¶305** Rev. Rul. 66-283, 1966-2 CB 297.

LIFE INSURANCE

4

TABLE OF CONTENTS

¶400 LIFE INSURANCE—GIFT TAX PERSPECTIVE

From the gift tax perspective, the transfer of a life insurance policy is just like the transfer of any other type of property. This means that a donor will face potential gift tax liability if he or she transfers a life insurance policy, the value of which exceeds $14,000 in 2014 and the transfer is treated as a transfer of a present interest [IRC Sec. 2503].

Gift tax consequences can also result if a donor owns a life insurance policy on his or her life and either:

- Irrevocably assigns or transfers the life insurance policy to another outright or in trust; or

- Irrevocably designates the beneficiary of the policy so that he or she has no right to cancel or change the beneficiary designation directly or indirectly, for example, by canceling the policy in whole or in part [Reg. Sec. 25.2511-1(h)(8)].[1]

If the donor continues to pay the premiums on a life insurance policy after transferring the policy, each premium payment will constitute a gift to the new owner of the policy unless the owner is an entity, in which case the gift is attributed to the beneficiaries of a trust or the shareholders of a corporation. The premium payment, however, qualifies for the annual per donee gift tax exclusion [see ¶901].

¶401 IRREVOCABLE LIFE INSURANCE TRUST

(a) Purpose. The irrevocable life insurance trust (ILIT) is a vehicle that estate planners use in an attempt to eliminate estate tax on life insurance proceeds. Remember that the proceeds of life insurance on the decedent's life that are payable to, or received by, the decedent's personal representative rather than the ILIT will be included in the decedent's gross estate [IRC Sec. 2042(1)]. See ¶403.

Irrevocable life insurance trusts offer a technique for removing life insurance proceeds from the taxable estate as well as the estate of the surviving spouse, provided neither spouse retains ownership over the policy.

(b) How to Revoke an ILIT. By definition, an irrevocable trust cannot be amended or modified in any way by the insured after execution. Modification through court proceedings can be difficult, if not impossible. In addition, the insured loses all control over the policy insuring his or her life, including the right to borrow against the policy's cash value or to change the policy's beneficiaries. The insured can retain no control over the assets owned by or transferred to the trust. The insured can, however, decide whether to provide the funds needed by the trustee to pay the life insurance premiums. If the premiums are not paid, the policy would lapse and the irrevocable life insurance trust would in essence be revoked.

(c) How to Fund the ILIT. There are two methods by which the trust becomes the policy owner.

Best Method: First, establish the irrevocable life insurance trust, then have the independent trustee of the trust apply for the life insurance on the insured's behalf. The trust then becomes both the owner and beneficiary of the life insurance policy and, on the insured's death, the trustee will invest the insurance proceeds and administer the trust on behalf of the beneficiaries.

Note that authorizing the trustee of the irrevocable trust to make loans for adequate security and purchase assets at their fair-market value in order to provide liquidity for the settler-insured's estate does not cause inclusion under IRC Sec. 2041(1), even if exercised. However, language in the trust instrument that permits the trustee to use life insurance proceeds for the payment of debts, taxes, or administrative expenses

---

[1] **¶400** Rev. Rul. 81-166, 1981-1 CB 477.

for less than adequate consideration causes inclusion in the settler-insured's gross estate to the extent that the trustee actually makes such payments.

Second Best Method: Transfer ownership of an existing life insurance policy to an irrevocable life insurance trust. This method will result in exclusion of the insurance proceeds from the insured's gross estate only if he survives the transfer by at least three years [IRC Sec. 2035(d)(2)]. If the insured dies within the three-year period, the proceeds will be included in his gross estate.

> ▶ **CAUTION:** A significant planning risk exists when the settler/insured severs all incidents of ownership with respect to the life insurance policy that he or she owns to an irrevocable trust within three years of his or her death. Under IRC Sec. 2035(d)(2), such a transfer causes the value of the policy to be included in the settler-insured's gross estate.

You can even make annual gift tax exclusion transfers to the trust each year to pay for the premiums without causing the proceeds to be taxed in the settler/insured's estate. You can do this by using a so-called *Crummy* power, which gives the holder a limited right to withdraw the premium funds transferred to the trust. This causes the transfer to meet the exclusion's present interest requirement [see ¶ 908]. The withdrawal power usually expires after about 30 days and is never expected to be exercised, although legally the beneficiary could exercise it.

> ▶ **CAUTION:** The courts have said that a policy purchased with funds furnished by the insured, but owned by another (such as an irrevocable life insurance trust) is not included in the decedent-insured's gross estate even if the insured dies within the three-year period. The even better news is that the IRS has announced that it will no longer litigate cases in this area.[1] The reason is that the insured never possessed any incidents of ownership over the life insurance policy once it was owned by the trust.

However, to the extent that the premiums paid during the three-year period prior to the insured's death generate a federal gift tax, the tax paid would be included in the insured's gross estate under IRC Sec. 2035(c). In addition, taxable gifts, specifically, the value of the gifts (i.e., the premiums) in excess of the annual per donee exclusion, if applicable, are included in the insured's gross estate under IRC Sec. 2001(b).

Life insurance will be included in the insured's taxable estate if the insured has any "incidents of ownership" in the policy. "Incidents of ownership" include rights to name the beneficiary, surrender or cancel the policy, assign the policy, pledge the policy for a loan, or otherwise enjoy the economic benefits of the policy [Reg. Sec. 20.2042-1(c)(2)]. See ¶ 1804.

When an ILIT holds the policy, the owner-settlor of the policy lacks any retained power to alter, amend, revoke, or terminate the trust. That is why it is called an irrevocable trust. It cannot be changed.

If a properly drafted ILIT exists, you can either transfer ownership of the policy into the trust and pray you are not snagged by the three-year rule [see ¶ 1804] or transfer money into the trust so the trustee can purchase the life insurance policy with the money (the better way to go if at all possible). According to the three-year rule, the

---

[1] ¶ **401** Estate of Headrick, 93 TC 171, *aff'd,* 918 F.2d 1263 (6th Cir. 1990), AOD 1991-012.

¶401

donor must live for at least three years after the transfer of an existing life insurance policy into the ILIT in order to remove the policy proceeds from the donor's estate [IRC Sec. 2035(d)(2)].

The irrevocable trust permits owner-settlors to accomplish the following estate-planning objectives:

1. Remove the proceeds of the life insurance policy from their (and hopefully their spouse's) gross estate; since removal of the life insurance proceeds from the insured-grantor's gross estate is the primary goal of an ILIT, be sure that the insured does not hold or retain any incidents of ownership over the insurance policies or possess any powers over the ILIT or its trustee that would cause the ILIT or the insurance proceeds to be included in the insured-grantor's gross estate for estate tax purposes;

2. Incur minimal federal gift tax on the funding of the trust and the subsequent payment of the premiums;

3. Preserve the federal income tax exclusion for the life insurance proceeds;

4. Create a cash resource accessible by loan for the payment of their federal estate tax and debts and expenses;

5. Enhance the transfer of wealth by reducing or eliminating the GST tax on life insurance proceeds passed down to successive generations. To achieve this goal, be sure that the spouse and other beneficiaries are not deemed to hold a retained interest in the ILIT as a result of a taxable release of a *Crummey* withdrawal right or the existence of a general power of appointment over the trust assets;

6. Add flexibility to an estate plan;

7. Allow for professional management of the insurance proceeds thus promoting the tax-free growth of the beneficiaries' inheritance;

8. Provide creditor and divorce protection to the beneficiaries;

9. Create liquidity for the grantor's estate without forcing survivors to sell a profitable business or family farm to pay the estate tax due on a parent's estate;

10. Allow for the payment of life insurance premiums while incurring little or no gift tax. A *Crummey* withdrawal right granted to each beneficiary will allow the grantor's payment of premiums to be free of gift tax provided the payments qualify for the annual gift tax exclusion under IRC Sec. 2503(b); and

11. Replace an amount given to a charity.

> **Example 1:** Husband has an antique furniture collection worth $5 million. Husband and Wife sign a will leaving the furniture to Wife. Husband gives cash to an ILIT, which buys a $2,750,000 joint and survivor life insurance policy on the lives of Husband and Wife. This policy pays the $2,750,000 benefit only after the death of the survivor. Husband dies first. After Wife dies, her estate owes estate tax of $2,750,000 on the furniture. She has no other money. Her executor can tap the ILIT to get the life insurance proceeds. As a result, Wife's executor can pay the estate tax and the furniture need not be sold to pay the estate tax.

(d) Gift Tax Consequences. A transfer to an ILIT is a completed gift provided the owner-settlor has not retained other interests or powers over the trust. An incomplete gift for federal gift tax purposes occurs if the owner-settlor reserves:

1. A power to change the beneficial enjoyment; or

2. Administrative or managerial powers over the trust [see ¶ 210].

The completed gift includes the transfer of both the life insurance policy itself and funds for the payment of the premiums on a life insurance policy owned by the trust. The transfer for the payment of policy premiums may be made directly to the insurer or indirectly to the trustee who applies the funds transferred to the premium payments.

The value of the gift equals either the interpolated terminal reserve value of the life insurance policy where the policy is transferred or the amount of each premium paid, directly or indirectly (see discussion of valuation of life insurance for gift tax purposes at ¶ 1915).

The transfer to the irrevocable life insurance trust generally represents a gift of a future interest that will not qualify for the annual per donee gift tax exclusion [see ¶ 902]. The gift is a future interest because the proceeds of the life insurance policy are not payable until some unknown time in the future when the insured dies.

Regardless of whether the property transferred is the life insurance policy or the funds needed to pay the premium on the insurance policy, in order for the transfer to a trust to qualify for the annual per donee exclusion, the trust must qualify as a present interest. In order to do so, the trust must be (1) a trust with *Crummey* powers [see ¶ 906] or (2) a trust for minors [see ¶ 907].

¶402 GIFTS OF COMMUNITY PROPERTY LIFE INSURANCE POLICIES

Gifts of community property life insurance policies can cause some unexpected gift tax issues.

First, if the policy is converted to the separate property of either spouse, it is sheltered from federal gift taxation by the unlimited federal gift tax marital deduction [see ¶ 1107].

Second, the revocable designation of a nonspouse as the beneficiary of the life insurance policy will on the death of the insured-spouse create a gift of one-half the amount of the death benefit by the surviving spouse to the nonspouse-beneficiary [Reg. Sec. 25.2511-1(h)(9)]. The noninsured surviving spouse is treated as making a gift of one-half of the proceeds less whatever interest the surviving spouse may possess in the proceeds. In other words, a spousal income interest for life is subtracted from the amount of the gift.

¶403 LIFE INSURANCE—ESTATE TAX PERSPECTIVE

Life insurance is entitled to all kinds of special tax breaks. The inside build-up of policies with an investment component is not subject to current income tax and in most cases the recipient of death benefits paid on a policy does not have to pay income tax on them. The bad news, however, is that the proceeds of a life insurance policy are included in the insured's gross estate for tax purposes if the proceeds are receivable by or for the benefit of the decedent's estate. But, with proper planning, the life insurance proceeds can pass to loved ones free of estate tax.

> ▶ **PRACTICE POINTER:** It is important to understand that the inclusion of life insurance in the decedent's taxable gross estate differs from the basic income tax principle of IRC Sec. 101(a), which provides generally that the proceeds of life insurance are excluded from the gross income of the recipient.

Life insurance for estate tax purposes means all kinds of life insurance, including (1) whole life policies; (2) term insurance; (3) group life insurance; (4) double indemnity, travel, and accident insurance; (5) endowment contracts (before being paid up); and (6) death benefits paid by fraternal beneficial societies operating under the lodge system [Reg. Sec. 20.2042-1(a)(1)].

The term "life insurance," however, does not include (1) refunds of life insurance premiums in case of suicide and (2) no-risk, single-premium policies combining annuities and life insurance [Reg. Sec. 20.2042-1(a)(2)].

Life insurance can be a valuable tool in the estate-planning process and can be used to achieve the following goals:

1. To provide estate liquidity and avoid forced sales of liquid assets at depressed prices to pay federal or state estate taxes and administration expenses;

2. To replace the lost income of the decedent and meet the immediate and future needs of the surviving family members;

3. To enlarge an existing estate or to create a sizable estate for decedents who otherwise would be leaving no estate or only a modest estate to loved ones; and

4. To provide a funding mechanism for buy-sell agreements, nonqualified deferred compensation agreements, and key-person insurance programs.

¶404 TESTS FOR INCLUSION

The death benefit (i.e., the proceeds) of a life insurance policy on a decedent's life are included in the decedent's gross estate if one of the three tests are satisfied:

1. The death benefit is payable to the executor or receivable by or for the benefit of the decedent's estate [IRC Sec. 2042(1)];

2. At the time of his or her death, the decedent possessed any incident of ownership in the insurance policy that was exercisable alone or in conjunction with any other person [IRC Sec. 2042(2)]; or

3. The decedent transferred a life insurance policy in which he or she had any incident of ownership within three years of his or her death [IRC Sec. 2035(d)(2)].

Each of these tests is considered in more detail below.

(a) Receipt by Executor. The scope of inclusion under the receipt by executor test is generally straightforward. The proceeds of a life insurance policy paid to or received by or for the benefit of the decedent's estate are included in the decedent's gross estate, regardless of whether the decedent owned the life insurance policy, possessed any incident of ownership, or paid any premium. Although most circumstances will make the application of this test easy, the application of the rule may be unclear in three instances.

First, the rule triggers inclusion when the life insurance proceeds are paid to a creditor in satisfaction of a debt of the decedent [Reg. Sec. 20.2042-1(b)(1)]. Thus, if the proceeds of a policy are receivable by a beneficiary, other than the decedent's executor or his or her estate, and are subject to a legal obligation on the beneficiary to pay taxes, debts, or other charges enforceable against the estate, the proceeds required for payment of these obligations are includable in the decedent's gross estate to the extent of the beneficiary's obligation.

Second, if state law requires that the proceeds be distributed to the decedent's surviving spouse or children, the proceeds will not be included in the decedent's gross estate, provided the decedent retained no incidents of ownership over the policy at the time of his or her death.[1]

Third, the proceeds of a life insurance policy owned by a third party that are paid to a revocable trust created by the decedent are not included in the decedent's gross estate.[2]

> **NOTE:** If the proceeds of an insurance policy payable to a decedent's estate are community property, then only one-half of the proceeds is considered to be received by or for the benefit of the decedent's estate [Reg. Sec. 20.2042-1(b)(2)].

(b) Incidents of Ownership. The value of the decedent's gross estate includes the value of all property to the extent of the amount receivable by all beneficiaries (other than the decedent's estate) as insurance under policies on the life of the decedent if the decedent possessed, at his death, any of the "incidents of ownership" [IRC Sec. 2042(2)].

As explained in Reg. Sec. 20.2042-1(c)(2), the term "incidents of ownership" is not limited in its meaning to ownership of the policies in the technical legal sense. The term also refers to the right of the insured or his estate to the "economic benefits of the policy." Thus, it includes the power to change the beneficiary, to surrender or cancel the policy, to assign the policy, to revoke an assignment, to pledge the policy for a loan, or to obtain from the insurer a loan against the surrender value of the policy. Possession of any of these incidents of ownership will cause the proceeds to be taxable to the holder of the incidents of ownership.[3]

---

[1] ¶**404** Margrave, 71 TC 13 (1978), *aff'd*, 618 F.2d 34 (8th Cir. 1975); Rev. Rul. 81-166, 1981-1 CB 477.

[2] Estate of Rockwell, TC Memo 1984-654, *aff'd in part and rev'd in part*, 779 F.2d 931 (3d Cir. 1985).

[3] Chase Nat'l Bank, 278 U.S. 327 (1929).

A decedent is considered to have an "incident of ownership" in an insurance policy on his life held in trust if, under the terms of the policy, the decedent has the power to change the beneficial ownership in the policy or its proceeds, or the time or manner of enjoyment thereof, even though the decedent has no beneficial interest in the trust [Reg. Sec. 20.2042-1(c)(4)].

Look at policy terms. A determination of whether the decedent possessed an incident of ownership is made by looking to the terms of the policy (e.g., whether the policy permits the owner to exercise such a right). Facts outside of the contract negating such "policy facts" are immaterial, except for actions taken by an insurance agent on his or her own initiative.

Incidents of ownership also include a reversionary interest in excess of 5 percent of the value of the policy, taking into account any incidents of ownership held by others [IRC Sec. 2042(2)].[4] A reversionary interest includes the possibility that the proceeds will be paid to the decedent's estate, the policy will return to the decedent, or the power to dispose of the policy (or its proceeds) will return to the decedent. However, the possibility that the decedent might inherit a policy on his life from someone else (e.g., a child who bought insurance on a parent's life and could die before the parent, leaving the policy to the parent) is not a reversionary interest or an incident of ownership. [Reg. Sec. 20.2042-1(c)(3)].

> **Example 1:** At age 51, Frank assigns a policy on his life to a trust he created to pay the income to his sister, Edith, age 47, for her life. The trust will terminate on Edith's death. At that time, the trust principal, including the insurance policy, will revert to Frank, if alive, or be distributed to his surviving son. Frank is survived by Edith. The insurance proceeds are includable in Frank's gross estate because actuarially he had a reversionary interest in the policy in excess of 5 percent of its value.

> **Example 2:** Assume the same facts as in Example 1, except that the trust instrument gives Edith the power to surrender the policy and obtain cash. Because of Edith's power to obtain the cash surrender value, Frank's reversionary interest does not amount to an incident of ownership.

The decedent's gross estate also includes life insurance proceeds paid directly to a decedent's former spouse if, under a decree of divorce, the decedent was required to name the divorced spouse as beneficiary of certain life insurance policies on the decedent's life and was required to maintain the policies until the former spouse's death or remarriage (at which time the proceeds would become payable to the decedent or the decedent's estate) [IRC Sec. 2042(2)]. However, a deduction is allowed from the gross estate for the obligation to pay the proceeds to the former spouse as an indebtedness of the estate [see ¶ 2001].

When incident of ownership considered exercised by owner. Beyond what constitutes an incident of ownership, a problem exists in delineating under what circum-

---

[4] Estate of Kahanic, TC Memo 2012-81.

¶404

stances an incident of ownership is considered exercised by the owner-insured. The following five situations are noteworthy:

1. Joint powers that are an incident of ownership exercisable by the decedent alone or in conjunction with any other person do not prevent inclusion in the decedent's gross estate. Tainted powers may be shared (A and B must act together), negative (A acts but B has a veto power with respect to much action),[5] or consensual (A acts but such action is invalid unless B consents).

2. Courts have crafted an exception (accepted by the IRS) for an incident of ownership held by the decedent in a fiduciary capacity. The IRS's position is that a decedent, acting as a fiduciary, is not considered to possess any incident of ownership in a life insurance policy in which the decedent is the insured, provided (1) the powers the decedent has over the policy cannot be exercised for his or her personal benefit, (2) the policy was not transferred by a decedent to a trust (or trust equivalent, such as, a custodial account under the UTMA); and (3) the decedent has not furnished any consideration for maintaining the policy.[6]

3. Facts and circumstances making it impossible for the decedent to exercise an incident of ownership are irrelevant. The test is couched in terms of the power to exercise an incident of ownership, not the ability of the insured-owner to exercise the power at any particular moment. Thus, courts have held that the decedent possessed an incident of ownership where (1) the policy was obtained moments before the decedent boarded a plane that crashed shortly thereafter[7] or (2) the decedent was incompetent.

4. Incidents of ownership may be attributed from an entity (e.g., a corporation) that owns the life insurance policy to the decedent where the decedent is the insured. Incidents of ownership held by a corporation of which the decedent was the sole or controlling shareholder (i.e., more than 50 percent of the combined voting power) are attributed to the decedent if the proceeds are not payable to the corporation or are not payable for a valid business purpose [Reg. Sec. 20.2042-1(c)(6)]. The decedent will be deemed to own stock held (1) by an agent or nominee, (2) jointly with another person where the co-owner's interest was acquired by gift from the decedent, (3) in a voting trust to the extent of the decedent's interest in the voting trust, or (4) in a grantor trust [Reg. Sec. 20.2042-1(c)(6)].

However, a decedent is not considered a controlling shareholder of a corporation owned by a husband and wife as community property.[8] A shareholder whose stock is community property (and thus one-half of community assets are deemed owned by the spouse, not the decedent) is unlikely to trigger inclusion of life insurance proceeds under the controlling shareholder regulation.

The proceeds of a life insurance policy owned by a partnership on the life of a partner are not includable in the insured partner's gross estate if the proceeds are payable to or for the benefit of the partnership. However, this only applies if the

---

[5] Rev. Rul. 75-70, 1975-1 CB 301.
[6] Estate of Skifter, 56 TC 1190 (1971), *aff'd*, 468 F.2d 699 (2d Cir. 1972), *nonacq.*, 1978-1 CB 3; Rev. Rul. 84-179, 1984-2 CB 195.

[7] Noel, 380 U.S. 678 (1965).
[8] Estate of Lee, 69 TC 860 (1978), *nonacq.*, 1980-1 CB 2.

partner, in his or her individual capacity, had no incidents of ownership in the policy.[9]

If the proceeds are payable other than to or for the benefit of the partnership, the proceeds are includable in the insured partner's gross estate. In this situation, the incidents of ownership in the policy held by the partnership are effectively held by the partners as individuals. Thus, the insured partner possesses incidents of ownership that are exercisable with the other partners.[10]

5. The gross estate includes a group life insurance policy taken out by an employer on the decedent's life if the decedent possessed the right to change the beneficiaries, the right to terminate the policy, or the right to prevent cancellation by purchasing the policy. In addition, a decedent's right to select a settlement option for the proceeds is generally an incident of ownership.

The power to terminate a policy solely by ending employment is not an incident of ownership and the value of the proceeds is not included in the gross estate.[11] Also, if the employee had the right to convert a group policy into an individual insurance policy at the end of employment and could transfer this right, the proceeds of the policy are not included in the gross estate if the decedent irrevocably transferred the policy to another and retained the conversion privilege. In this case, the conversion privilege is not an incident of ownership.[12]

(c) Impact of Substitution Power. In Rev. Rul. 2011-28,[13] the IRS examined the situation where a grantor had the power, exercisable at any time, to acquire any property held in the trust by substituting other property of equivalent value. The trust held a life insurance policy on the grantor's life. The IRS concluded that grantor's retention of the power, exercisable in a nonfiduciary capacity, to acquire an insurance policy held in trust by substituting other assets of equivalent value will not, by itself, cause the value of the insurance policy to be includible in the grantor's gross estate under IRC Sec. 2042, provided the trustee has a fiduciary obligation (under local law or the trust instrument) to ensure the grantor's compliance with the terms of this power by satisfying itself that the properties acquired and substituted by the grantor are in fact of equivalent value, and further provided that the substitution power cannot be exercised in a manner that can shift benefits among the trust beneficiaries. A substitution power cannot be exercised in a manner that can shift benefits if: (a) the trustee has both the power (under local law or the trust instrument) to reinvest the trust corpus and a duty of impartiality with respect to the trust beneficiaries; or (b) the nature of the trust's investments or the level of income produced by any or all of the trust's investments does not impact the respective interests of the beneficiaries, such as when the trust is

---

[9] Estate of Knipp, 25 TC 153, *acq.*, 1956-2 CB 6, *nonacq.* 1956-2 CB 10 (withdrawn), *acq. reinstated,* 1959-1 CB 4, *aff'd*, 244 F.2d 436 (4th Cir. 1957), *cert. denied*, 355 U.S. 827 (1957). See Ltr. Rul. 200111038 (insured did not hold any incidents of ownership in life insurance policies transferred to a partnership in which the insured held a limited partnership interest).

[10] Rev. Rul. 83-147, 1983-2 CB 158.

[11] Rev. Rul. 72-307, 1972-1 CB 307.

[12] Rev. Rul. 69-54, 1969-1 CB 221, *as modified by* Rev. Rul. 72-307, 1972-1 CB 307 and Rev. Rul. 84-130, 1984-2 CB 194.

[13] Rev. Rul. 2011-28, 2011-2 CB 830.

administered as a unitrust (under local law or the trust instrument) or when distributions from the trust are limited to discretionary distributions of principal and income.

> **Example 3:** The grantor had established and funded an irrevocable trust for the benefit of her descendants with cash. The trust purchased a life insurance policy on the grantor's life. The trust's terms prohibited her from serving as trustee. The grantor made gifts every year to the trust, and the trust paid the premium on the insurance policy. The trust's governing instrument provided the grantor with the power, exercisable at any time, to acquire any property held in trust by substituting other property of equivalent value. The trust instrument provided that the power was exercisable by her in a nonfiduciary capacity, without the approval or consent of any person acting in a fiduciary capacity. To exercise the power of substitution, she must certify in writing that the substituted property and the trust's property for which it is substituted are of equivalent value. The grantor's exercise of her power of substitution will not cause the value of the life insurance policy to be included in her gross estate.

(d) Life Insurance Purchased in Community Property State. If life insurance is acquired by a spouse domiciled in a community property state during marriage and premiums are paid from community funds, the incidents of ownership constitute community property rights. Under those circumstances, one-half of the proceeds is includible in the gross estate of the insured spouse [Reg. Sec. 20.2042-1(c)(5)]. In Rev. Rul. 2003-40,[14] the IRS explains the estate tax treatment of the proceeds of a life insurance policy purchased by a Louisiana resident on his life where the premiums were paid by his wife using community property. The IRS concluded that, taking into account a duty of consistency in reporting the tax treatment of life insurance policies in the estates of a husband and wife, the husband's estate must include 100 percent of the proceeds of the policy if the wife predeceased him and a community property share of the value of the policy was not included in her estate.

(e) Transfers within Three Years of Death. The proceeds of a life insurance policy are included in the decedent's gross estate for federal estate tax purposes if, within three years of death, the decedent:

- Irrevocably transferred a life insurance policy that was payable to the decedent's estate [IRC Sec. 2042(1)]; or

- Retained an incident of ownership in the policy under IRC Sec. 2042(2) [IRC Sec. 2035(d)(2); see ¶ 1804].

If the decedent made a completed gift of the policy and transferred all incidents of ownership more than three years before death, the policy is not included in the decedent's gross estate. For example, in Letter Ruling 201327010, the IRS concluded that proceeds of life insurance policies purchased by the insured's predeceased spouse, naming the purchasing spouse's estate as beneficiary, and held in a trust of which the insured is the trustee will not be included in the insured's gross estate if he relinquishes his role as a trustee and survives the three-year period of IRC Sec. 2035(a).

---

[14] Rev. Rul. 2003-40, 2003-1 CB 813.

An incident of ownership attributed from an entity owner to its deceased shareholder (or partner) is within the scope of IRC Sec. 2035(d)(2) if the entity transfers the life insurance policy within three years of the decedent's death. A transfer supported by a business purpose apparently is a recognized exception to this rule.[15]

> **NOTE:** The decedent's gross estate does not include any policy sold for adequate and full consideration in money or money's worth within three years of death [IRC Sec. 2035(b)(1)].

The payment of premiums by the decedent-insured on a life insurance policy irrevocably transferred by the decedent-insured within three years of death does not cause the life insurance proceeds to be included in the decedent's gross estate.[16] Only the amount of premiums paid by the insured within three years of his or her death is included in the decedent's gross estate.

(f) Right to Receive Life Insurance Policy Dividends. A decedent is considered to have an incident of ownership in an insurance policy on his life held in trust if, under the terms of the policy, the decedent has the power to change the beneficial ownership in the policy or its proceeds, or the time or manner of its enjoyment, even though the decedent has no beneficial interest in the trust [Reg. Sec. 20.2042-1(c)(4)].

Congress intended IRC Sec. 2042 to parallel IRC Secs. 2036, 2037, 2038, and 2041 which cause other property to be included in a decedent's gross estate.[17] In general, the term "incidents of ownership" relates to the right of the insured or his estate to the economic benefits of the insurance policy.

The question of whether "dividends paid on an insurance policy" is an economic benefit that would cause the value of the insurance proceeds to be includible in a decedent's gross estate was first considered by the Tax Court in *Estate of Bowers*.[18] In that case, the decedent agreed to carry life insurance on his life payable to his former wife as part of a settlement agreement in a divorce. The court held that the right to dividends, which may be applied against a current premium, is nothing more than a reduction in the amount of premiums paid rather than a right to the income of the policy. Therefore the court concluded in that case that upon the decedent's death, the value of the policies was not includible in his gross estate.

Similarly, in Chief Counsel Advice 201328030, the decedent was required to insure his life for a certain amount in conjunction with his property settlement agreement. Under the agreement, the decedent would pay all premiums, dues and assessments on the policies but he was not authorized to borrow against or pledge the policies. The decedent was also entitled to any dividends but, upon his death, his former spouse would receive the proceeds. The IRS concluded that the insurance proceeds were not includible in the decedent's gross estate because, at death, he held only a right to receive the policies' dividends which, pursuant to *Estate of Bowers*, were not considered to be an incident of ownership that would cause the value of a life insurance policy to be included in the decedent's gross estate.

---

[15] Rev. Rul. 82-141, 1982-2 CB 209; Rev. Rul. 90-21, 1990-1 CB 172.

[16] Estate of Headrick, 93 TC 171, *aff'd*, 918 F.2d 1263 (6th Cir. 1990), AOD 1991-012.

[17] S. Rep. No. 83-1622 (1954).

[18] Estate of Bowers, 23 TC 911 (1955); see also Estate of Jordahl, 65 TC 92 (1975) (the right to dividends not incident of ownership); Schwager, 64 TC 781 (1975).

¶405 INSURANCE ON ANOTHER'S LIFE

Only life insurance owned by the decedent-insured on his or her own life is included in his or her taxable gross estate. This means that a decedent's taxable gross estate does not include life insurance owned on someone else's life [IRC Sec. 2042].

¶406 RECOVERY OF ESTATE TAX FROM A BENEFICIARY

Unless the decedent's will provides otherwise, the executor can recover from a beneficiary any estate tax generated by insurance proceeds included in the gross estate and paid to the beneficiary [IRC Sec. 2206]. The beneficiary is liable to the estate for the fraction of the estate taxes represented by the amount of the proceeds divided by the taxable estate. If you do not want the taxes apportioned in this way, you can make different provisions in the language of the will or trust.

¶407 SPLIT-DOLLAR LIFE INSURANCE ARRANGEMENTS

A split-dollar life insurance arrangement is defined as any arrangement between an owner of a life insurance contract and a non-owner of the contract under which either party pays all or part of the premiums, and one of the parties paying the premiums is entitled to recover (either conditionally or unconditionally) all or any portion of those premiums and such recovery is to be made from, or is secured by, the proceeds of the contract [Reg. Sec. 1.61-22(b)]. Split-dollar life insurance is a perk that companies frequently provide for their executives. The split-dollar arrangement is a method of financing permanent life insurance that calls for a sharing of premium costs, cash values, and death benefits. In most split-dollar life insurance arrangements, employers and employees join in the purchase of life insurance for the employee and both parties share premium costs, cash values, and death benefits. In most situations, an employer pays the premiums on an employee's life insurance policy to the extent of the annual increase in the cash surrender value of the policy and the employee pays the balance. When the employee dies, the employer receives the cash surrender value and the balance is paid to the employee's beneficiaries.

Split-dollar insurance arrangements can also exist between family members in conjunction with family financial planning and wealth transfer. Split-dollar arrangements are used in estate planning because the amount of the gift made to the owner of the term portion of the policy is measured by the cost of pure term insurance, which will typically be much less than the cost of the life insurance premium.

(a) Tax Treatment. Determining the tax treatment of split-dollar arrangements is confusing because there are several sets of overlapping rules that depend on the type of arrangement and the date the split-dollar arrangement was created. There are three time frames as follows:

- Arrangements entered into prior to 1/28/02 which are governed by the rules in Notice 2002-8;[1]

- Arrangements entered into between 1/28/03 and 9/17/03 which are also governed by the rules in Notice 2002-8; and

- Arrangements entered into after 9/17/03 which are governed by the final regulations which address the income, employment, and gift tax treatment of split-dollar life insurance arrangements.

The tax treatment of parties to a split-dollar arrangement depends on what type of split-dollar life insurance plan exists. There are four types of split-dollar life insurance plans as follows: endorsement plans, collateral assignment plans, reverse split-dollar plans and private split-dollar plans.

(b) IRC Sec. 409A. IRC Sec. 409A generally provides that all amounts deferred under a nonqualified deferred compensation plan for all tax years are currently includible in gross income to the extent not subject to a substantial risk of forfeiture and not previously included in gross income, unless (a) the plan meets the distribution, acceleration of benefit and election requirements under IRC Sec. 409A, and (b) is operated in accordance with these requirements. If these requirements are not met, the deferred amounts will be included in the participants' gross income and the tax on this compensation will be increased by: (1) interest at the underpayment rate plus one percentage point; and (2) a 20 percent penalty.

Split dollar life insurance arrangements that provide only death benefits are outside the scope of IRC Sec. 409A, as are most split-dollar life insurance arrangements that are treated as loans. On the other hand, policies structured under the endorsement method, where the service recipient owns the policy but the service provider obtains a legally binding right to compensation that he or she will receive in future years are subject to IRC Sec. 409A.

In Notice 2007-34,[2] the IRS provides guidance regarding the application of IRC Sec. 409A to split-dollar life insurance arrangements. This Notice also provides that modifications of split-dollar life insurance arrangements that are required in order to comply with, or avoid application of IRC Sec. 409A will not be treated as a material modification to the split-dollar arrangement.

(c) Endorsement Plans. In an endorsement split-dollar plan, which is the traditional plan, the employer is formally designated as the owner and beneficiary of the life insurance contract. The employer pays the premiums and is treated as providing current life insurance protection and other economic benefits to the employee. As long as the plan is in place, there is an imputed economic benefit to the employee because of the continuing insurance protection provided to him by the employer. The employee will have taxable income under IRC Sec. 61 in the amount of term insurance cost. For plans entered into on or after January 28, 2002 but before September 17, 2003, the one-year term rates outlined in Table 2001 which is attached to Notice 2002-8 may be used to determine the measure of this economic benefit.

---

[1] ¶**407** Notice 2002-8, 2002-1 CB 398.   [2] Notice 2007-34, 2007-17 IRB 996.

In Notice 2002-8, the IRS provides rules to help taxpayers compute the value of the economic benefit received when life insurance is provided in split-dollar agreements and in qualified pension and profit-sharing plans. In the case of any split-dollar life insurance arrangement entered into on or before September 17, 2003, taxpayers may continue to rely on the revenue rulings described in Notice 2002-8, but only if the arrangement is not materially modified after September 17, 2003.

> **Example 1:** Employee is 53 years old and his employer establishes a split-dollar life insurance arrangement whereby the employer is treated as the owner. The cost of $3 million of term life insurance would be determined in Table 2001 in Notice 2002-8 based on a rate of $3.20 per $1,000. In the first policy year the employee would be taxed on $9,600. If he lives to age 65, the cost of the policy would increase to $11.90 per $1,000 and by age 99, the cost would increase to $281.05 per $1,000, or $843,150 per year of imputed income.

If the employer transfers an endorsement plan split-dollar insurance plan to the insured/employee, the employee would be taxed on the entire cash value of the policy under IRC Sec. 83, which deals with property received as compensation. [Reg. Sec. 1.83-3(e)].

For endorsement split-dollar plans entered into after September 17, 2003, the economic benefit regime applies to determine the value of the insurance benefit imputed to the employee. Under the economic benefit regime an owner is treated as providing economic benefits to a non-owner of the life insurance contract. The non-owner must take into account the full value of all economic benefits reduced by the consideration paid directly or indirectly by the non-owner to the owner for those economic benefits. Depending on the relationship between the owner and the non-owner, the economic benefits may constitute a payment of compensation, a dividend, a contribution to capital, a gift, or a transfer having a different tax character. Depending on the relationship between the parties, the economic benefits may be treated as provided from the owner to the non-owner and as separately provided from the non-owner to such other person or persons (for example, as a payment of compensation from an employer to an employee and as a gift from the employee to the employee's child) and those benefits must be accounted for fully and consistently by both the owner and the non-owner [Reg. Sec. 1.61-22(d)(1)].

   (d) Non-Equity Split-Dollar. The split-dollar final regulations provide that the value of the economic benefits provided to a non-owner for a taxable year under the non-equity split-dollar life insurance arrangement equals the following:

1. The cost of current life insurance protection provided to the non-owner which equals the excess of the death benefit of the life insurance contract (including paid-up additions thereto) over the total amount payable to the owner (including any outstanding policy loans that offset amounts otherwise payable to the owner) under the split-dollar life insurance arrangement, less the portion of the policy cash value actually taken into account or paid for by then on-owner for the current taxable year or any prior taxable year. The cost of current life insurance protection provided to the non-owner for any year equals the amount of the current life insurance protec-

tion provided to the non-owner multiplied by the life insurance premium factor published by the IRS [Reg. Sec. 1.61-22(d)(3)].

2. The amount of policy cash value to which the non-owner has current access. Policy cash value is determined disregarding surrender charges or other similar charges or reductions. Policy cash value includes policy cash value attributable to paid-up additions. A non-owner has current access to that portion of the policy cash value:

   • To which the non-owner has a current or future right under the arrangement; and

   • That currently is directly or indirectly accessible by the non-owner, inaccessible to the owner, or inaccessible to the owner's general creditors [Reg. Sec. 1.61-22(d)(4)].

3. The value of any economic benefits provided to the non-owner (to the extent not actually taken into account for a prior taxable year).

The amount of the current life insurance protection and the policy cash value shall be determined on the same valuation date. The valuation date is the last day of the non-owner's taxable year, unless the owner and non-owner agree to instead use the policy anniversary date as the valuation date. If the split-dollar life insurance arrangement terminates during the taxable year of the non-owner, the value of such economic benefits is determined on the day that the arrangement terminates. The owner and non-owner of the split-dollar life insurance arrangement must use the same valuation date. In addition, the same valuation date must be used for all years prior to termination of the split-dollar life insurance arrangement unless the parties receive IRS consent to change the valuation date [Reg. Sec. 1.61-22(d)(5)].

Example 2: On January 1 of year 1, R and E enter into the split-dollar life insurance arrangement. Under the arrangement, R pays all of the premiums on the life insurance contract until the termination of the arrangement or E's death. The arrangement provides that upon termination of the arrangement or E's death, R is entitled to receive the lesser of the aggregate premiums paid or the policy cash value of the contract and E is entitled to receive any remaining amounts. Under the terms of the arrangement and applicable state law, the policy cash value is fully accessible by R and R's creditors but E has the right to borrow or withdraw at any time the portion of the policy cash value exceeding the amount payable to R. To fund the arrangement, R purchases a life insurance contract with constant death benefit protection equal to $1.5 million. R makes premium payments on the life insurance contract of $60,000 in each of years 1, 2, and 3. The policy cash value equals $55,000 as of December 31 of year 1, $140,000 as of December 31 of year 2, and $240,000 as of December 31 of year 3. Under the terms of the split-dollar life insurance arrangement, E has the right for year 1 and all subsequent years to borrow or withdraw the portion of the policy cash value exceeding the amount payable to R. Thus, E has current access to such portion of the policy cash value for each year that the arrangement is in effect. In addition, because R pays all of the premiums on the life insurance contract, R provides to E all of the economic benefits that E receives under the arrangement. Therefore, E includes in gross income the value of all economic benefits provided to him under the arrangement. For year 1, E is provided $0 of policy cash value (excess of $55,000 policy cash value determined as of December 31 of year 1 over $55,000 payable to R). For year 1, *E* is also provided current life insurance protection of $1,445,000 ($1,500,000 minus $55,000 payable to R). Thus, *E* includes in gross income for year 1 the cost of $1,445,000 of current life insurance protection. For year 2, *E* is provided $20,000 of policy cash value ($140,000 policy cash value determined as of December 31 of year 2 minus $120,000 payable to *R*). For year 2, *E* is also provided current life insurance protection of $1,360,000 ($1,500,000 minus the sum of $120,000 payable to *R* and the aggregate of $20,000 of policy cash value that *E* actually includes in income on *E*'s year 1 and year 2 federal income tax returns). Thus, *E* includes in gross income for year 2 the sum of $20,000 of policy cash value and the cost of $1,360,000 of current life insurance protection. For year 3, *E* is provided $40,000 of policy cash value ($240,000 policy cash value determined as of December 31 of year 3 minus the sum of $180,000 payable to *R* and $20,000 of aggregate policy cash value that *E* actually included in gross income in year 1 and year 2). For year 3, *E* is also provided current insurance protection of $1,260,000 ($1,500,000 minus the sum of $180,000 payable to *R* and $60,000 of aggregate policy cash value that *E* actually includes in gross income in year 1, year 2, and year 3). Thus, *E* includes in gross income for year 3 the sum of $40,000 of policy cash value and the cost of $1,260,000 of current life insurance protection [Reg. Sec. 1.61-22(d)(6), ex. 1].

(e) Other Economic Benefit Tax Consequences. In a split-dollar life insurance arrangement taxed under the economic benefit regime, the non-owner has no investment in the contract [Reg. Sec. 1.61-22(f)(2)(i)]. Premiums paid by the owner are included in the owner's investment in the contract. Amounts received under a life insurance contract (other than death benefits), such as dividends, loan proceeds, or proceeds of a partial surrender, that are provided directly or indirectly to the non-owner are treated as paid by the insurance company to the owner and then by the owner to the non-owner. The owner is taxed on these amounts [Reg. Sec. 1.61-22(e)(1)]. The non-owner takes the amount into account as a payment or compensation, dividend, gift, etc., depending on his relationship to the owner. The amount taken into account is reduced, however, by economic benefits taken into account by the non-owner (with some adjustments) and consideration paid by the non-owner for economic benefits. Similar treatment applies to policy loans [Reg. Sec. 1.61-22(e)(3)].

Amounts paid to a non-owner beneficiary because of the insured's death are excludible from income to the extent allocable to current life insurance protection under the split-dollar arrangement, the cost of which was paid by the non-owner, or the value of which the non-owner actually took into account under the economic benefit rules [Reg. Sec. 1.61-22(f)(2)(ii)].

When a split-dollar policy is transferred, the transferee (the new owner) generally must take into account for federal income, employment, and gift tax purposes, the fair market value of the contract less the amount paid to the transferor and the value of all economic benefits already taken into account or paid for by the transferee [Reg. Sec. 1.61-22(f)(1)]. For this purpose, fair market value is the cash surrender value and the value of all other rights under the contract other than the value of the current life insurance protection [Reg. Sec. 1.61-22(f)(2)].

Transfers in exchange for services are governed by IRC Sec. 83 [Reg. Sec. 1.61-22(g)(3)]. Therefore there is no income recognition on a policy transfer from employer to employee until the employee's rights to the contract are substantially vested or the transferor elects to recognize the income. The employer's deduction is also deferred until the employee takes the transfer into income. The greater of the contract's fair market value or the amount paid by the transferee for the contract plus the amount of unrecovered economic benefits previously taken into account or paid for by the transferee, become the transferee's investment in the contract immediately after the transfer [Reg. Sec. 1.61-22(g)].

(f) Collateral Assignment Split-Dollar Plans. In the collateral assignment split-dollar plan, the employee is treated as the owner of the life insurance policy and may designate the beneficiary of the policy. In this situation, the premiums paid by the employer are treated as a series of loans made by the employer to the employee if the employee is obligated to repay the employer, whether out of contract proceeds or otherwise. Under the second regime, the loans are subject to the rules governing the original issue discount (OID) and the imputed interest rules of IRC Sec. 7872, which deals with below market loans. If the employee is not obligated to repay the premiums paid by the employer, these amounts are treated as compensation income to the employee at the time the premiums are paid by the employer.

For split-dollar arrangements in place on or after January 28, 2002 but before September 17, 2003, taxpayers may continue to use the one-year term rates found in Table 2001 to determine the value of current life insurance protection on a single life that is provided under a split-dollar life insurance arrangement, in a qualified retirement plan, or under employee annuity contracts. Taxpayers should make appropriate adjustments to these premium rates if the life insurance protection covers more than one life.

For collateral assigment split-dollar life insurance arrangements entered after September 17, 2003, the parties to the arrangement may treat premium or other payments by the sponsor as loans. In such cases, the IRS will not challenge reasonable efforts to comply with the OID and below-market interest rules. All payments by the sponsor from the inception of the arrangement (reduced by any repayments to the sponsor) before the first taxable year in which such payments are treated as loans for federal tax purposes must be treated as loans entered into at the beginning of that first year in which such payments are treated as loans.

Under the loan regime, a payment made under a collateral split-dollar life insurance arrangement is a split-dollar loan, and the policy owner and non-owner are treated, as borrower and lender, respectively, if [Reg. Sec. 1.7872-15(a)(2)(i)]:

1. The payment is made directly or indirectly by the non-owner to the owner;

2. The payment either is a loan under general federal tax law principles or a reasonable person would expect the payment to be repaid in full to the non-owner; and

3. Repayment is to be made from, or secured by, the policy's death benefit or cash surrender value.

   Example 3: Assume that an employee owns a life insurance policy under a split-dollar life insurance arrangement and the employer makes premium payments on this policy. There is a reasonable expectation that the payments will be repaid, and the repayments are secured by the policy. Each premium payment is a loan for federal tax purposes.

> **Example 4:** Assume an employee owns a life insurance policy under a split-dollar life insurance arrangement and the employer makes premium payments on this policy. The employer is entitled to be repaid 80 percent of each premium payment, and the repayments are secured by the policy. Under Reg. Sec. 1.7872-15(a)(2)(i), 20 percent of each premium payment is taxed as income. If there is a reasonable expectation that the remaining 80 percent of each payment will be repaid in full, the 80 percent is a loan for federal tax purposes. If less than 80 percent of a premium payment is reasonably expected to be repaid, then no part of the payment is treated as a loan for federal tax purposes and the entire premium payment is treated as taxable income [Reg. Sec. 1.7872-15(a)(2)(iv), ex. 2].

If a split-dollar loan does not provide for sufficient interest, it is a below market loan subject to IRC Sec. 7872 and Reg. Sec. 1.7872-15(e). Otherwise it is subject to the general rules for debt instruments, including the OID rules [Reg. Sec. 1.7872-15(a)(1)]. If a split-dollar loan is a below-market loan, then, generally, the loan is recharacterized as a loan with interest at the applicable federal rate (AFR), coupled with an imputed transfer by the lender to the borrower. The timing, amount, and characterization of the imputed transfer between the lender and borrower will depend on the relationship between them and whether the loan is a demand loan or a term loan. Thus, for example, the imputed transfer generally would be treated as a compensation payment if the lender were the borrower's employer [Reg. Sec. 1.7872-15(e)(1)].

(g) Split-Dollar Loans.

Split-dollar demand loans. *Testing for sufficient interest*—Each calendar year that a split-dollar demand loan is outstanding, the loan is tested to determine if the loan provides for sufficient interest. A split-dollar demand loan provides for sufficient interest for the calendar year if the rate (based on annual compounding) at which interest accrues on the loan's adjusted issue price during the year is no lower than the blended annual rate for the year. (The IRS publishes the blended annual rate in the Internal Revenue Bulletin in July of each year.) If the loan does not provide for sufficient interest, the loan is a below-market split-dollar demand loan for that calendar year. If the loan is below-market, the amount of forgone interest for the year is the annual interest at the appropriate AFR less any interest that accrues on the loan during the year. Generally, this excess amount is treated as transferred by the lender to the borrower and retransferred as interest by the borrower to the lender at the end of each calendar year that the loan remains outstanding [Reg. Sec. 1.7872-15(e)(3)].

Split-dollar term loans. *Testing a split-dollar term loan for sufficient interest.* A split-dollar term loan is tested on the day the loan is made to determine if the loan provides for sufficient interest. A split-dollar term loan provides for sufficient interest if the imputed loan amount equals or exceeds the amount loaned. The imputed loan amount is the present value of all payments due under the loan, determined as of the date the loan is made, using a discount rate equal to the AFR in effect on that date. The AFR must be appropriate for the loan's term (short-term, mid-term, or long-term) and for the compounding period used in computing the present value. If the split-dollar loan does not provide for sufficient interest, the loan is a below-market split-dollar term loan [Reg. Sec. 1.7872-15(e)(4)(ii)].

Payment schedule that minimizes yield. For purposes of determining a split-dollar loan's term, the borrower is projected to exercise or not exercise an option or combination of options in a manner that minimizes the loan's overall yield. Similarly, the lender is projected to exercise or not exercise an option or combination of options in a manner that minimizes the loan's overall yield. If different projected patterns of exercise or non-exercise produce the same minimum yield, the parties are projected to exercise or not exercise an option or combination of options in a manner that produces the longest term. If the borrower (or lender) does or does not exercise the option as projected, the split-dollar loan is treated as retired and reissued on the date the option is or is not exercised for an amount of cash equal to the loan's adjusted issue price on that date. The reissued loan must be retested using the appropriate AFR in effect on the date of reissuance to determine whether it is a below-market loan [Reg. Sec. 1.7872-15(e)(4)(iii)(B)(1)].

> **Example 5:** Employee *B* issues a 10-year split-dollar term loan to Employer *Y*. *B* has the right to prepay the loan at the end of year 5. Interest is payable on the split-dollar loan at 1 percent for the first 5 years and at 10 percent for the remaining 5 years. This arrangement is treated as a 5-year split-dollar term loan from *Y* to *B*, with interest payable at 1 percent [Reg. Sec. 1.7872-15(e)(4)(iii)(B)(3), ex. 1].

> **Example 6:** The facts are the same as the facts in Example 1 above, except that B does not in fact prepay the split-dollar loan at the end of year 5. The first loan is treated as retired at the end of year 5 and a new 5-year split-dollar term loan is issued at that time, with interest payable at 10 percent [Reg. Sec. 1.7872-15(e)(4)(iii)(B)(3), ex. 2].

(h) Terminating Split-Dollar. In the life insurance industry, the term "rollout" is used to describe termination of a split-dollar life insurance arrangement other than by the death of the insured employee. A rollout results in cancellation of the employer's premium payment obligation relating to the life insurance policy and leaves the insured employee as the sole owner and interest holder in the policy. When a rollout of a split-dollar life insurance arrangement occurs, the employer generally is entitled to be repaid or reimbursed by the insured-employee or owner of the insurance policy. The amount of the reimbursement is the lesser of the total premiums the employer paid on the related life insurance policy or the cash surrender value of the policy at the time of the rollout. Repayment is typically accomplished by having the policy owner withdraw from or borrow against the policy to generate the cash needed to repay the employer. These withdrawals cannibalize the policy. Withdrawals for collateral assignment arrangements are tax-free only up to the owner's basis which is the contributed or taxed economic benefit amounts.

¶407

In *Neff*,[3] the Tax Court concluded that the termination of a split-dollar life insurance arrangement resulted in compensation to an individual. Under the arrangement, the employer paid the premiums, the employee owned the policies and, if the arrangement terminated for any reason other than death, the employee would reimburse the employer for the lesser of the premiums paid or the cash value of the insurance policies. Although there was no formal "termination," the actions of the parties showed they had terminated the arrangement, which triggered the taxpayer's obligation to repay the premiums. However, rather than reimburse the employer for the premiums, the taxpayer paid an amount that represented the discounted value of the premiums at death. For split-dollar arrangements such as this one, entered prior to the revised regulatory scheme, the employee is taxed on the economic benefit received less any amount contributed by the employee.

¶408 PRIVATE SPLIT-DOLLAR LIFE INSURANCE

A private split-dollar life insurance arrangement is outside of the typical employer-employee setting. In a private split-dollar arrangement, the insured substitutes for the employer and the policy is owned by the irrevocable trust for the benefit of the insured's family. These policies are wealth transfer devices that are used by the insured to transfer wealth out of the taxable estate into the hands of beneficiaries.

In Ltr. Rul. 200825011, the IRS addressed the federal gift, estate and generation-skipping transfer tax consequences of a family split-dollar life insurance arrangement under Reg. Sec. 1.61-22, which are the final regulations that address the taxation of split-dollar life insurance arrangements. In the ruling, a husband and wife (grantors) established an irrevocable trust for the benefit of their three grandchildren. The initial trustee was child 3 and the grantors were prohibited from serving as trustees. The trustee initially was required to hold the trust property as three separate trusts with each established for the primary benefit of each of the three children.

Until the death of the last of the grantors to die, the trustee had discretion to distribute amounts of income and corpus to any of their descendants as the trustee deemed desirable (although no trustee could distribute any amounts to himself or herself other than in satisfaction of a *Crummey* withdrawal power). After the death of the last of the grantors to die, the trustee had discretion to distribute income and corpus to the beneficiary and his or her descendants, in such amounts as were necessary to provide for the beneficiary's or the beneficiary's descendants', health, support, maintenance, and education. Each trust established for a beneficiary who was a child of the grantors, was to terminate on the beneficiary's death, at which time the trust corpus was to be distributed pursuant to the exercise of a testamentary limited power of appointment granted to each beneficiary.

Thereafter, the trust bought, owned and paid the initial premiums on a second-to-die life insurance policy on the lives of the grantors. They proposed to enter into a nonequity, collateral assignment split-dollar arrangement, which provided that the husband and

---

[3] Neff, TC Memo 2012-244.

wife contributed 100% of the annual premium amounts to the trust and the trust paid the premium on the policy. The estate of the surviving grantor received the greater of the cash surrender value of the policy prior to termination or an amount equal to all premiums paid by the grantors. The trustee retained the balance of the insurance proceeds as part of the trust fund.

The trust was named the owner of the policy and had all ownership rights, but could only pledge or assign the policy for the sole purpose of securing a loan from the insurer or a third party for the purpose of repaying the husband and wife. All other incidents of ownership resided in the trustee.

The agreement could be terminated: (i) by the husband and wife acting jointly, or by the survivor; or (ii) by the trustee of the trust. The agreement also terminated on the personal bankruptcy of the husband and wife, their failure to pay premiums and the trustee's surrender or cancellation of the policy. If the agreement ended during the lifetimes of the husband and wife, or the lifetime of the survivor, then, within 60 days of termination, the trust was required to repay the husband and wife, or the survivor, an amount equal to the greater of the cash surrender value of the policy, or the premiums paid by the grantors, to the extent the cash surrender value of the policy was not sufficient to pay this amount.

The trustee executed a collateral assignment of the policy to the grantors in order to secure their interest in the policy. The trustee retained all rights of ownership in the policy subject to the right of the grantors or the estate of the survivor to receive repayment on termination of the agreement.

Based on these facts, the IRS concluded that:

1. The grantors are the deemed owners of the second-to-die life insurance policy under Reg. Sec. 1.61-22(c)(1)(ii)(A)(2) because the agreement provided life insurance protection as its only economic benefit;

2. If some or all of the cash surrender value is used (either directly, or indirectly through loans) to fund the trust's obligation to pay premiums, the grantors will be treated as making a gift at that time and IRC Sec. 2652(a) will apply; and

3. Because the couple did not retain any incidents of ownership in the policies under the agreement and the collateral assignment, the proceeds of the policies payable to the trust were not includible in the gross estate of the second to die under IRC Sec. 2042(2). However, the portion of the proceeds payable to the survivor's estate was includible under IRC Sec. 2042(1) and the estate of the first to die would include any amount that the estate was entitled to receive upon termination of the agreement.

Reverse private split-dollar life insurance arrangements. In Notice 2002-59,[1] the IRS provided standards for valuing private split-dollar life insurance arrangements used to transfer large sums of money to family members at death with little or no tax consequences. The notice attempts to crack down on split-dollar life insurance arrangements that are designed to "understate the value of benefits for income or gift tax purposes."

---

[1] ¶ **408** Notice 2002-59, 2002-2 CB 481.

¶408

Notice 2002-59 follows publicity in the media regarding use by the wealthy of a loophole to escape transfer by using private split-dollar life insurance rules to undervalue gifts made to beneficiaries. Here's how the technique works: A wealthy family member who wants to avoid tax on the transfer of his or her estate to the next generation establishes a life insurance trust or family limited partnership which purchases an expensive term life insurance policy on the life of the wealthy family member. The policy has an inappropriately inflated first-year premium price. Policies with first-year premiums of anywhere from $4.4 million to $40 million are not uncommon. The family member prepays all or most of the premiums on the life insurance policy. According to the gift tax annual exclusion, any premium paid on that life insurance in excess of $14,000 in 2014 is considered a gift to those heirs. On the gift tax return for the year that the premiums are paid, the far lower premium price (P.S. 58 rates) rather than the inflated premium price actually paid by the taxpayer is reported, thus lowering the gift tax due on the transfer. The insurer invests the difference between the inflated premium that was actually paid and the lower premium reported on the gift tax return. The investment grows tax-free inside the life insurance trust. When the insured dies, the trust or family partnership receives the death benefits and distributes them to the beneficiaries free of gift, estate, or income taxes.

In Notice 2002-59, the IRS concluded that reverse split-dollar life insurance arrangements are abusive techniques that distort estate and gift taxes by permitting taxpayers to abuse the term insurance rates or standardized rates from the IRS tables (P.S. 58 rates). The IRS points out that use of the P.S. 58 rates to understate the economic benefits provided under private split-dollar arrangements was never authorized by the IRS. Taxpayers had found support for their schemes in Letter Ruling 9636033, where the IRS concluded that a private reserve split-dollar life insurance arrangement did not result in gifts of the premium payments to the trust. In addition, the insurance proceeds payable to the trust and the insured's spouse were not includible in the insured's gross estate because he retained no incidents of ownership in the policy. The IRS goes on to say taxpayers "may not use the P.S. rates for reverse split-dollar life insurance arrangements or for split-dollar life insurance arrangements outside of the compensatory contest."

In Notice 2002-59, the IRS states that it will not respect any arrangement using inappropriately high current term insurance rates, prepayment of premiums, or other techniques to confer policy benefits other than current life insurance protection on another party. According to the IRS, the use of these techniques to understate the value of policy benefits distorts the gift tax consequences of the arrangement. Taxpayers who have employed the reverse split-dollar technique to reduce their transfer tax bill are now open to audit.

In Notice 2002-59, the IRS provides guidelines for parties participating in split-dollar life insurance arrangements. Taxpayers may value current life insurance protection using either the: (1) premium rates in Table 2001, "Interim Table of One Year Term Premiums for $1,000 of Life Insurance Protection," in Notice 2002-8; or (2) the insurer's published premium rates if the rates are lower than those in Table 2001. These rates may only be used when and to the extent that the life insurance protection is conferred as an economic benefit by one party on another party without regard to premiums paid. In other words, if one party has any right to current life insurance protection in a split-dollar arrangement, neither the rates in Table 2001, nor the insurer's lower published rates, may be used to value the party's current life insurance protection. For example, if a donor pays the premiums on a life insurance policy that is part of a split-dollar life insurance arrangement between the donor and a trust and, under the arrangement, the trust has the right to current life insurance protection, the current life insurance protection has been conferred as an economic benefit by the donor on the trust, and the donor is permitted to value the current life insurance protection using either the premium rates in Table 2001 or the insurer's lower published premium rates. In contract, if a donor pays the premiums on a life insurance policy that is part of a split-dollar life insurance arrangement between the donor and a trust, and the donor (or the donor's estate) has the right to current life insurance protection under the policy, neither the premium rates in Table 2001 nor the insurer's lower published premium rates may be relied upon to value the donor's current life insurance protection for the purpose of establishing the value of the policy benefits conferred upon the trust. If the trust pays for all or a portion of the policy benefits provided under the split-dollar life insurance arrangement, the result will be the same.

> **Example 1:** Grandpa pays the premium on a life insurance policy that is part of a split-dollar arrangement between him and a life insurance trust that exists to benefit his child and grandchildren. The trust has the right to current life insurance protection. Grandpa has conferred an economic benefit on the trust and may therefore value the benefit by using the premium rates in Notice 2002-8 or the insurer's lower published premium rates.

> **Example 2:** Same facts as Example 1, except that Grandpa or his estate (not the trust) has the right to current life insurance protection under the policy. In this situation, Grandpa cannot value the benefit conferred on the trust by relying on the rates in Table 1 or the insurer's lower published rates since those rates may understate the economic benefit provided by the arrangement and therefore the gift tax due.

¶409 CHARITABLE SPLIT-DOLLAR LIFE INSURANCE

The IRS no longer approves of charitable split-dollar insurance as it has in the past and that those promoting and participating in this popular tax-avoidance device can expect to face adverse tax consequences including interest and penalties.[1] The IRS warned that charitable split-dollar insurance transactions that allow wealthy taxpayers to pay for life insurance with tax-deductible dollars do not produce the tax benefits advertised by promoters. In the eyes of the IRS, charitable split-dollar life insurance arrangements are really abusive tax shelters.

Here's how a typical charitable split-dollar insurance transaction works: A wealthy taxpayer transfers funds to a charity with the understanding that the charity will use the

---

[1] **¶409** Notice 99-36, 1999-1 CB 1284.

funds to pay premiums on a cash value life insurance policy that will pay a small percentage of the death benefits to the charity and pay the bulk of the death benefits to the taxpayer's family. Central to this scheme tax-wise is the ability of the taxpayer making the transfer to characterize the transfer as a gift to a charity and thus claim a charitable contribution deduction for income tax purposes. The charity purchases a life insurance policy with the charity and members of the taxpayer's family as beneficiaries. They are not, however, equal beneficiaries. As a result when the donor dies, the charity receives a small portion of the death benefits but the donor's heirs get the lion's share, plus the added tax-free bonus of whatever has accumulated over time in the life insurance policy.

The IRS disapproves of this scheme for two reasons. First, on day one, the taxpayer is claiming a charitable contribution deduction for what essentially is the purchase of life insurance that benefits the taxpayer's heirs. Normally no deduction is allowed when a taxpayer pays a premium for the purchase of life insurance on his or her own life. A gift to a charity is only deductible to the extent that it exceeds the fair market value of the benefit that the donor receives in return [Reg. Sec. 1.170A-1(h)].

Second, according to the terms of the split-dollar agreement entered into between the charity and the donor, the donor and/or his family is often permitted after the charity has purchased the life insurance policy to borrow against the cash value of the policy, to partially or completely surrender the policy for cash, and to designate beneficiaries for specified portions of the death benefit. Although the terms of split-dollar agreements vary, the common feature, says the IRS, is that, over the life of the split-dollar agreement, the donor and his or her family has access to a disproportionately high percentage of the cash-surrender value and death benefit under the policy, compared to the percentage of premiums paid by the trust.

The IRS will look beyond the form of a charitable split-interest insurance transaction to determine its true substance. They will then disallow the charitable deduction you claimed when you initially transferred the money to the charity to enable them to purchase the cash value life insurance policy. The IRS says that having a charity briefly touch money on its way to buy life insurance, which primarily benefits a donor's heirs, does not justify a charitable tax deduction.

The IRS also warns that your charitable split-interest insurance transaction will be scrutinized no matter what intermediary is designated to purchase the life insurance— the charity, an irrevocable life insurance trust, a family limited partnership, or a member of the donor's family.

In addition, the IRS warns that charities may lose their tax-exempt status on private inurement or impermissible private benefit grounds. The IRS may also impose on the charity a variety of taxes, including taxes on excess benefit transactions under IRC Sec. 4958; taxes on self-dealing under IRC Sec. 4941; and taxes on taxable expenditures under IRC Sec. 4945. In addition, a charity that provides written substantiation of a charitable contribution in connection with a charitable split-dollar insurance transaction may be subject to penalties for aiding and abetting the understatement of tax liability under IRC Sec. 6701. The IRS is also considering whether to require charities to report participation in charitable split-dollar insurance transactions on their annual information return

Anyone else involved in the charity split-dollar insurance transaction including the donor and the promoter may face the accuracy-related penalty under IRC Sec. 6662, the return preparer penalty under IRC Sec. 6694, the promoter penalty under IRC Sec. 6700, and the penalty under IRC Sec. 6701 for aiding and abetting the understatement of tax liability.

Substantiation rule used to deny deduction. In *Addis*,[2] the Court of Appeals for the Ninth Circuit affirmed the Tax Court to conclude that married taxpayers who, through a family trust, made payments to an exempt organization that used those funds to pay premiums on a so-called charitable split-dollar life insurance policy on the life of the wife were denied charitable deductions for the donated monies. Pursuant to the policy, the charity would receive 56 percent and the family trust would receive 44 percent of the death benefit, with the charity paying the bulk of the premiums on the policy. No part of the taxpayers' purported contributions was deductible because the receipts provided by the organization for their donation premiums failed to meet the substantiation requirements of IRC Sec. 170(f)(8) and Reg. Sec. 1.170A-13(f)(6). IRC Sec. 170(f)(8) disallows charitable deductions in circumstances where the donee organization's contemporaneous written acknowledgement is erroneous and does not qualify as a good-faith estimate of the value of goods or services provided, and where the taxpayers use that erroneous statement to claim overstated deductions. The taxpayers and the organization in *Addis* had designed a scheme that purported to provide no benefits to the individuals in exchange for, or in consideration of, their payments. However, they received substantial benefits from the organization under the life insurance policy.

The court concluded that the receipts tendered to the couple by the organization, which stated that they received no consideration for their payments, were inaccurate and did not satisfy the IRC Sec. 170(f)(8) substantiation requirements. The charity's failure to make a good-faith estimate of the value of the benefits granted to the taxpayers precluded them from deducting their contributions.

---

[2] Addis, 118 TC 528 (2002), *aff'd*, 374 F.3d 881 (9th Cir. 2004), *cert. denied*, 543 U.S. 1151 (2005); Weiner, TC Memo 2002-153, *aff'd*, 2005-1 USTC ¶50,130 (9th Cir. 2004), *cert. denied*, 125 S. Ct. 1332 (2005); Estate of Roark, TC Memo 2004-271.

ANTI-FREEZE VALUATION RULES

TABLE OF CONTENTS

¶500 RATIONALE FOR ENACTMENT OF IRC SEC. 2701

Prior to October 8, 1990, individuals could pass wealth to future generations at no estate or gift tax cost by freezing the taxable value of their estates. The key was to transfer the future appreciation of certain property to junior family members while retaining present control over it.

Owners of closely held corporations frequently used one estate-freezing technique in which they would recapitalize the corporation so that it had both common and preferred stock. The preferred stock would soak up most of the company's value and the common stock would have a low value. Older family members would give the common stock to younger family at a low gift tax cost. Future appreciation in the value of the corporation would then go to the common shareholders—in this case, the junior family members—at no estate or gift tax costs. Similar results could be achieved through gifts of junior interests in partnerships and gifts of trust interests.

Congress considered these techniques to be abusive and enacted a whole new set of rules, which generally apply for transfers after October 8, 1990. Under the new rules, gifts with a retained interest (such as the preferred stock) are generally valued at the full value of the property transferred (both common and preferred) minus the value of the interest retained by the donor. In many cases under the rules, the retained

¶500

interest has no value. That, in turn, greatly increases the gift tax costs of the original transfer of the junior interest (the common stock).

Chapter 14 of the IRC (IRC Secs. 2701–2704) attempts to deal with a variety of situations in which gift tax valuation may be an issue. As discussed at ¶501, IRC Sec. 2701 provides valuation and deemed transfer rules applicable to intrafamily estate-freezing transactions involving corporate and partnership interests.

IRC Sec. 2702, discussed in detail at ¶602, sets forth valuation rules for grantor-retained income trusts and other term interests and for joint purchases of term and remainder interests by family members.

IRC Sec. 2703 provides rules for valuing property subject to buy-sell agreements [see ¶1909].

Finally, IRC Sec. 2704 [see ¶512] generally provides that the lapse of voting (or liquidation) rights in family corporations or partnerships will be treated as a taxable gift or testamentary transfer to the other shareholders or holders of partnership interests. A closer look at the specific rules follows.

¶501 VALUING TRANSFERRED INTERESTS IN CLOSELY HELD CORPORATIONS AND PARTNERSHIPS

To limit any abuse of the transfer tax system through the transfer of wealth to future generations, IRC Sec. 2701 provides rules to determine the amount of the gift that results when an equity interest in a corporation or partnership is transferred from an individual to a member of that individual's family (including the transferor's spouse, a lineal descendant of the transferor or the transferor's spouse, and the spouse of any such descendant) [Reg. Sec. 25.2701-1(a)]. For such rules to apply, "an applicable retained interest" (as discussed at ¶502) must be held by the transferor or an applicable family member (includes the transferor's spouse, an ancestor of the transferor or transferor's spouse, and the spouse of any such ancestor) immediately after this transfer [Reg. Sec. 25.2701-1(d)].

More specifically, IRC Sec. 2701 provides that if a person transfers an interest in a controlled corporation or partnership, to or for the benefit of a member of his or her family and retains an applicable retained interest immediately afterward, the value of the applicable retained interest equals $0. This zero value causes the residual interest transferred to have a higher value.

> **Example 1:** Dad holds all the outstanding stock of Eden Corp, a closely held corporation. Eden Corp's value equals $10 million. Dad recapitalizes Eden Corp by exchanging his Eden Corp Stock for 100 shares of 10 percent cumulative preferred stock and 100 shares of voting common stock. He then transfers the common stock to Daughter. Sec. 2701 applies to this transfer because Dad transferred an equity interest (common stock) to a member of his family (Daughter) and immediately afterwards holds an applicable retained interest (the preferred stock). Consequently, when Dad values the gift of common stock to Daughter, he must use the Sec. 2701 subtraction method of valuation. He

does this by subtracting his preferred stock's value from the value of the Eden Corp immediately before the transfer. For this purpose, Dad must value his preferred stock under the rules of Sec. 2701. He thus values the gift of the common stock to Daughter as follows: $10 million (value of the total entity being valued) less $0 (value of all preferred interests in the entity, calculated pursuant to Sec. 2701) equals $10 million (the value of the common stock gifted to Daughter).

The effect of IRC Sec. 2701 is to increase the value attributed to the gifted common stock to the junior family members by the value that otherwise would be attributed to the retained preferred stock, unless the preferred stock that the senior family member retains contains a qualified payment. Consequently, failure to satisfy IRC Sec. 2701 requires the payment of the wealth transfer tax at the time of the original gift as a gift tax, rather than at the subsequent transfer of the retained stock when the parent dies as an estate tax.

Amount of the gift. The amount of the gift that occurs is measured using the subtraction method of valuation as described in Regulation Sec. 25.2701-3. Using this method, the amount of the gift is determined by subtracting the value of any family-held applicable retained interest and other equity interests that have not been transferred from the aggregate value of family-held interests in the corporation or partnership [Reg. Sec. 25.2701-1(a)(2)].

When determining the value of any applicable retained interest held by the transferor or an applicable family member any put, call, or conversion right, right to compel liquidation, right to receive dividends is valued at zero if the right is an "extraordinary payment right." Any other right (including a qualified payment right) is valued as if any right valued at zero did not exist [Reg. Sec. 25.2701-1(a)(2)].

> **Example 2:** Alice holds all of the outstanding stock of ABCo. She exchanges her shares for 100 shares of 10-percent cumulative preferred stock and 100 shares of voting common stock. Alice transfers the common stock to her child. IRC Sec. 2701 applies to the transfer because Alice has transferred an equity interest (the common stock) to a member of her family, and immediately thereafter holds an applicable retained interest (the preferred stock). Her preferred stock is valued under the rules of IRC Sec. 2701. Her gift is determined under the subtraction method by subtracting the value of her preferred stock from the value of her interest in ABCo immediately prior to the transfer [Reg. Sec. 25.2701-1(a)(3)].

Definition of transfer. For purposes of IRC Sec. 2701, the term "transfer" includes a transaction that would not be a taxable gift under the gift tax provisions because it was for full and adequate consideration [Reg. Sec. 25.2701-1(b)(1)]. Pursuant to IRC Sec. 2701(e)(5) and Reg. Sec. 25.2701-1(b)(2), a contribution of capital to an existing entity or to a new entity would be considered a transfer for purposes of IRC Sec. 2701. A transfer also includes a redemption, a recapitalization or other change in capital structure, if: (1) the transferor or an applicable family member receives an applicable retained interest in the transaction; (2) the transferor or applicable family member who holds an applicable retained interest before the transaction surrenders a junior equity interest and receives property other than an applicable retained interest; or (3) the transferor or applicable family member who holds an applicable retained interest before the transaction surrenders an equity interest other than a subordinate interest and the fair market of the applicable retained interest is increased.

In addition, under IRC Sec. 2701(d)(5), the termination of an indirect holding in an entity (or a contribution to capital by an entity to the extent an individual holds an indirect interest in the entity) is considered to be a transfer, if the property is held in a trust with the indirect holder being treated as the owner or, if not treated as a transfer for this reason, then to the extent the value of the indirectly held interest would be included in the indirect holder's gross estate if he or she died immediately prior to the termination [Reg. Sec. 25.2701-1(b)(2)(i)(C)]. If the transfer of an indirect holding is treated as a transfer with respect to more than one indirect holder, the multiple attribution rules of Reg. Sec. 25.2701-1(b)(2)(ii) apply [see ¶ 511].

Excluded transactions. However, the term "transfer" does not apply for purposes of IRC Sec. 2701 to a capital structure transaction if, after the transaction, the transferor, each applicable family member, and each member of the transferor's family holds substantially the same interest as he or she held before the transaction. For this purpose, common stock with nonlapsing voting rights and nonvoting common stock are interests that are substantially the same [Reg. Sec. 25.2701-1(b)(3)(i)]. Nor does it apply to a shift of rights that occurs upon the execution of a qualified disclaimer under IRC Sec. 2518 or upon the exercise, release or lapse of a power of appointment (other than a general power under IRC Sec. 2514), except to the extent that such exercise, release, or lapse would constitute a transfer under the gift tax provisions [Reg. Sec. 25.2701-1(b)(3)(iii)].

¶502 DEFINITIONS

When dealing with tax law, the way terms are defined is always important. This is especially true with IRC Chapter 14, which uses a number of specialized terms. To assist in understanding Chapter 14's provisions, the following terms are defined:

- *Members of the transferor's family.* A member of the transferor's family includes the transferor's spouse, lineal descendants of the transferor (or transferor's spouse), and the spouse of any such lineal descendant [IRC Sec. 2701(e)(1); Reg. Sec. 25.2701-1(d)(1)].

- *Applicable family member.* An applicable family member (AFM) is defined as the transferor's spouse, any ancestor of the transferor (or transferor's spouse), and the spouse of any such ancestor [IRC Sec. 2701(e)(2); Reg. Sec. 25.2702-1(d)(2)].

- *Applicable retained interest.* Applicable retained interests are any corporate or partnership equity interests with respect to which there are either (1) extraordinary payment rights or (2) for controlled entities, distribution rights [IRC Sec. 2701(b)(1); Reg. Sec. 25.2701-1(b)(1)].

- *Extraordinary payment rights.* Generally, extraordinary payment rights are any put, call, or conversion rights; any rights to compel liquidation; or any similar rights the exercise or nonexercise of which affects the value of the transferred interest. For this purpose, call rights include all warrants, options, or other rights to acquire one or more equity interests [Reg. Sec. 25.2701-2(b)(2)]. However, extraordinary payment rights do not include any rights specifically excluded by Reg. Sec. 25.2701-2(b)(4).

- *Distribution rights.* Generally, distribution rights are rights to receive distributions on equity interests [IRC Sec. 2701(c)(1); Reg. Sec. 25.2701-2(b)(3)]. However, they do not include (1) rights to receive distributions on interests that are junior to the rights of the transferred interest; (2) extraordinary payment right (defined above); or (3) rights that Reg. Sec. 25.2701-2(b)(4) (discussed next) specifically excludes [IRC Sec. 2701(c)(1)(B)].

- *Rights that are neither extraordinary payment rights nor distribution rights.* Reg. Sec. 25.2701-2(b)(4) provides that the following rights are neither extraordinary payment rights nor distribution rights: (1) mandatory payment rights; (2) liquidation participation rights; (3) rights to IRC Sec. 707(c) guaranteed payments; and (4) nonlapsing conversion rights. For purposes of Reg. Sec. 25.2701-2(b)(4), mandatory payment rights are rights to receive payments required to be made at a specific time for a specific amount. For example, a mandatory redemption right in preferred stock requiring the corporation to redeem the stock at its fixed par value on a fixed date is a mandatory payment right. Therefore, such a payment is neither an extraordinary payment right nor a distribution right. Reg. Sec. 25.2701-2(b)(4)(i) specifies that rights to receive specified amounts on the death of the holder are mandatory payment rights.

- *Liquidation participation rights are rights to participate in liquidating distributions.* If the transferor, members of the transferor's family, or applicable family members can compel liquidation, they must value the liquidation participation right as if (1) the ability to compel liquidation did not exist or (2) if the "lower of" rule (discussed below) applies and is exercised in a way that is consistent with that rule [Reg. Sec. 25.2701-2(b)(4)(ii)].

- *Rights to IRC Sec. 707(c) guaranteed payments are of "fixed amounts" if their amounts are determined at fixed rates.* For this purpose, fixed rates include bearing a fixed relationship to a specified market interest rate. Payments that are contingent as to time or amount do not constitute guaranteed payments of fixed amounts [Reg. Sec. 25.2701-2(b)(4)(iii)].

- *Nonlapsing conversion rights for corporations are nonlapsing rights to convert corporate equity interests into a fixed number or percentage of shares of either (1) the same class as the transferred interest, or (2) a class that would be of the same class but for nonlapsing differences in voting rights.* However, such shares must be subject to (1) proportionate adjustments for changes in the corporation's equity ownership and (2) adjustments similar to the qualified payment compounding rules, discussed later in this section [IRC Sec. 2701(c)(2)(C); Reg. Sec. 25.2701-2(b)(4)(iv)(A)].

- *Nonlapsing conversion rights for partnerships are nonlapsing rights to convert partnership equity interests into specified interests (other than fixed dollar amount interests) of either (1) the same class as the transferred interest or (2) a class that would be of the same class but for nonlapsing differences in management rights or liability limitations.* However, such interests must be subject to (1) proportionate adjustments for changes in the partnership's equity ownership and (2) adjustments similar to the qualified payment compounding rules, discussed later in this section [IRC Sec. 2701(c)(2)(C); Reg. Sec. 25.2701-2(b)(4)(iv)(B)].

When determining which rights are neither extraordinary payment rights nor distribution rights under Reg. Sec. 25.2701-2(b)(4), corporate equity interests are subject to proportionate adjustments for equity ownership changes if the corporation must make proportionate adjustments for splits, combinations, reclassifications, and similar capital stock changes. Partnership equity interests are subject to proportionate adjustments for equity ownership changes if their equity interests are protected from dilution resulting from changes in the partnership structure [Reg. Sec. 25.2701-2(b)(4)(iv)(C)].

- *Controlled entity.* Generally for Sec. 2701 purposes, controlled entities are corporations or partnerships that are controlled immediately before the transfer by the transferor, AFMs, or any lineal descendants of the parents of the transferor or the transferor's spouse.

- *Controlled corporations.* Control of a corporation means the holding of at least 50 percent of either the corporation's (1) total voting power or (2) total fair-market value of its equity interest [IRC Sec. 2701(b)(2)(A); Reg. Sec. 25.2701-2(b)(5)(ii)(A)]. For this purpose, Sec. 2701 deems equity interests carrying no voting rights, other than on liquidation, merger, or a similar event, as lacking voting rights. Generally, voting rights are considered held by an individual to the extent that he or she, either alone or with others, may exercise the right. However, equity interests carrying voting rights held in a fiduciary capacity are considered held by each beneficial owner of the interest and by each permissible recipient of the interest's income. The fiduciary is not considered to hold such voting rights. Voting rights do not include rights subject to contingencies that have not yet occurred. However, such contingencies do not include contingencies within the control of the individual holding the right [Reg. Sec. 25.2701-2(b)(5)(ii)(B)].

- *Controlled partnerships.* Control of a partnership means the holding of at least 50 percent of either the partnership's capital interest or profits interest [IRC Sec. 2701(b)(2)(B)(i)]. For this purpose, disregard any rights to IRC Sec. 707(c) guaranteed payments of fixed amounts [Reg. Sec. 25.2701-2(b)(5)(iii)]. Also, for limited partnerships, control means the holding of any general partner equity interest [IRC Sec. 2701(b)(2)(B)(ii)].

- *Qualified payment right.* Qualified payment rights are rights to receive (1) dividends payable periodically (at least annually), on any cumulative preferred stock, determined at a fixed rate; (2) any other cumulative distributions payable periodically (at least annually) on an equity interest, payable at a fixed rate or as a fixed amount; or (3) any distribution right that an individual elects to treat as qualified payment right [IRC Sec. 2701(c)(3)]. For this purpose, a payment rate bearing a fixed relationship to a specified market interest rate constitutes a payment determined at a fixed rate [Reg. Sec. 25.2701-2(b)(6)].

Example 1: Dad transfers Willco Corporation nonvoting common stock to Daughter. Dad retains $100 par value preferred stock bearing a cumulative annual dividend of $10. Immediately before his transfer, Dad holds 100 percent of Willco's stock. Because Willco constitutes a controlled entity, Dad's dividend right constitutes a distribution right that is subject to Sec. 2701. Because the distribution right is an annual cumulative dividend, it constitutes a qualified payment right.

Example 2: The same facts as in Example 1, except that Dad's dividend right is noncumulative. Dad's dividend right constitutes a distribution right in a controlled entity. However, it does not constitute a qualified payment right because the dividend is noncumulative. Therefore, Dad must value the noncumulative dividend right at zero.

Example 3: The same facts as in Example 2, except that Willco is not a controlled entity. Here, Dad may value his dividend right, without regard to Sec. 2701.

¶503 EXCEPTIONS TO THE APPLICATION OF SEC. 2701

The special valuation rules of IRC Sec. 2701 do not apply in the following situations found in IRC Secs. 2701(a)(1) and (2) and Reg. Sec. 25.2701-1(c):

1. *Marketable transferred interests.* IRC Sec. 2701 does not apply if there are market quotations on an established securities market for the value of the transferred interest;

2. *Marketable retained interests.* The special valuation rules for retained interests under Reg. Sec. 25.2701-2 do not apply to any applicable retained interest if there are readily available market quotations on an established securities market for the value of the retained interests;

3. *Interests of the same class.* IRC Sec. 2701 does not apply if the retained interest is of the same class of equity as the transferred interest or if the retained interest is of a class that is proportional to the class of the transferred interest. A class is the same class as the transferred interest if the rights are identical to the rights of the transferred interest, except for nonlapsing differences in voting rights (or, for a partnership, nonlapsing differences with respect to management and limitations on liability). Nonlapsing provisions necessary to comply with the partnership allocation requirements of IRC Sec. 704(b) are nonlapsing differences with respect to limitations on liability. An interest in a partnership is not an interest in the same class as the transferred interest if the transferor or applicable family members have the right to alter the liability of the transferee;

4. *Proportionate transfers.* IRC Sec. 2701 does not apply to a transfer by an individual to a member of the individual's family of equity interests to the extent the transfer by that individual results in a proportionate reduction of each class of equity interest held by the individual and all applicable family members in the aggregate immediately before the transfer. Thus, for example, Section 2701 does not apply if P owns 50 percent of each class of equity interest in a corporation and transfers a portion of

each class to P's child in a manner that reduces each interest held by P and any applicable family members, in the aggregate, by 10 percent even if the transfer does not proportionately reduce P's interest in each class [see Reg. Sec. 25.2701-6 regarding indirect holding of interests].

¶504 APPLICATION OF SEC. 2701 IN VALUING TRANSFERRED BUSINESS INTERESTS

When analyzing whether IRC Sec. 2701 applies to the valuation of transferred business interests and, if so, what its impact will be, you should consider the following questions:

1. What types of transfers trigger Sec. 2701?
2. If Sec. 2701 applies, how does it generally affect valuation?
3. What are the qualified payment rules and how do they affect valuation under Sec. 2701?
4. How does the subtraction method work when calculating the value of gratuitous transfers under Sec. 2701?
5. What is the minimum value rule and how does it affect valuations of closely held businesses?
6. What happens if the entity fails to make qualified payments?
7. What are the Sec. 2701 attribution rules?

¶505 TRANSFERS THAT TRIGGER SEC. 2701

IRC Sec. 2701 applies when persons transfer interests in controlled corporations or partnerships to or for the benefit of members of their families and retain applicable retained interests immediately afterward. Thus, a transfer must occur before Sec. 2701 applies.

▶ **CAUTION:** Sec. 2701 applies to determine the existence and amount of any gift, regardless of whether the transfer would otherwise be a taxable gift. For example, it applies to transfers that would otherwise be taxable gifts because they are transfers for full and adequate consideration [Reg. Sec. 25.2701-1(b)(1)].

Reg. Sec. 25.2701-1(b)(2) provides that the following transactions constitute transfers for Sec. 2701 purposes:

1. Capital contributions to new or existing entities;
2. Redemptions, recapitalizations, or other capital structure changes ("capital structure transactions") if:

   • The transferor or an AFM receives an applicable retained interest (ARI) in the capital structure transaction;

   • The transferor or an AFM (1) holds an ARI before the capital structure transaction; (2) surrenders an equity interest that is junior to the ARI (a subordinate interest); and (3) receives property other than an ARI; or

- The transferor or an AFM (1) holds an ARI before the capital structure transaction; (2) surrenders a senior equity interest in the entity (other than a subordinate interest); and (3) the fair market value of the ARI increases; or

3. Terminations of indirect holdings in entities [Reg. Sec. 25.2701-6] (or contributions to capital by entities to the extent that an individual indirectly holds an interest in such entities) under the following circumstances:

   - The indirect holder holds the property indirectly through a grantor trust; or
   - The prior rule does not apply and the indirect holder dies immediately before the termination, then, to the extent his or her gross estate would have included the indirectly held interest's value for federal estate tax purposes.

Three types of transactions are not "transfers" and do not trigger Sec. 2701. First, capital structure transactions, except contributions to capital, where the transferor, each AFM, and each member of the transferor's family holds substantially the same interests before and after the transaction are not transfers subject to Sec. 2701 [IRC Sec. 2701(e)(5)]. For this purpose, Sec. 2701 treats common stock with nonlapsing voting rights and nonvoting common stock as interests that are substantially the same [Reg. Sec. 25.2701-1(b)(3)(i)].

Second, shifts of rights caused by qualified disclaimer executions do not constitute transfers [Reg. Sec. 25.2701-1(b)(3)(ii)].

Third, shifts of rights caused by releases, exercises, or lapses of powers of appointment [see ¶205] generally do not constitute transfers for purposes of Sec. 2701. However, this last exception does not apply to releases, exercises, or lapses of general powers of appointments that otherwise are transfers for gift tax purposes [Reg. Sec. 25.2701-1(b)(3)(iii)].

> **Example 1:** Daughter owns 100 percent of X Corporation, which has one class common stock. X Corporation's fair-market value equals $1 million. Dad contributes $1 million to X Corporation in exchange for newly issued X Corporation preferred stock. Dad's contribution constitutes a "transfer" that triggers Sec. 2701.

> **Example 2:** Same facts as in Example 1, except that originally, Daughter and Dad each own 50% of X Corporation's common stock, and X Corporation recapitalizes, issuing common stock to Daughter and preferred stock to Dad. Here, the recapitalization constitutes a "transfer" for Sec. 2701 purposes.

> **Example 3:** Same facts as Example 1, except that in X Corporation's recapitalization, Daughter and Dad each receive 100 shares of common stock and 100 shares of preferred stock. Here, the recapitalization does not constitute a "transfer" because both Daughter and Dad hold substantially the same interests that they held before the recapitalization.

> **Example 4:** Same facts as Example 1, except that in X Corporation's recapitalization, Daughter receives 100 shares of voting common stock and Dad receives 100 shares of nonvoting common stock. Other than different voting rights, both

classes of stock issued to Daughter and Dad are identical. Here, the recapitalization does not constitute a "transfer" because Sec. 2701 treats common stock with nonlapsing voting rights and nonvoting common stock as interests that are substantially the same.

¶506 SPECIAL VALUATION RULES

IRC Sec. 2701 values residual interests, for purposes of valuing gifts, by subtracting the value of all preferred interests from the entity's total value. However, you make the IRC Sec. 2701 subtraction calculation only after applying Sec. 2701's special valuation rules to interests that transferors and AFMs retain.

In applying the special valuation rules, all extraordinary payment rights are valued at zero [Reg. Sec. 25.2701-2(a)(1)]. Generally, extraordinary payment rights are put, call, or conversion rights, rights to compel liquidation, or any similar rights whose exercise or nonexercise affects the transferred interest's value. For this purpose, a call right includes any warrant, option, or other right to acquire one or more equity interests [Reg. Sec. 25.2701-2(b)(2)].

All distribution rights in controlled entities are valued at zero. However, this general rule does not apply to qualified payment rights [Reg. Sec. 25.2701-2(a)(2)]. Generally, distribution rights are rights to receive distributions on equity interests. However, distribution rights do not include (1) rights to receive distributions on interests that are of the same class as, or of a class that is subordinate to, the transferred interest or (2) extraordinary payment rights [Reg. Sec. 25.2701-2(b)(3)].

> **Example 1:** Mom owns 100 percent of Middlemarch Real Estate, which she operates as a sole proprietorship. Middlemarch's value equals $10 million. Mom contributes all of Middlemarch's assets to the M-Partnership and in exchange takes Class A and Class B interests in the M-Partnership. She immediately gives the Class B interest to Daughter. The Class A interest gives Daughter a noncumulative preferred return of 10 percent. The Class B interest is a residual interest, which gives Mom all income that exceeds Daughter's preferred return. Here, Daughter must value her retained Class A interest at $0 because the preferred stock she receives (1) gives her distribution rights that constitute rights to receive distributions on equity interests and (2) such rights are not rights to receive distributions on interests that are of the same class as, or of a class that is subordinate to, Mom's common stock.

Qualified payment rights are valued without regard to Sec. 2701 [Reg. Sec. 25.2701-2(a)(4)]. Qualified payments are distributions that are (1) dividends payable periodically (at least annually) on any cumulative preferred stock, determined at a fixed rate, (2) any other cumulative distributions payable periodically (at least annually) on an equity interest, payable at a fixed rate or as a fixed amount, or (3) any distribution right that an individual elects to treat as a qualified payment right [IRC Sec. 2701(c)(3); Reg. Sec. 25.2701-2(b)(6)].

¶506

▶ **OBSERVATION:** Congress was concerned with the possibility that entities might not make timely qualified payments. Such a failure would allow transactions to pass value, outside of the wealth transfer tax system equal to the time value of the delayed payment, to the holders of interests that are junior to the qualified payment interest. To address this possibility, Sec. 2701 contains special compounding rules discussed below.

When transferors retain both qualified payment rights and extraordinary payment rights, they must value all these rights by assuming that each extraordinary payment right is exercised in a way that results in the lowest total value being determined for all the rights. When making this valuation, they must use a consistent set of assumptions and give due regard to the entity's net worth, prospective earning power, and other relevant factors. This is called the "lower of" rule [Reg. Sec. 25.2701-2(a)(3)].

Example 2: Dad owns all 1,000 shares of E Corp's $1,000 par value preferred stock, which bears an annual cumulative dividend of $100 per share. Dad also holds all 1,000 shares of E Corp's voting common stock. He has the right to put all the preferred stock to E Corp anytime for $900,000. Dad gives the common stock to Daughter. When Dad gives the common stock to Daughter, E Corp's total value equals $1,500,000. At this time, the fair-market value of Dad's cumulative dividend right equals $1 million. Because the preferred stock confers both an extraordinary payment right (the put right) and a qualified payment right (the right to receive cumulative dividends), the "lower of" rule applies. Consequently, Dad must value these rights as if he will exercise the put right by assuming that he will exercise the put right immediately. The value of Dad's preferred stock is $900,000 (the lower of $1 million and $900,000). Thus, the gift amount equals $600,000 ($1,500,000 minus $900,000).

Finally, you must value all other rights (1) as if any right that Sec. 2701 values at zero does not exist and (2) as if the transferor exercises any right valued under the "lower of" rule in a manner consistent with the assumptions of that rule but otherwise without regard to Sec. 2701 [Reg. Sec. 25.2701-2(a)(4)]. In other words, if an ARI carries no rights that Sec. 2701 values at zero or under the "lower of" rule, its value for Sec. 2701 purposes equals its fair-market value.

¶507 QUALIFIED PAYMENT ELECTIONS

Transferors may irrevocably elect to waive qualified payment treatment, partially or entirely [IRC Sec. 2701(c)(3)(C)]. Transferors who make partial elections must exercise the election for a consistent part of each payment right for the class that the election has been made [Reg. Secs. 25.2701-2(c)(1), 25.2701-2(c)(2)].

Conversely, transferors may irrevocably elect to have certain distributions that Sec. 2701 would not otherwise classify as qualified payments, treated as qualified payments either partially or entirely [IRC Sec. 2701(c)(3)(C)(ii); Reg. Sec. 25.2701-2(c)(2)]. They may make such an election to the extent that the amounts and times specified as such are consistent with the underlying legal instrument [Reg. Sec. 25.2701-2(c)(2)(ii)]. If transferors make partial elections, they must exercise the election for a consistent part of each payment right for the class for which they have made the election [Reg. Secs. 25.2701-2(c)(1), 25.2701-2(c)(2)].

> ▶ **OBSERVATION:** Elections to treat nonqualified payments as qualified payments cannot cause an applicable retained interest's value for Sec. 2701 valuation purposes to exceed its fair-market value determined without regard to Sec. 2701 [Reg. Sec. 25.2701-2(c)(2)].

> **NOTE:** All elections to treat payments as either qualified payments or as non-qualified payments are irrevocable. Such elections may be revoked only with the IRS's consent [Reg. Sec. 25.2701-2(c)(3)].

Generally, payments that would otherwise be qualified payments do not qualify as qualified payments if the entity makes such payments to AFMs rather than to the transferor. However, such AFMs may elect to treat their payment rights as qualified payment rights [Reg. Sec. 25.2701-2(c)(4)].

Return preparation tips. You may elect qualified payment treatment by attaching statements to your IRS Form 709, "United States Gift (and Generation-Skipping Transfer) Tax Return," that you file for the transfer. The statement must do the following [Reg. Sec. 25.2701-2(c)(5)]:

1. State the electing individual's name, address, and taxpayer identification number, and that of the transferor, if different;

2. If the electing individual is not the transferor filing the return, state the relationship between the individual and the transferor;

3. Specifically identify the transfer disclosed on the return to which the election applies;

4. Describe in detail the distribution right to which the election applies;

5. State the specific provisions of the regulation under which the election applies;

6. If the election is being made under Reg. Sec. 25.2701-2(c)(2):

   - State the amounts that the election assumes will be paid and the times that the election assumes the payments will be made;

   - Contain a statement, signed by the electing individual, in which the electing individual agrees that:

     a. If payments are not made as provided in the election, the individual's subsequent taxable gifts or taxable estate will, on the occurrence of a taxable event (as defined in Reg. Sec. 25.2701-4(b)), be increased by an amount determined under Reg. Sec. 25.2701-4(c); and

     b. The individual will be personally liable for any increase in tax attributable thereto.

> **NOTE:** An election filed after the Form 709's due date does not constitute a valid qualified payment election [Reg. Sec. 25.2701-2(c)(5)].

¶507

¶508 CALCULATING VALUE OF GRATUITOUS TRANSFERS

Reg. Sec. 25.2701-3 determines gift valuations for IRC Sec. 2701 transfers using the subtraction method of valuation. This method first determines transfer amounts by determining the fair-market value of all family-held interests in the entity. Next, it subtracts the value of all family-held senior equity interests from the family-held interest values. You should make this valuation as of the time immediately before the transfer.

For this valuation, you must determine the value of the transferor's and the AFM's senior equity interests under IRC Sec. 2701. You must value other family-held senior equity interests and other family-held subordinate equity interests. Finally, you must adjust valuations by certain discounts and other appropriate reductions. The following discussion takes you through these steps.

Step 1—Valuation of family-held interests. You must first determine the fair-market value of all family-held equity interests in the entity immediately after the transfer [Reg. Sec. 25.2701-3(b)(1)]. This generally requires you to value the entire business. The regulations require you to determine the entity's fair-market value by assuming that one individual holds all the interests, using a consistent set of assumptions [Reg. Sec. 25.2701-3(b)(1)(i)].

A special rule applies for capital contributions. Specifically, for capital contributions you must determine the contribution's fair-market value [Reg. Sec. 25.2701-3(b)(1)(ii)].

Step 2—Subtract the value of senior equity interests. Under Step 2, you must subtract three amounts from the amount calculated in Step 1. These include (1) non-ARI senior equity interests, (2) excess ARIs, and (3) certain other ARIs.

First, you must subtract the value of non-ARI senior equity interests from the Step 1 amount. This amount equals the sum of the fair-market values of (1) all family-held senior equity interests (other than ARIs that the transferor or AFMs hold) and (2) any family-held equity interests of the same class or a subordinate class to the transferred interests held by persons other than the transferor, members of the transferor's family, and the transferor's AFMs. For purposes of this calculation, an interest's fair-market value equals its proportionate share of the fair-market value of all family-held senior equity interests of the same class. You determine this amount immediately after the transfer, by assuming that one individual holds all family-held senior equity interests [Reg. Sec. 25.2701-3(b)(2)(A)].

Essentially, this calculation removes all family-held interests that do not trigger IRC Sec. 2701. These interests include:

1. Senior equity interests that are not ARIs. These include guaranteed payments, voting rights, and preemptive subscription rights.

2. Senior equity interests that are "family-held" but that neither the transferor nor AFMs hold. These include distribution, liquidation, put, call, or conversion rights held by descendants, siblings, or descendants of siblings of the transferor or the transferor's spouse.

3. Equity interests of the same class or a junior class that neither the transferor, members of the transferor's family, nor AFMs hold.

Second, you must subtract the value of excess ARIs. More specifically, if the percentage of any class of ARIs that the transferor and AFMs hold exceeds the family interest percentage, you must treat the excess as a family-held interest that neither the transferor nor any AFM holds [Reg. Sec. 25.2701-3(b)(5)]. For this purpose, the family interest percentage equals the highest ownership percentage (based on relative fair-market values) of family-held interests in (1) any class of subordinate equity interest or (2) subordinate equity interests, valued in total.

Third, you must subtract the value of all ARIs the transferor or AFMs hold (other than interests received as consideration for the transfer). You must value these ARIs by applying the special IRC Sec. 2701 valuation rules.

Calculation Step 2 subtraction amount. The non-ARI senior equity interests to be subtracted from the value of family-held interests include:

1. The fair-market value of all family-held senior equity interests, other than ARIs that either the transferor or the AFMs hold;

2. The fair-market value of all family-held equity interests that are equal to or subordinate to the transferred interests held by parties other than the transfer or, members of the transferor's family, and AFMs;

3. The fair-market value of excess ARIs; and

4. The ARIs the transferor or AFMs hold (other than interests they receive as consideration for the transfer).

If you determine values in Step 1 under the rule for capital contributions, you must also subtract the value of any ARI the contributor receives in exchange for the contribution to capital [Reg. Sec. 25.2701-3(b)(2)(ii)].

Step 3—Allocate the remaining value among the transferred interests and other family-held subordinate equity interests. You must next allocate the value remaining after Step 2 between the transferred interests and other subordinate equity interests that the transferor, AFMs, and members of the transferor's family hold. When more than one class of family-held subordinate equity interest exists, you must make this allocation in the manner that most fairly approximates their value if all rights valued under IRC Sec. 2701 at zero did not exist.

You must make this allocation beginning with the most senior class of subordinate equity interest. If no clearly appropriate method of allocating the remaining value exists, you must allocate the remaining value to the interests in proportion to their fair-market values determined without regard to IRC Sec. 2701 [Reg. Sec. 25.2701-3(b)(3)].

Step 4—Determine the amount of the gift. In Step 4, you reduce the amount that Step 3 allocates to the transferred interests for (1) minority and other discounts, (2) adjustments for transfers with retained interests, and (3) consideration received for transferred interests [Reg. Sec. 25.2701-3(a)(4)(ii)].

Reduction for minority or similar discounts. Reg. Sec. 25.2701-3(b)(4)(ii) provides a formula to use to reduce IRC Sec. 2701 gift amounts for minority discounts. The reduction for minority discounts begins by calculating a prorated portion of the market value of the family-held interests of the same class. You should determine this amount by assuming that (1) one person holds all voting rights conferred by family-held equity interests and (2) such person has no interest in the entity other than such family-held interests of the same class, but otherwise without regard to IRC Sec. 2701. You should then subtract the value of the transferred interest determined without regard to IRC Sec. 2701.

Adjustment for retained interests. Reg. Sec. 25.2701-3(b)(4)(iii) provides that, if the value of transferor's gifts, determined without regard to IRC Sec. 2701, would be reduced under IRC Sec. 2702 to reflect the value of retained interest, then you must reduce the values determined under IRC Sec. 2701 by the same amount.

Reduction for consideration. Consideration that transferors receive reduces the amount of the IRC Sec. 2701 determined transfers [Reg. Sec. 25.2701-3(b)(4)(iv)]. However, this reduction cannot exceed the gift amount, determined without regard to IRC Sec. 2701. If the transferor receives such consideration in the form of an ARI, the transfer must determine such ARI's value under IRC Sec. 2701. However, for a contribution to capital, the Step 4 value of such an interest is zero.

> **Example 1:** EZ Corporation has 1,000 shares of $1,000 par value voting preferred stock outstanding. Each share carries a cumulative annual dividend of 8 percent and the right to put the stock to EZ for its par value at any time. EZ also has outstanding 1,000 shares of nonvoting common stock. A holds 600 shares of EZ preferred and 750 shares of EZ common stock. B, who is not related to A, holds the remaining EZ stock. The fair-market value of all of A's family-held interests in EZ equals $1 million.

Because EZ's preferred stock confers both a qualified payment right and an extraordinary payment right, A must value his rights under the "lower of" rule. Under this rule, A values his EZ preferred stock at $800.

A gives all of his common stock to C, his daughter. A's gift to C is valued as follows:

Step 1: First, determine the fair-market value of all family-held equity interests in EZ immediately after A's gift to C. Here, this amount equals $1 million.

Step 2: Second, subtract the value of senior interests from the amount determined in Step 1, or $480,000.

The Step 2 subtraction amount of $480,000, representing non-ARI senior equity interests to be subtracted from the value of family-held interests is calculated by adding the following:

1. $0 (the fair-market value of all family-held senior equity interests, other than ARIs that either the transferor or AFMs hold);

2. $0 (the fair-market value of all family-held equity interests that are equal to or subordinate to the transferred interests held by parties other than the transferor, members of the transferor's family, and AFMs);

3. $0 (the fair-market value of excess ARIs);

4. $480,000 (the ARIs that the transferor or AFMs hold, other than interests they receive as consideration for the transfer). This amount equals 600 shares times $800 (the IRC Sec. 2701 value of A's preferred stock, computed under the "lower of" rule).

¶508

Step 3: In Step 3, allocate the value remaining after Step 2 among the transferred interests and other subordinate equity interests that the transferor, AFMs, and members of the transferor's family hold. Here, the result of Step 2 is a balance of $520,000. Fully allocate this amount to the 750 shares of family-held common stock.

Step 4: Because no consideration was furnished for the transfer, the adjustment under Step 4 is limited to the amount of any appropriate minority or similar discount. Before the application of Step 4, A's gift is $520,000.

Example 2: The same facts as Example 1, except that before giving his common stock to C, A holds only 50 percent of EZ's common stock and B holds the remaining 50 percent. The fair-market value of A's 600 shares of preferred stock equals $600,000 and the value of A's family-held interests equals $980,000. Here, value A's gift to C as follows:

Step 1: First, determine the fair-market value of all family-held equity interests in EZ immediately after A's gift to C. Here, this amount equals $980,000.

Step 2: Second, subtract the value of senior interests from the amount determined in Step 1. The Step 2 subtraction amount of $500,000, representing non-ARI senior equity interests to be subtracted from the value of family-held interests, is calculated by adding the following:

1. $0 (the fair-market value of all family-held senior equity interests, other than the transferor or AFMs hold).

2. $0 (the fair-market value of all family-held interests that are equal or subordinate to the transferred interests held by parties other than the transferor, members of the transferor's family, and AFMs).

3. $100,000 (the fair-market value of excess ARIs, which is calculated by adding 60 percent (percentage of preferred class) and subtracting 50 percent (family interest percentage, i.e., the highest ownership percentage of family-held interests in any class of subordinate interest, or all subordinate equity interests valued in total). Then, 10 percent (Reg. Sec. 25.2701-3(b)(5) adjustment percentage) is multiplied by 100 (the excess ARI shares of preferred stock). Then, 100 is multiplied by $1,000 fair-market value per share) and equals $100,000 (the fair-market value of excess ARIs).

4. $400,000 (the ARIs the transferor or AFMs hold, other than interests they receive as consideration for the transfer). This amount equals 500 shares times $800 (i.e., the IRC Sec. 2701 value of A's preferred stock, computed under "lower of" rule).

Step 3: In Step 3, allocate the value remaining after Step 2 among the transferred interests that the transferor, AFMs, and members of the transferor's family hold. Here, the result of Step 2 is a balance of $480,000 ($980,000 minus $500,000) that is allocated to the family-held common stock. Because A transferred all of the family-held subordinate equity interests, allocate all of the value determined under Step 2 to the transferred shares.

Step 4: The adjustment under Step 4 is the same as in Example 11. Thus, the amount of the gift is $480,000.

¶508

¶509 MINIMUM VALUE RULE

IRC Sec. 2701 provides for a minimum value for junior equity interests. Congress intended this rule to reflect the "option value" of the right of the residual interest to future appreciation. Specifically, if junior equity interest transfers are subject to IRC Sec. 2701, the value assigned to such interests must equal or exceed an amount you would arrive at if the value of all junior equity interests in the entity equaled their proportionate part of 10 percent of the sum of:

1. The total value of the entity's equity; and

2. The entity's total debt to the transferor and AFMs [IRC Sec. 2701(a)(4); Reg. Sec. 25.2701-3(c)].

For purposes of the minimum value rule, a corporate junior equity interest is the corporation's common stock. For this purpose, common stock is the class (or classes) of stock entitled to share in the entity's reasonably anticipated residual growth. Partnership junior equity interests are any partnership interests under which the rights to income and capital are junior to the rights of all other classes of partnership interests [Reg. Sec. 25.2701-3(c)(2)]. The IRS has regulatory authority to treat a partnership interest with rights that are junior with respect to either income or capital as a junior equity interest [IRC Sec. 2701(a)(4)(B)(i)].

For minimum value rule purposes, debt that entities owe transferors or AFMs excludes:

1. Short-term indebtedness for the current conduct of the entity's trade or business;

2. Debt owed to third parties solely because the transferor or an AFM guaranteed it; and

3. Amounts permanently set aside in a qualified deferred compensation arrangement, to the extent the amounts are unavailable for use by the entity [Reg. Sec. 25.2701-3(c)(3)(i)].

For minimum value rule purposes, leases do not constitute debt if their payments represent full and adequate consideration for the use of the property. Lease payments are considered to be for full and adequate consideration if:

1. The parties make a good-faith effort to determine the fair rental value under the lease and

2. The lease terms conform to the value so determined. On the other hand, lease arrearages represent debt for minimum valuation rule purposes [Reg. Sec. 25.2701-3(c)(3)(ii)].

¶510 UNPAID UNQUALIFIED PAYMENTS—THE COMPOUNDING RULES

When Congress enacted IRC Sec. 2701 it was concerned with the possibility that entities would not pay qualified payments on a timely basis and that such failures would pass value outside the wealth transfer tax system. The value passing equals the time value of the delayed payment to the holders of interests that are junior to the qualified payment interest. To address this potential problem, Congress enacted special compounding rules as part of IRC Sec. 2701.

The compounding rules require an increase in the taxable estate or taxable gift of the transferor whenever a "taxable event" occurs [IRC Sec. 2701(d)(1)]. Taxable events are transfers of qualified payment interests, during life or at death, by individuals (the interest holder) in whose hands such interests are originally valued. Taxable events also include transfers by individuals that IRC Sec. 2701 deems treated in the same manner as interest holders. The taxable events include (1) the transferor's death, but only if the transferor's gross estate includes the ARI conferring the qualified payment, (2) the transfer of the qualified payment right, or (3) at the taxpayer's election payment after the four-year compounding rule grace period [IRC Sec. 2701(d)(3)]. If the taxable event is the transferor's death, the decedent's taxable gross estate must be increased. In all other cases, the transferor's taxable gift must be increased.

When an individual's qualified payment rights terminate, if the interest holder's gross estate would include the qualified payment right if he or she died immediately after its termination, the taxable transfer does not occur until the earlier of:

1. The time the individual's gross estate would no longer include the property; or

2. The individual dies [Reg. Sec. 25.2701-4(b)(2)].

If interest holders transfer qualified payment interests in taxable events to ARIs of individuals who made the transfer to which IRC Sec. 2701 applied, the compounding rules treat the transferee-AFM as the interest holder for late or unpaid qualified payments first due after the taxable event. However, this does not apply to transfers to the spouse of an individual transferring a qualified payment interest [Reg. Sec. 25.2701-4(b)(3)].

> **Example 1:** Son holds preferred stock in White Corporation. Son's preferred stock constitutes a qualified payment interest. Son received the stock from Dad. Son gives the stock to Grandpa. The gift constitutes a taxable event. Here, the compounding rules treat Son as the interest holder for the transfer year. In all future years, IRC Sec. 2701 treats Grandpa as the interest holder.

If the transferor's spouse receives the qualified payment right and no wealth transfer tax is due because of (1) the marital deduction [see ¶¶ 1107, 1100] or (2) the spouse pays adequate and full consideration [see ¶ 1811], no taxable event occurs. The compounding rules do not apply. If this spousal exception applies, the transferee spouse steps into the transferor's shoes and from then on the compounding rules treat the transferee as the transferor [IRC Sec. 2701(d)(3)(B); Reg. Sec. 25.2701-4(b)(3)(ii)]. In other words, no inclusion would occur on the transfer of an applicable retained interest to a spouse, but later transfers of an applicable retained interest by a spouse would be subject to inclusion.

It is helpful to have a checklist for the calculation of the increase in taxable estate or taxable gifts caused by a compounding rule taxable event [Reg. Sec. 25.2701-4(c)(1)]. To calculate the increase in a wealth holder's taxable estate or taxable gifts caused by a compounding rule taxable event, you should:

¶510

1. Add: the amount of qualified payments that the entity actually paid during the period beginning on the date of the transfer to which section 2701 applied (or, in the case of an individual treated as the interest holder, on the date the interest of the prior interest holder terminated) and ending on the date of the taxable event.

2. Add: the earnings on the qualified payments that the holder would have earned if the entity had made the qualified payment on the appropriate due dates and reinvested at a yield equal to the appropriate discount rate.

3. Subtract: qualified payments actually made, based on the appropriate discount rate.

4. Add: deemed earnings on qualified payments.

5. Subtract: adjustments to prevent double inclusion, consisting of the following: (1) the portion of the qualified payment fair-market value attributable to any right to receive unpaid qualified payments at the taxable event date; (2) the fair-market value of any entity equity interest that the holder received instead of qualified payments that the holder holds at the qualified payment date; (3) the amount by which the holder's failure to enforce his or her right to qualified payments increased the holder's taxable gifts.

The appropriate discount rate equals the rate used to determine the value of the qualified payment right at the time of the original IRC Sec. 2701 transfer [Reg. Sec. 25.2701-4(c)(3)].

The compounding rules apply to any payment made toward unpaid qualified payments first to satisfy the earliest unpaid qualified payments. Conversely, the compounding rules treat any overpaid qualified payments as prepayments of future qualified payments [Reg. Sec. 25.2701-4(c)(4)].

The compounding rules include a maximum limitation on their application. This maximum limitation limits the increase in the interest holder's taxable estate or taxable gifts. The following provides a checklist for calculation of compounding rules limitation [Reg. Sec. 25.2701-4(c)(6)]. You calculate the maximum limitation on the compounding rules as follows:

1. Add: fair-market value of all outstanding equity interests subordinate to the ARI determined as of the taxable event date without regard to accrued liability attributable to unpaid qualified payments.

2. Add: amounts the entity expended to acquire or redeem any equity interest subordinate to the ARI during the period beginning on the Sec. 2701 transfer date and ending on the taxable event date, reduced by any resale proceeds.

3. Subtract: fair-market value of all outstanding equity interests in the entity that are subordinate to the ARI, determined at the date of the original IRC Sec. 2701 transfer (or the date of the termination of the prior interest holder).

4. Multiply: the balance of (1), (2), and (3) by the applicable percentage. The applicable percentage for purposes of the compounding rule limitation is calculated by dividing (1) the number of shares/units of the ARI that the transferor or interest holder holds on the taxable event date by (2) the total number of such shares/units of ARI outstanding on the taxable event date.

¶510

If the interest holder holds two or more different ARIs on the taxable event date, then the applicable percentage equals the highest applicable percentage for any one class of ARI.

Taxpayers may elect to treat payments of qualified payments that are more than four years late as taxable events [Reg. Sec. 25.2701-4(d)].

¶511 ATTRIBUTION RULES

For IRC Sec. 2701 purposes, two attribution rules apply. The attribution rules subject indirect holdings and transfers to the reach of IRC Sec. 2701. A party is deemed to hold an interest to the extent that he or she holds such interest indirectly through a corporation, partnership, trust, or any other entity. Furthermore, a transfer of an interest in such an entity resulting in the holder no longer being treated as holding the underlying interest must be treated as a transfer of such underlying interest by the holder [IRC Sec. 2701(e)(3)(A); Reg: Sec. 25.2701-6(a)].

Also, for purposes of determining whether a party has "control," the individual is treated as holding any interest held by his or her siblings or lineal descendants [IRC Sec. 2701(e)(3)(B)].

¶512 LAPSING RIGHTS AND RESTRICTIONS

In addition to IRC Sec. 2701, another provision of the IRC that impacts on gift tax valuation of business entities is IRC Sec. 2704. For nontax reasons, the owners of a family business may wish to limit or restrict the voting rights or preferences a certain class of corporate stock will possess when a certain event occurs. The existence of such a restriction (e.g., a voting right which lapses on the death of holder of the stock), would depress the value of shares. IRC Sec. 2704 recognizes the appropriateness of the limitation or preference but seeks to prevent the value associated with this benefit from going untaxed for federal gift or estate purposes.

Under IRC Sec. 2704(a)(1), the lapse of any voting or liquidating right in a family-controlled corporation or partnership during the holder's lifetime is treated as a transfer by gift from the individual holding the lapsed right to the other owners. If the lapse occurs at the holder's death, then the lapse is a transfer includable in the holder's gross estate [IRC Sec. 2704(a)(1); Reg. Sec. 25.2704-1(a)].

IRC Sec. 2704 applies only if the Sec. 2704 interest-holder and members of the holder's family control the entity immediately before and after the lapse [IRC Sec. 2704(a)(1); Reg. Sec. 25.2704-1(a)]. A member of the family includes the following:

1. An individual's spouse;

2. The ancestor or lineal descendant of an individual or an individual's spouse;

3. The individual's sibling; or

4. The spouse of any person in Items 2 or 3 [IRC Sec. 2704(c)(2); Reg. Sec. 25.2702-2(a)(1)].

Control means the holding of at least 50 percent (by vote or value) of the shares of a corporation, the holding of at least 50 percent of a partnership's capital or profits interest, or the holding of any interest as a general partner in a limited partnership [IRC Sec. 2701(b)(2)].

As to such lapse, the amount of the transfer equals the excess (if any) of (1) the value of all interests in the entity that holder owned immediately before the lapse (determined as if the right were nonlapsing) over (2) the value of all interests in the entity that the holder owned immediately after the lapse (determined as if all such interests were held by one individual) [IRC Sec. 2704(a)(2); Reg. Sec. 25.2704-1(d)].

> **Example 1:** Dad and Daughter each own general and limited interests in a limited partnership. The general partnership interest carries with it the right to liquidate the partnership, which lapses after 10 years. The limited partnership interest lacks such a right. When Dad's liquidation right expires, he is deemed to make a gift to Daughter. The amount of the gift equals the excess of (1) the value of Dad's partnership interests immediately before the lapse over (2) the value of Dad's partnership interests immediately after the lapse.

In addition, if an individual transfers an interest in a family-controlled corporation or partnership to or for the benefit of a family member, any applicable restriction created after October 8, 1990, is disregarded for valuation purposes [IRC Sec. 2704(b); Reg. Sec. 25.2704-2(a)]. An applicable restriction is any restriction that:

1. Limits the ability of the corporation or partnership to liquidate if the limitation is more restrictive than a limitation under the state law; and

2. Either lapses after the transfer or may be removed by the transferor or any other family member immediately after the transfer [IRC Sec. 2704(b)(2); Reg. Sec. 25.2704-2(b)].

An applicable restriction does *not* include the following:

1. Any commercially reasonable restriction arising from financing with an unrelated party;

2. Any restriction imposed as a result of state or federal law; or

3. Any option, right to use property, or agreement subject to IRC Sec. 2703 [IRC Sec. 2704(b)(3); Reg. Sec. 25.2704-2(b)].

GRITs, GRATs, GRUTs

6

TABLE OF CONTENTS

¶600 IRC SEC. 2702—THE BASICS

IRC Sec. 2702 was created to prevent taxpayers from attempting to minimize the gift tax consequences when they transferred property to loved ones by creative use of the actuarial tables. In drafting IRC Sec. 2702, Congress intended to curb potential valuation abuse associated with intra-family transfers of wealth. Prior to the enactment of IRC Sec. 2702, taxpayers transferred property to loved ones but retained interests in the transferred property in order to reduce the value of the total gift. For example, a taxpayer would transfer property such as publicly traded common stock or closely held business stock that typically generates no income to a trust and retain the right to receive the hypothetical income from the property for a number of years. The taxpayer would then subtract the value of the retained interest based on the actuarial tables published by the IRS from the total value of the gift when determining the amount of the taxable gift. This device resulted in significant transfer tax savings. Congress thought this scheme abused the actuarial tables and enacted IRC Sec. 2702 to address that abuse.

In general, IRC Sec. 2702 provides that if a taxpayer retains an interest in transferred property, that interest reduces the gift only where the retained interest is in the form of an annuity (a fixed annual payment) or a unitrust (a fixed percentage of the value of the property determined annually). This provision fixed the perceived abuse because either a GRAT (grantor retained annuity trust) or a GRUT (grantor retained unitrust) generate payments to the interest holder and eliminate the opportunity to claim deductions for income that never existed.

IRC Sec. 2702 focuses on estate valuation freezing techniques involving the transfer of appreciated property to an irrevocable (unchangeable) trust by a donor-settlor who retains an income interest in the trust for a specified period of years (a grantor retained income trust (GRIT)) with a contingent remainder (remaining trust assets) passing to the donor's children or other named beneficiaries at the end of the trust term.

These estate-freezing techniques involve a big gamble. If the donor survives the term of the trust, the remainder passes to the donor's children and the device works exactly as planned. On the other hand, if the donor fails to survive the term, the property reverts to the donor's estate or is distributed as the donor directs under a general testamentary power of appointment, and the gamble has failed [see ¶ 1810].

IRC Sec. 2702 applies to a transfer in trust to or for the benefit of certain family members if the transferor (or applicable family member) retains an interest in the property transferred [IRC Sec. 2702(a); Reg. Sec. 25.2702-1].

IRC Sec. 2702 also applies to similar transactions involving nontrust property, such as property involving one or more term interests [IRC Sec. 2702(c)(1)]. Thus, if a parent transfers a remainder interest in real property to a child while retaining a legal life estate, the gift of the remainder is valued under IRC Sec. 2702.

A joint purchase of property by family members is also valued under IRC Sec. 2702 as if held in trust [IRC Sec. 2702(c)(2)]. For example, if an individual acquires a term interest in property and one or more family members also acquire interests in the same property, the acquirer of the term interest is treated as acquiring the entire property and then transferring to the other family members the interests acquired by them in exchange for any consideration they may have paid for their interests.

¶601 FIVE MAJOR EXCEPTIONS

The following five main exceptions exist to the zero value rule of IRC Sec. 2702:

1. The non-family-member exception;
2. The qualified interest exception;
3. The incomplete gift exception;
4. The personal residence exception; and
5. The tangible personal property exception.

Each of these exceptions is considered below.

Non-family-member exception. The definition of the term "family member" creates an exception to the zero value rule by excluding those outside the definition. IRC Secs. 2702(e) and 2704(c)(2) define the members of the grantor's family or "an applicable family member." Within the definition are the grantor's spouse, ancestors or lineal descendants of the grantor, the grantor's siblings (or siblings of the grantor's spouse), and their respective spouses. Thus, the non-family-member exclusion applies to anyone not within the described class, such as nephews and nieces.

Qualified interest exception. If a retained interest meets the requirements of a "qualified interest," the interest will be valued under the valuation tables found in IRC Sec. 7520 [IRC Sec. 2702(a)(2)(B)]. A "qualified interest" under IRC Sec. 2702(b) is:

1. Any interest that consists of the right to receive fixed amounts payable not less frequently than annually;

2. Any interest that consists of the right to receive amounts that are payable not less frequently than annually and are a fixed percentage of the fair market value of the trust (determined annually); and

3. Any non-contingent remainder interest if all of the other interests in the trust consist of interests described in paragraphs (1) or (2) [IRC Sec. 2702(b)].

The value of any interest that is not a "qualified interest" is treated as zero.

Incomplete transfer exception. The zero value rule of IRC Sec. 2702 does not apply where the transfer would be considered an incomplete gift, regardless of whether any consideration is paid [IRC Secs. 2702(a)(3)(A)(i), 2702(a)(3)(B)].

Personal residence exception. If the only property transferred to the trust is a "residence to be used as a personal residence by the persons holding term interests in the trust," the zero value of IRC Sec. 2702 does not apply [IRC Sec. 2702(a)(3)(A)(ii)]. The term holders generally are the grantor and possibly the grantor's spouse. Basically, two methods qualify for this exception: (1) the trust satisfying the test for a personal residence trust [Reg. Sec. 25.2702-5(b)]; or (2) the trust satisfying the test for a "qualified personal residence trust" (QPRT) [Reg. Sec. 25.2702-5(c)]. See detailed discussion of QPRT at ¶700.

Distinctions between these two forms are discussed below. Both types of trusts, however, share a common characteristic. At the root of both forms is the definition of a personal residence [Reg. Secs. 25.2702-5(b)(2), 25.2702-5(c)(2)]. The definition of a personal residence tracks (1) the IRC's definition of a primary residence for purposes of the exclusion of gain on the sale of a principal residence found in IRC Sec. 121, (2) the IRC's concept of a personal use dwelling unit that may also be used for business or rental purposes [IRC Sec. 280A], or (3) an undivided fractional interest in either items 1 or 2 [Reg. Secs. 25.2702-5(b)(2)(i), 25.2702-5(c)(2)(i)].

Thus, the residence that you occupy most of the time will be considered your principal residence. A vacation residence will qualify as a personal residence if you use it for a number of days that exceeds the greater of:

1. 14 days; or

2. 10 percent of the number of days during the year that the residence was rented at fair rental.

Alternatively, you could show that the vacation residence was used only by you and was available for your personal use at all times.

The definition of a personal residence also includes appurtenant structures and adjacent land used for residential purposes and an undivided interest in either. Excluded from the definition of a personal residence is personal property furniture or household furnishings [Reg. Secs. 25.2702-2(b)(2)(ii), 25.2702-5(c)(2)(ii)]. The requirements for a personal residence trust and then a qualified personal residence trust are considered below.

Personal residence trust. Regs. Sec. 25.2702-5(b) and (c) provide for two types of personal residence trust: the personal residence trust in Reg. Sec. 25.2702-5(b) and the more flexible and more commonly used qualified personal residence trust in Reg. Sec. 25.2702-5(c), which is discussed in detail in ¶700 below. The personal residence trust [Reg. Secs. 25.2702-5(b)(1), 25.2702-5(b)(3)] has three key points. First, this type of trust is limited to the property that qualifies as a personal residence. Only one personal residence may be held in the trust. However, the trust may also hold the proceeds resulting from damage to, destruction of, or involuntary conversion of the residence, provided the trust instrument requires that such proceeds be reinvested in a personal residence within two years from the date on which the proceeds are received (becoming qualified proceeds).

Second, the governing instrument for a personal residence trust must limit the personal residence to or for the use of the term holder, a spouse or dependent (becoming qualified use). When actually used by the term holder, a personal residence may be rented during any period when the house is not being used. When held "for the use of" the term holder, the personal residence must be available at all times for the term holder. If the term holder vacates the personal residence (e.g., for health reasons), no other person can "house sit." Expenses of the residence may be paid directly by the term holder generating an additional gift to the remainderperson [Reg. Sec. 25.2702-5(b)(1)].

Third, if during the original duration of the term interest, the residence may be sold, transferred, or used as something other than as a personal residence, the trust will fail to qualify [Reg. Sec. 25.2702-5(b)(1)].

Tangible personal property exception. When tangible personal property is transferred to a GRIT, the zero value rule does not apply [IRC Sec. 2702(c)(4)]. Tangible personal property is limited to personal property for which no depreciation or depletion deduction can be taken, such as a work of art. The value of the grantor's retained interest is determined by the willing buyer/willing seller test. Specifically, the value equals the amount a willing buyer would pay and a willing seller would sell the retained interest for each having reasonable knowledge of the circumstances and neither being under any compulsion to buy or sell [Reg. Sec. 25.2702-2(c)(1)]. The grantor has the burden of establishing the value of this type of trust. The best evidence of value is actual sale or rentals of comparable property [Reg. Sec. 25.2702-2(c)(3)].

▶ **CAUTION:** The inability of the grantor to secure comparable valuations for the tangible personal property makes the use of this exception very limited.

If the tangible personal property is subsequently converted to something other than a tangible personal property GRIT (e.g., cash), the conversion is treated as a gift of the term interest to the remainderperson [Reg. Sec. 25.2702-2(c)(4)].

Other exceptions. In addition to the above five exceptions, IRC Sec. 2702 does not apply to:

1. Transfers in trust to a member of the transferor's family if the remainder interest in the trust qualifies for the charitable deduction as a charitable remainder trust

[Reg. Sec. 25.2702-1(c)(3); see ¶ 1005 for further discussion of charitable remainder trusts];

2. Transfer to a charitable lead trust [Reg. Sec. 25.2702-1(c)(5); see ¶ 1004 for further discussion of charitable lead trusts];

3. Transfer to a pooled income fund [Reg. Sec. 25.2702-1(c)(4); see ¶ 1006 for further discussion of pooled income funds];

4. Transfers in trust pursuant to marital property settlements incident to divorce [Reg. Sec. 25.2702-1(c)(7)];

5. Transfer of a remainder interest, if the only retained interest of the transferor (or applicable family member) is as permissible income beneficiary in the sole discretion of an independent trustee (as defined in IRC Sec. 674(c)) [Reg. Sec. 25.2702-1(c)(6)]; and

6. Transfers or assignments by a non-U.S. citizen surviving spouse to a qualified domestic trust (QDOT) [Reg. Sec. 25.2702-1(c)(8); see ¶ 1106].

¶602 GRITs

GRITs are used to reduce wealth transfer costs by transferring property within the family. Typically, a senior family member transfers securities or other valuable property to an irrevocable trust from which the grantor is entitled to receive the income for a term of years with remainder to his or her children or other beneficiaries. At the end of the term the property passes outright to the designated remainder beneficiaries. The transfer of assets into the GRIT is valued at the time of the completed gift using the subtraction method. If the transfer is not tied to a lapse of right or some other contingency, the gift is complete when the trust is funded [see ¶ 206]. Because the grantor's retained interest pertains to the income interest, the transfer is complete only as to the remainder interest.

Following the subtraction method of valuation for the federal gift tax purposes, the value of the gift equals the difference between (1) the value of the property transferred and (2) the value of the grantor's retained income interest. Because the remainder person cannot immediately possess or enjoy the value of the remainder interest, the gift is not a present interest and will not qualify for the annual per donee exclusion [see ¶ 902].

IRC Sec. 2702 provides special rules to determine the amount of a gift when there has been a transfer to a GRIT that benefits a member of the grantor's family. A family member, for purposes of IRC Sec. 2702, includes:

1. The transferor's spouse;

2. Any ancestor or lineal descendant of the transferor (or the transferor's spouse);

3. The transferor's sibling;

4. A spouse of any individual described in Item 2 or 3 [IRC Secs. 2702(e), 2704(c)(2)].

Under IRC Sec. 2702, unless one of the exceptions listed below applies, the value of the grantor's retained interest is zero, making the value of the gifted remainder equal to the value of the assets transferred in trust.

¶603 THE BASIC GRAT

(a) Elements of a GRAT. A GRAT is a valuable estate planning tool created and sanctioned by IRC Sec. 2702. When an individual creates a GRAT, he or she has created a trust that pays an annuity for a specified period of time. At the expiration of the trust term, the trust property goes to a child or other individual named in the trust documents. Gift tax is payable, but only on the present value of the remainder interest, which is the value of the property transferred to the trust less the value of the retained interest.

> ▶ **PLANNING POINTER:** When interest rates are low, the value of the annuity retained by the grantor increases thus reducing the value of the gift of the remainder in the GRAT. Therefore, when interest rates are low, it is good time to consider GRATs.

A GRAT can be an effective means of moving assets with a potential for appreciation out of a taxpayer's estate free of gift tax because any portion of a transferred asset's future appreciation that exceeds the rate of return required by IRC Sec. 7520 (used by the IRS to value annuity interests) will not be exposed to gift tax. In order to achieve this transfer tax savings, the terms of the GRAT must satisfy the requirements set forth in Reg. Sec. 25.2702-3. If this is accomplished, the grantor's interest is a "qualified annuity interest" and the value of the gift to the remainder beneficiaries is determined under IRC Sec. 7520. If the grantor's interest fails to be a "qualified annuity interest," the gift tax value of the transfer will be the full value of the property transferred to the trust.

GRAT basics. IRC Sec. 2702 provides that, if an interest in a trust is transferred to a family member, the value of any interest retained by the grantor is valued at zero for purposes of determining the transfer tax value of the gift to the family member(s). This rule does not apply if the retained interest is a "qualified interest." A fixed annuity, such as the annuity interest retained by the grantor of a GRAT, is one form of "qualified interest," so the gift of the remainder interest in the GRAT is determined by deducting the present value of the retained annuity during the GRAT term from the fair market value of the property contributed to the trust.

Generally, a GRAT is an irrevocable trust funded with assets expected to appreciate in value, in which the grantor retains an annuity interest for a term of years that the grantor expects to survive. At the end of that term, the assets then remaining in the trust are transferred to (or held in further trust for) the beneficiaries, who generally are descendants of the grantor. If the grantor dies during the GRAT term, however, the trust assets (at least the portion needed to produce the retained annuity) are included in the grantor's gross estate for estate tax purposes. To this extent, although the beneficiaries will own the remaining trust assets, the estate tax benefit of creating the GRAT (specifically, the tax-free transfer of the appreciation during the GRAT term in excess of the annuity payments) is not realized.

Example 1: When the IRC Sec. 7520 interest factor is 1.4 percent, A transfers $1 million to a trust, which is to pay him an annual annuity of $80,000 for 10 years. At the end of the 10 years, the trust property goes to A's children. The value of A's retained annuity is $741,696. This figure is determined by multiplying

$80,000 by 9.2712, which is the annuity factor for a 10-year term and an interest rate of 1.4 percent. The value of the gift of the remainder is $258,304.

Example 2: Assume instead that the interest factor in the above example is 5 percent instead of 1.4 percent. In this case, the value of the retained annuity would be $617,736 ($80,000 times 7.7217) and the value of the gift would be $382,264.

(b) Required Provisions of Governing Instrument. The regulations require a GRAT's governing instrument to include the following provisions:

- The GRAT's annuity amount must be payable to the holder of the annuity interest at least annually. A fixed amount means (a) a stated dollar amount payable periodically, but not less frequently than annually, but only to the extent the amount does not exceed 120 percent of the stated dollar amount payable in the preceding year; or (b) a fixed fraction or percentage of the initial fair market value of the property transferred to the trust, payable periodically but not less frequently than annually, but only to the extent the fraction or percentage does not exceed 120 percent of the fixed fraction or percentage payable in the preceding year [Reg. Sec. 25.2701-3(b)(1)(ii)];

- If the terms of the GRAT's annuity are stated in terms of a fraction or a fixed percentage of the value of the trust assets, the trust terms must contain a provision requiring adjustment of annuity payments previously paid if an error was made by the trustee in valuing the assets [Reg. Sec. 25.2701-3(b)(2)];

- An annuity amount payable based on the anniversary date of the creation of the trust must be paid no later than 105 days after the anniversary date. An annuity amount payable based on the taxable year of the trust may be paid after the close of the taxable year, provided the payment is made no later than the date by which the trustee is required to file the income tax return of the trust for the taxable year (without regard to extensions) [Reg. Sec. 25.2701-3(b)];

- The GRAT's governing instrument must prohibit additional contributions to the trust [Reg. Sec. 25.2701-3(b)(5)];

- The GRAT's governing instrument must prohibit distributions from the trust to or for the benefit of any person other than the holder of the annuity interest [Reg. Sec. 25.2702-3(d)(3)];

- The GRAT's governing instrument must fix the term of the annuity interest. The term of the interest must be fixed and ascertainable at the creation of the trust [Reg. Sec. 25.2701-3(d)(4)]. The term chosen must be one of the following: the life of the term holder, a specified term of years, or the shorter of these periods. In addition, successive term interests for the benefit of the same individual are treated as the same term interest [Reg. Sec. 25.2702-3(d)(3)]. In *Estate of Focardi*,[1] the Tax Court held that the revocable spousal interests contained in four separate GRATs created by a husband and wife were not qualified interests under IRC Sec. 2702(b) because (1) the spousal interests were contingent and (2) the interests did not satisfy the

---

[1] ¶**603** Estate of Focardi, TC Memo 2006-56.

durational requirements of Reg. Sec. 25.2702-3(d)(3). The spousal interests created in the GRATs were not fixed and ascertainable at the inception of the GRATS within the meaning of Reg. Sec. 25.2702-3(d)(3) because, under the terms of the GRATs, the interests were payable only if the grantor predeceased the spouse during the applicable term. In addition, the spousal interests did not meet the duration requirement that a term extend for the life of the term holder, a term of years, or the shorter of those periods. Thus, the spousal interests were not IRC Sec. 2702 qualified interests.

The fixed payments may be made after the end of the taxable year but must be made prior to the due date for filing the grantor-annuitant's individual income tax return (without regard to extensions) [Reg. Sec. 25.2702-3(b)(1)(i)]. The "qualified annuity interest" must be payable, "for the life of the term holder, for a specified term of years, or for the shorter (but not longer) of those periods" [Reg. Sec. 25.2702-3(d)(3)]. Issuance of a note, other debt instrument, or option of other similar financial arrangement, directly or indirectly in satisfaction of the annuity amount does not constitute payment of the annuity amount [Reg. Sec. 25.2702-3(b)(1)(i)]. The step-transaction doctrine is applicable, even in the estate and gift tax context, where a series of transactions is used to achieve a result that is inconsistent with these regulations, such as where the trustee borrows cash from a bank to make the required annuity payment and then borrows cash from the grantor to repay the bank;

- The GRAT's governing instrument must prohibit commutation (prepayment) by the trustee of the annuitant's annuity interest [Reg. Sec. 25.2702-3(d)(5)];

- The GRAT's governing instrument must prohibit the trustee from issuing a note, other than a debt instrument, option, or other similar financial arrangement in satisfaction of the annuity or unitrust payment obligation [Reg. Sec. 25.2702-3(b)(1)(i)].

   (c) Qualified Interest Defined. Under IRC Sec. 2702(b), a "qualified interest" is defined as:

- An interest that consists of a right to receive fixed amounts payable not less frequently than annually, and the yearly amount must be paid by a specified date each year (a qualified annuity interest) [IRC Sec. 2702(b)(1); Reg. Sec. 25.2702-3(b)(1)];

- An interest that consists of a right, payable at least annually, to receive a fixed percentage of the net fair market value of the trust corpus determined annually (a qualified unitrust interest) [IRC Sec. 2702(b)(2)]; and

- A right to receive a noncontingent remainder interest if all other interests in the trust are qualified annuity or unitrust interests (a qualified remainder interest) [IRC Sec. 2702(b)(3)].

   ▶ **PLANNING TIP:** It is more favorable for taxpayers to establish a GRAT when interest rates are low. Why? A lower interest rate increases the value of the annuity retained by the grantor and therefore reduces the value of the gift of the remainder interest.

¶603

Treatment of revocable spousal interest. In *Cook*,[2] the Seventh Circuit affirmed the Tax Court to conclude that the interest of the surviving spouse as either an independent interest or as an expansion of the grantor's interest failed to qualify as a "qualified interest" under IRC Sec. 2702 because the spousal interests were too contingent. Reg. Sec. 25.2702-3(d)(3) requires that the term of the second annuity be fixed and ascertainable at the creation of the trust. Since the spousal interests failed both of these tests, the court held that the spousal interests were not "qualified interests" and therefore have a zero value. The court noted that even if the spousal interest was a qualifying interest, the retained power to terminate the spousal annuity could extend the term of the annuity beyond the mandated lesser of a term of years or the life of the term holder. The appellate court agreed that the spousal interests were not qualified interests because they may never vest.

In *Schott*,[3] the Court of Appeals for the Ninth Circuit examined the circumstances under which a revocable spousal interest will constitute a qualified interest. A qualified interest includes not only a qualified annuity interest or unitrust interest but also a power by the grantor to revoke a qualified annuity or unitrust interest payable to the grantor's spouse. In *Schott*, a husband and wife each set up a GRAT providing for annuity payments to the grantor for the shorter of 15 years or until the death of the grantor. If the grantor died prior to the end of the 15-year term, the grantor's spouse was to receive the annuity payments for the remaining balance of the 15-year term, unless the grantor had revoked the spouse's interest. The appellate court reversed the Tax Court and held that the annuity interest of each of the spouses was a qualified interest and that therefore the grantor's power of revocation of that annuity interest was also a qualified interest. The court based its holding that the spousal interests were qualified annuity interests on the fact that a two-life annuity table enables the value of the spouse's annuity interest to be ascertained.

The IRS regulation clarifies that the exception treating a spouse's revocable successor interest as a retained qualified interest applies only if the spouse's annuity or unitrust interest, standing alone, would constitute a qualified interest that meets the requirements of Reg. Sec. 25.2702-3(d)(3), but for the grantor's revocation power [Reg. Sec. 25.2702-2(a)(6)]. This regulation is a clarification of those parts of the regulations under IRC Sec. regulation 2702 addressing revocable spousal interests that were at issue in *Schott*[4] and *Cook*.

To illustrate this change, the IRS added the following two examples (examples 8 and 9) to Reg. Sec. 25.2702-3(d)(3):

Example 3: The grantor of a GRAT retains the right to an annuity for a term equal to the shorter of 10 years or the grantor's death. At the expiration of the 10-year term, or the grantor's prior death, an annuity is to be paid to the grantor's spouse, if then living for a term equal to the shorter of 10 years or the spouse's death. The grantor retains the right to revoke the spouse's annuity interest. Since the spouse's interest is a qualified annuity interest, the grantor's

[2] Cook, 115 TC 15 (2000), *aff'd*, 269 F.3d 854 (7th Cir. 2001).

[3] Schott, TC Memo 2001-110, *rev'd and rem'd*, 319 F.3d 1203 (9th Cir. 2003).

[4] Schott, TC Memo 2001-110, *rev'd and rem'd*, 319 F.3d 1203 (9th Cir. 2003).

retained power of revocation is also a qualified interest retained by the grantor [Reg. Sec. 25.2702-3(e), ex. 8].

> **Example 4:** The grantor of a GRAT retains the right to an annuity for a term equal to the shorter of 10 years or the grantor's death. If the grantor dies prior to the expiration of the 10-year term, the annuity is payable to the grantor's spouse, if then living, for the shorter of the balance of the 10-year term or the spouse's death. The grantor retains the right to revoke the spouse's annuity interest. The spouse's interest is not a qualified annuity interest because (1) it is not payable for either life, a specified term of years, and (2) the spouse's right to the payment of the annuity is not dependent solely on surviving the grantor but rather is dependent on an impermissible contingency—the failure of the grantor to survive the initial term. Accordingly, the spouse's interest is not a qualified interest and therefore is valued at zero [Reg. Sec. 25.2702-3(e), ex. 9].

(d) Fixed Amount Defined. The fixed amount may be stated (1) in dollars, but only to the extent that it does not exceed 120 percent of the stated dollar amount payable in the preceding year, or (2) a fixed fraction or percentage of the initial fair-market value of the transferred property payable periodically (but at least annually), but only to the extent that the fraction or percentage does not exceed 120 percent of the fixed fraction or percentage payable in the preceding year [Reg. Sec. 25.2702-3(b)(1)(ii)]. A GRAT may permit the payment of amounts in excess of the annuity to the grantor. However, the right to receive the excess amount is not taken into account in valuing the gift for gift tax purposes [Reg. Sec. 25.2703-3(b)(1)(iii)].

(e) Benefits of GRATs.

- The main benefit of the properly drafted GRAT is that it is a successful technique for shifting wealth to younger beneficiaries free of transfer tax. This objective will be achieved with minimal gift tax exposure if the value of the donor's retained annuity interest is close to the value of the asset transferred to the GRAT.

- The taxpayer can maintain control of the trust assets for the term of the trust.

- The value of the remainder interest can be determined for gift tax purposes with a degree of certainty if the grantor relates the amount of the annuity payment to a percentage of the transferred asset's value as finally determined for gift tax purposes. Any increase in value on audit would cause a corresponding increase in the amount of the annuity payment resulting in a very small increase in the value of the remainder interest, which is the measure of the gift.

- There is no need to make a gift to the trust of seed money.

- The requirements of a GRAT are clearly spelled out in the Internal Revenue Code and regulations, leaving little to chance.

(f) Disadvantages of GRATs.

- If the grantor dies during the term of the GRAT, the value of some or all of the assets in the GRAT will be includible in the grantor's estate under IRC Sec. 2036(a) because he or she has retained the right to enjoy the income from the transferred assets [Reg. Sec. 20.2036-1(c)(2)].

- A GST tax exemption cannot be allocated by the grantor to the transfer of assets into the GRAT until the grantor's interest terminates.

- The value of the retained interest is based on 120 percent of the federal mid-term rate, which is typically higher than the applicable federal rate which is used for determining the minimum to be paid on other wealth transfer devices like the installment sale to a grantor trust.

- Distributions from a GRAT may only be made to the holder of the annuity interest during the term of the interest.

(g) Estate and Gift Tax Consequences of GRAT Creation.

Gift tax consequences. At the expiration of the grantor's retained annuity interest, the trust assets are distributed to younger family members who are the remainder beneficiaries specified in the trust documents. This transfer of assets to the remainder beneficiaries will generally be subject to gift tax as of the time of the initial transfer of assets to the trust. The value of that gift is computed under IRC Sec. 2702 as the value of the transferred assets less the actuarial value of the grantors' retained annuity interest, provided the requirements contained in IRC Sec. 2702 and the regulations relating to the creation of a "qualified annuity interest" are satisfied.

The IRC Sec. 7520 tables are used to determine the present value of the grantor's retained interest. The interest rate used in the valuation process is equal to 120 percent of the federal mid-term rate in effect under IRC Sec. 1274 on the date the gift was made [IRC Sec. 2702(a)(2)(B)]. The interest rate changes monthly.

The grantor will be required to use a portion of his or her gift tax exemption equal to—or, to the extent insufficient exemption remains, to pay gift tax on—the value of the remainder interest determined when the grantor initially funds the trust. The annuity portion of a GRAT is valued using the procedures for valuing qualified interests outlined in IRC Sec. 7520. To value the remainder interest in a GRAT, the value of any qualified interest, as determined under IRC Sec. 7520, is subtracted from the value of the property transferred to the trust.

Estate tax consequences. Because the value of the transferor's gift to the remainder beneficiaries is determined at the time of the transfer to the GRAT, if trust property grows at a rate in excess of the growth rate assumed under IRC Sec. 7520, the excess appreciation generally will pass to the remainder beneficiaries without further gift tax consequences to the grantor. If, however, the grantor dies during the trust term, the retained assets or that portion of the trust necessary to satisfy the annuity amount will be included in the grantor's gross estate for estate tax purposes under IRC Sec. 2036 because the grantor has retained the right to enjoy the income from the transferred assets [Reg. Sec. 20.2036-1(c)]. This result will negate the original benefits of creating a GRAT. When calculating the portion of a GRAT that is includible in the grantor's estate when the grantor predeceases the termination of the trust term, Reg. Sec. 20.2036-1(c)(3) provides that the includible portion is the lesser of:

¶603

1. The fair market value of the trust corpus on the decedent's date of death, or

2. A computed amount. The computed amount equals the total of (a) the amount of corpus required to generate the annuity payable in the trust year when the decedent died, and (b) the present values of the amounts of corpus necessary to generate the graduated annuity balances for each trust year following the year when the decedent died.

Taxpayers also "zero out" their GRATs by structuring the trust so that the value of the annuity interest under IRC Sec. 7520 approximates the value of the property transferred to the trust. When this is done, the value of the remainder interest (which is computed by subtracting the value of the annuity as determined under IRC Sec. 7520 from the value of the property transferred to the trust)—and therefore the value of any gift that is subject to gift taxation—is deemed to be equal to or near zero. In reality, however, taxpayers often realize returns on trust assets in excess of the returns assumed under IRC Sec. 7520. Any such excess appreciation generally passes to the remainder beneficiaries without further transfer tax consequences [for further discussion of zeroed-out GRATs, see ¶ 604].

(h) Income Tax Consequences of GRAT Creation. The GRAT will be taxed for income tax purposes as a grantor trust under IRC Sec. 673(a) which provides that the grantor will be treated as the owner of a trust in which the grantor has a reversionary interest that exceeds 5 percent of the value of the trust [for further discussion of the tax treatment of grantor trusts, see ¶ 3100].

¶604 ZEROED-OUT GRAT

Creative taxpayers have found a way to avoid paying gift tax by creating the "zeroed-out" or tax-free GRAT where the annuity is set so that the present value of the grantor's retained annuity payments is equal to the fair market value of the transferred property. When this occurs no gift tax consequences result. The transferred interest and the retained interest zero each other out. However, if the retained annuity interest is not a "qualified interest" that satisfies certain requirements of IRC Sec. 2702, no value is assigned to it and gift tax is payable on the entire value of the property transferred to the trust.

The IRS signaled their disapproval of this technique in old Reg. Sec. 25.2702-3(e), Example 5, which provided that an individual's right to receive a unitrust amount for 10 years was a qualified interest to the extent of the right to receive the amount for 10 years or until the individual's death. In the example, the IRS clarified that the amount payable to the individual's estate if he or she dies during the 10-year period was not a qualified interest.

(a) Tax Court Invalidates Example 5 of Reg. Sec. 25.2702-3(e) in Walton. The Tax Court came to the rescue in *Walton*,[1] where the court considered a situation similar to that presented in old Example 5 and held in a unanimous reviewed-by-the-court opinion that old Example 5 was an unreasonable interpreta-

---

[1] ¶ **604** Walton, 115 TC 589 (2000), *appeal dismissed* (8th Cir. 2002), *acq. in result*, Notice 2003-72, 2003-2 CB 964.

tion and invalid extension of IRC Sec. 2702. The court concluded, contrary to old Example 5, that a retained annuity payable for a specified term of years to the grantor, or to the grantor's estate if the grantor dies before the expiration of the specified period, is a qualified interest for that period of time. In that case, the grantor established a GRAT, providing that the grantor was to receive an annuity for a term of 2 years. If the grantor died before the expiration of the 2-year term, the annuity was to be paid to the grantor's estate for the balance of the term. Upon expiration of the 2-year term, the trust corpus was to be distributed to a designated remainder beneficiary. After considering the legislative history and intent behind IRC Sec. 2702, the court held that old Example 5 was an unreasonable interpretation and invalid extension of the law as provided in IRC Sec. 2702. The court concluded that a retained annuity payable for a specified term of years to the grantor, or to the grantor's estate if the grantor dies prior to expiration of the term, is a "qualified interest" retained by the grantor and could be subtracted in computing the value of the remainder interest given to the remainder beneficiary. This resulted in a reduction in the value of the taxable gift to zero. In what can be hailed as a great planning opportunity for taxpayers and estate planners, the zeroed-out GRAT was thus sanctioned by the Tax Court in *Walton*. Moreover, the Tax Court specifically invalidated the famous Example 5 of Reg. Sec. 25.2702-3(e) in this opinion.

(b) Example 5 of Reg. Sec. 25.2702-3(e). Based on the Tax Court's decision, the IRS finally relented in its battle against zeroed-out GRATs and has formally acquiesced to the Tax Court's decision in *Walton*. Moreover, the IRS has revised Example 5 of Reg. Sec. 25.2702-3(e) to be consistent with the holding in *Walton*. Therefore the conclusion stated in Example 5 now provides that the unitrust payments retained by the grantor constitutes a qualified interest for the full stated term of 10 years. This means that the IRS will now treat the retained unitrust payable to an individual or an individual's estate as a "qualified interest" payable for a 10-year term. Best of all, the IRS has finally agreed to stop challenging zeroed-out GRATs. This means that an annuity should be valued as an annuity for a term of years, notwithstanding the possibility that the grantor might predecease the expiration of the full GRAT term.

Disputed regulation revised. The IRS has issued final regulations that conform the gift tax regulations defining a qualified interest under IRC Sec. 2702 to the Tax Court's decision in *Walton* where the court declared Example 5 of Reg. Sec. 25.2702-3(e) to be invalid. The final regulations amend the gift tax special valuation rules to provide that a unitrust or annuity interest payable for a specified term of years to the grantor, or to the grantor's estate if the grantor dies prior to the expiration of the term, is a qualified interest for the specified term. In accordance with this change, the last line of Example 5 of Reg. Sec. 25.2702-3(e) now provides that "[t]he interest of A (and A's estate) to receive the unitrust amount for the specified term of 10 years in all events is a qualified unitrust interest for a term of 10 years."

▶ **PLANNING IMPLICATIONS:** As a result of the Tax Court's approval of the zeroed-out GRAT in *Walton* and the IRS acquiescence in the case, tax payers should feel more comfortable creating zeroed-out GRATs that are free from gift tax. This creates tax planning opportunities for the transfer of property to loved ones free of transfer tax. The transfer will be tax-free if the present value of the GRAT payments is at least equal to the value of the property transferred, and if the annuity is payable to the grantor's estate for the remainder of the original term if he or she does not survive that term. In addition, when drafting the GRAT, the annuity must be expressed in terms of a percentage of the value of the property transferred to the GRAT. As a result, the value of the transferred property fluctuates with the value of the annuity.

(c) Administration Proposes Minimum 10-Year Term for GRATs. The Treasury Department's "General Explanations of the Administration's Fiscal Year 2014 Revenue Proposals" ("GreenBook") was released on April 10, 2013. One of the revenue-raising proposals was to require a minimum term for GRATs. The administration explained as follows:

Reasons for Change

GRATs have proven to be a popular and efficient technique for transferring wealth while minimizing the gift tax cost of transfers, providing that the grantor survives the GRAT term and the trust assets do not depreciate in value. The greater the appreciation, the greater the transfer tax benefit achieved. Taxpayers have become adept at maximizing the benefit of this technique, often by minimizing the term of the GRAT (thus reducing the risk of the grantor's death during the term), in many cases to two years, and by retaining annuity interests significant enough to reduce the gift tax value of the remainder interest to zero or to a number small enough to generate only a minimal gift tax liability.

Proposal

The proposal would require, in effect, some downside risk in the use of this technique by imposing the requirement that a GRAT have a minimum term of ten years and a maximum term of the life expectancy of the annuitant plus ten years. The proposal also would include a requirement that the remainder interest have a value greater than zero at the time the interest is created and would prohibit any decrease in the annuity during the GRAT term. Although a minimum term would not prevent "zeroing-out" the gift tax value of the remainder interest, it would increase the risk that the grantor fails to outlive the GRAT term and the resulting loss of any anticipated transfer tax benefit.[2]

To remedy this perceived abuse, the Obama administration wants to impose a 10-year minimum term for GRATs and a maximum term of the life expectancy of the annuitant plus ten years. In addition, the remainder interest must have a value greater than zero when the interest is created and any decrease in the annuity during the GRAT term would be prohibited. This proposal would increase the risk of the grantor dying during the GRAT term and an inability to benefit from any tax savings. The Treasury's rationale for the proposal was as follows: grantors often structure GRATs with short terms (two years) in order to minimize the risk that the grantor will die during the trust term which would result in all or part of the trust assets being included in the grantor's estate for estate tax purposes. Therefore, grantors

---

[2] General Explanations of the Administration's Fiscal Year 2014 Revenue Proposals (Greenbook), 142.

maintain multiple short-term, zeroed-out GRATs funded with different asset portfolios to improve the grantor's odds that at least one trust will outperform significantly the IRC Sec. 7520 rate assumptions and thereby allow the grantor to achieve a transfer to the remainder beneficiaries at little or no gift tax cost.

The Obama Administration's budget proposal was designed to introduce additional downside risk to the use of GRATs by imposing a requirement that GRATs have a minimum term of 10 years. The Obama Administration argues that a GRAT with a 10-year term would carry greater risk that the grantor would die during the trust term thereby eliminating the transfer tax benefit of appreciated assets and increasing the likelihood that the trust assets would be included in the grantor's estate for estate tax purposes.

The proposal would eliminate the use of shorter-term GRATs (i.e., GRATs with terms of less than 10 years) for gift tax avoidance. The proposal would not prevent the "zeroing-out" of a GRAT's remainder interest for gift tax purposes. Instead, the proposal introduces the specter of estate tax by increasing the likelihood that a grantor will die during the trust term and subject the trust assets to estate tax. Wealthy younger taxpayers may view the likelihood of dying during a 10-year trust term as remote and thus may be willing to establish one or more 10-year GRATs in an effort to avoid gift tax. The proposal might therefore encourage taxpayers to establish GRATs earlier in life. If the proposal becomes law, long-term GRATs would therefore become less attractive to taxpayers who become wealthy later in life.

¶605 GRUTs

A grantor-retained unitrust (GRUT) also satisfies the qualified interest test. With a GRUT, the grantor (or applicable family member) must have an irrevocable right to receive payments at least annually of a fixed fraction or percentage of the fair-market value of the property transferred to the trust, determined annually, and paid over a specified term [IRC Sec. 2702(b)(2); Reg. Secs. 25.2702-2(a)(7), 25.2702-3(c), and 25.2702-3(d)].

> ▶ **PLANNING POINTER:** Changes in interest rates do not have an impact on the value of a gift of a remainder interest in a GRUT because the retained unitrust interest is the right to receive a fixed percentage of the trust's assets and changes in rates affect the unitrust's beneficiary and remainderperson equally.

Similar to the GRAT, the payment of the amount due in a GRUT must be made no later than the due date for filing the grantor-annuitant's individual tax return (without regard to extensions). The fixed percentage is a fraction or percentage of the net fair-market value of the trust assets, determined annually, but only to the extent that the fraction or percentage does not exceed 120 percent of the fixed fraction or percentage payable in the preceding year [Reg. Sec. 25.2702-3(c)(1)].

Example 1: The grantor transfers property worth $1 million to an irrevocable trust and retains the right to receive 5 percent of the net fair-market value (valued annually) for a period of 15 years. At the end of the 15-year term, the trust and the payments terminate. The interest the grantor has is a qualified unitrust interest for the full 15-year term.

The value of the grantor's retained annuity or unitrust interest is determined in accordance with IRC Sec. 7520 (the "rate of the month" published by the IRS based on 120 percent of the applicable federal mid-term rate) for the month in which the transfer is made.

The value of the grantor's retained interest, however, is linked between the Sec. 7520 rate for the month of the transfer and the rate used to determine the annuity or unitrust interest the grantor will receive under the trust instrument. When the two rates are equal, the value of the completed gift equals the value of the remainder. However, where the Sec. 7520 rate exceeds or falls below the trust rate, a downward or upward adjustment in the value of the gifted remainder, as appropriate, is required.

A qualified remainder interest is a noncontingent remainder provided (1) all other interests in the trust are qualified annuity interests or qualified unitrust interests; and (2) the governing instrument does not permit the payment of income in excess of the annuity or unitrust amount to the holder of the qualified interest [IRC Sec. 2702(b)(3); Reg. Secs. 25.2702-2(a)(8), 25.2702-3(f)]. The interest must be a qualified remainder interest in every respect from the creation of the interest and it must be noncontingent [Reg. Sec. 25.2702-3(f)(1)(i)]. For this purpose, an interest is noncontingent only if it is payable to the beneficiary or the beneficiary's estate in all events.

> **Example 2:** Alice transfers property to an irrevocable trust. Alice's child has the right to receive the greater of the income of the trust or $10,000 per year. If Alice's child dies, the trust is to terminate and the trust corpus is to be paid to Alice. Alice's remainder interest is not a qualified remainder interest because the right of Alice's child to receive income in excess of the annuity amount is not a qualified interest [Reg. Sec. 25.2702-3(f)(3), Example (2)].

QUALIFIED PERSONAL RESIDENCE TRUSTS (QPRTs)

TABLE OF CONTENTS

¶700 QPRT BASICS

The qualified personal residence trust (QPRT) is an excellent statutorily permitted estate planning tool that is commonly used by wealthy taxpayers to transfer a personal residence to family members and also enjoy considerable transfer tax savings [IRC Sec. 2702(a)(3)(A)(ii); Reg. Sec. 25.2702-5(a)(1)]. A taxpayer creates a QPRT by transferring his or her personal residence and/or vacation home to an irrevocable trust(s) for the benefit of designated beneficiaries (typically his or her children), while retaining the right to live in and use the property rent free for a fixed number of years or until death. This right to occupy the residence is a retained income interest. When the trust expires, ownership of the residence will pass to the remainder beneficiaries of the trust. If the donor dies before the termination of the QPRT term, the trust will terminate and the residence will revert to the donor's estate.

The objective of the QPRT is to enable the donor to get a discount in computing the value of a taxable gift for the interests he retains. If the donor survives the QPRT term, the entire property is out of his estate, even though he paid gift tax on only a discounted value.

¶701 TAX BENEFITS OF QPRTs

1. *Reduced transfer taxes when residence transferred to trust.* The QPRT saves wealth transfer taxes if the transfer of the residence into the trust satisfies the requirements established in Reg. Sec. 25.2702-5, which are outlined in ¶702. Gift tax may be owed on the transfer, but the sum on which it is calculated will be much less than the full market value of the residence transferred into the trust because the taxpayer has made a gift of only a future or remainder interest in the home. A remainder or future interest is worth much less than the current fair market value of the residence according to IRC Sec. 2702(a); Reg. Sec. 25.2702-2(b)(2). When the residence is transferred to the QPRT, a gift of only the remainder interest is made because the taxpayer has retained a present interest which is the right to live in the residence until termination of the trust. The actuarial value of this retained interest (determined as of the date of the contribution of the property to the trust) is subtracted from the fair market value of the residence transferred to the trust. The value of the retained interest depends upon the grantor's age, the duration of the reserved interest, the fair market value of the property and the prevailing IRS interest rate, called the Section 7520 rate, which is 120 percent of the federal midterm rate. The actuarial values are calculated by referring to the valuation tables prescribed under IRC Sec. 7520, using the rate prescribed for the month of the transfer [¶1916]. If the grantor survives the trust term, the residence passes to the beneficiaries with no further transfer tax consequences. Moreover, all post-gift appreciation of the property escapes taxation with respect to the grantor.

> **Example 1:** A 75-year-old taxpayer transfers a home worth $2 million to his children. He has made a taxable gift of $2 million. If, however, he creates a QPRT and transfers his residence into the trust and retains a seven-year term interest during which he plans to live in the home, he has made a gift to his children of a remainder interest in the home of only $1.4 million. If he retains a contingent reversion, the taxable gift is reduced to about $966,000.

The value of the residence for gift tax purposes is calculated by taking the value of the home on the date the residence is transferred into the trust and subtracting the value of the interest retained by the parent living in the home which will be specified as a term of years in the language of the QPRT. Taxpayers use the interest rates released each month by the Treasury Department to determine the actuarial value of their retained interest or their right to reside in the home. If the interest rate is high and the term is long, the discount will be at its highest level and taxpayers will benefit most from a QPRT. A longer term that is retained to live in the home will result in a more valuable retained interest and consequently a lower remainder and ultimately a smaller gift to loved ones.

> **Example 2:** Dad transfers his personal residence worth $1 million to a QPRT for the benefit of his children, retains the right to live in the house for 15 years, and does not retain a contingent reversion interest. Dad has already used up his unified credit and his annual exclusions. To determine the value of the remainder interest, refer to Table B of IRS Pub. 1457. The applicable IRC Sec. 7520 rate

is 15 percent. Table B shows that the remainder factor for a 15-year discount rate is .362446. Dad multiplies this factor by the $1 million value of the home for a remainder interest of $362,446. This is the amount of the taxable gift that Dad has made to his children. The QPRT has enabled Dad to reduce the value of his taxable transfer from $1 million to $362,446. The QPRT has saved him $255,022 in gift taxes [($1 million – $362,446) × 40 percent].

Impact of actuarial tables on QPRTs. The IRS, as required by IRC Sec. 7520(c)(3), has updated its actuarial tables to reflect the new mortality data produced by the 2000 U.S. census. The value of life estates, term interests, remainders, and reversions for estate, gift, and income tax purposes is generally determined under tables promulgated under IRC Sec. 7520. The valuation depends on both an actuarial factor dependent on life expectancies and an interest factor. The new data reflects an increased life expectancy for all persons under age 95. The value of the grantor's reserved interest in a QPRT includes both the value of the right to use the residence for a fixed term of years and the value of the contingency reversionary interest if the grantor dies during the fixed term of years. The increased longevity under the new actuarial tables reduces slightly the value of the reversionary interest, because it is less likely that the grantor will die during the term of years. This will decrease the value of the grantor's retained interests and increase the amount of the taxable gift of the remainder interest making QPRTs slightly less desirable estate planning devices.

2. *Estate freezing device.* A QPRT acts as an estate freezing tool because any appreciation in the value of the residence transferred into the trust also passes to loved ones tax-free at end of the trust term.

> **Example 3:** Mom transfers a home worth $1 million into a QPRT with a 7-year trust term. Her children are the beneficiaries of the trust. At the time of the transfer, the IRS tables reveal that the value of the taxable gift is only $500,000. At the time of the transfer of the home into the QPRT, the home is removed from her taxable estate. At the termination of the trust term, when the value of the home has appreciated to $2.5 million, her children have an asset worth $2.5 million but gift tax was paid on an estate worth only $500,000.

3. *Opportunity for further estate reduction.* When the term of the QPRT expires and the parent wants to continue living in the residence that now belongs to the remainder beneficiaries, the parent must pay fair market value rent to the children thus affording another opportunity to transfer funds from his or her estate into the hand of the next generation. No gift tax will be owed on these rent payments. The rent payments will, however be taxed as income in the hands of the beneficiaries.

4. *Removes major investment from gross estate.* For many taxpayers, their residence or vacation home is their biggest investment. The QPRT offers taxpayers a way to permanently remove this asset plus appreciation from their taxable estate.

5. *Use of fractional discount.* If a fractional share discount is used in conjunction with a QPRT, gift taxes can be reduced even further. Here is how it works. If married taxpayers change title to their personal residence from joint tenancy by the entirety to

tenancy-in-common (if permitted by state law), each spouse will transfer his or her one-half ownership to a separate trust, thus making a fractional share discount available.

¶702 REQUIREMENTS FOR QPRT

To be a valid QPRT, the requirements set forth in Reg. Sec. 25.2702-5(c) must be satisfied as follows:

(a) Principal Residence Requirement. In order to create a QPRT, the donor must own and transfer a residence into a trust that qualifies as a "personal residence." In order to qualify as a personal residence, the residence must satisfy the following requirements:

- The personal residence must satisfy the "primary use" requirement
- The personal residence must qualify as either

  — the donor's principal residence, or
  — another residence.

Example 1: C maintains C's principal place of business in one room of C's principal residence. The residence is a personal residence [Reg. Sec. 2702-5(d), ex. 1].

Example 2: L owns a vacation condominium that L rents out for six months of the year, but which is treated as L's residence because L occupies it for at least 18 days per year. L provides no substantial services in connection with the rental of the condominium. L transfers the condominium to a QPRT and retains the right to use the condominium during L's lifetime. The trust is a qualified personal residence trust [Reg. Sec. 2702-5(d), ex. 2].

Example 3: W owns a 200-acre working farm. The farm includes a house, barns, equipment buildings, a silo, and enclosures for confinement of farm animals. W transfers the farm to a QPRT, retaining the use of the farm for 20 years, with the remainder to W's child. The trust is not a QPRT because the farm includes assets not meeting the requirements of a personal residence [Reg. Sec. 2702-5(d), ex. 3].

A facts and circumstances test is used to determine whether the donor's residence is his or her principal residence. As outlined in Reg. Sec. 1.121-1(b)(2), the IRS will consider the following factors in making this determination:

- The taxpayer's place of employment;
- The principal place of abode of the taxpayer's family members;
- The address listed on the taxpayer's federal and state tax returns, driver's license, automobile registration and voter registration card;
- The taxpayer's mailing address for bills and correspondence;

- The location of the taxpayer's banks; and

- The location of religious organizations and recreational clubs with which the taxpayer is affiliated.

A taxpayer may transfer his personal residence as well as an "other residence" that qualifies as a vacation home into a QPRT [Reg. Sec. 25.2702-5(c)(2)(i)]. A vacation home will constitute an "other residence" under IRC Sec. 280A(d)(1) if the donor uses the house for the greater of 14 days per year or 10 percent of the number of days it is rented [Reg. Sec. 25.2702-5(c)(2)(i)(B)]. The vacation home need not be located in the United States. The IRS approved the contribution of co-op stock to a QPRT in Letter Ruling 9151046. The fact that a residence is subject to a mortgage does not affect its status as a personal residence eligible for transfer to a QPRT.

Other property. A personal residence may include "appurtenant structures" used by the term holder for residential purposes and adjacent or surrounding land not in excess of that which is reasonably appropriate for residential purposes (taking into account the residence's size and location). The IRS liberally construed the term "appurtenant structures" to include a guesthouse, barn, boathouse, two sheds, a large pier and a dock in Letter Ruling 200241039. The IRS also approved a QPRT containing a caretaker's house, an indoor riding barn, tennis courts, a water treatment building, a pool and a pool house as well as an office/workshop in Letter Rulings 9730013 and 9739024. The only limitation is that the additional structures be used solely for residential rather than for commercial purposes. The IRS concluded that adjacent land may be placed in a QPRT provided the land use is equal in measure and size with that of surrounding lots and the land is used strictly for residential purposes in Letter. Rulings 199916030 and 9841015. Personal property such as household furnishings may not be transferred to the QPRT [Reg. Sec. 25.2702-5(c)(ii)].

(b) Primary Use Requirement. In order for a donor to transfer his or her residence into a QPRT, the donor must satisfy the two prongs of the primary use requirement as outlined in Reg. Sec. 25.2702-5(c)(iii). First, a residence is the donor's principal residence only if its primary use is as the donor's residence when the donor occupies it. Second, a residence is not a principal residence if during any time that the donor does not occupy the residence its primary use is other than as a residence. If the donor has guests that live with him or her in the house, the primary use test is still satisfied. The principal residence will not fail to qualify if a portion of the residence is used as a home office provided that such use is secondary to use of the residence as a residence. Disqualifying activities include providing transient lodging and substantial services (e.g., a hotel or a bed and breakfast) [Reg. Sec. 25.2702-5(c)(iii)]. In Letter Ruling 200626043, the IRS approved a QPRT when a vacation home was converted to a personal residence. A trust will cease to be a QPRT if the residence ceases to be used or held for use as a personal residence of the grantor, whether due to sale, damage or destruction [Reg. Sec. 25.2702-5(c)(7)].

(c) Trust Income. The governing instrument of the QPRT must require that any income of the trust be distributed to the term holder not less frequently than annually [Reg. Sec. 25.2702-5(c)(3)].

(d) Assets of QPRT. The QPRT cannot hold tangible personal property. The QPRT may hold cash in addition to the residence under the following limited situations [Reg. Sec. 25.2702-5(c)(5)(ii)]:

- The QPRT may permit additions of cash to the trust in an amount which does not exceed the amount required: (1) for payment of trust expenses (including mortgage payments) already incurred or reasonably expected to be paid by the trust within six months from the date the addition is made; (2) for improvements to the residence to be paid by the trust within six months from the date the addition is made; and (3) for purchase of the initial residence, within three months of the date the trust is created, provided the trustee has previously entered into a contract to purchase that residence; and (4) for purchase of a residence to replace another residence, within three months of the date the addition is made, provided the trustee has previously entered into a contract to purchase that residence.

- If the QPRT permits additions of cash to the trust, the trustee must determine, at least quarterly, the amounts held by the trust for payment of excess expenses and must require that those amounts be distributed to the term holder. In addition, the QPRT must require, upon termination of the term holder's interest in the trust, that any amounts held by the trust that are not used to pay trust expenses due and payable on the date of termination (including expenses directly related to termination) be distributed outright to the term holder within 30 days of termination.

(e) Improvements. The QPRT may permit improvements to the residence to be added to the trust and may permit the trust to hold such improvements, provided that the residence when improved still qualifies as a personal residence [Reg. Sec. 25.2702-5(c)(5)(B)].

(f) Sale Proceeds. The QPRT may sell the residence to a third party (except not to grantor or grantor's spouse as discussed below) and the trust may hold the sale proceeds in a separate account [Reg. Sec. 25.2702-5(c)(5)(C)]. In Letter Ruling 200919002, the IRS sustained a transfer of a residence to a QPRT where the remainder interest was sold to a second trust with no gift or estate tax consequences.

(g) Insurance and Insurance Proceeds. The QPRT may hold one or more insurance policies on the residence. In addition, the trust may hold, in a separate account, insurance proceeds payable to the trust as a result of damage or destruction of the residence. Amounts (other than insurance proceeds payable to the trust as a result of damage or destruction of the residence) received as a result of the involuntary conversion of the residence are treated as insurance proceeds [Reg. Sec. 25.2702-5(c)(5)(D)].

(h) Prepayment Prohibited. The QPRT must prohibit prepayment of the term holder's interest [Reg. Sec. 25.2702-5(c)(6)].

(i) Cessation of Use as Personal Residence. If the personal residence is sold, transferred, or used as something other than a personal residence, the trust instrument must require that within 30 days after the date on which the trust ceases to be a QPRT, either: (1) the trust be terminated and the assets be distributed to the grantor; or (2) the grantor's interest be converted to a qualifying annuity interest [Reg.

Sec. 25.2702-5(c)(8)]. The trustee has the option of choosing either of these two alternatives. At the end of the trust term, if the grantor is still alive, he may continue to live in the residence with the consent of the new owner, provided a fair market rental is paid. If a fair rental is not paid, the QPRT is revoked and the property is includible in the grantor's estate at death.

(j) Damage/Destruction of Personal Residence. The QPRT must provide that, if damage or destruction renders the residence unusable as a residence, the trust ceases to be a QPRT two years after the date of damage or destruction (or the date of termination of the term holder's interest in the trust, if earlier) unless, prior to such date replacement of or repairs to the residence are completed; or a new residence is acquired by the trust.

(k) Sale of Residence to Grantor Prohibited. Reg. Sec. 25.2702-5(c)(9) prohibits the QPRT from selling or transferring the residence, directly or indirectly, to the grantor, the grantor's spouse, a grantor trust of the grantor or grantor's spouse, or an entity controlled by the grantor or grantor's spouse. Reg. Sec. 25.2702-5(c)(9) eliminates a planning strategy that the IRS viewed as abusive. The grantor would often buy the home from the QPRT during the term of the trust so the residence would then be included in the decedent's gross estate and receive a step-up in basis equal to the fair-market value of the property. This tactic designed to manipulate the basis of the residence is now prohibited by Reg. Sec. 25.2702-5(c)(9)].

¶703 WHAT TO DO AT TERMINATION OF QPRT TERM

One of the biggest problems with establishing a QPRT is what happens at the end of the QPRT term. If the donor/parent survives the trust term, at the termination of the QPRT, the donor/parent no longer owns the residence and ownership passes to the remainder beneficiaries of the trust. This means that the parents no longer own the home they may have lived in for decades. These issues are often difficult for families to grasp. The tax issues, however, are clear. If the donor continues to occupy the residence rent-free after the end of the QPRT term, the residence will be fully includible in the donor's estate under IRC Sec. 2036 regardless of whether the understanding is express[1] or implied.[2] The only way around this is for the donor who survives the trust term to lease the residence from the remainder beneficiaries at a fair market rental. The IRS has consistently ruled that a QPRT may allow a grantor who survives the trust term to lease the residence from the remainder beneficiaries at a fair market rental.[3]

▶**PLANNING POINTER:** A wise drafter will build into QPRT trust instrument language providing that the donor/parent has the option to pay rent to the remainder beneficiaries/children at the end of the QPRT term. This will eliminate the IRC Sec. 2036 presumption.

---

[1] ¶703 Estate of Tehan, TC Memo 2005-128; Rev. Rul. 70-155, 1970-1 CB 189.

[2] Guynn, 437 F.2d 1148 (4th Cir. 1971); Rev. Rul. 78-409, 1978-2 CB 234.

[3] Priv. Ltr. Ruls. 9249014, 9433016, 9626041, 9714025, 9735011, 9735012.

In *Estate of Riese*,[4] the Tax Court concluded that a decedent's estate could exclude the value of her personal residence from the gross estate. The decedent's attorney created a three-year QPRT for the decedent's home. According to the terms of the QPRT, if the decedent survived the three-year period, the QPRT would terminate, and the residence would pass to two trusts for the benefit of the decedent's daughters. The decedent reported the transfer on a gift tax return. After the trust terminated, no deed was executed to transfer the residence to the trusts. The decedent's daughter contacted the attorney to inquire about the appropriate way in which she should calculate the fair market rent on the residence. However, the decedent died unexpectedly before a lease agreement could be created. Because the intent of the parties involved was to create a lease under which the decedent would pay rent after the termination of the QPRT, there was no express or implied agreement that the decedent would stay in the residence rent free. Thus, the decedent did not retain a life estate in the property and the residence was excluded from her gross estate underIRC Sec. 2036.

Return or reverse QPRT provides parent with right to use residence after termination of reserved life term and avoid leasing residence back from children. In a series of Private Letter Rulings, the IRS has approved a technique whereby, following the termination of a QPRT established by a grantor, the remainder beneficiaries transfer the residence to a new QPRT of their own, this one giving the original grantor another occupancy right for a term of years. Following the term of years, the second QPRT terminates and the house is distributed back to the remainder beneficiaries in equal shares as tenants in common. In the rulings, the IRS concluded that these reverse or return QPRTs qualify for the exception to the zero-value rule in IRC Sec. 2702(a), assuming the trusts comply with all of the statutory and regulatory requirements for a traditional QPRT as follows: (1) the trust was operated in a matter consistent with the terms of the trust instrument; (2) the trust was valid under applicable state law; and (3) the residence qualified as a personal residence under Reg. Sec. 25.2702-5(c)(2).

For example, the return or reverse QPRT has been approved by the IRS in Letter Rulings 200848003, 200848007, 200848008, 200901019, 200935004, 201019012, 201006012, 201014044, 201019006, 201019007, 201024012, 201118014, 201129017, 201131006 and 201144001.

> ▶**PLANNING POINTER:** The return QPRT is an alternative to the creation of a landlord-tenant relationship between children and parents, which can occur when the fixed term of years of the initial QPRT ends and the parents/grandparents still want to continue living in the residence and the children are forced to lease the residence back to them for a fair market rent. This type of leaseback arrangement, although not favored by clients, permits the original grantor to continue living in the residence in exchange for the payment of market rent. In contrast, the return QPRT will permit the original grantor to continue residing in the residence for the rest of his or her lifetime after the expiration of the initial reserved use term without the payment of rent or the establishment of the landlord-tenant relationship with family members. There is a risk, however, that the IRS could include the entire residence in the deceased grantor's gross estate

---

[4] Estate of Riese, TC Memo 2011-60.

¶703

under IRC Sec. 2036(a). In light of this risk, which has not been addressed to date by the IRS, the return QPRT may be inferior to a leaseback of the property to the grantor for a fair market rental, but it does avoid establishing a landlord-tenant relationship between a child and parent or grandparent.

Modification to QPRT. In Letter Ruling 201006012, the IRS concluded that a modification of the terms of a QPRT to allow a grantor and his spouse to live in the grantor's home for a specific number of years after the expiration of the QPRT term did not result in a taxable gift. The taxpayer created a QPRT which permitted the taxpayer and his spouse to live in the taxpayer's home for a specific number of years. The QPRT provided further that the trust was to be distributed to the grantor's children at the later of his death or a specified number of years. However, a prenuptial agreement between the grantor and his spouse allowed the spouse to occupy the home after the grantor's death.

The grantor modified the QPRT to give each of his four children a power of appointment over the trust corpus to allow the grantor to live in the house. The power of appointment was also subject to the terms of the prenuptial agreement (*i.e.*, the spouse's occupancy rights after the grantor's death). The taxpayer requested a ruling regarding whether IRC Sec. 2702 would apply to the proposed trust modification and result in a taxable gift.

The IRS ruled that IRC Sec. 2702 did not apply to the trust modification and therefore no taxable gift resulted, provided that: (1) the trust agreement was substantially similar to the sample QPRT provisions provided by the IRS; (2) the trust operated in a manner consistent with the trust instrument; (3) the trust was a valid trust under applicable local law; and (4) the residence qualified as a personal residence under Reg. Sec. 25.2702-5(c)(2). However, the IRS did not address whether the transfer of the residence to the grantor would result in the residence being included in the gross estate of the grantor under IRC Sec. 2036.

> ▶ **PRACTICE POINTER:** As a result of the IRS-sanctioned trust modification made by the taxpayers in Letter Ruling 201006012, at the expiration of the QPRT term, the parents have the opportunity to stay in the residence for the remainder of their lifetime and do not have to enter into an often uncomfortable lease agreement with their children. In conjunction with this prearranged leaseback of the residence to the parents, they were to pay their children a fair market rental and the residence should not be included in their gross estate when they die based on Letter Rulings 200822011, 200825004, and 199931028.

Income tax consequences of QPRT. Since a QPRT is a so-called grantor (flow-through) trust, all of the trust's income and expenses will be taxed as if the grantor owned the property. However, the grantor can deduct expenses such as mortgage interest and real estate taxes that are paid by the trust. In addition, the grantor will owe capital gains on any taxable gain realized by the trust if the residence is sold during the period when it is owned by the trust. For further discussion of grantor trusts, see ¶ 3100.

¶703

¶704 DISADVANTAGES OF QPRT

Taxpayers should be aware of the following disadvantages before using the QPRT as a tool to minimize transfer taxes:

- The donor's basis in the residence at the time of the transfer to the QPRT will carry over to the beneficiaries under IRC Sec. 1015. In contrast, a transfer at death would give the beneficiaries a stepped-up basis in the residence under IRC Sec. 1014 equal to the fair market value of the residence at the date of death. Reg. Sec. 25.2702-5(9) prevents donors from repurchasing the residence from the QPRT before the end of the term and holding it until death so the beneficiaries will have a basis step-up. As a result of the carry over basis rule, a big capital gains tax will result if the beneficiaries sell the residence if it has appreciated in value.

- There is a risk that the grantor may die before the expiration of the term of the reserved interest. If this occurs, the full fair market value of the residence will be included in his or her estate for federal estate tax purposes and all the well-intentioned estate planning schemes will not work as planned. Thus, the health of the homeowner must be considered before transferring his or her personal residence into a QPRT. It is not wise to establish a QPRT for a grantor who is terminally ill. The longer the retained interest, the greater the chance that the transferor will die prior to termination of the trust term and could risk having the entire value of the residence included in his or her gross estate. So planners must factor in a homeowner's health and life expectancy when choosing the duration of the trust term.

- Senior family members may be reluctant to transfer a home into the QPRT and lose control over their home. There is a way around this problem. Instead of transferring ownership of the property to the grantors' children at the termination of the QPRT, the remainder interest should be transferred to an irrevocable life insurance trust that is permitted to own both life insurance and other assets including a personal residence [see ¶400]. When the irrevocable life insurance trust is established, the grantors can name an independent trustee such as a bank or corporate trustee, attorney, or CPA. Alternatively, they could name a trustworthy family member or a reliable family friend. The law even permits the grantor to retain trustee removal powers provided the successor trustee is neither related nor subordinate to the grantors.[1] If the grantors continue to live in the residence after ownership is transferred to the irrevocable life insurance trust, the grantors would have to make fair market value rental payments to the trust. If the grantors decide instead to sell the home after it has been transferred to the irrevocable life insurance trust, the trustee of the QPRT could sell the home and any gain from the sale of the property would be taxable to the grantors. They could partially offset any gain from the sale with the $250,000 or $500,000 exclusion of gain from the sale of a principal residence as provided in IRC Sec. 121. After the sale, the trustee would have two years to buy a replacement property. If the trustee fails to do so, the excess must be distributed to the grantors who must pay tax on the income because the trust is subject to the grantor trust rules as discussed in ¶3100.

---

[1] ¶**704** Rev. Rul. 95-58, 1995-2 CB 191.

¶705 SAMPLE QPRT

In Rev. Proc. 2003-42,[1] the IRS released a sample declaration of trust and alternate provisions that meet the requirements for a QPRT. The sample declaration of trust is designed for a QPRT with one transferor for a term equal to the lesser of the term holder's life or a term of years. The alternate provisions relate to additions to the trust to purchase a personal residence and to the disposition of trust assets on cessation of its qualification as a QPRT. The IRS will recognize a trust as meeting all of the QPRT requirements if: (1) the trust instrument is substantially similar to the sample declaration or properly integrates one or more of the alternate provisions in a document that is substantially similar to the sample declaration; and (2) the trust operates in a manner consistent with the terms of the trust instrument and is a valid trust under applicable local law.

Even though there are some risks associated with transferring a residence into a QPRT, the planning tool still remains an excellent way to remove a taxpayer's home plus appreciation from his or her taxable estate, while allowing the taxpayer to live there as if nothing happened.

---

[1] **¶705** Rev. Proc. 2003-42, 2003-1 CB 993.

PENALTIES IMPOSED ON ESTATE AND GIFT TAX PREPARERS

TABLE OF CONTENTS

¶800 ACCURACY-RELATED PENALTY

Penalties that the IRS could apply for the failure to report a gift or for undervaluing an estate are the accuracy-related penalties of IRC Sec. 6662. The potential penalties involved are the negligence penalty [IRC Sec. 6662(b)(1)] and the valuation understatement penalty [IRC Sec. 6662(b)(5)]. Each of these penalties is imposed at 20 percent of the tax due, and interest runs on the penalty from the date the return was due. The maximum penalty that can be imposed under IRC Sec. 6662 is 20 percent, even if there is more than one accuracy related failure asserted. Negligence includes "any failure to make a reasonable attempt to comply with the tax laws and the term "disregard" includes any careless, reckless, or intentional disregard" [IRC Sec. 6662(c)].

IRC Sec. 6662(b)(5) imposes a penalty on an underpayment that is attributable to a "substantial estate or gift tax valuation understatement," which occurs when the value of any property listed on a return is 65 percent or less of the amount determined to be the correct value [IRC Sec. 6662(g)(1)]. Although the penalty is generally 20 percent, it may be increased to 40 percent if the value of property listed on a gift tax return is 40 percent or less of the amount determined to be the correct valuation amount [IRC Secs. 6662(h)(1) and 6662(h)(2)(C)]. For a discussion of situations where the IRS will waive an accuracy-related penalty if the taxpayer can show that he or she had reasonable cause for the return position and acted in good faith under IRC Sec. 6664(c)(1) and Reg. Sec. 1.6664-4(b)(1), see ¶805.

¶801 PENALTY FOR GROSS VALUATION MISSTATEMENTS

The 40-percent penalty for gross valuation misstatements is imposed where the property value claimed on the return is 40 percent (instead of 65 percent) or less of the correct amount [IRC Sec. 6662(h)(2)(C)].

In *Bergquist v. Commissioner,*[1] the Tax Court held that the doctors who donated stock in their medical practice to a newly formed tax-exempt professional services corporation were only entitled to a small portion of the charitable contribution deductions they claimed and each taxpayer was liable for the 40 percent accuracy-related penalty for gross valuation misstatement because they did not act in good faith and did not make a good-faith investigation as to the value of the donated stock. Despite the taxpayers' claimed reliance on appraisers and advisors, the taxpayers were well-educated and should have been aware of the problems in valuing the stock at so high a price when it was unlikely that the medical group would continue as an operating entity. The appraiser used the "going concern" method to value the stock and the court found that the taxpayers' reliance on this value was unreasonable in light of the facts that the taxpayers knew or had reason to know.

Limitation. No penalty will be imposed on a taxpayer for a substantial valuation understatement unless the portion of the underpayment for the tax year attributable to substantial valuation understatements exceeds $5,000.

¶802 SUBSTANTIAL GROSS VALUATION MISSTATEMENTS ATTRIBUTABLE TO INCORRECT APPRAISALS

A civil penalty is imposed on a person who prepares an appraisal that results in a substantial or gross valuation misstatement [IRC Sec. 6695A(a)]. The appraiser must know or should reasonably have known that the appraisal would be used in connection with a return or a claim for refund.

The same standards in IRC Sec. 6662 (relating to accuracy-related penalties) will be used in determining whether there is a substantial or gross valuation misstatement in an appraisal. For this purpose, a substantial valuation misstatement generally means a value claimed that is at least twice (200 percent or more) the amount determined to be the correct value, and a gross valuation misstatement generally means a value claimed that is at least four times (400 percent or more) the amount determined to be the correct value [IRC Secs. 6662(e) and (h)].

---

[1] ¶801 B.J. Bergquist, 131 TC 8 (2008).

The penalty amount is the lesser of:

1. The greater of $1,000 or 10 percent of the tax underpayment amount attributable to the misstatement; or
2. 125 percent of the gross income received by the appraiser for preparing the appraisal [IRC Sec. 6695A(b)].

The IRS can assess the appraiser a penalty for gross valuation misstatements regarding estate or gift taxes for appraisals prepared after May 25, 2007. A gross valuation misstatement for estate and gift taxes occurs when the claimed property value is 40 percent or less of the correct amount [IRC Sec. 6662(h)(2)(C)]. The appraiser penalty will be applied to situations where the claimed value of the appraised property results in a substantial estate or gift tax valuation understatement under IRC Sec. 6662(g) [IRC Sec. 6695A(a)]. For estate and gift taxes, a substantial valuation understatement occurs if the claimed value of any property on an estate, gift or generation skipping tax return is 65 percent or less of the amount determined to be the correct valuation amount [IRC Sec. 6662(g)(a)].

No penalty is imposed under IRC Sec. 6695A if the appraiser establishes that the appraised value was more likely than not the proper value [IRC Sec. 6695A(c)].

¶803 RETURN PREPARER PENALTIES

A penalty may be imposed against a gift or estate tax return preparer for each tax return or claim for refund that understates the taxpayer's liability due to an unreasonable position. The penalty is the greater of (a) $1,000 or (b) 50 percent of the income derived (or to be derived) by the preparer with respect to the return or refund claim [IRC Sec. 6694(a)]. The standard for undisclosed positions is a "reasonable belief" standard, which requires that:

1. The preparer knew, or reasonably should have known, of the position;
2. There was not a reasonable belief that the tax treatment of the position would more likely than not be the proper treatment; and
3. The position was not disclosed or there was not a reasonable basis for the position.

A reasonable cause exception applies if it is shown that there was a reasonable cause for the understatement and the preparer acted in good faith. The penalty increases to the greater of (a) $5,000 or (b) 50 percent of the income derived (or to be derived) by the preparer with respect to the return or refund claim if the understatement is willful or reckless [IRC Sec. 6694(b)]. The preparer penalty for willful or reckless conduct must be reduced by the amount of any penalty imposed for an unreasonable position relating to the same understatement.

¶804 FRAUD PENALTIES

IRC Sec. 6663 imposes a civil fraud penalty of 75 percent of any underpayment of wealth transfer taxes attributable to fraud [IRC Secs. 6663(a), 6663(b)]. However, if you can establish that part of the underpayment is not attributable to fraud, that portion is not subject to the 75 percent penalty, although it may be subject to the 20 percent accuracy-related penalty under IRC Sec. 6662(g). The portion coming under the 75 percent civil fraud penalty is not also subject to the accuracy-related penalty. The government will either impose the fraud penalty or the negligence penalty, but it cannot collect both. Fraud is defined as the intent to evade a tax the taxpayer knows he or she has an obligation to pay. The burden of proof is on the government to prove fraud.

¶805 REASONABLE CAUSE EXCEPTION TO UNDERPAYMENTS

Neither the accuracy-related penalty under IRC Sec. 6662 nor the fraud penalty under IRC Sec. 6663 is imposed with respect to any portion of an underpayment if it is shown that the taxpayer had reasonable cause for an underpayment and acted in good faith [IRC Sec. 6664(c)(1)].

Good faith/reasonable cause defense. Whether an underpayment of tax is made in good faith and due to reasonable cause will depend upon the facts and circumstances of each case [Reg. Sec. 1.6664-4(b)(1)]. The regulation provides that "the most important factor is the extent of the taxpayer's effort to assess the taxpayer's proper tax liability. Circumstances that may indicate reasonable cause and good faith include an honest misunderstanding of fact or law that is reasonable in light of all of the facts and circumstances, including the experience, knowledge, and education of the taxpayer."

To determine whether a taxpayer acted reasonably and in good faith in valuing property, the following factors should be considered: (1) the methodology and assumptions underlying the appraisal; (2) the appraised value; (3) the circumstances under which the appraisal was obtained; and (4) the appraiser's relationship to the taxpayer [Reg. Sec. 1.6664-4(b)(1)].[1]

Reliance on professional advice as a defense. Reg. Sec. 1.6664-4(b)(1) provides that reliance on professional advice can establish reasonable cause and good faith if, under all the circumstances, such reliance was reasonable and the taxpayer acted in good faith. Courts reviewing application of this safe harbor have said that the taxpayer must prove three things to establish reasonable reliance: (1) that the expert was a competent professional who had sufficient expertise to justify reliance; (2) that the expert provided the taxpayer with necessary and accurate information; and (3) that the taxpayer actually relied in good faith on the expert's judgment.[2]

Special rule for certain valuation overstatements. Effective for returns filed after August 17, 2006, the reasonable cause exception is unavailable for underpayments due to gross valuation misstatements of charitable deduction property unless the claimed value of the property was based on a qualified appraisal made by a qualified appraiser, and the taxpayer made a good faith investigation of the value of the contributed property [IRC Sec. 6664(c)(2)].

---

[1] ¶805 Estate of Giustina, TC Memo 2011-14.
[2] Alen, TC Memo 2013-235; Neonatology Assocs., 115 TC 43 (2000), aff'd, 299 F.3d 1203 (9th Cir. 2005); Giovacchini, TC Memo 2013-27; Charlotte's Office Boutique, Inc., 425 F.3d 1203 (9th Cir. 2005), aff'g 121 TC 89 (2003).

Reasonable cause defined. The determination of whether a taxpayer acted with reasonable cause and in good faith is made on a case-by-case basis, taking into account all pertinent facts and circumstances. Generally, the most important factor is the extent of the taxpayer's effort to assess the taxpayer's proper tax liability. Circumstances that may indicate reasonable cause and good faith include an honest misunderstanding of fact or law that is reasonable in light of all of the facts and circumstances, including the experience, knowledge, and education of the taxpayer. An isolated computational or transcriptional error generally is not inconsistent with reasonable cause and good faith.

Reliance on an information return or on the advice of a professional tax advisor or an appraiser does not necessarily demonstrate reasonable cause and good faith. Similarly, reasonable cause and good faith is not necessarily indicated by reliance on facts that, unknown to the taxpayer, are incorrect. Reliance on an information return, professional advice, or other facts, however, constitutes reasonable cause and good faith if, under all the circumstances, such reliance was reasonable and the taxpayer acted in good faith.

Reasonable cause and good faith ordinarily is not indicated by the mere fact that there is an appraisal of the value of property. Other factors to consider include the methodology and assumptions underlying the appraisal, the appraised value, the relationship between appraised value and purchase price, the circumstances under which the appraisal was obtained, and the appraiser's relationship to the taxpayer or to the activity in which the property is used.

A taxpayer's reliance on erroneous information reported on a Form W-2, Form 1099, or other information return indicates reasonable cause and good faith, provided the taxpayer did not know or have reason to know that the information was incorrect. Generally, a taxpayer knows, or has reason to know, that the information on an information return is incorrect if such information is inconsistent with other information reported or otherwise furnished to the taxpayer, or with the taxpayer's knowledge of the transaction. This knowledge includes, for example, the taxpayer's knowledge of the terms of his employment relationship or of the rate of return on a payor's obligation [Reg. Sec. 6664-4(b)(1)].

The courts generally follow the reasonable cause guidelines set out by the IRS and outlined in the IRS Manual. In determining whether a taxpayer exercised ordinary business care and prudence, the IRS will investigate:

1. The reason the taxpayer took or failed to take the action in question;

2. The taxpayer's compliance history;

3. The length of time between the event cited for noncompliance and subsequent compliance; and

4. Whether the noncompliance was due to circumstances beyond the taxpayer's control (whether the taxpayer could have anticipated the event) [Internal Revenue Manual, 20.1.1.3.1.2, August, 1998].

¶805

¶806 PENALTIES FOR AIDING AND ABETTING UNDERSTATEMENTS OF TAX LIABILITY

A penalty of $1,000 will be imposed on any person:

1. Who aids or assists in, procures, or advises with respect to, the preparation or presentation of any portion of a return, affidavit, claim, or other document;

2. Who knows (or has reason to believe) that such portion will be used in connection with any material matter arising under the internal revenue laws; and

3. Who knows that such portion (if so used) would result in an understatement of the liability for tax of another person [IRC Sec. 6701(a)].

¶807 CRIMINAL FRAUD PENALTIES

Criminal fraud penalties may be imposed on any person for making, assisting in, procuring, counseling, advising, delivering, or disclosing fraudulent returns, statements, or documents. The penalties may reach up to $100,000 for an individual and $500,000 for a corporation, and may include imprisonment for up to three years in addition to the costs of prosecution [IRC Sec. 7206].

¶808 FRAUDULENT RETURNS OR STATEMENTS

Willful delivery or disclosure of fraudulent lists, returns, accounts, statements, or other documents is a misdemeanor, punishable by a fine of not more than $10,000 ($50,000 for corporations), or imprisonment for not more than one year, or both [IRC Sec. 7207]. The same penalty applies to persons who willfully supply false information to the IRS with respect to self-employed persons' retirement plans and to persons who willfully fail to comply with the public inspection requirements for returns of private foundations. Persons willfully failing to comply with the public inspection requirements for tax-exempt organizations, including private foundations, are also subject to the penalty [IRC Sec. 7207].

¶809 FAILURE TO FILE

If a taxpayer fails to file a return when due (including extensions), IRC Sec. 6651(a)(1) imposes a penalty of five percent per month for up to five months, or a maximum of 25 percent. The penalty applies to the amount of tax due but unpaid. If the failure to file is fraudulent, the penalty is increased to 15 percent per month, with a maximum of 75 percent for five or more months [IRC Sec. 6651(f)]. If fraud is asserted, the government must prove the fraud by "clear and convincing evidence" [IRC Sec. 7454(a)]. IRC Sec. 6651(a) provides that failure to timely file a tax return and pay taxes owed will be subject to penalty "unless it is shown that such failure is due to reasonable cause and not due to willful neglect." In order for a taxpayer's illness to constitute reasonable cause excusing a late filing, the taxpayer's serious illness must be of a duration that is commensurate with the failure to timely file the tax return. In *Stine*,[1] the court concluded that a donor's health problems were not severe enough to establish reasonable cause for failure to timely file her gift tax return. The court specifically stated that "episodic or intermittent periods of disability are not sufficient to excuse a late tax filing—the disability must have rendered the taxpayer effectively unable to meet the obligation during the overall period of time relevant to the filing obligation."

¶810 FAILURE TO PAY

A separate failure to pay penalty could also be imposed. In general, the failure to pay penalty is half a percent per month, up to a maximum of 25 percent (for a delinquency of 50 months or more) [IRC Secs. 6651(a)(2) and (3)]. In any month when both the failure to file and the failure to pay penalties are assessed, the maximum penalty per month is five percent (absent fraud). Therefore, over a 50-month period, the total penalty can be as much as 47.5 percent of the tax [IRC Sec. 6651(c)]. These penalties are imposed in addition to any interest due. The penalties can be waived by the IRS on a showing that the failure to file or failure to pay is due to reasonable cause and not due to willful neglect [IRC Sec. 6651(a)]. The taxpayer must prove both to avoid the penalty. A taxpayer has reasonable cause to the extent that he exercised ordinary business care and prudence in providing for payment of his tax liability and was nevertheless unable to pay the tax (or would suffer an undue hardship by paying the tax on time) [Reg. Sec. 301.6651-1(c)(1)]. The Internal Revenue Manual 20.1.1.3.2. (Nov. 25, 2011) states: "Reasonable cause is based on all the facts and circumstances in each situation and allows the IRS to provide relief from a penalty that would otherwise be assessed. Reasonable cause relief is generally granted when the taxpayer exercised ordinary business care and prudence in determining their tax obligations but nevertheless failed to comply with those obligations."

In *Freeman, Exr.*,[1] the court concluded that an estate was liable for penalties and interest under IRC Sec. 6651(a)(1) for its failure to timely file its estate tax return because it did not have reasonable cause for filing the return after the deadline. The executor retained an attorney to represent the estate. However, the executor was unaware that the attorney was suffering from a number of physical and mental disorders, which led the attorney to neglect his duties and file and pay the estate tax three years after the due date. Because the executor's duty to timely file the estate tax return was nondelegable, the failure to file the return before the due date was not excused by the attorney's negligence.

In *Rossman, Exr.*,[2] the court concluded that an estate was liable for the IRC Sec. 6651 late payment penalty for its failure to timely pay the estate tax due. Eight months after the decedent's death, the estate requested and received an extension of time to pay the tax. Two additional extensions of time to pay were requested and granted. Although the estate made periodic payments on the tax due, the estate tax, interest,

---

[1] **¶809** Stein, Fed. Cl., 2012-2 USTC ¶60,655. [2] G. Rossman, Exr., Fed. Cl., 2012-1 USTC
[1] **¶810** T. Freeman, Exr., D.C. Pa., 2012-1 USTC ¶60,638.
¶60,636.

and penalties were not paid in full until almost four years after the decedent's death. The executor claimed that her failure to timely pay the estate tax was due to reasonable cause as a result of her grief from the death of both of her parents, unfavorable market conditions, and her accountant's failure to notify her about the option to elect to pay the estate tax in installments. However, the court found that by making the three timely requests for an extension of time to pay, the executor demonstrated her ability to meet the required standard of "ordinary business care and prudence" under Reg. Sec. 301.6651-1(c)(1). Moreover, since the executor's duty to file and pay the estate tax was nondelegable, the executor's reliance on her accountant did not excuse her from ensuring that the deadline to pay was met.

¶811 LIABILITY OF OTHERS

IRC Sec. 6901 provides for the assessment and collection of gift tax from a recipient or donee of the gifted property. In the case of an "original transferee" who is the donee of a gift, the tax can be assessed within one year after the expiration of the period of limitation for assessment against the transferor [IRC Sec. 6901(c)(1)]. If the period of limitations has not commenced to run because the gift has not been adequately disclosed on a gift tax return, the IRS can assess the tax against the transferee at any time, but typically will only do so if it cannot collect directly from the donor. IRC Sec. 6901 does not create a tax liability on the part of the transferee, only the procedure for assessing and collecting the tax.

TAX-FREE GIFTS

9

TABLE OF CONTENTS

¶900 TRANSFERS EXEMPT FROM GIFT TAX

You only pay tax on your "taxable gifts." They are the total amount of gifts made during the calendar year, less the charitable [see ¶910] and marital deductions [see

¶900

¶1107]. However, certain transfers are not counted as "taxable gifts." These exempt transfers include annual exclusion gifts that allow you to give away up to $14,000 in 2014 to an unlimited number of recipients [see ¶901]. There is also an educational exclusion and a medical exclusion that enable a generous wealthy friend or relative to directly pay someone else's qualifying tuition or medical bills without any gift tax consequences [see ¶908]. An additional tax-exempt gift opportunity is to transfer property to an IRC Sec. 529 College Savings Plan (Qualified State Tuition Program) as discussed further in ¶1708.

(a) The Lifetime Gift Tax Exclusion. The lifetime gift tax exclusion was increased to $5,340,000 in 2014. Therefore, wealthy married donors may give away as much as $10,680,000 to loved ones free of gift tax.

(b) Benefits of Lifetime Gifts.

- **Removal of Appreciation from Estate.** The fundamental motivation for making gifts during a donor's lifetime is to remove from the donor's estate for estate tax purposes the appreciation on and income from the property that is earned after the date of the gift because growth in the value of the gifted property is transferred to the donee totally free of gift and estate taxes. Even though the value of the gifted property is later added back to the donor's taxable estate as adjusted taxable gifts and factors into the estate tax calculation, the appreciation and income on the gifted assets are not included in the estate tax calculation. This aspect of gifting appreciating property can be very beneficial and donors should try to make gifts of their appreciating assets in order to take advantage of this tax-savings opportunity.

  Example 1: Dad owns $250,000 worth of stock which he transfers to his daughter and, as a result of the annual exclusion and the applicable credit amount, pays no gift tax. Dad dies 15 years later when the value of that stock has increased to $1 million. All appreciation subsequent to the date of the gift (from $250,000 to $1 million) has escaped estate and gift tax. If Dad had instead held that stock until his death, all $1 million of value would have been subject to estate tax.

- **Gift Tax Removed from Estate.** Under IRC Sec. 2035(b) if the donor pays gift tax on gifts made during his or her lifetime, the gift tax is not included in the donor's estate unless the gift tax was paid on a gift made within three years of the decedent's death. Thus, if the decedent made gifts in excess of the exclusion amount and paid a gift tax, the gift tax paid is removed from the decedent's estate for estate tax purposes after three years from the date the gift was made.

- **Tax Exclusive Nature of Gift Tax.** Although the gift tax rate is the same as the estate tax rate, it is less expensive from a tax perspective to make a gift than to bequeath the same amount upon death and pay estate tax on that amount. Why? Because gifts are tax exclusive (i.e., only the value of the property given as a gift is taxed), while the estate tax is tax inclusive (i.e., there is an estate tax on the estate tax, as well as on the bequeathed property). Therefore the effective rate of the gift tax is lower than the effective rate of the estate tax.

- **State Estate Tax Avoidance.** Lifetime federal exclusion gifts will save the donor substantial state estate taxes because most states do not impose a gift tax on lifetime gifts or on prior gifts at death.

- **Income Shifting.** Even with the Kiddie Tax, shifting income-producing assets to younger donees in lower income tax brackets will save income taxes. The Kiddie Tax rules provide that the amount of net unearned income of a child meeting certain statutory requirements that exceed an annual inflation-adjusted amount generally is taxed at the parents' highest marginal rate. For the kiddie tax to apply, the child must be younger than the person claiming the child as a qualifying child under IRC Sec. 152(c), and must fall into one of the following categories:

  — The child is younger than 18 years of age at the end of the year;

  — The child is younger than 19 years of age at the end of the year, and the child's earned income is one half or less of the child's support costs; or

  — The child is younger than 24 years of age, the child's earned income is one half or less of the child's support costs, and the child is a full-time student.

  [IRC Sec. 1(g)(2)(A)].

  Net unearned income of a child is the portion of adjusted gross income for the year that is not attributable to earned income, reduced by $1,000 in 2014, and by either (1) the standard deduction amount, which is $1,000 for 2014, or (2) the child's itemized deductions relating to the production of the unearned income. The combination of the $1,000 standard deduction for a child without earned income and the $1,000 used to calculate the net unearned income reported on the kiddie tax return shields $2,000 of a child's unearned income from tax at the parents' tax rate in 2014.

- **No GST.** If the donor allocates generation-skipping transfer tax exemption to lifetime gifts, the gifts and future appreciation will avoid exposure to estate and generation-skipping transfer (GST) tax. For a detailed discussion of the GST, see Chapter 25. The GST exemption amount in 2014 is $5,340,000. For further discussion of the GST tax exemption, see ¶ 2509.

(c) Disadvantages of Lifetime Gifts.

- **Carryover Basis.** The basis of property acquired by gift is the same as it would be in the hands of the donor, increased by the amount of gift tax (if any) paid [IRC Sec. 1015(a)]. This concept is called carryover basis. [For further discussion of the carryover basis rules, see ¶ 103]. Under the carryover basis rules, the basis of property transferred by a decedent to another person becomes the basis in the hands of the recipient; the decedent's basis is "carried over" to the recipient. If the gifted property appreciates, the recipient would face a significant capital gain on a later sale of the gifted property. Therefore, if appreciated assets are gifted and then sold by the donee, a substantial capital gains obligation may be incurred by the donee. On the other hand, under the step-up basis rules, the basis of property acquired from a decedent is stepped-up to the fair market value of the property at the date of the decedent's death [IRC Sec. 1014(a)]. The results produced when the stepped-up basis rules are applied to property acquired from a decedent contrast sharply with the results produced when the basis of property is computed under the carryover basis rules as illustrated in the examples below.

Example 2: When her mother died, Sally received 2,500 shares of ABCo stock from her mother's testamentary trust. At her death, Mother had a basis of $100 per share in the stock, and each share had a fair market value of $1,000. In each of the 2,500 shares received Sally will have a basis stepped up to its date of death value, that is, $1,000. If, upon receipt of her shares, Sally chooses to immediately sell them (assuming the value of each share is still $1,000), she will incur no taxable gain because her basis is equal to the stock's fair market value. Thus, the taxation of the $900 gain per share that had occurred during her mother's lifetime is permanently excused: none of Sally's $2.25 million gain (2,500 shares × $900) will be subject to capital gains tax.

Example 3: Assume the same facts as in the example above, except that Mother gave the 2,500 shares to Sally during her lifetime. The shares will have a carryover basis of $100 and if Sally sells her stock at $1,000 per share, she will incur a taxable gain of $900 per share times 2,500 shares for a total gain of $2.25 million.

- **Donor Loses Income.** When the donor gives away income-producing property, they lose the right to receive that income. This may present insurmountable obstacles to some donors who are reluctant to give up assets that might otherwise be available to them in case of financial emergencies. One way to generate income for the donors even after the assets are gifted away is to make installment sales to grantor trusts which are discussed in more detail below.

- **Donor Loses Control.** Some donors may find it difficult to lose control over their assets that they have spent a lifetime earning.

(d) How to Use the Lifetime Exclusion Amount. There are a number of techniques by which donors can best take advantage of the lifetime exclusion amount as outlined below:

- Pay off children's or grandchildren's home mortgages.

- A donor can fund a lifetime credit shelter trust with the applicable. exclusion amount. The trust can permit discretionary distributions to the client's spouse and/or other beneficiaries. The spouse can serve as trustee and have a limited power of appointment over the trust without causing adverse estate or gift tax consequences.

- Forgive previous loans and note balances on money lent and loans made to children or grandchildren.

- Equalize gifts to different family lines.

- Transfer retained interests such as general partnership interests in a family limited partnership in order to avoid inclusion of the interests in the taxable estate.

- Use the exclusion amount to prepay premiums for life insurance held in irrevocable life insurance trusts.

¶900

- Make outright cash gifts to children to help them pay off debt, start a business or buy a home.

- Make gifts in trust for the benefit of the donor's spouse and children (family trust) keeping in mind that the donor may not retain any powers over the trust and is not a permissible distributee. However, the donor's spouse and children may receive benefits for health, education, maintenance and support. In addition, the spouse could have the non-cumulative right to withdraw the greater of $5,000 or 5 percent of the trust value annually. The spouse could also have an inter vivos or testamentary limited power of appointment to direct trust funds to family members (not including the spouse, his or her estate, his or her creditors, or the creditors of his or her estate). Both spouses could create these trusts but they need to be aware of the reciprocal trust doctrine which will cause the inclusion of the trust assets in the grantor's gross estate under IRC Secs. 2036 and 2038. Reciprocal trusts are two basically identical trusts that are created by two people for the benefit of one another under a common plan.[1] To avoid the application of the reciprocal trust doctrine, the trusts should be created at different times, they should have materially different terms, and they should hold different assets. In addition, one trust could provide that one spouse held a power of appointment that was not granted to the other spouse. In *Estate of Levy*,[2] a husband and wife created mutual trusts naming the other as trustee. The Tax Court determined that the trusts were not interrelated because one spouse held a power of appointment that was not granted to the other spouse. The Tax Court concluded that the limited power of appointment was sufficiently significant as to create two separate and distinct trusts that were not reciprocal.

- Gifts could be made to grantor trusts where the donor is considered the owner or grantor of the trust for income tax purposes if the grantor or certain other individuals retain the powers described in IRC Secs. 674(a), 675 or 678. These gifts provide estate tax savings because the income of the trust is taxable to the grantor and is not considered an additional transfer for gift tax purposes.[3] See ¶ 3100 for further discussion of grantor trusts.

- Make installment sales to grantor trusts. This planning tool, which is often referred to as a "freezing technique," involves the sale by the donor of property at its fair market value to an irrevocable grantor trust in return for an installment note. Since the trust is a grantor trust, it will be disregarded for income tax purposes and no capital gains tax will be due on the sale.[4] In the typical situation, the grantor makes a gift to the trust and this gift of "seed" money should equal at least 10 percent of the value of the assets to be sold to the trust. This gift will use up a portion of the grantor's lifetime gift tax exemption. If the trust is designed as a GST trust, the grantor may allocate a portion of his/her GST exemption to the trust to cover the amount of the seed money gift. The technique freezes the value of the assets in the hands of the donor and when the donor dies, the grantor's estate includes only the value of the promissory note plus any accrued and unpaid interest. In addition, the appreciation in value of the grantor trust assets in excess of the payments required to

---

[1] ¶**900** Lehman, 109 F.2d 99 (2d Cir. 1939).

[2] Estate of Levy, TC Memo 1983-453. See also Ltr. Rul. 200426008.

[3] Rev. Rul. 2004-64, 2004-2 CB 7.

[4] Rev. Rul. 85-13, 1985-1 CB 184.

satisfy the promissory note passes to the remainder beneficiaries free of transfer taxes. However, the assets sold to the grantor trust will receive a carryover basis which can present a capital gains tax exposure if appreciated assets are sold by the grantor trust.

¶901 ANNUAL EXCLUSION GIFTS

IRC Sec. 2503(b) establishes the annual gift tax exclusion which provides that the first $14,000 of gifts made in 2014 to an unlimited number of donees will be free of gift tax as long as the gifts are gifts of a "present interest" rather than future interests. The following chart illustrates the gift tax annual exclusion amounts in effect for transfers made in 1939 through 2014.

Gift Tax Annual Exclusion Amounts

For Transfers Made in:	
1939 through 1942	4,000
1943 through 1981	3,000
1982 through 2001	10,000
2002 through 2005	11,000
2006 through 2008	12,000
2009 through 2012	13,000
2013 and 2014	14,000

Under Reg. Sec. 25.2503-3(b), a gift of a present interest requires that the donee have an "unrestricted right to immediate use, possession, or enjoyment of property or the income from property."[1]

▶ **PLANNING POINTER:** Gifts made during the donor's lifetime under the annual gift tax exclusion will have the most significant estate planning benefit if the donor gives away assets that are expected to appreciate substantially after the date of the gifts. Keep in mind, however, the donee receives the gift with a carry-over basis which is equal the donor's basis. This will result in gain when the donee goes to sell the appreciated asset.

The terms "use, possess or enjoy" connote the right to substantial present economic benefit, that is, meaningful economic, rather than paper rights. Thus, to qualify as a present interest, a gift must confer on the donee a substantial present economic benefit by reason of use, possession, or enjoyment (1) of property or (2) of income from the property. A gift in the form of an outright transfer of an equity interest in a business or property, such as a limited partnership interest, is not necessarily a present interest gift [See discussion at ¶901(d)]. When determining whether a gift is of a present interest, the IRS and the courts must examine all the facts and circumstances as they existed on the date of the gift. Thus, on each date of gift, the estate must show that the donees obtained use, possession, or enjoyment of the property or the income from the property. The donees' ability to use, possess or enjoy the property is spelled out in the trust document or the partnership agreement.

---

[1] **¶901** Fondren, 324 U.S. 18 (1945); Disston, 325 U.S. 442 (1945).

¶901

If you give an individual cash gifts in 2014 that are valued at more than $14,000, you must report the total gifts to the IRS and may have to pay tax on the gifts. Note that the person who received the gift does not have to report the gift to the IRS or pay gift or income tax on its value. Gifts include money and property, including the use of property without expecting to receive something of equal value in return. If you sell something at less than its value or make an interest-free or reduced-interest loan, you may be making a gift [For discussion of exceptions, see ¶ 200].

> **Example 1:** You give your niece a cash gift of $14,000 in 2014. If it is your only gift to her that year, the gift is not a taxable gift because it is excluded from tax by the annual gift tax exclusion.

If the gifts by an unmarried donor to a donee total more than $14,000 in 2014, they are taxable only to the extent they exceed $14,000.

> **Example 2:** You give your 25-year-old daughter $25,000 in 2014: The first $14,000 of your gift is not subject to the gift tax because of the annual gift tax exclusion. The remaining $11,000 is subject to gift tax.

Married donors are allowed to give away up to $28,000 a year in 2014 because each spouse is treated as if he or she had made one-half of the gift [IRC Sec. 2513]. This is called gift splitting. [See ¶ 902 for further discussion of gift splitting].

Why annual exclusion gifts make sense. If you are financially secure, you can significantly reduce your future estate tax bill by taking full advantage of the annual gift tax exclusion. By embarking on an annual gift-giving program, you can effectively deplete the value of your estate that otherwise would be subject to a hefty estate tax bill after your death. When you make annual exclusion gifts you not only remove the value of the gifted assets from your estate, but you also remove from your estate any future appreciation in the value of the gifted property. In addition, under IRC Sec. 2642(c)(1), transfers to grandchildren made as annual gift tax exclusion gifts will not be considered generation skipping transfers and will therefore not be subject to the GST tax. For further discussion, see ¶ 2510.

> **Example 3:** Dad gives $14,000 worth of stock to Son in 2014. Ten years later, when Dad dies, those shares are worth $54,000. The gift removed from Dad's taxable estate includes not only the $14,000 worth of stock but also the $40,000 of appreciation, for a total shifting of $54,000 which otherwise would have been subject to estate tax in Dad's estate.

Another reason an annual program of gift-giving makes sense is that a gift is less costly than a transfer at death. Why? The estate tax is paid out of the property transferred on a "tax inclusive" basis, but the gift tax is paid in addition to the transferred property on a "tax exclusive" basis.

> **Example 4:** Mom is in the 50 percent gift and estate tax bracket. She gives $50,000 to her child and pays a gift tax of $25,000 plus the gift of $50,000. This means that the gift cost her during her lifetime a total of $75,000. If she makes

¶901

the same $50,000 transfer at death, she would need $100,000 ($50,000 estate tax in the 50 percent bracket, plus the gift of $50,000). It costs Mom 25 percent more to make the transfer at death.

Example 5: Mom has a painting she bought at a flea market for $5. The painting is an impressionist masterpiece worth $1 million. She gives it to Son while still alive and he sells it for $1 million. Son's basis in the painting is $5 and he must pay tax on gain in the amount of $999,995. If Mom held the painting until she died and then gave it to Son, his basis would have been $1 million and his tax bill would have been zero.

(a) **Unlimited Number of Donees.** There is no limit on the number of donees for whom an annual exclusion may be taken or the number of years in which it may be taken. If you are wealthy and want to reduce the amount of estate and gift tax your family will have to pay when you die, you can make an unlimited number of annual exclusion gifts per year without owing a dime of gift tax.

For a gift in trust, each beneficiary is treated as a separate person for purposes of the exclusion [Reg. Sec. 25.2503-2(a)]. Thus, a donor who transfers property by gift in trust receives the exclusion for each trust beneficiary having a present interest in trust property.

(b) **Use It or Lose It.** The per donee gift tax exclusion renews annually and there is no carryover of any unused amount. If you fail to take advantage of your annual exclusion in any year, you lose it. This means that you can make an annual exclusion gift on December 31st and make another $14,000 gift to the same donee on January 1st of the following year.

(c) **Present Interest Requirement.** The annual gift tax exclusion is only available for *present*, not future interests in property. When you have the unrestricted right to the immediate use, possession, or enjoyment of property or income from property, you have a present interest in the property [Reg. Sec. 25.2503-3(b)].

Taxpayers claiming an annual exclusion must establish that the transfer in dispute conferred on the donee an unrestricted and noncontingent right to the immediate use, possession, or enjoyment of: (1) property, or (2) income from property so that the donee realizes a substantial economic benefit.

Contrast a present interest with a future interest in property, which is the right to use, possess, or enjoy money or property that will not commence until some future date or time. In general, gifts in trust and gifts of remainder or reversion interests will not qualify for the annual gift tax exclusion because they are future interests [Reg. Sec. 25.2503-3(a)]. An exception exists for certain gifts in trust made to minors. See ¶ 907 for a discussion of trusts for minors. Where the donee's use, possession, or enjoyment of the gifted property is postponed to the happening of a contingent or uncertain future event, such as where distributions of property or income will occur only at the discretion of a trustee or upon joint action of entity interest holders, or where there is otherwise no showing from facts and circumstances of a steady flow of funds from the trust or entity, the gift will fail to qualify for the IRC Sec. 2503(b) annual gift tax exclusion.

In order for the annual per donee exclusion to shelter a gift to a trust, the gift must be of a present interest in the trust.

> **Example 6:** Dad created a trust for Son and Daughter. The trustee was given discretion to distribute the income or accumulate and add it to principal. Transfers to the trust had to be communicated to the beneficiaries immediately, but only Son was given the power, within 90 days after a transfer, to withdraw the lesser of the amount transferred or $14,000 in 2014. The trust qualified for only one $14,000 annual exclusion for Son's interest but not for Daughter's. Reason: Daughter's interest was a future interest, but Son's withdrawal power made his interest a present interest. This withdrawal power, a so-called *Crummey* power, after the leading case approving its use, is discussed at ¶ 906.

As a general rule, the gift of a present right to all the income or principal from a trust (or a specific percentage of trust income or principal) for a defined period of time constitutes a present interest and the annual exclusion is allowed [Reg. Sec. 25.2503-3(b)]. If a gift creates both present and future interests in the same property, the present interest must be valued separately in order to determine the amount of the applicable annual exclusion. The valuation of term interests is discussed in detail at ¶ 1916.

Establishing the existence of a present interest has generated considerable controversy, usually involving the use of a trust. A future interest exists, for example, in the following cases:

1. The property is incapable of producing income. Even the inclusion of a clause in the trust instrument that authorizes the trustee to convert the non-income-producing property into income-producing property is not enough to create a present interest.[2]

2. A trustee can exercise such discretion over the transferred property that the beneficiary has no assurance of any distribution.[3] Thus, if the trustee has unlimited discretion to accumulate income for future distribution to a life income beneficiary, that beneficiary's interest does not constitute a present interest [Reg. Sec. 25.2503-3, Example (1)].

3. A trustee has the power to invade the trust principal and make distributions to the remainder person, in which case the life income beneficiary's interest is incapable of valuation and does not constitute a present interest.[4] However, if an income beneficiary's interest is limited by a spendthrift provision that does not sufficiently restrict the beneficiary's right to demand a present income distribution, then the interest qualifies as a present interest.[5]

The present-future interest problem can also arise whenever the donor attempts to make an indirect gift to a donee. For example, a gift to a corporation and to the

---

[2] Calder, 85 TC 713 (1985).

[3] Ritland, TC Memo 1986-298.

[4] Funkhouser Trusts, TC Memo 1958-222, *aff'd,* 275 F.2d 245 (4th Cir. 1960), *cert. denied,* 363 U.S. 804 (1960).

[5] Rev. Rul. 54-344, 1954-2 CB 319.

¶901

corporation's shareholders represents a gift to the extent of each shareholder's interest in the corporation [see ¶ 201]. The transfer must then be analyzed under the general present-future interest rules. Typically, the gift is a future interest because the shareholders do not have an immediate right to the possession and enjoyment of property until the corporation declares a dividend or liquidates its assets. However, if the donor's spouse is a shareholder, the gift qualifies for the gift tax marital deduction [see ¶ 1200] in proportion to the interest of the donor's spouse in the corporation.

(d) Gifts of LLCs and Other Closely Held Business Interests. In order for the gift/transfer of an ownership interest in a business entity to qualify for the annual gift tax exclusion, the transfer must qualify as a present (rather than a future) interest in property. What that means in the context of the transfer of an interest in an LLC was addressed by the Court of Appeals for the Seventh Circuit in affirming the Tax Court's decision in *Hackl*.[6] The court held that a husband and wife's gifts of units in a limited liability company (LLC) to their children and grandchildren failed to qualify for the annual gift tax exclusion because the gifts did not qualify as present interests. The court reasoned that the donees did not receive an "unrestricted and noncontingent" right to the immediate use, possession, or enjoyment of the transferred LLC units (or the income therefrom). To qualify as a gift of a present interest for purposes of the annual gift tax exclusion, the donee must receive not just vested rights in the transferred property, but a "substantial present economic benefit" from ownership of the property.

The court found that the restrictions in the LLC operating agreement prevented the donees from obtaining a substantial economic benefit from the LLC units because the donees, under the terms of the agreement, could not: (1) unilaterally withdraw their capital accounts; (2) sell or transfer their units without the consent of the LLC's manager; or (3) unilaterally effectuate a dissolution of the LLC. Moreover, there was no expectation that the LLC would produce immediate income and the distribution of any income that was generated was at the discretion of the manager. As a result, the donors were not entitled to the annual exclusions for their gifts of the LLC membership units.

In *Price*,[7] the Tax Court followed *Hackl* to conclude that the transfer of limited partnership (LP) interests by husband and wife donors to their adult children failed to qualify for the annual gift tax exclusion because the children did not have the unrestricted right to the immediate use, possession or enjoyment of their interests in the LP (or the income therefrom). In order to qualify as a gift of a present interest for purposes of IRC Sec. 2503(b), the children were required to receive not just all of the donors' legal rights in the transferred property, but a "substantial present economic benefit" derived from ownership of the property. Pursuant to the agreement, the children were prevented from obtaining a substantial economic benefit because:

- The agreement imposed restrictions on their ability to sell, assign or transfer their partnership interests to third parties without the written consent of all partners;

- The children were not properly characterized as limited partners of the partnership;

---

[6] Hackl, 118 TC 279, *aff'd*, 335 F.3d 664 (7th Cir. 2003).   [7] Price, TC Memo 2010-2.

- The children were not given an immediate unrestricted right to the partnership income because income distributed did not flow "steadily," nor could it be "readily ascertained" as the amount distributed was discretionary;

- The children had no unilateral right to withdraw their capital accounts;

- The children were prohibited from selling, assigning, or transferring their partnership interests to third parties or from otherwise encumbering or disposing of their partnership interests without the written consent of all partners;

- The record fails to establish that any ascertainable portion of the income would flow steadily to the donees. To the contrary, the record shows that the partnership's income did *not* flow steadily to the donees; in fact there were no distributions at all in some years.

Therefore, the donors gifts failed to qualify for the gift tax annual exclusion under IRC Sec. 2503(b) because the transfers were of a future interest rather than a present interest in the underlying property.

In *Fisher*,[8] a husband and wife transferred 4.76 percent membership interests in Good Harbor Partners, LLC to each of their seven children in each of four years. The primary asset of the LLC was an undeveloped plot of lakefront property. The operating agreement stated, in part, that the Fishers formed the LLC primarily to (1) invest in and hold real property; (2) select partners; (3) keep property held by the LLC for use by its members; (4) discourage business disputes among family members; (5) prevent partition of the lakefront property; and (6) protect the lakefront property from creditors. The IRS challenged the annual exclusion gifts alleging that the gifts were not gifts of a present interest.

On the annual exclusion gift issue, the district court held that the gifts did not qualify for the gift tax annual exclusion relying on *Hackl*.[9] Under the terms of the operating agreement, the donees' rights to receive distributions as well as their right to transfer their membership interests were significantly restricted, preventing them from retaining a "substantial present economic benefit" in the property. Thus, the gifts were not gifts of a present interest in the LLC, and failed to qualify for the annual gift tax exclusion under IRC Sec. 2503. The court noted that since the donee was not "entitled unconditionally to the present use, possession, or enjoyment of the property transferred," the gift was one of a future interest.

For example, even though the children had a unilateral right to transfer their interests, those transfers could be made only subject to the LLC's right of first refusal, which effectively prevented them from transferring their interests in exchange for immediate value, unless the transfer was to a family member. Therefore, transfers from the Fishers to their children were transfers of future interests in property and, therefore, not subject to the gift tax exclusion under IRC Sec. 2503(b)(1).

Limited partnership gifts qualified for gift tax exclusion. In *Wimmer*,[10] the decedent and his wife created a family limited partnership with the objective of (1) investing in property, including stock, bonds, notes, securities, and other personal property and real

---

[8] Fisher, 2010-1 USTC ¶ 60,588 (S.D. Ind. 2010).   [10] Estate of Wimmer, TC Memo 2012-157.

[9] See N. 6, 335 F.3d at 667.

estate, on a profitable basis, and of (2) sharing profits, losses, benefits and risks with the partners. The purpose of the partnership was to increase family wealth, control the division of family assets, restrict nonfamily rights to acquire such family assets and, by using the annual gift tax exclusion, transfer property to younger generations without fractionalizing family assets. The partnership was funded with publicly-traded and dividend-paying stock. The partnership received dividends from the stock and made gifts of limited partnership interests pursuant to transfer restrictions prescribed in the trust instrument to family members and to a trust benefiting family members. The Tax Court concluded that these gifts of limited partnership interests made during the decedent's lifetime were gifts of present interests and qualified for the gift tax annual exclusion under IRC Sec. 2503(b) because the estate proved that on the date of each gift: (1) the partnership would generate income, (2) some portion of that income would flow steadily to the donees, and (3) that a portion of income could be readily ascertained.[11]

> ▶ **PRACTICE POINTER:** The following drafting suggestions will make it easier for gifts to qualify for the annual gift tax exclusion:
>
> - Make sure that the partnership owns assets that generate or produce current income;
> - Make sure that the income from the property is distributed to the donee in all years;
> - Make sure that a portion of the income distributed to the donee can be readily ascertainable;
> - Do not include a prohibition on transfers but provide that any transferee will be subject to a right of first refusal, within reasonable time limits;
> - Do not explicitly favor reinvestments over distributions in the partnership agreement;
> - Make distributions annually and predictably;
> - Mandate distributions of net cash flow;
> - Specify that the general partner/manager owes fiduciary duties to the other partners/members;
> - Give donees a *Crummey* withdrawal power with respect to gifts of limited partnership interests that would enable donees to withdraw the fair market value of their limited partnership interests for a limited period of time after each gift. This is obviously an unusual provision to include in a partnership agreement. Such a right would reduce or eliminate any discount for lack of marketability or control with respect to that portion of each gift that qualified for the annual exclusion, but, depending on the context, that may be a modest penalty to pay for the entire elimination of the gift tax on the first $14,000 of gifts to each donee each year;
> - Give donee-partners a limited period of time to sell the interest to the partnership for its fair market value, determined without regard to the existence of the put right.

---

[11] Calder, 85 TC 713 (1985).

¶901

(e) Indirect Gifts Will Not Multiply Gift Tax Exclusion. Some aggressive taxpayers have tried to take advantage of the annual gift tax exclusion by using it as a loophole to avoid paying gift tax. Here's how the scheme works: The donor makes numerous annual exclusion gifts to several recipients who in turn make subsequent transfers to collateral donees who are more closely related to the donor. In reality, these transfers are really indirect transfers totaling more than $14,000 in 2014 to the intended recipients and were structured to avoid gift tax. These indirect transfers will be disallowed for purposes of the annual gift tax exclusion. The courts that have looked at this situation have held that if the transfers are direct in form but not in substance, the taxpayer is liable for the gift tax that would have resulted if the transfer had truly been direct.[12]

> ▶ **PLANNING TIP:** Avoid making annual exclusion transfers to multiple donees who have collateral agreements to transfer the gifts to subsequent donees who are your real intended beneficiaries in an attempt to avoid the payment of gift tax. To maximize use of your annual exclusion each year, keep in mind that the annual exclusion is available each year and you should therefore start an annual gift-giving program early on. In addition, married donors have the opportunity to double their excludable gifts by gift splitting and giving up to $28,000 per donee, in 2014. [See ¶ 902 for further discussion of gift splitting].

Example 7: A donor transfers stock to 29 beneficiaries, who subsequently transfer their shares to the donor's real intended beneficiaries. The original beneficiaries had entered into a collateral agreement to transfer their shares to other people chosen by the donor. These transfers will be viewed as indirect transfers of stock to the collateral beneficiaries done in a manner to avoid payment of gift tax on the transfers and as such will be disallowed by the IRS and the courts.

(f) Gifts of Life Insurance Policies. Whether the transfer of a life insurance policy or the payment of premiums qualifies for the annual per donee exclusion depends on the nature of the rights created or assigned. An outright transfer of the incidents of ownership to one donee, as absolute owner, constitutes the gift of a present interest and, therefore, the annual exclusion is usually available [Reg. Sec. 25.2503-3(a)].

The impact of restrictions on ownership can be seen in the case of a gift of a life insurance policy to more than one donee. Because a single owner cannot exercise all the ownership rights without the consent of his or her co-owners, the gift of a life insurance policy to several donees does not qualify as a gift of a present interest for gift tax exclusion purposes.[13]

Whether post-transfer premium payments made by the insured qualify for the annual gift tax exclusion turns on whether the beneficial owner of the policy has a present or future interest in the policy. If the owner has an unrestricted right to the policy, then

---

[12] Heyen, 731 F. Supp. 1488, *aff'd*, 945 F.2d 359 (10th Cir. 1991); Estate of Cidulka, TC Memo 1996-149; Estate of Bies, TC Memo 2000-338; Estate of Schuler, TC Memo 2000-392, *aff'd*, 282 F.3d 575 (8th Cir. 2002); Sather, TC Memo 1999-309, *aff'd and rev'd*, 251 F.3d 1168 (8th Cir. 2001).

[13] Skouras, 14 TC 523, *aff'd*, 188 F.2d 831 (2d Cir. 1951).

premiums paid on the policy by another would constitute a gift of a present interest, thereby qualifying for the annual exclusion [Reg. Sec. 25.2503-3, Example (6)].

Qualifying for the annual gift tax exclusion for gifts of a life insurance policy to a trust is more difficult than with outright gifts to individuals. For a variety of reasons, the assignment of a policy to a trust generally constitutes a gift of a future interest to the trust beneficiary, making the annual exclusion unavailable[14] [Reg. Sec. 25.2503-3(c), Example (2)]. Why? The lack of dividends under some term insurance policies make them unproductive assets in the hands of a trustee, and thus makes any interest in the trust inherently a future interest. You would get the same result if the trustee could use the dividends of a whole life insurance policy to pay policy premiums because the power would add a contingency to the trust beneficiary's interest in the income from the policy.

A gift of a future interest also exists if the trustee, in his or her discretion, can distribute the policy proceeds between or among named beneficiaries and the trust beneficiaries do not possess any incidents of ownership over the policy. For the same reasons, if a trust owns the policy, the insured's payment of a premium usually constitutes a gift of a future interest to the trust beneficiary, for which the annual exclusion is unavailable.[15]

For a transfer of a policy to an irrevocable life insurance trust to qualify for the annual gift tax exclusion, the trust must be:

1. A trust with *Crummey* powers [see ¶ 906]; or
2. A trust for minors [see ¶ 907].

Both types of trusts may also be used to qualify the payment of premiums for the annual exclusion.

(g) Giving Gifts Under a Power of Attorney. A durable power of attorney authorizes someone to handle your financial affairs if you become disabled or incompetent and are unable to act on your own behalf. The power is labeled "durable" because it is not revoked by incompetence and will continue in effect after your incapacity, permitting continued management of your affairs without the expense or complexity of obtaining authority to act through judicial process. If properly drafted, a power of attorney can authorize the attorney-in-fact (the person you have designated to act on your behalf) to make gifts for you. Thus your practice of making annual exclusion gifts can continue even after you become disabled provided the proper gift-giving language is used. Authorizing the person exercising the power to perform "any and all acts" without even specifically mentioning the power to make gifts may be sufficient.

Keep in mind, however, when considering gift giving under a durable power of attorney that the courts will be suspicious of gifts made by an agent under a durable power of attorney because of the opportunity for fraud and abuse. In fact, if the durable power of attorney does not expressly authorize making gifts, courts are reluctant to imply the existence of gift-giving privileges in the absence of a state statute authorizing such inference. If you intend for your agent to make gifts on your behalf after you have become incapacitated, be sure that your durable power of attorney includes explicit language expressly authorizing the agent to execute gifts on your behalf. You will not

---

[14] Rev. Rul. 79-47, 1979-1 CB 312.   [15] Rev. Rul. 76-490, 1976-2 CB 300.

be able to rely on loose language in a bank-drafted power of attorney to support gift-giving privileges. The courts will only uphold gifts by agents pursuant to durable powers of attorney where the power of attorney expressly authorizes the agent to make the gifts or where state statute implied that such power existed.[16] To be sure that gift-giving made on your behalf will qualify for the annual gift tax exclusion, your power of attorney should specifically give the attorney-in-fact the authority to make gifts on your behalf in order to take advantage of the annual gift tax exclusion. Be sure he or she is authorized "to make gifts in the pattern" you have used during your lifetime.

For example, in one case checks that the taxpayer's son wrote to family members acting pursuant to a durable power of attorney constituted valid gifts even though the power of attorney did not specifically authorize gifts. The gifts qualified because the father had a long history of making annual per donee exclusion gifts to these family members.[17] This history created an implied gift-giving power. The power of attorney contained a general grant of authority, empowering the son "to do, execute and perform all and every act, matter and thing . . . in relation to all or any part of my property, estate, affairs, and business of any kind or description, as fully and amply, and with the same effect, as I, myself, might or could do if acting personally." This broad, unencumbered power was enough to indicate a gift-giving intent.

Keep in mind when creating gift-giving powers under a power of attorney that the IRS and the courts are inherently suspicious of gifts made by a donor who is dead and therefore unable to corroborate or deny the claim. This is especially true when an agent pursuant to a durable power of attorney makes the gift and the opportunity for abuse and the conflict of interest exists. To ward off any claims of abuse, the power of attorney should expressly state that the agent has the authority to make gifts on behalf of the principal in order to take advantage of the annual gift tax exclusion. If the principal has engaged during his or her lifetime in making annual gift tax exclusion gifts, include in the power of attorney language authorizing the agent to make annual exclusion gifts in the pattern used during his or her lifetime. Failure to include these few sentences could have costly repercussions because gifts that fail to qualify for the annual gift tax exclusion will be included in the decedent's taxable estate.

For example, one court concluded that 38 deathbed gifts in the amount of $10,000 each made under a durable general power of attorney were void because the authority to make the gifts was not expressly authorized in the document and therefore the gifts were includible in the decedent's taxable gross estate under IRC Sec. 2038(a)(2).[18]

> **Example 8:** When Mom's health began to fail, she granted a durable general power of attorney to her nephew. The durable general power of attorney gave the nephew the legal authority to manage and dispose of Mom's property and to conduct business on her behalf. It was broad in the authority and discretion it purported to invest in the nephew and he had the sole discretion to determine

---

[16] Estate of Frank, TC Memo 1995-132; Townsend, 889 F. Supp. 369 (DC Neb. 1995); Estate of Pruitt TC Memo 2000-287.

[17] Estate of Ridenour, TC Memo 1993-41, *aff'd,* 36 F.3d 332 (4th Cir. 1994).

[18] Estate of Swanson, 2000-1 USTC ¶60,371 (Ct. Fed. Cl. 2000), *aff'd,* 2001-1 USTC ¶60,408 (CAFC 2001). See also Estate of Gaynor, TC Memo 2001-206.

¶901

when to invoke the powers conferred by the document. Shortly before her death, Mom's nephew wrote, signed and delivered 38 checks from her accounts to 38 separate individuals in the amount of $10,000 each. The nephew stated that the idea for the $10,000 checks arose in a discussion with Mom about minimizing the impact of the wealth transfer taxes on her estate. The nephew came up with a list of 40 potential recipients for the gifts and from her hospital bed, Mom approved of 38 of them by nodding her head when he read her each individual's name. She died a few days later. The court concluded that the deathbed gifts made under the durable general power of attorney were void because the power to make gifts was not expressly authorized in the document and that power could not be implied or inferred under state law. The court found that Mom's act of nodding approval at the names as her nephew read them to her was insufficient to ratify his act of writing $380,000 worth of checks from her accounts. According to the court, Mom or her estate could have recalled the gifts at any point. IRC Sec. 2038(a)(2) therefore draws the gifts back into the estate and the checks are includible in her taxable gross estate. The court acknowledged that although the power of attorney gave the nephew significant powers to manage and convey Mom's real and personal property, it could not give him the power to make gifts without expressly doing so.[19]

¶902 GIFT SPLITTING

Suppose your spouse does not have sufficient funds in his or her own name to take advantage of the annual gift tax exclusion. Does his or her annual gift tax exclusion go to waste? Absolutely not.

IRC Sec. 2513 allows a married couple to treat a gift to a third person as if each spouse had made one-half of the gift. In other words, when one spouse makes a gift to a third party with his or her own money, the IRC permits the nondonor spouse to join in the gift as if the nondonor spouse had put up the money for one-half of the gift. This is called gift splitting.

> **Example 1:** Mom gives $28,000 to Son in 2014. Dad consents to gift splitting. As a result, Mom is treated as if she gave Son $14,000 and Dad is treated as if he gave Son $14,000. No gift tax is owed that year because the annual per donee exclusion allowable to each spouse applies to the gift even though Mom put up all the money.

(a) Purpose. The gift-splitting option provides an excellent opportunity for spouses to double the amount of the annual exclusion available for a gift. An annual lifetime giving program can be an effective way of reducing the value of your taxable estate after you have died. By engaging in gift splitting, a married couple can take advantage of each spouse's annual gift tax exclusion.

---

[19] *Id.*

(b) Requirements. The gift-splitting provisions require the filing of an election for each calendar year in which a married couple split their gifts to third persons [IRC Secs. 2513(a) and 2513(b)]. If the spouses consent to gift splitting, all qualifying gifts made by either spouse during the year of the election must be split. The spouses may not pick and choose which gifts to split. Gifts made in previous or subsequent years may not be split unless gift splitting applies for these years. Use of the gift-splitting provision obligates each spouse, jointly and severally, to pay the combined gift taxes owed by both spouses. This means that each spouse is obligated to pay the entire gift tax imposed [IRC Sec. 2513(d)].

There are five requirements that must be satisfied in order to take advantage of the gift-splitting provisions [IRC Sec. 2513(a)]:

1. The donor and nondonor spouse must be married to each other at the time of the gift [IRC Sec. 2513(a)(1); Reg. Sec. 25.2513-1(a)]. If they are divorced during the year, they may still split the gift provided neither is married to anyone else at the end of the calendar year in which the gift takes place;

2. Each spouse must be a citizen or resident of the United States at the time of the gift [IRC Sec. 2513(a)(1); Reg. Sec. 25.2513-1(a)];

3. The donor spouse must transfer the gift to a third party (i.e., not between the spouses);

4. The nondonor spouse must not receive a general power of appointment [see ¶ 205] over the property transferred [IRC Sec. 2513(a)(1)];

5. Both spouses must make or consent to the election on the gift tax return in question. [IRC Sec. 2513(b); Reg. Sec. 25.2513-2(a)(1)]. The election applies to all gifts made by either spouse during the year and cannot be made selectively [IRC Sec. 2513(a)(2)].

An election to split gifts is made at the same time as the gift tax return is due (generally April 15th of the year following the year of the gift) and is irrevocable after that date [IRC Sec. 2513(b)(2); Reg. Sec. 25.2513-3(a)(1)]. See ¶ 1707.

(c) Consent. If both spouses file gift tax returns within the time for signifying consent, it is sufficient if:

1. The consent of the husband is signified on the wife's return and the consent of the wife is signified on the husband's return;

2. The consent of each spouse is signified on his or her own return; or

3. The consent of both spouses is signified on one of the returns [Reg. Sec. 25.2513-2(a)(1)].

If only one spouse files a gift tax return within the time provided for signifying consent, the consent of both spouses must be signified on that return.

If only one spouse has made gifts during the year and the spouses consent to gift splitting, the other spouse need not file a gift tax return provided:

1. The total value of gifts made to any one donee does not exceed $28,000 in 2014; and

2. The property transferred is not a gift of a future interest.

If gifts of a future interest or gifts exceeding $28,000 in 2014 are made to any one donee during the calendar year, then each spouse must file a separate gift tax return [Reg. Sec. 25.2513-1(c)].

(d) Splitting Gifts with a Decedent's Surviving Spouse. The executor of a deceased spouse can consent to gift splitting for gifts made during the year of death [Reg. Sec. 25.2513-2(c)]. Consent can be signified on:

1. The decedent's gift tax return; or

2. On the surviving spouse's gift tax return.

If the executor of a deceased spouse or the surviving spouse files a gift tax return without consenting to gift splitting, such consent cannot be given after the due date of the return [IRC Sec. 2513(b)(2)(A)].

In assessing whether to consent to gift splitting, the executor must consider the possibility of the imposition of additional gift tax liability on undisclosed gifts. If consent to gift splitting is signified in a particular year, the liability for the entire gift tax of each spouse during such year is joint and several [IRC Sec. 2513(d)]. If one of the spouses dies with the gift tax unpaid, the split gift liability can produce an IRC Sec. 2053 deduction for estate tax purposes [see ¶ 2001].

▶ **PRACTICE POINTER:** The executor should consider the following issues when deciding whether to split gifts between spouses:

1. Which spouse actually made the gift;

2. The amount of the unified credit available in each estate;

3. The differing amounts of assets in each spouse's individual estates; and

4. Whether the objective is to equalize the estate of the two spouses or to defer the estate tax.

When no savings to the decedent's estate would result from gift splitting, the surviving spouse should preserve his or her unified credit or low wealth transfer tax bracket by not consenting to gift splitting.

¶903 TRANSFERS TO MINORS

You may give property to minors using one of the following four methods:

1. An outright gift to a minor using the Uniform Transfers to Minors Act (UTMA) [see ¶ 904];

2. Present interest trusts [IRC Sec. 2503(b); see ¶ 905];

3. *Crummey* trusts [see ¶ 906]; and

4. Trusts for minors [IRC Sec. 2503(c); see ¶ 907].

The gift tax consequences that result from these various methods of making a gift to a minor are discussed below.

Compare the following benefits of a trust versus a gift to a minor using the UTMA [see ¶ 904]:

1. Fewer restrictions exist on the types of property that can be given to a minor using a trust.

2. A gift under the UTMA is always irrevocable; a trust can be made revocable if the donor retains control.

3. The donor's administrative powers are specified by the UTMA but designated by the donor in a trust.

4. Investment activities of the trustee and the custodian must both be judged by the "prudent person" standard; however, in most jurisdictions the trust instrument may provide for a more lenient standard providing a trust with more flexible investing powers than a transfer under the UTMA.

5. The UTMA restricts the use of the property to certain categories (e.g., the minor's support, education, and maintenance). Trusts are more flexible and may provide the trustee more discretion over use of the trust's income and principal.

6. The death of the minor under the UTMA causes the property to be distributed to the minor's estate resulting in expensive estate administration and the return of property to the parent-donor by intestacy. A trust may be structured to provide for a disposition without the possibility of reversion to the donor.

7. The trust may stipulate that distribution be postponed beyond age 21. Keep in mind that the UTMA requires distribution at age 21 (or the local jurisdiction's age of majority).

¶904 TRANSFERS UNDER THE UNIFORM TRANSFERS TO MINORS ACT (UTMA)

(a) Basics. In order to facilitate gifts to minors, all 50 states and the District of Columbia have adopted a uniform law regulating gifts to minors. Originally enacted as the Uniform Gifts to Minor Act (UGMA), the uniform law has undergone a series of refinements and has been replaced by the newer version, the Uniform Transfers to Minors Act (UTMA).

The UTMA provides a straightforward and inexpensive approach for making a gift of securities, cash, life insurance policies, or other eligible property to a minor. The transfer instrument must declare that the property is being transferred to an individual "as custodian for the minor-donee under the state Uniform Transfers to Minors Act." By statute, this language incorporates the entire uniform act as enacted in the locality. Thus, no other instrument need be executed.

The UTMA requires the custodian to deliver the custodial property to the minor-donee when the minor attains majority (as defined by local law), or to the minor's estate if the minor dies before reaching majority. The gift is irrevocable and vests legal title in the minor.

Transfers to minors via an UTMA account may be made during life, or through testamentary provisions in a will or revocable living trust of the parent or grandparent. An UTMA account is easy to establish because the terms are set by state law and most banks, credit unions or brokerage firms will have preprinted forms that interested taxpayers can complete to open an account.

An UTMA transfer constitutes a completed gift at the time of the transfer, subject to the gift tax,[1] to the extent of the full fair-market value of the property transferred and is considered a gift of a present interest in property qualifying for the $14,000 in 2014 annual per donee exclusion [see ¶ 901; IRC Sec. 2503(b)]. An UTMA transfer also qualifies for split-gift treatment by a married couple. [See ¶ 902 for discussion of gift splitting].

(b) Income Tax Consequences. Income earned on assets in an UTMA account is generally taxable to the child but it may be subject to the kiddie tax rules if the beneficiary is under age 18 or if the child is age 19-23 and his or her earned income does not exceed 50 percent of the support that he or she receives [see ¶ 900]. However, if a legal obligation to support a minor child is satisfied by the income from the UTMA account, the person with the legal obligation to support the child must recognize the income.[2]

¶ 905 SECTION 2503(b) TRUSTS

The present interest trust [IRC Sec. 2503(b)] combines the benefits of a trust [see ¶ 903] and the annual per donee gift tax exclusion [see ¶ 901]. To qualify for the annual per donee exclusion, property transferred into a trust for a minor-beneficiary must:

1. Constitute a transfer of a present interest (specifically, the unrestricted right to the immediate use, possession, or enjoyment of the income from the trust property); and

2. Have an ascertainable value.

Typically, the minor-beneficiary will be given an income interest for life, or for a defined period, which is paid annually no matter what happens.

The value of the present interest that qualifies for the exclusion equals the present value of the minor-beneficiary's income interest, as determined by reference to actuarial tables for a life estate or term certain [see ¶ 1916]. If the minor's present income interest is incapable of valuation, it will not qualify for the annual per donee gift tax exclusion [Reg. Sec. 25.2503-3(b)].[1]

As a result, if the trustee has an unlimited power to accumulate, rather than distribute, the trust income, the minor-beneficiary's income interest does not constitute a present interest [see ¶ 901]. In addition, if the distribution of income is entirely within the trustee's discretion, there is no present interest. If a trust provides that trust principal may be invaded in order to benefit someone other than the income beneficiary, the minor-income beneficiary does not possess a present interest because of the possibility that the income interest may be reduced and therefore is incapable of valuation.

---

[1] ¶ 904 Rev. Rul. 56-86, 1956-1 CB 449; Rev. Rul. 59-357, 1959-2 CB 212; Rev. Rul. 70-348, 1970-2 CB 193.

[2] Rev. Rul. 56-484, 1956-2 CB 23.

[1] ¶ 905 Funkhouser Trusts, TC Memo 1958-222, aff'd, 275 F.2d 245 (4th Cir. 1960), cert. denied, 363 U.S. 804 (1960).

¶906 TRUSTS WITH *CRUMMEY* POWERS

A trust that gives the trustee discretion to make distributions to a minor child before and after the child attains majority provides flexibility in the distribution of family wealth. Even though the minor child does not have a fixed right to receive distributions, the annual per donee gift tax exclusion is available for transfers to the trust, if the beneficiary is given the unrestricted power to withdraw specified funds from the trust. By using annual exclusion gifts to multiple trust beneficiaries, you can transfer significant wealth without being subject to estate or gift tax.

Thanks to a famous case where the taxpayer's name was Crummey,[1] we are blessed with a valuable estate-planning tool with a funny name that enables you to convert a gift made to a trust, which would otherwise qualify as a future interest, into a "present interest" qualifying for the annual gift tax exclusion. A present interest is an "unrestricted right of the immediate use, possession or enjoyment of property or income from property" [Reg. Sec. 25.2503-3(b)]. All you have to do is give the trust beneficiary the right to demand immediate distribution of money from the trust, even though he or she does not actually exercise the withdrawal right. Typically, the so-called *Crummey* power permits donees to make withdrawals or demand distribution of a particular amount from the trust within a limited time period (e.g., 30 days) after the gift has been made. As long as the power to exercise a withdrawal right exists even for a limited time period, the interest qualifies as a "present interest." It does not matter that, as a practical matter, minor children are unable to exercise the withdrawal right without the appointment of a guardian.

> **Example 1:** Uncle creates a trust for the benefit of his three nieces. When the last surviving niece has died, the trust assets will pass equally to the three girls. In 2014, Uncle gives $50,000 to the trust. Each of the nieces has the right to withdraw $14,000 in 2014 during the 30-day period following the gift. Uncle is entitled to a gift tax exclusion of $42,000.

In fact, in the actual facts of the *Crummey* case, a gift was made in trust for a minor child. This otherwise future interest was converted by the court into a present interest gift eligible for the annual gift tax exclusion because the minor had a legally unrestricted present right to demand that the trustee distribute the property to him free and clear. The transfers in trust were thus gifts of a present interest regardless of the fact that the minors would need a guardian to make the demand.

(a) Beware—The IRS Is Watching. In a broad interpretation of the *Crummey* case, the Tax Court held that a 15-day unrestricted demand right that a grandmother gave to each of her grandchildren who only had contingent remainder interests qualified as a present interest in the trust.[2] What this means is that a trust beneficiary

---

[1] **¶906** Crummey, TC Memo 1966-144, *aff'd and rev'd*, 397 F.2d 82 (9th Cir. 1968); Rev. Rul. 80-261, 1980-2 CB 279.

[2] Estate of Cristofani, 97 TC 74 (1991), *acq.* 1996-2 CB 1. See also Estate of Kohlsaat, TC Memo 1997-212 (gift tax exclusion available to 16 contingent remainder beneficiaries who held Crummey withdrawal rights and no present interest in the trust itself other than the withdrawal rights); Estate of Holland, TC Memo 1997-302.

need not have an absolute right to the money invested in the trust or the income it generates in order to qualify for the annual exclusion.

Even though the IRS issued a formal approval of the result in the case,[3] they also issued a warning to overly creative estate planners. In statements accompanying the approval, the IRS indicated that they intend to challenge aggressively gift tax exclusions arising out of the granting of *Crummey* powers.

The IRS stated that it "does not contest annual gift tax exclusions for *Crummey* powers where the trust instrument gives the power holders a bona fide unrestricted legal right to demand immediate possession and enjoyment of trust income or corpus." However, the IRS intends to deny "the exclusions for *Crummey* powers, regardless of the power holders' other interests in the trust where the withdrawal rights are not in substance what they purport to be in form."

This simply means that you can expect the IRS to take a closer look at your trust if you make contributions to trusts with multiple contingent beneficiaries having *Crummey* powers or with individuals having only *Crummey* powers and no other interests in the trust. They will look behind the form of the Crummey rights to see what their substance really is.

▶ **PRACTICE POINTERS:** A trust containing *Crummey* power provisions for a minor child must satisfy the following requirements:

1. *Be explicit about the guardianship.* Acknowledge that a guardian (the parent, a natural guardian, or a judicially appointed guardian) will be acting on behalf of the minor beneficiary. Be sure that nothing bars the appointment of a guardian for any beneficiary who is a minor child.

2. *Notice required.* Make sure beneficiaries are provided with actual notice[4] of the *Crummey* withdrawal powers and of their right to demand distribution from the trust. The notice should be given within a reasonable time after the date of the gift. An attempt should be made to give notice on the date of the gift transfer. In the case of a minor, the minor's guardian must receive actual notice of the beneficiary's right to demand distribution. The donee cannot waive his or her right to receive notice of the *Crummey* withdrawal rights.[5] In fact, taxpayers should carefully adhere to the *Crummey* requirements. Every time property is contributed to the trust, the donor should deliver written notice to each beneficiary and each beneficiary (or representative, if the beneficiary is a minor) should sign the notice to establish receipt. These documents should be kept with the trust records.

3. *Contents of Crummey Letter.* In order for a gift to a trust to qualify for the annual exclusion, the trust beneficiary must have actual notice of his or her withdrawal right. Otherwise the IRS could challenge the beneficiary's demand

---

[3] IRS Action on Decision (1996-010, 1996-29 IRB 4). The IRS acquiesced in result only. This means that it will continue to challenge, outside the Ninth Circuit where *Cristofani* was decided, *Crummey* powers held by contingent beneficiaries where there was "greater abuse."

[4] See Rev. Rul. 81-7, 1981-1 CB 474.

[5] Technical Advice Memorandum 9532001.

right as illusory.[6] This requirement can be satisfied by providing the beneficiary with written notice (called the *Crummey* Letter) which should include:

a. A statement that a gift was made to the trust for the benefit of the beneficiary;

b. The amount of the gift subject to the beneficiary's demand right;

c. The demand right exercise period;

d. A request that the beneficiary notify the trustee if the beneficiary wishes to exercise the demand right;

e. An attached acknowledgment with instructions that the beneficiary sign and return the acknowledgment, in order to provide documentation of the beneficiary's receipt of the notice.

Although written notice is always preferable, the IRS has concluded that actual notice suffices as long as the beneficiary has actual knowledge of the demand right.[7] However, in the absence of written notice, the donor-taxpayer bears the difficult burden of proof of proving that the beneficiary had actual knowledge of the demand right.[8]

4. *Give the beneficiary enough time to exercise withdrawal right before it lapses.* The beneficiary or his or her guardian must be afforded adequate time to exercise the withdrawal right. To play it safe, give the beneficiary at least 30 days to exercise the withdrawal right.[9] The IRS has approved *Crummey* withdrawal powers as short as 15 days in *Cristofani*[10] and as long as 60 days[11] and 90 days.[12] However, a three-day demand right was held to be insufficient in Rev. Rul. 81-7.[13] It is preferable for the lapse time of the withdrawal power to begin to run on the date of the gift transfer rather than the date of the notice. The IRS has indicated that a trust instrument created and funded on December 29 that gave a legally competent adult beneficiary the power to demand principal through December 31 of the same year did not qualify as a present interest eligible for the annual gift tax exclusion because it failed to afford the beneficiary sufficient time to exercise the withdrawal right.[14] The period during which the beneficiary can exercise the demand right should begin immediately on the date of the transfer, rather than on the date of notice.

5. *Avoid prearranged understanding.* No annual gift tax exclusion will be available if beneficiaries sign statements when the trust is created waiving not only their rights to withdraw the initial gift, but also their rights to receive notices regarding their rights to withdraw future gifts.[15]

6. *Make sure beneficiaries have more than just* Crummey *powers.* To avoid IRS scrutiny, trust beneficiaries with *Crummey* powers must have more than just the one-year

---

[6] Rev. Rul. 81-7, 1981-1 CB 474.

[7] Ltr. Ruls. 8008040, 8022048 and 9030005.

[8] Estate of Holland, TC Memo 1997-302; Ltr. Rul. 9030005.

[9] Ltr. Rul. 9030005; TAM 8901004; Ltr. Ruls. 200130030, 200123034, 200011054, 199912016 and 9311021.

[10] Estate of Cristofani, 97 TC 74 (1991), *acq.* 1996-2 CB 1.

[11] Ltr. Rul. 7939061.

[12] Ltr. Rul. 8044080.

[13] Rev. Rul. 81-7, 1981-1 CB 474.

[14] TAM 9628004; Rev. Rul. 81-7, 1981-1 CB 474.

[15] Rev. Rul. 85-24, 1985-1 CB 329; Rev. Rul. 81-7, 1981-1 CB 474; Ltr. Rul. 9532001.

power to withdraw annual trust contributions. They must have some beneficial interest in the trust. A slim chance that they will get some money some day if 10 other people do not get it first will not suffice. The IRS has held that a donor's transfers to eight trusts with seventeen different beneficiaries only qualified for the gift tax annual exclusion with respect to four of the trust's beneficiaries, even though all the beneficiaries were given the power to withdraw specified amounts during a one-year period starting on the date a contribution was made to the trust. The remaining beneficiaries were contingent beneficiaries, remotely contingent beneficiaries, or beneficiaries that had no other interest in the trust except for the one-year power to withdraw.[16] A contingent beneficiary only gets the money if others in line ahead of him do not get it all first.

7. *Funds in trust should be adequate to satisfy demand.* The trust funded with annual exclusion gifts should have sufficient assets that can be withdrawn by beneficiaries exercising their *Crummey* withdrawal rights. If the assets are unavailable to satisfy the potential claims, the IRS could argue that the withdrawal rights are mere illusory rights designed to avoid transfer taxes.

8. *Make sure that the Crummey withdrawal rights are enforceable and not merely illusory.* In Chief Counsel Advice 201208026, each beneficiary was given a right of withdrawal of an amount of property transferred to the trust based on the gift tax annual exclusion amount, but the trustee could void the right for any additions made to the trust. Furthermore, in accordance with the trust instrument, a beneficiary was not permitted to enforce his withdrawal right in a state court. If a beneficiary sought to enforce his or her withdrawal right, the beneficiary's interest in the trust would be terminated. Due to the threat of severe economic punishment if enforcement was pursued through a civil suit, the IRS found the withdrawal right to be illusory. Because the withdrawal rights under a trust instrument were not legally enforceable and, therefore, were not present interests, the gift tax annual exclusion was not allowed under IRC Sec. 2503(b)].

(b) The 5 or 5 Power. You can avoid having a current gift result from the lapse of a withdrawal power by limiting the beneficiary's withdrawal power in any one year to the greater of $5,000 or 5 percent of the property available to satisfy the withdrawal power [IRC Secs. 2514(b), 2514(e)]. Here is why it works.

The donor's transfer of property to a trust containing *Crummey* powers is viewed under the general rules relating to the taxation of a gift. What is unique about the *Crummey* power is the beneficiary's demand right. This demand right constitutes a general power of appointment. The release of a general power of appointment represents a gift of that property by the holder of the power [IRC Sec. 2514(b)]. The lapse of a general power of appointment is treated as a release and, therefore, as a taxable transfer to the extent that the value of the property subject to the power exceeds the greater of the following amounts:

1. $5,000; or

2. 5 percent of the aggregate value of the assets out of which, or the proceeds of which, the exercise of the lapsed power could be satisfied [IRC Sec. 2514(e)].

---

[16] TAM 9731004.

¶906

This is referred to as the "5 or 5 power." If the minor income beneficiary's power (demand right) extends to more than $5,000 or 5 percent of the trust principal and if the income beneficiary fails to exercise the power, that lapse will be deemed a gift, to the extent of the excess, to the other beneficiaries of the trust [see ¶205].

> **Example 2:** Grandpa creates a *Crummey* trust for the benefit of Son and transfers $10,000 to the trust. If Son had a right to demand $10,000, the lapse of the demand right would create a taxable gift of a future interest in the amount of $5,000. When Son receives both the income from and, eventually, the principal of the *Crummey* trust, no deemed transfer will result because one cannot make a completed gift to one's self. However, where the trust instrument provides for contingent remainder persons, as is usually the case, a deemed transfer of a taxable future interest by the beneficiary to such contingent remainder persons will result.

(c) Hanging Powers. If you want to make more than a $5,000 gift to a trust to pay the premiums on an insurance policy and avoid a lapse problem as illustrated in the example above, you would have to take advantage of hanging powers. These are powers that "hang around" until they can be used up. Here is how they work.

If you make a $25,000 *Crummey* gift per donee per year, each year the greater of $5,000 or 5 percent of the trust corpus will lapse after the 30-day withdrawal period. This lapsed part will not be a gift because it is simply disregarded. The withdrawal period for the remainder is just suspended or postponed until the 30-day withdrawal period the following year. This process goes on until the suspended remainder is all used up.

> **Example 3:** Alice contributes $10,000 to a trust in the first year for the sole benefit of her son, Jack. Jack's power to demand $10,000 can lapse as to $5,000 ($5,000 is greater than 5 percent of the value of the trust assets). The remaining $5,000 balance hangs over for future years. In the second and third years, if Alice contributes another $10,000 in each of the two years, in each of these years, Jack's power can lapse as to $5,000 with $5,000 hanging over. At the end of three years, a total of $15,000 would be left hanging over. If Alice subsequently contributes nothing else to the trust, Jack's power to demand payment is not measured by current contributions of additions to the trust, but by the 5 or 5 limitation applied to the $15,000 left hanging over. If Jack lives long enough for the annually lapsing 5 or 5 limitation to reduce the $15,000 to zero, Jack will not have made a taxable gift.

¶907 THE SECTION 2503(c) MINOR'S TRUST

IRC Sec. 2503(c) was enacted to permit transfers of a present interest to minors in trust. As a result, gifts in trust can be made to minors and still qualify for the gift tax exclusion without the minor needing a *Crummey* withdrawal right.

In order to qualify for the present interest exclusion for transfers to minors under IRC Sec. 2503(c), a trust must meet three requirements:

1. Both the transferred property and its income must be able to be expended by, or for the benefit of, the minor-beneficiary before he or she attains age 21. The terms of the trust may not impose any "substantial restrictions" upon the trustee's discretion to determine the amount of income or property distributed and the purposes for which the expenditure is made [Reg. Sec. 25.2503-4(b)];

2. Any unexpended balance of the property and its income must pass to the beneficiary when he or she attains age 21;

3. If the beneficiary dies before age 21, any unexpended balance of the property and its income must be payable to the beneficiary's estate (not the minor's descendants, heirs, or next of kin) or as the beneficiary may appoint under a testamentary general power of appointment even though the minor under local law cannot execute a valid will and thus cannot exercise the power [Reg. Sec. 25.2503-4(b)].

If a transfer in trust meets these requirements, it will qualify for the annual per donee gift tax exclusion.

The "no substantial restriction test" mentioned in Item 1 above will be satisfied if the trust property may be spent during the beneficiary's minority as necessary for the "support, care, education, comfort and welfare" of the child.[1] If, on the other hand, a trustee is required to consider the child's other available resources before distributing any trust corpus or income to him or her, the gift tax exclusion will be lost.[2] The annual exclusion will be lost in that situation because the trust instrument will contain a condition precedent that would substantially restrict the trustee's power to use the property for the minor's benefit.

The second requirement directs that the interest must pass to the beneficiary when he or she reaches 21 years of age. This has been interpreted to allow the beneficiary to extend the trust to a later date on reaching 21 and/or to allow the trust to contain language to require the beneficiary to give a written demand to terminate the trust within 30 days of his or her 21st birthday. If notice is not given, the trust would then continue until as provided in the trust instrument or until the beneficiary gives written notice to terminate the trust.[3]

> ▶ **PLANNING TIP:** *Compare Sec. 2503(c) trusts and UTMA trusts.* A Sec. 2503(c) trust may be preferable for the following reasons:
>
> 1. There are no restrictions on the property that may be transferred into a Sec. 2503(c) trust. Only gifts of securities, money, life insurance policies, or other eligible property may be transferred to an individual "as custodian for the minor donee under the state UTMA."
>
> 2. Under many state UTMA statutes, property must be distributed at age 21, which is the age of majority. The Sec. 2503(c) trust allows for post age-21 distributions.

---

[1] ¶ **907** Rev. Rul. 67-270, 1967-2, CB 349.
[2] Rev. Rul. 69-345, 1969-1 CB 226.

[3] Rev. Rul. 74-43, 1974-1 CB 285; Heidrich, 55 TC 746 (1971), *acq.* 1974-1 CB 2.

¶907

¶908 EXCLUSION FOR PAYMENTS OF EDUCATIONAL/MEDICAL EXPENSES

If you pay for someone else's education or pay their medical bills, you need not be concerned with any potential gift tax consequences. These acts of generosity are not subject to gift tax and do not use up any of your exclusions or exemptions [Reg. Sec. 25.2503-6(c)]. Unlike the annual per donee exclusions [see ¶901], no dollar limit exists on qualified educational or medical expense transfers [IRC Sec. 2503(e)]. This very effective and relatively easy estate reduction tool is a gift from Congress that taxpayers often overlook. Failure to take advantage of it just means that loved ones will have to pay more estate tax down the road.

> **Example 1:** Grandma pays the private school tuition and college tuition for her four grandchildren ($200,000) as well as the health insurance for the whole family ($50,000). She has removed $250,000 from her estate free of transfer tax and has used up none of her annual exclusion or her exemption equivalent available if she dies that year. The best news is that she can do it every year and reduce her taxable estate with no lawyer involvement or gift tax cost.

(a) Educational Expense Exclusion. All amounts that are paid on behalf of an individual as tuition directly to a qualifying educational institution to be used exclusively for the education or training of designated individuals are eligible for the unlimited gift tax exclusion [IRC Sec. 2503(e)(2)(A)]. The tuition exclusion applies to tuition expenses of full-time or part-time students. The tuition must be paid directly to the educational organization providing the education [Reg. Sec. 25.2503-6(b)(2)].

The exclusion for educational expenses applies to tuition for any educational organization, including nursery, elementary, secondary schools, colleges and universities. However, the exclusion does not cover books, rent, board, and other living expenses. The individual may be a full-time or part-time student [Reg. Sec. 25.2503-6(b)(2)]. A qualifying educational organization is an organization with a regular faculty and curriculum and a regularly enrolled body of students in attendance at the place where the educational activities are carried on [IRC Sec. 170(b)(1)(A)(ii)]. The school may be either domestic or foreign.

The payments must be made directly to the educational institution. Payments made by the donor to the donee who uses them (or is reimbursed) to pay for tuition at the school will fail to qualify for the gift tax exclusion.

Payments made to a trust with terms requiring the trustee to use the trust funds to pay tuition expenses will not qualify for the IRC Sec. 2503(e) exclusion because the payments are not a direct transfer to an educational organization. Reg. Sec. 25.2503-6(c), Example 2, considers a situation where a donor transfers $100,000 to a trust which requires the trustee to use the trust funds to pay tuition expenses for the donor's grandchildren. The example concludes that the donor's transfer to the trust is not a direct transfer to an educational organization and therefore fails to qualify for the unlimited gift tax exclusion available to taxpayers who pay for someone else's education.

¶908

In Letter Ruling 200602002, the IRS concluded that the prepaid tuition payments made by a grandmother directly to her grandchildren's private school qualified as tax-free gifts under IRC Sec. 2503(e)(2)(A) even though most of the payments were for tuition for years other than the year in which the payment was made because: (1) the prepaid tuition payments made by the grandmother were made directly to the school; (2) the agreements between the grandparent and the school provided that the prepayments were to be used for the payment of specified tuition costs for each designated grandchild; and (3) the payments were not refundable and would be forfeited if a respective grandchild did not attend the school.

▶**PRACTICE TIPS:** Unlike the annual per donee exclusion, which is limited to $14,000 per year per donee in 2014, no dollar limit exists on qualified educational expenses if payments are made directly to the school and are earmarked for the payment of a specific person's tuition [IRC Sec. 2503(e)]. Taxpayers with serious health problems or who have a shortened life expectancy and want to reduce future estate taxes and also pay the future tuition bills of loved ones can rely on Letter Ruling 200602002 to support making prepaid tuition payments to the educational institutions, provided the funds are earmarked for the tuition expenses of loved ones. By taking advantage of this technique they have accomplished a variety of objectives:

1. The prepaid tuition payments will be free of transfer tax;
2. These funds will be permanently removed from their taxable estate;
3. Their loved one's tuition worries are over;
4. The donors have avoided generation-skipping transfer taxes on the transfers;
5. The multiyear tuition prepayments fall outside the radar of the IRS because these gifts need not be reported to the IRS on any form or return;
6. The taxpayer's annual gift tax exclusion amount ($14,000 in 2014) is still available for other gifts even after the donor has made the multiyear tuition prepayments thus increasing the amount that the donor can remove from his or her taxable estate; and
7. The multiyear tuition prepayment technique is relatively easy to use because the donor has no need to hire an attorney to draft expensive and complicated documents in order to take advantage of this gift tax reduction tool.

Example 2: Dad, a widower, has one married daughter who has three children in college. Their total tuition for one year equals $120,000. Dad can pay his grandchildren's tuition free of gift tax provided he sends the tuition directly to the college. If he had transferred $120,000 to his daughter and son-in-law so they could pay the bills, only $28,000 would qualify for the annual per donee exclusion. However, the remainder would be subject to gift tax, forcing Dad to use up some of his unified credit or to pay gift tax [see ¶ 1400].

(b) Medical Expense Exclusion. Transfers qualifying under the medical expense exclusion [IRC Sec. 2503(e)] are limited to medical care expenses as defined under IRC Sec. 213(d). This includes amounts spent for the diagnosis, cure, mitigation, treatment, or prevention of disease, or for the purpose of affecting any structure or function of the body. In addition, transportation and certain lodging expenses necessary for medical care are included. You cannot, however, pay for medical treatment for cosmetic purposes unless the cosmetic surgery is to correct disfigurement due to birth defect, accident, or disease [Reg. Sec. 25.2503-6(b)(3)].

(c) Insurance Premiums Qualify. Keep in mind that a taxpayer can pay someone else's health care insurance premiums with no gift tax cost and without using up any of their annual exclusion or exemption equivalent. The big thing to keep in mind is that the insurance premiums and medical expenses must be paid directly to the medical service or care provider and not to an intermediary. Keep in mind, however, that the exclusion does not apply to amounts that the insurance company reimburses [Reg. Sec. 25.2503-6(b)(3)].

(d) Anyone Can Use the Exclusion. The educational or medical exclusion can be used by grandparents and other relatives, including parents, aunts, and uncles. You don't even have to be related to the person for whom gift-tax free medical or tuition payments are made because the education and medical exclusions exist without regard to the relationship between the donor and the donee.

▶**TAX RETURN TIP:** Transfers to educational organizations and for medical expenses do not have to be reported as gifts on Schedule A of IRS Form 709.

(e) Why This Provision Should Be Taken Advantage Of. You should take advantage of the tax-free ability to make unlimited payments for tuition and medical expenses of loved ones for the following reasons:

- You are investing in future of your loved ones;
- Your efforts will be greatly appreciated;
- No lawyers or accountants are involved;
- No expensive documents need be drafted;
- No actuarial tables need be consulted;
- You are reducing your taxable estate after you die with no estate or gift tax consequences die; and
- No gift tax return is required if you make qualified payments of tuition and medical expenses.

¶909 EXCLUSION FOR LOANS OF QUALIFIED WORKS OF ART

If you loan a "qualified work of art" (i.e., any archeological, historic, or creative tangible personal property) to an IRC Sec. 501(c)(3) organization that will use the work of art in furtherance of its exempt function, the loan is not treated as a transfer for gift tax purposes and therefore is not subject to gift tax [IRC Sec. 2503(g)].

Example 1: Darlene loans her Picasso painting to a local museum so they can include it in an upcoming Picasso exhibit. The transaction is not a transfer subject to gift tax.

¶910 DEDUCTION FOR CERTAIN TRANSFERS TO CHARITY

IRC Sec. 2522 provides that outright gifts made by a citizen or a permanent resident of the United States to, or for, the benefit of a qualified charity are deducted from the donor's taxable gifts. For charitable gifts by nonresident noncitizens, see ¶ 1500.

Generally, a qualified charity for the gift tax deduction falls into three basic categories:

1. The first category tracks the definition of a charity for federal income tax purposes [IRC Sec. 170(c)], namely, a religious, charitable, scientific, literary or educational organization or a governmental body organized to serve a public purpose. The organization's earnings cannot benefit a private shareholder or individual.

2. The second category covers fraternal organizations organized through a lodge system, provided the gifts are used exclusively for religious, charitable, scientific, literary, or education purposes.

3. The third category is devoted to U.S.-based nonprofit veteran groups [IRC Sec. 2522(a)].

Gifts to a charity in which the charity is the sole beneficiary receive an unlimited deduction for all outright transfers. The charitable deduction for federal gift tax purposes applies after the annual per donee gift tax exclusion, if applicable, has been deducted from the gift [IRC Sec. 2503(a)]. Thus, a gift of $16,000 to a university by an unmarried donor during the present calendar year is viewed as follows: the first $14,000 in 2014 is excluded from federal gift tax under the annual per donee exclusion [see ¶ 901] and the next $2,000 is subject to the unlimited gift tax charitable deduction.

Transfers subject to condition or power. If, at the date of the gift, a transfer to a qualified charity is contingent on a future act or occurrence, the deduction is allowed only if it is virtually certain that the transfer will become effective and the contingency can be ignored. Also, if the donee (or the trustee) possesses the power to direct any part of the property for a nondeductible use or purpose, only the part of the property not subject to this power is deductible [Reg. Sec. 25.2522(a)-2(b)].

CHARITABLE AND SPLIT INTEREST TRANSFERS

TABLE OF CONTENTS

Donors can transfer unlimited amounts to charities either during life or at death free of wealth transfer tax. Lifetime transfers are shielded from tax by the gift tax charitable deduction [see ¶910] and transfers at death are exempted by the estate tax charitable deduction [IRC Sec. 2055; Reg. Sec. 20.2055-1(a)]. IRC Sec. 2055(a) allows a federal estate tax deduction for the value of assets transferred to or for the use of a charitable organization operating exclusively for religious or charitable purposes. However, IRC Sec. 2055(c) reduces the charitable deduction by the amount of any federal and/or state death taxes payable out of the assets allocated to the charitable bequest. Only the value of assets actually going to the charity is eligible for the tax deduction.[1]

¶1000 VALUE OF RESTRICTIONS IMPOSED ON CHARITABLE BEQUESTS

The value of the taxable estate is determined by deducting from the value of the gross estate the amount of all bequests, legacies, devises, or transfers to or for the use of any corporation organized and operated exclusively for religious, charitable, scientific, literary, or educational purposes, including the encouragement of art. The estate may claim a charitable deduction provided: (1) no part of the contribution inures to the benefit of any private shareholder or individual; and (2) the contribution is not used to attempt to influence legislation or intervene in any political campaign on behalf of (or in opposition to) any candidate for public office.

Reg. Sec. 20.2055-1(a) provides that a deduction is allowed under IRC Sec. 2055(a) for the value of property included in the decedent's gross estate and transferred by the decedent to certain charitable entities. In general, the amount allowable as an estate tax charitable deduction under IRC Sec. 2055 is the fair market value of the property passing to charity without restriction. Under certain scenarios, however, this value may not be the same as the value included in a decedent's gross estate under IRC Sec. 2033. For example, the imposition of restrictions or other limitations imposed on charitable contributions of property may result in a reduction in the value of the charitable bequest and consequently a reduction in the amount of the charitable deduction.[1] In these situations, property encumbered by some restriction or condition limiting its marketability or use must be valued in light of this limitation. Not all restrictions, however, that are imposed on donees will result in a reduction of the charitable deduction. Carefully drafted restrictions on charitable bequests will have no impact on the value of the charitable bequest. For example, in Letter Ruling 200202032, the IRS concluded that despite the imposition of numerous restrictions on a charitable bequest of an art collection, the allowable estate tax charitable deduction was equal to the full fair market value of the artwork includable in the donor's gross estate. The following three factors were identified by the IRS to support this result:

---

[1] **Ch. 10** Estate of Bradford, TC Memo 2002-238.

[1] **¶1000** Ahmanson Foundation, 674 F.2d 761 (9th Cir. 1981), *on remand,* 733 F.2d 623 (9th Cir.

1984); Estate of Schwan, TC Memo 2001-174; Rev. Rul. 85-99, 1985-2 CB 83.

1. The museum could not be divested of its ownership of the collection;

2. The only restriction on the sale of works of art in the collection was that the use of the sale proceeds was limited to the acquisition of works of art that are typified by the collection and are equal to the value of the de-accessioned work of art; and

3. The museum was not prohibited from loaning works of art as long as the loans are made on a temporary basis in accordance with the museum's standard operating policies.

These restrictions, which the IRS accepted as not resulting in a reduction in the value of the charitable bequest, will serve as a model for other taxpayers imposing restrictions on future charitable bequests.

An estate tax charitable deduction is allowed for transfers to four types of beneficiaries where the contribution is used by:

1. The United States, any state, political subdivision of the state, or the District of Columbia, for exclusively public purposes [Reg. Sec. 20.2055-1(a)(1)];

2. Any corporation or association organized and operated exclusively for religious, charitable, scientific, literary, or educational purposes, including the encouragement of art and the prevention of cruelty to children or animals, or to foster national or international amateur sports competition without providing athletic facilities or equipment [Reg. Sec. 20.2055-1(a)(2)];

3. A trustee, or a fraternal society, order, or association operating under the lodge system if the transferred property is to be used exclusively for religious, charitable, scientific, literary, or educational purposes or for the prevention of cruelty to children or animals [Reg. Sec. 20.2055-1(a)(3)]; or

4. Any veterans' organization incorporated by Act of Congress, or any of its departments, local chapters, or posts [IRC Sec. 2055(a); Reg. Sec. 20.2055-1(a)(4)].

¶1001 CONSERVATION EASEMENTS

An estate tax deduction is also allowed for certain perpetual easements and restrictive covenants given to a qualified charitable organization or to the government for exclusively conservation purposes [IRC Sec. 2055(f); Reg. Secs. 20.2055-2(e)(2)(iv), 1.170A-14]. In order for this type of transfer to qualify for a deduction, the recipient must be either a governmental unit or a publicly supported charity [Reg. Sec. 1.170A-14(c)]. A conservation easement is a voluntary burden or restriction placed on the use of land, which is created to protect the land from future development. Typically, a donor and a charitable organization enter into a written agreement describing the restrictions that will limit the types of uses and activities that may be performed on the land. The agreement is recorded in the real estate records.

The deduction is not limited, in the case of estates of citizens or residents of the United States, to transfers to domestic corporations or associations, or to trustees for use within the United States [Reg. Sec. 20.2055-1(a)]. Furthermore, the deduction is not subject to the percentage limitations applicable for income tax purposes [Reg. Sec. 20.2055-1(a)]. However, the deduction cannot exceed the value of the property included in the decedent's gross estate [IRC Sec. 2055(d)].

If a transfer to a qualified charity depends on some act or occurrence, a deduction is allowable only if it is virtually certain that the transfer will become effective.

If the donee or trustee has the power to divert any part of the property or fund for a use or purpose that is not deductible, only the portion of the property or fund not subject to this power is deductible [Reg. Sec. 20.2055-2(a)].

The estate tax charitable deduction is limited to the amount actually available for charitable uses. If under the terms of a will or the provisions of local law, the federal estate tax or any other death tax is payable, in whole or in part, out of property transferred as a charitable deduction, the deduction equals the amount of the transferred property reduced by these taxes [IRC Sec. 2055(c); Reg. Sec. 20.2055-3].

¶1002 QUALIFIED CONSERVATION EASEMENT EXCLUSION

IRC Sec. 2031(c)(9) provides that the IRC Sec. 2055(f) conservation easement deduction is allowable even if the executor or the trustee of a trust holding the land grants the qualifying easement after the decedent's death so long as it is granted before the due date (with extensions) for filing the federal estate tax return. However, in the case of a qualified conservation easement contributed after a decedent's death, the estate tax deduction is allowed only if no income tax deduction is allowed to the estate or the qualified heirs with respect to the post-death grant of the conservation easement [IRC Sec. 2013(c)(9)].[1]

(a) Procedures. The election is made by: (1) filing Schedule U with a timely filed Form 706 (including extensions); (2) including all required information; and (3) excluding the applicable value of the land that is subject to the easement on Form 706. The transferee of land subject to a conservation easement that is acquired at death receives a carryover basis, to the extent that the value of land is excluded from the taxable estate. Once made, the election is irrevocable. To avoid the risk of audit and litigation, the donor of a conservation easement should be sure to obtain a qualified appraisal of the donated property.

(b) Amount of Exclusion. The executor is allowed to make an irrevocable election to exclude from the decedent's gross estate up to 40 percent (the "applicable percentage") of the value of the land that is subject to a qualified conservation easement. The executor must compute the "applicable percentage" when determining the amount of the decedent's conservation easement deduction [IRC Sec. 2013(c)(1)]. The applicable percentage means 40 percent reduced, but not below zero, by two percentage points for each percentage point (or fraction thereof) by which the value of the qualified conservation easement is less than 30 percent of the value of the land [IRC Sec. 2013(c)(2)]. For this purpose, the value of the land is determined without regard to the value of the easement and reduced by the value of any retained development rights. As a result, if the value of the easement is 10 percent or less of

---

[1] ¶**1002** S. Rep. No. 105-174, 105th Cong. 2d
Sess. 160 (1998).

¶**1002**

the value of the land before the easement, less the value of any retained development rights, the applicable percentage will be zero.

The maximum amount that may be excluded is $500,000 for decedent's dying in 2002 or thereafter [IRC Sec. 2031(c)(3)].

> **Example 1:** Dad owned 200 acres of forestland in Montana. He donated a conservation easement on 100 acres of the forestland in 2006. The easement reduces the value of the land from $2 million to $1 million. When Dad dies in 2014, the land is an asset included in his estate with a value of $1 million as a result of the easement. If the land had not been subject to the easement, it would have been worth $2 million. The easement therefore has a value of $1 million. This is greater than 30 percent of the property without the easement. Dad's executor is thus entitled to exclude 40 percent of the easement-protected value of the land or $400,000 (40 percent × $1 million). Even though the exclusion limit is $500,000, only $400,000 may be excluded from his estate.

(c) Definition of "Land" Subject to Easement. The exclusion for a qualified conservation easement will be available for: (1) qualified real property that is located in the United States or any possession of the United States; (2) that was owned by the decedent or a member of the decedent's family during the three-year period ending on the date of the decedent's death; and (3) is subject to a qualified conservation easement granted by the decedent or a member of the decedent's family [IRC Sec. 2031(c)(8)(A)].

Date used to determine values. The values used in calculating the value of the property subject to the easement and the value of the easement will be determined as of the date of the taxpayer's contribution [IRC Sec. 2031(c)(2)]. This clarification of the date used for determining the amount of the exclusion was made permanent for the estates of decedent's dying after December 31, 2012 by the American Taxpayer Relief Act of 2012.

(d) Ownership Requirements. To qualify for the exclusion, the land must have been owned by the decedent or by a member of his or family for the three-year period ending on the date of the decedent's death. Members of the decedent's family include the decedent's spouse; ancestors; lineal descendants of the decedent, lineal descendants of the decedent's spouse, and of the parents of the decedent; and the spouse of any lineal descendant. A legally adopted child of an individual is considered a child of the individual by blood [IRC Sec. 2031(c)(8)(D); IRC Sec. 2032A(e)(2)].

An interest in a partnership, corporation, or a trust will qualify for the exclusion provided at least 30 percent of the entity is owned, directly or indirectly, by the decedent [IRC Sec. 2031(c)(10); IRC Sec. 2057(e)(3)].

The IRS has concluded that a decedent's estate will be allowed an estate tax charitable deduction for the value of a conservation easement attributable to a tenancy in common interest includible in the decedent's gross estate.[2] At death, the decedent possessed a 68.8 percent beneficial interest in real estate titled in the name of a trust, with the

---

[2] Ltr. Rul. 200143011.

remaining interests held by two other individuals. The decedent's estate was permitted to claim the charitable deduction, despite the income tax deductions taken by the two other co-owners of the property, because: (1) the value of their interests was not included in the decedent's gross estate and was not subject to the election available for conservation easements; and (2) no estate tax charitable deduction was claimed for the conservation easement granted with respect to their property interests.

(e) "Qualified Conservation Contribution" Defined. To qualify for the exclusion, a (1) "qualified real property interest" must be contributed to a (2) "qualified organization" (3) "exclusively for conservation purposes" [IRC Sec. 2031(c)(8)(B); IRC Sec. 170(h)(1)]. Each of these terms of art will be discussed in detail below.

(f) "Qualified Real Property" Interest Defined. A "qualified real property interest" means either:

1. The entire interest of the donor, other than a qualified mineral interest;

2. A remainder interest; or

3. A restriction granted in perpetuity on how the land may be used [IRC Sec. 170(h)(2)]. The restriction must include a prohibition on anything more than a *de minimis* use of the land for commercial purposes [IRC Sec. 2031(c)(8)(B)]. Hopefully, the IRS will issue regulations describing in more detail what constitutes a *de minimis* use.

Contributed property must be debt-free. Debt-financed property is not eligible for the exclusion [IRC Sec. 2031(c)(4)(A)]. Debt-financed property is property with an acquisition indebtedness on the date of the decedent's death. Acquisition indebtedness includes the unpaid amount of:

1. Indebtedness incurred by the donor in acquiring the property;

2. Indebtedness incurred before the acquisition of the property if such indebtedness would not have been incurred but for such acquisition;

3. Indebtedness incurred after the acquisition of the property if such indebtedness would not have been incurred but for such acquisition and the indebtedness was reasonably foreseeable at the time of acquisition; and

4. The extension, renewal, or refinancing of an acquisition indebtedness [IRC Sec. 2031(c)(4)(B)].

(g) "Qualified Organization" Defined. The donation of a conservation easement must be made to a "qualified organization." Reg. Sec. 1.170A-14(c)(1) provides that the organization must (1) have a commitment to protect the conservation purposes of the donation, and (2) have the resources to enforce the restrictions. A conservation group organized or operated primarily or substantially for one of the conservation purposes specified in IRC Sec. 170(h)(4)(A) (listed above) will be considered to have the requisite commitment. The regulation expressly provides that the qualified organization need not set aside funds to enforce the restrictions that are the subject of the contribution. Included in the definition of "qualified organization" are governmental units, which include the United States, the District of Columbia, and the states and their political subdivisions. Also included are publicly-supported charities as defined in IRC Sec. 509(a)(1).

(h) "Conservation Purpose" Defined. A conservation easement will be considered to be have been granted for a conservation purpose if it furthers one or more of the following goals as articulated in IRC Sec. 170(h)(4)(A) and Reg. Sec. 170A-14(d):

1. the preservation of land areas for outdoor recreation by, or the education of, the general public;

2. the protection of a relatively natural habitat of fish, wildlife, or plants, or a similar ecosystem;

3. the preservation of open space (including farmland and forest land) where such preservation is—

   i. for the scenic enjoyment of the general public, *or*

   ii. made pursuant to a clearly delineated federal, state, or local government conservation policy that will yield a significant public benefit;

   or

4. the preservation of a historically important or a certified historic structure.

Public recreation or education. The donation of a qualified real property interest to preserve land areas for the outdoor recreation of the general public or for the education of the general public will meet the conservation purposes test [IRC Sec. 170(h)]. Thus, conservation purposes would include, for example, the preservation of a water area for the use of the public for boating or fishing, or a nature or hiking trail for the use of the public. The preservation of land areas for recreation or education will not meet the test of this section unless the recreation or education is for the substantial and regular use of the general public [Reg. Sec. 1.170A-14(d)(2)(i) and (ii)].

Protection of significant natural habitat. The donation of a qualified real property interest to protect a significant relatively natural habitat in which a fish, wildlife, or plant community, or similar ecosystem, normally lives will meet the conservation purposes test of IRC Sec. 170(h). The fact that the habitat or environment has been altered to some extent by human activity will not result in a deduction being denied under this section if the fish, wildlife, or plants continue to exist there in a relatively natural state. For example, the preservation of a lake formed by a man-made dam or a salt pond formed by a man-made dike would meet the conservation purposes test if the lake or pond were a natural feeding area for a wildlife community that included rare, endangered, or threatened native species [Reg. Sec. 1.170A-14(d)(3)(i)].

Significant habitats and ecosystems include, but are not limited to, habitats for rare, endangered, or threatened species of animals, fish, or plants; natural areas that represent high quality examples of a terrestrial community or aquatic community, such as islands that are undeveloped or not intensely developed where the coastal ecosystem is relatively intact; and natural areas which are included in, or which contribute to, the ecological viability of a local, state, or national park, nature preserve, wildlife refuge, wilderness area, or other similar conservation area [Reg. Sec. 1.170A-14(d)(3)(ii)].

Limitations on public access to property will not render the donation nondeductible. For example, a restriction on all public access to the habitat of a threatened native animal species would not cause the donation to be nondeductible [Reg. Sec. 1.170A-14(d)(3)(iii)].

Open space preservation. The donation of a qualified real property interest to preserve open space (including farmland and forest land) will meet the conservation purposes test of this section if such a preservation is (1) pursuant to a clearly delineated federal, state, or local governmental conservation policy and will yield a significant public benefit, or (2) for the scenic enjoyment of the general public and will yield a significant public benefit [Reg. Sec. 1.170A-14(d)(4)(i)].

Scenic easements. A contribution made for the preservation of open space may be for the scenic enjoyment of the general public if development of the property would impair the scenic character of the local rural or urban landscape or would interfere with a scenic panorama that can be enjoyed from a park, nature preserve, road, water-body, trail, or historic structure or land area, and such area or transportation way is open to, or utilized by, the public. "Scenic enjoyment" will be evaluated by considering all pertinent facts and circumstances germane to the contribution. Regional variations in topography, geology, biology, and cultural and economic conditions require flexibility in the application of this test, but do not lessen the burden on the taxpayer to demonstrate the scenic characteristics of a donation under this paragraph. The application of a particular objective factor to help define a view as "scenic" in one setting may in fact be entirely inappropriate in another setting.

Reg. Sec. 1.170A-14(d)(4)(ii)(A) provides that the following factors should be considered when determining whether a view over any given property qualifies as scenic:

- The compatibility of the land use with other land in the vicinity;
- The degree of contrast and variety provided by the visual scene;
- The openness of the land (which would be a more significant factor in an urban or densely populated setting or in a heavily wooded area);
- Relief from urban closeness;
- The harmonious variety of shapes and textures;
- The degree to which the land use maintains the scale and character of the urban landscape to preserve open space, visual enjoyment, and sunlight for the surrounding area;
- The consistency of the proposed scenic view with a methodical state scenic identification program, such as a state landscape inventory; and
- The consistency of the proposed scenic view with a regional or local landscape inventory made pursuant to a sufficiently rigorous review process, especially if the donation is endorsed by an appropriate state or local governmental agency.

To qualify for a scenic conservation purpose, the public must have visual (rather than physical) access to or across the property.

Easements pursuant to a governmental conservation policy. An easement that preserves open space must be pursuant to a clearly delineated federal, state, or local governmental policy. A general declaration of conservation goals by a single official or legislative body is not sufficient. The governmental conservation policy need not, however, identify particular lots or small parcels of individually owned property. In Reg. Sec.

1.170A-14(d)(4)(iii), the IRS provides that this requirement will be met by donations that further a specific, identified conservation project, such as the preservation of land within a state or local landmark district that is locally recognized as being significant to that district; the preservation of a wild or scenic river; the preservation of farmland pursuant to a state program for flood prevention and control; or the protection of the scenic, ecological, or historic character of land that is contiguous to, or an integral part of, the surroundings of existing recreation or conservation sites. A program need not be funded, but it must involve a significant commitment by the government with respect to the conservation project.

Impact of agency's acceptance. Acceptance of an easement by a government agency will not necessary mean that the IRS will find that the conservation purposes test has been satisfied. The IRS will take into account the government agency's review process. Reg. Sec. 1.170A-14(d)(4)(iii)(B) provides "the more rigorous the review process by the governmental agency, the more the acceptance of the easement tends to establish the requisite clearly delineated governmental policy."

Significant public benefit. In Reg. Sec. 1.170A-14(d)(4), the IRS provides that all contributions made for the preservation of open space must yield a significant public benefit. Public benefit will be evaluated by considering all pertinent facts and circumstances germane to the contribution. Among the factors to be considered are:

- The uniqueness of the property to the area;
- The intensity of land development in the vicinity of the property (both existing development and foreseeable trends of development);
- The consistency of the proposed open space use with public programs (whether federal, state or local) for conservation in the region, including programs for outdoor recreation, irrigation or water supply protection, water quality maintenance or enhancement, flood prevention and control, erosion control, shoreline protection, and protection of land areas included in, or related to, a government approved master plan or land management area;
- The consistency of the proposed open space use with existing private conservation programs in the area, as evidenced by other land, protected by easement or fee ownership by organizations, in close proximity to the property;
- The likelihood that development of the property would lead to or contribute to degradation of the scenic, natural, or historic character of the area;
- The opportunity for the general public to use the property or to appreciate its scenic values;
- The importance of the property in preserving a local or regional landscape or resource that attracts tourism or commerce to the area;
- The likelihood that the donee will acquire equally desirable and valuable substitute property or property rights;
- The cost to the donee of enforcing the terms of the conservation restriction;
- The population density in the area of the property; and
- The consistency of the proposed open space use with a legislatively mandated program identifying particular parcels of land for future protection.

The IRS notes that there is a connection between the "clearly delineated governmental policy" and "significant public benefit." Reg. Sec. 1.170A-(d)(4)(vi)(A) provides that although the two requirements must be met independently, the two requirements may also be related. The more specific the governmental policy with respect to the particular site to be protected, the more likely the governmental decision, by itself, will tend to establish the significant public benefit associated with the donation. For example, while a statute in State X permitting preferential assessment for farmland is, by definition, governmental policy, it is distinguishable from a state statute, accompanied by appropriations, naming the X River as a valuable resource and articulating the legislative policy that the X River and the relatively natural quality of its surroundings be protected. On these facts, an open space easement on farmland in State X would have to demonstrate additional factors to establish "significant public benefit." The specificity of the legislative mandate to protect the X River, however, would by itself tend to establish the significant public benefit associated with an open space easement on land fronting the X River.

Preservation of historic land areas or structures. The preservation of historic land areas or certified historic structures is the final permissible conservation purpose but since both the estate tax deduction under IRC Sec. 2055(f) and the estate tax exclusion under IRC Sec. 2031(c) can be claimed only if the conservation purpose is one other than historic preservation, this purpose will not be addressed in this treatise.

(i) Post-Mortem Easements. A post-mortem easement is defined as an easement that is donated by a decedent's executor, trustee, and/or the devisee of the property after the decedent has died. A post-mortem easement may be created even if the decedent failed to donate a conservation easement during his or her lifetime or upon death [IRC Secs. 2031(c)(8)(A)(iii), 2031(c)(8)(C) and 2031(c)(9)]. A post-mortem easement could be a valuable estate planning tool in situations where the decedent was either unaware that conservation easements were available under the law or if he or she was aware but failed to actually donate the conservation easement prior to death. Both of these instances could be addressed if the decedent's personal representative makes a post-mortem donation of a conservation easement.

The post-mortem donation of a conservation easement must be made within 15 months of the date of the decedent's death (assuming a six-month extension has been obtained prior to the nine-month Form 706 filing deadline). In addition, the executor must make the irrevocable conservation easement election on Schedule U of Form 706 within 15 months of the decedent's death provided the extension has been obtained.

Disclaimers are one of the post-mortem tools that could be used to make gifts of conservation easements.

Property passing to a charitable beneficiary as a result of a qualified disclaimer by the person to whom the property was devised also qualifies for the charitable deduction [Reg. Sec. 20.2055-2(c)(1); see Chapter 12 for a discussion of disclaimers]. Thus, the charitable deduction is allowed for amounts that are transferred to charitable organizations as a result of qualified disclaimers or the complete termination of a power to consume, invade, or appropriate property for an individual's benefit. The termination must occur within the time period (including extensions) for filing the decedent's estate tax return but before the power is exercised.

¶1003 CHARITABLE SPLIT INTERESTS

If taxpayers leave interests in the same property to both charitable and noncharitable beneficiaries providing an income interest to one and a remainder to the other, special requirements must be met in order to claim a charitable deduction.

Charitable lead trust. In the case of a charitable lead interest (CLT), the income interest must be a guaranteed annuity or a unitrust interest (i.e., a fixed percentage of the fair-market value of the property, determined and distributed yearly).

Charitable remainder trust. In the case of a charitable remainder interest (CRT), the income interest must be either a charitable remainder annuity trust (CRAT), a charitable remainder unitrust (CRUT), or a pooled income fund [IRC Sec. 2055(e); Reg. Sec. 20.2055-2]. These various types of transfers can be set up so that charitable-minded individuals can benefit their favorite charities and save estate taxes.

The IRS issues special tables for taxpayers to use in figuring the amount of the estate and gift tax deduction for these various charitable lead and charitable remainder interests. The tables change monthly based on changes in interest rates. The deduction can be figured using the table for the month in which death occurs or the table for either of the two prior months, whichever produces the largest deduction.

The split interest rule, requiring charitable split interests to be in specified forms, does not apply to the following type of transfers:

1. Transfers (not in trust) of a remainder interest in your personal residence or a farm; or

2. Transfers to an undivided portion of your entire interest in property [Reg. Sec. 20.2055-2(e)(2)(I), 20.2055-2(e)(2)(I)(ii), 20.2055-2(e)(2)(I)(iii)]. For a more detailed discussion of these special charitable split interests, see ¶¶ 1007 and 1008.

   NOTE: If the transfer of a charitable remainder interest in a personal residence or farm is in trust, the trust must comply with the split interest rule (e.g., a charitable remainder annuity trust or unitrust).

Perpetual easements and restrictive covenants do not have to be in the specified split interest forms either. In addition, a work of art and its copyright are treated as separate properties [IRC Sec. 2055(e)(4)]. Thus, a work of art can be transferred to certain charitable organizations and its copyright retained without following the split interest rule.

¶1004 CHARITABLE LEAD TRUSTS

When the charitable interest is placed first, the trust is referred to as a charitable lead trust. A charitable lead trust (CLT) is a useful tax strategy that pays income from property to a named charity for the lifetime of a designated individual (often the grantor or the grantor's spouse), after which the remainder interest is distributed to noncharitable beneficiaries, who usually are the donor's children. The charity's interest may be for a set number of years or for the life or lives of certain individuals living on the date the trust was created. A CLT is a great way to save estate and gift taxes while also leaving money to a charity and ultimately passing the assets on to family members at the end of the term of the required payments to charity, provided the grantor's family does not need the money immediately.

A properly drafted CLT generates a gift or estate tax charitable deduction for the present value of the charity's lead interest and possibly an income tax deduction equal to the present value of the amounts that must be paid to qualifying charities from the CLT during its term if the grantor is treated as the owner of the entire trust under the grantor trust rules [IRC Sec. 170(f)(2)(B); Reg. Sec. 1.170A-6(c)(1)]. Note that this income tax deduction may only be claimed in the year the CLT is established and that the donor receives no income tax deduction in subsequent years. However, the donor can carry forward any part of the deduction not used in the first year for an additional five years. During the term of the trust, the donor will be taxed on the income of the trust, despite the fact that he or she does not receive this income because it is distributed to the charity.

To qualify for estate or gift tax charitable deductions, the CLT must be in the form of:

- A charitable lead annuity trust (CLAT); or
- A charitable lead unitrust (CLUT) [IRC Sec. 2522(c)(2)(B)].

In a CLAT, the periodic payments to qualifying charities take the form of a guaranteed annuity, which the trust instrument can describe as either a fixed amount or a fixed percentage of the initial fair market value of the assets transferred to the CLAT. The CLAT pays a percentage of the value of its trust assets, determined annually, to a named charity for the charitable term. For example, if a CLAT held assets worth $10 million and provided for a guaranteed annuity of 5 percent paid annually, qualifying charities would receive $500,000 from the CLAT each year. The guaranteed annuity would remain unchanged whether the value of the assets of the CLAT decreased to $9 million or increased to $11 million [Reg. Sec. 20.2055-2(e)(2)(vi)].

In a CLUT, the periodic payments to qualifying charities are a fixed percentage of the fair market value of the assets of the CLUT determined annually. For example, if a CLUT had $10 million worth of assets and provided for a unitrust interest of 5 percent to be paid annually, qualifying charities would receive $500,000 in that year. If the value of the CLUT's assets decreased to $9 million, the unitrust payment would fall to $450,000 for that year, but if the value increased to $11 million, the unitrust payment would increase to $550,000 for that year [Reg. Sec. 20.2055-2(e)(2)(viii)(a)].

Impact of actuarial tables on CLTs. The IRS has updated its actuarial tables to reflect the new mortality data produced by the latest U.S. census. The value of life estates, term interests, remainders, and reversions for estate, gift, and income tax purposes is generally determined under tables promulgated under IRC Sec. 7520. The valuation depends on both an actuarial factor dependent on life expectancies and an interest factor. The new data reflects an increased life expectancy for all persons under age 95. Since a CLT pays an annuity or unitrust amount to named charities for the lifetime of a designated individual with the remainder interest going to designated individuals or trusts, the increased longevity under the new actuarial tables increases the value of the charity's annuity or unitrust interest and decreases the value of the noncharitable remainder interest. Therefore, the value of the deductions for a gift to a CLT will be increased because it is based on a longer life expectancy of the designated individual.

¶1004

(a) How the CLT Works. To qualify for a charitable deduction for gift or estate tax purposes, the CLT, whether in the form of a CLAT or CLUT, must satisfy the following basic elements:

- An irrevocable trust valid under state law (the governing instrument) must be created;

- Assets such as money, artwork, or securities must be transferred to the irrevocable trust;

- When a CLAT is created, the donor is treated as having made a gift to the noncharitable beneficiaries equal to the present value of the remainder interest at the time the trust is created. The value of the CLAT's remainder interest is determined by referring to IRS tables based on the relevant AFR at the time of the gift (or during either of the two months immediately preceding the gift);

- Nothing will be included in the donor's estate at death provided the donor does not retain any interest or control over the CLAT. The donor cannot therefore act as the trustee of the CLAT;

- The decedent receives an estate tax charitable deduction for the present value of the lead interest which is equal to the total value of the property transferred to the CLAT minus the present value of the lead interest owned by the charity;

- A qualifying income interest in the form of a guaranteed annuity or charitable unitrust must exist. Any amounts payable for a private purpose before the expiration of the charitable annuity or unitrust interest either must be in the form of a guaranteed annuity or unitrust interest, or must be payable from a separate group of assets devoted exclusively to private purposes [Reg. Secs. 1.170A-6(c)(2), 20.2055-2(e)(e), 25.2522(c)-3(c)(2)]. Each year, annual payments must be made from the trust to the designated charity;

- For tax purposes, the IRS uses a set rate to project the trust's growth. This determines the taxable gift that will pass to the heirs. If the trust grows beyond that amount, the gains will pass to heirs tax-free. To eliminate gift tax entirely on the assets passing to family members at the termination of the charity's interest, planners try to "zero-out" the trust, which means that the trust is structured so that the annual charitable payouts equal the original value of the assets put into trust;

- The governing instrument must have language that:

    — Prohibits the trust from engaging in actions which under IRC Sec. 508(e) would cause a private foundation to be taxed for federal income tax purposes (e.g., self-dealing); and

    — Restricts the use of the income of the charitable component of the trust to exclusively charitable purposes [Reg. Secs. 25.2522(c)-3(c)(2)(vi), 25.2522(c)-3(c)(2)(vii)].

The CLT saves wealth transfer taxes because only the "present value" of the family's remainder interest, rather than the entire value of the assets transferred to the trust, is considered a taxable gift. The amount of the taxable gift is computed by taking the fair market value of the assets transferred to the CLT and reducing it by the gift or estate tax charitable contribution deduction. A zeroed-out CLAT would be created when gift or estate tax is eliminated entirely. A zeroed out CLAT results when the term and guaranteed annuity payment provided under a CLAT are structured so that the present value of the charitable contribution deduction equals the fair market value of the assets transferred to the CLAT.

> ▶ **PRACTICE POINTER:** A basic rule of thumb emerges after you begin working with the government's actuarial factors to compute the value of the remainder interest. The larger the income interest and the longer the trust term, the more valuable the income interest becomes. Reason: the value of the taxable remainder interest diminishes dramatically and gift and estate taxes are likewise reduced.

Example 1: With a charitable trust term of 24 years and a rate of interest of 8 percent per year, the amount of tax savings is astounding. Assume that the trust were funded with $150 million. In this case, the taxable gift made to the trust would only be about $30 million.

Regulations prevent taxpayers from inflating transfer tax deductions for charitable lead trusts by fixing the charity's term to last for the life of an unrelated person who is seriously ill and can be expected to die prematurely. The regulations provide that only one or more of the following individuals may be used as measuring lives: the donor, the donor's spouse, and an individual who, with respect to all noncharitable remainder beneficiaries, is either a lineal ancestor of the spouse or a lineal ancestor of those beneficiaries. A trust satisfies the requirement that all noncharitable remainder beneficiaries be lineal descendants of the individual who is the measuring life, or that individual's spouse, if there is less than a 15 percent probability that individuals who are not lineal descendants will receive any trust corpus [Reg. Sec. 1.170A-6(c)(2); Reg. Sec. 20.2055-2(e)(2); Reg. Sec. 25.2522(c)-3(c)(2)].

Example 2: Alan sets up a CLAT that provides for the annuity to be paid to a charity for the life of Sally, who is age 75, on the date the CLAT is created. On Sally's death, the corpus is to pass to her only child, Bob, who was age 50, when the CLAT was created. If Bob predeceases his mother, the corpus is to pass to Bob's issue then living and if Bob has no living issue at that time, then to his mother's heirs at law (which class could include Sally's siblings, uncles, aunts, nieces, and nephews). Bob has no living children on the date the CLAT is created. Based on Life Table 90CM in Reg. Sec. 20.2031-7, the probability that Bob will predecease his mother, and the trust will pass to individuals who are not lineal descendants of Sally is 10.462 percent, taking into account the interests of remainder beneficiaries living at the time the trust was created. Since the probability that any trust corpus will pass to beneficiaries who are not lineal descendants of Sally is less than 15 percent, the CLAT will satisfy the requirement that all noncharitable remainder beneficiaries are lineal descendants of Sally or her spouse [T.D. 8923].

(b) Impact of Interest Rate Fluctuation on CLATs. The applicable federal rates (AFR) are at historic lows. Similarly, the IRC Sec. 7520 rate used to calculate the estate and gift tax values for many common interest-rate sensitive estate planning techniques are also at historic lows. These low interest rates present planning opportunities for estate planners seeking to assist clients in removing wealth from their estates and passing it tax-free to heirs. The current low IRC Sec. 7520 rates make it a good time to consider establishing a charitable lead trust because the lower interest rate results in a larger charitable income tax deduction for the annuity interest going to the charity and a lower gift tax value for any gift of the remainder interest that passes to family members. Moreover, any appreciation in the value of the charitable lead annuity trust's assets above the IRS's assumed rate of return passes to family members free of gift and estate tax.

Declining interest rates create a favorable economic environment for the creation of CLATs. Here's why: The value of the remainder interest is determined by referring to the term of the trust and the IRC Sec. 7520 rate or AFR for the month in which the trust is established (or the rate for either of the two preceding months). This rate is directly linked to current financial markets and predictions about the overall economy and the fluctuating bond rates. As the AFR goes down, the estate or gift tax deduction for the annuity interest going to the charity goes up and the value of the remainder interest going to the noncharitable beneficiaries after the term of years goes down. This reduces the value of the taxable gift that the donee makes to the noncharitable beneficiaries. An increase in the interest rate decreases the gift or estate tax deduction for the annuity interest going to the charity and increases the value of the taxable gift of the remainder interest going to a private beneficiary.

A rule of thumb is: the lower the AFR rate, the lower the value of the remainder interest and the lower the gift tax bill. If the tax planner couples a lower AFR rate with a long trust term (not advisable for elderly or ill donors), the value of the remainder interest can be significantly reduced. In fact, if the value of the lead interest is equal to the full value of the property transferred to the CLAT, the remainder interest can be reduced to zero. This is called a zeroed-out testamentary CLAT as discussed above. Consider the following three examples which illustrate how varying the AFR and the trust term will change the value of the remainder interest:

1. In the first example, Dad transfers $1 million to a CLAT that pays the charity eight percent annually for ten years. The remainder goes to Son. Assume an AFR of 5.8 percent. The value of the remainder interest in $406,576.

2. In the second example, the facts are the same except that the term of the CLAT is 20 years, the annual payout is 5.5 percent, and the AFR is 5.5 percent. The value of the remainder interest is $343,000.

3. In the final example, the facts are the same except that the term of the CLAT is 20 years and the AFR is 6.2 percent. The IRS tables show that the term certain annuity factor required to yield a zeroed-out CLAT for a 20-year term and a 6.2 percent AFR is 11.285993. Since the value of the lead interest equals the value of the annuity factor multiplied by the amount of the annual payments, the amount of the taxable gift in this zeroed-out CLAT is zero.

    (c) Ordering Provisions. Ordering provisions are often used when CLTs are drafted in order to achieve a desired tax effect. A provision in a trust, will or local law that specifically indicates the source out of which amounts are to be paid, permanently set aside, or used for a charitable purpose must have independent economic effect in addition to its income tax consequences if the allocation is to be respected for federal tax purposes [Reg. Sec. 1.642(c)-3(b)(2)]. If the applicable provision does not have

¶1004

economic effect independent of income tax consequences, income distributed will consist of the same proportion of each class of the items of income as the total of each class bears to the total of all classes [Reg. Sec. 1.643(a)-5(b)].

This rule targets charitable lead trusts which are split-interest trusts with a lead interest paid to charitable beneficiaries and a remainder interest passing to noncharitable beneficiaries. Any amounts that are not paid to charity through the annuity or unitrust payment are taxable to the charitable lead trust. The ordering rules in the charitable lead trust's governing instruments typically provide for the following ordering of classes of annuity or unitrust payment, until the class has been exhausted: (1) ordinary income, (2) capital gains, (3) other income (including tax-exempt income), and (4) corpus. These ordering rules benefit the charitable lead trust because they make certain that taxable income is fully allocated before nontaxable income is allocated. They, therefore, minimize the amount of the trust's income that would be taxed to the trust. The IRS has consistently challenged this ordering regime because, in their view, it does not have economic effect.

> **Example 3:** A charitable lead annuity trust has the calendar year as its tax year, and is to pay an annuity of $10,000 annually to a local charity. A provision in the trust governing instrument provides that the $10,000 annuity should be deemed to come first from ordinary income, second from short-term capital gain, third from fifty percent of the unrelated business taxable income, fourth from long-term capital gain, fifth from the balance of unrelated business taxable income, sixth from tax-exempt income, and seventh from principal. This provision in the governing instrument does not have economic effect independent of income tax consequences, because the amount to be paid to the charity is not dependent upon the type of income from which it is to be paid. Accordingly, the amount to which IRC Sec. 642(c) applies is deemed to consist of the same proportion of each class of the items of income of the trust as the total of each class bears to the total of all classes [Reg. Sec.1.642(c)-3(b)(2), ex. 1].

> **Example 4:** A trust instrument provides that 100 percent of the trust's ordinary income must be distributed currently to a local charity and that all remaining items of income must be distributed currently to a noncharitable beneficiary. This income ordering provision has economic effect independent of income tax consequences because the amount to be paid to the charitable organization each year is dependent upon the amount of ordinary income the trust earns within that taxable year. Accordingly, for purposes of IRC Sec. 642(c), the full amount distributed to charity is deemed to consist of ordinary income [Reg. Sec.1.642(c)-3(b)(2), ex. 2].

(d) Charitable Lead Annuity Trust ("CLAT"). The CLAT is a split-interest trust that pays a fixed annuity to a designated charity for a term of years or until the death of the donor. At the end of the set time period, the remaining property (the remainder interest) passes to one or more noncharitable beneficiaries (typically the donor's family) as stated in the irrevocable trust agreement.

¶1004

In a CLAT, the periodic payments to qualifying charities take the form of a guaranteed annuity, which the trust instrument can describe as either a fixed amount or a fixed percentage of the initial fair market value of the assets transferred to the CLAT either at the inception for a CLT created during life (*inter vivos*) or when the testator dies if the CLT is created by will (testamentary). The CLAT pays a percentage of the value of its trust assets, determined annually, to a named charity for the charitable term. For example, if a CLAT held assets worth $10 million and provided for a guaranteed annuity of 5 percent paid annually, qualifying charities would receive $500,000 from the CLAT each year. The guaranteed annuity paid to the charity would remain unchanged whether the value of the assets of the CLAT decreased to $9 million or increased to $11 million [Reg. Sec. 20.2055-2(e)(2)(vi)].

The "guaranteed annuity" method of payment grants the charity an irrevocable contractual right to receive a sum certain, payable at least annually, either for a preset number of years or term or for the life of an individual or individuals, who must be living at the date of the gift. No minimum or maximum annuity payments are required, so the donor may freely set the annuity guarantee at whatever level he or she desires. The annuity amount must be paid at least annually [Reg. Sec. 25.2522(c)-3(c)(2)(vi)].

> **NOTE:** A guaranteed annuity interest, not in trust, will be considered a guaranteed annuity only if it is paid by an insurance company or an organization regularly engaged in issuing annuity contracts [Reg. Sec. 25.2522(c)-3(c)(2)(vi)(c)].

Income in excess of the amount needed to pay the guaranteed annuity may be retained by the trust, distributed currently to the charity, or, where permitted by the governing instrument, paid to the family members.

Tax consequences of CLAT.

1. When the CLAT is created, the donor is treated as having made a gift to the noncharitable beneficiaries equal to the value of the remainder interest at the time the trust is created. The value of the CLAT's remainder interest is determined by referring to IRS tables based on the relevant AFR at the time of the gift (or during either of the two months immediately preceding the gift).

2. Nothing will be included in the donor's estate at death provided the donor does not retain any interest or control over the CLAT. The donor cannot therefore act as the trustee of the CLAT.

3. The decedent receives an estate tax charitable deduction for the present value of the lead interest which is equal to the total value of the property transferred to the CLAT minus the present value of the lead interest owned by the charity.

IRS provides sample forms for CLATs. In Rev. Proc. 2007-45,[1] the IRS supplied sample forms for the following two types of inter vivos CLATS: a nongrantor CLAT with a term of years annuity period; and one for a grantor CLAT. In addition to the sample forms, the revenue procedures provide annotations to the sample trust provisions and samples of certain alternate provisions. The alternate provisions for the inter vivos sample forms concern: (1) an annuity period for the life of an individual; (2) retention of the right to substitute the charitable lead beneficiary; (3)

---

[1] ¶ **1004** Rev. Proc. 2007-45, 2007-29 IRB 89.

apportionment of the annuity amount in the trustee's discretion; (4) the annuity amount as a specific dollar amount; (5) designation of an alternate charitable beneficiary; and (6) with respect to a grantor CLAT, restriction of the charitable beneficiary to a public charity.

In Rev. Proc. 2007-46,[2] the IRS supplied a sample form for a testamentary charitable lead annuity trust. In addition, the revenue procedure contains annotations to the sample trust provisions and samples of certain alternate provisions. The alternate provisions concern: (1) an annuity period for the life of an individual; (2) apportionment of the annuity amount in the trustee's discretion; (3) the annuity amount as a specific dollar amount; and (4) designation of an alternate charitable beneficiary.

According to the IRS safe harbor, assuming all other requirements are satisfied, the value of the charitable lead interest will be deductible under IRC Sec. 2522(c)(2)(B) and/or IRC Sec. 2055(e)(2)(B) if the trust: (1) is substantially similar to the sample trust (or properly integrates one or more alternate provisions into a document substantially similar to the sample trust); (2) is valid under applicable local law; and (3) operates in a manner consistent with the terms of the instrument. The IRS warns taxpayers that a trust that contains substantive provisions in addition to those included in the sample forms (other than properly integrated alternate provisions), or that omits any of the provisions of the sample forms, will not be assured of qualification for the appropriate charitable deductions.

The IRS has also released sample *inter vivos* nongrantor and grantor charitable lead unitrust (CLUT) forms in Rev. Proc. 2008-45[3] and a sample form testamentary charitable lead unitrust form in Rev. Proc. 2008-46.[4] These Rev. Procs. confirm that:

1. Estate taxes may be paid from assets passing to the CLUT; and

2. Unitrust percentages may be increased or decreased, provided the present value of the charitable interest is ascertainable at the decedent's death.

A form for a "grantor" CLUT is provided, with such status being provided by a power to reacquire trust assets in a person other than the grantor.

The IRS notes that it generally will not issue a letter ruling on whether a CLAT qualifies for estate and/or gift tax charitable deductions. However, the IRS generally will issue letter rulings relating to the tax consequences of the inclusion in a CLAT of substantive trust provisions other than those contained in the sample forms or alternate provisions.

▶ **PRACTICE POINTER:** Drafters of trust documents should not be lead into complacency just because the IRS has supplied sample forms and promised a safe harbor if a trust follows all the provisions outlined in the Revenue Procedures. Each sample form is merely a model which must be adapted to each taxpayer's individual set of circumstances.

(e) Charitable Lead Unitrust. In a CLUT, in contrast to a CLAT, the periodic payments to qualifying charities are a fixed percentage of the fair market value of the assets of the CLUT determined annually. For example, if a CLUT had $10 million worth of assets and provided for a unitrust interest of five percent to be paid

---

[2] Rev. Proc. 2007-46, 2007-29 IRB 102.
[3] Rev. Proc. 2008-45, 2008-30 IRB 224.
[4] Rev. Proc. 2008-46, 2008-30 IRB 238.

annually, qualifying charities would receive $500,000 in that year. If the value of the assets decreased to $9 million, the unitrust payment would fall to $450,000 for that year, but if the value increased to $11 million, the unitrust payment would increase to $550,000 for that year [Reg. Sec. 20.2055-2(e)(2)(viii)(a)].

Most investors choose the CLAT rather than the CLUT because the charitable payments are fixed and do not reflect the market gyrations that change the value of the unitrust. If the assets in the unitrust increase, the payouts to the charity also increase and therefore reduce the amount left for family members to inherit when the charitable interest terminates.

> **NOTE:** A unitrust interest, not in trust, is considered a unitrust interest only if it is paid by:
>
> 1. An insurance company; or
> 2. An organization regularly engaged in issuing interests otherwise meeting the requirements for a unitrust interest [Reg. Sec. 25.2522(c)-3(c)(2)(vii)(c)].

(f) Valuation of Charitable Lead Interest. A charitable lead interest, because it is immediately payable to a charity, is capable of accurate valuation, assuming the charitable and the private interests are separate and distinguishable. The transfer into the CLT is a completed gift for federal gift tax purposes [see ¶ 206].

The method for valuing an annuity interest in a CLT is set forth in Reg. Sec. 25.7250-2(b). In brief, the present value of the annuity is calculated by multiplying:

1. The amount of the annuity by
2. The appropriate annuity factor found in Table B (for term of years) or Table S (for the life of an individual) contained in IRS Publication 1457, Actuarial Values, Aleph Volume.

The annuity factor depends on the applicable IRC Sec. 7520 interest rate and the term of the annuity. For the donor to receive a full charitable deduction, the interest rate selected must be 120 percent of the federal mid-term rate (determined under IRC Sec. 7520) for the month in which the transfer occurs, compounded annually. IRC Sec. 7520(a) provides a special option that allows a donor to use the IRC Sec. 7520 rate for the month in which the transfer occurs or either of the two months preceding the month of the transfer.

The present value of a unitrust is determined by subtracting:

1. The present value of the remainder interest, from
2. The fair-market value of the transferred property at the date of the transfer [Reg. Sec. 25.2522(c)-3(d)(2)(v)].

Because the enjoyment of the noncharitable interest is postponed until the charitable income interest terminates, the remainder interest in a CLT is a future interest that does not qualify for the annual per donee gift tax exclusion [see ¶ 901].

(g) CLT Benefits. There are numerous benefits to using a CLT in an estate plan, including:

1. The decedent's estate gets a charitable estate tax deduction, which will greatly reduce the estate tax bite;

¶1004

2. If the property in the CLT appreciates in value, the beneficiaries will receive the property at its appreciated value at the termination of the trust term, without paying a dime of tax on the appreciation;

3. During the trust term when the charity has an income interest, the charity will use the income for its charitable purpose;

4. CLTs are not just for the super-rich. If you own real estate or a family business and have children or grandchildren who will not need your money immediately after you die, a CLT offers a way for you to leave money to charity but also pass the bulk of your estate intact to your family while saving a bundle on estate taxes;

5. CLTs offer a way for real estate or the family business to stay in the family.

¶1005 CHARITABLE REMAINDER TRUSTS

When the charitable interest follows the noncharitable interest, the trust is referred to as a charitable remainder trust (CRT). The charitable remainder trust (CRT) is the mirror image of the CLT [see ¶1004]. The beneficiaries, typically the donor's children or grandchildren, receive income for their lifetime from the assets the older generation has placed in either an annuity trust or a unitrust. After the younger generation dies, the assets in the CRT pass to the designated charity. CRTs are very popular estate planning tools because of the substantial benefits they provide to both the charity and the donor. CRTs allow the children and grandchildren of wealthy taxpayers to enjoy the income from property that will eventually go to a charity after the senior's death.

Contributions to the CRT are eligible for an income, gift, and estate tax charitable deduction equal to the fair-market value of the charity's remainder interest. The deduction is based on the age of each noncharitable beneficiary and the percentage of the trust assets that will be paid to the noncharitable beneficiaries annually. An increase in the interest rate decreases the income, estate, and gift tax deductions associated with a remainder interest going to a private beneficiary.

> **Example 1:** Grandma creates a CRT that distributes income to her grandchildren for their lifetimes. After the grandchildren die, the assets in the CRT pass to the National Kidney Foundation. In the year of creation, Grandma receives a charitable deduction equal to the fair-market value of the foundation's remainder interest. The deduction amount will be based on the age of each grandchild and the percentage of the trust assets that will be paid to them annually.

Excise tax imposed on UBTI. Charitable remainder trusts are subject to a 100 percent excise tax on their unrelated business taxable income (UBTI). [IRC Sec. 664(c)(2)(A); Reg. Sec. 1.664-1(c)(1)].

What is UBTI? IRC Sec. 512(a)(1) provides that UBTI is the gross income derived by an organization from any unrelated trade or business regularly carried on by it, less the deductions directly connected with the carrying on of such trade or business, both computed with certain modifications. Common sources of UBTI in CRTs are pass-through entities such as partnerships and debt-financed property (property held to produce income and with respect to which there is an acquisition indebtedness at any time during the tax year) held by the trust [Reg. Sec. 1.514(b)-1(a)].

CRT benefits. The following benefits will stem from a properly drafted CRT:

1. There is cash flow to the donor for a fixed number of years from the CRT.
2. The donor can claim an income tax deduction [IRC Sec. 170] in the year the assets are contributed to the CRT. The deduction is equal to the actuarial value of the remainder interest passing to the charity.
3. The donor's taxable estate is reduced by the value of the assets transferred to the CRT.
4. The donor has an opportunity to benefit a charity of his or her choice while benefiting himself or herself at the same time.
5. When appreciated assets fund the CRT, no tax is paid on this appreciation.

(a) CRT Varieties. Two types of CRTs are available. There is a charitable remainder annuity trust (CRAT) and a charitable remainder unitrust (CRUT).

A CRAT is a trust that must pay, at least annually, a specific dollar amount equal to at least 5 percent of the initial value of the trust assets to a noncharitable beneficiary for the life of an individual or for a term of years (not to exceed 20 years) with the remainder passing to a named charity.

▶ **PLANNING POINTER:** When interest rates are low, it is not a good time to establish a CRAT because a lower interest rate produces smaller income, gift and estate tax charitable deductions and a higher gift tax value for the gifted annuity interest.

A CRUT is similar except that the amount of the annual payments is a fixed percentage of the trust assets, valued annually [IRC Sec. 664(d)].

The IRS has issued eight Revenue Procedures[1] updating the sample trust forms for CRUTs. The IRS will recognize a CRUT as a qualified charitable remainder trust under IRC Sec. 664 if it is substantially similar to an IRS sample trust form. In the Revenue Procedures the IRS has provided detailed annotations to the provisions of the sample CRUT forms and includes many alternate provisions that can be integrated into the sample trust forms. Because of the very specific, complex and narrowly construed requirements of IRC Sec. 644, tax planners should closely follow these sample forms when drafting CRUTs. If an estate planner uses a sample IRS form and makes any modifications, he or she must make sure that the modifications do not inadvertently cause disqualification of the CRUT. Even if a sample IRS CRUT form is used, the following issues must be considered when preparing the trust document:

1. The objectives of the settlor in establishing the CRT;
2. Whether the CRT should be a CRAT or a CRUT;
3. The identity of the noncharitable and the charitable remainder beneficiaries;

---

[1] ¶1005 Rev. Proc. 2005-52, 2005-2 CB 326; Rev. Proc. 2005-53, 2005-2 CB 339; Rev. Proc. 2005-54, 2005-2 CB 353; Rev. Proc. 2005-55, 2005-2 CB 367; Rev. Proc. 2005-56, 2005-2 CB 383; Rev. Proc. 2005-57, 2005-2 CB 392; Rev. Proc. 2005-58, 2005-2 CB 402; Rev. Proc. 2005-59, 2005-2 CB 412.

¶**1005**

4. The naming of current and successor trustees;

5. The assets that will fund the CRT, and whether they will include marketable assets, which will subject the trust to special valuation rules;

6. The amount of the annual annuity or unitrust payment to the noncharitable beneficiaries;

7. The amount and availability of a charitable income, gift, and estate tax deduction;

8. Whether the transfer to the CRT is complete for gift tax purposes and whether the trust or any portion of it will be included in the settlor's estate;

9. Compliance with the minimum (5%) and maximum (50%) payment requirements applicable to annuity and unitrust payouts;

10. Compliance with the 10% remainder interest requirement, and the 5% probability of exhaustion rule generally applicable to CRATs payable for lfe;

11. The inclusion of various alternate provisions, such as the testamentary power of the settlor to revoke a noncharitable beneficiary's annuity or unitrust interest, the ability to provide a substitute charitable remainder beneficiary, or to allow the allocation or "sprinkling" of the annuity or unitrust payment; and

12. If the trust is a CRUT, whether the trust will be a NICRUT, a NIMCRUT, or a flit CRUT, and if so, whether post-contribution capital gain should be allocated to income.

Strict adherence to statutory requirements is critical when establishing a CRUT. In *Estate of Tamulis*,[2] the Court of Appeals for the Seventh Circuit held that the estate was not entitled to a deduction for a CRUT because the trust was not set up or reformed in accordance with the criteria for a CRUT as set forth in IRC Sec. 664(d)(2).

(b) Ordering Rules. IRC Sec. 664 contains the rules for the tax treatment of CRATs and CRUTs. In general, a CRT provides for a specified periodic distribution (CRT distribution) to one or more beneficiaries (at least one of which is a noncharitable beneficiary) for life or for a term of years, with an irrevocable remainder interest held for the benefit of charity. IRC Sec. 664(b) provides ordering rules for determining the character of CRT distributions in the hands of the recipient of those distributions. A CRT distribution is treated as being made from each category in the following order:

• First, as ordinary income to the extent of the trust's gross income other than gains from the sale of capital assets ("ordinary income") for the trust's taxable year and its undistributed ordinary income for prior years;

• Second, as capital gain to the extent of the trust's capital gain for the trust's taxable year and its undistributed capital gain for prior years;

• Third, as other income (that is, tax-exempt income) to the extent of the trust's other income for the trust's taxable year and its undistributed other income for prior years; and

• Finally, as a distribution of trust corpus [IRC Sec. 664(b); Reg. Sec. 1.664-1(d)(1)(ii)].

---

[2] Estate of Tamulis, 509 F.3d 343 (7th Cir. 2007).

¶1005

If the CRT has different classes of income in the ordinary income category, the distribution from that category is treated as being made from each class, in turn, until exhaustion of the class, beginning with the class subject to the highest federal income tax rate and ending with the class subject to the lowest income tax rate. If the trust has different classes of net gain in the capital gains category, the distribution from that category is treated as being made first from the short-term capital gain class and then from each class of long-term capital gain, in turn, until exhaustion of the class, beginning with the class subject to the highest tax rate and ending with the class subject to the lowest rate. If two or more classes within the same category are subject to the same current tax rate, but at least one of those classes will be subject to a different tax rate in a future year (for example, if the current rate sunsets), the order of that class in relation to other classes in the category with the same current tax rate is determined based on the future rate or rates applicable to those classes. Within each category, if there is more than one type of income in a class, amounts treated as distributed from that class are to be treated as consisting of the same proportion of each type of income as the total of the current and undistributed income of that type bears to the total of the current and undistributed income of all types of income included in that class. For example, if rental income and interest income are subject to the same current and future tax rate and therefore are in the same class, a distribution from that class will be treated as consisting of a proportional amount of rental income and interest income [Reg. Sec. 1.664-1(d)(1)(ii)(b)].

Netting of capital gains and losses. Reg. Sec. 1.664-1(d)(1)(iv) provides that capital gains of a CRT trust are determined on a cumulative net basis. Thus, for each taxable year, current and undistributed gains and losses within each class are netted to determine the net gain or loss for that class, and the classes of capital gains and losses are then netted against each other in the following order. A net loss from the class of short-term capital gain and loss offsets the net gain from each class of long-term capital gain and loss, in turn, until exhaustion of the class, beginning with the class subject to the highest income tax rate and ending with the class subject to the lowest tax rate. A net loss from a class of long-term capital gain and loss (beginning with the class subject to the highest tax rate and ending with the class subject to the lowest rate) is used to offset net gain from each other class of long-term capital gain and loss, in turn, until exhaustion of the class, beginning with the class subject to the highest tax rate and ending with the class subject to the lowest rate. A net loss from all the classes of long-term capital gain and loss (beginning with the class subject to the highest tax rate and ending with the class subject to the lowest rate) offsets any net gain from the class of short-term capital gain and loss.

Example 2: X, a CRAT is created and the annual annuity amount is $100. X's income for the 2014 tax year is as follows:

Interest income	$80
Qualified dividend income	$50
Capital gains and losses	$0
Tax-exempt income	$0

The year this income is received by the trust, qualified dividend income is subject to a different rate of federal income tax than interest income and is, therefore, a separate class of income in the ordinary income category. The annuity amount is deemed to be distributed from the classes within the ordinary income category, beginning with the class subject to the highest federal income tax rate and ending with the class subject to the lowest rate. Because qualified dividend income is taxed at a lower rate than interest income, the interest income is deemed distributed prior to the qualified dividend income. Therefore, in the hands of the recipient, the annuity amount has the following characteristics:

Interest income	$80
Qualified dividend income	$20

The remaining $30 of qualified dividend income that is not treated as distributed to the recipient is carried forward to the following year as undistributed qualified dividend income [Reg. Sec. 1.664-1(d)(1)(viii), ex. 1].

(c) Abuse of Ordering Rules. Creative taxpayers have abused these ordering rules by creating accelerated CRTs that try to convert appreciated assets into cash while avoiding most of the tax that would otherwise be imposed on the appreciation of the asset. The IRS has challenged these transactions that used CRUTs as a vehicle for converting appreciated assets into untaxed gains.

For example, the IRS viewed the steps of the following transaction as abusive:

1. An accelerated CRUT was funded with highly appreciated assets producing no income.

2. The CRUT made no distributions in Year 1.

3. The CRUT would sell all the appreciated assets at the beginning of Year 2.

4. The proceeds from the sale would then be used to pay the required distribution for Year 1.

Because the distribution related back to Year 1, it was treated as a nontaxable distribution of trust corpus under the ordering rules listed above [IRC Sec. 664(b)]. Planners could achieve this result because the trust did not realize any income during Year 1, because the sale did not occur until Year 2. As a result of combining the benefits available with the grace period permitted for making CRT payments under Reg. Sec. 1.664-2(a)(1)(i) and the ordering rules, the payment made early in Year 2 was allocated to Year 1.

> **Example 3:** Mom transferred assets with a fair-market value of $1 million and a zero basis to a CRUT on January 1 of Year 1. The assets paid no income and the trust term was two years. Mom reserved an annuity worth 80 percent of the fair-market value of the trust assets valued annually. In the first year, the CRUT was supposed to pay Mom $800,000, but no payments were actually made to Mom that year. On January 1 of the second year, the CRUT sold the property, generating capital gain of $1 million. On April 15 of the second year, the CRUT distributed to Mom the $800,000 unitrust amount that was due for the first year. In the second year, Mom was paid the payout amount of $160,000 (80 percent of $200,000 remaining in the trust). At the end of the second year, the trust terminated and the balance remaining in the trust was paid to charity. Proponents of this transaction treated Mom's $800,000 distribution on April 15 of the second year as a tax-free distribution of principal because the trust had no

¶1005

ordinary income, capital gain, or other income in Year 1 [IRC Sec. 664(b)(4)]. The $160,000 unitrust amount for the second year was characterized as capital gain, on which Mom paid capital gains tax. If Mom had sold the assets directly, she would have paid capital gain on $1 million gain and have to part with the trust principal. In the CRUT scheme, she pays capital gains tax on only $160,000 and winds up with nearly all of the trust principal back in her pocket.

The IRS deems this CRUT as abusive because it produced an essentially tax-free return of cash to the donor from the sale of appreciated assets. To limit these CRT planning schemes involving the use of appreciated assets to fund CRTs, the IRS now mandates that payment of any required annuity or unitrust amount by a CRT be made by the close of the year in which the payment is due [Reg. Secs. 1.664-2(a)(1)(i), 1.664-3(a)(1)(i)]. In addition, the IRS prevents individuals from using CRTs to cash in appreciated property tax-free by treating the CRT as having sold the appreciated assets in a deemed sale [Reg. Sec. 1.643(a)-8(b)(1)].

Reporting requirements. The CRT trustee must report each group of long-term capital gain separately on Form 5227, "Split-Interest Trust Information Return." The trustee may use any reasonable method for determining the amount of each type of gain within a group that has been distributed.

The following restrictions have been imposed on CRTs in an effort to curtail taxpayer abuse.

1. CRUTs and CRATs must meet 10 percent minimum remainder interest requirements. This means that the value of the charitable remainder must be at least 10 percent of the initial fair-market value of all trust assets on the date the property was contributed to the trust [IRC Secs. 664(d)(1), 664(d)(2)]. The 10 percent minimum test is measured on each transfer to the charitable remainder trust and consequently, a charitable remainder trust that meets the 10 percent test on the date of transfer will not subsequently fail to meet that test if interest rates have declined between the trust's creation and death of a measuring life. Similarly, when a charitable remainder trust is created for the joint lives of two individuals with a remainder to charity, the trust will not cease to qualify as a charitable remainder trust because the value of the charitable remainder was less than 10 percent of the trust's assets at the first death of these two individuals.

2. A CRT cannot have a maximum payout percentage in excess of 50 percent of the trust's fair-market value [IRC Sec. 664(d)(2)(A)]. In the case of a CRAT, this means that the annual payout cannot exceed 50 percent of the initial fair-market value of the trust's assets. In the case of a CRUT, it means that the annual payout cannot exceed 50 percent of the fair-market value of the trust assets determined annually. Trusts that fail this 50 percent test are treated as complex trusts and have all of their income taxed to the beneficiaries of the trust.

3. In order to encourage certain transfers to stock to employee stock option plans (ESOPs), in limited circumstances, an ESOP rather than a charitable organization may be the remainder beneficiary of a CRT without adverse tax affect [IRC Sec. 664(g)].

4. A CRT cannot hold S corporation stock as an electing small business trust.

(d) Relief Available for Failure to Qualify. Three types of relief are available for trusts that fail the 10 percent rule.

First, the governing instrument of the trust can be reformed or amended in order to reduce the payout rate or shorten the duration of any noncharitable beneficiary's interest (or both). The reformation must be made no later than the 90th day after the last date (including extensions) for filing the estate tax return, or if no estate tax return had to be filed, the last date (including extensions) for filing the income tax return for the last year that the trust must file a return.

Second, a trust that would qualify as a charitable remainder trust but for failure to meet the minimum value test may be declared void. As a result of this characterization, any transaction entered into by the trust before it was declared void would be treated as entered into by the transferor who would be denied the charitable deduction for the transfer and would be taxed on any income earned on the assets transferred to the trust.

Third, when an additional contribution is made to a trust that was a charitable remainder unitrust before the contribution, and the contribution would have the effect of causing the trust to violate the 10 percent rule, such contribution is treated as a transfer to a separate trust. As a result, the transfer does not affect the status of the original trust as a charitable remainder unitrust.

> ▶ **PLANNING TIP:** The attack on CRTs is focused on CRTs that seek to convert appreciated assets into cash, while avoiding the capital gains tax on the gain. The typical targeted transaction involves a taxpayer contributing greatly appreciated assets to a CRT for a short term and a high payout rate. The CRT trustee pays out the annuity in a calendar year before the trust's sale of the assets. As a result, the parties characterize the distribution as a tax-free return of corpus under IRC Sec. 664 rather than as taxable income. To avoid an audit, stay away from CRTs where substantially appreciated assets are contributed to a short-term charitable remainder unitrust having a high percentage unitrust amount.

To qualify for a charitable deduction for gift and estate tax purposes, the CRT, similar to its counterpart the CLT [see ¶ 1004], must satisfy the following requirements [IRC Secs. 2522(c)(2)(A), 664]:

1. An irrevocable trust effective under state law (the governing instrument) must be created. The IRS has released sample forms for the following types of CRATs: an inter vivos CRAT for one measuring life [Rev. Proc. 2003-53], an inter vivos CRAT for a term of years [Rev. Proc. 2003-54], an inter vivos CRAT providing consecutive interests for two measuring lives [Rev. Proc. 2003-55], an inter vivos CRAT providing for concurrent and consecutive interests for two measuring lives [Rev. Proc. 2003-56], a testamentary CRAT for one measuring life [Rev. Proc. 2003-57], a testamentary CRAT for a term of years [Rev. Proc. 2003-58], a testamentary CRAT providing for consecutive interests for two measuring lives [Rev. Proc. 2003-59], and a testamentary CRAT providing for concurrent and consecutive interests for two measuring lives [Rev. Proc. 2003-60]. The IRS promises to recognize a trust as a qualified CRAT if: (1) it operates in a manner consistent with the terms of the trust instrument, if the trust is a valid trust under applicable local law, and (2) if

the trust instrument is substantially similar to the sample forms in the revenue procedures listed above;

2. Property must be transferred to the irrevocable trust;

3. The governing instrument must create a qualified interest (e.g., a guaranteed annuity trust interest) [IRC Sec. 664(d)(1)] or a unitrust interest [IRC Sec. 664(d)(2)];

4. The governing instrument must create a lead/income interest payable to one or more noncharitable beneficiaries followed by an irrevocable disposition of the remainder interest to a charitable organization, effective from the time when the trust is funded for an *inter vivos* (lifetime) trust;

5. The language in the governing instrument:

   - Cannot restrict the trustee's ability to invest trust assets in income-producing property [Reg. Sec. 1.664-1(a)(3)];

   - Must bar anyone from altering, amending, revoking, or invading the trust in a manner that would jeopardize the charity's right to the remainder [Reg. Sec. 1.664-2(a)(4)]; and

   - Must prohibit the trust from engaging in actions that would cause a private foundation to be taxed for federal income tax purposes, for activities such as self-dealing [IRC Sec. 508(e)].

6. The grantor can retain a power to:

   - Accelerate the charitable remainder interest; and

   - Change the specific charity or charities to whom the remainder is paid;

7. Lifetime payments must be paid to and measured by the recipient's life and no one else's;

8. At the time of death of the last noncharitable beneficiary or at the end of a term of up to 20 years, the remainder interest must be paid to or held for the benefit of a qualified charitable organization [IRC Secs. 664(d)(1), 664(d)(2)]. In Rev. Rul. 2002-20[3] the IRS ruled that a trust may qualify as a CRUT where the unitrust amounts will be paid to a separate trust for the life of a "financially disabled individual," even though the regulations generally permit unitrust amounts to be paid to a second trust only for a term of 20 years or less. If payments are made to an individual, they may be made for the individual's life and are not limited by the 20-year rule; and

9. Careful attention must be paid to the administration of a CRT. The trustee of the CRT must be meticulous about following the terms of the trust and failure to do so will result in a denial of the estate tax charitable deduction. In *Estate of Atkinson*,[4] the Tax Court denied the charitable deduction under IRC Sec. 2055 because the trust's failure to make a required payment of the annuity amount to a beneficiary pursuant to the trust terms amounted to a failure to function as a valid CRT. These problems can be avoided if the drafting attorney creates an owner's manual to accompany the CRT. The manual should explain to all parties

---

[3] Rev. Rul. 2002-20, 2002-1 CB 794.

[4] Estate of Atkinson, 115 TC 26 (2000), *aff'd*, 309 F.3d 1290 (11th Cir. 2002), *cert. denied*, 540 U.S. 946 (2003).

¶1005

that the annuity must be paid in a timely manner and that the tax advantages sought by the trust will be forfeited if the instructions are not followed meticulously.

(e) Other Types of Charitable Remainder Interests. In addition to a CRAT or a CRUT, a charitable remainder interest may qualify as:

1. A pooled income fund [see ¶1006];

2. A remainder interest in a personal residence or farm [see ¶1007]; or

3. An undivided portion of the transferor's entire interest (or the transferor's entire partial interest) in the property, including a qualified conservation contribution [see ¶1008].

(f) Calculating the Amount of the Charitable Deduction. In a CRT, where the charitable interest follows the noncharitable income interests, the trust must have at least one noncharitable income beneficiary.

With an annuity trust, the present value of the charitable remainder interest is computed using the subtraction method discussed at ¶1003. The present value of the annuity is subtracted from the value of the gift to yield the value of the charitable deduction [Reg. Sec. 1.664-2(c)].

The income interest may be a term of years (or successive terms, if successive noncharitable income beneficiaries are involved) or for the life (or lives) of the noncharitable beneficiaries. Thus, the actuarial tables used depend on the term granted the income beneficiary or beneficiaries and the applicable interest rate. Similar to the charitable lead trust, IRC Sec. 7520 requires the use of an interest rate equal to 120 percent of the federal mid-term rate, compounded annually.

The donor may elect to use the rate in effect for either of the two months preceding the transfer [IRC Sec. 7520(a)]. Comprehensive tables for the valuation of charitable interest under IRC Sec. 7520 are available in IRS Publications 1547 (Actuarial Values, Aleph Volume) and 1548 (Actuarial Values, Beth Volume).

For a CRUT, the present value of the remainder interest is determined by:

1. Computing an "adjusted payout rate" (i.e., multiplying the fixed percentage provided in the unitrust instrument by a payout factor contained in Table F under Reg. Sec. 1.644-4(e)(6));

2. Applying a "valuation factor" to the net fair-market value of the assets placed in trust. You obtain the valuation factor by matching the adjusted payment rate with the appropriate term of years or the appropriate age of the measuring life [Table D or Table U(1) under Reg. Sec. 1.644-4(e)(6)]. Again, a fluctuating interest rate equal to 120 percent of the federal mid-term rate must be used.

(g) Annual Per Donee Exclusion. When the income is paid to some one other than the settlor-donor, a completed gift of the income interest has occurred [see ¶206] and is subject to federal gift tax. When the income interest is required to be paid currently to the first noncharitable income beneficiary and thus is immediate in possession and enjoyment, the gift is a present interest and qualifies for the annual per donee gift tax exclusion [see ¶901]. However, a succeeding noncharitable beneficiary's interest will not qualify for the annual per donee exclusion.

¶1005

(h) IRS Delays Application of Safe Harbor for CRTs Subject to Elective Share. Rev. Proc. 2005-24[5] provided a safe harbor procedure under which the IRS would disregard a surviving spouse's right of election to take against the grantor's will for purposes of determining whether the CRAT and CRUT met the requirements of IRC Sec. 664(d)(1)(B) or IRC Sec. 664(d)(2)(B) continuously since its creation. The revenue procedure applies to any CRAT or CRUT created by a grantor whose surviving spouse, under applicable state law, has a right of election exercisable on the grantor's death to receive an elective share of the grantor's estate that can be satisfied in whole or in part from assets of the CRAT or CRUT. The existence of the right to receive an elective share, where the share could include assets of the CRAT or CRUT, causes the trust to fail to qualify under IRC Sec. 664(d) because an amount other than the annuity or unitrust payments could be paid to, or used by, a person other than a tax-exempt organization.

The IRS agreed to disregard the right of election for determining whether a CRAT or CRUT within the scope of the revenue procedure satisfies the requirements of IRC Sec. 664(d) continuously from the date that the trust is created if the safe harbor requirements are satisfied. Specifically, the surviving spouse must irrevocably waive the right of election to the extent necessary to ensure that no part of the trust (other than the annuity or unitrust interest of which the surviving spouse is the named recipient) may be used to satisfy the elective share. A waiver will satisfy the safe harbor requirements if it is valid under applicable state law, in writing, and signed and dated by the surviving spouse.

For CRATs or CRUTs created on or after June 28, 2005, the surviving spouse must execute the waiver on or before the date that is six months after the due date of Form 5227, "Split-Interest Trust Information Return," for the year in which the later of the following occurs:

1. The creation of the trust;

2. The date of the grantor's marriage to the surviving spouse;

3. The date the grantor first becomes domiciled or a resident in a jurisdiction whose law provides a right of election that could be satisfied from trust assets; or

4. The effective date of applicable law creating a right of election.

For trusts created before June 28, 2005, the IRS will disregard the right of election, even without a waiver, so long as the surviving spouse does not exercise the right of election. In no event will the safe harbor procedure be available to a CRAT or CRUT if the surviving spouse exercises the right of election.

In Notice 2006-15,[6] the IRS provided that until further guidance is published regarding the effect of a spousal right of election on a trust's qualification as a CRAT or CRUT, the IRS will disregard the existence of such a right of election, even without a waiver as described in Rev. Proc. 2005-24, but only if the surviving spouse does not exercise the right of election.

Background on elective share statutes. In many jurisdictions, states have enacted laws, known as elective share statutes, to protect spouses from being disinherited. Elective share statutes give spouses the right to elect a statutory share of the grantor's

---

[5] Rev. Proc. 2005-24, 2005-1 CB 909.   [6] Notice 2006-15, 2006-1 CB 501

estate regardless of whether the grantor made any bequest to the spouse. The spouse's share under these statutes is often referred to as an elective share. The definition of an elective share in many states is broad enough to include the assets of a CRAT or a CRUT. In states that have adopted the elective share provisions of the Uniform Probate Code, spouses can elect to take a portion of the augmented estate. Assets of CRATs and CRUTs may be included in the augmented estates and can be used to satisfy a spouse's elective share amount.

Under IRC Sec. 664(d)(1)(B) and IRC Sec. 664(d)(2)(B), a CRAT or CRUT, respectively that makes payments to a person other than an organization eligible to receive tax-deductible charitable contributions will be disqualified. Thus, a CRT will be disqualified if a spouse can elect to receive an elective share that could be satisfied with CRT assets. Moreover, the CRT could be disqualified even if the spouse never elects to exercise the right.

(i) Division of One Trust into Two Trusts. In Rev. Rul. 2008-41,[7] the IRS provided taxpayers with guidelines on dividing a CRT into two or more separate and equal CRTs. The guidance presented two situations in which either a charitable remainder annuity trust (CRAT) or a charitable remainder unitrust (CRUT) was divided into separate trusts. In one case the trust was divided, *pro rata*, into as many separate and equal trusts as necessary to provide a separate trust for each recipient living at the time of the division, while, in the second case, the trust was divided pursuant to a divorce. In both cases, the *pro rata* division of the trust (1) did not terminate the trust's status as a trust described in, and subject to, the private foundation provisions of IRC Sec. 4947(a)(2); (2) did not result in the imposition of an excise tax under IRC Sec. 507(c); (3) did not cause the trust or any of the separate trusts to fail to qualify as a CRT; (4) was not a sale, exchange or other disposition producing gain or loss and, under IRC Sec. 1015, each separate trusts' basis in each asset was the same share of the basis of that asset in the hands of the trust immediately before the division and each separate trust's holding period for assets transferred to it included the holding period of the asset as held by the original trust immediately before division; (5) did not constitute an act of self-dealing under IRC Sec. 4941 or constitute a taxable expenditure under IRC Sec. 4945.

(j) Sale by Grantor of Retained Interest. In proposed regulations, the IRS has provided rules for determining a taxable beneficiary's basis in a term interest in a CRT upon a sale or other disposition of all interests in the trust to the extent that basis consists of a share of adjusted uniform basis. The regulations affect taxable beneficiaries of charitable remainder trusts. The proposed regulations are intended to curb perceived abuse which stems from a transaction described in Notice 2008-99,[8] as a "transaction of interest" which means that it has the potential for tax avoidance or evasion. The "abusive" transaction in Notice 2008-99 involved the following facts:

- The CRT grantor contributes assets to the CRT and claims a charitable donation deduction under IRC Sec. 170 for the portion of the fair market value (FMV) of the assets that is attributable to the CRT. This FMV generally exceeds the grantor's cost basis in the assets.

---

[7] Rev. Rul. 2008-41, 2008-30 IRB 170.   [8] Notice 2008-99, 2008-47 IRB 1194.

- The CRT sells or liquidates the contributed assets. The CRT is exempt from tax on any gain under IRC Sec. 664(c). The taxable beneficiary also does not recognize the gain.

- The CRT reinvests the proceeds in other assets such as a portfolio of marketable securities, with a basis equal to the portfolio's cost.

- The taxable beneficiary and charity subsequently sell all of their respective interests in the CRT to a third party. The taxable beneficiary takes the position that the entire interest in the CRT has been sold under IRC Sec. 1001(e)(3) and, therefore, IRC Sec. 1001(e)(1) does not apply to the transaction. As a result, the taxable beneficiary computes gain on the sale of his term interest by taking into account the portion of the uniform basis allocable to the term interest under Reg. Sec. 1.1014-5 and Reg. Sec. 1.1015-1(b). The taxable beneficiary takes the position that this uniform basis is derived from the basis of the new assets acquired by the CRT rather than the grantor's basis in the assets contributed to the CRT.

Uniform basis rule. Property acquired by a trust from a decedent or as a gift generally has a uniform basis. This means that property has a single basis even though more than one person has an interest in that property [see Reg. Secs. 1.1014-4(a)(1) and 1.1015-1(b)]. Generally, the uniform basis of assets transferred to a trust is determined under IRC Sec. 1015 for assets transferred by lifetime gift, or under IRC Secs. 1014 or 1022 for assets transferred from a decedent. Adjustments to uniform basis for items such as depreciation are made even though more than one person holds an interest in the property (adjusted uniform basis). When a taxable trust sells assets, any gain is taxed currently to the trust, to one or more beneficiaries, or apportioned among the trust and its beneficiaries. If the trust reinvests the proceeds from the sale in new assets, the trust's basis in the newly purchased assets is the cost of the new assets. Thus, the adjusted uniform basis of that taxable trust is attributable to the basis obtained with proceeds from sales that were subject to income tax.

Basis in term and remainder interests in a CRT. The basis of a term or remainder interest in a trust at the time of its sale or other disposition is determined under the rules provided in Reg. Sec. 1.1014-5 [see also Reg. Secs. 1.1015-1(b) and 1.1015-2(a)(2), which refer to the rules of Reg. Sec. 1.1014-5]. Specifically, Reg. Sec. 1.1014-5(a)(3) provides that, in determining the basis in a term or remainder interest in property at the time of the interest's sale or disposition, adjusted uniform basis is allocated using the factors for valuing life estates and remainder interests. Thus, the portions of the adjusted uniform basis attributable to the interests of the life tenant and remaindermen are adjusted to reflect the change in the relative values of such interests due to the lapse of time.

Proposed regulations. In order to prevent a taxable beneficiary of a CRT from benefiting from a basis step-up attributable to tax-exempt gains, the proposed regulations provide a special rule for determining the basis in certain CRT term interests in transactions to which IRC Sec. 1001(e)(3) applies. In these cases, the proposed regulations would provide that the basis of a term interest of a taxable beneficiary is the portion of the adjusted uniform basis assignable to that interest reduced by the portion of the sum of the following amounts assignable to that interest:

1. The amount of undistributed net ordinary income described in IRC Sec. 664(b)(1); and

2. The amount of undistributed net capital gain described in IRC Sec. 664(b)(2) [Prop. Reg. Sec. 1.1014-5(c)(1)].

The proposed regulations do not affect the CRT's basis in its assets, but rather are for the purpose of determining a taxable beneficiary's gain arising from a transaction described in IRC Sec. 1001(e)(3). The rules in the proposed regulations would be limited in application to charitable remainder annuity trusts (CRATs) and charitable remainder unitrusts (CRUTs) [Prop. Reg. Sec. 1.1014-5(c)(2)]. The regulations are proposed to apply to sales and other dispositions of interests in CRTs occurring on or after January 17, 2014, except for sales or dispositions occurring pursuant to a binding commitment entered into before that date.

¶1006 POOLED INCOME FUND

A gift tax charitable deduction is available when money or property is transferred to a pooled income fund, which is a collective investment vehicle typically used by donors to make charitable split-interest gifts [IRC Sec. 2522(c)(2)(A)]. A decedent can also receive an estate tax charitable deduction for the transfer of a remainder interest in property to a pooled income fund [IRC Sec. 2055(e)(2); Reg. Sec. 20.2055-2(e)(2)(v)].

A pooled income fund typically is a trust maintained by a charity to which wealth holders transfer money or property and receive a pro rata share of all income earned by the fund based on the amount that they contribute to the fund. The charity gets the remainder interest after the donor has died.

The holder of the lead/income interest receives "participation units" that fluctuate in value according to the performance of the assets in the pooled income fund. Think of a pooled income fund as a mutual fund that a charity maintains with the annual income going to a noncharitable beneficiary and the remainder going to the charity. When you make a split-interest contribution to a pooled income fund, you receive for life an income interest in that portion of the fund representing your percentage or unit interest. Since you have irrevocably contributed the remainder interest in your contribution to the charity maintaining the fund, when the income interest terminates, the units or percentage that produced the income are liquidated and the proceeds are paid to the charity.

The essential elements of a pooled income fund include the following organizational and operational requirements [IRC Sec. 642(c)(5)]:

1. You must irrevocably transfer your remainder interest in the money or property to a fund created by and for the exclusive benefit of a single public charitable organization [Reg. Sec. 1.642(c)-5(b)(1)];

2. The fund must be created by and for the exclusive benefit of a single public charitable organization [Reg. Sec. 1.642(c)-5(a)(5)(iv)];

3. The property transferred into the trust must generate taxable income;

4. Your transferred property, which generates income, must be commingled with property from other donors for investment purposes [Reg. Sec. 1.642(c)-5(b)(3)]; and

5. You must retain an income interest for life or create a life income interest for the benefit of one or more beneficiaries at the time of the transfer.

6. The governing instrument of the pooled income trust must prohibit the fund from accepting, holding or investing in tax-exempt investments [Reg. Sec. 1.642(c)-5(b)(4)].

7. The pooled income fund must be maintained by the same public charity that is the remainder beneficiary. This means that the public charity must exercise direct or indirect control over the fund. For example, this requirement of control must be met if the governing instrument of the trust contains provisions giving the charitable remainder beneficiary the ability to remove and replace the trustee and the donor must be prohibited from serving as trustee of the fund [Reg. Secs. 1.642(c)-5(b)(5) and (6)].

8. Every income interest retained or created in property transferred to a pooled income fund must be assigned a proportionate share of the annual income earned by the fund and each share or unit of participation must be based on the fair market value of such property on the date of transfer [Reg. Sec. 1.642(c)-5(c)(1)]. The fair market value of a unit in the fund at the time of the transfer shall be determined by dividing the fair market of all property in the fund by the number of units then in the fund. The initial fair market value of a unit in a pooled income fund shall be the fair market value of the property transferred to the fund divided by the number of units assigned to the income interest in that property. The value of each unit of participation will fluctuate with each new transfer of property to the fund in relation to the appreciation or depreciation in the fair market value of the property in the fund, but all units in the fund will always have equal value [Reg. Sec. 1.642(c)-5(c)(2)(i)(b)].

9. In order to provide an average market value for purposes of determining the annual rate of return of the pooled income fund, the fund must have at least four valuation dates per year. These so-called "determination dates" must be not more than three months apart, thus requiring quarterly valuation dates [Reg. Sec. 1.642(c)-5(a)(5)(vi)].

10. Each beneficiary entitled to income of any taxable year of the fund must receive such income in an amount determined by the rate of return earned by the fund for such taxable year with respect to his income interest. All income generated by the fund must be distributed during the calendar year or within 65 days after the close of the year. Income must be payable either up to the date of the beneficiary's death or up to the last income payment date preceding the beneficiary's death [Reg. Sec. 1.642(c)-5(b)(7)].

11. The trust's governing instrument must contain either a prohibition against investing in depreciable or depletable property or arequirement that a depreciation or depletion reserve be created in accordance with generally accepted accounting principles.[1]

   ▶**PRACTICE WARNING:** If the fund fails to satisfy these requirements not only will the transfer not receive the expected federal wealth and income tax benefits,

---

[1] ¶ 1006 Rev. Rul. 92-81, 1992-2 CB 119.

¶1006

the irrevocable nature of the transfer means that the donor will not be able to be get his or her property back.

If you are contemplating QTIP trusts, keep in mind that the IRS has ruled that a transfer to a pooled income fund can qualify for a QTIP marital deduction.[2]

(a) Drafting Tips Are Available. The IRS has issued drafting guidelines for pooled income funds and instruments of transfer. Consult these to avoid problems down the road.[3]

(b) How to Value a Gift for Gift Tax Purposes. You will get a gift tax deduction based on the value of the remainder interest that goes to the charity after you die provided the gift qualifies for the gift tax charitable deduction as discussed above [IRC Sec. 2522(c)(2)(A)]. To figure out the value of your gift for gift tax purposes, you must compute the present value of the remainder interest in the property transferred to the pooled income fund. To make this computation, which is based on your age at the time of the gift, you must consult IRS tables found in Reg. Sec. 1.642(e)-6.

¶1007 CHARITABLE REMAINDER INTERESTS IN A PERSONAL RESIDENCE OR FARM

You can contribute your remainder interest in either your farm or your personal residence and qualify for a gift tax charitable deduction [IRC Sec. 2522(c)(2)]. The gift of your personal residence or farm can take the form of a charitable remainder interest with you reserving a life estate or the successive life estate of your spouse, or transferring the life estate to someone else.

> **NOTE:** A transfer of the personal residence or farm into a trust (as distinguished from the retention of a life estate by deed) does qualify for the charitable deduction unless the trust qualifies as a charitable remainder annuity trust, unitrust, or pooled income fund [see ¶¶1005, 1006].[1]

Only the value of the real estate qualifies for the charitable deduction, not any accompanying nontrust gifts of other property. Thus, in a gift of the remainder interest in a personal residence and household furnishings, the value of household furnishings would not qualify for a charitable deduction.[2]

The term "personal residence" refers to property, including real and intangible personal property (e.g., shares of a cooperative corporation) used by the donor as a residence and is not restricted to the donor's principal residence [Reg. Secs. 25.2522(c)-3(c)(2)(ii), 20.2055-2(e)(2)(ii)]. The term "farm" includes agricultural products or livestock [Reg. Secs. 25.2522(c)-3(c)(2)(iii), 20.2055-2(e)(2)(iii)].

A donor may (1) split the remainder interest between the charity and a noncharity (e.g., 20 percent to the charity and 80 percent to a member of the donor's family) as

---

[2] Ltr. Rul. 9406013.

[3] See Rev. Rul. 82-38, 1982-1 CB 96; Rev. Rul. 85-57, 1985-1 CB 182; Rev. Rul. 90-103, 1990-2 CB 159; Rev. Rul. 92-81, 1992-2 CB 119.

[1] ¶1007 Rev. Rul. 76-357, 1976-2 CB 285.

[2] Rev. Rul. 76-165, 1976-1 CB 279.

tenants in common or (2) direct that the charity receive a specific portion of the donor's residence or farm.[3] In this situation, the charitable deduction is reduced to reflect the valuation of the cotenancy.[4]

¶1008 CONTRIBUTIONS OF FRACTIONAL INTERESTS IN TANGIBLE PROPERTY

Typically, a contribution of a partial interest in property to a qualified charitable organization of less than the donor's entire interest, does not qualify for the estate [IRC Sec. 2055(e)(2)] or gift tax [IRC Sec. 2522(c)(2)] charitable deduction. An exception is provided for a contribution of an undivided portion of the donor's entire interest in the property. For purposes of the charitable deduction, an undivided portion is a fraction or percentage of each and every substantial interest and right that the donor owns in the property for the entire time that the donor owns the property. The gift or estate tax deduction will be allowed if the donee-charity is given the right, as a tenant in common with the donor, to possession, dominion, and control of the property for the portion of each year corresponding to its interest in the property. For example, if a donor makes a gift of an undivided fractional one-quarter interest in a painting that entitles the charitable donee to possession during three months of each year, the donor may claim a deduction upon the donee's receipt of the deed of gift provided that the donee's initial possession is not deferred for longer than one year. An undivided interest will be treated as a present interest rather than a future interest for purposes of the charitable deduction if the donee has the right to possession, although not necessarily actual, physical possession, of the property during each year following the donation. In addition, a deduction is allowable in each subsequent year that an additional gift is made of an undivided interest in the same property.[1]

A donor may claim a deduction for a charitable contribution of a fractional interest in tangible personal property (such as a work of art), provided the donor satisfies the following requirements for deductibility:

1. Immediately before a contribution of a fractional interest in property by the donor, all the interests in the property are owned either (a) by the donor, or (b) by the donor and the donee organization [IRC Secs. 170(o)(1)(A) and 2522(e)(1)(A)]; and

2. In subsequent years the donor must make additional charitable contributions of interests in the same property.[2]

The IRS is authorized to make exceptions to the first rule in cases where all persons who hold an interest in the item make proportional contributions of undivided interests in their respective shares of such item to the donee organization [IRC Secs. 170(o)(1)(B) and 2522(e)(1)(B)]. For example, if A owns an undivided 40 percent interest in a painting and B owns an undivided 60 percent interest in the same

---

[3] Rev. Rul. 78-303, 1978-2 CB 122.
[4] Rev. Rul. 87-37, 1987-1 CB 295.

[1] ¶1008 Winokur, 90 TC 733 (1988), *acq.*, 1989-1 CB 1.
[2] Winokur, 90 TC 733 (1988), *acq.*, 1989-1 CB 1.

painting, the IRS may provide that A may take a deduction for a charitable contribution of less than the entire interest held by A, provided that both A and B make proportional contributions of undivided fractional interests in their respective shares of the painting to the same donee organization (e.g., if A contributes 50 percent of A's interest and B contributes 50 percent of B's interest).

(a) Consistent Valuation Required for Contributions of Fractional Interests. The value of a donor's charitable deduction for the initial contribution of a fractional interest in an item of tangible personal property, such as artwork, or collection of such items, will be based upon the fair market value of the artwork at the time of the contribution of the fractional interest and consideration of whether the use of the artwork will be related to the donee's exempt purposes.

(b) Recapture Rules. Any income tax or gift tax charitable deduction allowed for contributions of undivided interests in tangible personal property will be recaptured (with interest) if:

(1) the donor fails to contribute all of the remaining interests in the property to the donee (or another charitable organization if the donee is no longer in existence) before the earlier of the tenth anniversary of the initial fractional contribution or the donor's date of death; or

(2) the donee fails to take substantial physical possession of the property or fails to use the property in a manner related to the donee's exempt purpose during the period beginning after the initial fractional contribution and ending on the earlier of the tenth anniversary of the initial contribution or the donor's date of death [IRC Secs. 170(o)(3) and 2522(e)(3)(A)].

If an income tax or a gift tax charitable deduction is recaptured, as described above, an additional tax will be imposed in an amount equal to 10 percent of the amount recaptured [IRC Secs. 170(o)(3)(B) and 2522(e)(3)(B)].

(c) Contribution for Conservation Purposes. The contribution of a partial interest in real estate to a charitable organization for conservation purposes also qualifies for the gift tax charitable deduction [IRC Sec. 2522(d); Reg. Sec. 25.2522(c)-3(c)(2)(iv)].

To qualify for the deduction, the recipient must be either a governmental unit or a publicly supported charity [Reg. Sec. 1.170A-14(c)]. The amount of the gift of a conservation easement equals the amount by which the restricted use, that is, the preservation for conservation purposes, reduces the value of the donor's retained interest in the property.[3] Ownership by the donor of contiguous or adjacent property is usually immaterial, unless the contribution will enhance the value of the other property and thereby reduce the amount of the deduction [Reg. Sec. 1.170A-14(h)(3)(i)].

---

[3] Rev. Rul. 76-376, 1976-2 CB 53.

¶1008

¶1009 REFORMATION OF CHARITABLE SPLIT INTERESTS

The technical rules applicable to split interest transfers may result in defective transfers even where the wealth holder clearly intended the transfer to qualify for the charitable deduction. The following two approaches are available to salvage the charitable deduction:

1. A qualified disclaimer [IRC Sec. 2518]; or

2. Reforming the charitable split interest pursuant to IRC Sec. 2055(e)(3).

Disclaimer. Using a disclaimer to reshape a transfer to qualify for a wealth transfer tax deduction is a common post-mortem estate-planning technique. The disclaimer can be used to eliminate an undesired interest or power. [For further discussion, see Chapter 12].

> **Example 1:** Assume Mom transfers property to a trust that provides for the payment of an annuity to Dad for life and the remainder to a qualifying charity. The provisions of the trust, however, also permit Dad to invade or withdraw principal from the trust for his support. The existence of this power of invasion by the Dad will disqualify the transfer from qualifying as a charitable remainder annuity trust. To qualify the trust as a charitable remainder annuity trust, Dad could disclaim the power of invasion or withdrawal pursuant to IRC Sec. 2518.

Reformation of charitable split interest trust. Rules exist for reforming split interest trusts that do not qualify for the charitable deduction. Reformation of a testamentary trust must be retroactive to the date of death (and for a lifetime trust to the date of its creation). Provision must be made for correcting any overpayment or underpayment to a beneficiary.

For a charitable split interest trust, reformation requires the satisfaction of one of two requirements:

1. The governing instrument must provide for payments to noncharitable beneficiaries in specified dollar amounts or as a fixed percentage of the fair-market value [IRC Sec. 2055(e)(3)(C)(ii)]; or

2. Judicial reformation of the trust must be commenced within 90 days of the due date (including extensions) for:

   - The first trust income tax return for the trust (for transfers during life where no federal estate tax return is required); or

   - The federal estate tax return (for transfers where an estate tax return is required) [IRC Sec. 2055(e)(3)(C)(iii)].

Satisfaction of one of these two requirements makes the split interest a "reformable interest," the precondition to entering into the qualified reformation process.

> ▶ **CAUTION:** If the trust instrument does not provide for payments to noncharitable beneficiaries in specified dollar amounts or as a fixed percentage of fair-

market value, reformation proceedings must be commenced not later than 90 days after the due date of the estate tax return (including extensions) or, if no estate tax return is required, after the due date of the trust's first income tax return [IRC Sec. 2055(e)(3)(C)].

State law governs the reformation process. The IRC mandates that through the reformation process under state law, the following three guidelines must be satisfied [IRC Sec. 2055(e)(3)(B)]:

1. The reformation must be retroactive to the date of death (or the creation of a lifetime charitable split interest trust);

2. The reformation may not result in a change of more than 5 percent in the value of the reformable interest;

3. Except for the reduction of the term of the noncharitable interest from beyond 20 years to 20 years, the reformation cannot change the duration of the charitable and the noncharitable interests.

In other words, the IRC imposes limits on the extent of the reformation. For example, the difference in actuarial values of the charitable interests in the unreformed and reformed trusts cannot exceed 5 percent of the actuarial value of such interests in the unreformed trust. A noncharitable interest in a charitable remainder trust must terminate at the same time both before and after the reformation. However, a noncharitable interest for a term of more than 20 years can be reduced to 20 years. And for a charitable lead trust, the charitable interest must be of the same duration both before and after the reformation [IRC Sec. 2055(e)(3)(B)].

If all the noncharitable income beneficiaries die by the due date for filing the estate tax return (including extensions) and the property passes to the charity, the charitable deduction is allowed without reformation [IRC Sec. 2055(e)(3)(f)].

MARITAL DEDUCTION

TABLE OF CONTENTS

¶1100 MARITAL DEDUCTION BASICS

An individual can transfer unlimited amounts to his or her spouse either during life or at death free of wealth transfer taxes [IRC Sec. 2056(a)]. Lifetime transfers are shielded from tax by the unlimited gift tax marital deduction [see ¶1107] and transfers at death are exempted by the unlimited estate tax marital deduction which is our focus here. The marital deduction does not eliminate or reduce tax on the transfer of assets out of the marital unit, but merely postpones the payment of tax because property that qualifies for the marital deduction in the estate of the first spouse to die is includable in the estate of the surviving spouse unless it is spent or given away by the surviving spouse during his or her lifetime.

Transfers from one spouse to his or her surviving spouse, if these transfers satisfy the technical requirements listed below, will be deducted from the transferor spouse's gross estate for purposes of figuring his or her federal estate tax bill. The deduction is mandatory [IRC Sec. 2056(a)]. The marital deduction results in a deferral of the federal estate tax that is due when the first spouse dies. You may claim the marital deduction only for property interests that pass from the decedent to the surviving spouse and are included in the decedent's gross estate.

¶1101 REQUIREMENTS FOR MARITAL DEDUCTION

The following five technical requirements must be met in order for the transfer of an interest in property to qualify for the unlimited estate tax marital deduction:

1. The decedent was a United States citizen or resident;

2. The decedent must have been married and survived by a spouse who is a citizen of the United States [Reg. Sec. 20.2056(c)-2(e)]. The estate tax marital deduction is not available if the decedent's surviving spouse is not a U.S. citizen unless the spouse becomes a citizen before the estate tax return is filed or the property passes to a qualified domestic trust (QDOT) [IRC Secs. 2056(d) and 2056A];

3. The interest in property must be included in the decedent's gross estate;

4. The interest must "pass" to the decedent's surviving spouse [Reg. Secs. 20.2056(b)-5 through 20.2056(b)-8 and 20.2056(c)-1 through 20.2056(c)-3]; and

5. The interest must be a deductible one (i.e., it is not a nondeductible terminable interest) [Reg. Sec. 20.2056(a)-2].

(a) U.S. Citizen or Resident. The decedent must be a citizen or resident of the United States at the time of death [Reg. Sec. 20.2056(a)-1(a)].

(b) Survived by Spouse Who Is U.S. Citizen. The decedent must be survived by a spouse who is a citizen of the United States [IRC Sec. 2056(d); Reg. Sec. 20.2056(a)-1(b)(1)]. Although citizenship or residency status for the decedent is determined at death, the citizenship status of a surviving spouse is determined at the time of the filing of the decedent spouse's federal estate tax return, including extensions

[IRC Sec. 2056(d)(4)]. A surviving spouse who at the time of the decedent's death is not a citizen of the United States may become a citizen within the permissible period, thereby fulfilling this requirement.

Marital status is determined under state law at the time of the decedent's death. A legal separation or interlocutory decree of divorce that has not terminated the marriage would not affect the decedent's marital status.

> **NOTE:** A marital deduction for a citizen or permanent resident decedent of the United States with a noncitizen spouse is not entirely precluded. A marital deduction is possible through the use of a qualified domestic trust (QDOT), as described in IRC Sec. 2056A(a) and discussed in ¶1106.

Same-sex couples entitled to marital deduction. In *Windsor*[1] the Supreme Court held that a same-sex couple was entitled to claim the estate tax marital deduction because Section 3 of DOMA violated the equal protection clause and was therefore unconstitutional. DOMA defined the word marriage as "a legal union between one man and one woman as husband and wife, [and] the word 'spouse' [referred] only to a person of the opposite sex who [was] a husband or a wife."

In response to *Windsor*, the IRS released Rev. Rul. 2013-17,[2] which provides that the frequently-used terms "spouse," "husband and wife," "husband," "wife," "marriage," and "married" include an individual married to a person of the same sex if the individuals are lawfully married under state law. For federal tax purposes, the IRS adopts a general rule recognizing a marriage of same-sex individuals that was validly entered into in a state whose laws authorize the marriage of two individuals of the same sex even if the married couple is domiciled in a state that does not recognize the validity of same-sex marriages. For federal tax purposes, the terms "spouse," "husband and wife," "husband," and "wife" do not include individuals (whether of the opposite sex or the same sex) who have entered into a registered domestic partnership, civil union, or other similar formal relationship recognized under state law that is not denominated as a marriage under the laws of that state, and the term "marriage" does not include such formal relationships.

(c) Included in Decedent's Gross Estate. The interest in property must be included in the decedent's gross estate [IRC Sec. 2056(a)]. For example, life insurance proceeds on the life of the decedent paid to the surviving spouse from a policy owned by the surviving spouse would not be included in the decedent's gross estate. Thus, the proceeds from such a policy would not satisfy the inclusion requirement.

(d) Pass from Decedents to Surviving Spouse. The interest in property must pass from the decedent to his or her surviving spouse. The passing requirement [IRC Sec. 2056(a)] is broadly defined [IRC Sec. 2056(c)]. Decedents often pass property to their surviving spouses in one of the following ways: (1) bequest or devise; (2) inheritance; (3) dower or curtesy; (4) inter vivos transfer; (5) joint tenancy or right of survivorship; (6) the exercise or nonexercise of a power of appointment; and (7) policies of insurance on the decedent's life. Such interests are bequeathed or devised to such person by the decedent.

---

[1] ¶1101 Windsor, 570 U.S. —, 133 S. Ct. 2884, 186 L. Ed. 2d 932 (June 26, 2013).

[2] Rev. Rul. 2013-17, 2013-38 IRB 201.

Example 1: Mom devised real property to Dad for life, with remainder to her children. The life interest that passed to Dad does not qualify for the marital deduction because it will terminate at his death and the children will thereafter possess or enjoy the property.

Example 2: Mom purchased a joint and survivor annuity for herself and her husband who survived her. The value of her husband's annuity will qualify for the marital deduction to the extent that it is included in Mom's gross estate, because even though the interest will terminate on the husband's death, no one else will possess or enjoy any part of the property.

Spousal elections. Other interests passing to the surviving spouse include dower, curtesy, or statutory interests in place of dower or curtesy (if elected), as well as an interest under community property laws, even if the surviving spouse merely had an expectant interest prior to the decedent spouse's death [Reg. Secs. 20.2056(c)-1(a), 20.2056(c)-1(b)].

A property interest passes to a surviving spouse when a will requires an executor to satisfy a surviving spouse's debt for which the decedent had no liability. The amount of the devise needed to satisfy the debt qualifies for the marital deduction. Certain interests that pass to the surviving spouse do not qualify for the marital deduction including:

- A property interest transferred to the spouse to satisfy a claim against the estate;

- Commissions received by the surviving spouse as executor of the estate and which are deducted as an administration expense; and

- A property interest on which a deductible loss was incurred during the settlement of the estate [IRC Sec. 2056(b)(9); Reg. Sec. 20.2056(a)-2(b)].

An interest included in the decedent's estate is considered to pass from the decedent to the surviving spouse at death, regardless of the actual date of transfer [IRC Sec. 2056(c)(4)]. For example, a revocable trust qualifies for the federal estate tax deduction regardless of when the trust was established, provided the other marital deduction requirements are satisfied.

Two situations require further discussion:

- *Qualified disclaimer* [see Chapter 12]. The ability of a spouse or a third party to disclaim impacts on the passing requirement of the marital deduction. If the surviving spouse is the disclaimant, no interest is considered passing to the spouse because it is considered to pass to the person entitled to receive that interest as a result of the disclaimer. Therefore, no marital deduction is available. However, where a third party is the disclaimant and as a result of the disclaimer the property interest is considered to pass directly from the decedent to the surviving spouse, the marital deduction is available.

Will contests. An interest in property transferred to a surviving spouse as a consequence of enforceable rights by the spouse against the decedent's estate will qualify for the marital deduction [Reg. Sec. 20.2056(c)-2(d)(2)]. Thus, a claim under an antenuptial agreement by a surviving spouse who was left out of the decedent's will and did not elect against it, qualifies for the marital deduction as property passing from the decedent.[3]

Property relinquished by the surviving spouse in reaching a settlement will not, however, qualify [Reg. Sec. 20.2056(c)-2(d)(1)]. A property interest the surviving spouse assigns or surrenders in settlement of a will contest is not considered to pass from the decedent to the surviving spouse.

Value of Interest Passing to Surviving Spouse. The marital deduction is limited to the net value of property passing to the spouse [IRC Sec. 2056(b)(4)]. Death taxes, debts, and administration expenses payable from the marital bequest, mortgages on property passing to the spouse, and insufficient estate assets to fund the marital bequest all reduce the amount of the deduction [Reg. Sec. 20.2056(b)-4].

Impact of Administrative Expenses on Estate Tax Marital and Charitable Deductions. IRC Sec. 2056(b)(4)(B) provides that a marital deduction bequest is reduced when it is encumbered in any manner or where the surviving spouse incurs any obligation imposed by the decedent with respect to the passing of the interest. For example, if the principal is charged with an administrative expense (even if the estate deducts the expense for income tax purposes and not for estate tax purposes) the value of the marital deduction bequest passing under IRC Sec. 2056 or 2055 receives a corresponding reduction. The U.S. Supreme Court has held that the marital and charitable deductions must be reduced for administration expenses paid from income only if these payments would materially affect the interests of the charity or the surviving spouse.[4]

> **Example 3:** Mark Bell dies with an estate of $2 million. He leaves $1 million outright to his son and leaves the rest to his wife in a form that qualifies for the estate tax marital deduction. If there are no administration expenses, the marital deduction would be $1 million and the taxable estate would be $1 million. If the estate had a $100,000 administration expense that was deducted from the marital deduction as the IRS suggests, the taxable estate would be $1,100,000 ($2 million gross estate less $900,000 marital deduction). If the $100,000 administration expense was deducted instead from post-death income so that it does not constitute a "material limitation" on the spouse's right to receive income from the estate, as the Supreme Court required, the marital deduction remains at $1 million and the taxable estate would only be $1 million ($2 million gross estate less $1 million marital deduction).

In addition, the IRS has issued regulations addressing the effect of certain administration expenses on the valuation of property that qualifies for the estate tax marital or charitable deduction. The regulations provide that there must first be a material

---

[3] Rev. Rul. 68-271, 1968-1 CB 409.   [4] Estate of Hubert, 520 US 93 (1997).

limitation on income before any reduction in the marital deduction will be imposed as described in Reg. Sec. 20.2056(b)-4(a):

> In determining the value of the interest in property passing to the spouse an account must be taken of the effect of any material limitations upon her right to income from the property. An example of a case in which this rule may be applied is a bequest of property in trust for the benefit of the decedent's spouse but the income from the property from the date of the decedent's death until distribution of the property to the trustee is to be used to pay expenses incurred in the administration of the estate.

In addition, the regulations provide that for purposes of determining the marital deduction, the value of the marital share, which is the property passing from the estate which is eligible for the marital deduction, will not be reduced by estate transmission expenses [Reg. Sec. 20.2056(b)-4(d)(2)]. On the other hand, for purposes of determining the marital deduction, the value of the marital share shall not be reduced by the amount of estate management expenses attributable to and paid from the marital share. However, pursuant to IRC Sec. 2056(b)(9), the amount of the allowable marital deduction shall be reduced by the amount of these management expenses that are deducted on the decedent's federal estate tax return under IRC Sec. 2053 [Reg. Sec. 20.2056(b)-4(d)(3)].

Estate management expenses are defined as "expenses incurred in connection with the investment of the estate assets or with their preservation or maintenance during a reasonable period of administration." Examples of these expenses include investment advisory fees, stock brokerage commissions, custodial fees, and interest [Reg. Sec. 20.2056(b)-4(d)(1)(i)].

Estate transmission expenses are expenses that would not have been incurred but for the decedent's death and the consequent necessity of collecting the decedent's assets, paying the decedent's debts and death taxes, and distributing the decedent's property to those who are entitled to receive it. Estate transmission expenses include all expenses that are not estate management expenses, and include "expenses incurred in collecting estate assets, paying debts, estate and inheritance taxes, and distributing the decedent's property to those who are entitled to receive it." Examples of these expenses include executor commissions and attorney fees (except to the extent specifically related to investment, preservation, and maintenance of the assets), probate fees, expenses incurred in construction proceedings and defending against will contest, and appraisal fees [Reg. Sec. 20.2056(b)-4(d)(1)(ii)].

The regulations do not provide a test based on what constitutes a material limitation, but rather focus on the character of the administration expenses as illustrated in the following examples:

> **Example 4:** Dad dies and makes a bequest of shares of ABC Corp. stock to Child. The bequest provides that Child is to receive income from the shares from the date of Dad's death. The value of the bequeathed shares, on Dad's date of death, is $3 million. The residue of the estate is bequeathed to a trust that qualifies for the marital deduction. The value of the residue, on the date of Dad's death, before the payment of administration expenses and estate taxes, is

$6 million. Under applicable local law, the executor has the discretion to pay administration expenses from the income or principal of the residuary estate. All estate taxes are to be paid from the residue. The state estate tax equals the state tax credit available under IRC Sec. 2011. During the period of administration, the estate incurs estate transmission expenses of $400,000, which the executor charges to the residue. For purposes of determining the marital deduction, the value of the residue is reduced by the federal and state estate taxes and by the estate transmission expenses. If the transmission expenses are deducted on the federal estate tax return, the marital deduction is $3,500,000 ($6,000,000 minus $400,000 transmission expenses and minus $2,100,000 federal and state estate taxes). If the transmission expenses are deducted on the estate's income tax return rather than on the estate tax return, the marital deduction is $3,011,111 ($6,000,000 minus $400,000 transmission expenses and minus $2,588,889 federal and state estate taxes) [Reg. Sec. 20.2056(b)-4(d)(5), ex. 1].

Example 5: The facts are the same as in Example 2 above, except that, instead of incurring estate transmission expenses, the estate incurs estate management expenses of $400,000 in connection with the residue property passing for the benefit of the spouse. The executor charges these management expenses to the residue. In determining the value of the residue passing to the spouse for marital deduction purposes, a reduction is made for federal and state estate taxes payable from the residue but no reduction is made for the estate management expenses. If the management expenses are deducted on the estate's income tax return, the net value of the property passing to the spouse is $3,900,000 ($6,000,000 minus $2,100,000 federal and state estate taxes). A marital deduction is claimed for that amount and the taxable estate is $5,100,000 [Reg. Sec. 20.2056(b)-4(d)(5), ex. 2].

Example 6: The decedent has a gross estate of $3 million. Included in the gross estate are proceeds of $150,000 from a policy insuring the decedent's life and payable to the decedent's child as beneficiary. The applicable credit amount against the tax was fully consumed by the decedent's lifetime gifts. Applicable state law requires the child to pay any estate taxes attributable to the life insurance policy. Pursuant to the decedent's will, the rest of the decedent's estate passes outright to the surviving spouse. During the period of administration, the estate incurs estate management expenses of $150,000 in connection with the property passing to the spouse. The value of the property passing to the spouse is $2,850,000 ($3 million less the insurance proceeds of $150,000 passing to the child). For purposes of determining the marital deduction, if the management expenses are deducted on the estate's income tax return, the marital deduction is $2,850,000 ($3,000,000 less $150,000) and there is a resulting taxable estate of $150,000 ($3 million less a marital deduction of $2,850,000). Suppose instead, the management expenses of $150,000 are deducted on the estate's estate tax return under IRC Sec. 2053 as expenses of administration. In such a situation, claiming a marital deduction of $2,850,000 would be taking a deduction for the same $150,000 in property under both IRC Secs. 2053 and 2056 and would shield from estate taxes the $150,000 in insurance proceeds passing to the decedent's child. Therefore, in accordance with IRC Sec. 2056(b)(9), the marital deduction is limited to $2,700,000, and the resulting taxable estate is $150,000 [Reg. Sec. 20.2056(b)-4(d)(5), ex. 4].

▶ **PLANNING TIP:** As a result of the distinctions made in these regulations, it is now critical for estate planners to maintain thorough records that adequately allocate their fees and charges for services between the following two categories:

1. Estate transmission expenses, which are expenses incurred for the administration of the estate, payment of taxes and distribution of assets; and

2. Estate management expenses, which are expenses incurred in connection with the investment, maintenance or preservation of the estate.

(e) Terminable Interest Rule. The marital deduction may not be claimed if the surviving spouse receives a terminable interest. Terminable interests are interests that lapse after the passage of time, such as the right to income for life or for a stated number of years. The reason for the disallowance is that these interests would not be subject to estate taxation in the surviving spouse's estate. In other words, the marital deduction is designed to allow taxes to be deferred until the survivor disposes of the property by gift or dies and not to escape tax permanently.

However, there are exceptions to the terminable interest rule. These exceptions allow flexibility in planning for the needs of the decedent's spouse and children. At the same time, they ensure that the property will not ultimately go untaxed to your spouse unless, of course, he or she spends or consumes it all.

According to the IRC, an interest in property passing to the surviving spouse, when viewed at the time of the decedent's death, which may terminate or fail due to the lapse of time, the occurrence of an event or contingency, or the failure of an event or contingency to occur, is a terminable interest [IRC Sec. 2056(b)(1)]. A terminable interest is nondeductible if:

• For less than adequate and full consideration, the property interest passes from the decedent to someone other than the surviving spouse or the estate of the surviving spouse; and

• Because of the passing of the interest to another person, such person or his or her heirs or assigns may possess or enjoy any part of such property on the termination or failure of the surviving spouse's interest [IRC Sec. 2056(b)(1)].

Regardless of these two requirements, a terminable interest is nondeductible if the surviving spouse's interest is to be acquired for the surviving spouse pursuant to the decedent's directions, by the decedent's executor, or by a trustee [IRC Sec. 2056(b)(1)(C)]. Thus, no marital deduction is allowed for a property interest that the executor must convert into a terminable interest for the surviving spouse [Reg. Sec. 20.2056(b)-1(f)]. For example, a bequest of money is a nondeductible interest if the executor must use the money to purchase an annuity for the surviving spouse. An interest in property passing from the decedent to the surviving spouse and another person does not qualify for the marital deduction even though the other person's contingent interest will be extinguished before the alternate valuation date [see ¶1907] elected by the executor of the decedent's estate.[5]

[5] Rev. Rul. 70-400, 1970-2 CB 196.

In *Estate of Sansone*,[6] the Court of Appeals for the Ninth Circuit affirmed a district court holding that an inflation component to an annuity for which a QTIP estate tax marital deduction was elected did not increase the amount of the marital deduction. Rather, the deduction was limited to the value of the minimum annuity payable. Thus the marital deduction was limited to the starting annuity without adjustment for inflation.

Example 7: Dad devised a property named Blackacre to Mom, for her life with remainder over to Son. Mom's is a terminable interest because it will terminate on her death. No marital deduction is available because on its termination the remainder interest in Blackacre will pass to Son, who paid nothing for it.

Example 8: Dad bequeathed his residuary estate to Wife, if living on the date of distribution of his estate. Wife was living on the date of distribution and received the assets of the residuary estate. No marital deduction is allowable because her interest is a nondeductible terminable interest that could have been defeated by her failure to survive distribution. (But see below for an exception for survival for limited period.)

Example 9: Dad is the owner of joint and survivor annuity for a term of 40 years or the earlier death of the survivor of himself and Wife. He bequeathed the unexpired term of the annuity to Wife. The marital deduction is allowable. Reason: Dad passed his entire interest in the property to Wife and no one else will get the annuity after her death.

Example 10: Dad purchased a joint and survivor annuity contract payable to him for life and thereafter to Wife, including a "guarantee" that Daughters would receive the difference between the purchase price for the annuity and the sums paid to Mom and Dad. This annuity contract constitutes a nondeductible terminable interest because Daughters will possess the annuity, based on the guarantee, on Mom's death.

▶ **CAUTION:** The marital deduction is reduced if the group of assets available to satisfy the marital deduction contains nonqualified assets, such as terminable interests [IRC Sec. 2056(b)(2)].

Example 11: Mom, a surviving spouse, is to receive one-third of Husband's estate after the payment of all expenses. The value of his estate equals $150,000. Husband's estate includes a property interest valued at $120,000 that would be a nondeductible terminable interest if it passes to Mom. The executor has the right to satisfy the devise by transferring this entire property interest to Mom. The devise to Mom is nondeductible to the extent of $120,000.

---

[6] Estate of Sansone, 2001-1 USTC ¶60,399 (C.D. Cal. 2001), *aff'd*, 2002-2 USTC ¶60,442 (9th Cir. 2002).

Condition of survival for limited period. The passing of an interest to the surviving spouse conditioned on the survival for a period not exceeding six months is not a terminable interest [IRC Sec. 2056(b)(3)]. Technically, the terminable interest rule is *not* violated if:

1. The interest passing to the surviving spouse will terminate on the death of the surviving spouse within six months of the decedent's death or if the decedent and the surviving spouse die as a result of a common disaster; and

2. The condition does not, in fact, occur [Reg. Sec. 20.2056(b)-3(a)].

A devise to a spouse on the condition that the spouse does not die within six months of the decedent qualifies for the marital deduction if the spouse in fact survives the six-month period. A devise on the condition that the surviving spouse not die before a specified event also qualifies, provided the event is of such a nature that it could occur only within six months of the decedent's death and it did not in fact occur. If the condition is one that may occur either within or after the six-month period, the deduction will not be allowed, unless the condition relates to death as a result of a common disaster. However, a common disaster condition disqualifies the interest if state law can deprive the surviving spouse of the property interest at the time of the final audit of the estate tax return [Reg. Sec. 20.2056(b)-3(c)].

The six-month survivorship exception expires on the day of the sixth calendar month after the decedent's death that numerically corresponds to the day of the calendar month on which death occurs (e.g., December 15 for a June 15 date of death). Because it is possible for there to be no numerical correlation (no June 31 for a December 31 date of death), a 180-day period is often used.

> **Example 12:** Husband bequeaths 3,000 shares of stock to Wife, if she survives him by six months. If she does not survive him by six months, the shares are to go to his Husband's nephew. The nephew dies on February 1, and on August 1 Wife is still living. The bequest qualifies for the marital deduction.

> **Example 13:** Mom is the primary beneficiary of an insurance policy on Dad's life. Daughter is the contingent beneficiary. The policy provides that the interest of the primary beneficiary will fail if that beneficiary is not alive when the insurance company receives due proof of death of the insured. Dad dies, and the proceeds are paid to Mom. The insurance proceeds do not qualify for the marital deduction. Reason: Submission of proof of death could have occurred later than six months after Dad's death.[7]

A bequest under a self-prepared will qualified for the marital deduction even though one part of the will conditioned the bequest on the spouse's survival until distribution, in apparent violation of IRC Sec. 2056(b), which denies the marital deduction for a terminable interest. The court applied state (Washington) law, which provides that if it is determined that the testator intended a marital deduction gift, the will must be construed to comply with the marital deduction provisions of the Internal Revenue

---

[7] Rev. Rul. 54-121, 1954-1 CB 196.

Code. The court then examined the testator's intent when he drafted his will and found ample evidence to support the conclusion that he intended for the marital deduction to apply.[8]

¶1102 TRANSFERS QUALIFYING FOR MARITAL DEDUCTION

The following six types of transfers qualify for the estate tax marital deduction:

1. Outright transfers;
2. Estate trusts;
3. Life estate—general power of appointment trusts [IRC Sec. 2056(b)(5)];
4. Life insurance settlements with power of appointment [IRC Sec. 2056(b)(6)];
5. Interest in a qualified charitable remainder trusts [IRC Sec. 2056(b)(8)]; and
6. QTIP trusts [IRC Sec. 2056(b)(7); see ¶ 1103].

(a) Outright Transfers. Outright transfers, such as transfers of cash or of specific property, pose no particular problems [IRC Sec. 2056(c)]. Intestate dispositions in favor of the surviving spouse qualify, as well as nonprobate transfers to the surviving spouse, such as:

- Joint ownership between spouses, such as joint tenancy with right of survivorship, or tenancy by the entirety;
- Pseudo-joint property, such as Totten trusts;
- Spousal beneficiary designations, such as the "pay on death" designations frequently appearing on U.S. savings bonds; and
- Formal beneficiary designations associated with life insurance, annuities, and retirement plans.

(b) Estate Trusts. The marital deduction is allowed for a bequest in trust to pay income to the surviving spouse for life with remainder over to the surviving spouse's estate. This device is known as an estate trust. Derived from the parenthetical language in IRC Sec. 2056(b)(1) that the deduction is denied when the interest passes to any person other than the surviving spouse, this marital deduction form requires that the property interest (and any accumulated income) pass entirely to the surviving spouse's estate. This form of the deduction permits a marital deduction where property is likely to be non–income producing or where the decedent intends the trustee to accumulate income during the surviving spouse's lifetime. Thus, the estate trust qualifies for the marital deduction, even if payment of income to the surviving spouse during his or her lifetime is discretionary. However, the accumulated income, as well as principal, must be paid to the surviving spouse's estate.[1]

---

[8] Sowder, 2005-2 USTC ¶60,512 (D. Wash. 2005) *aff'd*, 2007-2 USTC ¶60,550 (9th Cir. 2007).

[1] **¶1102** Rev. Rul. 68-554, 1968-2 CB 412.

(c) Life Estate—General Power of Appointment Trusts. To qualify for the marital deduction, a life estate–general power of appointment trust must provide the surviving spouse with income from the trust for life and a general power of appointment over the trust property, which meets certain standards [IRC Sec. 2056(b)(5)]. Specifically, the following three requirements must be met:

1. Specific portion;

2. Frequency of income; and

3. Power of appointment.

Specific portion requirement. The surviving spouse must be entitled for life to all the income from the entire interest or all of the income from a specific portion of the trust [Reg. Sec. 20.2056(b)-5(a)(1)]. The right to income and the power of appointment [Reg. Sec. 20.2056(b)-5(c)] can apply to the trust as a whole or to an identifiable fractional or percentage portion. IRC Sec. 2056(b)(10) defines a specific portion only in terms of a fraction or percentage. A fixed dollar amount does not qualify.

Frequency of income requirement. The income from the trust must be paid to the surviving spouse at least annually or at more frequent intervals. The trust must give the surviving spouse the degree of enjoyment that a person designated as a life beneficiary of a trust has under state law. All the income from the marital deduction trust must be paid to the surviving spouse at least annually [Reg. Sec. 20.2056(b)-5(f)(1)]. Conditions or restrictions imposed on the income interest, such as conditioning the income interest on the surviving spouse not remarrying, will cause the trust to fail the frequency of income test. However, when the trust allows the trustee to accumulate income but provides that the surviving spouse can compel the trustee to distribute the income at least annually, the statutory requirements are met [Reg. Sec. 20.2056(b)-5(f)(8)].

Silence in the trust instrument as to the time for the payment of the income to the surviving spouse does not constitute a failure to meet this requirement unless local law permits the periodic payments to be made less frequently than annually [Reg. Sec. 20.2056(b)-5(e)].

Administrative powers must also be scrutinized to ensure that the frequency of income test is satisfied. These administrative powers emanate from local law. A trustee may be given discretionary power to allocate trust receipts and expenses between income and principal if the discretion is exercised fairly between the income beneficiary (the surviving spouse) and the remainderpersons. However, a power given to a trustee to allocate receipts, such as cash dividends and interest, to the trust principal indicates that the decedent did not intend the trust to supply the surviving spouse with the requisite income [Reg. Secs. 20.2056(b)-5(f)(2), 20.2056(b)-5(f)(3), 20.2056(b)-5(f)(4)].

Frequently, the funding of the marital deduction trust is deferred pending the administration of the decedent's estate. This delay does not prevent the trust from qualifying for the marital deduction, unless the delay is authorized or directed by decedent's will beyond the period reasonably necessary for the administration of the decedent's estate [Reg. Sec. 20.2056(b)-5(f)(9)].

Income that accrues but that is undistributed at the surviving spouse's death (the so-called "stub" income) must be subject to disposition by the surviving spouse. This can be satisfied if the stub income is paid to the spouse's estate or is subject to the spouse's power of appointment [Reg. Sec. 20.2056(b)-5(f)(8)].

Power of appointment requirements. The following power of appointment requirements must be met [IRC Sec. 2056(b)(5)]:

1. The surviving spouse must have a power to appoint the entire trust property or a specific portion to the surviving spouse or his or her estate [Reg. Sec. 20.2056(b)-5(g)(1)];

2. The trust principal must not be subject to a power in anyone else to appoint any part of the entire property or any specific portion thereof to any person other than the surviving spouse [Reg. Sec. 20.2056(b)-5(j)]; and

3. The power in the surviving spouse must be freely exercised by the surviving spouse alone and in all events [Reg. Sec. 20.2056(b)-5(g)(3)].

The first part of the power of appointment requirement is satisfied when the surviving spouse has the ability to direct that the property is paid to the surviving spouse or the surviving spouse's estate.

> **NOTE:** The power of appointment requirement of IRC Sec. 2056(b)(5) is often confused with IRC Sec. 2041, the estate tax general power of appointment provision. Although a surviving spouse who possesses a Sec. 2041 general power of appointment must include the property subject to the power in the spouse's gross estate for federal estate tax purposes, this property will not qualify for a federal estate tax marital deduction in the decedent's estate (i.e., the first spouse to die) unless this power expressly permits the surviving spouse to exercise it in favor of the surviving spouse or the surviving spouse's estate.

A qualifying power of appointment may be exercisable during the life of the surviving spouse, by the surviving spouse's last will, or a combination of the two. The decedent may limit the surviving spouse's exercise of the power during his or her life or by will [Reg. Sec. 20.2056(b)-5(g)(1)].

The marital deduction is available even if the decedent spouse has designated the beneficiaries who will take the trust property in default of an exercise of the power of appointment by the surviving spouse. However, an agreement cannot exist between the decedent and the surviving spouse that the surviving spouse will not exercise the power or will exercise the power in favor of certain persons [Reg. Sec. 20.2056(b)-5(g)(2)].

The trust principal must not be subject to anyone else's power. For example, the trustee may not possess the discretionary power to invade the trust principal and make distributions or divert the trust property to someone other than the surviving spouse, such as the decedent's children. If the trustee possesses such a power, the surviving spouse lacks the requisite unlimited power to appoint the entire principal free of the trust. The trustee may, however, possess the power to invade the trust property for the surviving spouse's benefit.

Beyond possessing the power of appointment, the surviving spouse must be able to exercise it freely and unconditionally. For example, a power that may be exercised for a limited purpose or a power to invade the trust principal, if restricted to the surviving spouse's support or reasonable needs, is not exercisable in all events [Reg. Sec. 20.2056(b)-5(g)(3)].

Certain formal limitations on the exercise of the power are, however, permitted. For example, the exercise of a lifetime power of appointment conditioned on the delivery of a written instrument to the trustee is permissible [Reg. Sec. 20.2056(b)-5(g)(4)].

The fact that the spouse is legally incapacitated and presently incapable of exercising the power of appointment under state law will not disallow the marital deduction.[2]

(d) Life Insurance Settlement with Power of Appointment. The insurance exception is similar to the one for a life estate with power of appointment. However, under this exception to the terminable interest rule, the payments must begin not later than 13 months after the decedent's death. The insurance contract must provide either that the proceeds be paid in installments or be held by the insurer subject to the payment of interest [IRC Sec. 2056(b)(6)].

(e) Interest in Qualified Charitable Remainder Trust. The marital deduction is allowable for an interest in a charitable remainder annuity trust or a charitable remainder unitrust [see ¶1005] that passes to the surviving spouse if the surviving spouse is the only noncharitable beneficiary of the trust [IRC Sec. 2056(b)(8)]. A noncharitable beneficiary means a trust beneficiary except an organization for which the charitable deduction is allowed.

The combination of a qualified income interest payable to the surviving spouse as income beneficiary of a charitable remainder trust and a charitable remainder interest results in a complete federal estate tax deduction of the property being transferred in the first-to-die spouse's estate regardless of the value of property being transferred. The income component qualifies for the federal estate tax marital deduction. The remainder will qualify for the charitable deduction under IRC Sec. 2055 [IRC Sec. 2056(b)(8)]. Thus, this arrangement involves no election or inclusion in the surviving spouse's estate.

¶1103 QUALIFIED TERMINABLE INTEREST PROPERTY (QTIP)—ESTATE TAX DEDUCTION

The QTIP trust is a popular estate-planning device because it enables a decedent to provide not only for the surviving spouse with income for the surviving spouse's lifetime but after the surviving spouse's death, to pass assets on to beneficiaries designated by the decedent. The beneficiaries frequently are the decedent's children from a prior marriage(s).

Purpose of QTIP trust. A QTIP trust can be particularly helpful in a second-marriage situation because the QTIP trust will help the decedent feel secure that his or her wishes for the ultimate disposition of assets will be honored no matter what the plans of the surviving spouse may be. For example, an individual may want to provide for her surviving spouse during her lifetime but also want to provide for her children from a prior marriage. A QTIP trust will permit the decedent to accomplish this objective while also providing income for a surviving spouse during the surviving spouse's lifetime. The surviving spouse does not have the power to change any beneficiary designations in the QTIP trust.

---

[2] Rev. Rul. 75-350, 1975-2 CB 366.

Example 1: Wife transfers $100,000 to a trust for the benefit of Husband. The terms of the trust provide that Husband will receive all of the net income annually from the trust for life. The trustee has the power to invade corpus for Husband's health, maintenance and support. When Husband dies, the balance of the trust passes to Wife's daughter from a previous marriage. Although Husband has a terminable interest in the trust, he has a qualifying income interest making the transfer eligible for the marital deduction. Wife may elect to treat the property as QTIP property and claim a marital deduction for the value of the property transferred. This election is made by listing the property on Form 709, Schedule A, Part 1, and deducting the value of the trust on Form 709, Schedule A, Part 4, line 4.

Although only a life interest actually passes from the first spouse to die to the surviving spouse, the entire QTIP qualifies for the marital deduction and escapes inclusion in the estate of the first spouse to die [IRC Sec. 2056(b)(7)]. However, the QTIP will be included in the estate of the surviving spouse either at the time of his or her death pursuant to IRC Sec. 2044(a), or upon a lifetime disposition of his or her qualifying income interest pursuant to IRC Sec. 2519. IRC Sec. 2519 addresses the gift tax consequences of dispositions of income interests from a QTIP trust [For a detailed discussion, see ¶ 1105]. Unique to the QTIP trust is the right of recovery from the *person receiving the property* of the federal estate or gift tax (and any related interest and penalties) paid as a result of the inclusion of the QTIP trust assets in the surviving spouse's gross estate [IRC Sec. 2207A]. For further discussion, see ¶ 1105.

For further discussion of the QTIP trust, see ¶ 1708 (gift tax) and ¶ 2425 (Form 706).

(a) Requirements for QTIP Trust. The following three requirements must be satisfied in order for terminable interest property to be eligible for the estate tax marital deduction and qualify as QTIP property:

1. The property funding the QTIP must pass directly from the decedent to the surviving spouse who is a U.S. citizen [IRC Secs. 2056(b)(7)(B)(i)(I), 2056(d)(1)];

2. The surviving spouse must have a qualifying income interest for life which means that he or she is entitled to receive all the income from the property payable annually or at more frequent intervals, and that no person has a power to appoint any part of the property to any person other than the surviving spouse [IRC Sec. 2056(b)(7)(B)(ii)(II)]. Therefore, an income interest granted for a term of years, a life estate that terminates upon the occurrence of an event such as remarriage or any other limiting provision will not qualify for the marital deduction. Any restriction on the surviving spouse's right to the income will result in a denial of the marital deduction in a QTIP trust. An income interest in a trust won't fail to constitute a qualifying income interest for life solely because the trustee has a power to distribute principal to or for the benefit of the surviving spouse. The fact that property distributed to a surviving spouse may be transferred by the spouse to another person does not result in a failure to satisfy IRC Sec. 2056(b)(7)(B)(ii)(II). However, if the surviving spouse is legally bound to transfer the distributed property to another person without full and adequate consideration in money or money's worth, the requirement of IRC Sec. 2056(b)(7)(B)(ii)(II) is not satisfied

[Reg. Sec. 20.2056(b)-7(d)(6)]. In *A. Baer Revocable Trust*[1] the IRS Associate Chief Counsel recommended that the IRS acquiesce in the result only of a decision by the U.S. District Court of Nebraska where the court held that the decedent's estate was entitled to a refund of the estate tax deficiency assessed against the value of certain contingent bequests. Following the decedent's death, the majority of his estate passed to a trust for the benefit of his surviving spouse. The terms of the trust provided for certain specific bequests to individuals, which were contingent upon the sale of the decedent's stock in a private equity company for a profit during the surviving spouse's lifetime. After transferring the private equity stock to the trust, the decedent's personal representative made a QTIP election. Upon review, the IRS denied the marital deduction for the value of the contingent bequests and assessed an estate tax deficiency.

Because the court found that the contingent bequests were essentially worthless, it concluded that the estate was entitled to a refund for the deficiency related to the bequests. The Associate Chief Counsel argued that the court erred as a matter of law because, under IRC Sec. 2056(b)(7)(B)(ii)(II), the contingent bequests rendered the value of the stocks ineligible for QTIP treatment. IRC Sec. 2056(b)(7)(B)(ii)(II) and Reg. Sec. 20.2056(b)-7(d)(6) provide that no person can have the power to appoint any property subject to the QTIP election to anyone other than the surviving spouse, even if the spouse is legally bound to transfer the distributed property for less than full and adequate consideration. However, because the court found that the contingent bequests had negligible value, the court's error did not impact the outcome of the case;

and

3. The executor of the estate of the first spouse to die must make an affirmative election on the decedent spouse's estate tax return to designate some or all of the trust property as QTIP property [IRC Sec. 2056(b)(7)(B)(i)(III)].

(b) Operation of QTIP Trust. A QTIP trust provides a qualified income interest to the surviving spouse for life and allows the decedent to name who receives the remainder interest in the trust assets when the surviving spouse dies. This ability of the decedent to direct who will be the ultimate beneficiary of the QTIP trust assets is the reason that QTIP trusts are used so frequently by estate planners. However, the property does not completely escape estate tax. The fair market value of the property at the date of the surviving spouse's death is included in the surviving spouse's estate under IRC Sec. 2044.

Right of recovery in the case of certain marital deduction property. If the surviving spouse's estate owes estate tax, its executor generally can recover from the person(s) receiving the property that portion of the tax attributable to the inclusion of the QTIP property in the gross estate from the QTIP property under IRC Sec. 2207A. However, if the surviving spouse specifically directs in his or her will that the estate tax attributable to the QTIP property is to be paid from other sources, the taxes are to be paid as provided in the will.

---

[1] **¶1103** D.C. Neb., 2012-1 USTC ¶60,590. AOD, 2012-001, 4/23/2012.

(c) Reverse QTIP Election. IRC Sec. 2652(a)(3) gives an executor or trustee who is making the QTIP election the choice to treat the property as if the QTIP election had not been made. As a result of this "reverse QTIP election" the decedent remains, for GST tax purposes, the transferor of the QTIP trust or property rather than the surviving spouse. Thus, the decedent's GST tax exemption may be allocated to the QTIP trust or property even though the QTIP is taxed in the estate of the surviving spouse [see ¶ 2502].

The reverse QTIP election must be made on the same return that the QTIP election is made [Reg. Sec. 26.2652-2(b)]. The election is irrevocable and must be made with respect to all the property in the trust to which the QTIP election applies [Reg. Sec. 26.2652-2(a)]. The reverse QTIP election should be made when executors want to avoid wasting any of the deceased spouse's available GST exemption.

(d) Late QTIP Election. In Rev. Proc. 2004-47,[2] the IRS released an alternate method for executors and trustees to make a late QTIP election under IRC Sec. 2652. The alternate method may be used in lieu of the letter ruling process. Relief for a late reverse QTIP is available under Rev. Proc. 2004-47 if the following requirements are met:

1. A valid IRC Sec. 2056(b)(7) QTIP election was made;

2. The reverse QTIP election was not properly made because the taxpayer relied on counsel who failed to advise the taxpayer of the need or proper method to make a reverse QTIP election;

3. The decedent has a sufficient amount of unused GST exemption;

4. The estate is not eligible for an automatic six-month extension;

5. The surviving spouse has not made a lifetime disposition of any part of the qualifying income interest for life in the QTIP property;

6. The surviving spouse is alive or no more than six months have passed since the surviving spouse's death; and

7. The estate files a request for more time to make a reverse QTIP election. The request must have a cover sheet that states "Request for Extension Filed Pursuant to Rev. Proc. 2004-47."

(e) Clayton Contingent QTIP Election. An alternative to the traditional reduce-to-zero marital deduction formula is the use of a *Clayton* contingent QTIP election, which permits a surviving spouse's income interest in a QTIP marital deduction trust to be contingent on the executor making a QTIP election to treat the marital trust property as QTIP property under IRC Sec. 2056(b)(7)(B)(i)(III) [Reg. Sec. 20.2056(b)-7(d)(3) and (h), ex. 6]. The regulations were changed to conform to the numerous court decisions that allowed an estate tax marital deduction for a surviving spouse's interest in property that was contingent upon the executor making a QTIP election.[3] In addition, the regulations clarify that the interest will not fail to qualify for

---

[2] Rev. Proc. 2004-47, 2004-2 CB 169.

[3] Estate of Clayton, 97 TC 327 (1991), *rev'd and rem'd*, 976 F.2d 1486 (5th Cir. 1992); Estate of Robertson, 98 TC 678 (1992), *aff'd*, 15 F.3d 779 (8th Cir. 1994); Estate of Spencer, TC Memo 1992-579, *rev'd and rem'd*, 43 F.3d 226 (6th Cir.

the marital deduction because the portion of the property for which the QTIP election is not made passes to or for the benefit of persons other than the surviving spouse [Reg. Sec. 20.2056(b)-7(d)(3)].

> **Example 2:** Dad's will establishes a trust provided that Mom is entitled to receive the income, payable at least annually, from that portion of the trust that the executor elects to treat as QTIP property. The portion of the trust that the executor does not elect to treat as QTIP property passes as of Dad's date of death to a trust for the benefit of Son, who is Dad's child from a prior marriage. The executor is not considered to have a power to appoint any part of the trust property to any person other than Mom during her lifetime and the marital deduction may be claimed for the value of the property subject to the QTIP election [Reg. Sec. 20.2056(b)-7(h), ex. 6].

The executor is permitted to determine, by means of the QTIP election, both the amount of the deceased spouse's estate that will qualify for the marital deduction and the nature of the beneficiaries' interests. This provides the executor with a great deal of after-death planning flexibility.

(f) Income Interest for Life Requirement. It is axiomatic that the QTIP must provide the surviving spouse with a qualifying income interest for life. The surviving spouse must be entitled to receive, for life, all the income from the entire interest or from a specific portion, payable annually or at more frequent intervals [IRC Sec. 2056(b)(7)(B)(ii)]. Providing the surviving spouse with an income interest for life that is limited by an ascertainable standard or is otherwise limited will not qualify. For example, in *Estate of Davis*,[4] the Court of Appeals for the Ninth Circuit found that the QTIP trust did not give the surviving spouse an unfettered interest in the income from the trust. It limited her to income necessary for her accustomed standard of living and therefore did not qualify for the marital deduction.

> ▶ **CAUTION:** Income interests granted for a term of years or life estates subject to termination if certain events occur (e.g., if the surviving spouse remarries) do not qualify for the marital deduction [Reg. Sec. 20.2056(b)-7(d)(3)].

In Rev. Rul. 2006-26,[5] the IRS described three situations where a surviving spouse has a qualifying income interest for life in an IRA or other qualified plan for purposes of electing to treat the IRA as qualified terminable interest property (QTIP) under IRC Sec. 2056(b)(7). In the three situations described in Rev. Rul. 2006-26, the income of the trust, excluding the IRA, and the income of the IRA were determined separately even though IRA distributions were made to the trust. In addition, the surviving spouse had the power to compel the trustee to withdraw from the IRA all the income earned on the IRA assets at least annually and distribute that amount to the spouse. In two of the situations, the income of the trust and IRA were determined pursuant to applicable state law. In the other situation, applicable state law (common or statutory) determined the amount of IRA income that the spouse could compel the trustee

---

(Footnote Continued)

1995); Estate of Clack, 106 TC 131 (1996), *acq.*, 1996-2 CB 1.

[4] Estate of Davis, TC Memo 2003-55, *aff'd*, 394 F.3d 1294 (9th Cir. 2005).

[5] Rev. Rul. 2006-26, 2006-1 CB 939.

to withdraw in accordance with the requirements of IRC Sec. 2056(b)(7)(B)(ii) and Reg. Sec. 20.2056(b)-5(f)(1).

The IRS has ruled that a distribution of income to a service provider (rather than payment to the spouse directly) "for the benefit of" an incapacitated surviving spouse was acceptable.[6] The payment to the surviving spouse for the use and benefit of individuals the spouse is legally obligated to support is permissible, but payment to the spouse for any other class of beneficiaries is not.[7]

(g) "Stub Income". "Stub income" is the income that accumulates between the time the surviving spouse dies and the date when the last quarterly income payment from the trust must be distributed to beneficiaries. The QTIP deduction will still be allowed even if this stub income is not distributed to the surviving spouse's estate [Reg. Sec. 20.2056(b)-7(d)(4)].[8] Keep in mind, however, that the amount of the stub income must still be included in the surviving spouse's taxable gross estate [Reg. Sec. 1.2044-1(d)(2)].

(h) No Beneficiaries Except Surviving Spouse. The QTIP trust can have no beneficiaries except the surviving spouse during the surviving spouse's lifetime. No one—not even the surviving spouse—may have a power to appoint or give the property to any other person during the surviving spouse's life [IRC Sec. 2056(b)(7)(B)(ii)(II)].

The surviving spouse is entitled to possess a testamentary general power of appointment because it is exercisable only after the surviving spouse's death [IRC Sec. 2056(b)(7)]. The surviving spouse may also be granted a nongeneral power of appointment exercisable in the spouse's favor during the spouse's lifetime without disqualifying the property from marital deduction treatment. Thus, the trust may permit the trustee to invade the trust principal for the benefit of the surviving spouse limited by an ascertainable standard. Or, the surviving spouse can be given the power to withdraw the greater of $5,000 or 5 percent of the trust principal annually.

> ▶ **OBSERVATION:** Often, the decisive factor in determining to use the QTIP trust rather than the life estate–general power of appointment trust is the absence of the power of appointment requirement. Its removal enables the trust property to qualify for the marital deduction without allowing the surviving spouse to determine who will ultimately enjoy the trust property.

One court has held that a provision allowing a deceased father's son to purchase property from a trust at a bargain price violated the QTIP requirement that "no person has a power to appoint any part of the property to any person than the surviving spouse" and thus prevented the trust from qualifying for the marital deduction as a QTIP.[9]

> ▶ **PRACTICE POINTER:** An executor can only make a QTIP election if the will and trust documents have been carefully drafted to comply with the precise requirements set forth in IRC Sec. 2056(b)(7). The estate-planning documents must meticulously adhere to these formal statutory requirements. There is no

---

[6] Estate of Rinaldi, 97-2 USTC ¶60,281 (Fed. Cl. Ct. 1997), *aff'd*,178 F.3d 1308 (Fed. Cir. 1998), *cert. denied*, 526 US 1006 (1999).

[7] Ltr. Rul. 8706008.

[8] Estate of Howard, 91 TC 329 (1988), *rev'd*, 910 F.2d 633 (9th Cir. 1990); Estate of Shelfer, 103 TC 10 (1994), *rev'd*, 86 F.3d 1045 (11th Cir. 1996).

[9] Ltr. Rul. 8701004

room for creativity. If your will falls short, the QTIP election will be denied because the IRS will find that the terms of the will set forth a framework directly contradictory to the statutory requirements for QTIP eligibility. Drafters should avoid placing limitations on distributions from QTIP trusts and on authorizing the sale of assets held in a QTIP trust at a discount.

(i) The QTIP Election. The executor must make an irrevocable election on the decedent spouse's estate tax return to claim a marital deduction for all or a portion of the property [IRC Sec. 2056(b)(7)(B)(i)(III)]. The election is irrevocable [IRC Sec. 2056(b)(7)(B)(v)].

IRC Sec. 2203 defines the term "executor" and includes, where an estate is not being administered, any person in actual or constructive possession of the decedent's property.

The election must be made on the decedent's estate tax return, that is, the last estate tax return filed on or before the due date (including extensions), or, if no timely return was filed, the first estate tax return filed after the due date [Reg. Sec. 20.2056(b)-7(b)(4)]. An untimely filed amended estate tax return cannot change the estate tax consequences of a QTIP election (or the failure to elect) after the estate filed a timely estate tax return.[10] An estate will only be allowed an extension of time to make a QTIP election at the discretion of the IRS in cases where the taxpayer demonstrates to the satisfaction of the IRS that (1) the taxpayer acted reasonably and in good faith, and (2) granting the relief will not prejudice the interest of the government [Reg. Sec. 301.9100-1(c)].[11]

An executor can make the QTIP election by simply listing the QTIP on Schedule M on the estate tax return and deducting its value. Thus, the procedure now requires action on the part of the executor to elect out of the QTIP marital deduction.

A joint and survivor annuity that is included in the decedent's gross estate under IRC Sec. 2039 (or, in the case of an interest in an annuity arising under the community property laws of a state, included in the gross estate of the decedent under IRC Sec. 2033) automatically qualifies as QTIP even though only the surviving spouse has the right to receive payments before the surviving spouse's death. An election is necessary only to refuse acceptance of QTIP treatment for this type of annuity [IRC Sec. 2056(b)(7)(C)]. The deductible interest is the specific portion of the property that (assuming the interest rate for valuing annuities) would produce income equal to the minimum amount payable annually to the surviving spouse [Reg. Sec. 20.2056(b)-7(e)(2)].

Example 3: $200,000 of a $500,000 trust paying $20,000 a year to the surviving spouse for life is treated as a qualifying income interest, assuming that the applicable interest rate under IRC Sec. 7520 is 10 percent [Reg. Sec. 20.2056(b)-7(h), ex. 11].

If all of the decedent's property was held jointly and there is no property to probate, the election process may seem confusing. However, the person in possession of the QTIP

---

[10] Ltr. Rul. 8746004.   [11] Ltr. Rul. 9848041.

property (e.g., the trustee of a living trust), has the responsibility for making the QTIP election.

> ▶ **OBSERVATION:** In case of doubt, you should open an estate, even when not otherwise required, to designate the person responsible for making the QTIP election. A protective QTIP election can be made if, at the time the estate tax return is filed, there is an issue concerning the includability of an asset in the decedent's gross estate or the nature of the property to which the surviving spouse is entitled [Reg. Sec. 20.2056(b)-7(c)].

(j) Planning Strategies. QTIP trusts offer great opportunities for estate planning, even after death. The first spouse will usually use a formula clause to figure how much will go to the QTIP. The amount shielded from tax by the unified credit will go to children, and the balance will go the QTIP. The executor normally elects the marital deduction for the entire QTIP, thereby deferring estate taxes until the surviving spouse's death. But if the first spouse failed to make use of his or her applicable exclusion amount, an executor may make only a partial QTIP election.

The executor can make a partial election of only a fractional or percentile share of the QTIP property [Reg. Sec. 20.2056(b)-7(b)(2)]. The controlling instrument should permit postmortem planning to determine the size, by fraction or percentage, of the QTIP property to which the election applies. Remember, a partial election, once made, is irrevocable.

Before making a QTIP election on a decedent's federal estate tax return, you should determine whether it would be more beneficial to forgo the election, incur an estate tax in the estate of the first spouse to die, and claim the Section 2013 credit in the surviving spouse's estate [see ¶ 2104].

This option should be considered particularly where the surviving spouse is elderly (or in poor health) or where the surviving spouse dies before the federal estate tax return is filed for the first spouse's estate. However, it is important to keep in mind that because the income from the trust will be accumulating in the surviving spouse's estate, there will be some point at which it is no longer beneficial to forgo the QTIP election and take the Section 2013 credit.

Because it usually is difficult to determine whether the surviving spouse will die before or after this crossover point, it may be advisable to submit an extension for filing the decedent's federal estate tax return and defer the decision for up to 15 months after the death of the first spouse to die. If the surviving spouse does not die within this period, you must assess the potential benefits of taking the Sec. 2013 credit in view of the surviving spouse's life expectancy.

(k) Relief from Unneeded QTIP Election Available. Relief is available for surviving spouses and their estates in situations where an unneeded QTIP election must be undone to save tax for the survivor's estate.[12] If the following steps are taken, the unneeded QTIP election will be treated as null and void for federal estate, gift, and generation-skipping transfer tax purposes. The taxpayer must produce a copy of

---

[12] Rev. Proc. 2001-38, 2001-1 CB 1335. See Ltr. Ruls. 201345006, 201338003, 200226020 (IRS disregarded QTIP election made on the decedent's estate tax return because it was unnecessary to reduce the estate tax liability to zero and, therefore, treated as null and void for estate, gift and GST purposes).

the estate tax return filed by the predeceased spouse's estate establishing that the election was not necessary to reduce the estate tax liability to zero, based on values as finally determined for federal estate tax purposes. This information, coupled with an explanation of why the election should be treated as void, should be submitted either with the Form 706 filed for the surviving spouse's estate, or with a request for a private letter ruling submitted at any time before filing the Form 706.

¶1104 QUALIFIED TERMINABLE INTEREST PROPERTY (QTIP)—GIFT TAX DEDUCTION

The following three requirements must be met for terminable interest property to be eligible for the gift tax marital deduction as a QTIP:

- The property funding the QTIP must be transferred by the donor spouse [IRC Sec. 2523(f)(2)(A)];
- The donee spouse must have a qualifying income interest for life [IRC Sec. 2523(f)(2)(B)]; and
- An irrevocable election must be made to treat the property as QTIP property [IRC Sec. 2523(f)(2)(B)].

The QTIP trust enables a donor spouse to provide, not only for the donee spouse with an income interest for the donee spouse's lifetime, but after the donee spouse's death to pass assets on to beneficiaries designated by the donor spouse. Although only a life interest actually passes from the donor to the donee, the entire QTIP qualifies for the marital deduction and escapes inclusion in the estate of the donor [IRC Secs. 2523(a), 2523(f)]. However, the QTIP will be included in the estate of the donee spouse either at the time of his or her death pursuant to IRC Sec. 2044(a) , or upon a lifetime disposition of his or her qualifying income interest pursuant to IRC Sec. 2519. For a detailed discussion of IRC Sec. 2519, which addresses the gift tax consequences of dispositions of income interests from a QTIP trust, see ¶1105.

The marital deduction defers tax until the donee spouse dies or otherwise disposes of the QTIP property. For further discussion of the QTIP trust, see ¶1105 (IRC Sec. 2519), and ¶2425 (Form 706).

IRC Sec. 2519 addresses the gift tax consequences of dispositions of income interests from a QTIP trust. For a detailed discussion, see ¶1105.

The QTIP election is made by listing the qualified terminable interest property on Schedule M of a timely filed gift tax return (Form 706) and deducting its value. The QTIP election, which is irrevocable, is presumed to have been made if the property is listed and deducted on Schedule M. A gift tax return is required to elect QTIP treatment for interspousal gifts, even though a gift tax return is not otherwise required for gifts qualifying for the marital deduction.

If a donor spouse gives a donee spouse a life interest in property, the gift generally is a terminable interest that does not qualify for the gift tax marital deduction. The donor spouse may, however, elect to treat the life interest as a QTIP for which the marital deduction is allowed. The QTIP election may be made for any property transferred to a donee spouse in which the spouse has a qualified income interest for life.

¶1104

The donee spouse has a qualified income interest for life if these four requirements are met [IRC Sec. 2523(f)]:

1. The donee spouse is entitled to all the income from the transferred property for life;

2. The income is payable to the donee spouse annually or at more frequent intervals;

3. During the donee spouse's lifetime, no person has the power to appoint any part of the property to any person except the donee spouse; and

4. Even though no person can appoint any part of the property during the donee spouse's lifetime, a trustee may invade the trust principal for the donee spouse's benefit.

¶1105 DISPOSITION OF QTIP LIFE INCOME INTEREST

In general, no gift tax marital deduction is available for the transfer of a "terminable interest" (e.g., a life estate) to a spouse. However, a marital deduction is available for transfers of QTIP under IRC Sec. 2523(f) (gift tax).

The following three requirements must be satisfied in order for terminable interest property to be eligible for the gift tax marital deduction and qualify as QTIP [see ¶1107]:

1. The property funding the QTIP must be transferred by the donor spouse [IRC Sec. 2523(f)(2)(A)];

2. The donee spouse must have a qualifying income interest for life [IRC Sec. 2523(f)(2)(B)]; and

3. An irrevocable election must be made to treat the property as QTIP property [IRC Sec. 2523(f)(2)(C)].

The QTIP trust enables a donor spouse to provide not only for the donee spouse with an income interest for the donee spouse's lifetime but after the donee spouse's death, to pass assets on to beneficiaries designated by the donor. Although only a life interest actually passes from the donor spouse to the donee, the entire QTIP qualifies for the marital deduction and escapes inclusion in the estate of the donor spouse [IRC Sec. 2523(f)]. However, the QTIP will be included in the estate of the surviving spouse either at the time of his or her death pursuant to IRC Sec. 2044(a) or upon a lifetime disposition of his or her qualifying income interest pursuant to IRC Sec. 2519. For further discussion of the QTIP trust, see ¶1107.

(a) IRC Sec. 2519—Dispositions of Qualifying Life Estate. A special provision [IRC Sec. 2519(b)(1)] applies to dispositions of income interests from a QTIP trust. IRC Sec. 2519(a) provides that where the surviving spouse disposes of all or a part of the qualifying income interest, such transfer is deemed a gratuitous transfer of the entire QTIP other than the qualifying income interest [Reg. Sec. 25.2519-1(a)]. For example, if the donee spouse gives away all or part of a qualifying income interest for life, the spouse will be treated under IRC Sec. 2519 as making a taxable gift of the entire trust other than the qualifying income interest for life. The amount of the gift will be the fair market value of the entire property minus the income interest. This means that the gift will be the value of the remainder interest. This gift will not be eligible for the annual gift tax exclusion because it is a gift of a future interest [Reg. Sec. 25.2519-1(c)].

Reg. Sec. 25.2519-1 provides for a "net gift" treatment on the deemed gift of a remainder that occurs when an individual makes a gift of some or all of his or her QTIP income interest. This means that the value of the transfer under IRC Sec. 2519 will be reduced by the amount of the gift tax to be paid by the donee.

Although IRC Sec. 2519 does not define a "disposition," Reg. Sec. 25.2519-1(f) provides that the sale of QTIP, followed by the payment to the surviving spouse of a portion of the proceeds equal to the value of the surviving spouse's income interest, is considered a disposition of the qualifying income interest. Not included as a disposition for purposes of IRC Sec. 2519 is the conversion of QTIP into other property in which the surviving spouse has a qualifying interest for life [Reg. Sec. 25.2519-1(f)]. Reg. Sec. 25.2519-1(f) provides that the sale and reinvestment of assets of a trust holding QTIP is not a disposition of the qualifying income interest, provided that the surviving spouse continues to have a qualifying income interest for life in the trust after the sale and reinvestment.

In *Kite*,[1] the Tax Court concluded that the sale of a decedent's interest in two QTIP trusts was subject to gift tax. In preparation for an annuity transaction, the decedent retroactively named her children trustees of two QTIP trusts, a marital deduction trust over which the decedent had a general power of appointment, and a residuary trust. The children, as trustees of the trusts, terminated the QTIP trusts and the marital deduction trust, with the assets passing to the decedent's revocable trust. The trust assets consisted entirely of family limited partnership (FLP) interests. A separate partnership owned by the children contributed assets to the FLP. The decedent's revocable trust then sold its entire interest in the FLP to the children in exchange for private annuities. The first annuity payments were scheduled to begin 10 years after the agreements were executed. The record established that the disposition of the QTIP trusts was "part of a prearranged and simultaneous transfer." Pursuant to Reg. Sec. 25.2519-1(f), the decedent disposed of her qualifying income interests, which were traceable from the FLP to the QTIP trusts.

The court found that by creating an intermediary step in the annuity transaction, i.e., terminating the QTIP trusts before selling the QTIP trust assets to the Kite children, Mrs. Kite's transfer of her ownership interests circumvented the QTIP regime and avoided any transfer tax imposed by IRC Sec. 2519. Therefore, the court found that the termination of the QTIP trusts and the following immediate transfer of the QTIP trust assets to the Kite children should be treated as a single transaction for purposes of IRC Sec. 2519. As discussed above, the sale of QTIP assets, followed by the payment to the surviving spouse of a portion of the proceeds equal to the value of the surviving spouse's income interest, is considered a disposition of the qualifying income interest [Reg. Sec. 25.2519-1(f)]. The court, therefore, concluded pursuant to Reg. Sec. 25.2519-1(c)(1) that the sale of the decedent's FLP interests that could be

---

[1] ¶ 1105 Estate of Kite, TC Memo 2013-43.

¶1105

traced to the QTIP trusts was subject to gift tax to the extent of the fair market value of the entire property subject to the decedent's qualifying income interest, as of the date of the annuity transaction, less the value of her qualifying income interest. Reg. Sec. 25.2519-1(c)(1) provides that the amount treated as a transfer under IRC Sec. 2519 is equal to the fair market value of the entire property subject to the qualifying income interest, determined on the date of the disposition, less the value of the qualifying income interest in the property on the date of the disposition.

Example 1: *Transfer of the spouse's life estate in residence.* Under D's will, a personal residence valued for estate tax purposes at $250,000 passes to S for life, and after S's death to D's children. D's executor made a valid election to treat the property as qualified terminable interest property. When the fair market value of the property is $300,000 and the value of S's life interest in the property is $100,000, S makes a gift of S's entire interest in the property to D's children. Pursuant to IRC Sec. 2519, S makes a gift in the amount of $200,000 (i.e., the fair market value of the QTIP of $300,000 less the fair market value of S's qualifying income interest in the property of $100,000). In addition, S makes a gift of $100,000 (i.e., the fair market value of S's income interest in the property) [Reg. Sec. 25.2519-1(g), ex. 1].

Example 2: *Sale of spouse's life estate.* The facts are the same as in Example 1 except that S sells S's interest in the property to D's children for $100,000. S makes a gift of $200,000 ($300,000 less the $100,000 value of the qualifying income interest in the property). S does not make a gift of the income interest, because the consideration received for S's income interest is equal to the value of the income interest [Reg. Sec. 25.2519-1(g), ex. 2].

Example 3: *Transfer of income interest in trust subject to partial election.* D's will established a trust valued for estate tax purposes at $500,000, all of the income of which is payable annually to S for life. After S's death, the principal of the trust is to be distributed to D's children. Assume that only 50 percent of the trust was treated as a QTIP. S makes a gift of all of S's interest in the trust to D's children at which time the fair market value of the trust is $400,000 and the fair market value of S's life income interest in the trust is $100,000. S makes a gift of $150,000 (the fair market value of the QTIP, 50 percent of $400,000, less the $50,000 income interest in the qualified terminable interest property). S also makes a gift pursuant to IRC Sec. 2511 of $100,000 (i.e., the fair market value of S's life income interest) [Reg. Sec. 25.2519-1(g), ex. 3].

(b) Right of Recovery of Tax. Unique to the QTIP trust is the right of recovery from the *person receiving the property* of the federal estate or gift tax (and any related interest and penalties) paid as a result of the inclusion of the QTIP trust assets in the surviving spouse's gross estate [IRC Sec. 2207A].

IRC Sec. 2207A provides that a spouse or a spouse's estate may recover from the recipient of the property (when transferred by the spouse or the spouse's estate) the gift tax paid on the remainder interest as a result of the lifetime transfer of the income

¶1105

interest, or the estate tax paid as a result of the inclusion of the value of the property in the spouse's gross estate. Reg. Sec. 20.2207A-1(a)(1) explains:

> If the gross estate includes the value of property that is includible by reason of IRC Sec. 2044 (relating to certain property in which the decedent had a qualifying income interest for life under IRC Sec. 2056(b)(7) or 2523(f)), the estate of the surviving spouse is entitled to recover from the *person receiving the property* . . . the amount of Federal estate tax attributable to that property.

Any penalties or interest attributable to the additional estate or gift tax paid may also be recoverable. The right of recovery arises when the federal estate tax with respect to the property includible in the gross estate is paid by the estate [Reg. Sec. 20.2207A-1(a)(1)].

(c) Waiver of Right of Recovery. The right of a surviving spouse's estate to recover any estate tax attributable to inclusion of a QTIP in the surviving spouse's estate from the person receiving the property may not be waived by a will provision specifying that all taxes shall be paid by the estate. In order to be effective, the waiver must specifically refer to the QTIP, the QTIP trust, IRC Sec. 2044, or IRC Sec. 2207A [IRC Sec. 2207A(a)(2)]. Similarly, the right of a decedent's estate to receive contributions for previously transferred property over which the decedent retained enjoyment or the right to income during life can only be waived by a specific indication in a will or trust document. However, a specific reference to IRC Sec. 2207B is no longer required [IRC Sec. 2207B(b)(2)]. As a result, a general provision specifying that all taxes be paid by the estate is no longer sufficient to waive the right of recovery with respect to a QTIP.

> **Example 4:** Husband's will created a trust to pay all the income quarterly to Wife, for life, with remainder over to his daughter. Husband bequeathed assets worth $1 million to the trust. The QTIP election was made and Husband's estate claimed an estate tax marital deduction. In 2014, when the trust was worth $1,212,000, and her life interest was worth $200,000, Wife assigned her life interest to her sister. Wife made no other transfers to her sister that year. Result: In 2014, Wife made a gift to her sister of $998,000. This consists of a gift of the trust worth $1,212,000 less the value of Wife's qualifying income interest of $200,000, and less the $14,000 annual gift tax exclusion available that year.

> **NOTE:** Wife can recover from her sister the gift tax attributable to the $998,000 transfer [IRC Sec. 2207A]. The amount of the gift tax attributable to the application of IRC Sec. 2519 equals the amount by which (1) the total gift tax for the year exceeds (2) the total gift tax that would have been payable if the value of the property treated as transferred under IRC Sec. 2519 had not been taken into account for gift tax purposes [IRC Sec. 2207A(b)].

In *Estate of Morgens*,[2] the Court of Appeals for the Ninth Circuit affirmed the Tax Court to conclude that a decedent was required to include in her gross estate the amount of gift tax paid by the trustees of the decedent's QTIP trusts. The decedent

---

[2] Estate of Morgens, 133 TC 402 (2009), *aff'd*, 678 F.3d 769, 2012-1 USTC ¶60,645 (9th Cir. 2012).

made gifts of the QTIP trusts' residual trust income interests within three years of her death. Pursuant to a previous agreement entered into by the remainder beneficiaries of the trusts indemnifying the decedent from gift or estate taxes related to gifts of her income interest, the trustees of the QTIP trusts paid the gift taxes. Because the decedent was considered the donor of interests in the QTIP trust, she was liable for the gift tax attributable to gifts made pursuant to IRC Sec. 2519. Furthermore, IRC Sec. 2235(b) requires that gift taxes paid by the decedent on any gift made during the last three years prior to death must be included in her gross estate. The court noted that even though IRC Sec. 2207A(b) allows for the recovery of gift tax from the QTIP, the law does not state that donees of the QTIP interest should be held liable for the gift tax. Therefore, the amount of gift taxes paid pursuant to gifts of residual trust income interests were included in the decedent's gross estate under IRC Sec. 2235(b). See also ¶ 1804.

¶1106 NONCITIZEN SPOUSES: QUALIFIED DOMESTIC TRUST (QDOT) ELIGIBLE FOR UNLIMITED MARITAL DEDUCTION

In order to claim an estate tax marital deduction for property passing from a U.S. decedent to a noncitizen surviving spouse, the property must pass to the surviving spouse in a qualified domestic trust (QDOT) [IRC Sec. 2056(d)(2)]. Property will be treated as passing to the surviving spouse in a QDOT if the property is transferred to the QDOT before the date on which an estate tax return is filed or if the property is irrevocably assigned to a QDOT under an irrevocable assignment made on or before the date the estate tax return is filed and that is enforceable under local law. The determination as to whether a trust is a QDOT is made as of the date that an estate tax return is filed or, if a judicial proceeding is commenced on or before the due date (including extensions) for filing an estate tax return to change the trust to a QDOT, as of the time when changes pursuant to that proceeding are made [IRC Sec. 2056(d)(5)].

The marital deduction will be denied for transfers of property passing to a surviving spouse who is not a citizen of the United States unless:

1. The surviving spouse was at all times subsequent to his or her spouse's death a permanent resident of the United States, and before the filing of deceased spouse's federal estate tax return, including extensions, the surviving spouse becomes a citizen of the United States [IRC Sec. 2056(d)(4)]; or

2. The property passes to the surviving spouse in a QDOT [IRC Sec. 2056(d)(2)(A)].

   (a) Why Noncitizens Are Singled Out. The reason that noncitizen spouses are singled out for different tax treatment under the law stems from the perception of Congress that opportunities for abuse existed when property was left by a decedent to a surviving spouse who was not a United States citizen. Lawmakers feared that, after the death of the first spouse, the surviving spouse who was not a United States citizen would leave the country and their heirs would be able to avoid paying estate tax on everything that the second spouse took with them. If the surviving spouse had been a U.S. citizen when he or she died, Uncle Sam could have taken a large chunk out of the estate. Congress enacted the QDOT laws to remedy this perceived abuse.

¶1106

(b) How QDOT Qualifies for Marital Deduction. To qualify as a QDOT, the trust must first have the characteristics of a trust that would qualify for a marital deduction if the surviving spouse were a United States citizen. Thus, it must be a QTIP trust, power of appointment trust, estate trust, or charitable remainder trust with the surviving spouse as the only noncharitable income beneficiary. Legal arrangements that have substantially the same effect as trusts will be treated as trusts [IRC Sec. 2056A(c)(3)]. The trust must satisfy the following requirements [IRC Sec. 2056A(a); Reg. Sec. 20.2056A-2]:

1. The trust must be maintained under the laws of a state or the District of Columbia, and the administration of the trust must be governed by the laws of a particular state or the District of Columbia. A trust may be established pursuant to an instrument executed under the laws of a foreign jurisdiction provided that the foreign instrument designates the laws of a particular state or the District of Columbia as governing the administration of the trust and such designation is effective under the law of the designated jurisdiction;

2. The trust instrument must provide that at least one trustee be a United States citizen or domestic corporation [IRC Sec. 2056A(a)(1)(A)];

3. No distribution (other than income) may be made from the trust unless the U.S. trustee has the right to withhold from such distribution the U.S. estate tax imposed on the distribution; and

4. The executor of the decedent's estate must make an irrevocable election on the estate tax return filed in respect of the decedent's estate to treat the property as QDOT property. The election is made by listing the QDOT on Schedule M "Bequests, etc., to Surviving Spouse)" of Form 706 "United States Estate (and Generation-Skipping Transfer) Tax Return" claiming the marital deduction. No election may be made on any return that is filed more than one year after the due date for such return, including extensions [IRC Sec. 2056A(d)]. Under Reg. Sec. 301.9100-1(c), the IRS has discretion to grant a reasonable extension of time for an executor to make an election. Reg. Sec. 301.9100-3 provides that requests for relief will be granted when the taxpayer provides the evidence to establish that the taxpayer acted reasonably and in good faith, and the grant of relief will not prejudice the interests of the government.

In Letter Ruling 201243012, an estate was granted an extension of time to complete the transfer of a retirement account into the QDOT. Due to intervening events beyond the spouse's control, there was a delay in making the transfer. Because the estate acted reasonably and in good faith and the interests of the government were not be prejudiced by granting such relief, the IRS granted an extension of 120 days to complete the transfer and file a supplementary estate tax return.

(c) Security Arrangements. IRS regulations impose additional requirements on QDOTs to ensure collection of the QDOT estate tax [Reg. Sec. 20.2056A-2(d)(1)]. Different requirements are imposed depending on whether the QDOT has assets of $2 million or less or more than $2 million.

If the fair market value of the QDOT's assets (determined without reduction for any indebtedness with respect to the assets) as finally determined for federal estate tax purposes is $2 million or less, the trust instrument must provide either that no more than 35 percent of the fair market value of the trust assets (determined annually on the last day of the trust's tax year) will consist of real property located outside the United States or that the trust will meet any of the security arrangements imposed on QDOTs with assets in excess of $2 million [Reg. Sec. 20.2056A-2(d)(1)(ii)]. If the value of foreign real property on the last day of the QDOT's tax year exceeds 35 percent of the fair market value of the trust's assets due to distributions of principal during that year, fluctuations in the value of the foreign currency in the jurisdiction where the real estate is located, or fluctuations in the fair market value of any assets held in the QDOT, the trust will have one year to comply with the 35 percent requirement or satisfy any of the security arrangements imposed on QDOTs with assets in excess of $2 million.

A QDOT that has assets with a fair market value in excess of $2 million may alternate among the three following security arrangements, provided at least one of the following three arrangements is operative at all times [Reg. Sec. 20.2056A-2(d)(1)(i)]:

1. The trust instrument must provide that whenever the Bank Trustee security alternative is used for the QDOT, at least one U.S. trustee must be a bank;

2. The trust instrument must provide that whenever the bond security arrangement alternative is used for the QDOT the U.S. trustee must furnish a bond in favor of the IRS in an amount equal to 65 percent of the fair market value of the trust assets (determined without regard to any indebtedness with respect to the assets) as finally determined for estate tax purposes; or

3. The trust instrument must provide that whenever the letter of credit security arrangement is used for the QDOT the U.S. trustee must furnish an irrevocable letter of credit issued by a bank incorporated and doing business in the U.S., a United States branch of a foreign bank, or a foreign bank with a confirmation by a bank incorporated and doing business in the U.S. for an amount equal to 65 percent of the fair market value of the trust assets (determined without regard to any indebtedness with respect to the assets) as finally determined for federal estate tax purposes.

(d) Duration of Bond or Letter of Credit. IRS regulations provide that the security arrangement must remain in effect until the trust ceases to function as a QDOT. A taxpayer filing a notice of failure to renew a bond or letter of credit must mail the notice to the IRS at least 60 days prior to the end of the term of the bond or letter of credit. The notice must also be mailed to the U.S. trustee of the QDOT.

(e) Personal Residence Exclusion. The value of the surviving spouse's personal residence and "related furnishings" up to a total value of $600,000 may be excluded in determining whether the $2 million threshold is exceeded [Reg. Sec. 20.2056A-2(d)(1)(iv)(A)]. A personal residence is either the surviving spouse's principal residence or one additional residence [Reg. Sec. 20.2056A-2(d)(1)(iv)(D)]. To qualify for the exclusion, a personal residence must be available at all times for use by the surviving spouse and may not be rented out to another party, even when not occupied by the surviving spouse. The term *related furnishings* means furniture, appliances, fixtures, decorative items and china. Rare artwork, valuable antiques and automobiles of any kind or class are specifically excluded [Reg. Sec. 20.2056A-2(d)(1)(iv)(E)].

¶1106

Annual reporting will be required where the residence that was previously subject to the exclusion is sold, or where the residence ceases to be used as a personal residence during the year.

(f) Cessation of Use. If the residence ceases to be used as a personal residence of the surviving spouse, or is sold during the term of the QDOT, the exclusion may be transferred to another residence that is held in either the same QDOT or in another QDOT, provided such residence is used as a personal residence of the surviving spouse. If the residence is sold and less than the entire adjusted sales price is reinvested in a new residence, the amount of the exclusion equals the amount reinvested in the new residence plus any amount previously allocated to a residence that continues to qualify for the exclusion, up to a total of $600,000 [Reg. Sec. 20.2056A-2(d)(1)(iv)(G)].

> **NOTE:** The marital deduction is allowed for a bequest to a noncitizen spouse who was a resident at the time of the decedent's death and becomes a citizen before the estate tax return is filed [IRC Sec. 2056(d)(4)]. Therefore the need to transfer property to a QDOT may be avoided if the surviving spouse becomes a U.S. citizen before the U.S. estate tax return must be filed.

(g) Surviving Spouse Creates QDOT. If the decedent fails to leave property to a noncitizen surviving spouse in a QDOT, the surviving spouse may transfer or irrevocably assign property to a QDOT before the decedent's estate tax return is filed (9 months after death) and before the QDOT election is required [IRC Sec. 2056(d)(2)(B); Reg. Sec. 20.2056A-2(b)(2)]. Even if the QDOT was not established when the decedent died, the trust may be reformed to satisfy the requirements of a QDOT [Reg. Sec. 20.2056A-4(a)]. The determination of whether a trust is a QDOT is made as of the date that an estate tax return is filed or, if a judicial proceeding is commenced on or before the due date (including extensions) for filing an estate tax return to change the trust to a QDOT, as of the time when changes pursuant to that proceeding are made. [IRC Sec. 2056(d)(5)].

(h) Calculating QDOT Tax. The tax treatment of the QDOT differs from the tax treatment afforded other marital trusts created for U.S. citizens. Normally marital trusts created for U.S. citizens enjoy freedom from tax until the surviving spouse dies. In sharp contrast, the QDOT tax is imposed on the value of distributions of principal (not income) made from a QDOT during the surviving spouse's lifetime (other than for hardship), and on all assets remaining in the trust when it ceases to qualify as a QDOT. These taxes are in addition to the tax imposed on those assets remaining in the QDOT at the surviving spouse's death. Don't expect to rely on the hardship exception to avoid the QDOT tax on principal distributions because the IRS will only grant a hardship exception in extraordinary circumstances.

The principal that is taken out of the QDOT trust is taxed as though it had been part of the estate of the first spouse to die. To make matters worse, the estate tax rate is calculated to include all prior distributions. As a result each successive withdrawal pushes the taxpayer into higher estate tax brackets. Note, however, that there is no estate tax due on distributions of income from a QDOT. Only principal distributions are taxed. In addition, payment of the tax on a distribution out of the trust is itself considered a distribution subject to the tax [IRC Sec. 2056A(b)(3), (b)(2)].

Before determination of the tax on the decedent's taxable estate, QDOTs are taxed at the highest estate tax rate, and any overpayment is refunded with interest after the correct tax bracket is determined. Multiple QDOTs are taxed at the highest tax rate in effect on the date of the decedent's death; and no hardship exemption is allowed, unless the executor designates a U.S citizen or a domestic corporation that meets regulatory tax collection requirements and is responsible for filing all estate tax returns and paying all taxes imposed. The entire trust is subject to the tax if it ceases to be a QDOT [IRC Sec. 2056A(b)].

The QDOT may also be taxed in the surviving spouse's gross estate, if the control the surviving spouse enjoys over the QDOT would cause estate tax inclusion under other IRC sections. Recognizing this possibility, IRC Sec. 2056(d)(3) allows a credit under IRC Sec. 2013 [see ¶2104] for the federal estate tax paid by the decedent on the QDOT without regard to the dates of the decedent's and the surviving spouse's deaths [Reg. Sec. 20.2056A-7].

QDOTs also enjoy the following estate tax benefits:

1. Alternate valuation date [see ¶1907];

2. Special use valuation [see ¶1908]; and

3. Extension of time to pay the estate tax [see ¶2001] [IRC Sec. 2056A(b)(10)].

   ▶ **IMPORTANT:** Even if the surviving spouse does not become a citizen of the United States within the prescribed time period [IRC Sec. 2056(b)(4)], a QDOT is taxed as a normal marital deduction trust provided the surviving spouse becomes a citizen of the United States before distributions are made to him or her and he or she is a resident of the United States at all times after the decedent's death [IRC Sec. 2056A(b)(12); Reg. Sec. 20.2056A-10].

¶1107 UNLIMITED GIFT TAX MARITAL DEDUCTION

Generally, property that a spouse gives to his or her spouse while both are still alive enjoys an unlimited exemption from federal gift tax as a result of the unlimited gift tax marital deduction [IRC Sec. 2523]. The gift tax marital deduction is comparable to the estate tax marital deduction found in IRC Sec. 2056 [see ¶1101].

You will qualify for the gift tax marital deduction if the following conditions are satisfied at the time the gift is made [IRC Sec. 2523]:

1. The donor and donee must be married to each other when the gift is made. This means that a gift to a person who becomes your spouse after you have made the gift does not qualify for the marital deduction.

2. The interest transferred to the donee spouse cannot be a "terminable interest." These are interests such as life estates, terms for years and annuities that will terminate or fail after a period of time or after the occurrence or failure to occur of a contingency. An exception is provided for a QTIP under IRC Sec. 2523(f), which is discussed further below.

3. The donee spouse must be a U.S. citizen [IRC Sec. 2523(i)]

(a) Outright Transfers. An outright gift by a citizen or permanent resident donor of the United States to a U.S. citizen spouse is fully deductible for federal gift tax purposes [IRC Sec. 2523(a)]. Outright transfers between spouses qualify without needing to meet any special requirements applicable to other types of transfers, such as transfers in trust, life estates, joint and survivor annuities, CRTs, or joint property interests.

(b) Transfers in Trust. Transfers in trust qualify for the unlimited gift tax marital deduction only if special requirements are met. These requirements are designed to ensure that the property will be taxed automatically when the donee spouse dies unless he or she has previously disposed of the property. In other words, the gift tax marital deduction generally does not allow wealth transfer taxation to be permanently avoided. Rather, it is aimed at providing tax deferral.

Specifically, terminable interest transfers is fully deductible if the U.S. citizen donee spouse receives a so-called "qualifying income interest" for life that can take one of three forms:

- Life estate with general power of appointment trust;
- A QTIP; or
- A joint and survivor annuity.

(c) Life Estate with Power of Appointment Trust. You are considered to have made a transfer that constitutes a "qualifying income interest" for the gift tax marital deduction if the transfer takes the form of a life estate with a power of appointment trust meeting the following requirements [IRC Sec. 2523(e)]:

1. The donee spouse is entitled to all the income from the transferred property (usually made by the donor spouse to a trust) for life.

2. The donee spouse must receive from the transferred property the income annually or at more frequent intervals.

3. No person has the power to appoint the property to anyone other than the donee spouse during the donee spouse's lifetime.

4. The donee spouse has a specified power of appointment over the gift property. The donee spouse must have the power, exercisable in his or her favor (or for his or her estate), to appoint the gift property. The donee spouse must be able to exercise the power alone (whether exercisable by will or during life) and in all events.

   NOTE: If either the right to income or the power of appointment given to the donee spouse pertains only to a specific portion, say, one-half of the entire interest, then only one-half of the property transferred qualifies for the gift tax marital deduction provided the other requirements are met. A partial interest in the property transferred is treated as a specific portion of an entire interest only if the rights of the donee spouse to the income and/or to the power of appointment constitute a fractional or percentile share of the entire property interest [Reg. Sec. 25.2523(e)-1(c)].

Joint and survivor annuity. A transfer of an interest in a joint and survivor annuity in which only the spouses have the right to receive any payments prior to the survivor's death qualifies for the gift tax marital deduction as a QTIP [IRC Sec.

2523(f)(6)]. However, for transfers made after December 31, 1981, transfers of a joint and survivor annuity do qualify for the gift tax marital deduction if the donor spouse elects out of QTIP treatment [IRC Sec. 2523(f)(6)(B)].

Charitable remainder trust. If you create a CRAT or CRUT [see ¶1604] in which the only noncharitable beneficiaries are you and your spouse, you can claim a gift tax marital deduction for the interest in the trust you transfer to your spouse [IRC Sec. 2523(g); Reg. Sec. 25.2523(g)-1].

Joint interests in property. If you transfer a property interest to your U.S. citizen spouse and you and your spouse are the only joint tenants (or are tenants by the entirety), you are not considered to have retained an interest in the property. You receive the gift tax marital deduction even if you may receive the property because your spouse dies or the tenancy is severed [IRC Sec. 2523(d)].

¶1108 GIFTS TO NONCITIZEN SPOUSES

For gifts made after July 13, 1988, the gift tax marital deduction is not allowed for transfers to a noncitizen spouse. However, the first $145,000 in 2014 (up from $143,000 in 2013) of present interest gifts made to a noncitizen spouse will not be taxed as a result of the special annual gift tax exclusion for such transfers [IRC Sec. 2523(i)(2)]. The special annual exclusion for transfers by gift to a noncitizen spouse is allowed only for transfers that would qualify for the marital deduction if the donee spouse were a citizen of the United States. For example, a transfer in trust must qualify as:

- A life estate with a power of appointment trust; or
- A QTIP trust.

    NOTE: A gift to a citizen donee spouse of the United States qualifies for the gift tax marital deduction if the other requirements are met, provided the donor spouse is a citizen or resident of the United States.

DISCLAIMERS—A POWERFUL POST-MORTEM TAX-PLANNING TOOL

TABLE OF CONTENTS

¶1200 DISCLAIMER BASICS

Everybody likes to inherit property from a deceased loved one, but there are situations when it may make sense from a tax perspective to say thanks, but no thanks. "Disclaimers" are the legal way to say thanks, but no thanks when you have inherited property under the terms of a will or trust from a decedent and want to pretend like you never did in an effort to save wealth transfer taxes or reorder the disposition of assets as a result of changed circumstances. All 50 states have enacted statutes that regulate beneficiaries who want to disclaim an inheritance. A qualified disclaimer will avoid gift tax consequences to the person disclaiming the gift. This may become necessary because of unexpected changes in the family dynamics or unexpected changes in the tax laws that occurred after the original documents were drafted.

Under IRC Sec. 2518(a), if a person makes a qualified disclaimer with respect to any interest in property, then for estate, gift, and generation-skipping transfer tax purposes, the disclaimed interest will be treated as if the interest was never transferred to the disclaimant. Instead, the interest will be considered as having passed directly from the decedent to the person entitled to receive the property as a result of the disclaimer. The person who disclaims the gift is treated as if he or she predeceased the decedent or donor so that the property passes directly to the next person in line. A qualified disclaimer is a written statement to the executor or donor refusing to accept the inheritance or gift [IRC Sec. 2518]. The qualified disclaimer must be made within 9 months of a decedent's death and before any benefits have been accepted. If the property is passing to a minor child, the child must make the disclaimer 9 months after the child's 21st birthday. See ¶1203 for further discussion of the requirements for a valid disclaimer.

One way to create the split estate plan and to provide for flexibility is to leave all assets outright to a surviving spouse and then provide that the surviving spouse has the option to make a qualified disclaimer of the amount that is necessary to fund the nonmarital share. This will afford the surviving spouse the opportunity to determine the size of the marital share based on his or her financial needs after the date of his or her spouse's death and to fund the nonmarital share with the amount of the unified credit in effect in the year of death. The disclaimed-based estate plan also enables the surviving spouse to take full advantage of the applicable exemption amount, the GST exemption, the state death tax exemption and any other laws that may be in effect at the time of the decedent's death. In essence, when disclaimers are judiciously used in estate planning, the surviving spouse is not locked into applying the law as it existed when the decedent spouse's estate planning documents were drafted.

There are three disadvantages to estate planning based on the surviving spouse disclaiming a portion of the amount received from the decedent. First, there are specific requirements that must be satisfied in order for the disclaimer to be qualified for estate and gift tax purposes. The disclaimer by the surviving spouse must be made in writing within nine months after the decedent's death and before any benefits from the disclaimed assets have been claimed. Second, surviving spouses may be reluctant to disclaim or give up assets that would otherwise be theirs to keep despite the wishes of their spouse. They may find it necessary in effect to disinherit their offspring in light of financial set-backs or the state of the economy or the stock market when their spouse dies. Finally, disclaimer-based estate planning is never a good idea when there are children from a prior marriage. A surviving spouse may find it particularly difficult to disclaim large sums of marriage assets to children from a deceased spouse's prior marriage.

¶1201 WHY DISCLAIMERS SAVE TAXES

Disclaimers can be extremely valuable estate-planning tools because they can provide you with a flexible way to save wealth transfer taxes when dealing with gifts and inheritances. As discussed further below, drafting of estate-planning documents should anticipate possible use of this effective technique.

There are two major advantages of using disclaimers in estate planning:

1. They permit you to postpone decision making on transfers of assets, property, interests and powers until you have had time to determine the impact of changes that occurred from the time a parent's or spouse's estate plan was originally

drafted and the date of their death. Disclaimers in effect give you an alternative estate plan that you can fall back on if circumstances mandate it.

2. They permit you to correct any drafting errors or omissions that existed in the original estate plan and afford you the opportunity to benefit from information that was not available at an earlier date.

Disclaimers can qualify property for the estate tax marital deduction so it passes tax-free to the decedent's surviving spouse. For example, in Letter Ruling 200626002, the IRS concluded that disclaimers made by a decedent's children and grandchildren would constitute qualified disclaimers within the meaning of IRC Sec. 2518. The decedent's three children, eight adult grandchildren, and two minor grandchildren, acting through a court-appointed guardian, disclaimed their interests in a family trust, resulting in the disclaimed interests passing pursuant to the trust instrument and applicable state law to the decedent's surviving spouse. The disclaimers were irrevocable, in writing, and delivered to the executors and co-trustees within nine months of the decedent's death. Moreover, the children and grandchildren had not received any benefit from the disclaimed property and there was no express or implied agreement between or among the disclaimants or the surviving spouse that the disclaimed property would be given to a person specified by the disclaimants. Consequently, the disclaimers by the children and grandchildren would be qualified disclaimers in accordance with Reg. Sec. 20.2056(d)-2(b), and the property passing to the spouse would be treated for estate tax marital deduction purposes under IRC Sec. 2056(a) as passing directly from the decedent to the spouse. Therefore, the property would qualify for the estate tax marital deduction.

Disclaimers can help achieve the objectives expressed in the decedent's will. For example, in Letter Ruling 200618017, a surviving spouse disclaimed interests in residential rental property, two certificates of deposit, and one-half of the interest in four financial accounts. The real estate and CDs were owned by the decedent and the financial accounts were held as joint tenants with right of survivorship by the couple. The surviving spouse did not contribute any funds to the rental property, certificates of deposit, or the financial accounts during the decedent's lifetime. The disclaimer was in writing and made within nine months of the decedent's death and the spouse did not accept any benefit or interest in the property being disclaimed, including any income earned after the decedent's death that was attributable to the disclaimed property. The IRS concluded that the disclaimer was valid and as a result, the disclaimed property would pass, pursuant to the decedent's will, to his two stepchildren.

¶1202 HOW DISCLAIMERS WORK

A surviving spouse may disclaim an interest in property that would otherwise pass to him or her in order to achieve various planning objectives. A properly drafted disclaimer will ensure that a property interest passes as if the person making the disclaimer predeceased the decedent. Thus, the disclaimed assets will pass to a person not originally designated to receive that interest. The identity of this recipient will be determined according to the terms of the will or, if the will is unclear, as provided under state law.

▶ **CAUTION:** The potential problem with disclaimers is that unless you are careful to comply with all the statutory requirements set forth below, you could wind up being treated as if you made a taxable gift to the person who ends up with the disclaimed property. Fortunately, you will not be treated as making a gift if you make a qualified disclaimer by complying with the statutory requirements that are discussed in detail below.

Multiple or "waterfall" disclaimers approved. In Letter Ruling 200442027, the IRS approved a disclaimer-based estate plan involving multiple disclaimers or so-called "waterfall" disclaimers made by a grantor's spouse of her interest in a series of trusts. The grantor established an irrevocable trust for the benefit of his spouse and descendants. The trust was to terminate nine months after the date of the first contribution to the trust. The trust agreement contemplated a series of disclaimers by the grantor's spouse, whereby property would pass to an additional four trusts. Within nine months of the creation of the initial trust, the grantor's spouse executed the contemplated disclaimers with respect to her trust interests, which had the effect of funding the additional four trusts in varying amounts. Two of the trusts required that income be paid to the grantor's spouse during her lifetime. With respect to the other two trusts, the trustee had discretion to distribute income to the grantor's spouse and living issue. All four trusts would terminate at the death of the grantor's spouse, at which time the trust principal would be divided into separate shares for the grantor's then living issue, *per stirpes*.

The IRS observed that the disclaimers by the grantor's spouse were executed in accordance with applicable state law, which required that a disclaimer (1) be in writing, (2) signed by the person disclaiming, and (3) filed in the appropriate court within nine months after the date of the disposition. As a result, the trust assets would pass to a series of trusts for the benefit of the grantor's spouse and issue without any direction on the part of the spouse. Accordingly, the IRS ruled that the spouse's disclaimers were qualified disclaimers under IRC Sec. 2518 and the property was treated as passing directly from the grantor according to the terms of the trust.

¶1203 REQUIREMENTS FOR VALID DISCLAIMER

A disclaimer is an irrevocable and unconditional refusal by a person to accept a gift or bequest of property [IRC Sec. 2518(a)]. The person doing the disclaiming is called the disclaimant under the disclaimer rules. For example, if Son disclaims property from Dad's estate, Son is the disclaimant and the property will pass under state law to whomever would take the property if Son had died intestate (without a will) immediately before Dad's death. The property is treated as if it was never transferred to Son who, although still very much alive, is treated for tax purposes as having died immediately prior to the event that caused the property to pass to him. As a result, the property is treated as going to someone else, usually the next beneficiary in line for the transfer, and the disclaimant is not regarded as making a gift to the person who receives the property provided the disclaimer is a qualified disclaimer under IRC Sec. 2518(a) [Reg. Sec. 25.2518-1(b)].

In order for the disclaimer to constitute a qualified disclaimer and avoid gift tax and/ or GST tax liability, the following five requirements must be met [Reg. Sec. 25.2518-2(a)]:

1. The disclaimer must be an irrevocable and unconditional legal refusal of a gift or inheritance;

2. The disclaimer must be made in writing;

3. The written disclaimer must be received by the transferor of the interest, the transferor's legal representative or the holder of the legal title to the property within 9 months of the owner's date of death. If the beneficiary is under the age of 21, he has 9 months from the date he turns 21 to provide the appropriate party with the same written notification. For IRAs, the receiver is generally the account's custodian;

4. The individual making the disclaimer must not have accepted the property or any benefits. Acceptance is described by the IRS as "an affirmative act that is consistent with the ownership of the interest in property";

5. The property must pass without direction on the part of the person making the disclaimer and the property must pass to someone other than the person making the disclaimer (unless it is the decedent's spouse).

(a) Irrevocable and Unconditional. The disclaimant must make an irrevocable, unconditional refusal to accept an interest in property. [IRC Sec. 2518(b); Reg. Sec. 25.2518-2(b)]. A written instrument manifesting the intent to disclaim an interest in property is required.[1]

(b) Written Refusal. The disclaimer must be in writing and must be signed by either the disclaimant or the disclaimant's legal representative [IRC Sec. 2518(b)(1)]. The form of the disclaimer should conform to the standards set forth in the applicable state statute. Generally, the disclaimer should describe the property being disclaimed, the nature of the disclaimer, and its extent. In addition, the disclaimer may have to be witnessed and acknowledged. This will be provided for in the state statute.

(c) Receipt/Delivery Requirement. The written disclaimer must be received by the transferor of the property interest or his or her legal representative. The delivery must be completed no later than nine months after the later of:

- The date on which the original transfer for federal wealth transfer purposes was made [Reg. Sec. 25.2518-2(c)(3)]; or

- The date nine months after the day on which the disclaimant attains the age of 21, or learned of the inheritance, whichever occurs later, if the beneficiary was a minor at the time of the transfer [IRC Sec. 2518(b)(2); Reg. Sec. 25.2518-2(c)].[2] In Letter Ruling 200150049, the IRS concluded that the nine-month time limit will begin to run from the date that the beneficiary learned of the inheritance even though it

---

[1] ¶1203 Estate of Chamberlain, 2001-1 USTC ¶60,407 (9th Cir. 2001), *aff'g* TC Memo 1999-181.

[2] Ltr. Ruls. 201403005, 201004006 (disclaimers made within nine months of reaching majority did not result in taxable gift).

¶1203

was well after nine months after his 21st birthday. Disclaimers of transfers made before January 1, 1977, need only be made within a reasonable time after the date the beneficiary/disclaimant first learns of the interest.[3]

Check local law to determine whether the disclaimer must be recorded or filed.

Because a disclaimer must be made in a timely manner, the date of the original transfer is important. When the transfers occur differs depending on the type of transfer involved as illustrated in the following situations:

- *Transfers made at death.* The nine-month period begins to run on the date of the wealth holder's death when the transfer occurs after someone has died. The starting date is not the date the will is admitted to probate or nine months after the expiration of the grantor's term interest in a qualified personal residence trust (QPRT). In *Breakiron*,[4] the taxpayer was incorrectly told by his attorney that he could disclaim his interest in a QPRT created by his parents within nine months of the expiration of the QPRT's terms. In actuality, pursuant to Reg. Sec. 25.2518-2(c)(3)(i), disclaimers must be made within nine months of the date on which the individual has a contingent, not a vested interest in the property. Thus, the transferor should have made the disclaimer within nine months of the *creation* of the QPRT. The U.S. District Court for the District of Massachusetts held that under state law, the disclaimer could be rescinded because the disclaimer was executed based on a mistake which frustrated the purpose of the transfer. Therefore the court rescinded the disclaimer.

- *Transfers by gift.* The starting date for lifetime transfers is the date the transfer of property occurred.

- *Transfers where transferor retained interest in the property.* If a lifetime transfer is included in the transferor's gross estate because the transferor retained an interest in the property (e.g., if a life income interest in a trust was retained [see ¶1807]), the person who received the interest in the property during the grantor's lifetime and another person who would receive an interest in the property on or after the grantor's death would each have nine months after the taxable transfer in which to disclaim.

Example 1: Sam transfers property in trust, with income to Alice for life, remainder to Bob. Sam reserves the power to revoke the trust. The transfer of Bob's remainder interest is incomplete for both federal gift and estate tax purposes as long as Sam has the power to revoke. Bob may disclaim her interest at any time within nine months after the earlier of Sam's death, Sam's relinquishment of the power to revoke, or the death of Alice if the termination of Alice's life estate eliminates Sam's power to revoke. Alice's income interest constitutes an incomplete transfer for federal gift tax purposes because of Sam's power to revoke. However, the gifts of income to Alice become complete when they are made from the trust. Therefore, Alice must make a qualified disclaimer with respect to any income distribution within nine months after any particular distribution [Reg. Sec. 25.2518-2(c)(5), Example (6)].

---

[3] Ltr. Rul. 201334001; Jewett, 455 U.S. 305 (1982).

[4] Breakiron v. Gudonis, 2010-2 USTC ¶60,597 (DC Mass. 2010).

¶1203

- *Transfers involving general power of appointment.* If your mother gave you a general power of appointment over property [see ¶205], you have nine months after the creation of the power to disclaim it. If your brother gets the property as a result of the disclaimer, your brother must disclaim the property nine months after you exercised your disclaimer [Reg. Sec. 25.2518-2(c)(3)].

- *Transfers involving special power of appointment.* In the case of a special or limited power of appointment (i.e., a power that specifically does not permit appointment so as to benefit the holder, directly or indirectly), the holder of the power, permissible appointees, and persons who take the property in default of appointment must disclaim within the nine-month period that begins at the time of the taxable transfer creating the power [Reg. Sec. 25.2518-2(c)(3)].

- *When is the disclaimer considered delivered?* A timely transmittal of your disclaimer will be treated as a timely delivery if you mailed your disclaimer on time even though it arrived at its destination late [IRC Sec. 7502; Reg. Sec. 25.2518-2(c)]. You can even mail your disclaimer at the last minute using certain qualifying private delivery services (PDS) other than the U.S. Postal Service and still qualify under the rule that a return or payment mailed on time is considered to be filed or received on time [IRC Sec. 7502(f)]. The IRS has designated the following PDS that can be used to file returns or pay tax with the assurance that they will be treated as filed or paid on time if you mailed them on time:[5]

  1. DHL Express (DHL): DHL Same Day Service; DHL Next Day 10:30 am; DHL Next Day 12:00 pm; DHL Next Day 3:00 pm; and DHL 2nd Day Service;

  2. Federal Express (FedEx): FedEx Priority Overnight, FedEx Standard Overnight, FedEx 2 Day, FedEx International Priority, and FedEx International First; and

  3. United Parcel Service (UPS): UPS Next Day Air, UPS Next Day Air Saver, UPS 2nd Day Air, UPS 2nd Day Air A.M., UPS Worldwide Express Plus, and UPS Worldwide Express.

(d) No Acceptance of Benefits. A qualified disclaimer cannot be made with respect to an interest in property if the disclaimant has accepted the interest or any of its benefits, expressly or impliedly, prior to making the disclaimer [Reg. Sec. 25.2518-2(d)(1)]. If a person receives any form of consideration for disclaiming an interest in property, he or she is deemed to have accepted the property and a qualified disclaimer cannot be made. In *Estate of Engelman*,[6] the Tax Court concluded that a disclaimer for the estate of trust property was not a qualified disclaimer because the decedent's exercise of the power of appointment document, which became effective on her death, was an acceptance of the property in trust under IRC Sec. 2518. The court found support for its position that execution of the power of appointment constituted an acceptance of benefits by citing Example (7) of Reg. Sec. 25.2518-(2)(d)(4), which provides:

Example 2: On January 1, 1980, *A* created an irrevocable trust in which *B* was given a testamentary general power of appointment over the trust's corpus. *B* executed a will on June 1, 1980, in which *B* provided for the exercise of the

---

[5] Notice 2004-83, 2004-2 CB 1030.   [6] Estate of Engleman, 121 TC 54 (2003).

power of appointment. On September 1, 1980, *B* disclaimed the testamentary power of appointment. Assuming the remaining requirements of IRC Sec. 2518(b) are satisfied, *B*'s disclaimer of the testamentary power of appointment is a qualified disclaimer.

Acceptance is manifested by an affirmative act that is consistent with ownership of the interest in the property [Reg. Sec. 25.2518-2(d)(1)]. Acts indicative of acceptance include:

- Using the property (except in a fiduciary capacity when the actions are directed towards preserving and protecting the property);

- Accepting dividends, interest, or rent;[7]

- Directing others to act with respect to the property or interest in the property;

- Receiving any consideration in return for making the disclaimer; or

- Entering into any agreement, express or implied, in which the disclaimed property is transferred to a person at the direction of the disclaimant.

However, a disclaimant is not considered to have accepted the property merely because, under applicable local law, title to the property vests immediately on the decedent's death in the disclaimant. Thus, taking delivery of title to the property (without any further action) in an individual capacity does not constitute the acceptance of benefits [Reg. Sec. 25.2518-2(d)].

The acceptance of one interest in the property will not, however, by itself constitute an acceptance of any other separate interests created by the transferor and held by the disclaimant in the same property [Reg. Sec. 25.2518-2(d)(1)]. For example, all of the income interests beneficially owned by a trust beneficiary are considered as one interest, while the beneficial interest in the trust principal represents a separate interest. A beneficiary may accept benefits from the income interest without accepting a benefit from the interest in trust principal. The Court of Appeals for the Fifth Circuit held that disclaimers were not unqualified merely because the disclaimers were made with the expectation of a future benefit or an implied promise of gifts in the future.[8] Even though the beneficiaries expected to receive some future benefit from the decedent's husband if they disclaimed their bequests, there was no contractual agreement or formal obligation between the parties. The "mere expectation" or an "implied promise" was not sufficient to disqualify the disclaimer.

Acceptance of RMD from decedent's IRA doesn't disqualify disclaimer. The IRS has concluded that a surviving spouse's acceptance of required minimum distributions (RMDs) from a retirement plan trust does not preclude the surviving spouse from making a qualified disclaimer of the deceased spouse's IRA.[9]

---

[7] Ltr. Rul. 201250001.

[8] Estate of Monroe, 104 TC 352 (1995), *rev'd and rem'd*, 124 F.3d 699 (5th Cir. 1997).

[9] Ltr. Rul. 201245004; Rev. Rul. 2005-36, 2005-1 CB 1368; Ltr. Rul. 201125009.

(e) Passage Without Direction by Disclaimant. The interest disclaimed must pass either:

- To the spouse of the decedent; or

- To a person other than the disclaimant without any direction on the part of the person making the disclaimer [IRC Sec. 2518(b)(4); Reg. Sec. 25.2518-2(e)].

If there is an express or implied agreement that the disclaimed interest in property is to be given or bequeathed to a person specified by the disclaimant, the disclaimant shall be treated as directing the transfer of the property:

a. The disclaimant, either alone or in conjunction with another, directs the redistribution or transfer of the property or interest in property to another person (or has the power to direct the redistribution or transfer of the property or interest in property to another person unless such power is limited by an ascertainable standard); or

b. The disclaimed property or interest in property passes to or for the benefit of the disclaimant as a result of the disclaimer [Reg. Sec. 25.2518-2(e)].

Disclaimer of IRA interest. In Rev. Rul. 2005-36,[10] the IRS concluded that a beneficiary's disclaimer of an interest in a decedent's individual retirement account (IRA) was a qualified disclaimer (assuming all other requirements are satisfied) although the disclaimant received the required minimum distribution (RMD) from the IRA for the year of the decedent's death. A qualified disclaimer may be made with respect to all, or a portion of, the balance of the IRA, except for the income attributable to the RMD. Specifically, a qualified disclaimer can be made if, when the disclaimer is made, the beneficiary entitled to receive the disclaimed amount is paid the disclaimed amount and the income attributable to such amount or the disclaimed amounts are segregated in a separate fund.

In Letter Ruling 200616041, a disclaimer of an interest in an IRA made on behalf of a decedent's wife was a qualified disclaimer. The wife was designated as the primary beneficiary of the decedent's IRA. Shortly after the decedent died, the wife died. Within nine months of the decedent's death, the wife's personal representative (one of the couple's two daughters) disclaimed the entire interest the wife or her estate had in the IRA. Pursuant to court order, the IRA beneficiary designation was reformed to name the decedent's daughters as the contingent beneficiaries of the IRA as the daughters were mistakenly omitted as contingent beneficiaries. In accordance with IRC Sec. 2518(b), the disclaimer was in writing and was executed within nine months of the decedent's death and the wife did not accept any of disclaimed interest. Therefore, the disclaimer constituted a qualified disclaimer. As a result, the wife would be treated as predeceasing the decedent with respect to the disclaimed interest. Because the reformation of the IRA was consistent with applicable state law, the IRA interests would pass to the couple's daughters as contingent beneficiaries of the IRA.

---

[10] Rev. Rul. 2005-36, 2005-1 CB 1368.

¶1204 PARTIAL DISCLAIMERS

Rules regarding the circumstances under which an individual may make a partial disclaimer which is a qualified disclaimer of less than the individual's entire interest in property and may accept the balance of the property are provided in IRC Sec. 2518(c)(1) and Reg. Sec. 25.2518-3. A disclaimer of an undivided portion of a separate interest in property that meets the other requirements of a qualified disclaimer is a qualified disclaimer [Reg. Sec. 25.2518-3(b)]. Each interest in property that is separately created by the transferor is treated as a separate interest in property. An undivided portion of a disclaimant's separate interest in property must consist of a fraction or percentage of each and every substantial interest or right owned by the disclaimant in the property and must extend over the entire term of the disclaimant's interest in the property and in other property into which the property is converted [Reg. Sec. 25.2518-3(b)].

You can make a partial disclaimer if severable property interests exist and an individual portion of an interest is disclaimed [Reg. Sec. 25.2518-3(a)(1)(i)]. Severable property is defined in Reg. Sec. 25.2518(a)(1)(ii) as property that can be divided and that, after severance, retains a complete and independent existence. For example, you could claim one-half of your interest in property, such as $300,000 of a $600,000 inheritance. If you inherited a farm, you could disclaim one-half of your interest in the farm, but you could not disclaim just the second floor of the farmhouse.

The disclaimer is a qualified partial disclaimer provided the disclaimer extends over the entire term of the disclaimant's interest in the property (and in other property into which the property is converted) and applies to each and every interest the disclaimant has in that property.

> **Example 1:** Albert conveys his farm to his daughter, Linda. Within nine months, before accepting any benefits from the property, Linda can properly disclaim one-half of her entire interest in the farm.

Although an interest in trust principal is distinguishable (and thus capable of being disclaimed) from an income interest, an income beneficiary cannot make a qualified disclaimer of the income derived from specific properties while accepting income derived from the remaining properties of the same trust. In addition, a disclaimer of both an income and a remainder interest in a specific trust asset is not a qualified disclaimer if the beneficiary retains interests in other trust property [Reg. Sec. 25.2518-3(a)(2)]. Property that can be severed into two or more separate and independent parts, such as a block of corporate shares, can be the subject of a qualified partial disclaimer [Reg. Secs. 25.2518-3(a)(1)(ii), 25.2518-3(d), Example (1)].

A power over property including a power of appointment, is treated as a separate interest in property. Thus, the income beneficiary of a trust, who has a power of appointment with respect to principal, may disclaim the power and retain the income interest [Reg. Sec. 25.2518-3(d), Example (21)]. However, the disclaimer of an interest, including a power, in property while retaining another power to direct the disposition of that property does not constitute a qualified disclaimer [IRC Sec. 2518(b)(4); Reg. Sec. 25.2518-2(e)(1)].

¶1204

Example 2: Janet, who is the income beneficiary and trustee of a trust, holds both the power to invade the trust principal for her health and support and a testamentary power of appointment. Her disclaimer of the power of invasion while retaining the testamentary power, is not a qualified disclaimer. However, if Janet were to disclaim the testamentary power and if her retained power of invasion were limited by an ascertainable standard, her disclaimer would be a qualified disclaimer.

You can also make a partial disclaimer by refusing to accept an "undivided" interest in property consisting of a fractional or percentile share of each and every substantial interest or right given to you [Reg. Secs. 25.2518-3(b), 25.2518-3(d) Example (15)]. This means that a donee or disclaimant can disclaim a percentage or fraction of an income interest from a trust. Similarly, the donee of an outright gift of realty or securities cannot carve out an income interest and disclaim the remainder [Reg. Sec. 25.2518-3(d), Example (2)].

Partial disclaimer of only part of split-interest trust not qualified disclaimer. In *Estate of Walshire*,[1] the court held that in order for a disclaimer to be valid, it must be made of an undivided interest in property and cannot be made of a remainder interest in the property while retaining a life estate. In *Walshire*, the decedent attempted to disclaim the remainder interest of his share of his deceased brother's residuary estate while reserving the income and use of the property for his life. The court concluded that the disclaimer was invalid because Reg. Sec. 25.2518-3(b) specifically precludes the decedent from dividing the property horizontally (i.e., retaining a life interest while disclaiming the remainder interest). Reg. Sec. 25.2518-3(b) requires disclaimer of an "undivided portion" of the disclaimed property. An "undivided" interest encompassed all of the rights associated with a fee interest, and did not include an interest solely in the remainder. As a result, the court concluded that the decedent failed to make a qualified disclaimer and the value of the property was includible in his estate for federal estate tax purposes.

In *Estate of Christiansen*,[2] the Court of Appeals for the Eighth Circuit affirmed the Tax Court to hold that no deduction was allowed for any portion of the property passing to a charitable lead annuity trust as a result of a disclaimer by a decedent's daughter because she failed to disclaim the contingent remainder interest in the trust. The court noted that Reg. Sec. 25.2518-3(b) provides that "A disclaimer of some specific rights while retaining other rights with respect to an interest in the property is not a qualified disclaimer of an undivided portion of the disclaimant's interest in property." The court said that the daughter's retaining a remainder interest while giving up present enjoyment fit neatly into this definition. The court found that the daughter's remainder interest was neither "severable property" nor "an undivided portion of the property." Thus, the daughter could not disclaim the present enjoyment of partnership units that passed to the trust but retain a remainder interest in such units. The daughter was not permitted to disclaim a "horizontal slice" of her interest in the property—in other words, she could not disclaim the income interest and keep the remainder. A savings clause in the disclaimer did not change the result because, no matter how the clause operated, it

---

[1] **¶1204** Walshire, 288 F.3d 342 (8th Cir. 2002), *aff'g* an unpublished decision (D.C. Iowa).

[2] Estate of Christiansen, 586 F.2d 1061 (8th Cir.2009), *aff'g* 130 TC 1 (2008).

would violate one of the requirements for a qualified disclaimer. Therefore, because the daughter did not make a qualified disclaimer as to any portion of the property passing to the trust, none of the property passing to the trust was eligible for a charitable deduction.

¶1205 FORMULA DISCLAIMER OF LIFETIME GIFTS

Defined value formula clauses are clauses in wills, trusts and gifts that express the beneficiary's interest in terms of a formula or a fixed dollar amount. For example, the interest passing to a surviving spouse, a QTIP trust, or to a marital deduction trust for the benefit of a surviving spouse can be determined by reference to a pecuniary formula clause or a fractional share formula clause. The use of defined value formula clauses is frequently used by estate planners to ensure the proper division of property, however, the terms of formula clauses must be reviewed in light of legislative changes to make certain that they continue to implement the testator's intent. A common problem is transferring too little or too much to the surviving spouse. Disclaimers can be used to cure any over- and underfunding problems. [For further discussion of defined values clauses, see ¶ 1918.]

Reg. Sec. 25.2518-3(d) provides an example of a disclaimer of a fractional share of the residuary estate calculated by defined value formula. Example (20) in this regulation provides as follows:

> A bequeathed his residuary estate to B. B disclaims a fractional share of the residuary estate. Any disclaimed property will pass to A's surviving spouse W. The numerator of the fraction disclaimed is the smallest amount which will allow A's estate to pass free of Federal estate tax and the denominator is the value of the residuary estate. B's disclaimer is a qualified disclaimer.

Before using formula disclaimers planners should be aware that the IRS generally ignores price adjustment clauses and, as it did in *Procter*,[1] will refuse to give effect to provisions that it believes impose a condition subsequent and hence violate public policy. But the courts have upheld the validity of defined value clauses in subsequent cases as discussed below.

In addition to the issue discussed previously regarding the partial disclaimer of an interest that passed to the charitable lead annuity trust, the Eighth Circuit also addressed the validity of a formula disclaimer in *Christianson*,[2] where the decedent's daughter, Hamilton, disclaimed a portion of the contingent remainder interest in her mother's estate. The result of the disclaimer was that 75 percent of the disclaimed property would pass to a charitable lead annuity trust and 25 percent would pass to her mother's private foundation. The formula disclaimer stated in pertinent part as follows:

> Partial Disclaimer of the Gift: Intending to disclaim a fractional portion of the Gift, Christine Christiansen Hamilton hereby disclaims that portion of the Gift determined by reference to a fraction, the numerator of which is the fair market value of the Gift (before payment of debts, expenses and taxes)

---

[1] **¶1205** Procter, 142 F.2d 824 (4th Cir. 1944), *cert. denied*, 323 U.S. 756 (1944); Ltr. Ruls. 200245053; 200337012.

[2] Estate of Christiansen, 586 F.3d 1061 (8th Cir. 2009), *aff'g* 130 TC 1 (2008).

on April 17, 2001, less Six Million Three Hundred Fifty Thousand and No/100 Dollars ($6,350,000.00) and the denominator of which is the fair market value of the Gift (before payment of debts, expenses and taxes) on April 17, 2001 ("the Disclaimed Portion"). For purposes of this paragraph, the fair market value of the Gift (before payment of debts, expenses and taxes) on April 17, 2001, shall be the price at which the Gift (before payment of debts, expenses and taxes) would have changed hands on April 17, 2001, between a hypothetical willing buyer and a hypothetical willing seller, neither being under any compulsion to buy or sell and both having reasonable knowledge of relevant facts.

The Court of Appeals for the Eighth Circuit affirmed the Tax Court in approving the validity of the formula disclaimer in *Christianson*. Now that the Eighth Circuit has approved of a defined value formula disclaimer of a testamentary gift in *Christianson*, planners should be more comfortable using defined value formula disclaimers of *inter vivos* gifts. A disclaimer of a lifetime gift may be useful in circumstances where the asset is hard to value and an increase in valuation for gift tax purposes may cause gift taxes to be due. If, for example, a donor makes a gift of closely-held stock to an irrevocable trust, the beneficiaries may be able to disclaim by formula that portion of the gift that exceeds the donor's remaining gift tax exemption. The trust instrument could provide that any disclaimed property would be returned to the donor or would pass outright or in a qualifying trust to charity. The disclaimer could specify that the amount disclaimed is a fractional portion of the gift determined by reference to a fraction, the numerator of which is the fair market value of the gift less the remaining gift tax exemption of the donor and the denominator of which is the fair market value of the gift. In this way, the formula disclaimer will most closely resemble the disclaimer approved by the court in *Christianson*.

Several issues must be carefully considered for this type of formula disclaimer to be fully effective. The beneficiary must not have accepted any of the benefits of the property transferred, so the trustees must carefully determine what, if any, distributions may be made from the trust. The trust agreement must be carefully drafted to assure that the disclaimer of any property will operate to redistribute the property to the donor rather than having the property pass to a subsequent generation. It may be advisable for the trustee to segregate the property in order to assure that sufficient assets remain for distribution to the donor should the property valuation be adjusted. The separate trust account should be retained until the gift tax statute of limitations has run.

In *Petter*,[3] the Tax Court approved the use of defined value formula clauses to reallocate property passing to charity. Property passing to two charities as a result of an adjustment in the value of units in an LLC qualified for a charitable deduction in an amount that reflected the increased valuation of the units. The donor transferred units in the LLC to her two children in trust through both gift and sale. She also transferred units to two charities. Both the gift documents and the sale documents assigned a number of units to the trusts and indicated that the intent was to transfer a specific value to the

---

[3] Estate of Petter, TC Memo 2009-280, *aff'd*, 653 F.3d 1012 (9th Cir. 2011); see also Hendrix, TC Memo 2011-133.

children's trusts. Any units transferred in excess of that value should be transferred to the charities instead. The documents were drafted to allow the donor to transfer the greatest number of units possible to the trusts without subjecting the donor to gift tax. The final number of units to be transferred was determined based on an appraisal. The IRS issued a notice of deficiency, and the donor and IRS eventually settled on a value in excess of the donor's original appraisal. After the new value was determined, the LLC units were reallocated between the trusts and the charities.

The Tax Court decided that the reallocation of the transfers was proper and that the transfer clauses in the gift and sale documents were valid formula clauses because the intent was to transfer a specific value to the trusts. The transfers to the charities followed the general public policy favoring charitable donations. The court found that the formula clauses were not against public policy.

For discussion of *Wandry*,[4] which involved a defined value clause but not a disclaimer, see ¶ 1918.

¶1206 DISCLAIMER TRUSTS

What if you want to disclaim an interest in property but find that you may still need the income that the disclaimed property generates? A disclaimer trust could be used to satisfy both needs. As long as the decedent's will provides for the establishment of a disclaimer trust, any income-generating assets that you disclaim would pass into a disclaimer trust, which provides under the terms of the trust that the income be distributed to you.

¶1207 WHEN TO USE DISCLAIMERS

Use a disclaimer as an estate-planning tool in the following situations:

- To cure deficiencies in the existing estate plans;
- To reduce the size of a taxable estate;
- To increase the amount that will pass to others free of transfer tax;
- To create a QTIP trust;
- To fund the unified credit fully;
- To reduce GST tax;
- To create, enlarge, or reduce charitable donations;
- To salvage a defective marital bequest; and
- To avoid inadvertent termination of S corporation status by passing S corporation stock to a nonqualified trust (i.e., one that has more than one beneficiary).

---

[4] Wandry, TC Memo 2012-88, *nonacq.*, 2012-46 IRB 1.

¶1208 HOW TO PREPARE FOR DISCLAIMERS IN ESTATE PLANNING

The possibility of a disclaimer should be carefully considered in the estate-planning discussions. For maximum flexibility, the possibility of a disclaimer trust should be anticipated and specifically provided for in the estate-planning documents [¶ 1809].

Considering and planning for a disclaimer early on is very important because you have only nine months from the date of the property transfer or the date of the decedent's death to make a qualified disclaimer. In addition, significant tax savings can be lost if the disclaimant accepts the property or benefits from it in any way. Once this has occurred, the disclaimant is precluded from making a qualified disclaimer with respect to that property.

¶1209 HOW TO DISCLAIM JOINTLY HELD PROPERTY

The disclaimer of jointly held property raises two thorny issues. The main problem is deciding when the jointly held property must be disclaimed—way back when the joint property interest was first created or when the first joint tenant dies and the property passes by operation of law to the survivor.

The second problem is whether a spouse can disclaim the one-half survivorship interest in property that he or she originally contributed.

The law provides that a joint tenancy with right of survivorship and a tenancy by the entirety between spouses must be disclaimed within nine months after the interest was *created* [IRC Sec. 2518(b)(2)].

The judicial response. The courts have held that the disclaimer of jointly held property made within nine months after the death of the first joint tenant was valid even though the joint interest was created several decades before the decedent died.[1] The court reasoned that because state law permitted the joint tenancy with right of survivorship to be unilaterally transferred by one of the joint tenants, the transfer of the entire property interest did not occur until the death of one of the joint property owners. Until that time, either of the joint tenants could transfer their undivided one-half interest and destroy the survivorship interest of the other joint tenant. Thus, as the law currently stands, the interest of a surviving tenant can be disclaimed nine months after the death of the first co-tenant even though the interest may have been created many years earlier.

The IRS response. The IRS agrees with the courts and has issued a formal response, called an Action on Decision[2] in which they make it clear that they will no longer argue that a disclaimer of jointly held property is invalid because it should have been done within nine months of the day the joint interest was originally created. The IRS also

---

[1] **¶1209** Kennedy, TC Memo 1986-3, *rev'd*, 804 F.2d 1332 (7th Cir, 1986); Estate of Dancy, 89 TC 550, *rev'd and rem'd*, 872 F.2d 84 (4th Cir. 1989); McDonald, 89 TC 293 (1987), *rev'd and rem'd*, 853 F.2d 1494 (8th Cir. 1988), *on remand*, TC Memo 1989-140, *cert. denied*, 4/3/89.

[2] Action on Decision CC-1990-06 (Feb. 7, 1990).

stated that a joint tenant may make a qualified disclaimer of any portion of the joint interest attributable to consideration that he or she furnished.

▶ **PRACTICE ALERT:** In order to ascertain whether a "qualified disclaimer" is a viable post-death planning option, local law must give the joint tenant the right to unilaterally sever the joint tenancy or cause the property to be partitioned. In states where a joint tenancy cannot be partitioned except by a voluntary act by both tenants, the "transfer" for IRC Sec. 2518 purposes occurs on the date the tenancy was created.

The IRS has issued regulations echoing the court view and the Action on Decision discussed above. According to the regulations, a surviving joint tenant may disclaim the one-half survivorship interest in property held in joint tenancy with right of survivorship or in tenancy by the entirety, within nine months of the death of the first joint tenant to die. This rule applies regardless of the following:

1. The portion of the property attributable to consideration furnished by the disclaimant;

2. The portion of the property that is included in the decedent's gross estate;

3. Whether the interest can be unilaterally severed under local law [Reg. Sec. 25.2518-2(c)(4)(i)].

▶ **PRACTICE POINTER:** These regulations are helpful to married couples who own property as tenants by the entirety. Now the surviving spouse can disclaim the interests that they held as joint tenants by the entirety within nine months of the death of the first tenant to die.

Example 1: Alice purchased real property with her own money. Title to the property was conveyed to Alice and Bob, as joint tenants with right of survivorship. Alice and Bob are not married. Under state law, the joint interest is unilaterally severable by either tenant. Bob dies eight years later and is survived by Alice. Just six months after Bob's death, Alice disclaims the one-half survivorship interest in the property to which Alice succeeds as result of Bob's death. Assuming that the other requirements of IRC Sec. 2518(b) are satisfied, Alice has made a qualified disclaimer of the one-half survivorship interest (but not the interest retained by Alice upon the creation of the tenancy, which may not be disclaimed by Alice). The result is the same whether or not Alice and Bob are married and regardless of the proportion of consideration furnished by Alice and Bob in purchasing the property [Reg. Sec. 25.2518-2(c)(5), Example (7)].

Example 2: Sally purchases a parcel of real property with her own money. Sally was married to Bob. The property was titled "Sally and Bob as tenants by the entirety." Assume Sally dies first. In order to be a qualified disclaimer, any disclaimer by Bob of Bob's interest in the land must be made within nine months of the date of Sally's death. The result is the same regardless of the proportion of consideration furnished by either spouse in purchasing the property [Reg. Sec. 25.2518-2(c)(5), Example (8)].

¶1209

Joint bank and brokerage accounts. For joint bank accounts and joint brokerage accounts, including mutual fund accounts, the Regulations provide that the nine-month period begins when the first joint tenant dies. A surviving joint tenant cannot disclaim any portion of the account attributable to the survivor's own contributions [Reg. Sec. 25.2518-2(c)(4)(iii)].

> **Example 3:** Alice opens a bank account that is held jointly with her husband Bob, and transfers $50,000 of her money to the account. Alice dies five years later and Bob disclaims the entire amount in the bank account just two months after Alice's death. Assuming that the remaining requirements of IRC Sec. 2518(b) are satisfied, Bob has made a qualified disclaimer because the disclaimer was made within nine months after Alice's death at which time Bob had succeeded to full dominion and control over the account. As a result of the disclaimer, Bob is treated as predeceasing Alice with respect to the disclaimed interest. The disclaimed account balance passes through Alice's probate estate. The result would be the same if Alice and Bob were not married [Reg. Sec. 25.2518-2(c)(5), Example (12)].

> **Example 4:** The facts are the same as in the example above except that Bob rather than Alice dies first. Alice may not make a qualified disclaimer with respect to any of the funds in the bank account because Alice furnished the funds for the entire account and Alice did not relinquish dominion and control over the funds [Reg. Sec. 25.2518-2(c)(5), Example (13)].

Result of disclaimer. If a qualified disclaimer is made with respect to a taxable transfer, the federal estate tax provisions apply with respect to the property interest disclaimed as if there had never been a gift or transfer of the property to the person making the disclaimer [Reg. Secs. 20.2046-1, 20.2046-1(a)]. The U.S. Supreme Court has held that an heir's disclaimer of his interest in an estate will not protect him from liens for federal taxes he owes.[3] This means that disclaimers cannot be used to thwart tax liens against the disclaimant's property from applying to the disclaimed interest.

Roadmap to disclaiming interests in joint accounts. In Letter Ruling 200832018 , the IRS provides a detailed roadmap for disclaiming interests in joint accounts at the death of a joint tenant. A couple had two joint accounts with a brokerage firm (Account 1 and Account 2). The husband was the sole contributor to Account 1 and both spouses contributed equally to Account 2. After the husband's death, the brokerage firm canceled the accounts and transferred the assets to new accounts in the wife's name (Wife Account 1 and Wife Account 2). The wife received distributions from Wife Account 1 and approved the purchase of new securities in Wife Account 2. After the wife met with her attorneys regarding her husband's estate, she set up two new brokerage accounts for the estate and conveyed to the accounts all of the assets which had been in Account 1, and one-half of the assets from Account 2, plus one-half of the new securities. The wife then disclaimed the assets from Account 1, minus the distributions received,

---

[3] Drye, 528 U.S. 49 (1999).

and her husband's one-half interest in Account 2, minus her husband's one-half interest in the new securities.

Because the husband retained the right to unilaterally withdraw his interest in both accounts, the IRS concluded that his prior contributions to Accounts 1 and 2 were incomplete gifts. Thus, the wife's survivorship interest was not created until the husband's death. The IRS also found that pursuant to Reg. Sec. 25.2518-2(d)(1), the wife had not accepted the benefit of the assets when she transferred them to Wife Accounts 1 and 2 because the mere transfer of title was not considered an acceptance of benefits. However, the wife had accepted the benefit of the distributions from Wife Account 1 and the new securities purchased in Wife Account 2. The IRS concluded that Reg. Sec. 25.2518-3(c) permitted both the amount of distributions and the value of the new securities to be segregated from the disclaimed amount.

Once disclaimed, the accounts' assets were distributed into a marital and family trust over which the wife held a testamentary non-general power of appointment. The IRS noted that in accordance with Reg. Sec. 25.2518-2(e)(2) and 25.2518-2(e)(5), Example (5), the wife's power of appointment must be disclaimed in order for her disclaimer of the assets from Accounts 1 and 2 to be qualified. As permitted by Reg. Sec. 25.2518-3(a)(iii), her power of appointment was treated as a separate interest, which was disclaimed independently from any other interests. Thus, the disclaimers of the wife's testamentary non-general power of appointment and the husband's interest in the assets in Accounts 1 and 2 were qualified disclaimers under IRC Sec. 2518.

¶1210 AFTER-DEATH PLANNING STRATEGIES

The use of a qualified disclaimer as a post-mortem planning device is wide and varied. The effect of a disclaimer is to treat the disclaiming party as though the interest being disclaimed had never been transferred to that party. Three areas warrant special attention:

1. The impact of a disclaimer on a general power of appointment held by the disclaimant;

2. The impact of a disclaimer on charitable giving; and

3. The impact of a disclaimer on marital gifts.

General powers of appointment. A general power of appointment is the power to appoint property to oneself, one's estate, one's creditors, or the creditors of one's estate that is not limited (1) by the standards of health, education, maintenance, or support, or (2) to an amount not greater than five percent of the principal or $5,000, determined on an annual basis, noncumulatively [IRC Sec. 2041; see¶ 1810].

If a holder renounces a general power of appointment by a qualified disclaimer, the disclaiming party is treated as never having had such a power and, therefore, will not be regarded as having such a power at death or as having exercised or released such a power. The property subject to the power will not be included in the disclaimant's gross estate.

The lapse or termination of a general power of appointment represents a separate interest in property. The Regulations provide for a nine-month period in which to make a qualified disclaimer following the lapse or termination of a general power of appointment [Reg. Sec. 25.2518-2(c)(3)].

When to disclaim. For purposes of a qualified disclaimer, the holder of a general power of appointment or the holder of a nongeneral power of appointment are treated alike. Because a taxable transfer occurs when the power is created, the time to disclaim begins with the creation date. Thus, for permissible appointees and for takers in default of the exercise of a general or nongeneral power of appointment, the time to disclaim begins with the creation date. For appointees and for takers in default after the exercise or lapse of a general power, the time to disclaim begins after the holder's exercise, on the lapse of the power [Reg. Sec. 25.2518-2(c)(3)].

Charitable gifts. If, as a result of a charitable disclaimer, an interest in a decedent's estate passes to a charitable beneficiary instead of a private beneficiary, the decedent's estate is entitled to a charitable deduction with respect to that interest [see ¶ 1000]. Under IRC Sec. 2055(a), a charitable deduction is allowable for property passing to a charitable devisee as a result of a qualified disclaimer. To obtain a deduction under IRC Sec. 2055(a), the disclaimant must satisfy the requirements for a qualified disclaimer set forth in IRC Sec. 2518, including the nine-month time limit.

> **Example 1:** Mom's will contains a devise to Son with the remainder of her property going to charity. A qualified disclaimer by Son would cause the amount of the devise to pass to the charity, thereby permitting Mom's estate to include the devise as part of her federal estate tax charitable deduction.

When a right of withdrawal from, or a power of invasion over, a trust would defeat the charitable deduction by rendering the amount passing to the charity unascertainable [see ¶ 1000], the right or power could be disclaimed to save the charitable deduction. Thus, a qualified disclaimer occurs where a power to consume, invade, or appropriate property for the benefit of an individual terminates prior to:

- The exercise of the power;
- The due date (including extensions) of the estate tax return in which the property subject to the power is included; and
- Within the nine-month time limit contained in IRC Sec. 2518(b)(2) [Reg. Sec. 20.2055-2(c)(1)]. If, as a result of the termination of the power, the property is distributed to a charity, a charitable gift occurs.

When a decedent's surviving spouse elects against the decedent's will, and, thus, the decedent's will is construed as though the surviving spouse were deceased, the election is treated as a disclaimer for purposes of IRC Sec. 2055(a)(2).[1] Again, the surviving spouse must comply with the requirements of IRC Sec. 2518, including the nine-month time limit.

Marital deduction. Disclaimers provide a valuable estate-planning tool to cure problems of under-funding or over-funding of the marital portion of an estate plan. A

---

[1] **¶ 1210** Ltr. Ruls. 7718017, 7724055.

recurring post-mortem application of a qualified disclaimer focuses on increasing or saving a marital deduction. If someone other than the surviving spouse makes a qualified disclaimer to the surviving spouse, the disclaimed property passes to the surviving spouse. Such property qualifies for the marital deduction because it is treated as passing from the decedent spouse to the surviving spouse [see ¶ 1100].

For example, as a result of intestate succession or poor estate planning, beneficiaries other than the surviving spouse may be entitled to the greater-than-desired part of the decedent's gross estate causing the estate to be subject to estate tax. By using a qualified disclaimer, the portions inherited by the surviving spouse and those of the other beneficiaries can be adjusted, thereby reducing or hopefully eliminating federal estate tax liability.

A qualified disclaimer can be used to shape a decedent's disposition so that it will qualify for QTIP treatment [see ¶ 1100]. A qualified disclaimer may be used to salvage a flawed QTIP trust by correcting drafting inadequacies or by supplying what the purported QTIP trust lacked.

¶1211 DECIDING WHETHER PROPERTY SHOULD BE DISCLAIMED

Before disclaiming property, you should carefully analyze the decedent's will, the provisions of will substitutes, and state law to determine who will receive the disclaimed property. This is important for two reasons.

First, as a prospective disclaimant, you should know who will receive the property. Second, the property must pass without direction by you to the decedent's spouse or a third party.

Unless the will provides otherwise, disclaimed property generally passes as if the disclaimant predeceased the decedent. You should analyze the following issues:

1. Does the will provide for a gift over in the event of a disclaimer? The will controls if the decedent specified the recipient of the disclaimed property.

2. Does the will require that the beneficiary survive? If the will provides for a gift over if the beneficiary predeceases the decedent, the disclaimed property passes to the alternative taker. If the will contains survivorship language but does not provide for a gift over, generally the gift lapses. A preresiduary devise generally falls into the residuary. If a portion of the residuary lapses, it must be determined, under state law, whether that portion passes to the other residuary beneficiaries or whether the property passes by intestacy.

3. If the will does not contain survivorship language or provide for a gift over in the event of a disclaimer, does an anti-lapse statute control? Most states have enacted anti-lapse statutes to avoid the common law rule that provides that a gift to a beneficiary who fails to survive does not pass to the beneficiary's descendants. Under an anti-lapse statute, if the beneficiary is within a certain degree of kinship to the decedent, the gift normally passes to the beneficiary's descendants unless the will expressly provides otherwise.

4. Is the transfer part of a class gift? Special rules apply to the lapse of a class gift with the anti-lapse statutes generally governing.

> **NOTE:** If the answer to these questions is in doubt, you should consider obtaining disclaimers from possible takers to achieve the desired result.

The above testamentary principles may not apply to will substitutes. The transfer of disclaimed interests in life insurance proceeds, retirement plan benefits, and other contractual rights may be controlled by the provisions of the contract or state statute. You should carefully check these provisions before disclaiming will substitute property.

FAMILY LIMITED PARTNERSHIPS (FLPs)

TABLE OF CONTENTS

¶1300 FAMILY LIMITED PARTNERSHIP BASICS

The family limited partnership (FLP) has become a popular estate planning tool for shifting the wealth of the older generation to the younger generation at a reduced estate tax cost. The FLP allows taxpayers to take advantage of substantial valuation discounts for lack of marketability and for lack of control over the business assets transferred into the FLP if a valid nontax purpose exists for establishing the FLP. These valuation discounts will result in reduced estate taxes. The family limited partnership (FLP) is a limited partnership controlled by members of a family. Typically, the older family members are general partners and their children are limited partners in a family-owned business. The use of FLPs has proliferated because, in addition to saving estate taxes, the FLP may: (1) offer great flexibility in structuring the ownership and control of family businesses; (2) insulate family assets from the claims of creditors and potential litigants; and (3) provide for centralized management of family businesses. From an income-tax standpoint, FLPs avoid the compressed tax rates imposed on trusts [¶2820] as well as the double taxation imposed at both the corporate and shareholder levels. In order for the FLP to be respected by the IRS, the partnership must be valid under state law, the entity must be respected by its partners and a valid business purpose (independent of saving wealth transfer taxes) must exist for its creation. FLPs most often run into trouble with the IRS when the principal assets are not a business but rather a portfolio of investments.

¶1300

¶1301 HOW FLPs WORK

In a typical FLP, the owner of a family business, who is a parent, transfers assets, such as stock, real estate or a business into the FLP formed with the children in exchange for both a general partnership interest and limited partnership interest. The parent keeps a small ownership interest and becomes the general partner, retaining control over the management of the business. The children often receive limited partnership interests with less control. Thus the value of their limited shares often can be discounted by at least 20 percent, thus lowering gift tax exposure.

The FLP remains in existence until the death of the parents, when the partnership is dissolved and assets are distributed to the children in accordance with their ownership interests. The tax savings exist because the interests of the limited partners are eligible for substantial valuation discounts which allow the limited partnership interests to be transferred at a fraction of the value of the underlying FLP assets, thereby creating transfer tax savings of between 30 to 60 percent for:

1. Lack of marketability because sales of interests in the FLP are usually restricted and would be difficult to sell outside the family, and

2. For minority discounts because the children who have received the interests are merely limited partners who cannot make major management decisions for the business.

   ▶ **PRACTICE POINTER:** With many pro-taxpayer decisions, the Tax Court has paved the way for taxpayers to claim up to a 40 percent discount for transfers of FLP interests. The FLP cannot only be a valuable income tax reduction tool, but can transfer wealth to children and grandchildren, generate substantial estate and gift tax valuation discounts, insulate family assets from the claims of creditors, provide for centralized management, and afford parents flexibility in controlling family businesses. Keep in mind, however, that the IRS is looking over your shoulder. The gift tax return (Form 709) contains a box that you must check to indicate that you are claiming a discount in your valuation of any property listed on the return. This makes it easier for the IRS to spot taxpayers making use of this valuable but controversial estate planning tool.

¶1302 BENEFITS OF FLPs

FLPs offer the following tax and nontax benefits:

- FLPs offer the potential for assets of a closely held family business that are transferred to the FLP to be eligible for valuation discounts for lack of control (ownership of a minority interest) and for lack of marketability.[1] The IRS has

---

[1] ¶**1302** Estate of Dailey, TC Memo 2001-263, costs and fees proceeding, TC Memo 2002-301 (40% aggregate discount for lack of marketability and minority interest); Estate of Jones, 116 TC 121 (2001) (44.8% discount for lack of marketability of 83% limited partnership interest); Shep- herd, 115 TC 376 (2000), *aff'd*, 283 F.3d 1258 (11th Cir. 2002) (15% discount for undivided 50% interest in leased real estate and in bank stock); Knight, 115 TC 506 (2000) (15% discount for lack of control and marketability of FLP); Kerr, 113 TC 449 (1999), *aff'd*, 292 F.3d 490 (5th Cir. 2002)

approved valuation discounts ranging from 8 percent to 40 percent where the facts of the case justify them and where the appraisers and attorneys adequately support the valuation discount with an appraisal report. Any valuation discount should be supported by a detailed and well-reasoned appraisal or valuation report by an appraiser qualified to value the property involved. In fact, in *Estate of Astleford*,[2] the Tax Court concluded that it was appropriate to apply multiple layers of discounts, or tiered discounts, where the taxpayer held a minority interest in an entity that, in turn, held a minority interest in another entity.

- FLPs can facilitate intrafamily wealth transfers when senior family members take advantage of their annual per-donee gift tax exclusion to make annual gifts to junior family members.

- FLPs can save income taxes because partnerships are pass-through entities, which means that income, gains, deduction, and losses flow through to the partners unlike corporations which are subject to double taxation at both the shareholder and corporate levels. Income shifting makes sense only if the children or the limited partners are in the lowest tax bracket and the parents or the general partners are in the highest tax bracket.

- Parents, as general partners, can use the FLP to manage and control assets in the hands of their inexperienced children who are the limited partners of the FLP.

- To some extent, FLPs can protect partnership assets from creditors of the partners.

- The FLP is flexible enough to be responsive to changes in the law and family situations. The partnership agreement can be amended to accommodate changed business and personal needs.

- The FLP can be used to consolidate diverse family assets in a single business entity.

- The FLP can be used to teach or train children about the management of a business and/or wealth.

The following example illustrates how the FLP can solve many of the tax and business concerns of a prosperous business owner with children. Mr. and Mrs. Able, who have three children in their twenties, own a widget-making business that they want to preserve as a family business. In addition, they own several large pieces of commercial real estate that they expect to appreciate in value. They have several objectives in mind. (1) They want to make substantial gifts of their assets to their children in the future so their children will eventually own the business and the real estate. In addition, they want to minimize their potential estate tax exposure. (2) They want to make maximum use of the annual gift tax exclusion by electing to gift-split so that they as a couple can give a total of $28,000 in 2014 to each child and grandchild.

(Footnote Continued)

(valuation discounts for lack of control and lack of marketability in the determination of fair market value for gifted FLP); Lappo, TC Memo 2003-258 (valuation discounts of 15% and 24% were applied for minority interest and lack of marketability); Estate of Stone, TC Memo 2003-309 (FLP discounts averaging 43%); Estate of Dunn, TC Memo 2003-176 (30% discount for lack of marketability and minority interest).

[2] Estate of Astleford, TC Memo 2008-128 (court upheld market absorption discount of about 20 percent; 30 percent discount for a 50 percent interest in a general partnership; and a combined discount of 34 percent and 36 percent for limited partnership interests).

(3) They doubt whether their children have the business acumen and financial sophistication to manage the business and the real estate. (4) They are worried that assets given directly to their children may be squandered or exposed to the claims of their children's creditors or ex-spouses in a divorce settlement.

The FLP will address these concerns. Here's how it works. The Ables establish an FLP in which they are the general partners and they make gifts of limited partnership interests to their children. To be recognized as completed gifts for tax purposes, the gifts would have to be complete and unrestricted. The Ables could retain no control over the gifts. The gifts by the Ables of limited partnership interests to their children would qualify for valuation discounts for lack of marketability and lack of control because the interests would be less than a majority interest and would be difficult to sell outside the family. The FLP agreement gives the Ables the exclusive right to control the partnership and to determine what gets distributed, while denying their children the right to liquidate or dissolve the partnership. As a result the transfers of limited partnership interests qualify for discounts ranging from 20 percent to 60 percent. Factors that impact on these discounts include the bundle of rights transferred to the children, such as the right to vote, to require distributions, and to force liquidations of the partnership. The IRS sanctioned the use of FLPs in Rev. Rul. 93-12,[3] where a minority discount was applied in the context of intrafamily transfers to value gifts of a minority block of stock in a closely held corporation.

As general partners, the Ables, rather than the children, will manage the business, determine how the FLP's assets are invested, and decide when distributions are made and management fees are paid. When assets are transferred to their children as limited partners of the FLP, the value of the limited partnership interests will be excluded from the Ables' taxable estate. Since the FLP is viewed as a flow-through entity, all FLP income will be taxed directly to the individual partners. This will result in an income tax savings if the limited partners are in a lower tax bracket than the general partners.

The Ables have the burden of proving the appropriate discount applicable to the transfer of the limited partnership interests to their children. A professional is needed to prepare an appraisal supporting the claimed valuation discount. The IRS Regulations suggest, but do not require, an appraisal for gifts of property other then cash or marketable securities with a value in excess of $5,000 [Reg. Sec. 1.170A-13C]. The Ables should select an appraiser who is trained, tested, and certified by a professional appraisal society.

¶1303 IRS SCRUTINY OF FLPs

The IRS has become increasingly hostile to the use by taxpayers of FLPs as an estate-planning tool and has vigorously litigated FLP cases perceived as abusive. When auditing an FLP, the IRS will focus on the actual operations of the partnership and will want to examine the books and records of the partnership, the partnership's bank statements, and the documents conveying assets into the partnerships. The IRS will ask if the distributions were made in accordance with the terms of the partner-

---

[3] Rev. Rul. 93-12, 1993-1 CB 202.

ship agreement. Their primary concern will be whether the partnership was operated as a separate legal entity or merely as a bank account for the decedent.

The IRS often attacks valuation discounts claimed by taxpayers for property transferred to FLPs. Taxpayers can thwart those attacks by demonstrating that the FLP can support the valuation discount with documentation of a well-reasoned appraisal prepared by a qualified appraiser before the return was filed. The valuation discounts frequently claimed are discounts for lack of control and lack of marketability. The purpose of these discounts is rarely disputed because a person acquiring an interest in an FLP typically lacks the ability to dictate how the partnership will be run and how distributions will be made. Moreover, in an FLP, there usually is no established market where the interests can be traded and the values readily established. The oft-litigated issue, however, is the amount of the valuation discount [see ¶1914 for further discussion of valuation discounts]. The courts have approved discounts to the value of property (including closely held stock, real estate, and companies) transferred to an FLP in the range of 15 percent[1] to 63 percent,[2] depending on the specific facts and circumstances.

The cases discussed below provide a roadmap for taxpayers who are considering using FLPs in their financial and estate planning.

IRS weapon of choice—IRC Sec. 2036(a). The IRS has successfully challenged FLP cases by arguing that under IRC Sec. 2036, the full fair market value of the FLP should be included in the decedent's estate because the decedent (1) transferred interests in the FLP for less than adequate and full value in money or money's worth, and (2) retained an interest in the FLP interests transferred. IRC Sec. 2036(a) includes in a transferor's gross estate the entire value of a lifetime transfer of property if he or she has retained, through explicit or implied agreements, one or more of the valuable economic benefits associated with property ownership such as the right to possess or enjoy the property, the right to income therefrom or the right to designate the person(s) who would enjoy such rights. Collectively, these rights can be classified as "prohibited right."

To avoid application of IRC Sec. 2036(a), an estate must show that either (1) the decedent transferred property in a *bona fide* sale for full and adequate consideration in money or money's worth (the *bona fide* sale exception); or (2) the decedent did not retain the possession or enjoyment or right to income from the property or the right to designate either alone or in conjunction with any person who shall possess or enjoy the property or its income (the "retained rights or interest exception").

(a) Legitimate Nontax Motive for FLP Creation. The Tax Court found a legitimate and actual nontax motive for a decedent's transfer of woodland parcels to an FLP in *Estate of Stone*.[3] The court was persuaded that the decedent's desire to have woodland parcels held and managed as a family asset constituted a legitimate nontax motive for the transaction. Several factors supported the estate's contention that a bona fide sale had occurred, specifically: (1) the decedent and her husband never received any distributions from the FLP; (2) the woodland parcels were, in fact, transferred to the FLP; (3) there was no commingling of the partners' personal funds with partnership funds; (4) the FLP interests were not discounted for gift tax

---

[1] ¶**1303** Knight, 115 TC 506 (2000).   [3] TC Memo 2012-48.
[2] Church, 268 F.3d 1063 (5th Cir. 2001).

purposes; and (5) the decedent and her husband were in good health at the time the woodland parcels were transferred to the FLP. The court ultimately ruled that the decedent's transfer was bona fide and for adequate and full consideration for purposes of IRC Sec. 2036, and, therefore, the values of the woodland parcels were not includible in the decedent's gross estate.

In *Estate of Kelly*,[4] the Tax Court found legitimate and significant nontax reasons for the creation of limited partnerships in a situation where the decedent, who owned 27 parcels of real property, was declared mentally incompetent due to Alzheimer's disease. The decedent's children, acting as her guardians, sought the advice of an attorney regarding liability issues surrounding a number of the parcels, the difficulty in managing the properties as guardians, and ensuring that the decedent's estate was divided equally among them. In order to address these concerns, the attorney created a plan to divide the real property among three limited partnerships, one for each living child. Because the decedent's children had legitimate nontax reasons for creating the partnerships and the decedent received partnership interests proportionate to the value of the property transferred, the court found that the transfer of assets to the partnerships was a bona fide sale for full and adequate consideration. As a result, the value of the transferred assets was not includible in the decedent's gross estate pursuant to IRC Sec. 2036. The nontax reasons for setting up the FLP were: (1) the need for effective management of the real estate assets transferred into the partnership; (2) the need to protect the assets against liability; and (3) the need to avoid controversy by ensuring equal distribution of the estate.

In a taxpayer victory, *Estate of Mirowski*,[5] the Tax Court concluded that assets including securities, patents and license agreements transferred to a family limited liability company (FLLC) by the decedent two weeks prior to her sudden and unexpected death were not includible in her gross estate under IRC Sections 2036(a) or 2038(a) because the decedent's transfers of property to the FLLC qualified as bona fide sales for full and adequate consideration under the exceptions to IRC Sections 2036(a) and 2038(a). The decedent had adequate and significant non-tax purposes for forming, and transferring assets to the FLLC which included:

1. Joint management of the family's assets by her daughters and eventually her grandchildren;

2. Maintenance of the bulk of the family's assets in a single pool in order to allow for investment opportunities that would not be otherwise available; and

3. Providing for each of her daughters and eventually each of her grandchildren on an equal basis.

Moreover, the court found it was sufficient that the FLLC was a valid functioning investment operation and that the FLLC did not need to rise to the level of a "business" under the federal income tax laws in order for the bona fide sale for an adequate and full consideration under IRC Sec. 2036(a) to occur. The court also concluded that decedent received an FLLC interest proportionate to the value of the property transferred and her capital account was properly credited with those assets. In the event of liquidation, she had the right to a distribution in accordance with her capital account. The decedent also maintained significant assets outside of the FLLC

---

[4] TC Memo 2012-73.   [5] Estate of Mirowski, TC Memo 2008-74.

to satisfy her personal obligations, including payment of the gift tax on the FLLC interests she gifted to her daughters. There was no express or implied agreement that the decedent would retain any interest in the FLLC interests she transferred to her daughters' trusts.

In *Estate of Black*,[6] the Tax Court concluded that stock transferred by a decedent to an FLP was not includible in the decedent's gross estate under IRC Sec. 2036(a) because the transfer was a bona fide sale for adequate and full consideration. The decedent and his advisers decided to create the FLP in order to consolidate and protect his stock holdings in an insurance company, namely by preventing his grandsons from selling their shares of stock and protecting his son's shares from potential claims incident to divorce. The creation of the FLP was the result of an arm's-length transaction. The court considered protection from creditors to be a legitimate and significant nontax reason for its creation. Furthermore, the decedent received an interest in the FLP that represented adequate and full consideration because:

1. The participants in the FLP received interests proportionate to the value of the property each contributed;
2. The respective contributed assets were properly credited to the transferors' capital accounts;
3. Distributions required negative adjustments to distributee capital accounts; and
4. There was a legitimate and significant nontax reason for formation of the FLP that included:

   - Adherence to the decedent's buy-and-hold investment philosophy that resulted in the increase in net asset value from $80 million when the FLP was formed to over $315 million 8 years later;
   - Preventing the decedent's son from selling or encumbering Erie stock;
   - Preventing the decedent's son from selling Erie stock at the urging of his wife whom the decedent thought was lazy and her parents who had suffered financial setbacks;
   - Preserving a seat for some member of the decedent's family on Erie's board of directors;
   - Preventing family members from losing any Erie shares upon a future divorce;
   - Consolidation of family assets; and
   - Providing for long-term centralized management of assets.

Therefore the court concluded that creating the FLP served the legitimate nontax purpose of consolidating and holding the family's Erie stock. This case joins a growing body of cases relying on buy and hold philosophy for family legacy assets.

In *Estate of Miller*,[7] the Tax Court concluded that a portion of a decedent's assets, which were transferred to a FLP were not includible in the decedent's gross estate under IRC Sec. 2036 because the transfer was a bona fide sale for adequate and full consideration. The bona fide sale for full and adequate consideration exception to IRC Sec. 2036 applied only to transfers of marketable securities to an FLP made about 13 months prior to the decedent's death. The court concluded that there were

---

[6] Estate of Black, 133 TC 340 (2009).   [7] Estate of Miller, TC Memo 2009 119.

legitimate and significant nontax reasons for the contributions to the partnership, finding credible the witnesses' testimony "that the driving force behind decedent's desire to form [the FLP] was to continue the management of family assets in accordance with Mr. Miller's investment strategy." The court emphasized that there was active management of the partnership's assets by the decedent's son as the general partner, that there was a change in the investment activity after formation of the FLP, and that the decedent retained sufficient assets for living expenses.

The court refused to apply the bona fide sale exception to additional contributions to the FLP made only 13 days before the decedent's death following very serious health problems, finding that "the decline in her health and the decision to reduce her taxable estate were clearly the driving forces" behind the subsequent contribution of assets to the FLP. Because the decedent's declining health appeared to be the prime motivation for the additional contributions, it was determined that there was no significant nontax reason for the later transfers to the FLP. Therefore, the later transfers to the FLP were includible in the decedent's gross estate at their fair market value.

In *Estate of Shurtz*,[8] the Tax Court held that an interest in a limited partnership and timberland, which was transferred to a FLP was not includible in the decedent's gross estate under IRC Sec. 2036(a) because the transfer was a bona fide sale for adequate and full consideration. The decedent and her husband created an FLP to hold the decedent's timberland property and her interest in a separate LP in order to protect the assets from potential litigation in Mississippi, to provide for their heirs, to ease the management of the assets, and to reduce the value of the estate. The court concluded that the creation of the FLP was a bona fide sale because protecting the assets from potential litigants and using the FLP to facilitate the active management of the assets were legitimate and significant nontax reasons for its creation.

The court concluded that the transfer of timberland interests to the FLP constituted a bona fide sale and that the decedent received an interest in the FLP that represented adequate and full consideration because: (1) the participants in the FLP received interests proportionate to the fair market value of the property each contributed; (2) the respective contributed assets were properly credited to the transferors' capital accounts; (3) distributions required negative adjustments to distributee capital accounts; and (4) there was a legitimate and significant nontax reason for formation of the FLP which included:

1. Preserving the family business;

2. Protecting the assets contributed to the FLP from potential litigation in Mississippi where "jackpot justice" prevails; and

3. Facilitating the management of the timberland.

Thus, the fair market value of the decedent's interest in the FLP, rather than the fair market value of the assets, which she contributed to the FLP was includible in her gross estate. Consequently, the estate's marital deduction for the interest in the FLP passing to the decedent's spouse, was to be calculated based on the value of the FLP, not on the value of its underlying assets.

---

[8] Estate of Shurtz, TC Memo 2010-21.

¶1303

(b) Bad Facts Lead to Bad Tax Results. In *Estate of Liljestrand*,[9] the value of assets that a decedent transferred to an FLP was includible in the decedent's gross estate under IRC Sec. 2036(a)(1). The decedent transferred real estate to the FLP in exchange for a 99.98-percent interest in the FLP. The Tax Court concluded that the decedent did not have a legitimate and significant nontax reason for transferring the assets to the FLP, and therefore the transfers were not bona fide sales. The transactions were not at arm's length and the FLP failed to follow basic partnership formalities. In addition, the court determined that the decedent did not contribute the real estate to the FLP for adequate and full consideration, noting that the FLP failed to maintain capital accounts upon the FLP's formation and did not use the fair market value of the real estate to establish the value of the FLP interests. Finally, the decedent retained enjoyment of the transferred assets, as evidenced by the direct use of FLP funds to pay the decedent's personal expenses, the commingling of FLP and the decedent's assets, and the large FLP distributions to the decedent. According to the court there was no significant change in the decedent's relationship with the assets before and after he formed the partnership. He received a disproportionate share of the partnership distributions, engineered a guaranteed payment equal to the partnership's expected annual income and benefited from the sale of the partnership assets. Although he retained some assets outside the partnership, the court found that the decedent lacked sufficient funds to maintain his lifestyle and satisfy his future obligations. He also commingled personal and partnership funds. The court viewed the FLP as an alternative testamentary vehicle to the trust and therefore concluded that the decedent retained enjoyment of the contributed property.

In *Estate of Jorgensen*,[10] the Tax Court concluded that the value of marketable securities transferred to two FLPs was includible in the decedent's gross estate because the transfers were not bona fide sales and there was an implied agreement that the decedent would retain the economic benefit from the property. In 1995, the decedent's deceased husband created an FLP and the couple each contributed marketable securities in exchange for a 50-percent limited partnership interest. The decedent's children and the decedent's deceased husband were the general partners. The couple then transferred limited partnership interests to their children and grandchildren. In 1997, after the decedent's husband's death, a second FLP was created and funded with cash and marketable securities from the decedent and the decedent's husband's estate. The decedent's children were the general partners. Over the course of the next several years, the decedent transferred small interests in the second FLP to her children and grandchildren.

The transfers of assets to the FLPs were not bona fide sales because of the following bad facts:

1. There was no legitimate nontax purpose for forming the FLPs and all purported nontax reasons were found to be insignificant;

2. The transactions were not at arm's length;

3. The partners failed to follow any partnership formalities, such as maintaining sufficient records and treating the FLPs as separate entities;

---

[9] Estate of Liljestrand, TC Memo 2011-256.

[10] Estate of Jorgensen, TC Memo 2009-66, *aff'd by unpub'd op.*, Estate of Erma v. Jorgensen, 2011 U.S. App. LEXIS 9203 (9th Cir., May 4, 2011).

4. There was an implied agreement that the decedent would retain an economic benefit from the property;

5. The decedent used partnership assets to make cash gifts to relatives; and

6. After the decedent's death, the partnership assets were used to pay the estate's transfer tax obligations and administrative expenses.

Since the decedent retained the use, benefit, and enjoyment from the assets, the court concluded that the property was includible in the decedent's estate for federal estate tax purposes under IRC Sec. 2036.

Similarly, in *Estate of Hurford*,[11] the Tax Court concluded that assets transferred to three FLPs were includible in the decedent's gross estate. Although the estate asserted several nontax reasons for creating the FLPs, the estate did not establish that any of these alleged reasons were the main motivation behind creating the FLPs. The transfer of assets to the FLPs was not motivated by a legitimate and significant nontax reason because the family disregarded partnership formalities, the decedent transferred nearly all of her personal assets to the FLP and commingled her own funds with partnership funds, and the FLPs were not functioning businesses and had no real economic activity. In addition, the value of the decedent's interest in each FLP was worth less than the value of the assets that she contributed. Therefore, the court concluded that the transfers to the FLPs were not bona fide sales for adequate and full consideration under IRC Sec. 2036.

More bad facts in *Estate of Malkin*[12] resulted in stock that was transferred to two family FLPs being included in the decedent's gross estate because the decedent retained possession and enjoyment of the stock. The court was unable to identify a legitimate and significant nontax reason for the transfers. The court therefore found that decedent's transfers of stock to the FLPs achieved nothing more than testamentary objectives and tax benefits, and, thus, those transfers did not qualify for the bona fide sale exception in IRC Sec. 2036(a). The following bad facts were present:

1. The grant of partnership interests to trusts for the decedent's children occurred before the partnership was funded;

2. The partnership was allegedly funded to pool investments; however, the decedent's children had substantial investments but did not contribute and were not asked to contribute any part of those to the partnership;

3. The partnership was allegedly formed to control certain stock owned by the decedent; although the decedent's son owned very large blocks of the same stock, the decedent never asked his son to contribute his stock to the partnership;

4. The intrafamily loans were not documented or enforced and the explanations for them were not credible; and

5. The decedent was the general partner of the partnerships.

Taxpayer victory in appellate court. In *Kimbell*,[13] an important case where the taxpayers were victorious, the Court of Appeals for the Fifth Circuit concluded that assets transferred to a FLP were not includible in a decedent's gross estate because

---

[11] Estate of Hurford, TC Memo 2008-278.

[12] Estate of Malkin, TC Memo 2009-212.

[13] Estate of Kimbell, 244 F. Supp. 2d 700 (D.C. Tex. 2002), *vac'd and rem'd*, 371 F.3d 257 (5th Cir. 2004).

the transfer qualified as a bona fide sale for adequate and full consideration. Before her death, Ruth Kimbell, through her revocable trust, contributed $2.5 million of various assets including working interests in oil and gas properties to an FLP in exchange for a 99 percent limited partnership interest. An LLC owned 50 percent by her and 25 percent each by her son and daughter-in-law, contributed $25,000 in cash, for a 1 percent general partnership interest in the FLP. When Mrs. Kimbell died, her estate claimed a 49 percent discount on the value of her interests in the FLP and the LLC for lack of control and marketability of the partnership interest. Transfers into an FLP will escape the grasp of IRC Sec. 2036(a) and thus avoid inclusion in the decedent's taxable estate if the transfer is a bona fide sale for full and adequate consideration ("bona fide sale exception") or if the decedent did not retain either the (1) possession, enjoyment, or rights to the transferred property, or (2) the right to designate the persons who would possess or enjoy the transferred property ("retained income or rights exception").

Kimbell's transfer to the partnership was for full and adequate consideration because:

1. The interests credited to each of the partners were proportionate to the fair-market value of the assets each partner contributed to the partnership;
2. The assets contributed by each partner to the partnership were properly credited to the respective capital accounts of the partners; and
3. On termination or dissolution of the partnership the partners were entitled to distributions from the partnership in amounts equal to their respective capital accounts.

The transfers were bona fide, even under the heightened scrutiny afforded intra-family transfers, because:

1. The decedent retained sufficient assets outside the partnership for her support and there was no commingling of partnership and personal assets;
2. Partnership formalities were satisfied and the assets contributed to the partnership were actually assigned to the partnership;
3. The assets contributed to the partnership (working interests in oil and gas properties) required active management thus constituting a credible nontax business reason for creation of the FLP;
4. Keeping the assets in one pool, under one management reduced administrative costs;
5. The partnership avoided costs associated with recording transfers of oil and gas properties as the property was passed from generation to generation. The decedent wanted to keep the asset in an entity that would preserve the property as separate property of her descendants;
6. The FLP avoided potential family disputes by providing for the management of assets in the event of the death or disability of the managing partner.

   ▶ **PRACTICE POINTER:** In *Estates of Stone, Keller, Mirowski, Black, Shurtz* and *Kimbell*, the courts have breathed new life into FLPs and have shown that these wealth transfer devices can still be used safely if the transfers to the FLP can be characterized as bona fide sales for adequate and full consideration in money or money's worth under IRC Sec. 2036(a). To support that position, the decedent's estate must be able to provide extensive evidence to support a legitimate and substantial nontax purposes for forming, and transferring assets to the FLP. The estate must be able to show that (1) the decedent received an interest in the FLP proportionate to the value of the assets transferred to it; (2) that the decedent's capital account was properly credited with those assets, and (3) in the event of a liquidation of the entity the decedent had the right to a distribution of property in accordance with his or her capital account.

(c) Bad Facts to Avoid. In the numerous cases involving transfers to FLPs where the IRS prevailed, the following so-called "bad facts" were present:

1. There was no legitimate business nontax purpose for creating the FLPs and all purported nontax reasons were insignificant;

2. The transactions were not at arm's length;

3. The partners failed to follow any partnership formalities, such as maintaining sufficient records and treating the FLP as a separate entity;

4. There was an implied agreement that the decedent would retain an economic benefit from the property;

5. The decedent used partnership assets to make cash gifts to relatives;

6. After the decedent's death, the partnership assets were used to pay the estate's transfer tax obligations and administrative expenses;

7. The taxpayers transferred substantially all of their assets to the partnership, leaving them with insufficient asserts to sustain their normal lifestyle;

8. The FLP paid the taxpayer's personal expenses directly;

9. The taxpayer continued to receive income or otherwise benefit from the assets transferred to the partnership;

10. The taxpayer was old and in poor health and formed the partnership shortly before death, with no independent business or investment purpose for establishing the FLP;

11. The taxpayer transferred a personal residence to a partnership and continued to live there for less than fair market rent thus triggering IRC Sec. 2036;[14]

12. The taxpayer transferred certain assets into an existing partnership contemporaneous with a gift of a partnership interest which is evidence of an indirect gift of the transferred asset;[15]

13. The taxpayer formed a partnership and transferred assets by the attorney-in-fact because the transferor was incapacitated, thus indicating to the court that the transaction was not a bona fide sale;[16] or

14. The taxpayer transferred assets into an FLP in a situation where the assets did not require active management or special protection. After the assets had been transferred into the FLP, no special investment strategy was implemented in managing the assets; the FLP did not prove to be more efficient in managing the assets; there was no litigation or threat of litigation among family members and therefore the FLP did not resolve conflict among children and grandchildren; the

---

[14] Estate of Disbrow, TC Memo 2006-34.   [16] Estate of Erickson, TC Memo 2007-107.

[15] Heckerman, 2009-2 USTC ¶60,578 (D.C. Wash.).

assets transferred into the FLP were not in need of special protection because of a troubled family member; there was no negotiation or meaningful bargaining with other parties involved in the transaction; the FLP was used to commingle personal assets and partnership funds; the transfers to the FLP occurred over an eight-month period rather than occurring within the same month as is normally the case; there were disproportionate distributions from the FLP to the transferor; the FLP used entity funds for personal expenses; and the purpose of the FLP was primarily focused on testamentary planning and minimizing estate taxes.[17]

The courts have relied on these facts to prove that while the decedents may have technically transferred title to the property to the FLP during life, they never actually parted with some or all of the valuable economic attributes associated with ownership, such as the right to income from or use of the property transferred into the FLP. Thus the courts have concluded that the property transferred by the decedent to the FLP must be included in the decedent's gross estate under IRC Sec. 2036(a) because the assets were not transferred through a bona fide sale for full and adequate consideration and the decedent continued to retain the possession or enjoyment of the assets until death.[18]

¶1304 FLP PRACTICE POINTERS

It should be apparent from these cases that the IRS is hostile to the use of FLPs to minimize estate and gift tax. Thus, taxpayers using them to limit wealth transfer tax, should proceed with extreme caution. They can be sure that the IRS will take a very close look at the deal. They will want to be sure that the FLP passes muster and makes good business sense rather than being just a savvy wealth transfer tax dodge. To avoid IRS scrutiny, taxpayers should heed the following advice when establishing an FLP:

1. Avoid deathbed formation of FLPs. Do not set up FLPs in situations where the taxpayer is gravely ill and is expected to die soon or where he or she is incapacitated.

2. Show a nontax business purpose for the formation of the limited partnership. For example, the desire to achieve centralized management of assets has been recognized as a valid business purpose for setting up an FLP.[1] The FLP must demonstrate a business purpose and conduct a legitimate business activity. This means doing more than managing a personal securities portfolio or owning a life insurance policy. Spell out your nontax reasons for setting up the FLP loud and

---

[17] Estate of Turner, TC Memo 2011-209, *supplemental decision*, 138 TC No. 14 (2012).

[18] Estate of Abraham, TC Memo 2004-39, *aff'd*, 408 F.3d 26 (1st Cir. 2005), *cert. denied*, 6/5/2006; Estate of Erickson, TC Memo 2007-107; Estate of Gore, TC Memo 2007-169 (supplemental decision TC Memo 2007-370); Estate of Bongard, 124 TC 95 (2005); Estate of Bigelow, TC Memo 2005-65, *aff'd*, 503 F.3d 955 (9th Cir. 2007); Estate of Schutt, TC Memo 2005-126; Estate of Rosen, TC Memo 2006-115; Estate of Korby, TC Memo 2005-102, *aff'd*, 471 F.3d 848 (8th Cir. 2006); Estate of Strangi, 115 TC 478 (2000), *aff'd in part and rev'd in part*, 293 F.3d 279 (5th Cir. 2000), *rem'd*, TC Memo 2003-145, *aff'd*, 417 F.3d 468 (5th Cir. 2005); Turner (Estate of Thompson), TC Memo 2002-246, *aff'd*, 382 F.3d 367 (3d Cir. 2004).

[1] ¶1304 Church, 2000-1 USTC ¶60,369 (W.D. Tex. 2000), *aff'd*, 268 F.3d 1063 (5th Cir. 2001).

clear. Save any letters or memos that document the business reasons for setting up the FLP. FLPs most often run into trouble with the IRS when the principal assets are not a business but rather a portfolio of investments. Some of the business reasons found relevant by the courts include the following:

- Facilitation of active and economical management for business interests transferred;
- Shielding assets from the grasp of creditors or ex-spouses;
- Continuation and preservation of assets;
- Reduction of administrative costs;
- Continuity of management;
- Potential dispute resolution among family member/owner;
- Increase family wealth;
- Establishment of a method of making annual gifts without fractionalizing family assets.

3. Avoid implied agreements between the partners that the decedent will retain possession and enjoyment of the assets transferred to the limited partnership. In *Estate of Reichardt*,[2] the Tax Court concluded that the value of assets transferred by a decedent to three family limited partnerships was includible in the decedent's estate because there was an implied agreement between the partners that the decedent would retain possession and enjoyment of the assets.

4. Respect the partnership's existence. Partners cannot treat the FLP as their alter ego. For example, the partners cannot commingle partnership assets with personal assets and use the money from the account to pay both personal and partnership expenses. Separate records must be kept for the partnership's money. In essence, the parties must respect the form of the partnership and follow all formalities required in forming the entity. The Tax Court has found in several cases[3] that the commingling of assets, the disproportional distributions to the decedent, the transfer of substantially all of the decedent's assets to the partnership, and the amount of control that the decedent retained over the partnership indicated that the decedent retained the economic benefits of the contributed assets. As a result the limited partnership formed by the decedents in these cases was defective and disregarded for tax purposes.

5. Make sure the partnership is legitimate. The formation of the partnership and transfer of the partnership interests cannot be sham transactions. Taxpayers creating FLPs should strictly adhere to all formalities in the creation, structure, and operation of the entity, including strict avoidance of any form of commingling of personal and entity assets.

6. Get a professional written appraisal of the assets transferred into the FLP. This appraisal should support the discount that you have claimed for the assets.

7. Avoid excessive valuation discounts that scream valuation abuse designed to avoid taxes.

---

[2] Estate of Reichardt, 114 TC 144 (2000); Estate of Schauerhamer, TC Memo 1997-242; Estate of Rector, TC Memo 2007-367.

[3] Estate of Harper, TC Memo 2002-121; Estate of Reichardt, 114 TC 144 (2000); Estate of Schauerhamer, TC Memo 1997-242.

8. The limited partnership agreement should be drafted to deal with the exigencies that arise in bankruptcy and under the income, estate, and gift tax laws.

9. The limited partnership should include one or more unrelated parties to give the appearance of a partnership operated at arm's length.

10. Ensure that the transferor retains sufficient assets to support himself or herself. Taxpayers who fail to heed this advise will risk the challenge that the assets of the transferee entity are being used to pay personal living expenses. All of the taxpayer's assets should not be transferred to the FLP.

11. To avoid inclusion of the transferred assets in the decedent's estate under IRC Sec. 2036(a), make sure that the transfer qualifies as a *bona fide* sale for full and adequate consideration in money or money's worth.

12. Taxpayers should strictly follow the letter of state law when transferring property to the entity. The transaction must be properly structured. The partnership should not be formed before the FLP creator contributes assets to the FLP. This so-called "delay in funding" could result in a delay in documentation and recordation of the transfer of assets to the FLP and eventual rejection of the FLP by the IRS. For example, in *Estate of Senda*,[4] the Court of Appeals for the Eighth Circuit concluded that a couple's transfers of stock to two FLPs were indirect gifts of stock to the couple's children for purposes of IRC Sec. 2511. The court concluded that the couple did not establish that they contributed the stock to the FLPs before they transferred the partnership interests to the children. In reaching this conclusion, the court found that: (1) the donors disregarded the formalities of the FLPs evidenced by the failure of the husband, as general partner, to maintain any records or books for the FLPs (other than tax returns) and the considerable delay in preparing certificates of ownership reflecting the transfer of the partnership interests; (2) the FLP tax returns were unreliable for determining whether the transfer of the stock to the FLPs occurred before or after the transfer of the partnership interests to the children because they were prepared months after the transfers of partnership interests; and (3) letters faxed to the couple's tax advisors were inconclusive as to what the partnership interests were before the funding or how the partnership interests were allocated among the partners' capital accounts at the time of the funding. Accordingly, the transfers of stock, coupled with the partnership interests, constituted indirect gifts of stock to the children.

But in *Estate of Holman*,[5] the Court of Appeals for the Eighth Circuit affirmed the Tax Court to conclude that a husband and wife's transfers of limited partnership (LP) units to a trust and a custodianship were not indirect gifts for purposes of IRC Sec. 2511 because the whole transaction was properly structured as follows: (1) transfers were not made first to the trust and custodianship and then to the partnership; and (2) the taxpayers did not simultaneously transfer the shares to the partnership and the LP units to the trustee and custodian. Moreover, the court found that the step transaction doctrine did not apply because the taxpayers bore a real economic risk of a change in value of the partnership for the six

---

[4] Estate of Senda, TC Memo 2004-160, *aff'd*, 433 F.3d 1044 (8th Cir. 2006).

[5] Estate of Holman, 130 TC 170 (2008), *aff'd*, 601 F.3d 763 (8th Cir. 2010). See also Linton,

2011-1 USTC ¶60,611 (9th Cir. 2011), *aff'g in part and rev'g in part*, 2009-2 USTC ¶60,575 (D.C. Wash. 2009).

days that separated the contribution to the LP and the gift of LP units. The step transaction doctrine treats multiple transactions as a single integrated transaction for tax purposes if all of the elements of at least one of three tests are satisfied: (1) the end result test, (2) the interdependence test, or (3) the binding commitment test. The step transaction doctrine has been described as combining a series of individually meaningless steps into a single transaction. The step transaction doctrine is a judicially created doctrine which treats a series of separate steps as a single transaction when the steps are integrated parts of a single plan. Under the end result test, the step transaction doctrine will be applicable if a series of formally separate transactions appear to be part of a single prearranged plan intended from its inception to reach the ultimate result. This test is based on the intent of the parties.

The interdependence test requires an evaluation as to whether the steps are so interdependent that the legal relationships created by one transaction would have been fruitless without the completion of the other steps in the plan. This test concentrates on the relationship between the transactions rather than on the end result. However, because the interdependence test requires a determination as to whether the steps have independent significance or whether the steps only have substance as part of a larger transaction, the interdependence test can be considered a variation of the end result test.

The binding commitment test is the narrowest of the step transaction alternatives. Under this test, the inquiry is whether after the first step is taken the parties are obligated to undertake later steps. This test was formulated to deal with the characterization of transactions that may span several years.

In *Estate of Gross*,[6] a taxpayer's transfers of securities to a family limited partnership were not indirect gifts of securities for purposes of IRC Sec. 2511 because the taxpayer complied with state law when structuring the transaction. In addition, as in *Estate of Holman*, the step transaction doctrine did not apply because the taxpayers bore a real economic risk of a change in value of the partnership for the 11 days that separated the contribution to the partnership and the gifts.

13. Capital accounts should be maintained for all partners. In addition, capital accounts should be credited for all contributions of property and/or services by all partners.

14. Taxpayers should operate the FLP like a legitimate business in substance as well as form. They should conduct appropriate business activities, keep proper books and records, hold partner meetings, keep minutes and enforce any rights and actions against the partners.

▶**WARNING: PROCEED WITH CAUTION:** The opportunity to save big dollars on wealth transfer taxes via an FLP is enticing. It can not only be a valuable income tax reduction tool, but can also transfer wealth to your children and grandchildren, generate substantial estate and gift tax valuation discounts, insulate family assets from the claims of creditors, provide for centralized management, and afford parents flexibility in controlling family businesses. But remember that the IRS is looking over your shoulder. The gift tax return (Form 709) contains a box that you must check to indicate that you are claiming a

---

[6] Estate of Gross, TC Memo 2008-221.

discount in your valuation of any property listed on the return. This makes it easier for the IRS to spot at a glance taxpayers who may be using FLPs to save gift tax.

To make matters worse, in a recent directive, the IRS has indicated that it will take a second look at FLPs if the following factors are present:

1. The partnership consists either entirely or predominately of liquid assets that can easily be valued and are entitled to no valuation discount;

2. Transfers were made to the limited partnership shortly before the family knew that the business owner/parent was going to die in the foreseeable future;

3. Transfers were made pursuant to a durable power of attorney.

Lawmakers have suggested the need for legislation that would put the kibosh on FLPs. Specifically, they seek to prohibit taxpayers from claiming valuation discounts when the subject of the valuation is liquid, easily valued passive investments such as publicly traded securities, cash, real property, and collectibles.

CALCULATION OF THE GIFT TAX

TABLE OF CONTENTS

¶1400 COMPUTATION OF GIFT TAX

Taxpayers compute their federal gift tax liability on a cumulative basis that takes into account taxable gifts that were made in both the current and prior years [IRC Sec. 2502(a)].

If prior taxable gifts were made. If the donor has made one or more taxable gifts in a prior year, the following steps should be observed:

1. Determine the amount of taxable gifts for the calendar year for which the computation is made;

2. Determine the aggregate sum of taxable gifts for each of the prior calendar years, considering only gifts made after June 6, 1932 (prior taxable gifts);

3. Aggregate all taxable gifts made during the donor's lifetime by adding taxable gifts made in the current calendar year (see description below) to the prior taxable gifts;

4. Calculate the tentative tax on the aggregate total of lifetime taxable gifts (determined in Step 3) by applying the current unified estate and gift tax rate schedule;

5. Calculate the tax on the prior taxable gifts by applying the unified rate schedule to the amount determined in Step 2;

6. Calculate the tentative gift tax for the computation year by subtracting the amount determined in Step 5 from the amount determined in Step 4; and

7. Subtract the available unified credit and any deceased spousal unused exclusion amount from the amount of the tentative gift tax computed under Step 6.

If no prior taxable gifts were made. If the donor has made no taxable gifts in the prior years, the following steps should be observed:

1. Determine the donor's total taxable gifts during the current year. If the donor and donor's spouse consent to gift splitting [see ¶902], only include the donor's one-half share of the gifts;

2. Subtract any amounts allowable under the annual per donee exclusion [see ¶ 901];

3. Subtract any charitable gifts [see ¶ 910] and gifts qualifying for the marital deduction [see ¶ 1107];

4. Determine the tentative gift tax payable from the unified estate and gift tax rate schedule [see below]; and

5. Subtract the unified credit and any deceased spousal unused exclusion amount from the tentative gift tax.

The following unified rate schedule is used to compute the tax on both cumulative and prior taxable gifts.

Unified Estate and Gift Tax Rate Schedule (After 2012)

(A) Amount subject to tax equal to or more than—	(B) Amount subject to tax less than—	(C) Tax on amount in column (A)	(D) Rate of tax on excess over amount in column (A)
			Percent
	$10,000		18
$10,000	20,000	$1,800	20
20,000	40,000	3,800	22
40,000	60,000	8,200	24
60,000	80,000	13,000	26
80,000	100,000	18,200	28
100,000	150,000	23,800	30
150,000	250,000	38,800	32
250,000	500,000	70,800	34
500,000	750,000	155,800	37
750,000	1,000,000	248,300	39
1,000,000		345,800	40

Current-year taxable gifts. The gift tax is imposed on taxable gifts made during the calendar year. The amount of taxable gifts is the total amount of gifts made during the calendar year, as reduced by the following exclusions and deductions:

1. *Annual Exclusion.* A donor's total gifts for the year are reduced by a $14,000 in 2014 per donee annual gift tax exclusion which is $14,000 in 2014, provided the gifts are present and not future interests in property [see ¶ 901]. The following chart illustrates the gift tax annual exclusion amounts in effect for transfers made from 1939 through 2014.

Gift Tax Annual Exclusion Amounts

For Transfers Made in:	
1939 through 1942	4,000
1943 through 1981	3,000
1982 through 2001	10,000
2002 through 2005	11,000
2006 through 2008	12,000
2009 through 2012	13,000
2013 and 2014	14,000

2. *Exclusion for Medical and Educational Expenses.* Transfers made by the taxpayer directly to educational institutions to pay tuition expenses and transfers to medical care providers to pay medical expenses are not subject to the gift tax and are not reported on the gift tax return. Thus, a donor's total gifts during the year are reduced for qualifying transfers for educational and medical expenses [see ¶ 908].

3. *Charitable Transfers.* A donor is allowed a gift tax charitable deduction for the value of property transferred to a qualified charity. When a donor makes an outright gift of his or her entire interest in the property, the full value of the transferred property (less annual exclusions) is reduced by the gift tax charitable deduction. When the donor transfers property to both charitable and noncharitable interests (i.e., split interest gifts), only the portion of the property transferred to a noncharitable beneficiary is subject to gift tax.

4. *Marital Transfers.* Gifts between spouses are eligible for the unlimited marital deduction. To qualify for the deduction, the spouses must be married, the spouse receiving the gift must be a U.S. citizen, and the interest transferred cannot be a nondeductible terminable interest. These gifts eligible for the unlimited marital deduction are not reported on the gift tax return [See ¶ 1107].

Gift tax applicable credit amount. An applicable credit amount is allowed against cumulative taxes imposed on lifetime transfers [IRC Sec. 2010]. Use of the available credit amount is mandatory and not refundable. The applicable credit amount for 2014 is the tentative tax on the sum of the $5,340,000 basic exclusion amount plus any unused exclusion amount allocated to the donor by a predeceased spouse. If there is no unused exclusion amount allocated by a deceased spouse, the maximum applicable credit amount for 2014 is $2,081,800. For decedents who die after 2012, any unused estate tax exclusion (DSUE) amount may be transferred to a surviving spouse. The ability to transfer the unused amount, commonly referred to as *portability*, is elected by the predeceased spouse's executor who must file a timely and complete estate tax return on Form 706 for the deceased spouse in order for the surviving spouse to take advantage of the deceased spouse's unused exclusion amount. The unused exclusion amount transferred from a predeceased spouse is added to the surviving spouse's basic exclusion amount to determine the lifetime transfers and transfer at death that the surviving spouse will be able to shelter from estate and gift tax. For further discussion of portability, see Chapter 15.

Reduction for portion of $30,000 specific exemption. If a donor previously used any of the $30,000 specific lifetime exemption (the predecessor to the unified credit and the applicable credit amount for taxable gifts made after September 8, 1976, and before January 1, 1977, the applicable credit amount is reduced by 20 percent of the specific exemption claimed [IRC Sec. 2505(b)].

Credit for foreign gift taxes. The United States has entered into death tax conventions with certain foreign countries to avoid double taxation. These conventions provide that credits are available to U.S. citizens and residents for part or all of gift taxes paid to the foreign country [IRC Sec. 2501(a)(3)(B)]. Gift tax conventions are in effect with Australia, Austria, Denmark, France, Germany, Japan, and the United Kingdom. To determine the amount of the foreign gift tax credit, the actual treaty should be consulted and a statement attached to the return which details the calculation of the credit and proof that taxes were actually paid to the foreign country.

¶1400

¶1401   WHY THE GIFT TAX IS CHEAPER THAN THE ESTATE TAX

A lifetime program of making tax-free gifts makes sense for a number of reasons as discussed in ¶901. One of the reasons is that a gift costs less than a transfer at death. Why? The gift tax is tax-exclusive, which means that the tax bill on the gift must be paid by the gift-giver and is payable from funds that are not part of the gift. The estate tax, in sharp contrast, is tax-inclusive, which means that the tax is imposed on the transferred property before the tax bill is paid and is payable out of the transferred property so the person inheriting the estate pays the tax and ends up with less money. The estate tax base is bigger because it includes the tax imposed on the property included in the estate or in tax terminology is "tax-inclusive" [IRC Sec. 2001]. The gift tax base is smaller because it excludes the tax imposed on the gifted property or is "tax-exclusive" [IRC Sec. 2501]:

> **Example 1:** Son inherits $1 million. Assume a 50 percent tax rate applies to the transfer. The estate tax bill on the transfer is $500,000. After the estate tax is paid, Son is left with $500,000.

> **Example 2:** Daughter receives a $1 million gift from Mom. Assume a 50 percent tax rate applies to the gift. The gift tax of $500,000 must be paid by Mom and Daughter ends up with the full $1 million.

Portability

15

TABLE OF CONTENTS

¶1500 PURPOSE AND OPERATION

The Tax Relief Act of 2010 dramatically changed the estate tax laws by amending IRC Sec. 2010(c), to add the portability feature which generally allows the surviving spouse to use the decedent's unused exclusion amount in addition to the surviving spouse's own basic exclusion amount if an election is made on a timely filed and complete estate tax return. Portability was designed to simplify estate planning by eliminating the need for spouses to retitle property and create credit shelter trusts solely to take full advantage of each spouse's applicable exclusion amount.

Example 1: Wife died in 2014 when the applicable exclusion amount is $5,340,000. During her life she made no taxable gifts. Her timely filed estate tax return includes a portability election. Husband also dies in 2014 and assuming he has made no taxable gifts, his applicable exclusion amount is $10,680,000 (his applicable exclusion amount of $5,340,000 plus her unused applicable exclusion amount of $5,340,000).

Portability now permanent. The concept of "portability" of a deceased spouse's unused exclusion (DSUE) amount was made permanent for the estates of decedents dying after December 31, 2012 by the American Taxpayer Relief Act of 2012. Portability applies to the gift tax exemption as well as the estate tax exemption. Portability does not, however, apply to the generation skipping transfer tax exemption.

¶1501 COMPUTING EXCLUSION AMOUNT OF SURVIVING SPOUSE

(a) Definition of "Applicable Exclusion Amount". The Tax Relief Act of 2010 created portability by redefining the term "applicable exclusion amount" to enable a surviving spouse to use the applicable exclusion amount that remains unused at the death of his or her predeceased spouse, in addition to his or her own applicable exclusion amount to reduce gift and estate tax liability. The term "applicable exclusion amount" is defined in IRC Sec. 2010(c)(2) as the sum of:

• The basic exclusion amount ($5,340,000 for 2014); and

• The aggregate deceased spousal unused exclusion (DSUE) amount (discussed below) [IRC Sec. 2010(c)(2)].

The basic exclusion amount is adjusted annually for inflation but once it is transferred to the surviving spouse, it is not adjusted for inflation. Any portion of the predeceased spouse's applicable exclusion amount that was used to reduce his or her estate tax liability may not be used to reduce the surviving spouse's estate tax liability.

The term "deceased spousal unused exclusion amount" (DSUE amount) is the lesser of:

• The basic exclusion amount, or

• The last deceased spouse's applicable exclusion amount, minus the amount with respect to which the tentative tax is determined under IRC Sec. 2001(b)(1) on the estate of such deceased spouse [IRC Sec. 2010(c)(4)].

Amounts on which gift taxes were paid by a decedent are excluded from adjusted taxable gifts for purposes of computing that decedent's DSUE amount. This avoids the use of the exclusion on amounts if: (1) gift tax was paid by the decedent on transfers that caused total taxable transfers to exceed the applicable exclusion amount at the time of the transfer and (2) the decedent's total adjusted taxable gifts are less than the applicable exclusion amount on the date of death [Temp. Reg. Sec. 20.2010-2T(c)(2)].

If the decedent is the last deceased spouse of a surviving spouse on the date of a transfer by the surviving spouse that is subject to estate or gift tax, the surviving spouse (or the estate) may take into account the decedent's DSUE amount in determining the surviving spouse's applicable exclusion amount when computing the surviving spouse's estate or gift tax liability on that transfer. The portability election by the decedent's estate is effective as of the decedent's date of death. Accordingly, it is not possible for individuals who have been married multiple times to tack on multiple applicable exclusion amounts of their predeceased spouses [Temp. Reg. Secs. 20.2010-3T(a) and 25.2505-2T(a)].

(b) Same-Sex Couples Entitled to Benefit from Portability. As a result of the Supreme Court decision in *Windsor*[1] and the IRS response in Rev. Rul. 2013-17,[2] the terms "spouse," "husband and wife," "husband," "wife" and "married" include an individual married to a person of the same sex if the individuals are lawfully married under state law. Therefore, same-sex couples can take advantage of portability. The IRS has adopted a state-of-celebration rule which recognizes a marriage of same-sex individuals that was validly entered into in a state whose laws authorize the marriage of two individuals of the same sex even if the married couple is domiciled in a state that does not recognize the validity of same-sex marriages. Individuals (whether of the opposite sex or the same sex) who have entered into a registered domestic partnership, civil union, or other similar formal relationship are not considered married for federal tax purposes.

(c) Portability Available Regardless of Size of Deceased Spouse's Estate. The deceased spouse can make a portability election and the surviving spouse can apply the DSUE of his or her last deceased spouse no matter the size of the estate. Consider the following examples:

Example 1: A decedent dies in 2014 with a $3 million taxable estate. If the decedent makes a portability election on Form 706, the decedent's surviving spouse will have use of the deceased spouse's unused exclusion amount in the amount of $2,340,000.

Example 2: A decedent dies in 2014 with a $20 million estate. He leaves $5 million to his children and $13 million to a surviving spouse and charity. If he makes a portability election on Form 706, the decedent's surviving spouse will have use of the decedent spouse's unused exclusion amount in the amount of $2,340,000.

(d) "Last Deceased Spouse" Limitation. The surviving spouse may only use the unused exclusion of his or her "last deceased spouse" who is defined as the most recently deceased person who was married to the surviving spouse at the time of that person's death [IRC Sec. 2010(c)(4)]. The Joint Committee on Taxation explains that the identity of the last deceased spouse is not impacted by whether the decedent's estate elected portability or whether the last deceased spouse had any DSUE amount available.[3] For example, if the last deceased spouse opted out of the portability election,

---

[1] **¶1501** Windsor, 570 U.S. —, 133 S. Ct. 2675, 186 L. Ed. 2d 808 (2013).
[2] Rev. Rul. 2013-17, 2013-38 IRB 201.

[3] Staff of the Joint Committee on Taxation, 111th Cong., 2d Sess., "Technical Explanation of the Revenue Provisions Contained in the Tax

the surviving spouse's DSUE amount is zero even if a prior spouse made a portability election. As a result of this rule, it is possible for a surviving spouse to lose his or her DSUE amount if he or she remarries and that next spouse opts out of the portability election.

> **Example 3:** Assume that Husband 1 dies in 2014 when the applicable exclusion amount is $5,340,000. He made taxable transfers of $3,340,000 and has no taxable estate. An election is made on Husband 1's estate tax return to permit Wife to use Husband 1's DSUE. As of Husband 1's death, Wife has made no taxable gifts. Thereafter, Wife's applicable exclusion amount is $7,430,000 (her $5,340,000 basic exclusion amount plus the $2 million DSUE from Husband 1), which she may use for lifetime gifts or for transfers at death.

> **Example 4:** Assume the same facts as in Example 4, except that Wife subsequently marries Husband 2. Husband 2 also predeceases Wife, having made $4 million in taxable transfers and having no taxable estate. An election is made on Husband 2's estate tax return to permit Wife to use Husband 2's DSUE. Only Husband 2's $1 million unused exclusion is available for use by Wife, because the DSUE is limited to the lesser of the basic exclusion amount or the unused exclusion of the last deceased spouse of the surviving spouse (here, Husband 2's $1 million unused exclusion). Thereafter, Wife's applicable exclusion amount is $6,340,000 (her $5,340,000 basic exclusion amount plus the $1 million deceased spousal unused exclusion amount from Husband 2), which she may use for lifetime gifts or for transfers at death.

> **Example 5:** Assume the same facts as in Examples 4 and 5, except that Wife predeceases Husband 2. Following Husband 1's death, Wife's applicable exclusion amount is $7,340,000 (her $5,340,000 basic exclusion amount plus $2 million deceased spousal unused exclusion amount from Husband 1). Wife made no taxable transfers and has a taxable estate of $3 million. An election is made on Wife's estate tax return to permit Husband 2 to use Wife's DSUE, which is $4,340,000 (Wife's $7,340,000 applicable exclusion amount less her $3 million taxable estate). Under the provision, Husband 2's applicable exclusion amount is increased by $4,340,000, i.e., the amount of DSUE of Wife.

(e) DSUE in Case of Multiple Spouses and Previously-Applied DSUE Amount. The temporary regulations address how to compute the DSUE amount included in the applicable exclusion amount of a surviving spouse who made gifts between the deaths of two decedents, each of whom were at separate times the last deceased spouse of such surviving spouse.

1. Temp. Reg. Sec. 25.2505-2T(b) creates an ordering rule by providing that, when a surviving spouse makes a taxable gift, the DSUE of the decedent who is the last

---

(Footnote Continued)

Relief, Unemployment Insurance Reauthoriza- tion and Job Creation Act of 2010," p. 52, Note 57 (Dec. 10, 2010).

deceased spouse of such surviving spouse will be considered to apply against the amount of the surviving spouse's taxable gifts for that calendar year before the surviving spouse's own applicable exclusion amount will apply.

2. Temp. Regs. Secs. 25.2505-2T(c) and 20.2010-3T(b), compute the DSUE available to such a surviving spouse or to his or her estate, respectively, as including both: (i) the DSUE of the surviving spouse's last deceased spouse, and (ii) any DSUE actually applied to taxable gifts to the extent the DSUE so applied was from a decedent who no longer is the last deceased spouse. Temp. Reg. Sec. 25.2505-2T provides that a surviving spouse may use the DSUE of a predeceased spouse as long as, for each transfer, such DSUE is from the surviving spouse's last deceased spouse at the time of that transfer. Thus, a spouse who has survived multiple spouses may use each last deceased spouse's DSUE before the death of that spouse's next spouse, and thereby may apply the DSUE of multiple deceased spouses in succession. However, this does not permit the surviving spouse to use the sum of the DSUE of those deceased spouses at one time, and a surviving spouse may not use the remaining DSUE of a prior deceased spouse following the death of a subsequent spouse.

> **Example 6:** Husband 1 (H1) dies on January 15, 2014, survived by Wife (W). Neither has made any taxable gifts during H1's lifetime. H1's executor elects portability of H1's DSUE amount. The DSUE amount of H1 as computed on the estate tax return filed on behalf of H1's estate is $5,340,000. On December 31, 2014, W makes taxable gifts to her children valued at $2,340,000. W reports the gifts on a timely-filed gift tax return. W is considered to have applied $2,340,000 of H1's DSUE amount to the amount of taxable gifts and therefore owes no gift tax. W has an applicable exclusion amount remaining in the amount of $8,340,000 ($3 million of H1's remaining DSUE amount plus W's own $5,340,000 basic exclusion amount). After the death of H1, W marries Husband 2 (H2). H2 dies in June 2015. H2's executor elects portability of H2's DSUE amount, which is $2 million. W dies in October 2015. The DSUE amount to be included in determining the applicable exclusion amount available to W's estate is $4 million, determined by adding the $2 million DSUE amount of H2 and the $2 million DSUE amount of H1 that was applied by W to W's 2014 taxable gifts. Thus, W's applicable exclusion amount is $9,340,000 [Temp. Reg. Sec. 20.2010-3T(b), ex. 2].

¶1502 HOW TO ELECT PORTABILITY

(a) How to Make Portability Election. The portability election is not automatic. In order for a decedent's surviving spouse to take into account that decedent's deceased spousal unused exclusion (DSUE) amount, the executor of the deceased spouse must elect portability on a timely-filed Form 706, "United States Estate (and Generation-Skipping Transfer) Tax Return" [Temp. Reg. Sec. 20.2010-2T(a)]. The portability election will be considered timely if it is filed 9 months after the decedent's date of death or the last day of the period covered by an extension (if an extension of time for filing has been obtained from the IRS) [Temp. Reg. Sec. 20.2010-2T(a)(1)]. Upon the timely filing of a complete and properly-prepared estate tax return, an executor of an estate of a decedent survived by a spouse will be deemed to have elected portability of the decedent's DSUE amount unless the executor opts out of the portability election as discussed below [Temp. Reg. Sec. 20.2010-2T(a)(2)].

The Instructions to Form 706 provide that if the executor is unable to file Form 706 by the due date, an automatic 6-month extension of time to file Form 706 will be available if the executor files Form 4768, "Application for Extension of Time to File a Return and/or Pay U.S. Estate (and Generation-Skipping Transfer) Taxes." An executor can only elect to transfer the DSUE amount to the surviving spouse if the Form 706 is filed within 9 months of the decedent's date of death or, if the executor has received an extension of time to file, before the 6-month extension period ends by filing Form 4768.

The last return filed by the return due date, including extensions actually granted, will supersede any previously-filed return. Thus, an executor generally may supersede a previously-filed portability election on a subsequent timely-filed estate tax return. Temp. Reg. Sec. 20.2010-2T(a)(4) provides that a portability election is irrevocable once the due date (as extended) of the return has passed. The timing requirement for filing a return applies to all estates electing portability regardless of the size of the gross estate [Temp. Reg. Sec. 20.2010-2T(a)(1)].

(b) How to Opt Out of Portability Election. The executor can opt out of the portability election in one of the two following ways: (1) The executor of the estate of a decedent who is survived by a spouse can opt out of the portability election by checking the box indicated in Section A of Part 6 on Form 706; (2) If no estate tax return is required for that decedent's estate under IRC Sec. 6018(a) because the estate is less than the exclusion amount in the year of the decedent's death, then the fact that the executor does not timely file an estate tax return will be deemed by the IRS to signify the decision not to make the portability election [Temp. Reg. Sec. 20.2010-2T(a)(3)].

(c) How Small Estates Can Extend Time to Make Portability Election. In Rev. Proc. 2014-18,[1] the IRS provided a simplified procedure for the executors of decedents who died before January 1, 2014 to obtain an extension of time to make an estate tax portability election under IRC Sec. 2010(c)(5)(A). Once the portability election has been made, the decedent's unused exclusion amount (deceased spousal unused exclusion amount, or DSUE amount) can be used by his or her surviving spouse to reduce tax liability. No user fee is required for submissions filed under Rev. Proc. 2014-18. The extension is only available in the following limited situations:

1. The taxpayer is the executor of the estate of a decedent described below:

   • The decedent has a surviving spouse;

   • The decedent died after December 31, 2010 and on or before December 31, 2013;

   • The decedent was a citizen or resident of the United States on the date of death.

2. The only reason the decedent will be filing Form 706 is to elect portability because the decedent is not otherwise required to file an estate tax return under IRC Sec.

---

[1] **¶ 1502** Rev. Proc. 2014-18, 2014-7 IRB 513.

6018(a) because the value of his or her gross estate and adjusted taxable gifts is less than the basic exclusion amount in effect in the year of the decedent's death ($5,250,000 in 2013); and

3. The taxpayer did not file an estate tax return within the time prescribed by Temp. Reg. Sec. 20.2010-2T(a)(1) to elect portability.

Taxpayers who fail to qualify for relief under Rev. Proc. 2014-18 may request an extension of time to make the portability election under IRC Sec. 2010(c)(5)(A) by requesting a letter ruling from the IRS under the provisions of Reg. Sec. 301.9100-3.

Relief procedures. The decedent's estate will be granted an extension of time to elect portability if:

1. The estate files a "complete and properly-prepared" Form 706 on or before December 31, 2014.

2. The person filing the Form 706 on behalf of the decedent's estate states at the top of the Form 706 that the return is "FILED PURSUANT TO REV. PROC. 2014-18 TO ELECT PORTABILITY UNDER § 2010(c)(5)(A)."

The taxpayer will receive an estate tax closing letter acknowledging receipt of the taxpayer's Form 706. If the requirements of Rev. Proc. 2014-18 are satisfied, the taxpayer's Form 706 will be deemed to have been timely filed, the estate will be deemed to meet the requirements for relief, and relief will be granted to extend the time to elect portability. If relief is granted pursuant to Rev. Proc. 2014-18 and it is later determined that the estate was required to file a federal estate tax return, based on the value of the gross estate, plus any adjusted taxable gifts, the extension of time granted to make the portability election is deemed null and void. The extension procedures outlined in Rev. Proc. 2014-18 do not apply to taxpayers that filed an estate tax return within the time prescribed by Temp. Reg. Sec. 20.2010-2T(a)(1) for the purpose of electing portability. These taxpayers either will have elected portability of the DSUE amount by timely filing that estate tax return or will have affirmatively opted out of portability in accordance with Temp. Reg. Sec. 20.2010-2T(a)(3)(i).

(d) "Complete and Properly Prepared" Form 706 Required. In Notice 2011-82,[2] the IRS provided that the estate of a decedent will be deemed to make the portability election upon the timely filing of a "complete and properly-prepared" estate tax return. Temp. Reg. Sec. 20.2010-2T(a)(2) likewise provides that the estate of a decedent (survived by a spouse) makes the portability election by timely filing a "complete and properly-prepared" estate tax return for the decedent's estate. An estate tax return prepared in accordance with all applicable requirements is considered a "complete and properly prepared" estate tax return [Temp. Reg. Sec. 20.2010-2T(a)(7)(i)].

(e) Simplified Reporting for Estates under Filing Threshold. A reprieve from the expense and burden of filing a "complete" estate tax return on Form 706 when all the executor wants to do is make a portability election is available in Temp. Reg. Sec. 20.2010-2T(a)(7)(ii) which provides that executors of estates that are not otherwise required to file an estate tax return do not have to report the value of certain

---

[2] Notice 2011-82, 2011-42 IRB 516.

property that qualifies for the marital or charitable deduction. In the instructions accompanying Form 706, Schedule B, the IRS explains the special reporting rule.

Instead of entering the value of assets that qualify for the marital or charitable deductions, the IRS directs taxpayers to refer to the instructions to determine how to estimate and report the value of these assets. The IRS explains that if the total value of the gross estate and adjusted taxable gifts is less than the basic exclusion amount and Form 706 is being filed only to elect portability of the DSUE amount, the estate is not required to report the value of property qualifying for the marital or charitable deduction. Instead, the executor may calculate his or her best estimate of the value exercising good faith and due diligence. The IRS provides in the Form 706 instructions, ranges of dollar values, and the executor must identify on the estate tax return the particular range within which falls the executor's best estimate of the total gross estate. An amount corresponding to this range must be included on the estate tax return, along with an indication of whether the total includes an estimate under this special rule. For example, if the total estimated value of the assets eligible for the special rule under Temp. Reg. Sec. 20.2010-2T(a)(7)(ii) is more than $1 million but less than or equal to $1,250,000 the IRS instructions direct executors to include $1,250,000 on lines 10 and 23 of Form 706. By signing the return, the executor will be certifying, under penalties of perjury, that the estimate falls within the identified range of values to the best of the executor's knowledge and belief.

> **Example 1:** Husband dies in 2013, survived by Wife. Husband's gross estate does not exceed $5.25 million. Executor timely files Form 706 solely to make the portability election. To establish the estate's entitlement to the marital deduction, Executor includes with the Form 706 evidence to verify the title of each jointly held asset, to confirm that Wife is the sole beneficiary of both the life insurance policy and the survivor annuity, and to verify that the annuity is exclusively for her life. Finally, Executor certifies on Form 706 his best estimate, determined by exercising due diligence, of the fair market value of the gross estate. This estimate was an amount corresponding to the particular range within which falls the executor's best estimate of the value of the decedent's total gross estate rounded to the nearest $250,000. The estate tax return is considered complete and properly prepared and Executor has elected portability [Temp. Reg. Sec. 20.2010-2T(a)(7)(ii)(C), ex. 1].

When simplified reporting unavailable. Executors of decedents may not take advantage of simplified reporting in the following situations where the value of property relates to, affects, or is needed to determine the value passing from the decedent to another beneficiary [Temp. Reg. Sec. 20.2010-2T(a)(7)(ii)]:

1. Only a portion of an interest in property qualifies for the marital or charitable deduction;

2. The value of property is needed to determine the estate's eligibility for the alternate valuation date under IRC Sec. 2032, the special use valuation under IRC Sec. 2032A, or installment payments of estate taxes under IRC Sec. 6166;

3. A partial disclaimer of marital or charitable deduction property is made; or

4. A partial qualified terminable interest property (QTIP) election is made.

¶1502

▶ **PLANNING POINTER:** In light of the expense and time associated with filing a complete estate tax return, practitioners should address in the estate planning documents whether the executor of the deceased spouse or the surviving spouse will pay for preparation of the estate tax return in situations where the only reason for filing the form is to elect portability. Since the benefit of filing the return to elect portability benefits the surviving spouse, it may make sense to charge the expense of filing the Form 706 against the surviving spouse's share of the estate.

(f) Effective Date of Portability Election. Temp. Reg. Sec. 20.2010-3T(c)(1) and Temp. Reg. Sec. 20.2010-2T(d)(1) provide that a portability election made by the executor of a decedent's estate is effective as of the date of the decedent's death. The DSUE of a decedent survived by a spouse may therefore be included in determining the applicable exclusion amount of the surviving spouse, subject to any applicable limitations, with respect to all transfers occurring after the death of the decedent, if the executor of the decedent's estate makes a portability election and the election is not superseded by the executor of the decedent's estate before the due date of the return, including extensions.

¶1503 AUTHORITY TO EXAMINE RETURN OF DECEASED SPOUSE

In determining the allowable DSUE, the IRS may examine any one or more returns of each deceased spouse of the surviving spouse whose executor elected portability even if the period of limitations on assessments under IRC Sec. 6501 has expired [IRC Sec. 2010(c)(5)(B)]. Upon examination, the IRS may adjust or eliminate the DSUE reported on a return. The ability of the IRS to examine returns of a deceased spouse applies to each transfer by the surviving spouse to which a DSUE has been applied. The returns and return information of a deceased spouse may be disclosed to the surviving spouse or the surviving spouse's estate [Temp. Reg. Secs. 20.2001-2T(a), 20.2010-2T(d), 20.2010-3T(d), and 25.2505-2T(e)].

¶1504 PORTABILITY AND NONRESIDENT NONCITIZENS

In order to make the portability election, both spouses must be United States citizens. An executor of the estate of a nonresident decedent who was not a citizen of the United States at the time of death may not make a portability election on behalf of that decedent [Temp. Reg. Sec. 20.2010-2T(a)(5)]. A nonresident surviving spouse who was not a citizen of the United States at the time of such surviving spouse's death may not take into account the DSUE of any deceased spouse of such surviving spouse, except to the extent allowed under a treaty obligation of the United States [Temp. Reg. Secs. 20.2010-3T(e), 25.2505-2T(f)].

¶1505 PORTABILITY AND QUALIFIED DOMESTIC TRUSTS (QDOTs)

A qualified domestic trust (QDOT) is a trust that qualifies for the estate tax marital deduction under IRC Sec. 2056(d)(2) even though the transferee spouse is not a citizen of the United States. Property passing to a surviving spouse who is not a U.S. citizen is otherwise ineligible for the estate tax marital deduction. [For further discussion of QDOTs, see ¶1106.] Temp. Reg. Sec. 20.2010-2T(c)(4) provides that the executor of a decedent's estate claiming a marital deduction for property passing to a QDOT must compute the decedent's DSUE on a preliminary basis on the decedent's estate tax return for the purpose of electing portability. The DSUE of such a decedent will be redetermined upon the final distribution or other taxable event on which estate tax is imposed, which is generally upon the death of the noncitizen surviving spouse or the earlier termination of all QDOTs created for that surviving spouse.

Temp. Reg. Sec. 20.2010-3T(c)(2) provides that the earliest date such a decedent's DSUE amount may be included in determining the applicable exclusion amount available to the noncitizen surviving spouse or the surviving spouse's estate is the date of the event that triggers the final estate tax liability of the decedent. Generally, this means that such a decedent's DSUE amount will be available for transfers occurring by reason of the noncitizen surviving spouse's death, but generally will not be available to the surviving spouse during life. Therefore, the noncitizen surviving spouse will generally not be entitled to use the decedent's DSUE to avoid gift taxes unless the surviving spouse made taxable gifts in the year of the surviving spouse's death, or, if the event terminating the QDOT occurs prior to the surviving spouse's death.

The following Example 3 from Temp. Reg. Sec. 25.2505-2T(c)(5), ex. 3, illustrates computation of DSUE amount when a QDOT has been created.

> **Example 1:** Husband, a U.S. citizen, makes his first taxable gift in 2002, valued at $1 million and reports the gift on a timely-filed gift tax return. No gift tax is due because the $1 million applicable exclusion amount for that year equals the fair market value of the gift. Husband dies in 2014 with a gross estate of $2 million. Wife is a U.S. resident but not a citizen of the United States and, under Husband's will, a pecuniary bequest of $1.5 million passes to a QDOT for the benefit of Wife. Husband's executor timely files an estate tax return and makes the QDOT election for the property passing to the QDOT, and Husband's estate is allowed a marital deduction of $1.5 million for the value of that property. Husband's taxable estate is $500,000. The executor computes his preliminary DSUE amount to be $3,840,000 (the lesser of the $5,340,000 basic exclusion amount in 2014, or the excess of Husband's $5,340,000 applicable exclusion amount over the sum of the $500,000 taxable estate and the $1 million adjusted taxable gifts). Wife dies in 2014 and the value of the assets of the QDOT has grown to $1.8 million. Husband's DSUE amount is redetermined to be $1,700,000 (the lesser of the $5,340,000 basic exclusion amount in 2014, or the excess of his $5,340,000 applicable exclusion amount over $3,300,000 (the sum of the $500,000 taxable estate augmented by the $1,800,000 of QDOT assets and the $1 million adjusted taxable gifts)).

¶1506 HOW PORTABILITY IMPACTS CREDIT SHELTER TRUSTS

Prior to the adoption of portability, the estate tax exemption of the first spouse to die was considered to be wasted unless the spouse (1) owned assets in his or her name alone equal to the exemption amount in the year of death and (2) left such assets to a beneficiary other than the surviving spouse or charity—such as the couple's children, or a "credit shelter" (bypass) trust for the life benefit of the surviving spouse. As a result of portability, credit shelter trusts no longer need to be created for this reason alone. Estate planning no longer has to focus so much attention on retitling assets solely to avoid wasting the deceased spouse's exclusion amount.

With portability, any applicable exclusion amount that remains unused as of the death of the last deceased spouse, which is called the deceased spousal unused exclusion amount, generally is available for use by the surviving spouse as an addition to the surviving spouse's own applicable exclusion amount.

¶1507 PROS AND CONS OF PORTABILITY

(a) Why Credit Shelter Trusts Still Make Sense After Portability. It still makes sense to create credit shelter trusts when the first spouse dies rather than rely solely on the portability provision because:

- Assets transferred to a credit shelter trust will escape the reach of the surviving spouse's creditors thus offering asset protection for the next generation;

- No estate tax return must be filed to use a credit shelter trust. In contrast, a decedent's executor must file a timely and complete estate tax return in order to elect portability even if the decedent's estate is below the federal filing threshold and a return is not even required;

- If the deceased spouse's estate includes hard-to-value assets or assets for which a valuation discount was taken, it may be preferable to use bypass trust planning rather than to elect portability because of IRC Sec. 2010(c) (5) (B) which provides that after a portability election has been made, even though the statute of limitations for assessing estate or gift tax of the predeceased spouse has expired, the IRS can examine a return of the deceased spouse to determine the appropriateness of the DSUE passing to the surviving spouse;

- The unused exclusion from a particular predeceased spouse will be lost if the surviving spouse remarries and survives his or her next spouse;

- Appreciation and accumulated income earned on amounts in the credit shelter trusts escape federal estate tax no matter how much they grow in value. Suppose for example, Husband died today and his executor puts $5 million into a credit shelter trust with the balance going outright to Wife. The trust assets grow to $10 million by the time the Wife dies in 2024. The good news is that none of the trust assets will be included in the Wife's gross estate and she still has her own exclusion amount to use;

- Amounts in the credit shelter trust cannot be touched by second spouses or children from a second marriage thus protecting those assets for children and grandchildren from a first marriage;

- There is no portability of the unused GST exemption to the surviving spouse, whereas credit shelter trusts can still be used to take advantage of the GST tax exemption of the first spouse to die;

- Creation of the credit shelter trust will avoid having to file an estate tax return for the predeceased spouse's estate if the estate is not so large as to otherwise require a return.

The trust entity offers many benefits including asset protection and professional management, and restricts transfers of assets by the surviving spouse. Portability cannot offer these advantages. However, if everything is left outright to the surviving spouse and portability is relied on, the advantages are simplicity and a step-up in basis when the surviving spouse dies.

     (b) Benefits of Portability. Portability offers the following advantages:

- Portability simplifies the estate planning process. With portability as an option for the executor of the deceased spouse, married couples can simply leave all property to the surviving spouse and the deceased spouse's exclusion amount will not be wasted. There is no need to divide assets between the spouses and retitle them in order to create the split estate plan that is required creation of a credit shelter trust;

- Portability is a good option if the decedent's estate includes retirement benefits because assets can escape estate tax liability in a retirement account without having to qualify the bypass as a designated beneficiary of the retirement benefits. With portability as an option, the decedent can name the surviving spouse as the designated beneficiary of the retirement account; and

- With a portability election in place, there will be two step ups in basis—once when assets pass to the surviving spouse and again when the surviving spouse dies and the assets pass to the beneficiaries. In contrast, when a credit shelter trust is involved, there will only be one step-up in basis when assets first pass to the surviving spouse but not again when the surviving spouse dies.

INHERITANCE TAXES IMPOSED ON TRANSFERS FROM EXPATRIATES

16

TABLE OF CONTENTS

¶1600 PURPOSE OF EXPATRIATION LAW

The expatriation laws were enacted to remove any incentive for U.S. citizens to relinquish their U.S. citizenship and to move to a foreign country in order to avoid exposure to the U.S. estate and gift tax laws. The expatriation laws therefore plug the loophole that had allowed wealthy Americans to avoid tax by "expatriating" or renouncing their U.S. citizenship to claim offshore tax havens as their new home.

¶1601 GIFT TAX IMPOSED ON EXPATRIATES

(a) **Importance of Date of Expatriation.** The expatriation rules which impose a U.S. gift tax on gifts made by a former U.S. citizen who had voluntarily or involuntarily relinquished his or her U.S. citizenship or long-term residency to become a foreign donor depend on the date that the donor expatriated or relinquished his or her United States citizenship. Expatriates who relinquish U.S. citizenship or long-term residency before June 17, 2008 are subject to one set of rules as discussed in ¶1602. Expatriates who relinquish U.S. citizenship or long-term residency after June 16, 2008 are subject to IRC Sec. 2801 as discussed in ¶1604.

¶1602 EXPATRIATION AFTER JUNE 3, 2004 AND BEFORE JUNE 17, 2008—GIFT TAX REGIME

(a) General Rule. Donors who (1) voluntarily or involuntarily relinquished their U.S. citizenship or long-term residence (expatriated) after June 3, 2004 and before June 17, 2008 are subject to U.S. gift tax on gifts made during the 10-year period beginning with the date of expatriation of real or tangible personal property situated in the United States, stock of a U.S. corporation, and debt instruments issued by U.S. obligors (including deposits in U.S. banks) if they satisfy the requirements set forth in IRC Sec. 877(a)(2) [IRC Sec. 2511(b)(2); Reg. Sec. 25.2511-3(b)(4)].

(b) Physical Presence in United States. If the expatriate is present in the United States for a period of 30 days or more in any calendar year that ends during the 10-year period following relinquishment of citizenship or long-term residency, IRC Sec. 877(g) provides that he or she will be treated as a resident of the United States for federal gift tax purposes. Therefore, all gifts, regardless of where the property is situated, made by the former citizen or long-term resident in that calendar year will be subject to the federal gift tax imposed under IRC Sec. 2501.

For purposes of these rules, an individual is treated as present in the United States on any day that he or she is physically present in the United States at any time during that day. However, under IRC Sec. 877(g)(2)(A), a day of physical presence in the United States is disregarded if the individual is performing services in the United States for his or her employer. This exception will not apply if the employer is related to the taxpayer within the meaning of IRC Sec. IRC Secs. 267 and 707(b). Not more than 30 days during any calendar year may be disregarded under this rule.

(c) Situs of Property. If the donor is an expatriate who is a nonresident alien (not a citizen of the United States), the gift tax will apply to the transfer of all property—real or personal, tangible or intangible—situated in the United States at the time of transfer [Reg. Sec. 25.2511-3(a)(2)].

- **Real property and tangible personal property.** Real property and tangible personal property constitute property within the United States only if physically situated in the United States [Reg. Sec. 25.2511-3(b)(1)].

- **Intangible personal property.** Intangible personal property constitutes property situated in the United States if it consists of a property right issued by or enforceable against a resident of the United States or a domestic corporation (public or private), regardless of where the written evidence of the property is physically located at the time of the transfer [Reg. Sec. 25.2511-3(b)(2)].

- **Shares of stock.** Regardless of where the stock certificates are physically located at the time of the transfer, shares of stock issued by a domestic corporation constitute property situated within the United States, and shares of stock issued by a corporation which is not a domestic corporation constitute property situated outside the United States [Reg. Sec. 25.2511-3(b)(3)].

- **Debt obligations.** A debt obligation, including a bank deposit, will constitute property situated in the United States if the primary obligor is a U.S. person, the United States, a state, or any U.S. political subdivision, the District of Columbia, or any agency or instrumentality of these government entities [Reg. Sec. 25.2511-3(b)(4)].

Example 1: Mom is a U.S. citizen who resides in France. In 2007, she renounces her U.S. citizenship. In 2010, Mom gives to Child interests in ABCo, a U.S. corporation with most of its assets and activities located in France. The gift is one of U.S.-situs intangible assets that should be deemed situated within the United States, and Mom must pay U.S. gift taxes on this transfer.

¶1603 GIFTS BY EXPATRIATES OF STOCK/DEBT OF FOREIGN CORPORATION

(a) General Rule. Gift tax is imposed on gifts made by an expatriate of stock or debt obligations of a foreign corporation under IRC Sec. 2501(a)(5) if during the 10-year period following relinquishment of citizenship or long-term residency:

1. The donor was an expatriate who expatriated after June 3, 2004 and before June 17, 2008 and who satisfies the IRC Sec. 877(a)(2) requirements as follows: (a) The individual's average net income tax liability for the prior five years exceeds $157,000 in 2014 (as adjusted for inflation); (b) the individual's net worth exceeds $2 million (including interests in trusts) (not adjusted for inflation); or (c) the individual fails to certify under penalty of perjury that he or she has complied with all federal tax obligations for the previous five years [IRC Secs. 2501(a)(5)(A), 877(b)];

2. Immediately before the transfer, the donor owned stock of the foreign corporation carrying at least 10 percent of the total combined voting power of all classes of stock entitled to vote [IRC Sec. 2501(a)(5)(B)(i)]; and

3. Immediately before the transfer, the donor owned (directly, indirectly, or constructively) stock of the foreign corporation representing more than 50 percent of either the total combined voting power of all classes of stock entitled to vote or the total value of all of the corporation's stock [IRC Sec. 2501(a)(5)(B)(ii)].

(b) Computation of Gift Tax. IRC Sec. 2501(a)(5)(C) provides that gift tax is imposed on that portion of the value of an expatriate's foreign stock on the date of the transfer that is associated with its U.S. situs assets. This portion is determined by a fraction the numerator of which is the fair market value of the U.S. assets owned by the foreign corporation and the denominator of which is the aggregate fair market value of all of the corporation's total worldwide assets [IRC Sec. 2501(a)(5)(C)(i)].

¶1604 RULES FOR EXPATRIATION ON OR AFTER JUNE 17, 2008

(a) General Rule. The Heroes Earnings Assistance and Relief Tax Act of 2008 imposed a new transfer tax on certain wealth transfers to United States citizens or residents by "covered expatriates" who relinquished U.S. citizenship or long-term residency on or after June 16, 2008.

(b) Tax Imposed on Recipients. IRC Sec. 2801(b) provides that the tax imposed by IRC Sec. 2801 must be paid by the person *receiving* the gift or bequest. It is *not* imposed on the donors. The IRC Sec. 2801 tax applies to gifts made at any time after the donor's expatriation—there is no 10-year limitation on the imposition of the tax.

(c) Computation of Tax. A United States citizen or resident receiving a "covered gift or bequest" must pay a tax equal to the value of the covered gift or bequest times the highest rate of federal estate or gift in effect on the date of the receipt of the gift (40 percent in 2014) [IRC Sec. 2801(a)]. The tax applies after the application of the annual gift tax annual exclusion under IRC Sec. 2503(b) ($14,000 in 2014) [IRC Sec. 2801(c)]. The amount of tax imposed is also reduced by any gift or estate tax paid to a foreign country with respect to the covered gift or bequest [IRC Sec. 2801(d)]. There is, however, no unified credit or applicable exclusion amount available to reduce the tax on a lifetime gift made by a covered expatriate who expatriated on or after June 17, 2008.

(d) "Covered Gift or Bequest". A "covered gift or bequest" is defined as any gift or bequest acquired directly or indirectly from a "covered expatriate" [IRC Sec. 2801(e)(1)]. The following property is excluded from the definition of a "covered gift or bequest" under IRC Sec. 2801(e)(2):

1. If the property is shown as a taxable gift on a timely filed gift tax return by the covered expatriate;

2. If the property is included in the gross estate of the covered expatriate for estate tax purposes and is shown on a timely filed estate tax return of the estate of the covered expatriate; and

3. If a charitable or marital deduction would have been allowed for the transfer of that property if the donor or decedent had been a U.S. person.

(e) "Covered Expatriate". A "covered expatriate" is defined an expatriate (a U.S. citizen who has relinquished citizenship or a long-term U.S. resident that ceases to be a lawful permanent resident) who:

1. Has an average annual net income tax liability for the five prior years of more than $157,000 in 2014 (as adjusted for inflation);

2. Has a net worth of $2 million or more (not adjusted for inflation); or

3. Fails to certify under penalties of perjury compliance with all federal tax obligations for the five prior years [IRC Secs. 877A(g)(1), 2801(f)].

A covered expatriate does not include: (1) a former dual citizen who continues to be taxed as a resident of the other country of citizenship and who was a U.S. resident for not more than 10 years during the 15-year period prior to expatriation or (2) an individual who relinquished citizenship or long-term residency prior to reaching the age of eighteen and one-half years and was a resident of the United States for not more than 10 years prior to the date of expatriation [IRC Sec. 2801(f) and IRC Sec. 877A(g)(a)(B)].

(f) Transfers in Trust.

Domestic trusts. A "covered gift or bequest" made to a domestic trust is subject to tax in the same manner as a U.S. citizen or resident described above and, as the recipient, the trust is required to pay the tax imposed [IRC Sec. 2801(e)(4)(A)].

Foreign trusts. A covered gift or bequest made to a foreign trust is also subject to tax, but only at the time a distribution (whether from income or principal) is made to a U.S. citizen or resident from the trust that is attributable to the covered gift or bequest [IRC Sec. 2801(e)(4)(B)(i)].

Deduction for tax paid by recipients. The recipient is allowed an income tax deduction under IRC Sec. 164 for the amount of tax paid or accrued under IRC Sec. 2801 by reason of a distribution from a foreign trust, but only to the extent the tax is imposed on the portion of the distribution included in the recipient's gross income [IRC Sec. 2801(e)(4)(B)(ii). For purposes of IRC Sec. 2801 only, a foreign trust may elect to be treated as a domestic trust [IRC Sec. 2801(e)(4)(B)(iii)]. This election may be revoked with the consent of the IRS. In Announcement 2009-57,[1] the IRS announced that it intends to issue guidance under IRC Sec. 2801 and a new Form 708 where taxpayers can report the receipt of gifts and bequests subject to IRC Sec. 2801. To date, the Form 708 has not been released.

---

[1] **¶1604** Announcement 2009-57, 2009-29 IRB 158.

THE GIFT TAX RETURN—FORM 709

TABLE OF CONTENTS

THE GIFT TAX RETURN

The gift tax applies to all gifts of real or personal property. Whether the gift is of tangible or intangible property, outright or in trust, direct or indirect, the donor may be required to file a gift tax return and pay gift taxes. This chapter examines who must pay the gift tax and various situations in which the gift tax applies.

IRS reports that number of gift tax returns filed in 2012 increased. The Statistics of Income (SOI) division of the IRS has released a statistical table consisting of data collected from Forms 709, "U.S. Gift (and Generation-Skipping Transfer) Tax Return," filed in 2012. The table includes information on total gifts, deductions, credits, and the net tax on current year gifts. Although the number of all returns filed in 2012 (258,393) was more than returns filed in 2011 (219,544), the number of taxable returns filed in 2012 (2,469) was significantly less than those filed in 2011 (10,982).

Nontaxable returns filed in 2012 (255,924) and total gifts for the current period ($122.297 billion) were higher than 2011 nontaxable returns (208,562) and total gifts for the current period ($29.067 billion). The IRS speculates that the higher applicable exclusion amount in combination with the uncertain state of the tax law in 2011 likely resulted in the higher number of returns filed and total gifts made.

¶1700 WHO MUST FILE A GIFT TAX RETURN

(a) **General Rule.** A gift tax return must be filed on Internal Revenue Service (IRS) Form 709, "United States Gift (and Generation-Skipping Transfer) Tax Return," by any person who is a U.S. citizen or resident and who makes a transfer subject to federal gift and certain generation-skipping transfer taxes during the calendar year. [See ¶1716 for the IRS Instructions for Form 709]. A husband and wife may not file a joint gift tax return. Each individual is responsible for his or her own Form 709.

Only individuals who are citizens or residents of the United States must file gift tax returns. The person who gives the gift (i.e., the donor) is the one who is responsible for paying the gift tax [IRC Sec. 2502(d); Reg. Sec. 25.2502-2]. If the donor dies before the gift tax is paid, the amount of the tax is a debt due the United States from the decedent's estate and the estate's executor or administrator is responsible for paying the tax out of the estate. If there is no executor or administrator, the heirs and distributees are liable for and are required to pay the tax to the extent of the value of their inheritances or distributive shares of the donor's estate [Reg. Sec. 25.2502-2].

Trusts, estates, corporations, and partnerships do not need to pay gift tax or file gift tax returns, but if a trust, estate, corporation, or partnership makes a gift, the individual beneficiaries, the partners, or the stockholders may be considered to have made that gift and they may be required to file a return and pay gift and GST taxes.

> **NOTE:** There is an exception for gifts to charity in IRC Sec. 6019(l). If the only gifts made during the year are deductible as gifts to charities, a return need not be filed as long as the donor's entire interest in the property was transferred to qualifying charities. If only a partial interest was transferred, or if part of the donor's interest was transferred to someone other than a charity, a gift tax return must still be filed and all of the gifts to charities must be reported. If the donor is required to file a return to report noncharitable gifts and the donor also made gifts to charities, all of the gifts to charities must be included on the return [see ¶1708 for further discussion of the treatment on Form 709 of gifts to charities].

(b) Exceptions. Form 709 need not be filed under the following circumstances:

1. *Gifts below $14,000 as discussed further at ¶901.* You need not file a gift tax return if the value of the gift is below the $14,000 annual exclusion amount in 2014 and the gift is a gift of a present interest. A gift made in trust is a future interest and therefore does not qualify for the annual exclusion unless the trust beneficiaries are given a limited right to withdraw the gifted property from the trust (a *Crummey* withdrawal right) [see ¶906].

2. *Tuition or medical expenses.* No gift tax return is required if the taxpayer paid someone else's medical or tuition expenses and these payments were made directly to the health care provider (e.g., doctor or hospital) or to a school or college [see ¶908]. Note that contributions to qualified state tuition programs do not qualify for the tuition expense exclusion [see ¶1708].

3. *Gifts to spouse.* No gift tax return must be filed to report gifts to a spouse who is a U.S. citizen regardless of the amount of these gifts and regardless of whether the gifts are present or future interests [¶1107].

4. *Political organizations.* No gift tax return is required if the gift was made to a political organization for the use of the organization, as defined in IRC Sec. 527(e)(1).

5. *Deductible gifts to charities.* No gift tax return must be filed if the only gifts made in the tax year were deductible gifts to charities and the taxpayer's entire interest in

the property was transferred to a qualifying charity. If only a partial interest was transferred to the charity, a gift tax return must be filed.

(c) Gift Splitting. If a married couple agrees to gift splitting, each spouse must file an individual gift tax return even though only one spouse actually made the gift. This rule applies when the value of the gift to any third-party donee during any one year exceeds $14,000 in 2014 or when part of the gift is a gift of a future interest [see ¶902]. Keep in mind that there is no such thing as a joint gift tax return for married couples. Each spouse must file an individual Form 709.

If neither of the above factors applies, the nondonor spouse does not have to file a separate gift tax return, but the nondonor spouse still must sign the gift tax return of the donor spouse to indicate consent to gift splitting. However, both spouses may wish to file a gift tax return if a generation-skipping transfer (GST) tax exemption is being allocated, so that both spouses can allocate an equal amount of exemption [see ¶1710].

▶**HELPFUL HINT:** Both spouses should file their individual tax returns in the same envelope to avoid IRS correspondence.

(d) Nonresidents Aliens (Not U.S. Citizens). Nonresident aliens (not citizens of the United States) are subject to gift and GST taxes for gifts of tangible property situated in the United States [IRC Sec. 2511]. A person is considered a nonresident (not a U.S. citizen) if he or she, at the time the gift is made, was domiciled in a United States possession and acquired citizenship solely by reason of birth or residence in the United States or the possession. The annual exclusion for gifts of present interests is available to a foreign donor but the foreign donor may not take advantage of the applicable exclusion amount to shelter lifetime transfers and may not take advantage of gift-splitting [IRC Sec. 2503(a)(1)]. Gifts of intangible property by a foreign donor are not subject to U.S. gift taxes, no matter where the physical situs of the documents establishing ownership of such property.

If a nonresident not a citizen of the United States made a gift subject to gift tax, he or she must file a Form 709 where:

- He or she gave any gifts of future interests;
- His or her gifts of present interests to any donee other than his or her spouse total more than $14,000 in 2014; or
- His or her outright gifts to a spouse who is not a U.S. citizen total more than $145,000 in 2014.

For a discussion of gift tax imposed on expatriates under IRC Sec. 2801, see ¶¶1601-1603.

(e) Subsequent Death of Donor. The executor or administrator of the estate must file the gift tax return for a donor who died after making a gift to someone but before filing the gift tax return. The executor or administrator also signs the return.

(f) Purpose of the Gift Tax Return. The gift tax return is used to report transfers that are subject either to the gift tax or to the GST tax (or both). Moreover, the gift tax return is used to compute gift and GST tax due, as well as to allocate GST exemption to property transferred during the transferor's lifetime [see ¶2509]. All gift

¶1700

and GST taxes must be computed and filed on a calendar year basis. The donor should list all reportable gifts made during the calendar year on one Form 709. The donor should not file more than one Form 709 for any one calendar year.

(g) File Protective Gift Tax Return to Limit IRS Attack. In order to limit the ability of the IRS, many years after a gift has been made, to revalue the gift for purposes of determining the applicable estate tax bracket and the available unified credit at death, it is a good idea to file a protective gift tax return where you adequately disclose gifts made that year [¶1910]. Why? Because the statute of limitations for assessing gift tax is normally three years after the gift tax return is filed (or due, if later) [IRC Sec. 6501(a)]. The statute runs for six years after the return is filed (or is due, if later) if the value of the gifts omitted from the gift tax return exceeds 25 percent of the total gifts reported in the year in question. But the three-year statute of limitations provided in IRC Sec. 6501 only applies to gifts made after August 5, 1997, if the gifts have been "adequately disclosed" on a gift tax return [IRC Sec. 6501(c)(9)]. The disclosure must be adequate to apprise the IRS of the nature of the transaction. [For further discussion of what constitutes "adequate disclosure" see Reg. Sec. 301.6501(c)-1(f)(2) as discussed further in ¶1910.]

The IRS cannot wait until the estate tax return is filed to revalue the gift and assess additional gift tax if the statute of limitations has run for the year in question. It thus behooves you to file a protective gift tax return disclosing the gifts in order to protect yourself from IRS attack many years after the gifts were made. If the three-year statute of limitations has expired for gift tax purposes on a gift that was adequately disclosed on a gift tax return, the IRS cannot indefinitely revalue the gift for purposes of determining the applicable estate tax bracket and the available unified credit at death [IRC Sec. 2001(f)(1)]. If you and the IRS cannot agree on the value of a gift, the U.S. Tax Court now has jurisdiction to issue a declaratory judgment on the value of the gift [IRC Sec. 7477].

¶1701 WHEN TO FILE A GIFT TAX RETURN

The Form 709, which is an annual return, must be filed on or after January 1 but not later than April 15 following the end of the calendar year in which the gift was made [IRC Sec. 6075(b)(1)]. The 2013 Form 709 was due on April 15, 2014.

> **Example 1:** On July 8, 2013, Joe gives $50,000 to his friend Jill. Joe must file his gift tax return by April 15, 2014.

There are exceptions to this requirement. For example, if the donor is granted an extension to file his or her income tax return, he or she will automatically receive an extension of time to file the gift tax return for that same year. The gift tax return and the income tax return will be due on the same date.

If the donor died during 2013, the executor is required to file the donor's 2013 Form 709 no later than the earlier of:

- The due date (with extensions) for filing the donor's estate tax return; or
- April 15, 2014, or the extended due date granted for filing the donor's gift tax return.

¶1702 EXTENSION OF TIME TO FILE FORM 709

An extension of time to file means that you may have an additional six months to file the gift tax return. Note that this is not, however, an extension of time to pay any gift taxes due.

Requesting an extension of time to file Form 709. There are two methods of extending the time to file the gift tax return. However, note that neither method extends the time to pay the gift or GST taxes. If an extension of time to pay the gift or GST taxes is necessary, the requests must be made separately [Reg. Sec. 25.6161-1]. The time for filing Form 709 can be extended by extending the donor's individual income tax return using Form 4868 or Form 2350, or by extending the gift tax return using Form 8892.

1. *File Form 4868.* IRC Sec. 6075(b)(2) provides that filing Form 4868, "Application for Automatic Extension of Time to File U.S. Individual Income Tax Return" to extend a donor's individual income tax return will automatically extend the time for filing the donor's Form 709 for six months. If gift or GST tax is due as a result of filing Form 4868, the donor must use Form 8892-V (Form 8892, Part III) as a payment voucher for paying the gift or GST tax. Form 4868 automatically extends the Form 709 (and the individual income tax return) for six months.

2. If a taxpayer has a tax home in a foreign country and expects to qualify for the foreign earned income exclusion (and/or the foreign housing exclusion or deduction), the taxpayer may request an extension of time to file Form 1040 by completing Form 2350, "Application of Time to File U.S. Income Tax Return." An extension of time granted to file an income tax return using Form 2350 will also extend the time to file Form 709. If gift or GST tax is due, the taxpayer must use Form 8892-V (Form 8892, Part III) as a payment voucher for the gift tax due.

3. *File Form 8892.* If the taxpayer does not request an extension for his or her income tax return, the taxpayer should use Form 8892, "Application for Automatic Extension of Time to File Form 709 and/or Payment of Gift/Generation-Skipping Transfer Tax," to request an automatic 6-month extension of time to file the gift tax return. In addition to containing an extension request, Form 8892 also serves as a payment voucher for a balance due on federal gift taxes for which the taxpayer has requested a filing extension.

   ▶ **CAUTION:** Even if the taxpayer was granted an extension to file the gift tax return, the taxpayer must still pay the tax due on the original due date.

¶1703 PENALTIES

For further discussion of penalties, see Chapter 8.

¶1704 WHAT'S NEW ON FORM 709

- **Increased gift tax audits.** The IRS is placing additional emphasis on gift tax audits.

- **Inflation adjustments.**
  - — The annual gift tax exclusion for 2013 and 2014 is $14,000.
  - — For gifts made to spouses who are not U.S. citizens, the annual exclusion increased to $145,000 in 2014 from $143,000 in 2013.
  - — The top rate for gifts and generation-skipping transfers in 2014 is 40 percent.
  - — The basic credit amount for 2014 is $2,081,800 (increased from $2,045,800 in 2013).
  - — The applicable exclusion amount consists of the basic exclusion amount ($5,340,000 in 2014, increased from $5,250,000 in 2013) and, in the case of a surviving spouse, any unused exclusion amount of the last deceased spouse (who died after December 31, 2010). The executor of the predeceased spouse's estate must have elected on a timely and complete Form 706 to allow the donor to use the predeceased spouse's unused exclusion amount.

¶1705 FACTS APPLICABLE TO SAMPLE GIFT TAX RETURN

Below is a line-by-line explanation of how to complete the gift tax return, Form 709, for gifts made in 2013. For a completed Form 709, see ¶¶1715-1717. The Instructions for Form 709 are reproduced at ¶1719.

The facts are for hypothetical gift tax returns filed by Maureen B. Gift and her husband, Michael A. Gift. Note that gift tax returns may not be filed jointly and each spouse must file his or her own gift tax return if they made reportable or taxable gifts. Maureen and Michael Gift were both married before and have children from prior marriages. On January 12, 2013, Michael gave $60,000 of ABCo stock to his grandson, Joel Gift. On February 23, 2013, Maureen gave her granddaughter, Amy Russ, a new car valued at $36,000. Maureen and Michael have agreed to split these two gifts to the grandchildren. Therefore, each spouse will be able to take advantage of his or her own $14,000 per donee exclusion which is available in 2013 regardless of who actually made the gift. Because Maureen and Michael have agreed to gift splitting, each must file a gift tax return because each was considered the donor of one-half of the gifts for gift tax purposes. Note that the returns for each spouse are different and each spouse must file his or her own individual gift tax return. They both want to allocate a portion of their GST exemption to the transfer and this can only be accomplished by filing a gift tax return. A gift tax return must be filed to allocate GST exemption even if the Form 709 will report that no gift tax is due.

On March 21, 2013, Michael established a trust that will pay all of its income to his son from a prior marriage, David Gift, for life. The trustee can invade principal for David's benefit, subject to an ascertainable standard. At David's death, the trust will terminate and the remainder will pass to Michael's grandson, Adam. The trust will be funded with $1 million of closely-held stock expected to appreciate in value. This trust established by Michael is a GST trust because it is an indirect skip under IRC Sec. 2632(c)(3)(A) because after the death of Michael's son, David, the remainder will be distributed to Michael's grandson, Adam, who is a skip person. An indirect skip is defined as a lifetime transfer (other than a direct skip) to a GST trust which is any trust that could have a generation-skipping transfer occur with respect to the transfer other than a trust that falls into one or more of six categories of trusts listed in IRC Sec. 2632(c)(3)(B) [see discussion at ¶2504]. Michael wants to preserve his GST exemption for a direct stock transfer to a trust for his grandchildren that he intends to establish next year. As a result, Michael wants to elect out of the deemed allocation of GST exemption. Michael therefore lists the gift to the trust in Part 3 of Schedule A and he checks the box in Column C of Part 3 of Schedule A. The box is marked 2632(c) election. IRC Sec. 2632(c) provides for the automatic allocation of the donor's unused GST exemption to indirect skips. There are three different elections that the transferor can make regarding the allocation of GST exemption as follows:

Election 1. The transferor may elect not to have the automatic allocation rules apply to the current transfer made to a particular trust. This election is timely if it is made on a timely filed gift tax return for the year the transfer was made or was deemed to have been made.

Election 2. The transferor may elect not to have the automatic rules apply to both the current transfer and any and all future transfers made to a particular trust. This election is timely if made on a timely filed gift tax return for the year for which the election is to become effective.

Election 3. The transferor may elect to treat any trust as a GST trust for purposes of the automatic allocation rules. This election is timely if made on a timely filed gift tax return for the year for which the election is to become effective.

To make these elections, check Column C next to the transfer to which the election applies and attach an explanation that describes the election being made and clearly identifies the trusts and/or transfers to which the election applies.

Michael is making Election 1 because he elects not to have automatic allocation apply to the current transfer. Instead he wants to preserve his GST exemption for a direct stock transfer to a trust for his grandchildren that he intends to establish next year. He attaches an Election Statement to his Form 709 explaining that he is electing out of automatic allocation of GST exemption to the transfer under IRC Sec. 2632(c). A copy of his Election Statement is reproduced at ¶1718.

On June 15, 2013, Maureen Gift established a trust that will pay all of its income to her daughter from a prior marriage, Emily Russ, for life. Twenty percent of the trust corpus will be paid to Emily when she reaches age 35, 45, and 55, respectively. At Emily's death, any remaining corpus will be distributed to Maureen's grandson, Andrew. The trust was funded with $700,000 of securities expected to appreciate in value. Maureen lists the transfer to the Maureen B. Gift Family Trust f/b/o Emily Russ in Part 3 of Schedule A because it is an indirect skip. The value of the trust at the date of the gift is $700,000 and she lists this amount in Columns F and H. Maureen wants to allocate GST exemption to the trust because the trust may be subject to GST when her daughter dies and the trust corpus is distributed to her granddaughter who is a skip person. Maureen checks the box in Column C of Part 3 of Schedule A on page 2 of Form 709. The box is marked 2632(c) election. IRC Sec. 2632(c) provides for the automatic allocation of the donor's unused GST exemption to indirect skips. As described above, there are three different elections that the transferor can make regarding the allocation of GST exemption. Maureen is making election 3 because she elects to treat the trust as a GST trust so GST exemption will automatically be applied to the transfer. By making Election 3, the transferor may elect to treat any trust as a

¶1705

GST trust for purposes of the automatic allocation rules. This election is timely if made on a timely filed gift tax return for the year for which the election is to become effective. Maureen attaches a Notice of Allocation to her Form 709 that describes the election being made, the amount of exemption she wants to allocate to the trust and clearly identifies the trusts and/or transfers to which the election applies [see ¶ 1717 for a copy of her Notice of Allocation].

What to include on the Notice of Allocation. According to Reg. Sec. 26.2632-1(b)(4)(i) and the Instructions to Form 709, the notice of allocation should identify the following: (1) the trust to which the allocation is made, including the trust's EIN, if known; (2) if applicable, the item number(s) from column A, Schedule A, Part 3 of the transfers; (3) if the allocation is late, the year the transfer was reported on Form 709; (4) the amount of GST tax exemption allocated to it; (5) the value of the gift; and (6) the inclusion ratio of the trust after the allocation.

The GST exemption allocated to the indirect skip is also listed on Schedule D, Part 2, line 5 on page 5 of Form 709.

¶1706 HOW TO COMPLETE FORM 709 IN THE PROPER ORDER

The following steps should be taken when contemplating the completion of Form 709:

1. Determine whether Form 709 must be filed for each spouse.
2. Figure out what gifts must be reported on the Form 709.
3. Decide whether the gifts will be split between spouses.
4. Complete the general information required on Form 709.
5. List each gift on Part 1, 2, or 3, of Schedule A as appropriate.
6. Complete Schedules B, C and D, if applicable.
7. If the gift was listed on Part 2 or 3 of Schedule A, complete the necessary portions of Schedule D.
8. Complete Schedule A, Part 4.
9. Complete Part 2—Tax Computation.
10. Sign and date the return.

> ▶ **PRACTICE POINTER:** If husband and wife are splitting gifts, be sure that line 18, in Part 1, page 1 of the husband's Form 709 is signed by the wife and vice versa.

¶1707 PART 1 ON PAGE 1—GENERAL INFORMATION

(a) General Information. In Part 1 on Page 1 of Form 709 the identifying information about the individual donor must be provided. Because gift tax returns are not jointly filed for married couples, each spouse who must file a gift tax return must file his or her own Form 709. Listed below is a line-by-line explanation of Part 1 of Form 709:

Line 1—Enter the donor's first name and middle initial.

Line 2—Enter the donor's last name. Remember to enter the name and address of only one donor on each return. Enter the donor's name even if he or she died after the gift was made but before the return was filed.

Line 3—Enter the donor's Social Security number.

Line 4—Enter the donor's street address, including the apartment number.

Line 5—Enter the legal residence (county and state) of the donor's domicile. A donor's domicile for tax purposes is the place where the donor resides and has the intention of remaining indefinitely. This may or may not be the place where the donor is actually living when the gift is made.

Line 6—Enter the city, state, and zip code where the donor lives.

Line 7—Enter the donor's citizenship.

> ■ In the hypothetical situation [see ¶1705], because Maureen B. and Michael Gift are U.S. citizens, they will enter "USA" on line 7.

Line 8—Death of donor. If you are filling out the return for a donor who died during the year for which the gift tax return is being filed, check the box on line 8 and enter the date of the donor's death. If the donor dies after the calendar year for which the return is being filed, do not check the box on line 8.

Line 9—Extension of time to file return. If you receive an extension of time to file the gift tax return, check the box on line 9. Be sure to attach Form 8892, "Application for Automatic Extension of Time to File Form 709 and/or Payment of Gift/Generation-Skipping Transfer Tax." See ¶1702 for further discussion of filing extensions.

> ▶ **CAUTION:** If you start filling out your gift tax return with the intention of filing it on time and later realize you need more time, make sure you go back and check this box.

Line 10—Number of donees. Enter the total of number of separate donees (counting each donee only once) listed on Schedule A.

> ■ Maureen B. and Michael A. Gift [see ¶1705] each enter 3 for the three separate donees listed on Schedule A (including the gift in trust).

Line 11a—Have you filed a gift tax return for any other year? If you previously filed a gift tax return on Form 709 for any other period, you should check the "Yes" box on line 11a and complete line 11b. Otherwise, you should check "No" and skip to line 12.

> ■ Maureen B. and Michael A. Gift [see ¶1705] each check the "Yes" box on line 11a to show that they had previously filed a gift tax return on Form 709.

Line 11b—Has your address changed since you filed previous Forms 709? Check "Yes" or "No" to show whether or not your address has changed since the last time you filed Form 709.

(b) Gift Splitting. Gifts by husband or wife to third parties (gift splitting)—Part 1, lines 12 though 18. For a further discussion of gift splitting, see ¶902.

¶1707

Line 12—Gifts by husband or wife to third parties—Consent to split gifts. If you make a gift that you would like to treat as being made one-half by you and the other half by your spouse, be sure to complete lines 13 through 18 and go to Schedule A. If the answer is no, skip the rest of Part 1.

▶**REMEMBER:** If you elect to split gifts with your spouse, the election will apply to all gifts made by either you or your spouse to children and other third parties (but not to each other) during the calendar year while you are married.

▶ **CAUTION:** If you split gifts with your spouse, and if you give more than $28,000 in 2013 or in 2014 to any third-party donee, or if any part of the gift is a future interest, your spouse will be required to file his or her own gift tax return, even if he or she did not make any of the gifts. If spouses elect to split gifts [see ¶902], each spouse must consent to gift splitting on the gift tax return.

■ Maureen B. Gift and her husband, Michael A. Gift [see ¶1705], have each consented to split the gifts reported on Schedule A and will therefore complete lines 13 through 18 of Part 1. In addition, each will file his or her own Form 709.

Line 13—Name of consenting spouse. Fill in the name of your spouse.

▶ **HELPFUL HINT:** If you are married to one spouse at the beginning of the calendar year and to a different spouse at a later point in the calendar year, you may only split gifts with the second spouse and then only gifts that you make while married to the second spouse. Gifts you made while married to the first spouse may not be split. However, you do not need to be married to the second spouse at the end of the calendar year in order to split gifts.

Line 14—Social Security number of consenting spouse. If your spouse agreed to split the gifts with you, enter his or her Social Security number.

Line 15—Marital status. Check "Yes" or "No" depending on whether or not you were married to the consenting spouse during the entire calendar year to which the consent applies.

■ Maureen B. and Michael Gift [see ¶1705] will each check the "Yes" box on line 15 to show that they were married during the whole year.

Line 16—Married, divorced, or widowed during the calendar year. You should only fill out this line if you checked "No" on line 15 and "Yes" on line 12. Check the "married" box on line 16 if you got married to the consenting spouse during the calendar year. Check the "divorced" box if you got divorced from the consenting spouse during the calendar year. Check the "widowed" box if the consenting spouse died during the year. You must also give the date of the marriage, divorce, or death.

▶ **NEW TAX LAW ALERT: Same-Sex Spouses.** In response to the U.S. Supreme Court ruling in *Windsor*,[1] the IRS recently ruled that same-sex couples who are

---

[1] ¶**1707** 570 U.S. —, 133 S. Ct. 2884, 186 L. Ed. 2d 932 (June 26, 2013).

¶1707

legally married according to their state law must be treated as married for federal tax law purposes regardless of where they live.[2]

Line 17—Will your spouse also file a gift tax return this year? If you checked "Yes" on line 12, then check "Yes" or "No" here to show whether your consenting spouse must also file a separate gift tax return for the same calendar year covered by your return.

▶**REMEMBER:** Your spouse must file a separate gift tax return if you give more than $28,000 in 2013 or 2014 to any third-party donee during the calendar year or part of the gift is a gift of a future interest.

▶**HELPFUL HINT:** If both of you are required to file separate gift tax returns, the two returns should be filed together in the same envelope.

Line 18—Consent of spouse. If your spouse consents to split gifts with you, the spouse must sign the consent for the gift-splitting election to be valid. The consent may generally be signed at any time after the end of the calendar year. However, there are two exceptions:

1. The consent may not be signed after April 15, following the end of the year in which the gift was made. But, if neither spouse has filed a gift tax return for the year on or before that date, the consent may be made on the first gift tax return for the year filed by either spouse.

2. The consent may not be signed after a notice of deficiency for the gift tax for the year has been sent to either spouse.

The executor for a deceased spouse or the guardian for a legally incompetent spouse may sign the consent.

▶ **CAUTION:** You are not allowed to split gifts that you make after the death of your spouse.

DO NOT COMPLETE PART 2 OF THE RETURN (lower portion of Part1) ON PAGE 1 OF FORM 709 UNTIL YOU HAVE COMPLETED SCHEDULES A, B, AND C OF FORM 709.

Line 19. Application of DSUE amount. If the donor is a citizen or resident of the United States and his or her spouse died after December 31, 2010, the donor may be eligible to use the deceased spouse's unused exclusion (DSUE) amount. The executor of his or her spouse's estate must have elected on Form 706 to allow use of the unused exclusion amount. [See instructions for Form 706, Part 6—Portability of the Deceased Spousal Unused Exclusion]. If the executor of the estate made this election, attach the Form 706 filed by the estate and include a calculation of the DSUE amount (either as an attachment or on Part 6—Portability of the Deceased Spousal Unused Exclusion). [For further discussion of portability, see Chapter 15]. Using the checkboxes provided, indicate whether the donor is applying or has applied a DSUE amount from a predeceased spouse to gifts reported on this or a previous Form 709. If so, complete Schedule C.

---

[2] Rev. Rul. 2013-17, 2013-38 IRB 201.

¶1707

¶1708 SCHEDULE A—COMPUTATION OF TAXABLE GIFTS

(a) Purpose of Schedule A—Computation of Taxable Gifts (Including Transfers in Trust).

- Schedule A, Part 1 of Form 709 is used to report taxable transfers if the transfer is subject only to the gift tax.
- Schedule A, Part 2 of Form 709 is used if the transfer is a direct skip that is subject to both the gift tax and the GST tax.
- Schedule A, Part 3 of Form 709 is used if the transfer is an indirect skip that is subject to the gift tax and may later be subject to the GST tax.

The following four categories should be used to report gifts on Schedule A of Form 709: (1) gifts to the donor's spouse, (2) gifts made to third parties that will be split with the donor's spouse, (3) charitable gifts, and (4) other gifts. Each gift should only be entered once—in Part 1, Part 2 or Part 3 of Schedule A, Form 709. If a transfer results in gifts to two or more individuals such as an income interest to one and a remainder interest to the other, each interest should be listed separately. A separate item number should be assigned to each transfer listed on Schedule A, Form 709.

All gifts of future interests to donees other than a spouse should be reported on Schedule A, Form 709 regardless of the value of the gifts. A future interest gift to a spouse should generally only be reported if the future interest is also a terminable interest that does not qualify as a life estate with power of appointment. If gift-splitting is elected, the entire amount of the gift should be included on Schedule A, Column F, even if the gift's value will be less than the annual exclusion ($14,000 for 2013 and 2014) after it is split. Include half of the split gift amount in Columns G and H.

Do not enter on Form 709, any transfer, gift or part of a gift that qualifies for the political organization, educational, or medical exclusions.

A. Valuation Discounts. At the top of Schedule A there is a box for the taxpayer to check to indicate whether the value of any item listed on Schedule A reflects a valuation discount. [For further discussion of valuation discounts, see ¶1914]. Valuation discounts that may be taken include the following:

1. Any discount for lack of marketability;
2. A minority interest;
3. A fractional interest in real estate;
4. Blockage; or
5. Market absorption.

If you claim any discount, you must attach an explanation giving the factual basis for the claimed discount and the amount of the discount you are taking.

■ Maureen B. and Michael Gift [see ¶1705] will each check "No" because they did not use valuation discounts when valuing the gifts at issue.

B. Qualified State Tuition Programs or College Savings Plans (Section 529 Plans). On Schedule A, item B should be checked if the donor wants to elect to treat transfers to a qualified tuition program as made ratably over a five-year period. If he

¶1708

made contributions in excess of $14,000 in 2014 (no change from 2013) to a college savings plan (529 plan) on behalf of any individual beneficiary, he may elect to treat up to $70,000 in 2014 of his total contributions as having been made ratably over a five-year period beginning with the first contribution year [IRC Sec. 529(c)(2)(B)]. If the donor made this election, he reports only 1/5 (20 percent) of his total contributions (up to $70,000 in 2014) on Form 709. He must then report an additional 20 percent of the total in each of the succeeding four years. To make the election he simply checks the box on line B at the top of Schedule A of Form 709. The donor must make the election for the calendar year in which the contribution is made. In addition, he should attach to his return the following information:

1. The total amount contributed per individual beneficiary;
2. The amount for which the election is being made;
3. The name of the individual for whom the contribution was made.

Estate and gift tax consequences. A contribution of $28,000 if made by a married couple in 2014, to a QSTP will be treated as a completed gift of a present interest from the contributor to the beneficiary at the time of the contribution. Annual contributions will therefore be eligible for the annual gift tax exclusion and are also excluded for purposes of the generation-skipping transfer tax [IRC Sec. 529(c)(2)(A)(i)].

If contributions exceed the annual exclusion limit for a year, the contributor may elect to have the contribution treated as if made ratably over five years beginning in the year the contribution is made.

> **Example 1:** In 2014, Dad makes a $30,000 contribution to a QSTP for his son and elects to have it treated as five annual contributions of $6,000. Dad could make up to $8,000 in other transfers to the beneficiary each year without gift tax exposure.

According to this five-year averaging rule, a donor may contribute up to $70,000 with no gift tax consequences to a QSTP for an unlimited number of donees. The donor must elect on Form 709 to treat up to $70,000 of the contribution for one donee as if it had been made ratably over a five-year period. The election allows the donor to apply the annual exclusion to a portion of the contribution in each of the five years beginning in 2014. A gift tax return must be filed with respect to any contribution in excess of the annual gift-tax exclusion limit, and the election for five-year averaging must be made on the contributor's gift tax return. If, in any of the four years following the election, the donor does not need to file Form 709 other than to report that year's portion of the election, the donor need not file or otherwise report that year's portion. In addition, IRC Sec. 529(c)(4)(A) provides that no amount shall be includible in the gross estate of any taxpayer because of his or her interest in a qualified tuition program. If, however, in 2014, a donor has made an over-$14,000 contribution and then dies during the five-year averaging period, the portion of the contribution that has not been allocated to the years prior to death is includible in the donor's taxable estate.

> **Example 2:** Beth Bell makes a $40,000 contribution to a QSTP in 2014 and elects to treat the transfer as being made over a five-year period. Beth dies the following year. $14,000 would be allocated to the year of contribution, another $14,000 would be allocated to the year of death, and the remaining $12,000 would be includible in Beth's estate.

For each of the five years, the donor must report in Part 1 of Schedule A one-fifth of the amount for which the election was made.

¶1708

(b) Schedule A, Part 1—Gifts Subject Only to Gift Tax (Gifts to Non-Skip Persons). Gifts to list. Before completing Schedule A you should determine which gifts made during the year are subject to the gift tax and therefore should be listed on Schedule A. Then divide these gifts as follows:

- Part 1—gifts subject only to the gift tax because they were made to "non-skip persons" [¶ 2503];
- Part 2—gifts subject to both the gift and GST taxes because the gifts were made to "skip persons" [¶ 2503];
- Part 3—gifts subject only to the gift tax at this time but which could later be subject to GST tax.

After dividing the gifts up into three parts as outlined above, follow the rules outlined below:

- Enter a gift in only one place—either Part 1, Part 2, or Part 3—not in multiple places.
- Do not enter any gift or part of a gift that qualifies for the political organization, educational, or medical exclusion.
- Enter gifts under "Gifts made by spouse" only if you have chosen to split gifts with your spouse and your spouse is required to file Form 709.
- In column F, enter the full value of the gift (including those made by your spouse, if applicable). If you have chosen to split gifts, that one-half portion of the gift is entered in column G.
- Enter all gifts of future interests made during the calendar year regardless of their value.
- If the total gifts of present interests to any donee are more than $14,000 in 2014, enter all such gifts made during the year to or on behalf of that donee, including those gifts that will be excluded under the annual exclusion. If the total is $14,000 or less in 2014, you need not enter on Schedule A any gifts (except gifts of future interests) that you made to that donee. Enter these gifts in the top half of Part 1, 2 or 3, as applicable.
- Enter on Schedule A the entire value of every gift made during the calendar year while you were married, even if the gift's value will be less than $14,000 in 2014 after it is split in Column G of Part 1, 2, or 3 of Schedule A.
- If you elected gift splitting and your spouse made gifts, list those gifts in the space below "Gifts made by spouse" in Part 1, 2 or 3. Report these gifts in the same way you report gifts you made.
- If all the terminable interests you gave to your spouse qualify as life estates with power of appointment you do not need to enter any of them on Schedule A. However, if you gave your spouse any terminable interests that does not qualify as a life estate with power of appointment, you must report on Schedule A all gifts of terminable interests you made to your spouse during the year.
- If your spouse is not a U.S. citizen and you gave him or her a gift of a future interest, you must report on Schedule A all gifts to your spouse for the year. If all gifts to your spouse were present interests, do not report on Schedule A any gifts to your spouse if

the total gifts for the year do not exceed $145,000 and all gifts in excess of $14,000 in 2014 would qualify for a marital deduction if your spouse were a U.S. citizen.

- If you make a gift to a charitable remainder trust and your spouse is the only noncharitable beneficiary (other than yourself), you do not need to include the gift to your spouse on Schedule A because the interest is not considered a terminable interest.

- Do not report a gift of a future interest to your spouse unless the future interest is also a terminable interest that is required to be reported as discussed above. However, if you gave a gift of a future interest to your spouse and you are required to report the gift on Form 709 because you gave the present interest to a donee other than your spouse, then you should enter the entire gift, including the future interest given to your spouse on Schedule A.

In Part 1, list the gifts subject only to the gift tax. This includes: all the gifts made to your spouse (that are required to be listed); gifts made to your children; gifts made to charitable organizations that are not subject to the GST tax and should therefore be listed only in Part 1. Group the gifts in four categories as follows: gifts made to your spouse; gifts made to third parties that are to be split with your spouse; charitable gifts (if you are not splitting gifts with your spouse); and other gifts. If a transfer results in gifts to two or more individuals (such as a life estate to one with remainder to the other), list the gift to each separately.

Column A, Part 1—Item number. Itemize and number each separate gift in Column A. List separately in Schedule A gifts of separate interests to two donees by one transfer.

■ Maureen and Michael A. Gift list nothing in Part 1 because they made no gifts in 2013 that are subject only to gift tax.

Column B, Part 1—Donee's name, relationship to donor, address, and description of the gift (CUSIP no. if stock). You should enter the donee's name, the donee's relationship to you, and the donee's address before the description of each gift. Describe each gift so that it can be easily identified. You may have to attach any documents, including an appraisal, that will adequately explain the gift and how it was valued. The IRS requires that descriptions of gifts on Form 709 provide sufficient detail to easily identify the property.

Direct skips that are subject to both the gift tax and the generation-skipping transfer tax are reported in Part 2.

Below is a guide that will help you describe certain types of property:

1. *Real estate.* For each parcel, provide:

- The legal description;

- The street number, name, and area of the city within which the property is located, and

- A short statement of the character of any improvements made to the property;

You should also include the basis on which you are valuing the property for gift tax purposes.

¶1708

2. *Seller's interest in land contracts.* Provide:

- Name of the buyer;
- Date of the contract;
- Description of the property;
- Sale price;
- Initial payment;
- Amounts of installment payments;
- Unpaid principal balance; and
- Interest rate and date (before the gift) to which interest has been paid.

3. *Stock.* Provide:

- Number of shares transferred;
- CUSIP number; and
- A statement regarding whether it is common or preferred stock.

For preferred stock:

- Give the issue;
- Par value;
- Quotation at which valued; and
- Principal name of issuer.

For listed stock, give the principal exchange on which it is traded. For stock that is not listed on an exchange, give the location of the corporation's principal business office and state and date of incorporation.

4. *Closely held or inactive stock.* You should attach balance sheets, especially one that is dated closest to the date of the gift. You should also attach statements of the net earnings or operating results and dividends paid for each of the five preceding years. If closely held entity, be sure to provide the employer identification number "EIN."

5. *Bonds.* Provide:

- The number of bonds transferred;
- The principal amount of the bonds;
- The name of the obligor;
- Date of maturity;
- Interest rate;
- Interest payment dates;
- Series number if more than one issue;
- Exchanges on which listed;
- Principal business office if not listed on an exchange; and
- CUSIP number which is the nine-digit number assigned by the American Banking Association to traded securities.

¶1708

6. *Notes.* Provide:

- Name of maker;
- Date on which given;
- Maturity date;
- Principal amount;
- Unpaid principal;
- Interest rate and whether it is simple or compound; and
- Date to which interest has been paid.

7. *Life insurance policies.* Provide:

- Name of insurer;
- Policy number;
- Life insurance statement Form 712 (issued by the insurance company); and
- If the surrender value of the policy exceeds its replacement cost, report the true economic value of the policy on Schedule A.

8. *Annuities.* Provide:

- Name of issuing company;
- Address of issuing company;
- If payable out of a trust or other fund, a description that will fully identify the trust or fund;
- Duration of the annuity if it is for a term of years;
- Date on which it began; and
- Person's date of birth if annuity is payable for person's lifetime.

9. *Property interests based on length of a person's life.* Provide the date of birth of that person.

10. *Gifts relating to a court judgment.* Provide:

- Title of the case;
- Name of the court;
- Date of judgment;
- Name and address of judgment debtor;
- Amount of judgment;
- Rate of interest on judgment; and
- The amount and dates of any payments made on the judgment.

11. *Gifts in trust.* Provide:

- Trust's identifying number;
- Attach a certified or verified copy of the trust instrument to your return on which you report your first transfer to the trust. However, to report subsequent transfers to the trust, you may attach a brief description of the terms of the trust or a copy of the trust instrument; and
- Attach any appraisal used to determine the value of real estate or other property owned by the trust.

¶1708

12. *Accrued income on property that happens to be included in your gift.* Provide the accrued income as a separate entry beneath the amount of the gift.

13. *Sales and exchanges of property for less than full and adequate consideration.* Provide fair-market value of:

- The property sold or exchanged; and
- The consideration received.

(Both values are determined as of the date of the sale or exchange.)

> ▶**HELPFUL HINTS:** If you received less than full and adequate consideration because you happened to make a bad bargain in an arm's-length business transaction, you have not made a gift that is subject to tax.

Column D, Part 1—Donor's adjusted basis of gift. For each gift, give your adjusted basis in the property as of the date of the gift. The adjusted basis is the value you would use to determine your income tax gain or loss if you had sold the property on the date you made the gift. The adjusted basis is usually the amount you paid for the item. Specific types of property are:

- *Stocks and bonds.* The amount for Column D will usually be the amount you paid for them. You must reduce the basis of the stock by all nontaxable distributions that you received before you gave away the stock. This includes nontaxable dividends that you receive from utility company stock and mutual funds. Do not forget to adjust the basis to account for stock splits.

- *Depreciable real estate and other depreciable property.* The amount for Column D is usually the amount that you paid for the property less any depreciation allowed or allowable.

- *Property acquired from a decedent.* The amount for Column D is usually the fair-market value of the property as of the date of death of the decedent.

Column E, Part 1—Date of gift. Enter the date on which you made the gift to the donee. This must be the date on which the gift is considered complete.

> ▶**HELPFUL HINTS:** If a gift is complete, it means that you no longer have any control over the property that you gave away.

The exact date of the gift is very important for gifts that fluctuate in value, such as stocks, because the value of the gift is the fair-market value on the date of the gift.

Column F, Part 1—Value at date of gift.

1. Enter the fair-market value of the gift on the date that you make the transfer. The fair market value is the price at which the property would change hands between a willing buyer and a willing seller, when neither is forced to buy or to sell, and when both have reasonable knowledge of all relevant facts. Fair market value may not be determined by a forced sale price, nor by the sale price of the item in a market other than that in which the item is most commonly sold to the public.

2. The value of property that is mortgaged or subject to another type of lien is reduced by the amount of the mortgage or other lien.

3. If you want the donee to pay the gift tax on the gift, the amount of the tax that the donee must pay reduces the value of the gift.

¶1708

4. Any transfer that you make for less than adequate and full consideration in money or money's worth will be considered a gift. The amount of the gift is computed as follows:

Value of the transferred property at date of sale or exchange	×	Amount of consideration received	=	Value of gift for gift tax purposes

5. Before completing Part 1 of Schedule A, be sure to note in the space provided the total of all gifts subject only to gift tax as listed in Part 1.

■ Maureen B. Gift [see ¶ 1705] enters $700,000 as the value at the date the gift was made to the trust.

Column G, Part 1—Split gifts. Enter an amount in this column only if you have elected to split gifts with your spouse. Generally, if you elect to split your gifts, you must split all gifts made by you and your spouse to third-party donees. The only exception is if you gave your spouse a general power of appointment over a gift you made.

Gift made by spouse—Schedule A—Part 1. If you have elected to split gifts with your spouse and your spouse has given a gift that is being split with you, enter it in this area of Part 1, information on the gift made by your spouse. If only you made gifts and you are splitting them with your spouse, do not make an entry in this area. Generally, if you elect to split your gifts, you must split all made by you and your spouse. An exception exists if you gave your spouse a general power of appointment over a gift you made.

(c) Schedule A, Part 2—Gifts That Are Direct Skips and Are Subject to Both Gift and GST. List only those gifts that are subject to both the gift tax and the GST tax in Part 2 of Schedule A. The GST tax that you must report on Form 709 is only the tax imposed on *inter vivos* direct skips (defined below).

1. Organize all the gifts into chronological order. You should list the oldest gift first.

2. Number the gifts, describe them and value them in the same way that you did for the gifts listed in Part 1 of Schedule A.

3. If you made a transfer to a trust that was a direct skip, list the entire gift as one line entry in Part 2. A direct skip occurs when property subject to either the estate or gift tax is transferred to a "skip person." Generally, skip persons are individuals two or more generations younger than the transferor (e.g., grandchildren). A transfer to a trust is a direct skip (occurring at the time of the transfer) if all of the beneficiaries with an interest in the trust are skip persons. Direct skips can occur during life or at death. However, only lifetime direct skip transfers are reported on Form 709.

4. For a lifetime direct skip transfer, a portion of the donor's unused GST exemption will automatically be allocated to the transfer under the deemed allocation rules. If the donor wants to allocate GST exemption to a direct skip transfer (including a split gift made by the donor's spouse), column C of Schedule A should be left blank. The value of the transfer listed on Schedule A, Part 2, column H should be entered on Schedule D, Computation of Generation-Skipping Transfer Tax, Part 1,

¶1708

column B. After reducing this amount by the annual GST exclusion, the net value of the transfer for GST purposes is entered in column D.

■ Because the gifts made by Michael and Maureen Gift are direct skips, they must be included on Schedule A, Part 2. In Michael's case, the ABCo stock would be listed at the top half of Part 2 and $30,000 of the gift would be included in column G (because it will be reported by Maureen) leaving a net transfer of $30,000 in column H. Maureen would also report the stock gift on her return in the section marked "Gifts made by spouse." The automobile that Maureen gave to her granddaughter is also listed in Part 2 of both returns because they agreed to gift-split this gift. The half of the gift ($18,000) that will be included on Maureen's Form 709 is included in column G, leaving a net transfer of $18,000 in column H.

Column C—2632(b) Election out. If you elect under IRC Sec. 2632(b)(3) not to have the automatic GST allocation rules of IRC Sec. 2632(b) apply to a direct skip, enter a check in column C next to the transfer. You must also attach a statement to Form 709 clearly describing the transaction and the extent to which the automatic allocation does not apply. Reporting a direct skip on a timely filed Form 709 and paying the GST tax due on the transfer, will qualify as such a statement.

Inter vivos **direct skip defined.** An "*inter vivos* direct skip" is (1) a transfer that is subject to the gift tax, (2) *of* an interest in property, and (3) made to a "skip person" [see ¶ 2503]. All three of these requirements must be met before the gift is subject to the GST tax. A gift is "subject to gift tax" if you must list it on Schedule A of Form 709. A "skip person" is a natural person who is assigned to a generation which is two or more generations below the generation assignment of the donor or a trust if all interests in the trust are held by skip persons. For example, a taxpayer's grandchildren or great-grandchildren are skip persons. See further discussion at ¶ 2504.

If you make a nontaxable gift to a trust for the benefit of a skip person, the transfer does not qualify for the annual exclusion but may be subject to the GST tax unless:

1. During the life of the beneficiary, no income or corpus may be distributed to anyone other than the beneficiary; and

2. If the beneficiary dies before the termination of the trust, the beneficiary's estate will include those trust assets. See IRC Sec. 2642(c) and ¶ 1710.

Now that you have completed Parts 1 and 2 of Schedule A, count how many different people you made gifts to and enter that number on line 10 of Part 1 of your return (Page 1).

(d) Schedule A, Part 3—Indirect Skips (Gifts to Trusts That Are Currently Subject to Gift Tax and May Later Be Subject to the GST Tax). On Schedule A, Part 3 of Form 709, the following indirect skips to a GST must be listed:

• Gifts made to trusts that are subject only to gift tax at the time of the transfer, later may be subject to GST tax. The GST tax could apply either at the time of a distribution from the trust, at the termination of the trust, or both.

• In general, an indirect skip is a transfer of property that is subject to gift tax (other than a direct skip) and is made to a GST trust [IRC Sec. 2632(c)]. A GST trust is a trust that could have a generation-skipping transfer with respect to the transferor,

¶1708

unless the trust provides for certain distributions of trust corpus to non-skip persons.

- List on Schedule A, Part 3 the transferor's total gifts that are indirect skips. Be sure to list the gifts in chronological order. The donee's name, relationship and a description of the gift are reported in column B. The donor's adjusted basis, the gift date and the gift's fair market value are listed in the appropriate columns. If gift-splitting is elected, the split-gift portion of the transfer reported by the transferor's spouse is listed in column G; only the net amount of the transfer attributable to the transferor is listed in column H. Similarly, split gifts by the transferor's spouse are listed in the lower half of Part 3, Schedule A.

Automatic allocation of GST exemption to indirect skips. Under the deemed allocation rules, the donor's GST exemption will automatically be allocated to indirect skip transfers made during the year. If the donor wants to allocate GST exemption to the indirect skip transfer, column C of Part 3, Schedule A should be left blank. The lesser of (1) the exemption amount equal to the value of the transfer in column H, or (2) the donor's remaining GST exemption should also be entered on Schedule D, Part 2, line 5, enabling the donor to track the amount used. IRC Sec. 2632(c) provides for the automatic allocation of the donor's unused GST exemption to indirect skips to the extent needed to produce the lowest possible inclusion ratio for the property. A donor has the option, however, to elect not to have the automatic allocation rules apply. There are three different elections that the transferor can make regarding the allocation of GST exemption as follows:

Election 1. The transferor may elect not to have the automatic allocation rules apply to the current transfer made to a particular trust. This election is timely if it is made on a timely filed gift tax return for the year the transfer was made or was deemed to have been made.

Election 2. The transferor may elect not to have the automatic rules apply to both the current transfer and any and all future transfers made to a particular trust. This election is timely if made on a timely filed gift tax return for the year for which the election is to become effective.

Election 3. The transferor may elect to treat any trust as a GST trust for purposes of the automatic allocation rules. This election is timely if made on a timely filed gift tax return for the year for which the election is to become effective.

To make an election, check column C next to the transfer to which the election applies. Be sure to attach an Election Statement or Notice of Allocation to Form 709 that describes the election you are making and that clearly identifies the trusts and/ or transfers to which the election applies.

> ■ In Part 3 of Schedule A, Maureen B. Gift [see ¶1705] lists the trust that she established on June 16, 2013 for the benefit of her daughter from a prior marriage, Emily Russ, for life. This transfer is an indirect skip because it is a gift to a trust that is currently subject to gift tax and may later be subject to GST tax. Maureen elects to allocate GST exemption to this transfer and attaches a Notice of Allocation which is reproduced after her return. Twenty percent of trust corpus will be paid to Emily when she reaches age 35, 45, and 55, respectively. At her death, any remaining

¶1708

corpus will be distributed to Maureen's grandson, Andrew. The trust was funded with $700,000 of highly appreciating securities.

■ In Part 3 of Schedule A, Michael A. Gift enters the information about the trust he established on March 21, 2013 for the benefit of his son from a prior marriage, David Gift, for life. The trustee can invade principal for David's benefit, subject to an ascertainable standard. At David's death, the trust remainder will pass to Michael's grandson, Adam. The trust will be funded with $1 million of closely held stock that is expected to appreciate in value. The trust is a GST trust. Since Michael Gift wants to preserve his GST exemption for a direct skip transfer to a trust for his grandchildren that he intends to make next year, he wants to elect out of the deemed allocation of GST exemption. He will therefore check column C of Part 3, Schedule A and attach an Election Statement to elect out of the deemed allocation rules [see ¶ 1718]. Since the transfer is not a direct skip transfer, Schedule D need not be completed for this item.

(e) Schedule A, Part 4—Taxable Gift Reconciliation (Page 3 of Form 709).

Line 1—Total value of gifts of donor. Add the totals from column H of Parts 1, 2 and 3 of Schedule A and enter the total in the space provided.

■ Maureen B. Gift [see ¶ 1705] enters $748,000 as the total value of gifts listed in Parts 1 and 2 of Schedule A. Michael enters $1,048,000.

Line 2—Total annual exclusions for gifts listed on line 1. Enter the total annual exclusions you are claiming for the gifts listed on Schedule A. If you split a gift with your spouse, the annual exclusion you claim against that gift may not be more than your half of the gift.

Annual Exclusion Gifts. If you elect to split gifts with a spouse, each spouse is entitled to claim a $14,000 per donee exclusion from taxable gifts in 2013 or 2014.

> **Example 3:** In 2014, you make a $30,000 gift to your daughter and gift splitting is elected. Both you and your spouse are considered to have made a gift of $15,000 to your daughter. A $14,000 exclusion is allowed on both your return and on your spouse's return in 2014.

All gifts made during the calendar year to a donee are fully excluded under the annual exclusion if they are all gifts of present interests and they total $14,000 in 2013 or 2014. A gift of a future interest cannot be excluded under the annual exclusion [see ¶ 901]. A gift is considered a present interest if the donee has all immediate rights to the use, possession, and enjoyment of the property or income from the property. A gift is considered a future interest if the donee's rights to the use, possession, and enjoyment of the property or income from the property will not begin until some future date. Future interests include reversions, remainders, and other similar interests or estates. A contribution to a qualified tuition plan on behalf of a designated beneficiary is considered a gift of a present interest and is therefore eligible for the annual exclusion.

¶1708

A gift to a minor will be considered a present interest if all the following conditions are met:

- Both the property and its income may be expended by, or for the benefit of, the minor before the minor reaches age 21;

- All remaining property and its income must pass to the minor on the minor's 21st birthday; and

- If the minor dies before the age of 21, the property and its income will be payable either to the minor's estate or to whomever the minor may appoint under a general power of appointment.

> ■ Maureen and Michael Gift each enter $14,000 on line 2 of Part 4. The gifts to the trust for both taxpayers are ineligible for the annual exclusion because they are gifts to trusts and are therefore future rather than present interests.

(f) Schedule A, Part 4—Deductions.

Unlimited marital deduction. On line 4 of Part 3 of Form 709, taxpayers have the opportunity to claim the unlimited marital deduction which is allowed for qualifying transfers to a spouse during their lifetime. IRC Sec. 2523(a) provides that the amount of the marital deduction is the fair market value of the property transferred to the spouse. There is no election that needs to be made in order to claim the unlimited marital deduction; if the requirements are satisfied, the deduction is mandatory.

Enter on line 4 all of the gifts to your spouse that you listed on Schedule A and for which you are claiming a marital deduction. Do not enter any gift that you did not include on Schedule A. On the dotted line on line 4, indicate which numbered items from Schedule A are gifts to your spouse for which you are claiming the marital deduction. Do not enter on line 4 any gifts to your spouse who was not a US citizen at the time of the gift. A marital deduction may not be claimed if the gift to a spouse is a terminable interest, which means that someone other than the donee spouse will have an interest in the property following the termination of the donee spouse's interest. Examples of terminable interests include: a life estate, an estate for a specified number of years, or any other property interest that after a period of time will terminate or fail.

For further discussion of the marital deduction, see ¶ 1107.

Requirements for marital deduction. Gifts between two spouses are eligible for the unlimited gift tax marital deduction under IRC Sec. 2523 if the following conditions are satisfied at the time the gift is made: (1) the spouses are married;[1] (2) the spouse receiving the gift is a U.S. citizen; (3) the interest transferred is not a nondeductible terminable interest; (4) the property interest transferred is not otherwise deducted for federal gift tax purposes; and (5) the gifts are included in the total taxable gifts for the year.

---

[1] **¶1708 Same-sex couples.** Beginning in 2013, same-sex couples who were legally married in a jurisdiction that recognizes same-sex marriages are entitled to claim the federal tax marital deduction even if they live in a jurisdiction that does not recognize same-sex marriages. However, couples in civil unions and domestic partnerships will not be treated as married for federal tax purposes and therefore may not claim the marital deduction. Rev. Rul. 2013-17, 2013-38 IRB 201.

¶1708

Nondeductible terminable interests. The marital deduction may not be claimed if the gift to a spouse is a terminable interest which is any interest that will fail or terminate because of the passage of time or the occurrence (or nonoccurrence) of an event or contingency. For example, annuities, copyrights, patents, terms of years, and life estates are all examples of terminable interests [Reg. Sec. 25.2523(b)-1(a)(3)]. Generally, terminable interests fall into one of the following three categories: (1) interests that cannot qualify for the marital deduction; (2) interests that qualify for the deduction without the need for an election; and (3) interests that do not qualify for the marital deduction unless the donor makes a QTIP election which is an election to treat the interest as a qualified terminable interest property.

Life estate with general power of appointment. Certain property interests, although terminable, will qualify for the marital deduction. A gift of a life estate, in trust or otherwise, to the donor's spouse will qualify for the marital deduction if the following requirements of IRC Sec. 2523(e) are satisfied: (1) all (or a specific part) of the net income from the entire interest (or specific part) is payable, at least annually, to the donee spouse for life; (2) the donee spouse has the power, alone and in all events, to appoint all (or a specific part) of the interest, including appointing the interest to himself or herself or his or her estate; and (3) no other person has the power to appoint the interest to anyone other than the donee spouse.

Claiming marital deduction for QTIP property. A donor may also elect under IRC Sec. 2523(f) to claim a gift tax marital deduction for all or a portion of an interest in qualified terminable interest property (QTIP) gifted to a spouse. The election is made by listing the QTIP on Schedule A of Form 709 and then deducting its value on Form 709, Schedule A, Part 4, line 4. The election must be made on the Form 709 for the calendar year in which the interest is transferred. The election is irrevocable once it has been made.

Qualified terminable interest property defined. QTIP property is defined as property passing from the decedent to a spouse who is entitled to all income from the property (or a portion thereof) for life, payable at least annually. Such an interest is known as a "qualified income interest" [IRC Sec. 2523(f)(2)(B)]. No person, including the donee spouse, has the power to appoint the assets to any person other than the donee spouse during the spouse's life. However, the creation or retention of powers over all or a portion of the corpus is permitted, provided that all such powers are exercisable only after the spouse's death.

> **Example 4:** Wife transferred $100,000 to an *inter vivos* trust for the benefit of Husband. The terms of the trust provide that Husband will receive all of the net income annually from the trust for life. The trustee also has the power to invade corpus for Husband's benefit. When Husband dies, the balance of the trust passes to Wife's daughter from a previous marriage. Although Husband has a terminable interest in the trust, he has a qualifying income interest making the transfer eligible for the marital deduction. Wife may elect to treat the property as QTIP property and claim a marital deduction for the value of the property transferred. This election is made by listing the property on Form 709, Schedule A, Part 1, and deducting the value of the trust on Form 709, Schedule A, Part 4, line 4.

¶1708

Election out of QTIP treatment of annuities for joint and survivor annuities. The transfer to a spouse of an interest in a joint and survivor annuity in which only the spouses have the right to receive payments prior to the death of the surviving spouse qualifies for the marital deduction. However, such a transfer does not qualify for a gift tax marital deduction if either the donor or the executor elects out of QTIP treatment under IRC Sec. 2523(f)(6). This election is irrevocable once it has been made. The donee's subsequent transfer of an interest in the annuity is treated as a transfer of all interest in the annuity other than the donor's interest. If the donee dies before the donor, no amount with respect to the annuity is includible in the estate of the donee.

The donor spouse can elect out of the automatic election by checking the box on Schedule A, Part 4, line 12, and entering the corresponding item number of the annuity in the space provided. If the spouse elects out of the automatic QTIP election, no annuity amount can be claimed as a marital deduction on Form 709, Schedule A, Part 4, line 4.

Line 7—Charitable deduction. You may deduct from the total gifts made during the calendar year all charitable gifts given to the following:

- The United States, a state or political subdivision of a state, or the District of Columbia, for exclusively public purposes;

- Any corporation, trust, community chest, fund, or foundation organized and operated only for religious, charitable, scientific, literary, or educational purposes, or to prevent cruelty to children or animals, or to foster national or international amateur sports competition (if none of its activities involve providing athletic equipment— unless it is a qualified amateur sports organization), as long as no part of the earnings benefit any one person, no substantial propaganda is produced, and no lobbying or campaigning for any candidate for public office is done;

- A fraternal society, order, or association operating under a lodge system, if the transferred property is to be used only for religious, charitable, scientific, literary, or educational purposes, including the encouragement of art and the prevention of cruelty to children or animals; and

- Any war veterans organization organized in the United States (or any of its possessions), or any of its auxiliary departments or local chapters or posts, as long as no part of any of the earnings benefits any one person.

On line 7, show your total charitable, public, or similar gifts (minus annual exclusions allowed). On the dotted line, indicate which numbered items from the top of Schedule A are charitable gifts.

> **Example 5:** Suppose you gave a gift of $50,000 to your church in 2014. On line 7, you would write down only $36,000, the net amount of the gift after the annual exclusion.

Line 8—Total deductions. Add line 6 and line 7 and enter the total on line 8.

Line 9—Total gifts less deductions. Subtract line 8 from line 3 and enter the difference on line 9.

¶1708

Line 10—GST taxes payable with Form 709. If you entered gifts on Part 2 of Schedule A or if you and your spouse elect gift splitting and your spouse made gifts that are subject to the GST tax that you are required to show on Form 709, then complete Schedule D. Enter on line 10 the total of Schedule D, Part 3, Column H. This tax is considered a gift and must be added to your other gifts reported on this return. See IRC Sec. 2515. Otherwise, enter "0" on line 10.

■ Maureen B. and Michael A. Gift [see ¶ 1705] each enter "0" on line 10 because no GST tax is payable with respect to the gifts they made last year.

Line 11—Taxable gifts. Add line 9 and line 10 and enter the sum on line 11. Also enter this figure on line 1 of the Tax Computation section on Page 1 of Form 709.

Qualified terminable interest property (QTIP) marital deduction. The QTIP election is automatic if it applies. There is no box to check.

If a trust or other property meets the requirements for a QTIP, and the trust (or other property) is listed on Schedule A, and the value of the trust (or other property) is entered in whole or in part as a deduction on line 4, Part 4 of Schedule A, then you will be treated as having made a QTIP election for this property.

▶ **CAUTION:** If you make the QTIP election, the terminable interest property involved will be included in your spouse's gross estate upon his or her death. If your spouse disposes (by gift or otherwise) of all or part of the qualifying life income interest, he or she will be considered to have made a transfer of the entire property that is subject to the gift tax.

▶**HELPFUL HINT:** If you want to elect out of QTIP treatment, you should not deduct its value on line 4, Part 4 of Schedule A.

Line 12—Election out of QTIP treatment of annuities. Check the box on line 12 if you want to elect NOT to treat any joint and survivor annuities that are reported on Schedule A as a QTIP. Enter the item numbers (from Schedule A) for the annuities for which you are making this election. IRC Sec. 2523(f)(6) creates an automatic QTIP election for gifts of joint and survivor annuities where the spouses are the only possible recipients of the annuity prior to the death of the last surviving spouse. The donor spouse has the option to elect out of QTIP treatment, however, by checking the box on line 13. If there is more than one joint and survivor annuity, the election need not be made for all of them.

▶ **CAUTION:** The election out of QTIP treatment is irrevocable once you make it.

¶1709 SCHEDULE B—GIFTS FROM PRIOR PERIODS AND SCHEDULE C—COMPUTATION OF DECEASED SPOUSAL UNUSED EXCLUSION (DSUE) AMOUNT

Schedule B—Gifts from Prior Periods

The amount of the donor's prior taxable gifts is computed on Form 709, Schedule B. Prior taxable gifts are important when computing the amount of gift tax owed by a donor because the gift tax is computed on a cumulative basis that takes into account taxable gifts made in both the current and prior years. For gifts made before 1977, taxable gifts are reduced by the $30,000 specific (lifetime) exemption allowable under former IRC Sec. 2521 without regard to whether the exemption was actually claimed.

If you checked the "Yes" box on line 11a of Part 1, page 1, because you filed gift tax returns for previous periods, you must complete Schedule B by listing the years or quarters in chronological order. If you have never filed a gift tax return before, skip ahead to Schedule D. Complete Schedule A before beginning Schedule B.

> ▶ **CAUTION:** If you made taxable gifts in prior years, but failed to file gift tax returns, you must write down the amount of those taxable gifts on Schedule B. You might also be required to file gift tax returns for these gifts.

(a) Schedule B—Column A—Calendar Year or Calendar Quarter.

1. List in chronological order (oldest date first) the years or calendar quarters in which you filed your previous gift tax returns.

2. You must also list the years or calendar quarters in which you made a taxable gift but did not file a gift tax return.

(b) Schedule B—Column B—IRS Office Where Prior Return Was Filed.

1. Identify the IRS office where you filed your earlier returns.

2. If you have changed your name since you filed one of the other gift tax returns, be sure to list the names under which you filed the other returns.

> ▶**HELPFUL HINT:** You should also list any variations of your name. For example, if you filed one return with an initial and another one with your full name, you should show that here.

(c) Schedule B—Column C—Amount of Unified Credit Against Gift Tax for Periods After December 31, 1976.
In this column, identify the amount of the unified credit against gift tax allowable on each gift tax return filed for prior periods after 1976. If prior gifts total more than $500,000, the unified credit in column C must be recomputed. Donors should not use the amount of unified credit that actually applied in prior periods. The instructions to Form 709 include a worksheet to use in making this calculation [see ¶ 1716].

(d) Schedule B—Column D—Specific Exemption for Prior Periods Before 1977.
In this column, identify the amount of the specific lifetime exemption claimed and allowed on each gift tax return filed for a prior period before 1977. Prior to 1977, taxable gifts were computed by reducing total gifts by (1) the allowable per donee annual exclusion ($5,000 before 1939, $4,000 from 1939 through 1942, and $3,000 from 1943 through 1981); (2) allowable marital and charitable deductions; and (3) any portion of the specific (lifetime) exemption that had not been used to offset prior gifts. The lifetime exemption was $50,000 for calendar years before 1936, $40,000 for calendar years 1936 through 1942, and $30,000 for calendar years after 1942 through the date of repeal (December 31, 1976).

When determining prior taxable gifts for years before 1977, the deduction allowed for the pre-1977 specific (lifetime) exemption is limited to $30,000 [IRC Sec. 2504(a)]. This limitation is applied by increasing prior taxable gifts by the amount by which the exemption (not the gift) previously claimed exceeds $30,000. The excess is entered on Schedule B, line 2.

The estate and gift tax systems were unified in 1977. After 1976, estate and gift taxes are based on the amount of cumulative transfers and computed using a unified rate schedule. The separate gift and estate tax exemptions were replaced with the unified credit and later the applicable credit amount. For 2013, each donor's applicable credit amount is $2,045,800 for gift tax purposes and the unified credit increases to $2,081,800 in 2014. This amount must be reduced by the amount of credit used to offset gift taxes payable in a prior year.

(e) Schedule B—Column E—Amount of Taxable Gifts. You should enter the correct amount of the taxable gift for each earlier period. This will be the amount finally determined as the taxable gifts. This will not always be the same as the amount reported on the earlier gift tax returns.

> ▶**HELPFUL HINT:** "Taxable gift" means the total value of all transfers subject to tax reduced by annual exclusions, deductions, and the specific exemption claimed and allowed for a preceding period before 1977.

You should explain any differences between the amount of taxable gifts listed in Column E and the amount on an earlier return.

Here are some rules to help you figure out the amount to enter in this column:

- If you filed a return showing the amount of the taxable gifts as one value and the amount was later determined to be either higher or lower as a result of an audit, you must show the amount finally determined as the total taxable gifts in this column.

- You only have to include transfers that were considered taxable gifts in the period in which you made the gift.

- You are only allowed to take the maximum annual exclusion that was in effect during the year in which you made the gifts. The maximum annual exclusions applicable to previous periods are:

1932–1938	$5,000
1939–1942	$4,000
1943–1981	$3,000
1982–2001	$10,000
2002–2005	$11,000
2006–2008	$12,000
2009–2012	$13,000

- You are only allowed to take the deductions that were allowable under the law when you made the gifts.

Line 1—Totals for prior periods. Add up the amounts in Columns C, D, and E and enter the totals in the spaces provided on line 1 for Columns C, D, and E.

> ▶**HELPFUL HINT:** The instruction "(without adjustment for reduced specific exemption)," refers to the rule that you are only allowed a $30,000 exemption for periods before 1977. Because you will make this adjustment on line 2, enter the

full total of specific exemption amounts on line 1 even if the total exceeds $30,000.

Line 2—Amount, if any, by which total specific exemption, line 1, Column D, is more than $30,000 . When you are computing taxable gifts for prior periods, remember that the maximum specific exemption allowed is $30,000. If the total specific exemption for prior periods before 1977 shown in Column D of line 1 is greater than $30,000, you must add the excess back to the taxable gifts on line 2. Follow this formula to determine what you should write down on line 2:

Amount from line 1, Column D	–	$30,000	=	Amount by which exemptions exceed $30,000

If the total from Column D, line 1 does not exceed $30,000, just enter zero on line 2.

Line 3—Total amount of taxable gifts for prior periods. Add line 2 and line 1 and enter the sum on line 3. This shows the amount of taxable gifts for prior periods. Remember to enter this amount on line 2 of Part 2, Tax Computation, on Page 1 of your return.

(f) Schedule C—Computation of Portability of Deceased Spousal Unused Exclusion (DSUE) Amount. Complete Schedule C if the donor is a surviving spouse who received a DSUE amount from one or more predeceased spouses.

Entry spaces with gray shading and columns and lines marked "Reserved" are inactive. Do not enter any information in these areas.

Schedule C requests information on all DSUE amounts received from the donor's last deceased spouse and any previously deceased spouses. Each line in the chart should reflect a different predeceased spouse.

The Tax Relief Act of 2010 authorized estates of decedents dying on or after January 1, 2011, to elect to transfer any unused estate tax exclusion amount to the surviving spouse. The American Taxpayer Relief Act of 2012 made this provision permanent. The amount received by the surviving spouse is called the deceased spousal unused exclusion, or DSUE, amount. If the executor of the decedent's estate elects transfer, or portability, of the DSUE amount, the surviving spouse can apply the DSUE amount received from the estate of his or her last deceased spouse (defined later) against any tax liability arising from subsequent lifetime gifts and transfers at death.

Complete Schedule A before beginning Schedule C.

> **NOTE:** A nonresident surviving spouse who is not a citizen of the United States may not take into account the DSUE amount of a deceased spouse, except to the extent allowed by a treaty with his or her country of citizenship.

For 2013, a decedent's DSUE amount is normally the *lesser* of [IRC Sec. 2010(c)(4)(B); Temp. Reg. Sec. 20.2010-2T(c)(1)]: (1) the basic exclusion amount in effect in the year of the decedent's death, or (2) the excess of the decedent's applicable exclusion amount over the amount of the taxable estate plus the amount of the decedent's adjusted taxable gifts. The unused exclusion amount transferred from a predeceased spouse is added to the surviving spouse's $5.25 million basic exclusion amount in 2013 (increasing to $5,340,000 in 2014) to determine the surviving spouse's applicable exclusion amount.

¶1709

(g) Last Deceased Spouse Limitation. The *last deceased spouse* is the most recently deceased person who was married to the surviving spouse at the time of that person's death. The identity of the last deceased spouse is determined as of the day a taxable gift is made and is not impacted by whether the decedent's estate elected portability or whether the last deceased spouse had any DSUE amount available. Remarriage also does not affect the designation of the last deceased spouse and does not prevent the surviving spouse from applying the DSUE amount to taxable transfers.

When a taxable gift is made, the DSUE amount received from the last deceased spouse is applied before the surviving spouse's basic exclusion amount. A surviving spouse who has more than one predeceased spouse is not precluded from using the DSUE amount of each spouse in succession. A surviving spouse may not use the sum of DSUE amounts from multiple predeceased spouses at one time nor may the DSUE amount of a predeceased spouse be applied after the death of a subsequent spouse.

When a surviving spouse applies the DSUE amount to a lifetime gift, the IRS may examine any return of a predeceased spouse whose executor elected portability to verify the allowable DSUE amount. The DSUE may be adjusted or eliminated as a result of the examination; however, the IRS may make an assessment of additional tax on the return of a predeceased spouse only within the applicable limitations period under section 6501.

(h) Schedule C—Part 1. DSUE Received from Last Deceased Spouse. In this Part, include information about the DSUE amount from the donor's most recently deceased spouse (whose date of death is after December 31, 2010). In column E, enter the total of the amount in column D that the donor has applied to gifts in previous years and is applying to gifts reported on this return. Do not make any entries in columns F or G.

(i) Schedule C—Part 2. DSUE Received from Other Predeceased Spouse(s). Enter information about the DSUE amount from the spouse(s), if any, who died prior to the donor's most recently deceased spouse (but not before January 1, 2011) if the prior spouse's executor elected portability of the DSUE amount. In column D, indicate the amount of DSUE received from the estate of each predeceased spouse. In column E, enter the portion of the amount of DSUE shown in column E that was applied to prior lifetime gifts or transfers.

Any remaining DSUE from a predeceased spouse cannot be applied against tax arising from lifetime gifts if that spouse is not the most recently deceased spouse on the date of the gift. This rule applies even if the last deceased spouse had no DSUE amount or made no valid portability election, or if the DSUE amount from the last deceased spouse has been fully applied to gifts in previous periods.

(j) Determining Applicable Credit. On line 1, enter the donor's basic exclusion amount; for 2013, this amount is $5,250,000. Add the amounts listed in column E from Parts 1 and 2 and enter the total on line 2. On line 4, enter the total of lines 1 and 2. Using the Table for Computing Gift Tax, later, determine the donor's applicable credit by applying the appropriate tax rate to the amount on line 4. Enter this amount on line 5 and on line 7 of Part 2—Tax Computation.

¶1709

NOTE: Lines 3, 6, 7, 8, 9, and 10 of this computation are marked "Reserved" and are inactive. Do not enter any amount on these lines.

■ Maureen B. and Michael A. Gift make no entries on Schedule C because they have no DSUE amount received from a predeceased spouse to a gift or gifts reported on this or a previous Form 709.

¶1710 SCHEDULE D—COMPUTATION OF GENERATION-SKIPPING TRANSFER TAX

(a) Part 1 of Schedule D—Computation of GST Tax. Schedule D deals with the GST tax.

Part 1—In this part of Form 709 you must show any GST that you listed on Part 2 of Schedule A.

Part 2—This part is used to reconcile the GST tax exemption on the current return with any GST exemption that you may have claimed on a prior return.

Part 3—Compute the GST tax in Part 3 if you make a GST that is subject to GST tax, but cannot be offset by the GST exclusion amount.

■ Under the deemed-allocation rules, Michael Gift's GST exemption will automatically be allocated to the transfers he made. As a result, they will carry over to Schedule D, Part 1.

Schedule D is then completed, so that the exemption amount used for the transfer can be tracked. If the transferor does not want to allocate GST exemption to the transfer, he or she can irrevocably elect out of the automatic IRC Sec. 2632(b)(3) exemption-allocation rules for direct skips. The election is made by checking column C in Part 2 of Schedule A and including the transfer's net value (from Schedule A, Part 2, column H) on Schedule D, Part 1, column B (split gifts made by the donor's spouse are listed in the lower portion of Schedule D, Part 1). Schedule D, Parts 1 and 3 are then completed to determine the GST tax due on the transfer.

Column A, Part 1 of Schedule D—Item number.

1. Enter all of the gifts that you listed on Part 2 of Schedule A in the same order that you listed them on Schedule A.

2. You may attach an extra piece of paper if you made more than six transfers that are generation-skipping transfers.

In the middle of Part 1, you will notice the line "Gifts made by spouse (for gift splitting only)." If you elected to split gifts with your spouse, enter one-half of the value of each gift here in Part 1. If you did not elect to split gifts with your spouse, enter zero in Column A.

Column B, Part 1 of Schedule D—Value. Enter the same amount that you used in Column H on Part 2 of Schedule A.

■ Maureen B. and Michael A. Gift [see ¶1705] each enter $30,000 and $18,000 in Column B, Part 1 of Schedule D for the two gifts to their grandchildren that they elected to split in 2013. They make the entries

¶1710

under the second part of Part 1, Schedule D, entitled "Gifts made by spouse (for gift-splitting only)."

Column C, Part 1 of Schedule D—Nontaxable portion of transfer. You may claim the $14,000 annual gift tax exclusion for your reported direct skips (other than certain direct skips to trusts in 2013 or in 2014). However, you must allocate the exclusion on a gift-by-gift basis for GST computation purposes. You must allocate the exclusion to each gift to the maximum allowable amount and in chronological order, beginning with the earliest gift that qualifies for the exclusion. Be sure that you do not claim a total exclusion of more than $14,000 per donee in 2013 or in 2014.

■ Maureen B. and Michael A. Gift each enter $14,000 for the gifts made to their grandchildren in 2013 in Column C, Part 1 of Schedule D. They make their entries under the second part of Part I, Schedule D, entitled "Gifts made by spouse (for gift-splitting only)." On Schedule D, Maureen enters $14,000 for Gift #1 and therefore allocates her entire exclusion to the first gift as the Form 709 Instructions mandate. Michael enters the same thing on his Schedule D.

Column D, Part 1 of Schedule D—Net transfer—subtract Column C from Column B.

(b) Part 2—GST Exemption Reconciliation (Section 2631) and Section 2652(a)(3) Election. *Line 1—Maximum allowable exemption.* Every donor may claim a lifetime GST exemption. The amount of the exemption is indexed for inflation. The maximum allowable GST tax exemption for transfers made through 1998 was $1 million. The increased exemption amounts are as follows:

Year	Amount
1999	$1,010,000
2000	$1,030,000
2001	$1,060,000
2002	$1,100,000
2003	$1,120,000
2004 and 2005	$1,500,000
2006–2008	$2,000,000
2009	$3,500,000
2010 and 2011	$5,000,000
2012	$5,120,000
2013	$5,250,000
2014	$5,340,000

Each annual increase can only be allocated to transfers made (or appreciation occurring) during or after the year of the transfer.

Example 1: A donor made $1,750,000 in GST transfers through 2005 and allocated all of his $1,500,000 of the GST exemption to those transfers. In 2013, the donor makes a $207,000 taxable GST transfer. The donor can allocate $207,000 of exemption to the 2013 transfer but cannot allocate the $3,543,000 of unused 2013 exemption to pre-2013 transfers. However, if in 2005, the donor had made a $1,750,000 transfer to a trust that was not a direct skip, but from which generation-skipping transfers could be made in the future, the donor could allocate the increased exemption to the trust, even though no additional transfers were made to the trust. See Reg. Sec. 26.2642-4 for details on the redetermination of the applicable fraction when additional exemption is allocated to the trust. Taxpayers should keep a record of transfers and exemption allocations to make sure that any future increases are allocated correctly.

Enter on line 1 of Part 2 the maximum GST exemption you are allowed. This will not necessarily be the highest indexed amount if you have made no GST transfer during the year of the increase. For example, if the taxpayer's last GST transfer was in 2009, the maximum available GST exemption would be $3,500,000. The GST exemption can be applied to *inter vivos* transfers made during the donor's lifetime on Form 709. The executor can apply the exemption on Form 709 to transfers taking effect at death. The allocation is irrevocable.

Special QTIP election. If you have elected QTIP treatment for any gifts in trust listed on Schedule A, then you may make an election on Schedule D to treat the entire trust as non-QTIP for purposes of the GST tax. The election must be made for the entire trust that contains the particular gift involved on this return. Be sure to identify by item number the specific gift for which you are making this special QTIP election. Check the box provided in the first line of Part 2 of Schedule D if you wish to make this special election. You would make this election where part of your GST exemption would otherwise be wasted. This election allows you to allocate part or all of your exemption to property that is in a QTIP trust that will end up being subject to the GST tax. If you do not use the reverse QTIP election, your spouse would have to use his or her own GST exemption when the QTIP trust terminates or when he or she transfers of the property out of the trust.

Line 2—Total GST exemption used for periods before filing this return. Enter the amount of the total GST tax exemption that you used for periods before filing this return.

   ■ Maureen and Michael Gift [see ¶ 1705] both enter zero here because they made no generation-skipping transfers in prior periods.

Line 3—Exemption available for this return. Subtract line 2 from line 1 and enter the difference here.

Line 4—Exemption claimed on this return. Enter the total GST exemption from Column C of Part 3 of Schedule D. You must fill out Part 3 of Schedule D before you can complete this line.

   ■ Michael Gift enters $34,000 on line 4 of Part 2 on page 5. This number is computed in Part 3—Tax Computation.

Line 5—Automatic allocation of exemption to transfers reported on Schedule A, Part 3. Enter on line 5 of Schedule D, Part 2, page 4, the amount of GST exemption you are applying to transfers reported in Part 3, Schedule A, page 2. As discussed at ¶ 1708, Part 3 of Schedule A is where you enter indirect skips which are gifts to trusts that are subject to gift tax at the time of the transfer and may later be subject to GST tax either at the time of a distribution from the trust, at the termination of the trust, or both. Under the automatic or deemed allocation rules of IRC Sec. 2632(c), the donor's GST unused

¶1710

exemption will automatically be allocated to indirect skip transfers made during the year to the extent needed to produce the lowest possible inclusion ratio for the property. If the donor wants to allocate GST exemption to the indirect skip transfer, column C of Schedule A, Part 3, page 2 should have been left blank. The lesser of: (1) the exemption amount equal to the value of the transfer in column H of Schedule A, Part 3, page 2, or (2) the donor's remaining GST exemption should also be entered on Schedule D, Part 2, line 5, enabling the donor to track the amount used. A donor has the option, however, to elect not to have the automatic allocation rules apply to both the current transfer and to any and all future transfers made to a particular trust. This election may be made on a timely filed gift tax return for the year for which the election is to become effective.

> ■ In Part 3, Schedule A, page 2, Michael A. Gift entered the information about the trust he established on March 21, 2013 for the benefit of his son from a prior marriage, David Gift. At David's death, the trust remainder will pass to Michael's grandson, Adam, and is therefore a GST trust. Since Michael Gift wants to preserve his GST exemption for a direct skip transfer to a trust for his grandchildren that he intends to make next year, he wants to elect out of the deemed allocation of GST exemption. He therefore checked column C of Part 3, Schedule A, page 2, and attached an Election Statement to his Form 709 [see ¶ 1718] to elect out of the deemed allocation rules. Michael therefore enters -0- on line 5 of Schedule D, page 4 because he has no allocation of GST exemption to indirect skips to report on this line.

Maureen B. Gift enters $700,000 on line 5 of Schedule D, page 4 because she had indirect skips to be entered on Schedule A, Part 3, page 2 and she wanted to allocate GST exemption to the transfers.

Line 6—Exemption allocated to transfers not shown on line 4 or 5, above ("Notice of Allocation" must be attached). On line 6 you may allocate GST exemption to transfers not reported on this return, such as a late allocation. To allocate your exemption to such transfers, attach a statement to Form 709 and entitle it "Notice of Allocation." The notice must contain the following for each trust (or other transfer):

* Clearly identify the trust, including the trust's employer identification number, if known;
* If this is a late allocation, the year the transfer was reported on form 709;
* The value of the trust assets at the effective date of the allocation;
* The amount of your GST exemption allocated to each gift (or a statement that you are allocating exemption by means of a formula such as "an amount necessary to produce an inclusion ratio of zero"); and
* The inclusion ratio of the trust after the allocation.

Total the exemption allocations and enter this total on line 6.

Line 7—Add lines 4, 5, and 6.

Line 8—Exemption available for future transfers. Subtract line 7 from line 3 and enter the balance on line 8.

■ Maureen A. Gift enters $4,516,000 on Line 8 which represents how much GST exemption she has available for future transfers.

(c) Part 3—Computation of GST Tax.

Column A, Part 3—Item number. In Part 3 you must enter every gift you listed in Part 1 of Schedule D. Use the same item numbers.

■ Maureen B. and Michael A. Gift [see ¶ 1705] each enter item numbers 1 and 2.

Column B, Part 3—Net transfer. Enter each amount from Schedule D, Part 1, Column D.

■ Maureen B. and Michael A. Gift each enter $16,000 and $18,000 in Column B of Part 3 of Schedule D. These figures represent the generation-skipping transfers identified in Part 1 of Schedule D. These entries are made under the subheading "Gifts made by spouse (for gift-splitting only)."

Column C, Part 3—GST exemption allocated. You are not required to allocate your available exemption to your gifts. You may allocate some, all, or none of your available exemption among the gifts listed in Part 3 of Schedule D. You may enter an amount in column C that is greater than the amount you entered in column B. If you do not allocate your exemption to your gifts, you might pay GST tax on those transfers.

■ Maureen B. and Michael A. Gift [see ¶ 1705] each allocate part of their lifetime GST tax exemption to these gifts.

Bottom of Column C, Part 3—Total exemption claimed. Add the amounts in Column C and enter the total at the bottom of Column C and also on line 4 of Part 2 of Schedule D. The total exemption claimed in Column C may not exceed the amount you entered on line 3 of Part 2 of Schedule D (exemption available for this return).

Column G, Part 3—Applicable rate. Multiply the inclusion ratio by zero in Column E by 40 percent.

Column H, Part 3—GST tax. The form states that the GST tax rate in 2013 is 40 percent.

Line at bottom of Column H, Part 3—Total GST tax. Add the GST tax amounts in Column H. Enter the total on the line at the bottom of Column H. Enter this amount on line 10 of Part 4 of Schedule A and on line 16 of the Tax Computation section in Part 1 on Page 2 of Form 709.

¶1711 PART 2—TAX COMPUTATION

You should now go back to Part 2 on Page 1 of Form 709 so you can complete the tax computation and finish your gift tax return.

Line 1—Amount from Schedule A, Part 4, line 11. Enter on line 1 the amount of taxable gifts from line 11 of Part 4 of Schedule A, which is on Page 3 of Form 709.

■ Maureen B. Gift enters $734,000 and Michael A. Gift enters $1,034,000 on line 1 of Part 2 on page 1 of Form 709.

Line 2—Amount from Schedule B, line 3. Enter on line 2 the amount of taxable gifts for prior periods from line 3 of Schedule B, which is on Page 3 of Form 709.

Both taxpayers enter 0 on line 2.

Line 3—Total taxable gifts. Add line 1 to line 2 and enter the sum on line 3.

■ Maureen B. Gift enters $734,000 and Michael A. Gift enters $1,034,000 on line 3 of Part 2 on page 1 of Form 709.

Line 4—Tax computed on amount on line 3. Use the Table for Computing Gift Tax on Page 17 of the 2013 Instructions to Form 709 to determine the rate and tax based on the amount listed in line 3. The table is reproduced below:

Table for Computing Gift Tax

Column A Taxable amount over	Column B Taxable amount not over—	Column C Tax on amount in Column A	Column D Rate of tax on excess over amount in Column A
—	$10,000	—	18%
$10,000	20,000	$1,800	20%
20,000	40,000	3,800	22%
40,000	60,000	8,200	24%
60,000	80,000	13,000	26%
80,000	100,000	18,200	28%
100,000	150,000	23,800	30%
150,000	250,000	38,800	32%
250,000	500,000	70,800	34%
500,000	750,000	155,800	37%
750,000	1,000,000	248,300	39%
1,000,000	----	345,800	40%

■ Maureen B. Gift enters $242,380 and Michael A. Gift enters $359,400 on line 4 of Part 2.

Line 5—Tax computed on amount in line 2. This is the gift tax on taxable gifts from prior periods. Again, use the Table for Computing Gift Tax on Page 17 of the 2013 Form 709 instructions to determine the applicable rate and tax due on the amount in line 2.

■ Both taxpayers enter 0 on line 5 of Part 2.

Line 6—Balance (current tax before unified credit). Subtract line 5 from line 4 and enter the result on line 6.

■ Maureen B. Gift enters $242,380 and Michael A. Gift enters $359,400 on line 6 of Part 2.

Line 7—Maximum unified credit. The maximum unified credit amount is the tentative tax on the applicable exclusion amount. For gifts made in 2013, the applicable exclusion amount equals:

- The basic exclusion amount of $5,250,000, PLUS
- Any deceased spousal unused exclusion (DSUE) amount.

Any taxpayer who is a citizen or resident of the United States must apply any available unified credit against gift tax. If the taxpayer is not eligible to use a DSUE from a predeceased spouse, enter $1,772,800 on line 7. Nonresident aliens many not claim the unified credit and should enter zero on line 7.

Deceased spousal unused exclusion amount. A surviving spouse who is a citizen or resident of the United States may be eligible to use his or her deceased spouse's unused exclusion amount if the spouse died after December 31, 2010. The executor of the deceased spouse's estate must have elected on the 2013 Form 706 to allow the surviving spouse to use the deceased spouse's unused exclusion amount. If the election was made, the surviving spouse must attach the 2013 Form 706 for the deceased spouse's estate to Form 709.

▶ **CAUTION:** Nonresident aliens may not claim the unified credit. Therefore, if you are a nonresident alien and are required to file a gift tax return, cross out the number preprinted on line 7 and write zero ("0") on line 7.

■ Maureen B. Gift enters $2,048,800, as does Michael A. Gift.

Line 8—Unified credit allowable for all prior periods. Enter the amount from Schedule B, Column C, line 1 of the form.

■ Both taxpayers enter 0 on line 8 of Part 2.

Line 9—Balance (unused unified credit). Subtract line 8 from line 7 and enter the result on line 9.

Line 10—20 percent of the amount allowed as a specific exemption for gifts made after September 8, 1976, and before January 1, 1977. Enter 20 percent of the amount allowed as a specific exemption for gifts that you made after September 8, 1976, and before January 1, 1977. (These amounts will be among those listed in Column D of Schedule B, for gifts made in the third and fourth quarters of 1976.)

■ Both taxpayers enter 0 on line 10 of Part 2.

Line 11—Balance (unified credit available to offset current tax). Subtract line 10 from line 9 and enter the balance on line 11.

Line 12—Unified credit. On line 12 enter the smaller of:

• The amount on line 6 (tax); or

• The amount on line 11 (balance of the unified credit).

■ Maureen B. Gift enters $242,380 and Michael A. Gift enters $359,400 on line 12 of Part 2.

Line 13—Credit for foreign gift taxes. Gift tax conventions are in effect with Australia, Austria, Denmark, France, Germany, Japan, and the United Kingdom. If you are claiming a credit for payment of foreign gift tax, figure the credit on another sheet of paper and attach evidence that the foreign taxes were paid.

■ Both taxpayers enter 0 on line 13 of Part 2.

Line 14—Total credits. Add lines 12 and 13 and enter the sum on line 14.

■ Maureen B. Gift enters $242,380 and Michael A. Gift enters $359,400 on line 14 of Part 2.

¶1711

Line 15—Balance (gift tax, current year). Subtract the amount on line 14 from the amount on line 6 and enter the balance on line 15. The amount on line 15 is the gift tax that you owe on taxable gifts for the current calendar year.

> ▶ **CAUTION:** The amount on line 15 may not be less than zero.

> ■ On line 15, Maureen B. Gift enters 0 and Michael A. Gift enters 0.

Line 16—GST taxes. Enter the total from Schedule D, Column H of Part 3 of that Schedule. This is the amount of GST taxes that you owe this year.

> ■ Both taxpayers enter 0 on line 16.

Line 17—Total (gift and GST) tax: Add lines 15 and 16 and enter the sum on line 17. This is the TOTAL amount of taxes that you owe.

> ■ On line 17, Maureen B. Gift enters 0 and Michael A. Gift enters 0.

Line 18—Gift and GST taxes prepaid with extension of time to file. Enter on line 18 the amount of any gift and GST taxes that you already paid because you had an extension of time in which to file the actual return.

> ▶ **CAUTION:** Even if you have an extension of time to file the return, you must still pay the tax due by the original due date—even without a return. Payment in full by the due date is necessary to prevent the imposition of penalties and interest charges.

*Lines 19 and 20—*Balance due or amount to be refunded.

> ■ Maureen B. Gift enters 0 and Michael A. Gift enters 0 on line 19 and sends a check payable to the United States Treasury in this amount.

- Compare the total tax on line 17 with the prepayment (if any) on line 18 to determine which is greater.

- If the total tax on line 17 is greater, subtract the prepayment on line 18 from the amount on line 17, enter the balance due on line 19, and leave line 20 blank.

- Attach a check or money order for the amount that you owe to the lower left-hand margin of Page 1 for the amount on line 19. Make your check or money order payable to the "United States Treasury." Write your Social Security number on the check or money order.

> ▶ **CAUTION:** You may not use an overpayment on your Form 1040 to offset the gift and GST taxes owed on Form 709.

- If the payment on line 18 is greater than the total tax due on line 17, subtract the tax on line 17 from the payment on line 18, enter the refund amount on line 20, and leave line 19 blank.

¶1712 FILING FORM 709

(a) Signature and Verification.

- DO NOT FORGET TO SIGN AND DATE YOUR RETURN IN THE SPACE PROVIDED ON PAGE 1.

¶1712

Any person, firm, or corporation who prepares your return for some type of compensation is required to sign the return on the line below your signature. They must also give their address in the space provided.

▶**HELPFUL HINT:** This verification is not required if the return is prepared by your regular full-time employee.

If you did not pay the person who prepared your gift tax return, they are not required to sign the return.

(b) Where To File. You must file Form 709 at the Cincinnati Service Center, regardless of whether you are located in the 50 states, the District of Columbia, a foreign country, American Samoa, Guam, the Virgin Islands, Puerto Rico, or have an APO or FPO address. The Cincinnati address is:

Department of the Treasury
Internal Revenue Service Center
Cincinnati, OH 45999

If Form 709 is being submitted by private delivery service, mail to:

Internal Revenue Service
201 West Rivercenter Boulevard
Covington, KY 41011

(c) Private Delivery Services. Taxpayers can use the following private delivery services designated by the IRS to meet the "timely mailing as timely filing/paying" rule for tax returns and payments:

- DHL Express (DHL)
  - DHL Same Day Service
- Federal Express (FedEx)
  - FedEx Priority Overnight
  - FedEx Standard Overnight
  - FedEx 2Day
  - FedEx International Priority
  - FedEx International First
- United Parcel Service (UPS)
  - UPS Next Day Air
  - UPS Next Day Air Saver
  - UPS 2nd Day Air
  - UPS 2nd Day Air A.M.
  - UPS Worldwide Express Plus
  - UPS Worldwide Express

(d) Paid Preparer Information. A paid tax return preparer who prepares all or substantially all of a tax return is required to obtain and annually renew a PTIN. All PTINs expire on December 31 of each year and can be applied for or renewed on the IRS website. A fee is required to obtain or renew a PTIN.

¶1712

¶1713 CHECKLIST OF ATTACHMENTS TO FORM 709

Below is a checklist of documents that you should attach to your completed Form 709.

■ Extension of time to file return—use IRS Form 4868, Form 2350, or Form 8892,

■ List of gifts that are not subject to tax:

- Transfers of property that are incomplete because you retained some power over the property—Submit evidence showing all relevant facts and include a copy of trust or other instrument of transfer.

- Transfers under certain property settlement agreements within three-year period beginning one year before divorce and ending two years after divorce—Attach a copy of the agreement to the return. Also, file a certified copy of the final divorce decree not later than 60 days after the divorce is granted.

- Transfers subject to the Chapter 14 rules which are not shown as gifts on a gift tax return—Attach a statement to the return disclosing the transfer in a manner adequate to apprise IRS of the existence of the item.

■ Any documents which are required to adequately explain, describe, and identify the gift and the basis for valuing it. A formal appraisal will satisfy this requirement. The requirements for various types of property are:

- *Real estate.* If you are basing the value of the real estate on an appraisal, attach the appraisal and an explanation of the basis of the appraisal.

- *Closely-held or inactive stock.* Attach balance sheets, especially ones that were done near to the date of the gift, and statements of the net earnings or operating results and dividends paid during the last five years.

- *Life insurance policies.* Attach IRS Form 712 for each policy that you listed on the return.

- *Gifts in trust.* Attach a copy of the trust document.

■ The piece of paper on which you calculated the foreign gift tax credit and any evidence that you paid the foreign gift tax.

■ The document that shows that you elected to not have the GST tax exemption automatically apply to property that you gave away during the year.

■ Notice to allocate GST tax exemption to a trust that is not involved in a transfer listed on Schedule A or D.

■ A check or money order for the balance of the gift and GST tax due.

■ Any attachments that are necessary because there was not enough room on the return to fully explain or list something

¶1713

¶1714 AUDITS OF GIFT TAX RETURNS

If your gift tax return is audited, the IRS agent will focus on the following things:

1. Verifying the total taxable gifts for the current period and all prior periods;
2. Looking for additional unreported gifts especially non-spousal transfers of real property; and
3. Verifying the correct gift tax computation.

The Audit Technique Handbook provides the following instructions to the auditor:

1. Check local real estate records to see whether fractional gifts were made in addition to current real estate gifts reported on Form 709.
2. Request Form 709 files for the donor's brothers and sisters if the donor's return includes gifts to nieces and nephews. A reciprocal gift situation may be disclosed requiring disallowance of annual exclusion.
3. Inspect income tax returns to see whether changes in income reflect unreported gifts.

(a) Statute of Limitations. The statute of limitations for assessing gift tax is normally three years after the gift tax return is filed (or due, if later) [IRC Sec. 6501(a); see ¶1701]. The statute runs for six years after the return is filed (or is due, if later) if the value of the gifts omitted from the gift tax return exceeds 25 percent of the total gifts reported in the year in question. But the three-year statute of limitations provided in IRC Sec. 6501 only applies if the gifts have been "adequately disclosed" on a gift tax return [IRC Sec. 6501(c)(9)]. The disclosure must be adequate to apprise the IRS of the nature of the transaction. [For further discussion of what constitutes "adequate disclosure," see Reg. Sec. 301.6501(c)-1(f)(2) as discussed further in ¶1910].

¶1714

¶1715 SAMPLE COMPLETED FORM 709 FOR MAUREEN B. GIFT

Form **709**	United States Gift (and Generation-Skipping Transfer) Tax Return	OMB No. 1545-0020
Department of the Treasury Internal Revenue Service	▶ Information about Form 709 and its separate instructions is at *www.irs.gov/form709*. (For gifts made during calendar year 2013) ▶ See instructions.	20**13**

Part 1—General Information

1 Donor's first name and middle initial Maureen B.	2 Donor's last name Gift	3 Donor's social security number 123-44-5678
4 Address (number, street, and apartment number) 1 Highland Court		5 Legal residence (domicile) Baltimore County, Maryland
6 City or town, state or province, country, and ZIP or foreign postal code Baltimore, Maryland 21231		7 Citizenship (see instructions) USA

		Yes	No
8	If the donor died during the year, check here ▶ ☐ and enter date of death _____ , _____		
9	If you extended the time to file this Form 709, check here ▶ ☐		
10	Enter the total number of donees listed on Schedule A. Count each person only once. ▶ 3		
11a	Have you (the donor) previously filed a Form 709 (or 709-A) for any other year? If "No," skip line 11b	✓	
b	Has your address changed since you last filed Form 709 (or 709-A)?		✓
12	**Gifts by husband or wife to third parties.** Do you consent to have the gifts (including generation-skipping transfers) made by you and by your spouse to third parties during the calendar year considered as made one-half by each of you? (see instructions.) (If the answer is "Yes," the following information must be furnished and your spouse must sign the consent shown below. **If the answer is "No," skip lines 13–18.**)	✓	
13	Name of consenting spouse **Michael A. Gift** **14** SSN **876-55-4321**		
15	Were you married to one another during the entire calendar year? (see instructions)	✓	
16	If 15 is "No," check whether ☐ married ☐ divorced or ☐ widowed/deceased, and give date (see instructions) ▶		
17	Will a gift tax return for this year be filed by your spouse? (If "Yes," mail both returns in the same envelope.)	✓	
18	**Consent of Spouse.** I consent to have the gifts (and generation-skipping transfers) made by me and by my spouse to third parties during the calendar year considered as made one-half by each of us. We are both aware of the joint and several liability for tax created by the execution of this consent.		

Consenting spouse's signature ▶   Date ▶

		Yes	No
19	Have you applied a DSUE amount received from a predeceased spouse to a gift or gifts reported on this or a previous Form 709? If "Yes," complete Schedule C		✓

Part 2—Tax Computation

1	Enter the amount from Schedule A, Part 4, line 11	1	734,000
2	Enter the amount from Schedule B, line 3	2	-0-
3	Total taxable gifts. Add lines 1 and 2	3	734,000
4	Tax computed on amount on line 3 (see *Table for Computing Gift Tax* in instructions)	4	242,380
5	Tax computed on amount on line 2 (see *Table for Computing Gift Tax* in instructions)	5	-0-
6	Balance. Subtract line 5 from line 4	6	242,380
7	Applicable credit amount. If donor has DSUE amount from predeceased spouse(s), enter amount from Schedule C, line 4; otherwise, see instructions	7	2,045,800
8	Enter the applicable credit against tax allowable for all prior periods (from Sch. B, line 1, col. C)	8	-0-
9	Balance. Subtract line 8 from line 7. Do not enter less than zero	9	2,045,800
10	Enter 20% (.20) of the amount allowed as a specific exemption for gifts made after September 8, 1976, and before January 1, 1977 (see instructions)	10	-0-
11	Balance. Subtract line 10 from line 9. Do not enter less than zero	11	2,045,800
12	Applicable credit. Enter the smaller of line 6 or line 11	12	242,380
13	Credit for foreign gift taxes (see instructions)	13	-0-
14	Total credits. Add lines 12 and 13	14	242,380
15	Balance. Subtract line 14 from line 6. Do not enter less than zero	15	-0-
16	Generation-skipping transfer taxes (from Schedule D, Part 3, col. H, Total)	16	-0-
17	Total tax. Add lines 15 and 16	17	-0-
18	Gift and generation-skipping transfer taxes prepaid with extension of time to file	18	-0-
19	If line 18 is less than line 17, enter **balance due** (see instructions)	19	-0-
20	If line 18 is greater than line 17, enter **amount to be refunded**	20	-0-

Sign Here

Under penalties of perjury, I declare that I have examined this return, including any accompanying schedules and statements, and to the best of my knowledge and belief, it is true, correct, and complete. Declaration of preparer (other than donor) is based on all information of which preparer has any knowledge.

May the IRS discuss this return with the preparer shown below (see instructions)? ☑ Yes ☐ No

▶ _____
Signature of donor   Date

Paid Preparer Use Only	Print/Type preparer's name	Preparer's signature	Date	Check ☐ if self-employed	PTIN
	Firm's name ▶			Firm's EIN ▶	
	Firm's address ▶			Phone no.	

Attach check or money order here.

For Disclosure, Privacy Act, and Paperwork Reduction Act Notice, see the instructions for this form.   Cat. No. 16783M   Form **709** (2013)

¶1715

Form 709 (2013) — Page **2**

SCHEDULE A   Computation of Taxable Gifts (Including transfers in trust) (see instructions)

A Does the value of any item listed on Schedule A reflect any valuation discount? If "Yes," attach explanation . . . . . . Yes ☐ No ☑

B ☐ ◄ Check here if you elect under section 529(c)(2)(B) to treat any transfers made this year to a qualified tuition program as made ratably over a 5-year period beginning this year. See instructions. Attach explanation.

Part 1—Gifts Subject Only to Gift Tax. Gifts less political organization, medical, and educational exclusions. (see instructions)

A Item number	B • Donee's name and address • Relationship to donor (if any) • Description of gift • If the gift was of securities, give CUSIP no. • If closely held entity, give EIN	C	D Donor's adjusted basis of gift	E Date of gift	F Value at date of gift	G For split gifts, enter ½ of column F	H Net transfer (subtract col. G from col. F)
1							

*Gifts made by spouse —complete **only** if you are splitting gifts with your spouse and he/she also made gifts.*

Total of Part 1. Add amounts from Part 1, column H . . . . ▶ | | | | | | |

Part 2—Direct Skips. Gifts that are direct skips and are subject to both gift tax and generation-skipping transfer tax. You must list the gifts in chronological order.

A Item number	B • Donee's name and address • Relationship to donor (if any) • Description of gift • If the gift was of securities, give CUSIP no. • If closely held entity, give EIN	C 2632(b) election out	D Donor's adjusted basis of gift	E Date of gift	F Value at date of gift	G For split gifts, enter ½ of column F	H Net transfer (subtract col. G from col. F)
1							

*Gifts made by spouse —complete **only** if you are splitting gifts with your spouse and he/she also made gifts.*

A	B	C	D	E	F	G	H
1	Joel Gift (Grandson) 550 shares of ABCo		40,000	1/12/13	60,000	30,000	30,000
	(CUSIP Number 987333)						
2	Amy Gift (Granddaughter)		36,000	2/23/13	36,000	18,000	18,000
	2013 Toyota Highlander Hybrid						48,000

Total of Part 2. Add amounts from Part 2, column H . . . . ▶ | | | | | | |

Part 3—Indirect Skips. Gifts to trusts that are currently subject to gift tax and may later be subject to generation-skipping transfer tax. You must list these gifts in chronological order.

A Item number	B • Donee's name and address • Relationship to donor (if any) • Description of gift • If the gift was of securities, give CUSIP no. • If closely held entity, give EIN	C 2632(c) election	D Donor's adjusted basis of gift	E Date of gift	F Value at date of gift	G For split gifts, enter ½ of column F	H Net transfer (subtract col. G from col. F)
1	Maureen B. Gift Family Trust f/b/o Emily Russ	✓	300,000	6/15/13	700,000	-0-	700,000

*Gifts made by spouse —complete **only** if you are splitting gifts with your spouse and he/she also made gifts.*

Total of Part 3. Add amounts from Part 3, column H . . . . ▶ | | | | | | 700,000 |

(If more space is needed, attach additional statements.)   Form **709** (2013)

Form 709 (2013)   Page **3**

Part 4—Taxable Gift Reconciliation

1	Total value of gifts of donor. Add totals from column H of Parts 1, 2, and 3	1	748,000
2	Total annual exclusions for gifts listed on line 1 (see instructions)	2	14,000
3	Total included amount of gifts. Subtract line 2 from line 1	3	734,000

Deductions (see instructions)

4	Gifts of interests to spouse for which a marital deduction will be claimed, based on item numbers _____ of Schedule A . .	4	-0-		
5	Exclusions attributable to gifts on line 4	5	-0-		
6	Marital deduction. Subtract line 5 from line 4	6	-0-		
7	Charitable deduction, based on item nos. _____ less exclusions .	7	-0-		
8	Total deductions. Add lines 6 and 7			8	-0-
9	Subtract line 8 from line 3			9	734,000
10	Generation-skipping transfer taxes payable with this Form 709 (from Schedule D, Part 3, col. H, Total) . .			10	-0-
11	**Taxable gifts.** Add lines 9 and 10. Enter here and on page 1, Part 2—Tax Computation, line 1			11	734,000

Terminable Interest (QTIP) Marital Deduction. (see instructions for Schedule A, Part 4, line 4)

If a trust (or other property) meets the requirements of qualified terminable interest property under section 2523(f), and:

   a. The trust (or other property) is listed on Schedule A, and

   b. The value of the trust (or other property) is entered in whole or in part as a deduction on Schedule A, Part 4, line 4,

then the donor shall be deemed to have made an election to have such trust (or other property) treated as qualified terminable interest property under section 2523(f).

If less than the entire value of the trust (or other property) that the donor has included in Parts 1 and 3 of Schedule A is entered as a deduction on line 4, the donor shall be considered to have made an election only as to a fraction of the trust (or other property). The numerator of this fraction is equal to the amount of the trust (or other property) deducted on Schedule A, Part 4, line 6. The denominator is equal to the total value of the trust (or other property) listed in Parts 1 and 3 of Schedule A.

If you make the QTIP election, the terminable interest property involved will be included in your spouse's gross estate upon his or her death (section 2044). See instructions for line 4 of Schedule A. If your spouse disposes (by gift or otherwise) of all or part of the qualifying life income interest, he or she will be considered to have made a transfer of the entire property that is subject to the gift tax. See *Transfer of Certain Life Estates Received From Spouse* in the instructions.

12   Election Out of QTIP Treatment of Annuities

☐   ◄Check here if you elect under section 2523(f)(6) **not** to treat as qualified terminable interest property any joint and survivor annuities that are reported on Schedule A and would otherwise be treated as qualified terminable interest property under section 2523(f). See instructions. Enter the item numbers from Schedule A for the annuities for which you are making this election ► _____

SCHEDULE B   Gifts From Prior Periods

If you answered "Yes," on line 11a of page 1, Part 1, see the instructions for completing Schedule B. If you answered "No," skip to the Tax Computation on page 1 (or Schedules C or D, if applicable). Complete Schedule A before beginning Schedule B. See instructions for recalculation of the column C amounts. Attach calculations.

A Calendar year or calendar quarter (see instructions)	B Internal Revenue office where prior return was filed	C Amount of applicable credit (unified credit) against gift tax for periods after December 31, 1976	D Amount of specific exemption for prior periods ending before January 1, 1977	E Amount of taxable gifts
1 Totals for prior periods **1**				

2	Amount, if any, by which total specific exemption, line 1, column D is more than $30,000	2	
3	Total amount of taxable gifts for prior periods. Add amount on line 1, column E and amount, if any, on line 2. Enter here and on page 1, Part 2—Tax Computation, line 2	3	

(If more space is needed, attach additional statements.)   Form **709** (2013)

¶1715

Form 709 (2013)

SCHEDULE C   Deceased Spousal Unused Exclusion (DSUE) Amount

Provide the following information to determine the DSUE amount and applicable credit received from prior spouses. Complete Schedule A before beginning Schedule C.

A Name of Deceased Spouse (dates of death after December 31, 2010 only)	B Date of Death	C Portability Election Made?		D If "Yes," DSUE Amount Received from Spouse	E DSUE Amount Applied by Donor to Lifetime Gifts (list current and prior gifts)	F Date of Gift(s) (enter as mm/dd/yy for Part 1 and as yyyy for Part 2)
		Yes	No			
Part 1—DSUE RECEIVED FROM LAST DECEASED SPOUSE						
Part 2—DSUE RECEIVED FROM PREDECEASED SPOUSE(S)						

TOTAL (for all DSUE amounts applied for Part 1 and Part 2)			

1	Donor's basic exclusion amount (see instructions)	**1**	
2	Total from column E, Parts 1 and 2	**2**	
3	Add lines 1 and 2	**3**	
4	Applicable credit on amount in line 3 (See *Table for Computing Gift Tax* in the instructions). Enter here and on line 7, Part 2—Tax Computation	**4**	

SCHEDULE D   Computation of Generation-Skipping Transfer Tax

Note. Inter vivos direct skips that are completely excluded by the GST exemption must still be fully reported (including value and exemptions claimed) on Schedule D.

Part 1—Generation-Skipping Transfers

A Item No. (from Schedule A, Part 2, col. A)	B Value (from Schedule A, Part 2, col. H)	C Nontaxable Portion of Transfer	D Net Transfer (subtract col. C from col. B)
1			
Gifts made by spouse (for gift splitting only)			
1	30,000	14,000	16,000
2	18,000	-0-	18,000

(If more space is needed, attach additional statements.)   Form **709** (2013)

Form 709 (2013)   Page **5**

Part 2—GST Exemption Reconciliation (Section 2631) and Section 2652(a)(3) Election

Check here ▶ ☐ if you are making a section 2652(a)(3) (special QTIP) election (see instructions)

Enter the item numbers from Schedule A of the gifts for which you are making this election ▶ ------------------------------

1	Maximum allowable exemption (see instructions)	1	5,250,000
2	Total exemption used for periods before filing this return	2	-0-
3	Exemption available for this return. Subtract line 2 from line 1	3	5,250,000
4	Exemption claimed on this return from Part 3, column C total, below	4	34,000
5	Automatic allocation of exemption to transfers reported on Schedule A, Part 3 (see instructions)	5	700,000
6	Exemption allocated to transfers not shown on line 4 or 5, above. **You must attach a "Notice of Allocation."** (see instructions)	6	-0-
7	Add lines 4, 5, and 6	7	734,000
8	Exemption available for future transfers. Subtract line 7 from line 3	8	4,516,000

Part 3—Tax Computation

A Item No. (from Schedule D, Part 1)	B Net Transfer (from Schedule D, Part 1, col. D)	C GST Exemption Allocated	D Divide col. C by col. B	E Inclusion Ratio (Subtract col. D from 1.000)	F Maximum Estate Tax Rate	G Applicable Rate (multiply col. E by col. F)	H Generation-Skipping Transfer Tax (multiply col. B by col. G)
1					40% (.40)		
					40% (.40)		
					40% (.40)		
					40% (.40)		
					40% (.40)		
					40% (.40)		
Gifts made by spouse (for gift splitting only)							
1	16,000	16,000	1	-0-	40% (.40)	-0-	-0-
2	18,000	18,000	1	-0-	40% (.40)	-0-	-0-
					40% (.40)		
					40% (.40)		
					40% (.40)		
					40% (.40)		
Total exemption claimed. Enter here and on Part 2, line 4, above. May not exceed Part 2, line 3, above		**Total generation-skipping transfer tax.** Enter here; on page 3, Schedule A, Part 4, line 10; and on page 1, Part 2—Tax Computation, line 16					-0-

(If more space is needed, attach additional statements.)   Form **709** (2013)

¶1715

¶1716 ELECTION STATEMENT FOR MAUREEN B. GIFT

NOTICE OF ALLOCATION OF GST EXEMPTION TO INDIRECT SKIP—REPORTED ON PART 3, SCHEDULE A—ITEM 1

Pursuant to IRC Sec. 2632(c)(1) and Reg. Sec. 26.2632-1(b)(4)(i), the taxpayer, Maureen B. Gift, hereby allocates $700,000 of GST exemption to the $700,000 worth of securities that she transferred to the Maureen B. Gift Family Trust f/b/o Emily Russ on June 15, 2013.

Trust Name—Maureen B. Gift Family Trust f/b/o Emily Russ

Trust ID No.—52-19202123

Amount of GST Allocation—$700,000

Describe Transfer—In Part 3, line 1 of Schedule A, the taxpayer reported the transfer of $700,000 worth of securities expected to appreciate to a newly-established family trust.

Maureen lists the transfer to the Maureen B. Gift Family Trust f/b/o Emily Russ in Part 3 of Schedule A because it is an indirect skip. The value of the trust at the date of the gift is $700,000 and she lists this amount in Columns F and H. Maureen wants to allocate GST exemption to the trust because the trust may be subject to GST when her daughter dies and the trust corpus is distributed to her granddaughter who is a skip person. Maureen checks the box in Column C of Part 3 of Schedule A on page 2 of Form 709. The box is marked 2632(c) election. IRC Sec. 2632(c) provides for the automatic allocation of the donor's unused GST exemption to indirect skips. There are three different elections that the transferor can make regarding the allocation of GST exemption. Maureen is making election 3 because she elects to treat the trust as a GST trust so GST exemption will automatically be applied to the transfer. By making Election 3, the transferor may elect to treat any trust as a GST trust for purposes of the automatic allocation rules. This election is timely if made on a timely filed gift tax return for the year for which the election is to become effective.

¶1716

¶1717 SAMPLE COMPLETED FORM 709 FOR MICHAEL A. GIFT

Form **709**	United States Gift (and Generation-Skipping Transfer) Tax Return	OMB No. 1545-0020

Department of the Treasury
Internal Revenue Service

▶ Information about Form 709 and its separate instructions is at *www.irs.gov/form709*.

(For gifts made during calendar year 2013)
▶ See instructions.

2013

1 Donor's first name and middle initial	2 Donor's last name	3 Donor's social security number
Michael A.	Gift	86755-4321

4 Address (number, street, and apartment number)	5 Legal residence (domicile)
1 highland Court	Baltimore County, Maryland

6 City or town, state or province, country, and ZIP or foreign postal code	7 Citizenship (see instructions)
Baltimore, Maryland 21231	USA

Part 1—General Information

		Yes	No
8	If the donor died during the year, check here ▶ ☐ and enter date of death ____		
9	If you extended the time to file this Form 709, check here ▶ ☐		
10	Enter the total number of donees listed on Schedule A. Count each person only once. ▶ 3		
11a	Have you (the donor) previously filed a Form 709 (or 709-A) for any other year? If "No," skip line 11b	✓	
b	Has your address changed since you last filed Form 709 (or 709-A)?		✓
12	Gifts by husband or wife to third parties. Do you consent to have the gifts (including generation-skipping transfers) made by you and by your spouse to third parties during the calendar year considered as made one-half by each of you? (see instructions.) (If the answer is "Yes," the following information must be furnished and your spouse must sign the consent shown below. If the answer is "No," skip lines 13–18.)	✓	
13	Name of consenting spouse Maureen B. Gift **14** SSN 123-44-5678		
15	Were you married to one another during the entire calendar year? (see instructions)	✓	
16	If 15 is "No," check whether ☐ married ☐ divorced or ☐ widowed/deceased, and give date (see instructions) ▶		
17	Will a gift tax return for this year be filed by your spouse? (If "Yes," mail both returns in the same envelope.)	✓	
18	Consent of Spouse. I consent to have the gifts (and generation-skipping transfers) made by me and by my spouse to third parties during the calendar year considered as made one-half by each of us. We are both aware of the joint and several liability for tax created by the execution of this consent.		

Consenting spouse's signature ▶   Date ▶

19	Have you applied a DSUE amount received from a predeceased spouse to a gift or gifts reported on this or a previous Form 709? If "Yes," complete Schedule C		

Part 2—Tax Computation

1	Enter the amount from Schedule A, Part 4, line 11	1	1,034,000
2	Enter the amount from Schedule B, line 3	2	-0-
3	Total taxable gifts. Add lines 1 and 2	3	1,034,000
4	Tax computed on amount on line 3 (see *Table for Computing Gift Tax* in instructions)	4	359,400
5	Tax computed on amount on line 2 (see *Table for Computing Gift Tax* in instructions)	5	-0-
6	Balance. Subtract line 5 from line 4	6	359,400
7	Applicable credit amount. If donor has DSUE amount from predeceased spouse(s), enter amount from Schedule C, line 4; otherwise, see instructions	7	2,045,800
8	Enter the applicable credit against tax allowable for all prior periods (from Sch. B, line 1, col. C)	8	-0-
9	Balance. Subtract line 8 from line 7. Do not enter less than zero	9	2,045,800
10	Enter 20% (.20) of the amount allowed as a specific exemption for gifts made after September 8, 1976, and before January 1, 1977 (see instructions)	10	-0-
11	Balance. Subtract line 10 from line 9. Do not enter less than zero	11	2,045,800
12	Applicable credit. Enter the smaller of line 6 or line 11	12	359,400
13	Credit for foreign gift taxes (see instructions)	13	
14	Total credits. Add lines 12 and 13	14	359,400
15	Balance. Subtract line 14 from line 6. Do not enter less than zero	15	-0-
16	Generation-skipping transfer taxes (from Schedule D, Part 3, col. H, Total)	16	-0-
17	Total tax. Add lines 15 and 16	17	-0-
18	Gift and generation-skipping transfer taxes prepaid with extension of time to file	18	-0-
19	If line 18 is less than line 17, enter **balance due** (see instructions)	19	-0-
20	If line 18 is greater than line 17, enter **amount to be refunded**	20	-0-

Under penalties of perjury, I declare that I have examined this return, including any accompanying schedules and statements, and to the best of my knowledge and belief, it is true, correct, and complete. Declaration of preparer (other than donor) is based on all information of which preparer has any knowledge.

Sign Here

May the IRS discuss this return with the preparer shown below (see instructions)? ☑Yes ☐No

▶ Signature of donor   Date

Paid Preparer Use Only

Print/Type preparer's name	Preparer's signature	Date	Check ☐ if self-employed	PTIN
Firm's name ▶			Firm's EIN ▶	
Firm's address ▶			Phone no.	

Attach check or money order here.

For Disclosure, Privacy Act, and Paperwork Reduction Act Notice, see the instructions for this form.   Cat. No. 16783M   Form **709** (2013)

¶1717

Form 709 (2013)   Page **2**

SCHEDULE A   **Computation of Taxable Gifts** (Including transfers in trust) (see instructions)

A   Does the value of any item listed on Schedule A reflect any valuation discount? If "Yes," attach explanation . . . . . .   Yes ☐   No ☐

B   ☐ ◄ Check here if you elect under section 529(c)(2)(B) to treat any transfers made this year to a qualified tuition program as made ratably over a 5-year period beginning this year. See instructions. Attach explanation.

Part 1—Gifts Subject Only to Gift Tax. Gifts less political organization, medical, and educational exclusions. (see instructions)

A Item number	B • Donee's name and address • Relationship to donor (if any) • Description of gift • If the gift was of securities, give CUSIP no. • If closely held entity, give EIN	C	D Donor's adjusted basis of gift	E Date of gift	F Value at date of gift	G For split gifts, enter ½ of column F	H Net transfer (subtract col. G from col. F)
1							

Gifts made by spouse —complete **only** if you are splitting gifts with your spouse and he/she also made gifts.

Total of Part 1. Add amounts from Part 1, column H . . . . ► | |

Part 2—Direct Skips. Gifts that are direct skips and are subject to both gift tax and generation-skipping transfer tax. You must list the gifts in chronological order.

A Item number	B • Donee's name and address • Relationship to donor (if any) • Description of gift • If the gift was of securities, give CUSIP no. • If closely held entity, give EIN	C 2632(b) election out	D Donor's adjusted basis of gift	E Date of gift	F Value at date of gift	G For split gifts, enter ½ of column F	H Net transfer (subtract col. G from col. F)
1							

Gifts made by spouse —complete **only** if you are splitting gifts with your spouse and he/she also made gifts.

2	Joel (Grandson) 550 shares of ABCo		40,000	1/12/13	60,000	30,000	30,000
	(CUSIP Number 987333)						
2	Amy Gift (Granddaughter)		36,000	2/23/13	36,000	18,000	18,000
	2013 Toyota Highlander Hybrid						

Total of Part 2. Add amounts from Part 2, column H . . . . ► | |

Part 3—Indirect Skips. Gifts to trusts that are currently subject to gift tax and may later be subject to generation-skipping transfer tax. You must list these gifts in chronological order.

A Item number	B • Donee's name and address • Relationship to donor (if any) • Description of gift • If the gift was of securities, give CUSIP no. • If closely held entity, give EIN	C 2632(c) election	D Donor's adjusted basis of gift	E Date of gift	F Value at date of gift	G For split gifts, enter ½ of column F	H Net transfer (subtract col. G from col. F)
1	Michael A. Gift Family Trust f/b/o David Gift	✓	450,000	3/21/13	1,000,000	-0-	1,000,000

Gifts made by spouse —complete **only** if you are splitting gifts with your spouse and he/she also made gifts.

Total of Part 3. Add amounts from Part 3, column H . . . . ► | 1,000,000

(If more space is needed, attach additional statements.)   Form **709** (2013)

¶1717

Part 4—Taxable Gift Reconciliation

1	Total value of gifts of donor. Add totals from column H of Parts 1, 2, and 3	1	1,048,000
2	Total annual exclusions for gifts listed on line 1 (see instructions)	2	14,000
3	Total included amount of gifts. Subtract line 2 from line 1	3	1,034,000

Deductions (see instructions)

4	Gifts of interests to spouse for which a marital deduction will be claimed, based on item numbers _____ of Schedule A . .	4		
5	Exclusions attributable to gifts on line 4	5		
6	Marital deduction. Subtract line 5 from line 4	6		
7	Charitable deduction, based on item nos. _____ less exclusions .	7		
8	Total deductions. Add lines 6 and 7		8	-0-
9	Subtract line 8 from line 3		9	1,034,000
10	Generation-skipping transfer taxes payable with this Form 709 (from Schedule D, Part 3, col. H, Total) . .		10	-0-
11	**Taxable gifts.** Add lines 9 and 10. Enter here and on page 1, Part 2—Tax Computation, line 1		11	1,034,000

Terminable Interest (QTIP) Marital Deduction. (see instructions for Schedule A, Part 4, line 4)

If a trust (or other property) meets the requirements of qualified terminable interest property under section 2523(f), and:

   a. The trust (or other property) is listed on Schedule A, and

   b. The value of the trust (or other property) is entered in whole or in part as a deduction on Schedule A, Part 4, line 4,

then the donor shall be deemed to have made an election to have such trust (or other property) treated as qualified terminable interest property under section 2523(f).

If less than the entire value of the trust (or other property) that the donor has included in Parts 1 and 3 of Schedule A is entered as a deduction on line 4, the donor shall be considered to have made an election only as to a fraction of the trust (or other property). The numerator of this fraction is equal to the amount of the trust (or other property) deducted on Schedule A, Part 4, line 6. The denominator is equal to the total value of the trust (or other property) listed in Parts 1 and 3 of Schedule A.

If you make the QTIP election, the terminable interest property involved will be included in your spouse's gross estate upon his or her death (section 2044). See instructions for line 4 of Schedule A. If your spouse disposes (by gift or otherwise) of all or part of the qualifying life income interest, he or she will be considered to have made a transfer of the entire property that is subject to the gift tax. See *Transfer of Certain Life Estates Received From Spouse* in the instructions.

12   Election Out of QTIP Treatment of Annuities

☐   ◀Check here if you elect under section 2523(f)(6) **not** to treat as qualified terminable interest property any joint and survivor annuities that are reported on Schedule A and would otherwise be treated as qualified terminable interest property under section 2523(f). See instructions. Enter the item numbers from Schedule A for the annuities for which you are making this election ▶ _____

SCHEDULE B   Gifts From Prior Periods

If you answered "Yes," on line 11a of page 1, Part 1, see the instructions for completing Schedule B. If you answered "No," skip to the Tax Computation on page 1 (or Schedules C or D, if applicable). Complete Schedule A before beginning Schedule B. See instructions for recalculation of the column C amounts. Attach calculations.

A Calendar year or calendar quarter (see instructions)	B Internal Revenue office where prior return was filed	C Amount of applicable credit (unified credit) against gift tax for periods after December 31, 1976	D Amount of specific exemption for prior periods ending before January 1, 1977	E Amount of taxable gifts

1	Totals for prior periods 1		
2	Amount, if any, by which total specific exemption, line 1, column D is more than $30,000 2		
3	Total amount of taxable gifts for prior periods. Add amount on line 1, column E and amount, if any, on line 2. Enter here and on page 1, Part 2—Tax Computation, line 2 3		-0-

(If more space is needed, attach additional statements.)   Form **709** (2013)

Form 709 (2013)   Page **4**

SCHEDULE C   **Deceased Spousal Unused Exclusion (DSUE) Amount**

Provide the following information to determine the DSUE amount and applicable credit received from prior spouses. Complete Schedule A before beginning Schedule C.

A Name of Deceased Spouse (dates of death after December 31, 2010 only)	B Date of Death	C Portability Election Made?		D If "Yes," DSUE Amount Received from Spouse	E DSUE Amount Applied by Donor to Lifetime Gifts (list current and prior gifts)	F Date of Gift(s) (enter as mm/dd/yy for Part 1 and as yyyy for Part 2)
		Yes	No			
Part 1—DSUE RECEIVED FROM LAST DECEASED SPOUSE						
Part 2—DSUE RECEIVED FROM PREDECEASED SPOUSE(S)						

TOTAL (for all DSUE amounts applied for Part 1 and Part 2)		

1	Donor's basic exclusion amount (see instructions)	**1**	
2	Total from column E, Parts 1 and 2	**2**	
3	Add lines 1 and 2	**3**	
4	Applicable credit on amount in line 3 (See *Table for Computing Gift Tax* in the instructions). Enter here and on line 7, Part 2—Tax Computation	**4**	

SCHEDULE D   **Computation of Generation-Skipping Transfer Tax**

Note. Inter vivos direct skips that are completely excluded by the GST exemption must still be fully reported (including value and exemptions claimed) on Schedule D.

Part 1—Generation-Skipping Transfers

A Item No. (from Schedule A, Part 2, col. A)	B Value (from Schedule A, Part 2, col. H)	C Nontaxable Portion of Transfer	D Net Transfer (subtract col. C from col. B)
1			
Gifts made by spouse (for gift splitting only)			
1	30,000	14,000	16,000
2	18,000	-0-	18,000

(If more space is needed, attach additional statements.)   Form **709** (2013)

¶1717

Part 2—GST Exemption Reconciliation (Section 2631) and Section 2652(a)(3) Election

Check here ▶ ☐ if you are making a section 2652(a)(3) (special QTIP) election (see instructions)

Enter the item numbers from Schedule A of the gifts for which you are making this election ▶ ----------------------------

1	Maximum allowable exemption (see instructions)	1	5,250,000
2	Total exemption used for periods before filing this return	2	-0-
3	Exemption available for this return. Subtract line 2 from line 1	3	5,250,000
4	Exemption claimed on this return from Part 3, column C total, below	4	34,000
5	Automatic allocation of exemption to transfers reported on Schedule A, Part 3 (see instructions)	5	-0-
6	Exemption allocated to transfers not shown on line 4 or 5, above. **You must attach a "Notice of Allocation."** (see instructions)	6	-0-
7	Add lines 4, 5, and 6	7	34,000
8	Exemption available for future transfers. Subtract line 7 from line 3	8	5,216,000

Part 3—Tax Computation

A Item No. (from Schedule D, Part 1)	B Net Transfer (from Schedule D, Part 1, col. D)	C GST Exemption Allocated	D Divide col. C by col. B	E Inclusion Ratio (Subtract col. D from 1.000)	F Maximum Estate Tax Rate	G Applicable Rate (multiply col. E by col. F)	H Generation-Skipping Transfer Tax (multiply col. B by col. G)
1					40% (.40)		
					40% (.40)		
					40% (.40)		
					40% (.40)		
					40% (.40)		
					40% (.40)		
Gifts made by spouse (for gift splitting only)							
1	16,000	16,000	1	-0-	40% (.40)	-0-	-0-
2	18,000	18,000	1	-0-	40% (.40)	-0-	-0-
					40% (.40)		
					40% (.40)		
					40% (.40)		
					40% (.40)		

Total exemption claimed. Enter here and on Part 2, line 4, above. May not exceed Part 2, line 3, above	**Total generation-skipping transfer tax.** Enter here; on page 3, Schedule A, Part 4, line 10; and on page 1, Part 2—Tax Computation, line 16	-0-

(If more space is needed, attach additional statements.)   Form **709** (2013)

¶1718 ELECTION STATEMENT FOR MICHAEL A. GIFT

ELECTION NOT TO HAVE THE AUTOMATIC GST—TAX EXEMPTION ALLO-CATION RULES APPLY TO CURRENT-YEAR TRANSFER REPORTED ON SCHEDULE A—PART 3, ITEM 1

Pursuant to IRC Sec. 2632(c)(5)(A)(i) and Reg. Sec. 26.2632-1(b)(2)(iii)(A)(2), the taxpayer, Michael A. Gift, hereby elects not to have the automatic GST allocation rules apply to the $1 million transferred to the Michael A Gift Family Trust f/b/o David Gift on March 21, 2013. The election out of the automatic allocation rules will be effective only for Michael A. Gift's March 21, 2013 transfer.

Trust Name—Michael A. Gift Family Trust f/b/o David Gift

Trust ID No.—52-19191919

Describe Transfer—In Part 3 of Schedule A, the taxpayer reported the transfer of $1 million worth of securities expected to appreciate to a newly-established family trust that will pay all of its income to his son from a prior marriage, David Gift for life. The trustee can invade principal for David's benefit, subject to an ascertainable standard. At David's death, the trust remainder will pass to Michael's grandson, Adam. The taxpayer has elected out of automatic allocation of GST exemption to this indirect skip by checking the box C in Part 3 of Schedule A. Box C is marked IRC Sec. 2632(c) election.

¶1719   IRS INSTRUCTIONS FOR FORM 709

20**13**

Department of the Treasury
Internal Revenue Service

Instructions for Form 709

United States Gift (and Generation-Skipping Transfer) Tax Return

For gifts made during calendar year 2013.

Section references are to the Internal Revenue Code unless otherwise noted.

Future Developments

For the latest information about developments related to Form 709 and its instructions, such as legislation enacted after they were published, go to *www.irs.gov/form709*.

For Disclosure, Privacy Act, and Paperwork Reduction Act Notice, see below.

For Gifts Made		Use Revision of Form 709 Dated
After	and Before	
-----	January 1, 1982	November 1981
December 31, 1981	January 1, 1987	January 1987
December 31, 1986	January 1, 1989	December 1988
December 31, 1988	January 1, 1990	December 1989
December 31, 1989	October 9, 1990	October 1990
October 8, 1990	January 1, 1992	November 1991
December 31, 1992	January 1, 1998	December 1996
December 31, 1997	-----	*

* Use the corresponding annual form.

What's New

- The annual gift exclusion for 2013 increased to $14,000. See *Annual Exclusion*, later.
- For gifts made to spouses who are not U.S. citizens, the annual exclusion has increased to $143,000. See *Nonresidents not Citizens of the United States*, later.
- The top rate for gifts and generation-skipping transfers has increased to 40%. See *Table for Computing Gift Tax*, later.
- The basic credit amount for 2013 is $2,045,800. See *Table of Basic Exclusion and Credit Amounts*, later.
- The applicable exclusion amount consists of the basic exclusion amount ($5,250,000 in 2013) and, in the case of a surviving spouse, any unused exclusion

Jan 14, 2014

amount of the last deceased spouse (who died after December 31, 2010). The executor of the predeceased spouse's estate must have elected on a timely and complete Form 706 to allow the donor to use the predeceased spouse's unused exclusion amount.

Photographs of Missing Children

The IRS is a proud partner with the National Center for Missing and Exploited Children. Photographs of missing children selected by the Center may appear in instructions on pages that would otherwise be blank. You can help bring these children home by looking at the photographs and calling 1-800-THE-LOST (1-800-843-5678) if you recognize a child.

General Instructions

Purpose of Form

Use Form 709 to report the following:
- Transfers subject to the federal gift and certain generation-skipping transfer (GST) taxes and to figure the tax due, if any, on those transfers, and
- Allocation of the lifetime GST exemption to property transferred during the transferor's lifetime. (For more details, see *Part 2—GST Exemption Reconciliation*, later, and Regulations section 26.2632-1.)

 All gift and GST taxes must be computed and filed on a calendar year basis. List all reportable gifts made during the calendar year on one Form 709. This means you must file a separate return for each calendar year a reportable gift is given (for example, a gift given in 2013 must be reported on a 2013 Form 709). Do not file more than one Form 709 for any one calendar year.

How To Complete Form 709

1. Determine whether you are required to file Form 709.

2. Determine what gifts you must report.

3. Decide whether you and your spouse, if any, will elect to split gifts for the year.

4. Complete lines 1 through 19 of Part 1—General Information.

Cat. No. 16784X

5. List each gift on Part 1, 2, or 3 of Schedule A, as appropriate.

6. Complete Schedules B, C, and D, as applicable.

7. If the gift was listed on Part 2 or 3 of Schedule A, complete the necessary portions of Schedule D.

8. Complete Schedule A, Part 4.

9. Complete Part 2—Tax Computation.

10. Sign and date the return.

> **TIP** *Remember, if you are splitting gifts, your spouse must sign line 18, in Part 1—General Information.*

Who Must File

In general. If you are a citizen or resident of the United States, you must file a gift tax return (whether or not any tax is ultimately due) in the following situations.
- If you gave gifts to someone in 2013 totalling more than $14,000 (other than to your spouse), you probably must file Form 709. But see *Transfers Not Subject to Gift Tax* and *Gifts to Spouse*, later, for more information on specific gifts that are not taxable.
- Certain gifts, called future interests, are not subject to the $14,000 annual exclusion and you must file Form 709 even if the gift was under $14,000. See *Annual Exclusion*, later.
- Spouses may not file a joint gift tax return. Each individual is responsible for his or her own Form 709.
- You must file a gift tax return to split gifts with your spouse (regardless of their amount) as described in *Part 1—General Information*.
- If a gift is of community property, it is considered made one-half by each spouse. For example, a gift of $100,000 of community property is considered a gift of $50,000 made by each spouse, and each spouse must file a gift tax return.
- Likewise, each spouse must file a gift tax return if they have made a gift of property held by them as joint tenants or tenants by the entirety.
- Only individuals are required to file gift tax returns. If a trust, estate, partnership, or corporation makes a gift, the individual beneficiaries, partners, or stockholders are considered donors and may be liable for the gift and GST taxes.

- The donor is responsible for paying the gift tax. However, if the donor does not pay the tax, the person receiving the gift may have to pay the tax.
- If a donor dies before filing a return, the donor's executor must file the return.

Who does not need to file. If you meet all of the following requirements, you are not required to file Form 709:
- You made no gifts during the year to your spouse,
- You did not give more than $14,000 to any one donee, and
- All the gifts you made were of present interests.

Gifts to charities. If the only gifts you made during the year are deductible as gifts to charities, you do not need to file a return as long as you transferred your entire interest in the property to qualifying charities. If you transferred only a partial interest, or transferred part of your interest to someone other than a charity, you must still file a return and report all of your gifts to charities.

If you are required to file a return to report noncharitable gifts and you made gifts to charities, you must include all of your gifts to charities on the return.

Transfers Subject to the Gift Tax

Generally, the federal gift tax applies to any transfer by gift of real or personal property, whether tangible or intangible, that you made directly or indirectly, in trust, or by any other means.

The gift tax applies not only to the free transfer of any kind of property, but also to sales or exchanges, not made in the ordinary course of business, where value of the money (or property) received is less than the value of what is sold or exchanged. The gift tax is in addition to any other tax, such as federal income tax, paid or due on the transfer.

The exercise or release of a general power of appointment may be a gift by the individual possessing the power. General powers of appointment are those in which the holders of the power can appoint the property under the power to themselves, their creditors, their estates, or the creditors of their estates. To qualify as a power of appointment, it must be created by someone other than the holder of the power.

The gift tax may also apply to forgiving a debt, to making an interest-free or below market interest rate loan, to transferring the benefits of an insurance policy, to certain property settlements in divorce cases, and to giving up of some amount of annuity in exchange for the creation of a survivor annuity.

Bonds that are exempt from federal income taxes are not exempt from federal gift taxes.

Sections 2701 and 2702 provide rules for determining whether certain transfers to a family member of interests in corporations, partnerships, and trusts are gifts. The rules of section 2704 determine whether the lapse of any voting or liquidation right is a gift.

Gifts to your spouse. You must file a gift tax return if you made any gift to your spouse of a terminable interest that does not meet the exception described in *Life estate with power of appointment*, or if your spouse is not a U.S. citizen and the total gifts you made to your spouse during the year exceed $143,000.

You must also file a gift tax return to make the Qualified Terminable Interest Property (QTIP) election described under *Line 12. Election Out of QTIP Treatment of Annuities*.

Except as described above, you do not have to file a gift tax return to report gifts to your spouse regardless of the amount of these gifts and regardless of whether the gifts are present or future interests.

Transfers Not Subject to the Gift Tax

Three types of transfers are not subject to the gift tax. These are:
- Transfers to political organizations,
- Payments that qualify for the educational exclusion, and
- Payments that qualify for the medical exclusion.

These transfers are not "gifts" as that term is used on Form 709 and its instructions. You need not file a Form 709 to report these transfers and should not list them on Schedule A of Form 709 if you do file Form 709.

Political organizations. The gift tax does not apply to a transfer to a political organization (defined in section 527(e)(1)) for the use of the organization.

Educational exclusion. The gift tax does not apply to an amount you paid on behalf of an individual to a qualifying domestic or foreign educational organization as tuition for the education or training of the individual. A qualifying educational organization is one that normally maintains a regular faculty and curriculum and normally has a regularly enrolled body of pupils or students in attendance at the place where its educational activities are regularly carried on. See section 170(b)(1)(A)(ii) and its regulations.

The payment must be made directly to the qualifying educational organization and it must be for tuition. No educational exclusion is allowed for amounts paid for books, supplies, room and board, or other similar expenses that are not direct tuition costs. To the extent that the payment to the educational organization was for something other than tuition, it is a gift to the individual for whose benefit it was made, and may be offset by the annual exclusion if it is otherwise available.

Contributions to a qualified tuition program (QTP) on behalf of a designated beneficiary do not qualify for the educational exclusion. See *Line B—Qualified Tuition Programs (529 Plans or Programs)* in the instructions for Schedule A, later.

Medical exclusion. The gift tax does not apply to an amount you paid on behalf of an individual to a person or institution that provided medical care for the individual. The payment must be to the care provider. The medical care must meet the requirements of section 213(d) (definition of medical care for income tax deduction purposes). Medical care includes expenses incurred for the diagnosis, cure, mitigation, treatment, or prevention of disease, or for the purpose of affecting any structure or function of the body, or for transportation primarily for and essential to medical care. Medical care also includes amounts paid for medical insurance on behalf of any individual.

The medical exclusion does not apply to amounts paid for medical care that are reimbursed by the donee's insurance. If payment for a medical expense is reimbursed by the donee's insurance company, your payment for that expense, to the extent of the reimbursed amount, is not eligible for the medical exclusion and you are considered to have made a gift to the donee of the reimbursed amount.

To the extent that the payment was for something other than medical care, it is a gift to the individual on whose behalf the payment was made and may be offset by the annual exclusion if it is otherwise available.

The medical and educational exclusions are allowed without regard to the relationship between you and the donee. For examples illustrating these exclusions, see Regulations section 25.2503-6(c).

Qualified disclaimers. A donee's refusal to accept a gift is called a *disclaimer*. If a person makes a qualified disclaimer of any interest in property, the property will be treated as if it had never been transferred to that person. Accordingly, the disclaimant is not regarded as making a gift to the person who receives the property because of the qualified disclaimer.

Requirements. To be a qualified disclaimer, a refusal to accept an interest in property must meet the following conditions:

-2-

1. The refusal must be in writing.

2. The refusal must be received by the donor, the legal representative of the donor, the holder of the legal title to the property disclaimed, or the person in possession of the property within 9 months after the later of:

   a. the day the transfer creating the interest is made or

   b. the day the disclaimant reaches age 21.

3. The disclaimant must not have accepted the interest or any of its benefits.

4. As a result of the refusal, the interest must pass without any direction from the disclaimant to either:

   a. the spouse of the decedent or

   b. a person other than the disclaimant, and

5. The refusal must be irrevocable and unqualified.

The 9-month period for making the disclaimer generally is determined separately for each taxable transfer. For gifts, the period begins on the date the transfer is a completed transfer for gift tax purposes.

Annual Exclusion

The first $14,000 of gifts of present interest to each donee during the calendar year is subtracted from total gifts in figuring the amount of taxable gifts. For a gift in trust, each beneficiary of the trust is treated as a separate donee for purposes of the annual exclusion.

All of the gifts made during the calendar year to a donee are fully excluded under the annual exclusion if they are all gifts of present interest and they total $14,000 or less.

Note. For gifts made to spouses who are not U.S. citizens, the annual exclusion has been increased to $143,000, provided the additional (above the $14,000 annual exclusion) $129,000 gift would otherwise qualify for the gift tax marital deduction (as described in the *Schedule A, Part 4, line 4* instructions, later).

A gift of a future interest cannot be excluded under the annual exclusion.

A gift is considered a present interest if the donee has all immediate rights to the use, possession, and enjoyment of the property or income from the property.

A gift is considered a future interest if the donee's rights to the use, possession, and enjoyment of the property or income from the property will not begin until some future date. Future interests include reversions, remainders, and other similar interests or estates.

A contribution to a QTP on behalf of a designated beneficiary is considered a gift of a present interest.

A gift to a minor is considered a present interest if all of the following conditions are met:

1. Both the property and its income may be expended by, or for the benefit of, the minor before the minor reaches age 21;

2. All remaining property and its income must pass to the minor on the minor's 21st birthday; and

3. If the minor dies before the age of 21, the property and its income will be payable either to the minor's estate or to whomever the minor may appoint under a general power of appointment.

The gift of a present interest to more than one donee as joint tenants qualifies for the annual exclusion for each donee.

Nonresidents not Citizens of the United States

Nonresidents not citizens of the United States are subject to gift and GST taxes for gifts of tangible property situated in the United States. A person is considered a *nonresident not a citizen of the United States* if he or she, at the time the gift is made, (1) was not a citizen of the United States and did not reside there or (2) was domiciled in a United States possession and acquired citizenship solely by reason of birth or residence in the possession. Under certain circumstances, they are also subject to gift and GST taxes for gifts of intangible property. See section 2501(a).

If you are a nonresident not a citizen of the United States who made a gift subject to gift tax, you must file a gift tax return where:
- You gave any gifts of future interests,
- Your gifts of present interests to any donee other than your spouse total more than $14,000, or
- Your outright gifts to your spouse who is not a U.S. citizen total more than $143,000.

Transfers Subject to the GST Tax

You must report on Form 709 the GST tax imposed on inter vivos direct skips. An *inter vivos direct skip* is a transfer made during the donor's lifetime that is:
- Subject to the gift tax,
- Of an interest in property, and
- Made to a skip person. (See *Gifts Subject to Both Gift and GST Taxes*, later.)

A transfer is subject to the gift tax if it is required to be reported on Schedule A of Form 709 under the rules contained in the gift tax portions of these instructions,

including the split gift rules. Therefore, transfers made to political organizations, transfers that qualify for the medical or educational exclusions, transfers that are fully excluded under the annual exclusion, and most transfers made to your spouse are not subject to the GST tax.

Transfers subject to the GST tax are described in further detail in the instructions.

 Certain transfers, particularly transfers to a trust, that are not subject to gift tax and are therefore not subject to the GST tax on Form 709 may be subject to the GST tax at a later date. This is true even if the transfer is less than the $14,000 annual exclusion. In this instance, you may want to apply a GST exemption amount to the transfer on this return or on a Notice of Allocation. For more information, see Schedule D, Part 2—GST Exemption Reconciliation and Schedule A, Part 3—Indirect Skips.

Transfers Subject to an Estate Tax Inclusion Period (ETIP)

Certain transfers that are direct skips receive special treatment. If the transferred property would have been includible in the donor's estate if the donor had died immediately after the transfer (for a reason other than the donor having died within 3 years of making the gift), the direct skip will be treated as having been made at the end of the ETIP rather than at the time of the actual transfer.

For example, if A transferred her house to her granddaughter, B, but retained the right to live in the house until her death (a retained life estate), the value of the house would be includible in A's estate if she died while still holding the life estate. In this case, the transfer to B is a completed gift (it is a transfer of a future interest) and must be reported on Part 1 of Schedule A. The GST portion of the transfer would not be reported until A died or otherwise gave up her life estate in the house.

Report the gift portion of such a transfer on Schedule A, Part 1, at the time of the actual transfer. Report the GST portion on Schedule A, Part 2, but only at the close of the ETIP. Use Form 709 only to report those transfers where the ETIP closed due to something other than the donor's death. (If the ETIP closed as the result of the donor's death, report the transfer on Form 706, United States Estate (and Generation-Skipping Transfer) Tax Return.)

If you are filing this Form 709 solely to report the GST portion of transfers subject to an ETIP, complete the form as you normally would with the following exceptions:

1. Write "ETIP" at the top of page 1;

2. Complete only lines 1 through 6, 8, and 9 of Part 1—General Information;

3. Complete Schedule A, Part 2, as explained in the instructions for that schedule;

4. Complete Schedule D. Complete Column B of Schedule D, Part 1, as explained in the instructions for that schedule;

5. Complete only lines 10 and 11 of Schedule A, Part 4; and

6. Complete Part 2—Tax Computation.

Section 2701 Elections

The special valuation rules of section 2701 contain three elections that you must make with Form 709:

1. A transferor may elect to treat a qualified payment right he or she holds (and all other rights of the same class) as other than a qualified payment right;

2. A person may elect to treat a distribution right held by that person in a controlled entity as a qualified payment right; and,

3. An interest holder may elect to treat as a taxable event the payment of a qualified payment that occurs more than 4 years after its due date.

The elections described in (1) and (2) above must be made on the Form 709 that is filed by the transferor to report the transfer that is being valued under section 2701. The elections are made by attaching a statement to Form 709. For information on what must be in the statement and for definitions and other details on the elections, see section 2701 and Regulations section 25.2701-2(c).

The election described in (3) above may be made by attaching a statement to the Form 709 filed by the recipient of the qualified payment for the year the payment is received. If the election is made on a timely filed return, the taxable event is deemed to occur on the date the qualified payment is received. If it is made on a late filed return, the taxable event is deemed to occur on the first day of the month immediately preceding the month in which the return is filed. For information on what must be in the statement and for definitions and other details on this election, see section 2701 and Regulations section 25.2701-4(d).

All of the elections may be revoked only with the consent of the IRS.

When To File

Form 709 is an annual return.

Generally, you must file the Form 709 no earlier than January 1, but not later than April 15, of the year after the gift was made. However, in instances when April 15 falls on a Saturday, Sunday, or legal holiday, Form 709 will be due on the next business day. See section 7503.

If the donor died during 2013, the executor must file the donor's 2013 Form 709 not later than the earlier of:
*   The due date (with extensions) for filing the donor's estate tax return, or
*   April 15, 2014, or the extended due date granted for filing the donor's gift tax return.

Extension of Time To File

There are two methods of extending the time to file the gift tax return. Neither method extends the time to pay the gift or GST taxes. If you want an extension of time to pay the gift or GST taxes, you must request that separately. See Regulations section 25.6161-1.

By extending the time to file your income tax return. Any extension of time granted for filing your calendar year 2013 federal income tax return will also automatically extend the time to file your 2013 federal gift tax return. Income tax extensions are made by using Form 4868, Application for Automatic Extension of Time To File U.S. Individual Income Tax Return, or Form 2350, Application for Extension of Time To File U.S. Income Tax Return. You may only use these forms to extend the time for filing your gift tax return if you are also requesting an extension of time to file your income tax return.

By filing Form 8892. If you do not request an extension for your income tax return, use Form 8892, Application for Automatic Extension of Time To File Form 709 and/or Payment of Gift/Generation-Skipping Transfer Tax, to request an automatic 6-month extension of time to file your federal gift tax return. In addition to containing an extension request, Form 8892 also serves as a payment voucher (Form 8892-V) for a balance due on federal gift taxes for which you are extending the time to file. For more information, see Form 8892.

Private delivery services

You can use certain private delivery services designated by the IRS to meet the "timely mailing as timely filing/paying" rule for tax returns and payments. These private delivery services include only the following:
*   DHL Express (DHL): DHL Same Day Service.
*   Federal Express (FedEx): FedEx Priority Overnight, FedEx Standard Overnight, FedEx 2Day, FedEx International Priority, FedEx International First.
*   United Parcel Service (UPS): UPS Next Day Air, UPS Next Day Air Saver, UPS 2nd Day Air, UPS 2nd Day Air A.M., UPS Worldwide Express Plus, and UPS Worldwide Express.

The private delivery service can tell you how to get written proof of the mailing date.

Where To File

File Form 709 at the following address:

Department of the Treasury
Internal Revenue Service Center
Cincinnati, OH 45999

If submitting Form 709 by private delivery service (discussed earlier), mail to:

Internal Revenue Service
201 West Rivercenter Boulevard
Covington, KY 41011

 See the Caution under Lines 12 – 18. Split Gifts, later, before you mail the return.

Adequate Disclosure

 To begin the running of the statute of limitations for a gift, the gift must be adequately disclosed on Form 709 (or an attached statement) filed for the year of the gift.

In general, a gift will be considered adequately disclosed if the return or statement includes the following:
*   A full and complete Form 709.
*   A description of the transferred property and any consideration received by the donor;
*   The identity of, and relationship between, the donor and each donee;
*   If the property is transferred in trust, the trust's employer identification number (EIN) and a brief description of the terms of the trust (or a copy of the trust instrument in lieu of the description); and
*   Either a qualified appraisal or a detailed description of the method used to determine the fair market value of the gift.

See Regulations section 301.6501(c)-1(e) and (f) for details, including what constitutes a qualified appraisal, the information required if no appraisal is provided, and the information required for transfers under sections 2701 and 2702.

Penalties

Late filing and late payment. Section 6651 imposes penalties for both late filing and late payment, unless there is reasonable cause for the delay.

Reasonable cause determinations. If you receive a notice about penalties after you file Form 709, send an explanation

-4-

and we will determine if you meet reasonable cause criteria. Do **not** attach an explanation when you file Form 709.

There are also penalties for willful failure to file a return on time, willful attempt to evade or defeat payment of tax, and valuation understatements that cause an underpayment of the tax. A substantial valuation understatement occurs when the reported value of property entered on Form 709 is 65% or less of the actual value of the property. A gross valuation understatement occurs when the reported value listed on the Form 709 is 40% or less of the actual value of the property.

Return preparer. Penalties may also be applied to tax return preparers, including gift tax return preparers.

The Small Business and Work Opportunity Tax Act of 2007 extended section 6694 income tax return preparer penalties to all tax return preparers, including gift tax return preparers. Now, gift tax return preparers who prepare any return or claim for refund with an understatement of tax liability due to willful or reckless conduct can be penalized $5,000 or 50% of the income received (or income to be received), whichever is greater, for each return. See section 6694, its regulations, and Ann. 2009-15, 2009-11 I.R.B. 687 (available at *www.irs.gov/pub/irs-irbs/irb09-11.pdf*) for more information.

Joint Tenancy

If you buy property with your own funds and the title to the property is held by you and a donee as joint tenants with right of survivorship and if either you or the donee may give up those rights by severing your interest, you have made a gift to the donee in the amount of half the value of the property.

If you create a joint bank account for yourself and a donee (or a similar kind of ownership by which you can get back the entire fund without the donee's consent), you have made a gift to the donee when the donee draws on the account for his or her own benefit. The amount of the gift is the amount that the donee took out without any obligation to repay you.

If you buy a U.S. savings bond registered as payable to yourself or a donee, there is a gift to the donee when he or she cashes the bond without any obligation to account to you.

Transfer of Certain Life Estates Received From Spouse

If you received a qualified terminable interest (see *Line 12. Election Out of QTIP Treatment of Annuities* in the instructions for Schedule A, later) from your spouse for which a marital deduction was elected on

your spouse's estate or gift tax return, you will be subject to the gift tax (and GST tax, if applicable) if you dispose of all or part of your life income interest (by gift, sale, or otherwise).

Generally, the entire value of the property transferred less:

1. The amount you received (if any) for the life income interest, and

2. The amount (if any) determined after the application of section 2702, valuing certain retained interests at zero, for the life income interest you retained after the transfer,

will be treated as a taxable gift.

That portion of the property's value that is attributable to the remainder interest is a gift of a future interest for which no annual exclusion is allowed. To the extent you made a gift of the life income interest, you may claim an annual exclusion, treating the person to whom you transferred the interest as the donee for purposes of figuring the annual exclusion.

Specific Instructions

Part 1—General Information

Lines 4 and 6. Address. Enter your current mailing address.

Foreign address. If your address is outside of the United States or its possessions or territories, enter the information as follows: city, province or state, and name of country. Follow the country's practice for entering the postal code. Do not abbreviate the country name.

Line 5. Legal residence (domicile). In general, your legal residence (also known as your domicile) is acquired by living in a place, for even a brief period of time, with no definite present intention of moving from that place.

Enter the state of the United States (including the District of Columbia) or a foreign country in which you legally reside or are domiciled at the time of the gift.

Line 7. Citizenship. Enter your citizenship.

The term *citizen of the United States* includes a person who, at the time of making the gift:
• Was domiciled in a possession of the United States,
• Was a U.S. citizen, and
• Became a U.S. citizen for a reason other than being a citizen of a U.S. possession or being born or residing in a possession.

A *nonresident not a citizen of the United States* includes a person who, at the time of making the gift:
• Was domiciled in a possession of the United States,
• Was a U.S. citizen, and
• Became a U.S. citizen only because he or she was a citizen of a possession or was born or resided in a possession.

Lines 12–18. Split Gifts

 A married couple may not file a joint gift tax return. However, if after reading the instructions below, you and your spouse agree to split your gifts, you should file both of your individual gift tax returns together (that is, in the same envelope) to help the IRS process the returns and to avoid correspondence from the IRS.

If you and your spouse agree, all gifts (including gifts of property held with your spouse as joint tenants or tenants by the entirety) either of you make to third parties during the calendar year will be considered as made one-half by each of you if:
• You and your spouse were married to one another at the time of the gift;
• If divorced or widowed after the gift, you did not remarry during the rest of the calendar year;
• Neither of you was a nonresident not a citizen of the United States at the time of the gift; and
• You did not give your spouse a general power of appointment over the property interest transferred.

If you transferred property partly to your spouse and partly to third parties, you can only split the gifts if the interest transferred to the third parties is ascertainable at the time of the gift.

The consent is effective for the entire calendar year; therefore, all gifts made by both you and your spouse to third parties during the calendar year (while you were married) must be split.

If the consent is effective, the liability for the entire gift tax of each spouse is joint and several.

If you meet these requirements and want your gifts to be considered made one-half by you and one-half by your spouse, check the "Yes" box on line 12; complete lines 13 through 17; and have your spouse sign the consent on line 18.

If you are not married or do not wish to split gifts, skip to line 19.

Line 15. If you were married to one another for all of 2013, check the "Yes" box and skip to line 17. If you were married for only part of the year, check the "No" box and go to line 16. If you were divorced or widowed after you made the

-5-

gift, you cannot elect to split gifts if you remarried before the end of 2013.

Line 16. Check the box that explains the change in your marital status during the year and give the date you were married, divorced, or widowed.

Consent of Spouse

Your spouse must sign the consent for your gift-splitting election to be valid. The consent may generally be signed at any time after the end of the calendar year. However, there are two exceptions.

1. The consent may not be signed after April 15 following the end of the year in which the gift was made. But, if neither you nor your spouse has filed a gift tax return for the year on or before that date, the consent must be made on the first gift tax return for the year filed by either of you.

2. The consent may not be signed after a notice of deficiency for the gift tax for the year has been sent to either you or your spouse.

The executor for a deceased spouse or the guardian for a legally incompetent spouse may sign the consent.

When the Consenting Spouse Must Also File a Gift Tax Return

In general, if you and your spouse elect gift splitting, then both spouses must file his or her own, individual, gift tax return.

However, only one spouse must file a return if the requirements of either of the exceptions below are met. In the exceptions below, *gifts* means transfers (or parts of transfers) that do not qualify for the political organization, educational, or medical exclusions.

Exception 1. During the calendar year:
• Only one spouse made any gifts,
• The total value of these gifts to each third-party donee does not exceed $28,000, and
• All of the gifts were of present interests.

Exception 2. During the calendar year:
• Only one spouse (the donor spouse) made gifts of more than $14,000 but not more than $28,000 to any third-party donee,
• The only gifts made by the other spouse (the consenting spouse) were gifts of not more than $14,000 to third-party donees other than those to whom the donor spouse made gifts, and
• All of the gifts by both spouses were of present interests.

If either of the above exceptions is met, only the donor spouse must file a return and the consenting spouse signifies consent on that return.

Specific instructions for *Part 2—Tax Computation* are discussed later. Because you must complete Schedules A, B, C, and D to fill out *Part 2*, you will find instructions for these schedules below.

Line 19. Application of DSUE Amount

If the donor is a citizen or resident of the United States and his or her spouse died after December 31, 2010, the donor may be eligible to use the deceased spouse's unused exclusion (DSUE) amount. The executor of his or her spouse's estate must have elected on Form 706 to allow use of the unused exclusion amount. See instructions for Form 706, Part 6—Portability of the Deceased Spousal Unused Exclusion. If the executor of the estate made this election, attach Form 706 filed by the estate and include a calculation of the DSUE amount (either as an attachment or on Part 6—Portability of the Deceased Spousal Unused Exclusion). See also section 2010(c)(4) and related regulations.

Using the checkboxes provided, indicate whether the donor is applying or has applied a DSUE amount from a predeceased spouse to gifts reported on this or a previous Form 709. If so, complete Schedule C before going to Part 2—Tax Computation.

Schedule A. Computation of Taxable Gifts

Do not enter on Schedule A any gift or part of a gift that qualifies for the political organization, educational, or medical exclusions. In the instructions below, *gifts* means transfers (or parts of transfers) that do not qualify for the political organization, educational, or medical exclusions

Line A. Valuation Discounts

If the value of any gift you report in either Part 1, Part 2, or Part 3 of Schedule A includes a discount for lack of marketability, a minority interest, a fractional interest in real estate, blockage, market absorption, or for any other reason, answer "Yes" to the question at the top of Schedule A. Also, attach an explanation giving the basis for the claimed discounts and showing the amount of the discounts taken.

Line B. Qualified Tuition Programs (529 Plans or Programs)

If in 2013, you contributed more than $14,000 to a Qualified Tuition Plan (QTP) on behalf of any one person, you may elect to treat up to $70,000 of the contribution for that person as if you had made it ratably over a 5-year period. The election allows you to apply the annual

exclusion to a portion of the contribution in each of the 5 years, beginning in 2013. You can make this election for as many separate people as you made QTP contributions.

You can only apply the election to a maximum of $70,000. You must report all of your 2013 QTP contributions for any single person that exceed $70,000 (in addition to any other gifts you made to that person).

For each of the 5 years, you report in Part 1 of Schedule A one-fifth (20%) of the amount for which you made the election. In column E of Part 1 (Schedule A) list the date of the gift as the calendar year for which you are deemed to have made the gift (that is, the year of the current Form 709 you are filing). Do not list the actual year of contribution for subsequent years.

However, if in any of the last 4 years of the election, you did not make any other gifts that would require you to file a Form 709, you do not need to file Form 709 to report that year's portion of the election amount.

Example. In 2013, D contributed $100,000 to a QTP for the benefit of her son. D elects to treat $70,000 of this contribution as having been made ratably over a 5-year period. Accordingly, for 2013, D reports the following:

$30,000	(the amount of the contribution that exceeded $70,000)
+ $14,000	(the $\frac{1}{5}$ portion from the election)
$44,000	the total gift to her son listed in Part 1 of Schedule A for 2013

In 2014, D gives a gift of $20,000 cash to her niece and no other gifts. On her 2014 Form 709, D reports in Part 1 of Schedule A the $20,000 gift to her niece and a $14,000 gift to her son (the one-fifth portion of the 2013 gift that is treated as made in 2014). In column E of Part 1 (Schedule A), D lists "2014" as the date of the gift.

D makes no gifts in 2015, 2016, or 2017. She is not required to file Form 709 in any of those years to report the one-fifth portion of the QTP gift, because she is not otherwise required to file Form 709.

You make the election by checking the box on line B at the top of Schedule A. The election must be made for the calendar year in which the contribution is made. Also attach an explanation that includes the following:
• The total amount contributed per individual beneficiary,
• The amount for which the election is being made, and
• The name of the individual for whom the contribution was made.

If you are electing gift splitting, apply the gift-splitting rules before applying the

-6-

¶1719

QTP rules. Each spouse would then decide individually whether to make this QTP election.

Contributions to QTPs do not qualify for the education exclusion.

How To Complete Parts 1, 2, and 3

After you determine which gifts you made in 2013 that are subject to the gift tax, list them on Schedule A. You must divide these gifts between:

1. Part 1—those subject only to the gift tax (gifts made to nonskip persons—see *Part 1—Gifts Subject Only to Gift Tax*),

2. Part 2—those subject to both the gift and GST taxes (gifts made to skip persons—see *Gifts Subject to Both Gift and GST Taxes* and *Part 2—Direct Skips*), and

3. Part 3—those subject only to the gift tax at this time but which could later be subject to GST tax (gifts that are indirect skips, see *Part 3—Indirect Skips*).

If you need more space, attach a separate sheet using the same format as Schedule A.

Use the following guidelines when entering gifts on Schedule A:

• *Enter a gift only once—in Part 1, Part 2, or Part 3;*
• *Do not enter any gift or part of a gift that qualified for the political organization, educational, or medical exclusion;*
• *Enter gifts under "Gifts made by spouse" only if you have chosen to split gifts with your spouse and your spouse is required to file a Form 709 (see* Part 1—General Information, Lines 12–18. Split Gifts*); and*
• *In column F, enter the full value of the gift (including those made by your spouse, if applicable). If you have chosen to split gifts, that one-half portion of the gift is entered in column G.*

Gifts to Donees Other Than Your Spouse

You must always enter all gifts of future interests that you made during the calendar year regardless of their value.

Gift splitting not elected. If the total gifts of present interests to any donee are more than $14,000 in the calendar year, then you must enter all such gifts that you made during the year to or on behalf of that donee, including those gifts that will be excluded under the annual exclusion. If the total is $14,000 or less, you need not enter on Schedule A any gifts (except gifts of future interests) that you made to that

donee. Enter these gifts in the top half of Part 1, 2, or 3, as applicable.

Gift splitting elected. Enter on Schedule A the entire value of every gift you made during the calendar year while you were married, even if the gift's value will be less than $14,000 after it is split in Column G of Part 1, 2, or 3 of Schedule A.

Gifts made by spouse. If you elected gift splitting and your spouse made gifts, list those gifts in the space below "Gifts made by spouse" in Part 1, 2, or 3. Report these gifts in the same way you report gifts you made.

Gifts to Your Spouse

Except for the gifts described below, you do not need to enter any of your gifts to your spouse on Schedule A.

Terminable interests. Terminable interests are defined in the instructions to *Part 4, line 4*. If all the terminable interests you gave to your spouse qualify as life estates with power of appointment (defined under *Life estate with power of appointment*), you do not need to enter any of them on Schedule A.

However, if you gave your spouse any terminable interest that does not qualify as a life estate with power of appointment, you must report on Schedule A all gifts of terminable interests you made to your spouse during the year.

Charitable remainder trusts. If you make a gift to a charitable remainder trust and your spouse is the only noncharitable beneficiary (other than yourself), the interest you gave to your spouse is not considered a terminable interest and, therefore, should not be shown on Schedule A. See section 2523(g)(1). For definitions and rules concerning these trusts, see section 2056(b)(8)(B).

Future interest. Generally, you should not report a gift of a future interest to your spouse unless the future interest is also a terminable interest that is required to be reported as described above. However, if you gave a gift of a future interest to your spouse and you are required to report the present interest to a donee other than your spouse, then you should enter the entire gift, including the future interest given to your spouse, on Schedule A. You should use the rules under *Gifts Subject to Both Gift and GST Taxes*, later, to determine whether to enter the gift on Schedule A, Part 1, Part 2, or Part 3.

Spouses who are not U.S. citizens. If your spouse is not a U.S. citizen and you gave him or her a gift of a future interest, you must report on Schedule A all gifts to your spouse for the year. If all gifts to your spouse were present interests, do not report on Schedule A any gifts to your

spouse if the total of such gifts for the year does not exceed $143,000 and all gifts in excess of $14,000 would qualify for a marital deduction if your spouse were a U.S. citizen (see the instructions for Schedule A, Part 4, line 4). If the gifts exceed $143,000, you must report all of the gifts even though some may be excluded.

Gifts Subject to Both Gift and GST Taxes

Definitions

Direct skip. The GST tax you must report on Form 709 is that imposed only on inter vivos direct skips. An *inter vivos direct skip* is a transfer that is:
• Subject to the gift tax,
• Of an interest in property, and
• Made to a skip person.
All three requirements must be met before the gift is subject to the GST tax.

A gift is "subject to the gift tax" if you are required to list it on Schedule A of Form 709. However, if you make a nontaxable gift (which is a direct skip) to a trust for the benefit of an individual, this transfer is subject to the GST tax unless:

1. During the lifetime of the beneficiary, no corpus or income may be distributed to anyone other than the beneficiary, and

2. If the beneficiary dies before the termination of the trust, the assets of the trust will be included in the gross estate of the beneficiary.

Note. If the property transferred in the direct skip would have been includible in the donor's estate if the donor died immediately after the transfer, see *Transfers Subject to an Estate Tax Inclusion Period (ETIP)*.

To determine if a gift "is of an interest in property" and "is made to a skip person," you must first determine if the donee is a "natural person" or a "trust," as defined below.

Trust. For purposes of the GST tax, a *trust* includes not only an ordinary trust, but also any other arrangement (other than an estate) that although not explicitly a trust, has substantially the same effect as a trust. For example, a *trust* includes life estates with remainders, terms for years, and insurance and annuity contracts. A transfer of property that is conditional on the occurrence of an event is a transfer in trust.

Interest in property. If a gift is made to a *natural person,* it is always considered a gift of an interest in property for purposes of the GST tax.

If a gift is made to a trust, a natural person will have an *interest in the property* transferred to the trust if that person either has a present right to receive income or corpus from the trust (such as an income interest for life) or is a permissible current recipient of income or corpus from the trust (for example, possesses a general power of appointment).

Skip person. A donee, who is a natural person, is a *skip person* if that donee is assigned to a generation that is two or more generations below the generation assignment of the donor. See *Determining the Generation of a Donee.*

A donee that is a trust is a skip person if all the interests in the property transferred to the trust (as defined above) are held by skip persons.

A trust will also be a skip person if there are no interests in the property transferred to the trust held by any person, and future distributions or terminations from the trust can be made only to skip persons.

Nonskip person. A *nonskip person* is any donee who is not a skip person.

Determining the Generation of a Donee

Generally, a generation is determined along family lines as follows:

1. If the donee is a lineal descendant of a grandparent of the donor (for example, the donor's cousin, niece, nephew, etc.), the number of generations between the donor and the descendant (donee) is determined by subtracting the number of generations between the grandparent and the donor from the number of generations between the grandparent and the descendant (donee).

2. If the donee is a lineal descendant of a grandparent of a spouse (or former spouse) of the donor, the number of generations between the donor and the descendant (donee) is determined by subtracting the number of generations between the grandparent and the spouse (or former spouse) from the number of generations between the grandparent and the descendant (donee).

3. A person who at any time was married to a person described in (1) or (2) above is assigned to the generation of that person. A person who at any time was married to the donor is assigned to the donor's generation.

4. A relationship by adoption or half-blood is treated as a relationship by whole-blood.

A person who is not assigned to a generation according to (1), (2), (3), or (4) above is assigned to a generation based on his or her birth date as follows:

1. A person who was born not more than 12½ years after the donor is in the donor's generation.

2. A person born more than 12½ years, but not more than 37½ years, after the donor is in the first generation younger than the donor.

3. Similar rules apply for a new generation every 25 years.

If more than one of the rules for assigning generations applies to a donee, that donee is generally assigned to the youngest of the generations that would apply.

If an estate, trust, partnership, corporation, or other entity (other than governmental entities and certain charitable organizations and trusts, described in sections 511(a)(2) and 511(b)(2), as discussed later) is a donee, then each person who indirectly receives the gift through the entity is treated as a donee and is assigned to a generation as explained in the above rules.

Charitable organizations and trusts, described in sections 511(a)(2) and 511(b)(2), and governmental entities are assigned to the donor's generation. Transfers to such organizations are therefore not subject to the GST tax. These gifts should always be listed in Part 1 of Schedule A.

Charitable Remainder Trusts

Gifts in the form of charitable remainder annuity trusts, charitable remainder unitrusts, and pooled income funds are not transfers to skip persons and therefore are not direct skips. You should always list these gifts in Part 1 of Schedule A even if all of the life beneficiaries are skip persons.

Generation Assignment Where Intervening Parent Is Deceased

If you made a gift to your grandchild and at the time you made the gift, the grandchild's parent (who is your or your spouse's or your former spouse's child) is deceased, then for purposes of generation assignment, your grandchild is considered to be your child rather than your grandchild. Your grandchild's children will be treated as your grandchildren rather than your great-grandchildren.

This rule is also applied to your lineal descendants below the level of grandchild. For example, if your grandchild is deceased, your great-grandchildren who are lineal descendants of the deceased grandchild are considered your grandchildren for purposes of the GST tax.

This special rule may also apply in other cases of the death of a parent of the transferee. If property is transferred to a descendant of the transferor and that person's parent (who is a lineal descendant of the parent of the transferor) is deceased at the time the transfer is

subject to gift or estate tax, then for purposes of generation assignment, the individual is treated as if he or she is a member of the generation that is one generation below the lower of:
• The transferor's generation, or
• The generation assignment of the youngest living ancestor of the individual who is also a descendant of the parent of the transferor.

The same rules apply to the generation assignment of any descendant of the individual.

This rule does not apply to a transfer to an individual who is not a lineal descendant of the transferor if the transferor at the time of the transfer has any living lineal descendants.

If any transfer of property to a trust would have been a direct skip except for this generation assignment rule, then the rule also applies to transfers from the trust attributable to such property.

Ninety-day rule. For assigning individuals to generations for purposes of the GST tax, any individual who dies no later than 90 days after a transfer occurring by reason of the death of the transferor is treated as having predeceased the transferor. The 90-day rule applies to transfers occurring on or after July 18, 2005. See Regulations section 26.2651-1(a)(2)(iii) for more information.

Examples

The GST rules can be illustrated by the following examples.

Example 1. You give your house to your daughter for her life with the remainder then passing to her children. This gift is made to a "trust" even though there is no explicit trust instrument. The interest in the property transferred (the present right to use the house) is transferred to a nonskip person (your daughter). Therefore, the trust is not a skip person because there is an interest in the transferred property that is held by a nonskip person, and the gift is not a direct skip. The transfer is an indirect skip, however, because on the death of the daughter, a termination of her interest in the trust will occur that may be subject to the GST tax. See the instructions for *Part 3—Indirect Skips* for a discussion of how to allocate GST exemption to such a trust.

Example 2. You give $100,000 to your grandchild. This gift is a direct skip that is not made in trust. You should list it in Part 2 of Schedule A.

Example 3. You establish a trust that is required to accumulate income for 10 years and then pay its income to your grandchildren for their lives and upon their deaths distribute the corpus to their

-8-

children. Because the trust has no current beneficiaries, there are no present interests in the property transferred to the trust. All of the persons to whom the trust can make future distributions (including distributions upon the termination of interests in property held in trust) are skip persons (that is, your grandchildren and great-grandchildren). Therefore, the trust itself is a skip person and you should list the gift in Part 2 of Schedule A.

Example 4. You establish a trust that pays all of its income to your grandchildren for 10 years. At the end of 10 years, the corpus is to be distributed to your children. Since for this purpose interests in trusts are defined only as present interests, all of the interests in this trust are held by skip persons (the children's interests are future interests). Therefore, the trust is a skip person and you should list the entire amount you transferred to the trust in Part 2 of Schedule A even though some of the trust's ultimate beneficiaries are nonskip persons.

Part 1—Gifts Subject Only to Gift Tax

List in Part 1 gifts subject only to the gift tax. Generally, all of the gifts you made to your spouse (that are required to be listed, as described earlier), to your children, and to charitable organizations are not subject to the GST tax and should, therefore, be listed only in Part 1.

Group the gifts in four categories:
• Gifts made to your spouse,
• Gifts made to third parties that are to be split with your spouse,
• Charitable gifts (if you are not splitting gifts with your spouse), and
• Other gifts.
If a transfer results in gifts to two or more individuals (such as a life estate to one with remainder to the other), list the gift to each separately.

Number and describe all gifts (including charitable, public, and similar gifts) in the columns provided in Schedule A.

Column B

Describe each gift in enough detail so that the property can be easily identified, as explained below.

For real estate, give:
• A legal description of each parcel;
• The street number, name, and area if the property is located in a city; and
• A short statement of any improvements made to the property.

For bonds, give:
• The number of bonds transferred;
• The principal amount of each bond;

• Name of obligor;
• Date of maturity;
• Rate of interest;
• Date or dates when interest is payable;
• Series number, if there is more than one issue;
• Exchanges where listed or, if unlisted, give the location of the principal business office of the corporation; and
• CUSIP number. The CUSIP number is a nine-digit number assigned by the American Banking Association to traded securities.

For stocks:
• Give number of shares;
• State whether common or preferred;
• If preferred, give the issue, par value, quotation at which returned, and exact name of corporation;
• If unlisted on a principal exchange, give the location of the principal business office of the corporation, the state in which incorporated, and the date of incorporation;
• If listed, give principal exchange; and
• CUSIP number.

For interests in property based on the length of a person's life, give the date of birth of the person. If you transfer any interest in a closely held entity, provide the EIN of the entity.

For life insurance policies, give the name of the insurer and the policy number.

Clearly identify in the description column which gifts create the opening of an ETIP as described under *Transfers Subject to an Estate Tax Inclusion Period (ETIP).* Describe the interest that is creating the ETIP. An allocation of GST exemption to property subject to an ETIP that is made prior to the close of the ETIP becomes effective no earlier than the date of the close of the ETIP. See *Schedule D. Computation of GST Tax.*

Column D. Donor's Adjusted Basis of Gifts

Show the basis you would use for income tax purposes if the gift were sold or exchanged. Generally, this means cost plus improvements, less applicable depreciation, amortization, and depletion.

For more information on adjusted basis, see Pub. 551, Basis of Assets.

Columns E and F. Date and Value of Gift

The value of a gift is the fair market value (FMV) of the property on the date the gift is made (valuation date). The FMV is the price at which the property would change

hands between a willing buyer and a willing seller, when neither is forced to buy or to sell, and when both have reasonable knowledge of all relevant facts. FMV may not be determined by a forced sale price, nor by the sale price of the item in a market other than that in which the item is most commonly sold to the public. The location of the item must be taken into account whenever appropriate.

The FMV of a stock or bond (whether listed or unlisted) is the mean between the highest and lowest selling prices quoted on the valuation date. If only the closing selling prices are available, then the FMV is the mean between the quoted closing selling price on the valuation date and on the trading day before the valuation date. If there were no sales on the valuation date, figure the FMV as follows:

1. Find the mean between the highest and lowest selling prices on the nearest trading date before and the nearest trading date after the valuation date. Both trading dates must be reasonably close to the valuation date.

2. Prorate the difference between mean prices to the valuation date.

3. Add or subtract (whichever applies) the prorated part of the difference to or from the mean price figured for the nearest trading date before the actual valuation date.

If no actual sales were made reasonably close to the valuation date, make the same computation using the mean between the bona fide bid and the asked prices instead of sales prices. If actual sales prices or bona fide bid and asked prices are available within a reasonable period of time before the valuation date but not after the valuation date, or vice versa, use the mean between the highest and lowest sales prices or bid and asked prices as the FMV.

Stock of close corporations or inactive stock must be valued on the basis of net worth, earnings, earning and dividend capacity, and other relevant factors.

Generally, the best indication of the value of real property is the price paid for the property in an arm's-length transaction on or before the valuation date. If there has been no such transaction, use the comparable sales method. In comparing similar properties, consider differences in the date of the sale, and the size, condition, and location of the properties, and make all appropriate adjustments.

The value of all annuities, life estates, terms for years, remainders, or reversions is generally the present value on the date of the gift.

-9-

¶1719

Sections 2701 and 2702 provide special valuation rules to determine the amount of the gift when a donor transfers an equity interest in a corporation or partnership (section 2701) or makes a gift in trust (section 2702). The rules only apply if, immediately after the transfer, the donor (or an applicable family member) holds an applicable retained interest in the corporation or partnership, or retains an interest in the trust. For details, see sections 2701 and 2702, and their regulations.

Column G. Split Gifts

Enter an amount in this column only if you have chosen to split gifts with your spouse.

Split Gifts—Gifts Made by Spouses

If you elected to split gifts with your spouse and your spouse has given a gift(s) that is being split with you, enter in this area of Part 1 information on the gift(s) made by your spouse. If only you made gifts and you are splitting them with your spouse, do not make an entry in this area.

Generally, if you elect to split your gifts, you must split all gifts made by you and your spouse to third-party donees. The only exception is if you gave your spouse a general power of appointment over a gift you made.

Supplemental Documents

To support the value of your gifts, you must provide information showing how it was determined.

For stock of close corporations or inactive stock, attach balance sheets, particularly the one nearest the date of the gift, and statements of net earnings or operating results and dividends paid for each of the 5 preceding years.

For each life insurance policy, attach Form 712, Life Insurance Statement.

Note for single premium or paid-up policies. In certain situations, for example, where the surrender value of the policy exceeds its replacement cost, the true economic value of the policy will be greater than the amount shown on line 59 of Form 712. In these situations, report the full economic value of the policy on Schedule A. See Rev. Rul. 78-137, 1978-1 C.B. 280 for details.

If the gift was made by means of a trust, attach a certified or verified copy of the trust instrument to the return on which you report your first transfer to the trust. However, to report subsequent transfers to the trust, you may attach a brief description of the terms of the trust or a copy of the trust instrument.

Also attach any appraisal used to determine the value of real estate or other property.

If you do not attach this information, Schedule A must include a full explanation of how value was determined.

Part 2—Direct Skips

List in Part 2 only those gifts that are currently subject to both the gift and GST taxes. You must list the gifts in Part 2 in the chronological order that you made them. Number, describe, and value the gifts as described in the instructions for Part 1.

If you made a transfer to a trust that was a direct skip, list the entire gift as one line entry in Part 2.

Column C. 2632(b) Election

If you elect under section 2632(b)(3) to not have the automatic allocation rules of section 2632(b) apply to a transfer, enter a check in column C next to the transfer. You must also attach a statement to Form 709 clearly describing the transaction and the extent to which the automatic allocation is not to apply. Reporting a direct skip on a timely filed Form 709 and paying the GST tax on the transfer will qualify as such a statement.

How to report generation-skipping transfers after the close of an ETIP. If you are reporting a generation-skipping transfer that was subject to an ETIP (provided the ETIP closed as a result of something other than the death of the transferor; see Form 706), and you are also reporting gifts made during the year, complete Schedule A as you normally would with the transfer subject to an ETIP listed on Schedule A, Part 2.

Column B. In addition to the information already requested, describe the interest that is closing the ETIP; explain what caused the interest to terminate; and list the year the gift portion of the transfer was reported and its item number on Schedule A that was originally filed to report the gift portion of the ETIP transfer.

Column E. Give the date the ETIP closed rather than the date of the initial gift.

Columns F, G, and H. Enter "N/A" in these columns.

The value is entered only in Column B of Part 1, Schedule D. See *Column B,* earlier.

Split Gifts—Gifts Made by Spouse

See this heading under Part 1.

Part 3—Indirect Skips

Some gifts made to trusts are subject only to gift tax at the time of the transfer but later may be subject to GST tax. The GST tax could apply either at the time of a distribution from the trust, at the termination of the trust, or both.

Section 2632(c) defines indirect skips and applies special rules to the allocation of GST exemption to such transfers. In general, an indirect skip is a transfer of property that is subject to gift tax (other than a direct skip) and is made to a GST trust. A GST trust is a trust that could have a generation-skipping transfer with respect to the transferor, unless the trust provides for certain distributions of trust corpus to nonskip persons. See section 2632(c)(3)(B) for details.

List in Part 3 those gifts that are indirect skips as defined in section 2632(c) or may later be subject to GST tax. This includes indirect skips for which election (2), described below, will be made in the current year or has been made in a previous year. You must list the gifts in Part 3 in the chronological order that you made them.

Column C. 2632(c) Election

Section 2632(c) provides for the automatic allocation of the donor's unused GST exemption to indirect skips. This section also sets forth three different elections you may make regarding the allocation of exemption.

Election 1. You may elect not to have the automatic allocation rules apply to the current transfer made to a particular trust.
Election 2. You may elect not to have the automatic rules apply to both the current transfer and any and all future transfers made to a particular trust.
Election 3. You may elect to treat any trust as a GST trust for purposes of the automatic allocation rules.

See section 2632(c)(5) for details.

When to make an election. Election 1 is timely made if it is made on a timely filed gift tax return for the year the transfer was made or was deemed to have been made.

Elections 2 and 3 may be made on a timely filed gift tax return for the year for which the election is to become effective.

To make one of these elections, check column C next to the transfer to which the election applies. You must also attach an explanation as described below. If you are making election 2 or 3 on a return on which the transfer is not reported, simply attach the statement described below.

If you are reporting a transfer to a trust for which election 2 or 3 was made on a previously filed return, do not make an entry in column C for that transfer and do not attach a statement.

Attachment. Attach a statement to Form 709 that describes the election you are making and clearly identifies the trusts and/or transfers to which the election applies.

Split Gifts—Gifts Made by Spouse

See this heading under Part 1.

Part 4—Taxable Gift Reconciliation

Line 2

Enter the total annual exclusions you are claiming for the gifts listed on Schedule A. See *Annual Exclusion*, earlier. If you split a gift with your spouse, the annual exclusion you claim against that gift may not be more than the smaller of your half of the gift or $14,000.

Deductions

Line 4. Marital deduction

Enter all of the gifts to your spouse that you listed on Schedule A and for which you are claiming a marital deduction. Do not enter any gift that you did not include on Schedule A. On the dotted line on line 4, indicate which numbered items from Schedule A are gifts to your spouse for which you are claiming the marital deduction.

 Do not enter on line 4 any gifts to your spouse who was not a U.S. citizen at the time of the gift.

You may deduct all gifts of nonterminable interests made during the year that you entered on Schedule A regardless of amount, and certain gifts of terminable interests as outlined below.

Terminable interests. Generally, you cannot take the marital deduction if the gift to your spouse is a terminable interest. In most instances, a terminable interest is nondeductible if someone other than the donee spouse will have an interest in the property following the termination of the donee spouse's interest. Some examples of terminable interests are:
• A life estate,
• An estate for a specified number of years, or
• Any other property interest that after a period of time will terminate or fail.

If you transfer an interest to your spouse as sole joint tenant with yourself or as a tenant by the entirety, the interest is not considered a terminable interest just because the tenancy may be severed.

Life estate with power of appointment. You may deduct, without an election, a gift of a terminable interest if all four requirements below are met:

1. Your spouse is entitled for life to all of the income from the entire interest;

2. The income is paid yearly or more often;

3. Your spouse has the unlimited power, while he or she is alive or by will, to appoint the entire interest in all circumstances; and,

4. No part of the entire interest is subject to another person's power of appointment (except to appoint it to your spouse).

If either the right to income or the power of appointment given to your spouse pertains only to a specific portion of a property interest, the marital deduction is allowed only to the extent that the rights of your spouse meet all four of the above conditions. For example, if your spouse is to receive all of the income from the entire interest, but only has a power to appoint one-half of the entire interest, then only one-half qualifies for the marital deduction.

A partial interest in property is treated as a specific portion of an entire interest only if the rights of your spouse to the income and to the power are a fractional or percentile share of the entire property interest. This means that the interest or share will reflect any increase or decrease in the value of the entire property interest. If the spouse is entitled to receive a specified sum of income annually, the capital amount that would produce such a sum will be considered the specific portion from which the spouse is entitled to receive the income.

Election to deduct qualified terminable interest property (QTIP). You may elect to deduct a gift of a terminable interest if it meets requirements (1), (2), and (4) earlier, even though it does not meet requirement (3).

You make this election simply by listing the qualified terminable interest property on Schedule A and deducting its value from Schedule A, Part 4, line 4. You are presumed to have made the election for all qualified property that you both list and deduct on Schedule A. You may not make the election on a late filed Form 709.

Line 5

Enter the amount of the annual exclusions that were claimed for the gifts listed on line 4.

Line 7. Charitable Deduction

You may deduct from the total gifts made during the calendar year all gifts you gave to or for the use of:

• The United States, a state or political subdivision of a state or the District of Columbia for exclusively public purposes;
• Any corporation, trust, community chest, fund, or foundation organized and operated only for religious, charitable, scientific, literary, or educational purposes, or to prevent cruelty to children or animals, or to foster national or international amateur sports competition (if none of its activities involve providing athletic equipment unless it is a qualified amateur sports organization), as long as no part of the earnings benefits any one person, no substantial propaganda is produced, and no lobbying or campaigning for any candidate for public office is done;
• A fraternal society, order, or association operating under a lodge system, if the transferred property is to be used only for religious, charitable, scientific, literary, or educational purposes, including the encouragement of art and the prevention of cruelty to children or animals; or
• Any war veterans' organization organized in the United States (or any of its possessions), or any of its auxiliary departments or local chapters or posts, as long as no part of any of the earnings benefits any one person.

On line 7, show your total charitable, public, or similar gifts (minus annual exclusions allowed). On the dotted line, indicate which numbered items from the top of Schedule A are charitable gifts.

Line 10. GST Tax

If GST tax is due on any direct skips reported on this return, the amount of that GST tax is also considered a gift and must be added to the value of the direct skip reported on this return.

If you entered gifts on Part 2, or if you and your spouse elected gift splitting and your spouse made gifts subject to the GST tax that you are required to show on your Form 709, complete Schedule D, and enter on line 10 the total from Schedule D, Part 3, column H. Otherwise, enter zero on line 10.

Line 12. Election Out of QTIP Treatment of Annuities

Section 2523(f)(6) creates an automatic QTIP election for gifts of joint and survivor annuities where the spouses are the only possible recipients of the annuity prior to the death of the last surviving spouse.

The donor spouse can elect out of QTIP treatment, however, by checking the box on line 12 and entering the item number from Schedule A for the annuities for which you are making the election. Any annuities entered on line 12 cannot also be entered on line 4 of Schedule A, Part 4. Any such annuities that are not listed on line 12 must be entered on line 4 of Part 4, Schedule A. If there is more than one such joint and survivor annuity, you are not required to make the election for all of them. Once made, the election is irrevocable.

Schedule B. Gifts From Prior Periods

If you did not file gift tax returns for previous periods, check the "No" box on page 1 of Form 709, line 11a of *Part 1—General Information*. If you filed gift tax returns for previous periods, check the "Yes" box on line 11a and complete Schedule B by listing the years or quarters in chronological order as described below. If you need more space, attach a separate sheet using the same format as Schedule B.

 Complete Schedule A before beginning Schedule B.

Column A. If you filed returns for gifts made before 1971 or after 1981, show the calendar years in column A. If you filed returns for gifts made after 1970 and before 1982, show the calendar quarters.

Column B. In column B, identify the IRS office where you filed the returns. If you have changed your name, be sure to list any other names under which the returns were filed. If there was any other variation in the names under which you filed, such as the use of full given names instead of initials, please explain.

Column C. To determine the amount of applicable credit (formerly unified credit) used for gifts made after 1976, use the *Worksheet for Schedule B, Column C (Credit Allowable for Prior Periods)*, later, unless your prior gifts total $500,000 or less.

Prior gifts totaling $500,000 or less. In column C, enter the amount of

applicable credit actually applied in the prior period.

Prior gifts totaling over $500,000. See *Redetermining the Applicable Credit,* later.

Column D. In column D, enter the amount of specific exemption claimed for gifts made in periods ending before January 1, 1977.

Column E. In column E, show the correct amount (the amount finally determined) of the taxable gifts for each earlier period.

See Regulations section 25.2504-2 for rules regarding the final determination of the value of a gift.

Redetermining the Applicable Credit.

To redetermine the Applicable Credit for prior gifts in excess of $500,000, use the Worksheet for Schedule B, Column C (Credit Allowable for Prior Periods).

Instructions for Worksheet for Schedule B, Column C (Credit Allowable for Prior Periods)

Beginning with the earliest year after 1976 in which gifts using a credit amount were made, determine the credit amount (at current rates) for each quarter/year as follows:	
Column	
A Period	Enter the quarter/year of the prior gift(s). Pre-1977 gifts will be on the first row.
B Taxable Gifts for Current Period	Enter the amount of all taxable gifts for the year in column A. The total of all pre-1977 gifts should be combined in the first row.
C Taxable Gifts for Prior Periods	Enter the amount from Column D of the *previous* row.
D Cumulative Taxable Gifts Including Current Period	Enter the sum of Columns B and C from the current row.
E Tax on Gifts for Prior Periods	Enter the amount from Column F of the *previous* row.
F Tax on Cumulative Gifts Including Current Period	Enter the tax based on the amount in Column D of the current row using the *Table for Computing Gift Tax.*
G Tax on Gifts for Current Period	Subtract the amount in Column E from the amount in Column F of the current row and enter here.
H DSUE Amount from Predeceased Spouse(s)	Enter the total Deceased Spousal Unused Exclusion amount (if any) received from the estate of the donor's last deceased spouse.
I Basic Exclusion Amount for Year of Gift	Enter the exclusion amount corresponding with the year listed in Column A of the current row. (See *Table of Exclusion and Credit Amounts*), later.
J Applicable Exclusion Amount	Add the amounts in Columns H and I of the current row and enter here.
K Applicable Credit Amount (based on Amount in Column J)	Using the *Table for Computing Gift Tax*, determine the credit corresponding to the amount in Column J of the current row and enter here. For each row in Column K, subtract 20 percent of any amount allowed as a specific exemption for gifts made after September 8, 1976, and before January 1, 1977.
L Applicable Credit Amount Used in Prior Periods	Enter the total of the amounts in Columns L and N of the *previous* row.
M Available Credit in Current Period	Subtract the amount in Column L from the amount in Column K of the current row and enter here.
N Credit Allowable	Enter the lesser of Column G or Column M of the current row.
Repeat this process for each prior year with taxable gifts. Do not enter less than zero.	

¶1719

Worksheet for Schedule B, Column C (Credit Allowable for Prior Periods).

Prior Years Credit Recalculation (for Form 709 Schedule B, Column C)
(Keep for your records.)

A Period	B Taxable Gifts for Current Period	C Taxable Gifts for Prior Periods[1]	D Cumulative Taxable Gifts Including Current Period (Col. B + Col. C)	E Tax on Gifts for Prior Periods (Col. C)[2],[3]	F Tax on Cumulative Gifts Including Current Period (Col. D)[3]	G Tax on Gifts for Current Period (Col. F - Col. E)	H DSUE from Predeceased Spouse(s)	I Basic Exclusion for Year of Gift[4]	J Applicable Exclusion Amount (Col. H + Col. I)	K Applicable Credit Amount based on Column J[3],[5]	L Applicable Credit Amount Used in Prior Periods[3],[6]	M Available Credit in Current Period (Col. K - Col. L)	N Credit Allowable (lesser of Col. G or Col. M)
Pre-1977													
YYYY													
YYYY													
YYYY													
Total Applicable Credit Used in Prior Periods (*Enter the Total of Column N on Schedule B, Line 1, Column C*):													

1. Column C: Enter amount from column D of the **previous** row.
2. Column E: Compute the tax on the amount in Column C or enter amount from column F of the **previous** row.
3. To compute tax or credit amount, see *Table for Computing Gift Tax*, later.
4. For years prior to 2010, the basic exclusion amount equals the applicable exclusion amount.
5. For each row in Column K, subtract 20 percent of any amount allowed as a specific exemption for gifts made after September 8, 1976, and before January 1, 1977.
6. Enter the total of Columns L and N of the **previous** row.

Example 1. Prior Years Credit Recalculation (for Form 709 Schedule B, Column C)
(Three post-1976 years involved. All have the same maximum credit available. Tentative tax exceeds available credit.)

A Period	B Taxable Gifts for Current Period	C Taxable Gifts for Prior Periods[1]	D Cumulative Taxable Gifts Including Current Period (Col. B + Col. C)	E Tax on Gifts for Prior Periods (Col. C)[2],[3]	F Tax on Cumulative Gifts Including Current Period (Col. D)[3]	G Tax on Gifts for Current Period (Col. F - Col. E)	H DSUE from Predeceased Spouse(s)	I Basic Exclusion for Year of the Gift[4]	J Applicable Exclusion Amount (Col. H + Col. I)	K Applicable Credit Amount based on Column J[3],[5]	L Applicable Credit Amount Used in Prior Periods[3],[6]	M Available Credit in Current Period (Col. K - Col. L)	N Credit Allowable (lesser of Col. G or Col. M)
Pre-1977													
2004	800,000	0	800,000	0	267,800	267,800	0	1,000,000	1,000,000	345,800	0	345,800	267,800
2007	300,000	800,000	1,100,000	267,800	385,800	118,000	0	1,000,000	1,000,000	345,800	267,800	78,000	78,000
2009	200,000	1,100,000	1,300,000	385,800	465,800	80,000	0	1,000,000	1,000,000	345,800	345,800	0	0
Total Applicable Credit Used in Prior Periods (*Enter the Total of Column N on Schedule B, Line 1, Column C*):													345,800

1. Column C: Enter amount from column D of the **previous** row.
2. Column E: Compute the tax on the amount in Column C or enter amount from column F of the **previous** row.
3. To compute tax or credit amount, see *Table for Computing Gift Tax*, later.
4. For years prior to 2010, the basic exclusion amount equals the applicable exclusion amount.
5. For each row in Column K, subtract 20 percent of any amount allowed as a specific exemption for gifts made after September 8, 1976, and before January 1, 1977.
6. Enter the total of Columns L and N of the **previous** row.

¶1719

	**Example 2. Prior Years Credit Recalculation (for Form 709 Schedule B, Column C)**													
	(Pre-1977 gifts plus 3 post-1976 years: Earlier years' gifts exceed credit then available. Last gift made after credit increased.)													
A	**B**	**C**	**D**	**E**	**F**	**G**	**H**	**I**	**J**	**K**	**L**	**M**	**N**
Period	Taxable Gifts for Current Period	Taxable Gifts for Prior Periods¹	Cumulative Taxable Gifts Including Current Period (Col. B + Col. C)	Tax on Gifts for Prior Periods (Col. C)²,³	Tax on Cumulative Gifts Including Current Period (Col. D)³	Tax on Gifts for Current Period (Col. F - Col. E)	DSUE from Predeceased Spouse(s)	Basic Exclusion for Year of the Gift⁴	Applicable Exclusion Amount (Col. H + Col. I)	Applicable Credit Amount based on Column J³,⁵	Applicable Credit Amount Used in Prior Periods³,⁶	Available Credit in Current Period (Col. K - Col. L)	Credit Allowable (lesser of Col. G or Col. M)
Pre-1977	200,000		200,000		54,800								
1987	600,000	200,000	800,000	54,800	267,800	213,000	0	600,000	600,000	192,800	0	192,800	192,800
1999	200,000	800,000	1,000,000	267,800	345,800	78,000	0	650,000	650,000	211,300	192,800	18,500	18,500
2002	100	1,000,000	1,000,100	345,800	345,840	40	0	1,000,000	1,000,000	345,800	211,300	134,500	40
Total Applicable Credit Used in Prior Periods *(Enter the Total of Column N on Schedule B, Line 1, Column C)*:													211,340

¹ Column C: Enter amount from column D of the *previous* row.
² Column E: Compute the tax on the amount in Column C or enter amount from column F of the *previous* row.
³ To compute tax or credit amount, see *Table for Computing Gift Tax*, later.
⁴ For years prior to 2010, the basic exclusion amount equals the applicable exclusion amount.
⁵ For each row in Column K, subtract 20 percent of any amount allowed as a specific exemption for gifts made after September 8, 1976, and before January 1, 1977.
⁶ Enter the total of Columns L and N of the *previous* row.

	Example 3. Prior Years Credit Recalculation (for Form 709 Schedule B, Column C)													
	($4M gift made within the applicable credit, $5M DSUE received prior to subsequent $4M gift in the same year.)													
A	**B**	**C**	**D**	**E**	**F**	**G**	**H**	**I**	**J**	**K**	**L**	**M**	**N**
Period	Taxable Gifts for Current Period	Taxable Gifts for Prior Periods¹	Cumulative Taxable Gifts Including Current Period (Col. B + Col. C)	Tax on Gifts for Prior Periods (Col. C)²,³	Tax on Cumulative Gifts Including Current Period (Col. D)³	Tax on Gifts for Current Period (Col. F - Col. E)	DSUE from Predeceased Spouse(s)	Basic Exclusion for Year of the Gift⁴	Applicable Exclusion Amount (Col. H + Col. I)	Applicable Credit Amount based on Column J³,⁵	Applicable Credit Amount Used in Prior Periods³,⁶	Available Credit in Current Period (Col. K - Col. L)	Credit Allowable (lesser of Col. G or Col. M)
Pre-1977													
2011	8,000,000	0	8,000,000	0	3,145,800	3,145,800	4,000,000	5,000,000	9,000,000	3,545,800	0	3,545,800	3,145,800
YYYY													
YYYY													
Total Applicable Credit Used in Prior Periods *(Enter the Total of Column N on Schedule B, Line 1, Column C)*:													3,145,800

¹ Column C: Enter amount from column D of the *previous* row.
² Column E: Compute the tax on the amount in Column C or enter amount from column F of the *previous* row.
³ To compute tax or credit amount, see *Table for Computing Gift Tax*, later.
⁴ For years prior to 2010, the basic exclusion amount equals the applicable exclusion amount.
⁵ For each row in Column K, subtract 20 percent of any amount allowed as a specific exemption for gifts made after September 8, 1976, and before January 1, 1977.
⁶ Enter the total of Columns L and N of the *previous* row.

¶1719

Example 4. Prior Years Credit Recalculation (for Form 709 Schedule B, Column C) (Prior gift exceeds applicable credit, $5M DSUE received prior to subsequent gift.)													
A	B	C	D	E	F	G	H	I	J	K	L	M	N
Period	Taxable Gifts for Current Period	Taxable Gifts for Prior Periods[1]	Cumulative Taxable Gifts Including Current Period (Col. B + Col. C)	Tax on Gifts for Prior Periods (Col. C)[2,3]	Tax on Cumulative Gifts Including Current Period (Col. D)[3]	Tax on Gifts for Current Period (Col. F - Col. E)	DSUE from Predeceased Spouse(s)	Basic Exclusion for Year of the Gift[4]	Applicable Exclusion Amount (Col. H + Col. I)	Applicable Credit Amount based on Column J[3,5]	Applicable Credit Amount Used in Prior Periods[3,6]	Available Credit in Current Period (Col. K - Col. L)	Credit Allowable (lesser of Col. G or Col. M)
Pre-1977													
2002	4,000,000	0	4,000,000	0	1,545,800	1,545,800	0	1,000,000	1,000,000	345,800	0	345,800	345,800
2011	4,000,000	4,000,000	8,000,000	1,545,800	3,145,800	1,600,000	4,000,000	5,000,000	9,000,000	3,545,800	345,800	3,200,000	1,600,000
YYYY													

Total Applicable Credit Used in Prior Periods (*Enter the Total of Column N on Schedule B, Line 1, Column C*): 1,945,800

[1] Column C: Enter amount from column D of the **previous** row.
[2] Column E: Compute the tax on the amount in Column C or enter amount from column F of the **previous** row.
[3] To compute tax or credit amount, see *Table for Computing Gift Tax,* later.
[4] For years prior to 2010, the basic exclusion amount equals the applicable exclusion amount.
[5] For each row in Column K, subtract 20 percent of any amount allowed as a specific exemption for gifts made after September 8, 1976, and before January 1, 1977.
[6] Enter the total of Columns L and N of the **previous** row.

Table of Basic Exclusion and Credit Amounts
(as Recalculated for 2013 Rates)

Period	Exclusion Amounts	Credit Amounts
1977 (Quarters 1 & 2)	$30,000	$6,000
1977 (Quarters 3 & 4)	$120,667	$30,000
1978	$134,000	$34,000
1979	$147,333	$38,000
1980	$161,563	$42,500
1981	$175,625	$47,000
1982	$225,000	$62,800
1983	$275,000	$79,300
1984	$325,000	$96,300
1985	$400,000	$121,800
1986	$500,000	$155,800
1987 through 1997	$600,000	$192,800
1998	$625,000	$202,050
1999	$650,000	$211,300
2000 and 2001	$675,000	$220,550
2002 through 2010	$1,000,000	$345,800
2011	$5,000,000	$1,945,800
2012	$5,120,000	$1,993,800
2013	$5,250,000	$2,045,800

Schedule C. Portability of Deceased Spousal Unused Exclusion (DSUE) Amount

Section 303 of the Tax Relief, Unemployment Insurance Reauthorization, and Job Creation Act of 2010 authorized estates of decedents dying on or after January 1, 2011, to elect to transfer any unused exclusion to the surviving spouse. The amount received by the surviving spouse is called the *deceased spousal unused exclusion, or DSUE,* amount. If the executor of the decedent's estate elects transfer, or portability, of the DSUE amount, the surviving spouse can apply the DSUE amount received from the estate of his or her last deceased spouse (defined later) against any tax liability arising from subsequent lifetime gifts and transfers at death.

 Complete Schedule A before beginning Schedule C.

Note. A nonresident surviving spouse who is not a citizen of the United States may not take into account the DSUE amount of a deceased spouse, except to the extent allowed by treaty with his or her country of citizenship.

Last Deceased Spouse Limitation

The *last deceased spouse* is the most recently deceased person who was married to the surviving spouse at the time of that person's death. The identity of the last deceased spouse is determined as of the day a taxable gift is made and is not impacted by whether the decedent's estate elected portability or whether the last deceased spouse had any DSUE amount available. Remarriage also does not affect the designation of the last deceased spouse and does not prevent the surviving spouse from applying the DSUE amount to taxable transfers.

When a taxable gift is made, the DSUE amount received from the last deceased spouse is applied before the surviving spouse's basic exclusion amount. A surviving spouse who has more than one predeceased spouse is not precluded from using the DSUE amount of each spouse in succession. A surviving spouse may not use the sum of DSUE amounts from multiple predeceased spouses at one time nor may the DSUE amount of a predeceased spouse be applied after the death of a subsequent spouse.

When a surviving spouse applies the DSUE amount to a lifetime gift, the IRS may examine any return of a predeceased spouse whose executor elected portability to verify the allowable DSUE amount. The DSUE may be adjusted or eliminated as a result of the examination; however, the IRS may make an assessment of additional tax on the return of a predeceased spouse only within the applicable limitations period under section 6501.

Completing Schedule C

Complete Schedule C if the donor is a surviving spouse who received a DSUE amount from one or more predeceased spouses.

 Entry spaces with gray shading and columns and lines marked "Reserved" are inactive. Do not enter any information in these areas.

Schedule C requests information on all DSUE amounts received from the donor's last deceased spouse and any previously deceased spouses. Each line in the chart should reflect a different predeceased spouse.

Part 1. DSUE Received From the Last Deceased Spouse

In this Part, include information about the DSUE amount from the donor's most recently deceased spouse (whose date of death is after December 31, 2010). In column E, enter the total of the amount in column D that the donor has applied to gifts in previous years and is applying to gifts reported on this return.

Part 2. DSUE Received From Other Predeceased Spouse(s)

Enter information about the DSUE amount from the spouse(s), if any, who died prior to the donor's most recently deceased spouse (but not before January 1, 2011) if the prior spouse's executor elected portability of the DSUE amount. In column D, indicate the amount of DSUE received from the estate of each predeceased spouse. In column E, enter the portion of the amount of DSUE shown in column D that was applied to prior lifetime gifts or transfers.

 Any remaining DSUE from a predeceased spouse cannot be applied against tax arising from lifetime gifts if that spouse is not the most recently deceased spouse on the date of the gift. This rule applies even if the last deceased spouse had no DSUE amount or made no valid portability election, or if the DSUE amount from the last deceased spouse has been fully applied to gifts in previous periods.

Determining the Applicable Credit Amount including DSUE

On line 1, enter the donor's basic exclusion amount; for 2013, this amount is $5,250,000. Add the amounts listed in column E from Parts 1 and 2 and enter the total on line 2. On line 3, enter the total of lines 1 and 2. Using the Table for Computing Gift Tax, later, determine the donor's applicable credit by applying the appropriate tax rate to the amount on line 3. Enter this amount on line 4 and on line 7 of Part 2—Tax Computation.

Schedule D. Computation of GST Tax

Part 1—Generation-Skipping Transfers

Enter in Part 1 all of the gifts you listed in Part 2 of Schedule A, in the same order and showing the same values.

Column B

If you are reporting a generation-skipping transfer that occurred because of the close of an ETIP, complete column B for such transfer as follows:

  1. If the GST exemption is being allocated on a timely filed (including extensions) gift tax return, enter the value as of the close of the ETIP.

  2. If the GST exemption is being allocated on a late filed (past the due date including extensions) gift tax return, enter the value as of the date the gift tax return was filed.

Column C

You are allowed to claim the gift tax annual exclusion currently allowable for your reported direct skips (other than certain direct skips to trusts—see *Note*), using the rules and limits discussed earlier for the gift tax annual exclusion. However, you must allocate the exclusion on a gift-by-gift basis for GST computation purposes. You must allocate the exclusion to each gift to the maximum allowable amount and in chronological order, beginning with the earliest gift that qualifies for the exclusion. Be sure that you do not claim a total exclusion of more than $14,000 per donee.

Note. You may not claim any annual exclusion for a transfer made to a trust unless the trust meets the requirements discussed under *Part 2—Direct Skips*.

Part 2—GST Exemption Reconciliation

Line 1

Every donor is allowed a lifetime GST exemption. The amount of the exemption for 2013 is $5,250,000. For transfers made through 1998, the GST exemption was $1 million. The exemption amounts for 1999 through 2013 are as follows:

Year	Amount
1999	$1,010,000
2000	$1,030,000
2001	$1,060,000
2002	$1,100,000
2003	$1,120,000
2004 and 2005	$1,500,000
2006, 2007, and 2008	$2,000,000
2009	$3,500,000
2010 and 2011	$5,000,000
2012	$5,120,000
2013	$5,250,000

In general, each annual increase can only be allocated to transfers made (or appreciation occurring) during or after the year of the transfer.

  Example. A donor made $1,750,000 in GSTs through 2005, and allocated all $1,500,000 of the exemption to those transfers. In 2013, the donor makes a $207,000 taxable generation-skipping transfer. The donor can allocate $207,000

of exemption to the 2013 transfer but cannot allocate the $3,543,000 of unused 2013 exemption to pre-2013 transfers.

  However, if in 2005, the donor made a $1,750,000 transfer to a trust that was not a direct skip, but from which generation-skipping transfers could be made in the future, the donor could allocate the increased exemption to the trust, even though no additional transfers were made to the trust. See Regulations section 26.2642-4 for the redetermination of the applicable fraction when additional exemption is allocated to the trust.

  Keep a record of your transfers and exemption allocations to make sure that any future increases are allocated correctly.

  Enter on line 1 of Part 2 the maximum GST exemption you are allowed. This will not necessarily be the highest indexed amount if you made no generation-skipping transfers during the year of the increase.

  The donor can apply this exemption to inter vivos transfers (that is, transfers made during the donor's life) on Form 709. The executor can apply the exemption on Form 706 to transfers taking effect at death. An allocation is irrevocable.

  In the case of inter vivos direct skips, a portion of the donor's unused exemption is automatically allocated to the transferred property unless the donor elects otherwise. To elect out of the automatic allocation of exemption, you must file Form 709 and attach a statement to it clearly describing the transaction and the extent to which the automatic allocation is not to apply. Reporting a direct skip on a timely filed Form 709 and paying the GST tax on the transfer will prevent an automatic allocation.

  Special QTIP election. If you elect QTIP treatment for any gifts in trust listed on Schedule A, then on Schedule D you may also elect to treat the entire trust as non-QTIP for purposes of the GST tax. The election must be made for the entire trust that contains the particular gift involved on this return. Be sure to identify the item number of the specific gift for which you are making this special QTIP election.

Line 5

Enter the amount of GST exemption you are applying to transfers reported in Part 3 of Schedule A.

  Section 2632(c) provides an automatic allocation to indirect skips of any unused GST exemption. The unused exemption is allocated to indirect skips to the extent necessary to make the inclusion ratio zero for the property transferred. You may elect

Table for Computing Gift Tax

Column A	Column B	Column C	Column D
Taxable amount over	Taxable amount not over—	Tax on amount in Column A	Rate of tax on excess over amount in Column A
- - - - -	$10,000	- - - - -	18%
$10,000	20,000	$1,800	20%
20,000	40,000	3,800	22%
40,000	60,000	8,200	24%
60,000	80,000	13,000	26%
80,000	100,000	18,200	28%
100,000	150,000	23,800	30%
150,000	250,000	38,800	32%
250,000	500,000	70,800	34%
500,000	750,000	155,800	37%
750,000	1,000,000	248,300	39%
1,000,000	- - - -	345,800	40%

out of this automatic allocation as explained in the instructions for Part 3.

Line 6

Notice of allocation. You may wish to allocate GST exemption to transfers not reported on this return, such as a late allocation.

To allocate your exemption to such transfers, attach a statement to this Form 709 and entitle it "Notice of Allocation." The notice must contain the following for each trust (or other transfer):
• Clear identification of the trust, including the trust's EIN, if known;
• If this is a late allocation, the year the transfer was reported on Form 709;
• The value of the trust assets at the effective date of the allocation;
• The amount of your GST exemption allocated to each gift (or a statement that you are allocating exemption by means of a formula such as "an amount necessary to produce an inclusion ratio of zero"); and
• The inclusion ratio of the trust after the allocation.

Total the exemption allocations and enter this total on line 6.

Note. Where the property involved in such a transfer is subject to an ETIP because it would be includible in the donor's estate if the donor died immediately after the transfer (other than by reason of the donor having died within 3 years of making the gift), an allocation of the GST exemption at the time of the transfer will only become effective at the end of the ETIP. For details, see *Transfers Subject to an Estate Tax Inclusion Period (ETIP)*, earlier, and section 2642(f).

Part 3—Tax Computation

You must enter in Part 3 every gift you listed in Part 1 of Schedule D.

Column C

You are not required to allocate your available exemption. You may allocate some, all, or none of your available exemption, as you wish, among the gifts listed in Part 3 of Schedule D. However, the total exemption claimed in column C may not exceed the amount you entered on line 3 of Part 2 of Schedule D.

You may enter an amount in column C that is greater than the amount you entered in column B.

Column D

Carry your computation to three decimal places (for example, "1.000").

Part 2—Tax Computation (Page 1 of Form 709)

Lines 4 and 5

To compute the tax for the amount on line 3 (to be entered on line 4) and the tax for the amount on line 2 (to be entered on line 5), use the *Table for Computing Gift Tax*, earlier.

Line 7

The applicable credit (formerly unified credit) amount is the tentative tax on the applicable exclusion amount. For gifts made in 2013, the applicable exclusion amount equals:
• The basic exclusion amount of $5,250,000, PLUS
• Any deceased spousal unused exclusion (DSUE) amount.

If you are a citizen or resident of the United States, you must apply any available applicable credit against gift tax. If you are not eligible to use a DSUE amount from a predeceased spouse, enter $2,045,800 on Line 7. Nonresidents not citizens of the United States may not claim

the applicable credit and should enter zero on line 7.

If you are eligible to use a DSUE amount from a predeceased spouse, complete Schedule C—Deceased Spousal Unused Exclusion (DSUE) Amount and enter the amount from line 4 of that schedule on line 7 of Part 2—Tax Computation.

Determine the tentative tax on the applicable exclusion amount using the rates in *Table for Computing Gift Tax*, above, and enter the result on Line 7.

Line 10

Enter 20% of the amount allowed as a specific exemption for gifts made after September 8, 1976, and before January 1, 1977. (These amounts will be among those listed in Schedule B, column D, for gifts made in the third and fourth quarters of 1976.)

Line 13

Gift tax conventions are in effect with Australia, Austria, Denmark, France, Germany, Japan, and the United Kingdom. If you are claiming a credit for payment of foreign gift tax, figure the credit and attach the calculation to Form 709, along with evidence that the foreign taxes were paid. See the applicable convention for details of computing the credit.

Line 19

Make your check or money order payable to "United States Treasury" and write the donor's social security number on it. You may not use an overpayment on Form 1040 to offset the gift and GST taxes owed on Form 709.

Signature

As a donor, you must sign the return. If you pay another person, firm, or corporation to prepare your return, that person must also sign the return as preparer unless he or she is your regular full-time employee.

Third-party designee. If you want to allow the return preparer (listed on the bottom of page 1 of Form 709) to discuss your 2013 Form 709 with the IRS, check the "Yes" box to the far right of your signature on page 1 of your return.

If you check the "Yes" box, you (and your spouse, if splitting gifts) are authorizing the IRS to call your return preparer to answer questions that may arise during the processing of your return. You are also authorizing the return preparer of your 2013 Form 709 to:
• Give the IRS any information that is missing from your return,
• Call the IRS for information about the processing of your return or the status of your payment(s),

-17-

¶1719

• Receive copies of notices or transcripts related to your return, upon request, and
• Respond to certain IRS notices about math errors, offsets, and return preparation.

You are not authorizing your return preparer to receive any refund check, to bind you to anything (including any additional tax liability), or otherwise represent you before the IRS. If you want to expand the authorization of your return preparer, see Pub. 947, Practice Before the IRS and Power of Attorney.

The authorization will automatically end three years from the date of filing Form 709. If you wish to revoke the authorization before it ends, see Pub. 947.

Disclosure, Privacy Act, and Paperwork Reduction Act Notice. We ask for the information on this form to carry out the Internal Revenue laws of the United States. We need the information to figure and collect the right amount of tax. Form 709 is used to report (1) transfers subject to the federal gift and certain GST taxes and to figure the tax, if any, due on those transfers, and (2) allocations of the lifetime GST exemption to property transferred during the transferor's lifetime.

Our legal right to ask for the information requested on this form is found in sections 6001, 6011, 6019, and 6061, and their regulations. You are required to provide the information requested on this form. Section 6109 requires that you provide your identifying number.

Generally, tax returns and return information are confidential, as stated in section 6103. However, section 6103 allows or requires the Internal Revenue Service to disclose or give such information shown on your Form 709 to the Department of Justice to enforce the tax laws, both civil and criminal, and to cities, states, the District of Columbia, and U.S. commonwealths or possessions for use in administering their tax laws. We may also disclose this information to other countries under a tax treaty, to federal and state agencies to enforce federal nontax criminal laws, or to federal law enforcement and intelligence agencies to combat terrorism.

We may disclose the information on your Form 709 to the Department of the Treasury and contractors for tax administration purposes; and to other persons as necessary to obtain information which we cannot get in any other way for purposes of determining the amount of or to collect the tax you owe. We may disclose the information on your Form 709 to the Comptroller General to review the Internal Revenue Service. We may also disclose the information on your Form 709 to Committees of Congress; federal, state, and local child support agencies; and to other federal agencies for the purpose of determining entitlement for benefits or the eligibility for, and the repayment of, loans.

If you are required to but do not file a Form 709, or do not provide the information requested on the form, or provide fraudulent information, you may be charged penalties and be subject to criminal prosecution.

You are not required to provide the information requested on a form that is subject to the Paperwork Reduction Act unless the form displays a valid OMB control number. Books or records relating to a form or its instructions must be retained as long as their contents may become material in the administration of any Internal Revenue law.

The time needed to complete and file this form will vary depending on individual circumstances. The estimated average time is:

Recordkeeping	52 min.
Learning about the law or the form	1 hr., 53 min.
Preparing the form	2 hrs., 21min.
Copying, assembling, and sending the form to the IRS	1 hr., 3 min.

If you have comments concerning the accuracy of these time estimates or suggestions for making this form simpler, we would be happy to hear from you. You can send us comments from _www.irs.gov/formspubs_. Click on "More Information" and then on "Comment on Tax Forms and Publications." Or you can also send your comments to the Internal Revenue Service, Tax Forms and Publications Division, 1111 Constitution Ave. NW, IR-6526, Washington, DC 20224. Do not send the tax form to this office. Instead, see _Where To File_, earlier.

¶1719

THE FEDERAL ESTATE TAX

TABLE OF CONTENTS

GROSS ESTATE

¶1800 IMPOSITION OF THE ESTATE TAX

An estate tax is imposed on the transfer of the taxable estate of every decedent who is a citizen or resident of the United States under IRC Sec. 2001(a). A resident for these purposes is defined as a decedent who had his or her domicile in the United States at the time of death [Reg. Sec. 20.0-1(b)]. If the decedent was domiciled in the United States at the time of death, the total value of all real or personal, tangible or intangible property, wherever situated, must be included in the decedent's gross estate [Reg. Sec. 20.2033-1(a)]. If the decedent was a nonresident and noncitizen, his or her taxable estate is subject to the estate tax under IRC Sec. 2101. In this situation, the value of the gross estate is only that part of the gross estate that was situated in the United States at the time of death [IRC Sec. 2103]. [See ¶1818 for further discussion.]

A gift tax is imposed on all lifetime transfers and an estate tax is imposed on all transfers that are occasioned by death.

A deceased person is known as a "decedent." The estate tax is imposed on a decedent's "taxable estate," which is his or her gross estate [see ¶1801], less applicable estate tax deductions [see ¶¶2000–2001]. To compute a decedent's taxable estate, you first add up all the property that the decedent owned at death and certain additional property transferred during his or her lifetime and subtract charitable gifts, transfers to a spouse, and all administrative expenses and debts.

A decedent's gross estate includes the following:

1. Property that the decedent owned at the time of death[1] [see Chapter 19 for discussion of valuation of that property];

2. Property that the decedent could obtain through the exercise of a power conferred by someone else, such as a general power of appointment [see ¶1810];

3. Property that the decedent uses as a testamentary substitute, such as an irrevocable trust established by the decedent-settlor, which provides a life income interest to the decedent-beneficiary; and

4. Property for which the federal estate tax was deferred at the death of a prior spouse, such as a marital deduction [see Chapter 11].

Deductions from the gross estate include:

1. Administrative expenses and claims;

2. Debts of the decedent;

3. Losses to property occurring during administration; and

4. Charitable devises and transfers to a surviving spouse.

These deductions are discussed in detail at Chapter 20.

A citizen or permanent resident of the United States is taxed on all of his or her property worldwide [IRC Sec. 2033].

---

[1] ¶1800 Estate of Richard, TC Memo 2012-173

In determining the rate of tax, the taxable estate is stacked on top of lifetime gifts to push transfers at death into a higher tax rate bracket. In other words, the amount of the decedent's post-1976 taxable gifts is added to the decedent's taxable estate [IRC Sec. 2001(b)] to reach the taxable amount. Gifts that are subject to inclusion in the decedent's gross estate because they were incomplete until the donor-decedent's death are not considered part of the decedent's gifts [IRC Sec. 2001(b)].

The rate schedule [see ¶2201] is applied to the taxable amount to arrive at the tentative estate tax.

¶1801 THE GROSS ESTATE: OVERVIEW

The decedent's gross estate is the starting point for figuring out how much estate tax is owed by the decedent.

General rule. IRC Sec. 2033 provides that "[t]he value of the gross estate shall include the value of all property to the extent of the interest therein of the decedent at the time of his death." IRC Sec. 2036(a) more clearly defines the types of property interests that will be included in the decedent's gross estate as follows:

> The value of the gross estate shall include the value of all property to the extent of any interest therein of which the decedent has at any time made a transfer (except in case of a bona fide sale for an adequate and full consideration in money or money's worth), by trust or otherwise, under which he has retained for his life or for any period not ascertainable without reference to his death or for any period which does not in fact end before his death—
>
> (1) the possession or enjoyment of, or the right to the income from, the property, or
>
> (2) the right, either alone or in conjunction with any person, to designate the persons who shall possess or enjoy the property or the income therefrom.

IRC Sec. 2036. The intent of IRC Sec. 2036 is to include in a decedent's gross estate transfers of property that are "essentially testamentary' in nature."[1] Testamentary transfers are defined as those "transfers which leave the transferor a significant interest in or control over the property transferred during his lifetime."[2] Therefore, IRC Sec. 2036 includes the value of assets in a decedent's gross estate when: (1) the decedent made an *inter vivos* transfer of property; (2) the decedent's transfer was not a bona fide sale for adequate and full consideration; and (3) the decedent retained an interest or right in the transferred property that she did not relinquish before her death.[3] In addition, IRC Sec. 2035(a) provides that a decedent's gross estate includes the value of any property with respect to which the decedent made a transfer or relinquished a power within three years of her death if the value of such property would have been included in her estate under IRC Sec. 2036 but for her transfer of an interest in the property or her relinquishment of a power with respect to the property.

---

[1] **¶1801** Ray, 762 F.2d 1361 (9th Cir. 1985).   [3] Estate of Bongard, 124 TC 95 (2005).
[2] Estate of Grace, 395 U.S. 316 (1969).

Bona fide sale exception. Property transferred with a retained interest during a decedent's lifetime will not be included in the decedent's estate under IRC Sec. 2036(a) if the transfer of property was part of a bona fide sale in exchange for full and adequate consideration. A bona fide sale is an arm's-length business transaction between a willing buyer and a willing seller.[4] Availability of the exception rests on two requirements: (1) a bona fide sale, meaning an arm's-length transaction, and (2) full and adequate consideration.[5] Transfers will only qualify for the bona fide sale exception is there is a significant nontax reason for the transfer.[6]

Retained interest. Whether a decedent retained an interest in transferred property depends upon whether "there is an express or implied agreement at the time of transfer that the transferor will retain lifetime possession or enjoyment of, or right to income from, the transferred property." To avoid characterization as a retained interest, the decedent must have "absolutely, unequivocally, irrevocably, and without possible reservations" parted with all of her title, possession, and enjoyment of the transferred assets.[7] The term "enjoyment" has been described as "synonymous with substantial present economic benefit."[8] Reg. Sec. 20.2036-1(b)(2) provides that use, possession, right to income, or other enjoyment of transferred property is considered as having been retained or reserved "to the extent that the use, possession, right to the income, or other enjoyment is to be applied toward the discharge of a legal obligation of the decedent, or otherwise for his pecuniary benefit." Enjoyment of the transferred property is retained for purposes of IRC Sec. 2036(a)(1) "if there is an express or implied understanding among the parties at the time of the transfer, even if the retained interest is not legally enforceable."[9]

The term "right" has been described for purposes of IRC Sec. 2036(a) as "an ascertainable and legally enforceable power."[10] Reg. Sec. 20.2036-1(b)(3) provides:

> With respect to such a power, it is immaterial (i) whether the power was exercisable alone or only in conjunction with another person or persons, whether or not having an adverse interest; (ii) in what capacity the power was exercisable by the decedent or by another person or persons in conjunction with the decedent; and (iii) whether the exercise of the power was subject to a contingency beyond the decedent's control which did not occur before his death * * *. The phrase, however, does not include a power over the transferred property itself which does not affect the enjoyment of the income received or earned during the decedent's life.   * * *

In *Estate of Trombetta*,[11] the Tax Court concluded that the value of the assets of a 15-year annuity trust and a 15-year residence trust that were required to pay the grantor a fixed amount a year for 15 years and then distribute the remainder to the grantor's children or grandchildren were includible in the decedent's estate because

---

[4] Estate of Reichardt, 114 TC 144 (2000).

[5] Estate of Trombetta, TC Memo 2013-234; Estate of Harper, TC Memo 2002-121.

[6] Thompson, 382 F.3d 367 (3d Cir. 2004).

[7] Estate of Church, 335 U.S. 632 (1949).

[8] Estate of McNichol, 265 F.2d 667 (3d Cir. 1959); Estate of Reichardt, 114 TC 144 (2000).

[9] Estate of Trombetta, TC Memo 2013-234; Estate of Rapelje, 73 TC 82 (1979); Estate of Turner, TC Memo 2011-209.

[10] Byrum, 408 U.S. 125 (1972).

[11] Estate of Trombetta, TC Memo 2013-234; Estate of Erickson, TC Memo 2007-107; Estate of Hurford, TC Memo 2008 278.

the grantor (1) impliedly retained the right to possession or enjoyment of the transferred properties, (2) made all decisions with respect to the trust assets, and the co-trustees generally did whatever she directed them to do, (3) had sole signatory authority with respect to the disposition of the properties, and (4) had the right to the excess income from the properties, and (5) used the income from the properties to discharge her personal legal obligations.

What's included in the decedent's gross estate. A decedent's gross estate consists of the following:

1. Property owned by the decedent;
2. Property subject to dower or curtesy;
3. Transfers that occurred within three years of death;
4. Transfers taking effect at death;
5. Transfers with retained interests;
6. Commercial annuities;
7. Joint tenancies;
8. Property over which the decedent possessed general powers of appointment;
9. Life insurance owned by the decedent at the time of death;
10. Transfers for insufficient consideration; and
11. Qualified terminable interest property.

Each of these items is discussed below.

   (a) Property Owned by the Decedent. All property, including future interests, in which the decedent had an interest at the time of death is included in the decedent's gross estate. The concept of an ownership interest includes a beneficial interest [see ¶ 1802].

   (b) Property Subject to Dower or Curtesy. The gross estate includes the value of dower, curtesy and all interests created by statute in lieu of dower or curtesy [IRC Sec. 2034; see ¶ 1803].

   (c) Transfers Within Three Years of Death. The gross estate includes the value of any interest in property transferred, in trust or otherwise, if the decedent retained the power to alter, amend, revoke, or terminate the interest, or if such power was relinquished within three years of death [IRC Sec. 2035(a)(2); see ¶ 1804]. In addition, the decedent's gross estate includes an interest in a life insurance policy that was transferred within three years of the decedent's death [IRC Sec. 2042; see ¶ 1804].

   (d) Transfers Taking Effect at Death. The gross estate includes all lifetime transfers by the decedent if (1) the recipient must survive the donor to obtain possession or enjoyment of the property, (2) the donor retains a reversionary interest in the property, and (3) the value of the reversionary interest just before the donor's death is over 5 percent of the value of the property [see ¶ 1805].

   (e) Transfers with Retained Interests. IRC Sec. 2036 provides that a decedent's gross estate includes all lifetime transfers where the decedent retained for his or her lifetime either explicitly or implicitly (for a period longer than the decedent's life expectancy), the right to (1) receive income from the transferred property, (2) possession or enjoyment of the transferred property, (3) alter the beneficial enjoyment of the transferred property, or (4) vote shares of a closely held corporation [see ¶¶ 1806, 1807].

In *Estate of Tehan*,[12] the Tax Court concluded that the decedent's estate included the value of a condominium unit that the decedent had purportedly transferred to his eight children in a series of fractional interest gifts during the three years preceding his death under IRC Sec. 2036(a) because the decedent retained the right to possess and enjoy the residence during his life as evidenced by the fact that he continued to live there at all times after the purported transfers, paid all of the monthly expenses with respect to the unit, and at no time sought the permission of his children in order to have guests in the unit or to redecorate it.

Similarly, in *Estate of Disbrow*,[13] the full value of a decedent's personal residence, which was transferred to a family general partnership (FGP) created by the decedent, her five children, and their spouses, was includible in her gross estate under IRC Sec. 2036(a)(1). Although the decedent later transferred her entire interest in the residence to the FGP, the decedent was guaranteed by the other partners that she could live in the residence as long as she furnished the funds necessary to maintain the home. The decedent retained possession and enjoyment of the residence pursuant to an express agreement recorded in lease agreements for each of the years that she resided in the home because the agreements gave her the same rights to use and enjoy the residence following the transfer to the FGP as she had before the transfer without requiring the decedent to pay the residence's fair rental value. In addition, the parties' conduct and the lease agreements established that an implied agreement existed between the decedent and the FGP allowing the continued possession and enjoyment of the residence. The implied agreement was evidenced by the following: (1) the FGP was not a business operated for profit but was a testamentary device; (2) the decedent's relationship to the property was not treated by the decedent or the FGP as that of a tenant to leased property; (3) the transfer was made when the decedent was almost 72 years old and in poor health; (4) the other partners wanted the decedent to live in the residence for as long as she could and enjoy the residence as she had before the transfer; and (5) the transfer was made on the advice of counsel to minimize estate tax. Accordingly, the value of the personal residence was includible in the decedent's gross estate under IRC Sec. 2036(a)(1).

In *Estate of Stewart*,[14] the decedent and her adult son lived on the first two floors of a five-story brownstone in Manhattan. After the mother was diagnosed with a terminal illness, she conveyed 49 percent of the Manhattan brownstone to her son and they owned the property as tenants in common. She died six months later. During that six-month period, mother and son continued to live in the lower two floors of the brownstone, and the decedent leased the remaining three floors to an unrelated third party. The decedent received 100% of the rent and paid most of the expenses. On her estate tax return, she included only 51% of her interest in her gross estate. The IRS issued a notice of deficiency stating that the decedent had retained possession or

---

[12] Estate of Tehan, TC Memo 2005-128; see also Estate of Van, TC Memo 2011-22; Estate of Adler, TC Memo 2011-28.

[13] Estate of Disbrow, TC Memo 2006-34; Estate of Rosen, TC Memo 2006-115.

[14] Estate of Stewart, 617 F.3d 148 (2d Cir. 2010), *rev'g and remanding*, TC Memo 2006-225.

enjoyment of the transferred 49% interest and that, therefore, under IRC Sec. 2036, the entire property was part of her estate for federal tax purposes. The Tax Court held that the full value of the Manhattan property was includible in the mother's estate because the decedent "retained . . . the possession or enjoyment of, or the right to the income from, the property." The Tax Court emphasized the fact that the decedent and her son never entered into a written agreement to allocate income and expenses according to the parties' ownership interests and that the decedent and her son had an implied agreement that the decedent would retain economic benefits of the property.

The Second Circuit remanded the case to the Tax Court finding that the Tax Court erred in including all of the Manhattan property in the decedent's gross estate when her son lived there and retained a 49% interest in the property. The court concluded that IRC Sec. 2036(a) applied to only that portion of the son's 49% interest in the brownstone that produced the rental income decedent received. As for the residential portion, since the son continued to share occupancy with his mother, the Second Circuit held that it should not have been included in her taxable gross estate under IRC Sec. 2036(a).

The court looked at the two different property rights (1) retained rights of possession and occupancy and (2) the retained right to economic benefit (rental income). The decedent retained 100% of the rents so she must include in gross estate 100% of the economic value of the property attributable to rental income from the property. But with respect to the portion used as a residence, the Second Circuit said that there was no evidence that she retained rights to occupy the son's 49% interest in the property.

The question was whether she retained the actual "possession or enjoyment" of her son's 49 percent interest. The decedent's formal retention of a 51 percent interest in the property does not, the court stressed, necessarily mean that she retained enjoyment of the transferred 49 percent interest. The joint use of the residential part of the brownstone by the decedent and her son does not suggest that she had either held exclusive use of that portion or excluded her son's use.

▶ **PRACTICE POINTER:** To avoid the adverse tax results in *Estate of Tehan*, *Estate of Disbrow* and *Estate of Stewart*, taxpayers transferring a residence to a partnership or trust and continuing to live there or receive other benefits from the property should be sure to follow these guidelines:

1. If the transferee is living in the property after it has been transferred to the trust, the transferee should be certain to pay rent at its fair rental value;

2. To determine fair rental value, an independent analysis of the property value based on comparables should be obtained and the rent charged the parent should be set at or above the fair rental value;

3. Formalities typically associated with lease agreements should be observed. For example, a separate account should be set up to deposit rent receipts and keep track of and pay expenses related to the property;

4. The taxpayer still living in the property should pay his or her rent regularly and on time;

5. Avoid implied agreements regarding the transferor retaining economic benefits of the property.

(f) Commercial Annuities. The gross estate includes annuities or other payments made or to be made to the decedent during the decedent's lifetime that meet the following requirements: (1) the payments are pursuant to a contract or agreement; and (2) someone other than the decedent receives the annuity payments as a result of surviving the decedent. Commercial annuities are discussed at ¶ 1808.

(g) Joint Tenancies. Property in which the decedent at the time of death held an interest either as a joint tenant or as a tenant by the entirety, with right of survivorship, are included in the decedent gross estate in varying amounts depending on how the property is titled [see ¶ 1809]. Community property is discussed at ¶ 1813.

(h) General Powers of Appointment. Generally, property subject to a general power of appointment is included in the decedent's gross estate if he or she (1) dies possessing the power to appoint property to himself or herself, his or her estate, his or her creditors or the creditors of his or her estate; or (2) has exercised or released such a power during life in such a manner that if it were a disposition of property owned by the decedent, the disposition would be treated as incomplete for estate tax purposes [see ¶ 1810].

(i) Life Insurance. The proceeds of life insurance on a decedent's life payable to a named beneficiary are included in the decedent's gross estate if the proceeds are payable to the insured's personal representative [IRC Sec. 2042(1)] or if the decedent possessed any "incidents of ownership" in the policy at the time of death [IRC Sec. 2042(2)]. "Incidents of ownership" include rights to name the beneficiary, surrender or cancel the policy, assign the policy, pledge the policy for a loan, or otherwise enjoy the economic benefits of the policy [Reg. Sec. 20.2042-1(c)(2)]. State law determines whether and to what extent a decedent holds incidents of ownership in a life insurance policy [Reg. Sec. 20.2042-1(c)(5)]. For further discussion of life insurance see ¶ 401.

(j) Transfers for Insufficient Consideration. A decedent's estate includes property that was transferred for insufficient consideration. Only the excess of the fair-market value of the property over the money received for it is subject to inclusion in the decedent's taxable gross estate [IRC Sec. 2043(a); see ¶ 1811].

(k) Qualified Terminable Interest Property (QTIP). A decedent's gross estate includes any property that was transferred to the decedent as a result of a qualified terminable interest property (QTIP) marital deduction [IRC Sec. 2044] [see ¶ ¶ 1812, 1101].

¶ 1802 THE GROSS ESTATE: IRC SECTION 2033

A decedent's gross estate includes all property, real or personal, tangible or intangible, that the decedent owned at his or her death [IRC Sec. 2033; Reg. Sec. 20.2033-1(a)].

Example 1: Mom owns a Picasso painting. If she has not given it away or sold it by the time she dies, it will be included in her gross estate.

The decedent's gross estate includes all property that the decedent owned an interest in and had the right to transfer at death. Interests that terminate on the decedent's death, such as life estates, are not included in the taxable gross estate under Internal Revenue Code (IRC) Section 2033. The gross estate includes, however, any undistributed trust income that the decedent's personal representative or executor can collect as a result of the decedent's life estate.

In *Estate of Fortunato*,[1] the IRS claimed under IRC Sec. 2033 that the decedent had an ownership interest for estate tax purposes in a family warehouse business even though he owned no stock in the company. Because the decedent created the company's business strategies, controlled the finances, had the employees reporting to him, and held himself out as the business owner, the IRS determined that the decedent held a 50-percent interest in the companies as a beneficial or uncertificated owner and issued an estate tax deficiency against the estate.

To determine the decedent's interest in the property, the Tax Court first looked to state law (California, Georgia and New Jersey) which provided that a legal owner of a corporation may be an uncertificated shareholder. However, in cases where an individual was found to be an uncertificated owner, both the corporation and the individual must take overt actions demonstrating that both parties want the individual to obtain an ownership interest in the corporation. However, the court found that the decedent and his brother never wanted him to be a shareholder because (1) they were fearful that if creditors were aware of any assets owned by them, they would attempt (forcibly or otherwise) to collect past debts, and (2) they were worried that a criminal past would hurt business. Consequently, the Tax Court held that the decedent's participation in the family business did not amount to an ownership interest for federal estate tax purposes under IRC Sec. 2033 even though he was instrumental in its success.

In *Estate of Frazier*,[2] the Court of Appeals for the Ninth Circuit held that several structures built on a decedent's land were not includible in the decedent's gross estate because the structures were removable trade fixtures under applicable state (California) law. Under California law, fixtures were removable from a leasehold if, considering the method of attachment, the fixtures were not an integral part of the real property. In cases such as the decedent's, where the entire building was the fixture, California courts had permitted the lessee to remove the buildings as trade fixtures, holding that the buildings had not become integral parts of the underlying land. Accordingly, the improvements to the decedent's land were removable trade fixtures under California law and not includible in the decedent's gross estate.

Laws exist that exempt from income taxation bonds, notes, bills, and certificates of indebtedness of the federal government or its agencies. However, these statutes do not apply to the estate tax because this tax is an excise tax on the transfer of wealth and not a tax on the property transferred [Reg. Sec. 20.2033-1(a)]. A statutory exemption from tax does not apply to the estate tax (or the gift tax or the generation-skipping transfer

---

[1] ¶**1802** Estate of Fortunato, TC Memo 2010-105.

[2] Estate of Frazier, TC Memo 1999-201, *rev'd and rem'd*, 2001-1 USTC ¶60,404 (9th Cir. 2001),

TC Memo 2002-120, *rev'd and rem'd*, 2003-2 USTC ¶60,473 (9th Cir. 2003).

¶1802

[GST] tax) unless it makes specific reference to the wealth transfer tax provisions of the IRC.

(a) Dividends. Outstanding dividends declared to shareholders of record on or before the date of death are included in the gross estate [Reg. Sec. 20.2033-1(b)]. Dividends declared after the date of death are not included in the gross estate.

(b) Interest. Similarly, interest accrued at the date of the decedent's death constitutes part of his or her gross estate [Reg. Sec. 20.2033-1(b)]. Thus, unpaid interest accruing from the date of the last interest payment to the date of death on savings certificates redeemable after death without forfeiture of interest, together with the face amount of the certificates, is includable in the gross estate.

(c) Joint Return with Spouse. If the estate is entitled to a refund because of the overpayment of income tax, the overpayment is an asset includable in the gross estate. If the estate and the decedent's surviving spouse are entitled to a refund because of the overpayment of income tax, part of the overpayment of income is includable in the gross estate. The includable amount equals the amount by which the decedent's payment of the joint income tax exceeds his or her income tax liability.

The decedent's income tax liability for the period covered by a joint return is calculated by:

1. Figuring the amount of income tax for which the decedent would have been liable on a separate return, as if a separate return had been filed;

2. Figuring the amount of income tax for which the surviving spouse would have been liable on a separate return; and

3. Multiplying the joint income tax liability by a fraction, the numerator of which is the amount in item 1 and the denominator of which the aggregate of the amounts in items 1 and 2.

Item 3 above represents the decedent's income tax liability for the period covered by the joint return. The excess of the decedent's payment of the joint income tax over this amount is includable in the gross estate.

(d) Damages. A claim for damages for pain and suffering is included in the decedent's gross estate because the decedent could have recovered it before death. However, a wrongful death claim brought by the decedent's heirs is generally not included because the decedent could not have recovered it.[3] Medical insurance reimbursements are included in the gross estate if the decedent had a right to the amount at death.

(e) Social Security Benefits. Social Security benefits payable after the decedent's death to his or her surviving spouse (or if none, to certain other persons) are excluded from the decedent's gross estate.[4]

---

[3] Rev. Rul. 75-127, 1975-1 CB 297; Rev Rul. 69-8, 1969-1 CB 219; Ltr. Rul. 9622035.

[4] Rev. Rul. 75-145, 1975-1 CB 298.

¶1803 PROPERTY SUBJECT TO DOWER OR CURTESY

A surviving spouse's dower or curtesy interests or a statutory interest in place of dower and curtesy (i.e., a right to some portion of the deceased spouse's estate) is included in the decedent's gross estate [IRC Sec. 2034; Reg. Sec. 20.2034-1].

A dower interest is the part of the deceased husband's real property allowed to his widow for her lifetime. A curtesy interest is a deceased wife's real property interest that passes on her death to her husband for his lifetime if they have had children who are able to inherit the property. However, these interests do not increase the decedent's taxable estate because they qualify for the marital deduction [see ¶ 1101].

¶1804 TRANSFERS WITHIN THREE YEARS OF DEATH

Gifts made within three years of the donor's death generally are not included in the donor's gross estate provided the donor has retained no rights with respect to the transfers [IRC Sec. 2035(a)].

(a) Transfers Included in Decedent's Gross Estate. However, according to the so-called "three-year rule," the following four types of transfers are included in the decedent's gross estate if made within three years of death [IRC Sec. 2035(a)(2)]:

1. Transfers where the donor retained the beneficial enjoyment of the property during life under IRC Sec. 2036 [see ¶ 1807];

2. Transfers where the gift became complete at the donor's death under IRC Sec. 2037 [see ¶ 1805];

3. Transfers where the donor retained the power to alter, amend, or revoke a previous lifetime transfer under IRC Sec. 2038 [see ¶ 1806];[1] or

4. Transfers where the donor possessed an "incident of ownership" over life insurance proceeds or if the proceeds were receivable by the donor's estate under IRC Sec. 2042 [see ¶ 412].

(b) What Are "Incidents of Ownership". A donor possesses incidents of ownership over life insurance proceeds if he or she retains any of the following powers:

1. The power to change the beneficiary;

2. The power to change the time or manner in which the beneficiary or owner receives the beneficial interest of the policy or the proceeds;

3. The power to borrow against the policy;

4. The power to pledge the policy as collateral for a loan;

5. The power to choose where to receive dividends or apply them to premiums;

---

[1] **¶ 1804** Estate of Trombetta, TC Memo 2013-234.

6. The power to surrender the policy;

7. The power to determine the form in which proceeds are to be paid; or

8. The power to change the owner [Reg. Sec. 20.2042-1(c)(2)].

> **Example 1:** Mom owns a life insurance policy on her life with the proceeds payable upon her death to her estate. One year before her death, Mom gives the life insurance policy to Son. Under the three-year rule, the policy is included in Mom's gross estate because the life insurance proceeds would have been included in her estate under IRC Sec. 2042(1). This provision states that life insurance proceeds payable to the insured's estate are included in the insured's taxable gross estate [IRC Sec. 2035(d)(2)].

▶ PRACTICE POINTERS:

- If you assigned all rights under the insurance policy to another person *more than* three years before your death, the proceeds are not included in your gross estate. If you think the insured does not have three years to live, it is better to set up an irrevocable life insurance trust and transfer money into the trust so the trustee can purchase the life insurance policy. This way you completely avoid running into problems with the three-year rule.

- As is true in the case of all lifetime transfers, the three-year inclusion rules do not apply to property transferred through a bona fide sale for adequate and full consideration [IRC Sec. 2035(d)].

A gift of an insurance policy is considered to be made within three years of death if each year you repurchase a policy that expires at the end of the policy year and reassign it. In this situation, the repurchase and reassignment constitutes a new transfer. However, the proceeds are not included in the gross estate if there is an option for an automatic renewal of a group term life insurance policy on payment of the premium and if the policy was assigned more than three years before death.

The three-year rule also taxes releases within three years of death of a retained interest that would cause inclusion if held at death.

> **Example 2:** Mom sets up a trust and reserves the right to the income from the trust for her life. The trust property is included in her estate under IRC Sec. 2036(a) because she has retained a life estate [see ¶ 1807]. She cannot escape inclusion by assigning her right to the income to Son within three years of her death.

A release of a power of revocation [see ¶ 1806] within three years of death is also includable.

(c) Gifts from Revocable Trusts Within Three Years of Death. The value of property transferred to a donee from a decedent's revocable trust within three years of the decedent's death is not includable in the decedent's gross estate [IRC Sec. 2035(e)]. In addition, the value of property in a revocable trust with respect to which the decedent's power to revoke is relinquished during the three years before death is not includable in the decedent's gross estate. As a result, gifts made by a trustee from a revocable trust are treated as if they were made by the decedent and are eligible for the annual gift tax exclusion. This rule, which is found in IRC Sec. 2035(e), codifies the rules set forth in recent case law.[2]

> ▶ **PRACTICE POINTERS:** As a result of the rule that treats gifts from revocable trusts as if they were made by the decedent, gifts from a revocable trust will remove assets from the estate for estate tax purposes.

Example 3: Mom set up a revocable trust and gave the trustee the power to make annual gifts of $10,000 to each of her children and grandchildren. Gifts from Mom's revocable trust are treated as if they were made by Mom and are eligible for the annual gift tax exclusion.

(d) Special Application of Three-Year Rule. For purposes of making the following special estate tax computations, the value of the gross estate includes the value of all property to the extent of any interest that the decedent had at any time made a transfer, by trust or otherwise, during the three-year period ending on the date of the decedent's death [IRC Sec. 2035(c)(1)]:

1. Determining eligibility for special use valuation of certain farms and land [see ¶ 1908].

2. Determining whether the estate meets the eligibility requirements for sale or exchange income tax treatment on the redemption of certain closely held stock to pay death taxes [IRC Sec. 303].

3. Determining eligibility for installment payment of estate taxes [see ¶ 2303]. The requirement that more than 35 percent of the adjusted gross estate be an interest in a closely held business must be met both with and without the application of the three-year inclusion rule in order to qualify to pay your estate tax over two to ten annual installments [IRC Secs. 2035(d)(4), 6166(k)(5)].

4. For purposes of imposing tax liens [IRC Sec. 6324].

Example 4: Dad owns all of the stock in a closely held company. Its value in relation to his other assets is not sufficient to qualify for special use valuation [see ¶ 1908] or installment payment of estate tax [see ¶ 2303], both of which require that the business consist of a certain percentage of his estate to qualify. So Dad makes lifetime gifts to Wife and Children of cash and other property. If Dad does not survive for three years after these gifts, they are included in his estate. And that could render the estate ineligible to use the special use valuation and installment payment of estate tax breaks.

(e) Gross-Up of Gift Tax. Under the so-called "gross-up rule" of IRC Sec. 2035(b), even though gifts made within three years of death are not generally included in the donor's gross estate, gift taxes paid on such transfers are included in the donor's gross estate whether paid by the donor or by the donor's estate and whether paid on gifts made by the donor or the donor's spouse [IRC Sec. 2035(b)]. The gift tax that a

---

[2] McNeely, 16 F.3d 303 (8th Cir. 1994); Estate of Kisling, TC Memo 1993-262, *rev'd*, 32 F.3d 1222 (8th Cir. 1994), *acq.*, 1995-2 CB 1.

¶1804

donee pays as a condition of a gift (a so-called net gift) made within three years of the donor's death is includable in the donor's gross estate because the gift tax is primarily the obligation of the donor.[3] In *Brown*,[4] the court explained the purpose and structure of the gross-up rule of IRC Sec. 2035(b) as follows:

> [IRC Sec. 2035(b)] is designed to recoup any advantage gained by so-called "death-bed" transfers in which a taxpayer, cognizant of impending mortality, transfers property out of her estate in order to reduce estate tax liability. Although these inter vivos transfers incur gift tax liability, opting to transfer assets prior to death still carries a tax advantage. Gift tax is calculated using a tax exclusive method (the applicable rate is applied to the net gift, exclusive of gift taxes), whereas estate taxes are calculated on a tax inclusive method (the applicable rate is applied to the gross estate, before taxes are deducted). [IRC Sec. 2035(b)] presumes that gifts made within three years of death are made with tax-avoidance motives and eliminates the tax advantage for those death bed transactions.

¶1805 TRANSFERS TAKING EFFECT AT DEATH

Property that the decedent gave away or transferred during his or her lifetime (except in a bona fide sale for full consideration) is included in the decedent's estate if:

1. The decedent had a "reversionary interest" in the property (i.e., a chance to get it back on the happening of a stated condition such as failure of someone else to survive him);

2. The reversionary interest, immediately before death, is worth more than 5 percent of the value of the property; and

3. The recipient must survive the decedent to possess or enjoy the transferred interest [IRC Sec. 2037; Reg. Sec. 20.2037-1]. The value of a reversionary interest is determined under Internal Revenue Service (IRS) tables [see ¶ 1916].

(a) "Reversionary Interest" Defined. A reversionary interest includes the possibility that the transferred property may return to the decedent or his or her estate or may be subject to his or her power of disposition. The transfer is taxable, whether the reversionary interest arises by operation of law or by virtue of an express reservation in the trust.

A reversionary interest is not (1) the reservation of a life estate [see ¶ 1807]; (2) the possible return of, or power of disposition over income alone from the property; or (3) the possibility that the decedent during his or her lifetime might have gotten back an interest in the transferred property by inheritance through the estate of another person [IRC Sec. 2037(b); Reg. Sec. 20.2037-1(c)(2)].

---

[3] Estate of Sachs, 88 TC 769 (1987), *aff'd and rev'd*, 856 F.2d 1158 (8th Cir. 1988). See Estate of Morgens, 133 TC 402 (2009), *aff'd*, 2012-1 USTC ¶ 60,645, 678 F.3d 769 (9th Cir. 2012).

[4] Brown, 2003-1 USTC ¶ 60,462, 329 F.3d 664, 667-68 (9th Cir. 2003).

NOTE: The transferred interest is not included in the taxable gross estate if the transfer was made for its full worth in money or something else of equal value.

Determining whether IRC Sec. 2037 applies to tax in a decedent's estate property that was already given away during the decedent's lifetime can be difficult, as illustrated by the following three examples:

Example 1: Dad transfers property into a trust with income to Wife for life, then at her death principal to Dad's children then living, and if there are no children, then to Dad's estate. Sec. 2037 does not apply because Dad's children do not have to survive Dad. As a result, the property is not included in his estate.

Example 2: Dad transfers property into a trust with income for Wife but only for Dad's life, then at Dad's death principal to Wife's children, if there are any living, and if not then to Wife's children. Wife's children must survive Dad to take. Sec. 2037 does not apply because Dad has no reversion. As a result, the property in the trust is not included in his estate.

Example 3: Dad transfers property into a trust with income to Wife for life, then income to Dad for life, if living, and remainder to Dad's children. The reversion is to income only; therefore, IRC Sec. 2037 does not apply. However, IRC Sec. 2036 applies, resulting in the inclusion of the trust in Dad's gross estate less the value of Wife's life estate.

(b) Death Benefit Under Employment Contract. An employment contract may provide that the employer will pay a death benefit during the term of the contract to the employee's spouse or to the employee's estate if the spouse dies first. This is a transfer that takes effect at death. The employee retained a reversionary interest in the death benefit. If the value of the reversionary interest in the death benefit at the moment before death was more than 5 percent of the payment, the value of the death benefit is included in the employee's gross estate.

Example 4: John entered into an employment contract with ABC Corp. The employment contract provides that ABC will pay a stated death benefit to John's wife if John is an employee of ABC at his death. If John's wife dies before him, the contract allows the benefit to be paid to his estate. After John's death, the death benefit was paid to his wife under the terms of the contract. The value of John's reversionary interest in the death benefit payment was more than 5 percent of the value of the payment at the moment before death. The value of the death benefit is includable in John's estate as a transfer taking effect at death.

To determine whether the reversionary interest is worth more than 5 percent of the payment, taxpayers should consult the actuarial tables published by the Treasury Department [Reg. Sec. 25.2512-5]. These tables are used to value interests that are limited in time, such as life estates and interests for a term of years.

¶1805

(c) Transfer of Reversionary Interest Within Three Years of Death.
The decedent's gross estate includes the value of the property transferred that meets all three conditions stated above. However, if the decedent transferred the reversionary interest more than three years before death, the value of the property is not includable in the gross estate. Conversely, if the transfer of the reversionary interest occurs within the three-year period before death, the value of the property is includable in the gross estate, whether or not a gift tax return was required to be filed [see ¶ 1804].

¶1806 REVOCABLE TRANSFERS

Property that the decedent gave away during his or her lifetime will be included in the decedent's taxable gross estate if at the time of death the decedent retained the power to alter, amend, revoke, or terminate the property interest [IRC Sec. 2038(a)]. The property is included in the decedent's gross estate because the decedent did not relinquish complete dominion and control over the property.[1]

> **Example 1:** Dad transferred property into a trust and names herself as the trustee with the power to decide who will receive income from the trust and to change the beneficiary designations. Dad dies and is still trustee of the trust. The value of the assets in the trust are included in Dad's gross estate.

It is immaterial when or from what source the decedent acquired the power. It can be either from an express provision of the transfer, by operation of law, or by an unrelated action at a later date [IRC Sec. 2038(a)(1)]. It does not matter whether the power can be exercised alone, or only with someone else, or even only with the consent of the trustee and a beneficiary.[2]

(a) Nature of Power. Property that the decedent transferred and that is subject to a power to alter, amend, revoke, or terminate is included in the decedent's gross estate, even if the power cannot be used to benefit the decedent,[3] or the power is exercisable only as a custodian (such as under the Uniform Transfers to Minors Act (the UTMA)).[4] The discretion to pay over or withhold the custodial property renders the property included in the estate of the donor-custodian.

> ▶ **OBSERVATION:** The donor should not name himself trustee or custodian of a gift to a minor under the UTMA [see ¶ 904]. Instead, a third party (not a spouse) should be named the custodian. If the donor dies while serving as custodian over the gifted funds, the value of the property will be included in the donor's estate and be subject to estate tax. This would defeat one of the advantages of making the transfer in the first place. The same problem could arise if the donor merely retains the power to appoint himself the custodian.

---

[1] ¶**1806** Estate of Sommers, TC Memo 2013-8.

[2] City Bank Farmers Trust Co., 296 U.S. 85 (1935), *reh'g denied*, 296 U.S. 664 (1935).

[3] Estate of Holmes, 326 U.S. 480 (1946), *reh'g denied*, 327 U.S. 813 (1946).

[4] Rev. Rul. 57-366, 1957-2 CB 618; Rev. Rul. 59-357, 1959-2 CB 212.

Also triggering inclusion is a power exercisable as a trustee.[5] Thus, discretionary powers granted to trustees may cause inclusion of the trust assets if the settlor is serving as trustee with the power to revoke the trust at his or her death. Even if the settlor possessing the power to alter, amend, revoke, or terminate a trust lacks the mental or physical capacity to exercise the power, the trust property will still be included in his or her gross estate.

Other powers that result in the transferred property being included in the estate are:

1. The power to change the beneficiaries;[6]

2. A settlor-trustee's power to invade the trust principal for the beneficiary, unless the power is limited by an ascertainable standard (health, education, maintenance, or support, or HEMS for short); and

3. A power to control income flows to a beneficiary, unless limited by an ascertainable standard.[7]

(b) Revocable Transfers Versus Retained Life Interest. In the case of a transfer with retained life estate, the transferred property is not includable in the decedent's gross estate unless the decedent, expressly or by implication, reserves an interest in the property [see ¶ 1807]. In the case of a revocable transfer, on the other hand, all that is necessary for inclusion is that the decedent be in possession of the taxable power at the time of death.[8]

> **NOTE:** This rule does not apply when the beneficiary, in an independent and unrelated transaction, retransfers the trust property back to the individual who created the trust.[9] Thus, IRC Sec. 2038(a)(1) applies only when the decedent's power comes from a direct reservation that the decedent retained at the time of the transfer of the property from him or her or from the conditions of the original transfer from the decedent.

(c) Trustee Removal Powers. If the decedent named another person trustee but retained the power to appoint himself or herself trustee, the property is includable in the decedent's gross estate. The decedent is considered to have the powers of the trustee [Reg. Sec. 20.2038-1(a)].

> **Example 2:** Mom transferred property to a trust and named Son as the trustee, but she reserved the right to remove Son as trustee and name herself as trustee. The trust property is included in her taxable gross estate.

If, however, the decedent had only the power to appoint himself or herself trustee under limited conditions that did not exist at the time of the decedent's death, the trust property would not be included in the taxable gross estate.

For example, IRC Sec. 2038 is not applicable to a power which was not exercised prior to the decedent's death, Therefore the value of trust property would not be included in the decedent's gross estate if the decedent had the power to replace the trustee if the

---

[5] O'Malley, 383 U.S. 627 (1966).

[6] Crile, 76-2 USTC ¶ 13,161 (Ct. Cl. 1976).

[7] Rev. Rul. 73-143, 1973-1 CB 407.

[8] Rev. Rul. 70-348, 1970-2 CB 193.

[9] Estate of Reed, 75-1 USTC ¶ 13,073 (M.D. Fla. 1975).

¶ 1806

trustee resigned or was disqualified and those contingencies failed to occur during the decedent's lifetime.

> **Example 3:** Mom transferred property to a trust and named Son as the trustee, but she reserved the right to remove Son as trustee and name herself as trustee if Son ever became unable to function as trustee. The trust property is not included in her taxable gross estate.

For a discussion of a settlor's reservation of the power to remove a trustee and appoint a successor trustee who is not related, see ¶ 1807.

(d) Amount Included. The amount included in the decedent's gross estate under IRC Sec. 2038 is the fair-market value of the property that is subject to the decedent's power, valued as of the valuation date (generally the date of the decedent's death or the alternate valuation date [see ¶ 1907]) [Reg. Sec. 20.2038-1(a)].

When the transfer of property or the relinquishment of the power to revoke is made for consideration in money or money's worth, the amount to be included in the gross estate equals only the excess of the value, at the valuation date, of the property transferred over the value of the consideration received for it by the decedent [IRC Sec. 2038(a)(1); Reg. Sec. 20.2038-1(a)(1)].

(e) Exceptions. When a beneficiary (or any person other than the decedent) has exclusive and sole power to revoke or terminate a trust, the trust property is not taxable in the estate of the person who set up the trust [Reg. Sec. 20.2038-1(a)].

The value of the property transferred is also not includable in the decedent's gross estate if the decedent can exercise the power to alter, amend, revoke, or terminate only with the consent of all parties having a vested or contingent interest in the transferred property—and this is permitted under local law [Reg. Sec. 20.2038-1(a)(2)]. In some states, such a power adds nothing because the settlor's creditors cannot reach the trust income or principal.[10] In other states, such a power exposes the trust income to the settlor's creditors. In that case, the transferred property is taxable.

Excluded are contingent rights and powers beyond the decedent's control that are not exercisable at death. Thus, if the use of a power to revoke, alter, or amend was limited by a condition beyond the decedent's control, such as the death of another person during the decedent's life, and that condition never occurred, the property is not included in the decedent's gross estate as a revocable transfer [Reg. Sec. 20.2038-1(b)].

¶1807 TRANSFERS WITH RETAINED LIFE ESTATE

Property that is transferred during the decedent's life is included in the decedent's gross estate if he or she retained the right to use or enjoy the property or receive income from it during his or her lifetime [IRC Sec. 2036(a)]. Even retaining a lifetime right (alone or in conjunction with someone else) to designate who will possess or enjoy

---

[10] Estate of German, 85-1 USTC ¶ 13,610 (Ct. Cl. 1985).

the transferred property or its income will cause the value of the property to be included in the decedent's gross estate [IRC Sec. 2036(a)(2); Reg. Sec. 20.2036-1(a)].

> **Example 1:** Dad transfers money into a trust to benefit his children. He retains the right to say who will receive income from the trust and in what amounts and when the distributions will be made. His power is not limited by any standard related to health, education, maintenance, or support. The property in the trust is included in Dad's taxable estate when he dies.

This is the case because the mere existence of the power in the hands of the decedent at death amounts to sufficient dominion and control over the trust property to be equated with the retention of the enjoyment and ownership of the property and results in taxation.

> **NOTE:** If the transfer of property was made for its full worth in money (or other equal value), it is not included in the gross estate [IRC Sec. 2036(a); Reg. Sec. 20.2036-1(a)].

(a) Rights or Interests. The retained rights or interests that will result in taxation include the use, possession, income, or other enjoyment of the transferred property, or the right to name persons who will possess or enjoy the transferred property or its income. Inclusion is not triggered by a power over transferred property that does not have an impact on the enjoyment of income received or earned during the decedent's life [Reg. Sec. 20.2036-1(b)(3)].

The right to designate may be exercisable alone, or with others. It does not matter if the others have adverse interests, or if they or the person that made the transfer (i.e., the transferor) acts in a special position, such as a trustee or agent [Reg. Sec. 20.2036-1(b)(3)].

The use, possession, right to the income, or other enjoyment of the property is considered retained by the decedent to the extent that this use is to be applied toward the discharge of a legal obligation of the decedent or otherwise for the decedent's profit. This includes a legal obligation to support a dependent prior to the decedent's death [Reg. Sec. 20.2036-1(b)(2)].

> **Example 2:** Mom transfers property to Children in trust, but reserves the right to receive the income from the trust, in quarterly payments, for life. However, the trust states that Mom's estate does not receive any income that accrues between the last quarterly payment and the date of her death. The value of the property is includable in Mom's gross estate. Reason: The period for which the income was reserved is tied to her death.

The retention need not be expressed. An implied retention causes the value of the transferred property to be included in the decedent's gross estate. The IRS often seeks to use the implied retention rule to tax a residence that a parent transfers to a child when the parent continues to live in the residence after the transfer. Cases have gone both ways on this issue. One winner: A residence transferred by a father to his son and daughter-in-law without restrictions was not included in the father's gross estate, even though he continued to live there and pay the property tax.[1]

A retained power to designate who shall possess or enjoy the transferred property or its income results in the value of the property being included in the transferor's gross estate, even though the power is retained in a fiduciary capacity [Reg. Sec. 20.2036-1(b)]. A settlor-trustee's power to accumulate income is regarded as a power to designate enjoyment.

> ▶ **OBSERVATION:** For the assets of an irrevocable trust to be included in the settlor's gross estate, the settlor must have retained an enforceable right to receive income. Giving an independent trustee absolute discretion to distribute income to the settlor is not enough. If the settlor is also a trustee, the discretion to invade principal for the beneficiaries is not considered a reserved right to designate who shall possess or enjoy the property if the discretion is limited by an ascertainable standard (e.g., the health, education, maintenance, or support of the beneficiaries).[2]

(b) Reciprocal Trusts. The grantor cannot get around the retained life interest rule by joining with someone else, perhaps a sibling, to set up identical trusts to benefit each other. If this is done, the value of the sibling's trust is included in the grantor's gross estate and vice versa if the arrangement leaves each sibling in about the same economic position as they would have been had they named themselves life beneficiaries.[3]

> **Example 3:** Sister transfers property to a trust giving income to Brother for life, remainder to her children. Brother transfers an identical amount of property to a trust giving income to Sister for life, remainder to his children. Each is treated as the settlor of the trust established by the other, so the trust established by Brother is included in Sister's estate and the trust established by Sister is included in Brother's estate.[4]

(c) Trustee Removal Powers. The IRS has held that the retention of the power by a grantor to remove a trustee and appoint an individual or successor trustee that is not related or subordinate to the decedent would not result in the grantor retaining the trustee's discretionary powers. Thus, the value of the trust property would not be included in the grantor's gross estate upon his or her death.[5]

> **Example 4:** Brother created an irrevocable trust to pay the income to Sister for life with remainder over to her children. He named Local Bank as trustee with power to accumulate income. Brother retained the right to remove the bank and

---

[1] ¶1807 Diehl, 68-1 USTC ¶12,506 (W.D. Tenn. 1967), *not followed by* Rev. Rul. 78-409, 1978-2 CB 234.

[2] Estate of Wier, 17 TC 409 (1951), *acq.*, 1952-1 CB 4, *nonacq.*, 1966-2 CB 8.

[3] Estate of Grace, 395 U.S. 316 (1961); Estate of Sather, TC Memo 1999-309, *aff'd and rev'd*, 251 F.3d 1168 (8th Cir. 2001).

[4] Estate of Grace, 395 U.S. 316 (1961); Rev. Rul. 74-533, 1974-2 CB 293.

[5] Rev. Rul. 95-58, 1995-2 CB 191.

appear a successor trustee. Upon Brother's death, the value of the trust assets will not be includable in his gross estate.

This approach follows the decisions of the Tax Court in a pivotal case, *Estate of Wall,*[6] where the court upheld a grantor's retained right to remove a corporate trustee and appoint another without having the trust property included in her taxable estate. The court refused to take what it called a "quantum leap" in equating a grantor's trustee-removal power with retention by the grantor of the trustee's decision-making powers. In the absence of a side agreement between the grantor and the new trustee (which would be fraudulent), the grantor's retention of trustee-removal powers did not amount to the grantor retaining the power to determine who will enjoy the trust property or result in estate tax consequences.

▶ **PRACTICE POINTERS:** Include trustee removal and replacement provisions in all trusts.

(d) Administrative and Managerial Powers. Under IRC Sec. 2036, administrative and managerial powers retained by the settlor are subject to the following test: Can the decedent manipulate the fiduciary powers held by the trustee so that the decedent designates the enjoyment of the property transferred into the trust? If the answer is "yes," then the property subject to the power will be included in the decedent's gross estate.[7] The U.S. Supreme Court has recognized that administrative or managerial powers subject to legal limits (such as fiduciary duties) are beyond the scope of IRC Sec. 2036(a).[8]

Courts will likely impose fiduciary restrictions on the settlor's actions thereby excluding the reserved powers from estate tax inclusion when the powers are generally exercised by a trustee in the administration of a trust.

Care must be exercised in this area because the regulations state that an individual is deemed to have retained an interest or right in transferred property for tax purposes if at the time of the transfer "there was an understanding, express, or implied, that the interest or right would later be conferred" [Reg. Sec. 20.2036-1(a)]. This turns on a factual issue as to whether there was an understanding between the settlor and the trustee that the trustee would permit the settlor to determine who will possess or enjoy the trust property. For purposes of Sec. 2036, it does not matter that the "understanding" is unenforceable, all that matters is that the understanding exists. This results in taxation.

> **Example 5:** Max, the decedent-settlor, transferred property in trust, naming Tom as trustee, and reserved the power to join with the trustee in exercising decisions with regard to the type of investments to be held in the trust and to allocate receipts between principal and income. These management powers would appear to enable the decedent-settlor to accomplish the same objectives of redistributing income and principal between income beneficiaries and re-

---

[6] Estate of Wall, 101 TC 300 (1993), *later proceeding* 102 TC 391 (1994).

[7] Old Colony Trust Co., 300 F. Supp. 1032 (D. Mass. 1969), *aff'd*, 423 F.2d 601 (1st Cir. 1970).

[8] Northern Trust Co., 278 U.S. 339 (1929).

¶1807

mainder persons through choice of investments and allocation of receipts and disbursements. Federal estate tax inclusion seems likely.

Additional caution should be exercised if the settlor appoints himself or herself trustee and then grants the trustee broad discretionary powers. If the discretion is tantamount to a right to designate the persons who will possess or enjoy the property or income, estate tax inclusion results under IRC Sec. 2036(a)(2).

(e) Right to Vote Stock. If the decedent gives shares of a "controlled corporation" and retains the right, directly or indirectly, to vote the transferred shares, you are deemed to have retained the right to determine enjoyment of the transferred shares [IRC Sec. 2036(b)]. As a result, the value of the transferred stock is included in the decedent's taxable gross estate.

The capacity in which the decedent can exercise voting power is immaterial. This means that even if a decedent's right to vote the stock is only in a fiduciary capacity, such as trustee, co-trustee, or as officer of a corporation, the stock will still be includable in the decedent's estate [Prop. Reg. Sec. 20.2036-2(c)].

Voting rights are indirectly retained if there is an agreement or arrangement with a trustee to vote the stock according to the transferor's directions. Voting rights may be indirectly retained under an oral agreement with the trustee even if there is no such agreement in the trust instrument. Stock that may vote only on extraordinary matters, such as mergers or liquidations, will be disregarded. Similarly, Treasury stock and stock that is authorized but unissued will be disregarded [Prop. Reg. Sec. 20.2036-2(d)(2)(i)].

A "controlled corporation" is a corporation in which the decedent and his or her relatives, directly or indirectly, owned, or had the power to vote stock having at least 20 percent of the total combined voting power of all classes of stock. The time frame considered is any time after the gift is made, provided it is less than three years before the donor's death [IRC Sec. 2036(b)(2)].

According to the attribution rules, the decedent is considered to own stock held by his spouse (unless the spouse is legally separated from the decedent by a court order), children, grandchildren, and parents [IRC Sec. 318(a)(1)].

> **Example 6:** Two years before he dies, Dad gives voting stock in his family business to a trust. Dad retains the right to vote the shares. The stock will be included in Dad's estate.

(f) Trusts for Minors. When the donor-parent serves as trustee of a trust for minors [see ¶ 907], adverse estate tax consequences to the well-intentioned parent may result. If the trustee possesses the discretionary power to distribute income and principal, a donor who serves as trustee will be deemed to have made a transfer that results in the inclusion of the value of the trust property in the donor-parent's gross estate. Under IRC Sec. 2036(a), the donor-trustee has retained the power to control the time of enjoyment of the trust property,

¶1807

(g) Joint (Split) Purchases of Property. Estate planners use a joint or split purchase to pass the property as well as its appreciation to younger family members without estate tax consequences. This result can be achieved if:

1. The senior family member pays the actuarially determined value for the life estate; and

2. The junior family member pays the actuarially determined value for the remainder.

Any potential estate tax savings would be jeopardized if:

1. The consideration the junior family member paid for the remainder could be traced to funds that his or her parent or grandparent supplied. Thus, a senior family member's contribution via the junior family member might be recast as a purchase of the entire property (both life estate and remainder) and a gift of the remainder to the junior family member. The senior family member arguably has retained an income interest in the property. This "retained income interest" would trigger the inclusion of the entire value of the property, as of the date of death, in senior's gross estate under IRC Sec. 2036(a)(1).

2. There is a misvaluation of the property. The incorrect valuation of the property would cause the consideration paid for the life estate interest and remainder interest in the property to be inaccurate. The IRS might assert that the senior family member "gifted" any overpayment for the life estate to the junior family member, retaining an income interest (tainted under IRC Sec. 2036(a)(1)) in the property, resulting in the property, valued as of date of death, being included in the senior family member's gross estate for tax purposes.

(h) Amount Included. If the decedent kept or reserved one or more of these rights or interests, the amount includable in the gross estate is the value of the property transferred, minus the value of any outstanding income interest not subject to the decedent's interest or right. For its value to be excluded from the gross estate, the income interest must actually be enjoyed by someone else at the time of the decedent's death. If the decedent kept or reserved an interest or right to only a part of the transferred property, the amount includable in the gross estate is a corresponding part of the entire value of the property [Reg. Sec. 20.2036-1(a)].

If trust property is included in a decedent's gross estate under IRC Sec. 2036 because the decedent retained a power over the trust income, any income accumulated in the trust at the date of the decedent's death is also included in his or her gross estate.

¶1808 COMMERCIAL ANNUITIES AND OTHER DEATH BENEFITS

Annuities require periodic payments for a specified period of time. There are many types of annuities. This section is concerned with the commercial annuities.

(a) Commercial Annuities. Commercial annuities are often purchased from insurance companies or banks as a tax-deferred investment because the income that an annuity earns is out of the reach of Uncle Sam until the money in the annuity is withdrawn [IRC Sec. 72]. The purchaser receives an annuity payment for a specified number of years that usually is the duration of the purchaser's lifetime. When the purchaser dies, the beneficiaries receive the remaining benefits. Annuities can be used to save for retirement and to provide something for loved ones to inherit after the purchaser of the annuity dies.

Annuities that will be included in the gross estate. The bad news about annuities is that an annuity is included in the purchaser's gross estate after he or she dies if:

- The decedent was entitled to receive either alone or in conjunction with others all or part of the annuity payments that did not end before his or her death; and

- The contract provides that an annuity or other payment is payable to a beneficiary because he or she survived the beneficiary [IRC Sec. 2039(a)].

Examples of items includable under this rule include retirement benefits, IRAs, amounts paid under an annuity contract, and amounts paid under an employment contract calling for retirement and survivor benefits. The agreement need not be in writing, but the decedent and the survivor-beneficiary must have some enforceable rights to the payment. The inclusion applies whether the beneficiary receives a lump sum or periodic payments [Reg. Sec. 20.2039-1(b)].

Amount included in the gross estate. The amount of survivor benefit included in your gross estate is proportionate to the consideration or contribution you furnished. In the case of an employee's annuity, an employer's contribution to an employee's plan is deemed consideration furnished by the employee [IRC Sec. 2039(b); Reg. Sec. 20.2039-1(c)].

> **Example 1:** Dad is receiving pension benefits from his former employer. On his death, Daughter will receive survivor benefits for the rest of her life. The value of these survivor benefits, at the time of Dad's death, will be included in his gross estate.

> **Example 2:** Husband and Wife purchased a joint and survivor annuity for $50,000. Each paid one-half of the cost. Wife's interest is worth $40,000 at the time of Husband's death. Since he paid for half of the annuity, half of its date of death value ($20,000) is included in his gross estate.

(b) Other Estate Tax Consequences of Death Benefits. The survivor benefit provisions do not apply to life insurance. (For the estate taxation of life insurance, see ¶ 412.) They apply only when you are in actual receipt of, or have a right to receive, benefits (other than wages or salary or other employment compensation) during your life and a surviving beneficiary receives benefits under the same arrangement [Reg. Sec. 20.2039-1(b)(1)]. A death benefit that is not taxed as a survivor benefit may still be taxed as property that you own at death.

Rule of thumb. If the decedent had any enforceable right at the time of death and as a result payment is made to a survivor or to the decedent's estate, the amount is includable in the decedent's gross estate under IRC Sec. 2039. The inclusion may come

¶1808

under either the rules for property owned at the time of death, a survivor benefit, a transfer taking effect at death, or other taxable life transfer.

On the other hand, if the decedent had no enforceable right but her employer makes a voluntary payment (or voluntary payments) to her surviving spouse or children or to any other person, the death benefit is not taxable under any estate tax provision.[1] It should also be remembered that taxable death benefits payable to a surviving spouse usually qualify for the estate tax marital deduction [see ¶ 1101].

> **Example 3:** Gary was an employee of ABC Corp. Every year ABC Corp. gives a bonus to a certain class of employees, of which Gary was one. To be eligible, the employee must be alive on the last day of the company's fiscal year. If an employee dies before the end of the fiscal year, the company has discretion to pay the bonus to the employee's widow or children. Gary died before the last day of the fiscal year, and the company paid the bonus to his daughter. Because Gary had no enforceable right to any part of the bonus on the date of his death, the amount paid to his daughter is not includible in his gross estate.

> **NOTE:** Certain death benefits paid by the government are not included in a decedent's gross estate because they are payable under statute rather than under contract or agreement. These include payments made under the Social Security Act, the Railroad Retirement Act, the Federal Coal Mine Health and Safety Act of 1969, and the Public Safety Officers' Benefit Act.[2]

(c) Lottery Winnings. There is a split in the federal circuits on whether the IRS valuation tables must be used when valuing the remaining payments due to a deceased winner of a lottery. Generally, lottery winnings are valued as an annuity. The estate tax value of a stream of annuity payments is determined under tables issued by the IRS in the regulations under IRC Sec. 7520. The value is therefore derived from application of standardized valuation tables used to value annuities found in IRC Sec. 7520(a). However, departure from the annuity valuation tables is appropriate when adherence to them would produce an obviously erroneous result, or would produce a substantially unrealistic and unreasonable result. A party challenging application of the tables bears the considerable burden of proving that the tables produce such an unrealistic and unreasonable result that they should not be used.

The basic issue on which the courts have disagreed is whether the IRC Sec. 7520 annuity tables produce an unrealistic and unreasonable result when valuing lottery payments with marketability restrictions.

---

[1] **¶ 1808** Estate of Barr, 40 TC 227 (1963), *acq.*, 1978-2 CB 1 (in result).

[2] Rev. Rul. 2002-39, 2002-2 CB 33 (accidental death benefits payable pursuant to New York City and New York state laws to specified beneficiaries of a deceased New York City firefighter or police officer who died in the line of duty are not includible in the decedent's gross estate, except to the extent the benefits represent a return of the decedent's contributions to the pension fund); Rev. Rul. 60-70, 1960-1 CB 372 (*as modified* by Rev. Rul. 73-316, 1973-2 CB 318); Rev. Rul. 76-102, 1976-1 CB 172 (amounts paid under the Federal Coal Mine Health & Safey Act of 1969 not includible in decedent's gross estate); Rev. Rul. 79-397, 1979-2 CB 322 (value of death benefits payable pursuant to federal law under the Public Safely Officers' Benefit Act to survivors of decedents who died in the line of duty are not includible in the gross estate); Rev. Rul. 81-82, 1981-2 CB 179.

¶1808

Following the Court of Appeals for the Ninth Circuit's opinion in *Estate of Shackleford*,[3] the Court of Appeals for the Second Circuit reversed the Tax Court in *Estate of Gribauskas*,[4] to hold that Lotto payments owed to an estate should not be valued using the IRC Sec. 7520 annuity tables when a more accurate valuation, which takes into account marketability restrictions, is available. The court found that it is appropriate, when valuing the Lotto winnings, to consider the fact that winners are forbidden from assigning or transferring their right to future installments to third parties. As one would expect, these prohibitions severely restricted the ability of winners to exchange contractually their rights to future payments for an up-front lump sum. In *Estate of Shackleford*, the Court of Appeals for the Ninth Circuit held that where the tables produce an unrealistic and unreasonable value, they are not an appropriate method of valuation. The court considered the lack of marketability for the transferred assets when valuing future payments and concluded that the tables should be ignored where they fail to take into consideration the decrease in value resulting from transfer restrictions.

Setting up the split in the circuits, the Court of Appeals for the Fifth Circuit held in *Cook*,[5] that a lottery prize should be characterized as a private annuity and that the nonmarketability of the payments did not cause the valuation under the Section 7520 tables to be unreasonable. According to the court, the value produced under the tables was not so unreasonble or unrealistic as to warrant using a different valuation method. The court concluded that the value of a lottery prize is the sum of the payments to be received, discounted because the payments are made over time. The tables provide a discount to account for this time delay and therefore must be used to value the prize for estate tax purposes.

In *Estate of Donovan*,[6] a U.S. District Court in Massachusetts held that nonassignable lottery winnings are valued, for estate tax purposes, under the IRS actuarial tables, without regard to their nonassignability. They agreed with the analysis of the Tax Court and the Fifth Circuit in *Cook*, and rejected the analysis adopted by the Second and Ninth Circuits in *Gribauskas* and *Shackleford*, respectively.

In *Estate of Davis*,[7] an estate's interest in future lottery payments was valued in accordance with the IRC Sec. 7520 annuity tables because the estate failed to prove that the tables produced an unrealistic and unreasonable result and, therefore, the payments should be calculated by another method. The district said that lack of marketability for the lottery payments was not a relevant factor in determining the value of the payments.

In *Estate of Negron*,[8] two decedents, together with a third party, jointly won an Ohio lottery prize of $20 million. Each winner was entitled to receive 26 annual payments of $256,000 for a total payment of approximately $6,667,000. When each of the two

---

[3] Estate of Shackleford, 99-2 USTC ¶60,356 (E.D. Cal. 1999), *aff'd*, 262 F.3d 1028 (9th Cir. 2001).

[4] Estate of Gribauskas, 116 TC 142 (2001), *rev'd and rem'd*, 342 F.3d 85 (2d Cir. 2003).

[5] Estate of Cook, TC Memo 2001-170, *aff'd*, 349 F.3d 850 (5th Cir. 2003); Estate of Anthony, 2005-2 USTC ¶60,504 (M.D. La. 2005), *aff'd*, 520 F.3d 374 (5th Cir. 2008).

[6] Estate of Donovan, 2005-1 USTC ¶50,322 (D. Mass. 2005).

[7] Estate of Davis, 491 F. Supp. 2d 192 (DC N.H. 2007).

[8] Estate of Negron, 2007-1 USTC ¶60,541 (DC Ohio 2007), *rev'd and rem'd*, 553 F.3d 1013 (6th Cir. 2008).

decedents died, each had received 11 lottery payments and had 15 more payments remaining. These payments were not assignable and could not be used as collateral for a loan. Each decedent's estate reported the value as $2,275,867 based upon the amount that each received from the Ohio Lottery Commission as a lump sum distribution. The Ohio Lottery Commission had determined the present value of the remaining payments using a 9 percent discount rate.

The IRS determined that the value of the remaining payments was $2,775,209 for one decedent and $2,668,118 for the second decedent based upon the IRC Sec. 7520 tables. The IRS appealed the district court's determination that a departure from the annuity tables would be warranted if the tables created an "unreasonable and unrealistic result" and there was a more reasonable and realistic means by which to determine the fair market value.

The Sixth Circuit reversed and remanded the district court decision to hold that the annuity tables in IRC Sec. 7520 accurately reflected the fair market value of future lottery payments. As a result of this decision, the disagreement between the Circuits on the valuation of lottery payments at a decedent's death continues.

▶ **PRACTICE POINTER:** A taxpayer who wins a lottery in one year but receives installment payments with no right to an accelerated lump sum, receives income in the year each installment is paid. If received after death, income in respect of decedent (IRD) must be recognized. The recipient of IRD, however, may claim an income tax deduction for federal estate tax attributable to the inclusion of IRD in the gross estate. See ¶ 2614 for a further discussion of IRD.

¶ 1809   JOINT PROPERTY AND QUALIFIED JOINT INTERESTS OF SPOUSES

(a) General Rule. The decedent's gross estate includes property held by the decedent and any other person as joint tenants with right of survivorship [IRC Sec. 2040; Reg. Secs. 20.2040-1(a), 20.2040-1(b)].

Example 1: Dad uses his own funds to buy property jointly with Son. They hold the property as joint tenants with right of survivorship. When Dad dies, the full date-of-death value of the property will be included in his gross estate.

A joint tenancy with right of survivorship is a form of ownership in which the survivor automatically becomes the owner of the property after the death of the first joint owner. The entire value of jointly held property is included in a decedent's gross estate unless one of the three exceptions apply:

1. If the executor submits facts sufficient to show that property was not acquired entirely with consideration furnished by the decedent, the portion representing the survivor's contribution is not included in the decedent's estate [IRC Sec. 2040(a)] (the "consideration furnished exception");

2. To the extent that the property was acquired by the decedent and the other joint owner by gift, devise, bequest, or inheritance, the decedent's fractional share of the

¶ 1809

property is included in his or her gross estate [Reg. Sec. 20.2040-1(a)(1)] (the fractional share test);

3. If the joint tenants are married, only one-half of a spouse's qualified joint interest is included in the deceased joint tenant's gross estate for federal estate tax purposes, regardless of who furnished the consideration. This interest is valued as of the valuation date [see ¶ 1907] [IRC Sec. 2040(b)] (qualified spousal interest test).

(b) Consideration Furnished Exception. If the executor can prove that the nonspousal survivor paid part of the property's cost, the portion representing the survivor's contribution is not included in the decedent's estate [IRC Sec. 2040(a)]. This so-called consideration furnished test applies regardless of whether the decedent-spouse is a citizen or resident of the United States.

Examples of the acceptable forms of consideration include:

1. Income from property gifted by the decedent, if the donee realizes and recognizes the income for federal income tax purposes [Reg. Sec. 20.2040-1(c)];
2. Gain from the sale of property gifted by the decedent;[1]
3. Appreciation on the original consideration;
4. Payments on a mortgage that financed the acquisition of the property;[2] and
5. One joint tenant providing the other joint tenant with a home for a considerable length of time could constitute sufficient consideration.[3]

The following examples illustrate the application of the consideration furnished test and in each of these examples, it is assumed that the other joint owner or owners survived the decedent:

1. If the decedent furnished the entire purchase price of the jointly held property, the value of the entire property is included in his gross estate;
2. If the decedent furnished only a part of the purchase price, only a corresponding portion of the value of the property is so included;
3. If the decedent furnished no part of the purchase price, no part of the value of the property is so included;
4. If the decedent, before the acquisition of the property by himself and the other joint owner, gave the latter a sum of money or other property which thereafter became the other joint owner's entire contribution to the purchase price, then the value of the entire property is so included, even if the other property may have appreciated in value due to market conditions between the time of the gift and the time of the acquisition of the jointly held property;
5. If the decedent, before the acquisition of the property by himself and the other joint owner, transferred to the latter for less than an adequate and full consideration other income-producing property, the income from which belonged to and became the other joint owner's entire contribution to the purchase price, then the value of

---

[1] ¶ **1809** Estate of Goldsborough, 70 TC 1077 (1978), *aff'd*, 49 AFTR ¶ 82-1469 (4th Cir. 1982).

[2] Rev. Rul. 79-302, 1979-2 CB 328.

[3] Estate of Concordia, TC Memo 2002-216.

¶1809

the jointly held property less that portion attributable to the income which the other joint owner did furnish is included in the decedent's gross estate;

6. If the property originally belonged to the other joint owner and the decedent purchased his interest from the other joint owner, only that portion of the value of the property attributable to the consideration paid by the decedent is included;

7. If the decedent and his spouse acquired the property by will or gift as tenants by the entirety, one half of the value of the property is included in the decedent's gross estate; and

8. If the decedent and his two brothers acquired the property by will or gift as joint tenants, one third of the value of the property is included in the decedent's gross estate [Reg. Sec. 1.20.2040(c)].

When computing how much to exclude from the decedent's estate for consideration furnished by the surviving joint tenant, you exclude "such part of the entire value" that is attributable to the amount of money paid by the other joint owner or owners. "Such part of the entire value" is that portion of the entire value of the property at the decedent's death that the money furnished by the other joint owner or owners bears to the total cost of acquisition and capital additions [Reg. Sec. 20.2040-1(a)(2)].

(c) Fractional Share Exception. To fall within the fractional share exception, the property must have been gratuitously transferred to the decedent and other(s) who are not married to each other as joint tenants. According to this exception, for property acquired by gift, devise, or inheritance, only the decedent's stated ownership share (or if unstated, the decedent's pro rata share) of the property is included in his or her gross estate [IRC Sec. 2040(a) (last sentence)].

> **Example 2:** If the decedent and his two brothers acquired the property by will or gifts as joint tenants, one-third of the value of the property is included in the decedent's gross estate.

The fractional interest rule is limited to the portion of the property that is acquired gratuitously. If consideration is furnished for improvements made to the property, but the consideration is not furnished proportionally by each joint tenant, the value of the improvements is governed by the consideration furnished test, discussed above.

The fractional share rule also applies to spousal joint interests created by a gift, devise, or inheritance from a third party. This same result occurs under IRC Sec. 2040(b).

> **NOTE:** Joint tenancy should not be confused with tenancy in common. In a tenancy in common, the deceased can transfer his or her share to whomever he or she desires. The property does not automatically go the surviving joint tenant. Only the fractional interest of the decedent is included in his or her gross estate.

> **Example 3:** Brother furnished $20,000 and Sister supplied $60,000 to purchase a piece of property as tenants in common. At the time of Brother's death, the property was worth $160,000. Because Brother held a 25 percent undivided interest in the property, $40,000 is includable in his gross estate ($160,000 × .25).

¶1809

(d) Qualified Spousal Interest Rule. The estate of the decedent includes one-half of any survivorship property owned with the decedent's spouse, regardless of which spouses's fund were used to purchase the property [IRC Sec. 2040(b)].

> **Example 4:** Mom and Dad own their home as tenants by the entirety. Dad's money was used to buy the house. Mom dies first. One-half of the fair-market value of the home on the date of death will be included in her estate even though her money was not used to purchase the house. After Mom's death, Dad owns the home.

"Qualified joint interest" means an interest held by only the spouses as tenants by the entirety or joint tenants with the right of survivorship [IRC Sec. 2040(b)(2)]. In addition to holding a qualified joint interest, the three other conditions must be met:

1. The decedent and the decedent's spouse must be married at the time of the decedent spouse's death;

2. The joint tenancy must have been created prior to the decedent's death; and

3. The surviving spouse must be a citizen of the United States.

Satisfying these conditions is straightforward in most instances. Federal law determines citizenship and state law determines the other conditions.

Because of the unlimited estate tax marital deduction [see ¶ 1101], qualified joint interest property passes tax-free to the surviving spouse. The cost basis for the property for income tax purposes in the hands of the survivor is:

1. The original cost as to one-half, plus

2. The estate tax value as to the balance.

> **Example 5:** Husband bought property with $50,000 of his own funds in the names of himself and Wife as joint tenants with the right of survivorship. Husband dies when the property is worth $80,000. One-half of the date-of-death value ($40,000) of the property is includable in Husband's gross estate. And that one-half has a stepped-up basis for income tax purposes when Wife sells the property. Thus, her basis becomes $65,000 ($25,000 + $40,000).

(e) Pre-1977 Rule. The consideration furnished test of IRC Sec. 2040(a) applies to spousal joint interests created prior to 1977. When one spouse furnished the entire consideration, the entire value of property is included in the spouse's gross estate for federal estate tax purposes. The property escapes immediate federal estate tax because of the unlimited estate tax marital deduction [see ¶ 1101]. The surviving spouse takes as his or her basis, for federal income tax purposes, the full value of the property as of the valuation date, thereby eliminating federal income tax consequences on the appreciation of the survivor's one-half of the joint property.[4] Thus, no income tax has to be paid on any of the appreciation in the value of the property occurring before the death of the

---

[4] Gallenstein, 91-2 USTC ¶60,088 (D. Ky. 1991), aff'd, 975 F.2d 286 (6th Cir. 1992); Patten, 96-1 USTC ¶60,231 (D. Va. 1996), aff'd, 116 F.3d 1029 (4th Cir. 1997).

¶1809

first joint tenant to die, provided that the deceased tenant furnished all the consideration.

> **Example 6:** Husband bought property with $50,000 of his own funds in the names of himself and Wife as joint tenants with the right of survivorship in 1982. Husband dies when the property is worth $80,000. One-half of the date-of-death value ($40,000) of the property is includable in Husband's gross estate. And that one-half has a stepped-up basis for income tax purposes when Wife sells the property. Thus, her basis becomes $65,000 ($25,000 + $40,000).

> **Example 7:** Assume the same facts as in example above except that Husband made the purchase in 1976. The full $80,000 would be included in his estate and Wife would get an $80,000 basis.

(f) Simultaneous Death of Co-Owners. When joint owners die simultaneously so who died first cannot really be determined, state law determines the disposition of the property. Generally, the governing state law is the Uniform Simultaneous Death Act, which provides that each joint tenant is deemed to have survived the other. Thus, each estate would include one half of the joint property under IRC Sec. 2033. The remaining one half of the property would be tested for inclusion under the consideration furnished test of IRC Sec. 2040(a).

When spouses perish simultaneously, the unlimited estate tax marital deduction [see ¶ 1101] for qualified joint interests should apply to the portion of the property tested under IRC Sec. 2040. Thus, only one-half of the value of the property is ultimately included in each spouse's gross estate.[5]

(g) Disclaimers of Jointly Held Property. The law provides that a joint tenancy with right of survivorship and a tenancy by the entirety between spouses must be disclaimed within nine months after the joint interest was *created* [IRC Secs. 2046, 2518(b)(2); see ¶ 1209]. This requirement is problematic because you have to figure out when the property interest was created—way back when the joint interest was originally created or when one of the joint property owners dies and the property passes by operation of law to the survivor.

A second big issue in disclaimer planning is deciding whether a spouse can disclaim the one-half survivorship interest in property that he or she originally contributed.

The judicial response. The courts have held that the disclaimer of jointly held property made within nine months after the death of the first joint tenant was valid even though the joint interest was created several decades earlier.[6] The courts have reasoned that because state law permitted the joint tenancy with right of survivorship to be unilaterally transferred by one of the joint tenants, the transfer of the entire property interest did not occur until the death of one of the joint property owners. Until that time,

---

[5] Rev. Rul. 76-303, 1976-2 CB 266.

[6] Kennedy, TC Memo 1986-3, *rev'd,* 804 F.2d 1332 (7th Cir. 1986); Dancy, 89 TC 550 (1987), *rev'd and rem'd,* 872 F.2d 84 (4th Cir. 1989); Mc-

Donald, 853 F.2d 1494 (8th Cir. 1988) *on remand,* TC Memo 1989-140, *cert. denied sub nom.* Cornelius, 490 U.S. 1005 (1989).

either of the joint tenants could transfer their undivided one-half interest and destroy the survivorship interest of the other joint tenant. Thus, as the law currently stands, the interest of a surviving tenant can be disclaimed nine months after the death of the first co-tenant even though the interest may have been created many years earlier.

The IRS response. The IRS agrees with the courts and has issued a formal response, called an Action on Decision,[7] in which they make it clear that they will no longer argue that a disclaimer of jointly held property is invalid because it should have been done within nine months of the day the joint interest was originally created. The IRS also stated that is okay for a joint tenant to make a qualified disclaimer of any portion of the joint interest attributable to consideration that he or she furnished.

▶**PRACTICE ALERT:** In order to ascertain whether a "qualified disclaimer" is a viable post-death planning option, local law must give the joint tenant the right to unilaterally sever the joint tenancy or cause the property to be partitioned. In states where a joint tenancy cannot be partitioned except by a voluntary act by both tenants, the "transfer" for IRC Sec. 2518 purposes occurs on the date the tenancy was created. Be sure to know the law in your state.

The IRS regulations echo the court view and the Action on Decision discussed above and provide that a surviving joint tenant may disclaim the one-half survivorship interest in property held in joint tenancy with right of survivorship or in tenancy by the entirety within nine months of the death of the first joint tenant to die. This rule applies regardless of the following:

1. The portion of the property attributable to consideration furnished by the disclaimant;
2. The property that is included in the decedent's gross estate; and
3. Whether the interest can be unilaterally severed under local law [Reg. Sec. 25.2518-2(c)(4)(i)].

▶ **PRACTICE POINTER:** These final regulations are helpful to married couples who own property as tenants by the entirety. Now the surviving spouse can disclaim the interests that they held as joint tenants by the entirety within nine months of the death of the first tenant to die.

Example 8: Alice purchased real property with her own money. Title to the property was conveyed to Alice and Bob, as joint tenants with right of survivorship. Alice and Bob are not married. Under state law, the joint interest is unilaterally severable by either tenant. Bob dies eight years later and is survived by Alice. Just six months after Bob's death, Alice disclaims the one-half survivorship interest in the property to which Alice succeeds as result of Bob's death. Assuming that the other requirements of IRC Sec. 2518(b) are satisfied, Alice has made a qualified disclaimer of the one-half survivorship interest (but not the interest retained by Alice upon the creation of the tenancy, which may not be disclaimed by Alice). The result is the same whether or not Alice and Bob are married and regardless of the proportion of consideration furnished by Alice and Bob in purchasing the property [Reg. Sec. 25.2518-2(c)(5), Example (7)].

---

[7] Action on Decision, CC-1990-06 (Feb. 7, 1990).

Example 9: Sally purchases a parcel of real property with her own money. Sally was married to Bob. The property was titled "Sally and Bob as tenants by the entirety." Assume Sally dies first. In order to be a qualified disclaimer, any disclaimer by Bob of Bob's interest in the land must be made within nine months of the date of Sally's death. The result is the same regardless of the proportion of consideration furnished by either spouse in purchasing the property [Reg. Sec. 25.2518-2(c)(5), Example (8)].

(h) Joint Bank and Brokerage Accounts. For joint bank accounts and joint brokerage accounts including mutual fund accounts, the regulations provide that the nine-month period begins when the first joint tenant dies. A surviving joint tenant cannot disclaim any portion of the account attributable to the survivor's own contributions [Reg. Sec. 25.2518-2(c)(4)(iii)].

Example 10: Alice opens a bank account that is held jointly with Bob, Alice's spouse, and transfers $50,000 of her money to the account. Alice dies five years later, and Bob disclaims the entire amount in the bank account just two months after Alice's death. Assuming that the remaining requirements of IRC Sec. 2518(b) are satisfied, Bob has made a qualified disclaimer because the disclaimer was made within nine months after Alice's death at which time Bob had succeeded to full dominion and control over the account. As a result of the disclaimer, Bob is treated as predeceasing Alice with respect to the disclaimed interest. The disclaimed account balance passes through Alice's probate estate. The result would be the same if Alice and Bob were not married [Reg. Sec. 25.2518-2(c)(5), Example (12)].

Example 11: The facts are the same as in the example above except that Bob dies first. Alice may not make a qualified disclaimer with respect to any of the funds in the bank account because Alice furnished the funds for the entire account and Alice did not relinquish dominion and control over the funds [Reg. Sec. 25.2518-2(c)(5), Example (13)].

Result of disclaimer. If a qualified disclaimer is made with respect to a taxable transfer, the federal estate tax provisions apply with respect to the property interest disclaimed as if there had never been a gift or transfer of the property to the person making the disclaimer [Reg. Secs. 20.2046-1, 20.2046-1(a)].

¶1810 TRANSFERS SUBJECT TO POWER OF APPOINTMENT

(a) Power of Appointment Defined. A power of appointment is a power enabling the holder of the power to determine who will own or enjoy the property subject to the power even if the holder of the power of appointment never owned the property [see ¶ 205]. It does not matter whether a power is actually called a power of appointment in a legal document. It also does not matter if the term is used in local property law. What matters is that the power exists in substance and effect [Reg. Sec. 20.2041-1(b)(1)].

Some powers do not in themselves constitute a power of appointment. For example, a power to amend only administrative provisions of a trust that cannot substantially affect the beneficial enjoyment of the trust property or income is not a power of appointment. A power to manage, invest, or control assets, or to allocate receipts and disbursements, when exercised only in a fiduciary capacity, also is not a power of appointment [Reg. Sec. 20.2041-1(b)(1)].

Powers of appointment are valuable in estate planning because they provide for flexibility to meet changed circumstances. For example, a testator may want to give a surviving spouse a power to give property to those of their children who are in the greatest need. The spouse would be able to respond to needs of different children as they arise. The estate tax consequences of powers of appointment vary depending on whether the power of appointment is a general power or a special power.

(b) General Powers of Appointment. A general power of appointment is a power created by someone other than the decedent-holder that is exercisable in favor of either the holder, the holder's estate, creditors, or creditors of the holder's estate [IRC Sec. 2041(b)(1); Reg. Sec. 20.2041-1(c)(1)]. A discretionary power to consume or to invade trust principal or interest (or both) for the benefit of the decedent-holder is also considered a general power of appointment, unless it is limited by an ascertainable standard relating to the decedent's health, education, maintenance, or support [IRC Sec. 2041(b)(1)(A); Reg. Sec. 20.2041-1(c)(2)].

There are many cases interpreting the meaning of "ascertainable standard." The IRS regards a power to use property for the comfort, welfare, or happiness of the decedent as not subject to an ascertainable standard and, therefore, as a general power of appointment [Reg. Sec. 20.2041-1(c)(2)]. However, one appellate court has said that a power to invade principal "as . . . required for the continued comfort, support, maintenance, or education of the beneficiary" was limited by an ascertainable standard and therefore was not a general power.[1]

The value of property over which a decedent had a general power of appointment at the time of his or her death is includable in his or her gross estate [IRC Sec. 2041(a)(2)]. The mere existence of a general power of appointment, without its exercise, will result in inclusion of the trust property in the decedent's gross estate. Property over which the decedent had a general power of appointment is taxable, even if the decedent was unaware of its existence[2] or was incompetent at all times after the power was conferred.[3] In determining the estate tax value of two blocks of stock in the same company, a block owned outright had to be aggregated with a block over which the individual possessed a general power of appointment, exercisable only in his will.[4]

---

[1] **¶1810** Estate of Vissering, 96 TC 749 (1991), *rev'd and rem'd*, 990 F.2d 578 (10th Cir. 1993).

[2] Estate of Freeman, 67 TC 202 (1976).

[3] Estate of Alperstein, 71 TC 351 (1978), *aff'd*, 613 F.2d 1213 (2d Cir. 1979), *cert. denied sub nom.* Greenberg, 446 U.S. 918 (1980).

[4] Estate of Fontana, 118 TC 318 (2002).

¶1810

In *Estate of Chancellor*,[5] the Tax Court concluded that a decedent's gross estate need not include the value of assets in a trust established by her spouse because the decedent did not have a general power of appointment over the trust assets. The decedent's power to invade the corpus was limited to, "the necessary maintenance, education, health care, sustenance, welfare or other appropriate expenditures needed by [the decedent] and the other beneficiaries of this trust taking into consideration the standard of living to which they are accustomed," which was an ascertainable standard. Under applicable state law the phrase, "welfare or other appropriate expenditures needed by," was construed narrowly to mean only support-related needs. Thus, the decedent's power was limited by an ascertainable standard that was related solely to health, education, support, or maintenance, which met the exception under IRC Sec. 2041(b)(1)(A) for general powers of appointment.

(c) Released and Lapsed Powers of Appointment. In some situations, property over which a decedent had a general power of appointment may be included in the decedent's gross estate even though the decedent released the power during his or her lifetime. Inclusion is required where the property would have been included in the gross estate had the decedent owned the property outright at death, instead of just having a general power of appointment, and similarly disposed of it [IRC Sec. 2041(a)(2); Reg. Sec. 20.2041-3(d)(1)].

> **Example 1:** Jim Johnson has a life income interest in a trust and a general power of appointment over the remainder. Less than three years before his death, Jim releases the power of appointment. The value of the trust is includible in his gross estate because it would have been includible as a transfer within three years of death if Jim were the owner of the trust assets [see ¶ 1804]. The release of the power would not result in any estate tax if Jim did not have an income interest in the trust.

The lapse of a power by failure to exercise it is treated as a release. However, in the case of a lapse, the property is included in the gross estate only to the extent that its value exceeds the greater of $5,000 or 5 percent of the value of the appointive property at the time of the lapse [IRC Sec. 2041(b)(2)]. Powers designed to take advantage of this limitation are sometimes referred to as "five or five" powers or "*Crummey*" powers [see ¶ 906]. A power holder who possesses a "five or five" power, exercisable at the time of death, faces inclusion in his or her gross estate of the greater of $5,000 or 5 percent of value of the trust property [Reg. Sec. 20.2041-3(d)(3)].

> **Example 2:** Husband created a trust for Wife and gave her a noncumulative power to make annual income withdrawals of $10,000. Wife died three years later, without ever exercising her power. The trust income in the year of Wife's death was $20,000. Assume the value of the trust remained constant at $200,000. There was a lapse of $10,000 (5 percent × $200,000) that is includible in Wife's

---

[5] Estate of Chancellor, TC Memo 2011-172.

¶1810

gross estate. The powers lapsed in prior years can be ignored because the amount that could be appointed each year did not exceed 5 percent of $200,000.

> **NOTE:** A qualified disclaimer [see ¶1203] of a general power of appointment is not a release or lapse of a general power.

(d) Special Powers of Appointment. A power of appointment that is exercisable in favor of a class of persons, not including the decedent, is a special power of appointment. Ordinarily, property subject to a special power of appointment is not includable in the holder's gross estate. However, the property is includable if the decedent exercises a special power by will (or by a transfer that is of such a nature that if the property had been the decedent's property, it would have been included in the decedent's gross estate) to create another power that, under state law, can be exercised to postpone the vesting of property or an interest in property without regard to the date the first power was created [IRC Sec. 2041(a)(3)].

(e) Joint Powers of Appointment. A power that is exercisable by the power holder only in conjunction with the creator of the power or with a person having a substantial and adverse interest in the property subject to the power is not considered a general power of appointment [IRC Sec. 2041(b)(1)(C)]. A trustee administrating a trust as a fiduciary does not have an adverse interest in the trust.

> **Example 3:** Hal Herbert created a trust to pay the income to Mary Oliver, whom he named trustee, for life. The trustee has the power to use the principal for the beneficiary as she sees fit. The power to access the principal of the trust, though, is exercisable only in conjunction with Hal. Mary did not have a general power of appointment because her power over the principal was exercisable only in conjunction with the creator of the power. Thus, the trust is not includible in her gross estate.

> **Example 4:** Gary created a trust to pay the income to Brother for life with the remainder over to Granddaughter. Brother could demand distributions of trust principal, but the trustee required Granddaughter's consent before he could make any distribution. Brother does not have a general power appointment because his power is exercisable only in conjunction with Granddaughter, a person having a substantial and adverse interest.

(f) Time of Creation of Powers of Appointment. A power of appointment created by will is generally considered created on the date of the creator's death [Reg. Sec. 20.2041-1(e)].

A power of appointment created by an *inter vivos* (lifetime) instrument that takes effect during your life is considered created on the date the instrument takes effect. Such a power is not considered as created at some future date merely because it is not exercisable immediately, because it is revocable, or because the identity of its holders cannot be determined until after the date the instrument takes effect. However, if the holder of a power exercises it by creating a second power, the second power is considered as created at the time of the exercise of the first [Reg. Sec. 20.2041 1(c)].

¶1810

(g) Decanting Powers. Decanting is the term used to describe the act of a trustee distributing or paying trust property directly to another trust. Decanting is used by trustees to achieve a variety of tax and non-tax objectives, including addressing changes in the law, trust administration problems, or changed circumstances. The term "decanting" is aptly used because the act of paying trust property to another trust is similar to the act of pouring wine from one container to another which is also referred to as decanting. Decanting is a valuable tool for trustees and beneficiaries because this device will enable them to change the terms of the trusts without having to petition a court to make necessary changes to trust terms or make corrections. Court proceedings should be avoided because they can be time-consuming, costly and the court may not agree to the requested trust modifications. For a detailed discussion of decanting, see ¶ 2827.

¶1811 TRANSFERS FOR INSUFFICIENT CONSIDERATION

If the decedent sold some property for fair-market value, the property is excluded from the decedent's taxable gross estate. If, however, the sale was not bona fide, that is, the decedent did not receive full and adequate consideration (money) for the property, the result is different. The law provides that a decedent's estate includes property that was transferred for insufficient consideration. Only the excess of the fair-market value of the property over the money received for it is subject to inclusion in the decedent's taxable gross estate [IRC Sec. 2043(a)].

> **Example 1:** Dad has a painting worth $1 million. He sells the painting to Daughter for $400,000. Dad has made a gift to Daughter of $600,000. The amount included in Dad's estate is $600,000, which is the $1 million value of the painting less the $400,000 which Daughter paid for it.

(a) Marital Rights. The relinquishment or promised relinquishment of marital rights, other than support rights,[1] is not treated as consideration for this purpose. As a result, the giving up of marital rights, including dower, curtesy, and any statutory estate created in lieu of such rights, does not reduce the estate tax value of the asset transferred.

> **Example 2:** Husband has a painting worth $1 million. He sells the painting to his estranged wife for $400,000 in exchange for her release of her right to support. The amount included in Husband's estate is $1 million because the wife's relinquishment of marital rights is not treated as consideration in this situation.

An exception exists in certain situations. If the property transfer is made under a written agreement in settlement of marital and property rights incident to divorce, it is consid-

---

[1] **¶1811** Rev. Rul. 77-314, 1977-2 CB 349; Rev. Rul. 68-379, 1968-2 CB 414.

ered to be made for full consideration if the spouses are divorced within three years beginning one year before the agreement is entered into. The agreement need not be approved by the divorce decree [IRC Secs. 2043(b), 2516; see ¶ 203].

> **Example 3:** Dad has a painting worth $1 million. He sells the painting to his ex-wife for $400,000 in accordance with their divorce decree, which provided that the bargain sale of the painting would be in exchange for her release of her right to support. The amount included in Dad's estate is $600,000 because the wife's relinquishment of marital rights is treated as consideration worth $400,000 in this situation.

(b) Installment Sale Transactions. The equality of consideration represents the key to the federal estate tax analysis of an installment sale transaction [see ¶ 204]. When the installment note represents full and adequate consideration in money or money's worth, the transferred property is not included in the seller-parent's gross estate under IRC Sec. 2043. However, the fair-market value of the installment note is included in the seller-parent's gross estate together with any interest accruing to the date of death. The seller-parent also includes in his or her gross estate the unconsumed prior payments made on the note.

If the buyer-child dies while the installment obligation remains outstanding, the principal balance of the note together with an accrued but unpaid interest is reported as a debt of the decedent under IRC Sec. 2053 [see ¶ 2001]. However, if, the buyer-child is not obligated on the installment note (e.g., the obligation is a nonrecourse note which carries no personal liability), the death of the buyer-child while the obligation is outstanding does not create a debt of the decedent deductible under IRC Sec. 2053. In either situation, the fair-market value of the transferred property is included in the decedent's (the buyer-child's) gross estate under IRC Sec. 2033.

¶1812 PROPERTY FOR WHICH MARITAL DEDUCTION WAS PREVIOUSLY ALLOWED

A married person can transfer unlimited amounts of property to his or her spouse either during life or at death free of wealth transfer taxes. Lifetime transfers are shielded from tax by the gift tax marital deduction [see ¶ 1103], and transfers at death are exempted by the estate tax marital deduction [see ¶ 1104]. Despite its name, the marital deduction is really a tax-postponer because property that qualifies for the martial deduction in the estate of the first spouse to die is includable in the estate of the surviving spouse, unless the surviving spouse spends it all first.

Congress did not want to take any chances that the property transferred free of transfer tax thanks to the QTIP trust rules would not be taxed in the estate of the surviving spouse. As a result, we have IRC Sec. 2044, which provides that the value of the gross estate will include the value of any property if a marital deduction was allowed in a deceased spouse's estate for property passing to the decedent in a QTIP trust. This means that the property transferred to the surviving spouse via the QTIP trust is automatically taxed in the estate of the surviving spouse if the decedent had a qualifying income interest for life. see ¶ 1103 for discussion of QTIP trusts.

Exception. If the trust is a QTIP trust, a special rule includes the value of the property in the surviving spouse's gross estate unless he or she made a lifetime disposition of the income interest [IRC Sec. 2044]. In that case, the lifetime disposition triggers a gift tax [see ¶ 1105]. Unless the decedent directs otherwise by will, the estate tax attributable to the inclusion of QTIP can be recovered from whomever receives the property, typically, the remainder persons [IRC Sec. 2207A].

The QTIP property bears the excess of (1) the surviving spouse's total estate tax over (2) the estate tax that the surviving spouse would have paid absent the QTIP property.

¶1813 COMMUNITY PROPERTY

Nine states (Arizona, California, Idaho, Louisiana, Nevada, New Mexico, Texas, Washington, and Wisconsin) have community property laws [see ¶ 209]. Community property is a form of property ownership that, like other forms of ownership such as individual ownership or tenancy in common, triggers inclusion in the decedent's gross estate for estate tax purposes under IRC Sec. 2033.

(a) Community Property Included in Gross Estate. Generally, one-half of the value of community property as it exists at the decedent's death is included in a decedent's gross estate [IRC Sec. 2033]. In addition, community property may also be included as part of the decedent's gross estate as a transfer by the decedent:

1. Within three years of death [IRC Sec. 2035; see ¶ 1804];

2. With a retained interest [IRC Secs. 2036 and 2038; see ¶ ¶ 1806 and 1807];

3. With a reversion [IRC Sec. 2037; see ¶ 1805]; or

4. With a retained power to effect beneficial enjoyment [IRC Sec. 2038; see ¶ 1807].

Two other federal estate tax inclusion provisions applicable to community property are:

1. *Using community property as a co-tenant in joint property.* When community property becomes a portion of joint property owned with a nonspouse (e.g., a child), one-half of the portion of the joint property attributed to community property is included in the decedent's gross estate under IRC Sec. 2033.

2. *Creating a general power of appointment over community property.* A general power of appointment over community property may arise when one spouse grants the other spouse such a power over the community property that they own together. If such a power be conferred, the death of the spouse holding the power would cause the portion of the community property subject to the power to be included in the decedent-spouse's gross estate under IRC Sec. 2041 [see ¶ 1810].

In most instances, the value of the decedent's interest in the community property for federal estate tax purposes equals one-half of the value of the community property. If the proceeds of a life insurance policy made payable to the decedent's estate are community property, then only one-half of the proceeds is considered to be receivable by or for the benefit of the decedent's estate [Reg. Sec. 20.2042-1(b)(2), 20.2042-1(c)(5)].

(b) Revocable Trusts. Estate planning with community property often involves the use of a revocable living trust. Two cases settled confusing points in this area. In one case,[1] the husband transferred the entire community property interest (not just his proportional interest) into a trust retaining a life income interest, giving a life interest to his wife and then to their children. The IRS argued that the transfer converted community property into separate property and, thus, the decedent-husband held a retained life estate over the entire trust, which was includable in his gross estate under IRC Sec. 2036. The Ninth Circuit rejected the government's argument and held that the creation of the revocable living trust did not change the character of the community property. Thus, only one-half of the value of the trust was included in the decedent-husband's gross estate.

In other cases,[2] irrevocable trusts have contained community property that the decedent-husband managed under the statutory powers conferred by state community property law. The courts have held that such a statutory power was not a power to alter, amend, or revoke (an IRC Sec. 2038 power). As a result, the normal rule applied and only one-half of the community property was included in the decedent's gross estate.

(c) Widow's Election. If the decedent spouse by will or the post-death provisions of a living trust attempts to dispose of the entire community property, including the stake of the surviving spouse in the community property, the surviving spouse is forced to either (1) accept the provisions made by the deceased spouse for the community property or (2) "elect" against the will (or living trust) and receive his or her interest in the community property.

Typically, a spouse places all the community property in a post-mortem trust that will pay the income to the surviving spouse for life and distribute the remainder to their children. Because the settlor-decedent spouse cannot transfer more than one-half of the community property, the surviving spouse must choose between (1) the provisions made for him or her under the governing instrument and (2) an outright ownership of his or her one-half of the community property.

"Voluntary" widow's election. Planning for a "voluntary" widow's election is also possible. This technique follows the design of the forced widow's election described above, except that the surviving spouse is typically granted (1) a testamentary power to appoint his or her share of the community property and/or (2) the right during the surviving spouse's lifetime to access his or her share of community property for any purpose.

Regardless of whether the surviving spouse elects to receive the property outright or accepts the provisions made for him or her by the deceased spouse, one-half of the community property is included in the deceased spouse's gross estate [IRC Sec. 2033]. The transfer of this interest qualifies for the estate tax marital deduction provided it is

---

[1] ¶ 1813 Katz, 382 F.2d 723 (9th Cir. 1967).

[2] Goodyear, 99 F.2d 523 (9th Cir. 1938); Overton, 138 F.2d 417 (9th Cir. 1943).

not a disqualified terminable interest [see ¶ 1103]. The surviving spouse's share of the community property is not part of the deceased spouse's gross estate.[3]

If, at the death of the first spouse, the surviving spouse elects to take his or her one-half community property outright, then on the surviving spouse's death, his or her outright ownership in the community property will be included in his or her gross estate under IRC Sec. 2033.

If the surviving spouse accepts the provisions made for him or her by the deceased spouse, then at the surviving spouse's death, the deceased spouse's share of the community property will be included in the surviving spouse's gross estate if:

1. The interest of the surviving spouse qualified for a marital deduction in the deceased spouse's estate [IRC Sec. 2056(b)(7)]; or

2. The surviving spouse has a general power of appointment over the deceased spouse's share that would make the interest subject to federal estate taxation under IRC Sec. 2041 [¶ 1810].

The surviving spouse's share of the community property is included in the surviving spouse's gross estate as a tainted retained income interest under IRC Sec. 2036(a). The surviving spouse is the grantor of his or her one-half interest, which remains in the trust [see ¶ 1807].

A transfer included in the decedent's gross estate under IRC Sec. 2036 is reduced by any consideration that the decedent receives in exchange for the transfer [IRC Sec. 2036(a)]. If the surviving spouse makes a widow's election, he or she is treated as if his or her one-half interest in the community property were transferred in exchange for a life income interest in the deceased spouse's one-half interest in the community property. Thus, if the consideration that the surviving spouse received in exchange for the transfer was adequate and full consideration, the surviving spouse's retained income interest in his or her one-half of the community property would not be included in the surviving spouse's gross estate.

One court[4] has held that the measure of full and adequate consideration in a widow's election is the value of one-half of the community property owned by the surviving spouse, not the value of the remainder in his or her community property. Thus, in order for the surviving spouse to receive adequate and full consideration in the making of a widow's election, the surviving spouse must receive the equivalent of both the income interest retained plus remainder interest transferred. Generally, the surviving spouse does not receive an interest in the remainder of the deceased spouse's one-half of the community property and, therefore, the adequate and full consideration requirement is not satisfied.

For federal tax purposes, two scenarios are noteworthy. First, if the surviving spouse accepts the provisions made for him or her by the deceased spouse, the surviving spouse has made a completed gift to the remainderperson(s) of the remainder interest in the surviving spouse's one-half of the community property. The life income interest that the surviving spouse receives in the deceased spouse's one-half of the community

---

[3] Pacific National Bank of Seattle, 40 BTA 128 (1939), *acq.*, 1939-2 CB 25.   [4] Gradow, 897 F.2d 516 (Fed. Cir. 1990).

¶ 1813

property constitutes consideration received in exchange for the gift. Thus, the value of this income interest reduces the value of the gift of the remainder interest.[5]

Second, the deceased spouse may grant the surviving spouse a general testamentary power of appointment over the remainder (specifically, the surviving spouse may receive a power to appoint the remainder to himself or herself or to his or her estate or the creditors of either) [IRC Sec. 2041]. The existence of this general power of appointment causes the gift to be incomplete for federal gift tax purposes until the surviving spouse dies [see ¶ 206].

¶1814 NONQUALIFIED DEFERRED COMPENSATION ARRANGEMENTS

Nonqualified deferred compensation plans offer benefits to a select group of management or highly compensated employees. These plans are designed to supplement the retirement benefits that these executives receive under their qualified retirement plans.

A nonqualified deferred compensation plan is defined as any plan that provides for the deferral of compensation except the following [IRC Sec. 409A(d)(1); Reg. Sec. 1.409A-1(a)]:

- A qualified employer plan including a qualified retirement plan, tax-deferred annuity, simplified employee pension, SIMPLE plan, a qualified governmental excess benefit arrangement and a deferred compensation plan that is also a qualified employer plan [IRC Sec. 409A(d)(2)];

- IRC Sec. 457(b) tax-exempt or governmental deferred compensation plans;

- Bona fide vacation leave, sick leave, compensatory time, disability pay, or a death benefit plan [IRC Sec. 409A(d)(1)];

- Incentive stock options;

- Nonqualified employer stock options with an exercise price that is not less than the fair market value of the underlying stock on the date of grant if the arrangement does not include a deferral feature other than the feature that the option holder has the right to exercise the option in the future;

- Employee stock purchase plans; and

- Amounts paid within 2½ months after the end of the tax year in which vesting occurs, using the later of the plan sponsors tax year or the participants tax year.

IRC Sec. 409A generally provides that all amounts deferred under a nonqualified deferred compensation plan for all tax years are currently includible in gross income to the extent not subject to a substantial risk of forfeiture and not previously included in gross income, unless (a) the plan meets the distribution, acceleration of benefit and election requirements under IRC Sec. 409A, and (b) is operated in accordance with these requirements. If these requirements are not met, the deferred amounts will be included in the participants' gross income and the tax on this compensation will be

---

[5] Siegel, 250 F.2d 339 (9th Cir. 1957).

increased by: (1) interest at the underpayment rate plus one percentage point; and (2) a 20 percent penalty [IRC Sec. 409A(a)(1)(B)(i)].

(a) Contractual Nonqualified Deferred Compensation. Most nonqualified deferred compensation arrangements are "contractual" in that they are subject to a contractual agreement between the business and the executive. A firm may offer a "noncontractual" arrangement in which the benefits are provided through the generosity of the business.

(b) Estate Tax Consequences. As a general rule, death benefits payable under contractual nonqualified deferred compensation arrangements are included in the deceased employee's gross estate under one or more of the following provisions:

1. IRC Sec. 2033 (property owned at death included in decedent's gross estate);

2. IRC Sec. 2036(a)(1) (the retention for life to the right to income, or to designate who may enjoy the income from the property) [see ¶ 1807];

3. IRC Sec. 2038 (the power to alter, amend, or revoke who will enjoy the death benefits) [see ¶ 1806]; and

4. IRC Sec. 2039 (an annuity payable to the decedent for life and then to someone else who survives in the decedent) [see ¶ 1808].

The terms of each individual plan determines which provision the IRS will try to use in an effort to include death benefits in the estates of deceased employees.

Death payments. Payments made under a nonqualified deferred compensation plan in the event of death are death payments not subject to FICA taxes to the extent the total benefits payable under the plan exceed the lifetime benefits payable under the plan. This excess is calculated by taking the present value of all benefits under the plan (other than disability payments) less the present value of the benefits payable to an employee, using the largest present value of the available options.

(c) Noncontractual Deferred Compensation. In contrast, a noncontractual death benefit payment is not included in the decedent's gross estate under any of these IRC provisions because (1) no transfer of property has occurred and (2) the decedent has no retained interest.

A noncontractual death benefit payment will escape federal estate tax inclusion unless the payment is made under circumstances where the firm's course of conduct creates a contract between the business and the executive. If the contract provides that the death benefits are payable to the decedent or the decedent possessed the right to receive the payment, either alone or in conjunction with another for his life, they will be included in the decedent's taxable gross estate [IRC Sec. 2039].[1]

---

[1] ¶ **1814** Neely, 613 F.2d 802 (Fed. Cl. Ct. 1980).

¶1814

¶1815 TRUSTS WITH *CRUMMEY* POWERS

If a beneficiary dies prior to the termination of a trust with *Crummey* powers, the right that the beneficiary retained to demand the withdrawal of trust principal may have estate tax consequences [for a detailed discussion of *Crummey* powers, see ¶ 906].

If the trust instrument provides that the beneficiary, or such beneficiary's estate at death, may receive the trust principal, the value of the entire trust is included in the beneficiary's gross estate [IRC Sec. 2033].

> **NOTE:** Be sure to draft the *Crummey* power to avoid adverse estate and gift tax consequences to the beneficiary. This can easily be accomplished by limiting the beneficiary's withdrawal right to the greater of $5,000 or 5 percent of the trust principal [IRC Secs. 2041(b)(2), 2514(e); see ¶¶ 906 and 1810].

If the trust instrument makes provision for contingent, alternative takers, the lapse of a power of appointment is treated as a release of such power to the extent the value of the property over which the power may be exercised exceeds the five or five limitation [IRC Sec. 2041(b)(2); see ¶ 1810]. The beneficiary's gross estate includes the value of any lapsed power in excess of the five or five limitation, which would be included in the beneficiary's gross estate if the beneficiary had transferred the power.

If the trust instrument provides that the beneficiary will receive all the trust income, the release of a withdrawal power over the trust principal in excess of the five or five limitation would constitute a transfer with a retained life interest under IRC Sec. 2036(a)(1).

Usually, however, the trust instrument gives the trustee discretionary powers to distribute trust income and principal. In this situation, all transfers resulting from released powers exceeding the five or five limitation that have occurred within three years of the beneficiary's death are included in his or her gross estate [IRC Secs. 2041(a)(1), 2035].

If the trust instrument provides that the beneficiary would have succeeded to the trust property in all events, had he or she died prior to the termination of the trust, the beneficiary's gross estate includes any transfers exceeding the five or five limitation [IRC Sec. 2037].

¶1816 NONMARITAL DEDUCTION (CREDIT SHELTER OR BYPASS) TRUSTS

The common estate planning practice is for a married couple to direct that when the first spouse dies, that spouse's estate should be divided into two parts. One part is equal to the estate tax exemption effective in the year of death ($5,340,000 in 2014). This amount will escape estate tax when the first spouse dies because of the unified or applicable estate tax credit. This part is typically placed in a credit shelter trust, with the surviving spouse as a beneficiary. If drafted properly, the credit shelter trust will also be excluded from the gross estate of the survivor. This trust is commonly referred to as a credit shelter or estate tax exemption trust because it is protected from tax by reason of the unified credit and the estate tax exemption. It may also be called the bypass trust because it bypasses the estate of the surviving spouse for estate tax purposes.

The second part of the decedent's estate usually passes to the surviving spouse outright or into a trust that qualified for the unlimited marital deduction trust in benefit for the surviving spouse. No tax is due when the second part passes to the surviving spouse regardless of the form because of the unlimited marital deduction. The property that passes to or in trust for the surviving spouse under the protection of the estate tax marital deduction is included in the gross estate of that surviving spouse when he or she dies unless it is consumed, given away or dissipated before the surviving spouse dies.

(a) How Portability Impacts Credit Shelter Trusts. Prior to the adoption of portability, the estate tax exemption of the first spouse to die was considered to be wasted unless the spouse

1. Owned assets in his or her name alone equal to the exemption amount in the year of death and

2. Left such assets to a beneficiary other than the surviving spouse or charity—such as the couple's children, or a credit shelter (bypass) trust for the life benefit of the surviving spouse.

As a result of portability, credit shelter trusts no longer need to be created for this reason alone. Estate planning no longer has to focus so much attention on avoiding wasting the deceased spouse's exemption. For a detailed discussion of the portability concept, see Chapter 15.

Now that portability exists, any applicable exclusion amount that remains unused as of the death of the last deceased spouse, the deceased spousal unused exclusion (DSUE) amount, generally is available for use by the surviving spouse, as an addition to the surviving spouse's own applicable exclusion amount which is $5,250,000 in 2013 and increases to $5,340,000 in 2014. The DSUE is not available automatically. The statute requires an election from the first deceased spouse's executor on a completed Form 706 even if the executor is not otherwise obligated to file a Form 706 because of the size of the deceased spouse's estate. For further discussion of the need to file a complete estate tax return on Form 706 in order to make the portability election, and for a sample completed Form 706, see Chapter 24.

(b) Why It Still Makes Sense To Create Credit Shelter Trusts. It still makes sense to create credit shelter trusts when the first spouse dies rather than rely solely on the portability provision because:

• The unused exclusion from a particular predeceased spouse will be lost if the surviving spouse remarries and survives his or her next spouse,

• Appreciation and accumulated income earned on amounts in the credit shelter trusts escape federal estate tax no matter how much they grow in value. Suppose, for example, Husband died today and his executor puts $5 million into a credit shelter trust with the balance going outright to Wife. The trust assets grow to $10 million by the time the Wife dies in 2024. The good news is that none of the trust assets will be included in the Wife's gross estate and she still has her own exclusion amount to use.

¶1816

- Amounts in the credit shelter trust cannot be touched by second spouses or children from a second marriage thus protecting those assets for children and grandchildren from a first marriage.
- There is no portability of the unused GST exemption to the surviving spouse, whereas credit shelter trusts can still be used to take advantage of the GST tax exemption of the first spouse to die.
- Creation of the credit shelter trust will avoid having to file an estate tax return for the predeceased spouse's estate if the estate is not so large as to otherwise require a return.
- Bypass trusts offer asset protection, professional management, and restrict transfers of assets by the surviving spouse. However, if everything is left outright to the surviving spouse and portability is relied on, the advantages are simplicity and a step-up in basis when the surviving spouse dies.

The bottom line is that few individuals will be willing to rely solely on portability of the estate tax exemption when planning their estates, because portability as it currently stands, only exists for two years and there are a variety of other reasons for continuing to draft bypass trusts.

(c) Tax Purpose for Credit Shelter (Bypass) Trust. One of the most commonly used estate-planning techniques for married taxpayers is the split estate plan. The split estate plan is popular because it ensures that each spouse will take full advantage of his or her unified credit and pays the least amount of estate tax. When you adopt the split estate plan, the "credit shelter" or "bypass trust" receives the value of the applicable exclusion amount in assets as provided in the decedent's will. After the applicable exclusion amount is left to nonspousal beneficiaries in a bypass trust, the balance is left to the surviving spouse in a manner qualifying for the unlimited marital deduction [¶1100]. Principal and interest generated by assets in the bypass trust may be used for the surviving spouse's health, education, maintenance and support and after the surviving spouse's death the balance is typically distributed to the children of the marriage. Often the surviving spouse is given a limited power of appointment in order to change the final distribution of assets at his or her death.

If structured properly, this scheme results in a zero tax bill for both spouses. The amounts in the bypass trust are not taxed when the first spouse dies because they are sheltered by his or her applicable exclusion amount. They are not subject to estate tax when the second spouse dies because he or she did not own or have control over the assets at death. The amount passing to the surviving spouse qualifies for the unlimited marital deduction when the first spouse dies [see ¶1100]. This so-called marital share is not subject to estate tax in the surviving spouse's gross estate to the extent that it does not exceed the surviving spouse's own applicable exclusion amount.

In order for the split estate plan to work, both spouses must set up identical trusts in their wills so that, regardless of who dies first, both can reduce or eliminate federal estate taxes. In addition, for this type of trust to avoid federal estate taxes, both spouses must own property in their own names rather than as joint tenants.

(d) Nontax Purpose for Credit Shelter (Bypass) Trust. In addition to offering the surviving spouse favorable estate tax consequences, the credit shelter trust may prove useful for a number of nontax purposes, including (1) serving as a

¶1816

contingent trust for children or a trust for grandchildren who are minors after the death of an adult; (2) providing management assistance for a surviving spouse; (3) allowing spouses the opportunity to impose a limitation on the surviving spouse's ability to direct the ultimate disposition of the property; and (4) providing for children of a previous marriage who benefit from the first-to die spouse's estate and the first-to die spouse does not want the surviving spouse disturbing this plan.

(e) Scope of Surviving Spouse's Power Over Credit Shelter Trust.

The scope of the surviving spouse's power over the credit shelter trust is defined by IRC Sec. 2041. In addition to the entire income generated by the trust, the surviving spouse may possess the following without adverse federal estate tax consequences:

- A power to invade the trust principal for the spouse's own benefit which is limited by an ascertainable standard relating to his or her health, education, maintenance or support;

- A special power of appointment by which the spouse may appoint the principal of the nonmarital trust to a preselected group of people not including the surviving spouse, his or her estate, his or her creditors, or the creditors of his or her estate. By giving a surviving spouse a special appointment over the nonmarital deduction trust, the remainderpersons' share remains available for a second look by the surviving spouse, thus providing flexibility in the distribution of the family wealth during the surviving spouse's lifetime or at the surviving spouse's death;

- A "five or five" power by which the spouse may invade the nonmarital deduction trust each year, noncumulatively, by the greater of 5 percent of the trust principal computed at the end of the year, or $5,000. A surviving spouse who possesses a five or five power, which is unexercised at the time of the surviving spouse's death, must include in his or her estate the greater of $5,000 or 5 percent of the value of the trust property [Reg. Sec. 20.2041-3(d)(3)].

  NOTE: If the surviving spouse declines to exercise the five or five power in any calendar year, no adverse gift tax consequence would result [IRC Sec. 2514(e)]. As discussed in ¶205, the lapse or the failure to exercise the five or five power is subject to gift taxation only to the extent that the property that could have been appointed by the exercise of the power exceeds the greater of $5,000 or 5 percent of the value of the assets out of which the exercise of the power could have been satisfied [Reg. Sec. 25.2514-3(c)(4)].

(f) Formula Clauses Need Periodic Review.

Formula clauses are clauses inserted in estate planning documents such as wills and trusts that express the beneficiary's interest in terms of a pecuniary or fractional formula. The use of formula clauses is frequently used by estate planners to ensure the proper division of property but it is extremely important that the wording in those formula clauses be reviewed, particularly in light of recent legislative changes to make certain that they continue to implement the testator's long-term intent for his or her loved-ones. A common problem is transferring too little or too much to the surviving spouse because of overfunding of the credit shelter trust in the typical split estate plan.

In the past, bypass trusts have been funded with a formula disposition that leaves the applicable exclusion amount to nonspousal beneficiaries and the balance to the surviving spouse. For example, in the past, the language to fund the bypass trust has typically been tied into the applicable exclusion amount or the amount necessary to "reduce estate tax to zero," or "to eliminate any federal estate tax." This language may result in the funding of the bypass trust with 100 percent of a decedent's estate and unwittingly impoverish the surviving spouse because nothing will be left to fund the marital share. Drafters must ask whether the surviving spouse will have sufficient assets to maintain his or her lifestyle if most or all of the family assets go to fund a bypass trust for the benefit of children. The surviving spouse only has an income interest in the bypass trust as well as a limited power to invade for health, education, maintenance or support. Anyone who drafts wills must review all formula clauses in estate planning documents in light of recent law changes.

Disclaimers may be used to cure some of these over- and underfunding problems that have resulted from formula clauses. For example, it may be better to leave everything outright to the surviving spouse and rely on a disclaimer to determine how to fund the bypass trust. The decedent's will could provide that anything the surviving spouse disclaims passes to a bypass trust. Keep in mind, however, that qualified disclaimers must be made within nine months of death as discussed further in ¶1203.

¶1817 RECAPITALIZATION: TRANSFERRED INTERESTS IN CLOSELY HELD CORPORATIONS AND PARTNERSHIPS

After a recapitalization of a corporation or partnership, the senior family member's ownership interest in the family business is included in the senior's gross estate [IRC Sec. 2033]. However, the federal estate tax also causes inclusion of the transferred interest (e.g., the common stock transferred to the junior family member), when the senior family member retains any of the following interests in the transferred property: (1) income, (2) the right to determine who will enjoy the income or the transferred asset itself, or (3) voting powers [IRC Secs. 2036, 2038; see ¶¶1806, 1807].

In a recapitalization, retained voting control over interests transferred by the senior family member frequently draws the most attention. Federal estate tax inclusion results when the senior family member retains either direct voting control or indirect control as the guardian or trustee for the benefit of the junior family member [IRC Sec. 2036(a)(2)].

¶1818 ESTATES OF NONRESIDENT NONCITIZENS

The gross estate of a nonresident alien consists of the same items as that of a citizen or resident of the United States [IRC Sec. 2103]. However, a nonresident estate is subject to the tax only with respect to property having a U.S. situs. Assets with U.S. situs include U.S. real property, tangible personal property located in the United States, stock in domestic corporations, and debt obligations of U.S. persons or governmental units. Also included are lifetime transfers of U.S. situs property if the nonresident alien still retains control over the property within the meaning of IRC Secs 2035-2038 and transfers within three years of death [IRC Sec. 2104(b)]. Property not included in the gross estate of a nonresident includes real and personal property located outside the United States; bank deposits (regardless of whether within or without the United States) not effectively connected with a U.S. trade or business; foreign stocks and debt obligations, including those of U.S. obligors if the interest is eligible for exemption under IRC Sec. 871(h)(1) for portfolio interest received by a nonresident individual from sources within the United States; and proceeds of an insurance policy on the life of a nonresident alien domiciliary. Also excluded are works of art on loan for exhibition [IRC Sec. 2105(c)].

For the estates of nonresidents who are not citizens of the United States (nonresident aliens), a return must be filed on Form 706-NA, "United States Estate (and Generation-Skipping Transfer) Tax Return, Estate of Nonresident, Not a Citizen of the United States," if the value of the decedent's gross estate located in the United States exceeds $60,000, reduced by (1) the amount of adjusted taxable gifts made by the decedent after December 31, 1976, and (2) the aggregate amount allowed as a specific exemption under IRC Sec. 2521 (as in effect before its repeal by the Tax Reform Act of 1976) with respect to gifts made by the decedent after September 8, 1976, and before January 1, 1977 [IRC Sec. 6018(a)(2); IRC Sec. 2106].

(a) Who Is a Nonresident Citizen. For estate tax purposes, a resident is someone who had a domicile in the United States at the time of death. A person acquires a U.S. domicile by living in the United States, for even a brief time period, with no present intention of moving from the United States [Reg. Sec. 20.0-1(b)(1)]. On the other hand, "residence without the requisite intention to remain indefinitely will not suffice to constitute domicile, nor will intention to change domicile effect such a change unless accompanied by actual removal" [Reg. Sec. 20.0-1(b)(1)]. This test requires a fact and circumstances analysis that looks into a variety of factors, such as citizenship in another country and the location of the taxpayer's investments, driver's registration, bank accounts, homes, etc. Domicile is presumed to continue in a foreign jurisdiction until it is established in the United States. In *Estate of Paquette*,[1] a decedent was found to be a nonresident of the United States at the time of his death even though he owned a home in Florida and wintered there for twenty-five years. The decedent's numerous contacts with Canada, such as citizenship, location of investment assets and driver's registration in that country supported the presumption of continuance of original (Canadian) domicile.

A person can establish a domicile in the United States even if he or she is subject to deportation. Thus, a person who is in the United States illegally and who lives here until death may be considered a resident of the United States for federal estate tax purposes.

If a person is a resident of any U.S. possession and is a citizen of the United States only because of birth, residence, or citizenship in that possession, he or she is considered a nonresident noncitizen for estate tax purposes [IRC Sec. 2209].

(b) Property Located in the United States. Both real property located in the United States and tangible personal property located in the United States have a U.S. situs. However, works of art lent to a public gallery or museum for exhibition in the United States are deemed not to be situated in the United States while being exhibited or transported for exhibition [IRC Sec. 2105(c)].

---

[1] ¶ **1818** Estate of Paquette, TC Memo 1983-571.

¶1818

Shares of domestic corporations have a U.S. situs, regardless of where the certificates are located. Debt obligations (e.g., bonds) of a citizen or resident of the United States, including a domestic partnership or corporation, the United States, or a state or political subdivision of the United States, are considered as situated in the United States [IRC Sec. 2104].

A nonresident alien's real property located in the U.S. is subject to estate tax under IRC Sec. 2101. IRC Sec. 2106(a)(1) provides for allowance of that proportion of the deductions specified in IRC Sec. 2053, relating to expenses, debt, and taxes, which is the relationship that part of the decedent's gross estate that is situated in the U.S. bears to the value of his entire gross estate, wherever situated. Deductions allowable in computing the taxable estate include amounts "for unpaid mortgages on the property where the value of the mortgage is included in the value of the gross estate." If the decedent's estate is liable for the mortgage or debt, the full value of the property subject to it must be included in the gross estate, with the amount of the mortgage or debt allowed as a deduction. But if the decedent's estate is not so liable, only the value of the property net of the mortgage or debt need be included in the value of the gross estate.

In *Estate of Fung*,[2] the estate of a deceased nonresident alien was required to include the full value, rather than the net equity value, of the decedent's interest in encumbered real property in the decedent's gross estate because he was personally liable for the indebtedness under the terms of the promissory note. Under both the promissory note and state (California) law, the lender had the option of imposing personal liability as an enforcement remedy. State law did not prohibit a lender holding a deed of trust on the subject property from seeking a deficiency judgment against the debtor. Therefore, pursuant to Reg. Sec. 20.2053-7, the full value of the property was includible in the decedent's estate, with a deduction allowed for the amount of the outstanding indebtedness.

Property with retained strings that is transferred during the nonresident alien's lifetime [IRC Secs. 2035–2038] will be included in the estates of the nonresident aliens if the property is located in the United States at the time of the transfer or the decedent's death [Reg. Sec. 20.2104-1(b)].

Property of a nonresident noncitizen is not considered located in the United States, if it is:

1. An amount receivable as insurance on the decedent's life;

2. Certain debt obligations of a domestic corporation; or

3. Certain bank deposits [IRC Secs. 2104(c)(2), 2105].

Situs rules for determining the location of property are also provided in bilateral tax treaties [Reg. Sec. 20.2104-1(c)].

(c) Short-Term Obligations Treated as Property Outside the United States.
U.S. debt obligations held by nonresident noncitizens that produce short-term original issue discount income are treated as property located outside the United States for purposes of the federal estate tax imposed on such individuals. As a

---

[2] Estate of Fung, 2003-1 USTC ¶60,460 (9th Cir. 2003), *aff'g* 117 TC 247 (2001).

result, qualified debt obligations will not be included in a nonresident noncitizen's gross estate [IRC Sec. 2105(b)(4)].

(d) Taxable Estate. A nonresident noncitizen's taxable estate equals his or her gross estate less:

1. A proportional deduction for expenses, indebtedness, taxes, and losses. The deductible portion of each item is limited to the amount of each item multiplied by a fraction, the numerator of which is the value of property located in the United States and the denominator of which is the value of the decedent's entire gross estate, wherever located [Reg. Sec. 20.2106-2(a)].

2. A charitable deduction for public, charitable, and religious uses in the United States as provided in IRC Sec. 2106(a)(2).

3. A marital deduction for property passing to a spouse who is a citizen of the United States [IRC Sec. 2106(a)(3)].

   NOTE: A deduction is allowed only if the executor discloses in the estate tax return the value of that part of the gross estate not located in the United States [IRC Sec. 2106(b)].

(e) Estate Tax Rates and Credits. The estates of nonresident noncitizen are taxed at the same rates as those of citizens and residents [IRC Sec. 2101]. However, they are allowed a unified credit of only $13,000, unless they are entitled to a greater amount under a treaty [IRC Sec. 2102(c)(3); Reg. Sec. 20.2102-1(c)(2)].

Estates of residents of U.S. possessions who become citizens of the United States because of their connection with the possession (e.g., birth or residence there) are taxed only with respect to property situated in the United States [IRC Sec. 2209]. The unified credit for such estates is the greater of:

1. $13,000 (which exempts the first $60,000 of the estate from estate tax); or

2. $46,800 multiplied by a fraction, the numerator of which is the value of the property situated in the United States and the denominator of which is the value of the gross estate worldwide [IRC Sec. 2102(c)(2); Reg. Sec. 20.2102-1(c)(3)].

¶1819 CHECKLIST OF AFTER-DEATH ESTATE TAX ELECTIONS AVAILABLE TO AN ESTATE

☐ Use of special valuation provisions to value a farm or closely-held business real property, including qualified woodlands (note that the maximum reduction in value for any estate is $1,090,000 in 2014 [¶1908].

☐ Deduction of administrative expenses on estate tax return or estate income tax return (election made on estate income tax return—Form 1041).

☐ Deduction of casualty losses on estate tax return or estate income tax return (election made on estate income tax return—Form 1041).

¶1819

☐ Deduction of medical expenses paid within one year of decedent's death on the estate tax return or on decedent's income tax return (election made on decedent's income tax return).

☐ Marital deduction for QTIP election [¶ 1103].

☐ Use of alternate valuation date (valuation of property six months after date of death) [¶ 1907].

☐ Postponement of tax reversionary or remainder interest [¶ 2304].

☐ Elect to pay estate tax attributable to a closely held business in up to ten annual installments and defer the first installment until five years after the decedent's death [IRC Section 6166]. This 15-year estate tax deferral is a valuable business tool. In lieu of a forced liquidation of business assets to pay estate taxes, the deferral can afford the decedent's survivors an opportunity to retain a business within a decedent's family. The deferral will give the estate time to raise the estate taxes, often from the profits of the business, itself [¶ 2303].

VALUATION

19

TABLE OF CONTENTS

¶1900 VALUATION OF ESTATE PROPERTY

Determining the fair market value of property which is transferred either by gift during someone's lifetime or as a result of someone's death is a fundamental concept in estate planning. Property is includible in the decedent's gross estate at its fair market value at the time of death or on the alternate valuation date, if elected [¶ see ¶1907 for further discussion of alternate valuation]. The fair market value of property for transfer tax purposes is based upon a fundamental test which requires a determination of the "price at which the property would change hands between a willing buyer and a willing seller, neither being under any compulsion to buy or to sell and both having reasonable knowledge of relevant facts" [Reg. Secs. 20.2031-1(b), 25.2512-1]. This standard is an "objective test using hypothetical buyers and sellers in the marketplace, and is not a personalized one which envisions a particular buyer and seller."[1] All relevant facts and elements of value as of the applicable valuation date shall be considered in every case" [Reg. Sec. 20.2031-1(b)]. These hypothetical persons are considered to know all relevant facts involving the property. Each of these hypothetical persons also is presumed to be aiming to achieve the maximum economic advantage (i.e., maximum profit) from the hypothetical sale of the property.

Special rules apply when valuing the stock of a closely held corporation. For detailed discussion of the valuation of closely held stock, see ¶1913.

---

[1] ¶1900 LeFrak, TC Memo 1993-526.

¶1900

An IRS determination of fair-market value is accepted as correct until the taxpayer proves it is wrong.[2] Events occurring after death are not considered in valuation unless they are foreseeable at the time of death. Keep in mind that the value of a decedent's interest in stock will be determined at the time of his death, and not at the time the stock passes to the estate.[3] Events that cause the price of the stock to change after death will generally be disregarded. For example, post-death events cannot be considered when valuing a deduction for unpaid income taxes taken on an estate tax return[4] or when valuing a claim deducted on a federal estate tax return.[5]

¶1901 VALUATION OF CLOSELY HELD STOCK

The valuation of closely held non-publicly traded stock is a complex task for the executor because the shares often have no ready market from which either sales or bid and asked prices may be obtained. Actual arm's-length sales on or close to the valuation date provide the best evidence of value. In the absence of actual sales, various factors, or a combination thereof, are used in arriving at fair market value. These factors include (but are not limited to) comparable sales, net worth, capitalization of earnings, price-earnings ratio, history of the enterprise, economic outlook of the particular industry, dividend-paying capacity, and good will. For discussion of buy-sell agreements, see ¶1913 and ¶1909.

The following discounts are generally taken into consideration when computing the estate tax in a closely held corporation:

• Discount for lack of marketability to reflect the difficulty that closely held corporations often experience when trying to convert shares to cash;

• Discount for lack of control to reflect the absence of power to make decisions regarding the closely held corporation;

• Pending litigation or the possibility of a stockholder suit; and

• Discount for built-in capital gains tax liability.

The following cases illustrate the application of these discounts when valuing closely held corporate stock for estate tax purposes.

In *Okerlund*,[1] the Court of Appeals for the Federal Circuit concluded that future risks cannot be taken into account when valuing a decedent's close corporation stock holdings. Generally, stock in a closely held company is valued for estate tax purposes by considering the company's net worth, potential earnings, capacity to pay dividends, and other factors on the valuation date. Events that occur after the valuation date are not considered. In *Okerlund,* the value of closely held stock transferred by sibling donors to trusts for the benefit of their respective children was determined by applying a 40-percent discount for lack of marketability and a five-percent discount for the lack of voting rights, resulting in a combined discount factor of 45 percent.

---

[2] Estate of Lyons, TC Memo 1976-136.

[3] Estate of McClatchy, 106 TC 206 (1996), *rev'd,* 147 F.3d 1089 (9th Cir. 1998).

[4] Estate of McMorris, TC Memo 1999-82, *rev'd and rem'd*, 243 F.3d 1254 (10th Cir. 2001)

[5] Estate of O'Neal, 258 F.3d 1265 (11th Cir. 2001), *on remand,* 228 F. Supp. 2d 1290 (N.D. Ala. 2002).

[1] **¶1901** Estate of Okerlund, 365 F.3d 1044 (Fed. Cir. 2004), *aff'g* 2002-2 USTC ¶60,447 (Fed. Cl. 2002).

The death of the company's founder and a salmonella outbreak, although identifiable risks, were unexpected occurrences that led to declines in the company's sales and income after the valuation date. Characterizing the death of the company's founder and the salmonella outbreak as "exogenous low-probability high-risk events," the court refused to consider them in valuing the gifts. The alternate valuation method is discussed at ¶1907. Real property used in farming or other closely held businesses may be eligible for a reduced valuation for estate tax purposes if the executor elects the special valuation method [see ¶1908].

¶1902 POST-DEATH SALE CONSIDERED

In *Estate of Noble*,[1] the Tax Court determined the fair market value of a decedent's interest in the stock of a closely held bank using the actual sales price of the stock in a transaction that occurred one year after the decedent's death. The court concluded that the best method to determine the value of the closely held stock was to examine any arm's-length sales near the valuation date. The two sales prior to the decedent's death were not indicative of the stock's fair market value because (1) the sellers of those shares were not knowledgeable, as the shares were sold for much less than the appraised value, and (2) those 17 shares were not comparable in number to the decedent's 116 shares. Moreover, the decedent's stock had special value because it was the only interest not owned by the other shareholder. The third sale, which occurred after the decedent's death, was the best measure of the fair market value of the decedent's interest because the sale was an arm's-length transaction consummated by unrelated parties. In addition, the shares that were the subject of the third sale constituted the actual interest owned by the decedent at her death. As a result, the fair market value of the decedent's shares for estate tax purposes under IRC Sec. 2031 was the post-death sales price.

¶1903 VALUE REDUCED BY BUILT-IN CAPITAL GAINS

The rationale for the built-in hypothetical capital gains tax discount is simple. A purchaser buying a corporation with appreciating assets will have to incur a second level capital gains tax on future appreciation that a purchaser of directly-owned assets will not have to bear. As a result, prospective purchasers should have to pay less to purchase the stock subject to the capital gains tax on future appreciation and an adjustment should be made to the value of the stock to reflect the financial burden of built-in gains tax attributable to its future appreciation.

The discount for hypothetical capital gains tax is allowed even though no liquidation or sale of the corporation or its assets is planned at the time the stock is received. Deducting an amount for this discount for gift tax purposes can represent a significant gift tax savings because it reduces the value of the gift.

The courts approving this discount have reasoned that the discount for potential capital gains liabilities was justified even though no liquidation of the company or

---

[1] ¶**1902** Estate of Noble, TC Memo 2005-2.

sale of its assets was planned or contemplated on the date of the gifts, because a hypothetical seller deciding on a purchase price for stock would reduce the purchase price by the amount of built-in capital gains taxes that would be incurred when the shares were sold.[1]

> **Example 1:** Dad owns ABCo stock with a value of $100,000 and a basis of $50,000. Assume a 20 percent tax rate. If Dad sold the stock he would pay capital gains tax of $10,000 on his $50,000 capital gain. Change the facts. Instead of selling the stock, Dad gave all the stock to Son, while Dad is still alive. In this situation, the $100,000 value of the stock Dad gave Son would be discounted to reflect the $10,000 built-in capital gains tax liability that would be due if Dad had sold the stock. The value of the gift would therefore be $90,000.

There are two general approaches for calculating the built-in gains discount:

- First, a dollar-for-dollar approach was allowed in the Eleventh Circuit in *Estate of Jelke*,[2] the Court of Appeals for the Fifth Circuit in *Estate of Dunn*;[3] and the Tax Court in *Estate of Jensen*;[4]

- Second, other courts have applied a present value analysis, considering when the corporation might sell appreciated assets and determining the present value of the additional corporate level capital gains costs as was done by the Tax Court in *Estate of Litchfield*;[5] however, the court therein specifically declined to say that this analysis should be applied in future cases. The court noted that both experts in *Litchfield* applied the present value analysis. The court emphasized that it was not deciding which of the two approaches was most appropriate, observing that the estate's expert did not ask the court to apply a full dollar-for-dollar valuation discount. "Therefore, we need not decide herein whether such an approach would be appropriate in another case where that argument is made."

In *Estate of Jelke III*,[6] the Court of Appeals for the Eleventh Circuit held that the date of death value of a decedent's 6.44-percent interest in a closely-held investment corporation should be discounted dollar-for-dollar for the corporation's built-in capital gains tax liability. The decedent owned, through a revocable trust, a 6.44-percent interest in a closely-held corporation that held and managed investments for its shareholders. The corporation's primary objective was long-term capital growth, resulting in low asset turnover and large, unrealized capital gains, which, at the time of the decedent's death, had grown into a $51 million potential tax liability.

The amount of the discount was based on a dollar-for-dollar approach, as set forth by the Court of Appeals for the Fifth Circuit in *Estate of Dunn*.[7] Under the dollar-for dollar approach, the value of the interest was determined by assuming that all assets in the

---

[1] ¶ **1903** Estate of Litchfield, TC Memo 2009-21.

[2] Estate of Jelke III, TC Memo 2005-131, *vac. and rem'd*, 507 F.3d 1317 (11th Cir. 2007) ("Jelke III").

[3] Dunn, TC Memo 2000-12, *rev'd and rem'd*, 301 F.3d 339 (5th Cir. 2002).

[4] Estate of Jensen, TC Memo 2010-182.

[5] Estate of Litchfield, TC Memo 2009-21.

[6] Estate of Jelke III, TC Memo 2005-131, *vac. and rem'd*, 507 F.3d 1317 (11th Cir. 2007) ("Jelke III").

[7] Dunn, TC Memo 2000-12, *rev'd and rem'd*, 301 F.3d 339 (5th Cir. 2002).

corporation were liquidated at the decedent's death, and 100 percent of the built-in capital gains tax liability was offset against the value of the stock. The court concluded that it was more logical to value the corporation based on the assumption that the liquidation occurred on the date of death than to estimate that it would occur some time in the future. Therefore, when determining the amount of the decedent's 6.44 percent interest, the value of the corporation was reduced by the $51 million capital gains tax liability.

In *Estate of Jensen*,[8] the Tax Court effectively permitted a dollar-for-dollar discount for built-in capital gains tax in computing the fair market value of the decedent's interest in a summer camp which was transferred into a revocable trust. If the assets had been sold on the date of death, there would have been a built-in long term capital gains tax to the corporation of nearly $1 million. The estate's appraiser took a dollar-for-dollar discount for the built-in capital gains tax from the net asset value of the camp on the Form 706. The appraiser concluded that a dollar-for-dollar discount for the built-in long term capital gains was appropriate because: "[t]he adjusted book value method is based on the inherent assumption that the assets will be liquidated, which automatically gives rise to a tax liability predicated upon the built-in capital gains that result from appreciation in the assets."

The Tax Court accepted the estate's valuation by first looking at a long line of cases in which a 100 percent dollar-for-dollar discount was allowed for long-term capital gains tax. The court used a discounted present value method to make its own calculation of the built-in capital gains tax. It first concluded that the capital gains would be incurred over a 17-year period. Next it determined the amount of that gain and then the amount of the tax. Then it used factors to discount the anticipated future built-in capital gains tax to present value. The results reached by the court were higher than the result reached by the taxpayer's expert in looking at a dollar-for-dollar reduction of the built-in capital gains tax.

No discount for beneficiaries' income tax liability attributable to IRAs. In *Estate of Kahn*,[9] the Tax Court concluded that the value of two IRAs included in a decedent's gross estate could not be reduced by the anticipated income tax liability that would be incurred by the beneficiaries upon distribution of the IRAs. For purposes of applying the willing seller-willing buyer test, the subject of a hypothetical sale was the underlying assets of the IRAs, not the IRAs themselves. The tax burden associated with distributing the assets in the IRAs would not be transferred to a hypothetical buyer. Therefore, the hypothetical buyer would not consider the income tax liability of the IRA beneficiary because the beneficiary, rather than the buyer, would pay the tax. In addition, it was inappropriate to apply a lack of marketability discount in valuing the IRAs because the underlying assets of the IRAs were marketable securities, unlike a situation involving closely-held stock. No reduction in value was warranted because the hypothetical sale of the marketable securities would not transfer any built-in tax liability or marketability restriction to a willing buyer, who would receive the securities free of any such burden. Because no discount applied, the IRAs were valued based on their respective account balances on the date of the decedent's death.

---

[8] Estate of Jensen, TC Memo 2010-182.   [9] Estate of Kahn, 125 TC 227 (2005).

¶1904 HOUSEHOLD AND PERSONAL EFFECTS

Household goods and personal effects are valued for estate tax purposes at their fair market value—that is, the price that a willing buyer would pay to a willing seller, with no compulsion to buy or sell and the parties having reasonable knowledge of relevant facts. A room-by-room itemization is desirable. All articles should be named specifically and a separate value given for each article. However, articles in the same room may be grouped if none of the articles has a separate value of over $100. In place of an itemized list, an executor may furnish a sworn written statement setting forth the aggregate value as appraised by a competent appraiser or a dealer in the class of property involved [Reg. Sec. 20.2031-6(a)].

Special rule for variables. If the decedent's estate includes household and personal effects that have a marked artistic or intrinsic value in excess of $3,000, the Regulations require an appraisal [Reg. Sec. 20.2031-6(b)]. The Regulations list the following examples of items that might require an appraisal: jewelry; furs; silverware; paintings; etchings; engravings; antiques; books; statuary; vases; oriental rugs; and coin or stamp collections. Specific rules are provided if an appraisal is involved [Reg. Sec. 20.2031-6(d)].

You must be certain that the appraiser is not only reputable but is qualified to appraise the particular item involved. In the appraisal, books in sets by standard authors must be listed in separate groups. When valuing paintings having artistic value, the size, subject and artist's name must be stated. In the case of oriental rugs, the size, make and general condition of the rug must be provided. Sets of silverware must be listed in separate groups. Groups or individual pieces of silverware must be weighed and the weights must be given in troy ounces. In arriving at the value of silverware, the appraisers must take into consideration its age, utility, desirability, condition and obsolescence [Reg. Sec. 20.2031-6].

Sales through dealers who buy tangible personal property, such as jewelry or automobiles, at a discount from the retail price are not indicative of fair-market value. Instead, the value of such items is their higher retail price [Reg. Sec. 20.2031-1(b)]. When this type of property is sold through the use of a public auction or classified advertisement, the amount received from the resulting sales is determinative of value.[1]

Works of art. The Art Advisory Panel assists the IRS by reviewing and evaluating the acceptability of appraisals submitted by taxpayers to support the valuation of works of art. The meetings of the panel are closed to the public in order to protect the confidentiality of tax returns. The IRS Art Advisory Panel is a collection of experts who are not paid (except for cost reimbursements) and who are not told whether an item is being valued for a charitable contribution deduction, estate tax valuation, or gift tax valuation.

---

[1] ¶1904 Rev. Proc. 65-19, 1965-2 CB 1002.

In *Stone*,[2] the Court of Appeals for the Ninth Circuit approved a five-percent discount on its undivided one-half interest in an art collection for estate tax purposes. The estate had claimed a 44 percent discount for lack of marketability and control. The court adopted the valuation prepared by the IRS Art Advisory Panel, rather than the estate's valuation prepared by Sotheby's. The court found the valuation prepared by the IRS Art Advisory Panel to be credible and unbiased. The court rejected the estate's valuation prepared by Sotheby's because it contained no description of how the valuations were determined and because the estate failed to introduce expert testimony to support the Sotheby's valuations.

¶1905 VALUATION STATEMENT

If the IRS does not accept the estate's property values, the IRS must furnish a valuation statement on written request of the executor. The statement must explain the basis of the valuation or proposed valuation, display any computation used in arriving at the valuation, and contain a copy of any expert appraisal made for the IRS. The statement must be furnished within 45 days after the request or after the IRS makes a determination or proposed determination, whichever is later [IRC Sec. 7517; Reg. Sec. 301.7517-1(a)].

¶1906 SPECIAL VALUATION RULES

There are special valuation rules for determining the fair-market value of various kinds of property including publicly traded stocks and bonds [see ¶ 1911], mutual funds [see ¶ 1912], closely held businesses [see ¶ 1913], notes, mortgages, and bonds with no recognized market [see ¶ 1912(b)], life insurance [see ¶ 1915], term interests (life estates, term of years, remainders, reversions, annuities) [see ¶ 1916], real property [see ¶ 1917], and household and personal effects. The valuation rules for estate tax purposes are generally the same as those for determining fair-market value of these items for gift tax purposes.

Flower bonds. Flower bonds (i.e., certain inheritable U.S. Treasury bonds issued before 1971 that were redeemable at par value plus accrued interest to the date of death to pay federal estate taxes), are included in the decedent's gross estate at par value even if the market value is less than par. The bonds were called flower bonds because they "blossomed" (i.e., were redeemable at par) upon death. The last bonds that qualified for redemption matured on November 15, 1998.

---

[2] Stone v. U.S., 2009-1 USTC ¶60,572 (9th Cir. 2009).

¶1907 ALTERNATE VALUATION METHOD

In general, fair-market value of the decedent's assets for estate tax purposes is determined as of the date of death unless the executor elects the alternate valuation method under IRC Sec. 2032(a) [Reg. Sec. 20.2031-1(b)]. If the value of the decedent's gross estate declines in the six months following the decedent's death and if electing to use the alternate valuation date for estate tax purposes would reduce the taxes due, the executor may elect under IRC Sec. 2032 to value the assets of the estate as of the date six months after the decedent's death.

If an executor elects the alternate valuation method under IRC Sec. 2032, the property included in the decedent's gross estate on the date of his death is valued as of whichever of the following dates is applicable:

1. Any property "distributed, sold, exchanged, or otherwise disposed of" [defined below] within 6 months after the decedent's death is valued as of the date on which it is first distributed, sold, exchanged, or otherwise disposed of;

2. Any property not distributed, sold, exchanged, or otherwise disposed of within 6 months after the decedent's death is valued as of the date 6 months after the date of the decedent's death; or

3. Any property, interest, or estate which is affected by mere lapse of time is valued as of the date of the decedent's death, but adjusted for any difference in its value not due to mere lapse of time as of the date 6 months after the decedent's death, or as of the date of its distribution, sale, exchange, or other disposition, whichever date first occurs [IRC Sec. 2032(a)(1); Reg. Sec. 20.2032-1(a)].

The election, however, is limited. The alternate valuation can be made only if it results in a reduction in both the value of the gross estate and the estate tax and the GST tax liability (reduced by credits allowable against these taxes) of the estate for which the election is made [IRC Sec. 2032(c)]. Reg. Sec. 20.2032-1(b)(1) provides that the determination of whether there has been a decrease in the sum (reduced by allowable credits) of the estate tax and GST tax liability is made with reference to the estate tax and GST tax payable by reason of the decedent's death. This avoids the problem of not being able to determine whether the election will reduce the sum of the two taxes if the GST tax will not be imposed until later on (e.g., in the event of a later taxable termination or a taxable distribution).

(a) Meaning of "Distributed, Sold, Exchanged, or Otherwise Disposed of". The phrase "distributed, sold, exchanged, or otherwise disposed of" comprehends all possible ways by which property ceases to form a part of the gross estate. For example, money on hand at the date of the decedent's death which is thereafter used in the payment of funeral expenses, or which is thereafter invested, falls within the term "otherwise disposed of." The term also includes the surrender of a stock certificate for corporate assets in complete or partial liquidation of a corporation. The term does not, however, extend to transactions that are mere changes in form. Thus, it does not include a transfer of assets to a corporation in exchange for its stock in a transaction with respect to which no gain or loss would be recognizable for income tax purposes under IRC Sec. 351. Nor does it include an exchange of stock or securities in a corporation for stock or securities in the same corporation or another corporation in a transaction, such as a tax-free merger, recapitalization, or reorganization under IRC Sec. 368 where no gain or loss is recognizable for income tax purposes [Reg. Sec. 20.2032-1(c)(1)].

How valuation discounts affect valuation of stock on alternate valuation date. In *Kohler v. Commissioner*,[1] the Tax Court held that valuation discounts attributable to restrictions imposed on closely-held corporate stock pursuant to a post-death reorganization of the Kohler Company should be taken into consideration in valuing stock on the alternate valuation date. In that case, approximately two months after the death of the decedent, the Kohler Company underwent a reorganization that qualified as a tax-free reorganization under IRC Sec. 368(a). The estate opted to receive new Kohler shares that were subject to transfer restrictions. The estate elected to use the alternate valuation method and took into account discounts attributable to the transfer restrictions on the stock in determining the value for federal estate tax purposes. The court agreed with the estate and, accordingly, the Kohler stock was not treated as disposed of on the date of the reorganization and is not valued as of the date of the reorganization, but, rather, on the alternate valuation date six months later.

The IRS disagreed and nonacquiesced to the Tax Court opinion in *Kohler* stating that it believed the Tax Court "had erred in focusing on whether a disposition had occurred rather than on whether it should take into account a change in the character of the property that had occurred during the alternate valuation period."

In response to the taxpayer victory in *Kohler*, the IRS has released Proposed Regulations, including examples, that amend Reg. Sec. 20.2032-1 to clarify that the election to use the alternate valuation method under IRC Sec. 2032 is only available to estates that experience a reduction in the value of the gross estate following the date of the decedent's death due to market conditions, but not due to other post-death events such as reorganizations.

Post-death market conditions. The election to use the alternate valuation method under IRC Sec. 2032 permits the property included in the gross estate to be valued as of the alternate valuation date to the extent that the change in value during the alternate valuation period is the result of market conditions. The term market conditions is defined as events outside of the control of the decedent (or the decedent's executor or trustee) or other person whose property is being valued that affect the fair market value of the property being valued. Changes in value due to mere lapse of time or to other post-death events other than market conditions will be ignored in determining the value of the decedent's gross estate under the alternate valuation method [Prop. Reg. Sec. 20.2032-1(f)(1)].

Post-death events. In order to eliminate changes in value due to post-death events other than market conditions, any interest or estate affected by post-death events other than market conditions is included in a decedent's gross estate under the alternate valuation method at its value as of the date of the decedent's death, with adjustment for any change in value that is due to market conditions. The term post-death events

---

[1] **¶1907** Kohler v. Commissioner, TC Memo 2006-152, *nonacq.*, IRB 2008-9 (March 3, 2008).

¶1907

includes, but is not limited to, a reorganization of an entity (for example, corporation, partnership, or limited liability company) in which the estate holds an interest, a distribution of cash or other property to the estate from such entity, or one or more distributions by the estate of a fractional interest in such entity [Prop. Reg. Sec. 20.2032-1(f)(3)].

> **Example 1:** Decedent's estate elects to value the gross estate under the alternate valuation method. At Decedent's death, he owned common stock in ABCo. At that time, the common stock was not subject to transfer restrictions. Decedent's stock was valued at $50X at the date of death. Two months after his death, Decedent's estate participated in a tax-free reorganization of ABCo where no gain or loss was realized. Pursuant to the reorganization, Decedent's estate opted to exchange its stock for stock subject to transfer restrictions. Although the value of the stock did not change during the alternate valuation period, discounts for lack of marketability and lack of control (totaling $20X) were applied in determining the value of stock held by Decedent's estate on the alternate valuation date and D's estate reported the value of the stock on that date as $30X. Because the claimed reduction in value is not attributable to market conditions, the discounts may not be taken into account in determining the value of the stock on the alternate valuation date and the value on that date is $50X [Prop. Reg. Sec. 20.2032-1(f)(3)(ii), ex. 1].

> **Example 2:** The facts are the same as in the example above except that the value of the stock declined from $50X to $40X during the alternate valuation period because of changes in market conditions during that period. Decedent's estate may report the value of the stock as $40X on the alternate valuation date. As in Example 1, however, no discounts resulting from the reorganization are allowed in computing the value on the alternate valuation date [Prop. Reg. Sec. 20.2032-1(f)(3)(ii), ex. 2].

Property may be "distributed" either by the executor, or by a trustee of property included in the gross estate. Property is considered as "distributed" upon the first to occur of the following:

1. The entry of an order or decree of distribution, if the order or decree subsequently becomes final;
2. The segregation or separation of the property from the estate or trust so that it becomes unqualifiedly subject to the demand or disposition of the distributee; or
3. The actual paying over or delivery of the property to the distributee [Reg. Sec. 20.2032-1(c)(2)].

Property may be "sold, exchanged, or otherwise disposed of" by:

1. The executor;
2. A trustee or other donee to whom the decedent during his lifetime transferred property included in his gross estate under IRC Secs. 2035 through 2038, or IRC Sec. 2041;
3. An heir or devisee to whom title to property passes directly under local law;

4. A surviving joint tenant or tenant by the entirety; or

5. Any other person [Reg. Sec. 20.2032-1(c)(3)].

If a binding contract for the sale, exchange, or other disposition of property is entered into, the property is considered as sold, exchanged, or otherwise disposed of on the effective date of the contract, unless the contract is not subsequently carried out substantially in accordance with its terms. The effective date of a contract is normally the date it is entered into (and not the date it is consummated, or the date legal title to the property passes) unless the contract specifies a different effective date.

(b) "Included Property" and "Excluded Property" for Alternate Valuation Purposes. If the executor elects the alternate valuation method, all property interests existing at the date of decedent's death which form a part of his gross estate are referred to as "included property." Furthermore, such property interests remain "included property" for the purpose of valuing the gross estate under the alternate valuation method even though they change in form during the alternate valuation period by being actually received, or disposed of, in whole or in part, by the estate. On the other hand, property earned or accrued after the date of the decedent's death and during the alternate valuation period, which does not represent a form of "included property" itself or the receipt of "included property" is excluded in valuing the gross estate under the alternate valuation method. Such property is referred to as "excluded property" [Reg. Sec. 1.2032-1(d)].

The following types of property are considered "included property" for alternate valuation purposes:

1. Interest-bearing obligations, such as bonds or notes, may comprise two elements of "included property" at the date of the decedent's death, namely, (i) the principal of the obligation itself, and (ii) interest accrued to the date of death. Each of these elements is to be separately valued as of the applicable valuation date. Interest accrued after the date of death and before the subsequent valuation date constitutes "excluded property" [Reg. Sec. 20.2032-1(d)(1)].

2. Leased realty included in the gross estate and with respect to which an obligation to pay rent has been reserved constitute "included property." Any rent accrued after the date of death and before the subsequent valuation date is "excluded property" [Reg. Sec. 20.2032-1(d)(2)].

3. Noninterest-bearing obligations sold at a discount, such as savings bonds, the principal obligation and the discount amortized to the date of death are property interests existing at the date of death and constitute "included property." The obligation itself is to be valued at the subsequent valuation date without regard to any further increase in value due to amortized discount. The additional discount amortized after death and during the alternate valuation period is the equivalent of interest accruing during that period and is, therefore, not to be included in the gross estate under the alternate valuation method [Reg. Sec. 20.2032-1(d)(3)].

4. Shares of stock in a corporation and dividends declared to stockholders of record on or before the date of the decedent's death and not collected at the date of death constitute "included property" of the estate. On the other hand, ordinary dividends out of earnings and profits (whether in cash, shares of the corporation, or other

property) declared to stockholders of record after the date of the decedent's death are "excluded property" and are not to be valued under the alternate valuation method. If, however, dividends are declared to stockholders of record after the date of the decedent's death with the effect that the shares of stock at the subsequent valuation date do not reasonably represent the same "included property" of the gross estate as existed at the date of the decedent's death, the dividends are "included property," except to the extent that they are out of earnings of the corporation after the date of the decedent's death. For example, if a corporation makes a distribution in partial liquidation to stockholders during the alternate valuation period which is not accompanied by a surrender of a stock certificate for cancellation, the amount of the distribution received on stock included in the gross estate is itself "included property," except to the extent that the distribution was out of earnings and profits since the date of the decedent's death. Similarly, if a corporation, in which the decedent owned a substantial interest and which possessed at the date of the decedent's death accumulated earnings and profits equal to its paid-in capital, distributed all of its accumulated earnings and profits as a cash dividend to shareholders of record during the alternate valuation period, the amount of the dividends received on stock includible in the gross estate will be included in the gross estate under the alternate valuation method. Likewise, a stock dividend distributed under such circumstances is "included property" [Reg. Sec. 20.2032-1(d)(4)].

(c) Value of Property Affected by Lapse of Time. In order to eliminate changes in value due only to mere lapse of time, IRC Sec. 2032(a)(3) provides that any interest or estate "affected by mere lapse of time" is included in a decedent's gross estate under the alternate valuation method at its value as of the date of the decedent's death, but with adjustment for any difference in its value as of the subsequent valuation date not due to mere lapse of time. Properties, interests, or estates which are "affected by mere lapse of time" include patents, estates for the life of a person other than the decedent, remainders, reversions, and other like properties, interests, or estates. The phrase "affected by mere lapse of time" excludes obligations for the payment of money, whether or not interest-bearing, the value of which changes with the passing of time [Reg. Sec. 20.2032-1(f)(2)].

> **Example 3:** Husband died owning an income interest in a trust for the duration of the life of Wife. On the date of Husband's death, Wife was 47 years and five months old, and the trust assets were valued at $2 million. Six months later, the trust assets were valued at $1,950,000. Furthermore, the fact that Wife is a half year older reduces the value of the income interest based on her life span. If Husband's executor uses the alternate valuation date, the reduction in the value of the life interest due to the mere lapse of time is not taken into account, but the lower value of the trust assets is used.

Valuation of life estates, remainders, and similar interests. The values of life estates, remainders, and similar interests are determined by applying the methods prescribed in Reg. Sec. 20.2031-1(f)(2)(i), using:

1. The age of each person, the duration of whose life may affect the value of the interest, as of the date of the decedent's death, and

2. The value of the property as of the alternate date.

Valuation of patents. To illustrate the alternate valuation of a patent, assume that the decedent owned a patent that, on the date of the decedent's death, had an unexpired term of ten years and a value of $78,000. Six months after the date of the decedent's death, the patent was sold, because of lapse of time and other causes, for $60,000. The alternate value would be determined by dividing $60,000 by 0.95 (ratio of the remaining life of the patent at the alternate date to the remaining life of the patent at the date of the decedent's death), and would, therefore, be $63,157.89 [Reg. Sec. 20.2032-1(f)(2)(ii)].

Keys to alternate valuation.

1. All assets in the decedent's gross estate are affected by the election and must be valued as of the alternate valuation date [Reg. Sec. 20.2032-1(d)]. In other words, the executor cannot elect the alternate valuation date for some assets and not others [Reg. Sec. 20.2032-1(b)(2)]. The executor may elect alternate valuation and also elect special use valuation, for real property [see ¶ 1908].[2]

2. The election is not available unless the valuation change will decrease both the federal estate tax (and the GST tax, where applicable) and the size of the decedent's gross estate [IRC Sec. 2032(c)].

3. Property that comes into existence after the decedent's death is not subject to the election. Thus, in general, most dividends declared to shareholders of record after the decedent's death generally are not included or valued under the alternate valuation method [Reg. Sec. 20.2032-1(d)(4)]. When a mutual fund declares and pays a capital gain dividend on its shares between the date of the decedent's death and the alternate valuation date, it is not includable in computing the value of the decedent's gross estate on the alternate valuation date. This rule applies provided the value of the mutual fund shares on the alternate valuation date reasonably represents the same property as existing at the date of death.[3]

4. Under IRC Sec. 2032(b), if alternate valuation is elected, deductions for losses [see ¶ 2001] are allowed only to the extent they are not reflected in the values used to determine the gross estate.

5. If the election is made and property is "distributed, sold, exchanged or otherwise disposed of" within the six-month period, the date of disposition is considered the alternate valuation date [IRC Sec. 2032(a)(1)].

(d) How to Elect. Alternate valuation is elected on the estate tax return (Form 706). The election is irrevocable and must be made on a timely filed return or the first late return filed within one year of the due date (including extensions) [IRC Sec. 2032(d)]. Estates that fail to make the alternate valuation election on the last estate tax return filed before the due date or the first return filed after the due date may request an extension of time to make the election. The requests must be made within one year after the return's due date (including filing extensions actually granted) [Reg. Sec.

---

[2] Rev. Rul. 83-31, 1983-1 CB 225.   [3] Rev. Rul. 76-234, 1976-1 CB 271.

20.2032-1(b)(3)]. In *Estate of Loree*,[4] a district court concluded that the decedent's alternate valuation election was not timely because it was made on an amended return that was filed more than six months after the due date for the return.

Protective elections. Estates may also make a protective election if, based on the tax return as filed, use of the alternate valuation method would not result in a decrease in both the value of the gross estate and the sum (reduced by allowable credits) of the estate/GST tax due with respect to the property includible in the decedent's gross estate, a protective election may be made to use the alternate valuation method if it is subsequently determined that such a decrease would occur. A protective election is made on the decedent's estate tax return. The protective election is irrevocable as of the due date of the return (including extensions of time actually granted). The protective election becomes effective on the date when use of the alternate valuation method would result in a decrease in both the value of the gross estate and in the sum (reduced by allowable credits) of the estate/GST tax due with respect to the property includible in the decedent's gross estate [Reg. Sec. 20.2032-1(b)(2)].

> ▶ **CAUTION:** Because the alternate valuation date is a key tax option available to the executor, you must file the estate tax return on time and obtain written acknowledgment of the filing from the IRS. The return should be sent by registered or certified mail at a U.S. Post Office or one of the private delivery services (PDSs) designated by the IRS [IRC Secs. 7502(c), 7502(f); Reg. Sec. 301.7502-1(c)]. For list of approved PDSs, see ¶ 2604.

The IRS has been consistently unsympathetic to executors who are late in making the alternate valuation election. In *Estate of Eddy*,[5] the Tax Court denied an executor's ability to make this election because it was made more than one year after the deadline (with extensions) for filing the estate tax return.

In certain situations, however, executors may find relief in Reg. Sec. 301.9100-1(c), which provides that the IRS may grant a reasonable extension of time to make a regulatory or statutory election (but no more than six months, unless the taxpayer is abroad). Reg. Sec. 301.9100-3 provides that relief will be granted when the taxpayer provides evidence that he or she acted reasonably and in good faith and the grant of relief will not prejudice IRS interests.

In Letter Ruling 200302007, an executor was entitled to an extension to make an alternate valuation election when a law firm failed to advise the executor about the availability of the election. The IRS concluded that the executor had acted reasonably and in good faith when the executor's law firm had failed to advise about the alternate dates. Therefore the IRS granted an extension of time to make the election.

In Letter Ruling 201033023, an executor was denied an extension to make an alternate valuation election because the election was not filed within one year of the due date of the return, thus violating IRC Sec. 2032(d)(1) which provides that no election under IRC Sec. 2032 is available if the return is filed more than one year after the time prescribed by law (including extensions) for filing the return.

Reg. Sec. 20.2032-1(b)(3) provides that a request for an extension of time to make the IRC Sec. 2032 election will not be granted unless the estate tax return is filed no later

---

[4] Estate of Loree, 2008-1 USTC ¶ 60,555 (D. N.J. 2008).

[5] Estate of Eddy, 115 TC 135 (2000). See also Ltr. Ruls. 201151003, 201216013, 201236002.

than one year after the due date of the return (including extensions to time actually granted).

(e) After-Death Planning Strategies. The IRC Sec. 2032 election allows you to reduce the amount of estate tax to be paid. However, its income tax consequences must be considered. Use of the election will result in a lower cost basis to the heirs and higher future income taxes.

If the executor must sell assets to meet the estate's cash requirements, the executor should make the sales during the six-month alternate valuation period. If the alternate valuation date is used, no loss is realized and recognized on the sale for income tax purposes. Usually, the estate tax savings from using the alternate valuation date are greater than the income tax savings resulting from the long-term capital loss that would be generated if the alternate valuation date were not used.

To minimize the estate tax value, the executor should not make any distributions during the six-month alternate valuation period. By making a distribution before the decline in value has occurred, the executor will forfeit the estate reduction that might be obtained by using the alternate valuation date.

The executor must also consider how the use of the alternate valuation method will effect the ability of an estate to satisfy the requirements for deferring the estate tax under IRC Sec. 6166 which depends on meeting a percentage test [see ¶2303].

¶1908 SPECIAL USE VALUATION

An executor may elect to value real property includible in a decedent's estate that is used for farming or for closely held business use on the basis of the property's actual use, rather than on the traditional basis of "highest or best" use, if certain conditions are met [IRC Sec. 2032A]. Before the enactment of IRC Sec. 2032A, heirs were often forced to sell property used in farming or in a closely held business for development purposes to meet the estate tax burden caused by valuing the property on an often inappropriate highest and best use basis. Thus, the purpose of the special use valuation provision is twofold—to benefit the estates of farmers and owners of closely held businesses by substantially reducing estate taxes and, in so doing, to encourage heirs to continue using the property for farming and other small business purposes. However, an estate is not required to show that farm real property has a highest and best use other than farming. Accordingly, qualified real farm property may be specially valued even if its higher fair market value is based on speculative agricultural use.[1]

The purpose of the special use valuation rules under IRC Sec. 2032A is "to encourage the continued operation of family farms and other small family businesses by permitting real property used for the farm or business to be valued based in its present use, rather than upon its highest and best use."[2] Specifically, "§ 2032A relieves taxpayers from having to sell an eligible family farm or business when the

---

[1] **¶1908** IRS News Release, IR-2160, September 10, 1979.

[2] Schuneman, 86-1 USTC ¶13,660, 783 F.2d 694 (7th Cir. 1986).

income from its present use is insufficient to pay the tax calculated upon its highest and best use."[3]

To make sure that the current use valuation rules are not abused, the IRC contains a provision for recapture of the lost taxes if, within 10 years, the property is no longer used for farming or closely held business purposes or is transferred to someone other than a family member or qualified heir [IRC Sec. 2032A(c)].

The maximum reduction in the value of real property resulting from an election under IRC Sec. 2032A is $1,090,000 for decedents dying in 2014.

The executor may elect to combine special use valuation with the alternate valuation date method [see ¶ 1907].[4] If both are elected, special use values and the $1,090,000 limitation in 2014 are determined as of the alternate valuation date.

Impact of special use valuation on basis of property. In *Van Alen*,[5] the Tax Court concluded that the alternate use valuation, which had been elected by the decedent's estate, determined the basis of the property that carried over to the trust that inherited the property, and then to the taxpayers who were the beneficiaries of the trust.

(a) Requirements. Special use valuation applies only to real property located in the United States and used for farming purposes or in a closely held business. To qualify for special use valuation, the following conditions must be met [IRC Sec. 2032A]:

1. The decedent must have been a citizen or resident of the United States at the time of death [IRC Sec. 2032A(a)(1)(A)].

2. The real estate must be located in the United States [IRC Sec. 2032A(b)(1)].

3. At the time of death, the real property must have been used in farming or in a closely held business by the decedent or a family member [IRC Sec. 2032A(b)(1)]. The concept of farming (and farming purposes) encompasses virtually all agricultural activities and qualified woodlands [IRC Secs. 2032A(e)(4), 2032(e)(5), and 2032(e)(13)].

   Any active business, such as manufacturing, mercantile, or service enterprises, falls within the scope of a business. The concept of a business under Sec. 2032A is narrower than the concept of a business for income tax purposes under IRC Sec. 162 and must comprise an activity engaged in for profit [Reg. Sec. 20.2032A-3(b)]. Thus, a business does not apply to passive investment activities or the passive rental of property to a party except to a member of the decedent's family [Reg. Sec. 20.2032A-3].

   Qualified real property includes residential buildings and other structures and real property improvements regularly occupied or used by the owner or lessee of real property (or by employees of the owner or lessee) to operate the farm or business. Qualified real property also includes roads, buildings, and other structures, and improvements functionally related to the qualified use. However, elements of value, such as mineral rights and hunting rights, that are not related

---

[3] Schuneman, 86-1 USTC ¶ 13,660, 783 F.2d 694 (7th Cir. 1986).

[4] Rev. Rul. 83-31, 1983-1 CB 225.

[5] Van Alen, TC Memo 2013-235.

to the farm or business use are not eligible for special use valuation [IRC Sec. 2032A(e)(3); Reg. Sec. 20.2032A-3(b)(2)].

The special use valuation method may apply to a decedent's indirect ownership of the real estate (e.g., if the decedent owns an interest in an entity that owns the real estate). The ownership qualification of the real estate is satisfied if the ownership tests of IRC Sec. 6166(b)(1) are met [see ¶ 2303].

If the indirect ownership is through a corporation, you have two ways to satisfy the test: (1) at least 20 percent of the value of the corporation's voting stock must be included in the gross estate, or (2) the corporation must have had no more than 45 shareholders.

If the indirect ownership is through a partnership, you have three ways to satisfy the test: (1) at least 20 percent of the partnership's total capital interest must be included in the gross estate, (2) the partnership must have had no more than 45 partners, or (3) the material participation test discussed below is in item 6 is fulfilled [Reg. Sec. 20.2032A-3(f)(1)].

Family members are defined to include:

- The taxpayer's ancestors (e.g., parents);
- Spouse;
- Lineal descendants (e.g., children); and
- Lineal descendants of the taxpayer's spouse or parents (e.g., siblings). A spouse of any of the taxpayer's descendants is also a family member. An adopted child is treated as a natural child [IRC Sec. 2032A(e)(2)].

4. The real property must pass to, or be acquired from the estate, by a member of the decedent's family, known as a qualified heir [IRC Secs. 2032A(b)(1), 2032A(e)(1)]. A qualified heir is defined as a member of the decedent's family who acquired the property or to whom the property passed from the decedent [IRC Sec. 2032A(e)(1)].

   The concept of property acquired (or passed) from the decedent encompasses virtually all transfers, at death and during life, of property included in the decedent's gross estate. Also included is property purchased from the decedent's estate or from a trust, to the extent the property is included in the decedent's gross estate [IRC Secs. 2032A(e)(9)(B) and 2032A(e)(9)(C)].

   Qualified property may pass to a qualified heir as a result of a qualified disclaimer [see Chapter 12].[6]

5. For purposes of the special use valuation rules, the term "qualified real property" means real property located in the United States which was acquired from or passed from the decedent to a qualified heir of the decedent and which, on the date of the decedent's death, was being used for a qualified use by the decedent or a member of the decedent's family, but only if **50 percent** or more of the adjusted value of the gross estate consists of the adjusted value of real or personal property which on the date of the decedent's death, was being used for a qualified use by the decedent or a member of the decedent's family, and was

---

[6] Rev. Rul. 82-140, 1982-2 CB 208.

¶1908

acquired from or passed from the decedent to a qualified heir of the decedent [IRC Sec. 2032A(b)(1)(A)].

The adjusted value of the decedent's gross estate equals the value of the gross estate less allowable deductions for mortgages or indebtedness with respect to the property [IRC Sec. 2032A(b)(3)(A)]. Valuation is determined on the date of death or the alternate valuation date [see ¶ 1907].

The adjusted value of the real or personal property is its fair-market value (without regard to the special use valuation) less any mortgage or other indebtedness against property in the estate [IRC Sec. 2032A(b)(3)(B)].

A decedent's estate takes into consideration property transferred by the decedent within three years of death for purposes of determining if the estate qualifies for special use valuation [IRC Sec. 2035(d)(3)(B)]. If this property continues to be used for a qualified use until the decedent's death, it may be used to meet the 50 percent requirement.[7]

NOTE: Personal property is taken into account to satisfy the 50 percent requirement provided it satisfies the qualified use test and the acquisition by a qualified heir test.[8]

6. For purposes of the special use valuation rules, the term "qualified real property" means real property located in the United States which was acquired from or passed from the decedent to a qualified heir of the decedent and which, on the date of the decedent's death, was being used for a qualified use by the decedent or a member of the decedent's family, but only if at least **25 percent** or more of the adjusted value of the gross estate consists of real property that (1) "was acquired from or passed from the decedent to a qualified heir of the decedent as provided in IRC Sec. 2032A(b)(1)(A)(ii)"; and (2) has been used for a qualified use for 5 of the 8 years preceding the decedent's death and for which there was material participation by the decedent or a member of the decedent's family in the operation of the farm as provided in IRC Sec. 2032A(b)(1)(C) [IRC Sec. 20.2032A(b)(1)(B)]. Reg. Sec. 20.2032A-8(a)(2) provides that while an estate need not elect special use valuation with respect to all of the qualifying property, the property actually elected for the special use valuation must constitute at least 25 percent of the adjusted value of the gross estate. In *Miller*,[9] the court found Reg. Sec. 20.2032A-8(a)(1) to be invalid explaining that even though a special use valuation "need not include all real property included in an estate which is eligible for special use valuation," it must include "sufficient property to satisfy the threshold requirements" of IRC Sec. 2032A(b)(1)(B).

The court in *Finfrock*[10] also found Reg. Sec. 20.2032A-8(a)(1) to be invalid because it conflicted with IRC Sec. 2032A which does not require that the special use valuation election be made for all or a certain percentage of the qualified property. The court found that the IRS was wrong in Reg. Sec. 20.2032A-8(a)(2) to add the substantive requirement that Congress did not add in the statute—that an estate could not elect special use valuation for less than 25 percent of the

---

[7] Rev. Rul. 87-122, 1987-2 CB 221.

[8] Rev. Rul. 85-168, 1985-2 CB 197.

[9] Miller, 88-1 USTC ¶ 13,757, 680 F. Supp. 1269 (C.D. Ill. 1988).

[10] Finfrock, 2012-1 USTC ¶ 60,641 (C.D. Ill. 2012).

adjusted gross estate. In light of this conflict, the court found Reg. Sec.20.2032A-8(a)(2) to be invalid.

A surviving spouse's interest in qualified real property held as community property is taken into account for purposes of meeting the 50 percent and 25 percent tests, but not for purposes of reducing the $1,090,000 limitation in 2014 [IRC Sec. 2032A(e)(10)]. Thus, if the decedent and the decedent's spouse at any time held qualified real property as community property, the special use valuation rules apply as if the property were not community property. The decedent's community property interest is treated in the same manner as a comparable common law interest. The full amount of the limitation applies to the decedent's qualified community property interest whether or not the decedent contributed to the purchase of the property.

7. In order to meet the 25 percent requirement, during at least five years of the eight-year period immediately preceding the decedent's death, the property must have been (1) owned by the decedent (or a family member) and (2) used by the decedent (or a family member) for farming or business activities in which there was material participation by the decedent (or a family member) [IRC Sec. 2032A(b)(1)(C)].

If, at the date of the decedent's death, the decedent was disabled or had retired, the eight-year period ends with the earlier of the beginning of the disability or retirement [IRC Sec. 2032A(b)(4)]. The substitute period appears only if the decedent were retired on Social Security or were disabled for a continuous period ending with his or her death.

Material participation is not defined in IRC Sec. 2032A. Instead, IRC Sec. 2032A(e)(6) provides that material participation is determined in a manner similar to the manner used in IRC Sec. 1402(a)(1), which defines the term "net earnings from self-employment" in connection with agricultural or horticultural activities.

No one factor connotes material participation, but physical work and participation in management decisions are the principal factors to be considered [Reg. Sec. 20.2032A-3(e)(2)].

To constitute material participation, the actual employment of the decedent or a member of the decedent's family must be substantially full-time. This means 35 hours a week or more or enough time to personally manage the farm or business in which the real property is used. For many farming operations that require only seasonal activity, material participation exists as long as necessary functions are performed even though little or no actual activity occurs during nonproducing seasons. In the absence of this direct involvement in the farm or other business, the activities of either the decedent or family member must meet the standards prescribed and subject the person to self-employment tax.

If participants are self-employed with respect to the farm or other business, their income from the farm or other business must be earned income for purposes of the tax on self-employment income before they are considered to be materially participating. Payment of the self-employment tax does not in itself indicate material participation. If no self-employment taxes have been paid, however, no material participation is considered to have occurred unless the executor demonstrates to the satisfaction of the IRS that material participation did in fact occur and informs the IRS of the reason why no tax was paid. In addition, all self-employment taxes (including interest and penalties) determined to be due must be paid, if they can be assessed at the time of the determination. Generally this means that any self-employment tax due for the previous three years must be paid [Reg. Sec. 20.2032A-3(e)(1)].

The decedent or family member must regularly advise or consult with the other managing party on the operation of the business. Although they need not make all final management decisions alone, the decedent or family member must participate in making a substantial number of these decisions.

The family participant should regularly look at the production activities on the land. The decedent or family member should also have advanced funds and have taken on financial responsibility for a substantial part of the expense involved in the operation of the farm or other business in which real property is used. An important factor in material participation, in the case of a farm, is whether the owner or other family members furnish a substantial part of the machinery, implements, and livestock used in the production activities.

When the business is a farm, hotel, or apartment building, a factor in material participation is whether the participating decedent or heir maintains his or her principal place of residence on the premises.

Material participation by the decedent or family members may exist even when a professional farm manager is used. However, the decedent or family member must materially participate under the terms of arrangement with the professional farm manager to satisfy this requirement [Reg. Sec. 20.2032A-3(e)(2)].

NOTE: Passively collecting rents, salaries, draws, dividends, or other income from the farm or other business is not material participation. Neither is merely advancing capital and reviewing a crop plan or other business proposal and financial reports each season or business year.

There is an alternative to the material participation requirement for estates of surviving spouses who receive property from a decedent in whose estate the real property was eligible for special use valuation. In other words, the surviving spouse's estate may elect special use valuation even if that valuation was not used by the estate of the first spouse who died. The surviving spouse is treated as having materially participated during the period when the surviving spouse (but not a family member) actively managed the farm or business [IRC Sec. 2032A(b)(5)]. "Active management" means the making of management decisions for a business, except daily operating decisions [IRC Sec. 2032A(e)(12)].

Active management, for farming purposes, includes the inspection of growing crops, review and approval of annual crop plans before planting, approval of large expenditures in advance, and making a large number of management decisions. Typical management decisions are deciding what crops to plant, where and when to market crops and other business products, how to finance operations, and what capital expenditures to make.

Special use valuation is allowed to the estate of a surviving spouse even if the surviving spouse did not materially participate in the operation of the farm or business, if the first deceased spouse materially participated in such management [IRC Sec. 2032A(b)(5)(A)]. IRC Sec. 2032A(b)(5) allows "tacking" of material participation by a retired spouse with active management by the surviving spouse to qualify the property for current use valuation in the surviving spouse's estate where the spouse survives the first decedent by fewer than eight years. For example, in Technical Advice Memorandum 200911009, the IRS concluded that a decedent's surviving spouse was deemed to have materially participated in a farming activity because the decedent had materially participated in the farming activity for five of the eight years preceding the decedent's retirement and the surviving spouse was retired from farming at the time of the decedent's death.

Example 1: Husband materially participated in the operations of his farm from January 2006 through February 2009 when he became disabled. After he became disabled, Wife actively managed the farm until her death. Husband died in 2013. Wife died in 2014. Husband's and Wife's work constitute sufficient material participation to qualify the farm for special use valuation (assuming the other requirements are met) in both estates. Reason: Husband materially participated for five out of eight years ending with the onset of his disability. In addition, Wife's three years of active management can be tacked onto Husband's material participation.

Tacking is permitted to satisfy the ownership and material participation requirements (as well as the qualified use test) for real estate exchanged in a like-kind exchange or converted in an involuntary conversion. The tacking allowed applies only to that portion of the replacement property that does not exceed the fair-market value of the replaced or exchanged property [IRC Sec. 2032A(e)(14)].

8. The qualified property must be designated in a written agreement signed by each person who has an interest in the property consenting to the application of the recapture tax discussed below [IRC Secs. 2032A(b)(1)(D), 2032A(d)(2)].

   (b) Valuation Methods. Assuming that the above seven requirements for the special use valuation method are satisfied, the IRC sets forth two methods for valuing the real estate:

1. Capitalization of rental income [IRC Sec. 2032A(e)(7)]; or

2. The five-factor method [IRC Sec. 2032A(e)(8)].

Capitalization of rental income. The capitalization of rental income approach is available only for valuing real estate used for farming purposes. To use this technique, you must (1) find the average annual net capital rental (gross cash rental less state and local real estate taxes) for comparable real property and (2) divide this figure by the average annual effective interest rate for all new Federal Land Bank loans [IRC Sec. 2032A(e)(7)(A)]. Each computation is made on the basis of the five most recent calendar years before the date of the decedent's death.

   NOTE: The capitalization of rental income approach method cannot be used if it is established that there is no comparable property from which the average annual gross cash rental (or net share rental) can be determined or if the executor elects to use the five-factor method.

¶1908

Five-factor method. The five-factor method is used to determine the special use valuation of qualifying real property used in a business other than farming [IRC Sec. 2032A(e)(8)]. You may also use the method for qualifying farm property if there is no comparable property from which cash rentals can be determined or if you elect to use this method for farm property. The five factors to be applied are as follows [IRC Sec. 2032A(e)(8)]:

1. Capitalization of income that the property can be expected to yield for farming or for closely held business purposes over a reasonable period of time with prudent management and traditional cropping patterns for the area, taking into account soil capacity, terrain configuration, and similar factors.

2. Capitalization of the fair rental value of the land for farming or for closely held business purposes.

3. Assessed land values in a state that provides a differential or use value assessment law for farmland or closely held business land.

4. Comparable sales of other farm or closely held business land in the same geographical area far enough removed from a metropolitan or resort area so that nonagricultural use is not a significant factor in the sales price.

5. Any other factor that fairly values the farm or closely held business value of the property.

The Tax Court has held that an estate was entitled to value a decedent's timberland and standing timber, as well as a parcel of pastureland that constituted "qualified woodland," pursuant to the special-use valuation formula method under IRC Sec. 2032A(e)(7), because the estate provided leases of comparable land for the five most recent calendar years ending before the date of the decedent's death.[11]

(c) How to Elect. Special use valuation must be elected on a timely filed estate tax return (Form 706) or on a late-filed Form 706 as long as it is the first return filed after the due date [IRC Sec. 2032A(d)(1); Reg. Sec. 20.2032A-8(a)]. See ¶2408. The election, once made, is irrevocable. In order to make a valid election, certain information is required to be included in the Notice of Election, and each person who has an interest in the property is required to sign an agreement consenting to the imposition of additional estate tax in the event of a failure to use the property for its qualified use within 10 years of the decedent's death.

Both a notice of election and an agreement by heirs must be attached to the estate tax return. The Notice of Election must contain the following information [Reg. Sec. 20.2032A-8(a)(3)]:

1. The decedent's name and taxpayer identification number as they appear on the estate tax return;

2. The relevant qualified use;

3. The items of real property shown on the estate tax return to be specially valued under the election (identified by schedule and item number);

---

[11] Estate of Rogers, TC Memo 2000-133.

4. The fair-market value of the property to be specially valued and the property's value based on its qualified use (both values determined without reduction for unpaid mortgages);

5. The adjusted value of all real property (after reduction for unpaid mortgages) that is used in a qualified use and that passes to a qualified heir, and the adjusted value of all real property to be specially valued;

6. The items of real property shown on the estate tax return that pass from a decedent to a qualified heir and that are used in a qualified use (identified by schedule and item number), and the total value of the personal property (reduced by unpaid mortgages);

7. The adjusted value of the gross estate (gross estate minus any unpaid mortgages);

8. The methods used for determining the special value based on use;

9. Copies of written appraisals of the fair-market value of the real property;

10. A statement that the decedent or a member of his or her family has owned all specially valued real property for at least five of the eight years immediately preceding the date of the decedent's death;

11. A statement listing any periods during the eight years preceding the date of the decedent's death during which the decedent or a member of his or her family did not own the property, use it in a qualified use, or materially participate in the operation of the farm or other business;

12. Affidavits describing the activities consisting of material participation and the identity of the material participant or participants; and

13. A legal description of the specially valued property.

The Notice of Election must include a consent agreement signed by all parties having an interest in the property being valued on its qualified use at the date of death. In addition to consenting to special use valuation, qualified heirs must agree to personal liability (or furnish a bond) for the recapture tax (discussed below), and other beneficiaries must agree to the collection of the recapture tax from the qualified real property.

The agreement must be binding on all parties having an interest in the property. The agreement must give the name and address of an agent with satisfactory evidence of authority to act for the parties in all dealings with the IRS on matters arising out of the agreement. The agent must agree to notify the IRS of any disposition or cessation of qualified use of the property [IRC Sec. 2032A(d)(2); Reg. Sec. 20.2032A-8(c)]. For a sample form of an agreement, see Revenue Procedure 81-14.[12]

An interest in property is an interest that, as of the date of the decedent's death, can be asserted under local law to affect the deposition of the specially valued property by the estate. Any person who at the decedent's death has any interest in the property, present or future, vested or contingent, must enter into the agreement [Reg. Sec. 20.2032A-8(c)(2)].

(d) Extension of Time to Make Election. An executor who fails to make an election to take advantage of the estate tax election to specially value qualified real

---

[12] Rev. Proc. 81-14, 1981-1 CB 669.

property can request an automatic 12-month extension under Reg. Sec. 301.9100-2(a)(2)(vii) provided the taxpayer takes corrective action as defined in Reg. Sec. 301.9100-2(c).

Under Reg. Sec. 301.9100-2(c), corrective action means taking the steps required to file the election in accordance with the statute, revenue ruling, revenue procedure, IRS notice or announcement. For those elections required to be filed with a return, corrective action includes filing an original or an amended return for the year the regulatory or statutory election should have been made and attaching the appropriate form or statement for making the election.

Reg. Sec. 301.9100-3 provides the standards used to determine whether the IRS will grant an extension of time to make an election. Requests for relief under Reg. Sec.301.9100-3 will be granted when the taxpayer provides the evidence to establish to the satisfaction of the IRS that the taxpayer acted reasonably and in good faith, and the grant of relief will not prejudice the interests of the IRS. Reg. Sec. 301.9100-3(b)(1)(i) provides that a taxpayer is deemed to have acted reasonably and in good faith if the taxpayer requests relief under this section before the failure to make the regulatory election is discovered by the IRS.[13] Reg. Sec.301.9100-3(b)(1)(v) provides that a taxpayer is deemed to have acted reasonably and in good faith if the taxpayer reasonably relied on a qualified tax professional, including a tax professional employed by the taxpayer, and the tax professional failed to make, or advise the taxpayer to make, the election.[14]

(e) Right to Correct Mistakes. If an election is timely filed and (1) the Notice of Election does not contain all of the required information or (2) the signature of one or more persons required to sign the agreement is missing or the agreement does not contain all the required information, the executor may provide the missing information or signatures within 90 days of being notified by the IRS [IRC Sec. 2032A(d)(3)].

(f) Protective Election. A protective election may be filed if it is uncertain whether the estate qualifies for special use valuation so that if the requirements are met during audit, the election will be available [Reg. Sec. 20.2032A-8(b)]. A protective election is made by a notice of protective election filed with the estate tax return stating that a protective election under IRC Sec. 2032A is being made pending the final determination of values.

> **NOTE:** The protective election must be made on a timely filed estate tax return. If you make a protective election, you complete the estate tax return by valuing all property at its fair-market value.

A protective election does not extend the time for payment of any amount of tax. If you wish to extend the time to pay the taxes, you should file IRS Form 4768 in adequate time before the return due date. If it is later determined that the estate qualifies for special use valuation, you must file a supplemental estate tax return within 60 days after date of this determination.

---

[13] Ltr. Rul. 201224019.   [14] Ltr. Rul. 201230023.

(g) Recapture of Estate Tax Benefits. The recapture tax is an additional estate tax that is imposed within 10 years after the decedent's death and before the death of the qualified heir if certain recapture events occur.

Requirements. The following three events must occur for the recapture to apply:

1. Any interest in qualified real property must be transferred to a non-family member.

2. The property must not be used for farming or other closely held business purposes.

> **NOTE:** The cash lease of specially valued real property by a lineal descendant of the decedent to a member of the lineal descendant's family, who continues to work the farm or closely held business, does not cause the recapture of the special use value for purposes of imposing the additional estate tax [IRC Sec. 2032A(c)(7)(E)]. Members of the lineal descendant's family include that individual's (1) ancestors; (2) spouse; (3) lineal descendants of the individual, of the individual's spouse, or of a parent of such individual; or (4) the spouse of any lineal descendant in (3) above.

> **Example 2:** Daughter inherits a farm from Father for which a special use valuation election is made, and she rents the farm to an unrelated neighbor on a crop share basis. Three years after her father's death, Daughter leases the qualified real property to her nephew on a net cash basis and the nephew continues to operate the farm. The lease of the farm to the nephew does not result in a cessation of qualified use because Daughter is a lineal descendant of her father, who is the decedent, and her nephew is a lineal descendant of her parent. Thus the nephew is a member of the family.

1. Within any eight-year period ending after the decedent's death (or before the death of a qualified heir), there were periods aggregating more than three years during which there was no material participation in the farming or business operation by the decedent (or a family member) or by a qualified heir (or a family member) [IRC Sec. 2032A(c)(1), 2032A(c)(6)]. The qualified heir has a two-year period after the decedent's death to begin putting the real property to a qualified use. The 10-year recapture period is extended by the length of any grace period that is used before qualified use begins [IRC Sec. 2032A(c)(7)].

For certain persons (so-called eligible qualified heirs [IRC Sec. 2032A(e)(7)(C)]), active management [IRC Sec. 2032A(e)(12)] is treated as material participation [IRC Sec. 2032A(c)(7)(B)].

> ▶ **OBSERVATION:** Because of the possible imposition of the recapture tax, all qualified heirs should be advised in writing to continue the qualified use of the property. This correspondence should explain all post-death requirements and warn the heirs not to make any changes in the ownership or use of the property without obtaining legal advice.

> **NOTE:** Two situations extinguish the possibility of the recapture tax: (1) the expiration of 10 years from the death of the decedent with no recapture event occurring; or (2) the death of the qualified heir before the occurrence of a recapture event. If qualified heirs have successive interests in the property,

termination of potential recapture tax liability cannot occur until the death of all qualified heirs.

Amount of additional tax. The amount of the recapture tax is the lesser of the following [IRC Sec. 2032A(c)(2)]:

1. The difference between the estate tax liability based on the special use valuation and what the estate tax liability would have been had special use valuation not been elected. If the special use valuation affected more than just the property for which tax is now recaptured, multiply the above by this fraction: the difference between the fair-market value and special use value of the property, divided by the difference between the fair-market value and the special use value of all qualified property; or

2. The excess of the amount realized on the sale of the interest or its fair-market value (in any case except its sale or exchange at arm's length) over the special use value.

     NOTE: A qualified heir may elect to increase the basis of specially valued real property to its fair-market value on the date of the decedent's death or alternate valuation date (if applicable) [see ¶1907] when the recapture tax is imposed. If the recapture event was a sale, for federal income tax purposes the qualified heir's recognized gain is therefore reduced because the basis increase is deemed to occur immediately before the recapture event [IRC Sec. 1016(c)].

Filing requirement and payment of additional tax. The qualified heir who has caused a recapture event to occur must file IRS Form 706-A and pay the additional tax within six months after a taxable disposition or the end of the qualified use unless the IRS grants an extension of time [IRC Sec. 2032A(c)(4)]. The form must be filed if there is an early disposition, an early cessation of qualified use, or an exchange or involuntary conversion of specially valued property, even if no additional tax is due.

No tax is due on an early disposition to a family member who signs an agreement to assume personal liability for any additional tax that may become due [IRC Sec. 2032A(c)(1)(A)]. Furthermore, no recapture tax is imposed if there is an involuntary conversion of qualified replacement property [IRC Sec. 2032A(h)]. No additional tax is imposed on an exchange of specially valued property for "qualified exchange property" (i.e., property that will be used for the same qualified use) as was applied to the property for which it was exchanged [IRC Sec. 2032A(I)].

Special lien. There is a special lien in favor of the United States on all qualified property for which an election to use the special valuation method has been made, including qualified replacement property [IRC Sec. 6324B]. The lien equals the adjusted tax difference attributable to the interest in the property [Reg. Sec. 20.6324B-1(a)]. The adjusted tax difference is the difference between the estate tax liability and what the estate tax liability would have been had the special use valuation not been elected. The attributable amount bears the same ratio to the adjusted tax difference as the excess fair-market value of the particular qualified property bears to the excess fair-market value of all qualified property. In other words, the adjusted tax difference is multiplied by a fraction, the numerator of which is the difference between the fair-market value and the special value of the property and the denominator of which is difference between the fair-market value and the special value of all qualified property [IRC Sec. 2032A(c)(2)(B)].

¶1908

The lien continues until the tax benefits are recaptured or potential liability ends [IRC Sec. 6324B(b)]. The lien may be:

1. Discharged by the substitution of adequate security [IRC Sec. 6324B(d)]; or

2. Subordinated to other liens if the IRS determines that the interests of the U.S. government will be adequately protected after subordination and there is an amount equal to the amount of the private lien paid over to the IRS [IRC Sec. 6325(d)(3)].

   (h) After-Death Planning Strategies. Before taking advantage of the special use valuation election, keep in mind that it can only be used if:

- The qualified heirs intend to use the property in the same manner for the next 10 years;

- All interested parties sign the necessary agreements; and

- The estate tax is reduced or eliminated because of the election.

An election need not include all real property included in the gross estate that is eligible for special use valuation. For instance, some acreage contained in a farm may be valued at its fair-market value if the heirs plan to sell that land, while other acreage may be valued at its special tax value. If qualified heirs receive a joint interest (e.g., as joint tenants) in the same property, an election for one heir's joint interest need not include any other heir's interest in the same property.

An executor should consider making a protective election that allows more time to decide whether to make the election if the estate qualifies.

   ▶ **PRACTICE POINTER:** Several disadvantages of a special valuation election are noteworthy:

1. If Sec. 2032A valuation is elected, the basis to the qualified heir for income tax purposes is the lower special use value.

2. If the unlimited estate tax material deduction [see ¶ 1100] is available on the first spouse's death, the marital deduction does eliminate the recapture tax if a disqualifying event occurs.

3. Use of the Sec. 2032A special use valuation may prevent an estate from qualifying for the deferral of the estate taxes under IRC Sec. 6166 [see ¶ 2303] because the special use valuation could reduce the value of a closely held business interest to the point where the estate no longer meets the more than 35 percent test.

¶ 1909 BUY-SELL AGREEMENTS AND VALUING CLOSELY HELD BUSINESSES

Buy-sell agreements can be useful estate-planning tools because they provide for the contractual purchase of closely held business interests at a set price when a business owner dies. Unlike publicly traded corporations, closely held businesses typically do not have a market eager to purchase a owner's interest after death. This can present a cash-flow problem for family members. Here are some of the benefits associated with the buy-sell agreements:

- They can prevent an unwanted dilution of control that occurs when outsiders become shareholders or partners in a closely held business.

- They can prevent a sale of the business to unwanted third parties.

- They can provide cash for what may otherwise be an illiquid estate of a deceased closely held business owner. Often a closely held business interest is the most valuable asset in the decedent's estate. The buy-sell agreement can help establish a value for that asset and prevent a forced sale of business assets following the death of the owner to provide funds for payment of estate taxes and administration expenses.

- They can prevent inadvertent termination of an S election or status as a professional corporation under state law.

- They can ensure a smooth transition of power or business ownership after the death, disability, or retirement of an owner.

- Protracted disputes between business owners can be avoided.

- They can establish the value of a deceased owner's interest for the federal estate tax return. The value of the business will also be important if the surviving owners want to sell the business and need to establish a purchase price.

- They provide certainty for the remaining business owners regarding the terms under which a deceased owner's interest will be purchased.

(a) Types of Buy-Sell Agreements. Buy-sell agreements usually take the form of either:

- A redemption; or

- A cross-purchase agreement.

In a redemption agreement or an entity purchase agreement, the corporation or partnership is obligated or has an option to purchase the ownership interest of the deceased owner.

In a cross-purchase agreement, the shareholders or partners must purchase or have an option to purchase, on a pro rata or other basis, all or part of the business interest of the deceased shareholder or partner.

When life insurance is being used to fund the purchase of a deceased owner, the existence of more than two owners may make use of a cross-purchase agreement impractical because each owner would be required to purchase a policy on the life of the other owners. For example, if there are 4 shareholders, 12 policies would be required in a cross-purchase plan according to the simple formula of $N \times (N - 1)$, where N is the number of shareholders $[4 \times (4 - 1) = 12]$. This problem can be solved if you use a trust to own and hold the one life insurance policy required for each shareholder. With four shareholders, the number of policies needed would be reduced to four.

(b) What Is Covered in a Typical Buy-Sell Agreement. The typical buy-sell agreement covers the following:

- Restricting all transfers, other than to permitted transferees, and defining both;
- Specifying the buy-sell triggering events, such as death, disability, retirement (voluntary), termination of employment (involuntary termination), and other circumstances that would cause continued association with the business difficult;
- Valuing the business interest (the price); and
- Providing a funding mechanism.

In addition to these essentials, a buy-sell agreement customarily includes:

- Allocation of enforcement costs;
- Specifics on when the agreement will terminate; and
- Rights of the departing owner where the entire purchase price is not paid in full at closing.

(c) How to Determine the Purchase Price. Determining the purchase price of a business interest is one of the most critical and often inexact aspects of a buy-sell agreement. The buy-sell agreement could provide for one of the following valuation methods:

- Appraisal by a business appraiser at the time of purchase;
- Capitalization of earnings;
- Book value that is the cost of assets less depreciation; or
- Fixed-price method, which requires periodic evaluation of the business after the analysis of the business' financial statements.

(d) Using Buy-Sell Agreements for Estate Tax Valuation Purposes. You must distinguish between buy-sell agreements entered into before October 9, 1990, and after October 8, 1990.

A buy-sell agreement entered into before October 9, 1990, may establish the estate tax value of a decedent's shares or partnership interest. The agreement must have a bona fide business purpose, not be a device to pass the decedent's share (or interest) to the natural objects of his or her bounty for less than full consideration, and be binding on the shareholder's (or partners) estate at death [Reg. Sec. 20.2031-2(h)].

Agreements entered into after October 8, 1990 (and prior agreements substantially modified after that date) may establish value for estate tax purposes only if they are bona fide business arrangements, arm's-length transactions, and not a device to transfer property to family members for less than full and adequate consideration [IRC Sec. 2703]. Thus, IRC Sec. 2703 imposes one added requirement on the previous criteria needed for the agreement to set a binding value for estate tax purposes—namely, the terms must be comparable to those found in an arm's-length transaction [Reg. Sec. 25.2703-1(b)(4)].

A safe harbor exists for agreements in which a majority of the interests in the closely held business (i.e., greater than 50 percent) are owned by nonfamily members [Reg. Sec. 25.2703-1(b)(3)]. In other words, the three requirements contained in IRC Sec. 2703(b) are considered met if more than 50 percent of the persons subject to the restrictions are not members of the transferor's family. A member of the transferor's family includes the persons described in Reg. Sec. 25.2701-2(b)(5) and any other individual who is a natural object of the transferor's bounty. Indirectly held interests (as defined in Reg. Sec. 25.2701-6) must also be considered.

¶1909

In *Estate of True*,[1] the Court of Appeals for the Tenth Circuit considered buy-sell agreement entered into prior to October 8, 1990 (when IRC Sec. 2703 was added to the law) and concluded that the prices which were based on tax book value were not controlling in valuing six different businesses for estate and gift tax purposes. As a result, the pre-October 9, 1990 buy-sell agreements were subject to the price control test embodied in Reg. Sec. 20.2031-2(h) to determine whether the stated price in the agreements would control for estate tax purposes. For further discussion, see ¶ 1913.

(e) Tax Treatment of Death Benefits from Employer-Owned Life Insurance.

Employers holding a life insurance policy that covers the life of an employee may exclude from income the proceeds from the policy when the employee dies. In general, the amount excluded by the employer is limited to the amount the employer paid for the policy as premiums or other payments [IRC Sec. 101(j)(1)]. However, the employer may exclude the full amount of the proceeds if it satisfies several requirements, including notice and consent requirements [IRC Sec. 101(j)(2)].

This exclusion rule applies to any person that is an "applicable policyholder" who is defined as a person (or entity) engaged in a trade or business owning a life insurance contract on an employee that is also directly or indirectly a beneficiary under the contract [IRC Sec. 101(j)(3)]. An applicable policyholder can also be a person related to the employer under IRC Sec. 267(b), a controlling partner of the employer under IRC Sec. 707(b)(1) or a corporation in a controlled group with the employer and engaged in the same trade or business [IRC Sec. 101(j)(3)(B)(ii)].

In order to exclude the full amount, the insured employee must have either been an employee of the employer at any time during the 12-month period before the death of the employee or, at the time the contract is issued, the insured must have been a director, a highly compensated employee or a highly compensated individual [IRC Sec. 101(j)(2)(A)].

An insured person will be considered to be a highly-compensated employee using the same definition as used in IRC Sec. 414(q) without regard to the election to base the determination on whether the insured was in the top-paid group of employees in the preceding year [IRC Sec. 101(j)(2)(A)(ii)(II)]. An insured person will be considered a highly compensated individual if he or she is one of the five highest paid officers, a shareholder holding more than 10 percent of the value of employer stock or among the highest paid 35 percent of all employees [IRC Sec. 101(j)(2)(A)(ii)(II)].

The employer will also be allowed to exclude the proceeds from income if the amount is paid to a member of the insured employee's family, the estate of the insured or a trust established for the benefit of a member of the insured's family. The exclusion will also apply if the amount is paid to any of the aforementioned parties to purchase an interest in the employer [IRC Sec. 101(j)(2)(B)].

Notice and consent requirements. In order for an employer to be eligible for the exclusion, the employer must satisfy the following notice and consent requirements:

1. The insured employee must be notified in writing that the employer intends to insure the employee's life and the maximum face amount for which the employee could be insured; the insured employee must then have provided written consent

---

[1] **¶1909** Estate of True, TC Memo 2001-167, *aff'd*, 390 F.3d 1210 (10th Cir. 2004).

to being insured and to the continuation of such coverage after employment terminates;

2. The insured must also be notified in writing that an applicable policyholder will be a beneficiary of any proceeds payable upon the death of the insured employee [IRC Sec. 101(j)(4)].

¶1910 VALUATION OF GIFTS AND BEQUESTS

The amount of a transfer that is subject to tax is clear when money is transferred—it's simply the amount of cash given. But when property other than money is transferred, the amount subject to tax raises many questions and requires some thought.

In general, the gift equals:

1. The fair-market value of the property at the time of the gift, less any payment made by the donee; or

2. The fair-market value of the property at the time of the decedent's death. Value cannot be arrived at arbitrarily. Instead, it must be determined under principles that the IRS prescribes.

(a) Overview. In general terms, the fair-market value of property is the price at which the property would change hands between a willing buyer and a willing seller, neither being under any compulsion to buy or sell and both having reasonable knowledge of relevant facts [Reg. Secs. 25.2512-1, 20.2031-1(b)].[1]

The fair-market value is not determined by a forced sale price and by the sale price of the item in a market other than that in which the item is most commonly sold to the public [Reg. Secs. 25.2512-1, 20.2031-1(b)].

For property that the public generally purchases in the retail market, the fair-market value equals the price at which the item or a comparable item would be sold at retail [Reg. Secs. 25.2512-1, 20.2031-1(b)]. The price tangible personal property brings at auction or is advertised at in a newspaper is presumed to be the retail price.[2] If property is sold at an auction, its value is the bid price plus any premium paid to the auction house.

> **Example 1:** An automobile is usually sold at retail so that the retail value, not the price a used car dealer would pay, equals the fair-market value.

Consideration of Subsequent Events. It is well established that "[v]aluation is not an exact science and each case necessarily turns on its own particular facts and circumstances."[3] Valuation could be characterized as an approximation derived from all the evidence and therefore boils down to the facts of the case. Fair market value has been characterized as a question of judgment rather than mathematics.[4] When valuing real estate, sales of comparable properties are credible evidence of real estate's fair market

---

[1] ¶1910 Frazee, 98 TC 554, 562 (1992).

[2] Rev. Proc. 65-19, 1965-2 CB 1002.

[3] Estate of Spruill, 88 TC 1197, 1228 (1987); Estate of Spicer, TC Memo 1974-13.

[4] Hamm, 325 F.2d 934, 940 (8th Cir. 1963), *aff'g* TC Memo 1961-347.

value within a reasonable time of the relevant valuation date(s). Even though subsequent events are generally irrelevant (and therefore inadmissible) in determining a property's fair market value as of a relevant valuation date, this rule is generally inapplicable when the subsequent event is a sale of the subject property itself within a reasonable time of the relevant valuation date.[5] The IRS will therefore will consider subsequent events which serve as evidence of a property's fair market value as of the relevant valuation date.[6]

When determining the gift and estate tax value of unique real estate, prices from sales of a portion of the property that occurred subsequent to the gift and estate tax valuation dates may be considered as evidenced in the following Tax Court case. In *Estate of Giovacchini*,[7] the decedent owned a mountainous 2,356-acre property in California near Lake Tahoe that was unique and difficult to value. The court found the previous appraisals on which the decedent and the estate had based the value of the property to be seriously flawed. Therefore, to determine the value of the property, the court started with the flawed earlier appraisal and made the following adjustments to the value in order to account for the flaws: (1) downward adjustments of 9 percent for estate tax purposes and 17 percent for gift tax purposes to correct for inflation, the time value of money, and increases in market prices; (2) a 20-percent reduction to reflect the generally unfavorable legal status of the existing access to the land; and (3) an 11-percent discount to resolve deficiencies relating to the appraisers' approach to parcel size matters.

Retail sale prices as evidence of value. A retail sales price will be considered the retail sales price of an item on the date of the gift (or the decedent's death) if the sale is made within a "reasonable time" following the gift (or the decedent's death) and there is no substantial change in market conditions or other circumstances affecting the value of similar items between the time of sale and the date of the gift (or the decedent's death).

For an actual sale transaction to be considered it must (1) occur within a reasonable time before or after the valuation date and (2) be within the property's usual and customary market for sale.[8] When an actual sale is unavailable, other approaches may be used including (1) comparable sales of similar property and (2) informal appraisals in probate proceedings on which state inheritance taxes are based.

> **NOTE:** An IRS determination of fair-market value is accepted as correct until the taxpayer proves it is wrong.[9]

(b) Use of Appraisals. Various regulations require the use of an appraisal to support the value placed on the wealth transfer tax return. [Reg. Secs. 20.2031-2(f), 20.2031-3, 20.2031-6(b), 25.2512-2(f), and 25.2512-3]. If the item to be valued includes assets that have marked artistic or intrinsic value that totals more than $3,000, Reg. Sec. 20.2031-6(b) requires an appraisal executed by the appraiser under oath, to be filed with the estate tax return. The regulations also require that the appraiser is reputable and recognized as competent to appraise the artistic assets. In *Estate of*

---

[5] Estate of Spruill, 88 TC 1197 (1987).

[6] Estate of Jung, 101 TC 412 (1993).

[7] Estate of Giovacchini, TC Memo 2013-27.

[8] First National Bank of Kenosha, 763 F.2d 891 (7th Cir. 1985).

[9] Estate of Lyons, TC Memo 1976-136.

Mitchell,[10] the Tax Court relied exclusively on the reports of art experts when appraising paintings that were difficult to value because the expert exhaustively researched all sales, had expertise in the relevant genre of art, and produced the most understandable report. The court explained that "experts consider several different criteria in valuing art that are not typically used in general property valuations. These include thematic appeal, period of work, style, overall quality, provenance, condition of artwork and market conditions (collectively, the art valuation factors)." When an appraisal is required, don't assume that an accountant who prepares the tax returns and keeps the books of a business will be qualified to provide an appraisal that will be deemed sufficient for estate tax purposes. The Tax Court has stated that a valuation by someone who is not a full-time business appraiser engaged in the business of valuing similar assets will be afforded minimal weight.[11] To be accepted for estate tax purposes, the appraisal should include the following beyond the recitation of value and the signature of the appraiser:

1. A specific description of the property being appraised;

2. The appraiser's qualifications and experience;

3. The method of appraisal; and

4. When the property is an art object, the cost, manner, and date of acquisition.[12]

(c) Appraiser Penalty Applies to Substantial Estate or Gift Tax Valuation Misstatements. A civil penalty is imposed against appraisers for certain types of valuation misstatements that result in tax underpayments. The penalty amount is the lesser of: (1) the greater of $1,000 or 10 percent of the tax underpayment amount attributable to the misstatement; or (2) 125 percent of the gross income received by the appraiser for preparing the appraisal. However, no penalty is imposed if the appraiser establishes that the appraised value was more likely than not the proper value [IRC Sec. 6695A(b) and (c)].

A person who prepares an appraisal of property value must pay the penalty if: (1) he or she knows, or reasonably should have known, that the appraisal would be used in connection with a federal tax return or refund claim; and (2) the claimed value of the appraised property results in a substantial valuation misstatement related to income tax under IRC Sec. 6662(e), a substantial estate or gift tax valuation understatement, or a gross valuation misstatement under IRC Sec. 6662(h) [IRC Sec. 6695A(a)].

The appraiser penalty must be assessed within three years after the return or refund claim with respect to which the penalty is assessed was filed. No court proceeding without assessment for the collection of the affected tax can begin after this period has expired [IRC Sec. 6696(d)(1)].

(d) Applicability of Valuation Principles. Generally, gift tax valuation principles apply for estate tax valuation purposes. Some special estate tax valuation rules such as alternate valuation date [see ¶1907] and special use valuation [see ¶1908] do not apply for gift tax purposes.

---

[10] Estate of Mitchell, TC Memo 2011-94.

[11] Estate of Ford, TC Memo 1993-580, *aff'd*, 53 F.3d 924 (8th Cir. 1995).

[12] Rev. Proc. 96-15, 1996-1 CB 627.

¶1910

Valuation date. A gift for federal gift tax purposes is valued at the date a completed transfer of the property takes place [Reg. Sec. 25.2512-1]. See ¶ 206 for an analysis of when a gratuitous transfer is complete for federal gift tax purposes.

Fair-market value is determined as of the date of the decedent's death unless the executor elects the alternate valuation date [see ¶ 1907].

Valuation of transfers of interests in single-member LLC. In *Pierre I*,[13] the Tax Court concluded that a donor's transfer of interests in a single-member limited liability company (LLC) to two trusts was valued for federal gift tax purposes as transfers of interests in the LLC and not as transfers of a proportionate share of the underlying assets of the LLC. Consequently, the transfers were eligible for valuation discounts for lack of marketability and control.

(e) Valuation Statement. If the IRS does not accept the property value listed on the wealth transfer tax return, the IRS must furnish a valuation statement on written request of the donor (or the executor). The statement must explain the basis of the valuation or proposed valuation, display any computation used in arriving at the valuation, and contain a copy of any expert appraisal made for the IRS. The statement must be furnished within 45 days after the request or after the IRS makes a determination or proposed determination, whichever is later [IRC Sec. 7517; Reg. Sec. 301.7517-1].

(f) Revaluation of Gifts by the IRS. The amount of any tax that is owed must generally be assessed within three years after the return was filed [IRC Sec. 6501]. However, effective for gifts made after August 5, 1997, IRC Sec. 6501(c)(9) provides that the three-year gift tax statute of limitations does not start running unless and until the gift is adequately disclosed on a gift tax return. This means that the IRS cannot revalue a gift for gift tax purposes for a three-year period beginning from the date that the gift was adequately disclosed on a gift tax return or was disclosed in a statement attached to the return, in a manner adequate to apprise the IRS of the nature of the gift [IRC Sec. 2001(f)]. IRC Sec. 2504(c) now provides that gift tax need not be paid to stop the IRS from revaluing the gift. Note that for gifts made on or before August 5, 1997, the old rules discussed previously apply.

▶ **PRACTICE TIP:** Once the three-year statute of limitations has passed, taxpayers can rest assured that the IRS will not challenge the value of a gift as disclosed on a gift tax return or on a statement attached to a return. This offers taxpayers protection against any IRS adjustment.

In determining the amount of prior taxable gifts for estate tax purposes, the value of such gifts is the value as finally determined, even if no gift tax was paid or assessed on the gift. A final determination of a gift's value will be the value: (1) reported on a gift tax return, or in a statement attached to the return, in a manner adequate to apprise the IRS of the nature of the item (if not challenged by the IRS prior to expiration of the statute of limitations); (2) determined by the IRS (if not challenged by the taxpayer in court); (3) determined by a court; or (4) agreed upon by the taxpayer and the IRS in a settlement agreement [IRC Sec. 2001(f)].

---

[13] Pierre I, 133 TC 24 (2009).

(g) Declaratory Judgment on Gift Tax Value. In order to revalue an adequately disclosed gift, the IRS must issue a final notice of redetermination of value within the statute of limitations for gift tax purposes. This rule applies even where the redetermination of value does not result in a gift tax being owed. A taxpayer who is mailed a final notice may challenge the redetermined value by filing a motion for declaratory judgment with the Tax Court within 90 days of the date of mailing of the final notice [IRC Sec. 7477].

In Reg. Sec. 301.7477-1 the IRS provides guidance on the declaratory judgment procedure available to a donor who fails to resolve a dispute with the IRS concerning the value of a transfer for gift tax purposes at the Examination level. The donor will be sent a notice of preliminary determination of value (Letter 950-G), inviting him or her to file a formal protest and to request consideration by the appropriate IRS Appeals office. Subsequently, the donor will be sent a notice of determination of value (Letter 3569) if:

1. The donor requests Appeals consideration in writing within 30 calendar days after the mailing date of the Letter 950-G, or by such later date as determined pursuant to IRS procedures, and the matter is not resolved by Appeals;

2. The donor does not request Appeals consideration within the time provided; or

3. The IRS does not issue a Letter 950-G.

The Letter 3569 will notify the donor of the adjustment(s) proposed by the IRS, and will advise the donor that the donor may contest the determination made by the IRS by filing a petition with the Tax Court before the 91st day after the date on which the Letter 3569 was mailed to the donor by the IRS. If the donor does not file a timely petition with the Tax Court, the IRS determination, as set forth in the Letter 3569, will be considered the final determination of value. If the donor files a timely petition with the Tax Court, the Tax Court will determine whether the donor has exhausted available administrative remedies. Under IRC Sec. 7477, the Tax Court is not authorized to issue a declaratory judgment unless the Tax Court finds that the donor has exhausted all administrative remedies within the IRS [Reg. Sec. 301.7477-1(b)(3)].

The Tax Court determines whether the donor has exhausted all administrative remedies available within the IRS for resolving the controversy. The IRS will consider a donor to have exhausted all administrative remedies if, prior to filing a petition in Tax Court, the donor timely requests consideration by Appeals and participates fully in the Appeals consideration process. A timely request for consideration by Appeals is a written request from the donor for Appeals consideration made within 30 days after the mailing date of the Letter 950-G, or by such later date for responding to the Letter 950-G as is agreed to between the donor and the IRS.

If the donor timely requests consideration by Appeals and Appeals does not grant that request, the IRS nevertheless will consider the donor to have exhausted all administrative remedies within the IRS upon the issuance of the Letter 3569 if the donor participates fully in the Appeals office consideration if offered by the IRS while the case is in docketed status.

If the IRS does not issue a Letter 950-G to the donor prior to the issuance of Letter 3569, the IRS nevertheless will consider the donor to have exhausted all administrative remedies within the IRS for purposes of section 7477 upon the issuance of the Letter 3569, if the IRS decision not to issue the Letter 950-G was not due to actions or

¶1910

inactions of the donor (such as a failure to supply requested information or a current mailing address to the Area Director having jurisdiction over the tax matter) and the donor, after the filing of a petition in Tax Court for a declaratory judgment, participates fully in the Appeals office consideration if offered by the IRS while the case is in docketed status.

The donor participates fully in the Appeals consideration process if the donor timely submits all information related to the transfer that is requested by the IRS in connection with the Appeals consideration and discloses to the Appeals office all relevant information regarding the controversy to the extent such information and its relevance is known or should be known by the donor or the qualified representative during the time the issue is under consideration by Appeals [Reg. Sec. 301.7477-1(d)(4)(vi)].

(h) What Constitutes "Adequate Disclosure" of Gifts. If the three-year statute of limitations has expired for gift tax purposes on a gift that was "adequately disclosed" on a gift tax return, the IRS is prohibited from revaluing the gift for purposes of determining the applicable estate tax bracket and the available unified credit at death [IRC Sec. 2001(f)(1)]. The IRS has issued guidelines on what constitutes "adequate disclosure" of transfers of property reported as gifts in Reg. Sec. 301.6501(c)-1(f)(2)(i)-(vi).

The IRS provides that a gift will be adequately disclosed on the gift tax return only if it is reported in a manner adequate to apprise the IRS of the nature of the gift and the basis for the reported value. The return must provide a complete and accurate description of the transaction including the following:

1. A description of the transferred property and any consideration received by the donor;

2. The identity of the transferor and each transferee;

3. The relationship between the donor and donee;

4. A detailed description of the method used to determine the fair-market value of the property transferred, including any financial data (for example, balance sheets, etc., with explanations of any adjustments) and a description of any discounts, such as discounts for blockage, minority or fractional interests, and lack of marketability, claimed in valuing the property;

5. In the case of the transfer of an interest that is not actively traded on an established market such as the New York Stock Exchange, the American Stock Exchange, the NASDAQ National Market, or a regional exchange in which quotations are published daily, including recognized foreign exchanges, recitation of the exchange where the interest is listed, the CUSIP number of the security, and the mean between the highest and lowest quoted selling prices on the applicable valuation date;

6. In the case of a transfer of an interest in an entity that is not actively traded, a description must be provided of any discount claimed in valuing the interests in the entity or any assets owned by the entity. Moreover, if the value of the entity or of the interests in the entity is properly determined based on the net value of assets held by the entity, a statement must be provided regarding the net fair market value of 100 percent of the entity (determined without regard to any

¶1910

discounts in valuing the entity or any assets owned by the entity), the pro rata portion of the entity subject of the transfer, and the fair market value of the transferred interest as reported on the return;

7. If the entity that is the subject of the transfer owns an interest in another actively traded entity (either directly or through ownership of an entity), valuation information must be provided for each entity if the information is relevant and material in determining the value of the interest;

8. If the property is transferred in trust, the trust's tax identification number and a brief description of the terms of the trust. In lieu of the description of the trust terms, a copy of the trust instrument could be included;

9. A statement describing any position you take that is contrary to any proposed, temporary, or final Treasury regulations or revenue rulings published at the time of the transfer; and

10. In the case of the transfer of an interest in an LLC, the description should include the number of units in the limited liability company, the class type, and the percentage of ownership interest that the gift represents.[14]

In lieu of the information listed above, Reg. Sec. 301.6501(c)-1(f)(3) permits the submission of an appraisal of the gift provided the appraisal satisfies the following requirements:

1. The appraisal is prepared by an appraiser who holds himself or herself out to the public as an appraiser or performs appraisals on a regular basis;

2. The appraiser is qualified to make the appraisals of the type of property being valued by virtue of the appraiser's qualifications, as described in the appraisal that details the appraiser's background, experience, education, and membership, if any, in professional appraisal associations; and

3. The appraiser is not the donor or the donee or a member of the family of the donor or donee, or any person employed by the donor, the donee, or a member of the family of either.

In addition, Reg. Sec. 301.6501(c)-1(f)(3) provides that the appraisal must contain the following information:

1. The date of the transfer, the date on which the transferred property was appraised, and the purpose of the appraisal;

2. A description of the property;

3. A description of the appraisal process used;

4. A description of the assumptions, hypothetical conditions, and any limiting conditions and restrictions on the transferred property that affect the analyses, opinions, and conclusions;

5. The information considered in determining the appraised value, including in the case of an ownership interest in a business, all financial data that was used in determining the value of the interest, which must be sufficiently detailed so that another person can replicate the process and arrive at the appraised value;

---

[14] Chief Counsel Advice 200221010.

¶1910

6. The appraisal procedures followed and the reasoning that supports the analyses, opinions, and conclusions;

7. The valuation method used, the rationale for the valuation method, and the procedure used in determining the fair market value of the asset transferred; and

8. The specific basis for the valuation, such as specific comparable sales or transactions, sales of similar interests, asset-based approaches or merger-acquisition transactions.

Example 2: Dad transfers 100 shares of common stock of XYZ Corp to Son. The common stock of XYZ Corp is actively traded on a major stock exchange. For gift tax purposes, the fair market value of one share of XYZ common stock on the date of the transfer, based on the mean between the highest and lowest quoted selling prices, is $150. On Dad's gift tax return, Form 709, for the year, Dad reports the gift to Son of 100 shares of common stock of XYZ Corp, with a value for gift tax purposes of $15,000. He specifies the date of the transfer, recites that the stock is publicly traded, identifies the stock exchange on which the stock is traded, lists the stock's CUSIP number, and lists the mean between the highest and lowest quoted selling prices for the date of transfer. Dad has adequately disclosed the transfer. Therefore, the period of assessment for the transfer under IRC Sec. 6501 will run from the time the return is filed [Reg. Sec. 301.6501(c)-1(f), Example 1].

Example 3: Dad owns 100 percent of the common stock of X, a closely held corporation. Dad does not hold an interest in any other entity that is not actively traded. Dad transfers 20 percent of the X stock to Son and Daughter. This transfer is not subject to the special valuation rules of IRC Sec. 2701. The transfer is made outright with no restrictions on ownership rights, voting rights and transfer rights. Based on generally applicable valuation principles, the value of X would be determined based on the net value of the assets owned by X. The reported value of the transferred stock incorporates the use of minority discounts and lack of marketability discounts. No other discounts were used in arriving at the fair market value of the transferred stock or any assets owned by X. On Dad's federal gift tax return, he includes a detailed description of the gift including a statement reporting the fair market value of 100 percent of X (before taking into account any discounts), the pro rata portion of X subject to the transfer, and the reported value of the transfer. He also attaches a statement regarding the determination of value that includes a discussion of the discounts claimed and how the discounts were determined. Dad has provided sufficient information such that the transfer will be considered adequately disclosed and the period of assessment for the transfer will run from the time the return is filed [Reg. Sec. 301.6501(c)-1(f), Example 3].

(i) Adequate Disclosure if Gift Not Reported on Form 709. The IRS explains in Rev. Proc. 2000-34[15] that taxpayers may begin the running of the period of limitations on assessment for a gift that was not adequately disclosed on a gift tax

---

[15] Rev. Proc. 2000-34, 2000-2 CB 186.

return, by filing an amended gift tax return for the calendar year in which the gift was made. The amended return must identify the transfer and provide all information required under Reg. Sec. 301.6501(c)-1(f)(2) that was not previously submitted with the original gift tax return. The amended return must be filed with the same Service Center where the donor filed the original. The top of the first page of the amended return must have the words "Amended Form 709 for gift(s) made in (the applicable calendar year) in accordance with Rev. Proc. 2000-34." Why is this important? Adequate disclosure of gifts is crucial because gift taxes can only be assessed for the three-year period from the return due date or filing date, whichever occurs later. This period will begin to run only if the donee submits the required information for the gift on an original or amended gift tax return.

¶1911 VALUATION OF PUBLICLY TRADED STOCKS AND BONDS

The fair-market value of listed securities, stocks, and bonds that are publicly traded on a recognized market (e.g., the New York Stock Exchange or NASDAQ) equals the average between the highest and the lowest quoted selling prices for the valuation date [Reg. Secs. 25.2512-2(b), 20.2031-2(b)]. For example, if on the date of death a particular stock had a high of $40 per share and a low of $39.00 per share, the price used to determine the date-of-death value is $39.50.

If there were no sales on the valuation date, the nearest sale dates within a reasonable period before and after the valuation date are used. The securities are valued at a weighted average of the mean between the highest and lowest prices on these dates. The average must be weighted inversely by the respective number of trading days between the selling dates and the valuation date [Reg. Secs. 25.2512-2(b), 20.2031-2(b)].

Example 1: Doris Doe died on Friday, June 15, leaving common stock in Rabbit Corporation. There were no sales on June 15. However, on June 13, the mean sale price per share was $10; it was $15 on June 20. These are the nearest dates before and after the valuation date on which there were sales of Rabbit stock, two trading days before and three after. The stock is valued at $12 per share, arrived at as follows:

$$\frac{(3 \times 10) + (2 \times 15)}{3 + 2} = 12$$

Example 2: Assume the same facts as in Example 1 except that the mean sale price per share was $15 on June 13 and $10 on June 20. The fair-market value on June 15 is $13, arrived at as follows:

$$\frac{(3 \times 15) + (2 \times 10)}{3 + 2} = 12$$

If no sales occurred within a reasonable period before and after the valuation date, the fair-market value is determined (1) by taking the mean between the bona fide bid and asked prices on the valuation date or (2) if none, by taking the weighted average of the means between the bona fide bid and asked prices on the nearest trading date before and the nearest trading date after the valuation date. Either of these dates must be within a reasonable time period of the valuation date [Reg. Secs. 25.2512-2(c), 20.2031-2(c)].

If no actual sale prices or bona fide bid and asked prices are available within a reasonable period before the valuation date, but are available a reasonable period after that date (or vice versa), then the mean between the highest and lowest available sale prices (or bid and asked prices) on that date may be taken as the fair market value [Reg. Secs. 25.2512-2(c), 20.2031-2(c)].

If the stock (or bond) is listed on more than one exchange, the records of the exchange where the shares (or bonds) are principally traded should be used, provided these records are available in a generally available listing or publication of general circulation. If these records are not available and the shares (or bonds) are in a composite listing of the combined exchanges that is generally available, these records should be used [Reg. Secs. 25.2512-2(b)(1), 20.2031-2(b)(1)].

(a) Shares Selling Ex-Dividend. If a dividend was declared on the stock before the valuation date and was payable after that date and if the stock is selling ex-dividend on the valuation date, the fair-market value of the stock equals (1) the ex-dividend (without dividend) quotation, plus (2) the amount of the dividend. If the decedent died on a weekend and the stock began selling ex-dividend on the following trading day, determine the weighted average by adding (1) the mean of the ex-dividend quotations, plus (2) the amount of the dividend [Reg. Sec. 20.2031-2(c)].

(b) Restricted Shares. Some shares cannot be resold immediately because they are restricted from resale under federal securities laws. These shares are known as restricted shares, unregistered shares, investment letter stock, or private placement shares. Rev. Rul. 77-287 provides guidelines for valuing restricted securities.[1] The following factors are relevant in valuing restricted securities:

1. Earnings;

2. Net assets, and net sales of the corporation;

3. The resale provisions of the restricted stock;

4. The relative bargaining strength of the buyers and sellers; and

5. The market experience of the corporation's freely tradable securities.[2]

(c) Adjustment to Value. An adjustment to the value determined under the method that the Regulations prescribe is permissible where the value does not reflect

---

[1] **¶1911** Rev. Rul. 77-287, 1977-2 CB 319, as *amplified* by Rev. Rul. 80-213, 1980-2 CB 101, as *amplified* by Rev. Rul. 83-120, 1983-2 CB 170

[2] Pree, 408 F.3d 855 (7th Cir. 2005).

the actual value of the stock or bond. In such a situation, the stock or bond is valued as if it was not traded on a recognized market [Reg. Secs. 25.2512-2(e), 20.2031-2(e)].

(d) Blockage Discount. A blockage discount is provided for transfers of large blocks of publicly traded stocks and securities. A blockage discount is allowed if the block of stock to be valued "is so large in relation to the actual sales on the market that it could not be liquidated in a reasonable time without depressing the market" [Reg. Secs. 25.2512-2(e), 20.2031-2(e)].

The size of the blockage discount, if allowed, depends on a variety of factors, including the size of the block in comparison with the corporation's total outstanding shares, the amount of shares the stock market will absorb, and the amount of time needed to liquidate the block without depressing the market.

> **NOTE:** If a donor makes simultaneous gifts to several donees, each gift to a different donee is treated separately in determining (1) whether a blockage discount is appropriate and (2) the amount of the blockage discount [Reg. Sec. 25.2512-2(e)].

(e) U.S. Savings Bonds. U.S. savings bonds are valued at their redemption value on the valuation date.[3]

¶ 1912 VALUATION OF INVESTMENTS

(a) Mutual Funds. The fair-market value of a share in a mutual fund (an open-ended investment company) equals the bid or redemption price. If no public redemption price is quoted for the valuation date, the fair-market value of the mutual fund share equals the last public redemption price quoted by the mutual fund for the first day before the valuation date for which there is a quotation [Reg. Secs. 25.2512-6(b), 20.2031-8(b)].

(b) Notes, Mortgages and Bonds with No Recognized Market. Notes and bonds that have no recognized market for resale are presumed to be worth their unpaid principal, plus accrued interest, subject to a showing of a lesser value [Reg. Secs. 25.2512-4, 20.2031-4]. Evidence demonstrating a lesser value consists of (1) a showing of insolvency by the maker of the note or bond, (2) a below-market interest rate, and (3) any collateral being insufficient to satisfy the debt.[1]

¶ 1913 VALUATION OF CLOSELY HELD BUSINESSES

The valuation of shares in a closely held corporation, an interest in a partnership or limited liability company, or a sole proprietorship is a complex task. Typically, these shares or interests have no ready market from which either sales or bid and asked

---

[3] Rev. Rul. 55-278, 1955-1 CB 471.

[1] **¶ 1912** Olster, 79 TC 456, *aff'd*, 751 F.2d 1168 (11th Cir. 1985).

prices may be obtained. Actual arm's-length sales on or close to the valuation date provide the best evidence of value.

In the absence of actual sales, the fair-market value of an interest in a closely held business equals the net amount that a willing buyer would pay a willing seller, where neither is under any compulsion to buy or sell and both have reasonable knowledge of the relevant facts [Reg. Sec. 20.2031-3].

Rev. Rul. 59-60[1] is the starting point for valuing closely held businesses where market quotes are not available. It sets forth the basic valuation factors planners must use when valuing such businesses.

> **NOTE:** Rev. Rul. 59-60 has been modified by Rev. Rul. 65-193[2] and further amplified by Rev. Rul. 77-287 (valuation of restricted securities)[3] and Rev. Rul. 83-120 (valuation of preferred and common stock).[4]

Rev. Rul. 59-60, which is widely accepted in the valuation community and which is regularly referenced by both the IRS and the Courts states that the

> Valuation of securities is, in essence, a prophesy as to the future and must be based on facts available at the required date of appraisal. As a generalization, the prices of stocks which are traded in volume in a free and active market by informed persons best reflect the consensus of the investing public as to what the future holds for the corporations and industries represented. When a stock is closely held, is traded infrequently, or is traded in an erratic market, some other measure of value must be used. In many instances, the next best measure may be found in the prices at which the stocks of companies engaged in the same or a similar line of business are selling in a free and open market. [Rev. Proc. 59-60, § 3.03, 1959-1 C.B. at 238.]

(a) Factors Established in Rev. Rul. 59-60. Rev. Rul. 59-60 states that in the absence of relevant market quotations, all available financial data and all relevant factors affecting fair market value must be considered in valuing the stock of a closely held corporation. The ruling lists as relevant eight specific factors. These factors, which are virtually identical to the factors referenced in Reg. Sec. 20.2031-2(f) are:

1. The nature of the business and the history of the enterprise from its inception;
2. The economic outlook in general and the condition and outlook of the specific industry in particular;
3. The book value of the stock and the financial condition of the business;
4. The earning capacity of the company;
5. The dividend-paying capacity;
6. Whether or not the enterprise has goodwill or other intangible value;
7. Sales of the stock and the size of the block of the stock to be valued;
8. The market price of stocks of corporations engaged in the same or a similar line of business having their stocks actively traded in a free and open market, either

---

[1] ¶1913 Rev. Rul. 59-60, 1959-1 CB 237.
[2] Rev. Rul. 65-193, 1965-2 CB 370.
[3] Rev. Rul. 77-287, 1977-2 CB 319.
[4] Rev. Rul. 83-120, 1983-2 CB 170.

on an exchange or over-the-counter. [Rev. Proc. 59-60, §4.01.] [See also Reg. Sec. 25.2512-2(f).]

Because the valuation of a closely held business is one of the most often contested in federal gift and estate tax matters, each of these factors is examined in more detail.

Business nature and history. Rev. Rul. 59-60 (§4.02(a)) sets forth the following guidelines, which should help you in evaluating the entity's future prospects by considering the entity's history:

- *Changes of form of organization.* When an entity changes its form of organization, you must consider the history of predecessor enterprises if the successor carries on the same or similar operations.

- *Detail of analysis required.* You should analyze events close in time to the appraisal more closely than more distant events. On the other hand, you should study gross income, net income, and dividends over a long period if possible.

- *Items of history to consider.* You should consider, among other items, both the historical nature of and the current condition of the business including its products or services, operating and investment assets, capital structure, plant facilities, sales record, and management.

- *Extraordinary items.* You should discount past events that are unlikely to recur in the future.

Economic outlook and industry outlook. Rev. Rul. 59-60 (§4.02(b)) also requires you to consider current and prospective economic conditions— both national economic conditions and the conditions of the entity's industry—at the valuation date. You should consider the following factors when examining current prospective economic conditions:

- *Comparison to industry competitors.* You must compare the entity's success with its competitors. You must know whether the entity is more or less successful than its competitors, and whether it is maintaining a stable position with respect to such competitors.

- *Comparison of industry to other industries.* You must also compare the entire industry's ability to compete with other industries.

- *Prospective competition.* You must consider the possibility of prospective competition that has not previously been a factor. For example, high profits due to a product's novelty and lack of competition often lead to increasing competition.

- *Price trends of commodities and securities.* You may assess the public's appraisal of future prospects by examining price trends in the commodities and securities markets. You may use this analysis for both industries and competitors within industries.

- *"One person" businesses.* You must assess the effect of the loss of the entity's manager on the future prospects of the business. For example, the loss of the manager of a so-called "one person" business may reduce the entity's value. This is particularly true if the entity lacks trained personnel capable of succeeding the manager. You must also assess the presence or absence of management-succession potentialities, as well as factors that offset the loss of the entity's key manager. For example, the business's nature may be such that if the entity loses its key manager, this loss will not impair the entity's value. Moreover, entities may compensate for such losses by obtaining adequate life insurance coverage. Alternatively, they may be able to employ competent management based on the former manager's compensation.

Book value and financial condition. Book value equals the historical accounting value of the entity's assets over its liabilities. Rev. Rul. 59-60 (§4.02(c)) states that normally you should view book value as a subordinate factor when determining market value of closely held entities. However, book value becomes much more important if the entity being valued is either (1) being liquidated or likely to be liquidated in the near future, (2) failing and owns assets with values greatly exceeding any earnings-derived value, (3) involves holding companies, or (4) falls within one of certain special industries such as auto dealerships and real estate development companies.

However, when such situations occur, you generally should adjust historical book value. For example, you may have to adjust fixed assets to fair-market value or correct excess depreciation.

You should take the following steps when analyzing an entity's book value and financial condition.

- *Obtain comparative balance sheets.* You should obtain the entity's comparative balance sheets for at least two years before the valuation date. You should also obtain a balance sheet as of the end of the month immediately preceding the valuation date.

- *Clarify balance sheet descriptions.* You must clarify any unclear balance sheet descriptions. You must also obtain supporting supplemental schedules for any balance sheet items composed of diverse assets or liabilities.

- *Conduct financial analysis.* You must conduct a financial analysis to determine the following for the entity: (1) liquid position (i.e., its ratio of current assets to current liabilities), (2) gross and net book value of principal classes of fixed assets, (3) working capital, (4) long-term debt, (5) capital structure, and (6) net worth.

- *Consider nonessential assets.* You should consider whether any assets are not essential to the business's operation. Examples of such assets include securities investments and real estate. Generally, such nonoperating assets give the entity a lower rate of return than operating assets.

- *Analyze changes over time.* You must compare the entity's balance sheets over several years. This may reveal several developments, including the acquisition of additional production facilities or subsidiary companies, improvement in financial position, and capital structure changes.

Entity's earning capacity. Rev. Rul. 59-60 (§4.02(d)) states that future earning power is the most important factor in valuing closely held entities. However, to determine the entity's future earning power, you should look at its past earnings history. To make such an evaluation, you should:

- *Obtain profit and loss statements.* You should obtain detailed profit and loss (P & L) statements at least five years immediately before the appraisal date.

- *Ensure that P & L statements reflect certain items.* You should ensure that the P & L statements obtained reflect the following items: (1) gross income by principal items, (2) principal deductions from gross income (including major operating expenses), (3) expenses for each long-term debt item, including interest, (4) depreciation, (5) officers' salaries (in total if they seem reasonable or in detail if they seem excessive), (6) net income available for dividends, (7) rates and amounts of dividends paid on each equity class, (8) remaining amounts of dividends paid on each equity class, (9) remaining amounts carried to retained earnings, and (10) adjustments to, and reconciliation with, retained earnings.

- *Adjust for nonoperating assets and nonrecurring events.* You must adjust the entity's earnings by removing nonrecurring factors (e.g., capital gains) before comparing its earnings with other entities. You must also separate any substantial nonoperating assets from the entity's operating entity because different rates of return apply to these income sources.

- *Note percentages of earnings retained for business expansion.* You should note the percentage of earnings the entity retains for business expansion. This is especially true when you consider the entity's dividend-paying capacity.

- *Earnings trends.* Prior earnings records are usually the most reliable guide as to the future income earnings. If the entity's earnings trend is up over five years, you should consider assigning a mathematically greater weight to the most recent years' earnings. For example, you may use a "weighted average" approach. If the entity has no definite earnings trend, it may be cyclical. Here, you may want to use an average of five years' earnings.

- *Deductions from earnings.* When judging risk, you should examine deductions from income and net income as percentages of sales.

Dividend paying capacity. Rev. Rul. 59-60 (§4.02(e)) requires consideration of the entity's dividend-paying capacity. Conversely, it also recognizes that businesses must retain a reasonable part of their profits to meet competition. This analysis focuses on the entity's capacity to pay dividends rather than the dividends actually paid. This results because past dividends may have no relation to the entity's dividend-paying capacity. For example, dividends that closely held businesses have paid may be determined by their owner's income needs or, for "C" corporations, the desire to avoid income taxes on dividends received. In such cases, dividends paid bears no relation to the ability to pay dividends.

In valuing controlling interests in entities, dividends are not a material factor. This results because controlling equity holders have discretionary control over distributions. The controlling equity holders can substitute salaries and bonuses for dividends. This reduces the entity's net income and understates its dividend-paying capacity. Therefore, in valuing controlling interests in entities, dividends are a less reliable criterion of fair-market value than other applicable factors.

Goodwill. Rev. Rul. 59-60 (§4.02(f)) notes that goodwill is the excess of the firm's net earnings beyond a fair return on its net tangible assets. Goodwill is based on the firm's earning capacity. However, other factors may also be important. Factors supporting the inclusion of goodwill value include the business's prestige and reputation, the ownership of trade or brand names, and a prolonged record of successful operations in a particular locality.

Sales of stock and size of block of stock being valued. Generally, market prices are the best indicia of value (Rev. Rul. 59-60, §4.02(g)). Unfortunately, there is often no or

¶1913

little market activity in closely held businesses. When such market activity does exist, you should consider the following when analyzing market prices:

- *Degree of market activity.* When market activity exists, you must carefully investigate sales of the business's equity interests to determine whether they represent arm's-length transactions. For example, forced sales, distress sales, and isolated sales of small amounts generally do not reflect fair-market value, especially when valuing controlling interests in businesses.

- *Size of the block of stock.* The size of the equity block is itself a relevant factor to be considered. For example, minority interests in a closely held corporation's stock are more difficult to sell than similar blocks of listed stock. Conversely, actual or effective control of a corporation represents an added element of value that may justify a higher value for a specific block of stock.

- *Proximity of sales to valuation date.* The closer the sales are to the valuation date, the greater weight you should place on such sales. You must also consider any material change in the business's financial condition during the interim.

- *Arm's-length sales.* You should place less weight on sales between family members or the business's insiders. Such sales generally do not provide a reliable indicator of value. For family members, wealth transfer tax considerations generally play an important role in such transfers. For insiders, the employer-employee relationship may distort the sales price.

Price of comparable entities. Rev. Rul. 59-60 (§4.02(h)) also requires consideration of the value of corporate shares listed on an exchange that are engaged in similar lines of business to the entity being valued. For this reason, Rev. Rul. 59-60 recommends analysis of shares listed on an exchange. When you cannot find sufficient comparable companies whose shares are listed on an exchange, you may use other comparable companies whose shares the public actively trades on the over-the-counter market.

> **NOTE:** In selecting corporations for comparative purposes, you must use care to select only comparable companies. In addition to selecting comparable corporations having similar lines of business, you must consider other relevant factors to ensure the most valid comparison possible is obtained.

(b) Application of Factors. Rev. Rul. 59-60 discusses how to apply the factors it sets forth. Specifically, it analyzes the following:

- Comparative weight to be given each factor;
- Determination of appropriate capitalization rates; and
- Averaging the results of several valuation approaches.

Weight accorded various factors. Consideration must be given to all the relevant factors that Rev. Rul. 59-60 (§5) discusses. In doing so, you must carefully determine the weight to place on each particular factor. Such weight varies depending on the facts in each case.

For example, earnings may be the most important value factor in some situations. In other cases, asset value will be the most important value criterion. You should place greater weight on earnings when valuing shares of companies that sell products or services to the public. Conversely, for investment or holding companies, you should place greater weight on the entity's underlying assets.

In valuing closely held investment or real estate holding companies, you must look closely at the underlying assets and determine the fair-market values of the company's underlying assets. When the underlying assets' market values are being determined, you should give weight to their potential earnings and dividends, capitalized at rates the investing public deems proper at the valuation date.

1. *Capitalization rates.* Rev. Rul. 59-60 (§6) recognizes that when various valuation factors are being applied, you must capitalize various results at appropriate rates. It also recognizes that determining a proper capitalization rate is one of the most difficult valuation problems and that there is no simple solution. Important factors you should consider when deciding on a capitalization rate in a particular situation include:

   - The business' nature;

   - The risk involved; and

   - The stability or irregularity of the entity's earnings.

2. *Average of factors.* Because you cannot make a valuation based on a prescribed formula, assigning mathematical weights to the different factors in any particular case is impossible. Therefore, Rev. Rul. 59-60 (§7) states that basing valuation on averages of several factors would be fruitless. It reasons that such a process would exclude consideration of other pertinent factors. It also states, under this approach, a realistic application of the significant facts cannot support the end result except by mere chance.

¶1914 VALUATION DISCOUNTS

An important and often confusing issue for gift tax purposes is determining the fair-market value of closely held non-publicly traded stock that a donor has gifted away to others. A number of courts have recently taken a giant step toward clearing up some of the confusion in this area. The Court of Appeals for the Second Circuit,[1] the Court of Appeals for the Fifth Circuit[2] and the Tax Court[3] have each concluded, and the IRS agrees,[4] that a donor is entitled to discount the value of gifted closely-held stock:

- To reflect lack of marketability;

- To reflect existence of a minority interest; and

- To reflect the hypothetical built-in capital gains tax the corporation would incur if it were to liquidate, distribute, or sell the gifted stock on the valuation date.

(a) Amount of Valuation Discount. When determining the amount of the valuation discount available for closely-held corporate stock, courts will examine the

---

[1] **¶1914** Eisenberg, 155 F.3d 50 (2d Cir. 1998), *acq. in part*, 1999-1 CB XIX.

[2] Estate of Dunn, TC Memo 2000-12, *rev'd and remanded*, 301 F.3d 339 (5th Cir. 2002); Jameson, TC Memo 1999-43, *vacated and remanded*, 267 F.3d 366 (5th Cir. 2001).

[3] Estate of Davis, 110 TC 530 (1998); Estate of Litchfield, TC Memo 2009-21.

[4] Action on Decision CC-1999-00.

¶1914

size of the interest being valued, the quality of the companies, and the relations among shareholders.[5] Discounts for lack of marketability have ranged from 5 percent to 40 percent[6] while discounts for lack of control have been as high as 20 percent.[7] See ¶ 1900 for further discussion.

(b) Lack of Marketability Discount. The lack of marketability discount is based on the premise that shares (or an interest) in a closely held business are less attractive and more difficult to sell than publicly traded stock of a comparable company.[8] The courts will uphold a lack of marketability discount only if it can be proven that the discount makes sense from a business standpoint. It should be noted that valuations containing discounts are targets for IRS audits and that the taxpayer has the burden of proof on this issue. Experts should be hired to relate market data to the facts and circumstances surrounding one's particular business. One of the following types of discount analysis may be used to support one's lack of marketability discount:

- Closely held non-publicly-traded business,
- Limited partnerships and LLCs,
- Restricted stock of public companies,
- Large stock interests subject to blockage,
- Undivided interests in real estate.

In *Ludwick*,[9] the Tax Court approved a 17 percent discount for lack of marketability for a vacation residence owned as tenants in common. The Tax Court determined the fair market value of the transferors' interests by taking into account the rate of return, cost of partition, annual operating costs, length of time to partition the property, and cost of selling the property. According to the court, a buyer would be willing to pay half of the fair market value of the property less the cost of maintaining and eventually disposing of the property, which could include the cost of partition. In addition, a buyer would discount the price of the property based on the marketability risk. The marketability discount was determined to be 10 percent. The long-term sustainable growth of the property was also taken into account. After taking into consideration all of the above-mentioned factors, a discount of approximately 17 percent was applied to the fractional interests.

▶ **PRACTICE POINTER:** The Tax Court's 17 percent discount in *Ludwick* is one of the lowest discounts allowed for tenancy-in-common interests in improved real estate. See other discounts allowed in other cases below:

- *Lefrak*[10] (30 percent discount for lack of marketability and control in partial interests in certain apartment buildings);

---

[5] Estate of Ford, TC Memo 1993-580, *aff'd*, 53 F.3d 924 (8th Cir. 1995); Estate of Andrews, 79 TC 938 (1982).

[6] Estate of Hall, 92 TC 312 (1998) (5% discount); Estate of Andrews, 79 TC 938 (1982) (20% discount); Ward, 87 TC 78 (1986) (33 1/3% combined marketability and minority interest discount); Okerlund, 53 Fed. Ct. 341 (Fed. Cl. 2002), *aff'd*, 365 F.3d 1044 (Fed. Cir. 2004) (40% discount for lack of marketability).

[7] Estate of Winkler, TC Memo 1989-231 (20% discount).

[8] Morrissey, TC Memo 1999-119, *rev'd and rem'd*, 243 F.3d 1145 (9th Cir. 2001).

[9] Ludwick, TC Memo 2010-104.

[10] Lefrak, TC Memo 1993-527.

- *Estate of Cervin*[11] (20 percent discount for undivided fractional interest in farm);

- *Estate of Stevens*[12] (25 percent discount for undivided fractional interest in improved real estate);

- *Estate of Williams*[13] (44 percent discount for undivided one-half interest in real estate);

- *Estate of Baird*[14] (55 percent discount for $^{14}/_{65}$ fractional interest in timberland);

- *Estate of Giustina*[15] (25 percent discount for lack of marketability and 12.25 percent rate to discount future cash flow to present value (reduced from 16.25 percent to reflect an assumption that cash flow from forestry operations would increase by four percent per year);

- *Estate of Gallagher*[16] (23 percent discount for a minority interest and 31 discount percent for lack of marketability for closely-held newspaper publishing company);

- *Estate of Koons*[17] (7.5 percent discount for lack of marketability allowed for transfer to LLC of proceeds of the sale of the family's Pepsi distributorship business); and

- *Estate of Tanenblatt*[18] (26 percent discount for lack of marketability allowed for transfer to LLC of commercial building).

(c) Minority Interest Discount. The minority interest discount is central to many estate planning techniques that involve the transfer of minority interests in limited liability companies, family limited partnerships, and closely held corporations to family members as part of a gift-giving program. If the IRS accepts the minority interest discount, it can result in a significant reduction in transfer taxes for the family.

> **Example 1:** Dad owns stock in a closely held business worth $1 million on the books. When Dad dies the stock is divided among his four children. If the executor of the estate applies a minority discount of 50 percent when the estate tax return is filed, the estate will only owe tax on $500,000 rather than $1 million.

The minority discount is based on the premise that holders of minority interests have little influence or control over business policy and affairs, for example, with respect to the payment of dividends or compelling the sale of the business. Because the owner of a minority interest in a closely held company lacks these benefits, the theory behind this oft-used wealth transfer tax technique is that a hypothetical buyer of these shares will pay less per share to acquire a minority interest than the hypothetical buyer would pay to acquire a controlling interest. For example, a minority discount may be appropriate if

---

[11] Estate of Cervin, TC Memo 1994-550, *rev'd on other grounds*, 111 F.3d 1252 (5th Cir. 1997).

[12] Estate of Stevens,TC Memo 2000-53.

[13] Estate of Williams, TC Memo 1998-59.

[14] Estate of Baird, 416 F.3d 224 (5th Cir. 2005).

[15] Estate of Giustina, TC Memo 2011-141.

[16] Estate of Gallagher, TC Memo 2011-148, *supplemented by* TC Memo 2011-244.

[17] Estate of Koons, TC Memo 2013-94.

[18] Estate of Tanenblatt, TC Memo 2013-263.

the block of stock does not enjoy the rights associated with control of the enterprise.[19] The application of the minority discount is only appropriate however, if, as a factual matter, the minority status of the interest would affect the value that a willing buyer would pay. Thus, the question of whether a discount for a lack of control is warranted depends, like the question of valuation generally, on the facts and circumstances of the case. Depending on the situation, minority discounts can range from a modest 20 percent to a more substantial 50 percent discount that is applied to the net asset value of the company.

For example, in *Estate of Godley*,[20] the Court of Appeals for the Fourth Circuit concluded that no minority discount for lack of control was applicable in valuing the decedent's 50-percent interest in partnerships. The partnerships operated housing projects for elderly tenants and held long-term contracts with the federal government which guaranteed that the partnerships would receive rental payments according to specified rates. The low-risk, steady income stream generated by the contracts, together with the passive nature of the operation, meant that the power to sell partnership assets or liquidate the partnership had minimal value to a potential investor. In addition, the decedent was guaranteed an annual distribution of income under the terms of the partnership agreements. In view of the guaranteed rental payments, the minority discount was not justified.

> **NOTE:** The lack of marketability discount and the minority discount are separate and distinct.[21] The discount for lack of marketability reflects the lack of a ready market for shares of a closely held corporation (or an interest in a closely held business). In contrast, the minority discount (or discount for lack of control) reflects the inability of a minority shareholder to compel the sale (or liquidation) and realize a pro rata share of the corporation's net asset value.

The application of the minority interest discount to a family-owned business has received consistent judicial support but until recently the IRS consistently objected to it. The IRS previously contended that the attribution rules applicable to family holdings were to be inferred in this context and thus disallowed the minority interest discount, if other family members owned shares in the company. The IRS then reversed its position. It now recognizes, for gift and estate tax purposes, minority interest discounts in valuing simultaneous transfers of shares in a family-controlled corporation to family members.[22] Consequently, a minority interest discount is not disallowed solely because a transferred minority interest, when aggregated with interests held by other family interests, would constitute a majority interest.

(d) **Control Premiums.** The degree of control represented by the shares or interest to be valued is one of the factors to be considered in determining fair-market value [Reg. Secs. 25.2512-2(f), 20.2031-2(f)]. Because a block of stock that represents a controlling interest in a closely held corporation may be worth more per share than a block of stock that does not grant the owner control, a control or swing vote premium may be added to the value of stock in a closely held corporation if those shares will

---

[19] Estate of Chenoweth, 88 TC 1577, 1582 (1987).

[20] Estate of Godley, TC Memo 2000-242, *aff'd*, 286 F.3d 210 (4th Cir. 2002).

[21] Estate of Newhouse, 94 TC 193, 249 (1990), *nonacq.*, 1991-1 CB 1.

[22] Rev. Rul. 93-12, 1993-1 CB 202.

vest control in the holder. In determining the size of a discount or premium, each situation is evaluated on its specific facts and circumstances. Empirical analytical support is needed to justify each discount or premium. The market, as analyzed by business valuation experts, determines the magnitude of the discount or premium.

In *Estate of Simplot*,[23] the Court of Appeals for the Ninth Circuit handed the taxpayers a huge valuation victory by concluding that the value of the decedent's voting stock of a closely held corporation could not be increased by a premium to reflect the additional value that prospective buyers might place on the decedent's stock. The court refused to value decedent's stock as the Tax Court and IRS had suggested by speculating as to the possible motivation or behavior of certain parties who might buy the stock. In addition, the court concluded that the per share value of a minority interest in a closely held company's voting stock was no greater than the value of a share of nonvoting stock. Even if a purchaser of those shares bought them with an eye to their increased value if combined with the shares owned by one or more other shareholders, such a future possibility played no role in determining the value of the shares on the decedent's date of death. A control premium could not be attributed to the voting stock based on possible future developments. The value of the transfer must be established at the moment of the transfer and not on the potential value that may be realized at a later date.

Similarly, the impact of hypothetical purchases was ignored in *Estate of True*,[24] where the court held that a swing vote premium should not be applied to reduce or eliminate a minority interest discount on the transfer of a minority interest in a closely held business owned entirely by a single family. The swing vote premium was rejected because it was unlikely that the hypothetical buyer would be able to form a coalition with other owners of the business who are all family members either to control the business or to block the other owners from controlling the business.

(e) Transfer Restrictions.   Transfer restrictions are frequently inserted in buy-sell agreements, stock purchase agreements and family limited partnership agreements for transfer tax valuation purposes. Taxpayers use the transfer restrictions to support valuation discounts because restrictions on the sale or use of property generally tend to reduce the marketability of the property. Sometimes, however, they serve actual business purposes and can legitimately minimize the tax consequences of gifts or transfers. Congress enacted IRC Sec. 2703(a) to address transfer restrictions used for valuation purposes in agreements created or substantially modified after October 8, 1990.

IRC Sec. 2703(a) provides that the value of property will be determined without regard to these transfer restrictions unless the taxpayer can prove that the transfer restrictions satisfy a three-part test:

1. The restrictions constitute "a bona fide business arrangement;"
2. The restrictions must not be "a device to transfer such property to members of the decedent's family for less than full and adequate consideration;" and
3. The terms of the restrictions must be "comparable to similar arrangements entered into by persons in an arms' length transaction."

[IRC Sec. 2703(b)(3)].

---

[23] Estate of Simplot, 112 TC 130 (1999), *rev'd and rem'd*, 249 F.3d 1191 (9th Cir. 2001).

[24] Estate of True, TC Memo 2001-167, *aff'd*, 390 F.3d 1210 (10th Cir. 2004).

In *Estate of Elkins*,[25] the decedent and his wife bought 64 famous works of art. They then each created a grantor retained income trust (GRIT) and each spouse contributed his or her community property interest in several pieces of art to his or her GRIT, retaining a ten-year right to use and enjoy the artwork, after which the artwork would pass to the other spouse (if the grantor died during the ten-year term) or to their children in equal shares (if the grantor was still alive at the end of the ten-year term). The decedent's wife died during her GRIT and the decedent husband survived his. The wife's' will left her 50 percent community property interests in the other 61 works of art outright to her husband, but he disclaimed a portion of those interests equal in value to the unused unified credit against estate tax available to her estate, so that the disclaimed portion could pass to their children free of estate tax. On the basis of appraisals, the decedent disclaimed a 26.945 percent interest in each of the 61 works. After executing the partial disclaimer, the decedent and his children entered into a co-tenants' agreement relating to the disclaimed artwork, which allocated use of the artwork among the co-tenants and required unanimous consent to sell any of the artwork, and waiving each co-tenant's unilateral right to partition. The agreement was amended to cover the GRIT art after termination of the decedent's GRIT.

On the estate tax return, the estate claimed valuation discounts for the partial interests in artwork of 44.75 percent from the *pro rata* portion of the total undiscounted value, reflecting the lack of marketability of a partial interest and the time and expense of a partition action, even if the co-tenants' agreement were unenforceable.

The Tax Court held that IRC Sec. 2703(a)(2) required that the artwork be valued without regard to the restrictions on transferability in the co-tenancy agreement. IRC Sec. 2703(a)(2) states that for estate and gift tax purposes, the value of any property should be determined without regard to any restrictions on the right to sell or use the property unless the right or restriction satisfied the three-part test in IRC Sec. 2703(b)(3) which the taxpayer failed to satisfy. The estate argued that the cotenants' agreement restricted the sale of each item of artwork, but did not restrict the sale of fractional interests owned by the cotenants, and thus should not be subject to IRC Sec. 2703(a). The court concluded that the cotenants' agreement had the effect of waiving the right of partition, and, therefore, was a restriction on the right to sell or use the property, within the meaning of IRC Sec. 2703(a)(2).Therefore the court ignored the transfer restrictions for estate tax valuation purposes.

Even without the restriction on partitioning the artwork, the Tax Court held that the interest was only entitled to a 10 percent discount to reflect the lessened marketability of a tenancy-in-common interest in art.

In *Holman*,[26] the Court of Appeals for the Eighth Circuit affirmed the Tax Court to conclude that transfer restrictions in a partnership agreement must be disregarded under IRC Sec. 2703 in valuing gifts of interests in a family limited partnership (FLP). The taxpayer, Thomas Holman acquired 70,000 shares of Dell stock while he was a

---

[25] Estate of Elkins, 140 TC No. 5 (2013); see also Stone, 2007-1 USTC ¶60,545 (N.D. Cal. 2007), *aff'd*, 2009-1 USTC ¶60,572 (9th Cir. 2009) (5% discount allowed); Estate of Scull, TC Memo 1994-211.

[26] Holman, 130 TC 170 (2008), *aff'd*, 601 F.3d 763 (8th Cir. 2010); see also Fisher, 2010-1 USTC ¶60,588 (S.D. Ind. 2010).

Dell Computer employee. As part of an overall estate planning strategy seeking to transfer wealth to their children, Thomas and his wife created an FLP which they funded with the Dell stock. The partnership agreement provided that the purposes of the partnership were (1) asset preservation, (2) asset protection, (3) long-term growth, and (4) teaching the children about basic investment principles including saving for their education.

The partnership agreement contained a number of commonly used transfer restrictions that included prohibiting limited partners from withdrawing from the partnership or assigning, encumbering or transferring all or part of their partnership interests without the consent of all partners; however transfers to certain family members were allowed. In addition, the partnership had the right to purchase non-permitted assignments of partnership interests at an appraised value.

Six days after the partnership was created, the taxpayer and his spouse made gifts of limited partner interests to their children. Additional annual exclusion gifts of limited partner interests were made by the taxpayer and his spouse in subsequent months.

On their gift tax return, the Holmans claimed overall discounts of slightly more than 49% relative to the then-prevailing market prices for the underlying Dell stock. The discounts were based on appraisals that considered minority status and lack of marketability. The discounts also took into account the perceived impact that the transfer restrictions had on the value of the limited partnership shares. The Holmans believed that the transfer restrictions would depress the value of the partnership shares relative to the value of the underlying assets.

The IRS audited the return applying IRC Sec. 2703 and disregarded the partnership agreement's transfer restrictions for valuation purposes which the taxpayer had used to depress the value of the stock. In the view of the IRS the partnership interests should be valued without regard to restrictions on the right to sell or use the partnership interest within the meaning of IRC Sec. 2703(a)(2).

The Tax Court held that the IRS correctly applied IRC Sec. 2703 and properly disregarded the transfer restrictions in the agreement because the partnership agreement failed both the IRC Sec. 2703(b)(1) (bona fide business arrangement test) and the IRC Sec. 2703(b)(2) (not a device to transfer property test). The court also applied smaller lack-of-marketability and minority-interest discounts than those claimed by the donors. It adopted instead the lack-of-marketability discount raised by the IRS's expert based on historical studies of restricted stock sales.

The Court of Appeals for the Eighth Circuit affirmed the Tax Court findings on the IRC Sec. 2703 issue. The court therefore disregarded the transfer restrictions when determining the value of the FLP units. Since the court held that the restrictions in the case were not a bona fide business arrangement, it addressed only the first part of the test.

The court noted that the couple's stated purposes for creating the FLP, which included estate planning, tax reduction, wealth transfer, protection against dissipation by their children, and wealth management education, were not a "bona fide business arrangement" as required in IRC Sec. 2703(b)(1). According to the court the transfer restrictions were merely a device for making gifts to members of the taxpayer's family, no different from the use of a partnership to hold a passbook savings or interest-bearing checking account.

¶1914

In *Estate of True*,[27] the Court of Appeals for the Tenth Circuit considered buy-sell agreements entered into prior to October 8, 1990 (when IRC Sec. 2703 was added to the law) and concluded that the prices which were based on tax book value were not controlling in valuing six different businesses for estate and gift tax purposes. As a result the pre-10/9/90 buy-sell agreements were subject to the price control test embodied in Reg. Sec. 20.2031-2(h) to determine whether the stated price in the agreements would control for estate tax purposes. The court rejected the prices in the buy-sell agreements because the agreements were testamentary substitutes unsupported by adequate consideration. The following factors supported a finding that the agreements were merely testamentary substitutes rather than valid stock purchase agreements:

1. The arbitrary manner in which the price term was selected, including the limited amount of professional advice sought by the decedent and the absence of independent appraisals or outside evaluations of the company;

2. The exclusion of the value of intangible assets in setting the price term;

3. The lack of a mechanism in the agreements by which the price terms could be reevaluated;

4. The lack of negotiations between the parties to the agreements; and

5. The exclusion of one of the decedent's children as a beneficiary of his estate after that child withdrew from the family businesses.

In determining whether the price terms in a buy-sell agreement control to set estate tax values, the court overruled *Brodrick v. Gore*,[28] to the extent it holds that the terms in a buy-sell agreement are wholly controlling for estate tax purposes when the agreement's restrictive terms bind all parties equally at life and death. Instead, the court stated that the terms in a buy-sell agreement should be controlling for estate tax valuation purposes only after a full and careful examination of all the factors laid out in the price term control test.

(f) Buy-Sell Agreements. In *Estate of Blount*,[29] the Court of Appeals for the Eleventh Circuit held that a buy-sell agreement between the decedent and his closely held corporation must be ignored in determining the value of the corporate shares because the decedent's control over the corporation rendered the agreement not fixed and binding during his lifetime. In addition, the estate failed to establish that the terms of the agreement were comparable to those that would be entered into among unrelated parties.

Buy-sell agreement fixed price of stock. In *Estate of Amlie*,[30] a buy-sell agreement restricting the sale of a decedent's stock in a bank fixed the fair market value of the stock in determining the value for estate tax purposes and satisfied the requirements of IRC Sec. 2703(b). The following factors were considered in reaching this conclusion: (1) the agreement reached between the prospective heirs fixed the value of all of the decedent's bank stock; (2) the agreement between the heirs and conservator was enforceable as proven by the court order approving the settlement and granting the

---

[27] Estate of True, TC Memo 2001-167, *aff'd*, 390 F.3d 1210 (10th Cir. 2004).

[28] Brodrick v. Gore, 224 F.2d 892 (10th Cir. 1955).

[29] Estate of Blount, TC Memo 2004-116, *aff'd in part, rev'd in part and rem'd in part*, 428 F.3d 1338 (11th Cir. 2005).

[30] Estate of Amlie, TC Memo 2006-76.

conservator the authority to effectuate the terms and conditions of the agreement; (3) the agreement furthered a business purpose to serve the decedent's best interest by minimizing the risk to the decedent of holding a minority interest in a closely held bank; (4) the agreement was not a testamentary device as the decedent received significant consideration under the agreement; and (5) the agreement was similar to comparable arm's-length transactions.

¶1915 LIFE INSURANCE VALUATION FOR GIFT TAX PURPOSES

The valuation of a life insurance policy is established by the cost of the specific policy (or comparable policy) on the valuation date [Reg. Secs. 25.2512-6(a), 20.2031-8(a)(1)]. Four types of policies must be distinguished.

First, a newly issued life insurance policy is the simplest to value. The value of this type of policy equals the initial premium paid for the policy [Reg. Sec. 25.2512-6(a), Example (1)]. The same rule applies to commercial annuity contracts that are defined as "an annuity issued by a company regularly engaged in the selling of contracts of that character... ." [Reg. Sec. 25.2512-6(a)].

Second, the value of a term insurance policy equals its un expired prepaid premium. However, if the insured's medical condition makes it likely that the insured will die during the coverage period because of a terminal illness, the policy's value equals the death benefit.

Third, for a single premium or paid-up life insurance policy that has been in effect for some time, the value of this type of policy equals the current cost for securing a comparable policy on a person the age of the insured. In other words, the value of the gift of this type of policy equals what the same insurer would charge for the same amount of insurance for a person of the insured's age as of the valuation date [Reg. Secs. 25.2512-6(a), Example (3), 20.2031-8(a)(3), Example (2)].

Fourth, for a whole life insurance policy that has been in force for some time and on which further premium payments must be made to keep the policy in force, the value of this type of policy equals the "interpolated terminal reserve" of the policy at the valuation date plus the proportionate part of the premium last paid that covers the period extending beyond the date of the transfer [Reg. Secs. 25.2512-6(a), 25.2512-6(a) Example (4), 20.2031-8(a)(2), 20.2031-8(a)(3) Example (3)]. The policy's interpolated terminal reserve, which must be obtained from the insurer, is roughly equivalent to the policy's cash surrender value.

The value of life insurance policy must be reduced by the amount of any loan outstanding against the policy, including any accrued interest.

> **NOTE:** When making a gift of a life insurance policy, the owner should request that the insurer furnish a Form 712, which contains the financial data pertaining to the policy prepared by the insurance company.

¶1916 VALUATION OF TERM INTERESTS

The value of all term interests, including life estates, term of years, remainders, and reversions, generally equals the present value of the interest on the valuation date.

The value of a life insurance contract or of a contract for the payment of an annuity issued by a company regularly engaged in the selling of contracts of that character is established through the sale of the particular contract by the company or through the sale by the company of comparable contracts. Since valuation of an insurance policy through sale of comparable contracts is not readily ascertainable when the gift is of a contract which has been in force for some time and on which further premium payments are to be made, the value may be approximated by adding to the interpolated terminal reserve at the date of the gift the proportionate part of the gross premium last paid before the date of the gift which covers the period extending beyond that date. If, however, because of the unusual nature of the contract such approximation is not reasonably close to the full value, this method may not be used [Reg. Secs. 25.2512-6(a), 20.2031-8(a)(1)].

Other forms of annuities (so-called "private annuities," discussed at ¶204) and term interests (life estates, term of years, reversions, and remainders—for example, a life estate in real property or a life income interest in a trust), are determined by reference to various tables. The tables you use depend on the date of the transfer.

First, if the transfer (by gift or death) was made after December 31, 1970, but before December 1, 1983, use the 6 percent tables found in former Reg. Sec. 25.2512-9(f).

Second, if the transfer occurred after November 30, 1983, but before May 1, 1989, use the 10 percent tables found in Reg. Sec. 20.2031-7A (Reg. Sec. 25.2512-5A(d)(6) refers to the tables in Reg. Sec. 20.2031-7A(d)(6)).

Third, if the transfer occurred after April 30, 1989, use the factors corresponding to the interest rates that the IRS publishes monthly. Use the table for the month in which the valuation is made. The tables round to the nearest 2/10th of 1 percent to yield an interest rate equal to 120 percent of the federal mid-term rate in effect under IRC Sec. 1274(d)(1) for the month in question [IRC Sec. 7520(a)(2)]. The tables of factors based on these rates are found in IRS Publications 1457 (Actuarial Values, Aleph Volume) and 1458 (Actuarial Values, Beth Volume). The publications include remainder, income, and annuity factors for one life, two lives, and term certain calculations. The publication also include factors for weekly, monthly, quarterly and semiannual payment periods. The IRS may, on request for a ruling, supply the factor for two lives situations not covered in these publications or for three or more lives situations [Reg. Sec. 25.7520-1(c)].

> **NOTE:** If a factor, computation, or ruling is needed to complete a tax return, request assistance by writing to: Internal Revenue Service, Associate Chief Counsel (Technical and International), Attention CC:CORT:T, P.O Box 7604, Ben Franklin Station, Washington, D.C. 20044.

(a) Life Estates. The present value of a life estate for the life of one individual is determined by reference to Table S (actuarial factors for one life) contained in Reg. Sec. 20.2031-7(d)(6). The value of the property is completed by using the IRC Sec. 7520 interest rate component described in Reg. Sec. 25.7520-1(b)(1) and the mortality component described in Reg. Sec. 25.7520-1(b)(2) multiplied by the applicable factor representing the income interests. The applicable factor is obtained by subtracting from 1.0 the appropriate remainder factor in Table 2 for the federal mid-term rate under IRC Sec. 1274(d)(1) for the month in which the transfer occurs, based on the number of years nearest to the actual age of the measuring life.

> **Example 1:** A transfers to B an income interest for A's life in property valued at $100,000 during a month in which the interest rate that is 120 percent of the applicable federal mid-term rate equals 8.8 percent. At the date of the gift B is 31 years and 3 months old.
>
> Under Table S at an applicable interest rate of 8.8 percent, the factor for determining the present value of the remainder interest at the death of an individual, age 31, is 0.05045. Subtracting the remainder factor (0.05045) from 1.0 equals 0.944955 (1.0 minus 0.05045), the factor needed to determine the present value of the income interest. The present value of A's gift to B equals $94,955 ($100,000 times 0.94955).

(b) Term of Years. The value of an income interest for a term of years is determined by multiplying the value of the property by the applicable factor representing the income interest. The applicable factor representing the income interest is obtained by subtracting from 1.0 the appropriate remainder factor in Table B [Reg. Sec. 20.2031-7(d)(6)] for the IRC Sec. 1274(d)(1) federal mid-term interest rate for the month in which the transfer occurs, opposite the number of years of the term [Reg. Secs. 25.7520-1(a)(1), 20.2031-7(d)(2)(iii)].

(c) Remainders or Reversions. The present value of a remainder or reversionary interest that follows a one-person life estate is determined under IRC Sec. 7520 by multiplying the value of the property by the figure in Table S [Reg. Sec. 20.2031-7(d)(6)] for the federal mid-term rate under IRC Sec. 1274(d)(1) for the month in which the transfer occurs, based on the number of years nearest to the life tenant's actual age [Reg. Sec. 20.2031-7(d)(6)]. If the remainder or reversion is to take effect at the end of a term of years, the present value of the remainder (or reversionary) interest is determined under IRS Sec. 7520 by multiplying the value of the property by the applicable actuarial factor in Table B [Reg. Sec. 20.2031-7(d)(2)(ii)] based on the IRC Sec. 1274(d)(1) federal mid-term interest rate for the month in which the transfer occurs, opposite the number of years representing the duration of the interest [Reg. Secs. 25.7520-1(a), 20.2031-7(d)(2)(ii)].

> **Example 2:** C transfers to D a remainder interest in a trust worth $100,000 subject to E's right to receive income from the trust for E's life. On the date of the creation of the trust, E's age is 31 years and 9 months. Assume that 120 percent of the federal mid-term rate equals 9.6 percent. The figure in Table S at 9.6 percent opposite age 32 is 0.04510. Thus, the present value of E's remainder interest equals $4,510 ($100,000 times 0.04510).

(d) Annuities. The present value of an annuity payable at the end of each year for a term of years is determined under IRC Sec. 7520 by multiplying the aggregate amount payable annually by an annuity factor from Table B (contained in Reg. Sec. 20.2031-7(d)(6), which provides the remainder factors for a term of years) based on the interest rate component on the valuation date [Reg. Secs. 25.7520-1(a)(1), 20.2031-7(d)(2)(iv)(A)]. The annuity factor is obtained in two steps by (1) subtracting from 1.0 the remainder factor in Table B [Reg. Sec. 20.2031-7(d)(6)] under the appropriate interest rate opposite the number of years representing the duration of the annuity and (2) then dividing the result in step (1) by the appropriate interest rate component expressed as a decimal number [Reg. Secs. 25.7520-1(a)(1), 20.2031-7(d)(2)(iv)(A)].

> **Example 3:** F is the beneficiary of an annuity of $25,000 to be paid at the end of the year for 30 years. F transfers the annuity to F's sister in a month in which 120 percent of the federal mid-term rate equals 9.6 percent. At the time of the gift on the last day of the year and immediately after receipt of the current year's payment, 25 additional payments will be made. Under Table B, at 9.6 percent, the remainder factor opposite 25 years is 0.101097. Subtracting this remainder factor of 0.101097 from 1.0 produces the income factor of 0.898903. The annuity factor (9.3636) equals (1) the income factor (0.898903) divided by (2) the interest rate component expressed as a decimal number (0.096). Thus, the present value of the 25-year annuity, which pays $25,000 at the end of each year, equals $234,089.32 ($25,000 times 9.3636).

If the annuity is to be paid at the end of a semi-annual, quarterly, monthly, or weekly period, an adjustment must be made to the value as determined under Table B (contained in Reg. Sec. 20.2031-7(d)(6)) [Reg. Sec. 20.2031-7(d)(3)(iv)(B)]. The Table B amount must be multiplied by an adjustment factor provided in Table K (contained in Reg. Sec. 20.2031-7(d)(6)), opposite the interest rate equal to 120 percent of the applicable federal mid-term interest rate.

> **Example 4:** F is the beneficiary of an annuity to be paid in amounts of $12,500, semiannually, for 30 years. F transfers the annuity to F's sister in a month in which 120 percent of the federal mid-term rate equals 9.6 percent. Fifty additional payments will be made on the annuity. The adjustment factor in Table K for 9.6 percent for semiannual intervals is 1.0235. The present value of the gift equals $239,591.12 ($25,000 (annual annuity amount) times 9.3636 times 1.0235).

If an annuity payment is to be made at the beginning of annual, semiannual, quarterly, monthly, or weekly periods for one or more lives, the value of the annuity equals the sum of (1) the first payment, plus (2) the present value of a similar annuity, the first payment of which is not to be made until the end of the payment period. If the first payment of an annuity for a specified term of years is due at the beginning of the payment period, the value of the annuity is calculated by (1) first multiplying the aggregate amount payable annually by the appropriate annuity factor based on the applicable federal mid-term rate opposite the number of years representing the duration of the annuity, and (2) then multiplying the product by the applicable adjustment factor set forth in Table J (contained in Reg. Sec. 20.2031-7(d)(6)) for payments made at the beginning of specified periods [Reg. Secs. 25.7520-1(a)(1), 20.2031 7(d)(2)(iv)(C)].

¶1916

(e) Exceptions to the Use of Valuation Tables. Generally, the 120 percent actuarial tables must be used to value any annuity, life incomes, term of years, remainder, or reversionary interest for transfers on or after May 1, 1989 [IRC Sec. 7520; Reg. Sec. 20.7520-1(a)(1)] subject to two exceptions.

First, if the beneficial interests are "restricted," these standard factors cannot be used for transfers or deaths occurring after December 31, 1995 [Reg. Sec. 20.7520-3(b)(3)]. The actuarial tables are inappropriate if an individual is "terminally ill," that is, if that individual is known to have an "incurable illness" or "deteriorating physical condition" such that there is at least a 50 percent probability that the individual will die within one year. If an individual who is a measuring life lives for 18 months or longer, then the individual is presumed not to be terminally ill "unless the contrary is established by clear and convincing evidence" [Reg. Sec. 20.7520-3(b)(3)(i)].

Second, if an interest in trust is transferred to or for the benefit of certain family members of the transferor and the transferor (or a family member) retains an interest in the trust, the value of the transferor's retained interest is determined under IRC Sec. 2702 [see ¶ 226]. Sec. 2702 also applies to certain transfers of an interest in property if one or more term interests (e.g., a life interest) in the property exist immediately after the transfer [IRC Sec. 2702(c)].

¶1917 VALUATION OF REAL PROPERTY

Since the IRS regulations do not contain special rules dedicated specifically to the valuation of gifts of real estate, taxpayers should refer to the general valuation principles in Reg. Sec. 25.2512-1 and the precepts contained in the various IRS rulings and court decisions when valuing transfers of real property.

Valuing real property can be difficult because each parcel is unique and its valuation cannot be determined by formula or rule. Each valuation must be fixed individually, in accordance with the requirements and circumstances of the particular situation. Expert testimony is preferred in order to address the local market conditions relative to the specific piece of land involved.

The following factors are important when determining valuation of real estate for gift tax purposes: market activity, comparable sales, rentals, and recent mortgages.

In general, the fair-market value of real property is based on its highest and best use.[1] The highest and best use of the real estate represents the hypothetical utilization of the real estate designed to produce the greatest return or benefit to the owner. For estate tax purposes, however, special rules exist for the valuation of certain real property under the "special use valuation." [see ¶ 1908]. Generally, in valuing real property you must distinguish between unimproved and improved realty

(a) Unimproved Real Property. You may own unimproved realty, that is, land without significant buildings or improvements that contribute to its value. The best indication of value of unimproved realty is the price paid for the property in an arm's-

---

[1] **¶1917** Frazee, 98 TC 554 (1992).

length transaction on or before the valuation date. If the property has not been the subject of a recent arm's-length transaction, use the comparable sales approach to arrive at its value.

Under the comparable sales method, an appraiser compares the subject property and other similar properties that have been sold. After the sales prices are adjusted to reflect a variety of differences, including date of sale, size, condition, and location, the comparable sales reflect the estimated fair-market value of the property being valued.

In using the comparable sales method, the appraiser must carefully consider the following factors:

1. Location, configuration, and restrictions on use or zoning;
2. Accessibility and road frontage, availability of utilities, and water rights;
3. Riparian rights, existing easements, and rights of way; and
4. Soil characteristics, vegetation cover, and status of mineral rights.

The appraiser should note the names of the buyer and seller, the legal and property description, the date of sale, the amount and terms of financing, the assessed value, the real property tax rate, and the assessor's appraised fair-market value of comparable properties. The appraiser should consider only comparable sales having the least adjustments in terms of the various items as comparable to the property being valued. The appraiser should use only the two or three adjusted sales that furnish the most reliable estimates of the fair-market value of the property being valued.

(b) Improved Real Property. In arriving at the value of improved real estate based on its highest and best use, four methods (or a combination thereof) are commonly used:

1. *Market data approach.* The "market value" approach relies first on actual sales that satisfy the relevancy test (i.e., timely, in an appropriate market, and auction). If no actual sales exist, then comparable sales are used. The appraiser uses such factors as location, configuration, restrictions on land use, and zoning to determine comparability.

2. *Capitalization of rental income approach.* When rent constitutes the primary factor in owning the property, then capitalization of rental income represents the most reliable valuation method. To use this technique, an appraiser must establish the present value of the future rental income stream the property will generate.[2] Performing this analysis requires the appraiser to estimate the highest sustainable rent as adjusted for normal vacancy rates and expenses and reduced by nonrecurring and extraordinary items.

3. *Replacement of cost approach.* Unique real estate may be appraised using the "replacement cost" approach. In using this approach, the appraiser must calculate the replacement cost of the property and then subtract the depreciation.[3]

4. *Tax assessed value approach.* For the tax assessed value approach, only assessments made by the local tax assessor's office equal to the full fair-market value of the property are relevant.

---

[2] Lefrak, TC Memo 1993-526.   [3] Scheidelman, TC Memo 1970-70.

(c) Valuing Fractional Interests. If the donor (or decedent) transfers a partial or fractional interest in real property, the valuation process must establish the value of the fractional interest. Valuing a fractional interest consists of the following three-step process:

1. *Determining the unadjusted value of the fractional interest.* The procedure for determining the unadjusted value of the fractional interest is simple, provided the real estate:

   - Is owned directly by the donor (or decedent) or by an entity owned by the donor (or decedent); and

   - Comprises the entity's primary asset.

     In these situations, the percentage of the donor's (or decedent's) interest transferred (or owned at death) is applied to the value of the real estate as a whole. When the entity owning the real estate has other significant assets, the appraiser must incorporate the valuation of the real estate into the entity's overall valuation and employ the procedures for valuing closely held business entities [see ¶ 1913].

     Assuming the real estate is directly owned by the donor (or decedent) or by an entity that the donor (or decedent) owns in which the real estate is the entity's primary asset, once the appraiser determines the unadjusted value of the fractional interest, the appraiser should apply the fractional interest discount and, if appropriate, the restriction discount. Both discounts, which are discussed below, are available to the donor (or decedent) regardless of whether:

   - The real estate is owned directly (e.g., as a cotenant in common with others or indirectly—for example, as a partner or shareholder of an entity which holds title to the real estate);

   - The donor's (or decedent's) interest is a majority or minority interest.

2. *Adjusting the unadjusted value of the fractional interest for a fractional interest discount.* The fractional interest discount recognizes what the hypothetical seller and buyer in the willing seller–willing buyer test would likely take into account in making a deal. These individuals would reduce the value of the real estate from its unadjusted value because the full value of the real estate cannot be obtained without the cooperation of the other owners or interest holders. The burden of substantiating the value, as adjusted, rests on the donor or the executor.

   In valuing directly owned real property, if the donor or the executor fails to offer any evidence that a fractional interest would sell for less than the donor's (or decedent's) proportionate share of the entire value of the real estate, the Tax Court has refused to allow any fractional interest discount.[4] However, expert testimony alone is insufficient. The Tax Court has allowed a fractional interest discount on directly owned real estate if:

   - Expert testimony presents such a discount and sales of comparable real estate support the expert testimony;[5] or

---

[4] Estate of Iacono, TC Memo 1980-520.   [5] Estate of Sels, TC Memo 1986-501.

- The taxpayer offers expert testimony that is unchallenged by the IRS.

- If the fractional interest in real estate is owned indirectly, such as where the donor (or decedent) owns an interest in a closely held business entity, the appraiser uses the fractional interest discount that is comparable to the minority interest discount [see ¶ 800] used to value an interest in a closely held business for which there is no recognized market.[6]

3. *Adjusting the unadjusted value of the fractional interest for restraints on the free transferability of the interest.* A restriction restraining the free transferability of the donor's (or decedent's) interest acts as a value inhibitor. The restriction may be established as part of the formation of the entity or later by agreement between or among the owners.

¶1918 DEFINED VALUE FORMULA CLAUSES

(a) Defined Value Formulas Defined. Defined value formula clauses are clauses contained in the language of wills, trusts and gifts that express the beneficiary's or donor's interest in terms of a formula or a fixed dollar amount. Think about going to the gas station and asking for $30 worth of gasoline rather than saying "fill it up." You have used a defined value clause at the gas station.

Taxpayers use defined value clauses to make certain that a certain dollar amount (rather than an asset of unknown value that could be challenged by the IRS) will go the taxpayer's intended beneficiaries. For example, in a defined value clause a taxpayer could specify that the exact dollar amount of the annual gift tax exclusion be gifted each year to his children.

> **Example 1:** Dad transfers stock to Son and the documents provide that Son should receive $100,000 worth of ABCo stock. Mom transfers stock to Son and the documents provide that Son should receive 1000 shares of ABCo stock. Dad has used a defined value clause in transferring stock to Son.

In order to avoid the valuation errors, some gift plans provide for a gift over to charity of the value of the donative property above a specified amount. For example, the language in the donor's gift plan could give the donor's children units in an LLC, but if the units are finally determined to have a value in excess of a specified amount, units equal in value to the excess will pass to a designated charity.

Defined value clauses could also include an adjustment or savings clause which would become operative if the IRS or a court of law determines that the value of the transferred units are different from the one used by the donor. If an appraisal resulted in an increase in the value of the gifted unit, the gift to the donee would equal its original stated amount and any excess in gift value over the dollar amount listed on the gift tax return would be returned to the taxpayer.

---

[6] Ward, 87 TC 78 (1986)

Even though it is clear that the IRS is not fond of defined value clauses and loves to challenge them, the courts have approved their validity in five cases discussed below. The IRS position on defined value clauses is evidenced in their refusal to accept formula clauses that provided for adjustments based upon finally determined values for gift tax purposes[1] and the fact that it had announced its nonacquiesence in *Wandry*,[2] which is a gift tax case and the first case to hold that a "formula transfer clause" was valid. The appellate court approved a dollar value formula clause when a charity was not involved. The case is discussed in detail below.

(b) Cases Involving Defined Value Formulas. In *Procter*,[3] which was the first case to consider the validity of defined value clauses, the Court of Appeals for the Fourth Circuit refused to enforce a formula clause on public policy grounds. The trust provision provided that if any portion of the transfer in trust were subject to gift tax as determined by "final judgment or order of a competent federal court of last resort" then the property subject to the tax was not to be included in the transfer and would remain the property of the settlor. The court held that the trust provision nullifying a transfer that would otherwise be subject to gift tax was a condition subsequent that was void as against public policy.

In *Hendrix*,[4] the Tax Court held that the value of stock in a closely-held corporation transferred by a husband and wife to family trusts and a charitable foundation was the value reached by using a defined value formula clause that was set forth in an assignment agreement. Because the stock in the closely-held corporation was difficult to value, the couple chose to use a defined value formula clause in their assignment agreement in order to set the value of the stock in dollars as opposed to percentages at the time of the transfer. The court upheld the defined value formula clause because it did not provide a condition subsequent that would defeat the transfer. The formula clause also furthered a public policy goal of encouraging gifts to charities. In addition, there was no evidence of collusion between any of the parties. The foundation was represented by independent counsel and had a fiduciary duty to make certain that it received the proper number of shares under the formula clause. Thus, the formula clause was a product of an arm's length transaction. Consequently, the couple was entitled to deduct the full value of the charitable contribution made to the foundation, and did not owe any additional gift tax for the transfer of stock in the closely-held corporation to the trusts.

In *McCord*,[5] the Court of Appeals for the Fifth Circuit reversed the Tax Court to uphold a defined value formula clause that was included in an assignment agreement entered into among members of a family limited partnership. The formula clause provided that the donor's children, trusts for the children, and a charitable organization received partnership interests of a total stated value and another charitable organization was to receive any value in excess of the stated amount.

---

[1] ¶ **1918** Ltr. Ruls. 2002245053, 200337012.

[2] Wandry, TC Memo 2012-88, *nonacq.*, 2012-46 IRB 1.

[3] Procter, 142 F.2d 824 (4th Cir. 1944), *cert. denied*, 323 U.S. 756 (1944).

[4] Hendrix, TC Memo 2011-133.

[5] McCord, 120 TC 358 (2003), *rev'd*, 461 F.3d 614 (5th Cir. 2006).

¶1918

In *Estate of Christiansen*,[6] the Tax Court upheld a formula clause similar to the one at issue in *McCord* and the decision was affirmed by the Court of Appeals for the Eighth Circuit. In that case, the taxpayer included "a fixed-dollar-amount partial disclaimer" in her will. This disclaimer is a type of defined value clause in which a charitable foundation had the right to receive 25 percent of those amounts in excess of $6.35 million. After the taxpayer's death, the taxpayer's experts valued the estate and a portion of that value that was mandated by the fixed-dollar-amount clause was transferred to a charitable foundation. The IRS argued that allowing this type of defined value clause to exist would decrease government revenue and increase valuation abuses. Based on this reasoning, the IRS urged the appellate court to "categorically disqualif[y]" the use of such clauses due to the detrimental effect on public policy. The Eighth Circuit rejected these arguments and upheld the validity of the defined value clause after pointing out that the defined value clause would not be detrimental to public policy.

In *Estate of Petter*,[7] the Tax Court again considered the validity of a formula clause where gifted property in excess of a defined value would pass to designated charitable organizations, and the Tax Court upheld the validity of the clause with the Court of Appeals for the Ninth Circuit affirming the decision. In that case, Anne Petter inherited UPS stock that was worth $22.6 million. In order to achieve her objective of giving as much of the stock as possible to her children without paying any transfer tax and with the remainder going to charity, she created a family LLC and transferred her UPS stock into the trust and provided that the remainder of the shares would be given to charity. This would enable her to pay zero gift tax and claim a charitable deduction for the amount going to charity.

The following defined value clause was used:

> "The trust agrees that, if the value of the Units it initially receives is finally determined for federal gift tax purposes to exceed the [federal gift tax exclusion] . . . Trustee will, on behalf of the Trust and as a condition of the gift to it, transfer the excess Units to the [charitable foundation] . . . as soon as practicable." "The [charitable foundation] . . . agrees that, if the value of the Units the Trust initially receives is finally determined for federal gift tax purposes to be less than the [federal gift tax exclusion], . . . [the charitable foundation] . . . will, as a condition of the gift to it, transfer the excess Units to the Trust as soon as practicable."

This language ensured that the exact amount of the taxpayer's gift tax exclusion would be used while transferring the stock to the taxpayer's children. The IRS challenged the arrangement saying that the defined value clause was against the law and the interests of the country.

The court disagreed with the IRS and found that it was clear from the documents how much was being donated to the donees. Even though the number of units was not initially known, "the foundations were always entitled to receive a predefined number of units, which the documents essentially expressed as a mathematical formula." In

---

[6] Estate of Christiansen, 130 TC 1 (2008), *aff'd*, 586 F.3d 1061 (2009).

[7] Estate of Petter, TC Memo 2009-280, *aff'd*, 653 F.3d 1012.

response to the IRS' public policy argument, the Eighth Circuit said that they did not believe the defined value clause would have the catastrophic effects predicted by the IRS and the Ninth Circuit upheld the validity of the defined value clause.

> ▶ **PLANNING POINTER:** *Petter* illustrates how effective defined value clauses can be when transferring assets that do not have an established fair market value and are difficult to value. This is particularly true with closely-held business stock. The use of the defined value clauses when transferring assets of this nature helps avoid audits and potential litigation.

In *Wandry*,[8] the taxpayers formed a limited liability partnership (LLP) which they funded with cash and marketable securities. The taxpayers then began making gifts of LLP membership units to their children and grandchildren. At issue in the case was the language of the gifting documents. Rather than give a certain number of units, the taxpayers' gave each donee a sufficient number of LLP membership units that equaled specific dollar amounts that used up the taxpayers' annual gift tax exclusion and their lifetime gift tax exclusion amount. The gift documents also contained a so-called adjustment or savings clause which would become operative if the IRS or a court of law determined that the value of the transferred units was different from the one used by the donor. If an appraisal resulted in an increase in the value of the gifted unit, any excess in gift value over the dollar amount listed on the gift tax return would be returned to the taxpayer by means of a reallocation of the LLP units. The IRS challenged the validity of the gifts saying that the interests should have been valued at a higher amount and that the formula did not work.

The Tax Court upheld the validity of the taxpayer's defined value clause citing *Estate of Christensen, Estate of Petter v. Comm'r* and *McCord v. Comm'r*, where formula clauses were all upheld. The court explained that the gifts were simply gifts of a certain dollar amount of assets rather than gifts of specific assets. They therefore held that individuals transferred gifts of a specified dollar value of membership units in an LLP to their children and grandchildren and rejected the IRS contention that the gifts were of fixed percentage interests in the LLP and void as against public policy. The court distinguished the formula clause from the savings clause, saying that a savings clause is void because it creates a situation where a donor is trying to take back property it has already given away. A formula clause, on the other hand, is valid because it merely transfers a "fixed set of rights with uncertain value."

The IRS has announced its nonacquiesence to the decision in *Wandry*. The IRS initially appealed the decision to the Court of Appeals for the Tenth Circuit but the IRS has withdrawn the appeal.

> ▶ **PLANNING POINTER:** Practitioners should take advantage of *Wandry* where it can be used efficiently, unless they are in the Fourth Circuit where the case of *Proctor* was decided, and the court invalidated what the court characterized as a savings clause. Wandry is an important case because it was the first Tax Court case which upheld the validity of formula clauses and did not involve charitable organizations as did *McCord, Christiansen, Petter* and *Hendrix*. Donors can therefore feel more comfortable using defined value clauses without the involvement of a charity.

---

[8] Wandry, TC Memo 2012-88, *nonacq.*, 2012-46 IRB 1.

(c) Disadvantages of Using Defined Value Formulas. The downside to using defined value clauses is the possibility of litigation in view of the fact that the IRS hates them and has continued to challenge them despite numerous court defeats. It is also possible that the IRS will release regulations or legislation that could make it difficult or nearly impossible for taxpayers to use defined value clauses when transferring property.

ESTATE TAX DEDUCTIONS

TABLE OF CONTENTS

¶2000 DEDUCTIONS FROM THE GROSS ESTATE

The estate tax is imposed on the taxable estate, which is the gross estate reduced by the following deductions [IRC Secs. 2051, 2053; Reg. Sec. 20.2051-1(a)]:

1. Funeral expenses paid out of the estate [see ¶2001];

2. Expenses of administering the estate [see ¶2001];

3. Debts owed at the time of death, including claims against the estate and unpaid mortgages on property included in the gross estate [see ¶2001];

4. Casualty and theft losses that occur during settlement of the estate [see ¶2001];

5. Charitable contributions made by the estate [see ¶1000];

6. The marital deduction, which is generally the value of the property that passes from the estate to the surviving spouse [see ¶1101]. The marital deduction is unlimited, so a decedent can pass any amount of property to the surviving spouse free of estate and gift tax;

7. A qualified domestic trust (QDOT) under IRC Sec. 2056A, which is a marital deduction trust created for property passing from a U.S. decedent to a noncitizen surviving spouse; and [For further discussion see ¶1106]

8. State death taxes under IRC Sec. 2058 to the extent applicable to the estates of decedents [see ¶2001].

These deductions reduce the amount of the taxable gross estate and therefore reduce the amount of estate taxes due.

¶2001 DEDUCTIONS FOR EXPENSES, CLAIMS AGAINST THE ESTATE, TAXES, AND LOSSES

Allowable expenses. In analyzing the estate tax deductions for expenses, indebtedness, and taxes, you must distinguish between:

1. Expenses incurred in administering property subject to creditors' claims (probate assets); and

2. Expenses incurred in administering property not subject to creditors' claims.

Pursuant to IRC Sec. 2053(a), the value of the taxable estate is determined by deducting from the value of the gross estate the following expenses:

- Funeral expenses;
- Administration expenses;
- Claims against the estate, unpaid mortgages; and
- Other indebtedness.

The amount of the deduction for these expenses is the amount allowable by the law of the jurisdiction where the decedent's estate is being administered [IRC Sec. 2053(a)]. The deduction, however, is limited to:

1. The value of property subject to claims included in the gross estate, plus

2. The amount paid out of property included in the gross estate but not subject to claims. This second amount must actually be paid within the time allowed for the filing of the estate tax return, including any extensions [IRC Sec. 2053(c)(2)].

A deduction is also allowed for the expenses of administering property not subject to creditors' claims (nonprobate assets included in the decedent's gross estate) if:

1. The expenses are paid before the expiration of the period for assessing estate tax deficiencies, which is generally three years from the due date for filing [IRC Sec. 6501; Reg. Sec. 20.2053-8]; and

2. The expense is allowable by the law governing the administration of the decedent's estate as if the property were subject to claims [IRC Sec. 2053(b)].

   ▶ **OBSERVATION:** If the estate's total expenses and debts exceed the probate assets, maximize the deductions by paying the items prior to the due date of the estate tax return out of nonprobate assets [Reg. Sec. 20.2053-1(c), Example (2)].

The applicable local law under which the estate is being administered determines which property is subject to creditors' claims and which property is not subject to creditors' claims. If under local law a particular property interest included in the decedent's gross estate would bear the burden for the payment of the expenses, then the property is considered property subject to claims. For this purpose, the value of this property is reduced by the amount of any deduction allowed for a casualty or theft loss to the property during the settlement of the estate [Reg. Sec. 20.2053-1(c)(2)].

¶2001

Expenses incurred in administering the entire community property are deductible in proportion to the decedent's interest in the community property. Expenses specifically allocable to the decedent's share of the community property are fully deductible.

The following sections consider more specifically five types of expenses: funeral, administration, claims against the estate, interest, and taxes.

(a) Funeral Expenses. Funeral expenses are allowed as a deduction from the gross estate under IRC Sec. 2053(a)(1) if they are actually paid, are allowable out of property subject to claims under local law, and satisfy the limitation for the total amount of expenses allowed for the items discussed in this section. Deductible funeral expenses may include the cost of a tombstone, monument, mausoleum, or a burial lot either for the decedent or the decedent's family, and a reasonable expenditure for its future care if allowable by the local law. The cost of transportation of the person bringing the body to the place of burial is deductible [Reg. Sec. 20.2053-2].

The estate is allowed a deduction if it is primarily liable under local law for the decedent's funeral expense. However, under local law, the husband may be primarily liable for the funeral expenses of his deceased wife. In this case, the estate would be allowed a deduction for these expenses only if the wife's will directs that these expenses be paid out of her estate.

In *Estate of Davenport*,[1] the Tax Court denied a deduction under IRC Sec. 2053(a)(1) to the estate of a 12-year-old for a lavish funeral luncheon because the estate failed to show sufficient proof of its reasonable relationship to the funeral.

(b) Administration Expenses. Administration expenses include executor's commissions [Reg. Sec. 20.2053-3(b)], attorneys' fees [Reg. Sec. 20.2053-3(c)] and trustee's commissions when a trustee performs services with respect to property subject to claims that the executor would normally perform [Reg. Sec. 20.2053-3(b)(3)]. Administration expense deductions against the gross estate are limited in Reg. Sec. 20.2053-3(a) to "expenses . . . actually and necessarily incurred in the administration of the decedent's estate.[2] To qualify for the deduction, the administrative expenses must satisfy the requirements of both state and federal law.[3] The expenses must be incurred in conjunction with the collection of assets, payment of debts, and distribution of property to the persons entitled to it." Reg. Sec. 20.2053-3(a) provides further that: "Expenditures not essential to the proper settlement of the estate, but incurred for the individual benefit of the heirs, legatees, or devisees, may not be taken as deductions."[4] Deductible administrative expenses could even include payments made to attorneys for their efforts in discovering the misappropriation of the decedent's assets.[5]

In *Estate of Koons*,[6] the Tax Court concluded that an estate was not entitled to deduct the projected interest expense on a loan from a limited liability company (LLC) to the decedent's revocable trust. In order to pay the decedent's estate tax liabilities, the

---

[1] **¶2001** Estate of Davenport, TC Memo 2006-215.

[2] Estate of Fujishima, TC Memo 2012-6.

[3] Estate of Grant, TC Memo 1999-396, *aff'd*, 294 F.3d 352 (2d Cir. 2002).

[4] Estate of Bates, TC Memo 2012-314.

[5] Estate of Glover, TC Memo 2002-186.

[6] Estate of Koons, TC Memo 2013-94; see also Estate of Huntington, 36 BTA 698 (1937); Gilman, TC Memo 2004-286.

decedent's revocable trust borrowed $10.75 million from an LLC in which the trust held a majority interest. Under the terms of the loan, the interest and principal payments were to be deferred for over 18 years. This deferral resulted in over $71 million in interest payments. It was unnecessary for the trust to have borrowed the money from the LLC. With a 70.42-percent voting interest, the trust could have forced the LLC to distribute a portion of it $200 million in liquid assets. Thus, because the loan was not necessary to the administration of the estate, it was not a deductible expense under Reg. Sec. 20.2053-3(a). The court explained that interest payments on loans can be deducted only if the loan is necessary to raise money to pay the estate tax without liquidating the assets of the estate at forced-sale prices.

The executor may deduct attorneys' fees and executor's commissions that have actually been paid or that, at the time of filing the estate tax return, may reasonably be expected to be paid [Reg. Secs. 20.2053-3(b), 20.2053-3(c)]. If the estimated attorney's fees and executor's commissions have not been paid by the time of the final audit, the deduction must be supported by an affidavit of the attorney or executor stating the amount claimed has been agreed on and will be paid.

Administration expenses also include selling expenses (e.g., brokerage fees and excise taxes on the sale) and other miscellaneous expenses (e.g., court costs, accountants' fees, appraisers' fees, costs of storing or maintaining the estate's property for a reasonable time period before the property is distributed) connected with the administration of the estate [Reg. Sec. 20.2053-3(d)].

(c) Claims Against the Estate. The IRS has issued final regulations relating to the amount deductible from a decedent's gross estate under IRC Sec. 2053. To resolve the inconsistency among the courts[7] regarding the extent post-death events are considered in valuing claims against a decedent's estate, especially claims being pursued in litigation pending at the date of the decedent's death, the regulations provide, in general, that post-death events should be considered in computing the amount deductible under IRC Sec. 2053 only if and when they are paid or ascertainable with reasonable certainty. [Reg. Sec. 20.2053-1(a)].

In *Estate of Saunders*,[8] the Tax Court concluded that a decedent's estate was only able to take a estate tax deduction for the amount of a claim against the estate that was actually paid, not the value claimed upon the date of death. Shortly before the decedent's death, a malpractice claim for $90 million was filed against the decedent's predeceased spouse's estate. The $30 million appraised value of the claim was deducted from the decedent's estate. Three years after the original claim was filed, the parties settled for $250,000. Pursuant to Reg. Sec. 20.2031-1(b)(3), a claim against the estate is deductible if the value of the claim is "ascertainable with reasonable certainty, and will be paid." The value of the claim was not certain at the time of the decedent's death. This is evidenced by the reports by the decedent's experts presented at trial, where the appraised values varied by almost $11 million. In addition, none of the experts stated that any specific amount would be paid by the estate, as required under Reg. Sec. 20.2031-1(b)(3). Thus, only the amount paid during

[7] The Fifth, Tenth and Eleventh Circuits have been unwilling to consider post-death events. See Estate of Smith, 198 F.3d 515 (5th Cir. 1999); Estate of McMarris, 243 F.3d 1254; O'Neal, 258 F.3d 1265. The Eighth Circuit has been more willing to do so. See Estate of Sachs, 856 F.2d 1158 (8th Cir. 1988).

[8] Estate of Saunders, 136 TC 406 (2011).

the administration of the estate could be deducted in accordance with Reg. Sec. 20.2031-1(b)(3).

The expenses may not be based upon a "vague or uncertain estimate." The regulations provide further that a claim or expense that is contested or contingent is not ascertainable with reasonable certainty and, therefore, may not be deducted prior to the time it is paid.

Estimated payments. A limitation on the type of claim that can be deducted on an estate tax return is provided in Reg. Sec. 20.2053-1(b)(3) which provides that "[a]n item may be entered on the return for deduction although its exact amount is not then known, provided it is ascertainable with reasonable certainty, and will be paid." However, "[n]o deduction may be taken upon the basis of a vague or uncertain estimate." In such a case, where the "liability was not ascertainable at the time of final audit of the return by the district director and, as a consequence, it was not allowed as a deduction in the audit, and subsequently the amount of the liability is ascertained, relief may be sought by a petition to the Tax Court or a claim for refund." Reg. Sec. 20.2053-4 provides that claims may be deducted only if they "represent personal obligations of the decedent existing at the time of his death, whether or not then matured, and interest thereon which had accrued at the time of death."

Court decrees. If a court reviews and approves expenditures for funeral expenses, administration expenses, claims against the estate or unpaid mortgages, a final judicial decision in that matter may be relied upon to establish the amount of a claim or expense that is otherwise deductible under IRC Sec. 2053 if the court actually passes upon the facts on which deductibility depends [Reg. Sec. 20.2053-1(b)(3)(i)].

Consent decrees. A local court decree rendered by consent may be relied on to establish the amount of a claim or expense that is otherwise deductible under IRC Sec. 2053 provided that the consent resolves a bona fide issue in a genuine contest. Consent given by all parties having interests adverse to that of the claimant will be presumed to resolve a bona fide issue in a genuine contest [Reg. Sec. 20.2053-1(b)(3)(iii)].

Settlements. A settlement may be relied on to establish the amount of a claim or expense (whether contingent or noncontingent) that is otherwise deductible under IRC Sec. 2053, if it resolves a bona fide issue in a genuine contest and is the product of arm's-length negotiations by parties having adverse interests with respect to the claim or expense. A deduction will not be denied for a settlement amount paid by an estate if the estate can establish that the cost of defending or contesting the claim or expense, or the delay associated with litigating the claim or expense, would impose a higher burden on the estate than the payment of the amount paid to settle the claim or expense [Reg. Sec. 20.2053-1(b)(3)(iv)]. Estates may only deduct the actual amount specified in a settlement agreement and not the potential income tax liability that could have been incurred. In *Marshall Naify Revocable Trust*,[9] the Ninth Circuit concluded that a decedent's estate was limited to a deduction for the amount of state income tax actually paid in settlement with the state taxing authority and not a deduction for the potential state income tax liability.

---

[9] Marshall Naify Revocable Trust, 672 F.3d 620 (9th Cir. 2012).

Exception for ascertainable amounts. A deduction will be allowed for a claim, even though it is not yet paid, provided that the amount to be paid is ascertainable with reasonable certainty and will be paid. For example, executors' commissions and attorneys' fees that are not yet paid are deemed to be ascertainable with reasonable certainty and may be deducted if such expenses will be paid. However, no deduction may be taken upon the basis of a vague or uncertain estimate. To the extent a claim or expense is contested or contingent, such a claim or expense cannot be ascertained with reasonable certainty [Reg. Sec. 20.2053-1(d)(4)].

Protective claims for refund. If the deduction is not determinable with reasonable certainty before the estate tax statute of limitations runs, the executor's recourse is to file a protective claim for refund. [For a discussion of new Schedule PC, Protective Claim for Refund, on Form 706, see ¶ 2433.] The estate may file this protective claim at any time before the expiration of the period of limitation prescribed in IRC Sec. 6511(a) for the filing of a claim for refund to preserve the estate's right to claim a refund. Although the protective claim need not state a particular dollar amount or demand an immediate refund, Reg. Sec. 20.2053-1(d)(5)(i) provides that a protective claim must identify the outstanding claim or expense that would have been deductible under IRC Sec. 2053(a) or (b) if such item already had been paid, and must describe the reasons and contingencies delaying the actual payment of the claim or expense. When the contingencies delaying actual payment are resolved, Reg. Sec. 20.2053-1(d)(5)(i) requires the fiduciary acting on behalf of the estate to notify the IRS within a reasonable period that the contingency has been resolved and that the amount deductible under Reg. Sec. 20.2053-1 has been established. A deduction will be allowed to the extent the claim or expense that was the subject of the protective claim satisfies the requirements for deductibility under IRC Sec. 2053 and the corresponding regulations, subject to any applicable limitations in Reg. Sec. 20.2053-1.

In Rev. Proc. 2011-48,[10] the IRS provides guidance related to the filing and resolution of a protective claim for refund of estate tax based on IRC Sec. 2053. A protective claim for refund must be filed before the expiration of the period of limitation prescribed in IRC Sec. 6511(a) for filing a claim for refund. IRC Sec. 6511(a) provides that a claim for refund must be filed by the taxpayer within three years from the time the return was filed or two years from the time the tax was paid, whichever expires later, or if no return was filed by the taxpayer, within two years from the time the tax was paid. The protective claim for refund must identify in detail the IRC Sec. 2053 expense claimed and contain documentary evidence to establish the authority of the individual filing the protective claim on behalf of the estate. A separate protective claim for refund must be filed for each claim or expense. When the IRC Sec. 2053 claim or expense that was subject to a protective claim for refund meets the requirements for deductibility under Reg. Sec. 20.2053-1, the estate must notify the IRS that the claim is ready for consideration. In order for a protective claim for refund to be properly filed, the outstanding claim or expense that forms the basis of a potential deduction under IRC Sec. 2053 must be clearly identified so that the IRS has notice of each claim or expense for which a deduction will be claimed. In addition, as provided in Reg. Sec. 20.2053-1(d)(5), proper identification of the claim or expense must include an explanation of the reasons and contingencies delaying the actual payment to be made in satisfaction of the claim or expense. Finally, claims or expenses related

---

[10] Rev. Proc. 2011-48, 2011-2 CB 527.

to but separate from a particular IRC Sec. 2053 claim or expense must be separately identified. The use of vague or broad language that does not describe a specific claim or expense that would be deductible under IRC Sec. 2053 does not provide clear identification of an IRC Sec. 2053 claim or expense.

Effect on the marital and charitable deductions. If a claim or expense is the subject of a protective claim for refund under IRC Sec. 2053 and is payable out of a fund that meets the requirements for a charitable or marital deduction, the charitable or marital deduction will not be reduced by the amount of the claim or expense until the amount is actually paid [Reg. Sec. 20.2053-1(d)(5)(ii)].

The IRS issued Notice 2009-84,[11] announcing its decision to limit the review of an estate tax return, in certain circumstances, when a timely-filed claim for refund of estate taxes that is based on a deduction under IRC Sec. 2053 ripens after the expiration of the limitations period on assessment [Reg. Sec. 20.2053-1(d)(5)]. The IRS will instead limit its examination to the deduction under IRC Sec. 2053 that was related to the protective claim. However, the IRS will recompute the estate tax liability based on its determination.

Reimbursements. An executor may certify on the estate tax return that no reimbursement is available for a claim or expense if the executor neither knows nor reasonably should have known of the availability of any reimbursement. In addition, the final regulations provide that an executor need not reduce the amount of a claim or expense deductible under IRC Sec. 2053 by the amount of a potential reimbursement if the executor provides a reasonable explanation on Form 706 for his or her reasonable determination that the burden of necessary collection efforts would outweigh the anticipated benefits from those efforts [Reg. Sec. 20.2053-1(b)(3)].

Claims and counterclaims. Reg. Sec. 20.2053-4(b) provides that the current value of a claim against the estate with respect to which there is one or more substantially-related claims or integrally-related assets that are included in a decedent's gross estate may be deducted on the estate tax return, provided that the related claim or asset of the estate constitutes at least 10 percent of the decedent's gross estate, the value of each such claim against the estate is determined from a "qualified appraisal" performed by a "qualified appraiser," and the value of each such claim against the estate is subject to adjustment to reflect post-death events.

Only bona fide expenses and claims. Reg. Sec. 20.2053-1(b)(2)(i) specifies that amounts deductible under IRC Sec. 2053(a) and IRC Sec. 2053(b) must be for bona fide expenses and claims. A deduction is not permitted to the extent the expense or claim is based on a donative transfer (e.g., "a mere cloak for a gift or bequest") except to the extent the deduction is for a claim that would be deductible under IRC Sec. 2055 as a charitable bequest. Reg. Sec. 20.2053-1(b)(2)(ii) lists the following five factors that will indicate the bona fide nature of a transaction:

1. The transaction underlying the claim or expense occurs in the ordinary course of business, is negotiated at arm's length, and is free from donative intent;

2. The nature of the claim or expense is not related to an expectation or claim of inheritance;

---

[11] Notice 2009-84, 2009-44 IRB 558.

3. The claim or expense originates pursuant to an agreement between the decedent and the family member, related entity, or beneficiary, and the agreement is substantiated with contemporaneous evidence;

4. Performance by the claimant is pursuant to the terms of an agreement between the decedent and the family member, related entity, or beneficiary and the performance and the agreement can be substantiated;

5. All amounts paid in satisfaction or settlement of a claim or expense are reported by each party for federal income and employment tax purposes, to the extent appropriate, in a manner that is consistent with the reported nature of the claim or expense.

Family member claims and expenses. Reg. Sec. 20.2053-1(b)(2)(ii) provides a nonexclusive list of factors indicative of the bona fide nature of a claim or expense involving a family member, related entity, or beneficiary of the estate of a decedent.

Recurring payments. The final regulations clarify that an obligation subject to death or remarriage is treated as a noncontingent obligation [Reg. Sec. 20.2053-4(d)(6)].

Penalties for failure to comply. Failure to deduct a claim or expense properly on Form 706 could result in the taxpayer being charged with negligence or with intentionally disregarding a regulation either of which would subject the taxpayer to a nondeductible 20 percent penalty of the amount of tax underpaid under IRC Sec. 6662. If the taxpayer is doubtful about the deduction, it would be a good idea to disclose on the return the basis for claiming it on Form 8275R. This may prevent the imposition of the penalty under IRC Sec. 6662 and may prevent the return preparer from becoming subject to a penalty under IRC Sec. 6694. Note, however, that attaching Form 8275R to disclose that the taxpayer has taken a position contrary to a regulation will only "automatically" prevent the penalty under IRC Sec. 6662 if it is a good faith challenge to the validity of a regulation [Reg. Sec. 1.6662-3].

(d) Unpaid Mortgages and Indebtedness. A mortgage or other secured debt is deducted from the gross estate if the underlying property is included in the estate [IRC Sec. 2053(a)(4)]. If the decedent was personally liable for the debt or it is enforceable against other estate property, the full value of the mortgaged property is included in the gross estate. Then a separate deduction is taken for the obligation. Election of special use valuation [see ¶1908] for the property does not bar the full deduction.[12]

If the estate is not liable on the obligation because the mortgage is a nonrecourse obligation, the mortgage is subtracted from the property's value. Only that net amount (i.e., the "equity of redemption") is included in the gross estate, and no separate deduction is allowed. In other words, a full recourse debt requires full inclusion; a nonrecourse debt requires inclusion of the "equity of redemption" [Reg. Sec. 20.2053-7].

> **NOTE:** Whether a mortgage (or other lien) is deducted as a debt or reduces the value of the encumbered property affects the value of the gross estate and may affect (1) the amount of the foreign death tax credit against the estate tax [see ¶2105] and (2) the availability of installment payments of the estate tax [see ¶2303].

---

[12] Rev. Rul. 83-81, 1983-1 CB 230.

¶2001

If the mortgage is on jointly held property, only part of the mortgage for which the decedent was liable and for which the estate must pay is deductible.[13]

If a decedent had made a transfer before death that must be included in the gross estate [see ¶ 1804], the value of the property that is included in the decedent's gross estate is not reduced by the amount of any mortgage that the donee (recipient) obtains on the property.

Insurance proceeds in estate deductible as debt. In *Estate of Kahanic*,[14] the Tax Court held that an estate may deduct, under IRC Sec. 2053(a)(4), life insurance proceeds payable to the decedent's ex-wife in connection with a divorce obligation because the insurance policy served as collateral for spousal support payments and was considered a debt by the court.

(e) Interest. A deduction is allowed for interest that had accrued on claims against the estate at the time of death even though the executor may elect the alternate valuation date [Reg. Sec. 20.2053-4; see ¶ 1907]. In such situations, if the decedent had lived, he or she would have been liable for the interest as well as for the principal. On the other hand, for interest that became payable after a decedent's death and that is attributable to an installment obligation that the decedent incurred, an administration expense is not allowed. In these cases, the interest is not actually and necessarily incurred in the administration of the decedent's estate, and it is therefore not allowable as an administration expense.

However, interest expenses incurred after the decedent's death are allowed as a deduction if they are reasonable and necessary to the administration of the estate (e.g., if incurred to preserve the estate).[15] To be deductible, the interest must be allowable under local law.

Interest accruing after death on taxes is generally deductible as an administration expense. Thus, the interest that accrues after death on federal and state income tax deficiencies while an executor contests the imposition of the taxes is deductible as an administration expense.[16]

Interest on a loan incurred to pay estate taxes is deductible as an administration expense when it accrues. A deduction is not allowed for estimated amounts that will accrue if repayment of the loan could be accelerated. Also, interest incurred as the result of a federal estate tax or gift tax deficiency is a deductible administration expense.[17]

In *Estate of Gilman*,[18] the court permitted a deduction for estate tax purposes for interest and closing costs paid on a *bona fide* loan to the extent that the loan was necessary to pay legitimately incurred obligations of the estate. The interest and closing costs associated with the portion of the loan used to pay nondeductible estate expenses were not deductible.

---

[13] Estate of Fawcett, 64 TC 889 (1975), *acq.*, 1978-2 CB 2.

[14] Estate of Kahanic, TC Memo 2012-81.

[15] Estate of Todd, 57 TC 288 (1971), *acq.*, 1973-2 CB 4; McKee, TC Memo 1996-362; Estate of Wheless, 72 TC 470 (1979), *nonacq.*, 1982-1 CB 1.

[16] Rev. Rul. 69-402, 1969-2 CB 176.

[17] Rev. Rul. 79-252, 1979-2 CB 333.

[18] Estate of Gilman, TC Memo 2004-286.

¶2001

If the executor elects installment payments for the estate tax, the interest payable on these installments is deductible provided the expenses are allowable under state law, the requirements of IRC Sec. 6166 are satisfied [see ¶2303], and an election has been properly made.[19] An estimate of the amount of interest payable is not deductible because it may be necessary to accelerate the payment of the tax. Therefore, this interest expense is deductible only when the interest accrues.[20]

The procedure for deducting interest on deferred installments of federal estate tax as an administration expense is set forth in Rev. Proc. 81-27.[21] At or after the time each installment of federal estate tax is paid, an additional estate tax return is filed with the words "Supplemental Information" typed on the top of Page 1. In each supplemental return, the amount of interest actually paid is claimed as an estate tax deduction, thereby reducing the amount of the federal estate tax and the amount of interest payable on it.

Interest incurred as the result of a late payment of the federal estate tax, a state death tax, or a foreign death tax is deductible as an administration expense. However, any penalty for failure to pay or failure to file is not deductible as an administration expense even if it is allowable under local law.[22]

Interest on the recapture tax under the special use valuation provisions [see ¶1908] is not deductible as an administration expense because the tax is imposed on the qualified heir as a result of his or her activity, not in connection with the transfer of estate property.[23]

(f) Deduction for Taxes. When computing a decedent's taxable estate, only certain taxes are deductible. In order for the property taxes to be deductible there must be an enforceable obligation of the decedent to pay them at the time of death [Reg. Sec. 20.2053-6(b)]. Only if the obligation to pay them was fixed prior to the decedent's death may they be deducted.[24] Property taxes that accrue after the decedent's death are not deductible from the decedent's gross estate.

State death tax deduction. A deduction is allowed for state death taxes but not federal or foreign death taxes. However, a credit is allowed for foreign death taxes [see ¶2105]. A deduction is allowable for the Canadian tax on appreciation on deemed disposition at death; but no credit is allowed.

Beginning in 2005, the state death tax credit was replaced by a deduction for state death taxes [IRC Sec. 2058]. Accordingly, for the estates of decedents dying on or after January 1, 2005, the value of a decedent's taxable estate will be determined by deducting from the gross estate the amount of any estate, inheritance, legacy or succession taxes actually paid to any state or the District of Columbia with respect to property included in the decedent's gross estate. A deduction for state taxes is allowed only for taxes actually paid and claimed as a deduction during the time period that ends before the later of:

---

[19] Rev. Rul. 78-125, 1978-1 CB 292; Ltr. Rul. 9123024.

[20] Rev. Rul. 80-250, 1980-2 CB 278.

[21] Rev. Proc. 81-27, 1981-2 CB 548.

[22] Rev. Rul. 81-154, 1981-1 CB 470; *but see* Rev. Rul. 90-8, 1990-1 CB 173, where interest expense was not deductible as administrative expense because not actually and necessarily incurred in the administration of the estate as required under IRC Sec. 2053(a)(2).

[23] Ltr. Rul. 8902002.

[24] Estate of Pardee, 49 TC 140 (1967), *acq.*, 1973-2 CB 3.

1. Four years after the filing of the estate tax return;

2. 60 days after the Tax Court decision becomes final if a timely petition for redetermination of a deficiency has been filed with the Tax Court;

3. The expiration date of the extension period if an extension of time has been granted under IRC Sec. 6161 or IRC Sec. 6166 for payment of the tax; or

4. If a timely claim for refund or credit of an overpayment of tax has been filed, the latest of:

   (a) 60 days after the IRS mails to the taxpayer by certified or registered mail a notice of disallowance of any part of the claim;

   (b) 60 days after a decision by a court of competent jurisdiction becomes final as to a timely suit started upon the claim; or

   (c) Two years after waiver of the notice of disallowance is filed under IRC Sec. 6532(a)(3) [IRC Sec. 2058(b)].

Gift tax deduction. Unpaid gift taxes on gifts made by a decedent before his death, however, are deductible. A deduction is available for excise taxes incurred in selling property of a decedent's estate if the sale is necessary in order to (1) pay the decedent's debts, expenses of administration, or taxes, (2) preserve the estate, or (3) effect distribution. Excise taxes incurred in distributing property of the estate in kind are also deductible.

Unpaid income taxes are deductible if they are on income properly includible in an income tax return of the decedent for a period before his death. Taxes on income received after the decedent's death are not deductible [Reg. Sec. 20.2053-6].

An election may be made to deduct foreign death taxes on a charitable transfer of property situated within a foreign country [IRC Sec. 2053(d); Reg. Sec. 20.2053-10]. The estate may elect to take a deduction for the payment of these taxes rather than the foreign death tax credit. The election must be made before the assessment period expires [Reg. Secs. 20.2053-9(c), 20.2053-10(c)]. An election to take a deduction constitutes a waiver of the right to claim an estate tax credit under any treaty or IRC Secs. 2011 and 2014, with respect to the amount deducted. When the deduction is claimed, the credit for foreign death taxes must be reduced to reflect that a portion of the tax is used as a deduction, not a credit [IRC Sec. 2011(e); Reg. Sec. 20.2011-2].

In a National Office Technical Advice Memorandum,[25] the IRS concluded that an estate could not claim an estate tax deduction under IRC Sec. 2053 for income taxes it paid on amounts the estate was "forced" to withdraw from the decedent's IRAs to pay estate tax because of a cash crunch.

Post-death adjustments of deductible tax liability. Post-death adjustments increasing a tax liability accrued prior to the decedent's death, including increases of taxes will increase the IRC Sec. 2053(a)(3) deduction for that tax liability. Similarly, any refund subsequently determined to be due to and received by the estate with respect to taxes deducted by the estate reduces the amount of the deduction taken for that tax liability under IRC Sec. 2053(a)(3). Expenses associated with defending the estate against the increase in tax liability or with obtaining the refund may also be deductible under Reg. Sec. 20.2053-3(d)(3). A protective claim for refund of estate taxes may

---

[25] Ltr. Rul. 20444021.

be filed before the expiration of the period of limitations for claims for refund in order to preserve the estate's right to claim a refund if the amount of a deductible tax liability may be affected by such an adjustment or refund [Reg. Sec. 20.2053-6(g)].

> **Example 1:** After the decedent's death, the IRS examines the gift tax return filed by the decedent in the year before the decedent's death and asserts a deficiency of $100x. The estate spends $30x in a non-frivolous defense against the increased deficiency. The final determination of the deficiency, in the amount of $90x, is paid by the estate. The estate may deduct $90x under IRC Sec. 2053(a)(3) and $30x under Reg. Sec. 20.2053-3(c)(2) or (d)(3) [Reg. Sec. 20.2053-6(g), ex. 1].

> **Example 2:** Decedent's estate timely files Decedent's individual income tax return for the year in which the decedent died. The estate timely pays the entire amount of the tax due, $50x, as shown on that return. The entire $50x was attributable to income received prior to the decedent's death. Decedent's estate subsequently discovers an error on the income tax return and files a timely claim for refund. Decedent's estate receives a refund of $10x. The estate is only allowed a deduction of $40x under IRC Sec. 2053(a)(3) for the income tax liability accrued prior to the decedent's death. If a deduction for $50x was allowed on the estate tax return prior to the receipt of the refund, it shall be the duty of the executor to notify the IRS of the change and to pay the resulting tax, with interest [Reg. Sec. 20.2053-6(g), ex. 2].

(g) Casualty or Theft Losses. A deduction is allowed for losses from theft and casualties such as fire and storms that are incurred during the administration of the estate. However these losses are allowed only to the extent they are not compensated by insurance or in another manner [IRC Sec. 2054; Reg. Sec. 20.2054-1]. An executor's inability to recover estate taxes from the beneficiary ultimately liable is not considered a loss.[26]

> ▶ **OBSERVATION:** You may waive the right to claim a loss for estate tax purposes if you want to claim the loss in computing the taxable income of the estate for income tax purposes.

(h) Palimony. In *Estate of Shapiro*,[27] the Court of Appeals for the Ninth Circuit reversed a federal district court to conclude that an estate was entitled to an IRC Sec. 2053 estate tax deduction for a palimony claim filed against the estate to the extent that the consideration was adequate and full in money or money's worth.

---

[26] Rev. Rul. 69-411, 1969-2 CB 177.

[27] Estate of Shapiro, 2011-1 USTC ¶ 60,614 (9th Cir. 2011).

¶2002 QUALIFIED FAMILY-OWNED BUSINESS INTEREST DEDUCTION

The qualified family-owned business interest (QFOBI) deduction under IRC Sec. 2057 was permanently repealed as a result of the elimination of the EGTRRA sunset provision by the American Taxpayer Relief Act of 2012. The QFOBI deduction was repealed because it is obsolete in light of the increased applicable exclusion amount allowed and was viewed as a burden to heirs.

Additional tax continues for recapture events. Although the QFOBI deduction was permanently repealed, the recapture tax provisions of IRC Sec. 2057(f)(2) are still applicable if a specified recapture event occurs within the 10-year period following the decedent's death and before the death of the qualified heir. The last day that a decedent's estate was entitled to elect QFOBI treatment was December 31, 2004. Thus, a recapture tax can be imposed until December 31, 2014, if an estate of a decedent dying on or before December 31, 2004, elected QFOBI treatment and a recapture event occurred within that time period.

An additional tax is imposed if any of the following recapture events occurs within 10 years of the decedent's death and before the qualified heir's death: (1) the qualified heir ceases to meet the material participation requirements; (2) the qualified heir disposes of any portion of his or her interest in the family-owned business, other than by a disposition to a member of the qualified heir's family or through a conservation contribution under IRC Sec. 170(h); (3) the principal place of business of the trade or business ceases to be located in the United States; or (4) the qualified heir loses U.S. citizenship. The amount of the tax is based upon when the recapture event occurs in relation to the decedent's death.

If the recapture event occurs within the first six years of material participation, 100 percent of the reduction in estate tax attributable to the heir's interest, plus interest, is recaptured. Thereafter, the applicable percentage is 80 percent in the seventh year, 60 percent in the eighth year, 40 percent in the ninth year and 20 percent in the tenth year. The total amount of tax potentially subject to recapture is the difference between the actual amount of estate tax liability for the estate and the amount of estate tax that would have been owed had the QFOBI deduction not been taken.

¶2003 AFTER-DEATH PLANING STRATEGIES: ESTATE TAX DEDUCTION VS. INCOME TAX DEDUCTION

You may not use amounts allowable as administration expenses or losses during administration of the estate as deductions in computing the taxable income of the estate for income tax purposes unless you waive the deduction for estate tax purposes [IRC Sec. 642(g)]. The total deductions, or the total amount of any deduction, does not have to be treated in the same way. One deduction, or a portion of a deduction, may be allowed for income tax purposes if the waiver is filed and another deduction or portion may be allowed for estate tax purposes [Reg. Sec. 1.642(g)-2].

NOTE: It is generally desirable to take the deductions on whichever return is in the higher tax bracket.

File the waiver, in duplicate, with the estate's income tax return in the year the expenses are claimed on the estate's return for income tax purposes [Reg. Sec. 1.642(g)-1]. This waiver is irrevocable.

The required statement need not be filed with the estate's income tax return but may be filed later at any time prior to the expiration of the statutory period for assessment [IRC Sec. 642(g); Reg. Sec. 1.642(g)-1].

NOTE: By not filing the statement with the estate's income tax return, two or three years are available to the executor to decide how many deductions should be shifted to the income tax returns.

Claiming the deduction on the estate tax return does not prevent the executor from later claiming them on estate income tax returns. Provided a timely filing of the necessary statement is made, the deductions remain viable for income tax purposes as long as they have not been finally allowed for estate tax purposes, which should occur when a prohibition on deductibility exists, for example, by a statute of limitations or closing agreement regarding the estate tax.

Taxes, interest, and business expenses. Taxes, interest, and business expenses accrued at the date of the decedent's death are deductible as claims against the estate on the estate tax return and also as deductions in respect of the decedent on the income tax return of the estate or a beneficiary who received the property subject to these expenses [Reg. Sec. 1.642(g)-2]. However, if these expenses were not accrued at the date of the decedent's death, they are administration expenses and are deductible only on the estate tax return unless you file the waiver under IRC Sec. 642(g), as discussed above.

Funeral expenses, claims against the estate, and federal gift and income taxes owed by the decedent are allowable only as deductions in computing the estate tax.

Medical expenses. If medical expenses are deducted only on the estate tax return, they are fully deductible as claims against the estate. In this case, if a waiver is filed under IRC Sec. 642(g), the expenses may be deducted on the decedent's income tax return for the year incurred. The deduction may be claimed only to the extent that the decedent's total medical deduction exceeds the applicable percentage limitation for the year incurred [IRC Sec. 213(a)].

If part of the medical expenses are deducted on the decedent's income tax return and part deducted on the estate tax return, the part deducted on the estate tax return may not include the amount that is not deductible for income tax purposes because of the percentage limitation.

Example 1: Mom died this year. She incurred $20,000 in medical expenses last year. These were the only medical expenses incurred during the year. Mom's income tax return for last year showed an adjusted gross income of $100,000. The executor paid the $20,000 in medical expenses within one year of Mom's death so they are treated as being paid last year. The executor elected to deduct $5,000 as a claim against the estate and filed an amended income tax return for the following year and attached the necessary waiver indicating that $15,000 had not been and would not be deducted for estate tax purposes. Only $7,500

($15,000 – $7,500 (7.5% × $100,000) is deductible on the decedent's income tax return for the following year. If the executor had deducted all the medical expenses as claims against the estate, $20,000 would be deductible for estate tax purposes.

Selling expenses. Selling expenses cannot be used to offset the sales price of property in determining gain or loss for income tax purposes if they have been deducted for estate tax purposes as an administration expense [IRC Sec. 642(g)]. Thus, the estate must elect to claim selling expenses either as:

1. An estate tax deduction under IRC Sec. 2053; or

2. As an offset against the selling price for purposes of determining gain or loss realized on the disposition of property for income tax purposes.

Alimony payments. The commuted value of alimony payments to be made by the estate is deductible as a claim against the estate if the court that issued the divorce decree had the power to settle all property rights. The alimony payments made by the fiduciary during the administration of the decedent's estate are deductible for income tax purposes. If the court did not have jurisdiction to settle all property rights, the value of the alimony payments would be deductible only to the extent that they do not exceed the reasonable value of the support rights of the ex-spouse.

Deductions in respect of the decedent. Certain payments may be validly claimed as both income *and* estate tax deductions. IRC Sec. 691(b) specifically provides for the deduction by the estate (so-called deductions in respect of the decedent) of various items for which the decedent was liable but which were not deductible on his or her last income tax return. This comes into play where the decedent was a cash method taxpayer for income tax purposes and, prior to his or her death, had accrued liability for certain otherwise deductible items. Thus, business expenses, investment expenses, interest, and taxes that the decedent owed on the date of death are deductible both:

1. As debts for estate tax purposes under IRC Sec. 2053; and

2. On the estate's income tax return because of IRC Sec. 691(b).

To qualify as a deduction in respect of a decedent, the payments must be an item (1) that would have been deductible by the decedent had it been paid, and (2) specified in IRC Sec. 691(b).

> **Example 2:** On July 1, 2014, Mom, a cash method taxpayer, borrows $10,000 and agrees to pay 10 percent simple interest on July 1, 2015. On December 31, 2014, Mom dies. Her estate may deduct $500 for both income and estate tax purposes because that much interest had "accrued" at the date of death as a claim against the estate and also as deductible interest in respect of a decedent.

¶2003

TAX CREDITS

TABLE OF CONTENTS

¶2100 TAX CREDITS

The following tax credits are allowed against the federal estate tax:

- **The credit for federal estate tax paid on prior transfers.** A credit is available for federal estate tax paid on prior transfers to the decedent from a person who died within 10 years before or two years after the decedent [IRC Sec. 2013]. The credit is limited to the lesser of the estate tax attributable to the transferred property in the transferor's estate or the estate tax attributable to the transferred property in the decedent's estate [IRC Sec. 2013]. If the transferor predeceased the decedent by more than two years, the allowable credit is a reduced by 20 percent for each full two-year period by which the death of the transferor preceded the decedent's death. The credit is claimed on Schedule Q on Form 706. See ¶2104;

- **The credit for foreign death taxes.** A credit against estate tax is available for foreign death taxes paid on property located in a foreign country but included in the gross estate of a U.S. citizen or resident [IRC Sec. 2014; see ¶2105]. The credit is limited to the lesser of the foreign or the U.S. tax attributable to the property. If a treaty exists with the foreign country, the credit provided for under the treaty or IRC Sec. 2014 may be used, whichever results in the lower amount of estate tax.The estate must file Form 706-CE, "Certificate of Payment of Foreign Death Tax," to claim the credit;

- **The credit for pre-1977 gifts.** For gifts made before 1977, the gift tax paid on gifts included in the gross estate is a credit to the estate tax. The credit is limited to the lesser of the gift tax paid or the estate tax attributable to inclusion of the gift in the gross estate [IRC Sec. 2012]. See ¶ 2103.

¶2101 UNIFIED CREDIT/APPLICABLE EXCLUSION AMOUNT

The estate and gift tax rates are unified in a single rate schedule effective for the estates of decedents dying, and for gifts made, after December 31, 1976. Lifetime transfers and transfers made at death are cumulated for gift and estate tax purposes.

The estate tax liability is determined by applying the unified rate schedule to the cumulated transfers and subtracting the gift taxes payable. The cumulated transfers to which the tentative tax applies is the sum of (1) the amount of the taxable estate and (2) the amount of the taxable gifts made by the decedent after 1976, other than gifts includible in the gross estate. Gift taxes to be subtracted in computing the estate tax include the aggregate gift tax payable on gifts made after December 31, 1976. For this purpose, the amount of gift taxes paid by a decedent after 1976 is to be determined as if the rate schedule in effect in the year of death was in effect in the year of the gift. However, with respect to certain gifts subsequently included in a decedent's gross estate, a credit is allowed [IRC Sec. 2012] for gift taxes paid on pre-1977 gifts.

Gift tax liability for any calendar quarter (for gifts made after 1970 and before 1982) or year (for gifts made before 1971 and after 1981) is determined by applying the unified rate schedule to cumulative lifetime taxable transfers and subtracting the taxes payable for prior taxable periods. Preceding calendar periods are: (1) calendar year 1932 (after June 6) and 1970 and all intervening calendar years, (2) the first calendar quarter of 1971 and all quarters between that quarter and the first quarter of 1982, and, (3) all calendar years after 1981 and before the year for which the tax is being computed. In computing cumulative taxable gifts for prior taxable periods, the donor's pre-1977 taxable gifts are to be taken into account, with the reduction for taxes previously paid to be based upon the unified rate schedule.

The pre-1977 $60,000 estate tax exemption and the $30,000 lifetime gift tax exemption were replaced in 1977 by a single unified credit that is subtracted after determining the taxpayer's estate or gift tax liability. In effect, the amount of the unified credit available at death will be reduced to the extent that any portion of the credit is used to offset gift taxes on lifetime transfers. Amounts allowed as lifetime exemptions on gifts made after September 8, 1976, but before January 1, 1977, reduce the unified credit allowable by 20 percent of the exemption used, to a maximum of $6,000.

The unified credit, as phased in by the Tax Reform Act of 1976 and the Taxpayer Relief Act of 1997, is as follows for years prior to 2002 (except that only $6,000 of the credit otherwise applicable to gifts made during the first six months of 1977 may actually be applied):

Year	Applicable Credit Amount	Applicable Exclusion Amount
1977	$ 30,000	$ 120,667
1978	34,000	134,000
1979	38,000	147,333

Year	Applicable Credit Amount	Applicable Exclusion Amount
1980	42,500	161,563
1981	47,000	175,625
1982	62,800	225,000
1983	79,300	275,000
1984	96,300	325,000
1985	121,800	400,000
1986	155,800	500,000
1987 through 1997	192,800	600,000
1998	202,050	625,000
1999	211,300	650,000
2000 and 2001	220,550	675,000

Law following EGTRRA. EGTRRA increased the *estate tax* applicable exclusion amount according to the following schedule: $1 million for decedents dying in 2002 and 2003; $1.5 million in 2004 and 2005; $2 million in 2006, 2007 and 2008; and $3.5 million in 2009.

EGTRRA also increased the *gift tax* applicable exclusion amount to $1 million, beginning with gifts made in 2002. However, unlike the gradual increase in the estate tax applicable exclusion amount in the years leading up to repeal of the estate tax, the gift tax applicable exclusion amount remained at $1 million and was not indexed for inflation. The amounts in effect for 2002 and 2003 are as follows:

Year	Applicable Credit Amount	Applicable Exclusion Amount
2002 and 2003	$ 345,800	$ 1,000,000

As a result of EGTRRA, beginning in 2004, the unified credit was no longer truly "unified," as the estate and gift tax applicable exclusion amounts differed. The estate tax applicable exclusion and credit amounts for years after 2003 are as follows:

Year	Applicable Credit Amount	Applicable Exclusion Amount
2004 and 2005	$ 555,800	$ 1,500,000
2006 - 2008	780,800	2,000,000
2009	1,455,800	3,500,000

Law following the Tax Relief Act of 2010. The Tax Relief Act of 2010 reinstated the estate and GST tax for decedents dying and GSTs made after December 31, 2009, and increased the applicable exclusion amount to $5 million for the estates of decedents dying after December 31, 2009. The Tax Relief Act of 2010 also reunified the estate and gift tax applicable exclusion amounts for decedents dying and gifts made after December 31, 2010. For taxable gifts made on or before December 31, 2010, the gift tax applicable exclusion amount is $1 million. In 2011, the estate and gift tax exclusion amounts were $5 million. In 2012, the estate and gift tax applicable exclusion amounts was adjusted for inflation to $5,120,000.

Election for decedents dying in 2010. The executors for estates of decedents dying after December 31, 2009 and before January 1, 2011, could elect to have the EGTRRA rules apply, with the result that such estates were exempt from the estate tax, and the heirs of the estate received a carryover basis (rather than a stepped-up basis) in property received from the decedent.

¶2101

Sunset provision. All transfer tax provisions in the Tax Relief Act of 2010 and EGTRRA were set to expire on the amended sunset date of December 31, 2012, meaning that the transfer tax laws in effect prior to the passage of EGTRRA would be revived in 2013.

Changes made to the law governing federal estate, gift, and GST taxes made by EGTRRA and the Tax Relief Act of 2010 that were set to expire with respect to the estates of decedents dying and gifts and GSTs made after December 31, 2012, by operation of the sunset provision of EGTRRA, were made permanent for estates of decedents dying, gifts made, or generation skipping transfers after December 31, 2012 by the American Taxpayer Relief Act of 2012.

Estate & Gift Applicable Credit and Basic Exclusion Amounts

Year	Applicable Credit Amount	Applicable Exclusion Amount
2011	$ 1,730,800	$ 5,000,000
2012	1,772,800	5,120,000
2013	2,045,800	5,250,000
2014	2,081,800	5,340,000

The unified credit (or applicable credit amount) is the amount that is subtracted from the tentative gift tax in computing the taxpayer's gift tax liability. Use of the credit to offset gift tax liability is mandatory. The credit is statutorily prescribed in IRC Sec. 2505. The amount of the unified credit that is available for gifts made in any one year must be reduced by the sum of the allowable credits in previous calendar periods. However, the allowable credit for any one year cannot exceed the gift tax liability for that calendar period [IRC Sec. 2505(c)].

The unified gift tax credit must be used to reduce a donor's gift tax liability in the gift tax period when the liability occurs. The amount of the gift tax credit that may be subtracted in any given period is computed on Form 709, "United States Gift (and Generation-Skipping Transfer) Tax Return" [see Chapter 17].

Unified credit. The unified credit amount was $192,800 for transfers made after 1986 and before 1998 (see chart, below). A chart indicating the unified credit amount and the "exemption equivalent" for 1977 through 1997 follows.

Unified Credits and "Exemption Equivalents"

Year	Unified Credit	Exemption Equivalent
Jan. 1, 1977 - June 30, 1977	$6,000	
July 1, 1977 - Dec. 31, 1977	30,000	$120,666
1978	34,000	134,000
1979	38,000	147,333
1980	42,500	161,563
1981	47,000	175,225
1982	62,800	225,000
1983	79,300	275,000
1984	96,300	325,000
1985	121,800	400,000
1986	155,800	500,000
1987-1997	192,800	600,000

A special adjustment (transitional) rule applies to gifts made during the period September 9, 1976, through December 31, 1976. To the extent that use was made of the $30,000 lifetime exemption during this period, the allowable unified gift tax credit is reduced by an amount equal to 20 percent of the exemption. Thus, if the full $30,000 exemption was used during this period, a maximum reduction of $6,000 would be made to the unified credit IRC Sec. 2505(b)].

Applicable credit amount. The Taxpayer Relief Act of 1997 replaced the unified credit amount with an applicable credit amount, effective for gifts made (and estates of decedents dying) after December 31, 1997. The table below provides the applicable credit and exclusion amounts for the period from 1998 to 2001:

Applicable Credit and Exclusion Amounts

Year	Applicable Credit	Applicable Exclusion
1998	$ 202,050	$ 625,000
1999	211,300	650,000
2000 and 2001	220,550	675,000

EGTRRA increased the gift tax applicable exclusion amount to $1 million, beginning with gifts made in 2002. EGTRRA also set the estate tax applicable exclusion amount at $1 million for estates of decedents dying in 2002 and 2003. The table below provides the applicable credit and applicable exclusion amounts for years 2002 and 2003:

Applicable Credit and Exclusion Amounts

Year	Applicable Credit	Applicable Exclusion
2002 and 2003	$ 345,800	$ 1,000,000

After 2003, the applicable exclusion amount for estate tax, but not *gift tax*, purposes gradually increases to $3.5 million by 2009. In contrast to the gradual increase in the estate tax applicable exclusion amount, the gift tax applicable exclusion amount remained at $1 million during this time. The table below provides the applicable credit and applicable exclusion amounts, *for gift tax purposes only*, for years 2004 through 2009:

Applicable Credit and Exclusion Amounts (Gift Tax Only)

Year	Applicable Credit	Applicable Exclusion
2004 through 2009	$ 345,800	$ 1,000,000

For years 2002 through 2009, the amount of the gift tax unified credit was equal to (1) the applicable credit amount in effect under IRC Sec. 2010(c) for such calendar year, determined as if the applicable exclusion amount were $1 million, reduced by (2) the sum of the amounts allowable as a credit under IRC Sec. 2505 for all preceding calendar periods [IRC Sec. 2505(a)].

Computation of credit for 2010. The Tax Relief Act of 2010 reunified the estate and gift tax applicable exclusion amounts at $5 million. However, in 2010 the gift tax applicable exclusion amount remained at $1 million with a maximum tax rate of 35 percent. The table below provides the applicable credit and applicable exclusion amounts, *for gift tax purposes only*, for 2010:

Applicable Credit and Exclusion Amounts (Gift Tax Only)

Year	Applicable Credit	Applicable Exclusion
2010	$ 330,800	$ 1,000,000

Gift tax liability for 2010 was determined by using the rate schedule created by the 2010 Act. The credit allowed against the gift tax for such years was equal to (1) the amount of the tentative tax that would be determined under the new gift tax-only rate schedule if the amount with respect to which such tentative tax is to be computed was $1 million, reduced by (2) the sum of the amounts allowable as a credit for all preceding calendar periods, using the rate table in IRC Sec. 2502(a)(2) [IRC Sec. 2505(a), as applicable to gifts made after December 31, 2009, but before January 1, 2011].

After 2010, the estate and gift tax applicable credit amounts were reunified. The table below provides the unified credit amount and the "exemption equivalent" for 2011 through 2014:

Unified Credits and "Exemption Equivalents"

Year	Unified Credit	Exemption Equivalent
2011	$ 1,730,800	$ 5,000,000
2012	1,730,800	5,120,000
2013	2,045,800	5,250,000
2014	2,081,800	5,340,000

For purposes of determining the amount of gift tax that would have been paid on one or more prior year gifts, the estate tax rates in effect under IRC Sec. 2001(c) are used to compute both (1) the gift tax imposed with respect to such gifts, and (2) the applicable credit allowed against such gifts under IRC Sec. 2505 (including the computation of the applicable credit amount under IRC Sec. 2505(a)(1) and the sum of amounts allowed as a credit for all preceding periods under IRC Sec. 2505(a)(2)).

¶2102 REPEAL OF CREDIT FOR STATE DEATH TAXES

The state death tax credit, allowed for estate, inheritance, legacy, or succession taxes paid to any state or the District of Columbia, was permanently repealed for the estates of decedents dying after December 31, 2012 by the American Taxpayer Relief Act of 2012. It was replaced by the state death tax deduction under IRC Sec. 2058 which was made permanent for the estates of decedents dying after December 31, 2012. Thus, the estates of decedents dying after December 31, 2012 will be able to deduct estate, inheritance, legacy, or succession taxes actually paid to any state or the District of Columbia from the value of the gross estate [see ¶2001 for further discussion of the state death tax deduction].

¶2103 PRE-1977 GIFT TAX CREDIT

A credit is allowed towards the payment of the federal estate tax for gift taxes actually paid on gifts made prior to 1977 on property included in the decedent's gross estate [IRC Sec. 2012].

Clarification. No credit is allowed for gift tax paid on gifts made after 1976 because the gift tax payable on post-1976 gifts is automatically reflected in determining the estate tax liability as a result of the unified transfer tax system.

The first requirement for the application of IRC Sec. 2012 is that property on which the federal gift tax was imposed be included in the decedent's gross estate [IRC Sec. 2012(a)]. For example, if the decedent had, in 1975, created an irrevocable trust in which he retained the income for life and gave the remainder to his child, a gift tax was due on the value of the remainder. If he died in 1997, the trust principal would be included in his gross estate under IRC Sec. 2036(a)(1) and his estate would be allowed to take the gift tax paid as a credit against the estate tax generated by the inclusion of the trust principal in his gross estate.

The second requirement for application of the credit is that the gift must have been made before 1977 [IRC Sec. 2012(e)].

> **NOTE:** Gift taxes payable on post-1976 gift that are included in a decedent's gross estate may be subtracted from the tentative estate tax due [IRC Sec. 2001(b)(2)]. This provides the equivalent of a credit for gift taxes on those post-1976 transactions that effectively parallels the operation of IRC Sec. 2012. The credit is limited to the lesser of:
>
> 1. The gift tax paid on the gift that is included in the decedent's gross estate, or
>
> 2. The amount of the estate tax attributable to the inclusion of the gift in the decedent's gross estate [IRC Sec. 2012(a); Reg. Sec. 20.2012-1].

Computational examples of these two limitations are provided in Reg. Secs. 20.2012-1(c) and 20.2012-1(d).

¶2104 CREDIT FOR TAX ON PRIOR TRANSFERS

The estate can claim a credit for federal estate tax paid on property transferred to the decedent by another decedent within ten years before or two years after death [IRC Sec. 2013]. This rule is intended to provide a break because the property was recently taxed in someone else's estate. Thus, if the estate tax marital deduction [see ¶1101] was allowed for the property received from the earlier decedent, the estate does not get the credit. In the case of transfers to a non-U.S. citizen surviving spouse for which the marital deduction was not available [IRC Sec. 2056(d)(1)], the prior transfer tax credit is allowable regardless of the date of death of the first decedent [IRC Sec. 2056(d)(3)]. The Tax Court has held that the IRC Sec. 2013 estate tax credit for tax on a prior transfer was not allowable to either estate of two spouses who were presumed to have died simultaneously in a plane crash because the life estate received by each spouse from the other had a value of zero.[1]

The amount of the credit is the lesser of:

1. The amount of the federal estate tax attributable to the transferred property in the transferor's estate [IRC Sec. 2013(b)], or

2. The amount of the federal estate tax attributable to the transferred property in the decedent's estate [IRC Sec. 2013(c)].

(a) How to Figure the Credit. The credit is calculated in two ways. The lesser of the two is the one allowed. Each imposes a different limit.

First way: The credit cannot exceed the proportion of the transferor's estate tax that the value of the transferred property that you received bore to the total adjusted taxable estate of the transferor [Reg. Sec. 20.2013-2(a)]. The first trial credit is figured by the following formula:

$$\text{Transferor's adjusted federal estate tax} \times \frac{\text{Value of transferred property}}{\text{Transferor's adjusted taxable estate}} = \text{Maximum credit that will be allowed}$$

The numerator of the fraction is the value of the property transferred to the decedent less any applicable death taxes paid there from as a result of the transfer [Reg. Secs. 20.2013-2(a), 20.2013-4(a) and 20.2013-4(b)]. The transferor's adjusted taxable estate, the denominator of the fraction, equals the amount of the transferor's taxable estate decreased by the amount of any death taxes paid with respect to the gross estate (and increased by the $60,000 exemption if the transferor died before 1977). Death taxes are the federal estate tax plus the net amount of all other estate, inheritance, legacy, succession, or similar taxes imposed by and paid to any taxing authority, whether or not within the United States [Reg. Sec. 20.2013-2(c)].

> **NOTE:** If the federal estate tax of the transferor is being paid in installments [see ¶2303], only the amount of the installments actually paid is used in computing the credit for tax on prior transferors for the estate of the transferee. As the transferor's estate makes the installment payments, the first limitation and the amount of the credit increase. The executor of the transferee's estate must file a protective claim for a refund of the entire amount of credit that may be due because of subsequent installment payments. The protective claim must be perfected by filing a claim for refund for the additional credit allowable on the payment of each installment of the transferor's estate tax.

Second way: The credit cannot exceed the proportion of the estate tax that the value of the property received from the transferor bears to the total of your estate. The second trial credit is figured as follows: The net estate tax payable on the estate is figured, without taking any credit for:

---

[1] ¶**2104** Estate of Harrison, 115 TC 161 (2000).

¶**2104**

1. The tax on prior transfers, and

2. Foreign death taxes claimed under the provisions of a death tax convention [Reg. Sec. 20.0-2(b)(5)].

From this figure is subtracted the estate tax that results when your estate is reduced by the value of the property transferred. The difference is the second trial credit [IRC Sec. 2013(c); Reg. Sec. 20.2013-3(a)]. In figuring this trial tax, any charitable deduction must be reduced. The amount is determined by multiplying the full charitable deduction by the ratio that the value of the transferred property bears to your adjusted gross estate (i.e., your gross estate less deductions for expenses and losses)[2] [IRC Sec. 2013(c)(1)(B); Reg. Sec. 20.2013-3(b)].

> ▶ **CAUTION:** The amount determined by comparing the two limitations is not necessarily the allowable credit. This amount is creditable only if the decedent and the transferor die within two years of each other. As discussed below, if the decedent dies more than two years and less than ten years after the transferor's death, then the credit is a percentage of the determined amount.

Tax Court addresses credit for tax on prior transfers. In *Estate of Le Caer*,[3] the Tax Court held that the amount of credit a wife's estate was allowed to claim for the federal estate taxes paid by the husband's estate was subject to the limitations of IRC Sec. 2013(b) and (c). The husband and his wife died within three months of each other. Both estates filed their tax returns and paid their estate taxes. The husband's estate made a QTIP election for one of the trust shares and, three years later, made an additional protective QTIP election. The wife received a life estate in the remaining portion of that share, but the portion purposefully did not qualify for the marital deduction and the husband's estate paid federal and state estate taxes. The wife's estate claimed a credit under IRC Sec. 2013 for estate taxes paid on transfers by the husband's estate. The IRS assessed deficiencies with respect to both estates arguing that the protective QTIP election was invalid and that the credit under IRC Sec. 2013 should be less than that claimed by the wife's estate. The court concluded that in calculating the amount of the husband's taxable estate for purposes of IRC Sec. 2013(b), the taxable estate is not reduced by the applicable exclusion amount. The court also held that the wife's estate could not receive a credit for state taxes paid by the husband's estate because IRC Sec. 2013(b) only allows a credit for federal estate tax paid on the first estate.

(b) Valuation of Transferred Property. In computing the two trial credits, the property transferred to you has the same value as it had in the transferor's estate for estate tax purposes. Specific property does not have to be identified. The value of property received from a transferor is presumed to be contained in your estate. But when the property transferred is encumbered in any way, or when you incur any obligation imposed by the transferor with respect to the property, its value is reduced by an equivalent amount. The value of the transferred property is also reduced by:

1. The amount of any death taxes (federal or state) payable out of the transferred property (or paid by the decedent in connection with it); and

2. The amount of any marital deduction allowed in the transferor's estate if the decedent was the transferor's spouse at the time of the transferor's death [IRC Sec. 2013(d); Reg. Sec. 20.2013-4].

---

[2] Rev. Rul. 61-208, 1961-2 CB 148.   [3] Le Caer, 135 TC 288 (2010).

The property does not need to be identifiable in your estate. Any transfer of a property interest that was included in another's gross estate qualifies [IRC Sec. 2013(e)].

Difficulties arise if the inherited interest is an income interest. Although the income generated by the trust will be included in the decedent's gross estate, the income interest will not be includable because it terminates on the decedent's death [IRC Sec. 2033; see ¶1803]. Nevertheless, a credit may be allowed for the actuarial value of the income interest [Reg. Secs. 20.2013-1(a), 20.2013-4(a) Example (2)]. The credit depends on the possibility of valuing the interest actuarially. The IRS has allowed a credit for a devise of a life estate within the credit period.[4] The IRS has also ruled that an income interest that will terminate on remarriage could be valued for credit purposes.[5] However, if the income interest is not susceptible of valuation, for instance, because the trustee has absolute discretion over the income payments, then no credit is allowed for any amounts that in fact were paid out by the trustee.[6]

(c) Tax Consequences of Certain Real Property. If the transferor's gross estate included certain real property, such as farm property, for which the special case valuation election was made [see ¶1908] and if an additional estate tax was imposed because the property was disposed of or ceased to be used for a qualified use, the additional tax is treated as a federal estate tax payable on the transfer of the decedent's estate and is eligible for credit under IRC Sec. 2013. The value of this property and the amount of the transferor's taxable estate is determined as if the special valuation had not been elected [IRC Sec. 2013(f)].

(d) Amount of Credit Allowed. The credit is allowed in full if you die within two years after the death of the transferor. If you die later than that, the credit is reduced by 20 percent every two years, so that no credit is allowed after the tenth year. The following table shows the percentage of the credit allowed [IRC Sec. 2013(a); Reg. Sec. 20.2013-1(c)].

Time interval between death of present decedent and transferor	Percentage of the full credit allowed against the present decedent's estate tax
0–2 years	100%
3–4 years	80
5–6 years	60
7–8 years	40
9–10 years	20
More than 10 years	0

(e) After-Death Planning Strategy. Before making a estate tax marital deduction QTIP election [see ¶1101] on a decedent's federal estate tax return, you should determine whether it would be more beneficial to forgo the election, incur an estate tax in the estate of the first spouse to die and take the Section 2013 credit in the surviving spouse's estate.

This option should be considered particularly when the surviving spouse is elderly (or in poor health) or where the surviving spouse dies before the federal estate tax

---

[4] Rev. Rul. 59-9, 1959-1 CB 232.   [6] Rev. Rul. 67-53, 1967-1 CB 265.
[5] Rev. Rul. 85-111, 1985-2 CB 196.

return is filed for the first spouse's estate. However, it is important to keep in mind that because the income from the trust will be accumulating in the surviving spouse's estate, there will be some point at which it is no longer beneficial to forgo the QTIP election and take the Sec. 2013 credit.

Because it usually is difficult to determine whether the surviving spouse will die before or after this crossover point, it may be advisable to submit an extension for filing the decedent's federal estate tax return and defer the decision for up to 15 months after the death of the first spouse to die. If the surviving spouse does not die within this period, you must assess the potential benefits of taking the Sec. 2013 credit in view of the surviving spouse's life expectancy.

¶2105 CREDIT FOR FOREIGN DEATH TAXES

The estate of a citizen or resident of the United States is allowed a credit for death tax paid by the decedent's estate to a foreign country or its political subdivision or to a possession of the United States. No credit is allowed for taxes paid for the estate of a person except the decedent [IRC Sec. 2014(a); see ¶2426]. No credit is allowed for interest or penalties relating to foreign death taxes [Reg. Sec. 20.2014-1(a)(1)].

When the credit is allowed. The credit is allowed only for property situated in the foreign country to which the tax is paid and included in the decedent's gross estate. Whether property was actually situated in the foreign country for the purposes of IRC Sec. 2014 is determined by using the rules for determining the situs of property owned by nonresidents who are not citizens of the United States [see ¶1818] [IRC Secs. 2014(a), 2104, and 2105]. For purposes of this credit, each possession of the United States is deemed to be a foreign country [IRC Sec. 2014(g)]. If the tax is imposed by a political subdivision of a foreign country, the credit may be allowed even though the property involved is situated in a political subdivision different from the one imposing the tax [Reg. Sec. 20.2014-1(a)(3)].

Calculating the credit. The credit equals the lesser of one of the following two limitations [IRC Sec. 2014(b)]:

1. *First limitation.* Calculate the amount of the foreign death tax attributable to property situated in the country imposing the tax and included in the decedent's gross estate for federal estate tax purposes. The first limitation on the amount of the credit equals the death tax imposed by the foreign country times a fraction of the tax imposed by the foreign country, without allowance for any credit for federal estate tax. The numerator of the fraction is the value of the property situated in the foreign country subject to the foreign tax and included in the decedent's gross estate for federal estate tax purposes. The denominator of the fraction is the value of all the property subjected to the death taxation in the foreign country [Reg. Sec. 20.2014-2].

2. *Second limitation.* Calculate the amount of the federal estate tax attributable to particular property situated in a foreign country, subject to death tax in that country, and included in the decedent's gross estate for federal estate tax purposes. The second limitation equals the federal estate tax liability (reduced by the unified credit, and any credit for gift tax but not the credit for prior transfers) times a fraction. The numerator of the fraction is the adjusted value of the

property situated in the foreign country, subjected to foreign death tax and included in the decedent's gross estate. The adjusted value of property situated in a foreign country is the value of the property in a foreign country meeting the requirements for the credit less the amount of any allowable charitable and marital deductions attributable to the property. The denominator of the fraction is the value of the gross estate reduced by the total amount allowed as a charitable deduction and as a marital deduction [Reg. Sec. 20.2014-3].

If a foreign death tax paid on property passing to charity is deducted under IRC Sec. 2053(d) [see ¶ 2001], then the value of that property is excluded from the numerator in the computation of both limitations [IRC Sec. 2014(f)].

▶ **OBSERVATION:** Sometimes credit is allowable for tax paid to more than one foreign country. If so, the credits are combined and the total amount is credited against the federal estate tax. The amount allowable is limited to the amount of the federal estate tax attributable to the property involved, determined according to the rules for computing the second limitation [Reg. Sec. 20.2014-4(c)].

NOTE: If a credit is allowable under the IRC or under the provisions of a tax treaty, the credit allowed is the one most beneficial to the estate [Reg. Sec. 20.2014-4(a)(1)].

When the credit must be claimed. The credit for foreign death taxes is limited to those taxes actually paid [Reg. Sec. 20.2014-6]. The requirements pertaining to the proof of the credit are set forth in Reg. Sec. 20.2014-5. The credit is limited to those taxes for which a credit is claimed within the later of:

1. Four years after filing the estate tax return;

2. Before date of the expiration of any extension of time for paying the federal estate tax; or

3. 60 days after a final decision of the Tax Court on a timely filed petition for a determination of a deficiency [IRC Sec. 2014(e); Reg. Sec. 20.2014-6]. If a foreign death tax for which the credit was allowed is refunded, the executor must report the refund to the IRS. No statute of limitations exists on this duty to report and pay the additional estate tax [IRC Sec. 2016].

COMPUTATION OF ESTATE TAX

TABLE OF CONTENTS

¶2200 ESTATE AND GST TAXES

Changes made to the law governing federal estate, gift, and GST taxes made by EGTRRA and the 2010 Tax Relief Act that were set to expire with respect to the estates of decedents dying and gifts and GSTs made after December 31, 2012, by operation of the sunset provision of EGTRRA, were made permanent for estates of decedents dying, gifts made, or generation skipping transfers after December 31, 2012 by the American Taxpayer Relief Act of 2012. However, the maximum transfer tax rate will now be 40 percent, rather than 35 percent, the rate under the 2010 Tax Relief Act.

The table below summarizes the estate, gift and GST taxes in 2013 and 2014:

Summary of Transfer Taxes in 2013 and 2014

- Maximum estate, gift, and GST tax rate: generally 40 percent [IRC Sec. 2001(c)(1)];

- Applicable exclusion amount for estate and gift taxes: $5,250,000 in 2013 and $5,340,000 in 2014 [IRC Sec. 2010];

- Exemption amount for GST tax: $5,250,000 in 2013 and $5,340,000 in 2014 [IRC Sec. 2631];

- Portability of the deceased spousal unused exclusion (DSUE) amount for estate and gift tax purposes is now permanent and available to reduce the estate and gift tax liability of the surviving spouse [IRC Sec. 2010(c)].

¶2201 UNIFIED ESTATE AND GIFT TAX RATES (AFTER 2012)

The basic rate structure that applied to the estates of decedents dying and gifts made during 2010 through 2012 will continue to apply to the estates of decedents dying and gifts made after December 31, 2012, with the exception of the rates applied to taxable estates in excess of $1 million. Accordingly, the maximum tax rate will now be 40 percent [IRC Sec. 2001].

The following chart illustrates the unified estate and gift tax rates in effect after 2012:

Unified Estate and Gift Tax Rates (After 2012)

(A) Amount subject to tax equal to or more than—	(B) Amount subject to tax less than—	(C) Tax on amount in column (A)	(D) Rate of tax on excess over amount in column (A) Percent
	$10,000		18
$10,000	20,000	$1,800	20
20,000	40,000	3,800	22
40,000	60,000	8,200	24
60,000	80,000	13,000	26
80,000	100,000	18,200	28
100,000	150,000	23,800	30
150,000	250,000	38,800	32
250,000	500,000	70,800	34
500,000	750,000	155,800	37
750,000	1,000,000	248,300	39
1,000,000		345,800	40

GST applicable rate matches estate tax rate. The "applicable rate" for GST purposes will be computed based on a maximum estate tax rate of 40 percent for GSTs occurring after December 31, 2012, up from 35 percent as it had been for GSTs occurring in 2011 and 2012 [IRC Sec. 2641]. Every individual is allowed a lifetime GST tax exemption equal to the "basic exclusion amount" in the calendar year of the allocation ($5,340,000 in 2014) [IRC Sec. 2631(a)]. The GST exemption may be allocated by the individual or his or her executor to the transfer of any property if the individual is the transferor [IRC Sec. 2631(a)]. Once made, the allocation of GST exemption is irrevocable [IRC Sec. 2631(b)]. The GST tax is assessed at the highest transfer tax rate in effect in the year of the event that triggered the GST tax. The tax rate is 40 percent in 2014. The tax is assessed in addition to any estate or gift tax that applies to the transfer [For further discussion of the GST tax exemption, see ¶2509].

The following chart illustrates the GST tax exemption amounts in effect from 1999-2014.

¶2201

GST Tax Exemption Amount

For Transfers Made in:	Exemption
1999	1,010,000
2000	1,030,000
2001	1,060,000
2002	1,100,000
2003	1,120,000
2004-2005	1,500,000
2006-2008	2,000,000
2009	3,500,000
2010-2011	5,000,000
2012	5,120,000
2013	5,250,000
2014	5,340,000

¶2202 COMPUTATION OF ESTATE TAX

The following step-by-step approach illustrates the computation of the estate tax under the unified transfer tax system in effect after 2012.

1. Compute the decedent's taxable estate [see ¶1801]. The taxable estate of a U.S. citizen or resident is determined by subtracting from the gross estate certain deductible items. The gross estate includes the value of all property owned in whole or in part by the decedent at the date of the decedent's death, unless the executor elects to exclude certain amounts. The estate of a decedent includes the gift tax paid on transfers made within three years of death, but does not generally include the value of the gift itself [IRC Sec. 2035].

2. Compute the "adjusted taxable gifts." These are the aggregate post-1976 lifetime taxable gifts, other than post-1976 gifts that are includible in the gross estate. The value of a gift is finally determined if the value is (1) reported on a gift tax return [Form 709] and is not challenged by the IRS prior to the expiration of the statute of limitations, (2) determined by the IRS and not challenged by the taxpayer in court, (3) determined by a court, or (4) agreed upon by the taxpayer and the IRS in a settlement.

3. Add the amounts computed in steps (1) and (2).

4. Determine the tentative tax by applying the rates in the unified estate and gift tax rate schedule [see ¶2201] to the total amount arrived at in step (3).

5. Subtract the total gift tax payable on gifts made after 1976 according to the rate schedule in effect in the year of the decedent's death (including the gift tax paid on transfers includible in the gross estate).

6. Subtract the applicable credits as shown in the following chart:

¶2202

Applicable Credit and Exclusion Amounts

For Transfers Made in:	Estates		Gifts	
	Maximum Credit	Exclusion Amount	Maximum Credit	Exclusion Amount
2006-2008	$ 780,800	$ 2,000,000	$ 345,800	$ 1,000,000
2009	1,455,800	3,500,000	345,800	1,000,000
2010	1,730,800*	5,000,000*	330,800	1,000,000
2011	1,730,800**	5,000,000**	1,730,800**	5,000,000**
2012	1,772,800**	5,120,000**	1,772,800**	5,120,000**
2013	2,045,800**	5,250,000**	2,045,800**	5,250,000**
2014	2,081,800**	5,340,000**	2,081,800**	5,340,000**

* Unless executor elected modified carryover basis rules.
** Increased by amount unused by first spouse that is transferred to a surviving spouse, if elected.

¶2203 REDUCED ESTATE TAX RATES

IRC Sec. 2201(b)(2) imposes a reduced estate tax rate on the estates of certain qualified decedents. The reduced estate tax rates have a top marginal rate of 20 percent. Only the following decedents are eligible for the reduced estate tax rate:

- Any U.S. citizen or resident who dies while in the line of duty from wounds, disease or injury suffered while serving in a combat zone in active service of the Armed Forces (as defined in IRC Sec. 112(c)) [IRC Sec. 2201(b)(1)];

- Any specified terrorist victim (as defined in IRC Sec. 692(d)(4)) [IRC Sec. 2201(b)(2)]; and

- Any astronaut whose death occurs in the line of duty [IRC Sec. 2201(b)(3)].

Definition of "specified terrorist victim." A "specified terrorist victim" is any decedent who: (1) dies as a result of the terrorist attacks against the United States on April 19, 1995, or September 11, 2001, or (2) dies as a result of illness incurred from an anthrax attack occurring during the period from September 11, 2001 to December 31, 2001.

Reduced rates unavailable to 9/11 spouse who committed suicide. In *Estate of Kalahasthi*,[1] a wife who committed suicide five weeks after her husband died in the September 11 terrorist attacks was not considered a "specified terrorist victim" for purposes of the reduced estate tax rates under IRC Sec. 2201, which includes any specified terrorist victim as defined in IRC Sec. 692(d)(4). Because it was determined that the reduced estate tax rate was equivalent to a tax deduction, the doctrine of strict construction applied and any ambiguity in the statutory definition of "specified terrorist victim" had to be resolved in favor of the government and against the estate.

---

[1] **¶2203** Estate of Kalahasthi, 2008-2 USTC ¶60,565 (CD Cal. 2008).

Interpreted narrowly, IRC Sec. 692(d)(4) requires that a specified terrorist victim suffer physical injury as a direct result of the terrorist attack. The wife's death neither resulted from a physical injury, nor was it a sufficiently direct result of the attacks to render her a specified terrorist victim.

¶2204 WHY ESTATE TAX MORE EXPENSIVE THAN GIFT TAX

It is cheaper to pay the gift tax than the estate tax because the gift tax is tax-exclusive, which means that the tax bill on the gift must be paid by the gift-giver and is payable out of his or her other property [see ¶1402]. The estate tax, in sharp contrast, is tax-inclusive, which means that the tax is imposed on the transferred property before the tax bill is paid and is payable out of the transferred property so the person inheriting the estate pays the tax and ends up with less money. What is actually happening here is a difference in the gift and estate tax bases. The estate tax base is bigger because it includes the tax or in tax terminology is "tax-inclusive" [IRC Sec. 2001]. The gift tax base is smaller because it excludes the tax or is "tax-exclusive" [IRC Sec. 2501]. This concept is easier to understand after you have read and compared the following examples:

Example 1: Son inherits $1 million. Assume a 50 percent tax rate applies to the transfer. The estate tax bill on the transfer is $500,000. After the estate tax is paid, Son is left with $500,000.

Example 2: Daughter is given a $1,000,000 gift. Assume a 50 percent tax rate applies to the gift. The gift tax of $500,000 must be paid by the person who gave Daughter the gift and she ends up with the full $1 million.

OPTIONS FOR PAYING THE ESTATE TAX

TABLE OF CONTENTS

¶2300 WHEN THE RETURN IS DUE

The executor must pay the estate tax when the estate tax return is due, which is generally nine months after the decedent's death [IRC Secs. 6075(a), 6151(a)]. An extension of time for filing the return does not extend the due date for paying the estate tax. Thus, taxpayers requesting an extension of time to file should accompany the extension request with a payment estimating the amount of estate and GST taxes that are due.

(a) Penalty Imposed for Late Filing. The Tax Code provides for the imposition of a penalty for filing a required tax return after its due date "unless it is shown that such failure is due to reasonable cause and not due to willful neglect" [IRC Sec. 6651(a)(1)]. The taxpayer has the "heavy burden" of proving that he was not willfully neglectful and had reasonable cause to excuse his late filing.[1] The regulations provide that reasonable cause exists where the taxpayer "exercised ordinary business care and prudence and was nevertheless unable to file the return within the prescribed time" [Reg. Sec. 301.6651-1(c)(1); for further discussion of the IRC Sec. 6651 penalty, see ¶809].

(b) Reliance on Tax Professional. A frequent source of litigation has been whether an executor's reliance on a tax professional to timely file the estate tax return constitutes reasonable cause for late filing of the return. The U.S. Supreme Court has said that the delegation of an executor's duty to comply with unambiguous and fixed filing requirements does not relieve the executor of his or her burden to ascertain the relevant filing deadlines and to ensure that they are met.[2] Therefore, if an executor relies on others to comply with these filing requirements, the executor's reliance will typically not constitute reasonable cause for a late filing of the estate tax return. Therefore, executors typically cannot avoid a late filing penalty by arguing that their attorney's mental and physical ailments constituted reasonable cause to excuse the late filing.[3] In *Estate of Liftin*,[4] however, the estate proved that its failure to timely file the estate tax return was due to reasonable cause. The decedent's surviving spouse applied for U.S. citizenship to enable the estate to claim the unlimited marital deduction. An attorney advised the executor that the estate could file the estate tax return after the extended due date and preserve the estate's full marital deduction. The estate tax return was filed almost two years after the extended due date and the IRS imposed a late filing penalty. The court concluded that the estate acted prudently by seeking and relying on the advice of a tax expert.

¶2301 AUTOMATIC EXTENSION

The executor may use Form 4768, "Application for Extension of Time to File a Return and/or Pay U.S. Estate (and Generation-Skipping Transfer) Taxes" to apply for an automatic 6-month extension of time to file the following forms:

- Form 706, "United States Estate (and Generation- Skipping Transfer) Tax Return";

- Form 706-A, "United States Additional Estate Tax Return";

- Form 706-D, "United States Additional Estate Tax Return Under Code Section 2057";

- Form 706-NA, "United States Estate (and Generation-Skipping Transfer) Tax Return, Estate of Nonresident Not a Citizen of the United States";

- Form 706-QDT, "United States Estate Tax Return for Qualified Domestic Trusts."

---

[1] **¶2300** Boyle, 469 U.S. 241 (1985).

[2] Boyle 469 U.S. 241 (1985).

[3] Knappe, 713 F.3d 1164 (9th Cir. 2013); Freeman, Exr., 2012-1 USTC ¶60,636 (D.C. Pa.); Rissman, Exr., 2012-1 USTC ¶60,638 (Fed. Cl.).

[4] Estate of Liftin, 2011-2 USTC ¶60,630 (Fed. Cl.).

In addition, Form 4768 can be used for the following purposes:

- To apply for a discretionary (additional) extension of time to file Form 706 (Part II of Form 4768);
- To apply for a discretionary (for cause) extension of time to file Form 706; or
- To apply for an extension of time to pay estate or generation-skipping taxes.

In accordance with Reg. Sec. 20.6081-1(c) the IRS has the discretion to grant requests for an extension of time with the showing of good cause, even if the request is made after the due date. However, the IRS's decision as to whether to grant an extension of time to file is subject to judicial review.

In *Estate of Proske*,[1] the New Jersey District Court found that the estate demonstrated good and sufficient cause for an extension of time to file the estate tax return and concluded that the IRS had abused its discretion in denying the request. The executor explained that he was unable to meet the original filing deadline because: (a) the amount of estate taxes due could not be ascertained as a result of family tensions; (b) the estate's attorney was missing a material document needed to calculate tax liability; (c) the estate's assets were largely illiquid preventing the taxpayer from paying estimated taxes until after the expiration of the original filing period; (d) there were a number of communications between decedent's widow and the estate regarding her bequest that complicated calculation of the tax liability; and (e) the estate was especially complex. After reviewing these facts, the court concluded that there was no indication of bad faith on the part of the estate and no showing of how the IRS's interests would be prejudiced by granting the extension. Therefore the court concluded that the estate was not liable for penalties and interest resulting from the late filing of the estate tax return.

In *Estate of Cederloff*,[2] the Maryland District Court concluded that the estate was liable for a late-filing penalty because the executor failed to prove that the late filing fell within the reasonable cause exception of IRC Sec. 6651(a)(1). The executor's failure to properly value the estate was not a sufficient justification for the delay. Although an estate tax return cannot be amended after the expiration of the extension, the court noted that Reg. Sec. 20.6081-1(d) states that supplemental information affecting the estate tax liability may be filed after the expiration of the extension period. Therefore, the executor should have filled out the estate tax return using the best information available at the time the return was due (including the six-month extension). The executor's claim of reliance upon the advice of a professional was also disregarded.

In *Baccei*,[3] the Court of Appeals for the Ninth Circuit held that late payment penalties were properly assessed against a decedent's estate because the executor of the estate did not request an extension of time to pay the estate tax. The decedent's executor retained a CPA to prepare the estate's Form 706. The accountant filed Form 4768 but neglected to complete Part III of Form 4768, "Extension of Time to Pay," and no entry was made in the box labeled "Extension date requested." Instead, the accountant attached a letter to Form 4768, which he titled "Request for extension of time to file and pay U.S. Estate Tax." The letter indicated that the estimated tax due could not be paid at that time and requested an extension of time to pay and that no penalty be

---

[1] **¶2301** Estate of Proske, 2010-1 USTC ¶60,594 (D.C. N.J. 2010).

[2] Estate of Cederloff, 2010-2 USTC ¶60,604 (D.C. Md. 2010).

[3] Baccei, 2011-1 USTC ¶60,612 (9th Cir. 2011).

¶2301

asserted against the estate. Six months after the original due date, the estate filed the Form 4768 and paid estate tax. The IRS assessed a late-payment penalty. The appellate court affirmed the decision of the U.S. District Court for the Northern District of California concluding that because the estate paid the tax late without receiving an extension from the IRS to do so, the penalties were properly imposed against the estate. An extension of time to pay could not be inferred from the request because the statutory requirements for an extension and the time allowed to pay the estate tax under Reg. Sec. 20.6161-1(a) differs from the statutory requirements for extensions to file under Reg. Sec. 20.6081(a). Accordingly, the assessment of the late-payment penalty was appropriate.

When asking for an automatic 6-month extension, taxpayers are not required to provide an explanation for the request. Unless the taxpayer is an executor out of the country, the maximum extension of time to file is 6 months from the original due date of the applicable return. Form 4768 must be filed by the original due date of the applicable return. The IRS will use Part B of Form 4768 to notify the executor whether his or her request for an extension of time to pay has been approved or denied, or requires other action.

The executor may also be able to pay the tax in installments if the estate consists of certain kinds of property [see ¶ 2303]. An extension for the payment of the federal estate tax attributable to a reversionary or remainder interest is also available [see ¶ 2304].

¶2302 EXTENSION FOR REASONABLE CAUSE

Deferral of federal estate tax is possible under IRC Sec. 6161, which provides for an extension for the payment of estate tax for 12 months from the date the tax is due [IRC Sec. 6161(a)(1); Reg. Sec. 20.6161-1(a)]. The IRS may also extend the time for payment of the federal estate tax for up to 10 years from the required due date [IRC Sec. 6161(a)(2)].

Either of these extensions are allowed if you can show reasonable cause. When you apply for the extension, you must show why it is impossible or impractical for you to pay the full amount of the estate tax on the due date.

(a) Reasonable Cause. Examples of reasonable cause include [Reg. Sec. 20.6161-1(a)(1)]:

1. Most of the estate's assets consist of rights to receive future payments, such as, accounts receivable, contingent fees, and the estate can not borrow against these assets without causing loss to the estate.

2. The estate includes a claim to substantial assets that cannot be collected without litigation.

3. The executor has made a reasonable effort to convert the decedent's assets (except an interest in a closely held business) to cash. As a result, the estate would be forced to borrow at an interest rate higher than generally available to have sufficient funds to (1) pay the estate tax when due, (2) provide a reasonable allowance for the decedent's surviving spouse and dependent children during

the administration of the estate, or (3) satisfy claims against the estate that are due and payable.

The following examples illustrate cases involving reasonable cause for granting an extension of time as required in Reg. Sec. 20.6161-1(a), examples 1-4:

Example 1: An estate includes sufficient liquid assets to pay the estate tax when otherwise due. The liquid assets, however, are located in several jurisdictions and are not immediately subject to the control of the executor. Consequently, such assets cannot readily be marshalled by the executor, even with the exercise of due diligence.

Example 2: An estate is comprised in substantial part of assets consisting of rights to receive payments in the future (i.e., annuities, copyright royalties, contingent fees, or accounts receivables). These assets provide insufficient present cash with which to pay the estate tax when otherwise due and the estate cannot borrow against these assets except upon terms which would inflict loss upon the estate.

Example 3: An estate includes a claim to substantial assets which cannot be collected without litigation. Consequently, the size of the gross estate is unascertainable as of the time the tax is otherwise due.

Example 4: An estate does not have sufficient funds (without borrowing at a rate of interest higher than that generally available) with which to pay the entire estate tax when otherwise due, to provide a reasonable allowance during the remaining period of administration of the estate for the decedent's widow and dependent children, and to satisfy claims against the estate that are due and payable. Furthermore, the executor has made a reasonable effort to convert assets in his possession (other than an interest in a closely held business to which IRC Sec. 6166 applies) into cash.

(b) Form to Use. Taxpayers should file Form 4768 to request an automatic six-month extension of time to pay the full amount of the estate or GST tax. The request should be filed by the original due date of the return under IRC Sec. 6161 [see ¶ 2303].

Executors should pay as much of the tax as possible by the original (not extended) due date of the return. Interest will be charged by the IRS on any estate and GST tax that is not paid in full by the original due date of the tax return. Payment should accompany Form 4768.

¶2303 DEFERRAL OF ESTATE TAX UNDER IRC SECTION 6166

Normally, any estate tax that is due must be paid within nine months after the date of the decedent's death. An executor may, however, elect to pay the estate tax attributable to a decedent's closely held business interest in 2 or more (but not exceeding 10) equal annual installments starting no later than five years after the regular due date for payment if: (1) a closely held business interest is included in the gross estate of a decedent who was a U.S. citizen or resident at the time of his death; and (2) the value of the business interest exceeds 35 percent of the decedent's gross estate [IRC Sec. 6166].[1] The maximum payment period is 14 rather than 15 years because the due date for the last payment of interest coincides with the due date for the first installment of tax. See line 3 of Part 3 of IRS Form 706 as discussed in ¶ 2409.

If the executor takes advantage of the deferral provision, the payment of that portion of the decedent's estate attributable to the estate's interest in one or more closely held businesses may be deferred for up to 14 years with the estate making annual payments of interest only for the first four years and paying the balance in 10 equal annual installments. The deferral period is 14 years rather than 15 years because the due date for the last payment of interest coincides with the due date for the first installment of tax.

(a) Purpose of Deferral. Congress enacted IRC Section 6166 to permit the deferral of the payment of federal estate tax when it would be necessary to sell the assets used in an on-going business to pay the estate tax at one time. The purpose of the deferral is to prevent a family-owned business from having to sell the business in order to raise the money required to pay the estate tax owed on that business. As a result of the deferral, family members have more time to save up the money from the profits generated by the family business to pay the estate tax. Deferral of tax is only available for the portion of the estate taxes attributable to closely held interests in an active trade or business owned by the decedent at the time of death.

The amount of estate tax attributable to the closely held business interest is determined by multiplying the tax imposed minus credits) by a fraction the numerator of which is the value of the closely held business interest included in the gross estate and the denominator of which is the value of the gross estate (reduced by expenses and losses) [IRC Sec. 6166(a)(2)].

Interest on deferral. A two-percent interest rate is imposed on the amount of deferred estate tax attributable to a farm or closely held business interest worth up to $1,450,000 (in 2014) [IRC Sec. 6601(j)(2)]. Forty-five percent of the underpayment rate of interest, as determined under IRC Sec. 6621, applies to the deferred estate tax attributable to the value of closely held business property that exceeds $1,450,000 in 2014 (up from $1,430,000 in 2013). The special two-percent interest rate is not available with respect to deferred estate tax payments on certain holding company stock and other non-readily-tradable business assets [IRC Sec. 6166(b)(7)(A)(iii) and IRC Sec. 6166(b)(8)(A)(iii)]. In these cases, the applicable interest rate is forty-five percent of the rate for underpayments of tax. No deduction is allowed for interest payments in this situation.

(b) Requirements. To qualify for the installment payment election, the following requirements must be satisfied:

---

[1] **¶ 2303** IRS Instructions for Form 706 United States Estate (and Generation-Skipping Transfer) Tax Return, p. 12.

¶2303

1. The decedent must have been a citizen or resident of the United States at the time of death;

2. The value included in the decedent's gross estate for either (i) "an interest in a closely held business"[2] or (ii) interests in two or more closely held businesses that are treated as an interest in a single closely held business exceeds 35 percent of the adjusted gross estate; and

3. The executor must elect to pay the estate tax attributable to the closely held business interest in two or more (but not more than 10) equal installments [IRC Sec. 6166(a)(1)].

For these purposes, the decedent's adjusted gross estate equals the value of the gross estate less expenses, indebtedness, taxes, and losses [see ¶ 2001].

If the decedent held interests in two or more closely held businesses, the interests are combined and are treated as an interest in one closely held business for purposes of the 35 percent test, if at least 20 percent or more of the total value of each business is included in the decedent's gross estate. Aggregation is available with respect to different types of interests in closely held businesses (e.g., a corporation and a partnership). The interest of the decedent's spouse is treated as owned by the decedent in satisfying the 20 percent requirement if the decedent and surviving spouse held the interests as community property, joint tenants, tenants by the entireties, or tenants in common [IRC Sec. 6166(c)].

Security requirement. In Notice 2007-90,[3] the IRS announced a change in its policy and provided interim guidance for estates making an election to pay all or part of the estate tax in installments. In order to protect the government's interest in the deferred estate tax, the IRS had required that when making an IRC Sec. 6166 election an estate must post a surety bond or grant the IRS an IRC Sec. 6324A special extended tax lien.

However, the Tax Court in *Estate of Roski*,[4] determined that the IRS had abused its discretion by requiring that every estate provide a bond or special tax lien in order to qualify for the IRC Sec. 6166 election. The court found that it was Congress's intent that the IRS would evaluate on a case-by-case basis whether the bond or special tax lien requirements were necessary. Until the IRS and the Treasury Department establish criteria to identify the estates that are at risk of not making the deferred payments, the IRS will consider the following non-exclusive factors: (1) the duration and stability of the closely held business on which the estate tax is deferred; (2) the estate's ability to timely pay installments of tax and interest; and (3) the estate's compliance history.

Notice 2007-90 applies to each estate (1) that timely elects to pay the estate tax in installments and timely files a return on or after November 13, 2007; (2) whose return was being classified, surveyed or audited by the IRS as of April 12, 2007; or (3) there is a reasonable belief that the collection of the tax and interest is sufficiently at risk to require a bond or special tax lien.

(c) Valuation. The value used for determining the gross estate is the value you must use in meeting the percentage requirements of purposes of qualifying to pay the

---

[2] Chief Counsel Advice 201302037.

[3] Notice 2007-90, 2007-2 CB 1003.

[4] Estate of Roski, 128 TC 113 (2007).

estate tax in installments [IRC Sec. 6166(b)(4)]. Thus, if the estate is valued at the alternate valuation date [see ¶ 1907] or under special use valuation method [see ¶ 1908], you must use this valuation to meet the percentage requirements.

(d) Transfers Before Death. In calculating the 35 percent requirement, the estate must include in the gross estate any gifts made by the decedent within three years of death [IRC Sec. 2035(d)(4)].

> **Example 1:** Mom made a $75,000 taxable gift within three years of death. If the value of her interest in a closely held business equals $130,000 and the value of her adjusted gross estate (including the value of the gift) equals $400,000, because the value of her business interest equals 32.5 percent of her adjusted gross estate, her estate cannot pay the estate tax in installments under Sec. 6166.

(e) Interests in Closely Held Businesses. IRC Section 6166 was enacted to permit the deferral of the payment of federal estate tax when it would be necessary to sell assets used in an on-going business (and thereby disrupt or destroy the business enterprise) to pay the estate tax at one time. The section was intended to permit deferral of tax on income-producing assets only where the assets formed a part of an interest in closely held active trade or business producing business income rather than income generated solely from the ownership of investment property [IRC Sec. 6166(a)(1)]. It is the level of activity that distinguishes an active trade or business from passively owning or managing investment property. In determining the level of business activity carried on by a corporation, the activities of its agents and/or employees are taken into account. The activities of independent contractors or lessees, however, are not taken into account.

An "interest in a closely held business" is defined for purposes of the extension and deferral of estate tax payments under IRC Sec. 6166 as:

1. A sole proprietorship;

2. A partnership interest, if at least 20 percent of the assets are included in the decedent's gross estate, or the partnership had no more than 45 partners [IRC Sec. 6166(b)(1)(B)(ii)]; or

3. Stock in a corporation, if least 20 percent or more of the voting stock is included in determining the decedent's gross estate or the corporation had no more than 45 shareholders [IRC Sec. 6166(b)(1)(C)(ii)].

In order to qualify for the deferral, the interest in the closely held business must be carried on by the decedent at the time of his or her death [IRC Sec. 6166(b)(2)(A)]. The maximum allowable number of partners or shareholders in a closely held business owned by a decedent at the time of his or her death will remain at 45 for the estates of decedents dying after December 31, 2012.

An interest in a closely held active trade or business for these purposes includes the following:

- *Interests in qualified lending and finance business interests.* For purposes of qualifying for an estate tax deferral, an executor may elect to treat any asset used in a "qualifying lending and finance business" as an asset which is used in carrying on a trade or business. In order to be considered a qualifying lending and finance business, the entity must have:

— Conducted substantial activity relating to the lending and finance business immediately prior to the decedent's death; or

— Employed at least one full-time manager and 10 full-time, non-owner employees during at least three of the five tax years prior to the decedent's death; and

— Earned at least $5 million in gross receipts from lending and finance activities [IRC Sec. 6166(b)(10)(B)(i)].[5]

In addition the term "lending and finance business" is defined as a business that is involved in:

1. Making loans;

2. Purchasing or discounting accounts receivable, notes or installment obligations;

3. Renting and leasing real estate and tangible personal property; and

4. Rendering services or making facilities available in the ordinary course of a lending or financing business.

The term also includes providing services or making facilities available in connection with the activities that are listed in (1) through (4) above that are carried on by a corporation rendering such services or making facilities available, or another corporation that is a member of an affiliated group, as defined in IRC Sec. 1504 (without regard to IRC Sec. 1504(b)(3)) [IRC Sec. 6166(b)(10)(B)(ii)]. However, the definition of a qualified lending and finance business does not include an interest in an entity if the stock or debt of that entity was readily tradable on an established securities market or secondary market at any time during the three years preceding the decedent's death [IRC Sec. 6166(b)(10)(B)(ii)].

The rule in IRC Sec. 6166(b)(10) that permits a decedent's estate to pay estate tax in installments with respect to interests attributable to businesses that are engaged in lending and finance activities has been permanently extended to apply to the estates of decedents dying after December 31, 2012. Thus, such stock held by the estate of a decedent who dies after December 31, 2012, will not be treated as a passive asset that does not qualify for inclusion in the property used to compute the percentage threshold necessary to satisfy the requirements for the election to pay estate taxes in installments.

Attribution rules. For purposes of determining whether a business is closely held, the following attribution rules apply:

• In determining the number of shareholders or partners, a stock or partnership interest is treated as owned by one shareholder or partner if it is: (1) community property, or (2) held by spouses as joint tenants, tenants by the entirety, or tenants in common [IRC Sec. 6166(b)(2)(B)].

---

[5] Ltr. Rul. 201343004 (leasing and management company qualified for IRC Sec. 6166 tax deferral).

- Property owned, directly or indirectly, by or for a corporation, partnership, estate, or trust is treated as owned proportionately by or for its shareholders, partners, or beneficiaries.

- A person will only be treated as a beneficiary of a trust if the person has a present interest in the trust [IRC Sec. 6166(b)(2)(C)].

- All stock and all partnership interests held by the decedent or by any member of his family will be treated as owned by the decedent [IRC Sec. 6166(b)(2)(D)]. Members of the decedent's family include his siblings, spouse, ancestors, and lineal descendants [IRC Sec. 267(c)(4)].

- For purposes of the 35 percent requirement, the interest in a closely held farm business includes an interest in the residential buildings and related improvements occupied on a regular basis by the owners, lessees, and employees operating or maintaining the farm [IRC Sec. 6166(b)(3)].

(f) Holding Company Stock. Under a special rule, an executor may elect to treat the portion of any holding company stock as an interest in a closely held business.[6] To gain this special treatment, the executor must elect to treat the portion of holding company stock representing direct ownership (or indirect ownership through one or more holding companies) by that company in a business company as business company stock [IRC Sec. 6166(b)(8)]. A holding company is defined as a corporation holding shares in another corporation. A business company is a corporation carrying on an active trade or business. In order to qualify for the deferral election under IRC Sec. 6166, the holding company must satisfy the same requirements that apply to elections made for closely-held business interests. Those requirements are:

- the corporation must have 45 shareholders or fewer; or

- at least 20 percent of the corporation's voting stock must be included in the decedent's gross estate [IRC Sec. 6166(b)(1)(C)].

In addition to the items listed above, the value of the business interest held by the holding company must exceed 35 percent of the value of the decedent's adjusted gross estate [IRC Sec. 6166(a)(1)]. The election to defer payments applies to stock that is "non-readily tradable," meaning there was no market for the stock, either on a stock exchange or over-the-counter, at the time of the decedent's death. In order to qualify for the election, only the stock of the holding company must be non-readily tradable, not the stock of the operating subsidiary [IRC Sec. 6166(b)(8)(B)].

The rule under IRC Sec. 6166(b)(8)(B) exempting the stock of operating subsidiaries of a holding company from the requirement that stock in a holding company must be non-readily tradable to qualify for purposes of the installment payment rules has been made permanent for estates of decedents dying after December 31, 2012, as a result of the elimination of the sunset provision of EGTRRA by the American Taxpayer Relief Act of 2012.

---

[6] IRS Instructions for Form 706, "United States Estate (and Generation-Skipping Transfer) Tax Return," pp. 10–11.

¶2303

(g) Deferral Unavailable for Passive Assets. The estate tax deferral under IRC Sec. 6166 is unavailable for closely held business interests attributable to passive assets held by the decedent [IRC Sec. 6166(b)(9)]. Thus, the estate tax deferral under IRC Sec. 6166 is only available for interests held by the decedent in an active trade or business and the decedent's mere ownership of passive investment property such as real estate will not count in determining: (1) the value of the closely held business, and (2) whether the 35 percent requirement is satisfied for purposes of qualifying for the IRC Sec. 6166 deferral [IRC Sec. 6166(b)(9)].

The term "passive asset" is defined in Code Sec. 6166(b)(9)(B)(i) as any asset other than an asset used in carrying on a trade or business. Thus, the estate tax deferral under Code Sec. 6166 is only available for interests held by the decedent in an active trade or business and the decedent's ownership of passive investment property such as real estate may not constitute ownership of a qualifying interest in a closely-held business.

Active trade or business requirement. In order for an interest in a business to qualify as an interest in a closely-held business under IRC Sec. 6166, a decedent must conduct an active trade or business, or must hold an interest in a partnership, LLC, or corporation that itself carries on an active trade or business as distinguished from the mere management of investment assets. To determine whether a decedent's interest in real property is an interest in an asset used in an active trade or business, the IRS will consider all the facts and circumstances, including the activities of agents and employees, the activities of management companies or other third parties, and the decedent's ownership interest in any management company or other third party.

When real estate interests qualify for deferral. A frequently contested issue between the IRS and taxpayers has been determining whether a decedent's real estate investments constitute an interest in an active trade or business for purposes of the estate tax deferral. After a series of rulings where the IRS concluded that the decedents' interest in real estate did not constitute an interest in a closely-held business because the decedents' interest represented a mere investment, in Rev. Rul. 2006-34,[7] the IRS provided taxpayers with a list of six factors (listed below) that the IRS will consider in determining whether a decedent's interest in real estate is an interest in an active trade or business so as to constitute an interest in a closely-held business for purposes of an estate tax deferral under IRC Sec. 6166.

Factors indicating real estate is active trade or business. The IRS will consider the following nonexclusive six factors in determining whether a decedent's interest in real property is an interest in an active trade or business:

1. The amount of time the decedent devoted to the trade or business;

2. Whether an office was maintained from which the activities of the decedent, partnership, LLC, or corporation were conducted or coordinated, and whether the decedent maintained regular business hours for that purpose;

---

[7] Rev. Rul. 2006-34, 2006-1 CB 1171. See Ltr. Rul. 201343004.

3. The extent to which the decedent was actively involved in finding new tenants and negotiating and executing new leases;

4. The extent to which the decedent provided landscaping, grounds care, or other services beyond the mere furnishing of leased premises;

5. The extent to which the decedent personally made, arranged for, performed, or supervised repairs and maintenance to the property (whether or not performed by independent contractors), including, without limitation, painting, carpentry, and plumbing; and

6. The extent to which the decedent handled tenant repair requests and complaints.

In each situation, the real property interests are included in the decedent's gross estate if they aggregate in value more than 35 percent of the decedent's adjusted gross estate within the meaning of IRC Sec. 6166(b)(6).

> **Example 2:** At the time of A's death, he owned a ten store strip mall titled in A's name. A personally handled the day-to-day operation, management and maintenance of the mall as well as most repairs. When unable to personally perform a repair, he hired a third-party independent contractor and reviewed and approved the work performed. A's activities went beyond those of a mere investor collecting profits from a passive asset. Moreover, even in situations in which A hired independent contractors to perform repairs that A could not perform personally, A was involved in the selection of the contractors and reviewed and approved the work performed. Under these circumstances, the use of independent contractors on occasions when A could not personally perform the work does not prevent A's activities from rising to the level of the conduct of an active trade or business. Thus, A's ownership of the strip mall qualifies as an interest in a closely-held business.

> **Example 3:** At the time of death, B owned a small office park titled in his name. The office park consisted of five separate two-story buildings, each of which had multiple tenants. B hired a property management company in which B had no ownership interest, to lease, manage, and maintain the office park, and B relied entirely on the company to provide all necessary services. The company provided a monthly accounting statement to B, along with a check for the rental income, net of expenses and fees. In this situation, B was not a proprietor in an active trade or business and B's interest in the office park does not qualify as an interest in a closely-held business because B relied on the management company to perform all necessary services.

> **Example 4:** Same as example above, except that B owned 20 percent in value of the stock of the management company. The management company provided all necessary services with regard to the management and maintenance of the office park, including advertising to attract new tenants, showing the property to prospective tenants, negotiating and administering leases, collecting the monthly rent, and arranging for third party independent contractors to provide all necessary services to maintain the buildings and grounds of the office park,

including snow removal, security, and janitorial services. These activities are sufficient to conclude that the management company was actively managing the office park. Because B owned a significant interest in the management company, the activities of the company with regard to the office park allow B's interest in the office park to qualify as an interest in a closely-held business.

Grouping assets together to satisfy threshold. Grouping together several passive real estate investments, all of which are income-producing assets, will not overcome the fact that the assets are passive in nature and fail to qualify for the estate tax deferral. For example, in Rev. Rul. 75-365,[8] a decedent individually maintained a fully equipped business office to collect rental payments on commercial and farm rental properties, receive payments on notes receivable, negotiate leases, make occasional loans, and direct the maintenance of the properties by contract. The IRS concluded that the decedent was merely an owner managing investment assets to obtain the income ordinarily expected from them, rather than conducting an active business. Therefore, the commercial and farm rental properties and notes receivable included in the decedent's gross estate did not constitute an interest in a closely-held business for purposes of claiming an estate tax deferral.

In several other rulings involving whether a decedent's real estate investments constituted an active trade or business, the IRS concluded that the level of activity that is required to qualify for the estate tax deferral existed. Taxpayers who own substantial closely held real estate investments should compare their activities to those in the situations considered by the IRS to make sure they would qualify for the deferral.

In Rev. Rul. 75-366,[9] the IRS found that the decedent's activities qualified as an active trade or business under IRC Sec. 6166 where the decedent owned and leased a farm to tenant farmers. The decedent paid 40 percent of the expenses, received 40 percent of the crops, made almost daily visits to inspect the property and discuss operations with the tenant, occasionally delivered supplies to the tenants, and actively participated in the important management decisions of the farm.

Similarly, in Rev. Rul. 75-367,[10] a decedent's ownership of a corporation that built homes constituted the active conduct of a trade or business. The decedent owned the land on which the houses were built and owned a business office and warehouses that were used by both the corporation and the decedent in the home-building activities. However, the decedent's ownership and rental of eight houses were considered merely the management of investment assets and failed to qualify as an active trade or business for purposes of the estate tax deferral.

In Letter Ruling 200340012, a decedent's interests in real estate qualified as closely held business interests for purposes of the estate tax deferral. The decedent, assisted by his son and five part-time employees, actively participated in the management, operation, and maintenance of the properties. The decedent's level of activity in connection with the properties went beyond that of an owner merely managing investment assets to obtain the rents ordinarily expected in the course of business. Consequently, the decedent's interests in the properties qualified as closely held business interests. In

---

[8] Rev. Rul. 75-365, 1975-2 CB 471.   [10] Rev. Rul. 75-367, 1975-2 CB 472.

[9] Rev. Rul. 75-366, 1975-2 CB 472.

addition, the decedent's interests as a proprietor in six of the properties and as a partner in partnerships that owned two other properties were treated as an interest in a single closely held business. Accordingly, the federal estate tax attributable to the decedent's interest in the closely held business was payable in installments under IRC Sec. 6166.

In Letter Ruling 200339043, the decedent owned through a revocable trust, all the stock of two S corporations that owned a commercial shopping center, an office building complex, three buildings used in research and development, two separate two-store office buildings, and a mountain top radio transmission site containing three buildings with attached radio towers. The corporations had ten full-time employees who conducted, on a day-to-day basis all aspects of their real estate business. The IRS measured the decedent's level of business involvement by examining the activities of agents and employees (not independent contractors or lessees) and determined that the activities regarding most of the properties constituted an active trade or business. The fact that one property was held as a passive assets, however did not render the overall activity passive under IRC Sec. 6166.

Ownership of shares in another corporation will constitute a passive asset and fail to constitute an active business interest unless:

1. The stock is treated as held by the decedent because of the election to treat holding company stock as business company stock, as discussed above; and

2. The stock qualifies under the 35 percent percentage requirement [IRC Sec. 6166(b)(9)(B)(ii)]. However, if a corporation owns at least 20 percent in value of the voting shares of another corporation (or the other corporation had no more than 45 shareholders) and at least 80 percent of the value of the assets of each of these corporations is attributable to assets used in carrying on a business, then these corporations are treated as one corporation and the stock held is not treated as a passive asset [IRC Sec. 6166(b)(9)(B)(iii)]. Shares held in the other corporation are not taken into account in determining the 80 percent requirement. In other words, by meeting these requirements, the parent corporation's stock is not treated as holding company stock but rather as shares of a corporation actively engaged in a business and will qualify for the estate tax deferral.

(h) Time for Payment. Under the deferral method, the executor may elect to defer the payment of the estate tax attributed to the ratio of:

1. The value of the closely held business to

2. The decedent's gross estate [IRC Sec. 6166(a)(2)].

The deferral of the estate tax (not the interest) is for up to five years from the original payment due date [IRC Sec. 6166(a)(3)].

After the first installment of the estate tax is paid, the executor must pay the remaining installments annually by the date one year after the due date of the preceding installment payment. There can be not more than 10 equal installment payments [IRC Secs. 6166(a)(1), 6166(a)(3)].

(i) Interest Not Deductible. Interest on the unpaid portion of the tax is not deferred and must be paid annually. Interest must be paid at the same time and as a part of each installment payment of the tax. No estate tax administration expense deduction

¶2303

is allowed for any interest payment on any unpaid portion of the estate tax for the period during which an extension of time for payment of the tax is in effect under IRC Sec. 6166 [IRC Sec. 2053(c)(1)(D)]. This provision eliminates the need to file supplemental estate tax returns and make complex computations to claim an estate tax deduction for interest paid.

> **NOTE:** No income tax deduction is allowable for any interest payable on any unpaid portion of the estate tax for the period during which an extension of time for payment of the tax is in effect under IRC Sec. 6166 [IRC Sec. 163(k)]. In CCA 200836027, the IRS concluded that estate tax interest payable due to an IRC Sec. 6166 deferral is not deductible for income tax purposes under IRC Sec. 163.

(j) Interest Computation. Under IRC Sec. 6601(j), the maximum amount of the estate tax that may be subject to the lower two-percent interest rate is the lesser of:

1. Estate tax owed on $1,450,000 in 2014 (increased from $1,430,000 in 2013); or

2. The amount of the estate tax that is attributable to the closely held business and that is payable in installments.

If you elect installment payments and the estate tax due is more than the maximum amount to which the 2 percent interest rate applies, each installment payment is deemed to comprise both tax subject to the 2 percent interest rate and tax subject to the regular interest rate that equals the short-term federal rate plus three points, compounded daily [IRC Secs. 6621, 6622]. The percentage of any installment subject to the 2 percent rate is the same percentage of the total tax payable in installments that is subject to the 2 percent rate.

(k) Acceleration of Payments. Under IRC Sec. 6166(g), the estate tax deferral is generally terminated if [IRC Sec. 6166(g)]:

1. The executor fails to pay an installment of principal or interest by the due date of any installment [IRC Sec. 6166(g)(3)];[11] or

2. 50 percent or more of the value of the decedent's interest in the closely held business is redeemed, sold, exchanged or otherwise disposed of or if money and other property attributable to that interest is withdrawn from the business. However, a disposition does not include the transfer of an interest because of the death of the original transferee, or a subsequent transferee, if it is transferred to a family member of the last transferor [IRC Sec. 6166(g)(1)(D)]. For example, if an interest for which an election had been made was inherited by a son and that son died, the transfer to a member of that son's family is not considered a disposition.

> ▶ **OBSERVATION:** A qualified redemption of stock under IRC Sec. 303 to pay death taxes, funeral costs, and administrative expenses is not considered a distribution or withdrawal for purposes of accelerating payments, but the value of the interest in the closely held business is reduced by the value of the stock redeemed [IRC Sec. 6166(g)(1)(B)].

The acceleration rules apply in the cases of the disposition of any interest in holding company stock, or any withdrawal of money or other property from the holding

---

[11] Estate of Ardell, TC Memo 2013-228 (estate tax deferral under IRC Sec. 6166 terminated for missed installment payments of interest).

company, if the election to treat holding company stock as business company stock had been made. If the election was made, the acceleration rules apply to any disposition of the business company stock by the holding company, or any withdrawal of any money or other property from the business company attributable to its stock by the holding company owning that stock [IRC Secs. 6166(g)(1)(E) and 6166(g)(1)(F)].

(l) Time and Manner of Election. The decedent's executor makes the election by attaching a Notice of Election to a timely filed estate tax return on IRS Form 706 (including extensions) [IRC Sec. 6166(d)]. The notice must contain the following information [Reg. Secs. 20.6166-1(b) and 20.6166-1(d)]:

1. The decedent's name and taxpayer identification number as they appear on the estate tax return;

2. The total amount of tax to be paid in installments;

3. The date elected for paying the first installment;

4. The number of annual installments, including the first installment, in which the tax is to be paid;

5. The properties shown on the estate tax return that make up the closely held business interest (identified by schedule and item number); and

6. Why the estate qualifies for installment payments.

If information for items 2, 3, and 4 is not included, the election is presumed to be for the maximum amount payable in installments and must be made in 10 equal installments, the first payment of which is due five years after the due date for paying the estate tax.

In *Estate of Woodbury*,[12] the Tax Court held that an estate was not entitled to pay its estate tax in installments because it failed to make a timely IRC Sec. 6166 election. The executor of the estate requested an extension of time to file the estate tax return and included a letter with the form expressing the estate's intent to make the installment payment election. A second request for an extension of time and similar letter were filed with the IRS. In its letters the estate did not specify the properties that constituted closely held business interests. Nearly three years after the original due date, the executor filed Form 706 and made the election to pay the estate tax in installments. The election was denied as untimely for failure to comply with Reg. Sec. 20.6166-1(b) which provides that a valid notice of election should include, among other items, the properties reported on the estate tax return that constitute the closely held business interest and the facts on which the executor relied to conclude that the estate qualifies for the installment payment election. The court found that the estate failed to identify the properties that constituted closely held business interests in the letters accompanying the requests for extensions of time to file and did not identify those properties until it filed the estate tax return. The court found that the executor did not provide a statement of the facts that formed the basis for the conclusion that the estate qualified for the election. Because of the threshold requirements of the election, the identity of the properties and the executor's statement were critical for both the executor and the government to determine if the estate qualified for the

---

[12] Estate of Woodbury, TC Memo 2014-66.

¶2303

election. The court found that the estate failed to provide essential information regarding the estate's closely held business interests.

The IRS can require the estate to post a bond in an amount up to double the amount of the tax deferred as additional security for the payment of the deferred obligation [IRC Sec. 6165]. An executor may elect a lien in favor of the United States [IRC Sec. 6324A] in lieu of the bond under IRC Sec. 6165. The executor makes such an election by filing a notice of election with the IRS office where the estate tax return is to be filed prior to the payment of the full amount of the deferred estate tax and any interest due plus any additions to tax, assessable penalties, and costs attributable to the deferred amount. The notice must be filed with a written agreement describing the property subject to the lien and signed by all persons with an interest in the property. The maximum value of the property that the IRS may require as lien property cannot exceed the sum of the amount of taxes deferred and the aggregate required interest amount [IRC Sec. 6324A].

(m) Protective Election. The decedent's executor may make a protective election to defer payment of any part of the estate tax that is still unpaid when the values are finally determined (or agreed to, following an examination of the return). This protective election also covers any deficiencies attributable to the closely held business interest [Reg. Sec. 20.6166-1(d)].[13] Extension of tax payments under this election depends on whether the final values meet the requirements for deferral under IRC Sec. 6166. However, a protective election does not extend the time for paying the tax. Such an extension must be granted under IRC Secs. 6161 [see ¶2302] or 6163 [see ¶2304].

The decedent's executor makes a protective election by filling a Notice of Protective Election with a timely filed estate tax return on Form 706. Within 60 days after the values are finally determined or agreed to, you must send a letter containing a final Notice of Election with the required information to the IRS office where you filled the estate tax return. The executor must pay any previously unpaid tax and interest now due, plus any unpaid tax and interest that is not attributable to a closely held business and that is not eligible for further extension (or currently extended) under IRC Secs. 6161 or IRC Sec. 6163.

> **NOTE:** If an actual or protective election was not made, the executor can still elect to pay a portion of any deficiency in installments within 60 days after notice and demand for payment [IRC Sec. 6166(h); Reg. Sec. 20.6166-1(c)]. This election must contain the same information as a notice of election filed with the original estate tax return.

(n) Deciding Whether to Make the Election. The clear advantage of an IRC Sec. 6166 deferred payment of taxes is the availability of the low two percent interest rate on deferred estate tax attributable to a farm or closely-held business interest worth $1,450,000 in 2014 (increased from $1,430,000 in 2013). The disadvantages of a Sec. 6166 election include:

1. **Beware:** The family cannot dispose of or withdraw cash out of the closely held business above certain levels without accelerating the full estate tax due.

---

[13] Chief Counsel Advice 201302037.

2. If the business interest exceeds $1,450,000 in 2014 (increased from $1,430,000 in 2013), interest must be paid at 45 percent of the current underpayment rate.

3. The estate may incur a bonding expense.

   ▶ **CAUTION:** Under IRC Sec. 2002, liability for payment of the estate tax is imposed on the executor. If the unpaid portion of the estate tax bears a substantial relationship to the value of the closely held business interests and if the estate does not have other substantial assets, a risk exists that a decline in the profits of the business would leave the executor in a position where he or she would have to sell the business to meet the installment payments. A sale of the business during a period of declining profits might result in a loss leaving the personal representative holding insufficient funds to pay the balance of the estate tax. In this situation, the executor would be personally liable for the balance of the estate tax owed.

(o) What to Do if Estate Is Ineligible for Election. If the IRS finds that an estate is ineligible for installment payment of estate tax, the executor may seek a declaratory judgment before the Tax Court regarding the estate's eligibility for installment payments [IRC Sec. 7479]. This provision applies to both the initial and continued eligibility to pay estate tax in installments. The Tax Court's jurisdiction to determine an estate's eligibility for the installment payment of estate taxes extends to the issue of which businesses that are includible in the decedent's gross estate are eligible for the deferral of tax [IRC Sec. 7479(a)]. Provided the IRS's adverse determination is sent by certified or registered mail, a pleading for a declaratory judgment must be filed with the Tax Court within 90 days of the IRS mailing [IRC Sec. 7479(b)(3)].

In order to be eligible for judicial review under IRC Sec. 7479, the estate must show that it exhausted all administrative remedies within the IRS. A taxpayer is deemed to have exhausted all available administrative remedies if the IRS fails to make a determination within 180 days of a request for determination, providing all reasonable steps to secure such determination have been made [IRC Sec. 7479(b)(2)].

In Rev. Proc. 2005-33,[14] the IRS provided guidance on exhausting administrative remedies before seeking a declaratory judgment pursuant to IRC Sec. 7479 where an executor has made an election under IRC Sec. 6166 to extend the time for payment of estate tax. To be deemed to have exhausted all administrative remedies, the applicant is required to complete the following steps:

1. The executor must timely file a Form 706 on behalf of the estate and attach the election to extend the time to pay pursuant to IRC Sec. 6166(a) and

2. Within 30 calendar days after the mailing date of a preliminary determination letter from the IRS, the applicant must request, in writing, a conference with the IRS's Appeals Office and fully participate in the conference.

After these actions are completed and a reasonable time has expired for the IRS to issue a final determination letter subsequent to the appeals conference (which is deemed to have ended on the 61st day after the conference), an applicant is deemed to have exhausted all administrative remedies. An applicant will also be deemed to have exhausted all administrative remedies in the following situations: (1) upon the

---

[14] Rev. Proc. 2005-33, 2005-1 CB 1231.

¶2303

issuance of a final determination letter where a preliminary determination letter was not received, as long as the failure to receive a preliminary letter was not due to the actions or inactions of the applicant; (2) where the applicant has not received a preliminary or final determination letter after 180 days has expired from the date a request for determination was made, and the failure is not due to any action or inaction on the applicant's part; or (3) at least 61 days after an appeals conference was requested in response to a preliminary determination letter and the IRS has not responded.

Assessments. After the return is filed, it is examined by the proper officials in the IRS. If the return is found to understate the tax, the IRS notifies the executor that it will issue a deficiency notice unless the matter is settled. If a deficiency notice is issued, the executor may petition the Tax Court for a redetermination or pay the tax and apply for a refund from the IRS. If the refund is denied, the taxpayer may apply to the U.S. District Court or the U.S. Claims Court. Collection is postponed during the pendency of the case, unless the assessment was a jeopardy assessment [Reg. Secs. 301.6212-1, 301.6213-1]. The IRS ordinarily has three years from the date a return is filed to make an estate, gift, or generation skipping transfer tax assessment [IRC Sec. 6501]. No proceeding in a court for the collection of an estate or gift tax can be begun without an assessment within the three-year period. If no return is filed, the tax may be assessed, or a suit commenced to collect the tax without assessment, at any time. If an estate or gift tax return is filed, and the amount of unreported items exceeds 25 percent of the amount of the reported items, the tax may be assessed or a suit commenced to collect the tax without assessment, within six years after the return was filed [IRC Sec. 6501(e)(2)].

Refunds. Refund claims must be filed within three years of the return's due date or two years of the payment of the tax, whichever is later. It should state the amount of refund claimed and the grounds on which the claim is based. [IRC Sec. 6511].

¶2304 ELECTION TO POSTPONE TAX ON REVERSIONS OR REMAINDERS

An IRC Sec. 6163 election allows an executor to postpone paying the estate tax attributable to reversions or remainder interests that are included in the decedent's gross estate. The tax can be postponed until six months after the reversion or remainder interest is in the hands of the decedent's estate or heirs [IRC Sec. 6163(a)]. The purpose of IRC Sec. 6163 is to provide relief for an estate that otherwise would be taxed on an asset that it does not yet have in its possession.

The IRS has the discretion to extend the payment date until three years following the expiration date of such postponement for "reasonable cause" [IRC Sec. 6163(b); see ¶2302].

The estate tax attributable to the reversion or remainder interest equals that portion of the tax that the net value of the future interest bears to the net value of the entire estate. The amount of tax that can be postponed equals the value of reversion divided by the amount of the gross estate times the net estate tax due. The formula also requires adjustments to both the numerator and denominator for certain claims, mortgages, or debts and all IRC Sec. 2054, 2055, or 2056 items directly on the remainder or reversion interest [Reg. Sec. 20.6163-1(c)].

Return preparation tip. Be sure to note on Form 706 that a Sec. 6163 election has been made [see ¶2433]. In addition, you should notify the District Director that a Sec. 6163 election has been made before the date prescribed for payment of the estate tax. Enclose a certified copy of the instrument creating the reversion or remainder along with the birth date(s) and name(s) of any intervening life or lives [Reg. Sec. 20.6163-1(b)].

You can revoke your Sec. 6163 election at any time. Once the election has been revoked, the executor can prepay the tax on the reversion or remainder without penalty.

The main advantage of IRC Sec. 6163 is that it allows for a tax deferral. Remember, that a deferral is not a savings. This is especially so because the deferred Sec. 6163 tax portion must bear current interest and may also incur a bond expense if the District Director requires a payment bond to be posted [IRC Secs. 6163(c), 6165].

THE ESTATE TAX RETURN—FORM 706

TABLE OF CONTENTS

¶2400 WHICH ESTATES MUST FILE FORM 706

The discussion in this chapter addresses the timely filing of the 2013 federal estate tax return for use by estates of decedents dying in 2013.

An estate tax return, Form 706, "United States Estate (and Generation-Skipping Transfer) Tax Return," must be filed by the executor for a decedent who was a U.S. citizen or resident in the following two situations:

1. If the amount of the decedent's gross estate on the date of death exceeds the applicable exclusion amount, reduced by the amount of the decedent's adjusted taxable gifts [IRC Sec. 6018(a)(1)]. The applicable exclusion amount is $5,250,000 in 2013 and increases to $5,340,000 in 2014.

2. A timely and **complete** Form 706 must also be filed for the predeceased spouse's estate even if there is no tax due because the estate is less than the applicable exclusion amount for the year of the decedent's death, in order to allow the executor to make the portability election to pass the decedent's unused estate and gift tax exclusion amount to a surviving spouse [See Chapter 15 for a detailed discussion of portability]. If an estate files a Form 706 but does not wish to make the portability election, the executor can opt out of the portability election by checking the box indicated in Section A of Part 6 on Form 706. If the executor is not required to file a federal estate tax return for the decedent, not filing Form 706 will avoid making the portability election.

Special rules for computing the value of decedent's estate.

• When computing the value of the decedent's assets for purposes of determining whether or not Form 706 must be filed, the decedent's estate is not reduced by outstanding recourse debts (decedent personally liable for repayment of the debt) and expenses. Therefore, some decedents may have to file Form 706 even though their taxable estate is below the $5,340,000 filing threshold in 2014 if their debts and expenses had been deducted.

¶2400

• If the decedent holds title to property jointly with another, only half the value of qualified joint interest property is included in the decedent's estate. For example, assume the decedent's gross estate's sole asset is jointly owned securities valued at $10 million on the date of death. The decedent would not be required to file Form 706 because the decedent's gross estate would only total $5 million.

Example 1: Joe dies in 2014 owning $7 million of investment real estate with a $6.5 million recourse mortgage that he still owes. Even though his net taxable estate is only $500,000, Joe's executor must still file Form 706 because the gross estate is over the threshold filing limit in 2014 of $5,340,000.

Example 2: A decedent dies in 2014 owning $6 million worth of securities jointly with his spouse. Form 706 is not required because the decedent's gross estate is worth only $3 million unless the surviving spouse wants to make the portability election discussed in 2., above. Under IRC Sec. 2040(b), only one-half of qualified joint spousal interests are included in the gross estate.

▶ **PRACTICE POINTER:** The value of the decedent's estate on the date of his death, not the alternate valuation date, determines whether an estate tax return is necessary.

Example 3: On Joe's date of death (March 11, 2014), his gross estate is valued at $4.9 million and at the alternate valuation date (six months later) it is valued at $6.5 million. Form 706 is not required because on the date of Joe's death (not the alternate valuation date), his gross estate was valued at $4.9 million, which is less than the $5,340,000 requisite filing threshold for 2014.

Example 4: On Jill's date of death (August 3, 2012), her gross estate is valued at $5.3 million, and at the alternate valuation date (six months later) it is only valued at $1.8 million. Unfortunately, Form 706 must be filed.

The amount of any pre-1976 Tax Reform Act (see former IRC Section 2521) $30,000 lifetime gift tax exemption allowed with respect to gifts made after September 8, 1976, but before January 1, 1977, also reduces the Form 706 filing threshold. These gifts were made after the 1976 Tax Reform Act was passed but before its effective date.

U.S. citizens or residents. File Form 706 for the estates of decedents who were either U.S. citizens or U.S. residents at the time of death. For estate tax purposes, a resident is a person who has had a domicile in the United States at the time of death. A person acquires a domicile by living in a place for even a brief period of time, as long as the person had no intention of moving from that place.

Nonresident noncitizens (nonresident aliens). For the estates of nonresidents who were neither domiciled in nor a citizen of the United States at the time of death (nonresident aliens), a return must be filed on Form 706-NA, "United States Estate (and Generation- Skipping Transfer) Tax Return, Estate of Nonresident, Not a Citizen of the United States," if the value of the decedent's gross estate located in the United States exceeds $60,000, reduced by (1) the amount of adjusted taxable gifts made by the

¶2400

decedent after December 31, 1976, and (2) the aggregate amount allowed as a specific exemption under IRC Sec. 2521 (as in effect before its repeal by the Tax Reform Act of 1976) with respect to gifts made by the decedent after September 8, 1976 [IRC Sec. 6018(a)(2)]. The Form 706-NA must be filed within nine months after the date of death unless an extension of time to file is requested [IRC Sec. 6075(a)]. The actual due date is nine months after the date of death (i.e., if the date of death is February 25, the due date is November 25). If there is no numerically corresponding day in the ninth month, the due date is the last day of the ninth month. For example, if the decedent died on May 31, the estate tax return would be due on the last day of February (i.e., February 28 or 29) since there are not 31 days in February. If the due date falls on a Saturday, Sunday, or a legal holiday, the due date is the next business day [Reg. Sec. 20.6075-1]. Form 706-NA is filed with the Department of the Treasury, Internal Revenue Service, Cincinnati, OH 45999. If the return is mailed, the author recommends that it be sent by registered or certified mail, with a return receipt requested or by a private delivery company designated by the IRS.

Exclusions, deductions and credits available on Form 706-NA. The following exclusions, deductions, or credits may be available to the decedent's estate on Form 706-NA:

- *Qualified Conservation Easement Exclusion (Schedule A).* Under IRC Sec. 2031(c), estates may make an irrevocable election to exclude the lesser of (1) the applicable percentage of the value of land (after certain reductions) subject to a qualified conservation easement or (2) $500,000. Attach Schedule U of Form 706.

- *Funeral and Administration Expenses, Debts and Liens (Schedule B, line 4).* The following items can be deducted: funeral expenses, administration expenses, claims against the estate, mortgages (if the full amount of the mortgaged property is included in the gross estate), other liens, and nonreimbursed casualty or theft losses incurred during the estate administration. The expenses need not be incurred in the United States.

- *Charitable Deduction (Schedule B, line 6).* Unless a treaty allows otherwise, this deduction is available only if the transfer was to a U.S. charity or for U.S. charitable purposes. Attach Schedule O of Form 706. If the deduction is claimed under a treaty, attach a computation of the deduction (and specify the treaty).

- *Marital Deduction (Schedule B, line 6).* Unless a treaty allows otherwise, this deduction is available only if the surviving spouse is a U.S. citizen or if the property passes to a qualified domestic trust (QDOT), and an election is made on Schedule M of Form 706. Attach Schedule M of Form 706 and attach a computation of the deduction.

- *State Death Tax Deduction (Schedule B, line 7).* A deduction is allowed for death taxes (estate, inheritance, legacy, or succession taxes) paid to any state or the District of Columbia related to property listed in Schedule A.

- *Unified Credit (Part II, line 7).* A credit is allowed for the smaller of the amount shown on line 6 of Part II or the maximum unified credit, which generally is $13,000.

- *Other Credits (Part II, line 9).* A credit for federal gift taxes may be allowed. Attach the computation of the credit. In addition, a Canadian marital credit may be allowed if

¶2400

all applicable elections are made. This nonrefundable marital credit is generally limited to the lesser of (1) the unified credit allowed to the estate before the reduction for any gift tax unified credit, or (2) the amount of estate tax that the U.S. would otherwise impose on the transfer of qualifying property to the surviving spouse. Attach the computation of the credit, and write "Canadian marital credit" to the left of the line 9 entry.

- *Generation-Skipping Transfer Tax (Part II, line 13).* If the answer to Part III, question 11 is yes, attach Schedules R and/or R-1 from Form 706. However, only include transfers of interests in property that are a part of the U.S. gross estate (i.e., those included on Schedule A).

The following items should be attached to Form 706-NA:

1. If the decedent died testate, a certified copy of the decedent's will.
2. Explanation if a certified copy of the will is not available.
3. Copy of the death certificate.
4. Copies of U.S. gift tax returns filed by the decedent.
5. For closely held or inactive corporate stock, five years of balance sheets, operating results, and dividend history.
6. Any other explanatory documents, such as appraisals.
7. English translations for any documents written in other languages.

Estate tax treaties. To avoid double taxation, the U.S. has entered into death tax conventions with the following foreign countries:

Australia	Finland	Ireland	Norway
Austria	France	Italy	South Africa
Canada	Germany	Japan	Switzerland
Denmark	Greece	Netherlands	United Kingdom

The death tax conventions make credits available to estates of U.S. citizens and residents for death taxes paid to the foreign countries. They also provide rules for determining the situs of property. Reg. Sec. 301.6114-1 provides that an estate claiming an estate tax position based on an estate tax treaty with another country, should attach an explanation of the treaty-based position to the estate tax return.

¶2401 WHEN TO FILE FORM 706

Form 706 must be filed to report estate tax and/or generation-skipping transfer tax within nine months after the date of a decedent's death unless (1) the IRS has granted an extension of time to file or (2) the estate has elected under IRC Sec. 6166 [see ¶ 2303] to pay in installments, or (3) the estate has elected under IRC Sec. 6163 [see ¶ 2304] to postpone the part of the tax attributable to a reversionary or remainder interest [see IRC Sec. 6075(a)]. These elections are made by checking lines 3 and 4 of Part 3, Elections by the Executor and attaching the required statements. The actual due date is nine months after the date of death (i.e., if the date of death is February 25, the due date is November 25). If there is no numerically corresponding day in the ninth month, the due date is the last day of the ninth month. For example, if the decedent died on May 31, the estate tax return would be due on the last day of February (i.e., February 28 or 29) since there are not 31 days in February. If the due date falls on a Saturday, Sunday, or a legal holiday, the due date is the next business day [Reg. Sec. 20.6075-1].

Extension of time to file. Use IRS Form 4768, "Application for Extension of Time to File and/or Pay U.S. Estate (and Generation-Skipping Transfer) Taxes," to apply for an automatic six-month extension of time to file Form 706, "United States Estate and Generation-Skipping Transfer Tax Return"; Form 706-A, "United States Additional Estate Tax Return" (used to report recapture of special use valuation); Form 706-D, "United States Additional Estate Tax Return under Code Sec. 2057" (used to report recapture of the qualified family-owned business deduction); Form 706-NA, "United States Estate (and Generation-Skipping Transfer) Tax Return" (used for estates of nonresident aliens); and Form 706-QDT, "United States Estate Tax Return for Qualified Domestic Trusts."

In addition, executors who are abroad may also request extensions beyond the automatic six-month period [Reg. Sec. 20.6081-1(b)(2)]. When asking for an automatic six-month extension, the taxpayer need not provide an explanation for the request. The executor must include with Form 706 a check or money order that estimates the full amount of estate and GST tax due [Reg. Sec. 20.6081-1(b)(1)]. An automatic extension of time for filing the return does not extend the time for paying the tax. If an extension of time to file a return is obtained, but no extension of time for payment of the tax is granted, interest will be due on the tax not paid by the due date and the estate will be subject to all applicable late payment penalties [Reg. Sec. 20.6081-1(e)].

The estate tax return on distributions to a noncitizen surviving spouse from a qualified domestic trust (QDOT) is due on April 15 of the year following the calendar year in which the distributions are made [IRC Sec. 2056A(b)(5)]. See ¶ 1106 for further discussion of QDOTs.

Delinquent estate tax returns. Where the estate tax return is not filed within nine months and no extension has been granted, the return is delinquent and the executor is subject to a personal penalty not exceeding $500 [IRC Sec. 7269]. The estate is subject to an *ad valorem* penalty of 5 percent of the tax for each month of delinquency, with a maximum penalty of 25 percent, unless it is shown that the failure to file was due to reasonable cause and not to willful neglect. There is also a penalty for failure to pay the tax shown on a return.

¶2402 WHAT'S NEW ON FORM 706

- **Portability election.** The ability for married individuals to elect to transfer a deceased spouse's unused exclusion to the surviving spouse is now permanent in the law. Therefore, Form 706, Part 6, was revised in 2013 so that the portability election can be reported directly on the decedent's Form 706.

- **Same-sex marriages.** Same-sex couples who were legally married in jurisdictions that recognize same-sex marriages will be treated as married for federal tax purposes, regardless of whether their state of residence recognizes same-sex marriage.
- **Inflation adjustments.**
  - The basic exclusion amount in 2013 is $5,250,000 (increasing to $5,340,000 in 2014).
  - The ceiling on special-use valuation is $1,070,000 (increasing to $1,090,000 in 2014).
  - The amount used in figuring the 2 percent portion of estate tax payable in installments is $1,430,000 (increasing to $1,450,000 in 2014).
- **Schedule PC Added.** Schedule PC, "Protective Claim for Refund" was added to Form 706. By filing Schedule PC, taxpayers can preserve their right to a refund of estate taxes paid when a claim or expense which is the subject of unresolved controversy at the time of filing the return later becomes deductible under IRC Sec. 2053.
- **Line 7 Worksheet.** The Line 7 Worksheet in the Form 706 instructions has been expanded to include the calculation for cumulative lifetime gifts on which tax was paid or payable. This amount is used in Section C of Part 6–Portability of Deceased Spousal Unused Exclusion (DSUE). Executors should submit a copy of the Line 7 worksheet. A copy of the Line 7 worksheet (if completed) should be submitted along with Form 706.

¶2403 CHECKLIST FOR COMPLETING FORM 706

- Do not forget to include Schedule F, "Other Miscellaneous Property Not Reportable Under Any Other Schedule," even if no assets were reported on that schedule. If the estate does not contain any of the assets specified in lines 1 through 9 of the Recapitulation on Page 3 of the return, place a "0" on that line. File only one Form 706 with the IRS.
- List items separately on each schedule, beginning with number 1 on each schedule. Do not list the assets consecutively throughout the whole return. Attach properly labeled continuation sheets if necessary. Form 706 contains one continuation sheet, which you can make copies of. Each schedule must have its own continuation sheet if necessary.
- Use whole dollar amounts to report values. Whole dollar amounts make the return easier to read and mistakes less likely. Round 50 cents or more up to the next whole dollar amount and round less than 50 cents down.
- Attach a certified copy of the decedent's will if he died testate (with a will). If not certified, explain why.
- If you received an extension of time to file and/or pay the tax, attach a copy of the extension to Form 706.
- Attach a copy of the decedent's death certificate.

- Attach any appraisals used to value property included on the return.
- Attach copies of all trust documents where the decedent was a grantor or a beneficiary.
- Attach a copy of any Form(s) 709, "Gift Tax Return," filed by the decedent.
- File form 712 if filing Schedule D.
- File form 706-CE if claiming a foreign death tax credit.
- Explanation of reasonable cause for late filing, if applicable.
- Complete Part 4, line 4, on page 2, if there is a surviving spouse.
- Complete and attach Schedule D to report insurance on the life of the decedent, even if its value is not included in the estate.
- Include any QTIP property received from a predeceased spouse.
- Enter the decedent's name, SSN, and "Form 706" on your check or money order.
- Complete Part 6, section A if the estate elects not to transfer any deceased spousal unused exclusion (DSUE) amount to the surviving spouse.
- Complete Part 6, section C if the estate elects portability of any DSUE amount.
- Complete Part 6, section D and include a copy of the Form 706 of any predeceased spouse(s) from whom a deceased spousal unused exclusion (DSUE) amount was received and applied.

¶2404 HOW TO COMPLETE FORM 706— HYPOTHETICAL FACTS FOR FORM 706

To demonstrate how to complete an estate tax return (Form 706), we present a line-by-line analysis of a hypothetical estate tax return to be filed by the executor for the estate of Dr. Mark F. Smith, a veterinarian.

Dr. Smith died on December 15, 2013, leaving a wife, Jane R. Smith and two sons (Albert and Gary Smith). He also had a sister named Beth Smith Bromley. Dr. Smith owned various parcels of land that he used in his veterinary practice, other pieces of property that he owned in joint tenancy with his wife, life insurance policies, annuities, shares of stock in several companies, liquid assets held in various bank accounts, and miscellaneous personal property.

Although the decedent named his surviving spouse, Jane R. Smith, as the executor of his estate, and she must file the Form 706, it will actually be prepared by the attorney or accountant for the estate, John P. Reed.

Protective claim for refund. Dr. Smith was sued by one of his patient's owners for malpractice. Dr. Smith died before a final judgment in the case had been rendered and before the Form 706 had to be filed by Dr. Smith's executor. If the lawsuit is successful, Dr. Smith's estate could be required to pay as much as $750,000; however his executor thinks that the two parties can ultimately settle for $600,000. Therefore, Dr. Smith's executor files Schedule PC with Dr. Smith's Form 706 as shown in ¶ 2436. The Schedule PC is explained in ¶ 2433.

¶2404

¶2405 PART 1, PAGE 1—DECEDENT AND EXECUTOR

Fill in all of the information requested in lines 1 through 10 of Part 1.

▶ **CAUTION:** If the decedent died testate (i.e., he had a will), the executor must attach a copy of the will to the Form 706 and check the box on line 8.

Do not fill out Part 2—Tax Computation until you have completed the rest of the return. [For a discussion of Tax Computation, see ¶2432].

¶2406 PART 3, PAGE 2—ELECTIONS BY EXECUTOR

In Part 3, you must check the "Yes" or "No" box to each of the following four questions that are discussed in detail at ¶¶2407-2410:

1. Did the executor use alternate valuation?

2. Did the executor elect a special-use valuation? If "Yes," you must complete and attach Schedule A-1.

3. Did the executor elect to pay the taxes in installments under IRC Sec. 6166? If "Yes," you must attach the additional information described in the instructions. As a result of electing to pay taxes in installments, the executor may be required to provide security for estate tax deferred under IRC Sec. 6166 and interest in the form of a surety bond or an IRC Sec. 6324A lien.

4. Do you elect to postpone the part of the taxes due to a reversionary or remainder interest as described in IRC Sec. 6163?

¶2407 PART 3—ELECTIONS BY EXECUTOR—LINE 1— ALTERNATE VALUATION ELECTION

You may make an election to value all gross estate property at a date six months after the date of death unless the property is sold or otherwise disposed of between the date of death and the alternate valuation date. If you do sell or dispose of the property, it will be valued for estate tax purposes as of the date of the sale or disposition. All other property will be valued at the alternate valuation date under IRC Sec. 2032. See ¶1907 for further discussion of the alternate valuation election.

Use this election if the decedent's estate experienced a decline in value shortly after death. You are only allowed to make this election if the decline in value decreases both the value of the gross estate and the net estate tax on the gross estate. The election must also decrease any generation-skipping tax that is due.

▶ **CAUTION:** You are not allowed to use this election to increase the value of the estate so that the heirs will get a step-up in basis for the value of the assets.

You elect alternate valuation by checking "Yes" on line 1 of Part 3 of Form 706 and then filing this Form 706. Once made, the alternate valuation election may not be revoked. The election may be made on a late filed Form 706 provided it is not filed later than one year after the due date (including extensions actually granted). If

¶2407

alternate valuation is elected, value the property as of six months after the date of the decedent's death. As part of each Schedule A through Schedule I, show the following:

1. What property is included in the gross estate on the date of the decedent's death;

2. What property was distributed, sold, exchanged, or otherwise disposed of within the 6-month period after the decedent's death, and the dates of these distributions;

3. The date of death value, entered in the appropriate value column with items of principal and includible income shown separately; and

4. The alternate value, entered in the appropriate value column with items of principal and includible income shown separately.

■ Dr. Smith's executor [see ¶ 2404] has not elected to use the alternate valuation date for his assets. Consequently, all values shown on his return reflect the value of the assets on the date of Dr. Smith's death.

¶2408 PART 3—ELECTIONS BY EXECUTOR—LINE 2— SPECIAL USE VALUATION ELECTION

In order to keep family farms and closely held family business property within the family, the property can be valued at its actual use value under IRC Sec. 2032A rather than the property's fair market value. The election prevents the necessity of selling the family farm or businesses to pay the estate tax. Taxpayers may elect both special use valuation and alternate valuation. See ¶ 1908 for further discussion of the special use valuation election.

Election procedure. To make the election, check "Yes" in the box on line 2 of Part 3 on Page 2 and complete and attach Schedule A-1 to the Form 706. You must attach Schedule A-1 and its required attachments with Form 706 in order for this election to be valid. You may make the election on a late filed return so long as it is the first return filed.

The total value of the property valued under IRC Sec. 2032A may not be decreased from fair market value by more than $1,070,000 in 2013 ($1,090,000 in 2014).

Answer Part 1 of Schedule A-1 by checking the box marked "Regular Election." If the percentage tests are close, you can make a protective election on Form 706. Make the protective election by checking the box marked "Protective Election." Under this election, whether or not you may ultimately use special use valuation depends upon values as finally determined (or agreed to following examination of the return) meeting the requirements of IRC Sec. 2032A.

If the protective election is being made:

1. Check "Yes" to line 2 of Part 3 and complete Schedule A-1. If you make a protective election, you should complete this Form 706 by valuing all property at its fair market value. Do not use special use valuation. Usually, this will result in higher estate and GST tax liabilities than will be ultimately determined if special use valuation is allowed. The protective election does not extend the time to pay the taxes shown on the return. If you wish to extend the time to pay the taxes, you should file Form 4768 in adequate time before the return due date, see ¶ 1908.

¶2408

2. If the estate qualifies for special use valuation under IRC Sec. 2032A based on the values as finally determined (or agreed to following examination of the return), you must file an amended Form 706 with the full attachments and a fully completed Schedule A-1 within 60 days of the determination. Complete this amended return using special use values under the rules of IRC Sec. 2032A and complete Schedule A-1 and attach all of the required statements.

Complete all of Part 2 on Schedule A-1.

1. Part 2 includes all of the items required by Reg. Sec. 20.2032A-8(a)(3) and is called the "Notice of Election."

2. Line 11 of Part 2 includes a box that will allow you to make the special woodlands election under IRC Sec. 2032A(e)(13) if certain requirements are met. Be sure to attach a statement indicating why you are entitled to the election.

3. Attach a legal description of all properties listed on line 2 of Part 2.

4. Attach copies of the appraisals showing the Column B value for properties listed in lines 2 and 3.

Complete all of Part 3 of Schedule A-1. Part 3 contains the agreement to use special use valuation, which must be signed by all qualified heirs and other interested parties. Identify the qualified real estate on other schedules in the return with the notation "IRC Section 2032A valuation."

¶2409 PART 3—ELECTIONS BY EXECUTOR—LINE 3— ELECTION TO PAY TAXES IN INSTALLMENTS AS DESCRIBED IN SECTION 6166

If more than 35 percent of the adjusted gross estate consists of an interest in a farm or other closely held business, an executor may elect to defer payments of tax attributable to the interest for five years (paying interest only) and thereafter pay the tax in equal installments over the next ten years [IRC Sec. 6166]. The maximum payment period, however, is 14 rather than 15 years because the due date for the last payment of interest coincides with the due date for the first installment of tax. For purposes of the 35 percent rule, the adjusted gross estate consists of the gross estate less debts, expenses, claims, and losses allowable as deductions under IRC Sec. 2053 or IRC Sec. 2054. The maximum amount that can be paid in installments is that part of estate tax that is attributable to the closely held business. In general, that amount is the amount of tax that bears the same ratio to the total estate tax that the value of the closely held business included in the gross estate bears to the total gross estate. For further discussion of the election to pay part of the estate tax in installments under IRC Sec. 6166, see ¶2303.

The election procedure is as follows:

1. Check the "Yes" box on line 3 in Part 3 on Page 2 of Form 706.

2. Attach a "Notice of Protective Election" to the Form 706 that contains the following information:

    • The decedent's name and Social Security number;

    • The amount of tax to be paid in installments;

- The due date of the first installment;

- The number of annual installments elected (always elect 10 because the number of installments cannot be increased but the tax can be prepaid);

- Identification of the IRC Sec. 6166 property items by cross reference to the respective Form 706 schedules and line item numbers; and

- A narrative of the facts supporting the basis for the conclusion that the estate qualifies for IRC Sec. 6166 relief.

A protective election is made by filing a "Notice of Protective Election" with Form 706 and checking the "Yes" box on line 3 of Part 3 of Form 706. Moreover, you can request that the Sec. 6166 election be treated in the alternative as a request for IRC Sec. 6161 relief if the estate fails to qualify for IRC Sec. 6166.

Section 6166 is revocable. The IRS allows the tax to be paid early without prepayment penalty. However, because IRC Sec. 6601(j) authorizes a special 2 percent interest rate on a certain part of the tax extended under Sec. 6166, it may be economically foolish to pay the tax early as follows:

1. Interest at the rate of 2 percent is imposed in 2013 on the first $1,430,000 ($1,450,000 in 2014) in taxable value, of the estate tax attributable to a closely held business when an estate elects the IRC Sec. 6166 extension of time for payment of the estate tax. The interest rate imposed on the amount of the deferred estate tax attributable to the taxable value of a closely held business in excess of the 2 percent portion is reduced to an amount equal to 45 percent of the rate applicable to underpayments of tax.

2. No deduction is allowed for estate or income tax purposes for the interest paid on estate taxes deferred under IRC Sec. 6166.

   ▶ **PRACTICE POINTER:** The interest on the unpaid portion is not deferred and must be paid annually.

   ▶ **CAUTION:** IRC Sec. 6166 does provide that the tax must be paid early if certain dispositions of the business or withdrawal of business funds occurs.

¶2410 PART 3—ELECTIONS BY EXECUTOR—LINE 4—ELECTION TO POSTPONE TAX ON REVERSIONS OR REMAINDERS

The estate may postpone paying the estate tax attributable to reversions or remainder interests that are included in the estate until six months after the reversion or remainder becomes possessory to the decedent's estate or heirs.

If the decedent's gross estate consists of both a reversionary or remainder interest in property and other property, tax attributable to the reversionary or remainder interest for purposes of postponing payment, is the amount that bears the same ratio to the total tax as the value of the reversionary or remainder interest bears to the entire gross estate.

In applying this ratio, the value of the reversionary or remainder interest and the value of the gross estate must be reduced. The value of the reversionary or remainder interest is reduced by:

- The amount of claims, mortgages, and indebtedness that is a lien upon the interest;

- Losses related to the interest during the settlement of the estate that are deductible under IRC Sec. 2054 (deductions from the gross estates of U.S. citizens or residents for uncompensated losses from casualties or theft) or IRC Sec. 2106(a) (deductions from the gross estates of nonresident noncitizens for expenses, losses, indebtedness, and taxes);

- Any amount deductible from the gross estate as transfers for public, charitable, and religious uses under IRC Sec. 2055 (U.S. citizens and residents) or IRC Sec. 2106(a)(2) (nonresident noncitizens); and

- The portion of the marital deduction allowed under IRC Sec. 2056 because of bequests or other transfers of the reversionary or remainder interests to the decedent's surviving spouse. The value of the gross estate, for purposes of applying the above ratio, is reduced by the deductions of this kind having a similar relationship to the items making up the gross estate.

[Reg. Sec. 20.6163-1(c)]

Definitions of key terms.

- *Reversion.* This is the possibility of a return of property to the original transferor after its enjoyment by another person. Persons who hold reversions are said to hold reversionary interests. Reversions are classified as future estates for purposes of local property law.

- *Remainder.* This is a residual or leftover interest in property held by someone other than the original transferor. The holder of the remainder interest will take the property after the property has been used by the lifetime user of the property. For example, if a farmer's will provides that upon his death his sons will receive the farm outright, the sons have a remainder interest in the farm.

Election procedure.

- Check the "Yes" box on line 4 in Part 3 on Page 2 of Form 706.

- Send a letter to the district director and enclose a certified copy of the instrument creating the reversion or remainder along with the birth date(s) and name(s) of any intervening life or lives.

- Attach a copy of the letter to Form 706.

The election is revocable because you can prepay the tax on the reversion or remainder at any time without penalty.

¶2411 PART 4, PAGES 2 AND 3—GENERAL INFORMATION

Fill in all of the information that is requested in lines 1 through 17 in Part 4, Pages 2 and 3.

Authorization. Completing the authorization on page 2 of Form 706 will authorize one attorney, accountant, or enrolled agent to represent the estate and receive confidential tax information, but will not authorize the representative to enter into closing agreement for the estate. If the executor wants to represent the estate, he must complete and sign the authorization. The executor must complete and sign Form 2848, "Power of Attorney and Declaration of Representative," to authorize someone to enter into closing agreements for the estate. Filing a completed Form 2848 with Form 706 may expedite processing of the Form 706.

Part 4—General Information, Lines 1 through 4

Lines 1 through 4 request general information about the decedent's death, occupation, marital status, and surviving spouse. Complete these lines as follows.

Line 1. Enter the decedent's death certificate number and issuing authority on line 1. A copy of the certificate should be attached to the return.

Line 2. Enter the decedent's occupation on line 2. If the decedent was retired, his former occupation should be entered and the box indicating the decedent was retired should be checked.

Line 3a and 3b. Enter the decedent's marital status at the date of death on line 3a. Use line 3b to report the following:

1. For all prior marriages, provide the name and social security number of each former spouse, the date(s) the marriage ended, and indicate whether the marriage ended by annulment, divorce, or death of a spouse (to the extent not already provided by the way other items on line 3 were answered).

2. If the prior marriage ended in death and the predeceased spouse died after 2010, complete Form 706, Part 6 (Portability of Deceased Spousal Unused Exclusion (DSUE)), Section D.

Lines 4a, 4b, and 4c. Complete line 4 by entering the surviving spouse's name, social security number, and an estimate of the amount of property the spouse received in the spaces indicated. If there was no surviving spouse, "none" should be entered on line 4a, and lines 4b and 4c should be left blank (i.e., line 4 should be completed even if there is no surviving spouse). The amount entered on line 4c need not be exact—a reasonable estimate is sufficient. Do not include any DSUE amount transferred to the surviving spouse in line 4c.

Changes on Form 706 to reflect portability. To reflect the introduction of portability into the law as discussed in Chapter 15, the IRS made changes to the instructions for Form 706 and they are contained in Part 4, Lines 3 and 4. The instructions for Line 3 regarding the decedent's marital status now require the executor to include if the decedent had more than one marriage, the name and Social Security Number of each former spouse, the date the marriage ended and whether the marriage ended by annulment, divorce, or death of the spouse. In addition, if the prior marriage ended in death and the predeceased spouse died after December 31, 2010, it must be indicated on the Explanation Line whether the executor of the estate of the predeceased spouse elected to allow the decedent to use the deceased spousal unused exclusion amount. If the executor of the predeceased spouse's estate made the election, the predeceased spouse's Form 706 must be attached to the return with a calculation of the deceased spousal unused exclusion amount.

¶2411

Form 706, Part 4—General Information, Line 5–page 2

The names of individuals (other than the surviving spouse), trusts, or estates who receive the decedent's property from the estate (other than a charity) are disclosed on line 5 of Part 4–General Information.

- **Name of individual.** The name of each beneficiary (including a trust or estate) receiving $5,000 or more from the estate directly as an heir, devisee, or legatee; or indirectly (i.e., as a shareholder of a corporation that was the beneficiary of a life insurance policy) should be listed in the designated column of line 5. Beneficiaries who received less than $5,000 need not be identified but can be combined and disclosed as distributions to unascertainable beneficiaries on the line provided.

- **Identifying number.** The beneficiary's social security number should be entered in the designated column of line 5. If the individual does not have a social security number, or if the number is not known, enter "none" or "unknown." For a trust or another estate, enter its tax identification number.

- **Relationship to decedent.** Enter the beneficiary's family relationship, if any, to the decedent in the designated column, including relationships by blood, adoption, or marriage (e.g., son, mother-in-law, etc.) on line 5. If there is no familial relationship, enter "none." If the beneficiary is a trust or another estate, enter "Trust" or "Estate."

- **Amount.** A reasonable estimate of the amount distributed (or to be distributed) to the beneficiary should be entered in the "Amount" column on line 5. This amount includes bequests received at the decedent's death, as well as transfers received by the beneficiary during the decedent's life that are included in the decedent's gross estate. The total listed in the "Amount" column should approximate the amount of the gross estate reduced by funeral and administration expenses, debts and mortgages, marital bequests, charitable bequests, and any federal or state estate and GST taxes paid on the amount of the estate distributed to the noncharitable estate beneficiaries. Note that the amount does not have to be exact. A reasonable estimate is sufficient.

Part 4—General Information, Lines 6 through 17

Line 6. If the estate is filing a protective claim for refund, check the "yes" box and attach two copies of a completed Schedule PC to Form 706 [For further discussion, see ¶2433].

Line 7. Check the "yes" box if the decedent held a qualifying interest in qualified terminable interest property (QTIP) at the time of death [For further discussion, see ¶1103, ¶1104, and ¶1105].

Lines 8a, 8b, and 8c. If the decedent filed gift tax returns (Form 709), check the "yes" box on line 8a and attach a copy of the returns to the estate tax return. Enter the periods covered by the gift tax returns on line 8b and the IRS office where they were filed on line 8c.

Line 9a. Check the "yes" box on line 9a and attach an explanation to Schedule D if an insurance policy on the decedent's life is excluded from the decedent's gross estate.

Line 9b. Check the "yes" box on line 9b and attach an explanation attached if the decedent owned any insurance on the life of another that is excluded from the decedent's gross estate.

¶2411

Line 10. Check the "yes" box on line 10 if less than the entire value of jointly owned property held with someone other than the decedent's spouse is included in the decedent's gross estate and complete and attach Schedule E.

Line 11a. Check the "yes" box on line 11a if the decedent owned an interest in a partnership (such as a family limited partnership), an unincorporated business (i.e., a sole proprietorship), a limited liability company, or owned any stock in an inactive or closely held corporation.

Line 11b. If the "yes" box was checked on line 11a, any discounts taken on Form 706, Schedule F or G with respect to the value of any interest listed in Line 11a must be disclosed. Therefore, if the decedent owned an interest in a partnership, unincorporated business, LLC, or a closely held corporation and the value reported on Form 706 Schedules F or G was discounted, the "yes" box on line 11b must be checked and the total accumulated or effective discounts must be reported on the applicable schedule.

Line 12. If the decedent made transfers as described in IRC Secs. 2035, 2036, 2037, or 2038, check the "yes" box on line 12 and attached completed Schedule G.

Line 13a. Check the "yes" box on line 13a and complete Schedule G if a trust was created during the decedent's lifetime.

Line 13b. Check the "yes" box on line 13b if the decedent during his or her lifetime possessed a power, beneficial interest, or trusteeship over a trust created by someone other than the decedent. The details of the trust ownership should be included on Schedule F.

Lines 13c and 13d. On the first line of line 13c, check the "yes" box if the decedent was receiving income from a trust created after October 22, 1986, by a parent or grandparent. On the second part of line 13c, indicate whether there was a GST taxable termination upon the death of the decedent under IRC Sec. 2612. If "yes" was checked, an explanatory statement and a copy of the documents creating the trust and the name, address, and phone number of the current trustee(s) must be attached to Form 706.

Line 13e. Check the "yes" box on line 13e if the decedent at any time during his or her lifetime transferred or sold an interest in a partnership, limited liability company, or closely held corporation to a trust described in question 13a or 13b. The EIN of the interest transferred must be provided.

Line 14. Check the "yes" box on line 14 if the decedent ever possessed, exercised, or released any general power of appointment. Schedule H of Form 706 must be completed if the answer was yes.

Line 15. Check the "yes" box on line 15 if the decedent had an interest in (or a signature or other authority over) a foreign financial account, such as a bank account, securities account, or other financial account.

Line 16. Check the "yes" box on line 16 and complete Schedule I if, immediately before death, the decedent was receiving an annuity.

Line 17. Check the "yes" box on line 17 if the decedent was the beneficiary of a qualified terminable interest trust (QTIP) trust that was not reported on Form 706. If "yes" was checked, an explanation must be attached.

¶2411

¶2412 SCHEDULE A—REAL ESTATE

When the total gross estate includes any real estate, Schedule A must be completed and filed with the return. On Schedule A list all real estate interests that the decedent owned or had contracted to purchase. Number each parcel in the left-hand column.

▶ **CAUTION:** Joint tenancy interests and real estate owned by a revocable trust are not disclosed on Schedule A; they are disclosed on Schedule E (Jointly Owned Property) or Schedule G (Transfers During Decedent's Life). Reversionary or remainder interests in land as well as real estate parcels that are part of a sole proprietorship are reported on Schedule F (Other Miscellaneous Property Not Reportable Under Any Other Schedule).

The following is a partial list of interests that must be listed on Schedule A:

• Land, along with all improvements and permanent fixtures attached to it, including decedent's community property interest in real estate;

▶ **PRACTICE POINTER:** Growing crops are listed on Schedule F. They are not apart of the real estate.

• Accrued rentals of land;

• Mineral interests, but not royalty interests;

• Easements on land;

• Extra cemetery lots that have market value;

NOTE: Do not include the lots for the burial of the decedent and his family members—they are not part of the gross estate.

• Condominium apartments;

▶ **CAUTION:** Co-op apartments are disclosed on Schedule B (Stocks and Bonds).

• The decedent's fractional share in any tenancy in common real estate;

• The deceased buyer's interest under a real estate sales contract. Report the full value of the contract on Schedule A, and any unpaid purchase price as debt on Schedule K (Debts of the Decedent and Mortgages and Liens).

Description of the property. Describe the land with enough detail so that the IRS can easily locate it for inspection and valuation:

1. *Vacant land.* Provide a full legal description of the property;

2. *City or town property.* Provide the street address and a full legal description of the property;

3. *Rural property.* Report the township, range, landmarks, etc.;

4. *Improved property.* Describe the improvements.

Valuation. Use the fair-market value of the property on the valuation date.

▶ **PRACTICE POINTER:** Fair-market value is the price at which the property would change hands between a willing buyer and seller, neither being under any compulsion to buy or sell, respectively, and both having reasonable knowledge of the relevant facts.

¶2412

The fair-market value of real estate is determined by its highest and best use and not its actual use. Report the whole value of the real estate without reduction for homestead, dower, curtesy, or elective share rights. Use an appraisal to explain how you determined the value of the real estate. Be sure to attach a copy of the appraisal to the return.

Attachments. Attach an appraisal of the property that contains a full legal description. Include photographs of improvements and maps for complex descriptions. Also attach a resume of credentials and a statement of impartiality from the appraiser. The appraiser should state that the value of the property had no effect on the cost of his or her services. Finally, attach copies of all leases, contracts, easements, and special zoning restrictions pertaining to the property.

> ■ John P. Reed, who is preparing Dr. Smith's estate tax return, lists all of the real estate that Dr. Smith owned at the time of his death on Schedule A. Notice that he uses legal descriptions of the property as well as the street address. The preparer also shows that he used an appraiser to value the property and attaches those appraisals as Exhibits to the return.

¶2413 SCHEDULE B—STOCKS AND BONDS

On Schedule B include all stocks and bonds that are in the decedent's name alone, any stocks and bonds in which the decedent has an interest as a tenant in common, or any stocks in which the decedent has a community property interest. Note that bonds that are exempt from Federal income tax are not exempt from estate tax and must be listed on Schedule B.

Simplified reporting for estates under the filing threshold. In the instructions accompanying Form 706, Schedule B, the IRS provides a special reporting rule for assets subject to the special rule of Temp. Reg. Sec. 20.2010-2T(a)(7)(ii). The IRS directs taxpayers not to enter any value in the last three columns of Schedule B of Form 706 and to refer to the instructions for line 10 of Part 5–Recapitulation for information on how to estimate and report the value of these assets. The IRS explains in line 10 of Part 5–Recapitulation, that under Temp. Reg. Sec. 20.2010-2T(a)(7)(ii), if the total value of the gross estate and adjusted taxable gifts is less than the basic exclusion amount and Form 706 is being filed only to elect portability of the decedent spouse's unused exclusion amount, the estate is not required to report the value of property qualifying for the marital or charitable deduction. Instead, the executor may calculate his or her best estimate of the value exercising good faith and due diligence. The IRS directs executors to list and describe property qualifying for this simplified reporting on the appropriate schedule but a specific dollar value is not reported either on the schedule or on lines 1 through 9 of the Recapitulation on Form 706, Part 5. Instead the estimated value of the assets subject to the special rule should be entered on Form 706, Part 5, lines 10 and 23 based on the following range of dollar values provided in the Form 706 instructions.

¶2413

Table of Estimated Values

If the total estimated value of the assets eligible for the special rule under Temp. Reg. Sec. 20.2010–2T(a)(7)(ii) is more than	But less than or equal to	Include this amount on lines 10 and 23:
$0	$250,000	$250,000
$250,000	$500,000	$500,000
$500,000	$750,000	$750,000
$750,000	$1,000,000	$1,000,000
$1,000,000	$1,250,000	$1,250,000
$1,250,000	$1,500,000	$1,500,000
$1,500,000	$1,750,000	$1,750,000
$1,750,000	$2,000,000	$2,000,000
$2,000,000	$2,250,000	$2,250,000
$2,250,000	$2,500,000	$2,500,000
$2,500,000	$2,750,000	$2,750,000
$2,750,000	$3,000,000	$3,000,000
$3,000,000	$3,250,000	$3,250,000
$3,250,000	$3,500,000	$3,500,000
$3,500,000	$3,750,000	$3,750,000
$3,750,000	$4,000,000	$4,000,000
$4,000,000	$4,250,000	$4,250,000
$4,250,000	$4,500,000	$4,500,000
$4,500,000	$4,750,000	$4,750,000
$4,750,000	$5,000,000	$5,000,000
$5,000,000	$5,250,000	$5,250,000

Example 1: Husband dies in 2013, survived by Wife. Husband's gross estate does not exceed $5.25 million. Executor timely files Form 706 solely to make the portability election. To establish the estate's entitlement to the marital deduction, Executor includes with the Form 706 evidence to verify the title of each jointly held asset, to confirm that Wife is the sole beneficiary of both the life insurance policy and the survivor annuity, and to verify that the annuity is exclusively for her life. Finally, Executor certifies on Form 706 his best estimate, determined by exercising due diligence, of the fair market value of the gross estate. This estimate was an amount corresponding to the particular range within which falls the executor's best estimate of the value of the decedent's total gross estate rounded to the nearest $250,000. The estate tax return is considered complete and properly prepared and Executor has elected portability [Temp. Reg. Sec. 20.2010-2T(a)(7)(ii)(C), ex. 1].

When simplified reporting unavailable. Estates may not take advantage of simplified reporting in the following situations where the value of property relates to, affects, or is needed to determine the value passing from the decedent to another beneficiary and [Temp. Reg. Sec. 20.2010-2T(a)(7)(ii)]:

¶2413

1. Only a portion of an interest in property qualifies for the marital or charitable deduction;
2. The value of property is needed to determine the estate's eligibility for the alternate valuation date under IRC Sec. 2032, the special use valuation under IRC Sec. 2032A, or installment payments of estate taxes under IRC Sec. 6166;
3. A partial disclaimer of marital or charitable deduction property is made; or
4. A partial qualified terminable interest property (QTIP) election is made.

▶ **PRACTICE POINTER:** Jointly held stocks and bonds are listed on Schedule E. Stocks and bonds that are held in a revocable trust are listed on Schedule G.

The following is a partial list of includable interests:

1. All kinds of stocks and bonds;
2. Shares in mutual funds;
3. Brokerage house money market accounts;
4. Traded or nontraded securities;
5. Government bonds;
6. Municipal bonds;
7. Co-op apartment shares;
8. Public housing bonds; and
9. All bearer obligations owned by the decedent.

Stock description. Include the following in the description of the stock:

1. The number of shares;
2. Whether the shares are common or preferred;
3. Price per share;
4. Principal exchange where traded (or the issuer's principal business address if the stock is not traded on a trading exchange);
5. Nine-digit CUSIP (Committee on Uniform Security Identification Procedure) number, which is a nine-digit number assigned to all stocks and bonds traded on major exchanges and many unlisted securities. The CUSIP number can usually be found on the back of the stock certificate. If the CUSIP number is not printed, it can be obtained from the company's transfer agent; and
6. Par value, where needed for identification.

Bond description. Include the following in the description of bonds:

1. The quantity and denomination;
2. Obligor's name;
3. Maturity date;
4. Interest rate;
5. Interest due date;
6. Nine-digit CUSIP number; and
7. Principal exchange, if listed on an exchange. If not listed, report the company's principal business office.

¶2413

Give the company's principal business address if the bond is not traded on a trading exchange.

Tax-exempt bonds are not exempt from federal estate tax and should be listed on Schedule B.

Valuation. The following guidelines apply to stocks, trust funds, money market cash funds, flower bonds, stocks of co-op apartments, open-end mutual funds, and bonds.

1. *Stock.*

- If the security is traded on a national, regional, or local exchange, use the mean of the high and low selling prices on the valuation date to determine the value.

- Use the values from the exchange on which the securities are principally traded if they are traded on more than one exchange or a composite of all exchanges where the security is traded.

- If the valuation date is not a business day with trades, use the averages of the high and low on each of the days with trades immediately before and after the valuation date.

The general formula for the value can be expressed as follows:

$$\frac{(Daf \times Pbef) + (Dbef \times Paf)}{Daf + Dbef}$$

Where:

Daf = Number of trading days after the valuation date until a date with trades

Dbef = Number of trading days before the valuation date since a date with trades

Paf = Average price on the following date with trades

Pbef = Average price on the preceding date with trades

▶ **CAUTION:** Do not use this method if the trades are not within a reasonable number of days.

1. *Decedent's participating interest in a common trust fund.* Use the weighted average method as shown above for stocks.

2. *Brokerage house money market cash funds.* These usually trade at $1 per share but you should check with the broker.

3. *Stocks of co-op apartments.* These stocks must be valued by a qualified real estate appraiser.

4. *Open-end mutual funds.* Value open-end mutual funds at the bid or public redemption price on the valuation date or on the date the last redemption price was quoted before the valuation date.

5. *U.S. Series E and EE bonds.* Use the government redemption table that is available at any commercial bank.

6. *U.S. Series H bonds.* Value at full face value.

List interest that has accrued to the date of death on all bonds as a separate item for each bond listed on Schedule B. List the accrued interest immediately below each respective bond. Use the heading "accrued interest thereon."

¶2413

Treatment of dividends. Include the dividends that are payable to the decedent's estate by reason of the fact that on or before the date of the decedent's death he was a shareholder of record. List dividends as a separate item on Schedule B. Do not include dividends declared before the decedent's death but payable to stockholders of record on a date after his or her death.

> ▶ **CAUTION:** If the stock is selling ex-dividend on the date of death, the dividend is added to the ex-dividend quotation in determining the value of the stock on the date of death.

Treatment of closely held stock. The following are factors that influence the value of closely held stock:

1. The history and uniqueness of the corporation to be valued. An appraiser should look at gross and net income, dividend history, sales records, products and services, assets, nature of the business, and significant events that have affected the corporation;

2. The economic outlook in general and in the specific industry;

3. The loss of a key manager;

4. Capacity to pay dividends;

5. Trades of stock of competing corporations;

6. Current and book values of the assets;

7. The extent of control that the decedent had before he or she died. There may be an argument for a minority discount;

8. A binding bona fide buy-sell agreement.

> ▶ **CAUTION:** Buy-sell agreements among family members may be ignored by the IRS for valuation purposes under IRC Sec. 2703. For further discussion of buy-sell agreements used to establish value for estate tax purposes, see ¶1909 and ¶1914.

1. Options or other restrictive agreements concerning the stock.

Attachments. The following attachments must be made to Schedule B:

1. Financial records for the last five years—balance sheets and statements of net earnings;

2. An appraiser's report;

3. A narrative of any significant irregular events.

   ■ The preparer lists the following items that Dr. Smith owned at the time of death: money market account; cash he had on his person when he died; certificate of deposit; and promissory note with the unpaid balance listed on Schedule C.

¶2414 SCHEDULE C—MORTGAGES, NOTES, AND CASH

On Schedule C, list mortgages, notes or cash payable **to the decedent** at the time of death, certificates of deposit (CDs) owned by the decedent at the time of death, bank accounts owned by the decedent at the time of death, and cash the decedent had at

¶2414

the time of death. Do not list on Schedule C mortgages and notes payable **by the decedent**. If these are deductible, list them on Schedule K.

Simplified reporting for estates under the filing threshold. In the instructions accompanying Form 706, Schedule C, the IRS provides a special reporting rule for assets subject to the special rule of Temp. Reg. Sec. 20.2010-2T(a)(7)(ii). The IRS directs taxpayers not to enter any value in the last three columns of Schedule C of Form 706 and to refer to the instructions for line 10 of Part 5–Recapitulation for information on how to estimate and report the value of these assets [For further discussion, see ¶2413].

▶ **PRACTICE POINTER:** List any cash that the decedent was carrying at the time of his or her death separately from the rest of the bank accounts.

List the items on Schedule C in the following order:

- Mortgages;
- Promissory notes;
- Contracts by decedent to sell land;
- Cash in possession; and
- Cash in banks, savings and loan associations, and other types of financial organizations.

The description of each mortgage must include:

1. Face value;
2. Unpaid balance;
3. Date of mortgage;
4. Maturity date;
5. Mortgagor's name;
6. Property mortgaged;
7. Interest rate; and
8. Payment dates.

Example 1: Enter in "Description" column: "Bond and mortgage of $50,000, unpaid balance: $17,000; dated: January 1, 1992; John Doe to Richard Roe; premises: 22 Clinton Street, Newark, NJ; due: January 1, 2014; interest payable at 10% a year—January 1 and July 1."

The description of each bank account must include:

1. Amount in the account (including accrued interest);
2. The bank in which the account was kept;
3. The account or serial number;
4. Unpaid interest accrued from date of last interest payment to the date of death; and
5. The type of account.

¶**2414**

Valuation. Value mortgages and notes at the full remaining indebtedness unless there is a good reason for taking some sort of discount. Make sure to include any accrued interest as of the date of death. Cash is valued at its full face value.

> ▶ **PRACTICE POINTER:** Any cash that has value as a collectible item should be listed on Schedule F.

Foreign currency should be valued per the official currency exchange rates on the valuation date. Value CDs at full face value even if the CD has several years to run.

> ▶ **PRACTICE POINTER:** A CD can be redeemed at full value without an interest penalty at the owner's death.

Attachments. Attach documentation to support the opinion that a mortgage or note should be valued at a discount. Also attach whatever documentation is necessary to support a market discount in valuing any of the other items on Schedule C.

> ■ The preparer lists all of the money market accounts, certificates of deposit and promissory notes that Dr. Smith owned at the time of his death. Also listed are unpaid interest accrued at death and cash he had on-hand when he died.

¶2415 SCHEDULE D—INSURANCE ON DECEDENT'S LIFE

On Schedule D, the executor must include:

- Insurance on the decedent's life receivable by or for the benefit of the estate; and

- Insurance on the decedent's life receivable by beneficiaries other than the estate.

The term "insurance" includes life insurance of every type, including death benefits paid by fraternal beneficiary societies operating under the lodge system, and death benefits paid under no-fault automobile insurance policies if the no-fault insurer was unconditionally bound to pay the benefit when the decedent died.

Simplified reporting for estates under the filing threshold. In the instructions accompanying Form 706, Schedule D, the IRS provides a special reporting rule for assets subject to the special rule of Temp. Reg. Sec. 20.2010-2T(a)(7)(ii). The IRS directs taxpayers not to enter any value in the last three columns of Schedule D of Form 706 and to refer to the instructions for line 10 of Part 5–Recapitulation for information on how to estimate and report the value of these assets [For further discussion, see ¶2413].

Insurance in favor of the estate. Include on Schedule D the full amount of the proceeds of insurance on the life of the decedent receivable by the executor or otherwise payable to or for the benefit of the estate. Insurance in favor of the estate includes insurance used to pay the estate tax, and any other taxes, debts, or charges that are enforceable against the estate. How the policy is drafted is immaterial provided there is an obligation, legally binding on the beneficiary, to use the proceeds to pay taxes, debts or charges. The full amount of the policy must be included on Schedule D even though the premiums may have been paid by a person other than the decedent.

¶2415

Insurance receivable by beneficiaries other than the estate. Include on Schedule D the proceeds of all insurance on the life of the decedent receivable by or for the benefit of the decedent's estate if the decedent possessed at death any of the incidents of ownership, exercisable either alone or in conjunction with any person. Incidents of ownership in a life insurance policy include the following:

* The right of the insured or estate to its economic benefits;
* The power to change the beneficiary;
* The power to surrender or cancel the policy;
* The power to assign the policy or to revoke an assignment;
* The power to pledge the policy for a loan;
* The power to obtain from the insurer a loan against the surrender value of the policy; and
* A reversionary interest if the value of the reversionary interest was more than 5 percent of the value of the policy immediately before the decedent died. An interest in an insurance policy is considered a reversionary interest if, for example, the proceeds become payable to the insured's estate or payable as the insured directs if the beneficiary dies before the insured.

> ▶ **CAUTION:** On Schedule F, report life insurance owned by the decedent on another's life. On Schedule G, report insurance policies on the decedent's life that are includable under the lifetime transfer provisions of IRC Secs. 2036-2038.

The insurance company that issued the policy can provide the value of the policy for estate tax purposes. This is done on IRS Form 712. Attach a Form 712 behind Schedule D for each insurance policy on the decedent's life, even if the policies are not includable in the decedent's estate. Answer "Yes" to question 8a of Part 4 on Page 3 of the return to show that policies on the decedent's estate are not included on the Form 706 even though you have a Form 712 for them and will attach these forms to the Form 706. Do not include the proceeds of a corporation-owned life insurance policy to the extent that they are payable to such corporation or third party for a valid business purpose.

> ■ The preparer lists the life insurance policies on Dr. Smith's life. However, because this policy was owned by Dr. Smith's wife and she was the beneficiary of the policy, none of the proceeds are payable to Dr. Smith's estate and therefore, are not includable in his estate.

¶2416 SCHEDULE E—JOINTLY OWNED PROPERTY

On Schedule E, report all joint ownership interests with rights of survivorship. These include:

* real estate;
* stocks;
* bonds;
* bank accounts; and

- cars, boats, and mobile homes in which the decedent held at the time of death an interest either as a joint tenant with right to survivorship or as a tenant by the entirety.

Simplified reporting for estates under the filing threshold. In the instructions accompanying Form 706, Schedule E, the IRS provides a special reporting rule for assets subject to the special rule of Temp. Reg. Sec. 20.2010-2T(a)(7)(ii). The IRS directs taxpayers not to enter any value in the last three columns of Schedule E of Form 706 and to refer to the instructions for line 10 of Part 5–Recapitulation for information on how to estimate and report the value of these assets [For further discussion, see ¶2413].

Do not list on Schedule E property that the decedent held as a tenant in common. Instead, report the value of the interest on Schedule A if real estate, or on the appropriate schedule if personal property. Community property held jointly by the decedent and spouse should be reported on the appropriate Schedules A through I. The decedent's interest in a partnership should not be reported on Schedule E unless the partnership interest is jointly owned. Solely owned partnership interests should be reported on Schedule F, "Other Miscellaneous Property Not Reportable Under Any Other Schedule."

Part 1. Qualified joint interests held by decedent and spouse. Enter on Part I joint interests that the decedent and the surviving spouse held as:

- Tenants by the entirety; or
- Joint tenants with right of survivorship if the decedent and the decedent's spouse are the only joint tenants.

Valuation. Value joint tenancy property using the same method that you would use for that type of property if it were not joint tenancy property. On Part 1 of Schedule E, include only one-half of the value of the property if the joint tenancy is solely between the decedent and the decedent's spouse.

> ▶ **PRACTICE POINTER:** The courts have held that a spousal joint interest in real estate created before 1977 is not subject to the 50 percent inclusion rule no matter when the spousal co-owner dies. Thus, 100 percent of the value of jointly held property was included in the decedent spouse's estate and the surviving spouse could claim a stepped-up basis equal to the date of death value with respect to the entire property.

Part 2. All other joint interests. Include nonspousal joint interests on Part 2 of Schedule E. Include the full value of the joint property unless you can establish that a part of the property originally belonged to or was contributed by the other tenant(s) (i.e., by proof of actual cash contributions or inheritance records).

> ▶ **PRACTICE POINTER:** Include the names and addresses of all joint tenants on the lines under 2(a) on Schedule E to indicate the surviving co-tenant.

The passing of title of jointly held property to a joint tenant at death is not a disposition for purposes of alternate valuation. Make sure that you answer the question on line 10 on Page 3 of Form 706 to disclose whether any nonspousal joint tenancy property was excluded from the gross estate. If you check "Yes," you must attach a description of the property, and a list that includes the names of the joint

¶2416

tenants, the total value of the property and the value of the part excluded, and the reason for the exclusion.

■ In Part 1 of Schedule E, the preparer lists all of the property that Dr. Smith and his wife own together [see ¶2404]. This includes the couple's residence, including the lot, as well as their joint savings and checking accounts held at Bank of America. Each asset is described and then its value at the date of Dr. Smith's death is listed. On line 1b of Part 1, the preparer divides the total value of the joint property in half to arrive at the amount that is included in Mr. Smith's gross estate. In Part 2 of Schedule E, the preparer lists all other joint interests owned by the decedent with surviving co-tenants other than his or her spouse.

In this instance, the decedent owned a brokerage account worth $500,000 at the date of death with his sister, Beth Smith Bromley. Her name and address are listed in Part 2, section 2a, Line A and the account number is listed below that. One-half of the date-of-death value ($250,000) is includible in the decedent's estate for tax purposes and is listed in Part 2, item 1.

¶2417 SCHEDULE F—OTHER MISCELLANEOUS PROPERTY NOT REPORTABLE UNDER ANY OTHER SCHEDULE

On Schedule F, list all the following property that is not reported on any other schedule including:

- partnership interests;
- all business interests including sole proprietorship interests;
- antiques;
- tangible personal property;
- art objects;
- remainder interests;
- royalties;
- insurance policies owned by the decedent on another's life (obtain and attach Form 712, "Life Insurance Statement," for each policy);
- firearms;
- vested interests in other estates and trusts;
- claims for refunds;
- unpaid commissions;
- bonuses or wages;
- coin collections;
- gold or silver bullion;
- precious metals;
- bankruptcy claims;

- books;
- cars;
- boats;
- clothing;
- growing crops;
- cattle;
- deferred compensation payments;
- jewelry;
- qualified terminable interest property;
- stamp collections;
- income tax refunds;
- any interest in an Archer medical savings account (MSA) or health savings account (HSA), unless such interest passes to the surviving spouse;
- all possible debts or claims due the decedent (other than notes and mortgages included on Schedule C); and
- real estate used as part of a sole proprietorship.

Simplified reporting for estates under the filing threshold. In the instructions accompanying Form 706, Schedule F, the IRS provides a special reporting rule for assets subject to the special rule of Temp. Reg. Sec. 20.2010-2T(a)(7)(ii). The IRS directs taxpayers not to enter any value in the last three columns of Schedule F of Form 706 and to refer to the instructions for line 10 of Part 5–Recapitulation for information on how to estimate and report the value of these assets [For further discussion, see ¶2413].

Valuation. Value the property items according to the usual valuation methods for property. The best way to do this is to hire an appraiser who is familiar with the different types of property. This may mean that you have to hire more than one appraiser before all of the items can be properly valued. The following guidelines apply to the valuation of household and personal effects, automobiles, and jewelry.

- *Household and personal effects.* Itemize these items room by room and value each item separately. You may group together items in the room, none of which exceeds $100 in value. You must file an appraisal under oath if the value of any one item exceeds $3,000 or if a collection of items exceeds $10,000.

  ▶ **PRACTICE POINTER:** Items referred to as "collectibles" on Schedule F are jewelry, furs, silverware, books, statuary, vases, oriental rugs, art, coin, and stamp collections.

- *Automobiles.* Value may be taken from the various books for used car prices. Use the average retail price, not the average wholesale price. If the car is in poor condition or has high mileage, you may reduce the value of the car below the average retail figure.

- *Jewelry.* Use fair-market value.

If you sell the decedent's property at auction or through the classified ads, the value of the property is the sales price, as long as there are no substantial changes between

¶2417

the date of death and the date of sale and the sale is within a reasonable time after the decedent's death.

Attachments. Attach a proper appraisal (under oath for items exceeding $3,000 or for a group exceeding $10,000) along with a statement signed by the executor under penalty of perjury that the property schedule is complete and the appraiser is disinterested. Attach business records for the last five years for sole proprietorships and partnerships. Also attach copies of wills or trust instruments for vested interests in other estates or trusts and a Form 712 for each life insurance policy that the decedent owned on another's life. Indicate on line 3 of Schedule F if there are any items of value in the decedent's safe deposit box that are not reported on the Form 706 and attach a list of those items and an explanation of why they were omitted.

An appraisal of property must include the following five items:

1. A summary of the appraiser's credentials.

2. A statement of value and the appraiser's definition of the value he or she has obtained.

3. The basis for the appraisal. This should include any restrictions, understandings, or covenants limiting the use or disposition of the property.

4. The valuation date (or dates if alternate valuation is applicable).

5. The date the appraisal was made.

General information from Form 706, Part 4 related to Schedule F. All estates must answer the questions found in lines 7, 9b, 11a, 11b, and 13b of Part 4 (General Information) of Form 706. These questions concern miscellaneous items of property includable on Schedule F (and on line 6 of the Recapitulation):

1. Line 7 asks whether the gross estate includes any qualified terminable interest property (QTIP) property that was received from a prior gift or estate. If the decedent was a surviving spouse, he or she may have received QTIP from the predeceased spouse for which the marital deduction was elected either on the predeceased spouse's estate tax return or on a gift tax return. If so, the "yes" box should be checked and the property must be listed on Schedule F. If the QTIP election was made and the surviving spouse retained his or her interest in the QTIP property at death, the full value of the QTIP property is includible in his or her estate, even though the qualifying interest terminated at death. It is valued as of the date of the surviving spouse's death, or the alternate valuation date, if applicable. The value of QTIP property included in the surviving spouse's gross estate is treated as passing from the surviving spouse and it therefore qualifies for the charitable and marital deductions on the surviving spouse's estate tax return if the interest satisfies the other requirements for those deductions [Reg. Sec. 20.2044-1; for further discussion of QTIP property, see ¶1103].

2. Line 9b asks whether the decedent owned any insurance on the life of another that is not included in the gross estate. If this question is answered "yes," the executor must attach a Form 712 (Life Insurance Statement) for each policy and an explanation of why the policy is not includable in the gross estate.

3. Line 11a asks whether the decedent owned any interest in a partnership, an unincorporated business, a limited liability corporation, or stock in an inactive or closely held corporation. Line 11b asks if the value of any such interest has been

discounted on the estate tax return. If the value is discounted, the Schedule F instructions require attaching a statement to the return that lists the item number from Schedule F and identifies the total accumulated discount taken. The statement should include an appraisal from a qualified appraiser and an explanation of the methodology used to support the discount.

4. Line 13b requires the executor to indicate whether the decedent at the time of death possessed any power, beneficial interest, or trusteeship under any existing trust created by another person. If this question is answered "yes," the executor must attach a copy of the trust instrument for each trust (even if the trust interest is not includable in the gross estate, e.g., a life interest terminating at death).

■ The preparer lists all of Dr. Smith's property [see ¶ 2404] that is not includable on any other schedule. This includes his Ford pick-up truck, his household goods and personal effects, his collection of antique books on veterinary procedures and his veterinary tools and surgical instruments used in his current practice. The value of the last two items is based on appraisals prepared by qualified appraisers. The appraisals are attached to the estate tax return.

¶2418   SCHEDULE G—TRANSFERS DURING DECEDENT'S LIFE

Transfers included on Schedule G. The decedent must complete Schedule G and file it with Form 706 if the decedent answered "Yes" to question 12 or 13a of Part 4–General Information or made any of the following lifetime transfers required to be included in the decedent's gross estate:

• Transfers with a retained life estate under IRC Sec. 2036 [for further discussion, see ¶ 1807];

• Transfers taking effect at death under IRC Sec. 2037 [for further discussion, see ¶ 1805];

• Revocable transfers under IRC Sec. 2038 [for further discussion, see ¶ 1806]; and

• Certain transfers made within three years of death under IRC Sec. 2035 [for further discussion, see ¶ 1804].

Simplified reporting for estates under the filing threshold. In the instructions accompanying Form 706, Schedule G, the IRS provides a special reporting rule for assets subject to the special rule of Temp. Reg. Sec. 20.2010-2T(a)(7)(ii). The IRS directs taxpayers not to enter any value in the last three columns of Schedule G of Form 706 and to refer to the instructions for line 10 of Part 5–Recapitulation for information on how to estimate and report the value of these assets [For further discussion, see ¶ 2413].

How to complete Schedule G. When completing Schedule G, all transfers (other than outright transfers not in trust and bona fide sales) made by the decedent at any time during life must be reported regardless of whether the transfers are subject to tax. Schedule G should be completed for each transfer that is included in the gross estate under IRC Secs. 2035(a), 2036, 2037, and 2039. In the "Item number" column, each transfer should be numbered consecutively beginning with "1." In the "Description" column, list the name of the transferee and the date of the transfer, and give a complete description of the property. Transfers included in the gross estate should be valued on the date of the decedent's death unless an alternate valuation date is elected under IRC Sec. 2032.

Attachments. Attach copies of all trust documents that affect Schedule G transfers. Include a Form 712 for each life insurance policy that is listed on Schedule G (i.e., life insurance policies on decedent's life transferred within three years of death, life insurance policies on decedent's life that are paid to a revocable living insurance trust, or life insurance policies owned by a revocable trust on the life of someone other than the decedent). Also attach appraisals or other documentation that indicates the value for underlying assets of the lifetime transfers. Finally, attach copies of the decedent's and the decedent's spouse's gift tax returns.

Item A on Schedule G asks you to include the gift tax paid by the decedent for all gifts made by the decedent or the decedent's spouse within three years before the decedent's death. This is to gross up the estate for gift taxes actually paid. The date of the gift and not the date of the gift tax payment controls.

> **Example 1:** Joe dies on March 1, 2014. The person who is preparing his estate tax return should gross up the estate for gift taxes paid on gifts made on or after March 1, 2011.

> ▶ **CAUTION:** Make sure to include any gift taxes that were paid by the donee of the gift by a so-called net gift.

> ■ The preparer lists all of the assets that Dr. Smith gave away during his life but may be included in his estate. Here, Dr. Smith gave two life insurance policies to his sons within three years of his death. Therefore, they are included in his gross estate.

¶2419 SCHEDULE H—POWERS OF APPOINTMENT

Complete Schedule H–Powers of Appointment, and file it with Form 706 if "Yes" was the answer to question 14 of Part 4–General Information.

Simplified reporting for estates under the filing threshold. In the instructions accompanying Form 706, Schedule H, the IRS provides a special reporting rule for assets subject to the special rule of Temp. Reg. Sec. 20.2010-2T(a)(7)(ii). The IRS directs taxpayers not to enter any value in the last three columns of Schedule H of Form 706 and to refer to the instructions for line 10 of Part 5–Recapitulation for information on how to estimate and report the value of these assets [For further discussion, see ¶2413].

On Schedule H, include the following:

1. The value of property for which the decedent possessed a general power of appointment under IRC Sec. 2041 on the date of his or her death [For further discussion, see ¶1810]. A power of appointment determines who will own or enjoy the property subject to the power and when they will own or enjoy it. The

power must be created by someone other than the decedent. It does not include a power created or held on property transferred by the decedent. A power of appointment includes all powers which have the same effect as powers of appointment, regardless how they are identified in the document. For example, if a settlor transfers property in trust for the life of his wife, with a power in the wife to appropriate or consume the principal of the trust, the wife has a power of appointment. A general power of appointment is a power that is exercisable in favor of the decedent, the decedent's estate, the decedent's creditors, or the creditors of the decedent's estate, except: (1) a power to consume, invade, or appropriate property for the benefit of the decedent that is limited by an ascertainable standard relating to health, education, support, or maintenance of the decedent; (2) a power exercisable by the decedent only in conjunction with the creator of the power or a person who has a substantial interest in the property subject to the power, which is adverse to the exercise of the power in favor of the decedent; and

2. The value of property for which the decedent possessed a general power of appointment that he or she exercised or released before death by disposing of it so that if it were a transfer of property owned by the decedent, the property would be includible in the decedent's gross estate as a transfer with a retained life estate, a transfer taking effect at death, or a revocable transfer.

Do not include property subject to a power of appointment if the decedent released the power completely and the decedent held no interest in or control over the property.

Some powers do not constitute powers of appointment. For example, a power to amend only administrative provisions of a trust that cannot substantially affect the beneficial enjoyment of the trust property or income is not a power of appointment. A power to manage, invest, or control assets, or to allocate receipts and disbursements when exercised only in a fiduciary capacity, is not a power of appointment.

Value the underlying assets that are subject to the power of appointment the same way that you would value other property that the decedent owned when he or she died. You must attach a copy of the instrument that created the power of appointment in the decedent.

¶2420 SCHEDULE I—ANNUITIES

Complete Schedule I–Annuities and file it with Form 706, if "Yes" was the answer to question 16 of Part 4–General Information.

Simplified reporting for estates under the filing threshold. In the instructions accompanying Form 706, Schedule I, the IRS provides a special reporting rule for assets subject to the special rule of Temp. Reg. Sec. 20.2010-2T(a)(7)(ii). The IRS directs taxpayers not to enter any value in the last three columns of Schedule I of Form 706 and to refer to the instructions for line 10 of Part 5–Recapitulation for information on how to estimate and report the value of these assets [For further discussion, see ¶2413].

¶2420

On Schedule I, list all annuities in which the decedent had an interest at the time of his or her death. The executor must include all or part of the value of any annuity that meets the following requirements:

1. It is receivable by a beneficiary following the death of the decedent and by reason of surviving the decedent;

2. The annuity is under a contract or agreement entered into after March 3, 1931;

3. The annuity was payable to the decedent (or the decedent possessed the right to receive the annuity) either alone or in conjunction with another, for the decedent's life or for any period not ascertainable without reference to the decedent's death or for any period that did not in fact end before the decedent's death; and

4. The contract or agreement is not a policy of insurance on the life of the decedent.

   ▶ **PRACTICE POINTER:** Some qualified plan benefits may be excludable from the estate based on certain elections made by the decedent before death. As certain whether the estate qualifies for this bonus.

Joint and survivor annuities in which only the surviving spouse can receive payments before his or her death automatically qualify for the marital deduction under IRC Sec. 2056(b)(7).

Valuation. Following are guidelines for the valuation of annuities and all types of qualified plans.

1. *Commercial annuities.* The company that issues the annuity will provide a valuation letter or Form 712 that details the annuity's current value.

2. *Other annuities (including private annuities).* The value can be found in Reg. Sec. 20.2039-1(c).

3. *All types of qualified plans.* The trustee of the plan will provide a letter of valuation.

Attachments. The following attachments must be filed with Schedule I.

1. Applicable valuation letter.

2. If you answer "Yes" to Question A on Schedule I, you must attach a statement of the name, address, and tax I.D. number of each beneficiary of the lump sum distribution, and state whether the beneficiary has made the lump sum distribution election.

   ■ The preparer lists all of the annuities in which Dr. Smith had an interest in at death. The values of the annuities or individual retirement accounts (IRAs) were obtained from the issuing bank and the letter from the bank will be attached to the return.

¶2421 SCHEDULE J—FUNERAL EXPENSES AND EXPENSES INCURRED IN ADMINISTERING PROPERTY SUBJECT TO CLAIMS

Schedule J–Funeral Expenses and Expenses Incurred in Administering Property Subject to Claims, should be completed if a deduction was claimed on Form 706, Part 5, Item 14–Recapitulation

Schedule PC-Protective claim for refund. A protective claim for refund can be filed on Schedule PC (Protective Claim for Refund) to preserve the estate's right to claim a refund of tax for an unresolved claim or expense that may not become deductible under Section 2053 until after the statute of limitations expires for filing a supplementary return. Once the claim or expense has been paid or otherwise becomes deductible, the executor notifies the IRS that the estate is ready to pursue the refund claim for the deductible expense.

What expenses are claimed on Schedule J. Funeral expenses and expenses incurred in administering property subject to claims are claimed on Schedule J. Deductible expenses include amounts paid as well as reasonable estimates of expenses not yet incurred at the time the return is filed. An election permits certain administration expenses to be deducted on either the estate tax return (Form 706) or the estate's income tax return (Form 1041).

Funeral expenses. On Schedule J, the executor should list funeral expenses that are deductible against the estate include the following:

1. Funeral expenses actually paid and allowable under local law;
2. Tombstone;
3. Mausoleum;
4. Burial plot;
5. Cost of shipping the body; and
6. Travel expenses for one person to accompany the body if it is shipped for burial and returning to the burial site for the stone setting [IRC Sec. 2053(a)(1); Reg. Sec. 20.2053-2].

No deduction is available for the amount set aside for perpetual care of a burial lot if it is allowed as a deduction under local probate law.

Administration expenses. Administration expenses are those incurred for collection of the decedent's assets, payment of claims, and distribution of the assets to the beneficiaries and include executor's commissions, attorney fees, and other miscellaneous expenses necessary to the estate administration [Reg. Sec. 20.2053-3(a)]. Administration expenses that are deductible against the estate include the following:

1. Attorney's fees;
2. Executor fees;
3. Interest expense incurred after the decedent's death as a result of a federal estate tax deficiency;
4. Appraiser fees;
5. Accountant fees;
6. Court fees;
7. Expense of publishing legal notices;
8. Costs for publications;
9. Costs for preservation of estate assets; and
10. Expenses of selling assets if the sales are necessary to pay taxes, debts, expenses, or to effect an orderly distribution.

¶2421

▶ **PRACTICE POINTER:** You may deduct any of these administration expenses on the estate's income tax return rather than on the Form 706 as long as the fiduciary files a statement waiving the right to deduct the expenses on Form 706 as required under IRC Sec. 642(g).

■ The preparer lists all the expenses that were incurred for Dr. Smith's funeral and burial. In addition, the preparer lists the administrative expenses incurred by the estate, including executors' commissions, attorney fees, and accountant fees. Also listed are amounts expended to obtain the various appraisals required in order to prepare the decedent's federal estate tax return, administer the estate in the probate court and maintain the real estate the decedent owned at the time of his death.

Attachments. If the fees are not paid by final audit, you should prepare IRS Form 4421, "Declaration–Executor's, Commissioner's and Attorney's Fees," which is a declaration of the executor's commissions and attorney's fees that will be paid. It is often requested to be signed by the estate tax examiner prior to closing the audit.

¶2422 SCHEDULE K—DEBTS OF THE DECEDENT, MORTGAGES, AND LIENS

Schedule K–Debts of the Decedent and Mortgages and Liens, must be completed if the decedent claimed deductions on either item 15 or item 16 of Part 5– Recapitulation.

IRC Sec. 2053(a)(3) provides that an estate is permitted to deduct claims representing personal obligations of the decedent that existed and were legally enforceable at the time of death, whether or not matured. The amount that may be deducted is unpaid principal note amount (outstanding balance) at the date of death even if the executor elects alternate valuation. Interest on the claims is deductible to the extent it had accrued at the date of death, even if the executor elects the alternate valuation date [Reg. Sec. 20.2053-4].

On Schedule K, the executor should list all valid debts that the decedent owed at the time of death. If the amount of the debt is disputed or the subject of litigation, deduct only the amount the estate concedes to be a valid claim. Enter the amount in contest in the column provided. You may deduct the interest that has accrued on the debt, but only up until the date of death even if you elect IRC Sec. 2032 alternate valuation. You may take a deduction for the decedent's share of personal income taxes accrued at death.

If the decedent was personally liable on any mortgages, you must disclose this on Schedule K. Do not reduce the amount of the mortgage where you have elected to use special use valuation. Describe the mortgaged property. List the mortgagee's name and address. List the original and unpaid balance, the interest rate, and the date and length of the debt.

▶ **PLANNING POINTER:** Taxes, interest, and business expenses accrued at the date of the decedent's death are deductible on both Schedule K and as deductions in respect of the decedent on the income tax return of the estate. If the executor chooses to deduct medical expenses of the decedent only on the estate tax return, they are fully deductible as claims against the estate. If, however, they are claimed on the decedent's final income tax return under IRC Sec. 213(c), they may not also be claimed on the estate tax return. The executor may not deduct on the estate tax return any amounts that were not deductible on the income tax return as a result of the percentage limitations.

On the upper portion of Schedule K under the heading "Debts of the Decedent," deduct all allowable unsecured claims against the decedent's estate. This will typically include credit card debt, amounts owed on utilities as of the date of death, unpaid subscriptions, unpaid professional fees, and money collected as agent to be distributed to its actual owners.

On the lower portion of Schedule K, all mortgages and liens are deducted. Enter the nature of the claim and the creditor's name for all claims listed. Any portion of a claim being contested by the estate is not deductible and should be entered in the designated column on Schedule K. The following obligations require additional information:

1. *Unsecured Notes.* Include the payee's name, face amount, the unpaid balance, term and date of the note, the interest rate and date to which interest was paid before death, and the nature of the claim.

2. *Claim for Services Performed.* Report the amount due, nature of the claim, the creditor's name, and the period covered by the claim.

3. *Contract for the Purchase of Property.* Report the unpaid balance due on the contract, and indicate the schedule and item number where the subject property is reported.

Deductibility of claims. Claims will only be deductible if they are bona fide claims that (1) represent personal obligations of the decedent existing at the time of the decedent's death, (2) are enforceable against the estate at the time of payment, and (3) are actually paid by the estate in settlement of the claim or meet the requirements for deducting ascertainable amounts under Reg. Sec. 20.2053-1(d)(4). No deduction is permitted for a potential or contested claim or a claim that has not yet matured [Reg. Sec. 20.2053-4(d)(1)]. A claim that has been the subject of litigation is deductible only to the extent of the amount conceded by the estate to be a valid claim. When a claim against an estate is based on a promise or agreement, the deduction is limited to the extent the liability was contracted in a bona fide transaction for full and adequate consideration [IRC Sec. 2053(c)(1)(A)]. Note that "love and affection" alone are considered adequate consideration.

Validity of claims between related parties. Reg. Sec. 20.2053-1(b)(2)(ii) provides that a claim involving a family member or related entity will only be bona fide and therefore deductible if the creditor can prove that the claim: (1) occurred in the ordinary course of business, is negotiated at arm's length, and is free from donative intent; (2) was unrelated to an expectation or claim of inheritance; (3) originated pursuant to an agreement between the decedent and family member (or related entity) and is documented contemporaneously; (4) was supported by the actual performance of the agreement that can be substantiated; or (5) was supported by consistent reporting of amounts for income or employment tax as appropriate.

¶2422

■ The preparer lists all of the debts that were incurred by Dr. Smith before his death but were not paid at the time of his death. These claims qualify for a deduction against the gross estate.

¶2423 SCHEDULE L—NET LOSSES DURING ADMINISTRATION AND EXPENSES INCURRED IN ADMINISTERING PROPERTY NOT SUBJECT TO CLAIMS

Complete Schedule L and file it with Form 706 if the decedent claimed deductions on either item 19 or item 20 of Part 5–Recapitulation.

Net losses during administration. On Schedule L, the executor deducts sudden, unforeseen losses that are not covered by insurance, including losses due to fire, storm, shipwreck, thefts, and sudden casualties. The losses will only be deductible if they occur during the settlement of the estate. There is no deductible floor for the estate tax casualty deduction. You should include a reference to the location on the Form 706 where the damaged property is included in the gross estate. The itemization on Schedule L should include a note that the damage is not covered by insurance, the date of the loss, the cause of the damage, and a description of the damage that will support the amount claimed.

▶ **CAUTION:** If the loss was partially covered by insurance, make sure to note the name and address of the insurer, the extent of coverage, and show that any insurance recovery was deducted from the claim.

Expenses incurred while administering nonprobate assets are deductible if they meet two requirements:

1. The expense would have been deductible if the property had been probate property and subject to estate administration; and

2. The expenses were paid before expiration of the statute of limitations.

Expenses incurred in administering property not subject to claims. The executor may deduct expenses incurred in administering property that is included in the gross estate but that is not subject to claims. The executor may only deduct these expenses if they were paid before the IRC Sec. 6501 period of limitations for assessment expired. Expenses normally deducted are those incurred in the administration of a trust established by the decedent before death. These expenses may also be incurred in the collection of other assets or in the transfer or clearance of title to other property included in the decedent's gross estate for estate tax purposes, but not included in the decedent's probate estate. The expenses deductible on this schedule are limited to those that are the result of settling the decedent's interest in the property or of vesting good title to the property in the beneficiaries [see Reg. Sec. 20.2053-8].

¶2423

¶2424 SCHEDULE M—BEQUESTS, ETC., TO SURVIVING SPOUSE (THE MARITAL DEDUCTION)

The executor must complete Schedule M and file it with the return if the marital deduction is claimed on item 21 of Part 5, Recapitulation. Schedule M is used to list each property interest included in the gross estate that passes from the decedent to the surviving spouse and for which the decedent is claiming a marital deduction. The amount of the marital deduction is computed on Schedule M. A marital deduction is allowed for the value of property included in the gross estate that "passes" to the surviving spouse under IRC Sec. 2056(a).

To be eligible for the marital deduction, the property interest that passes to the surviving spouse must be included in the decedent's gross estate. Thus, property over which the decedent possessed a limited power of appointment is not eligible for the marital deduction because it is not included in the decedent's gross estate. Generally, qualifying property interests are considered to "pass" to the surviving spouse if they are transferred to the surviving spouse: (1) by will (or by state law when there is no will), (2) by law as the decedent's surviving joint tenant or tenant by the entirety, (3) by contract under a life insurance policy or retirement plan, (4) under dower, curtesy, or other similar state law, (5) by the decedent's exercise of a general power of appointment, or (6) by the decedent's nonexercise of a general power of appointment where the surviving spouse is the default taker [For further discussion of the marital deduction, see Chapter 11].

What interests to list on Schedule M. The executor should list on Schedule M only those interests that the surviving spouse takes:

1. As the decedent's legatee, devisee, heir or donee;
2. As the decedent's surviving tenant by the entirety or joint tenant;
3. As an appointee under the decedent's exercise of power of appointment or as a taker in default at the decedent's nonexercise of a power;
4. As a beneficiary of insurance on the decedent's life;
5. As the surviving spouse taking under dower or curtesy or similar statutory interest; or
6. As a transferee of a transfer made by the decedent at any time.

The net value of the gift passing to the surviving spouse sets the value of the deduction. However, there is no limit on the allowable marital deduction.

Dower and elective share interests qualify for the marital deduction because they are a fixed right that accrues at the moment of death. However, family allowances to do not qualify because they are not a fixed right vested at death.

Not listed on Schedule M. The following property interests may not be listed on Schedule M:

1. The value of any property that does not pass from the decedent to the surviving spouse;
2. Property interests that are not included in the decedent's gross estate;

¶2424

3. The full value of a property interest for which a deduction was claimed on Schedules J through L. The value of the property interest should be reduced by the deductions claimed with respect to it;

4. The full value of a property interest that passes to the surviving spouse subject to a mortgage or other encumbrance or an obligation of the surviving spouse. Include on Schedule M only the net value of the interest after reducing it by the amount of the mortgage or other debt;

5. Nondeductible terminable interests; or

6. Any property interest disclaimed by the surviving spouse.

QTIP included on Schedule M. An executor may elect to claim a marital deduction for qualified terminable interest property (QTIP) or property interests. The QTIP election, which is irrevocable, is made by simply listing the qualified terminable interest property on Schedule M after item number A1 and deducting its value. If the election is made, the surviving spouse's gross estate will include the value of the qualified terminable interest property. See ¶1103 for a discussion of the QTIP election. Describe the instrument (including any clause or paragraph number) or provision of law under which each item passed to the surviving spouse. If possible, show where each item appears (number and schedule) on Schedules A through I.

QTIP requirements. A QTIP trust must meet the following requirements:

1. All trust accounting income must be payable to the surviving spouse at least annually for life [IRC Sec. 2056(b)(7)].

2. No one (including the surviving spouse) has a power to distribute or appoint the assets to any person other than the surviving spouse during the surviving spouse's lifetime [IRC Sec. 2056(b)(7)].

3. The trust may hold assets that do not generate income only if the trust document requires, or permits the surviving spouse to require, the trustee to either make the property productive or convert it to productive property within a reasonable time [Reg. Sec. 20.2056(b)-5(f)(5)].

4. The executor of the decedent's estate must elect on the estate tax return to have some or all of the trust property qualify for the marital deduction [IRC Sec. 2056(b)(7)].

   ■ The preparer lists all of Dr. Smith's property that is being given to his wife, Jane R. Smith including the following which qualify for the marital deduction: all items on Schedule E that were jointly owned by the decedent and his wife; cash bequests to the decedent's wife as provided in the decedent's will; and the amount passing to the surviving spouse under the decedent's will which established a marital trust providing that income be paid to the surviving spouse for life with remainder over to the surviving spouse's estate.

¶2424

¶2425 SCHEDULE O—CHARITABLE, PUBLIC, AND SIMILAR GIFTS AND BEQUESTS

Complete Schedule O and file it with Form 706 if the decedent claimed a deduction on item 22 of Part 5–Recapitulation. IRC Sec. 2055(a) provides that a decedent's estate is allowed a charitable deduction for the value of property included in the decedent's gross estate that passes to a qualified charity as a result of: (1) a bequest, legacy, devise, or other transfer, (2) a qualified disclaimer, or (3) the exercise of (or failure to exercise) a general power of appointment.

The executor should complete Schedule O to claim the charitable deduction for the value of property in the decedent's gross estate that was transferred by the decedent during life or by will to or for the use of any charitable organization. The contribution must be made to one of the following types of qualified organizations:

1. Any corporation or association organized and operated only for religious, charitable, educational, scientific, medical or literary purposes, or for the prevention of cruelty to animals or children. In addition, organizations that foster national or international amateur sports competitions qualify but only if no part of their activities involve the provision of athletic facilities or equipment [IRC Sec. 170(c)(2)];

2. War veterans' organizations including posts, auxiliaries, trusts, or foundations [IRC Sec. 170(c)(3)];

3. Domestic fraternal societies, orders, and associations operating under the lodge system [IRC Sec. 170(c)(4)];

4. The United States or any state, the District of Columbia, a U.S. possession (including Puerto Rico), a political subdivision of a state or U.S. possession, or an Indian tribal government or any of its subdivisions that perform substantial governmental functions [IRC Sec. 170(c)(1)]; or

5. A foreign government or its political subdivision when the use of such property is limited exclusively to charitable purposes.

List all IRC Sec. 2055 charitable deductions on Schedule O. Charitable deductions include:

1. Outright bequests;

2. Split-interest charitable remainder trusts; and

3. Property passing by court decree.

> ▶ **CAUTION:** An outstanding binding charitable pledge that is paid by the estate does not qualify for the estate tax charitable deduction under IRC Sec. 2055. However, if the pledge is valid and enforceable, it will be considered a claim against the decedent's estate that is deductible under IRC Sec. 2053, on Schedule K.

Valuation presents little or no problem for charitable bequests because there is no limit on the estate's charitable deduction against the estate tax. The assets are included in the gross estate and then an offsetting charitable deduction is taken.

¶2425

1. You must use the IRS valuation tables if the charitable gift is in the form of a charitable remainder trust.

2. You are allowed to take a marital deduction for the surviving spouse's interest in a charitable remainder trust if the spouse's interest is the only intervening interest before the charity's remainder. The value of the remainder will qualify for the charitable deduction.

You must reduce the value of the charitable deduction if the share passing to charity must bear a share of any tax liability.

Attachments. The following attachments must be made to Schedule O:

1. A copy of any disclaimer that results in property passing to a charity.

2. A certified or verified copy of the will or trust if the charitable transfer is made by these documents. You must also attach a certified or verified copy of the order admitting the will to probate.

3. A computation showing how the residuary value was obtained if the charity is a residuary beneficiary. This computation must show the reduction of all taxes charged to the charitable residue portion. Attach a statement that lists the date of birth of all life tenants or annuitants because the length of their lives may control the value of the interest passing to charity where the charity is a residuary beneficiary.

¶2426 SCHEDULE P—CREDIT FOR FOREIGN DEATH TAXES

IRC Sec. 2014 allows a credit against the gross estate tax for any estate, inheritance, legacy, or succession tax paid by the decedent's estate to a foreign country. The purpose of this credit is to minimize the impact of double taxation which could occur when estate tax is imposed on the worldwide assets of a U.S. citizen or resident and those assets are also subject to death taxes in another country. If a tax treaty exists between the United States and the foreign country taxing the decedent's property, a credit for death taxes may be allowable under more favorable terms.

Schedule P, Credit for Foreign Death Taxes is used to compute the amount of the credit under IRC Sec. 2014 for foreign death taxes. The credit is then carried to Form 706, Part 2, line 13. The death taxes paid to the foreign country must be converted to U.S. dollars by using the exchange rate in effect on the date of payment.

A decedent is allowed a tax credit on Form 706 for death taxes actually paid to a foreign country if:

1. The property is included in the decedent's gross estate; and

2. The tax paid to the foreign country is directly related to property located in the country imposing the tax.

For further discussion of the credit for foreign death taxes, see ¶2105.

> ▶ **CAUTION:** You must attach a separate Schedule P for each country in which you paid foreign death taxes

Limitations on amount of foreign death tax credit. The credit for foreign death taxes is subject to two separate limitations. The "first limitation" limits the amount of the foreign death tax credit to the amount of foreign death tax (1) attributable to property situated in the country imposing the tax, and (2) included in the decedent's gross estate [IRC Sec. 2014(b)(1)].The result of the first limitation should be entered on Schedule P (Credit for Foreign Death Taxes), line 1. A schedule detailing the calculation should be attached to the return.

The "second limitation" limits the credit to the amount of federal estate tax attributable to the foreign property [IRC Sec. 2014(b)(2)]. These two limitations determine the extent to which the decedent's property is subject to double taxation. The second limitation limits the foreign death tax credit to the amount of federal estate tax attributable to the foreign property. The second limitation applies a fraction to the gross federal estate tax reduced by the applicable credit amount and any credit for gift tax. The numerator of this fraction is the adjusted value of the foreign property subject to foreign death taxes (situated in that country) and included in the gross estate. The denominator is the value of the gross estate reduced by the total amount allowed as a charitable or marital deduction.

Use IRS Form 706-CE to certify the payment of foreign death tax.

1. Prepare Form 706-CE in triplicate for each country that is imposing a tax for which you are claiming a credit.

2. Send the original and one copy to the foreign country's tax official so that it may be signed and certified.

3. The foreign official must send the Form 706-CE directly to the IRS. The credit must be certified within four years after filing the Form 706.

4. Attach a copy of each Form 706-CE (one for each country) to the Form 706.

5. Keep one copy of the Form 706-CE. If the foreign government refuses to process Form 706-CE, you can meet the certification requirement by mailing your copy to the district director. You must then attach:

   - A statement under oath signed by the executor explaining the facts;

   - A copy of the foreign return; and

   - A photocopy of the front and back of the canceled check.

¶2427 SCHEDULE Q—CREDIT FOR TAX ON PRIOR TRANSFERS

Complete Schedule Q and file it with Form 706 if the decedent claimed a credit on Part 2–Tax Computation, line 14.

A percentage of the prior transfers credit is available if the decedent inherited property within the last 10 years from an estate and the property generated federal estate tax in the other estate [IRC Sec. 2013]. For further discussion of the credit for tax on prior transfers, see ¶2104. There is no requirement that the property be identified in the estate of the transferee or that it exist on the date of the transferee's death [Reg. Sec. 20.2013-1(a)]. The maximum credit is limited to the smaller of:

1. The amount of tax attributable to the transferred property in the transferor's estate (prior decedent); or

2. The amount of tax attributable to the transferred property in the decedent transferee's estate.

This graduated scale shows the percent of the maximum amount that you are allowed to take as a credit. It depends on how many years have elapsed between the date of death of the transferor and the decedent-transferee.

Prior Transfers Credit

Time Exceeding	Not Exceeding	Percent Allowable
—	2 years	100
2 years	4 years	80
4 years	6 years	60
6 years	8 years	40
8 years	10 years	20
10 years	—	none

A 100 percent credit is allowed if not more than two years have elapsed between the dates of death where the decedent-transferee predeceases the transferor. Use the worksheet that is contained in the instructions to the Form 706 to compute the credit. You may want to attach the worksheet to the Form 706 to aid in the examination process.

It is possible to obtain a prior transfer credit for property that passes through several successive estates.

> **Example 1:** Joe dies in 2010, devising his estate to Bill. Bill dies in 2011, devising his estate to George. George dies in 2012. George's estate will be able to avail itself of a prior transfer credit for taxes paid in Joe's estate.

Look for property received from two or more transferors that were not successive transferors, because a prior transfer credit is available from each transferor's estate.

¶2428 SCHEDULE R—GENERATION-SKIPPING TRANSFER TAX

Use Schedule R to compute the generation-skipping transfer (GST) tax that is payable by the estate. Unlike the estate tax, which is imposed on the value of the entire taxable estate regardless of who receives it, the GST tax is imposed only on the value of interests in property, wherever located, that actually pass to skip persons.

Consult the following chart to determine the filing requirements for the different types of GST transfers:

Filing Requirements for Generation-Skipping Transfers

The reporting requirements for GST grantors is dependent on what type of generation-skipping transfer is involved as illustrated in the following chart:

Type of GST Transfer	Where to Report	Who Must File	When Due
Inter vivos direct skip	Form 709 (Sch. D)	Transferor	When Form 709 due
Direct skip at death	Form 706 (Sch. R)	Executor	When Form 706 due
Direct skip at death from a trust	Form 706 (Sch. R-1)	Trustee	When Form 706 due
Taxable distribution	Form 706-GS(D) and (D-1)	Transferee Trustee	15th day of the fourth month following the calendar year in which the distribution occurs
Taxable termination	Form 706-GS(T)	Trustee	15th day of the fourth month following the calendar year in which the termination occurs

Skip person. A transferee who is a natural person is a skip person if that transferee is assigned to a generation that is two or more generations below the generation assignment of the decedent. A transferee who is a trust is a skip person if all the interests in the property transferred to the trust are held by skip persons. Thus, whenever a non-skip person has an interest in a trust, the trust will not be a skip person even though a skip person also has an interest in the trust. A trust will also be a skip person if there are no interests in the property transferred to the trust held by any person, and future distributions or terminations from the trust can be made only to skip persons. A non-skip person is any transferee who is not a skip person. For further discussion, see ¶ 2503.

The GST tax that is to be reported on Form 706 is imposed only on direct skips that occur at death. Schedule R is used to allocate the decedent's $5,250,000 GST exemption in 2013 (increasing to $5,340,000 in 2014) from GST tax.

- If the exemption is not allocated on the return, the IRS will automatically allocate the GST exemption under the deemed allocation at death rules of IRC Sec. 2632(c).

- The automatic allocation will occur whether or not you are required to file a return.

To avoid application of the deemed allocation rules, Form 706 and Schedule R must be filed to allocate the GST exemption to trusts that may later have taxable terminations or distributions under IRC Sec. 2612 even if the form is not required to be filed to report estate or GST tax. The GST tax is imposed on taxable transfers of interests in property located **outside the United States** as well as property located inside the United States.

The first step in computing the GST tax liability is to determine the property interest includible in the gross estate by completing Schedules A through I of Form 706.

The second step is to determine who the skip persons are. To do this, assign each transferee to a generation and determine whether each transferee is a "natural person" or a "trust" for GST purposes.

The third step is to determine which skip persons are transferees of "interests in property." If the skip person is a natural person, anything transferred is an interest in

¶2428

property. If the skip person is a trust, a person will have an interest in the property transferred to the trust if that person either has a present right to receive income or corpus from the trust (such as an income interest for life) or is a permissible current recipient of income or corpus from the trust (receives income or corpus at the discretion of the trustee).

The fourth step is to determine whether to enter the transfer on Schedule R or on Schedule R-1 as discussed in ¶ 2429.

The fifth step is to compute Schedules R and R-1 using the "How to Complete Schedules R and R-1" instructions, beginning on page 44 of the Instructions to Form 706.

Reverse QTIP election. Use Schedule R to make the reverse QTIP election. Generally, the donee spouse (surviving spouse) of a QTIP trust is treated as the transferor of the trust for GST tax purposes. Thus, the donor spouse's (decedent's) GST tax exemption may be wasted when the remainder beneficiary of the trust is a skip person (i.e., grandchildren). The irrevocable reverse QTIP election allows the donor spouse to be treated as the transferor of the trust property for GST tax purposes. Thus, the donor spouse's GST tax exemption can be allocated to the transfer [see ¶ 2502 for further discussion of the reverse QTIP election]. The QTIP election allows you to treat a QTIP as if the QTIP election had not been made for purposes of the GST tax [see ¶ 2502 for further discussion of the reverse QTIP election]. The decedent will be treated as the transferor of the QTIP property and his GST exemption may be allocated to the elected property. To make a reverse QTIP election under IRC Sec. 2652(a)(3), list qualifying property in Part 1, line 9 on Schedule R. Basically you should report all GST transfers on Schedule R unless they must be reported on Schedule R-1.

Valuation. The following are valuation guidelines:

1. Enter the estate tax value of the property interests that have been transferred; and

2. If you elected IRC Sec. 2032 or Sec. 2032A valuation, that value must be used.

Attachments. You may allocate GST exemption to a trust by clearly identifying the trust and the amount of the decedent's GST exemption allocated to the trust and attaching the Notice of Allocation.

■ The preparer makes no entries on this schedule because Dr. Smith made no transfers subject to the GST.

¶2429 SCHEDULE R-1—GENERATION-SKIPPING TRANSFER TAX (DIRECT SKIPS FROM A TRUST PAYMENT VOUCHER)

This schedule is used to compute the GST tax payable by certain trusts that are includable in the decedent's gross estate. You must send two copies of Schedule R-1 to the fiduciary of the trust by the due date of the Form 706 because you are notifying the trustee that a GST tax is due and that the trustee must pay it. Schedule R-1 serves as a payment voucher for the GST tax imposed on a direct skip from a trust, which the trustee of the trust must pay.

■ The preparer makes no entries on this schedule because Dr. Smith made no transfers subject to the GST.

¶2430 SCHEDULE U—QUALIFIED CONSERVATION EASEMENT EXCLUSION

▶ **CAUTION:** If at the time of the contribution of the conservation easement, the value of the easement, the value of the land subject to the easement, or the value of any retained development right, was different than the estate tax value, the executor must complete a separate computation in addition to completing Schedule U. A copy of Schedule U should be used as a worksheet for this separate computation. Complete lines 4 through 14 of the worksheet on Schedule U. However, the value used on lines 4, 5, 7 and 10 of the worksheet is the value for these items as of the date of the contribution of the easement, not the estate tax value. If the date of contribution and the estate tax values are the same, the separate computation is unnecessary. After completing the worksheet, enter the amount from line 14 of the worksheet on line 14 of Schedule U. Finish completing Schedule U by entering amounts on lines 4, 7, and 15 through 20 as discussed below. At the top of Schedule U, enter "Worksheet Attached" and be sure to attach the worksheet to the return.

On Schedule U, executors may make an irrevocable election under IRC Sec. 2031(c) to exclude up to 40 percent of the value of land that is subject to a qualified conservation easement. The qualified conservation easement exclusion for estates of decedents dying is the lesser of:

- The applicable percentage of the value of the land (after certain reductions) subject to a qualified conservation easement, or
- $500,000.

The election is made by filing Schedule U with a timely filed Form 706, including extensions, with all the required information and excluding the applicable value of the land that is subject to the easement on Part 5, Recapitulation, Page 3, at item 11. To elect the exclusion, the executor must include on Schedule A, B, E, F, G or H, as appropriate, the decedent's interest in the land that is subject to the exclusion [For further discussion of qualified conservation easement exclusions, see ¶1002].

Part 1—Election. If you are required to complete Schedule U you will be deemed to have made the election under IRC Sec. 2031(c)(6) if you file this schedule and exclude any qualifying conservation easements from the gross estate.

Part 2—General qualifications.

Line 1. Describe the land subject to the easement by using one or more of the item numbers on a Form 706 schedule. All you have to do is list the schedule and the item numbers.

Line 3. Describe the conservation easement by using the general rules for describing real estate. You will need to provide enough information so the IRS will be able to value the easement. You will need to give the date the easement was granted and by whom it was granted.

Part 3—Computation of exclusion.

Line 4. Enter the estate tax value of the land subject to the qualified conservation easement. This means you should enter the gross value at which the land was reported on the applicable assets schedule on Form 706. The value of the assets should be reduced by the amount of any mortgage outstanding. The estate tax value must be reported even if the easement was granted by the decedent or someone other than the decedent prior to the decedent's death.

Line 5. Enter the date of death value of any easements granted prior to the decedent's death.

Line 7. On line 8 you must enter the value of retained development rights on the land because the land value must be reduced by the value of any development rights retained by the donor in the conveyance of the easement. A development right is any right to use the land for any commercial purpose that is not subordinate to and directly supportive of the use of the land as a farm for farming purposes. No reduction will be required on this line if everyone with an interest in the land agrees to permanently extinguish the retained development right. To qualify for this safe harbor you must file a copy of the agreement with Form 706. The agreement must include the following:

- A statement that the agreement is made pursuant to IRC Sec. 2031(c)(5).

- A list of all persons in being holding an interest in the land that is subject to the qualified conservation easement, including each person's name, address, tax identifying number, relationship to the decedent, and a description of their interest.

- The items of real property shown on the estate tax return that are subject to the qualified conservation easement (identified by schedule and item number).

- A description of the retained development right that is to be extinguished.

- A clear statement of consent that is binding on all parties under applicable local law: (1) to take whatever action is necessary to permanently extinguish the retained development rights listed in the agreement; and (2) to be personally liable for additional taxes if the agreement is not implemented by the earlier of the date that is two years after the date of the decedent's death; or the date of sale of the land subject to the qualified conservation easement.

- A statement that in the event this agreement is not timely implemented, that they will report the additional tax on whatever return is required by the IRS and will file the return and pay the additional tax by the last day of the sixth month following the applicable date described above.

- All parties to the agreement must sign the agreement.

Line 10. On line 10 you enter the value as of the date of death of the qualified conservation easement for which the exclusion is being claimed. You could include here: (1) easements granted by the decedent or someone other than the decedent prior to the decedent's death; (2) easements granted by the executor after the decedent's death; or (3) a combination of these. You will need to explain how the value of the easement was determined. Be sure to attach copies of any appraisals. Typically, you should value a conservation easement by determining the fair-market value of the land both before and after the granting of the easement. The difference between the two will be the value of the easement.

Be sure to reduce the reported value of the easement by the amount of any consideration received for the easement. If the date of death value of the easement is different than the value at the time the consideration was received, you must reduce the value of the easement by the same proportion that the consideration received bears to the value of the easement at the time it was granted.

> **Example 1:** The value of the easement at the time it was granted was $200,000 and $20,000 was received in consideration for the easement. If the easement was worth $300,000 at the date of death, you must reduce the value of the easement by $30,000 ($20,000/$200,000 × $300,000) and report the value of the easement on line 11 as $270,000.

> ▶ **CAUTION:** Use the value of the easement as of the date of death, even if the easement was granted prior to the date of death. But, if the value of the easement was different at the time the easement was contributed than at the date of death, see the **CAUTION** at the beginning of ¶2430.

Line 15. If you have claimed a charitable contribution deduction for this land on Schedule O, you should enter the amount of the deduction here. If the easement was granted after the decedent's death, a contribution deduction may be taken on Schedule O, if it otherwise qualifies, as long as no income tax deduction was or will be claimed for the contribution by any person or entity.

Line 16. You must reduce the value of the land by the amount of any acquisition indebtedness on the land at the time of the decedent's death because debt-financed property is not eligible for the qualified conservation easement exclusion. Acquisition indebtedness includes the unpaid amount of:

1. Any indebtedness incurred by the donor in acquiring the property;

2. Any indebtedness incurred before the acquisition of the property if such indebtedness would not have been incurred but for such acquisition;

3. Any indebtedness incurred after the acquisition of the property if such indebtedness would not have been incurred but for such acquisition and the indebtedness was reasonably foreseeable at the time of acquisition; and

4. The extension, renewal, or refinancing of an acquisition indebtedness.

■ The preparer makes no entries on this schedule because Dr. Smith claimed no exclusions for qualified conservations easements.

¶2431 PART 5, PAGE 3—RECAPITULATION AND PART 6, PAGE 4—PORTABILITY

(a) **Part 5, Page 3—Recapitulation.** If you are required to file an estate tax return for the decedent's estate, you must complete Part 5–Recapitulation on Page 3 of Form 706. The Recapitulation is a summary of the assets included in the decedent's gross estate and the total deductions that may be claimed when computing the amount of the decedent's taxable estate.

¶2431

Items 1 through 9. An entry must be made in each of items 1 though 9 even if the entry is -0- because the gross estate does not contain any assets of the type specified by a given item. The total gross estate (less the qualified conservation easement exclusion) is computed on line 13 and carried to Part 2 (Tax Computation), line 1.

Item 10: Under Temp. Reg. Sec. 20.2010-2T(a)(7)(ii), if the total value of the gross estate and adjusted taxable gifts is less than the applicable exclusion amount ($5,250,000 in 2013 and increasing to $5,340,000 in 2014) and Form 706 is being filed only to elect portability of the DSUE amount, the estate is not required to report the value of certain property eligible for the marital or charitable deduction. For property being reported on Schedules A, B, C, D, E, F, G, H and I, the executor must calculate his or her best estimate of the value. Do not include the estimated value on the line corresponding to the schedule on which the property was reported. Instead, total the estimated value of the assets subject to the special rule and enter on line 10 the amount from the Table of Estimated Values [see ¶ 2413] that corresponds to that total.

Item 12: Enter the amount from Schedule U—Qualified Conservation Easement Exclusion. You use this schedule to elect to exclude a portion of the value of land that is subject to a qualified conservation easement. You make the election by filing Schedule U with all the required information and excluding the applicable value of the land that is subject to the easement on Part 5, Recapitulation, Page 3, item 12. In item 13 you subtract the exclusion from the decedent's total gross estate. You enter the result here and on line 1 of the Tax Computation.

Items 14-17: Total the amount in items 14 through 16 and enter the total on item 17.

Item 18: If item 17 is less than or equal to the value (at the time of the decedent's death) of the property subject to claims, enter the amount from item 17 on item 18. If the amount on item 17 is more than the value of the property subject to claims, enter the greater of:

- The value of the property subject to claims, or
- The amount actually paid at the time the return is filed.

   ▶ **CAUTION:** Do not enter a larger amount on item 18 than on item 17.

Items 19 and 20: These items reflect the Schedule L values of the net losses during administration and expenses of administering property not subject to claims.

Item 21: This item reflects the value of the marital deduction from Schedule M.

Item 22: This item reflects the value of the total amount of charitable, public, and similar gifts and bequests from Schedule O.

Item 23: Add all allowable deductions (items 18 through 23) and enter the total on line 23. Also enter this amount on line 2 of the Tax Computation which is on Page 1 of the form.

(b) Part 6, Page 4—Portability of Deceased Spousal Unused Exclusion (DSUE).

Part 6 of Form 706, page 4 is used for the following: (1) making a portability election, (2) opting out of the portability election, (3) addressing whether assets of the estate are being transferred to a qualified domestic trust (QDOT), (4) computing the deceased spousal unused exclusion (DSUE) amount, if any, that can be transferred to the surviving spouse, and (5) computing the DSUE amount that can be transferred to the surviving spouse

¶2431

Portability basics. The estates of decedents dying on or after January 1, 2011 may make an election to transfer any unused exclusion to the surviving spouse. The amount received by the surviving spouse is called the *deceased spousal unused exclusion*, or DSUE, amount. If the executor of the decedent's estate elects transfer, or portability, of the DSUE amount, the surviving spouse can apply the DSUE amount received from the estate of his or her last deceased spouse against any tax liability arising from subsequent lifetime gifts and transfers at death [See Chapter 15 for a detailed discussion of the DSUE amount].

> **NOTE:** A nonresident surviving spouse who is not a citizen of the United States may not take into account the DSUE amount of a deceased spouse, except to the extent allowed by treaty with his or her country of citizenship. Therefore, an executor of the estate of a nonresident decedent who was not a U.S. citizen at the time of death cannot elect to transfer DSUE to a surviving spouse [Temp. Reg. Sec. 20.2010-2T(a)(5)].

How to make the election. In order for portability of the DSUE amount to be available to the surviving spouse, the executor of the estate of the deceased spouse, regardless of the size of the estate, must elect portability of the DSUE amount on a timely-filed and complete Form 706, United States Estate (and Generation-Skipping Transfer) Tax Return. The estate must file Form 706 nine months after the decedent's date of death or the last day of the period covered by an extension (if an extension of time for filing has been obtained). Upon the timely filing of a complete and properly-prepared estate tax return, an executor of an estate of a decedent survived by a spouse will be deemed to have elected portability of the decedent's DSUE amount unless the executor opts out of portability by checking a box in Part 6, Section A of Form 706. The election is effective as of the decedent's date of death, so the DSUE amount received by a surviving spouse may be applied to any transfer occurring after the decedent's death. A portability election is irrevocable, unless an adjustment or amendment to the election is made on a subsequent return filed on or before the due date.

How to extend time to make portability election. In Rev. Proc. 2014-18,[1] the IRS provided a simplified procedure for the estates of decedents with smaller estates who died before January 1, 2014 to obtain an extension of time to make an estate tax portability election under IRC Sec. 2010(c)(5)(A). Once the portability election has been made, the decedent's unused exclusion amount (deceased spousal unused exclusion amount, or DSUE amount) can be used by his or her surviving spouse to reduce tax liability. No user fee is required for submissions filed under this revenue procedure.

The extension procedure is only available in the following limited situations:

1. The taxpayer is the executor of the estate of a decedent described below:

   - The decedent has a surviving spouse;
   - The decedent died after December 31, 2010, and on or before December 31, 2013;
   - The decedent was a citizen or resident of the United States on the date of death.

---

[1] ¶ **2431** Rev. Proc. 2014-18, 2014-7 IRB 513.

¶2431

2. The only reason the decedent will be filing Form 706 is to elect portability because the decedent is not otherwise required to file an estate tax return under IRC Sec. 6018(a) because the value of his or her gross estate and adjusted taxable gifts is less than the basic exclusion in effect in the year of the decedent's death ($5,250,000 in 2013);

3. The taxpayer did not file an estate tax return within the time prescribed by Temp. Reg. Sec. 20.2010-2T(a)(1) for filing an estate tax return required to elect portability.

Taxpayers who fail to qualify for relief under Rev. Proc. 2014-18 may request an extension of time to make the portability election under IRC Sec. 2010(c)(5)(A) by requesting a letter ruling from the IRS under the provisions of Reg. Sec. 301.9100-3.

The decedent's estate will be granted an extension of time to elect portability if:

1. The estate files a "complete and properly-prepared" Form 706 on or before December 31, 2014;

2. The person filing the Form 706 on behalf of the decedent's estate must state at the top of the Form 706 that the return is "FILED PURSUANT TO REV. PROC. 2014-18 TO ELECT PORTABILITY UNDER SEC. 2010(c)(5)(A)."

The taxpayer will receive an estate tax closing letter acknowledging receipt of the taxpayer's Form 706.

If these requirements are satisfied, the taxpayer's Form 706 will be considered to have been timely filed, the estate will be deemed to meet the requirements for relief, and relief will be granted to extend the time to elect portability. If relief is granted pursuant to Rev. Proc. 2014-18 and it is later determined that the estate was required to file a federal estate tax return, based on the value of the gross estate, plus any adjusted taxable gifts, the extension of time granted to make the portability election is deemed null and void. The new procedures outlined in Rev. Proc. 2014-18 do not apply to taxpayers that filed an estate tax return within the time prescribed by Temp. Reg. Sec. 20.2010-2T(a)(1) for the purpose of electing portability. These taxpayers either will have elected portability of the DSUE amount by timely filing that estate tax return or will have affirmatively opted out of portability in accordance with Temp. Reg. Sec. 20.2010-2T(a)(3)(i).

How to opt-out of portability election. If the executor does not desire to make the portability election to transfer the deceased spouse's unused exclusion amount to the surviving spouse, the executor has two options:

1. Opt-out of portability by checking a box in Part 6, Section A of Form 706. Do not complete Section B or C of Part 6;

2. Do not file a complete and timely Form 706 for the decedent. If the decedent's estate is below the basic exclusion amount and Form 706 need not be filed, and the executor does not file Form 706, the executor will be deemed to have opted out of portability.

Note that only the executor appointed, qualified, and acting on the estate's behalf can opt out of the portability election.

Computing the DSUE amount. An executor electing to transfer a decedent's unused exclusion amount (DSUE) is required to compute the amount of the DSUE on Form 706. The calculation is made in Section C, Part 6, of Form 706. For a decedent who dies in 2013, the DSUE amount that may be transferred to a surviving spouse is the lesser of:

1. $5.25 million which is the basic exclusion amount in 2013 (increasing to $5.34 million in 2014); or

2. The decedent's applicable exclusion amount less the amount on Part 2, line 5–Tax Computation of Form 706 for the Decedent's Estate. The amount on which gift taxes were paid is excluded from adjusted taxable gifts for the purpose of this computation.

DSUE of first spouse to die subject to review when surviving spouse dies. When the surviving spouse applies the DSUE amount to a lifetime gift or bequest at death, the IRS may examine any return of a predeceased spouse whose executor elected portability to verify the allowable DSUE amount. The IRS may adjust or eliminate the DSUE amount as a result of the examination, but the IRS may only make an assessment of additional tax on the return of the predeceased spouse within the statutory limitations period under IRC Sec. 6501.

Simplified Reporting for Estates under the Filing Threshold

Special rules where value of certain property need not be reported on Form 706. In the instructions accompanying Form 706, Part 6, the IRS refers to a special reporting rule for assets subject to the special rule of Temp. Reg. Sec. 20.2010-2T(a)(7)(ii). The temporary rules provide that executors of estates who are not otherwise required to file Form 706 under IRC Sec. 6018(a) because the decedent's estate is below the basic exclusion amount, do not need to report the value of certain property qualifying for the marital or charitable deduction. When computing the value of the property qualifying for the marital or charitable deduction that must be included in the gross estate, the executor may estimate the value exercising good faith and due diligence. The amount reported on Form 706 will correspond to a range of dollar values from the Table of Estimated Values (see below) and will be included in the value of the gross estate shown on line 1 of Part 2–Tax Computation, Page 1.

Table of Estimated Values

If the total estimated value of the assets eligible for the special rule under Temp. Reg. Sec. 20.2010-2T(a)(7)(ii) is more than	But less than or equal to	Include this amount on lines 10 and 23:
$0	$250,000	$250,000
$250,000	$500,000	$500,000
$500,000	$750,000	$750,000
$750,000	$1,000,000	$1,000,000
$1,000,000	$1,250,000	$1,250,000
$1,250,000	$1,500,000	$1,500,000
$1,500,000	$1,750,000	$1,750,000
$1,750,000	$2,000,000	$2,000,000
$2,000,000	$2,250,000	$2,250,000
$2,250,000	$2,500,000	$2,500,000
$2,500,000	$2,750,000	$2,750,000
$2,750,000	$3,000,000	$3,000,000

¶2431

If the total estimated value of the assets eligible for the special rule under Temp. Reg. Sec. 20.2010–2T(a)(7)(ii) is more than	But less than or equal to	Include this amount on lines 10 and 23:
$3,000,000	$3,250,000	$3,250,000
$3,250,000	$3,500,000	$3,500,000
$3,500,000	$3,750,000	$3,750,000
$3,750,000	$4,000,000	$4,000,000
$4,000,000	$4,250,000	$4,250,000
$4,250,000	$4,500,000	$4,500,000
$4,500,000	$4,750,000	$4,750,000
$4,750,000	$5,000,000	$5,000,000
$5,000,000	$5,250,000	$5,250,000

Section C. DSUE amount portable to the surviving spouse. The estate of the decedent making a portability election must calculate the amount of DSUE available to transfer to a surviving spouse. This amount is calculated in Part 6, Section C as follows:

Line 1. Enter the amount from Part 2, line 9c–Tax Computation. This amount is the sum of the basic exclusion amount for the year of death and, for a surviving spouse, any DSUE amount received from a predeceased spouse.

Line 2. Reserved.

Line 3. Enter the value of the cumulative lifetime gifts on which gift tax was paid or payable from line 6 of the Line 7 Worksheet, Part B as the total of Row (4) from the Line 7 Worksheet, Part A. Enter the amount as it appears on line 6 of the Line 7 Worksheet, Part B.

Line 4. Add the amounts on lines 1 and 3.

Line 5. Enter the amount from Part 2, line 10.

Line 6. Divide the amount on line 5 by 40 percent, but do not enter less than zero.

Line 7. Subtract line 6 from line 4.

Line 8. Enter the amount from Part 2, line 5.

Line 9. Figure the unused exclusion amount by subtracting line 8 from line 7 but do not enter less than zero. The DSUE amount available to the surviving spouse will be the lesser of this amount or the basic exclusion amount shown on line 9l of Part 2–Tax Computation.

Line 10. Enter the lesser of line 9 or the basic exclusion amount of Part 2–Tax Computation, line 9a.

Section D. DSUE amount received from a predeceased spouse(s). Section D of Part 6 should be completed if the decedent was a surviving spouse who received a DSUE amount from one of more predeceased spouse(s). On Section D, information must be supplied on all DSUE amounts received from the decedent's last deceased spouse and any previously deceased spouses. Information on the decedent's last deceased spouse is reported in Part 1. DSUE information for previously deceased spouses is included in Part 2.

Report information on DSUE the decedent received from a predeceased spouse in Section D, Part 1 or 2, as follows:

> Column A. Enter the name of the predeceased spouse (for spouses who died after December 31, 2010).
>
> Column B. Enter the spouse's date of death.
>
> Column C. Indicate whether the portability election was made by the predeceased spouse's estate.
>
> Column D. Enter the amount of DSUE transferred from the predeceased spouse if the portability election was made.
>
> Column E. Enter the amount of DSUE transferred from a predeceased spouse that was applied by the decedent to lifetime gifts. Temp. Reg. Sec. 20.2010-2T(c)(2) provides that the amount of the decedent's adjusted taxable gifts will exclude gifts for which gift taxes were paid.
>
> Column F. Enter the date(s) of the gift(s).
>
> Column G. Subtract the Column E amount from the Column D amount to determine the remaining DSUE amount.

Any remaining DSUE amount from a previously deceased spouse that was not used prior to a subsequent spouse's death is not available to apply against any taxable transfer.

> ■ The executor for the Smith Estate makes the portability election for the decedent, Mark F. Smith, in Part 6 by completing and timely filing Form 706 for his estate. No further action is required to elect portability of Smith's DSUE amount. To compute the DSUE amount that will be available to Smith's surviving spouse, the executor completes Section C of Part 6 of Form 706. After completing the 10-line computation, the executor computes the DSUE amount to be zero.

¶2432 PART 2, PAGE 1—TAX COMPUTATION

In Part 2–Tax Computation, on page 1 of Form 706, the executor calculates the decedent's estate tax.

Complete this part as follows:

Line 1: Enter the value of the total gross estate from Item number 13 of Part 5, Recapitulation on page 3 of the Form. Use the amount from the "Value at date of death" column unless you have chosen alternate valuation. A decedent's gross estate includes the value of all property, wherever situated, in which the decedent owned an interest at the time of death [IRC Sec. 2033]. This includes all property subject to transfer by will or pursuant to state intestacy laws, including real and personal property, and tangible and intangible property owned by the decedent [IRC Sec. 2031]. Property included in the decedent's gross estate is reported on Form 706, Schedules A through I and summarized on Part 5–Recapitulation, lines 1 through 10. The total property included in the gross estate from Part 5, line 13, which is adjusted for any qualified conservation easement reported on line 12, is entered on line 1 of Part 2 (Tax Computation).

◼ The executor for the Smith Estate enters $14,272,000 from Part 5, recapitulation, Page 3, item 13).

Line 2: Enter total allowable deductions as computed on Item 24, Part 5, Recapitulation, Page 3.

A decedent's gross estate is reduced by the following allowable deductions:

1. Funeral and administration expenses which are reported on Schedule J;

2. Debts of the decedent, including claims against the estate, mortgages and liens, which are reported on Schedule K;

3. Casualty and theft losses incurred during administration which are reported on Schedule L;

4. Transfers to the surviving spouse which are reported on Schedule M;

5. Charitable bequests and gifts which are reported on Schedule O;

6. State death taxes paid which are reported in Part 2, line 3b.

The total allowable deductions from Part 5–Recapitulation, line 24, are entered on line 2 of Part 2–Tax Computation.

◼ The executor for the Smith Estate enters $1,060,635.

Line 3: Subtract line 2 from line 1 to determine the tentative taxable estate (before state death tax deduction). The estates of decedents dying after December 31, 2004 will be allowed a deduction for state death taxes, instead of a credit. Beginning in 2005, the state death tax credit was repealed. The executor may take a deduction on line 3b for estate, inheritance, legacy, or succession taxes paid as the result of the decedent's death to any state or the District of Columbia. The executor must send the IRS the following evidence of the state death taxes paid:

1. A certificate of the proper officer of the taxing state, or the District of Columbia, showing:

   a. The total amount of tax imposed (before adding interest and penalties and before allowing discount);

   b. The amount of discount allowed;

   c. The amount of penalties and interest imposed or charged;

   d. Total amount actually paid in cash; and

   e. Date of payment;

2. Any additional proof the IRS specifically requests. The executor may claim an anticipated amount of deduction and figure the federal estate tax on the return before the state death taxes have been paid. However, the deduction cannot be finally allowed unless the state death taxes are paid and the deduction is claimed within 4 years after the return is filed if:

   a. A petition is filed with the Tax Court of the United States;

   b. You have an extension of time to pay; or

¶2432

3. You file a claim for refund or credit of an overpayment which extends the deadline for claiming the deduction. Note that the deduction is not subject to dollar limits.

■ The executor for the Smith Estate enters $13,211,365 on line 3a. On line 3b, the executor for the Smith Estate enters a state death tax deduction for Maryland death tax in the amount of $50,000. On line 3c, the executor enters $13,161,365 which is the decedent's taxable estate after reducing the tentative taxable estate by the state death tax deduction.

Line 4: Enter the amount of the adjusted taxable gifts that the decedent made after 1976 that are not includable in his or her gross estate. You should attach copies of the decedent's gift tax returns.

Because the estate and gift tax system are unified with respect to the tax rates for lifetime transfers and transfers at death, the same tax rates apply regardless of whether the decedent made the property transfer as a gift during his or her lifetime or it was made at death pursuant to the terms of a will or trust. In order to achieve this result, adjusted taxable gifts are added to the taxable estate to arrive at the tentative estate tax base on line 5.

Adjusted taxable gifts are total taxable gifts made by the decedent after 1976, other than gifts included in the gross estate [IRC Sec. 2001(b)]. Taxable gifts are the total amount of gifts made each year, less exclusions such as the annual exclusion amount, medical or educational exclusions and deductions for charitable and spousal gifts [IRC Sec. 2503(a)].

In order to reconcile the decedent's taxable gifts made before and after December 31, 1976, return preparers should use Worksheet TG. Worksheet TG, which is available in the IRS instructions to Form 706, is reproduced below.

Worksheet TG and Line 4 Worksheet

Worksheet TG— Taxable Gifts Reconciliation
(To be used for lines 4 and 7 of the Tax Computation)

		a. Calendar year or calendar quarter	b. Total taxable gifts for period (see Note)	Note. For the definition of a taxable gift, see section 2503. Follow Form 709. That is, include only the decedent's one-half of split gifts, whether the gifts were made by the decedent or the decedent's spouse. In addition to gifts reported on Form 709, you must include any taxable gifts in excess of the annual exclusion that were not reported on Form 709.			
Gifts made after June 6, 1932, and before 1977				c. Taxable amount included in col. b for gifts included in the gross estate	d. Taxable amount included in col. b for gifts that qualify for "special treatment of split gifts" described below	e. Gift tax paid by decedent on gifts in col. d	f. Gift tax paid by decedent's spouse on gifts in col. c
	1.	Total taxable gifts made before 1977					
Gifts made after 1976							
	2.	Totals for gifts made after 1976					

Worksheet TG is divided into two parts. Gifts made before 1977 should be entered on line 1. Gifts made after 1976 should be entered on line 2. Enter the decedent's taxable gifts on Worksheet TG, column b (line 1 or 2). Gifts made after 1976 that are included in the gross estate should be entered in column c. If the decedent and spouse elected gift splitting on any gifts included in column c, the gift tax paid by the decedent's spouse should be entered in column f. If any portion of the decedent's taxable gifts is eligible for special treatment, enter the eligible gifts in column d. Gift taxes paid by the decedent on gifts eligible for special treatment is entered in column e.

Use the totals from this worksheet on the Line 4 and Line 7 Worksheets (see Form 706 instructions) to determine the decedent's adjusted taxable gifts and taxes paid on post-1976 transfers.

Line 4 Worksheet. The Line 4 Worksheet (see Form 706 instructions), reproduced below, which is not filed with Form 706, is used to calculate the decedent's adjusted taxable gifts made after 1976. Gifts included in the decedent's gross estate (Worksheet TG, line 2, column c) and gifts qualifying for special treatment (Worksheet TG, line 2, column d) are subtracted from the decedent's total post-1976 taxable gifts (Worksheet TG, line 2, column b) to arrive at adjusted taxable gifts. (See line 5 of the Line 4 Worksheet.) The amount of these adjusted taxable gifts as computed on line 5 of the Line 4 Worksheet should be entered on Form 706, Page 1, line 4.

Line 4 Worksheet—Adjusted Taxable Gifts Made After 1976

1. Taxable gifts made after 1976. Enter the amount from Worksheet TG, line 2, column b	**1**
2. Taxable gifts made after 1976 reportable on Schedule G. Enter the amount from Worksheet TG, line 2, column c. **2**	
3. Taxable gifts made after 1976 that qualify for "special treatment." Enter the amount from Worksheet TG, line 2, column d. **3**	
4. Add lines 2 and 3	**4**
5. Adjusted taxable gifts. Subtract line 4 from line 1. Enter here and on Part 2—Tax Computation, line 4.	**5**

■ The executor for the Smith Estate enters -0-here.

Line 5: Add lines 3c and 4 and enter the total on line 5.

■ The executor for the Smith Estate enters $13,161,365.

Line 6: Compute and enter the tentative estate tax on the amount on line 5, using the unified rate schedule in Table A of the Instructions to Form 706 and reproduced below.

Table A—Unified Rate Schedule

Column A Taxable amount over	Column B Taxable amount not over	Column C Tax on amount in Column A	Column D Rate of tax on excess over amount in Column A
$0	$10,000	$0	18%
10,000	20,000	1,800	20%
20,000	40,000	3,800	22%
40,000	60,000	8,200	24%
60,000	80,000	13,000	26%
80,000	100,000	18,200	28%
100,000	150,000	23,800	30%
150,000	250,000	38,800	32%
250,000	500,000	70,800	34%
500,000	750,000	155,800	37%
750,000	1,000,000	248,300	39%
1,000,000	----	345,800	40%

¶2432

■ The executor for the Smith Estate computes the tax on $13,161,365 to be $5,210,346 using Table A of the 2013 Instructions for Form 706.

Line 7: Enter the total amount of gift taxes payable on gifts made by the decedent after 1976, including gift taxes payable by the decedent's spouse for such spouse's share of split gifts only if the decedent was the donor of these gifts and they are includible in the decedent's gross estate.

The IRS provides a Line 7 Worksheet to be completed and submitted with Form 706. The Line 7 Worksheet is used to allow the return preparer to reconcile the decedent's lifetime taxable gifts, taking into account gifts made after 1976, as well as the unified credit allowable for prior periods. The Line 7 Worksheet including the Taxable Gift Amount Table found in the Form 706 Instructions (pages 7 and 8) is reproduced below:

Line 7 Worksheet – Submit a copy with Form 706

	Line 7 Worksheet Part A- Used to determine Applicable Credit Allowable for Prior Periods after 1976				
(a)	Tax Period[1]	Pre-1977			
(b)	Taxable Gifts for Applicable Period				
(c)	Taxable Gifts for Prior Periods [2]				
(d)	Cumulative Taxable Gifts Including Applicable Period (add Row (b) and Row (c))				
(e)	Tax at Date of Death Rates for Prior Gifts (from Row (c))[3]				
(f)	Tax at Date of Death Rates for Cumulative Gifts including Applicable Period (from Row (d))				
(g)	Tax at Date of Death Rates for Gifts in Applicable Period (subtract Row (e) from Row (f))				
(h)	Total DSUE applied from Prior Periods and Applicable Period (from Line 2 of Schedule C of Applicable Period Form 709)				
(i)	Basic Exclusion for Applicable Period (Enter the amount from the Table of Basic Exclusion Amounts)				
(j)	Basic Exclusion amount plus Total DSUE applied in prior periods and applicable period (add Row (h) and Row (i))				
(k)	Maximum Applicable Credit amount based on Row (j) (Using Table A—Unified Rate Schedule)[4]				
(l)	Applicable Credit amount used in Prior Periods (add Row (l) and Row (n) from prior period)				
(m)	Available Credit in Applicable Period (subtract Row (l) from Row (k))				
(n)	Credit Allowable (lesser of Row (g) or Row (m))				
(o)	Tax paid or payable at Date of Death rates for Applicable Period (subtract Row (n) from Row (g))				
(p)	Tax on Cumulative Gifts less tax paid or payable for Applicable Period (subtract Row (o) from Row (f))				
(q)	Cumulative Taxable Gifts less Gifts in the Applicable Period on which tax was paid or payable based on Row (p) (Using the Taxable Gift Amount Table)				
(r)	Gifts in the Applicable Period on which tax was payable (subtract Row (q) from Row (d))				
Line 7 Worksheet Part B					
1	Total gift taxes payable on gifts after 1976 (sum of amounts in Row (o)).				
2	Gift taxes paid by the decedent on gifts that qualify for "special treatment." Enter the amount from Worksheet TG, line 2, col. (e).				
3	Subtract line 2 from line 1.				
4	Gift tax paid by decedent's spouse on split gifts included on Schedule G. Enter amount from Worksheet TG, line 2, col. (f).				
5	Add lines 3 and 4. Enter here and on Part 2—Tax Computation, line 7.				
6	Cumulative lifetime gifts on which tax was paid or payable. Enter this amount on line 3, Section C, Part 6 of Form 706 (sum of amounts in Row (r)).				

Footnotes:
[1] Row (a): For annual returns, enter the tax period as (YYYY). For quarterly returns enter tax period as (YYYY–Q).
[2] Row (c): Enter amount from Row (d) of the previous column.
[3] Row (e): Enter amount from Row (f) of the previous column.
[4] Row (k): Calculate the applicable credit on the amount in Row (j), using Table A — Unified Rate Schedule, and enter here. (For each column in Row (k), subtract 20 percent of any amount allowed as a specific exemption for gifts made after September 8, 1976, and before January 1, 1977.)

¶2432

Taxable Gift Amount Table

Column A	Column B	Column C	Column D
Amount in Row (p) Line 7 Worksheet over...	Amount in Row (p) Line 7 Worksheet not over...	Property Value on Amount in Column A	Rate (Divisor) on Excess of Amount in Column A
0	1,800	0	18%
1,800	3,800	$1,800	20%
3,800	8,200	20,000	22%
8,200	13,000	40,000	24%
13,000	18,200	60,000	26%
18,200	23,800	80,000	28%
23,800	38,800	100,000	30%
38,800	70,800	150,000	32%
70,800	155,800	250,000	34%
155,800	248,300	500,000	37%
248,300	345,800	750,000	39%
345,800	------	1,000,000	40%

The Line 7 Worksheet, Part A of Form 706 should be completed for each year in which the decedent made taxable gifts as follows:

• Row (a). Beginning with the earliest gift, enter the calendar year or quarter of the gifts;

• Row (b). Enter taxable gifts for the year (or quarter) listed in row (a). Enter the total of all pre-1977 gifts in the pre-1977 column (i.e., it is not necessary to list those individually);

• Row (c). Enter the amount from row (d) of the previous column;

• Row (d). Enter the total of rows (b) and (c) of the current column;

• Row (e). Enter the amount from row (f) of the previous column;

• Row (f). Enter the tax based on the amount in row (d) of the current column using the year of death rates;

• Row (g). Subtract the amount in row (e) from the amount in row (f), both current column;

• Row (h). Total DSUE applied from prior periods. See Form 709, Schedule C, line 2, for the year listed in row (a) for the amount to be entered here;

• Row (i). Enter the applicable credit equivalent amount from the Table of Basic Exclusion Amounts which can be found in the instructions to Form 706;

• Row (j). Enter the sum of rows (h) and (i);

• Row (k). Calculate the applicable credit on the amount in row (j) of the current column using the year of death tax rates;

• Row (l). Add the amounts in row (l) and row (n) from the previous column;

• Row (m). Subtract row (l) from row (k) to determine the amount of any available credit;

¶2432

- Row (n). Enter the lesser of row (g) or row (m) for the current column;
- Row (o). Subtract row (n) from row (g) for the current column;
- Row (p). Subtract row (o) from row (f) for the current column;
- Row (q). Enter the cumulative taxable gift amount based on the amount in row (p) using the Taxable Gift Amount Table (this table can be found on page 8 of the Form 706 Instructions and is reproduced above);
- Row (r). If row (o) is greater than zero in the applicable period, subtract row (q) from row (d). If row (o) is not greater than zero, enter zero.

Line 7: Worksheet, Part B. Once the total tax payable has been calculated, the credit for taxes on post-1976 gifts is determined on the 6-line Worksheet by subtracting the amount of taxes on gifts that receive "special treatment" and adding the taxes paid by the decedent's spouse on split gifts included in the decedent's estate.

Line 8: On line 8 of Part 2–Tax Computation, the decedent's gross estate tax is computed by subtracting the decedent's gift taxes payable on post-1976 transfers from the tentative tax calculated on line 6.

Line 9a: Enter the decedent's basic exclusion amount which is $5,250,000 in 2013.

Line 9b: If the decedent received any deceased spousal unused exclusion (DSUE) amount from a predeceased spouse, that amount is entered on line 9b.

Line 9c: The decedent's basic exclusion amount and allocated DSUE are combined to determine the decedent's applicable exclusion amount.

Line 9d: A tentative tax is calculated on the applicable exclusion amount from line 9c.

> ■ On line 9a, the executor for the Smith Estate enters $5,250,000 which is the applicable exclusion amount for 2013. The executor makes no entries on line 9b because the decedent did not have a spouse who predeceased him. On line 9c, the applicable exclusion amount is reentered. On line 9d the tentative tax imposed on the 2013 applicable exclusion amount of $5,250,000 is entered. That credit equivalent is $2,045,800.

Line 10: If the decedent made gifts (including gifts made by the decedent's spouse and treated as made by the decedent by reason of gift splitting) after September 8, 1976, and before January 1, 1977, for which the decedent claimed a specific $30,000 exemption, the unified credit on this estate tax return must be reduced. The reduction is figured by entering 20 percent of the specific exemption claimed for these gifts. If the decedent did not make any gifts between September 8, 1976 and January 1, 1977, or if the decedent made gifts during this period but did not claim the specific exemption, enter zero. The adjustment entered may not exceed $6,000.

Line 13: Enter the credit for foreign death taxes from Schedule(s) P. If you claim a credit on line 13, you must complete Schedule P and file it with the return. You must attach Form(s) 706-CE, "Certificate of Payment of Foreign Death Tax" to support any credit you claim.

Line 14: Enter the credit for tax on prior transfers from Schedule Q. IRC Sec. 2013 provides that a decedent's estate may claim a credit for federal estate taxes paid on the transfer of property to the decedent from a transferor who died within 10 years before or two years after the decedent's death. The transferred property need not be identified in the decedent's gross estate or even exist at the date of death.

Line 15: Enter total credits on line 15. You may also use line 15 to report credit taken for federal gift taxes paid on prior transfers the decedent made before January 1, 1977, that are included in the gross estate. In addition to using line 15 to report credit for federal gift taxes on pre-1977 gifts, you may also use line 15 to claim the Canadian marital credit, if applicable.

Line 16: The decedent's net estate tax is the amount of transfer tax imposed on the decedent's estate under the unified transfer tax system. It is determined by subtracting allowable credits (line 15) from the gross estate tax (line 12).

Line 17: Enter the amount of GST taxes from line 10 in Part 2 of Schedule R. The decedent's estate must pay GST tax on direct skips that occur at the decedent's death. The executor of the decedent's estate completes and files Schedule R of Form 706 to report these transfers and to compute the amount of GST tax payable on the transfer. A direct skip at death occurs when property that is included in the transferor's estate is transferred to a skip person.

Line 19: Enter the amount of any prior payments of transfer taxes that have been made to the IRS. If any prior payments have been made, attach a statement to the return explaining the payments.

Line 20: Enter balance due for overpayment of estate tax.

■ The executor for the Smith Estate enters $3,164,546 as the balance due and sends the IRS a check payable to the United States Treasury in this amount. He writes the decedent's name, Social Security number and "Form 706" on the check. The executor signs the return on the bottom of Page 1.

¶2433 PAYING THE ESTATE TAX

(a) Procedures for Paying Estate Tax. The executor should pay the tax due in cash or by check or money order made out to the United States Treasury. Make sure that you write the decedent's name, Social Security number, and "Form 706" on the check.

Payment of the estate tax is normally due when the tax return is due. Typically, the estate tax is due nine months after the decedent's death unless an extension of time for payment has been granted, or unless an election has been made to pay in installments under IRC Sec. 6166 or to postpone the part of the tax attributable to a reversionary or remainder interest under IRC Sec. 6163. The executor may elect to pay the estate tax on a reversionary or remainder interest six months after the termination of the precedent interest or interests in the property. See ¶2301 and ¶2302 for a discussion of filing extensions.

After the return is filed, it is examined by the proper officials in the IRS. If the return is found to understate the tax, the IRS will notify the executor that it will issue a deficiency notice unless the matter is settled. If a deficiency notice is issued, the executor may petition the Tax Court for a redetermination or pay the tax and apply for a refund from the IRS. If the refund is denied, the taxpayer may apply to the U.S. District Court or the U.S. Claims Court. Collection is postponed during pendency of the case, unless the assessment was a jeopardy assessment [Reg. Secs. 301.6212-1,

301.6213-1]. The IRS ordinarily has three years from the date a return is filed to make an estate, gift, or GST tax assessment [IRC Sec. 6501].

Refunds. Refund claims must be filed within three years of the return's due date or two years of the payment of the tax, whichever is later. It should state the amount of refund claimed and the grounds on which the claim is based. Expenses incurred in connection with the refund claim should also be claimed as a deduction [IRC Sec. 6501].

(b) Schedule PC—Protective Claim for Refund. Form 706 includes Schedule PC, Protective Claim for Refund, that should be filed to preserve the estate's right to claim a refund for an unresolved claim or expense that may not become deductible under IRC Sec. 2053 until after the statute of limitations period ends. Schedule PC is also used to notify the IRS that a refund is being claimed once the amount of the claim or expense is deductible [See ¶¶2001 and 2421 for further discussion of protective claims for refund].

▶ **PRACTICE POINTER:** Taxpayers should be sure to only use Schedule PC for protective claims for refund being filed with Form 706. If the initial notice of the protective claim for refund is being submitted after the Form 706 has been filed, use Form 843, Claim for Refund and Request for Abatement, to file the claim.

The estate must indicate whether the Schedule PC being filed is the initial notice of protective claim for refund, notice of partial claim for refund, or notice of the final resolution of the claim for refund. Each separate claim or expense requires a separate Schedule PC; therefore, more than one Schedule PC may be included with Form 706, if necessary.

Initial notice of claim. The first Schedule PC to be filed is the initial notice of protective claim for refund. The estate will receive a written acknowledgment of receipt of the claim from the IRS. The claim for refund will be rejected if:

- The claim was not timely filed;
- The claim was not filed by the fiduciary or other person with authority to act on behalf the estate;
- The acknowledgment of the penalties of perjury statement (on page 1 of Form 706) was not signed; or,
- The claim is not adequately described.

Related ancillary expenses. If a protective claim for refund has been adequately identified on Schedule PC, the IRS will presume that the claim includes certain expenses related to resolving, defending or satisfying the claim. These ancillary expenses may include attorneys' fees, court costs, appraisal fees, and accounting fees.

Notice of final resolution of claim. When an expense that was the subject of a protective claim for refund is finally determined, the estate must notify the IRS that the claim for refund is ready for consideration. The notification should provide facts and evidence substantiating the deduction and the resulting recomputation of the estate tax liability. A separate notice of final resolution for the claim must be filed with the IRS. The estate may notify the IRS of the resolution of the uncertainty that deprived the estate of the deduction when the Form 706 was filed. The estate may file a supplemental Form 706 with an updated Schedule PC and including each schedule affected by the allowance of the deduction. Page 1 of the Form 706 should contain the

¶2433

notation "Supplemental Information—Notification of Consideration of Section 2053 Protective Claim(s) for Refund" and include the filing date of the initial notice of the protective claim for refund. A copy of the initial notice of claim should also be submitted.

Alternatively, the estate may notify the IRS by filing an updated Form 843, Claim for Refund and Request for Abatement. Form 843 must contain the notation "Notification of Consideration of Section 2053 Protective Claim(s) for Refund," including the filing date of the initial notice of protective claim for refund, on page 1.

The estate should notify the IRS of resolution within 90 days of the date the claim or expense is paid or the date on which the amount of the claim becomes certain and no longer subject to contingency, whichever is later. Separate notifications must be submitted for every protective claim for refund that was filed. If the final claim or expense involves multiple or recurring payments, the 90-day period begins on the date of the last payment. The estate may also notify the IRS (not more than annually) as payments are being made and possibly qualify for a partial refund based on the amounts paid through the date of the notice.

Specific Instructions

Part 1. General Information. Complete Part 1 by providing information that is correct and complete as of the time the Schedule PC is filed. If filing an updated Schedule PC with a supplemental Form 706 or as notice of final resolution of the protective claim for refund, be sure to update the information from the original filing to ensure that it is accurate. Be particularly careful to verify that contact information (addresses and telephone numbers) and the reason for filing Schedule PC are indicated correctly. If the fiduciary is different from the executor identified on page 1 of the Form 706 or has changed since the initial notice of protective claim for refund was filed, attach letters testamentary, letters of administration, or similar documentation evidencing the fiduciary's authority to file the protective claim for refund on behalf of the estate. Include a copy of Form 56, Notice Concerning Fiduciary Relationship, if it has been filed.

Part 2. Claim Information. For a protective claim for refund to be properly filed and considered, the claim or expense forming the basis of the potential deduction must be clearly identified. Using the check boxes provided, indicate whether you are filing the initial claim for refund, a claim for partial refund or a final claim. On the chart in Part 2, give the Form 706 schedule and item number of the claim or expense. List any amounts claimed under exceptions for ascertainable amounts, claims and counter-claims in related matters, or claims under $500,000. Provide all relevant information as described including, most importantly, an explanation of the reasons and contingencies delaying the actual payment to be made in satisfaction of the claim or expense. Complete columns E and F only if filing a notice of partial or final resolution. Show the amount of ancillary or related expenses to be included in the claim for refund and indicate whether this amount is estimated, agreed upon, or has been paid. Also show the amount being claimed for refund.

Part 3. Other Schedules PC and Forms 843 Filed by the Estate. On the chart in Part 3, provide information on other protective claims for refund that have been previously filed on behalf of the estate (if any), whether on other Schedules PC or on Form 843. When the initial claim for refund is filed, only information from Form(s) 843 need be included in Part 3. However, when filing a partial or final claim for refund,

¶2433

complete Part 3 by including the status of all claims filed by or on behalf of the estate, including those filed on other Schedules PC with Form 706. For each such claim, give the place of filing, date of filing and amount of the claim.

■ **Protective Claim for Refund.** Dr. Smith was sued by one of his patient's owners, Julie Doglover for malpractice when the plaintiff's dog died during surgery performed by Dr. Smith. The plaintiff alleges in a malpractice suit filed before Dr. Smith died that his negligent surgery techniques were the proximate cause of her dog's death. When the decedent's Form 709 had to be filed by his executor, a final judgment in the case had not yet been rendered. If the lawsuit is successful, Dr. Smith's estate could be required to pay as much as $750,000 to Julie Doglover; however his executor thinks that the two parties can ultimately settle for $600,000. Therefore, Dr. Smith's executor files Schedule PC with his Form 706 as shown in ¶2436 and explains the situation on the form. He also attaches copies of the plaintiff's complaint, the decedent's answer and the court docket sheet.

(c) Where to File Form 706. File Form 706 at the following address regardless of whether the decedent was a United States' citizen residing in the U.S., a resident alien, or a nonresident U.S. citizen:

Department of the Treasury
Internal Revenue Service Center
Internal Revenue Service Center
Cincinnati, OH 45999

¶2434 SIGNATURES

Make sure that the executor signs and dates the return in the space provided at the bottom of Page 1. If there is more than one executor, all listed executors must verify and sign the return. All executors are responsible for the return as filed and are liable for penalties provided for erroneous or false returns.

If someone other than the executor prepared the return, then the preparer must sign the return and enter his or her address and the date in the spaces provided.

¶2435 AMENDING FORM 706

There is no provision in the law for filing an amended Form 706. However, if you find that you must change something on a return that has already been filed, you should file another Form 706 and write "Supplemental Information" across the top of Page 1 of the form. Attach a copy of pages 1, 2, and 3 of the original Form 706 that has already been filed. If you have already been notified that the return has been selected for examination, you should provide the additional information directly to the office conducting the examination.

¶2435

¶2436 SAMPLE COMPLETED FORM 706 FOR MARK F. SMITH

Form **706** (Rev. August 2013) Department of the Treasury Internal Revenue Service	**United States Estate (and Generation-Skipping Transfer) Tax Return** ► Estate of a citizen or resident of the United States (see instructions). To be filed for decedents dying after December 31, 2012. ► Information about Form 706 and its separate instructions is at *www.irs.gov/form706*.	OMB No. 1545-0015

Part 1—Decedent and Executor

1a Decedent's first name and middle initial (and maiden name, if any) Mark F.	**1b** Decedent's last name Smith	**2** Decedent's social security no. 655 11 6633

3a City, town, or post office; county; state or province; country; and ZIP or foreign postal code. Howard County	**3b** Year domicile established 1996	**4** Date of birth 5/01/34	**5** Date of death 12/15/2013

6a Name of executor (see instructions)
Jane R. Smith

6b Executor's address (number and street including apartment or suite no.; city, town, or post office; state or province; country; and ZIP or foreign postal code) and phone no.
1465 Green Road
Baltimore, Maryland 21277

6c Executor's social security number (see instructions)   214 77 9123
Phone no.   410-000-0000

6d If there are multiple executors, check here ☐ and attach a list showing the names, addresses, telephone numbers, and SSNs of the additional executors.

7a Name and location of court where will was probated or estate administered
Registrar of Wills for Howard County

7b Case number   4892

8 If decedent died testate, check here ► ☑ and attach a certified copy of the will.   **9** If you extended the time to file this Form 706, check here ► ☐

10 If Schedule R-1 is attached, check here ► ☐   **11** If you are estimating the value of assets included in the gross estate on line 1 pursuant to the special rule of Reg. section 20.2010-2T(a)(7)(ii), check here ► ☐

Part 2—Tax Computation

1	Total gross estate less exclusion (from Part 5—Recapitulation, item 13)	1	14,272,000
2	Tentative total allowable deductions (from Part 5—Recapitulation, item 24)	2	1,060,635
3a	Tentative taxable estate (subtract line 2 from line 1)	3a	13,211,365
b	State death tax deduction	3b	50,000
c	Taxable estate (subtract line 3b from line 3a)	3c	13,161,365
4	Adjusted taxable gifts (see instructions)	4	-0-
5	Add lines 3c and 4	5	13,161,365
6	Tentative tax on the amount on line 5 from Table A in the instructions	6	5,210,346
7	Total gift tax paid or payable (see instructions)	7	-0-
8	Gross estate tax (subtract line 7 from line 6)	8	5,210,346
9a	Basic exclusion amount	9a 5,250,000	
9b	Deceased spousal unused exclusion (DSUE) amount from predeceased spouse(s), if any (from Section D, Part 6—Portability of Deceased Spousal Unused Exclusion).	9b -0-	
9c	Applicable exclusion amount (add lines 9a and 9b)	9c 5,250,000	
9d	Applicable credit amount (tentative tax on the amount in 9c from Table A in the instructions)	9d 2,045,800	
10	Adjustment to applicable credit amount (May not exceed $6,000. See instructions.)	10 -0-	
11	Allowable applicable credit amount (subtract line 10 from line 9d)	11	2,045,800
12	Subtract line 11 from line 8 (but do not enter less than zero)	12	3,164,546
13	Credit for foreign death taxes (from Schedule P). (Attach Form(s) 706-CE.)	13 -0-	
14	Credit for tax on prior transfers (from Schedule Q)	14 -0-	
15	Total credits (add lines 13 and 14)	15	-0-
16	Net estate tax (subtract line 15 from line 12)	16	3,164,546
17	Generation-skipping transfer (GST) taxes payable (from Schedule R, Part 2, line 10)	17	-0-
18	Total transfer taxes (add lines 16 and 17)	18	3,164,546
19	Prior payments (explain in an attached statement)	19	-0-
20	Balance due (or overpayment) (subtract line 19 from line 18)	20	3,164,546

Under penalties of perjury, I declare that I have examined this return, including accompanying schedules and statements, and to the best of my knowledge and belief, it is true, correct, and complete. Declaration of preparer other than the executor is based on all information of which preparer has any knowledge.

Sign Here
► Signature of executor   Date ►
► Signature of executor   Date ►

Paid Preparer Use Only

Print/Type preparer's name	Preparer's signature	Date	Check ☐ if self-employed	PTIN
Firm's name ►			Firm's EIN ►	
Firm's address ►			Phone no.	

For Privacy Act and Paperwork Reduction Act Notice, see instructions.   Cat. No. 20548R   Form **706** (Rev. 8-2013)

¶2436

Form 706 (Rev. 8-2013)

Estate of: Mark F. Smith

Decedent's social security number		
655	11	6633

Part 3—Elections by the Executor

Note. For information on electing portability of the decedent's DSUE amount, including how to opt out of the election, see Part 6—Portability of Deceased Spousal Unused Exclusion.

Note. Some of the following elections may require the posting of bonds or liens.

Please check "Yes" or "No" box for each question (see instructions).

			Yes	No
1	Do you elect alternate valuation?	1		✓
2	Do you elect special-use valuation? If "Yes," you must complete and attach Schedule A-1	2		✓
3	Do you elect to pay the taxes in installments as described in section 6166?			✓
	If "Yes," you must attach the additional information described in the instructions.			
	Note. By electing section 6166 installment payments, you may be required to provide security for estate tax deferred under section 6166 and interest in the form of a surety bond or a section 6324A lien.	3		
4	Do you elect to postpone the part of the taxes due to a reversionary or remainder interest as described in section 6163? .	4		✓

Part 4—General Information

Note. Please attach the necessary supplemental documents. **You must attach the death certificate.** (See instructions)

Authorization to receive confidential tax information under Reg. section 601.504(b)(2)(i); to act as the estate's representative before the IRS; and to make written or oral presentations on behalf of the estate:

Name of representative (print or type)	State	Address (number, street, and room or suite no., city, state, and ZIP code)
John P. Reed	Md	123 Main Street Annapolis, Maryland 21222

I declare that I am the ☑ attorney/ ☐ certified public accountant/ ☐ enrolled agent (check the applicable box) for the executor. I am not under suspension or disbarment from practice before the Internal Revenue Service and am qualified to practice in the state shown above.

Signature	CAF number	Date	Telephone number
	1234-567897		

1. Death certificate number and issuing authority (attach a copy of the death certificate to this return).
   State of Maryland, Department of Health and Human Hygiene, Certificate #53554

2. Decedent's business or occupation. If retired, check here ▶ ☐   and state decedent's former business or occupation.
   Veterinarian

3a. Marital status of the decedent at time of death:
   ☑ Married   ☐ Widow/widower   ☐ Single   ☐ Legally separated   ☐ Divorced

3b. For all prior marriages, list the name and SSN of the former spouse, the date the marriage ended, and whether the marriage ended by annulment, divorce, or death. Attach additional statements of the same size if necessary.

4a Surviving spouse's name	4b Social security number	4c Amount received (see instructions)
Jane R. Smith	2 1 4 7 7 4 4 4	1,200,000

5. Individuals (other than the surviving spouse), trusts, or other estates who receive benefits from the estate (do not include charitable beneficiaries shown in Schedule O) (see instructions).

Name of individual, trust, or estate receiving $5,000 or more	Identifying number	Relationship to decedent	Amount (see instructions)
Family Trust u/w/o Mark F. Smith	52-0909090	Jane F. Smith, Trustee	1,000,000
Marital Trust u/w/o Mark F. Smith	52-0909091	Jane F. Smith, Trustee	250,000
Albert F. Smith	214-22-3103	Son	250,000
Gary O. Smith	398-33-0000	Son	250,000

All unascertainable beneficiaries and those who receive less than $5,000 . . . . ▶

| Total . . . . | | | 1,750,000 |

If you answer "Yes" to any of the following questions, you must attach additional information as described.

			Yes	No
6	Is the estate filing a protective claim for refund?		✓	
	If "Yes," complete and attach two copies of Schedule PC for each claim.			
7	Does the gross estate contain any section 2044 property (qualified terminable interest property (QTIP) from a prior gift or estate)? (see instructions)			✓
8a	Have federal gift tax returns ever been filed?		✓	
	If "Yes," attach copies of the returns, if available, and furnish the following information:			
b	Period(s) covered	c Internal Revenue office(s) where filed		
9a	Was there any insurance on the decedent's life that is not included on the return as part of the gross estate?			✓
b	Did the decedent own any insurance on the life of another that is not included in the gross estate?			✓

Page 2

¶2436

Form 706 (Rev. 8-2013)

Estate of: Mark F. Smith	Decedent's social security number		
	655	11	6633

Part 4—General Information *(continued)*

If you answer "Yes" to any of the following questions, you must attach additional information as described.	Yes	No
10 Did the decedent at the time of death own any property as a joint tenant with right of survivorship in which **(a)** one or more of the other joint tenants was someone other than the decedent's spouse, and **(b)** less than the full value of the property is included on the return as part of the gross estate? If "Yes," you must complete and attach Schedule E	✓	
11a Did the decedent, at the time of death, own any interest in a partnership (for example, a family limited partnership), an unincorporated business, or a limited liability company; or own any stock in an inactive or closely held corporation?		✓
b If "Yes," was the value of **any** interest owned (from above) discounted on this estate tax return? If "Yes," see the instructions on reporting the total accumulated or effective discounts taken on Schedule F or G		✓
12 Did the decedent make any transfer described in sections 2035, 2036, 2037, or 2038? (see instructions) If "Yes," you must complete and attach Schedule G		✓
13a Were there in existence at the time of the decedent's death any trusts created by the decedent during his or her lifetime? . .		✓
b Were there in existence at the time of the decedent's death any trusts not created by the decedent under which the decedent possessed any power, beneficial interest, or trusteeship?		✓
c Was the decedent receiving income from a trust created after October 22, 1986, by a parent or grandparent?		✓
If "Yes," was there a GST taxable termination (under section 2612) on the death of the decedent?		✓
d If there was a GST taxable termination (under section 2612), attach a statement to explain. Provide a copy of the trust or will creating the trust, and give the name, address, and phone number of the current trustee(s).		
e Did the decedent at any time during his or her lifetime transfer or sell an interest in a partnership, limited liability company, or closely held corporation to a trust described in lines 13a or 13b?		✓
If "Yes," provide the EIN for this transferred/sold item. ▶		
14 Did the decedent ever possess, exercise, or release any general power of appointment? If "Yes," you must complete and attach Schedule H		✓
15 Did the decedent have an interest in or a signature or other authority over a financial account in a foreign country, such as a bank account, securities account, or other financial account?		✓
16 Was the decedent, immediately before death, receiving an annuity described in the "General" paragraph of the instructions for Schedule I or a private annuity? If "Yes," you must complete and attach Schedule I . . .	✓	
17 Was the decedent ever the beneficiary of a trust for which a deduction was claimed by the estate of a predeceased spouse under section 2056(b)(7) and which is not reported on this return? If "Yes," attach an explanation		✓

Part 5—Recapitulation.
Note. If estimating the value of one or more assets pursuant to the special rule of Reg. section 20.2010-2T(a)(7)(ii), enter on both lines 10 and 23 the amount noted in the instructions for the corresponding range of values. (See instructions for details.)

Item no.	Gross estate		Alternate value	Value at date of death
1	Schedule A—Real Estate	**1**		2,997,550
2	Schedule B—Stocks and Bonds	**2**		2,400,000
3	Schedule C—Mortgages, Notes, and Cash	**3**		2,800,850
4	Schedule D—Insurance on the Decedent's Life (attach Form(s) 712)	**4**		-0-
5	Schedule E—Jointly Owned Property (attach Form(s) 712 for life insurance) .	**5**		1,025,000
6	Schedule F—Other Miscellaneous Property (attach Form(s) 712 for life insurance)	**6**		24,725
7	Schedule G—Transfers During Decedent's Life (att. Form(s) 712 for life insurance)	**7**		23,975
8	Schedule H—Powers of Appointment	**8**		-0-
9	Schedule I—Annuities	**9**		5,000,000
10	Estimated value of assets subject to the special rule of Reg. section 20.2010-2T(a)(7)(ii)	**10**		-0-
11	Total gross estate (add items 1 through 10)	**11**		14,272,100
12	Schedule U—Qualified Conservation Easement Exclusion	**12**		-0-
13	Total gross estate less exclusion (subtract item 12 from item 11). Enter here and on line 1 of Part 2—Tax Computation	**13**		14,272,100

Item no.	Deductions		Amount
14	Schedule J—Funeral Expenses and Expenses Incurred in Administering Property Subject to Claims	**14**	8,065
15	Schedule K—Debts of the Decedent	**15**	2,570
16	Schedule K—Mortgages and Liens	**16**	
17	Total of items 14 through 16	**17**	10,635
18	Allowable amount of deductions from item 17 (see the instructions for item 18 of the Recapitulation)	**18**	10,635
19	Schedule L—Net Losses During Administration	**19**	-0-
20	Schedule L—Expenses Incurred in Administering Property Not Subject to Claims	**20**	-0-
21	Schedule M—Bequests, etc., to Surviving Spouse	**21**	1,050,000
22	Schedule O—Charitable, Public, and Similar Gifts and Bequests	**22**	-0-
23	Estimated value of deductible assets subject to the special rule of Reg. section 20.2010-2T(a)(7)(ii) . . .	**23**	-0-
24	Tentative total allowable deductions (add items 18 through 23). Enter here and on line 2 of the Tax Computation	**24**	1,060,635

Page 3

¶2436

Form 706 (Rev. 8-2013)

Estate of: Mark F. Smith	Decedent's social security number		
	655	11	6633

Part 6—Portability of Deceased Spousal Unused Exclusion (DSUE)

Portability Election

A decedent with a surviving spouse elects portability of the deceased spousal unused exclusion (DSUE) amount, if any, by completing and timely-filing this return. No further action is required to elect portability of the DSUE amount to allow the surviving spouse to use the decedent's DSUE amount.

Section A. Opting Out of Portability

The estate of a decedent with a surviving spouse may opt out of electing portability of the DSUE amount. Check here and do not complete Sections B and C of Part 6 only if the estate opts **NOT** to elect portability of the DSUE amount. ☐

Section B. QDOT

	Yes	No
Are any assets of the estate being transferred to a qualified domestic trust (QDOT)?		✓

If "Yes," the DSUE amount portable to a surviving spouse (calculated in Section C, below) is preliminary and shall be redetermined at the time of the final distribution or other taxable event imposing estate tax under section 2056A. See instructions for more details.

Section C. DSUE Amount Portable to the Surviving Spouse (To be completed by the estate of a decedent making a portability election.)

Complete the following calculation to determine the DSUE amount that can be transferred to the surviving spouse.

1	Enter the amount from line 9c, Part 2—Tax Computation	1	5,250,000
2	Reserved	2	
3	Enter the value of the cumulative lifetime gifts on which tax was paid or payable (see instructions) . . .	3	-0-
4	Add lines 1 and 3	4	5,250,000
5	Enter amount from line 10, Part 2—Tax Computation	5	-0-
6	Divide amount on line 5 by 40% (0.40) (do not enter less than zero)	6	-0-
7	Subtract line 6 from line 4	7	5,250,000
8	Enter the amount from line 5, Part 2– Tax Computation	8	13,161,365
9	Subtract line 8 from line 7 (do not enter less than zero)	9	-0-
10	DSUE amount portable to surviving spouse (Enter lesser of line 9 or line 9a, Part 2 – Tax Computation) . .	10	-0-

Section D. DSUE Amount Received from Predeceased Spouse(s) (To be completed by the estate of a deceased surviving spouse with DSUE amount from predeceased spouse(s))

Provide the following information to determine the DSUE amount received from deceased spouses.

A Name of Deceased Spouse (dates of death after December 31, 2010, only)	B Date of Death (enter as mm/dd/yy)	C Portability Election Made?		D If "Yes," DSUE Amount Received from Spouse	E DSUE Amount Applied by Decedent to Lifetime Gifts	F Year of Form 709 Reporting Use of DSUE Amount Listed in col E	G Remaining DSUE Amount, if any (subtract col. E from col. D)
		Yes	No				
Part 1 — DSUE RECEIVED FROM LAST DECEASED SPOUSE							
Part 2 — DSUE RECEIVED FROM OTHER PREDECEASED SPOUSE(S) AND USED BY DECEDENT							

Total (for all DSUE amounts from predeceased spouse(s) applied) . . . . .

Add the amount from Part 1, column D and the total from Part 2, column E. Enter the result on line 9b, Part 2—Tax Computation . . . . ▶ _____

¶2436

Form 706 (Rev. 8-2013)

Estate of:	Mark F. Smith	Decedent's social security number		
		655	11	6633

SCHEDULE A—Real Estate

- For jointly owned property that must be disclosed on Schedule E, see instructions.
- Real estate that is part of a sole proprietorship should be shown on Schedule F.
- Real estate that is included in the gross estate under sections 2035, 2036, 2037, or 2038 should be shown on Schedule G.
- Real estate that is included in the gross estate under section 2041 should be shown on Schedule H.
- If you elect section 2032A valuation, you must complete Schedule A and Schedule A-1.

Note. If the value of the gross estate, together with the amount of adjusted taxable gifts, is less than the basic exclusion amount and the Form 706 is being filed solely to elect portability of the DSUE amount, consideration should be given as to whether you are required to report the value of assets eligible for the marital or charitable deduction on this schedule. See the instructions and Reg. section 20.2010-2T (a)(7)(ii) for more information. If you are not required to report the value of an asset, identify the property but make no entries in the last three columns.

Item number	Description	Alternate valuation date	Alternate value	Value at date of death
1	1,280 acres of farmland, west and north of Smith Road, west of Wharton; Deed reference #38989843; Value based on appraisal; A copy of the appraisal prepared by a qualified appraiser is attached			1,400,000
2	330 acres of farmland; south of Smith Road, west of Waterton; Deed reference #47834783; Value based on appraisal; A copy of the appraisal prepared by a qualified appraiser is attached			350,000
3	Decedent's one-half interest in real property held as tenants in common with spouse described as 220 acres with house, barn, pool, guest house known as Smith Road			1,238,500
	Total from continuation schedules or additional statements attached to this schedule . . .			-0-
	TOTAL. (Also enter on Part 5—Recapitulation, page 3, at item 1.)			2,997,500

(If more space is needed, attach the continuation schedule from the end of this package or additional statements of the same size.)

Schedule A—Page 5

¶2436

Form 706 (Rev. 8-2013)

Estate of: Mark F. Smith

Decedent's social security number		
655	11	6633

SCHEDULE A-1—Section 2032A Valuation

Part 1. Type of election (Before making an election, see the checklist in the instructions):

☐ **Protective election (Regulations section 20.2032A-8(b)).** Complete Part 2, line 1, and column A of lines 3 and 4. (see instructions)

☐ **Regular election.** Complete all of Part 2 (including line 11, if applicable) and Part 3. (see instructions)

Before completing Schedule A-1, see the instructions for the information and documents that must be included to make a valid election.

The election is not valid unless the agreement (that is, *Part 3. Agreement to Special Valuation Under Section 2032A*):

• Is signed by each qualified heir with an interest in the specially valued property and

• Is attached to this return when it is filed.

Part 2. Notice of election (Regulations section 20.2032A-8(a)(3))

Note. All real property entered on lines 2 and 3 must also be entered on Schedules A, E, F, G, or H, as applicable.

1   Qualified use—check one ▶   ☐ Farm used for farming, or

☐ Trade or business other than farming

2   Real property used in a qualified use, passing to qualified heirs, and to be specially valued on this Form 706.

A Schedule and item number from Form 706	B Full value (without section 2032A(b)(3)(B) adjustment)	C Adjusted value (with section 2032A (b)(3)(B) adjustment)	D Value based on qualified use (without section 2032A(b)(3)(B) adjustment)
Totals			

Attach a legal description of all property listed on line 2.

Attach copies of appraisals showing the column B values for all property listed on line 2.

3   Real property used in a qualified use, passing to qualified heirs, but not specially valued on this Form 706.

A Schedule and item number from Form 706	B Full value (without section 2032A(b)(3)(B) adjustment)	C Adjusted value (with section 2032A (b)(3)(B) adjustment)	D Value based on qualified use (without section 2032A(b)(3)(B) adjustment)
Totals			

If you checked "Regular election," you must attach copies of appraisals showing the column B values for all property listed on line 3.

(continued on next page)

Schedule A-1—Page 6

¶2436

Form 706 (Rev. 8-2013)

4	Personal property used in a qualified use and passing to qualified heirs.		
A Schedule and item number from Form 706	**B** Adjusted value (with section 2032A (b)(3)(B) adjustment)	**A (continued)** Schedule and item number from Form 706	**B (continued)** Adjusted value (with section 2032A (b)(3)(B) adjustment)
		"Subtotal" from Col. B, below left	
Subtotal		Total adjusted value . . .	

5   Enter the value of the total gross estate as adjusted under section 2032A(b)(3)(A). ▶ _____

6   **Attach a description of the method used to determine the special value based on qualified use.**

7   Did the decedent and/or a member of his or her family own all property listed on line 2 for at least 5 of the 8 years immediately preceding the date of the decedent's death? . . . .   ☐ Yes ☐ No

8   Were there any periods during the 8-year period preceding the date of the decedent's death during which the decedent or a member of his or her family:

		Yes	No
a	Did not own the property listed on line 2?		
b	Did not use the property listed on line 2 in a qualified use?		
c	Did not materially participate in the operation of the farm or other business within the meaning of section 2032A(e)(6)?		

    If you answered "Yes" to any of the above, attach a statement listing the periods. If applicable, describe whether the exceptions of sections 2032A(b)(4) or (5) are met.

9   **Attach affidavits describing the activities constituting material participation and the identity and relationship to the decedent of the material participants.**

10   Persons holding interests. Enter the requested information for each party who received any interest in the specially valued property. **(Each of the qualified heirs receiving an interest in the property must sign the agreement, to be found on Part 3 of this Schedule A-1, and the agreement must be filed with this return.)**

	Name	Address
A		
B		
C		
D		
E		
F		
G		
H		

	Identifying number	Relationship to decedent	Fair market value	Special-use value
A				
B				
C				
D				
E				
F				
G				
H				

    You must attach a computation of the GST tax savings attributable to direct skips for each person listed above who is a skip person. (see instructions)

11   **Woodlands election.** Check here ▶ ☐ if you wish to make a Woodlands election as described in section 2032A(e)(13). Enter the schedule and item numbers from Form 706 of the property for which you are making this election ▶ ---------------------------------

    Attach a statement explaining why you are entitled to make this election. The IRS may issue regulations that require more information to substantiate this election. You will be notified by the IRS if you must supply further information.

Schedule A-1—Page 7

¶2436

Form 706 (Rev. 8-2013)

Part 3. Agreement to Special Valuation Under Section 2032A

	Decedent's social security number		
Estate of: Mark F. Smith	655	11	6633

There cannot be a valid election unless:

• The agreement is executed by each one of the qualified heirs and

• The agreement is included with the estate tax return when the estate tax return is filed.

We (list all qualified heirs)

_____ ,

being all the qualified heirs and (list all other persons having an interest in the property required to sign this agreement)

_____

being all other parties having interests in the property which is qualified real property and which is valued under section 2032A of the Internal Revenue Code, do hereby approve of the election made by _____ ,
Executor/Administrator of the estate of _____ ,

pursuant to section 2032A to value said property on the basis of the qualified use to which the property is devoted and do hereby enter into this agreement pursuant to section 2032A(d).

The undersigned agree and consent to the application of subsection (c) of section 2032A with respect to all the property described on Form 706, Schedule A-1, Part 2, line 2, attached to this agreement. More specifically, the undersigned heirs expressly agree and consent to personal liability under subsection (c) of 2032A for the additional estate and GST taxes imposed by that subsection with respect to their respective interests in the above-described property in the event of certain early dispositions of the property or early cessation of the qualified use of the property. It is understood that if a qualified heir disposes of any interest in qualified real property to any member of his or her family, such member may thereafter be treated as the qualified heir with respect to such interest upon filing a Form 706-A, United States Additional Estate Tax Return, and a new agreement.

The undersigned interested parties who are not qualified heirs consent to the collection of any additional estate and GST taxes imposed under section 2032A(c) from the specially valued property.

If there is a disposition of any interest which passes, or has passed to him or her, or if there is a cessation of the qualified use of any specially valued property which passes or passed to him or her, each of the undersigned heirs agrees to file a Form 706-A, and pay any additional estate and GST taxes due within 6 months of the disposition or cessation.

It is understood by all interested parties that this agreement is a condition precedent to the election of special-use valuation under section 2032A and must be executed by every interested party even though that person may not have received the estate (or GST) tax benefits or be in possession of such property.

Each of the undersigned understands that by making this election, a lien will be created and recorded pursuant to section 6324B of the Code on the property referred to in this agreement for the adjusted tax differences with respect to the estate as defined in section 2032A(c)(2)(C).

As the interested parties, the undersigned designate the following individual as their agent for all dealings with the Internal Revenue Service concerning the continued qualification of the specially valued property under section 2032A and on all issues regarding the special lien under section 6324B. The agent is authorized to act for the parties with respect to all dealings with the Internal Revenue Service on matters affecting the qualified real property described earlier. This includes the authorization:

• To receive confidential information on all matters relating to continued qualification under section 2032A of the specially valued real property and on all matters relating to the special lien arising under section 6324B;

• To furnish the Internal Revenue Service with any requested information concerning the property;

• To notify the Internal Revenue Service of any disposition or cessation of qualified use of any part of the property;

• To receive, but not to endorse and collect, checks in payment of any refund of Internal Revenue taxes, penalties, or interest;

• To execute waivers (including offers of waivers) of restrictions on assessment or collection of deficiencies in tax and waivers of notice of disallowance of a claim for credit or refund; and

• To execute closing agreements under section 7121.

(continued on next page)

Schedule A-1— Page 8

¶2436

Form 706 (Rev. 8-2013)

Part 3. Agreement to Special Valuation Under Section 2032A *(continued)*

	Decedent's social security number		
Estate of: Mark F. Smith	655	11	6633

• Other acts (specify) ▶ _____

By signing this agreement, the agent agrees to provide the Internal Revenue Service with any requested information concerning this property and to notify the Internal Revenue Service of any disposition or cessation of the qualified use of any part of this property.

_____	_____	_____
Name of Agent	Signature	Address

The property to which this agreement relates is listed in Form 706, United States Estate (and Generation-Skipping Transfer) Tax Return, and in the Notice of Election, along with its fair market value according to section 2031 of the Code and its special-use value according to section 2032A. The name, address, social security number, and interest (including the value) of each of the undersigned in this property are as set forth in the attached Notice of Election.

IN WITNESS WHEREOF, the undersigned have hereunto set their hands at _____ ,

this _____ day of _____ .

SIGNATURES OF EACH OF THE QUALIFIED HEIRS:

_____	_____
Signature of qualified heir	Signature of qualified heir
_____	_____
Signature of qualified heir	Signature of qualified heir
_____	_____
Signature of qualified heir	Signature of qualified heir
_____	_____
Signature of qualified heir	Signature of qualified heir
_____	_____
Signature of qualified heir	Signature of qualified heir
_____	_____
Signature of qualified heir	Signature of qualified heir

_____
Signatures of other interested parties

_____
Signatures of other interested parties

Schedule A-1—Page 9

¶2436

Form 706 (Rev. 8-2013)

Estate of: Mark F. Smith	Decedent's social security number		
	655	11	6633

SCHEDULE B—Stocks and Bonds

(For jointly owned property that must be disclosed on Schedule E, see instructions.)

Note. If the value of the gross estate, together with the amount of adjusted taxable gifts, is less than the basic exclusion amount and the Form 706 is being filed solely to elect portability of the DSUE amount, consideration should be given as to whether you are required to report the value of assets eligible for the marital or charitable deduction on this schedule. See the instructions and Reg. section 20.2010-2T (a)(7)(ii) for more information. If you are not required to report the value of an asset, identify the property but make no entries in the last four columns.

Item number	Description, including face amount of bonds or number of shares and par value for identification. Give CUSIP number. If trust, partnership, or closely held entity, give EIN.		Unit value	Alternate valuation date	Alternate value	Value at date of death
		CUSIP number or EIN, where applicable				
1	2,500 shares of ABCo common stock NYSE	090909090	400			1,000,000
2	2,000 shares of PayCorp common stock NASDAQ	04398943	125			250,000
3	5,000 shares of Big Cap Mutual Fund	546464646	50			250,000
4	1,000 shares of XYZ common stock NYSE	345989389	500			500,000
5	10,000 shares of International Mutual	35252525	40			400,000
	Total from continuation schedules (or additional statements) attached to this schedule . . .					-0-
	TOTAL. (Also enter on Part 5—Recapitulation, page 3, at item 2.)					2,400,000

(If more space is needed, attach the continuation schedule from the end of this package or additional statements of the same size.)

¶2436

Form 706 (Rev. 8-2013)

Estate of: Mark F. Smith	Decedent's social security number
	655 : 11 : 6633

SCHEDULE C—Mortgages, Notes, and Cash

(For jointly owned property that must be disclosed on Schedule E, see instructions.)

Note. If the value of the gross estate, together with the amount of adjusted taxable gifts, is less than the basic exclusion amount and the Form 706 is being filed solely to elect portability of the DSUE amount, consideration should be given as to whether you are required to report the value of assets eligible for the marital or charitable deduction on this schedule. See the instructions and Reg. section 20.2010-2T (a)(7)(ii) for more information. If you are not required to report the value of an asset, identify the property but make no entries in the last three columns.

Item number	Description	Alternate valuation date	Alternate value	Value at date of death
1	Money market account #12322, First National Bank, Baltimore, MD 21200			2,500,000
	Unpaid interest accrued at death			500
2	Cash on decedent's person			100
3	$250,000 certificate of deposit, First National Bank, Baltimore, MD 21200			250,250
4	Promissory note of $100,000, unpaid balance of $50,000 dated 1/1/04 between decedent and son, Albert F. Smith. The son still owes decedent $50,000. The due date of the promissory note is 1/1/15 with interest payable at 7.5 percent per annum			50,000
	Total from continuation schedules (or additional statements) attached to this schedule . .			-0-
	TOTAL. (Also enter on Part 5—Recapitulation, page 3, at item 3.)			2,800,850

(If more space is needed, attach the continuation schedule from the end of this package or additional statements of the same size.)

Schedule C—Page 11

¶2436

Form 706 (Rev. 8-2013)

Estate of: Mark F. Smith	Decedent's social security number		
	655	11	6633

SCHEDULE D—Insurance on the Decedent's Life

You must list all policies on the life of the decedent and attach a Form 712 for each policy.

Note. If the value of the gross estate, together with the amount of adjusted taxable gifts, is less than the basic exclusion amount and the Form 706 is being filed solely to elect portability of the DSUE amount, consideration should be given as to whether you are required to report the value of assets eligible for the marital or charitable deduction on this schedule. See the instructions and Reg. section 20.2010-2T (a)(7)(ii) for more information. If you are not required to report the value of an asset, identify the property but make no entries in the last three columns.

Item number	Description	Alternate valuation date	Alternate value	Value at date of death
1	Nationwide Insurance Co. Life Insurance Policy #4848484 Owner Spouse: Jane R. Smith Beneficiary: Jane R. Smith Insured: Mark F. Smith This policy is not included in the decedent's taxable estate because the decedent did not own any interest in the policy within three years of the date of his death			
	Total from continuation schedules (or additional statements) attached to this schedule . .			
	TOTAL. (Also enter on Part 5—Recapitulation, page 3, at item 4.)			-0-

(If more space is needed, attach the continuation schedule from the end of this package or additional statements of the same size.)

Schedule D—Page 12

¶2436

Form 706 (Rev. 8-2013)

Estate of: Mark F. Smith	Decedent's social security number		
	655	11	6633

SCHEDULE E—Jointly Owned Property
(If you elect section 2032A valuation, you must complete Schedule E and Schedule A-1.)

PART 1. Qualified Joint Interests—Interests Held by the Decedent and His or Her Spouse as the Only Joint Tenants (Section 2040(b)(2))

Note. If the value of the gross estate, together with the amount of adjusted taxable gifts, is less than the basic exclusion amount and the Form 706 is being filed solely to elect portability of the DSUE amount, consideration should be given as to whether you are required to report the value of assets eligible for the marital or charitable deduction on this schedule. See the instructions and Reg. section 20.2010-2T (a)(7)(ii) for more information. If you are not required to report the value of an asset, identify the property but make no entries in the last three columns.

Item number	Description. For securities, give CUSIP number. If trust, partnership, or closely held entity, give EIN.		Alternate valuation date	Alternate value	Value at date of death
		CUSIP number or EIN, where applicable			
1	House and lot, 1424 Green Tree Road Baltimore, Maryland 21202 (lot z, square 122)				975,000
2	Bank of America Savings Account #2938493				375,000
3	Bank of America Checking Account #979898				225,000
	Total from continuation schedules (or additional statements) attached to this schedule				-0-
1a	Totals		**1a**		1,550,000
1b	Amounts included in gross estate (one-half of line 1a)		**1b**		775,000

PART 2. All Other Joint Interests

2a State the name and address of each surviving co-tenant. If there are more than three surviving co-tenants, list the additional co-tenants on an attached statement.

Name	Address (number and street, city, state, and ZIP code)
A. Beth Smith Bromley (Decedent's Sister)	1 North Main Street, Baltimore, Maryland 29999
B.	
C.	

Item number	Enter letter for co-tenant	Description (including alternate valuation date if any). For securities, give CUSIP number. If trust, partnership, or closely held entity, give EIN		Percentage includible	Includible alternate value	Includible value at date of death
			CUSIP number or EIN, where applicable			
1	A	Brokerage Account #9898, First National Bank Baltimore, Maryland. Decedent and co-tenant who was decedent's sister each contributed 50% of funds used to purchase securities held in account at First National Bank. The total value of the account is $500,000 and the decedent's one-half interest which is includible in his gross estate is $250,000. See attached list of securities held in account		50%		250,000
		Total from continuation schedules (or additional statements) attached to this schedule				
2b		Total other joint interests	**2b**			250,000
3		Total includible joint interests (add lines 1b and 2b). Also enter on Part 5—Recapitulation, page 3, at item 5	**3**			1,025,000

(If more space is needed, attach the continuation schedule from the end of this package or additional statements of the same size.)

Schedule E—Page 13

¶2436

Form 706 (Rev. 8-2013)

	Decedent's social security number
Estate of: Mark F. Smith	655 11 6633

SCHEDULE F—Other Miscellaneous Property Not Reportable Under Any Other Schedule

(For jointly owned property that must be disclosed on Schedule E, see instructions.)
(If you elect section 2032A valuation, you must complete Schedule F and Schedule A-1.)

Note. If the value of the gross estate, together with the amount of adjusted taxable gifts, is less than the basic exclusion amount and the Form 706 is being filed solely to elect portability of the DSUE amount, consideration should be given as to whether you are required to report the value of assets eligible for the marital or charitable deduction on this schedule. See the instructions and Reg. section 20.2010-2T (a)(7)(ii) for more information. If you are not required to report the value of an asset, identify the property but make no entries in the last three columns.

		Yes	No
1	Did the decedent own any works of art, items, or any collections whose artistic or collectible value at date of death exceeded $3,000?		✓
	If "Yes," submit full details on this schedule and attach appraisals.		
2	Has the decedent's estate, spouse, or any other person received (or will receive) any bonus or award as a result of the decedent's employment or death?		✓
	If "Yes," submit full details on this schedule.		
3	Did the decedent at the time of death have, or have access to, a safe deposit box?		✓
	If "Yes," state location, and if held jointly by decedent and another, state name and relationship of joint depositor.		

If any of the contents of the safe deposit box are omitted from the schedules in this return, explain fully why omitted.

Item number	Description. For securities, give CUSIP number. If trust, partnership, or closely held entity, give EIN	CUSIP number or EIN, where applicable	Alternate valuation date	Alternate value	Value at date of death
1	2008 Ford two-door pickup truck Vin/Serial #1G878787878 55,000 miles-Value based on appraisal prepared by qualified appraisers. See attached copy of appraisal				5,000
2	Household good and personal effects				10,300
3	Collection of antiquarian books on veterinary procedures Value based on appraisals prepared by qualified appraisers. See attached copy of appraisal				5,000
4	Veterinary tools and surgical instruments used in decedent's veterinary practice. Value based on appraisals prepared by qualified appraisers. See attached copy of appraisal				4,425
	Total from continuation schedules (or additional statements) attached to this schedule				-0-
	TOTAL. (Also enter on Part 5—Recapitulation, page 3, at item 6.)				24,725

(If more space is needed, attach the continuation schedule from the end of this package or additional statements of the same size.)

Schedule F—Page 14

¶2436

Form 706 (Rev. 8-2013)

Estate of: Mark F. Smith	Decedent's social security number		
	655	11	6633

SCHEDULE G—Transfers During Decedent's Life

(If you elect section 2032A valuation, you must complete Schedule G and Schedule A-1.)

Note. If the value of the gross estate, together with the amount of adjusted taxable gifts, is less than the basic exclusion amount and the Form 706 is being filed solely to elect portability of the DSUE amount, consideration should be given as to whether you are required to report the value of assets eligible for the marital or charitable deduction on this schedule. See the instructions and Reg. section 20.2010-2T (a)(7)(ii) for more information. If you are not required to report the value of an asset, identify the property but make no entries in the last three columns.

Item number	Description. For securities, give CUSIP number. If trust, partnership, or closely held entity, give EIN	Alternate valuation date	Alternate value	Value at date of death
A.	Gift tax paid or payable by the decedent or the estate for all gifts made by the decedent or his or her spouse within 3 years before the decedent's death (section 2035(b))	X X X X X		
B.	Transfers includible under sections 2035(a), 2036, 2037, or 2038:			
1	National Insurance Co. - Life insurance policy #98989 Insured: Deceased- Mark F. Smith Form 712 attached See exhibit #10			13,975
2	XYZlife Insurance Co. - Life Insurance policy #989898 Insured: Deceased- Mark F. Smith Form 712 attached See exhibit #11			10,000
	Total from continuation schedules (or additional statements) attached to this schedule . .			-0-
	TOTAL. (Also enter on Part 5—Recapitulation, page 3, at item 7.)			23,975

SCHEDULE H—Powers of Appointment

(Include "5 and 5 lapsing" powers (section 2041(b)(2)) held by the decedent.)

(If you elect section 2032A valuation, you must complete Schedule H and Schedule A-1.)

Note. If the value of the gross estate, together with the amount of adjusted taxable gifts, is less than the basic exclusion amount and the Form 706 is being filed solely to elect portability of the DSUE amount, consideration should be given as to whether you are required to report the value of assets eligible for the marital or charitable deduction on this schedule. See the instructions and Reg. section 20.2010-2T (a)(7)(ii) for more information. If you are not required to report the value of an asset, identify the property but make no entries in the last three columns.

Item number	Description	Alternate valuation date	Alternate value	Value at date of death
1				
	Total from continuation schedules (or additional statements) attached to this schedule . . .			
	TOTAL. (Also enter on Part 5—Recapitulation, page 3, at item 8.)			

(If more space is needed, attach the continuation schedule from the end of this package or additional statements of the same size.)

Schedules G and H—Page 15

¶2436

Form 706 (Rev. 8-2013)

	Decedent's social security number		
Estate of: Mark F. Smith	655	11	6633

SCHEDULE I—Annuities

Note. Generally, no exclusion is allowed for the estates of decedents dying after December 31, 1984 (see instructions).

Note. If the value of the gross estate, together with the amount of adjusted taxable gifts, is less than the basic exclusion amount and the Form 706 is being filed solely to elect portability of the DSUE amount, consideration should be given as to whether you are required to report the value of assets eligible for the marital or charitable deduction on this schedule. See the instructions and Reg. section 20.2010-2T (a)(7)(ii) for more information. If you are not required to report the value of an asset, identify the property but make no entries in the last three columns.

		Yes	No
A	Are you excluding from the decedent's gross estate the value of a lump-sum distribution described in section 2039(f)(2) (as in effect before its repeal by the Deficit Reduction Act of 1984)?		✓

If "Yes," you must attach the information required by the instructions.

Item number	Description. Show the entire value of the annuity before any exclusions	Alternate valuation date	Includible alternate value	Includible value at date of death
1	Individual Retirement Account #98989897			3,000,000
	Best Investors Bank of Baltimore, Baltimore, Maryland 21111			
	See attached list of marketable securities held in IRA			
2	First National Life Annuity Certificate #98989898			2,000,000
	Total from continuation schedules (or additional statements) attached to this schedule . .			-0-
	TOTAL. (Also enter on Part 5—Recapitulation, page 3, at item 9.)			5,000,000

(If more space is needed, attach the continuation schedule from the end of this package or additional statements of the same size.)

Schedule I—Page 16

¶2436

Form 706 (Rev. 8-2013)

Estate of: Mark F. Smith	Decedent's social security number
	655 : 11 : 6633

SCHEDULE J—Funeral Expenses and Expenses Incurred in Administering Property Subject to Claims

▶ Use Schedule PC to make a protective claim for refund due to an expense not currently deductible.

For such a claim, report the expense on Schedule J but without a value in the last column.

Note. Do not list expenses of administering property not subject to claims on this schedule. To report those expenses, see instructions.

If executors' commissions, attorney fees, etc., are claimed and allowed as a deduction for estate tax purposes, they are not allowable as a deduction in computing the taxable income of the estate for federal income tax purposes. They are allowable as an income tax deduction on Form 1041, U.S. Income Tax Return for Estates and Trusts, if a waiver is filed to forgo the deduction on Form 706 (see Instructions for Form 1041).

	Yes	No
Are you aware of any actual or potential reimbursement to the estate for any expense claimed as a deduction on this schedule? . .		✓
If "Yes," attach a statement describing the expense(s) subject to potential reimbursement. (see instructions)		

Item number	Description	Expense amount	Total amount
	A. Funeral expenses:		
1	Miller Funeral Home, Baltimore, Maryland 21111	1,000	
	Total funeral expenses . . . . ▶		1,000

B. Administration expenses:

	1 Executors' commissions—amount estimated/agreed upon/paid. (Strike out the words that do not apply.)		3,000
	2 Attorney fees—amount estimated/agreed upon/paid. (Strike out the words that do not apply.) . . .		2,265
	3 Accountant fees—amount estimated/agreed upon/paid. (Strike out the words that do not apply.) . .		1,000

	4 Miscellaneous expenses:	Expense amount	
a	Antique Appraisals, Inc., Baltimore, Maryland (appraisal of collection listed on Schedule F, item 3)	100	
b	ABC Appraisals, Inc., Baltimore, Maryland (appraisal of collection listed on Schedule F, item 4)	100	
c	Probate Court, Baltimore, Maryland (fees collected by court for administration of estate)	200	
d	Upkeep and maintenance of real estate listed on Schedule A, items 1 and 2	300	
e	Land Appraisals, Inc., Baltimore, Maryland (appraisal of farmland listed in Schedule A, item 1)	100	
	Total miscellaneous expenses from continuation schedules (or additional statements) attached to this schedule	-0-	-0-
	Total miscellaneous expenses . . . . ▶		800
	TOTAL. (Also enter on Part 5—Recapitulation, page 3, at item 14.) . . . . ▶		8,065

(If more space is needed, attach the continuation schedule from the end of this package or additional statements of the same size.)

Schedule J—Page 17

¶2436

Form 706 (Rev. 8-2013)

	Decedent's social security number
Estate of: Mark F. Smith	655 11 6633

SCHEDULE K—Debts of the Decedent, and Mortgages and Liens

▶ Use Schedule PC to make a protective claim for refund due to a claim not currently deductible.
For such a claim, report the expense on Schedule K but without a value in the last column.

	Yes	No
Are you aware of any actual or potential reimbursement to the estate for any debt of the decedent, mortgage, or lien claimed as a deduction on this schedule?		✓
If "Yes," attach a statement describing the items subject to potential reimbursement. (see instructions)		
Are any of the items on this schedule deductible under Reg. section 20.2053-4(b) and Reg. section 20.2053-4(c)? . .		✓
If "Yes," attach a statement indicating the applicable provision and documenting the value of the claim.		

Item number	Debts of the Decedent—Creditor and nature of debt, and allowable death taxes	Amount
1	Internal Revenue Service - federal income tax liability for 2012	1,200
2	Maryland Department of Revenue - state income tax liability for 2012	1,000
3	First National Bank, Baltimore, Maryland 21200- credit card purchases from 1/15/13- the date of death- 12/15/13	370
	Total from continuation schedules (or additional statements) attached to this schedule	-0-
	TOTAL. (Also enter on Part 5—Recapitulation, page 3, at item 15.)	2,570

Item number	Mortgages and Liens—Description	Amount
1		
	Total from continuation schedules (or additional statements) attached to this schedule	-0-
	TOTAL. (Also enter on Part 5—Recapitulation, page 3, at item 16.)	-0-

(If more space is needed, attach the continuation schedule from the end of this package or additional statements of the same size.)

Schedule K—Page 18

¶2436

Form 706 (Rev. 8-2013)

Estate of: Mark F. Smith	Decedent's social security number		
	655	11	6633

SCHEDULE L—Net Losses During Administration and Expenses Incurred in Administering Property Not Subject to Claims

▶ Use Schedule PC to make a protective claim for refund due to an expense not currently deductible.
For such expenses, report the expense on Schedule L but without a value in the last column.

Item number	Net losses during administration (**Note.** Do not deduct losses claimed on a federal income tax return.)	Amount
1		
	Total from continuation schedules (or additional statements) attached to this schedule	-0-
	TOTAL. (Also enter on Part 5—Recapitulation, page 3, at item 19.)	-0-

Item number	Expenses incurred in administering property not subject to claims. (Indicate whether estimated, agreed upon, or paid.)	Amount
1		
	Total from continuation schedules (or additional statements) attached to this schedule	-0-
	TOTAL. (Also enter on Part 5—Recapitulation, page 3, at item 20.)	-0-

(If more space is needed, attach the continuation schedule from the end of this package or additional statements of the same size.)

Schedule L—Page 19

¶2436

Form 706 (Rev. 8-2013)

Estate of: Mark F. Smith	Decedent's social security number
	655 11 6633

SCHEDULE M—Bequests, etc., to Surviving Spouse

Note. If the value of the gross estate, together with the amount of adjusted taxable gifts, is less than the basic exclusion amount and the Form 706 is being filed solely to elect portability of the DSUE amount, consideration should be given as to whether you are required to report the value of assets eligible for the marital or charitable deduction on this schedule. See the instructions and Reg. section 20.2010-2T (a)(7)(ii) for more information. If you are not required to report the value of an asset, identify the property but make no entry in the last column.

			Yes	No
1	Did any property pass to the surviving spouse as a result of a qualified disclaimer?	1		✓
	If "Yes," attach a copy of the written disclaimer required by section 2518(b).			
2a	In what country was the surviving spouse born? **United States**			
b	What is the surviving spouse's date of birth? **3/11/36**			
c	Is the surviving spouse a U.S. citizen?	2c	✓	
d	If the surviving spouse is a naturalized citizen, when did the surviving spouse acquire citizenship?			
e	If the surviving spouse is not a U.S. citizen, of what country is the surviving spouse a citizen?			
3	**Election Out of QTIP Treatment of Annuities.** Do you elect under section 2056(b)(7)(C)(ii) not to treat as qualified terminable interest property any joint and survivor annuities that are included in the gross estate and would otherwise be treated as qualified terminable interest property under section 2056(b)(7)(C)? (see instructions)	3		✓

Item number	Description of property interests passing to surviving spouse. For securities, give CUSIP number. If trust, partnership, or closely held entity, give EIN	Amount
	QTIP property:	
A1		
	All other property:	
B1	One-half of value of home and lot held as tenancy -by-entirety (Schedule E, Part 1, item 1)	475,000
B2	One-half of value of savings account (Schedule E- Part 1, item 2)	187,500
B3	One-half of value of checking account (Schedule E-Part 1, item 3)	112,500
B4	Cash bequest under Paragraph 10 of decedent's will	25,000
B5	Amount passing to surviving spouse (SS) under will of Mark F. Smith, establishing marital trust providing that trust pay income to SS with remainder to SS's estate	250,000
	Total from continuation schedules (or additional statements) attached to this schedule	-0-

4	**Total** amount of property interests listed on Schedule M	4	1,050,000
5a	Federal estate taxes payable out of property interests listed on Schedule M	5a	
b	Other death taxes payable out of property interests listed on Schedule M	5b	
c	Federal and state GST taxes payable out of property interests listed on Schedule M	5c	
d	Add items 5a, 5b, and 5c	5d	-0-
6	Net amount of property interests listed on Schedule M (subtract 5d from 4). Also enter on Part 5—Recapitulation, page 3, at item 21	6	1,050,000

(If more space is needed, attach the continuation schedule from the end of this package or additional statements of the same size.)

Schedule M—Page 20

¶2436

Form 706 (Rev. 8-2013)

Estate of: Mark F. Smith	Decedent's social security number		
	655	11	6633

SCHEDULE O—Charitable, Public, and Similar Gifts and Bequests

Note. If the value of the gross estate, together with the amount of adjusted taxable gifts, is less than the basic exclusion amount and the Form 706 is being filed solely to elect portability of the DSUE amount, consideration should be given as to whether you are required to report the value of assets eligible for the marital or charitable deduction on this schedule. See the instructions and Reg. section 20.2010-2T (a)(7)(ii) for more information. If you are not required to report the value of an asset, identify the property but make no entry in the last column.

		Yes	No
1a	If the transfer was made by will, has any action been instituted to contest or have interpreted any of its provisions affecting the charitable deductions claimed in this schedule? . . . . If "Yes," full details must be submitted with this schedule.		
b	According to the information and belief of the person or persons filing this return, is any such action planned? . If "Yes," full details must be submitted with this schedule.		
2	Did any property pass to charity as the result of a qualified disclaimer? . . . . If "Yes," attach a copy of the written disclaimer required by section 2518(b).		

Item number	Name and address of beneficiary	Character of institution	Amount
1			

Total from continuation schedules (or additional statements) attached to this schedule . . . .

3	Total	**3**	
4a	Federal estate tax payable out of property interests listed above	**4a**	
b	Other death taxes payable out of property interests listed above	**4b**	
c	Federal and state GST taxes payable out of property interests listed above .	**4c**	
d	Add items 4a, 4b, and 4c	**4d**	
5	Net value of property interests listed above (subtract 4d from 3). Also enter on Part 5—Recapitulation, page 3, at item 22	**5**	-0-

(If more space is needed, attach the continuation schedule from the end of this package or additional statements of the same size.)

Schedule O—Page 21

¶2436

Form 706 (Rev. 8-2013)

Estate of: Mark F. Smith	Decedent's social security number		
	655	11	6633

SCHEDULE P—Credit for Foreign Death Taxes

List all foreign countries to which death taxes have been paid and for which a credit is claimed on this return.

If a credit is claimed for death taxes paid to more than one foreign country, compute the credit for taxes paid to one country on this sheet and attach a separate copy of Schedule P for each of the other countries.

The credit computed on this sheet is for the _____
                                                                    (Name of death tax or taxes)

_____ imposed in _____
                                                                    (Name of country)

Credit is computed under the _____
                                                             (Insert title of treaty or statute)

Citizenship (nationality) of decedent at time of death

(All amounts and values must be entered in United States money.)

1	Total of estate, inheritance, legacy, and succession taxes imposed in the country named above attributable to property situated in that country, subjected to these taxes, and included in the gross estate (as defined by statute) .	**1**	
2	Value of the gross estate (adjusted, if necessary, according to the instructions)	**2**	
3	Value of property situated in that country, subjected to death taxes imposed in that country, and included in the gross estate (adjusted, if necessary, according to the instructions)	**3**	
4	Tax imposed by section 2001 reduced by the total credits claimed under sections 2010 and 2012 (see instructions)	**4**	
5	Amount of federal estate tax attributable to property specified at item 3. (Divide item 3 by item 2 and multiply the result by item 4.)	**5**	
6	Credit for death taxes imposed in the country named above (the smaller of item 1 or item 5). Also enter on line 13 of Part 2—Tax Computation	**6**	-0-

SCHEDULE Q—Credit for Tax on Prior Transfers

Part 1. Transferor Information

	Name of transferor	Social security number	IRS office where estate tax return was filed	Date of death
A				
B				
C				

Check here ▶ ☐ if section 2013(f) (special valuation of farm, etc., real property) adjustments to the computation of the credit were made (see instructions).

Part 2. Computation of Credit (see instructions)

Item	Transferor			Total A, B, & C
	A	B	C	
1 Transferee's tax as apportioned (from worksheet, (line 7 ÷ line 8) × line 35 for each column) . . .				
2 Transferor's tax (from each column of worksheet, line 20)				
3 Maximum amount before percentage requirement (for each column, enter amount from line 1 or 2, whichever is smaller)				
4 Percentage allowed (each column) (see instructions)	%	%	%	
5 Credit allowable (line 3 × line 4 for each column) .				
6 TOTAL credit allowable (add columns A, B, and C of line 5). Enter here and on line 14 of Part 2—Tax Computation				-0-

Form 706 (Rev. 8-2013)

SCHEDULE R—Generation-Skipping Transfer Tax

Note. To avoid application of the deemed allocation rules, Form 706 and Schedule R should be filed to allocate the GST exemption to trusts that may later have taxable terminations or distributions under section 2612 even if the form is not required to be filed to report estate or GST tax.

The GST tax is imposed on taxable transfers of interests in property located outside the United States as well as property located inside the United States. (see instructions)

Part 1. GST Exemption Reconciliation (Section 2631) and Special QTIP Election (Section 2652(a)(3))

You no longer need to check a box to make a section 2652(a)(3) (special QTIP) election. If you list qualifying property in Part 1, line 9 below, you will be considered to have made this election. See instructions for details.

1	Maximum allowable GST exemption	1
2	Total GST exemption allocated by the decedent against decedent's lifetime transfers	2
3	Total GST exemption allocated by the executor, using Form 709, against decedent's lifetime transfers	3
4	GST exemption allocated on line 6 of Schedule R, Part 2	4
5	GST exemption allocated on line 6 of Schedule R, Part 3	5
6	Total GST exemption allocated on line 4 of Schedule(s) R-1	6
7	Total GST exemption allocated to *inter vivos* transfers and direct skips (add lines 2–6)	7
8	GST exemption available to allocate to trusts and section 2032A interests (subtract line 7 from line 1)	8

9 Allocation of GST exemption to trusts (as defined for GST tax purposes):

A Name of trust	B Trust's EIN (if any)	C GST exemption allocated on lines 2–6, above (see instructions)	D Additional GST exemption allocated (see instructions)	E Trust's inclusion ratio (optional—see instructions)

9D Total. May not exceed line 8, above **9D**

10 GST exemption available to allocate to section 2032A interests received by individual beneficiaries (subtract line 9D from line 8). You must attach special-use allocation statement (see instructions) . **10** -0-

Schedule R—Page 23

¶2436

Form 706 (Rev. 8-2013)

Estate of: Mark F. Smith	Decedent's social security number		
	655	11	6633

Part 2. Direct Skips Where the Property Interests Transferred Bear the GST Tax on the Direct Skips

Name of skip person	Description of property interest transferred	Estate tax value

1	Total estate tax values of all property interests listed above	1	
2	Estate taxes, state death taxes, and other charges borne by the property interests listed above . .	2	
3	GST taxes borne by the property interests listed above but imposed on direct skips other than those shown on this Part 2 (see instructions)	3	
4	Total fixed taxes and other charges (add lines 2 and 3)	4	
5	Total tentative maximum direct skips (subtract line 4 from line 1)	5	
6	GST exemption allocated	6	
7	Subtract line 6 from line 5	7	
8	GST tax due (divide line 7 by 3.5)	8	
9	Enter the amount from line 8 of Schedule R, Part 3	9	
10	**Total GST taxes payable by the estate** (add lines 8 and 9). Enter here and on line 17 of Part 2—Tax Computation	10	-0-

Schedule R—Page 24

¶2436

Form 706 (Rev. 8-2013)

Estate of: Mark F. Smith	Decedent's social security number		
	655	11	6633

Part 3. Direct Skips Where the Property Interests Transferred Do Not Bear the GST Tax on the Direct Skips

Name of skip person	Description of property interest transferred	Estate tax value

1	Total estate tax values of all property interests listed above	1	
2	Estate taxes, state death taxes, and other charges borne by the property interests listed above . .	2	
3	GST taxes borne by the property interests listed above but imposed on direct skips other than those shown on this Part 3 (see instructions)	3	
4	Total fixed taxes and other charges (add lines 2 and 3)	4	
5	Total tentative maximum direct skips (subtract line 4 from line 1)	5	
6	GST exemption allocated	6	
7	Subtract line 6 from line 5	7	
8	GST tax due (multiply line 7 by .40). Enter here and on Schedule R, Part 2, line 9	8	

Schedule R—Page 25

¶2436

SCHEDULE R-1
(Form 706)
(Rev. August 2013)
Department of the Treasury
Internal Revenue Service

Generation-Skipping Transfer Tax

Direct Skips From a Trust
Payment Voucher

OMB No. 1545-0015

Executor: File one copy with Form 706 and send two copies to the fiduciary. Do not pay the tax shown. See instructions for details.
Fiduciary: See instructions for details. Pay the tax shown on line 6.

Name of trust	Trust's EIN

Name and title of fiduciary	Name of decedent	

Address of fiduciary (number and street)	Decedent's SSN	Service Center where Form 706 was filed

City, state, and ZIP or postal code	Name of executor	

Address of executor (number and street)	City, state, and ZIP or postal code	

Date of decedent's death	Filing due date of Schedule R, Form 706 (with extensions)	

Part 1. Computation of the GST Tax on the Direct Skip

Description of property interests subject to the direct skip	Estate tax value

1	Total estate tax value of all property interests listed above	1
2	Estate taxes, state death taxes, and other charges borne by the property interests listed above . .	2
3	Tentative maximum direct skip from trust (subtract line 2 from line 1)	3
4	GST exemption allocated	4
5	Subtract line 4 from line 3	5
6	**GST tax due from fiduciary** (divide line 5 by 3.5). **(See instructions if property will not bear the GST tax.)**	6

Under penalties of perjury, I declare that I have examined this document, including accompanying schedules and statements, and to the best of my knowledge and belief, it is true, correct, and complete.

Signature(s) of executor(s)	Date

	Date

Signature of fiduciary or officer representing fiduciary	Date

Schedule R-1—Page 26

¶2436

Form 706 (Rev. 8-2013)

Instructions for the Trustee

Introduction   Schedule R-1 (Form 706) serves as a payment voucher for the Generation-Skipping Transfer (GST) tax imposed on a direct skip from a trust, which you, the trustee of the trust, must pay. The executor completes the Schedule R-1 (Form 706) and gives you two copies. File one copy and keep one for your records.

How to pay   You can pay by check or money order or by electronic funds transfer.

To pay by check or money order:

- Make it payable to "United States Treasury."
- The amount of the check or money order should be the amount on line 6 of Schedule R-1.
- Write "GST Tax" and the trust's EIN on the check or money order.

To pay by electronic funds transfer:

- Funds must be submitted through the Electronic Federal Tax Payment System (EFTPS).
- Establish an EFTPS account by visiting *www.eftps.gov* or calling 1-800-555-4477.
- To be considered timely, payments made through EFTPS must be completed no later than 8 p.m. Eastern time the day **before** the due date.

Signature   You must sign the Schedule R-1 in the space provided.

What to mail   Mail your check or money order, if applicable, and the copy of Schedule R-1 that you signed.

Where to mail   Mail to the Department of the Treasury, Internal Revenue Service Center, Cincinnati, OH 45999.

When to pay   The GST tax is due and payable 9 months after the decedent's date of death (shown on the Schedule R-1). You will owe interest on any GST tax not paid by that date.

Automatic extension   You have an automatic extension of time to file Schedule R-1 and pay the GST tax. The automatic extension allows you to file and pay by 2 months after the due date (with extensions) for filing the decedent's Schedule R (shown on the Schedule R-1).

  If you pay the GST tax under the automatic extension, you will be charged interest (but no penalties).

Additional information   For more information, see section 2603(a)(2) and the Instructions for Form 706, United States Estate (and Generation-Skipping Transfer) Tax Return.

Schedule R-1—Page 27

¶2436

Form 706 (Rev. 8-2013)

Estate of: Mark F. Smith

	Decedent's social security number
	655 : 11 : 6633

SCHEDULE U—Qualified Conservation Easement Exclusion

Part 1. Election

Note. The executor is deemed to have made the election under section 2031(c)(6) if he or she files Schedule U and excludes any qualifying conservation easements from the gross estate.

Part 2. General Qualifications

1   Describe the land subject to the qualified conservation easement (see instructions) _____

2   Did the decedent or a member of the decedent's family own the land described above during the 3-year period ending on the date of the decedent's death? . . . . ☐ Yes ☐ No

3   Describe the conservation easement with regard to which the exclusion is being claimed (see instructions). _____

Part 3. Computation of Exclusion

4	Estate tax value of the land subject to the qualified conservation easement (see instructions) .	**4**	
5	Date of death value of any easements granted prior to decedent's death and included on line 10 below (see instructions)	**5**	
6	Add lines 4 and 5	**6**	
7	Value of retained development rights on the land (see instructions)	**7**	
8	Subtract line 7 from line 6	**8**	
9	Multiply line 8 by 30% (.30)	**9**	
10	Value of qualified conservation easement for which the exclusion is being claimed (see instructions)	**10**	
	Note. If line 10 is less than line 9, continue with line 11. If line 10 is equal to or more than line 9, skip lines 11 through 13, enter ".40" on line 14, and complete the schedule.		
11	Divide line 10 by line 8. Figure to 3 decimal places (for example, ".123")	**11**	
	Note. If line 11 is equal to or less than .100, stop here; the estate does not qualify for the conservation easement exclusion.		
12	Subtract line 11 from .300. Enter the answer in hundredths by rounding any thousandths up to the next higher hundredth (that is, .030 = .03, but .031 = .04)	**12**	
13	Multiply line 12 by 2	**13**	
14	Subtract line 13 from .40	**14**	
15	Deduction under section 2055(f) for the conservation easement (see instructions)	**15**	
16	Amount of indebtedness on the land (see instructions)	**16**	
17	Total reductions in value (add lines 7, 15, and 16)	**17**	
18	Net value of land (subtract line 17 from line 4)	**18**	
19	Multiply line 18 by line 14	**19**	
20	Enter the smaller of line 19 or the exclusion limitation (see instructions). Also enter this amount on item 12, Part 5—Recapitulation, page 3	**20**	-0-

Schedule U—Page 28

¶2436

Schedule **PC** (Rev. August 2013) Department of the Treasury Internal Revenue Service	**Protective Claim for Refund** ► To be used for decedents dying after December 31, 2011. File 2 copies of this schedule with Form 706 for each pending claim or expense under section 2053.	OMB No. 1545-0015

- Timely filing a protective claim for refund preserves the estate's right to claim a refund based on the amount of an unresolved claim or expense that may not become deductible under section 2053 until after the limitation period ends.

- Schedule PC can be used to file a protective claim for refund and, once the claim or expense becomes deductible, Schedule PC can be used to notify the IRS that a refund is being claimed.

- Schedule PC can be used by the estate of a decedent dying after 2011.

- Schedule PC must be filed with Form 706 and cannot be filed separately. (To file a protective claim for refund or notify the IRS that a refund is being claimed in a form separate from the Form 706, instead use Form 843, Claim for Refund and Request for Abatement.)

- Each separate claim or expense requires a separate Schedule PC (or Form 843, if not filed with Form 706).

- Schedule PC must be filed in duplicate (two copies) for each separate claim or expense.

Part 1. General Information

1. Name of decedent	2. Decedent's social security number
Mark F. Smith	655-11-6633

3. Name of fiduciary	4. Date of death
Jane R. Smith	12/15/2013

5a. Address (number, street, and room or suite no.)	5b. Room or suite no.
1465 Green Road	

5c. City or town, state, and ZIP or postal code	6. Daytime telephone number
Baltimore, Maryland 21277	

7. Number of Claims. Enter number of Schedules PC being filed with Form 706.   1

If the number is greater than one OR if another Schedule PC or Form 843 was previously filed by or on behalf of the estate, complete Part 3 of this Schedule PC.

8. Fiduciary   ☑ Check here if this Schedule PC is being filed with the original Form 706 or is being filed by the same fiduciary who filed the original Form 706 for decedent's estate. If a different fiduciary is filing this Schedule PC, see instructions for establishing the legal authority to pursue the claim for refund on behalf of the estate.

Part 2. Claim Information

Check the box that applies to this claim for refund.

a.   ☑ Protective claim for refund made for unresolved claim or expense.

   Amount in contest: _____750,000_____

b.   ☐ Partial refund claimed: partial resolution and/or satisfaction of claim or expense for which a protective claim for refund has been filed previously.

   Date protective claim for refund filed for this claim or expense: _____

   Amount of claim or expense partially resolved and/or satisfied and presently claimed as a deduction under section 2053 (do not include amounts previously deducted): _____

c.   ☐ Full and final refund claimed for this claim or expense: resolution and/or satisfaction of claim or expense for which a protective claim for refund has been filed previously.

   Date protective claim for refund filed for this claim or expense: _____

   Amount of claim or expense finally resolved and/or satisfied and presently claimed as a deduction under section 2053 (do not include amounts previously deducted): _____

Schedule PC—Page 29

¶2436

Form 706 (Rev. 8-2013)

				Decedent's social security number		
Estate of: Mark F. Smith				655	11	6633

A Form 706 Schedule and Item number	B Identification of the claim • Name or names of the claimant(s) • Basis of the claim or other description of the pending claim or expense • Reasons and contingencies delaying resolution •Status of contested matters •Attach copies of relevant pleadings or other documents	C Amount, if any, deducted under Treas. Reg. sections 20.2053-1(d)(4) or 20.2053-4 (b) or (c) for the identified claim or expense	D Amount presently claimed as a deduction under section 2053 for the identified claim	E Ancillary expenses estimated/ agreed upon/paid (Please indicate)	F Amount of tax to be refunded

Part 3. Other Schedules PC and Forms 843 Filed by Estate

If a Schedule PC or Form 843 was previously filed by the estate, complete Part 3 to identify each claim for refund reported.

A Date of death	B Internal Revenue office where filed	C Date filed	D Indicate whether (1) Protective Claim for Refund; (2) Partial Claim for Refund; or (3) Full and Final Claim for Refund	E Amount in Contest	
1					

To inquire about the receipt and/or processing of the protective claim for refund, please call (866) 699-4083.

(Rev. 8-2013)

Schedule PC—Page 30

¶2436

Form 706 (Rev. 8-2013) (Make copies of this schedule before completing it if you will need more than one schedule.)

			Decedent's social security number		
			655	11	6633

Estate of: Mark F. Smith

CONTINUATION SCHEDULE

Continuation of Schedule _____

(Enter letter of schedule you are continuing.)

Item number	Description. For securities, give CUSIP number. If trust, partnership, or closely held entity, give EIN.	Unit value (Sch. B, E, or G only)	Alternate valuation date	Alternate value	Value at date of death or amount deductible

TOTAL. (Carry forward to main schedule.) . . . .

Continuation Schedule—Page 31

¶2436

¶2437 IRS INSTRUCTIONS FOR FORM 706

Instructions for Form 706
(Rev. August 2013)

Department of the Treasury
Internal Revenue Service

For decendents dying after December 31, 2012

United States Estate (and Generation-Skipping Transfer) Tax Return

Section references are to the Internal Revenue Code unless otherwise noted.

Prior Revisions of Form 706

For Decedents Dying		Use Revision of Form 706 Dated
After	and Before	
December 31, 1998	January 1, 2001	July 1999
December 31, 2000	January 1, 2002	November 2001
December 31, 2001	January 1, 2003	August 2002
December 31, 2002	January 1, 2004	August 2003
December 31, 2003	January 1, 2005	August 2004
December 31, 2004	January 1, 2006	August 2005
December 31, 2005	January 1, 2007	October 2006
December 31, 2006	January 1, 2008	September 2007
December 31, 2007	January 1, 2009	August 2008
December 31, 2008	January 1, 2010	September 2009
December 31, 2009	January 1, 2011	July 2011
December 31, 2010	January 1, 2012	August 2011
December 31, 2011	January 1, 2013	August 2012

Contents

Future Developments

For the latest information about developments related to Form 706 and its instructions, such as legislation enacted after they were published, go to *www.irs.gov/form706.*

What's New

• Schedule PC—Protective Claim for Refund has been added to Form 706. By filing Schedule PC, taxpayers can preserve their right to a refund of estate taxes paid when a claim or expense which is the subject of unresolved controversy at the time of filing the return later becomes deductible under section 2053.

• Line 7 Worksheet in the instructions has been expanded to include the calculation for cumulative lifetime gifts on which tax was paid or payable. This amount is used in Section C of Part 6– Portability of Deceased Spousal Unused Exclusion (DSUE).

• Submit a copy of the Line 7 Worksheet (if completed) when you file Form 706.

• Various dollar amounts and limitations in the Form 706 are indexed for inflation. For decedents dying in 2013, the following amounts are applicable:

  a. The basic exclusion amount is $5,250,000.

  b. The ceiling on special-use valuation is $1,070,000.

  c. The amount used in figuring the 2% portion of estate tax payable in installments is $1,430,000.

The IRS will publish amounts for future years in annual revenue procedures.

Reminders

• Executors must provide documentation of their status.

• The credit for transfers made by lifetime gift has been reunified with the credit against transfers made at death. The applicable credit amount for 2013 is $2,045,800 (based on the basic exclusion amount of $5,250,000). This does not include any applicable credit resulting from DSUE amount received from a predeceased spouse.

Cat. No. 16779E

- Portability of Deceased Spousal Unused Exclusion

1. Part 6—Portability of Deceased Spousal Unused Exclusion (DSUE) was added to Form 706. The only action required to elect portability of the DSUE amount, if any, is to file a timely and complete Form 706. In this Part, taxpayers can opt out of electing to transfer any DSUE amount to a surviving spouse, calculate the amount of DSUE to be transferred in the event of an election, and/or account for any DSUE amount received from predeceased spouse(s).

2. Line 9 of Part 2—Tax Computation was replaced with lines 9a through 9d to calculate the applicable exclusion amount and applicable credit amount (formerly unified credit amount), factoring in any DSUE amount received from a predeceased spouse.

3. Executors of estates who are not required to file Form 706 under section 6018(a) but who are filing to elect portability of DSUE amount to the surviving spouse are not required to report the value of certain property eligible for the marital deduction under section 2056 or 2056A or the charitable deduction under section 2055 under the special rule of Reg. section 20.2010–2T(a)(7)(ii). However, the value of those assets must be estimated and included in the total value of the gross estate. The special rule does not apply to assets whose valuation is required for eligibility under section 2032, 2032A, 2652(a)(3), 6166 or other provision of the Code or Regulations.

- A timely and complete Form 706 must be filed by the executor of any estate who intends to transfer the DSUE amount to the decedent's surviving spouse, regardless of the amount of the gross estate. See instructions for Part 6—Portability of Deceased Spousal Unused Exclusion, below.
- Filing a timely and complete Form 706 with a DSUE amount will be considered an election to transfer the DSUE amount to the surviving spouse. An executor of an estate who files a Form 706 that does not elect to transfer the DSUE amount to the surviving spouse must affirmatively opt out of portability. See Part 6—Portability of Deceased Spousal Exclusion, Section A.

General Instructions

Purpose of Form

The executor of a decedent's estate uses Form 706 to figure the estate tax imposed by Chapter 11 of the Internal Revenue Code. This tax is levied on the entire taxable estate and not just on the share received by a particular beneficiary. Form 706 is also used to figure the generation-skipping transfer (GST) tax imposed by Chapter 13 on direct skips (transfers to skip persons of interests in property included in the decedent's gross estate).

Which Estates Must File

For decedents who died in 2013, Form 706 must be filed by the executor of the estate of every U.S. citizen or resident:

a. Whose gross estate, plus adjusted taxable gifts and specific exemption, is more than $5,250,000; or,

b. Whose executor elects to transfer the DSUE amount to the surviving spouse, regardless of the size of the decedent's gross estate. See instructions for Part 6—Portability of Deceased Spousal Unused Exclusion and sections 2010(c)(4) and (c)(5).

To determine whether you must file a return for the estate under test a above, add:

1. The adjusted taxable gifts (as defined in section 2503) made by the decedent after December 31, 1976;

2. The total specific exemption allowed under section 2521 (as in effect before its repeal by the Tax Reform Act of 1976) for gifts made by the decedent after September 8, 1976; and

3. The decedent's gross estate valued as of the date of death.

Gross Estate

The gross estate includes all property in which the decedent had an interest (including real property outside the United States). It also includes:
- Certain transfers made during the decedent's life without an adequate and full consideration in money or money's worth,
- Annuities,
- The includible portion of joint estates with right of survivorship (see instructions for Schedule E),
- The includible portion of tenancies by the entirety (see instructions for Schedule E),

- Certain life insurance proceeds (even though payable to beneficiaries other than the estate) (see instructions for Schedule D),
- Property over which the decedent possessed a general power of appointment,
- Dower or curtesy (or statutory estate) of the surviving spouse, and
- Community property to the extent of the decedent's interest as defined by applicable law.

Note. Under the special rule of Regulations section 20.2010–2T(a)(7)(ii), executors of estates who are not required to file Form 706 under section 6018(a), but who are filing to elect portability of DSUE amount to the surviving spouse, are not required to report the value of certain property eligible for the marital deduction under section 2056 or 2056A or the charitable deduction under section 2055. However, the value of those assets must be estimated and included in the total value of the gross estate. See instructions for Part 5—Recapitulation, lines 10 and 23, for more information.

For more specific information, see the instructions for Schedules A through I.

U.S. Citizens or Residents; Nonresident Noncitizens

File Form 706 for the estates of decedents who were either U.S. citizens or U.S. residents at the time of death. For estate tax purposes, a resident is someone who had a domicile in the United States at the time of death. A person acquires a domicile by living in a place for even a brief period of time, as long as the person had no intention of moving from that place.

File Form 706-NA, U.S. Estate (and Generation-Skipping Transfer) Tax Return, for the estates of nonresident alien decedents (decedents who were neither U.S. citizens nor U.S. residents at the time of death).

Residents of U.S. Possessions

All references to citizens of the United States are subject to the provisions of sections 2208 and 2209, relating to decedents who were U.S. citizens and residents of a U.S. possession on the date of death. If such a decedent became a U.S. citizen only because of his or her connection with a possession, then the decedent is considered a nonresident alien decedent for estate tax purposes, and you should file Form 706-NA. If such a decedent became a U.S. citizen wholly independently of his

General Instructions

or her connection with a possession, then the decedent is considered a U.S. citizen for estate tax purposes, and you should file Form 706.

Executor
The term *executor* includes the executor, personal representative, or administrator of the decedent's estate. If none of these is appointed, qualified, and acting in the United States, every person in actual or constructive possession of any property of the decedent is considered an executor and must file a return.

Executors must provide documentation proving their status. Documentation will vary, but may include documents such as a certified copy of the will or a court order designating the executor(s). A statement by the executor attesting to their status is insufficient.

When To File
You must file Form 706 to report estate and/or GST tax within 9 months after the date of the decedent's death. If you are unable to file Form 706 by the due date, you may receive an extension of time to file. Use Form 4768, Application for Extension of Time To File a Return and/or Pay U.S. Estate (and Generation-Skipping Transfer) Taxes, to apply for an automatic 6-month extension of time to file.

Note. An executor can only elect to transfer the DSUE amount to the surviving spouse if the Form 706 is filed timely; that is, within 9 months of the decedent's date of death or, if you have received an extension of time to file, before the 6-month extension period ends.

Private delivery services. You can use certain private delivery services designated by the IRS to meet the "timely mailing as timely filing/paying" rule for tax returns and payments. These private delivery services include only the following:
• DHL Express (DHL): DHL Same Day Service.
• Federal Express (FedEx): FedEx Priority Overnight, FedEx Standard Overnight, FedEx 2Day, FedEx International Priority, FedEx International First.
• United Parcel Service (UPS): UPS Next Day Air, UPS Next Day Air Saver, UPS 2nd Day Air, UPS 2nd Day Air A.M., UPS Worldwide Express Plus, and UPS Worldwide Express.

The private delivery service can tell you how to get written proof of the mailing date.

Where To File
File Form 706 at the following address:

> Department of the Treasury
> Internal Revenue Service Center
> Cincinnati, OH 45999

Paying the Tax
The estate and GST taxes are due within 9 months of the date of the decedent's death. You may request an extension of time for payment by filing Form 4768. You may also elect under section 6166 to pay in installments or under section 6163 to postpone the part of the tax attributable to a reversionary or remainder interest. These elections are made by checking lines 3 and 4 (respectively) of Part 3—Elections by the Executor, and attaching the required statements.

If the tax paid with the return is different from the balance due as figured on the return, explain the difference in an attached statement. If you have made prior payments to the IRS, attach a statement to Form 706 including these facts.

Paying by check. Make the check payable to the "United States Treasury." Please write the decedent's name, social security number (SSN), and "Form 706" on the check to assist us in posting it to the proper account.

Paying Electronically. Payment of the tax due shown on Form 706 may be submitted electronically through the Electronic Federal Tax Payment System (EFTPS). EFTPS is a free service of the Department of Treasury.

To be considered timely, payments made through EFTPS must be completed no later than 8 p.m. Eastern time the day before the due date. All EFTPS payments must be scheduled in advance of the due date and, if necessary, may be changed or cancelled up to two business days before the scheduled payment date.

To get more information about EFTPS or to enroll, visit *www.eftps.gov* or call 1–800–555–4477. Additional information about EFTPS is available in Publication 966, Electronic Federal Tax Payment System: A Guide to Getting Started.

Signature and Verification

 If there is more than one executor, all listed executors are responsible for the return. However, it is sufficient for only one of the co-executors to sign the return.

All executors are responsible for the return as filed and are liable for penalties imposed for erroneous or false returns.

If two or more persons are liable for filing the return, they should all join together in filing one complete return. However, if they are unable to join in making one complete return, each is required to file a return disclosing all the information the person has about the estate, including the name of every person holding an interest in the property and a full description of the property. If the appointed, qualified, and acting executor is unable to make a complete return, then every person holding an interest in the property must, on notice from the IRS, make a return regarding that interest.

The executor who files the return must, in every case, sign the declaration on page 1 under penalties of perjury.

Generally, anyone who is paid to prepare the return must sign the return in the space provided and fill in the Paid Preparer Use Only area. See section 7701(a)(36)(B) for exceptions.

In addition to signing and completing the required information, the paid preparer must give a copy of the completed return to the executor.

Note. A paid preparer may sign original or amended returns by rubber stamp, mechanical device, or computer software program.

Amending Form 706
If you find that you must change something on a return that has already been filed, you should:
• File another Form 706;
• Enter "Supplemental Information" across the top of page 1 of the form; and
• Attach a copy of pages 1, 2, 3, and 4 of the original Form 706 that has already been filed.

If you have already been notified that the return has been selected for examination, you should provide the additional information directly to the office conducting the examination.

Supplemental Documents

Note. You must attach the death certificate to the return.

If the decedent was a citizen or resident of the United States and died testate (leaving a valid will), attach a certified copy of the will to the return. If you cannot obtain a certified copy, attach a copy of the will and an explanation of why it is not certified. Other supplemental documents may be required as explained below. Examples include Forms 712, Life Insurance Statement; 709, United States Gift (and Generation-Skipping Transfer) Tax Return; and 706-CE, Certificate of Payment of Foreign Death Tax; trust and power of appointment instruments; and state certification of payment of death taxes. If you do not file these documents with the return, the processing of the return will be delayed.

If the decedent was a U.S. citizen but not a resident of the United States, you must attach the following documents to the return:

1. A copy of the inventory of property and the schedule of liabilities, claims against the estate, and expenses of administration filed with the foreign court of probate jurisdiction, certified by a proper official of the court;

2. A copy of the return filed under the foreign inheritance, estate, legacy, succession tax, or other death tax act, certified by a proper official of the foreign tax department, if the estate is subject to such a foreign tax; and

3. If the decedent died testate, a certified copy of the will.

Rounding Off to Whole Dollars

You may show the money items on the return and accompanying schedules as whole-dollar amounts. To do so, drop the cents from any amount with less than 50 cents and increase any amount with 50 to 99 cents to the next dollar. For example, $1.39 becomes $1 and $2.55 become $3. If you have to add two or more amounts to compute an item's value, include the cents when adding the amounts and round off only the total.

Penalties

Late filing and late payment. Section 6651 provides for penalties for both late filing and for late payment unless there is reasonable cause for the delay. The law also provides for penalties for willful attempts to evade payment of tax. The late filing penalty will not be imposed if the taxpayer can show that the failure to file a timely return is due to reasonable cause.

Reasonable cause determinations. If you receive a notice about penalties after you file Form 706, send an explanation and we will determine if you meet reasonable cause criteria. Do not attach an explanation when you file Form 706. Explanations attached to the return at the time of filing will not be considered.

Valuation understatement. Section 6662 provides a 20% penalty for the underpayment of estate tax that exceeds $5,000 when the underpayment is attributable to valuation understatements. A valuation understatement occurs when the value of property reported on Form 706 is 65% or less of the actual value of the property.

This penalty increases to 40% if there is a gross valuation understatement. A gross valuation understatement occurs if any property on the return is valued at 40% or less of the value determined to be correct.

Penalties also apply to late filing, late payment, and underpayment of GST taxes.

Return preparer. Estate tax return preparers, who prepare any return or claim for refund which reflects an understatement of tax liability due to willful or reckless conduct, are subject to a penalty of $5,000 or 50% of the income derived (or income to be derived), whichever is greater, for the preparation of each such return. See section 6694(b), the regulations thereunder, and Ann. 2009-15, 2009-11 I.R.B. 687 (available at *www.irs.gov/pub/irs-irbs/irb09-11.pdf*) for more information.

Obtaining Forms and Publications To File or Use

Internet. You can access the IRS website 24 hours a day, 7 days a week at *IRS.gov* to:

• Download forms, instructions, and publications;
• Order IRS products online;
• Research your tax questions online;
• Search publications online by topic or keyword; and
• Sign up to receive local and national tax news by email.

Other forms that may be required.
• Form SS-5, Application for a Social Security Card.

• Form 706-CE, Certificate of Payment of Foreign Death Tax.
• Form 706-NA, United States Estate (and Generation-Skipping Transfer) Tax Return, Estate of nonresident not a citizen of the United States.
• Form 709, United States Gift (and Generation-Skipping Transfer) Tax Return.
• Form 712, Life Insurance Statement.
• Form 2848, Power of Attorney and Declaration of Representative.
• Form 4768, Application for Extension of Time To File a Return and/or Pay U.S. Estate (and Generation-Skipping Transfer) Taxes.
• Form 4808, Computation of Credit for Gift Tax.
• Form 8821, Tax Information Authorization.
• Form 8822, Change of Address.

Additional Information. The following publications may assist you in learning about and preparing Form 706:
• Publication 559, Survivors, Executors, and Administrators.
• Publication 910, IRS Guide to Free Tax Services.

Note. For information about release of nonresident U.S. citizen decedents' assets using transfer certificates under Regulations section 20.6325-1, write to:

Internal Revenue Service
Cincinnati, OH 45999
Stop 824G

Specific Instructions

You must file the first four pages of Form 706 and all required schedules. File Schedules A through I, as appropriate, to support the entries in items 1 through 9 of Part 5—Recapitulation.

-4-

General, Specific, and Part Instructions

IF . . .	THEN . . .
you enter zero on any item of the Recapitulation,	you need not file the schedule (except for Schedule F) referred to on that item.
you are estimating the value of one or more assets pursuant to the special rule of Regulations section 20.2010–2T(a)(7)(ii),	you must report the asset on the appropriate schedule, but you are not required to enter a value for the asset. Include the estimated value of the asset in the totals entered on lines 10 and 23 of Part 5—Recapitulation.
you claim an exclusion on item 11,	complete and attach Schedule U.
you claim any deductions on items 14 through 22 of the Recapitulation,	complete and attach the appropriate schedules to support the claimed deductions.
you claim credits for foreign death taxes or tax on prior transfers,	complete and attach Schedule P or Q.
there is not enough space on a schedule to list all the items,	attach a Continuation Schedule (or additional sheets of the same size) to the back of the schedule (see the Continuation Schedule at the end of Form 706);
	photocopy the blank schedule before completing it, if you will need more than one copy.

Also consider the following:
• Form 706 has 31 numbered pages. The pages are perforated so that you can remove them for copying and filing.
• Number the items you list on each schedule, beginning with the number "1" each time, or using the numbering convention as indicated on the schedule (for example, Schedule M).
• Total the items listed on the schedule and its attachments, Continuation Schedules, etc.
• Enter the total of all attachments, Continuation Schedules, etc., at the bottom of the printed schedule, but do not carry the totals forward from one schedule to the next.
• Enter the total, or totals, for each schedule on page 3, Part 5—Recapitulation.
• Do not complete the "Alternate valuation date" or "Alternate value" columns of any schedule unless you elected alternate valuation on line 1 of Part 3—Elections by the Executor.

• When you complete the return, staple all the required pages together in the proper order.

Part 1—Decedent and Executor

Line 2
Enter the social security number (SSN) assigned specifically to the decedent. You cannot use the SSN assigned to the decedent's spouse. If the decedent did not have an SSN, the executor should obtain one for the decedent by filing Form SS-5, with a local Social Security Administration office.

Line 6a. Name of Executor
If there is more than one executor, enter the name of the executor to be contacted by the IRS and see line 6d.

Line 6b. Executor's Address
Use Form 8822 to report a change of the executor's address.

Line 6c. Executor's Social Security Number
Only one executor should complete this line. If there is more than one executor, see line 6d.

Line 6d. Multiple Executors
Check here if there is more than one executor. On an attached statement, provide the names, addresses, telephone numbers, and SSNs of any executor other than the one named on line 6a.

Line 11. Special Rule
If the estate is estimating the value of assets under the special rule of Regulations section 20.2010–2T(a)(7)(ii), check here and see the instructions for lines 10 and 23 of Part 5—Recapitulation.

Part 2—Tax Computation
In general, the estate tax is figured by applying the unified rates shown in Table A to the total of transfers both during life and at death, and then subtracting the gift taxes, as refigured based on the date of death rates. See Worksheet TG, Line 4 Worksheet, and Line 7 Worksheet.

Note. You must complete Part 2—Tax Computation.

Table A — Unified Rate Schedule

Column A Taxable amount over	Column B Taxable amount not over	Column C Tax on amount in Column A	Column D Rate of tax on excess over amount in Column A
$0	$10,000	$0	18%
10,000	20,000	1,800	20%
20,000	40,000	3,800	22%
40,000	60,000	8,200	24%
60,000	80,000	13,000	26%
80,000	100,000	18,200	28%
100,000	150,000	23,800	30%
150,000	250,000	38,800	32%
250,000	500,000	70,800	34%
500,000	750,000	155,800	37%
750,000	1,000,000	248,300	39%
1,000,000	----	345,800	40%

Line 1
If you elected alternate valuation on line 1, Part 3—Elections by the Executor, enter the amount you entered in the "Alternate value" column of item 13 of Part 5—Recapitulation. Otherwise, enter the amount from the "Value at date of death" column.

Line 3b. State Death Tax Deduction

 The estates of decedents dying after December 31, 2004, will be allowed a deduction for state death taxes, instead of a credit. The state death tax credit was repealed as of January 1, 2005.

You may take a deduction on line 3b for estate, inheritance, legacy, or succession taxes paid as the result of the decedent's death to any state or the District of Columbia.

You may claim an anticipated amount of deduction and figure the federal estate tax on the return before the state death taxes have been paid. However, the deduction cannot be finally allowed unless you pay the state death taxes and claim the deduction within 4 years after the return is filed, or later (see section 2058(b)) if:
• A petition is filed with the Tax Court of the United States,
• You have an extension of time to pay, or
• You file a claim for refund or credit of an overpayment which extends the deadline for claiming the deduction.

Worksheet TG and Line 4 Worksheet

Worksheet TG—Taxable Gifts Reconciliation
(To be used for lines 4 and 7 of the Tax Computation)

	a. Calendar year or calendar quarter	b. Total taxable gifts for period (see Note)	c. Taxable amount included in col. b for gifts included in the gross estate	d. Taxable amount included in col. b for gifts that qualify for "special treatment of split gifts" described below	e. Gift tax paid by decedent on gifts in col. d	f. Gift tax paid by decedent's spouse on gifts in col. c
Gifts made after June 6, 1932, and before 1977						
	1. Total taxable gifts made before 1977					
Gifts made after 1976						
2. Totals for gifts made after 1976						

Note. For the definition of a taxable gift, see section 2503. Follow Form 709. That is, include only the decedent's one-half of split gifts, whether the gifts were made by the decedent or the decedent's spouse. In addition to gifts reported on Form 709, you must include any taxable gifts in excess of the annual exclusion that were not reported on Form 709.

Line 4 Worksheet—Adjusted Taxable Gifts Made After 1976

1. Taxable gifts made after 1976. Enter the amount from Worksheet TG, line 2, column b			1	
2. Taxable gifts made after 1976 reportable on Schedule G. Enter the amount from Worksheet TG, line 2, column c	2			
3. Taxable gifts made after 1976 that qualify for "special treatment." Enter the amount from Worksheet TG, line 2, column d	3			
4. Add lines 2 and 3			4	
5. Adjusted taxable gifts. Subtract line 4 from line 1. Enter here and on Part 2—Tax Computation, line 4			5	

Note. The deduction is not subject to dollar limits.

If you make a section 6166 election to pay the federal estate tax in installments and make a similar election to pay the state death tax in installments, see section 2058(b) for exceptions and periods of limitation.

If you transfer property other than cash to the state in payment of state inheritance taxes, the amount you may claim as a deduction is the lesser of the state inheritance tax liability discharged or the fair market value (FMV) of the property on the date of the transfer. For more information on the application of such transfers, see the principles discussed in Revenue Ruling 86-117, 1986-2 C.B. 157, prior to the repeal of section 2011.

Send the following evidence to the IRS:

1. Certificate of the proper officer of the taxing state, or the District of Columbia, showing the:

a. Total amount of tax imposed (before adding interest and penalties and before allowing discount),

b. Amount of discount allowed,

c. Amount of penalties and interest imposed or charged,

d. Total amount actually paid in cash, and

e. Date of payment.

2. Any additional proof the IRS specifically requests.

File the evidence requested above with the return, if possible. Otherwise, send it as soon as possible after the return is filed.

Line 6

To figure the tentative tax on the amount on line 5, use Table A—Unified Rate Schedule, above, and put the result on this line.

Lines 4 and 7

Three worksheets are provided to help you figure the entries for these lines. Worksheet TG—Taxable Gifts Reconciliation allows you to reconcile the decedent's lifetime taxable gifts to figure totals that will be used for the Line 4 Worksheet and the Line 7 Worksheet.

You must have all of the decedent's gift tax returns (Forms 709) before completing Worksheet TG—Taxable Gifts Reconciliation. The amounts needed for Worksheet TG can usually be found on the filed returns that were subject to tax. However, if any of the returns were audited by the IRS, use the amounts that were finally determined as a result of the audits.

In addition, you must make a reasonable effort to discover any gifts in excess of the annual exclusion made by the decedent (or on behalf of the decedent under a power of attorney) for which no Forms 709 were filed. Include the value of such gifts in column b of Worksheet TG. The annual exclusion per donee for 1977 through 1981 was $3,000, $10,000 for 1981 through 2001, $11,000 for 2002 through 2005, $12,000 for 2006 through 2008, and $13,000 for 2009 through 2012. For 2013, the annual exclusion for gifts of present interest is $14,000 per donee.

Line 7 Worksheet – Submit a copy with Form 706

	Line 7 Worksheet Part A- Used to determine Applicable Credit Allowable for Prior Periods after 1976					
(a)	Tax Period[1]	Pre-1977				
(b)	Taxable Gifts for Applicable Period					
(c)	Taxable Gifts for Prior Periods [2]					
(d)	Cumulative Taxable Gifts Including Applicable Period (add Row (b) and Row (c))					
(e)	Tax at Date of Death Rates for Prior Gifts (from Row (c))[3]					
(f)	Tax at Date of Death Rates for Cumulative Gifts including Applicable Period (from Row (d))					
(g)	Tax at Date of Death Rates for Gifts in Applicable Period (subtract Row (e) from Row (f))					
(h)	Total DSUE applied from Prior Periods and Applicable Period (from Line 2 of Schedule C of Applicable Period Form 709)					
(i)	Basic Exclusion for Applicable Period (Enter the amount from the Table of Basic Exclusion Amounts)					
(j)	Basic Exclusion amount plus Total DSUE applied in prior periods and applicable period (add Row (h) and Row (i))					
(k)	Maximum Applicable Credit amount based on Row (j) (Using Table A—Unified Rate Schedule)[4]					
(l)	Applicable Credit amount used in Prior Periods (add Row (l) and Row (n) from prior period)					
(m)	Available Credit in Applicable Period (subtract Row (l) from Row (k))					
(n)	Credit Allowable (lesser of Row (g) or Row (m))					
(o)	Tax paid or payable at Date of Death rates for Applicable Period (subtract Row (n) from Row (g))					
(p)	Tax on Cumulative Gifts less tax paid or payable for Applicable Period (subtract Row (o) from Row (f))					
(q)	Cumulative Taxable Gifts less Gifts in the Applicable Period on which tax was paid or payable based on Row (p) (Using the Taxable Gift Amount Table)					
(r)	Gifts in the Applicable Period on which tax was payable (subtract Row (q) from Row (d))					
Line 7 Worksheet Part B						
1	Total gift taxes payable on gifts after 1976 (sum of amounts in Row (o)).					
2	Gift taxes paid by the decedent on gifts that qualify for "special treatment." Enter the amount from Worksheet TG, line 2, col. (e).					
3	Subtract line 2 from line 1.					
4	Gift tax paid by decedent's spouse on split gifts included on Schedule G. Enter amount from Worksheet TG, line 2, col. (f).					
5	Add lines 3 and 4. Enter here and on Part 2—Tax Computation, line 7.					
6	Cumulative lifetime gifts on which tax was paid or payable. Enter this amount on line 3, Section C, Part 6 of Form 706 (sum of amounts in Row (r)).					

Footnotes:
[1] Row (a): For annual returns, enter the tax period as (YYYY). For quarterly returns enter tax period as (YYYY–Q).
[2] Row (c): Enter amount from Row (d) of the previous column.
[3] Row (e): Enter amount from Row (f) of the previous column.
[4] Row (k): Calculate the applicable credit on the amount in Row (j), using Table A — Unified Rate Schedule, and enter here. (For each column in Row (k), subtract 20 percent of any amount allowed as a specific exemption for gifts made after September 8, 1976, and before January 1, 1977.)

¶2437

Taxable Gift Amount Table

Column A	Column B	Column C	Column D
Amount in Row (p) Line 7 Worksheet over...	Amount in Row (p) Line 7 Worksheet not over...	Property Value on Amount in Column A	Rate (Divisor) on excess of amount in Column A
0	1,800	0	18%
1,800	3,800	10,000	20%
3,800	8,200	20,000	22%
8,200	13,000	40,000	24%
13,000	18,200	60,000	26%
18,200	23,800	80,000	28%
23,800	38,800	100,000	30%
38,800	70,800	150,000	32%
70,800	155,800	250,000	34%
155,800	248,300	500,000	37%
248,300	345,800	750,000	39%
345,800	------	1,000,000	40%

How to complete line 7 worksheet.
Row (a). Beginning with the earliest year in which the taxable gifts were made, enter the tax period of prior gifts. If you filed returns for gifts made after 1981, enter the calendar year in Row (a) as (YYYY). If you filed returns for gifts made after 1976 and before 1982, enter the calendar quarters in Row (a) as (YYYY-Q).
Row (b). Enter all taxable gifts made in the specified year. Enter all pre-1977 gifts on the pre-1977 column.
Row (c). Enter the amount from Row (d) of the *previous* column.
Row (d). Enter the sum of Row (b) and Row (c) from the current column.
Row (e). Enter the amount from Row (f) of the *previous* column.
Row (f). Enter the tax based on the amount in Row (d) of the current column using Table A — Unified Rate Schedule, earlier.
Row (g). Subtract the amount in Row (e) from the amount in Row (f) for the current column.
Row (h). Complete this row only if a DSUE amount was received from predeceased spouse(s) and was applied to lifetime gifts. See line 2 of Schedule C on the Form 709 filed for the year listed in Row (a) for the amount to be entered in this row.
Row (i). Enter the applicable amount from the Table of Basic Exclusion Amounts.

Row (j). Enter the sum of Rows (h) and Row (i).
Row (k). Calculate the applicable credit on the amount in Row (j) using Table A — Unified Rate Schedule, and enter here.
Note. The entries in each column of Row (k) must be reduced by 20 percent of the amount allowed as a specific exemption for gifts made after September 8, 1976, and before January 1, 1977 (but no more than $6,000).
Row (l). Add the amounts in Row (l) and Row (n) from the *previous* column.
Row (m). Subtract the amount in Row (l) from the amount in Row (k) to determine the amount of any available credit. Enter result in Row (m).
Row (n). Enter the lesser of the amounts in Row (g) or Row (m).
Row (o). Subtract the amount in Row (n) from the amount in Row (g) for the current column.
Row (p). Subtract the amount in Row (o) from the amount in Row (f) for the current column.
Row (q). Enter the Cumulative Taxable Gift amount based on the amount in Row (p) using the Taxable Gift Amount Table.
Row (r). If Row (o) is greater than zero in the applicable period, subtract Row (q) from Row (d). If Row (o) is not greater than zero enter -0-.
Repeat for each year in which taxable gifts were made.

⚠ **CAUTION** *Remember to submit a copy of the Line 7 Worksheet when you file Form 706. If additional space is needed to report prior gifts, please attach additional sheets.*

Table of Basic Exclusion Amounts		
Period	Basic Exclusion Amount	Credit Equivalent at 2013 rates
1977 (Quarters 1 and 2)	$30,000	$6,000
1977 (Quarters 3 and 4)	$120,667	$30,000
1978	$134,000	$34,000
1979	$147,333	$38,000
1980	$161,563	$42,500
1981	$175,625	$47,000
1982	$225,000	$62,800
1983	$275,000	$79,300
1984	$325,000	$96,300
1985	$400,000	$121,800
1986	$500,000	$155,800
1987 through 1997	$600,000	$192,800
1998	$625,000	$202,050
1999	$650,000	$211,300
2000 and 2001	$675,000	$220,550
2002 through 2010	$1,000,000	$345,800
2011	$5,000,000	$1,945,800
2012	$5,120,000	$1,993,800
2013	$5,250,000	$2,045,800

Note. In figuring the line 7 amount, do not include any tax paid or payable on gifts made before 1977. The line 7 amount is a hypothetical figure used to calculate the estate tax.

Special treatment of split gifts.
These special rules apply only if:
• The decedent's spouse predeceased the decedent;
• The decedent's spouse made gifts that were "split" with the decedent under the rules of section 2513;
• The decedent was the "consenting spouse" for those split gifts, as that term is used on Form 709; and
• The split gifts were included in the decedent's spouse's gross estate under section 2035.

If all four conditions above are met, do not include these gifts on line 4 of the Tax Computation and do not include the gift taxes payable on these gifts on line 7 of the Tax Computation. These adjustments are incorporated into the worksheets.

Part Instructions

¶2437

Lines 9a through 9d. Applicable Credit Amount (formerly Unified Credit Amount)

The *applicable credit amount* is allowable credit against estate and gift taxes. It is calculated by determining the tentative tax on the *applicable exclusion amount*, which is the amount that can be transferred before an estate tax liability will be incurred.

The applicable exclusion amount equals the total of:
• Line 9a: The basic exclusion amount. In 2013, the basic exclusion amount, as adjusted for inflation under 2010(c)(3), is $5,250,000.
• Line 9b: The deceased spousal unused exclusion amount (DSUE). If the decedent had a spouse who died on or after January 1, 2011, whose estate did not use all of its applicable exclusion against gift or estate tax liability, a DSUE amount may be available for use by the decedent's estate. If the predeceased spouse died in 2011, the DSUE amount was calculated and attached to his or her Form 706. If the predeceased spouse died in 2012 or after, this amount is found in Part 6, Section C of the Form 706 filed by the estate of the decedent's predeceased spouse. The amount to be entered on line 9b is calculated in Part 6, Section D.

Line 10. Adjustment to Applicable Credit

If the decedent made gifts (including gifts made by the decedent's spouse and treated as made by the decedent by reason of gift splitting) after September 8, 1976, and before January 1, 1977, for which the decedent claimed a specific exemption, the applicable credit amount on this estate tax return must be reduced. The reduction is figured by entering 20% of the specific exemption claimed for these gifts.

Note. The specific exemption was allowed by section 2521 for gifts made before January 1, 1977.

If the decedent did not make any gifts between September 8, 1976, and January 1, 1977, or if the decedent made gifts during that period but did not claim the specific exemption, enter zero.

Line 15. Total Credits

Generally, line 15 is used to report the total of credit for foreign death taxes (line 13) and credit for tax on prior transfers (line 14).

However, you may also use line 15 to report credit taken for federal gift taxes imposed by Chapter 12 of the Code,

and the corresponding provisions of prior laws, on certain transfers the decedent made before January 1, 1977, that are included in the gross estate. The credit cannot be more than the amount figured by the following formula:

$$\frac{\text{Gross estate tax minus (the sum of the state death taxes and unified credit)}}{\text{Value of gross estate minus (the sum of the deductions for charitable, public, and similar gifts and bequests and marital deduction)}} \times \frac{\text{Value of included gift}}{}$$

When taking the credit for pre-1977 federal gift taxes:
• Include the credit in the amount on line 15 and
• Identify and enter the amount of the credit you are taking on the dotted line to the left of the entry space for line 15 on page 1 of Form 706 with a notation, "section 2012 credit."

For more information, see the regulations under section 2012. This computation may be made using Form 4808. Attach a copy of a completed Form 4808 or the computation of the credit. Also, attach all available copies of Forms 709 filed by the decedent to help verify the amounts entered on lines 4 and 7, and the amount of credit taken (on line 15) for pre-1977 federal gift taxes.

Canadian marital credit. In addition to using line 15 to report credit for federal gift taxes on pre-1977 gifts, you may also use line 15 to claim the Canadian marital credit, where applicable.

When taking the marital credit under the 1995 Canadian Protocol:
• Include the credit in the amount on line 15 and
• Identify and enter the amount of the credit you are taking on the dotted line to the left of the entry space for line 15 on page 1 of Form 706 with a notation, "Canadian marital credit."

Also, attach a statement to the return that refers to the treaty, waives QDOT rights, and shows the computation of the marital credit. See the 1995 Canadian income tax treaty protocol for details on figuring the credit.

Part 3—Elections by the Executor

Note. The election to allow the decedent's surviving spouse to use the decedent's unused exclusion amount is made by filing a timely and complete Form 706. See instructions for Part

6—Portability of Deceased Spousal Unused Exclusion, below, and sections 2010(c)(4) and (c)(5).

Line 1. Alternate Valuation

 See the example showing the use of Schedule B where the alternate valuation is adopted.

Unless you elect at the time the return is filed to adopt alternate valuation as authorized by section 2032, value all property included in the gross estate as of the date of the decedent's death. Alternate valuation cannot be applied to only a part of the property.

You may elect special-use valuation (line 2) in addition to alternate valuation.

You may not elect alternate valuation unless the election will decrease both the value of the gross estate and the sum (reduced by allowable credits) of the estate and GST taxes payable by reason of the decedent's death for the property includible in the decedent's gross estate.

Elect alternate valuation by checking "Yes," on line 1 and filing Form 706. You may make a protective alternate valuation election by checking "Yes," on line 1, writing the word "protective," and filing Form 706 using regular values.

Once made, the election may not be revoked. The election may be made on a late-filed Form 706 provided it is not filed later than 1 year after the due date (including extensions actually granted). Relief under sections 301.9100-1 and 301.9100-3 may be available to make an alternate valuation election or a protective alternate valuation election, provided a Form 706 is filed no later than 1 year after the due date of the return (including extensions actually granted).

If alternate valuation is elected, value the property included in the gross estate as of the following dates as applicable:
• Any property distributed, sold, exchanged, or otherwise disposed of or separated or passed from the gross estate by any method within 6 months after the decedent's death is valued on the date of distribution, sale, exchange, or other disposition. Value this property on the date it ceases to be a part of the gross estate; for example, on the date the title passes as the result of its sale, exchange, or other disposition.
• Any property not distributed, sold, exchanged, or otherwise disposed of within the 6-month period is valued as of 6 months after the date of the decedent's death.

Part Instructions   -9-

¶2437

• Any property, interest, or estate that is *affected by mere lapse of time* is valued as of the date of decedent's death or on the date of its distribution, sale, exchange, or other disposition, whichever occurs first. However, you may change the date of death value to account for any change in value that is not due to a "mere lapse of time" on the date of its distribution, sale, exchange, or other disposition.

The property included in the alternate valuation and valued as of 6 months after the date of the decedent's death, or as of some intermediate date (as described above) is the property included in the gross estate on the date of the decedent's death. Therefore, you must first determine what property was part of the gross estate at the decedent's death.

Interest. Interest accrued to the date of the decedent's death on bonds, notes, and other interest-bearing obligations is property of the gross estate on the date of death and is included in the alternate valuation.

Rent. Rent accrued to the date of the decedent's death on leased real or personal property is property of the gross estate on the date of death and is included in the alternate valuation.

Dividends. Outstanding dividends that were declared to stockholders of record on or before the date of the decedent's death are considered property of the gross estate on the date of death, and are included in the alternate valuation. Ordinary dividends declared to stockholders of record after the date of the decedent's death are not included in the gross estate on the date of death and are not eligible for alternate valuation. However, if dividends are declared to stockholders of record after the date of the decedent's death so that the shares of stock at the later valuation date do not reasonably represent the same property at the date of the decedent's death, include those dividends (except dividends paid from earnings of the corporation after the date of the decedent's death) in the alternate valuation.

On Schedules A through I, you must show:

1. What property is included in the gross estate on the date of the decedent's death;

2. What property was distributed, sold, exchanged, or otherwise disposed of within the 6 month period after the decedent's death, and the dates of these distributions, etc. (These two items should be entered in the "Description" column of each schedule. Briefly explain the status or disposition governing the alternate valuation date, such as: "Not disposed of within 6 months following death, ""Distributed," "Sold," "Bond paid on maturity," etc. In this same column, describe each item of principal and includible income);

3. The date of death value, entered in the appropriate value column with items of principal and includible income shown separately; and

4. The alternate value, entered in the appropriate value column with items of principal and includible income shown separately. (In the case of any interest or estate, the value of which is affected by lapse of time, such as patents, leaseholds, estates for the life of another, or remainder interests, the value shown under the heading "Alternate value" must be the adjusted value; for example, the value as of the date of death with an adjustment reflecting any difference in its value as of the later date not due to lapse of time.)

Note. If any property on Schedules A through I is being valued pursuant to the special rule of Regulations section 20.2010–2T(a)(7)(ii), values for those assets are not required to be reported on the Schedule. See Part 5—Recapitulation, line 10.

Distributions, sales, exchanges, and other dispositions of the property within the 6-month period after the decedent's death must be supported by evidence. If the court issued an order of distribution during that period, you must submit a certified copy of the order as part of the evidence. The IRS may require you to submit additional evidence, if necessary.

If the alternate valuation method is used, the values of life estates, remainders, and similar interests are figured using the age of the recipient on the date of the decedent's death and the value of the property on the alternate valuation date.

Line 2. Special-Use Valuation of Section 2032A

In general. Under section 2032A, you may elect to value certain farm and closely held business real property at its farm or business use value rather than its fair market value (FMV). Both special-use valuation and alternate valuation may be elected.

To elect special-use valuation, check "Yes," on line 2 and complete and attach Schedule A-1 and its required additional statements. You must file Schedule A-1 and its required attachments with Form 706 for this election to be valid. You may make the election on a late-filed return so long as it is the first return filed.

The total value of the property valued under section 2032A may not be decreased from FMV by more than $1,070,000 for decedents dying in 2013.

Real property may qualify for the section 2032A election if:

1. The decedent was a U.S. citizen or resident at the time of death;

2. The real property is located in the United States;

3. At the decedent's death, the real property was used by the decedent or a family member for farming or in a trade or business, or was rented for such use by either the surviving spouse or a lineal descendant of the decedent to a family member on a net cash basis;

4. The real property was acquired from or passed from the decedent to a qualified heir of the decedent;

5. The real property was owned and used in a qualified manner by the decedent or a member of the decedent's family during 5 of the 8 years before the decedent's death;

6. There was material participation by the decedent or a member of the decedent's family during 5 of the 8 years before the decedent's death; and

7. The property meets the following percentage requirements:

a. At least 50% of the adjusted value of the gross estate must consist of the adjusted value of real or personal property that was being used as a farm or in a closely-held business and that was acquired from, or passed from, the decedent to a qualified heir of the decedent, and

b. At least 25% of the adjusted value of the gross estate must consist of the adjusted value of qualified farm or closely-held business real property.

For this purpose, adjusted value is the value of property determined without regard to its special-use value. The value is reduced for unpaid mortgages on the property or any indebtedness against the property, if the full value of the decedent's interest in the property (not reduced by such mortgage or indebtedness) is included in the value of the gross estate. The adjusted value of the qualified real and personal property used in different businesses may be

Part Instructions

combined to meet the 50% and 25% requirements.

Qualified Real Property

Qualified use. *Qualified use* means use of the property as a farm for farming purposes or in a trade or business other than farming. Trade or business applies only to the active conduct of a business. It does not apply to passive investment activities or the mere passive rental of property to a person other than a member of the decedent's family. Also, no trade or business is present in the case of activities not engaged in for profit.

Ownership. To qualify as special-use property, the decedent or a member of the decedent's family must have owned and used the property in a qualified use for 5 of the last 8 years before the decedent's death. Ownership may be direct or indirect through a corporation, a partnership, or a trust.

If the ownership is indirect, the business must qualify as a closely-held business under section 6166. The indirect ownership, when combined with periods of direct ownership, must meet the requirements of section 6166 on the date of the decedent's death and for a period of time that equals at least 5 of the 8 years preceding death.

Directly owned property leased by the decedent to a separate closely-held business, is considered qualified real property if the business entity to which it was rented was a closely-held business (as defined by section 6166) for the decedent on the date of the decedent's death and for sufficient time to meet the "5 in 8 years" test explained above.

Structures and other real property improvements. Qualified real property includes residential buildings and other structures and real property improvements regularly occupied or used by the owner or lessee of real property (or by the employees of the owner or lessee) to operate a farm or other closely-held business. A farm residence which the decedent occupied is considered to have been occupied for the purpose of operating the farm even when a family member and not the decedent was the person materially participating in the operation of the farm.

Qualified real property also includes roads, buildings, and other structures and improvements functionally related to the qualified use.

Elements of value such as mineral rights that are not related to the farm or business use are not eligible for special-use valuation.

Property acquired from the decedent. Property is considered to have been acquired from or to have passed from the decedent if one of the following applies:
* The property is considered to have been acquired from or to have passed from the decedent under section 1014(b) (relating to basis of property acquired from a decedent);
* The property is acquired by any person from the estate; or
* The property is acquired by any person from a trust, to the extent the property is includible in the gross estate.

Qualified heir. A person is a *qualified heir* of property if he or she is a member of the decedent's family and acquired or received the property from the decedent. If a qualified heir disposes of any interest in qualified real property to any member of his or her family, that person will then be treated as the qualified heir for that interest.

A *member of the family* includes only:
* An ancestor (parent, grandparent, etc.) of the individual;
* The spouse of the individual;
* The lineal descendant (child, stepchild, grandchild, etc.) of the individual, the individual's spouse, or a parent of the individual; or
* The spouse, widow, or widower of any lineal descendant described above. A legally adopted child of an individual is treated as a child of that individual by blood.

Material Participation

To elect special-use valuation, either the decedent or a member of his or her family must have materially participated in the operation of the farm or other business for at least 5 of the 8 years ending on the date of the decedent's death. The existence of *material participation* is a factual determination. Passively collecting rents, salaries, draws, dividends, or other income from the farm or other business is not sufficient for material participation, nor is merely advancing capital and reviewing a crop plan and financial reports each season or business year.

In determining whether the required participation has occurred, disregard brief periods (that is, 30 days or less) during which there was no material participation, as long as such periods were both preceded and followed by substantial periods (more than 120

days) during which there was uninterrupted material participation.

Retirement or disability. If, on the date of death, the time period for material participation could not be met because the decedent was retired or disabled, a substitute period may apply. The decedent must have retired on social security or been disabled for a continuous period ending with death. A person is disabled for this purpose if he or she was mentally or physically unable to materially participate in the operation of the farm or other business.

The substitute time period for material participation for these decedents is a period totaling at least 5 years out of the 8-year period that ended on the earlier of:
* The date the decedent began receiving social security benefits or
* The date the decedent became disabled.

Surviving spouse. A surviving spouse who received qualified real property from the predeceased spouse is considered to have materially participated if he or she was engaged in the active management of the farm or other business. If the surviving spouse died within 8 years of the first spouse's death, you may add the period of material participation of the predeceased spouse to the period of active management by the surviving spouse to determine if the surviving spouse's estate qualifies for special-use valuation. To qualify for this, the property must have been eligible for special-use valuation in the predeceased spouse's estate, though it does not have to have been elected by that estate.

For additional details regarding material participation, see Regulations section 20.2032A-3(e).

Valuation Methods

The primary method of valuing special-use property that is used for farming purposes is the annual gross cash rental method. If comparable gross cash rentals are not available, you can substitute comparable average annual net share rentals. If neither of these is available, or if you so elect, you can use the method for valuing real property in a closely-held business.

Average annual gross cash rental. Generally, the special-use value of property that is used for farming purposes is determined as follows:

¶2437

1. Subtract the average annual state and local real estate taxes on actual tracts of comparable real property from the average annual gross cash rental for that same comparable property and

2. Divide the result in (1) by the average annual effective interest rate charged for all new Federal Land Bank loans. See Effective interest rate, below.

The computation of each average annual amount is based on the 5 most recent calendar years ending before the date of the decedent's death.

Gross cash rental. Generally, gross cash rental is the total amount of cash received in a calendar year for the use of actual tracts of comparable farm real property in the same locality as the property being specially valued. You may not use:
• Appraisals or other statements regarding rental value or areawide averages of rentals, or
• Rents paid wholly or partly in-kind, or
• Property for which the amount of rent is based on production.
The rental must have resulted from an arm's-length transaction and the amount of rent may not be reduced by the amount of any expenses or liabilities associated with the farm operation or the lease.

Comparable property. Comparable property must be situated in the same locality as the qualified real property as determined by generally accepted real property valuation rules. The determination of comparability is based on a number of factors, none of which carries more weight than the others. It is often necessary to value land in segments where there are different uses or land characteristics included in the specially valued land.

The following list contains some of the factors considered in determining comparability:
• Similarity of soil;
• Whether the crops grown would deplete the soil in a similar manner;
• Types of soil conservation techniques that have been practiced on the two properties;
• Whether the two properties are subject to flooding;
• Slope of the land;
• For livestock operations, the carrying capacity of the land;
• For timbered land, whether the timber is comparable;
• Whether the property as a whole is unified or segmented. If segmented, the availability of the means necessary for movement among the different sections;

• Number, types, and conditions of all buildings and other fixed improvements located on the properties and their location as it affects efficient management, use, and value of the property; and
• Availability and type of transportation facilities in terms of costs and of proximity of the properties to local markets.

You must specifically identify on the return the property being used as comparable property. Use the type of descriptions used to list real property on Schedule A.

Effective interest rate. See Tables 1 and 2 of Revenue Ruling 2013-19, 2013-39 I.R.B. 240, available at http://www.irs.gov/pub/irs-irbs/irb13-39.pdf, for the average annual effective interest rates in effect for 2013.

Net share rental. You may use average annual net share rental from comparable land only if there is no comparable land from which average annual gross cash rental can be determined. Net share rental is the difference between the gross value of produce received by the lessor from the comparable land and the cash operating expenses (other than real estate taxes) of growing the produce that, under the lease, are paid by the lessor. The production of the produce must be the business purpose of the farming operation. For this purpose, produce includes livestock.

The gross value of the produce is generally the gross amount received if the produce was disposed of in an arm's-length transaction within the period established by the Department of Agriculture for its price support program. Otherwise, the value is the weighted average price for which the produce sold on the closest national or regional commodities market. The value is figured for the date or dates on which the lessor received (or constructively received) the produce.

Valuing a real property interest in closely held business. Use this method to determine the special-use valuation for qualifying real property used in a trade or business other than farming. You may also use this method for qualifying farm property if there is no comparable land or if you elect to use it. Under this method, the following factors are considered:
• The capitalization of income that the property can be expected to yield for farming or for closely-held business purposes over a reasonable period of

time with prudent management and traditional cropping patterns for the area, taking into account soil capacity, terrain configuration, and similar factors;
• The capitalization of the fair rental value of the land for farming or for closely-held business purposes;
• The assessed land values in a state that provides a differential or use value assessment law for farmland or closely-held business;
• Comparable sales of other farm or closely-held business land in the same geographical area far enough removed from a metropolitan or resort area so that nonagricultural use is not a significant factor in the sales price; and
• Any other factor that fairly values the farm or closely-held business value of the property.

Making the Election

Include the words "section 2032A valuation" in the "Description" column of any Form 706 schedule if section 2032A property is included in the decedent's gross estate.

An election under section 2032A need not include all the property in an estate that is eligible for special-use valuation, but sufficient property to satisfy the threshold requirements of section 2032A(b)(1)(B) must be specially valued under the election.

If joint or undivided interests (that is, interests as joint tenants or tenants in common) in the same property are received from a decedent by qualified heirs, an election for one heir's joint or undivided interest need not include any other heir's interest in the same property if the electing heir's interest plus other property to be specially valued satisfies the requirements of section 2032A(b)(1)(B).

If successive interests (that is, life estates and remainder interests) are created by a decedent in otherwise qualified property, an election under section 2032A is available only for that property (or part) in which qualified heirs receive all of the successive interests, and such an election must include the interests of all of those heirs.

For example, if a surviving spouse receives a life estate in otherwise qualified property and the spouse's brother receives a remainder interest in fee, no part of the property may be valued under a section 2032A election.

¶2437

Where successive interests in specially valued property are created, remainder interests are treated as being received by qualified heirs only if the remainder interests are not contingent on surviving a nonfamily member or are not subject to divestment in favor of a nonfamily member.

Protective Election

You may make a protective election to specially value qualified real property. Under this election, whether or not you may ultimately use special-use valuation depends upon final values (as shown on the return determined following examination of the return) meeting the requirements of section 2032A.

To make a protective election, check "Yes," on line 2 and complete Schedule A-1 according to the instructions for Protective Election.

If you make a protective election, complete the initial Form 706 by valuing all property at its FMV. Do not use special-use valuation. Usually, this will result in higher estate and GST tax liabilities than will be ultimately determined if special-use valuation is allowed. The protective election does not extend the time to pay the taxes shown on the return. If you wish to extend the time to pay the taxes, file Form 4768 in adequate time before the due date of the return. See the separate instructions for Form 4768.

If the estate qualifies for special-use valuation based on the values as finally determined, you must file an amended Form 706 (with a complete section 2032A election) within 60 days after the date of this determination. Prepare the amended return using special-use values under the rules of section 2032A, complete Schedule A-1, and attach all of the required statements.

Additional information

For definitions and additional information, see section 2032A and the related regulations.

Line 3. Section 6166 Installment Payments

If the gross estate includes an interest in a closely-held business, you may be able to elect to pay part of the estate tax in installments under section 6166.

The maximum amount that can be paid in installments is that part of the estate tax that is attributable to the closely-held business; see Determine

how much of the estate tax may be paid in installments under section 6166, below. In general, that amount is the amount of tax that bears the same ratio to the total estate tax that the value of the closely-held business included in the gross estate bears to the adjusted gross estate.

Bond or lien. The IRS may require that an estate furnish a surety bond when granting the installment payment election. In the alternative, the executor may consent to elect the special lien provisions of section 6324A, in lieu of the bond. The IRS will contact you regarding the specifics of furnishing the bond or electing the special lien. The IRS will make this determination on a case-by-case basis, and you may be asked to provide additional information.

If you elect the lien provisions, section 6324A requires that the lien be placed on property having a value equal to the total deferred tax plus 4 years of interest. The property must be expected to survive the deferral period, and does not necessarily have to be property of the estate. In addition, all people with an interest in the designated property must consent to the creation of this lien.

Percentage requirements. To qualify for installment payments, the value of the interest in the closely-held business that is included in the gross estate must be more than 35% of the adjusted gross estate (the gross estate less expenses, indebtedness, taxes, and losses – Schedules J, K, and L of Form 706 (do not include any portion of the state death tax deduction)).

Interests in two or more closely-held businesses are treated as an interest in a single business if at least 20% of the total value of each business is included in the gross estate. For this purpose, include any interest held by the surviving spouse that represents the surviving spouse's interest in a business held jointly with the decedent as community property or as joint tenants, tenants by the entirety, or tenants in common.

Value. The value used for meeting the percentage requirements is the same value used for determining the gross estate. Therefore, if the estate is valued under alternate valuation or special-use valuation, you must use those values to meet the percentage requirements.

Transfers before death. Generally, gifts made before death are not included in the gross estate. However, the estate must meet the 35%

requirement by both including in and excluding from the gross estate any gifts made by the decedent in the 3-year period ending on the date of death.

Passive assets. In determining the value of a closely-held business and whether the 35% requirement is met, do not include the value of any passive assets held by the business. A passive asset is any asset not used in carrying on a trade or business. Any asset used in a qualifying lending and financing business is treated as an asset used in carrying on a trade or business; see section 6166(b)(10) for details. Stock in another corporation is a passive asset unless the stock is treated as held by the decedent because of the election to treat holding company stock as business company stock; see Holding company stock, below.

If a corporation owns at least 20% in value of the voting stock of another corporation, or the other corporation had no more than 45 shareholders and at least 80% of the value of the assets of each corporation is attributable to assets used in carrying on a trade or business, then these corporations will be treated as a single corporation, and the stock will not be treated as a passive asset. Stock held in the other corporation is not taken into account in determining the 80% requirement.

Interest in closely held business. For purposes of the installment payment election, an *interest in a closely-held business* means:
• Ownership of a trade or business carried on as a proprietorship,
• An interest as a partner in a partnership carrying on a trade or business if 20% or more of the total capital interest was included in the gross estate of the decedent or the partnership had no more than 45 partners, or
• Stock in a corporation carrying on a trade or business if 20% or more in value of the voting stock of the corporation is included in the gross estate of the decedent or the corporation had no more than 45 shareholders.

The partnership or corporation must be carrying on a trade or business at the time of the decedent's death. For further information on whether certain partnerships or corporations owning real property interests constitute a closely-held business, see Rev. Rul. 2006-34, 2006-26 I.R.B. 1171, available at *www.irs.gov/pub/irs-irbs/irb06-26.pdf*.

In determining the number of partners or shareholders, a partnership or stock interest is treated as owned by one partner or shareholder if it is community property or held by a husband and wife as joint tenants, tenants in common, or as tenants by the entirety.

Property owned directly or indirectly by or for a corporation, partnership, estate, or trust is treated as owned proportionately by or for its shareholders, partners, or beneficiaries. For trusts, only beneficiaries with present interests are considered.

The interest in a closely-held farm business includes the interest in the residential buildings and related improvements occupied regularly by the owners, lessees, and employees operating the farm.

Holding company stock. The executor may elect to treat as business company stock the portion of any holding company stock that represents direct ownership (or indirect ownership through one or more other holding companies) in a business company. A *holding company* is a corporation holding stock in another corporation. A *business company* is a corporation carrying on a trade or business.

In general, this election applies only to stock that is not readily tradable. However, the election can be made if the business company stock is readily tradable, as long as all of the stock of each holding company is not readily tradable.

For purposes of the 20% voting stock requirement, stock is treated as voting stock to the extent the holding company owns voting stock in the business company.

If the executor makes this election, the first installment payment is due when the estate tax return is filed. The 5-year deferral for payment of the tax, as discussed below under Time for payment, does not apply. In addition, the 2% interest rate, discussed below under Interest computation, will not apply. Also, if the business company stock is readily tradable, as explained above, the tax must be paid in five installments.

Determine how much of the estate tax may be paid in installments under section 6166. To determine whether the election may be made, you must calculate the adjusted gross estate. (See, Line 3 Worksheet —Adjusted Gross Estate, below.) To determine the value of the adjusted gross estate, subtract the deductions (Schedules J, K, and L) from the value of the gross estate.

To determine over how many installments the estate tax may be paid, please refer to sections 6166(a), (b)(7), (b)(8), and (b)(10).

Time for payment. Under the installment method, the executor may elect to defer payment of the qualified estate tax, but not interest, for up to 5 years from the original payment due date. After the first installment of tax is paid, you must pay the remaining installments annually by the date 1 year after the due date of the preceding installment. There can be no more than 10 installment payments.

Interest on the unpaid portion of the tax is not deferred and must be paid annually. Interest must be paid at the same time as and as a part of each installment payment of the tax.

Acceleration of payments. If the estate fails to make payments of tax or

interest within 6 months of the due date, the IRS may terminate the right to make installment payments and force an acceleration of payment of the tax upon notice and demand.

Generally, if any portion of the interest in the closely-held business which qualifies for installment payments is distributed, sold, exchanged, or otherwise disposed of, or money and other property attributable to such an interest is withdrawn, and the aggregate of those events equals or exceeds 50% of the value of the interest, then the right to make installment payments will be terminated, and the unpaid portion of the tax will be due upon notice and demand. See section 6166(g)(1)(A).

Interest computation. A special interest rate applies to installment payments. For decedents dying in 2013, the interest rate is 2% on the lesser of:
- $572,000 or
- The amount of the estate tax that is attributable to the closely-held business and that is payable in installments.

2% portion. The *2% portion* is an amount equal to the amount of the tentative estate tax (on $1,000,000 plus the applicable exclusion amount in effect) minus the applicable credit amount in effect. However, if the amount of estate tax extended under section 6166 is less than the amount figured above, the 2% portion is the lesser amount.

Inflation adjustment. The $1,000,000 amount used to calculate the 2% portion is indexed for inflation for the estates of decedents who died in a calendar year after 1998. For an estate of a decedent who died in 2013, the dollar amount used to determine the "2% portion" of the estate tax payable in installments under section 6166 is $1,430,000.

Computation. Interest on the portion of the tax in excess of the 2% portion is figured at 45% of the annual rate of interest on underpayments. This rate is based on the federal short-term rate and is announced quarterly by the IRS in the Internal Revenue Bulletin.

If you elect installment payments and the estate tax due is more than the maximum amount to which the 2% interest rate applies, each installment payment is deemed to comprise both tax subject to the 2% interest rate and tax subject to 45% of the regular underpayment rate. The amount of each installment that is subject to the 2% rate is the same as the percentage of total

Line 3 Worksheet—Adjusted Gross Estate

1	What is the value of the decedent's interest in closely-held business(es) included in the gross estate (less value of passive assets, as mentioned in section 6166(b)(9))?	_____
2	What is the value of the gross estate (Form 706, page 3, Part 5, line 13)?	_____
3	Add lines 18, 19, and 20 from Form 706, page 3, Part 5.	_____
4	Subtract line 3 from line 2 to calculate the adjusted gross estate.	_____
5	Divide line 1 by line 4 to calculate the value the business interest bears to the value of the adjusted gross estate. For purposes of this calculation, carry the decimal to the sixth place; the IRS will make this adjustment for purposes of determining the correct amount. If this amount is less than 0.350000, the estate does not qualify to make the election under section 6166.	_____
6	Multiply line 5 by the amount on line 16 of Form 706, page 1, Part 2. This is the maximum amount of estate tax that may be paid in installments under section 6166. (Certain GST taxes may be deferred as well; see section 6166(i) for more information.)	_____

tax payable in installments that is subject to the 2% rate.

 The interest paid on installment payments is not deductible as an administrative expense of the estate.

Making the election. If you check this line to make a final election, you must attach the notice of election described in Regulations section 20.6166-1(b). If you check this line to make a protective election, you must attach a notice of protective election as described in Regulations section 20.6166-1(d). Regulations section 20.6166-1(b) requires that the notice of election is made by attaching to a timely filed estate tax return the following information:
• The decedent's name and taxpayer identification number as they appear on the estate tax return;
• The amount of tax that is to be paid in installments;
• The date selected for payment of the first installment;
• The number of annual installments, including first installment, in which the tax is to be paid;
• The properties shown on the estate tax return that are the closely-held business interest (identified by schedule and item number); and
• The facts that formed the basis for the executor's conclusion that the estate qualifies for payment of the estate tax in installments.

You may also elect to pay certain GST taxes in installments. See section 6166(i).

Line 4. Reversionary or Remainder Interests

For details of this election, see section 6163 and the related regulations.

Part 4—General Information

Authorization

Completing the authorization will authorize one attorney, accountant, or enrolled agent to represent the estate and receive confidential tax information, but will not authorize the representative to enter into closing agreements for the estate. If you would like to authorize your representative to enter into agreements or perform other designated acts on behalf of the estate, you must file Form 2848 with Form 706.

Note. If you intend for the representative to represent the estate before the IRS, he or she must complete and sign this authorization.

Complete and attach Form 2848 if you would like to authorize:
• Persons other than attorneys, accountants, or enrolled agents to represent the estate, or
• More than one person to receive confidential information or represent the estate, or
• Someone to sign agreements, consents, waivers or other documents for the estate.
Filing a completed Form 2848 with this return may expedite processing of the Form 706.

If you wish only to authorize someone to inspect and/or receive confidential tax information (but not to represent you before the IRS), complete and file Form 8821.

Line 3

Enter the marital status of the decedent at the time of death by checking the appropriate box on line 3a. If the decedent was married at the time of death, complete line 4. If the decedent had one or more prior marriages, complete line 3b by providing the name and SSN of each former spouse, the date(s) the marriage ended, and specify whether the marriage ended by annulment, divorce decree, or death of spouse. If the prior marriage ended in death and the predeceased spouse died after December 31, 2010, complete Part 6 — Portability of Deceased Spousal Unused Exclusion, Section D if the estate of the predeceased spouse elected to allow the decedent to use any unused exclusion amount. For more information, see section 2010(c)(4) and related regulations.

Line 4

Complete line 4 whether or not there is a surviving spouse and whether or not the surviving spouse received any benefits from the estate. If there was no surviving spouse on the date of decedent's death, enter "None" in line 4a and leave lines 4b and 4c blank. The value entered in line 4c need not be exact. See the instructions for "Amount" under line 5 below.

Note. Do not include any DSUE amount transferred to the surviving spouse in the total entered on line 4c.

Line 5

Name. Enter the name of each individual, trust, or estate that received (or will receive) benefits of $5,000 or more from the estate directly as an heir, next-of-kin, devisee, or legatee; or indirectly (for example, as beneficiary of an annuity or insurance policy, shareholder of a corporation, or partner of a partnership that is an heir, etc.).

Identifying number. Enter the SSN of each individual beneficiary listed. If the number is unknown, or the individual has no number, please indicate "unknown" or "none." For trusts and other estates, enter the EIN.

Relationship. For each individual beneficiary, enter the relationship (if known) to the decedent by reason of blood, marriage, or adoption. For trust or estate beneficiaries, indicate "TRUST" or "ESTATE."

Amount. Enter the amount actually distributed (or to be distributed) to each beneficiary including transfers during the decedent's life from Schedule G required to be included in the gross estate. The value to be entered need not be exact. A reasonable estimate is sufficient. For example, where precise values cannot readily be determined, as with certain future interests, a reasonable approximation should be entered. The total of these distributions should approximate the amount of gross estate reduced by funeral and administrative expenses, debts and mortgages, bequests to surviving spouse, charitable bequests, and any federal and state estate and GST taxes paid (or payable) relating to the benefits received by the beneficiaries listed on lines 4 and 5.

All distributions of less than $5,000 to specific beneficiaries may be included with distributions to unascertainable beneficiaries on the line provided.

Line 6. Protective Claim for Refund

If you answered "Yes," complete Schedule PC for each claim. Two copies of each Schedule PC must be filed with the return.

A protective claim for refund may be filed when there is an unresolved claim or expense that will not be deductible under section 2053 before the expiration of the period of limitation under section 6511(a). To preserve the estate's right to a refund once the claim or expense has been finally determined, the protective claim must be filed before

¶2437

the end of the limitations period. For more information on how to file a protective claim for refund with this Form 706, see the instructions for Schedule PC, below.

Line 7. Section 2044 Property

If you answered "Yes," these assets must be shown on Schedule F.

Section 2044 property is property for which a previous section 2056(b)(7) election (QTIP election) has been made, or for which a similar gift tax election (section 2523) has been made. For more information, see the instructions for Schedule F, below.

Line 9. Insurance Not Included in the Gross Estate

If you answered "Yes," to either 9a or 9b, for each policy you must complete and attach Schedule D, Form 712, and an explanation of why the policy or its proceeds are not includible in the gross estate.

Line 11. Partnership Interests and Stock in Close Corporations

If you answered "Yes," on line 11a, you must include full details for partnerships (including family limited partnerships), unincorporated businesses, and limited liability companies on Schedule F (Schedule E if the partnership interest is jointly owned). Also include full details for fractional interests in real estate on Schedule A and for stock of inactive or close corporations on Schedule B.

Value these interests using the rules of Regulations section 20.2031-2 (stocks) or 20.2031-3 (other business interests).

A *close corporation* is a corporation whose shares are owned by a limited number of shareholders. Often, one family holds the entire stock issue. As a result, little, if any, trading of the stock takes place. There is, therefore, no established market for the stock, and those sales that do occur are at irregular intervals and seldom reflect all the elements of a representative transaction as defined by FMV.

Line 13. Trusts

If you answered "Yes," on either line 13a or line 13b, attach a copy of the trust instrument for each trust.

Complete Schedule G if you answered "Yes," on line 13a and Schedule F if you answered "Yes," on line 13b.

Line 15. Foreign Accounts

Check "Yes," on line 15 if the decedent at the time of death had an interest in or signature or other authority over a financial account in a foreign country, such as a bank account, securities account, an offshore trust, or other financial account.

Part 5—Recapitulation

Gross Estate—Items 1 through 11

Items 1 through 9. You must make an entry in each of items 1 through 9.

If the gross estate does not contain any assets of the type specified by a given item, enter zero for that item. Entering zero for any of items 1 through 9 is a statement by the executor, made under penalties of perjury, that the gross estate does not contain any includible assets covered by that item.

Do not enter any amounts in the "Alternate value" column unless you elected alternate valuation on line 1 of Part 3—Elections by the Executor on page 2 of the Form 706.

Note. If estimating the value of one or more assets pursuant to the special rule of Regulations section 20.2010–2T(a) (7)(ii), do not enter values for those assets in items 1 through 9. Total the estimated values for those assets and follow the instructions for item 10.

Which schedules to attach for items 1 through 9. You must attach:
- Schedule F. Answer its questions even if you report no assets on it;
- Schedules A, B, and C, if the gross estate includes any (1) Real Estate, (2) Stocks and Bonds, or (3) Mortgages, Notes, and Cash, respectively;
- Schedule D, if the gross estate includes any life insurance or if you answered "Yes," to question 9a of Part 4—General Information;
- Schedule E, if the gross estate contains any jointly-owned property or if you answered "Yes," to question 10 of Part 4;
- Schedule G, if the decedent made any of the lifetime transfers to be listed on that schedule or if you answered "Yes," to question 12 or 13a of Part 4;
- Schedule H, if you answered "Yes," to question 14 of Part 4; and
- Schedule I, if you answered "Yes," to question 16 of Part 4.

Item 10. Under Regulations section 20.2010-2T(a)(7)(ii), if the total value of the gross estate and adjusted taxable

gifts is less than the basic exclusion amount (see section 6018(a)) and Form 706 is being filed only to elect portability of the DSUE amount, the estate is not required to report the value of certain property eligible for the marital or charitable deduction. For this property being reported on Schedules A, B, C, D, E, F, G, H and I, the executor must calculate his or her best estimate of the value. Do not include the estimated value on the line corresponding to the schedule on which the property was reported. Instead, total the estimated value of the assets subject to the special rule and enter on line 10 the amount from the Table of Estimated Values, below, that corresponds to that total.

Note. The special rule does not apply if the valuation of the asset is needed to determine the estate's eligibility for the provisions of sections 2032, 2032A, 2652(a)(3), 6166, or any other provision of the Code or Regulations.

Note. As applies to all other values reported on Form 706, estimates of the value of property subject to the special rule of Regulations section 20.2010-2T(a)(7)(ii) must result from the executor's exercise of due diligence and are subject to penalties of perjury.

¶2437

Table of Estimated Values

If the total estimated value of the assets eligible for the special rule under Reg. section 20.2010–2T(a)(7)(ii) is more than	But less than or equal to	Include this amount on lines 10 and 23:
$0	$250,000	$250,000
$250,000	$500,000	$500,000
$500,000	$750,000	$750,000
$750,000	$1,000,000	$1,000,000
$1,000,000	$1,250,000	$1,250,000
$1,250,000	$1,500,000	$1,500,000
$1,500,000	$1,750,000	$1,750,000
$1,750,000	$2,000,000	$2,000,000
$2,000,000	$2,250,000	$2,250,000
$2,250,000	$2,500,000	$2,500,000
$2,500,000	$2,750,000	$2,750,000
$2,750,000	$3,000,000	$3,000,000
$3,000,000	$3,250,000	$3,250,000
$3,250,000	$3,500,000	$3,500,000
$3,500,000	$3,750,000	$3,750,000
$3,750,000	$4,000,000	$4,000,000
$4,000,000	$4,250,000	$4,250,000
$4,250,000	$4,500,000	$4,500,000
$4,500,000	$4,750,000	$4,750,000
$4,750,000	$5,000,000	$5,000,000
$5,000,000	$5,250,000	$5,250,000

Exclusion — Item 12

Item 12. Conservation easement exclusion. Complete and attach Schedule U (along with any required attachments) to claim the exclusion on this line.

Deductions — Items 14 through 23

Items 14 through 22. Attach the appropriate schedules for the deductions claimed.

Item 18. If item 17 is less than or equal to the value (at the time of the decedent's death) of the property subject to claims, enter the amount from item 17 on item 18.

If the amount on item 17 is more than the value of the property subject to claims, enter the greater of:
• The value of the property subject to claims or

• The amount actually paid at the time the return is filed.

In no event should you enter more on item 18 than the amount on item 17. See section 2053 and the related regulations for more information.

Item 23. Under Regulations section 20.2010-2T(a)(7)(ii), if the total value of the gross estate and adjusted taxable gifts is less than the basic exclusion amount (see section 6018(a)) and Form 706 is being filed only to elect portability of the DSUE amount, the estate is not required to report the value of certain property eligible for the marital or charitable deduction. For this property being reported on Schedule M or O, enter on line 23 the amount from line 10.

Part 6—Portability of Deceased Spousal Unused Exclusion (DSUE)

Section 303 of the Tax Relief, Unemployment Insurance Reauthorization, and Job Creation Act of 2010 authorized estates of decedents dying on or after January 1, 2011, to elect to transfer any unused exclusion to the surviving spouse. The amount received by the surviving spouse is called the *deceased spousal unused exclusion*, or DSUE, amount. If the executor of the decedent's estate elects transfer, or portability, of the DSUE amount, the surviving spouse can apply the DSUE amount received from the estate of his or her last deceased spouse (defined below) against any tax liability arising from subsequent lifetime gifts and transfers at death.

Note. A nonresident surviving spouse who is not a citizen of the United States may not take into account the DSUE amount of a deceased spouse, except to the extent allowed by treaty with his or her country of citizenship.

Last Deceased Spouse Limitation

The *last deceased spouse* is the most recently deceased person who was married to the surviving spouse at the time of that person's death. The identity of the last deceased spouse is determined as of the day a taxable gift is made, or in the case of a transfer at death, the date of the surviving spouse's death. The identity of the last deceased spouse is not impacted by whether the decedent's estate elected portability or whether the last deceased spouse had any DSUE amount available. Remarriage also does not affect the designation of the last deceased

spouse and does not prevent the surviving spouse from applying the DSUE amount to taxable transfers.

When a taxable gift is made, the DSUE amount received from the last deceased spouse is applied before the surviving spouse's basic exclusion amount. A surviving spouse may use the DSUE amount of the last deceased spouse to offset the tax on any taxable transfer made after the deceased spouse's death. A surviving spouse who has more than one predeceased spouse is not precluded from using the DSUE amount of each spouse in succession. A surviving spouse may not use the sum of DSUE amounts from multiple predeceased spouses at one time nor may the DSUE amount of a predeceased spouse be applied after the death of a subsequent spouse.

Making the Election

A timely-filed and complete Form 706 is required to elect portability of the DSUE amount to a surviving spouse. The filing requirement applies to all estates of decedents choosing to elect portability of the DSUE amount, regardless of the size of the estate. A timely-filed return is one that is filed on or before the due date of the return, including extensions.

The timely filing of a complete Form 706 with DSUE will be deemed a portability election if there is a surviving spouse. The election is effective as of the decedent's date of death, so the DSUE amount received by a surviving spouse may be applied to any transfer occurring after the decedent's death. A portability election is irrevocable, unless an adjustment or amendment to the election is made on a subsequent return filed on or before the due date.

Note. Under Regulations section 20.2010-2T(a)(5), the executor of an estate of a nonresident decedent who was not a citizen of the United States at the time of death cannot make a portability election.

If an executor is appointed, qualified, and acting with the United States on behalf of the decedent's estate, only that executor may make or opt out of a portability election. If there is no executor, see Regulations section 20.2010-2T(a)(6)(ii).

Opting Out

If an estate files a Form 706 but does not wish to make the portability election, the executor can opt out of the portability election by checking the box indicated in Section A of this Part. If no return is required under section 6018(a),

-17-

¶2437

not filing Form 706 will avoid making the election.

Computing the DSUE Amount

Regulations section 20.2010-2T(b)(1) requires that a decedent's DSUE be computed on the estate tax return. The DSUE amount is the lesser of (A) the basic exclusion amount in effect on the date of death of the decedent whose DSUE is being computed, or (B) the decedent's applicable exclusion amount less the amount on line 5 of Part 2–Tax Computation on the Form 706 for the estate of the decedent. Amounts on which gift taxes were paid are excluded from adjusted taxable gifts for the purpose of this computation.

When a surviving spouse applies the DSUE amount to a lifetime gift or bequest at death, the IRS may examine any return of a predeceased spouse whose executor elected portability to verify the allowable DSUE amount. The DSUE amount may be adjusted or eliminated as a result of the examination; however, the IRS may only make an assessment of additional tax on the return of the predeceased spouse within the applicable limitations period under section 6501.

Special Rule Where Value of Certain Property Not Required to Be Reported on Form 706

The temporary regulations provide that executors of estates who are not otherwise required to file Form 706 under section 6018(a) do not have to report the value of certain property qualifying for the marital or charitable deduction. For such property, the executor may estimate the value in good faith and with the due diligence to be afforded all assets includible in the gross estate. The amount reported on Form 706 will correspond to a range of dollar values and will be included in the value of the gross estate shown on line 1 of Part 2-Tax Computation. See instructions for lines 10 and 23 of Part 5-Recapitulation, above, for more details.

Specific Instructions

Portability Election. If you intend to elect portability of the DSUE amount, timely filing a complete Form 706 is all that is required. Complete section B if any assets of the estate are being transferred to a qualified domestic trust and complete section C of this Part to calculate the DSUE amount that will be transferred to the surviving spouse.

Section A. Opting Out of Portability. If you are filing Form 706 and do not wish to elect portability, then check the box indicated. Do not complete sections B or C.

Section B. Portability and Qualified Domestic Trusts. A *qualified domestic trust* (QDOT) allows the estate of a decedent to bequeath property to surviving spouse who is not a citizen of the United States and still receive a marital deduction. When property passes to a QDOT, estate tax is imposed under section 2056A as distributions are made from the trust. When a QDOT is established and there is a DSUE amount, the executor of the decedent's estate will determine a preliminary DSUE amount for the purpose of electing portability. This amount will decrease as section 2056A distributions are made. In estates with a QDOT, the DSUE amount generally may not be applied against tax arising from lifetime gifts because it will not be available to the surviving spouse until it is finally determined, usually upon the death of the surviving spouse or when the QDOT is terminated.

Check the appropriate box in this section and see the instructions for Schedule M if more information is needed about qualified domestic trusts.

Section C. DSUE Amount Portable to Decedent's Surviving Spouse. Complete section C only if electing portability of the DSUE amount to the surviving spouse.

On line 1, enter the decedent's applicable exclusion amount from Part 2—Tax Computation, line 9c. Under section 2010(c)(2), the *applicable exclusion amount* is the sum of the basic exclusion amount for the year of death and any DSUE amount received from a predeceased spouse, if applicable.

Line 2 is reserved.

On line 3, enter the value of the cumulative lifetime gifts on which gift tax was paid or payable. This amount is figured on line 6 of the Line 7 Worksheet Part B as the total of Row (r) from Line 7 Worksheet Part A. Enter the amount as it appears on line 6 of the Line 7 Worksheet Part B

Figure the unused exclusion amount on line 9. The DSUE amount available to the surviving spouse will be the lesser of this amount or the basic exclusion amount shown on line 9a of Part 2—Tax Computation. Enter the DSUE amount as determined on line 10.

Section D. DSUE Amount Received from Predeceased Spouse(s). Complete section D if the decedent was a surviving spouse who received a DSUE amount from one or more predeceased spouse(s).

Section D requests information on all DSUE amounts received from the decedent's last deceased spouse and any previously deceased spouses. Each line in the chart should reflect a different predeceased spouse; enter the calendar year(s) in column F. In Part 1, provide information on the decedent's last deceased spouse. In Part 2, provide information as requested if the decedent had any other predeceased spouse whose executor made the portability election. Any remaining DSUE amount which was not used prior to the death of a subsequent spouse is not considered in this calculation and cannot be applied against any taxable transfer. In column E, total only the amounts of DSUE received and used from spouses who died before the decedent's last deceased spouse. Add this amount to the amount from Part 1, column D, if any, to determine the decedent's total DSUE amount.

Schedule A—Real Estate

If there are any assets to which the special rule of Regulations section 20.2010–2T(a)(7)(ii) reported on this schedule, do not enter any value in the last three columns. See instructions for line 10 of Part 5– Recapitulation for information on how to estimate and report the value of these assets.

If the total gross estate contains any real estate, complete Schedule A and file it with the return. On Schedule A, list real estate the decedent owned or had contracted to purchase. Number each parcel in the left-hand column.

Describe the real estate in enough detail so that the IRS can easily locate it for inspection and valuation. For each parcel of real estate, report the area and, if the parcel is improved, describe the improvements. For city or town property, report the street and number, ward, subdivision, block and lot, etc. For rural property, report the township, range, landmarks, etc.

If any item of real estate is subject to a mortgage for which the decedent's estate is liable, that is, if the indebtedness may be charged against other property of the estate that is not subject to that mortgage, or if the decedent was personally liable for that

Part Instructions

Schedule A–Example 1

Item Number	Description	Alternate Valuation Date	Alternate Value	Value at date of death
	In this example, alternate valuation is not adopted; the date of death is January 1, 2013.			
1	House and lot, 1921 William Street, NW, Washington, DC (lot 6, square 481). Rent of $8,100 due at the end of each quarter, February 1, May 1, August 1, and November 1. Value based on appraisal, copy of which is attached			$550,000
	Rent due on item 1 for quarter ending November 1, 2012, but not collected at date of death . . .			8,100
	Rent accrued on Item 1 for November and December 2012			5,400
2	House and lot, 304 Jefferson Street, Alexandria, VA (lot 18, square 40). Rent of $1,800 payable monthly. Value based on appraisal, copy of which is attached			375,000
	Rent due on Item 2 for December 2012, but not collected at death			1,800

Schedule A–Example 2

Item Number	Description	Alternate Valuation Date	Alternate Value	Value at date of death
	In this example, alternate valuation is adopted; the date of death is January 1, 2013.			
1	House and lot, 1921 William Street, NW, Washington, DC (lot 6, square 481). Rent of $8,100 due at the end of each quarter, February 1, May 1, August 1, and November 1. Value based on appraisal, copy of which is attached. Not disposed of within 6 months of date of death	7/1/13	$535,000	$550,000
	Rent due on item 1 for quarter ending November 1, 2012, but not collected until February 1, 2013	2/1/13	8,100	8,100
	Rent accrued on Item 1 for November and December 2012, collected on February 1, 2013 . . .	2/1/13	5,400	5,400
2	House and lot, 304 Jefferson Street, Alexandria, VA (lot 18, square 40). Rent of $1,800 payable monthly. Value based on appraisal, copy of which is attached. Property exchanged for farm on May 1, 2013	5/1/13	369,000	375,000
	Rent due on Item 2 for December 2012, but not collected until February 1, 2013	2/1/13	1,800	1,800

mortgage, you must report the full value of the property in the value column. Enter the amount of the mortgage under "Description" on this schedule. The unpaid amount of the mortgage may be deducted on Schedule K.

If the decedent's estate is not liable for the amount of the mortgage, report only the value of the equity of redemption (or value of the property less the indebtedness) in the value column as part of the gross estate. Do not enter any amount less than zero. Do not deduct the amount of indebtedness on Schedule K.

Also list on Schedule A real property the decedent contracted to purchase. Report the full value of the property and not the equity in the value column. Deduct the unpaid part of the purchase price on Schedule K.

Report the value of real estate without reducing it for homestead or other exemption, or the value of dower, curtesy, or a statutory estate created instead of dower or curtesy.

Explain how the reported values were determined and attach copies of any appraisals.

Schedule A-1—Section 2032A Valuation

The election to value certain farm and closely-held business property at its special-use value is made by checking "Yes," on Form 706, Part 3—Elections by the Executor, line 2. Schedule A-1 is used to report the additional information that must be submitted to support this election. In order to make a valid election, you must complete Schedule A-1 and attach all of the required statements and appraisals.

For definitions and additional information concerning special-use valuation, see section 2032A and the related regulations.

Part 1. Type of Election

Estate and GST tax elections. If you elect special-use valuation for the estate tax, you must also elect special-use valuation for the Generation-Skipping Transfer (GST) tax and vice versa.

Protective election. To make the protective election described in the separate instructions for Part 3—Elections by the Executor, line 2, you must check the box in Part 1. Type of Election, enter the decedent's name and social security number in the spaces provided at the top of Schedule A-1, and complete Part 2.

Notice of Election, line 1 and lines 3 and 4, column A. For purposes of the protective election, list on line 3 all of the real property that passes to the qualified heirs even though some of the property will be shown on line 2 when the additional notice of election is subsequently filed. You need not complete columns B through D of lines 3 and 4. You need not complete any other line entries on Schedule A-1. Completing Schedule A-1 as described above constitutes a Notice of Protective Election as described in Regulations section 20.2032A-8(b).

Part 2. Notice of Election

Line 10. Because the special-use valuation election creates a potential tax liability for the recapture tax of section 2032A(c), you must list each person who receives an interest in the specially valued property on Schedule A-1. If there are more than eight persons who receive interests, use an additional sheet that follows the format of line 10. In the columns "Fair market value" and "Special-use value," enter the total respective values of all the specially valued property interests received by each person.

¶2437

GST Tax Savings

To figure the additional GST tax due upon disposition (or cessation of qualified use) of the property, each "skip person" (as defined in the instructions to Schedule R) who receives an interest in the specially valued property must know the total GST tax savings all interests in specially valued property received. The GST tax savings is the difference between the total GST tax that was imposed on all interests in specially valued property received by the skip person valued at their special-use value and the total GST tax that would have been imposed on the same interests received by the skip person had they been valued at their FMV.

Because the GST tax depends on the executor's allocation of the GST exemption and the grandchild exclusion, the skip person who receives the interests is unable to figure this GST tax savings. Therefore, for each skip person who receives an interest in specially valued property, you must attach a calculation of the total GST tax savings attributable to that person's interests in specially valued property.

How to figure the GST tax savings.
Before figuring each skip person's GST tax savings, complete Schedules R and R-1 for the entire estate (using the special-use values).

For each skip person, complete two Schedules R (Parts 2 and 3 only) as worksheets, one showing the interests in specially valued property received by the skip person at their special-use value and one showing the same interests at their FMV.

If the skip person received interests in specially valued property that were shown on Schedule R-1, show these interests on the Schedule R, Parts 2 and 3 worksheets, as appropriate. Do not use Schedule R-1 as a worksheet.

Completing the special-use value worksheets. On Schedule R, Parts 2 and 3, lines 2 through 4 and 6, enter -0-.

Completing the fair market value worksheets.
• *Schedule R, Parts 2 and 3, lines 2 and 3, fixed taxes and other charges.* If valuing the interests at FMV (instead of special-use value) causes any of these taxes and charges to increase, enter the increased amount (only) on these lines and attach an explanation of the increase. Otherwise, enter -0-.
• *Schedule R, Parts 2 and 3, line 6—GST exemption allocation.* If you completed Schedule R, Part 1, line 10, enter on line 6 the amount shown for the

skip person on the line 10 special-use allocation schedule you attached to Schedule R. If you did not complete Schedule R, Part 1, line 10, enter -0- on line 6.

Total GST tax savings. For each skip person, subtract the tax amount on line 10, Part 2 of the special-use value worksheet from the tax amount on line 10, Part 2 of the fair market value worksheet. This difference is the skip person's total GST tax savings.

Part 3. Agreement to Special Valuation Under Section 2032A

The agreement to special valuation is required under sections 2032A(a)(1)(B) and (d)(2) and must be signed by all parties who have any interest in the property being valued based on its qualified use as of the date of the decedent's death.

An interest in property is an interest that, as of the date of the decedent's death, can be asserted under applicable law so as to affect the disposition of the specially valued property by the estate. Any person who at the decedent's death has any such interest in the property, whether present, future, vested, or contingent, must enter into the agreement. Included are owners of remainder and executory interests; the holders of general or special powers of appointment; beneficiaries of a gift over in default of exercise of any such power; joint tenants and holders of similar undivided interests when the decedent held only a joint or undivided interest in the property or when only an undivided interest is specially valued; and trustees of trusts and representatives of other entities holding title to or any interests in the property. An heir who has the power under local law to challenge a will and thereby affect disposition of the property is not, however, considered to be a person with an interest in property under section 2032A solely by reason of that right. Likewise, creditors of an estate are not such persons solely by reason of their status as creditors.

If any person required to enter into the agreement either desires that an agent act for him or her or cannot legally bind himself or herself due to infancy or other incompetency, or due to death before the election under section 2032A is timely exercised, a representative authorized by local law to bind the person in an agreement of this nature may sign the agreement on his or her behalf.

The IRS will contact the agent designated in the agreement on all

matters relating to continued qualification under section 2032A of the specially valued real property and on all matters relating to the special lien arising under section 6324B. It is the duty of the agent as attorney-in-fact for the parties with interests in the specially valued property to furnish the IRS with any requested information and to notify the IRS of any disposition or cessation of qualified use of any part of the property.

Checklist for Section 2032A Election

 When making the special-use valuation election on Schedule A-1, please use this checklist to ensure that you are providing everything necessary to make a valid election.

To have a valid special-use valuation election under section 2032A, you must file, in addition to the federal estate tax return, (a) a notice of election (Schedule A-1, Part 2) and (b) a fully executed agreement (Schedule A-1, Part 3). You must include certain information in the notice of election. To ensure that the notice of election includes all of the information required for a valid election, use the following checklist. The checklist is for your use only. Do not file it with the return.

¶2437

☐ Does the notice of election include the decedent's name and social security number as they appear on the estate tax return?

☐ Does the notice of election include the relevant qualified use of the property to be specially valued?

☐ Does the notice of election describe the items of real property shown on the estate tax return that are to be specially valued and identify the property by the Form 706 schedule and item number?

☐ Does the notice of election include the FMV of the real property to be specially valued and also include its value based on the qualified use (determined without the adjustments provided in section 2032A(b)(3)(B))?

☐ Does the notice of election include the adjusted value (as defined in section 2032A(b)(3)(B)) of (a) all real property that both passes from the decedent and is used in a qualified use, without regard to whether it is to be specially valued, and (b) all real property to be specially valued?

☐ Does the notice of election include (a) the items of personal property shown on the estate tax return that pass from the decedent to a qualified heir and that are used in qualified use and (b) the total value of such personal property adjusted under section 2032A(b)(3)(B)?

☐ Does the notice of election include the adjusted value of the gross estate? (See section 2032A(b)(3)(A).)

☐ Does the notice of election include the method used to determine the special-use value?

☐ Does the notice of election include copies of written appraisals of the FMV of the real property?

☐ Does the notice of election include a statement that the decedent and/or a member of his or her family has owned all of the specially valued property for at least 5 years of the 8 years immediately preceding the date of the decedent's death?

☐ Does the notice of election include a statement as to whether there were any periods during the 8-year period preceding the decedent's date of death during which the decedent or a member of his or her family did not (a) own the property to be specially valued, (b) use it in a qualified use, or (c) materially participate in the operation of the farm or other business? (See section 2032A(e)(6).)

☐ Does the notice of election include, for each item of specially valued property, the name of every person who has an interest in that item of specially valued property and the following information about each such person: (a) the person's address, (b) the person's taxpayer identification number, (c) the person's relationship to the decedent, and (d) the value of the property interest passing to that person based on both FMV and qualified use?

☐ Does the notice of election include affidavits describing the activities constituting material participation and the identity of the material participants?

☐ Does the notice of election include a legal description of each item of specially valued property?

(In the case of an election made for qualified woodlands, the information included in the notice of election must include the reason for entitlement to the Woodlands election.)

Any election made under section 2032A will not be valid unless a properly executed agreement (Schedule A-1, Part 3) is filed with the estate tax return. To ensure that the agreement satisfies the requirements for a valid election, use the following checklist:

☐ Has the agreement been signed by each qualified heir having an interest in the property being specially valued?

☐ Has every qualified heir expressed consent to personal liability under section 2032A(c) in the event of an early disposition or early cessation of qualified use?

☐ Is the agreement that is actually signed by the qualified heirs in a form that is binding on all of the qualified heirs having an interest in the specially valued property?

☐ Does the agreement designate an agent to act for the parties to the agreement in all dealings with the IRS on matters arising under section 2032A?

☐ Has the agreement been signed by the designated agent and does it give the address of the agent?

Schedule B—Stocks and Bonds

If there are any assets to which the special rule of Regulations section 20.2010–2T(a)(7)(ii) reported on this schedule, do not enter any value in the last three columns. See instructions for line 10 of Part 5–Recapitulation for information on how to estimate and report the value of these assets.

TIP *Before completing Schedule B, see the examples illustrating the alternate valuation dates being adopted and not being adopted, below.*

If the total gross estate contains any stocks or bonds, you must complete Schedule B and file it with the return.

On Schedule B, list the stocks and bonds included in the decedent's gross estate. Number each item in the left-hand column.

Schedule B Examples

	Example showing use of Schedule B where the alternate valuation is not adopted; date of death, January 1, 2013				
Item number	Description, including face amount of bonds or number of shares and par value where needed for identification. Give CUSIP number. If trust, partnership, or closely-held entity, give EIN.	Unit value	Alternate valuation date	Alternate value	Value at date of death
	CUSIP number or EIN, where applicable				
1	$60,000-Arkansas Railroad Co. first mortgage 4%, 20-year bonds, due 2014. Interest payable quarterly on Feb. 1, May 1, Aug. 1, and Nov. 1; N.Y. Exchange XXXXXXXXX	100	- - - - - - -	$- - - - - -	$ 60,000
	Interest coupons attached to bonds, item 1, due and payable on Nov. 1, 2012, but not cashed at date of death	- - - - - - -	- - - - - - -	- - - - - - -	600
	Interest accrued on item 1, from Nov. 1, 2012, to Jan. 1, 2013	- - - - - - -	- - - - - - -	- - - - - - -	400
2	500 shares Public Service Corp., common; N.Y. Exchange . . XXXXXXXXX	110	- - - - - - -	- - - - - - -	55,000
	Dividend on item 2 of $2 per share declared Dec. 10, 2012, payable on Jan. 9, 2013, to holders of record on Dec. 30, 2012	- - - - - - -	- - - - - - -	- - - - - - -	1,000

	Example showing use of Schedule B where the alternate valuation is adopted; date of death, January 1, 2013				
Item number	Description, including face amount of bonds or number of shares and par value where needed for identification. Give CUSIP number. If trust, partnership, or closely-held entity, give EIN.	Unit value	Alternate valuation date	Alternate value	Value at date of death
	CUSIP number or EIN, where applicable				
1	$60,000-Arkansas Railroad Co. first mortgage 4%, 20-year bonds, due 2014. Interest payable quarterly on Feb. 1, May 1, Aug. 1, and Nov. 1; N.Y. Exchange XXXXXXXXX	100	- - - - - -	$- - - - - -	$ 60,000
	$30,000 of item 1 distributed to legatees on Apr. 1, 2013	99	4/1/13	29,700	- - - - - - -
	$30,000 of item 1 sold by executor on May 1, 2013	98	5/1/13	29,400	- - - - - - -
	Interest coupons attached to bonds, item 1, due and payable on Nov. 1, 2012, but not cashed at date of death. Cashed by executor on Feb. 2, 2013	- - - - - -	2/2/13	600	600
	Interest accrued on item 1, from Nov. 1, 2012, to Jan. 1, 2013. Cashed by executor on Feb. 2, 2013	- - - - - -	2/2/13	400	400
2	500 shares Public Service Corp., common; N.Y. Exchange . . XXXXXXXXX	110	- - - - - -	- - - - - - -	55,000
	Not disposed of within 6 months following death	90	7/1/13	45,000	- - - - - - -
	Dividend on item 2 of $2 per share declared Dec. 10, 2012, paid on Jan. 9, 2013, to holders of record on Dec. 30, 2012	- - - - - -	1/9/13	1,000	1,000

Note. Unless specifically exempted by an estate tax provision of the Code, bonds that are exempt from federal income tax are not exempt from estate tax. You should list these bonds on Schedule B.

Public housing bonds includible in the gross estate must be included at their full value.

If you paid any estate, inheritance, legacy, or succession tax to a foreign country on any stocks or bonds included in this schedule, group those stocks and bonds together and label them "Subjected to Foreign Death Taxes."

List interest and dividends on each stock or bond on a separate line.

Indicate as a separate item dividends that have not been collected at death and are payable to the decedent or the estate because the decedent was a stockholder of record on the date of death. However, if the stock is being traded on an exchange and is selling ex-dividend on the date of the decedent's death, do not include the amount of the dividend as a separate item. Instead, add it to the ex-dividend quotation in determining the FMV of the stock on the date of the decedent's death. Dividends declared on shares of stock before the death of the decedent but payable to stockholders of record on a date after the decedent's death are not includible in the gross estate for federal estate tax purposes and should not be listed here.

Description

Stocks. For stocks, indicate:
- Number of shares;
- Whether common or preferred;
- Issue;
- Par value where needed for identification;
- Price per share;
- Exact name of corporation;
- Principal exchange upon which sold, if listed on an exchange; and
- Nine-digit CUSIP number (defined below).

Bonds. For bonds, indicate:
- Quantity and denomination;

-22-

Part Instructions

¶2437

- Name of obligor;
- Date of maturity;
- Interest rate;
- Interest due date;
- Principal exchange, if listed on an exchange; and
- Nine-digit CUSIP number.

If the stock or bond is unlisted, show the company's principal business office.

If the gross estate includes any interest in a trust, partnership, or closely-held entity, provide the employer identification number (EIN) of the entity in the description column on Schedules B, E, F, G, M, and O. You must also provide the EIN of an estate (if any) in the description column on the above-noted schedules, where applicable.

The CUSIP (Committee on Uniform Security Identification Procedure) number is a nine-digit number that is assigned to all stocks and bonds traded on major exchanges and many unlisted securities. Usually, the CUSIP number is printed on the face of the stock certificate. If you do not have a stock certificate, the CUSIP may be found on the broker's or custodian's statement or by contacting the company's transfer agent.

Valuation

List the FMV of the stocks or bonds. The FMV of a stock or bond (whether listed or unlisted) is the mean between the highest and lowest selling prices quoted on the valuation date. If only the closing selling prices are available, then the FMV is the mean between the quoted closing selling price on the valuation date and on the trading day before the valuation date.

If there were no sales on the valuation date, figure the FMV as follows:

1. Find the mean between the highest and lowest selling prices on the nearest trading date before and the nearest trading date after the valuation date. Both trading dates must be reasonably close to the valuation date.

2. Prorate the difference between the mean prices to the valuation date.

3. Add or subtract (whichever applies) the prorated part of the difference to or from the mean price figured for the nearest trading date before the valuation date.

If no actual sales were made reasonably close to the valuation date, make the same computation using the

mean between the bona fide bid and asked prices instead of sales prices. If actual sales prices or bona fide bid and asked prices are available within a reasonable period of time before the valuation date but not after the valuation date, or vice versa, use the mean between the highest and lowest sales prices or bid and asked prices as the FMV.

For example, assume that sales of stock nearest the valuation date (June 15) occurred 2 trading days before (June 13) and 3 trading days after (June 18). On those days, the mean sale prices per share were $10 and $15, respectively. Therefore, the price of $12 is considered the FMV of a share of stock on the valuation date. If, however, on June 13 and 18, the mean sale prices per share were $15 and $10, respectively, the FMV of a share of stock on the valuation date is $13.

If only closing prices for bonds are available, see Regulations section 20.2031-2(b).

Apply the rules in the section 2031 regulations to determine the value of inactive stock and stock in close corporations. Attach to Schedule B complete financial and other data used to determine value, including balance sheets (particularly the one nearest to the valuation date) and statements of the net earnings or operating results and dividends paid for each of the 5 years immediately before the valuation date.

Securities reported as of no value, of nominal value, or obsolete should be listed last. Include the address of the company and the state and date of the incorporation. Attach copies of correspondence or statements used to determine the "no value."

If the security was listed on more than one stock exchange, use either the records of the exchange where the security is principally traded or the composite listing of combined exchanges, if available, in a publication of general circulation. In valuing listed stocks and bonds, you should carefully check accurate records to obtain values for the applicable valuation date.

If you get quotations from brokers, or evidence of the sale of securities from the officers of the issuing companies, attach to the schedule copies of the letters furnishing these quotations or evidence of sale.

Schedule C—Mortgages, Notes, and Cash

 If there are any assets to which the special rule of Regulations section 20.2010–2T(a)(7)(ii) reported on this schedule, do not enter any value in the last three columns. See instructions for line 10 of Part 5–Recapitulation for information on how to estimate and report the value of these assets.

Complete Schedule C and file it with your return if the total gross estate contains any:
- Mortgages,
- Notes, or
- Cash.

List on Schedule C:
- Mortgages and notes payable **to the decedent** at the time of death.
- Cash the decedent had at the date of death.

Note. Do not list mortgages and notes payable **by the decedent** on Schedule C. (If these are deductible, list them on Schedule K.)

List the items on Schedule C in the following order:

1. Mortgages;

2. Promissory notes;

3. Contracts by decedent to sell land;

4. Cash in possession; and

5. Cash in banks, savings and loan associations, and other types of financial organizations.

What to enter in the "Description" column:
For mortgages, list:
- Face value,
- Unpaid balance,
- Date of mortgage,
- Name of maker,
- Property mortgaged,
- Date of maturity,
- Interest rate, and
- Interest date.

Example to enter in "Description" column: "Bond and mortgage of $50,000, unpaid balance: $17,000; dated: January 1, 1992; John Doe to Richard Roe; premises: 22 Clinton Street, Newark, NJ; due: January 1, 2014; interest payable at 10% a year—January 1 and July 1."

For promissory notes, list in the same way as mortgages.

For contracts by the decedent to sell land, list:

Part Instructions

- Name of purchaser,
- Contract date,
- Property description,
- Sale price,
- Initial payment,
- Amounts of installment payment,
- Unpaid balance of principal, and
- Interest rate.

For cash on hand, list such cash separately from bank deposits.

For cash in banks, savings and loan associations, and other types of financial organizations, list:
- Name and address of each financial organization,
- Amount in each account,
- Serial or account number,
- Nature of account—checking, savings, time deposit, etc., and
- Unpaid interest accrued from date of last interest payment to the date of death.

Note. If you obtain statements from the financial organizations, keep them for IRS inspection.

Schedule D—Insurance on the Decedent's Life

 If there are any assets to which the special rule of Regulations section 20.2010–2T(a)(7)(ii) reported on this schedule, do not enter any value in the last three columns. See instructions for line 10 of Part 5– Recapitulation for information on how to estimate and report the value of these assets.

If you are required to file Form 706 and there was any insurance on the decedent's life, whether or not included in the gross estate, you must complete Schedule D and file it with the return.

Insurance you must include on Schedule D. Under section 2042, you must include in the gross estate:
- Insurance on the decedent's life receivable by or for the benefit of the estate; and
- Insurance on the decedent's life receivable by beneficiaries other than the estate, as described below.

The term "insurance" refers to life insurance of every description, including death benefits paid by fraternal beneficiary societies operating under the lodge system, and death benefits paid under no-fault automobile insurance policies if the no-fault insurer was unconditionally bound to pay the benefit in the event of the insured's death.

Insurance in favor of the estate. Include on Schedule D the full amount of the proceeds of insurance on the life of the decedent receivable by the executor or otherwise payable to or for the benefit of the estate. Insurance in favor of the estate includes insurance used to pay the estate tax, and any other taxes, debts, or charges that are enforceable against the estate. The manner in which the policy is drawn is immaterial as long as there is an obligation, legally binding on the beneficiary, to use the proceeds to pay taxes, debts, or charges. You must include the full amount even though the premiums or other consideration may have been paid by a person other than the decedent.

Insurance receivable by beneficiaries other than the estate. Include on Schedule D the proceeds of all insurance on the life of the decedent not receivable by, or for the benefit of, the decedent's estate if the decedent possessed at death any of the following incidents of ownership, exercisable either alone or in conjunction with any person or entity.

Incidents of ownership in a policy include:
- The right of the insured or estate to its economic benefits;
- The power to change the beneficiary;
- The power to surrender or cancel the policy;
- The power to assign the policy or to revoke an assignment;
- The power to pledge the policy for a loan;
- The power to obtain from the insurer a loan against the surrender value of the policy; and
- A reversionary interest if the value of the reversionary interest was more than 5% of the value of the policy immediately before the decedent died. (An interest in an insurance policy is considered a reversionary interest if, for example, the proceeds become payable to the insured's estate or payable as the insured directs if the beneficiary dies before the insured.)

Life insurance not includible in the gross estate under section 2042 may be includible under some other section of the Code. For example, a life insurance policy could be transferred by the decedent in such a way that it would be includible in the gross estate under section 2036, 2037, or 2038. See the instructions to Schedule G for a description of these sections.

Completing the Schedule

You must list every insurance policy on the life of the decedent, whether or not it is included in the gross estate.

Under "Description," list:
- The name of the insurance company, and
- The number of the policy.

For every life insurance policy listed on the schedule, request a statement on Form 712, Life Insurance Statement, from the company that issued the policy. Attach the Form 712 to Schedule D.

If the policy proceeds are paid in one sum, enter the net proceeds received (from Form 712, line 24) in the value (and alternate value) columns of Schedule D. If the policy proceeds are not paid in one sum, enter the value of the proceeds as of the date of the decedent's death (from Form 712, line 25).

If part or all of the policy proceeds are not included in the gross estate, explain why they were not included.

Schedule E—Jointly Owned Property

 If there are any assets to which the special rule of Regulations section 20.2010–2T(a)(7)(ii) reported on this schedule, do not enter any value in the last three columns. See instructions for line 10 of Part 5– Recapitulation for information on how to estimate and report the value of these assets.

If you are required to file Form 706, complete Schedule E and file it with the return if the decedent owned any joint property at the time of death, whether or not the decedent's interest is includible in the gross estate.

Enter on this schedule all property of whatever kind or character, whether real estate, personal property, or bank accounts, in which the decedent held at the time of death an interest either as a joint tenant with right to survivorship or as a tenant by the entirety.

Do not list on this schedule property that the decedent held as a tenant in common, but report the value of the interest on Schedule A if real estate, or on the appropriate schedule if personal property. Similarly, community property held by the decedent and spouse should be reported on the appropriate Schedules A through I. The decedent's interest in a partnership should not be entered on this schedule unless the

-24-   Part Instructions

¶2437

partnership interest itself is jointly-owned. Solely owned partnership interests should be reported on Schedule F, "Other Miscellaneous Property Not Reportable Under Any Other Schedule."

Part 1. Qualified joint interests held by decedent and spouse. Under section 2040(b)(2), a joint interest is a qualified joint interest if the decedent and the surviving spouse held the interest as:
• Tenants by the entirety, or
• Joint tenants with right of survivorship if the decedent and the decedent's spouse are the only joint tenants.

Interests that meet either of the two requirements above should be entered in Part 1. Joint interests that do not meet either of the two requirements above should be entered in Part 2.

Under "Description," describe the property as required in the instructions for Schedules A, B, C, and F for the type of property involved. For example, jointly held stocks and bonds should be described using the rules given in the instructions to Schedule B.

Under "Alternate value" and "Value at date of death," enter the full value of the property.

Note. You cannot claim the special treatment under section 2040(b) for property held jointly by a decedent and a surviving spouse who is not a U.S. citizen. Report these joint interests on Part 2 of Schedule E, not Part 1.

Part 2. All other joint interests. All joint interests that were not entered in Part 1 must be entered in Part 2.

For each item of property, enter the appropriate letter A, B, C, etc., from line 2a to indicate the name and address of the surviving co-tenant.

Under "Description," describe the property as required in the instructions for Schedules A, B, C, and F for the type of property involved.

In the "Percentage includible" column, enter the percentage of the total value of the property included in the gross estate.

Generally, you must include the full value of the jointly-owned property in the gross estate. However, the full value should not be included if you can show that a part of the property originally belonged to the other tenant or tenants and was never received or acquired by the other tenant or tenants from the decedent for less than adequate and full consideration in money or money's

worth. Full value of jointly-owned property also does not have to be included in the gross estate if you can show that any part of the property was acquired with consideration originally belonging to the surviving joint tenant or tenants. In this case, you may exclude from the value of the property an amount proportionate to the consideration furnished by the other tenant or tenants. Relinquishing or promising to relinquish dower, curtesy, or statutory estate created instead of dower or curtesy, or other marital rights in the decedent's property or estate is not consideration in money or money's worth. See the Schedule A instructions for the value to show for real property that is subject to a mortgage.

If the property was acquired by the decedent and another person or persons by gift, bequest, devise, or inheritance as joint tenants, and their interests are not otherwise specified by law, include only that part of the value of the property that is figured by dividing the full value of the property by the number of joint tenants.

If you believe that less than the full value of the entire property is includible in the gross estate for tax purposes, you must establish the right to include the smaller value by attaching proof of the extent, origin, and nature of the decedent's interest and the interest(s) of the decedent's co-tenant or co-tenants.

In the "Includible alternate value" and "Includible value at date of death" columns, enter only the values that you believe are includible in the gross estate.

Schedule F—Other Miscellaneous Property

 If there are any assets to which the special rule of Regulations section 20.2010–2T(a)(7)(ii) reported on this schedule, do not enter any value in the last three columns. See instructions for line 10 of Part 5– Recapitulation for information on how to estimate and report the value of these assets.

You must complete Schedule F and file it with the return.
On Schedule F, list all items that must be included in the gross estate that are not reported on any other schedule, including:
• Debts due the decedent (other than notes and mortgages included on Schedule C);
• Interests in business;

• Any interest in an Archer medical savings account (MSA) or health savings account (HSA), unless such interest passes to the surviving spouse; and
• Insurance on the life of another (obtain and attach Form 712, for each policy).

Note (for single premium or paid-up policies). In certain situations (for example, where the surrender value of the policy exceeds its replacement cost), the true economic value of the policy will be greater than the amount shown on line 59 of Form 712. In these situations, report the full economic value of the policy on Schedule F. See Rev. Rul. 78-137, 1978-1 C.B. 280 for details.

• Section 2044 property (see Decedent Who Was a Surviving Spouse, below);
• Claims (including the value of the decedent's interest in a claim for refund of income taxes or the amount of the refund actually received);
• Rights;
• Royalties;
• Leaseholds;
• Judgments;
• Reversionary or remainder interests;
• Shares in trust funds (attach a copy of the trust instrument);
• Household goods and personal effects, including wearing apparel;
• Farm products and growing crops;
• Livestock;
• Farm machinery; and
• Automobiles.

Interests. If the decedent owned any interest in a partnership or unincorporated business, attach a statement of assets and liabilities for the valuation date and for the 5 years before the valuation date. Also, attach statements of the net earnings for the same 5 years. Be sure to include the EIN of the entity. You must account for goodwill in the valuation. In general, furnish the same information and follow the methods used to value close corporations. See the instructions for Schedule B.

All partnership interests should be reported on Schedule F unless the partnership interest, itself, is jointly-owned. Jointly-owned partnership interests should be reported on Schedule E.

If real estate is owned by a sole proprietorship, it should be reported on Schedule F and not on Schedule A. Describe the real estate with the same detail required for Schedule A.

¶2437

Valuation discounts. If you answered "Yes," to Part 4—General Information, line 11b for any interest in a partnership, an unincorporated business, a limited liability company, or stock in a closely-held corporation, attach a statement that lists the item number from Schedule F and identifies the total effective discount taken (that is, XX.XX%) on such interest.

Example of effective discount:

a	Pro-rata value of limited liability company (before any discounts)	$100.00
b	Minus: 10% discounts for lack of control	(10.00)
c	Marketable minority interest value (as if freely traded minority interest value)	$90.00
d	Minus: 15% discount for lack of marketability	(13.50)
e	Non-marketable minority interest value	$76.50

Calculation of effective discount:

(**a** minus **e**) divided by **a** = effective discount
($100.00 - $76.50) ÷ $100.00 = 23.50%

Note. The amount of discounts are based on the factors pertaining to a specific interest and those discounts shown in the example are for demonstration purposes only.

If you answered "Yes," to line 11b for any transfer(s) described in (1) through (5) in the Schedule G instructions (and made by the decedent), **attach a statement to Schedule G** which lists the item number from that schedule and identifies the total effective discount taken (that is, XX.XX%) on such transfer(s).

Line 1. If the decedent owned at the date of death works of art or items with collectible value (for example, jewelry, furs, silverware, books, statuary, vases, oriental rugs, coin or stamp collections), check the "Yes," box on line 1 and provide full details. If any item or collection of similar items is valued at more than $3,000, attach an appraisal by an expert under oath and the required statement regarding the appraiser's qualifications (see Regulations section 20.2031-6(b)).

Decedent Who Was a Surviving Spouse

If the decedent was a surviving spouse, he or she may have received qualified terminable interest property (QTIP) from the predeceased spouse for which the marital deduction was elected either on the predeceased spouse's estate tax return or on a gift tax return, Form 709. The election is available for transfers made and decedents dying after December 31, 1981. List such property on Schedule F.

If this election was made and the surviving spouse retained his or her interest in the QTIP property at death, the full value of the QTIP property is includible in his or her estate, even though the qualifying income interest terminated at death. It is valued as of the date of the surviving spouse's death, or alternate valuation date, if applicable. Do not reduce the value by any annual exclusion that may have applied to the transfer creating the interest.

The value of such property included in the surviving spouse's gross estate is treated as passing from the surviving spouse. It therefore qualifies for the charitable and marital deductions on the surviving spouse's estate tax return if it meets the other requirements for those deductions.

For additional details, see Regulations section 20.2044-1.

Schedule G—Transfers During Decedent's Life

⚠ **CAUTION** *If there are any assets to which the special rule of Regulations section 20.2010–2T(a)(7)(ii) reported on this schedule, do not enter any value in the last three columns. See instructions for line 10 of Part 5– Recapitulation for information on how to estimate and report the value of these assets.*

Complete Schedule G and file it with the return if the decedent made any of the transfers described in (1) through (5) below, or if you answered "Yes," to question 12 or 13a of Part 4—General Information.

Report the following types of transfers on this schedule:

IF . . .	AND . . .	THEN . . .
the decedent made a transfer from a trust,	at the time of the transfer, the transfer was from a portion of the trust that was owned by the grantor under section 676 (other than by reason of section 672(e)) by reason of a power in the grantor,	for purposes of sections 2035 and 2038, treat the transfer as made directly by the decedent.
	Any such transfer within the annual gift tax exclusion is not includible in the gross estate.	

1. **Certain gift taxes (section 2035(b)).** Enter at item A of Schedule G the total value of the gift taxes that were paid by the decedent or the estate on gifts made by the decedent or the decedent's spouse within 3 years of death.

The date of the gift, not the date of payment of the gift tax, determines whether a gift tax paid is included in the gross estate under this rule. Therefore, you should carefully examine the Forms 709 filed by the decedent and the decedent's spouse to determine what part of the total gift taxes reported on them was attributable to gifts made within 3 years of death.

For example, if the decedent died on July 10, 2012, you should examine gift tax returns for 2012, 2011, 2010, and 2009. However, the gift taxes on the 2009 return that are attributable to gifts made on or before July 10, 2009, are not included in the gross estate.

Explain how you figured the includible gift taxes if the entire gift taxes shown on any Form 709 filed for gifts made within 3 years of death are not included in the gross estate. Also attach copies of any relevant gift tax returns filed by the decedent's spouse for gifts made within 3 years of death.

2. **Other transfers within 3 years of death (section 2035(a)).** These transfers include only the following:
• Any transfer by the decedent with respect to a life insurance policy within 3 years of death; or
• Any transfer within 3 years of death of a retained section 2036 life estate, section 2037 reversionary interest, or

Part Instructions

section 2038 power to revoke, etc., if the property subject to the life estate, interest, or power would have been included in the gross estate had the decedent continued to possess the life estate, interest, or power until death.

These transfers are reported on Schedule G, regardless of whether a gift tax return was required to be filed for them when they were made. However, the amount includible and the information required to be shown for the transfers are determined:

• For insurance on the life of the decedent using the instructions to Schedule D (attach Forms 712);
• For insurance on the life of another using the instructions to Schedule F (attach Forms 712); and
• For sections 2036, 2037, and 2038 transfers, using paragraphs (3), (4), and (5) of these instructions.

3. Transfers with retained life estate (section 2036). These are transfers by the decedent in which the decedent retained an interest in the transferred property. The transfer can be in trust or otherwise, but excludes bona fide sales for adequate and full consideration.

Interests or rights. Section 2036 applies to the following retained interests or rights:
• The right to income from the transferred property;
• The right to the possession or enjoyment of the property; and
• The right, either alone or with any person, to designate the persons who shall receive the income from, possess, or enjoy, the property.

Retained annuity, unitrust, and other income interests in trusts. If a decedent transferred property into a trust and retained or reserved the right to use the property, or the right to an annuity, unitrust, or other interest in such trust for the property for decedent's life, any period not ascertainable without reference to the decedent's death, or for a period that does not, in fact, end before the decedent's death, then the decedent's right to use the property or the retained annuity, unitrust, or other interest (whether payable from income and/or principal) is the retention of the possession or enjoyment of, or the right to the income from, the property for purposes of section 2036. See Regulations section 20.2036-1(c)(2).

Retained voting rights. Transfers with a retained life estate also include transfers of stock in a controlled corporation after June 22, 1976, if the decedent retained or acquired voting

rights in the stock. If the decedent retained direct or indirect voting rights in a controlled corporation, the decedent is considered to have retained enjoyment of the transferred property. A corporation is a *controlled corporation* if the decedent owned (actually or constructively) or had the right (either alone or with any other person) to vote at least 20% of the total combined voting power of all classes of stock. See section 2036(b)(2). If these voting rights ceased or were relinquished within 3 years of the decedent's death, the corporate interests are included in the gross estate as if the decedent had actually retained the voting rights until death.

The amount includible in the gross estate is the value of the transferred property at the time of the decedent's death. If the decedent kept or reserved an interest or right to only a part of the transferred property, the amount includible in the gross estate is a corresponding part of the entire value of the property.

A retained life estate does not have to be legally enforceable. What matters is that a substantial economic benefit was retained. For example, if a mother transferred title to her home to her daughter but with the informal understanding that she was to continue living there until her death, the value of the home would be includible in the mother's estate even if the agreement would not have been legally enforceable.

4. **Transfers taking effect at death (section 2037).** A transfer that takes effect at the decedent's death is one under which possession or enjoyment can be obtained only by surviving the decedent. A transfer is not treated as one that takes effect at the decedent's death unless the decedent retained a reversionary interest (defined below) in the property that immediately before the decedent's death had a value of more than 5% of the value of the transferred property. If the transfer was made before October 8, 1949, the reversionary interest must have arisen by the express terms of the instrument of transfer.

A *reversionary interest* is, generally, any right under which the transferred property will or may be returned to the decedent or the decedent's estate. It also includes the possibility that the transferred property may become subject to a power of disposition by the decedent. It does not matter if the right arises by the express terms of the

instrument of transfer or by operation of law. For this purpose, reversionary interest does not include the possibility that the income alone from the property may return to the decedent or become subject to the decedent's power of disposition.

5. **Revocable transfers (section 2038).** The gross estate includes the value of any transferred property which was subject to the decedent's power to alter, amend, revoke, or terminate the transfer at the time of the decedent's death. A decedent's power to change beneficiaries and to increase any beneficiary's enjoyment of the property are examples of this.

It does not matter whether the power was reserved at the time of the transfer, whether it arose by operation of law, or whether it was later created or conferred. The rule applies regardless of the source from which the power was acquired, and regardless of whether the power was exercisable by the decedent alone or with any person (and regardless of whether that person had a substantial adverse interest in the transferred property).

The capacity in which the decedent could use a power has no bearing. If the decedent gave property in trust and was the trustee with the power to revoke the trust, the property would be included in his or her gross estate. For transfers or additions to an irrevocable trust after October 28, 1979, the transferred property is includible if the decedent reserved the power to remove the trustee at will and appoint another trustee.

If the decedent relinquished within 3 years of death any of the includible powers described above, figure the gross estate as if the decedent had actually retained the powers until death.

Only the part of the transferred property that is subject to the decedent's power is included in the gross estate.

For more detailed information on which transfers are includible in the gross estate, see Regulations section 20.2038-1.

Special Valuation Rules for Certain Lifetime Transfers

Sections 2701 through 2704 provide rules for valuing certain transfers to family members.

Section 2701 deals with the transfer of an interest in a corporation or partnership while retaining certain distribution rights, or a liquidation, put, call, or conversion right.

Section 2702 deals with the transfer of an interest in a trust while retaining any interest other than a qualified interest. In general, a *qualified interest* is a right to receive certain distributions from the trust at least annually, or a noncontingent remainder interest if all of the other interests in the trust are distribution rights specified in section 2702.

Section 2703 provides rules for the valuation of property transferred to a family member but subject to an option, agreement, or other right to acquire or use the property at less than FMV. It also applies to transfers subject to restrictions on the right to sell or use the property.

Finally, section 2704 provides that in certain cases, the lapse of a voting or liquidation right in a family-owned corporation or partnership will result in a deemed transfer.

These rules have potential consequences for the valuation of property in an estate. If the decedent (or any member of his or her family) was involved in any such transactions, see sections 2701 through 2704 and the related regulations for additional details.

How To Complete Schedule G

All transfers (other than outright transfers not in trust and bona fide sales) made by the decedent at any time during life must be reported on Schedule G, regardless of whether you believe the transfers are subject to tax. If the decedent made any transfers not described in these instructions, the transfers should not be shown on Schedule G. Instead, attach a statement describing these transfers by listing:
• The date of the transfer,
• The amount or value of the transferred property, and
• The type of transfer.

Complete the schedule for each transfer that is included in the gross estate under sections 2035(a), 2036, 2037, and 2038 as described in the Instructions for Schedule G.

In the "Item number" column, number each transfer consecutively beginning with "1." In the "Description" column, list the name of the transferee and the date of the transfer, and give a complete description of the property. Transfers included in the gross estate should be valued on the date of the decedent's death or, if alternate valuation is elected, according to section 2032.

If only part of the property transferred meets the terms of section 2035(a), 2036, 2037, or 2038, then only a corresponding part of the value of the property should be included in the value of the gross estate. If the transferee makes additions or improvements to the property, the increased value of the property at the valuation date should not be included on Schedule G. However, if only a part of the value of the property is included, enter the value of the whole under the column headed "Description" and explain what part was included.

Attachments. If a transfer, by trust or otherwise, was made by a written instrument, attach a copy of the instrument to Schedule G. If the copy of the instrument is of public record, it should be certified; if not of public record, the copy should be verified.

Schedule H—Powers of Appointment

 If there are any assets to which the special rule of Regulations section 20.2010–2T(a)(7)(ii) reported on this schedule, do not enter any value in the last three columns. See instructions for line 10 of Part 5– Recapitulation for information on how to estimate and report the value of these assets.

Complete Schedule H and file it with the return if you answered "Yes," to question 14 of Part 4—General Information.

On Schedule H, include in the gross estate:
• The value of property for which the decedent possessed a general power of appointment (defined below) on the date of his or her death and
• The value of property for which the decedent possessed a general power of appointment that he or she exercised or released before death by disposing of it in such a way that if it were a transfer of property owned by the decedent, the property would be includible in the decedent's gross estate as a transfer with a retained life estate, a transfer taking effect at death, or a revocable transfer.

With the above exceptions, property subject to a power of appointment is not includible in the gross estate if the decedent released the power completely and the decedent held no interest in or control over the property.

If the failure to exercise a general power of appointment results in a lapse of the power, the lapse is treated as a

release only to the extent that the value of the property that could have been appointed by the exercise of the lapsed power is more than the greater of $5,000 or 5% of the total value, at the time of the lapse, of the assets out of which, or the proceeds of which, the exercise of the lapsed power could have been satisfied.

Powers of Appointment

A *power of appointment* determines who will own or enjoy the property subject to the power and when they will own or enjoy it. The power must be created by someone other than the decedent. It does not include a power created or held on property transferred by the decedent.

A power of appointment includes all powers which are, in substance and effect, powers of appointment regardless of how they are identified and regardless of local property laws. For example, if a settlor transfers property in trust for the life of his wife, with a power in the wife to appropriate or consume the principal of the trust, the wife has a power of appointment.

Some powers do not in themselves constitute a power of appointment. For example, a power to amend only administrative provisions of a trust that cannot substantially affect the beneficial enjoyment of the trust property or income is not a power of appointment. A power to manage, invest, or control assets, or to allocate receipts and disbursements, when exercised only in a fiduciary capacity, is not a power of appointment.

General power of appointment. A *general power of appointment* is a power that is exercisable in favor of the decedent, the decedent's estate, the decedent's creditors, or the creditors of the decedent's estate, except:

1. A power to consume, invade, or appropriate property for the benefit of the decedent that is limited by an ascertainable standard relating to health, education, support, or maintenance of the decedent.

2. A power exercisable by the decedent only in conjunction with:

   a. the creator of the power or

   b. a person who has a substantial interest in the property subject to the power, which is adverse to the exercise of the power in favor of the decedent.

A part of a power is considered a general power of appointment if the power:

Part Instructions

1. May only be exercised by the decedent in conjunction with another person and

2. Is also exercisable in favor of the other person (in addition to being exercisable in favor of the decedent, the decedent's creditors, the decedent's estate, or the creditors of the decedent's estate).

When there is a partial power, figure the amount included in the gross estate by dividing the value of the property by the number of persons (including the decedent) in favor of whom the power is exercisable.

Date power was created. Generally, a power of appointment created by will is considered created on the date of the testator's death.

A power of appointment created by an inter vivos instrument is considered created on the date the instrument takes effect. If the holder of a power exercises it by creating a second power, the second power is considered as created at the time of the exercise of the first.

Attachments

If the decedent ever possessed a power of appointment, attach a certified or verified copy of the instrument granting the power and a certified or verified copy of any instrument by which the power was exercised or released. You must file these copies even if you contend that the power was not a general power of appointment, and that the property is not otherwise includible in the gross estate.

Schedule I—Annuities

 If there are any assets to which the special rule of Regulations section 20.2010–2T(a)(7)(ii) reported on this schedule, do not enter any value in the last three columns. See instructions for line 10 of Part 5– Recapitulation for information on how to estimate and report the value of these assets.

Complete Schedule I and file it with the return if you answered "Yes," to question 16 of Part 4—General Information.

Enter on Schedule I every annuity that meets all of the conditions under General, below, and every annuity described in paragraphs (a) through (h) of Annuities Under Approved Plans, even if the annuities are wholly or partially excluded from the gross estate.

For a discussion regarding the QTIP treatment of certain joint and survivor

annuities, see the Schedule M, line 3 instructions.

General

These rules apply to all types of annuities, including pension plans, individual retirement arrangements, purchased commercial annuities, and private annuities.

In general, you must include in the gross estate all or part of the value of any annuity that meets the following requirements:
* It is receivable by a beneficiary following the death of the decedent and by reason of surviving the decedent;
* The annuity is under a contract or agreement entered into after March 3, 1931;
* The annuity was payable to the decedent (or the decedent possessed the right to receive the annuity) either alone or in conjunction with another, for the decedent's life or for any period not ascertainable without reference to the decedent's death or for any period that did not in fact end before the decedent's death; and
* The contract or agreement is not a policy of insurance on the life of the decedent.

Note. A *private annuity* is an annuity issued by a party not engaged in the business of writing annuity contracts, typically a junior generation family member or a family trust.

An annuity contract that provides periodic payments to a person for life and ceases at the person's death is not includible in the gross estate. Social security benefits are not includible in the gross estate even if the surviving spouse receives benefits.

An annuity or other payment that is not includible in the decedent's or the survivor's gross estate as an annuity may still be includible under some other applicable provision of the law. For example, see Powers of Appointment and the instructions for Schedule G—Transfers During Decedent's Life, above. See also Regulations section 20.2039-1(e).

If the decedent retired before January 1, 1985, see Annuities Under Approved Plans, below, for rules that allow the exclusion of part or all of certain annuities.

Part Includible

If the decedent contributed only part of the purchase price of the contract or agreement, include in the gross estate

only that part of the value of the annuity receivable by the surviving beneficiary that the decedent's contribution to the purchase price of the annuity or agreement bears to the total purchase price.

For example, if the value of the survivor's annuity was $20,000 and the decedent had contributed three-fourths of the purchase price of the contract, the amount includible is $15,000 (¾ × $20,000).

Except as provided under Annuities Under Approved Plans, contributions made by the decedent's employer to the purchase price of the contract or agreement are considered made by the decedent if they were made by the employer because of the decedent's employment. For more information, see section 2039(b).

Definitions

Annuity. An *annuity* consists of one or more payments extending over any period of time. The payments may be equal or unequal, conditional or unconditional, periodic or sporadic.

Examples. The following are examples of contracts (but not necessarily the only forms of contracts) for annuities that must be included in the gross estate:

1. A contract under which the decedent immediately before death was receiving or was entitled to receive, for the duration of life, an annuity with payments to continue after death to a designated beneficiary, if surviving the decedent.

2. A contract under which the decedent immediately before death was receiving or was entitled to receive, together with another person, an annuity payable to the decedent and the other person for their joint lives, with payments to continue to the survivor following the death of either.

3. A contract or agreement entered into by the decedent and employer under which the decedent immediately before death and following retirement was receiving, or was entitled to receive, an annuity payable to the decedent for life. After the decedent's death, if survived by a designated beneficiary, the annuity was payable to the beneficiary with payments either fixed by contract or subject to an option or election exercised or exercisable by the decedent. However, see Annuities Under Approved Plans, below.

Part Instructions   -29-

¶2437

4. A contract or agreement entered into by the decedent and the decedent's employer under which at the decedent's death, before retirement, or before the expiration of a stated period of time, an annuity was payable to a designated beneficiary, if surviving the decedent. However, see Annuities Under Approved Plans, below.

5. A contract or agreement under which the decedent immediately before death was receiving, or was entitled to receive, an annuity for a stated period of time, with the annuity to continue to a designated beneficiary, surviving the decedent, upon the decedent's death and before the expiration of that period of time.

6. An annuity contract or other arrangement providing for a series of substantially equal periodic payments to be made to a beneficiary for life or over a period of at least 36 months after the date of the decedent's death under an individual retirement account, annuity, or bond as described in section 2039(e) (before its repeal by P.L. 98-369).

Payable to the decedent. An annuity or other payment was payable to the decedent if, at the time of death, the decedent was in fact receiving an annuity or other payment, with or without an enforceable right to have the payments continued.

Right to receive an annuity. The decedent had the right to receive an annuity or other payment if, immediately before death, the decedent had an enforceable right to receive payments at some time in the future, whether or not at the time of death the decedent had a present right to receive payments.

Annuities Under Approved Plans

The following rules relate to whether part or all of an otherwise includible annuity may be excluded. These rules have been repealed and apply only if the decedent either:
• On December 31, 1984, was both a participant in the plan and in pay status (for example, had received at least one benefit payment on or before December 31, 1984) and had irrevocably elected the form of the benefit before July 18, 1984, or
• Had separated from service before January 1, 1985, and did not change the form of benefit before death.

The amount excluded cannot exceed $100,000 unless either of the following conditions is met:

• On December 31, 1982, the decedent was both a participant in the plan and in pay status (for example, had received at least one benefit payment on or before December 31, 1982) and the decedent irrevocably elected the form of the benefit before January 1, 1983, or
• The decedent separated from service before January 1, 1983, and did not change the form of benefit before death.

Approved Plans

Approved plans may be separated into two categories:
• Pension, profit-sharing, stock bonus, and other similar plans and
• Individual retirement arrangements (IRAs), and retirement bonds.

Different exclusion rules apply to the two categories of plans.

Pension, etc., plans. The following plans are approved plans for the exclusion rules:

a. An employees' trust (or a contract purchased by an employees' trust) forming part of a pension, stock bonus, or profit-sharing plan that met all the requirements of section 401(a), either at the time of the decedent's separation from employment (whether by death or otherwise) or at the time of the termination of the plan (if earlier);

b. A retirement annuity contract purchased by the employer (but not by an employees' trust) under a plan that, at the time of the decedent's separation from employment (by death or otherwise), or at the time of the termination of the plan (if earlier), was a plan described in section 403(a);

c. A retirement annuity contract purchased for an employee by an employer that is an organization referred to in section 170(b)(1)(A)(ii) or (vi), or that is a religious organization (other than a trust), and that is exempt from tax under section 501(a);

d. Chapter 73 of Title 10 of the United States Code; or

e. A bond purchase plan described in section 405 (before its repeal by P.L. 98-369, effective for obligations issued after December 31, 1983).

Exclusion rules for pension, etc., plans. If an annuity under an *approved plan* described in (a) through (e) above is receivable by a beneficiary other than the executor and the decedent made no contributions under the plan toward the cost, no part of the value of the annuity, subject to the $100,000 limitation (if

applicable), is includible in the gross estate.

If the decedent made a contribution under a plan described in (a) through (e) above toward the cost, include in the gross estate on this schedule that proportion of the value of the annuity which the amount of the decedent's contribution under the plan bears to the total amount of all contributions under the plan. The remaining value of the annuity is excludable from the gross estate subject to the $100,000 limitation (if applicable). For the rules to determine whether the decedent made contributions to the plan, see Regulations section 20.2039-1(c).

IRAs and retirement bonds. The following plans are approved plans for the exclusion rules:

f. An individual retirement account described in section 408(a),

g. An individual retirement annuity described in section 408(b), or

h. A retirement bond described in section 409(a) (before its repeal by P.L. 98-369).

Exclusion rules for IRAs and retirement bonds. These plans are approved plans only if they provide for a series of substantially equal periodic payments made to a beneficiary for life, or over a period of at least 36 months after the date of the decedent's death.

Subject to the $100,000 limitation (if applicable), if an annuity under a "plan" described in (f) through (h) above is receivable by a beneficiary other than the executor, the entire value of the annuity is excludable from the gross estate even if the decedent made a contribution under the plan.

However, if any payment to or for an account or annuity described in paragraph (f), (g), or (h) above was not allowable as an income tax deduction under section 219 (and was not a rollover contribution as described in section 2039(e) before its repeal by P.L. 98-369), include in the gross estate on this schedule that proportion of the value of the annuity which the amount not allowable as a deduction under section 219 and not a rollover contribution bears to the total amount paid to or for such account or annuity. For more information, see Regulations section 20.2039-5.

Rules applicable to all approved plans. The following rules apply to all approved plans described in paragraphs (a) through (h) above.

If any part of an annuity under a "plan" described in (a) through (h) above is receivable by the executor, it is generally includible in the gross estate to the extent that it is receivable by the executor in that capacity. In general, the annuity is receivable by the executor if it is to be paid to the executor or if there is an agreement (expressed or implied) that it will be applied by the beneficiary for the benefit of the estate (such as in discharge of the estate's liability for death taxes or debts of the decedent, etc.) or that its distribution will be governed to any extent by the terms of the decedent's will or the laws of descent and distribution.

If data available to you does not indicate whether the plan satisfies the requirements of section 401(a), 403(a), 408(a), 408(b), or 409(a), you may obtain that information from the IRS office where the employer's principal place of business is located.

Line A. Lump Sum Distribution Election

Note. The following rules have been repealed and apply only if the decedent:

• On December 31, 1984, was both a participant in the plan and in pay status (for example, had received at least one benefit payment on or before December 31, 1984) and had irrevocably elected the form of the benefit before July 18, 1984, or
• Had separated from service before January 1, 1985, and did not change the form of benefit before death.

Generally, the entire amount of any lump sum distribution is included in the decedent's gross estate. However, under this special rule, all or part of a lump sum distribution from a qualified (approved) plan will be excluded if the lump sum distribution is included in the recipient's income for income tax purposes.

If the decedent was born before 1936, the recipient may be eligible to elect special "10-year averaging" rules (under repealed section 402(e)) and capital gain treatment (under repealed section 402(a)(2)) in figuring the income tax on the distribution. For more information, see Pub. 575, Pension and Annuity Income. If this option is available, the estate tax exclusion cannot be claimed unless the recipient elects to forego the "10-year averaging" and capital gain treatment in figuring the income tax on the distribution. The recipient elects to forego this treatment by treating the distribution as taxable on his or her income tax return as

described in Regulations section 20.2039-4(d). The election is irrevocable.

The amount excluded from the gross estate is the portion attributable to the employer contributions. The portion, if any, attributable to the employee-decedent's contributions is always includible. Also, you may not figure the gross estate in accordance with this election unless you check "Yes" on line A and attach the name, address, and identifying number of the recipients of the lump sum distributions. See Regulations section 20.2039-4(d)(2).

How To Complete Schedule I

In describing an annuity, give the name and address of the grantor of the annuity. Specify if the annuity is under an approved plan.

IF . . .	THEN . . .
the annuity is under an approved plan,	state the ratio of the decedent's contribution to the total purchase price of the annuity.
the decedent was employed at the time of death and an annuity as described in Definitions, Annuity, Example 4, above, became payable to any beneficiary because the beneficiary survived the decedent,	state the ratio of the decedent's contribution to the total purchase price of the annuity.
an annuity under an individual retirement account or annuity became payable to any beneficiary because that beneficiary survived the decedent and is payable to the beneficiary for life or for at least 36 months following the decedent's death,	state the ratio of the amount paid for the individual retirement account or annuity that was not allowable as an income tax deduction under section 219 (other than a rollover contribution) to the total amount paid for the account or annuity.
the annuity is payable out of a trust or other fund,	the description should be sufficiently complete to fully identify it.
the annuity is payable for a term of years,	include the duration of the term and the date on which it began.
the annuity is payable for the life of a person other than the decedent,	include the date of birth of that person.
the annuity is wholly or partially excluded from the gross estate,	enter the amount excluded under "Description" and explain how you figured the exclusion.

Schedule J—Funeral Expenses and Expenses Incurred in Administering Property Subject to Claims

 Use Schedule PC to make a protective claim for refund for expenses which are not currently deductible under section 2053. For such a claim, report the expense on Schedule J but without a value in the last column.

General. Complete and file Schedule J if you claim a deduction on item 14 of Part 5—Recapitulation.

Part Instructions   -31-

¶2437

On Schedule J, itemize funeral expenses and expenses incurred in administering property subject to claims. List the names and addresses of persons to whom the expenses are payable and describe the nature of the expense. **Do not list expenses incurred in administering property not subject to claims on this schedule. List them on Schedule L instead.**

The deduction is limited to the amount paid for these expenses that is allowable under local law but may not exceed:

1. The value of property subject to claims included in the gross estate, plus

2. The amount paid out of property included in the gross estate but not subject to claims. This amount must actually be paid by the due date of the estate tax return.

The applicable local law under which the estate is being administered determines which property is and is not subject to claims. If under local law a particular property interest included in the gross estate would bear the burden for the payment of the expenses, then the property is considered property subject to claims.

Unlike certain claims against the estate for debts of the decedent (see the instructions for Schedule K), you cannot deduct expenses incurred in administering property subject to claims on both the estate tax return and the estate's income tax return. If you choose to deduct them on the estate tax return, you cannot deduct them on a Form 1041, U.S. Income Tax Return for Estate and Trusts, filed for the estate. Funeral expenses are only deductible on the estate tax return.

Funeral expenses. Itemize funeral expenses on line A. Deduct from the expenses any amounts that were reimbursed, such as death benefits payable by the Social Security Administration or the Veterans Administration.

Executors' commissions. When you file the return, you may deduct commissions that have actually been paid to you or that you expect will be paid. Do not deduct commissions if none will be collected. If the amount of the commissions has not been fixed by decree of the proper court, the deduction will be allowed on the final examination of the return, provided that:
• The Estate and Gift Tax Territory Manager is reasonably satisfied that the commissions claimed will be paid;

• The amount entered as a deduction is within the amount allowable by the laws of the jurisdiction where the estate is being administered; and
• It is in accordance with the usually accepted practice in that jurisdiction for estates of similar size and character.

If you have not been paid the commissions claimed at the time of the final examination of the return, you must support the amount you deducted with an affidavit or statement signed under the penalties of perjury that the amount has been agreed upon and will be paid.

You may not deduct a bequest or devise made to you instead of commissions. If, however, the decedent fixed by will the compensation payable to you for services to be rendered in the administration of the estate, you may deduct this amount to the extent it is not more than the compensation allowable by the local law or practice.

Do not deduct on this schedule amounts paid as trustees' commissions whether received by you acting in the capacity of a trustee or by a separate trustee. If such amounts were paid in administering property not subject to claims, deduct them on Schedule L.

Note. Executors' commissions are taxable income to the executors. Therefore, be sure to include them as income on your individual income tax return.

Attorney fees. Enter the amount of attorney fees that have actually been paid or that you reasonably expect to be paid. If, on the final examination of the return, the fees claimed have not been awarded by the proper court and paid, the deduction will be allowed provided the Estate and Gift Tax Territory Manager is reasonably satisfied that the amount claimed will be paid and that it does not exceed a reasonable payment for the services performed, taking into account the size and character of the estate and the local law and practice. If the fees claimed have not been paid at the time of final examination of the return, the amount deducted must be supported by an affidavit, or statement signed under the penalties of perjury, by the executor or the attorney stating that the amount has been agreed upon and will be paid.

Do not deduct attorney fees incidental to litigation incurred by the beneficiaries. These expenses are charged against the beneficiaries personally and are not administration expenses authorized by the Code.

Interest expense. Interest expenses incurred after the decedent's death are generally allowed as a deduction if they are reasonable, necessary to the administration of the estate, and allowable under local law.

Interest incurred as the result of a federal estate tax deficiency is a deductible administrative expense. Penalties are not deductible even if they are allowable under local law.

Note. If you elect to pay the tax in installments under section 6166, you may not deduct the interest payable on the installments.

Miscellaneous expenses. Miscellaneous administration expenses necessarily incurred in preserving and distributing the estate are deductible. These expenses include appraiser's and accountant's fees, certain court costs, and costs of storing or maintaining assets of the estate.

The expenses of selling assets are deductible only if the sale is necessary to pay the decedent's debts, the expenses of administration, or taxes, or to preserve the estate or carry out distribution.

Schedule K—Debts of the Decedent and Mortgages and Liens

 Use Schedule PC to make a protective claim for refund for expenses which are not currently deductible under section 2053. For such a claim, report the expense on Schedule K but without a value in the last column.

You must complete and attach Schedule K if you claimed deductions on either item 15 or item 16 of Part 5—Recapitulation.

Income vs. estate tax deduction. Taxes, interest, and business expenses accrued at the date of the decedent's death are deductible both on Schedule K and as deductions in respect of the decedent on the income tax return of the estate.

If you choose to deduct medical expenses of the decedent only on the estate tax return, they are fully deductible as claims against the estate. If, however, they are claimed on the decedent's final income tax return under section 213(c), they may not also be claimed on the estate tax return. In this case, you also may not deduct on the estate tax return any amounts that were

Part Instructions

¶2437

not deductible on the income tax return because of the percentage limitations.

Debts of the Decedent

List under "Debts of the Decedent" only valid debts the decedent owed at the time of death. List any indebtedness secured by a mortgage or other lien on property of the gross estate under the heading "Mortgages and Liens." If the amount of the debt is disputed or the subject of litigation, deduct only the amount the estate concedes to be a valid claim.

Generally, if the claim against the estate is based on a promise or agreement, the deduction is limited to the extent that the liability was contracted bona fide and for an adequate and full consideration in money or money's worth. However, any enforceable claim based on a promise or agreement of the decedent to make a contribution or gift (such as a pledge or a subscription) to or for the use of a charitable, public, religious, etc., organization is deductible to the extent that the deduction would be allowed as a bequest under the statute that applies.

Certain claims of a former spouse against the estate based on the relinquishment of marital rights are deductible on Schedule K. For these claims to be deductible, all of the following conditions must be met:
• The decedent and the decedent's spouse must have entered into a written agreement relative to their marital and property rights.
• The decedent and the spouse must have been divorced before the decedent's death and the divorce must have occurred within the 3-year period beginning on the date 1 year before the agreement was entered into. It is not required that the agreement be approved by the divorce decree.
• The property or interest transferred under the agreement must be transferred to the decedent's spouse in settlement of the spouse's marital rights.

You may not deduct a claim made against the estate by a remainderman relating to section 2044 property. Section 2044 property is described in the instructions to line 7 in Part 4—General Information.

Include in this schedule notes unsecured by mortgage or other lien and give full details, including:
• Name of payee,
• Face and unpaid balance,
• Date and term of note,
• Interest rate, and

Part Instructions

• Date to which interest was paid before death.

Include the exact nature of the claim as well as the name of the creditor. If the claim is for services performed over a period of time, state the period covered by the claim.

Example. Edison Electric Illuminating Co., for electric service during December 2010, $150.

If the amount of the claim is the unpaid balance due on a contract for the purchase of any property included in the gross estate, indicate the schedule and item number where you reported the property. If the claim represents a joint and separate liability, give full facts and explain the financial responsibility of the co-obligor.

Property and income taxes. The deduction for property taxes is limited to the taxes accrued before the date of the decedent's death. Federal taxes on income received during the decedent's lifetime are deductible, but taxes on income received after death are not deductible.

Keep all vouchers or original records for inspection by the IRS.

Allowable death taxes. If you elect to take a deduction for foreign death taxes under section 2053(d) rather than a credit under section 2014, the deduction is subject to the limitations described in section 2053(d) and its regulations. If you have difficulty figuring the deduction, you may request a computation of it. Send your request within a reasonable amount of time before the due date of the return to:

Department of the Treasury
Commissioner of Internal Revenue
Washington, DC 20224.

Attach to your request a copy of the will and relevant documents, a statement showing the distribution of the estate under the decedent's will, and a computation of the state or foreign death tax showing any amount payable by a charitable organization.

Mortgages and Liens

Under "Mortgages and Liens" list only obligations secured by mortgages or other liens on property included in the gross estate at its full value or at a value that was undiminished by the amount of the mortgage or lien. If the debt is enforceable against other property of the estate not subject to the mortgage or lien, or if the decedent was personally

-33-

liable for the debt, include the full value of the property subject to the mortgage or lien in the gross estate under the appropriate schedule and deduct the mortgage or lien on the property on this schedule.

However, if the decedent's estate is not liable, include in the gross estate only the value of the equity of redemption (or the value of the property less the amount of the debt), and do not deduct any portion of the indebtedness on this schedule.

Notes and other obligations secured by the deposit of collateral, such as stocks, bonds, etc., also should be listed under "Mortgages and Liens."

Description

Include under the "Description" column the particular schedule and item number where the property subject to the mortgage or lien is reported in the gross estate.

Include the name and address of the mortgagee, payee, or obligee, and the date and term of the mortgage, note, or other agreement by which the debt was established. Also include the face amount, the unpaid balance, the rate of interest, and date to which the interest was paid before the decedent's death.

Schedule L—Net Losses During Administration and Expenses Incurred in Administering Property Not Subject to Claims

 Use Schedule PC to make a protective claim for refund for expenses which are not currently deductible under section 2053. For such a claim, report the expense on Schedule L but without a value in the last column.

Complete Schedule L and file it with the return if you claim deductions on either item 19 or item 20 of Part 5—Recapitulation.

Net Losses During Administration

You may deduct only those losses from thefts, fires, storms, shipwrecks, or other casualties that occurred during the settlement of the estate. Deduct only the amount not reimbursed by insurance or otherwise.

Describe in detail the loss sustained and the cause. If you received insurance or other compensation for the loss, state the amount collected. Identify the property for which you are claiming the loss by indicating the schedule and item number where the property is included in the gross estate.

If you elect alternate valuation, do not deduct the amount by which you reduced the value of an item to include it in the gross estate.

Do not deduct losses claimed as a deduction on a federal income tax return or depreciation in the value of securities or other property.

Expenses Incurred in Administering Property Not Subject to Claims

You may deduct expenses incurred in administering property that is included in the gross estate but that is not subject to claims. Only deduct these expenses if they were paid before the section 6501 period of limitations for assessment expired.

The expenses deductible on this schedule are usually expenses incurred in the administration of a trust established by the decedent before death. They may also be incurred in the collection of other assets or the transfer or clearance of title to other property included in the decedent's gross estate for estate tax purposes, but not included in the decedent's probate estate.

The expenses deductible on this schedule are limited to those that are the result of settling the decedent's interest in the property or of vesting good title to the property in the beneficiaries. Expenses incurred on behalf of the transferees (except those described above) are not deductible. Examples of deductible and nondeductible expenses are provided in Regulations section 20.2053-8(d).

List the names and addresses of the persons to whom each expense was payable and the nature of the expense. Identify the property for which the expense was incurred by indicating the schedule and item number where the property is included in the gross estate. If you do not know the exact amount of the expense, you may deduct an estimate, provided that the amount may be verified with reasonable certainty and will be paid before the period of limitations for assessment (referred to above) expires. Keep all vouchers and receipts for inspection by the IRS.

Schedule M—Bequests, etc., to Surviving Spouse (Marital Deduction)

 If there are any assets to which the special rule of Regulations section 20.2010–2T(a)(7)(ii) reported on this schedule, do not enter any value in the last column. See instructions for line 23 of Part 5– Recapitulation for information on how to estimate and report the value of these assets.

General

You must complete Schedule M and file it with the return if you claim a deduction on Part 5—Recapitulation, item 21.

The marital deduction is authorized by section 2056 for certain property interests that pass from the decedent to the surviving spouse. You may claim the deduction only for property interests that are included in the decedent's gross estate (Schedules A through I).

Note. The marital deduction is generally not allowed if the surviving spouse is not a U.S. citizen. The marital deduction is allowed for property passing to such a surviving spouse in a qualified domestic trust (QDOT) or if such property is transferred or irrevocably assigned to such a trust before the estate tax return is filed. The executor must elect QDOT status on the return. See the instructions that follow for details on the election.

Property Interests That You May List on Schedule M

Generally, you may list on Schedule M all property interests that pass from the decedent to the surviving spouse and are included in the gross estate. However, do not list any *nondeductible terminable interests* (described below) on Schedule M unless you are making a QTIP election. The property for which you make this election must be included on Schedule M. See Qualified terminable interest property, below.

For the rules on common disaster and survival for a limited period, see section 2056(b)(3).

You may list on Schedule M only those interests that the surviving spouse takes:

1. As the decedent's legatee, devisee, heir, or donee;

2. As the decedent's surviving tenant by the entirety or joint tenant;

3. As an appointee under the decedent's exercise of a power or as a taker in default at the decedent's nonexercise of a power;

4. As a beneficiary of insurance on the decedent's life;

5. As the surviving spouse taking under dower or curtesy (or similar statutory interest); and

6. As a transferee of a transfer made by the decedent at any time.

Example—Listing Property Interests on Schedule M

Item number	Description of property interests passing to surviving spouse. For securities, give CUSIP number. If trust, partnership, or closely-held entity, give EIN.	Amount
	All other property:	
B1	One-half the value of a house and lot, 256 South West Street, held by decedent and surviving spouse as joint tenants with right of survivorship under deed dated July 15, 1975 (Schedule E, Part I, item 1)	$182,500
B2	Proceeds of Metropolitan Life Insurance Company policy No. 104729, payable in one sum to surviving spouse (Schedule D, item 3)	200,000
B3	Cash bequest under Paragraph Six of will	100,000

Property Interests That You May Not List on Schedule M

Do not list on Schedule M:

1. The value of any property that does not pass from the decedent to the surviving spouse;

2. Property interests that are not included in the decedent's gross estate;

3. The full value of a property interest for which a deduction was claimed on Schedules J through L. The value of the property interest should be reduced by the deductions claimed with respect to it;

4. The full value of a property interest that passes to the surviving spouse subject to a mortgage or other encumbrance or an obligation of the surviving spouse. Include on

¶2437

Schedule M only the net value of the interest after reducing it by the amount of the mortgage or other debt;

5. Nondeductible terminable interests (described below); or

6. Any property interest disclaimed by the surviving spouse.

Terminable Interests

Certain interests in property passing from a decedent to a surviving spouse are referred to as *terminable interests*. These are interests that will terminate or fail after the passage of time, or on the occurrence or nonoccurrence of a designated event. Examples are: life estates, annuities, estates for terms of years, and patents.

The ownership of a bond, note, or other contractual obligation, which when discharged would not have the effect of an annuity for life or for a term, is not considered a terminable interest.

Nondeductible terminable interests. Unless you are making a QTIP election, do not enter a terminable interest on Schedule M if:

1. Another interest in the same property passed from the decedent to some other person for less than adequate and full consideration in money or money's worth; and

2. By reason of its passing, the other person or that person's heirs may enjoy part of the property after the termination of the surviving spouse's interest.

This rule applies even though the interest that passes from the decedent to a person other than the surviving spouse is not included in the gross estate, and regardless of when the interest passes. The rule also applies regardless of whether the surviving spouse's interest and the other person's interest pass from the decedent at the same time.

Property interests that are considered to pass to a person other than the surviving spouse are any property interest that: (a) passes under a decedent's will or intestacy; (b) was transferred by a decedent during life; or (c) is held by or passed on to any person as a decedent's joint tenant, as appointee under a decedent's exercise of a power, as taker in default at a decedent's release or nonexercise of a power, or as a beneficiary of insurance on the decedent's life. See Regulations section 20.2056(c)-3.

For example, a decedent devised real property to his wife for life, with

remainder to his children. The life interest that passed to the wife does not qualify for the marital deduction because it will terminate at her death and the children will thereafter possess or enjoy the property.

However, if the decedent purchased a joint and survivor annuity for himself and his wife who survived him, the value of the survivor's annuity, to the extent that it is included in the gross estate, qualifies for the marital deduction because even though the interest will terminate on the wife's death, no one else will possess or enjoy any part of the property.

The marital deduction is not allowed for an interest that the decedent directed the executor or a trustee to convert, after death, into a terminable interest for the surviving spouse. The marital deduction is not allowed for such an interest even if there was no interest in the property passing to another person and even if the terminable interest would otherwise have been deductible under the exceptions described below for life estates, life insurance, and annuity payments with powers of appointment. For more information, see Regulations sections 20.2056(b)-1(f) and 20.2056(b)-1(g), Example (7).

If any property interest passing from the decedent to the surviving spouse may be paid or otherwise satisfied out of any of a group of assets, the value of the property interest is, for the entry on Schedule M, reduced by the value of any asset or assets that, if passing from the decedent to the surviving spouse, would be nondeductible terminable interests. Examples of property interests that may be paid or otherwise satisfied out of any of a group of assets are a bequest of the residue of the decedent's estate, or of a share of the residue, and a cash legacy payable out of the general estate.

Example. A decedent bequeathed $100,000 to the surviving spouse. The general estate includes a term for years (valued at $10,000 in determining the value of the gross estate) in an office building, which interest was retained by the decedent under a deed of the building by gift to a son. Accordingly, the value of the specific bequest entered on Schedule M is $90,000.

Life estate with power of appointment in the surviving spouse. A property interest, whether or not in trust, will be treated as passing to the surviving spouse, and will not be treated as a nondeductible terminable interest

if: (a) the surviving spouse is entitled for life to all of the income from the entire interest; (b) the income is payable annually or at more frequent intervals; (c) the surviving spouse has the power, exercisable in favor of the surviving spouse or the estate of the surviving spouse, to appoint the entire interest; (d) the power is exercisable by the surviving spouse alone and (whether exercisable by will or during life) is exercisable by the surviving spouse in all events; and (e) no part of the entire interest is subject to a power in any other person to appoint any part to any person other than the surviving spouse (or the surviving spouse's legal representative or relative if the surviving spouse is disabled. See Regulations section 20.2056(b)-5(a) and Revenue Ruling 85-35, 1985-1 C.B. 328). If these five conditions are satisfied only for a specific portion of the entire interest, see Regulations sections 20.2056(b)-5(b) and -5(c) to determine the amount of the marital deduction.

Life insurance, endowment, or annuity payments, with power of appointment in surviving spouse. A property interest consisting of the entire proceeds under a life insurance, endowment, or annuity contract is treated as passing from the decedent to the surviving spouse, and will not be treated as a nondeductible terminable interest if: (a) the surviving spouse is entitled to receive the proceeds in installments, or is entitled to interest on them, with all amounts payable during the life of the spouse, payable only to the surviving spouse; (b) the installment or interest payments are payable annually, or more frequently, beginning not later than 13 months after the decedent's death; (c) the surviving spouse has the power, exercisable in favor of the surviving spouse or of the estate of the surviving spouse, to appoint all amounts payable under the contract; (d) the power of appointment is exercisable by the surviving spouse alone and (whether exercisable by will or during life) is exercisable by the surviving spouse in all events; and (e) no part of the amount payable under the contract is subject to a power in any other person to appoint any part to any person other than the surviving spouse. If these five conditions are satisfied only for a specific portion of the proceeds, see Regulations section 20.2056(b)-6(b) to determine the amount of the marital deduction.

Charitable remainder trusts. An interest in a charitable remainder trust

¶2437

will not be treated as a nondeductible terminable interest if:

1. The interest in the trust passes from the decedent to the surviving spouse, and

2. The surviving spouse is the only beneficiary of the trust other than charitable organizations described in section 170(c).

A *charitable remainder trust* is either a charitable remainder annuity trust or a charitable remainder unitrust. (See section 664 for descriptions of these trusts.)

Election To Deduct Qualified Terminable Interests (QTIP)

You may elect to claim a marital deduction for qualified terminable interest property or property interests. You make the QTIP election simply by listing the qualified terminable interest property on Schedule M and inserting its value. You are presumed to have made the QTIP election if you list the property and insert its value on Schedule M. If you make this election, the surviving spouse's gross estate will include the value of the qualified terminable interest property. See the instructions for Part 4—General Information, line 7, for more details. **The election is irrevocable.**

If you file a Form 706 in which you do not make this election, you may not file an amended return to make the election unless you file the amended return on or before the due date for filing the original Form 706.

The effect of the election is that the property (interest) will be treated as passing to the surviving spouse and will not be treated as a nondeductible terminable interest. All of the other marital deduction requirements must still be satisfied before you may make this election. For example, you may not make this election for property or property interests that are not included in the decedent's gross estate.

Qualified terminable interest property. *Qualified terminable interest property* is property (a) that passes from the decedent, (b) in which the surviving spouse has a qualifying income interest for life, and (c) for which election under section 2056(b)(7) has been made.

The surviving spouse has a *qualifying income interest for life* if the surviving spouse is entitled to all of the income from the property payable annually or at more frequent intervals, or has a usufruct interest for life in the property, and during the surviving

spouse's lifetime no person has a power to appoint any part of the property to any person other than the surviving spouse. An annuity is treated as an income interest regardless of whether the property from which the annuity is payable can be separately identified.

Regulations sections 20.2044-1 and 20.2056(b)-7(d)(3) state that an interest in property is eligible for QTIP treatment if the income interest is contingent upon the executor's election even if that portion of the property for which no election is made will pass to or for the benefit of beneficiaries other than the surviving spouse.

The QTIP election may be made for all or any part of qualified terminable interest property. A partial election must relate to a fractional or percentile share of the property so that the elective part will reflect its proportionate share of the increase or decline in the whole of the property when applying section 2044 or 2519. Thus, if the interest of the surviving spouse in a trust (or other property in which the spouse has a qualified life estate) is qualified terminable interest property, you may make an election for a part of the trust (or other property) only if the election relates to a defined fraction or percentage of the entire trust (or other property). The fraction or percentage may be defined by means of a formula.

Election to Deduct Qualified Terminable Interest Property Under Section 2056(b)(7). If a trust (or other property) meets the requirements of qualified terminable interest property under section 2056(b)(7), and

1. The trust or other property is listed on Schedule M, and

2. The value of the trust (or other property) is entered in whole or in part as a deduction on Schedule M,

then unless the executor specifically identifies the trust (all or a fractional portion or percentage) or other property to be excluded from the election, the executor shall be deemed to have made an election to deduct such trust (or other property) treated as qualified terminable interest property under section 2056(b) (7).

If less than the entire value of the trust (or other property) that the executor has included in the gross estate is entered as a deduction on Schedule M, the executor shall be considered to have made an election only as to a fraction of the trust (or other property). The numerator of this fraction is equal to the amount of the trust (or

other property) deducted on Schedule M. The denominator is equal to the total value of the trust (or other property).

Qualified Domestic Trust Election (QDOT)

The marital deduction is allowed for transfers to a surviving spouse who is not a U.S. citizen only if the property passes to the surviving spouse in a *qualified domestic trust (QDOT)* or if such property is transferred or irrevocably assigned to a QDOT before the decedent's estate tax return is filed.

A *QDOT* is any trust:

1. That requires at least one trustee to be either a citizen of the United States or a domestic corporation;

2. That requires that no distribution of corpus from the trust can be made unless such a trustee has the right to withhold from the distribution the tax imposed on the QDOT;

3. That meets the requirements of any applicable regulations; and

4. For which the executor has made an election on the estate tax return of the decedent.

Note. For trusts created by an instrument executed before November 5, 1990, paragraphs 1 and 2 above will be treated as met if the trust instrument requires that all trustees be individuals who are citizens of the United States or domestic corporations.

You make the QDOT election simply by listing the qualified domestic trust or the entire value of the trust property on Schedule M and deducting its value. You are presumed to have made the QDOT election if you list the trust or trust property and insert its value on Schedule M. **Once made, the election is irrevocable.**

If an election is made to deduct qualified domestic trust property under section 2056A(d), provide the following information for each qualified domestic trust on an attachment to this schedule:

1. The name and address of every trustee;

2. A description of each transfer passing from the decedent that is the source of the property to be placed in trust; and

3. The employer identification number (EIN) for the trust.

The election must be made for an entire QDOT trust. In listing a trust for which you are making a QDOT election, **unless you specifically identify the**

Part Instructions

trust as not subject to the election, the election will be considered made for the entire trust.

The determination of whether a trust qualifies as a QDOT will be made as of the date the decedent's Form 706 is filed. If, however, judicial proceedings are brought before the Form 706's due date (including extensions) to have the trust revised to meet the QDOT requirements, then the determination will not be made until the court-ordered changes to the trust are made.

Election to Deduct Qualified Domestic Trust Property Under Section 2056A. If a trust meets the requirement of a qualified domestic trust under section 2056A(a), the return is filed no later than 1 year after the time prescribed by law (including extensions), and the entire value of the trust or trust property is listed and entered as a deduction on Schedule M, then unless the executor specifically identifies the trust to be excluded from the election, the executor shall be deemed to have made an election to have the entire trust treated as qualified domestic trust property.

Line 1

If property passes to the surviving spouse as the result of a qualified disclaimer, check "Yes," and attach a copy of the written disclaimer required by section 2518(b).

Line 3

Section 2056(b)(7)(C)(ii) creates an automatic QTIP election for certain joint and survivor annuities that are includible in the estate under section 2039. To qualify, only the surviving spouse can have the right to receive payments before the death of the surviving spouse.

The executor can elect out of QTIP treatment, however, by checking the "Yes," box on line 3. **Once made, the election is irrevocable.** If there is more than one such joint and survivor annuity, you are not required to make the election for all of them.

If you make the election out of QTIP treatment by checking "Yes," on line 3, you cannot deduct the amount of the annuity on Schedule M. If you do not elect out, you must list the joint and survivor annuities on Schedule M.

Listing Property Interests on Schedule M

List each property interest included in the gross estate that passes from the decedent to the surviving spouse and

for which a marital deduction is claimed. This includes otherwise nondeductible terminable interest property for which you are making a QTIP election. Number each item in sequence and describe each item in detail. Describe the instrument (including any clause or paragraph number) or provision of law under which each item passed to the surviving spouse. Indicate the schedule and item number of each asset.

In listing otherwise nondeductible property for which you are making a QTIP election, unless you specifically identify a fractional portion of the trust or other property as not subject to the election, the election will be considered made for the entire interest.

Enter the value of each interest before taking into account the federal estate tax or any other death tax. The valuation dates used in determining the value of the gross estate apply also on Schedule M.

If Schedule M includes a bequest of the residue or a part of the residue of the decedent's estate, attach a copy of the computation showing how the value of the residue was determined. Include a statement showing:
• The value of all property that is included in the decedent's gross estate (Schedules A through I) but is not a part of the decedent's probate estate, such as lifetime transfers, jointly-owned property that passed to the survivor on decedent's death, and the insurance payable to specific beneficiaries;
• The values of all specific and general legacies or devises, with reference to the applicable clause or paragraph of the decedent's will or codicil. (If legacies are made to each member of a class, for example, $1,000 to each of decedent's employees, only the number in each class and the total value of property received by them need be furnished);
• The date of birth of all persons, the length of whose lives may affect the value of the residuary interest passing to the surviving spouse; and
• Any other important information such as that relating to any claim to any part of the estate not arising under the will.

Lines 5a, 5b, and 5c. The total of the values listed on Schedule M must be reduced by the amount of the federal estate tax, the federal GST tax, and the amount of state or other death and GST taxes paid out of the property interest involved. If you enter an amount for state or other death or GST taxes on line 5b or 5c, identify the taxes and attach your computation of them.

Attachments. If you list property interests passing by the decedent's will on Schedule M, attach a certified copy of the order admitting the will to probate. If, when you file the return, the court of probate jurisdiction has entered any decree interpreting the will or any of its provisions affecting any of the interests listed on Schedule M, or has entered any order of distribution, attach a copy of the decree or order. In addition, the IRS may request other evidence to support the marital deduction claimed.

Schedule O—Charitable, Public, and Similar Gifts and Bequests

⚠️ *If there are any assets to which the special rule of Regulations section 20.2010–2T(a)(7)(ii) reported on this schedule, do not enter any value in the last column. See instructions for line 23 of Part 5– Recapitulation for information on how to estimate and report the value of these assets.*

General

You must complete Schedule O and file it with the return if you claim a deduction on item 22 of Part 5—Recapitulation.

You can claim the charitable deduction allowed under section 2055 for the value of property in the decedent's gross estate that was transferred by the decedent during life or by will to or for the use of any of the following:
• The United States, a state, a political subdivision of a state, or the District of Columbia, for exclusively public purposes;
• Any corporation or association organized and operated exclusively for religious, charitable, scientific, literary, or educational purposes, including the encouragement of art, or to foster national or international amateur sports competition (but only if none of its activities involve providing athletic facilities or equipment, unless the organization is a qualified amateur sports organization) and the prevention of cruelty to children and animals. No part of the net earnings may benefit any private individual and no substantial activity may be undertaken to carry on propaganda, or otherwise attempt to influence legislation or participate in any political campaign on behalf of any candidate for public office;
• A trustee or a fraternal society, order or association operating under the lodge system, if the transferred property is to

Part Instructions   -37-

¶2437

be used exclusively for religious, charitable, scientific, literary, or educational purposes, or for the prevention of cruelty to children or animals. No substantial activity may be undertaken to carry on propaganda or otherwise attempt to influence legislation, or participate in any political campaign on behalf of any candidate for public office;

• Any veterans organization incorporated by an Act of Congress or any of its departments, local chapters, or posts, for which none of the net earnings benefits any private individual; or

• Employee stock ownership plans, if the transfer qualifies as a *qualified gratuitous transfer of qualified employer securities* within the meaning provided in section 664(g).

For this purpose, certain Indian tribal governments are treated as states and transfers to them qualify as deductible charitable contributions. See section 7871 and Revenue Procedure 2008-55, 2008-39 I.R.B. 768, available at *www.irs.gov/pub/irs-irbs/irb08-39.pdf*, as modified and supplemented by subsequent revenue procedures, for a list of qualifying Indian tribal governments.

You may also claim a charitable contribution deduction for a qualifying conservation easement granted after the decedent's death under the provisions of section 2031(c)(9).

The charitable deduction is allowed for amounts that are transferred to charitable organizations as a result of either a qualified disclaimer (see Line 2. Qualified Disclaimer, below) or the complete termination of a power to consume, invade, or appropriate property for the benefit of an individual. It does not matter whether termination occurs because of the death of the individual or in any other way. The termination must occur within the period of time (including extensions) for filing the decedent's estate tax return and before the power has been exercised.

The deduction is limited to the amount actually available for charitable uses. Therefore, if under the terms of a will or the provisions of local law, or for any other reason, the federal estate tax, the federal GST tax, or any other estate, GST, succession, legacy, or inheritance tax is payable in whole or in part out of any bequest, legacy, or devise that would otherwise be allowed as a charitable deduction, the amount you may deduct is the amount of the

bequest, legacy, or devise reduced by the total amount of the taxes.

If you elected to make installment payments of the estate tax, and the interest is payable out of property transferred to charity, you must reduce the charitable deduction by an estimate of the maximum amount of interest that will be paid on the deferred tax.

For split-interest trusts or pooled income funds, only the figure that is passing to the charity should be entered in the "Amount" column. Do not enter the entire amount that passes to the trust or fund.

If you are deducting the value of the residue or a part of the residue passing to charity under the decedent's will, attach a copy of the computation showing how you determined the value, including any reduction for the taxes described above.

Also include:

• A statement that shows the values of all specific and general legacies or devises for both charitable and noncharitable uses. For each legacy or devise, indicate the paragraph or section of the decedent's will or codicil that applies. If legacies are made to each member of a class (for example, $1,000 to each of the decedent's employees), show only the number of each class and the total value of property they received;

• The date of birth of all life tenants or annuitants, the length of whose lives may affect the value of the interest passing to charity under the decedent's will;

• A statement showing the value of all property that is included in the decedent's gross estate but does not pass under the will, such as transfers, jointly-owned property that passed to the survivor on decedent's death, and insurance payable to specific beneficiaries; and

• Any other important information such as that relating to any claim, not arising under the will, to any part of the estate (that is, a spouse claiming dower or curtesy, or similar rights).

Line 2. Qualified Disclaimer

The charitable deduction is allowed for amounts that are transferred to charitable organizations as a result of a qualified disclaimer. To be a *qualified disclaimer*, a refusal to accept an interest in property must meet the conditions of section 2518. These are explained in Regulations sections 25.2518-1 through 25.2518-3. If property passes to a charitable

beneficiary as the result of a qualified disclaimer, check the "Yes," box on line 2 and attach a copy of the written disclaimer required by section 2518(b).

Attachments

If the charitable transfer was made by will, attach a certified copy of the order admitting the will to probate, in addition to the copy of the will. If the charitable transfer was made by any other written instrument, attach a copy. If the instrument is of record, the copy should be certified; if not, the copy should be verified.

Value

The valuation dates used in determining the value of the gross estate apply also on Schedule O.

Schedule P—Credit for Foreign Death Taxes

General

If you claim a credit on line 13 of Part 2—Tax Computation, complete Schedule P and file it with the return. Attach Form(s) 706-CE to Form 706 support any credit you claim.

If the foreign government refuses to certify Form 706-CE, file it directly with the IRS as instructed on the Form 706-CE. See Form 706-CE for instructions on how to complete the form and a description of the items that must be attached to the form when the foreign government refuses to certify it.

The credit for foreign death taxes is allowable only if the decedent was a citizen or resident of the United States. However, see section 2053(d) and the related regulations for exceptions and limitations if the executor has elected, in certain cases, to deduct these taxes from the value of the gross estate. For a resident, not a citizen, who was a citizen or subject of a foreign country for which the President has issued a proclamation under section 2014(h), the credit is allowable only if the country of which the decedent was a national allows a similar credit to decedents who were U.S. citizens residing in that country.

The credit is authorized either by statute or by treaty. If a credit is authorized by a treaty, whichever of the following is the most beneficial to the estate is allowed:

• The credit figured under the treaty;
• The credit figured under the statute; or

• The credit figured under the treaty, plus the credit figured under the statute for death taxes paid to each political subdivision or possession of the treaty country that are not directly or indirectly creditable under the treaty.

Under the statute, the credit is authorized for all death taxes (national and local) imposed in the foreign country. Whether local taxes are the basis for a credit under a treaty depends upon the provisions of the particular treaty.

If a credit for death taxes paid in more than one foreign country is allowable, a separate computation of the credit must be made for each foreign country. The copies of Schedule P on which the additional computations are made should be attached to the copy of Schedule P provided in the return.

The total credit allowable for any property, whether subjected to tax by one or more than one foreign country, is limited to the amount of the federal estate tax attributable to the property. The anticipated amount of the credit may be figured on the return, but the credit cannot finally be allowed until the foreign tax has been paid and a Form 706-CE evidencing payment is filed. Section 2014(g) provides that for credits for foreign death taxes, each U.S. possession is deemed a foreign country.

Convert death taxes paid to the foreign country into U.S. dollars by using the rate of exchange in effect at the time each payment of foreign tax is made.

If a credit is claimed for any foreign death tax that is later recovered, see Regulations section 20.2016-1 for the notice required within 30 days.

Limitation Period

The credit for foreign death taxes is limited to those taxes that were actually paid and for which a credit was claimed within the later of 4 years after the filing of the estate tax return, before the date of expiration of any extension of time for payment of the federal estate tax, or 60 days after a final decision of the Tax Court on a timely filed petition for a redetermination of a deficiency.

Credit Under the Statute

For the credit allowed by the statute, the question of whether particular property is situated in the foreign country imposing the tax is determined by the same principles that would apply in determining whether similar property of a nonresident not a U.S. citizen is situated within the United States for purposes of the federal estate tax. See the instructions for Form 706-NA.

Computation of Credit Under the Statute

Item 1. Enter the amount of the estate, inheritance, legacy, and succession taxes paid to the foreign country and its possessions or political subdivisions, attributable to property that is:
- Situated in that country,
- Subjected to these taxes, and
- Included in the gross estate.

The amount entered at item 1 should not include any tax paid to the foreign country for property not situated in that country and should not include any tax paid to the foreign country for property not included in the gross estate. If only a part of the property subjected to foreign taxes is both situated in the foreign country and included in the gross estate, it will be necessary to determine the portion of the taxes attributable to that part of the property. Also, attach the computation of the amount entered at item 1.

Item 2. Enter the value of the gross estate, less the total of the deductions on items 21 and 22 of Part 5—Recapitulation.

Item 3. Enter the value of the property situated in the foreign country that is subjected to the foreign taxes and included in the gross estate, less those portions of the deductions taken on Schedules M and O that are attributable to the property.

Item 4. Subtract any credit claimed on line 15 for federal gift taxes on pre-1977 gifts (section 2012) from line 12 of Part 2—Tax Computation, and enter the balance at item 4 of Schedule P.

Credit Under Treaties

If you are reporting any items on this return based on the provisions of a death tax treaty, you may have to attach a statement to this return disclosing the return position that is treaty based. See Regulations section 301.6114-1 for details.

In general. If the provisions of a treaty apply to the estate of a U.S. citizen or resident, a credit is authorized for payment of the foreign death tax or taxes specified in the treaty. Treaties with death tax conventions are in effect with the following countries: Australia, Austria, Canada, Denmark, Finland, France, Germany, Greece, Ireland, Italy, Japan, Netherlands, Norway, South Africa, Switzerland, and the United Kingdom.

A credit claimed under a treaty is in general figured on Schedule P in the same manner as the credit is figured under the statute with the following principal exceptions:
- The situs rules contained in the treaty apply in determining whether property was situated in the foreign country;
- The credit may be allowed only for payment of the death tax or taxes specified in the treaty (but see the instructions above for credit under the statute for death taxes paid to each political subdivision or possession of the treaty country that are not directly or indirectly creditable under the treaty);
- If specifically provided, the credit is proportionately shared for the tax applicable to property situated outside both countries, or that was deemed in some instances situated within both countries; and
- The amount entered at item 4 of Schedule P is the amount shown on line 12 of Part 2—Tax Computation, less the total of the credits claimed for federal gift taxes on pre-1977 gifts (section 2012) and for tax on prior transfers (line 14 of Part 2—Tax Computation). (If a credit is claimed for tax on prior transfers, it will be necessary to complete Schedule Q before completing Schedule P.) For examples of computation of credits under the treaties, see the applicable regulations.

Computation of credit in cases where property is situated outside both countries or deemed situated within both countries. See the appropriate treaty for details.

Schedule Q—Credit for Tax on Prior Transfers

General

Complete Schedule Q and file it with the return if you claim a credit on Part 2—Tax Computation, line 14.

The term *transferee* means the decedent for whose estate this return is filed. If the transferee received property from a transferor who died within 10 years before, or 2 years after, the transferee, a credit is allowable on this return for all or part of the federal estate tax paid by the transferor's estate for the transfer. There is no requirement that the property be identified in the estate of the transferee or that it exist on the date of the transferee's death. It is sufficient for the allowance of the credit that the transfer of the property was subjected to federal estate tax in the estate of the transferor and that the specified period

Part Instructions   -39-

¶2437

of time has not elapsed. A credit may be allowed for property received as the result of the exercise or nonexercise of a power of appointment when the property is included in the gross estate of the donee of the power.

If the transferee was the transferor's surviving spouse, no credit is allowed for property received from the transferor to the extent that a marital deduction was allowed to the transferor's estate for the property. There is no credit for tax on prior transfers for federal gift taxes paid in connection with the transfer of the property to the transferee.

If you are claiming a credit for tax on prior transfers on Form 706-NA, you should first complete and attach Part 5—Recapitulation from Form 706 before figuring the credit on Schedule Q from Form 706.

Section 2056(d)(3) contains specific rules for allowing a credit for certain transfers to a spouse who was not a U.S. citizen where the property passed outright to the spouse, or to a qualified domestic trust.

Property

The term *property* includes any interest (legal or equitable) of which the transferee received the beneficial ownership. The transferee is considered the beneficial owner of property over which the transferee received a general power of appointment. Property does not include interests to which the transferee received only a bare legal title, such as that of a trustee. Neither does it include an interest in property over which the transferee received a power of appointment that is not a general power of appointment. In addition to interests in which the transferee received the complete ownership, the credit may be allowed for annuities, life estates, terms for years, remainder interests (whether contingent or vested), and any other interest that is less than the complete ownership of the property, to the extent that the transferee became the beneficial owner of the interest.

Maximum Amount of the Credit

The *maximum amount of the credit* is the smaller of:

1. The amount of the estate tax of the transferor's estate attributable to the transferred property or

2. The amount by which:

a. An estate tax on the transferee's estate determined without the credit for tax on prior transfers exceeds

b. An estate tax on the transferee's estate determined by excluding from the gross estate the net value of the transfer.

If credit for a particular foreign death tax may be taken under either the statute or a death duty convention, and on this return the credit actually is taken under the convention, then no credit for that foreign death tax may be taken into consideration in figuring estate tax (a) or estate tax (b), above.

Percent Allowable

Where transferee predeceased the transferor. If not more than 2 years elapsed between the dates of death, the credit allowed is 100% of the maximum amount. If more than 2 years elapsed between the dates of death, no credit is allowed.

Where transferor predeceased the transferee. The percent of the maximum amount that is allowed as a credit depends on the number of years that elapsed between dates of death. It is determined using the following table:

Period of Time Exceeding	Not Exceeding	Percent Allowable
- - - - -	2 years	100
2 years	4 years	80
4 years	6 years	60
6 years	8 years	40
8 years	10 years	20
10 years	- - - - -	none

How To Figure the Credit

A worksheet for Schedule Q is provided to allow you to figure the limits before completing Schedule Q. Transfer the appropriate amounts from the worksheet to Schedule Q as indicated on the schedule. You do not need to file the worksheet with Form 706, but keep it for your records.

Cases involving transfers from two or more transferors. Part I of the worksheet and Schedule Q enable you to figure the credit for as many as three transferors. The number of transferors is irrelevant to Part II of the worksheet. If you are figuring the credit for more than three transferors, use more than one worksheet and Schedule Q, Part I, and combine the totals for the appropriate lines.

Section 2032A additional tax. If the transferor's estate elected special-use valuation and the additional estate tax of section 2032A(c) was imposed at any time up to 2 years after the death of the decedent for whom you are filing this return, check the box on Schedule Q. On lines 1 and 9 of the worksheet, include the property subject to the additional estate tax at its FMV rather than its special-use value. On line 10 of the worksheet, include the additional estate tax paid as a federal estate tax paid.

How To Complete the Schedule Q Worksheet

Most of the information to complete Part I of the worksheet should be obtained from the transferor's Form 706.

Line 5. Enter on line 5 the applicable marital deduction claimed for the transferor's estate (from the transferor's Form 706).

Lines 10 through 18. Enter on these lines the appropriate taxes paid by the transferor's estate.

If the transferor's estate elected to pay the federal estate tax in installments, enter on line 10 only the total of the installments that have actually been paid at the time you file this Form 706. See Rev. Rul. 83-15, 1983-1 C.B. 224, for more details.

Line 21. Add lines 11 (allowable applicable credit) and 13 (foreign death taxes credit) of Part 2—Tax Computation to the amount of any credit taken (on line 15) for federal gift taxes on pre-1977 gifts (section 2012). Subtract this total from Part 2—Tax Computation, line 8. Enter the result on line 21 of the worksheet.

Line 26. If you figured the marital deduction using the unlimited marital deduction in effect for decedents dying after 1981, for purposes of determining the marital deduction for the reduced gross estate, see Rev. Rul. 90-2, 1990-1 C.B. 169. To determine the "reduced adjusted gross estate," subtract the amount on line 25 of the Schedule Q Worksheet from the amount on line 24 of the worksheet. If community property is included in the amount on line 24 of the worksheet, figure the reduced adjusted gross estate using the rules of Regulations section 20.2056(c)-2 and Rev. Rul. 76-311, 1976-2 C.B. 261.

¶2437

Worksheet for Schedule Q—Credit for Tax on Prior Transfers

Part I Transferor's tax on prior transfers

Item	Transferor (From Schedule Q)			Total for all transfers (line 8 only)
	A	B	C	
1. Gross value of prior transfer to this transferee				
2. Death taxes payable from prior transfer				
3. Encumbrances allocable to prior transfer				
4. Obligations allocable to prior transfer . .				
5. Marital deduction applicable to line 1 above, as shown on transferor's Form 706 . . .				
6. **TOTAL.** Add lines 2, 3, 4, and 5 . . .				
7. **Net value of transfers.** Subtract line 6 from line 1.				
8. **Net value of transfers.** Add columns A, B, and C of line 7.				
9. Transferor's taxable estate. . . .				
10. Federal estate tax paid				
11. State death taxes paid				
12. Foreign death taxes paid				
13. Other death taxes paid				
14. **TOTAL taxes paid.** Add lines 10, 11, 12, and 13				
15. **Value of transferor's estate.** Subtract line 14 from line 9				
16. Net federal estate tax paid on transferor's estate				
17. Credit for gift tax paid on transferor's estate with respect to pre-1977 gifts (section 2012)				
18. Credit allowed transferor's estate for tax on prior transfers from prior transferor(s) who died within 10 years before death of decedent . .				
19. **Tax on transferor's estate.** Add lines 16, 17, and 18				
20. Transferor's tax on prior transfers ((line 7 ÷ line 15) × line 19 of respective estates).				

Part II Transferee's tax on prior transfers

Item		Amount
21. Transferee's actual tax before allowance of credit for prior transfers (see instructions)	21	
22. Total gross estate of transferee from line 1 of the Tax Computation, page 1, Form 706.	22	
23. Net value of all transfers from line 8 of this worksheet	23	
24. Transferee's reduced gross estate. Subtract line 23 from line 22	24	
25. Total debts and deductions (not including marital and charitable deductions) (line 3b of Part 2—Tax Computation, page 1 and items 18, 19, and 20 of the Recapitulation, page 3, Form 706)	25	
26. Marital deduction from item 21, Recapitulation, page 3, Form 706 (see instructions).	26	
27. Charitable bequests from item 22, Recapitulation, page 3, Form 706 . .	27	
28. Charitable deduction proportion ([line 23 ÷ (line 22 – line 25)] × line 27)	28	
29. Reduced charitable deduction. Subtract line 28 from line 27.	29	
30. Transferee's deduction as adjusted. Add lines 25, 26, and 29	30	
31. (a) Transferee's reduced taxable estate. Subtract line 30 from line 24	31(a)	
(b) Adjusted taxable gifts	31(b)	
(c) Total reduced taxable estate. Add lines 31(a) and 31(b)	31(c)	
32. Tentative tax on reduced taxable estate.	32	
33. (a) Post-1976 gift taxes paid	33(a)	
(b) Unified credit (applicable credit amount)	33(b)	
(c) Section 2012 gift tax credit. . . .	33(c)	
(d) Section 2014 foreign death tax credit .	33(d)	
(e) Total credits. Add lines 33(a) through 33(d)	33(e)	
34. Net tax on reduced taxable estate. Subtract line 33(e) from line 32	34	
35. Transferee's tax on prior transfers. Subtract line 34 from line 21	35	

Part Instructions   -41-

¶2437

Schedules R and R-1 – Generation-Skipping Transfer Tax

Introduction and Overview

Schedule R is used to figure the generation-skipping transfer (GST) tax that is payable by the estate. Schedule R-1 is used to figure the GST tax that is payable by certain trusts that are includible in the gross estate.

The GST tax reported on Form 706 is imposed only on direct skips occurring at death. Unlike the estate tax, which is imposed on the value of the entire taxable estate regardless of who receives it, the GST tax is imposed only on the value of interests in property, wherever located, that actually pass to certain transferees, who are referred to as *skip persons* (defined below).

For purposes of Form 706, the property interests transferred must be includible in the gross estate before they are subject to the GST tax. Therefore, the first step in figuring the GST tax liability is to determine the property interests includible in the gross estate by completing Schedules A through I of Form 706.

The second step is to determine who the skip persons are. To do this, assign each transferee to a generation and determine whether each transferee is a *natural person* or a *trust* for GST purposes. See section 2613 and Regulations section 26.2612–1(d) for details.

The third step is to determine which skip persons are transferees of *interests in property*. If the skip person is a natural person, anything transferred is an interest in property. If the skip person is a trust, make this determination using the rules under Interest in property, below. These first three steps are described in detail under the main heading, Determining Which Transfers Are Direct Skips, below.

The fourth step is to determine whether to enter the transfer on Schedule R or on Schedule R-1. See the rules under the main heading, Dividing Direct Skips Between Schedules R and R-1.

The fifth step is to complete Schedules R and R-1 using the How To Complete instructions for each schedule.

Determining Which Transfers Are Direct Skips

Effective dates. The rules below apply only for the purpose of determining if a transfer is a direct skip that should be reported on Schedule R or R-1 of Form 706.

In general. The GST tax is effective for the estates of decedents dying after October 22, 1986.

Irrevocable trusts. The GST tax will not apply to any transfer under a trust that was irrevocable on September 25, 1985, but only to the extent that the transfer was not made out of corpus added to the trust after September 25, 1985. An addition to the corpus after that date will cause a proportionate part of future income and appreciation to be subject to the GST tax. For more information, see Regulations section 26.2601-1(b)(1).

Mental disability. If, on October 22, 1986, the decedent was under a mental disability to change the disposition of his or her property and did not regain the competence to dispose of property before death, the GST tax will not apply to any property included in the gross estate (other than property transferred on behalf of the decedent during life and after October 21, 1986). The GST tax will also not apply to any transfer under a trust to the extent that the trust consists of property included in the gross estate (other than property transferred on behalf of the decedent during life and after October 21, 1986).

Under a mental disability means the decedent lacked the competence to execute an instrument governing the disposition of his or her property, regardless of whether there was an adjudication of incompetence or an appointment of any other person charged with the care of the person or property of the transferor.

If the decedent had been adjudged mentally incompetent, a copy of the judgment or decree must be filed with this return.

If the decedent had not been adjudged mentally incompetent, the executor must file with the return a certification from a qualified physician stating that in his opinion the decedent had been mentally incompetent at all times on and after October 22, 1986, and that the decedent had not regained the competence to modify or revoke the terms of the trust or will prior to his death or a statement as to why no such certification may be obtained from a physician.

Direct skip. The GST tax reported on Form 706 and Schedule R-1 is imposed only on direct skips. For purposes of

Form 706, a *direct skip* is a transfer that is:

- Subject to the estate tax,
- Of an interest in property, and
- To a skip person.

All three requirements must be met before the transfer is subject to the GST tax. A transfer is subject to the estate tax if you are required to list it on any of Schedules A through I of Form 706. To determine if a transfer is of an interest in property and to a skip person, you must first determine if the transferee is a natural person or a trust as defined below.

Trust. For purposes of the GST tax, a *trust* includes not only an ordinary trust (as defined in Special rule for trusts other than ordinary trusts), but also any other arrangement (other than an estate) which, although not explicitly a trust, has substantially the same effect as a trust. For example, a trust includes life estates with remainders, terms for years, and insurance and annuity contracts.

Substantially separate and independent shares of different beneficiaries in a trust are treated as separate trusts.

Interest in property. If a transfer is made to a natural person, it is always considered a transfer of *an interest in property* for purposes of the GST tax.

If a transfer is made to a trust, a person will have an interest in the property transferred to the trust if that person either has a present right to receive income or corpus from the trust (such as an income interest for life) or is a permissible current recipient of income or corpus from the trust (that is, may receive income or corpus at the discretion of the trustee).

Skip person. A transferee who is a natural person is a *skip person* if that transferee is assigned to a generation that is two or more generations below the generation assignment of the decedent. See Determining the generation of a transferee, below.

A transferee who is a trust is a skip person if all the interests in the property (as defined above) transferred to the trust are held by skip persons. Thus, whenever a non-skip person has an interest in a trust, the trust will not be a skip person even though a skip person also has an interest in the trust.

A trust will also be a skip person if there are no interests in the property transferred to the trust held by any person, and future distributions or terminations from the trust can be made only to skip persons.

Non-skip person. A *non-skip person* is any transferee who is not a skip person.

Determining the generation of a transferee. Generally, a generation is determined along family lines as follows:

1. Where the beneficiary is a lineal descendant of a grandparent of the decedent (that is, the decedent's cousin, niece, nephew, etc.), the number of generations between the decedent and the beneficiary is determined by subtracting the number of generations between the grandparent and the decedent from the number of generations between the grandparent and the beneficiary.

2. Where the beneficiary is a lineal descendant of a grandparent of a spouse (or former spouse) of the decedent, the number of generations between the decedent and the beneficiary is determined by subtracting the number of generations between the grandparent and the spouse (or former spouse) from the number of generations between the grandparent and the beneficiary.

3. A person who at any time was married to a person described in (1) or (2) above is assigned to the generation of that person. A person who at any time was married to the decedent is assigned to the decedent's generation.

4. A relationship by adoption or half-blood is treated as a relationship by whole-blood.

5. A person who is not assigned to a generation according to (1), (2), (3), or (4) above is assigned to a generation based on his or her birth date, as follows:

a. A person who was born not more than 12½ years after the decedent is in the decedent's generation.

b. A person born more than 12½ years, but not more than 37½ years, after the decedent is in the first generation younger than the decedent.

c. A similar rule applies for a new generation every 25 years.

If more than one of the rules for assigning generations applies to a transferee, that transferee is generally assigned to the youngest of the generations that would apply.

If an estate, trust, partnership, corporation, or other entity (other than certain charitable organizations and trusts described in sections 511(a)(2)

and 511(b)(2)) is a transferee, then each person who indirectly receives the property interests through the entity is treated as a transferee and is assigned to a generation as explained in the above rules. However, this look-through rule does not apply for the purpose of determining whether a transfer to a trust is a direct skip.

Generation assignment where intervening parent is deceased. A special rule may apply in the case of the death of a parent of the transferee. For terminations, distributions, and transfers after December 31, 1997, the existing rule that applied to grandchildren of the decedent has been extended to apply to other lineal descendants.

If property is transferred to an individual who is a descendant of a parent of the transferor, and that individual's parent (who is a lineal descendant of the parent of the transferor) is deceased at the time the transfer is subject to gift or estate tax, then for purposes of generation assignment, the individual is treated as if he or she is a member of the generation that is one generation below the lower of:

• The transferor's generation or
• The generation assignment of the youngest living ancestor of the individual, who is also a descendant of the parent of the transferor.

The same rules apply to the generation assignment of any descendant of the individual.

This rule does not apply to a transfer to an individual who is not a lineal descendant of the transferor if the transferor has any living lineal descendants.

If any transfer of property to a trust would have been a direct skip except for this generation assignment rule, then the rule also applies to transfers from the trust attributable to such property.

See examples in Regulations section 26.2651–1(c).

Ninety-day rule. For purposes of determining if an individual's parent is deceased at the time of a testamentary transfer, an individual's parent who dies no later than 90 days after a transfer occurring by reason of the death of the transferor is treated as having predeceased the transferor. The 90-day rule applies to transfers occurring on or after July 18, 2005. See Regulations section 26.2651-1, for more information.

Charitable organizations. Charitable organizations and trusts

described in sections 511(a)(2) and 511(b)(2) are assigned to the decedent's generation. Transfers to such organizations are therefore not subject to the GST tax.

Charitable remainder trusts. Transfers to or in the form of charitable remainder annuity trusts, charitable remainder unitrusts, and pooled income funds are not considered made to skip persons and, therefore, are not direct skips even if all of the life beneficiaries are skip persons.

Estate tax value. Estate tax value is the value shown on Schedules A through I of this Form 706.

Examples. The rules above can be illustrated by the following examples:

1. Under the will, the decedent's house is transferred to the decedent's daughter for her life with the remainder passing to her children. This transfer is made to a "trust" even though there is no explicit trust instrument. The interest in the property transferred (the present right to use the house) is transferred to a non-skip person (the decedent's daughter). Therefore, the trust is not a skip person because there is an interest in the transferred property that is held by a non-skip person. The transfer is not a direct skip.

2. The will bequeaths $100,000 to the decedent's grandchild. This transfer is a direct skip that is not made in trust and should be shown on Schedule R.

3. The will establishes a trust that is required to accumulate income for 10 years and then pay its income to the decedent's grandchildren for the rest of their lives and, upon their deaths, distribute the corpus to the decedent's great-grandchildren. Because the trust has no current beneficiaries, there are no present interests in the property transferred to the trust. All of the persons to whom the trust can make future distributions (including distributions upon the termination of interests in property held in trust) are skip persons (for example, the decedent's grandchildren and great-grandchildren). Therefore, the trust itself is a skip person and you should show the transfer on Schedule R.

4. The will establishes a trust that is to pay all of its income to the decedent's grandchildren for 10 years. At the end of 10 years, the corpus is to be distributed to the decedent's children. All of the present interests in this trust are held by skip persons. Therefore, the trust is a skip person and you should show this

transfer on Schedule R. You should show the estate tax value of all the property transferred to the trust even though the trust has some ultimate beneficiaries who are non-skip persons.

Dividing Direct Skips Between Schedules R and R-1

 Report all generation-skipping transfers on Schedule R unless the rules below specifically provide that they are to be reported on Schedule R-1.

Under section 2603(a)(2), the GST tax on direct skips from a trust (as defined for GST tax purposes) is to be paid by the trustee and not by the estate. Schedule R-1 serves as a notification from the executor to the trustee that a GST tax is due.

For a direct skip to be reportable on Schedule R-1, the trust must be includible in the decedent's gross estate.

If the decedent was a surviving spouse receiving benefits for his or her lifetime from a marital deduction power of appointment (or QTIP) trust created by the decedent's spouse, then transfers caused by reason of the decedent's death from that trust to skip persons are direct skips required to be reported on Schedule R-1.

If a direct skip is made "from a trust" under these rules, it is reportable on Schedule R-1 even if it is also made "to a trust" rather than to an individual.

Similarly, if property in a trust (as defined for GST tax purposes) is included in the decedent's gross estate under sections 2035, 2036, 2037, 2038, 2039, 2041, or 2042 and such property is, by reason of the decedent's death, transferred to skip persons, the transfers are direct skips required to be reported on Schedule R-1.

Special rule for trusts other than ordinary trusts. An *ordinary trust* is defined in Regulations section 301.7701-4(a) as "an arrangement created by a will or by an inter vivos declaration whereby trustees take title to property for the purpose of protecting or conserving it for the beneficiaries under the ordinary rules applied in chancery or probate courts." Direct skips from ordinary trusts are required to be reported on Schedule R-1 regardless of their size unless the executor is also a trustee (see Executor as trustee, below).

Direct skips from trusts that are trusts for GST tax purposes but are not

ordinary trusts are to be shown on Schedule R-1 only if the total of all tentative maximum direct skips from the entity is $250,000 or more. If this total is less than $250,000, the skips should be shown on Schedule R. For purposes of the $250,000 limit, *tentative maximum direct skips* is the amount you would enter on line 5 of Schedule R-1 if you were to file that schedule.

A liquidating trust (such as a bankruptcy trust) under Regulations section 301.7701-4(d) is not treated as an ordinary trust for the purposes of this special rule.

If the proceeds of a life insurance policy are includible in the gross estate and are payable to a beneficiary who is a skip person, the transfer is a direct skip from a trust that is not an ordinary trust. It should be reported on Schedule R-1 if the total of all the tentative maximum direct skips from the company is $250,000 or more. Otherwise, it should be reported on Schedule R.

Similarly, if an annuity is includible on Schedule I and its survivor benefits are payable to a beneficiary who is a skip person, then the estate tax value of the annuity should be reported as a direct skip on Schedule R-1 if the total tentative maximum direct skips from the entity paying the annuity is $250,000 or more.

Executor as trustee. If any of the executors of the decedent's estate are trustees of the trust, then all direct skips for that trust must be shown on Schedule R and not on Schedule R-1, even if they would otherwise have been required to be shown on Schedule R-1. This rule applies even if the trust has other trustees who are not executors of the decedent's estate.

How To Complete Schedules R and R-1

Valuation. Enter on Schedules R and R-1 the estate tax value of the property interests subject to the direct skips. If you elected alternate valuation (section 2032) and/or special-use valuation (section 2032A), you must use the alternate and/or special-use values on Schedules R and R-1.

How To Complete Schedule R

Part 1. GST Exemption Reconciliation

Part 1, line 6 of both Parts 2 and 3, and line 4 of Schedule R-1 are used to allocate the decedent's GST exemption. This allocation is made by filing Form

706 and attaching a completed Schedule R and/or R-1. Once made, the allocation is irrevocable. You are not required to allocate all of the decedent's GST exemption. However, the portion of the exemption that you do not allocate will be allocated by the IRS under the deemed allocation of unused GST exemption rules of section 2632(e).

For transfers made through 1998, the GST exemption was $1 million. The current GST exemption is $5,250,000. The exemption amounts for 1999 through 2012 are as follows:

Year of transfer	GST exemption
1999	1,010,000
2000	1,030,000
2001	1,060,000
2002	1,100,000
2003	1,120,000
2004 and 2005	1,500,000
2006, 2007, and 2008	2,000,000
2009	3,500,000
2010 and 2011	5,000,000
2012	$5,120,000

The amount of each increase can only be allocated to transfers made (or appreciation that occurred) during or after the year of the increase. The following example shows the application of this rule.

Example. In 2003, G made a direct skip of $1,120,000 and applied her full $1,120,000 of GST exemption to the transfer. G made a $450,000 taxable direct skip in 2004 and another of $90,000 in 2006. For 2004, G can only apply $380,000 of exemption ($380,000 inflation adjustment from 2004) to the $450,000 transfer in 2004. For 2006, G can apply $90,000 of exemption to the 2006 transfer, but nothing to the transfer made in 2004. At the end of 2006, G would have $410,000 of unused exemption that she can apply to future transfers (or appreciation) starting in 2007.

Special QTIP election. In the case of property for which a marital deduction is allowed to the decedent's estate under section 2056(b)(7) (QTIP election), section 2652(a)(3) allows you to treat such property for purposes of the GST tax as if the election to be treated as qualified terminable interest property had not been made.

The 2652(a)(3) election must include the value of all property in the trust for

Part Instructions

which a QTIP election was allowed under section 2056(b)(7).

If a section 2652(a)(3) election is made, then the decedent will, for GST tax purposes, be treated as the transferor of all the property in the trust for which a marital deduction was allowed to the decedent's estate under section 2056(b)(7). In this case, the executor of the decedent's estate may allocate part or all of the decedent's GST exemption to the property.

You make the election simply by listing qualifying property on line 9 of Part 1.

Line 2. These allocations will have been made either on Forms 709 filed by the decedent or on Notices of Allocation made by the decedent for inter vivos transfers that were not direct skips but to which the decedent allocated the GST exemption. These allocations by the decedent are irrevocable.

Also include on this line allocations deemed to have been made by the decedent under the rules of section 2632. Unless the decedent elected out of the deemed allocation rules, allocations are deemed to have been made in the following order:

1. To inter vivos direct skips and

2. Beginning with transfers made after December 31, 2000, to lifetime transfers to certain trusts, by the decedent, that constituted indirect skips that were subject to the gift tax.

For more information, see section 2632 and related regulations.

Line 3. Make an entry on this line if you are filing Form(s) 709 for the decedent and wish to allocate any exemption.

Lines 4, 5, and 6. These lines represent your allocation of the GST exemption to direct skips made by reason of the decedent's death. Complete Parts 2 and 3 and Schedule R-1 before completing these lines.

Line 9. Line 9 is used to allocate the remaining unused GST exemption (from line 8) and to help you figure the trust's inclusion ratio. Line 9 is a Notice of Allocation for allocating the GST exemption to trusts as to which the decedent is the transferor and from which a generation-skipping transfer could occur after the decedent's death.

If line 9 is not completed, the deemed allocation at death rules will apply to allocate the decedent's remaining unused GST exemption. The exemption will be first allocated to property that is

the subject of a direct skip occurring at the decedent's death, and then to trusts as to which the decedent is the transferor. To avoid the application of the deemed allocation rules, you should enter on line 9 every trust (except certain trusts entered on Schedule R-1, as described below) to which you wish to allocate any part of the decedent's GST exemption. Unless you enter a trust on line 9, the unused GST exemption will be allocated to it under the deemed allocation rules.

If a trust is entered on Schedule R-1, the amount you entered on line 4 of Schedule R-1 serves as a Notice of Allocation and you need not enter the trust on line 9 unless you wish to allocate more than the Schedule R-1, line 4 amount to the trust. However, you must enter the trust on line 9 if you wish to allocate any of the unused GST exemption amount to it. Such an additional allocation would not ordinarily be appropriate in the case of a trust entered on Schedule R-1 when the trust property passes outright (rather than to another trust) at the decedent's death. However, where section 2032A property is involved, it may be appropriate to allocate additional exemption amounts to the property. See the instructions for line 10 below.

 To avoid application of the deemed allocation rules, Form 706 and Schedule R should be filed to allocate the exemption to trusts that may later have taxable terminations or distributions under section 2612 even if the form is not required to be filed to report estate or GST tax.

Line 9, column C. Enter the GST exemption, included on lines 2 through 6 of Part 1 of Schedule R (discussed above), that was allocated to the trust.

Line 9, column D. Allocate the amount on line 8 of Part 1 of Schedule R in line 9, column D. This amount may be allocated to transfers into trusts that are not otherwise reported on Form 706. For example, the line 8 amount may be allocated to an inter vivos trust established by the decedent during his or her lifetime and not included in the gross estate. This allocation is made by identifying the trust on line 9 and making an allocation to it using column D. If the trust is not included in the gross estate, value the trust as of the date of death. Inform the trustee of each trust listed on line 9 of the total GST exemption you allocated to the trust. The trustee will need this information to figure the GST

tax on future distributions and terminations.

Line 9, column E. Trust's inclusion ratio. The trustee must know the trust's inclusion ratio to figure the trust's GST tax for future distributions and terminations. You are not required to inform the trustee of the inclusion ratio and may not have enough information to figure it. Therefore, you are not required to make an entry in column E. However, column E and the worksheet below are provided to assist you in figuring the inclusion ratio for the trustee if you wish to do so.

Inform the trustee of the amount of the GST exemption you allocated to the trust. Line 9, columns C and D may be used to figure this amount for each trust.

Note. This worksheet will figure an accurate inclusion ratio only if the decedent was the only settlor of the trust. Use a separate worksheet for each trust (or separate share of a trust that is treated as a separate trust).

WORKSHEET (inclusion ratio):

1	Total estate and gift tax value of all of the property interests that passed to the trust . . .	_____
2	Estate taxes, state death taxes, and other charges actually recovered from the trust . . .	_____
3	GST taxes imposed on direct skips to skip persons other than this trust and borne by the property transferred to this trust	_____
4	GST taxes actually recovered from this trust (from Schedule R, Part 2, line 8 or Schedule R-1, line 6)	_____
5	Add lines 2 through 4	_____
6	Subtract line 5 from line 1 . .	_____
7	Add columns C and D of line 9	_____
8	Divide line 7 by line 6	_____
9	Trust's inclusion ratio. Subtract line 8 from 1.000	_____

Line 10. Special-use allocation. For skip persons who receive an interest in section 2032A special-use property, you may allocate more GST exemption than the direct skip amount to reduce the additional GST tax that would be due when the interest is later disposed of or qualified use ceases. See Schedule A-1, above, for more details about this additional GST tax.

Enter on line 10 the total additional GST exemption available to allocate to all skip persons who received any interest in section 2032A property.

¶2437

Attach a special-use allocation statement listing each such skip person and the amount of the GST exemption allocated to that person.

If you do not allocate the GST exemption, it will be automatically allocated under the deemed allocation at death rules. To the extent any amount is not so allocated, it will be automatically allocated to the earliest disposition or cessation that is subject to the GST tax. Under certain circumstances, post-death events may cause the decedent to be treated as a transferor for purposes of Chapter 13.

Line 10 may be used to set aside an exemption amount for such an event. Attach a statement listing each such event and the amount of exemption allocated to that event.

Parts 2 and 3.

Use Part 2 to figure the GST tax on transfers in which the property interests transferred are to bear the GST tax on the transfers. Use Part 3 to report the GST tax on transfers in which the property interests transferred do not bear the GST tax on the transfers.

Section 2603(b) requires that unless the governing instrument provides otherwise, the GST tax is to be charged to the property constituting the transfer. Therefore, you will usually enter all of the direct skips on Part 2.

You may enter a transfer on Part 3 only if the will or trust instrument directs, by specific reference, that the GST tax is not to be paid from the transferred property interests.

Part 2, Line 3. Enter zero on this line unless the will or trust instrument specifies that the GST taxes will be paid by property other than that constituting the transfer (as described above). Enter on line 3 the total of the GST taxes shown on Part 3 and Schedule(s) R-1 that are payable out of the property interests shown on Part 2, line 1.

Part 2, Line 6. Do not enter more than the amount on line 5. Additional allocations may be made using Part 1.

Part 3, Line 3. See the instructions to Part 2, line 3 above. Enter only the total of the GST taxes shown on Schedule(s) R-1 that are payable out of the property interests shown on Part 3, line 1.

Part 3, Line 6. See the instructions to Part 2, line 6 above.

How To Complete Schedule R-1

Filing due date. Enter the due date of Form 706. You must send the copies of Schedule R-1 to the fiduciary before this date.

Line 4. Do not enter more than the amount on line 3. If you wish to allocate an additional GST exemption, you must use Schedule R, Part 1. Making an entry on line 4 constitutes a Notice of Allocation of the decedent's GST exemption to the trust.

Line 6. If the property interests entered on line 1 will not bear the GST tax, multiply line 6 by 40% (0.40).

Signature. The executor(s) must sign Schedule R-1 in the same manner as Form 706. See Signature and Verification, above.

Filing Schedule R-1. Attach to Form 706 one copy of each Schedule R-1 that you prepare. Send two copies of each Schedule R-1 to the fiduciary.

Schedule U—Qualified Conservation Easement Exclusion

 If at the time of the contribution of the conservation easement, the value of the easement, the value of the land subject to the easement, or the value of any retained development right was different than the estate tax value, you must complete a separate computation in addition to completing Schedule U.

Use a copy of Schedule U as a worksheet for this separate computation. Complete lines 4 through 14 of the worksheet Schedule U. However, the value you use on lines 4, 5, 7, and 10 of the worksheet is the value for these items as of the date of the contribution of the easement, not the estate tax value. If the date of contribution and the estate tax values are the same, you do not need to do a separate computation.

After completing the worksheet, enter the amount from line 14 of the worksheet on line 14 of Schedule U. Finish completing Schedule U by entering amounts on lines 4, 7, and 15 through 20, following the instructions below for those lines. At the top of Schedule U, enter "worksheet attached." Attach the worksheet to the return.

Under section 2031(c), you may elect to exclude a portion of the value of land that is subject to a qualified

conservation easement. You make the election by filing Schedule U with all of the required information and excluding the applicable value of the land that is subject to the easement on Part 5—Recapitulation, at item 12. To elect the exclusion, include on Schedule A, B, E, F, G, or H, as appropriate, the decedent's interest in the land that is subject to the exclusion. You must make the election on a timely filed Form 706, including extensions.

The exclusion is the lesser of:
- The applicable percentage of the value of land (after certain reductions) subject to a qualified conservation easement or
- $500,000.

Once made, the election is irrevocable.

General Requirements

Qualified Land

Land may qualify for the exclusion if all of the following requirements are met:
- The decedent or a member of the decedent's family must have owned the land for the 3-year period ending on the date of the decedent's death.
- No later than the date the election is made, a qualified conservation easement on the land has been made by the decedent, a member of the decedent's family, the executor of the decedent's estate, or the trustee of a trust that holds the land.
- The land is located in the United States or one of its possessions.

Member of Family

Members of the decedent's family include the decedent's spouse; ancestors; lineal descendants of the decedent, of the decedent's spouse, and of the parents of the decedent; and the spouse of any lineal descendant. A legally adopted child of an individual is considered a child of the individual by blood.

Indirect Ownership of Land

The qualified conservation easement exclusion applies if the land is owned indirectly through a partnership, corporation, or trust, if the decedent owned (directly or indirectly) at least 30% of the entity. For the rules on determining ownership of an entity, see Ownership rules, below.

Ownership rules. An interest in property owned, directly or indirectly, by or for a corporation, partnership, or trust is considered proportionately owned by

Part Instructions

or for the entity's shareholders, partners, or beneficiaries. A person is the beneficiary of a trust only if he or she has a present interest in the trust. For additional information, see the ownership rules in section 2057(e)(3).

Qualified Conservation Easement

A *qualified conservation easement* is one that would qualify as a qualified conservation contribution under section 170(h). It must be a contribution:
• Of a qualified real property interest,
• To a qualified organization, and
• Exclusively for conservation purposes.

Qualified real property interest. A *qualified real property interest* is any of the following:
• The entire interest of the donor, other than a qualified mineral interest;
• A remainder interest; or
• A restriction granted in perpetuity on the use that may be made of the real property. The restriction must include a prohibition on more than a de minimis use for commercial recreational activity.

Qualified organization. A *qualified organization* includes:
• Corporations and any community chest, fund, or foundation, organized and operated exclusively for religious, charitable, scientific, testing for public safety, literary, or educational purposes, or to foster national or international amateur sports competition, or for the prevention of cruelty to children or animals, without net earnings benefitting any individual shareholder and without activity with the purpose of influencing legislation or political campaigning, which

   a. Receives more than one-third of its support from gifts, contributions, membership fees, or receipts from sales, admissions fees, or performance of services, or

   b. Is controlled by such an organization.
• Any entity that qualifies under section 170(b)(1)(A)(v) or (vi).

Conservation purpose. An easement has a *conservation purpose* if it is for:
• The preservation of land areas for outdoor recreation by, or for the education of, the public;
• The protection of a relatively natural habitat of fish, wildlife, or plants, or a similar ecosystem; or
• The preservation of open space (including farmland and forest land) where such preservation is for the scenic enjoyment of the general public,

or under a clearly delineated federal, state, or local conservation policy and will yield a significant public benefit.

Specific Instructions

Line 1

If the land is reported as one or more item numbers on a Form 706 schedule, simply list the schedule and item numbers. If the land subject to the easement is only part of an item, however, list the schedule and item number and describe the part subject to the easement. See the Instructions for Schedule A — Real Estate for information on how to describe the land.

Line 3

Using the general rules for describing real estate, provide enough information so the IRS can value the easement. Give the date the easement was granted and by whom it was granted.

Line 4

Enter on this line the gross value at which the land was reported on the applicable asset schedule on this Form 706. Do not reduce the value by the amount of any mortgage outstanding. Report the estate tax value even if the easement was granted by the decedent (or someone other than the decedent) prior to the decedent's death.

Note. If the value of the land reported on line 4 was different at the time the easement was contributed than that reported on Form 706, see the *Caution* at the beginning of the Schedule U Instructions.

Line 5

The amount on line 5 should be the date of death value of any qualifying conservation easements granted prior to the decedent's death, whether granted by the decedent or someone other than the decedent, for which the exclusion is being elected.

Note. If the value of the easement reported on line 5 was different at the time the easement was contributed than at the date of death, see the *Caution* at the beginning of the Schedule U Instructions.

Line 7

You must reduce the land value by the value of any development rights retained by the donor in the conveyance of the easement. A *development right* is any right to use the land for any

commercial purpose that is not subordinate to or directly supportive of the use of the land as a farm for farming purposes.

Note. If the value of the retained development rights reported on line 7 was different at the time the easement was contributed than at the date of death, see the *Caution* at the beginning of the Schedule U Instructions.

You do not have to make this reduction if everyone with an interest in the land (regardless of whether in possession) agrees to permanently extinguish the retained development right. The agreement must be filed with this return and must include the following information and terms:

   1. A statement that the agreement is made under section 2031(c)(5);

   2. A list of all persons in being holding an interest in the land that is subject to the qualified conservation easement. Include each person's name, address, tax identifying number, relationship to the decedent, and a description of their interest;

   3. The items of real property shown on the estate tax return that are subject to the qualified conservation easement (identified by schedule and item number);

   4. A description of the retained development right that is to be extinguished;

   5. A clear statement of consent that is binding on all parties under applicable local law:

   a. To take whatever action is necessary to permanently extinguish the retained development rights listed in the agreement and

   b. To be personally liable for additional taxes under section 2031(c)(5)(C) if this agreement is not implemented by the earlier of:
      • The date that is 2 years after the date of the decedent's death or
      • The date of sale of the land subject to the qualified conservation easement;

   6. A statement that in the event this agreement is not timely implemented, that they will report the additional tax on whatever return is required by the IRS and will file the return and pay the additional tax by the last day of the 6th month following the applicable date described above.

All parties to the agreement must sign the agreement.

¶2437

For an example of an agreement containing some of the same terms, see Part 3 of Schedule A-1 (Form 706).

Line 10

Enter the total value of the qualified conservation easements on which the exclusion is based. This could include easements granted by the decedent (or someone other than the decedent) prior to the decedent's death, easements granted by the decedent that take effect at death, easements granted by the executor after the decedent's death, or some combination of these.

 Use the value of the easement as of the date of death, even if the easement was granted prior to the date of death. But, if the value of the easement was different at the time the easement was contributed than at the date of death, see the Caution at the beginning of the Schedule U Instructions.

Explain how this value was determined and attach copies of any appraisals. Normally, the appropriate way to value a conservation easement is to determine the FMV of the land both before and after the granting of the easement, with the difference being the value of the easement.

Reduce the reported value of the easement by the amount of any consideration received for the easement. If the date of death value of the easement is different from the value at the time the consideration was received, reduce the value of the easement by the same proportion that the consideration received bears to the value of the easement at the time it was granted. For example, assume the value of the easement at the time it was granted was $100,000 and $10,000 was received in consideration for the easement. If the easement was worth $150,000 at the date of death, you must reduce the value of the easement by $15,000 ($10,000/$100,000 × $150,000) and report the value of the easement on line 10 as $135,000.

Line 15

If a charitable contribution deduction for this land has been taken on Schedule O, enter the amount of the deduction here. If the easement was granted after the decedent's death, a contribution deduction may be taken on Schedule O, if it otherwise qualifies, as long as no income tax deduction was or

will be claimed for the contribution by any person or entity.

Line 16

Reduce the value of the land by the amount of any acquisition indebtedness on the land at the date of the decedent's death. Acquisition indebtedness includes the unpaid amount of:
• Any indebtedness incurred by the donor in acquiring the property;
• Any indebtedness incurred before the acquisition if the indebtedness would not have been incurred but for the acquisition;
• Any indebtedness incurred after the acquisition if the indebtedness would not have been incurred but for the acquisition and the incurrence of the indebtedness was reasonably foreseeable at the time of the acquisition; and
• The extension, renewal, or refinancing of acquisition indebtedness.

Schedule PC—Protective Claim for Refund

A *protective claim for refund* preserves the estate's right to a refund of tax paid on any amount included in the gross estate which would be deductible under section 2053 but has not been paid or otherwise will not meet the requirements of section 2053 until after the limitations period for filing the claim has passed. See section 6511(a).

 Only use Schedule PC for section 2053 protective claims for refund being filed with Form 706. If the initial notice of the protective claim for refund is being submitted after Form 706 has been filed, use Form 843, Claim for Refund and Request for Abatement, to file the claim.

Schedule PC may be used to file a section 2053 protective claim for refund by estates of decedents who died after December 31, 2011. It will also be used to inform the IRS when the contingency leading to the protective claim for refund is resolved and the refund due the estate is finalized. The estate must indicate whether the Schedule PC being filed is the initial notice of protective claim for refund, notice of partial claim for refund, or notice of the final resolution of the claim for refund.

Because each separate claim or expense requires a separate Schedule PC, more than one Schedule PC may be included with Form 706, if applicable. Two copies of

each Schedule PC must be included with Form 706.

Note. Filing a section 2053 protective claim for refund on Schedule PC will not suspend the IRS' review and examination of Form 706, nor will it delay the issuance of a closing letter for the estate.

Initial Notice of Claim

The first Schedule PC to be filed is the initial notice of protective claim for refund. The estate will receive a written acknowledgment of receipt of the claim from the IRS. If the acknowledgment is not received within 180 days of filing the protective claim for refund on Schedule PC, the fiduciary should contact the IRS at (866) 699-4083 to inquire about the receipt and processing of the claim. A certified mail receipt or other evidence of delivery is not sufficient to confirm receipt and processing of the protective claim for refund.

Note. The written acknowledgment of receipt does not constitute a determination that all requirements for a valid protective claim for refund have been met.

In general, the claim will not be subject to substantive review until the amount of the claim has been established. However, a claim can be disallowed at the time of filing. For example, the claim for refund will be rejected if:
• The claim was not timely filed;
• The claim was not filed by the fiduciary or other person with authority to act on behalf of the estate;
• The acknowledgment of the penalties of perjury statement (on page 1 of Form 706) was not signed; or,
• The claim is not adequately described.

If the IRS does not raise such a defect when the claim is filed, it will not be precluded from doing so in the later substantive review.

The estate may be given an opportunity to cure any defects in the initial notice by filing a corrected and signed protective claim for refund before the expiration of the limitations period in section 6511(a) or within 45 days of notice of the defect, whichever is later.

Related Ancillary Expenses

If a Section 2053 protective claim for refund has been adequately identified on Schedule PC, the IRS will presume that the claim includes certain expenses related to resolving, defending or satisfying the claim. These ancillary expenses may include attorneys' fees, court costs, appraisal fees, and accounting fees. The estate is not required to separately identify or substantiate these expenses; however, each expense must meet the requirements of section 2053 to be deductible.

Notice of Final Resolution of Claim

When an expense that was the subject of a section 2053 protective claim for refund is finally determined, the estate must notify the IRS that the claim for refund is ready for consideration. The notification should provide facts and evidence substantiating the deduction under section 2053 and the resulting recomputation of the estate tax liability. A separate notice of final resolution must be filed with the IRS for each resolved section 2053 protective claim for refund.

There are two means by which the estate may notify the IRS of the resolution of the uncertainty that deprived the estate of the deduction when Form 706 was filed. The estate may file a supplemental Form 706 with an updated Schedule PC and including each schedule affected by the allowance of the deduction under section 2053. Page 1 of Form 706 should contain the notation "Supplemental Information – Notification of Consideration of Section 2053 Protective Claim(s) for Refund" and include the filing date of the initial notice of protective claim for refund. A copy of the initial notice of claim should also be submitted.

Alternatively, the estate may notify the IRS by filing an updated Form 843, Claim for Refund and Request for Abatement. Form 843 must contain the notation "Notification of Consideration of Section 2053 Protective Claim(s) for Refund," including the filing date of the initial notice of protective claim for refund, on page 1. A copy of the initial notice of claim must also be submitted.

The estate should notify the IRS of resolution within 90 days of the date the claim or expense is paid or the date on which the amount of the claim becomes certain and no longer subject to contingency, whichever is later. Separate notifications must be submitted for every section 2053 protective claim for refund that was filed.

If the final section 2053 claim or expense involves multiple or recurring payments, the 90-day period begins on the date of the last payment. The estate may also notify the IRS (not more than annually) as payments are being made and possibly qualify for a partial refund based on the amounts paid through the date of the notice.

Specific Instructions
Part 1. General Information

Complete Part 1 by providing information that is correct and complete as of the time Schedule PC is filed. If filing an updated Schedule PC with a supplemental Form 706 or as notice of final resolution of the protective claim for refund, be sure to update the information from the original filing to ensure that it is accurate. Be particularly careful to verify that contact information (addresses and telephone numbers) and the reason for filing Schedule PC are indicated correctly. If the fiduciary is different from the executor identified on page 1 of Form 706 or has changed since the initial notice of protective claim for refund was filed, attach letters testamentary, letters of administration, or similar documentation evidencing the fiduciary's authority to file the protective claim for refund on behalf of the estate. Include a copy of Form 56, Notice Concerning Fiduciary Relationship, if it has been filed.

Part 2. Claim Information

For a protective claim for refund to be properly filed and considered, the claim or expense forming the basis of the potential 2053 deduction must be clearly identified. Using the check boxes provided, indicate whether you are filing the initial claim for refund, a claim for partial refund or a final claim. On the chart in Part 2, give the Form 706 schedule and item number of the claim or expense. List any amounts claimed under exceptions for ascertainable amounts (Regulations section 20.2053-1(d)(4)), claims and counterclaims in related matters (Regulations section 20.2053-4(b)), or claims under $500,000 (Regulations section 20.2053-4(c)). Provide all relevant information as described including, most importantly, an explanation of the reasons and contingencies delaying the actual payment to be made in satisfaction of the claim or expense. Complete columns E and F only if filing a notice of partial or final resolution. Show the amount of ancillary or related expenses to be included in the claim for refund and indicate whether this amount is estimated, agreed upon, or has been

paid. Also show the amount being claimed for refund.

Note. If you made partial claims for a recurring expense, the amount presently claimed as a deduction under section 2053 will only include the amount presently claimed, not the cumulative amount.

Part 3. Other Schedules PC and Forms 843 Filed by the Estate

On the chart in Part 3, provide information on other protective claims for refund that have been previously filed on behalf of the estate (if any), whether on other Schedules PC or on Form 843. When the initial claim for refund is filed, only information from Form(s) 843 need be included in Part 3. However, when filing a partial or final claim for refund, complete Part 3 by including the status of all claims filed by or on behalf of the estate, including those filed on other Schedules PC with Form 706. For each such claim, give the place of filing, date of filing and amount of the claim.

Continuation Schedule

When you need to list more assets or deductions than you have room for on one of the main schedules, use the Continuation Schedule at the end of Form 706. It provides a uniform format for listing additional assets from Schedules A through I and additional deductions from Schedules J, K, L, M, and O.

Please remember to:
• Use a separate Continuation Schedule for each main schedule you are continuing. Do not combine assets or deductions from different schedules on one Continuation Schedule.
• Make copies of the blank schedule before completing it if you expect to need more than one.
• Use as many Continuation Schedules as needed to list all the assets or deductions.
• Enter the letter of the schedule you are continuing in the space at the top of the Continuation Schedule.
• Use the Unit value column **only** if continuing Schedule B, E, or G. For all other schedules, use this space to continue the description.
• Carry the total from the Continuation Schedules forward to the appropriate line on the main schedule.

If continuing	Report	Where on Continuation Schedule
Schedule E, Pt. 2	*Percentage includible*	*Alternate valuation date*
Schedules J, L, M	*Continued description of deduction*	*Alternate valuation date* **and** *Alternate value*
Schedule O	*Character of institution*	*Alternate valuation date* **and** *Alternate value*
Schedule O	*Amount of each deduction*	*Amount deductible*

Privacy Act and Paperwork Reduction Act Notice. We ask for the information on this form to carry out the Internal Revenue laws of the United States. You are required to give us the information. We need it to ensure that you are complying with these laws and to allow us to figure and collect the right amount of tax. Subtitle B and section 6109, and the regulations require you to provide this information.

You are not required to provide the information requested on a form that is subject to the Paperwork Reduction Act unless the form displays a valid OMB control number. Books or records relating to a form or its instructions must be retained as long as their contents may become material in the administration of any Internal Revenue law. Generally, tax returns and return information are confidential as required by section 6103. However, section 6103 allows or requires the Internal Revenue Service to disclose information from this form in certain circumstances. For example, we may disclose information to the Department of Justice for civil or criminal litigation, and to cities, states, the District of Columbia, and U.S. commonwealths or possessions for use in administering their tax laws. We may also disclose this information to other countries under a tax treaty, to federal and state agencies to enforce federal non-tax criminal laws, or to federal law enforcement and intelligence agencies to combat terrorism. Failure to provide this information, or providing false information, may subject you to penalties.

The time needed to complete and file this form and related schedules will vary depending on individual circumstances. The estimated average times are:

Form	Recordkeeping	Learning about the law or the form	Preparing the form	Copying, assembling, and sending the form to the IRS
706	1 hr., 25 min.	1 hr., 50 min.	3 hr., 42 min.	48 min.
Schedule A	- - - -	15 min.	12 min.	20 min.
Schedule A-1	33 min.	31 min.	1 hr., 15 min.	1 hr., 3 min.
Schedule B	19 min.	9 min.	16 min.	20 min.
Schedule C	19 min.	1 min.	13 min.	20 min.
Schedule D	6 min.	6 min.	13 min.	20 min.
Schedule E	39 min.	6 min.	36 min.	20 min.
Schedule F	26 min.	8 min.	18 min.	20 min.
Schedule G	26 min.	21 min.	12 min.	13 min.
Schedule H	26 min.	6 min.	12 min.	13 min.
Schedule I	13 min.	30 min.	15 min.	20 min.
Schedule J	26 min.	6 min.	16 min.	20 min.
Schedule K	13 min.	9 min.	18 min.	20 min.
Schedule L	13 min.	4 min.	15 min.	20 min.
Schedule M	13 min.	34 min.	25 min.	20 min.
Schedule O	19 min.	12 min.	21 min.	20 min.
Schedule P	6 min.	15 min.	18 min.	13 min.
Schedule Q	- - - -	12 min.	15 min.	13 min.
Worksheet for Schedule Q	6 min.	6 min.	58 min.	20 min.
Schedule R	19 min.	45 min.	1 hr., 10 min.	48 min.
Schedule R-1	6 min.	46 min.	35 min.	20 min.
Schedule U	19 min.	26 min.	29 min.	20 min.
Continuation Schedule	19 min.	1 min.	13 min.	20 min.

If you have comments concerning the accuracy of these time estimates or suggestions for making this form simpler, we would be happy to hear from you. You can send us comments from *www.irs.gov/formspubs/*. Click on "More Information" and then on "Comment on Tax Forms and Publications." You can also send your comments to the Internal Revenue Service, Tax Forms and Publications Division, 1111 Constitution Ave. NW, IR-6526, Washington, DC 20224. Do not send the tax form to this address. Instead, see Where To File.

¶2437

Index

¶2437

Checklists for Completing Form 706

To ensure a complete return, review the following checklists before filing Form 706.

Attachments . . .

☐   Death Certificate

☐   Certified copy of the will—if decedent died testate, you must attach a certified copy of the will. If not certified, explain why.

☐   Appraisals—attach any appraisals used to value property included on the return.

☐   Copies of all trust documents where the decedent was a grantor or a beneficiary.

☐   Form 2848 or 8821, if applicable.

☐   Copy of any Form(s) 709 filed by the decedent.

☐   Copy of Line 7 worksheet, if applicable.

☐   Form 712, if any policies of life insurance are included on the return.

☐   Form 706-CE, if claiming a foreign death tax credit.

¶2437

Have you . . .

☐ Signed the return at the bottom of page 1?

☐ Had the preparer sign, if applicable?

☐ Obtained the signature of your authorized representative on Part 4, page 2?

☐ Entered a Total on all schedules filed?

☐ Made an entry on every line of the Recapitulation, even if it is a zero?

☐ Included the CUSIP number for all stocks and bonds?

☐ Included the EIN of trusts, partnerships, and closely held entities?

☐ Included the first 4 pages of the return and all required schedules?

☐ Completed Schedule F? It must be filed with all returns.

☐ Completed Part 4, line 4, on page 2, if there is a surviving spouse?

☐ Completed and attached Schedule D to report insurance on the life of the decedent, even if its value is not included in the estate?

☐ Included any QTIP property received from a predeceased spouse?

☐ Entered the decedent's name, SSN, and "Form 706" on your check or money order?

☐ Completed Part 6, section A if the estate elects not to transfer any deceased spousal unused exclusion (DSUE) amount to the surviving spouse?

☐ Completed Part 6, section C if the estate elects portability of any DSUE amount?

☐ Completed Part 6, section D and included a copy of the Form 706 of any predeceased spouse(s) from whom a deceased spousal unused exclusion (DSUE) amount was received and applied?

¶2437

GENERATION-SKIPPING TRANSFER TAX

TABLE OF CONTENTS

¶2500 PURPOSE OF THE GST TAX

(a) Impact of American Taxpayer Relief Act of 2012. On January 1, 2013, Congress passed the American Taxpayer Relief Act of 2012 ("2012 Taxpayer Relief Act"), and President Obama signed it into law on January 2, 2013. The new law makes permanent the $5 million GST tax exemption and indexes it for inflation (adjusting to $5,250,000 in 2013 and to $5,340,000 in 2014). In addition, the new law locks in a maximum 40-percent rate on GST tax transfers. The following GST provisions were also impacted by the 2012 Taxpayer Relief Act:

• **Deemed and Retroactive GST Allocation Provisions Made Permanent.** The deemed and retroactive GST allocation provisions under IRC Secs. 2632(c) and 2632(d) have been made permanent, effective for estates of decedents dying, gifts made or GSTs after December 31, 2012.

• **Qualified Severance Provision Made Permanent.** The 2012 Tax Relief Act made permanent the qualified severance provision of IRC Sec. 2642(a)(3) for estates of

¶2500

decedents dying, gifts made or GSTs after December 31, 2012. See ¶2518 for further discussion.

- **Clarification of Valuation Rules Made Permanent.** The 2012 Tax Relief Act made permanent the valuation rules under IRC Sec. 2642(b) with respect to the determination of the inclusion ratio for GST tax purposes effective for estates of decedents dying, gifts made or GSTs after December 31, 2012.

- **Provisions Providing Relief from Late GST Allocations and Elections Made Permanent.** The 2012 Tax Relief Act made permanent the provisions providing relief from late GST allocations and elections under IRC Sec. 2642(g)(1), as well as the provision pertaining to substantial compliance under IRC Sec. 2642(g)(2) for estates of decedents dying, gifts made, or GSTs after December 31, 2012. Taxpayers can obtain relief under IRC Sec. 2642(g) if they inadvertently failed to make a timely allocation of GST exemption to a transfer of property or where their allocation did not fully comply with the applicable statutory and regulatory requirements.

(b) Background on GST Tax. The GST tax was enacted to ensure that transfers of property would be subject to transfer tax at least once at each generation level. For years, wealthy individuals found advisors to help them create dynasty-type trusts that passed wealth down through the generations without ever paying a dime of wealth transfer taxes. These trusts were limited only by the rule against perpetuities and a lawyer's creativity. Here is how they worked. The parent placed the wealth in a trust in which the child and then the grandchild had the right to the income from the trust with the principal going to the great-grandchild. In this example, the parent would skip two generations of estate tax. No tax would be imposed at the child's level and no tax would be imposed when the grandchild died even though the child and grandchild had an income interest in the trust as well as substantial powers over the use, management, and disposition of the trust assets. While the tax advantages of generation-skipping trusts were theoretically available to all, in actual practice these devices were more valuable (in terms of tax savings) to wealthier families.

> **Example 1:** *Double taxation.* Father leaves commercial real estate to Son when he dies. Son wills the land to his children. By the time the land reaches Grandchildren, it has been taxed in two estates—both Father's and Son's.

> **Example 2:** *Classic GST trust.* In order to avoid this double taxation, lawyers draft a will for Father that puts the land in a trust. Son receives the trust income for his lifetime. When Son dies, the trust terminates and the land goes to Grandchildren. Without a GST tax, the land would be taxed in only one estate before reaching the grandchildren. Today this transfer would be subject to the GST tax. Keep in mind, however, that in every year except 2010 when the estate and GST tax do not exist, each person making a generation-skipping transfer has a GST exemption as discussed further at ¶2509.

Congress realized that generation-skipping was unfair because it enabled some families to pay these taxes only once every several generations, whereas other families who could not pay attorneys to create tax-saving trusts, paid these taxes every generation.

¶2500

Generation-skipping also reduced the progressive effect of the transfer taxes, because families with moderate levels of accumulated wealth might pay as much or more in cumulative transfer taxes as wealthier families who used generation-skipping devices.[1]

Rather than simply being a tax on the super-wealthy, the generation-skipping transfer (GST) tax applies across the board even to the transfers of many modestly situated taxpayers. It can apply, for example, to simple trusts used by middle income taxpayers to pass wealth on to grandchildren. In an arrangement that is common among middle-class taxpayers, the GST tax would apply to a trust in which a grandparent's children enjoy lifetime income from property that is left in trust for the grandchildren and the grandchildren inherit the trust assets when their parents die. Additionally, GST tax consequences must be considered anytime a grandchild holds an interest in a life insurance trust. Suffice it to say that this monster of a tax may apply when least expected.

A thorough understanding of the GST system's special vocabulary and an appreciation of when and how the tax applies are essential to minimize exposure to the GST tax. Good GST planning can reduce or possibly avoid the tax completely by enabling the taxpayer to take full advantage of the GST exemption, which is worth $5,340,000 in 2014 [See ¶ 2509 for further discussion of the GST tax exemption].

(c) How Generation-Skipping Transfers Are Taxed. Generation skipping transfers are taxed at a flat rate, which is equal to the highest federal transfer tax rate in existence at the time of the transfer. Consequently, unless a special rule, exception, or exemption applies, the maximum transfer tax rate is imposed on three types of generation-skipping transfers. The tax is imposed even if estate or gift tax is also imposed on the transfer. The three types of transfers subject to the GST are the direct skip [see ¶ 2504], taxable distribution [see ¶ 2506] and taxable termination [see ¶ 2505]. The GST tax applies to transfers that go directly to people who are two or more generations younger than the transferor (called skip persons) [see ¶ 2503].

This does not mean the GST tax applies to every gift or trust created for grandchildren. Married taxpayers may each make generation-skipping transfers free of the tax as a result of the GST tax exemption [IRC Sec. 2631; see ¶ 2509]. Married individuals who treat their gifts as made jointly can effectively double this exemption [see ¶ 2509]. Every individual is allowed a lifetime GST tax exemption equal to the "basic exclusion amount" in the calendar year of the allocation ($5,340,000 in 2014) [IRC Sec. 2631(a)]. The GST exemption may be allocated by the individual or his or her executor to the transfer of any property if the individual is the transferor [IRC Sec. 2631(a)]. Once made, the allocation of GST exemption is irrevocable [IRC Sec. 2631(b)]. The GST tax is assessed at the highest transfer tax rate in effect in the year of the event that triggered the GST tax. The tax rate is 40 percent in 2014. The tax is assessed in addition to any estate or gift tax that applies to the transfer [For further discussion of allocation of GST exemption see ¶ 2509]. Note that the GST tax does not apply to most small gifts, tuition payments, contributions to 529 college savings plans, and medical expense payments that skip a generation [see ¶ 2510].

---

[1] ¶ **2500** General Explanation of the Tax Reform Act of 1976, Committee Reports on the Act.

¶2500

(d) Application of GST Tax Provisions to Nonresidents, Noncitizens. An individual is a U.S. resident or citizen for GST tax purposes if that individual is a U.S. resident or citizen for gift or estate tax purposes. Every nonresident alien (NRA) transferor is allowed a $1 million GST tax exemption [Reg. Sec. 26.2663-2(a)].

If a nonresident makes a generation-skipping transfer, the GST tax applies to:

1. Direct skips to the extent that the transfer is subject to federal estate or gift tax (i.e., the transferred property is U.S. situs property) and

2. Taxable distributions and taxable terminations to the extent that the initial transfer of property to the trust was subject to federal estate or gift tax, regardless of the situs of the property at the time of the distribution or termination or the residency or citizenship of the skip persons [Reg. Sec. 26.2663-2(b)].[2]

For purposes of determining the applicable fraction and the inclusion ratio of a trust funded with U.S. situs property and foreign situs property, foreign situs property is treated as GST tax exempt [Reg. Sec. 26.2663-2(c)(2)].

(e) GST Tax Rates and Exemption Amounts. The following transfer tax exemptions and rates apply under current law:

Year	Top Estate Tax Rate	Estate Tax Exemption	GST Tax Rate	GST Exemption	Top Gift Tax Rate	Gift Tax Exemption
2009	45%	$3,500,000	45%	$3,500,000	45%	$1,000,000
2010	35%	$5 million	0%	$5 million	35%	$1,000,000
2011	35%	$5 million	35%	$5 million	35%	$5 million
2012	35%	$5,120,000	35%	$5,120,000	35%	$5,120,000
2013	40%	$5,250,000	40%	$5,250,000	40%	$5,250,000
2014	40%	$5,340,000	40%	$5,340,000	40%	$5,340,000

¶2501 HOW THE GST TAX WORKS—BASIC DEFINITIONS

The GST tax generally is imposed on transfers, either directly or in trust or similar arrangement, to a "skip person" [IRC Sec. 2601; see ¶ 2503]. As discussed further below, transfers subject to the GST tax include direct skips, taxable terminations, and taxable distributions [IRC Sec. 2611; see ¶ 2504, ¶ 2505 and ¶ 2506]. An exemption generally equal to the estate tax effective exemption amount is provided for each person making GSTs [see ¶ 2509]. The GST tax exemption may only be allocated by a transferor (or his or her executor) to transferred property [IRC Sec. 2631(a)]. The tax rate on GSTs is a flat rate of tax equal to the maximum estate and gift tax rate in effect at the time of the transfer multiplied by the inclusion ratio [IRC Sec. 2642; see ¶ 2513]. The inclusion ratio with respect to any property transferred in a GST indicates the amount of GST tax exemption allocated to a trust. The allocation of GST tax reduces the tax rate on a GST.

---

[2] Ltr. Rul. 201311004.

If an individual makes a direct skip during his or her lifetime, any unused GST tax exemption is automatically allocated to a direct skip to the extent necessary to make the inclusion ratio for such property equal to zero [IRC Sec. 2632(b)(1)]. An individual can elect out of the automatic allocation for lifetime direct skips [see ¶ 2509(c) for further discussion].

Taxable events. There are three types of generation-skipping transfers that can result in the imposition of the GST tax:

* Direct skip;

* Taxable termination; and

* Taxable distribution [IRC Sec. 2611(a); Reg. Sec. 26.2611-1].

These terms of art have special meaning for GST purposes and understanding how they work is critical.

Direct skip. A "direct skip," as discussed further at ¶ 2504, is any transfer subject to estate or gift tax of an interest in property directly to a "skip person" [IRC Sec. 2612(c); Reg. 26.2612-1]. The term "skip person" is defined as any individual assigned to a generation that is two or more generations below that of the transferor (grandchildren and great-grandchildren) [Reg. Sec. 26.2612-1(d)(1)]. Natural persons or certain trusts can be skip persons. Trusts are skip persons if (1) all interests in the trust are held by skip persons, or (2) no person holds an interest in the trust and at no time after the transfer may a distribution (including distributions and terminations) be made to a non-skip person. A taxable termination is a termination (by death, lapse of time, release of power, or otherwise) of an interest in property held in trust unless, immediately after such termination, a non-skip person has an interest in the property, or unless at no time after the termination may a distribution (including a distribution upon termination) be made from the trust to a skip person [IRC Sec. 2612(a); Reg. Sec. 26.2612-1(d)(2)]. The term "skip person" is explained at ¶ 2503.

When a grandparent makes a gift in excess of the annual exclusion amount to a grandchild, this is a direct skip unless the predeceased ancestor exception, as discussed at see ¶ 2507, applies. A direct skip will probably be subject to federal or gift tax in addition to the GST tax.

> **Example 1:** *Direct skip.* Grandfather gives his farm to his grandchildren. Because the transfer is a transfer to skip persons (his grandchildren) of property subject to federal gift tax, it is a direct skip [Reg. Sec. 26-2612-1(f), Example (1)].

> **Example 2:** *Direct skip of more than one generation.* Grandfather gives his farm to his great-grandchild. The transfer is a direct skip. Only one GST tax is imposed on the direct skip although two generations are skipped by the transfer [Reg. Sec. 26-2612-1(f), Example (2)].

Taxable termination. A "taxable termination," as discussed further at ¶ 2505, is the termination (by reason of death, lapse of time, release of power, or otherwise) of a beneficiary's interest held in trust if, immediately after the termination, all remaining interests are held by skip persons, unless at the time of the termination, a transfer subject to federal estate or gift tax occurs and a new transferor is determined for the property [IRC Sec. 2612(a)].

A taxable termination will not occur if the probability of a distribution to a skip person is so remote as to be negligible. This means that "it can be ascertained by actuarial standards that there is less than a 5 percent probability that the distribution will occur" [Reg. Sec. 26.2612-1(b)(1)(iii)].

> **Example 3:** *Taxable termination.* Grandfather's trust provides that income be paid to Child for life. When Child dies, the trust principal is to be paid to Grandchild. Because Child has an interest in the trust, the trust is not a skip person and the transfer to the trust is not a direct skip. If Child dies survived by Grandchild, a taxable termination occurs at Child's death because Child's interest in the trust terminates and thereafter the trust property is held by a skip person who occupies a lower generation than the child [Reg. Sec. 26.2612-1(f), Example (4)].

Taxable distribution. A "taxable distribution," as discussed further at ¶ 2506, is any distribution other than a direct skip or taxable termination of either income or principal from a trust to a skip person [IRC Sec. 2612(b)]. If a transferor allocates generation-skipping transfer tax exemption to a trust prior to the taxable distribution, generation-skipping transfer tax may be avoided. If any portion of GST tax (including penalties and interest) imposed on a distributee is paid from the distributing trust, the payment is an additional taxable distribution to the distributee. The additional distribution is treated as having been made on the last day of the calendar year in which the original taxable distribution is made [Reg. Sec. 26.2612-1(c)(1)].

> **Example 4:** Grandfather establishes an irrevocable trust under which the trust income is payable to Child for life. When Grandfather's grandchild attains 35 years of age, Grandchild is to receive one-half of the principal. The remaining one-half of the principal is to be distributed to Grandchild when Child dies. Assume that Child survives until Grandchild attains age 35. When the trustee distributes one-half of the principal to Grandchild on his 35th birthday, the distribution is a taxable distribution because it is a distribution to a skip person and is neither a taxable termination nor a direct skip.

Trust defined for GST tax purposes. A trust is generally defined as a legal relationship or arrangement under which an individual, who is called the settlor or grantor, transfers property to another person, who is called the trustee, so the property can be administered for the benefit of a third party, who is called the beneficiary [see ¶ 2800].

A trust is more broadly defined for GST tax purposes to include any arrangement (other than an estate) that has substantially the same effect as a trust [IRC Sec. 2652(b)]. For example, arrangements involving life estates and remainders, estates for years and life insurance and annuity contracts are considered to be trusts for GST tax purposes [IRC Sec. 2652(b)(3); Reg. Sec. 26.2652-1(b)(1)].

> **Example 5:** *Trust created by uniform gifts to minors transfers.* Grandmother transfers cash to an account in the name of Child, as custodian for Child's minor

child, Grandchild, under a state statute substantially similar to the Uniform Gifts/Transfers to Minors Act. For GST tax purposes, the transfer to the custodial account is treated as a transfer to a trust [Reg. Sec. 26.2652-1(b)(2), Example (1)].

Generally, a trust will exist even where the identity of the transferee is contingent upon the occurrence of an event. For GST tax purposes, however, where the identity of the transferee is contingent upon an event that must occur within six months of the settlor's death, a trust does not exist [Reg. Sec. 26.2652-1(b)(1)].

> **Example 6:** *Contingent transfer not a trust.* In her will, Grandmother leaves money to Daughter. The will provides that if Daughter does not survive Grandmother by more than six months, the bequest is payable to Grandchild. If Daughter dies four months after Grandmother, the bequest is not a transfer in trust because the contingency that determines the recipient of the bequest must occur within six months of grandmother's death. The bequest to Grandchild is a direct skip [Reg. Sec. 26.2652-1(b)(2), Example (2)].

> **Example 7:** *Contingent transfer that was a trust.* In her will, Grandmother leaves money to Daughter. The will provides that if Daughter does not survive Grandmother by more than 18 months, the bequest is payable to Grandchild. If Daughter dies four months after Grandmother, the bequest is a transfer in trust because the contingency that determines the recipient of the bequest did not have to occur within six months of Grandmother's death. The bequest to Grandchild is a taxable termination [Reg. Sec. 26.2652-1(b)(2), Example (3)].

Definition of trustee. A trustee is defined for GST tax purposes as the person designated as trustee under local law or, if no such person is designated, the person who actually or constructively possesses the property held in trust [IRC Sec. 2652(b)(2); Reg. Sec. 26.2652-1(c)].

Definition of executor. For GST tax purposes "executor" has the same meaning as it does for estate and gift tax purposes [IRC Sec. 2652(d)]. Despite this generalization, executor is defined for GST purposes as the executor or administrator of the decedent's estate. However, if no executor or administrator is appointed, qualified, or acting within the United States, the executor is the fiduciary who is primarily responsible for payment of the decedent's debts and expenses. If these is no such executor, administrator, or fiduciary, the executor is the person in actual or constructive possession of the largest portion of the value of the decedent's gross estate [Reg. Sec. 26.2652-1(d)].

¶2502 TRANSFEROR DEFINED

Any GST tax analysis must begin with a determination of who is the "transferor" of the property that is subject to the GST tax. Determining the identity of the transferor is important because application of the GST tax depends on generation assignments that all begin with the "transferor."

In general, the transferor is the person who most recently was subject to estate or gift taxes with respect to the property [IRC Sec. 2652(a); Reg. Sec. 26.2652-1(a)(1)]. For purposes of determining who is the transferor under the GST rules, it only matters if the taxpayer was *subject to* estate or gift taxes. Disregarded is the fact that no gift or estate tax is actually imposed as a result of an exclusion such as the annual per donee exclusion from gift tax or the exemption equivalent. The identity of the transferor is not affected just because some or all of the gift qualifies for an exclusion.

> **Example 1:** *Meaning of "subject to" gift tax:* Grandfather transfers $100,000 to a trust for the sole benefit of Grandchild. The transfer is a completed gift for gift tax purposes. For GST purposes, Grandfather is the transferor of the $100,000. It is immaterial that a portion of the transfer is excluded from the total amount of Grandfather's taxable gifts as a result of the annual gift tax exclusion. What matters is that the transfer is subject to gift tax making Grandfather the transferor [Reg. Sec. 26.2652-1(a)(5), Example (1)].

> **Example 2:** Grandfather creates an irrevocable trust for Child, age 12, and provides that Grandchild can withdraw one half of the trust fund at age 25. He reaches age 25 but does not withdraw any part of the trust. When the trust was created, Grandfather was the transferor of the entire trust, even after Grandson reaches age 25. Grandson does not become the transferor until a completed gift takes place or the property is subject to estate tax.

(a) Gift Splitting. When a married couple elect under IRC Sec. 2513 [see ¶ 902] to treat a gift as made equally by both of them for federal gift tax purposes, they have agreed to a practice known as gift splitting [see ¶ 2510]. This is a way for couples to reduce their taxable estate while they are still alive to see their children enjoy the money. In this situation, a husband and wife can give a total of $14,000 in 2014 annually to each child and/or grandchild. For GST purposes, each spouse is treated as the transferor of one-half of the entire value of the property transferred, even though only one of them actually transferred all the property under state law [Reg. Sec. 26.2652-1(a)(4)]. Gift splitting allows married couples to utilize both GST exemptions even though only one spouse owns all the property.

> **Example 3:** *How gift splitting affects identity of transferor.* Grandfather transfers $100,000 to a trust for the sole benefit of Grandchild. The transfer is a completed gift for gift tax purposes. Grandfather's spouse consents under Sec. 2513 to split the gift with him. For GST purposes, Grandfather and his spouse are each treated as the transferor of $50,000 to the trust [Reg. Sec. 26.2652-1(a)(5), Example (2)].

Generally, the transferor is the decedent in the case of a testamentary transfer. In the case of a transfer subject to gift taxes, the transferor is the donor. The two exceptions that will be discussed here are the special rule for certain qualified terminable interest property (QTIP) trusts and the exception for certain nongeneral powers of appointment.

¶2502

The IRS has held that if a gift is made by a member of a married couple who has elected to split all gifts, the deemed gift of the GST tax is treated as having been made equally by each of the spouses.[1]

(b) QTIP Election. In the case of a QTIP election [see discussion at ¶ 1103], the spouse who creates the QTIP trust is the transferor initially, but the surviving spouse becomes the new transferor of the property and the property becomes taxable in the surviving spouse's gross estate (provided no reverse QTIP election, as discussed below, is made) [Reg. Sec. 26.2652-1(a)(1)]. IRC Sec. 2044 provides that the gross estate of the surviving spouse in a QTIP trust includes the fair-market value of the trust funds or property in which the spouse has a life estate as their value is determined when the surviving spouse dies.

QTIP property is property that (1) passes from the decedent (2) in which the surviving spouse has a qualifying income interest for life and (3) to which an election under IRC Sec. 2056(b)(7) applies. Property for which a QTIP election is made is treated as passing to the surviving spouse for purposes of determining the decedent's taxable estate. A GST tax is imposed on all transfers, whether made directly or indirectly to skip persons. With respect to a QTIP, the decedent's surviving spouse will become the new transferor. Thus, a decedent's GST tax exemption is not automatically allocated to QTIP property.

> **Example 4:** *Change in identity of transferor.* Husband transfers $100,000 to a trust providing that all the net trust income is to be paid to Second Wife for her lifetime and upon her death it should pass to his children from his first marriage. He elects under IRC Sec. 2523(f) to treat the transfer as a transfer of qualified terminable interest property and he does not make a reverse QTIP election under IRC Sec. 2652(a)(3). When Second Wife dies, the trust property is included in her gross estate under IRC Sec. 2044. Thus she becomes the transferor at the time of her death [Reg. Sec. 26.2652-1(a)(5), Example (3)].

(c) Reverse QTIP Election. IRC Sec. 2652(a)(3) allows the executor or trustee making the QTIP election to treat the property as if the QTIP election had not been made. As a result of this "reverse QTIP election" the decedent remains, for GST tax purposes, the transferor of the QTIP trust or property, rather than the surviving spouse. Thus, the decedent's GST tax exemption may be allocated to the QTIP trust or property either by an affirmative allocation or by the automatic allocation of the decedent's remaining GST exemption. The decedent's GST tax exemption may be allocated to the QTIP trust or property even though the QTIP is taxed in the estate of the surviving spouse [Reg. Sec. 26.2652-2(b)]. The reverse QTIP election is made on the same return on which the QTIP election is made.

Result of reverse QTIP election: The surviving spouse will not be considered the transferor of QTIP property for GST tax purposes, if the executor for the deceased spouse or the donor or deceased spouse makes a reverse QTIP election under IRC Sec. 2652(a)(3). A reverse QTIP election simply means that the executor elects for the donor

---

[1] **¶2502** Technical Advice Memorandum 200147021.

¶2502

spouse to continue to be treated as the transferor of the property for GST tax purposes [IRC Sec. 2652(a)(3)]. In essence the donor or deceased spouse is electing to treat the QTIP property as if no QTIP election had been made for GST tax purposes [Reg. Sec. 26.2652-2(a)]. The donor or deceased spouse remains the transferor of the QTIP property for GST tax purposes even after the property is subject to estate or gift tax as a result of the death of the beneficiary or surviving spouse. You make the reverse QTIP election on the return where the QTIP election is made [Reg. Sec. 26.2652-2(b)]. The election is irrevocable and must be made with respect to all the property in the trust to which the QTIP election applies [Reg. Sec. 26.2652-2(a)]. You make the reverse QTIP election when you want to avoid wasting any of the deceased spouse's available GST exemption and when you still want to be able to take advantage of the ability to reduce estate taxes to zero when the surviving spouse dies.

> **Example 5:** *How reverse QTIP election changes identity of transferor.* Tom establishes a trust under his will. The terms of the trust provide that all trust income is payable to his surviving spouse, Sally, during her lifetime. Tom's executor makes an election to treat the trust property as qualified terminable interest property and also makes the reserve QTIP election. For GST tax purposes, Tom is the transferor with respect to the trust. When Sally dies, the then full fair-market value of the trust is included in her gross estate under IRC Sec. 2044. However, because of the reverse QTIP election, Sally does not become the transferor with respect to the trust. Tom continues to be treated as the transferor of the property after Sally's death for GST tax purposes [Reg. Sec. 26.2652-1(a)(5), Example (6)]. Because of the reverse QTIP election, if the trust principal is paid to a grandchild of Tom and Sally at Sally's death, a taxable termination rather than a direct skip occurs when Sally dies [Reg. Sec. 26.2652-2(d), Example (1)].

> **Example 6:** Dad died and in accordance with his will, $400,000 was transferred to a trust that will pay Wife all of its net income annually for her life. At her death, the trust principal will be distributed to Grandson. Executor makes the QTIP election for the value of the trust. Dad had $500,000 of unused GST tax exemption available at his death. Without a reverse QTIP election, Wife will be treated as the transferor of the property at her death and will have to use her GST tax exemption to offset the direct skip that occurs at her death. In effect, Dad's $500,000 of unused GST tax exemption would be wasted. If Executor makes the reverse QTIP election (so that Dad is treated as the transferor for GST purposes) and allocates $400,000 of Dad's exemption to the transfer, the trust will have a zero inclusion ratio and no part of the trust will be subject to the GST tax at Wife's death. In addition, it preserves $400,000 (or more if the QTIP trust appreciates in value) of her exemption that can be used for other transfers.

To make the reverse QTIP election, list the property in Part 1, line 9 on Schedule R.

IRS provides guidance on making late reverse QTIP election. In Rev. Proc. 2004-47,[2] the IRS provided an alternate method for executors and trustees to make a late

---

[2] Rev. Proc. 2004-47, 2004-2 CB 169.

reverse QTIP election under IRC Sec. 2652. The alternate method may be used in lieu of the letter ruling process. Relief for a late reverse QTIP is available under the new guidance if the following requirements are met:

1. A valid IRC Sec. 2056(b)(7) QTIP election was made;

2. The reverse QTIP election was not properly made because the taxpayer relied on attorneys who failed to advise the taxpayer of the need or proper method to make a reverse QTIP election;

3. The decedent has a sufficient amount of unused GST exemption;

4. The estate is not eligible for an automatic six-month extension;

5. The surviving spouse has not made a lifetime disposition of any part of the qualifying income interest for life in the QTIP property;

6. The surviving spouse is alive or no more than six months have passed since the surviving spouse's death; and

In addition the following procedural requirements must be satisfied:

1. The estate must file a request for more time to make a reverse QTIP election.

2. The request must have a cover sheet that states "Request for Extension Filed Pursuant to Rev. Proc. 2004-47." The following items must be attached:

    i. Copies of parts 1 through 5 and Schedule M of the original estate tax return filed with the IRS;

    ii. Schedule R, as required to make the reverse QTIP election;

    iii. A statement describing why the reverse QTIP election was not made previously;

    iv. Signed declaration by the executor; and

    v. Signed statement from the qualified tax professional.

(d) Powers of Appointment. A power of appointment [see discussion at ¶ ¶ 205 and 1810] is a power granted to someone enabling them to control or designate who will own the property subject to the power or benefit from its enjoyment. The property subject to the power of appointment is called the appointive property. A power of appointment must be created by someone other than the possessor (or holder) of the power. The power could be a general power of appointment or a special power of appointment. A special power of appointment can also be called a limited or nongeneral power of appointment. These two different types of powers have vastly different tax consequences.

General power of appointment. A general power of appointment is a power created by someone other than the decedent-holder that is exercisable in favor of either the holder, the decedent's estate, creditors, or creditors of the decedent's estate [IRC Sec. 2041(b)(1); Reg. Sec. 20.2041-1(c)(1)]. A general power of appointment includes the unlimited power to consume or invade the trust principal or income, or both, for the benefit of the holder of the power. The value of property over which someone has a general power of appointment at the time of death is subject to both estate and gift tax [IRC Secs. 2041(a)(2), 2514(c)(1)]. A general power of appointment does not include a

¶2502

power to consume, invade or appropriate property for the benefit of the holder if the power is limited by an ascertainable standard relating to health, education, support or maintenance of the decedent-holder [Reg. Sec. 20.2041-1(c)(2)]. The Tax Court has held that the holder of a general power of appointment over property includable in the estate of the holder for estate tax purposes is a transferor for purposes of the GST tax and will therefore be subject to GST tax.[3]

Special power of appointment. A power of appointment exercisable in favor of one or more persons or a class of persons, *not* including the decedent, the decedent's estate, creditors, or creditors of the decedent's estate, is called a special or limited power or nongeneral power of appointment [Reg. Sec. 25.2514-1(c)(1)]. Ordinarily, property subject to a special power of appointment is *not* subject to gift or estate tax [IRC Secs. 2041(b)(1)(A), 2514(c)(1)]. As a result, the holder of the limited power would not become the transferor of the appointive or trust property for GST tax purposes and would not be subject to GST tax.

¶2503 SKIP PERSON DEFINED

The GST tax is imposed on nonexempt transfers to people who are two or more generations below the settlor's generation. In GST tax parlance, these are known as "skip persons." The key to understanding and avoiding the GST tax is identification of skip persons. If no skip persons are involved in the transfer, the trust is not subject to the GST tax. Drafting a trust so that skip persons are intentionally avoided, if possible, could present an important planning opportunity.

A "skip person" is defined as an individual assigned to a generation that is two or more generations below that of the transferor [IRC Sec. 2613(a)(1); Reg. Sec. 26.2612-1(d)(1)]. An obvious skip person is a family member who is two or more generations below the transferor. For example, a grandchild is a skip person.

Individuals who are not lineal descendants may also be classified as skip persons. This determination is based on date of birth. For example, a person born within 12.5 years of the transferor's birth is considered part of the transferor's generation. An individual born more than 12.5 years after and no later than 37.5 years after the transferor's birth will be assigned to the first generation younger than the transferor. This means that a person who is more than 37.5 years younger than the transferor will be considered a skip person.

(a) Trust as Skip Person. In addition, a trust can be a skip person if (1) all interests in property held in trust are held by skip persons, or (2) if there is no non-skip person holding an interest in the trust and no distributions can be made from the trust to non-skip persons [IRC Sec. 2613(a)(2); Reg. Sec. 26.2612-1(d)]. A person will not have an interest in the property held in the trust, as required in (1) above, merely because his or her support obligation may be satisfied by a distribution that is within the discretion of a fiduciary or pursuant to the Uniform Gifts/Transfers to Minors Act [Reg.

---

[3] E. Peterson Marital Trust, 102 TC 790 (1994), *aff'd*, 78 F.3d 795 (2d Cir. 1996).

Sec. 26.2612-1(e)(2)(i)]. A trust meets the second part of this definition if the probability of a distribution to a non-skip person is "so remote as to be negligible," which the regulations define to mean that "it can be ascertained by actuarial standards that there is less than a 5 percent probability that the distribution will occur" [Reg. Sec. 26.2612-1(d)(2)(ii)].

> **Example 1:** *Support obligation.* Tom establishes an irrevocable trust for the benefit of his grandchild, Sam. The trustee has discretion to distribute property for Sam's support without regard to the duty or ability of Sam's parent to support him. Tom's child, Cathy, does not have an interest in the trust because the potential use of the trust property to satisfy her support obligation is within the discretion of a fiduciary. Cathy would be treated as having an interest in the trust if the trustee was required to distribute trust property for Sam's support [Reg. Sec. 26.2612-1(f), Example (13)].

(b) Non-Skip Persons. A non-skip person is any person (including a trust) who is not a skip person [IRC Sec. 2613(b)]. For example, a parent's child is a non-skip person.

> **Example 2:** *Non-skip person.* Tom creates a trust under his will. The trust provides that income will be distributed to his wife for her life and, at her death, the remainder will be split between Tom's daughter and grandson. The trust would not be a "skip person" because two non-skip persons hold an interest in the trust: Tom's wife and Tom's daughter.

For transfers to family members, generations are figured along family lines. All determinations are made relative to the transferor. That is why determining the identity of the transferor as discussed at ¶ 2502 is so important.

A person and his or her spouse and siblings are in one generation. Children (including adopted children), nieces, and nephews are in the first younger generation. Grandchildren, grandnieces, and grandnephews are in the second younger generation, and so on. A child who is adopted is treated identically to those related by blood [IRC Sec. 2651(b)(3)(A)].

> **Example 3:** *Skip person.* Alan has one brother, named Adam, who has no children. Alan has one child, named Bill, and Bill has a child named Charles. Adam makes gifts to his nephew Bill and grandnephew Charles. Bill is a non-skip person (only one generation below Adam) and therefore gifts by Adam to Bill are not GSTs. Gifts by Adam to Charles, however, are GSTs because Charles is a skip person to Adam.

For transfers made to nonfamily members, generations are measured from the date of the transferor's birth. Individuals whose ages are 12½ years younger than the transferor are treated as members of the same generation; individuals who are more than 12½ but not more than 37½ years younger are the first younger generation, and so on—a new generation every 25 years [IRC Sec. 2651(d)]. However, people who have

¶2503

ever been married to each other are always considered to be in the same generation, regardless of age [IRC Sec. 2651(c)].

If an estate, trust, partnership, or corporation is a beneficiary, the generation assignment is based on who owns the beneficial interest [IRC Sec. 2651(f)(2)].

¶2504 DIRECT SKIPS

The most common generation-skipping transfer is a direct skip. A direct skip is a taxable gift during life or a transfer at death from a transferor directly to a skip person who is someone two or more generations below the donor's generation [IRC Sec. 2612(c)]. A trust can also be a skip person and a direct skip gift to a trust is taxed like a direct skip gift to an individual. In the classic example, grandparent makes an outright gift to a grandchild or more remote descendant. This is treated as a direct skip because the grandparent has made a gift to someone two or more generations below his generation. The recipient of the gift is called a skip person. If the grandparent makes a transfer to a trust, this transfer is also a direct skip and the trust is considered a skip person if all the interests in the trust are held by skip persons. A direct skip is subject to both the generation-skipping tax and the estate or gift tax [IRC Sec. 2612(c)(1)].

The generation assignment of a person (who otherwise is a skip person) is redetermined by disregarding the intervening generation, if the intervening generation died before the transfer [IRC Sec. 2651(e)(1); Reg. Sec. 26.2612-1(a)(2)]. This is known as the "predeceased ancestor exception" and is discussed further at ¶ 2507.

> **Example 1:** Grandmother transfers property to Grandchild, and Child (Grandchild's parent) is deceased at the time. According to the predeceased ancestor exception, Grandchild will move up to the Child's generation so that the transfer will not be a direct skip subject to GST tax.

90-day rule. The rule has been modified to provide that if a descendant of the transferor dies within 90 days after the death of the transferor such descendant is treated as having predeceased the transferor for purposes of the predeceased ancestor exception to the extent that either the governing instrument or applicable local law so provides [Reg. Sec. 26.2612-1(a)(2)(i)]. This rule may avoid the tax being triggered by a transfer.

> **Example 2:** Dad dies. He leaves his estate to Child, but provides in his will that if Child does not survive him by at least 90 days, Child will be treated as predeceasing him, and Grandchild will take the estate. If Child dies one month after Mom dies, Grandchild will move up a generation and the transfer to the Grandchild will not result in a GST tax.

(a) **Direct Skips in Trust.** The following examples illustrate how a testamentary trust may constitute a direct skip.

¶2504

Example 3: Grandfather creates a trust under his will in the amount of $100,000 with income payable to his grandchild, Anna, until age 25, remainder to his grandchild, Billy. This testamentary trust constitutes a direct skip and is subject to GST tax. This particular trust is a skip person because all interests in the trust are held by skip persons [IRC Sec. 2613(a)(2)(A)].

Example 4: Grandfather creates a trust under his will in the amount of $100,000 with income payable to Grandchild, Anna, until age 25, remainder to Grandfather's adult child, Catherine. The entire value of the money in the trust is subject to GST tax (not just the actuarial value of the life estate) because the decedent left a life estate in the property to Anna, who was a skip person and a remainder interest to Catherine, who was a non-skip person. For purposes of the GST tax, the devise constituted a transfer to a deemed trust, and the trust was considered a skip person under IRC Sec. 2613(a)(2) and the transferee of a direct skip under the present interest rule of IRC Sec. 2652(c)(1)(A).[1] This trust is a skip person even though Catherine is a beneficiary assigned to only the first generation below Grandfather and therefore appears to give the trust a beneficiary who is not a skip person [IRC Sec. 2613(b)]. Catherine's future right to receive the corpus is ignored according to Sec. 2652(c)(1)(A), which provides that a person does not have an interest in trust for GST tax purposes if that person has only the future right to receive trust income or corpus. Because Catherine's interest is ignored, the trust is a skip person.

(b) Annual Exclusion Exception. Certain direct skips qualifying for the Section 2503(b) annual gift tax exclusion or the Section 2503(e) medical or education expense exclusion are exempt from gift tax as well as GST tax as discussed further at ¶ ¶ 2510 and 2511, respectively [IRC Sec. 2642(c)].

(c) Indirect Skips. An "indirect skip" is defined as any transfer of property (other than a direct skip) subject to the gift tax made to a GST trust [IRC Sec. 2632(c)(3)(A)]. A "GST trust" is defined as a trust that could have a GST with respect to the transferor *unless*:

1. The trust instrument provides that more than 25 percent of the trust corpus must be distributed to, or may be withdrawn by, one or more individuals who are nonskip persons (a) before the date that such individual attains age 46, (b) on or before one or more dates specified in the trust instrument that will occur before the date that such individual attains age 46, *or* (c) on the occurrence of an event that is reasonably expected to occur before the date that such individual attains age 46;

2. The trust instrument provides that more than 25 percent of the trust corpus must be distributed to, or may be withdrawn by, one or more individuals who are nonskip persons *and* who are living on the date of death of another person identified in the instrument (either by name or by class) who is more than 10 years older than such individuals;

---

[1] **¶2504** Technical Advice Memorandum 9105006.

¶2504

3. The trust instrument provides that, if one or more individuals who are nonskip persons die on or before a date or event described in (1) or (2) above, more than 25 percent of the trust corpus (a) must be distributed to the estate or estates of one or more of such individuals, *or* (b) is subject to a general power of appointment exercisable by one or more of such individuals;

4. Any portion of the trust would be included in the gross estate of a nonskip person (other than the transferor) if such person died immediately after the transfer;

5. The trust is a charitable lead annuity trust (per IRC Sec. 2642(e)(3)(A)), a charitable remainder annuity trust, or a charitable remainder unitrust (per IRC Sec. 664(d)); *or*

6. A gift tax charitable deduction was allowed under IRC Sec. 2522 with respect to the trust for the amount of an interest in the form of the right to receive annual payments of a fixed percentage of the net fair market value of the trust property (determined yearly) *and* which trust is required to pay principal to a nonskip person if such person is alive when the yearly payments for which the deduction was allowed terminate [IRC Sec. 2632(c)(3)(B)].

If an individual makes a lifetime indirect skip, any unused portion of the individual's GST tax exemption is automatically allocated to the property transferred to the extent necessary to make the inclusion ratio for such property equal to zero [IRC Sec. 2632(c)(1)]. If the amount of the indirect skip exceeds the unused portion, then the entire unused portion is allocated to the property transferred. For further discussion, see ¶ 2509.

Unused portion of GST tax exemption. For purposes of deemed allocations to lifetime indirect skips, the unused portion of an individual's GST tax exemption is the portion of the exemption that has not previously been (1) allocated by such individual, (2) treated as allocated under IRC Sec. 2632(b) with respect to a direct skip occurring during or before the calendar year in which the indirect skip is made, *or* (3) treated as allocated under IRC Sec. 2632(c)(1) with respect to a prior indirect skip.

> **Example 5:** A creates an irrevocable trust for the benefit of her lineal descendants. A has one child who is age 25. The trust instrument provides that (1) the trustee has discretion to distribute trust income to A during his lifetime, and (2) one-fifth of the trust corpus is to be distributed to child when he reaches age 45. At the child's death, the remaining corpus is to be distributed to the child's issue, *per stirpes*. The trust is a generation-skipping transfer trust because a generation-skipping transfer may occur with respect to Gertrude (child's issue) and the trust does not fall within any of the exceptions specified IRC Sec. 2632(c)(3)(B)(i)-(vi).

¶2505 TAXABLE TERMINATIONS

The termination of an interest held in trust, whether the termination occurs because of death, lapse of time, release of power, or otherwise, is a taxable termination if immediately after the termination all interests in the trust are held by skip persons [IRC Sec. 2612(a)].

Example 1: Dad creates a trust with income payable to Son for life, remainder to Grandchild. When the trust was created, it was not a GST taxable event, because the trust is not a skip person. It has a non-skip person (the son) as a beneficiary. However, when Son dies, a taxable termination occurs because Grandchild is a skip person who is a beneficiary of the trust.

The regulations specifically provide that a taxable termination will not occur if a transfer subject to federal estate or gift tax occurs with respect to the property held in the trust at the time of the termination and a new transferor is determined for the property [Reg. Sec. 26.2612-1(b)(1)(i)].

A taxable termination may not occur if the probability of a distribution to a skip person is so remote as to be negligible. This means that "it can be ascertained by actuarial standards that there is less than a 5 percent probability that the distribution will occur" [Reg. Sec. 26.2612-1(b)(1)(iii)].

(a) **Partial Termination.** If a distribution of a portion of trust property is made to a skip person because of a termination occurring on the death of a lineal descendant of the transferor, the termination is a taxable termination with respect to the distributed property [Reg. Sec. 26.2612-1(b)(2)].

Example 2: *Partial taxable termination.* Grandfather creates an irrevocable trust providing that trust income is to be paid to his two children, Alice and Bob, in such proportions as the trustee determines for their joint lives. When the first child dies, one-half of the trust principal is to be paid to Grandfather's then living grandchildren. The balance of the trust principal is to be paid to the grandchildren when Alice and Bob have both died. If Alice predeceases Bob, the distribution occurring on the termination of Alice's interest in the trust is a taxable termination and not a taxable distribution. It is a taxable termination because the distribution is a distribution of a portion of the trust that occurs as a result of the death of Alice, a lineal descendant of Grandfather. It is immaterial that a portion of the trust continues and that Bob, a person other than a skip person, thereafter holds an interest in the trust [Reg. Sec. 26.2612-1(f), Example (9)].

(b) **Simultaneous Termination.** A simultaneous termination of two or more interests creates only one taxable termination [Reg. Sec. 26.2612-1(b)(3)].

Example 3: *Simultaneous termination of interests of more than one beneficiary.* Grandfather establishes an irrevocable trust for the benefit of his child, grandchild, and great-grandchild. Under the terms of the trust, income and principal may be distributed to any or all of the living beneficiaries at the discretion of the trustee. Upon the death of the child, the trust property is to be distributed to the great-grandchild. If the child is survived by both the grandchild and the great-grandchild, both the child's and the grandchild's interests in the trust will terminate on the child's death. However, because both interests will terminate at the same time and as a result of one event, only one taxable termination occurs [Reg. Sec. 26.2612-1(f), Example (8)].

¶2506 TAXABLE DISTRIBUTIONS

A distribution from a trust is subject to GST tax if it is made to a skip person unless a direct skip or taxable termination also occurs on the distribution [IRC Sec. 2612(b)]. The distribution is taxable whether it comes from trust corpus or trust income. The trust beneficiaries can take an income tax deduction for GST tax imposed on an income distribution from a trust [IRC Sec. 164(a)(4)].

> **Example 1:** Grandfather creates a trust with income payable to Child for 10 years, corpus to Grandchild with power in the trustee to invade corpus for the benefit of Grandchild. The trustee exercises this power and distributes some trust corpus to Grandchild. The distribution of corpus constitutes a taxable distribution. Grandchild is a skip person and the distribution does not otherwise constitute a taxable termination or direct skip.

A transfer to a trust will be a taxable distribution only if the recipient trust itself (rather than its beneficiaries) is a skip person. In determining whether a trust is a skip person, trust interests disclaimed pursuant to qualified disclaimers described in IRC Sec. 2518 are not taken into account [Reg. Sec. 26.2612-1(e)(3)].

Note that both taxable terminations and direct skips take precedence over taxable distributions, in the sense that any transaction that constitutes either a taxable termination or a direct skip by definition is not a taxable distribution [IRC Sec. 2612(b)].

> **Example 2:** Grandfather creates a trust with income to Child for life, remainder to Grandchild. When Child dies, the trust is distributed to Grandchild. A taxable termination occurs when Child dies. Even though the distribution of corpus to Grandchild, a skip person, would otherwise constitute a taxable distribution, the transaction is treated only as a taxable termination. The distribution itself does not constitute a taxable event.

Taxable amount in case of taxable distribution. The taxable amount in the case of a taxable distribution is the value of the property received less tax-related expenses for determining the GST tax consequences [IRC Sec. 2621].

¶2507 GENERATION ASSIGNMENT WHERE INTERVENING PARENT IS DECEASED—THE PREDECEASED ANCESTOR EXCEPTION

The predeceased ancestor exception is a generation assignment rule in IRC Sec. 2651(e)(1) that may apply to determine whether the recipient of a transfer is a skip person and therefore if the transfer is subject to GST tax. The predeceased ancestor exception will apply if you make a gift to your grandchild and at the time you made the gift, the grandchild's parent is dead. In this situation, for purposes of generation assignment, the predeceased ancestor exception provides that your grandchild is considered to be your child rather than your grandchild. Similarly, your grandchild's children will be treated as your grandchildren rather than your great-grandchildren. Thus, if the recipient's parents died before the transfer, the generational assignment of a person (who otherwise is a skip person) is redetermined by disregarding the intervening generation [IRC Sec. 2651(e)(1); Reg. Sec. 26.2651-1(a)(2)]. The "predeceased ancestor exception" applies if both:

1. An individual is a descendant of a parent of the transfer (or the transferor's spouse or former spouse), and

2. The individual's parent who is the lineal descendant of the parent of the transferor (or the transferor's spouse or former spouse) died prior to the time the transferor is subject to estate or gift tax on the transfer from which an interest of that individual is established or derived.

An individual satisfying these criteria is treated as if the individual is a member of the generation that is one generation below the lower of either (a) the transferor's generation or (b) the generation assignment of the individual's youngest living lineal ancestor of the individual who is also a descendant of the parent of the transferor (or the transferor's spouse or former spouse).

> **Example 1:** Assume Grandfather makes a transfer to Grandson. Under the general rule, Grandson is a skip person because he is two generations below Grandfather. If Grandfather is Grandson's paternal grandfather and Grandson's father is deceased, the predeceased parent rule would assign Grandson to his father's generation. In that case, he would not be a skip person and this would not be a GST transfer. If Grandson's mother was deceased and his father was still living, however, Grandson would be a skip person and the predeceased ancestor exception would not apply.

> **Example 2:** Mom transfers property to Child and Grandchild. Child (i.e., Grandchild's parent) is deceased at the time of the transfer. According to the predeceased ancestor exception, Grandchild will move up to the Child's generation so that the Mom's transfer will not be a direct skip subject to GST tax.

When transferee's interest in property is established. For purposes of the predeceased ancestor exception, an individual's interest in property or a trust is established or derived when the transferor is subject to the estate or gift tax. If the property is subject to transfer tax on more than one occasion, then the individual's interest is considered established or derived on the earliest of these occasions. The interest of a remainder beneficiary of a trust for which a QTIP election under IRC Sec. 2523(f) or IRC Sec. 2056(b)(7) has been made, is deemed to have been established or derived, to the extent of the QTIP election, on the date when the value of the trust corpus is first subject to tax under IRC Sec. 2519 or IRC Sec. 2044. However, this rule does not apply to a trust to the extent that an election under IRC Sec. 2652(a)(3) (reverse QTIP election) has been made for the trust because, to the extent of a reverse QTIP election, the spouse who established the trust will remain the transferor of the trust for GST purposes [Reg. Sec. 26.2651-1(a)(3)].

¶2507

Ninety-day rule. For assigning individuals to generations for purposes of the GST tax, any individual who dies no later than 90 days after a transfer occurring because of the death of the transferor is treated as having predeceased the transferor [Reg. Sec. 26.2651-1(a)(2)(iii)]. A living person is not treated as having predeceased the transferor solely by reason of a provision of applicable local law; e.g., an individual who disclaims is not treated as a predeceased parent solely because state law treats a disclaimant as having predeceased the transferor for purposes of determining the disposition of the disclaimed property [Reg. Sec. 26.2651-1(a)(2)(iv)].

Predeceased ancestor exception and collateral heirs. The predeceased ancestor exception applies to transfers to collateral heirs, provided that the decedent has no living descendants at the time of the transfer [IRC Sec. 2651(e)(2)]. For example, the exception would apply to a transfer made by an individual (with no living lineal heirs) to a grandniece where the transferor's nephew or niece who is the parent of the grandniece is deceased at the time of the transfer. For the predeceased parent rule to apply to transfers to collateral heirs, the transferor must have no living lineal descendants at the time of the transfer [Reg. Sec. 26.2651-1(b)].

Application to taxable terminations and taxable distributions. The predeceased ancestor exception applies to taxable terminations and taxable distributions, provided the parent of the relevant beneficiary was deceased at the earliest time that the transfer (from which the beneficiary's interest in the property was established) was subject to estate or gift tax [IRC Sec. 2651(e)(1)]. For example, when a trust was established to pay an annuity to a charity for a term of years with a remainder interest granted to a grandson, the termination of the term for years would not be a taxable termination subject to the GST tax if the grandson's parent (who is the son or daughter of the transferor) is deceased at the time the trust was created and the transfer creating the trust was subject to estate or gift tax.

Adoptions. An individual will be treated as a member of the generation that is one generation below an adoptive parent for purposes of determining whether a transfer from the adoptive parent to the adopted individual is subject to GST tax if the individual is: (1) legally adopted by the adoptive parent; (2) a descendant of a parent of the adoptive parent or the adoptive parent's spouse; (3) under the age of 18 at the time of the adoption; and (4) not adopted primarily for GST tax-avoidance purposes [Reg. Sec. 26.2651-2(b)]. A legal adoption may create another generation assignment but will not substitute for the blood relationship.

> **Example 3:** T establishes an irrevocable trust, Trust, providing that trust income is to be paid to T's grandchild, GC, for 5 years. At the end of the 5-year period or on GC's prior death, Trust is to terminate and the principal is to be distributed to GC if GC is living or to GC's children if GC has died. At the time of the transfer, T's child, C, who is a parent of GC, is deceased. GC is treated as a member of the generation that is one generation below T's generation. As a result, GC is not a skip person and Trust is not a skip person. Therefore, the transfer to Trust is not a direct skip. Similarly, distributions to GC during the term of Trust and at the termination of Trust will not be GSTs [Reg. Sec. 26.2651-1(c), Example 1].

¶2507

Example 4: T transfers $100,000 to an irrevocable inter vivos trust that provides T with an annuity payable for four years or until T's prior death. When the trust terminates, the corpus is to be paid to T's grandchild, GC. The transfer is subject to gift tax and, at the time of the transfer, T's child, C, who is a parent of GC, is living. C dies two years later. In this case, C was alive at the time the transfer by T was subject to the GST tax. Therefore, the predeceased ancestor exception does not apply. When the trust subsequently terminates, the distribution to GC is a taxable termination that is subject to the GST tax to the extent the trust has an inclusion ratio greater than zero [Reg. Sec. 26.2651-1(c), Example 2].

Example 5: T dies testate and is survived by T's spouse, S, their children, C1 and C2, and C1's child, GC. Under the terms of T's will, a trust is established for the benefit of S and of T and S's descendants. Under the terms of the trust, all income is payable to S during S's lifetime and the trustee may distribute trust corpus for S's health, support and maintenance. At S's death, the corpus is to be distributed, outright, to C1 and C2. If either C1 or C2 has predeceased S, the deceased child's share of the corpus is to be distributed to that child's then-living descendants, *per stirpes*. The executor of T's estate makes the QTIP election with respect to the property but does not make the reverse QTIP election. C1 dies survived by S and GC. Two years later, S dies, and the trust terminates. The full fair market value of the trust is includible in S's gross estate and S becomes the transferor of the trust. GC's interest is considered established or derived at S's death, and because C1 is deceased at that time, GC is treated as a member of the generation that is one generation below the generation of the transferor, S. As a result, GC is not a skip person and the transfer to GC is not a direct skip [Reg. Sec. 26.2651-1(c), Example 3].

Example 6: T establishes an irrevocable trust providing that trust income is to be paid to T's grandniece, GN, for 5 years or until GN's prior death. At the end of the 5-year period or on GN's prior death, the trust is to terminate and the principal is to be distributed to GN if living, or if GN has died, to GN's then-living descendants, *per stirpes*. S is a sibling of T and the parent of N. N is the parent of GN. At the time of the transfer, T has no living lineal descendant, S is living, N is deceased, and the transfer is subject to gift tax. GN is treated as a member of the generation that is one generation below T's generation because S, GN's youngest living lineal ancestor who is also a descendant of T's parent, is in T's generation. As a result, GN is not a skip person and the transfer to the trust is not a direct skip. In addition, distributions to GN during the term of the trust and at the termination of the trust will not be GSTs [Reg. Sec. 26.2651-1(c), Example 5].

Example 7: T transfers $50,000 to a great-grandniece, GGN, who is the great-grandchild of B, a brother of T. At the time of the transfer, T has no living lineal descendants and B's grandchild, GN, who is a parent of GGN and a child of B's living child, N, is deceased. GGN will be treated as a member of the generation that is one generation below the lower of T's generation or the generation assignment of GGN's youngest living lineal ancestor who is also a descendant of the parent of the transferor. In this case, N is GGN's youngest living lineal ancestor who is also a descendant of the parent of T. Because N's generation assignment is lower than T's generation, GGN will be treated as a member of the generation that is one generation below N's generation assignment (i.e., GGN will be treated as a member of her parent's generation). As a result, GGN remains a skip person and the transfer to GGN is a direct skip [Reg. Sec. 26.2651-1(c), Example 6].

Example 8: T has a child, C. C and C's spouse, S, have a 20-year-old child, GC. C dies and S subsequently marries S2. S2 legally adopts GC. T transfers $100,000 to GC. GC is assigned to the generation that is two generations below T. However, since GC's parent, C, is deceased at the time of the transfer, GC will be treated as a member of the generation that is one generation below T. As a result, GC is not a skip person and the transfer to GC is not a direct skip [Reg. Sec. 26.2651-1(c), Example 7].

¶2508 TAXABLE AMOUNT

The amount of GST tax that is owed is determined by multiplying the "taxable amount" by the "applicable rate" [IRC Sec. 2602]. The "taxable amount" and who is responsible for paying the tax will change depending on whether the transfer is a direct skip, taxable distribution or taxable termination [IRC Sec. 2603].

Applicable rate. For GST purposes, the term "applicable rate" means the product of the maximum federal estate tax rate and the "inclusion ratio" that applies to the transfer [IRC Sec. 2641(a); see ¶ 2513].

(a) **Direct Skips.** The taxable amount in the case of a direct skip will be the value of the property received by the transferee [IRC Sec. 2623]. The donor or the transferor will be liable for the tax unless the direct skip is made from a trust, in which case the trustee will be liable for the tax [IRC Secs. 2603(a)(3), 2603(a)(2)].

The direct skip is the most economical of the GST transfers because, unlike taxable distributions and taxable terminations, direct skips do not include the GST tax in their tax base. The tax due on a direct skip is imposed on a tax-exclusive basis. This means that the tax is imposed only on the amount actually received. The GST tax is not part of the tax base. When the transferor pays the GST tax, the GST tax is treated as an additional gift for gift tax purposes [IRC Sec. 2515].

Example 1: Grandfather gives $2 million to Grandson in a transfer that constitutes a direct skip. Grandfather owes GST tax in the amount of $800,000 on the transfer in 2014 (40 percent × $2 million) because no GST exemption was allocated to the gift. Grandfather's payment of GST tax on the transfer is treated as an additional gift for gift tax purposes. As a result, the amount of his gift to Grandson equals $2,800,000 ($800,000 plus $2 million). Grandfather must pay the gift tax on this amount.

¶2508

(b) Taxable Terminations. The taxable amount in the case of a taxable termination will be the value of all property involved in the taxable termination, reduced by any deductions for expenses, indebtedness, and taxes [IRC Sec. 2622].

> **Example 2:** Grandfather creates a trust with $200,000 in corporate stock, with income to Son for life, remainder to Grandchild. When Son dies the trust property passing to Grandchild has a value of $500,000. The trustee's commissions are $10,000. The amount of the taxable termination is $490,000, or $500,000 reduced by the $10,000 commissions.

The trustee of the trust that produced the taxable termination will be liable for the tax [IRC Sec. 2603(a)(2)]. The GST tax on a taxable termination is determined by multiplying the taxable amount times the applicable rate [IRC Sec. 2602]. But the taxable amount is computed differently from the way in which you determine the taxable amount on a direct skip. Taxable terminations are taxed on a tax-inclusive basis. This means that you compute the GST tax by including in the tax base the property used to pay the tax. This makes the taxable termination more expensive than the direct skip.

> **Example 3:** Grandfather established a trust which paid income to Son until he reached age 50 and then the trust was to terminate with distribution to Grandchild. Grandfather allocated no GST exemption to the transfer of $500,000 into the trust. When Son reached age 50, the trust assets were worth $3 million, net of any indebtedness or expenses. The GST tax imposed in this taxable termination is $1,200,000 in 2014 ($3 million × 40 percent). The trustee of the trust is liable for the tax. Grandchild only received $1,800,000 after the GST tax was paid.

(c) Alternate Valuation Election Allowed. An alternate valuation election is permitted in the case of taxable termination occurring at death [IRC Sec. 2624(c)]. This election will enable the executor to value the trust property six months after death in accordance with IRC Sec. 2032.

(d) Taxable Distributions. The taxable amount in the case of a taxable distribution will be the value of the property received by the transferee reduced by any expenses incurred by the transferee in connection with the determination, collection, or refund of the GST tax [IRC Sec. 2621]. The recipient of the wealth or the transferee will be liable for the tax [IRC Sec. 2603(a)(1)]. If the trustee pays the GST tax (including penalties and interest) from the distributing trust, the payment of the tax will constitute an additional taxable distribution and is treated as having been made on the last day of the calendar year in which the original taxable distribution was made [IRC Sec. 2621(b); Reg. Sec. 26.2612-1(c)].

Like the taxable termination, the GST tax is imposed on a tax-inclusive basis. This means that the taxable amount includes the GST tax. As a result you compute the GST tax by including in the tax base the property used to pay the tax.

> **Example 4:** Grandfather established a trust that paid income and principal at the trustee's discretion to Child and then Grandson for 20 years and then

terminated in a final distribution to Grandson. Grandfather allocated no GST exemption to the transfer of $500,000 into the trust. In 2014, the trustee distributes $2 million to Grandson in a taxable distribution. Grandson is liable for the $800,000 GST tax (40 percent × $2 million) on the taxable distribution and he receives only $1,200,000 of the $2 million left for him by Grandfather.

¶2509 THE GST TAX EXEMPTION

Each person may escape GST tax on a portion of his generation-skipping transfers by taking advantage of the irrevocable GST exemption [IRC Sec. 2631(a)]. Judicious allocation of each person's GST tax exemption will also insulate from the GST tax all future appreciation and accumulated income earned by that money or property. Every individual is allowed a lifetime GST tax exemption equal to the "basic exclusion amount" in the calendar year of the allocation which is $5,340,000 in 2014 [IRC Sec. 2631(a)]. The GST exemption may be allocated by the individual or his or her executor to the transfer any property if the individual is the transferor [IRC Sec. 2631(a)]. Once made, the allocation of GST exemption is irrevocable [IRC Sec. 2631(b)]. The GST tax is assessed at the highest transfer tax rate which is 40 percent in 2014. The tax is assessed in addition to any estate or gift tax that applies to the transfer.

(a) Amount of GST Exemption. The GST tax exemption for generation-skipping transfers made in 2014 is $5,340,000 (increased from $5,250,000 in 2013). The following chart illustrates the GST tax exemption amounts in effect from 1999-2014.

GST Tax Exemption Amounts

For Transfers Made	Exemption
1999	1,010,000
2000	1,030,000
2001	1,060,000
2002	1,100,000
2003	1,120,000
2004–2005	1,500,000
2006–2008	2,000,000
2009	3,500,000
2010–2011	5,000,000
2012	5,120,000
2013	5,250,000
2014	5,340,000

(b) When to Allocate GST Exemption. The GST tax may only be allocated by a transferor or the transferor's executor to property transferred at any time from the date of the transfer through the due date for filing an estate tax return (with extensions), regardless of whether or not an estate tax return is required to be filed. The election is irrevocable [IRC Sec. 2632(a)(1); Reg. Sec. 26.2632-1(a)]. This grace period affords the executor at least 9 months, and up to 15 months if the maximum filing extension is granted, to allocate the GST exemption.

> **Example 1:** Grandfather transferred property worth $2 million to a trust and allocated $2 million of his GST tax exemption to the trust. That year, the value of the trust property increased to $5 million, at which time, a taxable termination occurred. Even though the trust property had increased in value, the entire $5 million of property is exempt from the GST tax on the taxable termination. If Grandfather had not made the $2 million allocation when he transferred the property, a late allocation could be made in the current year if Grandfather had any GST tax exemption available to allocate. Assuming Grandfather had $3 million of GST tax exemption remaining and made a late allocation, no GST tax would result [($5 million − $5 million GST tax exemption) × maximum estate tax rate] at the taxable termination.

An allocation of GST exemption during the transferor's lifetime can be made on a gift tax return (Form 709) filed any time prior to the due date of the transferor's estate tax return. A Form 709 is timely filed if it is filed on or before the date required for reporting the transfer if it were a taxable gift, including any extensions to file actually granted (the due date). The automatic allocation of GST exemption (or the election to prevent the allocation, if made) is irrevocable after the due date. An automatic allocation of GST exemption is effective as of the date of the transfer to which it relates. A Form 709 need not be filed to report an automatic allocation [Reg. Sec. 26.2632-1(b)(ii)].

The regulations provide that if property is held in trust, the allocation of GST exemption is made to the entire trust rather than to specific trust assets. If a transfer is a direct skip to a trust, the allocation of GST exemption to the transferred property is also treated as an allocation of GST exemption to the trust for purposes of future GSTs with respect to the trust by the same transferor [Reg. Sec. 26.2632-1(a)].

If the allocation is made on a Form 709 filed on or before the due date, the allocation is deemed to be timely filed and the values used in determining the applicable fraction and the resulting inclusion ratio are the values on the date of the transfer [IRC Sec. 2642(b)(1); Reg. Secs. 26.2632-1(b)(2)(ii), 26.2642-2(a)]. In such a case, the allocation is effective as of the date of the transfer.

(c) Requirements for Affirmative Allocation of GST Exemption. The regulations provide that an affirmative allocation of GST exemption must (i) clearly identify the trust to which the allocation is being made, (ii) disclose the amount of GST exemption allocated to it, and (3) if the allocation is late or if an inclusion ratio other than zero is claimed, list the value of the trust principal at the time of the allocation. The allocation should also state the inclusion ratio of the trust after the allocation Reg. Sec. 26.2632-1(b)(4)(i)].

"Notice of Allocation." In order for a transferor to make an effective allocation of GST exemption, Form 709 provides that a "Notice of Allocation" must be prepared for each trust or other transfer to which the transferor intends to allocate GST exemption. That statement should be attached to the Form 709 and must contain the following:

¶2509

1. Clear identification of the trust, including the trust's EIN, if known;
2. If a late allocation, the year the transfer was reported on Form 709;
3. The value of the trust assets at the effective date of the allocation;
4. The amount of the GST exemption allocated to each gift (or a statement that you are allocating exemption by means of a formula such as "an amount necessary to produce an inclusion ratio of zero"); and
5. The inclusion ratio of the trust after the allocation.

A timely allocation may be amended only if the amended allocation is also timely and clearly identifies the transfer and the nature and extent of the modification. Late allocations are effective on the date when the Form 709 is filed. If it is unclear whether an allocation on Form 709 is late or timely, the allocation takes place in the following order: (1) to any transfer to the trust disclosed on the return as to which the return is a timely return, (2) as a late allocation, (3) to any transfer to the trust not disclosed on the return as to which the return would be timely [Reg. Sec. 26.2632-1(b)(2)(ii)].

Property that is the subject of a late allocation of GST exemption must be valued as of the first day of the month during which the late allocate is made [Reg. Sec. 26.2642-2(a)(2)].

(d) Who Allocates the GST Tax Exemption. In general, only the transferor or his or her executor has the power to allocate GST tax exemption to any property [IRC Sec. 2632(a)(1); Reg. Sec. 26.2632-1(a)]. This limitation is important because a change in the identity of the transferor as discussed in ¶ 2502 will likewise change the persons who can allocate GST tax exemption. After the transferor has changed, any previous allocation of GST tax exemption becomes obsolete and only the new transferor or the new transferor's executor can allocate GST tax exemption to the transfer.

> **Example 2:** Husband transfers $1 million to a trust providing that all the net trust income is to be paid to his spouse for her lifetime and upon her death it should pass to his grandchildren. He elects underIRC Sec. 2523(f) to treat the transfer as a transfer of qualified terminable interest property and he does not make a reverse QTIP election under IRC Sec. 2652(a)(3). When the spouse dies, the trust property is included in her gross estate under IRC Sec. 2044 and she becomes the transferor at the time of her death. It is up to her or her spouse to allocate some or all of her GST tax exemption to the trust. If the husband had previously allocated GST tax exemption to this trust, the benefits of the allocation are now lost.

Automatic (deemed) GST exemption allocation. In addition to the transferor, the Internal Revenue Code has multiple sets of automatic allocation rules that automatically allocate the taxpayer's GST exemption to transfers made by the taxpayer without any additional action by the taxpayer. These rules are discussed in detail in ¶ 2509(e) (automatic allocation to direct skips) and ¶ 2509(f) (automatic allocation to indirect skips). Sometimes as a result of these automatic allocation rules, GST exemption will be allocated when the taxpayer would not have wanted it to be allocated. Taxpayers must be therefore be aware of the automatic GST allocation rules and how to elect out of the automatic allocations as discussed in ¶ 2509(f).

¶2509

(e) How the GST Tax Allocation Is Made. The GST tax exemption is cumulative over life and at death. If a taxpayer fails to use up all of the GST tax exemption he is entitled to while still alive, it can be allocated by the executor of the decedent's estate to transfers taking place at the taxpayer's death. If the GST tax exemption is not allocated during life or at death, it expires and is unavailable to anyone else. For discussion of securing an extension of time to allocate GST exemption, see ¶ 2509(h).

Allocation is irrevocable—but not until after due date. An allocation of GST tax exemption by an individual or by the executor of the individual's estate is irrevocable [IRC Sec. 2631(b)]. However, an allocation by an individual does not become irrevocable until after the due date (including any extensions for filing that have been actually granted) of the IRS Form 709, "United States Gift and Generation-Skipping Transfer Tax Return" [Reg. Sec. 26.2632-1(a)]. As a result, an allocation on a timely filed Form 709, "United States Gift and Generation-Skipping Transfer Tax Return" may be amended if the amended allocation is also timely and identifies the transfer and nature and extent of the modification [Reg. Sec. 26.2632-1(b)(2)(iii), Example (1)].

> **Example 3:** *Modification of allocation of GST tax exemption.* Grandfather transfers $100,000 to an irrevocable generation-skipping trust on December 1, 2013. The transfer to the trust is not a direct skip. The date prescribed for filing the gift tax return reporting the taxable gift is April 15, 2014. On February 10, 2014, Grandfather files a Form 709 allocating $50,000 of GST exemption to the trust. On April 10 of the same year, he files an amended Form 709 allocating $100,000 of GST exemption to the trust in a manner that clearly indicates the intention to modify and supersede the prior allocation with respect to the 2013 transfer. The allocation made on the April 10 return supersedes the prior allocation because it is made on a timely filed Form 709 that clearly identifies the trust and the nature and extent of the modification of GST exemption allocation. The allocation of $100,000 of GST exemption to the trust is effective as of December 1, 2013. The result would be the same if the amended Form 709 decreased the amount of the GST exemption allocated to the trust [Reg. Sec. 26.2632-1(b)(4)(iii), Example (1)].

> **Example 4:** *Ineffective modification.* The facts are the same as in the example above, except on July 10, 2014, the grandfather files a Form 709 attempting to reduce the earlier allocation. The return is not a timely filed return. The $100,000 GST exemption allocated to the trust, as amended on April 10, 2014, remains in effect because an allocation, once made, is irrevocable and may not be modified after the last date on which a timely filed Form 709 can be filed [Reg. Sec. 26.2632-1(b)(4)(iii), Example (2)].

(f) Automatic (Deemed) Allocation to Lifetime Direct Skips. If a direct skip occurs during the transferor's lifetime, any of the transferor's not previously allocated (unused) GST tax exemption will automatically be allocated to the transferred property (but not in excess of the fair-market value of the property on the date of the

¶2509

transfer) to the extent necessary to make the inclusion rate zero [IRC Sec. 2632(b)(1); Reg. Sec. 26.2632-1(b)].

Electing out of deemed allocation to direct skips. The transferor can prevent the automatic allocation of GST tax exemption by describing on a timely filed Form 709, "U.S. Gift (and Generation-Skipping Transfer) Tax Return," the transfer and the extent to which the automatic allocation should not apply [IRC Sec. 2632(b)(3)]. In addition, a timely filed Form 709 accompanied by payment of the GST tax (as shown on the return with respect to the direct skip) is sufficient to prevent an automatic allocation of GST exemption with respect to the transferred property [Reg. Sec. 26.2632-1(b)].

> **Example 5:** On December 1, 2013, T transfers $50,000 to an irrevocable GST Trust. The transfer to the trust is not a direct skip. On April 30, 2014, T and T's spouse, S, each file an initial gift tax return for 2013, on which they consent to have the gift treated as if one-half had been made by each. In spite of being made on a late-filed gift tax return for 2013, the election is valid because neither spouse had filed a timely gift tax return for that year. Previously, neither T nor S filed a timely gift tax return electing out of the automatic allocation rules. As a result of the gift-splitting election, which is retroactive to the date of T's transfer, T and S are each treated as the transferor of one-half of the property transferred in the indirect skip. Thus, $25,000 of T's unused GST exemption and $25,000 of S's unused GST exemption is automatically allocated to the trust. Both allocations are effective on and after the date that T made the transfer. The result would be the same if T's transfer constituted a direct skip subject to the automatic allocation rules [Reg. Sec. 26.2632-1(b)(2)(iii), Ex. 5].

No deemed allocation to nontaxable gifts. No deemed allocation of GST exemption will occur with respect to a nontaxable gift because the deemed allocations will be made only to the extent necessary to reduce the inclusion ratio of the transfer to zero. Since nontaxable gifts are automatically assigned an inclusion ratio of zero, they will not be the subject of deemed allocations. Nontaxable gifts include annual exclusion gifts under IRC Sec. 2503(b) as well as gifts for medical and educational expenses that are excluded from gift tax under IRC Sec. 2503(e) [IRC Sec. 2642(c)(3)].

> **Example 6:** Grandma transfers $250,000 to her grandchild in 2014 and has made no other transfers to the grandchild that year. The first $14,000 of the transfer qualifies for the annual exclusion, is a nontaxable gift, and therefore has a zero inclusion ratio. Therefore GST exemption would only be automatically allocated to the balance of the transfer which is $236,000.

(g) Automatic (Deemed) Allocation to Indirect Skips. If any individual makes an indirect skip during his or her lifetime, any unused portion of such individual's GST exemption will be automatically allocated to the property transferred to the extent necessary to make the inclusion ratio for such property zero. If the amount of the indirect skip exceeds such unused portion, the entire unused portion will be allocated to the property transferred [IRC Sec. 2632(c)(1)]. The deemed GST allocation provisions under IRC Sec. 2632(c) were made permanent effective for estates of decedents dying, gifts made, or generation-skipping transfers after December 31, 2012 by the American Taxpayer Relief Act of 2012.

The unused portion of an individual's GST tax exemption is the portion of the exemption that has not previously been: (1) allocated by such individual; (2) treated as allocated under IRC Sec. 2632(b) with respect to a direct skip occurring during or before the calendar year in which the indirect skip is made; or (3) treated as allocated under IRC Sec. 2632(c)(1) with respect to a prior indirect skip [IRC Sec. 2632(b)(2)]. This rule is similar to one that automatically allocates GST tax exemption to lifetime direct skips [IRC Sec. 2632(b)]. Those that do not want the automatic allocation to apply have the opportunity to elect out [IRC Sec. 2632(c)]. Taxpayers with irrevocable life insurance trusts (ILITs) already in place will benefit from extension of the automatic allocation rule to indirect skips because any future contributions to the ILIT could be insulated from tax by the GST tax exemption.

> ▶ **PLANNING POINTER:** As a result of this rule, allocation of the exemption will be automatic upon the making of the transfer, *unless* the transferor affirmatively *opts out* on that year's gift tax return. Here is what will happen if you fail to opt out: You are 40 years old and each year for the next 30 years you pay insurance premiums to fund your life insurance trust. After 20 years, your premiums total $500,000. This $500,000 will reduce your lifetime GST exemption. If you want to establish a trust for your grandchildren when you are 70 years old, your ability to apply GST exemption to the trust is reduced by $500,000.

An indirect skip is defined as any transfer of property (that is not a direct skip) subject to the gift tax that is made to a GST trust [IRC Sec. 2632(c)(3)(A)]. A GST trust is a trust that could have a generation-skipping transfer with respect to the transferor. The rule has six exceptions that will exclude a trust from being a GST trust. Therefore, an automatic allocation will not occur in the following six situations because the trusts in each situation fail to qualify as GST trusts:

1. The trust provides that more than 25 percent of the trust corpus must be distributed to, or may be withdrawn by, one or more individuals who are non-skip persons (a) before the date that the individual attains age 46, (b) on or before one or more dates specified in the trust instrument that will occur before the date that such individual attains age 46, or (c) upon the occurrence of an event that, in accordance with regulations prescribed by the Treasury Secretary, may reasonably be expected to occur before the date that such individual attains age 46;

2. The trust provides that more than 25 percent of the trust corpus must be distributed to, or may be withdrawn by, one or more individuals who are non-skip persons and who are living on the date of death of another person identified in the instrument (by name or by class) who is more than 10 years older than such individuals;

3. The trust provides that, if one or more individuals who are non-skip persons die on or before a date or event described in clause (1) or (2), more than 25 percent of the trust corpus either must be distributed to the estate or estates of one or more of such individuals or is subject to a general power of appointment exercisable by one or more of such individuals;

¶2509

4. If any portion of the trust would be included in the gross estate of a non-skip person (other than the transferor) if such person died immediately after the transfer;

5. The trust is a charitable lead annuity trust, a charitable remainder annuity trust or a charitable remainder unitrust; or

6. A gift tax charitable deduction was allowed under IRC Sec. 2522 with respect to the trust for the amount of an interest in the form of the right to receive annual payments of a fixed percentage of the net fair market value of the trust property (determined yearly) *and* which trust is required to pay principal to a nonskip person if such person is alive when the yearly payments for which the deduction was allowed terminate [IRC Sec. 2632(c)(3)(B)].

> **Example 7:** A creates an irrevocable trust for the benefit of her lineal descendants. A funds the trust with stock in 2014. A has one child, C. The trust instrument provides that the trustee has discretion to distribute trust income or principal to C during his lifetime. At A's death, the remaining corpus is to be distributed to A's issue, *per stirpes*. The trust is a "GST trust" because a GST may occur with respect to A and the trust does not fall within any of the exceptions specified in (1)–(6) above [IRC Sec. 2632(c)(3)(B)].

For purposes of determining whether a trust is a "GST trust," the value of transferred property is not considered to be includible in the gross estate of a non-skip person or subject to a right of withdrawal by reason of such person holding a right to withdraw an amount that does not exceed the IRC Sec. 2503(b) gift tax annual exclusion amount ($14,000 in 2014) with respect to any transferor. In addition, it is assumed that powers of appointment held by non-skip persons will not be exercised [IRC Sec. 2632(c)(3)(B)]. In addition, an indirect skip to which IRC Sec. 2642(f) applies is deemed to have been made only at the close of the estate tax inclusion period (ETIP). The value of such transfer is the fair market value of the trust property at the close of the ETIP [IRC Sec. 2632(c)(4)].

Electing out of deemed allocation to indirect skips. An individual may opt out of the deemed allocation rule for lifetime indirect skips. An individual may elect to have IRC Sec. 2632(c) not apply to

1. An indirect skip or

2. Any or all transfers made by the individual to a particular trust.

In addition, an individual may elect to treat any trust as a "GST trust" for purposes of IRC Sec. 2632(c) with respect to any and all transfers made by the individual to the trust [IRC Sec. 2632(c)(5)(A); see Reg. Sec. 26.2632-1(b)(3)].

An election to have IRC Sec. 2632(c) not apply to an indirect skip is deemed to be timely if it is filed on a timely filed gift tax return for the calendar year in which the transfer was made or deemed to have been made under IRC Sec. 2632(c)(4) (i.e., the close of the ETIP) [IRC Sec. 2632(c)(5)(B)(i)]. For other categories of elections permitted by IRC Sec. 2632(c)(5)(A), the election may be made on a timely filed gift tax return for the calendar year for which the election is to become effective [IRC Sec. 2632(c)(5)(B)(ii)].

¶2509

Example 8: A decides that he does not want any of his GST exemption allocated to the transfer to the trust described in the example above. On his 2014 Form 709, "U.S. Gift (and Generation-Skipping Transfer) Tax Return," A elects to have IRC Sec. 2632(c) not apply to the transfer of the stock.

Procedure for electing out. The transferor must attach an "election out" statement to a Form 709 filed on or before the due date for timely filing of the Form 709 for the calendar year in which the first transfer to be covered by the election out was made [Reg. Sec. 26.2632-1(b)(2)(iii)(C)] (special rules apply in the case of a transfer subject to an ETIP). The election out statement must identify the trust and specifically must provide that the transferor is electing out of the automatic allocation of GST exemption with respect to the described transfer(s) [Reg. Sec. 26.2632-1(b)(2)(iii)(B)]. In addition, the current-year transfers and/or future transfers to which the election out is to apply must be specifically described or otherwise identified.

A transferor may terminate an election out made on a Form 709 for a prior year, to the extent that the election out applied to future transfers or to a transfer subject to an ETIP. The transferor must attach a "termination" statement to a Form 709 filed on or before the due date of the Form 709 for the calendar year in which is made the first transfer to which the election out is not to apply. The termination statement must identify the trust, describe the prior election out that is being terminated, specifically provide that the prior election out is being terminated, and either describe the extent to which the prior election out is being terminated or describe any current-year transfers to which the election out is not to apply [Reg. Sec. 26.2632-1(b)(2)(iii)(E)].

Example 9: On November 15, 2013, T transfers $100,000 to an irrevocable GST trust. The transfer to the trust is not a direct skip. The date prescribed for filing the gift tax return reporting the taxable gift is April 15, 2014. On February 10, 2014, T files a Form 709 on which T properly elects out of the automatic allocation rules with respect to that transfer. On December 1, 2014, T files a Form 709 and allocates $50,000 to the trust. The allocation is effective as of December 1, 2014 [Reg. Sec. 26.2632-1(b)(4)(iii), Example 3].

Example 10: T transfers $100,000 to an irrevocable GST trust on December 1, 2013, in a transfer that is not a direct skip. On April 15, 2014, T files a Form 709 on which T properly elects out of the automatic allocation rules with respect to the entire transfer and T does not make an allocation of any GST exemption on the Form 709. On September 1, 2014, the trustee makes a taxable distribution from the trust to T's grandchild in the amount of $30,000. Immediately prior to the distribution, the value of the trust assets was $150,000. On the same date, T allocates GST exemption to the trust in the amount of $50,000. The allocation of GST exemption on the date of the transfer is treated as preceding in point of time the taxable distribution. At the time of the GST, the trust has an inclusion ratio of .6667 (1 − (50,000/150,000)) [Reg. Sec. 26.2632-1(b)(4)(iii), Example 4].

Extension of time to make election out of automatic allocation of GST exemption. The IRS will grant an extension of time to elect out of the automatic allocation of GST exemption if the request satisfies the requirements of IRC Sec. 2642(g) and Reg. Sec.

310.9100-3.[1] Requests for relief under IRC Sec. 2642(g)(1) will be granted when the taxpayer provides evidence to establish to the satisfaction of the IRS that the taxpayer acted reasonably and in good faith, and that the grant of relief will not prejudice the government's interests [Reg. Sec. 301.9100-3; Prop. Reg. Sec. 26.2642-7(d)(1)]. Reg. Sec. 301.9100-3(b)(1)(v) provides that a taxpayer is deemed to have acted reasonably and in good faith if the taxpayer reasonably relied on a qualified tax professional, including a tax professional employed by the taxpayer, and the tax professional failed to make, or advise the taxpayer to make, the election out of automatic allocation.

(h) Retroactive Allocation of Unused GST Tax Exemption. An individual may allocate his unused GST tax exemption to any previous transfer(s) made to a trust, on a chronological basis [IRC Sec. 2632(d)]. The retroactive GST allocation provisions under IRC Sec. 2632(d) were made permanent effective for estates of decedents dying, gifts made, or generation-skipping transfers after December 31, 2012 by the American Taxpayer Relief Act of 2012. This rule is designed to protect taxpayers when there is an "unnatural order of death" (such as when the second generation predeceases the first generation transferor) by allowing a transferor to allocate GST tax exemption retroactively to the date of a prior transfer to a trust.

Availability of retroactive allocation. An individual may make a retroactive allocation of GST tax exemption if:

1. A non-skip person has an interest or a future interest in a trust to which any transfer has been made;

2. Such person is a lineal descendant of a grandparent of the transferor or of a grandparent of the transferor's spouse or former spouse and such person is assigned to a generation below the generation assignment of the transferor; and

3. Such person predeceases the transferor.

[IRC Sec. 2632(d)(1)]

Future interest. A person has a "future interest" in a trust if the trust permits income or corpus to be paid to such person on a future date or dates [IRC Sec. 2632(d)(3)].

Retroactive allocation made in calendar year within which non-skip person's death occurs. If a transferor's retroactive allocation is made on a gift tax return (Form 709) that is filed on or before the date prescribed for gifts made within the calendar year within which the non-skip person's death occurred, then:

1. The value of such transfer(s) is determined as if such allocation had been made on a timely filed gift tax return (Form 709) for each calendar year within which each transfer was made;

2. Such allocation is effective immediately before the skip-person's death; and

3. The amount of the transferor's unused GST tax exemption that is available for allocation is determined immediately before the non-skip person's death. [IRC Sec. 2632(d)(2)]

---

[1] **¶2509** Ltr. Ruls. 201307004, 201314032 and 201345029.

Example 11: Father created an irrevocable trust for the primary benefit of Son, who was age 21. The trust instrument provided that (1) the trustee has discretion to distribute trust income to Son during his lifetime and (2) one-third of the trust corpus is to be distributed to Son at age 27, one-half of the remaining corpus at age 30, and the remainder of the corpus at age 35 (which will terminate the trust). If Son dies before reaching age 35, the corpus is to be distributed in equal shares to Son's children. Father made a transfer to the trust but did not allocate any of his GST tax exemption to the transfers on the gift tax returns reporting the transfers. Before reaching age 27, Son died, thus resulting in a taxable termination for GST tax purposes. Father may retroactively allocate unused GST tax exemption to the prior transfer to the trust and thereby exempt the trust property transferred to Son's children from the application of the GST tax.

(i) Extension of Time to Make Allocation of GST Exemptions. A

taxpayer can submit a ruling request in order to request that the IRS grant the taxpayer an extension of time to make an allocation of GST exemption. In determining whether to grant relief, the IRS is directed to take into account "all relevant circumstances," such as evidence of intent contained in the trust instrument or instrument of transfer [IRC Sec. 2642(g)(1)(B)].

In Notice 2001-50,[2] the IRS provided guidance regarding requests for the extensions of time covered by IRC Sec. 2642(g) and provided that taxpayers may seek an extension of time to allocate GST exemption to lifetime transfers and transfers at death, elect out of the automatic allocation rules, and elect to treat any trust as a GST trust, via the private letter ruling process under the provisions of Reg. Sec. 301.9100-3. In general, relief will be granted if the taxpayer establishes that he or she acted reasonably and in good faith and that the grant of relief will not prejudice the interests of the government.[3] If relief is granted and the allocation is made, the amount of GST exemption necessary to reduce the inclusion ratio to zero is based on the value of the property on the date of the transfer and the allocation is effective as of the date of the transfer.

In the private ruling request, the transferor or executor must submit a detailed affidavit describing the events that led to the failure to timely allocate GST exemption to a transfer or the failure to timely elect, and the events that led to the discovery of the failure. In addition, the transferor or executor must submit detailed affidavits from individuals who have knowledge or information about the events that led to the failure to allocate GST exemption or to elect, and/or to the discovery of the failure.

Substantial compliance. An allocation of GST exemption that demonstrated an intent to have the lowest possible inclusion ratio with respect to a transfer to a trust will be deemed to be an allocation of so much of the transferor's unused GST exemption as produces the lowest possible inclusion ratio [IRC Sec. 2642(g)(2)]. In determining whether there has been substantial compliance, "all relevant circumstances" are to be

---

[2] Notice 2001-50, 2001-2 CB 189.

[3] Ltr. Ruls. 201314017, 201314018, 201321002 and 201351007.

¶2509

considered, including evidence of intent contained in the trust instrument or instrument of transfer.[4]

The provisions providing relief from late GST allocations and elections under IRC Sec. 2642(g)(1), as well as the provision pertaining to substantial compliance in IRC Sec. 2642(g)(2) were made permanent by the American Taxpayer Relief Act of 2012.

Proposed regulations. In Proposed Regulations, the IRS has identified the standards that will apply in determining whether to grant a transferor or a transferor's estate an extension of time under IRC Sec. 2642(g)(1) to make a GST exemption allocation in the following situations:

1. To allocate GST exemption to a transfer;

2. To elect under IRC Sec. 2632(b)(3) not to have the deemed allocation of GST exemption apply to a direct skip;

3. To elect under IRC Sec. 2632(c)(5)(A)(i) not to have the deemed allocation of GST exemption apply to an indirect skip or transfers made to a particular trust; and

4. To elect under IRC Sec. 2632(C)(5)(A)(ii) to treat any trust as a GST trust. [Prop. Reg. Sec. 26.2642-7(a)]

When allocation is effective.

- If an extension of time to allocate GST exemption is granted, the allocation of GST exemption will be considered effective as of the date of the transfer, and the value of the property will determine the amount of GST exemption to be allocated.

- If an extension of time to elect out of the automatic allocation of GST exemption is granted, the election will be considered effective as of the date of the transfer.

- If an extension of time to elect to treat any trust as a GST trust is granted, the election will be considered effective as of the date of the first (or each) transfer covered by that election. [Prop. Reg. Sec. 26.2642-7(b)]

The amount of GST exemption that may be allocated to a transfer pursuant to an extension is limited to the amount of the transferor's unused GST exemption as of the date of the transfer. Thus, if the amount of GST exemption has increased since the date of the transfer, no portion of the increased amount may be applied by reason of the grant of relief to a transfer taking place in an earlier year and prior to the effective date of that increase [Prop. Reg. Sec. 26.2642-7(c)].

How to request relief. The transferor or the transferor's executor requesting relief needs to file a private letter ruling request following the procedures set forth in the Proposed Regulations and meeting the circumstances described therein. These circumstances include situations in which the transferor intended to allocate GST exemption or make an election and the failure to allocate or elect was inadvertent.

In a number of letter rulings, the IRS granted an extension of time ("Reg. Sec. 301.9100-3") to make allocations or elections with respect to the GST exemption or to take other related actions, such as the division of a trust.[5]

---

[4] Ltr. Ruls. 201027034, 200717002.

[5] Ltr. Ruls. 200905002, 200905003, 200906017, 200906023, 200908002, 200916002, 200919005, 200919013, 200921007, 200924007, 201036010, 201240010, 201302002.

Basis for relief. Requests for relief under IRC Sec. 2642(g)(1) will be granted when the taxpayer provides evidence to establish to the satisfaction of the IRS that the taxpayer acted reasonably and in good faith, and that the grant of relief will not prejudice the government's interests [Reg. Sec. 301.9100-3; Prop. Reg. Sec. 1.26.2642-7(d)(1)]. Reg. Sec. 301.9100-3(b)(1)(v) provides that a taxpayer is deemed to have acted reasonably and in good faith if the taxpayer reasonably relied on a qualified tax professional, including a tax professional employed by the taxpayer, and the tax professional failed to make, or advise the taxpayer to make, the election.

Reasonableness and good faith. The following nonexclusive list of factors will be used to determine whether a transferor or the executor of a transferor's estate acted reasonably and in good faith:

1. The intent of the transferor or the executor of the transferor's estate to timely allocate GST exemption or to timely make an election as evidenced in the trust instrument, instrument of transfer, or contemporaneous documents, such as federal gift or estate tax returns or correspondence;

2. The occurrence of intervening events beyond the control of the transferor, or of the executor of the transferor's estate that caused the failure to allocate GST exemption to a transfer or the failure to elect;

3. The lack of awareness by the transferor or the executor of the transferor's estate of the need to allocate GST exemption to a transfer after exercising reasonable diligence, taking into account the experience of the transferor or the executor of the transferor's estate and the complexity of the GST issue;

4. Evidence of consistency by the transferor in allocating (or not allocating) the transferor's GST exemption, although evidence of consistency may be less relevant if there is evidence of a change of circumstances or change of trust beneficiaries that would otherwise support a deviation from prior GST tax exemption allocation practices; and

5. Reasonable reliance by the transferor or the executor of the transferor's estate on the advice of a qualified tax professional retained or employed by either (or both) of them, and the failure of the transferor or executor, in reliance on or consistent with that advice, to allocate GST exemption to the transfer or to make an election. [Prop. Reg. Sec. 26.2642-7(d)(2)]

Prejudice to government interests. For purposes of determining whether a transferor or transferor's estate is entitled to an extension of time to make allocations of GST exemption under IRC Sec. 2642(g)(1), the following nonexclusive list of factors will be used to determine whether the interests of the government would be prejudiced:

1. The grant of requested relief would permit the use of hindsight to produce an economic advantage or other benefit that either would not have been available if the allocation or election had been timely made, or that results from the selection of one out of a number of alternatives (other than whether or not to make an allocation or election) that were available at the time the allocation or election could have been made timely;

2. If the transferor or the executor of the transferor's estate delayed the filing of the request for relief with the intent to deprive the IRS of sufficient time (by reason of

¶2509

the expiration or the impending expiration of the applicable statute of limitations or otherwise) to challenge the claimed identity of the transferor, the value of the transferred property that is the subject of the requested relief, or any other aspect of the transfer that is relevant for transfer tax purposes; and

3. A determination by the IRS that, in the event of a grant of relief, it would be unreasonably disruptive or difficult to adjust the GST tax consequences of a taxable termination or a taxable distribution that occurred between the time for making a timely allocation of GST exemption or a timely election and the time at which the request for relief was filed. [Prop. Reg. Sec. 26.2642-7(d)(3)]

Situations where standard of reasonableness, good faith, and lack of prejudice to government not met. The IRS will not grant an extension when the standard of reasonableness, good faith and lack of prejudice to the interests of the government is not met. This standard is not met in the following situations:

1. The transferor or the executor of the transferor's estate made an allocation of GST exemption or an election under Code Sec. 2632(b)(3) or (c)(5), on a timely filed federal gift or estate tax return, and the relief requested would decrease or revoke that allocation or election;

2. The transferor or the transferor's executor delayed in requesting relief in order to preclude the IRS, as a practical matter, from challenging the identity of the transferor, the value of the transferred interest on the federal estate or gift tax return, or any other aspect of the transaction that is relevant for federal estate or gift tax purposes;

3. The action or inaction that is the subject of the request for relief reflected or implemented the decision with regard to the allocation of GST exemption or an election that was made by the transferor or executor of the transferor's estate who had been accurately informed in all material respects by a qualified tax professional retained or employed by either (or both) of them; or

4. The IRS determines that the transferor's request is an attempt to benefit from hindsight. [Prop. Reg. Sec. 26.2642-7(e)]

Period of limitations. A request for relief does not reopen, suspend or extend the period of limitations on assessment of any estate, gift, or GST tax under IRC Sec. 6501. Thus, if the IRS requests that the transferor or the transferor's executor consent to an extension of the period of limitation on assessment or collection of gift and GST taxes for the transfers that are the subject of the requested relief, the transferor may refuse to extend the period of limitations or limit the extension to particular issues or to a particular period of time [Prop. Reg. Sec. 26.2642-7(f)].

Rev. Proc. 2004-46 provides alternate extension method. In Rev. Proc. 2004-46,[6] the IRS released a simple alternate method for taxpayers to obtain extensions of time to allocate the GST exemption in limited situations. The alternate method may be used in lieu of the letter ruling process and no user fee will be charged. Rev. Proc. 2004-46 applies only to a taxpayer who satisfies the following requirements:

---

[6] Rev. Proc. 2004-46, 2004-2 CB 142.

1. The taxpayer made or was deemed to have made a transfer by gift to a trust from which a GST may be made;

2. At the time the taxpayer files the request for relief, no taxable distributions have been made and no taxable terminations have occurred;

3. The transfer qualified for the annual gift tax exclusion and the amount of the transfer, when added to the value of all other gifts by the transferor to that donee in the same year, was equal to or less than the amount of the applicable annual exclusion for the year of the transfer;

4. No GST exemption was allocated to the transfer, whether or not a Form 709 was filed;

5. At the time the taxpayer files a request for relief, the taxpayer has unused GST exemption available to allocate to the transfer; and

6. All filing requirements for Form 709 were satisfied.

Procedural requirements. Rev. Proc. 2004-46 requires that Form 709 be filed for the year of the transfer to the trust, regardless of whether a Form 709 had been previously filed for that year. The notation "FILED PURSUANT TO REV. PROC. 2004-46" must appear across the top of the form. The value of the transferred property as of the date of the transfer must be reported and a statement captioned "Notice of Allocation" must be attached. The statement must contain the following information:

1. Clear identification of the trust, including the trust's identifying number;

2. The value of the property transferred as of the date of the transfer (adjusted to account for split gifts, if any);

3. The amount of the taxpayer's unused GST exemption at the time this Notice of Allocation is filed;

4. The amount of GST exemption allocated to the transfer;

5. The inclusion ratio of the trust after the allocation; and

6. A statement that all of the requirements stated in Rev. Proc. 2004-46 have been satisfied.

The Form 709 must be filed on or before the date prescribed for filing the federal estate tax return for the transferor's estate (determined with regard to any extensions actually obtained), regardless of whether an estate tax return is required to be filed.

(j) Automatic Allocation of GST Exemption at Death. If a transferor's GST exemption is not affirmatively allocated or deemed to be allocated during the transferor's lifetime and is not affirmatively allocated at the transferor's death by the executor either to lifetime transfers or transfers at death, IRC Sec. 2632(e) provides another way that the GST exemption can be allocated. Pursuant to IRC Sec. 2632(e), the decedent's remaining GST exemption is deemed allocated pro rate as follows:

1. To direct skips treated as occurring at the transferor's death; and the balance, if any, is allocated

2. To trusts where the decedent is the transferor and from which a taxable termination may occur or from which a taxable distribution may be made [Reg. Sec. 26.2632-1(d)(2)].

¶2509

A decedent's unused GST exemption is automatically allocated on the due date for filing Form 706 or Form 706NA to the extent not otherwise allocated by the decedent's executor on or before that date. The automatic allocation occurs whether or not a return is actually required to be filed [Reg. Sec. 26.2632-1(d)(2)]. The automatic allocation is irrevocable and an allocation made by the executor after the automatic allocation is made is ineffective. No automatic allocation of GST tax exemption will be made in the following circumstances:

1. To a trust that will have a new transferor with respect to the entire trust [Reg. Sec. 26.2642-1(d)(2)]. The new transferor or his or her executor would be the only people able to allocate GST exemption to that trust.

2. To a trust if, during the nine month period ending immediately after the death of the transferor no GST has occurred and at the end of the nine month period no future GST can occur [Reg. Sec. 26.2632-1(d)(2)].

¶2510 EXCLUSION FOR ANNUAL IRC SECTION 2503(b) GIFTS

There is an annual exclusion from gift tax of $14,000 in 2014 per donee for gifts of a *present interest* [IRC Sec. 2503(b); see ¶ 901]. Outright direct-skip transfers that qualify as nontaxable annual exclusion gifts are not subject to GST tax. In addition, if you make direct skip transfers to a qualified trust (as defined below) and the transfer qualifies as a nontaxable annual exclusion gift because of the annual gift tax exclusion under IRC Sec. 2503(b), the trust will have an inclusion ratio of zero and will thus not be subject to GST tax [IRC Sec. 2642(c)].

(a) Annual Per Donee Exclusion. The gift tax annual per donee exclusion operates by permitting the first $14,000 in 2014 in value of property or interest in property, other than future interests, which you transfer to any number of individuals, including those who are unrelated to you, to be excluded from current taxable gifts for federal gift tax purposes [IRC Sec. 2503(b)]. The best part of this gift from Congress is that there is no limit on the number of donees for whom an annual exclusion may be taken or the number of years in which it may be taken. Thus, as an estate planning tool, you can make an unlimited number of annual exclusion gifts each year without owing any gift tax. The per donee exclusion renews annually and there is no carryover of any unused amount.

The gift tax annual exclusion is only available for *present*, not future interests in property. The unrestricted right to the immediate use, possession, or enjoyment of property or income from property constitutes a present interest in property [Reg. Sec. 25.2503-3(b)]. A future interest is a right to use, possess, or enjoy money or property that will not commence until a future date or time. As result gifts in trust and gifts of remainder interests will not qualify for the annual exclusion.

(b) What Is a Qualified Trust for GST Annual Exclusion Purposes. A direct skip in trust, which is a nontaxable gift because of the annual gift tax exclusion, will be subject to GST tax as a taxable direct skip, unless the trust is a qualified trust. A trust will be qualified for these purposes if it complies with the following requirements:

1. During the life of the skip person, the trust must be for the current benefit of the skip person only. This means that no portion of the corpus or income of the trust may be distributed to (or for the benefit of) any person other than the skip person; and

2. If the trust does not terminate before the skip person dies, the assets of the trust will be includable in the skip person's gross estate [IRC Sec. 2642(c)(2); Reg. Sec. 26.2642-1(c)(3)].

Example 1: *Gift entirely nontaxable.* On December 31, 2014, Grandfather transfers $14,000 to an irrevocable trust for the benefit of Grandson, who possessed a right to withdraw any contribution to the trust such that the entire transfer qualifies for the annual gift tax exclusion. The income is to be paid to Grandson for 10 years or until his prior death. Upon the expiration of Grandson's income interest, the trust principal is payable to Grandson or Grandson's estate. The transfer to the trust is a direct skip. Grandfather made no prior gifts to or for the benefit of Grandson during the year. The entire $14,000 transfer is a nontaxable transfer. For purposes of computing the tax on the direct skip, the denominator of the applicable fraction is zero, and thus, the inclusion ratio is zero [Reg. Sec. 26.2642-1(d), Example (2)].

If the trust is partly taxable and partly nontaxable, it is divided into two parts as illustrated in the examples below. The nontaxable part has an inclusion ratio of zero and the taxable part has an inclusion ratio subject to the amount of GST exemption allocated to the transfer.

Example 2: *Gift nontaxable in part-GST tax exemption allocated.* Grandfather transfers $20,000 to an irrevocable trust for the benefit of Grandchild. Under the terms of the trust, the income to be paid to Grandchild for 10 years or until his prior death. Upon the expiration of Grandchild's income interest, the trust principal is payable to him or to his estate. Further, Grandchild has the right to withdraw $14,000 of any contribution to the trust because that amount qualifies for the annual exclusion. The amount of the nontaxable transfer is $14,000. Solely for purposes of computing the tax on the direct skip, Grandfather's transfer is divided into two portions. One portion is equal to the amount of the nontaxable transfer ($14,000) and has a zero inclusion ratio; the other portion is $6,000 ($20,000 – $14,000). With respect to the $6,000 portion, the denominator of the applicable fraction is $6,000. Assuming that Grandfather has sufficient GST tax exemption available, the numerator of the applicable fraction is $6,000 (unless Grandfather elects to have the automatic allocation provisions not apply). Thus, assuming Grandfather does not elect to have the automatic allocation not apply, the applicable fraction is one ($6,000/$6,000 = 1) and the inclusion ratio is zero (1 – 1 = 0) [Reg. Sec. 26.2642-1(d), Example (3)].

Change facts for different result—GST tax not allocated to taxable part. Assume the same facts as in the above example except that Grandfather files a timely Form 709 electing that the automatic allocation of GST tax exemption not apply to the $20,000 transferred in the direct skip. Grandfather's transfer is divided into two portions, a $14,000 portion with a zero inclusion ratio and a $6,000 portion with an applicable fraction of zero (0/$7,000 = 0) and an inclusion ratio of one (1 – 0 = 1) [Reg. Sec. 26.2642-1(d), Example (4)].

(c) Gift Splitting. If a spouse does not have sufficient funds to take advantage of his or her annual exclusion gift tax exclusion, his or her exclusion need not be wasted. The IRC allows two spouses to treat a gift to a third person made by either spouse as a gift made one half by each spouse [IRC Sec. 2652(a)(2)]. In other words, when one spouse makes a gift to a third party from his or her interest in property, the Internal Revenue Code permits the nondonor spouse to join in the gift as if the nondonor spouse had made one-half of the gift [IRC Sec. 2513]. Thus, if you transferred $28,000 to your son in 2014 and your spouse consents to gift splitting, the transfer is treated as made $14,000 by you and $14,000 by your spouse and no gift tax is owed because the annual per donee exclusion allowable to each spouse applies to the gift [see ¶ 901].

Because of the gift tax marital deduction [see ¶ 1107], married couples can freely transfer assets between them with no tax consequences. In order for both spouses to take advantage of the annual gift tax exclusion and to have each spouse become the "transferor" for purposes of allocating GST tax exemption, the spouse with more assets in his or her name can transfer property to the poorer spouse so he or she can become the transferor and make full use of the GST tax exemption. Remember that only the transferor can allocate GST tax exemption and each transferor has in year 2012, a $5,120,000 exemption from GST tax available to him or her. This may become important when considering generation assignments.

> **Example 3:** *Changing transferor.* Tom, age 70, and his spouse, Alice, age 65, want to give $100,000 to Pam, an unrelated blind woman who has befriended them. She is 31 years old. If Tom makes the gift it will be a direct skip because Pam is a skip person with respect to Tom because she is 39 years younger than Tom. If, instead, Tom transfers the money free of gift tax to his wife, Alice, and she makes the gift, it will not be subject to GST tax because Pam is not a skip person with respect to Alice. Because Pam is only 34 years younger than Alice, Pam is treated as being only one generation below Alice. Remember, the law provides that for transfers made to non-family members, generations are measured from the date of the transferor's birth. Individuals not more than $12^{1}/_{2}$ years younger than you are treated as members of your generation; more than $12^{1}/_{2}$ but not more than $37^{1}/_{2}$ years younger, first younger generation, and so on—a new generation every 25 years [IRC Sec. 2651(d)].

(d) What to Do If the Annual Exclusion Gift Fails to Qualify for the GST Tax Annual Exclusion. Just because a transfer qualifies for the annual gift tax exclusion doesn't mean that it will qualify for the GST tax annual exclusion under IRC Sec. 2642(c)(2). This can easily occur because the GST tax annual exclusion only applies to direct skips that are either direct skip transfers or transfers to a qualifying trust, as discussed above. Any transfer that fails to qualify as a direct skip will be ineligible for the GST tax annual exclusion.

¶2510

¶2511 EXCLUSION FOR PAYMENT OF MEDICAL AND TUITION EXPENSES

Distributions from trusts made directly to schools or hospitals to provide for a skip person's tuition or medical expenses are excluded from GST tax provided these payments are not reimbursed by insurance [IRC Sec. 2503(e); see ¶ 908]. The good news is that, unlike the annual gift tax exclusion, no dollar limit exists on qualified educational or medical expense transfers [see ¶ 908 and ¶ 2510].

Distributions from a trust will be excluded from GST only if the direct payment of someone else's medical and tuition expenses would have qualified for the IRC Sec. 2503(e) gift tax exclusion, if the payments had been made by an individual, rather than a trust [IRC Sec. 2611(b)(1)].

(a) Educational Expenses Covered. The exclusion for educational expenses is limited to tuition for educational institutions. An educational organization is an organization with a regular faculty and curriculum and a regularly enrolled body of students in attendance at the place where the educational activities are carried on [IRC Sec. 170(b)(1)(A)(ii)]. The educational organization may be domestic or foreign.

The education exclusion is not limited to college tuition but applies to tuition for any educational organization, including nursery, elementary, and secondary schools. However, the exclusion does not cover books, rent, board, and other living expenses. The individual may be a full- or part-time student [Reg. Sec. 25.2503-6(b)(2)].

(b) Payments Must Be Made to Educational Institution. Payments must be made directly to the educational institution. Payments to the donee who uses them (or is reimbursed) for education expenses will fail to qualify for the exclusion. This restriction is very important. If you give the money directly to your family and tell them to pay the tuition and hospital bills with the money, you will lose the exclusion. It's that simple.

> **Example 1:** *Tuition and medical expense exclusion.* Grandfather establishes a trust that will pay income and principal in the trustee's discretion to Grandfather's grandchildren. The trustee makes distributions from the trust directly to hospitals and schools to cover bills for medical and tuition, respectively. If Grandfather had paid the hospital and school bills directly, the payments would have qualified under IRC Sec. 2503(e) for the annual gift tax exclusion, regardless of amount. Therefore, the payments made by the trustee also qualify for the annual gift tax exclusion and transfers from the trust are not taxable distributions and are not subject to the GST tax.

Change facts for different result. If the trustee in the above example had made distributions from the trust directly to the grandchildren or their parents and told them to pay these bills as needed, the transfers would not have qualified for the gift tax annual exclusion under IRC Sec. 2503(e) and the transfers made by the trustee from the trust would be taxable distributions subject to GST tax.

¶2511

(c) Definition of Medical Care. Transfers qualifying under the medical expense exclusion [IRC Sec. 2503(e)] are limited to medical care as defined under IRC Sec. 213(d), more specifically, for the diagnosis, cure, mitigation, treatment, or prevention of disease, or for the purpose of affecting any structure or function of the body. Health care insurance premiums qualify.

Amounts must be paid directly to the medical service or care provider and not an intermediary. The exclusion does not apply to amounts that are reimbursed to the donee by insurance [Reg. Sec. 25.2503-6(b)(3)].

> **NOTE:** Although the educational or medical exclusion is particularly good for grandparents, other relatives, including parents, aunts, and uncles, can also take advantage of the exclusion. You don't even have to be related to the person for whom the medical or tuition payments are made because the education and medical exclusions exist without regard to the relationship between the donor and the donee.

(d) Qualified Tuition Programs (Section 529 Plans). Contributions made to qualified tuition programs (Section 529 plans) are treated as completed gifts of a present interest from the contributor to the beneficiary at the time of the contribution. Therefore, transfers made by taxpayers to Section 529 plans are not subject to the GST tax [Prop. Reg. Sec. 1.529-5(b)]. Annual contributions are eligible for the gift tax exclusion under IRC Sec. 2503(b) if the annual gift tax exclusion limit ($14,000 for a single individual, $28,000 for a married couple electing gift-splitting in 2014) is not exceeded. A contributor making a contribution in excess of the exclusion limit may elect to have the contribution treated as if made ratably over five years [Prop. Reg. Sec. 1.529-5(b)(2)(i)]. The maximum contribution is five times the IRC Sec. 2503(b) annual exclusion amount available in the calendar year of the contribution. Any excess may not be taken into account ratably and is treated as a taxable gift in the calendar year of the contribution. In addition, a donor and his or her spouse may agree to split the contributions in order to double the amount of the contribution. [Prop. Reg. Sec. 1.529-5(b)(2)(ii)]. The election is made on Form 709, "United States Gift (and Generation-Skipping Transfer) Tax Return, for the calendar year in which the contribution is made.

If in any year after the first year of the five-year period, the amount excludible under IRC Sec. 2503(b) is increased, the donor may make an additional contribution in any one or more of the four remaining years up to the difference between the exclusion amount as increased and the original exclusion amount for the year or years in which the original contribution was made.

> **Example 2:** In Year 1, when the annual exclusion was $12,000, Dad makes a contribution of $72,000 to a 529 plan for the benefit of Child. Dad elects under IRC Sec. 529(c)(2)(B) to account for the gift ratably over a five-year period beginning with the calendar year of contribution. Dad is treated as making an excludible gift of $12,000 in each of Years 1 through 5 and a taxable gift of $12,000 in Year 1. In Year 3, when the annual exclusion is increased to $14,000, he makes an additional contribution in the amount of $10,000. He is treated as making an excludible gift of $4,000 under IRC Sec. 2503(b); the remaining $6,000 is a taxable gift in Year 3 [Prop. Reg. Sec. 1.529-5(b)(2)(v)].

¶2511

If the contributor who has made a contribution in excess of the gift tax exclusion limit dies during the five-year period, the portion of the contribution that has not been allocated is included in the contributor's estate. If a beneficiary's interest is rolled over to another beneficiary or there is a change in beneficiary, no gift or GST tax consequences result, provided that the two beneficiaries are of the same generation. If a beneficiary's interest is rolled over to a beneficiary in a lower generation (e.g., parent to child or aunt to niece), the five-year averaging rule may be applied to exempt up to $72,000 of the transfer in 2013 when the annual exclusion amount is $14,000.

¶2512 THE GENERATION MOVE-DOWN RULE— TAXATION OF MULTIPLE SKIPS

A relief provision exists in the Internal Revenue Code to minimize multiple GST taxes from being imposed on the same transfer. It is called the generation move-down rule and it works by designating when future events involving property held in trust, after a GST has occurred, involve a skip person. By designating someone a non-skip person, no GST tax must be paid. The rule operates by lowering or moving down the generation assignment of the transferor so that people who would otherwise be skip persons are no longer treated as such. The generation move-down rule has the effect of an exclusion where a GST has already occurred at a generation level.

IRC Sec. 2653(a) provides that following a situation where property is held in trust immediately after a GST, solely for purposes of determining whether future events involve a skip person, the transferor is thereafter deemed to occupy the generation immediately above the highest generation of any person holding an interest in such trust immediately after the transfer. If no person holds an interest in the trust immediately after the GST, the transferor is treated as occupying the generation above the highest generation of any person in existence at the time of the GST who then occupies the highest generation level of any person who may subsequently hold an interest in the trust [IRC Sec. 2653(a); Reg. Sec. 26.2653-1(a)].

> **Example 1:** *Taxation of multiple skips as GST.* Grandfather transfers property to an irrevocable trust for the benefit Grandchild and Great-Grandchild. During Grandchild's life, the trust has the power to distribute trust income to the Grandchild and Great-Grandchild. At Grandchild's death, the trust property passes to Great-Grandchild. Both Grandchild and Great-Grandchild have an interest in the trust for GST purposes. The transfer by Grandfather to the trust is a direct skip, and the property is held in trust immediately after the transfer. After the direct skip, the transferor, who is Grandfather, is treated as being only one generation above Grandchild, the highest generation individual having an interest in the trust. Therefore, Grandchild is no longer a skip person and distributions to Grandchild are not taxable distributions. However, because Great-Grandchild occupies a generation that is two generations below the deemed generation of Grandfather, the Great-Grandchild is a skip person and distributions of trust income to Great-grandchild are taxable distributions [Reg. Sec. 26.2653-1(b), Example (1)].

Example 2: *Taxation of multiple skips not as GST.* Grandfather transfers property to an irrevocable trust providing that the income is to be paid to Child for life. When Child dies, the trust income is to be accumulated for 10 years and added to principal. At the end of the 10-year accumulation period, the trust income is to be paid to Grandchild for life. When Grandchild dies, the trust property is to be paid to Great-Grandchild or to his estate. A GST occurs when the Child dies. Immediately after Child's death and during the 10-year accumulation period, no person has an interest in the trust because no one can receive current distributions of income or principal. Immediately after Child's death, Grandfather is treated as occupying the generation above the generation of Grandchild (the trust beneficiary in existence at the time of the GST who then occupies the highest generation level of any person who may subsequently hold an interest in the trust). Thus subsequent income distributions to Grandchild are not taxable distributions because he is not a skip person [Reg. Sec. 26.2653-1(b), Example (2)].

¶2513 INCLUSION RATIO

When you allocate GST tax exemption to a direct skip or trust, the GST tax will be reduced or eliminated by means of a statutory device known as the inclusion ratio [IRC Sec. 2642]. This is the percentage of the outright transfer that exceeds the amount of GST tax exemption allocated to the transfer. The inclusion ratio for any property transferred in a GST is 1 minus the "applicable fraction" determined for the trust from which a generation-skipping transfer is made or, in the case of a direct skip, the applicable fraction determined for such a skip [IRC Sec. 2642(a)]. Simply stated, 1 minus the "applicable fraction" (see below) will equal your inclusion ratio, as follows:

Inclusion Ratio = 1 minus the applicable fraction

Your objective should be to get an inclusion ratio of zero because this will mean that the applicable rate of tax for the trust or transfer will be zero. You can accomplish this if the amount of GST tax exemption allocated to the trust or direct skip transfer equals the value of the trust or transfer at the time of the transfer even if the value of the assets appreciates over time.

Example 1: Bill created a trust with income distributed to his son, Sam, for life. When Sam died the trust was distributed to Sam's children. Bill transferred $1 million into the trust. On a timely filed gift tax return Bill allocated $1 million of his GST exemption to the trust. When his son died several years later, the value of the trust fund was $3 million. The inclusion ratio is zero because the GST exemption allocated to the trust is equal to the amount transferred even though the actual amount in the trust appreciated in value over time. The applicable rate is the maximum federal estate tax rate multiplied by the inclusion ratio of zero or zero percent. Therefore no GST tax is due on this taxable termination. If no GST exemption had been allocated to the trust, the applicable rate would be 40 percent, which is the maximum federal estate tax rate effective in 2013, multiplied by the inclusion ratio of one. The tax would be $1,200,000 ($3 million times 40 percent).

In connection with automatic allocations of the GST tax exemption, the value of the property for purposes of determining the inclusion ratio shall be its finally determined gift or estate tax value depending on the circumstances of the transfer. In the case of a GST tax exemption allocation deemed to be made at the conclusion of an estate tax inclusion period, the value for purposes of determining the inclusion ratio shall be its value at that time [IRC Sec. 2642(b)].

¶2514 THE APPLICABLE FRACTION

The numerator of the applicable fraction is the amount of the GST tax exemption allocated to the trust or the property transferred in the case of a direct skip not in trust [IRC Sec. 2642(a)(2)(A); Reg. Sec. 26.2642-1(b)(1)]. The rate of GST tax imposed on taxable distributions from a trust and on taxable terminations of interests in a trust is based on the inclusion ratio.

The denominator of the applicable fraction is the value of the property transferred to the trust (or involved in the direct skip) reduced by the sum of the following:

1. Any federal estate tax or state death tax actually recovered from the trust attributable to such property, and

2. Any charitable deduction allowed on the property [IRC Sec. 2642(a)(2)(B); Reg. Sec. 26.2642-1(c)(1)].

> **Example 1:** Grandfather gives $750,000 to Grandchild in a direct skip. If he allocates $750,000 of his GST exemption to this transfer and assuming there are no estate/death taxes and no charitable deductions, the inclusion ratio is zero, computed as follows: One minus $750,000/$750,000 equals zero. The tax rate on this transfer is thus zero and no GST tax is imposed [Reg. Sec. 26.2642-1(c)(2)].

> **Example 2:** Grandfather gives $750,000 to Grandchild in a direct skip. If Grandfather fails to allocate any GST tax exemption to the transfer, the inclusion ratio is one, computed as follows: One minus ($0/$750,000). Therefore at the 2013 maximum tax rate of 40 percent, a 40 percent GST tax is imposed on the transfer for a total GST tax bill of $300,000.

> **Example 3:** Grandfather leaves $2.5 million in trust for the benefit of Grandchildren. At the time of the transfer, $1 million GST tax exemption is allocated to the trust. Assuming there are no estate/death tax and charitable deductions, the calculation of the GST tax would be as follows: $1 million divided by the $2.5 million value of the property transferred equals 0.4. One minus 0.4 equals 0.6 which is the inclusion ratio. The GST tax rate is the product of the inclusion ratio of 0.6 and the maximum federal estate tax rate in 2013 at the time of the

transfer which is 40 percent. Thus the rate of tax on this transfer is 2.4 percent (40% × 0.6) [Reg. Sec. 26.2642-1(d), Example (1)].

(a) Valuation of Property—Lifetime Transfers. For purposes of determining the denominator of the applicable fraction, Reg. Sec. 26.2642-2(a)(1) provides that the value of property transferred during life is its fair market value on the effective date of the allocation of GST exemption. In the case of a timely allocation, the denominator of the applicable fraction is the fair market value of the property as finally determined for gift tax purposes.

Valuation rules. If an allocation of GST exemption to any transfer of property is made on a timely-filed gift tax return or is deemed to be made under IRC Sec. 2632(b)(1) (lifetime direct skips) or under IRC Sec. 2632(c)(1) (lifetime indirect skips), then

1. The value of the property for purposes of calculating the inclusion ratio will be the value of the property as finally determined for gift tax purposes, and

2. The allocation will be effective on and after the date of the transfer. In the case of an allocation deemed to have been made at the close of an estate tax inclusion period (ETIP), the value of the property for inclusion ratio purposes will be the value at the time of the close of the ETIP, and the allocation will be effective on and after the close of the ETIP [IRC Sec. 2642(b)(1)].

An ETIP is any period after a transfer during which the value of the transferred property would be includible in the gross estate of the transferor if he or she died [IRC Sec. 2642(f)(3)].

Similarly, the value of the transferred property for purposes of determining the inclusion ratio will be its value as finally determined for estate tax purposes. However, if the requirements respecting allocation of post-death changes in value are not met, the value of the property will be determined as of the time that the distribution occurred [IRC Sec. 2642(b)(2)(A)].

Special rule for late allocations during life. If a transferor makes a late allocation of GST exemption to a trust, Reg. Sec. 25.2642-2(a)(2) provides that the value of the property transferred to the trust is the fair market value of the trust assets determined on the effective date of the allocation of GST exemption. If a transferor makes a late allocation of GST exemption to a trust, the transferor may, solely for purposes of determining the fair market value of the trust assets, elect to treat the allocation as having been made on the first day of the month during which the late allocation is made (valuation date). This election is not effective with respect to a life insurance policy or a trust holding a life insurance policy, if the insured individual has died. The allocation is not effective until the election is made by stating on a gift tax return (Form 709) on which the allocation is made:

a. That the election is being made;

b. The applicable valuation date; and

c. The fair market value of the trust assets on the valuation date.

(b) Valuation of Property—Transfers at Death. For purposes of determining the denominator of the applicable fraction, Reg. Sec. 26.2642-2(b)(1) provides that

¶2514

the value of property included in the decedent's gross estate is its value for estate tax purposes. In the case of qualified real property with respect to which the election under IRC Sec. 2032A is made, the value of the property is the value determined under section 2032A provided the recapture agreement filed with the IRS specifically provides for the signatories' consent to the imposition of, and personal liability for, additional GST tax in the event an additional estate tax is imposed. If the recapture agreement does not contain these provisions, the value of qualified real property is the fair market value of the property determined without regard to special use valuation.

Special rule for pecuniary payments at death. If a pecuniary payment is satisfied with cash, the denominator of the applicable fraction is the pecuniary amount. If property other than cash is used to satisfy a pecuniary payment, the denominator of the applicable fraction is the pecuniary amount only if payment must be made with property on the basis of the value of the property on:

a. The date of distribution; or

b. A date other than the date of distribution, but only if the pecuniary payment must be satisfied on a basis that fairly reflects net appreciation and depreciation (occurring between the valuation date and the date of distribution) in all of the assets from which the distribution could have been made.

[Reg. Sec. 26.2642-2(b)(2)].

The denominator of the applicable fraction with respect to any property used to satisfy any other pecuniary payment payable in kind is the date of distribution value of the property.

> **Example 4:** Dad transfers $100,000 to a newly-created irrevocable trust. The trust provides that income is to be paid to Child for 10 years. At the end of the 10-year period, the trust principal is to be paid to Grandchild. Dad does not allocate any GST exemption to the trust on the gift tax return reporting the transfer. Thereafter, Dad files a late Form 709 allocating $50,000 of GST exemption to the trust. Because the allocation was made on a late-filed return, the value of the property transferred to the trust is determined on the date the allocation is filed. On the day of the late-filed Form 709, the value of the trust property is $150,000. Effective on that date, the applicable fraction with respect to the trust is .333 ($50,000 (the amount of GST exemption allocated to the trust) over $150,000 (the value of the trust principal on the effective date of the GST exemption allocation)), and the inclusion ratio is .667 (1.0 − .333) [Reg. Sec. 26.2642-2(c), Example (1)].

(c) Redetermination of Applicable Fraction. The applicable fraction for a trust will remain constant until some event occurs that mandates recomputation [Reg. Sec. 26.2642-4(a)]. These triggering events include:

- The allocation of additional exemption to the trust;
- Multiple transfers to a single trust;
- A consolidation of separate trusts; and
- The imposition of the special use valuation recapture tax.

¶2514

Including trust property in the original transferor's estate is only an event that requires recomputation of the inclusion ratio if additional GST exemption is allocated to the property.

1. *Allocation of additional exemption.* The applicable fraction will be redetermined whenever additional exemption is allocated to the trust. The numerator of the redetermined applicable fraction is the sum of the amount of GST tax exemption currently being allocated to the trust (if any) plus the value of the nontax portion of the trust. The denominator of the redetermined applicable fraction is the value of the trust principal immediately after the event occurs. The nontax portion of the trust is determined by multiplying the value of the trust assets, determined immediately prior to the event, by the then applicable fraction [Reg. Sec. 26.2642-4(a)].

> **Example 5:** *Allocation of additional exemption.* Grandfather transfers $200,000 to an irrevocable trust under which the income is payable to Child, for life. Upon the termination of the trust, the remainder is payable to Grandchild. Grandfather makes a timely allocation of $100,000 of GST tax exemption, resulting in an inclusion ratio of 50 percent. Subsequently, when the entire trust property is valued at $500,000, Grandfather allocated an additional $100,000 of his unused GST tax exemption to the trust. The inclusion ratio is recomputed at that time. The numerator of the applicable fraction is $350,000 ($250,000, which is the nontax portion as of the date of the allocation, plus the $100,000 GST tax exemption currently being allocated). The denominator is $500,000 (the date of allocation fair market value of the trust). The inclusion ratio is .30 (1 − .70) [Reg. Sec. 26.2642-4(b), Example (1)].

1. *Multiple transfers to a single trust.* When property is added to an existing trust, the denominator of the redetermined applicable fraction is the value of the trust immediately after the addition [Reg. Sec. 26.2642-4(a)(1)].

2. *Consolidation of separate trusts.* When separate trusts created by one transferor are consolidated into one trust, a single applicable fraction for the consolidated trust is determined. The numerator of the redetermined applicable fraction is the sum of the nontax portions of each trust immediately prior to the consolidation [Reg. Sec. 26.2642-4(a)(2)].

3. *Imposition of recapture tax under Section 2032A.* If an additional estate tax is imposed under the special use valuation provisions of IRC Sec. 2032A [see ¶ 1908], the applicable fraction with respect to the property is redetermined as of the date of death of the transferor. The special use valuation provisions of IRC Sec. 2032A allow an executor to elect that certain real estate such as the family farm included in a decedent's gross estate may be valued using a special valuation method designed to produce a lower valuation. This relief provision is targeted to small farmers and business owners. A recapture tax will be imposed, however, if ten years after a decedent's death, the real estate ceases to be used for farm or business purposes or is disposed of outside the decedent's family.

In redetermining the applicable fraction in this situation, any available GST exemption not allocated at the death of the transferor is automatically allocated to the property. The denominator of the applicable fraction is the fair market value of the property at the date of the transferor's death reduced by the following: (1) any federal estate and any state death tax incurred by reason of the transfer that is chargeable to the trust and is actually recovered from the trust; (2) the amount of any charitable deduction allowed on the transfer; and (3) the additional GST tax actually recovered from the trust [Reg. Sec. 26.2642-4(a)(4)].

(d) Property Included in Transferor's Gross Estate. If the trust property is included in the original transferor's estate, the inclusion ratio will only have to be recomputed if additional GST tax exemption is allocated to the property. If additional GST tax exemption is allocated, the numerator of the redetermined applicable fraction is the sum of the nontax portion of the trust immediately after the transferor's death and the amount of GST tax exemption allocated by the executor of the transferor's estate to the trust. If additional GST tax exemption is not allocated to the trust, the applicable fraction immediately before death is not changed. The denominator of the applicable fraction is reduced to reflect any federal or state estate or inheritance taxes paid from the trust [Reg. Sec. 26.2642-4(a)(3)].

Example 6: *No redetermination of inclusion ratio.* Grandfather transfers $1 million worth of life insurance policies to an irrevocable life insurance trust. He allocates $500,000 of GST tax exemption to the trust on a timely filed gift tax return. The trust therefore has an inclusion ratio of .5 (1 − ($500,000/$1 million)). Grandfather dies two years later and the value of the insurance policy, which is $1.5 million, is included in his gross estate because as provided under IRC Sec. 2035(d)(2) he died within three years of the transfer of the life insurance policy into the trust. No additional allocation of Grandfather's GST exemption was made by the executor to the trust. Therefore the trust's applicable fraction and inclusion ratio do not need to be redetermined.

Example 7: *Redetermination of inclusion ratio.* Same facts as above except that Grandfather's executor allocated Grandfather's unused $500,000 GST exemption to the life insurance trust. Now the applicable fraction and inclusion must be redetermined. The numerator is the nontax portion of the trust on the date of death (.5 × 1.5 million = $750,000) + additional GST exemption allocated to the trust in the amount of $500,000 = $1,250,000. The denominator is the value of the trust on the date of death which is $1,500,000. The applicable fraction is $1,250,000/$1,500,000 = 0.833. Therefore, the inclusion ratio is 1 − .833 = .167. The tax would be .167 × 40 percent × $1.5 million = $100,200.

(e) Special Allocation Rule for Lifetime Transfers Subject to an ETIP. In general, an individual or an executor may allocate a taxpayer's GST tax exemption at any time from the date of the transfer through the date for filing the individual's federal estate tax return (Form 706) (including any extensions for filing that have been actually granted) [Reg. Sec. 26.2632-1(a); see Chapter 2]. A special rule exists, however, for allocation of GST tax exemption to lifetime (*inter vivos*) transfers that would be included in the transferor's gross estate if he or she died. This includes transfers under IRC Sec. 2036 where the transferor has retained the right before his death to enjoy income from the transferred property.

The special allocation rule provides that no allocation of any portion of the transferor's exemption may be made by the transferor to any property that he or she has transferred during his or her lifetime that is includible in his or his spouse's gross estate until the end of the estate tax inclusion period (ETIP) [IRC Sec. 2642(f)]. This is important because an allocation of GST tax exemption can be effective no earlier than the end of the ETIP. An ETIP is the period during which, should death occur, the value of transferred property would be includible in the gross estate of the transferor or his or her spouse's estate [IRC Sec. 2642(f)(3); Reg. Sec. 26.2632-1(c)(2)]. The effect of this provision is to defer the effectiveness of the allocation of the exemption until the death of the transferor.

> **Example 8:** *Allocation of GST tax exemption during ETIP.* Tom transfers $100,000 to an irrevocable trust. The trust instrument provides that trust income is to be paid to Tom for nine years or until Tom's prior death. The trust principal is to be paid to Tom's grandchild on the termination of Tom's income interest. If Tom dies within the nine-year period, the value of the trust principal is includible in Tom's gross estate under IRC Sec. 2036(a) because he retained an income interest for life. Thus, the trust is subject to an ETIP because the trust would be included in Tom's gross estate if he were to die immediately after the initial transfer. Tom files a timely Form 709 reporting the transfer and allocating $100,000 of GST tax exemption to the trust. The allocation of GST tax exemption to the trust is not effective until the termination of the ETIP which continues from the date the trust is created until the date of Tom's death. The inclusion ratio for the trust is calculated as of the date of Tom's death [Reg. Sec. 26.2632-1(c)(5), Example (1)].

(f) Finality of Inclusion Ratio. The Internal Revenue Code provides no statute of limitations on the determination of an inclusion ratio, but the regulations provide the following rules regarding when the determination becomes final:

- *Direct skips.* The inclusion ratio applicable to a direct skip becomes final when no additional GST tax (including additional GST tax under the special use valuation rules of IRC Sec. 2032A) may be assessed with respect to the direct skip [Reg. Sec. 26.2642-5(a)].

- *Taxable distributions and taxable terminations.* With respect to taxable distributions and taxable terminations, the inclusion ratio becomes final on the later of the expiration of the period for assessment with respect to the first GST tax return filed using that inclusion ratio or the expiration of the period for assessment of federal estate tax with respect to the estate of the transferor. If an estate tax return is not required to be filed, the period for assessment is determined as if a return were required to be filed and as if the return were timely filed within nine months after the date of the decedent's death [Reg. Sec. 26.2642-5(b)].

(g) Valuation Rules. IRC Sec. 2642(b) spells out the valuation rules with respect to timely and automatic allocations of GST exemption. If an allocation of GST exemption to any transfer of property is made on a timely filed gift tax return or is deemed to be made under IRC Sec. 2632(b)(1) (lifetime direct skips) or IRC Sec. 2632(c)(1) (lifetime indirect skips), then (1) the value of the property for purposes of calculating the inclusion ratio will be the value of the property as finally determined for gift tax purposes and (2) the allocation will be effective on and after the date of the transfer. In the case of an allocation deemed to have been made at the close of an estate tax inclusion period (ETIP), the value of the property for inclusion ratio purposes will be the value at the time of the close of the ETIP, and the allocation will be effective on and after the close of the ETIP [IRC Sec. 2642(b)(1)].

Similarly, the value of the transferred property for purposes of determining the inclusion ratio will be its value as finally determined for estate tax purposes. However, if the requirements respecting allocation of post-death changes in value are not met, the value of the property will be determined as of the time that the distribution occurred [IRC Sec. 2642(b)(2)(A)].

The valuation rules under IRC Sec. 2642(b) with respect to the determination of the inclusion ratio for GST tax purposes were made permanent effective for estates of decedents dying, gifts made, or generation-skipping transfers after December 31, 2012, by the American Taxpayer Relief Act of 2012.

¶2515 COMPUTING THE GST TAX

If a generation-skipping transfer is fully subject to tax, the GST tax is computed by multiplying the amount of the transfer by the maximum federal estate tax rate effective in the year of death.

If part of your exemption has been allocated to a transfer, the calculation is more complicated. The amount transferred is multiplied by the maximum estate tax rate multiplied by the applicable fraction. This fraction is found by subtracting from the number one a fraction, the numerator of which is the amount of the exemption allocated to the gift and the denominator of which is the value of the property transferred [IRC Sec. 2642].

> **Example 1:** Grandfather transfers $1 million in trust for his granddaughter and allocates $250,000 of the GST exemption to the trust. The inclusion ratio is .75 (1 minus $250,000/$1,000,000). The GST tax would be $300,000 (which is .75 multiplied by the maximum 40 percent estate tax rate multiplied by $1,000,000.

> **NOTE:** There is a credit allowed against the GST tax for state generation-skipping taxes for transfers occurring at death, but the credit is limited to 5 percent of the federal GST imposed on the transfer [IRC Sec. 2604].

¶2516 EFFECTIVE DATE RULES

You must be aware of the effective date rules because they determine whether or not you need to even concern yourself with the GST tax. Some trusts may be protected from the GST tax simply because of the effective date rules.

The GST tax only applies to inter vivos transfers made after September 25, 1985 and any GSTs made after October 22, 1986, which is the date of enactment of the Tax Reform Act of 1986 [Reg. Sec. 26.2601-1]. The four types of transfers listed below are exempt from the GST tax under the effective date rules:

1. A GST under a trust that was irrevocable on September 25, 1985 (a "grandfathered trust"), but only to the extent that transfer is not made out of corpus added to the trust after September 25, 1985 (or out of income attributable to corpus so added). This exception is found in section 1433(b)(2)(A) of the Tax Relief Act of 1986.[1] Reg. Sec. 26.2601-1(b)(1)(i) provides that the grandfather rule does not apply to a transfer of property pursuant to the exercise, release, or lapse of a general power of appointment that is treated as a taxable transfer for estate or gift tax purposes. The transfer is made by the person holding the power at the time the exercise, release, or lapse of the power becomes effective, and is not considered a transfer under a trust that was irrevocable on September 25, 1985.

In *Estate of Gerson*,[2] the Court of Appeals for the Sixth Circuit affirmed the Tax Court to uphold the validity of Reg. Sec. 26.2601-1(b)(1)(i) and therefore concluded that the decedent's transfer of property by power of appointment to her grandchildren was subject to GST tax because the transfer was made by the exercise of a power of appointment after September 25, 1985, the deadline for being grandfathered. The husband established an irrevocable trust in 1973. His wife was given an unlimited general power of appointment over the trust property. The wife died in October 2000. In her Will, she exercised the power of appointment in favor of her grandchildren. The court found that the exercise of the power of appointment in 2000 was a transfer of property to the marital trust, followed by a GST to the grandchildren. Even though the trust was irrevocable prior to September 25, 1985, pursuant to a surviving spouse's exercise of a testamentary general power of appointment, it was subject to the tax under Reg. Sec. 26.2601-1(b)(1).

The effective date rules of Section 1433(b)(2)(A) of the Tax Reform Act of 1986 (P.L. 99-514) (TRA '86) provided an exception to the GST tax for transfers from a trust, which was irrevocable on September 25, 1985, to the extent that the transfer was not made out of corpus added to the trust after that date. Following an adverse decision in *Simpson*,[3] Reg. Sec. 26.2601-1(b)(1)(i) was amended to provide that a transfer of property pursuant to the exercise, release, or lapse of a general power of appointment was excepted from the transitional rules of TRA '86 if the transfer was treated as a taxable transfer by the power holder for federal estate or gift tax purposes.

---

[1] **¶2516** TRA '86, Pub. L. No. 99-514, § 1433(b)(2)(A).

[2] Estate of Gerson, 127 TC 139 (2006), *aff'd*, 507 F.3d 435 (6th Cir. 2007).

[3] Simpson, 183 F.3d 812 (8th Cir. 1999), *nonacq.* 2000-1 CB xvi.

The court in *Gerson* concluded that Reg. Sec. 26.2601-1(b)(1) was a reasonable and valid interpretation of Section 1433(b)(2)(A) of TRA '86. Therefore, the transfers made pursuant to the surviving spouse's exercise of her general power of appointment were subject to GST tax. The court followed *E. Norman Peterson Marital Trust*,[4] and distinguished *Simpson* and *Bachler*,[5] where the courts decided factual scenarios nearly identical to those in *Gerson* and held that a widow's exercise of a testamentary general power of appointment, over a trust created by her late husband upon his death in 1976, was not subject to GST tax, even though the assets passed to the widow's grandchildren, a skip generation.

Be careful not to ruin an otherwise exempt trust by making additions that would render the trust subject to the GST tax. The term "irrevocable trust" is strictly defined for these purposes. A trust will not be considered an irrevocable trust to the extent that on September 25, 1985, the creator of the trust (not his spouse) had the power, on the date of his death to alter, amend, revoke or terminate the trust so that it would be included in his taxable gross estate under IRC Sec. 2038 [Reg. Sec. 26.2601-1(b)(1)(ii)(B)]. In addition, any modification of a trust instrument that results in a change to the quality, value, or timing of any beneficial interest in the trust will cause the trust to lose exempt status. The IRS has concluded in a letter ruling, however, that trusts that were grandfathered from the GST tax would not lose their exemption merely because enjoyment of the interests of some beneficiaries (grandchildren of the grantor) was moved forward when other beneficiaries (their parents who were the children of the grantor) disclaimed their interests, and as a result, the trusts terminated.[6]

> **Example 1:** *Trust not irrevocable.* On September 25, 1985, Tom, the settlor of a trust that was created before September 25, 1985, held a testamentary power to add new beneficiaries to the trust. The testamentary power held by Tom would have caused the trust to be included in Tom's gross estate under IRC Sec. 2038 if Tom had died on September 25, 1985. Therefore, the trust is not an irrevocable trust for exemption purposes [Reg. Sec. 26.2601-1(b)(1)(D), Example (1)]. If instead Tom's spouse held the power to add new beneficiaries to the trust, and assuming that the trust was otherwise irrevocable, the power would not be an IRC Sec. 2038 power, and the trust would be considered an irrevocable trust for exemption purposes [Reg. Sec. 26.2601-1(b)(1)(D), Example (2)].

The IRS has issued regulations that provide four safe harbors for determining when a modification, judicial construction, settlement agreement or trustee action with respect to an irrevocable trust that is exempt from the GST tax under the grandfather rules, will allow the trust to retain its GST-exempt status as follows [Reg. Sec. 26.2601-1(b)(4)]:

- *Trustee's discretionary powers.* The distribution of trust principal from a GST-tax-exempt trust to a new trust will not cause the new trust to be subject to the GST tax if: (1) the terms of the governing instrument of the exempt trust authorize the trustee to make distributions to the new trust without the consent or approval of any

---

[4] E. Norman Peterson Marital Trust, 102 TC 790 (1994), *aff'd*, 78 F.3d 795 (2d Cir. 1996).

[5] Bachler, 2000-2 USTC ¶ 60,390, *rev'd and rem'd*, 281 F.3d 1078 (9th Cir. 2002).

[6] Ltr. Rul. 200034015.

¶2516

beneficiary or court, and (2) the terms of the governing instrument of the new trust do not extend the time for vesting of any beneficial interest beyond the period provided in the original trust;

- *Court-approved settlement.* A court-approved settlement of a bona fide controversy regarding the administration of the trust or the construction of terms of the governing instrument will not cause an exempt trust to be subject to the GST tax if: (1) the settlement is the product of arm's length negotiations, and (2) the settlement is within the range of reasonable outcomes under the governing instrument and applicable state law addressing the issues resolved by the settlement;

- *Court orders.* A judicial construction of a governing instrument to resolve an ambiguity in the terms of the instrument or to correct a typographical error will not cause an exempt trust to be subject to the GST tax if: (1) the court order involves a bona fide issue, and (2) the judicial interpretation is consistent with applicable state law that would be applied by the highest court of the state;

- *Other changes.* A modification of the governing instrument of an exempt trust by judicial reformation, or nonjudicial reformation that is valid under applicable state law, will not cause an exempt trust to be subject to the GST tax, but only if: (1) the modification does not shift a beneficial interest in the trust to any beneficiary who occupies a lower generation than the person or persons who held the beneficial interest prior to the modification, and (2) the modification does not extend the time for vesting of any beneficial interest in the trust beyond the period provided for in the original trust. The IRS has adopted the position in several letter rulings[7] that a modification to a grandfathered trust that "changes the quality, value or timing of any powers, beneficial interests, rights or expectancies originally provided for under the terms of the trust" forfeits the GST tax-exempt status of the trust. But the IRS has also concluded in several letter rulings that a proposed agreement to modify a trust would not cause it to lose its GST tax exempt status because the proposed amendment was administrative in nature and would not shift a beneficial interest in the trust to lower generations. The modification would not, therefore, cause the trust to lose its GST tax-exempt status.[8] If in doubt, one should request a private letter ruling on whether a proposed modification to a grandfathered trust will cause an undesirable GST tax to apply.

Example 2: *Construction of an ambiguous term in the instrument.* In 1980, Grantor established an irrevocable trust for the benefit of Grantor's children, A and B and their issue. The trust is to terminate on the death of the last to die of A and B, at which time the principal is to be distributed to their issue. However, the provision governing the termination of the trust is ambiguous regarding whether the trust principal is to be distributed only to the children of A and B or among the children, grandchildren, and more remote issue of A and B. The trustee files a constructive suit with the appropriate local court to resolve the ambiguity. The court issues an order construing the instrument to provide for distribution to the children, grandchildren, and more remote issue of A and B

---

[7] Ltr. Ruls. 8851017, 8927026, 9244019, and 9448024.

[8] Ltr. Ruls. 201322010, 201322015, 201345004, 201345026, 201345027, 201345028, 201345005.

living at the time the trust terminates. The court's construction is consistent with applicable state law as it would be interpreted by the highest court of the state and resolves a bona fide controversy regarding the property interpretation of the instrument. Therefore, the trust will not be subject to the GST tax [Reg. Sec. 26.2601-1(b)(4)(E), Example (3)].

Example 3: *Modification that does not shift an interest to a lower generation.* In 1980, Grantor established an irrevocable trust for the benefit of Grantor's grandchildren, A, B, and C. The trust provides that income is to be paid to A, B, and C, in equal shares for life. The trust further provides that, upon the death of the first grandchild to die, one-third of the principal is to be distributed to that grandchild's issue, *per stirpes.* Upon the death of the second grandchild to die, one-half of the remaining trust principal is to be distributed to that grandchild's issue, per stirpes, and upon the death of the last grandchild to die, the remaining principal is to be distributed to that grandchild's issue, *per stirpes.* At a later date, A became disabled. Subsequently, the trustee, with the consent of B and C, petitioned the appropriate local court and the court approved a modification of the trust that increased A's share of trust income. The modification does not shift a portion of the income interest to a beneficiary who occupies a generation lower than the generation occupied by A, B, and C, and does not extend the time for vesting of any beneficial interest in the trust beyond the period provided for in the original trust. Accordingly, the trust as modified will not be subject to the GST tax. However, the modification increasing A's share of trust income is a transfer by B and C to A for federal gift tax purposes [Reg. Sec. 26.2601-1(b)(4)(E), Example (7)].

2. A GST that occurred on or before September 25, 1985;

3. A GST under a will or revocable trust executed before October 22, 1986, if the testator died before January 1, 1987, without having amended, at anytime after October 21, 1986, the document in any way that created or increased the amount of a GST [Reg. Sec. 26.2601-1(b)(2)]. Mere administrative changes will not cause the GST under the will to be subject to the GST tax.

Example 4: *Administrative change.* Tom executed a will prior to October 22, 1986 and died on December 31, 1986. On November 1, 1986, Tom executed a codicil to his will removing one of the co-executors named in the will. Although the codicil may have the effect of lowering administrative costs and thus increasing the amount transferred, it is considered administrative in nature and thus does not cause GSTs under the will to be subject to the GST tax [Reg. Sec. 26.2601-1(b)(2)(vii), Example (1)].

4. Certain GSTs by individuals who were incompetent on October 22, 1986 and remained so until death [Reg. Sec. 26.2601-1(b)(3)]. This exemption for transfers from incompetents is strictly defined. It requires that the individual have been incompetent on October 22, 1986 and not regain competence before the date of his death. The incompetency exemption applies even if another person has the power to change the

¶2516

trust terms provided that the power is not exercised in a manner that creates, or increases the amount of a GST [Reg. Sec. 26.2602-1(b)(3)(v)].

> **Example 5:** *Incompetency exemption.* Tom was mentally incompetent on October 22, 1986, and remained so until his death in 1997. Prior to becoming incompetent, he created a revocable GST trust that was includible in his gross estate. Prior to October 22, 1986, the appropriate court issued an order under which Tom's son, Paul, who was charged with the care of his father's property, had the power to modify or revoke the revocable trust. Although Paul exercised the power after October 22, 1986, and while Tom was incompetent, the power was not exercised in a manner that created, or increased the amount of a GST. Thus, the existence and exercise of Paul's power did not cause the trust to lose its exempt status. The result would have been the same if the court order was issued after October 22, 1986 [Reg. Sec. 26.2601-1(b)(3)(vi), Example].

The incompetency exemption applies to direct skips occurring by reason of the death of the incompetent and to generation-skipping transfers from trusts included in the gross estate of the incompetent. Thus, the exemption would not apply to taxable terminations or taxable distributions from trusts, although those trusts would undoubtedly be grandfathered if created before the effective date.

¶2517   RETURN AND PAYMENT REQUIREMENTS

After you have determined that a GST has occurred and have figured how much tax is due you still have to decide who must pay the GST tax and file the return. The answers to these questions depend on: (1) whether a direct skip, taxable distribution, or taxable termination has occurred, and (2) when it has occurred. The estate tax procedural rules, including penalties, apply to the GSTs that occur at the same time as, and a result of, the death of the transferor [IRC Sec. 2661(2)]. The gift tax procedural rules apply to all other transfers [IRC Sec. 2661(1)].

(a) Form of Return. Returns are filed by the party liable for the GST tax [IRC Sec. 2662(a)(1)]. Which party is personally liable for the GST tax and for filing the return depends on the type of generation-skipping transfer involved [Reg. Sec. 26.2662-1].

Taxable distributions. Form 706GS(D) must be filed for any taxable distribution. The trust involved in a taxable distribution must file Form 706GS (D-1), which must be sent to each person receiving a distribution from the trust [Reg. Sec. 26.2662-1(b)(1)]. In a taxable distribution, the transferee is personally liable for the GST tax and must file the return, unless the governing instrument specifically directs otherwise [Reg. Sec. 26.2662-1(c)(1)(i)].

Taxable terminations. Form 706GS(T) must be filed for any taxable termination [Reg. Sec. 26.2662-(1)(b)2]. In a taxable termination, the trustee is personally liable for the GST tax and must file the return [Reg. Sec. 26.2662-1(c)(ii)].

***Inter vivos* or lifetime direct skips.** A federal gift tax return (Form 709) must be filed for any direct skip that occurs during the lifetime of the transferor [Reg. Sec.

26.2662-1(b)(3)(i)]. It is due on April 15 of the year following the calendar year in which the gift is made (plus extensions). The transferor in the case of an *inter vivos* direct skip is personally liable for the tax and must file the return [Reg. Sec. 26.2662-1(c)(1)(iii)].

> **Example 1:** *Inter vivos or lifetime direct skip.* Grandfather gives $3 million to Grandson. This GST is a direct skip and Grandfather is the transferor and must pay the tax on the gift.

Direct skips occurring at death. A federal estate tax return (Form 706) or Form 706NA must be filed by the executor for any direct skip that occurs when the decedent dies [Reg. Sec. 26.2662-1(b)(3)(ii)]. It is due nine months after the date of the decedent's death (plus extensions). The trustee in the case of a direct skip from an explicit trust or trust arrangement, or with respect to property that continues to be held in trust, is personally liable for the GST tax and must file the estate tax return [Reg. Sec. 26.2662-1(c)(1)(iv)]. Note that for these purposes, the term "trust" includes any "trust arrangement" even though an explicit trust has not been created [Reg. Sec. 26.2662-1(c)(2)(ii)]. This means that insurance and annuity contracts could be interpreted to be trust arrangements for these purposes.

The executor must pay the tax and file the return if the direct skip occurs at death [Reg. Sec. 26.2662-1(c)(1)(v)]. For these purposes "executor" is the administrator of the decedent's estate. If no executor or administrator has been appointed, the "executor" is the fiduciary who is primarily responsible for payment of the decedent's debts and expenses. If no such person, exists, the "executor" is the person in actual or constructive possession of the largest portion of the value of the decedent's gross estate [Reg. Sec. 26.2652-1(d)].

> **Example 2:** *Direct skips occurring at death.* In his will, Grandfather leaves $1 million to each of his grandchildren. These direct skips occur when Grandfather dies and his executor must pay the tax on the transfers. The tax will reduce the taxable amount of the direct skips going to the grandchildren.

(b) Time and Manner of Filing Return. Typically, the due date for filing GST tax returns generally coincides with the due dates for gift and estate tax returns [Reg. Sec. 26.2662-1]. Forms 706 (estate tax return), 706NA, 706GS(D), 706GS(D-1), 706GS(T), and 709 (gift tax return), and Schedule R-1 of Form 706 must be filed with the IRS office where the estate or gift tax return of the transferor must be filed [Reg. Sec. 26.2662-1(d)].

Direct skip. The time for filing for the return for a direct skip (other than from a trust) is on or before date on which an estate or gift tax return must be filed for the transfer [IRC Sec. 2662(a)(2)(A); Reg. Sec. 26.2662-1(d)(1)(i)]. For all other transfers, the return is due by the 15th day of the fourth month after the close of the calendar year in which the transfer occurs [IRC Sec. 2662(a)(2)(B); Reg. Sec. 26.2662-1(d)(1)(ii)]. Besides filing it with the IRS, the trustee must send a copy to each skip-person who receives a distribution from the trust.

See Appendix 25A for a chart summarizing relevant filing deadlines for 2010 events.

¶2517

(c) Automatic Allocation of GST Exemption. If a direct skip occurs during the transferor's lifetime, the transferor's GST exemption not previously allocated (unused GST exemption) is automatically allocated to the transferred property (but not in excess of the fair market value of the property on the date of the transfer). The transferor may prevent the automatic allocation of GST exemption by describing on a timely-filed United States Gift (and Generation-Skipping Transfer) Tax Return (Form 709) the transfer and the extent to which the automatic allocation is not to apply. In addition, a timely-filed Form 709 accompanied by payment of the GST tax (as shown on the return with respect to the direct skip) is sufficient to prevent an automatic allocation of GST exemption with respect to the transferred property.

Effective date of automatic allocation of GST exemption to direct skips. If a direct skip occurs during the transferor's lifetime, the transferor's GST exemption not previously allocated (unused GST exemption) is automatically allocated to the transferred property (but not in excess of the fair market value of the property on the date of the transfer). The transferor may prevent the automatic allocation of GST exemption by describing on a timely-filed United States Gift (and Generation-Skipping Transfer) Tax Return (Form 709) the transfer and the extent to which the automatic allocation is not to apply. In addition, a timely-filed Form 709 accompanied by payment of the GST tax (as shown on the return with respect to the direct skip) is sufficient to prevent an automatic allocation of GST exemption with respect to the transferred property [Reg. Sec. 26.2632-1(b)(1)].

A Form 709 is timely filed if it is filed on or before the date required for reporting the transfer if it were a taxable gift. The automatic allocation of GST exemption (or the election to prevent the allocation, if made) is irrevocable after the due date. An automatic allocation of GST exemption is effective as of the date of the transfer to which it relates. A Form 709 need not be filed to report an automatic allocation.

Effective date of automatic allocation to indirect skips. In the case of an indirect skip, the transferor's unused GST exemption is automatically allocated to the property transferred (but not in excess of the fair market value of the property on the date of the transfer). The automatic allocation is effective whether or not a Form 709 is filed reporting the transfer, and is effective as of the date of the transfer to which it relates. An automatic allocation is irrevocable after the due date of the Form 709 for the calendar year in which the transfer is made [Reg. Sec. 26.2632-1(b)(2)(i)].

The transferor may prevent the automatic allocation of GST exemption with regard to an indirect skip by making an election under IRC Sec. 2632(c)(5)(A) not to have the automatic allocation rules apply. See ¶ 2509. The transferor may also prevent the automatic allocation of GST exemption with regard to an indirect skip by making an affirmative allocation of GST exemption on a Form 709 filed at any time on or before the due date for the timely filing of an amount that is less than (but not equal to) the value of the property transferred as reported on that return [Reg. Sec. 26.2632-1(b)(2)(ii)].

> **Example 3:** *Effective date of late allocation of GST tax exemption.* Tom transfers $100,000 to an irrevocable GST on December 1, 2013. The transfer to the trust is not a direct skip. The date prescribed for filing the gift tax return reporting the taxable gift is April 17, 2014. On December 1, 2014, Tom files a Form 709 and

allocates $50,000 to the trust. The allocation is effective as of December 1, 2014 [Reg. Sec. 26.2632-1(b)(2)(iii), Example (3)].

Example 4: *Effective date of late allocation of GST tax exemption.* Tom transfers $100,000 to an irrevocable GST on December 1, 2014 in a transfer that is not a direct skip. Tom fails to make an allocation of GST exemption on a timely filed Form 709. On July 1, 2014, the trustee makes a distribution from the trust to Tom's grandchild in the amount of $30,000. Immediately prior to the distribution, the value of the trust assets was $150,000. On the same date, Tom allocates GST exemption to the trust in the amount of $50,000. The allocation of GST exemption on the date of the transfer is treated as preceding in point of time the taxable distribution. At the time of the GST, the trust has an inclusion ratio of .6667 (1 − (50,000/150,000)) [Reg. Sec. 26.2632-1(b)(2)(iii), Example (4)].

Allocations after the transferor's death. After someone dies, his or her unused GST tax exemption is automatically allocated on the due date for filing the estate tax return (Form 706) by the executor on or before that date. The automatic allocation occurs whether or not a return is actually required to be filed [Reg. Sec. 26.2632-1(d)(2)].

An allocation of GST tax exemption with respect to property included in the gross estate of a decedent is effective as of the date of death. A timely allocation of GST tax exemption by an executor for a lifetime transfer of property that is not included in the transferor's gross estate is made on a Form 709. A late allocation of GST tax exemption by an executor, with respect to a lifetime transfer of property, is made on Form 706 or 706NA and is effective as of the date the allocation is filed. An allocation of GST tax exemption to a trust is effective if the notice of allocation clearly identifies the trust and the amount of the decedent's GST tax exemption allocated to the trust [Reg. Sec. 26.2632-1(d)(1)].

¶2518 QUALIFIED SEVERANCE OF TRUSTS

IRC Sec. 2642(a) permits taxpayers to make "qualified severances." When a trust is severed in a "qualified severance," the resulting trusts will be treated as separate trusts thereafter for purposes of the GST tax [IRC Sec. 2642(a)(3)]. The qualified severance affords taxpayers the opportunity of having trusts that are either fully subject to GST tax (i.e., trusts with an inclusion ratio of one) or are completely exempt from GST tax (i.e., trusts with an inclusion ratio of zero), as opposed to having trusts that are partially exempt from GST tax (with an inclusion ratio between zero and one).

Transferors and executors of transferor's estates should be certain not to waste the valuable GST tax exemption on transfers that would not have been subject to GST tax in the first place. For example, it would be a waste of the GST tax exemption to allocate it to assets passing to non-skip persons or on transfers to charities that are not even subject to the GST tax. If a discretionary trust authorizes distributions to skip as well as non-skip persons, it would be wise to sever or split the single trust into two or more separate trusts with different beneficiaries. A single trust will be treated as a separate trust if (1) it consists of separate and independent shares for different beneficiaries, or

(2) there is more than one transferor with respect to the trust [Reg. Secs. 26.2654-1(a)(1) and 26.2654-1(a)(2)].

After severing the trust, GST exemption should be allocated to the trust with assets passing to skip persons so it would have an inclusion ratio of zero. The other trust would be subject to the GST tax and have an inclusion ratio of one. A split of the trusts would be required because prior to the split, allocation of GST tax exemption could only have been made to the entire trust rather than to the specific trust assets that would have been subject to the GST tax. After the trusts have been severed, the regulations authorize allocation of GST exemption to the assets that need protection from the GST tax [Reg. Sec. 26.2654-1(a)(3)].

> **Example 1:** *Segregation of assets into exempt and nonexempt trusts.* Grandfather transferred $2 million into a trust that provides that income will be provided to Son for life and on Son's death, the remainder will be split equally between Grandchild and a charity. Grandfather allocates $1 million of his available GST exemption to the trust. His inclusion ratio is 1 million divided by 2 million, which equals one-half. Thus his tax is 25 percent, or one half of 50 percent. When Son dies, the portion of the trust passing to Grandchild will be subject to GST tax at a rate of 25 percent. If the trust is worth $2 million, the tax bill on Grandchild's portion will be $250,000. The other half of the trust that passes to charity will not be subject to GST tax because transfers to charity are exempt from the GST tax.
>
> Grandchild could have avoided paying the GST tax if Grandfather had created two $1 million trusts instead of one. One trust would have been allocated $1 million GST exemption and would have had an inclusion ratio of zero, and the other one would have had an inclusion ratio of one. The exempt trust or the one with the inclusion ratio of zero would have passed to Grandchild and the nonexempt trust with the inclusion ratio of one would have passed to the charity.

> **NOTE:** The language of the trust should authorize the fiduciary to divide the trusts. In the absence of specific authority granted to the trustee, look to state law for authority in the trustee to split an existing trust into separate trusts. Some states will require a court order before a trust can be severed. If the trustee splits the trust without specific authority in the trust language or under state statute, the split will not be recognized for GST purposes. As a result, each new trust will have the same inclusion ratio as the original trust.

(a) Consequence of Qualified Severance. If a trust is divided in a qualified severance into two or more trusts, the separate trusts resulting from the severance will be treated as separate trusts for (GST) tax purposes and the inclusion ratio of each new resulting trust may differ from the inclusion ratio of the original trust [IRC Sec. 2642(a)(3)]. Because the post-severance resulting trusts are treated as separate trusts for GST tax purposes, certain actions with respect to one resulting trust will generally have no GST tax impact with respect to the other resulting trust(s). For example, GST exemption allocated to one resulting trust will not impact the inclusion ratio of the other resulting trust(s); a GST tax election made with respect to one resulting trust will not apply to the other resulting trust(s); the occurrence of a taxable distribution or termination with regard to a particular resulting trust will not have any GST tax impact on any other trust resulting from that severance [Reg. Sec. 26.2642-6(a)].

(b) Qualified Severance Defined. A "qualified severance" is defined as the division of a single trust and the creation (by any means available under the governing instrument or local law) of two or more trusts if: (1) the single trust is divided on a fractional basis and (2) the terms of the new trusts, in the aggregate, provide for the same succession of interests of beneficiaries as are provided for in the original trust [IRC Sec. 2642(a)(3)(B)(i)].[1] The qualified severance provision of IRC Sec. 2642(a)(3) has been made permanent effective for estates of decedents dying, gifts made, or generation-skipping transfers after December 31, 2012, by the American Taxpayer Relief Act of 2012.

Effective date of severance. A qualified severance is applicable as of the date of the severance, as defined in Reg. Sec. 26.2642-6(d)(3) and the resulting trusts are treated as separate trusts for GST tax purposes as of that date.

Time for making severance. A qualified severance under IRC Sec. 2642(a)(3) may be made at any time prior to the termination of the trust [IRC Sec. 2642(a)(3)(C); Reg. Sec. 26.2642-6(f)(1)]. Thus, provided that the separate resulting trusts continue in existence after the severance, a qualified severance may occur either before or after: (a) GST tax exemption has been allocated to the trust; (b) a taxable event has occurred with respect to the trust; or (c) an addition has been made to the trust. Because a qualified severance is effective as of the date of severance, a qualified severance has no effect on a taxable termination or a taxable distribution that occurred prior to the date of severance. A qualified severance shall be deemed to occur before a taxable termination or a taxable distribution that occurs by reason of the qualified severance [Reg. Sec. 26.2642-6(f)].

Nonqualified severances. Trusts resulting from a severance that does not meet the requirements of a qualified severance will be treated, after the date of the severance, as separate trusts for purposes of the GST tax, provided that such trusts are recognized as separate trusts under applicable state law [Reg. Sec. 26.2642-6(h)]. Separate trust treatment will generally permit the allocation of GST exemption, the making of various GST elections, and the occurrence of a taxable distribution or termination with regard to a particular resulting trust, with no GST tax impact on any other trust resulting from the severance. However, each trust resulting from a nonqualified severance will have the same inclusion ratio immediately after the severance as that of the original trust immediately before the severance.

(c) Requirements for a Qualified Severance. A qualified severance must satisfy each of the following requirements as provided in Reg. Sec. 26.2642-6(d):

1. The single trust is severed pursuant to the terms of the governing instrument, or pursuant to applicable local law;

2. The severance is effective under local law;

---

[1] **¶ 2518** Ltr. Ruls. 201238004, 200644015, 200508001, 200351010, 200213014.

¶2518

3. The date of severance is either the date selected by the trustee when the trust assets must be valued in order to determine the funding of the resulting trusts, or the court-imposed date of funding in the case of an order of the local court with jurisdiction over the trust ordering the trustee to fund the resulting trusts on or as of a specific date. The funding must commence immediately upon, and funding must occur within a reasonable time (but in no event more than 90 days) after, the selected valuation date;

4. The original trust is severed on a fractional basis, so that each new trust (resulting trust) is funded with a fraction or percentage of the original trust, and the sum of those fractions or percentages is one or one hundred percent, respectively. The fraction may be determined by means of a formula (for example, that fraction of the trust the numerator of which is equal to the transferor's unused GST tax exemption, and the denominator of which is the fair market value of the original trust's assets on the date of severance). The severance of a trust based on a pecuniary amount does not satisfy this requirement. For example, the severance of a trust is not a qualified severance if the trust is divided into two trusts, with one trust to be funded with $1,500,000 and the other trust to be funded with the balance of the original trust's assets. With respect to the particular assets to be distributed to each separate trust resulting from the severance, each such trust may be funded with the appropriate fraction or percentage (pro rata portion) of each asset held by the original trust. Alternatively, the assets may be divided among the resulting trusts on a non-pro rata basis, based on the fair market value of the assets on the date of severance. However, if a resulting trust is funded on a non-pro rata basis, each asset received by a resulting trust must be valued, solely for funding purposes, by multiplying the fair market value of the asset held in the original trust as of the date of severance by the fraction or percentage of that asset received by that resulting trust. Thus, the assets must be valued without taking into account any discount or premium arising from the severance, for example, any valuation discounts that might arise because the resulting trust receives less than the entire interest held by the original trust;

5. The terms of the resulting trusts must provide, in the aggregate, for the same succession of interests of beneficiaries as are provided in the original trust. This requirement is satisfied if the beneficiaries of the separate resulting trusts and the interests of the beneficiaries with respect to the separate trusts, when the separate trusts are viewed collectively, are the same as the beneficiaries and their respective beneficial interests with respect to the original trust before severance. With respect to trusts from which discretionary distributions may be made to any one or more beneficiaries on a non-pro rata basis, this requirement is satisfied if:

   a. The terms of each of the resulting trusts are the same as the terms of the original trust (even though each permissible distributee of the original trust is not a beneficiary of all of the resulting trusts);

   b. Each beneficiary's interest in the resulting trusts (collectively) equals the beneficiary's interest in the original trust, determined by the terms of the trust instrument or, if none, on a per-capita basis. For example, in the case of the severance of a discretionary trust established for the benefit of A, B, and C and their descendants with the remainder to be divided equally among those three families, this requirement is satisfied if the trust is divided into three

¶2518

separate trusts of equal value with one trust established for the benefit of A and A's descendants, one trust for the benefit of B and B's descendants, and one trust for the benefit of C and C's descendants;

    c. The severance does not shift a beneficial interest in the trust to any beneficiary in a lower generation than the person or persons who held the beneficial interest in the original trust; and

    d. The severance does not extend the time for the vesting of any beneficial interest in the trust beyond the period provided for in the original trust.

6. In the case of a qualified severance of a trust with an inclusion ratio of either one or zero, each trust resulting from the severance will have an inclusion ratio equal to the inclusion ratio of the original trust.

7. And:

- In the case of a qualified severance occurring after GST tax exemption has been allocated to the trust, the trust must have an inclusion ratio that is greater than zero and less than one;

- The trust is severed initially into only two resulting trusts. One resulting trust must receive that fractional share of the total value of the original trust as of the date of severance that is equal to the applicable fraction used to determine the inclusion ratio of the original trust immediately before the severance. The other resulting trust must receive that fractional share of the total value of the original trust as of the date of severance that is equal to the excess of one over the fractional share. The trust receiving the fractional share equal to the applicable fraction shall have an inclusion ratio of zero, and the other trust shall have an inclusion ratio of one. If the applicable fraction with respect to the original trust is .50, then, with respect to the two equal trusts resulting from the severance, the trustee may designate which of the resulting trusts will have an inclusion ratio of zero and which will have an inclusion ratio of one. Each separate trust resulting from the severance then may be further divided in accordance with the rules of this section;

- The trust is severed initially into more than two resulting trusts. One or more of the resulting trusts in the aggregate must receive that fractional share of the total value of the original trust as of the date of severance that is equal to the applicable fraction used to determine the inclusion ratio of the original trust immediately before the severance. The trust or trusts receiving such fractional share shall have an inclusion ratio of zero, and each of the other resulting trust or trusts shall have an inclusion ratio of one. (If, however, two or more of the resulting trusts each receives the fractional share of the total value of the original trust equal to the applicable fraction, the trustee may designate which of those resulting trusts will have an inclusion ratio of zero and which will have an inclusion ratio of one.) The resulting trust or trusts with an inclusion ratio of one must receive in the aggregate that fractional share of the total value of the original trust as of the date of severance that is equal to the excess of one over the fractional share described in the second sentence of this paragraph.

(d) Reporting a Qualified Severance. Reporting a qualified severance. A qualified severance is reported by filing Form 706-GS(T), "Generation-Skipping Transfer Tax Return for Terminations." The filer should write "Qualified Severance"

¶2518

at the top of the form and attach a Notice of Qualified Severance (Notice). The return and attached Notice should be filed by April 15th of the year immediately following the year during which the severance occurred or by the last day of the period covered by an extension of time, if an extension of time is granted, to file such form [Reg. Sec. 26.2642-6(e)].

The Notice should provide the following information regarding the original trust that was severed:

a. The name of the transferor;

b. The name and date of creation of the original trust;

c. The tax identification number of the original trust; and

d. The inclusion ratio before the severance [Reg. Sec. 26.2642-6(e)(2)].

The Notice should provide the following information with respect to each of the resulting trusts created by the severance:

a. The name and tax identification number of the trust;

b. The date of severance;

c. The fraction of the total assets of the original trust received by the resulting trust;

d. Other details explaining the basis for the funding of the resulting trust (a fraction of the total fair market value of the assets on the date of severance, or a fraction of each asset); and

e. The inclusion ratio [Reg. Sec. 26.2642-6(e)(3)].

(e) Treatment of Trusts Resulting from a Nonqualified Severance.

Trusts resulting from a nonqualified severance will be treated as separate trusts for purposes of the GST tax. The post-severance treatment of the resulting trusts as separate trusts for GST tax purposes generally permits the allocation of GST tax exemption, the making of various elections permitted for GST tax purposes, and the occurrence of a taxable distribution or termination with no GST tax impact on any other trust resulting from that severance. Each trust resulting from a severance, however, will have the same inclusion ratio immediately after the severance as that of the original trust immediately before the severance. Further, any trust resulting from a nonqualified severance may be severed subsequently [Reg. Sec. 26.2642-6(h)].

> **Example 2:** *Succession of interests.* T dies and his will establishes a testamentary trust (Trust) providing that income is to be paid to T's sister, S, for her life. On S's death, one-half of the corpus is to be paid to T's child, C (or to C's estate if C fails to survive S), and one-half of the corpus is to be paid to T's grandchild, GC (or to GC's estate if GC fails to survive S). On the Form 706, filed for T's estate, T's executor allocates all of T's available GST tax exemption to other transfers and trusts, such that Trust's inclusion ratio is one. Subsequent to filing the Form 706, the trustee divides Trust into two separate trusts, Trust 1 and Trust 2, with each trust receiving 50 percent of the value of the assets of the original trust as of the date of severance. Trust 1 provides that trust income is to be paid to S for life with remainder to C or C's estate, and Trust 2 provides that trust income is to be paid to S for life with remainder to GC or GC's estate. Because Trust 1 and Trust 2 provide for the same succession of interests in the aggregate as provided

¶2518

in the original trust, the severance constitutes a qualified severance [Reg. Sec. 26.2642-6(j), ex. 1].

Example 3: *Severance based on actuarial value of beneficial interests.* T establishes Trust, an irrevocable trust providing that income is to be paid to T's child C during C's lifetime. Upon C's death, Trust is to terminate and the assets of Trust are to be paid to GC, C's child, if living, or, if GC is not then living, to GC's estate. T properly elects not to have the automatic allocation rules apply with respect to T's transfers to Trust, and T does not otherwise allocate GST tax exemption with respect to Trust. Thus, Trust has an inclusion ratio of one. Three years later, the trustee of Trust divides Trust into two separate trusts, Trust 1 for the benefit of C (and on C's death to C's estate), and Trust 2 for the benefit of GC (and on GC's death to GC's estate). The document severing Trust directs that Trust 1 is to be funded with an amount equal to the actuarial value of C's interest in Trust prior to the severance. Similarly, Trust 2 is to be funded with an amount equal to the actuarial value of GC's interest in Trust prior to the severance. Trust 1 and Trust 2 do not provide for the same succession of interests as provided under the terms of the original trust. Therefore, the severance is not a qualified severance. Furthermore, because the severance results in no non-skip person having an interest in Trust 2, Trust 2 constitutes a skip person and, therefore, the severance results in a taxable termination subject to GST tax [Reg. Sec. 26.2642-6(j), ex. 3].

Example 4: *Severance of a trust with a 50% inclusion ratio.* T transfers $100,000 to a trust for the benefit of T's grandchild, GC. On a timely filed Form 709, reporting the transfer, T allocates all of T's remaining GST tax exemption ($50,000) to the trust. As a result of the allocation, the applicable fraction with respect to the trust is .50 [$50,000 (the amount of GST tax exemption allocated to the trust) divided by $100,000 (the value of the property transferred to the trust)]. The inclusion ratio with respect to the trust is .50 [1 – .50]. The next year, the trustee severs the trust into two trusts, Trust 1 and Trust 2, each of which is identical to the original trust and each of which receives a 50 percent fractional share of the total value of the original trust, valued as of the date of severance. Because the applicable fraction with respect to the original trust is .50 and the trust is severed into two equal trusts, the trustee may designate which resulting trust has an inclusion ratio of one, and which resulting trust has an inclusion ratio of zero. Accordingly, in the Notice of Qualified Severance reporting the severance, the trustee designates Trust 1 as having an inclusion ratio of zero, and Trust 2 as having an inclusion ratio of one. The severance constitutes a qualified severance [Reg. Sec. 26.2642-6(j), ex. 4].

Example 5: *Other severance that does not meet the requirements of a qualified severance.* (i) T establishes an irrevocable inter vivos trust (Trust) providing that Trust income is to be paid to T's children, A and B, in equal shares for their joint lives. Upon the death of the first to die of A and B, all Trust income will be paid to the survivor of A and B. At the death of the survivor, the corpus is to be

¶2518

distributed in equal shares to T's grandchildren, W and X (with any then-deceased grandchild's share being paid in accordance with that grandchild's testamentary general power of appointment). W is A's child and X is B's child. T elects not to have the automatic allocation rules apply with respect to T's transfers to Trust, but T allocates GST tax exemption to Trust resulting in Trust having an inclusion ratio of .30.

(ii) Five years later, the trustee divides Trust into Trust 1 and Trust 2. Trust 1 provides that trust income is to be paid to A for life and, on A's death, the remainder is to be distributed to W. Trust 2 provides that trust income is to be paid to B for life and, on B's death, the remainder is to be distributed to X. Because Trust 1 and Trust 2 do not provide A and B with the contingent survivor income interests that were provided to A and B under the terms of Trust, Trust 1 and Trust 2 do not provide for the same succession of interests in the aggregate as provided by Trust. Therefore, the severance is not a qualified severance. Trust 1 and Trust 2 will be recognized as separate trusts for GST tax purposes prospectively from the date of the severance but each has an inclusion ratio of .30 immediately after the severance, the same as the inclusion ratio of Trust prior to severance [Reg. Sec. 26.2642-6(j), ex. 12].

Example 6: *Qualified severance following a nonqualified severance.* Assume the same facts as in the example above except that, in the following year, the trustee of Trust 1 severs Trust 1 into two trusts, Trust 3 and Trust 4. The instrument severing Trust 1 provides that both resulting trusts have provisions identical to Trust 1. The terms of the instrument severing Trust 1 further provide that Trust 3 is to be funded on a pro rata basis with assets having a fair market value as of the date of severance equal to 70% of the value of Trust 1's assets on that date, and Trust 4 is to be funded with assets having a fair market value as of the date of severance equal to 30% of the value of Trust 1's assets on that date. The severance constitutes a qualified severance. Trust 3 will have an inclusion ratio of zero and Trust 4 will have an inclusion ratio of one [Reg. Sec. 26.2642-6(j), ex. 13].

(f) Practice Tips on Allocation of GST Tax Exemption.

- *Direct skips are more economical.* Remember that if you are forced into a situation involving a GST, direct skips are cheaper than taxable terminations or taxable distributions because direct skips do not include the GST tax in the tax base. Taxable distributions and taxable terminations, on the other hand, include the tax in the tax base. Given the choice always go for the direct skip.

- *Allocate GST exemption to appreciating assets.* Be sure to get the most leverage out of your GST tax exemption by allocating it to the extent possible to assets you expect to appreciate in value in the future. The properly allocated GST tax exemption will act as a shield and insulate the future appreciation from GST tax. For example, consider allocating GST tax exemption to trusts containing stocks, mutual funds, and life insurance.

- *Remember the reverse QTIP election.* Take advantage of the reverse QTIP election to avoid wasting any GST tax exemption. Here's how it works. Suppose someone's will creates a credit shelter or bypass trust that will contain assets worth the amount of the exemption equivalent with the balance of the estate passing to the surviving spouse in a QTIP trust. The deceased spouse's executor can allocate the amount of the GST tax exemption to the credit shelter or bypass trust, but the big question is what to do with the deceased spouse's remaining GST tax exemption. It's not wise planning to waste it. The deceased spouse's executor cannot allocate GST tax exemption to transfers under the surviving spouse's will because the deceased spouse will not be considered the "transferor" of those assets. Remember that only the "transferor" of property is eligible to allocate GST tax exemption. The surviving spouse will not be considered the transferor of QTIP property for GST tax purposes, if the executor for the deceased spouse makes a reverse QTIP election under IRC Sec. 2652(a)(3). A reverse QTIP election simply means that the executor elects for the deceased spouse to continue to be treated as the transferor of the property for GST tax purposes. The deceased spouse can thus apply the balance remaining on his GST exemption on the assets passing to the surviving spouse via the QTIP trust [IRC Sec. 2652(a)(3)].

- *Leverage your GST tax exemption with life insurance trusts.* Irrevocable life insurance trusts [see ¶ 401] offer you a technique for removing life insurance proceeds from your taxable estate as well as the estate of your surviving spouse, provided that you and your spouse do not own the policy. An irrevocable life insurance trust is an irrevocable trust that is both the owner and beneficiary of one or more life insurance policies. It is a device that can save you considerable amount of estate taxes. If any life insurance policy includes as a beneficiary a skip person such as a grandchild, the GST tax could be applicable and therefore must be considered. The objective with an irrevocable life insurance trust is to have it be fully exempt from the GST tax while using as little as possible of the donor's lifetime GST exemption. The two methods discussed below are available to ensure a zero inclusion ratio.

  Method One: If you allocate the grantor's GST tax exemption to the cash gifts given to the trustee each year to pay the life insurance premiums and to any life insurance policy transferred into the trust, you can shield from the GST tax not only the entire death benefit of a life insurance policy but also any amount that the policy owned by the trust appreciates in value. Using your GST tax exemption to avoid GST tax liability on the appreciation is called leveraging your GST tax exemption. It is this leveraging capability that makes life insurance trusts a very beneficial place to allocate GST tax exemption.

  You allocate the GST tax exemption to the cash gifts made to the life insurance trust by filing Form 709 on or before April 15 of each year. The allocation will apply GST exemption to all cash gifts made in the prior calendar year.

  Method Two: Rather than allocate GST exemption to the irrevocable life insurance trust on an annual basis equal to the amount contributed to the trust to pay the insurance premiums, the GST exemption could be allocated at a later date against the trust's fair market value at that time. If this method is used, the GST exemption would have to be alocated against all subsequent trust contributions to maintain the trust's exempt status. If this method is used, the GST exemption will be allocated to the trust as of the gift date, as long as (1) the donor files a gift

¶2518

tax return before the extended due date for that year, or (2) there is an automatic exemption allocation under IRC Sec. 2632(b)(1) or (c)(1).

- *Create a dynasty trust.* Use the GST rules to create a trust that lasts the maximum period permitted under the state law rule against perpetuities. By establishing the dynasty trust and allocating GST exemption as permitted by law, the grandparent will be able to pass assets from generation to generation free of estate tax and GST. Moreover, the assets in the trust have the opportunity to multiply in value. An added benefit to the dynasty trust is the ability to protect the assets in the trust from the reach of creditors and former spouses.

Example 7: Grandfather transfers assets worth up to $1.1 million to a trust that pays income to Child for life, with principal distributions for Child's heath, education, maintenance and support. Grandfather pays the gift tax that is owed. When Child dies, the trust is held for Grandchild with the same exact terms until the time limit provided by the rule against perpetuities if one exists in that state.

DECEDENT'S FINAL INCOME TAX RETURN

TABLE OF CONTENTS

¶2600 THE DECEDENT'S FINAL INCOME TAX RETURN—THE BASICS

One of the duties of the executor or personal representative of the deceased person's estate is to file an income tax return for the decedent's year of death. This return is called the decedent's final income tax return and it covers the period beginning on the first day of the decedent's regular tax year and ending with the day the decedent died [IRC Sec. 6012(b)].

If the person dies early in the calendar year, but before the April 15 filing deadline, the executor has a twofold filing responsibility:

1. File a regular income tax return for the tax year prior to the year the decedent died, and

2. File the final return for the year that the decedent died. This return will be due twelve months after the return mentioned in (1) above.

   Example 1: Mom died on March 15, 2014, before filing her 2013 federal income tax return, which was due on April 15, 2014. Her executor will have to file her 2013 federal income tax return by April 15, 2014. In addition, the executor must file a decedent's final income tax return on April 15, 2014, to report income that Mom received from January 1, 2014, until the date of her death, March 15, 2014.

If no executor or administrator has been appointed, the decedent's final income tax return must be filed by the person charged with the decedent's property such as the surviving spouse or heir [IRC Sec. 6012(b)(1); Reg. Sec. 1.6012-3(b)(1)].

¶2600

(a) Executor's Duty to Notify IRS. The decedent's executor has an obligation to notify the IRS of his or her status as the decedent's representative. This is accomplished on Form 56. The form should be filed when the relationship is created or when the first tax return is filed. Importantly, Form 56 notifies the IRS to mail correspondence concerning the decedent's taxes to the executor rather than to the decedent's last-known address. Once the executor's fiduciary capacity has terminated, a second Form 56 should be filed advising the IRS of the termination [Reg. Sec. 301.6903-1(c)].

(b) Questions the Executor Must Answer. The executor must address the following issues regarding the decedent's final return:

1. Do I have to file a final return on behalf of the decedent? [See ¶ 2601]

2. Should a joint return with a surviving spouse be filed? [See ¶ 2706]

3. Where do I deduct the decedent's medical expenses? [See ¶ ¶ 2609, 2740]

4. What do I do with the decedent's carryovers? [See ¶ ¶ 2610, 2720, and 2721]

5. What income should be reported on the decedent's final return? [See ¶ ¶ 2605, 2712]

6. How do I deal with life insurance proceeds received by the surviving spouse? [See ¶ 2701]

7. How do I treat the decedent's gains and losses from stocks, property and homes? [See ¶ ¶ 2720, 2721]

8. How do I treat the decedent's business income from partnerships and S corporations? [See ¶ ¶ 2606, 2720]

9. What tax benefits are available to the surviving spouse? [See ¶ 2709]

¶2601 IS A DECEDENT'S FINAL TAX RETURN NECESSARY

The threshold question to answer about filing a decedent's final return is whether it is necessary to file a return for the decedent. The same filing requirements that determine whether it is necessary to file a return for an individual determine if a final income tax return must be filed for a decedent. Consequently, whether or not the executor must file a return on behalf of the decedent depends on the decedent's filing status, age, and gross income. In most cases, the following outline can be used to determine whether it is necessary to file a final income tax return for a decedent who died in 2014.

Note that taxpayers must file as "Married Filing Jointly" if any of the following apply:

- The taxpayers were married at the end of 2014 even if they did not live together at the end of the year;

- One spouse died in 2014 and the surviving spouse did not remarry that year;

- The taxpayers were married at the end of 2014 and one of the spouses died in 2015 before filing a 2014 return.

¶2601

A taxpayer can file as "Qualifying Widower with Dependent Child" in 2014 and pay tax as if filing as joint taxpayers if all of the following apply:

- The widower's spouse died in 2012 or 2013 and the surviving spouse did not remarry by the end of 2014;

- The widower has a child or stepchild claimed as a dependent. This does not include a foster child;

- This child lived in the widower's home for all of 2014;

- The widower paid over half of the cost of keeping up his or her home;

- The widower could have filed a joint return with his or her spouse even if the widower did not actually do so.

Note that if the spouse died in 2014, the surviving spouse cannot file as "Qualifying Widower with Dependent Child" in 2014.

> ▶ **PRACTICE POINTER:** It is often preferable for the surviving spouse to file a joint income tax return because it will result in a lower overall income tax liability than if separate returns are filed. A joint return will allow the parties to fully take advantage of deductions which are attributable to a decedent's final taxable year. For example, consider the situation where the decedent had a net capital loss in his or her final taxable year and the surviving spouse had a net capital gain for the year. A net capital loss is deductible only to the extent of $3,000 ($1,500 if married taxpayers are filing separately). If a joint return is filed, the decedent's net capital loss could offset any capital gain realized by the surviving spouse during the taxable year before or after the decedent's death. Moreover, a decedent's net capital loss will be lost if not claimed on the decedent's final return.

Same-sex couples. Same-sex spouses who legally married on or before December 31, 2013 in a state that recognizes same-sex marriage must file as married filed jointly or married filing separately, even if they now live in a state that does not recognize same-sex marriage. For this purpose, "state" means any domestic or foreign jurisdiction having the legal authority to sanction marriages. Individuals who have entered into a registered domestic partnership, civil union, or other similar relationship that is not considered a marriage under state law are not considered married for federal tax purposes.

Form 1310 may be necessary. If you are filing a final return for a decedent and claiming a refund, in certain situations you must file Form 1310, "Statement of Person Claiming Refund due a Deceased Taxpayer," with the return. This form proves that you have authority to file the refund claim and receive the refund.

Form 1310 need **not** be filed if the person claiming the refund is:

- A surviving spouse filing an original or amended joint return with the decedent, or

- A court-appointed or certified personal representative filing Form 1040, Form 1040A, or Form 1040EZ for the decedent and a copy of the court certificate showing your appointment is attached to the return.

To avoid having to file the Form 1310, the personal representative must attach to the return a copy of the court certificate showing that he or she was appointed the personal representative for the decedent.

¶2601

¶2602 WHICH FORM TO USE

The executor will file the decedent's final income tax return on Form 1040, Form 1040A or Form 1040EZ. No matter which form is filed, all supporting schedules, such as Schedules A, B, and C should be attached to the form you file. Consult the lists below to determine which form should be filed for the decedent.

(a) Who Must File Form 1040. Anyone *can* use Form 1040, the so-called "long" form, but the decedent *must* use Form 1040 if:

- The decedent's taxable income was $100,000 or more;
- The decedent itemized deductions on Schedule A;
- The decedent had income that cannot be reported on Form 1040EZ or Form 1040A, including tax-exempt interest from private activity bonds issued after August 7, 1986;
- The decedent claims adjustments to gross income in addition to adjustments listed earlier under Form 1040A;
- The decedent's Form W-2, box 12, shows uncollected employee tax (social security and Medicare tax) on tips or group-term life insurance;
- The decedent received $20 or more in tips in any one month and did not report all of them to his or her employer;
- The decedent was a bona fide resident of Puerto Rico and excluded income from sources in Puerto Rico;
- The decedent claimed credits in addition to credits listed earlier under Form 1040A;
- The decedent owed excise tax on insider stock compensation from an expatriated corporation;
- The decedent's Form W-2 shows an amount in box 12 with a code Z;
- The decedent had a qualified health savings account funding distribution from an IRA;
- The decedent was an employee and the decedent's employer did not withhold social security and Medicare tax;
- The decedent must file other forms with the return to report certain exclusions, taxes, or transactions, such as Form 8959 or Form 8960;
- The decedent was a debtor in a bankruptcy case filed after October 16, 2005;
- The decedent must repay the first-time homebuyer credit;
- The decedent has AGI of more than $150,000 and must reduce the dollar amount of his or her exemptions.

(b) Who May File Form 1040A. The so-called short form, Form 1040A, is a simple way to file the decedent's final tax return. Form 1040A may be used if:

1. The decedent's income is only from:
   - Wages, salaries, and tips;
   - Interest;

- Ordinary dividends (including Alaska Permanent Fund dividends);
- Capital gain distributions;
- IRA distributions;
- Pensions and annuities;
- Unemployment compensation;
- Taxable social security and railroad retirement benefits; and
- Taxable scholarship and fellowship grants.

   NOTE: If the decedent received a capital gain distribution that includes unre-captured IRC Sec. 1250 gain, IRC Sec. 1202 gain, or collectibles (28%) gain, the decedent cannot use Form 1040A and must use Form 1040.

2. The decedent's taxable income is less than $100,000.

3. The decedent's only adjustments to income are for:

   - Educator expenses;
   - IRA deduction;
   - Student loan interest deduction;
   - Tuition and fees.

4. The decedent did not itemize deductions.

5. The decedent claimed only the following tax credits:

   - The credit for child and dependent care expenses;
   - The credit for the elderly or the disabled;
   - The education credits;
   - The retirement savings contribution credit;
   - The child tax credit;
   - The earned income credit;
   - The additional child tax credit.

6. The decedent did not have an AMT adjustment on stock acquired from the exercise of an incentive stock option.

The decedent can also use Form 1040A if he or she received employer-provided dependent care benefits or owed tax from the recapture of an education credit or the alternative minimum tax. The decedent must meet all these requirements to use Form 1040A.

(c) Who May File Form 1040EZ. Form 1040EZ, which is the simplest form to use, may be used if all of the following apply:

1. The decedent's filing status is single or married filing jointly. If the decedent was a nonresident alien at any time in 2013, the decedent's filing status must be married filing jointly;

2. The decedent and his or her spouse, if married filing a joint return, were under age 65 and not blind at the end of 2013;

3. The decedent does not claim any dependents;

4. The decedent's taxable income is less than $100,000;

¶2602

5. The decedent's income is only from wages, salaries, tips, unemployment compensation, Alaska Permanent Fund dividends, taxable scholarship and fellowship grants, and taxable interest of $1,500 or less;

6. The decedent does not claim any adjustments to income, such as a deduction for IRA contributions or student loan interest;

7. The decedent does not claim any credits other than the earned income credit;

8. The decedent does not owe any household employment taxes on wages paid to a household employee;

9. The decedent earned tips and they are included in boxes 5 and 7 of the decedent's Form W-2;

10. The decedent was not a debtor in a chapter 11 bankruptcy case filed after October 16, 2005.

The decedent must satisfy all of these requirements to use Form 1040EZ.

(d) What to File if Decedent Was Nonresident Alien. For a decedent who was a nonresident alien, Form 1040NR, "U.S. Nonresident Alien Income Tax Return," must be filed instead of any of the other forms mentioned above.

¶2603 DUE DATE OF DECEDENT'S FINAL RETURN

The decedent's final income tax return is due on the same day it would have been due if the decedent had not died. In other words, unless an extension is filed or the deadline falls on a Saturday, Sunday or holiday, the final return is due April 15 of the year following the year of death [Reg. Sec.1.6072-1(b)].

> **Example 1:** Dad died on December 15, 2013, his final income tax return was due April 15, 2014.

Automatic Six-Month Extension. Individual taxpayers may be able to use Form 4868, "Application for Automatic Extension of Time to File U.S. Individual Income Tax Return," to obtain an automatic six-month (four-month if out of the country) extension of time to file their tax returns without a reason or even a signature.

> ▶ **PRACTICE POINTER:** Form 4868 extends the time for filing a return, not the time for payment of the tax that is owed. So you may have to send a check by the original due date for filing the return with your Form 4868 in order to avoid an underpayment penalty [Reg. Sec. 1.6081-4(a)(4)]. If the tax is not properly estimated, the application for an extension will be disregarded. When filing an extension, keep in mind that interest will still be owed on any unpaid portion of the tax bill that is not paid in full by the due date.

¶2603

¶2604 WHERE TO FILE THE DECEDENT'S FINAL RETURN

If the decedent's final status is single or married filing separately, file the decedent's final income tax return with the IRS Service Center in the IRS district where the personal representative lives. If the decedent filed jointly, file the final return in the IRS district of the surviving spouse's residence [Reg. Sec. 1.6091-2(a)].

If the decedent was a nonresident alien and Form 1040NR was filed on his or her behalf, file the final return with the IRS Service Center, Philadelphia, PA 19255.

The timely mailed/timely filed rule. If a document or payment mailed to the IRS is delivered by the U.S. Postal Service in a postage prepaid, properly addressed envelope, it will be considered to be mailed on time if the date of the postmark is on or before the due date. This is known as the timely mailed/timely filed rule. In other words, if a taxpayer mailed his or her tax return or tax payment on time, it is considered to be filed or paid on time even though it arrived at its destination late. Taxpayers can use certain private delivery services designated by the IRS to meet the "timely mailing as timely filing/paying" rule for tax returns and payments. The following private delivery services have been approved by the IRS:[1]

- DHL Express (DHL)—DHL "Same Day" Service.
- Federal Express (FedEx)—FedEx Priority Overnight, FedEx Standard Overnight, FedEx 2Day, FedEx International Priority, and FedEx International First.
- United Parcel Service (UPS)—UPS Next Day Air, UPS Next Day Air Saver, UPS 2nd Day Air, UPS 2nd Day Air A.M., UPS Worldwide Express Plus, and UPS Worldwide Express.

    NOTE: Private delivery services cannot deliver items to P.O. boxes. Taxpayers must use the U.S. Postal Service to mail any item to an IRS P.O. box address.

¶2605 COMPUTING THE DECEDENT'S TAXABLE INCOME

When computing the decedent's taxable income for the year of death, use the same method of accounting that he or she last used while still alive. If the decedent did not use a regular accounting method while still alive, he is treated like a cash-basis decedent for reporting income items so that only items actually or constructively received (available without restriction) before death are reported on the final return [Reg. Sec. 1.451-1(b)(1)].

    (a) Cash Basis Taxpayer. If the deceased person was on the cash basis, as is usually the case, the final income tax return will include only income he or she actually or constructively received up to the end of the day of death. Income is constructively received if someone had use of the money without restriction. For example, an unclaimed paycheck that the decedent never picked up will be consid-

---

[1] **¶2604** Notice 2004-83, 2004-52 IRB 1030.

¶2604

ered constructively received and will be included in taxable income on the decedent's final return [Reg. Sec. 1.451-1(a)]. Income that accrues only because of death is not included on the decedent's final return. Any amount of gross income not reported on the return of the decedent is, when received, includible in the income of the person receiving such amounts by inheritance or survivorship. This may be the decedent's estate. Or, if the estate does not collect an item of income, but distributes the right to receive it to a testamentary trust or to the heir, next of kin, or devisee, it is included in the income of such trust, heir, next of kin, legatee or devisee [IRC Sec. 691(a); Reg. Sec. 1.691(a)-2].

A dividend is constructively received if it was available for use by the decedent before he died with no questions asked.[1] If the dividend recipient died between the time the dividend was declared and the time it was received in the mail (if the corporation customarily mails the dividend checks), the dividend is not constructively received and should not be included in the final return [Reg. Sec. 1.451-2(b)].[2]

Interest from coupons on bonds owned by the decedent is constructively received by the decedent if the coupons matured in the decedent's final tax year, but were not cashed.[3] Such interest should be included in the decedent's final income tax return.

Salary, commissions, wages, royalties, and bonuses received before death will be included in the decedent's final return [Reg. Sec. 1.451-1(a)]. A bonus received after the death of a cash basis taxpayer will not be reported on the final return, unless it was constructively received or could have been spent while the decedent was still alive.

Income items that the decedent was entitled to receive but did not receive before his death are called "income in respect of a decedent" (IRD) and are included in the gross income of the estate or the beneficiary who receives them [Reg. Sec. 1.691(a)-1(b)]. See ¶ 2614.

To be included on the final return of a cash basis decedent, the income must have been received or must have been available to the decedent prior to his or her death.

The depreciation recapture rules under IRC Secs. 1245 and 1250 apply to sales or other dispositions of property subject to those rules where the income therefrom is treated as income on the decedent's final return or as income in respect of a decedent under IRC Sec. 691. But these rules do not apply to transfers of depreciable property at death [IRC Secs. 1245(b)(2) and 1250(d)(2)].

(b) Accrual Basis Taxpayer. If the deceased person used the accrual method of accounting, his or her final income tax return will include only income or deductions that accrued up to and including the date of death. Income or deductions that accrue only because of death are not included in the final return [IRC Secs. 451(b), 461(b); Reg. Secs. 1.451-1(b), 1.461-1(b)]. Income that is received after death is not reported on the decedent's final return. This income is considered IRD and is taxed to the estate or the beneficiary receiving the income in the year of receipt. For discussion of IRD, see ¶ 2614.

---

[1] **¶ 2605** Avery, 292 U.S. 210 (1934).   [3] Loose, 15 BTA 169 (1929), *acq.*, 1929-2 CB 32.
[2] Avery, 292 U.S. 210 (1934).

¶2605

¶2606 REPORTING BUSINESS INCOME

(a) Partnership Income. If the decedent was a member of a partnership when he or she died, there are special rules to consider when determining the partnership income in the decedent's final taxable year. See ¶2720.

The death of a partner closes the tax year of the partnership [IRC Secs. 706(c), 708]. The partnership tax year, however, continues for both the remaining partners and the deceased partner's successor in interest [IRC Sec. 708(b)(1)]. The decedent's distributive share of partnership items must be figured as if the partnership's tax year ended on the date the partner died. IRC Sec. 706(c)(2)(A) provides that the taxable year of a partnership closes with respect to a partner whose entire interest in the partnership terminates, whether by death, liquidation, or otherwise [IRC Sec. 706(c)(2)(A)]. As a result, the deceased partner's income will be reported on the decedent's final income tax return.

> **Example 1:** Paula is a partner in a partnership and was entitled to a $100,000 distributive share of partnership income on the date of her death. She died on December 1. In addition, at the time of her death, she had personal deductions for mortgage interest and taxes in the amount of $25,000. Code Sec. 706(c)(2)(A) provides that Paula's partnership year will close when she dies and her share of partnership income will be reported on her final return and can be offset by her personal deductions.

To avoid an interim closing of the partnership books, the partners can agree to estimate the decedent's distributive share by prorating the amounts the partner would have included for the entire partnership tax year.

The decedent's final return must include the decedent's distributive share of partnership items for the following periods:

1. The partnership tax year that ended within or with the decedent's last tax year (the year ending on the date of death) [Reg. Sec.1.706-1(c)(3)(ii)].

2. The period, if any, from the end of that partnership tax year as described in item 1 above to the decedent's date of death.

> **Example 2:** Mom was a partner in a partnership and reported her income on a tax year ending December 31. The partnership uses a tax year ending June 30. Mom died on August 31, 2013 and her estate established its tax year ending August 31.
>
> The distributive share of taxable income from the partnership based on the decedent's partnership interest is reported as follows:
>
> (1) Final Return for the Decedent—January 1 through August 31, 2014, includes partnership items from
>
> > (a) the partnership tax year ending June 30, 2014, because the final Form 1040 of a deceased partner only includes her share of partnership taxable income for the partnership's taxable year ending with the last taxable year, which in this case ended on June 30, 2013, and

¶2606

(b) the partnership tax year beginning July 1, 2013, and ending August 31, 2014, which was the date of death;

(2) Income Tax Return of Mom's Estate—September 1, 2014 through August 31, 2015, includes partnership items for the period September 1, 2014 through June 30, 2015. The portion of income from the partnership for the period July 1, 2014 through August 31, 2014 is IRD and is included in the gross income of Mom's estate or the deceased partner's successor in interest who continues to share the partnership's profits and losses.

(b) S Corporation Income. If the decedent was a shareholder in an S corporation, the decedent's final return must include the decedent's share of S corporation income for the corporation's tax year that ends within or with the decedent's last tax year, ending on the date of death. The decedent's final return must also include the decedent's pro rata share of the S corporation's income for the period between the end of the corporation's last tax year and the date of death.

Amounts of income or loss from an S corporation during the year of the decedent's death are allocated between the decedent and the decedent's successor [IRC Sec. 1377(a)]. The income for the part of the S corporation's tax year after the shareholder's death is income to the estate or other person who has acquired the stock in the S corporation.

(c) Self-Employment Income. The decedent's final return must include the self-employment income that the decedent actually or constructively received or accrued, depending on the decedent's accounting method. For self-employment tax purposes only, the decedent's self-employment income will include the decedent's distributive share of a partnership's income or loss through the end of the month in which death occurred. For this purpose, the partnership income or loss is considered to be earned ratably over the partnership's tax year.

(d) Community Income. If the decedent was married and lived in a community property state, half of the income received and half of the expenses paid during the decedent's tax year by either the decedent or spouse may be considered to be the income and expenses of the other. The income and expenses must therefore be included on the decedent's final return.

(e) Coverdell Education Savings Account (ESA). Generally, the balance in a Coverdell ESA must be distributed within 30 days after the individual for whom the account was established reaches age 30, or dies, whichever is earlier. The treatment of the Coverdell ESA at the death of an individual under age 30 depends on who acquires the interest in the account. If the decedent's estate acquires the interest, the earnings on the account must be included on the final income tax return of the decedent. If a beneficiary acquires the interest, the Coverdell ESA becomes the person's Coverdell ESA.

Any other beneficiary (including a spouse or family member who is not the designated beneficiary) must include in income the earnings portion of the distribution. Any balance remaining at the close of the 30-day period is deemed to be distributed at that time. The amount included in income is reduced by any qualified education expenses of

¶2606

the decedent that are paid by the beneficiary within one year after the decedent's date of death.

The age 30 limit does not apply if the individual for whom the account was established, or the beneficiary that acquires the account, is an individual with special needs. This includes an individual who because of a physical, mental, or emotional condition (including a learning disability) requires additional time to complete his or education.

(f) HSA, Archer MSA, or a Medicare Advantage MSA. The treatment of a health savings account (HSA), an Archer MSA or a Medicare Advantage MSA, at the death of the account holder, depends on who acquires the interest in the account. If the decedent's estate acquires the interest, the fair market value of the assets in the account on the date of death is included in income on the decedent's final return. If the decedent's spouse is the designated beneficiary of the account, the account becomes that spouse's Archer MSA. Any other beneficiary (including a spouse that is not the designated beneficiary) must include in income the fair market value of the assets in the account on the decedent's date of death. This amount must be reported for the beneficiary's tax year that includes the decedent's date of death. The amount included in income is reduced by any qualified medical expenses for the decedent that are paid by the beneficiary within one year after the decedent's date of death.

¶2607 INTEREST AND DIVIDEND INCOME

The executor will usually receive the Forms 1099 that report interest and dividends for the decedent's entire year. Unless the decedent conveniently died on December 31, the Forms 1099 will include interest and dividends for the period after the decedent died. Only the income received by the decedent up to and including the date of death must be reported on the decedent's final return. The balance must be reported by either the decedent's estate or the person who received the asset or the right to receive the income from the asset after the death of the decedent [see ¶ ¶ 2713–2715].

There are two ways of handling this situation.

1. If you are the executor preparing the decedent's final return and you have received a Form 1099-INT or a Form 1099-DIV for the decedent that includes amounts belonging to the decedent and to the decedent's estate or a beneficiary, report the total interest shown on the Form 1099 on the appropriate schedule, then back out or deduct the income that was earned after the date of death. The result will be only the amount received by the decedent while still alive. The balance must be reported on the estate's income tax return or the return of the person who inherited the asset.

2. If the Forms 1099 do not reflect the proper amount of income received by the decedent prior to death, you the executor can request corrected Forms 1099 from the banks and brokerage houses that paid the interest. The corrected forms would need to separate out the income earned by the assets before and after death of the decedent.

¶2607

(a) Interest on Series EE U.S. Savings Bonds. Series EE U.S. Savings Bonds are issued at a 50 percent discount from face value. This means that you will buy a $100 face value Series EE U.S. Savings Bond for $50. The bond will increase in value as it matures and can be redeemed anytime after six months from the issue date. Bonds issued on or after May 1, 1995, earn 85 percent of the average of the six-month Treasury securities yield in the first five years. After five years, the bonds earn 85 percent of the average of the five-year Treasury securities yield. Interest is credited semiannually with new rates announced on May 1 and November 1.

The interest earned on Series EE U.S. Savings Bonds is subject to federal income tax but is not subject to state or local income taxes. You can defer federal income taxes on the interest earned on Series EE U.S. Savings Bonds.

(b) Election to Report Income from Bonds Annually. There are two methods for reporting interest on Series EE Savings Bonds for federal income tax purposes. The easiest method is to defer reporting the interest until the year in which the bond matures, is redeemed, or disposed of. There is no need to make a special election on the tax return to defer reporting the interest on Series EE Savings Bonds in this manner. Simply postpone reporting the interest until the bond is redeemed.

The other method is to make a special election to report the interest as it accrues each year. If the election is made, it will apply to all Series EE bonds owned at the time, as well as to all Series EE bonds acquired later. Once the election is made, the reporting method may not be changed without permission of the IRS [IRC Sec. 454(a); Reg. Sec. 1.454-1].

When a person dies owning Series EE U.S. Savings Bonds, there are tax consequences to consider when completing the decedent's final return. If the decedent-bond owner had elected to report the interest each year, and the bonds were transferred to someone at the decedent's death, the interest earned by the bonds in the year of death up to the date of death must be included on the decedent's final income tax return. The decedent's estate or the successor in interest of the bonds must only pay tax on the interest earned by the bonds after the date of the decedent's death.

If the decedent-bond owner was a cash method taxpayer who had not chosen to report the interest each year and had bought the bonds entirely with personal funds, the interest earned before death must be reported in one of two ways:

1. The executor elects to include in the decedent's final return all of the interest earned on the bonds before the decedent's death [IRC Sec. 454(a); Reg. Sec. 1.454-1]. The estate or beneficiary who inherits the bonds then includes on the tax return only the interest earned after the date of death;[1] or

2. The executor does not make the election described in (1). The interest earned up to the date of death is IRD [see ¶ 2614] and is not included in the decedent's final return. All of the interest earned before and after the decedent's death is income to the decedent's estate or to the successor in interest who inherits the bonds [Reg. Sec. 1.691(a)-2(b), Ex. (3)].

---

[1] **¶ 2607** Rev. Rul. 68-145, 1968-1 CB 203.

¶2607

A successor in interest of the bonds who uses the cash accounting method and who has not chosen to report the interest annually may defer reporting any of it until the bonds are cashed or until they mature, whichever is earlier. In the year the interest is reported, the beneficiary of the bonds may claim a deduction for any federal estate tax that was paid because interest from the bonds was included in the decedent's estate.[2]

> **Example 1:** Mom, a cash method taxpayer, died and left Son a $2,000 Series EE bond. Mom had paid $1,000 for the bond and had not chosen to report the increase in value (interest) each year. When she died, interest in the amount of $200 had accumulated and the $1,200 value of the bond at the date of her death was included in her estate. Mom's executor did not choose to include the $200 of interest in Mom's final return. Son is a cash method taxpayer and does not choose to report the increase in value each year as it is earned. If Son cashes in the bond when it reaches the maturity value of $2,000, Son would report $1,000 interest income (the difference between maturity value of $2,000 and the original cost of $1,000) that year. Son is also entitled to claim, in that year, a deduction for any federal estate tax resulting from the inclusion in Mom's estate of the $200 increase in value of the bond.

> ▶ **PRACTICE NOTE:** The IRS has ruled that neither an estate nor its charitable beneficiaries had to recognize income from Series E and HH U.S. savings bonds that had accrued untaxed interest at the time of the decedent's death.[3] The bonds in this situation escape income tax because they were left to charitable legatees. You should therefore be sure that wills specifically direct charitable bequests to be paid with IRD as much as possible. This will reduce both the taxable estate by the full value of the charitable bequest and allow the estate or noncharitable beneficiaries to avoid income taxation on IRD.

¶2608 EXEMPTIONS CLAIMED ON DECEDENT'S FINAL RETURN

The executor can claim the full amount of the personal exemption on the decedent's final income tax return. This means that the exemption amount does not have to be prorated if the decedent died before the end of the tax year [see ¶2748].

> **Example 1:** Mom dies on July 1. Her full personal exemptions are allowed on her final income tax return, even though she was alive for only one-half of the tax year.

The executor will not be able to claim any exemption on behalf of the decedent if the decedent can be claimed as a dependent* by another taxpayer. In this situation, the decedent's exemption amount is zero.

*__Definition of dependent:__ In order for a person to claim an exemption for a dependent, the dependent must be either a *qualifying child* or a *qualifying relative*.

---

[2] Rev. Rul. 64-104, 1964-1 CB 223. [3] Ltr. Rul. 9845026.

¶2608

Qualifying child defined. To be a *qualifying child*, the child must satisfy the following requirements:

- *Relationship.* The child must be the taxpayer's son, daughter, stepchild (whether by blood or adoption), foster child, brother, sister, stepbrother, stepsister, or a descendant of one of these (for example, the taxpayer's grandchild, niece or nephew);

- *Age.* The child must be under the age of 19 at the end of the tax year, or under the age of 24 if a full-time student for at least five months of the year, or be permanently and totally disabled at any time during the year. For 2009, the definition of a qualifying child is modified to include a new age test and a joint return test. According to the age test, the child must be younger than the taxpayer [IRC Sec. 152(c)(3)(A)];

- *Principal residence.* The child must have the same principal residence as the taxpayer for more than half of the year. Exceptions apply, in certain cases, for children of divorced or separated parents, kidnapped children, temporary absences, and for children who were born or died during the year;

- *Not self-supporting.* The child must *not* have provided over half of his or her own support for the year;

- *Joint return test.* A qualifying child cannot file a joint return with a spouse for a tax year beginning in the calendar year in which the tax year of the taxpayer claiming the qualifying child begins. However, a qualifying child is allowed to file a joint return for the limited purpose of obtaining a refund [IRC Sec. 152(c)(1)(E)].

Tie-breaking rules. If a child is claimed as a qualifying child by two or more taxpayers in a given year, the child will be the qualifying child of: (1) the parent; (2) if more than one taxpayer is the child's parent, the one with whom the child lived for the longest time during the year, or, if the time was equal, the parent with the highest AGI; (3) if no taxpayer is the child's parent, the taxpayer with the highest adjusted gross income (AGI).

The tie-breaker rules will apply whenever two or more taxpayers *can* claim the child as a qualifying child regardless of whether they actually do so [IRC Sec. 152(c)(4)(A)]. If the parents can claim the qualifying child but neither does so, another taxpayer may claim the child as his or her qualifying child but only if their adjusted gross income (AGI) is higher than the highest AGI of either of the qualifying child's parents [IRC Sec. 152(c)(4)(C)].

Qualifying relative defined. For purposes of claiming the dependency exemption, a *qualifying relative* must satisfy the following tests:

- *Relationship.* The following individuals can be classified as qualifying relatives: a child or a descendant of a child; a sibling, or stepsibling; parent and their ancestors and siblings; the taxpayer's stepparents and stepsiblings; and the taxpayer's son-in-law, daughter-in-law, father-in-law, mother-in-law, brother-in-law and sister-in-law. Qualifying relatives also include individuals, other than the taxpayer's spouse, who share an abode with the taxpayer and were members of the taxpayer's household during the year. An individual is not a member of the taxpayer's household if, at any time during the year, the relationship between the individual and the taxpayer violated local law;

¶2608

- *Gross income.* A dependent will be a qualifying relative if his or her gross income is less than the exemption amount which is $3,950 in 2014;
- *Support test.* In order to claim a person as a dependent the taxpayer must prove that he or she furnished over one half of the dependent's total support for the year;
- *Not a qualifying child.* An individual cannot be a qualifying child of the taxpayer or any other taxpayer for the year;
- A taxpayer cannot claim a dependency exemption for a married individual who files a joint return unless that joint return is filed solely in an attempt to claim a refund;
- If an individual is claimed as a dependent of another person, the dependent may not claim any dependents;
- A qualifying relative must be a United States citizen or national or a resident of the United States, Canada, or Mexico. However, a legally adopted child or an individual who is lawfully placed by the taxpayer for legal adoption need not satisfy this rule if for the tax year the child has the same principal place of residence as the taxpayer and is a member of the taxpayer's household and the taxpayer is a citizen or national of the United States.

Dependent's TIN. Taxpayers must provide a dependent's taxpayer identification number (TIN) in order to claim a dependency exemption for that person. An individual's TIN is generally that individual's social security number. An incorrect TIN is treated as a mathematical or clerical error, allowing the IRS to summarily assess any additional tax due as a result of the denied exemption. Any notification of additional tax is not treated as a notice of deficiency. Taxpayers apply for a social security number by filing Form SS-5 with the Social Security Administration.

¶2609 DEDUCTIONS CLAIMED ON DECEDENT'S FINAL RETURN

A decedent's deductions are treated in the same manner as the decedent's income, as discussed in ¶ 2605. In computing taxable income for the decedent's final year, the executor can only deduct the amounts properly deductible under the method of accounting used by the taxpayer [Reg. Sec. 1.461-1(b)].

If the decedent was on the cash basis, only those items of expense, interest, and taxes actually paid up to and including the date of death are deductible on the decedent's final return [Reg. Sec. 1.461-1(a)]. If the decedent was on the accrual basis, only those deductions properly accruable up to and including the date of death are claimed on the final return [Reg. Sec. 1.461-2(a)]. Deductions that accrue only because of the decedent's death are not allowed [IRC Sec. 461(b); Reg. Sec. 1.461-1(b)].

(a) Standard Deduction or Itemize. On the decedent's final return, the executor can claim either the full amount of the standard deduction or the total of all itemized deductions as computed on Schedule A. See ¶ 2739 for discussion and ¶ 2783 for a sample Schedule A.

▶RECOMMENDATION: If the total of the decedent's itemized deductions is more than the decedent's standard deductions, the decedent's final federal income tax bill will be less. The executor should therefore complete Schedule A to see if the decedent's itemized deductions exceed the available standard deduction.

The amount of the standard deduction for a decedent's final return is the same as it would have been if the decedent had not died. It does not have to be prorated based on the portion of the year that the decedent was alive. If the decedent was not 65 or older at the time of death, the higher standard deduction for age cannot be claimed.

If another taxpayer can claim the decedent as a dependent, the amount of the decedent's standard deduction may be limited in 2014 to the greater of (1) $1,000 or (2) the sum of $350 and the individual's earned income.

> **Example 1:** Betty was 17 when she died in 2014. She was single. Her parents claim an exemption for her on their income tax return. In the year of her death Betty had interest income of $850 and wages of $150. She had no itemized deductions. On Betty's final income tax return, her executor claimed a standard deduction of $1,000 for Betty because it is the greater of $1,000 and her earned income of $150 plus $3500.

(b) Medical Expenses. If the executor itemizes deductions, he or she may be able to deduct the decedent's medical expenses that were paid before the date of death. This includes expenses for the decedent as well as for the decedent's spouse and dependents. Individuals can deduct unreimbursed medical expenses only to the extent that they exceed 10 percent of the taxpayer's AGI in 2013 [IRC Sec. 213(a)]. The threshold for the itemized deduction for unreimbursed medical expenses increased from 7.5 percent of AGI to 10 percent of AGI beginning in 2013. However, in 2013, 2014, 2015 and 2016, if either the taxpayer or the taxpayer's spouse turns 65 before the end of the tax year, the increased threshold does not apply and the threshold remains at 7.5 percent of AGI [see ¶ 2740].

> ▶ **CAUTION:** Qualified medical expenses paid before death by the decedent are not deductible if paid with a tax-free distribution from an Archer MSA or health savings account.

(c) Election to Deduct Medical Expenses Paid One Year After Death. If the decedent's medical expenses are paid within one year after the decedent's death, the executor has the option of making a irrevocable election to treat these medical expenses as paid by the decedent at the time the medical services were provided and the expenses were incurred. This election results in the medical expenses being deducted on the decedent's final income tax return rather than on the federal estate tax return (Form 706) [IRC Sec. 213(c)]. See ¶ 2001 for further discussion.

> **Example 2:** In 2013, Taxpayer incurred, but did not pay, doctor and hospital bills totaling $400 for personal medical treatment. He files his return for the calendar year 2013 on January 15, 2014, and pays the tax shown to be due. Taxpayer dies in March 2014 without having paid the doctor and hospital bills. His estate pays them in August 2014. An amended return (or refund claim) can

be filed for 2013, and the allowable medical expenses can be deducted in that year.

The election to claim a deduction of a decedent's medical expenses in the year in which they were incurred applies only to expenses incurred for the deceased taxpayer. This election has no application to medical expenses which a decedent may have incurred on behalf of a dependent.

A decedent's estate will realize income in respect of a decedent under IRC Sec. 691(a) to the extent it is reimbursed by insurance for amounts deducted on the decedent's final return[1] [see ¶ 2614 for further discussion].

A surviving spouse who pays medical expenses is entitled to a deduction, on either a joint return or a separate return. The spouse may deduct the payments in the tax year in which they are made, regardless of whether they are paid before or after the death of the decedent. A decedent could also be a dependent of another, and that other person might be entitled to the deduction for medical expenses of a dependent.

▶ **PLANNING TIP:** Before making this election, the rates that apply to both returns should be compared so the best choice can be made.

To be able to take advantage of this irrevocable election, the decedent's medical expenses must be paid during the one-year period beginning with the day after the date of death. If the executor makes the election, the expenses incurred in the year of death can be deducted on the decedent's final income tax return or an amended return can be filed to claim a refund. The normal period for filing a claim for refund is three years after the return was filed or two years after the tax was paid, whichever is later [IRC Sec. 6511(a)].

AGI ceiling still applies. The amount that the executor can deduct for medical expenses on the income tax return is limited to the amount by which the expenses exceed 7.5 percent of adjusted gross income [IRC Sec. 213(a)]. The amounts not deductible because of this percentage cannot be claimed on the federal estate tax return.[2]

(d) How to Make the Election. The executor makes the election by filing with the decedent's income tax return, or amended return, a statement in duplicate stating that the amount has not been claimed as an estate tax deduction under IRC Sec. 2053, and that the estate waives the right to claim the amount as a deduction under IRC Sec. 2053 [IRC Sec. 213(c)(2)(B)].

This election applies only to expenses incurred for the medical care of the decedent, not to expenses incurred to provide medical care for dependents [IRC Sec. 213(c)(1)].

Example 3: Mom died this year with unpaid medical expenses of $3,000 from last year and $4,000 from this year. Her executor will pay the expenses in January of next year. The executor can file an amended return (Form 1040X) for last year deducting the $3,000 medical expenses, subject to the 7.5 percent adjusted gross income limit. The $4,000 medical expenses from this year can be deducted on this year's return, which will be Mom's final return, subject to the 7.5 percent limit. The executor must file a statement in duplicate with each

---

[1] **¶ 2609** Rev. Rul. 78-292, 1978-2 CB 233.   [2] Rev. Rul. 77-357, 1977-2 CB 328.

¶2609

return stating that these amounts have not been claimed on the federal estate tax return (Form 706), and waiving the right to claim such a deduction on Form 706 in the future.

¶2610 DEDUCTING SUSPENDED LOSSES ON DECEDENT'S FINAL RETURN

A decedent may have unused net operating loss (NOL) carryovers, capital loss carryovers, or suspended passive activity losses at the time of death. The executor needs to be aware of these when completing the decedent's final return because the following carryovers expire at death:

- Capital loss carryovers under IRC Sec. 1212.
- Net operating loss carryovers under IRC Sec. 172(b).
- Charitable contribution carryovers under IRC Sec. 172(d).
- Investment interest carryovers under IRC Sec. 162(d)(2).
- Home office expenses in excess of home office income under IRC Sec. 180A(c)(5).

These carryovers die with the decedent and cannot be deducted on the estate's income tax return or on a beneficiary's income tax return. The rule for suspended passive activity losses is different from the rule that applies to the other types of unused loss carryovers. The executor will be able to deduct the decedent's suspended passive activity losses on the final return but the loss is limited to the excess of the loss over the amount by which the basis of the passive asset is stepped-up at death as explained further below.

(a) Net Operating Loss. Tax liabilities are reduced in years that a profit was realized if there was an NOL. An NOL is created whenever business deductions exceed gross income [IRC Sec. 172(c)].

A decedent's NOL can be carried back, but not forward. On the decedent's final return, however, the decedent's NOL carryovers can be deducted. An NOL on the decedent's final income tax return can be carried back to prior years even if the final return is filed as a joint return.

▶ **PRACTICE TIP:** Any unused NOL carryover that is not claimed on the decedent's final return will be lost forever. NOL or capital loss carryovers sustained by the decedent before death cannot be deducted on the estate's income tax return or an heir's income tax return.[1] To make matters worse, if the decedent's spouse sustains an NOL after the decedent's death, any carryback to the joint returns will be limited to the portion of income on the joint return that is attributable to the surviving spouse.[2] In addition, if there is any NOL carryforward in the year of death on a joint return, only the surviving spouse's share can be carried to future returns.[3]

---

[1] **¶2610** Rev. Rul. 74-175, 1974-1 CB 52.
[2] Rev. Rul. 65-140, 1965-1 CB 127.

[3] York, 66-2 USTC ¶9628 (D.C. Tex. 1964); Zeeman, 275 F. Supp. 235 (D.C.N.Y. 1967), *aff'd in*

▶**RECOMMENDATION:** If a taxpayer dies with a big NOL carryover, it may be a good idea to file a joint return in the year of death so more of the otherwise lost NOL carryover can be claimed against the larger joint income of both the surviving spouse and the decedent.

Here's another possible way to salvage that NOL carryover. If a married decedent filed separately from a spouse in prior years, consider filing amended returns for the open years to file jointly and deduct the NOL against the joint income in those years [Reg. Secs. 1.6013-2(a)(1) and 1.172-1(d)].

(b) Capital Losses. Capital losses result when a taxpayer sells or otherwise disposes of a capital asset. A capital loss does not necessarily have to be the result of a sale or exchange of a capital asset, but can result where a specific Code provision, such as IRC Sec. 165(g), provides that a loss realized when a security becomes worthless will be treated as a capital loss.

(c) Limitations on Deduction of Capital Losses. Individuals can deduct capital losses only to the extent of any capital gains they have for the year, plus, ordinary income up to $3,000 [IRC Sec. 1211]. To determine whether a taxpayer can deduct capital losses, total all capital gains and losses (without distinguishing between long-term and short-term) incurred during the year. Then add up net long-term capital losses and net short-term capital losses and use the total to offset up to $3,000 of ordinary income. Unused capital losses may be carried over for an unlimited time until the loss is exhausted.

> **Example 1:** Mom has $25,000 of ordinary income, a net short-term loss of $2,000, and a net long-term capital loss of $2,000. Her capital loss deduction is limited to $3,000 and $1,000 is carried over to next year.

(d) Death Extinguishes Decedent's Capital Loss Carryovers. A capital loss sustained by a decedent during his or her last tax year (or carried over to that year from an earlier year) can be deducted only on that final income tax return filed for the decedent. A decedent's capital loss carryover is extinguished upon death. The unused capital loss of the decedent cannot be deducted by the estate[4] and it cannot be carried back unless it qualifies as an NOL as discussed above. Therefore the capital loss carryover must be deducted on the decedent's final return or be lost forever.

▶ **PRACTICE POINTER:** To take advantage of the expiring capital loss carryover, the decedent would have to file a joint return with a surviving spouse in the year of death. To generate capital gain, consider selling appreciated stock so the surviving spouse can offset the gain with the decedent's capital loss carryover on the decedent's final joint return.

(e) Passive Activity Losses. The passive activity rules provide that losses and credits from passive activities can generally be applied only against income and tax from passive activities. Thus passive losses and credits cannot be applied against

---

(Footnote Continued)

part, remanded, 395 F.2d 861 (2d Cir. 1968), *amended,* 69-1 USTC ¶ 9171 (D.C.N.Y. 1969); Rev. Rul. 71-382, 1971-2 CB 156.

[4] Rev. Rul. 74-175, 1974-1 CB 52.

(a) income from salaries, wages, professional fees, or a business in which the shareholder materially participates; (b) against portfolio income; or (c) against the tax related to any of these types of income. As a result of the passive loss rules, a decedent *cannot* use passive losses to absorb salaries, professional fees, interest, dividends, gains from the sale of stock and other capital assets, or the net income of businesses in which the taxpayer actively participates. Passive activity losses (PALs) that are not deducted are held in suspense or carried forward indefinitely to future years to be deducted against passive income in those years or held until the passive activity is sold, at which time they either reduce the gain or increase the loss from the sale [Reg. Sec. 1.469-1(f)(4)(i)].

Generally, passive activities include: (a) activities that involve the conduct of a trade or business in which the decedent did not materially participate, and (b) any rental activity even if the decedent materially participated. This means that rental activities are automatically deemed passive regardless of the level of the taxpayer's participation. As a result, real estate losses can only be used to offset income generated by other real estate investments. Real estate losses cannot be deducted against wages, interest, dividends, and other investment or "portfolio" income.

The following are not passive activities:

1. Trade or business activities in which the decedent materially participated for the tax year.

2. Any rental real estate activity in which the decedent materially participated if the decedent met both of the following conditions for the tax year: (a) more than one half of the personal services the decedent performed in trades and businesses were performed in real property trades or businesses in which he or she materially participated, and (b) the decedent performed more than 750 hours of serivces in real property trades or business in which he or she materially participated. A real property trade or business is any real property development, redevelopment, construction, reconstruction, acquisition, conversion, rental, operation, management, leasing or brokerage trade or business. Services the decedent performed as an employee are not treated as performed in a real property trade or business unless he or she owned more than 5 percent of the stock in the employer.

3. The rental of a dwelling unit used by the decedent for personal purposes during the year for more than the greater of 14 days or 10 percent of the number of days that the residence was rented at fair rental value.

4. Any activity of trading personal property for the account of owners of interest in the activity. For purposes of this rule, personal property means property that is actively traded, stocks, bonds, and other securities.

At the time of death, the decedent may have previously disallowed or suspended PALs. IRC Sec. 469(g) contains special rules to be used in determining the treatment of PALs when a taxpayer's interest in a passive activity is completely disposed of in the year of death. The rule is: Suspended PALs will be deductible in full provided (1) the sale is fully taxable which means that all gain or loss on the sale must be recognized [IRC Sec. 469(g)(1)], and (2) the taxpayer's interest is completely extinguished. If, however, the purchaser in the fully taxable sale mentioned in (1) above is a "related taxpayer" as defined in IRC Sec. 267(b) or IRC Sec. 707(b)(1), the suspended passive loss remains with the seller until the activity is transferred in a

¶2610

taxable transaction to someone unrelated to the original seller [IRC Sec. 469(g)(1)(B)]. Related taxpayers include the seller and his spouse, brother, sister, ancestor, lineal descendant, or a controlled corporation (direct or indirect ownership of more than 50 percent of stock value).

> **Example 2:** Mom sells her S corporation stock to Son for $20,000 at a time when her basis is $15,000 and her suspended passive losses with respect to the stock is $13,000. Her distributive share of passive income from the S corporation is $2,000 for the taxable year of the S corporation ending with respect to Mom because of her stock sale. Her suspended passive losses are reduced to $6,000 ($13,000 less $5,000 of gain, less $2,000). Even though Mom retains no interest in the activity she is left with $6,000 of suspended losses until such time as she may generate passive income from other sources or Son resells the stock in a taxable transaction to someone unrelated to Mom.

(f) Step-Up in Basis Results. When an interest in a passive activity is disposed of at death, the basis of the passive asset is stepped-up to its fair market value at the date of death in all years except 2010 when carry over basis applies if the executor makes an election. For further discussion, see ¶ 103 [IRC Sec. 1014(a)(1)]. The law provides that this step-up in the basis of the property results in a dollar-for-dollar reduction in the amount of suspended PALs that can be deducted on the decedent's final return.

As a result, the decedent's executor can only deduct suspended PALs to the extent that the PALs exceed the amount of the step-up in basis to the property's fair-market value at the date of death [IRC Sec. 469(g)(2)]. The good news is that the suspended PALs (subject to the limitation described above) may offset nonpassive income on the decedent's final return. The executor need not look for passive income against which to offset them. Any losses not claimed on the decedent's final return will be lost forever [IRC Sec. 469(g)(2)(B)].

> **Example 3:** At Mom's death last year she owned an apartment building with a basis of $500,000, a fair-market value of $700,000, and suspended PALs of $300,000. The terms of Mom's will provided that the asset pass to Daughter when Mom died. The basis of the asset in Daughter's hands is $700,000. On Mom's final income tax return, her executor wants to deduct the full amount of the $300,000 suspended PALs but is only entitled to a deduction in the amount of $100,000 (the amount of PALs remaining after being reduced by the $200,000 step-up in basis that resulted when Daughter inherited the building). Daughter's basis in the building will be increased by $200,000 to $900,000 to reflect the disallowed suspended PALs [IRC Sec. 469(j)(12)]. This will reduce any future gain or increase a future loss if she sells the building.

(g) How to Generate More Income on the Decedent's Final Return. The executor may encounter a problem in attempting to use the suspended PAL on the decedent's final return. There may not be sufficient income on the return to utilize all of the PALs. This will be important where the passive activity has been sold prior to death and there was no basis step-up. To generate more income, the executor may do one or more of the following:

1. Elect out of the installment sales treatment to generate more income on the final return so the suspended PAL can be used.

2. Elect joint return status with the surviving spouse if more passive income will be generated on the decedent's final return that way.

3. Determine if the PAL will qualify as a NOL and be eligible to be carried back to the prior two years of the decedent's return [IRC Sec. 172].

¶2611 CLAIMING CREDITS AND WITHHELD TAXES ON FINAL RETURN

On the decedent's final return, the executor can claim any of the tax credits that the decedent could claim while still alive.

(a) Earned Income Credit. On the decedent's final income tax return, the executor can claim the full amount of the available earned income credit even though the return covers less than 12 months provided the decedent was eligible for the credit while still alive. If the allowable credit exceeds the decedent's tax liability for the year, the IRS will refund the excess.

The earned income credit ("EIC") inflation adjustments for 2013 and 2014 are as follows:

2013 Earned Income Credit

| | Number of Qualifying Children | | | |
Item	One	Two	Three or More	None
Earned Income Amount	$ 9,560	$13,430	$13,430	$ 6,370
Maximum Amount of Credit	$ 3,250	$ 5,372	$ 6,044	$ 487
Threshold Phaseout Amount (Single, Surviving Spouse, or Head of Household)	$17,530	$17,530	$17,530	$ 7,970
Completed Phaseout Amount (Single, Surviving Spouse, or Head of Household)	$37,870	$43,038	$46,227	$14,340
Threshold Phaseout Amount (Married Filing Jointly)	$22,870	$22,870	$22,870	$13,310
Completed Phaseout Amount (Married Filing Jointly)	$43,210	$48,378	$51,567	$19,680

2014 Earned Income Credit

Number of Qualifying Children

Item	One	Two	Three or More	None
Earned Income Amount	$ 9,720	$13,650	$13,650	$ 6,480
Maximum Amount of Credit	$ 3,305	$ 5,460	$ 6,143	$ 496
Threshold Phaseout Amount (Single, Surviving Spouse, or Head of Household)	$17,830	$17,830	$17,830	$ 8,110
Completed Phaseout Amount (Single, Surviving Spouse, or Head of Household)	$38,511	$43,756	$46,997	$14,590
Threshold Phaseout Amount (Married Filing Jointly)	$23,260	$23,260	$23,260	$13,540
Completed Phaseout Amount (Married Filing Jointly)	$43,941	$49,186	$52,427	$20,020

Who can claim the credit? The earned income credit may be claimed if the decedent had at least one qualifying child and

- The decedent's filing status is not married filing separately and he or she had a valid social security number.

- The decedent's adjusted gross income must be less than the income amounts listed on the previous chart.

- The credit is based on earned income, which includes all wages, salaries, tips, and other employee compensation (including union strike benefits), plus the amount of the taxpayer's net earnings from self-employment taxes. Earned income is determined without regard to community property laws.

- Military families may elect to include excludable combat zone pay in their earned income for determining the credit amount.

- In addition, the taxpayer's investment income must be $3,350 in 2014 (increased from $3,300 in 2013). Investment income includes taxable interest, tax-exempt interest, dividend income, and capital gain net income.

When paid tax return preparers of federal income tax returns or claims for refund file returns claiming the EIC, the paid tax return preparers are required to file a due diligence checklist on Form 8867, "Paid Preparer's Earned Income Credit Checklist."

For further discussion of the definition of a qualifying child requirement and tie-breaking rules, see ¶ 2608.

(b) Credit for the Elderly or Disabled. The credit for the elderly or the disabled can also be claimed on Schedule R attached to a decedent's final income tax return if the decedent was age 65 or older or had retired before the end of the tax year on permanent and total disability. The 15 percent tax credit is figured on Schedule R of Form 1040, "Credit for the Elderly or the Disabled" and is claimed on line 48 of Form 1040.

To claim the credit, the decedent's adjusted gross income (as reported on line 37 of Form 1040) must be less than $17,500 for singles, heads of households and qualifying widow(er)s with dependent children. For married taxpayers filing separately, the

¶2611

income limit is $12,500. For married taxpayers filing jointly, the income limit is $20,000 if one spouse is elderly or disabled, or $25,000 if both spouses qualify. In addition, the nontaxable benefits the decedent received during the year (such as nontaxable Social Security, pension and disability benefits) must not exceed certain amounts. For taxpayers filing as single, head of household and qualifying widow(er)s, the benefits limit is $5,000. For married taxpayers filing separately, the benefits limit is $3,750. For married taxpayers filing jointly, the benefits limit is $5,000 if one spouse is elderly or disabled, or $7,500 if both spouses qualify.

The amount of the credit is 15 percent times the base amount after certain reductions. The base amount for the credit is $7,500 for joint filers, $5,000 for single filers, or $3,750 for married taxpayers filing separately. The base amount is reduced by nontaxable Social Security and other tax-free pensions. The credit will thus be worth up to $1,125 for joint filers, $750 for single filers, heads of households or a qualifying widow(er), and $563 for married taxpayers filing separately.

(c) General Business Tax Credit. The amount of the general business tax credit that can be claimed by any taxpayer, including the decedent on the final return, includes any unused credits that are carried back three years and then carried forward for up to 15 years. After the expiration of the 15-year period, a deduction may be allowed for any unused business credit. If the taxpayer dies before the end of the 15-year carryover period, the deduction generally is allowed in the year of death.

(d) Withheld Taxes. If the decedent paid estimated taxes or had income taxes withheld from salary, wages, pensions, or annuities while still alive, the decedent's executor should file a decedent's final return to have these taxes refunded if there was an overpayment.

¶2612 TAX FORGIVENESS FOR DEATHS DUE TO MILITARY OR TERRORIST ACTIONS

If the decedent was a member of the U.S. Armed Forces or a civilian employee of the United States, the decedent's income tax liability may be forgiven, or if already paid, refunded, if the decedent's death was due to active service in a combat zone or from wounds, disease, or other injury received in a combat zone, or from wounds or injury incurred in a terrorist or military action [IRC Sec. 692(a); Reg. Sec. 1.692-1(a)]. The tax forgiveness extends to the full calendar year in which the service member died, not just to the portion of the year when he or she was dead [Reg. Sec. 1.692-1(a)].

Note that these tax relief provisions apply with respect to:

- U.S. military and civilian employees killed in terrorist or military actions;
- Victims of specific domestic terrorist attacks; and
- Astronauts.

Income tax is also forgiven on amounts that would have been included in the decedent's gross income for the tax year of his death, but that are received after the decedent's death by another person or the decedent's estate. This would include, for example, amounts includible in the estate as income received in respect of a decedent [Reg. Sec. 1.692-1(a)(2)(ii)].

¶2612

Missing U.S. military or civilian personnel. If a U.S. military member or civilian employee is reported in a missing status (i.e., missing in action, interned in a foreign country, captured by a hostile force, or detained in a foreign country against his will) and it is later determined that he or she actually died at an earlier time, there is no federal income tax on income for the years after the year of death. This forgiveness applies to the year of death and to years after death that precede and include the year of determination of death [IRC Sec. 692(b)].

Tax-free military death gratuity payments. Any death gratuity paid to survivors of members of the armed forces is nontaxable.

(a) Death in Combat Zone.

(a) Death in Combat Zone. If a member of the Armed Forces of the United States dies while in active service in a combat zone or from wounds, disease, or injury incurred in a combat zone, the decedent's income tax liability is forgiven for the entire year in which death occurred and for any prior tax year ending on or after the first day the person served in a combat zone in active service [IRC Sec. 692(a)(1)]. For this purpose, a qualified hazardous duty area is treated as a combat zone.

If the tax for this period has already been collected, that tax will be credited or refunded as described in the procedures below.

(b) Death Due to Military or Terrorist Actions.

Relief available to U.S. military/civilian employees. The decedent's income tax liability is forgiven if, at death, he or she was a military or civilian employee of the United States who died because of wounds or injury incurred as a result of a military or terrorist action which a preponderance of the evidence indicates was directed against the United States or any of its allies [IRC Sec. 692(c)(2)].

The tax forgiveness applies to the tax year in which death occurred and for any prior tax year in the period, beginning with the year before the year in which the wounds or injury occurred [IRC Sec. 692(c)(1)(A)].

> **Example 1:** Bob dies in 2014 because of wounds he incurred while serving in the U.S. military in 2007. Bob's income tax liability will be forgiven for 2014 and for all prior tax years in the period from 2006–2014. Refunds are allowed for the tax years for which the period for filing a claim for refund has not ended.

Military or terrorist action is defined as follows:

1. Any terrorist activity which a preponderance of the evidence indicates was directed against the United States or any of its allies, and

2. Any military action involving the U.S. Armed Forces and resulting from violence or aggression against the United States or any of its allies, or the threat of such violence or aggression [IRC Sec. 692(c)(2)].

For these purposes, the term "military action" does not include training exercises [IRC Sec. 692(c)]. Any multinational force in which the United States is participating is treated as an ally of the United States [IRC Sec. 692(c)(3)].

The following types of income will be exempt from federal income tax under IRC Sec. 692(d)(2):

1. The decedent's final paycheck;
2. Dividends on stock held by the decedent that were paid to another person or the individual's estate after the date of death but before the end of the taxable year of the decedent (determined without regard to the death);
3. Payments of an individual's accrued vacation and accrued sick leave;
4. Qualified disaster relief payments made to cover personal, family, living, or funeral expenses incurred because of a terrorist attack;
5. Disability payments received for injuries sustained in a terrorist attack;
6. Death benefits paid by an employer to the survivor of an employee because the employee died as a result of a terrorist attack; and
7. Payments from the September 11th Victim Compensation Fund of 2001.

The following types of income may not be excluded from federal income tax under IRC Sec. 692(d)(3):

1. Deferred compensation which would have been payable after death if the individual had not died as a terrorist victim [IRC Sec. 692(d)(3)(A)];
2. Amounts payable in the taxable year that would not have been payable that year but for an action taken after September 11, 2001 [IRC Sec. 692(d)(3)(B)]. For example, the exemption does not apply to amounts payable from a qualified plan or IRA to the beneficiary or estate of the individual. Similarly, amounts payable only as death or survivor's benefits pursuant to deferred compensation preexisting arrangements that would have been paid if the death had occurred for another reason are not covered by the exemption;
3. Amounts payable because the individual's employer made adjustments to a plan or arrangement to accelerate the vesting of restricted property or the payment of nonqualified deferred compensation after the date of the particular attack; and
4. Amounts payable because the decedent's savings bonds were cashed.

Refund or credit of taxes already paid. IRC Sec. 692(d)(2) provides a minimum tax relief benefit of $10,000 to each terrorist victim regardless of the income tax liability of the individual for the eligible tax years. If an eligible individual's income tax for years eligible for the exclusion is less than $10,000, the individual is treated as having made a tax payment for such individual's last taxable year in an amount equal to the excess of $10,000 over the amount of tax not imposed under the provision.

(c) Claim for Credit or Refund. If any of these tax-forgiveness situations applies to a prior tax, any tax paid for which the period for filing a claim has not ended will be credited or refunded. If any tax is still due, it will be canceled. The normal period for filing a claim for credit or refund is three years after the return was filed or two years after the tax was paid, whichever is later [IRC Sec. 6511(a)]. The IRS will also provide penalty and interest relief for estates affected by the September 11, 2001 terrorist attacks. Affected taxpayers who have paid penalties and interest, should contact the IRS to obtain the necessary relief. Affected taxpayers include any taxpayers filing an estate tax return: (1) for which tax records necessary to meet the filing or payment deadline were located in the covered disaster area; or (2) signed and filed by a person whose principal residence, was located in the covered disaster area; or (3) signed and filed by a

¶2612

corporate fiduciary whose place of business from which the corporate fiduciary primarily administered estate matters was located in the covered area.

If death occurred in a combat zone or from wounds, disease, or injury incurred in a combat zone, the period for filing the claim is extended by:

1. The amount of time served in the combat zone (including any period in which the individual was considered to be missing in action); plus

2. The period of continuous qualified hospitalization for injury from service in the combat zone, if any; plus

3. The next 180 days [IRC Sec. 7508(a)(1)].

Qualified hospitalization means any hospitalization outside the United States, and any hospitalization in the United States of not more than five years.

The IRS will provide a free copy of prior year tax returns to survivors or executors of disaster victims' estates. The free copy can be obtained by filling out Form 4506, "Request for Copy or Transcript of Tax Form," writing "DISASTER" in the top margin, attaching Testamentary Letters or other evidence of authorization to act for the estate and mailing it as instructed in the form instructions. Additional guidance is available in IRS Pub. 3920, "Tax Relief for Victims of Terrorist Attacks."

(d) How to File a Claim. Use the following procedures from Rev. Proc. 2004-26[1] to file a claim for the decedent who was a member of the armed forces:

1. If a U.S. individual income tax return has not been filed, make a claim for refund of any withheld income tax or estimated tax payments by filing a tax return for the decedent on Form 1040 or Form 1040A. Form W-2 must accompany all returns.

2. If a U.S. individual income tax return has been filed, make a claim for refund by filing Form 1040X. A separate Form 1040X must be for each year in question.

File these returns and claims at the following address:

> Internal Revenue Service
> 333 W. Pershing, P5-6503
> Kansas City, MO 64108

Identify all returns and claims for refund by writing, for example, "Iraq-KIA," "Enduring Freedom-KIA," "Kosovo Operation-KIA," "Desert Storm-KIA" in bold letters on the top of page 1 of the return or claim. On Forms 1040 and 1040X the phrase, for example, "Desert Storm-KIA" or "Former Yugoslavia-KIA" must be written on the line for "total tax." If the individual was killed in a terrorist or military action outside the United States, write "KITA" on the front of the return and on the line for "total tax." An attachment should include a computation of the decedent's tax liability and a computation of the amount that is to be forgiven.

You must include the following necessary documents with all returns and claims for refund filed under these procedures:

---

[1] ¶ **2612** Rev. Proc. 2004-26, 2004-1 CB 890.

¶2612

1. Form 1310, "Statement of Person Claiming Refund Due a Deceased Taxpayer."

2. A certification from the Department of Defense or the Department of State that the death was due to military or terrorist action outside the United States. For civilian employees of all other agencies, certification must be a letter signed by the Director General of the Foreign Service, Department of State, or his or her delegate. The certification must include the individual's name and Social Security number, the date of injury, the date of death, and a statement that the individual died as the result of a miliary or terrorist action outside the United States and was an employee of the United States on the date of the injury and at the date of death.

(e) Joint Returns. If a joint return was filed, only the decedent's part of the income tax liability is eligible for the refund. Determine the decedent's tax liability as follows:

1. Figure the income tax for which the decedent would have been liable if a separate return had been filed.

2. Figure the income tax for which the spouse would have been liable if a separate return had been filed.

3. Multiply the joint tax liability by a fraction, the numerator of which is the amount in (1) above and the denominator is the total of (1) and (2).

The amount in (3) above is the decedent's tax liability that is eligible for the refund.

¶2613 BENEFITS FOR PUBLIC SAFETY OFFICERS' SURVIVORS

An amount paid as a survivor annuity to the spouse, former spouse, or child of a public safety officer killed in the line of duty is excludable from the recipient's gross income if the annuity is provided under a governmental plan that meets the requirements of IRC Sec. 401(a) [IRC Sec. 101(h)]. Public safety officers include police and law enforcement officers, fire fighters, ambulance crews, and rescue squads. The annuity is excludable to the extent it is attributable to the officer's service as a public safety officer.

The exclusion does not apply in the following circumstances:

1. The officer's death was caused by the officer's intentional misconduct.

2. The officer's death was caused by the officer's intent to bring about his death.

3. The officer was voluntarily intoxicated or was performing his duties in a grossly negligent manner at the time of death.

4. The recipient's actions were a substantial contributing factor to the death of the officer.

The exclusion is also available to a chaplain killed in the line of duty after September 10, 2001. The chaplain must have been responding to a fire, rescue, or police emergency as a member or employee of a fire or police department.

¶2613

¶2614 INCOME IN RESPECT OF A DECEDENT

Income in respect of a decedent (IRD) is any item of gross income that cannot properly be included in the decedent's final return, but to which the decedent had a right at the time of death and which the decedent would have received if he had not died. [IRC Sec. 691(a)] These amounts are included in the gross income of:

1. The decedent's estate under IRC Sec. 2033, if the estate received the IRD;

2. The beneficiary, if the beneficiary received the IRD; or

3. Anybody to whom the estate properly distributed the right to receive the IRD [IRC Sec. 691(a)(1); Reg. Sec. 1.691(a)-2].

> **Example 1:** Sally Brite was a sole proprietor who owned a dry cleaning business. She used the cash method of accounting. A local hotel owed Sally $4,000 for cleaning their draperies, but did not pay her before her death. Payment had not been made when estate was settled, and the estate transferred the right to the payment to Sally's surviving spouse, Brian. When Brian collects the $4,000, he must report that amount on his own federal income tax return as IRD. The payment is not reported on Sally's final return of the decedent nor on Sally's estate tax return.

> **Example 2:** If Sally in the Example 1 above used the accrual method of accounting, the amount accrued from cleaning the draperies would be included on her final return. Neither the estate nor Brian will realize IRD when the money is paid.

> **Example 3:** On June 1, Dad, a cash method taxpayer, sold his sailboat for $6,000, payable July of the same year. Dad's adjusted basis in the sailboat was $5,000. Dad died on June 15, before he received payment for the sailboat. The gain to be reported as IRD is the $1,000 difference between Dad's basis in the sailboat and the sale proceeds. Simply stated, the IRD is the gain Dad would have realized if he had lived.

> **Example 4:** Mom was entitled to a large salary payment at the date of her death. The amount was to be paid in five annual installments. Mom's estate collected two installments and distributed the right to the remaining installments to Son. No payments are included in Mom's return. The estate must include in its gross income the two installments it received, and Son must include each of the three remaining installments in his gross income as IRD.

> **Example 5:** Mom owned and operated a vineyard. During her lifetime, she sold and delivered 1,000 pounds of grapes to a winery, but did not receive payment for the grapes before her death. Mom also entered into negotiations to sell 4,000 pounds of grapes to a grape jam factory, but did not complete the sale before her death. After Mom died, the executor received payment from the winery.

¶2614

The executor also completed the sale to the jam factory and sold the factory another 1,200 pounds of grapes that were on hand when Mom died. After Mom died, the executor also harvested and transferred an additional 1,800 pounds of grapes. The gain from Mom's sale of grapes to the winery constitutes IRD when received. The gain from the sale of the grapes to the jam factory does not [Reg. Sec. 1.691(a)-2(b), Ex. (5)].

IRD refers to those amounts that a decedent was entitled to receive by the time he or she died but that were not actually received by that time and thus could not properly be included in the decedent's gross income prior to death [Reg. Sec. 1.691(a)-1(b)]. There need not be a legally enforceable right to receive the IRD item, but the payment must clearly represent a right of receipt that arose prior to death.

It is important to distinguish income that must be included on the decedent's final tax return and IRD, which is not included on the decedent's final return but is fully includible in the decedent's gross estate. A decedent's final return only includes items of gross income for the period prior to death under the appropriate method of accounting used by the decedent during life [IRC Sec. 691(a)(1)].

IRD includes the following:

- All accrued income of a decedent who reported his or her income on a cash method of accounting (e.g., accrued bond interest, declared but unpaid dividends, and accrued rents);
- Income accrued solely because of the decedent's death in the case of a decedent who reported his or her income on the accrual method of accounting (e.g., death benefit or lawsuit claim);
- Income to which the decedent had a contingent claim at the time of his or her death (e.g., lawsuit claim or commissions on premiums paid after the date of death); and
- Any retirement benefits the decedent owned [Reg. Sec. 1.691(a)-1(b)].

In other words, the income must be income earned by the decedent as a result of his or her personal labors, sales of property, or investment income that would have been taxable to the decedent if he or she had lived to receive it. It is important to know the difference between IRD and income resulting from appreciation in value of property owned by the decedent at the time of death. Appreciation in value is not IRD, even if the decedent's labors created the increase. An example of this would be stock that had appreciated in value between the date the taxpayer purchased it and the date he died. This appreciation is not IRD.[1]

(a) Examples of IRD. Examples of specific types of IRD include the following:

- Wages, unpaid bonuses or salary earned by the decedent but unpaid at the time of death [Reg. Sec. 1.691(a)-2(b), Ex. 1].[2] Vacation allowances and sick pay paid to an estate or beneficiary are also IRD. Wages paid as income in respect of a decedent are not subject to federal income tax withholding. However, if paid during the calendar year of death, they are subject to withholding for social security and Medicare taxes;

---

[1] **¶2614** Helvering v. Horst, 311 U.S. 112 (1940). [2] Rev. Rul. 59-64, 1959-1 CB 31.

- Promissory note payments due to the decedent but unpaid at the time of death;[3]

- Deferred compensation distributions;

- Dividends declared before the decedent's death but payable after death to holders of stock of record as of a date prior to death;

- Accrued interest and rents as of the time of the property owner's death;

- Installment obligations and commissions earned before death but not paid until later [IRC Sec. 691(a)(4)]. Persons who transfer the right to receive such amounts must include in income either what they get for the right, or its fair-market value, whichever is greater.

> **Example 6:** Dad, who died in November, kept his books on the cash basis. Shortly before his death, he was voted a salary payment of $10,000, to be paid in five $2,000 annual installments beginning the following January. Dad could not draw any of these payments before the actual payment date. His estate collected two installments and distributed the right to the remaining three installments to the residuary legatee. The $4,000 (two installments) must be included in the gross income of the estate, and the residuary legatee must include $6,000 (three installments) in his income when he receives it. However, if the estate had sold the right to the three remaining installments to a person not entitled to them as a legatee, devisee, or heir, or by reason of the death of the decedent, the estate would be required to include in its income the amount received or the fair-market value of the right, whichever was greater.

- The portion of a lump sum distribution to the beneficiary of a decedent's IRA that equals the balance in the IRA at the time of the owner's death is IRD. This includes unrealized appreciation and income accrued to that date, less the aggregate amount of the owner's nondeductible contributions to the IRA.[4] Such amounts are included in the beneficiary's gross income in the tax year that the distribution is received. In *Eberly*,[5] a retirement plan distribution constructively received by a son from his father's estate was not a death benefits payment; thus, it was not includible in the son's gross income as income in respect of a decedent (IRD). The receipt by the fund sponsor of a dated and signed withdrawal request from the decedent constituted an effective exercise by him of his right to a lump-sum distribution during his lifetime. The lump-sum distribution was income to the decedent and properly includible on his gross income. The fact that it was distributed and received by the son after the decedent's death did not make it IRD.

---

[3] Technical Advice Memorandum 200624065 (A portion of payments pursuant to a promissory note transferred to a spouse incident to a divorce was considered to be stated interest, but was not taxable to the spouse's estate as income in respect of a decedent (IRD) because the payments were payable directly to the beneficiaries rather than to the estate. The note provided that, in the event that the recipient spouse was not living on the date the note payments were due, the payments would be made in accordance with the recipient spouse's will or, if there were no will, equally to four beneficiaries); Payson, TC Memo 1959-158.

[4] Rev. Rul. 92-47, 1992-1 CB 198.

[5] Eberly, TC Summ. Op. 2006-45.

- Proceeds from the completed sale of farm crops, crop shares, and livestock. If the farmer died during a rent period, only the portion of the proceeds from the portion of the rent period ending with death is IRD. The proceeds of the rent period from the date after death to the end of the rent period are income of the estate. Cash rent or crop shares and livestock received as rent and reduced to cash by the decedent are includible in the final return even though the rent period did not end until after death.

  Example 7: Dad, who used the cash method of accounting, leased part of his farm for a one-year period beginning March 1. The rent was one-third of the crop, payable in cash when the crop share is sold at his direction. Dad died on June 30. He was alive during 122 days of the rental period. Seven months later, Dad's executor ordered the crop to be sold and was paid $1,500. Of the $1,500, 122/365, or $501, is IRD. The balance of the $1,500, or $999, is income to Dad's estate.

- Any part of a distributive share of partnership income of the estate or other successor in interest of a deceased partner that is for the period ending with the date of the decedent's death.

- Alimony arrearages paid to the estate of a deceased spouse by the surviving former spouse.[6]

- Life insurance commissions received from renewals of insurance that were sold by the decedent prior to death.[7]

- Uncollected interest on U.S. Savings Bonds: If a decedent was on the cash basis and did not elect under IRC Sec. 454(a) to report Series EE or E bond interest annually, the interest on the bonds is IRD that must be reported in one of the following ways: (1) The executor, administrator, or other person required to file the decedent's final return may make the IRC Sec. 454(a) election to include interest earned up to the date of death in the decedent's final return. If that is done, no part of the interest is IRD.[8] (2) If the election in (1) above is not made, the interest earned to date of the death is IRD and all of the interest earned before and after the decedent's death is income to the estate or other beneficiary receiving the bond [Reg. Sec. 1.691(a)-2(b), Example (3)].[9]

  ▶ **PRACTICE NOTE:** The IRS has ruled that neither an estate nor its charitable beneficiaries had to recognize income from Series E and HH U.S. savings bonds that had accrued untaxed interest at the time of the decedent's death.[10] The bonds in this situation escape income tax because they were left to charitable legatees. You should therefore be sure that wills specifically direct charitable bequests to be paid with IRD as much as possible. This will reduce both the taxable estate by the full value of the charitable bequest and allow the estate or noncharitable beneficiaries to avoid income taxation on IRD.

---

[6] Kitch, 104 TC 1 (1995), *aff'd*, 103 F.3d 104 (10th Cir. 1996); Estate of Narischkine, 14 TC 1128, *aff'd*, 189 F.2d 257 (2d Cir. 1951).

[7] Halliday, 655 F.2d 68 (5th Cir. 1981).

[8] Rev. Rul. 68-145, 1968-1 CB 203.

[9] Rev. Rul. 64-104, 1964-1 CB 223.

[10] Ltr. Rul. 9845026.

- Death benefits paid under annuity contract are taxed as IRD according to Rev. Rul. 2005-30,[11] where the IRS clarified that death-benefit payments from an annuity contract that had increased in value, to the beneficiary of the annuity before the annuity starting date, are IRD to the extent the payments exceed the deceased owner's investment in the contract. The beneficiaries may deduct the portion of the estate tax attributable to the IRD in the annuity contract. **Rationale**: If an individual surrenders an annuity contract and receives payments before the annuity starting date, the payments are taxable under IRC Sec. 72(e). Payments are deemed to be paid first from the income on the contract, and are includible in income. After all the income has been paid out, subsequent amounts are deemed to be a return of amounts invested in the contract. If an item of gross income was not taxed to a deceased individual, and the item is transferred to another person on the individual's death, the income is taxed to the recipient when it is paid. Under IRC Sec. 691(a), this item is identified as IRD.

Example 8: Dad purchases an annuity contract for $100. Payments on the contract will begin in 10 years. Mom is the beneficiary of the contract. In year 5, Dad dies and Mom receives the contract. At the time of Dad's death, the value of the contract's account is $150. Mom receives annual payments of $25 from the annuity contract. The $50 of income earned on the annuity contract would have been taxable if paid to Dad before he died. Since Dad died before receiving the income, the $50 is IRD and will be taxable to Mom. The first two payments to Mom of $25 are treated as payments of income and are includible in Mom's income. Subsequent payments are a nontaxable return of the amount invested by Dad. If Mom had chosen (or was allowed to chose) to receive the $150 in a lump sum, $50 would again be includible in her income, and $100 would be a return of the investment in the contract. Ordinarily, property received from an individual on the individual's death is entitled to a stepped-up basis, equal to the property's value on the date of death. However, the property's basis is not increased if the property includes a right to receive IRD. Because the payments to Mom are IRD, she does not receive a stepped-up basis for the fair market value of the annuity contract. However, Mom is entitled to a deduction under IRC Sec. 691(c). Mom can deduct the portion of any estate tax paid by Dad's estate that is attributable to the value of the annuity contract.

- In Letter Ruling 200744001, the IRS concluded that gain from a sale of real property by a decedent's revocable trust was not IRD and the basis of the property was determined under IRC Sec. 1014 to be the fair market value of the property. The trust contracted to sell a parcel of property before the decedent's death but the sale closed after decedent had died. The sale was delayed due to the discovery, after the signing of the contract, of a pipeline on the property, which created economically material contingencies that might have disrupted the sale prior to the death of the decedent.

- Distributions from qualified retirement plans to an estate or other successor that are made as a result of the decedent's death are IRD.[12] Any accrued income earned after the decedent's death is not IRD.

---

[11] Rev. Rul. 2005-30, 2005-1 CB 1015.

[12] Rev. Rul. 69-297, 1969-1 CB 131.

- Qualified distributions from a Roth IRA are not IRD. To be a qualified distribution, the distribution must be made after the five-tax year period that begins with the first tax year in which the owner (decedent) made a contribution [IRC Sec. 408A(d)(2)(B)]. If a distribution from a Roth is not qualified, the earnings from the Roth ending with the date of death are IRD. Earnings from the date of death are taxed as ordinary income to the recipient, but are not IRD.
- Accounts receivable held at death by a cash-basis taxpayer are IRD.

Example 9: Dad was a painter. At his death he was owed $10,000 for services performed for a client. As part of the settlement of the estate, the executor transferred the right to the payment to his widow. The $10,000 is IRD his widow, but not to the estate as the estate did not receive the money.

- The amount awarded in a patent infringement suit that began before the date of death, but was awarded after death, was IRD.[13]
- Medical expense reimbursements received after death for medical expenses that were deducted on the decedent's final return are IRD.[14]

(b) Character of Income. The character of IRD is the same as it would have been if the deceased person had remained alive and had actually received the money [IRC Sec. 691(a)(3)]. For example, if the income would have been capital gain if the decedent had received it, it will be capital gain as IRD. In addition, basis of an IRD item carries over from the decedent. As a result, any untaxed appreciation at death triggers taxable income when the appreciated asset is sold or disposed of.

(c) Installment Obligations. A deceased person's uncollected installment obligations, transmitted at his death directly to his estate or beneficiaries, are treated as IRD. The recipient reports the installment gain the same way the deceased person would have reported it [IRC Sec. 691(a)(4); Reg. Sec. 1.691(a)-5]. This means that an amount equal to the excess of the face value of the obligation over its basis in the hands of the decedent will be considered income in respect of a decedent.

Any previously unreported gain from an installment sale is recognized by a deceased seller's estate if the obligation (1) passes by bequest, devise or inheritance to the obligor, or (2) is canceled by the executor [IRC Sec. 691(a)(5)].

Example 10: Mom died and Son is entitled to collect an installment obligation with a face value of $100, a fair-market value of $80, and a basis in the hands of the decedent of $60. If Son collects the obligation at face value, the excess of the amount collected over the basis is considered IRD and is includable in Son's gross income. In this case, the includable amount would be $40 ($100 less $60). If Son collects the obligation at $90, an amount other than face value, the entire obligation is considered a right to receive income in respect of a decedent but the amount ordinarily required to be included in Son's gross income will be reduced by the amount of the basis of the obligation in the hands of the

---

[13] Rev. Rul. 55-463, 1955-2 CB 277.   [14] Rev. Rul. 78-292, 1978-2 CB 233.

decedent. In this case, the includable amount would be $30 ($90 less $60) [Reg. Sec. 1.691(a)-5(c), Example].

¶2615 DEDUCTIONS IN RESPECT OF A DECEDENT

Estates and other beneficiaries are allowed to claim on Form 1041 an income tax deduction for certain deductions in respect of a decedent that are the payments of certain liabilities that the decedent incurred but failed to pay prior to death. The following payments qualify as deductions in respect of a decedent even though they may not be claimed on the decedent's final income tax return:

- Business expenses deductible under IRC Sec. 162,
- Interest deductible under IRC Sec. 163,
- Taxes deductible under IRC Sec. 164,
- Investment expenses described in IRC Sec. 212 (in excess of 2 percent of AGI), and
- Percentage depletion allowed under IRC Sec. 611 when gross income from a mineral deposit or well is realized [IRC Sec. 691(b)].

In addition, a credit is available for payment of certain foreign income tax for which liability accrued before death [IRC Sec. 691(b)]. The decedent's successor in interest will claim the credit.

(a) Who Claims Deductions in Respect of a Decedent. Deductions in respect of a decedent are ordinarily deductible by the party who pays the bill. That party is either:

1. The decedent's estate, unless the estate is not obligated to pay the expense, or
2. The recipient of the interest in property subject to the liability who pays off the liability, if the decedent's estate is not liable to discharge the obligation to which the deduction or credit relates [IRC Sec. 691(b)(1); Reg. Sec. 1.691(b)-1(a)].

Example 1: Dad died owning property with an unpaid property tax bill. After Dad dies, his estate gets the property and pays the tax bill. The estate is entitled to deduct the property taxes Dad owed on the estate's income tax return [Reg. Sec. 1.691(b)-1(a)(1)].

The deduction in respect of a decedent is designed to avoid double taxation, which would occur when inherited assets are subjected to both federal income and estate taxes. In order to claim the deduction you must itemize your deductions. The deduction is claimed as a miscellaneous itemized deduction but, unlike other miscellaneous itemized deductions, it is deductible in full and is not subject to the two percent floor. In addition, the deduction is not subject to the alternative minimum tax. You determine if the deduction may be claimed by looking at the decedent's federal estate tax return. If federal estate tax is owed, you must recalculate the estate tax without the IRD asset and then subtract that amount from the actual estate tax bill. The deduction equals the difference between the two amounts.

¶2615

(b) Depletion Deduction. A deduction for percentage depletion is available only to the person who has an economic interest in the land or mineral that is eligible for the depletion. The person claiming the deduction need not own the property that generates the income [IRC Sec. 691(b)(2); Reg. Sec. 1.691(b)-1(b)].

> **Example 2:** Dad dies owning an iron mine. As a result of Dad's death, Son receives income from the sale of units of iron. Son is entitled to the deduction for percentage depletion with respect to that income. It doesn't matter that the only interest Son received in the mineral property was the income interest. If Dad did not compute his deduction for depletion on the basis of percentage depletion, any deduction for depletion to which the decedent was entitled at the date of death would be allowable in computing his or her taxable income for his last taxable year, and there can be no deduction in respect of the decedent by any other person for such depletion [Reg. Sec. 1.691(b)-1(b)].

¶2616 INCOME TAX DEDUCTION FOR ESTATE TAX PAID

In addition to being included in the income of IRD recipients, IRD is included in the decedent's gross estate for estate tax purposes under IRC Sec. 2033 as a property interest owned at the time of death. As a result, it is subject to double taxation. As a relief measure, the person who reports items of IRD may also deduct (not subject to the 2 percent-of-AGI floor) the estate tax paid with respect to such items [IRC Sec. 67(b)(7)]. The income recipient can deduct a proportionate share of the federal estate tax that is attributable to the IRD [IRC Sec. 691(c); Reg. Sec. 1.691(c)-1(a)]. Specifically, a taxpayer who includes an amount of IRD in gross income may deduct the portion of the estate tax on the decedent's estate that is attributable to the inclusion in the gross estate of the right to receive such income [IRC Sec. 691(c)(1)(A)].

In figuring the net long-term capital gains or the net capital loss, the amount of gain treated as IRD is reduced, but not below zero, by the amount of any deductible estate taxes attributable to a gain treated as IRD [IRC Sec. 691(c)(4)].

(a) How to Compute Deduction. To compute the deduction for estate taxes paid on IRD, go through the following four steps [IRC Sec. 691(c)(1)]:

1. Determine the total estate tax value of all items of gross income that constitute IRD.

2. Subtract the amount of any deduction in respect of a decedent for which a deduction was claimed on the estate tax return. Also subtract any foreign taxes claimed as credits by the estate or a beneficiary that were attributable to IRD items and allowed as estate tax deductions. The court held in *Estate of Cherry*,[1] that the income tax deduction under IRC Sec. 691(c) must be determined by first calculating the estate tax on the entire estate (including the ordinary consideration of the

---

[1] **¶2616** Estate of Cherry, 133 F. Supp. 2d 949 (D.C. Ky. 2001).

¶**2616**

marital share) and then making the recomputation by removing the IRD before proceeding in the customary fashion (including a recomputation of the marital share). This approach reduces double taxation by allowing a deduction from income tax for the portion of the estate tax fairly attributable to the presence of IRD in the estate.

3. You have now computed the net value for estate tax purposes of the IRD items. The estate tax attributable to inclusion of this net value is determined by using the marginal estate tax rate.

4. If more than one person receives items of IRD, the deduction he or she may claim is a fraction of the amount that you determined in Step 3 above. The numerator is the total amount received and the denominator is the total amount of all items of IRD before you reduced it for deductions in respect of a decedent [IRC Sec. 691(c)(1)(A)].

(b) Lump-Sum Distributions Under Qualified Plan. The amount of death benefits distributed to a beneficiary who receives a lump sum distribution under a qualified plan and elects special income averaging, is reduced by the amount of the estate tax deduction attributable to the distribution [IRC Sec. 691(c)(5)].

(c) Stock Option. Any estate tax resulting from including an employee stock option in a decedent's estate is deductible in the year the estate or beneficiary has income resulting from the sale of stock acquired under the option [IRC Sec. 421(c)(2)].

(d) Special Deduction for Surviving Annuitant. The portion of estate tax attributable to the survivor's annuity is allowable as a deduction to the surviving annuitant over his life expectancy period [IRC Sec. 691(d); Reg. Sec. 1.691(d)-1(a)].

(e) IRA Payments. An IRA account owned by a decedent at death is considered part of the decedent's estate for federal estate tax purposes [IRC Sec. 2039(a)]. Therefore, the estate must pay an estate tax on the value of the IRA. In addition, an income tax will be assessed against the beneficiaries of the accounts when the accounts are distributed [IRC Sec. 408(d)(1); IRC Sec. 691(a)(1)(B)]. To compensate (at least partially) for this potential double taxation, IRC Sec. 691(c) grants the recipient of an item of IRD an income tax deduction equal to the amount of federal estate tax attributable to that item of IRD.[2] Therefore, the decedent's beneficiaries will be allowed a deduction in the amount of the federal estate tax paid on the items of IRD included in the distributions to them from the IRA. The deduction is allowed in the same year the income is recognized—that is, when the IRA is actually distributed [IRC Sec. 691(c)(1)(A)].

In Letter Ruling 200316008, the IRS concluded that a surviving spouse and her estate and its beneficiaries who receive IRA distributions (which are IRD) are entitled to claim IRD deductions under IRC Sec. 691(c) for the estate tax attributable to the inclusion of the IRD items in the decedent spouse's gross estate. The deduction is calculated using the ratio in IRC Sec. 691(c)(1) multiplied by the estate tax attributable to the net value of the items of IRD.

---

[2] Estate of Smith, 391 F.3d 621 (5th Cir. 2004).

¶2616

¶2617 CHECKLIST OF FILING REMINDERS FOR DECEDENT'S FINAL RETURN

Be sure to follow these procedures when filing a decedent's final return in order to minimize the time the IRS takes to process the return and send a refund:

☐ Write "DECEASED," the decedent's name, and the date of death across the top of the tax return.

☐ If a personal representative has been appointed, the personal representative must sign the return. If no personal representative has been appointed, someone charged with the property of the decedent should sign the return.

☐ If the decedent was a minor or incompetent, the legal guardian responsible for the decedent should sign the return.

☐ If the decedent's spouse is filing a joint return with the decedent, he or she must write "Filing as surviving spouse" in the area where the filer's signature appears on the return. If a personal representative has been appointed, the personal representative must also sign the return.

☐ When claiming a refund for the decedent, take note of the following rules:

  • If you are the decedent's spouse filing a joint return with the decedent, file only the tax return to claim the refund.

  • If you are the personal representative and the return is not a joint return filed with the decedent's surviving spouse, file the return and attach a copy of the certificate that shows your appointment by the court. **(A power of attorney of attorney or a copy of the decedent's will is not acceptable evidence of your appointment as the personal representative.)** If you are filing an amended return, attach Form 1310 and a copy of the certificate of appointment (or, if you have already sent the certificate of appointment to IRS, write "Certificate Previously Filed" at the bottom of Form 1310).

  • If you are not filing a joint return as the surviving spouse, and a personal representative has not been appointed, file the return and attach Form 1310 and proof of death (generally, a copy of the death certificate).

☐ Remember that NOL and capital loss carryovers of decedent can only be deducted on the decedent's final return. They cannot be carried over and deducted by a successor in interest or to the decedent's estate.

☐ Remember that the taxable year of a partnership closes with respect to a partner on the date of the partner's death [IRC Sec. 706(c)(2)(A)]. Consequently, it is necessary to compute the deceased partner's share of partnership income up to the date of death as would be required if the partner had sold his or her partnership interest or had retired. The decedent's final return includes all partnership income from partnership year ending with or within his last taxable year.

☐ Check the rules for military personnel who die from injuries in a combat zone.

¶2617

SAMPLE OF DECEDENT'S FINAL INCOME TAX RETURN

TABLE OF CONTENTS

¶2700 PREPARATION OF THE DECEDENT'S FINAL INCOME TAX RETURN

In general, the preparation of the decedent's final income tax return is no different from the preparation of the income tax return for a living taxpayer. If the decedent used the cash method of accounting, which most people use, the decedent's final return must report all income that the decedent actually or constructively received before he or she died.

The decedent's income can be reduced by deductions that the decedent accrued before death. A special exception exists to enable the executor to deduct the decedent's medical expenses if they were paid within the one-year period beginning with the day after the date of death.

The deductions can take the form of the full standard deduction no matter when in the year death occurred or itemized deductions if the total of all itemized deductions is greater than the available standard deduction. In addition, the executor is entitled to claim a full personal exemption on behalf of the decedent no matter when in the year death occurred.

The decedent's final income tax return covers the tax year ending with the date of the decedent's death and must be prepared on a form for the year of death regardless of when during the year death occurred. If the decedent died after the close of the tax year, but before the return for that year was filed, the return for the year just closed will be a regular tax return rather than the decedent's final return. The executor must also file the decedent's final return for the year in which death occurred.

The decedent's final income tax return should be filed by the person who is in charge of the decedent's property. This person could be the surviving spouse, who has the option of filing a joint return with the decedent. The decedent's will may appoint an executor who has the job of administering the decedent's estate, distributing property as directed by the decedent, and winding up the decedent's affairs. In addition, the executor or personal representative has the task of filing the decedent's final income tax return. If the decedent died intestate (without a will), the final return can be prepared and filed by the decedent's personal representative or court-appointed administrator.

The final income tax return would be filed with the IRS center for the place where executor or personal representative preparing the return resides. The return can be filed electronically [see ¶2604].

¶2701 FACTS APPLICABLE TO SAMPLE RETURN

To demonstrate how to fill out a decedent's final return, we present a line-by-line analysis of a hypothetical final tax return to be filed for George E. King, who died on July 1, 2013, at age 55. For purposes of the discussion, assume the following facts. At the time of his death, George was married to Mary M. King. Mary was named executor of her husband's estate and therefore has the responsibility of filing the final income tax return on behalf of her husband.

At the time of his death, George was employed as a certified public accountant. According to the Form W-2 furnished by George King's employer, George received total compensation in the amount of $101,000 in 2013 prior to his death on July 1, 2013. George's employer withheld Medicare tax at a rate of 1.45 percent on all the wages as indicated on the W-2, box 6. The total Medicare tax withheld on George's wages of $101,000 in 2013 was $1,465. Mary King worked as a staff attorney in a real estate development corporation. Mary's W-2 indicated that she received compensation in the amount of $180,904 in 2013. Mary's employer withheld Medicare tax at a rate of 1.45 percent on all the wages as indicated on the W-2, box 6. The total Medicare tax withheld on Mary's wages of $180,904 in 2013 was $2,623. Mary and George King had total compensation of $281,904 in 2013 and total Medicare tax withheld of $4,088.

The Kings had two children, ages 8 and 10, living with them at home. They also supported Mary's elderly mother in a retirement home.

The Best Insurance Company gave Mary a check in the amount of $500,000 because she was the beneficiary named in the life insurance policy on George's life. Mary does not have to pay income tax on these life insurance proceeds because IRC Sec. 101(a)(1) provides that the proceeds of life insurance that are received under a life insurance policy and are paid by reason of the death of the insured are generally excluded from gross income.

George and Mary were joint owners of an office building in Kansas City. This rental property was leased the entire year of George's death for a total rental payment of $18,000. Under local law, George and Mary each had a half interest in the income from the property. George's will, however, provides that the entire rental income is to be paid directly to Mary. None of the rental income will be reported on the income tax return for the estate. Instead, Mary will report all the rental income and expenses on Schedule E [see ¶2786] of George's final income tax return.

George and Mary used the cash method of accounting and reported their income on a calendar-year basis. As executor of George's estate, Mary filed a joint final income tax return for George and herself. Since a joint tax return was filed, the decedent's final return will cover George's income and deductions for the period January 1, 2013 through July 1, 2013, and Mary's income and deductions for the full 2013 calendar year.

The final income tax return filed for George E. King is filed on Form 1040 because the Kings itemized their deductions and had taxable income in excess of $100,000. The completed Form 1040 and all necessary schedules filed on behalf of the decedent are reproduced starting at ¶2782. The Kings' various tax return entries are highlighted throughout the text.

¶2701

For discussion of whether you need to file a final return on behalf of the decedent, see ¶ 2601. For a discussion of whether to file Form 1040 or Form 1040A see ¶ 2602.

¶2702 TOP OF DECEDENT'S FINAL RETURN

At the very top of the decedent's final return Form 1040 [see ¶2782] write the following:

- "DECEASED"
- The decedent's name, and
- The date of death.

Include the same information on any Form 1040X, "Amended U.S. Individual Income Tax Return," that is filed on behalf of the decedent.

Report the decedent's name, address, and Social Security number at the top of Form 1040 [see ¶2782]. If you are filing a joint return for a decedent and the decedent's surviving spouse (who has not remarried before the end of the year of the decedent's death), you also report the surviving spouse's name, address, and Social Security number.

If you are filing a joint return on behalf of the decedent, and you received the forms from the Internal Revenue Service (IRS), simply peel off the mailing label on the front cover and affix it in the space provided for reporting report the decedent's name, address, and Social Security number. If necessary, make corrections on the label. If the Social Security number is wrong on the label, report the decedent's correct number in the appropriate box to the right of the label.

If a joint return is not being filed, write the decedent's name in the space provided for the taxpayer's name and the personal representative's name and address in the remaining space.

¶2703 WHAT'S NEW ON FORM 1040

Net investment income tax imposed on unearned income of individuals. Beginning in 2013, U.S. citizens and residents must pay a 3.8 percent net investment income (NII) tax on the lesser of: (1) NII for the year, or (2) the excess of modified adjusted gross income (MAGI) over the threshold amount ($250,000 for a joint return or surviving spouse, $125,000 for a married individual filing a separate return, and $200,000 for all others). These thresholds are not indexed for inflation. MAGI is defined as adjusted gross income (AGI) plus any amount excluded as foreign earned income under IRC Sec. 911(a)(1) (net of the deductions and exclusions disallowed with respect to the foreign earned income). The tax is reported for individuals, trusts and estates on Form 8960, "Net Investment Income Tax Individuals, Estates, and Trusts," which is attached to Form 1040 (individuals).

Net investment income is defined as: (1) interest, dividends, annuity income, royalties, and rents; (2) profits from a passive activity which is a trade or business where the taxpayer does not "materially participate"; A taxpayer who owns a business, either as a sole proprietorship or as part of a pass-through entity (partnership, LLC or S corporation) and who does not materially participate in the business is deemed to own an interest in a passive activity; (3) profits from a trade or business of trading in financial instruments or commodities, even if the taxpayer does materially participate, and (4) net gain from the disposition of property (e.g., capital gains from stock sales, mutual fund capital gain distributions, etc.) but not gains from selling property held in a trade or business where the taxpayer materially participates.

Increased payroll tax imposed on employees and self-employed taxpayers. Beginning in 2013, individual taxpayers must pay a 0.9% Additional Medicare Tax (hospital insurance tax) on employee compensation and self-employment income above the following thresholds: $250,000 for joint returns; $125,000 for married couples filing separately; and $200,000 in all other cases. These thresholds are not indexed for inflation. The 0.09 percent tax is in addition to the regular Medicare tax rate of 1.45 percent on wages for a total of 2.35 percent on wages received in a calendar year in excess of these threshold amounts. The tax only applies to the employee portion of the Medicare tax. The employer Medicare tax rate remains at 1.45 percent, and the employer and employee Social Security tax remain at 6.2 percent. Employers must begin withholding the additional Medicare tax from wages in excess of $200,000, even if the employee ultimately may not be liable for the additional tax (e.g., employee earns $210,000, his spouse earns $25,000 and they file a joint return).

The 0.9 percent additional Medicare tax also applies to self-employment income in excess of $200,000 ($250,000 of combined self-employment income on a joint return, $125,000 for married taxpayers filing a separate return), but the thresholds are reduced (but not below zero) by the amount of wages taken into account in determining the additional 0.9 percent tax on wages.

Taxpayers subject to the 0.9 percent tax must attach Form 8959, "Additional Medicare Tax" to their tax return. If taxpayers are filing Form 8959, they cannot file Form 1040A, Form 1040EZ or Form 1040NR-EZ. They must file any of the following forms: Form 1040, Form 1040NR, Form 1040-SS, Form 1040-PR. Taxpayers must file Form 8959 if their Medicare wages and tips on all Forms W-2, plus self-employment income, combined with a spouse's Medicare wages and tips and self-employment income if a joint return is filed, are more than the threshold amount for the taxpayer's filing status.

Higher individual income tax rates. For 2013 and subsequent years, the individual income tax rate schedules reflect a continuation of the rates under the "Bush-era" tax cuts, except for the addition of a new 39.6 percent rate for the highest bracket. The individual income tax rates for 2013 (and future years) are 10, 15, 25, 28, 33, 35 and 39.6 percent. For 2013, the starting point of the 39.6 percent rate is $400,000 for unmarried individuals; $425,000 for heads of households; $450,000 for married couples filing a joint return, and surviving spouses; and $225,000 for married couples filing separate returns.

Long-term capital gain and dividend tax rates increases. In 2013, the top tax rate for long-term capital gains and dividends increased to 20 percent for 2013 (up from 15 percent) for taxpayers that are taxed at a 39.6 percent rate as reflected in the following chart:

¶2703

Capital Gains Maximum Rates for 2013 and 2014

Type of Property	Period Held	Maximum Rate*
Capital assets, other than on gain attributable to Section 1250 recapture or collectibles	12 months or less	39.6%
	More than 12 months	0% if in 15% ordinary income tax rate bracket** 15% if in 28% or 33% ordinary income tax rate bracket 20% if in 39.6% ordinary income tax rate bracket

* Excluding the 3.8% net investment income tax that may apply.

** Only to the extent the gain would otherwise be in the 15% tax bracket.

Beginning in 2013, qualified dividends received by individuals, estates, and trusts will permanently be taxed at capital gains rates. The rate on unrecaptured depreciation remains at 25 percent and the rate on collectibles gains and IRC Sec. 1202 gains remain at 28 percent.

Impact of increased long-term capital gains and dividend tax rate and 3.8 percent NII tax. As previously mentioned, if an individual's AGI is over $200,000 ($250,000 if filing a joint return), then long-term capital gains and dividends are subject to the 3.8 percent NII tax. In 2013, the top tax rate for long-term capital gains and dividends increased to 20 percent (up from 15 percent) for taxpayers that are taxed at a 39.6 percent rate. This brings the effective tax rate to as high as 23.8 percent for taxpayers with long-term capital gains and they are in the 39.6 percent tax bracket and 18.8 percent for taxpayers in lower tax brackets with modified adjusted gross income over $200,000 ($250,000 joint).

Limitation on itemized deductions individuals reinstated. In 2013, taxpayers are required to reduce the amount of their itemized deductions if their AGI exceeds the following threshold amounts which will be adjusted for inflation after 2013: $300,000 if filing a joint return or as a surviving spouse, $275,000 if filing as head of household, $250,000 if filing as unmarried and not a surviving spouse or head of household, and $150,000 if a married individual filing a separate return. A taxpayer with AGI over the threshold amount will need to reduce his or her otherwise allowable itemized deductions by the lesser of: (1) three percent of the amount of the taxpayer's AGI in excess of the applicable threshold amount, or (2) 80 percent of the itemized deductions otherwise allowable for the tax year. Itemized deductions not subject to the limitation are medical expenses, investment interest expenses, casualty or theft losses, or gambling losses. The amount of itemized deductions that are cut back for regular income tax purposes are not cut back when calculating alternative minimum taxable income (AMTI).

Floor for deducting medical and dental expenses increased. Individuals can deduct unreimbursed medical expenses only to the extent that they exceed 10 percent of the taxpayer's adjusted gross income in 2013. The threshold for the itemized deduction for unreimbursed medical expenses increased from 7.5 percent of AGI to 10 percent of AGI beginning in 2013. However, in 2013, 2014, 2015 and 2016, if either the taxpayer or the taxpayer's spouse turns 65 before the end of the tax year, the increased threshold does not apply and the threshold remains at 7.5 percent of AGI.

¶2703

Health flexible spending arrangements. Health FSAs are benefit plans that employers sponsor in order to allow their employees to be reimbursed on a tax-favored basis for certain medical expenses that are not covered by the employer's major medical plan. Contributions to an FSA are not includible in the employee's income, and reimbursements from an FSA that are used to pay qualified medical expenses are not taxed. Employees who participate in their employers' health flexible spending accounts can only make a maximum contribution of $2,500 in 2013. In 2013, the IRS relaxed the long-standing "use-or-lose" rule for health FSAs so that for the first time, employees participating in health FSAs were allowed to amend cafeteria plans to provide that employees may carry over to the following year (instead of forfeiting) up to $500 of unused health FSA balances remaining at the end of a plan year. In addition, the existing option that allows plan sponsors to give employees a two and a half month grace period after the end of the plan year remains in place. However, a health FSA cannot offer employees both a $500 carryover option and a two and a half month grace period option. The plan can offer neither option, one or the other option, but cannot offer both options. Effective for plan years starting in 2013, employers should amend their cafeteria plan documents to provide for this new option. Any unused amount above $500 will be forfeited.

Personal exemption phaseout reinstated. The phaseout of otherwise allowable personal exemption deductions was also reinstated in 2013. Therefore, beginning in 2013, taxpayers are required to reduce the amount of their deductions for personal exemptions ($3,900 for 2013) when their AGI exceeds the following threshold levels which are adjusted for inflation after 2013: $300,000 if filing a joint return or as a surviving spouse, $275,000 if filing as head of household, $250,000 if filing as unmarried and not a surviving spouse or head of household, and $150,000 if married filing a separate return. The deduction for personal exemptions will be fully eliminated when AGI exceeds the threshold amount by more than $122,500 ($61,250 in the case of a married individual filing separately). For AMT purposes, there is no deduction for, or in lieu of, personal exemptions. Instead, the amount of personal exemptions actually deducted in calculating taxable income is added back to determine AMTI.

Same-sex marriages. Beginning in 2013, same-sex couples who are legally married in one of the 50 states, the District of Columbia, a U.S. territory or a foreign country that recognizes same-sex marriage will be treated as married for federal tax purposes regardless of where the couple resides. This is a "state of celebration" rule which means that a couple who married in a state that recognizes same-sex marriage will be treated as married regardless of where they live. The IRS does not, however, recognize as married for federal tax purposes couples who enter into registered domestic partnerships, civil unions or similar relationships.

Beginning in 2013, legally-married same-sex couples generally must file their federal income tax return using either the married filing jointly or married filing separately filing status. Individuals who were in same-sex marriages may, but are not required to, file original or amended returns choosing to be treated as married for federal tax purposes for one or more prior tax years still open under the statute of limitations. Generally, the statute of limitations for filing a refund claim is three years from the date the return was filed or two years from the date the tax was paid, whichever is later. As a result, refund claims can still be filed for tax years 2010, 2011 and 2012. Some taxpayers may have special circumstances, such as signing an agreement with the IRS to keep the statute of limitations open, that permit them to file refund claims for tax years 2009 and earlier.

Home office deduction simplified. Beginning in 2013, some taxpayers who qualified to claim a home office deduction may find it easier to rely on the new simplified safe harbor found in Rev. Proc. 2013-13 because the IRS revised Publication 587, "Business Use of Your Home," to reflect the safe harbor. To help taxpayers compute the amount of their deduction, the IRS also included the new Simplified Method Worksheet in the revised publication. This safe harbor method is an alternative for qualifying taxpayers and does not replace the existing method of calculating, allocating and substantiating actual home office expenses on the 43-line Form 8829, "Expenses for Business Use of Your Home."

Ponzi-type investment scheme. Taxpayers who want to claim a theft loss deduction under the safe harbors established in Rev. Proc. 2009-20, 2009-1CB 749 as modified by Rev. Proc. 2011-58 due to a Ponzi-type investment scheme must complete new Section C of Form 4684, "Casualties and Thefts." In Rev. Proc. 2011-58 the IRS modified the Madoff-type Ponzi scheme safe harbor found in Rev. Proc. 2009-20 so it would be easier for investors to claim a theft loss deduction under IRC Sec. 165 for "qualified losses" suffered when the lead figure in the Ponzi scheme had died.

Form 8949 used to report capital transactions. In 2013, there are changes in the way that taxpayers should report sales and exchanges of capital assets on the following three forms: (1) Form 1040, Schedule D; (2) Form 1120, Schedule D; and (3) Form 8949, "Sales and Other Dispositions of Capital Assets." In 2013, certain sale/other disposition transactions can be omitted from Form 8949 and reported directly on Schedule D. Prior to 2013, both corporations and electing large partnerships were required to report gain or loss from pass-through entities on Form 8949. In 2013, only corporations are required to report on Form 8949 and electing large partnerships report their gain on Schedule D.

New direct payment option for Form 1040 filers. In 2013, the IRS introduced a new direct payment option for Form 1040 filers. IRS Direct Pay will allow individual taxpayers with a valid Social Security number to make federal income tax payments directly from their checking or savings accounts. Unlike the current payment system, which uses third-party vendors that charge significant fees, the new payment option is free and provides an electronic payment confirmation. Only Form 1040 payments and associated penalties can be made through IRS Direct Pay. Individuals chosen to participate in the pilot will receive a flyer explaining the service with their balance due notices. Only taxpayers who receive a flyer can use IRS Direct Pay until the testing phase is completed. Taxpayers participating in the test who are unable to submit payments through IRS Direct Pay, should submit their payments through other electronic means.

Standard mileage rates. For 2013, the optional business standard mileage rate is 56.5 cents-per-mile. The optional standard mileage rate for qualified medical and moving expenses for 2013 is 24 cents-per-mile and the rate for charitable miles is 14 cents-per-mile. For 2014, the optional business standard mileage rate decreased to 56 cents-per-mile. The optional standard mileage rate for qualified medical and moving expenses also decreased for 2014 to 23.5 cents-per-mile. The rate for charitable miles driven is set by statute and remains unchanged for 2014.

¶2703

Credit for prior year minimum tax. Special rules generally allowed individuals with long-term unused minimum tax credits to claim an additional refundable minimum tax credit. These special rules expired after December 31, 2012. This AMT credit relief was enacted in 2006 and was intended primarily for individuals who exercised incentive stock options at a profit and sold the stock later when the stock price had significantly declined. Individuals would have had to pay an AMT on the profit in the year of the exercise, although they lost a large portion or all of the profit at the time of the stock sale. As a result, they could have ended up with a large amount of minimum tax credit that they may never be able to use even if carried forward.

Identity theft. As it has done in past filing seasons, the IRS is assigning IP PINs to victims of identity theft. A taxpayer uses the unique six-digit number on his or her return to show that they are the rightful filer of the return. If an IP PIN is assigned to a taxpayer for their 2013 return, the IP PIN must be used on any delinquent 2011 and 2012 returns filed during the 2014 calendar year.

¶2704 FILING STATUS

The decedent's filing status on the final return is the same filing status that the decedent would have used if he or she had been alive for the whole tax year. Report the decedent's filing status by checking one of the boxes on lines 1 through 5 of the Form 1040 [see ¶2782].

If the decedent was married at the time of death, and the surviving spouse does not remarry before year-end, and both taxpayers have the same tax year, a joint return may be made for the survivor and the deceased spouse. [IRC Sec. 6013(a)(3); Reg. Sec. 1.6013-1(d)]. A joint return filed on behalf of the decedent and a surviving spouse covers the entire tax year for the surviving spouse and the period ending with the date of death for the decedent [Reg. Sec. 1.6013-1(d)(1)].

Same-sex marriages. Beginning in 2013, same-sex couples who are legally married in one of the 50 states, the District of Columbia, a U.S. territory or a foreign country that recognize same-sex marriage will be treated as married for federal tax purposes regardless of where the couple resides. This is a "state of celebration" rule which means that a couple who married in a state that recognizes same-sex marriage will be treated as married regardless of where they live when they file their tax return. The IRS does not, however, recognize couples who enter into registered domestic partnerships, civil unions or similar relationships as married for federal tax purposes.

Beginning in 2013, legally-married same-sex couples generally must file their federal income tax return using either the married filing jointly or married filing separately filing status. Individuals who were in same-sex marriages may, but are not required to, file original or amended returns choosing to be treated as married for federal tax purposes for one or more prior tax years still open under the statute of limitations. Generally, the statute of limitations for filing a refund claim is three years from the date the return was filed or two years from the date the tax was paid, whichever is later. As a result, refund claims can still be filed for tax years 2010, 2011 and 2012. Some taxpayers may have special circumstances, such as signing an agreement with the IRS to keep the statute of limitations open, that permit them to file refund claims for tax years 2009 and earlier.

The decedent's filing status can affect many important parts of the return, including the following:

- The tax rates used to figure the ultimate tax bill;
- The number of exemptions claimed on the return;
- Whether or not the itemized deductions are reduced as a result of the adjusted gross income limitations;
- Who deducts the medical expenses; and
- The opportunity to use expiring losses, which may be not be available unless a joint return is filed and sufficient income is reported to cover the losses. A spouse filing separately after the death of his or her husband may not have sufficient income to cover the losses.

¶2705 LINE 1—SINGLE TAXPAYERS

The decedent files as a single taxpayer if (1) he or she was not married at year-end, and (2) he or she did not qualify as a surviving spouse, head of household, or widow(er) with a dependent child (see below). A decedent who was legally separated under state law at year-end, can file as a single taxpayer.

> ▶ **CAUTION:** A decedent who was living apart from his or her spouse will not be considered single for tax purposes. The separation must be under a court decree of separate maintenance. Anything less won't do. If the decedent and his or her spouse were simply living apart, unless the decedent was an abandoned spouse who can file as a head of household, the decedent can either file jointly with his or her estranged spouse or as a married person filing separately.

¶2706 LINE 2—JOINT RETURN

(a) Personal Representative Files the Return. The executor can file a joint income tax return for the decedent and the surviving spouse if:

1. The decedent and the surviving spouse were married at the time of the decedent's death.

2. The decedent and the surviving spouse had the same accounting period. This means that their tax years began on the same day and would have ended on the same day if the decedent had not died. If the tax year of either spouse is a fractional part of a year resulting from a change of accounting period, a joint return may not be filed [Reg. Sec. 1.6013-1(d)(2)].

Example 1: Mom and Dad file their returns on a calendar-year basis. Dad dies on March 1 and Mom receives permission from the IRS to change her accounting period to a fiscal year beginning June 1. As a result of the change in

¶2706

accounting period, Dad's executor may not file Dad's final income tax return as a joint return with Mom.

1. The decedent and the surviving spouse were U.S. citizens or residents for the tax year.
2. The surviving spouse must not have remarried before the close of the tax year in which the decedent died [Reg. Sec. 1.6013-1(d)(2)].

The election to file a joint return must be made by both the surviving spouse and the personal representative. If no personal representative has been appointed by the due date of the return, the surviving spouse may unilaterally make the election to file a joint return with the deceased spouse.

(b) Surviving Spouse Files the Return. If the surviving spouse has not remarried, he or she may file a joint return on behalf of himself or herself and the decedent if:

1. No return for the taxable year has been made by the decedent,
2. No executor or administrator has been appointed, and
3. No executor or administrator is appointed before the last day prescribed by law for filing the return of the surviving spouse [IRC Sec. 6013(a)(3); Reg. Sec. 1.6013-1(d)(3)].

(c) Consequences of Filing a Joint Return. Before filing a joint return on behalf of a decedent and a surviving spouse, be sure to consider the following consequences of filing a joint return:

• Electing joint status for the decedent's final return means that the return must include all of the income of the decedent earned prior to death, in addition to the surviving spouse's income for the entire taxable year [Reg. Sec. 1.6013-1(d)(1)].

   Example 2: Dad dies on September 15, 2013. If Dad's final income tax return is filed jointly with Mom, the return must include Dad's income and deductions for the period January 1, 2013, through the date of death, September 15, 2013, and Mom's income for the entire 2013 calendar year.

• How will the election to file a joint return affect the final tax bill? Be sure to take into consideration the tax rates for a joint return and the phase-out of the personal exemption when income reaches a certain level. If a joint return is not filed, each spouse must use the higher married filing separate tax rate and if one itemizes, the other must itemize [see ¶ 2707]. If certain requirements are met, the surviving spouse may be eligible for head of household status [see ¶ 2708].

• The decedent's estate becomes jointly and severally liable for the entire tax due on a jointly filed tax return [IRC Sec. 6013(d)(3)]. Consider whether the estate should be exposed to such liability.

• The unpaid income tax liability of a decedent's estate for income earned prior to death is deductible on the estate tax return [Reg. Sec. 20.2053-6(f)]. When a joint return is filed, the portion of the joint tax liability for which the estate will be liable is

¶2706

limited to the amount that the estate would be liable for under local law [Reg. Sec. 20.2053-6(f)]. This usually is the amount allocated to the decedent's percentage of income. The regulations set forth the following formula to use in determining how much of the tax should be allocable to the decedent:

Decedent's Separate Tax Both Separate Taxes × Joint Tax

> **Example 3:** On a final return decedent Husband and surviving Wife have a joint tax liability of $60,000. If they had filed separately, Husband's separate tax liability would have been $48,000 and Wife's would have been $24,000. Using the above formula, Husband's share of the joint tax liability is $40,000 ($48,000 divided by $72,000 times $60,000).

(d) Executor May Revoke Joint Return. If an executor or administrator of the decedent is appointed after the surviving spouse has filed a joint return with a deceased spouse, the executor or administrator has the option of revoking or disavowing that joint return.

This is accomplished if the executor files a separate return for the decedent within one year from the due date of the return (including any extensions). The joint return made by the surviving spouse will then become the separate return of that spouse by excluding the decedent's items and refiguring the tax liability [IRC Sec. 6013(a)(3); Reg. Sec. 1.6013-1(d)(5)].

> ▶**TAX RETURN TIP:** If the surviving spouse files a joint return with a deceased spouse, he or she should write "Filing as a surviving spouse" in the area at the bottom of the tax form where the taxpayer signs his or her name. If a separate tax form is filed for the deceased spouse, the person preparing the return should write "DECEASED" and the date of death in the name and address section of the tax form. The word "DECEASED" should also be written across the top of the form.

(e) Can You Change Your Mind. If a separate return was originally filed for the decedent and the due date for filing the return has expired, a change to a joint return can be made only by the decedent's executor or administrator. If no executor has been appointed, a joint return cannot be filed [IRC Sec. 6013(b)(1); Reg. Sec. 1.6013-2(b)].

The executor will not be able to switch from a separate return to a joint return in the following situations:

1. After the expiration of three years from the last date prescribed by law for filing the return;

2. Where either spouse has commenced a suit in any court for the recovery of any part of the tax for the tax year involved;

3. Where a notice of deficiency has been sent for the tax year involved and a timely petition has been filed with the Tax Court;

4. Where either spouse has entered into a closing agreement with respect to the tax for the tax year involved; or

¶2706

5. Where any civil or criminal case arising against either spouse with respect to the tax year involved has been compromised [IRC Sec. 6013(b)(2); Reg. Sec. 1.6013-2(b)].

■ Mary King, the executor of her husband's estate, files a joint final income tax return on behalf of her husband, George. This means that George's final return will cover his income and deductions for the period January 1, 2013, through the date of his death, July 1, 2013, and Mary's income and deductions for the full 2013 calendar year.

¶ 2707   LINE 3—MARRIED FILING SEPARATELY

If the decedent was married at the end of 2013 but the executor does not want the decedent to file a joint return with the surviving spouse, the executor can file the decedent's final return as a "married filing separately" return. However, before making the decision to file separately, check to see if the decedent can qualify as an abandoned spouse entitled to file as a head of household. Heads of households are taxed at more favorable tax rates than separate filers [see ¶ 2708].

Although joint filers enjoy more favorable tax rates than separate filers (separate filers are taxed at the highest rates—higher than singles and heads of households as well as joint filers), in some situations, filing separately may yield a more favorable tax result. Realizing tax savings by filing separately is most likely if the decedent had substantial deductions that are permitted only to the extent they exceed a percentage of adjusted gross income (AGI). For example, medical expenses are deductible only to the extent they exceed $7^1/_2$ percent of AGI.

Example 1: Sid and Nancy Smith each have adjusted gross income of $32,000. If Sid has unreimbursed medical expenses of $5,400 and Nancy has none, the deduction on Sid's separate return is $3,000 ($5,400 minus $2,400, or 7 percent of $32,000). On the other hand, the deduction on a joint return would be only $600 ($5,400 minus $4,800, or 7 percent of $64,000).

A married couple combining their AGIs on a joint return is also hit hard by the 2 percent-of-AGI floor for miscellaneous itemized deductions. Filing separately may make sense where the spouse with the lower AGI has a large amount of miscellaneous expenses. However, filing separate returns with one spouse taking medical and all other itemized deductions and the other spouse taking advantage of the standard deduction will not work. On separate returns, if one spouse itemizes, so must the other.

▶ **CAUTION:** In weighing the pros and cons of filing separately for a decedent and the decendent's surviving spouse, remember that separate filers lose the benefits of the joint return rates, and the ability to use up the decedent's net operation losses, capital losses, or charitable contribution carryforwards, or any other expiring deductions or credits.

¶ 2707

¶2708 LINE 4—HEAD OF HOUSEHOLD

A decedent who qualifies as head of household is taxed at a rate lower than the rate for single taxpayers (although higher than the rates for joint filers). This filing status is for unmarried individuals who provide a home for certain other persons described below.

Executors should check the box on line 4 only if the decedent was unmarried or legally separated (according to state law) under a decree of divorce or separate maintenance at year-end and either 1 or 2 below applies:

1. The decedent paid over half the cost of keeping up a home that was the main home for the entire year of a parent whom the decedent claimed as a dependent.* [*See "Definition of Dependent" below.] The parent does not have to live with the decedent;

2. The decedent paid over half the cost of keeping up a home in which the decedent lived and in which one of the following also lived for more than half of the year.

    a. Any person whom the decedent claimed as a dependent.* But do not include:

        i. The decedent's qualifying child* whom the decedent claimed as a dependent based on the rules for children of divorced or separated parents outlined below;

        ii. Any person who is the decedent's dependent* only because he or she lived with the decedent for the entire year; or

        iii. Any person claimed as a dependent* under a multiple support agreement.

    b. The decedent's unmarried qualifying child is who is not the decedent's dependent.

    c. The decedent's married qualifying child who is not the decedent's dependent only because the decedent can be claimed as a dependent on someone else's tax return for that year.

    d. The decedent's child who is neither the decedent's dependent nor his or her qualifying child because of the special rules for children of divorced or separated parents outlined below.

If the child is not the decedent's dependent, the executor should enter the child's name on line 4.

Exceptions to time lived with the decedent. Temporary absences for special circumstances, such as for school, vacation, medical care, military service, and detention in a juvenile facility, count as time lived in the home. If the person for whom the decedent kept up a home was born or died during the year, the decedent can still file as head of household as long as the home was that person's main home for the part of the year he or she was alive.

Married persons who live apart. Some married persons who live apart may be considered unmarried and be able to claim head of household status. Even if the decedent was not divorced or legally separated at the end of the year, the executor may be able to consider the decedent unmarried if all the following apply:

¶2708

- The decedent lived apart from his or her spouse for the last 6 months of the year. Temporary absences for special circumstances, such as for business, medical care, school, or military service, count as time lived in the home;
- The decedent filed a separate return from his or her spouse;
- The decedent paid over half the cost of keeping up the home for the year;*
- The decedent's home was the main home of the decedent's child, stepchild, or foster child (defined below) for more than half of the year;
- The decedent claimed this child as his or her dependent or the child's other parent claims his or her dependent under the special rules for children of divorced or separated parents outlined below under "Children of divorced or separated parents."

Adopted child. An adopted child is always treated as a taxpayer's own child. An adopted child includes a child lawfully placed with a taxpayer for legal adoption.

Foster child. A foster child is any child placed with the decedent by an authorized placement agency or by judgment, decree, or other order of any court of competent jurisdiction.

*Definition of "dependent." A dependent is either a *qualifying child* or a *qualifying relative*. To be a taxpayer's qualifying child for purposes of claiming head of household filing status, a person must satisfy the following tests:

- *Relationship test.* Qualifying children include the taxpayer's children, stepchild (whether by blood or adoption) foster child, sibling or stepsibling, or a descendant of one of these. An adopted child is defined as a child legally adopted by the taxpayer or lawfully placed with the taxpayer for legal adoption by the taxpayer. A qualifying child can also be an eligible foster child, defined as a person placed with the taxpayer by an authorized placement agency or by a judgment, decree, or other court order. There is no requirement that a foster child live with the taxpayer for the entire tax year;
- *Residence test.* Qualifying children have the same principal residence as the taxpayer for more than half the tax year. Exceptions apply for kidnapped children, temporary absences, and for children who were born or died during the year;
- *Age test.* Qualifying children must be under the age of 19 at the end of the year or under the age of 24 if a full-time student for at least five months of the year, or be permanently and totally disabled at any time during the year. In addition, the child must be younger than the taxpayer unless the child is permanently and totally disabled [IRC Sec. 152(c)(3)(A)];
- *Support test.* Qualifying children did not provide more than one-half of their own support during the year. If a child is claimed as a qualifying child by two or more taxpayers in a given year, the child will be the qualifying child of:
  - The parent;
  - If more than one taxpayer is the child's parent, the one with whom the child lived for the longest time during the year, or, if the time was equal, the parent with the highest AGI;
  - If no taxpayer is the child's parent, the taxpayer with the highest adjusted gross income;

¶2708

- *Joint return test.* A qualifying child cannot file a joint return with a spouse for a tax year beginning in the calendar year in which the tax year of the taxpayer claiming the qualifying child begins. However, a qualifying child is allowed to file a joint return for the limited purpose of obtaining a refund [IRC Sec. 152(c)(1)(E)].

For purposes of claiming the head of household status, a qualifying child who is married at the end of the year must also satisfy the following marital status and nationality tests:

- *Nationality.* A qualifying child who is married at the end of the year must be a U.S. citizen or national, or a resident of the United States, Canada, or Mexico. There is an exception for certain adopted children;

- *Marital status.* If married, a qualifying child may not file a joint return for that year, unless the return is filed only as a claim for refund and no tax liability would exist for either spouse if they had filed separate returns.

Children of divorced or separated parents. A child will be treated as being the qualifying child of his or her parent who has custody of the child for the greater part of the year. To be a custodial parent, the parent and the child must have shared the same principal place of abode for the greater portion of the tax year. In the event of a split custody, or if the divorce decree or agreement fails to establish who has custody, custody will be deemed to be with the parent who has physical custody of the child for the greater part of the year.

Tie-breaking rules for children of divorced or separated parents. Sometimes a child will satisfy the tests to be a qualifying child of more than one person. However, only one person can treat that child as a qualifying child. If two taxpayers (other than a spouse if filing jointly) have the same qualifying child, the two taxpayers can decide who will claim the child. If they cannot agree on who will claim the child and more than one person files a return using the same child, the IRS may disallow one or more of the claims using the tie-breaker rule explained in the following table:

IF . . .	THEN the child will be treated as the qualifying child of the . . .
only one of the persons is the child's parent,	parent.
both persons are the child's parent,	parent with whom the child lived for the longer period of time. If the child lived with each parent for the same amount of time, then the child will be treated as the qualifying child of the parent with the highest adjusted gross income (AGI).
none of the persons are the child's parent,	person with the highest adjusted gross income.

The tie-breaker rules will apply whenever two or more taxpayers can claim the child as a qualifying child regardless of whether they actually do so [IRC Sec. 152(c)(4)(A)]. The other modification is if the parents can claim the qualifying child but neither does so, another taxpayer may claim the child as his or her qualifying child but only if their adjusted gross income (AGI) is higher than the highest AGI of either of the qualifying child's parents [IRC Sec. 152(c)(4)(C)].

Note that only one person can claim head of household status.

¶2708

¶2709 LINE 5—QUALIFYING WIDOW(ER) WITH DEPENDENT CHILD

A surviving spouse who is left with a dependent child may be entitled to take advantage of the favorable joint return tax rates for the two years after the death of the decedent spouse if the following can be proved:

1. The decedent dies in 2011 or 2012 and the surviving spouse did not remarry in 2013;

2. The surviving spouse has a child or stepchild who qualifies as the surviving spouse's dependent for the tax year. This does not include a foster child;

3. The household of the surviving spouse is the main home of his or her child for all of the year (except for temporary absences for special circumstances, such as for school, vacation, medical care, military service, and detention in a juvenile facility);

4. The surviving spouse could have filed a joint return with his or her spouse the year he or she died, even if the surviving spouse did not actually do so;

5. The surviving spouse paid more than half the cost of maintaining his or her household the current tax year.

To use joint return tax rates for 2013, the executor must check the box on line 5 (filing status) of Form 1040 or Form 1040A and write in the year (during the last two years) of the decedent spouse's death.

> ▶ **CAUTION:** If you qualify to take advantage of the joint return tax rates, compute your tax bill using the joint tax tables. You are *not* entitled to file a joint return or claim an extra exemption or an increased standard deduction that would normally be available to joint filers. You are entitled to use the Tax Rate Schedule or the Column in the Tax Table for Married Filing Jointly, which gives you the benefit of filing jointly.

¶2710 LINES 6a AND 6b—PERSONAL EXEMPTIONS

For 2013, each personal exemption shelters $3,900 of taxable income. The full amount of the personal exemption may be claimed for the decedent on the final return. This means that the exemption amount does not have to be prorated if the decedent died before the end of the tax year.

The decedent may be entitled to claim an additional exemption on line 42 if he or her she provided housing to a person displaced by the midwestern storms, tornadoes or flooding.

> **Example 1:** Mom dies on July 1, 2013. Her full personal exemptions are allowed on her final income tax return, even though she was alive for only half of the tax year.

If the decedent was married at the time of death and a joint return is filed by the surviving spouse, a personal exemption may be claimed for both the decedent and the

¶2709

surviving spouse by checking the box on line 6b. However, the exemption for the decedent cannot be claimed if someone else is entitled to claim the decedent as a dependent.

■ On lines 6a and 6b of George King's final return, Mary King claims two personal exemptions—one for herself and one for George—even though her husband was only alive for six months of the year.

¶2711 LINES 6c THROUGH 6d—DEPENDENCY EXEMPTIONS

On the decedent's final return, the entire $3,900 exemption may be claimed for each person who was a dependent of the decedent in 2013 even if the decedent was alive for only a portion of the year. The exemption amount need not be prorated. Death has no impact on the rules regarding dependency exemptions.

(a) Who Is a Dependent. In order for a person to claim an exemption for a dependent, the dependent must be either a *qualifying child* or a *qualifying relative*.

Qualifying child defined. To be a *qualifying child*, the child must satisfy all of the following requirements:

- *Relationship.* The child must be the taxpayer's son, daughter, stepchild (whether by blood or adoption), foster child, brother, sister, stepbrother, stepsister, or a descendant of one of these (for example, the taxpayer's grandchild, niece or nephew);

- *Age.* The child must be under the age of 19 at the end of the year, or under the age of 24 if a full-time student for at least five months of the year, or be permanently and totally disabled at any time during the year. In addition, the child must be younger than the taxpayer unless the child is permanently and totally disabled [IRC Sec. 152(c)(3)(A)];

- *Principal Residence.* The child must have the same principal residence as the taxpayer for more than half of the year. Exceptions apply, in certain cases, for children of divorced or separated parents, kidnapped children, temporary absences, and for children who were born or died during the year;

- *Not Self-Supporting.* The child must *not* have provided over half of his or her own support for the year;

- *Joint Return Test.* A qualifying child cannot file a joint return with a spouse for a tax year beginning in the calendar year in which the tax year of the taxpayer claiming the qualifying child begins. However, a qualifying child is allowed to file a joint return for the limited purpose of obtaining a refund [IRC Sec. 152(c)(1)(E)].

Children of divorced or separated parents. The parent who has custody of the child for the greater part of the year is entitled to the dependency exemption. To be a custodial parent, the parent and the child must have shared the same principal place of abode for the greater portion of the tax year. In the event of a split custody, or if the divorce decree or agreement fails to establish who has custody, custody will be deemed to be with the parent who has physical custody of the child for the greater part of the year.

Exceptions to custodial parent rule. A child who receives more than one-half of his or her support during the year from a noncustodial parent will be treated as the qualifying child of the noncustodial parent if the parents' divorce or separation instrument provides that the noncustodial parent is entitled to the dependency exemption, or if the custodial parent provides the IRS with a signed written declaration on Form 8332, "Release of Claim to Exemption for Child of Divorced or Separated Parents" (or an equivalent document) waiving the child's dependency exemption. On Form 8332, the custodial parent may release the exemption for the child for the current tax year, for specific future years, or for all future years. The noncustodial parent must attach Form 8332 to his or her return for each year for which the exemption is claimed. A parent who never married his or her child's mother or father can also use Form 8332 to secure release of the dependency exemption from the custodial parent.

Multiple support agreement exception. The noncustodial parent may also be able to claim the dependency exemption for a child if a multiple support agreement provides that he or she is entitled to the dependency exemption. When two or more persons furnish more than half of the support of an individual, one of the contributing group is entitled to claim the dependency exemption if all of the following criteria are met: (1) No one person contributed more than half the dependent's support. Each member of the group, were it not for the support test, would have been entitled to claim the individual as a dependent; (2) The one claiming the deduction gave more than 10 percent of the dependent's support; (3) Every person (other than the one claiming the exemption) who gave more than 10 percent of the dependent's support files a written statement on Form 2120, "Multiple Support Declaration," providing that he or she will not claim the exemption in the same calendar year (or any tax year starting in the calendar year).

Pre-1985 exception. If the parents' divorce or separation instrument was executed before 1985, the noncustodial parent must also provide at least $600 in support during the calendar year.

Tie-breaking rules. If a child is claimed as a qualifying child by two or more taxpayers in a given year, the child will be the qualifying child of: (1) the parent; (2) if more than one taxpayer is the child's parent, the one with whom the child lived for the longest time during the year, or, if the time was equal, the parent with the highest AGI; (3) if no taxpayer is the child's parent, the taxpayer with the highest adjusted gross income (AGI). The first modification is that the tie-breaker rules will apply whenever two or more taxpayers *can* claim the child as a qualifying child regardless of whether they actually do so [IRC Sec. 152(c)(4)(A)]. If the parents can claim the qualifying child but neither does so, another taxpayer may claim the child as his or her qualifying child but only if their adjusted gross income (AGI) is higher than the highest AGI of either of the qualifying child's parents [IRC Sec. 152(c)(4)(C)].

Qualifying relative defined. For purposes of claiming the dependency exemption, a *qualifying relative* must satisfy the following tests:

• *Relationship.* The following individuals can be classified as qualifying relatives: son, daughter, foster child, or a descendant of any of them; a sibling or stepsibling or a son or daughter of either of them; parent and their ancestors and siblings; the taxpayer's stepparents and stepsiblings; and the taxpayer's son-in-law, daughter-in-law, father-in-law, mother-in-law, brother-in-law and sister-in-law. Qualifying relatives also include individuals, other than the taxpayer's spouse, who share an abode with the taxpayer and were members of the taxpayer's household during the year. An individual is not a member of the taxpayer's household if, at any time during the year, the relationship between the individual and the taxpayer violated local law;

- *Gross income.* A dependent will be a qualifying relative if his or her gross income for the year is less than the exemption amount ($3,900 in 2013);

- *Support test.* In order to claim a person as a dependent the taxpayer must prove that he or she furnished over one half of the dependent's total support for the year;

- *Not a qualifying child.* An individual cannot be a qualifying child of the taxpayer or any other taxpayer for the year;

- A taxpayer cannot claim a dependency exemption for a married individual who files a joint return unless that joint return is filed solely in an attempt to claim a refund;

- If an individual is claimed as a dependent of another person, the dependent may not claim any dependents;

- A qualifying relative must be a United States citizen or national or a resident of the United States, Canada, or Mexico. However, a legally adopted child or an individual who is lawfully placed by the taxpayer for legal adoption need not satisfy this rule if for the tax year the child has the same principal place of residence as the taxpayer and is a member of the taxpayer's household and the taxpayer is a citizen or national of the United States.

Dependent's TIN. Taxpayers must provide a dependent's taxpayer identification number (TIN) in order to claim a dependency exemption for that person. An individual's TIN is generally that individual's social security number. An incorrect TIN is treated as a mathematical or clerical error, allowing the IRS to summarily assess any additional tax due as a result of the denied exemption. Any notification of additional tax is not treated as a notice of deficiency. Taxpayers apply for a social security number by filing Form SS-5 with the Social Security Administration.

(b) Special Note About In-Laws. Once an in-law relationship has been established by marriage, it does terminate with death or divorce. This means that a decedent could claim a dependency exemption for a mother-in-law even after his or her spouse had died, as long as the decedent continued to support the mother-in-law until the decedent died.

On a joint return, the relationship test is satisfied if the dependent is related to either the decedent or the decedent's spouse.

(c) Filing Status. An individual generally cannot be claimed as the decedent's dependent for any year that he or she files a joint tax return. There is one exception: The decedent can claim an individual as a dependent if neither he nor his spouse was required to file a return, but they voluntarily filed simply to claim a refund of tax withheld.

¶2711

■ On the final return filed for George King, three dependency exemptions are claimed. One exemption is claimed for each of his two children and one is claimed for Mary's elderly mother whom the Kings support. The Kings can claim a dependency exemption for Mary's mother even though she did not live with them because she is a qualifying relative who had less than $3,900 of gross income for 2013 and relied on them for more than half of her support. Gross income for these purposes does not include nontaxable income such as welfare benefits or nontaxable Social Security benefits.

The requested information for each dependent is reported in columns 1 through 4 of line 6c. The Kings report "2" children living with them, "0" children not living with them, and "1" other dependent.

The personal exemptions claimed on line 6c are added up and the total number of exemptions claimed is entered on line 6d. On George King's final return, "5" is entered on line 6d (two exemptions for the parents, two for the children, and one for Mary King's mother).

¶2712 LINE 7—WAGES, SALARIES, TIPS, ETC.

The decedent's taxable income for the year of death is computed using the same method of accounting that the decedent last used while still alive. If the decedent had no regular accounting method while alive, he or she is treated as a cash-basis taxpayer for reporting income items. As a result, on line 7, the decedent's executor must report the total of all wages, salaries, fees, commissions, tips, bonuses, awards, and other amounts that the decedent actually or constructively received up to and including the date of death [Reg. Sec. 1.451-1(b)(1)].

Income is constructively received if the taxpayer had use of the money without restriction. For example, a paycheck that the decedent never picked up is considered constructively received (it was available with restriction) and must be included in the decedent's final income tax return [Reg. Sec. 1.451-1(a)].

Salary, commissions, wages, royalties, and bonuses received before death must be included in the decedent's final return [Reg. Sec. 1.451-1(a)]. A bonus that a cash-basis taxpayer received after death will not be reported on the final return, unless it was constructively received or could have been spent while the decedent was still alive.

Income items that the decedent was entitled to receive but did not receive while still alive are called "income in respect of a decedent" (IRD) and are included in the gross income of the decedent's estate or of the beneficiary who receives them [Reg. Sec. 1.691(a)-1(b)]. See ¶ 2614 for further discussion of IRD.

To be included on the final return of a cash-basis decedent, the income must have been received by or must have been available to the decedent prior to his or her death.

(a) Accrual Basis Taxpayer. If the deceased person used the accrual method of accounting, his or her final return will include only income or deductions that accrued up to and including the date of death. Income or deductions that accrue only because of death are not included in the decedent's final return [IRC Secs. 451(b),

461(b); Reg. Secs. 1.451-1(b), 1.461-1(b)]. Income that is received after death should not be reported on the decedent's final return. This income is considered IRD and is taxed to the estate or the beneficiary receiving the income in the year of receipt [see ¶ 2614].

In addition, the fair-market value of goods or services received by the decedent as compensation must be reported on line 7. These amounts are reported to the taxpayer in box 1 of the Form W-2 (withholding statement). If compensation that the decedent received from an employer is not shown on a Form W-2, it must be included in the amount entered on line 7. Attach an explanation of the origins of these extra income items.

(b) Fringe Benefits. The value of taxable fringe benefits (such as personal use of an employer's car) is also included in the amount reported on line 7 of Form 1040 [see ¶ 2782]. These amounts are generally listed in box 1 of Form W-2.

■ According to the Form W-2 furnished by George King's employer, George received compensation in 2013 of $101,000 prior to his death on July 1, 2013. George's employer withheld Medicare tax at a rate of 1.45 percent on all the wages as indicated on the W-2, box 6. The total Medicare tax withheld on George's wages in 2013 of $101,000 was $1,465.

Mary's W-2 indicated that she received compensation in the amount of $180,904 in 2013. Mary's employer withheld Medicare tax at a rate of 1.45 percent on all the wages as indicated on the W-2, box 6. The total Medicare tax withheld on Mary's wages in 2013 of $180,904 was $2,623. Mary and George E. King had total compensation of $281,904 in 2013 and total Medicare tax withheld of $4,088. After George's death, his employer sent Mary a check in the amount of $20,000 for accrued vacation time. Since the $20,000 representing unpaid vacation time was not paid to George before he died, the amount is not reported as income on his final return. It is reported on the estate's income tax return (Form 1041) for 2013. Because a joint return was filed, the return will cover George's income and deductions for the period January 1, 2013 through July 1, 2013 (the date of his death), and Mary's income and deductions for the full 2013 calendar year. The Kings enter total wages, tips and salaries for 2013 of $281,904 on line 7 of Form 1040.

¶2713 LINE 8a—TAXABLE INTEREST INCOME AND SCHEDULE B, PART I

All taxable interest that the decedent received prior to his or her death must be reported on line 8a of Form 1040 [see ¶ 2782]. The decedent must attach Schedule B if any of the following applies:

• The decedent received over $1,500 of taxable interest or ordinary dividends;

• The decedent received interest from a seller-financed mortgage and the buyer used the property as a personal residence;

• The decedent accrued interest from a bond;

- The decedent is reporting original issue discount (OID) in an amount less than the amount shown on Form 1099-OID;
- The decedent is reducing his or her interest income on a bond by the amount of amortizable bond premium;
- The decedent is claiming the exclusion of interest from series EE or I US savings bonds issued after 1989;
- The decedent received interest or ordinary dividends as a nominee; or
- The decedent had a financial interest in, or signature authority over a financial account in a foreign country or received a distribution from or was a grantor of, or a transferor to, a foreign trust.

(a) Where to Look. Taxpayers should receive information returns (Forms 1099) from their banks or other payers of interest. The decedent's Forms 1099 will show exactly how much taxable interest must be reported. Generally, interest income is reported on Form 1099-INT. Interest in the form of "original issue discount" (see below) is reported on Form 1099-OID. Interest from money market funds is reported on Form 1099-DIV.

One of the most common sources of taxable interest is interest on bank deposits. Bank deposit interest must be reported in the year it was credited to the decedent, even if the interest had not yet been entered in the decedent's passbook.

Other common sources of taxable interest income include:

- Bank certificates of deposit and money market accounts. This category of interest income includes interest on accounts with savings banks, savings and loan associations, and credit unions. Note that distributions from a nonbank money market account are generally reported as dividends, rather than interest.
- Corporate bonds.
- U.S. Treasury bonds, notes, and bills.
- Mortgages or other loans.

Tax refunds or dividends paid on insurance policies generally are not taxable interest. But part of the payment may include taxable interest.

(b) U.S. Savings Bonds. The interest on Series EE U.S. Savings Bonds (or their predecessors, Series E Bonds) is ordinarily taxed in the year the bonds mature or are redeemed. There are two methods of reporting interest on Series EE Savings Bonds for federal income tax purposes.

The easiest method is to defer reporting the interest until the year in which the bond matures, is redeemed, or disposed of. The taxpayer does not have to make a special election on his or her tax return in order to defer reporting the interest on Series EE Savings Bonds in this manner. The taxpayer simply postpones reporting the interest until the bond is redeemed.

The more complicated method is to elect to report the annual increase in the redemption value of the bonds as interest each year. Once made, the election applies to all Series E and EE Bonds the taxpayer owns or may acquire in the future, and it can be changed only after the taxpayer receives IRS approval. IRS approval can be obtained

¶2713

automatically by attaching a completed Form 3115, "Change in the Method of Accounting," to the tax return for the year of the switch.

When a person dies owning Series EE U.S. Savings Bonds, there are tax consequences to consider when completing the decedent's final return. These tax consequences turn on whether the decedent had elected to report the interest each year.

If the bonds were owned by an accrual-method taxpayer or by a cash-method taxpayer who had elected to report the interest each year and the bonds were transferred as a result of the decedent's death, the interest earned by the bonds in the year of death up to the date of death must be included on the decedent's final income tax return. The decedent's estate or the successor in interest of the bonds would pay tax only on the interest earned by the bonds after the date of the decedent's death.

If the discount bonds were owned by a cash-basis taxpayer who had not chosen to report the interest each year and had bought the bonds entirely with personal funds, the interest earned before death must be reported in one of the following ways:

1. The executor elects to include in the decedent's final return all of the interest earned on the bonds before the decedent's death [IRC Sec. 454(a); Reg. 1.454-1], and the estate or the beneficiary who inherits the bonds includes on the tax return only the interest earned after the date of death; or

2. The executor does not make the election described in (1) above, the interest earned to the date of death is considered IRD [see ¶ 2614] and is not included in the decedent's final return, and all of the interest earned before and after the decedent's death is considered income to the decedent's estate or the successor in interest who inherits the bond. [For further discussion, see ¶ 2607.]

> ■ George and Mary King received [see ¶ 2701] more than $1,500 of taxable interest income in the year of his death, so they must fill out Schedule B [see ¶ 2783]. In the year prior to his death, George received $600 on a short-term CD from Citizens Bank that matured in that year, $500 of interest on his savings and money market accounts at Thrifty Savings Bank, and $586 on an XYZ Corporation bond. He owned all these investments in his name alone. In addition, George received $120 from a Series EE U.S. Savings Bond that he owned in his name alone. George was a cash-basis taxpayer who did not report the interest accrued on the Series EE U.S. Savings Bonds on prior tax returns that he filed jointly with Mary. On George's final income tax return, Mary chooses to report the interest earned on these bonds before his death ($120). Mary reports all this information on line 1 of Part I of Schedule B [see ¶ 2783]. Mary then adds up the total amount of taxable interest she and George received and enters the result, $1,806, on line 2. Since the Kings did not take advantage of the interest exclusion for U.S. Savings Bonds used to pay for higher education, Mary leaves line 3 blank and carries the $1,806 to line 4 of Schedule B. Mary also enters this amount on line 8a of the Form 1040 [see ¶ 2782].

¶2713

¶2714 LINE 8b—TAX-EXEMPT INTEREST INCOME

All tax-exempt interest earned during the year from state and local municipal bonds (as well as from municipal bond mutual funds) must be reported on line 8b of Form 1040 [see ¶ 2782]. Death does not change this rule.

The decedent will not be taxed on the amount reported on line 8b, but the amount of tax-exempt interest received may have an impact on the decedent's overall tax bill. The decedent may have to pay tax on a portion of any Social Security benefits received or, depending on the types of municipal bonds held, may be subject to the alternative minimum tax.

■ George and Mary King received $7,500 of tax-exempt municipal bond interest in the year of death. This amount is reported on line 8b of Form 1040 [see ¶ 2782].

¶2715 LINE 9a—ORDINARY DIVIDENDS, LINE 9b, QUALIFIED DIVIDENDS, AND SCHEDULE B, PART II

The person preparing the decedent's final return must report on line 9a the total amount of ordinary dividends that the decedent actually or constructively received prior to death from corporate stock, mutual funds (including interest from nonbank money market accounts), or the decedent's share of ordinary dividends earned by a partnership, S corporation, estate, or trust.

A dividend is constructively received if it was available for the decedent's use without restriction. If the corporation normally mails its dividend checks, the dividend will be included in income when the check is received. If the taxpayer died between the time the dividend was declared and the time it was received in the mail, the decedent did not constructively receive the dividend before death, and the dividend should not be included in the decedent's final return.

If the decedent received over $1,500 in ordinary dividends during the year, list the sources and amount of dividend income in Part II of Schedule B [see ¶ 2783].

(a) **Where to Look.** The decedent's surviving spouse or personal representative should receive a Form 1099-DIV from every corporation or other payer that paid the decedent more than $10 worth of dividend income during the year. Taxable dividend income is reported in box 1b of Form 1099-DIV.

Line 9b: Qualified dividends. You should report the total amount of "qualified dividends" received by the decedent on line 9b of Form 1040. Dividends paid by most domestic and foreign corporations are called "qualified dividends" and will be shown in box 1b of Form 1099-DIV. They are eligible to be taxed at the capital gains tax rate. "Qualified dividends" received from either a domestic corporation or a "qualified foreign corporation" will be taxed at the same tax rates imposed on capital gains. Report the decedent's qualified dividends on Form 1040, line 9b or on Form 1040A, line 9b.

¶2714

(b) Exceptions. Some dividends may be reported as qualified dividends in Form Form 1099-DIV, box 1b, but are not qualified dividends. These include:

- Dividends the decedent received as a nominee;

- Dividends the decedent received on any share of stock that the decedent held for less than 61 days during the 121-day period that began 60 days before the ex-dividend date. The ex-dividend date is the first date following the declaration of a dividend on which the purchaser of a stock is not entitled to receive the next dividend payment. When counting the number of days the decedent held the stock, include the day the decedent disposed of the stock but not the date the decedent acquired it. Also, when counting the number of days the decedent held the stock, do not count certain days during which the decedent's risk of loss was diminished;

- Dividends attributable to periods totaling more than 366 days that the decedent received on any share of preferred stock held for less than 91 days during the 181-day period that began 90 days before the ex-dividend date. When counting the number of days the decedent held the stock, do not count certain days during which the decedent's risk of loss was diminished. Preferred dividends attributable to periods totaling less than 367 days are not subject to the 61-day holding period above;

- Dividends on any share of stock to the extent that the decedent was under an obligation (including a short sale) to make related payments with respect to positions in substantially similar or related property;

- Payments in lieu of dividends, but only if the decedent knew or had reason to know that the payments were not qualified dividends;

- Capital gain distributions;

- Dividends paid on deposits with mutual savings banks, cooperative banks, credit unions, U.S. building and loan associations, U.S. savings and loan associations, federal savings and loan associations, and similar financial institutions (report these amounts as interest income);

- Dividends from a corporation that is a tax-exempt organization or farmer's cooperative during the corporation's tax year in which the dividends were paid or during the corporation's previous tax year;

- Dividends paid by a corporation on employer securities which are held on the date of record by an employee stock ownership plan (ESOP) maintained by that corporation;

- Payments shown in Form 1099-DIV, box 1b, from a foreign corporation to the extent the decedent knew or had reason to know the payments were not qualified dividends.

> ■ The Kings received ordinary dividends totaling $8,000. The investments were held in joint name. When George died, Mary became the owner of the investments generating the dividends. The dividends reported on the return represent the total dividends received in the year of George's death. Mary King lists the sources and amounts of these dividends on line 5 of Schedule B, Part II [see ¶ 2783]. The Kings received the following dividends: $1,600 from Raynor Corp.; $1,340 from Styling, Inc.; $980 from Tornado Industries, Inc.; and $4,080 ordinary dividend and $100 capital gain distribution from U Growth Fund. When preparing their tax return, Mary writes the total of

¶2715

"$8,000" on lines 5 and 6 of Schedule B. The capital gain distribution is entered on line 13 of Schedule D. Mary King also enters $8,000 as ordinary dividend income on line 9a of Form 1040 [see ¶ 2782].

(c) Foreign Accounts and Trusts—Part III of Schedule B. Part III of Schedule B [see ¶ 2783] must be completed if the decedent (1) received more than $1,500 of taxable interest or ordinary dividends, (2) had a foreign bank account, or (3) created, transferred assets to, or was a beneficiary of a foreign trust.

If during the last year of his or her life, the decedent had a financial interest in or a signature authority over a financial account located in a foreign country, check the "Yes" box on line 7a even if the decedent was not required to file FinCEN Form 114, Report of Foreign Bank and Financial Accounts (FBAR). If the decedent checked the "Yes" box to Question 2 on line 7a, FinCEN Form 114 must be electronically filed with the Financial Crimes Enforcement Network (FinCEN). It should be attached to the decedent's return. In line 7b, the decedent is required to enter the name of the foreign country or countries if he or she is required to file FinCEN Form 114.

Financial account. A financial account includes but is not limited to, a securities, brokerage, savings, demand, checking, deposit, time deposit, or other account maintained with a financial institution. A financial account also includes a commodity futures or options account, an insurance policy with a cash value, an annuity policy with a cash value, and shares in a mutual fund or similar pooled fund.

Financial account located in a foreign country. A financial account is located in a foreign country if the account is physically located outside of the United States. For example, an account maintained with a branch of a United States bank that is physically located outside of the United States is a foreign financial account. An account maintained with a branch of a foreign bank that is physically located in the United States is not a foreign financial account.

Signature authority. Signature authority is the authority of an individual to control the disposition of assets held in a foreign financial account by direct communication to the bank or other financial institution that maintains the financial account.

Line 8 asks whether the taxpayer received a distribution from, or was the grantor of or transferor to, a foreign trust during the year. If the answer is "yes," the tax paper may have to file Form 3520.

■ The Kings have to complete Part III of Schedule B [see ¶ 2783] because line 4 of Schedule B was more than $1,500. However, they check the "No" Boxes on lines 7a and 8 because they did not have any interest in foreign bank accounts or trusts.

¶2716   LINE 10—STATE AND LOCAL INCOME TAX REFUNDS

If the decedent received a state or local income tax refund in 2013, the decedent will receive a Form 1099-G from the state or local government showing the amount of the refund. This amount may have to be reported as taxable income on line 10 of Form 1040 if the decedent claimed a deduction for state and local income taxes on his or her 2012 tax return. None of the refund is taxable, however, if in the year the decedent paid the tax, the decedent either (a) did not itemize deductions, or (b) elected to deduct state and local general sales taxes instead of state and local income taxes.

The refund is taxable only to the extent that the original deduction actually reduced the decedent's tax bill. Most taxpayers who received a refund and claimed a deduction on that year's return can use the abbreviated Worksheet for State and Local Income Tax Refunds in the Instructions to Form 1040. Others should use the full Worksheet in IRS Publication 525 to compute the amount they have to report on line 10.

■ The Kings did not receive a refund of Missouri income taxes in 2013 and therefore leave line 10 of Form 1040 blank.

¶2717 LINE 11—ALIMONY RECEIVED

If the decedent received alimony or separate maintenance payments under a court decree or a written separation agreement, the payments must be reported as income on line 11 of the decedent's final tax return. The amount of child support payments or property settlements received need not be included.

■ Neither George nor Mary King received alimony or separate maintenance payments, so no entry is made on line 11.

¶2718 LINE 12—BUSINESS INCOME OR LOSS AND SCHEDULE C

Self-employed taxpayers report their net business profit or loss on line 12 of Form 1040 [see ¶ 2782]. The amount of net profit or loss is figured on Schedule C or C-EZ of Form 1040.

■ Mary King does not complete Schedule C because neither she nor her husband, prior to his death, was self-employed.

¶2719 LINE 13—CAPITAL GAIN OR LOSS

If the decedent had a capital gain or loss, Schedule D and Form 8949 must be completed and attached to the decedent's return.

The following chart illustrates the capital gains tax rates in effect for 2013-2014.

Capital Gains Maximum Rates for 2013 and 2014

Type of Property	Period Held	Maximum Rate*
Capital assets, other than on gain attributable to Section 1250 recapture or collectibles	12 months or less More than 12 months	39.6% 0% if in 15% ordinary income tax rate bracket** 15% if in 28% or 33% ordinary income tax rate bracket 20% if in 39.6% ordinary income tax rate bracket

* Excluding the 3.8% net investment income tax that may apply.

** Only to the extent the gain would otherwise be in the 15% tax bracket.

▶ **FILING POINTER:** Complete Form 8949 before completing lines 1, 2, 3, 8, 9, or 10 of Schedule D of Form 1040 because the combined totals from all Forms 8949 are reported on Schedule D.

(a) Purpose of Schedule D. Schedule D (Form 1040), "Capital Gains and Losses," is used to report the following:

- The sale or exchange of a "capital asset" (defined below) not reported on another form or schedule.

- Gains from involuntary conversions (other than from casualty or theft) of capital assets not held for business or profit.

- Capital gain distributions not reported directly on Form 1040, line 13.

- Nonbusiness bad debts.

(b) Exceptions.

Exception 1. The decedent may not have to file Schedule D or Form 8949 if both of the following apply:

(1) The decedent had no capital losses and the only amounts to be reported on Schedule D are capital gain distributions from box 2a of Forms 1099-DIV or substitute statements.

(2) None of the Forms 1099-DIV or substitute statements have an amount in box 2b (unrecaptured IRC Sec. 1250 gain), box 2c (IRC Sec. 1202 gain), or box 2d (collectibles—28 percent gain).

Exception 2. The decedent must file Schedule D, but generally does not need to file Form 8949 if the exceptions (1) and (2) do not apply and the decedent's only capital gains and losses are:

- Capital gain distributions;

- A capital loss carryover from last year;

- A gain from Form 2439 or 6252, or Part I of Form 4797;

- A gain or loss from a partnership, S corporation, estate, or trust; or

- Gains and losses from transactions for which the decedent received a Form 1099-B that shows basis was reported to the IRS and the return preparer was not required to either make adjustments in column (g) of Form 8949 or enter any codes in column (f) of Form 8949.

¶2719

If Exception 1 applies, enter the total capital gain distribution (from box 2a of Form 1099-DIV) on line 13 and check the box on that line. If the decedent received capital gain distributions as a nominee (that is, they were paid to the decedent but actually belong to someone else), report on line 13 only the amount that belongs to the decedent. Attach a statement showing the full amount the decedent received and the amount the decedent received as a nominee.

If the decedent does not have to file Schedule D, be sure to use the "Qualified Dividends and Capital Gain Tax Worksheet" which can be found in the line 44 Instructions to Form 1040 to compute the amount of the decedent's tax.

(c) Key Concepts.

Capital asset. Schedule D defines a capital asset as most property that is owned and used for personal purpose, pleasure, or investment. For example, a taxpayer's house, furniture, car, stocks and bonds are capital assets. Excluded from the definition of capital asset are the following: (1) stock in trade or other property included in inventory or held mainly for sale to customers; (2) accounts or notes receivable for services performed in the ordinary course of a trade or business or as an employee or from the sale of any property described in (1) above; (3) depreciable property used in a trade or business even if fully depreciated; (4) real estate used in a trade or business; (5) copyrights, literary, musical, or artistic composition, letters or memoranda, or similar property; (6) U.S. Government publications; (7) certain commodities derivative financial instruments held by a dealer; (8) certain hedging transactions entered into in the normal course of a trade or business; and (9) supplies regularly used in a trade or business.

Capital gain distributions. Capital gain distributions are paid by a mutual fund (or other regulated investment company) or real estate investment trust from its net realized long-term capital gains. Distributions of net realized short-term capital gains are not treated as capital gains. Instead, they are included on Form 1099-DIV as ordinary dividends.

Exclusion of gain on sale of principal residence. A surviving spouse may exclude from income up to $500,000 on a joint return realized on the sale or exchange of a principal residence provided the ownership and use tests described below are satisfied. Keep in mind that the exclusion may only be claimed once every two years. The election to suspend the five-year test period for ownership and use of a main home may now be made by Peace Corps employees and volunteers serving outside the United States [IRC Sec. 121(d)(12)].

- *Ownership and use tests.* Gain may only be excluded if, during the five-year period that ends on the date of the sale or exchange, the individual owned and used the property as a principal residence for periods aggregating two years or more (i.e., a total of 730 days (365 × 2)). Short temporary absences for vacations or seasonal absences are counted as periods of use, even if the individual rents out the property during these periods of absence. However, an absence of an entire year is not considered a short temporary absence. The ownership and use tests may be met during nonconcurrent periods, provided that both tests are met during the five-year period that ends on the date of sale.

- *Gain from sale of principal residence allocated to nonqualified use ineligible for exclusion.* The homesale exclusion will not apply to the extent gain from the sale or

¶2719

exchange of a principal residence is allocated to periods of "nonqualified use" [IRC Sec. 121(b)(4)[5](A)]. A period of nonqualified use is any period during which the property is not used as the principal residence of the taxpayer, his or her spouse, or former spouse [IRC Sec. 121(b)(4)[5](C)(i)]. Gain is allocated between periods of qualified and nonqualified use on the basis of the respective amounts of time the property is used for qualified and nonqualified uses. Gain is allocated to periods of nonqualified use based on the ratio which the aggregate periods of nonqualified use during the period the property was owned by the taxpayer bears to the total period of time the property was owned by the taxpayer [IRC Sec. 121(b)(4)[5](B). There are several exceptions to the general definition of "period of nonqualified use" as follows:

1. Any portion of the five-year period ending on the date the property is sold that is after the last date that the property is used as the principal residence of the taxpayer or his or her spouse is not considered a period of nonqualified use;

2. Any period (not exceeding an aggregate period of 10 years) during which the taxpayer or his or her spouse is serving on "qualified official extended duty" as a member of the armed forces, as a Foreign Service officer, or as an employee of the intelligence community [IRC Sec. 121(b)(4)[5](C)(ii)(II)].

- *Period of ownership for home acquired in like-kind exchange.* When an individual acquires a principal residence in a like-kind exchange, the individual must own the property for at least five years prior to its sale or exchange in order for the exclusion of gain rule to apply.

- *Military personnel exception.* Uniformed and foreign service personnel called to active duty away from home may elect to suspend the five-year test period. The maximum length of the suspension is five years and it may only be made with respect to one property. If the election is made, the five-year period ending on the date of the sale of a principal residence does not include any period up to five years during which the serviceman or woman, or his or her spouse, is on qualified official extended duty. The individual may revoke the election at anytime. A "qualified official extended duty" is defined as any extended duty while serving at a duty station that is at least 50 miles from the individual's principal residence or while residing in government quarters under government orders. The term "extended duty" is any period of active duty due to a call or order to such duty for a period in excess of 90 days or for an indefinite time.

- *Portion not used as principal residence.* An individual cannot claim the exclusion for any portion of the gain that is allocable to the portion of the property that is separate from the actual residence (i.e., the "dwelling unit") and not used as a residence.

- *Married individuals.* The amount of excludable gain is $500,000 for married individuals filing jointly if: (1) either spouse meets the ownership test; (2) both spouses meet the use test; and (3) neither spouse is ineligible for exclusion by virtue of a sale or exchange of a residence within the prior two years.

- *Surviving spouses entitled to $500,000 exclusion of gain on home sales.* The $500,000 maximum exclusion of gain from sales or exchanges of principal residences that applies to joint return filers also applies to qualifying sales or exchanges by surviving spouses [IRC Sec. 121(b)(4)]. The increased exclusion amount

¶2719

applies to a sale or exchange of property by an unmarried individual whose spouse is deceased on the date of such sale if:

1. The sale occurs no later than two years after the date of death of such spouse;

2. Immediately before the date of death, either spouse met the two-out-of-five year ownership requirement, both spouses met the two-out-of-five year use requirement, and neither spouse was ineligible to claim the exclusion because of another sale or exchange within the prior two years that qualified for the exclusion; and

3. The surviving spouse did not remarry before the sale or exchange.

Thus, for the ownership and use requirements, only one spouse must have owned the property for periods aggregating two years or more during the five-year period immediately before the date of death. However, both spouses must have met the use requirement by using the property as a principal residence for periods aggregating two years or more during the five-year period immediately before the date of death [IRC Sec. 121(b)(2)(A)(i)].

> ▶ **PRACTICE POINTER:** The exclusion only applies to an *unmarried* taxpayer whose spouse is deceased on the date of sale of the principal residence. Thus, if the taxpayer *remarries* and sells the home within two years after the date of death of the first spouse, the taxpayer would not be entitled to the $500,000 maximum exclusion amount for surviving spouses. Further, it is unlikely that the taxpayer would be entitled to the $500,000 maximum exclusion amount for joint return filers because the new spouse would not have met the two-out-of-five year use requirement.

- *Deceased spouse.* When a spouse dies before the date of sale, the surviving spouse is considered to own and live in the home for the same period as the deceased spouse.

- *Divorced individuals.* When a residence is transferred to an individual incident to a divorce, the time during which the individual's spouse or former spouse owned the residence is added to the individual's period of ownership. An individual who owns a residence is deemed to use it as a principal residence during the time the individual's spouse or former spouse has use of the home under a divorce or separation agreement.

- *Hardship relief.* An individual who fails to meet the ownership and use requirements, or the minimum two-year time period for claiming the full exclusion (e.g., $250,000), may still be eligible for a partial exclusion when the primary reason for the sale of the home is due to: (1) a change in place of employment, (2) health reasons, or (3) unforeseen circumstances.

- *Reporting requirements.* An individual who is qualified to exclude all of the realized gain from the sale of a home is not required to report the sale on the tax return for the year of sale. However, if there is a portion of the realized gain that must be recognized, the taxpayer generally reports the entire gain in Part I (Short-Term) or Part II (Long-Term) of Schedule D, Form 1040. Then, directly below the line where realized gain is reported, the amount of the prorated exclusion is entered and identified as "Section 121 exclusion." The exclusion is shown as a loss in column (f). If the home was sold under the installment method and gain is recognized, Form 6252 "Installment Sale Income" has to be filed. If the home was

¶2719

used for business or to produce rental income during the year of sale, Form 4797 "Sale of Business Property" is filed.

- *Gain recognized to extent of depreciation.* The exclusion does not apply, and gain is recognized, to the extent of any depreciation claimed with respect to the rental or business use of a principal residence after May 6, 1997. Form 4797 is used to report the sale in this situation.

(d) Short-Term or Long-Term Gain. When completing Schedule D, separate the decedent's capital gains and losses according to how long the decedent held or owned the property. The long-term holding period is met if the decedent held or owned the assets more than 12 months. To figure the holding period, begin counting on the day after the decedent received the property and include the day the property was disposed of. The holding period for short-term capital gains and losses is one year or less. If the decedent disposed of property acquired by inheritance, report the disposition as long-term capital gain or loss regardless of how long the property was actually held. A nonbusiness bad debt must be treated as a short-term capital loss.

¶2720 FORM 8949

In 2013, the decedent may be able to combine certain transactions and report the totals directly on Schedule D. If this is done, the decedent should not include these transactions on Form 8949.

Form 8949, "Sales and Other Dispositions of Capital Assets," is used to report sales and exchanges of capital assets not reported on another form or schedule.

Individuals should use Form 8949 to report:

- The sale or exchange of a capital asset not reported on another form or schedule;
- Gains from involuntary conversions (other than from casualty or theft) of capital assets not held for business or profit; and
- Nonbusiness bad debts.

Corporations and partnerships. Corporations and partnerships should use Form 8949 to report:

- The sale or exchange of a capital asset not reported on another form or schedule,
- Nonbusiness bad debts, and
- Undistributed long-term capital gains from Form 2439.

Schedule D. Schedule D should be used:

- To figure the overall gain or loss from transactions reported on Form 8949;
- To report a gain from Form 6252, or Part I of Form 4797;
- To report a gain or loss from Form 4684, 6781, or 8824;
- To report capital gain distributions not reported directly on Form 1040, line 13 (or effectively connected capital gain distributions not reported directly on Form 1040NR, line 14);
- To report a capital loss carryover from the previous tax year to the current tax year;

- To report the decedent's share of a gain or (loss) from a partnership, S corporation, estate or trust. However, corporations must report this type of gain or (loss) on Form 8949;

- To report transactions reported to the decedent on a Form 1099-B showing basis was reported to the IRS and for which the decedent had no adjustments; and

- Individuals also use Schedule D to report undistributed long-term capital gains from Form 2439.

How to Complete Form 8949. On Form 8949, enter all sales and exchanges of capital assets, including stocks, bonds, etc. and real estate (if not reported on Form 4684, 4797, 6252, 6781 or 8824). These transactions must be included even if the decedent did not receive a Form 1099-B or 1099-S (or substitute statement) for the transaction. Report short-term gains or losses in Part 1. Report long-term gains and losses in Part II. The details of each transaction should be entered on a separate line of Form 8949.

Use a separate Part I for each of the following types of short-term transactions:

- Short-term transactions reported on Form 1099-B with an amount shown for cost or other basis **unless** the statement indicates that amount was not reported to the IRS. Check box A at the top of this Part I. If box 6b of Form 1099-B is not checked, which means basis was not reported to the IRS, report that transaction on Part I with box B, not box A, checked.

- Short-term transactions reported on Form 1099-B without an amount shown for cost or other basis. Check box B at the top of this Part I. If box 6b of Form 1099-B is not checked, which means basis was not reported to the IRS, report that transaction on Part I with box B, not box A, checked.

- Short-term transactions for which you cannot check box A or B because you did not receive a Form 1099-B (or substitute statement). Check box C at the top of this Part I.

Use a separate Part II for each of the following types of long-term transactions.

> ▶ **FILING POINTER:** Form 8949 must be completed before completing lines 1b, 2, 3, 8b, 9, or 10 of Schedule D of Form 1040 because the combined totals from all items reported on Form 8949 are reported on Schedule D.

- Long-term transactions reported on Form 1099-B with an amount shown for cost or other basis **unless** the statement indicates that amount was not reported to the IRS. Check box D at the top of this Part II. If box 6b of Form 1099-B is not checked, which means basis was not reported to the IRS, report that transaction on Part II with box E, not box D, checked.

- Long-term transactions reported on Form 1099-B without an amount shown for cost or other basis. Check box E at the top of this Part II. If box 6b of Form 1099-B is not checked, which means basis was not reported to the IRS, report that transaction on Part II with box E, not box D, checked.

- Long-term transactions without box D or E checked because the decedent did not receive a Form 1099-B (or substitute statement). Check box F at the top of this Part II.

> ▶ **FILING POINTER:** The decedent may not need to file Form 8949 for certain transactions. This is new in 2013. The return preparer may be able to aggregate

¶2720

those transactions and report them directly on either line 1a (for short-term transactions) or line 8a (for long-term transactions) of Schedule D. This option applies only to transactions (other than sales of collectibles) for which:

- The decedent received a Form 1099-B (or substitute statement) that shows basis was reported to the IRS and does not show a nondeductible wash sale loss in box 5; and

- The decedent does not need to make any adjustments to the basis of type of gain or loss (short-term or long-term) reported on Form 1099-B, or to your gain or loss.

If the decedent's return preparer decides to report these transactions directly on Schedule D, they do not need to be reported on Form 8949 and a statement does not need to be attached.

▶ **FILING POINTER:** Instead of reporting each transaction on a separate row on Form 8949, the return preparer can report them on an attached statement containing all the same information as Parts I and II and in a similar format with a description of property, dates of acquisition and disposition, proceeds, basis, adjustment and gains and losses. The combined totals from all attached statements should be entered on Parts I and II with the appropriate box checked.

Columns a-h of Form 8949. Enter in columns a-h the details regarding acquisition and sale of the asset.

Column (a)—Description of Property. For stock, use the stock ticker symbols or abbreviations to describe the property as long as they are based on the descriptions of the property as shown on Form 1099-B or Form 1099-S.

Column (b)—Date acquired. Enter in this column the date the decedent acquired the asset. Use the trade date for stocks and bonds traded on an exchange or over-the-counter market. For stock or the other property sold short, enter the date you acquired the stock or property delivered to the broker or lender to close the short sale.

Column (c)—Date sold. Enter in this column the date the decedent sold the assets. Use the trade date for stocks and bonds traded on an exchange or over-the-counter market. For stock or other property sold short, enter the date the decedent delivered the stock or property to the broker or lender to close the short sale.

Column (d)—Sales price. If the decedent sold stock or bonds and the decedent received a Form 1099-B from his or her broker that shows gross sales price, that amount should be entered in column (e). If Form 1099-B indicates that gross proceeds minus commissions and option premiums were reported to the IRS, enter that net amount in column (e).

Column (e)—Cost. The cost or other basis is the cost of the property plus purchase commissions and improvements, minus depreciation, amortization and depletion. If the property was inherited, received as a gift, or received in a tax-free exchange or involuntary conversion or in connection with a wash sale, the decedent may be able to use the actual cost as the basis.

Column (f)—Code. In order to explain any adjustment to gain or loss in column (g), enter the appropriate code(s) in column (f). See "How To Complete Form 8949, Columns (f) and (g)." If more than one code applies, enter all the codes that apply in alphabetical order (for example, "BOQ"). Do not separate the codes by a space or comma.

Column (g)—Adjustments. Enter in this column any necessary adjustments to gain or loss. Enter negative amounts in parentheses. Also enter a code in column (f) to explain the adjustment. See "How To Complete Form 8949, Columns (f) and (g)," below.

Include in this column any expense of sale, such as broker's fees, commissions, state and local transfer taxes, and option premiums, unless the net sales price was reported in column (e). If any expense of sale is included in this column, enter "0" in column (b).

Column (h)—Gain or (Loss). Figure gain or loss on each row. First, subtract the cost or other basis in column (e) from the proceeds (sales price) in column (d). Then take into account any adjustments in column (g). Enter the gain or (loss) in column (h). Enter negative amounts in parentheses.

> **Example 1—gain:** Column (d) is $6,000 and column (e) is $2,000. Enter $4,000 in column (h).

> **Example 2—loss:** Column (d) is $6,000 and column (e) is $8,000. Enter ($2,000) in column (h).

> **Example 3—adjustment:** Column (d) is $6,000, column (e) is $2,000, and column (g) is ($1,000). Enter $3,000 in column (h).

Lines 2 and 4. The total of the amounts in column (h) of line 2 of all Forms 8949 should equal the amount obtained by combining columns (d), (e), and (g) on the corresponding line of Schedule D.

How To Complete Form 8949, Columns (f) and (g)

For most transactions, you do not need to complete columns (f) and (g) and can leave them blank. You may need to complete columns (f) and (g) if you got a Form 1099-B or 1099-S (or substitute statement) that is incorrect, if you are excluding or postponing a capital gain, if you have a disallowed loss, or in certain other situations. Details are in the table below. If you enter more than one code in column (f), see *More than one code* in the instructions for column (g).

IF . . .	THEN enter this code in column (f) . . .	AND, . . .
You received a Form 1099-B (or substitute statement) and the basis shown in box 3 is incorrect	B	• If box B is checked at the top of Part I or if box E is checked at the top of Part II, enter the correct basis in column (e), and enter -0- in column (g). • If box A is checked at the top of Part I or if box D is checked at the top of Part II, enter the basis shown on Form 1099-B (or substitute statement) in column (e), even though that basis is incorrect. Correct the error by entering an adjustment in column (g). To figure the adjustment needed, see the *Worksheet for Basis Adjustments in Column (g)*. Also see *Example 4—adjustment for incorrect basis* in the instructions for column (h).
You received a Form 1099-B (or substitute statement) and the type of gain or loss (short-term or long-term) shown in box 1c is incorrect	T	Enter -0- in column (g). Report the gain or loss on the correct Part of Form 8949.
You received a Form 1099-B or 1099-S (or substitute statement) as a nominee for the actual owner of the property	N	Report the transaction on Form 8949 as you would if you were the actual owner, but also enter any resulting gain as a negative adjustment (in parentheses) in column (g) or any resulting loss as a positive adjustment in column (g). As a result of this adjustment, the amount in column (h) should be zero. However, if you received capital gain distributions as a nominee, report them instead as described under *Capital Gain Distributions* in the Instructions for Schedule D (Form 1040).
You sold or exchanged your main home at a gain, must report the sale or exchange on Part II of Form 8949 (as explained in *Sale of Your Home* in the Instructions for Schedule D (Form 1040)), and can exclude some or all of the gain	H	Report the sale or exchange on Form 8949 as you would if you were not taking the exclusion. Then enter the amount of excluded (nontaxable) gain as a negative number (in parentheses) in column (g). See the example in the instructions for column (g).
You sold or exchanged qualified small business stock and can exclude part of the gain	Q	Report the sale or exchange on Form 8949 as you would if you were not taking the exclusion and enter the amount of the exclusion as a negative number (in parentheses) in column (g). However, if the transaction is reported as an installment sale, see *Gain from an installment sale of QSB stock* in the Instructions for Schedule D (Form 1040).
You can exclude all or part of your gain under the rules explained in the Schedule D instructions for DC Zone assets or qualified community assets	X	Report the sale or exchange on Form 8949 as you would if you were not taking the exclusion. Then enter the amount of the exclusion as a negative number (in parentheses) in column (g).
You are electing to postpone all or part of your gain under the rules explained in the Schedule D instructions for any rollover of gain (for example, rollover of gain from QSB stock or publicly traded securities)	R	Report the sale or exchange on Form 8949 as you would if you were not making the election. Then enter the amount of postponed gain as a negative number (in parentheses) in column (g).

¶2720

IF . . .	THEN enter this code in column (f) . . .	AND. . .
You have a nondeductible loss from a wash sale	W	Report the sale or exchange on Form 8949 and enter the amount of the nondeductible loss as a positive number in column (g). See the Schedule D instructions for more information about wash sales. If you received a Form 1099-B (or substitute statement) and the amount of nondeductible wash sale loss shown (box 5 of Form 1099-B) is incorrect, enter the correct amount of the nondeductible loss as a positive number in column (g). If the amount of the nondeductible loss is less than the amount shown on Form 1099-B (or substitute statement), attach a statement explaining the difference. If no part of the loss is a nondeductible loss from a wash sale transaction, enter -0- in column (g).
You have a nondeductible loss other than a loss indicated by code W	L	Report the sale or exchange on Form 8949 and enter the amount of the nondeductible loss as a positive number in column (g). See Nondeductible Losses in the Instructions for Schedule D (Form 1040).
You received a Form 1099-B or 1099-S (or substitute statement) for a transaction and there are selling expenses or option premiums that are not reflected on the form or statement by an adjustment to either the proceeds or basis shown	E	Enter in column (d) the proceeds shown on the form or statement you received. Enter in column (e) any cost or other basis shown on Form 1099-B (or substitute statement). In column (g), enter as a negative number (in parentheses) any selling expenses and option premium that you paid (and that are not reflected on the form or statement you received) and enter as a positive number any option premium that you received (and that is not reflected on the form or statement you received). For more information about option premiums, see Gain or Loss From Options in the Instructions for Schedule D (Form 1040).
You had a loss from the sale, exchange, or worthlessness of small business (section 1244) stock and the total loss is more than the maximum amount that can be treated as an ordinary loss	S	See Small Business (Section 1244) Stock in the Schedule D (Form 1040) instructions.
You disposed of collectibles (see the Schedule D instructions)	C	Enter -0- in column (g). Report the disposition on Form 8949 as you would report any sale or exchange.
You report multiple transactions on a single row as described in Exception 1 or Exception 2 under Exceptions to reporting each transaction on a separate row	M	See Exception 1 and Exception 2 under Exceptions to reporting each transaction on a separate row. Enter -0- in column (g) unless an adjustment is required because of another code.
You have an adjustment not explained earlier in this column	O	Enter the appropriate adjustment amount in column (g). See the instructions for column (g).
None of the other statements in this column apply	Leave columns (f) and (g) blank.	

Column (h)—Gain or (Loss)

Figure gain or loss on each row. First, subtract the cost or other basis in column (e) from the proceeds (sales price) in column (d). Then take into account any adjustments in column (g). Enter the gain or (loss) in column (h). Enter negative amounts in parentheses.

Example 1—gain. Column (d) is $6,000 and column (e) is $2,000. Enter $4,000 in column (h).

Example 2—loss. Column (d) is $6,000 and column (e) is $8,000. Enter ($2,000) in column (h).

Example 3—adjustment. Column (d) is $6,000, column (e) is $2,000, and column (g) is ($1,000). Enter $3,000 in column (h).

Example 4—adjustment for incorrect basis. You sold stock for $1,000. You had owned the stock for 3 months. Your correct basis for the stock is $100, but you receive a Form 1099-B that shows your basis is $900 and shows your broker reported that basis to the IRS.

-7-

¶2720

■ On January 12, 2013, the Kings bought 100 shares of J Corp. preferred stock for $8,000. On May 3, 2013, they sold the J Corp. preferred stock for $10,570. They report the transaction on line 1 of Part 1 of Form 8949 (Short-term capital gains and losses). The Kings also purchased 50 shares of S Corp. common stock on January 16, 2013 for $3,500. They sold the stock on June 17, 2013 for $2,000.

■ The Kings bought 100 shares of Z Corp, preferred stock on April 4, 2011, for $3,500. They sold the stock on May 3, 2013 for $10,200. Enter this information on line 3 of Form 8949. The Kings owned two registered $1,000 M Corp. bonds that became worthless during the year. They purchased the bonds on February 1, 2009, which they enter in column (b). The basis of worthless stock or securities in registered form, or with interest coupons, can be written off on line 3 of Form 8949 in the year they became worthless. So they identify the bonds in column (a), enter the purchase date in column (b) and write 5/03/13 as the "Date sold" in column (c). They then enter a sales price of "-0-" in column (d). They enter their $2,000 purchase price in column (e).

¶2721 SCHEDULE D, PART I—SHORT-TERM CAPITAL GAINS AND LOSSES

Schedule D should be used by taxpayers:

* To figure the overall gain or loss from transactions reported on Form 8949;
* To report certain transactions you do not have to report on Form 8949;
* To report a gain from Form 2439 or 6252 or Part I of Form 4797;
* To report a gain or loss from Form 4684, 6781, or 8824;
* To report a gain or loss from a partnership, S corporation, estate or trust;
* To report capital gain distributions not reported directly on Form 1040, line 13 (or effectively connected capital gain distributions not reported directly on Form 1040NR, line 14); and
* To report a capital loss carryover from 2012 to 2013.

Complete all necessary pages of Form 8949 (see ¶2720) before you complete line 1b, 2, 3, 8b, 9, or 10 of Schedule D, "Capital Gains and Losses."

Lines 1a and 8a. Report on line 1a (for short-term transactions) or line 8a (for long-term transactions) the aggregate totals from any transactions (except sales of collectibles) for which:

* The decedent received a Form 1099-B that shows basis was reported to the IRS and does not show a nondeductible wash sale in box 5; and
* The decedent does not need to make any adjustments to the basis or type of gain or loss (short-term or long-term) reported on Form 1099-B or to gain or loss.

If the decedent's return preparer decides to report these transactions on lines 1a and 8a, the transactions do not need to be reported on Form 8949. In addition, no statement needs to be attached to explain the entries on lines 1a and 8a. Gain or loss should be computed on each line.

> **Example 1:** Sally received a Form 1099-B reporting the sale of stock she held for 3 years. It shows proceeds (in box 2a) of $6,000 and cost or other basis (in box 3) of $2,000. Box 6b is checked, meaning that basis was reported to the IRS. Sally does not need to make any adjustments to the amounts reported on Form 1099-B or enter any codes. This was her only 2013 transaction. Instead of reporting this transaction on Form 8949, she can enter $6,000 on Schedule D, line 8a, column (d), $2,000 in column (e), and $4,000 ($6,000 – $2,000) in column (h).

Lines 1b, 2, 3, 8b, 9, and 10, column (h) – Gain or Loss. The decedent should compute gain or loss on each line. First, subtract cost or other basis (column (e) from sales price (column (d)). Then take into account any adjustments in column (g). Enter the gain or loss in column (h). Enter negative amounts in parentheses.

Line 4. The sum of short-term gains and losses from different sources is entered on line 4.

Installment sale. If the decedent had capital gain from an installment sale in 2013, Form 6252 must be completed. Carry any short-term capital gain reported on Form 6252 to line 4 of Schedule D [see ¶ 2784]. When a taxpayer dies and an installment obligation is transferred to his estate or beneficiary, the transfer does not cause the unrecognized gain to be reported on the final return. Instead, the recipient of the installment obligation will receive IRD, which must be reported using the decedent's gross profit percentage [Reg. Sec. 1.691(a)-5(a)].

■ The Kings had no installment sales to report.

Casualty and theft. If the decedent had a casualty or theft in the year of death, complete Form 4684, attach it to the final return, and report any net short-term gain (there may be a gain from an insurance reimbursement) or loss on line 4 of Schedule D [see ¶ 2784].

■ The Kings had no casualties or thefts to report.

Straddles and Section 1256 contracts. Typically, IRC Sec. 1256 contracts are regulated futures and foreign currency contracts. In general, they are treated as sold at the end of the year, and 40 percent of the as-if gain or loss is treated as short-term gain or loss, regardless of how long the contracts have actually been held. A similar rule applies to straddles (taking offsetting long and short positions on the same property) unless the taxpayer elects not to have it apply. Form 6781 must be filed for IRC Sec. 1256 and straddle gains and losses. The 40 percent of gain or loss is entered on line 4, Schedule D [see ¶ 2784].

■ The Kings had no such transactions in the year George died.

Like-kind exchanges. Line 4 is used to report short-term gain or loss from like-kind exchanges entered on Form 8824.

■ The Kings did not have any property exchanges in the year George died.

¶2721

Line 5. Line 5 is used to enter the decedent's net short-term gain or loss from partnerships, S corporations, and estates and trusts as reported on Schedule(s) K-1.

■ The Kings did not receive any such gains or losses in the year George died.

Line 6. The maximum deduction for net short-term losses is $3,000 per year.

NOTE: A capital loss sustained by a decedent during his or her last tax year or a capital loss carryover from a prior year can only be deducted on the final income tax return filed for the decedent. The $3,000 capital loss limitation discussed above applies. The decedent's estate cannot deduct any of the loss or carry it over to following years.

■ The Kings had a net short-term capital loss of $4,000 last year and deducted $3,000 of the loss that year. Mary enters the $1,000 capital loss carryover on line 6 of the Kings' 2013 Schedule D [see ¶ 2784].

Line 7. Add the loss and gain amounts in columns (f) of lines 1 through 6, and enter the totals in column (f) of line 7b.

The decedent has net short-term capital gain of $70, which they enter on line 7 of Schedule D.

¶2722 SCHEDULE D, PART II—LONG-TERM CAPITAL GAINS AND LOSSES—ASSETS HELD MORE THAN ONE YEAR

Line 11: Gain from Form 4797, Part 1; long-term gain from Forms 2439 and 6252; and long-term gain or (loss) from Forms 4684, 6781, and 8824. Form 4797 must be completed and filed if the decedent sold or exchanged property, or had an involuntary conversion of property (e.g., an insured fire), and the property was used in the decedent's trade, business, or profession. Form 4797 must also be completed and filed if the decedent sold or exchanged depreciable and amortizable property; oil, gas, geothermal, or other mineral property; and Section 126 property. Form 4797 is used to take advantage of the favorable treatment afforded to business property and other special rules. Gains and losses on trade or business assets that are held one year or less are always treated as ordinary (rather than capital) gains or losses. Losses on assets used more than one year are generally ordinary losses (not subject to the $3,000 deduction limit on capital losses), but gains are generally taxed as capital gains. These gains are reported on line 11.

Nevertheless, gain from the sale of a business asset must be treated as ordinary income if depreciation is "recaptured." This ordinary income gain is also computed on Form 4797 but is reported on line 14 of Form 1040. For personal property used in a trade or business, gain is generally recaptured to the extent depreciation was claimed for the property.

Example 1: The decedent bought a piece of office furniture for $500 and claimed $300 worth of depreciation deductions. His adjusted basis in the property would be $200 ($500 less $300). If the decedent had sold the property for $600, he would have had a $400 gain. Of that $400, only $100 would be capital gain. The other $300 must be reported as ordinary income on line 14 of Form 1040.

The recapture rules are more liberal for real property. Gain is treated as ordinary income only to the extent accelerated depreciation deductions were claimed. Since the advent of (MACRS), real estate is written off on a straight-line basis. Therefore, as the decedent's personal representative, you do not have to worry about recapture for real property that was placed in service after 1986.

■ The Kings had no gains or losses reportable on Form 4797 and make no entry on line 11 on Schedule D.

Form 2439, "Notice to Shareholders of Undistributed Long-Term Capital Gains." If a mutual fund or REIT doesn't distribute all of the decedent's allocable share of net long-term capital gain, the fund must send the decedent a Form 2439 to identify the amount not distributed. That should be included on line 11.

■ The Kings had no undistributed mutual fund or REIT capital gain this year and make no entry on line 11 of Schedule D.

If the decedent had capital gain from an installment sale this year, you must complete Form 6252. You carry any short-term capital gain reported on Form 6252 to line 11 of Schedule D.

■ The Kings have no installment sale entry this year.

Use Form 4684 to report involuntary conversions of property due to casualty or theft and enter any long-term gain on line 11 of Schedule D.

Use Form 6781 to report gains and losses from Section 1256 contracts and straddles and enter any long-term gain on line 11 of Schedule D.

Use Form 8824 to report like-kind exchanges and report any long-term gains on line 11 of Schedule D.

Undistributed mutual fund capital gain. If a mutual fund does not distribute all of an investor's allocable share of its net long-term capital gain, the mutual fund must send the investor a Form 2439 informing him of the amount not distributed. That amount is entered on line 11. The investor can claim an offsetting credit for the tax paid on the undistributed amount on line 68 of Form 1040, but must attach a copy of Form 2439 to the return.

■ The Kings had no undistributed mutual fund capital gain in the year of George's death.

Line 12: Net long-term gain or (loss) from partnerships, S corporations, estates, and trusts from Schedule K-1. Use line 12 of Schedule D to report any long-term gain or loss generated from the decedent's investment in partnerships, S corporations, as well as estates and trusts. Look on the Schedule K-1 to see the amount of long-term gain realized.

Line 13: On line 13 enter the total capital gain distributions paid to the decedent during the year, regardless of how long the decedent held the investment. This amount will be shown in box 2a of Form 1099-DIV. Capital gain distributions are paid by a mutual fund (or other regulated investment company) or real estate investment trust from its net realized long-term capital gains. Distributions of net realized short-term capital gains are not treated as capital gains. Instead, they are included on Form 1099-DIV as ordinary dividends.

Mutual funds and other regulated investment companies often make capital gain distributions. The gain is treated as long-term regardless of how long you owned the mutual fund shares. Mutual fund distributions are reported on line 13 on Schedule D [see ¶ 2784]. Mutual funds and other regulated investment companies (RICs) and real estate investment companies (REITs) are special tax entities. The entities do not pay income taxes on the income and capital gains generated. Instead, the tax burden is passed through to its shareholders proportionately, according to the number of shares they own. This prevents the fund's income from being taxed twice, first at the fund level and then again at the shareholder level. On line 13, column (h), enter the total capital gain distributions paid to the decedent during the year, regardless of how long the decedent held the investment. This amount will be shown in box 2a of Form 1099-DIV.

■ In the year that George King died, the Kings received a $100 capital gain distribution from U Growth Fund. Mary King must report this here on line 13.

Line 14: Long-term capital loss carryover. Net capital losses, whether short-term or long-term, are subject to the same limitation. Only $3,000 may be deducted against ordinary income in a given year. If the decedent had unused net long-term losses from last year, he or she may get another chance to deduct them this year. Compute the amount of net long-term capital loss carryover on the Capital Loss Carryover Worksheet and enter the amount on line 14 of Schedule D.

■ Because the Kings have no long-term carryover, no entry is made on line 14.

Line 15: The next step is to offset the long-term loss in column (f) and the long-term gain in column (h) of lines 8 through 14.

■ The Kings end up with a $4,800 net long-term capital gain which is entered on line 15 of Schedule D.

¶2723 SCHEDULE D, PART III—SUMMARY

(a) **Summary.** This section is used to figure the amount of decedent's overall taxable net capital gain or deductible capital loss for the year.

Line 16. Combine the decedent's net short-term capital gain or loss from line 7 with the decedent's net long-term capital gain or loss from line 15 and enter the result. The decedent shows a $70 net short-term gain on line 7 and a $4,800 net long-term gain on line 15 and enters a $4,870 net capital gain on lines 16 and enters the same amount on line 13 of Form 1040.

Line 18. If the decedent checked "Yes" on line 17, complete the 28 percent Rate Gain Worksheet in the Instructions to Form D if either of the following situations apply for 2013:

- The decedent reported in Part II of Form 8949 an IRC Sec. 1202 exclusion from the eligible gain on qualified small business stock;

- The decedent reported in Part II of Form 8949 a collectibles gain or (loss). A collectibles gain or (loss) is any long-term gain or deductible long-term loss from the sale or exchange of a collectible that is a capital asset. Collectibles include works of art, rugs, antiques, metals (such as gold, silver or platinum bullion), gems, stamps, coins, alcoholic beverages and certain other intangible property.

Include on the worksheet any gain (but not loss) from the sale or exchange of an interest in a partnership, S corporation, or trust held for more than 1 year and attributable to unrealized appreciation of collectibles.

> ■ On the decedent's return, -0- is entered on line 18 because the decedent did not satisfy any of the conditions to complete the 28% Rate Gain Worksheet for line 18.

Line 19. If the decedent checked "Yes" on line 17, complete the Unrecaptured Section 1250 Gain Worksheet on page D-12 of the Instructions to Schedule D:

- The decedent sold or otherwise disposed of IRC Sec. 1250 property (generally, real property that the decedent depreciated) held more than 1 year;

- The decedent received installment payments for IRC Sec. 1250 property held for more than 1 year for which the decedent is reporting gain on the installment method;

- The decedent received a Schedule K-1 from an estate or trust, partnership, or S corporation that shows "Unrecaptured section 1250 gain;"

- The decedent received a Form 1099-DIV or Form 2439 from a real estate investment trust or regulated investment company (including a mutual fund) that reports "Unrecaptured section 1250 gain;"

- The decedent reported a long-term capital gain from the sale or exchange of an interest in a partnership that owned IRC Sec. 1250 property;

> ■ On the decedent's return, -0- is entered on line 19 because the decedent did not satisfy any of the conditions to complete the Unrecaptured Section 1250 Gain Worksheet for line 19.

Line 20. The Kings must complete the "Qualified Dividends and Capital Gain Tax Worksheet" in the Instructions for Form 1040, line 44, and enter the result on Form 1040, line 44 [see ¶ 2785 for completed Qualified Dividends and Capital Gain Tax Worksheet].

Line 21. Line 21 is normally used when a taxpayer has a capital loss carryover from 2013 to 2014 but the decedent's estate cannot deduct any of the loss or carry it over to following years and George King's estate leaves line 21 blank.

   (b) Worksheet. The executor should complete the Schedule D Tax Worksheet in the 2013 Instructions for Schedule D only if line 18 or line 19 of Schedule D is more than zero. Otherwise, complete the "Qualified Dividends and Capital Gain Tax Worksheet—Line 44" in the Instructions for Form 1040 to compute the decedent's tax.

The Kings complete the "Qualified Dividends and Capital Gain Tax Worksheet—Line 44" [¶ 2785] to compute the income tax owed.

¶2723

¶2724 LINE 14 OF FORM 1040—OTHER GAINS AND LOSSES

Ordinary gain or loss from the sale or exchange of property used in your business is figured in Part II of Form 4797. The result from Form 4797 is carried to line 14 of Form 1040.

(a) Property That Has Appreciated in Value. If the value of the property increased between the date the decedent acquired it and the date of decedent's death, the appreciation is not taxable on the decedent's last return. The fact that the decedent was on the cash or accrual basis does not change this result. The property becomes part of the decedent's estate and the appreciation in value is reflected in the property's increased value for estate tax valuation purposes.

> ■ Line 14 on the Kings' return is left blank because the Kings did not sell any business property in the year of George's death.

¶2725 LINES 15a AND 15b—IRA DISTRIBUTIONS

If, prior to death, the decedent withdrew funds from an individual retirement account (IRA), the distribution must be reported on line 15a of the decedent's final return. The decedent should receive a Form 1099-R showing the amount of any IRA distribution received that year. For purposes of line 15a and line 15b, IRA includes a traditional IRA, Roth IRA, simplified employee pension (SEP) IRA, and a savings incentive match plan for employees (SIMPLE) IRA. Report the taxable portion of the IRA distribution on line 15b unless one of the following exceptions applies:

Exception 1: Enter the total distribution on line 15a if the decedent rolled over part or all of the distribution from one: (a) IRA to another IRA of the same type (for example, from one traditional IRA to another traditional IRA), (b) SEP or SIMPLE IRA to a traditional IRA, or (c) IRA to a qualified plan other than an IRA.

Exception 2: If any of the following apply, enter the total distribution on line 15a and use Form 8606 to figure the amount to enter on line 15b:

(a) The decedent received a distribution from an IRA (other than a Roth IRA) and made nondeductible contributions to a traditional or SEP IRA for 2013 or an earlier year;

(b) The decedent received a distribution from a Roth IRA;

(c) The decedent converted part or all of a traditional, SEP, or SIMPLE IRA to a Roth IRA in 2013;

(d) The decedent had a 2012 or 2013 IRA contribution returned with the related earnings or less any loss, by the due date (including extensions) of the tax return for that year;

(e) The decedent made excess contributions to an IRA for an earlier year and had them returned in 2013;

(f) The decedent recharacterized part or all of a contributions to a Roth IRA as a traditional IRA contribution, or vice versa.

Exception 3: If the distribution is a qualified charitable distribution (QCD), enter the total distribution on line 15a. If the total amount distributed is a QCD, enter -0- on line 15a. If only part of the distribution is a QCD, enter the party that is not a QCD on line 15b unless Exception 2 above applies to that part. Enter "QCD" next to line 15b.

A QCD is a distribution made directly by the trustee of the decedent's IRA (other than an ongoing SEP or SIMPLE IRA) to an organization eligible to receive tax-deductible contributions. The decedent must have been at least age 70½ when the distributions were made. The total QCDs for the year cannot be more than $100,000. (On a joint return, the decedent's spouse can also have a QCD of up to $100,000.)

Exception 4: If the distribution is a qualified health savings account (HSA) funding distribution (HFD), enter the total distribution on line 15a. If the total amount distributed is an HFD and you elect to exclude it from income, enter -0- on line 15b. If only part of the distribution is an HFD and you elect to exclude that part from income, enter the part that is not an HFD on line 15b unless Exception 2 applies to that part. Enter "HFD" next to line 15b.

An HFD is a distribution made directly by the trustee of the decedent's IRA (other than an ongoing SEP or SIMPLE IRA) to the decedent's HSA. If eligible, the decedent can generally elect to exclude an HFD from income once in his or her lifetime. The decedent cannot exclude more than the limit on HSA contributions or more than the amount that would otherwise be included in his or her income.

More than one exception applies. If more than one exception applies, include a statement showing the amount of each exception, instead of making an entry next to line 15b. For example: "Line 15b-$1,000 Rollover and $500 HFD."

Penalty may apply. The decedent may owe a 10 penalty tax if:

- The decedent withdrew funds from his or her IRA before reaching age 59½. (If penalized, report the penalty on line 59 of Form 1040.) The penalty tax does not apply to IRA withdrawals used to pay medical expenses in excess of 7.5 percent of AGI. Also, unemployed individuals under age 59½ can make penalty-free IRA withdrawals for the payment of health insurance premiums if certain specified requirements are met [IRC Sec. 72(t)(2)(D)]. Penalty-free withdrawals may also be made from an IRA to pay for qualified higher education expenses. This includes tuition at a post-secondary educational institution, as well as room and board, fees, books, supplies, and necessary equipment. The expenses must be incurred by the decedent, the decedent's spouse, or any child or grandchild of the decedent or his or her spouse [IRC Sec. 72(t)(2)(E)].

- The 10 percent penalty tax does not apply if the decedent used the IRA distribution for certain expenses of a first-time homebuyer. Only $10,000 during the individual's lifetime may be withdrawn without incurring a penalty. Qualified expenses include acquisition costs, settlement charges and closing costs. The principal residence may be for the decedent or the decedent's spouse, child, or grandchild, or an ancestor of the decedent or the decedent's spouse. In order to be considered a first-time homebuyer, the person buying the residence (and spouse, if married) must not have

¶2725

had an ownership interest in a principal residence during the two-year period ending on the date that the new home is acquired [IRC Sec. 72(t)(2)(F)].

• The 10 percent penalty does not apply to the portion of the distribution that represents a return of nondeductible IRA contributions which represent the individual's cost basis in the IRA.

• The decedent was born before July 1, 1939, and received less than the minimum required distribution.

> ■ Lines 15a and 15b are blank because the decedent, prior to death, did not withdraw funds from an IRA.

¶2726 LINE 16—PENSION AND ANNUITY DISTRIBUTIONS

If the decedent received payments from a pension or annuity during the year of death, the decedent's personal representative should receive a Form 1099-R showing the taxable amount of the payments.

▶ **PRACTICE POINTER:** Be sure to attach the Form 1099-R to the decedent's final return if any federal income tax was withheld from the pension or annuity distributions.

(a) Fully Taxable Pensions and Annuities. If the pension or annuity payment was fully taxable, enter it on line 16b. Do not make an entry on line 16a. The payment will be fully taxable if either of the following applies:

1. The decedent did not contribute to the cost or net investment in the pension or annuity [see Form 1099R],

2. The decedent received his or her entire cost back tax-free before 2013.

(b) Special Rule—Unrecovered Investment in Pension. If the decedent was receiving a pension or annuity and died without a surviving annuitant, the executor can take a deduction on the decedent's final return for the amount of the decedent's investment in the pension or annuity contract that remained unrecovered at death. The deduction is a miscellaneous itemized deduction that is not subject to the 2 percent of AGI limit [IRC Secs. 72(b)(3)(A) and 67(b)(10)].

If Form 1099-R shows a taxable amount, report that amount on line 16b. But a lower taxable amount may be reported by using one of two special computation methods used to figure the tax-free part of each annuity payment using the annuitant's age when he or she starting receiving payments from the annuity. The two available methods are the General Rule and the Simplified Method.

(c) Partially Taxable Pensions and Annuities. If the decedent's pension or annuity is partially taxable and the Form 1099-R does not show the taxable part, use the General Rule to figure the taxable part. See IRS Publication 939 for an explanation of the General Rule.

If the date the decedent started receiving payouts from the annuity (called the "annuity starting date") was after July 1, 1986, he or she may qualify for the

¶2726

Simplified Method. If the decedent's "annuity starting date" was after November 18, 1996, the Simplified Method *must* be used to figure the taxable part if:

1. The payments were for the decedent's life or the life of the decedent and his or her beneficiary;

2. The payments were from a qualified employee plan, a qualified employee annuity, or a tax-sheltered annuity; and

3. At the time the pension or annuity payments began, either the decedent was under age 75 or the number of years of guaranteed payments was fewer than 5.

If all three apply, use the worksheet on Page 24 of the Instructions to Form 1040 to figure the taxable part of your pension or annuity. For further discussion of the Simplified Method, please see IRS Publication 575. An alternative is to ask the IRS to figure the tax for you as explained in IRS Publication 939.

For further discussion of the Simplified Method, see IRS Publication 575.

(d) Lump-Sum Distributions. A lump-sum distribution is the distribution or payment of a retiree's entire retirement account balance within a single tax year. The decedent's taxable lump-sum distributions are reported in box 2b of Form 1099-R.

No tax is owed on lump-sum distributions that the decedent reinvested in an IRA or another qualified plan. Enter the total distribution on line 16a and the taxable part on line 16b.

Special breaks may apply. The taxpayer may be able to elect optional methods of computing the tax on lump-sum distributions. For example, it may be possible to have the decedent's distribution taxed as if the payment had been received over 5 or 10 years. The decedent may also be eligible for special low capital gains rates on a portion of the payouts.

(e) Rollovers. No tax is owed if the decedent rolled over his or her pension or annuity distribution from one qualified employer's plan to another or to an IRA or SEP. Enter on line 16a the total distribution before income tax or other deductions were withheld. This amount will be shown in box 1 of Form 1099-R. Subtract from the total on line 16a any contributions (usually shown in box 5) that were taxable to the decedent when made. From that result, subtract the amount that the decedent rolled over either directly or within 60 days of receiving the distribution. Enter the remaining amount, even if zero, on line 16b. Write "Rollover" next to line 16b.

■ The Kings did not receive any pension or annuity distributions in the year of George's death, so this line is left blank.

¶2727 LINE 17—SCHEDULE E

Use Schedule E [see ¶2787] to report income or loss received by the decedent prior to death from rental real estate, royalties, partnerships, S corporations, estates, trusts, and residual interests in real estate mortgage investment conduits (REMICs). Then carry the total from line 41 of Schedule E to line 17 of Form 1040 [see ¶2782].

▶ **CAUTION:** The amounts deducted in Parts I, II, and III of Schedule E may be limited by the "at risk" or the "passive loss" rules [see ¶2729].

Net investment income tax. Beginning in 2013, individuals, estates and trusts may have to pay a 3.8 percent net investment income (NII) tax on the lesser of: (1) NII for the year, or (2) the excess of modified adjusted gross income (MAGI) over the threshold amount ($250,000 for a joint return or surviving spouse, $125,000 for a married individual filing a separate return, and $200,000 for all others). MAGI is defined as adjusted gross income (AGI) plus any amount excluded as foreign earned income under IRC Sec. 911(a)(1) (net of the deductions and exclusions disallowed with respect to the foreign earned income). Net investment income may include rental and royalty income, income from partnerships, S corporations and trusts and income from other passive activities reported on Schedule E. The tax is reported for individuals, trusts and estates on Form 8960, "Net Investment Income Tax Individuals, Estates, and Trusts," which is attached to Form 1040 (individuals) or Form 1041 (trusts and estates).

¶2728 SCHEDULE E, PART I—RENT AND ROYALTY INCOME

If the decedent owned rental property or rented out a vacation home for part of the year, use Part I of Schedule E [see ¶2786] to report rental income and to deduct various expenses relating to the property. Royalties from patents and copyrights, as well as oil, gas, and mineral royalties, are also reported in Part I.

(a) Line A and Line B. If the decedent made payments that would require him or her to file any Forms 1099, check the "Yes" box. Otherwise, check the "No" box. Generally, the decedent must file Form 1099-MISC if the decedent paid at least $600 in rents, services, prizes, medical and health care payments, and other income payments.

(b) Part I—Income or Loss from Rental Real Estate and Royalties. Use Part I to report the following:

a. Income and expenses from rental real estate (including personal property leased with real estate);

b. Royalty income and expenses;

c. For an estate or trust only, farm rental income and expenses based on crops or livestock produced by the tenant. Do not use Form 4835 or Schedule F (Form 1040) for this purpose.

If the decedent owned a part interest in a rental real estate property, report only the decedent's part of the income and expenses on Schedule E. Complete lines 1 and 2 for each rental real estate property. For royalty properties, line 2 and the address portion on line 1 should be left bank and the decedent should enter code "6" for royalty property.

Personal property. Do not use Schedule E to report income and expenses from the rental of personal property, such as equipment or vehicles. Instead, use Schedule C or C-EZ if the decedent was in the business of renting personal property. The decedent was in the business of renting personal property if the primary purpose for renting the property is income or profit and the decedent was involved in the rental activity with continuity and regularity.

Extraterritorial income exclusion. Even though gross income generally includes all income from whatever source derived, gross income, however, does not include extraterritorial income that is qualifying foreign trade income under certain circumstances. Use Form 8873 to figure the extraterritorial income exclusion and report it on Schedule E.

(c) Line 1a. On line 1a of Schedule E [see ¶2786] if the decedent had rental real estate property, show the street address, city or town, state, and ZIP code. If the property is located in a foreign country, enter the city, province or state, country, and postal code.

Line 1b. For the type of property, enter one of the codes listed under "Type of Property" in Part I of the form.

Self-rental. Enter code type "7" for self-rental if you rent property to a trade or business in which you materially participated.

Other. Enter code type "8" if the property is not one of the other types listed on the form. Attach a statement to your return describing the property.

> ■ George and Mary King were joint owners of an office building in Kansas City. The rental property was leased the entire year for a total rental payment of $18,000. Under local law, George and Mary each had a half interest in the income from the property. George's will, however, provides that the entire rental income is to be paid directly to Mary. None of the rental income will be reported on the income tax return for the estate. Instead, Mary will report all the rental income and expenses on Schedule E of George's final income tax return.

On Part I of Schedule E, Mary lists the office building as "Property A" on line 1. On line 1b, Mary enters "4" (commercial) which identifies the type of property that George owned at the time of his death.

(d) Line 2. For a decedent who rented out dwelling units that were also used for personal purposes, the decedent may not be able to deduct all the expenses for the rental part. List each property on line 1a, report the number of days in the year each property was rented at fair rental value and the number of days of personal use. The answer on line 2 depends on whether the decedent (or a member of his or her family) used the rental property more than the greater of 14 days or 10 percent of the total days it was rented at fair-market value during the year.

If the decedent (or a member of his or her family) did so, all other deductions must be allocated between personal and rental use. Both the rental use and personal use portions of mortgage interest and real estate taxes can be deducted, but only the rental use portion of all other expenses can be deducted. In addition, the deduction for rental expenses is limited to the rental income from the property.

> ■ The Kings did not use their rental property as a dwelling unit in the year of George's death, so Mary enters "-o-" in all the boxes for "Property A" on line 2. This means that she can deduct all of their expenses, as long as they are not limited by the "at risk" and "passive loss" rules.

¶2728

(e) Lines 3 and 4. If the decedent received rental income from real estate (including personal property leased with real estate), report the income on line 3. Use a separate column (A, B, or C) for each rental property. Include income received for renting a room or other space. If the decedent received services or property instead of money as rent, report the fair market value of what the decedent received as rental income on line 3.

If the decedent provided significant services to the rental, such as maid service, the decedent should report the rental activity on Schedule C or C-EZ, not on Schedule E. Significant services do not include the furnishing of heat and light, cleaning of public areas, trash collection or similar services.

If the decedent was a real estate dealer, include only the rent received from real estate (including personal property leased with this real estate) held by the decedent for the primary purpose of renting to produce income. Do not use Schedule E to report income and expenses from rentals of real estate held by the decedent for sale to customers in the ordinary course of the decedent's business as a real estate dealer. Instead use Schedule C or C-EZ for those rentals.

■ Mary King enters the $18,000 rent she and George received in the Column for "Property A" on line 3.

(f) Lines 5 Through 21. These lines are used to report the deductible expenses incurred by the decedent with respect to rental and royalty properties. Deductible expenses include property taxes, depreciation, mortgage interest, insurance, management fees, agent's commissions, and miscellaneous expenses (such as janitorial services and agents' fees), and the cost of repairs (such as painting or fixing the roof). However, the cost of improvements (such as installing a new roof) cannot all be deducted currently. Instead, those costs are recovered through depreciation. You can also deduct up to $15,000 of qualified costs paid or incurred during the year to remove architectural or transportation barriers affecting individuals with disabilities and the elderly.

■ The Kings report $600 of cleaning and maintenance expenses on line 7, $900 of insurance payments on line 9, $1,800 of mortgage interest on line 12, $700 of supplies on line 15, $3,000 of taxes on line 16, and $1,500 of utilities on line 17.

Line 18. Depreciation or depletion deductions for rental properties are reported on line 18. Complete Form 4562 to compute depreciation for any rental property first placed in service that year. You may be able to claim a deduction for depletion if the decedent owned an interest in mineral property or an oil, gas, or geothermal well.

▶ **TAX RETURN TIP:** A separate depreciation form (if required) must be completed for each business or activity.

■ The Kings can claim a $2,500 depreciation deduction on line 18. Mary combines this with $8,500 of all other currently deductible expenses and enters $11,000 of total rental expenses on line 20.

Line 19. Enter on line 19 any ordinary and necessary expenses not listed on lines 5 through 18. The executor may be able to deduct on line 19 part or all of the cost of modifying existing commercial buildings to make them energy efficient.

¶2728

Line 21. Subtract line 20 from line 3 (rents) and/or 4 (royalties). If the decedent had amounts for which he or she was not at risk, use Form 6198 to determine the amount of the deductible loss. Enter that amount in the appropriate column of Schedule E, line 21. In the space to the left of line 21, enter "Form 6198." Form 6198 should be attached to the decedent's return.

(g) Lines 22 Through 26.

Line 22. Do not complete line 22 if the amount on line 21 is from royalty properties. If the decedent had a rental real estate loss from a passive activity, the amount of his or her loss deduction may be limited by the passive activity loss rules. Form 8582 need not be completed to figure the amount of loss, if any, to enter on line 22.

If your rental real estate loss is not from a passive activity or if the decedent satisfied the exception for certain rental real estate activities, the executor for the decedent need not complete Form 8582. Enter the loss from line 21 on line 22. If the decedent has an unallowed rental real estate loss from a prior year that after completing Form 8582 can be deducted this year, include that loss on line 22.

Combine income and losses on line 26. If there are no other items to report on Schedule E (e.g., income or loss from a partnership), the taxpayer carries the rental or royalty income or loss to line 17 of Form 1040.

> ■ Mary King subtracts the Kings' total expenses of $11,000 (line 20) from their rents received (line 3) and enters their $7,000 income on line 21. As the Kings do not own any other rental properties, the $7,000 amount is carried to lines 24 and 26, as well as to line 40 in Part V. Mary also enters $7,000 on line 17 of the Kings' Form 1040.

¶2729 SCHEDULE E, PART II—INCOME OR LOSS FROM PARTNERSHIPS AND S CORPORATIONS

The decedent's share of income or loss from partnerships or S corporations is reported in Part II of Schedule E.

(a) Partnership Profit (or Loss).
In Part II of Schedule E of the decedent's final return, you must report the decedent's share of partnership income for the partnership's tax year that ends within or with the decedent's last tax year (the year ending on the date of death).

▶**LET SCHEDULE K-1 BE YOUR GUIDE:** Consult the Schedule K-1 from the partnership to determine where to report partnership items on the decedent's return. For example, the Schedule K-1 will tell you to report interest and dividends on Schedule B, capital gain or loss on Schedule D, and charitable contributions made by the partnership along with your personal contributions on Schedule A. If you are treating items on your tax return differently from the way the partnership or S corporation reported them on its return, Form 8082 may have to be filed.

Deceased partner's partnership tax year closes upon death. IRC Sec. 706(c)(2)(A) provides that the taxable year of a partnership closes with respect to a partner whose entire interest in the partnership terminates, whether by death, liquidation, or otherwise [IRC Sec. 706(c)(2)(A)]. As a result, the deceased partner's income must be reported on the decedent's final income tax return [see ¶ 2606].

(b) S Corporations. If the decedent was a shareholder in an S corporation, you must include on Part II of Schedule E of the decedent's final return the decedent's share of S corporation income for the corporation's tax year that ends within or with the decedent's last tax year (the year ending on the date of death). The final return must also include the decedent's pro rata share of the S corporation's income for the period between the end of the corporation's last tax year and the date of death.

The income for the part of the S corporation's tax year that follows the shareholder's death is income to the estate or other person who has acquired the stock in the S corporation.

(c) Loss Limitations. If the decedent's partnership or S corporation's business or rental activity produced a loss for the year, the decedent's deduction for his or her share of that loss may be limited as follows:

- Generally, a partner or S corporation shareholder cannot deduct a partnership or S corporation loss (including a capital loss) to the extent it exceeds his or her adjusted basis in the partnership interest or S corporation stock.

- The at-risk rules limit losses from trade or business or income-producing activities to the amount at risk in the activity. The decedent is considered to be at risk to the extent of the cash and the adjusted basis of property that he or she contributed to the activity and any amounts the decedent borrowed for use in the activity.

- The passive loss rules prevent passive investors in partnerships or S corporations from using losses to offset active income from other sources. Although rental losses are generally treated as passive, partners or shareholders who are active participants in the rental activity can use up to $25,000 of a loss to offset nonpassive income. This special $25,000 allowance is phased out for taxpayers with modified AGI over $100,000 ($50,000 if married filing separately).

  NOTE: Real estate professionals can deduct the net loss from all rental real estate activities in which they materially participated.

Normally, passive activity losses (PALs) that are not allowed in one tax year because of insufficient passive income to cover them, are carried forward to the next year. When a passive activity interest is transferred because the owner died, the accumulated unused PALs are allowed as a deduction against the decedent's income in the year of death. Losses are allowed only to the extent they are greater than the excess of the transferee's (recipient of the interest transferred) basis in the property over the decedent's adjusted basis in the property immediately before death. The portion of the losses that is equal to the excess is not allowed as a deduction for any tax year because carryovers die with the taxpayer.

■ George and Mary King had no interests in partnerships or S corporations, so there is no need to complete Part II of Schedule E.

¶2729

¶2730 SCHEDULE E, PART III—INCOME OR LOSS FROM ESTATES AND TRUSTS

If the decedent was the beneficiary of an estate or trust, report the decedent's distributable share of trust income and loss in Part III of Schedule E [see ¶2786].

■ The Kings had no interests in estates or trusts.

¶2731 SCHEDULE E, PART IV—INCOME OR LOSS FROM REMICs

If the decedent was a residual holder of a real estate mortgage investment conduit (REMIC), use Part IV of Schedule E to report the total share of the REMIC's taxable income or loss for each quarter included in the decedent's tax year.

■ The Kings do not fill out Part IV of Schedule E.

¶2732 SCHEDULE E, PART V—SUMMARY

Part V of Schedule E summarizes all the entries on the other parts of Schedule E. Total income or loss from the first four parts of Schedule E is entered on line 40. This amount is carried over to line 17 of Form 1040.

■ In the summary portion of Schedule E, Mary King enters total income of $7,000.

¶2733 LINE 18—FARM INCOME OR LOSS

If the decedent had any income from farming operations, fill out Schedule F and attach it to the decedent's final return. Farm income, as computed on Schedule F, is entered on line 18 of Form 1040.

■ The Kings did not have any farm income, so line 18 is left blank.

¶2734 LINE 19—UNEMPLOYMENT COMPENSATION

If the decedent received unemployment compensation in the year of death, he or she should receive a Form 1099-G reporting the amount. Enter the amount on line 19 of Form 1040.

■ The Kings did not receive any unemployment compensation benefits, so line 19 is left blank.

¶2734

¶2735 LINES 20a AND 20b—SOCIAL SECURITY BENEFITS

Social Security recipients must pay tax on their benefits if the benefits are more than a "base amount" of other income during the year. The "base amount" is $44,000 for married taxpayers filing jointly, and $34,000 for single taxpayers and heads of households.

If the decedent received Social Security benefits, he or she should receive a Form SSA-1099 showing the amount. Report this amount on line 20a of Form 1040. Then use the Social Security Benefits Worksheet in the Instructions to Form 1040 to figure the amount of taxable Social Security benefits, and enter the result on line 20b of Form 1040.

■ The Kings did not receive any Social Security benefits in the year of George's death, so lines 20a and 20b are left blank.

¶2736 LINE 21—OTHER INCOME

If the decedent had any other income and there is no other place for it on the return or other schedules, report it on line 21 of Form 1040. Income to report on this line includes the following:

* Taxable distributions from a Coverdell education savings account or a qualified tuition program. Distributions from these accounts may be taxable if they are more than the qualified higher education expenses of the designated beneficiary in 2013 and they were not included in a qualified rollover;

* Taxable distributions from a health savings account or an Archer MSA. Distributions from these accounts may be taxable if they are more than the unreimbursed qualified medical expenses of the account beneficiary or account holder and they were not included in a qualified rollover;

* Prizes and awards;

* Gambling, raffle, and lottery winnings;

* Jury duty fees;

* Reimbursements or other amounts the decedent recovered (such as bad debts) or received that were deducted in a prior year, such as medical expenses, real estate taxes, or home mortgage interest;

* Income from the rental of personal property if you engaged in the rental for profit but were not in the business of renting such property;

* Income from an activity not engaged in for profit;

* Alternate trade adjustment assistance payments. These payments should be shown in Form 1099-G, box 5;

* Alaska Permanent Fund dividends;

* Loss on certain corrective distributions of excess deferrals;

¶2735

- Dividends on insurance policies if they exceed the total of all net premiums paid for the contract;
- Recapture of a charitable contribution deduction relating to the contribution of a fractional interest in tangible personal property;
- Recapture of a charitable contribution deduction if the charitable organization disposes of the donated property within three years of the contribution; and
- Cancelled debts;
- Taxable part of disaster relief payments.

List type and amount of income on dotted line.

(a) Special Types of Income Not Taxed. Certain income or benefits received by the decedent would not be subject to tax, as follows:

- Child support;
- Payments received to help decedent pay for mortgage loan under the HFA Hardest Hit Fund or the Emergency Homeowner Loan Program or similar state programs;
- Any Pay-for-Performance Success Payments that reduced the principal balance of the decedent's home mortgage under the Home Affordable Modification Program;
- Life insurance proceeds received because of someone's death (other than from certain employer-owned life insurance contracts); and
- Gifts and bequests unless the gift or bequest is from a foreign person and is in excess of $15,102, in which case it must be reported on Form 3520, "Annual Receipt to Report Transactions With Foreign Trusts and Receipt of Certified Foreign Gifts," Part IV.

Income exclusion for restitution payments to victims of Nazi persecution. Payments made to a person or the heirs or estate of a person who was persecuted on the basis of race, religion, physical or mental disability, or sexual orientation by Nazi Germany, any other Axis regime, or any other Nazi-controlled or Nazi-allied country are excluded from gross income. In addition, these amounts are not taken into account for any provision of the Code that takes into account excludable gross income in computing adjusted gross income (e.g., the taxation of Social Security benefits). The basis of any property received by eligible individuals or their heirs or estate is the fair market value of such property at the time of receipt.

Cancellation of certain student loans. The cancellation of certain student loans is excluded from a taxpayer's income.

Damages. Only compensatory (nonpunitive) damages received on account of personal physical injury or personal physical sickness are excluded from gross income. All other types of damages are taxable.

Accelerated death benefits. A decedent who was terminally ill can exclude from income any accelerated death benefits he or she received prior to death from:

- A life insurance policy, or
- The viatical settlement proceeds from the sale or assignment of a life insurance policy.

¶2736

A terminally ill individual is a person who has been certified by a physician as having an illness or physical condition that can reasonably be expected to result in death within 24 months of the date of certification.

Tax-free treatment of accelerated death benefits or viatical settlement proceeds is also available to chronically ill persons, provided the payments are used to pay un-reimbursed qualifying long-term care costs and the policy meets certain require-ments. If a chronically ill person receives per diem payments without regard to actual long-term costs, the tax-free amount is limited to $330 per day in 2013 ($116,800 annually).

Survivor benefits of public safety officers. If a public safety officer is killed in the line of duty, a survivor annuity paid to the officer's spouse, former spouse, or child may be excluded from the recipient's gross income. The annuity must be provided under a government plan and is excludable to the extent that it is attributable to the officer's service as a public safety officer. The term "public safety officer" includes police and law enforcement officers, fire fighters, ambulance crews, and rescue squads.

The exclusion does not apply if the recipient's actions were responsible for the officer's death. It also does not apply in the following situations:

1. The death was caused by the intentional misconduct of the officer or by the officer's intention to cause such death,

2. The officer was voluntarily intoxicated at the time of death, or

3. The officer was performing his or her duties in a grossly negligent manner at the time of death.

   ■ Mary King leaves this line blank.

¶2737 LINE 22—TOTAL INCOME

Add all items of income listed on lines 7 through 21 to find total income, and enter this amount on line 22.

   ■ George and Mary King's total income is $303,580, and this amount is entered on line 22 of Form 1040.

¶2738 ADJUSTMENTS TO INCOME

Certain items can be deducted as "adjustments to income." These adjustments can be written off even if you do not itemize deductions on behalf of the decedent.

LINE 23—EDUCATOR EXPENSES

If the decedent was a teacher, instructor, counselor, principal, or aide in either a public or private elementary or secondary school, and worked at least 900 hours during the school year, the executor may subtract up to $250 of qualified expenses when calculating the decedent's adjusted gross income (AGI). Deductions need not be itemized to benefit from this deduction. If both the decedent and his or her spouse are filing jointly and are both eligible educators, the maximum deduction is $500.

Qualified expenses include ordinary and necessary expenses paid in connection with books, supplies, equipment (including computer equipment, software, and services), and other materials used in the classroom. An ordinary expense is one that is common and accepted in the teacher's educational field. The expense need not be required to be considered a necessary expense. Qualified expenses do not include expenses for home schooling or for nonathletic supplies for courses in health or physical education.

Qualified expenses must be reduced by the following amounts: (1) excludable U.S. series EE and I savings bond interest from Form 8815; (2) nontaxable qualified state tuition program earnings; (3) nontaxable earnings from Coverdell education savings accounts; and (4) any reimbursement received for these expenses that were not reported in box 1 of Form W-2.

An eligible teacher is a kindergarten through grade 12 teacher, instructor, counselor, principal, or aide who worked in the school for at least 900 hours during a school year.

■ The decedent had no educator expenses and leaves this line blank.

LINE 24—CERTAIN BUSINESS EXPENSES OF RESERVISTS, PERFORMING ARTISTS, AND FEE-BASIS GOVERNMENT OFFICIALS

Attach Form 2106 or 2106-EZ. Include the following deductions on line 24:

- Certain business expenses of National Guard and reserve members who traveled more than 100 miles from home to perform services as a National Guard or reserve member.
- Performing-arts-related expenses of a qualified performing artist.
- Business expenses of fee-basis state or local government officials.

■ The decedent had no expenses to enter on line 24.

LINE 25—HEALTH SAVINGS ACCOUNT DEDUCTION (ATTACH FORM 8889)

Eligible taxpayers were able to establish a tax-favored Health Savings Account (HSA) to help them save for qualified medical expenses on a tax-free basis. Contributions to HSAs are accumulated or distributed on a tax-free basis and may be used to pay or reimburse qualified medical expenses. An HSA is a tax-exempt trust or custodial account established exclusively for the purpose of paying qualified medical expenses of the account beneficiary who, for the months for which contributions are made to an HSA, is covered under a high-deductible health plan (HDHP). An HSA may be set up with a U.S. financial institution such as a bank or insurance company. The HSA allows taxpayers to pay or be reimbursed for certain medical expenses. They must attach Form 8889 to claim the deduction. In addition, contributions made by the taxpayer's employer (including contributions made through a cafeteria plan) will not be included in gross income and distributions will be tax-free if used to pay for qualified medical expenses.

■ The Kings did not establish HSAs in the year George died, so line 25 is left blank.

¶2738

LINE 26—MOVING EXPENSES

If the decedent made a job-related move this year, some, or even all, of his or her moving expenses may be deductible above-the-line. Calculate the moving expense deduction on Form 3903.

> **NOTE:** Employees who are reimbursed for their moving expenses by their employers must report the reimbursement as income on line 7 of Form 1040.

(a) How to Qualify. To qualify for a moving expense deduction, the taxpayer must pass a distance test and a time test. First, the new job must be at least 50 miles farther from the taxpayer's old home than the old job was. Second, the taxpayer must have been employed full-time at or near the new job location for 39 weeks during the 12 months following the move.

> **Example 1:** At the beginning of the year, Dad lived in Hometown, 10 miles from his job with Old Co. In February, he quit his job with Old Co. and took a new job with New Co. Because New Co.'s offices are located about 100 miles from Hometown, Dad and his family move to a home in Big City, about 10 miles away from his new job. Dad stays with New Co. until December 31, when he dies. Dad's executor can claim a deduction for the cost of moving himself and his family because: (1) the new job is 90 miles farther from his old home (a 100-mile commute) than his old job was (a 10-mile commute) (Part I, lines 1, 2 and 3, Form 3903), and (2) he had worked at his new job for the requisite 39 weeks by the end of the year.

(b) Additional Test for Self-Employeds. There is an additional time test for self-employed taxpayers. Self-employeds must work at or near the new job location for at least 78 weeks during the 24 months following their move.

(c) Military Personnel. Military personnel who make a required move can deduct their out-of-pocket moving expenses even if they do not meet the mileage test or the time test.

(d) How Much to Deduct. If the decedent qualifies for a moving expense deduction, all of his or her *direct* moving costs can be written off. Direct moving costs include the cost of moving household goods and personal effects from the old to the new home (Part I, line 4 on Form 3903). Direct moving costs also include reasonable expenses for travel by the decedent and his or her family, and for lodging en route, but not the cost of meals (Part I, line 5 on Form 3903).

■ The Kings did not move the year George died, so line 26 is left blank.

LINE 27—DEDUCTIBLE PART OF SELF-EMPLOYMENT TAX

Decedents who were self-employed at their time of death can take a deduction equal to 50 percent of their self-employment tax bill for the year of George's death.

■ Neither George nor Mary King was self-employed in the year George died, so line 27 of Form 1040 on their return is left blank.

¶2738

LINE 28—SELF-EMPLOYED SEP, SIMPLE, AND QUALIFIED PLAN CONTRIBUTIONS

SEP, SIMPLE, and qualified plans provide a way for taxpayers to save for their retirement. Employers may deduct contributions made to the plan for their employees. Sole proprietors can deduct contributions made to the plan for themselves. Typically, earnings on the contributions are tax-free until distributions are received from the plan. Self-employed taxpayers or partners may be able to claim a deduction for contributions made to self-employed SEPs, SIMPLE, and qualified plans on line 28 of Form 1040. Contributions made to fund employees' retirement benefits are deducted on Schedule C (for sole proprietors) or Schedule F (for farmers).

SEP and profit-sharing plans. Simplified employee pension (SEP) plans are qualified retirement plans specially designed for easy administration. Instead of setting up a profit-sharing or money purchase plan with a trust, taxpayers adopt a written SEP agreement and make contributions directly to a traditional individual retirement annuity or a traditional individual retirement account.

Elective deferrals. The maximum amount that may be contributed to a SEP, Section 401(k) plan (excluding SIMPLE plans) and deferred compensation plans of state or local governments and tax-exempt organizations in 2013 is $17,500.

Catch-up contributions. Participants who are age 50 or over at the end of the plan year may make an additional $5,500 catch-up contribution in 2013 to Section 401(k), 403(b) and 457 plans.

SIMPLE plan salary reduction contributions. A Savings Incentive Match Plan (SIMPLE) is a written arrangement that allows small business owners (who employ 100 or fewer employees earning at least $5,000 in compensation) to provide a retirement plan for their employees. The SIMPLE plan can be either an IRA for each employee or a qualified 401(k) plan. Under a SIMPLE plan, employees can choose to make salary reduction contributions rather than receiving these amounts as part of their regular pay. In addition, employers may contribute matching or nonelective contributions. The two types of SIMPLE plans are the SIMPLE IRA plan and the SIMPLE 401(k) plan. The limit on salary reduction contributions to a SIMPLE plan is $12,000 in 2013. Participants who are age 50 or over at the end of the year may make catch-up contributions of an additional $2,500 in 2013.

Plans covering self-employed taxpayers. In the past, the terms "Keogh plan" or "H.R. 10 Plan" were used to designate a retirement plan established by a self-employed individual as opposed to a plan established by a corporate or other business entity. Now, self-employed retirement plans are generally referred to by the name that is used for the particular type of plan such as SEP IRA, SIMPLE 401(k), or self-employed 401(k). Employers are entitled to deduct retirement plan contributions up to the applicable contribution limit. The applicable contribution limit is figured one of two ways, depending on whether the retirement plan was set up as a defined contribution or a defined benefit plan.

Defined contribution plans limits: If the retirement plan was set up as a defined contribution plan (e.g., a SEP-IRA), the contribution limit is the lesser of $51,000 in 2013 or 100 percent of compensation, which is limited to a maximum of $255,000 in 2013.

¶2738

Defined benefit plans: If the retirement plan was set up as a defined benefit plan, the contribution limit is the amount required to fund an annual benefit of up to the lesser of (1) the taxpayer's average compensation (as defined below) from self-employment for the three consecutive highest earning years, or (2) a dollar amount annually indexed to the cost of living ($205,000 in 2013).

Compensation: For purposes of calculating a self-employed taxpayer's contribution limit, "compensation" is the lesser of (1) a flat dollar amount ($255,000 in 2013), or (2) the taxpayer's net earnings from self-employment, adjusted to take into account the deduction for contributions the taxpayer made on his or her own behalf. Taxpayers should use the Worksheet in IRS Publication 560 to compute the contribution limit.

Timing contributions: As long as the retirement plan was set up before the end of the year, taxpayers have until the due date for filing their tax return, including extensions, to make contributions.

Timing contributions: Deductible SEP contributions can be made (and the SEP set up) as late as the due date for filing the return for the year (including extensions). Unlike a Keogh, a SEP can be set up until the due date of the return (including extensions).

Calculating the deduction for the self-employed. In IRS Publication 560, "Retirement Plans for the Small Business," the IRS provides the procedure for calculating deductible contributions to a SEP plan as follows:

1. The self-employed participant's net earnings from self-employment are reduced by 50 percent of the self-employment tax;

2. The net earnings as reduced in (1) are multiplied by the reduced contribution rate applicable to self-employed participants. The product is the deductible contribution of the participant.

How to compute the reduced contribution rate applicable to self-employeds. A reduction must be made for the deduction allowed for contributions made on behalf of the self-employed participant in a qualified plan. As a starting point, "earned income" is defined as net earnings from self-employment. However, in determining the amount of income upon which contributions and deductions are based, net earnings from self-employment must also be reduced by the following two adjustments:

1. A reduction must be made for the deduction allowed for contributions made on behalf of the self-employed participant. When the entire contribution is deductible, the equivalent of this reduction is achieved by limiting the contribution to a percentage of earned income (calculated without regard to the deduction) determined by dividing the nominal rate by the number 1 plus that rate. For example, if the plan calls for a contribution equal to 10 percent of each participant's compensation, the contribution on behalf of a self-employed participant is determined by dividing 10 percent by 1.10. The result of 9.0909 percent is the contribution rate for the self-employed individual.

2. A reduction must also be made for the deduction from gross income that is allowed for 50 percent of the self-employment tax paid by the self-employed participant.

In IRS Publication 560, the IRS provides a rate table that may be used to determine the reduced contribution that applies to a self-employed individual's contributions to a SEP

¶2738

or other type of defined contribution plan. For example, under the rate table, if the maximum plan contribution rate is 15 percent, the maximum deduction percentage for contributions to the self-employed individual's own plan is 13.0435 percent. The 15 percent rate applied to employees. Under the rate table, if the plan's maximum contribution rate is 25 percent, a 20 percent rate applies to the self-employed individual and the 25 percent rate applies to employees.

■ George and Mary King did not contribute to to a Keogh, SEP or SIMPLE plan the year George died because, prior to his death, George was an employee who contributed to his employer's 401(k) plan.

LINE 29—SELF-EMPLOYED HEALTH INSURANCE DEDUCTION

If a decedent was self-employed in the year of death, up to 100 percent of the cost of health insurance for the decedent and his or her family can be deducted if:

• The decedent had a net profit from a business for the year; or

• The decedent received wages from an S corporation in which he or she was a more-than-2-percent shareholder, health insurance benefits paid will be shown in Form W-2, box 14. The insurance plan must have been established under the decedent's business. But if the decedent was also eligible to participate in any subsidized health plan maintained by his or her employer or a spouse's employer for any month or part of a month in the year of death, amounts paid for health insurance coverage for that month cannot be used to figure the deduction.

(a) **Deduction Limit.** The deduction cannot exceed the sum of the decedent's net profit from the business (reduced by any Keogh, SEP, or SIMPLE deductions claimed on line 28 of Form 1040).

NOTE: The decedent cannot claim a deduction for the cost of providing health insurance coverage for employees on line 29. These costs are deductible as ordinary business expenses on Schedule C (for sole proprietors) or Schedule F (for farmers). Also, any amount claimed as a deduction on line 29 cannot be claimed again as an itemized medical expense deduction on Schedule A [see ¶2783].

■ Neither George nor Mary King was self-employed the year George died, so line 29 is left blank.

LINE 30—EARLY WITHDRAWAL PENALTY DEDUCTION

If the decedent withdrew funds from a time savings account (e.g., one-year bank CD) before the maturity date, you can deduct any early withdrawal penalty paid by the decedent. The amount of the penalty will be shown on the Form 1099-INT or Form 1099-OID sent by the bank or other financial institution.

■ In the year of George's death, the Kings did not forfeit any interest because of a premature withdrawal from a time savings account, so line 30 is left blank.

LINES 31a AND 31b—ALIMONY PAID

To qualify as deductible alimony, payments under a divorce or separation instrument must meet all five of the following requirements [IRC Sec. 71(b)(1)]:

¶2738

1. The payments must be in cash. Checks and money orders qualify as cash payments, but services and property do not;

2. The parties cannot designate that the payments are not to be treated as alimony. If a divorce or separation instrument designates that a payment that would otherwise qualify as alimony should not be treated as alimony (e.g., as a property settlement), the payment will not qualify as alimony;

3. The parties must live in separate households at the time the payments are made;

4. There must be no requirement that payments continue beyond the death of the recipient spouse or that any substitute payment (in cash or property) be made after the death of the payee spouse. This means that the payments must end when the recipient spouse dies;

5. The payments cannot be payments for the support of the payor's children. Child support payments are not deductible.

(a) How to Deduct. Enter the total amount deductible as alimony on line 31a. Also enter the recipient's Social Security number on line 31b. If the decedent paid alimony to more than one person, enter the Social Security number of one of the recipients on line 31b and attach a statement with the Social Security number of any other recipient to Form 1040.

■ The Kings did not make any alimony payments during the year, so lines 31 and 31b are left blank.

LINE 32—IRA DEDUCTION

If the decedent was qualified to make deductible IRA contributions in 2013, up to $5,500 or $6,500 if the decedent was age 50 or older at the end of the year can be deducted on line 32. To qualify for the deduction, either the decedent or the decedent's spouse must have earned income totaling at least $5,500 during the year. For IRA purposes, earned income includes compensation as well as alimony and separate maintenance payments. It does not include pensions, annuities or other forms of deferred compensation. If the decedent was a member of the U.S. armed forces, earned income includes any nontaxable combat pay that the decedent received. If the decedent was self-employed, earned income is generally net earnings from self-employment if personal services were a material income-producing factor.

Keep in mind that the IRA deduction may be limited or eliminated in certain situations. For example, if the decedent was age $70^1/2$ or older at the end of the year, any contributions he or she made to a traditional IRA are not deductible. In addition, contributions made to a Roth IRA are not deductible. But the decedent may be able to claim the retirement savings contribution credit. See line 53. In addition, IRA contributions may be limited if the decedent's income was above a certain level, or if the decedent or the decedent's spouse participated in an employer's retirement plan during the year.

►**CHECK IT OUT:** If you are not sure whether the decedent participated in an employer-sponsored plan, check his or her Form W-2. If the decedent participated, the employer will have checked "Retirement plan" in box 13 of the W-2. The decedent is considered covered by a plan for these purposes if he or she was self-employed and had a Keogh, SEP, or SIMPLE retirement plan.

¶2738

■ George and Mary King's AGI for the year exceeded the phase out range, so they did not qualify to make deductible IRA contributions in the year of George's death.

Inherited traditional IRA: Spouse. A surviving spouse may elect to treat the inherited traditional IRA as his or her own. One way to make the election is to have the account redesignated as an account with the surviving spouse as owner rather than beneficiary. Alternatively, the surviving spouse will be treated as having made this election if: (1) any amounts in the IRA are not distributed within the time period that applied to the decedent; or (2) the individual makes contributions (including rollover contributions) to the inherited IRA. In order to make the election, the surviving spouse must be the sole beneficiary of the IRA and have an unlimited right to withdraw amounts from the IRA [Reg. Sec. 1.408-8, Q&A-5]. When a trust is named as the beneficiary of the IRA, this requirement has not been satisfied even if the spouse is the sole beneficiary of the trust. When the surviving spouse makes the election, he or she is treated as the owner of the IRA for all purposes. If the election is not made, then the required minimum distribution (RMD) is determined as though the spouse was the beneficiary of the IRA.

Inherited Traditional IRA: Nonspouse. A nonspouse beneficiary who inherits an IRA cannot treat it as his or her own account, but must take RMDs from the IRA determined under the rules applicable to beneficiaries receiving distributions from a qualified plan. When an individual, other than the decedent's spouse, inherits a lump sum distribution from an IRA, the individual may not roll over that distribution into another IRA and the distribution, minus the aggregate amount of the owner's nondeductible IRA contributions, are taxed as ordinary income in the year the distribution is received [Rev. Rul. 92-47]. If the individual does not receive a lump sum distribution, then the RMDs are generally determined under the rules that apply to distributions from qualified plans.

Trust Named as Beneficiary. When a trust is named as the beneficiary of the IRA, the beneficiaries of the trust will be treated as the deceased individual's beneficiaries if certain requirements are met [Reg. Sec. 1.401(a)(9)-4, Q&A-5]. The requirements include: (1) validity of the trust; (2) identification of the trust's beneficiaries; and (3) the delivery of proper documentation to the plan administrator [Reg. Sec. 1.401(a)(9)-4, Q&A-6].

More Than One IRA. If an individual is required to receive an RMD from more than one traditional IRA in a calendar year, the amount of the minimum distribution from each IRA must be calculated separately and the separate amounts totalled. However, the total may be withdrawn from one or more of the IRAs in whatever amounts the individual chooses [Reg. Sec. 1.408-8, Q&A-9].

LINE 33—STUDENT LOAN INTEREST DEDUCTION

Qualifying individuals who have paid interest on qualified education loans may claim a deduction for such interest expenses, up to a maximum deduction of $2,500 in 2013. The deduction is phased out in 2013 for modified AGI of $75,000 if single, head of household, or qualifying widower; and $155,000 if married filing jointly. A qualified education loan is any indebtedness incurred to pay for the qualified higher education expenses of a taxpayer, the taxpayer's spouse, or any dependent of the taxpayer.

¶2738

Qualified higher education expenses generally include tuition, fees, room and board and related expenses such as books and supplies. The expenses must be for education in a degree, certificate, or similar program at an eligible educational institution, which includes most colleges, universities, and certain vocational schools. The expenses must be reduced by certain educational benefits excludable from gross income such as employer-provided educational assistance benefits not reported on W-2 forms; excludable U.S. series EE savings bond interest from Form 8815; nontaxable qualified state tuition program earnings; nontaxable earnings from Coverdell education savings accounts; any scholarship, educational assistance allowance or other payment (but not gifts or inheritances) excluded from income. These expenses must be paid or incurred within a reasonable period before or after the indebtedness is incurred and must be attributable to a period when the student is at least a half-time student enrolled in a degree, certificate, or other program leading to a recognized educational credential at an eligible educational institution.

■ The Kings did not qualify for this deduction and this line is left blank.

LINE 34—TUITION AND FEES DEDUCTION

Individuals may claim an above-the-line deduction on line 34 for their payments of tuition and fees required for themselves, their spouse, or any claimed dependent to enroll at or attend college. The maximum amount of the deduction is $4,000 for taxpayers whose adjusted gross income (with certain modifications) does not exceed $65,000 ($130,000 if they file a joint return) and $2,000 for taxpayers whose modified adjusted gross income does not exceed $80,000 ($160,000 if they file a joint return). See Form 8917, "Tuition and Fees Deduction."

Qualified tuition and fees do not include any of the following: (1) amounts paid for room and board, insurance, medical expenses (including student health fees), transportation, or other similar personal, living, or family expenses; (2) amounts paid for course-related books, supplies, equipment, and nonacademic activities, except for fees required to be paid to the institution as a condition of enrollment or attendance; (3) amounts paid for any course involving sports, games, or hobbies, unless such course is part of the student's degree program.

■ The Kings did not qualify for this deduction and this line is left blank.

LINE 35—DOMESTIC PRODUCTION ACTIVITIES DEDUCTION

On line 35 of Form 1040, the decedent may be able to deduct up to 9 percent of qualified production activities income from the following activities:

1. Construction of real property performed in the United States;

2. Engineering or architectural services performed in the United States for construction projects in the United States;

3. Any lease, rental, license, sale, exchange, or other disposition of:

    a. Tangible personal property, computer software, and sound recordings that the decedent manufactured, produced, grew, or extracted in whole or in significant part within the United States;

    b. Any qualified film produced by the decedent;

    c. Electricity, natural gas, or potable water produced in the United States.

¶2738

The deduction does not apply to income derived from:

1. The sale of food and beverages prepared at a retail establishment;
2. Property leased, licensed or rented for use by a related person; or
3. The transmission or distribution of electricity, natural gas, or potable water.
4. The lease, rental, license, sale or exchange, or other disposition of property.
   ■ The Kings have no qualified production activities income and have left this line blank.

LINE 36—WRITE-IN ADJUSTMENTS

On line 36 include any of the following write-in adjustments. On the dotted line next to line 36, enter the amount of the deduction and identify it as indicated:

- Deductible expenses related to income reported on line 21 from the rental of personal property engaged in for profit. Identify as "PPR."
- Reforestation amortization and expenses. Identify as "RFST."
- Repayment of supplemental unemployment benefits under the Trade Act of 1974. Identify as "Sub-Pay TRA."
- Contributions to section 501(c)(18)(D) pension plans. Identify as "501(c)(18)(D)."
- Contributions by certain chaplains to section 403(b) plans. Identify as "403(b)."
- Attorney fees and court costs for actions involving certain unlawful discrimination claims, but only to the extent of gross income from such actions. Identify as "UDC."
- Archer MSA deduction. Identify as "MSA."
- Jury duty pay if the decedent gave the pay to his or her employer because his or her employer paid his or her salary while the decedent served on the jury. Identify as "Jury Pay."
- Attorney fees and court costs paid by the decedent in connection with an award from the IRS for information provided that substantially contributed to the detection of tax law violations, up to the amount of the award includible in gross income. Identify as "WBF."
- Attorney fees and court costs for actions involving certain unlawful discrimination claims, but only to the extent of gross income from such actions. Identify as "UDC."

LINES 37 AND 38—ADJUSTED GROSS INCOME

Add all of the adjustments to gross income plus any other allowable adjustments (such as the amount of jury duty pay that the taxpayer had to turn over to his or her employer), and enter the total on line 36.

Subtract the line 36 amount from total income (from line 22) and enter the result on line 37. This is the taxpayer's AGI.

■ The Kings have no adjustments to income, so their AGI entered on line 37 is $303,580.

TAXABLE INCOME

The first step in computing the decedent's final tax bill is to figure his or her taxable income, just as would be done for any other taxpayer. To do this, reduce AGI by either (1) the standard deduction, or (2) the total of all itemized deductions as computed on Schedule A [see ¶ 2783], whichever yields a bigger deduction.

Reduce the remainder further by the deduction for personal and dependency exemptions. What's left is the taxable income for the year.

Line 39a. If the decedent was born before January 2, 1948, or was blind at the end of 2013, check the appropriate box(es) on line 39a. If the decedent was married and checked the box on Form 1040, line 6b, and the spouse was born before January 2, 1948, or was blind at the end of 2013, also check the appropriate box(es) for the decedent's spouse. Be sure to enter the total number of boxes checked. Do not check any box(es) for a spouse if the filing status is head of household.

Blindness. If the decedent was not totally blind as of December 31, 2013, the executor must get a statement certified by an ophthalmologist or optometrist that: (1) the decedent could not see better than 20/200 in his or her better eye with glasses or contact lenses, or (2) the decedent's field of vision is 20 degrees or less.

Line 39b. If the decedent's filing status is married filing separately (box 3 is checked), and the decedent's spouse itemizes deductions on his or her return, check the box on line 39b. Also check that box if the decedent was a dual-status alien. But if the decedent was a dual-status alien and filed a joint return with his or her spouse who was a U.S. citizen or resident alien at the end of 2013 and the executor and the surviving spouse agree to be taxed on their combined worldwide income, the box should not be checked.

¶2739 LINE 40—STANDARD OR ITEMIZED DEDUCTIONS

The decedent's executor may either claim the standard deduction or claim the "basic standard deduction." If the deductions are not itemized, the full amount of the appropriate standard deduction is allowed, regardless of the date of death [see ¶ 2609].

For 2013, the basic standard deductions are as follows:

- $12,200 for joint filers or qualifying widow(er)s;
- $8,950 for heads of households;
- $6,100 for singles, and married taxpayers filing separately.

(a) Who May Claim an Increased Standard Deduction. If the decedent and/or the decedent's spouse were/was age 65 at the beginning of the year, and either or both was/were legally blind at the beginning of the year, check the appropriate boxes on line 39a, and enter the number of boxes checked in the big box at the right. This entitles the decedent to increase the basic standard deduction by the "additional standard deduction." Each additional standard deduction for the aged or blind is $1,200 in 2013. For a single taxpayer or head of household, this amount increased to $1,500 in 2013.

The standard deduction for dependents in 2013 is the greater of $1,000 or the dependent's earned income plus $350, up to the applicable basic standard deduction.

¶2739

The decedent's executor cannot use the standard deduction if the surviving spouse files a separate return and itemizes deductions. In this situation, the executor must also itemize the deductions on the decedent's final return.

■ Mary King can enter the greater of the Kings' standard deduction or the Kings' itemized deductions on line 40. As a married couple filing a joint return, the Kings are entitled to a basic standard deduction of $12,200, even though George was only alive half of the year. Mary decides to itemize their deductions instead of claiming the standard deduction because itemizing results in a greater tax deduction and reduces her overall tax bill.

Itemized deductions. The decedent's itemized deductions are reported on Schedule A [see ¶2783] of Form 1040. If you choose to claim itemized deductions on behalf of the decedent, carry the total of itemized deductions from Schedule A to line 40 of Form 1040.

Limitation on itemized deductions for higher-income individuals reinstated. In 2013, the limitation on itemized deductions for higher-income individuals was reinstated. Therefore, higher-income taxpayers are required to reduce the amount of their itemized deductions in 2013 when their adjusted gross income exceeds $300,000 if filing a joint return or as a surviving spouse, $275,000 if filing as head of household, $250,000 if filing as unmarried and not a surviving spouse or head of household, and $150,000 if a married individual filing a separate return. A taxpayer with AGI over the threshold amount will need to reduce their otherwise allowable itemized deductions by the lesser of: (1) three percent of the amount of the taxpayer's AGI in excess of the applicable threshold amount, or (2) 80 percent of the itemized deductions otherwise allowable for the tax year. Itemized deductions not subject to the limitation are medical expenses, investment interest expenses, casualty or theft losses, and gambling losses. The amount of itemized deductions that are cut back for regular income tax purposes are not cut back when calculating alternative minimum taxable income (AMTI).

Itemized deductions worksheet. Decedent's should use the Itemized Deductions Worksheet to compute the amount to enter on line 29 of Schedule A, Itemized Deductions if the amount on Form 1040, line 38, is over $300,000 if married filing jointly or qualifying widow(er); $275,000 if head of household; $250,000 if single; or $150,000 if married filing separately [See ¶2783 for sample Itemized Deductions Worksheet–Line 29 prepared line-by-line for the decedent, George E. King].

The following paragraphs show how Mary King figured the Kings' itemized deductions on Schedule A [see ¶2783] of Form 1040.

¶2740 SCHEDULE A—MEDICAL AND DENTAL EXPENSES

Floor for deducting medical and dental expenses increased. Beginning in 2013, taxpayers (including decedents) may deduct only the part of their medical and dental expenses that exceed 10 percent of their adjusted gross income. However, in 2013, if either the taxpayer or the taxpayer's spouse turns 65 before the end of the tax year, the 10 percent threshold does not apply and the threshold remains at 7.5 percent of AGI.

Report all the unreimbursed medical and dental expenses paid on behalf of the decedent, his or her spouse, and his or her dependents on line 1 of Schedule A [see ¶¶2609, 2783].

▶ **CAUTION:** Qualified medical expenses paid before death by the decedent are not deductible if paid with a tax-free distribution from an MSA.

Dependents. A deduction is available for the unreimbursed medical expenses paid for those listed as a dependent on line 6c of Form 1040. Unreimbursed medical expenses paid for individuals claimed as dependents may also be deducted, unless the dependent earned more than $3,900 in 2013. Also, a divorced or legally separated parent who pays his or her child's medical expenses can claim those costs, even if the parent is not entitled to claim the child as a dependent.

Deductible expenses. A medical deduction may be claimed for almost any un-reimbursed expense for the diagnosis, cure, mitigation, treatment or prevention of disease, or for treatment affecting any part or function of the body. Unreimbursed amounts paid to participate in a program to stop smoking or for prescription medicines to alleviate nicotine withdrawal may be deducted. Nonprescription medicines, such as nicotine gum and certain nicotine patches are not deductible. Keep in mind that only the part of medical and dental expenses that exceeds 10 percent of adjusted gross income may be deducted unless either the decedent or the decedent's spouse turned 65 before the end of 2013, in which case the threshold is 7.5 percent.

Weight loss programs. The cost of attending a weight loss program designed as a treatment for a specific disease (including obesity) will be deductible provided the obesity is diagnosed by a doctor and weight loss is recommended to treat the obesity. The cost of the diet food will not be deductible.

Cosmetic surgery. Cosmetic surgery will not be deductible unless it was necessary to improve a deformity related to a congenital abnormality, an injury from an accident or trauma, or a disfiguring disease.

Day trips. The cost of going to and from a deductible medical treatment is also eligible for the medical deduction. This includes payments for bus, taxi, plane fare or ambulance services. If the taxpayer's own car is used, the out-of-pocket expenses of driving (gas, oil, parking, tolls) are eligible, but depreciation, insurance and general repairs are not. *Note:* The taxpayer need not maintain detailed records of actual medical-related car expenses. As long as the taxpayer keeps track of his or her trips, he or she may claim 24 cents a mile in 2013. Parking and tolls are deductible in addition to the automatic amount.

Overnight travel. If the taxpayer had to travel away from home to receive special medical treatment, he or she may deduct certain lodging expenses, up to $50 a night for each eligible individual.

Capital expenses. Generally, capital expenses (the cost of items that last more than one year) can be written off only over a period of time through depreciation deductions. However, capital expenses incurred primarily for medical care can be currently deducted. Examples: Eyeglasses, seeing eye dogs, artificial teeth and limbs, wheelchairs and crutches. Even a home improvement made for medical reasons is deductible to the extent it does not increase the value of the home.

Insurance premiums. The cost of insurance that provides reimbursement for medical care and prescription drugs is deductible. Deductible costs include: premiums for Blue Cross/Blue Shield, policies for dental care and to replace contact lenses; membership fees to join an HMO; the amount paid for Medicare A by taxpayers over age 65 and not covered by Social Security; the amount paid for Medicare B by those receiving Medicare health benefits.

Premiums for long-term care coverage. Depending on the taxpayer's age, all or part of his or her premium payments for a qualified long-term care policy are a deductible medical expense, subject to the 10 percent floor unless either the decedent or the decedent's spouse turned 65 before the end of 2013, in which case the floor is 7.5 percent. In 2013, the maximum annual deductible premium amounts are $360 if age 40 or under at the end of the year; $680 for those age 41 through 50; $1,360 for those age 51 through 60; $3,640 for those age 61 through 70; and $4,550 for those age 71 and older.

▶**SELF-EMPLOYEDS:** Self-employed taxpayers can deduct up to 100 percent of the cost of medical insurance from gross income on line 29 of Form 1040. The remainder of the premium can be deducted as a medical expense if total medical expenses exceed 10 percent of adjusted gross income unless either the decedent or the decedent's spouse turned 65 before the end of 2013 in which case the threshold is 7.5 percent [IRC Sec. 213(a)].

Nondeductible medical and dental expenses. The following medical and dental payments are not deductible:

- Life insurance or income protection policies, or policies providing payment for loss of life, limb, sight, etc.;
- Nursing care for a healthy baby. But the taxpayer may be able to claim a credit for child care expenses on line 48 of Form 1040;
- Illegal operations or drugs;
- Prescription drugs brought in or shipped from another country;
- Nonprescription medicines and toiletries (including nicotine gum and certain nicotine patches);
- Teeth whitening;
- Travel prescribed by a doctor;
- Health club dues;
- Bottled water;
- Maternity clothes;
- Baby sitting and childcare;
- Diaper service;
- Flexible spending account reimbursements (if contributions were on a pre-tax basis);
- Funeral, burial, or cremation costs.

¶2740

(a) One-Year Grace Period. If the decedent's medical bills (not those of the spouse and the dependent) are paid within one year after the decedent dies, a special rule allows the executor to make an irrevocable election to treat these medical expenses as paid by the decedent at the time the medical services were provided so that they can be deducted on the decedent's final income tax return rather than on the federal estate tax return (Form 706) [IRC Sec. 213(c)].

▶ **CAUTION:** The decedent's unreimbursed medical expenses paid within one year of death can be deducted either on the decedent's final income tax return or amended final income tax return, the decedent's regular return for the year before he or she died, the decedent's estate tax return (Form 706), but *not* on the estate income tax return (Form 1041) [Reg. Sec. 1.642(g)-2].

In order to take advantage of this election, the medical expenses for the decedent must be paid during the one-year period beginning with the day after death. If the executor makes the election, the expenses incurred in the year of death can be deducted on the decedent's final income tax return or an amended return can be filed in order to claim a refund. The normal period for filing a claim for refund is three years after the return was filed or two years after the tax was paid, whichever is later [IRC Sec. 6511(a)].

If you choose to take advantage of this election, be sure to attach a statement to the decedent's Form 1040 (or the decedent's amended return, Form 1040X) stating that the expenses have not been and will not be claimed on the estate tax return.

Example 1: Dad died in 2013 with unpaid medical expenses of $1,500 from 2012 and $5,000 from 2013. His executor will pay the expenses in January 2014. The executor can file an amended return for 2012 deducting the $1,500 medical expenses. The $5,000 medical expenses from 2013 can be included on Dad's final income tax return, which will be filed in 2014.

▶ **PLANNING TIP:** When you are deciding where to deduct the decedent's medical expenses, compare the tax rates that would be imposed on the decedent's final return and on the estate's return to help you determine on which return to deduct the decedent's medical expenses paid within one year of death.

(b) Funeral Expenses. Keep in mind that funeral, burial or cremation expenses cannot be deducted either on the decedent's final return or the estate's income tax return (Form 1041). They are deductible only on the federal estate tax return (Form 706).

(c) AGI Limits Apply. The decedent's medical and dental expenses are deductible only to the extent they exceed 10 percent of the decedent's AGI unless either the decedent or the decedent's spouse turned 65 before the end of 2013, in which case the floor is 7.5 percent.

Apply this limit by entering AGI (as reported on line 38 of Form 1040) on line 2 of Schedule A. Then multiply that amount by 10 percent (.10) (unless the decedent or the spouse turned 65 before the end of 2013, in which case the floor is 7.5 percent) and enter the result on line 3. Finally, subtract the amount on line 3 from the total amount of medical expenses on line 1, and enter the result on line 4. This is the amount of medical expenses you can deduct.

¶2740

■ The Kings (who were not yet 65) do not have unreimbursed medical or dental expenses in excess of 10 percent of their AGI, so lines 1 through 4 of Schedule A are left blank.

¶2741 SCHEDULE A—TAXES PAID

The decedent can deduct the following types of taxes paid during the year on lines 5 through 9 of Schedule A: (1) state and local income tax on line 5a; (2) state and local general sales taxes on line 5b; (3) real estate taxes on line 6; and (4) state and local personal property taxes on line 7. To claim the deduction, the decedent must have been liable for the tax paid. For example, the decedent can deduct the property taxes paid on his or her home, but not property taxes paid on his or her son's home.

Nondeductible taxes. The following taxes are not deductible:

- Federal income and most excise taxes.

- Social Security, Medicare, Federal unemployment (FUTA), and railroad retirement (RRTA) taxes.

- Customs duties.

- Federal estate and gift taxes.

- Certain state and local taxes, including: tax paid on gasoline, car inspection fees, assessments for sidewalks or other improvements to your property, or taxes paid for someone else, and license fees (marriage, driver's, dog, etc.).

(a) **State and Local Income Taxes.** The decedent can deduct state and local income taxes on line 5(a) of Schedule A.

Include on this line the state and local income taxes listed below:

- State and local income taxes withheld from the decedent's salary during the year as reflected on the decedent's W-2;

- State and local income taxes paid in 2013 for a prior year, such as taxes paid with the decedent's 2012 state or local income tax return. Do not include penalties or interest;

- State and local estimated tax payments made during 2013, including any part of a prior year refund that the decedent chooses to have credited to his or her 2013 state or local income taxes;

- Mandatory contributions made to the California, New Jersey, or New York Nonoccupational Disability Benefit Fund, Rhode Island Temporary Disability Benefit Fund, or Washington State Supplemental Workmen's Compensation Fund;

- Mandatory contributions to the Alaska, New Jersey, or Pennsylvania state unemployment fund.

- Mandatory contributions to state family leave programs, such as the New Jersey Family Leave Insurance (FLI) Program and the California Paid Family Leave program.

¶2741

The deduction should not be reduced by any:

- State or local income tax refund or credit the executor expects to receive on behalf of the decedent in 2013; or

- Refund of, or credit for, prior year state and local income taxes actually received in 2013.

   (b) State and Local General Sales Taxes. The decedent can elect to deduct state and local general sales taxes instead of state and local income taxes by checking box b on line 5 of Schedule A of Form 1040.

   ▶**WARNING:** Both cannot be deducted.

   To compute the amount of the deduction, the executor can use either actual expenses or the optional sales tax tables on page A-14 through A-16 of the Instructions to Form 1040.

Taxpayers also may add to the table amount any sales taxes paid on big ticket items such as:

- A motor vehicle, but only up to the amount of tax paid at the general sales tax rate; and

- An aircraft, boat, home (including mobile or prefabricated), or, in certain cases, a substantial addition to or major renovation of a home, if the tax rate is the same as the general sales tax rate.

Taxpayers should claim the deduction for state and local general sales taxes on Schedule A (Form 1040), line 5b, "State and local general sales taxes."

This option is available to all taxpayers regardless of where they live, though it's primarily designed to benefit residents of the seven states (Alaska, Florida, Nevada, South Dakota, Texas, Washington and Wyoming) without state and local income taxes.

AMT implications. Any state and local general sales taxes included on Schedule A, line 5b must be included when computing alternative minimum taxable income (AMTI). Therefore, like state and local income and property taxes, individuals cannot deduct sales tax when computing AMTI and may lose the benefit of the write-off if they are subject to the AMT. Practitioners must therefore compute the impact of AMT exposure before claiming a deduction for general sales taxes.

   (c) Real Estate Taxes. Most real estate taxes (state, local, or foreign) assessed on the decedent's home and other real property (not used in a business or an income-producing investment) are deductible on line 6 of Schedule A if the taxes were based on the assessed value of the property. In addition, the assessment must be made uniformly on property throughout the community, and proceeds must be used for general community or governmental purposes. If the decedent's mortgage payments include real estate taxes, the decedent may deduct only the amount the mortgage company actually paid to the taxing authority.

Tenant-stockholders in a cooperative housing corporation can deduct their share of real estate taxes paid by the corporation. However, there's no deduction if the corporation leases the building and pays taxes under the lease agreement.

Do not include the following items on line 6:

- Itemized charges for services to specific property or persons (for example, a $20 monthly charge per house for trash collection, a $5 charge for every 1,000 gallons of water consumed, or a flat charge for mowing a lawn that had grown higher than permitted under a local ordinance).

- Charges for improvements that tend to increase the value of your property (for example, an assessment to build a new sidewalk). The cost of a property improvement is added to the basis of the property. However, a charge is deductible if it is used only to maintain an existing public facility in service (for example, a charge to repair an existing sidewalk, and any interest included in that charge).

Refunds and rebates. If the decedent received a refund or rebate of real estate taxes paid in 2013, reduce the amount of the deduction by the amount of the refund or rebate. If the decedent received a refund or rebate this year of real estate taxes paid in an earlier year, do not reduce the deduction by this amount. Instead, include the refund or rebate in income on Form 1040, line 21 if the real estate taxes were deducted in an earlier year and the deduction reduced tax.

Apportioning taxes on a sale. For the year property is sold, real estate taxes are divided between the buyer and seller in proportion to the number of days each owned the property during the real property tax year (the period to which the tax relates). The seller pays the taxes through the date one day before the sale, and the buyer pays the taxes beginning with the date of sale. This allocation is mandatory for tax purposes. The tax allocation is usually provided in the closing statement.

(d) Personal Property Taxes. Enter the state and local personal property taxes paid by the decedent, but only if the taxes were based on value alone and were imposed on a yearly basis.

(e) Other Taxes. The decedent can deduct certain other taxes on line 8. Include here income tax paid to a foreign country or U.S. possession as well as state and local personal property taxes paid if the taxes were based on value alone and were imposed on a yearly basis.

■ During 2013, the Kings had withheld or paid a total of $7,807 in income taxes to Missouri and Kansas City. Mary enters this amount on line 5. The Kings paid $3,297 in real estate taxes on their home, which is reported on line 6, along with $2,000 of taxes they paid on a raw land investment for a total of $5,297 on line 6. Mary enters the total of all line 5 and line 6 amounts, $13,104, on line 9 of Schedule A [see ¶2783].

¶2742 SCHEDULE A—INTEREST PAID

Subject to certain limitations, you can deduct on lines 10 through 15 on Schedule A [see ¶2783] the interest paid by the decedent on:

1. A loan secured by the decedent's main home or second home. It includes first and second mortgages, home equity loans, and refinanced mortgages;
2. A loan the decedent took out to buy investments.

Interest on business debts is deducted on Schedule C (Schedule F for farmers), and interest incurred in connection with rental property is deducted on Schedule E.

¶2742

(a) Home Mortgage Interest. The decedent can deduct the interest on two kinds of home mortgage loans:

1. Home acquisition loans; and
2. Home equity loans.

Home acquisition loans are those used to buy, construct, or substantially improve a first or second home. You can deduct the interest on up to $1 million worth of home acquisition loans ($500,000 for a married taxpayer filing separately).

A home equity loan is any other loan secured by your first or second home. You can deduct the interest on up to $100,000 worth of home equity loans ($50,000 for a married taxpayer filing separately).

▶ **WHERE TO LOOK:** If the decedent's deductible mortgage interest was paid to a bank or other financial institution, the decedent should receive a Form 1098 showing the amount that was paid. Enter this amount on line 10.

▶ **CAUTION:** If any portion of the decedent's home mortgage interest is attributable to an office in his or her home, that portion is deducted on Schedule C. Do not include that portion in the mortgage interest deduction claimed on Schedule A.

(b) Private Loans. If the decedent obtained his or her mortgage from an individual rather than a bank or other financial institution, and the decedent did not receive a Form 1098, report the deductible mortgage interest on line 11. You must also write the name, address, and Social Security number of the lender on the dotted line to the left of the entry.

(c) Points. Many lenders require borrowers to prepay a certain percentage of interest on a mortgage loan to secure the loan. These payments are known as "points." The points will be deductible in full in the year paid if all the following requirements are met:

1. The taxpayer is legally liable for the debt and the main home in which the taxpayer lives most of the time secures the loan.
2. Paying points is an established business practice in the taxpayer's area.
3. The points paid were not more than the amount generally charged in that area.
4. The taxpayer uses the cash method of accounting, which means that income is reported in the year that it is received and expenses are deducted in the year they are paid.
5. The points were not paid for items that usually are separately stated on the settlement sheet such as appraisal fees, notary fees, inspection fees, title fees, attorney fees, and property taxes.
6. At or before closing the taxpayer provided funds that were at least as much as the points charged, not counting points paid by the seller. To be deductible, the points may be borrowed from the lender or mortgage broker.
7. The loan proceeds are used by the taxpayer to buy or build his or her main home.
8. The points were computed as a percentage of the principal amount of the mortgage.
9. The amount of the points paid is clearly shown on the settlement statement.

¶2742

Points paid solely to refinance a home mortgage usually must be deducted over the life of the loan. For a refinanced mortgage, the interest deduction for points is determined by dividing the points paid by the number of payments to be made over the life of the loan. Usually, this information is available from lenders. Taxpayers may deduct points only for those payments made in the tax year.

> **Example 1:** Taxpayer buys a new home and pays $2,000 in points on his 30-year mortgage. He must make 12 payments a year or 360 total payments on the mortgage and can deduct $5.56 per monthly payment, or $66.72 in one year.

If part of the refinanced mortgage money was used to finance improvements to the home and if the taxpayer meets certain other requirements, the points associated with the home improvements may be fully deductible in the year the points were paid. If a homeowner is refinancing a mortgage for a second time, the balance of points paid for the first refinanced mortgage may be fully deductible at time of pay-off.

> **Example 2:** Homeowner refinanced his house with a 30-year mortgage and paid $1,230 in points. On Schedule A, the taxpayer deducted $41 ($1,230 divided by 30) each year for 6 years. When the homeowner had deducted $246 of the total points paid, he refinanced again and paid off the entire previous loan including the points. He may deduct $984 in the year the mortgage ended.

Deduction of other closing costs. Other closing costs, such as appraisal fees and other non-interest fees generally are not deductible.

Points reported on Form 1098 are included in the amount reported on line10 of Schedule A. Points not reported on Form 1098 are reported on line 12.

If the points charged were excessive or were paid on a refinancing or a home equity loan used for purposes other than improving the decedent's home, they must be written off over the term of the loan.

> ■ The Kings paid no points in 2013 but did pay $11,000 in mortgage interest as reported to them on their Form 1098 from City Bank. That amount is entered on line 10 of their Schedule A [see ¶ 2783].

(d) Qualified Mortgage Insurance Premiums—Line 13 of Schedule A. On Line 13 the executor can enter the qualified mortgage insurance premiums paid under a mortgage insurance contract issued during 2013 in connection with home acquisition debt that was secured by the decedent's first or second home. Qualified mortgage insurance is mortgage insurance provided by the Department of Veterans Affairs, the Federal Housing Administration, or the Rural Housing Service, and private mortgage insurance.

Mortgage insurance premiums are not deductible if adjusted gross income (AGI) is more than $109,000 ($54,000 if married filing separately). If AGI is more than $100,000 ($50,000 if married filing separately), the deduction is limited and the worksheet on page A-7 of the Instructions to Form 1040 must be used to compute the amount of the deduction.

¶2742

(e) Investment Interest Expense Deduction—Line 14 of Schedule A.

The executor can write off interest paid by the decedent on a loan used to buy or carry investment property on line 14 of Schedule A. However, interest allocable to passive activities or to securities that generate tax-exempt income (such as municipal bonds) are generally not deductible.

The amount that can be deducted as investment interest is limited to the amount of net investment income (e.g., dividends, interest and net gain from the sale of investment property less investment expenses) reported on Form 1040 (reduced by any investment-related expenses that are written off).

Taxpayers generally figure their investment interest deduction on Form 4952 (Investment Interest Expense Deduction).

The decedent need not file Form 4952 if all three of the following apply:

1. The decedent's investment interest expense is not more than your investment income from interest and ordinary dividends minus any qualified dividends;

2. The decedent has no other deductible expenses connected with the production of the interest or dividends; and

3. The decedent has no disallowed investment interest expense from last year.

Instead, just enter the amount of your investment interest expenses on line 14 of Schedule A.

> ■ The Kings need not file Form 4952 because their investment interest expense is not more than their investment income. They had $9,567 in investment interest expense in 2013 and enter that amount on line 14 of Schedule A.

Qualified dividends and net capital gain from the disposition of property held for investment are excluded from investment income. But the decedent may elect to include part or all of these amounts in investment income on Form 4952, line 4g. If this election is made, the qualified dividends and net capital gain will be ineligible for taxation at capital gains tax rates. Once this election has been made, IRS consent must be obtained to revoke the election.

¶2743 SCHEDULE A—CHARITABLE CONTRIBUTIONS

Charitable contributions made in the decedent's final year should be deducted on his or her final income tax return. Keep in mind that charitable contributions and carryovers in excess of the decedent's AGI in the year of death will be lost forever. Any excess cannot be carried over to later years because the decedent's charitable contribution carryover dies with him.

> ▶ RECOMMENDATION: If the decedent alone has insufficient income to cover the deduction of charitable contributions and carryovers in the year of death, consider filing a joint return with the surviving spouse if he or she has income to report that will cover the carryover.

¶2743

(a) Charitable Contribution Basics. A qualified charity can be a governmental unit or an organization operated for religious, charitable, scientific, literary or educational purposes. An organization set up to foster national or international amateur sports also qualifies. Political campaign committees, social clubs, and labor unions are not qualified charitable organizations. The IRS publishes a full list of qualified charities in IRS Publication 78, "Cumulative List of Organizations."

▶ **CAUTION:** A charitable contribution is generally not deductible to the extent the donor receives a benefit in return for the contribution. In other words, only the excess over the value of the benefit is deductible. A special rule applies for contributions to a school's athletic program. If you received the right to purchase tickets in return for your contributions, 80 percent of the contribution qualifies as a charitable deduction.

(b) Cash Contributions. Cash contributions the decedent made (including any of out-of-pocket expenses) are reported on line 16 of Schedule A [see ¶2783]. To deduct any charitable donation of money, taxpayers must have a bank record or a written communication from the recipient. This rule applies regardless of the amount of the donation. The written proof must be provided at the time of the donation and must include the name of the charity, the date and location of the gift, and a detailed description of the property donated.

Out-of-pocket expenses incurred and paid by the decedent that are directly related to charitable activities are reported on line 17. These include:

- *Car costs.* The cost of the oil and gas that the decedent used while driving his or her car to perform charitable work can be deducted, provided adequate records were kept. The IRS requires that you show where the decedent drove, the charitable purpose of the trip, and how much money was spent. You can show how much was spent by either (1) keeping receipts of actual oil and gas costs, or (2) claiming an "automatic" deduction of 14 cents per mile in 2013. Parking fees and tolls are also deductible in addition to the amount computed under the cents-per-mile rule.

- *Travel.* The cost of the decedent's travel for charitable purposes is also deductible, as long as there is no significant element of personal pleasure, recreation, or vacation in such travel. Deductible costs would include transportation, lodging and 50 percent of meal expenses.

- *Exchange students.* You can deduct up to $50 for each month the decedent allowed a student (other than a dependent or relative) to live in his or her home. The student can be either an American or foreign exchange student and must be in the twelfth grade or lower.

(c) Property Contributions. Property contributions are reported on line 17 of Schedule A [see ¶2783]. To be deductible, clothing and household items donated to charity must be in good used condition or better. However, a taxpayer may claim a deduction of more than $500 for any single item, regardless of its condition, if the taxpayer includes a qualified appraisal of the item with the tax return on which the deduction is claimed. Household items include furniture, furnishings, electronics, appliances, and linens.

If the amount of the decedent's deduction was more than $500, Form 8283 must be completed and attached to the return. If the total deduction for contributions of

¶2743

property exceeds $5,000, an appraisal of the value of the donated property may be required. Use Form 8283.

(d) Appreciated Property. As a general rule, the full fair-market value of donated appreciated property is deductible. However, there are instances when the deductible amount is limited to the decedent's adjusted basis or cost in the property. For example, the deduction for appreciated property that would produce ordinary (rather than capital) gain is limited to the decedent's adjusted basis. This property includes: inventory, a work of art you created, depreciable property (to the extent depreciation would be recaptured if there had been a sale), and capital assets held for one year or less before donation.

For appreciated capital assets, the decedent's deduction depends on the type of property donated. You can deduct the fair-market value of intangible capital assets (such as stocks and bonds). But if the donated property is tangible personal property (e.g., cars, jewelry, art), and the charity does not use the property in a manner related to its tax-exempt function, the deduction is generally limited to the decedent's basis in the property.

(e) Tax-Free IRA Distributions to Charities. In 2013, IRA holders age $70^1/_2$ or older can make tax-free transfers of up to $100,000 per year from a traditional IRA or Roth IRA to an eligible charity [IRC Sec. 408(d)(8)]. Eligible IRA holders can take advantage of this provision, regardless of whether they itemize their deductions. Taxpayers may not claim a charitable deduction for this transfer. Funds must be contributed directly by the IRA trustee to the eligible charity. Transferred amounts are counted in determining whether the holder has satisfied the required minimum distribution rules. The recipient of the IRA funds must be a "50 percent organization." A church or a convention or association of churches is an eligible recipient. Other eligible charities include: educational institutions; hospitals; medical research organizations; organizations supporting governmental schools; governmental units; publicly supported organizations; common fund organizations; private operating foundations; and conduit foundations. Distributions to supporting organizations (i.e., organizations that support churches, educational institutions, hospitals, medical research organizations, organizations supporting government schools and publicly supported organizations) are not qualified distributions.

> ■ During 2013, the Kings gave $3,000 to the University of Missouri and $2,500 to the Heart Association. They also gave $700 to their church and $122 for door-to-door solicitations. Mary King served as a volunteer for a local charity. In performing her volunteer work, she drove 1,286 miles. Using the 14-cents-per-mile rate effective in 2013, gives her a deduction of $180. Mary enters the $6,502 total of their cash contributions (including the $180 out-of-pocket expenses) on line 16 of Schedule A [see ¶ 2783]. The Kings also donated clothing and furniture worth $240 to the Salvation Army. They got a receipt and an appraisal and Mary attached a statement to their return. This total is entered on line 17. If the Kings' total noncash charitable contributions had exceeded $500, a Form 8283 would have been completed and attached to the decedent's final income tax return. The Kings' 2013 charitable contributions total $6,742. Since they don't have a carryover from a prior year, Mary enters $6,742 on line 19 of Schedule A [see ¶ 2783].

¶2743

¶2744 SCHEDULE A, LINE 20—CASUALTY AND THEFT LOSSES

If the decedent's property (other than property used in a trade or business) was either stolen or destroyed by a casualty in 2013, the decedent may have suffered a deductible loss. You can deduct only losses for which the decedent was not reimbursed by insurance or otherwise. The decedent's loss for each casualty is deductible only to the extent it exceeds $100. In addition, the decedent's total casualty and theft losses are deductible only to the extent they exceed 10 percent of the decedent's AGI. Because of this limitation, many taxpayers cannot get a tax benefit for their theft and casualty losses.

To compute the decedent's casualty and theft loss, you should fill out Form 4684, and attach the form to Schedule A [see ¶2783]. Report the result on line 20 of Schedule A.

(a) How and When to Deduct. Generally, the decedent can only deduct casualty losses that occurred in 2013 on his or her 2013 return. However, theft losses that the decedent discovered in 2013, even if they occurred earlier, can be deducted on behalf of the decedent. If the decedent suffered a loss in an officially designated disaster area at any time during 2013, he must either file an amended 2012 return and claim the loss against 2012 income, or deduct the loss on the 2013 return.

To figure the amount of the decedent's casualty and theft deduction, start with the difference in value of the property before and after each casualty (up to the amount of the decedent's adjusted basis in the property). If the decedent received an insurance payment to cover the loss, reduce the difference by the amount of the payment. Then reduce the remainder by $100. Finally, add all the decedent's reduced casualty and theft losses for the year and subtract 10 percent of the decedent's AGI (as reported on line 37 of Form 1040). Do these calculations on Form 4684 and report the result on line 20 of the decedent's Schedule A [see ¶2783].

■ The Kings did not have casualty or theft losses in the year of George King's death, so line 20 of Schedule A is left blank.

¶2745 SCHEDULE A, LINE 21—UNREIMBURSED EMPLOYEE EXPENSES

A wide variety of items are deductible as miscellaneous expenses on Schedule A [see ¶2783], including employee business expenses and investment expenses.But most miscellaneous expenses are deductible only to the extent that they total more than 2 percent of the decedent's AGI.

(a) Unreimbursed Employee Business Expenses. Expenses that an employee incurs in connection with his or her job—and that are not paid for by the employer—are generally deductible. These expenses include the following: safety equipment, small tools, and supplies needed for work; uniforms required by the employer that are not suitable for ordinary wear; protective clothing required by the employer; physical exams required by the employer; dues to professional organizations and chambers of commerce; subscriptions to professional journals; fees to employment agencies and other costs to look for a new job in your present occupation, even if you do not get a new job; certain business use of part of your home; certain educational expenses; cost of business travel, professional association dues and entertaining associates.

Executors should compute the amount of the decedent's deduction for unreimbursed employee business expenses on Form 2106 and report the total on line 21 of Schedule A. However, if the decedent is not claiming transportation, travel, meal, or entertainment expenses, and the decedent did not receive a reimbursement for any other employee business expenses, the executor need not complete Form 2106 (or Form 2106-EZ) on behalf of the decedent.

The executor may use Form 2106-EZ if: (1) the decedent was not reimbursed for any expenses by his or her employer; and (2) the executor is claiming vehicle expenses on behalf of the decedent and the decedent owned his or her own vehicle, used the standard mileage rate this year and also used it for the year the vehicle was first placed in service. Deduct the business expenses directly on line 21 of Schedule A [¶ 2783].

> **NOTE:** Self-employed taxpayers report their deductible business expenses on Schedule C, rather than Schedule A.

> ■ *Tax return entry.* Mary King had $5,176 of unreimbursed employee business expenses and enters this amount on line 21 of Schedule A. She need not complete Form 2106 or Form 2106-EZ because she was not claiming transportation, travel, meal, or entertainment expenses, and received no reimbursement for these expenses.

(b) Tax Preparation Fees—Line 22. Enter on line 22 fees paid to a tax professional to prepare a decedent's tax return, including fees paid for filing electronically. If the tax was paid by credit card, do not include the convenience fee you were charged.

(c) Other Expenses—Line 23. Enter on line 23 the total amount paid to produce or collect taxable income and manage or protect property held for earning income. Do not include any personal expenses on this line. List the type and amount of each expense on the dotted line next to line 23. If more space is needed, attach a statement explaining the nature and amount of each expense. Expenses that are reported on line 23 of Schedule A include:

- Legal and accounting fees connected with tax or investment planning.

- Expenses incurred in connection with producing or collecting income, such as safe deposit boxes for storing income-producing securities, custodian fees, and investment advice.

- Clerical help and office rent.

- The taxpayer's share of the investment expenses of a regulated investment company.

- Certain losses on nonfederally insured deposits in an insolvent or bankrupt financial institution.

¶2745

- Casualty and theft losses of property used in performing services as an employee from Form 4684, or Form 4797.

- Deduction for repayment of amounts under a claim of right if $3,000 or less.

- Convenience fee charged by the card processor for paying income tax (including estimated tax payments) by credit or debit card. The deduction is claimed for the year in which the fee was charged to the taxpayer's card.

> ■ *Tax return entry.* In the year of George King's death the Kings paid $250 for a safe deposit box for storing their stocks and bonds. They also paid $936 to their accountant for preparation of their tax return. They enter $936 on line 22 and $250 on line 23.

> *Applying the 2 percent floor.* The Kings add their entries on lines 21, 22, and 23 and enter the total, $6,362, on line 24. They enter their $303,580 of AGI (as reported on line 38 of their Form 1040) on line 25 of Schedule A. They enter 2 percent of their AGI, $6,072, on line 26. Their miscellaneous expenses exceed 2 percent of their AGI by $290. They enter this amount on line 27 of Schedule A.

¶2746 SCHEDULE A—LINE 28—OTHER MISCELLANEOUS DEDUCTIONS

A few miscellaneous expenses are not subject to the 2 percent of AGI floor. If the taxpayer itemizes, these expenses can be claimed as deductions regardless of the amount of the taxpayer's AGI. Other miscellaneous expenses that can be deducted on line 28 of Schedule A include:

- Casualty and theft losses from income-producing property;

- Deduction for repayment of amounts under a claim of right if over $3,000;

- Certain unrecovered investment in a pension;

- Gambling losses (including but not limited to the cost of non-winning bingo, lottery, and raffle tickets), but only to the extent of gambling income;

- Impairment-related job expenses for the handicapped;

- Amortizable bond premium on bonds acquired before October 23, 1986; and

- Federal estate taxes due on income accrued by a deceased taxpayer before death (called income in respect of a decedent).

> ■ In the year of George's death, the Kings had no miscellaneous expenses not subject to the 2 percent floor, so line 28 of Schedule A is left blank.

¶2747 SCHEDULE A—TOTAL ITEMIZED DEDUCTIONS

The last step in completing Schedule A is to compute the amount to enter on line 29 which will be carried over to line 40, Form 1040.

¶2747

If the return preparer for the decedent elects to itemize deductions even though the itemized deductions are less than the standard deduction, the box on line 30 should be checked.

(a) Limitation on Itemized Deductions Reinstated. In 2013, taxpayers are required to reduce the amount of their itemized deductions in 2013 if their adjusted gross income exceeds the following amounts:

- $300,000 if filing a joint return or as a surviving spouse;

- $275,000 if filing as head of household;

- $250,000 if filing as unmarried and not a surviving spouse or head of household; and

- $150,000 if a married individual filing a separate return.

A taxpayer with AGI over these threshold amounts will need to reduce his or her otherwise allowable itemized deductions by the lesser of:

- Three percent of the amount of the taxpayer's AGI in excess of the applicable threshold amount; or

- 80 percent of the itemized deductions otherwise allowable for the tax year. Itemized deductions not subject to the limitation are medical expenses, investment interest expenses, casualty or theft losses, and gambling losses. The amount of itemized deductions that are cut back for regular income tax purposes are not cut back when calculating alternative minimum taxable income (AMTI).

(b) Itemized Deductions Worksheet. Decedents should use the Itemized Deductions Worksheet to compute the amount to enter on line 29 of Schedule A, Itemized Deductions, if the amount on Form 1040, line 38, is over the following thresholds:

- $300,000 if married filing jointly or qualifying widow(er);

- $275,000 if head of household;

- $250,000 if single; or

- $150,000 if married filing separately.

[See ¶2783 for a sample Itemized Deductions Worksheet–Line 29 prepared line-by-line for the decedent, George E. King].

> ■ *Tax return entry.* In order to determine the amount to enter on line 29 of Schedule A, the return preparer for the decedent George King and his surviving spouse must complete the Itemized Deduction Worksheet found in the instructions to Schedule A of Form 1040 because the King's AGI from line 38 of Form 1040 ($303,580) is over the $300,000 threshold for joint filers. After completing the Itemized Deduction Worksheet, they find that their total itemized deductions are $40,596 and this amount is entered on line 29, Schedule A and on line 40 of Form 1040.

¶2747

¶2748 LINE 42—EXEMPTION DEDUCTION

Regardless of when in the year the decedent died, he or she is entitled to a $3,900 deduction in 2013 for each personal or dependency exemption claimed on line 6 of Form 1040. The value of the exemption deduction could be reduced in 2013 depending on the decedent's AGI that year.

(a) Personal Exemption Phaseout Reinstated. Beginning in 2013, taxpayers are required to reduce the amount of their deductions for personal exemptions ($3,900 for 2013) if their AGI exceeds the following threshold levels which are adjusted for inflation after 2013:

- $300,000 if filing a joint return or as a surviving spouse;

- $275,000 if filing as head of household;

- $250,000 if filing as unmarried and not a surviving spouse or head of household; and

- $150,000 if married filing a separate return.

The deduction for personal exemptions will be fully eliminated when AGI exceeds the threshold amount by more than $122,500 ($61,250 in the case of a married individual filing separately). For AMT purposes, there is no deduction for, or in lieu of, personal exemptions. Instead, the amount of personal exemptions actually deducted in calculating taxable income is added back to determine AMTI.

(b) Deduction for Exemptions Worksheet—Line 42. In order to determine the amount to enter on line 42 of Form 1040, the return preparer for the decedent George King and his surviving spouse must complete the Deduction for Exemption Worksheet–Line 42 found in the instructions to Form 1040 because the King's AGI from line 38 of Form 1040 ($303,580) is over the $300,000 threshold for joint filers.

■ *Tax return entry.* The Kings claim 5 exemptions in 2013 and before the reduction, their exemption deduction would be $19,500 (5 × $3,900). After completing the Exemption Worksheet, they find that their total exemption deduction is reduced to $18,720 and this amount is entered on line 42 of Form 1040.

¶2749 LINE 43—TAXABLE INCOME

Subtract the amount of the exemption deduction on line 42 of Form 1040 from the amount on line 41, and enter the result on line 43. This is the decedent's taxable income.

■ The Kings' taxable income is $244,264.

¶2750 LINE 44—FIGURING THE DECEDENT'S PRE-CREDIT TAX

In general, you figure the decedent's tax liability by means of a tax table or tax rate schedule.

(a) High-Bracket Capital Gains. Taxpayers who have net long-term capital gain must use the Schedule D Tax Worksheet to compute their tax in order to take advantage of the lower capital gain tax rates. After computing the amount of tax owed by the taxpayer, enter the result on line 44 of Form 1040.

If you can use the tax tables to figure the decedent's tax bill, no arithmetic computation is required. The tax tables are found in the Instructions for Form 1040. The first two Columns of the tax table list income levels in $50 increments up to $100,000. Simply find the bracket for the decedent's taxable income (from line 43 on Form 1040) and then take the tax figure from the Column for the decedent's filing status.

If the amount of taxable income reported on line 43 exceeds $100,000, you need to consult the tax rate schedules to figure the amount of the decedent's tax. Which schedule is used depends on the filing status selected for the return.

(b) How to Complete Schedule D Tax Worksheet. The Kings have to figure their tax on the Schedule D "Qualified Dividends and Capital Gain Tax Worksheet—Line 44" [see ¶2785] found in the Instructions for Form 1040 because (1) they have a net capital gain, and (2) their taxable income is more than zero.

■ Mary enters the Kings' taxable income (from line 43 of Form 1040), $244,264 on line 1 of the "Dividends and Capital Gain Tax Worksheet" and after following the line-by-line directions ends up with a tax bill in the amount of $56,132, which is entered on line 44 of the Form 1040 [see ¶2782].

¶2751 LINE 44a—FORM 8814—KIDDIE TAX

Kiddie tax. In 2013, the first $1,000 of a child's unearned income is not taxable (this amount is equal to the standard deduction for dependents). The next $1,000 is taxed at the child's tax rate, and the amount greater than $2,000 is taxed at the parents' marginal tax rate.

Therefore, if a child's interest, dividends, and other investment income total more than $2,000 in 2013, part of that income may be taxed at the parent's tax rate instead of the child's tax rate. For these rules, the term "child" includes a legally adopted child and a stepchild. These rules apply whether or not the child is a dependent. Form 8814, "Parent's Election to Report Child's Interest and Dividends" is used by parents who make an election to report their child's income on their return. If a parent makes this election, the child will not have to file a return.

This tax is known as the Kiddie Tax.

■ Because George and Mary King's children had less than $2,000 of investment income in 2013, the kiddie tax is not an issue for them.

¶2752 LINE 44b—FORM 4972—ADDITIONAL TAXES

Complete Form 4972, "Tax on Lump-Sum Distributions," if the decedent received a lump sum distribution from a qualified retirement plan. If you complete this form check box b and enter the amount of tax the decedent owes on line 44.

■ The Kings did not pay this tax, so line 44b is left blank.

¶2753 LINE 45—ALTERNATIVE MINIMUM TAX

The alternative minimum tax (AMT) for individuals was originally enacted to ensure that all taxpayers, especially high-income taxpayers, paid at least a minimum amount of federal taxes. In addition to all other tax liabilities, a taxpayer is subject to the AMT to the extent that the taxpayer's tentative minimum tax exceeds the amount of regular income tax owed. The tentative minimum tax of an individual is generally equal to the sum of: (1) 26 percent of the first $179,500 of the taxpayer's alternative minimum taxable income (AMTI) ($89,750 for a married taxpayer filling a separate return); and (2) 28 percent of the taxpayer's remaining AMTI. AMTI is the individual's regular taxable income recomputed with certain adjustments and increased by certain tax preferences. Individuals pay the alternative minimum tax (AMT) to the extent that it exceeds their regular tax. Generally, alternative minimum taxable income (AMTI) is taxable income, plus or minus AMT adjustments, plus tax preferences.

The AMT exemption amount for individuals is increased for tax years beginning in 2013 to:

- $80,800 for married individuals filing a joint return and surviving spouses;
- $51,900 for unmarried individuals; and
- $40,400 for married individuals filing separate returns.

AMT exemption phaseout amounts. In 2013, the exemption phaseout threshold amounts are $153,900 for joint filers and qualifying widow(er)s, $115,400 for singles or heads-of-household, and $76,950 for married filing separately.

The AMT is figured on Form 6251. If AMTI is less than the exemption amount, no AMT will usually be owed.

■ The Kings owe no AMT.

¶2754 TAX CREDITS—IN GENERAL

Tax credits are amounts that directly reduce a decedent's tax liability. They include the credit for child and dependent care, the credit for the elderly and disabled, the child tax credit, education credits (Hope and Lifetime Learning Credits), retirement savings contribution credit, adoption credit, foreign tax credit, and others. You claim credits on behalf of the decedent on lines 47 through 54 of Form 1040. All the tax credits that a living taxpayer may claim may also be claimed on the final return of the decedent.

¶2755 LINE 47—FOREIGN TAX CREDIT

The foreign tax credit allows taxpayers including decedents to reduce their United States tax by the amount of tax they paid to a foreign country. The foreign tax credit is figured on Form 1116 and the result is reported on line 47 of Form 1040.

■ The Kings do not claim this credit.

¶2756 LINE 48—CHILD AND DEPENDENT CARE CREDIT

The child and dependent care credit gives a decedent a tax break if he or she paid someone to look after a dependent child under age 13 or a disabled dependent or spouse who could not care for himself or herself while the decedent worked. The credit for child and dependent care expenses may be claimed if the decedent paid someone to care for:

- His or her qualifying child under age 13 whom the decedent claimed as a dependent;

- A disabled spouse who could not care for himself or herself;

- Any disabled person not able to care for himself or herself whom the decedent claimed as a dependent (or could have claimed as a dependent except that person received $3,800 or more of gross income or filed a joint return);

- Any disabled person not able to care for himself or herself whom the decedent could have claimed as a dependent except that the decedent, or the decedent's spouse, if filing jointly, could be claimed as a dependent on someone else's 2013 return;

- The decedent's child whom the decedent could not claim as a dependent because of the rules for children or divorced or separated parents.

(a) **What Expenses Qualify.** "Qualified expenses" are defined as expenses for:

- Household services, and

- Caring for a parent if such expenses enabled the decedent to be gainfully employed. A credit may be claimed for expenses for the out-of-home care of a dependent other than a child if: (1) the dependent also spent at least 8 hours a day in the decedent's household; and (2) the care for the dependent was provided in a qualified dependent care center.

The decedent must have incurred the expenses to enable him or her to be gainfully employed either full time or part time. Work also includes actively looking for work. However, if the decedent did not find a job and had no earned income for the year, the credit may not be claimed. If the decedent worked all summer and paid a babysitter to care for a child or sent an under-age-13 child (or children) to day camp so the decedent could work productively, a credit may be claimed for a portion of those fees. Amounts paid for overnight camp do not qualify for the credit.

In 2013, if the decedent had adjusted gross income of less than $15,000, he or she may be able to claim a tax credit of up to 35 percent of up to $3,000 of employment-related expenses if the decedent had one qualifying child or dependent, or $6,000 if the decedent had two or more qualifying children or dependents. This means that taxpayers with incomes under $15,000 may claim a credit as high as $1,050 if they have one qualifying child or dependent and as much as $2,100 if they have two or more qualifying children or dependents. The credit will be reduced to 20 percent of up to $3,000 of "qualified expenses" if the decedent's adjusted gross income exceeds $43,000. These higher-earners may claim a credit of up to $600 if they have one dependent and up to $1,200 if they have two or more dependents. The following table outlines the maximum credits available to taxpayers through 2013:

		Maximum Credits	
Adjusted Gross Income	Applicable Percentage	One Qualifying Individual	Two or More Qualifying Individuals
$15,000 or less	35%	$1,050	$2,100
$15,001–17,000	34%	1,020	2,040
17,001–19,000	33%	990	1,980
19,001–21,000	32%	960	1,920
21,001–23,000	31%	930	1,860
23,001–25,000	30%	900	1,800
25,001–27,000	29%	870	1,740
27,001–29,000	28%	840	1,680
29,001–31,000	27%	810	1,620
31,001–33,000	26%	780	1,560
33,001–35,000	25%	750	1,500
35,001–37,000	24%	720	1,440
37,001–39,000	23%	690	1,380
39,001–41,000	22%	660	1,320
41,001–43,000	21%	630	1,260
43,001 and over	20%	600	1,200

(b) Payments to Relatives. The credit is available for child care payments made to a relative, provided the decedent is not eligible to claim a dependency exemption for the relative. If the relative is the decedent's child, the child must be at least 19 years of age.

(c) Filing Requirements. You compute the amount of the decedent's child and dependent care credit on Form 2441 and enter the result on line 48 of Form 1040. To claim the credit, report the name, address and taxpayer identification number (social security number for individuals; employer identification number for organizations) of the dependent care provider. To get this information, have the provider fill out Form W-10. If unable to furnish this information, you may still claim the credit if you can show to the IRS that you made a genuine effort to provide the information (for example, you retained a copy of the baby sitter's social security card on recently printed letterhead).

¶2756

(d) Special Rules. Married couples are allowed the credit only if they file a joint return. However, married taxpayers living apart are not considered married for this rule if the absent spouse was not a member of the household during the last six months of the tax year. So the spouse incurring the child care expenses can claim the credit even though a joint return is not filed, as long as he or she furnishes more than 50 percent of the cost of maintaining a household that was the principal place of abode of a qualifying individual for over one half of the tax year. For a child of divorced parents, the custodial parent can claim the credit even if that parent agrees to let the noncustodial parent claim the child's dependency exemption.

■ The Kings spent $10,400 on qualified child care expenses for their two children, both of whom were under age 13 at the end of the year. Their employers did not sponsor a dependent care assistance plan, so their child care expenses were not reimbursed. The Kings therefore are entitled to a credit of $1,200 as shown in the chart above. Mary King figures this credit on Form 2441 (not reproduced in this book) and reports the $1,200 total on line 48 of Form 1040.

¶2757 LINE 49—EDUCATION CREDITS

If the decedent or one of the decedent's dependents paid qualified expenses this year for himself, his or her spouse, or dependents to enroll in or attend an eligible educational institution, the decedent may be able to claim an education credit.

The decedent will be unable to claim an education credit if any of the following applies:

- The decedent, or the decedent's spouse if filing jointly, is claimed as a dependent on someone else's 2013 tax return;
- The decedent's filing status is married filing separately;
- The amount on Form 1040, line 38 is $90,000 or more ($180,000 or more if married filing jointly);
- The decedent is claiming a deduction for tuition and fees for the same student; or
- The decedent or the decedent's spouse were nonresident aliens for any part of 2013 unless the decedent's filing status is married filing jointly.

■ George and Mary King were ineligible to claim any education credits and therefore leave line 49 blank.

¶2758 LINE 50—RETIREMENT SAVINGS CONTRIBUTIONS CREDIT (SAVER'S CREDIT)

The decedent may be able to claim a nonrefundable credit of up to $1,000 for qualified contributions made to retirement savings plans in 2013. The decedent will be eligible to claim the credit for: (1) contributions made to a traditional or Roth IRA (other than rollover contributions); (2) elective deferrals to a 401(k), 403(b), 457, SEP, or SIMPLE plan; (3) voluntary employee contributions to a qualified retirement plan (including the Federal Thrift Savings Plan); or (4) voluntary contributions to a 501(c)(18)(D) plan. The credit may be claimed in addition to the exclusion or deduction claimed for making elective deferrals and IRA contributions. To be eligible for the credit, the decedent must have been at least 18 as of the close of the tax year, must *not* be claimed as a dependent on someone else's tax return, and must *not* be a student. The maximum credit rate is 50 percent, which is completely phased out when adjusted gross income exceeds $59,000 for joint return filers, $44,250 for head of household filers, and $29,500 for single and married filing separately filers. Form 8880 must be attached to the tax return where the credit is claimed.

■ *Tax return entry.* The Kings leave line 50 blank.

¶2759 LINE 51—CHILD TAX CREDIT

The decedent may be able to claim a child tax credit worth $1,000 for one or more qualifying child(ren) under the age of 18. The credit begins to phase out for single taxpayers and heads of households with AGI of $75,000 ($110,000 for joint filers and $55,000 for married taxpayers filing separately) and is fully phased out for single taxpayers and heads of households with AGI in excess of $84,000 ($120,000 for joint filers and $64,000 for married taxpayers filing separately).

■ George and Mary King were ineligible to claim the child care credit and therefore leave line 51 blank.

¶2760 LINE 52—RESIDENTIAL ENERGY CREDIT

(a) Nonbusiness Energy Property Credit. The decedent may be able to claim this credit by completing and attaching Form 5695 for any of the following types of improvements to his or her main home located in the United States in 2013 if the improvements are new and meet certain requirements for energy efficiency:

- Any insulation material or system primarily designed to reduce heat gain or loss in the home;
- Exterior windows (including skylights);
- Exterior doors;
- A metal roof or asphalt roof with pigmented coatings or cooling granules primarily designed to reduce the heat gain in the home.

The decedent may be able to claim the credit for the cost of the following items if the items meet certain performance and quality standards:

- Certain electric heat pump water heaters, electric heat pumps, central air conditioners, and natural gas, propane or oil water heaters;
- A qualified furnace or hot water boiler that uses natural gas, propane or oil;
- A stove that burns biomass fuel to heat the home or heat water for use in the home;
- An advanced main air circulating fan used in a natural gas, propane, or oil furnace.

¶2760

If a decedent was a member of a condominium management association for a condominium that the decedent owned or was a tenant-shareholder in a cooperative housing corporation, the decedent is treated as having paid his or her proportionate share of any costs of such association or corporation for purposes of this credit.

(b) Residential Energy Efficient Property Credit. The decedent may be able to claim this credit by completing and attaching Form 5695 if the decedent paid for any of the following during the year:

• Qualified solar electric property for use in his or her home located in the United States;

• Qualified solar water heating property for use in his or her home located in the United States;

• Qualified fuel cell property installed on or in connection with the decedent's main home located in the United States;

• Qualified small wind energy property for use in connection with the decedent's main home located in the United States;

• Qualified geothermal heat pump property installed on or in connection with the decedent's home located in the United States.

If a decedent was a member of a condominium management association for a condominium that the decedent owned or was a tenant-shareholder in a cooperative housing corporation, the decedent is treated as having paid his or her proportionate share of any costs of such association or corporation for purposes of this credit.

¶2761 LINE 53—CREDITS FROM OTHER FORMS

On line 53 include the following credits and check the appropriate boxes. If box c is checked, also enter the form number, if applicable.

• District of Columbia first-time homebuyer credit. See Form 8859;

• General business credit which consists of a number of credits that usually apply only to individuals that are partners, shareholders in an S corporation, self-employed or who have rental property. See Form 3800;

• Credit for prior year alternative minimum tax claimed on Form 8801;

• Qualified plug-in electric vehicle credit. The credit is claimed on Form 8834, Part II and is only available if the decedent had an electric vehicle passive activity credit carried forward from a prior year;

• Qualified plug-in electric drive motor vehicle credit. See Form 8936;

• Credit to holders of tax credit bonds. See Form 8912;

• Alternative motor vehicle credit claimed on Form 8910;

• Alternative fuel vehicle refueling property credit claimed on Form 8911;

• Credit for the elderly or the disabled. See Schedule R;

• Adoption credit. See Form 8839;

• Mortgage interest credit. If a state or local government gave the decedent a mortgage credit certificate, see Form 8396.

¶2761

■ The Kings do not claim any of these credits in the year of George King's death.

¶2762 LINE 54—TOTAL CREDITS

■ The Kings enter $1,200 as their total credits for the year on line 54.

¶2763 LINE 56—SELF-EMPLOYMENT TAX

If the decedent was a sole proprietor or a partner and his or her self-employment income from either the sole proprietorship or the partnership is $400 or more, he or she generally must fill in Schedule SE of Form 1040 and pay self-employment tax. This tax covers Social Security and Medicare benefits for the elderly and disabled.

In 2013, the self-employment tax imposed on self-employed people is:

- 12.4% OASDI on the first $113,700 of self-employment income, for a maximum tax of $14,098.80 (12.40% of $113,700), plus
- 2.90% Medicare tax on the first $200,000 of self-employment income ($250,000 of combined self-employment income on a joint return, $125,000 on a separate return) [IRC Sec. 1401(a), (b)], plus
- 3.8% (2.90% regular Medicare tax + 0.9% additional Medicare tax) on all self-employment income in excess of $200,000 ($250,000 of combined self-employment income on a joint return, $125,000 for married taxpayers filing a separate return).

(a) Schedule SE. Schedule SE has a Section A and a Section B. Section A is the short schedule. Section A is used to figure the tax unless the long schedule in Section B is used. The long schedule is required if the taxpayer (1) has wages as an employee in addition to earnings from self-employment, (2) is a minister or church employee, because the net earnings of such persons from self-employment do not include retirement benefits received from a church plan after retirement and the rental value of a home or an allowance for a home furnished after retirement, (3) has unreported tip income, or (4) wants to use an "optional method" to figure the self-employment tax.

■ Because none of the income earned by the Kings is from self-employment, Schedule SE is not required and line 56 is left blank.

¶2764 LINE 57—SOCIAL SECURITY AND MEDICARE TAX ON TIP INCOME NOT REPORTED TO EMPLOYER

Everybody, including the decedent in the year of death, must pay Social Security and Medicare tax (or Railroad Retirement tax) on earned income. Generally, these taxes are withheld from paychecks by employers. However, if the decedent received more than $20 a month of tip income that was not subject to payroll taxes, because it was not reported to the employer, the decedent must report the additional tax owed on line 57. Figure the amount owed on Form 4137 and Form 8919.

■ The Kings leave this line blank.

¶2765 LINE 58—TAX ON QUALIFIED PLANS, INCLUDING IRAs, AND TAX-FAVORED ACCOUNTS

The decedent may owe a tax reported on line 58 if he or she:

1. Received any early distribution from an IRA or other qualified retirement plan, an annuity or a modified endowment contract entered into after June 20, 1988 and the total distribution was not rolled over in a qualified rollover contribution.

2. Made excess contributions to IRAs, Coverdell education savings accounts, Archer MSAs or health savings accounts.

3. Received taxable distributions from Coverdell ESAs or qualified tuition programs.

4. Were born before July 1, 1942, and did not take the minimum required distribution from your IRA or other qualified retirement plan. Figure the amount of the penalty on Form 5329 and enter the result on line 58 of the Form 1040.

(a) Premature Distributions. Generally, the decedent will be subject to a penalty if he or she withdrew funds from an IRA, retirement plan, or qualified annuity before reaching age $59^1/_2$. These are called premature distributions. However, premature distributions do not include distributions that are: (1) part of a scheduled series of payments spread over the decedent's lifetime; (2) made to early retirees who are at least age 55; (3) made because of death or disability; (4) used to pay medical expenses that would qualify as deductible (i.e., in excess of the 10 percent floor for deductible medical expenses unless either the decedent or the decedent's spouse turned 65 before the end of 2013, in which case the floor is 7.5 percent); (5) used to pay for qualified higher education expenses. This includes tuition at a post-secondary educational institution, as well as room and board, fees, books, supplies, and necessary equipment. The expenses must be incurred by the decedent, his or her spouse, or any child or grandchild of the decedent or his or her spouse.

These payments are exempt from the penalty. Distributions that qualify as "rollovers" are also exempt.

■ None of these situations apply to the Kings, so they do not have to file Form 5329, and line 58 is left blank.

¶2765

¶2766 LINE 59a—HOUSEHOLD EMPLOYMENT TAXES

Employment taxes on wages paid to household employees, such as babysitters, drivers, caretakers, private nurses, nannies, housekeepers, and gardeners, are also reported on Form 1040, line 59b, using Schedule H.

Schedule H must be filed with the decedent's federal income tax return and household employment taxes must be paid on behalf of the decedent if the answer to any of the following questions is "Yes":

1. Did the decedent pay any one household employee cash wages of $1,800 or more in 2013? Cash wages include wages paid by check, money order, etc.
2. Did the decedent withhold federal income tax during 2012 for any household employee?
3. Did the decedent pay total cash wages of $1,000 or more in any calendar quarter of 2012 or 2013 to household employees?

Schedule H can be omitted from the decedent's tax return only if the answer to all three questions is "No."

The decedent does not have to pay Social Security tax if he or she paid wages of less than $1,800 to any household employee in a calendar year. However, if the decedent paid $1,800 or more in wages to any household worker in a calendar year, all wages (including the first $1,800) paid to that employee are subject to the FICA taxes.

The wages of domestic workers under age 18 are exempt from Social Security tax unless domestic work is their principal occupation. Consequently, there is no paperwork to complete or taxes to pay for part-time babysitters under age 18 employed by the decedent, even if the decedent paid them over $1,800 for the year. There is an exception, however, for full-time domestic workers who are under age 18.

> **Example 1:** Mom died on August 1, 2013. Before her death, Mom employed a nurse during the day. The nurse, Emily, was 17 years old. Nursing is a full-time profession. Before her death, Mom paid Emily $12,000. Mom must pay Social Security tax for the nurse.

> ■ The Kings do not employ any household employees or nannies, so line 59a is left blank.

¶2767 LINE 59b—FIRST-TIME HOMEBUYER CREDIT REPAYMENT

On line 59b–First-Time Homebuyer Credit Repayment, enter the first-time homebuyer credit the decedent has to repay.

Form 5405, line 16 (repayment of first-time homebuyer credit). The decedent will have to repay the credit if he or she:

- Disposed of the home within 36 months after buying it;
- Stopped using the home as his or her main home within 36 months after buying it; or
- Bought the home in 2008.

¶2767

See Form 5405 instructions for exceptions to the repayment rule.

■ The Kings did not claim the first-time homebuyer credit so box 59c is left blank.

¶2768   LINE 60 AND LINE 61—OTHER TAX AND TOTAL TAX

Use line 60 of Form 1040 to report any taxes not reported elsewhere on the return or other schedules including the following new taxes which became effective on January 1, 2013.

(a) Additional Medicare Tax on Earned Income. Beginning in 2013, an individual is liable for the 0.9 percent Additional Medicare Tax if the individual's wages, compensation, or self-employment income (together with that of his or her spouse if filing a joint return) exceed the threshold amount for the individual's filing status:

Filing Status	Threshold Amount
Married filing jointly	$250,000
Married filing separate	$125,000
Single	$200,000
Head of household (with qualifying person)	$200,000
Qualifying widow(er) with dependent child	$200,000

Employers are required to withhold from employee's wages and remit the increased employee portion of the Medicare tax to the IRS for each employee whose wages for Medicare tax purposes from the employer are over $200,000 [IRC Sec. 3102(f)(1)]. This rule applies regardless of the employee's filing status or other income. Thus, the employer disregards any amount of wages paid to the employee's spouse or any wages paid to the employee by another employer [Reg. Sec. 31.3202-1(g)(1)]. As a result of this tax, the employee portion of the Medicare tax is increased from 1.45 percent to 2.35 percent on wages received in a calendar year in excess of $200,000 ($250,000 for married couples filing jointly; $125,000 for married filing separately) [IRC Sec. 3101(b)(2)].

Example 1: Harry, who is married and files a joint return, receives $100,000 in wages from his employer for the calendar year. Ida, Harry's spouse, receives $300,000 in wages from her employer for the same calendar year. Harry's wages are not in excess of $200,000, so Harry's employer does not withhold Additional Medicare Tax. Ida's employer is required to collect 0.9 percent Additional Medicare Tax only with respect to wages it pays which are in excess of the $200,000 threshold (that is, $100,000) for the calendar year.

The employee is responsible for paying any of the 0.9 percent Additional Medicare Tax that was not withheld by an employer because the employee's wages were less than $200,000. The employee may still be subject to the 0.9 percent Additional Medicare Tax if, when combined with a spouse's wages, the couple's total wages exceed the $250,000 threshold [IRC Sec. 3102(f)(2); Reg. Sec. 31.3102-1(g)(2)]. Individuals must use Form 8959, "Additional Medicare Tax," to calculate their 0.9 percent Additional Medicare tax liability on line 18 which will be reported on line 60 of Form 1040 after checking Form 1040 box a. The total 0.9 percent Additional Medicare tax withholding (if any) from line 24 should also be included with their federal income tax withholding on line 62 of Form 1040.

The employee cannot request that the additional 0.9% Medicare tax be withheld from wages that are under the $200,000 threshold. However, he or she can make quarterly estimated tax payments or submit a new Form W-4 requesting additional income tax withholding that can offset the additional Medicare tax calculated and reported on the employee's personal income tax return [IRS FAQ 13].

> **Example 2:** Sally and Ann are married and will file a joint tax return in 2013. Sally's 2013 salary is $160,000, and Ann's 2013 wages are $130,000 so their total combined wage income in 2013 is $290,000 ($160,000 + $130,000). Since this amount is over $250,000, they owe the additional 0.9 percent Medicare tax on $40,000 ($290,000 − $250,000). The additional tax due is $360 ($40,000 × 0.9 percent). Neither Sally nor Ann's employer is liable for withholding and remitting the additional tax, because neither of them met the $200,000 wage threshold. Either Sally or Ann (or both) can submit a new Form W-4 to their employer that will result in additional income tax withholding to ensure that the $360 is properly paid during the year. Alternatively, they could make quarterly estimated tax payments. If the amount is not paid until their federal income tax return is filed, they may be responsible for the estimated tax penalty on any underpayment amount (whether the underpayment is actually income taxes or the additional Medicare taxes).

> ■ The decedent George E. King must file Form 8959 to report the 0.9 percent Additional Medicare Tax because the couple's total wages of $281,904 exceed the $250,000 filing threshold for joint filers. They must file Form 8959 even though the Form W-2 furnished by George King's employer, reported compensation of only $101,000 in 2013 and his surviving spouse, Mary King's W-2 indicated that she received compensation in the amount of $180,904 that year because their total compensation of $281,904 exceeds the $250,000 filing threshold for joint filers. [See ¶ 2788 for a completed Form 8959 with line-by-line explanations for the decedent George E. King and surviving spouse Mary King].

(b) Net Investment Income Tax on Unearned Income. Beginning in 2013, individuals are subject to a surtax of 3.8 percent of the lesser of: (1) net investment income, or (2) the excess of modified adjusted gross income (MAGI) over an unindexed threshold amount ($250,000 for joint filers or surviving spouses, $125,000 for a married individual filing a separate return, and $200,000 in any other case). Net investment income may include rental and royalty income, income from partnerships, S corporations and trusts, and income from other passive activities reported on a taxpayer's Schedule E. Taxpayers must use Form 8960, "Net Investment Income Tax—

¶2768

Individuals, Estates, and Trusts," to compute the amount of this tax. [See ¶ 2789 for a completed Form 8960 with line-by-line explanations for the decedent George E. King and surviving spouse Mary King].

In addition to all other taxes owed, there may be other special taxes that must be included in the amount reported on line 60. These include:

- *Recapture of the investment credit* (see Form 4255). Identify on dotted line as "ICR."

- *Recapture of the low-income housing credit* (see Form 8611). Identify on dotted line as "LIHCR."

- *Recapture of qualified plug-in electric drive motor vehicle credit* (see Form 8936). Identify as "8936R."

- *Recapture of the Indian employment credit.* Identify on dotted line as "IECR." See Form 8845.

- *Recapture of the new markets credit.* Identify on dotted line as "NMCR." See Form 8874.

- *Recapture of the credit for employer-provided child care facilities.* Identify on dotted line as "ECCFR." See Form 8882.

- *Recapture of the Federal Mortgage Subsidy.* If the decedent sold his or her home in 2013 and it was financed (in whole or in part) from the proceeds of any tax-exempt qualified mortgage bond or if the decedent claimed the mortgage credit, the decedent must recapture this benefit in 2013 (see Form 8828). Identify on dotted line as "FMSR."

- *Recapture of COBRA premium assistance.* If the decedent received premium assistance under COBRA continuation coverage that covered the decedent, his or her spouse, or any of his or her dependents, and the decedent's modified gross income is more than $125,000 ($250,000 if married filing jointly), see Pub. 502, Medical and Dental Expenses, subsection entitled COBRA Premium Assistance.

- *Recapture of the alternative motor vehicle credit.* Identify as "AMVCR."

- *Recapture of the alternative fuel vehicle refueling property credit.* Identify as "ARPCR."

- *Excess Benefits Tax.* Identify on dotted line as "Sec. 72(m)(5)."

- *Uncollected Social Security and Medicare or RRTA Tax on Tips or Group-Term Life Insurance.* This tax should be shown in box 12 of your Form W-2 with codes A and B or M and N. Identify on dotted line as "UT."

- *Golden Parachute Payments.* If the decedent received an excess parachute payment, a 20 percent tax is due on it. This tax should be shown in box 12 of your W-2 form with code K. If the decedent received a Form 1099-MISC, the tax is 20 percent of the EPP shown in box 13. Identify on dotted line as "EPP."

- *Tax on Accumulation Distribution of Trusts.* Enter the amount from Form 4970 and identify as "ADT."

- *Excise tax on insider stock compensation from an expatriated corporation.* The decedent may owe a 15 percent excise tax on the value of non-statutory stock options and certain other stock-based compensation held by the decedent or a member of his or her family from an expatriated corporation or its expanded affiliated group in which the decedent was an officer, director, or more-than-10 percent owner. Identify as "ISC."

- *Additional tax on health savings account distributions.* Identify as "HSA."

- *Additional tax on an HSA* because the decedent did not remain an eligible individual during the testing period. Identify as "HDHP."

- *Additional tax on Archer MSA distributions.* Identify as "MSA."

- *Additional tax on Medicare Advantage MSA distributions.* Identify as "Med MSA."

- *Additional tax on income the decedent received from a nonqualified deferred compensation plan that fails to meet certain requirements.* Identify as "NQDC."

- *Interest on the tax due on installment income from the sale of certain residential lots and timeshares.* Identify as "453(l)(3)" or "453A(c)," whichever applies.

- Interest on the deferred tax on gain from certain installment sales with sales price over $150,000. Identify as "453A(c)."

- *Additional tax on recapture of a charitable contribution deduction relating to a fractional interest in tangible property.* Identify as "FITPP."

- *Look-back interest under IRC Sec. 167(g) or IRC Sec. 460(b).*

- Any negative amount on Form 8885, line 7, because of advance payments of the health coverage tax credit the decedent received for months he or she was not eligible. Enter additional tax as a positive amount. Identify as "HCTC."

- Additional tax on compensation received from a nonqualified deferred compensation plan described in IRC Sec. 457A if the compensation would have been includible in income in an earlier year except that the amount was not determinable until 2013. The tax is 20 percent of the amount required to be included in income plus an interest amount determined under IRC Sec. 457A(c)(2). Identify as "457A."

- Tax on noneffectively connected income for any part of the year you were a nonresident alien. Identify as "From Form 1040NR."

■ Other than the entries from Form 8959 and Form 8960, the decedent George E. King and his surviving spouse Mary King do not owe any of the special taxes listed for line 60. Therefore, the return preparer checks box 60a on Form 8959 and box 60b on Form 8960 and adds a total tax of $926 which is the total of the tax due from both forms ($287 from line 18 of Form 8959 and $639 from line 17 of Form 8960).

¶2769 LINE 62—FEDERAL INCOME TAX WITHHELD

The decedent's final tax bill can be reduced by having taxes withheld from salary (as reported in box 2 of Form W-2), gambling winnings (from box 2 of Form W-2G), pension payments (from box 4 of Form 1099-R), or investment income (from box 2 of Form 1099-DIV, or box 4 of any other 1099 form). To do this, enter the total of all amounts withheld on line 61. If any of the amounts withheld were reported on a 1099-R form, attach a copy of the form to the return. Also attach a copy of Form W-2 or Form W-2G.

■ George's employer withheld $20,000 from his paycheck for federal income tax. Mary's employer withheld $10,000 from her salary for federal income tax. Mary enters the total, $30,000, on line 61 and attaches Copy B of both Form W-2s to the final return.

¶2770   LINE 63—ESTIMATED TAX PAYMENTS

A taxpayer who has died need not make quarterly estimated tax payments, but the taxpayer's surviving spouse remains liable for payment of any subsequent installments of joint estimated tax unless the surviving spouse creates an amended payment voucher stating the separate estimated tax for the tax year.

The decedent's ultimate tax bill can be offset by any estimated tax he or she paid during the year of death. When a joint income tax return is filed for the decedent and the surviving spouse, credit may be claimed by the surviving spouse for all estimated tax installments paid by either spouse.

If the spouses made joint payments of estimated taxes, but a joint return is not filed for the decedent and the surviving spouse, the estimated tax payments may be divided between the surviving spouse and the decedent's executor as agreed upon by the parties. If the parties cannot agree, the special allocation rule will apply. Accordingly, the surviving spouse will be entitled to that portion of the total amount of estimated tax payments as the amount of tax on the surviving spouse's separate tax return bears to the combined taxes shown on the separate returns of the surviving spouse and the decedent [Reg. Sec. 1.6654-2(e)(1)].

Example 1: Prior to Dad's death, Mom and Dad made total joint estimated tax payments of $20,000. Dad's executor decides to file Dad's final income tax return as married filing separately. The tax owed on Mom's separate return was $10,000. The tax owed on Dad's final return, filed separately, was $30,000. Mom is entitled to take a credit of $5,000 for the estimated tax payments ($10,000/$40,000 × $20,000 = $5,000).

Enter the amount of 2013 estimated tax paid by the decedent and the amount applied from the 2012 return on line 63.

■ Prior to his death, George King paid $12,000 in estimated tax payments for 2013. This amount is entered on line 63 of the final return filed for the decedent George E. and Mary King.

¶2771   LINES 64a AND 64b—EARNED INCOME CREDIT/NONTAXABLE COMBAT PAY ELECTION

The decedent may be eligible for the earned income credit even though he or she lived less than the full tax year. The earned income credit can be claimed by low-income taxpayers who work. The taxpayer need not have children living at home to qualify for the credit. To claim the credit on line 64a, Schedule EIC must be attached to Form 1040.

Nontaxable combat pay. If the decedent was a member of the U.S. Armed Forces who served in a combat zone, certain pay is excluded from his or her income. An election can be made to include this pay in earned income when figuring the EIC. The amount of the decedent's nontaxable combat pay should be shown in box 12 of Form(s) W-2 with code Q. If the decedent is filing a joint return and both the decedent and his or her spouse received nontaxable combat pay, they can each make their own election.

■ The Kings' income was too high to claim the EIC, so line 64a is left blank.

¶2772 LINE 65—ADDITIONAL CHILD TAX CREDIT

The executor may be able to claim the additional child tax credit on behalf of the decedent on line 65 if the decedent had three or more qualifying children. The additional child tax credit may result in a refund even if the decedent did not owe any tax. See discussion accompanying line 53 (¶ 2761). Use Form 8812 to compute the amount of the credit.

¶2773 LINE 66—AMERICAN OPPORTUNITY CREDIT

Use Form 8863, Education Credits (American Opportunity and Lifetime Learning Credits) to figure and claim the American Opportunity Credit which are based on qualified education expenses paid to an eligible postsecondary educational institution.

■ The Kings are not entitled to a refund of this credit.

¶2774 LINE 67—RESERVED

Line 47 on Form 1040 has been reserved for future use.

¶2775 LINE 68—AMOUNT PAID WITH EXTENSION TO FILE REQUEST

To obtain an automatic six-month (four, if out of the country) extension of time to file the decedent's final income tax return, file Form 4868 on or before April 15, 2010, and pay the tax that you expect the decedent to owe. To get credit for this payment on the return, enter the amount paid with Form 4868 on line 68.

■ The Kings did not apply for a filing extension, so they make no entry on line 68.

¶2776 LINE 69—EXCESS SOCIAL SECURITY AND TIER 1 RRTA TAX WITHHELD

If the decedent or his or her spouse is filing a joint return, had more than one employer in 2013 and together the employers paid them more than $113,700 in 2013 too much Social Security tax may have been withheld from their wages. A credit may be claimed on line 69 for the amount withheld in excess of $7,049.40. Figure the amount separately for the decedent and his or her spouse. There is a corresponding rule for railroad employees. To claim a refund for excess tier 2 railroad retirement tax, file Form 843.

■ Neither of the Kings worked for more than one employer in the year of George's death, so line 69 is left blank.

¶2777 LINE 70 AND LINE 71—OTHER CREDITS

If the decedent is entitled to a credit for the federal tax on fuels, include this amount on line 70 and attach a completed Form 4136 to the return.

Check the box(es) on line 71 to report any credit from Forms 2439, 8801 (line 27), or 8885. If you claim more than one of these credits, enter the total on line 71. If claiming a credit for repayment of amounts already included in income in an earlier year because it appeared the decedent had a right to the income, include the credit on line 71 and enter "IRC 1341" to the right of line 71.

■ The Kings do not claim either of these credits.

¶2778 LINES 73 THROUGH 75—REFUND OR BALANCE DUE

If the amount of taxes paid exceeds the total tax that is owed, enter the amount overpaid on line 73. Enter the amount of the overpayment to be refunded on line 74a.

(a) Steps to Follow to Obtain a Refund. You can obtain a refund on behalf of the decedent by following these procedures:

• If you are the decedent's spouse filing a joint return with the decedent, file only the decedent's final income tax return to claim the refund.

• If you are the decedent's personal representative, and the return is not a joint return filed with the decedent's surviving spouse, file the return and attach a copy of the certificate that shows your appointment by the court. (Keep in mind that a power of attorney or a copy of the decedent's is not acceptable proof of your appointment as the personal representative.) If you are filing an amended return, attach Form 1310, "Statement of Person Claiming Refund Due a Deceased Taxpayer," and a copy of the certificate of appointment. If you have already sent the certificate of appointment to the IRS, write "Certificate Previously Filed" at the bottom of Form 1310.

- If you are not filing a joint return as the surviving spouse and a personal representative has not been appointed, file the return and attach Form 1310 and proof of death. A copy of the death certificate will suffice.

  NOTE: Form 1310 cannot be used to claim a return of income taxes that have been paid on a previously filed return.

(b) How to Have the Refund Deposited. Instead of waiting for a check from the IRS to arrive, you can elect to have the refund deposited directly into the bank account of the surviving spouse (if a joint return was filed) or into the estate's bank account. To do so, instead of filing Form 8888 with the return for direct deposit of the refund, put the necessary account information on lines 73b, c, and d of the return. Contact the decedent's financial institution to obtain the correct routing number and account number.

Direct deposit of refunds. Taxpayers who choose direct deposit of their refunds can split their refunds among up to three accounts held by up to three different U.S. financial institutions, such as banks, mutual funds, brokerage firms or credit unions. To split their direct-deposit refunds among two or three different accounts of financial institutions, taxpayers should complete the new Form 8888, "Direct Deposit of Refund to More Than One Account." Taxpayers can also continue to use the direct deposit line on the Forms 1040 to electronically send their refunds to one account.

(c) What if the Decedent Owes Taxes. On the other hand, if the amount of tax that the decedent owes exceeds the amount already paid to the IRS, attach a check or money order for the full amount payable to the "United States Treasury." To help the IRS process your check, they ask that you enter the amount on the right side of the check like this: $XXX.XX. Do not use dashes or lines.

  ▶ **CAUTION:** Do not write just "IRS" on the check or money order. This could easily be changed to MRS. So-and-so if the check should fall into the wrong hands.

Be sure to write the decedent's or the surviving spouse's Social Security number, name, address, daytime phone number, and "2013 Form 1040" on the check or money order. Do not send cash. Complete Form 1040-V, "Payment Voucher," following the instructions on that form, and enclose it in the envelope with the tax payment.

(d) Tax Forgiveness for Deaths Due to Military or Terrorist Actions. The decedent's income tax liability may be forgiven if his or her death was due to service in a combat zone or to military or terrorist actions. For detailed discussion, see ¶2612.

  ■ On the final return filed by the decedent George E. and Mary King, the tax owed exceeds the total tax payments by $13,858. This amount is entered on line 76 and the executor for his estate, his surviving spouse, Mary King sends the IRS a check for this amount.

¶2778

¶2779 SIGNATURES

If an executor has been appointed, he or she must sign the decedent's final income tax return. If the final return is filed jointly with the surviving spouse, the surviving spouse must also sign the return.

Example 1: At the bottom of the return, the executor would sign "Frank Able, Administrator of the Estate of Betty Able, Deceased."

If the return is a joint return, both the executor and the surviving spouse should sign. If no administrator has been appointed, the surviving spouse should sign the return as the taxpayer and write in the signature area "Filing as surviving spouse." The surviving spouse should enter the date and his or her occupation.

If no personal representative has been appointed and there is no surviving spouse, the person in charge of the decedent's property must file and sign the return as "personal representative."

■ The executor of George's estate, his wife, Mary King, filed a joint return with her deceased husband. Mary signed the return on the "Your signature" line. She dated the return and wrote her occupation to the right of the date. On the spouse's signature line, she wrote, "Filing as surviving spouse."

¶2780 HOW TO PROMPTLY CLOSE THE ESTATE

If the executor wants to expedite the closing of the estate, he or she may request a prompt assessment of the decedent's income tax [IRC Sec. 6501(d)]. To request a prompt assessment of tax, file Form 4810 after filing the decedent's final return.

If Form 4810 is not used, you must clearly indicate that you are requesting a prompt assessment under IRC Sec. 6501(d) and specify the year(s) involved. File the request for prompt assessment separately from the decedent's final return. Address your request to the District Director and send it to the IRS office where the decedent's final return was filed.

Normally, the IRS has three years from the date an income tax return is filed (or due, if later) to assess additional tax. After the IRS has received the Form 4810, it has only 18 months to make an assessment.

By requesting a speedy assessment, the estate could be settled earlier and money and property distributed sooner to beneficiaries. This could be important if the surviving family members are strapped for cash.

▶ **CAUTION:** There is no relief available for fraud. Just because you request a prompt assessment of tax, do not assume that you have completely tied the hands of the IRS. The IRS can still come after you beyond the three years from the date the return was filed or due if (1) additional tax is owed because of a substantial omission of income or (2) a fraudulent return was filed.

¶2779

¶2781 RELEASE FROM PERSONAL LIABILITY

The executor can apply in writing for a discharge of personal liability under IRC Sec. 6905(a) after all relevant tax returns have been filed. The request can be filed on Form 5495. If Form 5495 is not used, the executor must clearly indicate that the request is for discharge from personal liability under IRC Sec. 6905.

Within nine months after receipt of the request, the IRS will notify the executor of the amount of taxes due. When this amount is paid, the executor will be discharged from personal liability for any future deficiencies. If the IRS fails to respond within nine months after the request is filed, the executor will still be discharged from personal liability at the end of the nine-month period [Reg. Sec. 301.6905-1(a)].

> ▶ **CAUTION:** Keep in mind that a release from personal liability will not relieve the estate from liability if there are assets in the executor's control or possession.

The executor should also notify the IRS of a termination of the fiduciary relationship on Form 56, "Notice Concerning Fiduciary Relation."

¶2782 FORM 1040, "U.S. INDIVIDUAL INCOME TAX RETURN" FOR DECEASED—GEORGE E. KING—JULY 1, 2013 AND DEDUCTION FOR EXEMPTIONS WORKSHEET—LINE 42

Form **1040**	Department of the Treasury—Internal Revenue Service (99)	**20 13**	OMB No. 1545-0074	IRS Use Only—Do not write or staple in this space.

U.S. Individual Income Tax Return

For the year Jan. 1–Dec. 31, 2013, or other tax year beginning _____ , 2013, ending _____ , 20 ____   See separate instructions.

Your first name and initial	Last name	Your social security number
George E. (deceased 7/01/2013)	King	1 0 0 0 9 0 6 0 3
If a joint return, spouse's first name and initial	Last name	Spouse's social security number
Mary M.	King	0 3 8 2 4 2 9 1 7

Home address (number and street). If you have a P.O. box, see instructions.   Apt. no.
189 Main Street

▲ Make sure the SSN(s) above and on line 6c are correct.

City, town or post office, state, and ZIP code. If you have a foreign address, also complete spaces below (see instructions).
Kansas City, Missouri 64138

Presidential Election Campaign
Check here if you, or your spouse if filing jointly, want $3 to go to this fund. Checking a box below will not change your tax or refund.   ☐ You ☐ Spouse

Foreign country name	Foreign province/state/county	Foreign postal code

Filing Status
Check only one box.

1 ☐ Single
2 ☑ Married filing jointly (even if only one had income)
3 ☐ Married filing separately. Enter spouse's SSN above and full name here. ▶
4 ☐ Head of household (with qualifying person). (See instructions.) If the qualifying person is a child but not your dependent, enter this child's name here. ▶
5 ☐ Qualifying widow(er) with dependent child

Exemptions

6a ☑ Yourself. If someone can claim you as a dependent, **do not** check box 6a
b ☑ Spouse

Boxes checked on 6a and 6b	2

c Dependents:

(1) First name Last name	(2) Dependent's social security number	(3) Dependent's relationship to you	(4) ✓ if child under age 17 qualifying for child tax credit (see instructions)
Julia A. King	1 0 0 4 2 4 8 8 8	Daughter	☐
Leonard B. King	9 9 0 7 7 6 3 8 7	Son	☐
Jane B. Trent	3 5 3 9 3 9 3 9 3	Mother	☐

If more than four dependents, see instructions and check here ▶ ☐

No. of children on 6c who:
• lived with you   2
• did not live with you due to divorce or separation (see instructions)
Dependents on 6c not entered above   1
Add numbers on lines above ▶   5

d Total number of exemptions claimed

Income

Attach Form(s) W-2 here. Also attach Forms W-2G and 1099-R if tax was withheld.

If you did not get a W-2, see instructions.

7	Wages, salaries, tips, etc. Attach Form(s) W-2	7	281,904
8a	Taxable interest. Attach Schedule B if required	8a	1,806
b	Tax-exempt interest. **Do not** include on line 8a	8b	7,500
9a	Ordinary dividends. Attach Schedule B if required	9a	8,000
b	Qualified dividends	9b	
10	Taxable refunds, credits, or offsets of state and local income taxes	10	
11	Alimony received	11	
12	Business income or (loss). Attach Schedule C or C-EZ	12	
13	Capital gain or (loss). Attach Schedule D if required. If not required, check here ▶ ☐	13	4,870
14	Other gains or (losses). Attach Form 4797	14	
15a	IRA distributions	15a	b Taxable amount	15b	
16a	Pensions and annuities	16a	b Taxable amount	16b	
17	Rental real estate, royalties, partnerships, S corporations, trusts, etc. Attach Schedule E	17	7,000
18	Farm income or (loss). Attach Schedule F	18	
19	Unemployment compensation	19	
20a	Social security benefits	20a	b Taxable amount	20b	
21	Other income. List type and amount	21	
22	Combine the amounts in the far right column for lines 7 through 21. This is your **total income** ▶	22	303,580

Adjusted Gross Income

23	Educator expenses	23	
24	Certain business expenses of reservists, performing artists, and fee-basis government officials. Attach Form 2106 or 2106-EZ	24	
25	Health savings account deduction. Attach Form 8889	25	
26	Moving expenses. Attach Form 3903	26	
27	Deductible part of self-employment tax. Attach Schedule SE	27	
28	Self-employed SEP, SIMPLE, and qualified plans	28	
29	Self-employed health insurance deduction	29	
30	Penalty on early withdrawal of savings	30	
31a	Alimony paid b Recipient's SSN ▶	31a	
32	IRA deduction	32	
33	Student loan interest deduction	33	
34	Tuition and fees. Attach Form 8917	34	
35	Domestic production activities deduction. Attach Form 8903	35	
36	Add lines 23 through 35	36	
37	Subtract line 36 from line 22. This is your **adjusted gross income** ▶	37	303,580

For Disclosure, Privacy Act, and Paperwork Reduction Act Notice, see separate instructions.   Cat. No. 11320B   Form **1040** (2013)

¶2782

Form 1040 (2013)   Page **2**

Tax and Credits	38	Amount from line 37 (adjusted gross income)		38	303,580
	39a	Check if: ☐ **You** were born before January 2, 1949, ☐ Blind. ☐ **Spouse** was born before January 2, 1949, ☐ Blind. **Total boxes checked ▶ 39a**			
Standard Deduction for—	b	If your spouse itemizes on a separate return or you were a dual-status alien, check here▶ **39b**☐			
	40	**Itemized deductions** (from Schedule A) **or** your **standard deduction** (see left margin) . .		40	40,596
• People who check any box on line 39a or 39b **or** who can be claimed as a dependent, see instructions.	41	Subtract line 40 from line 38		41	262,984
	42	**Exemptions.** If line 38 is $150,000 or less, multiply $3,900 by the number on line 6d. Otherwise, see instructions		42	18,720
	43	**Taxable income.** Subtract line 42 from line 41. If line 42 is more than line 41, enter -0- . .		43	244,264
	44	**Tax** (see instructions). Check if any from: **a** ☐ Form(s) 8814 **b** ☐ Form 4972 **c** ☐ ____		44	56,132
• All others:	45	**Alternative minimum tax** (see instructions). Attach Form 6251		45	
Single or Married filing separately, $6,100	46	Add lines 44 and 45 . . . . ▶		46	56,132
	47	Foreign tax credit. Attach Form 1116 if required	47		
Married filing jointly or Qualifying widow(er), $12,200	48	Credit for child and dependent care expenses. Attach Form 2441	48	1,200	
	49	Education credits from Form 8863, line 19	49		
	50	Retirement savings contributions credit. Attach Form 8880	50		
Head of household, $8,950	51	Child tax credit. Attach Schedule 8812, if required . . .	51		
	52	Residential energy credits. Attach Form 5695 . . .	52		
	53	Other credits from Form: **a** ☐ 3800 **b** ☐ 8801 **c** ☐	53		
	54	Add lines 47 through 53. These are your **total credits**		54	1,200
	55	Subtract line 54 from line 46. If line 54 is more than line 46, enter -0- . . . . ▶		55	54,932
Other Taxes	56	Self-employment tax. Attach Schedule SE		56	
	57	Unreported social security and Medicare tax from Form: **a** ☐ 4137 **b** ☐ 8919		57	
	58	Additional tax on IRAs, other qualified retirement plans, etc. Attach Form 5329 if required . .		58	
	59a	Household employment taxes from Schedule H		59a	
	b	First-time homebuyer credit repayment. Attach Form 5405 if required		59b	
	60	Taxes from: **a** ☑ Form 8959 **b** ☑ Form 8960 **c** ☐ Instructions; enter code(s) _____		60	926
	61	Add lines 55 through 60. This is your **total tax** . . . . ▶		61	55,858
Payments	62	Federal income tax withheld from Forms W-2 and 1099 .	62	30,000	
	63	2013 estimated tax payments and amount applied from 2012 return	63	12,000	
If you have a qualifying child, attach Schedule EIC.	64a	**Earned income credit (EIC)**	64a		
	b	Nontaxable combat pay election **64b**			
	65	Additional child tax credit. Attach Schedule 8812	65		
	66	American opportunity credit from Form 8863, line 8 . . .	66		
	67	Reserved	67		
	68	Amount paid with request for extension to file	68		
	69	Excess social security and tier 1 RRTA tax withheld . . .	69		
	70	Credit for federal tax on fuels. Attach Form 4136 . . .	70		
	71	Credits from Form: **a** ☐ 2439 **b** ☐ Reserved **c** ☐ 8885 **d** ☐	71		
	72	Add lines 62, 63, 64a, and 65 through 71. These are your **total payments** . . . . ▶		72	42,000
Refund	73	If line 72 is more than line 61, subtract line 61 from line 72. This is the amount you **overpaid**		73	
	74a	Amount of line 73 you want **refunded to you.** If Form 8888 is attached, check here . ▶ ☐		74a	
Direct deposit? ▶ See instructions.	b	Routing number ___ ▶ **c** Type: ☐ Checking ☐ Savings			
	d	Account number			
	75	Amount of line 73 you want **applied to your 2014 estimated tax** ▶	75		
Amount You Owe	76	**Amount you owe.** Subtract line 72 from line 61. For details on how to pay, see instructions ▶		76	13,858
	77	Estimated tax penalty (see instructions)	77		

Third Party Designee	Do you want to allow another person to discuss this return with the IRS (see instructions)? ☐ **Yes.** Complete below. ☐ **No**
	Designee's name ▶ _____ Phone no. ▶ _____ Personal identification number (PIN) ▶ ☐☐☐☐☐

Sign Here	Under penalties of perjury, I declare that I have examined this return and accompanying schedules and statements, and to the best of my knowledge and belief, they are true, correct, and complete. Declaration of preparer (other than taxpayer) is based on all information of which preparer has any knowledge.
Joint return? See instructions. Keep a copy for your records.	Your signature _____ Date _____ Your occupation _____ Daytime phone number _____
	Spouse's signature. If a joint return, **both** must sign. _____ Date _____ Spouse's occupation _____ If the IRS sent you an Identity Protection PIN, enter it here (see inst.) ☐☐☐☐☐☐

Paid Preparer Use Only	Print/Type preparer's name _____ Preparer's signature _____ Date _____ Check ☐ if self-employed PTIN _____
	Firm's name ▶ _____ Firm's EIN ▶ _____
	Firm's address ▶ _____ Phone no. _____

Form **1040** (2013)

2013 Form 1040—Lines 42 and 44

Deduction for Exemptions Worksheet—Line 42

Keep for Your Records

1.	Is the amount on Form 1040, line 38, more than the amount shown on line 4 below for your filing status?		
	☐ **No.** (STOP) Multiply $3,900 by the total number of exemptions claimed on Form 1040, line 6d, and enter the result on line 42.		
	☑ **Yes. Continue.**		
2.	Multiply $3,900 by the total number of exemptions claimed on Form 1040, line 6d	**2.**	19,500
3.	Enter the amount from Form 1040, line 38 .... **3.**	303,580	
4.	Enter the amount shown below for your filing status.		
	• Single —$250,000		
	• Married filing jointly or qualifying widow(er)—$300,000	**4.**	300,000
	• Married filing separately—$150,000		
	• Head of household—$275,000		
5.	Subtract line 4 from line 3. If the result is more than $122,500 ($61,250 if married filing separately), (STOP) Enter -0- on line 42 .... **5.**	3,580	
6.	Divide line 5 by $2,500 ($1,250 if married filing separately). If the result is not a whole number, increase it to the next higher whole number (for example, increase .00004 to 1) .... **6.**	2	
7.	Multiply line 6 by 2% (.02) and enter the result as a decimal .... **7.**		.04
8.	Multiply line 2 by line 7 .... **8.**		780
9.	**Deduction for exemptions.** Subtract line 8 from line 2. Enter the result here and on Form 1040, line 42 .... **9.**		18,720

Line 44

Tax

Include in the total on line 44 all of the following taxes that apply.

• Tax on your taxable income. Figure the tax using one of the methods described here.

• Tax from Form(s) 8814 (relating to the election to report child's interest or dividends). Check the appropriate box.

• Tax from Form 4972 (relating to lump-sum distributions). Check the appropriate box.

• Tax due to making a section 962 election (the election made by a domestic shareholder of a controlled foreign corporation to be taxed at corporate rates). See section 962 for details. Check box c and enter the amount and "962" in the space next to that box. Attach a statement showing how you figured the tax.

• Recapture of an education credit. You may owe this tax if you claimed an education credit in an earlier year, and either tax-free educational assistance or a refund of qualified expenses was received in 2013 for the student. See Form 8863 for more details. Check box c and enter the amount and "ECR" in the space next to that box.

• Any tax from Form 8621, line 16e, relating to a section 1291 fund. Check box c and enter the amount of the tax and "1291" in the space next to that box.

Do you want the IRS to figure the tax on your taxable income for you?

☐ **Yes.** See chapter 30 of Pub. 17 for details, including who is eligible and what to do. If you have paid too much, we will send you a refund. If you did not pay enough, we will send you a bill.

☐ **No.** Use one of the following methods to figure your tax.

Tax Table or Tax Computation Worksheet. If your taxable income is less than $100,000, you must use the Tax Table, later in these instructions, to figure your tax. Be sure you use the correct column. If your taxable income is $100,000 or more, use the Tax Computation Worksheet right after the Tax Table.

However, do not use the Tax Table or Tax Computation Worksheet to figure your tax if any of the following applies.

Form 8615. Form 8615 generally must be used to figure the tax for any child who had more than $2,000 of unearned income, such as taxable interest, ordinary dividends, or capital gains (including capital gain distributions), and who either:

1. Was under age 18 at the end of 2013,

¶2782

¶2783 SCHEDULE A—ITEMIZED DEDUCTIONS;
ITEMIZED DEDUCTION WORKSHEET—LINE 29;
SCHEDULE B—INTEREST AND DIVIDEND
INCOME

SCHEDULE A	Itemized Deductions	OMB No. 1545-0074
(Form 1040)	► Information about Schedule A and its separate instructions is at *www.irs.gov/schedulea*.	2013
Department of the Treasury Internal Revenue Service (99)	► Attach to Form 1040.	Attachment Sequence No. 07

Name(s) shown on Form 1040: George E (deceased) and Mary M. King   Your social security number: 100-09-0603

Medical and Dental Expenses		Caution. Do not include expenses reimbursed or paid by others.			
	1	Medical and dental expenses (see instructions)	1		
	2	Enter amount from Form 1040, line 38	2		
	3	Multiply line 2 by 10% (.10). But if either you or your spouse was born before January 2, 1949, multiply line 2 by 7.5% (.075) instead	3		
	4	Subtract line 3 from line 1. If line 3 is more than line 1, enter -0-		4	-0-
Taxes You Paid	5	State and local (check only one box): a ☑ Income taxes, or b ☐ General sales taxes	5	7,807	
	6	Real estate taxes (see instructions)	6	5,297	
	7	Personal property taxes	7		
	8	Other taxes. List type and amount ►	8		
	9	Add lines 5 through 8		9	13,104
Interest You Paid Note. Your mortgage interest deduction may be limited (see instructions).	10	Home mortgage interest and points reported to you on Form 1098	10	11,000	
	11	Home mortgage interest not reported to you on Form 1098. If paid to the person from whom you bought the home, see instructions and show that person's name, identifying no., and address ►	11		
	12	Points not reported to you on Form 1098. See instructions for special rules	12		
	13	Mortgage insurance premiums (see instructions)	13		
	14	Investment interest. Attach Form 4952 if required. (See instructions.)	14	9,567	
	15	Add lines 10 through 14		15	20,567
Gifts to Charity If you made a gift and got a benefit for it, see instructions.	16	Gifts by cash or check. If you made any gift of $250 or more, see instructions	16	6,502	
	17	Other than by cash or check. If any gift of $250 or more, see instructions. You **must** attach Form 8283 if over $500	17	240	
	18	Carryover from prior year	18		
	19	Add lines 16 through 18		19	6,742
Casualty and Theft Losses	20	Casualty or theft loss(es). Attach Form 4684. (See instructions.)		20	-0-
Job Expenses and Certain Miscellaneous Deductions	21	Unreimbursed employee expenses—job travel, union dues, job education, etc. Attach Form 2106 or 2106-EZ if required. (See instructions.) ►	21	5,176	
	22	Tax preparation fees	22	936	
	23	Other expenses—investment, safe deposit box, etc. List type and amount ►	23	250	
	24	Add lines 21 through 23	24	6,362	
	25	Enter amount from Form 1040, line 38	25	303,580	
	26	Multiply line 25 by 2% (.02)	26	6,072	
	27	Subtract line 26 from line 24. If line 26 is more than line 24, enter -0-		27	290
Other Miscellaneous Deductions	28	Other—from list in instructions. List type and amount ►		28	-0-
Total Itemized Deductions	29	Is Form 1040, line 38, over $150,000? ☐ **No.** Your deduction is not limited. Add the amounts in the far right column for lines 4 through 28. Also, enter this amount on Form 1040, line 40. ☑ **Yes.** Your deduction may be limited. See the Itemized Deductions Worksheet in the instructions to figure the amount to enter.		29	40,596
	30	If you elect to itemize deductions even though they are less than your standard deduction, check here ► ☐			

For Paperwork Reduction Act Notice, see Form 1040 instructions.   Cat. No. 17145C   Schedule A (Form 1040) 2013

¶2783

Itemized Deductions Worksheet—Line 29   *Keep for Your Records*

1.	Enter the total of the amounts from Schedule A, lines 4, 9, 15, 19, 20, 27, and 28	1. 40,703
2.	Enter the total of the amount from Schedule A, lines 4, 14, and 20, plus any gambling and casualty or theft losses included on line 28	2. 9,567

⚠ **CAUTION**   Be sure your total gambling and casualty or theft losses are clearly identified on the dotted lines next to line 28.

3.	Is the amount on line 2 less than the amount on line 1?	
	☐ **No.** 🛑 Your deduction is not limited. Enter the amount from line 1 above on Schedule A, line 29. **Do not** complete the rest of this worksheet.	
	☒ **Yes.** Subtract line 2 from line 1	3. 31,136
4.	Multiply line 3 by 80% (.80)	4. 24,909
5.	Enter the amount from Form 1040, line 38	5. 303,580
6.	Enter $300,000 if married filing jointly or qualifying widow(er); $275,000 if head of household; $250,000 if single; or $150,000 if married filing separately	6. 300,000
7.	Is the amount on line 6 less than the amount on line 5?	
	☐ **No.** 🛑 Your deduction is not limited. Enter the amount from line 1 above on Schedule A, line 29. **Do not** complete the rest of this worksheet.	
	☒ **Yes.** Subtract line 6 from line 5	7. 3,580
8.	Multiply line 7 by 3% (.03)	8. 107
9.	Enter the **smaller** of line 4 or line 8	9. 107
10.	**Total itemized deductions.** Subtract line 9 from line 1. Enter the result here and on Schedule A, line 29	10. 40,596

A-13

SCHEDULE B (Form 1040A or 1040) Department of the Treasury Internal Revenue Service (99)	Interest and Ordinary Dividends ▶ Attach to Form 1040A or 1040. ▶ Information about Schedule B (Form 1040A or 1040) and its instructions is at *www.irs.gov/scheduleb*.	OMB No. 1545-0074 2013 Attachment Sequence No. 08

Name(s) shown on return	Your social security number
George E. (Deceased) and Mary M. King	100-09-0603

Part I

Interest

(See instructions on back and the instructions for Form 1040A, or Form 1040, line 8a.)

Note. If you received a Form 1099-INT, Form 1099-OID, or substitute statement from a brokerage firm, list the firm's name as the payer and enter the total interest shown on that form.

			Amount
1	List name of payer. If any interest is from a seller-financed mortgage and the buyer used the property as a personal residence, see instructions on back and list this interest first. Also, show that buyer's social security number and address ▶		
	Citizens Band		500
	Thrifty Savings Bank		500
	XYZ Corp. Bank		586
	U.S. Series EE Savings Bonds		220
		1	
2	Add the amounts on line 1	2	1,806
3	Excludable interest on series EE and I U.S. savings bonds issued after 1989. Attach Form 8815	3	
4	Subtract line 3 from line 2. Enter the result here and on Form 1040A, or Form 1040, line 8a . . . . ▶	4	1,806

Note. If line 4 is over $1,500, you must complete Part III.

Part II

Ordinary Dividends

(See instructions on back and the instructions for Form 1040A, or Form 1040, line 9a.)

Note. If you received a Form 1099-DIV or substitute statement from a brokerage firm, list the firm's name as the payer and enter the ordinary dividends shown on that form.

			Amount
5	List name of payer ▶		
	Raynor Corp.		1,600
	Styling, Inc.		1,340
	Tornado Industries		980
	U Growth Fund		4,080
		5	8,000
6	Add the amounts on line 5. Enter the total here and on Form 1040A, or Form 1040, line 9a . . . . ▶	6	8,000

Note. If line 6 is over $1,500, you must complete Part III.

Part III

Foreign Accounts and Trusts

(See instructions on back.)

You must complete this part if you **(a)** had over $1,500 of taxable interest or ordinary dividends; **(b)** had a foreign account; or **(c)** received a distribution from, or were a grantor of, or a transferor to, a foreign trust.

		Yes	No
7a	At any time during 2013, did you have a financial interest in or signature authority over a financial account (such as a bank account, securities account, or brokerage account) located in a foreign country? See instructions		✓
	If "Yes," are you required to file FinCEN Form 114, Report of Foreign Bank and Financial Accounts (FBAR), formerly TD F 90-22.1, to report that financial interest or signature authority? See FinCEN Form 114 and its instructions for filing requirements and exceptions to those requirements		✓
b	If you are required to file FinCEN Form 114, enter the name of the foreign country where the financial account is located ▶		
8	During 2013, did you receive a distribution from, or were you the grantor of, or transferor to, a foreign trust? If "Yes," you may have to file Form 3520. See instructions on back		✓

For Paperwork Reduction Act Notice, see your tax return instructions.   Cat. No. 17146N   Schedule B (Form 1040A or 1040) 2013

¶2783

General Instructions

Section references are to the Internal Revenue Code unless otherwise noted.

Future Developments

For the latest information about developments related to Schedule B (Form 1040A or 1040) and its instructions, such as legislation enacted after they were published, go to www.irs.gov/scheduleb.

Purpose of Form

Use Schedule B if any of the following applies.

• You had over $1,500 of taxable interest or ordinary dividends.

• You received interest from a seller-financed mortgage and the buyer used the property as a personal residence.

• You have accrued interest from a bond.

• You are reporting original issue discount (OID) in an amount less than the amount shown on Form 1099-OID.

• You are reducing your interest income on a bond by the amount of amortizable bond premium.

• You are claiming the exclusion of interest from series EE or I U.S. savings bonds issued after 1989.

• You received interest or ordinary dividends as a nominee.

• You had a financial interest in, or signature authority over, a financial account in a foreign country or you received a distribution from, or were a grantor of, or transferor to, a foreign trust. Part III of the schedule has questions about foreign accounts and trusts.

Specific Instructions

 You can list more than one payer on each entry space for lines 1 and 5, but be sure to clearly show the amount paid next to the payer's name. Add the separate amounts paid by the payers listed on an entry space and enter the total in the "Amount" column. If you still need more space, attach separate statements that are the same size as the printed schedule. Use the same format as lines 1 and 5, but show your totals on Schedule B. Be sure to put your name and social security number (SSN) on the statements and attach them at the end of your return.

Part I. Interest

Line 1. Report on line 1 all of your taxable interest. Taxable interest should be shown on your Forms 1099-INT, Forms 1099-OID, or substitute statements. Include interest from series EE, H, HH, and I U.S. savings bonds. List each payer's name and show the amount. Do not report on this line any tax-exempt interest from box 8 or box 9 of Form 1099-INT. Instead, report the amount from box 8 on line 8b of Form 1040A or 1040. If an amount is shown in box 9 of Form 1099-INT, you generally must report it on line 12 of Form 6251. See the Instructions for Form 6251 for more details.

Seller-financed mortgages. If you sold your home or other property and the buyer used the property as a personal residence, list first any interest the buyer paid you on a mortgage or other form of seller financing. Be sure to show the buyer's name, address, and SSN. You must also let the buyer know your SSN. If you do not show the buyer's name, address, and SSN, or let the buyer know your SSN, you may have to pay a $50 penalty.

Nominees. If you received a Form 1099-INT that includes interest you received as a nominee (that is, in your name, but the interest actually belongs to someone else), report the total on line 1. Do this even if you later distributed some or all of this income to others. Under your last entry on line 1, put a subtotal of all interest listed on line 1. Below this subtotal, enter "Nominee Distribution" and show the total interest you received as a nominee. Subtract this amount from the subtotal and enter the result on line 2.

 If you received interest as a nominee, you must give the actual owner a Form 1099-INT unless the owner is your spouse. You must also file a Form 1096 and a Form 1099-INT with the IRS. For more details, see the General Instructions for Certain Information Returns and the Instructions for Forms 1099-INT and 1099-OID.

Accrued interest. When you buy bonds between interest payment dates and pay accrued interest to the seller, this interest is taxable to the seller. If you received a Form 1099 for interest as a purchaser of a bond with accrued interest, follow the rules earlier under Nominees to see how to report the accrued interest. But identify the amount to be subtracted as "Accrued Interest."

Original issue discount (OID). If you are reporting OID in an amount less than the amount shown on Form 1099-OID, follow the rules earlier under Nominees to see how to report the OID. But identify the amount to be subtracted as "OID Adjustment."

Amortizable bond premium. If you are reducing your interest income on a bond by the amount of amortizable bond premium, follow the rules earlier under Nominees to see how to report the interest. But identify the amount to be subtracted as "ABP Adjustment."

Line 3. If, during 2013, you cashed series EE or I U.S. savings bonds issued after 1989 and you paid qualified higher education expenses for yourself, your spouse, or your dependents, you may be able to exclude part or all of the interest on those bonds. See Form 8815 for details.

Part II. Ordinary Dividends

 You may have to file Form 5471 if, in 2013, you were an officer or director of a foreign corporation. You may also have to file Form 5471 if, in 2013, you owned 10% or more of the total (a) value of a foreign corporation's stock, or (b) combined voting power of all classes of a foreign corporation's stock with voting rights. For details, see Form 5471 and its instructions.

Line 5. Report on line 5 all of your ordinary dividends. This amount should be shown in box 1a of your Forms 1099-DIV or substitute statements. List each payer's name and show the amount.

Nominees. If you received a Form 1099-DIV that includes ordinary dividends you received as a nominee (that is, in your name, but the ordinary dividends actually belong to someone else), report the total on line 5. Do this even if you later distributed some or all of this income to others. Under your last entry on line 5, put a subtotal of all ordinary dividends listed on line 5. Below this subtotal, enter "Nominee Distribution" and show the total ordinary dividends you received as a nominee. Subtract this amount from the subtotal and enter the result on line 6.

 If you received dividends as a nominee, you must give the actual owner a Form 1099-DIV unless the owner is your spouse. You must also file a Form 1096 and a Form 1099-DIV with the IRS. For more details, see the General Instructions for Certain Information Returns and the Instructions for Form 1099-DIV.

Part III. Foreign Accounts and Trusts

 Regardless of whether you are required to file FinCEN Form 114 (FBAR), you may be required to file Form 8938, Statement of Specified Foreign Financial Assets, with your income tax return. Failure to file Form 8938 may result in penalties and extension of the statute of limitations. See www.irs.gov/form8938 for more information.

Line 7a–Question 1. Check the "Yes" box if at any time during 2013 you had a financial interest in or signature authority over a financial account located in a foreign country. See the definitions that follow. Check the "Yes" box even if you are not required to file FinCEN Form 114, Report of Foreign Bank and Financial Accounts (FBAR).

Financial account. A financial account includes, but is not limited to, a securities, brokerage, savings, demand, checking, deposit, time deposit, or other account maintained with a financial institution (or other person performing the services of a financial institution). A financial account also includes a commodity futures or options account, an insurance policy with a cash value (such as a whole life insurance policy), an annuity policy with a cash value, and shares in a mutual fund or similar pooled fund (that is, a fund that is available to the general public with a regular net asset value determination and regular redemptions).

Financial account located in a foreign country. A financial account is located in a foreign country if the account is physically located outside of the United States. For example, an account maintained with a branch of a United States bank that is physically located outside of the United States is a foreign financial account. An account maintained with a branch of a foreign bank that is physically located in the United States is not a foreign financial account.

Signature authority. Signature authority is the authority of an individual (alone or in conjunction with another individual) to control the disposition of assets held in a foreign financial account by direct communication (whether in writing or otherwise) to the bank or other financial institution that maintains the financial account. See the FinCEN Form 114 instructions for exceptions. Do not consider the exceptions relating to signature authority in answering Question 1 on line 7a.

Other definitions. For definitions of "financial interest," "United States," and other relevant terms, see the instructions for FinCEN Form 114.

Line 7a–Question 2. See FinCEN Form 114 and its instructions to determine whether you must file the form. Check the "Yes" box if you are required to file the form; check the "No" box if you are not required to file the form.

If you checked the "Yes" box to Question 2 on line 7a, FinCEN Form 114 must be electronically filed with the Financial Crimes Enforcement Network (FinCEN) at the following website: http://bsaefiling.fincen.treas.gov/main.html. Do not attach FinCEN Form 114 to your tax return. To be considered timely, FinCEN Form 114 **must be received** by June 30, 2014.

 If you are required to file FinCEN Form 114 but do not properly do so, you may have to pay a civil penalty up to $10,000. A person who willfully fails to report an account or provide account identifying information may be subject to a civil penalty equal to the greater of $100,000 or 50 percent of the balance in the account at the time of the violation. Willful violations may also be subject to criminal penalties.

Line 7b. If you are required to file FinCEN Form 114, enter the name of the foreign country or countries in the space provided on line 7b. Attach a separate statement if you need more space.

Line 8. If you received a distribution from a foreign trust, you must provide additional information. For this purpose, a loan of cash or marketable securities generally is considered to be a distribution. See Form 3520 for details.

If you were the grantor of, or transferor to, a foreign trust that existed during 2013, you may have to file Form 3520.

Do not attach Form 3520 to Form 1040. Instead, file it at the address shown in its instructions.

If you were treated as the owner of a foreign trust under the grantor trust rules, you are also responsible for ensuring that the foreign trust files Form 3520-A. Form 3520-A is due on March 17, 2014, for a calendar year trust. See the instructions for Form 3520-A for more details.

¶2784 SCHEDULE D—CAPITAL GAINS AND LOSSES

SCHEDULE D (Form 1040) Department of the Treasury Internal Revenue Service (99)	**Capital Gains and Losses** ► Attach to Form 1040 or Form 1040NR. ► Information about Schedule D and its separate instructions is at *www.irs.gov/scheduled*. ► Use Form 8949 to list your transactions for lines 1b, 2, 3, 8b, 9, and 10.	OMB No. 1545-0074 20**13** Attachment Sequence No. **12**

Name(s) shown on return	Your social security number
George E. (Deceased) and Mary M. King	100-09-0603

Part I Short-Term Capital Gains and Losses—Assets Held One Year or Less

See instructions for how to figure the amounts to enter on the lines below. This form may be easier to complete if you round off cents to whole dollars.	(d) Proceeds (sales price)	(e) Cost (or other basis)	(g) Adjustments to gain or loss from Form(s) 8949, Part I, line 2, column (g)	(h) Gain or (loss) Subtract column (e) from column (d) and combine the result with column (g)
1a Totals for all short-term transactions reported on Form 1099-B for which basis was reported to the IRS and for which you have no adjustments (see instructions). However, if you choose to report all these transactions on Form 8949, leave this line blank and go to line 1b .				
1b Totals for all transactions reported on Form(s) 8949 with **Box A** checked	12,570	11,500		1,070
2 Totals for all transactions reported on Form(s) 8949 with **Box B** checked				
3 Totals for all transactions reported on Form(s) 8949 with **Box C** checked				

4 Short-term gain from Form 6252 and short-term gain or (loss) from Forms 4684, 6781, and 8824 .	**4**	
5 Net short-term gain or (loss) from partnerships, S corporations, estates, and trusts from Schedule(s) K-1	**5**	
6 Short-term capital loss carryover. Enter the amount, if any, from line 8 of your **Capital Loss Carryover Worksheet** in the instructions	**6**	(1,000)
7 **Net short-term capital gain or (loss).** Combine lines 1a through 6 in column (h). If you have any long-term capital gains or losses, go to Part II below. Otherwise, go to Part III on the back	**7**	70

Part II Long-Term Capital Gains and Losses—Assets Held More Than One Year

See instructions for how to figure the amounts to enter on the lines below. This form may be easier to complete if you round off cents to whole dollars.	(d) Proceeds (sales price)	(e) Cost (or other basis)	(g) Adjustments to gain or loss from Form(s) 8949, Part II, line 2, column (g)	(h) Gain or (loss) Subtract column (e) from column (d) and combine the result with column (g)
8a Totals for all long-term transactions reported on Form 1099-B for which basis was reported to the IRS and for which you have no adjustments (see instructions). However, if you choose to report all these transactions on Form 8949, leave this line blank and go to line 8b .	10,200	5,500		4,700
8b Totals for all transactions reported on Form(s) 8949 with **Box D** checked				
9 Totals for all transactions reported on Form(s) 8949 with **Box E** checked				
10 Totals for all transactions reported on Form(s) 8949 with **Box F** checked.				

11 Gain from Form 4797, Part I; long-term gain from Forms 2439 and 6252; and long-term gain or (loss) from Forms 4684, 6781, and 8824	**11**	
12 Net long-term gain or (loss) from partnerships, S corporations, estates, and trusts from Schedule(s) K-1	**12**	
13 Capital gain distributions. See the instructions	**13**	100
14 Long-term capital loss carryover. Enter the amount, if any, from line 13 of your **Capital Loss Carryover Worksheet** in the instructions	**14**	( )
15 **Net long-term capital gain or (loss).** Combine lines 8a through 14 in column (h). Then go to Part III on the back	**15**	4,800

For Paperwork Reduction Act Notice, see your tax return instructions.   Cat. No. 11338H   Schedule D (Form 1040) 2013

¶2784

Part III   **Summary**

16	Combine lines 7 and 15 and enter the result	**16**	4,870

- If line 16 is a **gain,** enter the amount from line 16 on Form 1040, line 13, or Form 1040NR, line 14. Then go to line 17 below.
- If line 16 is a **loss,** skip lines 17 through 20 below. Then go to line 21. Also be sure to complete line 22.
- If line 16 is **zero,** skip lines 17 through 21 below and enter -0- on Form 1040, line 13, or Form 1040NR, line 14. Then go to line 22.

17   Are lines 15 and 16 **both** gains?
☑ **Yes.** Go to line 18.
☐ **No.** Skip lines 18 through 21, and go to line 22.

18   Enter the amount, if any, from line 7 of the **28% Rate Gain Worksheet** in the instructions . . ▶ | **18** |

19   Enter the amount, if any, from line 18 of the **Unrecaptured Section 1250 Gain Worksheet** in the instructions . . . . ▶ | **19** |

20   Are lines 18 and 19 **both** zero or blank?
☑ **Yes.** Complete the **Qualified Dividends and Capital Gain Tax Worksheet** in the instructions for Form 1040, line 44 (or in the instructions for Form 1040NR, line 42). **Do not** complete lines 21 and 22 below.

☐ **No.** Complete the **Schedule D Tax Worksheet** in the instructions. **Do not** complete lines 21 and 22 below.

21   If line 16 is a loss, enter here and on Form 1040, line 13, or Form 1040NR, line 14, the **smaller** of:

- The loss on line 16 or
- ($3,000), or if married filing separately, ($1,500)   . . . . | **21** | (   ) |

Note. When figuring which amount is smaller, treat both amounts as positive numbers.

22   Do you have qualified dividends on Form 1040, line 9b, or Form 1040NR, line 10b?

☐ **Yes.** Complete the **Qualified Dividends and Capital Gain Tax Worksheet** in the instructions for Form 1040, line 44 (or in the instructions for Form 1040NR, line 42).

☐ **No.** Complete the rest of Form 1040 or Form 1040NR.

¶2784

¶2785 FORM 1040—LINE 44

Qualified Dividends and Capital Gain Tax Worksheet—Line 44   *Keep for Your Records*

Before you begin:
- ✓ See the earlier instructions for line 44 to see if you can use this worksheet to figure your tax.
- ✓ Before completing this worksheet, complete Form 1040 through line 43.
- ✓ If you do not have to file Schedule D and you received capital gain distributions, be sure you checked the box on line 13 of Form 1040.

1.	Enter the amount from Form 1040, line 43. However, if you are filing Form 2555 or 2555-EZ (relating to foreign earned income), enter the amount from line 3 of the Foreign Earned Income Tax Worksheet .... **1.**	244,264
2.	Enter the amount from Form 1040, line 9b* .... **2.**	-0-
3.	Are you filing Schedule D?*	
	☐ **Yes.** Enter the **smaller** of line 15 or 16 of Schedule D. If either line 15 or line 16 is blank or a loss, enter -0-	4,800
	☐ **No.** Enter the amount from Form 1040, line 13 **3.**	
4.	Add lines 2 and 3 .... **4.**	4,800
5.	If filing Form 4952 (used to figure investment interest expense deduction), enter any amount from line 4g of that form. Otherwise, enter -0- .... **5.**	-0-
6.	Subtract line 5 from line 4. If zero or less, enter -0- .... **6.**	4,800
7.	Subtract line 6 from line 1. If zero or less, enter -0- .... **7.**	239,664
8.	Enter: $36,250 if single or married filing separately, $72,500 if married filing jointly or qualifying widow(er), $48,600 if head of household. } .... **8.**	72,500
9.	Enter the smaller of line 1 or line 8 .... **9.**	72,500
10.	Enter the smaller of line 7 or line 9 .... **10.**	72,500
11.	Subtract line 10 from line 9. This amount is taxed at 0% .... **11.**	-0-
12.	Enter the smaller of line 1 or line 6 .... **12.**	4,800
13.	Enter the amount from line 11 .... **13.**	-0-
14.	Subtract line 13 from line 12 .... **14.**	4,800
15.	Enter: $400,000 if single, $225,000 if married filing separately, $450,000 if married filing jointly or qualifying widow(er), $425,000 if head of household. } .... **15.**	450,000
16.	Enter the smaller of line 1 or line 15 .... **16.**	244,264
17.	Add lines 7 and 11 .... **17.**	239,664
18.	Subtract line 17 from line 16. If zero or less, enter -0- .... **18.**	4,600
19.	Enter the smaller of line 14 or line 18 .... **19.**	4,600
20.	Multiply line 19 by 15% (.15) .... **20.**	690
21.	Add lines 11 and 19 .... **21.**	4,600
22.	Subtract line 21 from line 12 .... **22.**	200
23.	Multiply line 22 by 20% (.20) .... **23.**	40
24.	Figure the tax on the amount on line 7. If the amount on line 7 is less than $100,000, use the Tax Table to figure the tax. If the amount on line 7 is $100,000 or more, use the Tax Computation Worksheet .... **24.**	55,402
25.	Add lines 20, 23, and 24 .... **25.**	56,132
26.	Figure the tax on the amount on line 1. If the amount on line 1 is less than $100,000, use the Tax Table to figure the tax. If the amount on line 1 is $100,000 or more, use the Tax Computation Worksheet .... **26.**	56,920
27.	**Tax on all taxable income.** Enter the **smaller** of line 25 or line 26. Also include this amount on Form 1040, line 44. If you are filing Form 2555 or 2555-EZ, do not enter this amount on Form 1040, line 44. Instead, enter it on line 4 of the Foreign Earned Income Tax Worksheet .... **27.**	56,132

*If you are filing Form 2555 or 2555-EZ, see the footnote in the Foreign Earned Income Tax Worksheet before completing this line.

¶2786 SCHEDULE E—SUPPLEMENTAL INCOME AND LOSS

SCHEDULE E (Form 1040)	**Supplemental Income and Loss**	OMB No. 1545-0074
Department of the Treasury Internal Revenue Service (99)	(From rental real estate, royalties, partnerships, S corporations, estates, trusts, REMICs, etc.) ▶ Attach to Form 1040, 1040NR, or Form 1041. ▶ Information about Schedule E and its separate instructions is at *www.irs.gov/schedulee*.	2013 Attachment Sequence No. **13**

Name(s) shown on return	Your social security number
George E. (Deceased) and Mary M. King	100-09-0603

Part I   **Income or Loss From Rental Real Estate and Royalties** Note. If you are in the business of renting personal property, use **Schedule C** or **C-EZ** (see instructions). If you are an individual, report farm rental income or loss from **Form 4835** on page 2, line 40.

A Did you make any payments in 2013 that would require you to file Form(s) 1099? (see instructions)   ☐ Yes ☑ No

B If "Yes," did you or will you file required Forms 1099?   ☐ Yes ☐ No

1a Physical address of each property (street, city, state, ZIP code)

A   17 Main Street, Kansas City, Missouri 64138

B

C

1b	Type of Property (from list below)	2	For each rental real estate property listed above, report the number of fair rental and personal use days. Check the **QJV** box only if you meet the requirements to file as a qualified joint venture. See instructions.		Fair Rental Days	Personal Use Days	QJV
A				A			☐
B				B			☐
C				C			☐

Type of Property:

1 Single Family Residence   3 Vacation/Short-Term Rental   5 Land   7 Self-Rental

2 Multi-Family Residence   4 Commercial   6 Royalties   8 Other (describe)

Income:	Properties:		A	B	C
3	Rents received	3	18,000		
4	Royalties received	4			
Expenses:					
5	Advertising	5			
6	Auto and travel (see instructions)	6			
7	Cleaning and maintenance	7	600		
8	Commissions.	8			
9	Insurance	9	900		
10	Legal and other professional fees	10			
11	Management fees	11			
12	Mortgage interest paid to banks, etc. (see instructions)	12	1,800		
13	Other interest.	13			
14	Repairs.	14			
15	Supplies	15	700		
16	Taxes	16	3,000		
17	Utilities	17	1,500		
18	Depreciation expense or depletion	18	2,500		
19	Other (list) ▶	19			
20	Total expenses. Add lines 5 through 19	20	11,000		
21	Subtract line 20 from line 3 (rents) and/or 4 (royalties). If result is a (loss), see instructions to find out if you must file **Form 6198**	21	7,000		
22	Deductible rental real estate loss after limitation, if any, on **Form 8582** (see instructions)	22	(	)(	)(	)

23a	Total of all amounts reported on line 3 for all rental properties	23a	18,000	
b	Total of all amounts reported on line 4 for all royalty properties	23b	-0-	
c	Total of all amounts reported on line 12 for all properties	23c	1,800	
d	Total of all amounts reported on line 18 for all properties	23d	2,500	
e	Total of all amounts reported on line 20 for all properties	23e	11,000	

24	**Income.** Add positive amounts shown on line 21. **Do not** include any losses	24	7,000
25	**Losses.** Add royalty losses from line 21 and rental real estate losses from line 22. Enter total losses here	25	( )
26	**Total rental real estate and royalty income or (loss).** Combine lines 24 and 25. Enter the result here. If Parts II, III, IV, and line 40 on page 2 do not apply to you, also enter this amount on Form 1040, line 17, or Form 1040NR, line 18. Otherwise, include this amount in the total on line 41 on page 2	26	7,000

For Paperwork Reduction Act Notice, see the separate instructions.   Cat. No. 11344L   Schedule E (Form 1040) 2013

¶2786

Schedule E (Form 1040) 2013		Attachment Sequence No. **13**	Page **2**

Name(s) shown on return. Do not enter name and social security number if shown on other side.

George E. (Deceased) and Mary M. King

Your social security number
100-09-0603

Caution. The IRS compares amounts reported on your tax return with amounts shown on Schedule(s) K-1.

Part II	Income or Loss From Partnerships and S Corporations	**Note.** If you report a loss from an at-risk activity for which

any amount is **not** at risk, you **must** check the box in column **(e)** on line 28 and attach **Form 6198.** See instructions.

27 Are you reporting any loss not allowed in a prior year due to the at-risk, excess farm loss, or basis limitations, a prior year unallowed loss from a passive activity (if that loss was not reported on Form 8582), or unreimbursed partnership expenses? If you answered "Yes," see instructions before completing this section. ☐ **Yes** ☑ **No**

28	**(a)** Name	**(b)** Enter **P** for partnership; **S** for S corporation	**(c)** Check if foreign partnership	**(d)** Employer identification number	**(e)** Check if any amount is not at risk
A			☐		☐
B			☐		☐
C			☐		☐
D			☐		☐

	Passive Income and Loss		Nonpassive Income and Loss		
	(f) Passive loss allowed (attach **Form 8582** if required)	**(g)** Passive income from **Schedule K–1**	**(h)** Nonpassive loss from **Schedule K–1**	**(i)** Section 179 expense deduction from **Form 4562**	**(j)** Nonpassive income from **Schedule K–1**
A					
B					
C					
D					
29a	Totals				
b	Totals				

30	Add columns (g) and (j) of line 29a	30	
31	Add columns (f), (h), and (i) of line 29b	31	( )
32	**Total partnership and S corporation income or (loss).** Combine lines 30 and 31. Enter the result here and include in the total on line 41 below	32	

Part III	Income or Loss From Estates and Trusts

33	**(a)** Name	**(b)** Employer identification number
A		
B		

	Passive Income and Loss		Nonpassive Income and Loss	
	(c) Passive deduction or loss allowed (attach **Form 8582** if required)	**(d)** Passive income from **Schedule K–1**	**(e)** Deduction or loss from **Schedule K–1**	**(f)** Other income from **Schedule K–1**
A				
B				
34a	Totals			
b	Totals			

35	Add columns (d) and (f) of line 34a	35	
36	Add columns (c) and (e) of line 34b	36	( )
37	**Total estate and trust income or (loss).** Combine lines 35 and 36. Enter the result here and include in the total on line 41 below	37	

Part IV	Income or Loss From Real Estate Mortgage Investment Conduits (REMICs)—Residual Holder

38	**(a)** Name	**(b)** Employer identification number	**(c)** Excess inclusion from **Schedules Q,** line 2c (see instructions)	**(d)** Taxable income (net loss) from **Schedules Q,** line 1b	**(e)** Income from **Schedules Q,** line 3b

39	Combine columns (d) and (e) only. Enter the result here and include in the total on line 41 below	39	

Part V	Summary

40	Net farm rental income or (loss) from **Form 4835.** Also, complete line 42 below	40	
41	**Total income or (loss).** Combine lines 26, 32, 37, 39, and 40. Enter the result here and on Form 1040, line 17, or Form 1040NR, line 18 ▶	41	7,000

42	**Reconciliation of farming and fishing income.** Enter your **gross** farming and fishing income reported on Form 4835, line 7; Schedule K-1 (Form 1065), box 14, code B; Schedule K-1 (Form 1120S), box 17, code V; and Schedule K-1 (Form 1041), box 14, code F (see instructions) . .	42	
43	**Reconciliation for real estate professionals.** If you were a real estate professional (see instructions), enter the net income or (loss) you reported anywhere on Form 1040 or Form 1040NR from all rental real estate activities in which you materially participated under the passive activity loss rules . .	43	

Schedule E (Form 1040) 2013

¶2787 FORM 8949—SALES AND OTHER DISPOSITIONS OF CAPITAL ASSETS

Form **8949**	**Sales and Other Dispositions of Capital Assets**	OMB No. 1545-0074
Department of the Treasury Internal Revenue Service	▶ Information about Form 8949 and its separate instructions is at *www.irs.gov/form8949*. ▶ File with your Schedule D to list your transactions for lines 1b, 2, 3, 8b, 9, and 10 of Schedule D.	20**13** Attachment Sequence No. **12A**

Name(s) shown on return	Social security number or taxpayer identification number
George E (Deceased) and Mary M. King	100-09-0603

Most brokers issue their own substitute statement instead of using Form 1099-B. They also may provide basis information (usually your cost) to you on the statement even if it is not reported to the IRS. Before you check Box A, B, or C below, determine whether you received any statement(s) and, if so, the transactions for which basis was reported to the IRS. Brokers are required to report basis to the IRS for most stock you bought in 2011 or later.

Part I   **Short-Term.** Transactions involving capital assets you held one year or less are short term. For long-term transactions, see page 2.

Note. You may aggregate all short-term transactions reported on Form(s) 1099-B showing basis was reported to the IRS and for which no adjustments or codes are required. Enter the total directly on Schedule D, line 1a; you are not required to report these transactions on Form 8949 (see instructions).

You *must* check Box A, B, *or* C below. Check only one box. If more than one box applies for your short-term transactions, complete a separate Form 8949, page 1, for each applicable box. If you have more short-term transactions than will fit on this page for one or more of the boxes, complete as many forms with the same box checked as you need.

- ☑ **(A)** Short-term transactions reported on Form(s) 1099-B showing basis was reported to the IRS (see **Note** above)
- ☐ **(B)** Short-term transactions reported on Form(s) 1099-B showing basis was **not** reported to the IRS
- ☐ **(C)** Short-term transactions not reported to you on Form 1099-B

1 (a) Description of property (Example: 100 sh. XYZ Co.)	(b) Date acquired (Mo., day, yr.)	(c) Date sold or disposed (Mo., day, yr.)	(d) Proceeds (sales price) (see instructions)	(e) Cost or other basis. See the **Note** below and see *Column (e)* in the separate instructions	Adjustment, if any, to gain or loss. If you enter an amount in column (g), enter a code in column (f). See the separate instructions.		(h) Gain or (loss). Subtract column (e) from column (d) and combine the result with column (g)
					(f) Code(s) from instructions	(g) Amount of adjustment	
Office Building	1/12/13	5/3/13	10,570	8,000			2,570
50 shares of S Corp. Stock	1/16/13	6/17/13	2,000	3,500			(1,500)
2 Totals. Add the amounts in columns (d), (e), (g), and (h) (subtract negative amounts). Enter each total here and include on your Schedule D, **line 1b** (if **Box A** above is checked), **line 2** (if **Box B** above is checked), or **line 3** (if **Box C** above is checked) ▶			12,570	11,500			1,070

Note. If you checked Box A above but the basis reported to the IRS was incorrect, enter in column (e) the basis as reported to the IRS, and enter an adjustment in column (g) to correct the basis. See *Column (g)* in the separate instructions for how to figure the amount of the adjustment.

For Paperwork Reduction Act Notice, see your tax return instructions.   Cat. No. 37768Z   Form **8949** (2013)

¶2787

Form 8949 (2013)   Attachment Sequence No. **12A**   Page **2**

Name(s) shown on return. (Name and SSN or taxpayer identification no. not required if shown on other side.)	Social security number or taxpayer identification number
George E. (Deceased) and Mary M. King	100-09-0603

Most brokers issue their own substitute statement instead of using Form 1099-B. They also may provide basis information (usually your cost) to you on the statement even if it is not reported to the IRS. Before you check Box D, E, or F below, determine whether you received any statement(s) and, if so, the transactions for which basis was reported to the IRS. Brokers are required to report basis to the IRS for most stock you bought in 2011 or later.

Part II   **Long-Term.** Transactions involving capital assets you held more than one year are long term. For short-term transactions, see page 1.

> **Note.** You may aggregate all long-term transactions reported on Form(s) 1099-B showing basis was reported to the IRS and for which no adjustments or codes are required. Enter the total directly on Schedule D, line 8a; you are not required to report these transactions on Form 8949 (see instructions).

You *must* check Box D, E, *or* F below. **Check only one box.** If more than one box applies for your long-term transactions, complete a separate Form 8949, page 2, for each applicable box. If you have more long-term transactions than will fit on this page for one or more of the boxes, complete as many forms with the same box checked as you need.

- ☐ **(D)** Long-term transactions reported on Form(s) 1099-B showing basis was reported to the IRS (see **Note** above)
- ☐ **(E)** Long-term transactions reported on Form(s) 1099-B showing basis was **not** reported to the IRS
- ☐ **(F)** Long-term transactions not reported to you on Form 1099-B

1					Adjustment, if any, to gain or loss. If you enter an amount in column (g), enter a code in column (f). See the separate instructions.		
(a) Description of property (Example: 100 sh. XYZ Co.)	(b) Date acquired (Mo., day, yr.)	(c) Date sold or disposed (Mo., day, yr.)	(d) Proceeds (sales price) (see instructions)	(e) Cost or other basis. See the **Note** below and see *Column (e)* in the separate instructions	(f) Code(s) from instructions	(g) Amount of adjustment	(h) Gain or (loss). Subtract column (e) from column (d) and combine the result with column (g)
100 shares of Z Corp.	4/4/11	5/3/13	10,200	3,500			6,700
2 $1,000 registered M Corp. bonds	2/01/09	5/3/13	-0-	2,000			(2,000)
2 Totals. Add the amounts in columns (d), (e), (g), and (h) (subtract negative amounts). Enter each total here and include on your Schedule D, **line 8b** (if **Box D** above is checked), **line 9** (if **Box E** above is checked), or **line 10** (if **Box F** above is checked) ▶							4,700

Note. If you checked Box D above but the basis reported to the IRS was incorrect, enter in column (e) the basis as reported to the IRS, and enter an adjustment in column (g) to correct the basis. See *Column (g)* in the separate instructions for how to figure the amount of the adjustment.

Form **8949** (2013)

¶2787

¶2788 FORM 8959—ADDITIONAL MEDICARE TAX

Use Form 8959, "Additional Medicare Tax," to compute the amount of Additional Medicare Tax owed by an employee, self-employed individual or recipient of compensation under the Railroad Retirement Tax Act (RRTA). Employees also use Form 8959 to compute the amount of Additional Medicare Tax that should be withheld by their employer. The amounts computed on Form 8959 should be carried over to the appropriate lines on the following returns: Form 1040, Form 1040NR, Form 1040-SS and Form 1040-PR. Form 8959 should be attached to Form 1040.

(a) 0.9 Percent Additional Medicare Tax on Earned Income.
Beginning in 2013, an individual is liable for the 0.9 percent Additional Medicare Tax if the individual's wages, compensation, or self-employment income (together with that of his or her spouse if filing a joint return) exceed the threshold amount for the individual's filing status as indicated below:

Filing Status	Threshold Amount
Married filing jointly	$250,000
Married filing separate	$125,000
Single	$200,000
Head of household (with qualifying person)	$200,000
Qualifying widow(er) with dependent child	$200,000

Employers are required to withhold from employee's wages and remit the increased employee portion of the Medicare tax to the IRS for each employee whose wages for Medicare tax purposes from the employer are over $200,000 [IRC Sec. 3102(f)(1)]. This rule applies regardless of the employee's filing status or other income. Thus, the employer disregards any amount of wages paid to the employee's spouse or any wages paid to the employee by another employer [Reg. Sec. 31.3202-1(g)(1)]. As a result of this tax, the employee portion of the Medicare taxes is increased from 1.45 percent to 2.35 percent on wages received in a calendar year in excess of $200,000 ($250,000 for married couples filing jointly; $125,000 for married filing separately) [IRC Sec. 3101(b)(2)].

All railroad retirement (RRTA) compensation that is currently subject to Medicare tax is subject to Additional Medicare Tax to the extent it exceeds the threshold amount for the employee's filing status. A railroad employer must withhold Additional Medicare Tax on compensation it pays to the employee in excess of $200,000 for the calendar year, regardless of the employee's filing status and regardless of wages or compensation paid by another employer.

If a taxpayer has both wages and self-employment income, the threshold amount for applying the Additional Medicare Tax on the self-employment income is reduced (but not below zero) by the amount of wages subject to Additional Medicare Tax. There is no equivalent rule for railroad retirement (RRTA) compensation.

If the taxpayer is a nonresident alien or a U.S. citizen living abroad, the taxpayer is required to pay the Additional Medicare Tax on Medicare wages, railroad retirement (RRTA) compensation, and self-employment income that exceed the threshold

¶2788

amount for the taxpayer's filing status, without regard to the taxpayer's domicile or citizenship.

Example 1: Harry, who is married and files a joint return, receives $100,000 in wages from his employer for the calendar year. Ida, Harry's spouse, receives $300,000 in wages from her employer for the same calendar year. Employers are required to withhold from employee's wages and remit the increased employee portion of the Medicare tax to the IRS for each employee whose wages for Medicare tax purposes from the employer are over $200,000. This rule applies regardless of the employee's filing status or other income. Harry's wages are not in excess of $200,000, so Harry's employer does not withhold Additional Medicare Tax. Ida's employer is required to collect 0.9 percent Additional Medicare Tax only with respect to wages it pays which are in excess of the $200,000 threshold (that is, $100,000) for the calendar year.

Example 2: Ann, a single filer, has $130,000 in self-employment income and $0 in wages. Ann is not liable to pay the Additional Medicare Tax and does not need to file Form 8959 because her self-employment income is less than the $200,000 threshold for single filers.

Example 3: Bob, a single filer, has $220,000 in self-employment income and $0 in wages. Bob is liable to pay the Additional Medicare Tax on $20,000 ($220,000 in self-employment income minus the threshold of $200,000). Bob must file Form 8959.

Example 4: Carl, a single filer, has $145,000 in self-employment income and $130,000 in wages. Carl's wages do not exceed $200,000. Therefore, Carl's employer did not withhold Additional Medicare Tax. However, the $130,000 of wages reduces the self-employment income threshold to $70,000 ($200,000 threshold minus the $130,000 of wages). Carl is liable to pay Additional Medicare Tax on $75,000 of self-employment income ($145,000 in self-employment income minus the reduced threshold of $70,000). Carl must file Form 8959.

Example 5: Don, who is married and files married filing separately, has $150,000 in self-employment income and $200,000 in wages. Don's wages do not exceed $200,000. Therefore, Don's employer did not withhold Additional Medicare Tax. However, the $200,000 of wages reduces the self-employment income threshold to $0 ($125,000 threshold minus the $200,000 of wages). Don is liable to pay the Additional Medicare Tax on $75,000 of wages ($200,000 in wages minus the $125,000 threshold for a married filing separately return) and on $150,000 of self-employment income ($150,000 in self-employment income minus the reduced threshold of $0). Don must file Form 8959.

Example 6: Erin and Frank are married and file jointly. Erin has $150,000 in wages and Frank has $175,000 in wages. Neither Erin nor Frank has wages that exceed $200,000. Therefore, their employers did not withhold the Additional Medicare Tax. However, their combined $325,000 in wages exceeds the $250,000 threshold for joint filers. Erin and Frank are liable to pay the Additional Medicare Tax on $75,000 of wages ($325,000 in wages minus the $250,000 threshold). Erin and Frank must file Form 8959.

Example 7: George and Helen are married and file jointly. George has $190,000 in wages and Helen has $150,000 in compensation subject to railroad retirement (RRTA) taxes. George and Helen do not combine their wages and railroad retirement (RRTA) compensation to determine whether they are in excess of the $250,000 threshold for a joint return. George and Helen are not liable to pay the Additional Medicare Tax because George's wages are not in excess of the $250,000 threshold and Helen's railroad retirement (RRTA) compensation is not in excess of the $250,000 threshold.

Example 8: Ishmael and Judy are married and file jointly. Ishmael has $160,000 in self-employment income and Judy has $140,000 in compensation subject to railroad retirement (RRTA) taxes. The $140,000 of railroad retirement (RRTA) compensation does not reduce the threshold at which Additional Medicare Tax applies to self-employment income. Ishmael and Judy are not liable to pay the Additional Medicare Tax because Ishmael's self-employment income is not in excess of the $250,000 threshold and Judy's railroad retirement (RRTA) compensation is not in excess of the $250,000 threshold.

The employee is responsible for paying any of the 0.9 percent Additional Medicare Tax that was not withheld by an employer because the employee's wages were less than $200,000. The employee may still be subject to the 0.9 percent Additional Medicare Tax if, when combined with a spouse's wages, the couple's total wages exceed the $250,000 threshold [IRC Sec. 3102(f)(2); Reg. Sec. 31.3102-1(g)(2)]. Individuals must use Form 8959, "Additional Medicare Tax," to calculate their 0.9 percent Additional Medicare tax liability on line 18 which will be reported on line 60 of Form 1040 after checking box a. The total 0.9 percent Additional Medicare tax withholding (if any) from line 24 should also be included with their federal income tax withholding on line 62 of Form 1040.

The employee cannot request that the additional 0.9% Medicare tax be withheld from wages that are under the $200,000 threshold. However, he or she can make quarterly estimated tax payments or submit a new Form W-4 requesting additional income tax withholding that can offset the additional Medicare tax calculated and reported on the employee's personal income tax return [IRS FAQ 13].

Example 9: Sally and Ann are married and will file a joint tax return in 2013. Sally's 2013 salary is $160,000, and Ann's 2013 wages are $130,000 so their total combined wage income in 2013 is $290,000 ($160,000 + $130,000). Since this amount is over $250,000, they owe the additional 0.9 percent Medicare tax on $40,000 ($290,000 − $250,000). The additional tax due is $360 ($40,000 × 0.9 percent). Neither Sally nor Ann's employer is liable for withholding and remitting the additional tax, because neither of them met the $200,000 wage threshold. Either Sally or Ann (or both) can submit a new Form W-4 to their employer that will result in additional income tax withholding to ensure that the $360 is properly paid during the year. Alternatively, they could make quarterly estimated tax payments. If the amount is not paid until their federal income tax return is filed, they may be responsible for the estimated tax penalty on any underpayment amount (whether the underpayment is actually income tax or the additional Medicare tax).

■ The decedent George E. King must file Form 8959 to report the 0.9 percent Additional Medicare Tax because their total wages of $281,904 exceed the $250,000 filing threshold for joint filers. They must file Form 8949 even though the Form W-2 furnished by George King's employer, reported his compensation of only $101,000 in 2013 and his surviving spouse, Mary King's W-2 indicated that she received compensation in the amount of $180,904 that year because their total compensation of $281,904 exceeds the $250,000 filing threshold for joint filers.

(b) How to Complete Form 8959.

Line 1—Enter the total of the taxpayers' Medicare wages and tips from box 5 of Form W-2. If the taxpayers have more than one Form W-2, enter the total of the amounts from box 5. If filing a joint return, include both spouse's wages and tips on line 1.

■ The decedent and his wife enter $281,905 which is the amount of their combined compensation as indicated on their W-2s for 2013 [see ¶ 2701].

Line 2—Enter unreported tips from line 6 of Form 4137, "Social Security and Medicare Tax on Unreported Tip Income." If filing a joint return, also include the amount from line 6 of the spouse's Form 4137.

Line 3—Enter wages from line 6 of Form 8919, "Uncollected Social Security and Medicare Tax on Wages." If filing a joint return, also include the amount from line 6 of the spouse's Form 8919.

Line 7—Multiply line 6 by 0.9% (.009). This is the amount of the taxpayer's Additional Medicare Tax on his or her wages. Enter the result on this line and go to Part II.

■ The Kings enter $287.

Part II—Additional Medicare Tax on Self-Employment (SE) Income

If the taxpayer and a spouse are filing a joint return did not have self-employment income, skip Part II and go to Part III.

Line 8—Enter self-employment income from Schedule SE, Section A, line 4 or Section B, line 6. Combine amounts from these lines if entries appear on both Section A, line 4 and Section B, line 6, or if the taxpayer has multiple Schedules SE.

Line 13—Multiply line 12 by 0.9% (.009). This is the amount of the individual's Additional Medicare Tax on self-employment income. Enter the result on this line and go to Part III.

Example 10: Kathleen and Liam are married and file a joint return. Kathleen has $130,000 in wages (included on line 4 of Form 8959). Liam has $140,000 in self-employment income (included on line 8 of Form 8959). The $130,000 of

Kathleen's wages reduces Liam's self-employment income threshold to $120,000 ($250,000 threshold minus the $130,000 of wages, as figured on lines 9 through 11 of Form 8959). Kathleen and Liam are liable to pay Additional Medicare Tax on $20,000 of Liam's self-employment income ($140,000 in self-employment income minus the reduced threshold amount of $120,000, as figured on line 12 of Form 8959). Kathleen and Liam owe Additional Medicare Tax of $180.00 ($20,000 × .009, as figured on line 13 of Form 8959).

Part III—Additional Medicare Tax on Railroad Retirement Tax Act (RRTA) Compensation

If the taxpayer and spouse are filing a joint return and did not have railroad retirement (RRTA) compensation, skip Part III and go to Part IV.

Line 14—Enter the total of your railroad retirement (RRTA) compensation and tips. The amount of RRTA compensation for a railroad employee is reported on Form W-2, box 14. If you have more than one Form W-2, enter the total of the RRTA compensation amounts from box 14 of all Forms W-2. If you are filing a joint return, also include your spouse's RRTA compensation. An employee representative subject to RRTA taxes should include the total compensation subject to Tier 1 Medicare tax as reported on line 2 of Form CT-2 (include the total of the compensation amounts from line 2 of all Forms CT-2 filed for 2013).

Line 17—Multiply line 16 by 0.9% (.009). This is your Additional Medicare Tax on railroad retirement (RRTA) compensation. Enter the result on this line and go to Part IV.

Part IV—Total Additional Medicare Tax

Line 18—Include the amount from line 18 on the following lines of the applicable tax return.

- Line 60 of Form 1040.
- Line 59 of Form 1040NR.
- Line 5 in Part I of Form 1040-SS.
- Line 5 in Part I of Form 1040-PR.

■ The Kings enter $287.

Part V—Withholding Reconciliation

Use Part V to figure the amount of Additional Medicare Tax on wages and railroad retirement (RRTA) compensation withheld by your employer. If the taxpayer and spouse are filing a joint return and did not have Medicare wages or railroad retirement (RRTA) compensation, leave Part V blank.

Line 19—Enter the amount of Medicare tax withheld, if any, which is reported on Form W-2, box 6. If the taxpayer has more than one Form W-2, add the amounts in box 6 of all Forms W-2 and enter the total on line 19. If filing a joint return, also include the spouse's Medicare tax withheld.

> **NOTE:** Both Medicare tax and Additional Medicare Tax withholding are reported together on Form W-2, box 6.

¶2788

■ The Kings enter $4,088 which is the Medicare Tax withheld at a rate of 1.45 percent on their total wages in 2013 of $281,904 ($281,904 × 1.45 percent).

Line 22—If line 22 is zero or less, enter zero.

Line 23—Enter the amount of Additional Medicare Tax withheld, if any, which is reported on Form W-2, box 14. If the taxpayer has more than one Form W-2, add the amounts in box 14 of all Forms W-2 and enter the total on line 23. If filing a joint return, also include the spouse's Additional Medicare Tax withheld. An employee representative subject to RRTA taxes should include the total Additional Medicare Tax paid as reported on line 3 of Form CT-2 (include the total Additional Medicare Tax paid from line 3 of all Forms CT-2 filed for 2013).

■ The Kings enter $363 which is their Additional Medicare Tax withholding on their wages. This will be entered on Form 1040, line 62.

Line 24—Include the amount from line 24 on the following line of the taxpayer's tax return. If the taxpayer files Form 1040, include this amount on line 62, combined with the taxpayer's federal income tax withholding.

(c) Sample Completed Form 8959—Additional Medicare Tax.

Form **8959**	**Additional Medicare Tax**	OMB No. 1545-0074

Department of the Treasury
Internal Revenue Service

▶ If any line does not apply to you, leave it blank. See separate instructions.
▶ Attach to Form 1040, 1040NR, 1040-PR, or 1040-SS.
▶ Information about Form 8959 and its instructions is at *www.irs.gov/form8959*.

20 13
Attachment Sequence No. **71**

Name(s) shown on Form 1040	Your social security number
George E. (deceased 07/01/13) and Mary M. King	100-09-0603

Part I   Additional Medicare Tax on Medicare Wages

1	Medicare wages and tips from Form W-2, box 5. If you have more than one Form W-2, enter the total of the amounts from box 5	**1**	281,905
2	Unreported tips from Form 4137, line 6	**2**	
3	Wages from Form 8919, line 6	**3**	
4	Add lines 1 through 3	**4**	
5	Enter the following amount for your filing status: Married filing jointly. . . . . $250,000 Married filing separately . . . . $125,000 Single, Head of household, or Qualifying widow(er) $200,000	**5**	250,000
6	Subtract line 5 from line 4. If the result is zero or less, enter -0-	**6**	31,905
7	Additional Medicare Tax on Medicare wages. Multiply line 6 by 0.9% (.009). Enter here and go to Part II	**7**	287

Part II   Additional Medicare Tax on Self-Employment Income

8	Self-employment income from Schedule SE (Form 1040), Section A, line 4, or Section B, line 6. If you had a loss, enter -0- (Form 1040-PR and Form 1040-SS filers, see instructions.)	**8**	
9	Enter the following amount for your filing status: Married filing jointly. . . . . $250,000 Married filing separately . . . . $125,000 Single, Head of household, or Qualifying widow(er) $200,000	**9**	
10	Enter the amount from line 4	**10**	
11	Subtract line 10 from line 9. If zero or less, enter -0- . . .	**11**	
12	Subtract line 11 from line 8. If the result is zero or less, enter -0-	**12**	
13	Additional Medicare Tax on self-employment income. Multiply line 12 by 0.9% (.009). Enter here and go to Part III	**13**	

Part III   Additional Medicare Tax on Railroad Retirement Tax Act (RRTA) Compensation

14	Railroad retirement (RRTA) compensation and tips from Form(s) W-2, box 14 (see instructions)	**14**	
15	Enter the following amount for your filing status: Married filing jointly. . . . . $250,000 Married filing separately . . . . $125,000 Single, Head of household, or Qualifying widow(er) $200,000	**15**	
16	Subtract line 15 from line 14. If zero or less, enter -0-	**16**	
17	Additional Medicare Tax on railroad retirement (RRTA) compensation. Multiply line 16 by 0.9% (.009). Enter here and go to Part IV	**17**	

Part IV   Total Additional Medicare Tax

18	Add lines 7, 13, and 17. Also include this amount on Form 1040, line 60, (Form 1040NR, 1040-PR, and 1040-SS filers, see instructions) and go to Part V	**18**	287

Part V   Withholding Reconciliation

19	Medicare tax withheld from Form W-2, box 6. If you have more than one Form W-2, enter the total of the amounts from box 6	**19**	4,088
20	Enter the amount from line 1	**20**	31,905
21	Multiply line 20 by 1.45% (.0145). This is your regular Medicare tax withholding on Medicare wages	**21**	463
22	Subtract line 21 from line 19. This is your Additional Medicare Tax withholding on Medicare wages	**22**	3,625
23	Additional Medicare Tax withholding on railroad retirement (RRTA) compensation from Form W-2, box 14 (see instructions)	**23**	-0-
24	**Total Additional Medicare Tax withholding.** Add lines 22 and 23. Also include this amount with federal income tax withholding on Form 1040, line 62 (Form 1040NR, 1040-PR, and 1040-SS filers, see instructions)	**24**	3,625

For Paperwork Reduction Act Notice, see your tax return instructions.   Cat. No. 59475X   Form **8959** (2013)

¶2789 FORM 8960—NET INVESTMENT INCOME TAX— INDIVIDUALS, ESTATES AND TRUSTS

(a) 3.8 Percent Net Investment Income Tax on Unearned Income.

Beginning in 2013, individuals are subject to a 3.8 net investment income tax on the lesser of: (1) net investment income, or (2) the excess of modified adjusted gross income (MAGI) over an unindexed threshold amount ($250,000 for joint filers or surviving spouses, $125,000 for a married individual filing a separate return, and $200,000 in any other case) [IRC Sec. 1411(a)(1); Reg. Sec. 14110-2(b)].

Net investment income consists of the sum of the following three groups of income reduced by any properly allocable deductions for each [Reg. Sec. 1.1411-4(a)]:

- Group 1: Gross income from interest, dividends, annuities, royalties, and rents, which is not derived in the ordinary course of an active trade or business, reduced by any properly allocable deductions.

- Group 2: Gross income from a trade or business that is a passive activity or a trade or business of trading in financial instruments or commodities reduced by any properly allocable deductions.

- Group 3: Net gain attributable to the disposition of nonbusiness property and property held in a passive business activity reduced by any properly allocable deductions. Net investment income may include rental and royalty income, income from partnerships, S corporations and trusts, and income from other passive activities reported on a taxpayer's Schedule E.

MAGI is defined in Reg. Sec. 1.1411-2(c) as adjusted gross income (AGI) less any net foreign earned income.

The MAGI threshold amounts are defined in IRC Sec.1411(b) as follows:

Filing Status	Threshold Amount
Married filing jointly or surviving spouse	$250,000
Married filing separate	$125,000
Single	$200,000
Head of household (with qualifying person)	$200,000
Qualifying widow(er) with dependent child	$200,000

In the case of an individual such as a decedent filing a final return who has a tax year consisting of less than 12 months (short tax year), the threshold amount is not reduced or prorated. For example, in the case of a married decedent who dies on July 1, the threshold amount is $250,000 for the decedent's short tax year that begins on January 1 and ends on July 1 and for which the decedent must file a final income tax return on Form 1040.

Example 1: Taxpayer who is single has net investment income of $100,000 and MAGI of $220,000. Taxpayer will pay 3.8 percent net investment income tax on $20,000, the amount by which Taxpayer's MAGI exceeds the $200,000 threshold since this is less than Taxpayer's net investment income of $100,000. Taxpayer's 3.8 percent net investment income tax will be $760 ($20,000 × 3.8 percent).

¶2789

■ The decedent George E. and Mary King will have to complete Form 8960 in 2013 because their modified adjusted gross income (MAGI) is over the threshold amount of $250,000 for joint filers.

Use Form 8960, "Net Investment Income Tax—Individuals, Estates, and Trusts," to compute the amount of the taxpayer's net investment income tax as follows.

Part I—Investment Income

Line 1—Taxable Interest. Interest income earned in the ordinary course of your non-section 1411 trade or business is excluded from net investment income. Self-charged interest income received from a partnership or S corporation that is a nonpassive activity (other than a trade or business of trading in financial instruments or commodities) is also excluded from net investment income.

■ The decedent George E. and Mary King enter taxable interest in the amount of $1,806 which comes from their Form 1040, line 8a.

Line 2—Ordinary Dividends. Enter the amount of ordinary dividends received.

■ The decedent George E. and Mary King enter ordinary dividends in the amount of $8,000 which comes from their Form 1040, line 9a.

Line 3—Annuities from Nonqualified Plans. Enter the gross income from all annuities received from nonqualified plans. Annuities received from both qualified and nonqualified plans are reported to the recipient on Form 1099-R. However, only those annuities received from nonqualified plans are subject to the NIIT. Examples of annuities from nonqualified plans include private annuities and purchased commercial annuities. Distributions from the following annuities/retirement plans are not included in calculating net investment income: Section 401—Qualified pension, profit-sharing, and stock bonus plans; Section 403(a)—Qualified annuity plans purchased by an employer for an employee; Section 403(b)—Annuities purchased by public schools or section 501(c)(3) tax-exempt organizations; Section 408—Individual Retirement Accounts; Section 408A—Roth IRAs; and Section 457(b)—Deferred compensation plans of a state or local government or tax-exempt organization.

Line 4a—Rental Real Estate, Royalties, Partnerships, S Corporations, Trusts, etc. See Form 1040, line 17 for the amount to enter on line 4a of Form 8960.

■ The decedent George E. and Mary King enter royalties in the amount of $7,000 from line 41 of Schedule E which is also entered on line 17 of Form 1040.

Line 4b—Adjustment for Net Income or Loss Derived in the Ordinary Course of a Non-Section 1411 Trade or Business. Enter the net positive or net negative amount for the following items included in line 4a that are not included in determining net investment income:

• Net income or loss from a trade or business that is not a passive activity and is not engaged in a trade or business of trading financial instruments or commodities,

• Net income or loss from a passive trade or business activity that is taken into account in determining self-employment income,

• Royalties derived in the ordinary course of a trade or business that is not a passive activity, and

¶2789

- Passive losses of a former passive activity that are allowed as a deduction in the current year.

In addition, use line 4b of Form 8960 to adjust for certain types of nonpassive rental income or loss derived in the ordinary course of a trade or business. For example, line 4b includes the following items:

- Nonpassive net rental income or loss of a real estate professional where the rental activity rises to a trade or business.

- Net rental income or loss that is a nonpassive activity because it was grouped with a trade or business under Reg. Sec. 1.469-4(d)(1).

- Other rental income or loss from a trade or business reported on Schedule K-1 (Form 1065), line 3, from a partnership, or Schedule K-1 (Form 1120S), line 3, from an S corporation, where the activity is not a passive activity.

- Net income that has been recharacterized as not from a passive activity under the passive loss rules and is derived in the ordinary course of a trade or business.

Part II—Investment Expenses Allocable to Investment Income and Modifications

Investment Expenses. Taxpayers should enter on Part II of Form 8960 any deductions and modifications to net investment income that are not otherwise included in Part I. Generally, expenses associated with a passive activity trade or business, or the trade or business of trading in financial instruments or commodities conducted through a pass-through entity are already included on line 4a because line 4a uses net income (loss) from Schedule E (Form 1040). Part II is used to report deductions that are, predominately, itemized deductions.

Line 9a—Investment Interest Expenses. Enter on Form 8960, line 9a, interest expense paid or accrued during the year from either Schedule A (Form 1040), line 14 or the amount from Form 4952, line 8.

Line 9b—State Income Tax. Include on line 9b any state or local income taxes, or foreign income taxes paid which are attributable to net investment income. This may be all or part of the amount reported on Schedule A (Form 1040), line 5a (or Form 1041, line 11). For purposes of line 9b, sales taxes are not deductible in computing net investment income. If the taxpayer claimed an income tax credit for foreign income taxes (generally, reported using Form 1116), those foreign taxes are not deductible in computing net investment income.

Line 9c—Miscellaneous Investment Expenses. Investment expenses you incur that are directly connected to the production of investment income are deductible expenses in determining net investment income. Generally, these amounts are reported on Form 4952, line 5.

Line 10—Additional Modifications. Use line 10 to report additional deductions and modifications to net investment income that are not otherwise reflected in lines 1–9. Enter amounts on line 10 as positive numbers. On line 10 only properly allocable deductions can be taken into account in determining a taxpayer's net investment income. These deductions cannot exceed the taxpayer's total amount of gross net investment income and net gain. The deductions are subtracted from affected gross income and gains in calculating a taxpayer's net investment income. Use line 10 to report properly allocable deductions such as:

- The penalty paid for an early withdrawal of savings,

- The amount treated as an ordinary loss by a holder of a contingency payment debt instrument,

- Net negative periodic payments paid on a national principal contract that is referenced to property that produces interest, dividends, royalties, or rents.

- Certain amounts reported on Schedule A (Form 1040), line 28 as follows:

  1. The amount of the deduction allowed to an annuitant for the annuitant's last tax year provided the income from the annuity would have been included in net investment income and not otherwise excluded as a distribution from a qualified plan

  2. Deduction for payment of amounts under a claim of right if over $3,000, to the extent that such repayments relate to items of income included in net investment income in a preceding year that began after 2012.

- The amount of the deduction allowable for the amortizable bond premium on a taxable bond. This amount of bond premium amortization is already taken into account in computing interest income on Form 8960, line 1.

- To the extent properly allocable to net investment income: all ordinary and necessary expenses paid or incurred during the tax year to determine, collect, or obtain a refund of any tax owed, but only to the extent the expenses are allocable to net investment income from Schedule A, Form 1040, line 22.

- **Deductions subject to AGI limitations under IRC Secs. 67 or 68.** Any deduction allowed against net investment income that, for purposes of computing income tax, is subject to either the 2% floor on miscellaneous itemized deductions under IRC Sec. 67 or the overall limitation on itemized deductions under IRC Sec. 68 is allowed in determining net investment income, but only to the extent the items are deductible after application of both limitations.

- **Miscellaneous itemized deductions.** The amount of miscellaneous itemized deductions, after application of the 2% floor but before application of the overall limitation, used in determining net investment income is the lesser of: (1) That portion of your miscellaneous itemized deductions before the application of the 2% floor that is properly allocable to net investment income, or (2) total miscellaneous itemized deductions allowed after the application of the 2% floor but before the application of the overall limitation on itemized deductions.

- **Itemized deductions.** The amount of itemized deductions allowed in determining net investment income after applying both the 2% floor and the overall limitation is the lesser of: (1) The sum of: (a) The amount of miscellaneous itemized deductions allowed as a deduction against net investment income (before application of the overall limitation), and (b) The total amount of itemized deductions not subject to the 2% floor and properly allocable to items of income or net gain for purposes of determining net investment income, or (2) The total amount of itemized deductions

¶2789

allowed after the application of both the 2% floor and the overall limitation on itemized deductions.

Part III—Tax Computation—Individuals

Individuals complete lines 13–17.

Line 13—Modified Adjusted Gross Income (MAGI). Enter the amount on line 38, Form 1040, unless the individual has any net foreign earned income which should be deducted from AGI to find MAGI.

Line 14—Threshold Based on Filing Status. Enter the threshold amount below based on filing status:

Filing Status	Threshold Amount
Married filing jointly or surviving spouse	$250,000
Married filing separate	$125,000
Single	$200,000
Head of household (with qualifying person)	$200,000
Qualifying widow(er) with dependent child	$200,000

■ The decedent George E. and Mary King enter the $250,000 threshold on line 14 of Part III of Form 8960 and compute their net investment income tax in the amount of $639 on line 17 of Part III of Form 8960 which they enter on Form 1040, line 60 after checking box 60b indicating that they have filed Form 8960. Note that box 60b on the Final Form 1040 filed for the decedent George E. and Mary King indicates that both Form 8959 and Form 8960 have been filed. The total amount included on line 60 of Form 1040 is $926 which represents the total of $287 from line 18 of Form 8959 and $639 from line 17 of Form 8960.

(b) Sample Completed Form 8960—Net Investment Income Tax—Individuals, Estates and Trusts.

Form **8960**	Net Investment Income Tax—Individuals, Estates, and Trusts	OMB No. 1545-2227
Department of the Treasury Internal Revenue Service (99)	▶ Attach to Form 1040 or Form 1041. ▶ Information about Form 8960 and its separate instructions is at *www.irs.gov/form8960*.	20**13** Attachment Sequence No. **72**

Name(s) shown on Form 1040 or Form 1041	Your social security number or EIN
George E. (deceased 07/01/13) and Mary M. King	100-09-0603

Part I Investment Income
☐ Section 6013(g) election (see instructions)
☐ Regulations section 1.1411-10(g) election (see instructions)

1	Taxable interest (Form 1040, line 8a; or Form 1041, line 1)	**1**	1,806
2	Ordinary dividends (Form 1040, line 9a; or Form 1041, line 2a)	**2**	8,000
3	Annuities from nonqualified plans (see instructions)	**3**	
4a	Rental real estate, royalties, partnerships, S corporations, trusts, etc. (Form 1040, line 17; or Form 1041, line 5)	**4a** 7,000		
b	Adjustment for net income or loss derived in the ordinary course of a non-section 1411 trade or business (see instructions)	**4b**		
c	Combine lines 4a and 4b	**4c**	7,000
5a	Net gain or loss from disposition of property from Form 1040, combine lines 13 and 14; or from Form 1041, combine lines 4 and 7	**5a**		
b	Net gain or loss from disposition of property that is not subject to net investment income tax (see instructions)	**5b**		
c	Adjustment from disposition of partnership interest or S corporation stock (see instructions)	**5c**		
d	Combine lines 5a through 5c	**5d**	
6	Changes to investment income for certain CFCs and PFICs (see instructions)	**6**	
7	Other modifications to investment income (see instructions)	**7**	
8	Total investment income. Combine lines 1, 2, 3, 4c, 5d, 6, and 7	**8**	16,806

Part II Investment Expenses Allocable to Investment Income and Modifications

9a	Investment interest expenses (see instructions)	**9a**		
b	State income tax (see instructions)	**9b**		
c	Miscellaneous investment expenses (see instructions)	**9c**		
d	Add lines 9a, 9b, and 9c	**9d**	
10	Additional modifications (see instructions)	**10**	
11	Total deductions and modifications. Add lines 9d and 10	**11**	-0-

Part III Tax Computation

12	Net investment income. Subtract Part II, line 11 from Part I, line 8. Individuals complete lines 13–17. Estates and trusts complete lines 18a–21. If zero or less, enter -0-	**12**	16,806
	Individuals:		
13	Modified adjusted gross income (see instructions)	**13** 303,580	
14	Threshold based on filing status (see instructions)	**14** 250,000	
15	Subtract line 14 from line 13. If zero or less, enter -0-	**15** 53,580	
16	Enter the smaller of line 12 or line 15	**16**	16,806
17	Net investment income tax for individuals. Multiply line 16 by 3.8% (.038). Enter here and on Form 1040, line 60	**17**	639
	Estates and Trusts:		
18a	Net investment income (line 12 above)	**18a**		
b	Deductions for distributions of net investment income and deductions under section 642(c) (see instructions)	**18b**		
c	Undistributed net investment income. Subtract line 18b from 18a (see instructions)	**18c**		
19a	Adjusted gross income (see instructions)	**19a**		
b	Highest tax bracket for estates and trusts for the year (see instructions)	**19b**		
c	Subtract line 19b from line 19a. If zero or less, enter -0- . . .	**19c**		
20	Enter the smaller of line 18c or line 19c	**20**	
21	Net investment income tax for estates and trusts. Multiply line 20 by 3.8% (.038). Enter here and on Form 1041, Schedule G, line 4	**21**	

For Paperwork Reduction Act Notice, see your tax return instructions.	Cat. No. 59474M	Form **8960** (2013)

¶2790 INSTRUCTIONS TO FORM 8960—NET INVESTMENT INCOME TAX—INDIVIDUALS, ESTATES AND TRUSTS

20**13**

Instructions for Form 8960

Net Investment Income Tax— Individuals, Estates, and Trusts

Department of the Treasury
Internal Revenue Service

Section references are to the Internal Revenue Code unless otherwise noted.

General Instructions

These instructions are based mostly on Regulations sections 1.1411-1 through 1.1411-10, which are effective for tax years beginning after 2013. However, you may rely on these instructions for your 2013 tax year.

Future Developments

For the latest information about developments related to Form 8960 and its instructions, such as legislation enacted after they were published, go to *www.irs.gov/form8960*.

Who Must File

Attach Form 8960 to your return if Form 8960, line 17, is greater than zero (individuals) or line 21 is greater than zero (estates and trusts).

Purpose of Form

Use Form 8960 to figure the amount of your Net Investment Income Tax (NIIT).

Definitions

Controlled foreign corporation (CFC). A corporation defined in section 953(c)(1)(B) or 957(a).

Excluded income. Excluded income means:
* Items of income excluded from gross income in IRC chapter 1,
* Items of income not included in net investment income, and
* Items of gross income and net gain specifically excluded by section 1411, related regulations, or other guidance published in the Internal Revenue Bulletin.

   Examples of excluded items are:
* Wages,
* Unemployment compensation,
* Alaska Permanent Fund Dividends,
* Alimony,
* Social Security benefits,
* Tax-exempt interest income,
* Income from certain qualified retirement plan distributions, and
* Income subject to self-employment taxes.

Net investment income. Net investment income is defined in section 1411(c) and Regulations section 1.1411-4. It is

adjusted according to the rules described in Regulations section 1.1411-10(c).

Passive foreign investment company (PFIC). A PFIC is as defined in section 1297(a).

Qualified electing fund (QEF). A QEF, as defined in section 1295, is a PFIC with respect to which an election under section 1295(b) is in effect.

Section 1.1411-10(g) election. An election made under Regulations section 1.1411-10(g)(section 1.1411-10(g) election). See *Regulations Section 1.1411-10(g) Election*, later.

Section 1411 trade or business. A trade or business described in section 1411(c)(2) and Regulations section 1.1411-5(a). Generally, a trade or business that is a passive activity, or is engaged in trading financial instruments or commodities.

Substitute interest or substitute dividends. Payments made to the transferor of a security in a securities lending transaction or a sale-repurchase transaction.

Recordkeeping

For the NIIT, certain items of investment income and investment expense receive different treatment than for the regular income tax. Therefore, you need to keep all records and worksheets for the items you need to include on Form 8960. Keep all records for the entire life of the investment to show how you calculated basis. Also, you will need to know what you did in prior years if the investment was part of a carryback or carryforward.

Application to Individuals

U.S. citizens and residents. Individuals who have for the tax year (a) modified adjusted gross income (MAGI) that is over an applicable threshold amount, and (b) net investment income, must pay 3.8% of the smaller of (a) or (b) as their NIIT.

   The applicable threshold amount is based on your filing status:
* Married Filing Jointly or Qualifying Widower with Dependent Child is $250,000,
* Married Filing Separately is $125,000, or
* Single or Head of Household is $200,000.

Nonresidents. The NIIT does not apply to nonresident alien (NRA) individuals. If you are a U.S. citizen or resident married to an NRA, your filing status will be married filing separately for purposes of determining your MAGI, net investment income, and whether you are subject to the NIIT. However, see information later about certain elections to file jointly with NRA spouses.

Dual-resident individual. If you are a dual-resident individual, within the meaning of Regulations section 301.7701(b)-7(a)(1), generally you will be treated as a U.S. resident for purposes of the NIIT. However, you will be treated as an NRA for purposes of the NIIT if:
* You determine you would be treated as a resident of a foreign country for purposes of an income tax treaty between the United States and that foreign country,
* You elect to be treated as a resident of the foreign country for purposes of computing your U.S. income tax liability, and
* You file Form 1040NR, U.S. Nonresident Alien Income Tax Return, and Form 8833, Treaty-Based Return Position Return Disclosure Under Section 6114 or 7701(b), as provided in Regulations section 301.7701(b)-7(b).

Dual-status individual. If you are a dual-status individual — i.e., an individual who was a resident of the United States for part of the year and an NRA for the other part of the year — you are subject to the NIIT only with respect to the portion of the year during which you were a U.S. resident. The relevant threshold amount is not reduced or prorated for a dual-status resident. For more information, see Pub. 519, U.S. Tax Guide for Aliens. If you file Form 1040NR and owe NIIT, include the tax from Form 8960, line 17, on Form 1040NR, line 59. Attach Form 8960 to Form 1040NR.

Election To File Jointly With Nonresident Spouse—Section 6013(g) or 6013(h)

If spouses elect to file a joint return under section:
* 6013(g) (where an NRA is married to a U.S. citizen or resident at the end of the tax year); or
* 6013(h) (where at least one spouse was an NRA at the beginning of the tax year, but is a U.S. citizen or resident married to

Feb 26, 2014

Cat. No. 53783S

a U.S. citizen or resident at the end of the tax year);

they can also elect to apply the joint return election for NIIT purposes.

If spouses make either election for NIIT purposes, spouses should use their combined items of income, gain, loss, and deduction from their joint return to figure their net investment income and MAGI, and use the married filing joint return applicable threshold amount ($250,000).

Additionally, if you make the election to file under section 6013(g), you must check the check-box near the top of Form 8960, Part I.

Once you make either election, its duration and termination is governed by sections 6013(g) and 6013(h), respectively, and related regulations.

You can make either election on an amended return only if the tax year for which you are making the election, and all tax years affected by the election, are not closed by the period of limitations on assessments under section 6501.

If you make a section 6013(g) election for NIIT purposes and later determine you did not meet the criteria for making that election at the time you made it, the original election will have no effect for that year and all future years. In that case, you must make adjustments to your return to reflect the ineffective election. However, if you meet the criteria for the same election in a later year, you will be considered to have made the original election in that later year unless you file (or amend) the return for that later year to report your NIIT without the original election.

Application to Estates and Trusts

Domestic estates and trusts. The NIIT applies to estates and trusts that have undistributed net investment income and adjusted gross income (AGI) in excess of the threshold amount. The NIIT is 3.8% of the lesser of:

• the undistributed net investment income for the tax year, or
• the excess, if any, of AGI (as defined in section 67(e)) over the applicable threshold amount.

The applicable threshold amount is the dollar amount at which the highest tax bracket in section 1(e) begins for the tax year. See Form 1041, U.S. Income Tax Return for Estates and Trusts, and its instructions for the highest tax bracket.

Exception for certain domestic trusts. The following trusts are not subject to the NIIT:

• Trusts that are exempt from income taxes imposed by Subtitle A of the Internal Revenue Code:

1. Charitable trusts and qualified retirement plan trusts exempt from tax under section 501, and

2. Charitable Remainder Trusts exempt from tax under section 664;

• A trust or decedent's estate in which all of the unexpired interests are devoted to one or more of the purposes described in section 170(c)(2)(B);
• Trusts that are classified as "grantor trusts" under sections 671-679;
• Electing Alaska Native Settlement Funds (described in section 646);
• Perpetual Care (Cemetery) Trusts (described in section 642(i)); and
• Trusts that are not classified as "trusts" for federal income tax purposes. For example:

1. Real Estate Investment Trusts, and

2. Common Trust Funds.

Special computational rules for qualified funeral trusts (QFTs). The NIIT applies to the QFT (as defined in section 685) by treating each beneficiary's interest in that beneficiary's contract as a separate trust. Complete one consolidated Form 8960 for all beneficiary contracts subject to NIIT.

If a QFT has one or more beneficiary contracts that have net investment income in excess of the threshold amount:

• Complete Form 8960, lines 1-12, using only the sum of the net investment income of the beneficiary contracts that have net investment income in excess of the threshold amount, and
• On line 19b:

1. Insert the number of beneficiary contracts that have net investment income in excess of the threshold amount next to the entry on the line, and

2. Multiply the number of beneficiary contracts that have net investment income in excess of the threshold amount by the threshold amount for the year and enter that amount on line 19b.

Example. A QFT has a beneficiary contract with $13,000 of interest income and another beneficiary contract with $12,000 of dividend income. Neither contract has any properly allocable deductions. The threshold amount for the year is $11,950. Therefore, the QFT has 2 beneficiary contracts with net investment income in excess of the threshold amount for the year.

The QFT will report $13,000 on line 1 (interest) and $12,000 on line 2 (dividends). Lines 12, 18a, and 19 would each be $25,000. Enter "2" on the dotted line at the end of line 19b and enter $23,900 ($11,950 × 2) on the entry line for 19b. Lines 19c and 20 will be $1,100 ($25,000 less $23,900). On line 21, enter

the NIIT liability of $41.80 ($1,100 × 3.8%).

Special computational rules for electing small business trusts (ESBTs). The NIIT has special computational rules for ESBTs. In general, ESBTs compute their NIIT in 3 steps:

1. The ESBT separately calculates the undistributed net investment income of the S portion and non-S portion according to the general rules for trusts under IRC chapter 1, and then combines the undistributed net investment income of the S portion and the non-S portion. In the case of an ESBT that has an S portion and a non-S portion, complete lines 1-11 of Form 8960 using the items from the non-S portion, and add undistributed net investment income of the S portion to net investment income on line 7.

2. The ESBT determines its AGI, solely for purposes of NIIT, by adding the net income or net loss from the S portion to the AGI of the non-S portion as a single item of income or loss. See instructions for line 19a for more information.

3. To determine whether the ESBT is subject to NIIT, the ESBT compares the combined undistributed net investment income with the excess of its AGI over the section 1(e) threshold.

See Regulations section 1.1411-3(c) for more details and examples.

Special computational rules for bankruptcy estates of an individual. A bankruptcy estate of an individual debtor is treated as an individual for purposes of the NIIT. Regardless of the actual marital status of the debtor, the applicable threshold for purposes of determining the NIIT is the amount applicable for a married person filing separately.

Distributions from foreign estates and foreign trusts. If you are a U.S. person who receives a distribution of income from a foreign estate or foreign trust, generally, you must include the distribution in your net investment income calculation to the extent that the income is included in your AGI for regular income tax purposes. However, you do not need to include any distributions of accumulated income that you receive from a foreign trust.

Note. The NIIT does not apply directly to foreign estates or foreign trusts.

Passive Activity

General Rules

Net investment income generally includes income and gain from passive activities. A passive activity for purposes of net investment income has the same meaning as under section 469. A passive activity includes any trade or business in which you do not materially participate. A passive activity also includes any rental activity, regardless of whether you materially participate. There are limited exceptions for rentals. See the discussion on rentals later. For more details on passive activities, see the Instructions for Form 8582, Passive Activity Loss Limitations, and Pub. 925, Passive Activity and At-Risk Rules.

Trade or Business Activities

The definition of trade or business for NIIT purposes is limited to a trade or business within the meaning of section 162. This is more restrictive than the definition of a trade or business activity for the purposes of the passive activity loss rules. For example, under the passive activity loss rules, a trade or business includes any activity conducted in anticipation of the commencement of a trade or business and any activity involving research or experimentation. In some cases, income from activities that are not passive activities under section 469 will be included in net investment income because the activity does not rise to the level of a trade or business within the meaning of section 162. The activity must be a trade or business within the meaning of section 162 and be nonpassive for the purposes of section 469 before the income is excluded from the NIIT. If you own an interest in a pass-through entity, the determination of whether that is a trade or business is made at the entity level.

Material Participation

A trade or business is a passive activity if you did not materially participate in the activity during the year. If you are an individual, you materially participate in your trade or business activity if you are involved in the operations of the activity on a regular, continuous, and substantial basis. You will be treated as materially participating in a trade or business only if you meet one of the following tests:

1. You participate in the activity for more than 500 hours,

2. Your participation was substantially all the participation in the trade or business of all individuals for the tax year, including the participation of individuals who did not own any interest in the trade or business,

3. You participated in the trade or business for more than 100 hours during the tax year, and you participated at least as much as any other individual (including individuals who did not own any interest in the trade or business) for the year,

4. The trade or business activity is a significant participation activity, and you participated in all significant participation activities for more than 500 hours. A significant participation activity is any trade or business activity in which you

participated for more than 100 hours during the year and in which you did not materially participate under any of the other material participation tests,

5. You materially participated in the activity for any 5 (whether or not consecutive) of the 10 immediately preceding tax years,

6. The trade or business is a personal service activity in which you materially participated for any 3 (whether or not consecutive) preceding tax years. A trade or business is a personal service activity if it involves the performance of personal services in the fields of health (including veterinary services), law, engineering, architecture, accounting, actuarial science, performing arts, consulting, or any other trade or business in which capital is not a material income-producing factor, or

7. Based on all the facts and circumstances, you participated in the trade or business on a regular, continuous, and substantial basis during the year.

You did not materially participate in the trade or business under the last test if you participated in the trade or business for 100 hours or less during the year. Your participation in managing the trade or business does not count in determining whether you materially participated under this test if any person other than you received compensation for managing the trade or business, or any individual spent more hours during the tax year managing the trade or business than you did.

There are special rules applicable to limited partners. If you owned an interest in a trade or business as a limited partner, you generally are treated as not participating in the trade or business. You can be treated as materially participating in the activity if you met the first, fifth, or sixth tests under the material participation tests, earlier.

Rental Activities

Generally, a rental activity is a passive activity regardless of whether you materially participate. A rental activity is an activity where payments are principally for the use of tangible property (real or personal) that is used or held for use by customers. However, your activity involving the use of tangible property is not a rental activity under Regulations section 1.469-1T(e)(3)(ii) if any of the following apply:
• The average period of customer use of the property is 7 days or less,
• The average period of customer use is 30 days or less and you provide significant personal services with the rental,
• You provide extraordinary personal services in connection with making such property available for customer use, or

• You provide the property for use in a nonrental activity in your capacity as an owner of an interest in the partnership, S corporation, or joint venture conducting that activity.

If you meet one of the exceptions listed above, the income will not be from a passive activity if you materially participated in the activity for the tax year. However, your income for the activity is included in net investment income even if you meet one of the exceptions and materially participated in the activity if it is not a trade or business within the meaning of section 162.

Real Estate Professionals

If you are a real estate professional for purposes of section 469(c)(7), your rental income, or loss will not be passive if you materially participated in the rental real estate activity. For additional information on real estate professionals, see section 469(c)(7) and Pub. 925.

However, your rental income is included in net investment income if the income is not derived in the ordinary course of a trade or business. Qualifying as a real estate professional does not necessarily mean you are engaged in a trade or business with respect to the rental real estate activities. If your rental real estate activity is not a section 162 trade or business or you do not materially participate in the rental real estate activities, the rental income will be included in NIIT.

Safe Harbor for Real Estate Professionals

You qualify for the safe harbor if you are a real estate professional for purposes of section 469 and you:
• Participate in each rental real estate activity for more than 500 hours during the tax year, or
• Participated in a rental real estate activity for more than 500 hours in any 5 tax years (whether or not consecutive) during the 10 tax years immediately prior to this tax year.
If you qualify, your gross rental income from your rental real estate activity is treated as though derived in the ordinary course of a trade or business and is not included in your net investment income. If you qualify in the year you dispose of the property used in the rental real estate activity, the amount of gain or loss from the disposition is also deemed to be derived from property used in the ordinary course of a trade or business and is not included in your net investment income.

Note. For real estate professionals with a Regulations section 1.469-9(g) election in effect, all of your rental real estate activities constitute a single activity for purposes of applying the 500-hour test described in *Safe Harbor for Real Estate Professionals*, earlier.

Note. If you are a real estate professional under section 469(c)(7), but you are unable to satisfy the qualifications for the safe harbor, you are not precluded from establishing that the gross income and gain or loss from the disposition of property associated with your rental real estate activity is not included in net investment income.

Recharacterization of Passive Income

The regulations under section 469 provide special rules that treat income from the following activities as not from a passive activity:
• Significant participation passive activities,
• Rental of property if less than 30% of the unadjusted basis of the property is subject to depreciation,
• Passive equity-financed lending activities,
• Rental of property incidental to a development activity,
• Rental of property to a nonpassive activity, or
• Acquisition of an interest in a pass-through entity that licenses intangible property.

The income from these activities may be included in net investment income if the income is not derived in the ordinary course of a trade or business and it constitutes income from interest, dividends, annuities, royalties, or rents. For more information on recharacterization of passive income, see Temporary Regulations section 1.469-2T(f), Regulations section 1.469-2(f), and Pub. 925.

Special Rules for Certain Rental Income

For income tax purposes, Regulations section 1.469-2(f)(6) generally recharacterizes what otherwise would be passive rental income from a taxpayer's property as nonpassive where the taxpayer rents the property for use in a trade or business in which the taxpayer materially participates. Similarly, for income tax purposes, a rental activity that is properly grouped with a trade or business activity in which the taxpayer materially participates under Regulations section 1.469-4(d)(1) is a nonpassive activity. For purposes of calculating your net investment income, the gross rental income in both of these situations is treated as though it is derived in the ordinary course of a trade or business. Further, upon the disposition of the assets associated with the rental activity, any gain or loss is also treated as gain or loss attributable to the disposition of property

held in a nonpassive trade or business and not included in your net investment income.

Treatment of Former Passive Activities

A former passive activity is any activity that was a passive activity in a prior tax year but it is not a passive activity in the current year. A prior tax year's unallowed loss from a former passive activity is allowed to the extent of current year income from the activity. For purposes of determining your net investment income, suspended losses from former passive activities are allowed as a properly allocable deduction, but only to the extent nonpassive income from the same activity is included in your net investment income in that year. For more information, see Regulations section 1.1411-4(g)(8) and examples.

Disposition of Entire Interest

If you disposed of your entire interest in a passive activity or a former passive activity to an unrelated person in a fully taxable transaction, your losses allocable to the activity for that year are not limited by the passive activity loss rules for income tax purposes. A fully taxable transaction is a transaction in which you recognize all realized gain or loss. For purposes of calculating your net investment income, these losses may be properly allocable deductions, depending on the underlying character and origin of the losses.

Note. If you dispose of an activity that has always been a passive activity, the suspended passive losses from that activity are allowed in full as a properly allocable deduction.

Note. If you dispose of an activity that is a former passive activity, any suspended passive losses allowed in the year of disposition by reason of section 469(f)(1)(A) are included as properly allocable deductions, but only to the extent the gain on the disposition of the activity is included in net investment income (before taking into account any suspended losses). Any suspended passive losses that are allowed by reason of section 469(g) are allowed as additional properly allocable deductions.

Economic Grouping

You can treat one or more trade or business activities, or rental activities, as a single activity if those activities form an appropriate economic unit for measuring gain or loss under the passive activity loss rules. For additional information on passive activity grouping rules, see Pub. 925.

Regrouping rules. The passive activity grouping rules determine the scope of

your trade or business and whether that trade or business is a passive activity for purposes of the NIIT. The proper grouping of a rental activity with a trade or business activity generally will not convert any gross income from rents into gross income derived from a trade or business.

Generally, you may not regroup activities unless your grouping was clearly inappropriate when originally made, or has become clearly inappropriate because of changed facts and circumstances. However, under the NIIT "fresh start" election you may regroup for the first tax year you are subject to the NIIT (without the effect of the regrouping). You may regroup only once under this election and that regrouping will apply to the tax year for which you regroup and all future tax years. If you are subject to the NIIT for 2013 and you do not regroup, you may make the election for the first tax year beginning after 2013 that you are subject to the NIIT.

Disclosure requirements. Regroupings under the NIIT "fresh start" are subject to the disclosure requirements of Rev. Proc. 2010-13.

Disposition of Partnership Interest or S Corporation Stock

In general, an interest in a partnership or S corporation is not property held for use in a trade or business and, therefore, gain or loss from the sale of a partnership interest or S corporation stock is included in your net investment income.

Adjustment

The amount of the gain or loss from the disposition for regular income tax purposes is included on Form 8960, line 5a, as a gain or loss. If you materially participated (as defined under the passive activity loss rules) in a trade or business activity of the partnership or S corporation (or one of its subsidiaries) and that trade or business activity is not the trade or business of trading in financial instruments or securities, then you must calculate the adjustment to report on line 5c. The adjustment described below only applies to dispositions of equity interests in partnerships and stock in S corporations and does not apply to gain or loss recognized on, for example, indebtedness owed to the taxpayer by a partnership or S corporation.

For tax year 2013, you may use the calculation and reporting methods from either the 2012 Proposed Regulations or the 2013 Proposed Regulations. For more information on how to calculate the adjustment to report on line 5c, see the 2012 Proposed Regulations section 1.1411-7 or the 2013 Proposed Regulations section 1.1411-7.

Note. If the tax basis of the interest in the partnership or S corporation for NIIT purposes is different than for regular income tax purposes due to certain adjustments associated with income from CFCs or QEFs, the amount of gain or loss may exceed the amount reported for regular income tax purposes.

Required statements. If your adjustment on line 5c is based on the 2012 Proposed Regulations, attach a statement to your return for the year of disposition. Your statement must include:
- A description of the disposed interest,
- The name and taxpayer identification number of the entity disposed of,
- The fair market value of each property of the entity,
- The entity's adjusted basis in each property,
- Your allocable share of gain or loss with respect to each property of the entity,
- Information regarding whether the property was held in a trade or business in which you materially participated and was not trading in financial instruments or commodities,
- The amount of gain you reported on line 5a, and
- The amount of your adjustment.

If your adjustment on line 5c is based on the 2013 Proposed Regulations, attach a statement to your return for the year of disposition. Your statement must include:
- The name and taxpayer identification number of the partnership or S corporation of which the interest was transferred,
- The amount of the transferor's gain or loss on the disposition of the interest for regular income tax purposes included on line 5a,
- The information provided by the partnership or S corporation to the transferor relating to the disposition (if any), and
- The amount of adjustment to gain or loss due to basis adjustments attributable to ownership in certain CFCs and QEFs.

Deferred recognition sales (install-ment sales and private annuities). If you disposed of a partnership interest or S corporation stock in an installment sale transaction to which section 453 applies, you need to calculate your adjustment to net gain in the year of the disposition, even if the disposition occurred prior to 2013. The difference between the amount reported for regular income tax and NIIT will be taken into account when each payment is received. You must attach the statement described above to your return in the first year you are subject to NIIT. In subsequent years, attach a statement to your return that provides "Adjustment relates to a deferred recognition sale first reported on line 5c of the (enter year) return."

Regulations Section 1.1411-10(g) Election

In general, you may make the election provided in Regulations section 1.1411-10(g) if you own stock of a CFC or QEF. If a section 1.1411-10(g) election is in effect for stock of a CFC or QEF, generally, the amounts you include in income for regular income tax purposes under sections 951 and 1293 from the stock of the CFC or QEF are included in net investment income, and distributions from the stock of the CFC or QEF described in section 959(d) or 1293(c) are excluded from net investment income.

Your election applies only to the specific stock of the CFC and QEF for which it is made and stock of the CFC or QEF that you subsequently acquire. If you own a CFC or QEF through certain domestic pass-through entities, such as a domestic partnership, the entity may make the election with respect to the stock of the CFC or QEF and you will be considered as having made the election with respect to the stock of the CFC or QEF owned or subsequently acquired by the pass-through entity. The election by the pass-through entity applies only to stock of the CFC or QEF held or subsequently acquired directly or indirectly by the pass-through entity. The pass-through entity's election does not apply to any stock of the CFC or QEF that you personally hold or subsequently acquire. If the entity does not make the election, you may make the election with respect to the stock of the CFC or QEF owned through the entity. For tax years beginning in 2013 only, a domestic partnership may make the election only if consent is received from all of the partners.

Timing of election. Your election applies to the tax year for which it is made and later tax years, and applies to all interests in the CFC or QEF that you later acquire. You cannot revoke the election. In general, the election must be made no later than the first tax year beginning after 2013, in which you include an amount in income for regular income tax purposes under section 951(a) or 1293(a) with respect to the stock of the CFC or QEF, and are subject to NIIT or would be subjected to NIIT if you made the election with respect to the stock of the CFC or QEF. The election may be made for a tax year beginning before January 1, 2014. The election can be made on an original or an amended return, provided that the tax year for which the election is made, and all tax years affected by the election, are not closed by the period of limitations on assessments under section 6501. For more information, see Regulations section 1.1411-10(g).

Example. If in 2014, a single individual acquires stock in a QEF, has a QEF

inclusion of $5,000, and has MAGI of $150,000, the individual would not have to make a section 1.1411-10(g) election for 2014 because section 1411 is not applicable. If in 2015, the individual has MAGI in excess of 200,000, and the individual would like to take QEF inclusions into account for purposes of section 1411 in the same manner and in the same tax year as those amounts are taken into account for IRC chapter 1 purposes, the individual must make the section 1.1411-10(g) election for 2015 in the time and manner described in Regulations section 1.1411-10(g).

Content requirements of election. If you are making the election, you must check the check-box for "Regulations section 1.1411-10(g) election" on the Form 8960 filed with your original or amended return for the tax year in which the election is made. In addition, you must attach a statement to your return which includes the following:
- Your name and SSN (individuals) or EIN (estates and trusts),
- A declaration that you elect under Regulations section 1.1411-10(g) to apply the rules in section 1.1411-10(g) to the CFCs and QEFs identified in the statement, and
- The following information with respect to each CFC and QEF for which an election is made:
    1. The name of the CFC or QEF, and
    2. Either the EIN of the CFC or QEF, or, if the CFC or QEF does not have an EIN, the reference ID number of the CFC or QEF.

Special Rule for Traders in Financial Instruments or Commodities

Gains and losses from your trade or business of trading in financial instruments or commodities are not subject to self-employment taxes. However, interest expense and other investment expenses are deducted by a trader on Schedule C (Form 1040), Profit or Loss From Business, if the expenses are from the trading business. A special rule may apply to a trader in financial instruments or commodities to reduce net investment income. The trader's interest and other investment expenses, to the extent the expenses are not used to reduce the trader's self-employment income, may be deductible for NIIT.

Specific Instructions

Part I—Investment Income

Elections for Investment Income

If you are making the section 6013(g) election (see *Election To File Jointly With Nonresident Spouse—Section 6013(g) or 6013(h)*, earlier), check the "Section 6013(g) Election" check-box.

Note. There is no check-box for the section 6013(h) election.

If you are making the section 1.1411-10(g) election (see *Regulations Section 1.1411-10(g) Election*, earlier), check the "Regulations section 1.1411-10(g) election" check-box and attach a statement to your return as described earlier under *Content requirements of election*.

Line 1—Taxable Interest

Enter the amount of interest received.

Interest income earned in the ordinary course of your non-section 1411 trade or business is excluded from net investment income. If this type of interest income is included in line 1, use line 7 to adjust your net investment income.

If line 1 includes self-charged interest income received from a partnership or S corporation that is a nonpassive activity (other than a trade or business of trading in financial instruments or commodities), see *Line 7—Other Modifications to Investment Income*, later, for a possible adjustment to net investment income.

Line 2—Ordinary Dividends

Enter the amount of ordinary dividends received.

Note. If line 2 includes dividends from employer securities held in an employee stock ownership plan (ESOP) that are deductible under section 404(k) or Alaska Permanent Fund Dividends, include those amounts as negative modifications on line 7. See *Line 7—Other Modifications to Investment Income*, later.

Line 3—Annuities

Enter the gross income from all annuities, except annuities paid from the following:
- Section 401 - Qualified pension, profit-sharing, and stock bonus plans;
- Section 403(a) - Qualified annuity plans purchased by an employer for an employee;
- Section 403(b) - Annuities purchased by public schools or Section 501(c)(3) tax-exempt organizations;

- Section 408 - Individual Retirement Accounts (IRAs) or Annuities;
- Section 408A - Roth IRAs;
- Section 457(b) - Deferred compensation plans of a state and local government and tax-exempt organization; and
- Amounts paid in consideration for services (for example, distributions from a foreign retirement plan that are paid in the form of an annuity and include investment income that was earned by the retirement plan).

Net investment income from annuities is reported to a recipient on Form 1099-R, Distributions From Pensions, Annuities, Retirement or Profit-Sharing Plans, IRAs, Insurance Contracts, etc. However, the amount reported on 1099-R may also include annuity payments from retirement plans that are exempt from NIIT.

Annuity amounts subject to NIIT should be identified with the special Distribution Code "D" in box 7 of Form 1099-R for "Annuity payments from nonqualified annuities and distributions from life insurance contracts that may be subject to tax under section 1411." If Distribution Code "D" is shown in box 7 of Form 1099-R, include on Form 8960, line 3, the taxable amount reported on Form 1099-R, box 2a. However, if the payor checks box 2b indicating the taxable amount cannot be determined, you may need to calculate the taxable portion of your distribution. See Pub. 939, General Rule for Pensions and Annuities, and Pub. 575, Pension and Annuity Income, for details.

Line 4b—Adjustment for Net Income or Loss Derived in the Ordinary Course of a Non-Section 1411 Trade or Business

Enter the net positive or net negative amount for the following items included in line 4a that are not included in determining net investment income:
- Net income or loss from a section 162 trade or business that is not a passive activity and is not engaged in a trade or business of trading financial instruments or commodities,
- Net income or loss from a passive section 162 trade or business activity that is taken into account in determining self-employment income,
- Royalties derived in the ordinary course of a section 162 trade or business that is not a passive activity, and
- Passive losses of a former passive activity that are allowed as a deduction in the current year by reason of section 469(f)(1)(A).

In addition, use line 4b to adjust for certain types of nonpassive rental income

or loss derived in the ordinary course of a section 162 trade or business. For example, line 4b includes the following items:
- Nonpassive net rental income or loss of a real estate professional where the rental activity rises to a section 162 trade or business. See *Real Estate Professionals*, earlier.
- Net rental income or loss that is a nonpassive activity because it was grouped with a trade or business under Regulations section 1.469-4(d)(1). See *Special Rules for Certain Rental Income*, earlier.
- Other rental income or loss from a section 162 trade or business reported on Schedule K-1 (Form 1065), Partner's Share of Income, Deductions, Credits, etc., line 3, from a partnership, or Schedule K-1 (Form 1120S), Shareholder's Share of Income, Deductions, Credits, etc., line 3, from an S corporation, where the activity is not a passive activity.
- Net income that has been recharacterized as not from a passive activity under the section 469 passive loss rules and is derived in the ordinary course of a section 162 trade or business. For example:

   1. Net income from property rented to a nonpassive activity. See *Special Rules for Certain Rental Income*, earlier,

   2. Net income from the rental of property with less than 30% of the unadjusted basis subject to depreciation that is a section 162 trade or business, or

   3. Net rental income or loss from a rental that meets an exception under Regulations section 1.469-1T(e)(3)(ii), the activity rises to a section 162 trade or business, and you materially participated in the activity.

Note. Any income attributable to an estate or trust reported on Part III of Schedule E (Form 1040), Supplemental Income and Loss, that excluded net investment income is taken into account on line 7 (using code "H" from box 14 of the Schedule K-1). Do not report any adjustments on line 4b.

 For line 4b adjustments, enter net positive amounts as a negative adjustment and enter net negative amounts as a positive adjustment.

Lines 5a-5d—Gains and Losses on the Dispositions of Property

Net investment income includes net gain attributable to the disposition of property that is taken into account in computing taxable income. Generally, the general income tax rules in IRC chapter 1 will determine whether there has been a

disposition of property for NIIT purposes. Generally, the term disposition means a:
- Sale,
- Exchange,
- Transfer,
- Conversion,
- Cash settlement,
- Cancellation,
- Termination,
- Lapse,
- Expiration,
- Deemed disposition, for example under section 877A, or
- Other disposition.

Net gain attributable to the sale, exchange, or other disposition of property not used in a trade or business is included in net investment income. Net gain or loss from the sale, exchange, or other disposition of property held in a passive activity or attributable to a trade or business of trading in financial instruments or commodities is also included in net investment income.

Gains and losses that are not taken into account in computing taxable income are not taken into account in computing net investment income. For example, gain that is not taxable by reason of section 121 (sale of a principal residence) or section 1031 (like-kind exchanges) is not included in net investment income.

See *Lines 5a-5d — Net Gains and Losses Worksheet*, later, for assistance in calculating net gain or loss includable in net investment income.

Line 5a—Gains and Losses From the Disposition of Property

If you incur gain or loss from a disposition that is not reported on Form 1040, U.S. Individual Income Tax Return, lines 13 and 14, or Form 1041, lines 4 and 7, report those gains on Form 8960, line 7. For example, gain or loss attributable to the disposition of a life insurance contract or gain attributable to the disposition of an annuity contract to the extent the sales price of the annuity exceeds the annuity's surrender value is considered net investment income, and should be reported on Form 8960, line 7.

Line 5b—Net Gain or Loss From Disposition of Property That Is Not Subject to Net Investment Income Tax

Use line 5b to adjust the amounts included on line 5a for gains and losses that are excluded from the calculation of net investment income. Enter the amount of gains (as a negative number) and losses (as a positive number) included on line 5a that are excluded from net investment

income. For example, line 5b will include amounts such as:
- Gain or loss from the sale of property held in a non-section 1411 trade or business.

1. However, if the losses are attributable to formerly suspended passive losses of the non-section 1411 trade or business, such gains and losses are excluded from net investment income to the extent the nonpassive income from the non-section 1411 trade or business is excluded from net investment income. See Regulations section 1.1411-4(g)(8) for more information and examples.

2. Gain or loss from the sale of property held in a non-section 1411 trade or business does not include substantially appreciated property that is recharacterized as portfolio income. See *Substantially appreciated property*, later.

- In the case of a QEF for which a section 1.1411-10(g) election is not in effect, enter the net long-term capital gain taken into account in computing taxable income by reason of section 1293(a)(1)(B).
- Gain attributable to net unrealized appreciation (NUA) in employer securities held by a qualified plan. See *Net gain attributable to NUA in employer securities held by a qualified plan*, later.
- Adjustments to your capital loss carryforwards for items of excluded loss. See *Adjustments to your capital loss carryforwards*, later.

Substantially appreciated property.

Generally, Regulations section 1.469-2(c)(2)(iii)(A) provides that if an interest in property previously used in a nonpassive activity but not used in a passive activity for more than 2 years prior to disposition is substantially appreciated at the time of disposition, any gain from the disposition is treated as not from a passive activity. The recharacterized gain may be taken into account under section 1411(c)(1)(A)(iii) if the gain is attributable to the disposition of property and recharacterized as portfolio income.

Net gain attributable to NUA in employer securities held by a qualified plan.

Any gain attributable to NUA (within the meaning of section 402(e)(4)) that you realize on a disposition of employer securities held by a qualified plan is a distribution within the meaning of section 1411(c)(5) and is not included in net investment income. However, any gain realized on a disposition of employer securities attributable to appreciation in the value of your employer securities after the distribution from a qualified plan is not a distribution within the meaning of section 1411(c)(5) and is included in net investment income.

Shareholders of CFCs and QEFs without a section 1.1411-10(g) election. In

the case of a QEF (other than a QEF held in a section 1411 trade or business) with respect to which a section 1.1411-10(g) election is not in effect, enter the amount treated as long-term capital gain for regular income tax purposes under section 1293(a)(1)(B).

Also, in the case of a disposition of a CFC or QEF (other than a CFC or QEF held in a section 1411 trade or business) with respect to which a section 1.1411-10(g) election is not in effect, enter the increase or decrease in the amount of gain or loss for NIIT purposes over the amount of gain or loss for regular income tax purposes. However, if the gain is higher (or the loss larger) for NIIT purposes compared to regular income tax purposes, in which case there is no impact to the adjustment for capital loss carryforwards for NIIT purposes, enter the difference on line 6.

Adjustments to your capital loss carryforwards. Starting in your 2nd tax year that begins after 2012 (generally, your 2014 tax year), capital loss carryforwards must be adjusted if any sum of all capital gain or loss amounts excluded from net investment income on lines 5b and 5c was a net loss (the sum of all excluded capital losses was greater than the sum of all excluded capital gains). Generally, the annual adjustment to your capital losses carryforward is the lesser of:
- The amount of your capital loss carryforward from the previous year (the sum of carryforward amounts reflected on Schedule D (Form 1040), Capital Gains and Losses, lines 6 and 14, or
- The amount of excluded capital losses in excess of excluded capital gain in the previous year.

See *Lines 5a-5d — Net Gains and Losses Worksheet*, later, for assistance with the calculation of capital loss carryforwards. In addition, see Proposed Regulations section 1.1411-4(d)(4)(iii) for more information and a comprehensive example of the application of this rule.

Pass-through entities. If you hold an interest in a pass-through entity, the determination of whether a trade or business exists is made at the entity level.

Line 5c—Adjustment From Disposition of Partnership Interest or S Corporation Stock

Enter the amount from the worksheet for lines 5a-5d, Part II, line 3d. Attach a statement as described in *Required statements*, earlier, to your return for the year of the disposition.

-7-

Lines 5a-5d — Net Gains and Losses Worksheet   *Keep for Your Records*

		(A) Capital gains/(losses) Form 1040, Line 13, or Form 1041, Line 4	(B) Ordinary gains/(losses) Form 1040, Line 14, or Form 1041, Line 7	Total of columns (A)+(B)
1.	**Beginning net gains and losses**	_____	_____	Enter this amount _____ on line 5a
2.	*Gains and losses excluded from net investment income*			
	(a) Enter net gains from the disposition of property used in a non-section 1411 trade or business (enter as negative amounts): Name of Trade or Business Amount _____ (_____) _____ (_____)	(_____)	(_____)	
	(b) Enter net losses from the disposition of property used in a non-section 1411 trade or business (enter as positive amounts): Name of Trade or Business Amount _____ _____ _____ _____	_____	_____	
	(c) Enter net losses from a former passive activity (FPA) allowed by reason of section 469(f)(1)(A)	_____	_____	
	(d) Gains recognized in the current year for payments received on an installment sale obligation or private annuity for the disposition of property used in a non-section 1411 trade or business	(_____)		
	(e) Enter the net gain attributable to the net unrealized appreciation (NUA) in employer securities	(_____)		
	(f) In the case of a QEF (other than a QEF held in a section 1411 trade or business) with respect to which a section 1.1411-10(g) election is not in effect, enter the amount treated as long-term capital gain for regular income tax purposes under section 1293(a)(1)(B)	(_____)		
	(g) Enter any other gains and losses included in net investment income that are not otherwise reported on Form 8960 and any other gains and losses excluded from net investment income reported on line 5a (enter excluded gains as a negative number and excluded losses as a positive number)	_____	_____	
	(h) If you do not have a capital loss carryover to the next year, skip this line and go to line 2(i). Otherwise, enter the lesser of (h)(1) or (h)(2) as a negative amount	(_____)		
	(h)(1) If the sum of the amounts reported on lines 2(a)-2(g) and line 3(d), column (A), is greater than zero, enter that amount here. Otherwise, enter -0- on line 2(h) and go to line 2(i) . . . . _____ **OR** **(h)(2)** The amount of capital loss carried over to the following year (Schedule D (Form 1040), line 16, less the amount allowed as a current deduction on Schedule D (Form 1040), line 21) entered as a positive number . . . . . . _____			
	(i) Enter the amount reported on line 2(h) of this worksheet from your prior year tax return calculations. Enter as a positive number	N/A in 2013 _____	_____	
	(j) Sum of lines 2(a) through 2(i)	_____	_____	Enter this amount _____ on line 5b

¶2790

Lines 5a-5d — Net Gains and Losses Worksheet—*continued*

		(A) Capital gains/(losses) Form 1040, Line 13, or Form 1041, Line 4	(B) Ordinary gains/ (losses) Form 1040, Line 14, or Form 1041, Line 7	Total of columns (A)+(B)
3.	*Adjustment for gains and losses attributable to the disposition of interests in partnerships and S corporations*			
(a) Net Gains	(i) Enter the amount of net gain from the disposition of a partnership or S corporation included in line 5a to which section 1411(c)(4)(A) applies			
	(ii) Enter the amount of net gain included in net investment income after the application of Regulations section 1.1411-7. (The sum of columns A and B of line 3(a)(ii) must be less than, or equal to, the sum of columns A and B of line 3(a)(i).)			
	(iii) Enter the difference between line 3(a)(i) and line 3(a) (ii)			
(b) Net Losses	(i) Enter the amount of net loss from the disposition of a partnership or S corporation included in line 5a to which section 1411(c)(4)(B) applies			
	(ii) Enter the amount of net loss included in net investment income after the application of Regulations section 1.1411-7. (The sum of columns A and B of line 3(b)(ii) must be less than, or equal to, the sum of columns A and B of line 3(b)(i).)			
	(iii) Enter the difference between line 3(b)(i) and line 3(b) (ii)			
(c) Deferred Sales	(i) Enter the amount of gain recognized in the current year attributable payments received on an installment sale obligation or private annuity that was attributable to the disposition of an interest in a partnership or an S corporation in a year preceding the current year. Also report any gain or loss associated with section 736(b) payments on this line			
	(ii) Enter the amount of adjustment attributable to such gain			
	(iii) Subtract 3(c)(ii) from 3(c)(i)			
(d)	Combine the amounts on lines 3(a)(iii), 3(b)(iii), and 3(c) (iii)			Enter this amount on line 5c
4.	*Sum of items reported on lines 5a-5c*			
	Add lines 1, 2(j), and 3(d)			Enter this amount on line 5d

TIP — *If the amount of gain for NIIT purposes is less than the amount of gain for regular income tax purposes, the entry on lines 3(a)(iii), 3(b)(iii), or 3(c)(iii) should be a negative number.*

If the amount of loss for NIIT purposes is less than the amount of loss for regular income tax purposes, the entry on lines 3(a)(iii), 3(b)(iii), or 3(c)(iii) should be a positive number.

¶2790

Line 6—Changes to Investment Income for Certain CFCs and PFICs

If you own stock, directly or indirectly, in a CFC or a PFIC (other than certain CFCs and PFICs held in a section 1411 trade or business), use line 6 for adjustments necessary to calculate your net investment income.

Income with respect to investments in CFCs and PFICs is generally included in the calculation of net investment income and, in many cases, will be included (in whole or in part) on other lines of Form 8960. Generally, dividends from a CFC or a PFIC that are included in your regular income tax base are included on Form 8960, line 2, and gains and losses derived with respect to the stock of a CFC or a PFIC that are included in your regular income tax base generally are included on Form 8960, line 5. Also, income derived with respect to CFCs and certain PFICs you hold in a section 1411 trade or business is generally reported on Form 8960, line 4a.

Line 6 is used for adjustments that are the result of additional rules. These additional rules may apply when you own an interest in a CFC or PFIC and may require you to subtract amounts not reported on Form 8960 or add amounts not reported on Form 8960. These additional rules vary depending upon the set of anti-deferral rules that apply to you for regular income tax purposes, and for CFCs and QEFs, and depending upon whether you have a section 1.1411-10(g) election in effect with respect to the CFC or QEF. For more information about determining the amount to report on line 6, see Regulations section 1.1411-10.

Mark to Market PFICs. Generally, if you are subject to the section 1296 mark to market rules with respect to a PFIC, you will include in net investment income any amounts included in income for regular income tax purposes under section 1296(a)(1) and deduct from net investment income any amounts deducted from income for regular income tax purposes under section 1296(a)(2). Use line 6 to make increases or decreases to net investment income as a result of this rule (with respect to items that are not otherwise reflected on Form 8960).

Section 1291 funds. If you are subject to the section 1291 rules with respect to a PFIC, you will include in net investment income any "excess distributions that are dividends for NIIT purposes as well as any gains that are treated as excess distributions for regular income tax purposes." Use line 6 to make the increases to net investment income as a result of the application of this rule (with

respect to items that are not otherwise reflected on Form 8960).

CFCs and QEFs with a section 1.1411-10(g) election in effect. If you have a section 1.1411-10(g) election in effect with respect to a CFC or QEF, you will include in net investment income any inclusions under section 951(a) or 1293(a) derived with respect to the CFC or QEF. Inclusions under section 1293(a)(1)(B) may be reported elsewhere on Form 8960, such as on line 5a. Use line 6 to make the increases to net investment income as a result of the application of this rule (with respect to items that are not otherwise reflected on Form 8960).

CFCs and QEFs without a section 1.1411-10(g) election in effect. If you do not have a section 1.1411-10(g) election in effect with respect to a CFC or QEF, generally, you will include in net investment income certain distributions of previously taxed income from the CFC or QEF that are not subject to regular income tax. In addition, other special rules may apply, including rules that provide, as applicable, alternative basis calculations with respect to your basis in the CFC or QEF, or your basis in a domestic partnership or S corporation that owns the interest in the CFC or QEF. Also, the amount of investment interest expense you take into account for NIIT purposes may be increased or decreased from the amount taken into account for regular income tax purposes. (For additional information on all of these rules, see Regulations section 1.1411-10.) As a result of these rules, you may need to include amounts in net investment income that aren't otherwise reported on Form 8960 or make adjustments to amounts reported elsewhere on Form 8960. For example, you may need to include distributions from a CFC or a QEF in net investment income. Use line 6 to make increases or decreases to net investment income as a result of the application of this rule (with respect to items that are not otherwise reflected on Form 8960).

Note. Use line 5b to deduct inclusions under section 1293(a)(1)(B) that are allowed on line 5a, or to adjust the amount of gain or loss derived from the disposition of shares of a CFC or QEF. However, if the gain included in net investment income is higher than the amount reported for regular income tax (or the loss is greater), report the adjustment on line 6.

Line 7—Other Modifications to Investment Income

Use line 7 to report additional net investment income modifications to net investment income that are not otherwise specified in lines 1-6. For example, use

line 7 to report additions and modifications to net investment income such as

• Section 1411 net operating loss (NOL) (enter as a negative amount). See *Section 1411 NOL*, later.

• Any deductions described in section 62(a)(1) that are properly allocable to a passive activity or trading business, but are not taken into account on lines 4a or 5a (enter as a negative amount). See *Other section 62(a)(1) deductions*, later.

• Adjustments for distributions from Estates and Trusts. See *Distributions from estates and trusts*, later.

• Section 404(k) dividends reported on line 2 (enter as a negative amount). See *Line 2—Ordinary Dividends*, earlier.

• Interest income reported on line 1 received from certain nonpassive activities (entered as a negative amount). See *Self-charged interest*, later.

• Recoveries of deductions taken on a prior year's Form 8960. See *Deduction recoveries*, later.

• Other items of net investment income (or properly allocable deductions) reported on Form 1040, line 21, or Form 1041, line 8. For example, these items could include:

1. Amounts reported on Form 8814, Parents' Election To Report Child's Interest and Dividends, line 21. See *Form 8814 election*, later,

2. Substitute interest and dividend payments (generally reported on Form 1099-MISC, Miscellaneous Income). and

3. Net positive periodic payments received from a notional principal contract (NPC) that is referenced to property (including an index) that produces (or would produce if the property were to produce income) interest, dividends, royalties, or rents. For example, an interest rate swap, cap, or floor and an equity swap would be treated as an NPC that produces net investment income.

• Gains and losses from the disposition of property not included on line 5a that are taken into account in computing taxable income. For example:

1. Gain or loss from the disposition of an annuity or life insurance contract. See *Line 3—Annuities From Nonqualified Plans*, earlier.

2. Casualty and theft losses reported on Schedule A (Form 1040), Itemized Deductions, line 20 (enter as a negative amount).

However, gains and losses attributable to assets held in a non-section 1411 trade or business are not included in net investment income. For more information, See *Line 5b—Net Gain or Loss From Disposition of Property That Is Not Subject to Net Investment Income Tax*, earlier.

¶2790

Other section 62(a)(1) deductions.
Use line 7 to report additional deductions attributable to a section 1411 trade or business that are not included on lines 4-6. Generally, these deductions are above-the-line deductions reported on Form 1040, lines 23-35.

Note. Expenses associated with the trade or business of trading in financial instruments or commodities that are reported on your Schedule C (Form 1040) are reported on Form 8960, line 10. See *Special rule for traders in financial instruments or commodities*, later.

Note. Early withdrawal penalty (Form 1040, line 30) is reported on Form 8960, line 10.

 Use line 7 to report the amount of your domestic production activities deduction from Form 1040, line 35, attributable to a section 1411 trade or business. Using Form 8903, Domestic Production Activities Deduction, as a worksheet, compute the domestic production activities deduction using only the information from your section 1411 trade or business. On line 7, enter the lesser of the amount on Form 1040, line 35 or the amount of the deduction reported on the recomputed Form 8903 worksheet. Keep the recomputed Form 8903 for your records; do not include it with your return.

Form 8814 election. Parents electing to include their child's dividends and capital gain distribution in their income by filing Form 8814 include on Form 8960, line 7, the amount on Form 8814, line 12, excluding Alaska Permanent Fund Dividends.

Distributions from estates and trusts. Enter the amount from Schedule K-1, Form 1041, Beneficiary's Share of Income, Deductions, Credits, etc., box 14, code "H."

Note. If the amount reported on Schedule K-1, Form 1041, box 14, with a code "H" is a positive number, enter the amount from box 14 on Form 8960, line 7, and increase your MAGI on Form 8960, line 13 (or Form 8960, line 19a) by the same amount.

If the amount reported on Schedule K-1, Form 1041, box 14, with a code "H" is a negative number, and the trust has indicated some (or all) of the adjustment also requires a MAGI adjustment, enter the amount from box 14 on Form 8960, line 7, and make the applicable increase or decrease to your MAGI on Form 8960, line 13 (or Form 8960, line 19a) as necessary.

Section 1411 NOL. If you have an NOL allowed under section 172 for purposes of determining your regular income tax, you may also be allowed to deduct some, or all, of the NOL in computing net investment income. Because NOLs are computed and carried over year by year, you must determine for each NOL year what portion of the NOL is attributable to net investment income. To determine how much of the accumulated NOL you can use in the current tax year as a deduction against your net investment income, you must first calculate your applicable portion of the NOL for each loss year. For more information and examples on the calculation of a section 1411 NOL and its use, see Regulations section 1.1411-4(h).

Note. No portion of an NOL incurred in a tax year beginning before 2013 is permitted to reduce net investment income.

Calculating your section 1411 NOL. In any tax year in which a taxpayer incurs an NOL, the section 1411 NOL is the lesser of:
• The amount of the NOL for the loss year the taxpayer would incur if only items of gross income that are used to determine net investment income and only properly allocable deductions (other than a section 1411 NOL) are taken into account in determining the NOL in accordance with sections 172(c) and 172(d), or
• The amount of the taxpayer's NOL for the loss year.

 For purposes of calculating the section 1411 NOL, compute your NOL using Form 1045, Application for Tentative Refund, Schedule A—NOL, with only items of income, gain, loss, and deduction on Form 8960 for that year. If this amount is less than your NOL computed for regular income tax purposes, then this amount is the applicable portion of your NOL. If this amount is equal to, or greater than, your NOL computed for regular income tax purposes, then your applicable portion is 100% of the regular income tax NOL (which means the entire NOL will be deductible in computing net investment income when the NOL is used for regular income tax purposes).

Using your section 1411 NOL. When you deduct an NOL that originated in a previous year against the current year income, a portion of the NOL will be deductible in computing net investment income for that year, regardless of whether you are subject to the NIIT in that year without the NOL deduction. The amount of the regular income tax NOL used in calculating net investment income is called the "applicable portion." The applicable portion is the percentage of the

regular income tax NOL that is a section 1411 NOL. Because NOLs are calculated on a year by year basis, the applicable portion of each NOL that is used in the current year may be different.

Note. If you incur an NOL in 2013 or 2014 and carry back that NOL to offset income in years preceding the imposition of the NIIT (for example, a carryback to calendar year 2011 and/or 2012), the amount of 1411 NOL that is included in the NOL carryback will be used (as an applicable portion) even though the NIIT was not in effect.

See *Example Calculation of Section 1411 NOL for NIIT*, later, for an illustration of the calculation and use of a section 1411 NOL for NIIT purposes.

Deduction recoveries. A recovery or refund of a previously deducted item increases net investment income in the year of the recovery. There are 2 exceptions to this general rule.

Generally, for purposes of determining the gross amount of the recovery, include the recovery of any amount that was deducted in a prior year, regardless of the application of the tax benefit rule (see section 111). For example, if a taxpayer receives a refund of state income taxes from a prior year, such a refund would be included in the taxpayer's gross income. However, if the taxpayer was subject to the alternative minimum tax in the year of the payment, the taxpayer may not have received any tax benefit under IRC chapter 1, and therefore section 111 may exclude some or all of the refund from gross income. However, the deductibility of state income taxes for NIIT is independent of the taxes for alternative minimum tax purposes. Therefore, the applicability of the recovery rule is determined without regard to whether the recovered amount was excluded from gross income by reason of section 111.

There are 2 exceptions to including recovered amounts in net investment income. The 2 exceptions apply the tax benefit rule of section 111 within the NIIT system, and therefore operate independently of the application of section 111 for IRC chapter 1 purposes. First, properly allocable deductions are not reduced in the year of the recovery if the amount deducted in the prior year did not reduce the amount of section 1411 liability. Second, properly allocable deductions are not reduced in the year of the recovery if the amount deducted in the prior year is included in net investment income.

Note. The total amount of recovery reported on Form 8960, line 7, cannot exceed the total amount of properly allocable deductions for the year.

¶2790

Example Calculation of Section 1411 NOL for NIIT

Assume an unmarried individual incurs the following NOLs:

NOL Origination Year	(A) Regular Income Tax NOL	(B) Section 1411 NOL	(C) Applicable Portion of NOL [Column B divided by Column A]
2012 Calendar Year	$150,000	None	0.00%
2013 Calendar Year	$100,000	$30,000	30.0%
2014 Calendar Year	$40,000	$40,000	100%
2015 Calendar Year	$120,000	$60,000	50.0%

Beginning in 2016, the unmarried individual begins to use the NOLs to offset his income:

Tax Year	NOL Origination Year	Regular Income	Applicable Portion	Section 1411 NOL
2016 Tax Year		$300,000		
	2012 NOL	($150,000)	0.00%	None
	2013 NOL	($100,000)	30.0%	($30,000)
	2014 NOL	($40,000)	100.0%	(40,000)
	2015 NOL	($10,000)	50.0%	($5,000)
Total Section 1411 NOL allowed as deduction against 2016 net investment income				($75,000)

In 2016, the regular income tax NOLs from 2012-2015 has caused the taxpayer's AGI ($0) to fall below the statutory threshold, therefore the individual is not subject to the NIIT.

Tax Year	NOL Origination Year	Regular Income	Applicable Portion	Section 1411 NOL
2017 Tax Year		$600,000		
	2015 NOL	($110,000)	50.0%	($55,000)
Total Section 1411 NOL allowed as deduction against 2017 net investment income				($55,000)

In 2017, the regular income tax NOL remaining from 2015 has reduced the taxpayer's income for regular income tax to $490,000. The individual is entitled to reduce his net investment income by $55,000 (entered as a negative on Form 8960, line 7).

 If the recovered amount relates to a deduction taken in a tax year beginning before 2013, none of the recovery is included in net investment income in the year of recovery.

 If the recovered amount relates to a deduction taken in a tax year beginning after 2012 and you were not subject to the NIIT because your MAGI (see Line 13—Modified Adjusted Gross Income (MAGI), *later), was below the applicable threshold on line 14, then none of the recovery is included in net investment income in the year of recovery. However, this rule does not apply if you incurred an NOL in the year of the deduction, and a portion of your NOL is a section 1411 NOL.*

 If the recovered amount is included in net investment income on line 1-6, none of the recovery is included in net investment income on line 7.

For more information and examples, see Regulations section 1.1411-4(g)(2). See *Line 7—Deduction Recoveries*

Worksheet, later, to determine the amount of recovery (if any) to include on line 7.

 In the case of multiple recoveries in a single year, complete this worksheet for each recovery. If multiple recoveries relate to a single deduction year, the amount reported on lines 8 and 9 of the first recovery worksheet will become lines 7 and 10, respectively, on the second recovery sheet.

Self-charged interest. The self-charged interest rules under section 469 (passive activity loss limitation) apply to lending transactions between a taxpayer and a pass-through entity in which the taxpayer owns a direct or indirect interest, or between certain pass-through entities. The section 469 self-charged interest rules apply only to items of interest income and interest expense that are recognized in the same tax year. The self-charged interest rules:
• Treat certain interest income resulting from these lending transactions as passive activity income,

• Treat certain deductions for interest expense that are properly allocable to the interest income as passive activity deductions, and
• Allocate the passive activity gross income and passive activity deductions resulting from this treatment among the taxpayer's activities.

The rules for computing net investment income adopt a similar rule with respect to self-charged interest. See Regulations section 1.1411-4(g)(5). Include on line 7 (as a negative amount) the amount of interest income you received that is equal to the amount of interest income that would have been considered passive income under the self-charged interest rules (Regulations section 1.469-7) had the nonpassive activity been considered a passive activity.

Note. This rule does not apply to interest received on loans made to a trade or business engaged in the trading of financial instruments or commodities.

Note. Do not include any adjustment for interest income on line 7 (as a negative amount) if the corresponding interest deduction is also taken into account in determining your self-employment income that is subject to tax under section 1401(b).

Part II—Investment Expenses Allocable to Investment Income and Modifications

Investment Expenses

Part II of Form 8960 includes deductions and modifications to net investment income that are not otherwise included in Part I. Generally, expenses associated with a passive activity trade or business, or the trade or business of trading in financial instruments or commodities conducted through a pass-through entity are already included on line 4a (because line 4a uses net income (loss) from Schedule E (Form 1040)), or on line 5a. Part II is used to report deductions that are, predominately, itemized deductions. For more information on what constitutes properly allocable deductions, see Regulations sections 1.1411-4(f)-(g).

Note. If you did not itemize your deductions for regular income tax purposes, you may not take any deductions that would be reported on Schedule A (Form 1040) on your Form 8960.

Reasonable method allocations. To the extent that you have a properly allocable deduction that is allocable to both net investment income and excluded income, you may use any reasonable

2013 Instructions for Form 8960

Line 7—Deduction Recoveries Worksheet   *Keep for Your Records*

1. Enter total amount of recovery included in gross income .... 1. _____

   • Do not include recoveries of items that are included in net investment income in the year of recovery (included on lines 1-6).
   • Do not include recoveries of items if the amount relates to a deduction taken in a tax year beginning before 2013.
   • Do not include recoveries of items if the amount relates to a deduction taken in a tax year beginning after 2012, and you were not subject to the NIIT solely because your MAGI was below the applicable threshold.

   > ⚠ *This rule does not apply if you incurred a net operating loss (NOL) in such year, and a portion of such NOL constitutes a section 1411 NOL.*

2. Amount of the recovery that would have been included in gross income but for the application of the tax benefit rule under section 111 .... 2. _____
3. Total amount of recovery (add lines 1 and 2) .... 3. _____
4. Enter the percentage of the deduction allocated to net investment income in the prior year. (If the deduction was not allocated between investment income and non-investment income, enter 100%.) .... 4. _____
5. Enter the lesser of (a) line 3 multiplied by line 4, or (b) the total amount deducted on the prior year Form 8960 attributable to item recovered (after any deduction limitations imposed by section 67 or 68) .... 5. _____

Calculation of recoveries when the deduction is not taken into account in computing your section 1411 NOL.

6. Multiply line 5 by .038 .... 6. _____
7. Enter the amount of net investment income in the year of the deduction (previous year's Form 8960, line 12) .... 7. _____
8. Add the amount of line 5 to line 7 .... 8. _____
9. Using the previous year's Form 8960, recalculate the NIIT for the year of the deduction by replacing the amount reported on line 12 with the amount reported on line 8 of this worksheet (do not use the net investment income reported on that year's Form 8960, line 12). Enter your recalculated NIIT here .... 9. _____
10. Enter the NIIT reported for the year of the deduction .... 10. _____
11. Subtract line 10 from Line 9 .... 11. _____
12. Enter the smaller of line 6 or Line 11 .... 12. _____
13. Divide line 12 by 3.8% (line 12 ÷ .038). Enter this amount on line 7 in the year of recovery .... 13. _____

Calculation of recoveries when the deduction is taken into account in computing your section 1411 NOL

14. Enter the amount of the section 1411 NOL in the year of the deduction (entered as a positive number) .... 14. _____
15. Enter the amount of the section 1411 NOL in the year of the deduction recomputed without the amount on line 5 (entered as a positive number, but not less than zero) .... 15. _____
16. Subtract line 15 from line 14. Enter this amount on line 7 in the year of recovery .... 16. _____

¶2790

method to determine that portion of the deduction that is properly allocable to net investment income. The 3 items that may be allocated between net investment income and excluded income are:

• State, local, and foreign income taxes deducted on Schedule A (Form 1040), line 5 (or Form 1041, line 11),

• All ordinary and necessary expenses paid or incurred during the tax year to determine, collect, or obtain a refund of any tax owed (Schedule A (Form 1040), line 22), and

• Amounts paid or incurred by the fiduciary of an estate or trust on account of administration expenses, including fiduciaries' fees and expenses of litigation, which are ordinary and necessary in connection with the performance of the duties of administration.

If you have more than one of the deductions described above, you may use a different method of allocation for each one. The reasonable method of allocation may differ from year to year.

Examples of reasonable methods of allocation include, but are not limited to, an allocation of the deduction based on the ratio of the amount of a taxpayer's gross investment income (Form 8960, line 8) to the amount of the taxpayer's AGI (Form 1040, line 38). In the case of an estate or trust, an allocation of a deduction pursuant to rules described in Regulations section 1.652(b)-3(b), and in the case of ESBT, Regulations section 1.641(c)-1(h), is also a reasonable method.

Note. If an estate or trust allocates expenses for regular income tax purposes under Regulations section 1.652(b)-3(b) or 1.641(c)-1(h), any deviation from that allocation may not be a reasonable allocation method for NIIT purposes.

Items not deductible in calculating net investment income. Unless a deduction is specifically identified as properly allocable to net investment income in the section 1411 regulations, or in supplemental guidance issued by the IRS in the Internal Revenue Bulletin, the deduction is not permitted. For example, the following items are not deductible in computing net investment income:

• Deductions for moving expenses (Form 1040, line 26),

• Expenses that are not deductible for regular income tax (for example, interest expense and investment expenses

associated with investments in tax-exempt bonds),

• Deduction for alimony paid (Form 1040, line 31),

• Deduction for contributions to IRAs or other qualified plans,

• The standard deduction,

• Personal exemptions (Form 1040, line 42),

• Deductions for charitable contributions (Schedule A (Form 1040), line 19),

• Deductions for medical expenses (Schedule A (Form 1040), line 4),

• Deductions for mortgage interest expense (Schedule A (Form 1040), lines 10-13),

• Deductions for real estate taxes or personal property taxes that do not constitute investment expenses under section 163(d)(4)(C) and are reported on Form 4952, Investment Interest Expense Deduction, line 5 (Schedule A (Form 1040), lines 6-7),

• Deductions for state and local sales tax (Schedule A (Form 1040), line 5), and

• Deductible contributions to Capital Contribution Funds under section 7518.

Line 9a—Investment Interest Expenses

Enter on Form 8960, line 9a, interest expense you paid or accrued during the tax year from either Schedule A (Form 1040), line 14 or the amount from Form 4952, line 8. For further details, see Form 4952 instructions or Pub. 550, Investment Income and Expenses.

Note. If Form 4952 includes investment interest expense that is deducted on Schedule E (Form 1040) and already taken into account on line 4a, do not include the same amount on line 9a.

Note. If you own a CFC or QEF with respect to which a section 1.1411-10(g) election is not in effect, you may calculate your section 163(d) investment expense deduction for NIIT purposes differently than for regular income tax purposes. See Regulations section 1.1411-10(c)(5) for additional guidance. Any modification to your section 163(d) investment expense deduction for NIIT purposes is taken into account on line 6.

Line 9b—State Income Tax

Include on line 9b any state or local income taxes, or foreign income taxes you

paid that are attributable to net investment income. This may be all or part of the amount you reported on Schedule A (Form 1040), line 5a (or Form 1041, line 11). For purposes of line 9b, sales taxes are not deductible in computing net investment income.

Foreign taxes. If you took an income tax credit for foreign income taxes (generally, reported using Form 1116, Foreign Tax Credit), those foreign taxes are not deductible in computing net investment income.

You can determine the portion of your state and local income taxes allocable to net investment income using any reasonable method. See *Reasonable method allocations*, earlier, and *Deductions subject to AGI limitations under section 67 or section 68*, later.

Note. Enter the amount of state, local, or foreign income taxes on Form 8960, line 9b, net of any deduction limitations imposed by section 68. See *Lines 9 and 10 — Application of Itemized Deduction Limitations on Deductions Properly Allocable to Investment Income Worksheet*, later, for assistance in figuring the amount to report on line 9b.

Line 9c—Miscellaneous Investment Expenses

Investment expenses you incur that are directly connected to the production of investment income are deductible expenses in determining your net investment income. Generally, these amounts are reported on Form 4952, line 5. See Form 4952 for the instructions for line 5 for more information. As in the case with line 5 of Form 4952, the amounts reported on line 9c are the amounts allowable after the application of the deduction limitations imposed by sections 67 and 68. See *Deductions subject to AGI limitations under section 67 or section 68*, later.

Note. Enter the amount of miscellaneous investment expenses on Form 8960, line 9c, net of any deduction limitations imposed by section 67 or section 68. See *Lines 9 and 10 — Application of Itemized Deduction Limitations on Deductions Properly Allocable to Investment Income Worksheet*, later, for assistance in figuring the amount to report on line 9c.

¶2790

Lines 9 and 10 — Application of Itemized Deduction Limitations on Deductions Properly Allocable to Investment Income Worksheet   *Keep for Your Records*

Part I — Application of Section 67 to Deductions Properly Allocable to Investment Income

1. Enter the amount of Miscellaneous Itemized Deductions properly allocable to investment income before any itemized deduction limitations (Description and Form 8960 line number where they will be reported):

	Description	Line	Amount
(a)	_____	_____	_____
(b)	_____	_____	_____

2. Enter the total of all items listed in line 1 .... **2.** _____

3. Enter the amount of all Miscellaneous Itemized Deductions after the application of the section 67 limitation (Schedule A (Form 1040), line 27) .... **3.** _____

4. Enter the lesser of the total reported on line 2 or line 3 .... **4.** _____

Part II — Application of Section 67 Limitation to Specific Deductions

(A) Reenter the amounts and descriptions from Part I, line 1.			**(B)** IF line 3 is less than line 2, **THEN** divide line 3 by line 2 **AND** enter the amount in column (B). IF amounts reported on Part I, lines 2 and 4 are equal, **THEN** enter 1.00 in column (B).	**(C)** Multiply the individual amounts in column (A) by the amount in column (B).
Description	Line	Amount		
(a) _____ _____ _____			× _____	= _____
(b) _____ _____ _____			× _____	= _____

TIP

Individuals — Use the amounts in column (C) on Part III, line 1, to determine the amount of these deductions that are allowable after the application of the section 68 limitation.

Estates or trusts — Enter the amounts in column (C) in the appropriate location on lines 9 and 10. Do not complete Parts III or IV of this worksheet.

¶2790

Lines 9 and 10 — Application of Itemized Deduction Limitations on Deductions Properly Allocable to Investment Income Worksheet— *continued*

Keep for Your Records

Part III — Application of Section 68 to deductions properly allocable to investment income (Individuals Only)

1. Enter the amount of Miscellaneous Itemized Deductions properly allocable to investment income from column (C) of Part II:

	Description	Line	Amount
(a)			
(b)			

2. Enter the amount of state, local, and foreign income taxes that are properly allocable to investment income. . . . .   **2.** _____

3. Enter the amounts of other Itemized Deductions subject to the section 68 limitation and properly allocable to investment income before any itemized deduction limitations (Description and Form 8960 line number):

	Description	Line	Amount
(a)			
(b)			

4. Enter the total deductions properly allocable to investment income subject to the section 68 limitation. Enter the sum of lines 1 through 3 . . . .   **4.** _____

5. Enter the amount of total itemized deductions reported on Form 1040, line 40 . . . .   **5.** _____

6. Enter all other itemized deductions allowed but not subject to the section 68 deduction limitation:

   (a) Investment Interest Expense . . . . _____

   (b) Casualty Losses (other than losses described in section 165(c)(1)) . . . . _____

   (c) Medical Expenses . . . . _____

   (d) Gambling Losses . . . . _____

   (e) Total of lines 6(a) through 6(d) . . . .   **6e.** _____

7. Subtract line 6e from line 5 . . . .   **7.** _____

8. Enter the lesser of line 7 or line 4 . . . .   **8.** _____

TIP *This is the amount of itemized deductions that are properly allocable to investment income after the application of the sections 67 and 68 deduction limitations. Use Part IV of this worksheet to reconcile this amount to the individual deduction amounts reported on Form 8960, lines 9 and 10.*

¶2790

Lines 9 and 10 — Application of Itemized Deduction Limitations on Deductions Properly Allocable to Investment Income Worksheet—
continued   *Keep for Your Records*

Part IV — Reconciliation of Schedule A Deductions to Form 8960, lines 9 and 10 (Individuals Only)		
(A) Reenter the amounts and descriptions from Part III, lines 1 – 3.	**(B)** **IF** Part III, line 8 is less than Part III, line 4, **THEN** divide line 8 by line 4 **AND** enter the amount in column (B). **IF** the amounts reported on Part III, lines 4 and 8 are equal, **THEN** enter 1.00 in column (B).	**(C)** Multiply the individual amounts in column (A) by the amount in column (B). Enter these amounts in the appropriate location on lines 9 and 10.
Miscellaneous Itemized Deductions properly allocable to investment income:		
Description Line Amount		
1. (a) _____ _____ _____	× _____	= _____
(b) _____ _____ _____	× _____	= _____
2. State, local, and foreign income taxes .... _____ _____	× _____	= _____
Itemized Deductions Subject to Section 68 included on Line 3 of Part III:		
3. (a) _____ _____ _____	× _____	= _____
(b) _____ _____ _____	× _____	= _____

Line 10—Additional Modifications

Use line 10 to report additional deductions and modifications to net investment income that are not otherwise reflected in lines 1-9. Enter amounts on line 10 as positive numbers.

Note. Enter the amount on line 10 after the application of section 67 or 68. See *Lines 9 and 10 — Application of Itemized Deduction Limitations on Deductions Properly Allocable to Investment Income Worksheet*, earlier, for assistance in figuring the amount to report on line 10.

You may use line 10 to report properly allocable deductions such as:
• The penalty paid for an early withdrawal of savings under section 62(a)(9) (Form 1040, line 30),
• The amount treated as an ordinary loss by a holder of a contingent payment debt instrument under Regulations section 1.1275-4(b) or an inflation-indexed debt instrument under Regulations section 1.1275-7(f)(1),
• Net negative periodic payments paid on a notional principal contract (NPC) that is referenced to property (including an index) that produces (or would produce if the property were to produce income) interest, dividends, royalties, or rents.
• Excess deductions allocated to a beneficiary upon the termination of an estate or trust under section 642(h)(2) that would otherwise have been allowable but

for the fact that the terminating trust or estate had negative net investment income upon termination. This amount may be some or all of the amount reported on Schedule K-1 (Form 1041), line 11a. See Regulations section 1.1411-4(g)(4)(iii),
• Certain amounts reported on Schedule A (Form 1040), line 28:

1. The amount of the deduction allowed to an annuitant for the annuitant's last tax year under section 72(b)(3), provided the income from the annuity (had the annuitant lived to receive such income) would have been included in net investment income and not otherwise excluded as a distribution from a qualified plan,

2. Deduction for payment of amounts under a claim of right if over $3,000, to the extent that such repayments relate to items of income included in net investment income in a preceding year that began after 2012. See Pub. 525, Taxable and Nontaxable Income, for details,

3. The amount of the deduction for estate taxes allowed by section 691(c) that is allocable to net investment income, except to the extent that the section 691(c) deduction is taken into account in computing net gain on line 5(a) (or line 7 if applicable), and

4. The amount of the deduction allowable under section 171(a)(1) for the amortizable bond premium on a taxable bond. Do not include the amount of bond

premium amortization that is used to offset interest income under section 171(e) on your Schedule B (Form 1040A or 1040), Interest and Ordinary Dividends. This amount of bond premium amortization is already taken into account in computing interest income on Form 8960, line 1.

• If you are a partner in an Electing Large Partnership and receive a Schedule K-1 (Form 1065-B), Partner's Share of Income (Loss) From an Electing Large Partnership, and box 2 contains a loss, report this loss on line 10,
• To the extent these items are properly allocable to net investment income. See *Reasonable method allocations*, earlier,

1. All ordinary and necessary expenses paid or incurred during the tax year to determine, collect, or obtain a refund of any tax owed, but only to the extent the expenses are allocable to net investment income (Schedule A (Form 1040), line 22), and

2. Amounts paid or incurred by the fiduciary of an estate or trust on account of administration expenses, including fiduciaries' fees and expenses of litigation, which are ordinary and necessary in connection with the performance of the duties of administration.

Special rule for traders in financial instruments or commodities. If your only business is trading in financial instruments or commodities, you may use the net loss amount on your Schedule C (Form 1040)

¶2790

Line 10—Worksheet for Traders in Financial Instruments That Maintain More Than One Trade or Business

Keep for Your Records

Use this worksheet to determine the amount on line 10.

1 Enter the total amount from Schedule SE (Form 1040), line 3.	1 _____
2 a If the amount on Schedule SE (Form 1040), line 3, is zero or greater, you cannot use the expenses from your trade or business to reduce your investment income. Stop here.	
b If the amount on Schedule SE (Form 1040), line 3, is a negative amount, enter your expenses from your trade or business of trading in financial instruments or commodities (entered as a positive amount).	2 b _____
3 Add line 1 to line 2b.	3 _____
a If the amount on line 3 of this worksheet is zero or less, include the trade or business expenses (line 2b of the worksheet) on Form 8960, line 10.	
b If the amount on line 3 of this worksheet is a positive number, convert the amount from Schedule SE (Form 1040), line 3 (line 1 of this worksheet) into a positive number and include it on Form 8960, line 10.	

as a deduction on line 10, and you do not need to complete Schedule SE (Form 1040), Self-Employment Tax.

If you have more than one trade or business, you must complete Schedule SE (Form 1040) to determine whether you can include some or all of the trading business Schedule C (Form 1040) expenses as a deduction on line 10. Complete the *Line 10—Worksheet for Traders in Financial Instruments That Maintain More Than One Trade or Business*, earlier.

Note. Although Schedule SE (Form 1040) must be completed to determine the amount of expenses that may be used as a modification on line 10, if Schedule SE (Form 1040), line 3, is a negative amount, do not file the Schedule SE (Form 1040) with your Form 1040. See the Instructions for Schedule SE (Form 1040) for who must file a Schedule SE (Form 1040). Retain the Schedule SE (Form 1040) and the worksheet used to determine the expenses included as a modification on line 10 with your records. Do not file the worksheet with Form 1040.

The amounts reported on line 10 are the amounts allowable after the application of the deduction limitations imposed by sections 67 and 68, as applicable. See *Deductions subject to AGI limitations under section 67 or section 68*, later.

Deductions subject to AGI limitations under section 67 or section 68. Any deduction allowed against net investment income that, for purposes of computing your regular income tax, is subject to either the 2% floor on miscellaneous itemized deductions (section 67) or the overall limitation on itemized deductions (section 68) is allowed in determining net investment income, but only to the extent the items are deductible after application of both limitations.

Miscellaneous itemized deductions. The amount of your miscellaneous itemized deductions, after application of the 2% floor but before application of the overall limitation, used in determining your net investment income is the lesser of:
• That portion of your miscellaneous itemized deductions before the application of the 2% floor that is properly allocable to net investment income, or
• Your total miscellaneous itemized deductions allowed after the application of the 2% floor but before the application of the overall limitation on itemized deductions.

Itemized deductions. The amount of your itemized deductions allowed in determining your net investment income after applying both the 2% floor and overall limitation is the lesser of:
• The sum of:
1. The amount of your miscellaneous itemized deductions allowed as a deduction against your net investment income (before application of the overall limitation), and
2. The total amount of your itemized deductions that are not subject to the 2% floor and are properly allocable to items of income or net gain for purposes of determining your net investment income, or
• The total amount of your itemized deductions allowed after the application of both the 2% floor and the overall limitation on itemized deductions.

For more information and examples, see Regulations section 1.1411-4(f)(7).

Part III—Tax Computation
Individuals
Individuals complete lines 13-17.

Line 13—Modified Adjusted Gross Income (MAGI)

If you did not exclude any amounts from your gross income under section 911 and you do not own a CFC or PFIC, your MAGI is your AGI as reported on Form 1040, line 38. If you exclude amounts under section 911 or own certain CFCs or PFICs, your MAGI is your AGI as modified by certain rules described in Regulations section 1.1411-10(e)(1).

Section 911. If you exclude amounts from income under section 911, to calculate your MAGI, you must increase your AGI by the excess of the amount excluded from income under section 911(a)(1) over the amount of any deductions (taken into account in computing AGI) or exclusions disallowed under section 911(d)(6) with respect to the amount excluded from income under section 911(a)(1). Use *Line 13 — MAGI Worksheet*, later, to compute your MAGI.

CFCs and PFICs. If you own, directly or indirectly, stock in a CFC or PFIC other than certain CFCs and PFICs held in a section 1411 trade or business or PFICs with respect to which an election under section 1296 is in effect, to calculate your MAGI, you may need to make certain adjustments to your AGI, as provided in Regulations section 1.1411-10(e)(1). Generally, these adjustments include:
• 1291 funds.
1. Increase AGI by the amount of any excess distributions derived from a PFIC that are dividends included in MAGI but not included in gross income for regular income tax purposes, and
2. Increase AGI by the amount of any gain treated as an excess distribution under section 1291 included in MAGI but not included in gross income for regular income tax purposes.

Line 13 — MAGI Worksheet   *Keep for Your Records*

1. Enter your Adjusted Gross Income	1. _____
2. Foreign Earned Income Exclusion:	
(a) Enter your Foreign Earned Income Exclusion (from Line 42 of Form 2555) .... _____	
(b) Enter the deductions reported on Line 44 of Form 2555 allocable to your Foreign Earned Income Exclusion .... (_____)	
(c) Combine Lines 2(a) and 2(b)	2. _____
3. Adjustments for Certain CFCs and Certain PFICs	3. _____
4. Enter the sum of Line 1, Line 2(c), and Line 3. (Enter this amount on Form 8960, Line 13.)	4. _____

- CFCs and QEFs without a section 1.1411-10(g) election in effect.

  1. Decrease AGI by the amount of any section 951(a) or 1293(a) inclusions,

  2. Increase AGI by the amount of any distributions described in section 959(d) or 1293(c) included in your net investment income as a dividend,

  3. Increase or decrease AGI (as appropriate) by the amount of any adjustment to gain or loss on the disposition of the CFC or QEF that results in an adjustment to your MAGI,

  4. Increase or decrease AGI (as appropriate) by the amount of any adjustment to gain or loss on the disposition of an interest in a domestic partnership or S corporation that holds a CFC or QEF that results in an adjustment to your MAGI,

  5. Increase or decrease AGI (as appropriate) by the amount of any adjustment to investment interest expense under Regulations section 1.1411-10(c)(5) that is taken into account in computing MAGI, and

  6. Enter the amount reported to you on Schedule K-1 (Form 1041) in box 14 with a code "H" that requires a MAGI adjustment.

- CFCs and QEFs held in a section 1411 trade or business or with a section 1.1411-10(g) election in effect.

  1. Enter the amount of any distributions described in section 959(d) or 1293(c) included in your net investment income as a dividend (not applicable to tax years beginning before 2014).

 TIP *If you do not own (directly or indirectly) any interests in CFCs or PFICs, and do not exclude any foreign earned income on Form 2555, Foreign Earned Income, enter your AGI from Form 1040, line 38 on line 13.*

Line 14—Threshold Based on Filing Status

The threshold amount is based on your filing status.

Filing Status	Threshold Amount
Married Filing Jointly	$250,000
Qualifying Widower with Dependent Child	$250,000
Married Filing Separately	$125,000
Single or Head of Household	$200,000

A bankruptcy estate of an individual enters $125,000 and uses Form 8960, lines 13-17, to compute the tax.

Estates and Trusts

Estates and trusts complete lines 18-21.

Line 18b—Deductions for Distributions of Net Investment Income and Deductions Under Section 642(c)

The undistributed net investment income of an estate or trust is its net investment income reported on line 18a, reduced by the net investment income included in the distributions to beneficiaries deductible by the estate or trust under section 651 or 661, and by the net investment income for which the estate or trust was entitled to a section 642(c) deduction, in each case as computed in accordance with Regulations section 1.642(c)-2 and the allocation and ordering rules under Regulations section 1.662(b)-2. Regulations section 1.1411-3(e) applies the class system of income categorization, generally embodied in sections 651 through 663 and related regulations, to arrive at the trust's net investment income reduction in the case of distributions that are comprised of both net investment income and net excluded income items. See Regulations section 1.1411-3(e) for more

information and examples on the calculation of undistributed net investment income.

Charitable deduction. Report the amount of net investment income distributed to beneficiaries of the estate or trust and the amount of net investment income allocated to distributions to charity pursuant to section 642(c). The amount of the deduction for net investment income distributed to charities under section 642(c) is the amount of the net investment income allocated to the charity in accordance with Regulations section 1.642(c)-2(b) and the allocation and ordering rules under Regulations section 1.662(b)-2.

 TIP *Form 1041, Schedule A, provides for a calculation of an estate's or trust's charitable deduction for regular income tax purposes. Form 1041, Schedule A, can be used as a worksheet to calculate the amounts of net investment income allocable to charitable distributions. For the worksheet, the Form 1041, Schedule A, line 2, includes both tax-exempt income and the difference between adjusted total income and Form 8960, line 18a.*

TIP *The amount of the deduction for net investment income distributed to beneficiaries should equal the sum of net investment income reported to the beneficiaries on their respective Schedules K-1 (Form 1041).*

Note. In general, the deduction for distributions of net investment income may not exceed the taxable income distributed to the beneficiary for regular income tax purposes. However, in the case of an estate or trust that owns an interest in certain CFCs or PFICs, the distribution of net investment income can exceed the distribution of taxable income when the amount of distributions exceed distributable net income for regular income tax purposes.

¶2790

Form 1041, Schedule B, provides for a calculation of an estate's or trust's income distribution deduction for regular income tax purposes. Form 1041, Schedule B can be used as a worksheet to calculate the income distribution deduction for NIIT purposes. For example, Form 1041, Schedule B can be used as a worksheet by replacing line 1 with the trust's net investment income (from Form 8960, line 18a) and line 2 includes both adjusted tax-exempt interest and the difference between Form 1041, Schedule B, line 1, and Form 8960, line 18a.

Line 19a—Adjusted Gross Income (AGI)

If the estate or trust does not own a CFC or PFIC, enter it's AGI for regular income tax purposes. See the Instructions for Form 1041, line 15c.

If the estate or trust owns a CFC or PFIC, it may need to make adjustments. See *Line 13—Modified Adjusted Gross Income (MAGI)*, earlier.

Line 19b—Highest Tax Bracket for Estates and Trusts

For the highest tax bracket for estates and trusts for the year, see Form 1041, Schedule G instructions for the tax rate schedule.

In the case of a QFT, see *Special computational rules for qualified funeral trusts (QFTs)*, earlier, to determine the amount to report on Form 8960, line 19b.

¶2790

INCOME TAXATION OF TRUSTS AND ESTATES

TABLE OF CONTENTS

¶2800 ESTATES AND TRUSTS—THE BASIC TERMS

It is essential for anyone involved in the area of estate planning and administration to have a basic understanding of the mechanics of the tax treatment of trusts and estates. Unfortunately, this area of the tax law can be extremely complex with many rules and terms of art.

Subchapter J of the Internal Revenue Code (the IRC) [IRC Secs. 641–692] contains all the rules regarding the tax treatment of trusts and estates. The objective of this chapter is to spell out the operation of the estate and trust tax rules in plain English. Examples will be provided to explain the operation of the law. The following sections provide some basic definitions of the terms you will have to know and understand.

(a) Estate Defined. When someone dies a new legal entity comes into being to handle the business, personal and financial affairs of the decedent. The legal entity is referred to as the decedent's estate and is established under the laws of the state in which the decedent lived. That state's probate court supervises and directs the administration of the decedent's estate. The decedent's estate consists of the decedent's real and personal property and is a separate legal entity for tax purposes. The estate may have to pay income tax on the income earned during the period of administration or settlement of the estate. [For a completed income tax return of an estate (Form 1041) see Chapter 30. The estate may also have to pay estate tax (Form 706) (see Chapter 24), gift tax (Form 709) (see Chapter 17) and/or generation-skipping transfer tax (see Chapter 25).]

(b) Executor Defined. An executor or a personal representative (PR) administers the affairs of the estate of a deceased person. The PR is appointed by the appropriate state court. The named executor, if there is a will, and the administrator, if there is no will, is the fiduciary in charge of an estate. They take charge of the decedent's probate property and wind up his or her affairs. The decedent's estate, like a trust, is a separate taxable entity and the fiduciary in charge has the same tax obligations as the trustee of a trust. The decedent's estate exists until the final distribution of its assets to the heirs and other beneficiaries.

An estate's executor has the following administrative duties:

- To collect the decedent's money and property;
- To pay the decedent's debts;
- To collect debts owed to the decedent;
- To pay all taxes due.

After these tasks are accomplished, the executor of the decedent's estate can distribute the decedent's money and other property to the decedent's heirs. The estate is required to follow the provisions in the decedent's will when distributing the remaining money and property. The estate is terminated at the end of the administration period when all the assets have been distributed to the heirs and beneficiaries of the estate.

(c) Trust Defined. A trust is a legal relationship or arrangement under which an individual, the settlor or grantor, transfers property to another person, the trustee, so the property can be administered for the benefit of a third party, the beneficiary. When trusts are created during the life of the settlor they are called *inter vivos* or living trusts. Trusts that are created according to the terms of a will when the settlor dies are called testamentary trusts.

To establish a trust, the following legal requirements must exist:

1. An intent to create a trust;
2. A designated trustee and beneficiaries;
3. Sufficiently identifiable property; and
4. Transfer of title to the trustee.

The subject matter of the trust is often referred to as the trust *res*, trust principal, trust property, or trust corpus. The most common types of property making up the trust principal or trust corpus are bonds, stocks, mortgages, titles to land, and bank accounts. The person who creates a trust is known as the grantor, creator, donor, or settlor of the trust.

All trusts have an identifiable home base or "*situs.*" A trust's "*situs*" is the state whose courts have primary jurisdiction over the trust. When a trust is drafted, it is important to consider which state's law will apply and how the application of the laws in that state will affect administration of the trust. It may be necessary to move the situs of the trust in order to find laws that are the most favorable to the trust's beneficiaries. The drafter of the trust should therefore add a provision of the trust which specifically authorizes a trustee to move the *situs* of the trust and to change the law governing the administration of the trust.

In the case of a testamentary trust, the creator is the testator or the person who executed the will. Once created, a trust becomes a separate taxable entity for which a return must be filed and taxes paid.

¶2800

(d) Types of Trusts.

Simple Trusts. There are two basic types of trusts: simple trusts and complex trusts. A simple trust is a trust that satisfies the following conditions:

- It is required to distribute all of its income currently;
- It is prohibited from the use of trust funds for charitable contributions;
- It does not distribute trust principal during the year.

For a further discussion of simple trusts, see ¶ 2817.

Complex Trusts. Complex trusts include all trusts that do not qualify as simple trusts. The determination of whether or not a trust is a simple or complex trust is made on an annual basis. For example, a simple trust will become a complex trust in any year that it distributes principal. Thus, a simple trust becomes a complex trust in the year of termination because principal is distributed in that year [Reg. Sec. 1.651(a)-1; for a further discussion of complex trusts, see ¶ 2818].

Qualified Disability Trust. A qualified disability trust is any nongrantor trust:

1. Established solely for the benefit of an individual under age 65 who is disabled, and
2. All the beneficiaries of the trust have been disabled for some part of the tax year.

A qualified disability trust is allowed a deduction equal to the exemption amount under IRC Sec. 151(d) by treating the trust as an unmarried individual with no dependent and by applying IRC Sec. 67(e) without reference to IRC Sec. 642(b). The deduction for qualified disability trusts is $3,950 in 2014. The deduction for the personal exemption for a qualified disability trust equals the personal exemption deduction allowed an individual under IRC Sec. 151(d), determined as if the trust was an unmarried individual who was not a surviving spouse or head of household [IRC Sec. 642(b)(2)(C)(i)]. Thus, a qualified disability trust's personal exemption equals that of the individual personal exemption for an unmarried individual with no dependents and is subject to the personal exemption phaseout which applies to that person if adjusted gross income exceeds a threshold amount. A trust with modified adjusted gross income above $254,200 in 2014 begins to lose part of the exemption deduction. No exemption is allowed for a qualified disability trust with modified adjusted gross income of $376,700 in 2014.

Electing Small Business Trusts. An electing small business trust (ESBT) is a special type of trust that qualifies to be a shareholder in an S corporation [IRC Sec. 1361(c)(2)(A)(v)]. S corporations are hybrid business entities that combine the flexibility of a partnership with the advantages of operating in the corporate format. However, unlike regular corporations, S corporations are generally not treated as taxable entities for federal income tax purposes. Instead, once an S corporation election has been made, the corporation's income passes through to the shareholders. Shareholders then pay tax on this income whether or not distributed. This pass-through-of-income principle parallels the tax treatment provided partnerships. An ESBT will qualify as an S corporation if if satisfies the following three requirements:

- An ESBT may only have the following types of beneficiaries: individuals; estates eligible to be S corporation shareholders; charitable organizations; or a state or local government that holds a contingent interest in the trust and is not a potential

¶2800

contingent beneficiary [IRC Sec. 1361(e)(1)(A)(i)]. Potential current beneficiaries of an ESBT are counted as shareholders of the S corporation for purposes of determining whether the corporation qualifies for the S corporation election. Powers of appointment, to the extent they are not exercised, are disregarded in determining the potential current beneficiaries of an ESBT. Thus, a potential current beneficiary does not include anyone by virtue of a power of appointment that remained unexercised during the relevant period [IRC Sec. 1361(e)(2)]. If potential current beneficiaries of an ESBT disqualify a corporation in which the ESBT holds stock from S corporation status, the ESBT can remedy the situation by disposing of the offending shares within one year [IRC Sec. 1361(e)(2)];

- No interest in the trust may be acquired by purchase which means any acquisition of property with a cost basis determined under IRC Sec. 1012 [IRC Sec. 1361(e)(1)(A)(ii)]. Thus, interests in qualifying trusts must be acquired by gift, bequest or other non-purchase acquisition; and

- The trustees must elect to be treated as an ESBT by filing a statement with the IRS. The statement must be filed with the same service center where the ESBT files its Form 1041. If the trust satisfies the ESBT requirements, the trust will be treated as an ESBT as of the date of the election [IRC Sec. 1361(e)].

An ESBT is taxed in a different manner than other trusts. First, the portion of the ESBT that consists of stock in one or more S corporations is treated as a separate trust for purposes of computing the income tax attributable to the S corporation stock held by the trust. This portion of the trust's income is taxed at the highest rate imposed on estates and trusts and includes:

1. The items of income, loss or deduction allocated to the trust as an S corporation shareholder under the rules of subchapter S;

2. Gain or loss from the sale of the S corporation stock; and

3. Any state or local income taxes and administrative expenses of the trust properly allocable to the S corporation stock.

Otherwise allowable capital losses are allowed only to the extent of capital gains. Moreover, no deduction is allowed for amounts distributed to beneficiaries, and, except as described above, no additional deductions or credits are allowed. Also, this income is not included in the distributable net income of the trust and, therefore, is not included in the beneficiaries' income. Furthermore, no item relating to the S corporation stock is apportioned to any beneficiary. Special rules apply upon termination of all or a part of the ESBT [IRC Sec. 641(c)].

Qualified Domestic Trust (QDOT). A qualified domestic trust (QDOT) is a special kind of trust that qualifies for the estate tax marital deduction even though the transferee spouse is not a U.S. citizen [IRC Sec. 2056A]. Property that is transferred from a U.S. citizen decedent to a nonresident alien spouse will not qualify for the estate tax marital deduction unless it is transferred from the decedent to a QDOT. For a detailed discussion of QDOTs, see ¶ 1106.

Business and Investment Trusts. A "business" or commercial trust is a type of trust created as a means of carrying on a profit-making business, usually using capital or property supplied by the beneficiaries. The trustees or other designated persons are, in effect, managers of the undertaking, whether appointed or controlled by the beneficiaries. This arrangement more closely resembles an association, which may be

¶2800

taxed as a corporation or a partnership and is distinguishable from the other type of trusts discussed in this chapter. The fact that beneficiaries do not supply the trust property is not sufficient to avoid the trust being classified and taxed as a business entity [Reg. Sec. 301.7701-4(b)].

An "investment" trust may also be taxed as an association, rather than a trust, if there is a power under the trust agreement to vary the investment of the certificate holders [Reg. Sec. 301.7701-4(c)]. However, if this power is lacking, the arrangement is taxed as a trust. Unit investment trusts, as defined in the Investment Company Act of 1940, that are set up to hold mutual fund shares for investors are also not taxed as trusts. Instead, their income is taxed directly to the investors [Reg. Sec. 1.851-7].

Liquidating Trust. A liquidating trust formed for the primary purpose of liquidating and distributing the assets transferred to it is taxed as a trust, and not as an association, even though the trust may have profits. All the activities of the trust must be reasonably necessary to, and consistent with, the accomplishment of the primary purpose of liquidation and distribution. The arrangement no longer qualifies as a liquidating trust if the liquidation is unreasonably prolonged, or if the liquidation purpose becomes so obscured by business activities that the declared purpose of liquidation no longer exists or has been abandoned [Reg. Sec. 301.7701-4(d)].

(e) Abusive Trusts. The IRS is aggressively targeting fraudulent trust schemes that advertise bogus tax benefits and are designed solely to minimize or evade taxes. This will occur when the trust has no true business purpose or economic substance. In light of an IRS scrutiny of abusive trusts, taxpayers should reconsider trust arrangements offered by overly zealous trust promoters who offer trust deals that are too good to be true. Taxpayers should be suspicious of any promoter who says that they can transfer a business or home into a trust and still retain full benefit from the assets transferred into the trust while also reducing or eliminating tax. Taxpayers should be especially wary of anyone who says that with a trust you can now deduct your personal living expenses or claim charitable contribution deductions for payments that really benefit you and your family. The big tip off is being told by a promoter that you can set up a trust, give up no control over your assets and pay zero tax. It just doesn't work that way. The IRS also warns that you should be suspicious of tax promoters who suggest that you need not check out a proposed trust arrangement with a tax advisor, such as an attorney or accountant, or with the IRS. If you have used one of the so-called abusive trusts to lower your tax bill in the past, the IRS advises you to file amended returns.

In Notice 97-24,[1] the IRS warned taxpayers to avoid abusive trust arrangements that promise to reduce or eliminate federal taxes in unauthorized ways. The IRS explained that promoters of abusive trust arrangements typically promise tax benefits with no meaningful change in the taxpayer's control over or benefit from the taxpayer's income or assets. The benefits promised could include: (1) reduction or elimination of income subject to tax; (2) deductions for personal expenses paid by the trust; (3) depreciation deductions of an owner's personal residence and furnishings; (4) a stepped-up basis for property transferred to the trust; (5) the reduction or elimination of self-employment taxes; and (6) the reduction or elimination of gift and estate taxes.

---

[1] **¶2800** Notice 97-24, 1997-1 CB 409; Treas. Dept., IRS Publication 2193, "Too Good to be True: Should Your Financial Portfolio Include Trusts" (1999).

¶2800

The IRS explained that abusive trust arrangements often use multiple trusts to hide the true ownership of assets and income or to disguise the substance of transactions. Typically funds flow from one trust to another by means of rental agreements, fees for services, purchase and sale agreements, and distributions that are legitimate only in their title or appearance.

In Notice 97-24, the IRS described the following five examples of abusive trust arrangements:

1. *The Business Trust.* The owner of a business transfers the business to a trust (sometimes described as an unincorporated business trust) in exchange for units or certificates of beneficial interest, sometimes described as units of beneficial interest or UBI's (trust units). The business trust makes payments to the trust unit holders or to other trusts created by the owner (characterized either as deductible business expenses or as deductible distributions) that purport to reduce the taxable income of the business trust to the point where little or no tax is due from the business trust. In addition, the owner claims the arrangement reduces or eliminates the owner's self-employment taxes on the theory that the owner is receiving reduced or no income from the operation of the business. In some cases, the trust units are supposed to be canceled at death or "sold" at a nominal price to the owner's children, leading to the contention by promoters that there is no estate tax liability.

2. *The Equipment or Service Trust.* The equipment trust is formed to hold equipment that is rented or leased to the business trust, often at inflated rates. The service trust is formed to provide services to the business trust, often for inflated fees. Under these abusive trust arrangements, the business trust may purport to reduce its income by making allegedly deductible payments to the equipment or service trust. Further, as to the equipment trust, the equipment owner may claim that the transfer of equipment to the equipment trust in exchange for the trust units is a taxable exchange. The trust takes the position that the trust has "purchased" the equipment with a known value (its fair market value) and that the value is the tax basis of the equipment for purposes of claiming depreciation deductions. The owner, on the other hand, takes the inconsistent position that the value of the trust units received cannot be determined, resulting in no taxable gain to the owner on the exchange. The equipment or service trust also may attempt to reduce or eliminate its income by distributions to other trusts.

3. *The Family Residence Trust.* The owner of the family residence transfers the residence, including its furnishings, to a trust. The parties claim inconsistent tax treatment for the trust and the owner (similar to the equipment trust). The trust claims the exchange results in a stepped-up basis for the property, while the owner reports no gain. The trust claims to be in the rental business and purports to rent the residence back to the owner; however, in most cases, little or no rent is actually paid. Rather, the owner contends that the owner and family members are caretakers or provide services to the trust and, therefore, live in the residence for the benefit of the trust. Under some arrangements, the family residence trust receives funds from other trusts (such as a business trust) which are treated as the income of the trust. In order to reduce the tax which might be due with respect to such income (and any income from rent actually paid by the owner), the trust

may attempt to deduct depreciation and the expenses of maintaining and operating the residence.

4. *The Charitable Trust.* The owner transfers assets to a purported charitable trust and claims either that the payments to the trust are deductible or that payments made by the trust are deductible charitable contributions. Payments are made to charitable organizations; however, in fact, the payments are principally for the personal educational, living, or recreational expenses of the owner or the owner's family. For example, the trust may pay for the college tuition of a child of the owner.

5. *The Final Trust.* In some multi-trust arrangements, the U.S. owner of one or more abusive trusts establishes a trust (the "final trust") that holds trust units of the owner's other trusts and is the final distributee of their income. A final trust often is formed in a foreign country that will impose little or no tax on the trust. In some arrangements, more than one foreign trust is used, with the cash flowing from one trust to another until the cash is ultimately distributed or made available to the U.S. owner, purportedly tax free.

The IRS promises that promoters of abusive trust arrangements will be subject to civil and/or criminal penalties.[2] For example, a husband and wife have been sentenced to the longest permissible prison term (11 years and $6^1/2$ years, respectively) for their role in an abusive trust scheme designed to defraud the IRS. Since there is no parole in the federal criminal system, the couple will be serving at least 85 percent of that prison term.[3]

Beware of fraudulent trust seminars. Fraudulent promoters conduct seminars where they advise taxpayers to create trusts to protect their assets from judgments, lawsuits, inheritance taxes, transfer taxes, and income taxes. The trusts are designed to enable taxpayers to deduct all of their personal living expenses that are otherwise nondeductible. It is well established that trusts cannot be used to transform a taxpayer's personal, living, or educational expenses into deductible items. The promoters for the creation and maintenance of these trusts charge exorbitant fees. The IRS is aware that as many as one million to two million taxpayers are concealing taxable income through extensive use of foreign entities like trusts, partnerships and offshore bank accounts.

(f) Basic Trust Tax Principles. In order to appreciate the fraudulent nature of some of the abusive trust schemes offered in the marketplace, an understanding of the basics of trust taxation is imperative. A trust is defined as a legal relationship or arrangement under which an individual transfers property to another person who is called the trustee, so the property can be administered for the benefit of a third party, who is called the beneficiary. The trust entity becomes the owner of the property so that the property can be controlled and managed by the designated independent trustee. Trusts are created to separate completely responsibility and control of assets from the benefits of ownership. All income received by the trust is taxable to the trust. Legitimate trusts may, in general, claim a deduction for distributions of income made to beneficiaries of the trust. As a result of this basic rule of trust taxation, trusts can eliminate income by making distributions of income to other trusts or other entities that are named as beneficiaries.

---

[2] Information Release 97-19, April 3, 1997.   [3] 2001 TNT 38-7 (Doc. 2001-5624).

In the fraudulent schemes, the IRS found that fraudulent expenses were charged against trust income at each trust layer resulting in a reduction of income from the trust that is ultimately reported to the IRS. The courts recognize that taxpayers have a legal right to structure transactions to minimize their tax obligations,[4] however, if a transaction is entered into solely for tax avoidance and does not have any economic, commercial, or legal effect other than the expected tax benefits, it constitutes an economic sham without effect for federal income tax purposes.[5]

Whether the IRS and courts will respect a taxpayer's characterization of a transaction depends on whether the characterization represents and is supported by a bona fide transaction with economic substance, compelled or encouraged by business or regulatory realities, and not shaped solely or primarily by tax avoidance features that have meaningless labels attached. No matter what label is attached to the trust, unless it has a true business purpose or economic substance, the IRS will consider the trust to be a sham. As a result of this characterization, the trust entity will be ignored and the transferor of the assets will be treated as the owner of the assets and must pay taxes on the trust's income.

In determining whether a trust has economic substance and should be respected for tax purposes, courts look to a variety of factors:

1. Whether the relationship of the grantors to the transferred property changes materially; if the taxpayer's relationship to the trust property before and after transfer to the trust is not materially different then the trust is most likely a sham that will be disregarded for tax purposes;

2. Whether any independent trustee exists to prevent the grantors from acting solely in their own interests; if no independent trustee has any meaningful role in the trust, then the trust is most likely a sham that will be disregarded for tax purposes;

3. Whether any economic interest in the trust assets passed to other beneficiaries; if the taxpayers fail to prove that any economic interest passes to any other beneficiary, the trust is most likely a sham that will be disregarded for tax purposes; and

4. Whether the trust imposes any restrictions on the grantors' use of the assets; if the taxpayers were not bound by any restrictions in the use of trust property, including the payment of fees to them for management services, the trust is most likely a sham that will be disregarded for tax purposes.[6]

Abusive trust arrangements often use the trust entity to hide the true ownership of assets and income or to disguise the substance of the transaction. These arrangements frequently involve more than one trust, each holding different assets of the taxpayer such as the taxpayer's business, business equipment, home, or automobile, as well as interests in other trusts. Funds may flow from one trust to another trust by way of rental agreements, fees for services, purchase and sale agreements, and distributions.

---

[4] Gregory v. Helvering, 293 U.S. 465 (1935).

[5] Frank Lyon Co., 435 U.S. 561 (1978); Gilman, 933 F.2d 143 (2d Cir. 1991); Nicole Rose Corp., 117 TC 328 (2001).

[6] Richardson, 509 F.3d 736 (6th Cir. 2007); Markosian, 73 TC 1235 (1980); Lund, 2002-2 USTC ¶ 50,507 (9th Cir. 2002), aff'g TC Memo 2000-334; Gouveia, TC Memo 2004-256.

Some trusts purport to involve charitable purposes. In some situations, one or more foreign trusts also may be part of the arrangement.

Tax basics ignored by promoters of abusive trusts. Abusive trust promoters typically ignore the following basic trust principles:

1. *Substance rather than form controls taxation.* This first basic principle is the "substance over form" rule. In analyzing trust arrangements to see if a sham exists, the IRS and the courts will examine the substance, rather than the form of the deal.[7] They will look to see if the taxpayer has engaged in the transaction solely to generate tax deductions and to determine if the transaction has a true business purpose or economic substance. The trust will be treated as a sham and will be ignored for tax purposes if the taxpayer was motivated by no business purpose other than obtaining tax benefits, and there was no reasonable possibility of making a profit.[8] For example, a transaction that can only be profitable when the tax benefits are taken into account is not entered into for profit. The following factors have been considered by the Tax Court to determine whether a purported trust lacks economic substance: (1) whether the taxpayer's relationship to the property differed materially before and after the trust's formation; (2) whether the trust had an independent trustee; (3) whether an economic interest passed to other beneficiaries of the trust; and (4) whether the taxpayer felt bound by any restriction imposed by the trust itself or by the law of trusts.[9]

2. *Grantors may be treated as owners of trusts.* The grantor trust rules provide that if the owner of property transferred to a trust retains an economic interest in, or control over, the trust, the owner is treated for income tax purposes as the owner of the trust property and all transactions by the trust are treated as transactions of the owner [IRC Secs. 671-677]. This means that all expenses and income of the trust would belong to, and must be reported by, the owner, and tax deductions and losses arising from transactions between the owner and the trust would be ignored.

    Moreover, because the owner and the trusts would be treated as the same taxpayer according to Rev. Rul. 85-13,[10] transfers between the two would not be taxable exchanges and would not give rise to a stepped-up basis in the assets transferred for depreciation purposes.

3. *Taxation of non-grantor trusts.* A trust is taxable on its income, reduced by amounts distributed to beneficiaries. The trust must (1) obtain a taxpayer identification number; (2) file annual returns reporting its income; and (3) report distributions to beneficiaries on a Form K-1, and the beneficiary must include the distributed income on the beneficiary's tax return [IRC Secs. 641, 651, 652, 661, and 662].

4. *Transfers to trusts may be subject to estate and gift taxes.* If the trust settlor retains the use of, enjoyment of, or income from the property placed in a trust, until his or

---

[7] Gregory v. Helvering, 293 U.S. 465 (1935), XIV-1 CB 193; Helvering v. Clifford, 309 U.S. 331 (1940), 1940-1 CB 105.

[8] Markosian, 73 TC 1235 (1980); Zmuda, 731 F.2d 1417 (9th Cir. 1984).

[9] Richardson, TC Memo 2006-69; Christal, TC Memo 1998-255; Markosian, 73 TC 1235 (1980); Gouveia, TC Memo 2004-256; Norton, TC Memo 2002-137; Castro, TC Memo 2001-115; Muhich, TC Memo 1999-192, *aff'd*, 238 F.3d 860 (7th Cir. 2001); Buckmaster, TC Memo 1997-236; Hanson, TC Memo 1981-675, *aff'd*, 696 F.2d 1232 (9th Cir. 1983).

[10] Rev. Rul. 85-13, 1985-1 CB 184.

her death, the property will be subject to federal estate tax under IRC Sec. 2036(a) when the transferor dies [See ¶ 1807 for further discussion of IRC Sec. 2036(a)].

5. *Personal expenses are generally not deductible.* Personal expenses such as those for home maintenance, education, and personal travel are not deductible unless expressly authorized by the tax laws. The courts have consistently held that non-deductible personal expenses cannot be transformed into deductible expenses by the use of trusts. Furthermore, the costs of creating these trusts are not deductible.[11]

6. *A genuine charity must benefit in order to claim a valid charitable deduction.* In order for a charitable trust to be tax-exempt it must strictly comply with the tax laws. Arrangements will not constitute tax-exempt charitable trusts if they do not satisfy the requirements of the tax law, including the requirement that their true purpose is to benefit charity. Furthermore, supposed charitable payments made by a trust are not deductible charitable contributions where the payments are really for the benefit of the owner or the owner's family members.[12]

7. *Special rules apply to foreign trusts.* If an arrangement involves a foreign trust, taxpayers should be aware that a number of special provisions apply to foreign trusts with U.S. grantors or U.S. beneficiaries. For example, a U.S. person that fails to report a transfer of property to a foreign trust or the receipt of a distribution from a foreign trust is subject to a tax penalty equal to 35 percent of the gross value of the transaction. Other examples of these provisions are the application of U.S. withholding taxes to payments to foreign trusts and the application of U.S. excise taxes to transfers of appreciated property to foreign trusts. [IRC Secs. 6048 and 6677; for further discussion see ¶ 3104].

8. *Civil and/or criminal penalties may apply.* The participants in and promoters of abusive trust arrangements may be subject to civil and/or criminal penalties in appropriate cases.[13]

(g) Red Flags Indicating Abusive Trust Arrangements. The telltale characteristics of an abusive trust arrangement include the following:

1. Ownership of assets or property has not really been transferred into the trust because the original owner has retained the authority to have income earned by those assets benefit him.

2. The trustee is the promoter, or a relative or friend of the owner who simply carries out the directions of the owner whether or not permitted by the terms of the trust.

3. The trustee gives the owner:

   • Checks that are pre-signed or back-dated by the trustee,

   • Checks that are accompanied by a rubber stamp of the trustee's signature, or

   • Credit or debit cards so cash can readily be obtained from the trust and used for the owner's benefit.

---

[11] Schulz, 686 F.2d 490 (7th Cir. 1982); Neely, 775 F.2d 1092 (9th Cir. 1985).

[12] Fausner, 55 TC 620 (1971).

[13] Buttorff, 761 F.2d 1056 (5th Cir. 1985); Krall, 835 F.2d 711 (8th Cir. 1987).

¶2800

4. The trustee gives the owner:

- Checks that are pre-signed or back-dated by the trustee,
- Checks that are accompanied by a rubber stamp of the trustee's signature, or
- Credit or debit cards so cash can readily be obtained from the trust and used for the owner's benefit.

5. The trust transforms a taxpayer's otherwise nondeductible personal, living, or educational expenses into deductible items.

6. The trust seeks to avoid tax liability by ignoring either the true ownership of the assets or the true substance of the transaction.

7. The trust name refers to constitutional issues, fairness, equity or patriotic themes. Alternatively, the trust could have labels that resemble common business organizations or nonabusive trusts.

8. Owners of the trust effectively retain control over trust assets but are promised tax benefits that are not legally available in conjunction with such control. Promoters of abusive trusts typically promise tax benefits that are unavailable under the law. The promised benefits often include: reduction or elimination of income subject to tax; deductions for personal expenses paid by the trust; depreciation deductions of an owner's personal residence and furnishings; a stepped-up basis for property transferred to the trust; the reduction or elimination of self-employment taxes; and the reduction or elimination of gift and estate taxes.

9. No independent trustee exists or the trust provides for unjustified replacement of the trustee.

10. The trust uses post office boxes for trust addresses.

11. High fees are charged for trust packages and the promoter promises to offset these expenses by tax benefits.

(h) Civil and/or Criminal Penalties Imposed on Abusive Trusts. Investors of abusive trust schemes that improperly evade tax are still liable for taxes, interest, and civil penalties. Violations of the Internal Revenue Code with the intent to evade income taxes may result in a civil fraud penalty or criminal prosecution. Civil fraud can include a penalty of up to 75 percent of the underpayment of tax attributable to fraud, in addition to the taxes owed. In addition a return preparer penalty may be imposed against a tax return preparer for each tax return or claim for refund that understates the taxpayer's liability due to an unreasonable position which includes a tax position relying on a sham trust arrangement. The penalty is the greater of (a) $1,000 or (b) 50 percent of the income derived (or to be derived) by the preparer with respect to the return or refund claim [IRC Sec. 6694(a)]. The standard for undisclosed positions is a "reasonable belief" standard, which requires that:

1. The preparer knew, or reasonably should have known, of the position;

2. There was not a reasonable belief that the tax treatment of the position would more likely than not be the proper treatment; and

3. The position was not disclosed or there was not a reasonable basis for the position.

¶2800

A reasonable cause exception applies if it is shown that there was a reasonable cause for the understatement and the preparer acted in good faith. The penalty increases to the greater of (a) $5,000 or (b) 50 percent of the income derived (or to be derived) by the preparer with respect to the return or refund claim if the understatement is willful or reckless [IRC Sec. 6694(b)]. The preparer penalty for willful or reckless conduct must be reduced by the amount of any penalty imposed for an unreasonable position relating to the same understatement.

Criminal convictions of promoters and investors may result in fines up to $250,000 and up to five years in prison. The following criminal statutes may apply:

- 18 USC 371, Conspiracy to Defraud the IRS
- IRC Sec. 7201, Tax Evasion
- IRC Sec. 7206(1), Subscription to a False Tax Return
- IRC Sec. 7206(2), Aiding or Assisting in a False Tax Return
- IRC Sec. 7212(a), Corrupt or Forcible Interference with the Administration of Internal Revenue Laws
- 31 USC 5314, Records and Reports on Foreign Financial Agency Transactions

¶2801 HOW ESTATES AND TRUSTS ARE TAXED

Estates and trusts are both separate taxpaying entities. The income earned by the assets in the estate or trust must be reported by the estate or trust. The fiduciary (an executor or administrator for an estate, a trustee for a trust) must file a tax return and pay any tax that may be due. The most important difference between the tax treatment of an individual and an estate or trust is that the estate or trust is treated as a hybrid pass-through entity. As a result, the estate or trust is taxed on undistributed trust income (DNI) and will be able to claim a deduction when income is distributed to beneficiaries who are required to include these distributions in income. For further discussion of DNI, see ¶2803.

In general, income received by the estate or trust is distributed to a beneficiary and is reported by the beneficiary or the fiduciary on IRS Form 1041 (U.S. Income Tax Return for Estates and Trusts). (See Chapter 29 for a completed Form 1041 for a trust and Chapter 30 for a completed Form 1041 for an estate. Each chapter includes line-by-line explanations of each entry.)

The fiduciary reports income, deductions, and credits on Form 1041 similar to the way these items are reported on a Form 1040. The IRS imposes penalties for failure to file a Form 1041 upon the fiduciary (personal representative or trustee) similar to the penalty imposed on an individual who failed to file a Form 1040 [Reg. Sec. 1.641(b)-2(a)].

Taxes for estates and trusts are computed by using a special rate schedule that differs from the one applicable to individuals or corporations [see ¶2935]. Except in the situation of grantor trusts [see ¶3100], the income of an estate or trust is taxed either to the estate or trust through its fiduciary, to the beneficiaries, or in part to each, depending upon the disposition of the income under the terms of the will or trust and state law. In this way, the entire taxable income of the estate or trust is taxed [see

¶2802]. The estate or trust will be entitled to a special deduction for amounts distributed or deemed to be distributed to beneficiaries as discussed further at ¶2814 [IRC Secs. 651, 661]. As a result, the estate or trust can be viewed as a conduit because it does not pay tax on amounts distributed or deemed distributed to beneficiaries.

The fiduciary of an estate (the executor or administrator, depending on whether there is a will) and the fiduciary of a trust (the trustee) must file Form 1041 and pay the tax of the estate or trust. The filing requirements are explained at ¶2820.

The fiduciaries must also file a separate Schedule K-1 for each beneficiary. The fiduciary of a trust or decedent's estate uses Schedule K-1 to report the beneficiary's share of the trust's or estate's income, deductions, credits, etc. The beneficiary must report items on his or her income tax return in the same way that the estate or trust treated the items on its return. For an estate, the executor or administrator, in addition to filing the estate's income tax return, generally files the decedent's final income tax return as well. The deceased person's final income tax return covers the period ending on the date of his or her death. The estate's income tax return covers the period beginning the day after death.

Multiple trusts. If several or multiple trusts are created in one instrument, they will be consolidated for tax purposes if:

1. The trusts have substantially the same grantor or grantors and substantially the same primary beneficiary or beneficiaries; and

2. A principal purpose of such trusts is the avoidance of tax [IRC Sec. 643(f)(2)]. For the purposes of this rule a husband and wife will be treated as one person.

To illustrate a situation where creative taxpayers could try to use multiple trusts to avoid paying tax, imagine a grantor creating ten $100,000 trusts. He would pay less tax than a grantor creating one $1 million trust, as a result of the progressive nature of the tax rate structure.[1] Where a trust is established with the principal purpose to avoid tax and the grantor and beneficiaries are substantially the same, then the trusts will be collapsed and treated as one for federal income tax purposes.[2]

The number of trusts that were created depends upon the intention of the creator of the trust (the trust settlor) as determined from the trust agreement.[3] The Supreme Court has held that separate trusts are created, even if there is only one trust instrument and the trust assets are not segregated, when each beneficiary has a separate account and is granted a fixed share in the trust property.[4]

> ▶ **PLANNING TIP:** Will drafters often create mirror reciprocal trusts in each spouse's will. To avoid having these mirror reciprocal trusts treated as one trust under IRC Sec. 643(f), one spouse's will should create a single discretionary trust for all descendants and the other spouse's will should create a separate trust for each child and the child's descendants.

---

[1] **¶2801** Committee Report on the Tax Reform Act of 1984 (Pub. L. No. 98-369).

[2] Committee Report on the Tax Reform Act of 1984 (Pub. L. No. 98-369).

[3] Fiduciary Trust Co., 36 F. Supp. 653 (S.D.N.Y. 1940); Boyce, 190 F. Supp. 950, *aff'd*, 296 F.2d 731 (5th Cir. 1961).

[4] United States Trust Co., 296 U.S. 481 (1936).

¶2801

¶2802 WHO PAYS TAX ON ESTATE AND TRUST INCOME

The beneficiary is generally taxed on distributions he or she receives, or is entitled to receive, from the estate or trust, but only to the extent of the beneficiary's share of either the trust or estate's "distributable net income" (DNI). The term DNI is a key concept unique to the world of estate and trust taxation [see ¶¶2803–2804].

A fiduciary is taxed on the income of the estate or trust. Taxable income is gross income [see ¶2805] less the deductions discussed at ¶2808 through ¶2815. In certain situations, the income of a trust is not taxed to either the beneficiaries or the fiduciary. Instead, it is taxed to the grantor or other persons who have control of the trust property or income. This type of trust is called a grantor trust and is discussed in further detail at ¶3100.

(a) An Estate's Taxable Year. Fiduciaries of estates have flexibility in choosing their taxable year. The estate's income must be reported annually on either a calendar or fiscal year basis. A fiscal year is a 12-month period ending on the last day of any month other than December [IRC Sec. 441(e)]. The fiscal year, however, cannot exceed 12 months from the date that the decedent died.

> **Example 1:** A taxpayer dies on June 1, 2013. The longest possible taxable year for his estate would start on June 2, 2014 and end on May 31, 2015.

Estates are afforded flexibility in choosing their taxable year and can, therefore, defer the payment of income tax because (1) estates generally do not last as long as trusts and (2) estate fiduciaries need to select an accounting period to coincide with the administration of the estate.

A fiscal year election is made on Form SS-4, at the time that the estate files for its tax identification number. In order to elect a fiscal year, the last month of the fiscal year should be inserted in box 11. The first fiscal year cannot exceed 12 months, and generally it is prudent to elect the month prior to the date of death as the fiscal year-end. For example, if the decedent dies on May 10, 2014, a fiscal year ending in April should be elected, making the first year May 10, 2014 to April 30, 2015.

The personal representative chooses the estate's accounting period when he or she files the first Form 1041 for the estate. The estate's first tax year can be any period that ends on the last day of a month and does not exceed 12 months. The first taxable year must be adopted by the due date (not including extensions) for filing the first return. After the personal representative has chosen the tax year, it cannot be changed without the permission from the IRS. In addition, on the first income tax return, the personal representative chooses either the cash or accrual accounting method that will be used to report the estate's income. After an accounting method has been chosen, it cannot be changed without the consent of the IRS. An application for change is filed on IRS Form 1128.

> ▶ **PLANNING TIP:** The ability of an estate to adopt a fiscal year as its taxable year provides a valuable income deferral opportunity. Using a fiscal year will enable a beneficiary to defer reporting taxable income from estate distributions

because estate income distributed or distributable to a beneficiary is taxable to the beneficiary for the tax year in which the tax year of the estate ends [IRC Sec. 662(c); Reg. 1.662(c)-1].

Example 2: Alice is the beneficiary of an estate that has a taxable year beginning June 1, 2013 and ending May 31, 2014. Alice is a calendar basis taxpayer. On June 1, 2013, Alice receives a distribution from the estate. She does not have to report any income resulting from this distribution until April 15, 2015, which is the due date of her 2014 tax return.

(b) A Trust's Taxable Year. Trusts, unlike estates, have no flexibility in choosing their taxable year. Trusts are not permitted to use fiscal tax years. Trusts must adopt the calendar year as their tax year [IRC Sec. 644(a)]. An exception is made for trusts exempt from tax under IRC Sec. 501(a) and wholly charitable trusts under IRC Sec. 4947(a). These two types of trust are not required to adopt the calendar year as their tax year.

A trust beneficiary is taxed on the distributions for the tax year or years of the estate or trust that end within or with his or her tax year [IRC Secs. 652(c), 662(c); Reg. Secs. 1.652(c)-1, 1.662(c)-1]. For a discussion of the taxable year of estates, see ¶ 3100.

(c) What Happens When a Trust Terminates. After a trust or the administration of an estate is terminated for federal income tax purposes, the gross income, deductions, and credits of the trust or estate are attributed to the beneficiaries of the estate or trust [Reg. 1.641(b)-3(d)]. However, a trust does not terminate automatically. A reasonable period is allowed for the trustee to wind up its affairs. During this period, the status of the trust income is determined under the terms of the trust instrument and state law [Reg. Sec. 1.641(b)-3; see ¶ 2943].

¶ 2803 DISTRIBUTABLE NET INCOME

Distributable net income (DNI) is an extremely important tax concept that is unique to the tax treatment of trusts and estates. The DNI of a trust is determined under IRC Sec. 643(a).

(a) Functions of DNI. DNI performs the following two critical functions:

- DNI measures the taxable income reportable by beneficiaries, even if the actual amount of trust or estate distributions is greater; and

- DNI limits the deductions allowed to a trust or estate for distributions made to its beneficiaries. DNI is also used to determine the character of distributions to the beneficiaries.

A beneficiary never reports more than his or her share of DNI. Moreover, the fiduciary's deduction for distributions cannot be more than the trust's DNI [IRC Secs. 643, 651(b), 652(a), 661(a), 662(a); Reg. Secs. 1.643(a)-0, 1.652(a)-2, 1.662(a)-2]. In addition, DNI provides the basis for allocating various classes of income among beneficiaries [IRC Secs. 652(b), 662(b)].

¶ 2803

Example 1: The taxpayer is the beneficiary of trust set up by his grandmother. The trust distributes $20,000 to the taxpayer in a year when DNI is computed to be $15,000. The taxpayer will report and pay taxes on only $15,000 even though he received $20,000 in cash. Similarly, the trust will only be able to deduct $15,000 as its distribution deduction even though it distributed $20,000, because the trust's deduction is limited to DNI.

(b) How to Compute DNI. To compute the amount of DNI, you start with the trust's or estate's taxable income (gross income minus deductions). Then, you make the adjustments described in ¶2803(d) below [IRC Sec. 643(a); Reg. Sec. 1.643(a)-0 to 1.643(a)-7].

(c) "Income" Defined for DNI Purposes. "Income" is defined as the amount of income of an estate or trust for the taxable year determined under the terms of the governing instrument and applicable local law. However, trust provisions that depart fundamentally from traditional principles of income and principal will generally not be recognized [Reg. Sec. 1.643(b)-1].

Thus, items such as dividends, interest, and rents are generally allocated to income and proceeds from the sale or exchange of trust assets are generally allocated to principal. However, an allocation of amounts between income and principal pursuant to applicable local law will be respected if local law provides for a reasonable apportionment between the income and remainder beneficiaries of the total return of the trust for the year, including ordinary and tax-exempt income, capital gains, and appreciation [Reg. Sec. 1.643(b)-1].

For example, a state statute providing that income is a unitrust amount of no less than 3 percent and no more than 5 percent of the fair market value of the trust assets, whether determined annually or averaged on a multiple year basis, is a reasonable apportionment of the total return of the trust. Similarly, a state statute that permits the trustee to make adjustments between income and principal to fulfill the trustee's duty of impartiality between the income and remainder beneficiaries is generally a reasonable apportionment of the total return of the trust [Reg. Sec. 1.643(b)-1].

Generally, these adjustments are permitted by state statutes when the trustee invests and manages the trust assets under the state's prudent investor standard, the trust describes the amount that may or must be distributed to a beneficiary by referring to the trust's income, and the trustee after applying the state statutory rules regarding the allocation of receipts and disbursements to income and principal, is unable to administer the trust impartially.

Allocations for apportioning the total return of a trust between income and principal will be respected regardless of whether the trust provides that the income must be distributed to one or more beneficiaries or may be accumulated in whole or in part, and regardless of which alternate permitted method is actually used, provided the trust complies with all requirements of the state statute for switching methods [Reg. Sec. 1.643(b)-1].

A switch between methods of determining trust income authorized by state statute will not result in a taxable gift from the trust's grantor or any of the trust's beneficiaries. A switch to a method not specifically authorized by state statute, but valid under state law

¶2803

(including a switch via judicial decision or a binding non-judicial settlement) may be taxable to the trust or its beneficiaries and may result in taxable gifts from the trust's grantor and beneficiaries [Reg. Sec. 1.643(b)-1].

The IRS will respect an allocation to income of all or a part of the gains from the sale or exchange of trust assets if the allocation is made either pursuant to the terms of the governing instrument and applicable local law, or pursuant to a reasonable and impartial exercise of a discretionary power granted to the fiduciary by applicable local law or by the governing instrument, if not prohibited by applicable local law [Reg. Sec. 1.643(b)-1].

(d) Computation of DNI. The distributable net income of a domestic estate or trust generally consists of the same items of gross income and deductions that make up the taxable income of the estate trust with the following critical modifications:

1. Distribution Deduction. No deduction for income distributions to beneficiaries under IRC Secs. 651 and 661 is allowed and must be added back to taxable income when computing DNI [Reg. Sec. 1.643(a)-1].

2. Personal Exemption. No deduction for the personal exemption is allowed and must be added back to taxable income when computing DNI [Reg. Sec. 1.643(a)-2; see ¶ 2809].

3. Capital Gains. Gains from the sale or exchange of capital assets are excluded from DNI to the extent that these gains are allocated to corpus and are not: (1) paid, credited, or required to be distributed to any beneficiary during the taxable year, or (2) paid, permanently set aside, or to be used for a charitable purpose [IRC Secs. 643(a)(3)]. Capital losses are excluded when computing DNI except to the extent that the losses are taken into account in determining the amount of gains from the sale or exchange of capital assets which are paid, credited, or required to be distributed to any beneficiary during the taxable year. The exclusion under IRC Sec. 1202 is no longer considered.

Capital gains will be included in DNI to the extent they are, pursuant to the terms of the governing instrument and local law, or pursuant to a reasonable and impartial exercise of discretion by the fiduciary: (a) allocated to income (if income under the state statute is defined as a unitrust amount, a discretionary power to allocate gains to income must also be exercised consistently and the amount so allocated may not be greater than the excess of the unitrust amount over the amount of DNI); (b) allocated to corpus but treated consistently by the fiduciary on the trust's books, records, and tax returns as part of a distribution to a beneficiary; or (c) allocated to corpus but actually distributed to the beneficiary or utilized by the fiduciary in determining the amount that is distributed or required to be distributed to a beneficiary [Reg. Sec. 1.643(a)-3(b)].

4. Tax-exempt interest. Tax-exempt interest on state and local bonds is included, reduced by amounts which would be deductible but for the disallowance of deductions on expenses and interest related to tax-exempt income.

5. Capital losses. Capital losses must first be netted at the trust level against any gains from the sale or exchange of capital assets, except for a capital gain that must be distributed to a particular beneficiary [Reg. Sec. 1.643(a)-3(d)].

6. Extraordinary dividends and taxable stock dividends. Extraordinary dividends (whether paid in cash or in kind) and taxable stock dividends of simple trusts (defined as trusts required to distribute all income currently; see ¶ 2805) which the fiduciary, acting in

¶2803

good faith, determines to be allocable to corpus under the terms of the governing instrument and applicable local law are not considered "income" when computing DNI [Reg. Secs. 1.643(b)-2, 1.643(a)-4, 1.643(d)-2].

7. Foreign trust income. A foreign trust's gross income from foreign sources, reduced by nondeductible expenses, is included in computing DNI [Reg. Sec. 1.643(a)-6].

Example 2: A trust has $40,000 gross income for the year, including $9,000 capital gain which, under the trust instrument, is to be distributed one-third to the beneficiary and two-thirds to trust corpus. Gross income also includes $5,000 domestic corporate dividends. The trust is entitled to deductions for interest, taxes, depreciation, and charitable contributions amounting to $8,000. In addition to the $40,000 gross income, the trust also receives $7,000 tax-exempt interest. DNI is $33,000, computed as follows:

Gross income	$40,000
Less: deductions	−8,000
Taxable income as modified	$32,000
Plus: tax-exempt interest	+ 7,000
	$39,000
Less: capital gain to be added to trust corpus (2/3)	−6,000
Distributable net income	$33,000

Example 3: Under the terms of Trust's governing instrument, all income is to be paid to A for life. Trustee is given discretionary powers to invade principal for A's benefit and to deem discretionary distributions to be made from capital gains realized during the year. During Trust's first taxable year, Trust has $5,000 of dividend income and $10,000 of capital gain from the sale of securities. Pursuant to the terms of the governing instrument and applicable local law, Trustee allocates the $10,000 capital gain to principal. During the year, Trustee distributes to A $5,000, representing A's right to trust income. In addition, Trustee distributes to A $12,000, pursuant to the discretionary power to distribute principal. Trustee does not exercise the discretionary power to deem the discretionary distributions of principal as being paid from capital gains realized during the year. Therefore, the capital gains realized during the year are not included in DNI and the $10,000 of capital gain is taxed to the trust. In future years, Trustee must treat all discretionary distributions as not being made from any realized capital gains [Reg. Sec. 1.643(a)-3(e), Example 1].

Example 4: The facts are the same as in *Example 2*, except that Trustee intends to follow a regular practice of treating discretionary distributions of principal as being paid first from any net capital gains realized by Trust during the year. Trustee evidences this treatment by including the $10,000 capital gain in DNI on Trust's federal income tax return so that it is taxed to A. This treatment of the capital gains is a reasonable exercise of Trustee's discretion. In future years

Trustee must treat all discretionary distributions as being made first from any realized capital gains. [Reg. Sec. 1.643(a)-3(e), Example 2].

Example 5: The facts are the same as in *Example 2*, except that Trustee intends to follow a regular practice of treating discretionary distributions of principal as being paid from any net capital gains realized by Trust during the year from the sale of certain specified assets or a particular class of investments. This treatment of capital gains is a reasonable exercise of Trustee's discretion. [Reg. Sec. 1.643(a)-3(e), Example 3].

Example 6: The facts are the same as in *Example 2*, except that pursuant to the terms of the governing instrument, capital gains realized by Trust are allocated to income. Because the capital gains are allocated to income pursuant to the terms of the governing instrument, the $10,000 capital gain is included in Trust's DNI [Reg. Sec. 1.643(a)-3(e), Example 4].

Example 7: The facts are the same as in *Example 2*, except that Trustee decides that discretionary distributions will be made only to the extent Trust has realized capital gains during the year and thus the discretionary distribution to A is $10,000, rather than $12,000. Because Trustee will use the amount of any realized capital gain to determine the amount of the discretionary distribution to the beneficiary, the $10,000 capital gain is included in Trust's DNI [Reg. Sec. 1.643(a)-3(e), Example 5].

Example 8: Trust's assets consist of Blackacre and other property. Trustee is directed to hold Blackacre for ten years and then sell it and distribute all the sales proceeds to A. Because Trustee uses the amount of the sales proceeds that includes any realized capital gain to determine the amount required to be distributed to A, any capital gain realized from the sale of Blackacre is included in Trust's distributable net income for the taxable year. [Reg. Sec. 1.643(a)-3(e), Example 6].

Example 9: Under the terms of Trust's governing instrument, all income is to be paid to A during the Trust's term. When A reaches 35, Trust is to terminate and all the principal is to be distributed to A. Because all the assets of the trust, including all capital gains, will be actually distributed to the beneficiary at the termination of Trust, all capital gains realized in the year of termination are included in DNI [Reg. Sec. 1.643(a)-3(e), Example 7].

Example 10: The facts are the same as in *Example 8*, except Trustee is directed to pay B $10,000 before distributing the remainder of Trust assets to A. Because the distribution to B is a gift of a specific sum of money none of Trust's DNI that includes all of the capital gains realized during the year of termination is allocated to B's distribution [Reg. Sec. 1.643(a)-3(e), Example 8].

¶2803

Example 11: The facts are the same as in *Example 8*, except Trustee is directed to distribute one-half of the principal to A when A reaches 35 and the balance to A when A reaches 45. Trust assets consist entirely of stock in corporation M with a fair market value of $1,000,000 and an adjusted basis of $300,000. When A reaches 35, Trustee sells one half of the stock and distributes the sales proceeds to A. All the sales proceeds, including all the capital gain attributable to that sale, are actually distributed to A and therefore all the capital gain is included in DNI [Reg. Sec. 1.643(a)-3(e), Example 9].

Example 12: The facts are the same as in *Example 8*, except when A reaches 35, Trustee sells all the stock and distributes one half of the sales proceeds to A. If authorized by the governing instrument and applicable state statute, Trustee may determine to what extent the capital gain is distributed to A. The $500,000 distribution to A may be treated as including a minimum of $200,000 of capital gain (and all of the principal amount of $300,000) and a maximum of $500,000 of the capital gain (with no principal). Trustee evidences the treatment by including the appropriate amount of capital gain in DNI on Trust's federal income tax return. If Trustee is not authorized by the governing instrument and applicable state statutes to determine to what extent the capital gain is distributed to A, one-half of the capital gain attributable to the sale is included in DNI [Reg. Sec. 1.643(a)-3(e), Example 10].

Example 13: The applicable state statute provides that a trustee may make an election to pay an income beneficiary an amount equal to four percent of the fair market value of the trust assets, as determined at the beginning of each taxable year, in full satisfaction of that beneficiary's right to income. State statute also provides that this unitrust amount shall be considered paid first from ordinary and tax-exempt income, then from net short-term capital gain, then from net long-term capital gain, and finally from return of principal. Trust's governing instrument provides that A is to receive each year income as defined under state statute. Trustee makes the unitrust election under state statute. At the beginning of the taxable year, Trust assets are valued at $500,000. During the year, Trust receives $5,000 of dividend income and realizes $80,000 of net long-term gain from the sale of capital assets. Trustee distributes to A $20,000 (4% of $500,000) in satisfaction of A's right to income. Net long-term capital gain in the amount of $15,000 is allocated to income pursuant to the ordering rule of the state statute and is included in DNI [Reg. Sec. 1.643(a)-3(e), Example 11].

Example 14: The facts are the same as in *Example 12*, except that neither state statute nor Trust's governing instrument has an ordering rule for the character of the unitrust amount, but leaves such a decision to the discretion of Trustee. Trustee intends to follow a regular practice of treating principal, other than capital gain, as distributed to the beneficiary to the extent that the unitrust amount exceeds Trust's ordinary and tax-exempt income. Trustee evidences this treatment by not including any capital gains in DNI on Trust's tax return so that the entire $80,000 capital gain is taxed to Trust. This treatment of the capital gains is a reasonable exercise of Trustee's discretion. In future years Trustee must consistently follow this treatment of not allocating realized capital gains to income [Reg. Sec. 1.643(a)-3(e), Example 12].

Example 15: The facts are the same as in *Example 12*, except that neither state statutes nor Trust's governing instrument has an ordering rule for the character of the unitrust amount, but leaves such a decision to the discretion of Trustee. Trustee intends to follow a regular practice of treating net capital gains as distributed to the beneficiary to the extent the unitrust amount exceeds Trust's ordinary and tax-exempt income. Trustee evidences this treatment by including $15,000 of the capital gain in distributable net income on Trust's Federal income tax return. This treatment of the capital gains is a reasonable exercise of Trustee's discretion. In future years Trustee must consistently treat realized capital gain, if any, as distributed to the beneficiary to the extent that the unitrust amount exceeds ordinary and tax-exempt income [Reg. Sec. 1.643(a)-3(e), Example 13].

Example 16: Trustee is a corporate fiduciary that administers numerous trusts. State statutes provide that a trustee may make an election to distribute to an income beneficiary an amount equal to four percent of the annual fair market value of the trust assets in full satisfaction of that beneficiary's right to income. Neither state statutes nor the governing instruments of any of the trusts administered by Trustee has an ordering rule for the character of the unitrust amount, but leaves such a decision to the discretion of Trustee. With respect to some trusts, Trustee intends to follow a regular practice of treating principal, other than capital gain, as distributed to the beneficiary to the extent that the unitrust amount exceeds the trust's ordinary and tax-exempt income. Trustee will evidence this treatment by not including any capital gains in DNI on the tax returns for those trusts. With respect to other trusts, Trustee intends to follow a regular practice of treating any net capital gains as distributed to the beneficiary to the extent the unitrust amount exceeds the trust's ordinary and tax-exempt income. Trustee will evidence this treatment by including net capital gains in DNI on the tax returns filed for these trusts. Trustee's decision with respect to each trust is a reasonable exercise of Trustee's discretion and, in future years, Trustee must treat the capital gains realized by each trust consistently with the treatment by that trust in prior years [Reg. Sec. 1.643(a)-3(e), Example 14].

¶2804 BENEFICIARY'S SHARE OF DISTRIBUTABLE NET INCOME

If DNI includes items with a special tax status, such as exempt interest, beneficiaries must determine how much of such items are included in their distribution. The reason for this is that such items have the same character in the hands of the beneficiary as in the hands of the trust [IRC Secs. 652(b), 662(b); Reg. Secs. 1.652(b)-1, 1.662(b)-1]. For example, according to this conduit principle, to the extent that a distribution includes exempt interest, beneficiaries can exclude it from their own tax returns.

(a) Method of Apportionment. To determine how much of each item is included in a given distribution, the net amount of each item (the gross amount of the item less the deductions allocable to it as discussed below) is apportioned among the beneficiaries on a simple proportional basis, unless the governing instrument or state law specially allocates different classes of income to different beneficiaries [IRC Secs. 652(b), 662(b); Reg. Secs. 1.652(b)-1, 1.662(b)-1].

> **Example 1:** Under the terms of the governing instrument, Alice, a beneficiary is to receive currently one-half of the trust income. Beneficiaries Bob and Carol are each to receive currently one-quarter. The DNI of the trust (after allocation of expenses) consists of dividends of $10,000, taxable interest of $10,000, and tax-exempt interest of $4,000. Alice will be deemed to have received $5,000 of dividends, $5,000 of taxable interest, and $2,000 of tax-exempt interest. Bob and Carol will each be deemed to have received $2,500 of dividends, $2,500 of taxable interest, and $1,000 of tax-exempt interest. However, if the terms of the trust specifically allocate different classes of income to different beneficiaries, entirely or in part, or if local law requires such an allocation, each beneficiary will be deemed to have received those items of income specifically allocated to him [Reg. Sec. 1.652(b)-2(a)].

The terms of the trust are considered specially to allocate different classes of income to different beneficiaries only to the extent that the allocation is required in the trust instrument and only to the extent that it has an economic effect independent of income tax consequences of the allocation. For example, if the trust instrument provides that the trustee has discretion to allocate different classes of income to different beneficiaries, it is not a specific allocation by terms of the trust instrument [Reg. Sec. 1.652(b)-2(b)].

(b) Allocation of Deductions. In determining the total of a particular item of DNI, the gross amount of each income item must be reduced by the deduction allocable to it. In the absence of specific instructions in the governing instrument, the deductions are allocated as follows [Reg. Sec. 1.652(b)-3]:

1. Any deduction directly allocable to a particular class of income is allocated to that class. For example, repairs to, taxes on, and other expenses directly attributable to the maintenance of rental property or the collection of rental income are allocated to rental income. Similarly, all expenditures directly attributable to a business carried on by a trust are allocated to the income from such business.

2. If the deduction directly attributable to a particular class of income exceeds the income, the excess may be applied against any other income class the trustee chooses, with these limitations:

- The income chosen must be included in figuring DNI;
- A proportionate share of nonbusiness deductions must be allocated to nontaxable income; and

¶2804

- Excess deductions attributable to tax-exempt income may not be used as an offset against any other class of income.

3. Expenses that are not directly allocable to any particular class of income (trustee's commissions, safe deposit rentals, state income and personal property taxes, for example) are treated the same as the excess deductions; see (2) above.

> **Example 2:** A trust has rents, taxable interest, dividends, and tax-exempt interest. Deductions directly attributable to the rents exceed the rental income. The excess may be allocated to the taxable interest and dividends in whatever proportions the trustee elects. However, if the excess deductions are attributable to the tax-exempt interest, they may not be allocated to the other income items.

(c) Charitable Contributions Adjustment. In determining the tax status of currently distributable income items in your hands, DNI is figured without regard to any part of a charitable deduction not attributable to income of the tax year. This prevents a charitable contribution from reducing the amount of current income otherwise taxable to a beneficiary, except to the extent the contribution is itself paid out of current income [IRC Sec. 662(b); Reg. Sec. 1.662(b)-2].

> **Example 3:** The Rose Family Trust provides that $30,000 of its income must be distributed currently to Alice Rose and the balance may either be distributed to Bruce Rose, distributed to a local charity, or accumulated. Accumulated income may be distributed to Bruce and to the charity. The trust for its taxable year has $40,000 of taxable interest and $10,000 of tax-exempt income, with no expenses. The trustee distributed $30,000 to Alice, $50,000 to the Kidney Foundation, and $10,000 to Bruce. DNI for the purpose of determining the character of the distribution to Alice is $30,000 (the charitable contributions deduction, for this purpose, being taken into account only to the extent of $20,000, the difference between the total income of the trust for the taxable year, $50,000, and the amount required to be distributed currently, $30,000). The charitable contributions deduction being taken into account, $20,000, is allocated proportionately to the items of income of the trust, $16,000 to taxable interest and $4,000 to tax-exempt income. The amount of income required to be distributed currently to Alice is $30,000, which consists of the balance of these items, $24,000 of taxable interest, and $6,000 of tax-exempt income [Reg. Sec. 1.662(b)-2, Example (1)].

> ▶ **OBSERVATION:** The charitable contributions deduction does not reduce the amount taxable to beneficiaries who receive currently distributable income, but it can reduce the amount taxable to beneficiaries who receive other amounts [Reg. Sec. 1.662(b)-2].

¶2805 GROSS INCOME OF ESTATES AND TRUSTS

The gross income of an estate or trust is determined in a manner that is similar to the computation of an individual's gross income [Reg. Sec. 1.641(a)-2]. Thus, the taxable gross income of an estate or trust consists of all items of gross income received during the taxable year, including the following:

- Income required to be distributed currently to beneficiaries;
- Income accumulated in trust for the benefit of unborn, unascertained, or contingent beneficiaries;
- Income accumulated or held for future distribution;
- Income collected by the guardian of an infant which is to be held or distributed as the court may direct;
- Income received by an estate of a deceased person during the period of administration or settlement of the estate; and
- Income which, in the discretion of the fiduciary, may be distributed to the beneficiaries or accumulated [IRC Sec. 641(a); Reg. Secs. 1.641(a)-1, 1.641(a)-2].

(a) Character of Income. In the hands of the beneficiaries, income retains the same character as it had when it was received by the estate or trust [IRC Secs. 652(b), 661(b), 662(b); Reg. Secs. 1.652(b)-2, 1.662(b)-2]. For example, to the extent that the amounts received consist of tax-exempt income, these amounts are not included in the beneficiary's gross income. Similarly, dividends distributed to a beneficiary retain their original character in the beneficiary's hands. As a result, the estate or trust is treated as a conduit through which income flows from its original source to the beneficiaries.

For an estate, title to personal property usually passes to the executor or administrator, but title to real property often passes to the heirs or persons named in a will at the decedent's death. Therefore, in most cases, the person who receives the real property reports the income produced by the property (such as rents), or the gain or loss from its sale. The only complication is the proper treatment of income accrued to a decedent at the time of his death.

(b) Transfer of Appreciated Property to Trust. The gain on the sale of property by a trust is taxed at the trust's marginal tax rates [see ¶ 2820 for trust tax rates].

(c) 3.8% Net Investment Income Tax. Beginning in 2013, estates and trusts must begin paying a 3.8 percent tax on net investment income (NII) on the lesser of:

1. Undistributed net investment income for the tax year, or
2. Any excess (if any) of AGI for the tax year (as determined under IRC Sec. 67(e)) over the dollar amount at which the highest tax bracket for estates and trusts begins for that year which is $12,150 in 2014 (increasing from $11,950 in 2013) [IRC Sec. 1411(a)(2); Reg. Sec. 1.1411-3(a)(ii)].

Note that unlike the threshold amounts for individuals, the amount used for trusts and estates to compute their net investment income will be adjusted annually for inflation because it is keyed to the highest bracket amount under IRC Sec. 1(e) for each year. Since the highest tax rate of 39.6 percent is imposed on all of an estate's or trust's income over $12,150 in 2014, trusts and estates should avoid accumulating income and consider distributing investment income to beneficiaries. Estates and trusts should also consider investing in tax-exempt and tax-deferred investments in order to reduce investment income subject to the tax.

¶2805

The NII tax is imposed in addition to all other taxes already imposed on that income such as income tax and the alternative minimum tax. Unfortunately, the 3.8 percent surtax may not be deducted anywhere on the federal income tax return. Taxpayers (including individuals and estate and trusts) subject to the NII tax should use Form 8960, "Net Investment Income Tax—Individuals, Estates and Trusts," to compute the 3.8 percent tax. Estates and trusts should report the tax on Form 1041, "U.S. Income Tax Return for Estates and Trusts."

Trusts subject to 3.8 percent NII tax. In general, trusts described in Reg. Sec. 301.7701-4(a) with taxable income over $12,150 in 2014 with net investment income are subject to the 3.8 percent NII tax. A special rule applies to an Electing Small Business Trust (ESBT) that owns stock of an S corporation. Reg. Sec. 1.1411-3(c)(1) provides that if a trust is an ESBT that owns stock of an S corporation, the $12,150 threshold amount that triggers the 3.8 percent NII tax is based on the total income of the trust rather than computed separately for the trust's S corporation income and the trust's other income.

Estates subject to 3.8 percent NII tax. In 2014, estates with net investment income and with taxable income over $12,150 will be subject to the net investment income tax.

AGI of estate or trust. The AGI of an estate or trust is generally determined in the same manner as for an individual [IRC Sec. 67(e)(2)]. However, the deductions permitted under IRC Sec. 642(b) (relating to the personal exemption of an estate or trust) and under IRC Secs. 651 and 661 (relating to amounts distributed to beneficiaries) are subtracted from gross income in computing the estate or trust's AGI. In addition, deductions for expenses incurred in the administration of a trust or estate that would not have been incurred if the property were not held in a trust or estate are allowable in computing AGI [IRC Sec. 67(e)(1)]. Therefore, expenses that cannot be deducted because they are subject to the two-percent floor may not be subtracted in arriving at AGI. The question of whether a trust-related expense is subject to the two-percent floor turns on a prediction about what would happen if the property were held by an individual rather than by a trust. Thus, costs are excepted from the two-percent floor if it would be uncommon, unusual, or unlikely for an individual owner of the property to incur them. However, costs do not have to be peculiar or unique to trusts in order to be excepted from the floor [See ¶2813 for discussion of *Michael J. Knight, Trustee of the William L. Rudkin Testamentary Trust*, where the Supreme Court addressed computation of a trust's AGI when trust expenses have been incurred].

Trusts not subject to NII tax. The following trusts are not subject to the NII tax [IRC Sec. 1411(e)(1); Reg. Sec. 1.1411-3(b)]:

- Trusts that are exempt from income tax include charitable trusts, private foundations, charitable remainder trusts, and qualified retirement plans including pension, profit-sharing and retirement plans, qualified pension, profit-sharing and stock bonus plans, IRAs, Roth IRAs, qualified annuity plans and deferred compensation plans and state and local government deferred compensation plans;

- A trust in which all of the unexpired interests are organized and operated exclusively for religious, charitable, scientific, literary, or educational purposes, or to foster national or international amateur sports competition (but only if no part of

¶2805

its activities involve the provision of athletic facilities or equipment), or for the prevention of cruelty to children or animals as described in IRC Sec. 170(c)(2)(B);

- Trusts that are classified as "grantor trusts" under IRC Secs. 671-679 [see ¶ 3100]; A grantor trust is treated as owned by the grantor for income tax purposes and all items of trust income, loss, credit and deduction are reported by the grantor on the grantor's tax return;

- Trusts that are not classified as "trusts" for federal income tax purposes such as real estate investment trusts (REITs) and common trust funds [IRC Sec. 1411(e)(2)];

- Electing Alaska Native Settlement Funds;

- Perpetual care (Cemetery) trusts;

- Foreign estates and trusts are generally not subject to the NIIT if they have little or no connection to the United States. However, to the extent the income is earned or accumulated for the benefit of, or distributed to, U.S. persons, the NII of a foreign estate or foreign trust will be subject to the tax [Reg. Sec. 1.1411-3(c)(3)].

Net investment income defined. Net investment income, which generally is defined in the same manner for estates and trusts as it is defined for individuals, includes the following:

1. Interest [IRC Sec. 1411(c)(1)(A)(i); Reg. Sec. 1.1411-1(d)(6)];

2. Dividends [IRC Sec. 1411(c)(1)(A)(i); Reg. Sec. 1.1411-1(d)(3)];

3. Annuity income [Reg. Sec. 1.1411-1(d)(1)];

4. Royalties received from mineral, oil and gas, and amounts received for the privilege of using patents, copyrights, secret processes and formulas, goodwill, trademarks, trade-brands, and franchises [IRC Sec. 1411(c)(1)(A)(i); Reg. Sec. 1.1411-1(d)(11)];

5. Rents that are derived from a passive rental activity that does not rise to the level of a trade or business; The material participation requirements under the IRC Sec. 469 passive loss rules are used for this purpose [IRC Sec. 1411(c)(2)(A)]; IRC Sec. 469(h)(1) defines material participation as an activity in which the taxpayer participates on a "regular, continuous, and substantial basis";

   Example 1: A, an unmarried individual, rents a commercial building to B for $50,000. A is not involved in the activity of the commercial building on a regular and continuous basis. Therefore, A's rental activity does not involve the conduct of a trade or business and, under IRC Sec. 469(c)(2), is considered a passive activity. Because A's rental activity does not rise to the level of a trade or business, A's rental income of $50,000 will constitute investment income from rents subject to the 3.8 percent NII tax.

6. Profits from a passive activity which is a trade or business where the taxpayer does not "materially participate"; A taxpayer who owns a business, either as a sole proprietorship or as part of a pass-through entity (partnership, LLC or S corporation) and who does not materially participate in the business, is deemed to own an interest in a passive activity;

7. Profits from a trade or business of trading in financial instruments or commodities, even if the taxpayer does materially participate; and

¶2805

8. Net gain from the disposition of property (e.g., capital gains from stock sales, mutual fund capital gain distributions, etc.) but not gains from selling property held in a trade or business where the taxpayer materially participates. Included are gains from the sales of stocks, bonds, mutual funds, investment real estate or a vacation home, and capital gain distributions from mutual funds. Also included are taxable gains attributable to cash distributions to partners or to S corporation shareholders that are greater than their basis in their partnership interests or S corporation stock.

Income/Gain excluded from definition of NII. The following income is *not* considered NII and therefore is not subject to the NII tax:

1. Income from active trades or businesses where the owner materially participates. If a taxpayer owns a trade or business (either as a sole proprietor or through a pass-through entity, such as an LLC, partnership or S corporation) and the taxpayer materially participates in the trade or business, then profits derived in the ordinary course of business will *not* be subject to the 3.8 percent NII tax. Whether an activity is a passive activity is determined under the IRC Sec. 469 passive loss limitations. Under these rules, the owner must generally have performed over 500 hours of work during the year in order for the activity to qualify as nonpassive;

2. Rental income of a real estate professional. A taxpayer qualifies as a real estate professional if (a) more than half of the personal services performed in trades or businesses by the taxpayer during the year are performed in real property trades or businesses in which the taxpayer materially participates; and (b) the taxpayer performs at least 750 hours in real property trades or businesses in which he or she materially participates. This is more than the 500 hours that is usually required to demonstrate "material participation" in a trade or business;

3. Gains attributable to the disposition of property held in a trade or business [IRC Sec. 1411(c)(1)(A)(iii); Reg. Sec. 1.1411-4(d)];

4. Tax-exempt income such as income earned on state and local bonds [Reg. Sec. 1.1411-1(d)(4)(i)];

5. Self-charged interest which occurs when the owner of an active business lends money to the business where he or she works [Reg. Sec. 1.1411-4(g)(5)];

6. Gains deferred under the IRC Sec. 453 installment sale rules, the IRC Sec. 1031 like-kind exchange provisions or the IRC Sec. 1033 involuntary conversion provisions;

7. Compensation and self-employment tax;

8. Qualified plan distributions including pension plans, profit-sharing plans, stock bonus plans, ESOPs, 401(k) plans, qualified annuity plans, IRAs, Roth IRAs, and state and local government deferred compensation plans;

9. Alimony income;

10. Lottery income and prizes; and

11. Social security benefits, unemployment compensation and Alaska Permanent Fund Distributions.

¶2805

(d) How Estates and Trusts Can Minimize Exposure to 3.8 Percent NII Tax.

1. *Reduce Modified Adjusted Gross Income.* If a trust or estate reduces MAGI below the thresholds, the trust or estate will not be subject to the 3.8 percent NII tax.

2. *Reduce NII.* If the trust or estate can reduce the amount of NII or convert NII into income that is not NII, then fewer dollars will be subject to the 3.8 percent NII tax. For example, a trust with taxable interest income could convert that income into tax-exempt bonds and tax-exempt bond mutual funds.

3. *Make Estate and Trust Distributions.* Estates and trusts can avoid exposure to the NIIT if the fiduciary (if permitted by the terms of the will or trust) makes income distributions to the beneficiaries because estates and trusts will only be subject to the surtax on "undistributed net investment income," which is defined in Reg. Sec. 1.1411-3(e)(2) as an estate or trust's NII determined just as it would be for an individual and then reduced by distributions of NII to beneficiaries and reduced further by any deductible charitable contributions. Distributions of income will accomplish two objectives: the beneficiaries will most likely be in a lower income tax bracket and may also have a MAGI below the threshold at which the NIIT becomes applicable.

4. *Change Estate and Trust Investments.* Estates and trusts should also consider investing in tax-exempt and tax-deferred investments in order to reduce income subject to the tax because these entities will be subject to the surtax if their AGI exceeds $12,150 in 2014.

5. *Establish Material Participation by Trust.* An estate or trust can minimize exposure to the 3.8 percent NII tax if the estate or trust's income does not constitute NII. IRC Sec. 1411(c)(1)(A)(ii) provides that the NII tax applies to income from a passive activity, but not from income generated by an activity in which the taxpayer materially participates. An estate or trust can establish material participation by satisfying one of the following two tests found in IRC Sec. 469(c)(7)(B): (1) More than half of the "personal services" performed in trades or businesses by the taxpayer during the year are performed in real-property trades or businesses in which the taxpayer materially participates; and (2) The taxpayer performs more than 750 hours of "services" during the year in real-property trades or businesses in which the taxpayer materially participates which means involvement in an activity on a regular, continuous and substantial basis.

Neither the Code nor the regulations explain how to determine whether an estate or trust materially participates in a business for purposes of the passive activity loss rules. The only guidance is in the legislative history which provides:

Special rules apply in the case of taxable entities that are subject to the passive loss rule. An estate or trust is treated as materially participating in an activity if an executor or fiduciary, in his capacity as such, is so participating .... The activities of ... [employees] are not attributed to the taxpayer.[1]

The first court opinion addressing how a trust establishes material participation for purposes of the PAL limitations was *Mattie K. Carter Trust*,[2] where the trust

---

[1] ¶2805 S. Rep. No. 99-313, 99th Cong., 2d Sess. 735 (1986).

[2] Mattie K. Carter Trust, 256 F. Supp. 2d 537 (N.D. Tex. 2003).

operated a 15,000 acre cattle ranch. The trustee hired a ranch manager to carry out the day-to-day operations of the ranch. The IRS maintained that the ranch manager's activities did not constitute material participation by the trust because the trust could only establish material participation by referring to the activities of a trustee. The district court disagreed and concluded that the trust's material participation should be determined by looking at the activities of all the people who conducted the business on behalf of the trust, including employees and trustees. The court reasoned that measuring the trust's participation by reference only to the trustee "finds no support within the plain meaning of the statute. Such a contention is arbitrary, subverts common sense, and attempts to create ambiguity where there is none." Therefore, the district court held that in determining material participation for trusts, the activities of the trust's fiduciaries, employees, and agents should be considered to determine whether the trust's participation is "regular, continuous, and substantial."

In Technical Advice Memorandum 200733023, the IRS considered whether a trust materially participated in the activities of a partnership. The trustees contracted with special trustees to perform services for the partnership, but the special trustees did not have the power to commit the trust to any course of action. The IRS ignored *Mattie K. Carter* to conclude that a trust materially participates only if its fiduciaries participate. Since the special trustees were not fiduciaries, their hours did not count toward satisfying the trust's material participation requirement.

In Technical Advice Memorandum 201317010, the trust owned stock in an S corporation. There was a trustee and a "special trustee" of the trust. The IRS argued that the trustee "did not materially participate in the day-to-day operations of the relevant activities" of the S corporation because the activities of the S corporation owners could not be attributed to the trusts. The IRS therefore concluded that the individual serving as special trustee and president was as an employee rather than as a fiduciary of the trust and therefore his work did not count for purposes of determining whether the trust materially participated in the trade or business activities of the company.

In *Frank Aragona Trust*,[3] the Tax Court concluded that (1) a trust that owned rental estate property participated in real-property trades or businesses and therefore was a real estate professional, (2) the trust satisfied the requirements of the IRC Sec. 469(c)(7) rental real estate exception; and (3) the trust's rental real-estate activities were not treated as *per se* passive activities. The court reached this conclusion after finding that services performed by trustees on behalf of the trust could be considered personal services performed by the trust so that the trust was considered to have materially participated in its real estate businesses. The Frank Aragona Trust owned rental real-estate and was involved in other real-estate business activities such as holding real estate and developing real estate. The grantor's five children plus an independent trustee were the trust's trustees. The trustees acted as a management board for the trust and made all major decisions regarding the trust's property. The trust owned an LLC that employed three of

---

[3] Frank Aragona Trust, Dec. 59,859, 142 TC No. 9 (2014).

the trustee-children full time. The LLC managed most of the trust's rental real-estate properties and had several other employees.

The trust conducted some of its rental real-estate activities directly, and the rest through entities that it wholly-owned. It conducted its real-estate holding and real-estate development operations through entities in which it owned majority or minority interests. The trust incurred losses from its rental real-estate activities which the trust reported on its income tax return as nonpassive activity losses. Therefore, the losses from these activities increased the trust's net operating losses, which the trust carried back to prior tax years. The IRS determined that the trust's rental real-estate activities were passive in nature and therefore the IRS disallowed the net-operating-loss carrybacks to prior tax years.

The Tax Court concluded that a trust is capable of performing personal services and therefore can qualify as a real estate professional under the IRC Sec. 469(c)(7) rental real estate exception. The court reasoned that trustees who are individuals can work in a trade or business as part of their trustee duties and therefore their work can be considered "work performed by an individual in connection with a trade or business" under Reg. Sec. 1.469-9(b)(4). The court noted that if Congress had wanted to exclude trusts from the IRC Sec. 469(c)(7) exception, it could have done so explicitly by limiting the exception to "any natural person." Instead, Congress used the word "taxpayer" in that provision, thus suggesting that Congress did not intend to exclude trusts. The Tax Court found that the trust materially participated in its real-estate operations because the court considered the activities of all six trustees in their roles as trustees and employees of the LLC. Their involvement in managing the day-to-day operations of the trust's various real-estate businesses was found to be "regular, continuous and substantial" thus satisfying the requirements of IRC Sec. 469(h).

6. *Use Installment Sales Method to Spread Out Taxable Gain.* One way to avoid exposure to the NII tax is to use the installment method of reporting to spread out taxable gain that would be subject to the NII tax and move the gain to years where the taxpayer is not exposed to the NII tax or has lower MAGI. An installment sale is defined as a sale of property where one or more payments are received after the close of the tax year in which the sale took place.

7. *Distributing Net Investment Income (NII).* For estates and trusts that are likely to be subject to the NIIT, the tax may be avoided or minimized by currently distributing the NII to its beneficiaries. The net investment income will be included in the individual beneficiaries' calculation when determining if the NIIT applies at their level. Because the NIIT threshold for taxability is much lower for estates and trusts than for individuals, distributing the net investment income to beneficiaries of the estate or trust may avoid the NIIT by both the fiduciary and the individual beneficiaries. This strategy will not apply to distributions of capital gains unless they are included in distributable net income (DNI). Usually, the capital gains are retained as principal and are not able to be currently distributed as income.

▶ **CAUTION:** Before distributing additional income to beneficiaries, the executor or trustee should determine that the distributions are authorized and appropriate, considering both tax and non-tax factors.

8. *Elect to Treat Distributed Amounts as Made During First 65 Days of Year.* The fiduciary of an estate or complex trust may elect to treat distributions made during the first 65 days after the close of the taxable year as if they had been made on the last day of the prior year [IRC Sec. 663(b)]. This election provides flexibility in determining when the income distribution deduction will have the optimal tax effect.

9. *Invest in Excluded Income.* To minimize net investment income for NIIT purposes, the fiduciary should consider investing in tax-exempt municipal bonds because their income is excluded from the NIIT. Additionally, the fiduciary may consider non-dividend paying growth stocks, which will not be included in net investment income until the stocks are sold. Tax-deferred annuities may provide accumulation of income, while giving flexibility to receive income in a lump-sum or as periodic payments, either currently or at some future date. Until the payments are received, the annuity's earnings grow tax-free (including NIIT-free).

¶2806 CAPITAL GAINS AND LOSSES

(a) Capital Gain. The gain on the sale or exchange of a capital asset by an estate or trust must be included in the trust or estate's gross income. The gain is either a short-term, if the capital asset was held less than 12 months, or long-term capital gain, if the capital asset was held more than 12 months [IRC Sec. 1222]. Begin counting the holding period the day after the asset was acquired. A special rule affords long-term treatment to the trust or estate if it acquired the property from the decedent and sold it within one year after the deceased person's death [IRC Sec. 1223(11)]. Any part of the gain that is properly paid, credited, or required to be distributed during the year to the beneficiary is deductible by the fiduciary. It is taxable to the beneficiary (to the extent of the DNI), even if allocated to corpus.

In 2014, the capital gains rates for estates and trusts are as reflected in the following chart:

Capital Gains, Holding Periods, and Maximum Tax Rates for 2013

Type of Property	Period Held	Maximum Rate[a]
Capital assets, except for assets listed below	12 months or less	39.6%
	More than 12 months	20%[b]
Gain attributable to depreciation on Section 1250 real property (unrecaptured Section 1250 gain) in excess of that subject to ordinary income recapture	12 months or less	39.6%
	More than 12 months	25%[c]
Collectibles (i.e., art, rugs, antiques, metal, gems, stamps, coins, alcoholic beverages, etc., that are capital assets)	12 months or less	39.6%
	More than 12 months	28%

Type of Property	Period Held	Maximum Rate[a]
Qualified small business stock issued after August 10, 1993	12 months or less	39.6%
	More than 12 months, but not more than 5 years	20%[d]
	More than 5 months	14%[e]

Notes:

[a] This rate does not include the 3.8 percent net investment income tax that may apply.

[b] Capital gains are taxed at 0 percent when an estate or trust is in the 15 percent ordinary tax rate bracket, but only to the extent the gain would otherwise be in the 15 percent tax bracket. The maximum long-term capital gain is 15 percent for estates and trusts in the 28 percent or 33 percent ordinary income tax rate bracket and 20 percent for those subject to the 39.6 percent ordinary income tax rate bracket (taxable income exceeding $11,950 in 2013 and increasing to $12,150 in 2014).

[c] Installment sales of Section 1250 real property may consist of both 25 percent and 15 percent tax rates.

[d] If qualified small business stock is held for more than five years, the taxpayer can exclude a portion or all of the gain on its sale or exchange, depending on when the stock was acquired, as follows:

[e] Date of Stock Acquisition	Allowable Gain Exclusion on Sale	Effective Maximum Capital Gains Rate (28% × Portion Subject to Gain)
After August 10, 1993, and before February 18, 2009	50%	14%
After February 17, 2009, and before September 28, 2010	75%	7%
After September 27, 2010, and before January 1, 2014	100%	0%

Qualified dividends received by an estate or trust from either a domestic corporation or a qualified foreign corporation are taxed at the same tax rates imposed on capital gains [IRC Sec. 1(h)(11)(B)(i)]. Thus, qualified dividends will be subject to tax at a 0-, 15-, or 20-percent capital gains tax rate in 2014, depending on the taxpayers ordinary income tax rate for the year.

(b) Capital Loss. A capital loss usually is deductible only by the estate or trust and not by the beneficiary.[1] The loss is either a short-term or long-term capital loss, and the rules for individuals apply. However, a special rule requires trusts and estates to treat losses as long-term even if the assets were sold soon after the deceased person's death. In most states, title to real property passes directly from the deceased person to the heirs (not to the executor). In such states, gain or loss on the sale of the property is reported directly by the heir. For treatment of an unused capital loss in the trust's or estate's year of termination, see ¶ 2802.

When a capital asset is disposed of in a manner requiring gain or loss to be taxed to an estate or trust, the fiduciary must file Schedule D, "Capital Gains and Losses," with the Form 1041, "Income Tax Return for Estates and Trusts."

---

[1] ¶ 2806 Beatty, 28 BTA 1286 (1933).

¶2806

(c) Unused Capital Loss Carryover. An unused capital loss carryover at the time of death, remaining on termination of an estate or trust is allowed to the beneficiaries succeeding to the property of the estate or trust [IRC Sec. 642(h)]. The carryovers are the same in the hands of noncorporate beneficiaries as in the hands of the estate or trust and are deductible from gross income in computing adjusted gross income.

(d) Asset Distributions in Lieu of Cash. When a fiduciary pays a *cash* legacy by transferring an asset to the beneficiary, it is treated as if a sale or exchange took place. Gain or loss to the fiduciary is equal to the difference between the property's fair market value at its transfer and its adjusted basis in the fiduciary's hands.[2]

> **Example 1:** Nations Bank must pay $50,000 to a deceased father's child when the child becomes 25. The bank is authorized to pay this amount in either cash or property worth $50,000. The bank elects to transfer securities worth $50,000 to satisfy the legacy. Assuming that the basis of the securities in the bank's hands was $40,000, a capital gain of $10,000 is recognized. If the property transferred was not a capital asset, the $10,000 gain would be taxable as ordinary income.

The person receiving the legacy, otherwise known as a legatee, is treated as the property's buyer. He or she has a basis equal to the fair market value of the property at the time of the distribution.[3] If the trustee distributes a capital asset with the same value as a required distribution of income, it is also treated as a sale or exchange. The value is deductible by the trustee and taxable to the beneficiary to the extent of the trust's DNI.[4] Special rules apply when the property involved is farm realty or closely held business realty [IRC Sec. 1040].

¶2807 BASIS OF PROPERTY TO ESTATE OR TRUST

(a) Sales to a Trust. Situations may occur where a trust may purchase property from an individual or entity. If a transfer to a trust during a taxpayer's lifetime is *for a valuable consideration,* the basis of the property to the trust is stepped-up to the basis of the property in the taxpayer's hands. Alternatively, the basis could be stepped-down if the property is sold to the trust at a loss.

(b) Gifts to a Trust. If the transfer is by *gift,* a different basis rule applies. The basis of the property in the hands of the trust will be the same as it would be in hands of the grantor [IRC Secs. 1015(a), 1015(b); Reg. Secs. 1.1015-1, -2]. This is called the "carry-over basis rule." These basis issues become important if the trust ever sells the property.

---

[2] Suisman v. Eaton, 15 F. Supp. 113, *aff'd per curiam,* 83 F.2d 1019, *cert. denied,* 299 U.S. 573 (1936); Kenan, 114 F.2d 217 (2d Cir. 1940); Rev. Rul. 66-207, 1966-2 CB 243.

[3] Ewing, 40 BTA 912.
[4] Rev. Rul. 67-74, 1967-1 CB 194.

Example 1: Mr. Brown bought $10,000 worth of bonds. That same year, in exchange for $15,000, he transferred the bonds to a trust. Brown's gain is $5,000, and the basis of the bonds to the trust is $15,000 (the basis of the bonds in the hands of Brown ($10,000) plus the gain recognized to Brown on the transfer ($5,000)).

(c) Property Acquired from a Decedent. Generally, the basis of property acquired from a decedent is stepped up to its fair market value or its special use value on the date of death. If the executor elects to use the alternate valuation date, the basis of the property is its value on that date [IRC Sec. 1014(a)(3)]. Under EGTRRA, effective for property acquired from a decedent dying after December 31, 2009, the income tax basis of property acquired from a decedent was generally to be carried over from the decedent [IRC Sec. 1022]. Therefore, the recipient of property was to receive a basis equal to the lesser of the adjusted basis of the property in the hands of the decedent, or the fair market value of the property on the date of the decedent's death.

The Tax Relief Act of 2010 replaced the modified carryover basis scheme enacted by EGTRRA with the stepped-up basis rules of IRC Sec. 1014 for decedents dying after December 31, 2009. Under the stepped-up basis rules, the income tax basis of property acquired from a decedent at death generally is stepped up (or stepped down) to equal its value as of the date of the decedent's death (or on the date six months after the date of death, if alternate valuation under IRC Sec. 2032 is elected on the decedent's estate tax return).

¶2808 DEDUCTIONS AND CREDITS OF ESTATES AND TRUSTS—IN GENERAL

Estates and trusts are generally entitled to the same deductions that are available to individuals [IRC Sec. 641(b); Reg. Sec. 1.641(b)-1]. Unlike individual taxpayers, however, estates or trusts cannot claim a standard deduction. Instead, they are entitled to an exemption as discussed further at ¶ 2809.

Another big difference between the tax treatment of individuals versus estates and trusts is that unlike individuals, estates and trusts are entitled to a deduction for income distributed or distributable to beneficiaries to the extent of DNI. This is discussed further at ¶ 2803.

(a) Deductions Available to Estates and Trusts. Estates and trusts can claim a deduction for the following expenses that are also deductible by individual taxpayers:

1. Ordinary and necessary business expenses incurred during the administration of the estate or trust can be deducted [IRC Sec. 162]. Don't overlook expenses associated with the sale of real property, including the broker's commission, title insurance, attorney's fees and expenses incurred in the upkeep of real property, including refinancing costs and the cost of insurance.

2. Interest paid or accrued on obligations by the estate or trust whether paid out of income or corpus can be deducted [IRC Sec. 163]. However, there are a number of

limitations on the deductibility of interest. Interest is not deductible on a debt incurred, or continued, to purchase or carry obligations the interest on which is wholly exempt from federal income taxes. Personal interest of an estate or trust is nondeductible. In addition, an estate or trust can only deduct interest on investment indebtedness up to the amount of net investment income during the year. Net investment income is defined as the excess of the investment income over the investment expenses [IRC Sec. 163(d)(4)]. Disallowed interest may be carried forward to future years to the extent of net investment income in those years. Net capital gain attributable to the disposition of property held for investment is generally excluded from investment income for purposes of computing this limitation. However, a special election is available to increase net capital gain includible in investment income by reducing the amount eligible for the maximum rate on capital gains [IRC Secs. 1(h) and 163(d)(4)(B)(iii)].

3. Taxes, including most state and local real estate taxes, personal property taxes, foreign real estate taxes, and foreign income taxes can be deducted [IRC Sec. 164]. Remember that property taxes on real estate sold must be apportioned between the seller and buyer according to the number of days in the year that each holds the property [IRC Sec. 164(d)]. No deduction is allowed for federal income taxes, gift and estate taxes, or for state death or succession taxes [IRC Sec. 275]. An exception exists, however, for the portion of federal estate taxes that are attributable to income in respect of a decedent, which may be deducted against income when it is received [IRC Sec. 691(c)].

4. Administrative expenses that were paid or incurred by the fiduciary to administer the estate or trust including fiduciary fees, commissions, amounts paid attorneys, tax return preparers, and litigation expenses can be deducted [IRC Sec. 212]. If you deduct these amounts for federal estate tax purposes, however, you cannot deduct them again in computing the taxable income of an estate or trust because double deductions are not allowed as discussed further below [IRC Sec. 642(b); see ¶2813].

5. Losses arising from casualty or theft during the administration of the estate can be deducted by the estate provided they have not already been claimed on the federal estate tax return (Form 706). Be sure to file the statement with the estate's income tax return waiving the deduction for estate tax purposes. In addition, losses incurred in a trade or business such as the sale of property or stock can be deducted [IRC Sec. 165]. Losses sustained by the estate or trust cannot be passed through to the beneficiary except in the year of termination when unused capital losses, net operating loss carryovers or deductions (except those for personal exemptions or charity) in excess of gross income for the last tax year can be deducted by the beneficiaries. The term "beneficiary" is defined in this context to include the following:

- The remaindermen of a trust;
- The heirs and next of kin of a person who dies without a will; and
- The residuary legatees (including a residuary trust) of a person leaving a will [IRC Sec. 642(h); Reg. Secs. 1.642(h)-1, 1.642(h)-3; see ¶2812].

(b) **Medical and Funeral Expenses.** No deduction can be taken for funeral expenses[1] or medical and dental expenses on the estate's income tax return (Form

---

[1] ¶2808 Yetter, 35 TC 737 (1961).

¶2808

1041) [Reg. Sec. 1.642(g)-2]. Funeral expenses are deductible only in determining the taxable estate for federal estate tax purposes on Form 706 [see Chapter 5 for sample federal estate tax return]. The medical and dental expenses of a decedent paid by the estate can only be deducted in figuring the taxable estate for federal estate tax purposes on Form 706. If these expenses are paid within the one-year period beginning with the day after the decedent's death, you can elect to deduct them on the decedent's final income tax return (Form 1040) for the year in which they were incurred [see ¶ 2740].

(c) Deductions in Year of Death. A taxpayer's taxable year ends on the date of his death [IRC Sec. 443(a)(2); Reg. Sec. 1.443-1]. When you compute taxable income for a taxpayer's final taxable year, you have to take into account the account-ing method that was used by the taxpayer. If the taxpayer reported on the cash basis, the allowable deductions would only be those actually paid. If the taxpayer used the accrual basis, a deduction would only be allowed for amounts that accrue up to the date of death. Deductions cannot be taken, however, for amounts that accrued only because of their death [IRC Sec. 461(b); Reg. Sec. 1.461-1(b)].

(d) Applying the Material Participation Standards to Nongrantor Trusts. For further discussion of how an estate or trust can establish material participation, see ¶ 2805(d).

¶ 2809 DEDUCTION FOR PERSONAL EXEMPTION

An estate or trust filing a tax return is entitled to a personal exemption similar to the one allowed individuals, but the amount varies depending on the nature of the entity seeking the exemption as follows [IRC Sec. 642(b); Reg. Sec. 1.642(b)-1]:

- An estate is allowed an exemption of $600 [IRC Sec. 642(b); Reg. Sec. 1.642(b)-1(a)].

- A simple trust (a trust required to distribute all income currently) is allowed an exemption of $300. Even though simple trusts that make distributions from princi-pal for a single year are called "complex trusts" for that taxable year, they are still entitled to a $300 exemption in the year of the distribution.

- All other trusts are allowed an exemption of $100 [IRC Sec. 642(b); Reg. Sec. 1.642(b)-1].

- No exemption is allowed in the year the estate or trust is terminated because the estate or trust must distribute all its income in the year of termination, and will not, therefore, have any income for the exemption to offset. A final Form 1041 must be filed once an estate or trust is terminated. An estate is terminated at the end of the administrative proceedings and after all remaining assets have been distrib-uted [Reg. Sec. 1.641(b)-3(a)]. A trust is also terminated when the assets have been distributed [Reg. Sec. 1.641(b)-3(b)].

NOTE: In contrast, on a deceased person's final income tax return (Form 1040), the executor can claim a full personal exemption for the decedent [IRC Sec. 151]. The exemption is allowed for the entire year even if the decedent did not live to the end of his last tax year. No proration is required.

¶2810 DEDUCTION FOR CHARITABLE CONTRIBUTIONS

An estate or a complex trust may claim an unlimited deduction for gross income which, under the terms of the will or trust, is paid or permanently set aside during the taxable year for charitable purposes [IRC Sec. 642(c)]. No deduction is available for unrelated business income of a trust. This deduction is in lieu of the charitable deductions allowed individuals under IRC Sec. 170(a). Unlike the charitable deduction allowed individuals, no limitation is placed on the amount that can be deducted by a trust or estate [Reg. Sec. 1.642(c)-2(a)]. In addition, a charitable deduction is only available if the source of the contribution is gross income and the contribution must be traced to determine its source [IRC Sec. 642(c)].

The tricky aspect of an estate or trust's deduction for charitable contributions is that the charitable contribution deduction is considered to consist of a proportionate part of each item of income. As a result, the deduction must be allocated proportionately among all items of income included in DNI. For example, if an estate or trust has taxable and nontaxable income, a proportionate part of the nontaxable income must be allocated to the amount paid or set aside for charitable purposes and is not allowed as a deduction [Reg. Secs. 1.642(c)-3(b), 1.643(a)-5].

> **Example 1:** A trust provides that $30,000 of income must be distributed currently to Alice and the balance must be distributed to a local charity. During the year the trust earned $30,000 of taxable interest and $10,000 of tax-exempt interest. The charitable contribution of $10,000 is allocated proportionately to the items of income of the trust as follows: $7,500 to taxable interest and $2,500 to tax-exempt interest. Thus the charitable deduction is limited to $7,500. Alice's $30,000 distribution consists of $22,500 of taxable interest and $7,500 of tax-exempt interest [Reg. Sec. 1.662(b)-2, Ex. (2)].

(a) Election to Treat Contributions as Paid in Preceding Taxable Year. To enable fiduciaries to act after they know the exact income for the year, they can elect to treat a current contribution as paid during the preceding tax year [IRC Sec. 642(c)(1); Reg. Sec. 1.642(c)-1(b)]. The election must be made no later than the due date (including extensions) for filing the income tax return for the succeeding tax year [Reg. Sec. 1.642(c)-1(b)(2)].

The election must be made by filing with the income tax return for the taxable year in which the contribution is treated as paid a statement containing the following:

• The name and address of the fiduciary;

• The estate or trust for which the fiduciary is acting;

- An indication that the fiduciary is making an election in respect of contributions treated as paid during such taxable year;
- The name and address of each organization to which any such contribution is paid; and
- The amount of each contribution and date of actual payment, or if applicable, the total amount of contributions paid to each organization during the succeeding taxable year, to be treated as paid in the preceding taxable year [Reg. Sec. 1.642(c)-1(b)(3)].

(b) Contributions from Gross Income. Generally, only contributions of items included in gross income are deductible by the estate or trust. This means that tax-exempt income does not qualify for the deduction.[1] Thus, no deduction will be allowed for a contribution out of the estate or trust corpus because these items are not included in gross income. However, a contribution from income allocable to corpus, such as capital gains, will qualify for the deduction, since such income is included in the gross income of the estate or trust. No deduction is allowed to a trust for contributions allocable to its unrelated business income for the tax year.

> **Example 2:** A trustee, under the terms of a will, is directed to pay to a charity half of the addition to corpus each year for the duration of the trust. The only addition to the corpus for the tax year consisted of $12,000 of capital gains, and the trustee distributed $6,000 to the charity. Capital gains allocated to corpus under the terms of the will are included in trust gross income, so a charitable contribution deduction will be allowed.

No charitable deduction for trust's donation of qualified conservation contribution. The IRS concluded in Rev. Rul. 2003-123[2] that a complex trust was not allowed a charitable deduction under IRC Sec. 642(c) or a distribution deduction under IRC Sec. 661(a)(2) for a contribution to charity of trust principal that meets the requirements of a qualified conservation contribution under IRC Sec. 170(h). The complex trust owned two adjacent parcels of property. One parcel was 20 acres of undeveloped land, and the other was 50 acres with improvements. The trust's governing instrument authorized the trustee to make contributions to charity, including contributions of the trust's gross income. The trustee conveyed a perpetual conservation easement in the 20 acre parcel to a state agency. The charitable deduction for the contribution under IRC Sec. 642(c) was denied because the trust's charitable contribution was made from the trust (real property), not from gross income. Since the conservation easement contribution was not made from gross income, the trust was not allowed a charitable deduction under IRC Sec. 642(c).

Trust allowed charitable deduction for partnership's contributions. In Rev. Rul. 2004-5,[3] the IRS ruled that a trust could deduct under IRC Sec. 642(c) its distributive share of charitable contributions from a partnership even if the trust instrument does not explicitly authorize charitable contributions. The requirement that all charitable

---

[1] **¶2810** Tyler Trust, 5 TC 729 (1945), *acq.*, 1945 CB 6.

[2] Rev. Rul. 2003-123, 2003-2 CB 1200; see also Rev. Rul. 68-667, 1968-2 CB 289.

[3] Rev. Rul. 2004-5, 2004-1 CB 295.

¶2810

contributions must be authorized by the governing trust instrument does not mean that the trust will be prevented from deducting its share of the contributions made by a partnership of which it is a member.

(c) Adjustment for Tax-Exempt Income. When a trust or estate has both taxable and tax-exempt income, the charitable deduction is allowed only for contributions considered to come from gross income. Unless the governing instrument makes a different allocation, the contribution that is considered to come from gross income bears the same proportion to the total contribution as the total gross income bears to the total income (including tax-exempt items) [Reg. Sec. 1.642(c)-3(b)].

▶ **OBSERVATION:** To enable the estate or trust to get the full benefit of the charitable deduction, the estate's or trust's governing instrument should specifically provide that contributions be payable out of ordinary taxable income, not from tax-exempt income or long-term capital gains.

Example 3: A trust had $8,000 of income—consisting of $5,000 rent and $3,000 tax-exempt interest on municipal bonds. The trustee was directed to pay 25 percent of the income to charity. He made a charitable contribution of $2,000 (25 percent of $8,000). If the trust instrument is silent on the income source of the contribution, the amount considered as coming from the gross income of the trust is $1,250 ($5,000/$8,000 × $2,000). Therefore, the trust can deduct $1,250. If the trustee had been directed to pay $2,000 of the rental income to charity, he could have deducted that amount.

(d) Filing Requirements. The charitable deduction is normally computed on Form 1041, Schedule A. When unrelated business income is involved, a separate schedule, rather than Schedule A, can be filed showing the computation of the deduction. Pooled income funds claiming the set-aside deduction for long-term capital gain are required to compute their deduction on a separate schedule, which is attached to the return.

Every trust claiming a charitable deduction under Code Sec. 642(c) (and every Code Sec. 4947(a)(2) split-interest trust, including a pooled income fund) is required to file an information return [IRC Sec. 6034]. The information return is usually filed on Form 1041-A, "U.S. Information Return Trust Accumulation of Charitable Amounts," due on or before April 15, 2013, for the 2012 calendar tax year. A nonexempt charitable trust, described in Code Sec. 4947(a)(1) and not treated as a private foundation, must also file a Form 990, "Return of Organization Exempt From Income Tax," if its gross receipts are normally more than $25,000. A tax-exempt trust may file a Form 990 to satisfy its Form 1041 filing requirement if the trust has zero taxable income. Both the trust and the trustee can be liable for a penalty of $10 per day up to a maximum of $5,000 for failure to timely file Form 1041-A [IRC Sec. 6652(c)(2)(A)]. Penalties also apply for filing a false or fraudulent return [IRC Sec. 6663]. When all trust net income must be distributed currently each year to the beneficiaries, the trust is relieved of filing Form 1041-A.

¶2811 DEDUCTION FOR DEPRECIATION AND DEPLETION

An estate or trust will be able to claim a deduction for depreciation and depletion from the date of the decedent's death if the entities hold qualified property after the decedent has died [IRC Sec. 642(e); Reg. Sec. 1.642(e)-1]. The available deduction must be apportioned among the estate or trust and the heirs, legatees, and devisees on the basis of the estate's income that is allocable to each [IRC Sec. 642(e)]. This means that an estate or trust will able to claim a deduction only after the deductions have been properly allocated to the beneficiaries. In this situation, the term "beneficiaries" includes charitable beneficiaries [Reg. Sec. 1.642(e)-1].

Same rules apply for depreciation and depletion deduction. The same rules used for figuring the amount of a trust's or estate's depreciation deduction apply in determining the amount of the trust's or estate's depletion deductions [IRC Sec. 611(b)(3); Reg. Sec. 1.611-1(c)(4)].

> **NOTE:** Estates and trusts cannot elect the expensing deduction available for certain depreciable business assets [IRC Sec. 179(d)(4)].

(a) Depreciation Deduction for Trust Property. The deduction for depreciation of trust property is divided between the income beneficiaries and the trustee as directed in the trust instrument. If the trust instrument makes no allocation, the deduction is apportioned on the basis of the trust income (determined under the trust instrument and state law) allocable to each [IRC Sec. 167(d)].

The regulations limit the allocation in the trust instrument. They provide that the share of the deduction allocated to either the trustee or a beneficiary ordinarily cannot be more than his or her pro rata share of the trust income. However, if the trust instrument or state law requires or allows the trustee to maintain a reserve for depreciation, the deduction is first allocated to the trustee for income set aside for the reserve. Any part of the deduction not used up is then divided between the beneficiaries and the trustee on the basis of the trust income (in excess of the amount set aside as a reserve) allocable to each [Reg. Secs. 1.167(h)-1(b), 1.642(e)-1].

> **Example 1:** If under the trust instrument or local law the income of a trust computed without regard to depreciation is to be distributed to a named beneficiary, the beneficiary is entitled to the deduction to the exclusion of the trustee [Reg. Sec. 1.167(h)-1(b)(1)].

> **Example 2:** If under the trust instrument or local law the income of a trust is to be distributed to a named beneficiary, but the trustee is directed to maintain a reserve for depreciation in any amount, the deduction is allowed to the trustee (except to the extent that income set aside for the reserve is less than the allowable deduction). The same result would follow if the trustee sets aside income for a depreciation reserve pursuant to discretionary authority to do so in the governing instrument [Reg. Sec. 1.167(h)-1(b)(2)].

Example 3: Dad establishes a trust for the benefit of Son and Daughter. The trust property includes an apartment house on which a depreciation allowance could be claimed. Under the terms of the trust instrument, the income of the trust is to be distributed to Son and Daughter in equal shares. The trust instrument also authorizes the trustee, in his discretion, to set aside income for a depreciation reserve. During the year, the trustee sets aside $2,000 income as a reserve. Depreciation on the trust property amounts to $2,500. The trustee gets a depreciation deduction of $2,000. Son and Daughter each get a deduction of $250.

> **NOTE:** If the income beneficiary is entitled to the entire income, and the instrument is silent on depreciation, the beneficiary gets the deduction. Even if the trust has no income during the year, the income beneficiary is still entitled to the deduction.[1]

The regulations also provide that no effect will be given to any allocation of the depreciation deduction which gives any beneficiary or the trustee a share of such deduction greater than his pro rata share of the trust income, irrespective of any provisions in the trust instrument, except when the trust instrument or local law requires or permits the trustee to maintain a reserve for depreciation [Reg. Sec. 1.167(h)-1(b)(2)].

(b) Depreciation Deductions for Estates. For an estate, the depreciation or depletion deduction is divided between the estate and the heirs, legatees and devisees on the basis of the income allocable to each [IRC Secs. 167(d), 611(b)(4); Reg. Secs. 1.167(h)-1(c), 1.611-1(c)(5)].

> ▶ **OBSERVATION:** If an estate or trust shares in depreciation or depletion of another trust or a partnership (or takes the deduction into account separately), the estate or trust divides the deduction among its own distributees on the same basis as it allocates its income.[2]

¶2812 DEDUCTION FOR NET OPERATING LOSS

Generally, estates and trusts are entitled to the net operating loss deduction when business losses are sustained [IRC Sec. 642(d); Reg. Sec. 1.642(d)-1]. Claiming a net operating loss may reduce DNI for the year to which the operating loss is carried back and therefore permit beneficiaries to recompute their shares of the estate or trust income for prior years and claim a refund.[1]

An estate's or trust's net operating loss is calculated in the same way as an individual's except that the estate or trust cannot avail itself of the deductions allowed for charitable contributions or distributions to beneficiaries [Reg. Sec. 1.642(d)-1(b)]. In addition, a trust also must exclude that portion of the income and deductions

---

[1] ¶**2811** Carol, 30 BTA 443 (1934), *acq.*, 1934-2 CB 4.

[2] Rev. Rul. 61-211, 1961-2 CB 124 as clarified by Rev. Rul. 66-278, 1966-2 CB 243; Rev. Rul. 74-71, 1974-1 CB 158.

[1] ¶**2812** Rev. Rul. 61-20, 1961-1 CB 248.

attributable to the grantor or any other person treated as substantial owners under the grantor trust rules [IRC Sec. 642(d); Reg. Sec. 1.642(d)-1(a)]. For further discussion of the grantor trust rules see ¶ 3100.

Unused net operating loss carryover. On termination of an estate or trust, any unused net operating loss carryovers are deductible by the beneficiaries succeeding to the estate or trust property [IRC Sec. 642(h); Reg. Sec. 1.642(h)-1]. The term "beneficiary" is limited to:

• The remaindermen of a trust;

• The heirs and next of kin of a person who dies without a will; and

• The residuary legatees (including a residuary trust) of a person leaving a will [IRC Sec. 642(h); Reg. Sec. 1.642(h)-3].

The net operating loss carryover is the same in the hands of a beneficiary as in the estate or trust, except that the capital loss carryover in the hands of a beneficiary that is a corporation is always treated as a short-term loss [Reg. Sec. 1.642(h)-1(b)]. The first taxable year of the beneficiary to which the loss can be carried over is the taxable year of the beneficiary in which the estate or trust terminates. However, for purposes of determining the number of years to which a net operating loss may be carried over by a beneficiary, the last taxable year of the estate of trust (whether or not a short taxable year) and the first taxable year of the beneficiary to which a loss is carried over each constitute a separate taxable year [Reg. Secs. 1.1212-1(a); 1.642(h)-1(b)].

> **Example 1:** A trust distributes all of its assets to Alice, the sole beneficiary, and terminates on December 31, when it has a capital loss carryover of $10,000. Alice, who reports on the calendar year basis, otherwise has ordinary income of $20,000 and capital gains of $4,000 for the year. She would offset her capital gains of $4,000 against the capital loss of the trust and, in addition, would use $3,000 of the capital loss to offset $3,000 of her ordinary income for the year in accordance with IRC Sec. 1211(b)(1). The $3,000 balance of the capital loss would then be carried to next year and later years until it is used up [Reg. Sec. 1.642(h)-1(c) Ex. (1)].

The net operating loss deduction of a common trust fund [see ¶ 2826] is allowed to the participants in the fund and not to the trust itself [IRC Sec. 584(g); Reg. Sec. 1.584-6].

¶2813 DEDUCTION FOR EXPENSES

The taxable income of a trust or estate is computed in the same manner as an individual, unless modified by the tax rules that are specific to trusts or estates. Just like an individual, an estate or trust can deduct ordinary and necessary expenses it pays or incurs, if the expenses are:

1. Trade or business expenses;

2. Expenses for the production or collection of income or for managing, conserving, or maintaining property held for the production of income;

¶2813

3. Reasonable administration expenses, including fiduciaries' fees and litigation expenses in connection with the duties of administration (except expenses allocable to the production or collection of tax-exempt income). Administrative expenses are deductible for income tax purposes only if they are not also claimed as deductions for estate tax purposes.[1] In fact, in order to deduct them in computing the taxable income of the estate for income tax purposes, the executor will have to file a statement (in duplicate) waiving the deduction for estate tax purposes as discussed below [IRC Sec. 642(g); Reg. Sec. 1.642(g)-1];

4. Expenses for the determination, collection, or refund of any tax [IRC Secs. 162(a), 212; Reg. Sec. 1.212-1].

A fiduciary can deduct counsel fees and other expenses of unsuccessfully contesting an income tax deficiency, or similar expenses relating to the final distribution from an expired trust.[2] Interest on overdue estate tax[3] or on legacies[4] is also deductible. However, there is no deduction for interest paid by an estate on deficiencies on state inheritance taxes which are not the estate's obligation under state law.[5] Similarly, no immediate deduction is available for expenses incurred in defending or protecting the estate's or trust's title to property. These expenses are treated as capital expenditures.

Deductible expenses chargeable only to trust corpus reduce DNI and thus the amount taxable to the beneficiary. However, these expenses do not reduce the amount of income available for the income beneficiary.[6] Fiduciaries must file Forms 1096 and 1099 if they make certain payments of $600 or more related to a trade or business.

> **NOTE:** Interest paid by a trust on an unpaid balance of estate tax liability that is deferred can qualify as an administrative expense deductible by the trust.[7]

(a) Expenses Incurred for Trust Investment Advice. Trustees who lack expertise in money management often seek professional advice to aid them in fulfilling their fiduciary duties and directing the investment of trust assets.

Background. IRC Sec. 67(a) provides that miscellaneous itemized deductions are allowed only to the extent they exceed 2 percent of adjusted gross income (AGI). For purposes of this floor, the AGI of an estate or trust is computed the same way as for an individual, subject to certain exceptions [IRC Sec. 67(e)]. A trust is allowed to deduct the following without regard to the two-percent limitation: (1) administrative expenses which were incurred as a result of the property being held in a trust, (2) distributions to beneficiaries, and (3) its personal exemption. Relevant to this discussion is the exception which provides that costs paid or incurred in connection with the administration of an estate or trust that wouldn't have been incurred if the property were not held in the estate or trust may be deducted when computing AGI [IRC Sec. 67(e)(1)].

---

[1] ¶ **2813** Rev. Rul. 63-27, 1963-1 CB 57.

[2] Erdman, 37 TC 119, *aff'd*, 315 F.2d 762 (7th Cir. 1963).

[3] Bingham, 325 U.S. 365 (1945).

[4] Penrose, 18 F. Supp. 413 (1937).

[5] Rev. Rul. 73-322, 1973-2 CB 44.

[6] Estate of McClatchy, 12 TC 370, *aff'd*, 179 F.2d 678 (9th Cir. 1950).

[7] Ungerman Revocable Trust, 89 TC 1131 (1987).

Supreme Court's decision in *Knight*. In *M. Knight, Trustee of W. Rudkin Testamentary Trust*,[8] the United States Supreme Court resolved years of litigation in a unanimous decision where the court held that fees for investment advice paid by a trust are not unique to trust administration and are therefore deductible as a miscellaneous deduction only to the extent that they exceed 2 percent of the trust's AGI pursuant to IRC Sec. 67(a). Since the Court concluded that the investment advice fees in question were not unique to the administration of a trust and are customarily incurred by individuals, they were subject to the 2-percent floor for miscellaneous deductions.

Note that the Supreme Court decision focuses on whether or not the expenses would have been incurred by an individual. A full deduction without consideration of the 2-percent floor will only be available if the taxpayer can prove that the expenses would not have been incurred by an individual.

The Court held that the proper reading of the language in IRC Sec. 67(e), which asks whether the expense "would not have been incurred if the property were not held in such trust or estate," requires an inquiry into whether a hypothetical individual who held the same property outside of a trust "customarily" or "commonly" would incur such expenses. Expenses that are "customarily" or "commonly" incurred by individuals are subject to the 2-percent floor.

Final regulations. The IRS has released final regulations under Reg. Sec. 1.67-4 that provide guidance on which costs incurred by estates or nongrantor trusts are subject to the 2-percent floor for miscellaneous itemized deductions under IRC Sec. 67(a). Under the final regulations, a cost is subject to the 2-percent floor to the extent that it (1) is included in the definition of miscellaneous itemized deduction under IRC Sec. 67(b), (2) is incurred by an estate or nongrantor trust, and (3) would "commonly or customarily" be incurred by a hypothetical individual holding the same property, based on the type of product or service rendered to the estate or trust [Reg. Sec. 1.67-4(a)].

"Commonly" or "customarily" defined. A cost will be considered to be "commonly" or "customarily" incurred if it is one that would be incurred by a hypothetical individual owning the same property. The focus should be on the type of product or service rendered to the estate or non-grantor trust in exchange for the cost, rather than the description of the cost of that product or service. Costs that are incurred commonly or customarily by individuals include, for example, costs incurred in defense of a claim against the estate, the decedent, or the non-grantor trust that are unrelated to the existence, validity, or administration of the estate or trust [Reg. Sec. 1.67-4(b)].

Ownership costs defined. Ownership costs include those that are commonly or customarily incurred by a property owner and include condo fees, insurance premiums, maintenance and lawn services, automobile registration and insurance costs. Other expenses such as real estate taxes, and trade or business expenses are fully deductible and are not subject to the 2-percent floor [Reg. Sec. 1.67-4(b)(2)].

Tax preparation fees. The costs relating to all estate and generation-skipping transfer tax returns, fiduciary income tax returns, and the decedent's final individual income tax returns are not subject to the 2-percent floor. The costs of preparing all other tax returns (for example, gift tax returns) are costs commonly and customarily incurred by individuals and thus are subject to the 2-percent floor [Reg. Sec. 1.67-4(b)(3)].

---

[8] Knight, 552 U.S. 181 (2008).

¶2813

Investment advisory fees. Investment advisory fees are incurred commonly or customarily by an individual investor and therefore are subject to the 2-percent floor. However, certain incremental costs of investment advice beyond the amount that normally would be charged to an individual investor are not subject to the 2-percent floor. These incremental costs are special, additional charges that are added solely because the investment advice is rendered to a trust or estate and are attributable to an unusual investment objective or the need for a specialized balancing of the interests of various parties. The portion of the investment advisory fees not subject to the 2-percent floor is limited to the amount of those fees, if any, that exceeds the fees normally charged to an individual investor [Reg. Sec. 1.67-4(b)(4)].

Appraisal fees. The appraisal fees incurred by an estate or a non-grantor trust to determine the fair market value of assets as of the date of the decedent's death, to determine value for purposes of making distributions, or as required to properly prepare the estate's or trust's tax returns are not incurred commonly or customarily by an individual and thus are not subject to the 2-percent floor [Reg. Sec. 1.67-4(b)(5)].

Certain fiduciary expenses. The following fiduciary expenses are not commonly or customarily incurred by individuals, and thus are not subject to the 2-percent floor: probate court fees and costs; fiduciary bond premiums; legal publication costs of notices to creditors or heirs; the cost of certified copies of the decedent's death certificate; and costs related to fiduciary accounts. [Reg. Sec. 1.67-4(b)(6)].

Bundled fees. A bundled fee is a single fee consisting of costs that are both subject to the 2-percent floor and those that are not. The final regulations require a bundled fee to be allocated between both costs [Reg. Sec. 1.67-4(c)(1)]. If a bundled fee is not computed on an hourly basis, only the portion attributable to investment advice is subject to the 2-percent floor [Reg. Sec. 1.67-4(c)(2)]. However, payments made to third parties out of the bundled fee that would have been subject to the 2-percent floor if they had been paid directly, and payments for expenses separately assessed by the fiduciary or other service provider that are commonly or customarily incurred by an individual, are subject to the 2-percent floor [Reg. Sec. 1.67-4(c)(3)].

Any reasonable method may be used to allocate a bundled fee between those costs that are subject to the 2-percent floor and those costs that are not, including the allocation of a portion of a fiduciary commission that is a bundled fee to investment advice. The following facts may be considered in determining whether an allocation is reasonable: the percentage of the value of the corpus subject to investment advice, whether a third party advisor would have charged a comparable fee for similar advisory services, and the amount of the fiduciary's attention to the trust or estate that is devoted to investment advice as compared to dealings with beneficiaries and distribution decisions and other fiduciary functions. The reasonable method standard does not apply to determine the portion of the bundled fee attributable to payments made to third parties for expenses subject to the 2-percent floor or to any other separately assessed expense commonly or customarily incurred by an individual, because those payments and expenses are readily identifiable without any discretion on the part of the fiduciary or return preparer [Reg. Sec. 1.67-4(c)(4)].

(b) Double Deductions Prohibited. Many of the deductions available to an estate or trust for income tax purposes can also be deducted for estate tax purposes. For example, an estate can deduct administrative expenses both on its income tax return (Form 1041) or on the estate tax return (Form 706). But you can't claim it in

¶2813

both places [IRC Sec. 642(g)]. In order to prevent double deductions, the law provides that amounts that qualify for both income tax and estate tax deductions will only be deductible for income tax purposes (or allowed as an offset against the sales price of property in determining gain or loss) if the executor waives the right to take the deduction for estate tax or generation-skipping tax purposes [IRC Sec. 642(g); Reg. Sec. 1.642(g)-1]. The fiduciary is therefore forced to decide whether to claim many of the available deductions as an estate tax deduction or as an income tax deduction.

(c) What Expenses Are Subject to Waiver. The law provides that amounts that are deductible for estate tax purposes under IRC Sec. 2053(a)(2) (relating to administration expenses) or Code Sec. 2054 (relating to losses during administration) may only be claimed as deductions in computing the taxable income of the estate (or any other person) if the deduction for estate tax purposes is waived [IRC Sec. 642(g); Reg. Sec. 1.642(g)-1]. Once the waiver is filed, it may not be revoked [Reg. Sec. 1.642(g)-1].[9]

The following expenses are subject to the no-double-dip rule:

- Executor's commissions;
- Attorney's fees;
- Accounting expenses;
- Certain costs of selling property incident to settlement of the estate or distribution of the trust;
- Some interest expenses, particularly on deferred payment of estate taxes;
- Expenses of administering an estate; and
- Casualty and theft losses.

(d) How to Waive the Estate Tax Deduction. The waiver statement should be filed in duplicate with the return for the year for which the deductions are claimed or with the IRS for the district in which the return was filed so the waiver can be paired up with the return. The statement may be filed at any time before the expiration of the statutory period of limitations applicable to the taxable year for which the deduction is sought.

After a waiver statement is filed for a particular item or portion of an item, the item cannot thereafter be allowed as a deduction for estate tax purposes since the waiver operates as a relinquishment of the right to have the deduction allowed at any time as a deduction from the taxable estate.

One deduction or only a portion of a deduction can be claimed for income tax purposes if the necessary waiver is filed, while another deduction or part of a deduction is claimed for estate tax purposes. The double deduction preclusion rule does not bar deductions related to income in respect of a decedent or for claims against the estate, such as payments under a divorce decree [IRC Sec. 642(g)].[10]

Fiduciaries managing a decedent's estate are afforded some flexibility when deciding whether to deduct an administration expense from the gross estate in figuring the

---

[9] Estate of Darby, 62-2 USTC ¶12,111 (D. Ok. 1962), *aff'd in part and rev'd in part*, 323 F.2d 792 (10th Cir. 1963); Rev. Rul. 63-240, 1963-2 CB 227.

[10] Rev. Rul. 67-304, 1967-2 CB 224.

federal estate tax on Form 706 or from the estate's gross income in figuring the estate's income tax on Form 1041. The law gives you some wiggle room by providing that you are not precluded from claiming a deduction when figuring the estate income tax just because the same deduction has already been claimed on the estate tax return. Keep in mind that the estate tax deduction may not be finally allowed and that you still may have time to file a waiver statement. The waiver statement can be filed at any time before the expiration of the statute of limitations that applies to the tax year for which the deduction is sought. In addition, the waiver also applies to casualty losses incurred during administration of the estate.[11]

(e) Exception for Accrued Expenses. The rule against double deductions under IRC Sec. 642(g) does *not* apply to deductions for taxes, interest, business expenses and other items *already accrued* at the date of a decedent's death. As a result these expenses are allowable as a deduction for estate tax purposes as claims against the estate, and are also allowable under IRC Sec. 691(b) as deductions in respect of a decedent for income tax purposes [see Chapter 7; Reg. Sec. 1.642(g)-2].[12]

> **Example 1:** On July 1, a cash basis taxpayer borrows $10,000 as a business loan and agrees to pay 10 percent on the loan the following July 1. On December 31, he dies. His estate may deduct $500 of interest for both income and estate tax purposes, because that much interest had accrued at the date of death as a claim against the estate.

Items *not* accrued at the date of the decedent's death so that they are allowable as deductions for estate tax purposes only as administration expenses, are not deductible in computing the taxable income of the estate, unless a statement is filed waiving the deduction for estate tax purposes [Reg. Sec. 1.642(g)-2].

(f) Domestic Production Activities by Trusts or Estates. A nongrantor trust or estate, and the beneficiaries of the trust or estate, may claim the deduction for qualified production activities (i.e., manufacturer's deduction). See discussion of Line 35 in ¶ 2738 [IRC Sec. 199(d)(1); Reg. Sec. 1.199-5(e)]. In computing the deduction, the qualified production activities income (QPAI) and W-2 wages of the trust or estate are allocated to each beneficiary and to the trust or estate based on the relative portion of the trust's or estate's distributable net income (DNI). If the trust or estate does not have any DNI for the tax year, QPAI and W-2 wages will be allocated entirely to the trust or estate.

Each beneficiary computes its Code Sec. 199 deduction by aggregating its share of QPAI and W-2 wages from the trust or estate with its share of QPAI and W-2 from other sources. For this purpose, a beneficiary's share of W-2 wages of a trust or estate is limited to the lesser of: (1) the beneficiary's allocable share of the W-2 wages of the trust or estate or (2) nine percent of the lesser of the taxpayer's taxable income (or an individual's AGI) or QPAI [IRC Sec. 199(a)(1)]. If the beneficiary's share of QPAI from

---

[11] IRS Publication 559, "Survivors, Executors, and Administrators," (for use in preparing 2012 tax returns) p. 18. See ¶ 105.

[12] IRS Publication 559, "Survivors, Executors, and Administrators," (for use in preparing 2012 tax returns) p. 18. See ¶ 105.

the trust or estate is not greater than zero, then the beneficiary may not take into account any W-2 wages of the trust or estate in computing its deduction.

¶2814 DEDUCTION FOR DISTRIBUTIONS TO BENEFICIARIES

The current policy is to tax the income of estates and trusts only once—either to the fiduciary, or to the beneficiary, or, in part, to each. This is accomplished by treating the estate or trust as a taxable entity, and by giving it a special deduction for amounts paid or payable to the beneficiary.

(a) Deductions Claimed by Simple Trusts. A simple trust is a trust that is required to distribute all of its income currently, regardless of whether the trustee actually does so, and has no provision in the trust instrument for charitable contributions. A simple trust is entitled to a deduction for trust income required to be distributed currently, whether or not distributed [IRC Sec. 651; Reg. Sec. 1.651(b)-1]. For asset distributions in lieu of cash, see ¶ 2806.

> **Example 1:** Grandpa's trust provides that income must be distributed to his grandson until he is age 21, at which time he will receive the entire principal remaining in the trust. This trust is a simple trust until the grandson turns age 21. At that time it will be called a complex trust.

> **Example 2:** The trust instrument requires all the income to be distributed currently. The trust has $10,000 income for 2013, of which $2,500 is collected in December. The trustee makes the usual quarterly payment of $2,500 to its sole beneficiary in January 2014. This simple trust can deduct $10,000 for 2013 because the trust was required to distribute $10,000 in 2013 regardless of whether or not it actually made the distribution.

The simple trust's deduction is limited to the amount of DNI [see ¶ 2804], even if the amount of income required to be distributed currently exceeds DNI. For this purpose, DNI does not include income items (adjusted for related deductions) not included in gross income [IRC Sec. 651; Reg. Sec. 1.651(b)-1].

> **Example 3:** Distributable net income is $99,000. This includes tax-exempt interest totaling $9,000. The deduction for distributions to beneficiaries cannot be more than $90,000.

(b) Deductions Claimed by Estates and Complex Trusts. A complex trust is any trust that is not a simple trust [see ¶ 2818]. Both an estate and a complex trust are allowed to claim a deduction for amounts paid, credited, or required to be distributed to the beneficiaries. A complex trust deducts, up to its DNI ceiling for the tax year, the sum of:

1. Any amount of income for the tax year required to be distributed currently to beneficiaries (including an amount payable out of income or corpus to the extent that it is paid out of income) [IRC Sec. 661(a)(1)]; and

2. Any other amounts paid, credited, or required to be distributed for the tax year. However, the deduction cannot exceed DNI of the trust [IRC Sec. 661(a)(2)].

The term "income required to be distributed currently" in IRC Sec. 661(a)(1) includes any amount required to be distributed which may be paid out of income or corpus (such as an annuity), to the extent it is paid out of income for the taxable year [Reg. Sec. 1.661(a)-2(b)]. The term also includes any amount used to discharge or satisfy any person's legal obligation [Reg. Sec. 1.661(a)-2(d)].

The term "any other amounts properly paid or credited or required to be distributed" in IRC Sec. 661(a)(2) includes all amounts properly paid, credited, or required to be distributed by an estate or trust during the taxable year other than income required to be distributed currently. Thus, the term includes the payment of an annuity to the extent it is not paid out of income for the taxable year, and a distribution of property in kind. Where the income of an estate or trust may be accumulated or distributed in the discretion of the fiduciary, or where the fiduciary has a power to distribute corpus to a beneficiary, any such discretionary distribution would qualify under IRC Sec. 661(a)(2). The term also includes an amount applied or distributed for the support of a dependent of a grantor or of a trustee or cotrustee out of corpus or out of other than income [Reg. Sec. 1.661(a)-2(c)]. The term also includes any amount used to discharge or satisfy any person's legal obligation [Reg. Sec. 1.661(a)-2(d)]. The term also includes amounts paid, or required to be paid, during the taxable year pursuant to a court order or decree or under local law, by a decedent's estate as an allowance or award for the support of the decedent's widow or other dependent for a limited period during the administration of the estate. Not included in the "any other amounts properly paid or credited or required to be distributed" is the value of any interest in real estate owned by a decedent, title to which passes under local law directly from the decedent to his heirs or devisees [Reg. Sec. 1.661(a)-2(e)].

A trust beneficiary must include in income the amount described in IRC Sec. 661(a) that is paid, credited or required to be distributed by the trust to the beneficiary [IRC Sec. 662(a)].

(c) **Character of Amounts Distributed.** In the absence of specific provisions in the governing instrument for the allocation of different classes of income, or unless local law requires such an allocation, the amount deductible for distributions to beneficiaries under IRC Sec. 661(a) is treated as consisting of the same proportion of each class of items entering into the computation of DNI as the total of each class bears to the total distributable net income [IRC Sec. 661(b); Reg. Sec. 1.661(b)-1].

Example 4: A trust has DNI of $100,000, consisting of $50,000 of taxable interest and $50,000 of royalties. The trust distributes $50,000 to beneficiary A. The deduction of $50,000 consists of $25,000 of taxable interest and $25,000 of royalties unless the trust instrument specifically provides for the distribution or accumulation of different classes of income or unless local law requires such an allocation [Reg. Sec. 1.661(b)-1].

¶2814

Limitation on deduction. An estate or trust is not allowed a deduction under IRC Sec. 661(a) for any amount which is treated as consisting of any item of DNI which is not included in the gross income of the estate or trust [Reg. Sec. 1.661(c)-1].

Charitable distributions. Any amount that is paid, permanently set aside, or used for a charitable purpose under IRC Sec. 642(c) is not allowed as an IRC Sec. 661 deduction to an estate or trust or treated as an amount distributed for purposes of determining the amounts includible in gross income of beneficiaries under IRC Sec. 662. Amounts paid, permanently set aside, or to be used for charitable, etc., purposes are deductible by estates or trusts only as provided in IRC Sec. 642(c) [IRC Sec. 663(a)(2); Reg. Sec. 1.663(a)-2].

Trust denied deduction for qualified conservation contributions of principal. In Rev. Rul. 2003-123,[1] the IRS concluded that a trust couldnot claim an IRC Sec. 661(a) distribution deduction for a contribution to charity of trust principal that satisfied the requirements of a qualified conservation contribution. Since the conservation easement contribution was made with respect to its principal (real property), not its gross income, the trust was not allowed a charitable deduction under IRC Sec. 642(c) for the contribution. The IRS noted that Reg. Sec. 1.663(a)-2 provides that any amount paid, permanently set aside, or allocated for charitable use and deductible under IRC Sec. 642(c) is not allowable as a deduction to an estate or trust under IRC Sec. 661. These amounts are deductible by estates and trusts only as provided in IRC Sec. 642(c).

¶2815 DEDUCTIONS IN TRANSACTIONS BETWEEN RELATED PARTIES

The law specifically prohibits the deduction of losses from sales and exchanges of property between certain related parties even if they intended for the transaction to be a bona fide business sale or exchange [IRC Sec. 267].

The term "related parties" for these purposes include, among others:

- Members of a family;
- A grantor and his trust fiduciary;
- Fiduciaries of two trusts having the same grantor;
- A fiduciary and a beneficiary of his trust;
- A fiduciary and a beneficiary of another trust with the same grantor;
- A fiduciary and a corporation over 50 percent of whose stock is owned, directly or indirectly, by or for the trust or the grantor;
- An executor of an estate and a beneficiary of the estate except in the case of a sale or exchange in satisfaction of a pecuniary bequest [IRC Sec. 267(b)].

---

[1] **¶2814** Rev. Rul. 2003-123, 2003-2 CB 1200; see also Rev. Rul. 68-667, 1968-2 CB 289.

¶2815

¶2816 CREDITS AGAINST TAX

Generally, estates and trusts are permitted the same credits that are available to individuals except for credits that only benefit individuals, such as the adoption credit and the earned income credit. Remember that tax credits reduce tax on a dollar-for-dollar basis (unlike deductions, which serve only to reduce the taxable income subject to tax).

The credits typically must be apportioned between the estate or trust and the beneficiaries on the basis of the income allocable to each. However, the foreign tax credit is allocated according to the proportionate share of the foreign taxes [IRC Sec. 642(a); Reg. Sec. 1.641(b)-1].

An estate or trust may claim the following tax credits on Form 1041:

1. Foreign tax credit (Attach Form 1116, "Foreign Tax Credit Individual, Estate or Trust" [IRC Sec. 642(a)];

2. Nonbusiness credits such as: the alternate motor vehicle credit; and the alternate fuel vehicle refueling property credit.

3. General Business Credit (Attach Form 3800, "General Business Credit") [IRC Sec. 38(a)]. This credit would be available to an estate or trust that is involved in a business. The general business tax credit is a limited nonrefundable credit against income tax that is claimed after all other nonrefundable credits are claimed. The amount of the general business tax credit may not exceed the "net income tax" minus the greater of the tentative minimum tax or 25 percent of the net regular tax liability over $25,000. For estates and trusts, the $25,000 amount must be reduced to an amount that bears the same ratio to $25,000 as the portion of the income of the estate or trust that is not allocated to the beneficiaries bears to the total income of the estate or trust [IRC Sec. 38(c)(5)(D)]. Any unused credit can be carried back one year and forward 20 years for credits that arose in tax years beginning after 1997, and back three years and forward 15 years for credits that arose in tax years before 1998 [IRC Sec. 39(a)(1)].

For a list of business credits, see ¶ 2935 and the 2013 Instructions for Form 1041 (reproduced at ¶ 2944). Estates and trusts are also entitled to claim various refundable tax credits, including the credit for federal income tax withheld on wages, the regulated investment company credit, the credit for federal excise taxes paid on fuels, and the credit for backup withholding.

¶2817 SIMPLE TRUSTS—DISTRIBUTIONS

When dealing with the tax treatment of distributions made to beneficiaries, the Internal Revenue Code makes a distinction between so-called "simple trusts" and "complex trusts." A simple trust, which is also called a "distributable" trust, is defined as one in which the trust terms:

1. Require that the trust distribute all of its income currently for the taxable year (it distributes no corpus),

2. Make no distribution from principal in the taxable year of the trust, and

3. Make no disbursements deductible as charitable contributions under IRC Sec. 642(c) [IRC Sec. 651; Reg. Sec. 1.651(a)-1].

A simple trust is primarily a conduit of income—the trust takes a deduction for the income that is required to be distributed currently, and the beneficiaries include that amount in their gross income, whether or not actually distributed. The terms of the trust instrument and state law determine what is income for this purpose.

(a) Income Taxable to Beneficiaries. Generally, beneficiaries must include in gross income all trust income required to be distributed to them, to the extent of the trust's DNI—regardless of whether the income is actually distributed [see ¶ 2803].[1] For asset distributions in lieu of cash, see ¶ 2806(d).

> **Example 1:** Mr. Brown placed certain securities in trust for the sole benefit of his wife. The trust instrument provided that all the income be distributed to her at least once a year, that no actual securities be distributed to her, and that no distributions be made to anyone else. This is a simple trust. Mrs. Brown must include the trust income in her gross income each year, whether or not the fiduciary actually makes the payment to her during the tax year.

If the income required to be distributed exceeds the DNI, beneficiaries are taxed only on their proportionate share of the DNI [IRC Sec. 652(a); Reg. Sec. 1.652(a)-2].

> **Example 2:** A simple trust provides that Mr. Black is to receive 60 percent of the trust income and Ms. Cox is to receive 40 percent. The trust has the following income and disbursements during the year: $9,000 interest on corporate bonds; $4,000 capital gains allocable to corpus; $1,500 commissions, legal fees and other deductible expenses allocable to corpus; and $400 expenses allocable to income.
>
> The trust income required to be distributed is $9,000 less $400, or $8,600. The trust's distributable net income is $9,000 (capital gains are excluded), less $1,900 (all deductible expenses), or $7,100. Although Black receives $5,160 ($8,600 × 60 percent), he will include only $4,260 ($7,100 × 60 percent) in income. Cox will receive $3,440 ($8,600 × 40 percent), but will include in income only $2,840 ($7,100 × 40 percent).

(b) Simple Trust Distribution Deduction. A simple trust may claim a distribution deduction under IRC Sec. 651 for the fiduciary accounting income (FAI) that the trust instrument requires it to distribute subject to the following two limitations:

1. The IRC Sec. 651 deduction cannot be greater than DNI of the trust, and

2. No deduction may be claimed for tax-exempt income [IRC Sec. 651(b)].

---

[1] **¶ 2817** Rev. Rul. 62-147, 1962-2 CB 151.

¶2817

If FAI exceeds DNI, the maximum amount of the distribution deduction is the DNI in that given year. If there is any tax-exempt interest in the trust, the net amount of tax-exempt interest minus expenses allocable to tax-exempt interest must be subtracted from DNI to arrive at the distribution deduction under IRC Sec. 651(b).

(c) Distributions of Corpus—Simple Trust Becomes Complex Trust.

A trust may be a simple trust one year and a complex trust another year [Reg. Sec. 1.651(a)-1]. For example, a trust will not qualify as a simple trust in any year in which the trustee is required to distribute amounts that exceed the trust's income for that year. In years when only income is distributed, the trust is a simple trust. However, if corpus is distributed, the trust becomes a complex trust for that year. When a trust ends, it is treated as a complex trust that year because corpus is distributed [Reg. Sec. 1.651(a)-3].

¶2818 COMPLEX TRUSTS AND ESTATES— DISTRIBUTIONS

(a) Complex Trusts and Estates Are Taxed Identically.

A complex trust is any trust that is not a simple trust. In other words, a complex trust may:

1. Accumulate income because it is not required to distribute all of its income currently;

2. Distribute corpus; or

3. Have a charitable beneficiary and therefore permit funds to be permanently set aside or used for charitable purposes.

> **Example 1:** Mom's trust directs the trustee to distribute net income monthly and gives the trustee discretion to invade principal for Son's education. Her trust will be treated as a complex trust for the taxable year in which the principal invasions occur.

> **Example 2:** Dad's trust directs the trustee not to distribute any income but to accumulate trust income. This trust is a complex trust for tax purposes.

An estate is treated as a complex trust. Therefore, a decedent's estate during its administration period and a complex trust are taxed identically. This means that both estates and complex trusts determine a beneficiary's income inclusions and a fiduciary's distribution deductions in the same manner [IRC Secs. 661 through 663; Reg. Sec. 1.661(a)-1].

(b) What Must Be Included in Gross Income.

The beneficiary of a complex trust or estate must include in gross income all income that is *required* to be distributed currently, whether or not it is actually distributed [IRC Sec. 662(a)]. Similarly, complex trusts and estates are allowed a deduction up to the amount of DNI for any amount of income required to be distributed currently and any other amounts properly paid or credited or required to be distributed [IRC Sec. 661(a)]. However, when an estate is being administered, income received by beneficiaries is not treated as "income required to be distributed currently."

If the amount of income required to be distributed currently to all beneficiaries exceeds the DNI (computed without the deduction under IRC Sec. 642(c) for amounts paid or permanently set aside for a charitable purpose), then the DNI is apportioned ratably among those beneficiaries [IRC Sec. 662(a)]. This so-called two-tier system is discussed later.

Exceptions—Items not includible in gross income. IRC Sec. 663(a) provides that the following items are *not* included in gross income for the current tax year and they are *not* deductible by a trust or estate as distributions [IRC Sec. 663(a)]:

1. *Gifts and bequests.* Any gift or bequest of a specific sum of money or of specific property which, under the terms of the governing instrument, is paid in a lump sum or in not more than three installments [IRC Sec. 663(a)(1). If, however, the instrument provides the gift or bequest is payable *only* from income (whether income for the payment year or income accumulated from a prior year), it will not be treated as a gift [Reg. Sec. 1.663(a)-1]. Instead, it will be deductible by the trust and taxable to the beneficiary [IRC Sec. 663(a)(1)].

> **Example 3:** Mom's will provides that her estate is to be divided equally between her two daughters. No provision was made in the will for the disposition of income of the estate during the period of administration. The estate had income of $50,000 for the taxable year. In accordance with an agreement among the beneficiaries that part of the assets of the estate would be distributed in-kind to the beneficiaries, stock in IBM was distributed to one daughter during the year. The fair market value of the stock was $40,000 on the date of distribution. No other distribution was made during the year. The distribution does not qualify as an exclusion within the meaning of IRC Sec. 663(a)(1), since it is not a specific gift to the daughter required by the terms of the will. Accordingly, the fair market value of the property ($40,000) represents a taxable distribution [Reg. Sec. 1.663(a)-1(b)(3), Example (2)].

A gift or bequest of a specific sum of money or of specific property is not disqualified solely because its payment is subject to a condition [Reg. Sec. 1.663(a)-1(b)(4)].

> **Example 4:** Dad's trust provides that Son receive $10,000 when he reaches age 25, and $10,000 when he reaches age 30, with payment over to Daughter of any amount not paid to Son if he dies. This is a gift to Son of a specific sum of money payable in two installments, even though the exact amount payable to Son cannot be ascertained with certainty under the terms of the trust instrument [Reg. Sec. 1.663(a)-1(b)(4)].

In determining whether a gift or bequest of a specific sum of money or of specific property is required to be paid or credited to a particular beneficiary in more than three installments, the following four bequests are disregarded:

• Gifts or bequests of articles for personal use, such as personal and household effects and automobiles are disregarded [Reg. Sec. 1.663(a)-1(c)(1)(i)].

¶2818

- Specifically devised real property which passes directly from the decedent to the devisee under local law, is disregarded [Reg. Sec. 1.663(a)-1(c)(1)(ii)].

- All gifts and bequests under a decedent's will for which no time of payment or credit is specified and which are to be paid or credited in the ordinary course of administration of the decedent's estate are considered as required to be paid or credited in a single installment [Reg. Sec. 1.663(a)-1(c)(1)(iii)].

- All gifts and bequests payable at any one specified time under the terms of the governing instrument are taken into account as a single installment.

Example 5: Under the terms of Dad's will, $10,000 in cash, household furniture, a watch, an automobile, 100 shares of IBM, 1,000 bushels of grain, 500 head of cattle, and a farm are left to Son. The title to the farm passes directly to Son under local law. The will also provides for the creation of a trust for the benefit of Son. The trust provides that Son be distributed the following: $10,000 in cash and 100 shares of AT&T when he reaches 25 years of age, $25,000 in cash and 200 shares of AT&T stock when he reaches 30 years of age and $50,000 in cash and 300 shares of AT&T stock when he reaches 35 years of age.

The furniture, watch, automobile and the farm are excluded under IRC Sec. 663(a)(1) in determining whether any gift or bequest "is required to be paid or credited" to Son in more than three installments. The $10,000 in cash, the shares of IBM stock, the grain, the cattle and the assets required to create the trust, to be paid or credited by the estate to Son and the trust are considered as "required to be paid or credited" in a single installment to each, regardless of the manner of payment or distribution by the executor, since no time of payment or crediting is specified in the will. The $10,000 in cash and shares of AT&T stock required to be distributed by the trust to Son when he is 25 years old are considered as required to be paid or distributed as one installment under the trust. Likewise, the distributions to be made by the trust to Son when he is 30 and 35 years old are each considered as one installment under the trust. Since the total number of installments to be made by the estate does not exceed three, all of the items of money and property distributed by the estate qualify for the IRC Sec. 663(a)(1) exclusion. Similarly, the three distributions by the trust qualify for the income exclusion.

2. *Charitable Distributions.* Any amount paid or permanently set aside or otherwise qualifying for the charitable deduction is not allowed as a deduction to an estate or trust or treated as an amount distributed for purposes of determining the amounts includible in gross income of beneficiaries [IRC Sec. 663(a)(2); Reg. Sec. 1.663(a)-2; but see ¶ 2810].

3. *Denial of Double Deduction.* Any distribution in the current tax year that was deducted by the estate or trust in a preceding tax year is excluded from a beneficiary's taxable income [IRC Sec. 663(a)(3); Reg. Sec. 1.663(a)-3].

(c) Allocation by Tiers—Overview. For estates and complex trusts, distributions are divided into two tiers so that an order or priority among beneficiaries is established [IRC Sec. 662(a)]. According to this tier system, the DNI of the estate or trust must first be allocated to tier one distributions and only the remaining balance of the DNI (if any) is allocated to tier two distributions.

Distributions are taxed to the extent of the DNI first to the beneficiaries to whom income must be currently distributed. These are known as first-tier beneficiaries. If distributions to these beneficiaries are greater than the DNI, their shares are prorated for tax purposes. All other beneficiaries eligible to receive income are second-tier beneficiaries. They are subject to income tax on their distributions only to the extent that the DNI is greater than the amount distributed to the first-tier beneficiaries [IRC Sec. 662(a)].

> **Example 6:** Ms. Ames, a first-tier beneficiary, is entitled to receive $15,000 as an annual distribution from an estate, and Ms. Bates is entitled to income in the discretion of the fiduciary.

- If the DNI is $30,000 and they each receive $15,000, each has taxable income of $15,000.
- If the DNI is $20,000 and they both receive the same $15,000 distributions, Ames still has taxable income of $15,000 but Bates is taxed on only $5,000. The remaining $10,000 that she receives is tax-free.

Distributions that exceed distributable net income. If the first-tier distributions to all beneficiaries exceed the DNI (figured without any deduction for charitable contributions), the amount to be included in each beneficiary's gross income is computed in the following manner [Reg. Sec. 1.662(a)-2(b)]:

$$\frac{\text{First-tier distributions to the beneficiary}}{\text{First-tier distributions to all beneficiaries}} \times \begin{array}{c}\text{Distributable net}\\\text{income (without}\\\text{deduction for}\\\text{charitable}\\\text{contributions)}\end{array} = \begin{array}{c}\text{Amount}\\\text{beneficiary}\\\text{includes in gross}\\\text{income}\end{array}$$

> **Example 7:** A trust is required to distribute one-half its current income for the tax year to Albert, the grantor's son; one-quarter to Bertha, the grantor's daughter; and one-quarter to Community Chest, a charity. The trust income is $10,000. The charitable contribution is $2,500 (× $10,000). The amount required to be distributed to Albert is $5,000, and the amount required to be distributed to Bertha is $2,500. Hence, the amount required to be distributed to all beneficiaries is $7,500, since the charity is not considered a beneficiary [IRC Sec. 663(a)(2)]. Assume the DNI of the trust is $7,000 before the charitable deduction is taken. Albert will include $4,666.67 ($5,000/$7,500 × $7,000) in his gross income. Bertha will include $2,333.33 ($2,500/$7,500 × $7,000) in her gross income.

(d) Allocation by Tiers—Other Distributions. Beneficiaries also must include in gross income all other amounts properly paid, credited, or required to be distributed to them (so-called second-tier distributions) [IRC Sec. 662(a)(2); Reg. Sec. 1.662(a)-3].

¶2818

▶ **OBSERVATION:** An amount is not treated as credited to a beneficiary, unless it is so definitely allocated to a beneficiary as to be beyond recall. Thus, "credit" for practical purposes is the equivalent of "payment." A mere entry on the books of the fiduciary will not serve as an amount credited to beneficiaries, unless it cannot be changed.[1]

Example 8: A trust provides that each year the fiduciary must distribute $3,000 of corpus to Mr. Brant, a beneficiary. Brant will include $3,000 in his gross income to the extent of the trust's DNI.

Distributions exceeding DNI. When the sum of the first-tier and second-tier distributions exceeds DNI, beneficiaries must include in gross income only a proportionate share of the DNI (less first tier distributions). The share is determined as follows [IRC Sec. 662(a)(2); Reg. Sec. 1.662(a)-3]:

$$\begin{array}{c}\text{Distributable net income,}\\\text{less first-tier distributions}\end{array} \times \begin{array}{c}\text{Second-tier distributions to}\\\text{the beneficiary Second-tier}\\\text{distributions to }all\\\text{beneficiaries}\end{array} = \begin{array}{c}\text{The beneficiary's share of}\\\text{distributable net income}\end{array}$$

▶ **OBSERVATION:** Beneficiaries are taxed on second-tier distributions only if the first-tier distributions fail to exhaust the DNI of the estate or trust. This is so, even if the second-tier distributions are made from income. To the extent that the DNI, reduced by first-tier distributions, is less than second-tier distributions, the second-tier distributions are prorated.

Example 9: A trust requires the distribution of $8,000 of income to A annually. Any remaining income may be accumulated or distributed to B, C, and D in the trustee's discretion. The trustee may also invade corpus for the benefit of any of the four beneficiaries. During the year, the trust has $20,000 of income after deducting expenses. Distributable net income is $20,000. The trustee distributes $8,000 of income to A. He also distributes $4,000 each to B and C, $2,000 to D, and an additional $6,000 to A. The amounts taxable to each are determined as follows:

Distributable net income	$20,000
Less: first-tier distribution to A	8,000
Available for second-tier distributions	$12,000
Second-tier distributions:	
A—$6,000/$16,000 × $12,000	$4,500
B—$4,000/$16,000 × $12,000	$3,000
C—$4,000/$16,000 × $12,000	$3,000
D—$2,000/$16,000 × $12,000	$1,500

A includes $12,500 in income ($8,000 first-tier distribution plus $4,500 second-tier distribution). B and C each include $3,000 in income. D includes $1,500.

---

[1] ¶ **2818** Stearns, 65 F.2d 371 (2d Cir. 1933), *cert. denied*, 290 U.S. 670 (1933).

(e) Separate Share Rule. The separate share rule exists in order to avoid the distortion of income that often results when a complex trust accumulates income for one beneficiary and makes taxable distributions to a different beneficiary. As a result, trusts with more than one beneficiary must use the "separate share rule," in order to provide different tax treatment of distributions to different beneficiaries. The separate share rule will reflect the income earned by different shares of the trust's corpus by treating substantially separate and independent shares of different beneficiaries in a single trust as though each share represented a separate trust [IRC Sec. 663(c)]. The rule is used to determine the amount of DNI of a trust that is allocable and taxable to a particular beneficiary. The separate share rule is important in situations where income is accumulated for beneficiary A but a distribution is made to beneficiary B of both income and corpus in an amount exceeding the share of income that would be distributable to beneficiary B had there been separate trusts or estates. The division of DNI into separate shares will limit the tax liability of B in this situation [Reg. Sec. 1.663(c)-1(a)].

> **Example 10:** Dad's will provides that all of the shares of his business, CDECorp, go to Daughter. The will also provides that all dividends paid to the estate by CDECorp should be paid only to Daughter. The will provides further that the payment of these dividends has no impact on any other amounts that Daughter is entitled to receive under the will. The separate share rule would apply in this situation.

Separate share rule applies to estates. According to the separate share rule, if an estate has multiple beneficiaries, substantially separate and independent shares of different beneficiaries (or classes of beneficiaries) are to be treated as separate estates only for purposes of computing distributable net income (DNI) [IRC Sec. 663(c)]. Separate shares exist when the governing instrument of the estate and applicable local law create separate economic interests in one beneficiary or class of beneficiaries in such a way that their economic interests neither affect nor are affected by the economic interests of another separate beneficiary or class of beneficiaries. The separate share rule is mandatory where separate shares exist. It requires that the estate's income and deductions be allocated among the separate shares as if they were separate estates. According to the separate share rule, a beneficiary is taxed only on the amount of income that belongs to that beneficiary's separate share. The Section 661 deduction to the estate and the Section 662 inclusion in the gross income of the beneficiary are limited by the DNI allocable to each separate share [Reg. Sec. 1.663(c)-2].

Separate share defined. A separate share generally is a separate economic interest in one beneficiary or class of beneficiaries of the decedent's estate. There would be separate economic interests where the economic interests of the beneficiary or class of beneficiaries neither affect nor are affected by economic interests accruing to another beneficiary or class of beneficiaries. Under this definition, a separate share generally exists only if it includes both corpus and the income attributable to that corpus and is independent from any other share [Reg. Sec. 1.663(c)-4(a)]. This means that income earned on assets in one share (the first share) and appreciation and depreciation in the value of those assets have no effect on any other share. Similarly, the income and changes in value of any other share have no effect on the first share. Note that a gift or bequest of a specific sum of money or of specific property is not a separate share [Reg. Sec. 1.663(c)-4(a)].

Surviving spouse's elective share. In general, an elective share statute gives the surviving spouse the right to claim a share of the deceased spouse's estate if he or she is disinherited or dissatisfied with the will bequest or inheritance. The regulations provide that the surviving spouse's elective share constitutes a separate share of the estate for the sole purpose of determining the amount of DNI in applying IRC Sec. 661(a) and IRC Sec. 662(a). This means that only the income that is (1) allocable to the surviving spouse's separate for a tax year, and (2) distributed to the surviving spouse in satisfaction of the elective share will be treated as a distribution subject to those provisions. This approach results in the surviving spouse being taxed on the estate's income earned during administration only to the extent of his or her right to share in the estate's income under state law.

Revocable trust as part of estate. The regulations provide that a qualified revocable trust that elects under IRC Sec. 645 to be treated as part of the decedent's estate for income tax purposes constitutes a separate share of the estate for the sole purpose of determining the amount of DNI in applying IRC Sec. 661(a) and IRC Sec. 662(a). For further discussion of election, see ¶ 2826 and Reg. Sec. 1.645-1.

The IRS regulations thus make it clear that the electing revocable trust itself may have two or more separate shares [Reg. Sec. 1.663(c)-4(a)]. Any pecuniary formula bequest that is entitled to income and to share in appreciation or depreciation under the governing instrument or local law constitutes a separate share under the general definition. Under a special rule, a pecuniary formula bequest that is not entitled to income or to share in appreciation or depreciation is also a separate share if the governing instrument does not provide that it must be paid or credited in more than three installments [Reg. Sec. 1.663(c)-4(b)].

No election required. The separate share rule is mandatory. No election is required. Thus, if a trust or estate is properly treated as having separate and independent shares, such treatment must prevail in all taxable years of the trust unless an event occurs which requires different treatment [Reg. Sec. 1.663(c)-1(d)].

Purpose of rule. The separate share rule exists for the sole purpose of determining the amount taxable to multiple beneficiaries of a single trust. The separate share rule cannot be used for any purpose other than the application of DNI. It does not, for instance, permit the treatment of separate shares as separate trusts for purposes of:

• The filing of returns and payment of tax;

• The deduction of personal exemption under IRC Sec. 642(b); or

• Allowing beneficiaries to claim excess deductions and unused net operating loss and capital loss carryovers on termination of the trust [IRC Sec. 663(c); Reg. Sec. 1.663(c)-1(b)].

The separate share rule may apply even though separate and independent accounts are not maintained and are not required to be maintained for each share on the books of account of the trust, and even though no physical segregation of assets is made or required [Reg. Sec. 1.663(c)-1(c)].

¶2818

Example 11: Mom's trust with two beneficiaries has DNI of $20,000. Trustee makes a mandatory distribution of one-half this amount, or $10,000, to Daughter. He accumulates the other $10,000 for future distribution to Son. He also makes a discretionary distribution of $10,000 out of corpus to Daughter. Under the tier system, the entire DNI would be allocated to Daughter, and she would be taxed on the $20,000 received. Her tax is being measured, in part, by $10,000 of current income that can only go to Son. If the trust is divided into two separate trusts, one for each beneficiary, each trust then will have DNI of $10,000. Assume that the Trustee of Daughter's trust distributes all the income of that trust and $10,000 of the corpus to her. The trustee of the trust for Son makes no distribution. Under these facts, Daughter would be taxed on $10,000. She actually received $20,000, but her taxable share may not exceed the trust's DNI. Son's trust makes no distributions, so its income of $10,000 is taxable to the trust. Application of the separate share rule in this situation prevents one beneficiary from being taxed on income payable to a separate class of beneficiaries.

▶ **OBSERVATION:** The "separate share" device achieves the two-trust result in a one-trust case. The two-trust result in the above example seems more equitable since it exempts the corpus distribution and limits the tax on the beneficiaries to current income.

(f) Sixty-Five Day Rule. The sixty-five day rule allows a trustee to make an election to treat all or part of amounts paid or credited in the first 65 days after the close of the tax year of a trust or estate to be attributed to the preceding tax year [IRC Sec. 663(b)(1); Reg. Sec. 1.663(b)-1]. This tax election simplifies the administration of estates but has no impact on a trustee's classification of income or principal on trust books and records. The election is limited to the trust's income. The election, which is made on Form 1041, is irrevocable for the year involved and is binding for that year only.

The 65-day rule applies only if the fiduciary or trustee elects this treatment. In addition, the election must be made within the time for filing a return for the year to which the election relates [IRC Sec. 663(b)(2); Reg. Secs. 1.663(b)-1, 1.663(b)-2]. If no return is due, a statement of election must be filed with the IRS where the return would normally be filed. In either case, it must be made within the time for filing the return for that year (including extensions) and cannot be revoked after the return due date [Reg. Sec. 1.663(b)-2].

Distributions eligible for the election cannot exceed the greater of: (1) the trust income for the tax year for which the election is made or (2) DNI for that year. The limitation is further reduced by distributions in that year, except those amounts for which the election was claimed in a preceding tax year [Reg. Sec. 1.663(b)-1].

Example 12: The Brotherhood Trust, a calendar year trust, has $1,000 of income and $800 of DNI in year 1. The trust properly paid $550 to a beneficiary, on January 11 of year 1, which the trustee elected to treat as paid on December 31 of the prior year. The trust also properly paid $600 to him on April 25 of year 1 and $450 on January 22 of year 2. For year 1, the maximum amount that can be elected as properly paid or credited on the last day of year 1 is $400 ($1,000 minus $600). The $550 paid on January 11 of year 1, does not reduce the maximum amount since it is treated as having been paid on December 31 of the prior year [Reg. Sec. 1.663(b)-1(a)(2), Example].

(g) Election for Property Distributed In-Kind.

Whenever an estate or trust distributes property "in-kind" (other than cash) significant tax consequences result which a fiduciary should consider carefully. For purposes of determining the distribution deduction available to the trust or estate and the amount includable by the beneficiary, the amount distributed is taken into account for DNI purposes only to the extent of the lesser of the property's basis or its fair market value at the time of distribution [IRC Sec. 643(e)(2)]. This means that the beneficiary's basis for the property will be the same as the trust's or estate's basis. This is called carryover basis. If the property has appreciated in value, this could lead to costly tax consequences down the road when the beneficiary goes to sell the appreciated property with a low basis. The beneficiary would recognize the previously untaxed gain on any subsequent disposition of the property.

Relief is available in IRC Sec. 643(e) which provides that the executor or trustee of a trust or estate may elect to have the property distributed in-kind to be treated as if the property had been sold to the beneficiary at its fair market value [IRC Sec. 643(e)(3)(A)]. If this election is made, the basis of the property in the beneficiary's hands is adjusted to reflect the gain or loss recognized by the estate or trust on the distribution [IRC Sec. 643(e)(1)]. The estate or trust will recognize any gain or loss as if the property had been sold to the beneficiary at its fair market value [IRC Sec. 643(e)(3)(A)(ii)]. The estate is also entitled to a distribution deduction equal to the property's fair market value [IRC Sec. 643(e)(3)(A)(iii)].

Election is irrevocable. This election is irrevocable (unless consent is obtained from Treasury) and applies to all distributions made by the estate or trust during a taxable year and must be made on the return of estate or trust for such taxable year [IRC Sec. 643(e)(3)(B)].

> **Example 13:** A trust has DNI equal to $10,000 and a capital asset with a basis of $4,000 and fair market value of $10,000 when distributed.
>
> *Without election.* There would be a DNI distribution deduction equal to the stock's basis of $4,000 and the trust would pay tax on income of $4,000. The beneficiary would receive property with a basis of $4,000 and have taxable income of $4,000. When he sells the property he will have capital gain of $6,000.
>
> *With election.* There would be a DNI distribution deduction of $10,000. The trust would have capital gain of $6,000 subject to tax. The beneficiary would receive property with basis of $10,000 ($4,000 estate basis plus $6,000 capital gain) and would pay tax on $10,000. The beneficiary would have no gain when he sells the asset.

¶ 2819 THROWBACK RULES

According to the throwback rules, which were repealed by the Taxpayer's Relief Act of 1997, a trust beneficiary was taxed on trust distributions of income that had been accumulated and taxed in prior years if the beneficiary's top average marginal tax rate during the previous five years was higher than that of the trust.[1] In a major simplification of the law, the throwback rules were repealed for most domestic trusts effective for all distributions made in tax years beginning after August 5, 1997.

The reason for the repeal is simple. The benefits of income shifting that were achieved by shifting income producing assets to trusts were eroded by the compressed income tax brackets that now apply to trusts [see ¶ 2935]. The throwback rules were created to limit the benefit that would otherwise occur from using the lower rates that once applied to trust income. Now that the trust tax rates have risen dramatically, the original purpose of the throwback rules no longer exists. The rules were generally eliminated for domestic trusts.

▶ **CAUTION:** Unfortunately, you can't forget about the throwback rules completely. The throwback rules continue to apply to:

1. Foreign trusts;

2. Trusts that were foreign trusts but became domestic trusts; and

3. Domestic trusts created before March 1, 1984, that would be treated as multiple trusts under IRC Sec. 643(f).

The discussion that follows applies only to trusts created before March 1, 1984 and foreign trusts. The throwback rules ordinarily apply only to complex trusts [Reg. Sec. 1.665(a)-0A]. But a simple trust that makes an accumulation distribution allocable to an earlier year is treated as a complex trust for that year for purposes of the throwback rules [Reg. Sec. 1.665(b)-1A].

(a) Why the Throwback Rules Were Created and Then Repealed. The throwback rules were designed to prevent tax avoidance at a time when the trust tax rates were lower than individual tax rates. As a result creative taxpayers used trusts to accumulate income and pay tax at a lower tax rate rather than distribute the income to a beneficiary and pay tax at the higher tax rate. When the income was distributed at a later date, little or no additional tax would be paid by the beneficiary because distributions in excess of DNI in the year of distribution are tax-exempt to the beneficiary.

The throwback rule taxes the beneficiaries as if the amounts had been distributed each year instead of accumulated and taxed at the trust tax rates. In other words, the rule "throws back" the accumulated income to the years in which it was accumulated. The throwback rules were repealed because the trust tax rates have increased dramatically to the point that it no longer makes sense to accumulate income in a trust. In addition, application of the throw-back rules rarely resulted in any additional tax due from a beneficiary on income that already had been taxed to a trust.

---

[1] **¶ 2819** Committee Report of the Taxpayer Relief Act of 1997 (P.L. 105-34), Act Sec. 507.

¶2819

(b) Operation of the Throwback Rules. The following concepts are basic to understanding the throwback rule:

- "Undistributed net income"; and

- "Accumulation distribution" [IRC Secs. 665(a), 665(b); Reg. Secs. 1.665(a)-1A, 1.665(b)-1A].

There can only be a throwback from a year with an accumulation distribution to a year with undistributed net income.

Undistributed net income. A trust has undistributed net income for a tax year when the amounts distributed are less than the DNI for the year [IRC Secs. 665(a)(2), 665(d); Reg. Sec. 1.665(a)-1A]. To find the undistributed net income:

1. Find the DNI of the trust [see ¶ 2803].

2. Subtract the following from the DNI:

    - The amount of *income* required to be distributed currently, including any amount that may be paid out of income or corpus to the extent it was paid out of trust income for the year;

    - Any other amounts paid, credited, or required to be distributed; and

    - The income tax on the undistributed portion of the trust's DNI. This is the same amount as the total tax paid by the trust (not including any alternative minimum tax) except when the trust has capital gains not included in distributable net income (for example, capital gains to corpus) [Reg. Sec. 1.665(d)-1A].

Example 1: Under the terms of a trust, the trustee must distribute $10,000 of income currently to Mr. Brown. He also has discretion to make additional distributions to Brown. In 1997, the trust's distributable net income of $30,100 was derived from royalties, and the trustee distributed $20,000 to Brown. The trust's taxable income is $10,000 (after subtracting out a $100 exemption) on which a tax must be paid. Compute the tax using the 1998 Tax Rate Schedule as follows: [$10,000 − $8,350 = $1,650 × 39.6% = 653 + $2,360 = $3,013.

The undistributed net income of the trust for 1998 is $7,087, computed as follows:

Distributable net income	$30,100
Less: Income currently distributable to Brown	10,000
Other amounts distributed to Brown	10,000
Tax attributable to undistributed net income	3,013
Undistributed net income	$ 7,087

Accumulation distribution. A trust has an accumulation distribution when it distributes more than the DNI for the year. To determine the accumulation distribution:

1. Find the total distribution for the tax year, reduced by the amount of income required to be distributed currently (including any amount that may be paid out of income or corpus to the extent it was paid out of trust income for the year);

¶2819

2. Subtract the DNI reduced (but not below zero) from the income required to be distributed currently.

The difference between (1) and (2) is the accumulation distribution for the tax year. A distribution made or required to be distributed by a trust that does not exceed the trust income for the year is not treated as an accumulation distribution for that year [IRC Sec. 665(b); Reg. Sec. 1.665(b)-1A].

> **Example 2:** During 1997, a trustee properly distributes $20,000 to a beneficiary, of which $7,000 is income required to be distributed currently to him. The distributable net income of the trust is $15,000. There is an accumulation distribution of $5,000, computed as follows:
>
> | | | |
> |---|---:|---:|
> | Total distribution | $20,000 | |
> | Less: Income required to be distributed currently | 7,000 | |
> | Other amounts distributed | | $13,000 |
> | Distributable net income | $15,000 | |
> | Less: Income required to be distributed currently | 7,000 | |
> | Balance of distributable net income | | 8,000 |
> | Accumulation distribution | | $5,000 |

(c) How to Handle the Throwback Rule. When a trust makes an accumulation distribution for any tax year, the distribution is thrown back to the earliest year the trust has undistributed net income, and so on, up to the year of the distribution. The accumulation being thrown back is deemed to have been distributed on the last day of the year to which it is thrown back, but only to the extent of the undistributed net income of that year. The rest of the accumulation distribution is then thrown back to the next succeeding year that had undistributed net income, and so on through the tax years until the accumulation distribution is used up [IRC Sec. 666(a); Reg. Sec. 1.666(a)-1A]. The trustee must file Schedule J (attached to Form 1041), showing the allocation of accumulation distribution to each beneficiary.

> ▶ **OBSERVATION:** The throwback rule can be avoided by electing to treat any distribution during the first 65 days of a trust year as an amount paid during the preceding year (¶ 2818(f)) [IRC Sec. 663(b); Reg. Secs. 1.663(b)-1, 2].

(d) Distributions to Minor Beneficiaries. Generally, the throwback rules do not apply to any distributions of income accumulated by a trust (other than a foreign trust) for a beneficiary before his birth or before he is 21 years old [IRC Sec. 665(b)]. These accumulated distributions are not taxable to the beneficiary.

> **NOTE:** There are special rules regarding distributions allocated to preceding years as they relate to multiple trusts and foreign trusts [IRC Secs. 665(c), 665(d)].

(e) Lack of Records. If records are not available to determine the trust's undistributed net income of any tax year, the accumulation distribution is deemed to have been determined on December 31, 1969, or the earliest subsequent date the trust was in existence. If the trustee establishes that the loss of records for some tax years

¶2819

was beyond his control, the accumulation distribution is first allocated to the tax years for which he has adequate records of the trust's existence [IRC Sec. 666(d); Reg. Sec. 1.666(d)-1A].

(f) Taxes Added to Distribution. When an accumulation distribution is thrown back to a particular year, all or part of the taxes imposed on the trust for that year (other than the alternative minimum tax) are also deemed distributed. This is done because the accumulation deemed distributed in the throw-back year would have increased the trust's distribution deduction in that year, and thereby reduced or eliminated the trust's taxes. If the accumulation distribution thrown back to a particular year is at least as much as the undistributed net income for that year, the taxes paid by the trust for that year are also deemed distributed and are added to the distribution [IRC Sec. 666(b); Reg. Sec. 1.666(b)-1A]. If the accumulation distribution thrown back is *less than* the undistributed net income, only a portion of the taxes is added to the accumulation. This portion is determined as follows [IRC Sec. 666(c); Reg. Sec. 1.666(c)-1A]:

$$\begin{array}{c}\text{Taxes (except} \\ \text{alternative} \\ \text{minimum tax) on} \\ \text{trust year to} \\ \text{which throwback} \\ \text{is made}\end{array} \times \begin{array}{c}\dfrac{\begin{array}{c}\text{Accumulation} \\ \text{distribution} \\ \text{thrown back to} \\ \text{particular year}\end{array}}{\begin{array}{c}\text{Undistributed net} \\ \text{income for that} \\ \text{particular year}\end{array}} \end{array} = \begin{array}{c}\text{The amount of} \\ \text{taxes deemed to} \\ \text{have been} \\ \text{distributed on the} \\ \text{last day of that} \\ \text{particular year}\end{array}$$

Example 3: A trust created on January 1, 1989, makes an accumulation distribution of $7,000 in 1997. For 1989 the trust's undistributed portion of distributable net income was $12,100, and its tax attributable to the undistributed net income was $2,712. Therefore, its undistributed net income for 1989 was $9,388 ($12,100 − $2,712). Since the entire amount of the accumulation distribution for 1997 ($7,000) is less than the undistributed net income for 1989 ($9,388), an additional amount of $2,022 ($7,000/$9,388 × $2,712) is deemed distributed to the beneficiary on the last day of 1989.

(g) Effect of Distributions in Intervening Years. The undistributed net income, for any year to which a later accumulation distribution may be thrown back, is reduced by accumulation distributions in intervening years that must be thrown back to such year [Reg. Sec. 1.665(a)-1A(c)]. To allocate an accumulation distribution to a prior year, that year's undistributed net income is reduced by the amount deemed distributed in an accumulation distribution made in any intervening years [Reg. Secs. 1.666(a)-1A(d); 1.666(c)-2A]. Also, when a throwback results in taxes paid by the trust being deemed distributed to beneficiaries, the taxes imposed on the trust attributable to any remaining undistributed net income are reduced by the taxes deemed distributed [Reg. Sec. 1.665(d)-1A(b)(2)].

(h) Tax Paid by Beneficiaries on Excess Distribution. The beneficiary must pay an additional tax (in the year in which the accumulation distribution is actually paid, credited, or required to be distributed) on the amount deemed to have been distributed to him or her by the trust in any year to which the throwback is made. The

¶2819

beneficiary is taxed on the accumulation distribution thrown back to a particular year and also an amount equal to the tax paid by the trust on that accumulation distribution. The tax on the beneficiary in the year the accumulation is actually distributed is the sum of:

1. The partial tax on the beneficiary's taxable income computed without regard to the accumulation distribution, and

2. The partial tax on the accumulation distribution [IRC Sec. 667].

The partial tax in (2) is computed on a three-year average basis, as follows:

First, the beneficiary takes his or her taxable income for the five years immediately preceding the distribution year, and disregards the lowest and highest years. If a beneficiary has a loss year in any of the five preceding years, the taxable income for the loss year is deemed to be zero for a *corporate* beneficiary for all computation purposes. However, an *individual* beneficiary's taxable income for any tax year starting after 1976 is deemed to be not less than his standard deduction for the year, and zero for earlier tax years.

Second, using the averaging device, add an amount equal to the trust income accumulation distribution, divided by the number of years the trust earned it, to the taxable income for the remaining three years and figure a tax for each year.

Finally, multiply the average increase in tax for the three-year period by the number of years the trust earned the income. The result is the beneficiary's tax on the accumulation [IRC Sec. 667(b)]. The tax may be offset by a credit for any taxes previously paid by the trust with respect to this income, and the remaining tax liability is then payable by the beneficiary in the distribution year. But no refund or credit is allowed as a result of accumulation distribution. Special rules apply to multiple trusts [IRC Sec. 667(c)].

(i) Adjustment for Estate and Generation-Skipping Transfer Taxes.
The beneficiary may reduce the partial tax (determined in the usual way) by the amount of the tax attributable to pre-death or pre-transfer accumulations in proportion to the transfer tax on the accumulation distribution [IRC Sec. 667(b)(6)].

Credit for tax paid by trust. As explained above, the beneficiary can deduct or offset the taxes paid by the trust in figuring his or her partial tax due on an accumulation distribution. However, the tax law sets an overall limit to the effect that a beneficiary or trust is not entitled to any refund or credit as a result of any accumulation distributions [IRC Sec. 666(e)]. Thus, if the partial tax is less than the amount of the tax deemed distributed, the excess cannot be used as a tax credit against the beneficiary's tax liability that arises from other sources of income. Nor can that excess give rise to a tax refund.

(j) Foreign Trusts.
U.S. beneficiaries receiving distributions from foreign trusts not taxed under the grantor trust rules [see ¶ 3100] are, with certain exceptions, subject to the throwback provisions generally as discussed above. However, foreign trusts are not allowed an exclusion from the throwback rule for accumulation distributions covering years before the beneficiary was born or reached age 21 [IRC Sec. 665(c)].

The character of capital gains is disregarded for purposes of taxing accumulation distributions to the beneficiary. But the character of income from which trust accumulation distributions are made to nonresident aliens and foreign corporate beneficiaries should be retained in the case of accumulation distributions to them [IRC Secs. 643(a)(6)(C), 667(e)]. Foreign trust beneficiaries who receive accumulation distributions must add to the distribution allocable foreign taxes paid by the trust before figuring additional tax due.

> **NOTE:** There are special rules for claiming the trust's foreign tax credit [IRC Sec. 665(d), 667(d)] and for distributions by foreign trusts not created by a U.S. person [IRC Sec. 665(c); Reg. Sec. 1.665(c)-1A].

¶2820 RATES AND RETURNS

(a) Who Must File Estate or Trust Tax Return. A Form 1041 (U.S. Income Tax Return for Estates and Trusts) must be filed for a domestic estate or trust by the fiduciary in the following situations:

1. If a domestic estate has gross income of $600 or more during a tax year;

2. If one or more of the beneficiaries of the domestic estate is a nonresident alien individual, Form 1041 must be filed even if the gross income of the estate is less than $600;

3. If the trust has any taxable income or has gross income of $600 or more, regardless of the amount of taxable income; or

4. If the estate of a bankrupt individual has gross income equal to or more than the sum of the exemption amount plus the basic standard deduction for a married individual filing a separate return. In 2014, the amount is $10,150 [IRC Sec. 6012(a)(8)].

Trusts and estates of decedents are separate legal entities which must file tax returns. Returns are generally filed by fiduciaries for trusts, and for a decedent's estate which comes into existence at the time of death of an individual.

Decedents. If a decedent would have been required to file a return, then the executor, administrator, legal representative, or survivor must file a final return. The return is made on Form 1040, 1040EZ, or 1040A. The final return covers the period from the beginning of the decedent's tax year, up to and including, the date of death [IRC Sec. 443(a)(2); Reg. Sec. 1.443-1(a)(2)]. See Chapter 26 for further discussion of the decedent's final income tax return.

Estates. The fiduciary of a domestic decedent's estate, trust, or bankruptcy estate (if gross income of bankrupt estate exceeds $10,150 in 2014) uses Form 1041 to report the following:

- The income, deductions, gains, losses, etc. of the estate or trust;

- The income that is either accumulated or held for future distribution or distributed currently to the beneficiaries;

- Any income tax liability of the estate or trust; and

- Employment taxes on wages paid to household employees.

The fiduciary must file Form 1041 for the estate of a domestic decedent that has:

- Gross income for the tax year of $600 or more [IRC Sec. 6012(a)(3)]; or

- A beneficiary who is a nonresident alien [IRC Sec. 6012(a)(5); Reg. Sec. 1.6012-3(a)].

(b) When to File. For calendar year estates and trusts, file Form 1041 and Schedule K-1 on or before April 15, following the close of the trust's calendar year. For fiscal year estates and trusts, file Form 1041 by the 15th day of the 4th month following the close of the tax year.

An estate or trust can obtain an automatic extension of time to file Form 1041 by timely filing Form 7004, "Application for Automatic Extension of Time to File Certain Business Income Tax, Information, and Other Returns." The automatic extension period is five months.

(c) Liability of Fiduciaries. Any fiduciary (other than a trustee acting under Chapter 11 of the Bankruptcy Code) who pays any debt due by the decedent or the estate, before paying federal estate tax obligations becomes personally liable for the tax of the estate to the extent of such payments.

Exceptions:

1. The fiduciary is not liable for amounts paid out for debts that have priority over the federal taxes due and owing on the estate, such as a decedent's funeral expenses or probate administration costs [Reg. Sec. 1.641(b)-2].

2. An executor or administrator who pays other debts is not personally liable unless the executor or administrator has either personal knowledge of a tax due the United States or knowledge that would put a reasonably prudent person on inquiry that such tax debts exist. Discharge of the fiduciary does not terminate the fiduciary's personal liability for the payment of other debts of the estate without satisfying prior tax claims.

(d) Forms That Must Be Filed. The fiduciary must file a separate Schedule K-1 (or an appropriate substitute) for each beneficiary, showing that beneficiary's share of income, deductions and credits. The fiduciary must also send a copy of Schedule K-1 to each beneficiary. An ancillary executor or administrator must file an information return on Form 1041 for the part of the estate he or she controls [Reg. Sec. 1.6012-3(a)(3)]. Any estate or trust fiduciary must furnish return information to the beneficiaries [IRC Sec. 6034A]. Penalties are provided for failure to comply.

In the first return, the fiduciary chooses the accounting period for the estate. This may be either a calendar year or *any* fiscal year which he or she selects. Estate gross income is figured from the day following the deceased person's death [Reg. Sec. 1.443-1]. Thus, a return may have to be filed for the short period from that date to the start of the estate's regular tax year.

▶ **OBSERVATION:** Although current law restricts a *trust's* ability to defer income taxation through the selection of trusts' tax years, the treatment of an *estate's* tax year is not affected [see ¶2802].

Trusts. The fiduciary of a trust must file Form 1041 for the estate of a domestic decedent that has:

- Any amount of taxable income for the tax year; or
- Gross income of $600 or more; or
- A beneficiary who is a nonresident alien [IRC Sec. 6012(a)(4); Reg. Sec. 1.6012-3(a)].

Split-interest trusts where the trust claims charitable deductions for amounts paid or permanently set aside for charity are required to file Form 5227, "Split-Interest Trust Information Return." The return is due by April 15th following the close of the trust's calendar year. The trustee must file a Schedule K-1 for each beneficiary. The failure-to-file-penalty under IRC Sec. 6652(c)(2)(C) will be imposed on a split-interest trust for failure to file timely, completely, or correctly unless the failure is due to reasonable cause. The penalty is $20 for each day the failure continues with a maximum of $10,000 for any one return. However, if the trust has gross income greater than $250,000, the penalty is $100 for each day the failure continues with a maximum of $500,000 for any one return.

(e) Consistency Requirement Imposed on Beneficiaries. Beneficiaries of a trust or estate are required to file their returns in a manner consistent with the manner reported on the trust or estate's return, or must file a notice that identifies the inconsistency [IRC Sec. 6034A(c)]. If a beneficiary fails to identify the inconsistent treatment, any adjustment necessary in order to make the treatment of the items by the beneficiary consistent with the treatment of the items on the entity's return will be treated as a mathematical or clerical error that will be subject to summary assessment procedures [IRC Sec. 6034A(c)(3)(B)]. In addition, a negligence penalty will be imposed [IRC Sec. 6034A(c)(5)].

(f) Estates and Trusts Tax Rates. See ¶ 2935 for the 2013 and 2014 tax rate schedule for estates and trusts.

(g) Tax Planning with Compressed Trust and Estate Tax Rates. The two highest income tax rates imposed on estates and trusts are 33 percent and 39.6 percent rates start at relatively low income levels, respectively, $8,900 and $12,150 of trust taxable income in 2014. With all trust income over $12,150 taxed at the maximum 39.6 percent rate in 2014, it becomes very expensive for beneficiaries to accumulate funds in trusts. By comparison, married couples filing jointly are not subject to the highest tax rate of 39.6 percent until their income exceeds $457,600 in 2014. You should therefore rethink the strategy behind employing the trust vehicle to accumulate money and consider the following strategies to avoid the impact of the tax rates:

- Examine any trust that permits the accumulation of funds with an eye to reducing or eliminating tax at the highest rate. Rather than accumulating income in the trust, consider distributing income to beneficiaries who are in lower tax brackets. Remember that all trust distributions need not be made by year-end to reduce trust income for the year. (To implement these objectives, the trust document should afford the trustee maximum flexibility to make discretionary distributions). Distributions made by a trust or estate in the first 65 days of a tax year are treated as made on the last day of the trust's prior tax year. For example, a distribution on March 1, 2014 will reduce the trust's taxable income for 2013 assuming the trust's tax year closes on December 31, 2013.

  ▶**ALERT:** A decedent's estate may elect to treat distributions made within 65 days after the close of its tax year as if they were made on the last day of the tax year [IRC Sec. 663(b)].

¶2820

- Generate income tax deductions by paying estate or trust expenses prior to the end of the estate's or trust's tax year (65 day rule does *not* apply to these expenses).

- Select investment vehicles that generate growth rather than current income. The objective is to reduce trust income thereby avoiding tax at the highest tax rate. Consideration should be given to investing in tax-exempt bonds, keeping in mind, however, that the eventual yield may be less with tax-exempt investments than with other investments. The trust creator's objectives should be kept in mind when changing the investment strategy of a trust.

- An alternative to accumulating income in the trust would be to establish custodial accounts for minors pursuant to your state's Uniform Transfer to Minors Act or Uniform Gifts to Minors Act. Income from these accounts would be taxed at the child's tax rate if the child is 18 years of age or older. These accounts are not only simple to administer but also qualify as gifts of a present interest and thus are eligible for the annual gift tax exclusion of $14,000 per donee in 2014. In addition, the custodian of the account can make expenditures for the minor's benefit until the minor reaches age 21, which is the age of majority in most states. The downside to the Minor's Trusts, however, is that the child has access to the funds when he or she reaches age 21.

- If trusts are being used to hold gift transfers that are expected to generate large amounts of income, be sure to set up a separate trust for each beneficiary rather than a single trust for multiple beneficiaries.

(h) Discharge from Personal Liability. As an executor or administrator, you can apply for release from personal liability for a decedent's income and gift taxes after you have filed the returns for these taxes. You file the application at the office where the estate tax return is to be filed. If no return is required, you file the application where the decedent's last income tax return is to be filed. The IRS must notify you within nine months after receiving the application of the amount of taxes due. You are then relieved from any future deficiencies on paying the amount. You are also discharged if the IRS does not notify you within the nine-month period [IRC Secs. 6905(a), 6905(b); Reg. Sec. 301.6905-1].

¶2821 ALTERNATIVE MINIMUM TAX

The alternative minimum tax (AMT) is a tax directed at high-bracket taxpayers who offset their income either wholly or partially through the clever use of deductions and other items that receive preferential treatment under the tax laws. The AMT, which is a backup tax to the regular taxing system, ensures that these taxpayers pay at least a minimum amount of income tax. Estates and trusts are subject to the same basic AMT rules that apply to individual taxpayers.

The AMT is a separately computed tax that is paid only if it exceeds a trust's or estate's regular tax bill. If the AMT applies to a trust or estate, the entity is taxed at a lower rate but on a much broader base of income. The AMT has a base tax rate of 26 percent on alternative minimum taxable income (AMTI) up to $175,000 and of 28 percent on AMTI over $175,000. To determine whether the trust or estate is subject to the AMT, first you must figure the entity's federal income tax under the regular rules.

Then compute the tax under the rules of the alternative tax. If the entity owes more under the AMT than it owes under the regular tax, it must pay the higher alternative minimum tax.

Calculating the AMT. To calculate the AMT, start with the entity's regular taxable income and add back any adjustments and preferences [IRC Secs. 56(a), 56(b), 57, 59(c)]. These are the tax breaks that are available under the regular tax rules but are disallowed or adjusted for purposes of the AMT [IRC Sec. 56(a)(1)]. In addition to having to add back all the deductions applicable to individuals as listed below, trusts and estates must add back miscellaneous itemized deductions [IRC Sec. 56(b)(1)(A)] including the personal exemption deduction allowed in IRC Sec. 642(b). [IRC Sec. 56(b)(1)(E); see ¶ 2809].

For a list of the items you will have to add back or adjust in your AMT computation see ¶ 2938.

After adding back all these preference items to the entity's taxable income, subtract the entity's standard AMT exemption to get its AMT income (AMTI). An estate or trust is entitled to an exemption of $23,500 in 2014 (increased from $23,100 in 2013). The AMT exemption amount for an estate or trust is reduced in 2014 by 25 percent for each $1 of AMTI in excess of $78,250 (50% of the exemption phaseout threshold amount for marrieds-filing-jointly/surviving spouse) [IRC Sec. 55(d)(3)].

Finally, you will compare your AMT bill with the entity's regular tax bill, and pay whichever is higher. Estates and trusts must pay the alternative minimum tax (AMT) to the extent the AMT exceeds the regular tax liability. Estates and trusts compute the alternative minimum tax on Schedule H (Alternative Minimum Tax) of Form 1041 [see Chapter 29].

¶ 2822 PAYMENT BY ESTATES AND TRUSTS

An estate or trust must pay estimated income tax for 2014 if it expects to owe, after subtracting any withholding and credits, at least $1,000 in tax, and it expects the withholding and credits to be less than the smaller of:

1. 90 percent of the tax shown on the 2014 tax return, or

2. 100 percent of the tax shown on the 2013 tax return (110 percent of that amount for tax years beginning in 2013 if the estate's or trust's adjusted gross income on that return is more than $150,000, and less than two-thirds of the gross income for 2013 or 2014 is from farming or fishing).

However, if a return was not filed for 2013 or that return did not cover a full 12 months, the second requirement does not apply.

Exceptions: Estimated tax payments are not required from:

1. An estate of a domestic decedent or a domestic trust that had no tax liability for the full 12-month 2013 tax year [IRC Sec. 6654(i)(2)(A)];

2. A decedent's estate for any tax year ending before the date that is two years after the decedent's death; or

3. A trust that was treated as owned by the decedent if the trust will receive the residue of the decedent's estate under the will (or if no will

is admitted to probate, the trust primarily responsible for paying debts, taxes, and expenses of administration) for any tax year ending before the date that is two years after the decedent's death.

(a) How Payments of Estimated Tax Are Made. Estates and trusts make payments of estimated tax on Form 1041-ES. This form is used to calculate and pay the estimated tax. The installment payments are due April 15, June 15, September 15, and January 15 of the following year. See ¶ 2930.

(b) Section 643(g) Election. Fiduciaries of trusts that pay estimated tax may elect under IRC Sec. 643(g) to have any portion of their estimated tax payments allocated to any of the beneficiaries. In this case, the estimated tax payments will not be treated as payments made by the trust. The election is made on Form 1041-T (Allocation of Estimated Tax Payments to Beneficiaries) and must be filed on or before the 65th day after the close of the trust's tax year [IRC Sec. 643(g)].

The fiduciary of a decedent's estate may make a Sec. 643(g) election only for the final year of the estate.

¶ 2823 GRANTOR TRUST RULES

In a grantor trust, the grantor possesses sufficient specifically enumerated rights and/or interests in or over a trust to be considered the owner of the trust. Therefore, all or part of the income of a trust will be taxed to the person who set it up or the "grantor" rather than to the trust and its beneficiaries. For detailed discussion of the grantor trust rules, see Chapter 31.

¶ 2824 PRE-NEED QUALIFIED FUNERAL TRUSTS

A pre-need qualified funeral trust (QFT) is an arrangement where someone purchases funeral services or merchandise from a funeral home prior to death. The person enters into a contract with the provider of the funeral services or merchandise and selects the services or merchandise to be provided upon his or her death, and agrees to pay for them in advance of death. Such amounts are held in trust during the person's lifetime and are paid to the funeral home when he or she dies.[1]

IRC Sec. 685 provides that the trustee of a QFT can elect special tax treatment for the trust.

QFTs are taxed at the entity level, with one simplified annual return (Form 1041-QFT) filed by the trustee reporting the aggregate income from all such trusts he or she administered.

If the trustee of a pre-need funeral trust elects the special tax treatment available under IRC Sec. 685, the trust will not be treated as a grantor trust and the tax on the annual earnings of the trust must be paid by the trustee. The tax will be imposed

---

[1] ¶ 2824 Committee Report of the Taxpayer Relief Act of 1997 (Pub. L. No. 105-34), Act Sec. 1309.

according to the income tax rate schedule generally applicable to trusts and estates [see ¶ 2820].

Even though the trustee will report the aggregate income from all pre-need funeral trusts that he or she administers on a single annual trust return (Form 1041-QFT), each beneficiary's interest will be treated as a separate trust. No deduction for personal exemption under IRC Sec. 642(b) will be allowed in calculating the tax. The trustee will have to make a separate election for each trust.

Conditions for QFT status. The following trusts qualify for the special pre-need funeral trust election [IRC Sec. 685(b)]:

1. The trust arises as the result of a contract with a person engaged in the trade or business of providing funeral or burial services or property necessary to provide such services;

2. The sole purpose of the trust is to hold, invest, and reinvest the trust funds and to use the funds solely to make payments for such services or property for the beneficiaries of the trust;

3. The only beneficiaries of the trust are individuals who have entered into contracts to have such services or merchandise provided upon their death;

4. The only contributions to the trust are contributions by or for the benefit of the trust's beneficiaries;

5. A qualified funeral trust cannot accept aggregate contributions by or for the benefit of an individual without regard to a dollar limitation [IRC Sec. 685(c)].

For this purpose, "contributions" include all amounts transferred to the trust, regardless of how denominated in the contract. Contributions do not include, however, income or gain earned by the property in the trust. A trust will be deemed to exceed the contribution limit if the trust is determined, over the anticipated life of the trust, to receive projected contributions (based upon existing contributions, the applicable state law trust contribution requirements, and any expected contributions in excess of the state law requirements) that exceed the contribution limit. The determination is made at the inception of the trust and is made again when the amount of the projected contributions used in the previous determination changes. For example, a trust that is determined at its inception to exceed the contribution limit during the life of the trust will be deemed to exceed the contribution limit at inception. However, a trust that is determined at its inception not to exceed the contribution limit but exceeds the contribution limit in a future year, due to a change in projected contributions, will be deemed to exceed the contribution limit at the time of the change in projected contributions. A trust loses its QFT status at the time that it is deemed to exceed the contribution limit;

6. A trustee may elect QFT status by filing Form 1041-QFT. The election must be filed no later than the due date, with extensions, for filing the trust income tax return for the year of election. The election applies to each trust reported in the QFT return. A QFT election, once made, cannot be revoked without the consent of the IRS;[2]

---

[2] Notice 98-6, 1998-1 CB 337; see also Notice 98-66, 1998-2 CB 810.

7. A QFT will continue to qualify for the election during the 60-day period beginning on the date of the grantor's death, even though the death of the grantor
causes the trust to no longer qualify as a grantor trust [IRC Sec. 685(b)].

¶2825 COMMON TRUST FUNDS

A common trust fund consists of money held by a bank, in a single federally
regulated account, exclusively for investment by the bank in its capacity as a
fiduciary for a number of beneficiaries. The fund is exempt from tax [IRC Sec. 584(b);
Reg. Sec. 1.584-1].

Each participant in the fund, however, is taxed on his or her share of the fund's
income, whether distributed or not [Reg. Sec. 1.584-2]. Consequently, the bank must
file an information return for the fund [IRC Sec. 6032; Reg. Sec. 1.6032-1]. The fund
computes its taxable income in the same manner as an individual, except that capital
gains and losses are segregated, and the fund cannot deduct charitable contributions
or net operating loss [IRC Sec. 584(d); Reg. Secs. 1.584-3, 1.584-6]. The partnership
return Form 1065 may be used [Reg. Sec. 1.6032-1].

When participants in a common trust fund compute taxable income, they take into
account the proportionate share of the capital gains or losses, and the taxable income
or net loss of the fund. Excludable interest is allocated to the participants, as is the
fund's net operating loss [IRC Sec. 584(c); Reg. Sec. 1.584-2]. Participants must also
account for their pro rata share of the fund's items of tax preference subject to the
alternative minimum tax [Reg. Sec. 1.58-5].

(a) Withdrawal of Participating Interest. No gain or loss is realized by the
fund on the admission or withdrawal of participants. But the withdrawal of a
participating interest by a participant is treated as a sale or exchange of their interest
resulting in a recognized gain or loss to them [IRC Sec. 584(e)]. A transfer into a new
trust is not a withdrawal of a participating interest.[1]

(b) Tax-Free Transfers to Regulated Investment Companies. A common trust fund can transfer substantially all of its assets to one or more regulated
investment companies (RICs) without gain or loss being recognized by the fund or its
participants. The fund must transfer its assets to the RICs solely in exchange for
shares of the RICs and the fund must distribute the RIC shares to the fund's
participants in exchange for the participants' interests in the fund. The basis of any
RIC shares received by a fund participant are an allocable portion of the participant's
basis in the interests exchanged [IRC Sec. 584(h)].

¶2826 LIVING TRUSTS (REVOCABLE TRUSTS)

Living trusts are commonly referred to as the panacea for all estate planning woes.
Also known as revocable trusts, living trusts have been aggressively marketed in

---

[1] ¶**2825** Wiggin, 59-1 USTC ¶9309 (D. Mass.
1959); Rev. Rul. 60-256, 1960-2 CB 193.

advertisements, seminars, and in mass mailings. Living trusts, however, are not for everyone and they do *not* solve all estate planning problems. In fact, if improperly used, living trusts can cause some unintended results and may end up costing the very dollars the grantor had hoped to leave to the heirs. There are some advantages to living trusts but promoters of these trusts often overrate the benefits or make blatant generalizations regarding the benefits that are inapplicable to most taxpayers. See ¶ 300.

(a) What Is a Living Trust. A living trust or revocable trust allows an individual to provide for the management of his or her assets in case of mental or physical disability. It is also used to remove assets from a decedent's probate estate. The trust is established during the grantor's lifetime with the grantor as trustee and another person or financial institution named as successor trustee.

The trust is revocable, which means the grantor retains the right to amend or revoke the trust at any time before death or disability. For example, the grantor can change the beneficiaries or the trustee, or alter or amend the terms of the trust agreement while the grantor is still alive. The living trust only becomes irrevocable when the grantor dies or becomes disabled. At the time of the grantor's death, the assets in it are disposed of as provided in the trust agreement, which essentially becomes a will substitute. This means that the living trust will provide for the disposition of the grantor's assets at death but the terms of the disposition will not be a matter of public record.

(b) Election to Treat Revocable Trust as Part of Estate. Executors have the option to make an irrevocable election to treat and tax a qualified revocable trust (QRT) as part of the deceased person's probate estate (rather than a separate trust) for federal income tax purposes [IRC Sec. 645(a)]. If the election is made, an estate is able to keep the revocable trust as is, instead of having to reregister it to the estate. If an estate tax return is required, the election is effective for all tax years of the estate ending after the date of the decedent's death and before the date that is six months after the date of the final determination of estate tax liability [IRC Sec. 645(b)(2)(B)]. However, if no estate tax return is required to be filed, the election is effective for the two years from the date of the decedent's death [IRC Sec. 645(b)(2)(A)].

The election is irrevocable and must be made by both the trustee of the revocable trust and the executor of the decedent's estate by the due date for filing the estate's income tax return for its first tax year (including extensions) [IRC Sec. 645(c)]. Once the deadline for the tax filing due date has passed, it is too late to make this election.

Why is this election a good idea? The election to treat a QRT as part of an estate makes sense because the election will make it possible for the QRT to take advantage of income tax breaks that are only available to estates. The election is designed to ease the estate administrative burdens. If the election to treat a revocable trust as part of the estate is made, only one Form 1041 must be filed, rather than separate returns for the trust and the estate.

Treating a revocable trust as part of a decedent's estate can save taxes because estates receive more favorable tax-treatment than revocable trusts receive for the following reasons:

1. Estates are allowed a charitable deduction for amounts permanently set aside for charitable purposes while post death revocable trusts are allowed a charitable deduction only for amounts paid to charities [IRC Sec. 642(c)];

2. The active participation requirement imposed by the passive loss rules is waived in the case of estates (but not revocable trusts) for two years after the owner's death;

3. Estates (but not revocable trusts) can qualify for the amortization of reforestation expenditures under IRC Sec. 194; and

4. Trusts are required to use calendar years, but estates are not [see ¶ 1802]. By electing to be treated as part of the estate, a qualified revocable trust effectively can have a non-calendar or fiscal tax year during that period and engage in income deferral to postpone the payment of taxes.

5. Another reason for making the election is to avoid the generation-skipping transfer tax. While the election is in effect, the trust is not subject to the generation-skipping transfer tax.

6. The election to combine the revocable trust and the estate can simplify the winding up process traditionally associated with settling an estate. It may even eliminate the need to file a separate income tax return for the revocable trust.

7. Electing qualified revocable trusts may deduct up to $25,000 in real estate passive losses for active rental real estate activities [IRC Sec. 469(i)(4)]. Trusts are typically not entitled to this deduction but qualified revocable trusts electing to be treated as part of an estate would be able to deduct active rental losses realized by the trust on the estate tax return.

8. Electing qualified revocable trusts may qualify for the $600 personal exemption deduction under IRC Sec. 642(b).

9. In a situation where the revocable trust uses a pecuniary formula to fund a testamentary trust (such as a credit shelter or a marital trust), the funding of such trust will cause either a gain or a loss if the assets have changed in value since the date of death. If the assets have declined in value, the loss that results from the funding can only be used if a Section 645 election is in place.

How to make the election. The election may be made whether or not an executor is appointed. If an executor is appointed, the executor and the trustee of the QRT make the election by filing Form 8855, "Election to Treat a Qualified Revocable Trust as Part of an Estate." If an executor is not appointed, the trustee makes the election by filing Form 8855 [Reg. Sec. 1.645-1(c)]. If an executor has been appointed, Form 8855 must be filed no later than the time for filing the Form 1041 for the first tax year of the combined electing trust and related estate. If no executor exists, Form 8855 must be filed no later than the first tax year of the electing trust regardless of income. If an extension is granted for the filing of the Form 1041 for the first tax year of the combined electing trust and related estate, Form 8855 will be timely if it is filed by the extended time for filing Form 1041 [Reg. Sec. 1.634-1(c)].

The fiduciaries of the electing trust and the fiduciaries of the related estate each continue to have a responsibility for filing returns and paying the tax due for their respective entities even though an election to treat a QRT as part of the estate has been made. The executor must file a complete, accurate, and timely Form 1041 for the combined related estate and electing trust for each tax year during the election period. The trustee of the electing trust must timely provide the executor of the related estate with all the trust information necessary to permit the executor to file a complete, accurate, and timely Form 1041 for the combined electing trust and related estate for each tax year during the election period. The trustee and the executor must allocate the tax burden of the combined electing trust and related estate in a manner that reasonably reflects the respective tax obligations of the electing trust and related estate or gifts may result [Reg. Sec. 1.645-1(c)].

The trustee of an electing trust for which an election will be made must obtain a taxpayer identification number (TIN) on the death of the decedent and must furnish it to the payors of the trust. The trustee must also use this TIN to file Forms 1041 as an estate during the election period. If an election will be made for a QRT, its trustee need not file a Form 1041 for the short tax year beginning with the decedent's date of death and ending December 31 of that year [Reg. Sec. 1.645-1(d)].

(c) What Revocable Trusts Qualify for the Election. To qualify for the election, the revocable trust must be a "qualified revocable trust." A QRT is defined as any trust, or portion of a trust, that on the date of the death of the decedent was treated as owned by the decedent because of a power held by the decedent [IRC Sec. 645(b)(1)]. Retained powers could include the power to revoke the trust or the power to affect beneficial enjoyment of the income for a period commencing after the occurrence of some stated event [IRC Sec. 676]. A power, exercisable by the decedent with the approval or consent of a nonadverse party does not prevent the trust from being treated as a QRT [Reg. Sec. 1.645-1(b)(1)]. Conversely, if only the spouse, and not the decedent, holds power to revoke, the trust is not a QRT.

> **Example 1:** Dad was diagnosed with Alzheimer's disease. Before he became incapacitated, he created a revocable trust. Mom retained the right to change the income beneficiaries after Dad became incapacitated. This trust will not qualify for the election to be treated as part of Dad's probate estate after his death because the power over the trust was held by Mom rather than Dad.

You still need a will. Living trusts should always be accompanied by a pour-over will, which will dispose of all assets which were not transferred into the trust. In addition, the will can accomplish things that cannot be achieved with a trust. This includes appointing guardians for minor and/or disabled children and appointing an executor to handle any probate assets.

In order for the revocable trust to be able to manage your assets when you become disabled, during your lifetime you must transfer everything you own into the trust. The terms of the trust designate the trustee and govern the management and disposition of the assets in the trust by directing how they are to be invested and indicating who will receive income and principal distributions from the trust.

The trustee will hold legal title to all property transferred into the trust and in his or her capacity as a fiduciary, is bound by the terms of the trust document. When the trust terminates or is changed, legal title reverts back to you or vests in the beneficiaries designated in the trust document. In most living trusts the trust grantor (person transferring property into the trust) is the trustee of his own living trust. It is only after the grantor becomes incapacitated or dies that a successor trustee is appointed.

¶2826

The trustee can be an individual, a bank, or a financial institution. It is advisable to name one or more alternate trustees and to name a financial institution as a final alternate trustee. Otherwise, if a sole trustee dies or otherwise becomes unable to serve as trustee, court proceedings will be required to administer the terms of the living trust.

(d) Who Is a Good Candidate for a Living Trust. You should consider a revocable trust whenever you expect someone to become incapacitated or experience decreased mental acuity as a result of illness or a disease. Someone with a terminal illness would be a good candidate for a living trust because they can expect to experience physical or mental incapacity before death.

> ▶ **PRACTICE WARNING: Retitle all your assets.** The only way for the living trust to be effective in providing for the management of your assets when needed, is to be sure that your assets are transferred into the trust. This means that you must retitle all your assets into the name of the trustee of your living trust. For example, your bank accounts should be retitled to read, "Your Name, Trustee under the Trust Agreement of Your Name, dated 10/25/14." It is critical that this often expensive and time-consuming step not be overlooked.

All securities, brokerage accounts, cars, deeds to property, and bank accounts must be retitled so they will be owned by the trustee of the living trust, not you individually. If you own real estate it must be transferred into your living trust. This means that you will have to draw up a new deed in the name in the trustee and record it in the land records office. If the property is mortgaged, the lender's approval will be required to transfer ownership of the property to the trustee and avoid triggering an acceleration clause in the mortgage.

In addition, if you own an interest in a partnership or closely held corporation, you will need permission of the other partners or shareholders to transfer your interest to your living trust. In addition, you should be aware that a transfer of S corporation stock to a living trust could jeopardize the S election after your death. The living trust can only continue to hold your S corporation stock for two years after you die [IRC Sec. 1361(c)(2)(A)]. An estate, in contrast, can hold the S corporation stock for a reasonable period of administration, which will usually be longer than two years.

Other problems may arise if you want to transfer your interest in a co-operative apartment to your living trust. You will need permission of the co-op's board and this will often be denied. You will then be forced to sell your co-op interest to the trustee of your living trust and pay the resulting closing costs, transfer fees, and attorney's fees.

(e) What Not to Transfer. You should avoid transferring ownership of your life insurance policy and your retirement accounts into your living trust. The life insurance proceeds will be subject to estate tax if you own the policy directly or control the policy through your living trust. To avoid estate tax on the life insurance proceeds, it is preferable to have an irrevocable life insurance trust own your policy. Retirement accounts should not be transferred into your living trust. A better bet if you are married, is to name your spouse as beneficiary. He or she can then roll over your retirement account into his or her own retirement account and achieve continued tax-free income accumulation on the assets.

(f) Myths and Realities About Living Trusts.

Living trusts are commonly referred to as the panacea for all estate planning woes. Also known as revocable trusts, living trusts are often aggressively promoted in advertisements, estate planning seminars, and in mass mailings directed to seniors. Living trusts, however, are not suitable for everyone and taxpayers need to aware the do *not* solve all estate planning problems and can even have adverse tax consequences. In fact, if used inappropriately, living trusts can cause some unintended results and may end up costing the very dollars the decedent had hoped to leave to loved ones. There are some advantages to living trusts but promoters of these trusts often overrate the benefits, understate the disadvantages, and make blatant generalizations that are inapplicable to most taxpayers. The following discussion aims to dispell some of the myths and misconceptions commonly associated with living trusts.

Myth and Misconception. Living trusts are appropriate for all taxpayers.

Reality. A living trust can be a useful estate planning tool when used to provide for the management of assets when a taxpayer becomes mentally or physically incapacitated. The trust must be established during the lifetime of the grantor (the person creating the trust) with the grantor as trustee and another person or financial institution named as successor trustee. This management feature makes the living trust an attractive option for taxpayers who do not want to manage their own property.

The grantor transfers property into the trust and when appropriate, the trustee manages the assets. The living trust is revocable, which means the grantor retains the right to amend or revoke the trust at any time before death or disability. For example, the grantor can change the beneficiaries or the trustee, or alter or amend the terms of the trust agreement while still alive. The living trust only becomes irrevocable when the grantor dies or is physically or mentally unable to manage his or her affairs. At the time of the grantor's death, assets that have been transferred into the trust are disposed of as provided in the trust agreement, which essentially becomes a will substitute.

A living trust is suitable for a person in poor physical or mental health or one who doesn't have the desire or ability to make prudent investment decisions. This feature of the living trust is its biggest selling point and affords a valuable commodity— peace of mind. Without a living trust, if a person becomes incapacitated, his or her family may be forced to iniate court proceedings to appoint a guardian or conservator of the person's property. These court proceedings can be inconvenient, time-consuming, and emotionally draining.

A living trust is also suitable for a taxpayer who owns real estate in two or more states because ownership of property in more than one state would require the filing of probate documents in each state. To avoid these ancillary probate proceedings, the taxpayer can transfer title of the real estate from the state, other than the state of domicile, into the living trust. Be sure, however, to check the laws in the other states to determine exposure to transfer tax.

Myth and Misconception. After the living trust has been created no additional steps are necessary to implement the objectives of the trusts.

Reality. A living trust will only be effective in providing for the management of assets when needed if the grantor transfers all assets to be managed into the trust.

¶2826

This means that all assets must be retitled into the name of the trustee of the living trust. For example, all bank accounts should be retitled to read, "Name of fill in name of grantor, Trustee under the Trust Agreement of fill in name of grantor, dated fill in date living trust created." It is critical that this often expensive and time-consuming step not be overlooked. All securities, brokerage accounts, cars, real estate, and bank accounts must be retitled and transferred into the living trust. In the case of real estate, a new deed in the name in the trustee must be drafted and recorded in the land records office. If the property is mortgaged, the lender's approval will be required to transfer ownership of the property to the trustee and avoid triggering a mortgage acceleration clause.

In addition, if the grantor owns an interest in a partnership or closely held corporation, the grantor will need permission of the other partners or shareholders to transfer ownership of his or her pro rata share to a living trust. Keep in mind that transfer of S corporation stock to a living trust could jeopardize the S election after death of the grantor. The living trust can only continue to hold S corporation stock for two years after the death of the grantor whereas an estate can hold the S corporation stock for a reasonable period of administration, which will usually be longer than two years [IRC Sec. 1361(c)(2)(A)].

Prior to the transfer of an interest in a co-operative apartment to a living trust, the grantor will need permission of the board of directors of the co-op. Some co-ops do not allow ownership interests to be transferred into a living trust and permission may be denied. If this occurs, the grantor will be forced to sell his or her co-op interest to the trustee of the living trust and pay any resulting closing costs, transfer fees, and attorney's fees.

Myth and Misconception. The grantor should transfer all assets into the revocable trust.

Reality. The grantor should avoid transferring ownership of his or her life insurance policy and retirement accounts into the living trust. The life insurance proceeds will be subject to estate tax if at the time of death, the grantor owns the policy directly or controls the policy indirectly through the living trust. To avoid a costly estate tax bill on the life insurance proceeds, it is preferable to have an irrevocable life insurance trust own the life insurance policy.

Retirement accounts should not be transferred into a living trust. A better choice if the grantor is married, is to name his or her spouse as beneficiary. The surviving spouse can then roll over the retirement account into his or her own retirement account and achieve continued tax-free income accumulation on the assets.

Myth or Misconception. Living trusts will reduce estate taxes.

Reality. Taxpayers should forget everything they have ever heard about living trusts reducing estate tax. Living trusts do *not* reduce estate taxes. The assets in a living trust are fully includible in the decedent's taxable estate upon death because the assets remain under the decedent's control under IRC Sec. 2036.

Myth or Misconception. Living trusts will reduce federal income taxes for the grantor prior to and after death.

Reality. A living trust does not achieve any federal income tax savings because it is considered a grantor trust for federal income tax purposes as a result of the grantor's retention of control over the property in the trust. This means that while the grantor is living, all the income, capital gains, deduction and credits of the trust must be included in determining the grantor's federal income tax liability as if the trust did not exist.

After the grantor's death, living trusts have the following federal income tax consequences:

1. A living trust must report income on the calendar year basis, whereas an estate may select a fiscal year. The ability to select a fiscal year enables an estate to defer recognition of post-death income for up to 11 months, thus deferring the payment of federal income tax for an entire year;

2. A living trust is only entitled to a $100 exemption, unless the trust instrument requires that all income be distributed each year, in which case the exemption is increased to $300. An estate, in contrast, is entitled to a $600 personal exemption each year;

3. The trustees of a living trust must make estimated income tax payments after the decedent's death unless what is left of the estate passes under the pour-over will into the living trust. An estate, in contrast, need not pay estimated income tax for the first two fiscal years after the decedent's death;

4. If the decedent had passive activity losses attributable to active participation in rental real estate, the living trust may not deduct those losses whereas the decedent's estate may deduct up to $25,000 of those passive activity losses.

▶**PLANNING POINTER: Election to Treat Qualified Revocable Trust Part of Decedent's Estate.** A personal representative or executor settling the estate of the decedent may make an irrevocable election to treat a qualified revocable trust (QRT) as part of the decedent's estate (rather than a separate trust) for federal income tax purposes [IRC Sec. 645(a)]. A QRT is defined as any trust, or portion of a trust, that on the date of the death of the decedent was treated as owned by the decedent because of a power held by the decedent [IRC Sec. 645(b)(1)]. Retained powers could include the power to revoke the trust or the power to affect beneficial enjoyment of the income for a period commencing after the occurrence of some stated event [IRC Sec. 676].

If an estate tax return is required, the election is effective for all tax years of the estate ending after the date of the decedent's death and before the date that is six months after the date of the final determination of estate tax liability [IRC Sec. 645(b)(2)(B)]. However, if no estate tax return must be filed, the election is effective for the two years from the date of the decedent's death [IRC Sec. 645(b)(2)(A)]. The election may be made whether or not an executor is appointed. If an executor is appointed, the executor and the trustee of the QRT make the election by filing Form 8855, "Election to Treat a Qualified Revocable Trust as Part of an Estate." If an executor is not appointed, the trustee makes the election by filing Form 8855 no later than the first tax year of the electing trust regardless of income. If an extension is granted for the filing of the Form 1041 for the first tax year of the combined electing trust and related estate, Form 8855 will be timely if it is filed by the extended time for filing Form 1041 [Reg. Sec. 1.634-1(c)].

The election to treat a QRT as part of an estate makes sense because the election will ease administrative burdens and make it possible for the QRT to take

¶2826

advantage of income tax breaks that are only available to estates. For example, if the election is made, only one Form 1041 must be filed for both the trust and the estate. In addition, if an election is made, the trustees need not file a Form 1041 for the short tax year beginning with the decedent's date of death and ending December 31 of that year [Reg. Sec. 1.645-1(d)].

Making an election to treat a QRT as part of a decedent's estate can save federal income taxes for the following reasons:

1. Estates are allowed a charitable deduction for amounts permanently set aside for charitable purposes whereas QRTs are allowed a charitable deduction only for amounts paid to charities [IRC Sec. 642(c)].

2. Estates (but not revocable trusts) can qualify for the amortization of reforestation expenditures under IRC Sec. 194.

3. Trusts are required to use calendar years, but estates are not. By electing to be treated as part of the estate, a QRT effectively can have a non-calendar or fiscal tax year during that period and engage in income deferral to postpone the payment of taxes.

4. While the election is in effect, the trust is not subject to the generation-skipping transfer tax.

5. The election to combine the QRT and the estate can simplify the winding up process traditionally associated with settling an estate.

6. Electing QRTs may deduct up to $25,000 in real estate passive losses for active rental real estate activities [IRC Sec. 469(i)(4)]. Trusts are typically not entitled to this deduction but QRTs electing to be treated as part of an estate would be able to deduct active rental losses realized by the trust on the estate tax return.

7. Electing QRTs may qualify for the $600 personal exemption deduction under IRC Sec. 642(b).

8. In a situation where the revocable trust uses a pecuniary formula to fund a testamentary trust (such as a credit shelter or marital trust), the funding of such trust will cause either a gain or a loss if the assets change in value after the date of death. If the assets have declined in value, the resulting loss can only be used if an election to treat a QRT as part of the decedent estate under IRC Sec. 645 election is in place.

Myth or Misconception. Living trusts act as will substitutes and no will is needed.

Reality. Living trusts should always be accompanied by a pour-over will, which will dispose of all assets which were not transferred into the trust. In addition, a will is still needed for administrative tasks such as nominating guardians for minor and/or disabled children, exercising testamentary powers of appointment (designating to whom property should be distributed after death), and to be sure that all property that was not transferred into the living trust is distributed according to the taxpayer's wishes after death. Even if the grantor is meticulous about transferring all assets into the living trust, often overlooked are inheritances, debts that are finally repaid, or lottery winnings. As a result the "pour-over" will has the job of pouring over any forgotten assets into the living trusts to be distributed according to the terms of the trust.

¶2826

Myth or Misconception. Living trusts provide protection from creditors.

Reality. The question of whether the trust assets are protected from the claims of creditors depends upon local law. In general, assets transferred to a living trust are not protected from the reach of creditors because most states provide that the grantor's creditors can reach the assets of a revocable living trust during the grantor's lifetime. After the grantor's death, creditors typically have three years from the date of death to make a claim against the assets held in a trust. Under the Medicaid rules, assets held in a grantor's living trust must be used to pay the grantor's expenses to the same extent as if the grantor owned the assets in his or her name alone.

Another consideration is the loss of protection from creditors that can result from transferring assets into a living trust. In some states, special protection is available by statute for certain assets owned by a husband and wife as tenants by the entirety (t-by-e). This means that a creditor of one spouse may not seek satisfaction of the debt from assets owned t-by-e. Taxpayers who split their t-by-e assets into tenancy in common interests to transfer them into a living trust will lose the benefit of this protection.

Myth and Misconception. Living trusts will avoid the complicated, expensive probate process.

Reality. Only the property that a taxpayer owns at death in his or her name alone is subject to probate which is the process whereby a court supervises the distribution of the assets that a person owns individually, as opposed to assets that pass automatically upon death to beneficiaries or joint owners, such as life insurance proceeds, retirement plan proceeds, and jointly owned assets.

Probate is not all bad; it can serve a useful purpose if the decedent's estate has debts or claims from creditors. The probate process provides a forum for settling those claims without a lawsuit and allows supervision of estate administration by the probate court providing notice to beneficiaries, who are given an opportunity to object. In contrast, a beneficiary of a living trust may have to sue a trustee in order to challenge the trustee's actions.

Although living trust promoters often advertise that living trusts will avoid probate entirely, this is not always true. Although a living trust will avoid probate on the assets that have been transferred into the trust (because the grantor no longer owns the assets after they have been transferred into the trust) the executor will still have to probate the assets not transferred into the trust. These are the assets covered by the pour-over will.

Another myth that must be dispelled is one regarding the high costs of probating an estate. Even though the probate fee structure differs from state to state making it difficult to generalize, it is fair to say that the fees charged by many probate courts are not exorbitant and they may even be deductible. Although there definitely are court costs and legal fees associated with the probate process, these future costs may be less than the costs associated with setting up the living trust. Taxpayers who want to avoid probate entirely, rather than resorting to a living trust, should jointly own property with another person so that upon death, the joint owner will own the property by operation of law without any further judicial intervention.

Myth and Misconception. Living trusts will reduce legal and accounting fees.

Reality. The costs, related fees and administrative burdens associated with creating a living trust, pour-over will, and transferring all assets into the trust are likely to exceed the cost of drafting a typical will and durable power of attorney.

Myth and Misconception. A living trust will afford the taxpayer privacy.

Reality. Promoters of living trusts often argue that living trusts will shield the nature of the taxpayer's assets and the identity of the taxpayer's beneficiaries from the public view because no probate will be involved. Although it is true that a living trust need not be filed in the probate court and thus expose the decedent's personal business to public scrutiny, taxpayers are often required to reveal the contents of a living trust to banks, financial institutions, or brokerage houses before opening an account. If privacy is a major concern, rather than creating a living trust, the executor should have a court seal the records of an estate including the will.

Myth and Misconception. Living trusts are the only legal device available to manage a taxpayer's financial affairs after he or she becomes physically or mentally incapacitated.

Reality. The durable power of attorney can achieve many of the same objectives of the living trust with much less expense and paperwork. Taxpayers should make certain, however, that their power of attorney is "durable" and remains in effect after the taxpayer has become incapacitated or otherwise unable to make decisions on his or her own. A power of attorney is simply an authorization in writing for one person to act in the place of another. The person granting the authorization is called the "principal" and the person receiving the authorization is called the "agent" or the "attorney-in-fact." With the proper authorization, the attorney-in-fact can deposit, write and endorse checks, pay bills, buy and sell property or investments, and even mortgage and convey real estate in the name of the principal.

Myth and Misconception. Living trusts eliminate delays associated with estate settlement and property distribution.

Reality. After the decedent's death, property will not be distributed to beneficiaries any faster from a living trust than from a will. No property will be distributed until all property has been valued and the estate taxes paid because trustees of a living trust and executors under a will are personally liable for any federal estate tax that may be due and will not make a final distribution until those taxes have been paid.

In conclusion, before taxpayers create living trusts they should consult an estate planning expert and carefully address all the advantages and disadvantages associated with these estate planning devices.

¶ 2827 TRUST REFORMATION

When trust documents no longer accomplish their intended goal, state law must first be consulted to determine how and when the terms of the trust can be modified. The trust document will typically specify which state's law should apply. The following five methods are available under state law: (1) construction, (2) reformation, (3) amendment, (4) division, and (5) decanting.

(a) Construction Proceedings. One way of modifying estate planning documents, including trusts, is in a construction proceeding which gives the court an opportunity to determine a testatrix's or a settlor's intent when the words of the will or trust are ambiguous or when the term of the document fail to account for a particular contingency that has occurred.

(b) Reformation. In a reformation proceeding, a court is faced with unambiguous language that fails to accomplish what the court concludes the settlor intended in the document. The court does not, in a reformation proceeding, determine what the settlor intended by the words that were used but, rather, is attempting to determine what words would have been used if settlor had been aware of a particular set of circumstances or laws.

(c) Amendment. The terms of a trust instrument or state statute will typically specify whether the trustees or beneficiaries have the power to amend a trust instrument.

(d) Division. The ability to divide a trust may emanate from common law, state statute, or the terms of the trust agreement. Dividing a trust may be useful to accomplish both tax and non-tax objectives.

(e) Decanting. Decanting is the term used to describe the act of a trustee distributing or paying trust property directly to another trust with updated or changed terms in order to achieve a variety of favorable tax and non-tax objectives. In general, decanting is the discretionary authority to distribute some or all the assets of one trust (a "Distributing Trust") to another (often new) trust (a "Receiving Trust") pursuant to a power or appointment, the governing instrument, or applicable state law, without the need for prior court approval or the prior consent of any beneficiary of the trust.

Decanting can be used to deal with changes in law, reform the terms of a trust, address trust administration problems or handle changed circumstances. The term "decanting" is aptly used because the act of paying trust property to another trust is similar to the act of pouring wine from one container to another which is also referred to as decanting. Decanting is a valuable tool for trustees and beneficiaries because this device will enable them to change the terms of trusts without having to petition a court to make necessary changes to trust terms or make corrections. Court proceedings should be avoided because they can be time-consuming, costly and the court may not agree to the requested trust modifications.

The first court to address decanting was the Supreme Court of Florida (the highest court of the state) in *Phipps v. Palm Beach Trust. Co.,*[1] where the court held that a trustee could invade trust property by paying it over to another trust for the beneficiary. This decision suggests that decanting may be also available under the common law of other states. No court has held that there is no such fiduciary power under common law. It may, however, be advisable to proceed with decanting only if authorized under specific state statute.

There are at least 21 states that adopted decanting statutes but not all state decanting statutes are alike. Some state decanting statutes permit decanting only if the trustee's

---

[1] ¶ 2827 Phipps v. Palm Beach Trust Co., 142 Fla. 782, 196 So. 299 (1940) (citing Restatement of Trusts §17); Wiedenmayer v. Johnson, 106 N.J. Super. 161, 164-65 (App. Div.), *aff'd sub. nom.* Wiedenmayer v. Super, 55 N.J. 81 (1969). See also In re Estate of Spencer, 232 N.W.2d 491 (Iowa 1975); Morse v. Kratt, 466 Mass. 92 (2013).

power to invade the trust is absolute or broad rather than being limited to health, education, maintenance and support. Most expressly require that an income interest cannot be eliminated but must be preserved. Some, but not all, statutes provide that the decanting power cannot be used to extend the term of the trust beyond the applicable rule against perpetuities.

The act of decanting is similar to the exercise of a special power of appointment over trust property or to the discretionary distribution of property from a trust by the trustee to a beneficiary. Some states expressly state that the power to invade is a special power of appointment while other states expressly state that the power is not exercisable in favor of the trustee, the trustee's estate, the trustee's creditors or the creditors of the trustee's estate. The restriction is intended to avoid having the power to decant treated as a general power of appointment includible in the gross estate under IRC Sec. 2041.

Trust terms authorizing decanting. The terms of a trust agreement may grant the trustee the power to distribute assets to another trust. In a state where state statute does not authorize decanting or, if the state law requirements regarding decanting are not acceptable to the settlor, it is advisable to give the trustee power to decant in the trust document.

Reasons for decanting. Decanting can be used to:

- Update or modify trust provisions;
- Improve trust administration or management;
- Correct drafting errors without the necessity of going to court;
- Address changed circumstances, such as changes in applicable fiduciary law or changes in family circumstances or dynamics;
- Remove unworkable restrictions;
- Change provisions relating to trust powers and succession;
- Achieve tax savings;
- Change trust situs;
- Combine or divide trusts;
- For GST planning;
- Protect the tax treatment of a trust;
- Grant a beneficiary a power of appointment, presently exercisable or otherwise;
- Reduce administrative costs;
- Alter trusteeship provisions such as the identity or manner of appointing fiduciaries;
- Extend the termination date of a trust;
- Convert a nongrantor trust to a grantor trust or the reverse;
- Change a trust's governing law;
- Divide trust property to create separate trusts;
- Reduce potential liability;
- Convert a trust into a supplemental needs trust to permit a beneficiary to qualify for certain governmental benefits;
- Make trust interests spendthrift or the reverse; and
- Modify administrative provisions, such as restrictions on investment powers or to create a directed trust.

SAMPLE INCOME TAX RETURNS FOR TRUSTS

TABLE OF CONTENTS

¶2900 PREPARATION OF FORM 1041: INCOME TAX RETURN FOR TRUSTS—FILING BASICS

The fiduciary of a trust is obligated to pay income tax on the income earned by the trust because, in general, estates and trusts are separate taxpaying entities [IRC Sec. 641(b)]. An exception exists for a special class of trusts known as grantor trusts, which are not considered separate legal entities for federal tax purposes. In a grantor trust the person creating the trust is treated as the owner of the trust assets for tax purposes. See ¶¶3100–3105 for a further discussion.

Fiduciaries use IRS Form 1041, "U.S. Income Tax Return for Estates and Trusts," to report the income earned by a trust and to pay the tax that is due.

The fiduciary must report the following on Form 1041:

1. The income, deductions, gains, losses, etc. of the estate or trust;

2. The income that is either accumulated or held for future distribution or distributed currently to the beneficiaries;

3. Any income tax liability of the estate or trust;

4. Any employment taxes on wages paid to household employees; and

5. Net investment income tax owed by the trust.

> ▶ **PRACTICE POINTER:** Do not be fooled into thinking that estates and trusts are taxed identically just because they use the same tax return (i.e., Form 1041) for filing purposes. They are subject to different tax rules, which will be discussed in detail in this chapter. The rules regarding an income tax return for an estate and a completed income tax return for an estate can be found in Chapter 30.

Checklist of forms. For a checklist of important forms and due dates that an executor, administrator, or personal representative must keep in mind, see ¶3040, IRS Publication 559, Survivors, Executors, and Administrators, Table A, Page 39.

Period covered. The 2013 Form 1041 should be filed for calendar year 2013 and fiscal years beginning in 2013 and ending in 2014. If the return is for a fiscal year or a short tax year (less than 12 months), fill in the tax year space at the top of Form 1041.

The 2013 Form 1041 may also be used for a tax year beginning in 2014 if:

1. The trust has a tax year of less than 12 months that begins and ends in 2014; and

2. The 2014 Form 1041 is not available at the time the trust is required to file its tax return. However, the trust must show its 2014 tax year on the 2013 Form 1041 and incorporate any tax law changes that are effective for tax years beginning after December 31, 2013.

(a) Role of Personal Representative. The responsibilities of the trust fiduciary or personal representative of the decedent's estate include:

- Collecting all of the decedent's assets;
- Paying all of the decedent's creditors;
- Limiting shrinkage of the estate so more assets can be distributed to the decedent's heirs and other beneficiaries;
- Religiously following the dictates of the decedent's will and trusts;
- Filing necessary tax returns when due; and
- Paying the tax that is due up to the date the personal representative is discharged from duties.

The personal representative, who is responsible for settling or handling the administrations of someone's estate, could be either an individual or an organization such as a bank or trust company. Keep in mind when choosing a personal representative that the person must be organized, responsible, and capable of understanding and managing complex financial matters, maintaining detailed records, and attending to all of the details involved with administering an estate. Choose a trusted individual. Winding up someone's affairs is not an easy job, and if no one in the family is up to it, select an attorney or the trust department of a bank that specializes in estate administration.

(b) Form 56—Notice of Fiduciary Relations. The first thing the trust fiduciary must do since he or she is acting on behalf of another person in a fiduciary capacity is to give the District Director of the Internal Revenue Service written notice of the existence of that fiduciary relationship [Reg. Sec. 301.6903-1(a)]. The term "fiduciary" means a guardian, trustee, executor, administrator, receiver, conservator, or any person acting in any fiduciary capacity for another person [IRC Sec. 7701(a)(6); Reg. Sec. 301.6903-1(d)].

The notice may be filed on IRS Form 56, "Notice Concerning Fiduciary Relationship," with the IRS Service Center where the person for whom the fiduciary is acting is required to file tax returns.

Form 56 must state the name and address of the person for whom the fiduciary is acting and the nature of the liability. As soon as this notice is filed, the fiduciary will assume the powers, duties, rights, and privileges imposed under the law. The fiduciary must file satisfactory evidence of his or her authority to act on behalf of another. If the fiduciary role exists by order of court, a certified copy of the court order should be filed.

When the fiduciary role has terminated, the IRS should be notified of the termination so the fiduciary will be relieved of any further duty or liability. The notice of termination must be accompanied by written evidence of the termination [Reg. Sec. 1.301.6903-1(b)].

¶2900

(c) What's New on the 2013 Form 1041.

- *Net Investment Income Tax.* Beginning in 2013, a new 3.8 percent tax is imposed on trusts with net investment income over $11,950 ($12,150 in 2014) [See ¶2935—Form 1041, Schedule G, line 4, Net investment income tax from Form 8960, line 21 for further discussion. See ¶2790 for a copy of the IRS Instructions for Form 8960 and ¶2947 for a sample completed Form 8960 for the Trent Trust. See ¶2948 for background discussion of the NII tax and ¶2949 for a line-by-line discussion of how to complete Form 8960 for the Trent Trust].

- *Form 8960 Required for Estates and Trusts with Net Investment Income.* Beginning in 2013, trusts with net investment income must attach Form 8960, "Net Investment Income Tax—Individuals, Estates and Trusts" to their return [see ¶2935].

- *New Income Tax Rates.* In 2013, the top fiduciary income tax rate increased from 35 percent in 2012 to 39.6 percent in 2013. The top income tax rate imposed on estates and trusts applies to income over $11,950 in 2013 and increases to $12,150 in 2014.

- *New Capital Gains and Qualified Dividend Tax Rates.* In 2013, the maximum tax rate for long-term capital gains and qualified dividends is 20 percent (increased from 15 percent). The 20 percent rate applies to amounts above $11,950. The 0 percent and 15 percent rates continue to apply to certain threshold amounts. The 0% rate applies to amounts up to $2,450. The 15 percent rate applies to amounts above $2,450 and up to $11,950.

- *Form 8949 Required for Trusts.* Beginning in 2013, trusts must use Form 8949, "Sales and Other Dispositions of Capital Assets" to report most capital gains and losses. In prior years, those transactions would have been reported by trusts on Form 1041, Schedule D or Schedule D-1.

- *Higher Tax Rate Imposed on Trusts.* The income tax rates for nongrantor trusts in 2013 was 15 percent, 25 percent, 28 percent, 33 percent and 39.6 percent in 2013. A nongrantor trust will be subject to the top income tax rate of 39.6 percent in 2013 on any taxable income in excess of $11,950.

- *Long-Term Capital Gain and Dividend Tax Rates Increase.* In 2013, the top tax rate for long-term capital gains and qualified dividends increased to 20 percent, up from 15 percent for trusts if the entities sell capital assets that are held for more than 12 months. Beginning in 2013, qualified dividends received by trusts will permanently be taxed at capital gains rates. The 20 percent capital gains tax rate applies to trusts with income above $11,950 in 2013.

- *Item F. Net Operating Loss (NOL) Carryback.* The IRS added a new net operating loss carryback check box in Item F of the heading. Taxpayers should check the box if an amended return is filed for an NOL carryback.

- *Item G. Section 645 Election.* If the estate has made an IRC Sec. 645 election (an election to treat a revocable trust as part of the decedent's estate), the executor must check Item G and provide the taxpayer identification number (TIN) of the electing trust with the greatest assets in the box provided. The executor must also attach a statement to Form 1041 providing the following information for each electing trust: (a) the name of the electing trust, (b) the TIN of the electing trust, and (c) the name and address of the trustee of the electing trust.

¶2900

- *Net Operating Loss Deduction (NOLD).* The IRS revised line 15b to report NOLDs. NOLDs were previously reported on line 15a.

- *Miscellaneous Itemized Deductions.* Miscellaneous itemized deductions subject to the 2 percent floor are now reported on new line 15c.

- *Form 1041 E-Filing.* For tax year 2013, Form 1041 can be e-filed through the Legacy Electronic Management System (EMS) or through Modernized e-File (MeF). Form 8453-F, "U.S. Estate or Trust Income Tax Declaration and Signature for Electronic Filing," will be used for EMS e-filed returns and new Form 8453-FE, "U.S. Estate or Trust Declaration for an IRS E-File Return," will be used for MeF e-filing.

- *Bankruptcy Estate Filing Threshold.* For tax years beginning in 2013, the requirement to file a return for a bankruptcy estate applies only if gross income is at least $10,000.

- *Qualified Disability Trusts.* In 2013, qualified disability trusts can claim an exemption of up to $3,900. A trust with modified adjusted gross income above $250,000 begins to lose part of the exemption deduction. No exemption is allowed for a trust with modified adjusted gross income of $372,500 or more.

- *AMT Tax Brackets Increased on Form 1041, Schedule I.* The threshold for the 28 percent AMT tax bracket increased to amounts over $179,500 in 2013.

- *AMT Exemption Amount and Phase-Out on Form 1041, Schedule I.* In 2013, the AMT exemption amount increased to $23,100. The exemption amount begins to be phased-out at amounts over $76,950 and is completely phased-out at $169,350.

- *Form 1041, Schedule I—Part IV—Line 52 Computation Using Maximum Capital Gains Rates.* Lines were added and lines involving the computation were revised to reflect the changes to the capital gains rates and thresholds.

¶2901 WHICH TRUSTS MUST FILE FORM 1041

The trustee must file Form 1041 for a taxable domestic trust in the following situations:

1. If the trust has taxable income in any amount for the tax year;

2. If the trust has gross income of $600 or more for the year, whether or not it has any taxable income; or

3. If the trust has any beneficiary who is a nonresident alien [IRC Secs. 6012(a)(4), 6012(a)(5)].

(a) Definition of Domestic Trust. A trust is a domestic trust if a U.S. court is able to exercise primary supervision over the administration of the trust, and one or more U.S. persons have the authority to control all substantial decisions of the trust.

(b) Filing Requirements for Nonresident Alien Beneficiaries. Instead of Filing Form 1041, a resident fiduciary of a "foreign trust" (i.e., any trust that is not a domestic trust) must file IRS Form 1040-NR, "U.S. Nonresident Alien Income Tax Return."

(c) Employer Identification Number. Every trust that is required to file Form 1041 must also have an employer identification number (EIN). An EIN is required for filing returns with the IRS and for making tax payments. A new EIN must be obtained when any of the following occurs:

- A trust is created with funds from an estate and the trust is not considered a continuation of the estate;
- A trust changes to an estate;
- A living or inter vivos trust changes to a testamentary trust; or
- A living trust terminates by distributing its property to a residual trust.

A new EIN is not necessary for the following events:

- The fiduciary changes a name or address; or
- The fiduciary or the beneficiaries of a trust change.

The fiduciary of a trust can obtain an EIN by one of the following methods:

- By going to www.irs.gov/businesses and clicking the "Employer ID Numbers" link. The EIN is issued immediately after the application information is validated; or
- By mailing or faxing Form SS-4, "Application for Employer Identification Number." Fiduciaries should be aware that the EIN may take 4–6 weeks if they are applying for the EIN by mail or fax.

If the trust has not received an EIN by the time the return is due, they should write "Applied for" and the application date in the space for the EIN. A social security number should never be substituted for the EIN on a tax return.

¶2902 FACTS APPLICABLE TO SAMPLE INCOME TAX RETURN FOR TRUST

This chapter provides a completed Form 1041, "U.S. Income Tax Return for Estates and Trusts," that has been prepared for a simple trust. A line-by-line explanation of each entry on the form and all supporting schedules are provided.

To take you through a line-by-line explanation of a sample income tax return for a trust, we will guide you through the income tax return to be filed on behalf of the trust created in the will of Jane B. Trent, who died on June 30, 2012. In her will, Jane created a "testamentary trust," which simply means that the trust came into being after Jane died.

Jane's will provides that all of the income from her trust would be payable to her only child, Mary King, for the duration of Mary's life. After Mary dies, anything left in the trust (called the remainder) will be distributed to Mary's two children, Julia and Leonard King.

This type of trust is called a "simple trust" because the trust was required to distribute all its income currently to a beneficiary, Mary King, and was not required to permanently set any money aside for charitable purposes [see ¶2817].

¶2902

The Best Bank was the trustee of Jane Trent's Trust, and the trustee distributed the trust's assets to the trust on February 1, 2013. The trust reports its income on a calendar-year basis and filed its first tax return on Form 1041 for tax year 2013.

The Best Bank must file a Form 1041 for Jane Trent's Trust because it had taxable income for its tax year, which began on February 1, 2013 and ended on December 31, 2013. Form 1041 must be filed by the Best Bank by the fifteenth day of the fourth month following the close of the short tax year [IRC Sec. 6072(a)].

In 2013, the Trent Trust received the following income:

- $2,000 in taxable interest;
- $16,000 in dividends;
- $2,000 in rent from an apartment building that Jane Trent owned when she died;
- $10,000 in net long-term capital gain from the sale of 1,000 shares of XYZ, Inc. stock held for more than 12 months. The trust received a Form 1099-B reporting the transaction and reporting the trust's basis in the stock. Local law provides that capital gains are allocated to trust principal.

The trustee's fees for the year were $4,000. Because local law provides that one-half of the trustee's fees must be paid from trust income and one-half from trust principal, $2,000 of the trustee fees are chargeable against the trust's income. As a result, only $18,000 of the $20,000 in income that the Trent Trust received that year from interest, ordinary dividends, and rent was distributed to the trust beneficiary, Mary King.

The Trent Trust uses the cash receipts and disbursements method of accounting in keeping its books and records. On the first income tax return, the fiduciary must choose the accounting method (cash, accrual, or other) that will be used to report the trust's income. In most situations, the fiduciary will compute taxable income using the method of accounting regularly used in keeping the trust's books and records. The only restriction is that the method chosen must clearly reflect income. Once a method has been selected, it cannot be changed without the consent of the IRS.

In order to change the accounting method, the fiduciary must request IRS approval on IRS Form 3115, "Application for Change in Accounting Method."

The trustee is also required to file a separate Schedule K-1 for each trust beneficiary along with the Form 1041. See ¶3040 for a completed Schedule K-1 for Mary King, the beneficiary of the Trent Trust.

¶2903 TOP OF INCOME TAX RETURN FOR TRUST—FORM 1041

The first line on the top of Form 1041 asks for information regarding the taxable year for which the income tax return for the trust is being filed. If the return is for the calendar year, as is usually the case, leave the space blank. If the return is for a fiscal year or a short tax year (less than 12 months), fill in the tax year space at the top of Form 1041.

Calendar year trusts. All trusts must use a calendar year for accounting purposes [IRC Sec. 644(a)]. The only exceptions are:

1. Trusts exempt from tax under IRC Sec. 501(a); or

2. A charitable trust described in IRC Sec. 4947(a)(1).

A trust that is treated as wholly owned by a grantor (grantor trust) is not required to use a calendar year. Application of the rules of IRC Sec. 644 is not necessary with respect to grantor trusts, because grantor trusts are disregarded for tax purposes and grantors must report the gross income from trust property as if the trust did not exist. See ¶3100 for further discussion of grantor trusts. See ¶2826 for further discussion of revocable living trusts.

If the return is for a short tax year or if a fiscal year is chosen for any one of the three types of trust mentioned above that are eligible for a fiscal year, enter the beginning and ending dates in the spaces for taxable year at the top of Form 1041.

Fiscal year trusts. For fiscal year trusts, file Form 1041 by the fifteenth day of the fourth month following the close of the tax year [IRC Sec. 6072(a); Reg. Sec. 1.6072-1(a)]. If the due date falls on a Saturday, Sunday, or legal holiday, file on the next regular business day [IRC Sec. 7503].

> ■ For the income tax return filed for the Trent Trust the spaces for tax year at the top of the form are left blank because the trust uses the calendar year.

Box A—Type of entity. Check the appropriate box that describes the entity for which the return is being filed. The following options are available:

Decedent's estate. See ¶3002 for explanation.

Simple trust. A simple trust satisfies the following requirements:

1. It is required to distribute all the trust income currently;

2. It does not provide that any amounts are to be paid, permanently set aside, or used for charitable purposes; and

3. It does not distribute amounts allocated to the corpus of the trust [Reg. Sec. 1.651(a)-1].

> ▶ **PRACTICE POINTER:** A trust can be a simple trust for one year and a complex trust for another year. This could occur if, for example, the trust that is required to distribute all income currently is also required in the year of termination to distribute corpus. In that final year, the trust would be a complex trust.

Complex trust. A complex trust is any trust that does not qualify as a simple trust. See ¶2818 for further discussion.

Qualified disability trust. A qualified disability trust is any nongrantor trust:

1. Established solely for the benefit of an individual under 65 years of age who is disabled; and

2. All the beneficiaries of which are determined by the Commissioner of Social Security to have been disabled for some part of the tax year.

A trust will not fail to meet #2 above just because the trust's corpus may revert to a person who is not disabled after the trust ceases to have any disabled beneficiaries. See ¶2925 for exemptions allowed to a qualified disability trust.

ESBT (S Portion Only). The S portion of an electing small business trust (ESBT) is the portion of the trust that consists of S corporation stock and that is not treated as owned by the grantor or another person. The S portion of an ESBT is the portion of the trust that consists of stock in one or more S corporations and is not treated as a grantor type trust.

Grantor type trust. A grantor type trust is a trust where the person creating the trust is treated as the owner of the trust assets so that the trust is not treated as a separate taxpayer. See ¶¶ 3100–3105 for further discussion of grantor trusts.

Bankruptcy estate. See ¶ 3002, for explanation.

Pooled income fund. A pooled income fund is a split-interest trust maintained by a charity to which wealthy individuals transfer money or property and receive in return a pro rata share of all income earned by the fund based on the amount contributed to the pooled income fund. The charity gets the remainder interest after the individual's death [see IRC Sec. 642(c)].

The holder of the lead/income interest receives "participation units," which fluctuate in valuation according to the performance of the pooled income fund. Think of a pooled income fund as a mutual fund maintained by a charity with the annual income going to a noncharitable beneficiary and the remainder going to the charity.

A pooled income fund must file an income tax return and attach a statement to support the following:

- The calculation of the yearly rate of return;
- The computation of the deduction for distributions to the beneficiaries; and
- The computation of any charitable deduction.

Schedule A or B of Form 1041 need not be completed, but Form 5227, "Split-Interest Trust Information Return" must be filed for the pooled income fund. However, if all the amounts were transferred in trust before May 27, 1969, or if an amount was transferred to the trust after May 26, 1969, for which no deduction was allowed, then Form 5227 need not be filed. Form 1041-A is no longer filed by pooled income funds.

If the pooled income fund has accumulations of income, file Form 1041-A unless the fund is required to distribute all of its net income to beneficiaries currently.

■ The Trent Trust marks an X in the Simple Trust box. The Trent Trust qualifies as a simple trust because:

1. The trust is required to distribute all the trust income currently;
2. It does not provide that any amounts are to be paid, permanently set aside, or used for charitable purposes; and
3. It does not distribute amounts allocated to the corpus of the trust [Reg. Sec. 1.651(a)-1].

Name of trust. When completing the name box at the top of Form 1041, be sure to copy the exact name of the trust from IRS Form SS-4, "Application for Employer Identification Number." This form is completed when the fiduciary applies for the employer identification number (EIN).

If the trust is a grantor trust (not separate taxpaying entity), be sure to include the name, identification number, and address of the grantor(s) or other owner(s) in parentheses after the name of the trust.

¶2903

Address of trust fiduciary. Be sure to include the number, street, and room or suite number of the fiduciary in the appropriate box on the top of Form 1041. Only include a P.O. box number if the Post Office does not deliver mail to the street address.

Box B: Number of Schedules K-1 attached. Every trust claiming an income distribution deduction on Page 1, line 18, of Form 1041 must enter the number of Schedules K-1 (Form 1041) that are attached to Form 1041.

■ The Trent Trust enters "1" in box B because the trust has one beneficiary and files only one Schedule K-1.

Box C: Employer identification number. Every trust that is required to file Form 1041 must also have an employer identification number (EIN). The fiduciary of a trust can obtain an EIN by one of the following methods:

- By going to www.irs.gov/businesses and clicking the "Employer ID Numbers" link. The EIN is issued immediately after the application information is validated;

- By telephone (1-800-829-4933); or

- By mailing or faxing Form SS-4, "Application for Employer Identification Number." Fiduciaries should be aware that the EIN may take 4–6 weeks if they are applying for the EIN by mail or fax.

If the trust has not received an EIN by the time the return is due, they should write "Applied for" and the application date in the space for the EIN. A social security number should never be substituted for the EIN on a tax return.

Box D: Date entity created. Enter the date the trust was created in box D. A trust comes into existence and is treated as a separate taxpayer when all the elements of a valid trust under state law are present. To establish a trust, the following legal requirements must exist:

1. An intent to create a trust;

2. A designated trustee and beneficiaries;

3. Sufficiently identifiable property; and

4. Transfer of title to the trustee.

■ The Trent Trust enters "02/01/13," the date The Best Bank, the trustee of Jane Trent's Trust, distributed the trust's assets to the trust and thus created the trust.

Box E: Nonexempt charitable and split-interest trusts.

IRC Section 4947(a)(1) trust. Check this box if the trust is a nonexempt charitable trust within the meaning of IRC Sec. 4947(a)(1).

A nonexempt charitable trust is defined as:

1. A trust that is not exempt from tax under IRC Sec. 501(a);

2. A trust in which all of the unexpired interests are devoted to one or more charitable purposes described in IRC Sec. 170(c)(2)(B); and

3. A trust for which a deduction was allowed under IRC Sec. 170 (for individual taxpayers) or for personal holding companies, foreign personal holding companies, or estates or trusts (including a deduction for estate or gift tax purposes).

¶2903

Not a private foundation. Check this box if the charitable trust is not treated as a private foundation under IRC Sec. 509. See Reg. Sec. 53.4947-1.

IRC Section 4947(a)(2) trust. Check this box if the trust is a split-interest trust under IRC Sec. 4947(a)(2) as follows:

1. The trust is not exempt from tax under IRC Sec. 501(a);
2. The trust has some unexpired interests that are devoted to purposes other than religious, charitable, or similar purposes; and
3. The trust has amounts transferred in trust after May 26, 1969, for which a deduction was allowed.

The fiduciary of a split-interest trust must also file Form 5227 for amounts transferred in trust after May 26, 1969, and Form 1041-A if the trust's governing instrument does not require that all of the trust's income be distributed currently.

■ The Trent Trust leaves these boxes blank because they do not apply.

Box F: Initial return, amended return, final return, change in fiduciary and change in fiduciary's name.

Initial return. If this is the first return filed by the trust, enter an "X" in the box marked "Initial return" in Section F.

Final return. The "Final return" box would be checked if this was the final return filed on behalf of a trust that was terminated. A trust is considered terminated when it ends as a separate taxable entity and no longer reports gross income or claims deductions or credit [Reg. Sec. 1.641(b)-3(b)]. After a trust has terminated, the IRS should be notified on Form 56 that the fiduciary relationship has ended.

Amended return. If this is an amended return check the "Amended return" box. The entire return should be completed with the new information reported on the appropriate lines. The trust's tax liability should be refigured. Attach a sheet explaining the reason for the changes and identify the lines and amounts being changed on the amended return.

If the amended return results in a change to income, or a change in distribution of any income or other information provided to a beneficiary, file an amended Schedule K-1 (Form 1041) along with the amended Form 1041. Check the "Amended K-1" box at the top of the amended Schedule K-1.

Net operating loss (NOL) carryback. Taxpayers should check the box if an amended return is filed for an NOL carryback.

Change in trust's name. If the name of the trust has changed from the name shown on the prior year's return (or Form SS-4 if this is the first return filed), be sure to check this box.

Change in fiduciary. If a different fiduciary enters his or her name on the line for *Name and title of fiduciary* than was shown on the prior year's return (or Form SS-4 if this is the first return being filed) and Form 8822-B, "Change of Address or Responsible Party—Business," was not filed, be sure to check this box. If there is a change in the fiduciary whose address is used as the mailing address for the trust after the return is filed, use Form 8822-B, to notify the IRS.

Change in fiduciary's address. Check the appropriate box if the same fiduciary who filed the prior year's return (or Form SS-4 if this is the first return being filed) files the

¶2903

current year's return and changed the address on the return (including a change to an "in care of" name and address) and did not report the change on Form 8822-B. If the address shown on Form 1041 changes after the form is filed (including a change to an "in care of" name and address) file Form 8822-B to notify the IRS of the change.

■ The Trent Trust enters an "X" in the box in item F that says "Initial return" because this is the first return filed by the trust.

Box G: Section 645 election. If the estate has made an IRC Sec. 645 election (an election to treat a revocable trust as part of the decedent's estate) by filing Form 8855, "Election to Treat a Qualified Revocable Trust as Part of an Estate," the executor must check Item G and provide the taxpayer identification number (TIN) of the electing trust with the greatest assets in the box provided. The executor must also attach a statement to Form 1041 providing the following information for each electing trust: (a) the name of the electing trust, (b) the TIN of the electing trust, and (c) the name and address of the trustee of the electing trust [For further discussion, see ¶ 2826].

¶2904 INCOME—IN GENERAL

A significant amount of income that is reported by trusts is from investments and retirement accounts. In order to properly report investment income, the taxpayer must be careful about having the correct classification for the income, report it in the correct tax year and attribute it to the correct taxpayer. A trust may also receive insurance proceeds when it is named as the beneficiary of an insurance policy or when no beneficiary has been named upon the insured's death. Beginning in 2013, trusts may be subject to an additional tax, the net investment income tax (NII tax), if they have undistributed net investment income that exceeds a certain threshold. In general, most of the income reported by trusts will constitute net investment income and whether or not the income is subject to the NII tax will depend on whether the income exceeds $11,950 in 2013 or $12,150 in 2014 [For further discussion, see ¶ 2935].

Blind Trusts. Taxpayers who are reporting income from a qualified blind trust (under the Ethics in Government Act of 1978) should write "Blind Trust" at the top of page 1 and complete the return as provided in the instructions. The taxpayer should not identify the payer of any income to the trust.

Extraterritorial Income Exclusion. The extraterritorial income exclusion is not allowed for transactions beginning in 2007. However, income from certain long-term sales and leases may still qualify for the exclusion. The estate or trust must report the extraterritorial income exclusion on line 15a of Form 1041, page 1. Although the extraterritorial income exclusion is entered on line 15a, it is an exclusion from income and should be treated as tax-exempt income when completing other parts of the return.

¶2905 LINE 1—INTEREST INCOME

On line 1 of Form 1041, report the trust's share of all taxable interest income that was received during the tax year. A trust could receive interest income from the following sources:

1. Accounts, including certificates of deposits and money market accounts, with banks, credit unions, and brokerage houses;

2. Notes, loans, and mortgages;

3. U.S. Treasury bills, notes, and bonds;

4. U.S. savings bonds;

5. Original issue discount; and

6. Income received as a regular interest holder of a real estate mortgage investment conduit (REMIC).

   NOTE: For taxable bonds acquired after 1987, amortizable bond premium is treated as an offset to the interest income instead of as a separate interest deduction.

   ■ The Trent Trust earned $4,000 in taxable interest income and that figure is entered here.

¶2906 LINE 2a—ORDINARY DIVIDENDS AND LINE 2b—QUALIFIED DIVIDENDS

Line 2a: Ordinary Dividends. Report the trust's share of all ordinary dividends received during the tax year on line 2a. But note that capital gain distributions should be reported on Schedule D (Form 1041), line 9. For the year of the decedent's death, Forms 1099-DIV issued in the decedent's name may include dividends earned after the date of death that should be reported on the income tax return of the decedent's estate.

   ■ The Trent Trust earned $20,000 in taxable ordinary dividends in the year the trust was created and that figure is entered on line 2a.

Line 2b: Qualified Dividends. Qualified dividends are dividends that are taxed at a lower tax rate. They are typically paid by a U.S. or qualified foreign corporation on stocks that have been held for the requisite period of time. Enter the beneficiary's allocable share of qualified dividends on line 2b(1) and enter the trust's allocable share on line 2b(2). If the trust received qualified dividends that were derived from income in respect of a decedent, you must reduce the amount on line 2b(2) by the portion of the estate tax deduction claimed on Form 1041, page 1, line 19, that is attributable to those qualified dividends. Do not reduce the amounts on line 2b by any other allocable expenses.

Dividends paid by most domestic and foreign corporations are called "qualified dividends" and are reported to the trust in box 1b of Form 1099-DIV. They are eligible for the capital gains tax rate. Corporate stock dividends that are passed through to investors by a mutual fund or other regulated investment company (RIC), partnership, real estate investment trust (REIT), or held by a common trust fund qualify for the lower tax rates assuming the distribution would otherwise be classified as "qualified dividend income."

Exceptions: The following types of dividend income may be reported to the trust as qualified dividends in box 1b of Form 1099-DIV but are specifically excluded from

¶2906

the definition of "qualified dividend income" and are therefore ineligible for the reduced tax rate:

- Dividends paid by a credit unions, mutual savings banks, savings and loans, domestic building and loans, mutual insurance companies, farmers' cooperatives, tax-exempt cemetery companies, tax-exempt corporations, nonprofit voluntary employee benefit associations (VEBAs).

- Dividends paid by employee stock ownership plans (ESOPs).

- Dividends paid by stock owned for less than 61 days during the 121-day period that began 60 days before the ex-dividend date which is the first date following the declaration of a dividend on which the purchase of a stock is entitled to receive the next dividend payment. When counting the number of days the stock was held, include the day the trust disposed of the stock but not the day it acquired the stock. However, you cannot count days during which the trust's risk of loss was diminished.

- Dividends paid by stock purchased with borrowed funds if the dividend was included in investment income in claiming an interest deduction.

- Dividends on any share of stock to the extent that the trust is under an obligation (including a short sale) to make related payments with respect to positions in substantially similar or related property. This situation most frequently arises in connection with short sales where the taxpayer borrows stock from a broker to sell. After this initial sale, the short seller hopes the price of the stock goes down so he can replace the borrowed stock with identical shares purchased at a lower price, pocketing the difference. In this situation, the broker delivers shares that it was holding for another customer in "street name." Any subsequent dividends paid on the stock will go to the buyer but the account of the customer whose shares were borrowed must be credited with a payment in lieu of dividend equal to the amount of the dividend. Payments in lieu of dividends are not eligible for taxation at lower capital gains rates.

- Dividends paid into a tax-free fund, such as a company retirement plan, traditional IRA or 401(k) plan.

- Payments in lieu of dividends, but only if you know or have reason to know that the payments are not qualified dividends.

- Dividends attributable to periods totaling more than 366 days that the trust received on any share of preferred stock held for less than 91days during the 181-day period that began 90 days before the ex-dividend date. When counting the number of days the trust held the stock, include the date the trust disposed of the stock but not the day it acquired the stock. However, you cannot count certain days during which the trust's risk of loss was diminished.

■ The Trent Trust earned no qualified dividends and leaves line 2b blank.

¶2906

¶2907 LINE 3—BUSINESS INCOME OR LOSS

If the trust operated a business, report the income and expenses on Schedule C (Form 1040) or Schedule C-EZ and enter the net profit or (loss) from Schedule C or Schedule C-EZ on line 3.

■ The Trent Trust has no business income or loss and leaves line 3 blank.

¶2908 LINE 4—CAPITAL GAIN OR LOSS

Enter the capital gain from Schedule D (Form 1041), Part III, line 19, Column (3) or the loss from Part IV, line 20, on line 4 of Schedule D (Form 1041). Gains and losses from the sale or exchange of capital assets are computed and allocated between the fiduciary and the beneficiaries on Schedule D, Form 1041 [see ¶2936].

▶ **CAUTION:** Do not substitute Schedule D (Form 1040) for Schedule D (Form 1041). These are different forms.

■ The Trent Trust earned $10,000 in capital gain from the sale of 1,000 shares of XYZ, Inc. stock. Because local law provides that capital gains are allocated to trust principal, the $10,000 capital gain earned by the trust is allocated to principal, rather than being distributed to beneficiaries. Do not include this gain in lines 3 and 4 of Schedule K-1 as an amount distributed to beneficiaries. The income, nevertheless, is taxable to the trust and is therefore included on line 4.

¶2909 LINE 5—RENTS, ROYALTIES, PARTNERSHIPS, OTHER ESTATES AND TRUSTS, ETC.

Use Schedule E (Form 1040—**not Form 1041**), "Supplemental Income and Loss," to report the trust's share of income or losses from rents, royalties, partnerships, S corporations, other estates and trusts and real estate mortgage investment conduits (REMICs). Enter the net profit or loss from Schedule E (Form 1040) on line 5 of Form 1041.

■ The Trent Trust received $6,000 in rent from a residential apartment building that the trust owned. This income was reported on Schedule E (Form 1040) as explained at ¶2939.

¶2910 LINE 6—FARM INCOME OR LOSS

If the trust operated a farm, use Schedule F (Form 1040), "Profit or Loss from Farming" to report farm income and expenses. Enter the net profit or (loss) from Schedule F on line 6.

■ The Trent Trust leaves line 6 blank.

¶2907

¶2911   LINE 7—ORDINARY GAIN OR LOSS

Enter from line 17, IRS Form 4797, "Sales of Business Property" the ordinary gain or loss from the sale or exchange of property other than capital assets and also from involuntary conversions (other than casualty or theft).

■ The Trent Trust leaves line 7 blank.

¶2912   LINE 8—OTHER INCOME

Enter other items of income not included on lines 1, 2a, and 3 through 7. Do not include tax-exempt income on this line. List the type and amount on the dotted line and attach a schedule if the trust has more than one item on this line. Include items such as any part of a total distribution shown on IRS Form 1099-R, "Distributions From Pensions, Annuities, Retirement or Profit-Sharing Plans, IRAs, Insurance Contracts, etc.," that is treated as ordinary income.

■ The Trent Trust leaves line 8 blank.

Line 9—Total income. Enter the total income on line 9.

■ The total income earned by the Trent Trust in the year the trust was created was $40,000 and that figure is reported on line 9.

¶2913   REPORTING THE TRUST'S DEDUCTIONS

When a trust computes taxable income, it is generally allowed the same types of deductions that are available to individual taxpayers. For further discussion, see ¶2808. A trust is not, however, allowed to make an election under IRC Sec. 179 to expense tangible property in a taxpayer's trade or business. Another difference between the deductions available to trusts and individual taxpayers is that a trust is allowed a deduction for amortization, depletion, and depreciation only to the extent the deductions are not apportioned to the beneficiaries.

(a) How Trusts Report Depreciation Deductions. For a trust, the depreciation deduction is apportioned between the income beneficiaries and the trust on the basis of the trust income allocable to each, unless the governing instrument (or local law) requires or permits the trust to maintain a reserve of deprecation in any amount. If the trustee is required to maintain a reserve, the deduction is first allocated to the trust to the extent that income is set aside for a depreciation reserve, and any part of the deduction in excess of the income set aside for the reserve is apportioned between the income beneficiaries and the trust on the basis of the trust income (in excess of the income set aside for the reserve) allocable to each. For example:

1. If, under the trust instrument or local law, the income of a trust computed without regard to depreciation is to be distributed to a named beneficiary, the beneficiary is entitled to the deduction to the exclusion of the trustee.

2. If, under the trust instrument or local law, the income of a trust is to be distributed to a named beneficiary, but the trustee is directed to maintain a

¶2913

reserve for depreciation in any amount, the deduction is allowed to the trustee (except to the extent that income set aside for the reserve is less than the allowable deduction). The same result would follow if the trustee sets aside income for a depreciation reserve pursuant to discretionary authority to do so in the governing instrument.

No effect should be given to any allocation of the depreciation deduction which gives any beneficiary or the trustee a share of such deduction greater than his pro rata share of the trust income, irrespective of any provisions in the trust instrument, except as otherwise provided in this paragraph when the trust instrument or local law requires or permits the trustee to maintain a reserve for depreciation [Reg. Sec. 1.167(h)-1(b)].

(b) How Trusts Report Depletion Deductions. If a mineral property or timber property is held in trust, the allowable deduction for depletion is to be apportioned between the income beneficiaries and the trust on the basis of the trust income from such property allocable to each, unless the governing instrument (or local law) requires or permits the trust to maintain a reserve for depletion in any amount. In the latter case, the deduction is first allocated to the trust to the extent that income is set aside for a depletion reserve, and any part of the deduction in excess of the income set aside for the reserve shall be apportioned between the income beneficiaries and the trust on the basis of the trust income (in excess of the income set aside for the reserve) allocable to each. For example:

1. If, under the trust instrument or local law, the income of a trust computed without regard to depletion is to be distributed to a named beneficiary, the beneficiary is entitled to the deduction to the exclusion of the trustee.

2. If, under the trust instrument or local law, the income of a trust is to be distributed to a named beneficiary, but the trustee is directed to maintain a reserve for depletion in any amount, the deduction is allowed to the trustee (except to the extent that income set aside for the reserve is less than the allowable deduction). The same result would follow if the trustee sets aside income for a depletion reserve pursuant to discretionary authority to do so in the governing instrument.

No effect will be given to any allocation of the depletion deduction which gives any beneficiary or the trustee a share of such deduction greater than his pro rata share of the trust income, irrespective of any provisions in the trust instrument. An exception is available when the trust instrument or local law requires or permits the trustee to maintain a reserve for depletion [Reg. Sec. 1.611-1(c)(4)].

(c) How Trusts Report Amortization Deductions. The deduction for amortization is apportioned between a trust and its beneficiaries under the same principles for apportioning the deductions for depreciation and depletion as discussed above.

(d) How the Passive Activity Loss Rules Affect Trusts. The passive activity loss rules limit the amount that a trust can deduct from a passive activity to the amount of income generated by passive activities [IRC Sec. 469(a)(1); Reg. Sec. 1.469-1. For further discussion, see ¶2808]. Similarly, credits from passive activities are generally limited to the tax attributable to those activities. These limitations are

¶2913

first applied at the trust level and then passed through to the trustee or beneficiary level. Use Form 8582, "Passive Activity Loss Limitations" to compute the amount of losses allowed from passive activities.

For purposes of the passive activity loss rule, taxable income is divided into three parts: (1) regular income from wages and salary or professional fees; (2) portfolio (or investment) income, such as dividends, bond interest, and gains on the sale of shares of stock (portfolio income does not include gross income, interest, or royalties derived in the ordinary course of a trade or business of lending money or credit to customers); and (3) passive income, such as is generated by most tax shelters and other types of passive investments. As a general rule, there will be no traffic across these three parts. In other words, a passive loss cannot be deducted against "active" income (e.g., salary or self-employment earnings) or "portfolio" income (e.g., dividends or interest income). Any disallowed or excess loss is suspended and carried forward to the following year or years until used, or until deducted in the year the trust sells or otherwise disposes of its entire interest in the activity in a fully taxable transaction [IRC Sec. 469(b)].

The following activities are not passive activities and are therefore not subject to the passive activity loss limitations.

- Trade or business activities in which the taxpayer "materially participated" for the tax year. To satisfy this test and deduct losses in full from a trade or business, the taxpayer must materially participate on a regular, continuous and substantial basis [IRC Sec. 469(h)(1)].

- A working interest in an oil or gas well held directly or through an entity that does not limit liability (such as a general partner interest in a partnership). It does not matter whether the taxpayer materially participated in the activity for the tax year [IRC Sec. 469(c)(3)(A)].

- The rental of a dwelling unit used for personal purposes during the year for more than the greater of 14 days or 10 percent of the number of days during the year that the home was rented at a fair rental.

    (e) How the At-Risk Rules Affect Trusts. The at-risk rules limit the trust's ability to deduct losses from an activity only to the extent that the trust is at risk for the activity at the close of the taxable year [IRC Sec. 465]. The amount at risk in an activity is the amount that could actually be lost as a result of the investment.

Like the passive loss rules, Congress created the "at-risk" rules to limit tax shelter investors from offsetting wages and dividends with losses generated from activities financed by nonrecourse loans where investors were not personally liable for the amount invested in circular investment schemes. For purposes of the at-risk rule, the term "loss" means the excess of the deductions allocable to the specific activity for the year, without regard to the at-risk limitation, over the income received or accrued by the investor during the same year from the same activity [IRC Sec. 465(d)].

Any loss disallowed because it exceeds the amount at risk in one year is suspended and may be deducted in the succeeding tax years, subject to the at-risk limits in each of those years [IRC Sec. 465(a)(2)]. There is no limit to the number of years it may be carried over [Reg. Sec. 1.465-2(b)]. The amount of loss which is deductible in a particular year reduces the amount at risk (but not below zero) for that activity for subsequent tax years. Thus, if a loss exceeds a trust's at-risk amount, it will not be

¶2913

allowed in the next year unless the at-risk amount is also increased by the investment of more money in the activity. The amount of loss which is allowed for a taxable year cannot reduce the amount at risk below zero [Reg. Sec. 1.465-3(a)].

■ The Trent Trust computes its deductions on lines 10 through 21 of Form 1041.

¶2914 LINE 10—INTEREST

Enter the amount of interest (subject to limitations) paid or incurred by the trust on amounts borrowed by the trust, or on debt acquired by the trust that is not claimed elsewhere on the trust's income tax return.

Personal interest is not deductible. This includes the following:

1. Interest paid on revolving charge accounts;
2. Installment loans on personal use property;
3. Personal notes for money borrowed from a bank, credit union, or other person; and
4. Underpayments of federal, state, or local income taxes.

Include on line 10 the following types of interest:

1. Investment interest;
2. Qualified residence interest (the beneficiary must have a present interest in the trust or an interest in the residuary of the trust in order for the interest to be "qualified residence interest" [IRC Sec. 163(h)(3)];
3. Interest payable on any unpaid portion of the estate tax attributable to the value of a reversionary or remainder interest in property, or an interest in a closely held business for the period during which an extension of time for payment of such tax is in effect.

Qualified mortgage insurance premiums. Enter (on the worksheet on page 23 of the 2013 Instructions to Form 1041) the qualified mortgage insurance premiums paid under a mortgage insurance contract issued during the year in connection with qualified residence debt that was secured by a first or second residence. If at least one other person was liable for and paid the premiums in connection with the loan, and the premiums were reported on Form 1098, include the trust's share of the premiums on the worksheet. Qualified mortgage insurance is mortgage insurance provided by the Department of Veterans Affairs, the Federal Housing Administration, or the Rural Housing Service, and private mortgage insurance.

Limit on deduction. If the trust's AGI is more than $100,000, its deduction is limited and the worksheet on page 23 of the Instructions to Form 1041 must be used to figure the amount of the deduction.

Prepaid mortgage insurance. If the trust paid premiums for qualified mortgage insurance that are allocable to periods after the end of its tax year, such premiums must be allocated over the shorter of:

• The stated term of the mortgage; or
• 84 months, beginning with the month the insurance was obtained.

¶2914

The premiums are treated as paid in the year to which they are allocated. If the mortgage is satisfied before its term, no deduction is allowed for the unamortized balance.

These allocation rules are inapplicable to qualified mortgage insurance provided by the Department of Veterans Affairs or the Rural Housing Service.

No deduction is allowed for the unamortized balance if the mortgage is satisfied before its term.

■ The Trent Trust leaves line 10 blank.

¶2915 LINE 11—TAXES

Enter any deductible taxes paid or incurred during the tax year that are not deductible by the trust elsewhere on Form 1041. Deductible taxes include:

1. State, and local income taxes unless you elect to deduct state and local general sales taxes. You cannot deduct both.

2. State and local general sales taxes which can be deducted instead of state and local income taxes. A trust cannot use the Optional Sales Tax Tables for individuals in the 2013 Schedule A (Form 1040) Instructions to compute its deduction.

3. State, local and foreign real property taxes;

4. State and local personal property taxes;

5. Foreign or U.S. possession income taxes unless you claim a credit for the tax instead of the deduction; and

6. Generation-skipping transfer tax imposed on income distributions.

Do *not* deduct:

1. Federal income taxes;

2. Estate, inheritance, legacy, succession, and gift taxes;

3. Federal duties and excise taxes.

Instead, treat these taxes as part of the cost of the property.

■ The Trent Trust leaves line 11 blank.

¶2916 LINE 12—FIDUCIARY FEES

The total amount of deductible fees paid to the fiduciary for administering the trust during the tax year should be entered on line 12. Fiduciary fees deducted on Form 706 cannot be deducted on Form 1041.

■ The Trent Trust's trustee's fees for the year the trust was created were $4,000. The $4,000 trustee fees are deductible without regard to the 2 percent floor for miscellaneous deductions. For further discussion of the deduction of trust advice fees, see ¶2813.

¶2916

¶2917 LINE 13—CHARITABLE DEDUCTION (FROM SCHEDULE A, LINE 7)

Only a complex trust would have an entry on this line because a simple trust is not even entitled to claim the charitable deduction [IRC Sec. 642(c)(1)]. A simple trust is required by definition to distribute all of its income to its beneficiaries [see ¶2817].

A complex trust may claim an unlimited deduction for gross income that, under the terms of the will or trust, is paid or permanently set aside during the taxable year for charitable purposes [IRC Sec. 642(c)]. Unlike the charitable deduction allowed individuals, no limitation is placed on the amount that can be deducted by a trust [Reg. Sec. 1.642(c)-2(a)]. The amount of the deduction is computed on Schedule A of Form 1041.

The tricky aspect of a trust's deduction for charitable contributions is that the charitable contribution deduction is considered to consist of a proportionate part of each item of income. As a result, the deduction must be allocated proportionately among all items of income included in distributable net income (DNI). For example, if a trust has taxable and nontaxable income, a proportionate part of the nontaxable income must be allocated to the amount paid or set aside for charitable purposes and is not allowed as a deduction [Reg. Secs. 1.642(c)-3(b), 1.643(a)-5]. For further discussion, see ¶2810.

■ The Trent Trust is a simple trust and therefore has no charitable deduction and leaves line 13 blank.

¶2918 LINE 14—ATTORNEY, ACCOUNTANT, AND RETURN PREPARER FEES

On this line, enter the total deductible fees paid to attorneys, accountants, and return preparers. If the fees paid to these professionals are ordinary and necessary fees incurred in connection with the administration of the trust, they will be deductible.

■ The Trent Trust has no entry on this line.

¶2919 LINE 15a—OTHER DEDUCTIONS NOT SUBJECT TO THE 2 PERCENT FLOOR

Attach a schedule and list by type and amount all allowable deductions that are not deductible elsewhere on Form 1041. Do not include any losses on worthless bonds and similar obligations and nonbusiness bad debts. Report these losses on Form 8949, "Sales and Other Dispositions of Capital Assets." Do not deduct medical or funeral expenses on Form 1041. Medical expenses of the decedent paid by the estate may be deductible on the decedent's income tax return for the year incurred. Funeral expenses are deductible only on Form 706.

Report the following on line 15a:

1. Bond premiums;

2. Casualty and theft losses. Trusts should use Form 4684, "Casualties and Thefts," to compute any deductible casualty and theft losses;

3. Domestic production activities deduction. The trust may be entitled to deduct up to 9 percent of its share of qualified production activities income from the following activities:

   (i) Construction performed in the United States;

   (ii) Engineering or architectural services performed in the United States for construction projects in the United States;

   (iii) Any lease, rental, license, sale, exchange, or other disposition of:

   • Tangible personal property, computer software, and sound recordings that the trust manufactured in whole or in significant part in the United States;

   • Any qualified film the trust produced; or

   • Electricity, natural gas, or potable water the trust produced in the United States.

4. The trust's share of amortization, depreciation, and depletion not claimed elsewhere;

   ■ The Trent Trust leaves line 15a blank.

¶2920 LINE 15b—NET OPERATING LOSS DEDUCTION AND LINE 15c—ALLOWABLE MISCELLANEOUS ITEMIZED DEDUCTIONS SUBJECT TO THE 2 PERCENT FLOOR

Line 15b—Net operating loss deduction. A trust may claim a net operating loss deduction (NOLD) under IRC Sec. 172.

Line 15c—Allowable miscellaneous itemized deductions subject to the 2% floor. Miscellaneous itemized deductions are deductible only to the extent that the aggregate amount of such deductions exceeds 2 percent of the trust's adjusted gross income. Deduct on line 15c expenses for the production or collection of income (e.g., investment advisory fees, subscriptions to investment advisory publications, and the cost of safe deposit boxes).

Miscellaneous itemized deductions do not include the following deductions:

1. Interest under IRC Sec. 163;

2. Taxes under IRC Sec. 164;

3. The amortization of bond premium under IRC Sec. 171;

4. Estate taxes attributable to income in respect of a decedent under IRC Sec. 691(c);

5. Expenses paid or incurred in connection with the administration of the trust that would not have been incurred if the property were not held in trust.

   ■ The Trent Trust leaves line 15b blank.

¶2920

¶2921 LINE 16—TOTAL DEDUCTIONS

Add lines 10 through 15b to compute the total deductions available to the trust to reduce total income as stated on line 9.

■ Because the Trent Trust has no other deductions, its total deductions equal $4,000.

¶2922 LINE 17—ADJUSTED TOTAL INCOME OR LOSS

Subtract line 16 from line 9 and enter the result on line 17.

■ The Trent Trust subtracts line 16 ($4,000) from line 9 ($40,000) and enters the result ($36,000) on line 17.

¶2923 LINE 18—INCOME DISTRIBUTION DEDUCTION

If the trust was required to distribute income currently or if it paid, credited, or was required to distribute any other amounts to beneficiaries during the tax year, complete Schedule B to determine the trust's income distribution deduction.

Cemetery perpetual care fund. One line 18, deduct no more than $5 per gravesite for the amount paid for maintenance of cemetery property. To the right of the entry space for line 18, enter the number of gravesites. Also write "Section 642(i) trust" in parentheses after the trust's name at the top of Form 1041. Taxpayers need not complete Schedules B of Form 1041 or K-1 (Form 1041).

▶ **PRACTICE POINTERS:** If the trust claims an income distribution deduction, be sure to complete and attach Parts I and II of Schedule I to refigure the deduction on a minimum tax basis and Schedule K-1 (Form 1041) for each beneficiary who received an income distribution.

■ The Trent Trust enters the $18,000 income distribution deduction from Schedule B, line 15. For a further explanation, see ¶2934.

¶2924 LINE 19—ESTATE TAX DEDUCTION (INCLUDING CERTAIN GENERATION-SKIPPING TRANSFER TAXES)

If the trust includes income in respect of a decedent (IRD) in its gross income, and this amount was also included in the decedent's estate for estate tax purposes, the trust is entitled to deduct, in the same tax year the income is included, that portion of the estate tax imposed on the decedent's estate that is attributable to the inclusion of the IRD in the decedent's estate [Reg. Sec. 1.691(c)-1. For further discussion, see ¶2615].

A deduction is also available for the generation-skipping transfer tax imposed as a result of a taxable termination or a direct skip occurring as a result of the death of the transferor [IRC Sec. 691(c)(3)].

■ The Trent Trust leaves line 19 blank.

¶2925 LINE 20—EXEMPTION

A trust filing a tax return is entitled to a personal exemption similar to the one allowed individuals, but the amount varies depending on the nature of the entity seeking the exemption as follows:

- A simple trust (a trust required to distribute all income currently as discussed in ¶2817) is allowed to claim an exemption in the amount of $300. Even though simple trusts that make distributions from principal for a single year are called "complex trusts" for that taxable year, they are still entitled to a $300 exemption in the year of the distribution;

- Most other trusts are allowed an exemption of $100 [IRC Sec. 642(b); Reg. Sec. 1.642(b)-1];

- For 2013, qualified disability trusts can claim an exemption of up to $3,900. A trust with modified adjusted gross income above $250,000 begins to lose part of the exemption deduction. No exemption is allowed for a trust with modified adjusted gross income of $372,500 or more. The term "qualified disability trust" is defined as (1) any trust established solely for the benefit of an individual under 65 years of age who is disabled, and (2) all of whose beneficiaries (except holders of a remainder or reversionary interest) are disabled for some portion of the taxable year [IRC Sec. 642(b)(2)(C)(ii)];

- No exemption is allowed in the year the trust is terminated because the trust must distribute all its income in the year of termination, and will not, therefore, have any income for the exemption to offset [IRC Sec. 642(b); Reg. Sec. 1.642(b)-1]. See ¶2809.

  ■ The Trent Trust is a simple trust because its governing instrument requires that all income be distributed currently. It therefore is allowed a $300 exemption, even if it distributed amounts other than income during the tax year. All other types of trusts are allowed a $100 exemption [Reg. Sec. 1.642(b)-1].

¶2926 LINE 21—TOTAL DEDUCTIONS

To find the amount of the total deductions, add lines 18, 19, and 20.

■ The total deductions for the Trent Trust are $18,300.

¶2927 LINE 22—TAXABLE INCOME

The trust's taxable income is entered on line 22. This is computed by subtracting line 21 from line 17. If line 22 is a loss, the trust may have a net operating loss ("NOL"). Do not include the deductions claimed on lines 13 (charitable), 18 (income distribution), and 20 (exemption) when figuring the amount of the NOL. Generally, an NOL may be carried back to the prior two tax years and forward for up to 20 years. The two-year carryback period does not apply to the portion of an NOL attributable to an eligible loss, a farming loss, a qualified disaster, GO Zone, or disaster recovery assistance loss, or a specified liability loss. An estate or trust may also elect to carry an NOL forward only, instead of first carrying it back.

Complete Schedule A of Form 1045 to figure the amount of the NOL that is available for carryback or carryover. Use Form 1045 or file an amended return to apply for a refund based on an NOL carryback. For more details, see Pub. 536, Net Operating Losses (NOLs) for Individuals, Estates, and Trusts.

On the termination of the trust, any unused NOL carryover that would be allowable to the trust in a later tax year, but for the termination, is allowed to the beneficiaries succeeding to the property of the trust [See the instructions for Schedule K-1 (Form 1041), box 11, codes D and E].

■ The taxable income for the Trent Trust is $17,700.

¶2928 LINE 23—TOTAL TAX (FROM SCHEDULE G, LINE 7)

The total tax, as computed on Schedule G, line 7 [using Schedule D (Form 1041)], is entered on line 23. For a discussion of Schedule G, see ¶2935.

■ The total tax for the Trent Trust in the amount of $3,746, as computed on Schedule D and Schedule G, is entered on line 23 of Form 1041.

¶2929 LINE 24—PAYMENTS: ESTIMATED TAX PAYMENTS AND AMOUNT APPLIED FROM PREVIOUS RETURN

Trusts are required to make quarterly estimated income tax payments in much the same way as individual taxpayers [IRC Sec. 6654(l)]. The big exception, however, is that certain grantor trusts do not have to pay estimated taxes for tax years ending before the date that is two years after the grantor's death [IRC Sec. 6654(l)(2)(B)(i)].

The estimated taxes are figured on IRS Form 1041-ES (Estimated Income Tax for Estates and Trusts), and the taxes are paid with Form 1041-ES payment vouchers. After the IRS receives the first payment voucher from the fiduciary, the trust will receive a 1041-ES package with the name, address, and employer identification number preprinted on the vouchers for the next tax year.

Electronic deposits of estimated tax. The fiduciary of the decedent's estate, trust or bankruptcy estate must deposit all estimated taxes of certain trusts and excise tax electronically using the Electronic Federal Payment System (EFTPS). A financial institution that maintains a Treasury Tax and Loan (TT&L) account, and administers at least 200 taxable trusts that are required to pay tax, are required to deposit the estimated tax payments electronically using EFTPS.

A fiduciary that is not required to make electronic deposits of estimated tax on behalf of a trust or the fiduciary of an estate may voluntarily participate in EFTPS.

In order for deposits using EFTPS to be on time, the deposit must be initiated by 8:00 p.m. Eastern time the day before the date the deposit is due. If a third party is used to make the deposits on behalf of the trust, the third party may have a different cut-off time.

Failure of a fiduciary to use EFTPS on behalf of a trust will subject the trust to a 10 percent penalty. A trust that is not required to make electronic deposits of estimated tax may use either the payment vouchers (Form 1041-ES) or voluntarily participate in EFTPS. In order for deposits made by EFTPS to be considered on time, the trust fiduciary must initiate the transaction at least one business day before the date the deposit is due.

(a) When Are Estimated Taxes Due.
Calendar year trusts must pay estimated taxes in four installments, which are due on or before the following dates [IRC Sec. 6654(c)]:

1st installment	April 15 of the current tax year
2nd installment	June 15 of the current tax year
3rd installment	September 15 of the current tax year
4th installment	January 15 of the following tax year

Fiscal year trusts must pay estimated taxes on or before the following dates [IRC Sec. 6654(k)(1)]:

1st installment	15th day of the fourth month of fiscal year
2nd installment	15th day of the sixth month of fiscal year
3rd installment	15th day of the ninth month of fiscal year
4th installment	15th day after the end of the fiscal year

A trust that has a short tax year (a period of less than 12 months) must pay installments of estimated tax on or before the following dates:

1st installment	15th day of the fourth month of tax year
2nd installment	15th day of the sixth month of tax year
3rd installment	15th day of the ninth month of tax year
4th installment	15th day of the first month of the next tax year

The payments due in the sixth and/or ninth month of the short tax year (but not the payment due on the fifteenth day of the first month of the succeeding tax year) are not required to be paid if the short tax year ended during or before the sixth and/or ninth months.

¶2929

Example 1: A trust has a short tax year beginning April 1 and ending December 31. The trust's installments of estimated tax are due as follows: The first payment is due on July 15, the second payment is due on September 15, the third payment is due on December 15, and the fourth payment is due on January 15.

Example 2: A trust has a short tax year beginning June 1 and ending December 31. The trust's installments of estimated tax are due as follows: The first payment is due on September 15, the second payment on November 15, no third payment is due because there is no ninth month of the tax year, and the fourth payment is due on January 15.

(b) How Much Is Due. The amount of any required installment of estimated tax is 25 percent of the required annual payment, even for a short tax year [IRC Sec. 6654(d)(1)(A)].

(c) Which Trusts Have to Pay Estimated Taxes. A trust must pay estimated tax for 2014 if it expects to owe, after subtracting any withholding and credits, at least $1,000 in tax, and it expects the withholding and credits to be less than the smaller of:

1. 90 percent of the tax shown on the 2014 tax return; or
2. 100 percent of the tax shown on the 2013 tax return (110 percent of that amount if the trust's adjusted gross income on that return is more than $150,000 and less than 2/3 of gross income for 2013 or 2014 is from farming or fishing).

However, if a return was not filed for 2013 or if that return did not cover a full 12 months, item 2 above does not apply. For this purpose, include household employment taxes in the tax shown on the tax return, but only if either of the following is true:

- The trust will have federal income tax withheld for 2014; or
- The trust would be required to make estimated tax payments for 2014 even if it did not include household employment taxes when figuring estimated tax.

Note also that foreign trusts are also required to make estimated tax payments.

(d) Exceptions. The fiduciary need not make estimated tax payments in the following circumstances:

1. A domestic trust had no tax liability for the entire previous tax year;
2. The trust is treated as a grantor trust that will receive the residue of the decedent's estate under the will for any tax year ending before the date that is two years after the decedent's death.

(e) How to Figure Estimated Tax. To figure out how much estimated tax to pay, the fiduciary should use the Estimated Tax Worksheet contained in Form 1041-ES (Estimated Income Tax For Estates and Trusts) and the current Tax Rate Schedule in Form 1041-ES.

The trust's tax return from last year should be used as a guide for figuring next year's estimated tax. If the trust receives its income unevenly throughout the year, it may be

¶2929

able to lower or eliminate the amount of its required estimated tax payment for one or more periods by using the annualized income installment method [IRC Sec. 6654(d)(2)(A)]. For further discussion of the annualized income installment, see IRS Publication 505, Tax Withholding and Estimated Tax.

(f) Line 24b—Allocation of Estimated Taxes to Beneficiaries. Fiduciaries of trusts that pay estimated tax may also elect to have any portion of their estimated tax payments allocated to any of the beneficiaries [IRC Sec. 643(g)(1)]. They need not wait until the final tax year of the trust to make the election. The trust's election must be filed on or before the 65th day after the close of its tax year [IRC Sec. 643(g)(2)]. Once the election is made, it is irrevocable [Reg. Sec. 301.9100-8(a)(4)(i)].

■ Estimated tax payments made by the trustee of the Trent Trust in the amount of $2,000 are entered on lines 24a and 24c.

Line 25—Total payments. To compute the amount of the total payments, add lines 24c through 24e and 24h.

■ The Trent Trust made total tax payments in the amount of $2,000, and this amount is entered on line 25.

¶2930 LINE 26—ESTIMATED TAX PENALTY

If line 27 is at least $1,000 and more than 10 percent of the tax shown on Form 1041, or the trust underpaid its 2013 estimated tax liability for any payment period, it may owe a penalty. See IRS Form 2210 to determine whether the trust owes a penalty and to figure the amount of the penalty.

(a) Waiver of Penalty. The underpayment penalty may be waived under the following circumstances:

1. The trustee did not make a payment because of a casualty, disaster, or other unusual circumstance and it would be inequitable to impose the penalty; or

2. The trustee retired (after reaching age 62) or became disabled during the tax year a payment was due or during the preceding tax year, and both the following requirements are met:

   • The trustee had a reasonable cause for not making the payment; and

   • The trustee's underpayment was not due to willful neglect.

Federally declared disaster. Certain estimated tax payment deadlines for taxpayers who live or work in a federally declared disaster area are postponed for a period during and after the disaster. During the processing of the tax return, the IRS automatically identifies taxpayers located in a covered disaster area and applies the appropriate penalty relief. The taxpayer should not file Form 2210 if the underpayment was due to a federally declared disaster. Trusts not in a covered disaster area but whose books, records, or tax professionals' officers are in a covered area are also entitled to relief. Also eligible are relief workers affiliated with a recognized government or charitable organization assisting in the relief activities in a covered disaster area.

(b) How to Request Penalty Waiver. To request a waiver, you must complete Form 2210. The IRS will review the information provided and will decide whether or not to grant the waiver request.

(c) Exception. No penalty applies to a trust that was treated as owned by the decedent if the trust will receive the residue of the decedent's estate under the will (or if no will is admitted to probate, the trust is primarily responsible for paying debts, taxes, and expenses of administration) for any tax year ending before the date that is two years after the decedent's death.

¶2931 LINE 27—TAX DUE

The amount of tax owed by the trust is entered on line 27. The fiduciary of a trust must pay any income tax due in full when the return is filed. The filing due date is the fifteenth day of the fourth month following the close of the tax year. The fiduciary should pay the tax in cash or by check or money order payable to the "United States Treasury." Employer identification numbers should be written on checks or money orders. In addition, "2013 Form 1041" should be written on the check.

(a) Forms of Payment. The fiduciary of the trust may pay any income tax owed in cash or by bank check or money order or by any commercially acceptable means deemed appropriate by the IRS [IRC Sec. 6311]. This includes, for example, electronic funds transfers, including those arising from credit cards, debit cards and charge cards [Reg. Sec. 301.6311-2].

Electronic deposits of estimated tax. The fiduciary may also voluntarily use the Electronic Federal Tax Payment System (EFTPS) to pay the tax due for a trust. In order for deposits made by EFTPS to be considered timely, the trust fiduciary must initiate the transaction at least one business day before the date the deposit is due. See the discussion at ¶ 2929.

(b) Interest and Penalties. Failure to pay by the due date will result in the imposition of interest and penalties.

Interest. Interest is compounded daily on taxes not paid by the due date, even if an extension of time to file is granted [IRC Secs. 6601(a), 6601(b)(1), 6622]. Interest will also be charged beginning on the return due date (including extensions) on civil penalties such as the failure-to-file penalty, the accuracy-related penalty, and the fraud penalty. The interest charge will stop on the date the penalty is paid [IRC Secs. 6601(e)(2)(A), 6601(e)(2)(B)]. The interest charge will be equal to the federal short-term rate plus 3 percentage points [IRC Sec. 6621(a)(2)].

Penalty for failure to file. For the late filing of a return, a penalty will be imposed in the amount of 5 percent of the tax due for each month, or part of a month, for which a return is not filed up to a maximum of 25 percent of the tax due (15 percent for each month, or part of a month, up to a maximum of 75 percent if the failure to file is fraudulent). The penalty will not be imposed if the fiduciary can show that the failure to file on time was due to reasonable cause. A statement explaining what reasonable cause resulted in the return being filed late should be attached to the return.

Penalty for failure to pay. If the fiduciary fails to pay the tax when due, in addition to interest charges on late payments, a late penalty of one-half of 1 percent of the unpaid tax shown on the return will be imposed for each month (or part of a month) that the tax remains unpaid up to a maximum of 25 percent of the unpaid amount, unless failure to pay timely is due to reasonable cause [IRC Sec. 6651(a)(2)]. Any penalty is in addition to interest charges or late payments.

(c) Timely Mailed/Timely Filed Rule. The general rule is that a tax return or tax payment that is delivered by the U.S. Postal Service after the due date in a postage prepaid, properly addressed envelope, will be considered to be mailed on time if the date of the postmark is on or before the due date [IRC Sec. 7502(a)]. This is known as the timely mailed/timely filed rule. In other words, if you used the U.S. Postal Service to mail your return or tax payment on time, it will be considered to be filed or paid on time even though it arrived at its destination late. You can file at the last minute using a private delivery services (PDS) other than the U.S. Postal Service and still qualify under the rule that a return mailed on time is considered to be filed on time [IRC Sec. 7502(f)]. The IRS has designated the following PDSs that can be used to file returns or pay tax with the assurance that they will be treated as filed or paid on time if you mailed them on time:

- DHL Express (DHL): DHL "Same Day" Service;

- Federal Express (FedEx): FedEx Priority Overnight, FedEx Standard Overnight, FedEx 2Day, FedEx International Priority, and FedEx International First;

- United Parcel Service (UPS): UPS Next Day Air, UPS Next Day Air Saver, UPS 2nd Day Air, UPS 2nd Day Air A.M., UPS Worldwide Express Plus, and UPS Worldwide Express.

(d) Extension of Time to File. If more time is needed to file Form 1041 for a trust, use Form 7004, "Application for Automatic Extension of Time to File Certain Business Income Tax, Information, and Other Returns," to apply for an automatic five-month extension of time to file.

■ The Trent Trust owes the IRS $1,746 after subtracting the $2,000 total payments made from the $3,746 total tax due.

¶2932 WHERE TO FILE FORM 1041

All trusts including charitable and split-interest trusts (other than charitable remainder trusts) should mail Form 1041 to the IRS Service Center listed in the chart below which is found on page 8 of the 2013 Instructions to Form 1041:

Where To File

For all estates and trusts, including charitable and split-interest trusts (other than Charitable Remainder Trusts).

IF you are located in ...	THEN use this address if you:	
	Are not enclosing a check or money order ...	**Are enclosing a check or money order ...**
Connecticut, Delaware, District of Columbia, Florida, Georgia, Illinois, Indiana, Kentucky, Maine, Maryland, Massachusetts, Michigan, New Hampshire, New Jersey, New York, North Carolina, Ohio, Pennsylvania, Rhode Island, South Carolina, Tennessee, Vermont, Virginia, West Virginia, Wisconsin	Department of the Treasury Internal Revenue Service Cincinnati, Ohio 45999-0048	Department of the Treasury Internal Revenue Service Cincinnati, Ohio 45999-0148
Alabama, Alaska, Arizona, Arkansas, California, Colorado, Hawaii, Idaho, Iowa, Kansas, Louisiana, Minnesota, Mississippi, Missouri, Montana, Nebraska, Nevada, New Mexico, North Dakota, Oklahoma, Oregon, South Dakota, Texas, Utah, Washington, Wyoming	Department of the Treasury Internal Revenue Service Ogden, Utah 84201-0048	Department of the Treasury Internal Revenue Service Ogden, Utah 84201-0148
A foreign country or United States possession	Internal Revenue Service P.O. Box 409101 Ogden, Utah 84409	Internal Revenue Service P.O. Box 409101 Ogden, Utah 84409

Electronic filing. Applications to become an IRS e-file provider must be submitted online. The IRS is no longer accepting paper applications on Form 8633, "Application to Participate in the IRS e-file Program." Qualified fiduciaries or transmitters may be able to file Form 1041 and related schedules electronically. To become an *e-file* provider complete the following steps: (1) Create an IRS e-Services account; (2) Submit an e-file provider application online; and (3) Pass a suitability check. Existing *e-file* providers must now use e-Services to make account updates.

¶2932

Form 1041 e-filing. For tax year 2013, both Form 8453-F, "U.S. Estate or Trust Income Tax Declaration and Signature for Electronic Filing," and new Form 8453-FE, "U.S. Estate or Trust Declaration for an IRS E-File Return," must be used when the trust e-files. Trusts that file Form 1041 electronically may have the trustee sign the return electronically by using a personal identification number (PIN) [See Form 8879-F, "IRS e-file Signature Authorization for Form 1041," for details]. If the trustee does not sign the electronically filed return by using a PIN, the trustee must file Form 8453-F, "U.S. Estate or Trust Income Tax Declaration and Signature for Electronic Filing." Form 8453-F may also be used as a transmittal if the trustee needs to attach certain forms or other documents that cannot be electronically filed. If Form 1041 is *e-filed* and there is a balance due, the trustee may authorize an electronic funds withdrawal with the return.

¶2933 SCHEDULE A—CHARITABLE DEDUCTION

If any part of the gross income of a trust other than a simple trust is paid (or treated as paid) during the tax year for a charitable purpose, the trust is entitled to claim a charitable deduction. The amount of that charitable deduction is computed on Schedule A of Schedule 1041.

> **NOTE:** Foreign charities are okay. The charitable organization need not be created or organized in the United States.

A simple trust or a pooled income fund need not complete Schedule A of Form 1041. This schedule must be completed by trusts such as complex trusts that claim a charitable deduction [IRC Sec. 642(c)(1)]. A simple trust is required by definition to distribute all of its income to its beneficiaries and therefore makes no charitable contributions.

A pooled income fund, a nonexempt charitable trust treated as a private foundation, or a trust with unrelated business income should attach a separate sheet to Form 1041 instead of using Schedule A of Form 1041 to compute the amount of the charitable deduction.

The confusing aspect of a trust's deduction for charitable contributions is that the charitable contribution deduction is considered to consist of a proportionate part of each item of income. As a result, the deduction must be allocated proportionately among all items of income included in DNI. For further discussion, see ¶2803.

Election to treat contributions as paid in prior tax year. The fiduciary of a trust may elect to treat a current contribution as paid during the previous tax year [IRC Sec. 642(c)(1); Reg. Sec. 1.642(c)-1(b)]. The election must be made no later than the due date (including extensions) for filing the income tax return for the succeeding tax year [Reg. Sec. 1.642(c)-1(b)(2)].

For example, if a calendar year trust makes a qualified charitable contribution on April 1, 2014, from income earned in 2013 or prior, then the fiduciary can elect to treat the contribution as paid in 2013.

The election must be made by filing a statement with the income tax return for the taxable year in which the contribution is treated as paid. The statement must contain the following:

1. The name and address of the fiduciary;

2. The estate or trust for which the fiduciary is acting;

3. An indication that the fiduciary is making an election under IRC Sec. 642(c)(1) in respect of contributions treated as paid during such taxable year;

4. The name and address of each organization to which any such contribution is paid; and

5. The amount of each contribution and date of actual payment, or if applicable, the total amount of contributions paid to each organization during the succeeding taxable year, to be treated as paid in the preceding taxable year [Reg. Sec. 1.642(c)-1(b)(3)].

The election must be filed by the due date (including extensions) for Form 1041 for the next year. See ¶ 2810.

Schedule A, Line 1—Amounts paid or permanently set aside for charitable purposes from gross income. A complex trust may claim an unlimited deduction for gross income that, under the terms of the will or trust, is paid or permanently set aside during the taxable year for charitable purposes [IRC Sec. 642(c)]. Unlike the charitable deduction allowed individuals, no limitation is placed on the amount that can be deducted by a trust [Reg. Sec. 1.642(c)-2(a)].

On line 1, enter the amounts that were paid for a charitable purpose out of the trust's gross income, including any capital gains that are attributable to income under the trust's governing instrument or local law. Include amounts paid during the tax year from gross income received in a prior tax year, but only if no deduction was allowed for any prior tax year for these amounts.

Schedule A, Line 2—Tax-exempt income allocable to charitable contributions. On line 2, enter the amount of the charitable deduction that was allocable to tax-exempt income. Unless the trust agreement provides otherwise, determine the amount of tax-exempt income allocable to charitable contributions by multiplying line 1 by a fraction, the numerator of which is the total tax-exempt income of the trust, and the denominator of which is the gross income of the trust. Do not include in the denominator any losses allocated to corpus.

Schedule A, Line 3. Subtract line 2 from line 1.

Schedule A, Line 4—Capital gains for the tax year allocated to corpus and paid or permanently set aside for charitable purposes. Enter the total of all capital gains for the tax year that are:

• Allocable to corpus; and

• Paid or permanently set aside for charitable purposes.

Schedule A, Line 5. Add lines 3 and 4.

Schedule A, Line 6—IRC Section 1202 exclusion available to capital gains paid or permanently set aside for charitable purposes. If the exclusion of gain from the sale or exchange of qualified small business stock was claimed, enter the part of the gain included on Schedule A, lines and 4, that was excluded under Sec. 1202.

Schedule A, Line 7—Charitable deduction. Subtract line 6 from line 5.

■ The Trent Trust does not complete Schedule A because it is a simple trust and claims no charitable deductions.

¶2933

¶2934 SCHEDULE B—INCOME DISTRIBUTION DEDUCTION

If the trust was required to distribute income currently or if it paid, credited, or was required to distribute any other amounts to beneficiaries during the tax year, complete Schedule B of Form 1041 to determine the amount of the trust's income distribution deduction.

Separate share rule. If the trust has more than one beneficiary, and if different beneficiaries have substantially separate and independent shares, their shares are treated as separate trusts for the sole purpose of determining the DNI allocable to the respective beneficiaries [IRC Sec. 663(c)]. If the separate share rule applies, figure the DNI allocable to each beneficiary on a separate sheet and attach the sheet to this return. Any deduction or loss that is applicable solely to one separate share of the trust is not available to any other share of the same estate. For a discussion of the separate share rule, see ¶2818.

Lines 1 through 7 of the Schedule B are used to determine the amount of a trust's DNI. See ¶2803 for a further discussion.

Briefly, DNI is important because it not only is a ceiling on the fiduciary's distributions deduction but is also a ceiling on the amounts taxable to beneficiaries. It is also used to determine the character of the distributions to the beneficiaries as indicated on Schedule K-1.

Schedule B, Line 1—Adjusted total income. Enter the amount of adjusted total income from line 17, page 1 of Form 1041. The instructions to Form 1041 provide that if this amount is a loss that is attributable wholly or in part to the capital loss limitation rules of IRC Sec. 1211(b) (line 4), then the trust should enter as a negative number on line 1 of Schedule B the lesser of the loss from line 17, page 1, or the loss from line 4, Page 1 of Form 1041. If the line 17 loss is not attributable to the capital loss on line 4, enter zero.

If Schedule B is being completed for a simple trust, subtract from adjusted total income any extraordinary dividends or taxable stock dividends included on Page 1, line 2, and determined under the governing instrument and applicable local law to be allocable to corpus.

> ■ The $36,000 adjusted total income of the Trent Trust from Page 1, line 17 is entered on line 1 of Schedule B of Form 1041.

Schedule B, Line 2—Adjusted tax-exempt interest. To compute the amount of adjusted tax-exempt interest, add the following:

- Tax-exempt interest income on line 2 of Schedule A;

- Any expenses allowable under IRC Sec. 212 allocable to tax-exempt interest; and

- Any interest expense allocable to tax-exempt interest.

Then subtract the Step 1 total from the amount of tax-exempt interest (including exempt-interest dividends) received.

Schedule B, Line 3. Total net gain from Schedule D (Form 1041), line 16, Column (1).

¶2934

Schedule B, Line 4. Enter amount from Schedule A, line 4 (reduced by any allocable Section 1202 exclusion).

Schedule B, Line 5. Enter capital gains for the tax year included on Schedule A, line 1.

Schedule B, Line 6. Enter any gain from page 1, line 4, as a negative number.

■ The $10,000 capital gain realized by the Trent Trust is entered on line 6 as a negative number.

Schedule B, Line 7. Distributable net income.

■ DNI for the Trent Trust is computed on line 7 by combining $36,000 from line 1 and ($10,000) from line 6 for a DNI of $26,000.

Schedule B, Line 8—Accounting income. If filing for a simple trust, skip this line. If filing for a complex trust, enter the income for the tax year determined under the terms of the governing instrument and applicable local law. Do not include extraordinary dividends or taxable stock dividends determined under the governing instrument and applicable local law to be allocable to corpus.

Schedule B, Lines 9 and 13. The amounts of income of the trust required to be distributed currently to each beneficiary, whether distributed or not, and any other amounts paid, credited, or required to be distributed during the tax year, are entered on line 9 and 10 of Schedule B, Page 2.

■ The Trent Trust had $20,000 of ordinary income and trustee's fees in the amount of $4,000. The $4,000 trustee fees are deductible without regard to the 2 percent floor for miscellaneous deductions because the fees were only incurred because the trust existed. See ¶2813 for a further explanation. Because local law provides that one-half of the trustee's fees are paid from trust income and one-half from trust principal, $2,000 of the trustee fees are chargeable against the trust's income. As a result only $18,000 was distributed to Mary and $18,000 is entered for line 9, line 11, and line 13.

Schedule B, Line 14—Tentative income distribution deduction. Subtract line 2 from line 7. If zero or less, enter -0-.

■ The Trent Trust's tentative income distribution deduction in the amount of $26,000 is entered on line 14. You figure this amount by subtracting line 2 (-0-) from line 7 ($26,000).

Schedule B, Line 15—Income distribution deduction. Enter the smaller of line 13 or line 14 here and on Page 1, line 18.

■ The Trent Trust enters $18,000.

¶2935 SCHEDULE G—TAX COMPUTATION

Schedule G (Form 1041), Line 1a—Tax rate schedule. The tax computation for the trust is made on Schedule G of Form 1041. If the trust had no capital gain, you would figure the tax using the 2013 Tax Rate Schedule below (included also is the 2014 tax rate schedule for planning purposes):

¶2935

2013 Tax Rate Schedule for Estates and Trusts

If taxable income is:	*The tax is:*
Not over $2,450	15% of the taxable income
Over $2,450 but not over $5,700	$367.50 plus 25% of the excess over $2,450
Over $5,700 but not over $8,750	$1,180 plus 28% of the excess over $5,700
Over $8,750 but not over $11,950	$2,034 plus 33% of the excess over $8,750
Over $11,950	$3,090 plus 39.6% of the excess over $11,950

2014 Tax Rate Schedule for Estates and Trusts

If taxable income is:	*The tax is:*
Not over $2,500	15% of the taxable income
Over $2,500 but not over $5,800	$375 plus 25% of the excess over $2,500
Over $5,800 but not over $8,900	$1,200 plus 28% of the excess over $5,800
Over $8,900 but not over $12,150	$2,068 plus 33% of the excess over $8,900
Over $12,150	$3,140.50 plus 39.6% of the excess over $12,150

If the trust had both net capital gain and any taxable income, complete Part V of Schedule D (Form 1041), enter the tax from line 35 of Schedule D (Form 1041).

■ The Trent Trust computed its tax bill on Schedule D (Form 1041) and on Form 8949 as discussed at ¶ 2936. The resulting tax bill in the amount of $3,527 is entered on lines 1a, 1d, 3, and 7 of Schedule G (Form 1041).

Schedule D and Schedule D Tax Worksheet. Use Part V of Schedule D (Form 1041) or the Schedule D Tax Worksheet, whichever is applicable to figure the trust's tax if the trust files Schedule D and has:

- A net capital gain and any taxable income, or

- Qualified dividends on line 2b(2) of Form 1041 and any taxable income.

Qualified Dividends Tax Worksheet. If the trust does not have to file Part I or Part II of Schedule D (Form 1041) and the trust has an amount entered on line 2b(2) of Form 1041, and any taxable income (line 22), Schedule G, then figure the tax using the worksheet on page 31 of the 2013 Form 1041 Instructions and enter the tax on line 1a. The amount entered on line 2b(2) of Form 1041 must be reduced by the portion of IRC Sec. 691(c) deduction claimed on line 19 of page 1 of Form 1041 if the trust received qualified dividends that were income in respect of a decedent.

Schedule G (Form 1041), Line 2a—Foreign tax credit. Attach Form 1116 "Foreign Tax Credit (Individual, Estate or Trust)" if the trust elects to claim credit for income or profits taxes paid or accured to a foreign country or a U.S. possession. The trust may claim credit for that part of the foreign taxes not allocable to beneficiaries (including charitable beneficiaries). Enter the trust's share of the credit on line 2a.

Schedule G (Form 1041), Line 2b—General business credit. Enter on line 2b the trust's total general business credit allowed for the year from Form 3800 which must be filed to claim any of the general business credits. If the trust's only source of credits listed in Part I of Form 3800 is from pass through entities, the trust may not be required to complete the source credit form. For a list of available credits, see the Instructions for Form 3800.

¶2935

Do not include any amounts that are allocated to a beneficiary. Credits that are allocated between the trust and the beneficiaries are listed in the instructions for Schedule K-1, box 13. Generally, these credits are apportioned on the basis of the income allocable to the trust and the beneficiaries.

Schedule G (Form 1041), Line 2c—Credit for prior year minimum tax. A trust that paid alternative minimum tax in a previous year may be eligible for a minimum tax credit this year. [See Form 8801, "Credit for Prior Year Minimum Tax—Individuals, Estates and Trusts."]

Schedule G (Form 1041), Line 2d—Bond credits. Complete and attach Form 8912, "Credit to Holders of Tax Credit Bonds," if the trust claims a credit for holding a tax credit bond. Be sure to include the credit in interest income.

Schedule G (Form 1041), Line 3—Total credits. To claim a credit other than the credits entered on lines 2a through 2d, include the credit in the total for line 3. Complete and attach the appropriate form and write the form number and amount of the credit on the dotted line to the left of the entry space.

Schedule G (Form 1041), Line 4—Net investment income tax from Form 8960, line 21. Enter on Line 4 of Schedule G (Form 1041), the amount of net investment income (NII) tax owed by the trust and attach Form 8960, "Net Investment Income Tax—Individuals, Estates, and Trusts" to Form 1041. Trusts use Form 8960 to report their NII tax and to calculate the amount of NII tax that the trust owes [See ¶2790 for a copy of the IRS Instructions for Form 8960 and ¶2947 for a sample completed Form 8960 for the Trent Trust. See ¶2948 for background discussion of the NII tax and see ¶2949 for a line-by-line discussion of how to complete Form 8960 for the Trent Trust].

■ The Trent Trust must complete Form 8960 [See ¶2790 for a copy of the IRS Instructions for Form 8960 and ¶2947 for a sample completed Form 8960 for the Trent Trust. See ¶2948 for background discussion of the NII tax and see ¶2949 for a line-by-line discussion of how to complete Form 8960 for the Trent Trust].

After completing Form 8960, the Trent Trust multiplies $5,750 by 3.8 percent to yield a NII tax owed by the trust in 2013 of $218.50 (rounded to $219) which the Trent Trust enters on line 21 (Form 8960) and on Schedule G, line 4 (Form 1041).

Schedule G (Form 1041), Line 5—Recapture taxes. Include the following recapture taxes on line 5: recapture of investment credit; recapture of low-income housing credit; recapture of qualified electric vehicle; recapture of the Indian employment credit; recapture of the new markets credit; recapture of the credit for the employment-provided child care facilities; and recapture of the alternative motor vehicle credit and the alternative fuel vehicle refueling property credit.

Schedule G (Form 1041), Line 6—Household employment taxes. The trust will owe household employment tax and must file Schedule H with the estate tax return if the answer to any of the following questions is "Yes":

1. Did the trust pay any one household employee cash wages of $1,800 or more in 2013? Cash wages include wages paid by check, money order, etc. When figuring the amount of cash wages paid, combine cash wages paid by the trust with cash wages paid to the household employee in the same calendar year by the house-

hold of the decedent or beneficiary for whom the administrator, executor, or trustee is acting.

2. Did the trust withhold federal income tax during 2013 for any household employee at the request of any household employee?

3. Did the trust pay total cash wages of $1,000 or more in any calendar quarter of 2012 or 2013 to household employees?

Schedule H can be omitted from the trust's tax return only if the answer to all three questions is "No."

Schedule G (Form 1041), Line 7—Total tax. Add the following taxes computed on the following forms to the total tax entered on line 7:

- Interest on deferred tax attributable to installment sales of certain timeshares and residential lots and certain nondealer real property installment obligations.

- Form 4970, "Tax on Accumulation Distribution of Trusts."

- Tax on electing small business trusts (ESBTs). For further discussion of ESBTs, see ¶ 2800.

- Form 8697, "Interest Computation Under the Look-Back Method for Completed Long-Term Contracts."

- Form 8866, "Interest Computation Under the Look-Back Method for Property Depreciated Under the Income Forecast Method."

- Interest on deferrral of gain from certain constructive ownership transactions.

- Form 5329, "Additional Taxes on Qualified Plans (including IRAs) and Other Tax-Favored Accounts."

¶2936 SCHEDULE D (FORM 1041)—CAPITAL GAINS AND LOSSES AND FORM 8949—SALES AND OTHER DISPOSITIONS OF CAPITAL ASSETS

(a) Report Capital Gains on Schedule D (Form 1041) and/or Form 8949. Beginning in 2013, trusts must use Form 8949, "Sales and Other Dispositions of Capital Assets" to report sales and exchanges of capital assets not reported on another form or schedule. The use of Form 8949 by trusts is new in 2013. Many transactions that, in previous years, would have been reported by estates and trusts on Schedule D (Form 1041) or Schedule D-1 (Form 1041) must be reported on Form 8949 if they have to be reported on a 2013 tax return form. Certain transactions may be combined and the totals reported on line 1a or line 8a of Schedule D (Form 1041) without completing Form 8949. Filers that use Form 8949 must complete Form 8949 before completing line 1b, 2, 3, 8b, 9 or 10 of Schedule D (Form 1041). Beginning in 2013, Schedule D-1 (Form 1041) will no longer be used [For a completed Form 8949 and Schedule D (Form 1041) see ¶ 2945. The IRS Instructions for Form 8949 are reproduced in ¶ 2944].

▶ **WARNING:** Do not substitute Schedule D (Form 1040) for Schedule D (Form 1041). They are different forms.

¶2936

(b) Capital Gains Tax Rates. The following chart illustrates the capital gains tax rates in effect for 2013-2014.

Capital Gains Maximum Rates for 2013 and 2014

Type of Property	Period Held	Maximum Rate*
Capital assets, other than on gain attributable to Section 1250 recapture or collectibles	12 months or less More than 12 months	39.6% 0% if in 15% ordinary income tax rate bracket** 15% if in 28% or 33% ordinary income tax rate bracket 20% if in 39.6% ordinary income tax rate bracket

* Excluding the 3.8% net investment income tax that may apply.

** Only to the extent the gain would otherwise be in the 15% tax bracket.

(c) Purpose of Schedule D, Capital Gains and Losses. Schedule D (Form 1041) should be used for the following purposes:

- To report the overall capital gains or losses from transactions reported on Form 8949.

- To report certain transactions that the trust does not have to report on Form 8949.

- To report gain from Part I of Form 4797, "Sales of Business Property."

- To report capital gain from Form 6252, "Installment Sale Income."

- To report capital gain or loss from Form 6781, "Gains and Losses From Section 1256 Contracts and Straddles."

- To report capital gain or loss from Form 8824, "Like-Kind Exchanges."

- To report undistributed long-term capital gains from Form 2439, "Notice to Shareholder of Undistributed Long-Term Capital Gains."

- To report capital gain or loss from partnerships, S corporations, or other estates or trusts.

(d) Form 8949, Sales and Other Dispositions of Capital Assets. Form 8949 should be completed as follows:

- On Part I of Form 8949 summarize three categories (A, B, and C) of short-term capital gains and losses.

- On Part II summarize three categories (D, E, and F) of long-term capital gains and losses.

- A separate Form 8949 should be completed for each category type.

- The capital gains and losses will be included in category A or D if the investment's cost or other basis is shown in box 3 of Form 1099-B.

- The capital gains and losses will be included in category B or E if no investment basis is shown in box 3 of Form 1099-B.

- The capital gains and losses will be included in category C or F if none of the other boxes are checked. When completed, the summarized Form 8949 information is transferred to Form 1041 Schedule D (Capital Gains and Losses).

¶2936

- A trust's share of capital gains (losses) from a partnership, S corporation, or another trust is reported only on Schedule D (1041) (i.e., not on Form 8949).

- Instead of reporting each of the transactions on a separate line of Form 8949, they can be reported on an attached statement containing all the same information as Form 8949 and in a similar format, using as many attached statements as needed. The combined totals from all the attached statements should be entered on a Form 8949 with the appropriate box checked. For example, report on Part II of Form 8949 with box D checked, all long-term gains and losses from transactions reported by the broker on a statement showing that the basis of the property sold was reported to the IRS. If there are statements from more than one broker, report the totals from each broker on a separate line. Do not enter "available upon request" and summary totals instead of reporting the details of each transaction on Form(s) 8949 or attached statements.

    (e) Form 8949—Line 1—Part I. On Form 8949, enter all sales and exchanges of capital assets, including stocks, bonds, etc. and real estate (if not reported on Form 4684, 4797, 6252, 6781 or 8824). Report short-term (held 1 year or less) gains or losses in Part I. Report long-term (held 1 year or more) gains and losses in Part II. The details of each transaction should be entered on a separate line of Form 8949. Note that Form 8949 must be completed before completing lines 1b, 2, 3, 8b, 9, or 10 of Schedule D (Form 1041) because the combined totals from all Forms 8949 are reported on Schedule D.

When computing the holding period begin counting on the date after the entity received the property and include the day the entity disposed of it.

Use a separate Part I for each of the following types of short-term transactions:

- Short-term transactions reported on Form 1099-B with an amount shown for cost or other basis unless the statement indicates that amount was not reported to the IRS. Check box A at the top of this Part I. If box 6b of Form 1099-B is not checked, which means basis was not reported to the IRS, report that transaction on Part I with box B, not box A, checked.

- Short-term transactions reported on Form 1099-B without an amount shown for cost or other basis. Check box B at the top of Form 8949-Part I. If box 6b of Form 1099-B is not checked, which means basis was not reported to the IRS, report that transaction on Part I with box B, not box A, checked.

- Short-term transactions for which the fiduciary cannot check box A or B because the fiduciary did not receive a Form 1099-B (or substitute statement). Check box C at the top of this Part I.

Use a separate Part II for each of the following types of long-term transactions:

- Long-term transactions reported on Form 1099-B with an amount shown for cost or other basis unless the statement indicates that that amount was not reported to the IRS. Check box D at the top of this Part II. If box 6b of Form 1099-B is not checked, which means that basis was not reported to the IRS, report that transaction on Part II with box E, not box D checked.

- Long-term transactions reported on Form 1099-B without an amount shown for cost or other basis. Check box E at the top of Part II. If box 6b of Form 1099-B is not

¶2936

checked, which means that basis was not reported to the IRS, report that transaction on Part II with box E, not box D, checked.

- Long-term transactions without box D or E checked because the trust did not receive a Form 1099-B (or substitute statement). Check box F at the top of Part II.

  ▶ **FILING POINTER:** The fiduciary may not need to file Form 8949 for certain transactions. This is new in 2013. The return preparer may be able to aggregate those transactions and report them directly on either line 1a (for short-term transactions) or line 8a (for long-term transactions) of Schedule D (Form 1041). This option applies only to transactions (other than sales of collectibles) for which:

  - The entity received a Form 1099-B (or substitute statement) that shows basis was reported to the IRS and does not show a nondeductible wash sale loss in box 5, and

  - The entity does not need to make any adjustments to the basis of type of gain or loss (short-term or long-term) reported on Form 1099-B, or to your gain or loss.

If the fiduciary decides to report these transactions directly on Schedule D, they do not need to be reported on Form 8949 and a statement does not need to be attached.

  ▶ **FILING POINTER:** Instead of reporting each transaction on a separate row on Form 8949, the return preparer can report them on an attached statement containing all the same information as Parts I and II and in a similar format with a description of property, dates of acquisition and disposition, proceeds, basis, adjustment and gains and loss. The combined totals from all attached statements should be entered on Parts I and II with the appropriate box checked.

Columns (a)–(h) of Form 8949. Enter in columns (a)–(h) the details regarding the entity's acquisition and sale of the asset.

- Column (a)—Description of Property. For stock, use the stock ticker symbols or abbreviations to describe the property as long as they are based on the descriptions of the property as shown on Form 1099-B or Form 1099-S.

- Column (b)—Date acquired. Enter in this column the date the entity acquired the asset. Use the trade date for stocks and bonds traded on an exchange or over-the-counter market. For stock or the other property sold short, enter the date the entity acquired the stock or property delivered to the broker or lender to close the short sale.

- Column (c)—Date sold or disposed. Enter in this column the date the entity sold or disposed of the property. Use the trade date for stocks and bonds traded on an exchange or over-the-counter market. For stock or other property sold short, enter the date the entity delivered the stock or property to the broker or lender to close the short sale.

- Column (d)—Proceeds (sales price). If the entity sold stock or bonds and received a Form 1099-B listing gross sales price, that amount should be entered in column (e). If Form 1099-B indicates that gross proceeds minus commissions and option premiums were reported to the IRS, enter that net amount in column (e).

¶2936

- Column (e)—Cost or other basis.

  — **Basis of trust property.** Special rules apply when determining the basis of trust property. Generally, the basis of property acquired by gift is the same as its basis in the hands of the donor. However, if the FMV of the property at the time it was transferred to the trust is less than the transferor's basis, then the FMV is used to determine any loss upon disposition. The cost or other basis is the cost of the property plus purchase commissions and improvements, minus depreciation, amortization and depletion. If the property was transferred to the trust after 1976, and a gift tax was paid, then the donor's basis should be increased as follows: Multiply the amount of the gift paid by a fraction, the numerator of which is the net appreciation in value of the gift and the denominator of which is the amount of the gift. For this purpose the net appreciation in value of the gift is the amount by which the FMV of the gift exceeds the donor's adjusted basis.

- Column (f)—Codes. In order to explain any adjustment to gain or loss in column (g), enter the appropriate code(s) in column (f). [See "How To Complete Form 8949, Columns (f) and (g)" which is found on pages 6 and 7 of Form 8949 (reproduced below).] If more than one code applies, enter all the codes that apply in alphabetical order (for example, "BOQ"). Do not separate the codes by a space or comma.

- Column (g)—Adjustments to gain or loss. Enter in this column any necessary adjustments to gain or loss. Enter negative amounts in parentheses. Also enter a code in column (f) to explain the adjustment. [See "How to Complete Form 8949, Columns (f) and (g)," which is found on pages 6 and 7 of Form 8949 (reproduced below).] Include in this column any expense of sale, such as broker's fees and commissions, state and local transfer taxes, option premiums, reinvested gains or dividends that were previously reported as income, costs that were capitalized and original issue discount that has been previously reported as income unless the net sales price was reported in column (e). If any expense of sale is included in this column, enter "0" in column (b). The following items may decrease the basis of the property owned by the trust prior to computing the gain or loss from the sale, exchange, or other disposition of the property:

  — Nontaxable distributions that consist of return of capital;

  — Deductions previously allowed or allowable for depreciation;

  — Casualty or theft loss deductions.

    ■ The Trent Trust makes no adjustments to basis and leaves boxes (f) and (g) blank.

- Column (h)—Gain or (Loss). Figure gain or loss on each row. First, subtract the cost or other basis in column (e) from the proceeds (sales price) in column (d). Then take into account any adjustments in column (g). Enter the gain or (loss) in column (h). Enter negative amounts in parentheses.

The total of the amounts in columns (d), (e), (g) , and (h) on Form 8949 are added and the total is entered on Part II, line 2 of Form 8949. That total is then entered on Schedule D of Form 1041 depending on whether box D, E, or F was checked at the beginning of Part II as follows:

- If box D was checked (long-term transaction reported on Form 1099-B showing basis was reported to the IRS), enter the total on Schedule D, Form 1041, line 8b.

¶2936

- If box E was checked (long-term transaction reported on Form 1099-B showing basis was not reported to the IRS), enter the total on Schedule D, Form 1041, line 9.
- If box F was checked (long-term transaction not reported on Form 1099-B) enter the total on Schedule D, Form 1041, line 10.

   ■ The Trent Trust checked box D because their long-term capital gain was reported on Form 1099-B showing basis was reported to the IRS. They therefore enter the $10,000 total from Part II, line 2 of Form 8949 on line 8b of Form 1041, Schedule D.

How To Complete Form 8949, Columns (f) and (g)

For most transactions, you do not need to complete columns (f) and (g) and can leave them blank. You may need to complete columns (f) and (g) if you got a Form 1099-B or 1099-S (or substitute statement) that is incorrect, if you are excluding or postponing a capital gain, if you have a disallowed loss, or in certain other situations. Details are in the table below. If you enter more than one code in column (f), see *More than one code* in the instructions for column (g).

IF . . .	THEN enter this code in column (f) . . .	AND. . .
You received a Form 1099-B (or substitute statement) and the basis shown in box 3 is incorrect	B	• If box B is checked at the top of Part I or if box E is checked at the top of Part II, enter the correct basis in column (e), and enter -0- in column (g). • If box A is checked at the top of Part I or if box D is checked at the top of Part II, enter the basis shown on Form 1099-B (or substitute statement) in column (e), even though that basis is incorrect. Correct the error by entering an adjustment in column (g). To figure the adjustment needed, see the *Worksheet for Basis Adjustments in Column (g)*. Also see *Example 4—adjustment for incorrect basis* in the instructions for column (h).
You received a Form 1099-B (or substitute statement) and the type of gain or loss (short-term or long-term) shown in box 1c is incorrect	T	Enter -0- in column (g). Report the gain or loss on the correct Part of Form 8949.
You received a Form 1099-B or 1099-S (or substitute statement) as a nominee for the actual owner of the property	N	Report the transaction on Form 8949 as you would if you were the actual owner, but also enter any resulting gain as a negative adjustment (in parentheses) in column (g) or any resulting loss as a positive adjustment in column (g). As a result of this adjustment, the amount in column (h) should be zero. However, if you received capital gain distributions as a nominee, report them instead as described under *Capital Gain Distributions* in the Instructions for Schedule D (Form 1040).
You sold or exchanged your main home at a gain, must report the sale or exchange on Part II of Form 8949 (as explained in *Sale of Your Home* in the Instructions for Schedule D (Form 1040)), and can exclude some or all of the gain	H	Report the sale or exchange on Form 8949 as you would if you were not taking the exclusion. Then enter the amount of excluded (nontaxable) gain as a negative number (in parentheses) in column (g). See the example in the instructions for column (g).
You sold or exchanged qualified small business stock and can exclude part of the gain	Q	Report the sale or exchange on Form 8949 as you would if you were not taking the exclusion and enter the amount of the exclusion as a negative number (in parentheses) in column (g). However, if the transaction is reported as an installment sale, see *Gain from an installment sale of QSB stock* in the Instructions for Schedule D (Form 1040).
You can exclude all or part of your gain under the rules explained in the Schedule D instructions for DC Zone assets or qualified community assets	X	Report the sale or exchange on Form 8949 as you would if you were not taking the exclusion. Then enter the amount of the exclusion as a negative number (in parentheses) in column (g).
You are electing to postpone all or part of your gain under the rules explained in the Schedule D instructions for any rollover of gain (for example, rollover of gain from QSB stock or publicly traded securities)	R	Report the sale or exchange on Form 8949 as you would if you were not making the election. Then enter the amount of postponed gain as a negative number (in parentheses) in column (g).

¶2936

IF . . .	THEN enter this code in column (f) . . .	AND . . .
You have a nondeductible loss from a wash sale	W	Report the sale or exchange on Form 8949 and enter the amount of the nondeductible loss as a positive number in column (g). See the Schedule D instructions for more information about wash sales. If you received a Form 1099-B (or substitute statement) and the amount of nondeductible wash sale loss shown (box 5 of Form 1099-B) is incorrect, enter the correct amount of the nondeductible loss as a positive number in column (g). If the amount of the nondeductible loss is less than the amount shown on Form 1099-B (or substitute statement), attach a statement explaining the difference. If no part of the loss is a nondeductible loss from a wash sale transaction, enter -0- in column (g).
You have a nondeductible loss other than a loss indicated by code W	L	Report the sale or exchange on Form 8949 and enter the amount of the nondeductible loss as a positive number in column (g). See *Nondeductible Losses* in the Instructions for Schedule D (Form 1040).
You received a Form 1099-B or 1099-S (or substitute statement) for a transaction and there are selling expenses or option premiums that are not reflected on the form or statement by an adjustment to either the proceeds or basis shown	E	Enter in column (d) the proceeds shown on the form or statement you received. Enter in column (e) any cost or other basis shown on Form 1099-B (or substitute statement). In column (g), enter as a negative number (in parentheses) any selling expenses and option premium that you paid (and that are not reflected on the form or statement you received) and enter as a positive number any option premium that you received (and that is not reflected on the form or statement you received). For more information about option premiums, see *Gain or Loss From Options* in the Instructions for Schedule D (Form 1040).
You had a loss from the sale, exchange, or worthlessness of small business (section 1244) stock and the total loss is more than the maximum amount that can be treated as an ordinary loss	S	See *Small Business (Section 1244) Stock* in the Schedule D (Form 1040) instructions.
You disposed of collectibles (see the Schedule D instructions)	C	Enter -0- in column (g). Report the disposition on Form 8949 as you would report any sale or exchange.
You report multiple transactions on a single row as described in *Exception 1* or *Exception 2* under *Exceptions to reporting each transaction on a separate row*	M	See *Exception 1* and *Exception 2* under *Exceptions to reporting each transaction on a separate row*. Enter -0- in column (g) unless an adjustment is required because of another code.
You have an adjustment not explained earlier in this column	O	Enter the appropriate adjustment amount in column (g). See the instructions for column (g).
None of the other statements in this column apply	Leave columns (f) and (g) blank.	

¶2936

(f) Schedule D (Form 1041).

Schedule D (Form 1041)—Lines 1a and 8a—Transactions Not Reported on Form 8949. The entity can report on line 1a (for short-term transactions) or line 8a (for long-term transactions) the aggregate totals from any transactions (except sales of collectibles) in the following situations:

- The trust received a Form 1099-B (or substitute statement) that shows basis was reported to the IRS and does not show a nondeductible wash sale loss in box 5, and

- The trust does not need to make any adjustments to the basis or type of gain or loss (short term or long term) reported on Form 1099-B (or substitute statement), or to its gain or loss.

If the trust chooses to report these transactions on lines 1a and 8a, the trust should not report them on Form 8949. The return preparer does not need to attach a statement to explain the entries on lines 1a and 8a. The amount of gain or loss should be computed on each line. First, subtract the cost or other basis in column (e) from the proceeds (sales price) in column (d). Enter the gain or loss in column (h). Enter negative amounts in parentheses.

Schedule D (Form 1041)—Lines 1b, 2, 3, 8b, 9 and 10—Transactions Reported on Form 8949. The trust should report the gain or loss on each line. First, subtract the cost of other basis in column (e) from the proceeds (sales price) in column (d). Then combine the result with any adjustments in column (g). Enter the gain or loss in column (h).

Line 8b. The trust can report on 8b the gain from any long-term gain transactions reported on Form 8949.

■ The Trent Trust enters $10,000 on line 8b because the Trent Trust checked Box D on Form 8949 which indicated that their long-term capital gain was reported on Form 1099-B and showed that basis was reported to the IRS. They therefore enter the $10,000 total from Part II, line 2 of Form 8949 on line 8b of Form 1041, Schedule D.

Schedule D (Form 1041)—Line 13—Capital Gain Distributions. On Line 13, column (h), enter as a long-term capital gain distributions paid during the year, regardless of how long the entity held its investment. This amount is reported in box 2a of Form 1099-DIV.

Schedule D (Form 1041)—Line 16—Net Long-Term Capital Gain or (Loss).

■ The Trent Trust carried the $10,000 figure to this line.

Part III—Summary of Parts I and II.

Line 17, Column 1—Beneficiaries' Net Short-Term Capital Gain or Loss. Enter the amount of net short-term capital gain or loss allocable to the beneficiary or beneficiaries. Include only those short-term capital losses that are taken into account in determining the amount of gain from the sale or exchange of capital assets that is paid, credited, or required to be distributed to any beneficiary during the tax year. If the losses from the sale or exchange of capital assets are more than the gains, all of the losses must be allocated to the trust and none are allocated to the beneficiaries.

¶2936

Line 17, Column 2—Trust's Net Short-Term Capital Gain or Loss. Enter the amount of the net short-term capital gain or loss allocable to the trust. Include any capital gain paid or permanently set aside for a charitable purpose.

Line 17, Column 3—Total. Enter the total of the amounts entered in columns 1 and 2. The amount in column 3 should be the same as the amount on line 7.

Line 18a, Net Long-Term Capital Gain or Loss. Allocate the net long-term capital gain or loss on line 18 in the same manner as the net short-term capital gain or loss on line 17. However, do not take the Section 1202 exclusion on gain from the sale or exchange of a qualified small business into account when figuring net long-term capital gain or loss allocable to the beneficiaries.

■ The Trent Trust carries the $10,000 figure from line 16 down to line 18 in Columns (2) and (3).

Line 18b—Unrecaptured Section 1250 Gain. Complete the worksheet found on page 5 of the separate Instructions to Schedule D (Form 1041) if any of the following apply:

1. The trust during the year sold or otherwise disposed of Section 1250 property (generally real property that was depreciated) held more than 1 year.

2. The trust received installment payments during the tax year for Section 1250 property held more than 1 year for which it is reporting gain on the installment method.

3. The trust received a Schedule K-1 from an estate, trust, partnership or S corporation that shows "unrecaptured Section 1250 gain" reportable for the tax year.

4. The trust received a Form 1099-DIV (or Form 2439) from a real estate investment trust or regulated investment company (including a mutual fund) that reports "unrecaptured Section 1250 gain" for the tax year.

5. The trust reported a long-term capital gain from the sale or exchange of an interest in a partnership that owned Section 1250 property.

Line 18c—28 Percent Gain or Loss. Complete the 28 percent rate gain worksheet found on page 8 of the Instructions to Schedule D (Form 1041) if lines **18a** and 19 for column 3 are both greater than zero and at least one of the following apply:

1. The trust reports in Part II, column f, a Section 1202 exclusion from the eligible gain on qualified small business stock; or

2. The trust reports in Part II, column f, a "collectibles" (see definition below) gain or loss. Also report here gain (but not loss) from the sale or exchange of an interest in a partnership, S corporation, or trust held for more than 1 year and attributable to unrealized appreciation of collectibles.

"Collectibles" defined. A collectibles gain or loss is any long-term gain or deductible long-term loss from the sale or exchange of a collectible that is a capital asset. Collectibles include works of art, rugs, antiques, metals (such as gold, silver, and platinum bullion), gems, stamps, coins, alcoholic beverages, and certain other tangible property.

Line 19—Total net gain or loss.

■ The Trent Trust carries the $10,000 figure from line **18a** to line **19** in columns (2) and (3).

¶2936

Part IV of Schedule D (Form 1041)—Capital Loss Limitation. If the sum of all the capital losses is more than the sum of all the capital gains, then these capital losses are allowed as a deduction only to the extent of the smaller of the net loss or $3,000. For any year (including the final year) in which capital losses exceed capital gains, the trust may have a capital loss carryover. Use the Capital Loss Carryover Worksheet found on page 9 of the Instructions for Schedule D (Form 1041) to figure any capital loss carryover. A capital loss carryover may be carried forward indefinitely. Capital losses keep their character as either short-term or long-term when carried over to the following year.

Part V of Schedule D (Form 1041)—Tax Computation Using Maximum Capital Gains Rates. Complete this part only if: (1) both lines **18a** and **19** in Column (2) of Schedule D (Form 1041) are gains; or (2) an amount is entered in Part I or Part II and there is an entry on Form 1041, line 2b(2); and (3) Form 1041, line 22 is more than zero.

■ Jane B. Trent's Trust earned $10,000 in capital gain from the sale of 1,000 shares of XYZ, Inc. stock held for more than 12 months. Because local law provides that capital gains are allocated to trust principal, the $10,000 capital gain earned by the trust is allocated to principal, rather than being distributed to beneficiaries. Thus you will not include this gain on Schedule K-1. The income, nevertheless is taxable to the trust as computed here on Schedule D (Form 1041).

■ The Trent Trust enters the $10,000 on line 22 of Part V of Schedule D (Form 1041).

Line 45—Tax on all taxable income. If the tax using the maximum capital gains rates is less than the regular tax, enter the amount from line 45 on line 1a of Schedule G, Form 1041.

■ The Trent Trust enters $3,527 which is the smaller of line 43 or line 44. That amount is also entered on line 1a of Schedule G, Form 1041.

¶2937 OTHER INFORMATION ON PAGE 2 OF FORM 1041

Question 1. Did the trust receive tax-exempt income? If "Yes," attach a computation of the allocation of expenses.

■ The Trent Trust received no tax-exempt income, so enter an X in the "No" column.

Question 2. Did the trust receive all or any part of the earnings (salary, wages, and other compensation) of any individual by reason of a contract assignment or similar arrangement?

■ The Trent Trust received no part of the earnings of any individual by reason of a contract assignment or similar arrangement, so enter X in the "No" column.

¶2937

Question 3. At any time during calendar year 2013, did the trust have an interest in or a signature or other authority over a bank, securities, or other financial account in a foreign country?

■ The Trent Trust had no interest in or a signature or other authority over a bank account, securities, or other financial account in a foreign country, so enter X in the "No" column.

Question 4. During the tax year, did the trust receive a distribution from, or was it the grantor of, or transferor to, a foreign trust?

■ This year the Trent Trust did not receive a distribution from, and was not the grantor of, or the transferor to a foreign trust, so enter X in the "No" column.

Question 5. Did the trust receive, or pay, any qualified residence interest on seller-provided financing?

■ The Trent Trust did not receive or pay any seller-financed mortgage interest, so enter X in the "No" column.

Question 6. If this is a complex trust making the IRC Sec. 663(b) election, check here.

■ Leave this box blank because the Trent Trust was not a complex trust making the Sec. 663(b) election to treat any amount paid or credited to a beneficiary within 65 days following the close of the tax year as being paid or credited on the last day of that tax year.

Question 7. To make an IRC Sec. 643(e)(3) election, attach Schedule D (Form 1041), and check here.

IRC Sec. 643(e)(3) election. Whenever a trust distributes property "in-kind" (other than cash) significant tax consequences result that a fiduciary should consider carefully. For purposes of determining the distribution deduction available to the trust and the amount includible by the beneficiary, the amount distributed is taken into account for DNI purposes only to the extent of the lesser of the property's basis or its fair market value at the time of distribution [IRC Sec. 643(e)(2)]. This means that the beneficiary's basis for the property will be the same as the trust's basis. This is called carryover basis. If the property has appreciated in value, this could lead to costly tax consequences down the road when the beneficiary goes to sell appreciated property with a low basis. The beneficiary would recognize the previously untaxed gain on any subsequent disposition of the property.

Relief is available in IRC Sec. 643(e), which provides that a fiduciary may elect to have distributed noncash property treated as if the property had been sold to the beneficiary at its fair market value [IRC Sec. 643(e)(3)(A)]. If this election is made, the basis of the property in the beneficiary's hands is adjusted to reflect the gain or loss recognized by the trust on the distribution [IRC Sec. 643(e)(1)]. The trust will recognize any gain or loss as if the property had been sold to the beneficiary at its fair market value [IRC Sec. 643(e)(3)(A)(ii)]. The trust is also entitled to a distribution deduction equal to the property's fair market value [IRC Sec. 643(e)(3)(A)(iii)].

This election is irrevocable (unless consent is obtained from Treasury) and applies to all distributions made by the estate or trust during a taxable year and must be made on the return of estate or trust for such taxable year [IRC Sec. 643(e)(3)(B)].

¶2937

Example 1: A trust has DNI equal to $10,000 and a capital asset with a basis of $4,000 and fair market value of $10,000 when distributed. *Without election*—there would be a DNI distribution deduction equal to the stock's basis of $4,000 and the trust would pay tax on income of $4,000. The beneficiary would receive property with a basis of $4,000 and have taxable income of $4,000. When he sells the property he will have capital gain of $6,000. *With election*—there would be a DNI distribution deduction of $10,000. The trust would have capital gain of $6,000 subject to tax. The beneficiary would receive property with basis of $10,000 ($4,000 estate basis plus $6,000 capital gain) and would pay tax on $10,000. The beneficiary would have no gain when he sells the asset.

■ Leave this box blank because the Trent Trust was not making the IRC Sec. 643(e)(3) election to recognize gain on property distributed in kind.

Line 8. If the decedent's estate has been open for more than two years, check here.

■ Leave this box blank because the Trent Trust was not an estate.

Question 9. Are any present or future trust beneficiaries skip persons?

A beneficiary is a skip person is the beneficiary is in a generation that is two or more generations below the generations of the transferor to the trust. To determine if a beneficiary that is a trust is a skip person, see the definition of a skip person at ¶ 2503. Also see the instructions for Schedule R of Form 706.

■ There are no trust beneficiaries of the Trent Trust who are skip persons, so the "No" box is marked in line 9.

¶2938 SCHEDULE I—ALTERNATIVE MINIMUM TAX

Schedule I must be completed to compute: (1) the trust's alternative minimum taxable income; (2) the income distribution deduction on a minimum tax basis; and (3) the trust's alternative minimum tax.

Who must complete Schedule I:

- Complete Schedule I, Parts I and II if the trust is required to complete Schedule B, Income Distribution Deduction.

- Complete Schedule I if the trust's share of alternative minimum taxable income (Part I, line 29) exceeds $23,100.

- Complete Schedule I if the trust claims any general business credit and line 6 or line 3 of Part III of Form 3800 is more than zero.

Part I—Trust's share of alternative minimum taxable income. There are three parts to Schedule I, Form 1041, AMT. The trust computes its share of alternative minimum taxable income in Part I. Its income distribution deduction on a minimum tax basis is computed in Part II, and its AMT liability is computed in Part III. If the trust's share of alternative minimum taxable income is $23,100 or less, enter -0- on Schedule G, line 1c because the trust is not liable for the alternative minimum tax (AMT).

Part I and Part II of Schedule I must be completed for any year for which an income distribution deduction on line 18 of page 1 of Form 1041 has been claimed, regardless of whether or not there is an alternative minimum tax liability.

Part III must be completed if the trust's share of alternative minimum taxable income from line 12 of Part I exceeds $23,100.

Line 1—Adjusted total income or loss. Enter the amount from line 17 of Form 1041.

■ The Trent Trust's adjusted total income from Page 1, line 17 is $36,000, which is entered here.

Lines 2 through 23—Adjustments and tax preference items. Add back the trust's adjustments and tax preference items that are listed in lines 2 through 23. These adjustments and tax preferences items are figured in substantially the same manner as they are for individuals.

Optional write-off for certain expenditures. No AMT adjustment will be needed for the following items if the trust elects to deduct them ratably over the period of time shown for the regular tax and the election is made in the year the expenditure was made:

1. Circulation expenditures—3 years;

2. Research and experimental expenditures—10 years;

3. Intangible drilling costs—60 months;

4. Mining exploration and development costs—10 years.

NOTE: Election may only be revoked with IRS consent.

Line 2—Interest. When computing AMTI, qualified residence interest is not allowed. Only "qualified housing interest" is deductible for AMT purposes [IRC Sec. 56(b)(1)(C)(i)].

- *Qualified housing interest defined.* "Qualified housing interest" is interest paid or accrued during the year on a debt incurred to buy, build, or substantially rehabilitate the taxpayer's principal residence or a second residence [IRC Sec. 56(e)(1)(B)]. The residence could be a house, apartment, cooperative apartment, condominium, or mobile home provided the mobile home is not used on a transient basis [IRC Sec. 56(e)(2)].

  Example 1: To finance a beneficiary's college education, a trust borrows against the equity in a home owned by the trust. Interest paid on this type of debt is deductible when computing regular tax but is not deductible in calculating AMT because the debt is not "qualified housing interest."

- *Refinanced debt.* The term "qualified housing interest" includes interest on any indebtedness resulting from the refinancing of a debt if: (1) the debt was incurred to buy, build, or substantially improve your principal or second residence; and (2) the refinancing does not exceed the amount of the refinanced debt immediately before the refinancing [IRC Sec. 56(e)(1)].

- *Mortgage prior to July 1, 1982.* Interest on a mortgage debt incurred before July 1, 1982 will qualify for an AMT deduction if the mortgage was secured by the taxpayer's

¶2938

principal residence or any other home used by the taxpayer or a family member at any time the mortgage was taken out [IRC Sec. 56(e)(3)].

Line 3—Taxes. Enter any state, local or foreign real property taxes; state or local personal taxes; state, local or foreign income taxes; and any state and local general sales taxes that were included on line 11 of page 1. Do not include any new motor vehicle taxes.

Line 5—Refund of taxes. Enter any refunds received in the year the trust was created of taxes described for line 3 above and included in income.

Line 6—Depletion. The trust must refigure depletion deductions for purposes of the AMTI computation. This means that the trust must use only income and deductions allowed for the AMT when refiguring the limit based on taxable income from the property under IRC Section 613(a) and the limit based on taxable income, with certain adjustments, under IRC Section 613A(d)(1). In addition, the trust's depletion deduction for mines, wells, and other natural deposits under IRC Section 611 is limited to the property's adjusted basis at the end of the year, as refigured for the AMT, unless the trust is an independent producer or royalty owner claiming percentage depletion for oil and gas wells under IRC Section 613A(c). This limit must be figured separately for each property. When refiguring the property's adjusted basis, take into account any AMT adjustments made this year or in previous years that affect basis (other than current year depletion).

The excess of the deduction for depletion under IRC Section 611 over the adjusted basis of the depletion property at the end of the taxable year (determined without regard to the depletion deduction for the taxable year) is a tax preference item and must be added back to regular income when computing AMTI [IRC Sec. 57(a)(1)].

> **Example 2:** A trust claimed a deduction for percentage depletion of $50 with respect to property having a basis of $10 (disregarding the percentage depletion deduction). When computing AMTI, the trust would have a tax preference item in the amount of $40.

Line 7—Net operating loss deduction. When computing AMTI, the alternative tax net operating loss deduction is allowed in lieu of the net operating loss (NOL) deduction allowed under IRC Section 172 [IRC Sec. 56(a)(4)]. The NOL for AMT purposes is figured the same way as for regular tax purposes with one exception: the operating loss is subject to the AMT adjustments and preferences, but preferences are taken into account only to the extent they increased the NOL for regular tax purposes [IRC Secs. 56(d)(1)(A) and (B)].

> **Example 3:** A trust has gross income of $20,000 and deductions of $35,000, of which $10,000 are due to AMT adjustments and preference items. The trust's NOL for regular tax purposes is $15,000. However, the AMT net operating loss for the year is limited to $5,000 [$20,000 − ($35,000 − $10,000)]. The trust can carry the $5,000 loss forward or back to reduce income that is subject to AMT in those years

Line 8—Interest from specified private activity bonds exempt from the regular tax. When figuring AMTI, add back tax-exempt interest on certain specified private activity bonds, which means any private bond issued after August 7, 1986 where the interest is tax exempt [IRC Sec. 57(a)(5)]. Tax-exempt dividends paid by a regulated investment company (RIC), (mutual fund) are treated as interest on specified private activity bonds to the extent the dividends are attributable to interest on the bonds received by the company, minus an allocable share of the expenses paid or incurred by the company in earning the interest.

Do not include on line 8 interest on qualified Gulf Opportunity Zone bonds described in IRC Sec. 1400N(a) or interest on qualified Midwestern disaster area bonds because these are not tax preference items.

Line 9—Qualified small business stock. IRC Sec. 1202 provides that noncorporate investors may exclude up to 50 percent of the gain they realize on the disposition of qualified small business stock issued after August 10, 1993, and held for more than five years. The percentage exclusion is increased to 75 percent for stock acquired after February 17, 2009 and before September 28, 2010. The percentage exclusion is increased to 100 percent for stock acquired after September 27, 2010. The exclusion was scheduled to end for stock acquired after December 31, 2011, but it has been extended for two years. The exclusion now applies to stock acquired before January 1, 2014, and held for more than five years. The percentage exclusion increase does not apply to the sale or exchange of certain empowerment zone stock.

In order for gain on its stock to qualify for the exclusion, a corporation must be a C corporation other than:

(1) a DISC or former DISC;

(2) a regulated investment company (RIC);

(3) a real estate investment trust (REIT);

(4) a real estate mortgage investment conduit (REMIC);

(5) a cooperative; or

(6) a corporation electing the Puerto Rico and possessions tax credit or having a direct or indirect subsidiary so electing.

Increased exclusion for empowerment zone stock sales. The exclusion of gain from the sale or exchange of qualified small business stock is increased to 60 percent in the case of the sale or exchange of certain empowerment zone stock. Thus, 60 percent of the gain from the sale of qualified small business stock is not recognized if:

(1) the stock is acquired after December 21, 2000;

(2) the stock is in a corporation that is a qualified business entity during substantially all of the taxpayer's holding period for such stock; and

(3) the stock is held for more than five years.

A "qualified business entity" means a corporation that satisfies the requirements of a qualifying business under the empowerment zone rules during substantially all of the taxpayer's holding period. The most important of these requirements are that the corporation conduct all its businesses within an empowerment zone, that it derive at

¶2938

least 50 percent of its total gross income from such businesses, and that at least 35 percent of its employees are residents of an empowerment zone.

If the trust claimed the exclusion under IRC Sec. 1202 for gain on qualified small business stock held for more than 5 years, multiply the excluded gain (as shown on Schedule D (Form 1041)) by 7 percent. Enter the result on line 9 as a positive amount.

Line 10—Exercise of incentive stock options. An incentive stock option (ISO) is an option granted by a corporation to its key executives to purchase stock of the corporation at a certain price. A corporation "grants" an employee an option when it completes the corporate action constituting the offer. The employee "exercises" a stock option when he or she accepts the offer to sell the stock subject to the option. A promise to pay the option price is not an exercise of the option unless the employee is personally liable to sell at that time. ISOs defer tax until the shares of option stock are sold, and turn what would otherwise be compensation (ordinary income) into long-term capital gains, which is eligible for favorable tax treatment. If a taxpayer including a trust holds onto ISOs for at least two years after receipt, the difference between pre-set "the exercise price" and the stock selling price is taxed as capital gain. This amount, which is called the "bargain element," is considered an adjustment for alternative minimum tax purposes [IRC Sec. 56(b)(3)].

Generally, the stock's fair market value is determined without regard to any restrictions except those that will never lapse [IRC Sec. 422(c)(7)]. Also, a change in an option's terms to make it nontransferable so that it qualifies as an ISO will be treated as the granting of a new option [IRC Sec. 424(h)].

ISOs may be subject to any condition not inconsistent with the qualification requirements of the options [IRC Sec. 422(c)(4)].

Although no taxable income is recognized when an ISO is granted or exercised, the difference between the fair market value of the stock and the exercise price is an item of AMT tax preference and can trigger a significant AMT liability in the year of exercise if a large amount of appreciated stock is involved [IRC Sec. 56(b)(3)]. The trust must generally include on line 10 the excess, if any, of:

1. The fair market value of the stock acquired through exercise of the option (determined without regard to any lapse restriction) when its rights in the acquired stock first become transferable or when these rights are no longer subject to a substantial risk of forfeiture, over

2. The amount paid for the stock, including any amount paid for the option used to acquire the stock.

If the trust acquired stock by exercising an ISO and it disposed of that stock in the same year, the tax treatment under the regular tax and the AMT is the same, and no adjustment is required.

Be sure to increase the AMT basis of any stock acquired through the exercise of an ISO by the amount of the adjustment.

Line 11—Other estates and trusts. If the trust is the beneficiary of another estate or trust, enter the adjustment for minimum tax purposes from box 12, Code A, Schedule K-1 (Form 1041).

¶2938

Line 12—Electing large partnerships. If the trust is a partner in an electing large partnership, enter on line 12 the amount from Schedule K-1 (Form 1065-B), box 6. Take into account any amount from Schedule K-1 (Form 1065-B), box 5, when figuring the amount to enter on line 15.

Line 13—Disposition of property. Use this line to report any AMT adjustment related to the disposition of property resulting from refiguring the following:

1. Gain or loss from the sale, exchange, or involuntary conversion of property reported on Form 4797, "Sales of Business Property."

2. Casualty gain or loss to business or income-producing property reported on Form 4684, "Casualties and Thefts."

3. Ordinary income from the disposition of property not taken into account in 1 or 2 above or on any other disposition of stock acquired in a prior year by exercising an ISO; and

4. Capital gain or loss (including any carryover that is different for the AMT) reported on Schedule D (Form 1041).

Line 14—Depreciation of assets placed in service after 1986.

Depreciation claimed as a deduction for regular tax purposes is an item of tax adjustment to the extent that it exceeds the depreciation allowable for alternative minimum tax purposes. This means that the ability of taxpayers to claim depreciation deductions is severely limited for purposes of the AMTI computation.

1. *What depreciation must be refigured for AMT purposes?* For purposes of the AMTI computation, you must refigure depreciation, including depreciation allocable to costs for:

   • Property placed in service after December 31, 1998, that is depreciated for the regular tax using the 200 percent declining balance method (generally 3-, 5-, 7-, and 10-year property under the modified accelerated cost recovery system (MACRS)),

   • Tangible property placed in service after 1986 and before 1999. If the transitional election was made, this rule applies to property placed in service after July 31, 1986.

   • IRC Section 1250 property placed in service after 1998 that is not depreciated for the regular tax using the straight line method.

2. *What depreciation is not refigured for AMT purposes?* You need not refigure depreciation for the AMT for:

   • Residential rental property placed in service after December 31, 1998.

   • Nonresidential real property with a class life of 27.5 years or more placed in service after 1998 that is depreciated for the regular tax using the straight line method.

   • Other Section 1250 property placed in service after 1998 that is depreciated for the regular tax using the straight-line method.

¶2938

- Property other than Section 1250 property, placed in service after 1998 that is depreciated for the regular tax using the 150 percent declining balance method or the straight line method.
- Property for which you elected to use the alternative depreciation system for the regular tax.
- Property that is qualified property eligible for the special depreciation allowance. The special allowance is deductible for the AMT and there is also no adjustment required for any depreciation figured on the remaining basis of the qualified property.
- Motion picture films, videotapes, or sound recordings.
- Property depreciated under the unit-of-production method or any other method not expressed in a term of years.
- Qualified Indian reservation property.
- A natural gas gathering line placed in service after April 11, 2005.

3. *How is depreciation refigured for AMT purposes?* If the property was placed in service before 1999, refigure depreciation for the AMT using the alternative depreciation system (ADS) of IRC Section 168(f), with the same convention used for the regular tax. If the property was placed in service after 1998 and the property was depreciated for the regular tax using the 200 percent declining balance method, for AMT purposes, use the 150 percent declining balance method. You should switch to the straight-line method the first tax year if it gives a larger deduction [IRC Sec. 56(a)(1)(A)(ii)].

Line 15—Passive activities. Passive activity gains and losses must be refigured for AMT purposes by taking into account all adjustments, preferences, and any suspended losses that apply to that activity. For example, deductions for post-1986 depreciation and tax-exempt interest would not be allowed and would reduce the amount of any passive activity loss, thus increasing taxable income.

> **Example 4:** The trust is a partner in a partnership and the Schedule K-1 (Form 1065) that you received from the partnership shows the following:
>
> - A passive activity loss of $10,000;
> - A depreciation adjustment of $1,000 on post-1986 property; and
> - An adjustment of $1,000 for adjusted gain or loss.

Because the adjustments are not allowed for the AMT, you must first reduce the passive activity loss by those amounts. The result is a passive activity loss for the AMT of $8,000. This amount would be used to refigure the allowable passive activity loss for the AMT.

Publicly traded partnership (PTP). If the trust has losses from a PTP, you will have to refigure the loss using any AMT adjustments and preferences and any AMT prior year unallowed loss.

Line 16—Loss limitations. Refigure losses for AMT purposes from activities for which the trust was not at risk. Enter the difference between the loss reported for regular tax purposes and the AMT loss. If the AMT loss is more than the loss reported for regular tax purposes, enter the adjustment as a negative amount.

Line 17—Circulation expenses. For the regular tax, circulation expenditures may be deducted in full when paid or incurred, but when computing AMT, these expenditures must be amortized over 3 years, thus reducing the amount of the deduction allowed in any one year. When computing AMTI, add back the difference between the regular tax and AMT deduction. If the AMT deduction is greater, enter the difference as a negative amount. There is no AMT adjustment for circulation expenditures if you elect to deduct them ratably over 3 years as provided in IRC Section 173 [IRC Sec. 59(e)].

Line 18—Long-term contracts. For AMT purposes, the percentage of completion method of accounting must be used unless a home construction contract is involved. Enter the difference between the AMT and regular tax income. If the AMT income is smaller, enter the difference as a negative number.

Line 19—Mining costs. For regular income tax, you may be able to deduct fully mining exploration and development costs incurred during the year. Current writeoffs are not allowed for AMT purposes. Instead, you must ratably amortize costs incurred after 1986 over a 10-year period beginning with the year the expenditures were paid or incurred [IRC Sec. 56(a)(2)(A). However, if the mine is abandoned as worthless, an immediate writeoff is allowed for both the regular tax and the AMT [IRC Sec. 56(a)(2)(B)]. Enter the difference between the amount allowed for AMT purposes and the amount allowed for regular tax purposes. If the amount allowed for AMT purposes exceeds the amount deducted for regular tax purposes, enter the difference as a negative number.

> **NOTE:** There is no AMT adjustment for mining exploration and development costs if you elect to deduct them ratably over 10 years as provided in IRC Sections 616(a) and 617(a) [IRC Sec. 59(e)].

Line 20—Research and experimental costs. Research and experimental expenditures that are deducted for regular tax purposes may be amortized over 10 years for AMT purposes. If the amount for AMT purposes exceeds the amount allowed for regular tax purposes, enter the difference as a negative number. If the trust had a loss on property for which research and experimental costs have not been fully amortized for the AMT, the AMT deduction is the smaller of (a) the loss allowable for the costs had they remained capitalized, or (b) the remaining costs to be amortized for the AMT.

Line 21—Income from certain installment sales before January 1, 1987. The installment method does not apply for AMT purposes to any nondealer disposition of property that occurred after August 16, 1986, but before the first day of your tax year that began in 1987, if an installment obligation to which the proportionate disallowance rule applied arose from the disposition. Enter on line 21 the amount of installment sale income that was reported for regular tax purposes.

Line 22—Intangible drilling costs. If you claim deductions for intangible drilling costs (IDCs) of oil, gas, or geothermal wells, you will have to refigure your IDCs for purposes of the AMT. When computing AMTI, add back the amount by which the "excess intangible drilling costs" exceed 65 percent of your "net income from the oil, gas or geothermal properties." Be sure to figure the preference for all oil and gas properties separately from the preference for all geothermal properties.

¶2938

Example 5: Mary has $100 of net oil and gas income (and a $65 net income offset) and $80 of excess intangible drilling costs. She would add back a tax preference in the amount of $15.

The term "net income from oil, gas, and geothermal properties" is determined without regard to deductions for excess intangible drilling costs [IRC Sec. 57(a)(2)(C)]. The amount of "excess intangible drilling costs" is the amount of the excess, if any, of the taxpayer's regular tax deduction for such costs [deductible under IRC Section 263(c) or 291(b)] over the amount that would have been allowable if the taxpayer had amortized the cost over ten years on a straight-line method [IRC Sec. 57(a)(2)(B)].

Steps to Follow in Figuring Excess IDCs. Figure excess IDCs as follows:

Step 1. Determine the amount of IDCs allowed for the regular tax under IRC Section 263(c), but do not include any Section 263(c) deduction for nonproductive wells.

Step 2. Subtract the amount that would have been allowed had you amortized these IDCs over a 12-month period starting with the month the well was placed in production.

Net income is determined by taking the gross income received or accrued during the tax year from all oil, gas, and geothermal wells and reducing the gross income by the deductions allocable to these properties (reduced by the excess IDCs). When refiguring net income, use only income and deductions allowed for the AMT.

There is no AMT adjustment for intangible drilling costs if you elect to deduct them ratably over 60 months as provided in IRC Section 263(c) [IRC Sec. 59(e)].

Exception for independent oil producers. Note that independent oil and gas producers [not integrated oil companies as defined in IRC Section 291(b)(4)], do not have to compute preference items for excess percentage depletion deductions because the preference for IDCs from oil and gas wells does not apply to them [IRC Sec. 57(a)(2)(E)].

Line 23—Other adjustments. Enter on line 23 the total of any other adjustments that apply including the following:

1. **Accelerated depreciation of property acquired before 1987.** If real property was acquired before 1987, the difference between the depreciation that would have been allowable if the straight-line method had been used and the accelerated depreciation that you claimed for regular tax purposes is considered a tax preference item [IRC Sec. 57(a)(6)]. As a result, when computing AMTI, you must use the straight-line method to figure depreciation on real property if for regular tax purposes you had used accelerated depreciation using pre-1987 rules. This means that you must use a recovery period of 19 years for 19-year real property and 15 years for low-income housing. For leased personal property other than recovery property, add back the amount by which your regular tax depreciation using the pre-1987 rules exceeds the depreciation allowable using the straight-line method. For leased 10-year recovery property and leased 15-year public utility property, add back the amount by which your regular tax depreciation exceeds the depreciation allowable using the straight-line method with a half-year convention, no salvage value, and a recovery period of 15 years (22 years for 15-year public utility property) [IRC Sec. 57(a)(6)].

¶2938

2. **Patron's adjustment.** Distributions the trust received from a cooperative may be includible in income. Unless the distributions are nontaxable, include on line 23 the total AMT patronage dividend adjustment reported to the trust from the cooperative.

3. **Amortization of pollution control facilities.** For regular tax purposes, you may be able to write off the cost of a pollution control facility (e.g., septic tank) over a 60-month amortization period [IRC Sec. 169]. For property placed in service before 1999, the election to amortize the basis of a certified pollution control facility over a 60-month period is not available for AMT purposes. Thus, for facilities placed in service before 1999, figure the AMT deduction using the alternative depreciation system [IRC Sec. 56(a)(5)]. For property placed in service after 1998, figure the AMT depreciation adjustment for pollution control facilities amortized under IRC Section 169 using the straight-line method.

4. **Tax shelter farm activities.** Losses from any tax shelter farm activity are disallowed when computing AMTI [IRC Sec. 58(a)(2)(A)]. A tax shelter farm activity is defined as a partnership or any other enterprise other than a corporation which is not an S corporation engaged in the trade or business of farming, if: (1) At any time interest in such partnership or enterprise has been offered for sale in any offering required to be registered with any federal or state agency having authority to regulate the offering of securities for sale; or (2) More than 35 percent of the losses during any period are allocable to limited partners or limited entrepreneurs [IRC Sec. 464(c)(1)]. A loss that is disallowed under the tax shelter farm activity rule may be carried forward for AMT purposes [IRC Sec. 58(a)(1)(B)]. More specifically, deductions in excess of the gross income allocable to each passive farm activity are disallowed. Each farm is treated as a separate activity. Income from one passive farm activity cannot be netted against another passive farm activity loss. Thus, each activity is treated as a separate basket for purposes of the farm activity loss rule. In applying the limitations on losses from passive activities or tax shelter farming activities, the amount of losses subject to limitation under IRC Section 58 is reduced by the amount (if any) of the taxpayer's insolvency at the close of the taxable year. Pursuant to IRC Section 108(d)(3), "insolvency" is the excess of liabilities over the fair market value of the taxpayer's assets. Since IRC Sec. 58(a)(1) denies a deduction for farm loss from any tax shelter farm activity in the computation of your AMTI, you must refigure any gain or loss from a tax shelter passive farm activity taking into account all AMT adjustments and preferences and any AMT prior year disallowed losses. If the amount is a gain, include it on the AMT Form 8582. If the amount is a loss, instead of including it on the form, carry the loss forward to next year to see if you can use it against gains or losses from tax shelter passive farm activities that year.

5. **Biofuel producer credit and biodiesel/renewable diesel fuels credit.** If the adjusted total income (Form 1041, page 1, line 17) includes the amount of the biofuel producer credit or biodiesel and renewable diesel fuels credit, include that amount as a negative amount on line 23.

6. **Related adjustments.** AMT adjustments and tax preference items may affect deductions that are based on an income limit other than adjusted gross income or

¶2938

modified adjusted gross income. Refigure these deductions using the income limit as modified for the AMT. Include the difference between the regular tax and AMT deduction on line 23. If the AMT deduction is more than the regular tax deduction, include the difference as a negative amount.

■ The Trent Trust has no adjustments and tax preference items.

Line 24—Alternative tax net operating loss deduction. Enter the alternative tax net operating loss deduction (ATNOLD) on line 24. To figure the ATNOLD, take the regular net operating loss (NOL) and modify it as follows:

1. Add back the AMT adjustments, or subtract them if the adjustments are negative; and

2. Reduce the NOL by any item of tax preference except the appreciated charitable contribution preference items. For a trust that held a residual interest in a REMIC, figure the ATNOLD without regard to any excess inclusion.

Line 25—Adjusted alternative minimum taxable income.

■ Because the Trent Trust has no adjustments and tax preference items, the adjusted alternative minimum taxable income is $36,000.

Line 26—Income distribution deduction. Enter the amount from line 44.

■ As computed on line 44, the Trent Trust's income distribution deduction on a minimum tax basis is $18,000.

Line 28. Add lines 26 and 27.

■ Because there is no estate tax deduction on lines 26 and 27, line 28 is $18,000.

Line 29—Trust's share of alternative minimum taxable income. Enter here the adjusted alternative minimum taxable income from the appropriate line as determined by the trust's income.

■ Subtract line 28 ($18,000) from line 25 ($36,000) to get $18,000, which is the Trent Trust's share of alternative minimum taxable income. Because this amount is less than $23,100 in 2013, enter -0- on Schedule G, line 6 because the Trent Trust is not liable for the AMT.

Part II—Income distribution deduction on a minimum tax basis.

Line 30—Adjusted alternative minimum taxable income. Enter the amount from line 1.

■ The Trent Trust's adjusted alternative minimum taxable income from line 25 of Part I is $36,000.

Line 35—Capital gains computed on a minimum tax basis.

■ The Trent Trust's $10,000 capital gain is expressed here as a negative number.

Line 37—Distributable net alternative minimum taxable income.

■ The Trent Trust subtracts $10,000 from $36,000 to get $26,000.

¶2938

Lines 43 and 44—Income distribution deduction on a minimum tax basis.

■ The Trent Trust subtracts line 31 (-0-) from line 37 ($26,000) to get $26,000, which is entered on line 43. To compute the income distribution deduction on a minimum basis, enter the smaller of line 42 ($18,000) or line 43 ($26,000). The Trent Trust enters $18,000 on line 44 and on line 26 of Schedule I. Completion of Parts III and IV of Schedule I reveal that the Trent Trust is not liable for the AMT because line 29 of Part I is less than $23,100 in 2013.

¶2939 SCHEDULE E (FORM 1040)—SUPPLEMENTAL INCOME AND LOSS

Schedule E (Form 1040) must be completed by a trust to report supplemental income from rents and royalties received by the trust. Carry the total from line 40 of Schedule E to line 5 of Form 1041.

▶ **WATCH OUT:** The amounts deducted in Parts I, II, and III of Schedule E may be limited by the "at risk" or the "passive loss" rules.

Schedule E, Part I: Rent and royalty income. If the trust owned rental property or rented out a vacation home for part of the year, use Part I of Schedule E to report rental income and to deduct various expenses relating to the property. Royalties from patents and copyrights, as well as oil, gas and mineral royalties, are also reported in Part I.

Is this the right form? If the trust received rental income in connection with a real estate sales business or provided significant services to tenants (e.g., maid or food services), do not use Schedule E to report the rent. These rentals are reported as business income on Schedule C or C-EZ. Also, report income from an operating oil, gas, or mineral interest on Schedule C (or C-EZ), rather than Schedule E.

Rental or royalty income received through a partnership or S corporation is reported in Part II of Schedule E.

Income or loss from estates and trusts is reported on Part III of Schedule E and income or loss from Real Estate Mortgage Investment Conduits (REMICS) is reported on Part IV.

Line A and Line B. If the decedent made payments that would require him or her to file any Forms 1099, check the "Yes" box. Otherwise, check the "No" box. Generally, the decedent must file Form 1099-MISC if the decedent paid at least $600 in rents, services, prizes, medical and health care payments, and other income payments.

Part I—Income or Loss from Rental Real Estate and Royalties. Use Part I to report the following:

a. Income and expenses from rental real estate (including personal property leased with real estate);

b. Royalty income and expenses;

c. For an estate or trust only, farm rental income and expenses based on crops or livestock produced by the tenant. Do not use Form 4835 or Schedule F (Form 1040) for this purpose.

¶2939

If the decedents owned a part interest in a rental real estate property, report only the decedent's part of the income and expenses on Schedule E.

Complete lines 1 and 2 for each rental real estate property. For royalty properties, line 2 and the address portion on line 1 should be left blank and the decedent should enter code "6" for royalty property.

Do not use Schedule E to report income and expenses from the rental of personal property, such as equipment or vehicles. Instead, use Schedule C or C-EZ if the decedent was in the business of renting personal property. The decedent was in the business of renting personal property if the primary purpose for renting the property is income or profit and the decedent was involved in the rental activity with continuity and regularity.

If the decedent had rental real estate property, show the street address, city or town, state, and ZIP code. If the property is located in a foreign country, enter the city, province or state, country, and postal code.

For the type of property, enter one of the codes listed under "Type of Property" in Part I of the form.

▪ Schedule E (Form 1040) must be completed by the Trent Trust to report the rental income received by the trust from the residential apartment building that the trust owns.

Line 1a and Line 1b. On line 1a and line 1b of Schedule E, identify the physical address and the type of each rental property. If the trust has more than three rental properties, fill out as many copies of Schedule E as needed to report them all—but total the figures from all properties on only one schedule. If you need to fill out other portions of Schedule E, use the copy that contains the rental property totals.

▪ On Part I of Schedule E, the Trent Trust lists the apartment building as property "A" on line 1aA. For the type of property, the Trent Trust enters "2" for multi-family residence on line 1bA. The trust uses column A on line 3 as discussed below to report rental income and expenses from this property.

Line 2. For taxpayers who rented out dwelling units, line 2 asks whether the trust used the rental property more than the greater of:

1. 14 days; or

2. 10 percent of the total days it was rented at fair-market value during the year.

If so, all other deductions must be allocated between personal and rental use. Both the rental and personal use portions of mortgage interest and real estate taxes can be deducted, but only the rental use portion of all other expenses can be deducted. What's more, the deduction for rental expenses is limited to the rental income from the property.

▪ Because Jane Trent's family did not use the apartment building for any personal purposes for more than the greater of 14 days or 10 percent of the total days rented at fair-rental value during the year, nothing is entered for line 2. Therefore, they can deduct all of their expenses, as long as they are not limited by the "at risk" and "passive loss" rules.

If the trust was a real estate dealer, include only the rent received from real estate (including personal property leased with this real estate) held by the decedent for the

¶2939

primary purpose of renting to produce income. Do not use Schedule E to report income and expenses from rentals of real estate held by the decedent for sale to customers in the ordinary course of the decedent's business as a real estate dealer. Instead use Schedule C or C-EZ for those rentals.

■ The $6,000 rent that the Trent trust received from the apartment building is listed on line 3, Coulmn A. Because there are no expenses listed in lines 5 through 18, the figure is carried down to line 21, line 24, and line 26.

■ The Trent Trust received no royalty income and leaves line 4 blank.

Lines 5 through 21—Expenses. These lines are used to report the deductible expenses that the trust incurred with respect to rental and royalty properties. This includes property taxes, mortgage interest, miscellaneous expenses (e.g., janitorial services and agent's fees) and the cost of repairs (e.g., painting or fixing the roof). However, the cost of improvements (e.g., installing a new roof) cannot be deducted currently. Instead, these costs are recovered through depreciation.

■ The Trent Trust incurred no expenses and therefore leaves these lines blank.

Line 18—Depreciation expense or depletion. Depreciation expense or depletion for rental properties are reported on line 18. Complete IRS Form 4562 to compute depreciation for any rental property first placed in service in 2013. However, for property placed in service before 2013, simply enter depreciation in the appropriate column on line 18.

■ A separate depreciation form (if required) must be completed for each business or activity.

Line 20. Add lines 5 through 19. Enter the total of expenses for each rental property in the appropriate column, and the total for all properties in the far right column on line 20.

Line 21. If the trust suffered a loss, the fiduciary may have to file IRS Form 6198 to apply the "at risk" limits. Form 6198 is required if the loss exceeds the amount at risk in the activity. If the trust had a loss from any rental properties, enter the amount of the loss (after applying the at-risk limits, if necessary) on line 21.

IRS Form 8582 must be completed if the trust had a rental real estate loss from a passive activity and the amount of that loss is limited by the passive activity loss rules. Form 8582 must be completed to figure the amount of that loss.

Enter the total income amounts reported on line 24.

Combine income and losses on line 26 and enter on line 41 on page 2 of Form 1040, Schedule E. If the trust has no other items to report on Schedule E (e.g., income or loss from a partnership), carry the rental or royalty income or loss to line 5 on Page 1 of Form 1041.

■ The Trent Trust enters $6,000 of income on line 26. Because they do not own any other properties, they carry this amount to line 41 on page 2 of Form 1040, Schedule E and then also enter $6,000 on line 5 on Page 1 of Form 1041.

Line 27—Income or loss from partnerships and S corporations. On Line 27, the IRS wants to know if the taxpayer is reporting losses not allowed in prior years due to the

¶2939

at-risk or basis limitations. They have in mind passive losses not reported on Form 8582, or unreimbursed partnership expenses. If you are reporting these losses, follow special instructions outlined on the Instructions to Schedule E. Failure to follow these instructions could result in the IRS sending out a notice of additional tax because the amounts reported on Schedule K-1 do not match the amounts reported on the tax return.

¶2940 SCHEDULE K-1—BENEFICIARY'S SHARE OF INCOME, DEDUCTIONS, CREDITS, ETC.

Use Schedule K-1 (Form 1041) to report each beneficiary's share of trust income, deductions, and credits that must be included in the beneficiary's gross income on his or her personal income tax return. The fiduciary (or one of the joint fiduciaries) must file Schedule K-1. A copy of each beneficiary's Schedule K-1 should be attached to the Form 1041 filed with the IRS, and each beneficiary should be given a copy of his or her respective Schedule K-1. The beneficiary should keep a copy of Schedule K-1 for his or her records but it need not be filed with the beneficiary's tax return, unless backup withholding was reported in box 13, code B.

In addition, the fiduciary must provide a Schedule K-1 (Form 1041) for each beneficiary who receives a distribution of property or an allocation from the trust. A penalty of $50 (not to exceed $100,000 for any calendar year) will be imposed on the fiduciary for each failure to furnish Schedule K-1 to each beneficiary unless reasonable cause for each failure is established.

Treatment of items must be consistent. Beneficiaries of a trust are required to report items on a Schedule K-1 in a manner consistent with the manner in which the item was reported on the Form 1041. If the treatment is inconsistent, they must file IRS Form 8082, "Notice of Inconsistent Treatment or Administrative Adjustment Request," with the original or amended return to identify and explain any inconsistencies [IRC Sec. 6034A(c)]. If a beneficiary fails to identify the inconsistent treatment, any adjustment necessary to make the treatment of the items by the beneficiary consistent with the treatment of the items on the entity's return will be treated as a mathematical or clerical error that will be subject to summary assessment procedures [IRC Sec. 6034A(3)]. In addition, a negligence penalty will be imposed [IRC Sec. 6034A(5)].

If Form 8082 must be filed but the trustee fails to do so, he or she may be subject to the accuracy-related penalty. This penalty is in addition to any tax that results from the inconsistent treatment. Any deficiency that results from making the amounts consistent may be assessed immediately.

■ The Trent Trust completes a Schedule K-1 for Mary King, who is the decedent's daughter and a beneficiary of the trust.

Use the following three-step process in order to compute the amounts to enter on Schedule K-1. See Reg. Sec. 1.652(c)-4(f) for a comprehensive example (reproduced below).

¶2940

Reg. Sec. 1.652(c)-4(f), Illustration of the provisions of Sections 651 and 652.—The rules applicable to a trust required to distribute all of its income currently and to its beneficiaries may be illustrated by the following example:

Example. (a) Under the terms of a simple trust all of the income is to be distributed equally to beneficiaries A and B and capital gains are to be allocated to corpus. The trust and both beneficiaries file returns on the calendar year basis. No provision is made in the governing instrument with respect to depreciation. During the taxable year, the trust had the following items of income and expense:

Rents	$25,000
Dividends of domestic corporations	50,000
Tax-exempt interest on municipal bonds	25,000
Long-term capital gains	15,000
Taxes and expenses directly attributable to rents	5,000
Trustee's commissions allocable to income account	2,600
Trustee's commissions allocable to principal account	1,300
Depreciation	5,000

(b) The income of the trust for fiduciary accounting purposes is $92,400, computed as follows:

Rents		$25,000
Dividends		50,000
Tax-exempt interest		25,000
Total		$100,000
Deductions: Expenses directly attributable to rental income	$5,000	
Trustee's commissions allocable to income account	2,600	7,600
Income computed under section 643(b)		$92,400

One-half ($46,200) of the income of $92,400 is currently distributable to each beneficiary.

(c) The distributable net income of the trust computed under section 643(a) is $91,100, determined as follows (cents are disregarded in the computation):

Rents		$25,000
Dividends		50,000
Tax-exempt interest	$25,000	
Less: Expenses allocable thereto (25,000/100,000 × $3,900)	975	24,025
Total		$99,025
Deductions:		
Expenses directly attributable to rental income	$5,000	
Trustee's commissions ($3,900 less $975 allocable to tax-exempt interest)	2,925	$7,925
Distributable net income		$91,100

In computing the distributable net income of $91,100, the taxable income of the trust was computed with the following modifications: No deductions were allowed for distributions to the beneficiaries and for personal exemption of the trust (IRC Secs. 643(a)(1) and (2)); capital gains were excluded and no deduction under IRC Sec. 1202 (relating to the 50 percent deduction for long-term capital gains) was taken into account (IRC Sec. 643(a)(3)); the tax-exempt interest (as adjusted for expenses) and the dividend exclusion of $50 were included (IRC Secs. 643(a)(5) and (7)). Since all of the income of the trust is required to be currently distributed, no deduction is allowable for depreciation in the absence of specific provisions in the governing instrument providing for the keeping of the trust corpus intact. See IRC Sec. 167(h) and the regulations thereunder.

¶2940

(d) The deduction allowable to the trust under IRC Sec. 651(a) for distributions to the beneficiaries is $67,025, computed as follows:

Distributable net income computed under section 643(a) (see paragraph (c))		$91,100
Less:		
Tax-exempt interest as adjusted	$24,025	
Dividend exclusion	50	24,075
Distributable net income as determined under IRC Sec. 651(b)		$67,025

Since the amount of the income ($92,400) required to be distributed currently by the trust exceeds the distributable net income ($67,025) as computed under IRC Sec. 651(b), the deduction allowable under IRC Sec. 651(a) is limited to the distributable net income of $67,025.

(e) The taxable income of the trust is $7,200 computed as follows:

Rents		$25,000
Dividends ($50,000 less $50 exclusion)		49,950
Long-term capital gains		15,000
Gross income		$89,950
Deductions:		
Rental expenses	$5,000	
Trustee's commissions	2,925	
Capital gain deduction	7,500	
Distributions to beneficiaries	67,025	
Personal exemption	300	82,750
Taxable income		$7,200

The trust is not allowed a deduction for the portion ($975) of the trustee's commissions allocable to tax-exempt interest in computing its taxable income.

(f) In determining the character of the amounts includible in the gross income of A and B, it is assumed that the trustee elects to allocate to rents the expenses not directly attributable to a specific item of income other than the portion ($975) of such expenses allocated to tax-exempt interest. The allocation of expenses among the items of income is shown below:

	Rents	Dividends	Tax-exempt interest	Total
Income for trust accounting purposes	$25,000	$50,000	$25,000	$100,000
Less:				
Rental expenses	5,000			5,000
Trustee's commissions	2,925		975	3,900
Total deductions	7,925	0	975	8,900
Character of amounts in the hands of the beneficiaries	17,075	50,000	24,025	91,100[1]

[1] Distributable net income.

Inasmuch as the income of the trust is to be distributed equally to A and B, each is deemed to have received one-half of each item of income; that is, rents of $8,537.50, dividends of $25,000, and tax-exempt interest of $12,012.50. The dividends of $25,000 allocated to each beneficiary are to be aggregated with his other dividends (if any) for purposes of the dividend exclusion provided by section 116 and the dividend received credit allowed under section 34. Also, each beneficiary is allowed a deduction of $2,500 for depreciation of rental property attributable to the portion (one-half) of the income of the trust distributed to him. [Reg. Sec. 1.652(c)-4]

Step one for Trent Trust. To begin, in step one, list all items of income of the trust entering into the computation of DNI, including tax-exempt interest. You will find these items on lines 1 through 8 of Form 1041, Page 1. The beneficiary of a simple trust must include in gross income the amount of the income required to be distributed currently, whether or not distributed, or if the income required to be distributed currently to all beneficiaries exceeds the distributable net income (DNI). The determination of whether trust income is required to be distributed currently depends on the terms of the trust instrument and applicable local law. The beneficiary's income is considered to have the same proportion of each class of items entering into the computation of DNI that the total of each class has to the DNI. For example, if the income of the trust is half dividends and half interest, the beneficiary's income will consist of half dividends and half interest. The following income items should be listed separately:

1. Income from rental activities;

2. Income from rental real estate activities;

3. Income from business activities that are passive activities; and

4. Income from business activities that are not passive activities.

Here's how the Trent Trust complies with Step 1.

■ The Trent Trust first enters $4,000. This figure is taken from line 1, Page 1 of Form 1041.

■ The Trent Trust then enters ordinary dividends in the amount of $20,000. This comes from line 2a, Page 1 of Form 1041.

■ The Trent Trust enters rents in the amount of $6,000. This comes from Schedule E, line 26.

Allocation of Income and Deductions:

Type of Income	Amount	Deductions	Balance of Distributable Net Income
Interest	$ 4,000	$ 533	$ 3,467
Ordinary Dividends	$20,000	$2,666	$17,334
Rentals	$ 6,000	$ 800	$ 5,200

NOTE: Capital gains and losses: Capital gains are not included in DNI unless they are:

1. Allocated to income under the governing instrument or local law;

2. Allocated to corpus and actually distributed to beneficiaries during the taxable year;

3. Used, under the governing instrument or the practice followed by the fiduciary, in determining the amount that is distributed or required to be distributed; or

4. Paid or to be used for charitable purposes so that a contributions deduction is allowed.

Capital losses are excluded from the computation of DNI. But if capital gains are distributed, the capital losses are offset against the gains to determine the net capital gains distributed.

■ Even though the Trent Trust earned $10,000 in capital gain from the sale of 1,000 shares of XYZ, Inc. stock held for more than 12 months, local

¶2940

law provides that capital gains are allocated to trust principal. Therefore, the $10,000 capital gain earned by the trust is allocated to principal, rather than being distributed to beneficiaries. Thus, do not include this gain in your Step 1 computation.

Step 2. The amount and character of income passed through to beneficiaries is based on the DNI of the trust. Thus, the amount of income entered onto the worksheet in Step 1 must be reduced by deductions and losses shown on Page 1 of Form 1041, which enters into the computation of DNI.

In Step 2, you allocate and subtract the deductions. Determine the amount of your deduction by multiplying each income item above by a percentage that is determined by dividing the total trust deductions from line 16 on Page 1 of Form 1041 ($4,000) by the total trust income minus capital gains [subtract line 4 from line 9 on Page 1 of Form 1041 ($30,000)]. In the example above, divide $4,000 by $30,000 to get 13.33 percent. You then take that percentage and multiply it by each income item to allocate the deductions among them. For example, $4,000 times 13.33 percent equals $533, which is entered in the deductions column above. Then subtract $533 from $4,000 to yield $3,467, which you enter in the third column. Perform the same process for each income item.

The IRS instructions for Form 1041 (pages 41-42) provide that generally items of deductions that enter into the computation of DNI are allocated among the items of income in the following order:

1. All deductions directly attributable to a specific class of income are deducted from that income;

2. Deductions that are not directly attributable to a specific class of income generally may be allocated to any class of income, as long as a reasonable portion is allocated to any tax-exempt income. Deductions considered not directly attributable to a specific class of income under this rule include fiduciary fees, safe deposit box rental charges, and state, income, and personal property taxes. The charitable deduction, however, must be ratably apportioned among each class of income included in DNI;

3. Any excess deductions that are directly attributable to a class of income may be allocated to another class of income. In no case can excess deductions from a passive activity be allocated to income from a nonpassive activity or to portfolio income earned by the trust. Excess deductions attributable to tax-exempt income cannot offset any other class of income.

Next, the Trent Trust complies with Step 3.

Step 3. Allocation of Distribution to be reported on Schedule K-1 (Form 1041) for the decedent's daughter, Mary.

Inclusion of amounts in beneficiaries income. The beneficiary of a decedent's trust must include in his or her gross income the sum of:

1. The amount of the income required to be distributed currently, or if the income required to be distributed currently to all beneficiaries exceeds the DNI (figured without taking into account the charitable deduction), his or her proportionate share of the DNI (as so figured); and

¶2940

2. All other amounts properly paid, credited, or required to be distributed, or if the sum of the income required to be distributed currently and other amounts properly paid, credited, or required to be distributed to all beneficiaries exceeds the DNI, his or her proportionate share of the excess of DNI over the income required to be distributed currently.

To compute the amount of the income allocation that must be entered on Schedule K-1, multiply the balance of the DNI for each income item after subtracting the deduction above in Column two times a fraction that is the total amount of the income distribution deduction from Schedule B, line 15 over the DNI from Schedule B, line 7 as shown below:

Interest: $3,467 × $18,000/$18,000 = $3,467 (enter in Box 1)

Dividends: $17,334 × $18,000/$18,000 = $17,334 (enter in Box 2a)

Rental Income: $5,200 × $18,000/$18,000 = $5,200 (enter in Box 7)

Top of Schedule K-1 (Form 1041). The return preparer is asked to fill in the tax year of the trust on the top of Schedule K-1. Note that this refers to the tax year of the trust rather than the tax year of the beneficiary. This should be the same tax year as was entered at the top of Page 1 of Form 1041.

Name of trust. Enter the name of the trust.

Beneficiary's taxpayer identification number (TIN). A trustee who distributes taxable income to beneficiaries is required to request and provide a proper taxpayer identification number (TIN) for each recipient of income. Enter the beneficiary's identifying number on this line of the Schedule K-1. Individuals and business recipients are responsible for giving the trustee their TIN upon request.

Use IRS Form W-9, "Request for Taxpayer Identification Number and Certification," to request the beneficiary's identifying number. Trustees will be charged a $50 penalty for each failure to provide a required TIN, unless reasonable cause is established for not providing it. Explain any reasonable cause in a signed affidavit and attach it to this return.

Box 1 of Schedule K-1—Interest Income. Enter the beneficiary's share of the taxable income minus allocable deductions.

> ■ Because the Trent Trust is a simple trust, the beneficiary of the trust must include in his or her gross income the amount of the income required to be distributed currently, whether or not it is actually distributed. Mary King's share of the trust taxable interest income minus deductions that are allocated against all items of income on a pro rata basis is entered on line 1. The amount entered is $3,467 as computed in the three-step process above.

Box 2a and 2b—Ordinary Dividends and Qualified Dividends. Enter the beneficiary's share of total ordinary dividends minus allocable deductions in Box 2a. In Box 2b enter the beneficiary's share of qualified dividends minus allocable deductions.

> ■ Mary King's share of ordinary dividend income minus allocable deductions is entered in Box 2a. The amount entered is $17,334 as computed in the three-step process described above.

Box 3—Net Short-Term Capital Gain. Enter the beneficiary's share of the net short-term capital gain from line 13, Column (1), Schedule D (Form 1041), minus allocable

¶2940

deductions. Do not enter a loss on line 3. If, for the final year of the trust, there is a capital loss carryover, enter the beneficiary's share of short-term capital loss carryover in Box 11, using code B.

Box 4a through 4c—Net Long-Term Capital Gain. Enter the beneficiary's share of the net long-term capital gain from lines 14a through 14c, Column (1), Schedule D (Form 1041) minus allocable deductions. Do not enter a loss on lines 4a through 4c. If, for the final year of the trust, there is a capital loss carryover, enter in Box 11, using code C.

Gains and losses from the complete or partial disposition of a rental, rental real estate, or trade or business activity that is a passive activity must be shown on an attachment to Schedule K-1.

> ■ Even though the Trent Trust earned $10,000 in capital gain from the sale of 1,000 shares of XYZ, Inc. stock held for more than 12 months, local law provides that capital gains are allocated to trust principal. Therefore, the $10,000 capital gain earned by the trust is allocated to principal, rather than being distributed to beneficiaries. Thus do not include this gain in Box 4 of Schedule K-1. The income nevertheless is taxable to the trust and was listed in line 4 of the Income portion of Page 1 of Form 1041.

Box 5—Other Portfolio and Nonbusiness Income. Enter the beneficiary's share of annuities, royalties, or any other income, minus allocable deductions (other than directly apportionable deductions), that are NOT subject to any passive activity loss limitation rules at the beneficiary level. Use Boxes 6 through 8 to report income items subject to the passive activity rules at the beneficiary's level.

Boxes 6 through 8—Ordinary Business Income, Rental Real Estate, and Other Rental Income. Enter the beneficiary's share of trade or business, rental real estate, and other rental income, minus allocable deductions (other than directly apportionable deductions).

> ■ Enter Mary King's share of the apartment building's rental income ($6,000) minus 13.33 percent allocable deductions (other than directly apportionable deductions) in Box 7. The amount entered is $5,200 as computed in the three-step process above.

Box 9—Directly Apportioned Deductions. Enter the beneficiary's share of directly apportioned deductions using code A through C.

Depreciation (code A). Enter the beneficiary's share of the depreciation deductions attributable to each activity reported on Boxes 5 through 8. For a trust, the depreciation deduction is apportioned between the income beneficiaries and the trust on the basis of the trust income allocable to each, unless the governing instrument requires or permits the trustee to maintain a depreciation reserve. If the reserve is required, the deduction is first allocated to the trust up to the amount of the reserve. Any excess is allocated among the beneficiaries and the trust in the same manner as the accounting income.

Depletion (code B). Enter the beneficiary's share of the depletion deduction under IRC Sec. 611 directly apportioned to each activity reported in Boxes 5 through 8.

Amortization (code C). Itemize the beneficiary's share of the amortization deductions directly apportioned to each activity reported in Boxes 5 through 8.

¶2940

■ Because all of the trust's income was distributed to Mary, all of the $2,000 depreciation allowable for the apartment building is allocated to Mary and cannot be deducted by the trust. Consequently, the $2,000 does not appear on Schedule E. Mary King's $2,000 share of the depreciation deductions attributable to the apartment building are entered in Box 9 with code A.

Box 10—Estate Tax Deduction (including Certain Generation-Skipping Transfer Taxes). If the distribution deduction consists of any IRD, and the trust was allowed a deduction under IRC Sec. 691(c) for the estate tax paid as a result of the inclusion of this item, then the beneficiary is allowed an estate tax deduction in proportion to his or her share of the distribution that consists of such income.

Box 11, Code A—Excess deductions on termination. If this is the final return of the trust, and there are excess deductions on termination, enter the beneficiary's share of the excess deductions in Box 11, using Code A. Excess deductions on termination occur only during the last tax year of the trust when the total deductions (excluding the charitable deduction and exemption) are greater than the gross income during that tax year.

Box 12—Alternative Minimum Tax Adjustment. Enter the beneficiary's share of the adjustment for minimum tax purposes using the codes that are listed in the 2011 Instructions to Form 1041 (reproduced at ¶ 2944).

Adjustments and Code for Box 12.

* AMT adjustment attributable to qualified dividends, net short-term capital gains, or net long-term capital gains (codes B through D)

* AMT adjustment attributable to unrecaptured section 1250 gain or 28 percent rate gain (codes E and F)

* Accelerated depreciation, depletion, and amortization (codes G through I)

* Exclusion items (code J)

Box 13—Credits and Credit Recapture. Enter the beneficiary's share of the credits and credit recapture using the applicable codes that are listed on pages 34–35 of the 2011 Instructions to Form 1041 and page 2 of Schedule K-1 (Form 1041) (reproduced at ¶ 2944 and ¶ 2945, respectively).

Box 14—Other (itemize). Enter the dollar amounts and applicable codes for the items listed under Other Information on page 2 of Schedule K-1 (reproduced at ¶ 2945).

¶2941 THE THROWBACK RULES—ACCUMULATION DISTRIBUTION FOR A COMPLEX TRUST

First, we begin with a basic explanation of the throwback rules and continue with a sample fact pattern for the completed Schedule J, Form 1041, which appears at ¶ 2946.

According to the throwback rules, which were generally repealed by the Taxpayer's Relief Act of 1997, a trust beneficiary of a domestic complex trust was taxed on trust distributions of income that had been accumulated and taxed in prior years if the beneficiary's top average marginal tax rate during the previous five years was higher than that of the trust. In a major simplification of the law, the throwback rules were repealed for most domestic trusts effective for all distributions made in tax years beginning after August 5, 1997.

▶ **PRACTICE WARNING:** Unfortunately, you cannot forget about the throwback rules completely. The throwback rules continue to apply to certain types of trusts and Schedule J must be used to report an accumulation distribution for the following trusts:

1. Domestic complex trust that was previously treated at any time as a foreign trust,

2. Domestic trusts created before March 1, 1984, that would be treated as multiply trusts under IRC Sec. 643(f).

An accumulation distribution is the excess of amounts properly paid, credited, or required to be distributed (other than income required to be distributed currently) over the DNI of the trust reduced by income required to be distributed currently. To have an accumulation distribution, the distribution must exceed the accounting income of the trust.

No throwback for Trent Trust. The throwback rules are not triggered by the Trent Trust because no accumulation distribution was made. Accumulation distributions can only be made by a tier two distribution. The Trent Trust is a simple trust that made no tier two distributions during 2013.

Nevertheless, a completed Schedule J with instructions for a taxpayer unrelated to the Trent Trust is included at ¶2946.

Two throwback concepts are basic to understanding the rule:

1. "Undistributed net income"; and

2. "Accumulation distribution" [IRC Secs. 665(a), 665(b); Reg. Secs. 1.665(a)-1A, 1.665(b)-1A].

There can only be a throwback from a year with an accumulation distribution to a year with undistributed net income.

(a) Undistributed Net Income. A trust has undistributed net income for a tax year when the amounts distributed are less than the DNI for the year [IRC Secs. 665(a)(2), 665(d); Reg. Sec. 1.665(a)-1A]. To find the undistributed net income:

1. Find the DNI of the trust [see ¶2903]. The trust's DNI is the trust's current taxable income before any deduction is taken for distributions to beneficiaries [IRC Sec. 643(a)]. DNI serves the following three purposes:

   • It limits the amount of income that can be taxed to the beneficiaries. All distributions made in a tax year of the trust are treated as income items to the beneficiaries to the extent they do not exceed DNI;

   • It limits the amount of the distribution deduction to the trust or estate;

   • It determines the character of the income distributed to the beneficiaries and retained by the trust.

2. Subtract the following from the DNI:

   • The amount of *income* required to be distributed currently, including any amount that may be paid out of income or corpus to the extent it was paid out of trust income for the year;

¶2941

- Any other amounts paid, credited, or required to be distributed; and

- The income tax on the undistributed portion of the trust's DNI. This is the same amount as the total tax paid by the trust (not including any AMT) except when the trust has capital gains not included in distributable net income (e.g., capital gains to corpus) [Reg. Sec. 1.665(d)-1A].

(b) Accumulation Distribution. A trust has an accumulation distribution when it distributes more than the DNI for the year. To determine the accumulation distribution:

1. Find the total distribution for the tax year, reduced by the amount of income required to be distributed currently (including any amount that may be paid out of income or corpus to the extent it was paid out of trust income for the year); and

2. Subtract the DNI reduced (but not below zero) from the income required to be distributed currently.

The difference between (1) and (2) is the accumulation distribution for the tax year. A distribution made or required to be distributed by a trust that does not exceed the trust income for the year is not treated as an accumulation distribution for that year [IRC Sec. 665(b); Reg. Sec. 1.665(b)-1A].

(c) How to Handle the Throwback Rule. When a trust makes an accumulation distribution for any tax year, the distribution is thrown back to the earliest year that the trust has undistributed net income, and so on, up to the year of the distribution. The accumulation being thrown back is deemed to have been distributed on the last day of the year to which it is thrown back, but only to the extent of the undistributed net income of that year. The rest of the accumulation distribution is then thrown back to the next succeeding year that had undistributed net income, and so on through the tax years until the accumulation distribution is used up [IRC Sec. 666(a); Reg. Sec. 1.666(a)-1A]. The trustee must file Schedule J (attached to Form 1041), showing the allocation of accumulation distribution to each beneficiary.

(d) Distributions to Minor Beneficiaries. Generally, the throwback rules do not apply to any distributions of income accumulated by a trust (other than a foreign trust) for a beneficiary before his birth or before he is 21 years old [IRC Sec. 665(b)]. These accumulated distributions are not taxable to the beneficiary.

NOTE: There are special rules regarding distributions allocated to preceding years as they relate to multiple trusts and foreign trusts [IRC Secs. 667(c), 667(d)].

(e) Lack of Records. If records are not available to determine the trust's undistributed net income of any tax year, the accumulation distribution is deemed to have been determined on December 31, 1969, or the earliest subsequent date the trust was in existence. If the trustee establishes that the loss of records for some tax years was beyond his or her control, the accumulation distribution is first allocated to the tax year for which the trustee has adequate records of the trust's existence [IRC Sec. 666(d); Reg. Sec. 1.666(d)-1A].

(f) Taxes Added to Distribution. When an accumulation distribution is thrown back to a particular year, all or part of the taxes imposed on the trust for that year (other than the AMT) are also deemed distributed. This is done because the

¶2941

accumulation deemed distributed in the throwback year would have increased the trust's distribution deduction in that year, and thereby reduced or eliminated the trust's taxes. If the accumulation distribution thrown back to a particular year is at least as much as the undistributed net income for that year, the taxes that the trust paid for that year are also deemed distributed and are added to the distribution [IRC Sec. 666(b); Reg. Sec. 1.666(b)-1A]. If the accumulation distribution thrown back is *less than* the undistributed net income, only a portion of the taxes is added to the accumulation. This portion is determined as follows [IRC Sec. 666(c); Reg. Sec. 1.666(c)-1A]: Taxes (except AMT) on the trust for the year to which the throwback is made TIMES the accumulation distribution thrown back to particular year DIVIDED BY the undistributed net income for that particular year EQUALS the amount of taxes deemed to have been distributed on last day of that particular year.

To show how much of the accumulation distribution is "thrown back" to prior years, the undistributed net income (UNI) of the trust must be computed for each preceding year. The amount thrown back is the amount by which DNI for a given tax year exceeds the sum of:

1. Any amount of income for such tax year required to be distributed currently;

2. Any other amounts properly paid or credited or required to be distributed in such tax year; and

3. The amount of tax imposed on the trust with respect to such undistributed net income. [IRC Sec. 665(a)].

Facts for Sample Schedule J, Form 1041. The John Brown Trust is subject to the throwback rules because it is a domestic trust that previously was a foreign trust. The trust makes a $20,000 accumulation distribution in 2013 to the trust's beneficiary, Pam Brown.

> ▶ **PRACTICE POINTER:** Keep in mind that amounts accumulated before a beneficiary reaches 21 years of age are not subject to the additional tax on accumulation distributions [IRC Sec. 665(b)].

The trustee had discretion to make additional income distributions to Pam. During each of the tax years of 2008 to 2012, the trust had DNI of $42,000. The trustee made distributions of $24,000 ($2,000 times 12 months) to Pam. The taxable income of the trust was $17,900 [$18,000 taxable income minus $100 exemption] each year. The following amount of tax should have been imposed on that amount of income ($17,900) based on the trust income tax rates in effect for the appropriate tax year:

- $5,284 for 2008,

- $5,242 for 2009,

- $5,241 for 2010,

- $5,230 for 2011, and

- $5,199 for 2012.

In 2013, the trustee paid Pam $100,000 from the trust in addition to her monthly distribution, so she could open a new business. The DNI of the trust in 2013 was $42,000.

¶2941

The UNI of the Brown Trust for 2008 is computed as follows:

• DNI:	$42,000

Less the sum of the following items:

• Income currently distributable:	$20,000
• Other amounts distributed:	$4,000
• Taxes imposed on the trust income of $17,900:** (based on tax rates in effect in 2008)	$5,284
• Therefore, UNI for 2008 is	$12,716

**[The trust income of $17,900 is computed by taking $42,000 DNI and subtracting the $24,000 income distributed to get $18,000 and subtracting a $100 exemption amount].

The UNI of the Brown Trust for 2009 is computed as follows:

• DNI:	$42,000

Less the sum of the following items:

• Income currently distributable:	$20,000
• Other amounts distributed:	$4,000
• Taxes imposed on the trust income of $17,900:*** (based on tax rates in effect in 2009)	$5,242
• So, for 2009, UNI is	$12,758

*** [The trust income of $17,900 is computed by taking $42,000 DNI and subtracting the $24,000 income distributed to get $18,000 and subtracting a $100 exemption amount].

The UNI of the Brown Trust for 2010 is computed as follows:

• DNI:	$42,000

Less the sum of the following items:

• Income currently distributable:	$20,000
• Other amounts distributed:	$4,000
• Taxes imposed on the trust income of $17,900:**** (based on tax rates in effect in 2010)	$5,241
• So, for 2010, UNI is	$12,759

**** [The trust income of $17,900 is computed by taking $42,000 DNI and subtracting the $24,000 income distributed to get $18,000 and subtracting a $100 exemption amount].

The UNI of the Brown Trust for 2011 is computed as follows:

• DNI:	$42,000

Less the sum of the following items:

• Income currently distributable:	$20,000
• Other amounts distributed:	$ 4,000
• Taxes imposed on trust income of $17,900:* (based on tax rates in effect in 2011)	$5,230
• Therefore, UNI for 2011 is	$12,770

* [The trust income of $17,900 is computed by taking $42,000 DNI and subtracting the $24,000 income distributed to get $18,000 and subtracting a $100 exemption amount].

¶2941

The UNI of the Brown Trust for 2012 is computed as follows:

• DNI:	$42,000

Less the sum of the following items:

• Income currently distributable:	$20,000
• Other amounts distributed:	$ 4,000
• Taxes imposed on trust income of $17,900:* (based on tax rates in effect in 2012)	$5,199
• Therefore, UNI for 2012 is	$12,801

---

* [The trust income of $17,900 is computed by taking $42,000 DNI and subtracting the $24,000 income distributed to get $18,000 and subtracting a $100 exemption amount].

The first thing you do is throw back the 2013 accumulation distribution of $58,500 to 2008 and apply it against the UNI of $12,716 for that year, leaving a remainder to be used in each succeeding year to absorb that year's UNI until you run out of dollars. When you reach the final year you add up all remaining accumulation distribution if the UNI exceeds the remaining distribution. This is why the UNI for the last throwback year (2012) is only $7,497 rather than $12,801, which is the UNI for 2012. This is reflected in line 13 of Schedule J as discussed further below.

The taxes that have been paid for the years 2008–2012 will be deemed distributed to distributees who must pay tax on the income. The tax paid in 2012, however, must be prorated to reflect the fact that the accumulation thrown back to that year was less than the amount of 2012 UNI. This computation is reflected in line 14 of Schedule J.

Pam Brown is taxed on the trust income deemed distributed in prior years.

¶2942 SCHEDULE J (FORM 1041)—BENEFICIARY'S SHARE OF INCOME, DEDUCTIONS, CREDITS, ETC.

Top of form—Name of trust. Enter the name and employer identification number of the trust.

Line 1—Distribution under IRC Sec. 661(a)(2). Enter the amount properly paid, credited, or required to be distributed other than the amount of income for the current tax year required to be distributed currently.

■ The Brown Trust enters $80,000 for 2013.

Line 2—Distributable net income. Enter the amount of DNI for the current tax year.

■ The Brown Trust enters $41,500.

Line 3—Distribution under IRC Section 661(a)(1). Enter the amount of income for the current tax year required to be distributed currently.

■ The Brown Trust enters $20,000.

Line 4. Subtract line 3 from line 2.

■ The Brown Trust enters $21,500.

Line 5—Accumulation distribution. Subtract line 4 from line 1 for the accumulation distribution for 2013. Keep in mind that amounts accumulated before a beneficiary reaches age 21 may be excluded by the beneficiary.

■ The accumulation distribution for the Brown Trust is $58,500.

Part II—Ordinary income accumulation distribution.

Line 6—Distributable net income for earlier years. Enter the applicable amounts as follows:

Throwback year(s)	Amount from line
1969–1977	Schedule C, Form 1041, line 5
1978–1979	Form 1041, line 61
1980	Form 1041, line 60
1981–1982	Form 1041, line 58
1983–1996	Schedule B, Form 1041, line 9
1997–2012	Schedule B, Form 1041, line 7

■ The Brown Trust enters $42,000 for all five years.

Line 7—Distributions made during earlier years. Enter the applicable amounts as follows:

Throwback year(s)	Amount from line
1969–1977	Schedule C, Form 1041, line 8
1978	Form 1041, line 64
1979	Form 1041, line 65
1980	Form 1041, line 64
1981–1982	Form 1041, line 62
1983–1996	Schedule B, Form 1041, line 13
1997–2012	Schedule B, Form 1041, line 11

■ The Brown Trust enters $24,000 for all five years.

Line 8. Subtract line 7 from line 6.

■ The Brown Trust enters $18,000 for all five years.

Line 9. Enter the amount of tax that would have been imposed on the undistributed net income if it would have been distributed in the appropriate years.

■ The Brown Trust enters the amounts from line 25 on Page 2.

Line 10. To find the undistributed net income, subtract line 9 from line 8.

Line 11—Prior accumulation distribution thrown back to any throwback year. Enter the amount of prior accumulation distributions thrown back to the throwback years. Do not enter distributions excluded for gifts or bequests.

■ The Brown Trust enters 0 for all entries.

Line 13—How to throwback the accumulation distribution. Allocate the accumulation distribution on line 5 of Schedule J to the earliest applicable year first, but do not allocate more than the amount on line 12 for any throwback year. An accumulation distribution is thrown back first to the earliest preceding tax year in which there is UNI. Then, it is thrown back beginning with the next earliest year to any remaining preceding tax years of the trust. The portion of the accumulation distribution allocated to the earliest preceding tax year is the amount of the UNI for that year. The portion of the accumulation distribution allocated to any remaining preceding tax year is the amount by which the accumulation distribution is larger than the total of the UNI for all earlier preceding tax years.

■ The Brown Trust allocates $12,716 to 2008, $12,758 to 2009, $12,759 to 2010, $12,770 to 2011 and the remaining $7,497 to 2012, the final year.

Line 14. Divide line 13 by line 10 and multiply result by amount on line 9.

Line 15. Add lines 13 and 14.

■ The Brown Trust enters $18,000 in all columns except the last one, where it enters $10,542.

Lines 16—Tax-exempt interest included on line 13. For each throwback year, divide line 15 by line 6 and multiply the result by the following:

Throwback year(s)	Amount from line
1969–1977	Schedule C, Form 1041, line 2(a)
1978–1979	Form 1041, line 58(a)
1980	Form 1041, line 57(a)
1981–1982	Form 1041, line 55(a)
1983–2012	Schedule B, Form 1041, line 2

■ The Brown Trust enters nothing because it had no tax-exempt interest.

Line 17. Subtract line 16 from line 15.

■ The Brown Trust enters $18,000 in all columns except the last one, where it enters $10,542.

Part III—Taxes imposed on undistributed net income. (See line 10.)

Line 18—Regular tax. Enter the applicable amounts as follows:

Throwback year(s)	Amount from line
1969–1976	Form 1041, Page 1, line 24
1977	Form 1041, Page 1, line 26
1978–1979	Form 1041, line 27
1980–1984	Form 1041, line 26c
1985–1986	Form 1041, line 25c
1987	Form 1041, line 22c
1988–2012	Schedule G, Form 1041, line 1a

■ The Brown Trust enters the amount of tax that would have been imposed on trust income of $17,900, which is computed by taking $42,000 DNI and subtracting the $24,000 income distributed to get $18,000 and subtracting the $100 exemption and then using the trust tax rates in effect for the tax years in issue.

Line 19—Trust's share of net short-term gain. For each throwback year, enter the smaller of the capital gain from the two lines indicated. If there is a capital loss or a zero on either or both of the lines indicated, enter zero on line 19.

■ The Brown Trust enters nothing in line 19.

Line 20—Trust's share of net long-term gain. Enter the applicable amount for each year.

  ■ The Brown Trust enters nothing in line 20.

Line 21. Add lines 19 and 20.

  ■ The Brown Trust enters nothing in line 21.

Line 22—Taxable income. Enter the trust's taxable income.

  ■ The taxable income of the John Brown Trust was $17,900 (i.e., $18,000 taxable income minus $100 exemption) each year. This amount was entered in each column of line 22. The instructions to line 22 found in ¶ 2944 list where to find the trust's taxable income for each of the throwback years.

Line 23—Enter percent. Divide line 21 by line 22, but do not enter more than 100 percent.

  ■ The John Brown Trust has no entry on this line.

Line 24. Multiply line 18 by the percentage on line 23.

  ■ The John Brown Trust has no entry on this line.

Line 25—Tax on undistributed net income. Subtract line 24 from line 18. Enter the result on line 25 and on Page 1, line 9.

  ■ The Brown Trust enters the same amount from line 18 because line 24 is zero.

Lines 26–31. These lines are completed only if the trust has elected the alternative tax on long-term capital gain.

  ■ Because the Brown Trust has not made this election, the lines are left blank.

Part IV—Allocation to beneficiary.

  NOTE: Be sure to complete IRS Form 4970, "Tax on Accumulation Distribution of Trusts," to figure the tax on the distribution. The beneficiary also uses Form 4970 for the IRC Sec. 667(b)(6) tax adjustment if an accumulation distribution is subject to estate or generation-skipping transfer tax. This is required because the trustee may not be the estate or generation-skipping transfer tax return filer.

Complete Part IV for each beneficiary. If the accumulation distribution is allocated to more than one beneficiary, attach an additional copy of Schedule J with Part IV completed for each additional beneficiary. Give each beneficiary a copy of his or her respective Part IV information. If more than five throwback years are involved, use another Schedule J, completing Parts II and III for each additional throwback year.

  ■ The Brown Trust enters the beneficiary's name, Social Security number, and address in the appropriate lines.

Lines 32–37. Enter the appropriate amount of the beneficiary's share of the accumulation distribution for each of the throwback years.

  ■ The Brown Trust enters the entire amount from line 13 for each year in lines 32a through 36a because Pam was the sole beneficiary. Similarly, the John Brown Trust enters the entire amount from line 14 for each year in lines 32b through 36b because Pam was the sole beneficiary. The amounts

¶2942

in Columns a and b are totaled in lines 37a and 37b. These amounts must be carried over to Form 4970 to determine the amount of tax Pam Brown owes on the accumulation distribution.

¶2943 TERMINATION OF TRUSTS

A trust is recognized as a taxable entity until trust property has been distributed to successors, plus a reasonable time after this event necessary for the trustee to complete the administration of the trust. Thus, a trust does not automatically terminate when a certain event (e.g., the death of the life beneficiary), occurs, even though this event is used in the trust language to measure the duration of the trust. A trust is considered terminated when all the assets have been distributed except for a reasonable amount set aside in good faith to pay unascertained or contingent liabilities and expenses (other than a claim by a beneficiary in that capacity) [Reg. Sec. 1.641(b)-3(b)]. Once an estate or trust is considered terminated for tax purposes, its gross income, credits, and deductions subsequent to termination are considered to be the gross income, credits, or deductions of the person or persons who succeed to the property [Reg. Sec. 1.641(b)-3(d)].

Definition of a reasonable time. For example, if under the terms of the governing instrument, the trust is to terminate upon the death of the life beneficiary and the corpus is to be distributed to the remainderman, the trust continues after the death of the life beneficiary for a period reasonably necessary to accomplish a proper winding up of the affairs of the trust [Reg. Sec. 1.641(b)-3(b)].

The law provides that the winding up of a trust cannot be unduly postponed and if the distribution of the trust corpus is unreasonably delayed, the trust will be considered terminated for federal income tax purposes after the expiration of a reasonable period for the trustee to complete the administration of the trust. In addition, a trust will be considered terminated when all the assets have been distributed except for a reasonable amount that is set aside in good faith for the payment of unascertained or contingent liabilities and expenses [Reg. Sec. 1.641(b)-3(b)].

During the period between an event that causes a trust to terminate and the time when a trust is actually terminated, the income and the excess of capital gains over capital losses of the trust are considered to be amounts required to be distributed for the year in which they are received.

> **Example 1:** A trust provides for the payment of income to Mom during her life, and upon her death for the payment of the corpus to Son. The trust reports on the calendar year basis. Mom dies on November 1, 2013, but no distribution is made to Son until January 15, 2014. The income of the trust and the excess of capital gains over capital losses for the entire year 2013, to the extent not paid, credited, or required to be distributed to Mom or Mom's estate, is treated as amounts required to be distributed to Son for the year 2013 [IRC Secs. 661, 662; Reg. Sec. 1.641(b)-3(c)(2)(ii)].

Why does termination matter? Determining when a trust is terminated is important because once termination is deemed to have occurred, the income, deductions, and credits of the trust are taxable directly to the trust beneficiaries who succeed to the property of the trust [Reg. Sec. 1.641(b)-3(d)]. If the fiduciary unduly prolongs the administration of a trust, the items on the fiduciary return will be allocated to the beneficiaries who would receive the property when the trust terminates.

In addition, an unused net operating loss carryover or capital loss carryover existing upon termination of the trust may be claimed by the beneficiaries succeeding to the property of the estate [IRC Sec. 642(h); Reg. Sec. 1.642(h)-1(b)]. This means that the losses can be claimed on the beneficiary's tax return if a carryover would have been allowed to the trust in a later tax year if the estate had not been terminated.

The first tax year to which the loss is carried is the beneficiary's tax year in which the trust terminates. If the loss can be carried to more than one tax year, the trust's last tax year (whether or not a short tax year) and the beneficiary's first tax year to which the loss is carried each constitute a tax year for figuring the number of years to which a loss may be carried [Reg. Sec. 1.642(h)-1(b)].

How individuals take advantage of trust's excess deductions. If the trust has deductions in its last tax year (other than deductions for personal exemptions and charitable contributions) that exceed gross income for the year, the beneficiaries succeeding to the trust's property can claim the excess as a deduction in figuring their own taxable income. In order to take advantage of these deductions, the following steps must be followed:

1. A return must be filed for the trust along with a schedule showing the computation of each type of deduction and the allocation of each deduction to the beneficiaries;

2. The individual beneficiary must itemize deductions to benefit from the excess deductions;

3. The deductions must be claimed on Schedule A, Form 1040, as miscellaneous itemized deductions subject to the 2 percent of adjusted gross income limit [IRC Sec. 67];

4. The excess deductions can only be claimed by the beneficiaries for the tax year in which the trust terminates, whether the year of termination is a normal year or a short tax year;

5. If there are more than one successor beneficiaries, the excess deductions must be allocated among the beneficiaries according to each one's share in income and loss as provided in the trust;

6. An item of income or deduction cannot be deducted twice by a beneficiary. This simply means that a net operating loss deduction cannot be deducted once as an excess deduction and again as a loss carryover.

When a trust is terminated, the fiduciary should take the following steps to file Form 1041:

1. Check box for "Final return" on Form 1041, area F;

2. Check box for "Final K-1" on Schedule K-1 of Form 1041; if any excess deductions, capital loss carryover, or net operating loss carryover would have been

¶2943

allowed in future years had the trust continued, the succeeding beneficiary may be able to take these deductions. Enter the amounts on Schedule K-1 (Form 1041), box 11;

3. Check box E on Schedule K-1 (Form 1041) to show this is the final Form 1041 for the trust.

¶2944 INSTRUCTIONS FOR FORM 1041 AND SCHEDULES A, B, G, J AND K-1; INSTRUCTIONS FOR SCHEDULE D (FORM 1041); INSTRUCTIONS FOR SCHEDULE I (FORM 1041); INSTRUCTIONS FOR FORM 8949

20**13**

Department of the Treasury
Internal Revenue Service

Instructions for Form 1041 and Schedules A, B, G, J, and K-1

U.S. Income Tax Return for Estates and Trusts

Section references are to the Internal Revenue Code unless otherwise noted.

Future Developments

For the latest information about developments related to Form 1041 and Schedules A, B, G, J, K-1 and its instructions, such as legislation enacted after they were published, go to *www.irs.gov/form1041*.

What's New

Income tax brackets. Beginning in 2013, the top income tax bracket for estates and trusts is 39.6%, as amended by the American Taxpayer Relief Act of 2012 (ATRA), P.L. 112–240.

Capital gains and qualified dividends. Beginning in 2013, the maximum rate for long-term capital gains and qualified dividends is 20%, as amended by ATRA. For tax year 2013, the 20% rate applies to estates and trusts with income above $11,950. The 0% and 15% rates continue to apply to certain threshold amounts.

Net investment income tax. This tax applies to certain investment income of estates and trusts. Use Form 8960 and its instructions to figure your net investment income tax. Form 8960 is new for 2013. See *Net Investment Income Tax*, later, for more information.

Item F. Net operating loss (NOL) carryback. We added a new *Net operating loss carryback* check box in Item F of the heading. If an amended return is filed for an NOL carryback, check the box. See *Amended Return*, later, for complete information.

Item G. Section 645 election. If the estate has made a section 645 election

the executor must check Item G and provide the taxpayer identification number (TIN) of the electing trust with the highest total asset value in the box provided.

The executor must also attach a statement to Form 1041 providing the following information for each electing trust (including the electing trust provided in Item G): (a) the name of the electing trust, (b) the TIN of the electing trust, and (c) the name and address of the trustee of the electing trust.

Net operating loss deduction (NOLD). We revised line 15b to report net operating loss deductions. NOLDs were previously reported on line 15a.

Note. Miscellaneous itemized deductions subject to the 2% floor are now reported on new line 15c.

Form 1041 *E-filing*. For tax year 2013, both Form 8453-F, U.S. Estate or Trust Income Tax Declaration and Signature for Electronic Filing, and new Form 8453-FE, U.S. Estate or Trust Declaration for an IRS *e-file* Return will be used for *e-filing*. See the instructions for these forms for additional information. Also see Form 8879-F, IRS *e-file* Signature Authorization for Form 1041, and its instructions.

For more information about the *e-file* program, see Publication 1437, Procedures for the Form 1041 *e-file* Program, U.S. Income Tax Returns for Estates and Trusts for Tax Year 2013, and Publication 4164, Modernized e-File (MeF) Guide for Software Developers And Transmitters, Processing Year 2014.

Bankruptcy estate filing threshold. For tax years beginning in 2013, the requirement to file a return for a bankruptcy estate applies only if gross income is at least $10,000.

Qualified disability trust. For tax year 2013, a qualified disability trust can claim an exemption of up to $3,900. A trust with modified adjusted gross income above $250,000 loses part of the exemption deduction. See the

Feb 18, 2014   Cat. No. 11372D

instructions for *Line 20—Exemption*, later, for more details.

Reminders

• Review a copy of the will or trust instrument, including any amendments or codicils, before preparing an estate's or trust's return.

• We encourage you to use Form 1041-V, Payment Voucher, to accompany your payment of a balance of tax due on Form 1041, particularly if your payment is made by check or money order.

Item A. Type of Entity. On page 1 of Form 1041, Item A, taxpayers should select more than one box, when appropriate, to reflect the type of entity.

Specified domestic entity. The IRS anticipates issuing regulations that will require a domestic entity to file Form 8938 if the entity is formed or availed of to hold specified foreign financial assets and the value of those assets exceeds the appropriate reporting threshold. Until the IRS issues such regulations, only individuals must file Form 8938.

Online IRS *e-file* provider application. Applications to become an IRS *e-file* provider must be submitted online. The IRS is no longer accepting paper applications on Form 8633, Application to Participate in the IRS *e-file* Program. See *Electronic Filing*, later, for complete information.

Section 67(e) regulations. The proposed regulations under section 67(e) are not yet final. These regulations clarify which costs, such as investment advisory and bundled fiduciary fees, incurred by estates and nongrantor trusts are not exempt from the 2% floor for miscellaneous itemized deductions. Notice 2011-37 (available at *www.irs.gov/irb/2011-20_IRB/ar08.html*) extends the existing interim guidance providing that taxpayers will not be required to determine the portion of a bundled fiduciary fee that is subject to the 2% floor under section 67 for taxable years that begin before the publication of final regulations. If the regulations are finalized later in the filing season, an update will be posted at *www.irs.gov/form1041.*

Photographs of Missing Children

The Internal Revenue Service is a proud partner with the National Center for Missing and Exploited Children. Photographs of missing children selected by the Center may appear in instructions on pages that would otherwise be blank. You can help bring these children home by looking at the photographs and calling 1-800-THE-LOST (1-800-843-5678) if you recognize a child.

Unresolved Tax Issues

If you have attempted to deal with an IRS problem unsuccessfully, you should contact the Taxpayer Advocate Service (TAS). The Taxpayer Advocate independently represents the estate's or trust's interests and concerns within the IRS by protecting its rights and resolving problems that have not been fixed through normal channels.

While Taxpayer Advocates cannot change the tax law or make a technical tax decision, they can clear up problems that resulted from previous contacts and ensure that the estate's or trust's case is given a complete and impartial review.

The estate's or trust's assigned personal advocate will listen to its point of view and will work with the estate or trust to address its concerns. The estate or trust can expect the advocate to provide:

• An impartial and independent look at your problem,

• Timely acknowledgment,

• The name and phone number of the individual assigned to its case,

• Updates on progress,

• Timeframes for action,

• Speedy resolution, and

• Courteous service.

When contacting the Taxpayer Advocate, you should provide the following information:

• The estate's or trust's name, address, and employer identification number (EIN).

• The name and telephone number of an authorized contact person and the hours he or she can be reached.

• The type of tax return and year(s) involved.

• A detailed description of the problem.

• Previous attempts to solve the problem and the office that had been contacted.

• A description of the hardship the estate or trust is facing and supporting documentation (if applicable).

You can contact a Taxpayer Advocate as follows:

• Call the Taxpayer Advocate's toll-free number: 1-877-777-4778.

• Call, write, or fax the Taxpayer Advocate office in its area (see Pub. 1546, Taxpayer Advocate Service, Your Voice At The IRS, for addresses and phone numbers).

• TTY/TDD help is available by calling 1-800-829-4059.

• Visit the website at *www.irs.gov/advocate*.

How To Get Forms and Publications

 Internet. You can access the IRS website 24 hours a day, 7 days a week, at *IRS.gov* to:

• Download forms, including talking tax forms, instructions, and publications;

• Order IRS products;

• Use the online Internal Revenue Code, regulations, and other official guidance;

• Research your tax questions;

• Search publications by topic or keyword;

• Apply for an Employer Identification Number (EIN); and

• Sign up to receive local and national tax news by email.

 Phone. You can order forms and publications by calling 1-800-TAX-FORM (1-800-829-3676). If you have access to TTY/TDD equipment, you can call 1-800-829-4059 to ask tax questions or order forms and publications. The TTY/TDD telephone number is for people who are deaf, hard of hearing, or have a speech disability. These individuals can also contact the IRS through relay services such as the Federal Relay Service available at *www.gsa.gov/fedrelay*.

 Walk-in. You can also get most forms and publications at your local IRS office.

General Instructions

Purpose of Form

The fiduciary of a domestic decedent's estate, trust, or bankruptcy estate uses Form 1041 to report:

• The income, deductions, gains, losses, etc. of the estate or trust;

• The income that is either accumulated or held for future distribution or distributed currently to the beneficiaries;

• Any income tax liability of the estate or trust; and

• Employment taxes on wages paid to household employees.

• Net Investment Income Tax. See Schedule G, line 4, and the Instructions for Form 8960.

Income Taxation of Trusts and Decedents' Estates

A trust or a decedent's estate is a separate legal entity for federal tax purposes. A decedent's estate comes into existence at the time of death of an individual. A trust may be created during an individual's life (*inter vivos*) or at the time of his or her death under a will (testamentary). If the trust instrument contains certain provisions, then the person creating the trust (the grantor) is treated as the owner of the trust's assets. Such a trust is a grantor type trust. See *Grantor Type Trusts*, later, under *Special Reporting Instructions*.

A trust or decedent's estate figures its gross income in much the same manner as an individual. Most deductions and credits allowed to individuals are also allowed to estates and trusts. However, there is one major distinction. A trust or decedent's estate is allowed an income distribution deduction for distributions to beneficiaries. To figure this deduction, the fiduciary must complete Schedule B. The income distribution deduction determines the amount of any distributions taxed to the beneficiaries.

For this reason, a trust or decedent's estate sometimes is referred to as a "pass-through" entity. The beneficiary, and not the trust or decedent's estate, pays income tax on his or her distributive share of income. Schedule K-1 (Form 1041) is used to notify the beneficiaries of the amounts to be included on their income tax returns.

Before preparing Form 1041, the fiduciary must figure the accounting income of the estate or trust under the will or trust instrument and applicable local law to determine the amount, if any, of income that is required to be distributed, because the income distribution deduction is based, in part, on that amount.

Abusive Trust Arrangements

Certain trust arrangements claim to reduce or eliminate federal taxes in ways that are not permitted under the law. Abusive trust arrangements typically are promoted by the promise of tax benefits with no meaningful change in the taxpayer's control over or benefit from the taxpayer's income or assets. The promised benefits may include reduction or elimination of income subject to tax; deductions for personal expenses paid by the trust; depreciation deductions of an owner's personal residence and furnishings; a stepped-up basis for property transferred to the trust; the reduction or elimination of self-employment taxes; and the reduction or elimination of gift and estate taxes. These promised benefits are inconsistent with the tax rules applicable to trust arrangements.

Abusive trust arrangements often use trusts to hide the true ownership of assets and income or to disguise the substance of transactions. These arrangements frequently involve more than one trust, each holding different assets of the taxpayer (for example, the taxpayer's business, business equipment, home, automobile, etc.). Some trusts may hold interests in other trusts, purport to involve charities, or are foreign trusts. Funds may flow from one trust to another trust by way of rental agreements, fees for services, purchase agreements, and distributions.

Some of the abusive trust arrangements that have been identified include unincorporated business trusts (or organizations), equipment or service trusts, family residence trusts, charitable trusts, and final trusts. In each of these trusts, the original owner of the assets nominally subject to the trust effectively retains the authority to cause financial benefits of the trust to be directly or indirectly returned or made available to the owner. For example, the trustee may be the promoter, a relative, or a friend of the owner who simply carries out the directions of the owner whether or not permitted by the terms of the trust.

When trusts are used for legitimate business, family, or estate planning purposes, either the trust, the beneficiary, or the transferor of assets to the trust will pay the tax on income generated by the trust property. Trusts cannot be used to transform a taxpayer's personal, living, or educational expenses into deductible items, and cannot seek to avoid tax liability by ignoring either the true ownership of income and assets or the true substance of transactions. Therefore, the tax results promised by the promoters of abusive trust arrangements are not allowable under the law, and the participants in and promoters of these arrangements may be subject to civil or criminal penalties in appropriate cases.

For more details, including the legal principles that control the proper tax treatment of these abusive trust arrangements, see Notice 97-24, 1997-1 C.B. 409.

For additional information about abusive tax arrangements, visit the IRS website at IRS.gov and type "Abusive Trusts" in the search box.

Definitions

Beneficiary. A beneficiary includes an heir, a legatee, or a devisee.

Decedent's estate. The decedent's estate is an entity that is formed at the time of an individual's death and generally is charged with gathering the decedent's assets, paying the decedent's debts and expenses, and distributing the remaining assets. Generally, the estate consists of all the property, real or personal, tangible or intangible, wherever situated, that the decedent owned an interest in at death.

Distributable net income (DNI). The income distribution deduction allowable to estates and trusts for amounts paid, credited, or required to be distributed to beneficiaries is limited to DNI. This amount, which is figured on Schedule B, line 7, is also used to determine how much of an amount paid, credited, or required to be distributed to a beneficiary will be includible in his or her gross income.

Income, deductions, and credits in respect of a decedent.

Income. When completing Form 1041, you must take into account any items that are income in respect of a decedent (IRD).

In general, IRD is income that a decedent was entitled to receive but that was not properly includible in the decedent's final income tax return under the decedent's method of accounting.

IRD includes:
* All accrued income of a decedent who reported his or her income on the cash method of accounting,
* Income accrued solely because of the decedent's death in the case of a decedent who reported his or her income on the accrual method of accounting, and
* Income to which the decedent had a contingent claim at the time of his or her death.

Some examples of IRD for a decedent who kept his or her books on the cash method are:
* Deferred salary payments that are payable to the decedent's estate,
* Uncollected interest on U.S. savings bonds,
* Proceeds from the completed sale of farm produce, and

2013 Instructions for Form 1041   -3-

¶2944

• The portion of a lump-sum distribution to the beneficiary of a decedent's IRA that equals the balance in the IRA at the time of the owner's death. This includes unrealized appreciation and income accrued to that date, less the aggregate amount of the owner's nondeductible contributions to the IRA. Such amounts are included in the beneficiary's gross income in the tax year that the distribution is received.

The IRD has the same character it would have had if the decedent had lived and received such amount.

Deductions and credits. The following deductions and credits, when paid by the decedent's estate, are allowed on Form 1041 even though they were not allowable on the decedent's final income tax return.
• Business expenses deductible under section 162.
• Interest deductible under section 163.
• Taxes deductible under section 164.
• Investment expenses described in section 212 (in excess of 2% of adjusted gross income (AGI)).
• Percentage depletion allowed under section 611.
• Foreign tax credit.

For more information on IRD, see section 691 and Pub. 559, Survivors, Executors, and Administrators.

Income required to be distributed currently. Income required to be distributed currently is income that is required under the terms of the governing instrument and applicable local law to be distributed in the year it is received. The fiduciary must be under a duty to distribute the income currently, even if the actual distribution is not made until after the close of the trust's tax year. See Regulations section 1.651(a)-2.

Fiduciary. A fiduciary is a trustee of a trust, or an executor, executrix, administrator, administratrix, personal representative, or person in possession of property of a decedent's estate.

Note. Any reference in these instructions to "you" means the fiduciary of the estate or trust.

Trust. A trust is an arrangement created either by a will or by an *inter vivos* declaration by which trustees take title to property for the purpose of protecting or conserving it for the beneficiaries under the ordinary rules applied in chancery or probate courts.

Revocable living trust. A revocable living trust is an arrangement created by

a written agreement or declaration during the life of an individual and can be changed or ended at any time during the life of an individual. A revocable living trust is generally created to manage and distribute property. Many people use this type of trust instead of (or in addition to) a will.

Because this type of trust is revocable, it is treated as a grantor type trust for tax purposes. See *Grantor Type Trusts* under *Special Reporting Instructions*, later, for special filing instructions that apply to grantor trusts.

 Be sure to read Optional Filing Methods for Certain Grantor Type Trusts. *Generally, most people that have revocable living trusts will be able to use Optional Method 1. This method is the easiest and least burdensome way to meet your obligations.*

Who Must File

Decedent's Estate

The fiduciary (or one of the joint fiduciaries) must file Form 1041 for a domestic estate that has:

1. Gross income for the tax year of $600 or more, or

2. A beneficiary who is a nonresident alien.

An estate is a domestic estate if it is not a foreign estate. A foreign estate is one the income of which is from sources outside the United States that is not effectively connected with the conduct of a U.S. trade or business and is not includible in gross income. If you are the fiduciary of a foreign estate, file Form 1040NR, U.S. Nonresident Alien Income Tax Return, instead of Form 1041.

Trust

The fiduciary (or one of the joint fiduciaries) must file Form 1041 for a domestic trust taxable under section 641 that has:

1. Any taxable income for the tax year,

2. Gross income of $600 or more (regardless of taxable income), or

3. A beneficiary who is a nonresident alien.

Two or more trusts are treated as one trust if the trusts have substantially the same grantor(s) and substantially the same primary beneficiary(ies) and a principal purpose of such trusts is avoidance of tax. This provision applies only to that portion of the trust that is

attributable to contributions to corpus made after March 1, 1984.

A trust is a domestic trust if:
• A U.S. court is able to exercise primary supervision over the administration of the trust (court test), and
• One or more U.S. persons have the authority to control all substantial decisions of the trust (control test).

See Regulations section 301.7701-7 for more information on the court and control tests.

Also treated as a domestic trust is a trust (other than a trust treated as wholly owned by the grantor) that:
• Was in existence on August 20, 1996,
• Was treated as a domestic trust on August 19, 1996, and
• Elected to continue to be treated as a domestic trust.

A trust that is not a domestic trust is treated as a foreign trust. If you are the trustee of a foreign trust, file Form 1040NR instead of Form 1041. Also, a foreign trust with a U.S. owner generally must file Form 3520-A, Annual Information Return of Foreign Trust With a U.S. Owner.

If a domestic trust becomes a foreign trust, it is treated under section 684 as having transferred all of its assets to a foreign trust, except to the extent a grantor or another person is treated as the owner of the trust when the trust becomes a foreign trust.

Grantor Type Trusts

If all or any portion of a trust is a grantor type trust, then that trust or portion of a trust must follow the special reporting requirements discussed later, under *Special Reporting Instructions*. See *Grantor Type Trust* under *Specific Instructions* for more details on what makes a trust a grantor type trust.

Note. A trust may be part grantor trust and part "other" type of trust, for example, simple or complex, or electing small business trust (ESBT).

Qualified subchapter S trusts (QSSTs). QSSTs must follow the special reporting requirements for these trusts discussed later, under *Special Reporting Instructions*.

Special Rule for Certain Revocable Trusts

Section 645 provides that if both the executor (if any) of an estate (the related estate) and the trustee of a qualified revocable trust (QRT) elect the

2013 Instructions for Form 1041

¶2944

treatment in section 645, the trust must be treated and taxed as part of the related estate during the election period. This election may be made by a QRT even if no executor is appointed for the related estate.

In general, Form 8855, Election To Treat a Qualified Revocable Trust as Part of an Estate, must be filed by the due date for Form 1041 for the first tax year of the related estate. This applies even if the combined related estate and electing trust do not have sufficient income to be required to file Form 1041. However, if the estate is granted an extension of time to file Form 1041 for its first tax year, the due date for Form 8855 is the extended due date.

Once made, the election is irrevocable.

Qualified revocable trusts. In general, a QRT is any trust (or part of a trust) that, on the day the decedent died, was treated as owned by the decedent because the decedent held the power to revoke the trust as described in section 676. An electing trust is a QRT for which a section 645 election has been made.

Election period. The election period is the period of time during which an electing trust is treated as part of its related estate.

The election period begins on the date of the decedent's death and terminates on the earlier of:
• The day on which the electing trust and related estate, if any, distribute all of their assets, or
• The day before the applicable date. To determine the applicable date, first determine whether a Form 706, United States Estate (and Generation-Skipping Transfer) Tax Return, is required to be filed as a result of the decedent's death. If no Form 706 is required to be filed, the applicable date is 2 years after the date of the decedent's death. If Form 706 is required, the applicable date is the later of 2 years after the date of the decedent's death or 6 months after the final determination of liability for estate tax. For additional information, see Regulations section 1.645-1(f).

Taxpayer identification number (TIN). All QRTs must obtain a new TIN following the death of the decedent whether or not a section 645 election is made. (Use Form W-9, Request for Taxpayer Identification Number and Certification, to notify payers of the new TIN.)

An electing trust that continues after the termination of the election period does not need to obtain a new TIN following the termination unless:
• An executor was appointed and agreed to the election after the electing trust made a valid section 645 election, and the electing trust filed a return as an estate under the trust's TIN, or
• No executor was appointed and the QRT was the filing trust (as explained later).

A related estate that continues after the termination of the election period does not need to obtain a new TIN.

For more information about TINs, including trusts with multiple owners, see Regulations sections 1.645-1 and 301.6109-1(a).

General procedures for completing Form 1041 during the election period.

If there is an executor. The following rules apply to filing Form 1041 while the election is in effect.
• The executor of the related estate is responsible for filing Form 1041 for the estate and all electing trusts. The return is filed under the name and TIN of the related estate. Be sure to check the Decedent's estate box at the top of Form 1041 and Item G if the estate has made a section 645 election. The executor continues to file Form 1041 during the election period even if the estate distributes all of its assets before the end of the election period.
• The Form 1041 includes all items of income, deduction, and credit for the estate and all electing trusts.
• For Item G, the executor must provide the TIN of the electing trust with the highest total asset value.
• The executor must attach a statement to Form 1041 providing the following information for each electing trust (including the electing trust provided in Item G): (a) the name of the electing trust, (b) the TIN of the electing trust, and (c) the name and address of the trustee of the electing trust.
• The related estate and the electing trust are treated as separate shares for purposes of computing DNI and applying distribution provisions. Also, each of those shares can contain two or more separate shares. For more information, see *Separate share rule*, later, and Regulations section 1.645-1(e)(2)(iii).
• The executor is responsible for insuring that the estate's share of the combined tax obligation is paid.

For additional information, including treatment of transfers between shares and charitable contribution deductions, see Regulations section 1.645-1(e).

If there is no executor. If no executor has been appointed for the related estate, the trustee of the electing trust files Form 1041 as if it was an estate. File using the TIN that the QRT obtained after the death of the decedent. The trustee can choose a fiscal year as the trust's tax year during the election period. Be sure to check the Decedent's estate box at the top of Form 1041 and Item G if the filing trust has made a section 645 election. For Item G, the filing trustee must provide the TIN of the electing trust with the highest total asset value. The electing trust is entitled to a single $600 personal exemption on returns filed for the election period.

If there is more than one electing trust, the trusts must appoint one trustee as the filing trustee. Form 1041 is filed under the name and TIN of the filing trustee's trust. A statement providing the same information about the electing trusts (except the filing trust) that is listed under, *If there is an executor,* above must be attached to these Forms 1041. All electing trusts must choose the same tax year.

If there is more than one electing trust, the filing trustee is responsible for ensuring that the filing trust's share of the combined tax liability is paid.

For additional information on filing requirements when there is no executor, including application of the separate share rule, see Regulations section 1.645-1(e). For information on the requirements when an executor is appointed after an election is made and the executor does not agree to the election, see below.

Responsibilities of the trustee when there is an executor (or there is no executor and the trustee is not the filing trustee). When there is an executor (or there is no executor and the trustee is not the filing trustee), the trustee of an electing trust is responsible for the following during the election period.
• To timely provide the executor with all the trust information necessary to allow the executor to file a complete, accurate, and timely Form 1041.
• To ensure that the electing trust's share of the combined tax liability is paid.

The trustee does not file a Form 1041 during the election period (except for a final return if the trust terminates during the election period as explained later).

Procedures for completing Form 1041 for the year in which the election terminates.

If there is an executor. If there is an executor, the Form 1041 filed under the name and TIN of the related estate for the tax year in which the election terminates includes (a) the items of income, deduction, and credit for the related estate for its entire tax year, and (b) the income, deductions, and credits for the electing trust for the period that ends with the last day of the election period. If the estate will not continue after the close of the tax year, indicate that this Form 1041 is a final return.

At the end of the last day of the election period, the combined entity is deemed to distribute the share comprising the electing trust to a new trust. All items of income, including net capital gains, that are attributable to the share comprising the electing trust are included in the calculation of DNI of the electing trust and treated as distributed. The distribution rules of sections 661 and 662 apply to this deemed distribution. The combined entity is entitled to an income distribution deduction for this deemed distribution, and the "new" trust must include its share of the distribution in its income. See Regulations sections 1.645-1(e)(2)(iii) and 1.645-1(h) for more information.

If the electing trust continues in existence after the termination of the election period, the trustee must file Form 1041 under the name and TIN of the trust, using the calendar year as its accounting period, if it is otherwise required to file.

If there is no executor. If there is no executor, the following rules apply to filing Form 1041 for the tax year in which the election period ends.
• The tax year of the electing trust closes on the last day of the election period, and the Form 1041 filed for that tax year includes all items of income, deduction, and credit for the electing trust for the period beginning with the first day of the tax year and ending with the last day of the election period.
• The deemed distribution rules discussed above apply.
• Check the box to indicate that this Form 1041 is a final return.
• If the filing trust continues after the termination of the election period, the trustee must obtain a new TIN. If the trust meets the filing requirements, the trustee must file a Form 1041 under the

new TIN for the period beginning with the day after the close of the election period and, in general, ending December 31 of that year.

Responsibilities of the trustee when there is an executor (or there is no executor and the trustee is not the filing trustee). In addition to the requirements listed above under this same heading, the trustee is responsible for the following.
• If the trust will not continue after the close of the election period, the trustee must file a Form 1041 under the name and TIN of the trust. Complete the entity information and items A, C, D, and F. Indicate in item F that this is a final return. Do not report any items of income, deduction, or credit.
• If the trust will continue after the close of the election period, the trustee must file a Form 1041 for the trust for the tax year beginning the day after the close of the election period and, in general, ending December 31 of that year. Use the TIN obtained after the decedent's death. Follow the general rules for completing the return.

Special filing instructions.

When the election is not made by the due date of the QRT's Form 1041. If the section 645 election has not been made by the time the QRT's first income tax return would be due for the tax year beginning with the decedent's death, but the trustee and executor (if any) have decided to make a section 645 election, then the QRT is not required to file a Form 1041 for the short tax year beginning with the decedent's death and ending on December 31 of that year. However, if a valid election is not subsequently made, the QRT may be subject to penalties and interest for failure to file and failure to pay.

If the QRT files a Form 1041 for this short period, and a valid section 645 election is subsequently made, then the trustee must file an amended Form 1041 for the electing trust, excluding all items of income, deduction, and credit of the electing trust. These amounts are then included on the first Form 1041 filed by the executor for the related estate (or the filing trustee for the electing trust filing as an estate).

Later appointed executor. If an executor for the related estate is not appointed until after the trustee has made a valid section 645 election, the executor must agree to the trustee's election and they must file a revised Form 8855 within 90 days of the

appointment of the executor. If the executor does not agree to the election, the election terminates as of the date of appointment of the executor.

If the executor agrees to the election, the trustee must amend any Form 1041 filed under the name and TIN of the electing trust for the period beginning with the decedent's death. The amended returns are still filed under the name and TIN of the electing trust, and they must include the items of income, deduction, and credit for the related estate for the periods covered by the returns. Also, attach a statement to the amended Forms 1041 identifying the name and TIN of the related estate, and the name and address of the executor. Check the Final return box on the amended return for the tax year that ends with the appointment of the executor. Except for this amended return, all returns filed for the combined entity after the appointment of the executor must be filed under the name and TIN of the related estate.

If the election terminates as the result of a later appointed executor, the executor of the related estate must file Forms 1041 under the name and TIN of the related estate for all tax years of the related estate beginning with the decedent's death. The electing trust's election period and tax year terminate the day before the appointment of the executor. The trustee is not required to amend any of the returns filed by the electing trust for the period prior to the appointment of the executor. The trust must file a final Form 1041 following the instructions above for completing Form 1041 in the year in which the election terminates and there is no executor.

Termination of the trust during the election period. If an electing trust terminates during the election period, the trustee of that trust must file a final Form 1041 by completing the entity information (using the trust's EIN), checking the Final return box, and signing and dating the form. Do not report items of income, deduction, and credit. These items are reported on the related estate's return.

Alaska Native Settlement Trusts

The trustee of an Alaska Native Settlement Trust may elect the special tax treatment for the trust and its beneficiaries provided for in section 646. The election must be made by the due date (including extensions) for filing the trust's tax return for its first tax year ending after June 7, 2001. Do not use

¶2944

Form 1041. Use Form 1041-N, U.S. Income Tax Return for Electing Alaska Native Settlement Trusts, to make the election. Additionally, Form 1041-N is the trust's income tax return and satisfies the section 6039H information reporting requirement for the trust.

Bankruptcy Estate

The bankruptcy trustee or debtor-in-possession must file Form 1041 for the estate of an individual involved in bankruptcy proceedings under chapter 7 or 11 of title 11 of the United States Code if the estate has gross income for the tax year of $10,000 or more. See *Bankruptcy Estates*, later, for details.

Charitable Remainder Trusts

A section 664 charitable remainder trust (CRT) does not file Form 1041. Instead, a CRT files Form 5227, Split-Interest Trust Information Return. If the CRT has any unrelated business taxable income, it also must file Form 4720, Return of Certain Excise Taxes Under Chapters 41 and 42 of the Internal Revenue Code.

Common Trust Funds

Do not file Form 1041 for a common trust fund maintained by a bank. Instead, the fund may use Form 1065, U.S. Return of Partnership Income, for its return. For more details, see section 584 and Regulations section 1.6032-1.

Electing Small Business Trusts

Electing small business trusts file Form 1041. However, see *Electing Small Business Trusts (ESBTs)*, later, for a discussion of the special reporting requirements for these trusts.

Pooled Income Funds

Pooled income funds file Form 1041. See *Pooled Income Funds*, later, for the special reporting requirements for these trusts. Additionally, pooled income funds must file Form 5227, Split-Interest Trust Information Return.

Qualified Funeral Trusts

Trustees of pre-need funeral trusts who elect treatment under section 685 file Form 1041-QFT, U.S. Income Tax Return for Qualified Funeral Trusts. All other pre-need funeral trusts, see *Grantor Type Trusts*, later, for Form 1041 reporting requirements.

Qualified Settlement Funds

The trustee of a designated or qualified settlement fund (QSF) generally must file Form 1120-SF, U.S. Income Tax

Return for Settlement Funds, instead of Form 1041.

Special election. If a QSF has only one transferor, the transferor may elect to treat the QSF as a grantor type trust.

To make the grantor trust election, the transferor must attach an election statement to a timely filed Form 1041, including extensions, that the administrator files for the QSF for the tax year in which the settlement fund is established. If Form 1041 is not filed because *Optional Method 1 or 2* was chosen, attach the election statement to a timely filed income tax return, including extensions, of the transferor for the tax year in which the settlement fund is established.

Election statement. The election statement may be made separately or, if filed with Form 1041, on the attachment described under *Grantor Type Trusts*, later. At the top of the election statement, write "Section 1.468B-1(k) Election" and include the transferor's:
• Name,
• Address,
• TIN, and
• A statement that he or she will treat the qualified settlement fund as a grantor type trust.

Widely Held Fixed Investment Trust (WHFITs)

Trustees and middlemen of WHFITs do not file Form 1041. Instead, they report all items of gross income and proceeds on the appropriate Form 1099. For the definition of a WHFIT, see Regulations section 1.671-5(b)(22). A tax information statement that includes the information given to the IRS on Forms 1099, as well as additional information identified in Regulations section 1.671-5(e) must be given to trust interest holders. See the General Instructions for Certain Information Returns for more information.

Electronic Filing

 Applications to become an IRS e-file provider must be submitted online. The IRS no longer accepts paper applications on Form 8633, Application to Participate in the IRS e-file Program.

Qualified fiduciaries or transmitters may be able to file Form 1041 and related schedules electronically. To become an e-file provider complete the following steps:

1. Create an IRS *e-Services account.*

2. Submit your *e-file provider application* online.

3. Pass a *suitability check.*

The online application process takes 4-6 weeks to complete.

Note. Existing *e-file* providers must now use *e*-Services to make account updates.

Help is available at IRS.gov or through the e-Help Desk at 1-866-255-0654 (512-416-7750 for international calls), Monday through Friday, 6:30 a.m. - 6:00 p.m. (CST). *Frequently asked questions* and online *Tutorials* are available to answer questions or to guide users through the application process.

If you file Form 1041 electronically, you may now sign the return electronically by using a personal identification number (PIN). See Form 8879-F, IRS *e-file* Signature Authorization for Form 1041, for details.

If you do not sign the electronically filed return by using a PIN, you must file Form 8453-F, U.S. Estate or Trust Income Tax Declaration and Signature for Electronic Filing.

Note. Form 8453-F may also used as a transmittal if you need to attach certain forms or other documents that cannot be electronically filed. See Form 8453-F and its instructions for more details.

 For 2013, new Form 8453-FE, U.S. Estate or Trust Declaration for an IRS e-file Return will also be used for electronic filing. Form 8453-FE cannot be used as a transmittal to attach forms and documents.

For more information about *e-filing* your return, see Publication 1437, Procedures for the Form 1041 *e-file* Program, U.S. Income Tax Returns for Estates and Trusts for Tax Year 2013, Publication 1438, File Specifications, Validation Criteria and Record Layouts for the Form 1041 E-file Program, U.S. Income Tax Return for Estates and Trusts for Tax Year 2013, and Publication 4164, Modernized e-file (MeF) Guide for Software Developers And Transmitters, Processing Year 2014.

If Form 1041 is *e-filed* and there is a balance due, the fiduciary may authorize an electronic funds withdrawal with the return.

Private Delivery Services

You can use certain private delivery services designated by the IRS to meet

¶2944

Where To File

For all estates and trusts, including charitable and split-interest trusts (other than Charitable Remainder Trusts).

IF you are located in ...	THEN use this address if you:	
	Are not enclosing a check or money order ...	Are enclosing a check or money order ...
Connecticut, Delaware, District of Columbia, Florida, Georgia, Illinois, Indiana, Kentucky, Maine, Maryland, Massachusetts, Michigan, New Hampshire, New Jersey, New York, North Carolina, Ohio, Pennsylvania, Rhode Island, South Carolina, Tennessee, Vermont, Virginia, West Virginia, Wisconsin	Department of the Treasury Internal Revenue Service Cincinnati, Ohio 45999-0048	Department of the Treasury Internal Revenue Service Cincinnati, Ohio 45999-0148
Alabama, Alaska, Arizona, Arkansas, California, Colorado, Hawaii, Idaho, Iowa, Kansas, Louisiana, Minnesota, Mississippi, Missouri, Montana, Nebraska, Nevada, New Mexico, North Dakota, Oklahoma, Oregon, South Dakota, Texas, Utah, Washington, Wyoming	Department of the Treasury Internal Revenue Service Ogden, Utah 84201-0048	Department of the Treasury Internal Revenue Service Ogden, Utah 84201-0148
A foreign country or United States possession	Internal Revenue Service P.O. Box 409101 Ogden, Utah 84409	Internal Revenue Service P.O. Box 409101 Ogden, Utah 84409

the "timely mailing as timely filing/paying" rule for tax returns and payments. These private delivery services include only the following.
• DHL Express (DHL): DHL Same Day Service.
• Federal Express (FedEx): FedEx Priority Overnight, FedEx Standard Overnight, FedEx 2Day, FedEx International Priority, and FedEx International First.
• United Parcel Service (UPS): UPS Next Day Air, UPS Next Day Air Saver, UPS 2nd Day Air, UPS 2nd Day Air A.M., UPS Worldwide Express Plus, and UPS Worldwide Express.

For the IRS mailing address to use if you are using a private delivery service, go to IRS.gov and enter "private delivery service" in the search box.

The private delivery service can tell you how to get written proof of the mailing date.

 Private delivery services cannot deliver items to P.O. boxes. You must use the U.S. Postal Service to mail any item to an IRS P.O. box address.

When To File

For calendar year estates and trusts, file Form 1041 and Schedule(s) K-1 on or before April 15, 2014. For fiscal year estates and trusts, file Form 1041 by the 15th day of the 4th month following the close of the tax year. For example, an estate that has a tax year that ends on June 30, 2014, must file Form 1041 by October 15, 2014. If the due date falls on a Saturday, Sunday, or legal holiday, file on the next business day.

Extension of Time To File

If more time is needed to file the estate or trust return, use Form 7004, Application for Automatic Extension of Time To File Certain Business Income Tax, Information, and Other Returns, to

apply for an automatic 5 month extension of time to file.

Note. Beginning June 24, 2011, the automatic extension of time to file a bankruptcy estate return was increased to 6 months.

Period Covered

File the 2013 return for calendar year 2013 and fiscal years beginning in 2013 and ending in 2014. If the return is for a fiscal year or a short tax year (less than 12 months), fill in the tax year space at the top of the form.

The 2013 Form 1041 may also be used for a tax year beginning in 2014 if:

1. The estate or trust has a tax year of less than 12 months that begins and ends in 2014, and

2. The 2014 Form 1041 is not available by the time the estate or trust is required to file its tax return. However, the estate or trust must show its 2014 tax year on the 2013 Form 1041 and incorporate any tax law changes that are effective for tax years beginning after December 31, 2013.

Who Must Sign

Fiduciary

The fiduciary, or an authorized representative, must sign Form 1041. If there are joint fiduciaries, only one is required to sign the return.

A financial institution that submitted estimated tax payments for trusts for which it is the trustee must enter its EIN in the space provided for the EIN of the fiduciary. Do not enter the EIN of the trust. For this purpose, a financial institution is one that maintains a Treasury Tax and Loan (TT&L) account. If you are an attorney or other individual functioning in a fiduciary capacity, leave this space blank. Do not enter your individual social security number (SSN).

Paid Preparer

Generally, anyone who is paid to prepare a tax return must sign the return and fill in the other blanks in the "Paid Preparer Use Only" area of the return.

The person required to sign the return must:
• Complete the required preparer information,
• Sign it in the space provided for the preparer's signature (a facsimile signature is acceptable), and
• Give you a copy of the return for your records.

-8-

2013 Instructions for Form 1041

If you, as fiduciary, fill in Form 1041, leave the "Paid Preparer Use Only" space blank.

If someone prepares this return and does not charge you, that person should not sign the return.

Paid Preparer Authorization

If the fiduciary wants to allow the IRS to discuss the estate's or trust's 2013 tax return with the paid preparer who signed it, check the "Yes," box in the signature area of the return. This authorization applies only to the individual whose signature appears in the *Paid Preparer Use Only* area of the estate's or trust's return. It does not apply to the firm, if any, shown in that section.

If the "Yes," box is checked, the fiduciary is authorizing the IRS to call the paid preparer to answer any questions that may arise during the processing of the estate's or trust's return. The fiduciary is also authorizing the paid preparer to:
* Give the IRS any information that is missing from the estate's or trust's return,
* Call the IRS for information about the processing of the estate's or trust's return or the status of its refund or payment(s), and
* Respond to certain IRS notices that the fiduciary has shared with the preparer about math errors, offsets, and return preparation. The notices will not be sent to the preparer.

The fiduciary is not authorizing the paid preparer to receive any refund check, bind the estate or trust to anything (including any additional tax liability), or otherwise represent the estate or trust before the IRS.

The authorization will automatically end no later than the due date (without regard to extensions) for filing the estate's or trust's 2014 tax return. If the fiduciary wants to expand the paid preparer's authorization or revoke the authorization before it ends, see Pub. 947, Practice Before the IRS and Power of Attorney.

Accounting Methods

Figure taxable income using the method of accounting regularly used in keeping the estate's or trust's books and records. Generally, permissible methods include the cash method, the accrual method, or any other method authorized by the Internal Revenue Code. In all cases, the method used must clearly reflect income.

Generally, the estate or trust may change its accounting method (for income as a whole or for any material item) only by getting consent on Form 3115, Application for Change in Accounting Method. For more information, see Pub. 538, Accounting Periods and Methods.

Accounting Periods

For a decedent's estate, the moment of death determines the end of the decedent's tax year and the beginning of the estate's tax year. As executor or administrator, you choose the estate's tax period when you file its first income tax return. The estate's first tax year may be any period of 12 months or less that ends on the last day of a month. If you select the last day of any month other than December, you are adopting a fiscal tax year.

To change the accounting period of an estate, use Form 1128, Application To Adopt, Change, or Retain a Tax Year.

Generally, a trust must adopt a calendar year. The following trusts are exempt from this requirement:
* A trust that is exempt from tax under section 501(a);
* A charitable trust described in section 4947(a)(1); and
* A trust that is treated as wholly owned by a grantor under the rules of sections 671 through 679.

Rounding Off to Whole Dollars

You may round off cents to whole dollars on the estate's or trust's return and schedules. If you do round to whole dollars, you must round all amounts. To round, drop amounts under 50 cents and increase amounts from 50 to 99 cents to the next dollar. For example, $1.39 becomes $1 and $2.50 becomes $3.

If you have to add two or more amounts to figure the amount to enter on a line, include cents when adding the amounts and round off only the total.

Estimated Tax

Generally, an estate or trust must pay estimated income tax for 2014 if it expects to owe, after subtracting any withholding and credits, at least $1,000 in tax, and it expects the withholding and credits to be less than the smaller of:

1. 90% of the tax shown on the 2014 tax return, or

2. 100% of the tax shown on the 2013 tax return (110% of that amount if the estate's or trust's adjusted gross income on that return is more than $150,000, and less than ⅔ of gross income for 2013 or 2014 is from farming or fishing).

However, if a return was not filed for 2013 or that return did not cover a full 12 months, item 2 does not apply.

For this purpose, include household employment taxes in the tax shown on the tax return, but only if either of the following is true:
* The estate or trust will have federal income tax withheld for 2014 (see the instructions for line 24e), or
* The estate or trust would be required to make estimated tax payments for 2014 even if it did not include household employment taxes when figuring estimated tax.

Exceptions

Estimated tax payments are not required from:

1. An estate of a domestic decedent or a domestic trust that had no tax liability for the full 12-month 2013 tax year;

2. A decedent's estate for any tax year ending before the date that is 2 years after the decedent's death; or

3. A trust that was treated as owned by the decedent if the trust will receive the residue of the decedent's estate under the will (or if no will is admitted to probate, the trust primarily responsible for paying debts, taxes, and expenses of administration) for any tax year ending before the date that is 2 years after the decedent's death.

For more information, see Form 1041-ES, Estimated Income Tax for Estates and Trusts.

Electronic Deposits

A financial institution that has been designated as an authorized federal tax depository, and acts as a fiduciary for at least 200 taxable trusts that are required to pay estimated tax, is required to deposit the estimated tax payments electronically using the Electronic Federal Tax Payment System (EFTPS).

A fiduciary that is not required to make electronic deposits of estimated tax on behalf of a trust or an estate may voluntarily participate in EFTPS. To enroll in or get more information about EFTPS, visit the EFTPS website at *www.eftps.gov* or call 1-800-555-4477. Also, see Pub. 966, Electronic Federal Tax Payment System: A Guide to Getting Started.

¶2944

Depositing on time. For a deposit using EFTPS to be on time, the deposit must be scheduled by 8:00 p.m. Eastern time the day before the due date of the deposit.

Section 643(g) Election

Fiduciaries of trusts that pay estimated tax may elect under section 643(g) to have any portion of their estimated tax payments allocated to any of the beneficiaries.

The fiduciary of a decedent's estate may make a section 643(g) election only for the final year of the estate.

Make the election by filing Form 1041-T, Allocation of Estimated Tax Payments to Beneficiaries, by the 65th day after the close of the estate's or trust's tax year. Then, include that amount on Schedule K-1 (Form 1041), box 13, code A, for any beneficiaries for whom it was elected.

If Form 1041-T was timely filed, the payments are treated as paid or credited to the beneficiary on the last day of the tax year and must be included as an other amount paid, credited, or required to be distributed on Form 1041, Schedule B, line 10. See the instructions for Schedule B, line 10, later.

Failure to make a timely election will result in the estimated tax payments not being transferred to the beneficiary(ies) even if you entered the amount on Schedule K-1.

See the instructions for line 24b for more details.

Interest and Penalties

Interest

Interest is charged on taxes not paid by the due date, even if an extension of time to file is granted.

Interest is also charged on penalties imposed for failure to file, negligence, fraud, substantial valuation misstatements, substantial understatements of tax, and reportable transaction understatements. Interest is charged on the penalty from the due date of the return (including extensions). The interest charge is figured at a rate determined under section 6621.

Late Filing of Return

The law provides a penalty of 5% of the tax due for each month, or part of a month, for which a return is not filed up to a maximum of 25% of the tax due (15% for each month, or part of a

month, up to a maximum of 75% if the failure to file is fraudulent). If the return is more than 60 days late, the minimum penalty is the smaller of $135 or the tax due.

The penalty will not be imposed if you can show that the failure to file on time was due to reasonable cause. If you receive a notice about penalty and interest after you file this return, send us an explanation and we will determine if you meet reasonable-cause criteria. Do **not** attach an explanation when you file Form 1041.

Late Payment of Tax

Generally, the penalty for not paying tax when due is ½ of 1% of the unpaid amount for each month or part of a month it remains unpaid. The maximum penalty is 25% of the unpaid amount. The penalty applies to any unpaid tax on the return. Any penalty is in addition to interest charges on late payments.

 If you include interest on either of these penalties with your payment, identify and enter these amounts in the bottom margin of Form 1041, page 1. Do not include the interest or penalty amount in the balance of tax due on line 27.

Failure To Provide Information Timely

You must provide Schedule K-1 (Form 1041), on or before the day you are required to file Form 1041, to each beneficiary who receives a distribution of property or an allocation of an item of the estate.

For each failure to provide Schedule K-1 to a beneficiary when due and each failure to include on Schedule K-1 all the information required to be shown (or the inclusion of incorrect information), a $100 penalty may be imposed with regard to each Schedule K-1 for which a failure occurs. The maximum penalty is $1.5 million for all such failures during a calendar year. If the requirement to report information is intentionally disregarded, each $100 penalty is increased to $250 or, if greater, 10% of the aggregate amount of items required to be reported, and the $1.5 million maximum does not apply.

The penalty will not be imposed if the fiduciary can show that not providing information timely was due to reasonable cause and not due to willful neglect.

Underpaid Estimated Tax

If the fiduciary underpaid estimated tax, use Form 2210, Underpayment of

Estimated Tax by Individuals, Estates, and Trusts, to figure any penalty. Enter the amount of any penalty on Form 1041, line 26.

Trust Fund Recovery Penalty

This penalty may apply if certain excise, income, social security, and Medicare taxes that must be collected or withheld are not collected or withheld, or these taxes are not paid. These taxes are generally reported on Forms 720, 941, 943, 944, or 945. The trust fund recovery penalty may be imposed on all persons who are determined by the IRS to have been responsible for collecting, accounting for, or paying over these taxes, and who acted willfully in not doing so. The penalty is equal to the unpaid trust fund tax. See the Instructions for Form 720, Pub. 15 (Circular E), Employer's Tax Guide, or Pub. 51 (Circular A), Agricultural Employer's Tax Guide, for more details, including the definition of responsible persons.

Other Penalties

Other penalties can be imposed for negligence, substantial understatement of tax, and fraud. See Pub. 17, Your Federal Income Tax, for details on these penalties.

Other Forms That May Be Required

Form W-2, Wage and Tax Statement, and Form W-3, Transmittal of Wage and Tax Statements.

Form 56, Notice Concerning Fiduciary Relationship. You must notify the IRS of the creation or termination of a fiduciary relationship. You may use Form 56 to provide this notice to the IRS.

Form 706, United States Estate (and Generation-Skipping Transfer) Tax Return, or Form 706-NA, United States Estate (and Generation-Skipping Transfer) Tax Return, Estate of nonresident not a citizen of the United States.

Form 706-GS(D), Generation-Skipping Transfer Tax Return for Distributions.

Form 706-GS(D-1), Notification of Distribution From a Generation-Skipping Trust.

Form 706-GS(T), Generation-Skipping Transfer Tax Return for Terminations.

Form 709, United States Gift (and Generation-Skipping Transfer) Tax Return.

Form 720, Quarterly Federal Excise Tax Return. Use Form 720 to report environmental excise taxes, communications and air transportation taxes, fuel taxes, luxury tax on passenger vehicles, manufacturers' taxes, ship passenger tax, and certain other excise taxes.

Caution. See *Trust Fund Recovery Penalty* earlier.

Form 926, Return by a U.S. Transferor of Property to a Foreign Corporation. Use this form to report certain information required under section 6038B.

Form 940, Employer's Annual Federal Unemployment (FUTA) Tax Return. The estate or trust may be liable for FUTA tax and may have to file Form 940 if it paid wages of $1,500 or more in any calendar quarter during the calendar year (or the preceding calendar year) or one or more employees worked for the estate or trust for some part of a day in any 20 different weeks during the calendar year (or the preceding calendar year).

Form 941, Employer's QUARTERLY Federal Tax Return. Employers must file this form quarterly to report income tax withheld on wages and employer and employee social security and Medicare taxes. Certain small employers must file Form 944, Employer's ANNUAL Federal Tax Return, instead of Form 941. For more information, see the Instructions for Form 944. Agricultural employers must file Form 943, Employer's Annual Federal Tax Return for Agricultural Employees, instead of Form 941, to report income tax withheld and employer and employee social security and Medicare taxes on farmworkers.

Caution. See *Trust Fund Recovery Penalty* earlier.

Form 945, Annual Return of Withheld Federal Income Tax. Use this form to report income tax withheld from nonpayroll payments, including pensions, annuities, IRAs, gambling winnings, and backup withholding.

Caution. See *Trust Fund Recovery Penalty* earlier.

Form 1040, U.S. Individual Income Tax Return.

Form 1040NR, U.S. Nonresident Alien Income Tax Return.

Form 1041-A, U.S. Information Return Trust Accumulation of Charitable Amounts.

Form 1042, Annual Withholding Tax Return for U.S. Source Income of Foreign Persons, and Form 1042-S, Foreign Person's U.S. Source Income Subject to Withholding. Use these forms to report and transmit withheld tax on payments or distributions made to nonresident alien individuals, foreign partnerships, or foreign corporations to the extent such payments or distributions constitute gross income from sources within the United States that is not effectively connected with a U.S. trade or business. For more information, see sections 1441 and 1442, and Pub. 515, Withholding of Tax on Nonresident Aliens and Foreign Entities.

Forms 1099-A, B, INT, LTC, MISC, OID, Q, R, S, and SA. You may have to file these information returns to report acquisitions or abandonments of secured property; proceeds from broker and barter exchange transactions; interest payments; payments of long-term care and accelerated death benefits; miscellaneous income payments; original issue discount; distributions from Coverdell ESAs; distributions from pensions, annuities, retirement or profit-sharing plans, IRAs (including SEPs, SIMPLEs, Roth IRAs, Roth Conversions, and IRA recharacterizations), insurance contracts, etc.; proceeds from real estate transactions; and distributions from an HSA, Archer MSA, or Medicare Advantage MSA.

Also, use certain of these returns to report amounts received as a nominee on behalf of another person, except amounts reported to beneficiaries on Schedule K-1 (Form 1041).

Form 8275, Disclosure Statement. File Form 8275 to disclose items or positions, except those contrary to a regulation, that are not otherwise adequately disclosed on a tax return. The disclosure is made to avoid parts of the accuracy-related penalty imposed for disregard of rules or substantial understatement of tax. Form 8275 is also used for disclosures relating to preparer penalties for understatements due to unrealistic positions or disregard of rules.

Form 8275-R, Regulation Disclosure Statement, is used to disclose any item on a tax return for which a position has been taken that is contrary to Treasury regulations.

Form 8288, U.S. Withholding Tax Return for Dispositions by Foreign Persons of U.S. Real Property Interests,

and Form 8288-A, Statement of Withholding on Dispositions by Foreign Persons of U.S. Real Property Interests. Use these forms to report and transmit withheld tax on the sale of U.S. real property by a foreign person. Also, use these forms to report and transmit tax withheld from amounts distributed to a foreign beneficiary from a "U.S. real property interest account" that a domestic estate or trust is required to establish under Regulations section 1.1445-5(c)(1)(iii).

Form 8300, Report of Cash Payments Over $10,000 Received in a Trade or Business. Generally, this form is used to report the receipt of more than $10,000 in cash or foreign currency in one transaction (or a series of related transactions).

Form 8855, Election To Treat a Qualified Revocable Trust as Part of an Estate. This election allows a qualified revocable trust to be treated and taxed (for income tax purposes) as part of its related estate during the election period.

Form 8865, Return of U.S. Persons With Respect to Certain Foreign Partnerships. The estate or trust may have to file Form 8865 if it:

1. Controlled a foreign partnership (that is, owned more than a 50% direct or indirect interest in a foreign partnership);

2. Owned at least a 10% direct or indirect interest in a foreign partnership while U.S. persons controlled that partnership;

3. Had an acquisition, disposition, or change in proportional interest in a foreign partnership that:

    a. Increased its direct interest to at least 10%;

    b. Reduced its direct interest of at least 10% to less than 10%; or

    c. Changed its direct interest by at least a 10% interest.

4. Contributed property to a foreign partnership in exchange for a partnership interest if:

    a. Immediately after the contribution, the estate or trust owned, directly or indirectly, at least a 10% interest in the foreign partnership or

    b. The fair market value (FMV) of the property the estate or trust contributed to the foreign partnership, for a partnership interest, when added to other contributions of property made to the foreign partnership during the preceding 12-month period, exceeds $100,000.

Also, the estate or trust may have to file Form 8865 to report certain dispositions by a foreign partnership of property it previously contributed to that foreign partnership if it was a partner at the time of the disposition.

For more details, including penalties for failing to file Form 8865, see Form 8865 and its separate instructions.

Form 8886, Reportable Transaction Disclosure Statement. Use Form 8886 to disclose information for each reportable transaction in which the trust participated, directly or indirectly. Form 8886 must be filed for each tax year that the federal income tax liability of the estate or trust is affected by its participation in the transaction. The estate or trust may have to pay a penalty if it has a requirement to file Form 8886 but you fail to file it. The following are reportable transactions.
• Any transaction that is the same as or substantially similar to tax avoidance transactions identified by the IRS as listed transactions.
• Any transaction offered under conditions of confidentiality and for which the estate or trust paid a minimum fee (confidential transaction).
• Any transaction for which the estate or trust or a related party has contractual protection against disallowance of the tax benefits (transaction with contractual protection).
• Any transaction resulting in a loss of at least $2 million in any single year or $4 million in any combination of years ($50,000 in any single year if the loss is generated by a section 988 transaction) (loss transactions).
• Any transaction substantially similar to one of the types of transactions identified by the IRS as a transaction of interest.

See the Instructions for Form 8886 for more details and exceptions.

Form 8918, Material Advisor Disclosure Statement. Material advisors who provide material aid, assistance, or advice on organizing, managing, promoting, selling, implementing, insuring, or carrying out any reportable transaction, and who directly or indirectly receive or expect to receive a minimum fee, must use Form 8918 to disclose any reportable transaction under Regulations section 301.6111-3. For more information, see Form 8918 and its instructions.

Form 8939, Allocation of Increase in Basis for Property Acquired From a Decedent. This form is used to allocate any additional basis when an executor

makes the special section 1022 election for property acquired from a decedent who died in 2010.

Form 8960, Net Investment Income Tax—Individuals, Estates, and Trusts.

Additional Information

The following publications may assist you in preparing Form 1041:
• Pub. 550, Investment Income and Expenses,
• Pub. 559, Survivors, Executors, and Administrators,
• Pub. 590, Individual Retirement Arrangements (IRAs), and
• Pub. 4895, Tax Treatment of Property Acquired From a Decedent Dying in 2010.

Assembly and Attachments

Assemble any schedules, forms, and attachments behind Form 1041 in the following order:

1. Schedule I (Form 1041);
2. Schedule D (Form 1041);
3. Form 4952;
4. Schedule H (Form 1040);
5. Form 3800;
6. Form 4136;
7. Form 8855;
8. Form 8960;
9. All other schedules and forms; and
10. All attachments.

Attachments

If you need more space on the forms or schedules, attach separate sheets. Use the same size and format as on the printed forms. But show the totals on the printed forms.

Attach these separate sheets after all the schedules and forms. Enter the estate's or trust's EIN on each sheet.

Do not file a copy of the decedent's will or the trust instrument unless the IRS requests it.

Special Reporting Instructions

Grantor type trusts, the S portion of electing small business trusts (ESBTs), and bankruptcy estates all have reporting requirements that are significantly different than other Subchapter J trusts and decedent's estates. Additionally, grantor type trusts have optional filing methods available. Pooled income funds have many similar

reporting requirements that other Subchapter J trusts (other than grantor type trusts and electing small business trusts) have but there are some very important differences. These reporting differences and optional filing methods are discussed below by entity.

Grantor Type Trusts

A trust is a grantor trust if the grantor retains certain powers or ownership benefits. This can also apply to only a portion of a trust. See *Grantor Type Trust*, later, for details on what makes a trust a grantor trust.

In general, a grantor trust is ignored for income tax purposes and all of the income, deductions, etc., are treated as belonging directly to the grantor. This also applies to any portion of a trust that is treated as a grantor trust.

Note. If only a portion of the trust is a grantor type trust, indicate both grantor trust *and* the other type of trust, for example, simple or complex trust, as the type of entities checked in Section A on page 1 of Form 1041.

 The following instructions apply only to grantor type trusts that are not using an optional filing method.

How to report. If the entire trust is a grantor trust, fill in only the entity information of Form 1041. Do not show any dollar amounts on the form itself; show dollar amounts only on an attachment to the form. Do not use Schedule K-1 (Form 1041) as the attachment.

If only part of the trust is a grantor type trust, the portion of the income, deductions, etc., that is allocable to the non-grantor part of the trust is reported on Form 1041, under normal reporting rules. The amounts that are allocable directly to the grantor are shown only on an attachment to the form. Do not use Schedule K-1 (Form 1041) as the attachment. However, Schedule K-1 is used to reflect any income distributed from the portion of the trust that is not taxable directly to the grantor or owner.

The fiduciary must give the grantor (owner) of the trust a copy of the attachment.

Attachment. On the attachment, show:
• The name, identifying number, and address of the person(s) to whom the income is taxable;
• The income of the trust that is taxable to the grantor or another person under sections 671 through 678. Report the

income in the same detail as it would be reported on the grantor's return had it been received directly by the grantor; and

• Any deductions or credits that apply to this income. Report these deductions and credits in the same detail as they would be reported on the grantor's return had they been received directly by the grantor.

The income taxable to the grantor or another person under sections 671 through 678 and the deductions and credits that apply to that income must be reported by that person on their own income tax return.

Example. The John Doe Trust is a grantor type trust. During the year, the trust sold 100 shares of ABC stock for $1,010 in which it had a basis of $10 and 200 shares of XYZ stock for $10 in which it had a $1,020 basis.

The trust does not report these transactions on Form 1041. Instead, a schedule is attached to the Form 1041 showing each stock transaction separately and in the same detail as John Doe (grantor and owner) will need to report these transactions on his Form 8949, Sales and Other Dispositions of Capital Assets and Schedule D (Form 1040). The trust does not net the capital gains and losses, nor does it issue John Doe a Schedule K-1 (Form 1041) showing a $10 long-term capital loss.

QSSTs. Income allocated to S corporation stock held by the trust is treated as owned by the income beneficiary of the portion of the trust that owns the stock. Report this income following the rules discussed above for grantor type trusts. A QSST cannot elect any of the optional filing methods discussed below.

However, the trust, and not the income beneficiary, is treated as the owner of the S corporation stock for figuring and attributing the tax results of a disposition of the stock. For example, if the disposition is a sale, the QSST election ends as to the stock sold and any gain or loss recognized on the sale will be that of the trust. For more information on QSSTs, see Regulations section 1.1361-1(j).

Optional Filing Methods for Certain Grantor Type Trusts

Generally, if a trust is treated as owned by one grantor or other person, the trustee may choose *Optional Method 1* or *Optional Method 2* as the trust's method of reporting instead of filing Form 1041. A husband and wife will be treated as one grantor for purposes of these two optional methods if:
• All of the trust is treated as owned by the husband and wife, and
• The husband and wife file their income tax return jointly for that tax year.

Generally, if a trust is treated as owned by two or more grantors or other persons, the trustee may choose *Optional Method 3* as the trust's method of reporting instead of filing Form 1041.

Once you choose the trust's filing method, you must follow the rules under *Changing filing methods* if you want to change to another method.

Exceptions. The following trusts cannot report using the optional filing methods.
• A common trust fund (as defined in section 584(a)).
• A foreign trust or a trust that has any of its assets located outside the United States.
• A qualified subchapter S trust (as defined in section 1361(d)(3)).
• A trust all of which is treated as owned by one grantor or one other person whose tax year is other than a calendar year.
• A trust all of which is treated as owned by one or more grantors or other persons, one of which is not a U.S. person.
• A trust all of which is treated as owned by one or more grantors or other persons if at least one grantor or other person is an exempt recipient for information reporting purposes, unless at least one grantor or other person is not an exempt recipient and the trustee reports without treating any of the grantors or other persons as exempt recipients.

Optional Method 1. For a trust treated as owned by one grantor or by one other person, the trustee must give all payers of income during the tax year the name and TIN of the grantor or other person treated as the owner of the trust and the address of the trust. This method may be used only if the owner of the trust provides the trustee with a signed Form W-9, Request for Taxpayer Identification Number and Certification. In addition, unless the grantor or other person treated as owner of the trust is the trustee or a co-trustee of the trust, the trustee must give the grantor or other person treated as owner of the trust a statement that:
• Shows all items of income, deduction, and credit of the trust;

• Identifies the payer of each item of income;
• Explains how the grantor or other person treated as owner of the trust takes those items into account when figuring the grantor's or other person's taxable income or tax; and
• Informs the grantor or other person treated as the owner of the trust that those items must be included when figuring taxable income and credits on his or her income tax return.

 Grantor trusts that have not applied for an EIN and are going to file under Optional Method 1 do not need an EIN for the trust as long as they continue to report under that method.

Optional Method 2. For a trust treated as owned by one grantor or by one other person, the trustee must give all payers of income during the tax year the name, address, and TIN of the trust. The trustee also must file with the IRS the appropriate Forms 1099 to report the income or gross proceeds paid to the trust during the tax year that shows the trust as the payer and the grantor, or other person treated as owner, as the payee. The trustee must report each type of income in the aggregate and each item of gross proceeds separately. The due date for any Forms 1099 required to be filed with the IRS by a trustee under this method is February 28, 2014 (March 31, 2014, if filed electronically).

In addition, unless the grantor, or other person treated as owner of the trust, is the trustee or a co-trustee of the trust, the trustee must give the grantor or other person treated as owner of the trust a statement that:
• Shows all items of income, deduction, and credit of the trust;
• Explains how the grantor or other person treated as owner of the trust takes those items into account when figuring the grantor's or other person's taxable income or tax; and
• Informs the grantor or other person treated as the owner of the trust that those items must be included when figuring taxable income and credits on his or her income tax return. This statement satisfies the requirement to give the recipient copies of the Forms 1099 filed by the trustee.

Optional Method 3. For a trust treated as owned by two or more grantors or other persons, the trustee must give all payers of income during the tax year the name, address, and TIN of the trust. The trustee also must file with the IRS

2013 Instructions for Form 1041

-13-

the appropriate Forms 1099 to report the income or gross proceeds paid to the trust by all payers during the tax year attributable to the part of the trust treated as owned by each grantor, or other person, showing the trust as the payer and each grantor, or other person treated as owner of the trust, as the payee. The trustee must report each type of income in the aggregate and each item of gross proceeds separately. The due date for any Forms 1099 required to be filed with the IRS by a trustee under this method is February 28, 2014 (March 31, 2014, if filed electronically).

In addition, the trustee must give each grantor or other person treated as owner of the trust a statement that:
• Shows all items of income, deduction, and credit of the trust attributable to the part of the trust treated as owned by the grantor or other person;
• Explains how the grantor or other person treated as owner of the trust takes those items into account when figuring the grantor's or other person's taxable income or tax; and
• Informs the grantor or other person treated as the owner of the trust that those items must be included when figuring taxable income and credits on his or her income tax return. This statement satisfies the requirement to give the recipient copies of the Forms 1099 filed by the trustee.

Changing filing methods. A trustee who previously had filed Form 1041 can change to one of the optional methods by filing a final Form 1041 for the tax year that immediately precedes the first tax year for which the trustee elects to report under one of the optional methods. On the front of the final Form 1041, the trustee must write "Pursuant to section 1.671-4(g), this is the final Form 1041 for this grantor trust," and check the Final return box in item F.

For more details on changing reporting methods, including changes from one optional method to another, see Regulations section 1.671-4(g).

Backup withholding. The following grantor trusts are treated as payors for purposes of backup withholding.

1. A trust established after 1995, all of which is owned by two or more grantors (treating spouses filing a joint return as one grantor).

2. A trust with 10 or more grantors established after 1983 but before 1996.

The trustee must withhold a certain percentage of reportable payments

made to any grantor who is subject to backup withholding.

For more information, see section 3406 and its regulations.

Pooled Income Funds

If you are filing for a pooled income fund, attach a statement to support the following:
• The calculation of the yearly rate of return,
• The computation of the deduction for distributions to the beneficiaries, and
• The computation of any charitable deduction.
See section 642 and the regulations thereunder for more information.

You do not have to complete Schedules A or B of Form 1041.

Also, you must file Form 5227, Split-Interest Trust Information Return, for the pooled income fund. However, if all amounts were transferred in trust before May 27, 1969, or if an amount was transferred to the trust after May 26, 1969, for which no deduction was allowed under any of the sections listed under section 4947(a)(2), then Form 5227 does not have to be filed.

Note. Form 1041-A is no longer filed by pooled income funds.

Electing Small Business Trusts (ESBTs)

Special rules apply when figuring the tax on the S portion of an ESBT. The S portion of an ESBT is the portion of the trust that consists of stock in one or more S corporations and is not treated as a grantor type trust. The tax on the S portion:
• Must be figured separately from the tax on the remainder of the ESBT (if any) and attached to the return,
• Is entered to the left of the Schedule G, line 7, entry space preceded by "Sec. 641(c)," and
• Is included in the total tax on Schedule G, line 7.

The tax on the remainder (non-S portion) of the ESBT is figured in the normal manner on Form 1041.

Tax computation attachment. Attach to the return the tax computation for the S portion of the ESBT.

To compute the tax on the S portion:
• Treat that portion of the ESBT as if it were a separate trust;
• Include only the income, losses, deductions, and credits allocated to the ESBT as an S corporation shareholder and gain or loss from the disposition of S corporation stock;

• Aggregate items of income, losses, deductions, and credits allocated to the ESBT as an S corporation shareholder if the S portion of the ESBT has stock in more than one S corporation;
• Deduct state and local income taxes and administrative expenses directly related to the S portion or allocated to the S portion if the allocation is reasonable in light of all the circumstances;
• Deduct interest expense paid or accrued on indebtedness incurred to acquire stock in an S corporation;
• Do not claim a deduction for capital losses in excess of capital gains;
• Do not claim an income distribution deduction or an exemption amount;
• Do not claim an exemption amount in figuring the AMT; and
• Do not use the tax rate schedule to figure the tax. The tax is 39.6% of the S portion's taxable income except in figuring the maximum tax on qualified dividends and capital gains.

For additional information, see Regulations section 1.641(c)-1.

Other information. When figuring the tax and DNI on the remaining (non-S) portion of the trust, disregard the S corporation items.

Do not apportion to the beneficiaries any of the S corporation items.

If the ESBT consists entirely of stock in one or more S corporations, do not make any entries on lines 1–22 of page 1. Instead:
• Complete the entity portion;
• Follow the instructions above for figuring the tax on the S corporation items;
• Carry the tax from line 7 of Schedule G to line 23 on page 1; and
• Complete the rest of the return.

The grantor portion (if any) of an ESBT will follow the rules discussed under *Grantor Type Trusts*, earlier.

Bankruptcy Estates

The bankruptcy estate that is created when an individual debtor files a petition under either chapter 7 or 11 of title 11 of the U.S. Code is treated as a separate taxable entity. The bankruptcy estate is administered by a trustee or a debtor-in-possession. If the case is later dismissed by the bankruptcy court, the individual debtor is treated as if the bankruptcy petition had never been filed.

A separate taxable entity is not created if a partnership or corporation files a petition under any chapter of title 11 of the U.S. Code.

For additional information about bankruptcy estates, see Pub. 908, Bankruptcy Tax Guide.

Who Must File

Every trustee (or debtor-in-possession) for an individual's bankruptcy estate under chapter 7 or 11 of title 11 of the U.S. Code must file a return if the bankruptcy estate has gross income of $10,000 or more for tax years beginning in 2013.

Failure to do so may result in an estimated Request for Administrative Expenses being filed by the IRS in the bankruptcy proceeding or a motion to compel filing of the return.

 The filing of a tax return for the bankruptcy estate does not relieve the individual debtor(s) of his, her, or their individual tax obligations.

EIN

Every bankruptcy estate of an individual required to file a return must have its own EIN. The SSN of the individual debtor cannot be used as the EIN for the bankruptcy estate.

Accounting Period

A bankruptcy estate is allowed to have a fiscal year. However, this period cannot be longer than 12 months.

When To File

File Form 1041 on or before the 15th day of the 4th month following the close of the tax year. Use Form 7004 to apply for an automatic 6-month extension of time to file.

Disclosure of Return Information

Under section 6103(e)(5), tax returns of individual debtors who have filed for bankruptcy under chapters 7 or 11 of title 11 are, upon written request, open to inspection by or disclosure to the trustee.

The returns subject to disclosure to the trustee are those for the year the bankruptcy begins and prior years. Use Form 4506, Request for Copy of Tax Return, to request copies of the individual debtor's tax returns.

If the bankruptcy case was not voluntary, disclosure cannot be made before the bankruptcy court has entered an order for relief, unless the court rules that the disclosure is needed for determining whether relief should be ordered.

Transfer of Tax Attributes From the Individual Debtor to the Bankruptcy Estate

The bankruptcy estate succeeds to the following tax attributes of the individual debtor:

1. Net operating loss (NOL) carryovers;

2. Charitable contribution carryovers;

3. Recovery of tax benefit items;

4. Credit carryovers;

5. Capital loss carryovers;

6. Basis, holding period, and character of assets;

7. Method of accounting;

8. Unused passive activity losses;

9. Unused passive activity credits; and

10. Unused section 465 losses.

Income, Deductions, and Credits

Under section 1398(c), the taxable income of the bankruptcy estate generally is figured in the same manner as that of an individual. The gross income of the bankruptcy estate includes any income included in property of the estate as defined in U.S. Code, title 11, sections 541 and 1115.

Under section 1115 of title 11, property of the bankruptcy estate includes (a) earnings from services performed by the debtor after the beginning of the case (both wages and self-employment income) and before the case is closed, dismissed, or converted to a case under a different chapter and (b) property described in section 541 of title 11 and income earned therefrom that the debtor acquires after the beginning of the case and before the case is closed, dismissed, or converted. If section 1115 of title 11 applies, the bankruptcy estate's gross income includes, as described above, (a) the debtor's earnings from services performed after the beginning of the case and (b) the income from property acquired after the beginning of the case.

The income from property owned by the debtor when the case began is also included in the bankruptcy estate's gross income. However, if this property is exempted from the bankruptcy estate or is abandoned by the trustee or debtor-in-possession, the income from the property is not included in the bankruptcy estate's gross income. Also included in income is gain from the sale of the bankruptcy estate's property. To figure gain, the trustee or debtor-in-possession must determine the correct basis of the property.

To determine whether any amount paid or incurred by the bankruptcy estate is allowable as a deduction or credit, or is treated as wages for employment tax purposes, treat the amount as if it were paid or incurred by the individual debtor in the same trade or business or other activity the debtor engaged in before the bankruptcy proceedings began.

Administrative expenses. The bankruptcy estate is allowed a deduction for any administrative expense allowed under section 503 of title 11 of the U.S. Code, and any fee or charge assessed under chapter 123 of title 28 of the U.S. Code, to the extent not disallowed under an Internal Revenue Code provision (for example, section 263, 265, or 275).

Administrative expense loss. When figuring an NOL, nonbusiness deductions (including administrative expenses) are limited under section 172(d)(4) to the bankruptcy estate's nonbusiness income. The excess nonbusiness deductions are an administrative expense loss that may be carried back to each of the 3 preceding tax years and forward to each of the 7 succeeding tax years of the bankruptcy estate. The amount of an administrative expense loss that may be carried to any tax year is determined after the NOL deductions allowed for that year. An administrative expense loss is allowed only to the bankruptcy estate and cannot be carried to any tax year of the individual debtor.

Carryback of NOLs and credits. If the bankruptcy estate itself incurs an NOL (apart from losses carried forward to the estate from the individual debtor), it can carry back its NOLs not only to previous tax years of the bankruptcy estate, but also to tax years of the individual debtor prior to the year in which the bankruptcy proceedings began. Excess credits, such as the foreign tax credit, also may be carried back to pre-bankruptcy years of the individual debtor.

Exemption. A bankruptcy estate is allowed a personal exemption of $3,900, for tax year 2013.

2013 Instructions for Form 1041   -15-

¶2944

Note. The personal exemption is subject to phaseout. See the Instructions for Form 1040, Line 42, regarding the personal exemption phaseout for a taxpayer using the married filing separately status.

Standard deduction. A bankruptcy estate that does not itemize deductions is allowed a standard deduction of $6,100, for tax year 2013.

Discharge of indebtedness. In a title 11 case, gross income does not include amounts that normally would be included in gross income resulting from the discharge of indebtedness. However, any amounts excluded from gross income must be applied to reduce certain tax attributes in a certain order. Attach Form 982, Reduction of Tax Attributes Due to Discharge of Indebtedness (and Section 1082 Basis Adjustment), to show the reduction of tax attributes.

Tax Rate Schedule

Figure the tax for the bankruptcy estate using the tax rate schedule below. Enter the tax on Form 1040, line 44.

If taxable income is:

Over—	But not over—	The tax is:	Of the amount over—
$0	$8,925	10%	$0
8,925	36,250	$892.50 + 15%	8,925
36,250	73,200	4,991.25 + 25%	36,250
73,200	111,525	14,228.75 + 28%	73,200
111,525	199,175	24,959.75 + 33%	111,525
199,175	225,000	53,884.25 + 35%	199,175
225,000	......	62,923.00 + 39.6%	225,000

Prompt Determination of Tax Liability

To request a prompt determination of the tax liability of the bankruptcy estate, the trustee or debtor-in-possession must file a written request for the determination with the IRS. The request must be submitted in duplicate and executed under penalties of perjury. The request must include a statement indicating that it is a request for prompt determination of tax liability and: (a) the return type, and all the tax periods for which prompt determination is sought; (b) the name and location of the office where the return was filed; (c) the debtor's name; (d) the debtor's SSN, TIN, or EIN; (e) the type of bankruptcy estate; (f) the bankruptcy case number; and (g) the court where the bankruptcy is pending. Send the request to the Centralized Insolvency Operation, P.O. Box 7346, Philadelphia, PA 19101-7346

(marked "Request for Prompt Determination").

The IRS will notify the trustee or debtor-in-possession within 60 days from receipt of the request if the return filed by the trustee or debtor-in-possession has been selected for examination or has been accepted as filed. If the return is selected for examination, it will be examined as soon as possible. The IRS will notify the trustee or debtor-in-possession of any tax due within 180 days from receipt of the request or within any additional time permitted by the bankruptcy court.

See Rev. Proc. 2006-24, 2006-22 I.R.B. 943, available at *www.irs.gov/irb/2006-22_IRB/ar12.html*, modified by Announcement 2011–77, available at *www.irs.gov/irb/2011-51_IRB/ar13*.

Special Filing Instructions for Bankruptcy Estates

Use Form 1041 only as a transmittal for Form 1040. In the top margin of Form 1040 write "Attachment to Form 1041. DO NOT DETACH." Attach Form 1040 to Form 1041. Complete only the identification area at the top of Form 1041. Enter the name of the individual debtor in the following format: "John Q. Public Bankruptcy Estate." Beneath, enter the name of the trustee in the following format: "Avery Snow, Trustee." In item D, enter the date the petition was filed or the date of conversion to a chapter 7 or 11 case.

Enter on Form 1041, line 23, the total tax from line 61 of Form 1040. Complete lines 24 through 29 of Form 1041, and sign and date it.

In a chapter 11 case filed after October 16, 2005, the bankruptcy estate's gross income may be affected by section 1115 of title 11 of the U.S. Code. See *Income, Deductions, and Credits* earlier. The debtor may receive a Form W-2, 1099-INT, 1099-DIV, or 1099-MISC or other information return reporting wages or other income to the debtor for the entire year, even though some or all of this income is includible in the bankruptcy estate's gross income under section 1115 of title 11 of the U.S. Code. If this happens, the income reported to the debtor on the Form W-2 or 1099, or other information return (and the withheld income tax shown on these forms) must be reasonably allocated between the debtor and the bankruptcy estate. The debtor-in-possession (or the chapter 11 trustee, if one was

appointed) must attach a schedule that shows (a) all the income reported on the Form W-2, Form 1099, or other information return, (b) the portion of this income includible in the bankruptcy estate's gross income, and (c) all the withheld income tax, if any, and the portion of withheld tax reasonably allocated to the bankruptcy estate. Also, the debtor-in-possession (or the chapter 11 trustee, if one was appointed) must attach a copy of the Form W-2, if any, issued to the debtor for the tax year if the Form W-2 reports wages to the debtor and some or all of the wages are includible in the bankruptcy estate's gross income because of section 1115 of title 11 of the U.S. Code. For more details, including acceptable allocation methods, see Notice 2006-83, 2006-40 I.R.B. 596, available at *www.irs.gov/irb/2006-40_IRB/ar12.html*.

Specific Instructions

Name of Estate or Trust

Copy the exact name of the estate or trust from the Form SS-4, Application for Employer Identification Number, that you used to apply for the EIN. If the name of the trust was changed during the tax year for which you are filing, enter the trust's new name and check the *Change in trust's name* box in item F.

If a grantor type trust (discussed later), write the name, identification number, and address of the grantor(s) or other owner(s) in parentheses after the name of the trust.

Name and Title of Fiduciary

Enter the name and title of the fiduciary. If the name entered is different than the name on the prior year's return, see *Change in Fiduciary's Name* and *Change in Fiduciary*, later.

Address

Include the suite, room, or other unit number after the street address. If the post office does not deliver mail to the street address and the fiduciary has a P.O. box, show the box number instead.

If you want a third party (such as an accountant or an attorney) to receive mail for the estate or trust, enter on the street address line "C/O" followed by the third party's name and street address or P.O. box.

If the estate or trust has had a change of address (including a change

-16-

to an "in care of" name and address) and did not file Form 8822-B, Change of Address or Responsible Party — Business, check the *Change in fiduciary's address* box in item F.

If the estate or trust has a change of mailing address (including a new "in care of" name and address) or responsible party after filing its return, file Form 8822-B to notify the IRS of the change.

A. Type of Entity

Check the appropriate box(es) that describes the entity for which you are filing the return.

In some cases, more than one box is checked. Check **all** boxes that apply to your trust. For example, if only a portion of a trust is a grantor type trust or if only a portion of an electing small business trust is the S portion, then more than one box is checked.

Note. Determination of entity status is made on an annual basis.

 There are special reporting requirements for grantor type trusts, pooled income funds, electing small business trusts, and bankruptcy estates. See Special Reporting Instructions, *earlier.*

Decedent's Estate

An estate of a deceased person is a taxable entity separate from the decedent. It generally continues to exist until the final distribution of the assets of the estate is made to the heirs and other beneficiaries. The income earned from the property of the estate during the period of administration or settlement must be accounted for and reported by the estate.

Simple Trust

A trust may qualify as a simple trust if:

1. The trust instrument requires that all income must be distributed currently;

2. The trust instrument does not provide that any amounts are to be paid, permanently set aside, or used for charitable purposes; and

3. The trust does not distribute amounts allocated to the corpus of the trust.

Complex Trust

A complex trust is any trust that does not qualify as a simple trust as explained above.

Qualified Disability Trust

A qualified disability trust is any nongrantor trust:

1. Described in 42 U.S.C. 1396p(c)(2)(B)(iv) and established solely for the benefit of an individual under 65 years of age who is disabled, and

2. All the beneficiaries of which are determined by the Commissioner of Social Security to have been disabled for some part of the tax year within the meaning of 42 U.S.C. 1382c(a)(3).

A trust will not fail to meet item 2 above just because the trust's corpus may revert to a person who is not disabled after the trust ceases to have any disabled beneficiaries.

ESBT (S Portion Only)

The S portion of an ESBT is the portion of the trust that consists of S corporation stock and that is not treated as owned by the grantor or another person. See *Electing Small Business Trusts (ESBTs)*, earlier, for more information about an ESBT.

Grantor Type Trust

A grantor type trust is a legal trust under applicable state law that is not recognized as a separate taxable entity for income tax purposes because the grantor or other substantial owners have not relinquished complete dominion and control over the trust.

Generally, for transfers made in trust after March 1, 1986, the grantor is treated as the owner of any portion of a trust in which he or she has a reversionary interest in either the income or corpus therefrom, if, as of the inception of that portion of the trust, the value of the reversionary interest is more than 5% of the value of that portion. Also, the grantor is treated as holding any power or interest that was held by either the grantor's spouse at the time that the power or interest was created or who became the grantor's spouse after the creation of that power or interest. See *Grantor Type Trusts*, earlier, for more information.

Pre-need funeral trusts. The purchasers of pre-need funeral services are the grantors and the owners of pre-need funeral trusts established under state laws. See Rev. Rul. 87-127, 1987-2 C.B. 156. However, the trustees of pre-need funeral trusts can elect to file the return and pay the tax for qualified funeral trusts. For more information, see Form 1041-QFT, U.S. Income Tax Return for Qualified Funeral Trusts.

Nonqualified deferred compensation plans. Taxpayers may adopt and maintain grantor trusts in connection with nonqualified deferred compensation plans (sometimes referred to as "rabbi trusts"). Rev. Proc. 92-64, 1992-2 C.B. 422, provides a "model grantor trust" for use in rabbi trust arrangements. The procedure also provides guidance for requesting rulings on the plans that use these trusts.

QSSTs. The beneficiary of a qualified subchapter S trust is treated as the substantial owner of that portion of the trust which consists of stock in an S corporation for which an election under section 1361(d)(2) has been made. See *QSSTs*, earlier.

Bankruptcy Estate

A chapter 7 or 11 bankruptcy estate is a separate and distinct taxable entity from the individual debtor for federal income tax purposes. See *Bankruptcy Estates*, earlier.

For more information, see section 1398 and Pub. 908, Bankruptcy Tax Guide.

Pooled Income Fund

A pooled income fund is a split-interest trust with a remainder interest for a public charity and a life income interest retained by the donor or for another person. The property is held in a pool with other pooled income fund property and does not include any tax-exempt securities. The income for a retained life interest is figured using the yearly rate of return earned by the trust. See section 642(c) and the related regulations for more information.

B. Number of Schedules K-1 Attached

Every trust or decedent's estate claiming an income distribution deduction on page 1, line 18, must enter the number of Schedules K-1 (Form 1041) that are attached to Form 1041.

C. Employer Identification Number

Every estate or trust that is required to file Form 1041 must have an EIN. An EIN may be applied for:

• Online by clicking on the EIN link at *www.irs.gov/businesses/small*. The EIN is issued immediately once the application information is validated.

• By mailing or faxing Form SS-4, Application for Employer Identification Number.

If the estate or trust has not received its EIN by the time the return is due, write "Applied for" and the date you applied in the space for the EIN. For more details, see Pub. 583, Starting a Business and Keeping Records.

D. Date Entity Created

Enter the date the trust was created, or, if a decedent's estate, the date of the decedent's death.

E. Nonexempt Charitable and Split-Interest Trusts

Section 4947(a)(1) Trust

Check this box if the trust is a nonexempt charitable trust within the meaning of section 4947(a)(1).

A nonexempt charitable trust is a trust:
• That is not exempt from tax under section 501(a);
• In which all of the unexpired interests are devoted to one or more charitable purposes described in section 170(c)(2)(B); and
• For which a deduction was allowed under section 170 (for individual taxpayers) or similar Code section for personal holding companies, foreign personal holding companies, or estates or trusts (including a deduction for estate or gift tax purposes).

Nonexempt charitable trust treated as a private foundation. If a nonexempt charitable trust is treated as though it were a private foundation under section 509, then the fiduciary must file Form 990-PF, Return of Private Foundation, in addition to Form 1041.

If a nonexempt charitable trust is treated as though it were a private foundation, and it has no taxable income under Subtitle A, it may check the box on Form 990-PF, Part VII-A, line 15 and enter the tax-exempt interest received or accrued during the year on that line, instead of filing Form 1041 to meet its section 6012 filing requirement for that tax year.

Excise taxes. If a nonexempt charitable trust is treated as a private foundation, then it is subject to the same excise taxes under chapters 41 and 42 that a private foundation is subject to. If the nonexempt charitable trust is liable for any of these taxes (except the section 4940 tax), then it reports these taxes on Form 4720, Return of Certain Excise Taxes Under Chapters 41 and 42 of the Internal Revenue Code. Taxes paid by the trust on Form 4720 or on Form 990-PF (the section 4940 tax)

cannot be taken as a deduction on Form 1041.

Not a Private Foundation

Check this box if the nonexempt charitable trust (section 4947(a)(1)) is not treated as a private foundation under section 509. For more information, see Regulations section 53.4947-1.

Other returns that must be filed. If a nonexempt charitable trust is not treated as though it were a private foundation, the fiduciary must file Form 990, Return of Organization Exempt From Income Tax, or Form 990-EZ, Short Form Return of Organization Exempt from Income Tax, in addition to Form 1041, if the trust meets the filing requirements for either of those forms.

If a nonexempt charitable trust is not treated as though it were a private foundation, and it has no taxable income under Subtitle A, it may answer "Yes" on Form 990, Part V, line 12a and enter the tax-exempt interest received or accrued during the year on Form 990, Part V, line 12b instead of filing Form 1041 to meet its section 6012 filing requirement for that tax year (or if Form 990-EZ is filed instead of Form 990, you may check the box on Form 990-EZ, line 43 and enter the tax-exempt interest received or accrued during the year on that line).

Section 4947(a)(2) Trust

Check this box if the trust is a split-interest trust described in section 4947(a)(2).

A split-interest trust is a trust that:
• Is not exempt from tax under section 501(a);
• Has some unexpired interests that are devoted to purposes other than religious, charitable, or similar purposes described in section 170(c)(2)(B); and
• Has amounts transferred in trust after May 26, 1969, for which a deduction was allowed under section 170 (for individual taxpayers) or similar Code sections for personal holding companies, foreign personal holding companies, or estates or trusts (including a deduction for estate or gift tax purposes).

Other returns that must be filed. The fiduciary of a split-interest trust must file Form 5227. However, see the Instructions for Form 5227 for the exception that applies to split-interest trusts other than section 664 charitable remainder trusts.

F. Initial Return, Amended Return, etc.

Amended Return

If you are filing an amended Form 1041:
• Check the "Amended return" box in Item F,
• Complete the entire return,
• Correct the appropriate lines with the new information, and
• Refigure the estate's or trust's tax liability.

Note. If you are amending the return for an NOL carryback, also check the "Net operating loss carryback" box in Item F.

If the total tax on line 23 is larger on the amended return than on the original return, you generally should pay the difference with the amended return. However, you should adjust this amount if there is any increase or decrease in the total payments shown on line 25.

Attach a sheet that explains the reason for the amendments and identifies the lines and amounts being changed on the amended return.

Amended Schedule H (Form 1040). If you discover an error on a Schedule H that you previously filed with Form 1041, file an "Amended" Form 1041 and attach a corrected Schedule H.

In the top margin of your corrected Schedule H, write "Amended," (using red ink, if possible) and the date you discovered the error. Also, on an attachment explain the reason for your correction. If you owe tax, pay the tax in full with your amended Form 1041. If you overpaid tax on a previously filed Schedule H, depending on whether you choose the adjustment or claim for refund process to correct the error, you must either repay or reimburse the employee's share of social security and Medicare tax or get the employee's consent to the filing of a refund claim for their share. See Pub. 926, Household Employer's Tax Guide, for more information.

Amended Schedule K-1 (Form 1041). If the amended return results in a change to income, or a change in distribution of any income or other information provided to a beneficiary, an amended Schedule K-1 (Form 1041) must also be filed with the amended Form 1041 and given to each beneficiary. Check the "Amended K-1" box at the top of the amended Schedule K-1.

2013 Instructions for Form 1041

¶2944

Final Return

Check this box if this is a final return because the estate or trust has terminated. Also, check the "Final K-1" box at the top of Schedule K-1.

If, on the final return, there are excess deductions, an unused capital loss carryover, or an NOL carryover, see the instructions for Schedule K-1, box 11, later.

Change in Trust's Name

If the name of the trust has changed from the name shown on the prior year's return (or Form SS-4 if this is the first return being filed), be sure to check this box.

Change in Fiduciary

If a different fiduciary enters his or her name on the line for *Name and title of fiduciary* than was shown on the prior year's return (or Form SS-4 if this is the first return being filed) and you did not file a Form 8822-B, be sure to check this box. If there is a change in the fiduciary whose address is used as the mailing address for the estate or trust after the return is filed, use Form 8822-B to notify the IRS.

Change in Fiduciary's Name

If the fiduciary changed his or her name from the name that he or she entered on the prior year's return (or Form SS-4 if this is the first return being filed), be sure to check this box.

Change in Fiduciary's Address

If the same fiduciary who filed the prior year's return (or Form SS-4 if this is the first return being filed) files the current year's return and changed the address on the return (including a change to an "in care of" name and address), and did not report the change on Form 8822-B, check this box.

If the address shown on Form 1041 changes after you file the form (including a change to an "in care of" name and address), file Form 8822-B to notify the IRS of the change.

G. Section 645 Election

If a section 645 election was made by filing Form 8855, check the box in item G. See *Special Rule for Certain Revocable Trusts* under *Who Must File* and Form 8855 for more information about this election.

Income

Special Rule for Blind Trust

If you are reporting income from a qualified blind trust (under the Ethics in Government Act of 1978), do not identify the payer of any income to the trust but complete the rest of the return as provided in the instructions. Also write "Blind Trust" at the top of page 1.

Extraterritorial Income Exclusion

The extraterritorial income exclusion is not allowed for transactions after 2006. However, income from certain long-term sales and leases may still qualify for the exclusion. For details and to figure the amount of the exclusion, see Form 8873, Extraterritorial Income Exclusion, and its separate instructions. The estate or trust must report the extraterritorial income exclusion on line 15a of Form 1041, page 1.

Although the extraterritorial income exclusion is entered on line 15a, it is an exclusion from income and should be treated as tax-exempt income when completing other parts of the return.

Line 1—Interest Income

Report the estate's or trust's share of all taxable interest income that was received during the tax year. Examples of taxable interest include interest from:
* Accounts (including certificates of deposit and money market accounts) with banks, credit unions, and thrift institutions;
* Notes, loans, and mortgages;
* U.S. Treasury bills, notes, and bonds;
* U.S. savings bonds;
* Original issue discount; and
* Income received as a regular interest holder of a real estate mortgage investment conduit (REMIC).

For taxable bonds acquired after 1987, amortizable bond premium is treated as an offset to the interest income instead of as a separate interest deduction. See Pub. 550.

For the year of the decedent's death, Forms 1099-INT issued in the decedent's name may include interest income earned after the date of death that should be reported on the income tax return of the decedent's estate. When preparing the decedent's final income tax return, report on Schedule B (Form 1040A or 1040), line 1 the total interest shown on Form 1099-INT. Under the last entry on line 1, subtotal all the interest reported on line 1. Below the subtotal, write "Form 1041" and the name and address shown on Form 1041 for the decedent's estate. Also, show the part of the interest reported on Form 1041 and subtract it from the subtotal.

Line 2a—Total Ordinary Dividends

Report the estate's or trust's share of all ordinary dividends received during the tax year.

For the year of the decedent's death, Forms 1099-DIV issued in the decedent's name may include dividends earned after the date of death that should be reported on the income tax return of the decedent's estate. When preparing the decedent's final income tax return, report on Schedule B (Form 1040A or 1040), line 5 the ordinary dividends shown on Form 1099-DIV. Under the last entry on line 5, subtotal all the dividends reported on line 5. Below the subtotal, write "Form 1041" and the name and address shown on Form 1041 for the decedent's estate. Also, show the part of the ordinary dividends reported on Form 1041 and subtract it from the subtotal.

 Report capital gain distributions on Schedule D (Form 1041), Line 13.

Line 2b—Qualified Dividends

Enter the beneficiary's allocable share of qualified dividends on line 2b(1) and enter the estate's or trust's allocable share on line 2b(2).

If the estate or trust received qualified dividends that were derived from IRD, you must reduce the amount on line 2b(2) by the portion of the estate tax deduction claimed on Form 1041, page 1, line 19, that is attributable to those qualified dividends. Do not reduce the amounts on line 2b by any other allocable expenses.

Note. The beneficiary's share (as figured above) may differ from the amount entered on line 2b of Schedule K-1 (Form 1041).

Qualified dividends. Qualified dividends are eligible for a lower tax rate than other ordinary income. Generally, these dividends are reported to the estate or trust in box 1b of Form(s) 1099-DIV. See Pub. 550 for the definition of qualified dividends if the estate or trust received dividends not reported on Form 1099-DIV.

Exception. Some dividends may be reported to the estate or trust as in box 1b of Form 1099-DIV but are not qualified dividends. These include:
* Dividends received on any share of stock that the estate or trust held for less than 61 days during the 121-day period that began 60 days before the

ex-dividend date. The ex-dividend date is the first date following the declaration of a dividend on which the purchaser of a stock is not entitled to receive the next dividend payment. When counting the number of days the stock was held, include the day the estate or trust disposed of the stock but not the day it acquired the stock. However, you cannot count certain days during which the estate's or trust's risk of loss was diminished. See Pub. 550 for more details.

• Dividends attributable to periods totaling more than 366 days that the estate or trust received on any share of preferred stock held for less than 91 days during the 181-day period that began 90 days before the ex-dividend date. When counting the number of days the stock was held, include the day the estate or trust disposed of the stock but not the day it acquired the stock. However, you cannot count certain days during which the estate's or trust's risk of loss was diminished. See Pub. 550 for more details. Preferred dividends attributable to periods totaling less than 367 days are subject to the 61-day holding period rule above.

• Dividends on any share of stock to the extent that the estate or trust is under an obligation (including a short sale) to make related payments with respect to positions in substantially similar or related property.

• Payments in lieu of dividends, but only if you know or have reason to know that the payments are not qualified dividends.

 If you have an entry on line 2b(2), be sure you use Schedule D (Form 1041), the Schedule D Tax Worksheet, or the Qualified Dividends Tax Worksheet, whichever applies, to figure the estate's or trust's tax. Figuring the estate's or trust's tax liability in this manner will usually result in a lower tax.

Line 3—Business Income or (Loss)

If the estate operated a business, report the income and expenses on Schedule C (Form 1040), Profit or Loss From Business (or Schedule C-EZ (Form 1040), Net Profit From Business). Enter the net profit or (loss) from Schedule C (or Schedule C-EZ) on line 3.

Line 4—Capital Gain or (Loss)

Enter the gain from Schedule D (Form 1041), Part III, line 19, column (3) or the loss from Part IV, line 20.

 Do not substitute Schedule D (Form 1040) for Schedule D (Form 1041).

Line 5—Rents, Royalties, Partnerships, Other Estates and Trusts, etc.

Use Schedule E (Form 1040), Supplemental Income and Loss, to report the estate's or trust's share of income or (losses) from rents, royalties, partnerships, S corporations, other estates and trusts, and REMICs. Also use Schedule E (Form 1040) to report farm rental income and expenses based on crops or livestock produced by a tenant. Enter the net profit or (loss) from Schedule E on line 5. See the Instructions for Schedule E (Form 1040) for reporting requirements.

If the estate or trust received a Schedule K-1 from a partnership, S corporation, or other flow-through entity, use the corresponding lines on Form 1041 to report the interest, dividends, capital gains, etc., from the flow-through entity.

Line 6—Farm Income or (Loss)

If the estate or trust operated a farm, use Schedule F (Form 1040), Profit or Loss From Farming, to report farm income and expenses. Enter the net profit or (loss) from Schedule F on line 6.

 If an estate or trust has farm rental income and expenses based on crops or livestock produced by a tenant, report the income and expenses on Schedule E (Form 1040). Do not use Form 4835, Farm Rental Income and Expenses, or Schedule F (Form 1040) to report such income and expenses and do not include the net profit or (loss) from such income and expenses on line 6.

Line 7—Ordinary Gain or (Loss)

Enter from line 17, Form 4797, Sales of Business Property, the ordinary gain or loss from the sale or exchange of property other than capital assets and also from involuntary conversions (other than casualty or theft).

Line 8—Other Income

Enter other items of income not included on lines 1, 2a, and 3 through 7. List the type and amount on an attached schedule if the estate or trust has more than one item.

Items to be reported on line 8 include:
• Unpaid compensation received by the decedent's estate that is IRD, and

• Any part of a total distribution shown on Form 1099-R, Distributions From Pensions, Annuities, Retirement or Profit-Sharing Plans, IRAs, Insurance Contracts, etc., that is treated as ordinary income. For more information, see Form 4972, Tax on Lump-Sum Distributions, and its instructions.

Deductions

Depreciation, Depletion, and Amortization

A trust or decedent's estate is allowed a deduction for depreciation, depletion, and amortization only to the extent the deductions are not apportioned to the beneficiaries. An estate or trust is not allowed to make an election under section 179 to expense depreciable business assets.

The estate's or trust's share of depreciation, depletion, and amortization is generally reported on the appropriate lines of Schedule C (or C-EZ), E, or F (Form 1040), the net income or loss from which is shown on lines 3, 5, or 6 of Form 1041. If the deduction is not related to a specific business or activity, then report it on line 15a.

Depreciation. For a decedent's estate, the depreciation deduction is apportioned between the estate and the heirs, legatees, and devisees on the basis of the estate's income allocable to each.

For a trust, the depreciation deduction is apportioned between the income beneficiaries and the trust on the basis of the trust income allocable to each, unless the governing instrument (or local law) requires or permits the trustee to maintain a depreciation reserve. If the trustee is required to maintain a reserve, the deduction is first allocated to the trust, up to the amount of the reserve. Any excess is allocated among the income beneficiaries and trust in the same manner as the trust's accounting income. See Regulations section 1.167(h)-1(b).

Depletion. For mineral or timber property held by a decedent's estate, the depletion deduction is apportioned between the estate and the heirs, legatees, and devisees on the basis of the estate's income from such property allocable to each.

For mineral or timber property held in trust, the depletion deduction is apportioned between the income beneficiaries and the trust based on the trust income from such property allocable to each, unless the governing instrument (or local law) requires or permits the trustee to maintain a reserve for depletion. If the trustee is required to maintain a reserve, the deduction is first allocated to the trust, up to the amount of the reserve. Any excess is allocated among the beneficiaries and the trust in the same manner as the trust's accounting income. See Regulations section 1.611-1(c)(4).

Amortization. The deduction for amortization is apportioned between an estate or trust and its beneficiaries under the same principles used to apportion the deductions for depreciation and depletion.

The deduction for the amortization of reforestation expenditures under section 194 is allowed only to an estate.

Allocable share from a pass-through entity. Depreciation, depletion, and amortization received from a pass-through entity on a Schedule K-1 is apportioned and reported in the same manner as discussed above. A section 179 expense received from a pass-through entity on a Schedule K-1 is not deductible by the estate or trust.

Allocation of Deductions for Tax-Exempt Income

Generally, no deduction that would otherwise be allowable is allowed for any expense (whether for business or for the production of income) that is allocable to tax-exempt income. Examples of tax-exempt income include:
- Certain death benefits (section 101),
- Interest on state or local bonds (section 103),
- Compensation for injuries or sickness (section 104), and
- Income from discharge of indebtedness in a title 11 case (section 108).

Exception. State income taxes and business expenses that are allocable to tax-exempt interest are deductible.

Expenses that are directly allocable to tax-exempt income are allocated only to tax-exempt income. A reasonable proportion of expenses indirectly allocable to both tax-exempt income and other income must be allocated to each class of income.

Deductions That May Be Allowable for Estate Tax Purposes

Administration expenses and casualty and theft losses deductible on Form 706 may be deducted, to the extent

otherwise deductible for income tax purposes, on Form 1041 if the fiduciary files a statement waiving the right to deduct the expenses and losses on Form 706. The statement must be filed before the expiration of the statutory period of limitations for the tax year the deduction is claimed. See Pub. 559 for more information.

Accrued Expenses

Generally, an accrual basis taxpayer can deduct accrued expenses in the tax year that: (a) all events have occurred that determine the liability; and (b) the amount of the liability can be figured with reasonable accuracy. However, all the events that establish liability are treated as occurring only when economic performance takes place. There are exceptions for recurring items. See section 461(h).

Limitations on Deductions

At-Risk Loss Limitations

Generally, the amount the estate or trust has "at-risk" limits the loss it can deduct for any tax year. Use Form 6198, At-Risk Limitations, to figure the deductible loss for the year and file it with Form 1041. For more information, see Pub. 925, Passive Activity and At-Risk Rules.

Passive Activity Loss and Credit Limitations

In general. Section 469 and the regulations thereunder generally limit losses from passive activities to the amount of income derived from all passive activities. Similarly, credits from passive activities are generally limited to the tax attributable to such activities. These limitations are first applied at the estate or trust level.

Generally, an activity is a passive activity if it involves the conduct of any trade or business, and the taxpayer does not materially participate in the activity. Passive activities do not include working interests in oil and gas properties. See section 469(c)(3).

Note. Material participation standards for estates and trusts have not been established by regulations.

For a grantor trust, material participation is determined at the grantor level.

If the estate or trust distributes an interest in a passive activity, the basis of the property immediately before the distribution is increased by the passive activity losses allocable to the interest,

and such losses cannot be deducted. See section 469(j)(12).

 Losses from passive activities are first subject to the at-risk rules. When the losses are deductible under the at-risk rules, the passive activity rules then apply.

Rental activities. Generally, rental activities are passive activities, whether or not the taxpayer materially participates. However, certain taxpayers who materially participate in real property trades or businesses are not subject to the passive activity limitations on losses from rental real estate activities in which they materially participate. For more details, see section 469(c)(7).

For tax years of an estate ending less than 2 years after the decedent's date of death, up to $25,000 of deductions and deduction equivalents of credits from rental real estate activities in which the decedent actively participated are allowed. Any excess losses or credits are suspended for the year and carried forward.

Portfolio income. Portfolio income is not treated as income from a passive activity, and passive losses and credits generally may not be applied to offset it. Portfolio income generally includes interest, dividends, royalties, and income from annuities. Portfolio income of an estate or trust must be accounted for separately.

Forms to file. See Form 8582, Passive Activity Loss Limitations, to figure the amount of losses allowed from passive activities. See Form 8582-CR, Passive Activity Credit Limitations, to figure the amount of credit allowed for the current year.

Transactions Between Related Taxpayers

Under section 267, a trust that uses the accrual method of accounting may only deduct business expenses and interest owed to a related party in the year the payment is included in the income of the related party. For this purpose, a related party includes:

1. A grantor and a fiduciary of any trust;

2. A fiduciary of a trust and a fiduciary of another trust, if the same person is a grantor of both trusts;

3. A fiduciary of a trust and a beneficiary of such trust;

4. A fiduciary of a trust and a beneficiary of another trust, if the same person is a grantor of both trusts;

¶2944

5. A fiduciary of a trust and a corporation more than 50% in value of the outstanding stock of which is owned, directly or indirectly, by or for the trust or by or for a person who is a grantor of the trust; and

6. An executor of an estate and a beneficiary of that estate, except for a sale or exchange to satisfy a pecuniary bequest (that is, a bequest of a sum of money).

Line 10—Interest

Enter the amount of interest (subject to limitations) paid or incurred by the estate or trust on amounts borrowed by the estate or trust, or on debt acquired by the estate or trust (for example, outstanding obligations from the decedent) that is not claimed elsewhere on the return.

If the proceeds of a loan were used for more than one purpose (for example, to purchase a portfolio investment and to acquire an interest in a passive activity), the fiduciary must make an interest allocation according to the rules in Temporary Regulations section 1.163-8T.

Do not include interest paid on indebtedness incurred or continued to purchase or carry obligations on which the interest is wholly exempt from income tax.

Personal interest is not deductible. Examples of personal interest include interest paid on:
• Revolving charge accounts used to purchase personal use property;
• Personal notes for money borrowed from a bank, credit union, or other person;
• Installment loans on personal use property; and
• Underpayments of federal, state, or local income taxes.

Interest that is paid or incurred on indebtedness allocable to a trade or business (including a rental activity) should be deducted on the appropriate line of Schedule C (or C-EZ), E, or F (Form 1040), the net income or loss from which is shown on line 3, 5, or 6 of Form 1041.

Types of interest to include on line 10 are:

1. Any investment interest (subject to limitations—see below);

2. Any qualified residence interest (see later); and

3. Any interest payable under section 6601 on any unpaid portion of the estate tax attributable to the value of

a reversionary or remainder interest in property for the period during which an extension of time for payment of such tax is in effect.

Investment interest. Generally, investment interest is interest (including amortizable bond premium on taxable bonds acquired after October 22, 1986, but before January 1, 1988) that is paid or incurred on indebtedness that is properly allocable to property held for investment. Investment interest does not include any qualified residence interest, or interest that is taken into account under section 469 in figuring income or loss from a passive activity.

Generally, net investment income is the excess of investment income over investment expenses. Investment expenses are those expenses (other than interest) allowable after application of the 2% floor on miscellaneous itemized deductions.

The amount of the investment interest deduction may be limited. Use Form 4952, Investment Interest Expense Deduction, to figure the allowable investment interest deduction.

If you must complete Form 4952, check the box on line 10 of Form 1041 and attach Form 4952. Then, add the deductible investment interest to the other types of deductible interest and enter the total on line 10.

Qualified residence interest. Interest paid or incurred by an estate or trust on indebtedness secured by a qualified residence of a beneficiary of an estate or trust is treated as qualified residence interest if the residence would be a qualified residence (that is, the principal residence or the secondary residence selected by the beneficiary) if owned by the beneficiary. The beneficiary must have a present interest in the estate or trust or an interest in the residuary of the estate or trust. See Pub. 936, Home Mortgage Interest Deduction, for an explanation of the general rules for deducting home mortgage interest.

See section 163(h)(3) for a definition of qualified residence interest and for limitations on indebtedness.

Qualified mortgage insurance premiums. Enter (on the worksheet later) the qualified mortgage insurance premiums paid under a mortgage insurance contract issued after December 31, 2006, in connection with qualified residence acquisition debt that was secured by a principal or secondary residence. See *Prepaid mortgage insurance* below if the estate or trust

paid any premiums allocable after 2013. If at least one other person was liable for and paid the premiums in connection with the loan, and the premiums were reported on Form 1098, Mortgage Interest Statement, include the estate's or trust's share of the 2013 premiums on the worksheet later.

Qualified mortgage insurance is mortgage insurance provided by the Department of Veterans Affairs, the Federal Housing Administration, or the Rural Housing Service, and private mortgage insurance (as defined in section 2 of the Homeowners Protection Act of 1998 as in effect on December 20, 2006).

Mortgage insurance provided by the Department of Veterans Affairs and the Rural Housing Service is commonly known as a funding fee and guarantee fee, respectively. These fees can be deducted fully in 2013 if the mortgage insurance contract was issued in 2013. Contact the mortgage insurance issuer to determine the deductible amount if it is not included in box 4 of Form 1098.

Prepaid mortgage insurance. If the estate or trust paid mortgage insurance premiums allocable to periods after 2013, such premiums must be allocated over the shorter of:
• The stated term of the mortgage, or
• 84 months, beginning with the month the insurance was obtained.

The premiums are treated as paid in the year to which they are allocated. If the mortgage is satisfied before its term, no deduction is allowed for the unamortized balance. See Pub. 936 for details. These allocation rules do not apply to qualified mortgage insurance provided by the Department of Veterans Affairs or the Rural Housing Service.

Limit on the amount that is deductible. The estate or trust cannot deduct mortgage insurance premiums if the estate's or trust's AGI is more than $109,000. If the estate's or trust's AGI is more than $100,000, its deduction is limited and you must use the worksheet later to figure the deduction. See *How to figure AGI for estates and trusts*, later, for information on figuring AGI.

Line 11—Taxes

Enter any deductible taxes paid or incurred during the tax year that are not deductible elsewhere on Form 1041. Deductible taxes include the following:
• State and local income taxes. You can deduct state and local income taxes unless you elect to deduct state and

Qualified Mortgage Insurance Premiums Deduction Worksheet

Keep for Your Records

1.	Enter the total premiums the estate or trust paid in 2013 for qualified mortgage insurance for a contract issued after December 31, 2006	1. _____
2.	Enter the estate's or trust's AGI	2. _____
3.	Enter $100,000	3. _____
4.	Is the amount on line 2 more than the amount on line 3?	
	No. The deduction is not limited. Include the amount from line 1 above on Form 1041, line 10. **Do not** complete the rest of this worksheet.	
	Yes. Subtract line 3 from line 2. If the result is not a multiple of $1,000, increase it to the next multiple of $1,000. For example, increase $425 to $1,000, increase $2,025 to $3,000, etc.	4. _____
5.	Divide line 4 by $10,000. Enter the result as a decimal. If the result is 1.0 or more, enter 1.0	5. . _____
6.	Multiply line 1 by line 5	6. _____
7.	**Qualified mortgage insurance premiums deduction.** Subtract line 6 from line 1. Enter the result here and include the amount on Form 1041, line 10	7. _____

local general sales taxes. You cannot deduct both.

• State and local general sales taxes. You can elect to deduct state and local general sales taxes instead of state and local income taxes. Generally, you can elect to deduct the actual state and local general sales taxes (including compensating use taxes) you paid in 2013 if the tax rate was the same as the general sales tax rate. However, sales taxes on food, clothing, medical supplies, and motor vehicles are deductible as a general sales tax even if the tax rate was less than the general sales tax rate. Sales taxes on motor vehicles are also deductible as a general sales tax if the tax rate was more than the general sales tax rate, but the tax is deductible only up to the amount of tax that would have been imposed at the general sales tax rate. Motor vehicles include cars, motorcycles, motor homes, recreational vehicles, sport utility vehicles, trucks, vans, and off-road vehicles. Also include any state and local general sales taxes paid for a leased motor vehicle.

Do not include sales taxes paid on items used in a trade or business. An estate or trust **cannot** use the Optional Sales Tax Tables for individuals in the Instructions for Schedule A (Form 1040), Itemized Deductions, to figure its deduction.

• State, local, and foreign real property taxes.

• State and local personal property taxes.

• Foreign or U.S. possession income taxes. You may want to take a credit for the tax instead of a deduction. See the instructions for Schedule G, line 2a, later, for more details.

• The generation-skipping transfer (GST) tax imposed on income distributions.

Do not deduct:

• Federal income taxes;

• Estate, inheritance, legacy, succession, and gift taxes; or

• Federal duties and excise taxes.

Line 12—Fiduciary Fees

Enter the deductible fees paid or incurred to the fiduciary for administering the estate or trust during the tax year.

TIP *Fiduciary fees deducted on Form 706 cannot be deducted on Form 1041.*

Line 15a—Other Deductions Not Subject to the 2% Floor

Attach your own schedule, listing by type and amount all allowable deductions that are not deductible elsewhere on Form 1041.

Do not include any losses on worthless bonds and similar obligations and nonbusiness bad debts. Report these losses as applicable on Form 8949, Sales and Other Dispositions of Capital Assets.

Do not deduct medical or funeral expenses on Form 1041. Medical expenses of the decedent paid by the estate may be deductible on the decedent's income tax return for the year incurred. See section 213(c). Funeral expenses are deductible only on Form 706.

The following are examples of deductions that are reported on line 15a.

Bond premium(s). For taxable bonds acquired before October 23, 1986, if the fiduciary elected to amortize the premium, report the amortization on this line. If you made the election to amortize the premium, the basis in the taxable bond must be reduced by the amount of amortization.

For tax-exempt bonds, you cannot deduct the premium that is amortized. Although the premium cannot be deducted, you must amortize the premium and reduce the estate's or trust's basis in the tax-exempt bond by the amount of premium amortized.

For more information, see section 171 and Pub. 550.

If you claim a bond premium deduction for the estate or trust, figure the deduction on a separate sheet and attach it to Form 1041.

Casualty and theft losses. Use Form 4684, Casualties and Thefts, to figure any deductible casualty and theft losses.

Domestic production activities deduction. The estate or trust may be able to deduct up to 9% of its share of qualified production activities income (QPAI) from the following activities.

1. Construction performed in the United States.

2. Engineering or architectural services performed in the United States for construction projects in the United States.

3. Any lease, rental, license, sale, exchange, or other disposition of:

¶2944

a. Tangible personal property, computer software, and sound recordings that the estate or trust manufactured, produced, grew, or extracted in whole or in significant part within the United States;

b. Any qualified film the estate or trust produced; or

c. Electricity, natural gas, or potable water the estate or trust produced in the United States.

In certain cases, the United States includes the Commonwealth of Puerto Rico.

The deduction does not apply to income derived from:
• The sale of food and beverages the estate or trust prepared at a retail establishment;
• Property the estate or trust leased, licensed, or rented for use by any related person; or
• The transmission or distribution of electricity, natural gas, or potable water.

The deduction cannot exceed 9% of modified AGI or 50% of certain Form W-2 wages. QPAI, as well as Form W-2 wages, must be apportioned between the trust or estate and its beneficiaries. For more details, see Form 8903, Domestic Production Activities Deduction, and its separate instructions.

Special rule for oil-related QPAI. If the estate or trust has oil-related QPAI, the domestic production activities deduction is reduced by 3% of the smallest of:
• Oil-related QPAI,
• QPAI, or
• Modified AGI.

See Form 8903 for details.

Estate's or trust's share of amortization, depreciation, and depletion not claimed elsewhere. If you cannot deduct the estate's or trust's apportioned share of amortization, depreciation, and depletion as rent or royalty expenses on Schedule E (Form 1040), or as business or farm expenses on Schedule C, C-EZ, or F (Form 1040), itemize the estate's or trust's apportioned share of the deductions on an attached sheet and include them on line 15a.

Note. Do not report the beneficiary's apportioned share of depreciation, depletion, and amortization on line 15a. Report the beneficiary's apportioned share of deductions on Schedule K-1 (Form 1041), box 9.

Itemize each beneficiary's apportioned share of the deductions

and report them in the appropriate box of Schedule K-1 (Form 1041).

Line15b—Net Operating Loss Deduction

An estate or trust is allowed a net operating loss deduction (NOLD) under section 172.

If you claim a NOLD for the estate or trust, figure the deduction on a separate sheet and attach it to the return.

Line 15c—Allowable Miscellaneous Itemized Deductions Subject to the 2% Floor

Miscellaneous itemized deductions are deductible only to the extent that the aggregate amount of such deductions exceeds 2% of AGI.

Among the miscellaneous itemized deductions that must be included on line 15c are expenses for the production or collection of income under section 212, such as investment advisory fees, subscriptions to investment advisory publications, and the cost of safe deposit boxes.

Miscellaneous itemized deductions do not include deductions for:
• Interest under section 163,
• Taxes under section 164,
• The amortization of bond premium under section 171,
• Estate taxes attributable to IRD under section 691(c), or
• Expenses paid or incurred in connection with the administration of the estate or trust that would not have been incurred if the property were not held in the estate or trust.

For other exceptions, see section 67(b).

How to figure AGI for estates and trusts. You figure AGI by subtracting the following from total income on line 9 of page 1:

1. The administration costs of the estate or trust (the total of lines 12, 14, and 15a to the extent they are costs incurred in the administration of the estate or trust) that would not have been incurred if the property were not held by the estate or trust;

2. The income distribution deduction (line 18);

3. The amount of the exemption (line 20);

4. The domestic production activities deduction claimed on line 15a; and

5. The NOLD claimed on line 15b.

For those estates and trusts whose income distribution deduction is limited to the actual distribution, and not the DNI (that is, the income distribution is less than the DNI), when computing the AGI, use the amount of the actual distribution.

For those estates and trusts whose income distribution deduction is limited to the DNI (that is, the actual distribution exceeds the DNI), the DNI must be figured taking into account the allowable miscellaneous itemized deductions (AMID) after application of the 2% floor. In this situation there are two unknown amounts: (a) the AMID and (b) the DNI.

Computing line 15c. To compute line 15c, use the equation below:

AMID = Total miscellaneous itemized deductions – (.02(AGI))

The following example illustrates how algebraic equations can be used to solve for these unknown amounts.

Example. The Malcolm Smith Trust, a complex trust, earned $20,000 of dividend income, $20,000 of capital gains, and a fully deductible $5,000 loss from XYZ partnership (chargeable to corpus) in 2013. The trust instrument provides that capital gains are added to corpus. Fifty percent of the fiduciary fees are allocated to income and 50% to corpus. The trust claimed a $2,000 deduction on line 12 of Form 1041. The trust incurred $1,500 of miscellaneous itemized deductions (chargeable to income), which are subject to the 2% floor. There are no other deductions. The trustee made a discretionary distribution of the accounting income of $17,500 to the trust's sole beneficiary.

Because the actual distribution can reasonably be expected to exceed the DNI, the trust must figure the DNI, taking into account the allowable miscellaneous itemized deductions, to determine the amount to enter on line 15c.

The trust also claims an exemption of $100 on line 20.

Using the facts in this example:

AMID = 1,500 – (.02(AGI))

In all situations, use the following equation to compute the AGI:

AGI = (line 9) – (the total of lines 12, 14, and 15a to the extent they are costs incurred in the administration of the estate or trust that would not have been incurred if the property were not held by the estate or trust) – (line 15b) – (line 18) – (line 20).

-24-

Note. There are no other deductions claimed by the trust on line 15a that are deductible in arriving at AGI.

Figuring AGI in this example, we get:

AGI = 35,000 − 2,000 − DNI − 100

Since the value of line 18 is not known because it is limited to the DNI, you are left with the following:

AGI = 32,900 − DNI

Substitute the value of AGI in the equation:

AMID = 1,500 − (.02(32,900 − DNI))

The equation cannot be solved until the value of DNI is known. The DNI can be expressed in terms of the AMID. To do this, compute the DNI using the known values. In this example, the DNI is equal to the total income of the trust (less any capital gains allocated to corpus or plus any capital loss from line 4); less total deductions from line 16 (excluding any miscellaneous itemized deductions); less the AMID.

Thus, DNI = (line 9) − (line 19, column (2) of Schedule D (Form 1041)) − (line 16) − (AMID)

Substitute the known values:

DNI = 35,000 − 20,000 − 2,000 − AMID

DNI = 13,000 − AMID

Substitute the value of DNI in the equation to solve for AMID:

AMID = 1,500 − (.02(32,900 − (13,000 − AMID)))

AMID = 1,500 − (.02(32,900 − 13,000 + AMID))

AMID = 1,500 − (658 − 260 + .02AMID)

AMID = 1,102 − .02AMID

1.02AMID = 1,102

AMID = 1,080

DNI = 11,920 (i.e., 13,000 − 1,080)

AGI = 20,980 (i.e., 32,900 − 11,920)

Note. The income distribution deduction is equal to the smaller of the distribution ($17,500) or the DNI ($11,920).

Enter the value of AMID on line 15b (the DNI should equal line 7 of Schedule B) and complete the rest of Form 1041 according to the instructions.

If the 2% floor is more than the deductions subject to the 2% floor, no deductions are allowed.

Line 18—Income Distribution Deduction

If the estate or trust was required to distribute income currently or if it paid,

credited, or was required to distribute any other amounts to beneficiaries during the tax year, complete Schedule B to determine the estate's or trust's income distribution deduction. However, if you are filing for a pooled income fund, do not complete Schedule B. Instead, attach a statement to support the computation of the income distribution deduction. For more information, see *Pooled Income Funds*, earlier.

If the estate or trust claims an income distribution deduction, complete and attach:
• Part I (through line 26) and Part II of Schedule I (Form 1041) to refigure the deduction on a minimum tax basis, and
• Schedule K-1 (Form 1041) for each beneficiary to which a distribution was made or required to be made.

Cemetery perpetual care fund. On line 18, deduct the amount, not more than $5 per gravesite, paid for maintenance of cemetery property. To the right of the entry space for line 18, enter the number of gravesites. Also write "Section 642(i) trust" in parentheses after the trust's name at the top of Form 1041. You do not have to complete Schedules B of Form 1041 and K-1 (Form 1041).

Do not enter less than zero on line 18.

Line 19—Estate Tax Deduction (Including Certain Generation-Skipping Transfer Taxes)

If the estate or trust includes IRD in its gross income, and such amount was included in the decedent's gross estate for estate tax purposes, the estate or trust is allowed to deduct in the same tax year that the income is included that portion of the estate tax imposed on the decedent's estate that is attributable to the inclusion of the IRD in the decedent's estate. For an example of the computation, see Regulations section 1.691(c)-1 and Pub. 559.

If any amount properly paid, credited, or required to be distributed by an estate or trust to a beneficiary consists of IRD received by the estate or trust, do not include such amounts in determining the estate tax deduction for the estate or trust. Figure the deduction on a separate sheet. Attach the sheet to your return.

 If you claim a deduction for estate tax attributable to qualified dividends or capital gains, you may have to adjust the amount on Form 1041, page 1, line 2b(2), or Schedule D (Form 1041), line 22.

Also, a deduction is allowed for the GST tax imposed as a result of a taxable termination or a direct skip occurring as a result of the death of the transferor. See section 691(c)(3). Enter the estate's or trust's share of these deductions on line 19.

Line 20—Exemption

Decedents' estates. A decedent's estate is allowed a $600 exemption.

Trusts required to distribute all income currently. A trust whose governing instrument requires that all income be distributed currently is allowed a $300 exemption, even if it distributed amounts other than income during the tax year.

Qualified disability trusts. A qualified disability trust is allowed a $3,900 exemption if the trust's modified AGI is less than or equal to $250,000. If its modified AGI exceeds $250,000, complete the worksheet, later, to figure the amount of the trust's exemption. To figure modified AGI, follow the instructions for figuring AGI for line 15c earlier, except use zero as the amount of the trust's exemption when figuring AGI.

A qualified disability trust is any trust:

1. Described in 42 U.S.C. 1396p(c)(2)(B)(iv) and established solely for the benefit of an individual under 65 years of age who is disabled, and

2. All of the beneficiaries of which are determined by the Commissioner of Social Security to have been disabled for some part of the tax year within the meaning of 42 U.S.C. 1382c(a)(3).

A trust will not fail to meet item 2 above just because the trust's corpus may revert to a person who is not disabled after the trust ceases to have any disabled beneficiaries.

All other trusts. A trust not described above is allowed a $100 exemption.

Tax and Payments

Line 22—Taxable Income

Minimum taxable income. Line 22 cannot be less than the larger of:
• The inversion gain of the estate or trust, as figured under section 7874, if

Exemption Worksheet for Qualified Disability Trusts Only—Line 20   *Keep for Your Records*

Note: *If the trust's modified AGI* is less than or equal to $250,000, enter $3,900 on Form 1041, line 20. Otherwise, complete the worksheet below to figure the trust's exemption.*	

1. Maximum exemption **1.** $3,900

2. Enter the trust's modified AGI* . . . . **2.** _____

3. Threshold amount **3.** $250,000

4. Subtract line 3 from line 2 . . . . **4.** _____

Note: *If line 4 is more than $122,500, enter -0- on line 8 below.* **Do not** *complete lines 5 through 7.*

5. Divide line 4 by $2,500. If the result is not a whole number, increase it to the
   next higher whole number (for example, increase 0.0004 to 1) . . . . **5.** _____

6. Multiply line 5 by 2% (.02) and enter the result as a decimal . . . . **6.** _____

7. Multiply line 1 by line 6 . . . . **7.** _____

8. **Exemption.** Subtract line 7 from line 1. Enter the result here and on Form 1041, line 20 . . . . **8.** _____

   *Figure the trust's modified AGI in the same manner as AGI is figured in the line 15c instructions earlier, ***except*** *use zero when figuring the amount of the trust's exemption.*

---

the estate or trust is an expatriated entity or a partner in an expatriated entity, or
- The sum of the excess inclusions of the estate or trust from Schedule Q (Form 1066), Quarterly Notice to Residual Interest Holder of REMIC Taxable Income or Net Loss Allocation, line 2c.

Net operating loss (NOL). If line 22 (figured without regard to the minimum taxable income rule stated above) is a loss, the estate or trust may have an NOL. Do not include the deductions claimed on lines 13, 18, and 20 when figuring the amount of the NOL.

Generally, an NOL may be carried back to the prior 2 tax years and forward for up to 20 years. The 2-year carryback period does not apply to the portion of an NOL attributable to an eligible loss; a farming loss; a qualified disaster, GO Zone, or disaster recovery assistance loss; or a specified liability loss. An estate or trust may also elect to carry an NOL forward only, instead of first carrying it back. For more information, see the Instructions for Form 1045, Application for Tentative Refund.

Complete Schedule A of Form 1045 to figure the amount of the NOL that is available for carryback or carryover. Use Form 1045 or file an amended return to apply for a refund based on an NOL carryback. For more details, see Pub. 536, Net Operating Losses (NOLs) for Individuals, Estates, and Trusts.

On the termination of the estate or trust, any unused NOL carryover that would be allowable to the estate or trust in a later tax year, but for the termination, is allowed to the beneficiaries succeeding to the property

of the estate or trust. See the instructions for Schedule K-1 (Form 1041), box 11, codes D and E, later.

Excess deductions on termination. If the estate or trust has for its final year deductions (excluding the charitable deduction and exemption) in excess of its gross income, the excess is allowed as an itemized deduction to the beneficiaries succeeding to the property of the estate or trust.

In general, an unused NOL carryover that is allowed to beneficiaries (as explained above) cannot also be treated as an excess deduction. However, if the final year of the estate or trust is also the last year of the NOL carryover period, the NOL carryover not absorbed in that tax year by the estate or trust is included as an excess deduction. See the instructions for Schedule K-1 (Form 1041), box 11, code A, later.

Line 24a—2013 Estimated Tax Payments and Amount Applied From 2012 Return

Enter the amount of any estimated tax payment you made with Form 1041-ES for 2013 plus the amount of any overpayment from the 2012 return that was applied to the 2013 estimated tax.

If the estate or trust is the beneficiary of another trust and received a payment of estimated tax that was credited to the trust (as reflected on the Schedule K-1 issued to the trust), then report this amount separately with the notation "section 643(g)" in the space next to line 24a and include this amount in the amount entered on line 24a.

 Do not include on Form 1041 estimated tax paid by an individual before death. Instead, include those payments on the decedent's final income tax return.

Line 24b—Estimated Tax Payments Allocated to Beneficiaries

The trustee (or executor, for the final year of the estate) may elect under section 643(g) to have any portion of its estimated tax treated as a payment of estimated tax made by a beneficiary or beneficiaries. The election is made on Form 1041-T, Allocation of Estimated Tax Payments to Beneficiaries, which must be filed by the 65th day after the close of the trust's tax year. Form 1041-T shows the amounts to be allocated to each beneficiary. This amount is reported on the beneficiary's Schedule K-1 (Form 1041), box 13, code A.

Attach Form 1041-T to your return only if you have not yet filed it; however, attaching Form 1041-T to Form 1041 does not extend the due date for filing Form 1041-T. If you have already filed Form 1041-T, do not attach a copy to your return.

Failure to file Form 1041-T by the due date (March 6, 2014, for calendar year estates and trusts) will result in an invalid election. An invalid election will require the filing of amended Schedules K-1 for each beneficiary who was allocated a payment of estimated tax.

¶2944

Line 24d—Tax Paid With Form 7004

If you filed Form 7004 to request an extension of time to file Form 1041, enter the amount that you paid with the extension request.

Line 24e—Federal Income Tax Withheld

Use line 24e to claim a credit for any federal income tax withheld (and not repaid) by: (a) an employer on wages and salaries of a decedent received by the decedent's estate; (b) a payer of certain gambling winnings (for example, state lottery winnings); or (c) a payer of distributions from pensions, annuities, retirement or profit-sharing plans, IRAs, insurance contracts, etc., received by a decedent's estate or trust. Attach a copy of Form W-2, Form W-2G, or Form 1099-R to the front of the return.

 Except for backup withholding (as explained below), withheld income tax cannot be passed through to beneficiaries on either Schedule K-1 or Form 1041-T.

Backup withholding. If the estate or trust received a 2013 Form 1099 showing federal income tax withheld (that is, backup withholding) on interest income, dividends, or other income, check the box and include the amount withheld on income retained by the estate or trust in the total for line 24e.

Report on Schedule K-1 (Form 1041), box 13, code B, any credit for backup withholding on income distributed to the beneficiary.

Line 24f—Credit for Tax Paid on Undistributed Capital Gains

Attach Copy B of Form 2439, Notice to Shareholder of Undistributed Long-Term Capital Gains.

Line 24g—Credit for Federal Tax on Fuels

Enter any credit for federal excise taxes paid on fuels that are ultimately used for nontaxable purposes (for example, an off-highway business use). Attach Form 4136, Credit for Federal Tax Paid on Fuels. See Pub. 510, Excise Taxes, for more information.

Line 26—Estimated Tax Penalty

If line 27 is at least $1,000 and more than 10% of the tax shown on Form 1041, or the estate or trust underpaid its 2013 estimated tax liability for any payment period, it may owe a penalty. See Form 2210 to determine whether

the estate or trust owes a penalty and to figure the amount of the penalty.

Note. The penalty may be waived under certain conditions. See Pub. 505, Tax Withholding and Estimated Tax, for details.

Line 27—Tax Due

You must pay the tax in full when the return is filed. You may pay by EFTPS. For more information about EFTPS, see *Electronic Deposits*, earlier. Also, you may pay by check or money order or by credit or debit card.

To pay by check or money order. If you pay by check or money order:
• Make it payable to "United States Treasury",
• Make sure the name of the estate or trust appears on the payment,
• Write the estate's or trust's EIN and "2013 Form 1041" on the payment,
• Consider completing the 2013 Form 1041-V, and
• Enclose, but do not attach, the payment (and Form 1041-V, if completed) with Form 1041.

To pay by credit or debit card. For information on paying your taxes electronically, including by credit or debit card, go to *www.irs.gov/e-pay.*

Line 29a—Credited to 2014 Estimated Tax

Enter the amount from line 28 that you want applied to the estate's or trust's 2014 estimated tax.

Schedule A—Charitable Deduction

General Instructions

Generally, any part of the gross income of an estate or trust (other than a simple trust) that, under the terms of the will or governing instrument, is paid (or treated as paid) during the tax year for a charitable purpose specified in section 170(c) is allowed as a deduction to the estate or trust. It is not necessary that the charitable organization be created or organized in the United States.

A pooled income fund or a section 4947(a)(1) nonexempt charitable trust treated as a private foundation must attach a separate sheet to Form 1041 instead of using Schedule A of Form 1041 to figure the charitable deduction.

Additional return to be filed by trusts. Trusts, other than split-interest trusts or nonexempt charitable trusts, that claim a charitable deduction also file Form 1041-A unless the trust is

required to distribute currently to the beneficiaries all the income for the year determined under section 643(b) and related regulations.

Pooled income funds and charitable lead trusts also file Form 5227. See Form 5227 for information about any exceptions.

Election to treat contributions as paid in the prior tax year. The fiduciary of an estate or trust may elect to treat as paid during the tax year any amount of gross income received during that tax year or any prior tax year that was paid in the next tax year for a charitable purpose.

For example, if a calendar year estate or trust makes a qualified charitable contribution on February 7, 2014, from income earned in 2013 or prior, then the fiduciary can elect to treat the contribution as paid in 2013.

To make the election, the fiduciary must file a statement with Form 1041 for the tax year in which the contribution is treated as paid. This statement must include:

1. The name and address of the fiduciary;

2. The name of the estate or trust;

3. An indication that the fiduciary is making an election under section 642(c)(1) for contributions treated as paid during such tax year;

4. The name and address of each organization to which any such contribution is paid; and

5. The amount of each contribution and date of actual payment or, if applicable, the total amount of contributions paid to each organization during the next tax year, to be treated as paid in the prior tax year.

The election must be filed by the due date (including extensions) for Form 1041 for the next tax year. If the original return was filed on time, you may make the election on an amended return filed no later than 6 months after the due date of the return (excluding extensions). Write "Filed pursuant to section 301.9100-2" at the top of the amended return and file it at the same address you used for your original return.

For more information about the charitable deduction, see section 642(c) and related regulations.

Specific Instructions

Line 1—Amounts Paid or Permanently Set Aside for Charitable Purposes From Gross Income

Enter amounts that were paid for a charitable purpose out of the estate's or trust's gross income, including any capital gains that are attributable to income under the governing instrument or local law. Include amounts paid during the tax year from gross income received in a prior tax year, but only if no deduction was allowed for any prior tax year for these amounts.

Estates, and certain trusts, may claim a deduction for amounts permanently set aside for a charitable purpose from gross income. Such amounts must be permanently set aside during the tax year to be used exclusively for religious, charitable, scientific, literary, or educational purposes, or for the prevention of cruelty to children or animals, or for the establishment, acquisition, maintenance, or operation of a public cemetery not operated for profit.

For a trust to qualify, the trust may not be a simple trust, and the set aside amounts must be required by the terms of a trust instrument that was created on or before October 9, 1969.

Further, the trust instrument must provide for an irrevocable remainder interest to be transferred to or for the use of an organization described in section 170(c); or the trust must have been created by a grantor who was at all times after October 9, 1969, under a mental disability to change the terms of the trust.

Also, certain testamentary trusts that were established by a will that was executed on or before October 9, 1969, may qualify. See Regulations section 1.642(c)-2(b).

Do not include any capital gains for the tax year allocated to corpus and paid or permanently set aside for charitable purposes. Instead, enter these amounts on line 4.

Line 2—Tax-Exempt Income Allocable to Charitable Contributions

Any estate or trust that pays or sets aside any part of its income for a charitable purpose must reduce the deduction by the portion allocable to any tax-exempt income. If the governing instrument specifically provides as to the source from which amounts are paid, permanently set aside, or to be used for charitable purposes, the specific provisions control. In all other cases, determine the amount of tax-exempt income allocable to charitable contributions by multiplying line 1 by a fraction, the numerator of which is the total tax-exempt income of the estate or trust, and the denominator of which is the gross income of the estate or trust. Do not include in the denominator any losses allocated to corpus.

Line 4—Capital Gains for the Tax Year Allocated to Corpus and Paid or Permanently Set Aside for Charitable Purposes

Enter the total of all capital gains for the tax year that are:
- Allocated to corpus, and
- Paid or permanently set aside for charitable purposes.

Line 6—Section 1202 Exclusion Allocable to Capital Gains Paid or Permanently Set Aside for Charitable Purposes

If the exclusion of gain from the sale or exchange of qualified small business (QSB) stock was claimed, enter the part of the gain included on Schedule A, lines 1 and 4, that was excluded under section 1202.

Schedule B—Income Distribution Deduction

General Instructions

If the estate or trust was required to distribute income currently or if it paid, credited, or was required to distribute any other amounts to beneficiaries during the tax year, complete Schedule B to determine the estate's or trust's income distribution deduction.

Note. Use Schedule I (Form 1041) to compute the DNI and income distribution deduction on a minimum tax basis.

Pooled income funds. Do not complete Schedule B for these funds. Instead, attach a separate statement to support the computation of the income distribution deduction. See *Pooled Income Funds*, earlier, for more information.

Separate share rule. If a single trust or an estate has more than one beneficiary, and if different beneficiaries have substantially separate and independent shares, their shares are treated as separate trusts or estates for the sole purpose of determining the DNI allocable to the respective beneficiaries.

If the separate share rule applies, figure the DNI allocable to each beneficiary on a separate sheet and attach the sheet to this return. Any deduction or loss that is applicable solely to one separate share of the trust or estate is not available to any other share of the same trust or estate.

For more information, see section 663(c) and related regulations.

Withholding of tax on foreign persons. The fiduciary may be liable for withholding tax on distributions to beneficiaries who are foreign persons. For more information, see Pub. 515, Withholding of Tax on Nonresident Aliens and Foreign Entities, and Forms 1042 and 1042-S.

Specific Instructions

Line 1—Adjusted Total Income

Generally, enter on line 1, Schedule B, the amount from line 17 on page 1 of Form 1041. However, if both line 4 and line 17 on page 1 of Form 1041 are losses, enter on line 1, Schedule B, the smaller of those losses. If line 4 is zero or a gain and line 17 is a loss, enter zero on line 1, Schedule B.

If you are filing for a simple trust, subtract from adjusted total income any extraordinary dividends or taxable stock dividends included on page 1, line 2, and determined under the governing instrument and applicable local law to be allocable to corpus.

Line 2—Adjusted Tax-Exempt Interest

To figure the adjusted tax-exempt interest:

Step 1. Add tax-exempt interest income on line 2 of Schedule A, any expenses allowable under section 212 allocable to tax-exempt interest, and any interest expense allocable to tax-exempt interest.

Step 2. Subtract the Step 1 total from the amount of tax-exempt interest (including exempt-interest dividends) received.

Section 212 expenses that are directly allocable to tax-exempt interest are allocated only to tax-exempt interest. A reasonable proportion of section 212 expenses that are indirectly allocable to both tax-exempt interest and other income must be allocated to each class of income.

Figure the interest expense allocable to tax-exempt interest according to the guidelines in Rev. Proc. 72-18, 1972-1 C.B. 740.

See Regulations sections 1.643(a)-5 and 1.265-1 for more information.

Line 3

Include all capital gains, whether or not distributed, that are attributable to income under the governing instrument or local law. For example, if the trustee distributed 50% of the current year's capital gains to the income beneficiaries (and reflects this amount in column (1), line 19 of Schedule D (Form 1041)), but under the governing instrument all capital gains are attributable to income, then include 100% of the capital gains on line 3. If the amount on Schedule D (Form 1041), line 19, column (1), is a net loss, enter zero.

If the exclusion of gain from the sale or exchange of QSB stock was claimed, do not reduce the gain on line 3 by any amount excluded under section 1202.

Line 5

In figuring the amount of long-term and short-term capital gain for the tax year included on Schedule A, line 1, the specific provisions of the governing instrument control if the instrument specifically provides as to the source from which amounts are paid, permanently set aside, or to be used for charitable purposes.

In all other cases, determine the amount to enter by multiplying line 1 of Schedule A by a fraction, the numerator of which is the amount of net capital gains that are included in the accounting income of the estate or trust (that is, not allocated to corpus) and are distributed to charities, and the denominator of which is all items of income (including the amount of such net capital gains) included in the DNI.

Reduce the amount on line 5 by any allocable section 1202 exclusion.

Line 8—Accounting Income

If you are filing for a decedent's estate or a simple trust, skip this line. If you are filing for a complex trust, enter the income for the tax year determined under the terms of the governing instrument and applicable local law. Do not include extraordinary dividends or taxable stock dividends determined under the governing instrument and applicable local law to be allocable to corpus.

Lines 9 and 10

Do not include any:
- Amount that was deducted on the prior year's return that was required to be distributed in the prior year;
- Amount that is paid or permanently set aside for charitable purposes or otherwise qualifying for the charitable deduction; or
- Amount that is properly paid or credited as a gift or bequest of a specific amount of money or specific property.

Note. An amount that can be paid or credited only from income is not considered a gift or bequest. Also, to qualify as a gift or bequest, the amount must be paid in three or fewer installments.

Line 9—Income Required To Be Distributed Currently

Line 9 is to be completed by all simple trusts as well as complex trusts and decedent's estates that are required to distribute income currently, whether it is distributed or not. The determination of whether trust income is required to be distributed currently depends on the terms of the governing instrument and the applicable local law.

The line 9 distributions are referred to as first tier distributions and are deductible by the estate or trust to the extent of the DNI. The beneficiary includes such amounts in his or her income to the extent of his or her proportionate share of the DNI.

Line 10—Other Amounts Paid, Credited, or Otherwise Required To Be Distributed

Line 10 is to be completed only by a decedent's estate or complex trust. These distributions consist of any other amounts paid, credited, or required to be distributed and are referred to as second tier distributions. Such amounts include annuities to the extent not paid out of income, mandatory and discretionary distributions of corpus, and distributions of property in kind.

If Form 1041-T was timely filed to elect to treat estimated tax payments as made by a beneficiary, the payments are treated as paid or credited to the beneficiary on the last day of the tax year and must be included on line 10.

Unless a section 643(e)(3) election is made, the value of all noncash property actually paid, credited, or required to be distributed to any beneficiaries is the smaller of:

1. The estate's or trust's adjusted basis in the property immediately before distribution, plus any gain or minus any loss recognized by the estate or trust on the distribution (basis of beneficiary), or

2. The FMV of such property.

If a section 643(e)(3) election is made by the fiduciary, then the amount entered on line 10 will be the FMV of the property.

A fiduciary of a complex trust or a decedent's estate may elect to treat any amount paid or credited to a beneficiary within 65 days following the close of the tax year as being paid or credited on the last day of that tax year. To make this election, see the instructions for Question 6, later.

The beneficiary includes the amounts on line 10 in his or her income only to the extent of his or her proportionate share of the DNI.

Complex trusts. If the second tier distributions exceed the DNI allocable to the second tier, the trust may have an accumulation distribution. See the line 11 instructions below.

Line 11—Total Distributions

If line 11 is more than line 8, and you are filing for a complex trust that has previously accumulated income, see the instructions for Schedule J, later, to see if you must complete Schedule J (Form 1041).

Line 12—Adjustment for Tax-Exempt Income

In figuring the income distribution deduction, the estate or trust is not allowed a deduction for any item of the DNI that is not included in the gross income of the estate or trust. Thus, for purposes of figuring the allowable income distribution deduction, the DNI

¶2944

(line 7) is figured without regard to any tax-exempt interest.

If tax-exempt interest is the only tax-exempt income included in the total distributions (line 11), and the DNI (line 7) is less than or equal to line 11, then enter on line 12 the amount from line 2.

If tax-exempt interest is the only tax-exempt income included in the total distributions (line 11), and the DNI is more than line 11 (that is, the estate or trust made a distribution that is less than the DNI), then figure the adjustment by multiplying line 2 by a fraction, the numerator of which is the total distributions (line 11), and the denominator of which is the DNI (line 7). Enter the result on line 12.

If line 11 includes tax-exempt income other than tax-exempt interest, figure line 12 by subtracting the total of the following from tax-exempt income included on line 11:

1. The charitable contribution deduction allocable to such tax-exempt income, and

2. Expenses allocable to tax-exempt income.

Expenses that are directly allocable to tax-exempt income are allocated only to tax-exempt income. A reasonable proportion of expenses indirectly allocable to both tax-exempt income and other income must be allocated to each class of income.

Schedule G—Tax Computation

Line 1a

2013 tax rate schedule. For tax years beginning in 2013, figure the tax using the Tax Rate Schedule below and enter the tax on line 1a. However, see the Instructions for Schedule D (Form 1041) and the *Qualified Dividends Tax Worksheet* later.

2013 Tax Rate Schedule

If taxable income is:			
Over—	But not over—	Its tax is:	Of the amount over—
$0	$2,450	15%	$0
2,450	5,700	$367.50 + 25%	2,450
5,700	8,750	1,180.00 + 28%	5,700
8,750	11,950	2,034.00 + 33%	8,750
11,950	-----	3,090.00 + 39.6%	11,950

Schedule D (Form 1041) and Schedule D Tax Worksheet. Use Part V of Schedule D (Form 1041) or the *Schedule D Tax Worksheet*, whichever is applicable, to figure the estate's or trust's tax if the estate or trust files Schedule D (Form 1041) and has:
- A net capital gain and any taxable income, or
- Qualified dividends on line 2b(2) of Form 1041 and any taxable income.

Qualified Dividends Tax Worksheet. If you do not have to complete Part I or Part II of Schedule D and the estate or trust has an amount entered on line 2b(2) of Form 1041 and any taxable income (line 22), then figure the estate's or trust's tax using the worksheet, later, and enter the tax on line 1a.

Note. You must reduce the amount you enter on line 2b(2) of Form 1041 by the portion of the section 691(c) deduction claimed on line 19 of Form 1041 if the estate or trust received qualified dividends that were IRD.

Line 1c—AMT. Attach Schedule I (Form 1041) if:
- The estate or trust must complete Schedule B.
- The estate or trust claims a credit on line 2b, 2c, or 2d of Schedule G.
- The estate's or trust's share of alternative minimum taxable income (line 29 of Schedule I (Form 1041)) exceeds $23,100.

Enter the amount from line 56 of Schedule I (Form 1041) on line 1c.

Line 2a—Foreign Tax Credit

Attach Form 1116, Foreign Tax Credit (Individual, Estate, or Trust), if you elect to claim credit for income or profits taxes paid or accrued to a foreign country or a U.S. possession. The estate or trust may claim credit for that part of the foreign taxes not allocable to the beneficiaries (including charitable beneficiaries). Enter the estate's or trust's share of the credit on line 2a. See Pub. 514, Foreign Tax Credit for Individuals, for details.

Line 2b—General Business Credit

⚠️ **CAUTION** *Do not include any amounts that are allocated to a beneficiary. Credits that are allocated between the estate or trust and the beneficiaries are listed in the instructions for Schedule K-1, box 13, later. Generally, these credits are apportioned on the basis of the income*

allocable to the estate or trust and the beneficiaries.

Enter on line 2b the estate's or trust's total general business credit allowed for the current year from Form 3800. The estate or trust must file Form 3800 to claim any of the general business credits. Generally, if the estate's or trust's only source of a credit is from a pass-through entity and the beneficiary is not entitled to an allocable share of a credit, you are not required to complete the source form for that credit. However, certain credits have limitations and special computations that may require you to complete the source form. See the Instructions for Form 3800 for more information.

Line 2c—Credit for Prior Year Minimum Tax

An estate or trust that paid AMT in a previous year may be eligible for a minimum tax credit in 2013. See Form 8801, Credit for Prior Year Minimum Tax—Individuals, Estates, and Trusts.

Line 2d—Bond Credits

Complete and attach Form 8912, Credit to Holders of Tax Credit Bonds, if the estate or trust claims a credit for holding a tax credit bond. Also, be sure to include the credit in interest income.

Line 2e—Total Credits

To claim a credit allowable to the estate or trust other than the credits entered on lines 2a through 2d, include the allowable credit in the total for line 2e. Complete and attach the appropriate form and write the form number and amount of the allowable credit on the dotted line to the left of the entry space.

Line 4—Net Investment Income Tax

Enter the amount of net investment income tax calculated and attach Form 8960. See the Instructions for Form 8960 to calculate the tax and *Net Investment Income Tax*, later, for more information.

Line 5—Recapture Taxes

Recapture of investment credit. If the estate or trust disposed of investment credit property or changed its use before the end of the recapture period, see Form 4255, Recapture of Investment Credit, to figure the recapture tax allocable to the estate or trust. Include the tax on line 5 and write "ICR" on the dotted line to the left of the entry space.

Qualified Dividends Tax Worksheet—Schedule G, line 1a   *Keep for Your Records*

Caution: *Do not* use this worksheet if the estate or trust must complete Schedule D (Form 1041).

1.	Enter the amount from Form 1041, line 22	**1.** _____
2.	Enter the amount from Form 1041, line 2b(2) .... **2.** _____	
3.	If you are claiming investment interest expense on Form 4952, enter the amount from line 4g; otherwise enter -0- .... **3.** _____	
4.	Subtract line 3 from line 2. If zero or less, enter -0-	**4.** _____
5.	Subtract line 4 from line 1. If zero or less, enter -0-	**5.** _____
6.	Enter the **smaller** of the amount on line 1 or $2,450	**6.** _____
7.	Enter the **smaller** of the amount on line 5 or line 6	**7.** _____
8.	Subtract line 7 from line 6. If zero or less, enter -0-. This amount is taxed at 0%	**8.** _____
9.	Enter the **smaller** of line 1 or line 4	**9.** _____
10.	Subtract line 8 from line 4	**10.** _____
11.	Enter the **smaller** of line 1 or $11,950	**11.** _____
12.	Add lines 5 and 8	**12.** _____
13.	Subtract line 12 from line 11. If zero or less, enter -0-	**13.** _____
14.	Enter the **smaller** of line 10 or line 13	**14.** _____
15.	Multiply line 14 by 15% (.15)	**15.** _____
16.	Enter the amount from line 9	**16.** _____
17.	Add lines 8 and 14	**17.** _____
18.	Subtract line 17 from line 16. If zero or less, enter -0-	**18.** _____
19.	Multiply line 18 by 20% (.20)	**19.** _____
20.	Figure the tax on the amount on line 5. Use the 2013 Tax Rate Schedule	**20.** _____
21.	Add lines 15, 19 and 20	**21.** _____
22.	Figure the tax on the amount on line 1. Use the 2013 Tax Rate Schedule	**22.** _____
23.	**Tax on all taxable income.** Enter the **smaller** of line 21 or line 22 here and on Sch. G, line 1a	**23.** _____

Recapture of low-income housing credit. If the estate or trust disposed of property (or there was a reduction in the qualified basis of the property) on which the low-income housing credit was claimed, see Form 8611, Recapture of Low-Income Housing Credit, to figure any recapture tax allocable to the estate or trust. Include the tax on line 5 and write "LIHCR" on the dotted line to the left of the entry space.

Recapture of qualified electric vehicle credit. If the estate or trust claimed the qualified electric vehicle credit in a prior tax year for a vehicle that ceased to qualify for the credit, part or all of the credit may have to be recaptured. See Regulations section 1.30-1(b) for details. If the estate or trust owes any recapture tax, include it on line 5 and write "QEVCR" on the dotted line to the left of the entry space.

Recapture of the Indian employment credit. Generally, if the estate or trust terminates a qualified employee less

than 1 year after the date of initial employment, any Indian employment credit allowed for a prior tax year by reason of wages paid or incurred to that employee must be recaptured. See Form 8845 for details. If the estate or trust owes any recapture tax, include it on line 5 and write "IECR" on the dotted line to the left of the entry space.

Recapture of the new markets credit. If the estate or trust owes any new markets recapture tax, include it on line 5 and write "NMCR" on the dotted line to the left of the entry space. For more information, including how to figure the recapture amount, see section 45D(g).

Recapture of the credit for employer-provided child care facilities. If the facility ceased to operate as a qualified child care facility or there was a change in ownership, part or all of the credit may have to be recaptured. See Form 8882 for details. If the estate or trust owes any recapture tax, include it

on line 5 and write "ECCFR" on the dotted line to the left of the entry space.

Recapture of the alternative motor vehicle credit. See section 30B(h)(8) for details. Include the tax on line 5 and write "AMVCR" on the dotted line to the left of the entry space.

Recapture of the alternative fuel vehicle refueling property credit. See section 30C(e)(5) for details. Include the tax on line 5 and write "ARPCR" on the dotted line to the left of the entry space.

Line 6—Household Employment Taxes

If any of the following apply, get Schedule H (Form 1040), Household Employment Taxes, and its instructions, to see if the estate or trust owes these taxes.

1. The estate or trust paid any one household employee cash wages of $1,800 or more in 2013. Cash wages include wages paid by checks, money

2013 Instructions for Form 1041   -31-

¶2944

orders, etc. When figuring the amount of cash wages paid, combine cash wages paid by the estate or trust with cash wages paid to the household employee in the same calendar year by the household of the decedent or beneficiary for whom the administrator, executor, or trustee of the estate or trust is acting.

2. The estate or trust withheld federal income tax during 2013 at the request of any household employee.

3. The estate or trust paid total cash wages of $1,000 or more in any calendar quarter of 2012 or 2013 to household employees.

Note. See *Amended Schedule H (Form 1040)* under *F. Initial Return, Amended Return, etc.*, earlier for information on filing an amended Schedule H (Form 1040) for a Form 1041.

Line 7—Total Tax

Tax on ESBTs. Attach the tax computation to the return. To the left of the line 7 entry space, write "Sec. 641(c)" and the amount of tax on the S corporation items. Include this amount in the total tax on line 7.

See *Electing Small Business Trusts (ESBTs)*, earlier, for the special tax computation rules that apply to the portion of an ESBT consisting of stock in one or more S corporations.

Interest on deferred tax attributable to installment sales of certain time-shares and residential lots and certain nondealer real property installment obligations. If an obligation arising from the disposition of real property to which section 453(l) or 453A applies is outstanding at the close of the year, the estate or trust must include the interest due under section 453(l)(3)(B) or 453A(c), whichever is applicable, in the amount to be entered on line 7 of Schedule G, Form 1041, with the notation "Section 453(l) interest" or "Section 453A(c) interest," whichever is applicable. Attach a schedule showing the computation.

Form 4970, Tax on Accumulation Distribution of Trusts. Include on this line any tax due on an accumulation distribution from a trust. To the left of the entry space, write "From Form 4970" and the amount of the tax.

Form 8697, Interest Computation Under the Look-Back Method for Completed Long-Term Contracts. Include the interest due under the look-back method of section 460(b)(2).

To the left of the entry space, write "From Form 8697" and the amount of interest due.

Form 8866, Interest Computation Under the Look-Back Method for Property Depreciated Under the Income Forecast Method. Include the interest due under the look-back method of section 167(g)(2). To the left of the entry space, write "From Form 8866" and the amount of interest due.

Interest on deferral of gain from certain constructive ownership transactions. Include the interest due under section 1260(b) on any deferral of gain from certain constructive ownership transactions. To the left of the entry space, write "1260(b)" and the amount of interest due.

Form 5329, Additional Taxes on Qualified Plans (Including IRAs) and Other Tax-Favored Accounts. If the estate or trust fails to receive the minimum distribution under section 4974, use Form 5329 to pay the excise tax. To the left of the entry space, write "From Form 5329" and the amount of the tax.

Net Investment Income Tax

For taxable years beginning after December 31, 2012, certain estates and trusts may be subject to the Net Investment Income Tax (NIIT). Estates and trusts use Form 8960 to report their Net Investment Income (NII) and calculate the tax. The amount of NIIT payable by the estate or trust is reported on Form 1041, Schedule G, line 4.

The NIIT is imposed on estates and trusts to the extent that they have undistributed net investment income and adjusted gross income (AGI) exceeding $11,950. See instructions to line 15c for the calculation of an estate or trust's AGI. The following types of estates and trusts may owe the NIIT in addition to their regular income tax liability:

• Decedent's estates,
• Simple and complex trusts,
• Electing small business trusts (ESBTs),
• Pooled income funds, and
• Bankruptcy estates.

However, in the case of bankruptcy estates, the adjusted gross income threshold is $125,000.

Calculation of Net Investment Income. In general, an estate or trust's NII is calculated in the same way as an

individual. However, there are special rules for the calculation of NII in the case of an ESBT. See instructions to Form 8960 and Regulations section 1.1411-3(e) for information on the calculation (and Regulations section 1.1411-3(c)(1) for information on the ESBT calculation).

Distributions on Net Investment Income. The NIIT is imposed on estates and trusts to the extent it has undistributed net investment income. In order to arrive at the estate or trust's undistributed net investment income, the estate or trust's NII is reduced for (1) distributions of NII to beneficiaries, and (2) NII allocable to charities when the estate or trust is allowed a deduction under section 642(c). Instructions for Form 8960, line 18, provide more information on the calculation of undistributed net investment income.

NII allocable to the deduction under section 642(c). An estate, trust, or pooled income fund's NII is reduced by the amount of NII allocable to the charitable deduction allowed under section 642(c). In the case of an estate, trust, or pooled income fund that has NII and non-NII income in a year when a section 642(c) deduction is claimed, the amount of the NII deduction allocable to the section 642(c) deduction will be less than the amount reported on Form 1041, Schedule A, line 7 (or on the separate calculation in the case of a pooled income fund).

Beneficiary reporting. In general, the amount of the income distribution deduction (from Form 1041, Schedule B, line 15) that reduces the estate or trust's NII will be the amount of NII that will be taxable to the beneficiaries on their Schedules K-1(Form 1041).

The Schedule K-1 has a new code H in box 14 to report the amount of net investment income distributed to the beneficiary. The amount reported in code H represents an adjustment (either positive or negative) that the beneficiary must use in completing its Form 8960 (if necessary). In the case where the trust's income distribution deduction allowed in calculating undistributed net investment income is less than the amount on Schedule B, line 15, then code H will show a negative number that is the difference between the two amounts. In the case of an estate or trust that issues more than one Schedule K-1 for a year, the sum of the amounts reported in code H on all of the Schedules K-1 will be the difference between Schedule B, line 15, and the amount deducted on

Form 8960, line 18b, for amounts of NII distributed to a beneficiary.

 The beneficiary's NII will equal all taxable amounts reported on the Schedule K-1, adjusted by the amount reported in box 14, code H.

 The only instance where code H will be a positive number is when:
• *The estate or trust owns directly, or indirectly, an (a) interest in a section 1291 fund, or (b) interest in a controlled foreign corporation or qualified electing fund and no election under Regulations section 1.1411–10(g) has been made with respect to that interest, and*
• *The distribution from one of the entities described above is (a) net investment income to the estate or trust, but not included in its taxable income, and (b) the distributions from the estate or trust to the beneficiary(s) in the year exceed the amount of the income distribution deduction allowed for regular tax purposes (from Schedule B, line 15).*

Special rules. In the final year of an estate or trust, deductions in excess of income may be reported to the beneficiary on Schedule K-1, box 11. These deductions may also be deductible by the beneficiary for NIIT purposes. In this situation, the terminating estate or trust should provide the beneficiary information regarding whether the amounts reported in box 11, codes A through D, include any amounts that are deductible for NIIT purposes. See Regulations section 1.1411-4(g)(4).

Other Information

Question 1

If the estate or trust received tax-exempt income, figure the allocation of expenses between tax-exempt and taxable income on a separate sheet and attach it to the return. Enter only the deductible amounts on the return. Do not figure the allocation on the return itself. For more information, see the instructions for *Allocation of Deductions for Tax-Exempt Income*, earlier.

Report the amount of tax-exempt interest income received or accrued in the space provided below Question 1.

Also, include any exempt-interest dividends the estate or trust received as a shareholder in a mutual fund or other regulated investment company.

Question 2

All salaries, wages, and other compensation for personal services must be included on the return of the person who earned the income, even if the income was irrevocably assigned to a trust by a contract assignment or similar arrangement.

The grantor or person creating the trust is considered the owner if he or she keeps "beneficial enjoyment" of or substantial control over the trust property. The trust's income, deductions, and credits are allocable to the owner.

If you checked "Yes" for Question 2, see *Special Reporting Instructions*, earlier.

Question 3

Check the "Yes" box and enter the name of the foreign country if either 1 or 2 below applies.

1. The estate or trust owns more than 50% of the stock in any corporation that owns one or more foreign bank accounts.

2. At any time during the year the estate or trust had an interest in or signature or other authority over a bank, securities, or other financial account in a foreign country.

Exception. Check "No" if either of the following applies to the estate or trust:
• The combined value of the accounts was $10,000 or less during the whole year, or
• The accounts were with a U.S. military banking facility operated by a U.S. financial institution.

If you checked "Yes" for Question 3, electronically file FinCEN Form 114, Report of Foreign Bank and Financial Accounts (FBAR) (formerly Form TD F 90–22.1) by June 30, 2014, with the Department of the Treasury using the FinCEN's BSA E-Filing Sytem. Because FinCEN Form 114 is not a tax form, do not file it with Form 1041.

See *www.fincen.gov* for more information.

 If you are required to file FinCEN Form 114 but do not, you may have to pay a penalty of up to $10,000 (or more in some cases).

Question 4

The estate or trust may be required to file Form 3520, Annual Return To Report Transactions With Foreign Trusts and Receipt of Certain Foreign Gifts, if:

• It directly or indirectly transferred property or money to a foreign trust. For this purpose, any U.S. person who created a foreign trust is considered a transferor;
• It is treated as the owner of any part of the assets of a foreign trust under the grantor trust rules; or
• It received a distribution from a foreign trust.

 An owner of a foreign trust must ensure that the trust files an annual information return on Form 3520-A, Annual Information Return of Foreign Trust With a U.S. Owner.

Question 5

An estate or trust claiming an interest deduction for qualified residence interest (as defined in section 163(h)(3)) on seller-provided financing must include on an attachment to the 2013 Form 1041 the name, address, and TIN of the person to whom the interest was paid or accrued (that is, the seller).

If the estate or trust received or accrued such interest, it must provide identical information on the person liable for such interest (that is, the buyer). This information does not need to be reported if it duplicates information already reported on Form 1098.

Question 6

To make the section 663(b) election to treat any amount paid or credited to a beneficiary within 65 days following the close of the tax year as being paid or credited on the last day of that tax year, check the box. This election can be made by the fiduciary of a complex trust or the executor of a decedent's estate. For the election to be valid, you must file Form 1041 by the due date (including extensions). Once made, the election is irrevocable.

Question 7

To make the section 643(e)(3) election to recognize gain on property distributed in kind, check the box and see the Instructions for Schedule D (Form 1041).

Question 9

Generally, a beneficiary is a skip person if the beneficiary is in a generation that is two or more generations below the generation of the transferor to the trust.

To determine if a beneficiary that is a trust is a skip person, and for exceptions to the general rules, see the definition of a skip person in the instructions for Schedule R of Form 706.

Schedule J (Form 1041) — Accumulation Distribution for Certain Complex Trusts

General Instructions

Use Schedule J (Form 1041) to report an accumulation distribution for a domestic complex trust that was:
• Previously treated at any time as a foreign trust (unless an exception is provided in future regulations), or
• Created before March 1, 1984, unless that trust would not be aggregated with other trusts under the rules of section 643(f) if that section applied to the trust.

An accumulation distribution is the excess of amounts properly paid, credited, or required to be distributed (other than income required to be distributed currently) over the DNI of the trust reduced by income required to be distributed currently. To have an accumulation distribution, the distribution must exceed the accounting income of the trust.

Specific Instructions

Part I—Accumulation Distribution in 2013

Line 1—Distribution Under Section 661(a)(2)

Enter the amount from Form 1041, Schedule B, line 10, for 2013. This is the amount properly paid, credited, or required to be distributed other than the amount of income for the current tax year required to be distributed currently.

Line 2—DNI

Enter the amount from Form 1041, Schedule B, line 7, for 2013. This is the amount of DNI for the current tax year determined under section 643(a).

Line 3—Distribution Under Section 661(a)(1)

Enter the amount from Form 1041, Schedule B, line 9, for 2013. This is the amount of income for the current tax year required to be distributed currently.

Line 5—Accumulation Distribution

If line 11 of Form 1041, Schedule B, is more than line 8 of Form 1041, Schedule B, complete the rest of Schedule J and file it with Form 1041, unless the trust has no previously accumulated income.

Generally, amounts accumulated before a beneficiary reaches age 21 may be excluded by the beneficiary. See sections 665 and 667(c) for exceptions relating to multiple trusts. The trustee reports to the IRS the total amount of the accumulation distribution before any reduction for income accumulated before the beneficiary reaches age 21. If the multiple trust rules do not apply, the beneficiary claims the exclusion when filing Form 4970, as you may not be aware that the beneficiary may be a beneficiary of other trusts with other trustees.

For examples of accumulation distributions that include payments from one trust to another trust, and amounts distributed for a dependent's support, see Regulations section 1.665(b)-1A(b).

Part II—Ordinary Income Accumulation Distribution

Enter the applicable year at the top of each column for each throwback year.

Line 6—DNI for Earlier Years

Enter the applicable amounts as follows:

Throwback year(s)	Amount from line
1969–1977	Form 1041, Schedule C, line 5
1978–1979	Form 1041, line 61
1980	Form 1041, line 60
1981–1982	Form 1041, line 58
1983–1996	Form 1041, Schedule B, line 9
1997–2012	Form 1041, Schedule B, line 7

For information about throwback years, see the instructions for line 13. For purposes of line 6, in figuring the DNI of the trust for a throwback year, subtract any estate tax deduction for IRD if the income is includible in figuring the DNI of the trust for that year.

Line 7—Distributions Made During Earlier Years

Enter the applicable amounts as follows:

Throwback year(s)	Amount from line
1969–1977	Form 1041, Schedule C, line 8
1978	Form 1041, line 64
1979	Form 1041, line 65
1980	Form 1041, line 64
1981–1982	Form 1041, line 62
1983–1996	Form 1041, Schedule B, line 13
1997–2012	Form 1041, Schedule B, line 11

Line 11—Prior Accumulation Distribution Thrown Back to Any Throwback Year

Enter the amount of prior accumulation distributions thrown back to the throwback years. Do not enter distributions excluded under section 663(a)(1) for gifts, bequests, etc.

Line 13—Throwback Years

Allocate the amount on line 5 that is an accumulation distribution to the earliest applicable year first, but do not allocate more than the amount on line 12 for any throwback year. An accumulation distribution is thrown back first to the earliest preceding tax year in which there is undistributed net income (UNI). Then, it is thrown back beginning with the next earliest year to any remaining preceding tax years of the trust. The portion of the accumulation distribution allocated to the earliest preceding tax year is the amount of the UNI for that year. The portion of the accumulation distribution allocated to any remaining preceding tax year is the amount by which the accumulation distribution is larger than the total of the UNI for all earlier preceding tax years.

A tax year of a trust during which the trust was a simple trust for the entire year is not a preceding tax year unless (a) during that year the trust received outside income, or (b) the trustee did not distribute all of the trust's income that was required to be distributed currently for that year. In this case, UNI for that year must not be more than the greater of the outside income or income not distributed during that year.

The term "outside income" means amounts that are included in the DNI of the trust for that year but that are not "income" of the trust as defined in Regulations section 1.643(b)-1. Some examples of outside income are: (a) income taxable to the trust under section 691; (b) unrealized accounts receivable that were assigned to the trust; and (c) distributions from another trust that include the DNI or UNI of the other trust.

Line 16—Tax-Exempt Interest Included on Line 13

For each throwback year, divide line 15 by line 6 and multiply the result by the following:

¶2944

Throwback year(s)	Amount from line
1969–1977	Form 1041, Schedule C, line 2(a)
1978–1979	Form 1041, line 58(a)
1980	Form 1041, line 57(a)
1981–1982	Form 1041, line 55(a)
1983–2012	Form 1041, Schedule B, line 2

Part III—Taxes Imposed on Undistributed Net Income

For the regular tax computation, if there is a capital gain, complete lines 18 through 25 for each throwback year. If the trustee elected the alternative tax on capital gains, complete lines 26 through 31 instead of lines 18 through 25 for each applicable year. If there is no capital gain for any year, or there is a capital loss for every year, enter on line 9 the amount of the tax for each year identified in the instruction for line 18 and do not complete Part III. If the trust received an accumulation distribution from another trust, see Regulations section 1.665(b)-1A.

Note. The alternative tax on capital gains was repealed for tax years beginning after December 31, 1978. The maximum rate on net capital gain for 1981, 1987, and 1991 through 2012 is not an alternative tax for this purpose.

Line 18—Regular Tax

Enter the applicable amounts as follows:

Throwback year(s)	Amount from line
1969–1976 . . .	Form 1041, page 1, line 24
1977	Form 1041, page 1, line 26
1978–1979 . . .	Form 1041, line 27
1980–1984 . . .	Form 1041, line 26c
1985–1986 . . .	Form 1041, line 25c
1987	Form 1041, line 22c
1988–2012 . . .	Form 1041, Schedule G, line 1a

Line 19—Trust's Share of Net Short-Term Gain

For each throwback year, enter the smaller of the capital gain from the two lines indicated. If there is a capital loss or a zero on either or both of the two lines indicated, enter zero on line 19.

Throwback year(s)	Amount from line
1969–1970 . . .	Schedule D, line 10, column 2, or Schedule D, line 12, column 2
1971–1978 . . .	Schedule D, line 14, column 2, or Schedule D, line 16, column 2
1979	Schedule D, line 18, column (b), or Schedule D, line 20, column (b)
1980–1981 . . .	Schedule D, line 14, column (b), or Schedule D, line 16, column (b)
1982	Schedule D, line 16, column (b), or Schedule D, line 18, column (b)
1983–1996 . . .	Schedule D, line 15, column (b), or Schedule D, line 17, column (b)
1997–2002 . . .	Schedule D, line 14, column (2), or Schedule D, line 16, column (2)
2003	Schedule D, line 14a, column (2), or Schedule D, line 16a, column (2)
2004–2012 . . .	Schedule D, line 13, column (2), or Schedule D, line 15, column (2)

Line 20—Trust's Share of Net Long-Term Gain

Enter the applicable amounts as follows:

Throwback year(s)	Amount from line
1969–1970	50% of Schedule D, line 13(e)
1971–1977	50% of Schedule D, line 17(e)
1978	Schedule D, line 17(e), or line 31, whichever is applicable, less Form 1041, line 23
1979	Schedule D, line 25 or line 27, whichever is applicable, less Form 1041, line 23
1980–1981	Schedule D, line 21, less Schedule D, line 22
1982	Schedule D, line 23, less Schedule D, line 24
1983–1986	Schedule D, line 22, less Schedule D, line 23
1987–1996	Schedule D, the smaller of any gain on line 16 or line 17, column (b)
1997–2001	Schedule D, the smaller of any gain on line 15c or line 16, column (2)
2002	Schedule D, the smaller of any gain on line 15a or line 16, column (2)
2003	Schedule D, the smaller of any gain on line 15a or line 16a, column (2)
2004–2012	Schedule D, the smaller of any gain on line 14a or line 15, column (2)

Line 22—Taxable Income

Enter the applicable amounts as follows:

Throwback year(s)	Amount from line
1969–1976	Form 1041, page 1, line 23
1977	Form 1041, page 1, line 25
1978–1979	Form 1041, line 26
1980–1984	Form 1041, line 25
1985–1986	Form 1041, line 24
1987	Form 1041, line 21
1988–1996	Form 1041, line 22
1997	Form 1041, line 23
1998–2012	Form 1041, line 22

Line 26—Tax on Income Other Than Long-Term Capital Gain

Enter the applicable amounts as follows:

Throwback year(s)	Amount from line
1969	Schedule D, line 20
1970	Schedule D, line 19
1971	Schedule D, line 50
1972–1975	Schedule D, line 48
1976–1978	Schedule D, line 27

Line 27—Trust's Share of Net Short-Term Gain

If there is a loss on any of the following lines, enter zero on line 27 for the applicable throwback year. Otherwise, enter the applicable amounts as follows:

Throwback year(s)	Amount from line
1969–1970	Schedule D, line 10, column 2
1971–1978	Schedule D, line 14, column 2

Line 28—Trust's Share of Taxable Income Less Section 1202 Deduction

Enter the applicable amounts as follows:

Throwback year(s)	Amount from line
1969	Schedule D, line 19
1970	Schedule D, line 18
1971	Schedule D, line 38
1972–1975	Schedule D, line 39
1976–1978	Schedule D, line 21

Part IV—Allocation to Beneficiary

Complete Part IV for each beneficiary. If the accumulation distribution is allocated to more than one beneficiary, attach an additional copy of Schedule J with Part IV completed for each additional beneficiary. Give each beneficiary a copy of his or her respective Part IV information. If more than 5 throwback years are involved, use another Schedule J, completing Parts II and III for each additional throwback year.

¶2944

If the beneficiary is a nonresident alien individual or a foreign corporation, see section 667(e) about retaining the character of the amounts distributed to determine the amount of the U.S. withholding tax.

The beneficiary uses Form 4970 to figure the tax on the distribution. The beneficiary also uses Form 4970 for the section 667(b)(6) tax adjustment if an accumulation distribution is subject to estate or generation-skipping transfer tax. This is because the trustee may not be the estate or generation-skipping transfer tax return filer.

Schedule K-1 (Form 1041)— Beneficiary's Share of Income, Deductions, Credits, etc.

General Instructions

Use Schedule K-1 (Form 1041) to report the beneficiary's share of income, deductions, and credits from a trust or a decedent's estate.

 Grantor type trusts do not use Schedule K-1 (Form 1041) to report the income, deductions, or credits of the grantor (or other person treated as owner). See Grantor Type Trusts, *earlier.*

Who Must File

The fiduciary (or one of the joint fiduciaries) must file Schedule K-1. A copy of each beneficiary's Schedule K-1 is attached to the Form 1041 filed with the IRS, and each beneficiary is given a copy of his or her respective Schedule K-1. One copy of each Schedule K-1 must be retained for the fiduciary's records.

Beneficiary's Identifying Number

As a payer of income, you are required to request and provide a proper identifying number for each recipient of income. Enter the beneficiary's number on the respective Schedule K-1 when you file Form 1041. Individuals and business recipients are responsible for giving you their TINs upon request. You may use Form W-9 to request the beneficiary's identifying number.

Penalty. You may be charged a $100 penalty for each failure to provide a required TIN, unless reasonable cause is established for not providing it. Explain any reasonable cause in a signed affidavit and attach it to this return.

Substitute Forms

You do not need IRS approval to use a substitute Schedule K-1 if it is an exact copy of the IRS schedule. The boxes must use the same numbers and titles and must be in the same order and format as on the comparable IRS Schedule K-1. The substitute schedule must include the OMB number and the 6-digit form ID code in the upper right-hand corner of the schedule.

You must provide each beneficiary with the Instructions for Beneficiary Filing Form 1040 or other prepared specific instructions for each item reported on the beneficiary's Schedule K-1.

Inclusion of Amounts in Beneficiaries' Income

Simple trust. The beneficiary of a simple trust must include in his or her gross income the amount of the income required to be distributed currently, whether or not distributed, or if the income required to be distributed currently to all beneficiaries exceeds the DNI, his or her proportionate share of the DNI. The determination of whether trust income is required to be distributed currently depends on the terms of the trust instrument and applicable local law. See Regulations section 1.652(c)-4 for a comprehensive example.

Estates and complex trusts. The beneficiary of a decedent's estate or complex trust must include in his or her gross income the sum of:

1. The amount of the income required to be distributed currently, or if the income required to be distributed currently to all beneficiaries exceeds the DNI (figured without taking into account the charitable deduction), his or her proportionate share of the DNI (as so figured), and

2. All other amounts properly paid, credited, or required to be distributed, or if the sum of the income required to be distributed currently and other amounts properly paid, credited, or required to be distributed to all beneficiaries exceeds the DNI, his or her proportionate share of the excess of DNI over the income required to be distributed currently.

See Regulations section 1.662(c)-4 for a comprehensive example.

For complex trusts that have more than one beneficiary, and if different beneficiaries have substantially separate and independent shares, their shares are treated as separate trusts for

the sole purpose of determining the amount of DNI allocable to the respective beneficiaries. A similar rule applies to treat substantially separate and independent shares of different beneficiaries of an estate as separate estates. For examples of the application of the separate share rule, see the regulations under section 663(c).

Gifts and bequests. Do not include in the beneficiary's income any gifts or bequests of a specific sum of money or of specific property under the terms of the governing instrument that are paid or credited in three installments or less.

Amounts that can be paid or credited only from income of the estate or trust do not qualify as a gift or bequest of a specific sum of money.

Past years. Do not include in the beneficiary's income any amounts deducted on Form 1041 for an earlier year that were credited or required to be distributed in that earlier year.

Character of income. The beneficiary's income is considered to have the same proportion of each class of items entering into the computation of DNI that the total of each class has to the DNI (for example, half dividends and half interest if the income of the estate or trust is half dividends and half interest).

Allocation of deductions. Generally, items of deduction that enter into the computation of DNI are allocated among the items of income to the extent such allocation is not inconsistent with the rules set out in section 469 and its regulations, relating to passive activity loss limitations, in the following order.

First, all deductions directly attributable to a specific class of income are deducted from that income. For example, rental expenses, to the extent allowable, are deducted from rental income.

Second, deductions that are not directly attributable to a specific class of income generally may be allocated to any class of income, as long as a reasonable portion is allocated to any tax-exempt income. Deductions considered not directly attributable to a specific class of income under this rule include fiduciary fees, safe deposit box rental charges, and state income and personal property taxes. The charitable deduction, however, must be ratably apportioned among each class of income included in DNI.

2013 Instructions for Form 1041

¶2944

Finally, any excess deductions that are directly attributable to a class of income may be allocated to another class of income. However, in no case can excess deductions from a passive activity be allocated to income from a nonpassive activity, or to portfolio income earned by the estate or trust. Excess deductions attributable to tax-exempt income cannot offset any other class of income.

In no case can deductions be allocated to an item of income that is not included in the computation of DNI, or attributable to corpus.

You cannot show any negative amounts for any class of income shown in boxes 1 through 8 of Schedule K-1. However, for the final year of the estate or trust, certain deductions or losses can be passed through to the beneficiary(ies). See the instructions for box 11 for more information on these deductions and losses. Also, the beneficiary's share of depreciation and depletion is apportioned separately. These deductions may be allocated to the beneficiary(ies) in amounts greater than his or her income. See *Depreciation, Depletion, and Amortization,* earlier, and Rev. Rul. 74-530, 1974-2 C.B. 188.

Beneficiary's Tax Year

The beneficiary's income from the estate or trust must be included in the beneficiary's tax year during which the tax year of the estate or trust ends. See Pub. 559 for more information, including the effect of the death of a beneficiary during the tax year of the estate or trust.

General Reporting Information

If the return is for a fiscal year or a short tax year, fill in the tax year space at the top of each Schedule K-1. On each Schedule K-1, enter the information about the estate or trust and the beneficiary in Parts I and II (items A through H). In Part III, enter the beneficiary's share of each item of income, deduction, credit, and any other information the beneficiary needs to file his or her income tax return.

Codes. In box 9 and boxes 11 through 14, identify each item by entering a code in the column to the left of the entry space for the dollar amount. These codes are identified in these instructions and on the back of the Schedule K-1.

Attached statements. Enter an asterisk (*) after the code, if any, in the column to the left of the dollar amount

entry space for each item for which you have attached a statement providing additional information. For those informational items that cannot be reported as a single dollar amount, enter the code and asterisk in the left-hand column and enter "STMT" in the entry space to the right to indicate that the information is provided on an attached statement. More than one attached statement can be placed on the same sheet of paper and should be identified in alphanumeric order by box number followed by the letter code (if any). For example: "Box 9, Code A—Depreciation" (followed by the information the beneficiary needs).

Too few entry spaces on Schedule K-1? If the estate or trust has more coded items than the number of spaces in box 9 or boxes 11 through 14, do not enter a code or dollar amount in the last entry space of the box. In the last entry space, enter an asterisk in the left column and enter "STMT" in the entry space to the right. Report the additional items on an attached statement and provide the box number, code, description, and dollar amount or information for each additional item. For example: "Box 13, Code H—Biofuel Producer Credit, $500.00."

Specific Instructions

Part I. Information About the Estate or Trust

On each Schedule K-1, enter the name, address, and identifying number of the estate or trust. Also, enter the name and address of the fiduciary.

Item D

If the fiduciary of a trust or decedent's estate filed Form 1041-T, you must check this box and enter the date it was filed.

Item E

If this is the final year of the estate or trust, you must check this box.

Note. If this is the final K-1 for the beneficiary, check the "Final K-1" box at the top of Schedule K-1.

Part II. Information About the Beneficiary

Complete a Schedule K-1 for each beneficiary. On each Schedule K-1, enter the beneficiary's name, address, and identifying number.

Item H

Check the foreign beneficiary box if the beneficiary is a nonresident alien individual, a foreign corporation, or a foreign estate or trust. Otherwise, check the domestic beneficiary box.

Part III. Beneficiary's Share of Current Year Income, Deductions, Credits, and Other Items

Box 1—Interest

Enter the beneficiary's share of the taxable interest income minus allocable deductions.

Box 2a—Total Ordinary Dividends

Enter the beneficiary's share of ordinary dividends minus allocable deductions.

Box 2b—Total Qualified Dividends

Enter the beneficiary's share of qualified dividends minus allocable deductions.

Box 3—Net Short-Term Capital Gain

Enter the beneficiary's share of the net short-term capital gain from Schedule D (Form 1041), line 17, column (1), minus allocable deductions. Do not enter a loss on line 3. If, for the final year of the estate or trust, there is a capital loss carryover, enter in box 11, code B, the beneficiary's share of short-term capital loss carryover. However, if the beneficiary is a corporation, enter in box 11, code B, the beneficiary's share of all short- and long-term capital loss carryovers as a single item. See section 642(h) and related regulations for more information.

Boxes 4a through 4c—Net Long-Term Capital Gain

Enter the beneficiary's share of the net long-term capital gain from Schedule D (Form 1041), lines 18a through 18c, column (1), minus allocable deductions.

Do not enter a loss in boxes 4a through 4c. If, for the final year of the estate or trust, there is a capital loss carryover, enter in box 11, code C, the beneficiary's share of the long-term capital loss carryover. (If the beneficiary is a corporation, see the instructions for box 3.) See section 642(h) and related regulations for more information.

Gains or losses from the complete or partial disposition of a rental, rental real estate, or trade or business activity that

¶2944

is a passive activity must be shown on an attachment to Schedule K-1.

Box 5—Other Portfolio and Nonbusiness Income

Enter the beneficiary's share of annuities, royalties, or any other income, minus allocable deductions (other than directly apportionable deductions), that is not subject to any passive activity loss limitation rules at the beneficiary level. Use boxes 6 through 8 to report income items subject to the passive activity rules at the beneficiary's level.

Boxes 6 through 8—Ordinary Business Income, Rental Real Estate, and Other Rental Income

Enter the beneficiary's share of trade or business, rental real estate, and other rental income, minus allocable deductions (other than directly apportionable deductions). To assist the beneficiary in figuring any applicable passive activity loss limitations, also attach a separate schedule showing the beneficiary's share of income derived from each trade or business, rental real estate, and other rental activity.

Box 9—Directly Apportioned Deductions

 The limitations on passive activity losses and credits under section 469 apply to estates and trusts. Estates and trusts that distribute income to beneficiaries are allowed to apportion depreciation, depletion, and amortization deductions to the beneficiaries. These deductions are referred to as "directly apportionable deductions."

Rules for treating a beneficiary's income and directly apportionable deductions from an estate or trust and other rules for applying the passive loss and credit limitations to beneficiaries of estates and trusts have not yet been issued.

Any directly apportionable deduction, such as depreciation, is treated by the beneficiary as having been incurred in the same activity as incurred by the estate or trust. However, the character of such deduction may be determined as if the beneficiary incurred the deduction directly.

To assist the beneficiary in figuring any applicable passive activity loss limitations, also attach a separate schedule showing the beneficiary's share of directly apportionable

deductions derived from each trade or business, rental real estate, and other rental activity.

Enter the beneficiary's share of directly apportioned deductions using codes A through C.

Depreciation (code A). Enter the beneficiary's share of the depreciation deductions directly apportioned to each activity reported in boxes 5 through 8. See the instructions under *Deductions*, earlier, for a discussion of how the depreciation deduction is apportioned between the beneficiaries and the estate or trust. Report any AMT adjustment or tax preference item attributable to depreciation separately in box 12, using code G.

Note. An estate or trust cannot make an election under section 179 to expense certain depreciable business assets.

Depletion (code B). Enter the beneficiary's share of the depletion deduction under section 611 directly apportioned to each activity reported in boxes 5 through 8. See *Depreciation, Depletion, and Amortization*, earlier, for a discussion of how the depletion deduction is apportioned between the beneficiaries and the estate or trust. Report any tax preference item attributable to depletion separately in box 12, using code H.

Amortization (code C). Itemize the beneficiary's share of the amortization deductions directly apportioned to each activity reported in boxes 5 through 8. Apportion the amortization deductions between the estate or trust and the beneficiaries in the same way that the depreciation and depletion deductions are divided. Report any AMT adjustment attributable to amortization separately in box 12, using code I.

Box 10—Estate Tax Deduction (Including Certain Generation-Skipping Transfer Taxes)

If the distribution deduction consists of any IRD, and the estate or trust was allowed a deduction under section 691(c) for the estate tax paid attributable to such income (see the line 19 instructions), then the beneficiary is allowed an estate tax deduction in proportion to his or her share of the distribution that consists of such income. For an example of the computation, see Regulations section 1.691(c)-2. Figure the computation on a

separate sheet and attach it to the return.

Box 11, Code A—Excess Deductions on Termination

If this is the final return of the estate or trust, and there are excess deductions on termination (see the instructions for line 22), enter the beneficiary's share of the excess deductions in box 11, using code A. Figure the deductions on a separate sheet and attach it to the return.

Excess deductions on termination occur only during the last tax year of the trust or decedent's estate when the total deductions (excluding the charitable deduction and exemption) are greater than the gross income during that tax year.

Generally, a deduction based on an NOL carryover is not available to a beneficiary as an excess deduction. However, if the last tax year of the estate or trust is also the last year in which an NOL carryover may be taken (see section 172(b)), the NOL carryover is considered an excess deduction on the termination of the estate or trust to the extent it is not absorbed by the estate or trust during its final tax year. For more information, see Regulations section 1.642(h)-4 for a discussion of the allocation of the carryover among the beneficiaries.

Only the beneficiary of an estate or trust that succeeds to its property is allowed to deduct that entity's excess deductions on termination. A beneficiary who does not have enough income in that year to absorb the entire deduction may not carry the balance over to any succeeding year. An individual beneficiary must be able to itemize deductions in order to claim the excess deductions in determining taxable income.

Box 11, Codes B and C—Unused Capital Loss Carryover

Upon termination of the trust or decedent's estate, the beneficiary succeeding to the property is allowed as a deduction any unused capital loss carryover under section 1212. If the estate or trust incurs capital losses in the final year, use the *Capital Loss Carryover Worksheet* in the Instructions for Schedule D (Form 1041) to figure the amount of capital loss carryover to be allocated to the beneficiary.

Box 11, Codes D and E—NOL Carryover

Upon termination of a trust or decedent's estate, a beneficiary succeeding to its property is allowed to deduct any unused NOL (and any ATNOL) carryover for regular and AMT purposes if the carryover would be allowable to the estate or trust in a later tax year but for the termination. Enter in box 11, using codes D and E, the unused carryover amounts.

Box 12—AMT Items

Adjustment for minimum tax purposes (code A). Enter the beneficiary's share of the adjustment for minimum tax purposes.

To figure the adjustment, subtract the beneficiary's share of the *income distribution deduction* figured on Schedule B, line 15, from the beneficiary's share of the *income distribution deduction on a minimum tax basis* figured on Schedule I (Form 1041), line 44. The difference is the beneficiary's share of the adjustment for minimum tax purposes.

Note. Schedule B, line 15 equals the sum of all Schedules K-1, boxes 1, 2a, 3, 4a, 5, 6, 7, and 8.

AMT adjustment attributable to qualified dividends, net short-term capital gains, or net long-term capital gains (codes B through D). If any part of the amount reported in box 12, code A, is attributable to qualified dividends (code B), net short-term capital gain (code C), or net long-term capital gain (code D), enter that part using the applicable code.

AMT adjustment attributable to unrecaptured section 1250 gain or 28% rate gain (codes E and F). Enter the beneficiary's distributive share of any AMT adjustments to the unrecaptured section 1250 gain (code E) or 28% rate gain (code F), whichever is applicable, in box 12.

Accelerated depreciation, depletion, and amortization (codes G through I). Enter any adjustments or tax preference items attributable to depreciation, depletion, or amortization that were directly apportioned to the beneficiary. For property placed in service before 1987, report separately the accelerated depreciation of real and leased personal property.

Exclusion items (code J). Enter the beneficiary's share of the adjustment for minimum tax purposes from

Schedule K-1, box 12, code A, that is attributable to exclusion items (Schedule I (Form 1041), lines 2 through 6 and 8).

Box 13—Credits and Credit Recapture

Enter each beneficiary's share of the credits and credit recapture using the applicable codes. Listed below are the credits that can be allocated to the beneficiary(ies). Attach a statement if additional information must be provided to the beneficiary as explained below.

• Credit for estimated taxes (code A)—Payment of estimated tax to be credited to the beneficiary (section 643(g)).

 See the instructions for line 24b before you make an entry to allocate any estimated tax payments to a beneficiary. If the fiduciary does not make a valid election, then the IRS will disallow the estimated tax payment that is reported on Schedule K-1 and claimed on the beneficiary's return.

• Credit for backup withholding (code B).

 Income tax withheld on wages cannot be distributed to the beneficiary.

• The low-income housing credit (code C). Attach a statement that shows the beneficiary's share of the amount, if any, entered on line 6 of Form 8586, Low-Income Housing Credit, with instructions to report that amount on Form 8586, line 4 or Form 3800, Part III, line 1d, if the beneficiary's only source for the credit is a pass-through entity. Also, show the beneficiary's share of the amount, if any, entered on line 13 of Form 8586 with instructions to report that amount on Form 8586, line 11 or Form 3800, Part III, line 4d, if the beneficiary's only source for the credit is a pass-through entity.
• Rehabilitation credit and energy credit (code D). Attach a statement that shows the beneficiary's apportioned share of basis, expenditures, and other information that is necessary for the beneficiary to complete Form 3468, Investment Credit, for the rehabilitation credit and the energy credit. See the Instructions for Form 3468 for more information.
• Other qualifying investment credit (code E). Attach a statement that shows the beneficiary's apportioned share of qualified investment and other

information that is necessary for the beneficiary to complete Form 3468 for the qualifying advanced coal project credit, qualifying gasification project credit, and qualifying advanced energy project credit. See the Instructions for Form 3468 for more information.
• Work opportunity credit (code F).
• Credit for small employer health insurance premiums (code G).
• Biofuel producer credit (code H). See the instructions for Form 6478, Biofuel Producer Credit, for more information.
• Credit for increasing research activities (code I).
• Renewable electricity, refined coal, and Indian coal production credit (code J). Attach a statement that shows the amount of the credit the beneficiary must report on line 9 and line 29 of Form 8835, in case the beneficiary is required to file that form in addition to Form 3800.
• Empowerment zone and renewal community employment credit (code K).
• Indian employment credit (code L).
• Orphan drug credit (code M).
• Credit for employer provided child care and facilities (code N).
• Biodiesel and renewable diesel fuels credit (code O). If the credit includes the small agri-biodiesel credit, attach a statement that shows the beneficiary's share of the small agri-biodiesel credit, the number of gallons claimed for the small agri-biodiesel credit, and the estate's or trust's productive capacity for agri-biodiesel.
• Nonconventional source fuel credit (code P).
• Credit to holders of tax credit bonds (code Q).
• Agricultural chemicals security credit (code R).
• Energy efficient appliance credit (code S).
• Credit for employer differential wage payments (code T).
• Recapture of credits (code U). On an attached statement to Schedule K-1, provide any information the beneficiary will need to report recapture of credits.

Box 14—Other Information

Enter the dollar amounts and applicable codes for the items listed under Other Information.

Foreign taxes (code B). Enter the beneficiary's allocable share of taxes paid or accrued to a foreign country. Attach a statement reporting the beneficiary's share of foreign tax (paid or accrued) and income by category including interest, dividends, rents and royalties, and other income. See Form

¶2944

1116 and Pub. 514 for more information.

Domestic production activities information. The estate or trust allocates QPAI (whether positive or negative) and Form W-2 wages based on the relative proportion of the estate's or trust's DNI that is distributed or required to be distributed to the beneficiary. If the estate or trust has no DNI for the tax year, QPAI and Form W-2 wages are allocated entirely to the estate or trust.

Qualified production activities income (code C). Enter the beneficiary's share, if any, of the estate's or trust's QPAI from all activities. The QPAI will be less than zero if the cost of goods sold and deductions allocated and apportioned to domestic production gross receipts (DPGR) is more than the estate's or trust's DPGR. If any of the QPAI is oil-related QPAI, attach a statement that shows the amount of oil-related QPAI. See Form 8903, Domestic Production Activities Deduction, and its instructions for more details.

Form W-2 wages (code D). Use code D to report the beneficiary's share, if any, of Form W-2 wages. Do not enter more than 9% of the beneficiary's share, if any, of the estate's or trust's QPAI. See Form 8903 and its instructions for more details.

Foreign trading gross receipts (code G). Enter the beneficiary's share, if any, of foreign trading gross receipts. See Form 8873, Extraterritorial Income Exclusion, for more information.

Net investment income tax (code H). Use code H to identify the amount of the beneficiary's adjustment for section 1411 net investment income or deductions. See the Instructions for Form 8960. An attachment may be provided with the K-1 informing the beneficiary of the detailed items to be reported on Form 1040. See *Net Investment Income Tax,* earlier, for more information on these amounts.

Other information (code I). List on a separate sheet the tax information the beneficiary will need to complete his or her return that is not entered elsewhere on Schedule K-1.

For example, if the estate or trust participates in a transaction that must be disclosed on Form 8886 (see earlier), both the estate or trust and its beneficiaries may be required to file Form 8886. The estate or trust must determine if any of its beneficiaries are required to disclose the transaction and provide those beneficiaries with information they will need to file Form 8886. This determination is based on the category(ies) under which a transaction qualified for disclosure. See the Instructions for Form 8886 for details.

In addition, if the beneficiary is a "covered person" in connection with a foreign tax credit splitter arrangement under section 909, attach a statement that identifies the arrangement including the foreign taxes paid or accrued.

¶2944

Paperwork Reduction Act Notice. We ask for the information on this form to carry out the Internal Revenue laws of the United States. You are required to give us the information. We need it to ensure that you are complying with these laws and to allow us to figure and collect the right amount of tax.

You are not required to provide the information requested on a form that is subject to the Paperwork Reduction Act unless the form displays a valid OMB control number. Books or records relating to a form or its instructions must be retained as long as their contents may become material in the administration of any Internal Revenue law. Generally, tax returns and return information are confidential, as required by Code section 6103.

The time needed to complete and file this form and related schedules will vary depending on individual circumstances. The estimated average times are:

	Form 1041	Schedule D	Schedule I	Schedule J	Schedule K-1	Form 1041-V
Recordkeeping	38 hr., 58 min.	26 hr., 33 min.	17 hr., 42 min.	11 hr., 00 min.	6 hr., 27 min.	43 min.
Learning about the law or the form	16 hr., 11 min.	4 hr., 5 min.	4 hr., 22 min.	1 hr., 27 min.	35 min.	- - - -
Preparing the form	30 hr., 34 min.	5 hr., 37 min.	4 hr., 51 min.	2 hr., 37 min.	43 min.	- - - -
Copying, assembling, and sending the form to the IRS	3 hr., 45 min.	51 min.	- - - -	16 min.	- - - -	- - - -

If you have comments concerning the accuracy of these time estimates or suggestions for making this form and related schedules simpler, we would be happy to hear from you. You can send your comments to Internal Revenue Service, Tax Forms and Publications Division,1111 Constitution Ave. NW, IR-6526, Washington, DC 20224. Do not send the tax form to this address. Instead, see *Where To File*, earlier.

¶2944

Index

¶2944

20**13**

Department of the Treasury
Internal Revenue Service

Instructions for Schedule D (Form 1041)

Capital Gains and Losses

Section references are to the Internal Revenue Code unless otherwise noted.

Future Developments

For the latest information about developments related to Schedule D and its instructions, such as legislation enacted after they were published, go to *www.irs.gov/form1041*.

What's New

Form 8949. The use of Form 8949 by estates and trusts is new for tax year 2013. Many transactions that, in previous years, would have been reported on Schedule D (Form 1041) or Schedule D-1 (Form 1041) must now be reported on Form 8949, Sales and Other Dispositions of Capital Assets. Certain transactions may be combined and the totals reported on line 1a or 8a of Schedule D (Form 1041) without completing Form 8949. For additional information, see the instructions for *Lines 1a and 8a—Transactions Not Reported on Form 8949*, later. Filers that use Form 8949 must complete Form 8949 before completing line 1b, 2, 3, 8b, 9, or 10 of Schedule D (Form 1041).

Note. Beginning in tax year 2013, Schedule D-1 will no longer be used.

Capital gains and qualified dividends. Beginning in 2013, the maximum rate for long-term capital gains and qualified dividends is 20%, as amended by the American Taxpayer Relief Act of 2012 (ATRA), P.L. 112–240. For 2013, the 20% rate applies to estates and trusts with income above $11,950. The 0% and 15% rates continue to apply to certain threshold amounts.

E-filing. For tax year 2013, Forms 1041 can be e-filed through the Legacy Electronic Management System (EMS) or through Modernized e-File (MeF). Form 8453-F, U.S. Estate or Trust Income Tax Declaration and Signature for Electronic Filing, will be used for EMS e-filed returns and new Form 8453-FE, U.S. Estate or Trust Declaration for an IRS e-file Return, will be used for MeF e-filing.

For returns e-filed through MeF. If Form 1041 is e-filed through MeF, then Schedule D must also be e-filed through MeF. Additionally, all Forms 8949 must be e-filed with the 1041 MeF return.

For more information about e-filing returns through MeF, see Publication 4164, Modernized e-File (MeF) Guide for Software Developers And Transmitters, Processing Year 2014.

For returns e-filed through Legacy EMS. If Form 1041 is e-filed through Legacy EMS, then Schedule D must also be e-filed with Form 1041. Form 8949 cannot be e-filed with a Form 1041 filed via the Legacy system. If applicable, Form 8949 must be submitted as an attachment to Form 8453-F, which can be used as a transmittal document.

For more information about e-filing returns through Legacy EMS, see Publication 1437, Procedures for the Form 1041 *e-file* Program, U.S. Income Tax Returns for Estates and Trusts for Tax Year 2013.

General Instructions

Note. Any reference in these instructions to "you" means the fiduciary of the estate or trust.

Purpose of Schedule

These instructions explain how to complete Schedule D (Form 1041). Complete Form 8949 before you complete line 1b, 2, 3, 8b, 9, or 10 of Schedule D.

Use Schedule D to report the following.

• The overall capital gains and losses from transactions reported on Form 8949.

• Certain transactions that the estate or trust does not have to report on Form 8949.

• Gain from Part I of Form 4797, Sales of Business Property.

• Capital gain or loss from Form 4684, Casualties and Thefts.

• Capital gain from Form 6252, Installment Sale Income.

• Capital gain or loss from Form 6781, Gains and Losses From Section 1256 Contracts and Straddles.

• Capital gain or loss from Form 8824, Like-Kind Exchanges.

• Undistributed long-term capital gains from Form 2439.

• Capital gain or loss from partnerships, S corporations, or other estates or trusts.

Note. For more information, see Pub. 544, Sales and Other Dispositions of Assets, and Instructions for Form 8949.

Other Forms You May Have To File

Use Form 8949 to report the sale or exchange of a capital asset (defined later) not reported on another form or schedule. Complete all necessary pages of Form 8949 before you complete line 1b, 2, 3, 8b, 9, or 10 of Schedule D (Form 1041). See *Lines 1a and 8a*, later, for more information about when Form 8949 is needed and when it is not.

Use Form 4797, Sales of Business Property, to report the following.

1. The sale or exchange of:

a. Property used in a trade or business;

b. Depreciable and amortizable property;

c. Oil, gas, geothermal, or other mineral property; and

d. Section 126 property.

2. The involuntary conversion (other than from casualty or theft) of property used in a trade or business and capital assets held for business or profit.

3. The disposition of noncapital assets other than inventory or property held primarily for sale to customers in the ordinary course of a trade or business.

4. Ordinary loss on the sale, exchange, or worthlessness of small business investment company (section 1242) stock.

5. Ordinary loss on the sale, exchange, or worthlessness of small business (section 1244) stock.

Jan 15, 2014

Cat. No. 11378R

Use Form 4684, Casualties and Thefts, to report involuntary conversions of property due to casualty or theft.

Use Form 6781, Gains and Losses From Section 1256 Contracts and Straddles, to report gains and losses from section 1256 contracts and straddles.

Use Form 8824, Like-Kind Exchanges, if the estate or trust made one or more *like-kind* exchanges. A like-kind exchange occurs when the estate or trust exchanges business or investment property for property of a like kind.

Special Rules for Determining Basis of Estate and Trust Property

Basis of trust property. Generally, the basis of property acquired by gift is the same as its basis in the hands of the donor. However, if the FMV of the property at the time it was transferred to the trust is less than the transferor's basis, then the FMV is used to determine any loss upon disposition.

If the property was transferred to the trust after 1976, and a gift tax was paid under Chapter 12, then increase the donor's basis as follows:

Multiply the amount of the gift tax paid by a fraction, the numerator of which is the net appreciation in value of the gift (defined below), and the denominator of which is the amount of the gift. For this purpose, the net appreciation in value of the gift is the amount by which the FMV of the gift exceeds the donor's adjusted basis.

Basis of decedent's estate property. Generally, the basis of property acquired by a decedent's estate is the FMV of the property at the date of the decedent's death, or the alternate valuation date if the executor elected to use an alternate valuation under section 2032.

See Pub. 551 and the Instructions for Form 706 for a discussion of the valuation of qualified real property under section 2032A.

Basis of property acquired from a decedent who died in 2010. See Pub. 4895, Tax Treatment of Property Acquired From a Decedent Dying in 2010, for details about determining the basis of property acquired from a decedent who died in 2010.

Basis of assets held on January 1, 2001, where an election to recognize gain was made. If you elected on behalf of an estate or trust to recognize gain on an asset held on January 1, 2001, the basis in the asset is its closing market price or FMV, whichever applies, on the date of the deemed sale and reacquisition, whether the deemed sale resulted in a gain or an unallowed loss.

Carryover basis. Carryover basis determined under repealed section 1023 applies to property acquired from a decedent who died after December 31, 1976, and before November 7, 1978, only if the executor made a timely filed election on Form 5970-A, Election of Carryover Basis.

Capital Asset

Each item of property held by the estate or trust (whether or not connected with a trade or business) is a capital asset, *except* the following:
* Stock in trade, inventory or property held primarily for sale to customers.
* Depreciable or real property used in a trade or business, even if it is fully depreciated.
* Copyrights; literary, musical, or artistic compositions; letters or memoranda; or similar property eligible for copyright protection that the trust received from someone whose personal efforts created them or for whom they were created in a way (such as by gift) that entitled the trust to the basis of the previous owner. In the case of letters, memoranda, or similar property, such property may also be prepared or produced for the trust.

Note. Under section 1221(b)(3), the trust can elect to treat musical compositions and copyrights in musical works as capital assets if it acquired the assets under circumstances entitling it to the basis of the person who created the property or for whom it was prepared or produced.
* Accounts or notes receivable acquired in the ordinary course of a trade or business for services rendered or from the sale of inventoriable assets or property held primarily for sale to customers.
* Certain U.S. Government publications not purchased at the public sale price.
* Certain "commodities derivative financial instruments" held by a dealer (see section 1221(a)(6)).
* Certain hedging transactions entered into in the normal course of a trade or business (see section 1221(a)(7)).
* Supplies regularly used in a trade or business.

You may find additional helpful information in the following publications.

* Pub. 544, Sales and Other Dispositions of Assets.
* Pub. 551, Basis of Assets.

Short-Term or Long-Term

Separate the capital gains and losses according to how long the estate or trust held or owned the property. The holding period for short-term capital gains and losses is 1 year or less. The holding period for long-term capital gains and losses is more than 1 year. Property acquired from a decedent is treated as held for more than 1 year.

Note. Long-term treatment may not apply to property acquired from a decedent who died in 2010 where the estate elected the use of carryover basis if the property was held less than 1 year. See Pub. 4895 for details.

To figure the length of the period the estate or trust held property, begin counting on the day after the estate or trust acquired the property and include the day it was disposed. Use the trade dates for the dates of acquisition and sale of stocks and bonds traded on an exchange or over-the-counter market.

Section 643(e)(3) Election

For in-kind noncash property distributions, a fiduciary may elect to have the estate or trust recognize gain or loss in the same manner as if the distributed property had been sold to the beneficiary at its fair market value (FMV). The distribution deduction is the property's FMV. This election applies to all distributions made by the estate or trust during the tax year. Once the election is made, it may only be revoked with IRS consent.

Note. Section 267 does not allow a trust or a decedent's estate to claim a deduction for any loss on property to which a section 643(e)(3) election applies. In addition, when a trust or a decedent's estate distributes depreciable property, section 1239 applies to deny capital gains treatment for any gain on property to which a section 643(e)(3) election applies.

Related Persons

A trust cannot deduct a loss from the sale or exchange of property directly or indirectly between any of the following:
* A grantor and a fiduciary of a trust,
* A fiduciary and a fiduciary or beneficiary of another trust created by the same grantor,
* A fiduciary and a beneficiary of the same trust,

¶2944

• A trust fiduciary and a corporation of which more than 50% in value of the outstanding stock is owned directly or indirectly by or for the trust or by or for the grantor of the trust, or

• An executor of an estate and a beneficiary of that estate, except when the sale or exchange is to satisfy a pecuniary bequest (that is, a bequest of a sum of money).

Items for Special Treatment

• Bonds and other debt instruments. See Pub. 550, Investment Income and Expenses.

• A nonbusiness bad debt must be treated as a short-term capital loss and can be deducted only in the year the debt becomes totally worthless. See Pub. 550 for details.

• Wash sales of stock or securities (including contracts or options to acquire or sell stock or securities) (section 1091).

• Gain or loss on options to buy or sell. See Pub. 550.

• Certain real estate subdivided for sale that may be considered a capital asset (section 1237).

• Gain on disposition of stock in an interest charge domestic international sales corporation (DISC) (section 995(c)).

• Gain on the sale or exchange of stock in certain foreign corporations (section 1248).

• Sales of stock received under a qualified public utility dividend reinvestment plan. See Pub. 550 for details.

• Transfer of appreciated property to a political organization (section 84).

• Amounts received by shareholders in corporate liquidations. See Pub. 550.

• Cash received in lieu of fractional shares of stock as a result of a stock split or stock dividend. See Pub. 550.

• Load charges to acquire stock in a regulated investment company (including a mutual fund), which may not be taken into account in determining gain or loss on certain dispositions of the stock if reinvestment rights were exercised. See Pub. 550.

• The sale or exchange of S corporation stock or an interest in a trust held for more than 1 year, which may result in collectibles gain (28% rate gain). See the instructions for line 18c.

• The sale or other disposition of a partnership interest may result in ordinary income, collectibles gain, or unrecaptured section 1250 gain.

• Gain or loss on the disposition of securities futures contracts. See Pub. 550.

• Gains from certain constructive ownership transactions. Gain in excess of the gain the estate or trust would have recognized if the estate or trust held a financial asset directly during the term of a derivative contract must be treated as ordinary income. See section 1260 for details.

• If qualified dividends include extraordinary dividends, any loss on the sale or exchange of the stock is a long-term capital loss to the extent of the extraordinary dividends. An extraordinary dividend is a dividend that is at least 10% (5% in the case of preferred stock) of the basis in the stock.

Constructive Sales Treatment for Certain Appreciated Positions

Generally, the estate or trust must recognize gain (but not loss) on the date it enters into a constructive sale of any appreciated position in stock, a partnership interest, or certain debt instruments as if the position were disposed of at FMV on that date.

The estate or trust is treated as making a constructive sale of an appreciated position when it (or a related person, in some cases) does one of the following:

• Enters into a short sale of the same or substantially identical property (that is, a "short sale against the box"),

• Enters into an offsetting notional principal contract relating to the same or substantially identical property,

• Enters into a futures or forward contract to deliver the same or substantially identical property, or

• Acquires the same or substantially identical property (if the appreciated position is a short sale, offsetting notional principal contract, or a futures or forward contract).

Exception. Generally, constructive sale treatment does not apply if:

• The estate or trust closed the transaction before the end of the 30th day after the end of the year in which it was entered into,

• The estate or trust held the appreciated position to which the transaction relates throughout the 60-day period starting on the date the transaction was closed, and

• At no time during that 60-day period was the estate's or trust's risk of loss reduced by holding certain other positions.

For details and other exceptions to these rules, see Pub. 550.

Exclusion of Gain on Qualified Small Business (QSB) Stock (Section 1202)

Section 1202 provides for an exclusion of 50% of the eligible gain on the sale or exchange of QSB stock. This exclusion can be up to 60% for certain empowerment zone business stock. The section 1202 exclusion applies only to QSB stock held for more than 5 years.

To be QSB stock, the stock must meet all of the following tests:

1. It must be stock in a C corporation (that is, not S corporation stock).

2. It must have been originally issued after August 10, 1993.

3. As of the date the stock was issued, the corporation was a QSB. A QSB is a domestic C corporation with total gross assets of $50 million or less (a) at all times after August 9, 1993, and before the stock was issued, and (b) immediately after the stock was issued. Gross assets include those of any predecessor of the corporation. All corporations that are members of the same parent-subsidiary controlled group are treated as one corporation.

4. The estate or trust acquired the stock at its original issue (either directly or through an underwriter), either in exchange for money or other property or as pay for services (other than as an underwriter) to the corporation. In certain cases, the estate or trust may meet the test if it acquired the stock from another person who met this test (such as by gift or inheritance) or through a conversion or exchange of QSB stock the estate or trust held.

5. During substantially all the time the estate or trust held the stock:

a. The corporation was a C corporation,

b. At least 80% of the value of the corporation's assets was used in the active conduct of one or more qualified businesses (defined below), and

c. The corporation was not a foreign corporation, DISC, former DISC, corporation that has made (or that has a subsidiary that has made) a section 936 election, regulated investment company, real estate investment trust, REMIC, FASIT, or cooperative.

Note. A specialized small business investment company (SSBIC) is treated as having met test 5b above.

¶2944

Qualified business. A qualified business is any business other than the following:

• One involving services performed in the fields of health, law, engineering, architecture, accounting, actuarial science, performing arts, consulting, athletics, financial services, or brokerage services;

• One whose principal asset is the reputation or skill of one or more employees;

• Any banking, insurance, financing, leasing, investing, or similar business;

• Any farming business (including the raising or harvesting of trees);

• Any business involving the production of products for which percentage depletion can be claimed; or

• Any business of operating a hotel, motel, restaurant, or similar business.

For more details about limits and additional requirements that may apply, see Pub. 550 or section 1202.

Empowerment zone business stock. Generally, the estate or trust can exclude up to 60% of its gain on certain QSB stock if it meets the following additional requirements.

1. The stock sold or exchanged was stock in a corporation that qualified as an empowerment zone business during substantially all of the time the estate or trust held the stock.

2. The estate or trust acquired the stock after December 21, 2000.

Requirement 1 will still be met if the corporation ceased to qualify after the 5-year period that began on the date the estate or trust acquired the stock. However, the gain that qualifies for the 60% exclusion cannot be more than the gain the estate or trust would have had if it had sold the stock on the date the corporation ceased to qualify.

See section 1397C for more details.

Pass-through entities. If the estate or trust held an interest in a pass-through entity (a partnership, S corporation, mutual fund, or other regulated investment company) that sold QSB stock, the estate or trust generally must have held the interest on the date the pass-through entity acquired the QSB stock and at all times thereafter until the stock was sold to qualify for the exclusion.

How to report. Report the sale or exchange of QSB stock on Form 8949, Part II, with the appropriate box checked, as it would be reported if the exclusion was not taken. Then enter "Q" in column (f) and enter the amount of

the excluded gain as a negative number in column (g). Put it in parentheses to show it is negative. Complete all remaining columns. See the Instructions for Form 8949, columns (f), (g), and (h). On line 2 of the *28% Rate Gain Worksheet*, include an amount equal to the 50% exclusion (⅔ of the exclusion if a 60% exclusion was claimed). Also, see the Instructions for Schedule I (Form 1041), line 9, for information on the amount of the exclusion to include on Schedule I (Form 1041).

Gain from Form 1099-DIV. If the estate or trust received a Form 1099-DIV, Dividends and Distributions, with a gain in box 2c, part or all of that gain (which is also included in box 2a) may be eligible for the section 1202 exclusion. In column (a) of Form 8949, Part II, enter the name of the corporation whose stock was sold. In column (f), enter "Q" and in column (g) enter the amount of the excluded gain as a negative number. See the Instructions for Form 8949, columns (f), (g), and (h). Also, include the amount of the 50% exclusion as a gain on line 2 of the *28% Rate Gain Worksheet* (include ⅔ of the exclusion if a 60% exclusion was claimed).

Gain from Form 2439. If the estate or trust received a Form 2439, Notice to Shareholder of Undistributed Long-Term Capital Gains, with a gain in box 1c, part or all of that gain (which is also included in box 1a) may be eligible for the section 1202 exclusion. In column (a) of Form 8949, Part II, enter the name of the corporation whose stock was sold. In column (f), enter "Q" and in column (g) enter the amount of the excluded gain as a negative number. See the Instructions for Form 8949, columns (f), (g), and (h). Also, include the amount of the 50% exclusion as a gain on line 2 of the *28% Rate Gain Worksheet* (include ⅔ of the exclusion if a 60% exclusion was claimed).

Gain from an installment sale of QSB stock. If all payments are not received in the year of sale, a sale of QSB stock that is not traded on an established securities market generally is treated as an installment sale and is reported on Form 6252, Installment Sale Income. Part or all of any gain from the sale that is reported on Form 6252 for the current year may be eligible for the section 1202 exclusion. In column (a) of Form 8949, Part II, enter the name of the corporation whose stock was sold. In column (f), enter "Q" and in column (g) enter the amount of the allowable

exclusion as a negative number. See the Instructions for Form 8949, columns (f), (g), and (h). Also, include the amount of the 50% exclusion as a gain on line 2 of the *28% Rate Gain Worksheet* (include ⅔ of the exclusion if a 60% exclusion was claimed).

Alternative minimum tax. You must enter 7% of the estate's or trust's allowable exclusion for the year on line 9 of Schedule I (Form 1041).

Rollover of gain from QSB stock. If the estate or trust held QSB stock (as defined earlier) for more than 6 months, it may elect to postpone gain if it purchased other QSB stock during the 60-day period that began on the date of the sale.

The estate or trust must recognize gain to the extent the sale proceeds exceed the cost of the replacement stock. Reduce the basis of the replacement stock by any postponed gain.

The estate or trust must make the election no later than the due date (including extensions) for filing Form 1041 for the tax year in which the stock was sold. If the original Form 1041 was filed on time, the election may be made on an amended return filed no later than 6 months after the due date of the original return (excluding extensions). Write "Filed pursuant to section 301.9100-2" at the top of the amended return, and file it at the same address used for the original Form 1041.

How to report. To make the election, report the sale on Part I or Part II of Form 8949 (depending on how long the estate or trust owned the stock), as it would be reported if the election was not made. Then enter "R" in column (f) and the amount of the postponed gain from the section 1045 rollover as a negative number in column (g). Complete all remaining columns. See the Instructions for Form 8949, columns (f), (g), and (h).

Rollover of Gain From Publicly Traded Securities. The estate or trust may elect to postpone gain from the sale of publicly traded securities by purchasing common stock or a partnership interest in a specialized small business investment company during the 60-day period that began on the date of the sale. See Pub. 550.

How to report. To make the election to postpone gain, report the sale in Part I or Part II of Form 8949 (depending on how long the estate or trust owned the stock), as it would be reported if the election was not made. Then enter "R" in column (f). Enter the amount of the postponed gain as a negative number in column (g). Put the amount in column (g) in parentheses to show it is negative. Complete all remaining columns. See the Instructions for Form 8949, columns (f), (g), and (h).

Exclusion of gain from DC Zone assets or qualified community assets. If the estate or trust sold or exchanged a District of Columbia Enterprise Zone asset or a qualified community asset that it held for more than 5 years, it may be able to exclude the amount of qualified capital gain that it would otherwise include in income. The exclusion of gain from DC Zone assets applies to an interest in, or property of, certain businesses operating in the District of Columbia. See section 1400B for more details on this exclusion. The exclusion of gain from qualified community assets applies to an interest in, or property of, certain renewal community businesses. See section 1400F for more details on this exclusion.

How to report. Report the sale or exchange of a "DC Zone asset" or "qualified community asset" on Form 8949, Part II, with the appropriate box checked, as it would be reported if the exclusion was not taken. Enter "X" in column (f) and the amount of the allowable exclusion as a negative number in column (g). Put the amount in column (g) in parentheses to show it is negative. Complete all remaining columns. See the Instructions for Form 8949, columns (f), (g), and (h).

Specific Instructions

 The instructions below assume the estate or trust is a cash basis calendar year taxpayer.

Rounding Off Whole Dollars

You can round off cents to whole dollars on your Schedule D (Form 1041). If you do round to whole dollars, you must round all amounts. To round, drop amounts under 50 cents and increase amounts from 50 to 99 cents to the next dollar. For example, $1.39 becomes $1 and $2.50 becomes $3.

If you have to add two or more amounts to figure the amount to enter on a line, include cents when adding the amounts and round off only the total.

Lines 1a and 8a—Transactions Not Reported on Form 8949

The estate or trust can report on line 1a (for short-term transactions) or line 8a (for long-term transactions) the aggregate totals from any transactions (except sales of collectibles) for which:

• The estate or trust received a Form 1099-B (or substitute statement) that shows basis was reported to the IRS and does not show a nondeductible wash sale loss in box 5, and

• The estate or trust does not need to make any adjustments to the basis or type of gain or loss (short term or long term) reported on Form 1099-B (or substitute statement), or to its gain or loss.

See *How To Complete Form 8949, Columns (f) and (g),* in the Form 8949 instructions for details about possible adjustments to your gain or loss.

If the estate or trust chooses to report these transactions on lines 1a and 8a, do not report them on Form 8949. You do not need to attach a statement to explain the entries on lines 1a and 8a.

Figure gain or loss on each line. First, subtract the cost or other basis in column (e) from the proceeds (sales price) in column (d). Enter the gain or loss in column (h). Enter negative amounts in parentheses.

Example 1 – basis reported to the IRS. The estate or trust received a Form 1099-B reporting the sale of stock held for 3 years. It shows proceeds (in box 2a) of $6,000 and cost or other basis (in box 3) of $2,000. Box 6b is checked, meaning that basis was reported to the IRS. The estate or trust does not need to make any adjustments to the amounts reported on Form 1099-B or enter any codes. This was the estate or trust's only 2013 transaction. Instead of reporting this transaction on Form 8949, the estate or trust can enter $6,000 on Schedule D, line 8a, column (d), $2,000 in column (e), and $4,000 ($6,000–$2,000) in column (h).

Example 2 – basis not reported to the IRS. The estate or trust received a Form 1099-B showing proceeds (in box 2a) of $6,000 and cost or other basis (in box 3) of $2,000. Box 6b is not checked, meaning that basis was not reported to the IRS. Do not report this transaction on line 1a or line 8a. Instead, report the transaction on Form 8949. Complete all necessary pages of Form 8949 before completing line 1b, 2, 3, 8b, 9, or 10 of Schedule D (Form 1041).

Example 3 – adjustment. The estate or trust received a Form 1099-B showing proceeds (in box 2a) of $6,000 and cost or other basis (in box 3) of $2,000. Box 6b is checked, meaning that basis was reported to the IRS. However, the basis shown in box 3 is incorrect. Do not report this transaction on line 1a or line 8a. Instead, report the transaction on Form 8949. See the instructions for Form 8949, columns (f), (g), and (h). Complete all necessary pages of Form 8949 before completing line 1b, 2, 3, 8b, 9, or 10 of Schedule D (Form 1041).

Lines 1b, 2, 3, 8b, 9, and 10, Column (h)—Transactions Reported on Form 8949

Figure gain or loss on each line. First, subtract the cost or other basis in column (e) from the proceeds (sales price) in column (d). Then combine the result with any adjustments in column (g). Enter the gain or loss in column (h). Enter negative amounts in parentheses.

Example 1 – gain. Column (d) is $6,000 and column (e) is $2,000. Enter $4,000 in column (h).

Example 2 – loss. Column (d) is $6,000 and column (e) is $8,000. Enter ($2,000) in column (h).

Example 3 – adjustment. Column (d) is $6,000, column (e) is $2,000, and column (g) is ($1,000). Enter $3,000 ($6,000 – $2,000 – $1,000) in column (h).

Lines 4 and 11

Undistributed capital gains. Include on line 11, column (h), the amount from box 1a of Form 2439. This amount represents the estate's or trust's share of undistributed long-term capital gains from a regulated investment company (mutual fund) or real estate investment trust.

If there is an amount in box 1b of Form 2439, include that amount on line 11 of the *Unrecaptured Section 1250 Gain Worksheet,* later, if you are required to complete line 18b, column (2) of the schedule. If there is an amount in box 1c of Form 2439, see *Exclusion of Gain on Qualified Small Business (QSB) Stock (Section 1202),* earlier. If there is an amount in box 1d of Form 2439, include that amount on line 4 of the *28% Rate Gain Worksheet.*

Enter on Form 1041, line 24f the tax paid as reported in box 2 of Form 2439. Increase the basis of the stock by the excess of the amount included in income over the amount of the credit for tax paid. See Pub. 550 for more details.

¶2944

Installment sales. If the estate or trust sold property (other than publicly traded stocks or securities) at a gain during the tax year and will receive a payment in a later tax year, you generally report the sale on the installment method and file Form 6252, unless you elect not to do so.

Also, use Form 6252 to report any payment received in 2013 from a sale made in an earlier tax year that was reported on the installment method.

To elect out of the installment method, report the full amount of the gain on Form 8949 on a timely filed return (including extensions) for the year of the sale. If the original return was filed timely, the election may be made on an amended return filed no later than 6 months after the due date of the original return (*excluding* extensions). Write "Filed pursuant to section 301.9100-2" at the top of the amended return, and file it at the same address as the original Form 1041.

Exchange of "like-kind" property. Generally, no gain or loss is recognized when property held for productive use in a trade or business or for investment is exchanged solely for property of a like kind to be held either for productive use in a trade or business or for investment. However, if a trust exchanges like-kind property with a related person (see *Related Persons*, earlier) and within 2 years of the last transfer that was part of the exchange, the related person disposes of the property, or the trust disposes of the property received in exchange from the related person, then the original exchange will not qualify for nonrecognition. See section 1031(f) for exceptions.

Complete and attach Form 8824, Like-Kind Exchanges, to Form 1041 for each exchange.

Line 13—Capital Gain Distributions

Enter as a long-term capital gain on line 13, column (h), the total capital gain distributions paid during the year, regardless of how long the estate or trust held its investment. This amount is reported in box 2a of Form 1099-DIV. If there is an amount in box 2b, include that amount on line 11 of the *Unrecaptured Section 1250 Gain Worksheet*, later, if the worksheet is required. If there is an amount in box 2c, see *Exclusion of Gain on Qualified Small Business (QSB) Stock (Section 1202)*, earlier. If there is an amount in box 2d of Form 1099-DIV, include the amount on line 4 of the *28% Rate Gain Worksheet*.

Line 17, Column (1)—Beneficiaries' Net Short-Term Capital Gain or Loss

Enter the amount of net short-term capital gain or loss allocable to the beneficiary or beneficiaries. Include only those short-term capital losses that are taken into account in determining the amount of gain from the sale or exchange of capital assets that is paid, credited, or required to be distributed to any beneficiary during the tax year. See Regulations section 1.643(a)-3 for more information about allocation of capital gains and losses.

If the losses from the sale or exchange of capital assets are more than the gains, the net loss must be allocated to the estate or trust and not to the beneficiaries.

Line 17, Column (2)—Estate's or Trust's Net Short-Term Capital Gain or Loss

Enter the amount of the net short-term capital gain or loss allocable to the estate or trust. Include any capital gain paid or permanently set aside for a charitable purpose specified in section 642(c).

Line 17, Column (3)—Total

Enter the total of the amounts entered in columns (1) and (2). The amount in column (3) should be the same as the amount on line 7.

Line 18a—Net Long-Term Capital Gain or Loss

Allocate the net long-term capital gain or loss on line 18a in the same manner as the net short-term capital gain or loss on line 17. However, do not take the section 1202 exclusion on gain from the sale or exchange of qualified small business stock into account when figuring net long-term capital gain or loss allocable to the beneficiaries.

Line 18b—Unrecaptured Section 1250 Gain

Complete the *Unrecaptured Section 1250 Gain Worksheet*, later, if any of the following apply.
- During the tax year, the estate or trust sold or otherwise disposed of section 1250 property (generally, real property that was depreciated) held more than 1 year.
- The estate or trust received installment payments during the tax year for section 1250 property held more than 1 year and is reporting gain on the installment method.
- The estate or trust received a Schedule K-1 from an estate or trust, partnership, or S corporation that reports "unrecaptured section 1250 gain" for the tax year.
- The estate or trust received a Form 1099-DIV or Form 2439 from a real estate investment trust or regulated investment company (including a mutual fund) that reports "unrecaptured section 1250 gain" for the tax year.
- The estate or trust reported a long-term capital gain from the sale or exchange of an interest in a partnership that owned section 1250 property.

Instructions for the Unrecaptured Section 1250 Gain Worksheet

Lines 1 through 3. If the estate or trust had more than one property, complete lines 1 through 3 for each property on a separate worksheet. Next, enter the total amount for all properties on line 3, then go to line 4.

Line 4. To figure the amount to enter on line 4, follow the steps below for each installment sale of trade or business property held more than 1 year.

Step 1. Figure the smaller of (a) the depreciation allowed or allowable or (b) the total gain for the sale. This is the smaller of line 22 or line 24 of the 2013 Form 4797 (or the comparable lines of Form 4797 for the year of sale) for that property.

Step 2. Reduce the amount figured in step 1 by any section 1250 ordinary income recapture for the sale. This is the amount from line 26g of the 2013 Form 4797 (or the comparable line of Form 4797 for the year of sale) for that property. The result is the total unrecaptured section 1250 gain that must be allocated to the installment payments received from the sale.

Step 3. Generally, the amount of section 1231 gain on each installment payment is treated as unrecaptured section 1250 gain until the total unrecaptured section 1250 gain figured in step 2 has been used in full. Figure the amount of gain treated as unrecaptured section 1250 gain for installment payments received during the tax year as the smaller of (a) the amount from line 26 or line 37 of the 2013 Form 6252, whichever applies, or (b) the amount of unrecaptured section

Unrecaptured Section 1250 Gain Worksheet—Line 18b   *Keep for Your Records*

> **If the estate or trust is not reporting a gain on Form 4797, line 7, skip lines 1 through 9 and go to line 10.**
>
> **1.** If the estate or trust has a section 1250 property in Part III of Form 4797 for which you made an entry in Part I of Form 4797 (but not on Form 6252), enter the **smaller** of line 22 or line 24 of Form 4797 for that property. If the estate or trust did not have any such property, go to line 4. If it had more than one such property, see instructions .... **1.** _____
>
> **2.** Enter the amount from Form 4797, line 26g, for the property for which you made an entry on line 1 .... **2.** _____
>
> **3.** Subtract line 2 from line 1 .... **3.** _____
>
> **4.** Enter the total unrecaptured section 1250 gain included on line 26 or line 37 of Form(s) 6252 from installment sales of trade or business property held more than 1 year (see instructions) .... **4.** _____
>
> **5.** Enter the total of any amounts reported to the estate or trust on a Schedule K-1 from a partnership or an S corporation as "unrecaptured section 1250 gain" .... **5.** _____
>
> **6.** Add lines 3 through 5 .... **6.** _____
>
> **7.** Enter the **smaller** of line 6 or the gain from Form 4797, line 7 .... **7.** _____
>
> **8.** Enter the amount, if any, from Form 4797, line 8 .... **8.** _____
>
> **9.** Subtract line 8 from line 7. If zero or less, enter -0- .... **9.** _____
>
> **10.** Enter the amount of any gain from the sale or exchange of an interest in a partnership attributable to unrecaptured section 1250 gain (see instructions) .... **10.** _____
>
> **11.** Enter the total of any amounts reported to the estate or trust on a Schedule K-1, Form 1099-DIV, or Form 2439 as "unrecaptured section 1250 gain" from an estate, trust, real estate investment trust, or mutual fund (or other regulated investment company) .... **11.** _____
>
> **12.** Enter the total of any unrecaptured section 1250 gain from sales (including installment sales) or other dispositions of section 1250 property held more than 1 year for which you did not make an entry in Part I of Form 4797 for the year of sale (see instructions) .... **12.** _____
>
> **13.** Add lines 9 through 12 .... **13.** _____
>
> **14.** If the estate or trust had any section 1202 gain or collectibles gain or (loss), enter the total of lines 1 through 4 of the *28% Rate Gain Worksheet.* Otherwise, enter -0- .... **14.** _____
>
> **15.** Enter the (loss), if any, from Schedule D, line 7. If Schedule D, line 7, is zero or a gain, enter -0- .... **15.** (_____)
>
> **16.** Enter the estate's or trust's long-term capital loss carryovers from Schedule D, line 15, and from Schedule K-1 (Form 1041), box 11, code C, from another estate or trust .... **16.** (_____)
>
> **17.** Combine lines 14 through 16. If the result is a (loss), enter it as a positive amount. If the result is zero or a gain, enter -0- .... **17.** _____
>
> **18. Unrecaptured section 1250 gain.** Subtract line 17 from line 13. If zero or less, enter -0-. Enter the result here and in the appropriate columns of Schedule D, line 18b .... **18.** _____

1250 gain remaining to be reported. This amount is generally the total unrecaptured section 1250 gain for the sale reduced by all gain reported in prior years (excluding section 1250 ordinary income recapture). However, if you chose not to treat all of the gain from payments received after May 6, 1997, and before August 24, 1999, as unrecaptured section 1250 gain, use only the amount you chose to treat as unrecaptured section 1250 gain for those payments to reduce the total unrecaptured section 1250 gain remaining to be reported for the sale. Include this amount on line 4.

Line 10. Include on line 10 the estate's or trust's share of the partnership's unrecaptured section 1250 gain that would result if the partnership had transferred all of its section 1250 property in a fully taxable transaction immediately before the estate or trust sold or exchanged its interest in that partnership. If the estate or trust recognized less than all of the realized

gain, the partnership will be treated as having transferred only a proportionate amount of each section 1250 property.

Line 12. An example of an amount reported on line 12 as an "other disposition" includes unrecaptured section 1250 gain from the sale of a vacation home previously used as a rental property that was converted to personal use before the sale. To figure the amount to enter on line 12, follow the applicable instructions below.

Installment sales. To figure the amount to include on line 12, follow the steps below for each installment sale of property held more than 1 year for which you did not make an entry in Part I of Form 4797 for the year of sale.

Step 1. Figure the smaller of (a) the depreciation allowed or allowable or (b) the total gain for the sale. This is the smaller of line 22 or line 24 of the 2013 Form 4797 (or comparable lines of Form 4797 for the year of sale) for that property.

Step 2. Reduce the amount figured in step 1 by any section 1250 ordinary income recapture for the sale. This is the amount from line 26g of the 2013 Form 4797 (or the comparable line of Form 4797 for the year of sale) for that property. The result is the total unrecaptured section 1250 gain that must be allocated to the installment payments received from the sale.

Step 3. Generally, the amount of capital gain on each installment payment is treated as unrecaptured section 1250 gain until the total unrecaptured section 1250 gain figured in step 2 has been used in full. Figure the amount of gain treated as unrecaptured section 1250 gain for installment payments received during the tax year as the smaller of (a) the amount from line 26 or line 37 of the 2013 Form 6252, whichever applies, or (b) the amount of unrecaptured section 1250 gain remaining to be reported. This amount is generally the total unrecaptured section 1250 gain for the

¶2944

28% Rate Gain Worksheet—Line 18c   *Keep for Your Records*

1. Enter the total of all collectibles gain or (loss) from items reported on Form 8949, Part II . . . .   1. _____

2. Enter as a positive number the amount of any section 1202 exclusion reported in column (g) of Form 8949, Part II, with code "Q" in column (f), for which you excluded 50% of the gain, plus $\frac{2}{3}$ of any section 1202 exclusion in column (g) of Form 8949, Part II, with code "Q" in column (f), for which you excluded 60% of the gain. . . . .   2. _____

3. Enter the total of all collectibles gain or (loss) from Form 4684, line 4 (but only if Form 4684, line 15 is more than zero); Form 6252; Form 6781, Part II; and Form 8824 . . . .   3. _____

4. Enter the total of any collectibles gain reported to the estate or trust on:
   - Form 1099-DIV, box 2d;
   - Form 2439, box 1d; and
   - Schedule K-1 from a partnership, S corporation, estate, or trust.   } . . . .   4. _____

5. Enter the estate's or trust's long-term capital loss carryovers from Schedule D, line 15, and from box 11, code C of Schedule K-1 (Form 1041) from another estate or trust . . . .   5. (_____)

6. If Schedule D, line 7 is a (loss), enter that (loss) here. Otherwise, enter -0- . . . .   6. (_____)

7. Combine lines 1 through 6. If zero or less, enter -0-. If more than zero, also enter this amount in the appropriate columns of Schedule D, line 18c . . . .   7. _____

sale reduced by all gain reported in prior years (excluding section 1250 ordinary income recapture). However, if you chose not to treat all of the gain from payments received after May 6, 1997, and before August 24, 1999, as unrecaptured section 1250 gain, use only the amount you chose to treat as unrecaptured section 1250 gain for those payments to reduce the total unrecaptured section 1250 gain remaining to be reported for the sale. Include this amount on line 12.

Other sales or dispositions of section 1250 property. For each sale of property held more than 1 year (for which an entry was not made in Part I of Form 4797), figure the smaller of (a) the depreciation allowed or allowable or (b) the total gain for the sale. This amount is

the smaller of line 22 or line 24 of Form 4797 for that property. Then, reduce that amount by any section 1250 ordinary income recapture for the sale. This is the amount from line 26g of Form 4797 for that property. The result is the total unrecaptured section 1250 gain for the sale. Include this amount on line 12.

Line 18c—28% Rate Gain

Complete the *28% Rate Gain Worksheet*, earlier, if lines 18a and 19 of column (3) are both greater than zero and at least one of the following applies:
- The estate or trust reported in Part II of Form 8949 a section 1202 exclusion from the eligible gain on qualified small business stock (as discussed earlier), or
- The estate or trust reported in Part II of Form 8949 a collectibles gain or loss.

A collectibles gain or loss is any long-term gain or deductible long-term loss from the sale or exchange of a collectible that is a capital asset.

Collectibles include works of art, rugs, antiques, metals (such as gold, silver, and platinum bullion), gems, stamps, coins, alcoholic beverages, and certain other tangible property.

Also include gain (but not loss) from the sale or exchange of an interest in a partnership, S corporation, or trust held for more than 1 year that is attributable to the unrealized appreciation of collectibles. For details, see Regulations section 1.1(h)-1. Attach the statement required under Regulations section 1.1(h)-1(e) to Schedule D.

¶2944

Capital Loss Carryover Worksheet

Keep for Your Records

Use this worksheet to figure the estate's or trust's capital loss carryovers from 2013 to 2014 if Schedule D, line 20 is a loss and (a) the loss on Schedule D, line 19, col. (3) is more than $3,000 or (b) Form 1041, page 1, line 22 is a loss.

1. Enter taxable income or (loss) from Form 1041, line 22 .... **1.** _____

2. Enter the loss from line 20 of Schedule D as a positive amount .... **2.** _____

3. Enter amount from Form 1041, line 20 .... **3.** _____

4. Adjusted taxable income. Combine lines 1, 2, and 3. If zero or less, enter -0- .... **4.** _____

5. Enter the **smaller** of line 2 or line 4 .... **5.** _____

   Note: *If line 7 of Schedule D is a loss, go to line 6; otherwise, enter -0- on line 6 and go to line 10.*

6. Enter loss from Schedule D, line 7 as a positive amount .... **6.** _____

7. Enter gain, if any, from Schedule D, line 16. If that line is blank or shows a loss, enter -0- .... **7.** _____

8. Add lines 5 and 7 .... **8.** _____

9. **Short-term capital loss carryover to 2014.** Subtract line 8 from line 6. If zero or less, enter -0-. If this is the final return of the estate or trust, also enter on Schedule K-1 (Form 1041), box 11, using code B .... **9.** _____

   Note: *If line 16 of Schedule D is a loss, go to line 10; otherwise, skip lines 10 through 14.*

10. Enter loss from Schedule D, line 16, as a positive amount .... **10.** _____

11. Enter gain, if any, from Schedule D, line 7. If that line is blank or shows a loss, enter -0- .... **11.** _____

12. Subtract line 6 from line 5. If zero or less, enter -0- .... **12.** _____

13. Add lines 11 and 12 .... **13.** _____

14. **Long-term capital loss carryover to 2014.** Subtract line 13 from line 10. If zero or less, enter -0-. If this is the final return of the estate or trust, also enter on Schedule K-1 (Form 1041), box 11, using code C .... **14.** _____

Part IV—Capital Loss Limitation

If the sum of all capital losses is more than the sum of all capital gains, the capital losses are allowed as a deduction, but only to the extent of the smaller of the net loss or $3,000.

For any year (including the final year) in which capital losses exceed capital gains, the estate or trust may have a capital loss carryover. Use the *Capital Loss Carryover Worksheet*, earlier, to figure any capital loss carryover. A capital loss carryover may be carried forward indefinitely. Capital losses keep their character as either short-term or long-term when carried over to the following year.

Part V—Tax Computation Using Maximum Capital Gains Rates

Line 26

If the estate or trust received qualified dividends or capital gains as income in respect of a decedent and a section 691(c) deduction was claimed, you must reduce the amount on Form 1041, page 1, line 2b(2), or Schedule D, line 22, (line 7 of the Schedule D Tax Worksheet, if applicable) by the portion of the section 691(c) deduction claimed on Form 1041, page 1, line 19 that is attributable to the estate's or trust's portion of qualified dividends or capital gains.

Line 45

If the tax using the maximum capital gains rates is less than the regular tax, enter the amount from line 45 on line 1a of Schedule G, Form 1041.

Schedule D Tax Worksheet

If you completed the *Schedule D Tax Worksheet* instead of Part V of Schedule D, be sure to enter the amount from line 44 of the worksheet on line 1a of Schedule G, Form 1041.

¶2944

Schedule D Tax Worksheet

Keep for Your Records

Complete this worksheet only if:
- On Schedule D, line 18b, column (2), **or** line 18c, column (2), is more than zero, **or**
- Both line 2b(1) of Form 1041 **and** line 4g of Form 4952 are more than zero.

Exception: Do not use this worksheet to figure the estate's or trust's tax if line 18a, column (2), or line 19, column (2), of Schedule D or Form 1041, line 22 is zero or less; instead, see the Instructions for Form 1041, Schedule G, line 1a.

1. Enter the estate's or trust's taxable income from Form 1041, line 22	1. _____
2. Enter qualified dividends, if any, from Form 1041, line 2b(2) . . . . 2. _____	
3. Enter the amount from Form 4952, line 4g . . . . 3. _____	
4. Enter the amount from Form 4952, line 4e* . . . . 4. _____	
5. Subtract line 4 from line 3. If zero or less, enter -0- . . . . 5. _____	
6. Subtract line 5 from line 2. If zero or less, enter -0- . . . . 6. _____	
7. Enter the **smaller** of line 18a, col. (2) or line 19, col. (2) from Sch. D . . . . 7. _____	
8. Enter the **smaller** of line 3 or line 4 . . . . 8. _____	
9. Subtract line 8 from line 7. If zero or less, enter -0- . . . . 9. _____	
10. Add lines 6 and 9	10. _____
11. Add lines 18b, column (2) and 18c, column (2) from Schedule D . . . . 11. _____	
12. Enter the **smaller** of line 9 or line 11	12. _____
13. Subtract line 12 from line 10.	13. _____
14. Subtract line 13 from line 1. If zero or less, enter -0-.	14. _____
15. Enter the **smaller** of line 1 or $2,450 . . . . 15. _____	
16. Enter the **smaller** of line 14 or line 15 . . . . 16. _____	
17. Subtract line 10 from line 1. If zero or less, enter -0- . . . . 17. _____	
18. Enter the **larger** of line 16 or line 17	18. _____
19. Subtract line 16 from line 15. This amount is taxed at 0%	19. _____
If lines 1 and 15 are the same, skip lines 20 through 40 and go to line 41. Otherwise, go to line 20.	
20. Enter the **smaller** of line 1 or line 13	20. _____
21. Enter the amount from line 19 (if line 19 is blank, enter -0-)	21. _____
22. Subtract line 21 from line 20. If zero or less, enter -0-	22. _____
23. Enter the **smaller** of line 1 or $11,950	23. _____
24. Add lines 18 and 19 . . . . 24. _____	
25. Subtract line 24 from line 23. If zero or less, enter -0-	25. _____
26. Enter the **smaller** of line 22 or line 25	26. _____
27. Multiply line 26 by 15%	27. _____
28. Reserved . . . . 28. _____	
29. Add lines 19 and 26 . . . . 29. _____	
If lines 1 and 29 are the same, skip lines 30 through 40 and go to line 41. Otherwise, go to line 30	
30. Subtract line 29 from line 20. If zero or less, enter -0-	30. _____
31. Multiply line 30 by 20%	31. _____
32. Enter the **smaller** of line 9 (above) or line 18b, col. (2) (from Schedule D) . . . . 32. _____	
33. Add lines 10 and 18 . . . . 33. _____	
34. Enter the amount from line 1 above . . . . 34. _____	
35. Subtract line 34 from line 33. If zero or less, enter -0- . . . . 35. _____	
36. Subtract line 35 from line 32. If zero or less, enter -0-	36. _____
37. Multiply line 36 by 25% (.25)	37. _____
If Schedule D, line 18c, column (2) is zero or blank, skip lines 38 through 40 and go to line 41. Otherwise, go to line 38.	
38. Add lines 18, 19, 26, 30, and 36 . . . . 38. _____	
39. Subtract line 38 from line 1 . . . . 39. _____	
40. Multiply line 39 by 28% (.28)	40. _____
41. Figure the tax on the amount on line 18. Use the 2013 Tax Rate Schedule in the Instructions for Form 1041	41. _____
42. Add lines 27, 31, 37, 40 and 41	42. _____
43. Figure the tax on the amount on line 1. Use the 2013 Tax Rate Schedule in the Instructions for Form 1041	43. _____
44. **Tax on all taxable income (including capital gains and qualified dividends).** Enter the **smaller** of line 42 or line 43 here **and** on Form 1041, Schedule G, line 1a	44. _____

*If applicable, enter instead the smaller amount entered on the dotted line next to line 4e of Form 4952.

¶2944

20**13**

Instructions for Schedule I (Form 1041)

Alternative Minimum Tax—Estates and Trusts

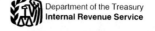
Department of the Treasury
Internal Revenue Service

Section references are to the Internal Revenue Code unless otherwise noted.

Future Developments

For the latest information about developments related to Schedule I and its instructions, such as legislation enacted after they were published, go to *www.irs.gov/form1041.*

What's New

AMT tax brackets. The threshold for the 28% AMT tax bracket increased to amounts over $179,500.

AMT exemption amount and phase-out. The AMT exemption amount increased to $23,100. The exemption amount begins to be phased-out at amounts over $76,950 and is completely phased-out at $169,350.

Capital gains and qualified dividends. Beginning in 2013, the maximum tax rate for long-term capital gains and qualified dividends is 20%, as amended by the American Taxpayer Relief Act of 2012 (ATRA), P.L. 112-240.

For tax year 2013, the 20% rate applies to amounts above $11,950. The 0% and 15% rates continue to apply to certain threshold amounts. The 0% rate applies to amounts up to $2,450. The 15% rate applies to amounts above $2,450 and up to $11,950.

In *Part IV—Line 52 Computation Using Maximum Capital Gains Rates*, we added and revised lines to the computation to reflect the changes to the capital gains rates and thresholds.

We also added a worksheet to compute the amount to enter on line 70. See *Line 70 Worksheet*, later.

General Instructions

Purpose of Schedule

Use Schedule I (Form 1041) to figure:
• The estate's or trust's alternative minimum taxable income;
• The income distribution deduction on a minimum tax basis; and
• The estate's or trust's alternative minimum tax (AMT).

Dec 20, 2013

Who Must Complete Schedule I (Form 1041)

• Complete Parts I and II if the estate or trust is required to complete Form 1041, Schedule B, Income Distribution Deduction.
• Complete Schedule I if the estate's or trust's share of alternative minimum taxable income (Part I, line 29) exceeds $23,100.
• Complete Schedule I if the estate or trust claims any general business credit and line 6 of Part I or line 3 of Part III of Form 3800, General Business Credit, is more than zero.

Recordkeeping

Schedule I contains adjustments and tax preference items that are treated differently for regular tax and AMT purposes. If you, as fiduciary for the estate or trust, completed a form to figure an item for regular tax purposes, you may have to complete it a second time for AMT purposes. Generally, the difference between the amounts on the two forms is the AMT adjustment or tax preference item to enter on Schedule I. Except for Form 1116, Foreign Tax Credit, any additional form completed for AMT purposes does not have to be filed with Form 1041.

For regular tax purposes, some deductions and credits may result in carrybacks or carryforwards to other tax years. Examples are investment interest expense, a net operating loss deduction (NOLD), a capital loss, and the foreign tax credit. Because these items may be refigured for the AMT, the carryback or carryforward amount may be different for regular and AMT purposes. Therefore, you should keep records of these different carryforward and carryback amounts for the AMT and regular tax. The AMT carryforward will be important in completing Schedule I for 2014.

Credit for Prior Year Minimum Tax

Estates and trusts that paid AMT in 2012, or had a minimum tax credit carryforward from the 2012 Form 8801, Credit for Prior Year Minimum

Cat. No. 51559W

Tax—Individuals, Estates, and Trusts, may be eligible for a minimum tax credit in 2013. See Form 8801.

Partners and Shareholders

An estate or trust that is a partner in a partnership or a shareholder in an S corporation must take into account its share of items of income and deductions that enter into the computation of its adjustments and tax preference items.

Allocation of Deductions to Beneficiaries

The distributable net alternative minimum taxable income (DNAMTI) of the estate or trust does not include amounts of depreciation, depletion, and amortization that are allocated to the beneficiaries, just as the distributable net income of the estate or trust does not include these items for regular tax purposes.

Report separately in box 12 of Schedule K-1 (Form 1041), Beneficiary's Share of Income, Deductions, Credits, etc., any adjustments or tax preference items attributable to depreciation (code G), depletion (code H), and amortization (code I) that were allocated to the beneficiaries.

Optional Write-Off for Certain Expenditures

There is no AMT adjustment for the following items if the estate or trust elects to deduct them ratably over the period of time shown for the regular tax.
• Circulation expenditures—3 years (section 173).
• Research and experimental expenditures—10 years (section 174(a)).
• Intangible drilling costs—60 months (section 263(c)).
• Mining exploration and development costs—10 years (sections 616(a) and 617(a)).

The election must be made in the year the expenditure was made and may be revoked only with IRS consent. See section 59(e) and Regulations section 1.59-1 for more details.

Specific Instructions

Part I—Estate's or Trust's Share of Alternative Minimum Taxable Income

Line 2—Interest

In determining the alternative minimum taxable income, qualified residence interest (other than qualified housing interest defined in section 56(e)) is not allowed.

If you completed Form 4952, Investment Interest Expense Deduction, for regular tax purposes, you may have an adjustment on this line. Refigure your investment interest expense on a separate AMT Form 4952 as follows.

Step 1. On line 1 of the AMT Form 4952, follow the instructions for that line, but also include the following amounts.
• Any qualified residence interest (other than qualified housing interest) that was paid or accrued on a loan or part of a loan that is allocable to property held for investment as defined in section 163(d)(5) (for example, interest on a home equity loan whose proceeds were invested in stocks or bonds).
• Any interest that would have been deductible if interest on specified private activity bonds had been included in income. See the instructions for line 8 for the definition of specified private activity bonds.

Step 2. On line 2, enter the AMT disallowed investment interest expense from 2012.

Step 3. When completing Part II of the AMT Form 4952, refigure gross income from property held for investment, any net gain from the disposition of property held for investment, net capital gain from the disposition of property held for investment, and any investment expenses, taking into account all AMT adjustments and tax preference items that apply. Include any interest income and investment expenses from private activity bonds issued after August 7, 1986.

When completing line 4g of the AMT Form 4952, enter the smaller of:
• The amount from line 4g of the regular tax Form 4952, or
• The total of lines 4b and 4e of the AMT Form 4952.

Step 4. Complete Part III.

Enter on Schedule I, line 2 the difference between line 8 of the AMT Form 4952 and line 8 of the regular tax

Form 4952. If the AMT deduction is greater, enter the difference as a negative amount.

Line 3—Taxes

Enter any state, local, or foreign real property taxes; state or local personal property taxes; state and local general sales taxes; and any state, local, or foreign income taxes that were included on Form 1041, page 1, line 11.

Line 5—Refund of Taxes

Enter any refunds received in 2013 of taxes described for line 3 above and included in income.

Line 6—Depletion

Refigure the depletion deduction for AMT purposes by using only the income and deductions allowed for the AMT when refiguring the limit based on taxable income from the property under section 613(a) and the limit based on taxable income, with certain adjustments, under section 613A(d)(1). Also, the depletion deduction for mines, wells, and other natural deposits under section 611 is limited to the property's adjusted basis at the end of the year, as refigured for the AMT, unless the estate or trust is an independent producer or royalty owner claiming percentage depletion for oil and gas wells. Figure this limit separately for each property. When refiguring the property's adjusted basis, take into account any AMT adjustments made this year or in previous years that affect basis (other than the current year's depletion).

Enter on line 6 the difference between the regular tax and AMT deduction. If the AMT deduction is more than the regular tax deduction, enter the difference as a negative amount.

Line 7—Net Operating Loss Deduction

Enter any NOLD from line 15b of page 1 of the Form 1041 as a positive amount.

Line 8—Interest From Specified Private Activity Bonds Exempt From the Regular Tax

Enter the interest earned from specified private activity bonds reduced (but not below zero) by any deduction that would have been allowable if the interest were includible in gross income for regular tax purposes. Each payer of this type of interest should send a Form 1099-INT, Interest Income, to the estate or trust showing the amount of this interest in box 9. Generally, specified private activity bonds are any qualified bonds (as defined in section 141) issued after

August 7, 1986, and before 2009 or after 2010, the interest on which is not includible in gross income for the regular tax. See section 57(a)(5) for more information.

Do not include interest on qualified Gulf Opportunity Zone bonds described in section 1400N(a) or qualified Midwestern disaster area bonds.

Exempt-interest dividends paid by a regulated investment company are treated as interest from specified private activity bonds to the extent the dividends are attributable to interest on the bonds received by the company, minus an allocable share of the expenses paid or incurred by the company in earning the interest. This amount should also be reported to the estate or trust on Form 1099-INT in box 9.

Line 9—Qualified Small Business Stock

If the estate or trust claimed the exclusion under section 1202 for gain on qualified small business stock held more than 5 years, multiply the excluded gain (as shown on Form 8949 in column (g)) by 7% (.07). Enter the result on line 9 as a positive amount.

Line 10—Exercise of Incentive Stock Options

For regular tax purposes, no income is recognized when an incentive stock option (as defined in section 422(b)) is exercised. However, this rule does not apply for AMT purposes. Instead, the estate or trust must generally include on line 10 the excess, if any, of:

1. The fair market value (FMV) of the stock acquired through exercise of the option (determined without regard to any lapse restriction) when its rights in the acquired stock first become transferable or when these rights are no longer subject to a substantial risk of forfeiture, over

2. The amount paid for the stock, including any amount paid for the option used to acquire the stock.

 Even if the estate's or trust's rights in the stock are not transferable and are subject to a substantial risk of forfeiture, you may elect to include in AMT income the excess of the stock's FMV (determined without regard to any lapse restriction) over the exercise price upon the transfer to the estate or trust of the stock acquired through exercise of the option. See section 83(b) for more details. The

election must be made no later than 30 days after the date of transfer.

If the estate or trust acquired stock by exercising an option and it disposed of that stock in the same year, the tax treatment under the regular tax and the AMT is the same, and no adjustment is required.

Increase the AMT basis of any stock acquired through the exercise of an incentive stock option by the amount of the adjustment.

Note. If a Form 3921, Exercise of an Incentive Stock Option Under Section 422(b), was received, it may help you figure the adjustment.

Line 11—Other Estates and Trusts

If the estate or trust is the beneficiary of another estate or trust, enter the adjustment for minimum tax purposes from box 12, code A, Schedule K-1 (Form 1041).

Line 12—Electing Large Partnerships

If the estate or trust is a partner in an electing large partnership, enter on line 12 the amount from Schedule K-1 (Form 1065-B), Partner's Share of Income (Loss) From an Electing Large Partnership, box 6. Take into account any amount from Schedule K-1 (Form 1065-B), box 5, when figuring the amount to enter on line 15.

Line 13—Disposition of Property

Use this line to report any AMT adjustment related to the disposition of property resulting from refiguring:

1. Gain or loss from the sale, exchange, or involuntary conversion of property reported on Form 4797, Sales of Business Property;

2. Casualty gain or loss to business or income-producing property reported on Form 4684, Casualties and Thefts;

3. Ordinary income from the disposition of property not taken into account in 1 or 2 above or on any other line on Schedule I, such as a disqualifying disposition of stock acquired in a prior year by exercising an incentive stock option; and

4. Capital gain or loss (including any carryover that is different for the AMT) reported on Form 8949, Sales and Other Dispositions of Capital Assets, or Schedule D (Form 1041), Capital Gains and Losses.

 The $3,000 capital loss limitation for the regular tax applies separately for the AMT.

First, figure any ordinary income adjustment related to 3 above. Then, refigure Form 4684, Form 4797, Form 8949, and Schedule D (Form 1041) for the AMT, if applicable, by taking into account any adjustments you made this year or in previous years that affect the estate's or trust's basis or otherwise result in a different amount for AMT. If the estate or trust has a capital loss after refiguring Schedule D for the AMT, apply the $3,000 capital loss limitation separately to the AMT loss. For each of the four items listed above, figure the difference between the amount included in taxable income for the regular tax and the amount included in income for the AMT. Treat the difference as a negative amount if (a) both the AMT and regular tax amounts are zero or more and the AMT amount is less than the regular tax amount or (b) the AMT amount is a loss, and the regular tax amount is a smaller loss, or zero or more.

Enter on line 13 the combined adjustments for the four items earlier.

Line 14—Depreciation on Assets Placed in Service After 1986

This section describes when depreciation must be refigured for the AMT and how to figure the amount to enter on line 14.

Do not include on this line any depreciation adjustment from:
● An activity for which the estate or trust is not at risk or income or loss from a partnership or an S corporation if the basis limitations under section 704(d) or 1366(d) apply. Take this adjustment into account on line 16;
● A tax shelter farm activity. Take this adjustment into account on line 23; or
● A passive activity. Take this adjustment into account on line 15.

What depreciation must be refigured for the AMT? Generally, you must refigure depreciation for the AMT, including depreciation allocable to inventory costs, for:
● Property placed in service after 1998 that is depreciated for the regular tax using the 200% declining balance method (generally 3-, 5-, 7-, or 10-year property under the modified accelerated cost recovery system (MACRS));
● Section 1250 property placed in service after 1998 that is not depreciated for the regular tax using the straight line method, and

● Tangible property placed in service after 1986 and before 1999. If the transitional election was made under section 203(a)(1)(B) of the Tax Reform Act of 1986, this rule applies to property placed in service after July 31, 1986.

What depreciation is not refigured for the AMT? Do not refigure depreciation for the AMT for the following items.
● Residential rental property placed in service after 1998.
● Nonresidential real property with a class life of 27.5 years or more placed in service after 1998 that is depreciated for the regular tax using the straight line method.
● Other section 1250 property placed in service after 1998 that is depreciated for the regular tax using the straight line method.
● Property (other than section 1250 property) placed in service after 1998 that is depreciated for the regular tax using the 150% declining balance method or the straight line method.
● Property for which you elected to use the alternative depreciation system (ADS) of section 168(g) for the regular tax.
● Qualified property that is or was eligible for the special depreciation allowance if the depreciable basis of the property for the AMT is the same as for the regular tax. This applies to any special depreciation allowance, including those for qualified disaster assistance property, qualified reuse and recycling property, qualified cellulosic biofuel plant property, qualified New York Liberty Zone property, qualified Gulf Opportunity Zone property, and Kansas disaster area qualified recovery assistance property. The special allowance is deductible for the AMT, and there also is no adjustment required for any depreciation figured on the remaining basis of the qualified property if the depreciable basis of the property for the AMT is the same as for the regular tax. Property for which an election is in effect to not have the special allowance apply is not qualified property.
● Motion picture films, videotapes, or sound recordings.
● Property depreciated under the unit-of-production method or any other method not expressed in a term of years.
● Qualified Indian reservation property.
● A natural gas gathering line placed in service after April 11, 2005.

Property placed in service before 1999. Refigure depreciation for the

AMT using ADS with the same convention used for the regular tax. See the table below for the method and recovery period to use.

How is depreciation refigured for the AMT?

Property Placed in Service Before 1999	
IF the property is...	THEN use the...
Section 1250 property.	Straight line method over 40 years.
Tangible property (other than section 1250 property) depreciated using straight line for the regular tax.	Straight line method over the property's AMT class life.
Any other tangible property.	150% declining balance method, switching to straight line the first tax year it gives a larger deduction, over the property's AMT class life.

Property placed in service after 1998. Use the same convention and recovery period used for the regular tax. For property other than section 1250 property, use the 150% declining balance method, switching to straight line the first tax year it gives a larger deduction. For section 1250 property, use the straight line method.

How is the AMT class life determined? The class life used for the AMT is not necessarily the same as the recovery period used for the regular tax. The class lives for the AMT are listed in Rev. Proc. 87-56, 1987-2 C.B. 674, and in Pub. 946, How To Depreciate Property. Use 12 years for any tangible personal property not assigned a class life.

 See Pub. 946 for optional tables that can be used to figure AMT depreciation. Rev. Proc. 89-15, 1989-1 C.B. 816, has special rules for short tax years and for property disposed of before the end of the recovery period.

How is the line 14 adjustment figured? Subtract the AMT deduction for depreciation from the regular tax deduction and enter the result. If the AMT deduction is more than the regular tax deduction, enter the difference as a negative amount.

In addition to the AMT adjustment to your deduction for depreciation, you must also adjust the amount of depreciation that was capitalized, if any,

to account for the difference between the rules for the regular tax and the AMT. Include on this line the current year adjustment to taxable income, if any, resulting from the difference.

Line 15—Passive Activities

 Do not enter again elsewhere on this schedule any AMT adjustment or tax preference item included on this line.

For AMT purposes, the rules described in section 469 apply, except that in applying the limitations, minimum tax rules apply.

Refigure passive activity gains and losses on an AMT basis. Refigure a passive activity gain or loss by taking into account all AMT adjustments or tax preference items that pertain to that activity.

You may complete a second Form 8582, Passive Activity Loss Limitations, to determine the passive activity losses allowed for AMT purposes, but do not send this AMT Form 8582 to the IRS.

Enter the difference between the loss reported on page 1 and the AMT loss, if any.

 The amount of any passive activity loss that is not deductible (and is therefore carried forward) for AMT purposes is likely to differ from the amount (if any) that is carried forward for regular tax purposes. Therefore, it is essential that you retain adequate records for both AMT and regular tax purposes.

Publicly traded partnerships (PTPs). If the estate or trust had a loss from a PTP, refigure the loss using any AMT adjustments, tax preference items, and any AMT prior year unallowed loss.

Line 16—Loss Limitations

 If the loss is from a passive activity, use line 15 instead. If the loss is from a tax shelter farm activity (that is not passive), use line 23.

Refigure your allowable losses for AMT purposes from activities for which you are not at risk and basis limitations applicable to interests in partnerships and stock in S corporations by taking into account your AMT adjustments and tax preference items. See sections 59(h), 465, 704(d), and 1366(d).

Enter the difference between the loss reported for regular tax purposes and the AMT loss. If the AMT loss is more than the loss reported for regular tax

purposes, enter the adjustment as a negative amount.

Line 17—Circulation Costs

 Do not make this adjustment for expenditures for which you elected the optional 3-year write-off period for regular tax purposes.

Circulation expenditures deducted under section 173(a) for regular tax purposes must be amortized for AMT purposes over 3 years beginning with the year the expenditures were paid or incurred.

Enter the difference between the regular tax and AMT deduction. If the AMT deduction is greater, enter the difference as a negative amount.

If the estate or trust had a loss on property for which circulation expenditures have not been fully amortized for the AMT, the AMT deduction is the smaller of (a) the amount of the loss allowable for the expenditures had they remained capitalized or (b) the remaining expenditures to be amortized for the AMT.

Line 18—Long-Term Contracts

For AMT purposes, the percentage of completion method of accounting described in section 460(b) generally must be used. However, this rule does not apply to any home construction contract (as defined in section 460(e) (6)).

Note. Contracts described in section 460(e)(1)(B) are subject to the simplified method of cost allocation of section 460(b)(4).

Enter the difference between the AMT and regular tax income. If the AMT income is smaller, enter the difference as a negative amount.

Line 19—Mining Costs

 Do not make this adjustment for costs for which you elected the optional 10-year write-off period under section 59(e) for regular tax purposes.

Expenditures for the development or exploration of a mine or certain other mineral deposits (other than an oil, gas, or geothermal well) deducted under sections 616(a) and 617(a) for regular tax purposes must be amortized for AMT purposes over 10 years beginning with the year the expenditures were paid or incurred.

Enter the difference between the amount allowed for AMT purposes and the amount allowed for regular tax purposes. If the amount allowed for AMT purposes exceeds the amount deducted for regular tax purposes, enter the difference as a negative amount.

If the estate or trust had a loss on property for which mining expenditures have not been fully amortized for the AMT, the AMT deduction is the smaller of (a) the amount of the loss allowable for the expenditures had they remained capitalized or (b) the remaining expenditures to be amortized for the AMT.

Line 20—Research and Experimental Costs

 Do not make this adjustment for costs paid or incurred in connection with an activity in which the estate or trust materially participated under the passive activity rules or for costs for which you elected the optional 10-year write-off for research and experimental expenditures under section 59(e) for regular tax purposes.

Research and experimental expenditures deducted under section 174(a) for regular tax purposes generally must be amortized for AMT purposes over 10 years beginning with the year the expenditures were paid or incurred.

Enter the difference between the amount allowed for AMT purposes and the amount allowed for regular tax purposes. If the amount for AMT purposes exceeds the amount allowed for regular tax purposes, enter the difference as a negative amount.

If the estate or trust had a loss on property for which research and experimental costs have not been fully amortized for the AMT, the AMT deduction is the smaller of (a) the loss allowable for the costs had they remained capitalized or (b) the remaining costs to be amortized for the AMT.

Line 21—Income From Certain Installment Sales Before January 1, 1987

The installment method does not apply for AMT purposes to any nondealer disposition of property that occurred after August 16, 1986, but before the first day of your tax year that began in 1987, if an installment obligation to which the proportionate disallowance rule applied arose from the disposition. Enter on line 21 the amount of

installment sale income that was reported for regular tax purposes.

Line 22—Intangible Drilling Costs Preference (IDCs)

 Do not make this adjustment for costs for which you elected the optional 60-month write-off under section 59(e) for regular tax purposes.

IDCs from oil, gas, and geothermal wells are a preference to the extent that the excess IDCs exceed 65% of the net income from the wells. Figure the preference for all oil and gas properties separately from the preference for all geothermal properties.

Figure excess IDCs as follows:

1. Determine the amount of the estate's or trust's IDCs allowed for the regular tax under section 263(c), but do not include any section 263(c) deduction for nonproductive wells, then

2. Subtract the amount that would have been allowed had you amortized these IDCs over a 120-month period starting with the month the well was placed in production.

 Cost depletion can be substituted for the amount allowed using amortization over 120 months.

Net income. Determine net income by reducing the gross income that the estate or trust received or accrued during the tax year from all oil, gas, and geothermal wells by the deductions allocable to those wells (reduced by the excess IDCs). When refiguring net income, use only income and deductions allowed for the AMT.

Exception. The preference for IDCs from oil and gas wells does not apply to taxpayers who are independent producers (that is, not integrated oil companies as defined in section 291(b)(4)). However, this benefit may be limited. First, figure the IDC preference as if this exception did not apply. For purposes of this exception, complete and combine lines 1 through 23, including the IDC preference. If the amount of the IDC preference exceeds 40% of the total of lines 1 through 23, enter the excess on line 22 (the benefit of this exception is limited). Otherwise, do not enter an amount on line 22 (the estate's or trust's benefit from this exception is not limited).

Line 23—Other Adjustments

Enter on line 23 the total of any other adjustments that apply including the following.

• **Depreciation figured using pre-1987 rules.** For AMT purposes, use the straight line method to figure depreciation on real property. Use a recovery period of 19 years for 19-year real property and 15 years for low-income housing. Enter the excess of depreciation claimed for regular tax purposes over depreciation refigured using the straight line method. Figure this amount separately for each property and include on line 23 only positive amounts.

For leased personal property other than recovery property, enter the amount by which the regular tax depreciation using the pre-1987 rules exceeds the depreciation allowable using the straight line method. For leased 10-year recovery property and leased 15-year public utility property, enter the amount by which the depreciation deduction determined for regular tax purposes is more than the deduction allowable using the straight line method with a half-year convention, no salvage value, and a recovery period of 15 years (22 years for 15-year public utility property). Figure this amount separately for each property and include on line 23 only positive amounts.

• **Patron's adjustment.** Distributions the estate or trust received from a cooperative may be includible in income. Unless the distributions are nontaxable, include on line 23 the total AMT patronage dividend adjustment reported to the estate or trust from the cooperative.

• **Amortization of pollution control facilities.** The amortization deduction under section 169 must be refigured for the AMT. For facilities placed in service after 1986 and before 1999, figure the amortization deduction for the AMT using the ADS described in section 168(g). For facilities placed in service after 1998, figure the AMT deduction under MACRS using the straight line method. Enter the difference between the regular tax and AMT deduction. If the AMT amount is greater, enter the difference as a negative amount.

• **Tax shelter farm activities.** Figure this adjustment only if the tax shelter farm activity (as defined in section 58(a)(2)) is not a passive activity. If the activity is passive, include it with any other passive activities on line 15.

Refigure all gains and losses reported for the regular tax from tax

¶2944

shelter farm activities by taking into account any AMT adjustments and preferences. Determine tax shelter farm activity gain or loss for the AMT using the same rules used for the regular tax with the following modifications. No refigured loss is allowed, except to the extent an estate or trust is insolvent (see section 58(c)(1)). A refigured loss may not be used in the current tax year to offset gains from other tax shelter farm activities. Instead, any refigured loss must be suspended and carried forward indefinitely until (a) the estate or trust has a gain in a subsequent tax year from the same activity or (b) the activity is disposed of.

The AMT amount of any tax shelter farm activity loss that is not deductible and is carried forward is likely to differ from the regular tax amount. Keep adequate records for both the AMT and regular tax.

Enter the difference between the amount that would be reported for the activity on Schedule E (Form 1040), Supplemental Income and Loss, or Schedule F (Form 1040), Profit or Loss From Farming, for the AMT and the regular tax amount. If (a) the AMT loss is more than the regular tax loss, (b) the AMT gain is less than the regular tax gain, or (c) there is an AMT loss and a regular tax gain, then enter the adjustment as a negative amount.

Enter any adjustment for amounts reported on Form 8949, Schedule D (Form 1041), Form 4684, or Form 4797 for the activity on line 13 instead.

● **Biofuel producer credit and biodiesel and renewable diesel fuels credit.** If the adjusted total income (Form 1041, page 1, line 17) includes the amount of the biofuel producer credit or biodiesel and renewable diesel fuels credit, include that amount as a negative amount on line 23.

● **Related adjustments.** AMT adjustments and tax preference items may affect deductions that are based on an income limit other than adjusted gross income (AGI) or modified AGI (for example, farm conservation expenses). Refigure these deductions using the income limit as modified for the AMT. Include the difference between the regular tax and AMT deduction on line 23. If the AMT deduction is more than the regular tax deduction, include the difference as a negative amount.

 Do not make an adjustment on line 23 for an item you refigured on another line of Schedule I (for example, line 6).

Line 24—Alternative Tax Net Operating Loss Deduction

The ATNOLD is the sum of the alternative tax net operating loss (ATNOL) carryovers and carrybacks to the tax year, subject to the limitation explained below.

The net operating loss (NOL) under section 172(c) is modified for alternative tax purposes by (a) taking into account the adjustments made under sections 56 and 58 and (b) reducing the NOL by any item of tax preference under section 57. For an estate or trust that held a residual interest in a real estate mortgage investment conduit (REMIC), figure the ATNOLD without regard to any excess inclusion.

If this estate or trust is the beneficiary of another estate or trust that terminated in 2013, include any ATNOL carryover that was reported in box 11, code E of Schedule K-1 (Form 1041).

The estate's or trust's ATNOLD may be limited. To figure the ATNOLD limitation, first figure alternative minimum taxable income (AMTI) without regard to the ATNOLD and any domestic production activities deduction. For this purpose, figure a tentative amount for line 6 of Schedule I (Form 1041) by treating line 24 as if it were zero. Then, figure a tentative total by combining lines 1–23 of Schedule I (Form 1041) using the line 6 tentative amount. Add any domestic production activities deduction to this tentative total. The ATNOLD limitation is 90% of the result.

However, the 90% limit does not apply to an ATNOL that is attributable to qualified disaster losses (as defined in section 172(j)), qualified Gulf Opportunity Zone losses as defined in section 1400N(k)(2), qualified recovery assistance losses as defined in Pub. 4492-A, Information for Taxpayers Affected by the May 4, 2007, Kansas Storms and Tornadoes), qualified disaster recovery assistance losses (as defined in Pub. 4492-B, Information for Affected Taxpayers in the Midwestern Disaster Areas) or a 2008 or 2009 loss that you elected to carryback more than 2 years under section 172(b)(1)(H). If an ATNOL that is carried back or carried forward to a tax year is attributable to any of those losses, the ATNOLD for the tax year is limited to the sum of:

1. The smaller of:

a. The sum of the ATNOL carrybacks and carryforwards to the tax year attributable to NOLs other than the losses described in 2a below, or

b. 90% of AMTI for the tax year (figured without regard to the ATNOLD and any domestic production activities deduction, as discussed earlier), plus

2. The smaller of:

a. The sum of the ATNOL carrybacks and carryforwards to the tax year attributable to qualified disaster losses, qualified Gulf Opportunity Zone losses, qualified recovery assistance losses, qualified disaster recovery assistance losses, and any 2008 or 2009 loss that you elected to carry back more than 2 years under section 172(b)(1)(H), or

b. 100% of AMTI for the tax year (figured without regard to the ATNOLD and any domestic production activities deduction, as discussed earlier) reduced by the amount determined under 1, above.

Enter on line 24 the smaller of the ATNOLD or the ATNOLD limitation.

Any ATNOL not used may be carried back 2 years or forward up to 20 years (15 years for loss years beginning before 1998). In some cases, the carryback period is longer than 2 years; for details, see Pub. 536, Net Operating Losses (NOLs) for Individuals, Estates, and Trusts.

The treatment of ATNOLs does not affect your regular tax NOL.

 If you elected under section 172(b)(3) to forego the carryback period for regular tax purposes, the election will also apply for the AMT.

Line 29—Estate's or Trust's Share of Alternative Minimum Taxable Income

For an estate or trust that held a residual interest in a REMIC, line 29 may not be less than the estate's or trust's share of the amount on Schedule E (Form 1040), line 38, column (c). If that amount is larger than the amount you would otherwise enter on line 29, enter that amount instead and write "Sch. Q" on the dotted line next to line 29.

Part II—Income Distribution Deduction on a Minimum Tax Basis

Line 30—Adjusted Alternative Minimum Taxable Income

Generally, enter on line 30, Schedule I, the amount from line 25, Schedule I. However, if Form 1041, page 1, line 4 and line 25 are losses, enter on line 30 the smaller of those losses. If Form 1041, line 4 is zero or a gain and line 25 is a loss, enter zero on line 30.

Line 31—Adjusted Tax-Exempt Interest

To figure the adjusted tax-exempt interest (including exempt-interest dividends received as a shareholder in a mutual fund or other regulated investment company), subtract the total of any:

1. Tax-exempt interest from Form 1041, Schedule A, line 2 figured for AMT purposes, and

2. Section 212 expenses allowable for AMT purposes allocable to tax-exempt interest, from the amount of tax-exempt interest received.

Do not subtract any deductions reported on lines 2 through 4.

Section 212 expenses that are directly allocable to tax-exempt interest are allocated only to tax-exempt interest. A reasonable proportion of section 212 expenses that are indirectly allocable to both tax-exempt interest and other income must be allocated to each class of income.

Line 33

Reduce the amount on line 33 by any allocable section 1202 exclusion (as refigured for AMT purposes).

Line 34

Enter any capital gains that were paid or permanently set aside for charitable purposes from the current year's income included on line 1 of Form 1041, Schedule A. Reduce the amount on line 34 by any allocable section 1202 exclusion (as refigured for AMT purposes).

Lines 35 and 36

Capital gains and losses must take into account any basis adjustments from line 13, Part I.

Line 41—Adjustment for Tax-Exempt Income

In figuring the income distribution deduction on a minimum tax basis, the estate or trust is not allowed a deduction for any item of DNAMTI (line 37) that is not included in the gross income of the estate or trust figured on an AMT basis. Thus, for purposes of figuring the allowable income distribution deduction on a minimum tax basis, the DNAMTI is figured without regard to any tax-exempt interest (except for amounts from line 8).

If tax-exempt interest is the only tax-exempt income included in the total distributions (line 40), and the DNAMTI (line 37) is less than or equal to line 40, then enter on line 41 the amount from line 31.

If tax-exempt interest is the only tax-exempt income included in the total distributions (line 40), and the DNAMTI is more than line 40 (that is, the estate or trust made a distribution that is less than the DNAMTI), then figure the adjustment by multiplying line 31 by a fraction, the numerator of which is the total distributions (line 40), and the denominator of which is the DNAMTI (line 37). Enter the result on line 41.

If line 40 includes tax-exempt income other than tax-exempt interest (except for amounts from line 8), figure line 41 by subtracting the total expenses allocable to tax-exempt income that are allowable for AMT purposes from tax-exempt income included on line 40.

Expenses that are directly allocable to tax-exempt income are allocated only to tax-exempt income. A reasonable proportion of expenses indirectly allocable to both tax-exempt income and other income must be allocated to each class of income.

Line 44—Income Distribution Deduction on a Minimum Tax Basis

Allocate the income distribution deduction figured on a minimum tax basis among the beneficiaries in the same manner as income was allocated for regular tax purposes. You need the allocated income distribution deduction figured on a minimum tax basis to figure the beneficiary's adjustment for minimum tax purposes, as explained under *Box 12—AMT Items* in the Schedule K-1 instruction section of the Instructions for Form 1041 and Schedules A, B, G, J, and K-1.

Part III—Alternative Minimum Tax Computation

Line 53—Alternative Minimum Foreign Tax Credit

 To see if you need to figure the estate's or trust's AMT foreign tax credit, fill in line 55 of Schedule I as instructed. If the amount on line 55 is greater than or equal to the amount on line 52, the estate or trust does not owe the AMT. Enter zero on line 56 and see Who Must Complete *earlier to find out if you must file Schedule I with Form 1041. However,*

even if the estate or trust does not owe AMT, you may need to complete line 53 to see if you have an AMT foreign tax credit carryback or carryforward to other tax years.

To figure the AMT foreign tax credit, follow the steps discussed below.

Step 1. Complete and attach a separate AMT Form 1116, with the notation at the top "Alt Min Tax" for each separate limitation category specified at the top of Form 1116.

Note. When applying the separate limitation categories, use the applicable AMT rate instead of the regular tax rate to determine if any income is "high-taxed."

Step 2. If you (on behalf of the estate or trust) previously made or are making the *Simplified limitation election* (as discussed later), skip Part I and enter on the AMT Form 1116, line 17, the same amount you entered on that line for the regular tax. If you did not complete Form 1116 for the regular tax and you previously made or are making the simplified limitation election (on behalf of the estate or trust), complete Part I and lines 15 through 17 of the AMT Form 1116 using regular tax amounts.

If the election does not apply, complete Part I, using only income and deductions allowed for the AMT that are attributable to sources outside the United States. If the estate or trust has any foreign source qualified dividends or foreign source capital gains or losses, use the instructions under *Step 3* to determine whether you must make adjustments to those amounts before you include the amounts on line 1a or line 5 of the AMT Form 1116.

Step 3. Follow the instructions below, if applicable, to determine the amount of foreign source qualified dividends and foreign source capital gains and losses to include on line 1a and line 5 of the AMT Form 1116.

Foreign qualified dividends. You must adjust the estate's or trust's foreign source qualified dividends before you include those amounts on line 1a of the AMT Form 1116 if:
* Line 62 of Schedule I (Form 1041) is greater than zero,
* Line 79 of Schedule I (Form 1041) is smaller than line 80, and
* The exception for foreign qualified dividends below does not apply.

But, you do not need to make any adjustments if:

• The estate or trust qualifies for the adjustment exception under *Qualified Dividends Tax Worksheet (Estates and Trusts)* or *Schedule D Filers* in the Instructions for Form 1116 and
• Line 62 of Schedule I (Form 1041) is not more than $179,500.

Note. Use the estate's or trust's capital gains and losses as refigured for the AMT to determine whether your total amounts are less than the $20,000 threshold under the adjustment exception.

To adjust foreign source qualified dividends, multiply the estate's or trust's foreign source qualified dividends in each separate category by 0.5357 if the foreign source qualified dividends are taxed at a rate of 15%. Include the results on line 1a of the AMT Form 1116.

If they are taxed at a rate of 20%, multiply your foreign source qualified dividends in each separate category by 0.7143. Include the results on line 1a of the AMT Form 1116.

You adjust the estate's or trust's foreign source qualified dividends taxed at the 0% rate by **not** including them on line 1a of Form 1116. Amounts taxed at the 0% rate are on line 8 of the Qualified Dividends Tax Worksheet in the Instructions for Form 1041, line 30 of Schedule D (Form 1041), or line 19 of the Schedule D Tax Worksheet in the Instructions for Schedule D (Form 1041).

 Do not adjust the amount of any foreign source qualified dividends you elected to include on line 4g of the AMT Form 4952.

Foreign capital gains or losses. If any capital gain or loss from U.S. or foreign sources is different for the AMT, use the refigured amounts to complete this step.

To figure the adjustment for the estate's or trust's foreign source capital gains or losses, you must first determine whether you can use *Worksheet A* or *Worksheet B* in the Instructions for Form 1116. Otherwise, you must use the instructions for *Capital Gains and Losses* in Pub. 514, Foreign Tax Credit for Individuals, to figure the adjustments you must make to the estate's or trust's foreign source capital gains and losses.

Use Worksheet A if the estate or trust has foreign source capital gains or losses in no more than two separate

categories, and any of the following apply.
• You were not required to make adjustments to the estate's or trust's foreign source qualified dividends under the rules described earlier (or if the estate or trust had foreign source qualified dividends, you would not have been required to make those adjustments).
• Schedule D (Form 1041), line 18a, column (2) or line 19, column (2), as refigured for the AMT if necessary, is zero or a loss.
• On the AMT Schedule D Tax Worksheet for Form 1041, a) line 17 is zero, b) line 9 is zero, or c) line 42 is equal to or greater than line 43.
• On the AMT Part V of Schedule D (Form 1041), a) line 22 of that AMT Part V minus the amount on Form 4952, line 4e, that you elected to include on Form 4952, line 4g, is zero or less, b) line 27 of that AMT Part V of Schedule D (Form 1041) is zero, or c) line 43 of that AMT Part V is equal to or greater than line 44.

Use Worksheet B if you:
• Cannot use Worksheet A,
• Have foreign source capital gains and losses in no more than two separate categories,
• Did not have any item of unrecaptured section 1250 gain or any item of 28% rate gain or loss for either regular tax or AMT, and
• Did not have any capital gains taxed at a rate of 0% or 20%.

Instructions for Worksheets A and B. When you complete Worksheet A or B, use foreign source capital gains and losses as refigured for the AMT, if necessary, and do not use any foreign source capital gains that you elected to include on line 4g of the AMT Form 4952. If you must complete a Schedule D (Form 1041) for the AMT, use line 19 of that AMT Schedule D (Form 1041) to complete line 3 of Worksheet A or line 4 of the Line 2 Worksheet for Worksheet B. Use 0.5357 instead of 0.3788 to complete lines 11, 13, and 15 of Worksheet B and to complete lines 8, 11, and 17 of the Line 15 Worksheet for Worksheet B.

If the estate or trust does not qualify to use Worksheet A or Worksheet B, use the instructions for *Capital Gains and Losses* in Pub. 514 to determine the adjustments you make.

Step 4. Complete Part II and lines 9 through 14 of the AMT Form 1116. Use the estate's or trust's AMT foreign tax credit carryover, if any, on line 10.

Step 5. If the simplified limitation election does not apply, complete lines 15 through 17 of the AMT Form 1116.

Step 6. If you did not complete Part IV of Schedule I (Form 1041), enter the amount from Schedule I (Form 1041), line 29 on line 18 of the AMT Form 1116 and go to Step 7 later.

If you completed Part IV of Schedule I (Form 1041), complete an AMT Worksheet for Line 18 in the Instructions for Form 1116 to figure the amount to enter on Form 1116, line 18, if:
• Line 62 of Schedule I (Form 1041) is greater than zero, and
• Line 79 of Schedule I (Form 1041) is smaller than line 80.

But you do not need to complete the Worksheet for Line 18 if:
• The estate or trust qualifies for the adjustment exception discussed in the Instructions for Form 1116 and
• Line 62 of Schedule I (Form 1041) is not more than $179,500.

Note. Use the estate's and trust's capital gains and losses as refigured for the AMT to determine if its total amounts are less than the $20,000 threshold under the adjustment exception.

If you do not have to complete an AMT Worksheet for Line 18, enter the amount from line 29 of Schedule I on line 18 of the AMT Form 1116.

Instructions for completing an AMT Worksheet for Line 18. To complete an AMT Worksheet for Line 18 in the Instructions for Form 1116, follow these instructions.

1. Enter the amount from Schedule I (Form 1041), line 29 on line 1 of the worksheet.

2. Skip lines 2 and 3 of the worksheet.

3. Enter the amount from Schedule I (Form 1041), line 77 on line 4 of the worksheet.

4. Multiply line 4 of the worksheet by 0.1071 (instead of 0.3687) and enter the results on line 5 of the worksheet.

5. Enter the amount from Schedule I (Form 1041), line 74 on line 6 of the worksheet.

6. Multiply line 6 of the worksheet by 0.2857 (instead of 0.4949) and enter the result on line 7 of the worksheet.

7. Enter the amount from Schedule I (Form 1041), line 71 on line 8 of the worksheet.

¶2944

8. Multiply line 8 of the worksheet by 0.4643 (instead of 0.6212). Enter the result on line 9 of the worksheet.

9. Enter the amount from Schedule I, line 68, on line 10 of the worksheet.

10. Complete lines 11 and 12 of the worksheet as instructed on the worksheet.

Step 7. Enter the amount from Schedule I (Form 1041), line 52 on the AMT Form 1116, line 20. Complete lines 19, 21, and 22 of the AMT Form 1116.

Step 8. Complete Part IV of the first AMT Form 1116 only.

Enter on line 53 of Schedule I the amount from line 30 of the first AMT Form 1116.

Attach to the estate's or trust's return all AMT Forms 1116 you used to figure your AMT Foreign Tax Credit.

AMT foreign tax credit carryback and carryforward. If the AMT foreign tax credit is limited, any unused amount can be carried back or forward under section 904(c). The election to forego the carryback period for regular tax purposes also applies for the AMT.

Simplified limitation election. The estate or trust may elect to use a simplified section 904 limitation to figure its AMT foreign tax credit. To do so, use the estate's or trust's regular tax income for Form 1116, Part I, instead of refiguring the estate's or trust's foreign source income for the AMT, as described in Step 2 in the instructions for line 53, earlier. The estate or trust must make the election for the first tax year after 1997 for which it claims an AMT foreign tax credit. If it does not make the election for that year, it may not make it for a later year. Once made, the election applies to all later tax years and may be revoked only with IRS consent.

Part IV—Line 52 Computation Using Maximum Capital Gains Rates

Lines 58, 59, and 60

If you used Schedule D (Form 1041), the Schedule D Tax Worksheet in the Instructions for Schedule D (Form 1041), or the Qualified Dividends Tax Worksheet in the Instructions for Form 1041, you generally may enter the amounts as instructed on Schedule I, lines 58, 59, and 60. But do not use those amounts if any of the following apply.

1. The gain or loss from any transaction reported on Form 8949 or Schedule D (Form 1041) is different for the AMT (for example, because the AMT basis was different due to depreciation adjustments or an incentive stock option adjustment or the AMT capital loss carryover from 2012 was different).

2. You did not complete Part V of Schedule D (Form 1041), the Schedule D Tax Worksheet in the Instructions for Schedule D (Form 1041), or the Qualified Dividends Tax Worksheet in the Instructions for Form 1041 because Form 1041, line 22, was zero or less.

3. The estate or trust received a Schedule K-1 (Form 1041) that shows an amount in box 12 with code B, C, D, E, or F. If this applies, see *If the estate or trust is a beneficiary of another estate or trust,* later.

If 1 above applies, complete an AMT Form 8949. Next, if 1 or 3 applies, complete Parts I through IV of an AMT Schedule D (Form 1041) by refiguring the amounts of your gains and losses for the AMT. Then, if 1, 2, or 3 applies, complete the following lines of the applicable schedule or worksheet:
- Lines 22 through 26 of an AMT Schedule D (Form 1041),
- Lines 2 through 13 of an AMT Schedule D Tax Worksheet in the Instructions for Schedule D (Form 1041), or
- Lines 2 through 4 of a Qualified Dividends Tax Worksheet in the Instructions for Form 1041.
If you were required to complete an AMT Form 4952, use it to figure the amount to enter on line 25 of the AMT Schedule D (Form 1041), lines 3 and 4 of the AMT Schedule D Tax Worksheet in the Instructions for Schedule D (Form 1041), and line 3 of the Qualified Dividends Tax Worksheet. Use amounts from the AMT Schedule D (Form 1041),

AMT Schedule D Tax Worksheet in the Instructions for Schedule D (Form 1041) or Qualified Dividends Tax Worksheet in the Instructions for Form 1041 to complete Schedule I (Form 1041), lines 58, 59, and 60. Keep the AMT Form 8949, AMT Schedule D (Form 1041) and applicable AMT worksheet for your records, but do not attach any of them to Form 1041.

 Do not decrease the estate's or trust's section 1202 exclusion by the amount, if any, included on line 9 of Schedule I (Form 1041).

If the estate or trust is a beneficiary of another estate or trust. If the estate or trust received a Schedule K-1 (Form 1041) from another estate or trust that shows an amount in box 12 with code B, C, D, E, or F, follow the instructions in the table below.

IF the code in box 12 is...	THEN include that amount in the total on...
B	line 2 of an AMT Qualified Dividends Tax Worksheet in the Instructions for Form 1041; line 23 of an AMT Schedule D (Form 1041); or line 2 of an AMT Schedule D Tax Worksheet in the Instructions for Schedule D (Form 1041), whichever applies.
C	line 5, column (h), of an AMT Schedule D (Form 1041).
D	line 12, column (h), of an AMT Schedule D (Form 1041).
E	line 11 of an AMT Unrecaptured Section 1250 Gain Worksheet in the Instructions for Schedule D (Form 1041).
F	line 4 of an AMT 28% Rate Gain Worksheet in the Instructions for Schedule D (Form 1041).

¶2944

Line 70

Complete the Line 70 Worksheet to
figure the amount to enter on this line.

Line 70 Worksheet	*Keep for Your Records*

1. Enter $11,950 .... **1.** _____
2. Enter the amount from Schedule I (Form 1041), line 66 .... **2.** _____
3. Enter the amount from line 27 of Schedule D (Form 1041), line 18 of the Schedule D Tax Worksheet, or line 5 of the of the Qualified Dividends Tax Worksheet, whichever applies (as figured for the regular tax). If you did not complete Schedule D or either worksheet for the regular tax, enter the amount from Form 1041, line 22; but do not enter less than -0-. .... **3.** _____
4. Add line 2 and line 3. .... **4.** _____
5. Subtract line 4 from line 1 and enter the result here and on line 70; but do not enter less than -0- ...... **5.** _____

¶2944

2013

Instructions for Form 8949

Sales and Other Dispositions of Capital Assets

Department of the Treasury
Internal Revenue Service

Section references are to the Internal Revenue Code unless otherwise noted.

Future Developments

For the latest information about developments related to Form 8949 and its instructions, such as legislation enacted after they were published, go to *www.irs.gov/form8949*.

What's New

Direct reporting on Schedule D. For 2013, you may be able to combine certain transactions and report the totals directly on Schedule D. If you choose to do that, you do not need to include these transactions on Form 8949. For additional information, see *Exception 3* under the instructions for line 1.

Estates and trusts. The use of Form 8949 by estates and trusts is new. Many transactions that, in previous years, would have been reported by estates and trusts on Schedule D or Schedule D-1 must be reported on Form 8949 if they have to be reported on a 2013 form.

General Instructions

File Form 8949 with the Schedule D for the return you are filing. This includes Schedule D of Forms 1040, 1041, 1065, 1065-B, 8865, 1120, 1120S, 1120-C, 1120-F, 1120-FSC, 1120-H, 1120-IC-DISC, 1120-L, 1120-ND, 1120-PC, 1120-POL, 1120-REIT, 1120-RIC, 1120-SF, and certain Forms 990-T.

Complete Form 8949 before you complete line 1b, 2, 3, 8b, 9, or 10 of Schedule D.

Purpose of Form

Use Form 8949 to report sales and exchanges of capital assets. Form 8949 allows you and the IRS to reconcile amounts that were reported to you and the IRS on Form 1099-B or 1099-S (or substitute statement) with the amounts you report on your return. If you received Form 1099-B or 1099-S (or substitute statement), always report the proceeds (sales price) shown on that form (or statement) in column (d) of Form 8949. If Form 1099-B (or substitute statement) shows that the cost or other basis was reported to the IRS, always report the basis shown on that form (or statement) in column (e). If any correction or adjustment to these amounts is needed, make it in

column (g). See *How To Complete Form 8949, Columns (f) and (g)*, later, for details about these adjustments.

If all Forms 1099-B you received (and all substitute statements) show basis was reported to the IRS and if no correction or adjustment is needed, you may not need to file Form 8949. See *Exception 3* under the instructions for line 1.

Individuals. Individuals use Form 8949 to report:
* The sale or exchange of a capital asset not reported on another form or schedule,
* Gains from involuntary conversions (other than from casualty or theft) of capital assets not held for business or profit, and
* Nonbusiness bad debts.

If you file a joint return, complete as many copies of Form 8949 as you need to report all of your and your spouse's transactions. You and your spouse may list your transactions on separate forms or you may combine them. However, you must include on your Schedule D the totals from all Forms 8949 for both you and your spouse.

Corporations and partnerships. Corporations and partnerships use Form 8949 to report:
* The sale or exchange of a capital asset not reported on another form or schedule,
* Nonbusiness bad debts, and
* Undistributed long-term capital gains from Form 2439.

Corporations also use Form 8949 to report their share of gain or (loss) from a partnership, estate, or trust.

For corporations and partnerships meeting certain criteria, an exception to some of the normal requirements for completing Form 8949 has been provided. See *Exception 2* under the instructions for line 1.

Estates and trusts. Estates and trusts use Form 8949 to report the sale or exchange of a capital asset not reported on another form or schedule.

Schedule D. Use Schedule D for the following purposes.
* To figure the overall gain or loss from transactions reported on Form 8949.
* To report a gain from Form 6252 or Part I of Form 4797.
* To report a gain or loss from Form 4684, 6781, or 8824.
* To report capital gain distributions not reported directly on Form 1040, line 13 (or

effectively connected capital gain distributions not reported directly on Form 1040NR, line 14).
* To report a capital loss carryover from the previous tax year to the current tax year.
* To report your share of a gain or (loss) from a partnership, S corporation, estate, or trust. (However, corporations report this type of gain or (loss) on Form 8949.)
* To report transactions reported to you on a Form 1099-B (or substitute statement) showing basis was reported to the IRS and for which you have no adjustments, as explained under *Exception 3*, later.

Individuals, estates, and trusts also use Schedule D to report undistributed long-term capital gains from Form 2439.

Additional information. See the instructions for the Schedule D you are filing for detailed information about the following.
* Other forms you may have to file.
* The definition of capital asset.
* Reporting capital gain distributions, undistributed capital gains, the sale of a main home, the sale of capital assets held for personal use, or the sale of a partnership interest.
* Capital losses, nondeductible losses, and losses from wash sales.
* Traders in securities.
* Short sales.
* Gain or loss from options.
* Installment sales.
* Demutualization of life insurance companies.
* Exclusion or rollover of gain from the sale of qualified small business stock.
* Any other rollover of gain, such as gain from the sale of publicly traded securities.
* Exclusion of gain from the sale of DC Zone assets or qualified community assets.
* Certain other items that get special treatment.
* Special reporting rules for corporations, partnerships, estates, and trusts in certain situations.

For more information about reporting on Forms 6252, 4797, 4684, 6781, and 8824, see the instructions for those forms. See Pub. 544 and Pub. 550 for more details.

Basis and Recordkeeping

Basis is the amount of your investment in property for tax purposes. The basis of

Dec 10, 2013   Cat. No. 59421Z property you buy is usually its cost. You need to know your basis to figure any gain or loss on the sale or other disposition of the property. You must keep accurate records that show the basis and, if applicable, adjusted basis of your property. Your records should show the purchase price, including commissions; increases to basis, such as the cost of improvements; and decreases to basis, such as depreciation, nondividend distributions on stock, and stock splits.

For more information on basis, see the instructions for column (e), later, and these publications.
• Pub. 550, Investment Income and Expenses (Including Capital Gains and Losses).
• Pub. 551, Basis of Assets.

If you lost or did not keep records to determine your basis in securities, contact your broker for help. If you receive a Form 1099-B (or substitute statement), your broker may have reported your basis for these securities in box 3.

 The IRS partners with companies that offer Form 8949 software that can import trades from many brokerage firms and accounting software that can help you keep track of your adjusted basis in securities. To find out more, go to *www.irs.gov/efile*.

Short Term or Long Term

Separate your capital gains and losses according to how long you held or owned the property.

The holding period for short-term capital gains and losses is 1 year or less. Report these transactions on Part I of Form 8949 (or line 1a of Schedule D if you can use *Exception 3* under the instructions for Form 8949, line 1).

The holding period for long-term capital gains and losses is more than 1 year. Report these transactions on Part II of Form 8949 (or line 8a of Schedule D if you can use *Exception 3* under the instructions for Form 8949, line 1).

To figure the holding period, begin counting on the day after you received the property and include the day you disposed of it. If you receive a Form 1099-B (or substitute statement), box 1c may help you determine whether the gain or loss is short-term or long-term.

Generally, if you disposed of property that you acquired by inheritance, report the disposition as a long-term gain or loss regardless of how long you held the property.

A nonbusiness bad debt must be treated as a short-term capital loss. See Pub. 550 for what qualifies as a

nonbusiness bad debt and how to enter it on Part I of Form 8949.

Corporation's Gains and Losses from Partnerships, Estates, or Trusts

Report a corporation's share of capital gains and losses from investments in partnerships, estates, or trusts on the appropriate Part of Form 8949. Report a net short-term capital gain or (loss) on Part I (with box C checked) and a net long-term capital gain or (loss) on Part II (with box F checked). In column (a), enter "From Schedule K-1 (Form 1065)," "From Schedule K-1 (Form 1065-B)," or "From Schedule K-1 (Form 1041)," whichever applies; enter the gain or (loss) in column (h); and leave all other columns blank.

If more than one Schedule K-1 is received, report each on a separate row. Include additional identifying information, such as "Partnership X."

Rounding Off to Whole Dollars

You can round off cents to whole dollars on Form 8949. If you do round to whole dollars, round all amounts. To round, drop cent amounts under 50 cents and increase cent amounts over 49 cents to the next dollar. For example, $1.49 becomes $1 and $1.50 becomes $2.

Specific Instructions

Report short-term gains and losses on Part I. Report long-term gains and losses on Part II.

Line 1

Enter all sales and exchanges of capital assets, including stocks, bonds, and real estate (if not reported on line 1a or 8a of Schedule D or on Form 4684, 4797, 6252, 6781, or 8824). Include these transactions even if you did not receive a Form 1099-B or 1099-S (or substitute statement) for the transaction. However, if the property you sold was your main home, see *Sale of Your Home* in the Instructions for Schedule D (Form 1040).

Enter the details of each transaction on a separate row (unless one of the *Exceptions to reporting each transaction on a separate row* described later applies to you).

Part I. Use a separate Part I for each type of short-term transaction described in the text for one of the boxes (A, B, or C) at the top of Part I. Include on each Part I only transactions described in the text for the box you check (A, B, or C). Check only one box on each Part I. For example, if you check box A in one Part I, include on that Part I only short-term transactions reported to you on a statement showing basis was reported to the IRS. Complete

as many copies of Part I as you need to report all transactions of each type (A, B, or C).

Box A. Report on a Part I with box A checked all short-term transactions reported to you on Form 1099-B (or substitute statement) with an amount shown for cost or other basis **unless** the statement indicates that amount was not reported to the IRS. If your statement shows cost or other basis but indicates it was not reported to the IRS (for example, if box 6b of Form 1099-B is not checked), see *Box B*, below.

 If you do not need to make any adjustments to the basis or type of gain or loss (short-term or long-term) reported to you on Form 1099-B (or substitute statement) or to your gain or loss for any transactions you normally would report on Form 8949 with box A checked, you do not have to include those transactions on Form 8949. Instead, you can report them directly on Schedule D. For more information, see Exception 3, later.

Box B. Report on a Part I with box B checked all short-term transactions reported to you on Form 1099-B (or substitute statement) without an amount shown for cost or other basis or showing that cost or other basis was not reported to the IRS. If your statement shows cost or other basis for the transaction was reported to the IRS (for example, if box 6b of Form 1099-B is checked), see *Box A*, above.

Box C. Report on a Part I with box C checked all short-term transactions for which you cannot check box A or B because you did not receive a Form 1099-B (or substitute statement).

Part II. Use a separate Part II for each type of long-term transaction described in the text for one of the boxes (D, E, or F) at the top of Part II. Include on each Part II only transactions described in the text for the box you check (D, E, or F). Check only one box on each Part II. For example, if you check box D in one Part II, include on that Part II only long-term transactions reported to you on a statement showing basis was reported to the IRS. Complete as many copies of Part II as you need to report all transactions of each type (D, E, or F).

Box D. Report on a Part II with box D checked all long-term transactions reported to you on Form 1099-B (or substitute statement) with an amount shown for cost or other basis **unless** the statement indicates that amount was not reported to the IRS. If your statement shows cost or other basis but indicates it was not reported to the IRS (for example,

-2-

if box 6b of Form 1099-B is not checked), see *Box E.*

 If you do not need to make any adjustments to the basis or type of gain or loss (short-term or long-term) reported to you on Form 1099-B (or substitute statement) or to your gain or loss for any transactions you normally would report on Form 8949 with box D checked, you do not have to include those transactions on Form 8949. Instead, you can report them directly on Schedule D. For more information, see Exception 3, later.

Box E. Report on a Part II with box E checked all long-term transactions reported to you on Form 1099-B (or substitute statement) without an amount shown for cost or other basis or showing that cost or other basis was not reported to the IRS. If your statement shows cost or other basis for the transaction was reported to the IRS (for example, if box 6b of Form 1099-B is checked), see *Box D.*

Box F. Report on a Part II with box F checked all long-term transactions for which you cannot check box D or E because you did not receive a Form 1099-B (or substitute statement).

You do not need to complete and file an entire copy of Form 8949 (Part I and Part II) if you can check a single box to describe all your transactions. In that case, complete and file either Part I or Part II and check the box that describes the transactions. Otherwise, complete a separate Part I or Part II for each category of your transactions, as described above.

Include on your Schedule D the totals from all your Parts I and Parts II. Form 8949 and Schedule D explain how to do this.

Exceptions to reporting each transaction on a separate row. There are three exceptions to the rule that you must report each of your transactions on a separate row of Part I or Part II.

Exception 1. Instead of reporting each of your transactions on a separate row of Part I or Part II, you can report them on an attached statement containing all the same information as Parts I and II and in a similar format (i.e., description of property, dates of acquisition and disposition, proceeds, basis, adjustment and code(s), and gain or (loss)). Use as many attached statements as you need. Enter the combined totals from all your attached statements on Parts I and II with the appropriate box checked.

For example, report on Part I with box B checked all short-term gains and losses from transactions your broker reported to you on a statement showing basis was not reported to the IRS. Enter the name of the broker followed by the words "see attached statement" in column (a). Leave columns (b) and (c) blank. Enter "M" in column (f). If other codes also apply, enter all of them in column (f). Enter the totals that apply in columns (d), (e), (g), and (h). If you have statements from more than one broker, report the totals from each broker on a separate row.

Do not enter "Available upon request" and summary totals in lieu of reporting the details of each transaction on Part I or II or attached statements.

Exception 2. You may enter summary totals instead of reporting the details of each transaction on a separate row of Part I or II or on attached statements if:

1. You must report more than five transactions for that Part, and

2. You file Form 1120S, 1065, or 1065-B or are a taxpayer exempt from receiving Form 1099-B, such as a corporation or exempt organization, under Regulations section 1.6045-1(c)(3)(i)(B).

If this exception applies to you, enter the summary totals on line 1. For short-term transactions, check box C at the top of Part I even if the summary totals include transactions described in the text for box A or B. For long-term transactions, check box F at the top of Part II even if the summary totals include transactions described in the text for box D or E. Enter "Available upon request" in column (a). Leave columns (b) and (c) blank. Enter "M" in column (f). If other codes also apply, enter all of them in column (f). Enter the totals that apply in columns (d), (e), (g), and (h).

Do not use a separate row for the totals from each broker. Instead, enter the summary totals from all brokers on a single row of Part I (with box C checked) or Part II (with box F checked).

Exception 3. Form 8949 is not required for certain transactions. You may be able to aggregate those transactions and report them directly on either line 1a (for short-term transactions) or line 8a (for long-term transactions) of Schedule D. This option applies only to transactions (other than sales of collectibles) for which:

• You received a Form 1099-B (or substitute statement) that shows basis was reported to the IRS and does not show a nondeductible wash sale loss in box 5, and

• You do not need to make any adjustments to the basis or type of gain or loss (short-term or long-term) reported on Form 1099-B (or substitute statement), or to your gain or loss.

If you choose to report these transactions directly on Schedule D, you do not need to include them on Form 8949 and do not need to attach a statement. For more information, see the Schedule D instructions.

If you qualify to use *Exception 3* and also qualify to use *Exception 1* or *Exception 2*, you can use both (*Exception 3* plus either *Exception 1* or *Exception 2*). Report the transactions that qualify for *Exception 3* directly on either line 1a or 8a of Schedule D, whichever applies. Report the rest of your transactions as explained in *Exception 1* or *Exception 2*, whichever applies.

E-file. If you *e-file* your return but choose not to report each transaction on a separate row on the electronic return, you must either (a) include Form 8949 as a PDF attachment to your return or (b) attach Form 8949 to Form 8453 (or the appropriate form in the Form 8453 series) and mail the forms to the IRS. You can attach one or more statements containing all the same information as Form 8949, instead of attaching Form 8949, if the statements are in a format similar to Form 8949.

However, this does not apply to transactions that qualify for *Exception 2* or *Exception 3*. In those cases, neither an attachment, a statement, nor Form 8453 is required.

Charitable gift annuity. If you are the beneficiary of a charitable gift annuity and receive a Form 1099-R showing an amount in box 3, report the box 3 amount on a Part II with box F checked. Enter "Form 1099-R" in column (a). Enter the box 3 amount in column (d). Also complete column (h).

Form 2438. Enter any net short-term capital gain from line 4 of Form 2438 on a Part I with box C checked. Enter "Net short-term capital gain from Form 2438, line 4" in column (a), enter the gain in column (h), and leave all other columns blank.

Enter any amount from line 12 of Form 2438 on a Part II with box F checked. Enter "Undistributed capital gains not designated (from Form 2438)" in column (a), enter the amount of the gain in column (h), and leave all other columns blank.

Form 2439. Corporations and partnerships report undistributed long-term capital gains from Form 2439 on a Part II with box F checked. Enter "From Form 2439" in column (a), enter the gain in column (h), and leave all other columns blank. Individuals report undistributed long-term capital gains from Form 2439 on line 11 of Schedule D (Form 1040). Estates and trusts report those amounts on line 11 of Schedule D (Form 1041).

Nondividend distributions. Distributions from a corporation that are a return of your cost (or other basis) are not taxed until you recover your cost (or other

-3-

basis). Reduce your cost (or other basis) by these distributions, but not below zero. After you have recovered your entire cost (or other basis), any later nondividend distribution is taxable as a capital gain. Enter the name of the payer of any taxable nondividend distributions in column (a) on a Part I with box C checked or Part II with box F checked (depending on how long you held the stock). Enter the taxable part of the distribution in columns (d) and (h). Each payer of a nondividend distribution should send you a Form 1099-DIV showing the amount of the distribution in box 3.

Other gains or losses where sales price or basis is not known. If you have another gain or loss for which you do not know the sales price or basis (such as a long-term capital gain from Form 8621), enter a description of the gain or loss in column (a) on a Part I with box C checked or Part II with box F checked (depending on how long you held the property). If you have a gain, enter it in columns (d) and (h). If you have a loss, enter it in columns (e) and (h). Complete any other columns you can.

Column (a)—Description of Property

For stock, include the number of shares. You can use stock ticker symbols or abbreviations to describe the property as long as they are based on the descriptions of the property as shown on Form 1099-B or 1099-S (or substitute statement).

If you inherited the property from someone who died in 2010 and the executor of the estate made the election to file Form 8939, also enter "INH-2010" in column (a).

Column (b)—Date Acquired

Enter in this column the date you acquired the property. Enter the trade date for stocks and bonds you purchased on an exchange or over-the-counter market. For a short sale, enter the date you acquired the property delivered to the broker or lender to close the short sale. For property you previously elected to treat as having been sold and reacquired on January 1, 2001 (or January 2, 2001, for readily tradeable stock), enter the date of the deemed sale and reacquisition.

Inherited property. Generally, if you disposed of property that you acquired by inheritance, report the sale or exchange on a Part II with the appropriate box checked (D, E, or F). Enter "INHERITED" in column (b).

Stock acquired on various dates. If you sold a block of stock (or similar property) that you acquired through several different purchases, you may report the sale on one row and enter "VARIOUS" in column (b). However, you still must report the short-term gain or (loss) on the sale on Part I and the long-term gain or (loss) on Part II.

Column (c)—Date Sold or Disposed

Enter in this column the date you sold or disposed of the property. Use the trade date for stocks and bonds traded on an exchange or over-the-counter market. For a short sale, enter the date you delivered the property to the broker or lender to close the short sale.

Column (d)—Proceeds (Sales Price)

Follow the instructions below that apply to your transaction(s).

You did not receive a Form 1099-B or 1099-S (or substitute statement). If you did not receive a Form 1099-B or 1099-S (or substitute statement) for a transaction, enter in column (d) the net proceeds. The net proceeds equal the gross proceeds minus any selling expenses (such as broker's fees, commissions, and state and local transfer taxes). If you sold a call option and it was exercised, you must also adjust the sales price of the property sold under the option for any option premiums (as instructed in *Gain or Loss From Options* in the instructions for Schedule D (Form 1040)).

You received a Form 1099-B or 1099-S (or substitute statement). If you received a Form 1099-B or 1099-S (or substitute statement) for a transaction, enter in column (d) the proceeds (sales price) shown on the form or statement you received. If there are any selling expenses or option premiums that are not reflected on the form or statement you received (by an adjustment to either the proceeds or basis shown), enter "E" in column (f) and the necessary adjustment in column (g). See the example under *Column (g)—Adjustments to Gain or Loss*, later.

If the proceeds you received were more than shown on Form 1099-B or 1099-S (or substitute statement), enter the correct proceeds in column (d). This might happen if, for example, box 4 on Form 1099-S is checked.

You should not have received a Form 1099-B (or substitute statement) for a transaction merely representing the return of your original investment in a nontransferable obligation, such as a savings bond or a certificate of deposit. But if you did, report the proceeds (sales price) shown on Form 1099-B (or substitute statement) in both columns (d) and (e).

Column (e)—Cost or Other Basis

The basis of property you buy is usually its cost, including the purchase price and any costs of purchase, such as commissions. You may not be able to use the actual cost as the basis if you inherited the property, got it as a gift, or received it in a tax-free exchange or involuntary conversion or in connection with a "wash sale." If you do not use the actual cost, attach an explanation of your basis.

The basis of property acquired by gift is generally the basis of the property in the hands of the donor. The basis of inherited property is generally the fair market value at the date of death. See Pub. 551 for details. However, if you sold property that you inherited from someone who died in 2010 and the executor made the election to file Form 8939, see Pub. 4895.

If you elected to recognize gain on property held on January 1, 2001, your basis in the property is its closing market price or fair market value, whichever applies, on the date of the deemed sale and reacquisition, whether the deemed sale resulted in a gain or an unallowed loss.

For more details, see Pub. 551 or Pub. 550.

Adjustments to basis. Before you can figure any gain or loss on a sale, exchange, or other disposition of property, you usually must make certain adjustments (increases and decreases) to the basis of the property. Increase the basis of your property by capital improvements. Decrease it by depreciation, amortization, and depletion.

If you sold stock, adjust your basis by subtracting all the nondividend distributions you received before the sale. Also adjust your basis for any stock splits. See Pub. 550 for details.

Increase the cost or other basis of an original issue discount (OID) debt instrument by the amount of OID that you have included in gross income for that instrument. See Pub. 550 for details.

If you elect to currently include in income the market discount on a bond, increase the basis of the bond by the market discount that has been included in income for that bond. See Pub. 550 for details.

Reduce the basis of a taxable bond by any bond premium amortization that has been permitted for that bond as either an offset to interest income or as a deduction. See Pub. 550 for details. Reduce the basis of a tax-exempt bond by any bond premium amortization that has been permitted for that bond as an offset to interest. See Pub. 550 for details.

-4-

¶2944

If a charitable contribution deduction is allowable because of a bargain sale of property to a charitable organization, you must allocate your basis in the property between the part sold and the part contributed based on the fair market value of each. See Pub. 544 for details.

Average basis. You can use the average basis method to determine the basis of shares of stock if the shares are identical to each other, you acquired them at different prices and left them in an account with a custodian or agent, and either:

• They are shares in a mutual fund (or other regulated investment company (RIC)), or

• You acquired them after 2010 in connection with a dividend reinvestment plan (DRP).

Shares are identical if they have the same CUSIP number, except that shares of stock in a DRP are not identical to shares of stock that are not in a DRP, even if they have the same CUSIP number. If you are using the average basis method and received a Form 1099-B (or substitute statement) that shows an incorrect basis, enter "B" in column (f), enter the basis shown on Form 1099-B (or substitute statement) in column (e), and see *How To Complete Form 8949, Columns (f) and (g)*, later. For details on making the election and figuring average basis, see Pub. 550 or Regulations section 1.1012-1(e).

Form 1099-B. If the property you sold was a covered security, its basis should be shown in box 3 of the Form 1099-B (or substitute statement) you received from your broker. Generally, a covered security is stock acquired after 2010 (after 2011 if in a mutual fund or other regulated investment company, or acquired through a dividend reinvestment plan).

If box 6a on Form 1099-B is checked, the property sold was not a covered security.

Enter the basis shown on Form 1099-B (or substitute statement) in column (e). If the basis shown on Form 1099-B (or substitute statement) is not correct, see *How To Complete Form 8949, Columns (f) and (g)*, later, for the adjustment you must make.

If no basis is shown on Form 1099-B (or substitute statement), enter the correct basis of the property in column (e).

Column (f)—Code

In order to explain any adjustment to gain or loss in column (g), enter the appropriate code(s) in column (f). See *How To Complete Form 8949, Columns (f) and (g)*, later. If more than one code applies, enter all the codes that apply in alphabetical order (for example, "BOQ"). Do not separate the codes by a space or comma.

Column (g)—Adjustments to Gain or Loss

Enter in this column any necessary adjustments to gain or loss. Enter negative amounts in parentheses. Also enter a code in column (f) to explain the adjustment. See *How To Complete Form 8949, Columns (f) and (g)*, later.

More than one code. If you entered more than one code in column (f) on the same row, enter the net adjustment in column (g). For example, if one adjustment is $5,000 and another is ($1,000), enter $4,000 ($5,000 – $1,000).

Example. You sold your main home in 2013 for $320,000 and received a Form 1099-S showing the $320,000 gross proceeds. The home's basis was $100,000. You had selling expenses of $20,000. Under the tests described in *Sale of Your Home* in the Instructions for Schedule D (Form 1040), you can exclude the entire $200,000 gain from income. On Form 8949, Part II, check box F at the top. Complete columns (a), (b), and (c). Enter $320,000 in column (d) and $100,000 in column (e). Enter "EH" in column (f). In column (g), enter $220,000 ($20,000 selling expenses + $200,000 exclusion) as a negative number. Put it in parentheses to show it is negative. In column (h), enter -0- ($320,000 – $100,000 – $220,000). If this is your only transaction on this Part II, enter $320,000 in column (d) on line 10 of Schedule D (Form 1040), $100,000 in column (e), ($220,000) in column (g), and -0- in column (h).

¶2944

How To Complete Form 8949, Columns (f) and (g)

For most transactions, you do not need to complete columns (f) and (g) and can leave them blank. You may need to complete columns (f) and (g) if you got a Form 1099-B or 1099-S (or substitute statement) that is incorrect, if you are excluding or postponing a capital gain, if you have a disallowed loss, or in certain other situations. Details are in the table below. If you enter more than one code in column (f), see *More than one code* in the instructions for column (g).

IF . . .	THEN enter this code in column (f) . . .	AND. . .
You received a Form 1099-B (or substitute statement) and the basis shown in box 3 is incorrect	B	• If box B is checked at the top of Part I or if box E is checked at the top of Part II, enter the correct basis in column (e), and enter -0- in column (g). • If box A is checked at the top of Part I or if box D is checked at the top of Part II, enter the basis shown on Form 1099-B (or substitute statement) in column (e), even though that basis is incorrect. Correct the error by entering an adjustment in column (g). To figure the adjustment needed, see the *Worksheet for Basis Adjustments in Column (g)*. Also see *Example 4—adjustment for incorrect basis* in the instructions for column (h).
You received a Form 1099-B (or substitute statement) and the type of gain or loss (short-term or long-term) shown in box 1c is incorrect	T	Enter -0- in column (g). Report the gain or loss on the correct Part of Form 8949.
You received a Form 1099-B or 1099-S (or substitute statement) as a nominee for the actual owner of the property	N	Report the transaction on Form 8949 as you would if you were the actual owner, but also enter any resulting gain as a negative adjustment (in parentheses) in column (g) or any resulting loss as a positive adjustment in column (g). As a result of this adjustment, the amount in column (h) should be zero. However, if you received capital gain distributions as a nominee, report them instead as described under *Capital Gain Distributions* in the Instructions for Schedule D (Form 1040).
You sold or exchanged your main home at a gain, must report the sale or exchange on Part II of Form 8949 (as explained in *Sale of Your Home* in the Instructions for Schedule D (Form 1040)), and can exclude some or all of the gain	H	Report the sale or exchange on Form 8949 as you would if you were not taking the exclusion. Then enter the amount of excluded (nontaxable) gain as a negative number (in parentheses) in column (g). See the example in the instructions for column (g).
You sold or exchanged qualified small business stock and can exclude part of the gain	Q	Report the sale or exchange on Form 8949 as you would if you were not taking the exclusion and enter the amount of the exclusion as a negative number (in parentheses) in column (g). However, if the transaction is reported as an installment sale, see *Gain from an installment sale of QSB stock* in the Instructions for Schedule D (Form 1040).
You can exclude all or part of your gain under the rules explained in the Schedule D instructions for DC Zone assets or qualified community assets	X	Report the sale or exchange on Form 8949 as you would if you were not taking the exclusion. Then enter the amount of the exclusion as a negative number (in parentheses) in column (g).
You are electing to postpone all or part of your gain under the rules explained in the Schedule D instructions for any rollover of gain (for example, rollover of gain from QSB stock or publicly traded securities)	R	Report the sale or exchange on Form 8949 as you would if you were not making the election. Then enter the amount of postponed gain as a negative number (in parentheses) in column (g).

¶2944

IF . . .	THEN enter this code in column (f) . . .	AND. . .
You have a nondeductible loss from a wash sale	W	Report the sale or exchange on Form 8949 and enter the amount of the nondeductible loss as a positive number in column (g). See the Schedule D instructions for more information about wash sales. If you received a Form 1099-B (or substitute statement) and the amount of nondeductible wash sale loss shown (box 5 of Form 1099-B) is incorrect, enter the correct amount of the nondeductible loss as a positive number in column (g). If the amount of the nondeductible loss is less than the amount shown on Form 1099-B (or substitute statement), attach a statement explaining the difference. If no part of the loss is a nondeductible loss from a wash sale transaction, enter -0- in column (g).
You have a nondeductible loss other than a loss indicated by code W	L	Report the sale or exchange on Form 8949 and enter the amount of the nondeductible loss as a positive number in column (g). See *Nondeductible Losses* in the Instructions for Schedule D (Form 1040).
You received a Form 1099-B or 1099-S (or substitute statement) for a transaction and there are selling expenses or option premiums that are not reflected on the form or statement by an adjustment to either the proceeds or basis shown	E	Enter in column (d) the proceeds shown on the form or statement you received. Enter in column (e) any cost or other basis shown on Form 1099-B (or substitute statement). In column (g), enter as a negative number (in parentheses) any selling expenses and option premium that you paid (and that are not reflected on the form or statement you received) and enter as a positive number any option premium that you received (and that is not reflected on the form or statement you received). For more information about option premiums, see *Gain or Loss From Options* in the Instructions for Schedule D (Form 1040).
You had a loss from the sale, exchange, or worthlessness of small business (section 1244) stock and the total loss is more than the maximum amount that can be treated as an ordinary loss	S	See *Small Business (Section 1244) Stock* in the Schedule D (Form 1040) instructions.
You disposed of collectibles (see the Schedule D instructions)	C	Enter -0- in column (g). Report the disposition on Form 8949 as you would report any sale or exchange.
You report multiple transactions on a single row as described in *Exception 1* or *Exception 2* under *Exceptions to reporting each transaction on a separate row*	M	See *Exception 1* and *Exception 2* under *Exceptions to reporting each transaction on a separate row*. Enter -0- in column (g) unless an adjustment is required because of another code.
You have an adjustment not explained earlier in this column	O	Enter the appropriate adjustment amount in column (g). See the instructions for column (g).
None of the other statements in this column apply	Leave columns (f) and (g) blank.	

Column (h)—Gain or (Loss)

Figure gain or loss on each row. First, subtract the cost or other basis in column (e) from the proceeds (sales price) in column (d). Then take into account any adjustments in column (g). Enter the gain or (loss) in column (h). Enter negative amounts in parentheses.

Example 1—gain. Column (d) is $6,000 and column (e) is $2,000. Enter $4,000 in column (h).

Example 2—loss. Column (d) is $6,000 and column (e) is $8,000. Enter ($2,000) in column (h).

Example 3—adjustment. Column (d) is $6,000, column (e) is $2,000, and column (g) is ($1,000). Enter $3,000 in column (h).

Example 4—adjustment for incorrect basis. You sold stock for $1,000. You had owned the stock for 3 months. Your correct basis for the stock is $100, but you receive a Form 1099-B that shows your basis is $900 and shows your broker reported that basis to the IRS.

-7-

¶2944

Enter $900 on line 1 of the *Worksheet for Basis Adjustments in Column (g)*. Enter $100 on line 2 of the worksheet. Since line 1 is larger than line 2, leave line 3 blank and enter $800 ($900 − $100) as a positive number on line 4. Also enter $800 in column (g) of a Part I with box A checked at the top. Enter "B" in column (f). Enter $1,000 in column (d) and $900 in column (e). To figure your gain or loss, subtract $900 from $1,000. Combine the result, $100, with the $800 adjustment in column (g). Your gain is $900 ($100 + $800). Enter $900 in column (h).

Worksheet for Basis Adjustments in Column (g)   *Keep for Your Records*

If the basis shown on Form 1099-B (or substitute statement) is not correct, do the following.		
• If the basis was not reported to the IRS, enter the correct basis in column (e) and enter -0- in column (g) (unless you must make an adjustment for some other reason).		
• If the basis was reported to the IRS, enter the reported basis shown on Form 1099-B (or substitute statement) in column (e) and use this worksheet to figure the adjustment to include in column (g).		
1. Enter the cost or other basis shown on Form 1099-B (or substitute statement)	1.	_____
2. Enter the correct cost or other basis	2.	_____
3. If line 1 is larger than line 2, leave this line blank and go to line 4. If line 2 is larger than line 1, subtract line 1 from line 2. Enter the result here and in column (g) as a negative number (in parentheses)	3.	_____
4. If line 1 is larger than line 2, subtract line 2 from line 1. Enter the result here and in column (g) as a positive number	4.	_____

Line 2

The total of the amounts in column (h) of line 2 of all your Forms 8949 should equal the amount you get by combining columns (d), (e), and (g) on the corresponding line of Schedule D. For example, the total of the amounts in column (h) of line 2 of all your Forms 8949 with box A checked should equal the amount you get by combining columns (d), (e), and (g) on line 1b of Schedule D. The total of the amounts in column (h) of line 2 of all your Forms 8949 with box E checked should equal the amount you get by combining columns (d), (e), and (g) on line 9 of Schedule D.

-8-

¶2944

¶2945 SAMPLE COMPLETED FORM 1041 FOR JANE B. TRENT TRUST

Form **1041**	Department of the Treasury—Internal Revenue Service **U.S. Income Tax Return for Estates and Trusts**	20**13**	OMB No. 1545-0092

▶ Information about Form 1041 and its separate instructions is at *www.irs.gov/form1041.*

A Check all that apply:	For calendar year 2013 or fiscal year beginning , 2013, and ending , 20	**C** Employer identification number
☐ Decedent's estate	Name of estate or trust (If a grantor type trust, see the instructions.)	52-00000
☑ Simple trust	**Trust u/w Jane B. Trent**	**D** Date entity created
☐ Complex trust	Name and title of fiduciary	02/01/13
☐ Qualified disability trust	**Best Bank of Missouri**	**E** Nonexempt charitable and split-interest trusts, check applicable box(es), see instructions.
☐ ESBT (S portion only)	Number, street, and room or suite no. (If a P.O. box, see the instructions.)	
☐ Grantor type trust		☐ Described in sec. 4947(a)(1). Check here if not a private foundation . . ▶ ☐
☐ Bankruptcy estate-Ch. 7	**123 Charles Street**	
☐ Bankruptcy estate-Ch. 11	City or town, state or province, country, and ZIP or foreign postal code	☐ Described in sec. 4947(a)(2)
☐ Pooled income fund	**Kansas City, Missouri 64233**	

B Number of Schedules K-1 attached (see instructions) ▶

F Check applicable boxes: ☑ Initial return ☐ Final return ☐ Amended return   ☐ Change in trust's name ☐ Change in fiduciary ☐ Change in fiduciary's name ☐ Change in fiduciary's address

G Check here if the estate or filing trust made a section 645 election . . . . . . ▶ ☐ Trust EIN ▶

Income

1	Interest income	**1**		4,000
2a	Total ordinary dividends	**2a**		20,000
b	Qualified dividends allocable to: **(1)** Beneficiaries _____ **(2)** Estate or trust _____			
3	Business income or (loss). Attach Schedule C or C-EZ (Form 1040)	**3**		
4	Capital gain or (loss). Attach Schedule D (Form 1041)	**4**		10,000
5	Rents, royalties, partnerships, other estates and trusts, etc. Attach Schedule E (Form 1040) .	**5**		6,000
6	Farm income or (loss). Attach Schedule F (Form 1040)	**6**		
7	Ordinary gain or (loss). Attach Form 4797	**7**		
8	Other income. List type and amount	**8**		
9	**Total income.** Combine lines 1, 2a, and 3 through 8 . . . . ▶	**9**		40,000

Deductions

10	Interest. Check if Form 4952 is attached ▶ ☐	**10**		
11	Taxes	**11**		
12	Fiduciary fees	**12**		4,000
13	Charitable deduction (from Schedule A, line 7)	**13**		
14	Attorney, accountant, and return preparer fees	**14**		
15a	Other deductions **not** subject to the 2% floor (attach schedule)	**15a**		
b	Net operating loss deduction (see instructions)	**15b**		
c	Allowable miscellaneous itemized deductions subject to the 2% floor	**15c**		
16	Add lines 10 through 15c . . . . ▶	**16**		4,000
17	Adjusted total income or (loss). Subtract line 16 from line 9 . . .	**17**	36,000	
18	Income distribution deduction (from Schedule B, line 15). Attach Schedules K-1 (Form 1041)	**18**		18,000
19	Estate tax deduction including certain generation-skipping taxes (attach computation) . . .	**19**		
20	Exemption	**20**		300
21	Add lines 18 through 20 . . . . ▶	**21**		18,300
22	Taxable income. Subtract line 21 from line 17. If a loss, see instructions	**22**		17,700
23	**Total tax** (from Schedule G, line 7)	**23**		3,746

Tax and Payments

24	**Payments: a** 2013 estimated tax payments and amount applied from 2012 return	**24a**		2,000
b	Estimated tax payments allocated to beneficiaries (from Form 1041-T)	**24b**		-0-
c	Subtract line 24b from line 24a	**24c**		2,000
d	Tax paid with Form 7004 (see instructions)	**24d**		-0-
e	Federal income tax withheld. If any is from Form(s) 1099, check ▶ ☐	**24e**		
	Other payments: **f** Form 2439 _____ ; **g** Form 4136 _____ ; Total ▶	**24h**		
25	**Total payments.** Add lines 24c through 24e, and 24h . . . . ▶	**25**		
26	Estimated tax penalty (see instructions)	**26**		
27	**Tax due.** If line 25 is smaller than the total of lines 23 and 26, enter amount owed . . .	**27**		1,746
28	**Overpayment.** If line 25 is larger than the total of lines 23 and 26, enter amount overpaid . .	**28**		
29	Amount of line 28 to be: **a** Credited to 2014 estimated tax ▶ ; **b** Refunded ▶	**29**		

Sign Here

Under penalties of perjury, I declare that I have examined this return, including accompanying schedules and statements, and to the best of my knowledge and belief, it is true, correct, and complete. Declaration of preparer (other than taxpayer) is based on all information of which preparer has any knowledge.

▶ _____ ▶ _____
Signature of fiduciary or officer representing fiduciary   Date   EIN of fiduciary if a financial institution

May the IRS discuss this return with the preparer shown below (see instr.)? ☐ Yes ☐ No

Paid Preparer Use Only

Print/Type preparer's name	Preparer's signature	Date	Check ☐ if self-employed	PTIN
Firm's name ▶			Firm's EIN ▶	
Firm's address ▶			Phone no.	

For Paperwork Reduction Act Notice, see the separate instructions.   Cat. No. 11370H   Form **1041** (2013)

Form 1041 (2013)   Page **2**

	Schedule A	Charitable Deduction. Do not complete for a simple trust or a pooled income fund.		
1		Amounts paid or permanently set aside for charitable purposes from gross income (see instructions)	1	
2		Tax-exempt income allocable to charitable contributions (see instructions)	2	
3		Subtract line 2 from line 1	3	
4		Capital gains for the tax year allocated to corpus and paid or permanently set aside for charitable purposes	4	
5		Add lines 3 and 4	5	
6		Section 1202 exclusion allocable to capital gains paid or permanently set aside for charitable purposes (see instructions)	6	
7		**Charitable deduction.** Subtract line 6 from line 5. Enter here and on page 1, line 13	7	

	Schedule B	Income Distribution Deduction		
1		Adjusted total income (see instructions)	1	36,000
2		Adjusted tax-exempt interest	2	
3		Total net gain from Schedule D (Form 1041), line 19, column (1) (see instructions)	3	
4		Enter amount from Schedule A, line 4 (minus any allocable section 1202 exclusion)	4	
5		Capital gains for the tax year included on Schedule A, line 1 (see instructions)	5	
6		Enter any gain from page 1, line 4, as a negative number. If page 1, line 4, is a loss, enter the loss as a positive number	6	(10,000)
7		**Distributable net income.** Combine lines 1 through 6. If zero or less, enter -0-	7	26,000
8		If a complex trust, enter accounting income for the tax year as determined under the governing instrument and applicable local law 8		
9		Income required to be distributed currently	9	18,000
10		Other amounts paid, credited, or otherwise required to be distributed	10	
11		Total distributions. Add lines 9 and 10. If greater than line 8, see instructions	11	18,000
12		Enter the amount of tax-exempt income included on line 11	12	
13		Tentative income distribution deduction. Subtract line 12 from line 11	13	18,000
14		Tentative income distribution deduction. Subtract line 2 from line 7. If zero or less, enter -0-	14	26,000
15		**Income distribution deduction.** Enter the smaller of line 13 or line 14 here and on page 1, line 18	15	18,000

	Schedule G	Tax Computation (see instructions)				
1	**Tax: a**	Tax on taxable income (see instructions)	1a	3,527		
	b	Tax on lump-sum distributions. Attach Form 4972	1b			
	c	Alternative minimum tax (from Schedule I (Form 1041), line 56)	1c			
	d	**Total.** Add lines 1a through 1c			1d	3,527
2a		Foreign tax credit. Attach Form 1116	2a			
b		General business credit. Attach Form 3800	2b			
c		Credit for prior year minimum tax. Attach Form 8801	2c			
d		Bond credits. Attach Form 8912	2d			
e		**Total credits.** Add lines 2a through 2d			2e	-0-
3		Subtract line 2e from line 1d. If zero or less, enter -0-			3	3,527
4		Net investment income tax from Form 8960, line 21			4	219
5		Recapture taxes. Check if from: ☐ Form 4255 ☐ Form 8611			5	
6		Household employment taxes. Attach Schedule H (Form 1040)			6	
7		**Total tax.** Add lines 3 through 6. Enter here and on page 1, line 23			7	3,746

	Other Information	Yes	No
1	Did the estate or trust receive tax-exempt income? If "Yes," attach a computation of the allocation of expenses. Enter the amount of tax-exempt interest income and exempt-interest dividends ▶ $ _____		✓
2	Did the estate or trust receive all or any part of the earnings (salary, wages, and other compensation) of any individual by reason of a contract assignment or similar arrangement?		✓
3	At any time during calendar year 2013, did the estate or trust have an interest in or a signature or other authority over a bank, securities, or other financial account in a foreign country?		✓
	See the instructions for exceptions and filing requirements for FinCEN Form 114. If "Yes," enter the name of the foreign country ▶		
4	During the tax year, did the estate or trust receive a distribution from, or was it the grantor of, or transferor to, a foreign trust? If "Yes," the estate or trust may have to file Form 3520. See instructions		✓
5	Did the estate or trust receive, or pay, any qualified residence interest on seller-provided financing? If "Yes," see the instructions for required attachment		✓
6	If this is an estate or a complex trust making the section 663(b) election, check here (see instructions) ▶ ☐		
7	To make a section 643(e)(3) election, attach Schedule D (Form 1041), and check here (see instructions) ▶ ☐		
8	If the decedent's estate has been open for more than 2 years, attach an explanation for the delay in closing the estate, and check here ▶ ☐		
9	Are any present or future trust beneficiaries skip persons? See instructions		✓

Form **1041** (2013)

SCHEDULE I (Form 1041)	Alternative Minimum Tax—Estates and Trusts	OMB No. 1545-0092
Department of the Treasury Internal Revenue Service	► Attach to Form 1041. ► Information about Schedule I (Form 1041) and its separate instructions is at *www.irs.gov/form1041.*	2013

Name of estate or trust	Employer identification number
Trust u/w Jane B. Trent	52-0000000

Part I   Estate's or Trust's Share of Alternative Minimum Taxable Income

1	Adjusted total income or (loss) (from Form 1041, line 17)	1	36,000
2	Interest	2	
3	Taxes	3	
4	Miscellaneous itemized deductions (from Form 1041, line 15c)	4	
5	Refund of taxes	5	( )
6	Depletion (difference between regular tax and AMT)	6	
7	Net operating loss deduction. Enter as a positive amount	7	
8	Interest from specified private activity bonds exempt from the regular tax	8	
9	Qualified small business stock (see instructions)	9	
10	Exercise of incentive stock options (excess of AMT income over regular tax income)	10	
11	Other estates and trusts (amount from Schedule K-1 (Form 1041), box 12, code A)	11	
12	Electing large partnerships (amount from Schedule K-1 (Form 1065-B), box 6)	12	
13	Disposition of property (difference between AMT and regular tax gain or loss)	13	
14	Depreciation on assets placed in service after 1986 (difference between regular tax and AMT)	14	
15	Passive activities (difference between AMT and regular tax income or loss)	15	
16	Loss limitations (difference between AMT and regular tax income or loss)	16	
17	Circulation costs (difference between regular tax and AMT)	17	
18	Long-term contracts (difference between AMT and regular tax income)	18	
19	Mining costs (difference between regular tax and AMT)	19	
20	Research and experimental costs (difference between regular tax and AMT)	20	
21	Income from certain installment sales before January 1, 1987	21	( )
22	Intangible drilling costs preference	22	
23	Other adjustments, including income-based related adjustments	23	
24	Alternative tax net operating loss deduction (See the instructions for the limitation that applies.)	24	( )
25	Adjusted alternative minimum taxable income. Combine lines 1 through 24	25	36,000
	Note: *Complete Part II below before going to line 26.*		
26	Income distribution deduction from Part II, line 44 ... **26** 18,000		
27	Estate tax deduction (from Form 1041, line 19) ... **27**		
28	Add lines 26 and 27	28	18,000
29	Estate's or trust's share of alternative minimum taxable income. Subtract line 28 from line 25	29	18,000

If line 29 is:
• $23,100 or less, stop here and enter -0- on Form 1041, Schedule G, line 1c. The estate or trust is not liable for the alternative minimum tax.
• Over $23,100, but less than $169,350, go to line 45.
• $169,350 or more, enter the amount from line 29 on line 51 and go to line 52.

Part II   Income Distribution Deduction on a Minimum Tax Basis

30	Adjusted alternative minimum taxable income (see instructions)	30	36,000
31	Adjusted tax-exempt interest (other than amounts included on line 8)	31	
32	Total net gain from Schedule D (Form 1041), line 19, column (1). If a loss, enter -0-	32	
33	Capital gains for the tax year allocated to corpus and paid or permanently set aside for charitable purposes (from Form 1041, Schedule A, line 4)	33	
34	Capital gains paid or permanently set aside for charitable purposes from gross income (see instructions)	34	
35	Capital gains computed on a minimum tax basis included on line 25	35	(10,000)
36	Capital losses computed on a minimum tax basis included on line 25. Enter as a positive amount	36	
37	Distributable net alternative minimum taxable income (DNAMTI). Combine lines 30 through 36. If zero or less, enter -0-	37	26,000
38	Income required to be distributed currently (from Form 1041, Schedule B, line 9)	38	18,000
39	Other amounts paid, credited, or otherwise required to be distributed (from Form 1041, Schedule B, line 10)	39	
40	Total distributions. Add lines 38 and 39	40	18,000
41	Tax-exempt income included on line 40 (other than amounts included on line 8)	41	
42	Tentative income distribution deduction on a minimum tax basis. Subtract line 41 from line 40	42	18,000

For Paperwork Reduction Act Notice, see the Instructions for Form 1041.   Cat. No. 51517Q   Schedule I (Form 1041) (2013)

¶2945

Part II	Income Distribution Deduction on a Minimum Tax Basis *(continued)*		
43	Tentative income distribution deduction on a minimum tax basis. Subtract line 31 from line 37. If zero or less, enter -0-	43	26,000
44	**Income distribution deduction on a minimum tax basis.** Enter the smaller of line 42 or line 43. Enter here and on line 26	44	18,000

Part III	Alternative Minimum Tax					
45	Exemption amount			45	$23,100	00
46	Enter the amount from line 29	46	18,000			
47	Phase-out of exemption amount	47	$76,950	00		
48	Subtract line 47 from line 46. If zero or less, enter -0-	48				
49	Multiply line 48 by 25% (.25)			49	-0-	
50	Subtract line 49 from line 45. If zero or less, enter -0-			50	23,100	
51	Subtract line 50 from line 46			51	-0-	
52	Go to Part IV of Schedule I to figure line 52 if the estate or trust has qualified dividends or has a gain on lines 18a and 19 of column (2) of Schedule D (Form 1041) (as refigured for the AMT, if necessary). Otherwise, if line 51 is— • $179,500 or less, multiply line 51 by 26% (.26). • Over $179,500, multiply line 51 by 28% (.28) and subtract $3,590 from the result			52	-0-	
53	Alternative minimum foreign tax credit (see instructions)			53	-0-	
54	Tentative minimum tax. Subtract line 53 from line 52			54	-0-	
55	Enter the tax from Form 1041, Schedule G, line 1a (minus any foreign tax credit from Schedule G, line 2a)			55	3,248	
56	**Alternative minimum tax.** Subtract line 55 from line 54. If zero or less, enter -0-. Enter here and on Form 1041, Schedule G, line 1c			56		

Part IV	Line 52 Computation Using Maximum Capital Gains Rates					
	Caution: *If you did not complete Part V of Schedule D (Form 1041), the Schedule D Tax Worksheet, or the Qualified Dividends Tax Worksheet in the Instructions for Form 1041, see the instructions before completing this part.*					
57	Enter the amount from line 51			57	-0-	
58	Enter the amount from Schedule D (Form 1041), line 26, line 13 of the Schedule D Tax Worksheet, or line 4 of the Qualified Dividends Tax Worksheet in the Instructions for Form 1041, whichever applies (as refigured for the AMT, if necessary)	58	10,000			
59	Enter the amount from Schedule D (Form 1041), line 18b, column (2) (as refigured for the AMT, if necessary). If you did not complete Schedule D for the regular tax or the AMT, enter -0-	59	-0-			
60	If you did not complete a Schedule D Tax Worksheet for the regular tax or the AMT, enter the amount from line 58. Otherwise, add lines 58 and 59 and enter the **smaller** of that result or the amount from line 10 of the Schedule D Tax Worksheet (as refigured for the AMT, if necessary) . .	60	-0-			
61	Enter the **smaller** of line 57 or line 60			61	-0-	
62	Subtract line 61 from line 57			62	-0-	
63	If line 62 is $179,500 or less, multiply line 62 by 26% (.26). Otherwise, multiply line 62 by 28% (.28) and subtract $3,590 from the result . . . . ▶			63	-0-	
64	Maximum amount subject to the 0% rate	64	$2,450	00		
65	Enter the amount from line 27 of Schedule D (Form 1041), line 14 of the Schedule D Tax Worksheet, or line 5 of the Qualified Dividends Tax Worksheet in the Instructions for Form 1041, whichever applies (as figured for the regular tax). If you did not complete Schedule D or either worksheet for the regular tax, enter the amount from Form 1041, line 22; but do not enter less than -0-	65	7,700			
66	Subtract line 65 from line 64. If zero or less, enter -0-	66	-0-			
67	Enter the **smaller** of line 57 or line 58	67	-0-			
68	Enter the **smaller** of line 66 or line 67. This amount is taxed at 0% . .	68	-0-			
69	Subtract line 68 from line 67	69	-0-			

¶2945

Part IV   Line 52 Computation Using Maximum Capital Gains Rates *(continued)*

70	Enter the amount from the Line 70 Worksheet in the instructions . .	70	-0-		
71	Enter the **smaller** of line 69 or 70	71	-0-		
72	Multiply line 71 by 15% (.15) . . . . ▶			72	-0-
73	Add lines 68 and 71	73	-0-		
	If lines 73 and 57 are the same, skip lines 74 through 78 and go to line 79. Otherwise, go to line 74.				
74	Subtract line 73 from line 67	74			
75	Multiply line 74 by 20% (.20) . . . . ▶			75	
	If line 59 is zero or blank, skip lines 76 through 78 and go to line 79. Otherwise, go to line 76.				
76	Add lines 62, 73, and 74	76	-0-		
77	Subtract line 76 from line 57	77	-0-		
78	Multiply line 77 by 25% (.25) . . . . ▶			78	-0-
79	Add lines 63, 72, 75, and 78			79	-0-
80	If line 57 is $179,500 or less, multiply line 57 by 26% (.26). Otherwise, multiply line 57 by 28% (.28) and subtract $3,590 from the result			80	-0-
81	Enter the **smaller** of line 79 or line 80 here and on line 52			81	-0-

¶2945

Form **8949**	**Sales and Other Dispositions of Capital Assets**	OMB No. 1545-0074
Form **8949**	▶ Information about Form 8949 and its separate instructions is at *www.irs.gov/form8949*.	20**13**
Department of the Treasury Internal Revenue Service	▶ File with your Schedule D to list your transactions for lines 1b, 2, 3, 8b, 9, and 10 of Schedule D.	Attachment Sequence No. **12A**

Name(s) shown on return	Social security number or taxpayer identification number
Trust u/w/ Jane B. Trent	52-0000000

Most brokers issue their own substitute statement instead of using Form 1099-B. They also may provide basis information (usually your cost) to you on the statement even if it is not reported to the IRS. Before you check Box A, B, or C below, determine whether you received any statement(s) and, if so, the transactions for which basis was reported to the IRS. Brokers are required to report basis to the IRS for most stock you bought in 2011 or later.

Part I | **Short-Term.** Transactions involving capital assets you held one year or less are short term. For long-term transactions, see page 2.

Note. You may aggregate all short-term transactions reported on Form(s) 1099-B showing basis was reported to the IRS and for which no adjustments or codes are required. Enter the total directly on Schedule D, line 1a; you are not required to report these transactions on Form 8949 (see instructions).

You *must* check Box A, B, *or* C below. Check only one box. If more than one box applies for your short-term transactions, complete a separate Form 8949, page 1, for each applicable box. If you have more short-term transactions than will fit on this page for one or more of the boxes, complete as many forms with the same box checked as you need.

- ☐ **(A)** Short-term transactions reported on Form(s) 1099-B showing basis was reported to the IRS (see **Note** above)
- ☐ **(B)** Short-term transactions reported on Form(s) 1099-B showing basis was **not** reported to the IRS
- ☐ **(C)** Short-term transactions not reported to you on Form 1099-B

1 (a) Description of property (Example: 100 sh. XYZ Co.)	(b) Date acquired (Mo., day, yr.)	(c) Date sold or disposed (Mo., day, yr.)	(d) Proceeds (sales price) (see instructions)	(e) Cost or other basis. See the **Note** below and see *Column (e)* in the separate instructions	Adjustment, if any, to gain or loss. If you enter an amount in column (g), enter a code in column (f). See the separate instructions. (f) Code(s) from instructions	(g) Amount of adjustment	(h) Gain or (loss). Subtract column (e) from column (d) and combine the result with column (g)

2 Totals. Add the amounts in columns (d), (e), (g), and (h) (subtract negative amounts). Enter each total here and include on your Schedule D, **line 1b** (if **Box A** above is checked), **line 2** (if **Box B** above is checked), or **line 3** (if **Box C** above is checked) ▶

Note. If you checked Box A above but the basis reported to the IRS was incorrect, enter in column (e) the basis as reported to the IRS, and enter an adjustment in column (g) to correct the basis. See *Column (g)* in the separate instructions for how to figure the amount of the adjustment.

For Paperwork Reduction Act Notice, see your tax return instructions.   Cat. No. 37768Z   Form **8949** (2013)

¶2945

Form 8949 (2013)   Attachment Sequence No. **12A**   Page **2**

Name(s) shown on return. (Name and SSN or taxpayer identification no. not required if shown on other side.)	Social security number or taxpayer identification number

Most brokers issue their own substitute statement instead of using Form 1099-B. They also may provide basis information (usually your cost) to you on the statement even if it is not reported to the IRS. Before you check Box D, E, or F below, determine whether you received any statement(s) and, if so, the transactions for which basis was reported to the IRS. Brokers are required to report basis to the IRS for most stock you bought in 2011 or later.

Part II **Long-Term.** Transactions involving capital assets you held more than one year are long term. For short-term transactions, see page 1.

Note. You may aggregate all long-term transactions reported on Form(s) 1099-B showing basis was reported to the IRS and for which no adjustments or codes are required. Enter the total directly on Schedule D, line 8a; you are not required to report these transactions on Form 8949 (see instructions).

You *must* check Box D, E, *or* F below. Check only one box. If more than one box applies for your long-term transactions, complete a separate Form 8949, page 2, for each applicable box. If you have more long-term transactions than will fit on this page for one or more of the boxes, complete as many forms with the same box checked as you need.

- [x] **(D)** Long-term transactions reported on Form(s) 1099-B showing basis was reported to the IRS (see **Note** above)
- [ ] **(E)** Long-term transactions reported on Form(s) 1099-B showing basis was **not** reported to the IRS
- [ ] **(F)** Long-term transactions not reported to you on Form 1099-B

1

(a) Description of property (Example: 100 sh. XYZ Co.)	(b) Date acquired (Mo., day, yr.)	(c) Date sold or disposed (Mo., day, yr.)	(d) Proceeds (sales price) (see instructions)	(e) Cost or other basis. See the **Note** below and see *Column (e)* in the separate instructions	Adjustment, if any, to gain or loss. If you enter an amount in column (g), enter a code in column (f). See the separate instructions.		(h) Gain or (loss). Subtract column (e) from column (d) and combine the result with column (g)
					(f) Code(s) from instructions	(g) Amount of adjustment	
1,000 shares of XYZ, Inc. stock	2/01/06	2/01/13	30,000	20,000			10,000
2 Totals. Add the amounts in columns (d), (e), (g), and (h) (subtract negative amounts). Enter each total here and include on your Schedule D, **line 8b** (if **Box D** above is checked), **line 9** (if **Box E** above is checked), or **line 10** (if **Box F** above is checked) ▶			30,000	20,000			10,000

Note. If you checked Box D above but the basis reported to the IRS was incorrect, enter in column (e) the basis as reported to the IRS, and enter an adjustment in column (g) to correct the basis. See *Column (g)* in the separate instructions for how to figure the amount of the adjustment.

Form **8949** (2013)

¶2945

SCHEDULE D (Form 1041) Department of the Treasury Internal Revenue Service	**Capital Gains and Losses** ▶ Attach to Form 1041, Form 5227, or Form 990-T. ▶ Use Form 8949 to list your transactions for lines 1b, 2, 3, 8b, 9 and 10. ▶ Information about Schedule D and its separate instructions is at *www.irs.gov/form1041*.	OMB No. 1545-0092 2013

Name of estate or trust	Employer identification number
Trust u/w Jane B. Trent	52-0000000

Note: *Form 5227 filers need to complete* **only** *Parts I and II.*

Part I — Short-Term Capital Gains and Losses—Assets Held One Year or Less

See instructions for how to figure the amounts to enter on the lines below. This form may be easier to complete if you round off cents to whole dollars.	(d) Proceeds (sales price)	(e) Cost (or other basis)	(g) Adjustments to gain or loss from Form(s) 8949, Part I, line 2, column (g)	(h) Gain or (loss) Subtract column (e) from column (d) and combine the result with column (g)
1a Totals for all short-term transactions reported on Form 1099-B for which basis was reported to the IRS and for which you have no adjustments (see instructions). However, if you choose to report all these transactions on Form 8949, leave this line blank and go to line 1b .				
1b Totals for all transactions reported on Form(s) 8949 with **Box A** checked				
2 Totals for all transactions reported on Form(s) 8949 with **Box B** checked				
3 Totals for all transactions reported on Form(s) 8949 with **Box C** checked				

4 Short-term capital gain or (loss) from Forms 4684, 6252, 6781, and 8824	**4**	
5 Net short-term gain or (loss) from partnerships, S corporations, and other estates or trusts . . .	**5**	
6 Short-term capital loss carryover. Enter the amount, if any, from line 9 of the 2012 Capital Loss Carryover Worksheet	**6**	( )
7 **Net short-term capital gain or (loss).** Combine lines 1a through 6 in column (h). Enter here and on line 17, column (3) on the back . . . . ▶	**7**	

Part II — Long-Term Capital Gains and Losses—Assets Held More Than One Year

See instructions for how to figure the amounts to enter on the lines below. This form may be easier to complete if you round off cents to whole dollars.	(d) Proceeds (sales price)	(e) Cost (or other basis)	(g) Adjustments to gain or loss from Form(s) 8949, Part II, line 2, column (g)	(h) Gain or (loss) Subtract column (e) from column (d) and combine the result with column (g)
8a Totals for all long-term transactions reported on Form 1099-B for which basis was reported to the IRS and for which you have no adjustments (see instructions). However, if you choose to report all these transactions on Form 8949, leave this line blank and go to line 8b .				
8b Totals for all transactions reported on Form(s) 8949 with **Box D** checked	30,000	20,000	-0-	10,000
9 Totals for all transactions reported on Form(s) 8949 with **Box E** checked				
10 Totals for all transactions reported on Form(s) 8949 with **Box F** checked.				

11 Long-term capital gain or (loss) from Forms 2439, 4684, 6252, 6781, and 8824	**11**	
12 Net long-term gain or (loss) from partnerships, S corporations, and other estates or trusts . . .	**12**	
13 Capital gain distributions	**13**	
14 Gain from Form 4797, Part I	**14**	
15 Long-term capital loss carryover. Enter the amount, if any, from line 14 of the 2012 Capital Loss Carryover Worksheet	**15**	( )
16 **Net long-term capital gain or (loss).** Combine lines 8a through 15 in column (h). Enter here and on line 18a, column (3) on the back . . . . ▶	**16**	10,000

For Paperwork Reduction Act Notice, see the Instructions for Form 1041.   Cat. No. 11376V   Schedule D (Form 1041) 2013

¶2945

Schedule D (Form 1041) 2013   Page **2**

Part III Summary of Parts I and II		(1) Beneficiaries' (see instr.)	(2) Estate's or trust's	(3) Total
Caution: *Read the instructions **before** completing this part.*				
17 Net short-term gain or (loss)	**17**			
18 Net long-term gain or (loss):				
a Total for year	**18a**		10,000	10,000
b Unrecaptured section 1250 gain (see line 18 of the wrksht.) .	**18b**			
c 28% rate gain	**18c**			
19 **Total net gain or (loss).** Combine lines 17 and 18a . . ▶	**19**		10,000	10,000

Note: *If line 19, column (3), is a net gain, enter the gain on Form 1041, line 4 (or Form 990-T, Part I, line 4a). If lines 18a and 19, column (2), are net gains, go to Part V, and **do not** complete Part IV. If line 19, column (3), is a net loss, complete Part IV and the **Capital Loss Carryover Worksheet,** as necessary.*

Part IV Capital Loss Limitation		
20 Enter here and enter as a (loss) on Form 1041, line 4 (or Form 990-T, Part I, line 4c, if a trust), the **smaller** of:		
a The loss on line 19, column (3) **or b** $3,000	**20** (	)

Note: *If the loss on line 19, column (3), is more than $3,000, **or** if Form 1041, page 1, line 22 (or Form 990-T, line 34), is a loss, complete the **Capital Loss Carryover Worksheet** in the instructions to figure your capital loss carryover.*

Part V Tax Computation Using Maximum Capital Gains Rates

Form 1041 filers. Complete this part **only** if both lines 18a and 19 in column (2) are gains, or an amount is entered in Part I or Part II and there is an entry on Form 1041, line 2b(2), **and** Form 1041, line 22, is more than zero.

Caution: *Skip this part and complete the **Schedule D Tax Worksheet** in the instructions if:*
* *Either line 18b, col. (2) or line 18c, col. (2) is more than zero, or*
* *Both Form 1041, line 2b(1), and Form 4952, line 4g are more than zero.*

Form 990-T trusts. Complete this part **only** if both lines 18a and 19 are gains, or qualified dividends are included in income in Part I of Form 990-T, **and** Form 990-T, line 34, is more than zero. Skip this part and complete the **Schedule D Tax Worksheet** in the instructions if either line 18b, col. (2) or line 18c, col. (2) is more than zero.

21	Enter taxable income from Form 1041, line 22 (or Form 990-T, line 34) .	**21**	17,700			
22	Enter the **smaller** of line 18a or 19 in column (2) but not less than zero	**22**	10,000			
23	Enter the estate's or trust's qualified dividends from Form 1041, line 2b(2) (or enter the qualified dividends included in income in Part I of Form 990-T)	**23**	-0-			
24	Add lines 22 and 23	**24**	10,000			
25	If the estate or trust is filing Form 4952, enter the amount from line 4g; otherwise, enter -0- . . ▶	**25**	-0-			
26	Subtract line 25 from line 24. If zero or less, enter -0-	**26**	10,000			
27	Subtract line 26 from line 21. If zero or less, enter -0-	**27**	7,700			
28	Enter the **smaller** of the amount on line 21 or $2,450	**28**	2,450			
29	Enter the **smaller** of the amount on line 27 or line 28	**29**	2,450			
30	Subtract line 29 from line 28. If zero or less, enter -0-. This amount is taxed at 0% . . . . . ▶	**30**			-0-	
31	Enter the smaller of line 21 or line 26	**31**	10,000			
32	Subtract line 30 from line 26	**32**	10,000			
33	Enter the **smaller** of line 21 or $11,950	**33**	11,960			
34	Add lines 27 and 30	**34**	7,700			
35	Subtract line 34 from line 33. If zero or less, enter -0-	**35**	4,260			
36	Enter the **smaller** of line 32 or line 35	**36**	4,260			
37	Multiply line 36 by 15% . . . . ▶			**37**	639	
38	Enter the amount from line 31	**38**	10,000			
39	Add lines 30 and 36	**39**	4,260			
40	Subtract line 39 from line 38. If zero or less, enter -0-	**40**	5,740			
41	Multiply line 40 by 20% . . . . ▶			**41**	1,148	
42	Figure the tax on the amount on line 27. Use the 2013 Tax Rate Schedule for Estates and Trusts (see the Schedule G instructions in the instructions for Form 1041) . .	**42**	1,740			
43	Add lines 37, 41, and 42	**43**	3,527			
44	Figure the tax on the amount on line 21. Use the 2013 Tax Rate Schedule for Estates and Trusts (see the Schedule G instructions in the instructions for Form 1041) . .	**44**	5,637			
45	**Tax on all taxable income.** Enter the **smaller** of line 43 or line 44 here and on Form 1041, Schedule G, line 1a (or Form 990-T, line 36) . . . . ▶			**45**	3,527	

Schedule D (Form 1041) 2013

SCHEDULE E (Form 1040) Department of the Treasury Internal Revenue Service (99)	**Supplemental Income and Loss** (From rental real estate, royalties, partnerships, S corporations, estates, trusts, REMICs, etc.) ▶ Attach to Form 1040, 1040NR, or Form 1041. ▶ Information about Schedule E and its separate instructions is at *www.irs.gov/schedulee*.	OMB No. 1545-0074 20**13** Attachment Sequence No. **13**

Name(s) shown on return	Your social security number
Trust u/w Jane B. Trent	52-00000

Part I   **Income or Loss From Rental Real Estate and Royalties**   **Note.** If you are in the business of renting personal property, use **Schedule C** or **C-EZ** (see instructions). If you are an individual, report farm rental income or loss from **Form 4835** on page 2, line 40.

A Did you make any payments in 2013 that would require you to file Form(s) 1099? (see instructions)   ☐ Yes   ☑ No
B If "Yes," did you or will you file required Forms 1099?   ☐ Yes   ☑ No

1a   Physical address of each property (street, city, state, ZIP code)

A   123 Main Street Kansas City, Missouri 64123
B
C

1b	Type of Property (from list below)	2	For each rental real estate property listed above, report the number of fair rental and personal use days. Check the **QJV** box only if you meet the requirements to file as a qualified joint venture. See instructions.		Fair Rental Days	Personal Use Days	QJV
A				A			☐
B				B			☐
C				C			☐

Type of Property:
1 Single Family Residence   3 Vacation/Short-Term Rental   5 Land   7 Self-Rental
2 Multi-Family Residence   4 Commercial   6 Royalties   8 Other (describe)

Income:		Properties:		A	B	C
3	Rents received	3		6,000		
4	Royalties received	4				
Expenses:						
5	Advertising	5				
6	Auto and travel (see instructions)	6				
7	Cleaning and maintenance	7				
8	Commissions.	8				
9	Insurance	9				
10	Legal and other professional fees	10				
11	Management fees	11				
12	Mortgage interest paid to banks, etc. (see instructions)	12				
13	Other interest.	13				
14	Repairs.	14				
15	Supplies	15				
16	Taxes	16				
17	Utilities	17				
18	Depreciation expense or depletion	18				
19	Other (list) ▶ _____	19				
20	Total expenses. Add lines 5 through 19 . . .	20				
21	Subtract line 20 from line 3 (rents) and/or 4 (royalties). If result is a (loss), see instructions to find out if you must file **Form 6198**	21		6,000		
22	Deductible rental real estate loss after limitation, if any, on **Form 8582** (see instructions)	22	(	) (	) (	)

23a	Total of all amounts reported on line 3 for all rental properties	23a		
b	Total of all amounts reported on line 4 for all royalty properties	23b		
c	Total of all amounts reported on line 12 for all properties	23c		
d	Total of all amounts reported on line 18 for all properties	23d		
e	Total of all amounts reported on line 20 for all properties	23e		
24	**Income.** Add positive amounts shown on line 21. **Do not** include any losses	24	6,000
25	**Losses.** Add royalty losses from line 21 and rental real estate losses from line 22. Enter total losses here	25	( )
26	**Total rental real estate and royalty income or (loss).** Combine lines 24 and 25. Enter the result here. If Parts II, III, IV, and line 40 on page 2 do not apply to you, also enter this amount on Form 1040, line 17, or Form 1040NR, line 18. Otherwise, include this amount in the total on line 41 on page 2	26	6,000

For Paperwork Reduction Act Notice, see the separate instructions.   Cat. No. 11344L   Schedule E (Form 1040) 2013

¶2945

Schedule E (Form 1040) 2013 | Attachment Sequence No. **13** | Page **2**

Name(s) shown on return. Do not enter name and social security number if shown on other side. | Your social security number

Trust u/w Jane B. Trent | 52-0000000

Caution. The IRS compares amounts reported on your tax return with amounts shown on Schedule(s) K-1.

Part II   **Income or Loss From Partnerships and S Corporations**   **Note.** If you report a loss from an at-risk activity for which **any** amount is **not** at risk, you **must** check the box in column **(e)** on line 28 and attach **Form 6198.** See instructions.

27 Are you reporting any loss not allowed in a prior year due to the at-risk, excess farm loss, or basis limitations, a prior year unallowed loss from a passive activity (if that loss was not reported on Form 8582), or unreimbursed partnership expenses? If you answered "Yes," see instructions before completing this section.   ☐ **Yes**   ☐ **No**

28

(a) Name	(b) Enter **P** for partnership; **S** for S corporation	(c) Check if foreign partnership	(d) Employer identification number	(e) Check if any amount is not at risk
A		☐		☐
B		☐		☐
C		☐		☐
D		☐		☐

	Passive Income and Loss		Nonpassive Income and Loss		
	(f) Passive loss allowed (attach **Form 8582** if required)	(g) Passive income from **Schedule K-1**	(h) Nonpassive loss from **Schedule K-1**	(i) Section 179 expense deduction from **Form 4562**	(j) Nonpassive income from **Schedule K-1**
A					
B					
C					
D					
29a Totals					
b Totals					

30 Add columns (g) and (j) of line 29a . . . . | **30** |
31 Add columns (f), (h), and (i) of line 29b . . . . | **31** (|)
32 **Total partnership and S corporation income or (loss).** Combine lines 30 and 31. Enter the result here and include in the total on line 41 below . . . . | **32** |

Part III   **Income or Loss From Estates and Trusts**

33

(a) Name	(b) Employer identification number
A	
B	

	Passive Income and Loss		Nonpassive Income and Loss	
	(c) Passive deduction or loss allowed (attach **Form 8582** if required)	(d) Passive income from **Schedule K-1**	(e) Deduction or loss from **Schedule K-1**	(f) Other income from **Schedule K-1**
A				
B				
34a Totals				
b Totals				

35 Add columns (d) and (f) of line 34a . . . . | **35** |
36 Add columns (c) and (e) of line 34b . . . . | **36** (|)
37 **Total estate and trust income or (loss).** Combine lines 35 and 36. Enter the result here and include in the total on line 41 below . . . . | **37** |

Part IV   **Income or Loss From Real Estate Mortgage Investment Conduits (REMICs)—Residual Holder**

38

(a) Name	(b) Employer identification number	(c) Excess inclusion from **Schedules Q,** line 2c (see instructions)	(d) Taxable income (net loss) from **Schedules Q,** line 1b	(e) Income from **Schedules Q,** line 3b

39 Combine columns (d) and (e) only. Enter the result here and include in the total on line 41 below | **39** |

Part V   **Summary**

40 Net farm rental income or (loss) from **Form 4835.** Also, complete line 42 below . . . . . . | **40** |
41 Total income or **(loss).** Combine lines 26, 32, 37, 39, and 40. Enter the result here and on Form 1040, line 17, or Form 1040NR, line 18 ▶ | **41** | 6,000
42 **Reconciliation of farming and fishing income.** Enter your **gross** farming and fishing income reported on Form 4835, line 7; Schedule K-1 (Form 1065), box 14, code B; Schedule K-1 (Form 1120S), box 17, code V; and Schedule K-1 (Form 1041), box 14, code F (see instructions) . . | **42** |
43 **Reconciliation for real estate professionals.** If you were a real estate professional (see instructions), enter the net income or (loss) you reported anywhere on Form 1040 or Form 1040NR from all rental real estate activities in which you materially participated under the passive activity loss rules . . | **43** |

Schedule E (Form 1040) 2013

¶2945

661113

| ☐ Final K-1 | ☐ Amended K-1 | OMB No. 1545-0092 |

Schedule K-1
(Form 1041)
Department of the Treasury
Internal Revenue Service

2013

For calendar year 2013,
or tax year beginning _____ , 2013,
and ending _____ , 20 _____

Beneficiary's Share of Income, Deductions, Credits, etc.   ► See back of form and instructions.

Part III	Beneficiary's Share of Current Year Income, Deductions, Credits, and Other Items

1	Interest income 3,467	11	Final year deductions
2a	Ordinary dividends 17,334		
2b	Qualified dividends		
3	Net short-term capital gain		
4a	Net long-term capital gain		
4b	28% rate gain	12	Alternative minimum tax adjustment
4c	Unrecaptured section 1250 gain		
5	Other portfolio and nonbusiness income		
6	Ordinary business income		
7	Net rental real estate income 5,200	13	Credits and credit recapture
8	Other rental income		
9	Directly apportioned deductions 2,000		
		14	Other information
10	Estate tax deduction		

Part I   Information About the Estate or Trust

A Estate's or trust's employer identification number

52-0000000

B Estate's or trust's name

Trust u/w Jane B Trent

C Fiduciary's name, address, city, state, and ZIP code

Best Bank of Missouri 123 Charles Street Kansas City, MO 64138

D ☐ Check if Form 1041-T was filed and enter the date it was filed
_____

E ☐ Check if this is the final Form 1041 for the estate or trust

Part II   Information About the Beneficiary

F Beneficiary's identifying number

G Beneficiary's name, address, city, state, and ZIP code

Mary M. King 189 Main Street Kansas City, MO 63138

H ☒ Domestic beneficiary   ☐ Foreign beneficiary

*See attached statement for additional information.

Note. A statement must be attached showing the beneficiary's share of income and directly apportioned deductions from each business, rental real estate, and other rental activity.

For IRS Use Only

For Paperwork Reduction Act Notice, see the Instructions for Form 1041.   IRS.gov/form1041   Cat. No. 11380D   Schedule K-1 (Form 1041) 2013

¶2945

This list identifies the codes used on Schedule K-1 for beneficiaries and provides summarized reporting information for beneficiaries who file Form 1040. For detailed reporting and filing information, see the Instructions for Schedule K-1 (Form 1041) for a Beneficiary Filing Form 1040 and the instructions for your income tax return.

	Report on
1. **Interest income**	Form 1040, line 8a
2a. **Ordinary dividends**	Form 1040, line 9a
2b. **Qualified dividends**	Form 1040, line 9b
3. **Net short-term capital gain**	Schedule D, line 5
4a. **Net long-term capital gain**	Schedule D, line 12
4b. **28% rate gain**	28% Rate Gain Worksheet, line 4 (Schedule D Instructions)
4c. **Unrecaptured section 1250 gain**	Unrecaptured Section 1250 Gain Worksheet, line 11 (Schedule D Instructions)
5. **Other portfolio and nonbusiness income**	Schedule E, line 33, column (f)
6. **Ordinary business income**	Schedule E, line 33, column (d) or (f)
7. **Net rental real estate income**	Schedule E, line 33, column (d) or (f)
8. **Other rental income**	Schedule E, line 33, column (d) or (f)
9. **Directly apportioned deductions**	
Code	
A Depreciation	Form 8582 or Schedule E, line 33, column (c) or (e)
B Depletion	Form 8582 or Schedule E, line 33, column (c) or (e)
C Amortization	Form 8582 or Schedule E, line 33, column (c) or (e)
10. **Estate tax deduction**	Schedule A, line 28
11. **Final year deductions**	
A Excess deductions	Schedule A, line 23
B Short-term capital loss carryover	Schedule D, line 5
C Long-term capital loss carryover	Schedule D, line 12; line 5 of the wksht. for Sch. D, line 18; and line 16 of the wksht. for Sch. D, line 19
D Net operating loss carryover — regular tax	Form 1040, line 21
E Net operating loss carryover — minimum tax	Form 6251, line 11
12. **Alternative minimum tax (AMT) items**	
A Adjustment for minimum tax purposes	Form 6251, line 15
B AMT adjustment attributable to qualified dividends	
C AMT adjustment attributable to net short-term capital gain	
D AMT adjustment attributable to net long-term capital gain	
E AMT adjustment attributable to unrecaptured section 1250 gain	See the beneficiary's instructions and the Instructions for Form 6251
F AMT adjustment attributable to 28% rate gain	
G Accelerated depreciation	
H Depletion	
I Amortization	
J Exclusion items	2014 Form 8801

13. **Credits and credit recapture**	
Code	*Report on*
A Credit for estimated taxes	Form 1040, line 63
B Credit for backup withholding	Form 1040, line 62
C Low-income housing credit	
D Rehabilitation credit and energy credit	
E Other qualifying investment credit	
F Work opportunity credit	
G Credit for small employer health insurance premiums	
H Biofuel producer credit	
I Credit for increasing research activities	
J Renewable electricity, refined coal, and Indian coal production credit	
K Empowerment zone and renewal community employment credit	
L Indian employment credit	See the beneficiary's instructions
M Orphan drug credit	
N Credit for employer-provided child care and facilities	
O Biodiesel and renewable diesel fuels credit	
P Nonconventional source fuel credit	
Q Credit to holders of tax credit bonds	
R Agricultural chemicals security credit	
S Energy efficient appliance credit	
T Credit for employer differential wage payments	
U Recapture of credits	
14. **Other information**	
A Tax-exempt interest	Form 1040, line 8b
B Foreign taxes	Form 1040, line 47 or Sch. A, line 8
C Qualified production activities income	Form 8903, line 7, col. (b) (also see the beneficiary's instructions)
D Form W-2 wages	Form 8903, line 17
E Net investment income	Form 4952, line 4a
F Gross farm and fishing income	Schedule E, line 42
G Foreign trading gross receipts (IRC 942(a))	See the Instructions for Form 8873
H Adjustment for section 1411 net investment income or deductions	Form 8960, line 7 (also see the beneficiary's instructions)
I Other information	See the beneficiary's instructions

Note. If you are a beneficiary who does not file a Form 1040, see instructions for the type of income tax return you are filing.

¶2946 SAMPLE COMPLETED SCHEDULE J (FORM 1041) FOR JOHN BROWN TRUST

SCHEDULE J (Form 1041)	**Accumulation Distribution for Certain Complex Trusts**	OMB No. 1545-0092
Department of the Treasury Internal Revenue Service	▶ Attach to Form 1041. ▶ Information about Schedule J (Form 1041) and its separate instructions is at *www.irs.gov/form1041.*	20**13**

Name of trust	Employer identification number
John Brown Trust	12-3456789

Part I   Accumulation Distribution in 2013

Note: *See the Form 4970 instructions for certain income that minors may exclude and special rules for multiple trusts.*

1	Other amounts paid, credited, or otherwise required to be distributed for 2013 (from Form 1041, Schedule B, line 10)	1	80,000
2	Distributable net income for 2013 (from Form 1041, Schedule B, line 7) **2** 41,500		
3	Income required to be distributed currently for 2013 (from Form 1041, Schedule B, line 9) **3** 20,000		
4	Subtract line 3 from line 2. If zero or less, enter -0-	4	21,500
5	Accumulation distribution for 2013. Subtract line 4 from line 1	5	58,500

Part II   Ordinary Income Accumulation Distribution (Enter the applicable throwback years below.)

Note: *If the distribution is thrown back to more than 5 years (starting with the earliest applicable tax year beginning after 1968), attach additional schedules. (If the trust was a simple trust, see Regulations section 1.665(e)-1A(b).)*		Throwback year ending 2008	Throwback year ending 2009	Throwback year ending 2010	Throwback year ending 2011	Throwback year ending 2012
6	Distributable net income (see the instructions)	**6** 42,000	42,000	42,000	42,000	42,000
7	Distributions (see the instructions)	**7** 24,000	24,000	24,000	24,000	24,000
8	Subtract line 7 from line 6 .	**8** 18,000	18,000	18,000	18,000	18,000
9	Enter amount from page 2, line 25 or line 31, as applicable	**9** 5,284	5,242	5,241	5,230	5,199
10	Undistributed net income Subtract line 9 from line 8 .	**10** 12,716	12,758	12,759	12,770	12,801
11	Enter amount of prior accumulation distributions thrown back to any of these years	**11** -0-	-0-	-0-	-0-	-0-
12	Subtract line 11 from line 10 .	**12** 12,716	12,758	12,759	12,770	12,801
13	Allocate the amount on line 5 to the earliest applicable year first. Do not allocate an amount greater than line 12 for the same year (see the instructions)	**13** 12,716	12,758	12,759	12,770	7,497
14	Divide line 13 by line 10 and multiply result by amount on line 9	**14** 5,284	5,242	5,241	5,230	3,045
15	Add lines 13 and 14 . . .	**15** 18,000	18,000	18,000	18,000	10,542
16	Tax-exempt interest included on line 13 (see the instructions)	**16** -0-	-0-	-0-	-0-	-0-
17	Subtract line 16 from line 15 .	**17** 18,000	18,000	18,000	18,000	10,542

For Paperwork Reduction Act Notice, see the Instructions for Form 1041.   Cat. No. 11382Z   Schedule J (Form 1041) 2013

¶2946

Schedule J (Form 1041) 2013   Page **2**

Part III   **Taxes Imposed on Undistributed Net Income** (Enter the applicable throwback years below.) (See the instructions.)

Note: *If more than 5 throwback years are involved, attach additional schedules. If the trust received an accumulation distribution from another trust, see Regulations section 1.665(d)-1A.*

If the trust elected the alternative tax on capital gains (repealed for tax years beginning after 1978), **skip** lines 18 through 25 and **complete** lines 26 through 31.		Throwback year ending 2008	Throwback year ending 2009	Throwback year ending 2010	Throwback year ending 2011	Throwback year ending 2012
18	Regular tax	18	5,284	5,242	5,241	5,230	5,199
19	Trust's share of net short-term gain	19	-0-	-0-	-0-	-0-	-0-
20	Trust's share of net long-term gain	20	-0-	-0-	-0-	-0-	-0-
21	Add lines 19 and 20 . . .	21	-0-	-0-	-0-	-0-	-0-
22	Taxable income	22	17,900	17,900	17,900	17,900	17,900
23	Enter percent. Divide line 21 by line 22, but do not enter more than 100%	23	0 %	0 %	0 %	0 %	0 %
24	Multiply line 18 by the percentage on line 23 . . .	24	-0-	-0-	-0-	-0-	-0-
25	Tax on undistributed net income. Subtract line 24 from line 18. Enter here and on page 1, line 9	25	5,284	5,242	5,241	5,230	5,199

Do not complete lines 26 through 31 unless the trust elected the alternative tax on long-term capital gain.						
26	Tax on income other than long-term capital gain . . .	26					
27	Trust's share of net short-term gain	27					
28	Trust's share of taxable income less section 1202 deduction	28					
29	Enter percent. Divide line 27 by line 28, but do not enter more than 100%	29	%	%	%	%	%
30	Multiply line 26 by the percentage on line 29 . . .	30					
31	Tax on undistributed net income. Subtract line 30 from line 26. Enter here and on page 1, line 9	31					

Part IV   **Allocation to Beneficiary**

Note: *Be sure to complete **Form 4970**, Tax on Accumulation Distribution of Trusts.*

Beneficiary's name				Identifying number	

Beneficiary's address (number and street including apartment number or P.O. box)			**(a)** This beneficiary's share of line 13	**(b)** This beneficiary's share of line 14	**(c)** This beneficiary's share of line 16
City, state, and ZIP code					
32	Throwback year 2008	32	12,716	5,284	-0-
33	Throwback year 2009	33	12,758	5,242	-0-
34	Throwback year 2010	34	12,759	5,241	-0-
35	Throwback year 2011	35	12,770	5,230	-0-
36	Throwback year 2012	36	7,497	3,045	-0-
37	Total. Add lines 32 through 36. Enter here and on the appropriate lines of Form 4970	37	58,500	24,042	-0-

Schedule J (Form 1041) 2013

¶2946

¶2947 SAMPLE COMPLETED FORM 8960 FOR JANE B. TRENT TRUST

Form **8960**	**Net Investment Income Tax—**	OMB No. 1545-2227
Department of the Treasury Internal Revenue Service (99)	**Individuals, Estates, and Trusts** ▶ Attach to Form 1040 or Form 1041. ▶ Information about Form 8960 and its separate instructions is at *www.irs.gov/form8960.*	20**13** Attachment Sequence No. **72**

Name(s) shown on Form 1040 or Form 1041	Your social security number or EIN
Trust u/w Jane B. Trent	52-000000

Part I Investment Income

☐ Section 6013(g) election (see instructions)
☐ Regulations section 1.1411-10(g) election (see instructions)

1	Taxable interest (Form 1040, line 8a; or Form 1041, line 1)			**1**	4,000
2	Ordinary dividends (Form 1040, line 9a; or Form 1041, line 2a)			**2**	20,000
3	Annuities from nonqualified plans (see instructions)			**3**	
4a	Rental real estate, royalties, partnerships, S corporations, trusts, etc. (Form 1040, line 17; or Form 1041, line 5)	**4a**	6,000		
b	Adjustment for net income or loss derived in the ordinary course of a non-section 1411 trade or business (see instructions)	**4b**			
c	Combine lines 4a and 4b			**4c**	6,000
5a	Net gain or loss from disposition of property from Form 1040, combine lines 13 and 14; or from Form 1041, combine lines 4 and 7	**5a**	10,000		
b	Net gain or loss from disposition of property that is not subject to net investment income tax (see instructions)	**5b**			
c	Adjustment from disposition of partnership interest or S corporation stock (see instructions)	**5c**			
d	Combine lines 5a through 5c			**5d**	10,000
6	Changes to investment income for certain CFCs and PFICs (see instructions)			**6**	
7	Other modifications to investment income (see instructions)			**7**	
8	Total investment income. Combine lines 1, 2, 3, 4c, 5d, 6, and 7			**8**	40,000

Part II Investment Expenses Allocable to Investment Income and Modifications

9a	Investment interest expenses (see instructions)	**9a**	5,000		
b	State income tax (see instructions)	**9b**			
c	Miscellaneous investment expenses (see instructions)	**9c**			
d	Add lines 9a, 9b, and 9c			**9d**	
10	Additional modifications (see instructions)			**10**	3,000
11	Total deductions and modifications. Add lines 9d and 10			**11**	8,000

Part III Tax Computation

12	Net investment income. Subtract Part II, line 11 from Part I, line 8. Individuals complete lines 13–17. Estates and trusts complete lines 18a–21. If zero or less, enter -0-			**12**	32,000
	Individuals:				
13	Modified adjusted gross income (see instructions)	**13**			
14	Threshold based on filing status (see instructions)	**14**			
15	Subtract line 14 from line 13. If zero or less, enter -0-	**15**			
16	Enter the smaller of line 12 or line 15			**16**	
17	Net investment income tax for individuals. Multiply line 16 by 3.8% (.038). Enter here and on Form 1040, line 60			**17**	
	Estates and Trusts:				
18a	Net investment income (line 12 above)	**18a**	32,000		
b	Deductions for distributions of net investment income and deductions under section 642(c) (see instructions)	**18b**			
c	Undistributed net investment income. Subtract line 18b from 18a (see instructions)	**18c**	32,000		
19a	Adjusted gross income (see instructions)	**19a**	17,700		
b	Highest tax bracket for estates and trusts for the year (see instructions)	**19b**	11,950		
c	Subtract line 19b from line 19a. If zero or less, enter -0- . . .	**19c**	5,750		
20	Enter the smaller of line 18c or line 19c			**20**	5,750
21	Net investment income tax for estates and trusts. Multiply line 20 by 3.8% (.038). Enter here and on Form 1041, Schedule G, line 4			**21**	219

For Paperwork Reduction Act Notice, see your tax return instructions.   Cat. No. 59474M   Form **8960** (2013)

¶2947

¶2948 BACKGROUND DISCUSSION ON NII TAX

    (a) NII Tax Basics. On Schedule G (From 1041), Line 4, trusts and estates must enter the amount of net investment income (NII) tax owed by the entity. This NII tax is computed on Form 8960, "Net Investment Income Tax—Individuals, Estates, and Trusts," and the trust or estate must attach Form 8960 to Form 1041 if they owe the NII tax.

For tax years beginning in 2013, certain trusts may be subject to an additional 3.8 percent tax on the lesser of the (1) undistributed NII or (2) excess of AGI [as defined in IRC Sec. 67(e)] over the dollar amount at which the highest trust income tax bracket begins [IRC Sec. 1411(a)(2); Reg. Sec. 1.1411-3(1)(ii)]. This dollar amount is $11,950 in 2013 and increases to $12,150 in 2014. If the trust has a short tax year (less than 12 months), the threshold amount is not reduced or prorated [Reg. Sec. 1.1411-3(a)(2)].

Undistributed NII is the trust's net investment income (NII) determined under Reg. Sec. 1.1411-4, reduced by distributions of NII to beneficiaries and allowable deductions, such as the charitable contribution deduction and the income distribution deduction [Reg. Sec. 1.1411-3(e)(2)].

    (b) What Trusts Subject to NII Tax. The 3.8 percent NII tax applies to all trusts with undistributed NII exceeding $11,950 in 2013 and $12,150 in 2014 except for the following trusts which are not subject to the NII tax [Reg. Sec. 1.1411-3(b) and (d)]:

1. A trust devoted to religious, charitable, scientific, literary, or educational purposes, or to foster national or international amateur sports competition, or for the prevention of cruelty to children or animals;

2. Charitable trusts exempt from tax under IRC Sec. 501;

3. Charitable remainder trusts exempt from tax under IRC Sec. 664;

4. Tax-exempt trusts, such as charitable trusts and qualified retirement plan trusts and any other trust statutorily exempt from taxes (such as HSAs, Coverdell accounts, and 529 tuition programs);

5. Grantor trusts (but not beneficiaries);

6. Electing Alaska Native Settlement Trusts subject to tax under IRC Sec. 646;

7. Cemetery Perpetual Care Funds under IRC Sec. 642(i); However, qualified funeral trusts (QFTs) are subject to the NII tax, with each beneficiary's interest in his or her contract treated as a separate trust [Reg. Sec. 1.1411-3(b)(2)(i)]. However, because the individual contracts are typically under $10,000, their annual investment income should be below the NII tax threshold amount ($11,950 for 2013 and increasing to $12,150 in 2014);

8. Foreign trusts (distributions to U.S. beneficiaries are not excluded) [Reg. Sec. 1.1411-3(b)];

9. Trusts not classified as trusts for federal income tax (e.g., real estate trusts and common trust funds);

10. Simple trusts because they are required to distribute all current income [see ¶ 2800]. Therefore, there would be no undistributed NII and all income taxes would

¶2948

apply at the beneficiary, rather than the trust, level. However, if the trust has capital gains that exceed the threshold amount, the NII tax will likely apply.

(c) Computing the Amount of NII. When computing the amount of NII, the following income and gains are included [IRC Sec. 1411(c)(1) and (c)(3); Reg. Secs. 1.1411-4(a), 1.1411-5, and 1.1411-7]:

1. Investment Income—including dividends, interest (not including tax-free interest such as municipal bond interest), annuities from nonqualified plans (e.g., private annuities and purchased commercial annuities), royalties, and rents that are not derived in the ordinary course of business. All income from the investment of working capital is treated as investment income, regardless of whether the working capital is used in a trade or business;

2. Passive Income and Gains—including income and gains from a trade or business in which the taxpayer does not materially participate [see ¶ 2805], rental income, allocations of income or gains from a partnership or S corporation in which the fiduciary does not materially participate, and gains from the sale of such properties;

3. Gain on Investment Property—including gains from the sale of stocks, bonds, and mutual funds, capital gain distributions from mutual funds, gain from the sale of investment real estate, and gains from the business of trading in financial instruments or commodities (regardless of whether the taxpayer materially participates).

(d) Income/Gains Excluded from NII. The following categories of income are excluded when computing NII [IRC Sec. 1411(c); Reg. Secs. 1.1411-4(b) and 1.1411-4(d)(4)]:

1. Operating income or gains on disposition from trade or business activities that are not passive with respect to the taxpayer. For NIIT purposes, the determination of a trade or business is made under IRC Sec. 162;

2. Distributions from tax-favored retirement accounts, e.g., 401(k) plans, pension plans, traditional IRAs, and Roth IRAs;

3. Tax-exempt income;

4. Any income or gain that is not recognized for income tax purposes within the tax year (e.g., because of an installment sale, like-kind exchange, or involuntary conversion);

5. Certain gains from the disposition of partnership interests and S corporations stock (those for which the entity is engaged in a trade or business that is not a passive activity with respect to the owner (i.e., the business does not involve renting property, and the fiduciary materially participates in the business)). If any of the partnership or S corporation activity is considered an active trade or business to the estate or trust (and not in the business of trading in financial instruments or securities), an adjustment is necessary to exclude that portion of gain or loss from NII. (If the partnership or S corporation activities were entirely passive to the estate or trust, no adjustment is necessary.)

(e) Allowable Deductions. Reg. Sec. 1.1411-4(f) provides that only "properly allocable deductions" can be taken into account in determining NII for purposes of NII

¶2948

tax. Only deductions that are allowed for regular income tax purposes can reduce NII. If the deductions or losses are disallowed for regular tax (e.g., investment interest expense, passive activity losses, or losses subject to at-risk limitations), they are not allowed when calculating the current year NII.

Examples of properly allocable deductions that can be subtracted from NII include:

1. Investment interest expense;

2. State income tax;

3. Investment advisory and brokerage fees;

4. Expenses related to rental and royalty income;

5. Expenses allocable to passive business activities and/or the business of trading in securities or commodities;

6. The IRC Sec. 691(c) deduction allocable to net investment income, except to the extent it is deducted in determining net gain (i.e., as required under IRC Sec. 691(c)(4) for income in respect of a decedent taxed at capital gain rates);

7. Amortizable bond premiums on taxable bonds;

8. Fiduciary administration expenses, such as fiduciaries' fees and the expense of litigation, to the extent they are allocable to NII;

9. Net casualty and abandonment losses that are deductible under IRC Sec. 165, except to the extent they are used to determine net gain for NII purposes (i.e., otherwise, they would be deducted twice);

10. Net operating loss deduction determined under Reg. Sec. 1.1411-4(h).

(f) How to Calculate NII Tax. To calculate NII tax, the threshold amount applicable to trusts ($11,950 for 2013 and increasing to $12,150 in 2014) is subtracted from the trust's AGI which is the total income of the trust reduced by (1) the deductible administration costs, (2) the income distribution deduction, and (3) the exemption amount. Expenses that are limited by the 2 percent floor cannot be subtracted in determining AGI. Therefore only the expenses that exceed the 2-percent floor can be deducted.

If the AGI reduced by the threshold amount is zero or less, the NII tax does not apply. If the amount is greater than zero, it must be compared to the amount of undistributed NII. The lesser of these two amounts is multiplied by 3.8 percent to determine the NII tax. This amount is reported on Form 8960, "Net Investment Income Tax—Individuals, Estates, and Trusts," and added to the trust's other taxes on Schedule G (Form 1041).

(g) How to Report and Pay NII Tax. Trusts calculate the NIIT on Form 8960, "Net Investment Income Tax—Individuals, Estates, and Trusts," and report the amount of tax, along with their regular income tax, on Schedule G (Form 1041), line 4. If the trust is subject to estimated tax payments, the amount of the estimated tax payments should be adjusted to include the NIIT.

For a qualified funeral trust (QFT), each beneficiary's interest in that beneficiary's contract is treated as a separate trust for NII tax purposes. However, if the QFT has one or more beneficiary contracts that have NII of more than $11,950 (for 2013), or $12,150

¶2948

(in 2014), a consolidated Form 8960 must be completed for all beneficiary contracts subject to the NII tax.

(h) Special Rules for Electing Small Business Trusts (ESBTs).

Special rules apply for calculating what portion of an electing small business trusts (ESBT) is subject to the NII tax. To calculate undistributed NII of an ESBT, the S corporation and non-S corporation portions (as defined in Reg. Sec. 1.641(c)-1(b)(2) and (3)) of the trust must be treated separately. However, the trust is treated as a single trust when determining the NII tax [Reg. Sec. 1.1411-3(c)(1)(i)]. A three-step method for determining the ESBT's NII tax liability is included in Reg. Sec. 1.1411-3(c)(2):

Step one: The S portion and non-S portion computes each portion's undistributed NII as separate trusts and then combines these amounts to calculate the ESBT's undistributed NII.

Step two: The ESBT calculates its AGI which is the AGI of the non-S portion, increased or decreased by the net income or net loss of the S portion, after taking into account all deductions, carryovers, and loss limitations applicable to the S portion, as a single item of ordinary income (or ordinary loss).

Step three: The ESBT pays tax on the lesser of (a) The ESBT's total undistributed NII or (b) The excess of the ESBT's AGI over the dollar amount at which the highest tax bracket begins for that tax year.

> **Example 1:** In Year 1 the non-S portion of an ESBT, has dividend income of $15,000, interest income of $10,000, and capital loss of $5,000. Trust's S portion has net rental income of $21,000 and a capital gain of $7,000. The Trustee's annual fee of $1,000 is allocated 60% to the non-S portion and 40% to the S portion. Trust makes a distribution from income to a single beneficiary of $9,000.
>
> *Step one*: Trust must compute the undistributed NII or the S portion and non-S portion as described above. The undistributed NII for the S portion is $20,600 and is determined as follows:

Net Rental Income	$21,000
Capital Gain	$ 7,000
Trustee Annual Fee	($400)
Total S portion undistributed NII	$27,600

> The undistributed NII for the non-S portion is $12,400 and is determined as follows:

Dividend Income	$15,000
Interest Income	$10,000
Deductible Capital Loss	($3,000)
Trustee Annual Fee	($600)
Distributable NII	($9,000)
Total non-S portion undistributed NII	$12,400

¶2948

Trust combines the undistributed NII of the S portion and non-S portions above to arrive at Trust's combined undistributed NII.

S portion's undistributed NII	$27,600
Non-S portion's undistributed NII	$12,400
Combined undistributed NII	$40,000

Step two: The ESBT calculates its AGI which is the non-S portion's AGI increased or decreased by the net income or net loss of the S portion. The AGI for the ESBT is $38,000 and is determined as follows:

Dividend Income		$15,000
Interest Income		$10,000
Deductible Capital Loss		($3,000)
Trustee Annual Fee		($600)
Distributable Net Income Distribution		($9,000)
S Portion Income		$27,600
	AGI	$40,000

The S portion's single item of ordinary income used in the ESBT's AGI calculation is $27,600. This item of income is determined by starting with net rental income of $21,000 and capital gain of $7,000 and reducing it by the S portion's $400 share of the annual trustee fee.

Step three: Trust pays tax on the lesser of (a) the combined undistributed NII ($40,000); or (b) the excess of AGI ($40,000) over the dollar amount at which the highest tax bracket applicable to a trust begins for the tax year [Reg. Sec. 1.1411-3(c)(3)].

(i) Special Rules for Charitable Remainder Trusts. Although charitable remainder trusts (CRT) are not subject to the NII tax, certain special rules apply to the annuity or unitrust distributions made from CRTs [Reg. Secs. 1.1411-3(b)(1)(iii), 1.1411-3(d)]. Annuity and unitrust distributions from a CRT to noncharitable beneficiaries are ordered for regular income tax purposes according to the IRC Sec. 664 four-tier system category and class system which characterizes CRT distributions as generally coming first from ordinary income, second from capital gains, third from tax-exempt income, and last from trust corpus or principal [Reg. Sec. 1.1411-31(d)(2)]. This same ordering rule is used when categorizing and distributing NII to noncharitable remainder beneficiaries. However, a simplified method may be elected that does not follow the four-tier ordering rule for the NIIT computation. CRTs are required to keep track of their undistributed income from prior tax years (reported on Part II of Form 5227) and their accumulated NII. If there are multiple beneficiaries of the CRT, the NII must be apportioned among the noncharitable beneficiaries based on their respective shares of the total annuity or unitrust amount paid by the trust for that tax year. In Reg. Sec. 1.1411-3(d)(2)(iii), ex. 1, the IRS illustrates these rules.

Example 2: In 2009, A formed CRT as a charitable remainder annuity trust. The trust document requires an annual annuity payment of $50,000 to A for 15 years. As of January 1, 2013, the CRT has the following items of undistributed income within its Reg. Sec. 1.664-1(d)(1) categories and classes:

Category	Class	Tax Rate	Amount
Ordinary Income	Interest	39.6%	$4,000
	Net Rental Income	39.6%	$8,000
	Non-Qualified Dividend Income	39.6%	$2,000
	Qualified Dividend Income	20.0%	$10,000
Capital Gain	Short-Term	39.6%	$39,000
	Unrecaptured Section 1250 Gain	25.0%	$1,000
	Long-Term	20.0%	$560,000
Other Income			None
Total undistributed income as of January 1, 2013			$624,000

Pursuant to Reg. Sec. 1.1411-3(d)(1)(iii), none of the $624,000 of undistributed income is accumulated net investment income (ANII) because none of it was received by the CRT after December 31, 2012. Thus, the entire $624,000 of undistributed income is excluded income. During 2013, the CRT receives $7,000 of interest income, $9,000 of qualified dividend income, $4,000 of short-term capital gain, and $11,000 of long-term capital gain. Prior to the 2013 distribution of $50,000 to A, CRT has the following items of undistributed income:

Category	Class	Excluded/ANII	Tax Rate	Amount
Ordinary Income				
	Interest	NII	43.4%	$7,000
	Interest	Excluded	39.6%	$4,000
	Net Rental Income	Excluded	39.6%	$8,000
	Non-Qualified Dividend Income	Excluded	39.6%	$2,000
	Qualified Dividend Income	NII	23.8%	$9,000
	Qualified Dividend Income	Excluded	20.0%	$10,000
Capital Gain				
	Short-Term	NII	43.4%	$4,000
	Short-Term	Excluded	39.6%	$39,000
	Unrecaptured Section 1250 Gain	Excluded	25.0%	$1,000
	Long-Term	NII	23.8%	$11,000
	Long-Term	Excluded	20.0%	$560,000
Other Income				None

The $50,000 distribution to A for 2013 will include the following amounts:

Category	Class	Excluded/ANII	Tax Rate	Amount
Ordinary Income				
	Interest	NII	43.4%	$7,000
	Interest	Excluded	39.6%	$4,000
	Net Rental Income	Excluded	39.6%	$8,000
	Non-Qualified Dividend Income	Excluded	39.6%	$2,000
	Qualified Dividend Income	NII	23.8%	$9,000
	Qualified Dividend Income	Excluded	20.0%	$10,000
Capital Gain				
	Short-Term	NII	43.4%	$4,000
	Short-Term	Excluded	39.6%	$6,000
	Unrecaptured Section 1250 Gain	Excluded	25.0%	None
	Long-Term	NII	23.8%	None
	Long-Term	Excluded	20.0%	None

The amount included in A's 2013 net investment income is $20,000. This amount is comprised of $7,000 of interest income, $9,000 of qualified dividend income, and $4,000 of short-term capital gain. As a result, as of January 1, 2014, the CRT has the following items of undistributed income within its Reg. Sec. 1.664-1(d)(1) categories and classes:

Category	Class	Excluded/ANII	Tax Rate	Amount
Ordinary Income				
	Interest			None
	Net Rental Income			None
	Non-Qualified Dividend Income			None
	Qualified Dividend Income			None
Capital Gain				
	Short-Term	Excluded	39.6%	$33,000
	Unrecaptured Section 1250 Gain	Excluded	25.0%	$1,000
	Long-Term	ANII	23.8%	$11,000
	Long-Term	Excluded	20.0%	$560,000
Other Income				None

¶2948

¶2949 LINE-BY-LINE DISCUSSION OF HOW TO COMPLETE FORM 8960 FOR TRENT TRUST

Part I—Line 1—Taxable Interest. Enter taxable interest income earned in the ordinary course of the trust's non-IRC Sec. 1411 trade or business. Interest income earned in the ordinary course of non-IRC Sec. 1411 trade or business is excluded from net investment income. If this type of interest income is included in line 1, use line 7 to adjust net investment income. If line 1 includes self-charged interest income received from a partnership or S corporation that is a nonpassive activity (other than a trade or business of trading in financial instruments or commodities), see Line 7—Other Modifications to Investment Income, for a possible adjustment to net investment income.

■ The Trent Trust enters taxable interest in the amount of $4,000 which comes from Form 1041, line 1.

Line 2—Ordinary Dividends. Enter the amount of ordinary dividends received.

■ The Trent Trust enters ordinary dividends in the amount of $20,000 which comes from Form 1040, line 2a.

Line 3—Annuities from Nonqualified Plans. Enter the gross income from all annuities received from nonqualified plans. Annuities received from both qualified and nonqualified plans are reported to the recipient on Form 1099-R. However, only those annuities received from nonqualified plans are subject to the NIIT. Examples of annuities from nonqualified plans include private annuities and purchased commercial annuities. Distributions from the following annuities/retirement plans are not included in calculating net investment income: Section 401—qualified pension, profit-sharing, and stock bonus plans; Section 403(a)—qualified annuity plans purchased by an employer for an employee; Section 403(b)—annuities purchased by public schools or section 501(c)(3) tax-exempt organizations; Section 408—Individual Retirement Accounts; Section 408A—Roth IRAs; and Section 457(b)—deferred compensation plans of a state or local government or tax-exempt organization.

Line 4a—Rental Real Estate, Royalties, Partnerships, S Corporations, Trust, etc. See Form 1040, line 17 for the amount to enter on line 4a of Form 8960.

■ The Trent Trust enters royalties in the amount of $6,000 from line 41 of Schedule E.

Line 4b—Adjustment for Net Income or Loss Derived in the Ordinary Course of a Non-Section 1411 Trade or Business. Enter the net positive or net negative amount for the following items included in line 4a that are not included in determining net investment income:

• Net income or loss from a trade or business that is not a passive activity and is not engaged in a trade or business of trading financial instruments or commodities;

• Net income or loss from a passive trade or business activity that is taken into account in determining self-employment income;

• Royalties derived in the ordinary course of a trade or business that is not a passive activity; and

¶2949

- Passive losses of a former passive activity that are allowed as a deduction in the current year.

In addition, use line 4b of Form 8960 to adjust for certain types of nonpassive rental income or loss derived in the ordinary course of a trade or business. For example, line 4b includes the following items:

- Nonpassive net rental income or loss of a real estate professional where the rental activity rises to a trade or business;

- Net rental income or loss that is a nonpassive activity because it was grouped with a trade or business under Reg. Sec. 1.469-4(d)(1);

- Other rental income or loss from a trade or business reported on Schedule K-1 (Form 1065), line 3, from a partnership, or Schedule K-1 (Form 1120S), line 3, from an S corporation, where the activity is not a passive activity; and

- Net income that has been recharacterized as not from a passive activity under the passive loss rules and is derived in the ordinary course of a trade or business.

Line 5a–5d—Net Gain from Disposition of Property from Form 1041. Enter on Lines 5a–5d any net gain attributable to the disposition of property that is taken into account in computing taxable income. The amount entered on Line 5a comes from Form 1041. The term disposition includes a sale, transfer, conversion, cash settlement, cancellation, termination, lapse, expiration, deemed disposition, for example under IRC Sec. 877A, or other disposition. Net gain attributable to the sale, exchange, or other disposition of property not used in a trade or business is included in net investment income. Net gain or loss from the sale, exchange, or other disposition of property held in a passive activity or attributable to a trade or business of trading in financial instruments or commodities is also included in NII.

Gains and losses that are not taken into account in computing taxable income are not taken into account in computing NII. For example, gain that is not taxable because of the home sale exclusion in IRC Sec. 121 or the like-kind exchange provision in IRC Sec. 1031 is not included in NII.

■ The Trent Trust entered $10,000 on Line 5a. This amount comes from Line 4 of Form 1041 and Schedule D (Form 1041).

Part II—Investment Expenses Allocable to Investment Income and Modifications. Trusts and estates should enter on Part II of Form 8960 any deductions and modifications to net investment income that are not otherwise included in Part I. Generally, expenses associated with a passive activity trade or business, or the trade or business of trading in financial instruments or commodities conducted through a pass-through entity are already included on line 4a because line 4a uses net income (loss) from Schedule E (Form 1040). Part II is used to report deductions that are, predominately, itemized deductions.

Line 9a—Investment Interest Expenses. Enter on Form 8960, line 9a, interest expense paid or accrued during the year from Form 4952, line 8. If, however, Form 4952 includes investment interest expense that is deducted on Schedule E and already taken into account on line 4a of Form 8960, do not include the same amount on line 9a of Form 8960.

■ The Trent Trust enters $5,000 on Line 9a of Form 8960.

¶2949

Line 9b—State Income Tax. Include on line 9b any state or local income tax, or foreign income tax paid by the trust or estate which is attributable to NII. This may be all or part of the amount reported on Form 1041, line 11. For purposes of line 9b, sales tax is not deductible in computing net investment income. If the taxpayer claimed an income tax credit for foreign income tax (generally reported on Form 1116), those foreign taxes are not deductible in computing net investment income.

Line 9c—Miscellaneous Investment Expenses. Enter on Line 9c investment expenses incurred by the trust that are directly connected to the production of investment income because these expenses are deductible when computing NII. Generally, these amounts are reported on Form 4952, line 5. The amounts reported on Line 9c are the amounts allowed after the application of the deduction limits imposed by IRC Secs. 67 and 68.

Line 10—Additional Modifications. Use line 10 to report additional deductions and modifications to net investment income that are not otherwise reflected on lines 1-9. Enter amounts on line 10 as positive numbers. On line 10 only *properly allocable deductions* can be taken into account in determining a taxpayer's net investment income. These deductions cannot exceed the taxpayer's total amount of gross net investment income and net gain. The deductions are subtracted from affected gross income and gains in calculating a taxpayer's net investment income. Use line 10 to report properly allocable deductions such as:

- The penalty paid for an early withdrawal of savings;

- The amount treated as an ordinary loss by a holder of a contingency payment debt instrument;

- Net negative periodic payments paid on a notional principal contract that is referenced to property that produces interest, dividends, royalties, or rents;

- The amount of the deduction allowable for the amortizable bond premium on a taxable bond. This amount of bond premium amortization is already taken into account in computing interest income on Form 8960, line 1;

- To the extent properly allocable to net investment income all ordinary and necessary expenses paid or incurred during the tax year to determine, collect, or obtain a refund of any tax owed, but only to the extent the expenses are allocable to net investment income from Schedule A, Form 1040, line 22.

- *Deductions subject to AGI limitations under IRC Secs. 67 or 68.* Any deduction allowed against net investment income that, for purposes of computing income tax, is subject to either the 2% floor on miscellaneous itemized deductions under IRC Sec. 67 or the overall limitation on itemized deductions under IRC Sec. 68 is allowed in determining net investment income, but only to the extent the items are deductible after application of both limitations.

- *Miscellaneous itemized deductions.* The amount of miscellaneous itemized deductions, after application of the 2% floor but before application of the overall limitation, used in determining net investment income is the lesser of: (1) That portion of your miscellaneous itemized deductions before the application of the 2% floor that is properly allocable to net investment income, or (2) total miscellaneous itemized deductions allowed after the application of the 2% floor but before the application of the overall limitation on itemized deductions.

¶2949

- *Itemized deductions.* The amount of itemized deductions allowed in determining net investment income after applying both the 2% floor and overall limitation is the lesser of: (1) The sum of: (a) The amount of miscellaneous itemized deductions allowed as a deduction against net investment income (before application of the overall limitation), and (b) The total amount of itemized deductions not subject to the 2% floor and properly allocable to items of income or net gain for purposes of determining net investment income, or (2) The total amount of itemized deductions allowed after the application of both the 2% floor and the overall limitation on itemized deductions.

■ The Trent Trust enters on Line 10 advisory fees in the amount of $3,000 that were paid to investment advisors in 2013.

Part III—Tax Computation—Estates and Trusts. Estates and trusts complete lines 18-21.

Line 18b—Deductions for Distributions of NII and Deductions under IRC Sec. 642(c). Enter on line 18a the undistributed NII of an estate or trust. This is the entity's NII reduced by the NII included in the distributions to beneficiaries deductible by the estate or trust under IRC Sec. 651 or 661 and by the NII for which the estate or trust was entitled to an IRC Sec. 642(c) deduction for amount permanently set aside for charity. Report on line 18b the amount of NII distributed to beneficiaries of the estate or trust and the amount of NII allocated to distributions to charity pursuant to IRC Sec. 642(c). The amount of the deduction for NII distributed to charities under IRC Sec. 642(c) is the amount of the NII allocated to the charity. In general, the deduction for distributions of NII may not exceed the taxable income distributed to the beneficiary for regular income tax purposes.

Line 19a—Adjusted Gross Income (AGI). The Instructions for Form 8960 tell return preparers to consult the IRS Instructions for line 15c (Form 1041) to compute the amount of the estate or trust's AGI. These instructions provide that estates and trusts compute AGI by subtracting the following from the entity's total income on line 9 of page 1 (Form 1041):

1. The administration costs of the estate or trust (the total of lines 12, 14, and 15a to the extent they are costs incurred in the administration of the estate or trust) that would not have been incurred if the property were not held by the estate or trust;

2. The income distribution deduction (line 18—Form 1041);

3. The amount of the exemption (line 20—Form 1041)

4. The domestic production activities deduction claimed on line 15a; and

5. The NOLD claimed on line 15b.

■ The Trent Trust computes AGI as follows: They take the amount on line 9 (Form 1041)—$40,000 and then they subtract $4,000 from line 12 (Form 1041), $18,000 from line 18 (Form 1041), the $300 exemption from line 20 (Form 1041) for a total AGI of $17,700 which they enter on 19a (Form 8960).

¶2949

Line 19b—Highest Tax Bracket for Estates and Trusts. [See ¶ 2935].

■ The Trent Trust enters $11,950 which was the income amount exposed to the highest tax bracket for estates and trusts in 2013.

Line 21—Net Investment Income Tax for Estates and Trusts. The entity must multiply the amount on line 20 by 3.8 percent and enter the result on line 21 (Form 8960) and on Schedule G, line 4 (Form 1041).

■ The Trent Trust multiplies $5,750 by 3.8 percent to yield a NII tax in 2013 of $218.50 (rounded to $219) which the Trent Trust enters on line 21 (Form 8960) and on Schedule G, line 4 (Form 1041).

¶2949

SAMPLE INCOME TAX RETURN FOR ESTATES

TABLE OF CONTENTS

¶3000 PREPARATION OF FORM 1041: INCOME TAX RETURN FOR AN ESTATE—FILING BASICS

The personal representative or executor of a decedent's estate is obligated to pay income tax on the income earned by an estate because estates are separate tax-paying entities [IRC Sec. 641(b)]. The estate's taxable income is the income that the estate received during the period of administration or settlement, which is the period actually required by the executor to perform the ordinary duties of administration, such as the collection of assets and the payment of debts, taxes, legacies, and bequests [Reg. Sec. 1.641(b)-3(a)].

¶3000

Executors must use IRS Form 1041, "U.S. Income Tax Return for Estates and Trusts," to report the income earned by the estate and to pay the tax that is due. Liability for the payment of the tax on the taxable income of an estate becomes the legal responsibility of the executor [Reg. Sec. 1.641(b)-2(a)].

The executor of the decedent's estate must report the following on Form 1041:

1. The income, deductions, gains, losses, etc. of the estate;

2. The income that is either accumulated or held for future distribution or distributed currently to the beneficiaries;

3. Any income tax liability of the estate;

4. Any employment taxes on wages paid to household employees; and

5. Net investment income tax owed by the estate.

▶ **PRACTICE ALERT:** Don't be fooled into thinking that estates and trusts are taxed identically just because they use the same tax return (Form 1041) for filing purposes. They are subject to different tax rules. The rules regarding an income tax return for a trust and a completed income tax return for a trust can be found in Chapter 29.

(a) Checklist of Forms. For a checklist of important forms and due dates that an executor, administrator, or personal representative must keep in mind, see ¶3040, IRS Publication 559, Survivors, Executors, and Administrators, Table A, Page 42.

(b) Period Covered. The 2013 Form 1041 should be filed for calendar year 2013 and fiscal years beginning in 2013 and ending in 2014. If the return is for a fiscal year or a short tax year (less than 12 months), fill in the tax year space at the top of Form 1041.

The 2013 Form 1041 may also be used for a tax year beginning in 2014 if:

1. The estate has a tax year of less than 12 months that begins and ends in 2014; and

2. The 2013 Form 1041 is not available by the time the estate is required to file its tax return. However, the estate must show its 2014 tax year on the 2014 Form 1041 and incorporate any tax law changes that are effective for tax years beginning after December 31, 2013.

(c) Role of Personal Representative. The responsibilities of the executor of the decedent's estate include the following:

• Collect all of the decedent's assets;

• Pay all of the decedent's creditors;

• Limit shrinkage of the estate so more assets can be distributed to the decedent's heirs and other beneficiaries;

• Religiously follow the dictates of the decedent's will;

• File necessary tax returns when due; and

• Pay the tax that is due up to the date the executor is discharged from duties.

The executor, who is responsible for settling or handling the administration of someone's estate, could be an individual or an organization such as a bank or trust company. Keep in mind when choosing an executor that the person must be organ-

¶3000

ized, responsible, and capable of understanding and managing complex financial matters, maintaining detailed records, and attending to all of the details involved with administering an estate. Choose a trusted individual. Winding up someone's affairs is not an easy job and if no one in the family is up to it, select an attorney or the trust department of a bank that specializes in estate administration.

(d) Form 56—Notice of Fiduciary Relations. The first thing the executor must do if he or she is acting on behalf of another person in a fiduciary capacity is to give the district director of the Internal Revenue Service (the IRS) written notice of the existence of that fiduciary relationship [Reg. Sec. 301.6903-1(a)]. The term "fiduciary" means a guardian, trustee, executor, administrator, receiver, conservator, or any person acting in any fiduciary capacity for another person [IRC Sec. 7701(a)(6); Reg. Sec. 301.6903-1(d)]. The notice may be filed on IRS Form 56, "Notice Concerning Fiduciary Relationships," with the IRS Service Center where the person for whom the fiduciary is acting is required to file tax returns.

Form 56 must state the name and address of the person for whom the fiduciary is acting and the nature of the liability. As soon as this notice is filed, the fiduciary will assume the powers, duties, rights, and privileges imposed under the law. The fiduciary must file satisfactory evidence of his or her authority to act on behalf of another. If the fiduciary role exists by order of court, a certified copy of the court order should be filed.

When the fiduciary role has terminated, notify the IRS of the termination so the fiduciary will be relieved of any further duty or liability. The notice of termination must be accompanied by written evidence of the termination [Reg. Sec. 1.301.6903-1(b)].

(e) Employer Identification Number. Every estate that is required to file Form 1041 must also have an employer identification number (EIN). An EIN is required for filing returns with the IRS and for making tax payments. A new EIN must be obtained when any of the following occur:

- A trust is created with funds from an estate and the trust is not considered a continuation of the estate
- An estate is created due to the death of the decedent
- The estate continues to operate a business after the owner's death.

A new EIN is not necessary for the following events:

- The fiduciary changes a name or address
- The fiduciary or the beneficiaries of a trust change.

The fiduciary of an estate can obtain an EIN by one of the following methods:

- By going to www.irs.gov/businesses and clicking the "Employer ID Numbers" link. The EIN is issued immediately after the application information is validated; or
- By mailing or faxing Form SS-4, "Application for Employer Identification Number." Fiduciaries should be aware that the EIN may take 4–6 weeks if they are applying for the EIN by mail or fax.

¶3000

If the estate has not received an EIN by the time the return is due, they should write "Applied for" and the application date in the space for the EIN. A social security number should never be substituted for the EIN on a tax return.

(f) What's New on the 2013 Form 1041.

- *Net Investment Income Tax.* Beginning in 2013, a new 3.8 percent tax is imposed on estates with net investment income over $11,950 (increasing to $12,150 in 2014). See Form 1041, Schedule G, line 4, Net investment income tax from Form 8960, line 21.

- *Form 8960 Required for Estates with Net Investment Income.* Beginning in 2013, estates with net investment income must attach Form 8960, "Net Investment Income Tax—Individuals, Estates and Trusts" to their return.

- *New Tax Rates.* Beginning in 2013, the top fiduciary income tax rate increased from 35 percent in 2012 to 39.6 percent in 2013. In addition, the maximum capital gain tax rate increased from 15 percent to 20 percent for estates in the 39.6 percent tax bracket.

- *Form 8949 Required for Estates.* Beginning in 2013, estates must use Form 8949, "Sales and Other Dispositions of Capital Assets" to report most capital gains and losses. In prior years, those transactions would have been reported by estates on Form 1041, Schedule D or Schedule D-1.

- *Higher Tax Rate Imposed on Estates.* The income tax rates for estates in 2013 were 15 percent, 25 percent, 28 percent, 33 percent and 39.6 percent in 2013. An estate will be subject to the top income tax rate of 39.6 percent in 2013 on any taxable income in excess of $11,950 (increasing to $12,150 in 2014).

- *Long-Term Capital Gain and Dividend Tax Rates Increase.* In 2013, the top tax rate for long-term capital gains and qualified dividends increased to 20 percent (up from 15 percent) if the estate sells capital assets that are held for more than 12 months. Beginning in 2013, qualified dividends received by estates will permanently be taxed at capital gains rates. The 20 percent capital gains tax rate applies to estates with income above $11,950 in 2013 (increasing to $12,150 in 2014).

- *Item F. Net Operating Loss (NOL) Carryback.* The IRS added a new NOL carryback check box in Item F of the heading. Taxpayers should check the box if an amended return is filed for an NOL carryback.

- *Item G. Section 645 Election.* If the estate has made an IRC Sec. 645 election (an election to treat a revocable trust as part of the decedent's estate), the executor must check Item G and provide the taxpayer identification number (TIN) of the electing trust with the greatest assets in the box provided. The executor must also attach a statement to Form 1041 providing the following information for each electing trust: (a) the name of the electing trust, (b) the TIN of the electing trust, and (c) the name and address of the trustee of the electing trust.

- *Net Operating Loss Deduction (NOLD).* The IRS revised line 15b to report NOLDs. NOLDs were previously reported on line 15a.

- *Miscellaneous Itemized Deductions.* Miscellaneous itemized deductions subject to the 2 percent floor are now reported on new line 15c.

- *Form 1041 E-Filing.* For tax year 2013, both Form 8453-F, "U.S. Estate or Trust Income Tax Declaration and Signature for Electronic Filing," and new Form

¶3000

8453-FE, "U.S. Estate or Trust Declaration for an IRS E-file Return," will be used for e-filing.

- *Bankruptcy Estate Filing Threshold.* For tax years beginning in 2013, the requirement to file a return for a bankruptcy estate applies only if gross income is at least $10,000.

¶3001 FORM 1041—COMPLETED U.S. INCOME TAX RETURN FOR ESTATES

This chapter provides a completed income tax return for a decedent's estate on IRS Form 1041 together with a line-by-line explanation of every entry on the form and supporting schedules.

For a line-by-line explanation of an estate's income tax return, you will be guided through the Form 1041 filed for the estate of Alan P. Barber, who died on February 9, 2013, at the age of 72. Barber did not reside in a community property state. He used the cash method of accounting for income tax reporting purposes. Barber's will names his daughter executor or personal representative of the estate.

Apply for employer identification number. After the court has approved the executor's appointment as executor, he or she must first obtain an employer identification number (EIN) for the estate. The executor should apply for this number as soon as possible because he or she needs to enter it on returns, statements, and other documents that he or she files concerning the estate. In addition, the executor has to give the number to payors of interest and dividends and other payors who must file a return concerning the estate. The executor applies for the number on Form SS-4, "Application for Employer Identification Number," which is available from the IRS and the Social Security Administration offices.

Next, the executor should notify the IRS Service Center where he or she will file the tax estate's tax returns that he or she has been appointed the decedent's executor. For this, the executor will use IRS Form 56, "Notice Concerning Fiduciary Relationship."

Relevant portions of will. Barber's last will and testament provides that all of the shares of stock in Generous Investors that he owned at the time of death should be given to the Child Abuse Center in Baltimore, Maryland. The will also provides that $5,000 in cash be given to Barber's sister, Louise Barber. Barber's will named his surviving spouse and his sister, Louise, as beneficiaries.

Estate's receipts. The following receipts apply to the Barber estate:

1. Barber's employer sent a check to Barber's surviving spouse in the amount of $10,000, which represented unpaid salary and payment for accrued vacation time. No amount was withheld for income tax. The check was made out to the estate, so it was received by the executor. Accordingly, the executor enters $10,000 on line 8 of Page 1 of Form 1041.

2. A dividend check in the amount of $600 was received from ZZZ Company on December 31, 2013. The executor enters $600 on line 2 of Page 1 of Form 1041.

3. The estate received an IRS Form 1099-INT showing $1,000 interest paid by the bank on the savings account in 2013 after Barber died. The executor enters $1,000 on line 1 of Form 1041.

A rare book collector pays $5,000 for the decedent's book collection on December 1, 2013. The estate has a $500 long-term capital gain from the sale of the rare books. This gain is computed by taking the excess of the sale price ($5,000) over the value of the collection at the date of Barber's death ($4,500). This gain must be reported on Schedule D (Form 1041) when the estate's income tax return is filed. Note that inherited property sold or disposed of within one year after the decedent's death is considered to have been held for more than one year regardless of how long the property was actually held by the estate. Thus, the sale of such property will qualify for long-term capital gains tax rates. The sale of the rare book collection by the Barber estate is thus entered in Part II under the long-term capital gain subheading of Form 8949 [see ¶ 3034 for a further discussion of Form 8949].

Estate's deductions. The following deductions apply to the Barber estate:

1. Real estate taxes on the primary residence—$3,000.
2. Real estate taxes on the beach-front rental property—$1,000. These taxes are deducted on Schedule E (IRS Form 1040) and not on line 11 of Form 1041.
3. Attorney's fees paid in connection with administration of the estate—$1,000. This is an expense of administration and is deducted on line 14 (Form 1041). In order to claim this deduction, however, the executor files with the return a statement in duplicate that such expense has not been claimed as a deduction from the gross estate for figuring the federal estate tax on IRS Form 706, and that all rights to claim that deduction are waived.

Estate's distributions. According to the terms of Barber's will, the executor makes a distribution in the amount of $5,000 to Barber's sister, Louise. The distribution was made from current income of the estate. The income distribution deduction is figured on Schedule B of Form 1041 and deducted on line 18 (Form 1041).

¶3002 WHICH ESTATES MUST FILE FORM 1041

A decedent's estate is created when someone dies. The estate exists until all the deceased person's money and other assets are distributed by the personal representative to the decedent's heirs and other beneficiaries and a local court sanctions termination of the estate.

A Form 1041 must be filed if the estate consisted of probate property, which is property owned in the decedent's name alone. If all of the decedent's assets consists of nonprobate assets, such as jointly held property, which pass to the survivor by operation of law when they died, no taxable estate is created and no fiduciary return need be filed.

A Form 1041 must be filed for a taxable domestic estate in the following situations:

1. If a domestic estate has gross income of $600 or more during a tax year;
2. If one or more of the beneficiaries of the domestic estate are nonresident alien individuals, in which case Form 1041 must be filed even if the gross income of the estate is less than $600;

3. If the estate of an individual involved in a bankruptcy proceeding under Chapter 7 or Chapter 11 of the Bankruptcy Code, has gross income equal to or more than $10,000 for tax years beginning in 2013 [IRC Sec. 6012(a)(8)].

Example 1: Betty, an individual using a calendar year, is declared bankrupt. She dies in 2013. Her bankrupt estate must file a return that year if it has income in excess of $10,000.

¶3003 TOP OF FORM 1041

The first line on the top of Form 1041 asks for information regarding the year for which the income tax return for the decedent's estate is being filed. If the return is for the calendar year, leave the space blank. If the return is for a short tax year or a fiscal year, enter the beginning and ending dates in these spaces.

The income that the assets earned during the estate administration period must be reported by the estate annually on either a calendar or fiscal tax year beginning on the date that the decedent dies. The estate's first tax year may be any period of 12 months or less that ends on the last day of a month. You do not need IRS permission to select the initial taxable period of an estate.

A fiscal tax year is selected when the executor or administrator chooses the last day of any month other than December. If such a fiscal tax year option is chosen by the executor, the due date for the return is generally the fifteenth day of the fourth month following the close of the year.

Example 1: If an estate has a fiscal tax year that ends on May 31, 2013, the fiduciary must file the estate tax return and pay any tax due by September 15, 2013.

Example 2: Alice is the beneficiary of an estate that has a fiscal year beginning June 1, 2013, and ending May 31, 2014. Alice is a calendar-basis taxpayer. On June 1, 2013, Alice receives a distribution from the estate. She does not have to report any income resulting from this distribution until April 15, 2014, which is the due date of her 2013 tax return.

Example 3: Decedent dies on October 15, 2013, and the estate receives substantial income in November and December of 2013. If the estate selects a calendar year and distributes the income to the beneficiary in 2013, the income will be taxed to the beneficiary in his 2013 calendar year and the tax will be due on April 15, 2014. If, however, the executor had selected an initial fiscal year ending January 31, 2014, and then distributed the income to the beneficiaries in February 2014, the beneficiaries may defer paying the tax on the income distributed until April 15, 2015, the due date of their 2014 Form 1040. Instead of having to pay a tax on the distributed income just a few months after it was received, the beneficiary of the estate that selects the January 31, 2014, fiscal year pays the tax a year after the distribution was received.

The estate's personal representative chooses the estate's accounting period when he or she files the estate's first Form 1041. This flexibility afforded estates in choosing either the calendar or fiscal year accounting periods leaves room for tax planning and creative use of the estate's year-end to postpone the payment of tax.

> **Example 4:** Decedent dies on September 15, 2013, and the estate receives substantial income in October 2013. Remember that the first tax year of an estate begins at the moment of the decedent's death and ends on the last day of the month selected by the fiduciary, but cannot exceed 12 months. If the estate selects a calendar year and distributes income to a beneficiary in 2013, the income will be taxed on April 15, 2014, only a few months after it was received. But if you select an initial fiscal year ending January 31, 2014, and then distribute the income in February 2014, you can defer the payment of tax on income received by the beneficiary until May 15, 2015.

> ▶ **PRACTICE TIP:** Pay careful attention to adopting either a calendar or fiscal year for the estate because this fixes the estate's tax year for subsequent periods. You cannot change the taxable year end after you have made your selection unless the estate gets permission from the IRS to make the change. The accounting period of an estate can be changed by filing IRS Form 1128, "Application To Adopt, Change, or Retain a Tax Year."

> ■ For the Barber Estate, the executor decides to use the calendar year and the cash method of accounting to report the estate's income. As a result, the first tax year of the estate begins on the date of death, which was February 9, 2013, and ends on December 31, 2013. The return is due by April 15, 2014. Therefore, the spaces for tax year at the top of the form are left blank.

Box A—Type of entity. Check the appropriate box that describes the entity for which you are filing the return. The following options that relate to estates are available:

Decedent's estate. The decedent's estate is created when someone dies. The decedent's estate is treated as a taxpayer that is separate and distinct from the deceased person. It generally continues to exist until all estate assets have been distributed to the heirs and other beneficiaries. The income earned from the property of the estate during the period of administration or settlement must be accounted for and reported by the estate on Form 1041.

Bankruptcy estate. A Chapter 7 or Chapter 11 bankruptcy estate is a separate taxable entity that is created when someone in debt files a petition for bankruptcy under either Chapter 7 or Chapter 11 of the Bankruptcy Code. The bankruptcy estate is administered by a trustee or a debtor-in-possession who must file an income tax return on Form 1041 if the bankruptcy estate has gross income of $10,000 or more for tax years beginning in 2013. The individual debtor must still file an individual tax return even though a tax return was filed for the bankrupt estate.

> ■ The Barber estate checks the first box marked "Decedent's estate."

Name of estate. When completing the name box at the top of Form 1041, be sure to enter the exact name of the estate from the Form SS-4, "Application for Employer Identification Number." This form is completed when the executor applies for the EIN.

¶**3003**

Address of estate. Enter the address of the executor in this space. Be sure to include the suite, room, or other unit number after the street address unless the mail cannot be delivered to the street address. In this situation, enter the executor's Post Office box number instead of the street address.

Box B—Number of Schedules K-1 attached. Every estate claiming an income distribution deduction on Page 1, line 18, of Form 1041 must enter the number of Schedules K-1 (Form 1041) that are attached to Form 1041. The Barber estate enters -1- in box B.

Box C—Employer identification number. Every estate must have an EIN [see ¶ 3000(e)].

Box D—Date entity created. On a decedent's estate return, enter the date of the decedent's death.

■ The Barber estate enters 2/9/13, the date Alan Barber died and thus the date the decedent's estate was created.

Box F—Initial return, amended return, final return, or change in fiduciary's name or address. *Initial return.* If this is the first return filed by the estate, enter an "X" in the box marked "Initial return" in Section F.

Final return. The "Final return" box would be checked if this was the final return filed on behalf of an estate that was terminated. An estate is considered terminated when it ends as a separate taxable entity and no longer reports gross income or claims deductions or credit [Reg. Sec. 1.641(b)-3(b)]. After an estate has terminated, the IRS should be notified on Form 56 that the fiduciary relationship has ended.

Amended return. If this is an amended return, check the "Amended return" box. The entire return should be completed with the new information reported on the appropriate lines. The estate's tax liability should be refigured. Attach a sheet explaining the reason for the changes and identify the lines and amounts being changed on the amended return.

If the amended return results in a change to income, or a change in distribution of any income or other information provided to a beneficiary, file an amended Schedule K-1 (Form 1041) along with the amended Form 1041. Check the "Amended K-1" box at the top of the amended Schedule K-1.

Change in fiduciary. If a different fiduciary enters his or her name on the line for *Name and title of fiduciary* than was shown on the prior year's return (or Form SS-4 if this is the first return being filed) and Form 3822-B, "Change of Address or Responsible Party—Business," was not filed, be sure to check this box. If there is a change in the fiduciary whose address is used as the mailing address for the trust after the return is filed, use Form 3822-B to notify the IRS.

Change in fiduciary's address. Check the appropriate box if the same fiduciary who filed the prior year's return (or Form SS-4 if this is the first return being filed) files the current year's return and changed the address on the return (including a change to an "in care of" name and address) and did not report the change on Form 3822-B. If the address shown on Form 1041 changes after the form is filed (including a change to an "in care of" name and address) file Form 3822-B to notify the IRS of the change.

■ The Barber estate marks the first box marked "Initial box" because this is the first return filed by the decedent's estate.

¶3003

¶3004 REPORTING THE ESTATE'S INCOME: LINE 1 OF FORM 1041—INTEREST INCOME

On line 1 of Form 1041, report the estate's share of all taxable interest income that was received during the tax year. An estate could receive interest income from the following sources:

1. Accounts including certificates of deposits and money market accounts with banks, credit unions, and brokerage houses;

2. Notes, loans, and mortgages;

3. U.S. Treasury bills, notes, and bonds;

4. U.S. savings bonds;

5. Original issue discount; and

6. Income received as a regular interest holder of a real estate mortgage investment conduit (REMIC).

> ■ The Barber estate earned $1,000 in interest income and that figure is entered here. It is not necessary to list the type of interest or the payer of the interest.

¶3005 LINE 2a—TOTAL ORDINARY DIVIDENDS AND LINE 2b—QUALIFIED DIVIDENDS

Line 2a: Total Ordinary Dividends. Report the estate's share of all ordinary dividends received during the tax year on line 2a. Note that for the year of the decedent's death, Forms 1099-DIV issued in the decedent's name may include dividends earned after the date of death that should be reported on the income tax return of the decedent's estate. When preparing the decedent's final income tax return, report on Schedule B (Form 1040), or Schedule 1 (Form 1040A), the ordinary dividends shown on Form 1099-DIV. Under the last entry on Schedule B or Schedule 1 as the case may be, subtotal all the dividends reported. Below the subtotal, write "Form 1041" and the name and address shown on Form 1041 for the decedent's estate. Also, show the part of the ordinary dividends reported on Form 1041 and subtract it from the subtotal.

Capital gains distributions should be reported on Schedule D (Form 1041).

> ■ The Barber estate earned $600 in ordinary dividends and that figure is entered on line 2a. It is not necessary to list the source of the dividends.

Line 2b: Qualified Dividends. Qualified dividends are dividends that are taxed at a lower tax rate. They are typically paid by a U.S. or qualified foreign corporation on stocks that have been held for the requisite period of time. Enter the beneficiary's allocable share of qualified dividends on line 2b(1) and enter the estate's allocable share on line 2b(2). If the estate received qualified dividends that were derived from income in respect of a decedent, reduce the amount on line 2b(2) by the portion of the estate tax deduction claimed on Form 1041, page 1, line 19, that is attributable to those qualified dividends. Do not reduce the amounts on line 2b by any other allocable expenses.

Dividends paid by most domestic and foreign corporations are called "qualified dividends" and are reported to the estate in box 1b of Form 1099-DIV. They are eligible for the capital gains tax rate. Corporate stock dividends that are passed through to investors by a mutual fund or other regulated investment company (RIC), partnership, real estate investment trust (REIT), or held by a common trust fund qualify for the lower tax rates assuming the distribution would otherwise be classified as "qualified dividend income."

Exceptions: The following types of dividend income may be reported to the estate as qualified dividends in box 1b of Form 1099-DIV but are specifically excluded from the definition of "qualified dividend income" and are therefore ineligible for the reduced tax rate:

- Dividends paid by a credit unions, mutual savings banks, savings and loans, domestic building and loans, mutual insurance companies, farmers' cooperatives, tax-exempt cemetery companies, tax-exempt corporations, nonprofit voluntary employee benefit associations (VEBAs).

- Dividends paid by employee stock ownership plans (ESOPs).

- Dividends paid by stock owned for less than 61 days during the 121-day period that began 60 days before the ex-dividend date. The ex-dividend date is the first date following the declaration of a dividend on which the purchaser or a stock is not entitled to receive the next dividend payment. When counting the number of days the estate held the stock, include the day the estate disposed of the stock but not the day it acquired the stock. However, you cannot count certain days during which the estate's risk of loss was diminished.

- Dividends paid by stock purchased with borrowed funds if the dividend was included in investment income in claiming an interest deduction.

- Dividends on any share of stock to the extent that the estate is under an obligation (including a short sale) to make related payments with respect to positions in substantially similar or related property. This situation most frequently arises in connection with short sales where the taxpayer borrows stock from a broker to sell. After this initial sale, the short seller hopes the price of the stock goes down so he can replace the borrowed stock with identical shares purchased at a lower price, pocketing the difference. In this situation, the broker delivers shares that it was holding for another customer in "street name." Any subsequent dividends paid on the stock will go to the buyer but the account of the customer whose shares were borrowed must be credited with a payment in lieu of dividend equal to the amount of the dividend. Payments in lieu of dividends are not eligible for taxation at lower capital gains rates.

- Dividends paid into a tax-free fund, such as a company retirement plan, traditional IRA or 401(k) plan.

¶3005

- Dividends attributable to periods totaling more than 366 days that the estate received on any share of preferred stock held for less than 91 days during the 181-day period that began 90 days before the ex-dividend date. When counting the number of days the estate held the stock, include the date the estate disposed of the stock but not the day it acquired the stock. However, you cannot count certain days during which the estate's risk of loss was diminished.

- Payments in lieu of dividends, but only if you know or have reason to know that the payments are not qualified dividends.

  ■ The Barber estate leaves line 2 blank.

¶3006 LINE 3—BUSINESS INCOME OR LOSS

If the estate operated a business, report the income and expenses on Schedule C (Form 1040) or Schedule C-EZ and enter the net profit or (loss) from Schedule C or Schedule C-EZ on line 3.

  ■ The Barber estate leaves line 3 blank.

¶3007 LINE 4—CAPITAL GAIN OR LOSS

Enter the capital gain from Schedule D (Form 1041), Part III, line 19, Column (3) or the loss from Part IV, line 20 of Form 1041. Gains and losses from the sale or exchange of capital assets are computed and allocated between the fiduciary and the beneficiaries on Schedule D, Form 1041.

  ▶ **WARNING:** Do not substitute Schedule D (Form 1040) for Schedule D (Form 1041).

Inherited property sold or disposed of by the estate within one year after the decedent's death is considered to have been held for more than one year and thus qualifies for capital gains tax rates. The Barber estate earned $500 in capital gain from the sale of a rare book collection, which was treated as a long-term capital asset. An asset in the hands of the estate generally retains the same character as it had in the hands of the decedent before death. A rare book collector paid $5,000 for the book collection on December 1, 2012. The $500 long-term capital gain from this sale is computed by taking the excess of the sale price ($5,000) over the value of the collection at the date of Barber's death ($4,500). Barber paid $3,000 for the book collection on May 15, 2003 but the estate acquired the collection on the date of Alan P. Barber's death, which was February 9, 2012.

  ▶ **BASIC BASIS FACTS:** Under the stepped-up basis rules, the income tax basis of property acquired from a decedent at death generally is stepped up (or stepped down) to equal its value as of the date of the decedent's death (or on the date six months after the date of death, if alternate valuation under IRC Sec. 2032 is elected on the decedent's estate tax return). The stepped-up basis at death rules will continue to apply to estates of decedents dying before and after 2012.

  ■ In the Barber example, the estate's basis in the book collection is stepped up to $4,500, which was the expert's valuation of the collection on the date of Alan Barber's death, which was February 9, 2012. The $500 gain is reported on Schedule D (Form 1041), Part II, line 12.

¶3008 LINE 5—RENTS, ROYALTIES, PARTNERSHIPS, OTHER ESTATES AND TRUSTS, ETC.

Use Schedule E (Form 1040—**not Form 1041**), "Supplemental Income and Loss," to report the estate's share of income or losses from rents, royalties, partnerships, S corporations, other estates and trusts, and real estate mortgage investment conduits (REMICs). Enter the net profit or loss from Schedule E (Form 1040) on line 5 of Form 1041.

■ The Barber estate leaves line 5 blank.

¶3009 LINE 6—FARM INCOME OR LOSS

If the estate operated a farm, use Schedule F (Form 1040) to report farm income and expenses. Enter the net profit or (loss) from Schedule F on line 6.

■ The Barber estate leaves line 6 blank.

¶3010 LINE 7—ORDINARY GAIN OR LOSS

Enter from line 17, Form 4797, "Sales of Business Property," the ordinary gain or loss from the sale or exchange of property other than capital assets and also from involuntary conversions (other than casualty or theft).

■ The Barber estate leaves line 7 blank.

¶3011 LINE 8—OTHER INCOME

Enter other items of income not included on lines 1, 2a, and 3 through 7. Do not include tax-exempt income on this line. List the type and amount on the dotted line and attach a schedule if the estate has more than one item on this line. Include items such as unpaid salary and bonuses received by the decedent's estate that is income in respect of a decedent as discussed in Chapter 7 and any part of a total distribution shown on Form 1099-R, "Distributions From Pensions, Annuities, Retirement or Profit-Sharing Plans, IRAs, Insurance Contracts, etc.," that is treated as ordinary income.

■ For the Barber estate, enter the $10,000 that Barber's employer paid the estate after Barber died. This represented unpaid salary and accrued vacation pay and is income in respect of decedent.

¶3008

Line 9—Total income. Enter the total income on line 9.

■ The total income earned by the estate was $12,100 and that figure is reported on line 9.

¶3012 REPORTING THE ESTATE'S DEDUCTIONS

When a decedent's estate computes taxable income, it is generally allowed the same types of deductions that are available to individual taxpayers. For further discussion see ¶ 2808. An estate is not, however, allowed to make an election under IRC Sec. 179 to expense tangible property in a taxpayer's trade or business. Another difference between the deductions available to estates and individual taxpayers is that an estate is allowed an income distribution deduction for distributions to beneficiaries.

In addition, deductions for amortization, depletion, and depreciation are only allowed to the extent the deductions are not apportioned to the beneficiaries.

(a) How Estates Report Depreciation Deductions. For a decedent's estate, the depreciation deduction is apportioned between the estate and the heirs, legatees, and devisees on the basis of the estate's income allocable to each [Reg. Sec. 1.167(h)-1(b)].

(b) How Estates Report Depletion Deductions. For mineral or timber property held by a decedent's estate, the depletion deduction is apportioned between the estate and the heirs, legatees, and the devisees on the basis of the estate's income from such property allocable to each [Reg. Sec. 1.611-1(c)(4)].

(c) How Estates Report Amortization Deductions. The deduction for amortization is apportioned between an estate and its beneficiaries under the same principles for apportioning the deduction for depreciation and depletion discussed above.

NOTE: **Amortization of reforestation expenses.** The deduction for amortization of reforestation expenses under IRC Sec. 194 is only available to an estate.

(d) How Passive Activity Loss Rules Affect Estates. The passive activity loss rules limit the amount that an estate can deduct from a passive activity to the amount of income generated by passive activities [IRC Sec. 469(a)(1); Reg. Sec. 1.469-1]. Similarly, credits from passive activities are generally limited to the tax attributable to those activities. These limitations are first applied at the estate level and then passed through to the beneficiary level. Use Form 8582, "Passive Activity Loss Limitations" to compute the amount of losses allowed from passive activities.

For purposes of the passive activity loss rule, taxable income is divided into three parts: (1) regular income from wages and salary or professional fees; (2) portfolio (or investment) income, such as dividends, bond interest, and gains on the sale of shares of stock. Portfolio income does not include gross income, interest, or royalties derived in the ordinary course of a trade or business of lending money or credit to customers; and (3) passive income, such as is generated by most tax shelters and other types of passive investments. As a general rule, there will be no traffic across these three parts. In other words, a passive loss cannot be deducted against "active" income (e.g., salary or self-employment earnings) or "portfolio" income (e.g., dividends or interest income). Any disallowed or excess loss is suspended and carried forward to the following year or years until used, or until deducted in the year the estate sells or otherwise disposes of its entire interest in the activity in a fully taxable transaction [IRC Sec. 469(b)].

The following activities are not passive activities and are therefore not subject to the passive activity loss limitations.

- Trade or business activities in which the taxpayer "materially participated" for the tax year. To satisfy this test and deduct losses in full from a trade or business, the taxpayer must materially participate on a regular, continuous and substantial basis [IRC Sec. 469(h)(1)].

- A working interest in an oil or gas well held directly or through an entity that does not limit liability (such as a general partner interest in a partnership). It does not matter whether the taxpayer materially participated in the activity for the tax year [IRC Sec. 469(c)(3)(A)].

- The rental of a dwelling unit used for personal purposes during the year for more than the greater of 14 days or 10 percent of the number of days during the year that the home was rented at a fair rental.

(e) How At-Risk Rules Affect Estates. The at-risk rules limit the estate's ability to deduct losses from an activity only to the extent that the estate is at risk for the activity at the close of the taxable year [IRC Sec. 465]. The amount at risk in an activity is the amount that could actually be lost as a result of the investment.

Like the passive loss rules, Congress created the "at-risk" rules to limit tax shelter investors from offsetting wages and dividends with losses generated from activities financed by nonrecourse loans where investors were not personally liable for the amount invested in circular investment schemes. For purposes of the at-risk rule, the term "loss" means the excess of the deductions allocable to the specific activity for the year, without regard to the at-risk limitation, over the income received or accrued by the investor during the same year from the same activity [IRC Sec. 465(d)].

Any loss disallowed because it exceeds the amount at risk in one year is suspended and may be deducted in the succeeding tax years, subject to the at-risk limits in each of those years [IRC Sec. 465(a)(2)]. There is no limit to the number of years it may be carried over [Reg. Sec. 1.465-2(b)]. The amount of loss which is deductible in a particular year reduces the amount at risk (but not below zero) for that activity for subsequent tax years. Thus, if a loss exceeds an estate's at-risk amount, it will not be allowed in the next year unless the at-risk amount is also increased by the investment of more money in the activity. The amount of loss which is allowed for a taxable year cannot reduce the amount at risk below zero [Reg. Sec. 1.465-3(a)].

¶3013 LINE 10—INTEREST

Enter the amount of interest (subject to limitations) paid or incurred by the estate on amounts borrowed by the estate, or on debt acquired by the estate that is not claimed elsewhere on the estate's income tax return.

¶3013

Personal interest is not deductible. This includes the following:

1. Interest paid on revolving charge accounts;
2. Personal notes for money borrowed from a bank, credit union, or other person;
3. Underpayments of federal, state, or local income taxes.

Include on line 10 the following types of interest:

1. Investment interest;
2. Qualified residence interest;
3. Interest payable on any unpaid portion of the estate tax attributable to the value of a reversionary or remainder interest in property, or an interest in a closely held business for the period during which an extension of time for payment of such tax is in effect;

    Qualified mortgage insurance premiums. Enter (on worksheet on page 23 of the 2013 Instructions to Form 1041) the qualified mortgage insurance premiums paid under a mortgage insurance contract issued during the year in connection with qualified residence debt that was secured by a first or second residence. If at least one other person was liable for and paid the premiums in connection with the loan, and the premiums were reported on Form 1098, include the estate's share of the premiums on the worksheet. Qualified mortgage insurance is mortgage insurance provided by the Department of Veterans Affairs, the Federal Housing Administration, or the Rural Housing Service, and private mortgage insurance.

    Limit on deduction. If the estate's AGI is more than $100,000, its deduction is limited and the worksheet on page 23 of the 2013 Instructions to Form 1041 must be used to figure the amount of the deduction;

    Prepaid mortgage insurance. If the estate paid premiums for qualified mortgage insurance that are allocable to periods after the end of its tax year, such premiums must be allocated over the shorter of:

    • The stated term of the mortgage; or
    • 84 months, beginning with the month the insurance was obtained.

    The premiums are treated as paid in the year to which they are allocated. If the mortgage is satisfied before its term, no deduction is allowed for the unamortized balance. These allocation rules are inapplicable to qualified mortgage insurance provided by the Department of Veterans Affairs or the Rural Housing Service.

    ■ The Barber estate leaves line 10 blank.

¶3014 LINE 11—TAXES

Enter any deductible taxes paid or incurred during the tax year that are not deductible by the estate elsewhere on Form 1041. Deductible taxes include:

1. State, and local income taxes unless you elect to deduct state and local general sales taxes. You cannot deduct both.
2. State and local general sales taxes which can be deducted instead of state and local income taxes. An estate cannot use the Optional Sales Tax Tables for individuals in the 2013 Schedule A (Form 1040) Instructions to compute its deduction.

¶3014

3. State, local and foreign real property taxes

4. State and local personal property taxes

5. Foreign or U.S. possession income taxes unless you claim a credit for the tax instead of the deduction; and

6. Generation-skipping transfer tax imposed on income distributions.

Do *not* deduct:

1. Federal income taxes;

2. Estate, inheritance, legacy, succession, and gift taxes;

3. Federal duties and excise taxes.

Instead, treat these taxes as part of the cost of the property.

■ The Barber estate deducts the $3,000 the estate paid for real estate taxes on the primary residence. The $1,000 real estate taxes paid on the beach-front rental property are deducted on Schedule E of Form 1040. They are not deducted on line 11 of Form 1041.

¶3015 LINE 12—FIDUCIARY FEES

The total amount of deductible fees paid to the fiduciary for administering the estate during the tax year should be entered on line 12.

■ The Barber estate leaves line 12 blank.

¶3016 LINE 13—CHARITABLE DEDUCTION (FROM SCHEDULE A, CHARITABLE DEDUCTION, LINE 7)

An estate is entitled to a deduction for gross income, which, under the terms of the will, is paid or permanently set aside during the taxable year for charitable purposes [IRC Sec. 642(c)]. The percentage limitations applicable to individuals do not apply to estates. The charitable organization need not be created or organized in the United States [Reg. Sec. 1.642(c)-1(a)(2)].

The amount of the charitable deduction is entered on line 13 of Form 1041 and the amount of the deduction is computed on Schedule A as discussed below.

The deduction is allowed only for amounts of gross income. Contributions out of corpus (other than gross income allocated to corpus) do not qualify for a deduction on the estate's income tax return.

Gross income includes amounts received by the estate as income in respect of a decedent. A charitable contribution will be deductible even though made out of income accumulated in earlier years, provided that no deduction has already been allowed for any previous year for any amount currently contributed [Reg. Sec. 1.642(c)(1)]. No deduction is allowed, to the extent it is made out of corpus other than taxable income allocated to corpus [Reg. Sec. 1.642(c)-3].

¶3015

Election to treat contributions as paid in the prior year. Fiduciaries of an estate may make an election to treat payments made up to the end of the following tax year as having been paid in the prior tax year for deduction purposes. This election is not available for any payment or amount that was deducted in any previous tax year or that was deducted in the tax year in which the amount was paid [IRC Sec. 642(c)(1)].

This election must be made not later than the time, including extensions, prescribed by law for filing the income tax return for the tax year following the tax year for which the election is made. The election may be revoked, without IRS consent, within the time prescribed for making it. Thereafter, the election for any tax year is binding and irrevocable for that particular year [Reg. Sec. 1.642(c)-1(b)(2)].

The election is made by attaching a statement to the return (or to an amended return) for the tax year in which the fiduciary chooses to claim the contribution deduction. The statement must contain the following information:

1. The name and address of the fiduciary and the name of the trust or estate;

2. A clear indication that the fiduciary is making an election under IRC Sec. 642(c)(1) for the tax year;

3. The name of each charitable organization to which a contribution was paid in respect of which the election applies; and

4. The amount and date of the actual payment of each contribution or contributions to which the election applies.

Example 1: A calendar year estate makes a contribution on February 7, 2012 from income earned in 2011. The fiduciary can elect to treat the contribution as paid in 2011. To make this election, the fiduciary must file a statement with Form 1041 for the tax year in which the contribution is treated as paid.

Schedule A, Line 1—Amounts paid or permanently set aside for charitable purposes from gross income. Enter amounts that were paid for a charitable purpose out of the estate's gross income, including any capital gains that are attributable to income under the governing instrument or local law. Include amounts paid during the tax year from gross income received in a prior tax year, but only if no deduction was allowed for any prior tax year for these amounts.

Claim a deduction here for amounts the estate permanently set aside during the tax year from gross income. Charitable purpose includes religious, charitable, scientific, literary, or educational purposes, or for the prevention of cruelty to children or animals, or for the establishment, acquisition, maintenance, or operation of a public cemetery not operated for profit.

■ The Barber estate enters $1,000 on line 1. This represents the dividends the estate received during the current taxable year from Generous Investors. Alan Barber's will provided that all shares of stock that he owned at the time of death in Generous Investors would be given to the Child Abuse Center in Baltimore, Maryland. Because under local law, the Child Abuse

Center is entitled to all dividends from the shares that are received by the estate during the administration period of the estate, the dividends are considered to be permanently set aside for charitable purposes during the current tax year.

The $5,000 cash bequest in Barber's will to the National Kidney Foundation is not deductible on the estate's income tax return because it was not required to be paid out of the gross income of the estate. The deduction for the contribution to the Kidney Foundation, however, may be claimed on the federal estate tax return.

Schedule A, Line 2—Tax-exempt income allocable to charitable contributions. The estate that pays or sets aside any part of its income for a charitable purpose must reduce the deduction by the portion allocable to any tax-exempt income. If the governing instrument specifically provides the source from which amounts are permanently set aside for charitable purposes, the specific provisions control. In all other cases, determine the amount of tax-exempt income allocable to charitable contributions by multiplying line 1 by a fraction where the numerator is the total tax-exempt income of the estate, and the denominator is the gross income of the estate. Do not include in the denominator any losses allocated to corpus.

■ The Barber estate does not allocate any part of its tax-exempt interest to the charitable contribution because the source of the contribution ($1,000 dividends from Generous Investors) is determined under Alan Barber's will.

Schedule A, Line 3. Subtract line 2 from line 1 and enter the total on line 3.

■ The Barber estate enters $1,000.

Schedule A, Line 4—Capital gains for the tax year allocated to corpus and paid or permanently set aside for charitable purposes. Enter the total of all capital gains for the tax year that are:

- Allocated to corpus, and

- Paid or permanently set aside for charitable purposes.

■ The Barber estate enters nothing.

Schedule A, Line 6—Section 1202 Exclusion allocable to capital gains paid or permanently set aside for charitable purposes. If the exclusion of gain from the sale or exchange of qualified small business stock was claimed, enter the part of the gain included on Schedule A, lines 1 and 4, that was excluded under IRC Sec. 1202. For further discussion of this exclusion, see ¶ 3034.

Schedule A, Line 7—Charitable deduction. Subtract line 6 from line 5 enter the result here and on Page 1, line 13.

■ The Barber estate enters $1,000 here and on Form 1041, Page 1, line 13.

¶3016

¶3017 LINE 14—ATTORNEY, ACCOUNTANT, AND RETURN PREPARER FEES

Enter here the total deductible fees paid by the executor of the estate to attorneys, accountants, and return preparers. Reasonable attorney's and accountant's fees paid or incurred by the fiduciary are deductible if they are ordinary and necessary in connection with the administration of the estate.

No deduction is allowed for expenses allocable to tax-exempt income or expenses allowed as a deduction for federal estate tax purposes. The deduction may also be limited by the 2 percent floor on miscellaneous itemized deductions.

■ The Barber estate paid the estate's attorney and accountant total fees of $2,000 during the taxable year. The portion of these fees allocable to tax-exempt income is $500. The balance of $1,500 is deducted on line 14.

¶3018 LINE 15a—OTHER DEDUCTIONS NOT SUBJECT TO THE 2 PERCENT FLOOR

Attach a schedule and list by type and amount all allowable deductions that are not deductible elsewhere on Form 1041. Do not include any losses on worthless bonds and similar obligations and nonbusiness bad debts. Report these losses on Form 8949, "Sales and Other Dispositions of Capital Assets."

Do not deduct medical or funeral expenses on Form 1041.

Report on line 15a the following:

1. Bond premium;
2. Casualty and theft losses; estates should use Form 4684, "Casualties and Thefts," to compute any deductible casualty and theft losses;
3. Domestic production activities deduction; the estate may be entitled to deduct up to 9 percent of its share of qualified production activities income from the following activities:

    a. Construction performed in the United States;
    b. Engineering or architectural services performed in the United States for construction projects in the United States;
    c. Any lease, rental, license, sale, exchange, or other disposition of:

       • Tangible personal property, computer software, and sound recordings that the estate manufactured in whole or in significant part in the United States;
       • Any qualified film the estate produced; or
       • Electricity, natural gas, or potable water the estate produced in the United States.

4. Estate's share of amortization, depreciation, and depletion not claimed elsewhere.

    ■ The Barber estate had no entry on this line.

¶3018

¶3019 LINE 15b—NET OPERATING LOSS DEDUCTION AND LINE 15c—ALLOWABLE MISCELLANEOUS ITEMIZED DEDUCTIONS SUBJECT TO THE 2 PERCENT FLOOR

Line 15b—Net operating loss deduction. An estate may claim a net operating loss deduction (NOLD) under IRC Sec. 172.

Line 15c—Allowable miscellaneous itemized deductions subject to the 2% floor. Miscellaneous itemized deductions are deductible only to the extent that the aggregate amount of such deductions exceeds 2 percent of the estate's adjusted gross income. Deduct on line 15c expenses for the production or collection of income, such as investment advisory fees, subscriptions to investment advisory publications, and the cost of safe deposit boxes.

Miscellaneous itemized deductions do not include the following deductions:

- Interest under IRC Sec. 163;
- Taxes under IRC Sec. 164;
- The amortization of bond premium under IRC Sec. 171;
- Estate taxes attributable to income in respect of a decedent (IRD) under IRC Sec. 691(c) (see ¶ 2614 for discussion of IRD); or
- Expenses paid or incurred in connection with the administration of the estate that would not have been incurred if the property were not held by the estate.

    ■ The Barber estate had no entry on this line.

¶3020 LINE 16—TOTAL DEDUCTIONS

Add lines 10 through 15b to compute the total deductions available to the estate to reduce total income as stated on line 9.

    ■ Because there were no other deductions, the total deductions for the Barber estate is $5,500.

¶3021 LINE 17—ADJUSTED TOTAL INCOME OR LOSS

Subtract line 16 from line 9 and enter the result on line 17.

    ■ Subtract line 16 ($5,500) from line 9 ($12,100) and enter the result $6,600 on line 17.

¶3019

¶3022 LINE 18—INCOME DISTRIBUTION DEDUCTION

If the estate was required to distribute income currently or if it paid, credited, or was required to distribute any other amounts to beneficiaries during the tax year, complete Schedule B to determine the estate's income distribution deduction.

Cemetery perpetual care fund. On line 18, deduct no more than $5 per gravesite for the amount paid for maintenance of cemetery property. To the right of the entry space for line 18, enter the number of gravesites. Also write "Section 642(i) trust" in parentheses after the trust's name at the top of Form 1041. Taxpayers need not complete Schedules B of Form 1041 or K-1 (Form 1041).

▶ **PRACTICE POINTER:** If the estate claims an income distribution deduction, be sure to complete and attach Parts I and II of Schedule I to refigure the deduction on a minimum tax basis and Schedule K-1 (Form 1041) for each beneficiary who received an income distribution.

■ The Barber estate enters the $5,000 income distribution deduction computed on Schedule B, line 15.

¶3023 LINE 19—ESTATE TAX DEDUCTION (INCLUDING CERTAIN GENERATION-SKIPPING TAXES)

If the estate includes income in respect of a decedent (IRD) in its gross income, and this amount was also included in the decedent's estate for estate tax purposes, the estate is entitled to deduct in the same tax year the income is included, that portion of the estate tax imposed on the decedent's estate that is attributable to the inclusion of the IRD in the decedent's estate [Reg. Sec. 1.691(c)-1]. For further discussion, see ¶2615.

A deduction is also available for the generation-skipping transfer tax imposed as a result of a taxable termination or a direct skip occurring as a result of the death of the transferor [IRC Sec. 691(c)(3)].

■ The Barber estate leaves this line blank.

¶3024 LINE 20—EXEMPTION

A decedent's estate filing a tax return is entitled to a personal exemption in the amount of $600 [see ¶2809].

■ The Barber estate claims a $600 exemption on line 20.

¶3025 LINE 21—TOTAL DEDUCTIONS

To find the amount of the total deductions, add lines 18, 19, and 20.

■ The total deductions for the Barber estate are $5,600.

¶3026   LINE 22—TAXABLE INCOME

The estate's taxable income is entered on line 22. This is computed by subtracting line 21 ($5,600) from line 17 ($6,600). The result ($1,000) is entered on line 22. If line 22 is a loss, the estate may have a net operating loss ("NOL"). Do not include the deductions claimed on lines 13 (charitable), 18 (income distribution), and 20 (exemption) when figuring the amount of the NOL. Generally, an NOL may be carried back to the prior two tax years and forward for up to 20 years. The two-year carryback period does not apply to the portion of an NOL attributable to an eligible loss, a farming loss, a qualified disaster, GO Zone, or disaster recovery assistance loss, or a specified liability loss. An estate may also elect to carry an NOL forward only, instead of first carrying it back.

Complete Schedule A of Form 1045 to figure the amount of the NOL that is available for carryback or carryover. Use Form 1045 or file an amended return to apply for a refund based on an NOL carryback. For more details, see Pub. 536, Net Operating Losses (NOLs) for Individuals, Estates, and Trusts.

On the termination of the estate, any unused NOL carryover that would be allowable to the estate in a later tax year, but for the termination, is allowed to the beneficiaries succeeding to the property of the estate. [See the instructions for Schedule K-1 (Form 1041), box 11, codes D and E.]

■ The taxable income for the Barber estate is $1,000.

¶3027   LINE 23—TOTAL TAX (FROM SCHEDULE G, LINE 7)

The total tax owed by the Barber estate in the amount of $75 as computed on Schedule G, line 7 is entered on line 23. For discussion of Schedule G, see ¶3033.

¶3028   LINE 24a—PAYMENTS: ESTIMATED TAX PAYMENTS AND AMOUNT APPLIED FROM PREVIOUS RETURN

Estates make estimated tax payments only for the tax years ending two or more years after the decedent's death [IRC Sec. 6654(l)(2)(A)]. The estimated taxes are figured on IRS Form 1041-ES (Estimated Income Tax for Estates and Trusts) and the taxes are paid with Form 1041-ES payment vouchers. After the IRS receives the first payment voucher from the fiduciary, the estate will be sent a Form 1041-ES package with the name, address, and EIN preprinted on the vouchers for the next tax year. Mail the payment voucher to the following address:

> Internal Revenue Service
> P.O. Box 804526
> Cincinnati, OH 45280-4526

Do not send the payment voucher to the IRS Center where Form 1041 is filed.

(a) When Are Estimated Taxes Due. Calendar year estates must pay estimated taxes in four installments, which are due on or before the following dates [IRC Sec. 6654(c)]:

1st installment	April 15 of the current tax year
2nd installment	June 15 of the current tax year
3rd installment	September 15 of the current tax year
4th installment	January 15 of the following tax year

Fiscal year estates must pay estimated taxes on or before the following dates [IRC Sec. 6654(k)(1)]:

1st installment	fifteenth day of the fourth month of fiscal year
2nd installment	fifteenth day of the sixth month of fiscal year
3rd installment	fifteenth day of the ninth month of fiscal year
4th installment	fifteenth day after the end of the fiscal year

An estate that has a short tax year (a period of less than 12 months) must pay installments of estimated tax on or before the following dates:

1st installment	fifteenth day of the fourth month of tax year
2nd installment	fifteenth day of the sixth month of tax year
3rd installment	fifteenth day of the ninth month of tax year
4th installment	fifteenth day of the first month of the next tax year

The payments due in the sixth and/or ninth month of the short tax year (but not the payment due on the fifteenth day of the first month of the succeeding tax year) are not required to be paid if the short tax year ended during or before the sixth and/or ninth months.

Example 1: An estate has a short tax year beginning April 1 and ending December 31. The estate's installments of estimated tax are due as follows: the first payment is due on July 15, the second payment is due on September 15, the third payment is due on December 15, and the fourth payment is due on January 15.

Example 2: An estate has a short tax year beginning June 1 and ending December 31. The estate's installments of estimated tax are due as follows: the first payment is due on September 15, the second payment on November 15, no third payment is due because there is no ninth month of the tax year, and the fourth payment is due on January 15.

(b) How Much Is Due. The amount of any required installment of estimated tax is 25 percent of the required annual payment even for a short tax year [IRC Sec. 6654(d)(1)(A)].

(c) Which Estates Must Pay Estimated Taxes. An estate must pay estimated tax for 2014 if it expects to owe, after subtracting any withholding and credits, at least $1,000 in tax, and it expects the withholding and credits to be less than the smaller of:

¶3028

1. 90 percent of the tax shown on the 2014 tax return; or

2. 100 percent of the tax shown on the 2013 tax return (110 percent of that amount if the estate's adjusted gross income on that return is more than $150,000, and less than 2/3 of gross income for 2013 or 2014 is from farming or fishing).

However, if a return was not filed for 2013 or that return did not cover a full 12 months, item 2 above does not apply. For this purpose, include household employment taxes in the tax shown on the return, but only if either of the following is true:

• The estate will have federal income tax withheld for 2014; or

• The estate would be required to make estimated tax payments for 2014 even if it did not include household employment taxes when figuring estimated tax.

(d) Exceptions. The fiduciary need not make estimated tax payments in the following circumstances:

1. An estate of a domestic decedent had no tax liability for the entire previous tax year;

2. A decedent's estate is for any tax year that ends before the date that is two years after the decedent's death.

Example 3: Bill died on May 1, 2013, and his estate adopted a calendar year as its tax year. The estate does not have to make estimated tax payments for its short tax year ending December 31, 2013, or its tax year beginning January 1, 2014, and ending December 31, 2014, because both of these tax years end before May 1, 2014, which is two years after Bill's death. However, the estate is subject to a penalty if it fails to pay estimated taxes promptly or in sufficient amounts for its tax year beginning January 1, 2014, and ending December 31, 2014, because this is the estate's first tax year ending two or more years after Bill's death.

(e) How to Figure Estimated Tax. To figure out how much estimated tax to pay, the fiduciary should use the Estimated Tax Worksheet contained in Form 1041-ES, "Estimated Income Tax For Estates and Trusts" and the current Tax Rate Schedule in Form 1041-ES [see ¶ 2935].

The estate's tax return from last year should be used as a guide for figuring next year's estimated tax. If the estate receives its income unevenly throughout the year, it may be able to lower or eliminate the amount of its required estimated tax payment for one or more periods by using the annualized income installment method [IRC Sec. 6654(d)(2)(A)]. For further discussion of the annualized income installment, get IRS Publication 505, "Tax Withholding and Estimated Tax."

(f) Line 24b—Allocation of Estimated Taxes to Beneficiaries. Allocation to estates in final tax year: In the final tax year of the estate only, the fiduciary of a decedent's estate may make an IRC Sec. 643(g) election to have any portion of their estimated tax payments allocated to any of the beneficiaries [IRC Sec. 643(g)(3)]. The amount of estimated tax allocated to each beneficiary is treated as paid or credited to the beneficiary on the last day of the estate's final tax year and must be reported on Schedule K-1 (Form 1041).

¶3028

The fiduciary makes the election by completing the following steps:

1. Complete and file IRS Form 1041-T, "Allocation of Estimated Tax Payments to Beneficiaries" with the IRS Center where the estate tax return for the year was filed;

2. Attach Form 1041-T to the Form 1041 only if Form 1041-T was not filed before the Form 1041 was filed; and

3. Complete the line on Schedule K-1 of Form 1041 for each beneficiary to whom the estimated tax payments are allocated.

   ■ The Barber estate enters nothing for estimated tax payments.

Line 25—Total payments. To compute the amount of the total payments, add lines 24c through 24e, and 24h.

¶3029 LINE 26—ESTIMATED TAX PENALTY

If line 27 is at least $1,000 and more than 10 percent of the tax shown on Form 1041, or the estate underpaid its 2013 estimated tax liability for any payment period, the estate may owe a penalty. See Form 2210 to determine whether the estate owes a penalty and to figure the amount of the penalty.

No penalty applies in either of the following situations:

• The taxpayer was a decedent's estate for any tax year ending before the date that is two years after the decedent's death;

• The estate had no tax liability last year, the taxpayer was an estate of a domestic decedent and last year's tax return covered (or would have if the taxpayer would have been required to file) a full 12 months.

   (a) Waiver of Penalty. The underpayment penalty may be waived under the following circumstances:

1. A payment was not made because of a casualty, disaster, or other unusual circumstance and it would be inequitable to impose the penalty; or

2. The executor retired (after reaching age 62) or became disabled during the tax year a payment was due or during the preceding tax year, and both the following requirements are met:

   • Reasonable cause exists for not making the payment; and

   • The underpayment was not due to willful neglect.

Federally declared disaster. Certain estimated tax payment deadlines for taxpayers who live or work in a federally declared disaster area are postponed for a period during and after the disaster. During the processing of the tax return, the IRS automatically identifies taxpayers located in a covered disaster area and applies the appropriate penalty relief. The taxpayer should not file Form 2210 if the underpayment was due to a federally declared disaster. Trusts not in a covered disaster area but whose books, records, or tax professionals' offices are in a covered area are also entitled to relief. Also eligible are relief workers affiliated with a recognized government or charitable organization assisting in the relief activities in a covered disaster area.

(b) How to Request Penalty Waiver. To request a penalty waiver, you must complete Form 2210. The IRS will review the information you provide and will decide whether or not to grant your request for waiver.

(c) Exception. The penalty does not apply to a decedent's estate for any tax year ending before the date that is two years after the decedent's death.

¶3030 LINE 27—TAX DUE

The amount of tax owed by the estate is entered on line 27.

The executor of an estate must pay any income tax due in full when the return is filed. The filing due date is the fifteenth day of the fourth month following the close of the tax year.

Pay the tax in cash or by check or money order drawn to the order of the "United States Treasury." Do not write simply "IRS." EINs should be written on checks or money orders. In addition, "2013 Form 1041" should be written on the check.

(a) Forms of Payment. The fiduciary of the estate may pay any income tax owed in cash or by bank check or money order or by any commercially acceptable means deemed appropriate by the IRS [IRC Sec. 6311]. This includes, for example, electronic funds transfers, including those arising from credit cards, debit cards and charge cards [Reg. Sec. 301.6311-2].

Electronic deposits. A fiduciary of an estate that is not required to make electronic deposits of estimated tax may voluntarily participate in the Electronic Federal Tax Payment System (EFTPS). In order to enroll, fiduciaries should visit the EFPTS website. In order for deposits made using EFTPS to be on time, the deposit must be initiated by 8:00 p.m. Eastern time the date before the date the deposit is due. If a third party is used to make the deposit, a different cut-off time may be imposed.

(b) Interest and Penalties. Failure to pay by the due date will result in the imposition of interest and penalties.

Interest. Interest is compounded daily on taxes not paid by the due date, even if an extension of time to file is granted [IRC Secs. 6601(a), 6601(b)(1), 6622]. Interest will also be charged beginning on the return due date (including extensions) on civil penalties such as the failure-to-file penalty, the accuracy-related penalty, and the fraud penalty. The interest charge will stop on the date the penalty is paid [IRC Secs. 6601(e)(2)(A), 6601(e)(2)(B)]. The interest charge will be equal to the federal short-term rate plus three percentage points [IRC Sec. 6621(a)(2)].

Penalty for failure to file. For the late filing of a return, a penalty will be imposed in the amount of 5 percent of the tax due for each month, or part of a month, for which a return is not filed up to a maximum of 25 percent of the tax due (15 percent for each month, or part of a month, up to a maximum of 75 percent if the failure to file is fraudulent). The penalty will not be imposed if the fiduciary can show that the failure to file on time was due to reasonable cause. A statement explaining what reasonable cause resulted in the return being filed late should be attached to the return.

¶3030

Penalty for failure to pay. If the fiduciary fails to pay the tax when due, in addition to interest charges on late payments, a late penalty of one-half of 1 percent of the unpaid tax shown on the estate's return will be imposed for each month (or part of a month) that the tax remains unpaid up to a maximum of 25 percent of the unpaid amount, unless failure to pay timely is due to reasonable cause [IRC Sec. 6651(a)(2)]. Any penalty is in addition to interest charges on late payments.

(c) Timely Mailed/Timely Filed Rule. The general rule is that a tax return or tax payment that is delivered by the U.S. Postal Service after the due date in a postage prepaid, properly addressed envelope, will be considered to be mailed on time if the date of the postmark is on or before the due date [IRC Sec. 7502(a)]. This is known as the timely mailed/timely filed rule [see ¶ 2931(b)]. In other words, if you used the U.S. Postal Service to mail your return or tax payment on time, it will be considered to be filed or paid on time even though it arrived at its destination late. You can file at the last minute using a private delivery services (PDS) other than the U.S. Postal Service and still qualify under the rule that a return mailed on time is considered to be filed on time [IRC Sec. 7502(f)]. The IRS has designated the following PDSs that can be used to file returns or pay tax with the assurance that they will be treated as filed or paid on time if you mailed them on time:

- DHL Express (DHL): DHL "Same Day" Service;

- Federal Express (FedEx): FedEx Priority Overnight, FedEx Standard Overnight, FedEx 2Day, FedEx International Priority, and FedEx International First;

- United Parcel Service (UPS): UPS Next Day Air, UPS Next Day Air Saver, UPS 2nd Day Air, UPS 2nd Day Air a.m., UPS Worldwide Express Plus, and UPS Worldwide Express.

(d) Extension of Time to File. If more time is needed to file the Form 1041 estate tax return for any estate other than a bankruptcy estate, use Form 7004, "Application for Automatic Extension of Time to File Certain Business Income Tax, Information and Other Returns," to apply for an automatic five-month extension of time to file. Bankruptcy estates only are entitled to an automatic six-month extension if they file Form 7004.

■ The Barber estate owes $150 in tax.

¶3031 WHERE TO FILE FORM 1041

All estates should mail Form 1041 to the IRS Service Center listed in the chart below which is found on page 8 of the 2013 Instructions to Form 1041.

Where To File

For all estates and trusts, including charitable and split-interest trusts (other than Charitable Remainder Trusts).

IF you are located in ...	THEN use this address if you:	
	Are not enclosing a check or money order ...	Are enclosing a check or money order ...
Connecticut, Delaware, District of Columbia, Florida, Georgia, Illinois, Indiana, Kentucky, Maine, Maryland, Massachusetts, Michigan, New Hampshire, New Jersey, New York, North Carolina, Ohio, Pennsylvania, Rhode Island, South Carolina, Tennessee, Vermont, Virginia, West Virginia, Wisconsin	Department of the Treasury Internal Revenue Service Cincinnati, Ohio 45999-0048	Department of the Treasury Internal Revenue Service Cincinnati, Ohio 45999-0148
Alabama, Alaska, Arizona, Arkansas, California, Colorado, Hawaii, Idaho, Iowa, Kansas, Louisiana, Minnesota, Mississippi, Missouri, Montana, Nebraska, Nevada, New Mexico, North Dakota, Oklahoma, Oregon, South Dakota, Texas, Utah, Washington, Wyoming	Department of the Treasury Internal Revenue Service Ogden, Utah 84201-0048	Department of the Treasury Internal Revenue Service Ogden, Utah 84201-0148
A foreign country or United States possession	Internal Revenue Service P.O. Box 409101 Ogden, Utah 84409	Internal Revenue Service P.O. Box 409101 Ogden, Utah 84409

Electronic filing. Applications to become an IRS e-file provider must be submitted online. The IRS is no longer accepting paper applications on Form 8633, "Application to Participate in the IRS e-file Program." Qualified fiduciaries or transmitters may be able to file Form 1041 and related schedules electronically. To become an *e-file* provider complete the following steps: (1) Create an IRS e-Services account; (2) Submit an *e-file* provider application online; and (3) Pass a suitability check. Existing e-file providers must now use e-Services to make account updates.

¶3031

Form 1041 E-filing. For tax year 2013, both Form 8453-F, "U.S. Estate or Trust Income Tax Declaration and Signature for Electronic Filing," and new Form 8453-FE, "U.S. Estate or Trust Declaration for an IRS e-file Return," must be used for the estate e-files. Estates that file Form 1041 electronically may now have the executor sign the return electronically by using a personal identification number (PIN). [See Form 8879-F, "IRS e-file Signature Authorization for Form 1041," for details.] If the executor does not sign the electronically filed return by using a PIN, the executor must file Form 8453-F, "U.S. Estate or Trust Income Tax Declaration and Signature for Electronic Filing." Form 8453-F may also used as a transmittal if the executor needs to attach certain forms or other documents that cannot be electronically filed. If Form 1041 is *e-filed* and there is a balance due, the executor may authorize an electronic funds withdrawal with the return.

¶3032 SCHEDULE B—INCOME DISTRIBUTION DEDUCTION

Schedule B must be completed to determine the estate's income distribution deduction if the estate was required to distribute income currently or if it paid, credited, or was required to distribute any other amounts to beneficiaries during the tax year.

Separate share rule. If the estate has more than one beneficiary, and if different beneficiaries have substantially separate and independent shares, their shares are treated as separate estates for the sole purpose of determining the DNI allocable to the respective beneficiaries [IRC Sec. 663(c)]. If the separate share rule applies, figure the DNI allocable to each beneficiary on a separate sheet and attach the sheet to this return. Any deduction or loss that is applicable solely to one separate share of the estate is not available to any other share of the same estate. See ¶ 2818 for further discussion of the separate share rule.

Schedule B, Line 1—Adjusted total income. Enter the amount of adjusted total income from line 17, Page 1 of Form 1041.

■ The $6,600 adjusted total income of the Barber Estate from Page 1, line 17 is entered on line 1.

Schedule B, Line 6—Capital gain entered as a negative number. The $500 capital gain entered by the Barber estate on Page 1, line 4, is entered on line 6 as a negative number.

Schedule B, Line 7—Distributable net income. Distributable net income (DNI) is computed on line 7 by combining $6,600 from line 1 and ($500) from line 6 for a DNI of $6,100.

Schedule B, Line 9—Income required to be distributed currently. The amount of income of the estate required to be distributed currently to each beneficiary, whether or not actually distributed during the tax year, is entered on line 9, Page 2 of Schedule B.

■ The Barber estate is not required to distribute any income currently and line 9 is blank.

Schedule B, Line 10—Other amounts paid, credited, or otherwise required to be distributed currently. The total of all amounts, other than those entered on line 11, that were actually paid, credited, or required to be distributed in the tax year, are entered on line 10. These amounts are included on line 10 whether paid from current or accumulated income or from corpus. These distributions are referred to as "second tier" distributions and include annuities to the extent not paid out of income, discretionary distributions of corpus, and distributions of property in kind. The beneficiary includes such amounts in income only to the extent of his or her proportionate share of DNI.

The following items are excluded from lines 9 and 10:

- Amounts deducted on prior year's return that were required to be distributed in the prior year;

- Amounts that are properly paid or credited as a gift or bequest of a specific amount of money or specific property. To qualify as a gift or specific bequest, the amount must be paid in three or fewer installments. An amount that can be paid or credited only from income is not considered a gift or bequest;

- Amount paid or permanently set aside for charitable purposes of otherwise qualifying for the charitable deduction.

    ■ The Barber estate enters on line 10 the $5,000 that Alan Barber's will provided was to be distributed to his sister, Louise. The distribution was made from current income of the estate.

Schedule B, Line 11—Total distributions. Add lines 9 and 10.

    ■ The Barber estate enters $5,000 on line 11.

Schedule B, Line 13—Tentative income distribution deduction. Subtract line 12 from 11.

    ■ The Barber estate enters $5,000 on line 13.

Schedule B, Line 14—Tentative income distribution deduction. Subtract line 2 from line 7.

    ■ The Barber estate's tentative income distribution deduction in the amount of $6,100 is entered on line 14. You figure this amount by subtracting line 2 (0) from line 7 ($6,100).

Schedule B, Line 15—Income distribution deduction. Enter the smaller of line 13 or line 14. The income distribution deduction determines the amount of income that will be taxed to the beneficiaries. The total amount of income for regular tax purposes that is reflected on line 8 of the individual beneficiaries' Schedule K-1 should equal the amount claimed on line 15.

    ■ The Barber estate is allowed an income distribution deduction of $5,000 on line 15 and this amount is entered on Page 1, line 18.

¶3033 TAX COMPUTATION—SCHEDULE G, LINE 1a

Schedule G, Line 1a. The tax computation for the Barber estate is made on Schedule G using Schedule D because the estate had both net capital gain and taxable income.

¶3033

You would figure the tax using the following 2013 Tax Rate Schedules (included also is the 2014 tax rate schedule for planning purposes):

2013 Tax Rate Schedule for Estates and Trusts

If taxable income is:	*The tax is:*
Not over $2,450	15% of the taxable income
Over $2,450 but not over $5,700	$367.50 plus 25% of the excess over $2,450
Over $5,700 but not over $8,750	$1,180 plus 28% of the excess over $5,700
Over $8,750 but not over $11,950	$2,034 plus 33% of the excess over $8,750
Over $11,950	$3,090 plus 39.6% of the excess over $11,950

2014 Tax Rate Schedule for Estates and Trusts

If taxable income is:	*The tax is:*
Not over $2,500	15% of the taxable income
Over $2,500 but not over $5,800	$375 plus 25% of the excess over $2,500
Over $5,800 but not over $8,900	$1,200 plus 28% of the excess over $5,800
Over $8,900 but not over $12,150	$2,068 plus 33% of the excess over $8,900
Over $12,150	$3,140.50 plus 39.6% of the excess over $12,150

Schedule D and Schedule D Tax Worksheet. Use Part V of Schedule D (Form 1041) or the "Schedule D Tax Worksheet," whichever is applicable to figure the estate's tax if the estate files Schedule D and has:

- A net capital gain and any taxable income, or

- Qualified dividends on line 2b(2) of Form 1041 and any taxable income.

Qualified Dividends Tax Worksheet. If the estate does not have to file Part I or Part II of Schedule D (Form 1041) and has entered an amount on line 2b(2) of Form 1041, and any taxable income (line 22), then figure the estate's tax using the worksheet on page 31 of the 2013 Form 1041 Instructions and enter the tax on Schedule G, line 1a. The amount entered on line 2b(2) of Form 1041 must be reduced by the portion of IRC Sec. 691(c) deduction claimed on line 19 of page 1 of Form 1041 if the estate received qualified dividends that were income in respect of a decedent.

Schedule G, Line 2a—Foreign Tax Credit. Attach Form 1116 "Foreign Tax Credit (Individual, Estate or Trust)" if the estate elects to claim credit for income or profits taxes paid or accrued to a foreign country or a U.S. possession. The estate may claim credit for that part of the foreign taxes not allocable to beneficiaries (including charitable beneficiaries). Enter the estate's share of the credit on line 2a.

Schedule G, Line 2b—General Business Credit. Enter on line 2b the estate's total general business credit allowed for the year from Form 3800 which must be filed to claim any of the general business credits. If the estate's only source of credits listed in Part I for Form 3800 is from pass through entities, the estate may not be required to complete the source credit form. For list of available credits, see Instructions for Form 3800.

Do not include any amounts that are allocated to a beneficiary. Credits that are allocated between the estate and the beneficiaries are listed in the instructions for Schedule K-1, box 13. Generally, these credits are apportioned on the basis of the income allocable to the estate and the beneficiaries.

Schedule G, Line 2c—Credit for Prior Year Minimum Tax. An estate that paid alternative minimum tax in a previous year may be eligible for a minimum tax credit this year. [See Form 8801, "Credit for Prior Year Minimum Tax-Individuals, Estates and Trusts."]

Schedule G, Line 2d—Bond Credits. Complete and attach Form 8912, "Credit to Holders of Tax Credit Bonds," if the estate claims a credit for holding a tax credit bond. Be sure to include the credit in interest income.

Schedule G, Line 3—Total Credits. To claim a credit other than the credits entered on lines 2a through 2d, include the credit in the total for line 3. Complete and attach the appropriate form and write the form number and amount of the credit on the dotted line to the left of the entry space.

Schedule G, Line 4—Net Investment Income Tax from Form 8960, Line 21. For tax years beginning in 2013, certain estates will be subject to an additional 3.8 percent net investment income (NII) tax on the lesser of the (1) undistributed NII for the tax year, or (2) excess of AGI [as defined in IRC Sec. 67(e)] over the dollar amount at which the highest estate income tax bracket begins [IRC Sec. 1411(a)(2); Reg. Sec. 1.1411-3(1)(ii)]. This dollar amount is $11,950 in 2013 and increases to $12,150 in 2014. If the estate has a short tax year (less than 12 months), the threshold amount is not reduced or prorated [Reg. Sec. 1.1411-3(a)(2)]. Estates use Form 8960 to report their NII tax and to calculate the amount of the NII tax. See ¶ 2790 for a copy of the IRS Instructions for Form 8960 and ¶ 2947 for a sample completed Form 8960 for a trust (the Barber Trust does not owe NII tax in 2013 because its NII is below the filing threshold). See ¶ 2949 for a line-by-line discussion of how to complete Form 8960 for the Trent Trust.

Decedent's estates and bankruptcy estates may owe the NII tax in addition to their regular tax liability. However, in the case of bankruptcy estates, the adjusted gross income threshold is $125,000.

Undistributed NII is the estate's NII determined under Reg. Sec. 1.1411-4, reduced by distributions of NII to beneficiaries and allowable deductions, such as the charitable contribution deduction and the income distribution deduction [Reg. Sec. 1.1411-3(e)(2)].

Special computational rules for bankruptcy estates of an individual. A bankruptcy estate of an individual debtor is treated as an individual for purposes of the NIIT. Regardless of the actual marital status of the debtor, the applicable threshold for purposes of determining the NIIT is the amount applicable for a married person filing separately.

Distributions from foreign estate. A U.S. person who receives a distribution of income from a foreign estate, generally, must include the distribution in his or her net investment income calculation to the extent that the income is included in AGI for regular income tax purposes. However, he or she need not include any distributions of accumulated income received from a foreign estate because the NIIT does not apply directly to foreign estates.

¶3033

Schedule G, Line 5—Recapture Taxes. Include the following recapture taxes on line 5: recapture of investment credit; recapture of low-income housing credit; recapture of qualified electric vehicle; recapture of the Indian employment credit; recapture of the new markets credit; recapture of the credit for the employment-provided child care facilities; recapture of the alternative motor vehicle credit; and the alternative fuel vehicle refueling property credit.

Schedule G, Line 6—Household Employment Taxes. The estate owes household employment tax and Schedule H must be completed and filed with the estate tax return if the answer to any of the following questions is "Yes":

1. Did the estate pay any one household employee cash wages of $1,800 or more in 2013? Cash wages include wages paid by check, money order, etc. When figuring the amount of cash wages paid, combine cash wages paid by the estate with cash wages paid to the household employee in the same calendar year by the household of the decedent or beneficiary for whom the administrator, executor, or trustee of the estate is acting.

2. Did the estate withhold federal income tax during 2013 for any household employee at the request of any household employee?

3. Did the estate pay total cash wages of $1,000 or more in any calendar quarter of 2012 or 2013 to household employees?

Schedule H can be omitted from the estate's tax return only if the answer to all three questions is "No."

Schedule G, Line 7—Total Tax. Add to total tax due on line 7 the interest or taxes computed on the following forms:

- Interest on deferred tax attributable to installment sales of certain timeshares and residential lots and certain nondealer real property installment obligations

- Form 4970, "Tax on Accumulation Distribution of Trusts"

- Tax on electing small business trusts (ESBTs). For further discussion of ESBTs, see ¶ 2800

- Form 8697, "Interest Computation Under the Look-Back Method for Completed Long-Term Contracts"

- Form 8866, "Interest Computation Under the Look-Back Method for Property Depreciated Under the Income Forecast Method"

- Interest on deferrral of gain from certain constructive ownership transactions

- Form 5329, "Additional Taxes on Qualified Plans (including IRAs) and Other Tax-Favored Accounts"

   ■ The Barber Trust computed its tax bill on Schedule D (Form 1041) and Form 8949 (¶ 3039) as discussed in ¶ 3034. The resulting tax bill in the amount of $75 is entered on lines 1a, 1d, 3 and 7 of Schedule G (Form 1041).

¶3033

¶3034 SCHEDULE D (FORM 1041)—CAPITAL GAINS AND LOSSES AND FORM 8949—SALES AND OTHER DISPOSITIONS OF CAPITAL ASSETS

(a) Report Capital Gains on Schedule D (Form 1041) and/or Form 8949. Beginning in 2013, estates must use Form 8949, Sales and Other Dispositions of Capital Assets to report sales and exchanges of capital assets not reported on another form or schedule. The use of Form 8949 by estates is new in 2013. Many transactions that, in previous years, would have been reported by estates on Schedule D or Schedule D-1 must be reported on Form 8949. Certain transactions may be combined and the totals reported on line 1a or line 8a of Schedule D (Form 1041) without completing Form 8949. Filers that use Form 8949 must complete Form 8949 before completing line 1b, 2, 3, 8b, 9 or 10 of Schedule D (Form 1041). Beginning in 2013 Schedule D-1 (Form 1041) will no longer be used.

■ The Barber Estate must complete both Schedule D (Form 1041) and Form 8949. [See ¶ 3039 for a completed Form 8949 for the Barber Estate.]

(b) Capital Gains Tax Rates. The following chart illustrates the capital gains tax rates in effect for 2013–2014.

Capital Gains Maximum Rates for 2013 and 2014

Type of Property	Period Held	Maximum Rate*
Capital assets, other than on gain attributable to Section 1250 recapture or collectibles	12 months or less	39.6%
	More than 12 months	0% if in 15% ordinary income tax rate bracket**
		15% if in 28% or 33% ordinary income tax rate bracket
		20% if in 39.6% ordinary income tax rate bracket

* Excluding the 3.8% net investment income tax that may apply.

** Only to the extent the gain would otherwise be in the 15% tax bracket.

▶ **PRACTICE WARNING:** Do not substitute Schedule D (Form 1040) for Schedule D (Form 1041).

(c) Purpose of Schedule D, Capital Gains and Losses. Schedule D of Form 1041 should be used for the following purposes:

- To report the overall capital gains or losses from transactions reported on Form 8949.

- To report certain transactions that the estate does not have to report on Form 8949.

- To report gain from Part I of Form 4797, "Sales of Business Property."

- To report capital gain or loss from Forms 4684, "Casualties and Thefts."

- To report capital gain from Form 6252, "Installment Sale Income."

- To report capital gain or loss from Form 6781, "Gains and Losses From Section 1256 Contracts and Straddles."

- To report capital gain or loss from Form 8824, "Like-Kind Exchanges."

¶3034

- To report undistributed long-term capital gains from Form 2439, "Notice to Shareholder of Undistributed Long-Term Capital Gains."

- To report capital gain or loss from partnerships, S corporations, or other estates or trusts.

   (d) Form 8949, Sales and Other Dispositions of Capital Assets. Form 8949 should be completed as follows:

- On Part I of Form 8949, summarize three categories (A, B, and C) of short-term capital gains and losses.

- On Part II, summarize three categories (D, E, and F) of long-term capital gains and losses.

- A separate Form 8949 should be completed for each category type.

- The capital gains and losses will be included in category A or D if the investment's cost or other basis is shown in box 3 of Form 1099-B.

- The capital gains and losses will be included in category B or E if no investment basis is shown in box 3 of Form 1099-B.

- The capital gains and losses will be included in category C or F if none of the other boxes are checked. When completed, the summarized Form 8949 information is transferred to Form 1041 Schedule D (Capital Gains and Losses).

- An estate's share of capital gains (losses) from a partnership, S corporation, or another estate is reported only on Schedule D (Form 1041) (i.e., not on Form 8949).

- Instead of reporting each of the transactions on a separate line of Form 8949, they can be reported on an attached statement containing all the same information as Form 8949 and in a similar format, using as many attached statements as needed. The combined totals from all the attached statements should be entered on a Form 8949 with the appropriate box checked. For example, report on Part II of Form 8949 with box D checked, all long-term gains and losses from transactions reported by the broker on a statement showing that the basis of the property sold was reported to the IRS. If there are statements from more than one broker, report the totals from each broker on a separate line. Do not enter "available upon request" and summary totals instead of reporting the details of each transaction on Form(s) 8949 or attached statements.

   (e) Form 8949—Line 1—Part I. On Form 8949, enter all sales and exchanges of capital assets, including stocks, bonds, etc. and real estate (if not reported on Form 4684, 4797, 6252, 6781 or 8824). Report short-term (held 1 year or less) gains or losses in Part I. Report long-term (held 1 year or more) gains and losses in Part II. The details of each transaction should be entered on a separate line of Form 8949. Note that Form 8949 must be completed before completing lines 1b, 2, 3, 8b, 9, or 10 of Schedule D (Form 1041) because the combined totals from all Forms 8949 are reported on Schedule D. When computing the holding period, begin counting on the date after the entity received the property and include the day the entity disposed of it. Use a separate Part I for each of the following types of short-term transactions:

- Short-term transactions reported on Form 1099-B with an amount shown for cost or other basis unless the statement indicates that amount was not reported to the IRS. Check box A at the top of this Part I. If box 6b of Form 1099-B is not checked,

¶3034

which means basis was not reported to the IRS, report that transaction on Part I with box B, not box A, checked.

- Short-term transactions reported on Form 1099-B without an amount shown for cost or other basis. Check box B at the top of Form 8949—Part I. If box 6b of Form 1099-B is not checked, which means basis was not reported to the IRS, report that transaction on Part I with box B, not box A, checked.

- Short-term transactions for which the estate cannot check box A or B because the estate did not receive a Form 1099-B (or substitute statement). Check box C at the top of this Part I.

Use a separate Part II for each of the following types of long-term transactions:

- Long-term transactions reported on Form 1099-B with an amount shown for cost or other basis unless the statement indicates that amount was not reported to the IRS. Check box D at the top of this Part II. If box 6b of Form 1099-B is not checked, which means that basis was not reported to the IRS, report that transaction on Part II with box E, not box D checked.

- Long-term transactions reported on Form 1099-B without an amount shown for cost or other basis. Check box E at the top of Part II. If box 6b of Form 1099-B is not checked, which means that basis was not reported to the IRS, report that transaction on Part II with box E, not box D, checked.

- Long-term transactions without box D or E checked because the estate did not receive a Form 1099-B (or substitute statement). Check box F at the top of Part II.

  ▶ **FILING POINTER:** The estate may not need to file Form 8949 for certain transactions. This is new in 2013. The estate may be able to aggregate those transactions and report them directly on either line 1a (for short-term transactions) or line 8a (for long-term transactions) of Schedule D (Form 1041). This option applies only to transactions (other than sales of collectibles) for which:

  - The estate received a Form 1099-B (or substitute statement) that shows basis was reported to the IRS and does not show a nondeductible wash sale loss in box 5, and

  - The estate does not need to make any adjustments to the basis of type of gain or loss (short-term or long-term) reported on Form 1099-B, or to your gain or loss.

If the estate decides to report these transactions directly on Schedule D, they do not need to be reported on Form 8949 and a statement does not need to be attached.

  ▶ **FILING POINTER:** Instead of reporting each transaction on a separate row on Form 8949, the estate can report them on an attached statement containing all the same information as Parts I and II and in a similar format with a description of property, dates of acquisition and disposition, proceeds, basis, adjustment and gains and loss. The combined totals from all attached statements should be entered on Parts I and II with the appropriate box checked.

Columns (a)–(h) of Form 8949. Enter in columns (a)–(h) the details regarding the estate's acquisition and sale of the asset.

¶3034

- Column (a)—Description of Property. For stock, use the stock ticker symbols or abbreviations to describe the property as long as they are based on the descriptions of the property as shown on Form 1099-B or Form 1099-S.

- Column (b)—Date acquired. Enter in this column the date the entity acquired the asset. Use the trade date for stocks and bonds traded on an exchange or over-the-counter market. For stock or the other property sold short, enter the date the entity acquired the stock or property delivered to the broker or lender to close the short sale.

- Column (c)—Date sold or disposed. Enter in this column the date the entity sold or disposed of the property. Use the trade date for stocks and bonds traded on an exchange or over-the-counter market. For stock or other property sold short, enter the date the entity delivered the stock or property to the broker or lender to close the short sale.

- Column (d)—Proceeds (Sales price). If the entity sold stock or bonds and received a Form 1099-B listing gross sales price, that amount should be entered in column (e). If Form 1099-B indicates that gross proceeds minus commissions and option premiums were reported to the IRS, enter that net amount in column (e).

- Column (e)—cost or other basis.

  Basis of decedent's estate property. Generally, the basis of property acquired by a decedent's estate is the FMV of the property on the date of the decedent's death, or the alternate valuation date if the executor elected to use an alternate valuation under IRC Sec. 2032.

- Column (f)—Code. In order to explain any adjustment to gain or loss in column (g), enter the appropriate code(s) in column (f). See "How To Complete Form 8949, Columns (f) and (g)" which is found on pages 6 and 7 of Form 8949 (reproduced below). If more than one code applies, enter all the codes that apply in alphabetical order (for example, "BOQ"). Do not separate the codes by a space or comma.

- Column (g)—Adjustments to gain or loss. Enter in this column any necessary adjustments to gain or loss. Enter negative amounts in parentheses. Also enter a code in column (f) to explain the adjustment. See "How to Complete Form 8949, Columns (f) and (g)," which is found on pages 6 and 7 of Form 8949 (reproduced below). Include in this column any expense of sale, such as broker's fees and commissions, state and local transfer taxes, option premiums, reinvested gains or dividends that were previously reported as income, costs that were capitalized and original issue discount that has been previously reported as income unless the net sales price was reported in column (e). If any expense of sale is included in this column, enter "0" in column (b). The following items may decrease the basis of the property owned by the estate prior to computing the gain or loss from the sale, exchange, or other disposition of the property:

  — Nontaxable distributions that consist of return of capital;

  — Deductions previously allowed or allowable for depreciation;

  — Casualty or theft loss deductions.

- Column (h)—Gain (or Loss). Figure gain or loss on each row. First, subtract the cost or other basis in column (e) from the proceeds (sales price) in column (d).

¶3034

Then take into account any adjustments in column (g). Enter the gain (or loss) in column (h). Enter negative amounts in parentheses.

The total of the amounts in columns (d), (e), (g), and (h) on Form 8949 are added and the total is entered on Part II, line 2 of Form 8949. That total is then entered on Schedule D of Form 1041 depending on whether box D, E, or F was checked at the beginning of Part II as follows:

- If box D was checked (long-term transaction reported on Form 1099-B showing basis was reported to the IRS), enter the total on Schedule D, Form 1041, line 8b.

- If box E was checked (long-term transaction reported on Form 1099-B showing basis was not reported to the IRS), enter the total on Schedule D, Form 1041, line 9.

- If box F was checked (long-term transaction not reported on Form 1099-B) enter the total on Schedule D, Form 1041, line 10.

■ The Barber estate earned $500 in capital gains from the sale of the rare book collection on December 1, 2013. The estate did not receive a Form 1099-B reporting the transactions to them. The estate therefore enters the transaction in Part II (Form 8949) and checks box F to indicate that the long-term transaction was not reported to them on Form 1099-B.

In column (a) of Part II (Form 8949), the estate describes the asset as "Rare Book Collection." The entry is made in Part II of Form 8949 because inherited property, if sold within one year of the decedent's death, will be considered held long term even if held less than one year.

In column (b) of Part II (Form 8949), the estate enters the date the book collection was acquired. Because the book collection was acquired by the estate on the date of Alan Barber's death, the estate enters 2/9/13, the date of his death.

In column (c) of Part II (Form 8949), the Barber Estate enters 12/1/13, the date the book collection was sold.

In column (d) of Part II (Form 8949), the Barber estate enters the $5,000 which was the sales price the estate received from the sale of the rare books.

In column (e) of Part II (Form 8949), the Barber estate enters the $4,500 cost basis for the assets.

In column (f) of Part II (Form 8949), the Barber estate enters C because the estate disposed of collectibles.

In column (g) of Part II (Form 8949), the Barber estate entered -0- as provided in "How to Complete Form 8949, Columns (f) and (g)" which can be found on pages 6 and 7 of the Instructions to Form 8949.

In column (h) of Part II (Form 8949), the Barber estate enters $500 which is amount of the long-term capital gain realized by the estate on the sale of the rare book collection. The estate's cost basis in the books was $4,500 and they sold for $5,000.

The amounts entered in columns (d), (e), (g), and (h) are added together and entered on Schedule D, line 8b, Form 1041, if box D was checked, line 9 if box E was checked, or line 10 if box F was checked.

¶3034

How To Complete Form 8949, Columns (f) and (g)

For most transactions, you do not need to complete columns (f) and (g) and can leave them blank. You may need to complete columns (f) and (g) if you got a Form 1099-B or 1099-S (or substitute statement) that is incorrect, if you are excluding or postponing a capital gain, if you have a disallowed loss, or in certain other situations. Details are in the table below. If you enter more than one code in column (f), see *More than one code* in the instructions for column (g).

IF...	THEN enter this code in column (f)...	AND...
You received a Form 1099-B (or substitute statement) and the basis shown in box 3 is incorrect	B	• If box B is checked at the top of Part I or if box E is checked at the top of Part II, enter the correct basis in column (e), and enter -0- in column (g). • If box A is checked at the top of Part I or if box D is checked at the top of Part II, enter the basis shown on Form 1099-B (or substitute statement) in column (e), even though that basis is incorrect. Correct the error by entering an adjustment in column (g). To figure the adjustment needed, see the *Worksheet for Basis Adjustments in Column (g)*. Also see *Example 4—adjustment for incorrect basis* in the instructions for column (h).
You received a Form 1099-B (or substitute statement) and the type of gain or loss (short-term or long-term) shown in box 1c is incorrect	T	Enter -0- in column (g). Report the gain or loss on the correct Part of Form 8949.
You received a Form 1099-B or 1099-S (or substitute statement) as a nominee for the actual owner of the property	N	Report the transaction on Form 8949 as you would if you were the actual owner, but also enter any resulting gain as a negative adjustment (in parentheses) in column (g) or any resulting loss as a positive adjustment in column (g). As a result of this adjustment, the amount in column (h) should be zero. However, if you received capital gain distributions as a nominee, report them instead as described under *Capital Gain Distributions* in the Instructions for Schedule D (Form 1040).
You sold or exchanged your main home at a gain, must report the sale or exchange on Part II of Form 8949 (as explained in *Sale of Your Home* in the Instructions for Schedule D (Form 1040)), and can exclude some or all of the gain	H	Report the sale or exchange on Form 8949 as you would if you were not taking the exclusion. Then enter the amount of excluded (nontaxable) gain as a negative number (in parentheses) in column (g). See the example in the instructions for column (g).
You sold or exchanged qualified small business stock and can exclude part of the gain	Q	Report the sale or exchange on Form 8949 as you would if you were not taking the exclusion and enter the amount of the exclusion as a negative number (in parentheses) in column (g). However, if the transaction is reported as an installment sale, see *Gain from an installment sale of QSB stock* in the Instructions for Schedule D (Form 1040).
You can exclude all or part of your gain under the rules explained in the Schedule D instructions for DC Zone assets or qualified community assets	X	Report the sale or exchange on Form 8949 as you would if you were not taking the exclusion. Then enter the amount of the exclusion as a negative number (in parentheses) in column (g).
You are electing to postpone all or part of your gain under the rules explained in the Schedule D instructions for any rollover of gain (for example, rollover of gain from QSB stock or publicly traded securities)	R	Report the sale or exchange on Form 8949 as you would if you were not making the election. Then enter the amount of postponed gain as a negative number (in parentheses) in column (g).

¶3034

IF . . .	THEN enter this code in column (f) . . .	AND . . .
You have a nondeductible loss from a wash sale	W	Report the sale or exchange on Form 8949 and enter the amount of the nondeductible loss as a positive number in column (g). See the Schedule D instructions for more information about wash sales. If you received a Form 1099-B (or substitute statement) and the amount of nondeductible wash sale loss shown (box 5 of Form 1099-B) is incorrect, enter the correct amount of the nondeductible loss as a positive number in column (g). If the amount of the nondeductible loss is less than the amount shown on Form 1099-B (or substitute statement), attach a statement explaining the difference. If no part of the loss is a nondeductible loss from a wash sale transaction, enter -0- in column (g).
You have a nondeductible loss other than a loss indicated by code W	L	Report the sale or exchange on Form 8949 and enter the amount of the nondeductible loss as a positive number in column (g). See *Nondeductible Losses* in the Instructions for Schedule D (Form 1040).
You received a Form 1099-B or 1099-S (or substitute statement) for a transaction and there are selling expenses or option premiums that are not reflected on the form or statement by an adjustment to either the proceeds or basis shown	E	Enter in column (d) the proceeds shown on the form or statement you received. Enter in column (e) any cost or other basis shown on Form 1099-B (or substitute statement). In column (g), enter as a negative number (in parentheses) any selling expenses and option premium that you paid (and that are not reflected on the form or statement you received) and enter as a positive number any option premium that you received (and that is not reflected on the form or statement you received). For more information about option premiums, see *Gain or Loss From Options* in the Instructions for Schedule D (Form 1040).
You had a loss from the sale, exchange, or worthlessness of small business (section 1244) stock and the total loss is more than the maximum amount that can be treated as an ordinary loss	S	See *Small Business (Section 1244) Stock* in the Schedule D (Form 1040) instructions.
You disposed of collectibles (see the Schedule D instructions)	C	Enter -0- in column (g). Report the disposition on Form 8949 as you would report any sale or exchange.
You report multiple transactions on a single row as described in *Exception 1* or *Exception 2* under *Exceptions to reporting each transaction on a separate row*	M	See *Exception 1* and *Exception 2* under *Exceptions to reporting each transaction on a separate row.* Enter -0- in column (g) unless an adjustment is required because of another code.
You have an adjustment not explained earlier in this column	O	Enter the appropriate adjustment amount in column (g). See the instructions for column (g).
None of the other statements in this column apply	Leave columns (f) and (g) blank.	

-7-

¶3034

(f) Schedule D (Form 1041).

Part I—Schedule D (Form 1041)—Short-term. The estate should enter in Part I of Schedule D any short-term capital gains and losses that were reported on Form 8949. The line that the gain is entered on reflects whether or not box A, B, or C was checked on Form 8949. These boxes reflect whether or not basis was reported to the taxpayer or the IRS on Form 1099-B. The estate should report the sales proceeds in column (d), the cost of other basis in column (e), any adjustments in column (g) and the gain or loss in column (h).

Part II—Schedule D (Form 1041)—Long-term. The estate should enter in Part II of Schedule D any long-term capital gains and losses that were reported on Form 8949. The line that the gain is entered on reflects whether or not box D, E or F was checked on Form 8949. These boxes reflect whether or not basis was reported to the taxpayer or the IRS on Form 1099-B. The estate should report the sales proceeds in column (d), the cost of other basis in column (e), any adjustments in column (g) and the gain or loss in column (h).

■ The Barber estate enters the totals from Part II of Form 8949 on line 10 because box F (Form 8949) was checked (long-term transactions not reported to the estate on Form 1099-B). In column (d), the estate enters $5,000. In column (e), the estate enters $4,500 and in column (h), the estate enters gain in the amount of $500.

Schedule D (Form 1041)—Line 13—Capital Gain Distributions. On Line 13, column (h), enter long-term capital gain distributions paid during the year, regardless of how long the entity held its investment. This amount is reported in box 2a of Form 1099-DIV.

Part III—Summary of Parts I and II.

Schedule D, Line 17, Column 1—Beneficiaries' Net Short-Term Capital Gain or Loss. Enter the amount of net short-term capital gain or loss allocable to the beneficiary or beneficiaries. Include only those short-term capital losses that are taken into account in determining the amount of gain from the sale or exchange of capital assets that is paid, credited, or required to be distributed to any beneficiary during the tax year. If the losses from the sale or exchange of capital assets are more than the gains, all of the losses must be allocated to the estate and none are allocated to the beneficiaries.

Schedule D, Line 17, Column 2—Estate's Net Short-Term Capital Gain or Loss. Enter the amount of the net short-term capital gain or loss allocable to the estate. Include any capital gain paid or permanently set aside for a charitable purpose.

Schedule D, Line 17, Column 3—Total. Enter the total of the amounts entered in columns 1 and 2. The amount in column 3 should be the same as the amount on line 7.

Schedule D, Line 18a—Net Long-Term Capital Gain or Loss. Allocate the net long-term capital gain or loss on line 18a in the same manner as the net short-term capital gain or loss on line 17. However, do not take the Section 1202 exclusion on gain from the sale or exchange or qualified small business account into account when figuring net long-term capital gain or loss allocable to the beneficiaries.

¶3034

Schedule D, Line 18b—Unrecaptured Section 1250 Gain. Complete the worksheet found on page 7 of the separate Instructions for Schedule D (Form 1041) if any of the following apply:

- The estate during the year sold or otherwise disposed of Section 1250 property (generally real property that was depreciated) held more than 1 year.

- The estate received installment payments during the tax year for Section 1250 property held more than 1 year for which it is reporting gain on the installment method.

- The estate received a Schedule K-1 from an estate, trust, partnership or S corporation that shows "unrecaptured section 1250 gain" reportable for the tax year.

- The estate received a Form 1099-DIV (or Form 2439) from a real estate investment trust or regulated investment company (including a mutual fund) that reports "unrecaptured section 1250 gain" for the tax year.

- The estate reported a long-term capital gain from the sale or exchange of an interest in a partnership that owned Section 1250 property.

Schedule D, Line 18c—28 Percent Gain or Loss. Complete the 28 percent rate gain worksheet found on page 8 of the separate Instructions for Schedule D (Form 1041) if lines 18a and 19 for column 3 are both greater than zero and at least one of the following apply:

- The estate reports in Part II, column f, an Section 1202 exclusion from the eligible gain on qualified small business stock, or

- The estate reports in Part II, column f, a "collectibles" (see definition below) gain or loss. Also report here gain (but not loss) from the sale or exchange of an interest in a partnership, S corporation, or trust held for more than 1 year and attributable to unrealized appreciation of collectibles.

   ■ The Barber estate enters the $500 realized on the sale of the rare book collection here on line 18c(2) because the rare books qualify as collectibles.

"Collectibles" defined. A collectibles gain or loss is any long-term gain or deductible long-term loss from the sale or exchange of a collectible that is a capital asset. Collectibles include works of art, rugs, antiques, metals (such as gold, silver, and platinum bullion), gems, stamps, coins, alcoholic beverages, and certain other tangible property including rare books.

Part IV of Schedule D (Form 1041)—Capital Loss Limitation. If the sum of all the capital losses is more than the sum of all the capital gains, then these capital losses are allowed as a deduction only to the extent of the smaller of the net loss or $3,000. For any year (including the final year) in which capital losses exceed capital gains, the estate may have a capital loss carryover. Use the Capital Loss Carryover Worksheet found on page 9 of the separate Instructions for Schedule D (Form 1041) to figure any capital loss carryover. A capital loss carryover may be carried forward indefinitely. Capital losses keep their character as either short-term or long-term when carried over to the following year.

Part V of Schedule D (Form 1041)—Tax computation using maximum capital gains rates. Complete this part only if: (1) both lines 18a and 19 in Column (2) of Schedule D (Form 1041) are gains or an amount is entered in Part I or Part II and there is an entry on Form 1041, line 2b(2); and (2) Form 1041, line 22 is more than zero.

¶3034

Part V of Schedule D (Form 1041) is skipped and the Schedule D Tax Worksheet is completed if:

- Either line 18b, column (2) or line 18c, column (2) is more than zero, or
- Both Form 1041, line 2b(1) and Form 4952, line 4g are more than zero.

■ The Barber estate does not complete Part V of Schedule D (Form 1041) because line 18c, column (2) of Schedule D (Form 1041) is more than zero. Instead, the estate completes the Schedule D Tax Worksheet which can be found on page 10 of the 2013 Instructions for Schedule D (Form 1041). After completion of this Worksheet, the estate computes the tax on its taxable income to be $150 which is entered on Schedule G, line 1a (Form 1041).

¶3035 OTHER INFORMATION

Go back to Page 2 of Form 1041.

Question 1. Did the estate receive tax-exempt income? If "Yes," attach a computation of the allocation of expenses.

The Barber estate received no tax-exempt income, so the estate enters an X in the "No" column.

Question 2. Did the estate receive all or any part of the earnings (salary, wages, and other compensation) of any individual by reason of a contract assignment or similar arrangement?

The Barber estate received no part of the earnings of any individual by reason of a contract assignment or similar arrangement, so the estate enters X in the "No" column.

Question 3. At any time during calendar year 2013, did the estate have an interest in or a signature or other authority over a bank, securities, or other financial account in a foreign country?

The Barber estate had no interest in or a signature or other authority over a bank, securities, or other financial account in a foreign country, so the estate enters X in the "No" column.

Question 4. During the tax year, did the estate receive a distribution from, or was it the grantor of, or transferor to, a foreign trust?

The Barber estate did not receive a distribution from, and was not the grantor of or the transferor to a foreign trust, so the estate enters X in the "No" column.

Question 5. Did the estate receive, or pay, any qualified residence interest on seller-provided financing?

The Barber estate did not receive or pay any seller-financed mortgage interest, so the estate enters X in the "No" column.

Question 6. If this is an estate making the IRC Sec. 663(b) election, check here.

This box is left blank because the Barber estate did not make the IRC Sec. 663(b) election to treat any amount paid or credited to a beneficiary within 65 days following the close of the tax year as being paid or credited on the last day of that tax year.

Question 7. To make an IRC Sec. 643(e)(3) election, attach Schedule D (Form 1041), and check here.

This box is left blank because the Barber estate was not making the IRC Sec. 643(e)(3) election to recognize gain on property distributed in kind. For further discussion of the IRC Sec. 643(e)(3) election, see ¶2937.

Question 8. If the decedent's estate has been open for more than two years, attach an explanation for the delay and check here.

This box is left blank because the Barber estate had not been open for more than two years and there was thus no need to attach an explanation for the delay in closing the estate.

Question 9. Are any present or future trust beneficiaries skip persons?

In the Barber estate, there are no trust beneficiaries who are skip persons, so the "No" box is checked next to line 9. To determine if a beneficiary that is a trust is a skip person, see the definition of a skip person at ¶2503.

¶3036 SCHEDULE I—ALTERNATIVE MINIMUM TAX

Schedule I must be completed to compute: (1) the estate's alternative minimum taxable income; (2) the income distribution deduction on a minimum tax basis; and (3) the estate's alternative minimum tax.

When to complete Schedule I:

- Complete Schedule I, Parts I and II if the estate must complete Schedule B, Income Distribution Deduction.

- Complete Schedule I if the estate's share of alternative minimum taxable income (Part I, line 29) exceeds $23,100.

- Complete Schedule I if the estate or trust claims any general business credit and line 6 of Part I or line 3 of Part III of Form 3800 is more than zero.

Schedule I, Part I—Estate's share of alternative minimum taxable income. There are three parts to Schedule I, Form 1041, Alternative Minimum Tax. The estate computes its share of alternative minimum taxable income in Part I, its income distribution deduction on a minimum tax basis in Part II, and its alternative minimum tax liability in Part III.

If the estate's share of alternative minimum taxable income is $23,100 or less, enter -0- on Schedule G, line 1c because the estate is not liable for the alternative minimum tax. Part I and Part II of Schedule I have to be completed for any year for which an income distribution deduction on line 18 of Form 1041 has been claimed, regardless of whether or not there is an alternative minimum tax liability. Part III must be completed if the estate's share of alternative minimum taxable income from line 12 of Part I of Schedule I exceeds $23,100.

Schedule I, Line 1—Adjusted total income or loss. The Barber estate's adjusted total income from Form 1041, line 17 is $6,600, which is entered here.

¶3036

Schedule I, Lines 2 through 23—Adjustments and tax preference items. Add back the trust's adjustments and tax preference items that are listed in lines 2 through 23. These adjustments and tax preferences items are figured in substantially the same manner as they are for trusts. For detailed discussion of these items see ¶ 2938.

On line 3 you enter any state, local, or foreign real property taxes; state or local personal property taxes; and state, local, or foreign income taxes that were included on line 11 of Page 1 of Form 1041. Do not include any new motor vehicle taxes.

■ The Barber estate paid $3,000 in real estate taxes in the Barber primary residence as indicated on line 11 of Page 1. The estate therefore enters $3,000 on line 3 of Schedule I. The Barber estate has no other adjustments and tax preference items.

Schedule I, Line 24—Alternative tax net operating loss deduction. Enter the alternative tax net operating loss deduction (ATNOLD) on line 24. To figure the ATNOLD, take the regular net operating loss (NOL) and modify it as follows:

1. Add back the AMT adjustments, or subtract them if the adjustments are negative; and

2. Reduce the NOL by any item of tax preference except the appreciated charitable contribution preference items. For a trust that held a residual interest in a REMIC, figure the ATNOLD without regard to any excess inclusion.

Schedule I, Line 25—Adjusted alternative minimum taxable income. The estate combines lines 1 through 24 and enters the total on line 25.

■ The Barber Estate enters $9,600.

Schedule I, Line 26—Income distribution deduction. Enter the amount from Part II (Form 1041, Schedule I) line 44.

■ As computed on line 44, the Barber Estate's income distribution deduction on a minimum tax basis is $5,000.

Schedule I, Line 29—Estate's share of alternative minimum taxable income. Subtract line 28 ($5,000) from line 25 ($9,600) to get $4,600, which is the estate's share of alternative minimum taxable income. Because this amount is less than $23,100 in 2013, the Barber estate enters -0- on Schedule G, line 1(c) because the estate is not liable for the alternative minimum tax.

Schedule I, Part II—Income distribution deduction on a minimum tax basis.

Schedule I, Line 30—Adjusted alternative minimum taxable income. The Barber estate's adjusted alternative minimum taxable income from line 25 of Part I is $9,600.

Schedule I, Line 32—Total net gain from Schedule D (Form 1041), line 16a, Column (1). The Barber estate enters $500.

Schedule I, Line 35—Capital gains computed on a minimum tax basis included on line 25. The Barber estate's $500 capital gain from line 4, Page 1 is expressed here as a negative number.

Schedule I, Line 37—Distributable net alternative minimum taxable income. Combine lines 30 through 36. The Barber estate enters $9,600 on line 37.

Schedule I, Line 42—Tentative income distribution deduction on a minimum tax basis. The Barber estate enters $5,000.

¶3036

Schedule I, Line 44—Income distribution deduction on a minimum tax basis. Enter the smaller of line 42 ($5,000) or line 43 ($9,600). The Barber estate enters $5,000 on line 44 and on line 26.

Completion of Parts III and IV of Schedule I reveal that the estate is not liable for the alternative minimum tax because line 29 of Part I is less than $23,100 in 2013.

¶3037 SCHEDULE K-1—BENEFICIARY'S SHARE OF INCOME, DEDUCTIONS, CREDITS, ETC.

The fiduciary of an estate uses Schedule K-1 (Form 1041) as an information return to report each beneficiary's share of income, deductions, and credits from an estate. That income must be included in the beneficiary's gross income and reported on his or her personal income tax return. Three copies of Schedule K-1 should be prepared for each beneficiary. The fiduciary must file one copy of the Schedule K-1 with the Form 1041 and retain one copy for the records.

In addition, the fiduciary should provide a Schedule K-1 (Form 1041) to each beneficiary who receives a distribution of property or an allocation from the estate. A penalty of $50 (not to exceed $100,000 for any calendar year) will be imposed on the fiduciary for each failure to furnish Schedule K-1 to each beneficiary unless reasonable cause for each failure is established. The beneficiary need not file Schedule K-1 with his or her tax return because the IRS already has a copy of that form.

Inconsistent treatment of items. The beneficiary receiving the Schedule K-1 must report items shown on the Schedule K-1 (and any attached schedules) the same way they were treated on the Form 1041. If the treatment on the original or amended return is inconsistent with the estate's treatment, or if the estate was required to but has not filed a return, the beneficiary must file IRS Form 8082 (Notice of Inconsistent Treatment or Administrative Adjustment Request) with the original or amended return to identify and explain any inconsistency (or to note that a return has not been filed).

If the fiduciary is required to file Form 8082 but fails to do so, the accuracy-related penalty may be imposed. This penalty is in addition to any tax that results from making your amount or treatment of the item inconsistent with that shown on the estate's return. Any deficiency that results from making the amounts consistent may be assessed immediately.

■ The Barber estate completes a Schedule K-1 for Louise Barber, the decedent's sister and a beneficiary of the estate. The terms of the decedent's will provides that a distribution in the amount of $5,000 was to be made out of current income to his sister, Louise. The distribution of $5,000 must be allocated and reported on Schedule K-1 (Form 1041).

Use the following three-step procedures in order to compute the amounts to enter on Schedule K-1. See Reg. Sec. 1.652(c)-4(f) for a comprehensive example (reproduced at ¶2940).

1. List all items of income of the estate entering into the computation of distributable net income, including tax-exempt interest. You will find these items on lines 1 through 8 of Form 1041, Page 1. The beneficiary of a decedent's estate must

include in his or her gross income the sum of: (a) the amount of the income required to be distributed currently, or if the income required to be distributed currently to all beneficiaries exceeds the DNI (figured without taking into account the charitable deduction), his or her proportionate share of the DNI; and (b) all other amounts properly paid, credited, or required to be distributed, or if the sum of the income required to be distributed currently and other amounts properly paid, credited, or required to be distributed to all beneficiaries exceeds the DNI, his or her proportionate share of the excess of DNI over the income required to be distributed currently.

2. Use a worksheet such as the one below to group items of income. The following income items should be shown separately:

- Income from rental activities;
- Income from rental real estate activities;
- Income from business activities that are passive activities; and
- Income from business activities that are not passive activities.

   ■ Here's how the Barber estate complies with Step One:

- The Barber estate enters $1,000 in the interest column. This figure is taken from line 1, Page 1 of Form 1041.
- The Barber estate enters $600 in the ordinary dividends column. This comes from line 2a, Page 1 of Form 1041.
- The Barber estate enters $10,000 for income in respect of decedent in the next column. This comes from line 8, Page 1 of Form 1041.

Step One. Allocation of income and deductions:

Type of Income	Amount	Deductions	Balance of Distributable Net Income
Interest	$1,000	$474	$526
Ordinary Dividends	$600	$284	$316
Income in respect of decedent (IRD)	$10,000	$4,741	$5,259

Note about capital gains and losses. Capital gains are not included in DNI unless they are:

1. Allocated to income under the governing instrument or local law;
2. Allocated to corpus and actually distributed to beneficiaries during the taxable year;
3. Used, under the governing instrument or the practice followed by the fiduciary, in determining the amount which is distributed or required to be distributed; or
4. Paid or to be used for charitable purposes so that a contributions deduction is allowed.

Capital losses are excluded from the computation of DNI. But if capital gains are distributed, the capital losses are offset against the gains to determine the net capital gains distributed.

¶3037

■ The $500 capital gains that the Barber estate received when they sold the rare book collection do not enter into the DNI computation because the money was not distributed to Louise.

Step Two. The amount and character of income passed through to beneficiaries is based on the DNI of the estate. Thus, the amount of income entered onto the worksheet in Step One must be reduced by deductions and losses shown on Page 1 of Form 1041, which enter into the computation of DNI.

In Step Two, the estate allocates and subtracts the deductions. You determine the amount of your deduction by multiplying each income item above by a percentage, which is determined by dividing the total estate deductions from line 16 on Page 1 of Form 1041 ($5,500) by the total income distributed by the estate (from line 9 of Page 1 of Form 1041—$12,100) minus capital gain (from line 4 of Page 1 of Form 1041—$500) for a total of $11,600.

In the example above, the percentage is 47.41 percent. Divide $5,500 by $11,600 to get 47.41 percent. Then take that percentage and multiply if by each income item to allocate the deductions among them. For example, multiply the $1,000 interest amount times 47.41 percent (.4741) to equal $474. Enter $474 in the deductions column of Step One above. Then subtract $474 from 1,000 to get $526, which is the balance of DNI remaining after the deduction. Enter $526 in the third column. Do the same with the $600 dividend amount to yield $284.46. Subtract $284.46 from $600 to yield $315.54 which is entered in the third column.

The IRS instructions for Form 1041 (page 40) provide that generally items of deductions that enter into the computation of DNI are allocated among the items of income in the following order:

1. All deductions directly attributable to a specific class of income are deducted from that income. For example, rental expenses, to the extent allowable, are deducted from rental income;

2. Deductions that are not directly attributable to a specific class of income generally, may be allocated to any class of income, as long as a reasonable portion is allocated to any tax-exempt income. Deductions considered not directly attributable to a specific class of income under this rule include fiduciary fees, safe deposit box rental charges, and state, income and personal property taxes. The charitable deduction, however, must be ratably apportioned among each class of income included in DNI;

3. Any excess deductions that are directly attributable to a class of income may be allocated to another class of income. In no case can excess deductions from a passive activity be allocated to income from a nonpassive activity or to portfolio income earned by the estate. Excess deductions attributable to tax-exempt income cannot offset any other class of income.

■ Next, the Barber estate complies with Step Three:

Step Three. Allocation of distribution to be reported on Schedule K-1 (Form 1041) for the decedent's sister, Louise.

Inclusion of amounts in beneficiaries income. The beneficiary of a decedent's estate must include in his or her gross income the sum of:

¶3037

1. The amount of the income required to be distributed currently, or if the income required to be distributed currently to all beneficiaries exceeds the DNI (figured without taking into account the charitable deduction), his or her proportionate share of the DNI (as so figured); and

2. All other amounts properly paid, credited, or required to be distributed, or if the sum of the income required to be distributed currently and other amounts properly paid, credited, or required to be distributed to all beneficiaries exceeds the DNI, his or her proportionate share of the excess of DNI over the income required to be distributed currently.

To compute the amount of the income allocation to enter on Schedule K-1, multiply the balance of the DNI for each income item after subtracting the deduction above in column two times a fraction that is the total amount of the income distribution deduction from Schedule B, line 15 over the DNI from Schedule B, line 7.

Interest on line 1 of Schedule K-1: $526 × $5,000/$6,100 = $431

Dividends on line 2 of Schedule K-1: $316 × $5,000/$6,100 = $259

Other Income on line 5a of Schedule K-1: $5,259 × $5,000/$6,100 = $4,311

Top of Schedule K-1. Keep in mind that the reference to the tax year at the top of Schedule K-1 is to the tax year of the estate and not to the tax year of the beneficiary. The tax year should therefore be the same tax year as shown at the top of Page 1 of Form 1041. The Barber estate used the calendar year as the tax year.

Enter in the appropriate spaces at the top of Schedule K-1, the beneficiary's Social Security number or other identifying number, name and address. Also enter at the top of Schedule K-1 the name and employer identification number of the estate and the name and address of the fiduciary.

Beneficiary's Taxpayer Identification Number (TIN). The executor of the decedent's estate is required to request and provide a taxpayer identification number (TIN) for each recipient of income from the estate. Enter the beneficiary's number on the respective Schedules K-1 when Form 1041 is filed. Individuals and business recipients are responsible for giving you their TIN upon request.

Use Form W-9, "Request for Taxpayer Identification Number and Certification," to request the beneficiary's TIN. IRC Sec. 6723 provides that the executor is charged a $50 penalty for each failure to provide a required TIN, unless reasonable cause is established for failure to provide it. Explain any reasonable cause in a signed affidavit and attach it to the return.

Box 1 of Schedule K-1—Interest Income. Enter the beneficiary's share of the taxable income minus allocable deductions.

■ The Barber Estate enters $431 as computed above.

Box 2a and 2b—Ordinary Dividends and Qualified Dividends. Enter the beneficiary's share of total ordinary dividends minus allocable deductions in box 2a. In box 2b enter the beneficiary's share of qualified dividends minus allocable deductions. Mary King's share of ordinary dividend income minus allocable deductions is entered in box 2a. The amount entered is $12,800 as computed in the three-step process described above.

■ The Barber Estate enters $259 as computed above.

¶3037

Box 3—Net Short-Term Capital Gain. Enter the beneficiary's share of the net short-term capital gain from line 13, Column (1), Schedule D (Form 1041), minus allocable deductions. Do not enter a loss on line 3. If, for the final year of the trust, there is a capital loss carryover, enter the beneficiary's share of short-term capital loss carryover in box 11, using code B.

Box 4a through 4c—Net Long-Term Capital Gain. Enter the beneficiary's share of the net long-term capital gain from lines 14a through 14c, Column (1), Schedule D (Form 1041) minus allocable deductions. Do not enter a loss on lines 4a through 4c. If, for the final year of the trust, there is a capital loss carryover, enter in box 11, using code C.

Gains and losses from the complete or partial disposition of a rental, rental real estate, or trade or business activity that is a passive activity must be shown on an attachment to Schedule K-1.

Box 5—Other Portfolio and Nonbusiness Income. Enter the beneficiary's share of annuities, royalties, or any other income, minus allocable deductions (other than directly apportionable deductions), that are NOT subject to any passive activity loss limitation rules at the beneficiary level. Use boxes 6 through 8 to report income items subject to the passive activity rules at the beneficiary's level.

■ Enter Louise Barber's share of the $10,000 salary and vacation pay received by the decedent. Enter $4,311.

Boxes 6 through 8—Ordinary Business Income, Rental Real Estate, and Other Rental Income. Enter the beneficiary's share of trade or business, rental real estate, and other rental income, minus allocable deductions (other than directly apportionable deductions).

Box 9—Directly Apportioned Deductions. Enter the beneficiary's share of directly apportioned deductions using code A through C.

Depreciation (code A). Enter the beneficiary's share of the depreciation deductions attributable to each activity reported on boxes 5 through 8. For a decedent's estate, the depreciation deduction is apportioned among the estate and the devisees, heirs and legatees on the basis of the estate's income allocable to each.

Depletion (code B). For a decedent's estate, the depletion deduction is apportioned among the estate and the heirs, legatees, and devisees on the basis of the estate's income allocable to each.

Amortization (code C). For a decedent's estate, the amortization deduction is apportioned among the estate and the heirs, legatees, and devisees on the basis of the estate's income allocable to each.

Box 10—Estate Tax Deduction (including Certain Generation-Skipping Transfer Taxes). If the distribution deduction consists of any IRD, and the estate was allowed a deduction under IRC Sec. 691(c) for the estate tax paid as a result of the inclusion of this item, then the beneficiary is allowed an estate tax deduction in proportion to his or her share of the distribution that consists of such income.

Box 11, Code A—Excess deductions on termination. If this is the final return of the estate, and there are excess deductions on termination, enter the beneficiary's share of the excess deductions in box 11, using Code A. Excess deductions on termination occur only during the last tax year of the decedent's estate when the total deductions

¶3037

(excluding the charitable deduction and exemption) are greater than the gross income during that tax year.

Box 12—Alternative Minimum Tax Adjustment. Enter the beneficiary's share of the adjustment for minimum tax purposes using the applicable codes that are listed in the 2012 Instructions to Form 1041 (reproduced at ¶ 2944).

Adjustments and Code for Box 12

- AMT adjustment attributable to qualified dividends, net short-term capital gains, or net long-term capital gains (codes B through D)
- AMT adjustment attributable to unrecaptured section 1250 gain or 28 percent rate gain (codes E and F)
- Accelerated depreciation, depletion, and amortization (codes G through I)
- Exclusion items (code J)

Box 13—Credits and Credit Recapture. Enter the beneficiary's share of the credits and credit recapture using the applicable codes that are listed on pages 34–35 of the 2011 Instructions to Form 1041 and page 2 of Schedule K-1 (Form 1041) (reproduced at ¶ 2944).

Line 14—Other (itemize). Itemize in box 14 the beneficiary's tax information not entered elsewhere on Schedule K-1. This includes:

- Domestic production activities information;
- Tax-exempt interest income;
- Net investment income (IRC Sec. 163(d));
- Gross farming and fishing income;
- Qualified production activities income;
- Foreign taxes;
- Employer's W-2 wages;
- Foreign trading gross receipts as defined in IRC Sec. 942(a).

Upon termination of an estate, any suspended passive activity losses (PALs) relating to an interest in a passive activity cannot be allocated to the beneficiary. Instead, the basis in such activity is increased by the amount of any PALs allocable to the interest, and no losses are allowed as a deduction on the estate's final Form 1041.

¶3038 TERMINATION OF ESTATE

An estate is recognized as a taxable entity only during the period of administration or settlement (i.e., the period actually required by the executor or administrator to perform the ordinary duties of administration, such as collection of assets, payment of debts and legacies, etc.). This is true whether the period is longer or shorter than that specified under local law for the settlement of estates. However, the administration of an estate may not be unduly prolonged. For federal tax purposes, the estate will be considered terminated after the expiration of a reasonable period for the performance of the duties of administration or when all the assets of the estate have been distributed except for a reasonable amount set aside in good faith for the payment of contingent liabilities and expenses. If the estate has joined in making a valid election to treat a qualified revocable trust as part of the estate, then it does not terminate prior to the termination of the election period [Reg. Sec. 1.641(b)-3(a)].

The termination of an estate generally is marked by the end of the "period of administration" or settlement and by the distribution of the assets to the beneficiaries under the terms of the will or under the laws of succession of the state if there is no will.

The law provides that the period of administration or settlement is the period actually required by the administrator or executor to perform the ordinary duties of administration. These duties include the collection of assets and the payment of debts, taxes, legacies, and bequests, whether the period required is longer or shorter than the period specified under local law for the settlement of estates [Reg. Sec. 1.641(b)-3(a)].

> **Example 1:** An executor is also named as trustee under a will. The executor fails to obtain his discharge as executor. The period of administration continues only until the duties of administration are complete and he or she actually assumes his or her duties as trustee, whether or not pursuant to a court order [Reg. Sec. 1.641(b)-3(a)].

The law provides that if the period of administration of an estate is unduly prolonged, the estate will be considered terminated for federal income tax purpose after the expiration of a reasonable period for the performance by the executor of all the duties of administration [Reg. Sec. 1.641(b)-3(a)]. The time that is required for the settlement of a decedent's estate will vary with the complexity of the estate and the nature of its assets.

Fiduciaries may be able to justify prolonging the administration of an estate if pending litigation makes it impossible to make a final distribution of the estate's assets. Other acceptable reasons for prolonging the administration of an estate include keeping the estate open to defer payment of estate taxes under IRC Sec. 6166.

The estate will be considered terminated when the executor makes a complete distribution of all assets except for a reasonable amount that is set aside in good faith for the payment of unascertained or contingent liabilities and expenses [Reg. Sec. 1.641(b)-3(a)]. The fiduciary should obtain a receipt from the beneficiaries stating that all assets of the estate have been distributed.

Why does termination matter? Determining when an estate has been terminated is important because once an estate is deemed to have been terminated, its income, deductions, and credits are taxable directly to the estate beneficiaries who succeed to the estate's assets [Reg. Sec. 1.641(b)-3(d)]. In addition, an unused net operating loss carryover or capital loss carryover existing upon termination of the estate is allowed to the beneficiaries succeeding to the property of the estate [IRC Sec. 642(h)]. This means that the losses can be claimed on the beneficiary's tax return if a carryover would have been allowed to the estate in a later tax year if the estate had not been terminated.

The first tax year to which the loss is carried is the beneficiary's tax year in which the estate terminates. If the loss can be carried to more than one tax year, the estate's last tax year (whether or not a short tax year) and the beneficiary's first tax year to which

¶3038

the loss is carried each constitute a tax year for figuring the number of years to which a loss may be carried.

How individuals take advantage of the estate's excess deductions. If the estate has deductions in its last tax year (other than deductions for personal exemptions and charitable contributions) that exceed the estate's gross income for the year, the beneficiaries succeeding to the estate's property can claim the excess as a deduction in figuring their own taxable income. In order to take advantage of these deductions, the following steps must be followed:

1. A return must be filed for the estate along with a schedule showing the computation of each type of deduction and the allocation of each deduction to the beneficiaries;

2. The individual beneficiary must itemize deductions to benefit from the excess deductions;

3. The deductions must be claimed on Schedule A, Form 1040, as a miscellaneous itemized deductions subject to the 2 percent of adjusted gross income limit [IRC Sec. 67];

4. The excess deductions can only be claimed by the beneficiaries for the tax year in which the estate terminates, whether the year of termination is a normal year or a short tax year;

5. If there are more than one successor beneficiaries, the excess deductions must be allocated among the beneficiaries according to each one's share in income and loss as provided in the decedent's will;

6. An item of income or deduction cannot be deducted twice by a beneficiary. This simply means that a net operating loss deduction cannot be deducted once as an excess deduction and again as a loss carryover.

¶3039 SAMPLE COMPLETED FORM 1041 FOR ESTATE OF ALAN P. BARBER

Form **1041**	Department of the Treasury – Internal Revenue Service		

Form 1041 U.S. Income Tax Return for Estates and Trusts **2013** OMB No. 1545-0092

▶ Information about Form 1041 and its separate instructions is at *www.irs.gov/form1041.*

A Check all that apply:	For calendar year 2013 or fiscal year beginning , 2013, and ending , 20	
☑ Decedent's estate	Name of estate or trust (If a grantor type trust, see the instructions.)	**C** Employer identification number
☐ Simple trust	Estate of Alan P. Barber	52-1234567
☐ Complex trust	Name and title of fiduciary	**D** Date entity created
☐ Qualified disability trust	Betty B. Barber, Executor	02/09/13
☐ ESBT (S portion only)	Number, street, and room or suite no. (If a P.O. box, see the instructions.)	**E** Nonexempt charitable and split-interest trusts, check applicable box(es), see instructions.
☐ Grantor type trust		
☐ Bankruptcy estate-Ch. 7	123 Main Street	☐ Described in sec. 4947(a)(1). Check here ▶ ☐
☐ Bankruptcy estate-Ch. 11	City or town, state or province, country, and ZIP or foreign postal code	if not a private foundation
☐ Pooled income fund	Baltimore, Maryland 21201	☐ Described in sec. 4947(a)(2)

B Number of Schedules K-1 attached (see instructions) ▶	F Check applicable boxes:	☑ Initial return	☐ Final return	☐ Amended return	☐ Net operating loss carryback
		☐ Change in trust's name	☐ Change in fiduciary	☐ Change in fiduciary's name	☐ Change in fiduciary's address

G Check here if the estate or filing trust made a section 645 election . . . . . ▶ ☐   Trust EIN ▶

Income

1	Interest income	1	1,000
2a	Total ordinary dividends	2a	600
b	Qualified dividends allocable to: **(1)** Beneficiaries _____ **(2)** Estate or trust _____		
3	Business income or (loss). Attach Schedule C or C-EZ (Form 1040)	3	
4	Capital gain or (loss). Attach Schedule D (Form 1041)	4	500
5	Rents, royalties, partnerships, other estates and trusts, etc. Attach Schedule E (Form 1040)	5	
6	Farm income or (loss). Attach Schedule F (Form 1040)	6	
7	Ordinary gain or (loss). Attach Form 4797	7	
8	Other income. List type and amount _____	8	10,000
9	**Total income.** Combine lines 1, 2a, and 3 through 8 . . . . ▶	9	12,100

Deductions

10	Interest. Check if Form 4952 is attached ▶ ☐	10	
11	Taxes	11	3,000
12	Fiduciary fees	12	
13	Charitable deduction (from Schedule A, line 7)	13	1,000
14	Attorney, accountant, and return preparer fees	14	1,500
15a	Other deductions **not** subject to the 2% floor (attach schedule)	15a	
b	Net operating loss deduction (see instructions)	15b	
c	Allowable miscellaneous itemized deductions subject to the 2% floor	15c	
16	Add lines 10 through 15c . . . . ▶	16	5,500
17	Adjusted total income or (loss). Subtract line 16 from line 9 . . . **17**		
18	Income distribution deduction (from Schedule B, line 15). Attach Schedules K-1 (Form 1041)	18	5,000
19	Estate tax deduction including certain generation-skipping taxes (attach computation) . . .	19	
20	Exemption	20	600
21	Add lines 18 through 20 . . . . ▶	21	5,600

Tax and Payments

22	Taxable income. Subtract line 21 from line 17. If a loss, see instructions	22	1,000
23	Total tax (from Schedule G, line 7)	23	150
24	**Payments: a** 2013 estimated tax payments and amount applied from 2012 return	24a	-0-
b	Estimated tax payments allocated to beneficiaries (from Form 1041-T)	24b	-0-
c	Subtract line 24b from line 24a	24c	-0-
d	Tax paid with Form 7004 (see instructions)	24d	-0-
e	Federal income tax withheld. If any is from Form(s) 1099, check ▶ ☐	24e	-0-
	Other payments: **f** Form 2439 _____; **g** Form 4136 _____; Total ▶	24h	-0-
25	**Total payments.** Add lines 24c through 24e, and 24h . . . . ▶	25	-0-
26	Estimated tax penalty (see instructions)	26	
27	**Tax due.** If line 25 is smaller than the total of lines 23 and 26, enter amount owed	27	150
28	**Overpayment.** If line 25 is larger than the total of lines 23 and 26, enter amount overpaid . . .	28	
29	Amount of line 28 to be: **a** Credited to 2014 estimated tax ▶ _____; **b** Refunded ▶	29	

Sign Here

Under penalties of perjury, I declare that I have examined this return, including accompanying schedules and statements, and to the best of my knowledge and belief, it is true, correct, and complete. Declaration of preparer (other than taxpayer) is based on all information of which preparer has any knowledge.

▶

Signature of fiduciary or officer representing fiduciary	Date	EIN of fiduciary if a financial institution	May the IRS discuss this return with the preparer shown below (see instr.)? ☐ Yes ☐ No

Paid Preparer Use Only

Print/Type preparer's name	Preparer's signature	Date	Check ☐ if self-employed	PTIN
Firm's name ▶			Firm's EIN ▶	
Firm's address ▶			Phone no.	

For Paperwork Reduction Act Notice, see the separate instructions.   Cat. No. 11370H   Form **1041** (2013)

¶3039

Form 1041 (2013)   Page **2**

	Schedule A	**Charitable Deduction.** Do not complete for a simple trust or a pooled income fund.		
1		Amounts paid or permanently set aside for charitable purposes from gross income (see instructions)	1	1,000
2		Tax-exempt income allocable to charitable contributions (see instructions)	2	
3		Subtract line 2 from line 1	3	1,000
4		Capital gains for the tax year allocated to corpus and paid or permanently set aside for charitable purposes	4	
5		Add lines 3 and 4	5	1,000
6		Section 1202 exclusion allocable to capital gains paid or permanently set aside for charitable purposes (see instructions)	6	
7		**Charitable deduction.** Subtract line 6 from line 5. Enter here and on page 1, line 13	7	1,000

	Schedule B	**Income Distribution Deduction**		
1		Adjusted total income (see instructions)	1	6,600
2		Adjusted tax-exempt interest	2	-0-
3		Total net gain from Schedule D (Form 1041), line 19, column (1) (see instructions)	3	
4		Enter amount from Schedule A, line 4 (minus any allocable section 1202 exclusion)	4	
5		Capital gains for the tax year included on Schedule A, line 1 (see instructions)	5	
6		Enter any gain from page 1, line 4, as a negative number. If page 1, line 4, is a loss, enter the loss as a positive number	6	(500)
7		**Distributable net income.** Combine lines 1 through 6. If zero or less, enter -0-	7	6,100
8		If a complex trust, enter accounting income for the tax year as determined under the governing instrument and applicable local law [8]		
9		Income required to be distributed currently	9	-0-
10		Other amounts paid, credited, or otherwise required to be distributed	10	5,000
11		Total distributions. Add lines 9 and 10. If greater than line 8, see instructions	11	5,000
12		Enter the amount of tax-exempt income included on line 11	12	-0-
13		Tentative income distribution deduction. Subtract line 12 from line 11	13	5,000
14		Tentative income distribution deduction. Subtract line 2 from line 7. If zero or less, enter -0-	14	6,100
15		**Income distribution deduction.** Enter the smaller of line 13 or line 14 here and on page 1, line 18	15	5,000

	Schedule G	**Tax Computation** (see instructions)			
1	**Tax: a**	Tax on taxable income (see instructions)	1a	150	
	b	Tax on lump-sum distributions. Attach Form 4972	1b		
	c	Alternative minimum tax (from Schedule I (Form 1041), line 56)	1c		
	d	**Total.** Add lines 1a through 1c	1d		150
2a		Foreign tax credit. Attach Form 1116	2a		
b		General business credit. Attach Form 3800	2b		
c		Credit for prior year minimum tax. Attach Form 8801	2c		
d		Bond credits. Attach Form 8912	2d		
e		**Total credits.** Add lines 2a through 2d	2e		
3		Subtract line 2e from line 1d. If zero or less, enter -0-	3		150
4		Net investment income tax from Form 8960, line 21	4		
5		Recapture taxes. Check if from: ☐ Form 4255 ☐ Form 8611	5		
6		Household employment taxes. Attach Schedule H (Form 1040)	6		
7		**Total tax.** Add lines 3 through 6. Enter here and on page 1, line 23	7		150

	Other Information	**Yes**	**No**
1	Did the estate or trust receive tax-exempt income? If "Yes," attach a computation of the allocation of expenses. Enter the amount of tax-exempt interest income and exempt-interest dividends ▶ $ _____		✓
2	Did the estate or trust receive all or any part of the earnings (salary, wages, and other compensation) of any individual by reason of a contract assignment or similar arrangement?		✓
3	At any time during calendar year 2013, did the estate or trust have an interest in or a signature or other authority over a bank, securities, or other financial account in a foreign country?		✓
	See the instructions for exceptions and filing requirements for FinCEN Form 114. If "Yes," enter the name of the foreign country ▶ _____		
4	During the tax year, did the estate or trust receive a distribution from, or was it the grantor of, or transferor to, a foreign trust? If "Yes," the estate or trust may have to file Form 3520. See instructions		✓
5	Did the estate or trust receive, or pay, any qualified residence interest on seller-provided financing? If "Yes," see the instructions for required attachment		✓
6	If this is an estate or a complex trust making the section 663(b) election, check here (see instructions) ▶ ☐		
7	To make a section 643(e)(3) election, attach Schedule D (Form 1041), and check here (see instructions) ▶ ☐		
8	If the decedent's estate has been open for more than 2 years, attach an explanation for the delay in closing the estate, and check here ▶ ☐		
9	Are any present or future trust beneficiaries skip persons? See instructions		✓

Form **1041** (2013)

¶3039

SCHEDULE I (Form 1041) Department of the Treasury Internal Revenue Service	**Alternative Minimum Tax—Estates and Trusts** ▶ Attach to Form 1041. ▶ Information about Schedule I (Form 1041) and its separate instructions is at *www.irs.gov/form1041*.	OMB No. 1545-0092 20**13**

Name of estate or trust	Employer identification number
Estate of Alan P. Barber	52-1234567

Part I   Estate's or Trust's Share of Alternative Minimum Taxable Income

1	Adjusted total income or (loss) (from Form 1041, line 17)	1	6,600
2	Interest	2	
3	Taxes	3	3,000
4	Miscellaneous itemized deductions (from Form 1041, line 15c)	4	
5	Refund of taxes	5	( )
6	Depletion (difference between regular tax and AMT)	6	
7	Net operating loss deduction. Enter as a positive amount	7	
8	Interest from specified private activity bonds exempt from the regular tax	8	
9	Qualified small business stock (see instructions)	9	
10	Exercise of incentive stock options (excess of AMT income over regular tax income)	10	
11	Other estates and trusts (amount from Schedule K-1 (Form 1041), box 12, code A)	11	
12	Electing large partnerships (amount from Schedule K-1 (Form 1065-B), box 6)	12	
13	Disposition of property (difference between AMT and regular tax gain or loss)	13	
14	Depreciation on assets placed in service after 1986 (difference between regular tax and AMT)	14	
15	Passive activities (difference between AMT and regular tax income or loss)	15	
16	Loss limitations (difference between AMT and regular tax income or loss)	16	
17	Circulation costs (difference between regular tax and AMT)	17	
18	Long-term contracts (difference between AMT and regular tax income)	18	
19	Mining costs (difference between regular tax and AMT)	19	
20	Research and experimental costs (difference between regular tax and AMT)	20	
21	Income from certain installment sales before January 1, 1987	21	( )
22	Intangible drilling costs preference	22	
23	Other adjustments, including income-based related adjustments	23	
24	Alternative tax net operating loss deduction (See the instructions for the limitation that applies.)	24	( )
25	Adjusted alternative minimum taxable income. Combine lines 1 through 24	25	9,600
	Note: *Complete Part II below before going to line 26.*		
26	Income distribution deduction from Part II, line 44 . . . **26** 5,000		
27	Estate tax deduction (from Form 1041, line 19) . . . **27**		
28	Add lines 26 and 27	28	5,000
29	Estate's or trust's share of alternative minimum taxable income. Subtract line 28 from line 25	29	4,600

If line 29 is:
- $23,100 or less, stop here and enter -0- on Form 1041, Schedule G, line 1c. The estate or trust is not liable for the alternative minimum tax.
- Over $23,100, but less than $169,350, go to line 45.
- $169,350 or more, enter the amount from line 29 on line 51 and go to line 52.

Part II   Income Distribution Deduction on a Minimum Tax Basis

30	Adjusted alternative minimum taxable income (see instructions)	30	9,600
31	Adjusted tax-exempt interest (other than amounts included on line 8)	31	
32	Total net gain from Schedule D (Form 1041), line 19, column (1). If a loss, enter -0-	32	500
33	Capital gains for the tax year allocated to corpus and paid or permanently set aside for charitable purposes (from Form 1041, Schedule A, line 4)	33	
34	Capital gains paid or permanently set aside for charitable purposes from gross income (see instructions)	34	
35	Capital gains computed on a minimum tax basis included on line 25	35	(500)
36	Capital losses computed on a minimum tax basis included on line 25. Enter as a positive amount	36	
37	Distributable net alternative minimum taxable income (DNAMTI). Combine lines 30 through 36. If zero or less, enter -0-	37	9,600
38	Income required to be distributed currently (from Form 1041, Schedule B, line 9)	38	-0-
39	Other amounts paid, credited, or otherwise required to be distributed (from Form 1041, Schedule B, line 10)	39	5,000
40	Total distributions. Add lines 38 and 39	40	5,000
41	Tax-exempt income included on line 40 (other than amounts included on line 8)	41	-0-
42	Tentative income distribution deduction on a minimum tax basis. Subtract line 41 from line 40	42	5,000

For Paperwork Reduction Act Notice, see the Instructions for Form 1041.   Cat. No. 51517Q   Schedule I (Form 1041) (2013)

¶3039

Schedule I (Form 1041) (2013)   Page **2**

Part II	**Income Distribution Deduction on a Minimum Tax Basis** *(continued)*			
43	Tentative income distribution deduction on a minimum tax basis. Subtract line 31 from line 37. If zero or less, enter -0-	**43**		9,600
44	**Income distribution deduction on a minimum tax basis.** Enter the smaller of line 42 or line 43. Enter here and on line 26	**44**		5,000

Part III	**Alternative Minimum Tax**				
45	Exemption amount			**45**	$23,100 00
46	Enter the amount from line 29	**46**			
47	Phase-out of exemption amount	**47**	$76,950 00		
48	Subtract line 47 from line 46. If zero or less, enter -0-	**48**			
49	Multiply line 48 by 25% (.25)			**49**	
50	Subtract line 49 from line 45. If zero or less, enter -0-			**50**	
51	Subtract line 50 from line 46			**51**	
52	Go to Part IV of Schedule I to figure line 52 if the estate or trust has qualified dividends or has a gain on lines 18a and 19 of column (2) of Schedule D (Form 1041) (as refigured for the AMT, if necessary). Otherwise, if line 51 is— • $179,500 or less, multiply line 51 by 26% (.26). • Over $179,500, multiply line 51 by 28% (.28) and subtract $3,590 from the result			**52**	
53	Alternative minimum foreign tax credit (see instructions)			**53**	
54	Tentative minimum tax. Subtract line 53 from line 52			**54**	
55	Enter the tax from Form 1041, Schedule G, line 1a (minus any foreign tax credit from Schedule G, line 2a)			**55**	
56	**Alternative minimum tax.** Subtract line 55 from line 54. If zero or less, enter -0-. Enter here and on Form 1041, Schedule G, line 1c			**56**	

Part IV	**Line 52 Computation Using Maximum Capital Gains Rates**			
	Caution: *If you did not complete Part V of Schedule D (Form 1041), the Schedule D Tax Worksheet, or the Qualified Dividends Tax Worksheet in the Instructions for Form 1041, see the instructions before completing this part.*			
57	Enter the amount from line 51		**57**	
58	Enter the amount from Schedule D (Form 1041), line 26, line 13 of the Schedule D Tax Worksheet, or line 4 of the Qualified Dividends Tax Worksheet in the Instructions for Form 1041, whichever applies (as refigured for the AMT, if necessary)	**58**		
59	Enter the amount from Schedule D (Form 1041), line 18b, column (2) (as refigured for the AMT, if necessary). If you did not complete Schedule D for the regular tax or the AMT, enter -0-	**59**		
60	If you did not complete a Schedule D Tax Worksheet for the regular tax or the AMT, enter the amount from line 58. Otherwise, add lines 58 and 59 and enter the **smaller** of that result or the amount from line 10 of the Schedule D Tax Worksheet (as refigured for the AMT, if necessary)	**60**		
61	Enter the **smaller** of line 57 or line 60		**61**	
62	Subtract line 61 from line 57		**62**	
63	If line 62 is $179,500 or less, multiply line 62 by 26% (.26). Otherwise, multiply line 62 by 28% (.28) and subtract $3,590 from the result ▶		**63**	
64	Maximum amount subject to the 0% rate	**64**	$2,450 00	
65	Enter the amount from line 27 of Schedule D (Form 1041), line 14 of the Schedule D Tax Worksheet, or line 5 of the Qualified Dividends Tax Worksheet in the Instructions for Form 1041, whichever applies (as figured for the regular tax). If you did not complete Schedule D or either worksheet for the regular tax, enter the amount from Form 1041, line 22; but do not enter less than -0-	**65**		
66	Subtract line 65 from line 64. If zero or less, enter -0-	**66**		
67	Enter the **smaller** of line 57 or line 58	**67**		
68	Enter the **smaller** of line 66 or line 67. This amount is taxed at 0%	**68**		
69	Subtract line 68 from line 67	**69**		

Schedule I (Form 1041) (2013)

Schedule I (Form 1041) (2013) Page 3

Part IV Line 52 Computation Using Maximum Capital Gains Rates *(continued)*

70	Enter the amount from the Line 70 Worksheet in the instructions	70			
71	Enter the **smaller** of line 69 or 70	71			
72	Multiply line 71 by 15% (.15) ▶			72	
73	Add lines 68 and 71	73			
	If lines 73 and 57 are the same, skip lines 74 through 78 and go to line 79. Otherwise, go to line 74.				
74	Subtract line 73 from line 67	74			
75	Multiply line 74 by 20% (.20) ▶			75	
	If line 59 is zero or blank, skip lines 76 through 78 and go to line 79. Otherwise, go to line 76.				
76	Add lines 62, 73, and 74	76			
77	Subtract line 76 from line 57	77			
78	Multiply line 77 by 25% (.25) ▶			78	
79	Add lines 63, 72, 75, and 78			79	
80	If line 57 is $179,500 or less, multiply line 57 by 26% (.26). Otherwise, multiply line 57 by 28% (.28) and subtract $3,590 from the result			80	
81	Enter the **smaller** of line 79 or line 80 here and on line 52			81	

Schedule I (Form 1041) (2013)

Form **8949**	**Sales and Other Dispositions of Capital Assets**	OMB No. 1545-0074
Department of the Treasury Internal Revenue Service	▶ Information about Form 8949 and its separate instructions is at *www.irs.gov/form8949*. ▶ File with your Schedule D to list your transactions for lines 1b, 2, 3, 8b, 9, and 10 of Schedule D.	20**13** Attachment Sequence No. **12A**

Name(s) shown on return	Social security number or taxpayer identification number
Estate of Alan P. Barber	52-1234567

Most brokers issue their own substitute statement instead of using Form 1099-B. They also may provide basis information (usually your cost) to you on the statement even if it is not reported to the IRS. Before you check Box A, B, or C below, determine whether you received any statement(s) and, if so, the transactions for which basis was reported to the IRS. Brokers are required to report basis to the IRS for most stock you bought in 2011 or later.

Part I   **Short-Term.** Transactions involving capital assets you held one year or less are short term. For long-term transactions, see page 2.

Note. You may aggregate all short-term transactions reported on Form(s) 1099-B showing basis was reported to the IRS and for which no adjustments or codes are required. Enter the total directly on Schedule D, line 1a; you are not required to report these transactions on Form 8949 (see instructions).

You *must* **check Box A, B, *or* C below. Check only one box.** If more than one box applies for your short-term transactions, complete a separate Form 8949, page 1, for each applicable box. If you have more short-term transactions than will fit on this page for one or more of the boxes, complete as many forms with the same box checked as you need.

- ☐ **(A)** Short-term transactions reported on Form(s) 1099-B showing basis was reported to the IRS (see **Note** above)
- ☐ **(B)** Short-term transactions reported on Form(s) 1099-B showing basis was **not** reported to the IRS
- ☐ **(C)** Short-term transactions not reported to you on Form 1099-B

1 **(a)** Description of property (Example: 100 sh. XYZ Co.)	**(b)** Date acquired (Mo., day, yr.)	**(c)** Date sold or disposed (Mo., day, yr.)	**(d)** Proceeds (sales price) (see instructions)	**(e)** Cost or other basis. See the **Note** below and see *Column (e)* in the separate instructions	Adjustment, if any, to gain or loss. If you enter an amount in column (g), enter a code in column (f). See the separate instructions.		**(h)** Gain or (loss). Subtract column (e) from column (d) and combine the result with column (g)
					(f) Code(s) from instructions	**(g)** Amount of adjustment	

2 Totals. Add the amounts in columns (d), (e), (g), and (h) (subtract negative amounts). Enter each total here and include on your Schedule D, **line 1b** (if **Box A** above is checked), **line 2** (if **Box B** above is checked), or **line 3** (if **Box C** above is checked) ▶

Note. If you checked Box A above but the basis reported to the IRS was incorrect, enter in column (e) the basis as reported to the IRS, and enter an adjustment in column (g) to correct the basis. See *Column (g)* in the separate instructions for how to figure the amount of the adjustment.

For Paperwork Reduction Act Notice, see your tax return instructions.   Cat. No. 37768Z   Form **8949** (2013)

¶3039

Form 8949 (2013)   Attachment Sequence No. **12A**   Page **2**

Name(s) shown on return. (Name and SSN or taxpayer identification no. not required if shown on other side.)	Social security number or taxpayer identification number

Most brokers issue their own substitute statement instead of using Form 1099-B. They also may provide basis information (usually your cost) to you on the statement even if it is not reported to the IRS. Before you check Box D, E, or F below, determine whether you received any statement(s) and, if so, the transactions for which basis was reported to the IRS. Brokers are required to report basis to the IRS for most stock you bought in 2011 or later.

Part II   **Long-Term.** Transactions involving capital assets you held more than one year are long term. For short-term transactions, see page 1.

Note. You may aggregate all long-term transactions reported on Form(s) 1099-B showing basis was reported to the IRS and for which no adjustments or codes are required. Enter the total directly on Schedule D, line 8a; you are not required to report these transactions on Form 8949 (see instructions).

You *must* **check Box D, E,** *or* **F below. Check only one box.** If more than one box applies for your long-term transactions, complete a separate Form 8949, page 2, for each applicable box. If you have more long-term transactions than will fit on this page for one or more of the boxes, complete as many forms with the same box checked as you need.

- ☐ **(D)** Long-term transactions reported on Form(s) 1099-B showing basis was reported to the IRS (see **Note** above)
- ☐ **(E)** Long-term transactions reported on Form(s) 1099-B showing basis was **not** reported to the IRS
- ☑ **(F)** Long-term transactions not reported to you on Form 1099-B

1

(a) Description of property (Example: 100 sh. XYZ Co.)	(b) Date acquired (Mo., day, yr.)	(c) Date sold or disposed (Mo., day, yr.)	(d) Proceeds (sales price) (see instructions)	(e) Cost or other basis. See the **Note** below and see *Column (e)* in the separate instructions	Adjustment, if any, to gain or loss. If you enter an amount in column (g), enter a code in column (f). See the separate instructions.		(h) Gain or (loss). Subtract column (e) from column (d) and combine the result with column (g)
					(f) Code(s) from instructions	(g) Amount of adjustment	
Rare Book Collection	02/08/13	12/01/13	5,000	4,500	C	-0-	500
2 Totals. Add the amounts in columns (d), (e), (g), and (h) (subtract negative amounts). Enter each total here and include on your Schedule D, **line 8b** (if **Box D** above is checked), **line 9** (if **Box E** above is checked), or **line 10** (if **Box F** above is checked) ▶			5,000	4,500		-0-	500

Note. If you checked Box D above but the basis reported to the IRS was incorrect, enter in column (e) the basis as reported to the IRS, and enter an adjustment in column (g) to correct the basis. See *Column (g)* in the separate instructions for how to figure the amount of the adjustment.

Form **8949** (2013)

¶3039

SCHEDULE D (Form 1041)	Capital Gains and Losses	OMB No. 1545-0092
Department of the Treasury Internal Revenue Service	▶ Attach to Form 1041, Form 5227, or Form 990-T. ▶ Use Form 8949 to list your transactions for lines 1b, 2, 3, 8b, 9 and 10. ▶ Information about Schedule D and its separate instructions is at *www.irs.gov/form1041*.	2013

Name of estate or trust	Employer identification number
Estate of Alan P. Barber	52-1234567

Note: *Form 5227 filers need to complete **only** Parts I and II.*

Part I   Short-Term Capital Gains and Losses—Assets Held One Year or Less

See instructions for how to figure the amounts to enter on the lines below. This form may be easier to complete if you round off cents to whole dollars.	(d) Proceeds (sales price)	(e) Cost (or other basis)	(g) Adjustments to gain or loss from Form(s) 8949, Part I, line 2, column (g)	(h) Gain or (loss) Subtract column (e) from column (d) and combine the result with column (g)
1a Totals for all short-term transactions reported on Form 1099-B for which basis was reported to the IRS and for which you have no adjustments (see instructions). However, if you choose to report all these transactions on Form 8949, leave this line blank and go to line 1b .				
1b Totals for all transactions reported on Form(s) 8949 with **Box A** checked				
2 Totals for all transactions reported on Form(s) 8949 with **Box B** checked				
3 Totals for all transactions reported on Form(s) 8949 with **Box C** checked				

4 Short-term capital gain or (loss) from Forms 4684, 6252, 6781, and 8824	**4**	
5 Net short-term gain or (loss) from partnerships, S corporations, and other estates or trusts . . .	**5**	
6 Short-term capital loss carryover. Enter the amount, if any, from line 9 of the 2012 Capital Loss Carryover Worksheet	**6**	( )
7 **Net short-term capital gain or (loss).** Combine lines 1a through 6 in column (h). Enter here and on line 17, column (3) on the back . . . . ▶	**7**	

Part II   Long-Term Capital Gains and Losses—Assets Held More Than One Year

See instructions for how to figure the amounts to enter on the lines below. This form may be easier to complete if you round off cents to whole dollars.	(d) Proceeds (sales price)	(e) Cost (or other basis)	(g) Adjustments to gain or loss from Form(s) 8949, Part II, line 2, column (g)	(h) Gain or (loss) Subtract column (e) from column (d) and combine the result with column (g)
8a Totals for all long-term transactions reported on Form 1099-B for which basis was reported to the IRS and for which you have no adjustments (see instructions). However, if you choose to report all these transactions on Form 8949, leave this line blank and go to line 8b .				
8b Totals for all transactions reported on Form(s) 8949 with **Box D** checked				
9 Totals for all transactions reported on Form(s) 8949 with **Box E** checked				
10 Totals for all transactions reported on Form(s) 8949 with **Box F** checked.	5,000	4,500	-0-	500

11 Long-term capital gain or (loss) from Forms 2439, 4684, 6252, 6781, and 8824	**11**	
12 Net long-term gain or (loss) from partnerships, S corporations, and other estates or trusts . . .	**12**	
13 Capital gain distributions	**13**	
14 Gain from Form 4797, Part I	**14**	
15 Long-term capital loss carryover. Enter the amount, if any, from line 14 of the 2012 Capital Loss Carryover Worksheet	**15**	( )
16 **Net long-term capital gain or (loss).** Combine lines 8a through 15 in column (h). Enter here and on line 18a, column (3) on the back . . . . ▶	**16**	

For Paperwork Reduction Act Notice, see the Instructions for Form 1041.   Cat. No. 11376V   Schedule D (Form 1041) 2013

¶3039

Schedule D (Form 1041) 2013   Page **2**

Part III Summary of Parts I and II		**(1)** Beneficiaries' (see instr.)	**(2)** Estate's or trust's	**(3)** Total
	Caution: *Read the instructions **before** completing this part.*			
17	**Net short-term gain or (loss)** **17**			
18	**Net long-term gain or (loss):**			
a	Total for year **18a**			
b	Unrecaptured section 1250 gain (see line 18 of the wrksht.) . **18b**			
c	28% rate gain **18c**		500	500
19	**Total net gain or (loss).** Combine lines 17 and 18a . . ▶ **19**		500	500

Note: *If line 19, column (3), is a net gain, enter the gain on Form 1041, line 4 (or Form 990-T, Part I, line 4a). If lines 18a and 19, column (2), are net gains, go to Part V, and **do not** complete Part IV. If line 19, column (3), is a net loss, complete Part IV and the **Capital Loss Carryover Worksheet,** as necessary.*

Part IV	**Capital Loss Limitation**		
20	Enter here and enter as a (loss) on Form 1041, line 4 (or Form 990-T, Part I, line 4c, if a trust), the **smaller** of:		
a	The loss on line 19, column (3) **or b** $3,000	**20**	( )

Note: *If the loss on line 19, column (3), is more than $3,000, or if Form 1041, page 1, line 22 (or Form 990-T, line 34), is a loss, complete the **Capital Loss Carryover Worksheet** in the instructions to figure your capital loss carryover.*

Part V	**Tax Computation Using Maximum Capital Gains Rates**

Form 1041 filers. Complete this part **only** if both lines 18a and 19 in column (2) are gains, or an amount is entered in Part I or Part II and there is an entry on Form 1041, line 2b(2), **and** Form 1041, line 22, is more than zero.

Caution: *Skip this part and complete the **Schedule D Tax Worksheet** in the instructions if:*
- *Either line 18b, col. (2) or line 18c, col. (2) is more than zero, or*
- *Both Form 1041, line 2b(1), and Form 4952, line 4g are more than zero.*

Form 990-T trusts. Complete this part **only** if both lines 18a and 19 are gains, or qualified dividends are included in income in Part I of Form 990-T, **and** Form 990-T, line 34, is more than zero. Skip this part and complete the **Schedule D Tax Worksheet** in the instructions if either line 18b, col. (2) or line 18c, col. (2) is more than zero.

21	Enter taxable income from Form 1041, line 22 (or Form 990-T, line 34) . .	**21**		
22	Enter the **smaller** of line 18a or 19 in column (2) but not less than zero	**22**		
23	Enter the estate's or trust's qualified dividends from Form 1041, line 2b(2) (or enter the qualified dividends included in income in Part I of Form 990-T)	**23**		
24	Add lines 22 and 23	**24**		
25	If the estate or trust is filing Form 4952, enter the amount from line 4g; otherwise, enter -0- . ▶	**25**		
26	Subtract line 25 from line 24. If zero or less, enter -0-	**26**		
27	Subtract line 26 from line 21. If zero or less, enter -0-	**27**		
28	Enter the **smaller** of the amount on line 21 or $2,450	**28**		
29	Enter the **smaller** of the amount on line 27 or line 28	**29**		
30	Subtract line 29 from line 28. If zero or less, enter -0-. This amount is taxed at 0% . . . . . ▶	**30**		
31	Enter the smaller of line 21 or line 26	**31**		
32	Subtract line 30 from line 26	**32**		
33	Enter the **smaller** of line 21 or $11,950	**33**		
34	Add lines 27 and 30	**34**		
35	Subtract line 34 from line 33. If zero or less, enter -0-	**35**		
36	Enter the **smaller** of line 32 or line 35	**36**		
37	Multiply line 36 by 15% . . . . ▶	**37**		
38	Enter the amount from line 31	**38**		
39	Add lines 30 and 36	**39**		
40	Subtract line 39 from line 38. If zero or less, enter -0-	**40**		
41	Multiply line 40 by 20% . . . . ▶	**41**		
42	Figure the tax on the amount on line 27. Use the 2013 Tax Rate Schedule for Estates and Trusts (see the Schedule G instructions in the instructions for Form 1041) . .	**42**		
43	Add lines 37, 41, and 42	**43**		
44	Figure the tax on the amount on line 21. Use the 2013 Tax Rate Schedule for Estates and Trusts (see the Schedule G instructions in the instructions for Form 1041) . .	**44**		
45	**Tax on all taxable income.** Enter the **smaller** of line 43 or line 44 here and on Form 1041, Schedule G, line 1a (or Form 990-T, line 36) . . . . ▶	**45**		

Schedule D (Form 1041) 2013

661113

| | Final K-1 | | Amended K-1 | OMB No. 1545-0092 |

Schedule K-1
(Form 1041)
Department of the Treasury
Internal Revenue Service

2013

For calendar year 2013,
or tax year beginning _____, 2013,
and ending _____, 20 _____

Beneficiary's Share of Income, Deductions, Credits, etc.   ▶ See back of form and instructions.

| **Part I** | **Information About the Estate or Trust** |

A Estate's or trust's employer identification number

52-1234567

B Estate's or trust's name

Estate of Alan P. Barber
123 Main Street
Baltimore, Maryland 21201

C Fiduciary's name, address, city, state, and ZIP code

D ☐ Check if Form 1041-T was filed and enter the date it was filed
_____

E ☐ Check if this is the final Form 1041 for the estate or trust

| **Part II** | **Information About the Beneficiary** |

F Beneficiary's identifying number

52-3456789

G Beneficiary's name, address, city, state, and ZIP code

Betty B. Barber
123 Main Street
Baltimore, Maryland 21201

H ☒ Domestic beneficiary   ☐ Foreign beneficiary

Part III	**Beneficiary's Share of Current Year Income, Deductions, Credits, and Other Items**	
1 Interest income	431	**11** Final year deductions
2a Ordinary dividends	259	
2b Qualified dividends		
3 Net short-term capital gain		
4a Net long-term capital gain		
4b 28% rate gain		**12** Alternative minimum tax adjustment
4c Unrecaptured section 1250 gain		
5 Other portfolio and nonbusiness income	4,311	
6 Ordinary business income		
7 Net rental real estate income		
8 Other rental income		**13** Credits and credit recapture
9 Directly apportioned deductions		
		14 Other information
10 Estate tax deduction		

*See attached statement for additional information.

Note. A statement must be attached showing the beneficiary's share of income and directly apportioned deductions from each business, rental real estate, and other rental activity.

For IRS Use Only

For Paperwork Reduction Act Notice, see the Instructions for Form 1041.   IRS.gov/form1041   Cat. No. 11380D   **Schedule K-1 (Form 1041) 2013**

¶3039

This list identifies the codes used on Schedule K-1 for beneficiaries and provides summarized reporting information for beneficiaries who file Form 1040. For detailed reporting and filing information, see the Instructions for Schedule K-1 (Form 1041) for a Beneficiary Filing Form 1040 and the instructions for your income tax return.

	Report on
1. Interest income	Form 1040, line 8a
2a. Ordinary dividends	Form 1040, line 9a
2b. Qualified dividends	Form 1040, line 9b
3. Net short-term capital gain	Schedule D, line 5
4a. Net long-term capital gain	Schedule D, line 12
4b. 28% rate gain	28% Rate Gain Worksheet, line 4 (Schedule D Instructions)
4c. Unrecaptured section 1250 gain	Unrecaptured Section 1250 Gain Worksheet, line 11 (Schedule D Instructions)
5. Other portfolio and nonbusiness income	Schedule E, line 33, column (f)
6. Ordinary business income	Schedule E, line 33, column (d) or (f)
7. Net rental real estate income	Schedule E, line 33, column (d) or (f)
8. Other rental income	Schedule E, line 33, column (d) or (f)
9. Directly apportioned deductions	
Code	
A Depreciation	Form 8582 or Schedule E, line 33, column (c) or (e)
B Depletion	Form 8582 or Schedule E, line 33, column (c) or (e)
C Amortization	Form 8582 or Schedule E, line 33, column (c) or (e)
10. Estate tax deduction	Schedule A, line 28
11. Final year deductions	
A Excess deductions	Schedule A, line 23
B Short-term capital loss carryover	Schedule D, line 5
C Long-term capital loss carryover	Schedule D, line 12; line 5 of the wksht. for Sch. D, line 18; and line 16 of the wksht. for Sch. D, line 19
D Net operating loss carryover — regular tax	Form 1040, line 21
E Net operating loss carryover — minimum tax	Form 6251, line 11
12. Alternative minimum tax (AMT) items	
A Adjustment for minimum tax purposes	Form 6251, line 15
B AMT adjustment attributable to qualified dividends	
C AMT adjustment attributable to net short-term capital gain	
D AMT adjustment attributable to net long-term capital gain	
E AMT adjustment attributable to unrecaptured section 1250 gain	See the beneficiary's instructions and the Instructions for Form 6251
F AMT adjustment attributable to 28% rate gain	
G Accelerated depreciation	
H Depletion	
I Amortization	
J Exclusion items	2014 Form 8801

13. Credits and credit recapture	
Code	*Report on*
A Credit for estimated taxes	Form 1040, line 63
B Credit for backup withholding	Form 1040, line 62
C Low-income housing credit	
D Rehabilitation credit and energy credit	
E Other qualifying investment credit	
F Work opportunity credit	
G Credit for small employer health insurance premiums	
H Biofuel producer credit	
I Credit for increasing research activities	
J Renewable electricity, refined coal, and Indian coal production credit	
K Empowerment zone and renewal community employment credit	
L Indian employment credit	See the beneficiary's instructions
M Orphan drug credit	
N Credit for employer-provided child care and facilities	
O Biodiesel and renewable diesel fuels credit	
P Nonconventional source fuel credit	
Q Credit to holders of tax credit bonds	
R Agricultural chemicals security credit	
S Energy efficient appliance credit	
T Credit for employer differential wage payments	
U Recapture of credits	
14. Other information	
A Tax-exempt interest	Form 1040, line 8b
B Foreign taxes	Form 1040, line 47 or Sch. A, line 8
C Qualified production activities income	Form 8903, line 7, col. (b) (also see the beneficiary's instructions)
D Form W-2 wages	Form 8903, line 17
E Net investment income	Form 4952, line 4a
F Gross farm and fishing income	Schedule E, line 42
G Foreign trading gross receipts (IRC 942(a))	See the Instructions for Form 8873
H Adjustment for section 1411 net investment income or deductions	Form 8960, line 7 (also see the beneficiary's instructions)
I Other information	See the beneficiary's instructions

Note. If you are a beneficiary who does not file a Form 1040, see instructions for the type of income tax return you are filing.

¶3039

GRANTOR TRUSTS 31

TABLE OF CONTENTS

¶3100 GRANTOR TRUST RULES

(a) What is a Grantor Trust. A grantor trust is a trust, whether revocable or irrevocable, in which the grantor has retained sufficient specifically enumerated rights and/or interests in or over the trust to be considered the owner of the trust for

)

federal income tax purposes. A "grantor" is defined to include any person who either creates a trust or, directly or indirectly, makes a gratuitous transfer of property to a trust [Reg. Sec. 1.671-2(e)(1)].

The grantor trust rules are found in IRC Secs. 671 through 679 and provide generally that a grantor will be treated as the owner of a trust and thus taxed on its income where he or she retains substantial dominion and control over the assets transferred into the trust. Congress created these rules so it would be impossible for the grantor to escape tax on the income from property transferred into a trust if the grantor retained sufficient control over the transferred property.

(b) Treatment of Income from Grantor Trust. IRC Sec. 671 provides that when the grantor or another person is treated as the owner of a portion of a trust, the grantor must report the trust's income, deductions, gain, loss and/or credits on his or her individual tax return as if there were no trust because a grantor trust is not recognized as a separate taxable entity for income tax purposes. The grantor, there-fore, computes his or her taxable income and credits by taking into account the trust items of income, deduction, and credit which are attributable to that portion of the trust. When items of income, deduction or credit are attributed to a grantor trust, they are treated as if they had been received or paid directly to the grantor and the character of the item is treated as if it had been received or paid directly by the grantor. The existence of the trust does not change or "filter" the character of the item. This means that capital gain items will pass through the trust to the grantor as capital gain items.

(c) No Advance Ruling on Grantor Trust Status. The IRS will not issue advance rulings as to whether the grantor will be considered the owner of any portion of a trust when: (1) substantially all of the trust corpus consists, or will consist, of insurance policies on the life of the grantor or the grantor's spouse, (2) the trustee or any other person has a power to apply the trust's income or corpus to the payment of premiums on policies of insurance on the life of the grantor or the grantor's spouse, (3) the trustee or any other person has a power to use the trust's assets to make loans to the grantor's estate or to purchase assets from the grantor's estate, and (4) there is a right or power in any person that would cause the grantor to be treated as the owner of all or a portion of the trust under IRC Secs. 673 to 677.[1]

(d) How to Terminate Grantor Trust Status. The grantor may find it necessary to terminate or turn off grantor trust status, if, for example the income generated by the trust presents too great a tax burden for the grantor. The grantor alone should hold the power to terminate grantor trust status so that he or she need not rely on someone else to execute the termination. Grantor trust status could be terminated if the trust documents provide that the grantor has the power to release one of the retained powers such as the power of corpus substitution.

(e) President Obama's Proposed Changes to Tax Treatment of Grantor Trusts. In the Obama Administration's Fiscal 2013 budget proposals and in the Treasury Department's "Greenbook," which is formally known as the "General Explanation of the Administration's Fiscal Year 2013 Revenue Proposals" (Depart-ment of the Treasury, April 2013), the Obama administration explains proposals to

---

[1] ¶**3100** Rev. Proc. 2014-3, 2014-1 IRB 111.

¶3100

close the gap between the income and transfer tax rules applicable to grantor trusts. The administration explains that the lack of coordination between the two sets of rules creates tax planning opportunities to structure transactions between the deemed owner and the trust that can result in the transfer of significant wealth without gift or estate tax consequences. The Obama administration makes the following proposals:

> "If a person who is a deemed owner under the grantor trust rules of all or a portion of a trust engages in a transaction with that trust that **constitutes a sale, exchange, or comparable transaction that is disregarded for income tax purposes by reason of the person's treatment as a deemed owner of the trust** (emphasis added), then the portion of the trust attributable to the property received by the trust in that transaction (including all retained income therefrom, appreciation thereon, and reinvestments thereof, net of the amount of the consideration received by the person in that transaction)

> "(1) will be subject to estate tax as part of the gross estate of the deemed owner,

> "(2) will be subject to gift tax at any time during the deemed owner's life when his or her treatment as a deemed owner of the trust is terminated, and

> "(3) will be treated as a gift by the deemed owner to the extent any distribution is made to another person (except in discharge of the deemed owner's obligation to the distributee) during the life of the deemed owner.

> "The proposal would reduce the amount subject to transfer tax by any portion of that amount that was treated as a prior taxable gift by the deemed owner. The transfer tax imposed by this proposal would be payable from the trust. The proposal would not change the treatment of any trust that is already includable in the grantor's gross estate under existing provisions of the Internal Revenue Code, including without limitation the following: grantor retained income trusts; grantor retained annuity trusts; personal residence trusts; and qualified personal residence trusts. Similarly, it would not apply to any trust having the exclusive purpose of paying deferred compensation under a nonqualified deferred compensation plan if the assets of such trust are available to satisfy claims of general creditors of the grantor. It also would not apply to any trust that is a grantor trust solely by reason of IRC Sec. 677(a)(3). The proposal would be effective with regard to trusts that engage in a described transaction on or after the date of enactment. Regulatory authority would be granted, including the ability to create exceptions to this provision."

Consequences of the Obama administration's proposal. If enacted as proposed, this change would be the death knell to installment sales to Intentionally Defective Grantor Trusts (IDGTs) because the new law would eliminate all estate tax savings associated with this technique. If the assets that are sold have appreciated in value, that appreciation would be subject to estate tax no matter how long the grantor has lived and whether or not the note is paid off. Even attempts to thwart this result by terminating grantor trust status or making distributions from the trust during the grantor's life would be subject to gift tax. The only hope for planners lies in the proposal's last line which grants the IRS regulatory authority to "create exceptions to this provision" and the planning opportunities that lie therein.

Significantly, the President's fiscal year 2014 proposal specifically excludes from its scope the following trusts:

- Grantor retained income trusts (GRITs);
- Grantor retained annuity trusts (GRATs);
- Personal residence trusts;
- Qualified personal residence trusts (QPRTs);
- Trusts having the exclusive purpose of paying deferred compensation under a nonqualified deferred compensation plan if the assets of such trust are available to satisfy claims of general creditors of the grantor. This is a reference to "rabbi trusts;" and
- Any trust that is a grantor trust solely by reason of IRC Sec. 677(a)(3). This exception refers to the application of income from the grantor trust to pay life insurance premiums. Therefore, certain irrevocable life insurance trusts would not be subject to estate tax inclusion merely because they are grantor trusts, if the income from the trust is used to pay premiums on policies of insurance on the life of the grantor or the grantor's spouse.

  ▶ **PLANNING POINTER:** Taxpayers who are considering estate planning transactions that involve leveraged transfers to grantor trusts should proceed as soon as possible because it may be impossible to do so in the years ahead if the legislation proposed by the Obama Administration regarding grantor trusts is enacted. The proposal provides that transfers to grantor trusts that occur prior to enactment of the proposed legislation would be unaffected by the new legislation. The need to act is therefore now.

¶3101 OVERVIEW OF GRANTOR TRUST RULES

If the grantor retains one or more of the following specifically enumerated rights and interests that are found in IRC Sec. 673 through IRC Sec. 678, the trust will be classified as a "grantor trust" and the grantor will be treated as the trust's owner and taxed on its income [Reg. Sec. 1.671-1(a)]:

- If the grantor holds a reversionary interest at the time of the trust's creation that is more than 5 percent of the value of the trust estate under IRC Sec. 673. For further discussion, see ¶3101(a).
- If the grantor or a nonadverse person as defined in IRC Sec. 672(a) has the power to determine the beneficial enjoyment of either corpus or income under IRC Sec. 674. For further discussion, see ¶3101(b).
- If the trust instrument grants certain administrative powers that are viewed as exercisable for the grantor's benefit under IRC Sec. 675. These administrative powers include the power to deal with trust assets for less than adequate and full consideration under IRC Sec. 675(1), the power to borrow trust assets without adequate interest and security under IRC Sec. 675(2), actual borrowing of trust assets without adequate interest or security and repayment during the tax year

under IRC Sec. 675(3) and certain administrative powers exercisable in a nonfiduciary capacity under IRC Sec. 675(4). For further discussion, see ¶ 3101(c).

- If the grantor or the grantor's spouse has the power to revoke the trust without the consent of an adverse party under IRC Sec. 676. For further discussion, see ¶ 3101(d).

- If the grantor or a nonadverse party has the power to use the trust income for the benefit of the grantor or the grantor's spouse under IRC Sec. 677. For further discussion, see ¶ 3101(e) or

- If a person other than the grantor has the sole power to vest income or principal in himself or herself so he or she is treated as a trust grantor [IRC Sec. 678(a)]. For further discussion, see ¶ 3101(f).

(a) Reversionary Interests. A trust is treated as a grantor trust when the grantor has a reversionary interest whose value at the time of the transfer of the property into the trust amounts to more than 5 percent of the value of the transferred property [IRC Sec. 673(a)].

Grantor's spouse. If the grantor's spouse retains a reversionary interest, the grantor is deemed to retain a reversionary interest as well. This rule applies if the spouse is living with the grantor at the time the interest is created. It also holds true if the individual became the grantor's spouse after the interest was created—but only for the period after the individual became a spouse. The grantor is treated as holding any power or interest held by the grantor's spouse not only for reversionary interests but generally for all the interests retained by a grantor that would make the grantor subject to tax [IRC Sec. 672(e)]. An individual legally separated from his spouse under a decree of divorce or of separate maintenance will not be considered married for purposes of this rule [IRC Sec. 672(e)(2)].

The possibility that an interest may return to the grantor or his spouse solely by inheritance under the intestacy laws is, however, not considered a reversionary interest and the grantor-trust rules will not apply.

Neither is it deemed a reversionary interest if all that the grantor or spouse retains is an interest that can become effective only after the death on or before the age of 21 of a minor beneficiary who is a lineal descendant of the grantor and holds all of the present interest of any portion of the trust [IRC Sec. 673(b)].

> **Example 1:** You transferred some rental property to a trust, the income from which is payable to your brother for 15 years, after which the money reverts to you. Your reversionary interest (using the valuation table) is valued at more than 5 percent of the value of the property. You are treated as the owner of the trust property and all income of the trust will be taxed to you and you will be able to claim all deductions [IRC Sec. 673(a)].

> **Example 2:** Dad transferred some rental property to a trust, the income from which is payable to his son until he reaches age 21, after which the money will be distributed to him outright. If the son dies before age 21, the property will revert back to Dad. Dad's reversionary interest (using the valuation table) is valued at more than 5 percent of the value of the property. Dad is not treated as

the owner of the trust property because his reversionary interest will only become effective if his son dies before the age of 21 [IRC Sec. 673(b)].

(b) Power to Control Beneficial Enjoyment. In general, the grantor is treated as the owner of any portion of a trust over which the grantor, a nonadverse party, or both, have the power to dispose of the beneficial enjoyment of the trust's income or corpus without the approval or consent of an adverse party [IRC Sec. 674(a); Reg. Sec. 1.674(a)-1]. In applying this rule, a grantor is treated as holding a power held by a spouse. Ten powers, however, are excluded from this general rule. An adverse party is any person having a substantial beneficial interest in the trust that would be adversely affected by the exercise or nonexercise of the power which he possesses over the trust. For example, a person having a general power of appointment over the trust property will be deemed to have a beneficial interest in the trust [IRC Secs. 672(a), 672(b); Reg. Sec. 1.672(a)-1]. In Letter Ruling 201326011, the IRS ruled that because the grantor had a limited testamentary power of appointment over the corpus of a trust, the grantor would be treated as the owner of the trust under IRC Sec. 674(a).

> **Example 3:** Mom creates a trust for the benefit of her two daughters but retains the power to change the beneficiaries. Mom will be treated as the owner of the trust's corpus and will be taxed on its income. Mom would not be treated as the owner if she needed the consent of both daughters to change the beneficiaries.

Beneficial interest. A beneficial interest in the trust includes both mandatory and discretionary interests, as well as interests in income or principal or both. A beneficial interest may be either a present or future interest. Thus, a remainder beneficiary has a beneficial interest in the trust, though it is adverse to the exercise of any power over the principal, but not to the exercise of a power over income preceding the remainder interest [Reg. Sec. 1.672(a)-1(d)]. There are no attribution rules applied to determine whether a beneficiary has an interest in the trust, or to determine its substantiality. Thus, a beneficiary is not deemed to own interests held by his or her family members.

Substantiality. An interest is a substantial interest if its value in relation to the total value of the property subject to the power is not insignificant [Reg. Sec. 1.672(a)-1(a)]. An interest may be substantial for purposes of the grantor trust rules, even if it is not vested under state law [Reg. Sec. 1.672(a)-1(c)]. Any contingencies that may prevent the beneficiary from actually receiving the use and enjoyment of the trust fund must be considered when deciding whether or not the interest is substantial. The value of a beneficiary's interest that will vest only if the beneficiary survives another individual or individuals can be ascertained actuarially.

Adverse to exercise. An adverse party's substantial beneficial interest in the trust must be of such a nature as to be adversely affected by the exercise of the power in question. A trustee is not an adverse party merely because of his interest as trustee, including the trustee's right to compensation [Reg. Sec. 1.672(a)-1(a)]. A person having a general power of appointment over trust property is deemed to have a beneficial interest in the trust [IRC Sec. 672(a); Reg. Sec. 1.672(a)-1(a)]. Ordinarily, a beneficiary is an adverse party, but a beneficiary whose share of income or corpus of a trust is limited to only a part may be an adverse party only as to that part [Reg. Sec. 1.672(a)-1(b)]. Thus, for example, the interest of an ordinary income beneficiary of a trust may not be adverse with respect to the exercise of a power over principal.

Exceptions for certain powers. There are ten exceptions to the general rule, which provides that the grantor will be treated as the owner of any portion of a trust over which the grantor, a nonadverse party, or both, have a power to dispose of the beneficial enjoyment of the trust's income or corpus without the approval or consent of an adverse party [IRC Sec. 674(a)]. The ten excluded powers are as follows:

1. *Power to apply income to support of a dependent.* The power to use trust income for the support of a beneficiary whom the grantor is legally obligated to support will not cause the grantor to be treated as the owner except to the extent that the income is in fact used for support. This exception applies even if the power is held by the grantor provided that the grantor is acting as trustee or co-trustee [IRC Sec. 674(b)(1); Reg. Sec. 1.674(b)-1(b)(1)].

2. *Power affecting beneficial enjoyment only after occurrence of event.* A power to affect enjoyment only after the occurrence of an event would not cause the grantor to be treated as the owner. However, this exception does not prevent the grantor from being treated as the owner after the occurrence of the event unless the power is relinquished [IRC Sec. 674(b)(2); Reg. Sec. 1.674(b)-1(b)(2)]. The grantor will be taxed if he has more than a five percent reversionary interest.

   Example 4: Taxpayer set up a trust when the interest factor for valuing reversions was 5 percent. Income is to be paid to Son for 10 years. At the expiration of 10 years, Taxpayer will have discretion to determine who receives income. This power does not cause Taxpayer to be taxed on trust income paid to Son because the reversion has a value not in excess of 5 percent. However, unless relinquished, the power would cause Taxpayer to be taxed on trust income when Son's income interest expires.

3. *Power exercisable only by will.* A power exercisable only by will does not cause the grantor to be treated as owner of the trust. This does not protect income that may be accumulated at the discretion of the grantor or a nonadverse party, or both, and ultimately given away by the grantor's will [IRC Sec. 674(b)(3); Reg. Sec. 1.674(b)-1(b)(3)].

   Example 5: Taxpayer sets up a trust giving himself discretion to accumulate income. The trust instrument further provides that any income that is actually accumulated may be given away by him in his will. Taxpayer's power over the accumulated income does not qualify as an excepted power and he will be treated as owner of the trust.

4. *Power to allocate among charitable beneficiaries.* A power to determine the beneficial enjoyment of the corpus or income of a trust will not cause the grantor to be treated as the owner of the trust if the corpus or income is irrevocably payable for a charitable purpose or to an employee stock ownership plan in a qualified gratuitous transfer [IRC Sec. 674(b)(4); Reg. Sec. 1.674(b)-1(b)(4)].

¶3101

Example 6: Taxpayer sets up a trust, which provides that the income will be irrevocably payable solely to the National Kidney Foundation. Taxpayer will not be treated as owner of this trust and therefore will not be taxed on trust income.

5. *Power to distribute corpus.* A power to distribute corpus that is limited by a reasonably definite standard described in the trust instrument will not cause the grantor to be treated as owner of the trust [IRC Sec. 674(b)(5)]. This type of permissible power may be exercisable in favor of a single beneficiary, multiple beneficiaries, or a class of beneficiaries. A power to distribute corpus for the education, support, maintenance, or health of the beneficiary would be subject to a definite standard and, thus, would qualify as an excepted power. However, a power to distribute corpus for the pleasure, desire, or happiness of the beneficiary would not be subject to a definite standard and, thus, would not qualify as an excepted power [Reg. Sec. 1.674(b)-1(b)(5)(i)]. A power that is not limited by a reasonably definite standard may nonetheless qualify as an excepted power if distributions of corpus may be made only to current income beneficiaries and any distribution is chargeable against the proportionate share of corpus held in trust for the beneficiary [Reg. Sec. 1.674(b)-1(b)(5)(ii)].

Example 7: A trust instrument provides for payment of the income to the grantor's two brothers for life, and for payment of the corpus to the grantor's nephews in equal shares. The grantor reserves the power to distribute corpus to pay medical expenses that may be incurred by his brothers or nephews. The grantor is not treated as an owner because the power is limited by a reasonably definite standard which is set forth in the trust instrument. However, if the power were also exercisable in favor of a person (for example, a sister) who was not otherwise a beneficiary of the trust, the grantor would be treated as an owner [Reg. Sec. 1.674(b)-1(b)(5)(iii), Example 1].

Example 8: The facts are the same as in Example 7 except that the grantor reserves the power to distribute any part of the corpus to his brothers or his nephews for their happiness. The grantor is treated as the owner of the trust because the power is not limited by a reasonably definite standard and because the power to distribute corpus permits a distribution of corpus to persons other than current income beneficiaries [Reg. Sec. 1.674(b)-1(b)(5)(iii), Example 2].

Example 9: A trust instrument provides for payment of income to the grantor's two adult sons in equal shares for ten years, after which the corpus is to be distributed to his grandchildren in equal shares. The grantor reserves the power to pay over to each son up to one-half of the corpus during the ten-year period, but these payments reduce proportionately subsequent income and corpus payments made to the son receiving the corpus. Thus, if one-half of the corpus is paid to one son, all the income from the remaining half is thereafter payable to the other son. The grantor is not treated as an owner because of this power

¶3101

because it qualifies under the exception of IRC Sec. 674(b)(5)(B) [Reg. Sec. 1.674(b)-1(b)(5)(iii), Example 3].

6. *Power to withhold income temporarily.* A power to distribute or accumulate income to or for a current income beneficiary qualifies as an excepted power only if the accumulated income satisfies either one of the following two tests [IRC Sec. 674(b)(6); Reg. Sec. 1.674(b)-1(b)(6)]:

   a. The accumulated income must ultimately be payable to the beneficiary, his estate, or his appointees (or to designated alternate takers). The beneficiary's power of appointment generally must be exercisable in favor of anyone except that the power does not have to be exercisable in favor of the beneficiary himself, his estate, his creditors, or the creditors of his estate;

   b. The accumulated income must ultimately be payable upon termination of the trust or, in conjunction with a disposition of corpus which contains the accumulated income, to the current income beneficiaries in irrevocably specified shares. Accumulated income is considered to be ultimately payable in accordance with these rules even though the trust provides for payment to other persons if the primary beneficiary fails to survive the date fixed for distribution if this date may reasonably be expected to occur within the lifetime of the primary beneficiary. The other persons may be either the deceased beneficiary's appointees or other alternate recipients (but not the grantor or his estate) who were irrevocably designated in advance. A power does not qualify for this exception if any person has the power to add beneficiaries (other than to provide for after-born or after-adopted children).

Example 10: A trust instrument provides that the income shall be paid in equal shares to the grantor's two adult daughters, but the grantor reserves the power to withhold from either beneficiary any part of that beneficiary's share of income and to add it to the corpus of the trust until the younger daughter reaches the age of 30 years. When the younger daughter reaches the age of 30, the trust terminates and the corpus is divided equally between the two daughters or their estates. Although exercise of this power may permit the shifting of accumulated income from one beneficiary to the other (since the corpus with the accumulations is to be divided equally) the power is excepted under IRC Sec. 674(b)(6)(B) [Reg. Sec. 1.674(b)-1(b)(6)(ii), Example 1].

Example 11: The facts are the same as in Example 1, except that the grantor of the trust reserves the power to distribute accumulated income to the beneficiaries in such shares as he chooses. The combined powers are not excepted by IRC Sec. 674(b)(6)(B) since income accumulated pursuant to the first power is neither required to be payable only in conjunction with a corpus distribution nor required to be payable in shares specified in the trust instrument [Reg. Sec. 1.674(b)-1(b)(6)(ii), Example 2].

Example 12: A trust provides for payment of income to the grantor's adult son with the grantor retaining the power to accumulate the income until the grantor's death, when all accumulations are to be paid to the son. If the son predeceases the grantor, all accumulations are, at the death of the grantor, to be paid to his daughter, or if she is not living, to alternate takers (which do not include the grantor's estate) in specified shares. The power is excepted under IRC Sec. 674(b)(6)(A) since the date of distribution (the date of the grantor's death) may, in the usual case, reasonably be expected to occur during the beneficiary's (the son's) lifetime. It is not necessary that the accumulations be payable to the son's estate or his appointees if he should predecease the grantor for this exception to apply [Reg. Sec. 1.674(b)-1(b)(6)(ii), Example 3].

7. *Power to withhold income during disability of a beneficiary.* A power to withhold income during the period of a beneficiary's disability or prior to the beneficiary attaining age 21 will not cause the grantor to be treated as owner of the trust [IRC Sec. 674(b)(7); Reg. Sec. 1.674(b)-1(b)(7)]. This exception applies even though the income may not be paid to the beneficiary from whom it was withheld. The income may be added to corpus and ultimately paid to others. A power does not qualify for this exception if any person has the power to add beneficiaries, except where such action is to provide for after-born or after-adopted children.

8. *Power to allocate between corpus and income.* A power to allocate receipts and disbursements as between corpus and income, even though expressed in broad language will not cause the grantor to be treated as the owner of the trust [IRC Sec. 674(b)(8); Reg. Sec. 1.674(b)-1(b)(8)].

9. *Exception for certain powers of independent trustees.* A power will not cause the grantor to be treated as the owner of a trust if it is solely exercisable (without the approval or consent of anyone) by a trustee or trustees:

   a. To distribute, apportion, or accumulate income to or for a beneficiary or beneficiaries, or to, for, or within a class of beneficiaries; or

   b. To pay out corpus to or for a beneficiary, beneficiaries, or class of beneficiaries. This exception does not apply if the grantor or his spouse is a trustee or more than one-half of the trustees are related or subordinate parties who are subservient to the wishes of the grantor [IRC Sec. 674(c); Reg. Sec. 1.674(c)-1]. A power does not qualify for this exception if any person has the power to add beneficiaries (other than to provide for after-born or after-adopted children).

10. *Power to allocate income if limited by a standard.* A power solely exercisable (without the approval or consent of any other person) by a trustee or trustees, none of whom is the grantor or a spouse living with the grantor, to distribute, apportion, or accumulate income to a beneficiary, or to a class of beneficiaries shall not cause the grantor to be treated as the owner of the trust if such power is limited by a reasonably definite external standard which is set forth in the trust instrument. This exception does not apply if the grantor or his spouse is a trustee [IRC Sec. 674(d); Reg. Sec. 1.674(d)-1]. A power does not qualify for this exception if any person has the power to add beneficiaries (other than to provide for after-born or after-adopted children).

¶3101

(c) Administrative Powers. The grantor is taxable on the trust income when administrative control of the trust may be exercised primarily for his or her benefit instead of for the benefit of the beneficiaries [IRC Sec. 675; Reg. Sec. 1.675-1]. The following situations illustrate this type of administrative control:

- Power in the grantor or a nonadverse party, or both, without the approval of any adverse party, to deal with the trust property or income for less than an adequate consideration;

- Power in the grantor or a nonadverse party, or both, that enables the grantor (or grantor's spouse) to borrow the corpus or income without adequate interest or security, except when a trustee (other than the grantor) is authorized to make loans to *any* persons without regard to interest or security;

- When the grantor has borrowed the corpus or income and has not repaid the loan before the start of the tax year, unless the loan was made for adequate interest and security by a trustee (other than the grantor or a trustee subservient to the grantor);

- General powers of administration exercisable by anyone in a nonfiduciary capacity so as to benefit the grantor individually rather than the beneficiaries.

(d) Power to Revoke. If the grantor of a trust reserves the power to take back title to the trust funds for himself, he is considered the owner of the trust, whether or not he actually exercises that power [IRC Sec. 1.676(a)]. The grantor is taxed if he can exercise the power alone, if it can be exercised only by a nonadverse party, or if it can be exercised by both the grantor and a nonadverse party together [IRC Sec. 676(a); Reg. Sec. 1.676(a)-1]. The grantor is not taxed if the power can be exercised only by or with consent of an adverse party [IRC Secs. 672(a), 676(a); Reg. Sec. 1.676(a)-1].

An adverse party is any person with a substantial beneficial interest in the trust (including a general power of appointment over trust property) which would be adversely affected by the exercise or non-exercise of his power with regards to the trust [IRC Sec. 672(a)]. A beneficiary is ordinarily an adverse party [Reg. Sec. 1.672(a)-1(b)]. A nonadverse party has either no beneficial interest, or one that is not substantial, or one which would not be adversely affected by the exercise of his power with regard to the trust [IRC Sec. 672(b); Reg. Sec. 1.672(b)-1].

> **Example 13:** Son transferred property to a trust under which the income is payable to his elderly mother. Son does not have the power to revoke, but the trustee, a local attorney, does possess a power to revoke. Since the attorney is a nonadverse party, Son will be treated as the owner of the trust and taxed on its income.

(e) Income for Benefit of Grantor, Spouse, or Dependent. The grantor is taxed on the income of a trust when, without the consent of an adverse party, the income is, or may be, paid or accumulated for the grantor's benefit, or used to pay his or her life insurance premiums (except on policies irrevocably payable to charity).[1] In

---

[1] ¶**3101** Ltr. Rul 201326011 (grantor treated as owner of trust because net income of trust must be paid to grantor).

addition, the grantor is taxed on the income from property transferred in trust for the benefit of his spouse. In transfers for the benefit of himself or his spouse, the grantor is treated as the owner of the property transferred [Reg. Sec. 1.677(a)-1].

A discretionary power to use trust income to discharge a grantor's legal support obligations will cause the grantor to be treated as the owner of the trust [IRC Sec. 677(b)]. However, a discretionary power to use the income from the trust to discharge the grantor's legal obligation to support an individual other than a spouse, such as a child, will not cause the grantor to be treated as the owner of the trust. The grantor is treated as the owner of the trust only to the extent that the income is actually used to discharge the obligation [IRC Sec. 677(b)]. This would include using trust income to pay a child's college tuition.[2] [IRC Sec. 677; Reg. Secs. 1.677(a)-1, 1.677(b)-1].

For an alimony or support trust, the wife is taxed on the payments (including any tax preference items) except to the extent the payments are for the support of minor children [IRC Sec. 682; Reg. Secs. 1.682(a)-1, 1.682(b)-1, 1.682(c)-1]. Some courts hold that tax-exempt income received by an alimony trust is not taxed when it is distributed to the wife,[3] but the IRS disagrees[4] as do other courts.[5]

    (f) Income Taxable to Person Other Than Grantor. A person other than the grantor may be taxed on the trust income if he or she has a power to acquire the corpus or income of the trust. Thus, a person who has exclusive power to vest the corpus or income of a trust in himself, or who has released such power but retained controls similar to those discussed above, is taxed on the trust income [IRC Sec. 678; Reg. Sec. 1.678(a)-1], subject to these modifications:

1. If the grantor of the trust is taxed as the owner, the other person will not be taxed under the above rule;

2. If the other person can merely use trust income to support a dependent, he or she will be taxed only to the extent it is so used [Reg. Sec. 1.678(c)-1];

3. If the other person renounces the power within a reasonable time after learning of it, he or she will not be taxed on the trust income [Reg. Sec. 1.678(d)-1].

IRC Sec. 678 would be triggered, for example, if a child had the unilateral right to withdraw all property in a trust created under the will of the child's deceased parent. This unilateral power of withdrawal would cause the child to be treated as the trust's owner under IRC Sec. 678(a) so that the income, deductions and credits against tax of the trust would be attributed directly to the child.

---

[2] Morrill, 228 F. Supp. 734 (D. Me. 1964).

[3] Ellis, 416 F.2d 894 (6th Cir. 1969); Stewart, 9 TC 195 (1947), *acq.,* 1947-2 CB 4, *and nonacq.,* 1965-2 CB 7.

[4] Rev. Rul. 65-283, 1965-2 CB 25.

[5] Kitch, 104 TC 1 (1995), *aff'd,* 103 F.3d 104 (10th Cir. 1996).

¶3102 USE OF GRANTOR TRUSTS

Estate planners create grantor trusts for the following reasons:

1. Grantor trusts allow wealthy taxpayers to shift additional wealth to future generations free of transfer tax but still retain some level of control or economic interest in the trust property.

2. Assets invested in a grantor trust will be allowed to grow on a tax-free basis for the benefit of future generations.

3. Transactions between a grantor and the grantor trust will be ignored for federal income tax purposes according to Rev. Rul. 85-13[1] because the grantor is treated as the owner of the trust property for income tax purposes and the IRS disregards any transfers of property between the grantor and the trust. Therefore, neither the grantor nor the grantor trust recognizes gain or loss on the sale or exchange of assets between them.[2] This well-established principle affords estate planners the opportunity to sell appreciated assets to a grantor trust without the recognition of gain.

4. As a result of the compression of the tax rate brackets for trusts and estates, it takes very little income for a trust or estate to be taxed at the highest income tax bracket. For example, in 2014, trusts and estates reach the top income tax rate of 39.6 percent if they have $12,150 of income, but individuals filing joint returns do not reach the 39.6 percent tax rate until they have $457,600 of income. Grantors therefore use the grantor trust rules to make sure that the trust income is taxed to the grantor at individual tax rates rather than be taxed to the trust at the trust's higher income tax rate.

5. Grantor trusts allow the grantor to make a completed gift for gift and estate tax purposes, while the grantor continues to be treated as the owner of the trust property for income tax purposes. In Rev. Rul. 2004-64,[3] the IRS concluded that the grantor who pays the income tax attributable to inclusion of the trust's income in his or her taxable income is not deemed to have made a gift in the amount of the taxes paid because the grantor, rather than the trust, is responsible for payment of these taxes. If, however, the trust's governing instrument or local law requires the trust to reimburse the grantor for income taxes paid by the grantor on the trust's income, the full value of the trust's assets are includible in the grantor's gross estate under IRC Sec. 2036(a)(1) because the grantor has retained the right to have trust property expended in discharge of the grantor's legal obligation. However, if the trust's governing instrument or local law provides that the trustee has only the discretion to reimburse the grantor for the taxes paid, regardless of whether the discretion is exercised, the mere existence of such discretion will not cause the trust's assets to be included in the grantor's gross estate. In the latter case, the presence of other facts, such as a pre-existing understanding or arrangement

---

[1] **¶3102** Rev. Rul. 85-13, 1985-1 CB 184.

[2] Chief Counsel Advice 201343021 (grantor trust disregarded for all purposes including dis-allowance of losses under IRC Secs. 267 and 707(b)(1)(A)).

[3] Rev. Rul. 2004-64, 2004-2 CB 7.

between the grantor and the trustee with respect to reimbursement may result in inclusion of the trust's assets in the grantor's estate.

The issues addressed in Rev. Rul. 2004-64 were the subject of IRS Ltr. Rul. 200944002 where the trust agreement prohibited the trustee from paying the grantor or the grantor's executors any income or principal of the trust for the purpose of discharging the grantor's income tax liability. The IRS reasoned that because the trustee was prohibited from reimbursing the grantor for taxes the grantor paid, the grantor had not retained a reimbursement right that would cause the trust corpus to be includible in the grantor's gross estate under IRC Sec. 2036. The IRS found that the trustee's discretionary authority to distribute income and/or principal to the grantor did not, by itself, cause the trust corpus to be includible in the grantor's gross estate under IRC Sec. 2036.

6. A gift of an installment note to a grantor trust is not regarded as a disposition of the note that causes the grantor to recognize gain under IRC Sec. 453B because the transfer is not recognized for income tax purposes.[4] If the gift had not been to a grantor trust, IRC Sec. 453B(a)(2) provides that a gift of an installment note is a taxable disposition of the note that results in gain recognition to the donor to the extent the fair market value of the note exceeds the basis.

Example 1: Mom created a trust in 2010 which was a grantor trust under the grantor trust rules. By 2014, the trust had earned $50,000 of interest income which would be taxable to the trust in the absence of the grantor trust rules. However, as a result of the application of the grantor trust rules to this trust, the interest income is taxable to Mom.

Example 2: Dad creates a grantor trust for the benefit of his children. The trust is initially funded with a $1 million gift. Later, Dad sells the trust some property and realizes a $600,000 gain. Under Rev. Rul. 85-13, no gain is recognized on the sale because Dad is deemed to be the same taxpayer as the trust.

7. When the grantor is taxed on the income of the trust, he or she is allowed the deductions, credits and exclusions (including home sale exclusions under IRC Sec. 121)[5] related to the income [IRC Sec. 671; Reg. Sec. 1.671-3(a)]. The tax year and method of accounting used by the trust are disregarded. The gross income from the trust properties is determined by the grantor as if the trust had not been created.[6]

Example 3: Sally lives in an assisted living facility. Prior to living there, she had lived in a private residence for 18 years. Sally's mother had established a trust that holds fee simple title to the residence, which is the only asset in the trust. Sally is the income beneficiary of the trust and does not have the power to vest the trust corpus or income from the trust in any person. When Sally dies, the residence goes to her children who are over the age of 21. The house has never

---

[4] Rev. Rul. 81-98, 1998-1 CB 40; Rev. Rul. 74-613, 1974-2 CB 153.

[5] Ltr. Rul. 20001802.

[6] Rev. Rul. 57-390, 1957-2 CB 326.

generated any income for Sally and the trustees sell it at a gain. The gain realized from the sale of the home by the trustee is not eligible for exclusion under IRC Sec. 121 because Sally was not considered the owner of the trust as required under IRC Sec. 121. IRC Sec. 678(a) provides that a person other than the grantor will be treated as the owner of a trust if the person has power exercisable solely by himself to vest the corpus or the income from the trust in himself. Based on the trust language, Sally never had the power to vest trust corpus or income from the trust in herself and therefore could not be treated as the owner of the trust for federal income tax purposes. She was therefore ineligible to claim an exclusion for the gain realized by the trust when the trustee sold the home.

¶3103 INTENTIONALLY DEFECTIVE GRANTOR TRUSTS

A popular income and estate tax planning technique involves creating an intentionally defective grantor trust (IDGT) that deliberately triggers the grantor trust rules set forth in IRC Secs. 671-679. Transfers by the grantor to the IDGT will be complete for gift and estate tax purposes but incomplete for income tax purposes. Therefore, if the trust is drafted properly, the income and gains of the trust will be taxable to the grantor, but the assets transferred to the trust by the grantor will be excluded from the grantor's gross estate upon death. The IDGT allows wealthy families to minimize estate tax as well as reduce the income tax burden imposed on income-generating assets held in trust for future generations.

Best grantor trust power for IDGT. The power used to make a trust an IDGT must not be one that would cause the trust property to be included in the grantor's estate under IRC Sec. 2036(a)(1) and/or IRC Sec. 2038. One of the best powers to use is an IRC Sec. 675(4)(c) power to substitute assets of equal value. The IRS ruled in Letter Ruling 200603040 that retention of this power did not cause estate inclusion. Another good choice is the IRC Sec. 675(2) power to borrow without adequate security or interest. Other techniques that will produce an intentional grantor trust that is excluded from the grantor's gross estate is to pair a nonadverse trustee's power to alter the beneficial enjoyment of the trust income and principal under IRC Sec. 674(a) with a power to add beneficiaries (other than after-born or after-adopted children). IRC Sec. 674(a) treats the grantor as the owner of any portion of a trust as to which the grantor or a nonadverse party, or both, holds a power to alter the beneficial enjoyment of the corpus or income, without the consent of an adverse party. In order to avoid causing the trust to be included in the grantor's gross estate under IRC Sec. 2036 or 2038, this power should not be held by the grantor. See ¶ 2825 for further discussion of the IRC Sec. 674(a) power to control beneficial enjoyment. 3101

Nonfiduciary power to substitute assets (IRC Sec. 675(4)(c)). The nonfiduciary power to substitute assets of equal value under IRC Sec. 675(4)(c) has received a shot in the arm from Rev. Rul. 2008-22[1] where the IRS concluded that an inter vivos trust will not be included in a grantor's taxable estate under IRC Sec. 2036 or 2038 if the grantor retains a nonfiduciary power to substitute property of equivalent value, as discussed in detail below. As a result of Rev. Rul. 2008-22, the nonfiduciary power to substitute assets under IRC Sec. 675(4)(c) is now the preferred power to use to create an intentional grantor trust.

IRC Sec. 675(4)(c) provides that the grantor will be treated as the owner of any portion of a trust in respect of which a power of administration is exercisable in a nonfiduciary capacity by any person without the approval or consent of any person in a fiduciary capacity. For this purpose, a "power of administration" includes a power to "reacquire" the trust corpus by substituting other property of equivalent value. The power to substitute assets must be held in a nonfiduciary capacity. A power to substitute assets held by someone who is a trustee may be held in a nonfiduciary capacity, but the regulations presume that the power is exercisable in a fiduciary capacity primarily in the interests of the beneficiaries. This presumption may be rebutted only by clear and convincing proof that the power is not exercisable primarily in the interests of the beneficiaries [Reg. Sec. 1.675-1(b)(4)(iii)]. To rebut this presumption, one should show that the trust instrument and state law do not impose on the holder of the power any fiduciary responsibility, and that the power holder can act without regard to the beneficiaries' best interests.

Tax benefits of IDGTs. The following consequences result from the proper drafting of an IDGT:

1. The IDGT requires creation of an irrevocable trust that intentionally violates one or more of the grantor trust rules set forth in IRC Secs. 671-679 so the grantor is treated as the owner of the trust and therefore taxed on the income generated by the trust at individual tax rates rather than the trust tax rates. This is an important distinction and typically will save the grantor income tax because of the compression of the tax rate brackets for trusts and estates vis-à-vis the rates for individual taxpayers. Here is why it works: In 2014, trusts and estates will reach the top income tax rate of 39.6 percent when they have taxable income over $12,150. To make matters worse, in 2014, the new Medicare tax of 3.8 percent tax on net investment income (also known as the net investment income (NII) tax) will also kick in for trusts with modified adjusted gross income (MAGI) over $12,150. This will bring the top trust income tax rate to 43.4 percent in 2014. In contrast, married taxpayers will not reach the 39.6 percent tax rate until they have taxable income over $457,600 in 2014. The new 3.8 percent Medicare tax on net investment income will kick in for single individuals with MAGI over $200,000, married individuals filing jointly with MAGI over $250,000, and married individuals filing separately with MAGI over $125,000.

---

[1] ¶3103 Rev. Rul. 2008-22, 2008-16 IRB 796. See also Estate of Jordahl, 65 TC 92 (1975), *acq. in result*, 1977-2 CB 1.

¶3103

2. The IDGT can be used to freeze the value of the property transferred by the grantor into the trust as of the date of the transfer. This will result in removing all future appreciation from the grantor to the trust beneficiaries.

3. If assets transferred into the IDGT include closely-held business interests, partnership interests or LLC interests, the transfers may be eligible for valuation discounts for lack of control or lack of marketability.

4. The grantor can make installment sales to the IDGT. This popular wealth transfer planning technique works because of Rev. Rul. 85-13,[2] where the IRS held that an apparent sale between a grantor trust and its grantor would not be regarded as a sale for income tax purposes. Therefore the grantor recognizes no gain or loss on the transaction because the grantor and the trust are considered one and the same taxpayer for income tax purposes. For example, if the grantor sells appreciated assets to the trust, the grantor recognizes no gain under IRC Sec. 1001 because the sale is ignored for income tax purposes. The IRS further blessed this transaction in Rev. Rul. 2004-64,[3] which provides that the grantor's payment of income taxes attributable to the trust will not constitute a gift for federal gift tax purposes because the grantor is discharging his own legal obligation.

In the typical installment sale to an IDGT, the grantor creates an irrevocable grantor trust for the benefit of descendants. The grantor can assign generation skipping transfer (GST) tax exemption to the trust so the assets will pass to grandchildren free of GST tax. The grantor makes a gift to the trust of so-called "seed" money that should be equal to at least 10 percent of the value of the assets to be sold to the trust. This seed gift will use up a portion of the grantor's lifetime gift tax exemption. The grantor then sells assets to the grantor trust in an installment sale where there is no down payment but interest is payable annually on the note. Ideally, the assets sold to the trust would generate income (to make the interest payments) and would also qualify for valuation discounts for lack of control and lack of marketability. For example, non-voting interests in an LLC or an S corporation are often good assets to sell to a grantor trust. A grantor trust is also an eligible Subchapter S stockholder [IRC Sec. 1361(c)(2)(A)(i)]. As a result of this installment sale to the grantor trust, the grantor recognizes no gain or loss on the sale because of Rev. Rul. 85-13. However, the trust's basis in the assets purchased is the same as the grantor's basis. The grantor is not taxed on the interest payments he or she receives. If the total return on the assets sold to the trust exceeds the interest rate on the note, the assets are transferred tax-free to the trust's beneficiaries.

¶3104 FOREIGN TRUST WITH U.S. BENEFICIARY

(a) Grantor Treatment for U.S. Person Transferring Property to Foreign Trust with U.S. Beneficiary. IRC Sec. 679 provides that any U.S. person who transfers property to a foreign trust that has a U.S. beneficiary is treated as the owner of the portion of the trust that is attributable to the transferred property unless one of the

---

[2] Rev. Rul. 85-13, 1985-1 CB 184.

[3] Rev. Rul. 2004-64, 2004-2 CB 7.

exceptions discussed below applies [Reg. Sec. 1.679-1(a)]. Accordingly, the income received by the trust with respect to such transferred property is taxable to the transferor under the grantor trust rules. See ¶ 3100 for discussion of the grantor trust rules. These rules apply to transfers of property by any U.S. person, including transfers by U.S. citizens or residents, by domestic partnerships, by domestic corporations, and by estates or trusts that are not foreign estates or trusts.

> **Example 1:** A U.S. citizen transfers $50,000 to an existing trust in Canada on June 1. The U.S. citizen's son, who is also a U.S. citizen, is a beneficiary of the trust. The transfer increases the trust's principal to $100,000. The U.S. citizen must report his income on a calendar-year basis, and is required each year to report one-half of the income earned by the trust.

(b) Foreign Trust Transfers Covered by Grantor Trust Rules. The grantor trust rules apply to both direct and indirect transfers of property to a foreign trust [IRC Sec. 679(a)(1); Reg. Sec. 1.679-3(a)]. A transfer by a domestic or foreign entity in which a U.S. person has an interest may be regarded as an indirect transfer to the foreign trust by a U.S. person if the entity merely serves as a conduit for the transfer by the U.S. person or if the U.S. person has sufficient control over the entity to direct the transfer by the entity.

Likewise, an indirect transfer can occur if a foreign trust borrows money or other property and a U.S. person guarantees the loan. Transfers by U.S. persons are subject to the grantor trust rules regardless of whether the transfers are made without consideration from the trust or whether the transfers are sales or exchanges and include tax-free exchanges of property to the trust.

Transfers of property to a foreign trust with U.S. beneficiaries do not result in the treatment of the grantor as owner of the trust if the trust paid fair market value to the transferor for the property transferred [IRC Sec. 679(a)(2)(B)]. Obligations issued by the trust, by any grantor, owner, or beneficiary of the trust, or any person related to any grantor, owner, or beneficiary are generally not taken into account when applying this exception except as provided for in regulations [IRC Sec. 679(a)(3)]. Any obligation that bears arm's-length terms would qualify for the exception. Principal payments by the trust on any such obligations are taken into account on and after the date of the payment in determining the portion of the trust attributable to the property transferred [IRC Sec. 679(a)(3)(B)].

A foreign grantor who becomes a U.S. resident within five years of directly or indirectly transferring property to a foreign trust is also subject to the foreign grantor trust rule [IRC Sec. 679(a)(4)]. Such a person is treated as transferring the property to a foreign trust on the grantor's residency starting date. The amount deemed transferred is the portion of the trust attributable to the property previously transferred. Undistributed net income for periods before the grantor's residency starting date is taken into account in determining the portion of the trust that is attributable to the property transferred by the grantor to the trust, but is not otherwise taken into account [IRC Sec. 679(a)(4)(B)].

A U.S. citizen or resident who transfers property to a trust that becomes a foreign trust while the individual is alive is treated as transferring property to a foreign trust on the date the trust became a foreign trust. The amount of the deemed transfer is the portion of the trust attributable to the property previously transferred. Consequently, the individual generally is treated as the owner of that portion of the trust in any tax year in which the trust had U.S. beneficiaries [IRC Sec. 679(a)(5)].

(c) Exceptions. Transfers of property to a foreign trust with U.S. beneficiaries do not result in the transferor being treated as the trust owner if:

1. Any transfer of property to a foreign trust resulted from the death of the transferor;
2. Any transfer of property is to employee trusts which were created and organized outside the United States;
3. The transfer of property was made to a tax-exempt foreign trust (without regard to the requirements of Section 508(a)); or
4. The trust paid fair market value to the transferor for the property transferred to a foreign trust with U.S. beneficiaries.

[IRC Sec. 679(a)(2)(B); Reg. Sec. 1.679-4(a)]

If a foreign trust acquires a U.S. beneficiary in any tax year and has undistributed net income (accumulated income taxable to a beneficiary upon distribution) at the close of the tax year prior to the year that the beneficiary is acquired, the transferor of property is treated as having received additional income in the first tax year in which he becomes subject to the grantor trust rules. The amount of the additional income is equal to the undistributed net income attributable to the transferred property remaining in the trust at the end of the last tax year before the trust had a U.S. beneficiary [IRC Sec. 679(b)].

(d) When Foreign Trust Has U.S. Beneficiary. For purposes of IRC Sec. 679, a foreign trust will be treated as having a U.S. beneficiary for the tax year unless:

1. Under the terms of the trust, no part of the income or corpus of the trust may be paid or accumulated during the tax year to or for the benefit of a U.S. person [IRC Sec. 679(c)(1)(A)], and
2. If the trust is terminated at any time during the tax year, no part of the income or corpus of the trust may be paid to or for the benefit of a U.S. person [IRC Sec. 679(c)(1)(B); Reg. Sec. 1.679-2(a)(1)].

A trust also is considered as having a U.S. beneficiary: (1) if the trust has a controlled foreign corporation as a beneficiary, (2) the trust has a foreign partnership as a beneficiary when the partnership has a U.S. person as a partner, either directly or indirectly; and (3) if the foreign trust or estate has as its beneficiary another foreign trust or foreign estate that has a U.S. beneficiary [IRC Sec. 679(c)(2)]. A beneficiary is not treated as a U.S. beneficiary if the beneficiary first became a U.S. person more than five years after the date of the transfer of property to a foreign trust [IRC Sec. 679(c)(3)].

A year-by-year determination is to be made as to whether a foreign trust has a U.S. beneficiary. A trust has a U.S. beneficiary if the trust instrument includes existing U.S. persons as beneficiaries or if the trust instrument (taken together with any related written or oral agreements between the trustee and persons transferring property to the trust) gives to any person the authority to distribute income or corpus to unnamed persons generally or to any class of persons which includes U.S. persons [Reg. Sec. 1.679-2].

IRC Sec. 679(c)(1) provides that an amount is treated as accumulated for the benefit of a U.S. person even if the U.S. person's interest in the trust is contingent on a future event [IRC Sec. 679(c)(1); Reg. Sec. 1.679-2(a)(2)].

IRC Sec. 679(c)(4) provides that if any person has the discretion (by authority given in the trust agreement, by power of appointment, or otherwise) to make a distribution from the trust to or for the benefit of any person, the trust is treated as having a beneficiary who is a United States person unless (a) the terms of the trust specifically identify the class of persons to whom such distributions may be made, and (b) none of those persons are United States persons during the taxable year [IRC Sec. 679(c)(4)].

IRC Sec. 679(c)(5) provides that if any U.S. person who directly or indirectly transfers property to the trust is directly or indirectly involved in any agreement or understanding (whether written, oral, or otherwise) that may result in the income or corpus of the trust being paid or accumulated to or for the benefit of a U.S. person, the agreement or understanding is treated as a term of the trust [IRC Sec. 679(c)(5)]. It is assumed, for these purposes, that a transferor of property to the trust is generally directly or indirectly involved with agreements regarding the accumulation or disposition of the trust income and corpus.

For transfers of property after March 18, 2010, new IRC Sec. 679(d) provides that if a United States person directly or indirectly transfers property to a foreign trust (other than a trust described in IRC Sec. 6048(a)(3)(B)(ii)) the IRS may treat such trust as having a United States beneficiary for purposes of applying IRC Sec. 679 to the transfer unless the person demonstrates otherwise to the satisfaction of the IRS [IRC Sec. 679(d)].

For loans made, and uses of property, after March 18, 2010, pursuant to IRC Sec. 679(c)(6), for purposes of IRC Sec. 679(c), a loan of cash or marketable securities (or the use of any other trust property) directly or indirectly to or by any United States person (whether or not a beneficiary under the terms of the trust) is treated as paid or accumulated for the benefit of a United States person. However, this does not apply to the extent that the United States person repays the loan at a market rate of interest (or pays the fair market value of the use of such property) within a reasonable period of time [IRC Sec. 679(c)(6)].

(e) Is Trust Domestic or Foreign. A trust is treated as domestic if:

1. A U.S. court (federal, state, or local) exercises primary supervision over the administration of the trust ("the court test"); and

2. One or more U.S. individuals including fiduciaries have the authority to control all substantial decisions of the trust ("the control test") [IRC Sec. 7701(a)(30)(E); Reg. Sec. 301.7701-7(a)(1)].

A foreign trust means any trust other than a trust described under either "the court test" or "the control test" described above [IRC Sec. 7701(a)(31)(B)].

In addition, a U.S. trust may be treated as a foreign trust for purposes of the reporting requirements if it has substantial activities or holds substantial property outside the U.S.

¶3104

"Court test" safe harbor. A trust will be treated as a domestic trust for purposes of the court test if:

1. The trust instrument does not direct that the trust be administered outside the U.S.;
2. The trust is in fact administered exclusively in the U.S.; and
3. The trust has no automatic migration provision that either permits or requires the trust to essentially shift jurisdictions when certain events occur [Reg. Sec. 301.7701-7(c)(1)].

> **Example 2:** Alan creates a trust for the equal benefit of his two children, Bob and Carol. The trust instrument provides that ABCo, a Maryland state corporation, is the trustee of the trust. ABCo administers the trust exclusively in Maryland. The trust instrument is silent as to where the trust is to be administered. Even though this is so the trust is not subject to an automatic migration provision described above and the trust satisfies the court test safe harbor [Reg. Sec. 301.7701-7(c)(2), Example].

The following four specific situations are examples of situations that meet the court test [Reg. Sec. 301.7701-7(c)(4)]:

- **Uniform Probate Code.** A trust meets the court test if the trust is registered by an authorized fiduciary or fiduciaries of the trust in a court within the U.S. pursuant to a state statute that has provisions substantially similar to Article VII, *Trust Administration*, of the Uniform Probate Code.

- **Testamentary trust.** In the case of a trust created pursuant to the terms of a will probated within the U.S., if all fiduciaries of the trust have been qualified as trustees of the trust by a court within the U.S., the trust meets the court test.

- ***Inter vivos* trust.** In the case of a trust other than a testamentary trust, if the fiduciaries and/or beneficiaries take steps with a U.S. court that cause the administration of the trust to be subject to the primary supervision of the court, the trust meets the court test.

- **A U.S. court and a foreign court are able to exercise primary supervision over the administration of the trust.** If both a U.S. court and a foreign court are able to exercise primary supervision over the administration of the trust, the trust meets the court test.

"Control test" substantial decisions defined. In the "control test" discussed above, the term substantial decisions means those decisions that persons are authorized or required to make under the terms of the trust instrument and applicable law and that are not ministerial. Decisions that are ministerial include decisions regarding details such as the bookkeeping, the collection of rents, and the execution of investment decisions. Substantially decisions include, but are not limited to, decisions concerning the following: (1) whether and when to distribute income or corpus; (2) the amount of any distributions; (3) the selection of a beneficiary; (4) whether a receipt is allocable to income or principal; (5) whether to terminate the trust; (6) whether to compromise, arbitrate, or abandon claims of the trust; (7) whether to sue on behalf of the trust or to defend suits against the trust; (8) whether to remove, add, or replace a trustee; (9)

¶3104

whether to appoint a successor trustee to succeed a trustee who has died, resigned, or otherwise ceased to act as a trustee; and (10) investment decisions; however, if a U.S. person hires an investment advisor for the trust, investment decisions made by the investment advisor will be considered substantial decisions controlled by the U.S. person if the U.S. person can terminate the investment advisor's power to make investment decisions at will [Reg. Secs. 301.7701-7(d)(1)(ii)(A) through (J)].

> **Example 3:** Assume that a trust has three fiduciaries, Alice, Bob, and Carol. Alice and Bob are both U.S. citizens but Carol is a nonresident alien. No persons except the fiduciaries have authority to make any decisions of the trust. The trust instrument provides that no substantial decisions of the trust can be made unless there is unanimity among the fiduciaries. The control test is not satisfied because U.S. persons do not control all the substantial decisions of the trust. No substantial decisions can be made without Carol's agreement.

> **Example 4:** Same facts as Example 2 above, except that the trust instrument provides that all substantial decisions of the trust are to be decided by a majority vote among the fiduciaries. The control test is satisfied because a majority of the fiduciaries are U.S. persons and therefore U.S. persons control all the substantial decisions of the trust.

> **Example 5:** Same facts as in Example 3 above, except that the trust instrument directs that Carol is to make all the trust's investment decisions, but that Alice and Bob may veto Carol's investment decisions. Alice and Bob cannot act to make the investment decisions on their own. The control test is not satisfied because the U.S. persons, Alice and Bob, do not have the power to make all of the substantial decisions of the trust.

> **Example 6:** Same facts as in Example 4 above, except that Alice and Bob may accept or veto Carol's investment decisions and can make investments that Carol has not recommended. The control test is satisfied because the U.S. persons control all substantial decisions of the trust [Reg. Sec. 301.7701-7(d)(1)(v), Examples 1 through 4].

Safe harbor for employee benefit trusts and investment trusts. Regulations provide that the following types of trusts would satisfy the "control test" and would thus be considered domestic rather than foreign trusts and would not be subject to the onerous burdens imposed on foreign trusts: (1) a group trust described in Rev. Rul. 81-100,[1] which includes trusts that are components of qualified retirement plans and IRAs that pool their assets in a group trust; (2) an investment trust provided: (a) the all trustees are U.S. persons and at least one of the trustees is a bank, a U.S. government-owned agency, or enterprise; (b) all sponsors are U.S. persons; and (c) the beneficial interests

---

[1] **¶3104** Rev. Rul. 81-100, 1981-1 CB 326, *as modified by* Rev. Rul. 2004-67, 2004-2 CB 28.

¶3104

are widely offered for sale primarily in the U.S. to U.S. persons [Reg. Sec. 301.7701-7(d)(1)(iv)].

> **Example 7:** Trust is a testamentary trust with three fiduciaries, A, B, and C. A and B are U.S. citizens and C is a nonresident alien. No persons except the fiduciaries have authority to make any decisions of the trust. The trust instrument provides that no substantial decisions of the trust can be made unless there is unanimity among the fiduciaries. The control test is not satisfied because U.S. persons do not control all the substantial decisions of the trust. No substantial decisions can be made without C's agreement and C is an on resident alien.

(f) Reporting Requirements. The opportunity for tax avoidance from unreported transactions involving foreign trusts was so great, that lawmakers beefed up the information reporting requirements for both U.S. persons making transfers to foreign trusts and U.S. owners of foreign trusts.[2] As a result, anyone making any gratuitous transfers to a foreign trust is required to file information returns with the IRS when certain triggering events occur. Use IRS Form 3520, "Annual Return to Report Transactions with Foreign Trusts and Receipt of Certain Foreign Gifts," to comply with the reporting requirements on a single form.

Gratuitous transfer defined. A gratuitous transfer is any transfer other than a transfer for fair market value or a distribution from a corporation or partnership. A transfer may be considered gratuitous without regard to whether it would qualify as a gift for gift tax purposes. A transfer is for fair market value only to the extent that the value of the property received, services rendered, or right of use is equal to the fair market value of the property transferred. Thus, rents, royalties and compensation paid to a trust are transfers for fair market value only if the payments reflect an arm's-length price for the use of the property of, or services rendered by, the trust.

While nongratuitous transfers are generally not reportable under IRC Sec. 6048(a), any transfer in exchange for an obligation treated as a qualified obligation must also be reported. An obligation includes any bond, note, debenture, certificate, receivable or annuity contract. An obligation is a qualified obligation only if:

1. It is reduced to writing by written agreement;

2. Its term is five years or less;

3. All payments are denominated in U.S. dollars;

4. The yield to maturity is between 100 percent and 130 percent;

5. The tax (income and transfer) assessment period is extended to at least three years beyond the maturity date of the obligation; and

6. The U.S. transferor reports the status of the obligation, including principal and interest payments, on Form 3520 for each year that the obligation is outstanding.[3]

---

[2] Notice 97-34, 1997-1 CB 422. For reporting requirements for individuals holding interests in Canadian retirement plans, see Notice 2003-75, 2003-2 CB 1204.

[3] Notice 97-34, 1997-1 CB 422.

Trust grantors are required to file information returns with the IRS when the following "reportable events" occur:

- Creation of any foreign trust by a U.S. person;
- Direct and indirect transfer of any money or property to a foreign trust, including a transfer by reason of death;
- Death of a U.S. citizen or resident if the decedent was treated as the owner of any portion of a foreign trust or any portion of a foreign trust was included in a decedent's gross estate [IRC Sec. 6048(a)(3)];

Excluded from the definition of reportable transfers are fair market value sales to a foreign trust and transfers involving deferred compensation and charitable trusts [IRC Sec. 6048(a)(3)(B)].

The "responsible party" must file a written notice on or before the 90th day after one of these "reportable events" occurs. A "responsible party" includes the following people:

- Grantor, for the creation of an *inter vivos* trust;
- Transferor, in the case of a money or property transfer (except by reason of death); or
- Executor of a decedent's estate.

[IRC Sec. 6048(a)(4)]

Responsibilities of U.S. owner of foreign trust. A U.S. person who is treated as the owner of any portion of a foreign trust under the grantor trust rules is responsible for ensuring that the trust:

1. files a return containing a full and complete accounting of trust activities, the name of the U.S. agent for the trust, and any other required information, and
2. furnishes prescribed information to each U.S. person who is treated as owner of the trust or who receives a distribution from the trust.

[IRC Sec. 6048(b)(1)]

Penalties are imposed under IRC Sec. 6677(b) for failure to comply with these reporting requirements.

Reporting requirements imposed on U.S. beneficiaries of foreign trusts. If any United States person receives (directly or indirectly) a distribution from a foreign trust, the person must file a return which reports the name of such trust and the aggregate amount of the distributions received for the tax year [IRC Sec. 6048(c)(a)]. If the records provided are not adequate to determine the proper treatment of the distribution, the distribution will be treated as an accumulation distribution, unless the foreign trust elects to maintain a U.S. agent for the limited purpose of accepting service of process [IRC Sec. 6048(c)(2)]. If the accumulation distribution rules are applied, the accumulation distribution is deemed to come from the trust's average year (i.e., half the number of years the trust has been in existence).

> ►**PRACTICE ALERT:** Beware: "beneficiary" has broad meaning. The definition of beneficiary is important under the reporting requirements because a U.S. beneficiary who receives a distribution, directly or indirectly, from a foreign trust must report the name of the trust and the amount of the distribution if he

¶3104

knows or has reason to know that the trust is a foreign trust. The term "benefici-ary" is defined very broadly to include any person that could possibly benefit, directly or indirectly, from a foreign trust at any time. This includes persons who could benefit if the trust were amended, whether or not the person is named in the trust instrument as a beneficiary or whether or not the person is eligible to receive a distribution in the current year.

Civil penalty imposed for failure to file foreign trust information returns. Certain events with respect to foreign trusts require responsible parties to comply with reporting requirements. Reportable events include:

1. The creation of a foreign trust by a U.S. person;

2. The transfer of money or property (either directly or indirectly) to a foreign trust by a U.S. person; and

3. The death of a U.S. citizen or resident if the decedent was treated as the owner of any portion of a foreign trust under the grantor trust rules or a portion of the foreign trust was includible in the decedent's gross estate.

After any of these events, the responsible party is generally required to provide the IRS with information on the amount of money or property transferred and the identity of the trust, trustee and each beneficiary [IRC Sec. 6048(a)(3)(A)]. IRC Sec. 6048 further requires that any U.S. person who receives any distribution from a foreign trust, either directly or indirectly, report such distribution to the IRS [IRC Sec. 6048(c)].

If the information required by IRC Sec. 6048 is not timely filed or is incomplete or incorrect, a penalty of 35 percent of the gross reportable amount is imposed against the foreign trust. If the failure continues for more than 90 days after the IRS mails notice of the failure, an additional penalty of $10,000 is imposed for each 30-day period or portion thereof. The penalty may not exceed the reportable amount [IRC Sec. 6677(a)]. Deficiency procedures do not apply for the assessment and collection of this penalty [IRC Sec. 6677(e)].

Civil penalty for failure by grantor trust to file foreign trust information returns. A U.S. person who is treated as the owner of any portion of a foreign trust under the grantor trust rules is responsible for ensuring that the trust: (1) files a return containing a full and complete accounting of trust activities, provides the name of the U.S. agent for the trust, and any other information the Secretary prescribes; and (2) furnishes other information that the IRS may prescribe to each U.S. person who is treated as owner of the trust or who receives a distribution from the trust [IRC Sec. 6048(b)(1)].

If a U.S. grantor fails to ensure compliance with reporting requirements by a foreign trust, the penalty of five percent rather than 35 percent of the gross reportable amount is imposed. If the failure continues for more than 90 days after the IRS mails notice of the failure, an additional penalty of $10,000 for each 30-day period (or portion thereof) is imposed. The penalty may not exceed the reportable amount [IRC Sec. 6677(b)].

Reasonable cause exception. There is a reasonable cause exception to the penalty imposed for failure to file the required information returns. Thus, if the failure to file is due to reasonable cause and not to willful neglect, no penalty is imposed. The fact that a foreign jurisdiction would impose a civil or criminal penalty on the taxpayer for disclosing the required information is not considered reasonable cause [IRC Sec. 6677(d)].

Examples: Assume the following facts exist: A is a U.S. citizen. DC is a domestic corporation. DT is a domestic trust. FT is a foreign trust.

Example 8: *Contribution to FT.* A contributed cash to FT, through a broker, in exchange for units in FT. The value of the units in FT is disregarded in determining whether A has received fair market value. The contribution by A is therefore a gratuitous transfer and must be reported.

Example 9: *Interest payment to FT.* A borrows cash from FT, an unrelated foreign trust. Arm's-length interest payments by A will not be treated as gratuitous transfers. Thus, A is not required to report the interest payments.

Example 10: *Trust distribution to FT.* A created and funded DT. After A's death, DT distributes cash to FT, which is a beneficiary of DT. The trust distribution by DT is a gratuitous transfer. DT must report the distribution.

Example 11: *Dividend payment to FT.* A creates and funds FT, which owns stock of DC, a publicly traded company, which pays a dividend to FT. The dividend is not a gratuitous transfer and need not be reported.

(g) Foreign Person as Trust Grantor. In an effort to stop foreign persons from using the grantor trust rules to avoid tax, foreign trusts are treated as taxable entities and U.S. beneficiaries are subject to federal income tax on distributions from these trusts [IRC Sec. 672(f)]. The inbound trust rules in IRC Sec. 672 govern the tax treatment of U.S. persons who benefit from offshore trusts created by foreign persons.

The U.S. grantor trust rules generally do not apply to any portion of a trust that would otherwise be deemed to be owned by a foreign person. Rather, the grantor trust rules are generally applied only when the rules result in amounts being taken into account, either directly or indirectly through an entity, in computing the income of a U.S. citizen or resident or a domestic corporation. The grantor trusts rules apply to the extent that any portion of a trust is treated as owned by a U.S. citizen or resident or domestic corporation [IRC Sec. 672(f)(1); Reg. Sec. 1.672(f)-1(a)(1)].

The grantor trust rules also apply in the following limited situations:

1. To revocable trusts where the power to revest absolutely in the grantor title to the trust property is exercisable solely by the grantor and not conditioned on approval or consent of any person, and the grantor has such power for at least 183 days during the tax year of the trust;
2. To trusts where distributions of income or corpus during the grantor's lifetime are only distributable to the grantor or the grantor's spouse;

¶3104

3. To compensatory trusts, such as nonexempt employees' trusts or "rabbi trusts," and any other trusts designated by the IRS; and

4. To trusts owned by the grantor or another person [IRC Sec. 672(f)(2); Reg. Sec. 1.672(f)-3].

A taxpayer is treated as the true grantor of a foreign trust and is therefore taxed on the income of the foreign trust if that person:

1. Is the trust's beneficiary; and

2. Made direct or indirect gifts to the supposed foreign grantor who otherwise would have been treated as the owner under the grantor trust rules. This rule applies, however, only to the extent it results, directly or indirectly, in income being taken currently into account in computing the income of a U.S. citizen or resident or a domestic corporation [IRC Sec. 672(f)(1)]. Therefore, trust income from a foreign grantor trust will be taxable to the U.S. beneficiary when distributions are made to the U.S. beneficiary.

The IRS has issued regulations governing the tax treatment of U.S. persons who benefit from offshore trusts created by foreign trusts (inbound trusts) [Reg. Sec. 1.672(f)-1]. The result is that many foreign trusts treated as grantor trusts under prior law will now be treated as nongrantor trusts, subjecting the beneficiaries to U.S. tax.

The rules subject beneficiaries to tax on amounts received directly or indirectly from a foreign trust and cover the circumstances under which a distribution from a foreign trust received through an intermediary will be treated as having been received directly from the foreign trust.

The amount will be deemed to have been paid directly by the foreign trust if one of the three following conditions is satisfied:

1. The intermediary is a related party to the U.S. beneficiary or the foreign trust and transfers property received from the trust;

2. The intermediary would not have made the transfer except for receiving property from the trust; or

3. The intermediary received the property from the trust as part of a plan to avoid U.S. tax.

   NOTE: The rule does not apply if the intermediary is the grantor of the portion of the trust from which the distribution was made.

(h) Tax Treatment of Transfers by U.S. Person of Property to Foreign Trusts/Estates.
Any transfer of property by a U.S. person to a foreign trust or estate is treated as a sale or exchange of the property for its fair market value (FMV). The U.S. transferor must recognize gain equal to the excess of the property's FMV over its adjusted basis in the hands of the transferor under IRC Sec. 684(a). This immediate recognition-of-gain rule will not apply to a transfer to a trust by a United States person to the extent that any person is treated as the owner of such trust under the grantor trust rules of IRC Sec. 671 [IRC Sec. 684(b)]. An exception is also provided if a trust which is not a foreign trust becomes a foreign trust. In this situation, the trust will be treated as having transferred, immediately before becoming a foreign trust, all of its assets to the foreign trust [IRC Sec. 684(c)].

If a trust which is not a foreign trust becomes a foreign trust, the trust will be treated as having transferred, immediately before becoming a foreign trust, all of its assets to the foreign trust [IRC Sec. 684(c)].

The following examples from Reg. Sec. 1.684-1(d), illustrate these rules. In all examples, A is a U.S. person and FT is a foreign trust:

Example 12: *Transfer to foreign trust.* A transfers property that has a fair market value of $1,000 to FT. A's adjusted basis in the property is $400. FT has no U.S. beneficiary and no person is treated as owning any portion of FT. A recognizes gain at the time of the transfer equal to $600.

Example 13: *Transfer of multiple properties.* A transfers property Q, with a fair market value of $1,000, and property R, with a fair market value of $2,000, to FT. At the time of the transfer, A's adjusted basis in property Q is $700, and A's adjusted basis in property R is $2,200. A recognizes the $300 of gain attributable to property Q. A does not recognize the $200 loss attributable to property R, and may not offset that loss against the gain attributable to property Q.

Example 14: *Transfer for less than fair market value.* A transfers property that has a fair market value of $1,000 to FT in exchange for $400 of cash. A's adjusted basis in the property is $200. A recognizes gain at the time of the transfer equal to $800.

Example 15: *Exchange of property for private annuity.* A transfers property that has a fair market value of $1,000 to FT in exchange for FT's obligation to pay A $50 per year for the rest of A's life. A's adjusted basis in the property is $100. A is required to recognize gain equal to $900 immediately upon transfer of the property to the trust. This result applies even though A might otherwise have been allowed to defer recognition of gain under another provision of the Code.

¶3105 REPORTING REQUIREMENTS FOR GRANTOR TRUSTS

Generally, the trustee must file a return on Form 1041 and report only the part of the income that is taxable to the trust. When a grantor trust exists, the return preparer should attach a separate sheet of paper to the Form 1041 in order to report the following:

- The income of the trust that is taxable to the grantor or another person;
- The name, identifying number, and address of the person(s) to whom the income is taxable; and
- Any deductions or credits applied to this income [Reg. Sec. 1.671-4(a)].

The income that is taxable to the grantor or another person and the deductions and credits applied to the income must be reported on the Form 1040 filed by grantor.

(a) Optional Filing Methods for Certain Grantor Type Trusts. Three optional filing methods are available for certain grantor type trusts. The optional methods are alternatives to filing Form 1041 for these trusts. The three optional methods are discussed below [Reg. Sec. 1.671-4].

Method 1. For a trust treated as owned by one grantor or by one other person, the trustee must give all payors of income during the tax year the name and taxpayer identification number (TIN) of the grantor or other person treated as the owner of the trust and the address of the trust [Reg. Sec. 1.671-4(b)(1)]. This method may be used only if the owner of the trust provides the trustee with a signed Form W-9, "Request for Taxpayer Identification Number and Certification." In addition, unless the grantor or other person treated as owner of the trust is the trustee or a co-trustee of the trust, the trustee must give the grantor or other person treated as owner of the trust a statement that:

1. Shows all items of income, deduction, and credit of the trust;
2. Identifies the payor of each item of income;
3. Explains how the grantor or other person treated as owner of the trust takes those items into account when figuring the grantor's or other person's taxable income or tax; and
4. Informs the grantor or other person treated as the owner of the trust that those items must be included when figuring taxable income and credits on his or her income tax return.

Method 2. For a trust treated as owned by one grantor or by one other person, the trustee must give all payors of income during the tax year the name, address, and TIN of the trust [Reg. Sec. 1.671-4(b)(2)]. The trustee also must file with the IRS the appropriate Forms 1099 to report the income or gross proceeds paid to the trust during the tax years that shows the trust as the payor and the grantor or other person treated as owner as the payee. The trustee must report each type of income in the aggregate and each item of gross proceeds separately. In addition, unless the grantor, or other person treated as owner of the trust is the trustee or a co-trustee of the trust, the trustee must give the grantor or other person treated as owner of the trust a statement that:

1. Shows all items of income, deduction, and credit of the trust;
2. Explains how the grantor or other person treated as owner of the trust takes those items into account when figuring the grantor's or other person's taxable income or tax; and
3. Informs the grantor or other person treated as the owner of the trust that those items must be included when figuring income and credits on his or her income tax return. This statement satisfies the requirement to give the recipient copies of the Forms 1099 filed by the trustee.

Method 3. For a trust treated as owned by two or more grantors or other persons, the trustee must give all payors of income during the tax year the name, address, and TIN of the trust [Reg. Sec. 1.671-4(b)(3)]. The trustee also must file with the IRS the appropriate Forms 1099 to report the income or gross proceeds paid to the trust by all payors during the tax year attributable to the part of the trust treated as owned by each grantor or other person, showing the trust as the payor and each grantor or other person treated as owner of the trust as the payee. The trustee must report each type of income in the aggregate and each item of gross proceeds separately. In addition, the trustee must give each grantor or other person treated as owner of the trust a statement that:

1. Shows all items of income, deduction, and credit of the trust attributable to the part of the trust treated as owned by the grantor or other person;

2. Explains how the grantor or other person treated as owner of the trust takes those items into account when figuring the grantor's or other person's taxable income tax; and

3. Informs the grantor or other person treated as the owner of the trust that those items must be included when figuring taxable income and credits on his or her income tax return. This statement satisfies the requirement to give the recipient copies of the Form 1099 filed by the trustee.

(b) Which Trusts Are Eligible to Use Optional Filing Methods. The following trusts cannot use the optional filing methods [Reg. Sec. 1.671-4(b)(6)]:

- A common trust fund [IRC Sec. 584(a)];
- A foreign trust or a trust that has any of its assets located outside the United States;
- A qualified subchapter S trust [IRC Sec. 1361(d)(3)];
- A grantor trust with an owner not on the calendar year;
- A grantor trust with an owner who is not a U.S. person;
- A grantor trust if at least one grantor or other person is an exempt recipient for information reporting purposes, unless at least one grantor or other person is not an exempt recipient and the trustee reports without treating any of the grantors or other persons as exempt recipients.

(c) Reporting Requirements for Widely Held Fixed Investment Trusts. The IRS has provided guidance on investment trusts that are not considered business entities for tax purposes [Reg. Sec. 1.671-5]. These trusts are classified as either widely held fixed investment trusts (WHFITs) or widely held mortgage trusts (WHMTs). Even though the "check-the-box" regulations [Reg. Sec. 301.7701-4(c)] classify these entities as trusts, they are treated as a grantor trust and items of income, deduction, and credit must be reported to the unit interest holder. WHMTs and WHFITs are treated as grantor trusts because the beneficial interests are divided into unit interests frequently owned by many beneficiaries but controlled by a "middleman" [Reg. Sec. 1.671-5(b)(22)]. The trustees communicate with the middlemen and often do not know the identities of or communicate with the beneficial owners. The middleman is therefore required to make reports of the WHFIT/WHMT tax information to the IRS and provide the same information to the individual beneficiaries [Reg. Sec. 1.671-5(d) and Reg. Sec. 1.671-5(c)]. The trustees of the WHFIT/WHMT must provide the information required under Reg. Sec. 1.671-5(d) to middlemen and other parties, but will no longer be required to file a Form 1041 under Reg. Sec. 1.671-4(a).

¶3105

General reporting requirements. In general, the trustees and middlemen of widely held fixed investment trusts (WHFITs) are required to report the following:

1. Information identifying the WHFIT including the classification as either a widely held mortgage trust (WHMT) or a non-mortgage widely held fixed investment trust (NMWHFIT);

2. Items of income, expense and credit;

3. Non pro-rata principal payments;

4. Asset sales and dispositions;

5. Redemptions and sales of WHFIT interests;

6. Information regarding bond premiums;

7. Information regarding market discount; and

8. Other information necessary for a beneficial owner of a trust interest to report, with reasonable accuracy, the items attributable to the portion of trust treated as owned by the beneficial owner under IRC Sec. 671 and Reg. Sec. 1.671-5(c)(2).

Reg. Sec. 1.671-5(f) has rules regarding the safe harbor reporting requirements for WHFITs. Included in the safe harbor information is specific guidance for the reporting of income and expenses, original issue discount (OID), asset sales and redemptions, or sales in secondary markets. WHMTs have their own safe harbor in Reg. Sec. 1.671-5(g). Included in the safe harbor information is specific guidance for the reporting of income, expenses, principal receipts, sales and dispositions of mortgages, OID, market discount information, and premium information.

APPENDIX

GLOSSARY OF TERMS

A Trust Another term for the marital deduction trust; the complement of the so-called B or family trust.

Accuracy-Related Penalty IRC Sec. 6662 imposes an accuracy-related penalty on any portion of an underpayment attributable to one or more of the following:

(1) Negligence or disregard of the rules and regulations [IRC Sec. 6662(c)];

(2) Any substantial understatement of income tax [IRC Sec. 6662(d)];

(3) Any substantial valuation misstatement [IRC Sec. 6662(e)];

(4) Any substantial overstatement of pension liabilities [IRC Sec. 6662(f)]; and

(5) Any substantial estate or gift tax valuation understatement [IRC Sec. 6662(g)].

The amount of the penalty is 20 percent of the portion of the underpayment resulting from the misconduct. Only a single 20 percent penalty may be imposed on any portion of an underpayment, even if that portion is attributable to more than one of the prohibited behaviors; stacking penalties is not permitted. For example, if a portion of an underpayment is attributable to both negligence and a substantial understatement of income tax, the maximum accuracy-related penalty is 20 percent of that portion [Reg. Sec. 1.6662-1(c)]. Further, no accuracy-related penalty is imposed for a failure to collect and pay over tax under IRC Sec. 6672, or an attempt to evade or defeat tax. The rate of the penalty is increased to 40 percent for "gross valuation misstatements" [IRC Sec. 6662(h)].

Actuarial Tables Tables used to determine the life expectancies of individuals in order to value property for purposes of annuities or remainders. The Treasury Department publishes extensive tables for estate and gift tax purposes, as well as for determining the taxability of annuity payments.

Additional Estate Tax Return IRS Form 706-A, used to report additional federal estate taxes due to an early disposition or cessation of use of property that qualified for special use evaluation.

Administration, Estate The activity of an executor or administrator in supervising and in winding up a decedent's estate. The term begins on the date of death and ends with the complete distribution of the estate's assets and the discharge of the liabilities.

Administration Expenses Expenses incurred in the administration of the decedent's estate, including executors' or administrators' commissions, attorney's fees, and miscellaneous expenses [Reg. Sec. 20.2053-3]. Administration expenses will be allowed even if the expense has not been fixed in amount [Reg. Sec. 20.2053-1(b)(3)]. Such expenses are allowable for estate taxes or income taxes, but not both [IRC Sec. 642(g); Reg. Sec. 1.642(g)-1].

Appendix A

Administrative Powers Powers held by a grantor of a trust (or a nonadverse party, or both) to deal with trust income or corpus for less than adequate consideration [IRC Sec. 675]. The existence of administrative powers result in taxation to the grantor. The principal powers are to borrow on inadequate terms (i.e., too low an interest rate, or with inadequate security) and to engage in unfair sales or exchanges with the trust. In addition IRC Sec. 675(4) taxes grantors who can acquire options over trust property or who can direct investments and voting power over corporations identified with the grantor. In addition, failure to repay loans from the trust by year-end causes the grantor (or spouse) to be taxed on unpaid balances.

Administrator An individual or entity appointed to undertake the administration or supervision of a decedent's estate. Administrators are judicially appointed, whereas an executor (sometimes "executrix" in the case of a female) is designated by will. This phrase also refers to persons who administer employee benefit plans.

Administratrix A female administrator of a decedent's estate.

Adverse Interest The interest of a party whose interests would be negatively affected by the exercise or nonexercise by someone else of their interest.

Adverse Party A party who has substantial beneficial interest that could be negatively affected by the exercise or nonexercise of a power granted by a trust instrument [IRC Sec. 672(a); Reg. Sec. 1.672(a)-1(a)]. The term is significant for questions of whether income earned by a trust should be taxed to the grantor, or to the trust and its beneficiaries. Beneficiaries and persons with general powers of appointment are generally considered to be adverse parties, although a party is always only adverse to the extent of his or her share of the income or corpus of the trust [Reg. Sec. 1.672(a)-1(b)].

Alternate Valuation Date The date six months after the decedent's death [IRC Sec. 2032].

Alternate Valuation Date Election An election permitting the executor or administrator of a decedent's estate to value all the assets of the estate on the alternative valuation date, which is six months after decedent's death [IRC Sec. 2032]. The executor cannot make the election on an item-by-item basis. All the assets are valued either immediately after death or six months later. The election can be made only if the value of the gross estate and the estate tax (after credits) decline as a result of its use. The purpose of the statute is to give relief in situations where values decline rapidly after someone dies.

Alternative Minimum Tax (AMT) The AMT is a parallel tax system designed to ensure that taxpayers pay "enough" income tax. Originally targeted against only very wealthy taxpayers, the AMT now reaches deep into the middle class, and disallows many tax benefits in computing the AMT. Taxpayers pay AMT if it exceeds their "regular" tax.

Annual Exclusion Amount In 2014, the first $14,000 of gifts made to any person by the donor during the calendar year is not included in the total amount of gifts made by the donor for purposes of IRC Sec. 2503(a). If a donor elects to split gifts with his spouse, the first $28,000 of gifts to a particular individual during a calendar year are excluded from the gift tax. The amount of this exclusion, set forth in IRC Sec. 2503(b), is referred to as the gift tax "annual exclusion amount." If a donor does not make gifts of over $14,000 to any one person during the year, there will be no potential gift

Appendix A

tax liability. In the case of gifts in trust, the trust beneficiaries (rather than the trust or trustees) are treated as the donees for the purpose of determining the number of annual exclusions allowable to the donor.

Annual Gift Tax Exclusion An Internal Revenue Code provision under which a donor may exclude the first $14,000 in 2014 of total gifts made during each calendar year to an unlimited number of donees. The exclusion is not allowed if the gift is of a future interest or if the value of a present interest is not ascertainable. In the case of joint gifts (often referred to as split gifts) by married persons, the annual exclusion is $28,000 in 2013 per donee, regardless of who actually supplied or owned the property [IRC Sec. 2503(b)]. Unused annual gift tax exclusions cannot be carried forward to the next year.

Annuity An annuity is a fixed amount which is typically payable for a period of years, the annuitant's lifetime, or a combination of the two. Annuities offer the certainty of a steady income stream for investors. *See also* Private Annuity.

Applicable Exclusion Amount The amount that each person is allowed to transfer of a certain amount of property that will not be subject to the estate tax. This amount is referred to in the tax code as the applicable exclusion amount. (The applicable exclusion amount is translated into an applicable credit amount in actually computing the estate and gift tax.) The applicable exclusion amount is determined by the year of death. In 2013 the applicable exclusion amount is $5,250,000 (increased from $5,120,000 in 2012). Also referred to as the exemption equivalent.

Applicable Federal Rate (AFR) The AFR is computed by the IRS as provided in IRC Sec. 1274(d) and is published monthly for use in connection with various provisions, including, but not limited to, IRC Sec. 42, IRC Sec. 382, IRC Sec. 483, IRC Sec. 642, IRC Sec. 807, IRC Sec. 846, IRC Sec. 1288, IRC Sec. 6621, IRC Sec. 7520 and IRC Sec. 7872. The AFR is computed monthly on the basis of the average market yield on outstanding marketable short-term, mid-term, and long-term obligations of the United States. The short-term AFR applies to debt instruments with terms not over three years, the mid-term AFR applies to debt instruments with terms over three years but not over nine years, and the long-term AFR applies to debt instruments with terms over nine years [IRC Sec. 1274(d)(1)(A)]. The deemed interest rate that a lender and a borrower must use for a below-market term loan is to be determined by reference to the term of the loan and the AFR corresponding to the term of the loan. In the case of a term loan, the applicable federal rate is the AFR in effect under IRC Sec. 1274(d) as of the day on which the loan was made. In the case of a demand loan, the AFR is the short-term rate in effect under IRC Sec. 1274(d) for the period for which the amount of the forgone interest is being determined. In the case of a below-market demand loan of a fixed principal amount that remains outstanding for the entire calendar year, IRC Sec. 7872(e)(2) provides a special formula for computing the interest amount.

Applicable Fraction, Generation-Skipping Transfer A fraction whose numerator is the amount of generation-skipping transfer GST exemption and whose denominator is the total value of a transferor's GST [IRC Sec. 2642(a)(2)]. The value of a GST is determined at the time of transfer, and deductions are permitted for charitable contributions and state or federal estate taxes paid from the property. When the fraction is subtracted from one, the result is the inclusion ratio for purposes of the GST tax. The inclusion ratio times the maximum federal estate tax rate equals the so-

Appendix A

called applicable rate. The applicable rate times the taxable amount equals the tax imposed by the GST tax.

Applicable Rate, Generation-Skipping Transfer Tax The rate of GST tax applied to the value of property transferred in generation-skipping transfers. The rate is calculated by multiplying the maximum federal estate tax rate at the time of the transfer, by the inclusion ratio.

Appreciation in Value The increase in value of property due to market conditions. When you sell appreciated property, you pay tax on the appreciation that has occurred from the date you bought or inherited the property.

Art Advisory Panel An Internal Revenue Service (IRS) panel of experts who meet periodically to assign values to particular works of art for federal income, estate, and gift tax purposes.

Ascertainable Standard, Power of Appointment Powers to consume, invade, or appropriate property for the benefit of the donee or decedent that are limited by an ascertainable standard relating to the health, education, support, or maintenance of the donee or decedent. For example, comfort, welfare, and happiness do not qualify as ascertainable standards, but maintaining an accustomed standard of living does [Reg. Secs. 25.2514-1(c)(2) (gift taxes), 20.2041-1(c)(2) (estate taxes)].

Audit An IRS examination of your tax return. The audit period is generally limited to the three-year period after you file your return.

B Trust Another term for the family trust, which is the trust established for the disposition of assets to children in order to keep the decedent's assets out of the surviving spouse's gross estate. It is the complement of the so-called A or marital deduction trust.

Basis A tax term that generally refers to the amount that you paid for property. In order to figure out your gain or loss when you sell property you will need to know the basis.

Beneficial Enjoyment, Control Over The power to direct beneficial enjoyment of a trust. IRC Section 674 taxes the grantor (or his or her spouse) of a trust if the grantor or a nonadverse party, or both, can dispose of trust income or corpus without the consent of an adverse party. Included are retained powers to change beneficiaries, or to change remainder interests.

Blockage Rule A theory applied in valuing property to account for the depressive price effect of suddenly placing a large amount of property on the market. It is commonly applied in valuing stocks and securities for federal estate tax purposes. The fair-market value of stock and securities applying the blockage rule is the price obtainable in a reasonable time without depressing the market [Reg. Secs. 20.2031-2(e), 25.2512-2(e)].

Borrowing of Trust Funds, Grantor Trust Rules Any direct or indirect borrowing of the income of a trust, by a grantor, without repaying the loan and the interest in its entirety, before the beginning of the taxable year. The grantor making such a loan is treated as the owner of the portion of the trust from which the money is borrowed [IRC Sec. 675(3)].

Buy-Sell Agreement In a buy-sell agreement, a corporation or individual (usually another stockholder) promises to buy stock, and the stockholder promises to sell,

Appendix A

upon the happening of some event, usually the death of a stockholder. If the parties to the buy-sell agreement are not related, the price contained in the agreement will set the estate tax value of the stock if: (1) the price of the stock is fixed or determined by a formula within the agreement; (2) the estate is required to sell the stock at the fixed price; and (3) the agreement represents a bona fide business arrangement, rather than serving as a device for passing the shares to the "natural objects of [the decedent's] bounty" for less than full and adequate consideration. If the decedent-shareholder sells stock during his life, he must sell the shares at the price fixed by the agreement. A buy-sell agreement between family members that was created, or substantially modified after October 8, 1990, will not set the estate tax value unless it can be shown that the agreement: (1) is a bona fide business arrangement; (2) is not a device for passing the property to the natural objects of the decedent's bounty for less than full and adequate consideration; and (3) is comparable to similar agreements entered into by persons in an arm's length transaction [Reg. Sec. 25.2703-1(b)]. These three requirements will be considered to have been satisfied where more than 50 percent of the value of the property subject to the agreement is owned by individuals who are not members of the decedent's family.

Bypass Trust *See* Credit Shelter Trust.

Calendar Year A taxable year that ends on December 31.

Carryover Basis A concept that is used to determine a taxpayer's gain or loss. According to carryover basis, the donor's basis in property generally carries over to the donee, adjusted as provided in IRC Sec. 1015.

Charitable Lead Trust (CLT) A valuable estate-planning tool that commits income from property to charity for a fixed number of years, after which the remainder interest is distributed to noncharitable beneficiaries, usually the donor's children. Each year the trustees distribute a fixed amount to the designated charities. When the charity's interest terminates, the trust assets will pass to your heirs. There are numerous benefits to the charitable lead trust. First, the estate gets a charitable estate tax deduction, which will greatly reduce estate taxes. The charitable lead trust also saves taxes because only the "present value" of the family's remainder interest, rather than the entire value of the assets transferred to the trust, are transferred to your children. You can make the taxable remainder interest practically vanish by combining the right set of numbers. A basic rule of thumb emerges after you begin working with the government's actuarial factors to compute the value of the remainder interest. The larger the income interest and the longer the trust term, the more valuable the income interest becomes and the value of the taxable remainder interest diminishes and taxes are reduced. Second, if the property in trust appreciates in value, at the termination of the charity's interest, the grandchildren will receive the property at its increased value, without paying tax on the appreciation. Finally, during the period when the charitable foundation has an income interest, the distributions to charity will benefit others.

Charitable Remainder Trust (CRT) A split-interest trust in which the remainder interest goes to a charitable donee so the estate can claim a charitable deduction [IRC Sec. 2055(e)]. Charitable remainder trusts can either be in the form of a *charitable remainder annuity trust (CRAT)*, a *charitable remainder unitrust (CRUT)* or a *pooled income fund*. A *CRAT* is a trust from which a sum certain or a specified amount must be paid to the income beneficiary or beneficiaries. When current payments terminate,

Appendix A

the trust's assets must go to or for the use of a charitable organization. The value of the remainder interest can qualify as a current charitable contribution [IRC Sec. 170(f)(2)]. These trusts are not subject to tax, unless they have unrelated business taxable income [IRC Sec. 664(d)(1)]. IRC Sec. 2055(e) authorizes an estate tax deduction. A *CRUT* is a trust providing that the trustee must pay to one or more noncharitable beneficiaries for life, or for a term not greater than 20 years, a sum which is no greater than 50 percent of the value of the trust fund, with the remainder of the property transferred to a charitable organization [IRC Sec. 664(d)]. CRUTs and CRATs must meet 10 percent minimum remainder interest requirements. This means that the value of the charitable remainder must be at least 10 percent of the initial fair-market value of all trust assets on the date the property was contributed to the trust [IRC Secs. 664(d)(1), 664(d)(2)].

Charitable Trust An exempt organization operated exclusively for charitable and other purposes described in IRC Sec. 501(c)(3). The creation of, or addition to, a charitable trust may entitle the donor or settlor of the trust to an estate tax deduction or an income tax deduction.

Check-The-Box Regulation A regulation adopted in December 1996, Reg. Sec. 301.7701-3, that allows an unincorporated business entity the discretion to choose whether the entity will be taxed as a corporation or a partnership.

Closely Held Corporation A corporation whose stock is owned by a relatively small group of shareholders, often family members. The IRS often subjects closely held corporations to special scrutiny and statutory control because of their potential for tax abuse.

Code Sec. 7520 Interest Rate The Code Sec. 7520 interest rate is the key interest rate used to value private annuities, life interests or interests for terms of years and remainder or reversionary interests for estate and gift tax purposes. The Code Sec. 7520 interest rate is based on market rates and recalculated monthly by the IRS. Transfer taxes are partly based on the Code Sec. 7520 interest rate, thus impacting the timing of certain asset transfers and estate planning strategies. Certain trusts and private annuity arrangements thrive when the interest rate is low.

College Savings Plan A college savings plan is a program established and maintained by a state instrumentality (such as a brokerage house) under which a person may make cash contributions to an account established solely for meeting the qualified higher education expenses of the designated beneficiary of the account [IRC Sec. 529(b)(1)]. Two types of college savings plans are available under IRC Sec. 529: the college savings plan and the "qualified state tuition program." (See definition in this Glossary under "Qualified State Tuition Program"). Taxpayers may not contribute to both on behalf of the same beneficiary. The more popular college funding option is the college savings plan. With this plan your contributions are invested by the brokerage house pursuant to any option you choose and the account balance is available to pay tuition and other educational expenses of the beneficiary when needed. Funds in the plan can be used to pay for "qualified higher education expenses" at any eligible college, university, or vocational school in the United States [IRC Sec. 529(b)(1)]. Contributions to college savings plans are not deductible and all distributions including the earnings are tax-free provided they are used to pay for "qualified higher education expenses" [IRC Sec. 529(c)(1)]. Distributions not used for qualified higher education expenses are subject to tax as well as an additional 10

Appendix A

percent penalty tax. Amounts in a qualified tuition program may be rolled over tax-free to an account for another individual who is a member of the family of the beneficiary. The tax code provides a lengthy list of family members who qualify, including the beneficiary's spouse, parents, children, stepchildren, grandchildren, siblings, cousins, nieces and nephews, aunts and uncles, and in-laws.

Community Property A marital property regime followed by nine states (Arizona, California, Idaho, Louisiana, Nevada, New Mexico, Texas, Washington and Wisconsin) under which a husband and wife own equal interests in property acquired during marriage.

Complex Trust Any trust that is not a simple trust. This means that a complex trust may (1) accumulate income because it is not required to distribute all of its income currently, (2) distribute corpus, or (3) have a charitable beneficiary and therefore permit funds to be permanently set aside or used for charitable purposes [IRC Secs. 661–663].

Conservation Easement A voluntary burden or restriction placed on the use of land that is created to protect the land from future development. Typically, a donor and a charitable organization enter into a written agreement describing the restrictions that will limit use of the land. The agreement is recorded in the real estate records.

Covered Expatriate A "covered expatriate" for purposes of the expatriation tax rules under IRC Sec. 877A is any U.S. citizen who relinquishes citizenship and any long-term U.S. resident who ceases to be a lawful permanent resident of the United States, if the individual: (1) has an average annual net income tax liability for the five preceding years ending before the date of the loss of U.S. citizenship or lawful permanent residency that exceeds $157,000 in 2014 ("tax liability test"); (2) has a net worth of $2 million or more on that date ("net worth test"); or (3) fails to certify under penalties of perjury that he or she has complied with all U.S. tax obligations for the preceding five years or fails to submit evidence of compliance as required by the IRS.

Credit for Tax on Prior Transfers A credit allowed against the federal estate tax for all or a part of the estate tax paid with respect to the transfer of property to the present decedent by or from a person who died within ten years before, or two years after the decedent [IRC Sec. 2013(a); Reg. Sec. 20.2013-1(a)]. The tax is computed on Schedule Q, "Credit for Tax on Prior Transfers" of IRS Form 706, "United States Estate (and Generation-Skipping Transfer) Tax Return."

Credit Shelter Trust A trust that receives the value of the exemption equivalent in assets as provided in a decedent's will. It absorbs the unified transfer tax credit and is a basic estate-planning technique. Also called the bypass trust.

Crummey **Trust Provision** The language in a trust, giving the beneficiary (usually a minor) the right to demand a withdrawal of funds from the trust for some reasonable period of time, which usually is 30 or 60 days. When additions to the trust are made, the trustee informs the beneficiary in writing of this withdrawal right. Then the beneficiary either declines to exercise the right by notifying the trustee in writing or by failing to respond to the trustee's letter within the prescribed time. A *Crummey* trust provision permits the grantor's transfer to the trust to qualify for the annual gift tax exclusion because transfers subject to such demand powers are gifts of present interests.

Appendix A

Crummey **Trusts** A gift of the right to demand a portion of trust corpus which qualifies as a gift of a present interest, provided that the donee-beneficiary is aware of the right to make the demand.

Current Use Valuation of Qualified Real Estate A reference to the provisions of IRC Sec. 2032A, permitting family farms and real estate used in a closely held business to be valued in a decedent's gross estate at its value under current use, rather than its full fair-market value (highest and best use).

Currently Distributable Income of Estate Income that the fiduciary has a duty to distribute to beneficiaries under the terms of the decedent's last will. Such distributions may be deducted from the estate's taxable income and may be payable from the income or corpus [IRC Sec. 661(a)(1); Reg. Secs. 1.661(a)(2), 1.651(a)-2(a)].

Curtesy A husband's right, usually dependent on the birth of children, to a life estate in the property of his deceased wife, created by statutes in noncommunity property states. A wife's counterpart to curtesy is dower. Treasury Regulations Sec. 20.2034-1 provides that the full value of real estate subject to curtesy is included in the decedent-wife's gross estate without deduction for the curtesy interest of the surviving husband.

Custodial Account An easy account to establish with a bank or securities firm pursuant to a state's Uniform Transfers/Gifts to Minor Act. Custodial accounts are used to shift income-producing assets to your child, who is named as the beneficiary. An adult is named as custodian to hold property for the minor's benefit. No trust is required. The custodian may pay income to or for the minor, or simply accumulate the funds. The child for whom the account is established is taxed on and entitled to income from the account and becomes entitled to the principal and undistributed income when he or she attains majority, which is age 21 in most states. Gifts to custodial accounts qualify as gifts of a present interest and will be eligible for the annual gift tax exclusion.

Custodian Someone who has been lawfully appointed to take custody of a thing or person. The Uniform Transfers/Gifts to Minors Act requires that property in a custodial account that is held for the benefit of a minor be managed by a custodian.

Decanting The term generally used to describe the distribution of trust property to another trust in order to address changes in the law, trust administration problems or changed circumstances.

Deceased Spousal Unused Exclusion Amount (DSUE) This term represents the amount of unused applicable exclusion amount of the last predeceased spouse and is used in the context of portability.

Decedent Someone who has died.

Decedent's Estate An entity that is formed at the time of an individual's death and generally is charged with gathering the decedent's assets, paying the decedent's debts and expenses, and distributing the remaining assets. Generally, the estate consists of all the property, real or personal, tangible or intangible, wherever situated, that the decedent owned an interest in at death.

Decedent's Final Return A return on IRS Form 1040 or IRS Form 1040A that must be filed for a decedent who would have been required to file an income tax return if he had not died. The decedent's final return covers that part of the year during which the decedent was alive and is filed by the executor or any other person responsible

Appendix A

for the decedent's affairs. Even if the decedent was not alive the entire year, the executor may file a separate or joint return with the decedent's surviving spouse and may claim the same filing benefits (e.g., extra standard deduction for being over age 65) as the decedent would have claimed if he had not died [Reg. Sec. 1.443-1(a)(2)].

Decoupling This term refers to the process whereby states untie themselves from the federal wealth transfer tax system.

Deduction for Estate Tax An income tax deduction allowed for federal estates taxes imposed on post-death income of a decedent, which income was included for federal estate tax purposes [IRC Sec. 691(c)]. The deduction is claimed by the person (or estate) required to report income in respect of a decedent [IRC Sec. 691(c)(1); Reg. Sec. 1.691(c)-1(a)].

Deductions in Respect of a Decedent Deductions such as business expenses, income-producing expenses, interest, and taxes, for which the decedent was liable but which are not deductible on the decedent's final income tax return because of the decedent's accounting method. When paid, these expenses may be deducted by the estate or if the estate is not liable for the expenses, the person, who because of the decedent's death acquired the decedent's property subject to the liability [IRC Sec. 691(b)].

Deemed Allocation, Generation-Skipping Transfer Tax An allocation of the GST exemption allowed when a transferor fails to make a timely allocation. For direct skips during the lifetime of an individual, any unused portion of the transferor's GST exemption is automatically applied in an amount equal to the value of the property transferred, unless the transferor elects to exclude that transfer [IRC Sec. 2632(b)]. For unallocated portions of the GST exemption remaining after filing of the transferor's estate tax return, allocations are deemed to be made first to direct skips occurring at the death of the transferor, and then to trusts that may produce taxable distributions or terminations [IRC Sec. 2632(c)].

Defective Grantor Trust A term used to describe a trust where the current income is taxable to the grantor. Sometimes this is done on purpose as a tax-planning technique. *See also* **Intentional Grantor Trust**.

Defined Value Clause A defined value clause is designed to mitigate adverse gift tax consequences when the donor gives away hard-to-value property. With such a clause, the gift's value typically equals a fixed dollar amount. If the IRS argues that the property is undervalued, the clause reallocates the donor's excess gift to another beneficiary (such as a charity); if a charity is not involved, the formula effectively reallocates the excess to the donor.

Direct Skip The most common GST. A direct skip is a taxable gift during life or a transfer at death from a transferor directly to a skip person who is someone two or more generations below the donor's generation [IRC Sec. 2612(c)]. A trust can also be a skip person and a direct skip gift to a trust is taxed like a direct skip gift to an individual. In the classic example, grandparent makes an outright gift to a grandchild or more remote descendant. This is treated as a direct skip because the grandparent has made a gift to someone two or more generations below his or her generation. The recipient of the gift is called a skip person. If the grandparent makes a transfer to a trust, this transfer is also a direct skip and the trust is considered a skip person if all

Appendix A

the interests in the trust are held by skip persons. A direct skip is subject to both the GST tax and the estate or gift tax [IRC Sec. 2612(c)(1)].

Disclaimer, Estate and Gift Taxation A refusal to accept a gift or a bequest, devise, or inheritance. To make an effective disclaimer, called a qualified disclaimer, and thus prevent federal estate, gift, or generation-skipping transfer tax liability, the conditions set forth in IRC Sec. 2518(b) must be met. If a person makes a "qualified disclaimer," the disclaimed interest in property will be treated as if it had never been transferred to the person making the disclaimer for federal transfer tax purposes. Rather, the property will be treated as passing directly from the transferor to the person entitled to receive the property as a result of the disclaimer. Thus, a person who makes a qualified disclaimer (the "disclaimant") is not treated as having made a gift to the person who receives the disclaimed property.

Disclaimer Trust A trust used as a kind of receptacle to collect property that a beneficiary of a decedent's estate rejects, usually by means of a qualified disclaimer. It is an estate-planning tool.

Discounts Applied in Valuing Closely Held Stock Discounts are often applied in valuing closely held stock. It is generally recognized that the value of closely held stock may be discounted to reflect a minority interest, lack of marketability, pending litigation or the possibility of a stockholder suit, and there may be also be a discount for built-in capital gains tax liability.

Discretionary Trust A trust that empowers the trustee, alone or in combination with others, to accumulate income for the later distributions to the income beneficiaries, for addition to the trust's corpus, for the benefit of the remainderman, or both. Such trusts are considered complex trusts.

Distributable Net Income (DNI) An extremely important tax concept unique to trust and estate taxation. DNI serves the following two functions: (1) measures the taxable income reportable by beneficiaries, even if the actual amount of trust or estate distributions is greater; and (2) limits the deductions allowed to a trust or estate for distributions made to its beneficiaries. It is also used to determine the character of distributions to the beneficiaries. Compute DNI by starting with the trust's or estate's taxable income and make the following adjustments: (1) add back the deduction for income distributions to beneficiaries; (2) add back the deduction for the personal exemption; (3) exclude capital gains to the extent that they are allocated to corpus unless they are: (a) allocated to income under the terms of the governing instrument or local law by the fiduciary on its books or by notice to the beneficiary, (b) paid, credited, or required to be distributed as capital gains to a beneficiary in the taxable year; or (c) paid, permanently set aside, or to be used for charitable purposes; (4) exclude capital losses except to the extent they are taken into account in determining the amount of capital gains that are paid, credited, or required to be distributed to beneficiaries currently; (5) include tax-exempt interest but reduce it by: (a) any portion of the interest that is paid or set aside for charitable purposes, and, by (b) nondeductible expenses (such as commissions and general expenses) related to the tax-exempt interest; (6) exclude extraordinary dividends (whether paid in cash or in kind) and taxable stock dividends of simple trusts allocated to corpus by a trustee or fiduciary; and (7) include a foreign trust's gross income from foreign sources, reduced by nondeductible expenses.

Domestic Trust A trust other than a foreign trust [IRC Sec. 7701(a)(30)(D)].

Appendix A

Donative Intent A legal standard used to determine whether someone has made a gift. The intent called for is simply the desire to make a gift. You will not pay income taxes if you receive a gift that arises out of "detached or disinterested generosity" and is made "out of affection, respect, admiration, charity or like impulses."

Donee The recipient of a gift or a power of appointment.

Donor The person who makes a gift or transfer of a power of appointment.

Donor-Advised Fund A donor-advised fund is a charitable fund that is typically run by a community trust or a financial institution. The donor's contribution goes into a separate account and is eligible for a current income tax deduction even though the dollars may not be currently paid to charity. The fund is treated as a public charity which means that the donor is entitled to a larger income tax deduction but is subject to many rules and restrictions.

Dower A wife's right, often found in the statutes of noncommunity property states, to a life estate in the real property of her deceased husband or any like interest created in lieu of dower. A husband's counterpart to dower is curtesy. The full value of reality subject to dower is included in the decedent husband's gross estate without deduction for the dower interest of the surviving wife [Reg. Sec. 20.2034-1].

Electing Small Business Trusts An electing small business trust (ESBT) is a special type of trust that qualifies to be a shareholder in an S corporation [IRC Sec. 1361(c)(2)(A)(v)]. An ESBT may only have the following types of beneficiaries: individuals; estates eligible to be S corporation shareholders; charitable organizations; or a state or local government that holds a contingent interest in the trust and is not a potential contingent beneficiary [IRC Sec. 1361(e)(1)(A)(i)]. No interest in the trust may be acquired by purchase which means any acquisition of property with a cost basis determined under IRC Sec. 1012 [IRC Sec. 1361(e)(1)(A)(ii)]. Thus, interests in qualifying trusts must be acquired by gift, bequest or other non-purchase acquisition. The trustees must elect to be treated as an ESBT by filing a statement with the IRS. The statement must be filed with the same service center where the ESBT files its Form 1041. If the trust satisfies the ESBT requirements, the trust will be treated as an ESBT as of the date of the election [IRC Sec. 1361(e)]. An ESBT is taxed in a different manner than other trusts. First, the portion of the ESBT that consists of stock in one or more S corporations is treated as a separate trust for purposes of computing the income tax attributable to the S corporation stock held by the trust. This portion of the trust's income is taxed at the highest rate imposed on estates and trusts and includes: (1) the items of income, loss or deduction allocated to the trust as an S corporation shareholder under the rules of subchapter S; (2) gain or loss from the sale of the S corporation stock; and (3) any state or local income taxes and administrative expenses of the trust properly allocable to the S corporation stock. Otherwise allowable capital losses are allowed only to the extent of capital gains. Moreover, no deduction is allowed for amounts distributed to beneficiaries, and, except as described above, no additional deductions or credits are allowed. Also, this income is not included in the distributable net income of the trust and, therefore, is not included in the beneficiaries' income. Furthermore, no item relating to the S corporation stock is apportioned to any beneficiary. Special rules apply upon termination of all or a part of the ESBT [IRC Sec. 641(c)].

Employer Identification Number Every trust that is required to file a Form 1041 must also have an employer identification number (EIN). An EIN is required for

Appendix A

filing returns with the IRS and for making tax payments. A new EIN must be obtained when any of the following occur:

- A trust is created with funds from an estate and the trust is not considered a continuation of the estate;
- A trust changes to an estate;
- A living or inter vivos trust changes to a testamentary trust; or
- A living trust terminates by distributing its property to a residual trust.

A new EIN is not necessary if the following events occur:

- The fiduciary changes a name or address; or
- The fiduciary or the beneficiaries of a trust change.

The fiduciary of a trust can obtain an EIN by one of the following methods:

- By going to www.irs.gov/businesses and clicking the "Employer ID Numbers" link. The EIN is issued immediately after the application information is validated; or
- By mailing or faxing Form SS-4, "Application for Employer Identification Number." Fiduciaries should be aware that the EIN may take 4-6 weeks if they are applying for the EIN by mail or fax.

If the trust has not received an EIN by the time the return is due, they should write "Applied for" and the application date in the space for the EIN. A social security number should never be substituted for the EIN on a tax return.

Estate The new legal entity that comes into being when someone dies to handle the business, personal and financial affairs of the decedent. The legal entity is referred to as the decedent's estate and is established under the laws of the state in which the decedent lived. That state's probate court supervises and directs the administration of the decedent's estate.

Executor The person (also called personal representative (PR)) appointed to by the state court to administer the affairs of a deceased person's estate. The named executor, if there is a will, and the administrator, if there is no will, is the fiduciary in charge of an estate. They take charge of the decedent's probate property and wind up his or her affairs. The decedent's estate, like a trust, is a separate taxable entity and the fiduciary in charge has the same tax obligations as the trustee of a trust. The decedent's estate exists until the final distribution of its assets to the heirs and other beneficiaries.

Exemption Equivalent The amount that each person is allowed to transfer (the value of the property) that will not be subject to the estate tax. This amount is referred to in the tax code as the applicable exclusion amount. (The applicable exclusion amount is translated into an applicable credit amount in actually computing the estate tax.) For purposes of the estate tax, the exemption equivalent is determined by the year of death.

Expatriation to Avoid Estate and Gift Tax If a former citizen or long-term resident dies within 10 years of relinquishment of citizenship or residency, an estate tax is imposed on the transfer of U.S-situs property, including the decedent's pro rata share of the U.S. property held by a foreign corporation pursuant to IRC Sec. 2107(b). The estate tax is computed on the taxable estate, as determined by IRC Sec. 2106, using

Appendix A

the same estate tax rate schedule used for the estate of a U.S. citizen or resident [IRC Sec. 2107(a)]. The expatriate alternate estate tax regime applies, without regard to tax motivation, to any former U.S. citizen or long-term resident: (i) whose net worth as of the date of loss of citizenship or termination of long-term resident status equals or exceeds $2 million, (ii) whose average annual net income tax liability for the five preceding taxable years exceeds $157,000 in 2014, or (iii) who fails to certify under penalties of perjury, that he or she has complied with all U.S. tax obligations for the preceding five years and has provided evidence of compliance as required by the IRS [IRC Sec. 877(a)(2)(C)].

Expatriation Date The date that the individual relinquishes his or her U.S. citizenship or in the case of a long-term U.S. resident, ceases to be a lawful permanent resident is the expatriation date [IRC Sec. 877A(g)(1)-(g)(3); IRC Sec. 877(a)(2)(A), (B) and (C)].

Extension of Time to Pay for Closely Held Business Interests The estate of an individual who dies owning a closely held business interest may qualify for a special elective method of paying the estate tax attributable to the interest. If the value of an "interest in a closely held business" exceeds 35 percent of the adjusted gross estate, the executor may elect to pay the estate tax attributable to the interest in up to ten equal installments [IRC Sec. 6166]. The first such installment is due no later than five years after the date that the tax was otherwise due (generally, nine months after death). Each remaining installment is due one year after the preceding installment. Thus, an executor can defer the full payment of the tax attributable to the closely held business interest for a maximum period of 14 years. Interest must be paid on the estate tax that is paid in installments. The interest must be paid on an annual basis. Therefore, if the executor elects the maximum ten-year extension, the estate will make annual payments of interest only for the first four years, and pay the balance in ten annual installments of principal and interest.

Family Limited Partnership (FLP) A business and tax-planning tool used by senior family members to facilitate business succession and estate planning. The senior creates a limited partnership and transfers property such as business interests or real estate to it. Keep in mind that the IRS wants to see that the creation of the partnership had a legitimate business purpose and that it was created well before the death of the senior. The senior is the general partner and in that capacity makes all the management decisions for the partnership and is subjected to unlimited liability. Limited partnership interests are given to children, grandchildren, or to trusts created on their behalf. The limited partners are not responsible for the debts of the partnership, but they must pay income tax on their share of partnership income. They have no voice in management and are entitled to receive only distributions that are declared by the general partners. Typically, they are in a lower income tax bracket than the parents, so using the partnership approach lowers overall income and wealth transfer taxes for the family. The gift of the partnership interest qualifies for the annual gift tax exclusion. In addition, because the limited partners don't control the FLP, and their rights to sell their interests may be limited, discounts for lack of control and marketability may be claimed on the value of the business interest passing to the children when the parents die. Better yet, all appreciation in the value of the limited partnership shares that occurs after the gifts also escapes estate and gift taxation.

Fiscal Year A 12-month period ending on the last day of any month other than December [IRC Sec. 7701(a)(24)].

Appendix A

Formula Clauses (also called Defined Value Formula Clauses) Formula clauses are clauses of a will or trust that express the beneficiary's interest in terms of a formula. For example, the interest passing to a surviving spouse, a QTIP trust, or to a marital deduction trust for the benefit of a surviving spouse is often determined by reference to a pecuniary formula clause or a fractional share formula clause. The use of a formula clause is frequently used by estate planners to ensure the proper division of property but formula clauses must frequently be reviewed to make certain that they implement the testator's intent.

Funeral Expenses Funeral expenses are allowed as a deduction from the gross estate to the extent that: (1) they are actually expended, (2) they are allowable out of property subject to claims under local law, and (3) they satisfy the requirements of Reg. Sec. 20.2053-1. A reasonable expenditure for a tombstone, monument, mausoleum, or burial lot is deductible as a funeral expense if allowable under local law.

GST Exemption A term referring to the GST tax exemption which is adjusted annually to reflect the applicable exclusion amount.

GST Tax Deduction An income tax deduction allowed for GST tax imposed on an income distribution from a trust [IRC Sec. 164(a)(5)].

General Power of Appointment The power the donor of property confers on a donee enabling the donee to determine who will enjoy or own the property down the road. IRC Section 2041(b) defines a general power as one exercisable "in favor of the decedent, his estate, his creditors, or the creditors of his estate." If the decedent possesses a general power, he or she will be treated as the owner of the property subject to the power, and the property will be included in the gross estate at death. A power of amendment or revocation so that the donor may substitute himself as trustee is a general power, as are other arrangements that are tantamount to general powers [Reg. Sec. 20.2041(b)(1)]. There are two major exceptions to the definition of a general power. First, the power to consume, to invade, or to appropriate property for the benefit of the decedent limited by an ascertainable standard relating to health, education, support, or maintenance of the decedent is not a general power [IRC Sec. 2041(b)(1)(A)]. Second, certain jointly held powers are not general powers [IRC Secs. 2041(b)(1)(B), 2041(b)(1)(C)].

Generation for GST Tax Purposes Basically, an individual who is in a different generation from another individual by reference to generations from his or her grandparent's generation, or by arbitrary chronological references. Property transfers that skip a generation are subject to the GST tax. For transfers to family members, generations are figured along family lines. You, your spouse, and siblings are in one generation. Children (including adopted children), nieces, and nephews are in the first younger generation. Grandchildren, grandnieces, and grandnephews are in the second younger generation, and so on. A child who is adopted is treated identically to those related by blood [IRC Sec. 2651(b)(3)(A)]. For transfers made to nonfamily members, generations are measured from the date of your birth. Individuals not more than 12 years younger than you are treated as members of your generation; more than 12 but not more than 37 years younger, first younger generation, and so on—a new generation every 25 years [IRC Sec. 2651(d)]. However, anyone who has ever been married to you is always considered to be in your generation, regardless of age [IRC Sec. 2651(c)].

Appendix A

Generation-Skipping Transfer A transfer of an interest in property to someone two or more generations below the transferor. The transfer is often accomplished via a trust that distributes income to the transferor's child for life, leaving the corpus to the grandchildren. Taxable GSTs are either taxable distributions, taxable terminations, or direct skips [IRC Sec. 2611(a)].

Generation-Skipping Transfer Exemption An exemption that is applied against the value of property transferred in GSTs to determine the applicable rate for purposes of the GST tax. In effect, the amount of the exemption will escape tax, and everything above that is subject to the highest transfer tax rate, subject to minor adjustments. A gift tax return may not be required in order to allocate the exemption to the gift [IRC Sec. 2642(b)]. If allocations are not made prior to filing of the transferor's estate tax return, the unused portion will be deemed allocated in an order specified by the Internal Revenue Code [IRC Sec. 2632(b)]. Once an allocation is made, it is irrevocable. Transferors will want to allocate their exemption as soon as possible because any appreciation in value of the property covered by an allocated exemption remains covered by the exemption.

Generation-Skipping Transfer Tax A tax imposed to ensure that wealth transfers are taxed at least once in each generation [IRC Sec. 2601]. GSTs are taxed at a flat rate that is equal to the highest federal transfer tax rate in existence at the time of the transfer. Consequently, unless a special rule, exception or exemption applies, the tax is imposed on three types of GSTs, even if estate or gift tax is also imposed on the transferor upon making the transfer. The three types of transfers are the direct skip [see ¶2504], taxable distribution [see ¶2506]and taxable termination [see ¶2505]. The GST tax applies to transfers that go directly to people who are two or more generations younger than you (called skip persons) [see ¶2503]. Each transferor is entitled to one exemption and a married couple can double the amount of the exemption [IRC Secs. 2631, 2652]. All generation-skipping transfers are subject to the tax, and to avoid taxation, exemption must be allocated to the generation-skipping transfer on a properly filed gift tax return [IRC Sec. 2632].

Generation-Skipping Transfer Tax Transferor The GST transferor's identity is important because the generation assignment is determined with reference to the transferor in IRC Sec. 2651. Also, only the transferor or the transferor's executor (in the case of an estate) may allocate the GST tax exemption to the transferred property [IRC Sec. 2631].

Gift A direct or indirect lifetime transfer by a competent donor, in trust or otherwise, for less than full and adequate consideration in money or money's worth [Reg. Sec. 25.2511]. If property is transferred for less than full and adequate consideration in money or money's worth, then the amount by which the value of the property exceeds the value of the consideration is a gift, although a sale or exchange made in the ordinary course of business in an arm's-length transaction is not a gift [IRC Sec. 2512(b); Reg. Sec. 25.2512-8]. Donative intent is not mandatory. Gifts can arise in various indirect manners such as placing title to property in joint name with someone else, the lapse of a power of appointment, which results in another's receiving a beneficial interest in the appointive property, and a refusal to accept property, which results in another's receipt of a beneficial interest in the disclaimed property [IRC. Secs. 2514, 2515, 2518].

Appendix A

Gift, Income Taxation A transfer excluded from gross income if the dominant motive for the transfer is "detached and disinterested generosity" arising "out of affection, respect, admiration, charity, or like impulses" [IRC Sec. 102].

Gift Loans Loans at below market rates (using the applicable federal rate) where the forgone interest is in the nature of a gift to the borrower [IRC Sec. 7872(f)(3)].

Gift Splitting A device whereby a spouse makes a gift to a third party and, in order to obtain two annual gift tax exclusions with respect to the one gift, the other spouse consents to treat the gift as being made one half by each spouse [IRC Sec. 2513]. Both spouses must be citizens of the United States or resident aliens, both must be married at the time of the gift, and the donor spouse cannot remarry during the year of the gift.

Gift Tax A cumulative, progressive excise tax imposed on the donor of a gift of property. The gift tax applies only to individuals. The tax exists to prevent the avoidance of estate taxes by giving property away before death. The gift tax is incorporated in the unified transfer tax.

Gift Tax Credit A credit against the federal estate tax liability based on federal gift taxes previously paid. The credit arises when property is first subject to a gift tax, then to an estate tax because it was the subject of an inter vivos transfer that was ineffective in removing it from the decedent's estate [IRC Sec. 2012].

Gift Tax Marital Deduction You may deduct from the total amount of gifts you make during the calendar year an unlimited amount of otherwise taxable gifts you make to your spouse provided the four following conditions are met at the time the gift is made. First, the individuals must be married to each other. Thus, a gift to a person who becomes your spouse after you make the gift does not qualify for the marital deduction. Second, the interest transferred to the donee spouse is not a nondeductible terminable interest. Third, the donor is a U.S. citizen or resident [Reg. Sec. 25.2523(a)-1(a)]. Fourth, the donee spouse is a U.S. citizen [IRC Sec. 2523].

Grantor A person who transfers property to a trustee also known as a settlor.

Grantor Retained Annuity Trust (GRAT) An irrevocable trust designed to reduce gift taxes and remove valuable assets from your taxable estate. You transfer property to an irrevocable trust, taking back an interest in the form of an annuity, which pays you a fixed amount each year. At the end of the term, the assets pass to your heirs. To benefit from this type of trust, you must outlive the trust so that the assets are given to the named beneficiaries and removed from your taxable estate.

Grantor Retained Income Trust (GRIT) An irrevocable trust designed to reduce gift taxes and remove highly valued assets from your taxable estate. You receive income from the assets placed in the trust for a set period. At the end of the term, the assets pass to your heirs. Assets placed in the trust may be your personal residence or other income-producing assets. To benefit from this type of trust, you must outlive the trust so that the assets are given to the named beneficiaries and removed from your taxable estate.

Grantor Retained Unitrust (GRUT) A trust in which the grantor retains a unitrust interest. Instead of getting a fixed dollar amount each year, the grantor gets a fixed percent of the amount given with assets each year. GRUTs can be valuable estate-planning tools.

Appendix A

Grantor Trust A trust that is considered owned by the grantor, who must pay tax on the income generated by the trust [IRC Secs. 671-679].

Grantor Trust Rules The provisions of IRC Secs. 671-679, which explain whether the grantor of a trust, as opposed to the trust, its beneficiaries, or both, is taxed on income of the trust. If the grantor has parted with sufficient dominion and control over the trust property, the grantor avoids tax on the trust's income. The grantor is treated as the owner and is taxed on any portion of the trust or its income if the grantor has access to or control over the trust property.

Gross Estate The total value of all interests held at the time of death by someone who was a citizen of the United States or resident alien and who has died [IRC Secs. 2033-2044].

Gross-up, Estate Tax A rule embodied in IRC Sec. 2035 providing that the decedent's gross estate must be increased by gift taxes paid by the decedent or the decedent's estate on gifts made by the decedent or the decedent's spouse after 1976 and during the three-year period that ends with the decedent's death [IRC Sec. 2035(c)].

Hanging Power A power to withdraw some or all of the addition to a trust up to the maximum annual gift tax exclusion, which power lapses at the end of the notice period mandated for withdrawals using a 5 and 5 power. The remaining part of the power "hangs" rather than disappears and is designed to solve estate and gift tax problems associated with paying the premiums owed on large life insurance policies that are held in trust.

Incidents of Ownership For federal estate tax purposes, the right of the insured or his or her estate to one or more of the economic benefits of a life insurance policy. IRC Sec. 2042 requires inclusion in the decedent's gross estate of life insurance on the decedent's life, even though the proceeds are not receivable by or for the benefit of the decedent's estate, if at the date of death the decedent possessed incidents of ownership in the policy, exercisable alone or in conjunction with another person. Examples of fatal incidents of ownership include the legal power to change the beneficiary, to surrender, to pledge the policy for a loan, or to obtain from the insurer a loan against the surrender value of the policy and a revisionary interest in the policy or its proceeds. Sometimes incidents of ownership held by a corporation are attributable to a decedent through stock ownership [Reg. Sec. 20.2042-1(c)(2)].

Inclusion Ratio, GST Tax A ratio determined by subtracting the applicable fraction under the GST tax from one. When multiplied by the maximum federal estate tax rate, it results in the rate at which the GST tax is imposed [IRC Sec. 2642]. The applicable fraction is:

$$\frac{\text{GST exemption allocable to transfer}}{\text{value of property}} = \text{(death taxes and charitable deduction)}$$

Income for the Taxable Year Required to Be Distributed Currently, Estate or Trust Amounts the fiduciary is required to distribute currently, even if made after the close of the taxable year, often called first-tier distributions. Such amounts are generally deductible under IRC Sec.651(a) for simple trusts and under IRC Section 661(a) (but, when combined with certain discretionary payments, not in excess of distributable net income) for complex trusts and estates, and are taxable to beneficiaries to the

Appendix A

extent of distributable net income [IRC Secs. 651(b), 661(a)]. In the case of complex trusts and estate, the deduction is the lesser of first- and second-tier distributions or distributable net income [IRC Sec. 661(a)].

Income in Respect of a Decedent (IRD) All gross income that cannot properly be included in the decedent's final return, but to which the decedent had a right and would have received if he not died [IRC Sec. 691(a)]. These amounts are included in the gross income of the deceased person's estate or the person who receives the income [IRC Sec. 691(a)(1); Reg. Secs. 1.691(a)-1, 1.691(a)-2]. Examples of IRD include the decedent's final paycheck that was earned but not yet received at the time of death.

Income Interest A right to, or interest in, a stream of income. An example is a beneficiary of a trust who is entitled to a share of its income.

Income Shifting or Splitting A tax planning strategy designed to move taxable income from a taxpayer in a higher bracket (typically a parent or grandparent) to a taxpayer (typically a child) who is in a lower tax bracket.

Income, Trusts and Estates Generally, income of a trust or estate as determined under the terms of the governing instrument (trust document or will) and local law.

Installment Sales to Grantor Trusts This is a tax strategy that can provide valuable income, gift and estate tax benefits and is most advantageous when interest rates are low. In a typical situation, the grantor creates an irrevocable trust for the benefit of descendants. The trust is designed so that the grantor is taxed on the trust's income, but the trust assets are not taxed in the grantor's estate. The trust can also be designed as a generation-skipping (dynasty) trust so that any trust assets remaining at a child's death pass free of estate tax to grandchildren even if they have appreciated in value. The grantor makes a gift to the trust of so-called "seed" money that should be equal to at least 10 percent of the value of the assets to be sold to the trust. This seed gift will use up a portion of the grantor's lifetime gift tax exemption. If the trust is designed as a GST trust, the grantor must allocate a portion of his/her GST exemption to the trust to cover the amount of the seed money gift. The GST exemption is the same amount as the estate tax exemption, and the allocation is reported on the grantor's gift tax return (Form 709). The grantor then sells assets to the trust that are expected to outperform the interest rate on the note. Typically, there is no down payment, interest is payable annually on the note, and a balloon payment would be due at the end of a set term ranging from 9–30 years. Ideally, the assets sold to the trust would generate income (to make the interest payments), and would also qualify for valuation discounts for lack of control and lack of marketability. For example, non-voting interests in an LLC or a Subchapter S corporation are often good assets to sell to a grantor trust. A grantor trust is also an eligible Subchapter S stockholder. The interest rate on the note is fixed for the entire note term at the lowest rate allowed under the tax law. This rate is known as the applicable federal rate (AFR) and is published monthly by the Department of the Treasury. The installment sale to a grantor trust is a popular wealth transfer planning technique being used today because the IRS has said in Rev. Rul. 85–13 [1985-1 CB 184], that the grantor recognizes no gain or loss on the sale. The reason is that the grantor and the trust are considered one and the same person for income tax purposes. However, the trust's basis in the assets purchased is not the purchase price paid for the assets, but instead the same as the grantor's basis. The grantor is not taxed separately on the interest

Appendix A

payments the grantor receives. The future growth (equity) in the trust provides additional equity with which to support future installment sales within the 10 percent test referred to above.

Intentional Grantor Trust A popular estate planning tool because it allows wealthy families to minimize estate tax as well as the income tax burden imposed on income-generating assets held in trust for future generations. The intentional grantor trust involves setting up a trust that will accumulate income and will purposely give the grantor a right or power that will cause him to be taxed on the trust's income under the grantor trust rules. The power must not be one that would cause the trust property to be included in the grantor's estate. The end result is that the trust's income will be taxed at the grantor's presumably lower tax rates. In addition, the value of the assets contributed to the trust are frozen at the contribution date for estate tax purposes. The highly compressed tax brackets for trusts make it very difficult to use trusts as a vehicle for saving taxes where trust income is accumulated, rather than distributed. An intentional grantor trust can reduce the income tax liability for families who want to accumulate income in a trust because under an intentional grantor trust, the grantor is taxed on the trust income at tax rates that are lower than those that would be imposed at the trust level. Also called the "intentionally defective" grantor trust.

In Terrorem Clause An *in terrorem* clause is a clause in a will or trust that threatens to disinherit anyone challenging the document. Courts are usually reluctant to enforce no-contest clauses and construe statutes authorizing them very narrowly. In some jurisdictions, they are unenforceable.

Inter Vivos During life as opposed to by will. For example, trusts may be established during the life of the grantor (inter vivos trust), or by will (testamentary trust).

Inter Vivos **Trust** A revocable or irrevocable trust, created during the life of the grantor, often called a living trust.

Interest in a Closely Held Business An "interest in a closely held business" is defined for purposes of the extension of time to pay for closely held business interests as: (1) an interest in a proprietorship or a trade or business carried on as a proprietorship; (2) an interest as a partner in a partnership carrying on a trade or business if: (a) at least 20 percent of the partnership's total capital interest is included in the decedent's gross estate, or (b) such partnership had 45 or fewer partners; or (3) stock in a corporation carrying on a trade or business if: (a) at least 20 percent of the corporation's voting stock is included in the decedent's gross estate, or (b) such corporation had 45 or fewer shareholders [IRC Sec. 6166(b)(1)].

Intestacy The death of an individual without a will, so that the decedent's property passes under state laws of intestate succession.

Intestate Succession In accordance with state law, the disposition of property as a result of someone dying without a will or intestate.

Invasion of Corpus Usually, a trustee's taking of the principal of a trust for a beneficiary.

Irrevocable Trust A trust created during the lifetime of the settlor that cannot be revoked by the settlor. If properly drafted, the settlor will not be taxed on the income of the irrevocable trust. The trust instrument must be carefully drafted to avoid taxation to the settlor as a result of the grantor trust rules. Keep in mind that a

Appendix A

transfer to a irrevocable trust will generally be subject to gift tax unless the gift is a present interest and qualifies for the annual gift tax exclusion. Use of the *Crummey* powers can turn a gift in trust that is normally a future interest into a present interest eligible for the annual gift tax exclusion.

Joint Tenancy Undivided ownership of property by two or more persons with the right of survivorship (i.e., a right giving the surviving owner full ownership of the decedents' interest in the property).

Lack of Marketability Discount A discount most frequently applied in valuing closely held stock to reflect the fact that the stock cannot easily be sold. There have been numerous cases where courts have had to determine the proper size of such discounts for estate and gift tax purposes. Frequently, the courts are confronted with appraisals submitted by valuation experts for both the taxpayer and the IRS and must determine which report is more credible and persuasive. Often the courts will appear to split the difference, arriving at a value that falls somewhere between the values claimed by the two sides. Because the approach to valuing closely held stock, including the issue of discounts, is intensely fact-specific and highly dependent on the particular circumstances involved, earlier valuation cases offer little guidance in resolving current disputes. However, the case law can provide insight into the factors the courts consider to be of greatest importance in resolving valuation disputes.

Life Estate A property right that entitles the holder, commonly a beneficiary of a trust, to the income or enjoyment of the property for his or her lifetime. When the holder of the life estate dies, the right to the income interest may pass to another such person, or the corpus may pass to a remainderman or revert to the initial transferor. The term also refers to a life tenant's interest in real or personal property.

Life Estate Coupled with a Power of Appointment An exception to the terminable interest rule, whereby the property interest passing from the decedent to the surviving spouse qualifies for the unlimited marital deduction, provided that five conditions are met: (1) the surviving spouse is entitled for life to all the income from the entire interest; (2) income payable to the spouse is payable annually or more often; (3) the spouse has the power to appoint the entire interest or the specific portion to either him or herself or his or her estate; (4) the spouse's power is exercisable by him or her alone and (whether by will or during life) is exercisable in all events; and (5) the entire interest or the specific portion is not subject to a power in any other person to appoint anyone other than the surviving spouse [IRC Secs. 2056(b)(5), 2056(b)(6); Reg. Sec. 20.2056(b)-5(c)].

Life Insurance Trust If you are the owner of life insurance on your own life, proceeds from a life insurance policy will be taxed as part of your estate at your death. A life insurance trust is an irrevocable trust to which an insured transfers a life insurance policy so that the death benefits are excluded from the insured's gross estate, minimizing estate taxes and avoiding probate. A life insurance trust usually grants a surviving spouse a life income interest, which is not includable in his or her estate [IRC Sec.2041]. Provided the insured transfers the policy more than three years prior to death and retains no incidents of ownership, the insured's estate will not include the death benefits.

Limited Power of Appointment *See* Special Power of Appointment.

Appendix A

Living Trusts Also called revocable trusts. A living trust is trust established during your lifetime to manage your assets in case of your disability or incapacity. You are the trustee and another person or financial institution is named as successor trustee. The trust is revocable, which means that you retain the right to change or revoke the trust at any time prior to death. The terms of the trust designate the trustee and govern the management and disposition of the assets in the trust by directing how they are to be invested and indicating who will receive principal and income from the trust. In addition, the trust provides who will receive the trust assets after you die. The only way for the living trust to be effective in providing for the management of your assets during your lifetime is to be sure that all your assets are transferred into the trust. The bad news is that the value of the assets in your living trust are fully includable in your taxable gross estate when you die. The primary advantages of living trusts are probate avoidance and the ability to anticipate and provide for your physical and mental incapacity in later years. By transferring your property while you are competent to a trustee whose powers will not be revoked by your subsequent incapacity, you have made sure that your financial affairs will be managed after you are no longer able to handle them yourself.

Living Will A document that sets forth a person's directions regarding their health care when the person is no longer able to make those decisions on his or her own.

Marital Deduction An unlimited estate and gift tax deduction available for interspousal transfers provided the four following conditions are met at the time the gift is made. First, the individuals must be married to each other. Thus, a gift to a person who becomes your spouse after you make the gift does not qualify for the marital deduction. Second, the interest transferred to the donee spouse is not a nondeductible terminable interest. Third, the donor is a U.S. citizen or resident [Reg. Sec. 25.2523(a)-1(a)]. Fourth, the donee spouse is a U.S. citizen [IRC Sec. 2523].

Marital Deduction Trust A testamentary trust that qualifies for a marital deduction. These trusts are created for the benefit of a surviving spouse [IRC Sec. 2056(a)]. Examples of such trusts include marital estate trusts, qualified terminable interest property (QTIP) trusts, power of appointment trusts, and any other present interests transferred in trust.

Marital Estate Trust A testamentary trust, in which the spouse holds all the beneficiary interests. All or part of the income of the marital estate trust must be accumulated during the surviving spouse's life and added to corpus, with the accumulated income and corpus to be paid to the estate of the surviving spouse at death. Transfers to such trusts qualify for the unlimited marital deduction because the surviving spouse's interest in the trust is not terminable, and no interest that may take effect on the occurrence or nonoccurrence of any contingency has passed from the decedent to any person other than the spouse or the spouse's estate and because the transfer is to a surviving spouse [Reg. Sec. 20.2056(e)-2(b)(1)(iii)].

Medical and Tuition Expenses, Gift Tax Exclusion Medical and tuition payments (so-called qualified transfers) made directly to the service provider free of federal gift taxes. Qualifying medical expenses are those incurred for the diagnosis, cure, mitigation, treatment, or prevention of disease, including drugs and medical insurance. The medical payments must be paid directly by the donor to the individual or organization providing medical services. No gift tax exclusion is available if the donee is simply reimbursed or serves as an intermediary for the hospital or school. The

Appendix A

unlimited exclusion from gift taxes is not permitted for amounts that are reimbursed by insurance. Qualifying tuition means only tuition paid on behalf of an individual directly to an educational organization. The educational institution must maintain a regular faculty and curriculum and must have a regularly enrolled body of pupils or students in attendance at the place where its educational activities are regularly carried on. No exclusion is provided for books, supplies, and dormitory fees. The gift tax exemption extends to foreign educational institutions.

Minority Interest Discount A discount most frequently applied in valuing closely held stock to reflect the fact that the stock at issue only represents a minority interest in the closely held corporation and thus does not afford the buyer much control over the company's business affairs. There have been numerous cases where courts have had to determine the proper size of such discounts for estate and gift tax purposes. Frequently, the courts are confronted with appraisals submitted by valuation experts for both the taxpayer and the IRS and must determine which report is more credible and persuasive. Often, the courts will appear to split the difference, arriving at a value that falls somewhere between the values claimed by the two sides. Because the approach to valuing closely held stock, including the issue of discounts, is intensely fact-specific and highly dependent on the particular circumstances involved, earlier valuation cases offer little guidance in resolving current disputes. However, the case law can provide insight into the factors the courts consider to be of greatest importance in resolving valuation disputes.

Multiple Trusts Trusts that have (1) no substantially independent purposes; (2) substantially the same grantor or grantors and substantially the same primary beneficiary or beneficiaries; and (3) the avoidance, mitigation, or deferral of tax as a principal purpose [Reg. Sec. 1.641(a)-0(c)]. Such trusts must be aggregated and treated as one trust [IRC Sec. 632(e)].

Net Gift A gift in connection with which the donee pays the gift tax. When the donee pays the gift tax, the donor has a taxable gain equal to the gift tax paid by the donee minus the donor's basis in the property.

Net Investment Income (NII) Tax Beginning in 2013, U.S. citizens and residents must pay a 3.8 percent net investment income (NII) tax on the lesser of: (1) NII for the year, or (2) the excess of modified adjusted gross income (MAGI) over the threshold amount ($250,000 for a joint return or surviving spouse, $125,000 for a married individual filing a separate return, and $200,000 for all others). These thresholds are not indexed for inflation. MAGI is defined as adjusted gross income (AGI) plus any amount excluded as foreign earned income under IRC Sec. 911(a)(1) (net of the deductions and exclusions disallowed with respect to the foreign earned income). The tax is reported for individuals, trusts and estates on Form 8960, "Net Investment Income Tax Individuals, Estates, and Trusts," which is attached to Form 1040 (individuals).

Net investment income is defined as: (1) interest, dividends, annuity income, royalties, and rents; (2) profits from a passive activity which is a trade or business where the taxpayer does not "materially participate;" A taxpayer who owns a business, either as a sole proprietorship or as part of a pass-through entity (partnership, LLC or S corporation) and who does not materially participate in the business is deemed to own an interest in a passive activity; (3) profits from a trade or business of trading in financial instruments or commodities, even if the taxpayer does materially partici-

Appendix A

pate, and (4) net gain from the disposition of property (e.g., capital gains from stock sales, mutual fund capital gain distributions, etc.) but not gains from selling property held in a trade or business where the taxpayer materially participates.

Nonprobate Asset Property that is not subject to probate under local law, such as property the decedent held as a joint tenant with a right of survivorship, or insurance proceeds payable directly to a named beneficiary. These assets are not subject to probate because they pass to the survivor by operation of law upon the death of the first joint property owner.

Non-skip Person A GST tax term that refers to a person other than a skip-person [IRC Sec. 2613(b)]. An example of a nonskip person is a person assigned to a generation one level below the transferor or to the same, or higher, level than the transferor. This means a transferor's ancestors, children, and spouse are nonskip persons. A trust is a nonskip person if a nonskip person holds an interest in the trust, even if other interests in the trust are held by skip persons. Also, a trust is a nonskip person if a distribution may be made to a nonskip person.

Ordering Provisions Ordering provisions are the language in a governing instrument or in local law that specifically identify the source out of which amounts are to be paid, permanently set aside or used for a specific purpose. They are often used when charitable lead trusts are drafted in order to achieve a desired tax effect. They are typically respected only if there is an economic effect independent of the income tax consequences of the provision [Prop. Reg. Sec. 1.642(C)-3(b)(2)].

Per Stirpes A decedent's estate is distributed per stirpes if each branch of the family is to receive an equal share of an estate. When the heir in the first generation of a branch predeceased the decedent, the share that would have been given to the heir would be distributed among the heir's issue in equal shares. For example, A's will specifies that his estate is to be divided among his descendants in equal shares per stirpes. A has three children, B, C, and D. B is already dead, but has left two children (grandchildren of A), B1 and B2. When A's will is executed, under a distribution per stirpes, C and D each receive one-third of the estate, and B1 and B2 each receive one-sixth. B1 and B2 constitute one "branch" of the family, and collectively receive a share equal to the shares received by C and D as branches.

Personal Exemption, Trusts and Estates Annual amounts ranging from $600 for an estate to $100 for a complex trust, allowed as a deduction by the trust [IRC Sec. 642(b)]. These deductions are allowed so returns will not have to be filed for trusts and estates that generate only a small amount of income each year.

Personal Residence Trust A trust that holds only a personal residence for use by term holders. This is an estate-planning device because the zero value rule does not apply to retained interests in personal residence trusts and qualified personal residence trusts [IRC Sec. 2702(a)(3)(A)(ii)].

Pooled Income Fund A pooled income fund is a collective investment vehicle, similar to a mutual fund or a common trust fund, except that it is maintained by a charity in order to make it easier for people to donate remainder interests in property to the charity. The pooled income fund combines the contributions of all donors for investment purposes, and each donor's contribution is converted into a percentage or unit interest in the fund. Each donor's unit interest in the fund fluctuates as the

Appendix A

current return on the underlying assets changes. Pooled income funds must satisfy the organizational and operational requirements set forth in IRC Sec. 642(c)(5).

Portability of Unused Exemption Between Spouses IRC Sec. 2010(c)(2) embodies the portability concept and provides that the estate tax applicable exclusion amount is (1) the "basic exclusion amount" ($5,340,000 in 2014), plus (2) for a surviving spouse, the "deceased spousal unused exclusion amount (DSUE)." Any applicable exclusion amount that remains unused as of the death of the last deceased spouse is available for use by the surviving spouse, as an addition to the surviving spouse's own applicable exclusion amount.

If a surviving spouse is predeceased by more than one spouse, the amount of unused exclusion that is available for use by the surviving spouse is limited to the lesser of (1) the basic exclusion amount or (2) the basic exclusion amount of the surviving spouse's *last* deceased spouse over the combined amount of the deceased spouse's taxable estate plus adjusted taxable gifts.

The term "basic exclusion amount" limits the unused exclusion to the amount of the basic exclusion amount. Therefore, if the estate tax exclusion amount decreases by the time of the surviving spouse's death, the lower basic exclusion amount would be the limit on the unused exclusion of the predeceased spouse that could be used by the surviving spouse.

Post-mortem Estate Planning Tax planning after the death of the decedent. The typical tax issues involve special use valuation, disclaimers, installment payment of estate taxes and use of the alternate valuation date in order to minimize federal estate taxes.

Power of Administration, Grantor Trust Rules The ability of an individual to exercise any one of the following three powers over a trust without the consent of any person in a fiduciary capacity: (1) the power to control the voting of any securities of a corporation in which the grantor's and the trust's holdings are significant in terms of voting control; (2) the power to control the investment of the trust's funds to the extent that the funds include securities of corporations in which the grantor's and the trust's holdings are significant in terms of voting control; or (3) the power to reacquire the trust's property by substituting other property of an equivalent value [IRC Sec. 675(4)]. The grantor of a trust will be treated as the owner of the portion of the trust over which the grantor has such powers [IRC Sec. 675].

Power of Appointment A power that one person confers on another (a donee) to select the person who is to enjoy a property interest upon the death of the donor of the power, or on the death of the donee. The distinction between a general power of appointment and a nongeneral or special power of appointment has tax significance because IRC Sec. 2041 includes in the gross estate of one who possesses a general power of appointment the value of the property subject to that power. Special powers of appointment are outside the scope of IRC Sec. 2041. The exercise or release of a power of appointment may result in a taxable gift [IRC Sec. 2514].

Power of Appointment Trust A trust that provides for a power of appointment in a beneficiary. Property passing to a surviving spouse under a power of appointment trust that meets the following requirements will qualify for the marital deduction despite the terminable interest rule: (1) the surviving spouse must get all the income for life; (2) the income must be payable at least annually; (3) the surviving spouse

Appendix A

must have the right to appoint the property to herself or her estate; (4) the power, whether exercisable by will or during her life, must be exercisable by her alone and in all events; and (5) no one else may have a power to appoint any part of the interest to any person other than the surviving spouse [IRC Sec. 2056(b)(5)].

Power of Attorney A power of attorney is a document wherein an individual (the "principal") names someone else to act as his or her attorney-in-fact and transfer business on his or her behalf. A durable power of attorney is effective when executed and remains so even if the principal becomes incompetent. A springing power of attorney does not become effective until a stated event occurs, such as the principal's incompetence. Any power of attorney ends at the principal's death.

Power of Invasion A power held by a trustee to withdraw corpus from a trust. The power exists to the extent granted by the trust instruments or local law.

Power of Withdrawal An estate-planning term referring to a power granted a beneficiary of a trust to extract some or all of the principal. The most common type of power of withdrawal is limited to the greater of $5,000 or 5 percent of the value of the trust's principal.

Power to Borrow Without Adequate Interest or Security, Grantor Trust Rules A power exercisable by the grantor of a trust, or a nonadverse party, that enables the grantor to borrow the corpus or income at below market interest rates or with inadequate collateral [IRC Sec. 675(2)]. The grantor of a trust is deemed the owner of the portion of the trust where this power exists [IRC Sec. 675].

Power to Deal for Less Than Adequate and Full Consideration, Grantor Trust Rules An administrative power exercisable by the grantor of a trust, a nonadverse party, or both, without the consent of any adverse party, enabling the grantor to deal with or dispose of the corpus of the trust, or the income from the corpus, for less than an adequate consideration [IRC Sec. 675(1)]. The grantor of a trust is deemed the owner of the portion of the trust over which he or she has such a power.

Power to Revoke, Estate Taxes Any power under which the grantor has the right to take possession of the property he or she transferred to another. When the grantor of a property interest reserves the power to revoke, and that power is possessed or exercised at the date of the grantor's death, then the property is included in the decedent's gross estate [IRC Sec. 2038].

Power to Revoke, Grantor Trust Rules A power that the grantor, a nonadverse party, or both may exercise over a trust to revest the title to any portion of the trust in the grantor [IRC Sec. 676(a)]. Such a power causes the grantor to be treated as the owner of that portion of a trust.

Power to Terminate A power whereby the grantor of a trust can end a trust before the life interest or term interest ends. If a grantor of a property interest reserves the power to terminate the income interest and he or she holds or exercises that power at the date of death, then the property is included in the grantor-decedent's gross estate under IRC Sec. 2038.

Private Annuity An exchange of money or property for an unsecured promise by the transferee (the obligor) to pay the transferor (the annuitant) specific annual or other periodic payments for the rest of the annuitant's lifetime. A private annuity transaction usually occurs between related parties and its tax advantages include both the

Appendix A

exclusion of the transferred property from the annuitant's gross estate, and deferral of income tax on the unpaid portions of the annuity.

Probate The state proceeding for the administration and disposition of certain assets belonging to a decedent. The assets that constitute the decedent's estate for probate purposes include assets or interests that are titled in the decedent's sole name. Nonprobate assets include joint property, such as life insurance or pension proceeds, which pass to designated beneficiaries independently of the terms of the will.

Probate Court The terminology for the estate or local court responsible for supervising the administration of decedents' estates.

Probate Estate A nontax term describing property of a decedent that is subject to probate administration. Only assets you own in your name alone are included in your probate estate. The disposition of your probate estate is determined by your will. The probate estate is not the same as the gross estate for federal estate tax purposes.

Property in Which the Decedent Had an Interest The value of all property, whether real, personal, tangible, or nontangible, that the decedent beneficially owned at the time of death [IRC Sec. 2033]. The regulations include in the decedent's gross estate federally exempt notes, bonds, bills, and certificates of indebtedness, as well as notes or other claims held by the decedent (even though canceled by the decedent's will), interest and rents accrued as of the date of the decedent's death, and dividends payable to the decedent or his or her estate because he or she was a shareholder of record, but which were uncollected as of time of death [Reg. Sec. 20.2033-1].

QTIP An acronym for qualified terminable interest property. See listing below.

QTIP Election An irrevocable election made on Schedule M of IRS Form 706 to treat certain property passing to the decedent's spouse as not part of the decedent's gross estate. The QTIP election is made by simply listing the QTIP property on Schedule M and deducting its value. The election can only be made for property that meets the QTIP requirements as listed below.

QTIP Trust A qualified terminable interest property (QTIP) trust qualifies for the marital deduction and therefore postpones estate tax. The surviving spouse must receive all the trust's income at least annually and may receive principal distributions at the trustee's discretion, if the trust so provides. When the surviving spouse dies, the trust is taxable in his or her estate. After taxes, the property passes according to the trust terms, as designated by the predeceased spouse. QTIP trusts are often used in second marriage situations when the predeceasing spouse wants to provide for his or her surviving spouse, but also wants to ensure that the children from his or her first marriage receive any remaining property when the surviving spouse dies.

Qualified Appraisal An appraisal prepared by a qualified appraiser and containing: (1) a description of property; (2) its fair-market value on date of its charitable contribution and specific basis for valuation; (3) a statement that an appraisal was prepared for income tax purposes; (4) appraiser's qualifications; (5) appraiser's signature and identifying number; and (6) such additional information as the regulations may acquire.

Qualified Appraiser An appraiser who is qualified to make an appraisal of the type of property donated. The following people are not qualified appraisers: the taxpayer, a party to the transaction in which the taxpayer acquired the property; the donee; any

Appendix A

person employed by any of the above-listed persons, or who bears a relationship to any of the above-listed persons; or any person whose relationship to the taxpayer would cause a reasonable person to question the appraiser's independence.

Qualified Disability Trust Any trust (1) established solely for the benefit of an individual under 65 years of age who is disabled, and (2) all of whose beneficiaries (except holders of a remainder or reversionary interest) are disabled for some portion of the taxable year [IRC Sec. 642(b)(2)(C)(ii)]. A "qualified disability trust," whether taxed as a simple or complex trust, can claim, in lieu of the $100 or $300 exemption, an exemption in the amount that a single individual taxpayer can claim [IRC Sec. 642(b)(2)(C)]. If a final distribution of assets has been made during the year, all income of the estate or trust must be reported as distributed to the beneficiaries, without reduction for the amount claimed for the exemption.

Qualified Disclaimer A qualified disclaimer is an irrevocable and unqualified refusal by a person to accept an interest in property if it meets the following four conditions: (1) the refusal is in writing; (2) the writing is received by the transferor, his legal representative, or the holder of legal title no more than nine months after the later of: (a) the day on which the transfer creating the interest is made, or (b) the day on which the person reach the age of 21; (3) the person making the disclaimer has not accepted the property or any of its benefits; and (4) the interest passes without any direction on the part of the person making the disclaimer to either: (a) the spouse of the decedent, or (b) a person other than the person making the disclaimer [IRC Sec. 2518(b)].

Qualified Domestic Trust (QDOT) A kind of trust that qualifies for the estate tax marital deduction even though the transferee spouse is not a citizen of the United States. This type of trust is necessary because property passing to a surviving spouse who is not a U.S. citizen is not eligible for the estate tax marital deduction unless the property passes through a QDOT. To qualify as a QDOT: (1) at least one trustee must be a citizen of the United States or domestic corporation, and that person or corporation must be able to block distributions from the trust; (2) the surviving spouse must get all income of the trust at least annually, unless the trust would qualify for the marital deduction if the spouse were a citizen; (3) the trust must be structured to ensure that a U.S. estate tax is imposed on the alien spouse's death; and (4) the executor must make an irrevocable election on the estate's tax return with respect to the marital deduction [IRC Sec. 2056A].

Qualified Family-Owned Business Interest Deduction The deduction for qualified family owned-business interests under IRC Sec. 2057 has been repealed.

Qualified Funeral Trust A trust is a qualified funeral trust (QFT) if it meets the following requirements: (1) the trust arises as the result of a contract with a person engaged in the trade or business of providing funeral or burial services or property necessary to provide such services; (2) the sole purpose of the trust is to hold, invest, and reinvest the trust funds and to use the funds solely to make payments for such services or property for the beneficiaries of the trust; (3) the only beneficiaries of the trust are the individuals with respect to whom such services or property are to be provided at their death under the contract; and (4) the only contributions to the trust are contributions by or for the benefit of the trust's beneficiaries. There is no dollar limit on contributions to a qualified funeral trust.

Qualified Personal Residence Trust (QPRT) A trust into which you transfer your principal residence or vacation home. You reserve the right to live in and use the

Appendix A

property rent free for a fixed number of years, which is called your "reserved interest." You pay all the expenses associated with maintaining the property just like any tenant would. If you live beyond the reserved interest, the residence held in the trust, which is called the "remainder interest" will pass to your children or to a trust for the benefit of your children, free of transfer tax even if the property has appreciated in value. If you still want to live in the home after the expiration of the reserved interest period, you have to rent the property from your children, who are now the new owners, at the fair-market value. If, on the other hand, you die before the end of the reserved interest period, the property would be included in your estate at its date-of-death value. The QPRT saves estate and gift taxes because you are leveraging the value of the remainder interest as determined by the IRS valuation tables. When you transfer the residence to the trust, you have made a taxable gift of only the remainder interest, because you have reserved the right to live in the residence until the trust terminates. You determine the value of the gift you have made by taking the value of the home on the date the gift was made and subtracting the actuarial value of your retained interest or your right to reside in the home as determined by the IRS valuation tables. A longer term that you reserve to live in the home will result in a more valuable retained interest and consequently a lower remainder and ultimately a smaller gift to your children. The longer you make your reserved interest, the greater the chance that you will die prior to its expiration and risk having the entire value of the residence included in your taxable estate. So, you must factor in your life expectancy when choosing the length of your reserved interest. The QPRT must satisfy the following requirements. First, you can only transfer a principal or vacation home into the trust. You cannot transfer other assets, except for a small amount of cash as needed for utilities, repairs, and maintenance, improvements, and other necessary expenses. Second, any income generated by the trust must be distributed to you at least annually. Because a QPRT is a so-called grantor (flow-through) trust, all of the trust's income and expenses will be taxed as if you (the grantor) owned the property. You can deduct expenses such as mortgage interest and real estate taxes that are paid by the trust. Third, if you (the grantor) stop living in the residence, the trust documents must require that either: (1) the trust be terminated and the residence be distributed to you; or (2) your interest be converted to a qualified annuity interest. The trustee can have the option of choosing either of the two alternatives [Reg. Sec. 25.2702-5].

Qualified State Tuition Program A "qualified state tuition program" is a program established and maintained by a state, state agency, or state instrumentality (such as a brokerage house) under which a person: (1) may purchase, in cash, tuition credits or certificates on behalf of a "designated beneficiary" that entitle the beneficiary to the waiver or payment of "qualified higher education expenses" of the beneficiary; or (2) may make cash contributions to an account established solely for meeting the qualified higher education expenses of the designated beneficiary of the account [IRC Sec. 529(b)(1)]. See also "College Savings Plan" in this Glossary.

Qualified Terminable Interest Property Trust (QTIP) A type of trust that can ensure that, after the death of the first spouse, children from a first marriage are not disinherited by a second spouse [IRC Sec. 2056(b)(7)]. A QTIP trust can protect the decedent's estate in case the surviving spouse remarries. The grantor places his or her property in a trust. When the grantor dies, the surviving spouse does not inherit the property, but receives income from the trust at least annually. When the surviving

Appendix A

spouse dies, the value of any assets remaining in the trust are taxed in that person's estate. Then the assets are distributed to the beneficiaries named in the trust, usually children from the previous marriage. If certain conditions are met, a life interest granted to a surviving spouse will not be treated as a terminable interest and will qualify for the marital deduction. To qualify: (1) the executor must make a QTIP election; (2) the surviving spouse must be entitled to all of the income from the property (or a portion thereof) for life, payable at least annually; and (3) no one, including the spouse, may have the power to appoint any part of the property that produces the income to anyone other than the surviving spouse during the life of the surviving spouse.

Qualifying Income Interest for Life An interest in property passing to a spouse from a decedent in which (1) the surviving spouse is entitled to all the income from property (or a portion of the property), payable annually or at more frequent intervals, and (2) no one has the power of appointment over any part of the property to any person other than the surviving spouse [IRC Sec. 2056(b)(7)(B)(ii)].

Reciprocal Trusts Reciprocal trusts are usually created by related grantors pursuant to an arrangement whereby each grantor transfers property to a trust at about the same time, and gives the other grantor the lifetime right to enjoy the property as a beneficiary. For example, suppose Ann and Brian agree that Ann will contribute $100,000 to an irrevocable trust that provides Brian with a life income interest if Brian will do the same and name Ann the life income beneficiary. Application of the reciprocal trust doctrine will cause the inclusion of the trust assets in the grantor's gross estate under IRC Secs. 2036 and 2038. To avoid the application of the reciprocal trust doctrine, the trusts should be created at different times, they should have materially different terms, and they should hold different assets. In addition, one trust could provide that one spouse held a power of appointment that was not granted to the other spouse.

Redemption of Stock to Pay Death Taxes When a portion of the stock held in the gross estate of a decedent in a corporation is redeemed, the redemption is treated as a tax-free exchange, rather than a taxable distribution, if the value of decedent's stock equals at least 35 percent of the decedent's adjusted gross estate [IRC Sec. 303]. Only the amount of the redemption proceeds payable to the decedent's estate up to the amount of the estate's inheritance, succession, and estate taxes, funeral expenses, and administration expenses are eligible for exchange treatment.

Remainder Interest A residual or leftover interest in property held by someone other than the original transferor. The holder of the remainder interest will take the property after the property has been used by the lifetime user of the property. For example, if a farmer's will provides that upon his death his sons will receive the farm outright, the sons have a remainder interest in the farm.

Required Minimum Distribution (RMD) Annual distributions that an account owner must start taking from an IRA when the IRA owner reaches age $70^1/_2$.

Return Preparer Penalty A penalty imposed against a gift or estate return preparer for each tax return or claim for refund that understates the taxpayer's liability due to an unreasonable position. The penalty is the greater of (a) $1,000 or (b) 50 percent of the income derived (or to be derived) by the preparer with respect to the return or refund claim [IRC Sec. 6694(a)]. The standard for undisclosed positions is a "reasonable belief" standard, which requires that: (1) the preparer knew, or reasonably should

Appendix A

have known, of the position; (2) there was not a reasonable belief that the tax treatment of the position would more likely than not be the proper treatment; and (3) the position was not disclosed or there was not a reasonable basis for the position. A reasonable cause exception applies if it is shown that there was a reasonable cause for the understatement and the preparer acted in good faith. The penalty increases to the greater of (a) $5,000 or (b) 50 percent of the income derived (or to be derived) by the preparer with respect to the return or refund claim if the understatement is willful or reckless [IRC Sec. 6694(b)]. The preparer penalty for willful or reckless conduct must be reduced by the amount of any penalty imposed for an unreasonable position relating to the same understatement.

Reverse QTIP Election IRC Sec. 2652(a)(3) allows the executor or trustee to make a QTIP election to treat the property as if the QTIP election had not been made. As a result of this "reverse QTIP election" the decedent remains, for GST tax purposes, the transferor of the QTIP trust or property rather than the surviving spouse. Thus, the decedent's GST tax exemption may be allocated to the QTIP trust or property even though the QTIP is taxed in the estate of the surviving spouse. The reverse QTIP election must be made on the same return that the QTIP election is made [Reg. Sec. 26.2652-2(b)]. The election is irrevocable and must be made with respect to all the property in the trust to which the QTIP election applies [Reg. Sec. 26.2652-2(a)]. The reverse QTIP election should be made when executors want to avoid wasting any of the deceased spouse's available GST exemption.

Reversion The possibility of a return of property to the original transferor after its enjoyment by another person. Persons who hold reversions are said to hold reversionary interests. Reversions are classified as future estates for purposes of local property law.

Revocable Transfer A property interest transferred by the decedent in trust or otherwise if the enjoyment of the interest was subject, on the date of the decedent's death, to any change through the exercise of a power by the decedent to alter, amend, revoke, or terminate, or if the decedent relinquished such a power within three years of death [IRC Sec. 2038]. Such amounts are included in the decedent's gross estate, except (1) to the extent that a transfer was for adequate and full consideration in money or money's worth; (2) if the decedent's power could be exercised only with consent of all parties having an interest in the transferred property, and if the power added nothing to the rights of the parties under local law; or (3) if the power was held solely by a person other than the decedent [Reg. Sec. 20.2038-1].

Revocable Trust Also called a living trust. A revocable trust is a trust created during the life of the settlor or grantor to manage assets in the case of disability. This type of trust is set up with the settlor as the trustee and another person named as successor trustee. The settlor has complete control over the assets in the trust until becoming disabled or incapacitated. When this occurs, the trust becomes irrevocable and the successor trustee takes over, using proceeds from the trust to care for the settlor and distributing the assets in the trust after the death of the settlor as directed in the trust agreement. A revocable trust should be accompanied by a "pour-over" will, which directs that any assets not held in the trust be added to the trust at the settlor's death. A revocable trust does not offer income nor estate tax savings. Because the settlor retains control over the assets in the trust, upon his or her death, the fair-market value of the assets in the trust as of the date of death are included in his or her taxable

Appendix A

gross estate. Property transferred to a revocable trust is not part of a decedent's probate estate and thus avoids the procedure and costs of probate.

S Corporation Subchapter S or S corporations are hybrid business entities that combine the flexibility of a partnership with the advantages of operating in the corporate format. However, unlike regular corporations, S corporations are generally not treated as taxable entities for federal income tax purposes. Instead, once an S corporation election has been made, the corporation's income passes through to the shareholders. Shareholders then pay tax on this income whether or not distributed. This pass-through-of-income principle parallels the tax treatment provided partnerships. A qualifying ESBT may be an S corporation.

Same-Sex Marriages Beginning in 2013, same-sex couples who are legally married in one of the 50 states, the District of Columbia, a U.S. territory or a foreign country that recognizes same-sex marriage will be treated as married for federal tax purposes regardless of where the couple resides. This is a "state of celebration" rule which means that a couple who married in a state that recognizes same-sex marriage will be treated as married regardless of where they live. The IRS does not, however, recognize couples who enter into registered domestic partnerships, civil unions or similar relationships as married for federal tax purposes. Beginning in 2013, legally-married same-sex couples generally must file their federal income tax return using either the married filing jointly or married filing separately filing status. Individuals who were in same-sex marriages may, but are not required to, file original or amended returns choosing to be treated as married for federal tax purposes for one or more prior tax years still open under the statute of limitations. Generally, the statute of limitations for filing a refund claim is three years from the date the return was filed or two years from the date the tax was paid, whichever is later. As a result, refund claims can still be filed for tax years 2010, 2011 and 2012. Some taxpayers may have special circumstances, such as signing an agreement with the IRS to keep the statute of limitations open, that permits them to file refund claims for tax years 2009 and earlier.

Second-to-Die or Survivorship Life Insurance A type of life insurance. Instead of buying individual life insurance for either a husband or wife, the life insurance purchased covers both spouses with the policy only paying a benefit after the second spouse dies. The premiums payable for second-to-die policies are often lower than they would be for single life insurance policies because the death benefit on the second-to-die policy is delayed until after the second spouse dies, thus affording the insurance company more time to invest the premiums. The downside, however, is that even though the annual premiums may be smaller, they may be payable for a much longer time. Second-to-die policies make sense where life insurance proceeds are needed to provide liquidity to pay estate taxes at the death of the surviving spouse. This can be important in situations where the bulk of the estate consists of illiquid assets such as a family business, farm, or an art collection, which otherwise would have to be sold to pay the estate tax. With the second-to-die policy in place, the estate taxes can be paid and the remainder of the estate left intact for the heirs. Buying second-to-die policies also makes sense if one of the spouses is sick. The cost of buying life insurance once someone has become sick may be prohibitive, whereas spreading the risk over the lives of a healthy spouse and an unhealthy one will result in lower premiums.

Appendix A

Section 2503(c) Trust Named after the Internal Revenue Code section creating them, Section 2503(c) trusts enable parents or grandparents to make gifts in trust to children so that the gifts qualify as a present interest and are eligible for the annual gift tax exclusion. The trust must meet the following requirements. First, principal and income must be available for distribution to or for the benefit of the minor before age 21. Second, when the minor becomes 21, all trust property must be made available to him. Third, if the minor dies before reaching age 21, the assets must be payable to the minor's estate or to whomever the minor appoints under a general power of appointment. A general power of appointment is a power granted to the minor permitting him to apply the trust proceeds in favor of himself, his or her estate, or his or her creditors. A Section 2503(c) trust is treated as a separate taxpayer, so accumulated income is taxed to the trust rather than the minor or the donor.

Self-Cancelling Installment Note (SCIN) A self-cancelling installment note (SCIN) is a debt obligation containing a provision canceling the liability upon the death of the holder. If the holder dies prior to the expiration of the term of the SCIN, the automatic cancellation feature may operate to remove a significant amount of assets from what would otherwise be includible in the holder's estate.

Settlor A party who transfers property to a trust. Also called the grantor.

7520 Rate The 7520 rate is an interest rate that the IRS publishes monthly. It is an assumed rate of return and is used to determine the present value of items like annuities, life estates, and income and remainder interests. For example, the 7520 rate is used to determine the present value of an annuity in a GRAT and the present value of the retained interest in a QPRT.

Simple Trust Also called "distributable" trust. A simple trust is one in which the trust terms (1) require that the trust distribute all of its income currently for the taxable year (it distributes no corpus), and (2) do not provide that any amounts may be paid, permanently set aside, or used for charitable purposes [IRC Sec. 651; Reg. Sec. 1.651(a)-1]. A simple trust is primarily a conduit of income. Therefore the trust takes a deduction for the income that is required to be distributed currently, and the beneficiaries include that amount in their gross income, whether or not actually distributed. The terms of the trust instrument and state law determine what is income for this purpose.

Skip Person, Generation-Skipping Transfer Tax An individual two generations or more below a transferor of property. A trust can be a skip person if (1) all the interests in the trust are held by skip persons, or (2) if there is no such person with an interest in the trust, at no time after the transfer made in trust may a distribution (even in termination) be made to a non-skip person.

Special Power of Appointment A term that refers to a power conferred upon a donee to select whomever the donee may select to enjoy an interest in property, provided the donee may not appoint him or herself, his or her estate, creditors, or the creditors of the estate. Special powers of appointment are outside the scope of IRC Sec. 2041, which includes in the gross estate of one who possesses a general power of appointment the value of the property subject to that power.

Special Use Valuation An election that enables an executor to elect to value, for federal estate tax purposes, certain qualified real property, including standing timber in qualified woodlands, and property devoted to farming or other trade or business

Appendix A

(qualified use) on the basis of its actual use, rather than its highest and best use [IRC Sec. 2032A].

Specified Terrorist Victim A "specified terrorist victim" is any decedent who: (1) dies as a result of the terrorist attacks against the United States on April 19, 1995 or September 11, 2001, or (2) dies as a result of illness incurred from an anthrax attack occurring during the period from September 11, 2001, to December 31, 2001. IRC Sec. 2201(b)(2) imposes a reduced estate tax rate on the estates of certain qualified decedents. The reduced estate tax rates have a top marginal rate of 20 percent. Only the following decedents are eligible for the reduced estate tax rate:

- Any U.S. citizen or resident who dies while in the line of duty from wounds, disease or injury suffered while serving in a combat zone in active service of the Armed Forces (as defined IRC Sec. 112(c)) [IRC Sec. 2201(b)(1)];

- Any specified terrorist victim (as defined in IRC Sec. 692(d)(4)) [IRC Sec. 2201(b)(2)]; and

- Any astronaut whose death occurs in the line of duty [IRC Sec. 2201(b)(3)].

Spendthrift Trust Also called a Minor's trust. Use a spendthrift trust if you are worried that your heirs will not be able to manage the estate, either because they are too young or might spend it unwisely. The terms of the trust can specify the investment objectives that the trustee must follow. In addition, the trust terms can spell out the criteria for eventually distributing the estate to the heirs, often when they reach a certain age.

Split Gifts An election by a husband or wife to treat gifts of property as made one-half by each, if both spouses consent. The result is to double the annual gift tax exclusion. To illustrate: Mom gives her car, worth $28,000 in 2014, to Son. If Mom and Dad both elect to split the gift, they can treat the car as half Dad's and half Mom's. As a result, they can take full advantage of the gift tax exclusion available that year [IRC Sec. 2513(a)(1)].

Sprinkling Trust A trust that authorizes trustees to select the amounts of income or principal to be distributed to particular beneficiaries each year. Also called spray trusts. Although sprinkling powers create flexibility, they may cause the grantor to be taxed as the owner of the trust under the grantor trust rules.

State Death Tax Credit The Economic Growth and Tax Relief Reconciliation Act of 2001 (EGTRRA) phased out the IRC Sec. 2011 state death tax credit between 2002 and 2004 and repealed the state death tax credit for the estates of decedents dying after December 31, 2004. Prior to its repeal, IRC Sec. 2011 allowed a credit against the federal estate tax for state death taxes.

State Death Tax Deduction Beginning in 2005, the state death tax credit was replaced by a deduction for state death taxes [IRC Sec. 2058]. Accordingly, for the estates of decedents dying after December 31, 2004, the value of a decedent's taxable estate is determined by deducting from the gross estate the amount of any estate, inheritance, legacy or succession taxes actually paid to any state or the District of Columbia with respect to property.

Step-Up in Basis A phrase used to describe the increased basis in property that occurs when someone dies and the basis of property passing at death is increased to the fair-market value of the property on the date of death [IRC Sec. 1014]. Achieving

Appendix A

a step-up in basis will be desirable because it enhances depreciation deductions and tax credits and reduces taxable gains on later sales or other dispositions of the property.

Substantial Gross Valuation Misstatements Attributable To Incorrect Appraisals A civil penalty imposed on a person who prepares an appraisal that results in a substantial or gross valuation misstatement [IRC Sec. 6695A(a)]. The appraiser must know or reasonably should have known that the appraisal would be used in connection with a return or a claim for refund. A substantial valuation misstatement generally means a value claimed that is at least twice (200 percent or more) the amount determined to be the correct value, and a gross valuation misstatement generally means a value claimed that is at least four times (400 percent or more) the amount determined to be the correct value [IRC Secs. 6662(e) and (h)]. The penalty amount is the lesser of:

(1) The greater of $1,000 or 10 percent of the tax underpayment amount attributable to the misstatement; or

(2) 125 percent of the gross income received by the appraiser for preparing the appraisal.

[IRC Sec. 6695A(b)].

The IRS can assess the appraiser penalty for gross valuation misstatements regarding estate or gift taxes. A gross valuation misstatement for estate and gift taxes occurs when the claimed property value is 40 percent or less of the correct amount [IRC Sec. 6662(h)(2)(C)]. The appraiser penalty will be applied to situations where the claimed value of the appraised property results in a substantial estate or gift tax valuation understatement under IRC Sec. 6662(g) [IRC Sec. 6695A(a)]. For estate and gift taxes, a substantial valuation understatement occurs if the claimed value of any property on an estate, gift or generation skipping tax return is 65 percent or less of the amount determined to be the correct valuation amount [IRC Sec. 6662(g)(a)]. No penalty is imposed under IRC Sec. 6695A if the appraiser establishes that the appraised value was more likely than not the proper value [IRC Sec. 6695A(c)].

Super GRIT Tax term for a grantor retained income trust that provides that, if the grantor should die before the income interest ends, assets in the GRIT revert to the estate of the grantor. This makes cash available to the estate to pay estate taxes.

Support Trust A trust used to support another person. The grantor is taxed to the extent that the income discharges a legal obligation of support [IRC Secs. 677(a)(1), 677(b), 678(c)].

Surviving Spouse A spouse who outlives the spouse to whom he or she was married. People who remarry cease to be considered surviving spouses [IRC Sec. 2(a)(1); Reg. Sec. 1.2-2].

Survivorship The right to property on the death of a co-owner of the property.

Taxable Estate The gross estate of a decedent after you have subtracted all available deductions provided in IRC Secs. 2052-2057 [IRC Sec. 2051]. The unified gift and estate tax is imposed on a decedent's taxable estate.

Taxable Gifts The total amounts of gifts made during the calendar year, less the deductions for marital gifts and charitable contributions [IRC 2503(a)]. For this purpose, the total amount of gifts equals the aggregate value of all gifts of present

Appendix A

interests made in the calendar year less any annual gift tax exclusions [Reg. Sec. 25.2503-1]. Qualified transfers for tuition and medical care are excluded, as are waivers of certain pension benefits and loans of qualified works of art to public charities and private operating foundations. Taxable gifts are the base on which the federal gift tax rates apply [IRC Sec. 2502(a)].

Taxable Termination, Generation-Skipping Transfer Tax A category of GSTs (other than a direct skip) consisting of terminations of interests in trust property (by reason of death, lapse of time, release of power, or otherwise) that result in distributions to, or those interests passing to, some skip person two or more generations below the transferor of property to that trust [IRC Sec. 2612(a)]. If a non-skip person succeeds to or continues to hold an interest, no taxable termination occurs. Also, if no distributions can be made at any time to skip persons from the trust property, no taxable termination occurs [IRC Sec. 2612(a)(1)]. A taxable termination may still occur even if the probability of a distribution to a skip person is so remote as to be negligible. This means that "it can be ascertained by actuarial standards that there is less than a 5 percent probability that the distribution will occur" [Reg. Sec. 26.2612-1(b)(1)(iii)].

Tenancy by the Entirety Property held in the name of both husband and wife is held as tenancy by the entirety. When one spouse dies, the surviving spouse receives the entire interest in his or her name alone.

Terminable Interest Property with a limited legal life. Generally, transfers of terminable interests, such as life estates, terms for years, annuities, etc., do not qualify for the marital deduction. An exception is provided for a qualified terminable interest property (QTIP) [IRC Sec. 2056(b)(7)]. See definition above. A terminable interest is an interest in property that will terminate or fail with the passage of time or occurrence or nonoccurrence of some event or contingency. The contingency need not actually occur or fail in order for the interest to be terminable.

Testamentary Trust Trusts that are created according to the terms of a will when someone (the settlor) dies are called testamentary trusts.

3.8 Percent Tax on Net Investment Income (NII) Beginning in 2013, U.S. citizens and residents must pay a 3.8 percent net investment income (NII) tax on the lesser of: (1) NII for the year, or (2) the excess of modified adjusted gross income (MAGI) over the threshold amount ($250,000 for a joint return or surviving spouse, $125,000 for a married individual filing a separate return, and $200,000 for all others). These thresholds are not indexed for inflation. MAGI is defined as adjusted gross income (AGI) plus any amount excluded as foreign earned income under IRC Sec. 911(a)(1) (net of the deductions and exclusions disallowed with respect to the foreign earned income). The tax is reported for individuals, trusts and estates on Form 8960, "Net Investment Income Tax Individuals, Estates, and Trusts," which is attached to Form 1040 (individuals).

Throwback Rules According to the devilishly complex throwback rules, which were repealed by the Taxpayer's Relief Act of 1997, a trust beneficiary was taxed on trust distributions of income that had been accumulated and taxed in prior years if the beneficiary's top average marginal tax rate during the previous five years was higher than that of the trust. In a major simplification of the law, the throwback rules were repealed for most domestic trusts effective for all distributions made in tax years beginning after August 5, 1997. The reason for the repeal is simple. The benefits of income shifting that were achieved by shifting income-producing assets to trusts

Appendix A

were eroded by the compressed income tax brackets that now apply to trusts [see ¶2819]. The throwback rules were created to limit the benefit that would otherwise occur from using the lower rates that once applied to trust income. Now that the trust tax rates have risen dramatically, the original purpose of the throwback rules no longer exists. The rules were generally eliminated for domestic trusts. **Warning:** Unfortunately, you can't forget about the throwback rules completely. The throwback rules continue to apply to (1) foreign trusts, (2) trusts that were foreign trusts but became domestic trusts, and (3) domestic trusts created before March 1, 1984, that would be treated as multiple trusts under IRC Sec. 643(f).

Transfer Taking Effect at Death Any transfer of an interest in property from the decedent, in trust or otherwise (except to the extent for full and adequate consideration in money or money's worth), if three conditions are met: (1) possession or enjoyment of the property could have been obtained only by surviving the decedent; (2) the decedent had retained a revisionary interest in the event the donee predeceased the transferor; and (3) the value of the reversionary interest immediately before the decedent's death exceeded 5 percent, actuarially determined, of the value of the entire property [Reg. Sec. 20.2037-1]. Property transfers taking effect at death are included in the decedent's gross estate.

Transfer with a Retained Life Estate Any property interest that the decedent has transferred in trust or otherwise (except to the extent that the transfer was for full and adequate consideration in money or money's worth) if a decedent retained or reserved such interest (1) for life, (2) for any period not ascertainable without reference to his or her death, or (3) for any period that does not in fact end before his or her death, the use, possession, right to income, or other enjoyment of the transferred property, or the right, either alone or in conjunction with any other person, to designate the person who will enjoy the transferred property or its income [IRC Sec. 2036(a)]. If the decedent retained or reserved an interest or right with respect to all of the property transferred, the amount included in the decedent's gross estate is the value of the entire property interest. If the decedent retained or reserved an interest or right with respect to only a part of the property, the amount to be included in the decedent's gross estate is only that portion of the property [Reg. Sec. 20.2036-1(a)].

Transferor, Generation-Skipping Transfer Tax A critical term in any GST tax analysis because application of the GST tax depends on generation assignments that all begin with the "transferor." In general, the transferor is the person who most recently was subject to estate or gift taxes with respect to the property [IRC Sec. 2652(a); Reg. Sec. 26.2652-1(a)(1)]. It only matters if the taxpayer was *subject to* estate or gift taxes. Disregarded is the fact that no gift or estate tax is actually imposed as a result of an exclusion such as the annual gift tax exclusion or the exemption equivalent. The identity of the transferor is not affected just because some or all of the gift qualifies for an exclusion.

Trust A legally recognized and enforceable arrangement, established by will (testamentary trust) or during one's lifetime (inter vivos trust), whereby one or more persons (trustees) take title to property in order to protect or conserve it for one or more beneficiaries designed in the document [Reg. Sec. 301.7701-4(a)].

Trustee A person who holds legal title to property for the purpose of protecting or conserving it for the benefit of others (beneficiaries) under the rules of courts of

Appendix A

equity. Trustees are held to particularly high standards of fiduciary duties [Reg. Sec. 301.7701-4(a)].

Undistributed Net Income The basis on which the throwback tax is imposed on distributions of prior accumulations of trust income. The term is defined on a cumulative year-by-year basis as distributable net income (DNI), minus various taxes imposed on the trust with respect to the undistributed DNI and required and discretionary (first- and second-tier) distributions for the year [IRC Sec. 665(a)]. All or a portion of taxes (other than the alternative minimum tax) imposed on the trust for the throwback year attributable to an accumulation distribution are deemed distributed along with the accumulation distribution [IRC Sec. 665(d); Reg. Sec. 1.665(d)-1]. Once undistributed net income (UNI) for prior years is determined, the beneficiary's tax is determined on the basis of deemed distributions of UNI from prior years.

Unified Credit Exemption Equivalent Trust An old term (now called annual exclusion trust) used to refer to a testamentary trust created according to the terms of a person's will after he or she dies, typically consisting of one spouse's separate property, and half the total property owned by both spouses in an amount equal to an equivalent of the unified credit amount (see listing for "unified gift and estate tax credit" below). This type of trust may grant the surviving spouse an income interest for life, but not a general power of appointment over trust property nor any power to withdraw trust assets. These powers would result in inclusion of the assets in the trust in the estate of the surviving spouse.

Unified Credit Trust A commonly used trust that is established for the benefit of the widow or widower of the decedent in order to use up the remainder of the lifetime exemption equivalent from the estate and gift taxes. The trust will generally be for the benefit of the survivor for his or her lifetime, with the remainder passing to the children.

Unified Gift and Estate Tax Credit The amount that is subtracted from the taxpayer's gift or estate tax liability [IRC Sec. 2505].

Unified Transfer Tax or Unified Rate Schedule The combined federal estate and gift tax system applicable to gratuitous transfers of an individual's wealth by gift and at death [IRC Sec. 2001(c)]. The unified transfer tax is separate from the tax on generation-skipping transfers.

Uniform Gifts/Transfers to Minors Act (UGMA, UTMA) State laws that authorize the transfer of property to a custodian who holds the property for a minor, distributing all property and income when the minor reaches adulthood under local law (usually age 21 in most states). Income earned on the property is taxed to the minor, except to the extent the income is used to discharge a duty of support owed to the minor by another. Although the kinds of property that can be accepted is limited, establishing a custodial arrangement is easy because custodians can be parents and need not have special skills. The custodial funds can be spent for the benefit of the minor or can be retained in the custodian's discretion until majority.

Unitrust Amount An amount payable, at least annually, equal to a fixed percentage of the net fair-market value of the trust's assets to the beneficiary of a charitable remainder unitrust [Reg. Sec. 1.664-3(a)(2)]. If the proper unitrust amount is not disbursed from the trust, then the grantor of the trust could lose income, estate, or gift tax deductions for the transfer to the trust. The trust instrument may direct the

Appendix A

trustee to pay the lesser of the trust income or the stated annual percentage payout. These trusts are often referred to as net income or income-only unitrusts. They are commonly used to fund charitable remainder trusts, whose payouts are deferred until the grantor retires.

Unitrust Interest An irrevocable right, established by the trust instrument, to receive payment, whether out of income or corpus, of a fixed percentage of the net fair-market value of the trust's assets, determined annually. Fair value may be determined on the basis of several valuation dates [Reg. Sec. 1.170A-6(c)(2)(ii)]. Gifts of remainder interests in trusts that are unitrust interests qualify for charitable contribution deductions [IRC Sec. 170(f)(2)(B)].

Unrelated Business Taxable Income (UBTI) The taxable income that is unrelated to a tax-exempt entity's purpose and will trigger an excise tax.

Valuation, Estate and Gift Taxes The process of determining the fair-market value of transferred property. Fair-market value is the amount for which the property would change hands between a willing buyer and a willing seller, neither being under any compulsion to buy or sell, both having reasonable knowledge of the relevant facts [Reg. Secs. 20.2031-1(b) (valuation of a gross estate), 25.2512-1 (valuation of gift property)]. A gift is valued on the date the gift is made. An estate is valued immediately after the decedent's death or, if an alternate valuation date election is made, six months after the date of decedent's death [IRC Sec. 2032(a)].

Zero Out GRAT A grantor retained annuity trust (GRAT) that gives the grantor a tiny or zero retained interest by carefully structuring the remainder interest.

Zero Value Rule A nickname for an estate freeze concept under which a retained interest is not assigned any value, and therefore, increases the gift tax liability of the transferor because the transferred property is not reduced by the retention. The zero value rule does not apply to qualified interests [IRC Sec. 2702(b)], but does apply in cases of incomplete transfers and transfers to certain trusts holding personal residences where the resident has a term interest in the trust [IRC Secs. 2702(a)(2)(A) and 2702(a)(3)].

Appendix A

INDEX

References are to paragraph (¶) numbers

A

Abusive Trust . . . 2800(e)
. civil and/or criminal penalties . . . 2800(h)
. overview . . . 2800(e)
. red flags . . . 2800(g)
. tax principles . . . 2800(f)

Accountant's Fees
. estates, income tax deduction . . . 3017
. trusts, income tax deduction . . . 2918

Accrual Basis Taxpayer
. decedent's final income tax return . . . 2605(b), 2712(a)
. decedent's taxable income computation . . . 2605(b)

Actuarial Tables
. charitable lead trusts . . . 1004
. charitable remainder interests . . . 1005(f)
. life estates . . . 1916(a)
. present interest trust . . . 905
. private annuity . . . 204(c)
. QPRT . . . 701
. self-canceling installment notes . . . 204(b)

Adjusted Gross Estate . . . 2000

Adjusted Gross Income (Form 1040) . . . 2738

Administrative Expenses
. estate and trust deductions . . . 2808(a), 2813
. estate tax
. . deductions . . . 2001, 2001(b)
. . marital and charitable deductions . . . 2001(c)
. Form 706, Schedule L . . . 2423
. Form 1041 deduction . . . 2916

Administrator. See Executors and Administrators

Adoptions . . . 2507

AFR. See Applicable Federal Rate (AFR)

After-Death Planning Strategies
. credit for tax on prior transfers . . . 2104
. . after-death planning strategy . . . 2104(e)
. . amount allowed . . . 2104(d)
. . computation of credit . . . 2104(a)
. . federal estate tax paid on . . . 2100
. . real property . . . 2104(c)
. . valuation of property . . . 2104(b)
. estate tax deduction vs. income tax deduction . . . 2003
. estate tax disclaimers . . . 1210
. QTIP trusts . . . 1103

Aliens. See Nonresident Alien

Alimony. See also Divorce
. decedent's final income tax return . . . 2717
. deduction (Form 1040) . . . 2738
. estate tax deduction . . . 2003

Alternate Valuation Election . . . 1907(a), 2508(c)

Alternate Valuation Method . . . 1907
. after-death planning strategies . . . 1907(e)
. date . . . 1907(a)
. distributed, sold, exchanged, or otherwise disposed of . . . 1907(a)
. election of . . . 1907(d)
. excluded property . . . 1907(b)
. generation-skipping transfer tax . . . 2508(c)
. included property . . . 1907(b)

Alternate Valuation Method—continued
. value affected by lapse of time . . . 1907(c)

Alternative Minimum Tax (AMT)
. estate or trust income tax . . . 2821
. Form 1040 . . . 2703, 2753
. Form 1041 . . . 2938, 3036

American Opportunity Credit (Form 1040) . . . 2773

American Taxpayer Relief Act of . . . 2012
. changes made by . . . 101
. estate tax computation . . . 2200
. gift tax rules . . . 200(a)
. GST tax . . . 2500(a)
. qualified family-owned business interest deduction . . . 2002

Amortization Deductions . . . 2913(c), 3012(c)

AMT. See Alternative Minimum Tax (AMT)

Annual Exclusion Gifts . . . 901
. closely held business interests . . . 901(d)
. direct skips . . . 2504(c)
. giving gifts under a power of attorney . . . 901(g)
. indirect gifts . . . 901(e)
. life insurance policies . . . 901(f)
. LLCs . . . 901(d)
. present interest requirement . . . 901(c)
. unlimited number of donees . . . 901(a)
. use it or lose it . . . 901(b)

Annuity
. charitable lead annuity trust . . . 1004(d)
. charitable remainder annuity trust . . . 1005(a)
. commercial annuities . . . 1801(f), 1808(a)
. decedent's income tax deduction for estate tax paid . . . 2616(d)
. Form 706, Schedule I . . . 2420
. Form 1040 reporting . . . 2726
. fully taxable . . . 2726(a)
. grantor retained annuities. See Grantor Retained Annuity Trust (GRAT)
. joint and survivor annuity, transfer of interest
. . unlimited gift tax marital deduction . . . 1107(c)
. . zeroed-out GRAT . . . 604
. lottery winnings . . . 1808(c)
. lump-sum distributions . . . 2726(d)
. partially taxable . . . 2726(c)
. private annuity
. . actuarial tables . . . 204(c)
. . charitable gift annuities . . . 204(c)
. . estate tax consequences . . . 204(c)
. . gift tax consequences . . . 204(c)
. . income tax treatment . . . 204(c)
. . intrafamily transactions . . . 204(c)
. rollovers . . . 2726(e)
. unrecovered investment in pension . . . 2726(b)
. valuation . . . 1916(d)

Anti-Freeze Valuation Rules Ch. 5
. attribution rules . . . 511
. closely held corporations . . . 501
. definitions . . . 502
. gratuitous transfers, calculating value of . . . 508
. lapsing rights and restrictions . . . 512
. minimum value rule . . . 509
. overview . . . 500
. partnerships . . . 501

APP

References are to paragraph (¶) numbers

CHA

References are to paragraph (¶) numbers

CHA

DEB

References are to paragraph (¶) numbers

References are to paragraph (¶) numbers

DEP

References are to paragraph (¶) numbers

References are to paragraph (¶) numbers

EST

References are to paragraph (¶) numbers

EST

EST

References are to paragraph (¶) numbers

EST

References are to paragraph (¶) numbers

FOR

References are to paragraph (¶) numbers

FOR

References are to paragraph (¶) numbers

FOR

References are to paragraph (¶) numbers

FOR

FUN

References are to paragraph (¶) numbers

References are to paragraph (¶) numbers

References are to paragraph (¶) numbers

GRA

References are to paragraph (¶) numbers

References are to paragraph (¶) numbers

INT

References are to paragraph (¶) numbers

LOS

References are to paragraph (¶) numbers

References are to paragraph (¶) numbers

RES

References are to paragraph (¶) numbers

TAX

References are to paragraph (¶) numbers

TAX

References are to paragraph (¶) numbers

TRU

References are to paragraph (¶) numbers

TRU

References are to paragraph (¶) numbers

VAL

WAG